MUSIC MASTER

PRICE GUIDE FOR RECORD COLLECTORS

Edited By Nick Hamlyn

Published By MBC Information
Services, London.

First Edition February 1991.

Published by Music Master (a division of MBC Information Services Ltd), Music House, 1 De Cham Avenue, Hastings, East Sussex, England. TN37 6HE.

Editorial enquiries: 0424 715181 Fax: 0424 422805.
Advertising enquiries: 081 490 0049.

Book trade enquiries: Harrap Publishing Group Ltd, Chelsea House, 26 Market Square, Bromley, Kent. BR1 1NA. Telephone: 081 313 3484. Fax: 081 313 0702.

Record trade enquiries: Music Master, Music House, 1 De Cham Avenue, Hastings, East Sussex. TN37 6HE. Telephone: 0424 715181. Fax: 0424 422805.
A full list of our distributors worldwide is published at the back of this book.

ISBN 0 904520 56 0

Printed and bound by Collins, Glasgow, Scotland.

MUSIC MASTER PRICE GUIDE FOR RECORD COLLECTORS

CONTENTS

Music Master titles .... Page 4
Introduction .... Page 5
Prefixes .... Page 15
Acetates sold at auction .... Page 17
Unreleased material .... Page 19
Abbreviations .... Page 21
Price Guide .... Page 25
List of plates .... Page 813

MUSIC MASTER TITLES

Many other **new** titles are now available from the Music Master range. All the books referred to below are currently in print and can be obtained by contacting Music Master, Music House, 1 De Cham Avenue, Hastings, East Sussex, England. TN37 6HE. Telephone: (0424) 715181. Fax: (0424) 422805. Watch out too for more new titles in 1991 and 1992.

MUSIC MASTER FILMS AND SHOWS CATALOGUE
First published in December, 1990, this book contains all your favourite recordings from the top film and stage musicals. In addition there are literally hundereds of tracks which have featured in popular films over the years. ***464 pages. £7.95.***

MUSIC MASTER HEAVY METAL CATALOGUE
First published in September, 1990, this is a must for all enthusiasts of heavy metal music. All the top bands are here, plus a few not so well known ones. With an interesting introduction by respected music journalist Neil Jeffries of Kerrang!, the ***624 pages*** represent superb value at only ***£6.95.***

MUSIC MASTER JAZZ CATALOGUE
First published in July, 1990, this book was edited by Graham Langley, Librarian of the British Institute of Jazz. His expert knowledge helped us to produce this popular book, which has since proved to be a top selling title. WIth over 25,000 entries and many interesting and informative biographies, the book's ***960 pages*** retail at ***£9.95.***

MUSIC MASTER MUSIC ON VIDEO CATALOGUE
Aimed at the specialist but ever increasingly popular music video market, this book was first pubished in February, 1990. A must for all enthusiasts of music videos, the book has more than 2,500 entries. ***320 pages. £4.45.***

Other new titles planned include the **Music Master Country Music Catalogue** and the updated edition of the Music Master Record Catalogue, last published in December, 1989.

For details of how to advertise in any of our books, telephone: 071 490 0049.

INTRODUCTION

It is like a disease. Those of us who suffer from it are often described as being "vinyl junkies" and the phrase is an apt one. As a student, with limited funds, I often had to choose between buying records and buying food. I ate a lot of bread and margarine, but my record collection was larger than anyone else's I knew. Of course, several of the records were bought second-hand. In those days there were no collectors' shops and a deleted record was, by definition, a cheap record. Imagine, for example, seeing a copy of "The Cheerful Insanity Of Giles, Giles And Fripp" for seventy-five pence, when you have just bought a copy of "In The Court Of The Crimson King" and fallen in love with it! (Imagine too the fascination at discovering that King Crimson's roots lay in a kind of updated music hall whimsy). It was two or three years later that I first discovered a shop full of deleted records that were not cheap. It certainly looked like a second-hand record shop - its shabby South London premises in drastic need of a coat of paint - but the prices were all two or three times as high as for new records. A few of the stock items I even had in my own collection....

I left quickly, convinced I had wandered into a madhouse! That bold pioneer is no longer there, but it was only a few years afterwards that I saw an advertisement in the paper for a "Record Fair". The prospect of being able to explore a room full of literally thousands of records was too great to resist. Here again many of the prices were high, but this time it did not seem so unreasonable. With the passing of time, so many records had now been issued that it was impossible for record companies to keep more than a fraction of their back catalogues available. I knew that the expensive collector's items on offer could not be bought at any ordinary record shop. There, for example, was a copy of the "Giles, Giles And Fripp" LP again, but it had gone up in value a little from the seventy-five pence I had paid for my copy! The really high prices, however, seemed to be reserved for rock'n'roll records - London label singles with gold print on the black background; Elvis Presley singles and albums on the HMV label; original recordings by Gene Vincent.

Finding a number of ridiculously cheap LPs - many of them long deleted and all in excellent condition - at a car boot sale inspired me to try my luck at a Record Fair as a dealer. At the stall next to mine a copy of "God Save The Queen" by the Sex Pistols on the A&M label was on offer. Near the end of the day it was sold - for £75, (this was in 1982). My own stall had nothing in that league, but LPs by artists as diverse as Grapefruit, Billy Fury, and Man went well, while an original album by H.P.Lovecraft went for a very respectable £10.

These days, running a collectors' record shop, it is possible to see how changes in fashion affect the collectors' market in the same way as in anything else. The values of most rock'n'roll records have barely kept pace with inflation and any in less than pristine condition are likely to languish unsold in the racks for months on end. Enough time has now passed since these records were made for long-term collectors to have already found most of what they need. Now they are merely seeking to upgrade the playing quality of their collection. Meanwhile, the collectability of the well-known names from the sixties and early seventies has been leap-frogged in recent years by the obscurities from the same period. Legendary items like David Bowie's "dress cover" LP and the albums issued by Kaleidoscope and Trees, which peaked early on, have hardly increased in value at all in the last few years. Records by the likes of Mellow Candle, A - Austr, and Apple, however, seem to be locked into a spiral of value that winds ever upwards. These, of course, are records that are genuinely rare, in that their sales at the time of their original release were miniscule (and unsold copies would, in all probability, have been destroyed).

An alternative collecting trend in recent years has been the tremendous growth in special format, limited edition releases - picture discs, coloured vinyls, exotic packagings, and so on. These records are rare because they are only issued in small quantities to begin with. The record companies intend the records to be instant collectors' items for which the usual process of waiting for time to create the rarity is circumvented. Although this aspect of record collecting could be viewed as being rather artificial, it does enable fans of artists too recently successful to have much of a history to assemble a real collection.

Even a short history, however, can yield valuable collectors' items of the "traditional" sort these days. Since it is common practice for record companies to delete singles within a few months of their release, these can become quite scarce very quickly - especially where the record company is an independent and the original sales were small. Whenever a new group hits the charts, it usually turns out that they have one or two unsuccessful singles behind them. For this reason, records of very recent vintage can achieve a surprisingly high value.

Every major town now has its regular Record Fair - the cities have several. Specialist collectors' record shops abound and the record companies are responding by showing far more interest in their own back catalogues than has ever been the case before. A number of specialist labels are now devoted to restoring long-deleted records to the market place and the resultant exposure has made the original pressings more sought after than ever. All of this activity betokens a record collectors' market that has grown from virtually nothing to a substantial industry in the space of less than two decades. Nevertheless, as a collectors' record dealer I am continually bombarded with enquiries from customers with regard to the value of records that they have in their collections. Many are extremely surprised to discover how high this value is - they have had no idea that their old records could be of interest to anybody. There are of course a number of magazines and other publications dealing with a small part of the collectors' field at a time, but no comprehensive guide covering it in its entirety - until now.

What kind of music is covered by the guide?

This is a price guide to collectable rock records, but the word "rock" has been interpreted very widely. It naturally includes rock'n'roll, beat, progressive, heavy metal and punk, and all other kinds of rock and pop music, but it also covers soul, R&B, funk, reggae, and folk, as well as a number of country, jazz (especially the British variety), blues, and even a few classical records. When considering a particular artist for inclusion, the criterion was always: is this artist likely to be of interest to any collector of rock music? My intuition in this respect led me to include Karlheinz Stockhausen and Mike Westbrook, but not Frank Sinatra or Dimitri Tiomkin. My apologies to anyone who feels that the decision should have been the other way round!

What records are collectable?
To qualify as collectable, a lower price limit was set. All the LPs included in the guide are valued at £10 or over; double LPs are £12 or over; 7" singles and EPs are £4 or over; 12", cassette and CD singles start at £6; CD albums start at £15. Arguably, any deleted record in mint condition has a value equal to that of a new record; a collectors' record is one whose value is at least a small margin above this figure. The small number of limited edition records whose retail price when new is already higher than the lower price limit are not included in the guide.

How important is the condition of a record?
The values quoted are for records in at least excellent condition. Such a record has no scratches or any other mark producing an audible effect that should not be there. The cover is free from tears and has no more than very slight scuffing or creasing. In the case of a single that should have a picture sleeve, this is present (from the late seventies onwards, virtually all singles were issued in picture sleeves; exceptions are noted in the guide). For a record in worse condition than this, the value will be substantially less than the figure listed. This cannot be stressed too strongly. A record whose music is interrupted by a click that repeats thirty-three or forty-five times every minute is likely to be of interest to a collector only as a stop-gap until he can obtain a better copy. He will certainly not pay more than half the top value for such a record, and maybe not even as much as half. A record whose music is accompanied by what sounds like a frying breakfast is practically worthless. Nor is it possible to use a record's age as an excuse. In many cases, hundreds of thousands of copies of a record may have been sold originally, but a relatively high value is given in the guide precisely because copies in excellent condition are scarce. At the other end of the scale, a record in truly mint condition (i.e. in the same condition as when it first left the factory) may sometimes fetch a little more than the listed value.

How is it possible to identify an original pressing?
The date of publication or the copyright date given on a record usually relates to the original release date, which is not necessarily the date of issue of the particular piece of vinyl in question. Where a record is given a reissue, after having been unavailable for a time, it is usually (though not always, unfortunately) given a new catalogue number. Catalogue numbers are therefore a considerable aid in identifying original pressings, and these are given in the guide wherever possible. Where a record remains in a company's catalogue over an extended period of time, changes in label design can make the first issues distinctive. In the UK, record companies clearly felt that the arrival of the Beatles and the other Merseybeat groups heralded a new age, for most of them started to use new labels around 1963. At the end of the decade they changed again - photographs of various label designs are shown within the guide.

The construction of the cover in the case of UK LPs is a further aid in dating a record. During the fifties and sixties, the cardboard edges of the front cover were turned over the outside of the back cover; from the late sixties the edges were glued inside the back cover. In addition, LP covers from the fifties seem to be made of a much thinner, flimsier cardboard than used subsequently.

Values given in this guide are for original pressings. Later pressings may not be collectable at all, although if the record in question is not available in any form, then a later pressing may still command some kind of collectors' value, although this will obviously be rather less than for the original.

What about records from other countries?

The majority of items listed in the guide are UK issues. A few releases from other countries have also been included where it is felt that these are of particular interest to the UK collector. The majority of these consist of recordings by British artists (by birth or by adoption) that were not actually released in Britain. The rest are a selection of records by artists from other countries that are of particular appeal to collectors in the UK. In addition, a large number of US albums have been included. This is easily justified on two counts.

American LPs have always been imported into Britain in quite large numbers so that they frequently turn up for sale in the collectors' market. More importantly, with so much rock music being American in origin, the first pressing of a large number of releases is actually an American record. As a general rule, US albums have been included in this guide either if they have no exact UK equivalent, or if the American pressing has a rather higher value than its British counterpart. (American pressings of many UK original albums are actually less valuable in the UK, especially where the label is a key factor in the collectability of the British record).

As regards the listed values of these records, they are weighted towards the going rates in their home country. Although dealers in Britain may sometimes set a higher price than this, there seems little reason why collectors should not be able to obtain American sale lists and purchase directly from these. There is no real justification for a UK dealer to charge over the odds for an American pressing merely on the grounds that copies actually in the UK are scarce. The world availability should be what matters.

How accurate are the values listed in the guide?

The title of this book means what it says: it is a guide to the values of collectable records. Within any collectors' field, an item is essentially worth whatever a collector is prepared to pay for it. When considering items of which several copies are potentially available, however, as is the case with collectors' records, a few points need to be kept in mind.

Let us suppose that Steve Crick, a collector of extraordinary tastes, is desperate to obtain a copy of "My Old Killarney Hat" by Sister Mary Gertrude. This is not a record that features very often in dealers' lists, so Steve advertises that he is prepared to pay fifty pounds for a copy. Four dealers eventually manage to come across the elusive record: one is delighted to receive £50 from an equally delighted Steve Crick, but the other three find that they are unable to interest anyone at all in the record, at any price. So what is the value of "My Old Killarney Hat"?

At the other end of the scale, there must be numerous collectors who would like to obtain a copy of the Beatles fan club album, "From Then To You". This is a record with a listed value of £250 - it is scarce, but copies do turn up, and most dealers will have had at least one passing through their hands. Dave Conroy is a keen Beatles collector and he does not have a copy of "From Then To You". On the other hand, he does have the actual music in his collection, as he was able to buy an American counterfeit of the record quite cheaply a few years ago. When he sees the real thing in his local collectors' record shop with a price tag of £250, he argues that he has waited twenty years for the record, so he might as well wait a little longer for a copy that is more "reasonably" priced. In the event, the shop is unable to find a customer for the record. The manager reduces the price to £200, and after a few weeks, with the record still unsold, Dave Conroy offers £175, which is accepted. So again, what is the value of "From Then To You"?

A junk shop, selling all kinds of second-hand goods from shabby premises, and with a box of old records in the corner, would find in all probability that the records would remain unsold if priced according to the values given in this guide. An efficient specialist mail-order company, on the other hand, with a large number of customers in Scandinavia, Germany, and Japan, could well be regularly managing to obtain prices in excess of those listed in the guide.

To these considerations must be added the fact that the collectors' market is a volatile one. The success of a new group in the charts can send the values of their back catalogue spiralling upwards (although a later fall from favour can just as easily send them tumbling back down again); an influential disc jockey can create a collectors' item out of an obscurity simply by deciding to play it (particularly in the case of soul records); or else the reissue of a scarce album can increase the value of the original merely by making more people aware of its existence. On the other hand, the discovery of a warehouse full of copies of a previously rare record is likely to make the price fall dramatically; or a similar effect can simply result from several people deciding to sell their cherished copies of the same record at the same time. It happens!

To repeat, therefore, this book is a guide to the values of collectable records. A large amount of research, however, has gone into making it as accurate as possible, much of it being first-hand - the result of actually selling the records through a successful collectors' record shop to both the home and the international market over a period of several years. The values are based on actual sales and, within the constraints detailed above, the margin of error is not likely to be large. Comments and corrections are always welcome, though.

It should be mentioned at this point that "value" means the price that a collector might be expected to pay for a copy of the record concerned in excellent condition. The price that a dealer might pay for the record is another matter altogether. A dealer has to cover the cost of his overheads, (which include the rent, rates, and other running expenses of the shop - staff salaries, advertising expenses and the time and effort spent acquiring the knowledge that he must have), before he can even begin to make a profit. A 10% or 20% slice of the record's value is too little to justify the outlay involved. In general, dealers expect to pay around half the anticipated selling price for a record, but this figure may be increased in the case of an item for which there is a waiting customer and decreased for an item whose appeal is rather specialised; it is likely to be decreased too for items at the bottom of the collectors' price scale and which therefore only just qualify.

How can a counterfeit record be recognised?
It is a sad fact that many of the rarer records have been counterfeited by unscrupulous individuals wishing to pass off their copies as the real thing. Recognising a counterfeit can sometimes be a problem. Often the label or the cover simply looks "too new", or the colour or some feature of the design simply does not look quite right. This is no help, however, where one has no idea what the original record should look like. In the case of UK pressings a good indication is provided by the matrix number, which is to be found on the vinyl in the space occupied by the run-out groove, next to the label. If this is printed, then the record is likely to be genuine; if, however, the number is hand scratched, then the record is likely to be a counterfeit. One should also always be suspicious of a record offered for sale far too cheaply, especially if the record is a well-known collectors' item and the dealer is not one with a reputable name. (Although genuine bargains can always be found, of course, amongst the stock of dealers who are simply unaware of its value. It's a matter of judgement).
Recently, a large number of unofficial reissues of scarce albums from the sixties and early seventies have appeared on the market, but the manufacturers of these take care to remove the original record company names from the cover and identification is not a problem.

A bootleg recording, incidentally, is a somewhat different animal. Bootlegs contain either a live performance or else studio out-takes; they do not duplicate any official record-company release and the issue of whether or not they are genuine does not arise. They are illegal because of the lack of record company involvement, (occasionally the artist is involved, however, and may even get some royalty payment), but they are often keenly sought by collectors for the sake of the otherwise unavailable music they contain. Popular titles are constantly reissued by different manufacturers and there is little interest in "originals" - any pressing will normally satisfy a collector. In so far, therefore, as the value of bootleg records stays at around the £10 to £20 figure they fetch when new, they are outside the scope of this guide.

Does it make any difference if a record is mono or stereo?
Where there is a considerable difference in the values of mono and stereo pressings of a record, this is indicated in the listings. If no mention is made of which is meant, then both mono and stereo pressings are implied. The catalogue number given could be either - a table is given on page 15 of this book showing how the prefixes differ for mono and stereo versions of the same record. Note that in the early days of stereo, the two versions could have numbers that were completely different from one another, but in general these alternatives are given in the listings. Some collectors value the stereo pressings over the mono for older records (those from the fifties and early sixties); for later records (from the late sixties) mono pressings may be thought more desirable. In these cases, therefore, a slight premium over the value listed might be in order.

During the seventies, a number of quadraphonic albums were issued. In general, these are worth more than the stereo equivalents, but all those that are of interest to collectors are listed separately. Similarly, a number of "super-stereo", audiophile albums were issued in the late seventies and eighties, and these are also listed in the guide. These are mastered at half the usual speed from a tape playing at half the usual speed, which is supposed to create a superior sound quality when played back normally. The records are also pressed on to virgin vinyl, with a high degree of quality control. Despite this, it is actually quite difficult to distinguish most audiophile recordings from their ordinary stereo equivalents on a blindfold test.

What about promotional and demonstration records?
For every record made, there are in principal three stages of pressing prior to the one that is sold in the record shops. An acetate is cut quickly on to hard, brittle plastic, (or sometimes it is made of metal with a thin vinyl coating), in order to give the artist or other interested party some idea of how the finished recording will sound. A test pressing is made on ordinary vinyl to literally test the fidelity of each component involved, from the master tape itself through to the setting of the cutting equipment. Finally, the first copies of the finished records to leave the pressing plant are sent to reviewers and radio stations and are often given special labels or numbers, identifying the records as "demonstration" copies.

If a particular record is collectable, then all of these versions of it will be too. As a general rule, demonstration copies have a value twice that of a regular pressing, while test pressings have two to three times the value. Where the values are higher than this formula would suggest, then they are listed in the guide separately.

Acetates have not been listed - normally there would be fewer than five copies of each one and they are therefore too rare to be given a realistic value. Lists are given on page 17 of this book of prices that have been reached at auction by an assortment of acetates. The most valuable of these are inevitably acetates of recordings that were never actually released as finished records. It should be noted, by the way, that acetates and test pressings are the easiest of all records to counterfeit.

In the case of shaped picture discs, there is another early version of the record, namely the rectangular piece of vinyl from which the finished shape is cut. These "uncut picture discs" are perhaps the trendiest collectors' items at the time of writing, and they sell for around three times the price of the normal shaped disc.

Special promotional releases have long been a feature of the record industry and in the eighties in particular, a large number have been issued.The major target for these is the radio stations and they often consist of formats or mixes not available to the general public. Keeping track of exactly what has been issued is a considerable undertaking and there are likely to be omissions within the guide. As many as possible, however, have been included.

Deliberately left out are the BBC transcription discs. In order to sell its programmes to radio stations abroad, the BBC records them on to LPs, which can be easily used for broadcast purposes. The records of interest to rock music collectors consist of live recordings from programmes like Radio One's "In Concert". Essentially, anyone who is anyone in the eighties has at least one side of one of these records devoted to their music, while a large number of seventies artists are also represented. The BBC itself does not approve of the sale of its transcription discs and will not provide any kind of discography. As a general rule, however, if you have heard a rock concert on the radio, there is probably a transcription disc of it in existence. Values of these records on the collectors' market are kept relatively low by the existence of bootlegs and counterfeits, (any BBC record with a black and white label is definitely a counterfeit - original labels are green and white), the average being around £50 - £60. Exceptions to this average are the artists one would expect - "The Beatles At The Beeb" set sells for £400, for example.

The American equivalents of the BBC transcription discs are mostly the products of two companies: Westwood One and King Biscuit Flower Hour. Originally issued as two and three LP sets, they are now coming out as compact discs. Either way the values are on a par with the BBC discs, at around £50 to £60 for the average album set or CD, (with the same obvious exceptions). These recordings consist of live concerts interspersed with advertisements, ready for broadcast in the US. Other radio show albums contain a mixture of music (some of it previously issued studio material) and interviews. These have lower values than the all-live sets, going down to as little as £10, depending on the amount of unreleased live material they contain.

Also excluded from individual listings in the guide are the series of Disco Mix Club LPs. These were issued to accredited disc jockeys who paid to join the club, at the rate of two albums per month from the early eighties. The first of these monthly issues is of no interest to collectors, being merely a compilation of recently issued tracks. The second, however, contains various remixes and megamixes of previously released material, much of it being unavailable anywhere else. These albums sell for prices in the range of £10 to £50, (depending on the artists involved), on the rare occasions when they come on to the open market.

What about 78's?
To most rock collectors, 78rpm recordings are of little interest. They break much too easily for one thing; and hardly anyone has the means to play them these days for another. A very small number of them, however, can be found within the pages of this guide, these being either records by particularly collectable artists, like Elvis Presley and Cliff Richard, or else the handful of rock'n'roll and R&B songs that were not given a 45rpm release in the fifties. Apart from these, the general rule is that 78's have a value of about a quarter of their seven-inch single equivalent.

How is the price guide organised?
The artists are listed alphabetically, and for each one the collectable records are also listed alphabetically, format by format, (all the LPs are together, all the 7" singles, and so on). It must be remembered that the listings are not complete discographies, but only a catalogue of those items that are valuable enough to be considered collectable. As far as possible, it is the A side that is listed in the case of singles, but if a certain title cannot be found, it is always worth checking to see if the B side has been listed instead. Similarly, where a record has a different artist on each side, (a common practice with sixties reggae and ska singles), it will only be listed under one of them. Records featuring several different artists are usually listed under the "Various" heading.

A small number of abbreviations have been used. These are as follows:-
cass: cassette. *cass-s:* cassingle. *CD-s:* compact disc single. *PS:* picture sleeve. *r-reel:* reel to reel tape.

The format "EP" is reserved for the seven-inch, picture sleeved records that were issued in the fifties and sixties as junior versions of the LP. Modern singles of the seven or twelve inch variety are described as "singles", whatever the record company might wish to call them.

Acknowledgements

As a finale to this introduction I would like to offer my grateful thanks to the various dealers and collectors who have helped with information, advice, and record sleeves for photographing. These include Malcolm Alsopp, Gerald Claridge, Alan Harrington, Nick Haycock, Jo and Steve Horne, Dave Kirby, Alan Lavender, David Reed, Allen Souster, John Wagstaff, David Walker-Collins, and Terry Walpole. A special big thanks for the special big help I have received from Michael Gerzon, Natalie Hill, Richard Sefton, Phil Walker, and my family - Liz, David and Eileen, Catherine and Fred.

Nick Hamlyn

Errata

Page 95
BOND, OLIVER
Knock on Wood.................................. artist should be BONE, OLIVER

Page 313
GROUNDHOGS
I'll Never Fall in Love Again .... artist is JOHN LEE'S GROUNDHOGS

Page 418
LEE, JACKIE
The following are recordings by another artist named Jackie Lee, and are not related to the listings which appear on this page:-

I know, Know, Know	7"	Columbia	DB7860	1966	£4
Lonely Clown	7"	Columbia	DB7685	1965	£4
Town I Live In	7"	Columbia	DB8052	1966	£4

Page 426
LIFE
The following are recordings by another artist named Life, and are not related to the listings which appear on this page:-

Cat's Eyes	7"	Phillips	6006280	1973	£10

Page 639
SHERMAN, FLAMMA
Should be Flamma Sherman

UK MONO AND STEREO LP PREFIXES

Label	Mono	Stereo
Ace Of Clubs	ACL	SCL
Apple	APCORS	APCOR
Atlantic	587	58
Bell	BLLS	BLL
Brunswick	LAT	STA
CBS	BPG	SBPG
Capitol	T	ST
Chess	CRL	CRLS
Columbia	(33)SX	SCX
Decca	LK	SLK
Deram	DML	SML
Elektra	EKL	EKS
Fontana	TFL	SFL
Fontana	TL	STL
HMV	CLP	CSD
Immediate	IMLP	IMSP
Island	ILP	ILPS
Liberty	LBL	LBS
London	HA	SAH
Major Minor	MMLP	SMLP
Marble Arch	MAL	MALS
Marmalade	607	608
Nova	DN	SND
Page One	POL	POLS
Parlophone	PMC	PCS
Philips	BL	SBL
President	PTL	PTLS
Pye	NPL	NSPL
RCA	RD	SF
Regal Zonophone	LRZ	SLRZ
Reprise	RLP	RSLP
Stateside	SL	SSL
Tamla Motown	TML	STML
Track	612	613
United Artists	ULP	SULP
Vanguard	VRL	SVRL
Verve	VLP	SVLP
Warner Brothers	WM	WS

US MONO AND STEREO LP PREFIXES

Label	Mono	Stereo
A&M	LP	SP
Ascot	ALM	ALS
Autumn	LP	SLP
Bang	BLP	BLPS
Brunswick	BL	BL7
Buddah	BDM	BDS
Buena Vista	BV	BVS or STER
Cadence	CLP3	CLP25
Camden	CAL	CAS
Cameo	C	SC
Capitol	MAL	SMAL
Capitol	MAS	SMAS
Caprice	LP	SLP
Carlton	LP	STLP
Challenge	CHL	CHS
Chancellor	CHL	CHLS
Checker	LP	LPS
Chess	LP	LPS
Colgems	COL	COS

Colpix	CP	SCP
Columbia	CL	CS
Coral	CRL	CRL7
Crown	CLP	CST
Decca	DL	DL7
Del-Fi	DFLP	DFST
Deram	DE	DES
Dolton	BLP	BST
Duke	DLP	DLPS
Elektra	EKL	EKS
End	LP	LPS
Epic	LN	BN
Era	EL	ELS
Everest	D	SD
Everest	LPBR	BRST
Folkways	FV	FVS
Fontana	MGF	SRF
Forecast	FT	FTS
Gee	GLP	SGLP
Hickory	LPM	LPS
Jamie	JLP	LP70
Kama Sutra	KLP	KLPS
Kapp	KL	KS
Kent	KLP	KST
King	K or LP	KS
Laurie	LLP	SLP
Liberty	LRP	LST
London	LL	PS
MGM	E	SE
Mercury	MG	SR
Monument	MLP	SLP
OKeh	M	S
Parkway	P	SP
Parrot	PAR	PAS
Philips	PC	PCC
Phillips	PHM	PHS
RCA	LOC	LSO
RCA	LPM	LSP
Red Bird	RB	RBS
Reprise	R	R9 or RS
Roulette	R	SR
Scepter	S	SS
Specter	SP	SPS
Sidewalk	T	DTorST
Smash	MGS	SRS
Stax	ST	STS
Swan	LP	LPS
Top Rank	RM	RS
Tower	T	DT or ST
Twentieth Century	TFM	TFS
United Artists	UAL	UAS
Vanguard	VRS	VSD
Vault	LP	VS
Vee Jay	LP	SR, VJS, or LPS
Verve	V	V6
Wand	WD	WDS
Warner Brothers	W	WS
Wing	MGW	SRW
World Artists	WAM	WAS
World Pacific	WP	WPS

Other companies have a prefix for stereo, but no prefix for mono.

ACETATES SOLD AT AUCTION IN LONDON

Artist	Title	Price	Year
BADFINGER	Apple LP	£200	(1987)
BAND AID	Do They Know It's Christmas	£80	(1988)
BEATLES	Across The Universe (unrel'd mono mix)	£500	(1985)
BEATLES	All My Lovin	£110	(1986)
BEATLES	All Together Now	£280	(1990)
BEATLES	Ballad Of John And Yoko (with count-in)	£400	(1985)
BEATLES	Best Of The Beatles (unis'ed double LP)	£2000	(1988)
BEATLES	Blue Jay Way	£110	(1986)
BEATLES	Day Tripper	£55	(1984)
BEATLES	Do You Want To Know A Secret	£350	(1987)
BEATLES	Fool On The Hill	£110	(1986)
BEATLES	Fool On The Hill	£280	(1990)
BEATLES	Get Back	£450	(1988)
BEATLES	Girl (US)	£100	(1986)
BEATLES	Hello Goodbye	£280	(1990)
BEATLES	Hello Little Girl/Like Dreamers Do	£2500	(1986)
BEATLES	Hey Jude	£220	(1987)
BEATLES	I Am The Walrus	£280	(1989)
BEATLES	I Feel Fine/She's A Woman	£140	(1986)
BEATLES	I Feel Fine/She's A Woman	£380	(1990)
BEATLES	Kenny Everett Interview	£260	(1985)
BEATLES	Lady Madonna/Let It Be out-takes	£240	(1985)
BEATLES	Like Dreamers Do	£1000	(1988)
BEATLES	Little Child	£380	(1984)
BEATLES	Long And Winding Road	£260	(1988)
BEATLES	Long And Winding Road (Paul solo)	£400	(1986)
BEATLES	One And One	£250	(1985)
BEATLES	Only A North	£280	(1990)
BEATLES	Please Please Me	£300	(1984)
BEATLES	Please Please Me	£420	(1987)
BEATLES	Revolution No.9 (alternate version)	£800	(1988)
BEATLES	Some Other Guy (live at Cavern)	£1100	(1982)
BEATLES	Some Other Guy/Beautiful Dreamer/Keep Your Hands	£1400	(1990)
BEATLES	Taste Of Honey/Do You Want To Know A Secret	£380	(1985)
BEATLES	Twelve Bar Original 13.12.65	£1300	(1988)
BEATLES	Yesterday	£520	(1987)
BEATLES	Yesterday (alternate take)	£770	(1989)
BEATLES	Yesterday (US)	£100	(1986)
BEE GEES	And The Sun Will Shine	£40	(1989)
BECK, JEFF	Plynth	£35	(1988)
BOLAN, MARC	Hot Love	£120	(1990)
BOWIE, DAVID	Golden Years (LP)	£95	(1987)
BOWIE, DAVID	Liza Jane/Louie Louie	£220	(1987)
BOWIE, DAVID	Love You Till Tuesday	£350	(1988)
BOWIE, DAVID	Up The Hill Backwards/Crystal Japan	£35	(1990)
DAVIS, SPENCER, & GR'M BOND	9 track audition	£180	(1989)
DYLAN, BOB	Got My Mind Made Up	£70	(1990)
FERRY AID	Let It Be	£55	(1988)
FURY, BILLY	Radio Luxembourg show	£260	(1990)
HALEY, BILL	Fool Such As I (US)	£100	(1989)
HARRIS, JET	Trouble In Mind/Banks Of The Ohio	£30	(1988)
HARRIS, JET	Worried Man Blues/untitled track	£30	(1988)
HIGH NUMBERS	Zoot Suit	£280	(1988)
HOLLY, BUDDY	Peggy Sue	£380	(1987)
HOT CHOCOLATE	Give Peace A Chance	£45	(1988)
JACKSON, MICHAEL	Bad	£220	(1989)
JOHN, ELTON	I Can't Go On Living Without You	£160	(1988)

JOHN, ELTON	Skyline Pigeon	£154	(1989)
JOHN, ELTON	Tide Will Turn For Rebecca	£250	(1988)
LENNON, JOHN	'Cold Turkey (US)	£150	(1988)
LENNON, JOHN	God Save Us	£600	(1982)
LENNON, JOHN	Happy Christmas (War Is Over)	£240	(1985)
LENNON, JOHN	Imagine	£600	(1987)
LENNON, JOHN	Love (alternate take)	£260	(1986)
MADONNA	True Blue	£65	(1989)
MARLEY, BOB	Jamming	£90	(1988)
MORTIMER	Dedicated Music Man (Apple)	£80	(1989)
ONO, YOKO	Open Your Box	£250	(1987)
PET SHOP BOYS	Always On My Mind	£100	(1989)
PINK FLOYD	Chapter Twenty-Four	£200	(1990)
PINK FLOYD	Money (alternate take)	£250	(1989)
PINK FLOYD	See Emily Play	£154	(1989)
PRESLEY, ELVIS	Good Rockin' Tonight (WHBZ Radio)	£3000	(1990)
PRESLEY, ELVIS	Heartbreak Hotel	£450	(1987)
PRESLEY, ELVIS	Heartbreak Hotel	£320	(1989)
PRESLEY, ELVIS	Suspicion/Girl Of My Best Friend	£60	(1988)
QUICKLY, TOMMY	Tip Of My Tongue	£55	(1989)
RICHARD, CLIFF	Breathless/Lawdy Miss Clawdy	£2800	(1985)
RICHARD, CLIFF	Breathless/Lawdy Miss Clawdy	£1000	(1986)
RICHARD, CLIFF	Deep Purple	£320	(1986)
RICHARD, CLIFF	Summer Holiday (1 sided LP)	£80	(1987)
RICHARD, CLIFF	Taxi Taxi Take Me To My Baby	£480	(1988)
RICHARD, CLIFF	Who's Gonna Take You Home/Let's Stick Together	£420	(1986)
ROLLING STONES	Angie/Silver Train	£55	(1988)
ROLLING STONES	Get Yer Ya-Yas Out	£520	(1988)
ROLLING STONES	Get Yer Ya-Yas Out (double LP)	£650	(1985)
ROLLING STONES	Road Runner/Diddley Daddy	£1500	(1988)
ROLLING STONES	Soon Forgotten/Close Together/Can't Judge A Book	£6000	(1988)
ROLLING STONES	Soon Forgotten/Close Together/Can't Judge A Book	£4000	(1989)
ROLLING STONES	You Can Make It	£140	(1988)
ROLLING STONES	You Can't Always Get What You Want	£140	(1988)
SEX PISTOLS	Anarchy In The UK	£95	(1985)
SEX PISTOLS	Anarchy In The UK	£120	(1987)
SEX PISTOLS	Anarchy In The UK	£240	(1987)
SEX PISTOLS	God Save The Queen	£170	(1987)
SEX PISTOLS	God Save The Queen	£85	(1988)
SEX PISTOLS	My Way	£220	(1987)
SEX PISTOLS	Pretty Vacant	£200	(1987)
SHADOWS	Savage (alternate take)	£220	(1988)
TOURISTS	Loneliest Man In The World	£32	(1989)
TOWNSHEND, PETE	Lazy Fat People	£250	(1985)
VINCENT, GENE	Temptation Baby	£75	(1989)
WHO	Tommy Live	£240	(1990)
YARDBIRDS	Certain Girl/I Wish You Would/Can't Judge A Book	£240	(1989)

OTHER ACETATES, OF UNRELEASED MATERIAL, KNOWN TO EXIST

AYERS, KEVIN,	Sing a song In The Morning (with Syd Barrett)
BEATLES	Bad To Me
BEATLES	Get Back (first single mix)
BEATLES	Get Back (LP)
BEATLES	Goodbye (Paul solo)
BEATLES	Hey Bulldog/ All Together Now
BEATLES	How Do You Do It
BEATLES	I Want You, I Need You
BEATLES	Let It Be (alternate take)
BEATLES	Love Me Do (audition)
BEATLES	Magical Mystery Tour (set of discs)
BEATLES	Not Guilty
BEATLES	Some Other Guy (Granada TV)
BEATLES	Some Other Guy (Hamburg)
BEATLES	Strawberry Fields Forever (take six)
BEATLES	Strawberry Fields Forever (take seven)
BEATLES	Taxman
BEATLES	That'll Be The Day/In Spite Of All The Danger (as Quarrymen)
BEATLES	Till There Was You/Hello Little Girl
BEATLES	You're Gonna Lose That Girl
BEATLES & WALLY	Fever
BEATLES & WALLY	Fever/Summertime
BOLAN, MARC	Chateau In Virginia Waters (hand-painted)
BOLAN, MARC	Road I'm On Gloria (as Toby Tyler)
BOWIE, DAVID	Rarities (compilation LP)
BUFFALO SPRINGFIELD	Bluebird (long version)
BUFFALO SPRINGFIELD	First LP alternate takes
DEEP PURPLE	Love Help Me (as Roundabout)
DYLAN, BOB	As It Is Before/Time And Again (demo)
DYLAN, BOB	Can You Please Crawl Out Your Window (longer version)
DYLAN, BOB	Celebration For A Passage Of Time (demo)
DYLAN, BOB	Death By Fire/To Care At All (demo)
DYLAN, BOB	Just A Little Glass Of Water
DYLAN, BOB	Lonesome Whistle Blues
DYLAN, BOB	Milk Cow Blues
DYLAN, BOB	Never Have Met
DYLAN, BOB	Phantom Engineer
DYLAN, BOB	Red Wing Reform School
DYLAN, BOB	When You Were Full Of Wonder/Mad Lydia's Waltz (demo)
DYLAN, BOB	Who Killed Davy Moore
DYLAN, BOB	You Gotta Go
FURY, BILLY	At This Stage (alternate take)
FURY, BILLY	Be Mine Tonight
FURY, BILLY	Communication/Bring It Back
FURY, BILLY	Devil Or Angel/Your Words
FURY, BILLY	Forget Him/Let Me Go Lover
FURY, BILLY	Hard Times
FURY, BILLY	Hurting All Over/Lovesick Blues + 3
FURY, BILLY	I Call For My Rose/You'll Break My Heart In Two
FURY, BILLY	I'll Be Your Sweetheart
FURY, BILLY	I'll Show You
FURY, BILLY	Love Or Money
FURY, BILLY	Please Love Me
FURY, BILLY	River And The Sun
FURY, BILLY	Will The Real Man Please Stand Up/The Stage
GENESIS	In The Beginning
GENESIS	Silver Song
GENESIS	Watcher Of The Skies
GOULDMAN, GRAHAM	Cry All Night
HACKETT, STEVE	Cell 151

HACKETT, STEVE	Cell 151/Time Lapse In Milton Keynes
HACKETT, STEVE	Walking Through Walls
HAWKWIND	Motorhead
HENDRIX, JIMI	14 track audition demo
HERMAN'S HERMITS	Wings Of Love/Big Man
HERMAN'S HERMITS	Train/Ride On The Water
JOEL, BILLY	Spring Harbor Is Cold (live LP)
JOHN, ELTON	In The Morning
JOHN, ELTON	Sarah's Coming Back
KINKS	You Still Want Me/You Do Something To Me (alternate takes)
LENNON, JOHN	Woman
LOMAX, JACKIE	How The Web Was Woven
LOMAX, JACKIE	Eagle Laughs At You
McCARTNEY, PAUL	The Man (with Michael Jackson)
OSBOURNE, OZZY	Crazy Train (live)
PINK FLOYD	Run Like Hell
RICHARD, CLIFF	Don't Bug Me Baby
ROLLING STONES	Ride On Baby
SEX PISTOLS	Belsen Was A Gas
SEX PISTOLS	Bodies
SEX PISTOLS	Did You No Wrong
SEX PISTOLS	EMI
SEX PISTOLS	God Save The Sex Pistols (LP)
SEX PISTOLS	Live At The Electric Circus (LP)
SEX PISTOLS	Seventeen
SLADE	Thanks For The Memory (original lyrics)
SPRINGSTEEN, BRUCE	Darkness On The Edge Of Town (US LP with Don't Look Back
SPRINGSTEEN, BRUCE	Greetings From Asbury..(US LP with Visitation at Fort Horn)
SPRINGSTEEN, BRUCE	River (US double LP with Help Up Without A Gun)
STEVENS, CAT	Hurt
YARDBIRDS	Boom Boom
YARDBIRDS	Goodnight Sweet Josephine (alternate take)

LABEL ABBREVIATIONS USED IN THIS BOOK

ABBREVIATION	LABEL
208 Luxem.	208 Luxembourg
ABC-Para	ABC-Paramount
Ace Of H.	Ace Of Hearts
Ad. In Reality	Adventures In Reality
All T. Madmen	All The Madmen
Alt. Tentacles	Alternative Tentacles
Amalgam.	Amalgamated
Am. Phonogram	American Phonogram
Angelic Up.	Angelic Upstarts
Ashes & Sands	Ashes And Sands
Audio Fid.	Audio Fidelity
Barking P.	Barking Pumpkin
Battle Of B.	Battle Of The Bands
Beggars B.	Beggars Banquet
Berry M.Co.	Berry Music Co.
Blanco Y.N.	Blanco Y Negro
Bludgeon Riff.	Bludgeon Riffola
Blue Mount.	Blue Mountain
Bristol Rec.	Bristol Recorder
B. Of Brains	Bucketful Of Brains
Bundestag	Bundestagrucksache
Cadet Conc.	Cadet Concept
Cameo Park.	Cameo Parkway
Castle Commu.	Castle Communications
Casual Ab.	Casual Abandon
Cause For C.	Cause For Concern
Charis/Vir	Charisma/Virgin
Chatham Sq.	Chatham Square
Chatta.	Chattahoochee
Chemical Im.	Chemical Imbalance
Chiltern Snd.	Chiltern Sound
C.C. Train	Choo Choo Train
Commu. Blur	Communication Blur
Contemp.	Contemporary
Con. Tapes	Conventional Tapes
Criminal D.	Criminal Damage
Custom Fid.	Custom Fidelity
Dead G.D.P.	Dead Good Dolly Platters
Dep Int.	Dep International
Deptford F.C.	Deptford Fun City
Deutsche G.	Deutsche Grammophon
Diamond A.	Diamond Age
Don't Fall Off...	Don't Fall Off The Mountain

Ecstatic P. . . . . Ecstatic Peace
Edinburgh S.C. . . . . Edinburgh Students Charity
Elektra/Met. . . . . Elektra/Metronome
Elstree S. . . . . Elstree Studios
Fast Prod. . . . . Fast Products
F. Dutchman . . . . Flying Dutchman
Forbidden F. . . . . Forbidden Fruit
F. Exposure . . . . Forced Exposure
For-Me-Not . . . . Forget-Me-Not
Genesis Publications . . . . Genesis Pub.
Ghetto R. . . . . Ghetto Rockers
GNP-Cres. . . . . GNP-Crescendo
Golden Guin. . . . . Golden Guinea
Gold Throat . . . . Golden Throat
G.T. Jazz . . . . Good Time Jazz
Good Vibs . . . . Good Vibrations
Graphic Snd. . . . . Graphic Sound
G. Truckers . . . . Greasy Truckers
H. Barbera . . . . Hanna Barbera
Hits & Corr. . . . . Hits & Corruption
H. Of Hits . . . . Home Of The Hits
Hook, L & S . . . . Hook, Line & Sinker
H. Of Dolls . . . . House Of Dolls
H. Of Snds . . . . House Of Sounds
Int. Allied . . . . International Allied
Int. Artists . . . . International Artists
Island/Trans. . . . . Island/Transatlantic
Isle Of L. . . . . Isle Of Light
JCP Rec. . . . . JCP Recording
Jet/United Art . . . . Jet/United Artists
Kaleid. Snd . . . . Kaleidoscope Sound
Keele Univ. . . . . Keele Univercity
Limited Ed. . . . . Limited Edition
Malicious D. . . . . Malicious Damage
Mark 56 Rec . . . . Mark 56 Records
Marks & Spen. . . . . Marks & Spencer
M. Melodies . . . . Massacred Melodies
Merciful Rel. . . . . Merciful Release
Mobile Fid. . . . . Mobile Fidelity
Mole Emb. . . . . Mole Embalming
Morgan B.T. . . . . Morgan Blue Town
Mnt. Vernon . . . . Mount Vernon
Music For N. . . . . Music For Nations
Music Is M. . . . . Music Is Medicine
N. Calypso . . . . National Calypso
N. Hormones . . . . New Hormones

N. Pleasures	New Pleasures
Ohio Rec. S.	Ohio Recording Service
One L.Ind.	One Little Indian
Original Snd.	Original Sound
O. Galaxie	Outer Galaxie
Parlo/Apple	Parlophone/Apple
Parta. M.	Partadiddle Music
Pav. In Splen.	Pavilioned In Splendour
Peckham A.G.	Peckham Action Group
P. Farthing	Penny Farthing
Phoenix F.	Phoenix Future
P. Elephant	Pink Elephant
Plastic F.	Plastic Fantastic
Pop Schall.	Pop Schallplaten
P. Exchange	Power Exchange
Press. Beat	Pressure Beat
Pr. Buster	Prince Buster
P. Stock	Private Stock
Radio Record	Radio Rec.
Raw TV Prod.	Raw TV Products
Reading R.R.	Reading Rag Record
Rec. Factory	Record Factory
Regal S.	Regal Starline
Regal Z.	Regal Zonophone
Rhythm O.L.	Rhythm Of Life
Ricordi Int.	Ricordi International
Rock T. House	Rock The House
Roll & Butt.	Roll & Butter
Rollin' D.	Rollin' Danny
R. Stones	Rolling Stones
S.F. Sound	San Francisco Sound
Scotti Bros.	Scotti Brothers
S. Immolation	Self Immolation
Sexual Ph.	Sexual Photography
Small Wond.	Small Wonder
Sordide S.	Sordide Sentimentale
S. Ceremony	Sound Ceremony
Snd. Of Ind.	Sound Of Industry
S.O. Leics.	Sound Of Leicester
Sound Rec.	Sound Recording
S.O. Hawaii	Sounds Of Hawaii
S. Circular	South Circular
Straight M.	Straight Music
Strang.Inf.S.	Stranglers Information Servic
Sudden D.	Sudden Death
Svensk Illum.	Svensk Illuminations

Syn. Chap. . . . . Syndicate Chapter
T. Motown . . . . Tamla Motown
Tetra Gramm . . . . Tetragrammaton
Texas Rev. . . . . Texas Revolution
Theatre Pros. . . . . Theatre Projects
3 Circles . . . . Three Circles
Throbbing G. . . . . Throbbing Gristle
Troll Kitch. . . . . Troll Kitchen
U. Impress. . . . . Underground Impressionios
Uni. S.L. . . . . Universal Spiritual League
W. Ulbricht . . . . Walter Ulbricht
W. Bros . . . . Warner Brothers
Wond. W.O. . . . . Wonderful World Of
Wooden N. . . . . Wooden Nickel
W. Artists . . . . World Artists
W. Pacific . . . . World Pacific
W. Rec. Club . . . . World Record Club
W.W.Artists . . . . World Wide Artists
Xciting P. . . . . Xciting Plastic

A

A - AUSTR

It is appropriate that the first record listed in this guide should be one that typifies exactly what collecting rare records is all about. Produced as a labour of love on an independent label created for the purpose, the record came complete with lavish packaging and sold hardly at all! The music, which is thoughtful and pastoral, is interesting enough to give the record a cult reputation, and the mystique is enhanced for record collectors today by the album being reissued in a very limited facsimile edition, itself being sold at something of a collectors' price.

Title	Format	Label	Number	Year	Price	Notes
A - Austr	LP	Holyground	113	1970	**£350**	

A CERTAIN RATIO

Title	Format	Label	Number	Year	Price	Notes
All Night Party	7"	Factory	FAC5	1979	**£5**	
Double 12"	12"	Factory	FAC42	1981	**£6**	export, double
Graveyard And The Ballroom	cass	Factory	FACT16	1980	**£10**	in orange purse, insert

A-HA

Title	Format	Label	Number	Year	Price	Notes
Cry Wolf	12"	W. Bros	W8500TP	1986	**£6**	pic disc
Hunting High And Low	12"	W. Bros	W6663TP	1986	**£6**	pic disc
Living Daylights	12"	W. Bros	W8305TP	1987	**£8**	pic disc
Sun Always Shines On TV	7"	W. Bros	W8846P	1986	**£8**	shaped pic disc
Take On Me	7"	W. Bros	W9006	1985	**£5**	black & white PS
Take On Me	7"	W. Bros	W9006	1985	**£5**	colour PS, booklet
Take On Me	7"	W. Bros	W9146	1984	**£10**	
Take On Me	12"	W. Bros	W9006T	1985	**£6**	black & white PS
Take On Me	12"	W. Bros	W9146T	1984	**£20**	
Train Of Thought	7"	W. Bros	W8736P	1986	**£8**	shaped pic disc

AARDVARK

Title	Format	Label	Number	Year	Price	Notes
Aardvark	LP	Nova	SDN17	1970	**£40**	

ABACUS

Title	Format	Label	Number	Year	Price	Notes
Abacus	LP	Polydor	2371215	1971	**£45**	
Everything You Need	LP	Zebra	2949002	1972	**£30**	German
Indian Dancer	7"	York	YR207	1973	**£8**	
Just A Day's Journey Away	LP	Polydor	2371270	1972	**£30**	
Midway	LP	Zebra	2949013	1974	**£30**	German

ABBA

Title	Format	Label	Number	Year	Price	Notes
Arrival	LP	Nautilus	NR20	1981	**£12**	US audiophile
Chiquitita (Spanish version)	7"	Vogue	45X1188	1978	**£5**	French
Estoy Sonando	7"	Vogue	101235	1979	**£5**	French
Lay All Your Love On Me	7"	Epic	EPCA1456DJ	1980	**£5**	1 sided promo
One Of Us	7"	Epic	EPCA1740	1981	**£4**	pic disc
Ring Ring	LP	Polar	POLS242	1973	**£10**	Swedish
Ring Ring	7"	Polar	POS1171	1973	**£10**	Swedish label & language
Ring Ring	7"	Polydor	2040105	1973	**£20**	sung in German
Singles, The First Ten Years	LP	Epic	ABBOX2	1983	**£20**	2 pic discs, boxed
Slipping Through My Fingers	7"	Discomate			**£30**	Japan Coca-Cola pic disc
Slipping Through My Fingers	12"	Discomate			**£45**	Japan Coca-Cola pic disc
Super Trouper	LP	Epic	ABBOX1	1980	**£15**	boxed, book, poster
Voulez Vous	LP	Epic	EPC86086	1979	**£50**	pic disc
Waterloo	7"	Polar	POS1186	1974	**£10**	Swedish label & language
Waterloo	7"	Polydor	2040116	1974	**£20**	sung in German
Waterloo	7"	Vogue	103104	1974	**£20**	sung in French
Winner Takes It All	12"	Epic	EPC138835	1980	**£10**	gatefold PS

ABBEY TAVERN SINGERS

Collectors of records on a particular label often find themselves buying albums or singles that are not at all to their taste! "We're Off To Dublin InThe Green" by the Abbey Tavern Singers is an LP of Irish pub songs that just happens to have been released on a subsidiary of Tamla Motown.

Title	Format	Label	Number	Year	Price	Notes
We're Off To Dublin In The Green	LP	VIP	VS402	1966	**£12**	US

ABBOTT, BILL & THE JEWELS

Title	Format	Label	Number	Year	Price	Notes
Groovy Baby	7"	Cameo Park	P874	1963	**£8**	

ABICAIR, SHIRLEY

In the quest to find increasingly rare grooves, some very strange artists become included within the domain of Northern Soul. Hence the unlikely inclusion here of Shirley Abicair, a lady who used to sing rather twee songs on Children's Television, to the accompaniment of a strummed autoharp.

Am I Losing You	7"	Piccadilly	7N35364	1967	**£5**	

ABRAHAMS, MICK

At Last	LP	Chrysalis	CHR1005	1972	**£15**	
Learning To Play Guitar With	LP	SRT	SRTM73313	1975	**£10**	
Mick Abrahams	LP	Chrysalis	ILPS9147	1971	**£15**	

ABSALOM, MIKE

Hector And Other Peccadillos	LP	Philips		1973	**£15**	
Mike Absalom	LP	Vertigo	6360053	1971	**£50**	spiral label
Save The Last Gherkin For Me	LP	Saydisc	SDL162	1969	**£20**	

ABSOLUTE ELSEWHERE

Earthbound	7"	W. Bros	K16697	1976	**£4**	
In Search Of Ancient Gods	LP	W. Bros	K56192	1976	**£10**	

AC/DC

Albert Archives	LP	Albert	APLP037	1979	**£15**	Australian
Can I Sit Next To You Girl	7"	Albert	AP10551	197-	**£10**	Australian
Danger	7"	Atlantic	A9532P	1985	**£6**	shaped pic disc
Danger	7"	Atlantic	A9532W	1985	**£4**	poster sleeve
Dirty Deeds Done Dirt Cheap	7"	Atlantic	K10899	1977	**£5**	
Flick Of The Switch Interview Album	LP	Atlantic	PR562	1983	**£15**	US promo
For Those About To Rock	12"	Atlantic	K11721T	1982	**£6**	
Girl's Got Rhythm	7"	Atlantic	K11406E	1979	**£10**	envelope sleeve
Girl's Got Rhythm	7"	Atlantic	SAM113	1979	**£10**	1 sided promo
Guns For Hire	7"	Atlantic	A9774P	1983	**£6**	shaped pic disc
Heatseeker	CD-s	Atlantic	A9136CD	1988	**£6**	
High Voltage	7"	Atlantic	K10860	1976	**£6**	PS
Highway To Hell	LP	Atlantic	K50628	1979	**£15**	test press, different cover
It's A Long Way To The Top	7"	Atlantic	K10745	1976	**£8**	
Jailbreak	7"	Atlantic	K10805	1976	**£15**	
Jailbreak	7"	Atlantic	K10805	1980	**£6**	
Japan Tour '81	LP	Atlantic	SAM155	1981	**£50**	promo pic disc
Let There Be Rock	7"	Atlantic	K11018	1977	**£4**	
Let's Get It Up	12"	Atlantic	K11706T	1982	**£6**	
Live From The Atlantic Studios	LP	Atlantic	LAAS001	1978	**£50**	US promo
Nervous Shakedown	cass-s	Atlantic	A9651C	1984	**£5**	
Nervous Shakedown	7"	Atlantic	A9651P	1984	**£6**	shaped pic disc
Rock'n'Roll Ain't Noise Pollution	12"	Atlantic	K11630T	1980	**£6**	
Rock'n'Roll Damnation	12"	Atlantic	K11142T	1978	**£8**	
Shake A Leg	7"	Atlantic	K11600	1979	**£20**	wrong A side
Shake Your Foundations	7"	Atlantic	A9474P	1986	**£6**	shaped pic disc
Whole Lotta Rosie	7"	Atlantic	K11207	1978	**£4**	
Whole Lotta Rosie	7"	Atlantic	K11207	1980	**£4**	
Whole Lotta Rosie	12"	Atlantic	K11207T	1978	**£15**	

ACADEMY

Pop Lore According To	LP	Morgan B.T.	5001	1969	**£50**	
Rachel's Dream	7"	Morgan B.T.	BTS2	1969	**£12**	

ACCENT

Red Sky At Night	7"	Decca	F12679	1967	**£40**	

ACCENTS

Wiggle Wiggle	7"	Coral	Q72351	1959	**£8**	

ACCIDENTS

Blood Spattered With Guitars	7"	Hook, L. & S.	HOOK1	1980	**£4**	

ACCOLADE

Accolade 1	LP	Columbia	SCX6405	1970	**£20**	
Accolade 2	LP	Regal Z.	SLRZ1024	1971	**£20**	
Natural Day	7"	Columbia	DB8688	1970	**£8**	

ACE, BUDDY

Buddy Ace	7" EP	Vocalion	VEP170164	1965	**£12**	

Got To Get Myself Together	7"	Action	ACT4504	1968	**£4**	
Got To Get Myself Together	7"	Action	ACT4504	1968	**£12**	demo

ACE, JOHNNY

Johnny Ace	7" EP	Vogue	VE170150	1962	**£20**	
Memorial Album	LP	Duke	DLP71	1956	**£75**	US
Memorial Album	LP-10"	Duke	DLP70	1955	**£200**	US
Pledging My Love	7"	Vogue	V9180	1961	**£15**	

ACE, RICHARD

Don't Let The Sun Catch You Crying	7"	Coxsone	CS7031	196-	**£10**	
Hang 'Em High	7"	Trojan	TR654	1969	**£6**	
I Need You	7"	Studio One	SO2022	196-	**£10**	
More Reggae	7"	Studio One	SO2072	196-	**£10**	

ACES

But Say It Isn't So	7"	Parlophone	R5108	1964	**£6**	
Wait Till Tomorrow	7"	Parlophone	R5094	1963	**£6**	

ACES (2)

One Way Street	7"	Etc.	ETC1	1982	**£6**	

ACHES & PAINS

Again And Again	7"	Page One	POF008	1966	**£4**	

ACID GALLERY

Dance Around The Maypole	7"	CBS	4608	1969	**£20**	

ACKLES, DAVID

If the musical worth of a record had any bearing on its value as a collectors' item, then "American Gothic" by David Ackles would be one of the most valuable records of all. Ackles is a singer-songwriter, but he is also an arranger of skill and considerable imagination. Every track on "American Gothic is memorable, while the lengthy "Montana", with its echoes of Aaron Copland, is little short of a masterpiece. The album is produced by Bernie Taupin, as it happens.

American Gothic	LP	Elektra	K42112	1972	**£10**	
David Ackles	LP	Elektra	EKS74002	1968	**£20**	
Down River	7"	Elektra	EKSN45039	1968	**£4**	
Five and Dime	LP	CBS	32466	1973	**£15**	US
Laissez Faire	7"	Elektra	EKSN45054	1969	**£4**	
Subway To The Country	LP	Elektra	EKS74060	1970	**£20**	
Subway To The Country	7"	Elektra	EKSN45079	1969	**£4**	

ACKLIN, BARBARA

Am I The Same Girl	7"	MCA	MU1071	1969	**£4**	
Love Makes A Woman	7"	MCA	MU1038	1968	**£4**	

ACKLIN, BARBARA & GENE CHANDLER

Little Green Apples	7"	MCA/Soul Bag	BAG1	1969	**£4**	

ACT

Absolutely Immune	12"	ZTT	VIMM1	1987	**£10**	
I Can't Escape From You	CD-s	ZTT	CDIMM2	1987	**£6**	
I Can't Escape From You	cass-s	ZTT	VIMM2	1987	**£5**	
Snobbery And Decay	CD-s	ZTT	ZCID28	1987	**£6**	
Snobbery And Decay	cass-s	ZTT	CTIS28	1987	**£6**	
Snobbery And Decay	12"	ZTT	12XACT28	1987	**£12**	
Snobbery And Decay	12"	ZTT	12ZACT28	1987	**£6**	gatefold sleeve
Snobbery And Decay	12"	ZTT	CT01	1987	**£20**	promo

ACT (2)

Cobbled Streets	7"	Columbia	DB8179	1967	**£6**	
Here Come Those Tears	7"	Columbia	DB8261	1967	**£8**	
Just A Little Bit	7"	Columbia	DB8331	1968	**£5**	

ACTION

The Action were a mod group with a similar soul/R&B sound to the Who, except that, according to those who saw the group live, the Action were better. Not that this is particularly apparent from the group's records, which are, for the most part, worthy cover versions, but lacking the extra spark of star quality. Sadly, the Action never did get to make an album.

Baby You've Got It	7"	Parlophone	R5474	1966	**£15**	
Harlem Shuffle	7"	Hansa	14321AT	1968	**£20**	German
I'll Keep On Holding On	7"	Parlophone	R5410	1966	**£12**	
Land Of 1000 Dances	7"	Parlophone	R5354	1965	**£12**	
Never Ever	7"	Parlophone	R5572	1967	**£12**	

Title	Format	Label	Number	Year	Price	Notes
Shadows And Reflections	7"	Parlophone	R5610	1967	**£15**	

ACTIVE RESTRAINT

Title	Format	Label	Number	Year	Price	Notes
Terror In My Home	7"	Sticky	PEELOFF3	1983	**£8**	

ACTRESS

Title	Format	Label	Number	Year	Price	Notes
Good Job With Prospects	7"	CBS	4016	1969	**£20**	

ACUFF, ROY

Title	Format	Label	Number	Year	Price	Notes
Favorite Hymns	LP	MGM	E3707	1958	**£12**	US
Old Time Barn Music	LP-10"	Columbia	CL9010	195-	**£20**	US
Songs Of The Smokey Mountains	LP	Capitol	T617	1955	**£12**	US
Songs Of The Smokey Mountains	LP-10"	Columbia	CL9004	195-	**£20**	US

AD CONSPIRACY

Title	Format	Label	Number	Year	Price	Notes
Ad Conspiracy	LP	Diamond A.		1979	**£20**	

ADAM & THE ANTS

Title	Format	Label	Number	Year	Price	Notes
A.N.T.S.	7"	Lyntone	LYN9285	1981	**£4**	Flexipop flexi
Antrap	7"	CBS	A111738	1981	**£4**	pic disc
Antrap	7"	CBS	A1738	1981	**£4**	advent calendar PS
Zerox	7"	Do-It	DUN8	1979	**£5**	MP B side plays 'Physical'

ADAM'S APPLES

Title	Format	Label	Number	Year	Price	Notes
Don't Take It Out On This World	7"	Brunswick	BR42	1977	**£4**	

ADAM, MIKE & TIM

Title	Format	Label	Number	Year	Price	Notes
Flowers On The Wall	7"	Columbia	DB7836	1966	**£4**	
Little Baby	7"	Decca	F12040	1964	**£4**	
Little Pictures	7"	Decca	F12221	1965	**£4**	
Most Peculiar Man	7"	Columbia	DB7902	1966	**£4**	
That's How I Feel	7"	Decca	F12112	1965	**£4**	

ADAMS, ARTHUR K.

Title	Format	Label	Number	Year	Price	Notes
She Drives Me Out Of My Mind	7"	Blue Horizon	573136	1968	**£10**	

ADAMS, FAYE

Title	Format	Label	Number	Year	Price	Notes
I'll Be True	7"	London	HLU8339	1956	**£30**	
Shake A Hand	LP	Warwick	2031	1961	**£40**	US

ADAMS, GLADSTON

Title	Format	Label	Number	Year	Price	Notes
Dollars And Cents	7"	Trojan	TR659	1969	**£6**	

ADAMS, GLEN

Title	Format	Label	Number	Year	Price	Notes
Hold Down Miss Winey	7"	Island	WI3100	1967	**£8**	
Rent Too High	7"	Trojan	TR621	1969	**£6**	
She	7"	Island	WI3083	1967	**£8**	
She Is Leaving	7"	Blue Cat	BS126	1968	**£10**	
She Is So Fine	7"	Island	WI3120	1967	**£8**	
Silent Lover	7"	Island	WI3072	1967	**£8**	

ADAMS, JOHNNY

Title	Format	Label	Number	Year	Price	Notes
Come On	7"	Top Rank	JAR192	1959	**£4**	
Reconsider Me	7"	Polydor	56775	1969	**£8**	

ADAMS, LLOYD

Title	Format	Label	Number	Year	Price	Notes
I Wish Your Picture Was You	7"	Blue Beat	BB366	1965	**£10**	

ADAMS, MARIE

Title	Format	Label	Number	Year	Price	Notes
What Do You Want To...	7"	Capitol	CL14963	1958	**£5**	

ADAMS, RITCHIE

Title	Format	Label	Number	Year	Price	Notes
Back To School	7"	London	HLU9200	1960	**£6**	

ADAMS, WOODROW

Title	Format	Label	Number	Year	Price	Notes
Baby You Just Don't Know	7"	Blue Horizon	451001	1965	**£20**	

ADDERLEY, CANNONBALL

Title	Format	Label	Number	Year	Price	Notes
Mercy Mercy Mercy	7"	Capitol	CL15489	1967	**£4**	
Why (Am I Treated So Bad)	7"	Capitol	CL15500	1967	**£5**	

ADDICTS

Title	Format	Label	Number	Year	Price	Notes
Here She Comes	7"	Decca	F11902	1964	**£5**	

ADDICTS (2)

Title	Format	Label	Cat. No.	Year	Price	Notes
Bad Boy	7"	Razor	RZLP104	1983	**£5**	pic disc
Lunch With The Addicts	7"	Dining Out	TUX1	1981	**£10**	

ADENO, BOBBY

Title	Format	Label	Cat. No.	Year	Price	Notes
Hands Of Time	7"	Vocalion	VP9279	1966	**£8**	

ADLIBS

Title	Format	Label	Cat. No.	Year	Price	Notes
Boy From New York City	7"	Red Bird	RB10102	1966	**£8**	
Giving Up	7"	Deep Soul	DS9102	1970	**£4**	
Neighbour Neighbour	7"	Fontana	TF584	1965	**£4**	

ADMIRALS

Title	Format	Label	Cat. No.	Year	Price	Notes
Promised Land	7"	Fontana	TF597	1965	**£25**	

ADRIAN & THE SUNSETS

Title	Format	Label	Cat. No.	Year	Price	Notes
Breakthrough	LP	Sunset	63601	1963	**£30**	US
Breakthrough	LP	Sunset	63601	1963	**£50**	US, multi-coloured vinyl

ADVERTS

Title	Format	Label	Cat. No.	Year	Price	Notes
Crossing The Red Sea	LP	Bright	BRL201	1978	**£10**	Chart LP
Crossing The Red Sea	LP	Bright	BRL201	1978	**£25**	red vinyl
Crossing The Red Sea	LP	Butt	ALSO002	1981	**£12**	red vinyl
Gary Gilmore's Eyes	7"	Anchor	ANC1043	1977	**£6**	chart single
One Chord Wonders	7"	Stiff	BUY13	1977	**£6**	
Safety In Numbers	7"	Anchor	ANC1047	1977	**£4**	

ADVOCATES

Title	Format	Label	Cat. No.	Year	Price	Notes
Advocates	LP	Dovetail		1973	**£30**	

AEROSMITH

Title	Format	Label	Cat. No.	Year	Price	Notes
Draw The Line	7"	CBS	AS2	1977	**£5**	promo
Dream On	7"	CBS	4000DJ	1976	**£5**	promo
Get Your Wings	LP	Columbia	KCQ32847	1974	**£15**	US quad
Rats In The Cellar	7"	CBS	AS1	1976	**£6**	promo
Rocks	LP	Columbia	PCQ34165	1976	**£15**	US quad
Toys In The Attic	LP	Columbia	JCQ33479	1975	**£15**	US quad

AESOPS FABLE

Title	Format	Label	Cat. No.	Year	Price	Notes
In Due Time	LP	Cadet Conc.	LPS323	1969	**£20**	US

AFEX

Title	Format	Label	Cat. No.	Year	Price	Notes
She Got The Time	7"	King	KG1058	196-	**£15**	

AFFINITY

Title	Format	Label	Cat. No.	Year	Price	Notes
Affinity	LP	Vertigo	6360004	1970	**£40**	spiral label
Eli's Comin'	7"	Vertigo	6059018	1970	**£10**	

AFO EXECUTIVES

Title	Format	Label	Cat. No.	Year	Price	Notes
Compendium	LP	AFO	LP0002		**£75**	US

AFRICAN BEAVERS

Title	Format	Label	Cat. No.	Year	Price	Notes
Find My Baby	7"	RCA	RCA1447	1965	**£4**	

AFRICAN MESSENGERS

Title	Format	Label	Cat. No.	Year	Price	Notes
High Life Piccadilly	7"	Page One	POF043	1967	**£4**	
Niger Blues	7"	Carnival	CV7021	1965	**£4**	

AFROTONES

Title	Format	Label	Cat. No.	Year	Price	Notes
All For One	7"	High Note	HS23	196-	**£8**	
Freedom Sound	7"	Duke	DU19	196-	**£8**	
Things I Love	7"	Trojan	TR655	1969	**£6**	

AFTER TEA

Title	Format	Label	Cat. No.	Year	Price	Notes
After Tea	LP	Ace Of Clubs	ACL1251	1967	**£15**	

AFTER THE FIRE

Title	Format	Label	Cat. No.	Year	Price	Notes
80F	7"	Epic	XPR104	1980	**£6**	promo
Batteries Not Included	LP	CBS	85135	1982	**£10**	
Love Will Always Make You Cry	7"	Epic	EPC8394	1980	**£6**	
One Rule For You	7"	CBS	7205	1979	**£4**	red vinyl
Signs Of Change	LP	Rapid	RR001	1978	**£20**	

AFTERSHAVE

Title	Format	Label	Cat. No.	Year	Price	Notes
Skin Deep	LP	Splendid		1972	**£120**	gatefold sleeve

AGGREGATION

Title	Format	Label	Cat. No.	Year	Price	Notes
Mind Odyssey	LP	L.H.I.	12008	1967	**£40**	US

AGINCOURT

Title	Format	Label	Cat. No.	Year	Price	Notes
Fly Away	LP	Merlin		1970	**£600**	

AGITATION FREE

Title	Format	Label	Cat. No.	Year	Price	Notes
Malesch	LP	Vertigo	6360607	1972	**£10**	
Second Album	LP	Vertigo	6360615	1973	**£10**	

AGNES STRANGE

Title	Format	Label	Cat. No.	Year	Price	Notes
Clever Fool	7"	Birds Nest	BN1	1975	**£10**	
Strange Flavour	LP	Birdsnest	BRL9000	1975	**£40**	

AIRFORCE

Airforce was put together by Ginger Baker as the archetypal supergroup.Graham Bond, Denny Laine, Steve Winwood, Harold McNair, Rick Grech, and Chris Wood rubbed shoulders within a big band - and achieved very much less than their talents might suggest they should have.

Title	Format	Label	Cat. No.	Year	Price	Notes
Airforce 1	LP	Polydor	2662001	1970	**£20**	double
Airforce 2	LP	Polydor	2383029	1970	**£12**	Chart LP
Man Of Constant Sorrow	7"	Polydor	56380	1970	**£4**	

AIRTO

Airto Moreira is a Brazilian percussionist who was a vital part of the Miles Davis band that virtually invented fusion music in 1969-70. His own records present an immensely appealing, danceable form of jazz, in which many of the key names of the genre are also involved - most notably Airto's singing wife, Flora Purim.

Title	Format	Label	Cat. No.	Year	Price	Notes
Branches	7"	CTI	CTS4003	1973	**£4**	
Fingers	LP	CTI	CTI18	1973	**£10**	
Free	LP	CTI	6020	1972	**£10**	US
In Concert	LP	CTI	CTI21	1974	**£10**	
Seeds To The Ground	LP	Polydor	2310040	1972	**£12**	
Virgin Land	LP	CTI	CTI23	1974	**£10**	

AITKEN, BOBBY

Title	Format	Label	Cat. No.	Year	Price	Notes
Keep On Pushing	7"	Doctor Bird	DB1071	1967	**£10**	
Kiss Bam Bam	7"	Island	WI3028	1967	**£8**	
Shame And Scandal	7"	Blue Beat	BB369	1965	**£10**	
Sweets For My Sweet	7"	Doctor Bird	DB1077	1967	**£10**	
Thunderball	7"	Ska Beat	JB252	1966	**£10**	
What A Fool	7"	Giant	GN11	1967	**£8**	

AITKEN, LAUREL

Title	Format	Label	Cat. No.	Year	Price	Notes
Aitken's Boogie	7"	Kalypso	XX16	1962	**£8**	
Avengers	7"	Unity	UN506	1969	**£6**	
Baby Don't Do It	7"	Rio	R92	196-	**£8**	
Bad Minded Woman	7"	Rio	R13	196-	**£8**	
Be Mine	7"	Columbia	DB7280	1964	**£8**	
Bewildered And Blue	7"	Rainbow	RAI106	196-	**£8**	
Boogie In My Bones	7"	Island	WI198	1965	**£8**	
Boogie In My Bones	7"	Starlite	ST45011	1960	**£8**	
Boogie Rock	7"	Blue Beat	BB1	1960	**£10**	
Clementine	7"	Blue Beat	BB340	1965	**£10**	
Drinking Whisky	7"	Starlite	ST45014	1960	**£8**	
Fire In Your Wire	7"	Doctor Bird	DB1187	196-	**£10**	
For Sentimental Reasons	7"	Fab	FAB45	196-	**£8**	
Green Banana	7"	Ska Beat	JB239	1966	**£10**	
Hailie Selasie	7"	New Beat	NB032	1968	**£8**	
How Can I Forget You	7"	Island	WI252	1965	**£8**	
How Can I Forget You	7"	Rio	R91	196-	**£8**	
I'm Still In Love With You Girl	7"	Columbia	DB106	1967	**£8**	
Jamaica	7"	Dice	CC28	1964	**£8**	
Jamboree	7"	Ska Beat	JB232	1966	**£10**	
Last Night	7"	Rainbow	RAI101	196-	**£8**	
Lawd Doctor	7"	New Beat	NB033	1968	**£8**	
Leave Me Standing	7"	Rio	R36	196-	**£8**	
Love Me Baby	7"	Starlite	ST45034	1961	**£8**	
Low Down Dirty Girl	7"	Duke	DK1002	1963	**£8**	
Mabel	7"	Dice	CC1	1962	**£8**	

Title	Format	Label	Cat. No.	Year	Price	Notes
Marylee	7"	Melodisc	1570	196-	**£8**	
Mash Potato Boogie	7"	Blue Beat	BB40	1961	**£10**	
Nebuchnezer	7"	Kalypso	XX15	196-	**£8**	
Never You Hurt	7"	Fab	FAB5	196-	**£8**	
Nursery Rhyme Boogie	7"	Blue Beat	BB52	1961	**£10**	
Pretty Face	7"	Columbia	DB8914	1972	**£4**	
Propaganda	7"	Ska Beat	JB236	1966	**£10**	
Pussy Price	7"	New Beat	NB046	1968	**£8**	
Railroad Track	7"	Blue Beat	BB22	1961	**£10**	
Revival	7"	Rio	R99	196-	**£8**	
Rise And Fall	7"	Doctor Bird	DB1197	196-	**£10**	
Rock Steady	7"	Columbia	DB102	1967	**£8**	
Run Powell Run	7"	New Beat	NB035	1968	**£8**	
Seven Lonely Nights	7"	Rio	R60	196-	**£8**	
Suffering Still	7"	New Beat	NB025	1969	**£8**	
Sweet Precious Love	7"	Rainbow	RAI111	196-	**£8**	
Tribute To Collie Smith	7"	Kalypso	XX19	196-	**£8**	
We Shall Overcome	7"	Rio	R97	196-	**£8**	
Weary Wanderer	7"	Blue Beat	BB142	1962	**£10**	
Woppi King	7"	New Beat	NB024	1968	**£8**	
You Left Me Standing	7"	Dice	CC31	1965	**£8**	

AKENS, JEWEL

Title	Format	Label	Cat. No.	Year	Price	Notes
Birds And The Bees	LP	London	HAN8234	1965	**£10**	
Birds And The Bees	7"	London	HLN9954	1965	**£4**	chart single
Dancing Jenny	7"	Ember	EMBS219	1966	**£6**	
Georgie Porgie	7"	London	HLN9969	1965	**£4**	

AKRYLYKZ

Title	Format	Label	Cat. No.	Year	Price	Notes
Spyderman	7"	Red Rhino	RED2	1980	**£5**	

AL & THE VIBRATORS

Title	Format	Label	Cat. No.	Year	Price	Notes
Move Up	7"	Doctor Bird	DB1085	1967	**£10**	
Move Up Calypso	7"	High Note	HS007	196-	**£8**	

AL, ROLANDO & THE SOUL BROTHERS

Title	Format	Label	Cat. No.	Year	Price	Notes
Doctor Ring A Ding	7"	Doctor Bird	DB1023	1966	**£10**	
From Russia With Love	7"	Doctor Bird	DB1010	1966	**£10**	
I Love You	7"	Doctor Bird	DB1035	1966	**£10**	
Phoenix City	7"	Doctor Bird	DB1020	1966	**£10**	
Sufferer's Choice	7"	Doctor Bird	DB1011	1966	**£10**	
Sugar And Spice	7"	Doctor Bird	DB1017	1966	**£10**	
VC10	7"	Doctor Bird	DB1008	1966	**£10**	

ALAIMO, STEVE

Title	Format	Label	Cat. No.	Year	Price	Notes
Everyday I Have To Cry	7"	Pye	7N25174	1963	**£15**	
So Much Love	7"	HMV	POP1531	1966	**£4**	

ALARM

Title	Format	Label	Cat. No.	Year	Price	Notes
Absolute Reality	7"	IRS	ALARMD1	1985	**£6**	double
Deceiver	7"	IRS	IRS103	1984	**£5**	clear vinyl
Deceiver	7"	IRS	IRS103	1984	**£50**	mustard vinyl
Deceiver	7"	IRS	IRSD103	1984	**£12**	double
Knife Edge	7"	IRS	IRMD112	1986	**£5**	double
Marching On	7"	IRS	ILS0032	1982	**£15**	
Rain In The Summertime	CD-s	IRS	DIRM144	1987	**£20**	promo
Spirit Of '76	12"	IRS	IRMTD109	1986	**£6**	double
Stand	7"	IRS	PFP1014	1983	**£4**	
Stand	12"	IRS	PFPX1014	1983	**£6**	
Strength	7"	IRS	IPM104	1985	**£4**	poster sleeve
Unsafe Buildings	7"	White Cross	001	1981	**£60**	gatefold PS

ALBERT, EDDIE

Title	Format	Label	Cat. No.	Year	Price	Notes
Come Pretty Little Girl	7"	London	HL8136	1955	**£6**	

ALBERT, EDDIE & SANDRA LEE

Title	Format	Label	Cat. No.	Year	Price	Notes
Jenny Kissed Me	7"	London	HLU8241	1956	**£6**	

ALBERTO Y LOS TRIOS PARANOIAS

Title	Format	Label	Cat. No.	Year	Price	Notes
Snuff Rock	7"	Stiff	LAST2	1977	**£6**	
Snuff Rock	12"	Stiff	LAST2	1977	**£10**	promo

ALBION BAND
Battle Of The Field .... LP .... Island .... HELP25 .... 1976 ...... **£10** ....

ALCAPONE, DENNIS
Belch It Off .... 7" .... Pyramid .... PYR7008 .... 1973 .... **£4** ....
Cassius Clay .... 7" .... Jackpot .... JP808 .... 197- .... **£4** ....
Musical Alphabet .... 7" .... Bread .... BR1121 .... 1973 .... **£4** ....
Ripe Cherry .... 7" .... Dynamic .... DYN422 .... 197- .... **£4** ....

ALDO, STEVE
Can I Get A Witness .... 7" .... Decca .... F12041 .... 1964 .... **£6** ....
Everybody Has To Cry .... 7" .... Parlophone ..... R5432 .... 1966 .... **£8** ....

ALEXANDER'S TIMELESS BLOOZBAND
Alexander's Timeless Bloozband .... LP .... Smack .... 1001 .... 1967 ...... **£65** .... US

ALEXANDER, ARTHUR
Alexander The Great .... 7" EP .... London .... RED1364 .... 1963 ...... **£10** ....
Anna .... 7" .... London .... HLD9641 .... 1962 .... **£6** ....
Black Night .... 7" .... London .... HLD9899 .... 1964 .... **£6** ....
For You .... 7" .... London .... HLU10023 .... 1966 .... **£6** ....
Go Home Girl .... 7" .... London .... HLD9667 .... 1963 .... **£6** ....
Soldier Of Love .... 7" EP .... London .... RED1401 .... 1963 ...... **£10** ....
Soldier Of Love .... 7" .... London .... HLD9566 .... 1962 .... **£6** ....
You Better Move On .... LP .... London .... HAD2457 .... 1962 ...... **£20** ....
You Better Move On .... 7" .... London .... HLD9523 .... 1962 .... **£6** ....

ALFIE & HARRY
Trouble With Harry .... 7" .... London .... HLU8242 .... 1956 .... **£6** .... chart single

ALFORD, CLEM
Electronic Sitar Of... .... LP .... Columbia .... 1974 ...... **£30** ....

ALFRED & MELMOTH
I Want Someone .... 7" .... Island .... WI3130 .... 1967 .... **£8** ....

ALFRED, SANDRA
Rocket And Roll .... 7" .... Oriole .... CB1408 .... 1958 .... **£4** ....

ALIEN SEX FIEND
Dead And Buried .... 7" .... Anagram .... EANA23 .... 1984 .... **£4** .... pic disc
Ignore The Machine .... 7" .... Anagram .... PANA11 .... 1985 .... **£4** .... pic disc

ALKATRAZ
Doing A Moonlight .... LP .... Rockfield .... UAS30001 .... 1976 ...... **£10** ....

ALL ABOUT EVE
All About Eve .... 12" .... Mercury .... MERH119 .... 1988 ...... **£15** ...... 4 track promo sampler
Ballads .... CD-s .... Mercury .... EVCDJ8 .... 1988 ...... **£10** .... promo
D For Desire .... 12" .... Eden .... EDEN1 .... 1985 ...... **£60** ....
December (edited) .... 7" .... Mercury .... EVNDJ11 .... 1989 .... **£8** .... promo
December (Narnia Mix) .... 10" .... Mercury .... EVENB11 .... 1989 .... **£6** .... with poster
December .... 7" .... Eden .... EVENP11 .... 1989 .... **£4** .... pic disc
December .... cass-s .. Mercury .... EVEMC11 .... 1989 .... **£8** .... with badge
Every Angel .... 7" .... Eden .... EVENG7 .... 1988 .... **£6** .... gatefold PS
Every Angel .... 10" .... Mercury .... EVEN710 .... 1988 ...... **£10** .... boxed with poster
Flowers In Our Hair (edited) .... 7" .... Eden .... EVENDJ4 .... 1987 ...... **£10** .... promo
Flowers In Our Hair .... 7" .... Eden .... EVEN4 .... 1987 ...... **£12** ....
Flowers In Our Hair .... 12" .... Eden .... EVENX4 .... 1987 ...... **£12** ....
Flowers In Our Hair .... 12" .... Mercury .... EVEN112 .... 1988 ...... **£10** 1 sided promo LP sampler
In The Clouds .... 12" .... Eden .... EDEN2 .... 1986 ...... **£25** ....
In The Clouds .... 12" .... Eden .... EDEN2 .... 1986 ...... **£40** .... with poster
In The Clouds .... 7" .... Mercury .... EVEN5 .... 1987 .... **£8** ....
In The Clouds .... 7" .... Mercury .... EVENP5 .... 1987 ...... **£15** .... with poster
n The Clouds .... 12" .... Mercury .... EVENX5 .... 1987 ...... **£12** ....
Martha's Harbour .... cass-s .. Mercury .... EVENM8 .... 1988 .... **£8** ....
Martha's Harbour .... 12" .... Mercury .... EVNXB8 .... 1988 ...... **£15** .... boxed with poster
Martha's Harbour .... 12" .... Mercury .... EVNXB8 .... 1988 ...... **£25** ..... as above, autographed
Our Summer .... 7" .... Eden .... EVEN3 .... 1987 ...... **£12** ....
Our Summer .... 12" .... Eden .... EVENX3 .... 1987 ...... **£20** ....
Road To Your Soul (edited) .... 7" .... Mercury .... EVNDJ10 .... 1989 .... **£6** .... promo
Road To Your Soul .... CD-s .... Mercury .... EVCDX10 .... 1989 .... **£6** .... in wallet

Road To Your Soul	12"	Mercury	EVENXP10	1989	**£6**	with print
Scarlet (Live)	12"	Mercury	EVENXL12	1990	**£6**	gatefold PS, with poster
What Kind Of Fool (Autumn Rhapsody)	12"	Mercury	EVENXB9	1988	**£8**	boxed with poster
What Kind Of Fool (Synthesis Mix)	12"	Mercury	EVENX99	1988	**£8**	
What Kind Of Fool	CD-s	Mercury	EVNCD99	1988	**£10**	envelope pack with cards
What Kind Of Fool	10"	Mercury	EVEN910	1988	**£8**	gatefold PS, with booklet
Wild Hearted Woman	12"	Mercury	EVENX622	1988	**£15**	boxed, with badge
Wild Hearted Woman	12"	Mercury	EVENX6	1988	**£6**	

ALL DAY

York Pop Music Project	LP	private		1973	**£300**	

ALLEN & MILTON

It Is I	7"	Blue Beat	BB348	1965	**£10**	
Someone Like You	7"	Blue Beat	BB353	1965	**£10**	

ALLEN, ANNISTEEN

Don't Nobody Move	7"	Brunswick	05639	1957	**£6**	
Fujiyama Mama	7"	Capitol	CL14264	1955	**£6**	

ALLEN, DAEVID

Banana Moon	LP	Caroline	C1512	1975	**£10**	
Good Morning	LP	Virgin	V2054	1976	**£15**	
It's The Time Of Your Life	7"	Virgin	VS123	1975	**£10**	promo

ALLEN, DAVE

Color Blind	LP	Int. Artists	IALP11	1969	**£20**	US
Good Earth	7"	Philips	BF1748	1969	**£4**	

ALLEN, DEAN

Ooh Ooh Baby Baby	7"	London	HLM8698	1958	**£8**	

ALLEN, LEE

Cat Walk	7"	Top Rank	JAR265	1960	**£5**	
Sweet Beat	7" EP	Top Rank	JKR8007	1959	**£15**	
Walking With Mr.Lee	LP	Ember	ELP200	1958	**£75**	US
Walking With Mr.Lee	7"	HMV	POP452	1958	**£15**	
Walking With Mr.Lee	7" EP	Top Rank	JKR8020	1959	**£15**	

ALLEN, MAURICE

Oooh Baby	7"	Pye	7N15128	1958	**£4**	

ALLEN, REX

This Ole House	7"	Brunswick	05341	1954	**£10**	

ALLEY CATS

Snap Crackle And Pop	7"	Vogue	V9155	1959	**£5**	

ALLISON, GENE

Hey Hey I Love You	7"	London	HLU8605	1958	**£20**	

ALLISON, MOSE

Baby Please Don't Go	7"	Fontana	H292	1961	**£4**	
I Love The Life I Live	7"	Columbia	DB7330	1964	**£4**	

ALLISONS

Allisons	7" EP	Fontana	TFE17339	1961	**£6**	
Are You Sure	LP	Fontana	TFL5135	1961	**£10**	
Are You Sure	7"	Fontana	H294	1961	**£4**	chart single
Lessons In Love	7"	Fontana	H362	1962	**£4**	chart single
Words	7"	Fontana	H304	1961	**£4**	chart single

ALLMAN BROTHERS BAND

Allman Brothers Band	LP	Capricorn	228033	1969	**£10**	
Black Hearted Woman	7"	Atco	226013	1970	**£4**	
Brothers And Sisters	LP	Capricorn	2429102	1973	**£10**	Chart LP
Eat A Peach	LP	Capricorn	CP40102	1972	**£20**	US quad
Eat A Peach	LP	Capricorn	K67501	1972	**£12**	double
Eat A Peach	LP	Mobile Fid.	MFSL2157	1983	**£20**	US audiophile
Idlewind South	LP	Capricorn	2400032	1970	**£10**	
Jessica	7"	Capricorn	2089006	1974	**£4**	
Live At Fillmore East	LP	Capricorn	2659005	1971	**£12**	double

Midnight Rider	7"	Atlantic	2091070	1971	**£4**	
Revival	7"	Atlantic	2091040	1970	**£4**	

ALLMAN JOYS

Allman Joys	LP	Mercury	6398005	1973	**£20**	

ALLMAN, DUANE

Anthology	LP	Capricorn	K67502	1972	**£12**	double
Anthology Vol.2	LP	Capricorn	2659037	1974	**£12**	double

ALLSUP, TOMMY

Buddy Holly Songbook	LP	Reprise	R6182	1965	**£25**	US

ALMOND LETTUCE

Magic Circle	7"	Philips	BF1764	1969	**£4**	
Tree Dog Song	7"	Columbia	DB8442	1968	**£4**	

ALMOND, JOHNNY

Decca, forever branded as the label that turned down the Beatles, spent the rest of the sixties signing up potential stars in such numbers that few could be promoted properly (with a handful of notable exceptions, such as the Rolling Stones). Decca let Genesis go after only one album, and It was the same story with their subsidiary label, Deram, which could do nothing with Johnny Almond, whose two Music Machine LPs are wonderfully inventive. A switch of labels did the trick - at any rate in the US - for a revamped Music Machine, now named Mark-Almond.

Hollywood Blues	LP	Deram	SML1057	1970	**£20**	
Patent Pending	LP	Deram	SML1043	1969	**£20**	
Solar Level	7"	Deram	DM266	1969	**£5**	

ALMOND, MARC

Boy Who Came Back	12"	Some Bizarre	BZS2312	1984	**£6**	
Love Letter	10"	Some Bizarre	BONK210	1985	**£12**	
Stories Of Johnny	10"	Some Bizarre	BONK110	1985	**£15**	
Tenderness Is A Weakness	10"	Some Bizarre	BZS2510	1984	**£15**	
Woman's Story	10"	Some Bizarre	GLOW210	1986	**£10**	
You Have	10"	Some Bizarre	BZS2410	1984	**£15**	

ALONE AGAIN OR

Drum The Beat	7"	All One	ALG1	1984	**£10**	

ALOVE & PAXTON

Wickeder	7"	Blue Cat	BS168	196-	**£10**	

ALPHONSO, CARLTON

I Have Changed	7"	New Beat	NB004	1968	**£8**	
Where In This World	7"	Pama	PM700	196-	**£8**	

ALPHONSO, CLYDE

Good Enough	7"	Studio One	SO2076	196-	**£10**	

ALPHONSO, ORVILLE

Belly Lick	7"	Caribou	CRC1	196-	**£8**	

ALPHONSO, ROLAND

Cat	7"	Pyramid	PYR6008	1967	**£10**	
Crime Wave	7"	R&B	JB164	1964	**£10**	
Devoted To You	7"	Island	WI264	1966	**£10**	
El Pussy Cat	7"	Island	WI217	1965	**£10**	
Feeling Fine	7"	Island	WI146	1964	**£10**	
Guantanamera Ska	7"	Pyramid	PYR6009	1967	**£10**	
Jazz Ska	7"	Rio	R58	196-	**£10**	
Jericho Chain	7"	Blue Beat	BB356	1965	**£10**	
Jungle Bit	7"	Pyramid	PYR6007	1967	**£10**	
Middle East	7"	Pyramid	PYR6003	1967	**£10**	
Never To Be Mine	7"	Trojan	TR001	196-	**£10**	
Nimblefoot	7"	Ska Beat	JB210	1965	**£10**	
Nothing For Nothing	7"	Pyramid	PYR6011	1967	**£10**	
Nuclear Weapon	7"	Ska Beat	JB216	1965	**£10**	
On The Move	7"	Pyramid	PYR6006	1967	**£10**	
Peace And Love	7"	Pyramid	PYR6023	1969	**£10**	
Phoenix City	7"	Trojan	TRM9010	1974	**£4**	
Reggae In The Grass	7"	Coxsone	CS7077	196-	**£10**	
Rinky Dink	7"	Ska Beat	JB231	1966	**£10**	
Roland Plays The Prince	7"	Blue Beat	BB286	1964	**£10**	

Shanty Town Curfew	7"	Island	WI3055	1967	**£8**	
Ska Au Go-Go	LP	Coxsone	CSL8003	196-	**£80**	
Sock It To Me	7"	Pyramid	PYR6018	1967	**£10**	
Song For My Father	7"	Pyramid	PYR6010	1967	**£10**	
Stream Of Life	7"	Pyramid	PYR6016	1967	**£10**	
Thousand Tons Of Megaton	7"	Gas	GAS112	196-	**£8**	
Whiter Shade Of Pale	7"	Pyramid	PYR6022	1968	**£10**	
Woman Of The World	7"	Pyramid	PYR6005	1967	**£10**	
Yard Broom	7"	Ska Beat	JB183	1965	**£10**	

ALTERNATIVE TV

Action Time Vision	LP	Deptford F.C.	DLP05	1980	**£12**	
An Ye As Well	cass	Con. Tapes	CON14	1981	**£12**	
Force Is Blind	7"	Deptford F.C.	DFC010	1979	**£4**	
How Much Longer	7"	Deptford F.C.	DFC02	1977	**£12**	
Image Has Cracked	LP	Deptford F.C.	DLP01	1978	**£12**	
Life After Life	7"	Deptford F.C.	DFC04	1978	**£4**	
Live At The Rat Club	LP	Crystal	CLP01	1979	**£20**	
Love Lies Limp	7"	Deptford F.C.	DFC05	1978	**£4**	
Love Lies Limp	7"	Sniffin' Glue	75RPS	1979	**£5**	flexi
Vibing Up The Senile Man	LP	Deptford F.C.	DLP03	1978	**£12**	

ALTERNATIVE TV & HERE AND NOW

What You See Is What You Are	LP	Deptford F.C.	DLP02	1978	**£12**	

ALTON & EDDY

Muriel	7"	Blue Beat	BB17	1961	**£10**	

ALTON & PHYLLIS

Love Letters	7"	Trojan	TR622	1969	**£6**	

ALTON & THE FLAMES

Blessings Of Love	7"	Doctor Bird	DB1044	1966	**£10**	
Dance Crasher	7"	Island	WI239	1965	**£10**	
Preacher	7"	Doctor Bird	DB1049	1966	**£10**	
Shake It	7"	Doctor Bird	DB1055	1966	**£10**	

AMALGAM

Play Blackwell And Higgins	LP	A Records		1973	**£20**	
Prayer For Peace	LP	Transatlantic	TRA196	1969	**£20**	

AMAZIAH

Straight Talker	LP	Sunrise		1973	**£200**	

AMAZING BLONDEL

Alleluia	7"	Island	WIP6153	1972	**£4**	
Amazing Blondel	LP	Bell	SBLL131	1970	**£100**	
Bad Dreams	LP	DJM	DJF20472	1976	**£10**	
Blondel	LP	Island	ILPS9257	1973	**£12**	
England '72	LP	Island	ILPS9205	1972	**£12**	
Evensong	LP	Island	ILPS9136	1970	**£12**	
Fantasia Lindum	LP	Island	ILPS9156	1971	**£12**	
Inspiration	LP	DJM	DJF20446	1975	**£10**	
Live In Tokyo	LP	DJM	DJF20503	1977	**£10**	
Mulgrave Street	LP	DJM	DJF20442	1974	**£10**	

AMAZING DANCE BAND

Deep Blue Train	7"	Verve	VS567	1968	**£8**	

AMAZING FRIENDLY APPLE

Water Woman	7"	Decca	F12887	1969	**£5**	

AMBER SQUAD

Can We Go Dancing?	7"	Deadgood	DEAD17	1980	**£6**	
Put My Finger On You	7"	S'nd Of Leic.	ST1	1980	**£8**	

AMBOY DUKES

In order to appreciate the Amboy Dukes' tendency to overdo everything, one need look no further than the seminal punk (sixties style) compilation, "Nuggets". Here the group turns "Tobacco Road" into a totally unsuitable vehicle for guitar excess. Lead guitarist Ted Nugent has followed more or less the same approach ever since.

All I Need	7"	Polydor	56172	1967	**£8**	
Amboy Dukes	LP	Fontana	STL4560	1968	**£20**	

Title	Format	Label	Cat. No.	Year	Price	Notes
Call Of The Wild	LP	Discreet	K59203	1974	**£10**	
He Came To Me Yesterday	7"	Polydor	56281	1968	**£8**	
High Life In Whitley Wood	7"	Polydor	56190	1967	**£8**	
Journey To The Centre Of The Mind	LP	London	HAK8378	1968	**£20**	
Judy In Disguise	7"	Polydor	56228	1968	**£8**	
Let's Go Get Stoned	7"			196-	**£8**	
Marriage On The Rocks	LP	Polydor	244012	1970	**£15**	US
Migration	LP	London	HAK8392	1969	**£20**	
Simon Says	7"	Polydor	56243	1968	**£8**	
Survival Of The Fittest	LP	Polydor	2675141	1974	**£10**	
Tooth,Fang & Claw	LP	Discreet	K59205	1975	**£10**	
Turn Back To Me	7"	Polydor	56149	1966	**£8**	

AMBROSE SLADE

Ambrose Slade was the original name of Slade, back in the days when they were being marketed as the first skinhead group (despite the fact that the group's music had nothing in common with the likes of "Skinhead Moonstomp"). The reissue of the group's LP, on Contour, is as rare as the original - it was withdrawn shortly after release - but the US version of the record, retitled "Ballzy" and given an appropriate cover, is rather more common.

Title	Format	Label	Cat. No.	Year	Price	Notes
Ballzy	LP	Fontana	SRF67598	1969	**£60**	US
Beginnings	LP	Contour	6870678	1975	**£60**	
Beginnings	LP	Fontana	STL5492	1969	**£200**	
Genesis	7"	Fontana	TF1015	1969	**£130**	

AMBROSE, SAMMY

Title	Format	Label	Cat. No.	Year	Price	Notes
Monkey See Monkey Do	7"	Stateside	SS399	1965	**£20**	
This Diamond Ring	7"	Stateside	SS385	1965	**£30**	

AMEN CORNER

Title	Format	Label	Cat. No.	Year	Price	Notes
Bend Me Shape Me	7"	Deram	DM172	1968	**£4**	chart single
Farewell Magnificent Seven	LP	Immediate	IMSP028	1969	**£10**	
Get Back	7"	Immediate	IM083	1969	**£4**	
Gin House Blues	7"	Deram	DM136	1967	**£4**	chart single
Half As Nice	7"	Immediate	IM073	1969	**£4**	chart single
Hello Suzie	7"	Immediate	IM081	1969	**£4**	chart single
High In The Sky	7"	Deram	DM197	1968	**£4**	chart single
National Welsh Coast Live	LP	Immediate	IMSP023	1969	**£10**	Chart LP
Round Amen Corner	LP	Deram	DML1021	1968	**£10**	Chart LP
World Of Broken Hearts	7"	Deram	DM151	1967	**£4**	chart single

AMENDS

Title	Format	Label	Cat. No.	Year	Price	Notes
Making Up	7"	UNI	UN511	1969	**£4**	

AMERICAN BLUES

The only UK release of the second American Blues album is a 1987 reissue on the See For Miles label. Although the record is a typically inventive chunk of psychedelia, its real interest, and the reason for the collectibility of the original, lies in the fact that two thirds of American Blues later became two thirds of ZZ Top.

Title	Format	Label	Cat. No.	Year	Price	Notes
American Blues Is Here	LP	Karma	KLP1001	1967	**£75**	US
Do Their Thing	LP	Uni	73044	1969	**£30**	US

AMERICAN BREED

Title	Format	Label	Cat. No.	Year	Price	Notes
American Breed	LP	Dot	DOLP255	1967	**£10**	
Bend Me Shape Me	LP	Dot	SLPD502	1968	**£10**	
Bend Me Shape Me	7"	Stateside	SS2078	1968	**£4**	chart single
Green Light	7"	Dot	101	1968	**£5**	
Lonely Side Of The City	LP	Atlantic	38008	1968	**£10**	
Pumpkin Powder,Scarlet And Green	LP	Atlantic	38006	1968	**£10**	
Ready, Willing, And Able	7"	Dot	106	1968	**£5**	
Step Out Of Your Mind	7"	CBS	2888	1967	**£8**	
Step Out Of Your Mind	7"	CBS	2972	1967	**£5**	

AMERICAN GYPSY

Title	Format	Label	Cat. No.	Year	Price	Notes
Gypsy	LP	CBS	66270	1971	**£10**	

AMERICAN POETS

Title	Format	Label	Cat. No.	Year	Price	Notes
She Blew A Good Thing	7"	London	HLC10037	1966	**£12**	

AMERICAN SPRING

Title	Format	Label	Cat. No.	Year	Price	Notes
American Spring	LP	United Artists	UAS29363	1972	**£15**	
Good Time	7"	United Artists	UP35376	1972	**£4**	
Mama Said	7"	United Artists	UP35421	1972	**£4**	
Shyin' Away	7"	CBS	1590	1973	**£5**	

AMERICAN YOUTH CHOIR

Title	Format	Label	Cat. No.	Year	Price	Notes
Together We Can Make It	7"	Polydor	2066013	1971	**£10**	

AMES BROTHERS

Title	Format	Label	Cat. No.	Year	Price	Notes
Best Of The Ames Bros.	7" EP	RCA	RCX1047	1959	**£6**	
Exactly Like You	7" EP	HMV	7EG8237	1957	**£6**	
Naughty Lady Of Shady Lane	7"	HMV	7M281	1955	**£5**	chart single

AMES, NANCY

Title	Format	Label	Cat. No.	Year	Price	Notes
Cry Softly	7"	Columbia	DB8039	1966	**£20**	

AMIN, IDI

Title	Format	Label	Cat. No.	Year	Price	Notes
Amazin' Man	7"	Transatlantic	BIG527	1973	**£4**	

AMM

AMM are probably the only group to have received mention in books on Rock, Jazz, Classical, and Avant Garde musics. In truth, they are all of these - and none, playing in a unique free improvised style, incorporating both instrumental and found sounds. Cornelius Cardew went on to form the Scratch Orchestra, which featured musicians performing on instruments that they had never learnt to play!

Title	Format	Label	Cat. No.	Year	Price	Notes
AMM Music	LP	Elektra	EUKS7256	1967	**£30**	
At The Roundhouse	7"	Incus	EP1	197-	**£10**	

AMM & MEV

Title	Format	Label	Cat. No.	Year	Price	Notes
Live Electronic Music Improvised	LP	Mainstream	MS5002		**£20**	US

AMMONS, ALBERT

Title	Format	Label	Cat. No.	Year	Price	Notes
Albert Ammons	7" EP	Vogue	EPV1071	195-	**£8**	
Boogie Woogie Stomp	7"	Brunswick	2187	1954	**£5**	
Boogie Woogie Stomp	7" EP	Brunswick	OE9325	1957	**£8**	

AMMONS, ALBERT, PETE JOHNSON, MEADE LUX LEWIS

Title	Format	Label	Cat. No.	Year	Price	Notes
Boogie Woogie Trio	LP	Storyville	SLP184	196-	**£12**	
Shout For Joy	7" EP	Columbia	SEG7528	1955	**£8**	

AMMONS, GENE

Title	Format	Label	Cat. No.	Year	Price	Notes
Ammons Boogie	7"	Starlite	ST45017	1960	**£5**	
Anna	7"	Starlite	45097	1963	**£4**	

AMON DUUL

Title	Format	Label	Cat. No.	Year	Price	Notes
Amon Duul	LP	Prophesy	1003	1969	**£20**	
Collapsing	LP	Metronome	SMLP012	1969	**£20**	
Disaster	LP	BASF	2929079	1971	**£20**	German
Minnelied	LP	Brain	0040149	1975	**£15**	German
Paradieswarts Duul	LP	Ohr	56068	1969	**£20**	German
This Is Amon Duul	LP	Brain	200146	1973	**£15**	German

AMON DUUL II

Amon Duul II were originally a splinter group away from Amon Duul, following an ideological disagreement, but they rapidly became rather better known than the parent group. Essentially, the group is a German version of Hawkwind, with a similar mystical outlook and fascination with spacey noises. Equally, the music is at root very simply constructed, with single chords being worried half to death for minutes at a time.

Title	Format	Label	Cat. No.	Year	Price	Notes
Almost Live	LP	Nova	623305	1977	**£10**	German
Carnival In Babylon	LP	United Artists	UAG29327	1972	**£10**	
Dance Of The Lemmings	LP	United Artists	60003/4	1971	**£12**	double
Hi Jack	LP	Atlantic	K50136	1974	**£10**	
Lemmingmania	LP	United Artists	UAS29723	1975	**£10**	
Live In London	LP	United Artists	UAS29466	1974	**£10**	
Made In Germany	LP	Atlantic	K50182	1975	**£10**	
Made In Germany	LP	Nova	628350	1975	**£15**	German, double
Only Human	LP	Vinyl	LV1004	1978	**£10**	
Phallus Dei	LP	Liberty	LBS83279	1969	**£20**	
Pyragony	LP	Nova	622890	1976	**£10**	German
Viva La Trance	LP	United Artists	UAS29504	1973	**£10**	
Wolf City	LP	United Artists	UAG29406	1972	**£10**	
Yeti	LP	Liberty	LSP101/2	1970	**£12**	double

AMOR VIVI

Title	Format	Label	Cat. No.	Year	Price	Notes
Dirty Dog	7"	Big Shot	BI534	1973	**£5**	

ANCIENT GREASE

Title	Format	Label	Cat. No.	Year	Price	Notes
Women And Children First	LP	Mercury	6338033	1970	**£25**	

AND ALSO THE TREES

Title	Format	Label	Cat. No.	Year	Price	Notes
Secret Sea	7"	Reflex	RE6	1984	**£8**	
Shantell	7"	Reflex	FS9	1984	**£8**	

ANDERSEN, ERIC

Title	Format	Label	Cat. No.	Year	Price	Notes
'Bout Changes & Things	LP	Vanguard	VSD79206	1966	**£15**	US
'Bout Changes & Things Take 2	LP	Fontana	STFL6068	1968	**£15**	
Avalanche	LP	W. Bros	WS1748	1970	**£12**	US
Be True To You	LP	Arista	ARTY114	1975	**£10**	
Best Of...	LP	Vanguard	VSD7/8	1973	**£15**	US, double
Best Songs	LP	Arista	4128	1977	**£10**	US
Blue River	LP	CBS	65145	1973	**£12**	
Country Dream	LP	Vanguard	VSD6540	1969	**£15**	US
Eric Andersen	LP	W. Bros	WS1806	1970	**£12**	US
More Hits From Tin Can Alley	LP	Vanguard	VSD79271	1968	**£15**	US
Stage	LP	CBS	65571	1974	**£12**	US
Sweet Surprise	LP	Arista	4075	1976	**£10**	US
Today Is The Highway	LP	Fontana	TFL6061	1965	**£15**	

ANDERSON'S ALL STARS

Title	Format	Label	Cat. No.	Year	Price	Notes
Intensified Girls	7"	Blue Cat	BS132	1968	**£10**	

ANDERSON, ERNESTINE

Title	Format	Label	Cat. No.	Year	Price	Notes
Jerk And Twine	7"	Mercury	MF912	1965	**£5**	
Keep An Eye On Love	7"	Sue	WI309	1964	**£10**	
Somebody Told You	7"	Stateside	SS455	1965	**£5**	

ANDERSON, IAN A.

Title	Format	Label	Cat. No.	Year	Price	Notes
Book Of Changes	LP	Fontana	STL5542	1970	**£15**	
Royal York Crescent	LP	Village Thing	VTS3	1970	**£12**	
Singer Sleeps On	LP	Village Thing	VTS18	1972	**£12**	
Stereo Death Breakdown	LP	Liberty	LBS83242	1969	**£20**	
Vulture Is Not A Bird You Can Trust	LP	Village Thing	VTS9	1971	**£12**	

ANDERSON, IAN A. & MIKE COOPER

Title	Format	Label	Cat. No.	Year	Price	Notes
Inverted World	LP	Matchbox	SDM159	1968	**£20**	

ANDERSON, JON

Title	Format	Label	Cat. No.	Year	Price	Notes
Evening With Jon Anderson	LP	Atlantic	PR285	1976	**£15**	US promo
Flight Of The Moorglade	7"	Atlantic	K10840	1976	**£4**	

ANDERSON, MILLER

Miller Anderson was the lead guitarist and singer with the Keef Hartley Band. His solo LP uses the band musicians (but not Hartley himself) to rather less effect than on "Little Big Band", which was released at the same time.

Title	Format	Label	Cat. No.	Year	Price	Notes
Bright City	LP	Deram	SDL3	1971	**£10**	
Bright City	7"	Deram	DM337	1971	**£4**	

ANDERSON, REUBEN

Title	Format	Label	Cat. No.	Year	Price	Notes
Christmas Time Again	7"	Doctor Bird	DB1045	1966	**£10**	

ANDERSON, SONNY

Title	Format	Label	Cat. No.	Year	Price	Notes
Lonely Lonely Train	7"	London	HLP9036	1960	**£15**	

ANDERSON, UDELL T.

Title	Format	Label	Cat. No.	Year	Price	Notes
Love Ain't Love	7"	Direction	584212	1969	**£4**	

ANDREWS, CHRIS

Title	Format	Label	Cat. No.	Year	Price	Notes
Hold On	7"	Decca	F22668	1967	**£4**	
I'll Walk To You	7"	Decca	F22597	1967	**£4**	
Man With The Red Balloon	7"	Pye	7N17617	1968	**£4**	
Pretty Belinda	7"	Pye	7N17727	1969	**£4**	
Something On My Mind	7"	Decca	F22365	1966	**£4**	chart single
Stop That Girl	7"	Decca	F22472	1966	**£4**	chart single
That's What She Said	7"	Decca	F22521	1966	**£4**	
To Whom It Concerns	7"	Decca	F22285	1965	**£4**	chart single
Whatcha Gonna Do Now	7"	Decca	F22404	1966	**£4**	chart single
Yesterday Man	7"	Decca	F12236	1965	**£4**	chart single

ANDREWS, ERNIE

Title	Format	Label	Cat. No.	Year	Price	Notes
Where Were you	7"	Capitol	CL15407	1965	**£5**	

ANDREWS, HARVEY

Title	Format	Label	Cat. No.	Year	Price	Notes
Fantasies From A Corner Seat	LP	Transatlantic	TRA298	1975	**£10**	
Friends Of Mine	LP	Fly	HIFLY15	1973	**£10**	
Harvey Andrews	7" EP	Transatlantic	TRAEP133	1965	**£20**	
Places And Faces	LP	Decca	SND9	1970	**£15**	
Soldier	7"	Cube	BUG20	1971	**£4**	
Someday	LP	Transatlantic	TRA329	1976	**£10**	
Writer Of Songs	LP	Cube	HIFLY10	1972	**£10**	

ANDREWS, JOHN & THE LONELY ONES

Title	Format	Label	Cat. No.	Year	Price	Notes
Rose Grows In The Ruins	7"	Parlophone	R5455	1966	**£15**	

ANDREWS, LEE & THE HEARTS

Title	Format	Label	Cat. No.	Year	Price	Notes
Teardrops	7"	London	HLM8546	1958	**£20**	
Try The Impossible	7"	London	HLU8661	1958	**£15**	

ANDREWS, TIM

Title	Format	Label	Cat. No.	Year	Price	Notes
Sad Simon Lives Again	7"	Parlophone	R5656	1967	**£5**	
Tiny Goddess	7"	Parlophone	R5824	1970	**£4**	
Your Tea Is Strong	7"	Parlophone	R5695	1968	**£4**	

ANDREWS, TIM & PAUL KORDA

Title	Format	Label	Cat. No.	Year	Price	Notes
Angel Face	7"	Parlophone	R5746	1968	**£4**	
Discovery	7"	Parlophone	R5769	1969	**£4**	
Makin' Love To Him	7"	Parlophone	R5714	1968	**£4**	

ANDROMEDA

Title	Format	Label	Cat. No.	Year	Price	Notes
Andromeda	LP	RCA	SF8031	1969	**£80**	
Go Your Way	7"	RCA	RCA1854	1969	**£10**	

ANDWELLA

Title	Format	Label	Cat. No.	Year	Price	Notes
Are You Ready	7"	Reflection	RS6	1970	**£6**	
Peoples People	LP	Reflection	REFL10	1971	**£15**	
World's End	LP	Reflection	REF1010	1970	**£15**	

ANDWELLA'S DREAM

Title	Format	Label	Cat. No.	Year	Price	Notes
Every Little Minute	7"	Reflection	RS1	1970	**£6**	
Love And Poetry	LP	CBS	63673	1969	**£70**	
Midday Sun	7"	CBS	4301	1969	**£6**	
Mr.Sunshine	7"	CBS	4634	1969	**£10**	
Mrs.Man	7"	CBS	4469	1969	**£10**	
Songs By...	LP	private			**£100**	

ANDY, BOB

Title	Format	Label	Cat. No.	Year	Price	Notes
Experience	7"	Studio One	SO2063	196-	**£10**	
Going Home	7"	Studio One	SO2075	196-	**£10**	
Stay In My Lonely Arms	7"	Rio	R126	196-	**£10**	

ANGEL

Title	Format	Label	Cat. No.	Year	Price	Notes
Ain't Gonna Eat Out My Heart	7"	Casablanca	CAN125	1978	**£4**	
Angel	LP	Casablanca	CBC4007	1976	**£10**	
Feelings	7"	Casablanca	CBX522	1976	**£4**	
Helluva Band	LP	Casablanca	CBC4010	1976	**£10**	
Live Without A Net	LP	Casablanca	CALH2703	1980	**£15**	double
On And On	7"	Casablanca	CBX514	1976	**£4**	
On Earth As It Is In Heaven	LP	Casablanca	CAL2002	1977	**£10**	
Sinful	LP	Casablanca	7127	1979	**£10**	US
That Magic Touch	7"	Casablanca	CAN104	1977	**£4**	
Twentieth Century Foxes	7"	Casablanca	CAN193	1980	**£4**	
White Hot	LP	Casablanca	CSL2023	1978	**£10**	
Winter Song	7"	Casablanca	CAN113	1977	**£4**	

ANGEL PAVEMENT

Title	Format	Label	Cat. No.	Year	Price	Notes
Baby You've Gotta Stay	7"	Fontana	TF1059	1969	**£8**	
Tell Me What I've Got To Do	7"	Fontana	TF1072	1970	**£8**	

ANGELA & THE FANS

Title	Format	Label	Cat. No.	Year	Price	Notes
Love Ya Illya	7"	Pye	7N17108	1966	**£6**	

ANGELIC UPSTARTS

Title	Format	Label	Cat. No.	Year	Price	Notes
I'm An Upstart	7"	W. Bros	K17354	1979	**£4**	green vinyl
Murder Of Liddle Towers	7"	Angelic Up.	AU1024	1978	**£15**	

Teenage Warning ... 7" ... W. Bros ... K17426 ... 1979 ... **£4** ... red vinyl

ANGELO, BOBBY & THE TUXEDOS

Baby Sitting ... 7" ... HMV ... POP892 ... 1961 ... **£4** ... chart single

ANGELOU, MAYA

Miss Calypso ... LP ... London ... HAU2062 ... 1957 ... **£10** ...

ANGELS

And The Angels Sing ... LP ... Caprice ... LP1001 ... 1962 ... **£20** ... US
Everybody Loves A Lover ... 7" ... Pye ... 7N25150 ... 1962 ... **£4** ...
Greatest Hits ... LP ... Ascot ... AM13009 ... 1964 ... **£12** ... US
Halo To You ... LP ... Smash ... MGS27048 ... 1964 ... **£15** ... US
I Adore Him ... 7" ... Mercury ... AMT1215 ... 1963 ... **£4** ...
My Boyfriend's Back ... 7" ... Mercury ... AMT1211 ... 1963 ... **£4** ... chart single
My Boyfriend's Back ... LP ... Smash ... MGS27039 ... 1963 ... **£20** ... US

ANGELWITCH

Sweet Danger ... 7" ... EMI ... EMI5064 ... 1980 ... **£4** ... chart single
Sweet Danger ... 12" ... EMI ... 125064 ... 1980 ... **£8** ...

ANGLIANS

Friend Of Mine ... 7" ... CBS ... 202489 ... 1967 ... **£4** ...

ANGLOS

The marvelous "Incense" by the Anglos was issued four times during the sixties and by some means still managed to avoid becoming a hit. The group, however, was purely a studio creation, the intensely soulful singer being Steve Winwood, and the musicians probably the members of the Spencer Davis Group.

Incense ... 7" ... Brit ... WI1004 ... 1965 ... **£15** ...
Incense ... 7" ... Fontana ... TF589 ... 1965 ... **£10** ...
Incense ... 7" ... Island ... WIP6061 ... 1969 ... **£6** ...
Incense ... 7" ... Sue ... WI4033 ... 1967 ... **£20** ... possibly unreleased

ANIMALS

As with the Beatles and the Rolling Stones, the British and American LPs by the Animals have numerous differences, even where the titles are the same. Five tracks on the first UK album were replaced in the US by the songs from the first two singles, together with a track, "Blue Feeling", that never did get a British release. The second album, called "Animal Tracks" in the UK, had three of its songs removed and four different ones added for the US version, which was retitled "The Animals On Tour". An American LP called "Animal Tracks" was also issued, but this was a different record altogether, being a compilation of various singles and LP tracks not already released in the US. The two hits anthologies are inevitably different - the British "Most Of The Animals" (not to be confused with a later Music For Pleasure release with a greatly inferior selection) has fourteen tracks, while the American "Best Of The Animals" has only eleven - and only nine are to be found on both records. "Animalisms" and "Animalization" have four differences in their running orders; the American "Animalism" LP has no British equivalent at all. Of its eleven tracks, nine were not released in the UK, while a tenth, "Outcast", is a different take to the version found on "Animalisms".

Animal Tracks ... LP ... Columbia ... 33SX1708 ... 1965 ... **£20** ... Chart LP
Animal Tracks ... 7" EP ... Columbia ... SEG8499 ... 1966 ... **£6** ...
Animal Tracks ... LP ... MGM ... SE4305 ... 1965 ... **£20** ... US
Animalisms ... LP ... Decca ... LK4797 ... 1966 ... **£20** ... Chart LP
Animalisms ... LP ... MGM ... SE4414 ... 1966 ... **£20** ... US
Animalization ... LP ... MGM ... SE4384 ... 1966 ... **£20** ... US
Animals ... LP ... Columbia ... 33SX1669 ... 1964 ... **£20** ... Chart LP
Animals ... 7" EP ... Columbia ... SEG8400 ... 1965 ... **£6** ...
Animals ... LP ... MGM ... SE4264 ... 1964 ... **£20** ... US
Animals Are Back ... 7" EP ... Columbia ... SEG8452 ... 1965 ... **£6** ...
Animals Is Here ... 7" EP ... Columbia ... SEG8374 ... 1964 ... **£6** ...
Animals No.2 ... 7" EP ... Columbia ... SEG8439 ... 1965 ... **£6** ...
Animals On Tour ... LP ... MGM ... SE4281 ... 1965 ... **£20** ... US
Baby Let Me Take You Home ... 7" ... Columbia ... DB7247 ... 1964 ... **£4** ... chart single
Best Of... ... LP ... MGM ... SE4324 ... 1966 ... **£15** ... US
Bring It On Home To Me ... 7" ... Columbia ... DB7539 ... 1965 ... **£4** ... chart single
Don't Bring Me Down ... 7" ... Decca ... F12407 ... 1966 ... **£5** ... chart single
Don't Let Me Be Misunderstood ... 7" ... Columbia ... DB7445 ... 1965 ... **£4** ... chart single
Help Me Girl ... 7" ... Decca ... F12502 ... 1966 ... **£5** ... chart single
House Of The Rising Sun ... 7" ... Columbia ... DB7301 ... 1964 ... **£4** ... chart single
I Just Want To Make Love To You ... 7" EP ... Graphic S'nd ... ALO10867 ... 1963 ... **£50** ...
I'm Crying ... 7" ... Columbia ... DB7354 ... 1964 ... **£4** ... chart single
In The Beginning There Was Early... ... 7" EP ... Decca ... DFE8643 ... 1965 ... **£6** ...
Inside Looking Out ... 7" ... Decca ... F12332 ... 1966 ... **£5** ... chart single
It's My Life ... 7" ... Columbia ... DB7741 ... 1965 ... **£4** ... chart single
Mama Told Me Not To Come ... 7" ... Decca ... F12502 ... 1966 ... **£30** ...

Most Of The Animals	LP	Columbia	SX6035	1966	**£20**	Chart LP
We've Gotta Get Out Of This Place	7"	Columbia	DB7639	1965	**£4**	chart single

ANIMALS & OTHERS

Get Yourself A College Girl	LP	MGM	E4273	1964	**£15**	US

ANIMATED EGG

Animated Egg	LP	Marble Arch	MAL890	1969	**£20**	

ANKA, PAUL

Anka Again	7" EP	Columbia	SEG7801	1958	**£5**	
Can't Get You Out Of My Mind	7"	RCA	RCA1676	1968	**£20**	
Diana	7"	Columbia	DB3980	1957	**£4**	chart single
Diana	7" EP	Columbia	SEG7747	1957	**£5**	
Fly Me To The Moon	7" EP	RCA	RCX7127	1964	**£4**	
Four Golden Hits	7" EP	RCA	RCX7152	1964	**£4**	
Paul Anka	LP	Columbia	33SX	1958	**£15**	
Sing Sing Sing	7" EP	Columbia	SEG7890	1959	**£4**	
Sings His Big 15	LP	Columbia	33SX1282	1960	**£10**	
Sings Songs From Girls Town	7" EP	Columbia	SEG7985	1960	**£4**	
Sylvia	7" EP	RCA	RCX7170	1964	**£4**	
To Wait For Love	7"	RCA	RCA1434	1965	**£4**	PS
Young,Alive And In Love	LP	RCA	SF5129	1962	**£10**	

ANKA, PAUL, SAM COOKE & NEIL SEDAKA

Three Great Guys	LP	RCA	RD7608	1963	**£12**	

ANN, BARBARA

You've Lost That Loving Feeling	7"	Piccadilly	7N35221	1965	**£4**	

ANN, BEVERLY

You've Got Your Mind On Other things	7"	RCA	RCA2655	1976	**£5**	+ 2 tracks by others

ANNETTE

Annette	LP	Buena Vista	BV3301	1959	**£30**	US
Annette And Hayley Mills	LP	Buena Vista	BV3508	196-	**£50**	US
Annette At Bikini Beach	LP	Buena Vista	BV3324	1964	**£20**	US
Annette Funicello	LP	Buena Vista	BV4037	1962	**£25**	US
Annette On Campus	LP	Buena Vista	BV3320	1964	**£20**	US
Annette Sings Anka	LP	Buena Vista	BV3302	1960	**£25**	US
Annette Sings Golden Surfin' Hits	LP	Buena Vista	BV3327	1964	**£20**	US
Annette's Beach Party	LP	Buena Vista	BV3316	1963	**£20**	US
Annette's Pajama Party	LP	Buena Vista	BV3325	1964	**£20**	US
Babes In Toyland	LP	Buena Vista	BV4022	1961	**£15**	US
Best Of Broadway	LP	Disneyland	DQ1267	1965	**£15**	US
Dance Annette	LP	Buena Vista	BV3305	1961	**£25**	US
First Name Initial	7"	Top Rank	JAR233	1959	**£4**	
Hawaiiannette	LP	Buena Vista	BV3303	1960	**£25**	US
How To Stuff A Wild Bikini	LP	Wand	671	1965	**£10**	US
Italiannette	LP	Buena Vista	BV3304	1960	**£25**	US
Lonely Guitar	7"	Top Rank	JAR137	1959	**£4**	
Merlin Jones	7"	HMV	POP1322	1964	**£4**	
Monkey's Uncle	7"	HMV	POP1447	1965	**£4**	
Muscle Beach Party	LP	Buena Vista	BV3314	1963	**£20**	US
Muscle Beach Party	7"	HMV	POP1270	1964	**£4**	
O Dio Mio	7"	Top Rank	JAR343	1960	**£4**	
Parent Trap	LP	Buena Vista	BV3309	1961	**£15**	US
Pineapple Princess	7"	Pye	7N25061	1960	**£4**	
Something Borrowed, Something Blue	LP	Buena Vista	BV3328	1964	**£20**	US
Songs From Annette	LP	Mickey Mouse	MM24	196-	**£30**	US
State And College Songs	LP	Disneyland	DQ1293	1967	**£15**	US
Story Of My Teens	LP	Buena Vista	BV3312	1962	**£30**	US
Tall Paul	7" EP	Gala	45XP1046	196-	**£4**	
Teen Street	LP	Buena Vista	BV3313	1962	**£25**	US
Thunder Alley	LP	Sidewalk	T5902	1967	**£10**	US
Tubby The Tuba	LP	Disneyland	DQ1287	1966	**£15**	US
Walt Disney's Wonderful World Of Color	LP	Disneyland	DQ1245	1964	**£15**	US

ANNIS

Don't Play Your Games	7"	GTO	266	1979	**£8**	

ANNO DOMINI

On The New Day	LP	Deram	SLM1085	1971	**£50**	

ANONYMOUSLY YOURS

Get Back	7"	Trojan	TR680	1969	**£6**	
It's Your Thing	7"	Trojan	TR681	1969	**£6**	
Organism	7"	Duke	DU40	196-	**£8**	

ANOTHER PRETTY FACE

All The Boys Love Carrie	7"	N. Pleasures	Z1	1979	**£20**	green & white sleeve
All The Boys Love Carrie	7"	N. Pleasures	Z1	1979	**£12**	red & white sleeve
Heaven Gets Closer Every Day	7"	Chicken Jazz	JAZZ1	1980	**£15**	
I'm Sorry That I Beat You	cass	Chicken Jazz	JAZZ2	1981	**£30**	with badge & book
Soul To Soul	7"	Chicken Jazz	JAZZ3	1981	**£20**	gatefold PS
Whatever Happened To The West	7"	Virgin	VS320	1980	**£6**	

ANSWERS

It's Just A Fear	7"	Columbia	DB7847	1966	**£10**	
That's What You're Doing To Me	7"	Columbia	DB7953	1966	**£8**	

ANT TRIP CEREMONY

Twenty-Four Hours	LP	C.R.C.	2129	1967	**£100**	US

ANTEEKS

I Don't Want You	7"	Philips	BF1471	1966	**£10**	

ANTELL, PETER

Times They Are A-Changin'	7"	Pye	7N25329	1965	**£5**	

ANTHONY, BILLIE

Lay Down Your Arms	7"	Columbia	DB3818	1956	**£4**	
Rock A Billy	7"	Columbia	DB3935	1957	**£5**	
Something's Gotta Give	7"	Columbia	SCM5184	1955	**£5**	
Sweet Old Fashioned Girl	7"	Columbia	SCM5286	1956	**£4**	
Teach Me Tonight	7"	Columbia	SCM5155	1954	**£5**	
This Ole House	7"	Columbia	SCM5143	1954	**£8**	chart single
Tweedle Dee	7"	Columbia	SCM5174	1955	**£6**	

ANTHONY, DAVE

All Night	7"	Island	WI3148	1968	**£8**	
Race With The Wind	7"	Mercury	MF1031	1968	**£6**	

ANTHONY, DAVE, MOODS

New Directions	7"	Parlophone	R5438	1966	**£4**	

ANTHONY, RAY

Flip Flop	7"	Capitol	CL14525	1956	**£5**	
Girl Can't Help It	7" EP	Capitol	EAP1823	1957	**£8**	
Hernando's Hideaway	7"	Capitol	CL14354	1955	**£5**	
Learning The Blues	7"	Capitol	CL14321	1955	**£4**	
Rock And Roll With...	7" EP	Capitol	EAP1958	1957	**£8**	
Rock Around The Rockpile	7"	Capitol	CL14689	1957	**£5**	

ANTHONY, RAYBURN

There's No Tomorrow	7"	London	HLS9167	1960	**£4**	

ANTHRAX

Among The Living	LP	Island	PILPS9865	1987	**£10**	pic disc
Indians	12"	Island	12ISP325	1987	**£6**	pic disc
Madhouse	12"	Island	12ISP285	1986	**£6**	pic disc

ANTI-NOWHERE LEAGUE

Streets Of London	7"	WXYZ	ABCD1	1982	**£5**	chart single

ANTOINETTE

Lullaby Of Love	7"	Piccadilly	7N35310	1966	**£5**	

ANTON, REY

Don't Worry Boy	7"	Parlophone	R5420	1966	**£5**	
Girl You Don't Know Me	7"	Parlophone	R5274	1965	**£5**	
Heard It All Before	7"	Parlophone	R5172	1964	**£6**	
Nothing Comes Easy	7"	Parlophone	R5310	1965	**£5**	

Premeditation .... 7" .... Parlophone ..... R5358 .... 1965 .... **£5**
Things Get Better .... 7" .... Parlophone ..... R5487 .... 1966 .... **£4**
Wishbone .... 7" .... Parlophone ..... R5245 .... 1965 .... **£5**
You Can't Judge A Book By The Cover . 7" .... Parlophone ..... R5132 .... 1964 .... **£8**

ANVIL FLUTES & CAPRICORN VOICES

April Showers .... 7" .... Deram .... DM208 .... 1968 .... **£6**
Something New Is Coming .... LP .... Deram .... SML1026 .... 1968 .... **£20**

ANY TROUBLE

Any Trouble's first LP was released to a fanfare of critical acclaim. It was as though after bravely withstanding the onslaught of punk for three years or so, the rock weeklies were delighted to find a new group that actually played "real tunes". Unfortunately, Any Trouble's material was not really strong enough to take the weight of the praise heaped on it, and although the group carried on for a few years, it was with diminishing success. Clive Gregson, the group's leader, has since established himself in the folk circuit as half a duo with Christine Collister - the pair also finding useful employment as part of the Richard Thompson band.

Live At The Venue .... LP .... Stiff .... TRUBZ1 .... 1980 .... **£20**
Nice Girls .... 7" .... Pennine .... PSS165 .... 1979 .... **£10**

APARTMENT ONE

Open House .... LP .... P. Elephant .... 1970 .... **£15**

APEX RHYTHM & BLUES ALL STARS

John Lever was, until the arrival of the chains forced its closure, the best known record shop in Northampton. It was also, via its own independent label, responsible for the recording debut of Ian Hunter, of later Mott The Hoople and solo fame - the only member of the Apex Rhythm And Blues All Stars to ever live up to the group's optimistic name.

.... 7" EP .... John Lever .... 196- **£50**

APHRODITE'S CHILD

To choose a name taken from Greek mythology was rather par for the course in the late sixties - but since the members of Aphrodite's Child did actually come from Greece, they were more entitled than most. Best known for the pop hit, "Rain And Tears", the group was perhaps an unlikely signing to the progressive Vertigo label. But the group was always something of a compromise between the diverse interests of the singer and the keyboards player - the pop sensibilities of Demis Roussos versus the ambition of Vangelis. Both, of course, became rather better known after the group split up.

666, Apocalypse Of John .... LP .... Vertigo .... 6673001 .... 1972 .... **£20** .... spiral label, double
Break .... 7" .... Vertigo .... 6032900 .... 1975 .... **£5**
End Of The World .... LP .... Mercury .... SMCL20140 .... 1969 .... **£12**
End Of The World .... 7" .... Mercury .... MF1079 .... 1969 .... **£4**
I Want To Live .... 7" .... Polydor .... 56769 .... 1969 .... **£5**
It's Five O'Clock .... 7" .... Polydor .... 56791 .... 1970 .... **£4**
Let Me Love Let Me Live .... 7" .... Polydor .... 56785 .... 1969 .... **£5**
Rain And Tears .... 7" .... Mercury .... MF1039 .... 1968 .... **£4** .... chart single

APOLLOS

Rocking Horse .... 7" .... Mercury .... AMT1096 .... 1960 .... **£4**

APOSTLES

Hour Of Prayer .... LP .... Sound Rec. ..... 1245 .... **£75** .... US

APOSTOLIC INTERVENTION

Have You Ever Seen Me .... 7" .... Immediate .... IM043 .... 1967 .... **£20**

APPALACHIANS

Look Away .... 7" .... Mercury .... MF930 .... 1965 .... **£4**

APPELL, DAVE & APPLEJACKS

Applejack .... 7" .... Columbia .... DB3894 .... 1957 .... **£12**

APPLE

Apple A Day .... LP .... Page One .... POLS016 .... 1968 .... **£450**
Dr.Rock .... 7" .... Page One .... POF110 .... 1968 .... **£30**
Let's Take A Trip Down The Rhine .... 7" .... Page One .... POF101 .... 1968 .... **£30**
Thank U Very Much .... 7" .... **£30** .... US

APPLEJACKS

Applejacks .... LP .... Decca .... LK4635 .... 1964 .... **£60**
Chim Chim Cheree .... 7" .... Decca .... F12050 .... 1965 .... **£15**
I Go To Sleep .... 7" .... Decca .... F12216 .... 1965 .... **£15**
I'm Through .... 7" .... Decca .... F12301 .... 1965 .... **£8**
It's Not A Game .... 7" .... Decca .... F12106 .... 1965 .... **£10**

Like Dreamers Do	7"	Decca	F11916	1964	**£4**	chart single
Tell Me When	7"	Decca	F11833	1964	**£4**	chart single
Three Little Words	7"	Decca	F11981	1964	**£4**	chart single
You've Been Cheatin'	7"	CBS	202615	1967	**£10**	

APPLEJACKS (2)

Mexican Hat Rock	7"	London	HLU8753	1958	**£4**	
Rock A Conga	7"	London	HLU8806	1959	**£4**	

APPLETREE THEATRE

Playback	LP	Polydor	2353051	1968	**£15**	

AQUARIAN AGE

Ten Thousand Words In A Cardboard...	7"	Parlophone	R5700	1968	**£20**	

AQUATONES

Aquatones Sing	LP	Fargo	3001	1964	**£100**	US
You	7"	London	HLO8631	1958	**£12**	

AQUILA

Aquila	LP	RCA	SF8126	1970	**£20**	

ARBORS

I Can't Quit Her	7"	CBS	4379	1969	**£4**	
Letter	7"	CBS	4137	1969	**£4**	
Motet Overture	7"	CBS	4640	1969	**£4**	
Symphony For Susan	7"	CBS	202410	1966	**£4**	
Valley Of The Dolls	7"	CBS	3221	1968	**£4**	

ARBRE

Time And Again	LP	DJM	DJF20480	1976	**£10**	

ARC

Arc At This	LP	Decca	SKLR5077	1971	**£15**	

ARCADIA

Election Day (Cryptic Cut)	12"	EMI		1985	**£10**	1 sided promo
Election Day (Re-election Day)	12"	EMI		1985	**£12**	1 sided promo
Election Day (remix)	12"	EMI	12NSR1	1985	**£10**	
Election Day	12"	EMI		1985	**£8**	promo in foil PS
Promise (remix)	12"	EMI	12NSR2	1986	**£10**	

ARCADIUM

Breathe Awhile	LP	Middle Earth	MDLS302	1969	**£120**	
Sing My Song	7"	Middle Earth	MDS102	1969	**£20**	

ARCHIES

Sugar Sugar	7"	RCA	RCA1872	1969	**£4**	chart single

ARCHITECTS OF DISASTER

Cucumber Sandwich	7"	Neuter	NEU1	1982	**£8**	with insert, polythene bag

ARDLEY, NEIL

The high prices being fetched by British jazz albums from the sixties and early seventies reflects the fact that, with many of the same musicians being involved in both jazz and rock recordings, LPs like those of Neil Ardley are very much part of the progressive rock scene. Certainly, drummer Jon Hiseman viewed his role within Neil Ardley's big band as being no different from that in his own group, Colosseum (most of whose members also played with Neil Ardley). Side two of "Symphony of Amaranths" includes, by way of a contrast, the delightfully eccentric Ivor Cutler reciting Edward Lear's "The Dong With The Luminous Nose", with Ardley's band performing a suitable accompaniment.

Dejeuner Sur L'Herbe	LP	Verve	SVLP9236	1969	**£100**	
Harmony Of The Spheres	LP	Decca	TXSR133	1979	**£10**	
Symphony Of Amaranths	LP	Regal Z.	SLRZ1028	1972	**£100**	
Western Union	LP	Decca	LK4690	1965	**£100**	

ARDLEY, NEIL, IAN CARR & DON RENDELL

Greek Variations	LP	Columbia	SCX6414	1970	**£100**	

ARDLEY, NEIL, IAN CARR & MIKE GIBBS

Will Power	LP	Argo		1974	**£150**	double

AREA CODE 615

Area Code 615, a group made up of Nashville session musicians, are perhaps best known in the UK as the creators of "Stone

Fox Chase" (included on "Trip In The Country), which was used as the signature tune of TV's "Old Grey Whistle Test".

Area Code 615	LP	Polydor	583572	1969	**£10**	
Area Code 615/Trip in The Country	LP	Polydor	2683040	1974	**£12**	double
Ruby	7"	Polydor	56546	1970	**£4**	
Stone Fox Chase	7"	Polydor	2066249	1973	**£4**	
Trip In The Country	LP	Polydor	2425023	1970	**£10**	

ARGENT

Argent was formed by the Zombies' keyboard player, Rod Argent, and the group's first LP takes the earlier group's posthumous hit, "Time Of The Season", as a stylistic jumping-off point. "Argent" emerges, in effect, as the follow up to the Zombies excellent "Odyssey and Oracle". Subsequent Argent releases were less distinctive, although the group was quite successful in sales terms. Rod Argent's colleagues included Russ Ballard and Bob Henrit, both of whom had been members of the Roulettes.

All Together Now	LP	Epic	64962	1972	**£10**	Chart LP
Argent	LP	CBS	63781	1970	**£15**	
Circus	LP	Epic	80691	1975	**£10**	
Counterpoints	LP	RCA	RS1020	1975	**£10**	
Encore	LP	Epic	88063	1974	**£15**	double
In Deep	LP	Epic	65475	1973	**£10**	Chart LP
In Deep	LP	Epic	Q65475	1974	**£15**	quad
Nexus	LP	Epic	65924	1974	**£10**	
Ring Of Hands	LP	Epic	64190	1971	**£12**	

ARIZONA SWAMP COMPANY

Train Keeps Rollin'	7"	Parlophone	R5841	1970	**£12**	

ARLON, DEKE

Can't Make Up My Mind	7"	Columbia	DB7194	1964	**£8**	
Hard Times For Young Lovers	7"	Columbia	DB7841	1966	**£5**	
I Need You	7"	HMV	POP1340	1964	**£15**	
If I Didn't Have A Dime	7"	Columbia	DB7487	1965	**£8**	
Little Piece Of Paper	7"	Columbia	DB7753	1965	**£5**	

ARMAGEDDON

Armageddon	LP	A&M	AMLH64513	1975	**£20**	

ARMATRADING, JOAN

Live At The Bijou, Philadelphia	LP	A&M	SP8414	1977	**£20**	US promo
Talk Under Ladders	LP	A&M	SAMP12	1981	**£15**	promo

ARMS & LEGS

Heat Of The Night	7"	MAM	MAM147	1976	**£8**	
Is There Any More Wine	7"	MAM	MAM156	1977	**£8**	
Janice	7"	MAM	MAM140	1976	**£8**	

ARMSTRONG, FRANKIE

Lovely On The Water	LP	Topic	12TS216	1972	**£10**	

ARNELL, GINNY

Just Like A Boy	7"	MGM	MGM1270	1965	**£4**	
Little Bit Of Love	7"	MGM	MGM1283	1965	**£4**	

ARNEZ, CHICO

Yashmak	7"	Pye	7N15196	1959	**£15**	

ARNOLD, CALVIN

Funky Way	7"	MGM	MGM1378	1968	**£4**	
Mama In Law	7"	MGM	MGM1449	1968	**£4**	

ARNOLD, EDDIE

All-Time Favorites	LP	RCA	LPM1223	1955	**£15**	US
All-Time Favorites	LP-10"	RCA	LPM3117	1953	**£20**	US
All-Time Hits From The Hills	LP-10"	RCA	LPM3031	1952	**£20**	US
American Institution	LP-10"	RCA	LPM3230	1954	**£20**	US
Anytime	LP	RCA	LPM1224	1955	**£15**	US
Anytime	LP-10"	RCA	LPM3027	1952	**£20**	US
Chapel On The Hill	LP	RCA	LPM1225	1955	**£15**	US
Chapel On The Hill	LP-10"	RCA	LPM3219	1954	**£20**	US
Dozen Hits	LP	RCA	LPM1293	1956	**£15**	US
Have Guitar, Will Travel	LP	RCA	LPM1928	1959	**£10**	US
Little On The Lonely Side	LP	RCA	LPM1377	1956	**£15**	US
Make The World Go Away	7"	RCA	RCA1496	1966	**£4**	chart single

My Darling, My Darling	LP	RCA	LPM1575	1957	**£15**	US
Praise Him, Praise Him	LP	RCA	LPM1733	1958	**£12**	US
Wanderin'	LP	RCA	LPM1111	1955	**£15**	US
When They Were Young	LP	RCA	LPM1484	1957	**£15**	US

ARNOLD, P.P.

Pat Arnold tried hard for solo success with a number of releases on the Immediate label. Despite producing several fondly remembered tracks, however, it was her backing group, the Nice, that achieved the most success. P.P.Arnold returned to session work, although she achieved a brief revival at the end of the eighties. She had originally been a member of Ike and Tina Turner's backing group, the Ikettes.

Angel Of The Morning	7"	Immediate	IM067	1968	**£5**	chart single
Everything's Gonna Be Alright	7"	Immediate	IM040	1966	**£30**	
First Cut Is The Deepest	7"	Immediate	IM047	1967	**£5**	chart single
First Cut Is The Deepest	7"	Immediate	IM079	1969	**£4**	
First Lady Of Immediate	LP	Immediate	IMSP11	1967	**£10**	
If You Think You're Groovy	7"	Immediate	IM061	1968	**£5**	chart single
Kafunta	LP	Immediate	IMSP17	1968	**£10**	
Time Has Come	7"	Immediate	IM055	1967	**£4**	chart single

ARRANBEE POP SYMPHONY ORCHESTRA

Today's Pop Symphony	LP	Immediate	IMSP003	1966	**£30**	

ARRIVAL

Arrival	LP	CBS	64733	1972	**£10**	
Arrival	LP	Decca	SKL5055	1970	**£10**	
Friends	7"	Decca	F12986	1969	**£4**	chart single
Heartbreak Kid	LP	CBS	70125	1973	**£10**	

ARRIVALS

Scooby Doo	7"	Pye	7N17761	1969	**£4**	

ARROWS

Apache '65	7"	Capitol	CL15386	1965	**£5**	

ARROWS (2)

Mercy	7"	Pye	7N17756	1969	**£4**	

ARS NOVA

Ars Nova	LP	Elektra	EKS74020	1968	**£10**	US
Fields Of People	7"	Elektra	EKSN45034	1968	**£4**	
Sunshine And Shadows	LP	Atlantic	588196	1969	**£10**	
Zoroaster	7"	Elektra	EKSN45029	1968	**£4**	

ART

When Chris Blackwell of Island records decided to expand his sphere of operations by entering the rock market place, he demonstrated from the start a remarkable sureness of touch in his decisions regarding which artists to sign. If Island albums seldom reach the high prices regularly achieved by Vertigo and Deram releases, then that is not because their music is uninteresting, but because the company was rather more successful at selling it. The Art LP is a relative obscurity, however, perhaps because the group itself immediately added an extra member and mutated into the rather better known Spooky Tooth.

Supernatural Fairytales	LP	Island	ILP967	1968	**£30**	
What's That Sound	7"	Island	WIP6019	1967	**£15**	
What's That Sound	7"	Island	WIP6224	1975	**£4**	

ART ATTACKS

I Am A Dalek	7"	Albatross	TIT1	1978	**£6**	
Punk Rock Stars	7"	Fresh	FRESH3	1979	**£4**	

ART BEARS

Coda To Man And Boy	7"	Re	RE6622	1981	**£6**	pic disc
Coda To Man And Boy	7"	Re	RE6622	1981	**£8**	PD signed & numbered
Hopes And Fears	LP	Re	2188	1978	**£10**	
Winter Songs	LP	Re	REO618	1979	**£10**	

ART MOVEMENT

For As Long As You Need Me	7"	Columbia	DB8651	1970	**£4**	
Game Of Love	7"	Decca	F12768	1968	**£4**	
Loving Touch	7"	Decca	F12836	1968	**£5**	
Sooner I Get You	7"	Columbia	DB8697	1970	**£4**	
Yes Sir No Sir	7"	Columbia	DB8602	1969	**£4**	

ART NOUVEAUX

Extra Terrestrial Visitations	7"	Fontana	TF483	1964	**£6**	

Extra Terrestrial Visitations ... 7" ... Fontana ... TF843 ... 1967 ... **£4**

ART OF NOISE

Close (To The Edit) ... cass-s .. ZTT ... CTIS106 ... 1984 ... **£6**
Close (To The Edit) ... 7" ... ZTT ... PZTPS01 ... 1984 ... **£5** ... pic disc
Close Up ... 12" ... ZTT ... 12ZTPS01 ... 1985 ... **£8** ... green label promo
Closely Closely ... 12" ... ZTT ... 12ZTPS01 ... 1984 ... **£6** ... 2 versions
Edited ... 12" ... ZTT ... 12PZTPS01 ... 1984 ... **£6** ... pic disc
Extended Versions Of Close (To ....) ... 12" ... ZTT ... 12ZTPS1 ... 1985 ... **£6** ... white label promo
Into Battle With the Art Of Noise ... cass-s .. ZTT ... CTIS100 ... 1983 ... **£12**
Into Battle With the Art Of Noise ... 12" ... ZTT ... ZTIS100 ... 1983 ... **£10**
Love Beat ... 12" ... ZTT ... 12ZTPS02 ... 1985 ... **£6** ... with poster
Moments In Love ... cass-s .. ZTT ... CTIS109 ... 1985 ... **£8**
Moments In Love ... 7" ... ZTT ... PZTPS02 ... 1985 ... **£5** ... shaped pic disc

ARTERY

Cars In Motion ... 7" ... Aardvark ... AARD5 ... 1981 ... **£4**
Mother Moon ... 7" ... Limited Ed. ... TAKE1 ... 1979 ... **£12**
Unbalanced ... 7" ... Aardvark ... STEAL3 ... 1980 ... **£5**
Unbalanced ... 7" ... Aardvark ... STEAL3 ... 1980 ... **£8** ... double

ARTHUR, DAVE & TONI

Lark In The Morning ... LP ... Topic ... 1969 ... **£20**

ARTISTICS

Girl I Need you ... 7" ... Coral ... Q72492 ... 1967 ... **£10**
I'm Gonna Miss You ... 7" ... Coral ... Q72488 ... 1966 ... **£8**
I'm Gonna Miss You ... 7" ... MCA ... MU1117 ... 1970 ... **£4**

ARTWOODS

The Artwoods were typical of the many R&B and beat groups that spent years slogging round the British club circuit without ever really gaining much success. Unlike many, however, two of the group's members did achieve success later - drummer Keef Hartley, who used his stint with John Mayall's Bluesbreakers as a springboard to forming his own band; and organist Jon Lord, the founder member of Deep Purple and Whitesnake. As for poor Art Wood himself, he has been rather eclipsed by his more famous brother, Ron Wood.

Art Gallery ... LP ... Decca ... LK4830 ... 1966 ... **£100**
Art Gallery ... LP ... Eclipse ... ECS2025 ... 1974 ... **£30**
Artwoods ... LP ... Spark ... SRLM2006 ... 1973 ... **£30**
Goodbye Sisters ... 7" ... Decca ... F12206 ... 1965 ... **£20**
I Feel Good ... 7" ... Decca ... F12465 ... 1966 ... **£20**
I Take What I Want ... 7" ... Decca ... F12384 ... 1966 ... **£20**
Jazz In Jeans ... 7" EP ... Decca ... DFE8654 ... 1966 ... **£200**
Oh My Love ... 7" ... Decca ... F12091 ... 1965 ... **£20**
Sweet Mary ... 7" ... Decca ... F12015 ... 1964 ... **£20**
What Shall I Do ... 7" ... Parlophone ... R5590 ... 1967 ... **£20**

ARZACHEL

The Arzachel LP only received a limited release, but it is a fine and innovative recording. As would be expected from the musicians involved - guitarist Steve Hillage and keyboard wizard Dave Stewart, with Clive Brooks and Hugh Montgomery-Campbell in support. In other words, this is Egg, augmented by guitar.

Arzachel ... LP ... Evolution ... Z1003 ... 1969 ... **£120**

ASGARD

Children Of A New Born Age ... 7" ... Threshold ... TH10 ... 1972 ... **£6**
In The Realm Of Asgard ... LP ... Threshold ... THS6 ... 1972 ... **£20**
In The Realm Of Asgard ... 7" ... Threshold ... TH15 ... 1973 ... **£6**

ASH RA TEMPLE

Ash Ra Temple ... LP ... Ohr ... OMM556013 ... 1971 ... **£20** ... German
Join In ... LP ... Ohr ... OMM556032 ... 1973 ... **£15** ... German
Schwingungen ... LP ... Ohr ... OMM556020 ... 1972 ... **£20** ... German
Seven Up ... LP ... Komische ... KM58001 ... 1973 ... **£15** ... German
Starring Rosi ... LP ... Komische ... KM58007 ... 1973 ... **£15** ... German

ASH, DANIEL

Daniel Ash ... 12" ... 4AD ... BAD203 ... 1982 ... **£10**

ASHBY, IRVING

Big Guitar ... 7" ... London ... HLP8578 ... 1958 ... **£5**

ASHKAN

In From The Cold ... LP ... Nova ... SRNR1 ... 1970 ... **£40**

ASHLEY, TYRONE

Title	Format	Label	Cat. No.	Year	Price	Notes
Nothing Short Of A Miracle	7"	Pye	7N25710	1976	**£4**	

ASHTON & LORD

Title	Format	Label	Cat. No.	Year	Price	Notes
First Of The Big Bands	LP	Purple	TPS3507	1974	**£15**	

ASHTON, GARDNER & DYKE

Title	Format	Label	Cat. No.	Year	Price	Notes
Ashton, Gardner & Dyke	LP	Polydor	583081	1969	**£12**	
Can You Get It	7"	Capitol	CL15684	1971	**£4**	
Maiden Voyage	7"	Polydor	56306	1969	**£4**	
Resurrection Shuffle	7"	Capitol	CL15665	1970	**£4**	chart single
What A Bloody Long Day It's Been	LP	Capitol	EAST862	1972	**£12**	
Worst Of...	LP	Capitol	EST563	1971	**£12**	

ASHTON, TONY

Title	Format	Label	Cat. No.	Year	Price	Notes
Celebration	7"	Purple	PUR109	1972	**£4**	
You, Me And A Friend Of Mine	7"	Capitol	CL15702	1971	**£4**	

ASHTON, TONY & JON LORD

Title	Format	Label	Cat. No.	Year	Price	Notes
We're Gonna Make It	7"	Purple	PUR121	1974	**£4**	

ASIA

Title	Format	Label	Cat. No.	Year	Price	Notes
Don't Cry	7"	Geffen	WA3580	1982	**£6**	shaped pic disc
Only Time Will Tell	7"	Geffen	GEFA112228	1982	**£6**	pic disc
Smile Has Left Your Eyes	12"	Geffen	TA3836	1983	**£6**	red vinyl

ASSAGAI

Title	Format	Label	Cat. No.	Year	Price	Notes
	LP	Vertigo	6360058		**£40**	test pressing
Assagai	LP	Vertigo	6360030	1971	**£20**	spiral label
Telephone Girl	7"	Vertigo	6059034	1971	**£6**	
Zimbabwe	LP	Philips	6308079	1972	**£12**	

ASSEMBLED MULTITUDE

Title	Format	Label	Cat. No.	Year	Price	Notes
Assembled Multitude	LP	Atlantic	2466004	1971	**£10**	
Medley From Jesus Christ Superstar	7"	Atlantic	2091052	1971	**£4**	
Overture From Tommy	7"	Atlantic	2091022	1970	**£4**	

ASSOCIATES

Title	Format	Label	Cat. No.	Year	Price	Notes
39 Lyon Street	12"	RSO	X78	1981	**£6**	
Affectionate Punch	7"	Fiction	FICS11	1980	**£4**	
Boys Keep Swinging	7"	Double Hip	DHR1	1980	**£40**	
Boys Keep Swinging	7"	MCA		1980	**£25**	promo
Even Dogs In The Wild	7"	Lyntone	LYN11649	1982	**£4**	Flexipop flexi
Kitchen Person	7"	Situation 2	SIT7	1981	**£4**	
Kitchen Person	12"	Situation 2	SIT7	1981	**£6**	
Message Oblique Speech	7"	Situation 2	SIT10	1981	**£4**	
Message Oblique Speech	12"	Situation 2	SIT10	1981	**£6**	
Q Quarters	7"	Situation 2	SIT4	1981	**£4**	
Q Quarters	12"	Situation 2	SIT4	1981	**£6**	
Tell Me Easter's On Friday	7"	Situation 2	SIT1	1981	**£4**	
Tell Me Easter's On Friday	12"	Situation 2	SIT1	1981	**£6**	
White Car In Germany	7"	Situation 2	SIT11	1981	**£4**	
White Car In Germany	12"	Situation 2	SIT11	1981	**£6**	

ASSOCIATION

Most of the successful Californian groups that emerged during the late sixties had backgrounds rooted in folk music and naturally tended to favour melodic material and close harmony singing. The Association were very much a case in point, sustaining a six year career on the back of four tuneful singles, which if not exactly classics, are at any rate fondly remembered. "Along Comes Mary", "Cherish", "Windy", and "Never My Love" are to be found scattered through their LP releases alongside similar fare, although, the vagueries of the pop charts being what they are, it was the much less well known "Time For Living" that scored in a small way in the UK.

Title	Format	Label	Cat. No.	Year	Price	Notes
Along Comes Mary	7"	London	HLT10054	1966	**£5**	
And Then...Along Came Association	LP	London	HAT8305	1966	**£15**	
Association	LP	W. Bros	WS1800	1969	**£12**	US
Birthday	LP	W. Bros	WS1733	1968	**£12**	US
Cherish	7"	London	HLT10074	1966	**£4**	
Everything That Touches You	7"	W. Bros	WB7163	1968	**£4**	
Goodbye Columbus	LP	W. Bros	WS1786	1969	**£12**	US
Goodbye Columbus	7"	W. Bros	WB7267	1969	**£4**	
Greatest Hits	LP	W. Bros	WS1767	1969	**£12**	US

Title	Format	Label	Cat. No.	Year	Price	Notes
Insight Out	LP	London	MHAT8342	1967	**£15**	
Just About The Same	7"	W. Bros	WB7372	1970	**£4**	
Live	LP	W. Bros	2WS1868	1970	**£20**	US
Never My Love	7"	London	HLT10157	1967	**£4**	
No Fair At All	7"	London	HLT10118	1967	**£4**	
Pandora's Golden Heebie Jeebies	7"	London	HLT10098	1966	**£6**	
Renaissance	LP	London	HAT8313	1967	**£15**	
Six Man Band	7"	W. Bros	WB7229	1968	**£4**	
Stop The Motor	LP	W. Bros	WS1927	1971	**£12**	US
Time For Living	7"	W. Bros	WB7195	1968	**£4**	chart single
Waterbeds In Trinidad	LP	CBS	65009	1972	**£10**	
Windy	7"	London	HLT10140	1967	**£4**	
Windy	7"	W. Bros	WB7119	1969	**£4**	

ASTLEY, EDWIN, ORCHESTRA

Title	Format	Label	Cat. No.	Year	Price	Notes
Danger Man Theme	7"	RCA	RCA1492	1965	**£6**	

ASTORS

Title	Format	Label	Cat. No.	Year	Price	Notes
Candy	7"	Atlantic	584245	1969	**£4**	
Candy	7"	Atlantic	AT4037	1965	**£10**	

ASTRAL NAVIGATION

Title	Format	Label	Cat. No.	Year	Price	Notes
Astral Navigation	LP	Holyground	130	1971	**£150**	

ASTRONAUTS

Title	Format	Label	Cat. No.	Year	Price	Notes
Banana	7"	Hala Gala	HG14	196-	**£10**	
Before You Leave	7"	Hala Gala	HG9	1966	**£10**	
Before You Leave	7"	Island	WI3065	1967	**£8**	
I'll Be There	7"	Hala Gala	HG13	196-	**£10**	
Oh Why I Still Love You	7"	Hala Gala	HG12	196-	**£10**	

ASTRONAUTS (2)

Title	Format	Label	Cat. No.	Year	Price	Notes
Astronauts Go Go Go	LP	RCA	LPM3307	1965	**£12**	US
Astronauts Orbit Campus	LP	RCA	LPM2903	1964	**£12**	US
Baju	7"	RCA	RCA1349	1963	**£4**	
Competition Coupe	LP	RCA	LPM2858	1964	**£12**	US
Down The Line	LP	RCA	LPM3454	1965	**£12**	US
Everything Is A-OK	LP	RCA	LPM2782	1964	**£12**	US
Favorites For You, Our Fans, From Us	LP	RCA	LPM3359	1965	**£12**	US
Out Of Sight	LP	Decca	DL4751	1966	**£10**	US
Rockin' With The Astronauts	LP	RCA	PRM183	1964	**£12**	US
Surf Party	LP	20th Century	TFM3131	1964	**£12**	US
Surfin' With The Astronauts	LP	RCA	LPM2760	1963	**£15**	US
Travelin' Men	LP	RCA	LPM3733	1967	**£10**	US
Wild On The Beach	LP	RCA	LPM3441	1965	**£10**	US
Wild Wild Winter	LP	Decca	DL4699	1966	**£10**	US

AT LAST THE 1958 ROCK'N'ROLL SHOW

Title	Format	Label	Cat. No.	Year	Price	Notes
I Can't Drive	7"	CBS	3349	1968	**£8**	

ATHENIANS

Title	Format	Label	Cat. No.	Year	Price	Notes
I've Got Love If You Want It	7"	Waverley	SLP532	1964	**£15**	PS
Thinking Of Our Love	7"	Waverley	SLP533	1965	**£15**	PS
You Tell Me	7"	Edinburgh.SC.	ESC1	1964	**£15**	

ATHENS, GLENN & THE TROJANS

Title	Format	Label	Cat. No.	Year	Price	Notes
	7" EP	Spot			**£60**	

ATKIN, PETE

Pete Atkin was the author of some half dozen LPs, whose stylish and intelligent singer-songwriting was somehow never as popular as it should have been. In the collectors' market too this remains the case, as such classics of the genre as "A King At Nightfall" and "The Road Of Silk" steadfastly refuse to fetch even moderate collectors' prices, despite being long deleted. Not that Atkin himself should worry, having forged a satisfying career as a television producer. The lyricist on the records has done rather well for himself too - his name is Clive James - yes, it is the same one!

Title	Format	Label	Cat. No.	Year	Price	Notes
Be Careful When They Offer You	7"	Philips	6006050	1970	**£4**	
Beware Of The Beautiful Stranger	LP	Fontana	6309011	1970	**£15**	
Driving Through Mythical America	LP	Philips	6308070	1971	**£12**	

ATKINS, CHET

Title	Format	Label	Cat. No.	Year	Price	Notes
At Home	LP	RCA	LPM1544	1957	**£15**	US
Chet Atkins' Gallopin' Guitar	LP-10"	RCA	LPM3079	1952	**£30**	US

Finger Style Guitar	LP	RCA	LPM1383	1956	**£15**	US
Guitar Genius	7" EP	RCA	RCX7118	1963	**£4**	
Hi Fi In Focus	LP	RCA	LPM1577	1957	**£15**	US
In Three Dimensions	LP	RCA	LPM1197	1956	**£15**	US
Picks On The Beatles	LP	RCA	SF7813	1966	**£12**	
Session With Chet Atkins	LP	RCA	LPM1090	1955	**£15**	US
String Dustin'	LP-10"	RCA	LPM3167	1953	**£25**	US
Stringin' Along	LP	RCA	LPM1236	1956	**£15**	US
Stringin' Along	LP-10"	RCA	LPM3169	1953	**£25**	US
Teen Scene	LP	RCA	SF7602	1963	**£10**	
Teensville	LP	RCA	RD27168	1960	**£12**	

ATLANTIC BRIDGE

Atlantic Bridge	LP	Dawn	DNLS3014	1970	**£10**	
I Can't Lie To You	7"	Dawn	DNX2507	1971	**£4**	

ATLANTIC OCEAN

Tranquility Bay	LP	Love		1970	**£60**	Swedish

ATLANTIS

Atlantis	LP	Polydor	2391176	1974	**£10**	
Atlantis	LP	Vertigo	6360609	1973	**£20**	spiral label
Get On Board	LP	Venus	1011	1975	**£10**	US
It's Getting Better	LP	Vertigo	6360614	1974	**£12**	
Live	LP	Vertigo	6623900	1974	**£15**	
Oh Baby	LP	Vertigo	6360621	1974	**£12**	
Top Of The Bill	LP	Venus	F1002	1976	**£10**	US

ATMOSPHERES

Fickle Chicken	7"	London	HLW8977	1959	**£8**	
Telegraph	7"	London	HLW9091	1960	**£6**	

ATOMIC ROOSTER

Atomic Rooster	LP	B&C	CAS1010	1970	**£15**	Chart LP
Death Walks Behind You	LP	B&C	CAS1026	1970	**£15**	Chart LP
Friday The 13th	7"	B&C	CB121	1970	**£4**	
In Hearing Of	LP	Pegasus	PEG1	1971	**£15**	Chart LP
Made In England	LP	Dawn	DNLS3038	1972	**£12**	
Made In England	LP	Dawn	DNLS3038	1972	**£15**	denim cover
Nice And Greasy	LP	Dawn	DNLS3049	1973	**£15**	
Save Me	7"	Dawn	DNS1029	1972	**£4**	
Stand By Me	7"	Dawn	DNS1027	1972	**£4**	
Tell Your Story - Sing Your Song	7"	Decca	FR13503	1974	**£6**	export

ATTACK

The Attack were best known as the performers of the other version of "Hi Ho Silver Lining", but unfortunately for them, despite receiving fairly extensive radio play, they lost out to Jeff Beck. The guitarist with the Attack was David O'List who subsequently became a member of the Nice.

Created By Clive	7"	Decca	F12631	1967	**£10**	
Hi Ho Silver Lining	7"	Decca	F12578	1967	**£8**	
Neville Thumbcatch	7"	Decca	F12725	1968	**£12**	
Please Mr.Phil Spector	7"	Philips	BF1585	1967	**£12**	
Try It	7"	Decca	F12550	1967	**£15**	

ATTILA

Attila was a duo - Billy Joel and a drummer.

Attila	LP	Epic	E30030	1970	**£20**	US

ATTITUDES

Attitudes	LP	Dark Horse	AMLH22008	1975	**£12**	
Good News	LP	Dark Horse	K56385	1977	**£10**	

ATTRACTIONS

Party Line	7"	Columbia	DB8010	1966	**£10**	
Stupid Girl	7"	Columbia	DB7936	1966	**£8**	

ATTRACTIONS (2)

Mad About The Wrong Boy	LP	F-Beat	XXLP8	1980	**£10**	with 7" (COMB1)

ATTRITION

Monkey In A Bin	12"	Uniton	19841	1984	**£6**	

Two Traces	7"	Ad. In Reality	AINR2	1982	**£8**	flexi

AU GO-GO SINGERS

San Francisco Bay Blues	7"	Columbia	DB7493	1965	**£6**	
They Call Us The Au Go-Go Singers	LP	Roulette	R25280	1964	**£25**	US

AUBREY SMALL

Aubrey Small	LP	Polydor	2383048	1971	**£40**	

AUDIENCE

As label-mates of Genesis and Van Der Graaf Generator, Audience played very much the same kind of complex structured but essentially melodic material, although with rather less commercial success. The real Audience rarity, however, is the first LP, recorded for Polydor. The scarcity of this record has led some dealers to conclude that the record was withdrawn soon after its release, although the truth is that it was simply deleted after a short time, due to its sales being rather poor.

Audience	LP	Polydor	583065	1969	**£70**	
Belladonna Moonshine	7"	Charisma	CB126	1971	**£4**	
Friends Friends Friends	LP	Charisma	CAS1012	1970	**£20**	
House On The Hill	LP	Charisma	CAS1032	1971	**£12**	
Indian Summer	7"	Charisma	CB141	1971	**£5**	PS
Lunch	LP	Charisma	CAS1054	1972	**£12**	
Stand By The Door	7"	Charisma	CB185	1972	**£4**	
You Can't Beat Them	LP	Charisma	CS7	1973	**£10**	
You're Not Smiling	7"	Charisma	CB156	1971	**£4**	

AUDREY

Getting Ready For A Heartache	7"	Trend	6099006	1970	**£5**	
Love Me Tonight	7"	Downtown	DT414	196-	**£8**	
Lovers' Concerto	7"	Downtown	DT418	196-	**£8**	
Oh I Was Wrong	7"	Downtown	DT454	196-	**£8**	
Sweeter Than Sugar	7"	Downtown	DT452	196-	**£8**	
You'll Lose A Good Thing	7"	Downtown	DT436	196-	**£8**	

AUGER, BRIAN

Brian Auger's long career as a jazz-rock organist peaked on the recordings made jointly with singer Julie Driscoll. For just a short while, Auger was more than just the skilled craftsman of his recordings before and since, becoming part of a group with real innovative power. Nothing Julie Driscoll and the Brian Auger Trinity recorded together could quite match the brilliance of "This Wheel's On Fire", but all the Marmalade recordings contain much worthwhile and memorable music.

Befour	LP	RCA	SF8101	1970	**£15**	
Better Land	LP	Polydor	2383062	1971	**£12**	
Closer To It	LP	CBS	65625	1973	**£12**	
Definitely What	LP	Marmalade	607003	1968	**£20**	
Encore	LP	W. Bros	K56458	1978	**£10**	
Fool Killer	7"	Columbia	DB7590	1965	**£8**	
Green Onions '65	7"	Columbia	DB7715	1965	**£6**	
Happiness Heartache	LP	W. Bros	K56326	1977	**£10**	
I Don't Know Where You Are	7"	Marmalade	598006	1968	**£4**	
I Want To Take You Higher	7"	RCA	RCA1947	1970	**£4**	
Live Oblivion	LP	RCA	0645	1974	**£12**	US
Oblivion Express	LP	RCA	SF8170	1971	**£15**	
Red Beans And Rice	7"	Marmalade	598003	1967	**£4**	
Reinforcements	LP	RCA	1210	1974	**£12**	US
Second Wind	LP	Polydor	2383104	1972	**£12**	
Straight Ahead	LP	CBS	80058	1974	**£12**	
Tiger	7"	Columbia	DB8163	1967	**£6**	
What You Gonna Do	7"	Marmalade	598015	1969	**£4**	

AUGER, BRIAN, JIMMY PAGE & SONNY BOY WILLIAMSON

Don't Send Me No Flowers	LP	Marmalade	608004	1968	**£30**	

AUM

Bluesvibes	LP	London	HAK8401	1969	**£15**	
Resurrection	LP	Fillmore	30002	1969	**£15**	US

AUNT MARY

Aunt Mary	LP	Polydor		1971	**£80**	
Janus	LP	Vertigo		1973	**£100**	
Loaded	LP	Philips		1971	**£150**	

AUSTIN, PATTI

Are You Ready For Love	7"	CBS	7180	1971	**£4**	

AUSTIN, PETER

Title	Format	Label	Cat. No.	Year	Price	Notes
Your Love	7"	Caltone	TONE125	196-	**£8**	

AUSTIN, REG

Title	Format	Label	Cat. No.	Year	Price	Notes
My Saddest Day	7"	Pye	7N15885	1965	**£12**	

AUSTIN, SIL

Title	Format	Label	Cat. No.	Year	Price	Notes
Band With The Beat	7" EP	Mercury	MEP9540	1958	**£8**	
Don't You Just Know It	7"	Mercury	7MT220	1958	**£10**	
Go Sil Go	7" EP	Mercury	MEP9541	1958	**£8**	
Hey Eula	7"	Mercury	7MT225	1958	**£8**	

AUSTRALIAN PLAYBOYS

Title	Format	Label	Cat. No.	Year	Price	Notes
Black Sheep R.I.P.	7"	Immediate	IM054	1967	**£50**	

AUTOSALVAGE

The one LP recorded by Autosalvage is a little like Jefferson Airplane and a little like The Lovin' Spoonful, but with more ambitious arranging than either (including the use of Medieval instruments, though not a Medieval sound). Unfortunately, the songs are not as strong as they might be, but the record is still very interesting. Frank Zappa is supposed to have had a hand in the group's discovery.

Title	Format	Label	Cat. No.	Year	Price	Notes
Autosalvage	LP	RCA	LSP3940	1968	**£15**	US

AUTRY, GENE

Title	Format	Label	Cat. No.	Year	Price	Notes
At The Rodeo	LP-10"	Columbia	JL8001	1949	**£25**	US
Champion Western Adventures	LP	Columbia	CL677	1955	**£15**	US
Christmas With Gene Autry	LP	Challenge	CHL600	1958	**£15**	US
Gene Autry Sings Peter Cottontail	LP-10"	Columbia	CL2568	1955	**£25**	US
Golden Hits	LP	RCA	LPM2623	1962	**£12**	US
Greatest Hits	LP	Columbia	CL1575	1961	**£15**	US
Little Johnny Pilgrim	LP-10"	Columbia	MJV83	195-	**£25**	US
Merry Christmas	LP-10"	Columbia	CL2547	1955	**£25**	US
Rusty The Rocking Horse	LP-10"	Columbia	MJV94	195-	**£25**	US
Stampede	LP-10"	Columbia	JL8009		**£25**	US
Story Of The Nativity	LP-10"	Columbia	MJV82	195-	**£25**	US
Western Classic, Vol.1	LP-10"	Columbia	HL9001	195-	**£25**	US
Western Classic, Vol.2	LP-10"	Columbia	HL9002	195-	**£25**	US

AVALANCHE

Title	Format	Label	Cat. No.	Year	Price	Notes
Finding My Way Home	7"	Parlophone	R5890	1971	**£4**	

AVALON, FRANKIE

Title	Format	Label	Cat. No.	Year	Price	Notes
And Now About Mr.Avalon	LP	Chancellor	CHL5022	1961	**£10**	US
Christmas Album	LP	Chancellor	CHL5031	1962	**£12**	US
Cleopatra	LP	Chancellor	CHL5032	1963	**£12**	US
Darling	7"	London	HL8636	1958	**£6**	
Dede Dinah	7"	HMV	POP453	1958	**£8**	
Don't Throw Away All Those Teardrops	7"	HMV	POP727	1960	**£4**	chart single
Fifteen Greatest Hits	LP	United Artists	UAL3382	1964	**£10**	US
Frankie Avalon	LP	Chancellor	CHL5001	1958	**£20**	US
Frankie Avalon	7" EP	HMV	7EG8471	1958	**£6**	
Frankie Avalon No.2	7" EP	HMV	7EG8482	1958	**£6**	
Frankie Avalon No.3	7" EP	HMV	7EG8507	1958	**£6**	
Gingerbread	7"	HMV	POP517	1958	**£6**	chart single
Italiano	LP	Chancellor	CHL5025	1962	**£10**	US
Songs From Muscle Beach Party	LP	United Artists	UAL3371	1964	**£10**	US
Summer Scene	LP	Chancellor	CHL5011	1960	**£12**	US
Swingin' On A Rainbow	LP	Chancellor	CHLX5004	1959	**£15**	US
Venus	7"	HMV	POP603	1959	**£4**	chart single
Whole Lot Of Frankie	LP	Chancellor	CHL5018	1961	**£12**	US
Why	7"	HMV	POP688	1960	**£4**	chart single
You Are Mine	LP	Chancellor	CHL5027	1962	**£10**	US
Young And In Love	LP	Chancellor	CHL69801	1960	**£20**	US
Young Frankie Avalon	LP	Chancellor	CHL5002	1959	**£15**	US

AVALONS

Title	Format	Label	Cat. No.	Year	Price	Notes
Every Day	7"	Island	WI263	1966	**£8**	

AVANT-GARDE

Title	Format	Label	Cat. No.	Year	Price	Notes
Naturally Stoned	7"	CBS	1333160	1975	**£4**	
Naturally Stoned	7"	CBS	3704	1968	**£6**	

AVENGERS

Everyone's Gonna Wonder	7"	Parlophone	R5661	1968	**£6**	

AVENGERS (2)

American In Me	12"	White Noise	WNR002	1979	**£12**	
American In Me	12"	White Noise	WNR002	1981	**£12**	different PS
We Are The One	7"	Dangerhouse	SFD400	1977	**£25**	PS in plastic bag, red vinyl
Real Cool Hits	LP	Mark 56 Recs		1965	**£60**	US

AVON CITIES SKIFFLE GROUP

Hey Hey Daddy Blues	7"	Tempo	A146	1956	**£4**	
How Long Blues	7"	Tempo	A156	1957	**£4**	
Lonesome Day Blues	7"	Tempo	A157	1957	**£4**	
Ray Bush & Avon Cities Skiffle Group	7" EP	Tempo	EXA40	195-	**£5**	
Ray Bush & Avon Cities Skiffle ...No.2	7" EP	Tempo	EXA50	195-	**£5**	
This Little Light Of Mine	7"	Tempo	A149	1956	**£4**	

AVON, ALAN & THE TOY SHOP

Night To Remember	7"	Concord	CONC005	1974	**£8**	

AVONS

Seven Little Girls Sitting In The...	7"	Columbia	DB4363	1959	**£4**	chart single

AVONS (2)

Avons	LP	Hull	HLP1000	1960	**£150**	US

AXELROD, DAVID

Auction	LP	MCA	MCF2664	1974	**£10**	
Earth Rot	LP	Capitol		1970	**£12**	US
Rock Messiah	LP	RCA	4636	1972	**£12**	US
Seriously Deep	LP	Polydor	2391193	1975	**£10**	
Songs Of Innocence	LP	Capitol	ST2982	1968	**£15**	

AXTON, HOYT

Greenback Dollar	LP	Stateside	SL10082	1964	**£15**	
Thunder And Lightnin'	LP	Stateside	SL10096	1964	**£15**	

AYERS, KEVIN

As one of the founders of the "English eccentric" school of rock music, Kevin Ayers still makes records for the loyal army of fans who have followed his activities since his days as bass player for the Soft Machine. The two earliest albums contain what is arguably his most interesting music, with telling contributions from the supporting musicians, who include Soft Machine on "Joy Of A Toy", and on "Shooting At The Moon", saxophonist Lol Coxhill, composer/arranger David Bedford (here playing keyboards), and the youthful Mike Oldfield.

Bananamour	LP	Harvest	SHVL807	1973	**£12**	
Caribbean Moon	7"	Harvest	HAR5071	1973	**£4**	
Caribbean Moon	7"	Harvest	HAR5100	1975	**£4**	
Confessions Of Dr.Dream	LP	Island	ILPS9263	1974	**£10**	
Joy Of A Toy	LP	Harvest	SHVL763	1970	**£15**	
Odd Ditties	LP	Harvest	SHSM2005	1976	**£10**	
Oh Wot A Dream	7"	Harvest	HAR5064	1972	**£4**	
Puis-Je?	7"	Harvest	HAR5027	1970	**£6**	
Shooting At The Moon	LP	Harvest	SHSP4005	1971	**£15**	
Singing A Song In The Morning	7"	Harvest	HAR5011	1970	**£8**	
Stranger In Blue Suede Shoes	7"	Harvest	HAR5042	1971	**£6**	
Sweet Deceiver	LP	Island	ILPS9322	1975	**£10**	
Whatevershebringswesing	LP	Harvest	SHVL800	1973	**£12**	
Yes We Have No Mananas	LP	Harvest	SHSP4057	1976	**£10**	

AYERS, ROY

Evolution	7"	Polydor	2066671	1976	**£4**	

AYSHEA

Another Night	7"	Polydor	56302	1969	**£4**	
Only Your Love Can Save Me	7"	Polydor	56276	1968	**£6**	
Peep My Love	7"	Fontana	TF627	1965	**£4**	

AZTEC CAMERA

Just Like Gold	7"	Postcard	81-3	1981	**£12**	
Just Like Gold	7"	Postcard	81-3	1981	**£15**	lyric postcard
Mattress Of Wire	7"	Postcard	81-8	1981	**£15**	PS
Pillar To Post	7"	Rough Trade	RT112	1982	**£4**	

Pillar To Post .... 7" .... Rough Trade .. RT112P .... 1982........ **£8** .... pic disc

AZTECS

Live At The Ad-Lib Club .... LP .... World Artists ... WAM2001 .... 1964...... **£50** .... US

B

B MOVIE

Title	Format	Label	Cat. No.	Year	Price	Notes
Marilyn Dreams	12"	Some Bizarre	DMX443	1981	**£6**	
Marilyn Dreams	7"	Some Bizarre	DM443	1981	**£4**	
Nowhere Girl	12"	Dead Good	BIGDEAD9	1980	**£15**	
Nowhere Girl	7"	Some Bizarre	BZZ8	1982	**£4**	chart single
Nowhere Girl	12"	Some Bizarre	BZZ8	1982	**£6**	
Remembrance Day	12"	Some Bizarre	DMX437	1981	**£6**	
Take Three	7"	Dead Good	DEAD9	1980	**£20**	

B-52'S

Title	Format	Label	Cat. No.	Year	Price	Notes
Future Generation	7"	Island	ISD107	1983	**£6**	double
Planet Claire	7"	Island	WIP6551	1980	**£5**	pic disc
Rock Lobster	7"	Boofant	DB52	1978	**£10**	US
Rock Lobster	7"	Island	PSR438	1979	**£5**	
Strobe Light	7"	Island	WIP6665	1980	**£4**	plastic sleeve
Wild Planet	LP	Island	ILPS9622	1980	**£12**	with carrying bag, badge

B.B.BLUNDER

"Worker's Playtime" is the often overlooked third LP by the Blossom Toes, and shares many of the inventive qualities of its predecessors. The cover is a delight, being a parody of the Radio Times, with all the song lyrics and credits disguised as programme information.

Title	Format	Label	Cat. No.	Year	Price	Notes
Sticky Living	7"	United Artists	UP5203	1971	**£4**	
Workers Playtime	LP	United Artists	UAS29156	1971	**£10**	

BABE RUTH

Title	Format	Label	Cat. No.	Year	Price	Notes
Amar Caballero	LP	Harvest	SHVL812	1973	**£10**	
Babe Ruth	LP	Harvest	SHSP4038	1975	**£10**	

BABY

Title	Format	Label	Cat. No.	Year	Price	Notes
Heartbreaker	7"	Spark	SRL1030	1971	**£4**	

BACHDENKEL

Title	Format	Label	Cat. No.	Year	Price	Notes
Lemmings	LP	Initial	IRL001	1977	**£10**	
Stalingrad	LP	Initial	IRL002	1977	**£10**	

BACHELOR, JOHNNY

Title	Format	Label	Cat. No.	Year	Price	Notes
Mumbles	7"	London	HLN9074	1960	**£20**	

BACK ALLEY CHOIR

Title	Format	Label	Cat. No.	Year	Price	Notes
Back Alley Choir	LP	York		1972	**£60**	

BACK DOOR

Title	Format	Label	Cat. No.	Year	Price	Notes
Activate	LP	W. Bros	K56243	1976	**£10**	
Another Fine Mess	LP	W. Bros	K56098	1975	**£10**	
Back Door	LP	Blakey	BLP5989	1972	**£20**	
Back Door	LP	W. Bros	K46231	1973	**£10**	
Dashing White Sergeant	7"	W. Bros	K16490	1975	**£4**	
Eighth Street Nites	LP	W. Bros	K46265	1973	**£10**	

BACK PORCH MAJORITY

Title	Format	Label	Cat. No.	Year	Price	Notes
Ramblin' Man	7"	Columbia	DB7627	1965	**£4**	

BACK STREET BAND

Title	Format	Label	Cat. No.	Year	Price	Notes
This Ain't The Road	7"	Ember	EMBS277	1970	**£4**	

BACK STREET CRAWLER

Title	Format	Label	Cat. No.	Year	Price	Notes
Band Plays On	LP	Atlantic	K50173	1975	**£10**	
Second Street	LP	Atlantic	K50267	1976	**£10**	

BACON FAT

Title	Format	Label	Cat. No.	Year	Price	Notes
Evil	7"	Blue Horizon	573181	1971	**£5**	
Grease One For Me	LP	Blue Horizon	763858	1970	**£20**	
Nobody But You	7"	Blue Horizon	573171	1970	**£5**	
Tough Dude	LP	Blue Horizon	2431001	1971	**£40**	

BACON, GAR

Title	Format	Label	Cat. No.	Year	Price	Notes
Chains Of Love	7"	Felsted	AF107	1958	**£4**	
Marshall Marshall	7"	Fontana	H196	1959	**£8**	

BAD COMPANY

Title	Format	Label	Cat. No.	Year	Price	Notes
Deal With The Preacher	7"	Island	BCDJ1	1976	**£25**	1 sided promo
Desolation Angels	12"	Swansong		1980	**£10**	promo

BADFINGER

Title	Format	Label	Cat. No.	Year	Price	Notes
Airwaves	LP	Elektra	K52129	1979	**£10**	
Apple Of My Eye	7"	Apple	49	1974	**£6**	
Ass	LP	Apple	SAPCOR27	1974	**£30**	
Badfinger	LP	W. Bros	K56023	1974	**£10**	
Come And Get It	7"	Apple	20	1969	**£8**	PS
Day After Day	7"	Apple	40	1972	**£4**	chart single
Day After Day	7"	Apple	40	1972	**£10**	PS
Love Is Easy	7"	W. Bros	K16323	1973	**£4**	
Magic Christian Music	LP	Apple	SAPCOR12	1970	**£30**	
No Dice	LP	Apple	SAPCOR16	1970	**£30**	
No Matter What	7"	Apple	31	1970	**£6**	PS
Say No More	LP	Radio Rec.	16030	1981	**£10**	
Straight Up	LP	Apple	SAPCOR19	1972	**£30**	
Wish You Were Here	LP	W. Bros	2827	1975	**£15**	US

BADGER

Badger was the group formed by Tony Kaye after his departure from Yes. "One Live Badger" has a pop-up cover - a badger (naturally) stands up when the gatefold sleeve is opened.

Title	Format	Label	Cat. No.	Year	Price	Notes
One Live Badger	LP	Atlantic	K40473	1973	**£15**	
White Lady	LP	Epic	80009	1974	**£12**	
White Lady	7"	Epic	EPC2326	1974	**£4**	

BAEZ, JOAN

Title	Format	Label	Cat. No.	Year	Price	Notes
Any Day Now	LP	Vanguard	55/66	1968	**£12**	double
Baptism	LP	Vanguard	SVRL19000	1968	**£10**	
Blessed Are	LP	Vanguard	VSD6570/1	1971	**£12**	double
Carry It On	LP	Vanguard	VSD519042	1972	**£10**	
Come From The Shadows	LP	A&M	AMLH64339	1972	**£10**	
David's Album	LP	Vanguard	SVRL19050	1969	**£10**	
Farewell Angelina	LP	Fontana	STFL6058	1965	**£10**	chart LP
Farewell Angelina	7"	Fontana	TF639	1965	**£4**	chart single
In Concert 1	LP	Fontana	STFL6033	1962	**£10**	
In Concert 2	LP	Fontana	STFL6035	1963	**£10**	chart LP
It's All Over Now Baby Blue	7"	Fontana	TF604	1965	**£4**	chart single
Joan	LP	Fontana	STFL6082	1967	**£10**	
Joan Baez 1	LP	Fontana	STFL6002	1960	**£10**	chart LP
Joan Baez 2	LP	Fontana	STFL6025	1961	**£10**	
Joan Baez 5	LP	Fontana	STFL6043	1964	**£10**	chart LP
Night They Drove Old Dixie Down	7"	Vanguard	VS35138	1971	**£4**	chart single
Noel	LP	Fontana	STFL6078	1966	**£10**	
One Day At A Time	LP	Vanguard	VSD23010	1970	**£10**	
Portrait	LP	Fontana	STFL6077	1966	**£10**	
There But For Fortune	7"	Fontana	TF587	1965	**£4**	chart single
We Shall Overcome	7"	Fontana	TF564	1965	**£4**	chart single

BAILEY, BURR

Title	Format	Label	Cat. No.	Year	Price	Notes
San Francisco Bay	7"	Decca	F11686	1963	**£4**	

BAKER, GINGER

Title	Format	Label	Cat. No.	Year	Price	Notes
Eleven Sides Of Baker	LP	Mountain	5005	1977	**£10**	
Fela Ransome Kuti with...	LP	Regal Z.	SLRZ1023	1972	**£10**	
Stratavarious	LP	Polydor	2383133	1972	**£10**	

BAKER, GLEN

Title	Format	Label	Cat. No.	Year	Price	Notes
Brief Encounter	LP	The Stand	THESTAND3	1985	**£100**	

BAKER, JEANETTE

Title	Format	Label	Cat. No.	Year	Price	Notes
Crazy With You	7"	Vogue	V9143	1959	**£15**	

BAKER, LAVERN

Title	Format	Label	Cat. No.	Year	Price	Notes
Best Of	LP	Atlantic	ATL5002	1964	**£20**	
Best Of Lavern	7" EP	Atlantic	AET6009	1965	**£12**	

Title	Format	Label	Cat. No.	Year	Price	
Blues Ballads	LP	Atlantic	8030	1959	**£30**	US
Bumble Bee	7"	London	HLK9252	1960	**£12**	
Game Of Love	7"	London	HLE8442	1957	**£30**	
Get Up Get Up	7"	London	HLE8260	1956	**£30**	
Humpty Dumpty Heart	7"	London	HLE8524	1957	**£20**	
I Can't Love You Enough	7"	London	HLE8396	1957	**£20**	
I Cried A Tear	7"	London	HLE8790	1959	**£15**	
I've Waited Too Long	7"	London	HLE8871	1959	**£10**	
Jim Dandy	7"7"	Columbia	DB3879	1957	**£40**	
Lavern	LP	Atlantic	8002	1956	**£60**	US
Lavern Baker	LP	Atlantic	8007	1957	**£40**	US
Learning To Love	7"	London	HLE8638	1958	**£15**	
Precious Memories	LP	Atlantic	8036	1959	**£30**	US
Rock And Roll With...	LP	London	HAE2107	1958	**£60**	
Saved	LP	London	HAE2422	1961	**£30**	
Saved	7"	London	HLK9343	1961	**£15**	
See See Rider	LP	Atlantic	587133	1968	**£10**	
See See Rider	LP	London	HAK8074	1963	**£20**	
See See Rider	7"	London	HLK9649	1963	**£10**	
Sings Bessie Smith	LP	London	LJZ-K15139	1958	**£30**	
So High So Low	7"	London	HLE8945	1959	**£10**	
That Lucky Old Sun	7"	London	HLA8199	1955	**£30**	
Tiny Tim	7"	London	HLE9023	1960	**£10**	
Tweedle Dee	7"	Columbia	SCM5172	1955	**£45**	
Voodoo Voodoo	7"	London	HLK9468	1961	**£15**	
Whipper Snapper	7"	London	HLE8672	1958	**£15**	

BAKER, LAVERN & JIMMY RICKS

Title	Format	Label	Cat. No.	Year	Price	
You're The Boss	7"	London	HLK9300	1961	**£10**	

BAKER, MICKEY

Title	Format	Label	Cat. No.	Year	Price	
But Wild	LP	King	K839	1963	**£30**	US
Wildest Guitar	LP	Atlantic	8035	1959	**£60**	US

BAKER, TWO TON

Title	Format	Label	Cat. No.	Year	Price	
Clink Clank	7"	London	HL8121	1955	**£25**	

BAKERLOO

Bakerloo (originally Bakerloo Blues Line) were one of the many guitarist-led blues groups to surface in the wake of the pioneering work carried out by the various editions of John Mayall's Bluesbreakers. This one featured Dave "Clem" Clempson, whose name has graced many album sleeves since - most notably during his time as a member of Humble Pie.

Title	Format	Label	Cat. No.	Year	Price	
Bakerloo	LP	Harvest	SHVL762	1969	**£50**	
Driving Backwards	7"	Harvest	HAR5004	1969	**£8**	

BALAAM & THE ANGEL

Title	Format	Label	Cat. No.	Year	Price	
World Of Light	12"	Chapter 22	CH22001	1984	**£8**	

BALANCE

Title	Format	Label	Cat. No.	Year	Price	
Balance	LP	Incus		1973	**£25**	

BALDRY, LONG JOHN

John Baldry, known as "long" because he is indeed something like six foot six tall, has for most of his career sung the blues, for which his distinctive, smokey voice is an ideal instrument. He is featured on Alexis Korner's "R&B At The Marquee" album, and was a member of Cyril Davies' group. When Davies died, Baldry became the leader of the group, which now became called the Hoochie Coochie Men. The earliest recordings in Baldry's name are by this group. With the switch to Pye, Baldry made what was probably a wrong career move when he decided to start singing middle-of-the-road ballad material. Four hits followed, but then nothing, and his attempts to recapture his blues audience in the seventies were not very successful.

Title	Format	Label	Cat. No.	Year	Price	
Cuckoo	7"	United Artists	UP1158	1966	**£5**	
Drifter	7"	United Artists	UP1136	1966	**£5**	
Everything Stops For Tea	LP	W. Bros	K46160	1972	**£10**	
How Long Will It Last	7"	United Artists	UP1107	1965	**£5**	
I'm On To You Baby	7"	United Artists	UP1078	1965	**£6**	
Iko Iko	7"	W. Bros	K16175	1972	**£4**	
It Ain't Easy	LP	W. Bros	K46008	1971	**£10**	
Let Me Go	7"	United Artists	UP1204	1967	**£4**	
Let The Heartaches Begin	LP	Pye	NSPL18208	1968	**£10**	
Let There Be Long John	LP	Pye	NSPL18228	1968	**£10**	
Long John's Blues	LP	United Artists	ULP1081	1964	**£30**	
Long John's Blues	7" EP	United Artists	UEP1013	1965	**£8**	
Looking At Long John	LP	United Artists	SULP1146	1966	**£30**	
Unseen Hands	7"	United Artists	UP1124	1966	**£5**	

Up Above My Head ..... 7" ..... United Artists .. UP1056 ..... 1964 ..... **£8**

BALDWIN
Land At Rainbow's End ..... 7" ..... Decca ..... F22624 ..... 1967 ..... **£4**

BALFOUR, KEITH
Dreaming ..... 7" ..... Studio One ..... SO2079 ..... 196- **£10**

BALL, EDWARD L'ORANGE MECHANIK
Symphony ..... 7" ..... Artpop ..... POP44 ..... 1985 ..... **£4**

BALLARD, FLORENCE
Doesn't Matter How I Say It ..... 7" ..... Stateside ..... SS2113 ..... 1968 ..... **£8**

BALLARD, FRANK
Rhythm And Blues Party ..... LP ..... Philips ..... 1985 ..... 1962 ..... **£240** ..... US

BALLARD, HANK & THE MIDNIGHTERS
1963 Sound Of Hank Ballard ..... LP ..... King ..... 815 ..... 1963 ..... **£20** ..... US
Biggest Hits ..... LP ..... King ..... 867 ..... 1963 ..... **£20** ..... US
Continental Walk ..... 7" ..... Parlophone ..... R4771 ..... 1961 ..... **£6**
Finger Popping Time ..... 7" ..... Parlophone ..... R4682 ..... 1960 ..... **£8**
Glad Songs, Sad Songs ..... LP ..... King ..... 927 ..... 1966 ..... **£10** ..... US
Hoochi Coochi Coo ..... 7" ..... Parlophone ..... R4728 ..... 1961 ..... **£6**
Jumpin' Hank Ballard ..... LP ..... London ..... HA8101 ..... 1963 ..... **£20**
Let's Go Again ..... LP ..... King ..... 748 ..... 1961 ..... **£20** ..... US
Let's Go Again ..... 7" ..... Parlophone ..... R4762 ..... 1961 ..... **£8**
Let's Go Let's Go Let's Go ..... 7" ..... Parlophone ..... R4707 ..... 1960 ..... **£6**
Midnighters ..... LP ..... Federal ..... 395541 ..... 1956 ..... **£150** ..... US
Midnighters ..... LP-10" .. Federal ..... 29590 ..... 1954 ..... **£300** ..... US
Midnighters ..... LP ..... King ..... 395541 ..... 1958 ..... **£50** ..... US
Midnighters Vol.2 ..... LP ..... Federal ..... 395581 ..... 1957 ..... **£100** ..... US
Midnighters Vol.2 ..... LP ..... King ..... 395581 ..... 1958 ..... **£50** ..... US
Mr.Rhythm And Blues ..... LP ..... King ..... 700 ..... 1960 ..... **£20** ..... US
One And Only Hank Ballard ..... LP ..... King ..... 674 ..... 1960 ..... **£20** ..... US
Sing Along ..... LP ..... King ..... 759 ..... 1961 ..... **£20** ..... US
Singin' And Swingin' ..... LP ..... King ..... 618 ..... 1959 ..... **£20** ..... US
Spotlight On Hank Ballard ..... LP ..... King ..... 740 ..... 1961 ..... **£20** ..... US
Star In Your Eyes ..... LP ..... King ..... 896 ..... 1964 ..... **£20** ..... US
Those Lazy Lazy Days ..... LP ..... King ..... 913 ..... 1965 ..... **£15** ..... US
Twist ..... 7" ..... Parlophone ..... R4558 ..... 1959 ..... **£12**
Twist ..... 7" ..... Parlophone ..... R4688 ..... 1960 ..... **£6**
Twistin' Fools ..... LP ..... King ..... 781 ..... 1962 ..... **£20** ..... US

BALLOON FARM
Question Of Temperature ..... 7" ..... London ..... HLP10185 ..... 1968 ..... **£6**

BALLS
Much was expected of the alliance between Denny Laine and the Move's Trevor Burton, but in the end, Balls could only manage one single. This was later reissued under Burton's name.

Fight For My Country ..... 7" ..... Wizard ..... WIZ101 ..... 1971 ..... **£5**

BALTIMORE & OHIO MARCHING BAND
Lapland ..... 7" ..... Stateside ..... SS2065 ..... 1967 ..... **£30**
Lapland ..... 7" ..... Stateside ..... SS2065 ..... 1967 ..... **£75** ..... demo

BAMBIS
Baby Blue ..... 7" ..... CBS ..... 201778 ..... 1965 ..... **£8**

BAMBOO SHOOTS
Fox Has Gone To Ground ..... 7" ..... Columbia ..... DB8370 ..... 1968 ..... **£40**

BANANAMEN (CRAMPS)
Crusher ..... 7" ..... Big Beat ..... NS88 ..... 1983 ..... **£4**

BANANARAMA
Aie A Mwana ..... 7" ..... Demon ..... D1010 ..... 1981 ..... **£8**

BANCO
Banco ..... LP ..... Manticore ..... K53507 ..... 1975 ..... **£10**
Banco Del Mutuo Soccorso ..... LP ..... Orizzonte ..... ORL8041 ..... 1972 ..... **£12** ..... Italian
Carofano Rosso ..... LP ..... Orizzonte ..... ORL8334 ..... 1976 ..... **£12** ..... Italian

Come In Un Ultima Cena	LP	Manticore	28004	1976	**£25**	
Darwin	LP	Orizzonte	ORL8094	1972	**£20**	Italian
Di Terra	LP	Dischi	SMRL6226	1978	**£10**	Italian
Lo Sono Nato Libero	LP	Orizzonte	ORL8202	1973	**£25**	Italian

BAND

Band	LP	Capitol	EST132	1969	**£10**	chart LP
Cahoots	LP	Capitol	EAST651	1971	**£10**	chart LP
Islands	LP	Capitol	EST11602	1977	**£10**	
Life Is A Carnival	7"	Capitol	CL15700	1971	**£4**	
Moondog Matinee	LP	Capitol	ESW11241	1973	**£15**	
Music From Big Pink	LP	Capitol	ST2955	1968	**£10**	
Music From Big Pink	LP	Capitol	T2955	1968	**£12**	mono
Northern Lights Southern Cross	LP	Capitol	EST11440	1975	**£10**	
Rag Mama Rag	7"	Capitol	CL15629	1970	**£4**	chart single
Rock Of Ages	LP	Capitol	ESTSP11	1972	**£15**	double
Shape I'm In	7"	Capitol	CL15675	1971	**£4**	
Stage Fright	LP	Capitol	EASW425	1970	**£10**	chart LP
Time To Kill	7"	Capitol	CL15659	1970	**£4**	
Up On Cripple Creek	7"	Capitol	CL15613	1969	**£4**	
Weight	7"	Capitol	CL15559	1968	**£4**	chart single

BAND AID

Do They Know It's Christmas?	7"	Mercury	FEEDP1	1985	**£4**	shaped pic disc

BAND OF ANGELS

A Band Of Angels wore straw boaters to emphasise their Harrow origins, and it would have been surprising if at least some of them had not achieved success. First up was singer Mike D'Abo, who became the lead singer with Manfred Mann after the departure of Paul Jones. Later, however, the group's guitarist and manager founded EG management, amongst whose signings were King Crimson and Roxy Music.

Gonna Make A Woman Of You	7"	United Artists	UP1066	1964	**£10**	
Invitation	7"	Piccadilly	7N35292	1966	**£10**	
Leave It To Me	7"	Piccadilly	7N35279	1966	**£8**	
Not True As Yet	7"	United Artists	UP1049	1964	**£12**	

BANGOR FLYING CIRCUS

Bangor Flying Circus	LP	Stateside	SSL5022	1969	**£15**	

BANKS, BESSIE

Go Now	7"	Red Bird	BC106	196-	**£15**	
Go Now	7"	Soul City	SC105		**£4**	
Go Now	7"	Soul City	SC105		**£20**	demo
I Can't Make It	7"	Verve	VS563	1967	**£8**	

BANKS, DARRELL

Angel Baby	7"	Atlantic	584120	1967	**£6**	
Just Because Your Love Is Gone	7"	Stax	STAX124	1969	**£4**	
Open The Door To Your Heart	7"	London	HL10070	1966	**£140**	demo only
Open The Door To Your Heart	7"	Stateside	SS536	1966	**£5**	
Open The Door To Your Heart	7"	Stateside	SS536	1966	**£25**	demo

BANKS, HOMER

Hooked By Love	7"	Liberty	LIB12060	1967	**£5**	
Lot Of Love	7"	Liberty	LIB12028	1966	**£8**	
Me Or Your Mama	7"	Minit	MLF11015	1969	**£5**	
Round The Clock Lover	7"	Minit	MLF11004	1968	**£5**	
Sixty Minutes Of Your Love	7"	Liberty	LIB12047	1967	**£8**	
Sixty Minutes Of Your Love	7"	Minit	MLF11007	1968	**£5**	

BANKS, LARRY

I Don't Wanna Do It	7"	Stateside	SS579	1967	**£4**	

BANKS, LLOYD

We'll Meet Again	7"	Reaction	591008	1966	**£6**	

BANKS, PETER

Peter Banks & Jan Akkerman	LP	Sovereign	SVNA7250	1972	**£20**	
Peter Banks	LP	Sovereign	SVNA7256	1973	**£20**	

BANKS, TONY

For A While	7"	Charisma	CB344	1979	**£4**	
For A While	7"	Charisma	CB365	1980	**£4**	PS

BANNED

Little Girl .... 7" .... Can't Eat .... EAT1UP .... 1977 .... **£10** ....

BANSHEES

The Banshees' "I Got A Woman" is one of a number of classic beat singles that somehow failed to achieve chart success, although the group's singer re-emerged for a very successful career throughout the seventies. His name was Bryan Ferry.

Big Buildin' .... 7" .... Columbia .... DB7530 .... 1965 .... **£15** ....
I Got A Woman .... 7" .... Columbia .... DB7361 .... 1964 .... **£25** ....
Yes Indeed .... 7" .... Columbia .... DB7752 .... 1965 .... **£20** ....

BARBARA & BRENDA

Never Love A Robin .... 7" .... Direction .... 583799 .... 1968 .... **£5** ....

BARBARIANS

Are You A Boy Or Are You A Girl? .... LP .... Laurie .... LLP2033 .... 1966 .... **£30** .... US
Are You A Boy Or Are You A Girl? .... 7" .... Stateside .... SS449 .... 1965 .... **£10** ....
Moulty .... 7" .... Stateside .... SS497 .... 1966 .... **£8** ....

BARBER, CHRIS

Battersea Rain Dance .... LP .... Marmalade .... 608009 .... 1969 .... **£15** ....
Battersea Rain Dance .... 7" .... Marmalade .... 598013 .... 1969 .... **£4** ....
Catcall .... 7" .... Marmalade .... 598005 .... 1967 .... **£20** ....
Chris Barber Skiffle Group .... 7" EP .... Pye .... NJE1025 .... 1957 .... **£5** ....
Doin' My Time .... 7" .... Pye .... 7NJ2014 .... 1958 .... **£4** ....

BARCLAY JAMES HARVEST

Barclay James Harvest .... LP .... Harvest .... SHVL770 .... 1970 .... **£10** ....
Breathless .... 7" .... Harvest .... HAR5095 .... 1975 .... **£4** ....
Brother Thrush .... 7" .... Harvest .... HAR5003 .... 1969 .... **£8** ....
Capricorn .... 7" .... Polydor .... POSP140 .... 1980 .... **£4** ....
Early Morning .... 7" .... Parlophone .... R5693 .... 1968 .... **£12** ....
Hymn .... 7" .... Polydor .... 2058904 .... 1977 .... **£4** ....
I'm Over You .... 7" .... Harvest .... HAR5051 .... 1972 .... **£5** ....
Just A Day Away .... 7" .... Polydor .... POPPX585 .... 1983 .... **£6** .... shaped pic disc
Live EP .... 7" EP .... Polydor .... 2229198 .... 1977 .... **£5** .... chart single
Love On The Line .... 7" .... Polydor .... POSP97 .... 1979 .... **£4** .... chart single
Loving Is Easy .... 7" .... Polydor .... POSP012 .... 1978 .... **£5** ....
Loving Is Easy .... 7" .... Polydor .... POSP012 .... 1978 .... **£4** .... blue vinyl
Mocking Bird .... 7" .... Harvest .... HAR5034 .... 1971 .... **£5** ....
Once Again .... LP .... Harvest .... Q4SHVL0788 .... 1971 .... **£15** .... quad
Poor Boy Blues .... 7" .... Polydor .... 2058474 .... 1974 .... **£4** ....
Rock And Roll Woman .... 7" .... Harvest .... HAR5068 .... 1973 .... **£5** .... PS
Taking Some Time On .... 7" .... Harvest .... HAR5025 .... 1970 .... **£5** ....
Thank You .... 7" .... Harvest .... HAR5058 .... 1972 .... **£5** ....
Titles .... 7" .... Polydor .... 2058660 .... 1975 .... **£4** ....
Victims Of Circumstance .... 7" .... Polydor .... POSPP674 .... 1984 .... **£6** .... pic disc

BARCLAY JAMES HARVEST (BOMBADIL)

Breathless .... 7" .... Harvest .... HAR5056 .... 1972 .... **£5** ....

BARCLAY, RUE & PEGGY DUNCAN

Tongue Tied Boy .... 7" .... London .... HL8033 .... 1954 .... **£8** ....

BARDENS, PETER

Answer .... LP .... Transatlantic .... TRA222 .... 1970 .... **£15** ....
Peter Bardens .... LP .... Transatlantic .... TRA243 .... 1971 .... **£15** ....

BARDOT, BRIGITTE

Harley Davidson .... 7" .... Pye .... 7N25450 .... 1968 .... **£5** ....
Mr.Sun .... 7" .... Vogue .... VRS7018 .... 1966 .... **£5** ....

BARDS

Owl And The Pussycat .... 7" .... Capitol .... CL15556 .... 1968 .... **£4** ....

BARE, BOBBY

Five Hundred Miles Away From Home .... LP .... RCA .... LPM2835 .... 1963 .... **£10** .... US
I'm Hanging Up My Rifle .... 7" .... Top Rank .... JAR310 .... 1960 .... **£5** ....

BARKAYS

Give Everybody Some .... 7" .... Stax .... 601025 .... 1967 .... **£4** ....
Hard Day's Night .... 7" .... Stax .... 601036 .... 1968 .... **£4** ....
Soul Finger .... 7" .... Atlantic .... 584244 .... 1969 .... **£4** ....

Soul Finger	7"	Stax	601014	1967	**£4**	chart single

BARNES, BARNEY J. & THE INTRO

It Must Be Love	7"	Decca	F12662	1967	**£4**	

BARNES, J.J.

Daytripper	7"	Polydor	56722	1967	**£4**	
Real Humdinger	7"	T. Motown	TMG870	1973	**£4**	
Real Humdinger	7"	T. Motown	TMG870	1973	**£10**	demo

BARNES, J.J. & STEVE MANCHA

J.J.Barnes And Steve Mancha	LP	Stax	SXATS1012	1969	**£12**	

BARNES, MAE

Songs By Mae Barnes	LP-10"	Atlantic	ALS404	195-	**£75**	US

BARNET, ERIC

Horse	7"	Gas	GAS100	196-	**£8**	
Te Ta Toe	7"	Gas	GAS106	196-	**£8**	

BARNETT, BARRY

All I Have To Do Is Dream	7"	HMV	POP487	1958	**£4**	
When	7"	HMV	POP511	1958	**£4**	

BARNUM, H.B.

Record	7"	Capitol	CL15391	1965	**£8**	

BAROCK & ROLL ENSEMBLE

"Eine Kleine Beatlemusik" by the Barock and Roll Ensemble consists of tunes written by the Beatles arranged for a small group of strings as though the music was by Mozart. The joke - perpetrated by musicologist Fritz Spiegl - is a good one, and the record works as music too. The B side is less successful, however; Spiegl knows his Mozart but not his rock music and his arrangements of themes by Wagner as if they were pieces by the Shadows are simply feeble.

Eine Kleine Beatlemusik	7" EP	HMV	7EG8887	1965	**£6**	

BARON & HIS POUNDING PIANO

Is A Bluebird Blue	7"	Sue	WI398	1965	**£20**	

BARONS

Cossack	7"	Oriole	CB1608	1961	**£8**	
Don't Walk Out	7"	London	HLP8391	1957	**£50**	
Samurai	7"	Oriole	CB1620	1961	**£8**	

BARRACUDAS

Plane View	LP	Justice	143	1968	**£75**	US

BARRACUDAS (2)

I Want My Woody Back	7"	Cells	CELLOUT1	1979	**£8**	
Inside Mind	7"	Flicknife	FLS207	1982	**£4**	

BARRETT, RICHARD

Come Softly To Me	7"	HMV	POP609	1959	**£4**	

BARRETT, RITCHIE

Some Other Guy	7"	London	HLK9552	1962	**£8**	

BARRETT, SYD

Syd Barrett was eased out of the Pink Floyd due to his increasingly unreliable behaviour - a guitarist with a tendency to stand still on stage without actually playing anything was something of a liability. Nevertheless, the rest of the Floyd bore him no malice and were happy to turn up to lend support to Barrett's solo recordings (as did Soft Machine too). Whether these records are the work of a brilliant eccentric or merely the last gasp of semi-coherency from an unmitigated loony probably depends on the listener's point of view.

Barrett	LP	Harvest	SHSP4007	1970	**£15**	
Madcap Laughs	LP	Harvest	SHVL765	1970	**£15**	chart LP
Octopus	7"	Harvest	HAR5009	1969	**£50**	

BARRETTO, RAY

Acid	7"	London	HL10262	1969	**£4**	
El Watusi	LP	Island	ILP946	1967	**£40**	
El Watusi	7"	Columbia	DB7684	1965	**£4**	

BARRIER

Georgie Brown	7"	Eyemark	EMS1013	196-	**£10**	

Spot The Lights	7"	Philips	BF1731	1968	**£8**	
Tide Is Turning	7"	Philips	BF1692	1968	**£8**	

BARRON KNIGHTS

Barron Knights	LP	Columbia	SX6007	1966	**£12**	
Call Up The Groups	LP	Columbia	33SX1648	1964	**£15**	
Call Up The Groups	7"	Columbia	DB7317	1964	**£4**	chart single
Come To The Dance	7"	Columbia	DB7375	1964	**£4**	chart single
Coming Home Baby	7"	Columbia	DB7188	1964	**£4**	
Guying The Top Pops	7" EP	Columbia	SEG8424	1965	**£5**	
Jo Anne	7"	Columbia	DB7108	1963	**£4**	
Merry Gentle Pops	7"	Columbia	DB7780	1965	**£4**	chart single
Never Miss A Chance	7"	Fontana	H368	1962	**£4**	
Olympic Record	7"	Columbia	DB8485	1968	**£4**	chart single
Pop Go The Workers	7"	Columbia	DB7525	1965	**£4**	chart single
Scribed	LP	Columbia	SCX6176	1967	**£10**	
Those Versatile Barron Knights	7" EP	Columbia	SEG8526	1966	**£5**	
Under New Management	7"	Columbia	DB8071	1966	**£4**	chart single

BARROW POETS

The Barrow Poets were a poetry and music group, a little like the Liverpool Scene, but with much less of a rock sound. Where the Liverpool Scene played on the John Peel programme, the Barrow Poets would have turned up on Radio Four. Essentially the records are an extension of the fifties and sixties jazz-and-poetry experiments, in which the words are by far the most important element. Fortunately, they are always well worth hearing.

Entertainment Of Poetry And Music	LP	Argo	PLP1072	197-	**£15**	
Joker	LP	RCA		1970	**£15**	
Letter In A Bottle	7"	Fontana	TF939	1968	**£4**	
Outpatients	LP	Argo	ZSW508	1972	**£15**	

BARRY SISTERS

Baby Come A Little Closer	7"	London	HLA8248	1956	**£5**	
Intrigue	7"	London	HLA8304	1956	**£5**	

BARRY, DAVE & SARAH BERNER

Out Of This World With Flying Saucers	7"	London	HLU8324	1956	**£20**	

BARRY, JOE

Fool To Care	7" EP	Mercury	ZEP10130	1962	**£12**	
I Started Loving You Again	7"	Stateside	SS2127	1969	**£6**	
I'm A Fool To Care	7"	Mercury	AMT1149	1961	**£4**	chart single

BARRY, JOHN

Barry Theme Successes	7" EP	Columbia	SEG8255	1963	**£4**	
Beat For Beatniks	7"	Columbia	DB4446	1960	**£4**	chart single
Bees Knees	7"	Parlophone	R4488	1958	**£4**	
Big Beat	7" EP	Parlophone	GEP8737	1958	**£6**	
Big Guitar	7"	Parlophone	R4418	1958	**£4**	
Black Stockings	7"	Columbia	DB4554	1960	**£4**	chart single
Cutty Sark	7"	Columbia	DB4806	1962	**£4**	chart single
Every Which Way	7"	Parlophone	R4394	1958	**£8**	
From Russia With Love	7"	Ember	S181	1963	**£4**	chart single
Goldfinger	7"	United Artists	UP1068	1964	**£4**	
Hideaway	7"	Parlophone	R4453	1958	**£4**	
Hit Or Miss	7"	Columbia	DB4414	1960	**£4**	chart single
James Bond Theme	7"	Columbia	DB4898	1962	**£4**	chart single
John Barry Sound	7" EP	Columbia	SEG8069	1961	**£6**	
Little John	7"	Parlophone	R4560	1959	**£4**	
Long John	7"	Parlophone	R4530	1959	**£4**	
Magnificent Seven	7"	Columbia	DB4598	1961	**£4**	chart single
Menace	7"	Columbia	DB4659	1961	**£4**	
Never Let Go	7"	Columbia	DB4480	1960	**£4**	chart single
Starfire	7"	Columbia	DB4699	1961	**£4**	
Stringbeat	LP	Columbia	33SX1358	1961	**£30**	
Twelfth Street Rag	7"	Parlophone	R4582	1959	**£4**	
Walk Don't Run	7"	Columbia	DB4505	1960	**£4**	chart single
Zip Zip	7"	Parlophone	R4363	1957	**£10**	

BARRY, LEN

1-2-3	7"	Brunswick	05942	1965	**£4**	chart single
1-2-3	LP	Decca	DL4720	1965	**£12**	US
Hearts Are Trumps	7"	Cameo Park.	C969	1965	**£4**	

I Struck It Rich	7"	Brunswick	05966	1966	£4	
It's That Time Of The Year	7"	Brunswick	05962	1966	£4	
Like A Baby	7"	Brunswick	05949	1966	£4	chart single
Somewhere	7"	Brunswick	05955	1966	£4	

BARRY, LEN & THE DOVELLS

Having A Good Time	7" EP	Cameo Park	CPE556	1966	£4	

BARRY, SANDRA

End Of The Line	7"	Pye	7N15753	1965	£5	
Question	7"	Pye	7N15840	1965	£5	
Stop Thief	7"	Pye	7N17102	1966	£6	

BARRY, SANDRA & THE BOYS

"Really Gonna Shake" by Sandra Barry And The Boys represents the first recording by the group that became (without Ms. Barry) the Action.

Really Gonna Shake	7"	Decca	F11851	1964	£15	

BARTHOLOMEW, DAVE

Fats Domino Presents...	LP	Imperial	LP9162	1961	£20	US
New Orleans House Party	LP	Imperial	LP9217	1963	£20	US

BARTLEY, CHRIS

Sweetest Thing This Side Of Heaven	7"	Cameo Park	P101	1962	£15	

BARTOK, EVA

Broken Blossoms	7"	Philips	BF1589	1967	£4	

BASES

Home Sweet Home	7"	Coxsone	CS7062	196-	£10	
I Don't Mind	7"	Studio One	SO2056	196-	£10	
River Jordan	7"	Coxsone	CS7030	196-	£10	

BASS, BILLY

I'm Coming Too	7"	Pama	PM761	196-	£8	

BASS, FONTELLA

Fontella Bass & Bobby McClure	7" EP	Chess	CRE6025	1966	£6	
Fontella's Hits	7" EP	Chess	CRE6015	1966	£6	
I Can't Rest	7"	Chess	CRS8032	1966	£4	
I Can't Rest	7" EP	Chess	CRE6020	1966	£6	
New Look	LP	Chess		1966	£15	US
Recovery	7"	Chess	CRS8027	1966	£4	chart single
Rescue Me	7"	Chess	CRS8023	1965	£5	chart single
Rescue Me	7"	Chess	CRS8090	1969	£4	
Safe And Sound	7"	Chess	CRS8042	1966	£4	

BASS, FONTELLA & BOBBY MCLURE

Don't Mess Up A Good Thing	7"	Chess	CRS8007	1965	£5	
Don't Mess Up A Good Thing	7"	Chess	CRS8007	1965	£6	Oliver Sain B-side

BATFISH BOYS

Swamp Liquor	7"	Batfish Inc.	BF102	1984	£4	
Swamp Liquor	12"	Batfish Inc.	USS101	1984	£6	

BATS

Accept It	7"	Columbia	DB7429	1964	£5	
Listen To My Heart	7"	Decca	F22534	1966	£5	
Take Me As I Am	7"	Decca	F22616	1967	£4	
You Will Won't You	7"	Decca	F22568	1967	£4	

BATT, MIKE

I See Wonderful Things In You	7"	Liberty	LBF15122	1968	£4	
Mr.Poem	7"	Liberty	LBF15093	1968	£4	
Your Mother Should Know	7"	Liberty	LBF15210	1969	£4	

BATTERED ORNAMENTS

The Battered Ornaments was the group originally brought together by poet Pete Brown. Without him, they still did not have an effective vocalist, but the "Mantle Piece" LP is an interesting and worthwhile addition to the Harvest catalogue.

Mantle Piece	LP	Harvest	SHVL758	1969	£40	

BATTIN, SKIP

Title	Format	Label	Cat. No.	Year	Price	Notes
Skip	LP	Signpost	SG4255	1973	**£15**	

BAUHAUS

Title	Format	Label	Cat. No.	Year	Price	Notes
1979-1983	LP	Beggars B.	BEGA64	1985	**£10**	with numbered insert
Bela Lugosi's Dead	12"	Small Wond.	TEENY2	1979	**£20**	white vinyl
Burning From The Inside	LP	Beggars B.	BEGA45P	1983	**£12**	pic disc
Dark Entries	7"	4AD	AD3	1980	**£6**	blue label
Dark Entries	7"	4AD	BEG37	1980	**£8**	
Dark Entries	7"	Axis	AXIS3	1980	**£15**	
Dark Entries	7"	Beggars B.	BEG37	1980	**£20**	
God In An Alcove	7"	Lyntone	023/LYN12106	1982	**£4**	Flexipop flexi
Kick In The Eye	12"	Beggars B.	BEG54T	1981	**£15**	
Kick In The Eye	12"	Beggars B.	BEG54T	1981	**£12**	white label, stamped sleeve
Kick In The Eye	12"	Beggars B.	BEG74TA1	1983	**£20**	mispress with 'Poison Pen'
Passion Of Lovers	7"	Beggars B.	BEG59	1981	**£4**	lyric sheet
Sanity Assassin	7"	Fan Club		1983	**£80**	
She's In Parties	7"	Beggars B.	BEG91P	1983	**£10**	pic disc
Sky's Gone Out	LP	Beggars B.	BEGA42	1982	**£15**	with LP BEGA38
Spirit	7"	Beggars B.	BEG79P	1982	**£10**	pic disc
Telegram Sam	7"	4AD	AD17	1980	**£6**	
Telegram Sam	12"	4AD	AD17T	1980	**£10**	
Terror Couple Kill Colonel	7"	4AD	AD7	1980	**£6**	
Terror Couple Kill Colonel	7"	4AD	AD7	1980	**£12**	different versions

BAUMSTAM

Title	Format	Label	Cat. No.	Year	Price	Notes
	LP	private		197-	**£120**	

BAXTER, DAVID

Title	Format	Label	Cat. No.	Year	Price	Notes
Goodbye Dave	LP	Reflection		1970	**£40**	

BAYTOWN SINGERS

Title	Format	Label	Cat. No.	Year	Price	Notes
Walkin' Down The Line	7"	Decca	F12160	1965	**£6**	

BBC RADIOPHONIC WORKSHOP

Title	Format	Label	Cat. No.	Year	Price	Notes
Dr.Who	7"	BBC	RESL11	1974	**£4**	
Dr.Who	7"	Decca	F11837	1964	**£5**	

BEACH BOYS

For a group as long-lived and as popular as the Beach Boys, there are surprisingly few hard-core rarities, although all their original issues from the sixties are inevitably collectable. The ultimate Beach Boys rarity has still not been released in full - the LP "Smile" was cancelled by Brian Wilson and would perhaps have included tracks to rival the masterworks "Good Vibrations", "Heroes and Villains", and "Surf's Up", which were all destined for inclusion on the lost album. For collectors who do not actually feel the need to own every note that the group has produced, it should be noted that the World Record Club boxed set "The Capitol Years" is a particularly well assembled compilation of the group's sixties work, with no major omissions. A bonus LP, moreover, assembles a number of Brian Wilson productions which are otherwise rather difficult to find.

Title	Format	Label	Cat. No.	Year	Price	Notes
20 Golden Greats	LP	EMI	EMTV1	1977	**£10**	blue vinyl
20 Golden Greats Promo	7"	EMI	PSR402	1976	**£10**	promo
20/20	LP	Capitol	EST133	1969	**£10**	chart LP
All Summer Long	LP	Capitol	T2110	1964	**£15**	
All Summer Long	7"	Capitol	CL15384	1965	**£5**	
All Summer Long	7"	Capitol	CL15384	1965	**£25**	demo
Barbara Ann	7"	Capitol	CL15432	1965	**£20**	demo
Barbara Ann	7"	Capitol	CL15432	1966	**£4**	chart single
Barbara Ann	7"	Capitol	CMS2	1972	**£4**	
Beach Boy Interviews	LP	Caribou	XPR1204	1980	**£20**	promo
Beach Boys Concert	LP	Capitol	T2198	1964	**£15**	
Beach Boys Concert	7" EP	Capitol	EAP42198	1964	**£6**	
Beach Boys Party	LP	Capitol	T2398	1965	**£12**	chart LP
Beach Boys Today	LP	Capitol	T2269	1965	**£12**	chart LP
Beach Boys' Hits	7" EP	Capitol	EAP120781	1964	**£6**	
Bluebirds Over The Mountain	7"	Capitol	CL15572	1968	**£4**	chart single
Bluebirds Over The Mountain	7"	Capitol	CL15572	1968	**£15**	demo
Break Away	7"	Capitol	CL15598	1969	**£4**	chart single
Break Away	7"	Capitol	CL15598	1969	**£12**	demo
California Girls	7"	Capitol	CL15409	1965	**£4**	chart single
California Girls	7"	Capitol	CL15409	1965	**£25**	demo
California Saga - California	7"	Reprise	K14232	1973	**£4**	chart single

Title	Format	Label	Cat. No.	Year	Price	Notes
California/Sail On Sailor	7"	Reprise	K14346	1974	**£4**	
Capitol Years	LP	W. Rec. Club	SM651-7	1981	**£50**	7 LPs, boxed
Carl & The Passions - So Tough	LP	Reprise	K44184	1972	**£10**	chart LP
Christmas Album	LP	Capitol	T2164	1964	**£15**	
Cottonfields	7"	Capitol	CL15640	1970	**£4**	chart single
Cottonfields	7"	Capitol	CL15640	1970	**£10**	demo
Dance Dance Dance	7"	Capitol	CL15370	1965	**£4**	chart single
Dance Dance Dance	7"	Capitol	CL15370	1965	**£25**	demo
Darlin'	7"	Capitol	CL15527	1968	**£4**	chart single
Darlin'	7"	Capitol	CL15527	1968	**£15**	demo
Deluxe Set	LP	Capitol	DTCL2813	1967	**£35**	US, triple, stereo
Deluxe Set	LP	Capitol	TCL2813	1967	**£60**	US, triple, mono
Do It Again	7"	Capitol	CL15554	1968	**£4**	chart single
Do It Again	7"	Capitol	CL15554	1968	**£15**	demo
Don't Go Near The Water	7"	Stateside	SS2194	1971	**£4**	
Don't Go Near The Water	7"	Stateside	SS2194	1971	**£12**	demo, PS
Four By The Beach Boys	7" EP	Capitol	EAP15267	1964	**£6**	
Friends	LP	Capitol	ST2895	1968	**£10**	chart LP
Friends	7"	Capitol	CL15545	1968	**£4**	chart single
Friends	7"	Capitol	CL15545	1968	**£15**	demo
Fun Fun Fun	7"	Capitol	CL15339	1964	**£5**	
Fun Fun Fun	7"	Capitol	CL15339	1964	**£25**	demo
Fun Fun Fun	7" EP	Capitol	EAP120603	1964	**£6**	
God Only Knows	7"	Capitol	CL15459	1966	**£4**	chart single
God Only Knows	7"	Capitol	CL15459	1966	**£20**	demo
God Only Knows	7" EP	Capitol	EAP62458	1967	**£6**	
Good Vibrations	7"	Capitol	CL15475	1966	**£4**	chart single
Good Vibrations	7"	Capitol	CL15475	1966	**£20**	demo
Help Me Rhonda	7"	Capitol	CL15392	1965	**£4**	chart single
Help Me Rhonda	7"	Capitol	CL15392	1965	**£25**	demo
Here Comes The Night	12"	Caribou	127204	1979	**£6**	blue vinyl
Heroes And Villains	7"	Capitol	CL15510	1967	**£4**	chart single
Heroes And Villains	7"	Capitol	CL15510	1967	**£20**	demo
Holland	LP	Reprise	K54008	1973	**£10**	includes 7", chart LP
Holland	LP	Reprise	MS2118	1973	**£150**	US test pressing with 'We Got Love'
I Can Hear Music	7"	Capitol	CL15584	1969	**£4**	chart single
I Can Hear Music	7"	Capitol	CL15584	1969	**£12**	demo
I Get Around	7"	Capitol	CL15350	1964	**£4**	chart single
I Get Around	7"	Capitol	CL15350	1964	**£25**	demo
L.A. (Light Album)	LP	Caribou	CRB1186081	1979	**£12**	pic disc
Little Deuce Coupe	LP	Capitol	T1998	1963	**£15**	
Little Girl I Once Knew	7"	Capitol	CL15425	1965	**£5**	
Little Girl I Once Knew	7"	Capitol	CL15425	1965	**£25**	demo
Long Promised Road	7"	Stateside	SS2190	1971	**£4**	
Long Promised Road	7"	Stateside	SS2190	1971	**£10**	demo
Pet Sounds	LP	Capitol	T2458	1966	**£10**	chart LP
Shut Down Vol.2	LP	Capitol	T2027	1964	**£15**	
singles Collection	7"	Capitol	BBP26	1979	**£60**	26 singles, boxed
Sloop John B	7"	Capitol	CL15441	1966	**£4**	chart single
Sloop John B	7"	Capitol	CL15441	1966	**£20**	demo
Smiley Smile	LP	Capitol	ST82891	1968	**£75**	US, record club issue
Smiley Smile	LP	Capitol	ST9001	1967	**£10**	chart LP
Stack-O-Tracks	LP	Capitol	DKAO2893	1968	**£60**	US, with booklet
Summer Days & Summer Nights	LP	Capitol	T2354	1965	**£12**	chart LP
Summertime Blues	LP	Sears	SPS609	1970	**£50**	US
Sunflower	LP	Capitol	SKAO93352	1970	**£20**	US, record club issue
Sunflower	LP	Stateside	SSLA8251	1970	**£10**	chart LP
Surf's Up	LP	Asylum	R113793	1971	**£50**	US, record club issue
Surfer Girl	LP	Capitol	T1981	1963	**£15**	chart LP
Surfin' Safari	LP	Capitol	T1808	1962	**£15**	
Surfin' Safari	7"	Capitol	CL15273	1962	**£8**	
Surfin' Safari	7"	Capitol	CL15273	1962	**£30**	demo
Surfin' USA	LP	Capitol	T1890	1963	**£15**	chart LP
Surfin' USA	7"	Capitol	CL15305	1963	**£6**	chart single
Surfin' USA	7"	Capitol	CL15305	1963	**£25**	demo
Surfin' USA	7" EP	Capitol	EAP120540	1963	**£6**	
Susie Cincinnatti	7"	Reprise	K14411	1976	**£30**	demo
Tears In The Morning	7"	Stateside	SS2181	1970	**£4**	
Tears In The Morning	7"	Stateside	SS2181	1970	**£10**	demo
Ten Little Indians	7"	Capitol	CL15285	1963	**£15**	

Ten Little Indians	7"	Capitol	CL15285	1963	**£50**	demo
Then I Kissed Her	7"	Capitol	CL15502	1967	**£4**	chart single
Then I Kissed Her	7"	Capitol	CL15502	1967	**£15**	demo
When I Grow Up	7"	Capitol	CL15361	1964	**£4**	chart single
When I Grow Up	7"	Capitol	CL15361	1964	**£25**	demo
Wild Honey	LP	Capitol	ST2859	1968	**£10**	chart LP
Wild Honey	7"	Capitol	CL15517	1967	**£60**	
Wild Honey	7"	Capitol	CL15521	1967	**£4**	chart single
Wild Honey	7"	Capitol	CL15521	1967	**£15**	demo
Wouldn't It Be Nice	7"	Capitol	CMS1	1972	**£4**	
You Need A Mess of Help	7"	Reprise	K14173	1972	**£4**	PS

BEACH NUTS

Out In The Sun	7"	London	HL9988	1965	**£5**	

BEACHCOMBERS

An instrumental group whose drummer was Keith Moon, who left to join the High Numbers just as the latter decided to revert to their earlier name of the Who.

Mad Goose	7"	Columbia	DB7124	1963	**£8**	
Night Train	7"	Columbia	DB7200	1964	**£10**	

BEACON STREET UNION

Blue Suede Shoes	7"	MGM	MGM1416	1968	**£6**	
Clown Died In Marvin Gardens	LP	MGM	SE4568	1968	**£15**	US
Eyes Of The...	LP	MGM	8069	1968	**£15**	

BEAN & LOOPY'S LOT

Haywire	7"	Parlophone	R5458	1966	**£5**	

BEAN, GEORGE

Sad Story	7"	Decca	F11922	1964	**£4**	
Secret Love	7"	Decca	F11762	1963	**£5**	
She Belongs To Me	7"	Decca	F12228	1965	**£4**	
Will You Be My Lover Tonight	7"	Decca	F11808	1964	**£6**	

BEAR

Greetings Children Of Paradise	LP	Verve	FTS3059	1968	**£15**	

BEARD, DEAN & THE CREWCUTS

On My Mind Again	7"	London	HLE8463	1957	**£40**	

BEARZ

She's My Girl	7"	Axis	AXIS2	1980	**£8**	

BEAS

Dr.Goodfoot And His Bikini Machine	7"	Pama	PM744	196-	**£8**	

BEASLEY, JIMMY

Fabulous...	LP	Crown	CLP5014	1957	**£20**	US
Fabulous...	LP	Modern	LMP1214	1956	**£50**	US

BEASTIE BOYS

Polly Wog Stew	12"	Rat Cage	MOTR21	1982	**£6**	

BEAT BOYS

That's My Plan	7"	Decca	F11730	1963	**£12**	

BEAT BROTHERS

Nick Nack Hully Gully	7"	Polydor	NH52185	1963	**£25**	

BEAT CHICS

Skinny Minny	7"	Decca	F12016	1964	**£5**	

BEAT MERCHANTS

Pretty Face	7"	Columbia	DB7367	1964	**£12**	
So Fine	7"	Columbia	DB7492	1965	**£12**	

BEAT SIX

Bernadine	7"	Decca	F12011	1964	**£6**	

BEATLES

The Beatles sold so many copies of their singles that it should come as no surprise that few of them have acquired much of a value in the collectors' market. It is a different matter with their LPs, however, especially as so many original copies have been extremely well played over the years! There are also a number of rarer items. The Polydor singles and LP are the first pressings of the material that the Beatles recorded in Germany in 1962 - mainly as a backing group to singer Tony Sheridan, although "Ain't She Sweet" features a typically gritty John Lennon vocal, and "Cry For A Shadow" is George Harrison's instrumental tribute to Hank Marvin and company. The Christmas flexi-disc singles were issued each year to members of the fan-club and feature specially recorded material not otherwise available, although not very much of this is actually musical. "From Then To You" gathers all these singles together on a highly sought-after LP, which forms the apex of any Beatles collection, alongside three other rarities: the limited edition package which combined the "Let It Be" album with a substantial book; first pressings of the "Please Please Me" LP, which have the old Parlophone label design, with gold lettering (the stereo version of this is especially rare); and the notorious American "butcher cover", hastily withdrawn after the initial release of "Yesterday And Today".

Title	Format	Label	Cat. No.	Year	Price	Notes
	7"	W. Rec. Club		1980	**£10**	promo flexi
1962-1970	7"	Lyntone		1977	**£10**	promo flexi
1962-66	LP	Apple	PCSPR717	1978	**£15**	red vinyl, double
1967-70	LP	Apple	PCSPR718	1978	**£12**	blue vinyl, double
Abbey Road	r-reel	Apple	TAPMC7088	1970	**£50**	mono
Abbey Road	r-reel	Apple	TDPCS7088	1970	**£20**	stereo
Abbey Road	LP	Apple	PCS7088	1978	**£20**	green vinyl
Abbey Road	LP	Apple	PHO7088		**£250**	pic disc
Abbey Road	LP	Apple	SO383	1969	**£10**	US
Abbey Road	LP	Capitol	SEAX11900	1978	**£15**	US pic disc
Abbey Road	LP	EMI	5CP06204243	1979	**£12**	German pic disc
Abbey Road	CD	EMI	BEACD25/7	1987	**£20**	badge, booklet, 2 posters
Abbey Road	LP	Mobile Fid.	MFSL1023	1979	**£35**	US audiophile
Abbey Road	CD	Odeon	CP353016	1986	**£80**	Japanese
All My Loving	7" EP	Parlophone	GEP8891	1964	**£5**	
All You Need Is Love	7"	Parlophone	R5620	1967	**£4**	chart single
All You Need Is Love	7"	Parlophone	R5620	1967	**£125**	demo
All You Need Is Love	7"	Parlophone	R5620	1967	**£12**	not TV transmission
All You Need Is Love	7"	Parlophone	RP5620	1987	**£8**	pic disc
Amazing Beatles	LP	Clarion	601	1966	**£40**	US, mono
Amazing Beatles	LP	Clarion	SD601	1966	**£60**	US, stereo
And I Love Her	78	Parlophone		196-	**£250**	Indian
Another Beatles Christmas Record	7"	Lyntone	LYN757	1964	**£40**	PS, flexi
Back In The USSR	7"	Parlophone	R6016	1976	**£15**	demo
Ballad Of John And Yoko	7"	Apple	R5786	1969	**£4**	chart single
Ballad Of John And Yoko	7"	Apple	R5786	1969	**£125**	demo
Ballad Of John And Yoko	7"	Apple	RP5786	1989	**£8**	pic disc
Beatles & Frank Ifield On Stage	LP	Vee Jay	LP1085	1964	**£800**	US, Beatles on cover
Beatles & Frank Ifield On Stage	LP	Vee Jay	LP1085	1964	**£50**	US, old man on cover, mono
Beatles & Frank Ifield On Stage	LP	Vee Jay	LPS1085	1964	**£150**	US, old man on cover, stereo
Beatles '65	LP	Apple	ST2228	1970	**£10**	US, 'a subsidiary of Capitol'
Beatles '65	LP	Capitol	ST2228	1964	**£15**	US, stereo
Beatles '65	LP	Capitol	T2228	1964	**£20**	US, mono
Beatles 1962	7"	Baktabak	TABOKS1001	1988	**£30**	15 singles, boxed
Beatles	LP	Apple	PCS7067/8	1968	**£15**	stereo, chart LP
Beatles	LP	Apple	PCS7067/8	1968	**£150**	test pressing
Beatles	LP	Apple	PCS7067/8	1978	**£25**	white vinyl
Beatles	LP	Apple	PMC7067/8	1968	**£30**	mono, chart LP
Beatles	LP	Apple	SWBO101	1968	**£20**	US, double
Beatles	CD	EMI	BEACD25/4	1987	**£35**	HMV box, badge, booklet
Beatles	LP	Mobile Fid.	MFSL2072	1982	**£25**	US audiophile
Beatles	LP	Parlophone	PCSJ7067/8	1968	**£400**	double export
Beatles	LP	Parlophone	PPCS7067/8	1968	**£400**	double export
Beatles At The Beeb	LP	BBC	CN3970	1982	**£400**	transcription disc
Beatles At The Hollywood Bowl	7"	Parlophone	EMTV4	1977	**£50**	promo boxed set
Beatles Box	7"	Lyntone	LYN8982	1980	**£10**	promo flexi
Beatles Box	LP	W. Rec. Club	WRCSM701-8	1980	**£50**	8 LPs, boxed
Beatles Collection	7"	Lyntone	LYNSF165	1978	**£10**	promo flexi, poster
Beatles Collection	LP	Mobile Fid.		1982	**£250**	US audiophile, 14 LPs, boxed
Beatles Collection	7"	W. Rec. Club		1977	**£50**	25 singles, boxed
Beatles Collection	7"	W. Rec. Club		1978	**£50**	26 singles, boxed
Beatles Fifth Christmas Record	7"	Lyntone	LYN1360	1967	**£40**	PS, flexi
Beatles For Sale	LP	Mobile Fid.	MFSL1104	1984	**£15**	US audiophile
Beatles For Sale	r-reel	Parlophone	TAPMC1240	1965	**£20**	mono
Beatles For Sale	r-reel	Parlophone	TDPCS3062	1965	**£20**	stereo
Beatles For Sale	LP	Parlophone	PCS3062	1964	**£15**	stereo, chart LP
Beatles For Sale	LP	Parlophone	PMC1240	1964	**£20**	mono, chart LP

Title	Format	Label	Number	Year	Price	Notes
Beatles For Sale	7" EP	Parlophone	GEP8931	1965	**£5**	
Beatles For Sale No.2	7" EP	Parlophone	GEP8938	1965	**£5**	
Beatles Fourth Christmas Record	7"	Lyntone	LYN1145	1966	**£40**	PS, flexi
Beatles Greatest Hits	LP	Parlophone	EMTVS34	1982	**£30**	double, test pressing
Beatles Hits	7" EP	Parlophone	GEP8880	1963	**£5**	
Beatles Million Sellers	7" EP	Parlophone	GEP8946	1965	**£5**	
Beatles Mono Collection	LP	Parlophone	BMC10	1982	**£80**	10 LPs, boxed
Beatles No.1	7" EP	Parlophone	GEP8883	1963	**£5**	
Beatles Second Album	LP	Apple	ST2080	1970	**£10**	US, 'a subsidiary of Capitol'
Beatles Second Album	LP	Capitol	ST2080	1964	**£15**	US, stereo
Beatles Second Album	LP	Capitol	ST82080	1964	**£50**	US, Record Club issue
Beatles Second Album	LP	Capitol	T2080	1964	**£20**	US, mono
Beatles Seventh Christmas Record	7"	Lyntone	LYN1970/1	1969	**£40**	PS, flexi
Beatles Seventh Christmas Record	7"	Lyntone	LYN1970/1	1969	**£75**	PS, test pressing
Beatles singles Collection	7"	EMI	BSC1	1982	**£40**	26 singles, boxed
Beatles singles Collection	7"	EMI	BSCP1	1982	**£50**	27 singles, boxed, export
Beatles singles Collection	7"	Lyntone	LYNSF1291	1977	**£10**	promo flexi, poster
Beatles singles Collection	7"	Parlo./Apple	BS24	1976	**£50**	24 singles, boxed
Beatles Sixth Christmas Record	7"	Lyntone	LYN1743/4	1968	**£40**	PS, flexi
Beatles Story	LP	Apple	ST2222	1970	**£10**	US, 'a subsidiary of Capitol'
Beatles Story	LP	Capitol	STBO2222	1964	**£20**	US, stereo
Beatles Story	LP	Capitol	TBO2222	1964	**£25**	US, mono
Beatles Third Christmas Record	7"	Lyntone	LYN948	1965	**£40**	PS, flexi
Beatles VI	LP	Apple	ST2358	1970	**£10**	US, 'a subsidiary of Capitol'
Beatles VI	LP	Capitol	ST2358	1965	**£15**	US, stereo
Beatles VI	LP	Capitol	ST82358	1965	**£50**	US, Record Club issue
Beatles VI	LP	Capitol	T2358	1965	**£20**	US, mono
Beatles VI	LP	Parlophone	CPCS104	1974	**£200**	export
Beatles VI	LP	Parlophone	CPCS105	1974	**£200**	export
Beatles Vs. The Four Seasons	LP	Vee Jay	DX30	1964	**£300**	US double
Beatles With Tony Sheridan	LP	MGM	E4215	1964	**£40**	US, mono
Beatles With Tony Sheridan	LP	MGM	SE4215	1964	**£90**	US, stereo
Beatles' Christmas Album	LP	Apple	SBC100	1970	**£200**	US
Beatles' Christmas Record	7"	Lyntone	LYN492	1963	**£100**	PS, flexi
Beatles' Movie Medley	7"	Parlophone	R6055	1982	**£10**	demo
Beatles' Rock'n'Roll Medley	7"	EMI	PSR401	1976	**£20**	1 sided promo
Beatles' Second Album	LP	Parlophone	CPCS103	1974	**£200**	export
Can't Buy Me Love	7"	Parlophone	R5114	1964	**£4**	chart single
Can't Buy Me Love	7"	Parlophone	R5114	1964	**£150**	demo
Can't Buy Me Love	7"	Parlophone	RP5114	1984	**£8**	pic disc
Collection Of Beatles Oldies	r-reel	Parlophone	TAPMC7016	1967	**£20**	mono
Collection Of Beatles Oldies	r-reel	Parlophone	TDPCS7016	1967	**£20**	stereo
Collection Of Oldies	LP	Parlophone	PCS7016	1967	**£15**	stereo, chart LP
Collection Of Oldies	LP	Parlophone	PMC7016	1967	**£20**	mono, chart LP
Day Tripper	7"	Parlophone	R5389	1965	**£4**	chart single
Day Tripper	7"	Parlophone	R5389	1965	**£130**	demo
Early Beatles	LP	Apple	ST2309	1970	**£10**	US, 'a subsidiary of Capitol'
Early Beatles	LP	Capitol	ST2309	1965	**£15**	US, stereo
Early Beatles	LP	Capitol	T2309	1965	**£20**	US, mono
From Me To You	7"	Parlophone	R5015	1963	**£4**	chart single
From Me To You	7"	Parlophone	R5015	1963	**£250**	demo
From Me To You	7"	Parlophone	RP5015	1983	**£8**	pic disc
From Then To You	LP	Apple	LYN2154	1970	**£250**	
Get Back	7"	Apple	R5777	1969	**£4**	chart single
Get Back	7"	Apple	R5779	1969	**£125**	demo
Get Back	7"	Apple	RP5777	1989	**£8**	pic disc
Hard Day's Night	LP	Mobile Fid.	MFSL1103	1984	**£15**	US audiophile
Hard Day's Night	7" EP	Parlophone	GEP8920	1964	**£5**	
Hard Day's Night	r-reel	Parlophone	TAPMC1230	1964	**£20**	mono
Hard Day's Night	r-reel	Parlophone	TDPCS3058	1964	**£20**	stereo
Hard Day's Night	LP	Parlophone	PCS3058	1964	**£15**	stereo, chart LP
Hard Day's Night	LP	Parlophone	PMC1230	1964	**£20**	mono, chart LP
Hard Day's Night	7"	Parlophone	R5160	1964	**£4**	chart single
Hard Day's Night	7"	Parlophone	R5160	1964	**£150**	demo
Hard Day's Night	7"	Parlophone	RP5160	1984	**£8**	pic disc
Hard Day's Night	LP	United Artists	SP2359	1964	**£200**	US promo with script

Title	Format	Label	Cat. No.	Year	Price	Notes
Hard Day's Night	LP	United Artists	UAL3366	1964	**£25**	US, mono
Hard Day's Night	LP	United Artists	UAS6366	1964	**£20**	US, stereo
Hard Day's Night No.2	7" EP	Parlophone	GEP8924	1964	**£5**	
Hello Goodbye	7"	Parlophone	R5655	1967	**£4**	chart single
Hello Goodbye	7"	Parlophone	R5655	1967	**£125**	demo
Hello Goodbye	7"	Parlophone	RP5655	1987	**£8**	pic disc
Help	LP	Apple	ST2386	1970	**£10**	US, 'a subsidiary of Capitol'
Help	LP	Capitol	MAS2386	1965	**£20**	US, mono
Help	LP	Capitol	SMAS2386	1965	**£15**	US, stereo
Help	LP	Capitol	SMAS82386	1965	**£50**	US, Record Club issue
Help	LP	Mobile Fid.	MFSL1105	1984	**£15**	US audiophile
Help	r-reel	Parlophone	TAPMC1255	1965	**£20**	mono
Help	r-reel	Parlophone	TDPCS3071	1965	**£20**	stereo
Help	LP	Parlophone	PCS3071	1965	**£15**	stereo, chart LP
Help	LP	Parlophone	PMC1255	1965	**£20**	chart LP
Help	7"	Parlophone	RP5305	1985	**£8**	pic disc
Help	7"	Parlophone	R5305	1965	**£4**	chart single
Help	7"	Parlophone	R5305	1965	**£130**	demo
Help,Rubber Soul,Revolver	CD			198-	**£100**	export
Help/Rubber Soul/Revolver	CD	EMI	BEACD25/2	1987	**£75**	HMV red box, magazine
Hey Jude	LP	Apple	SW385	1970	**£10**	US, 'a subsidiary of Capitol'
Hey Jude	7"	Apple	R5722	1968	**£4**	chart single
Hey Jude	7"	Apple	RP5722	1988	**£8**	pic disc
Hey Jude	12"	Apple	12RP5722	1988	**£10**	pic disc
Hey Jude	LP	Parlophone	CPCS106	1974	**£15**	export
Hey Jude	LP	Parlophone	PCSJ149		**£15**	export
Hey Jude	7"	Parlophone	DP570	1968	**£30**	export
Hey Jude	7"	Parlophone	R5722	1968	**£150**	demo
Hey Jude/The Beatles Again	LP	Apple	SO/SW385	1970	**£12**	US
History Of Rock Vol.26	LP	Orbis	HRL026	1984	**£15**	double
I Feel Fine	7"	Parlophone	R5200	1964	**£4**	chart single
I Feel Fine	7"	Parlophone	R5200	1964	**£150**	demo
I Feel Fine	7"	Parlophone	RP5200	1984	**£8**	pic disc
I Want To Hold Your Hand	7"	Parlophone	R5084	1963	**£4**	chart single
I Want To Hold Your Hand	7"	Parlophone	R5084	1963	**£175**	demo
I Want To Hold Your Hand	7"	Parlophone	RP5084	1983	**£8**	pic disc
If I Fell	78	Parlophone		196-	**£250**	Indian
If I Fell	7"	Parlophone	DP562	1964	**£50**	export
In The Beginning	LP	Polydor	244504	1970	**£12**	US, red label
Introducing The Beatles	LP	Vee Jay	LP1062	1963	**£300**	US, with Love Me Do, blank back cover, mono
Introducing The Beatles	LP	Vee Jay	LP1062	1963	**£100**	US, with Love Me Do, songs listed on back
Introducing The Beatles	LP	Vee Jay	LP1062	1964	**£50**	US, with Please Please Me, mono
Introducing The Beatles	LP	Vee Jay	LPS1062	1963	**£600**	US, with Love Me Do, blank back cover, stereo
Introducing The Beatles	LP	Vee Jay	LPS1062	1964	**£300**	US, with Please Please Me, stereo
Lady Madonna	7"	Parlophone	R5675	1968	**£4**	chart single
Lady Madonna	7"	Parlophone	R5675	1968	**£125**	demo
Lady Madonna	7"	Parlophone	RP5675	1988	**£8**	pic disc
Let It Be	CD			198-	**£120**	promo, pic label, boxed
Let It Be	r-reel	Apple	TAPMC7096	1970	**£50**	mono
Let It Be	r-reel	Apple	TDPCS7096	1970	**£20**	stereo
Let It Be	LP	Apple	AR34001	1970	**£10**	US, 'a subsidiary of Capitol'
Let It Be	LP	Apple	PCS7096	1978	**£20**	white vinyl
Let It Be	LP	Apple	PXS1	1970	**£150**	boxed with book
Let It Be	7"	Apple	R5833	1970	**£4**	chart single
Let It Be	7"	Apple	R5833	1970	**£125**	demo
Let It Be	7"	Apple	R5833	1970	**£8**	PS
Let It Be	7"	Apple	RP5833	1990	**£8**	pic disc
Let It Be	CD	EMI	BEACD25/8	1987	**£25**	HMV boxed set, poster, booklet, badge
Let It Be	LP	Mobile Fid.	MFSL1109	1984	**£15**	US audiophile

Title	Format	Label	Cat. No.	Year	Price	Notes
Long Tall Sally	78	Parlophone	DPE164	196-	**£250**	Indian
Long Tall Sally	7" EP	Parlophone	GEP8913	1964	**£5**	
Love Me Do	7"	Parlophone	R4949	1962	**£400**	demo
Love Me Do	7"	Parlophone	R4949	1962	**£20**	red label, chart single
Love Me Do	7"	Parlophone	R4949	1963	**£5**	black label
Love Me Do	7"	Parlophone	R4949	1982	**£20**	Ardmore & Beechwood credit
Love Me Do	7"	Parlophone	RP4949	1982	**£25**	Ardmore & Beechwood credit, pic disc
Love Me Do	7"	Parlophone	RP4983	1982	**£25**	pic disc, same pic both sides
Magical Mystery Tour	LP	Apple	SMAL2835	1970	**£10**	US, 'a subsidiary of Capitol'
Magical Mystery Tour	LP	Capitol	MAL2835	1967	**£50**	US, mono
Magical Mystery Tour	LP	Capitol	SMAL2835	1967	**£12**	US, stereo, chart LP
Magical Mystery Tour	CD	EMI	BEACD25/6	1987	**£30**	HMV box, badge, booklet, poster
Magical Mystery Tour	LP	Mobile Fid.	MFSL1047	1981	**£20**	US audiophile
Magical Mystery Tour	LP	Parlophone	PCTC255	1978	**£20**	yellow vinyl
Magical Mystery Tour	7" EP	Parlophone	MMT1	1967	**£8**	double, mono
Magical Mystery Tour	7" EP	Parlophone	SMMT1	1967	**£6**	double, stereo
Meet The Beatles	LP	Apple	ST2047	1970	**£10**	US, 'a subsidiary of Capitol'
Meet The Beatles	LP	Capitol	ST2047	1964	**£20**	US, brown title, stereo
Meet The Beatles	LP	Capitol	ST2047	1964	**£15**	US, green title, stereo
Meet The Beatles	LP	Capitol	ST82047	1964	**£50**	US, Record Club issue
Meet The Beatles	LP	Capitol	T2047	1964	**£25**	US, brown title, mono
Meet The Beatles	LP	Capitol	T2047	1964	**£20**	US, green title, mono
Michelle	7"	Parlophone	DP564	1966	**£50**	export
Nowhere Man	7" EP	Parlophone	GEP8952	1966	**£5**	
Paperback Writer	7"	Parlophone	R5452	1966	**£4**	chart single
Paperback Writer	7"	Parlophone	R5452	1966	**£125**	demo
Paperback Writer	7"	Parlophone	RP5452	1986	**£8**	pic disc
Past Masters Vol.1	CD	EMI	BEACD25/9	1987	**£20**	HMV box, booklet, badge
Past Masters Vol.2	CD	EMI	BEACD25/10	1987	**£20**	HMV box, booklet, badge
Penny Lane	7"	Parlophone	R5570	1967	**£4**	chart single
Penny Lane	7"	Parlophone	R5570	1967	**£125**	demo
Penny Lane	7"	Parlophone	R5570	1967	**£20**	PS
Penny Lane	7"	Parlophone	RP5570	1987	**£8**	pic disc
Please Please Me	LP	Mobile Fid.	MFSL1101	1984	**£15**	US audiophile
Please Please Me	r-reel	Parlophone	TAPMC1202	1963	**£20**	mono
Please Please Me	r-reel	Parlophone	TDPCS3042	1963	**£20**	stereo
Please Please Me	LP	Parlophone	PCS3042	1963	**£800**	gold label stereo
Please Please Me	LP	Parlophone	PCS3042	1963	**£15**	stereo, chart LP
Please Please Me	LP	Parlophone	PMC1202	1963	**£20**	mono, chart LP
Please Please Me	LP	Parlophone	PMC1202	1963	**£100**	gold label
Please Please Me	78	Parlophone		196-	**£250**	Indian
Please Please Me	7"	Parlophone	R4983	1963	**£4**	black label, chart single
Please Please Me	7"	Parlophone	R4983	1963	**£300**	demo
Please Please Me	7"	Parlophone	R4983	1963	**£20**	red label
Please Please Me	7"	Parlophone	RP4983	1983	**£8**	pic disc
Please Please Me/With.../ Hard Day's Night/For Sale	CD	EMI	BEACD25	1987	**£150**	HMV black box, book, leaflet
Rarities	LP	Capitol	SN12009	1978	**£35**	US green label
Reel Music	LP	Capitol	SV12199	1982	**£12**	US gold vinyl
Reel Music	LP	Capitol	SV12199	1982	**£25**	US gold vinyl, numbered
Revolver	LP	Apple	ST2576	1970	**£10**	US, 'a subsidiary of Capitol'
Revolver	LP	Capitol	ST2576	1966	**£15**	US, stereo
Revolver	LP	Capitol	ST82576	1966	**£50**	US, Record Club issue
Revolver	LP	Capitol	T2576	1966	**£20**	US, mono
Revolver	LP	Mobile Fid.	MFSL1107	1984	**£15**	US audiophile
Revolver	r-reel	Parlophone	TAPMC7009	1966	**£20**	mono
Revolver	r-reel	Parlophone	TDPCS7009	1966	**£20**	stereo
Revolver	LP	Parlophone	PCS7009	1966	**£15**	stereo, chart LP
Revolver	LP	Parlophone	PMC7009	1966	**£20**	mono, chart LP

Title	Format	Label	Number	Year	Price	Notes
Rubber Soul	LP	Apple	ST2442	1970	**£10**	US, 'a subsidiary of Capitol'
Rubber Soul	LP	Capitol	ST2442	1965	**£15**	US, stereo
Rubber Soul	LP	Capitol	ST82442	1965	**£50**	US, Record Club issue
Rubber Soul	LP	Capitol	T2442	1965	**£20**	US, mono
Rubber Soul	LP	Mobile Fid.	MFSL1106	1984	**£15**	US audiophile
Rubber Soul	r-reel	Parlophone	TAPMC1267	1966	**£20**	mono
Rubber Soul	r-reel	Parlophone	TDPCS3075	1966	**£20**	stereo
Rubber Soul	LP	Parlophone	PCS3075	1966	**£15**	stereo, chart LP
Rubber Soul	LP	Parlophone	PMC1267	1966	**£20**	mono, chart LP
Searchin'	7"	AFE	AFS1	1982	**£6**	
Sgt.Pepper	LP	Apple	SMAS2653	1970	**£10**	US, 'a subsidiary of Capitol'
Sgt.Pepper	LP	Capitol	MAS2653	1967	**£30**	US, mono
Sgt.Pepper	LP	Capitol	SEAX11840	1978	**£15**	US pic disc
Sgt.Pepper	LP	Capitol	SMAS2653	1967	**£12**	US, stereo
Sgt.Pepper	CD	EMI	BEACD25/3	1987	**£25**	HMV box, badge, booklet, cutouts
Sgt.Pepper	LP	Mobile Fid.	MFSL1100	1982	**£15**	US audiophile
Sgt.Pepper	LP	Mobile Fid.	UHQR1100	1982	**£200**	US audiophile, quarter-inch thick vinyl
Sgt.Pepper	r-reel	Parlophone	TAPMC7027	1967	**£20**	mono
Sgt.Pepper	r-reel	Parlophone	TDPCS7027	1967	**£20**	stereo
Sgt.Pepper	LP	Parlophone	PCS7027	1967	**£15**	stereo, chart LP
Sgt.Pepper	LP	Parlophone	PHO7027	1979	**£12**	pic disc
Sgt.Pepper	LP	Parlophone	PMC7027	1967	**£25**	mono, chart LP
Sgt.Pepper	LP	Parlophone	PMC7027	1982	**£15**	from BMC10, but with stereo B side
Sgt.Pepper	7"	Parlophone	R6022	1978	**£10**	demo
She Loves You	7"	Parlophone	R5055	1963	**£4**	chart single
She Loves You	7"	Parlophone	R5055	1963	**£200**	demo
She Loves You	7"	Parlophone	RP5055	1983	**£8**	pic disc
Something	7"	Apple	R5814	1969	**£4**	chart single
Something	7"	Apple	R5814	1969	**£125**	demo
Something	7"	Apple	RP5814	1989	**£8**	pic disc
Something New	LP	Apple	ST2108	1970	**£10**	US, 'a subsidiary of Capitol'
Something New	LP	Capitol	ST2108	1964	**£15**	US, stereo
Something New	LP	Capitol	ST82108	1964	**£50**	US, Record Club issue
Something New	LP	Capitol	T2108	1964	**£20**	US, mono
Something New	LP	Parlophone	CPCS101	1965	**£200**	export
Something New	LP	Parlophone	CPCS102	1974	**£200**	export
Songs, Pictures And Stories	LP	Vee Jay	LP1092	1964	**£75**	US, fold-open cover
Tell Me Why	78	Parlophone	DPE172	196-	**£250**	Indian
Ticket To Ride	7"	Parlophone	R5265	1965	**£4**	chart single
Ticket To Ride	7"	Parlophone	R5265	1965	**£150**	demo
Ticket To Ride	7"	Parlophone	RP5265	1985	**£8**	pic disc
Twist And Shout	7"	Lingasong	NB1	1977	**£10**	
Twist And Shout	7"	Lingasong	NB1	1977	**£15**	demo, details B-side only
Twist And Shout	7"	Lingasong	NB1	1977	**£20**	demo, details both sides
Twist And Shout	7" EP	Parlophone	GEP8882	1963	**£5**	
We Can Work It Out	7"	Parlophone	RP5389	1985	**£8**	pic disc
White Album	r-reel	Apple	DTAPMC7067/8	1969	**£30**	mono
White Album	r-reel	Apple	DTDPCS7067/8	1969	**£30**	stereo
With The Beatles	LP	Mobile Fid.	MFSL1102	1984	**£40**	US audiophile
With The Beatles	r-reel	Parlophone	TAPMC1206	1964	**£20**	mono
With The Beatles	r-reel	Parlophone	TDPCS3045	1964	**£20**	stereo
With The Beatles	LP	Parlophone	PCS3045	1963	**£15**	stereo, chart LP
With The Beatles	LP	Parlophone	PMC1206	1963	**£20**	mono, chart LP
Yellow Submarine	r-reel	Apple	TAPMC7070	1969	**£25**	mono
Yellow Submarine	r-reel	Apple	TDPCS7070	1969	**£20**	stereo
Yellow Submarine	LP	Apple	PMC7070	1969	**£25**	mono, chart LP
Yellow Submarine	LP	Apple	SW153	1968	**£10**	US
Yellow Submarine	CD	EMI	BEACD25/5	1987	**£40**	HMV box, badge, cutout, leaflet
Yellow Submarine	LP	Mobile Fid.	MFSL1108	1984	**£15**	US audiophile
Yellow Submarine	7"	Parlophone	R5493	1966	**£4**	chart single
Yellow Submarine	7"	Parlophone	R5493	1966	**£125**	demo
Yellow Submarine	7"	Parlophone	RP5493	1986	**£8**	pic disc

Title	Format	Label	Cat. No.	Year	Price	Notes
Yesterday	7"	Parlophone	DP563	1965	**£50**	export
Yesterday	7"	Parlophone	R6013	1976	**£15**	demo
Yesterday	7" EP	Parlophone	GEP8948	1966	**£5**	
Yesterday And Today	LP	Apple	ST2553	1970	**£10**	US, 'a subsidiary of Capitol'
Yesterday And Today	LP	Capitol	ST2553	1966	**£3000**	US, peeled butcher sleeve, stereo
Yesterday And Today	LP	Capitol	ST2553	1966	**£15**	US, stereo
Yesterday And Today	LP	Capitol	ST2553	1966	**£600**	US, unpeeled butcher sleeve, stereo
Yesterday And Today	LP	Capitol	ST82553	1966	**£50**	US, Record Club issue
Yesterday And Today	LP	Capitol	T2553	1966	**£800**	US peeled butcher sleeve
Yesterday And Today	LP	Capitol	T2553	1966	**£200**	US unpeeled butcher sleeve
Yesterday And Today	LP	Capitol	T2553	1966	**£20**	US, mono

BEATLES & OTHERS

Title	Format	Label	Cat. No.	Year	Price	Notes
Our First Four	7"	Apple		1968	**£400**	promo, pack with 4 x 7"

BEATLES WITH TONY SHERIDAN

Title	Format	Label	Cat. No.	Year	Price	Notes
Ain't She Sweet	LP	Atco	33169	1964	**£60**	US, mono
Ain't She Sweet	LP	Atco	SD33169	1964	**£75**	US, stereo
Ain't She Sweet	7"	Polydor	NH52317	1964	**£25**	chart single
Beatles First	CD	Polydor	8237012	1985	**£55**	withdrawn sleeve with wrong line-up
Beatles' First	LP	Polydor	236201	1964	**£40**	
Cry For A Shadow	7"	Polydor	NH52275	1964	**£30**	
My Bonnie	7"	Polydor	NH66833	1962	**£25**	chart single
Sweet Georgia Brown	7"	Polydor	NH52906	1964	**£30**	
Tony Sheridan With The Beatles	7" EP	Polydor	EPH21610	1963	**£40**	

BEATLES/WINGS

Title	Format	Label	Cat. No.	Year	Price	Notes
Get Back	7"	Apple	R5777	1978	**£8**	mispress - B side plays 'I've Had Enough'

BEATMEN

Title	Format	Label	Cat. No.	Year	Price	Notes
Now The Sun Has Gone	7"	Pye	7N15792	1965	**£5**	
You Can't Sit Down	7"	Pye	7N15659	1964	**£5**	

BEATSTALKERS

Title	Format	Label	Cat. No.	Year	Price	Notes
Everybody's Talkin' About My Baby	7"	Decca	F12259	1965	**£8**	
Everything Is You	7"	CBS	3557	1968	**£12**	
Left Right Left	7"	Decca	F12352	1966	**£8**	
Love Like Yours	7"	Decca	F12460	1966	**£8**	
My One Chance	7"	CBS	2732	1967	**£10**	
Silver Tree Top School For Boys	7"	CBS	3105	1967	**£15**	
When I'm Five	7"	CBS	3936	1969	**£12**	

BEATTY, E.C.

Title	Format	Label	Cat. No.	Year	Price	Notes
Ski King	7"	Felsted	AF127	1959	**£4**	

BEAU

C.J.T.Midgley (Beau) was a singer songwriter whose songs would have benefited from more fully worked out arrangements than they actually get. No doubt John Peel's Dandelion label could not afford the expense of a cast of session musicians. Nevertheless, "1917 Revolution" with its taut strummed twelve string guitar echoing across the sound-stage is quite wonderful.

Title	Format	Label	Cat. No.	Year	Price	Notes
1917 Revolution	7"	Dandelion	4403	1969	**£4**	
Beau	LP	Dandelion	63751	1969	**£20**	
Creation	LP	Dandelion	DAN8006	1971	**£20**	

BEAU BRUMMELS

The natural response of America to the initial furore surrounding the Beatles was for the record-buying public to embrace a number of home-grown talents, whose sound and style owed everything to their Liverpudlian rivals. The Beau Brummels were probably the most successful of these, although they inevitably meant little in Britain. As a result, one of the classic albums of the late sixties has been largely ignored - for "Triangle" is an immaculate collection of imaginatively arranged songs to rival Love's "Forever Changes".

Title	Format	Label	Cat. No.	Year	Price	Notes
Beau Brummels 66	LP	W. Bros	WS1644	1966	**£20**	US
Beau Brummels	LP	Pye	NPL28062	1965	**£25**	
Beau Brummels Vol.2	LP	Autumn	SLP104	1966	**£20**	US
Best Of	LP	Vault	LPS114	1967	**£15**	US
Bradley's Barn	LP	W. Bros	WS1760	1968	**£20**	US

Don't Talk To Strangers	7"	Pye	7N25333	1965	**£5**	
Good Time Music	7"	Pye	7N25342	1966	**£5**	
Just A Little	7"	Pye	7N25306	1965	**£5**	
Laugh Laugh	7"	Pye	7N25293	1965	**£6**	
Triangle	LP	W. Bros	WS1692	1967	**£20**	US
Vol.44	LP	Vault	LPS121	1967	**£20**	US
You Tell Me Why	7"	Pye	7N25318	1965	**£5**	

BEAUMARKS

Clap Your Hands	7"	Top Rank	JAR377	1960	**£4**	

BEAUMONT, JIMMY

You Got Too Much Going For You	7"	London	HLZ10059	1966	**£12**	

BEAVER, PAUL

Perchance To Dream	LP	Rapture	11111		**£15**	US

BEAVER-KRAUSE

Paul Beaver and Bernie Krause were the other pair of synthesiser pioneers, but, unlike the records by Tonto's Expanding Headband, theirs mix the electronics with conventional instruments. The "Guide To Electronic Music" is by way of being an aural handbook, recorded for an avant-garde classical label.

All Good Men	LP	W. Bros	K46184	1972	**£10**	
Gandharva	LP	W. Bros	K46130	1971	**£10**	
Guide To Electronic Music	LP	Nonesuch	K73018	1975	**£10**	
In A Wild Sanctuary	LP	W. Bros	WS1850	1970	**£12**	US
Ragnarok Electronic Funk	LP	Limelight	86069	1969	**£15**	US
Real Slow Drag	7"	W. Bros	K16237	1972	**£4**	

BEAZERS (CHRIS FARLOWE)

Blue Beat	7"	Decca	F11827	1964	**£10**	

BEBOP DELUXE

Between Two Worlds	7"	Harvest	HAR5091	1975	**£40**	
Live In The Air Age	LP	Harvest	SHVL816	1977	**£10**	with 7" (PSR412), chart LP
Teenage Archangel	7"	Smile	LAFS001	1973	**£20**	

BECK, GORDON

Beck-Matthewson-Humair Trio	LP	Dire	FO341	1972	**£30**	
Experiments With Pops	LP	Major Minor	SMLP22	1969	**£40**	
Gyroscope	LP	Morgan	MJ1	1968	**£30**	
Plays Dr.Doolittle	LP	Major Minor	SML88	1968	**£30**	
Plays Half A Jazz Sixpence	LP	Major Minor	SMLP22	1968	**£30**	

BECK, JEFF

When the Observer surveyed a number of well-known rock guitarists to discover who the "guitarists' guitarist" was, the consensus of opinion chose Jeff Beck. Notoriously difficult to work with, Beck's career has been notable for the instability of his group line-ups and also for his apparent difficulty in deciding on the best music style to display his talents. He has, nevertheless, managed to create the occasional masterpiece along the way, of which the most obvious examples are the electric jazz album "Blow By Blow" (too common to be valuable, unfortunately) and the blues-rock "Truth". This record, which included Rod Stewart and Ron Wood as members of a fine band,was a direct influence on Led Zeppelin, whose guitarist Jimmy Page used to very much model his guitar playing on that of Jeff Beck.

Beck-ola	LP	Columbia	SCX6351	1969	**£12**	chart LP
Blow By Blow	LP	Epic	PEQ33409	1975	**£15**	US quad
Hi Ho Silver Lining	7"	Columbia	DB8151	1967	**£6**	chart single
Hi Ho Silver Lining	7"	RAK	RRP3	1982	**£6**	pic disc
Jeff Beck Group	LP	Epic	EQ31331	1974	**£15**	US quad
Live	LP	Epic	PEQ34433	1977	**£15**	US quad
Love Is Blue	7"	Columbia	DB8359	1968	**£6**	chart single
Plinth	7"	Columbia	DB8590	1968	**£40**	promo only
Rough And Ready	LP	Epic	Q64619	1974	**£15**	quad
Tallyman	7"	Columbia	DB8227	1967	**£10**	chart single
Truth	LP	Columbia	SCX6293	1968	**£15**	
Truth	7"	Columbia	PSR317	1968	**£20**	promo
Wired	LP	Epic	PEQ33849	1976	**£15**	US quad

BECK,BOGERT & APPICE

Live In Japan	LP	CBS/Sony	ECPJ11/12	1973	**£25**	Japanese double

BECKETT, HAROLD

Harold Beckett is a jazz trumpeter whose playing seems to be included somewhere on most British rock LPs made in the early seventies! His own records, which feature the usual familiar jazz faces of the period, are actually remarkably free from rock influence, which is the reason for their relatively low collectors' values today.

Title	Format	Label	Cat. No.	Year	Price	Notes
Flare Up	LP	Philips	6308026	1971	**£20**	
Joy Unlimited	LP	Cadillac	SGC1004	1975	**£15**	
Theme For Fega	LP	RCA	SF8264	1973	**£20**	
Warm Smiles	LP	RCA	SF8225	1972	**£20**	

BECKFORD, KEITH

Title	Format	Label	Cat. No.	Year	Price	Notes
Suzy Wong	7"	Big Shot	BI521	1973	**£5**	

BECKFORD, LYNN

Title	Format	Label	Cat. No.	Year	Price	Notes
Combination	7"	Island	WI3144	1968	**£8**	

BECKFORD, THEO

Title	Format	Label	Cat. No.	Year	Price	Notes
If Life Was A Thing	7"	Island	WI246	1965	**£10**	
On Your Knees	7"	Blue Beat	BB287	1964	**£10**	
Trench Town People	7"	Island	WI238	1965	**£10**	
What A Woe	7"	Island	WI248	1965	**£10**	
You Are The One	7"	Island	WI243	1965	**£10**	

BEDFORD, DAVID

David Bedford is an avant-garde composer whose sympathy for rock music has led to his gaining much employment as an arranger. In particular, he has worked extensively with Mike Oldfield, producing an orchestral version of "Tubular Bells" and writing a guitar concerto for him (the superb "Star's End", which should be required listening for Jon Lord, Keith Emerson, and other rock-classical fusionists whose ideas of how classical music is constructed are still rooted in the nineteenth century). "Nurses Song With Elephants" is less accessible than later Bedford works, but is still crammed with original ideas.

Title	Format	Label	Cat. No.	Year	Price	Notes
Music For Albion Moonlight (other side Elizabeth Lutyens)	LP	Argo	ZRG638	1970	**£15**	
Nurses Song With Elephants	LP	Dandelion	2310165	1972	**£20**	

BEDROCKS

Title	Format	Label	Cat. No.	Year	Price	Notes
Hit Me On The Head	7"	Columbia	DB8669	1970	**£4**	
Lovedene Girls	7"	Columbia	DB8539	1969	**£4**	
Ob La Di Ob La Da	7"	Columbia	DB8516	1968	**£4**	chart single
Stone Cold Dead In The Market	7"	Columbia	DB8699	1970	**£4**	
Wonderful World	7"	Columbia	DB8620	1969	**£4**	

BEE GEES

Title	Format	Label	Cat. No.	Year	Price	Notes
Alive	7"	Polydor	2058304	1972	**£4**	
Bee Gees First	LP	Polydor	583012	1967	**£10**	chart LP
Boogie Child	7"	RSO	2090224	1977	**£10**	promo only
Charade	7"	RSO	2090136	1974	**£4**	
Cucumber Castle	LP	Polydor	2383010	1970	**£12**	chart LP
Don't Forget To Remember	7"	Polydor	56343	1969	**£4**	chart single
First Of May	7"	Polydor	56304	1969	**£4**	chart single
Horizontal	LP	Polydor	583020	1968	**£10**	chart LP
How Can You Mend A Broken Heart	7"	Polydor	2058115	1971	**£4**	
I've Gotta Get A Message To You	7"	Polydor	56273	1968	**£4**	chart single
I.O.I.O.	7"	Polydor	56377	1970	**£4**	chart single
Idea	LP	Polydor	583036	1968	**£10**	chart LP
Jumbo	7"	Polydor	56242	1968	**£4**	chart single
Life In A Tin Can	LP	RSO	2394102	1973	**£12**	
Lonely Days	7"	Polydor	2001104	1970	**£4**	chart single
Massachusetts	7"	Polydor	56192	1967	**£4**	chart single
Mr.Natural	LP	RSO	2394132	1974	**£12**	
Mr.Natural	7"	RSO	2090128	1974	**£4**	
My World	7"	Polydor	2058185	1972	**£4**	chart single
New York Mining Disaster 1941	7"	Polydor	56161	1967	**£4**	chart single
Night Fever	7"	RSO	SNF1	1978	**£6**	1 sided promo
Night Fever	12"	RSO	PPSP1	1978	**£8**	promo
Odessa	LP	Polydor	583049/050	1969	**£15**	felt sleeve, chart LP
Odessa	7"	Polydor	56304	1969	**£20**	
Rare Precious & Beautiful Vol.1	LP	Polydor	236221	1968	**£10**	
Rare Precious & Beautiful Vol.2	LP	Polydor	236513	1968	**£10**	
Rare Precious & Beautiful Vol.3	LP	Polydor	236556	1969	**£10**	
Run To Me	7"	Polydor	2058255	1972	**£4**	chart single
Saturday Night Fever	12"	RSO	PPSP12	1978	**£12**	promo
Saw A New Morning	7"	RSO	2090105	1973	**£4**	
Short Cuts	LP	RSO	BGPLP1	1979	**£10**	promo
Sing & Play 14 Barry Gibb Songs	LP	Calendar	R66241	1968	**£40**	Australian reissue
Sing & Play 14 Barry Gibb Songs	LP	Leedon	LL31801	1965	**£120**	Australian
Spicks And Specks	7"	Polydor	56727	1967	**£8**	

Spicks And Specks	LP	Spin	EL32031	1966	**£20**	Australian
Spirits Having Flown	LP	Nautilus	NR17	1981	**£12**	US audiophile
Spirits Having Flown	LP	RSO	13041	1979	**£10**	US pic disc
To Love Somebody	7"	Polydor	56178	1967	**£4**	chart single
To Whom It May Concern	LP	Polydor	2383139	1972	**£12**	
Tomorrow Tomorrow	7"	Polydor	56331	1969	**£4**	chart single
Trafalgar	LP	Polydor	2383052	1971	**£12**	
Two Years On	LP	Polydor	2310069	1970	**£12**	
Words	7"	Polydor	56229	1968	**£4**	chart single
World	7"	Polydor	56220	1967	**£4**	chart single
Wouldn't I Be Someone	7"	RSO	2090111	1973	**£4**	

BEE, EDWIN

I've Been Loving You	7"	Decca	F12781	1968	**£6**	

BEE, MOLLY

Since I Met You Baby	7"	London	HLD8400	1957	**£6**	
single Girl Again	7"	MGM	MGM1280	1965	**£4**	

BEEFEATERS

Meet You There	LP	Sonet	SPLP1509	1969	**£20**	
Please Let Me Love You	7"	Elektra	2101007	1970	**£10**	
Please Let Me Love You	7"	Pye	7N25277	1964	**£50**	

BEES

Jesse James Rides Again	7"	Columbia	DB101	1967	**£8**	
Prisoner From Alcatraz	7"	Columbia	DB111	1968	**£8**	

BEES MAKE HONEY

Knee Trembler	7"	EMI	EMI2078	1973	**£6**	
Music Every Night	LP	EMI	EMC3013	1972	**£20**	

BEGGARS OPERA

Act One	LP	Vertigo	6360018	1970	**£20**	spiral label
Classical Gas	7"	Vertigo	6059105	1974	**£6**	
Get Your Dog Off Me	LP	Vertigo	6360090	1973	**£15**	
Hobo	7"	Vertigo	6059060	1972	**£6**	
Pathfinder	LP	Vertigo	6360073	1972	**£20**	spiral label
Sarabande	7"	Vertigo	6059026	1970	**£8**	
Two Timing Woman	7"	Vertigo	6059088	1973	**£6**	
Waters Of Change	LP	Vertigo	6360054	1971	**£20**	spiral label

BEGINNING OF THE END

Funky Nassau	7"	Atlantic	2091097	1971	**£4**	

BEL CANTOS

Feel Alright	7"	R&B	MRB5003	1965	**£8**	

BELFAST GYPSIES

Gloria's Dream	7"	Island	WI3007	1966	**£10**	

BELIEVERS

Money In The Rock	7"	Masters Time	MT001	196-	**£6**	

BELL & ARC

The pattern whereby a young group records an impressive first album, followed by increasingly less inspired subsequent records, becomes to some extent disguised when the group changes its name. Bell & Arc is essentially Skip Bifferty, but some four years down the road, the fire is definitely burning low.

Bell And Arc	LP	Charisma	CAS1053	1971	**£10**	
She Belongs To Me	7"	Charisma	CB170	1971	**£4**	

BELL BROTHERS

Tell Him No	7"	Action	ACT4510	1968	**£5**	
Tell Him No	7"	Action	ACT4510	1968	**£15**	demo

BELL SOUNDS

Marching Guitars	7"	HMV	POP685	1959	**£4**	

BELL, ALEXANDER

Alexander Bell Believes	7"	CBS	2977	1967	**£8**	

BELL, ARCHIE & THE DRELLS

I Can't Stop Dancing	7"	Atlantic	584217	1968	**£4**	
Tighten Up	7"	Atlantic	584185	1968	**£4**	

BELL, FREDDY & THE BELL BOYS

Bells Are Swinging	LP	20th Century	4146	1964	**£10**	US
Giddy-Up-A-Ding-Dong	78	Mercury	MT122	1956	**£4**	chart single
Rock And Roll - All Flavors	LP	Mercury	MG20289	1958	**£50**	US
Rock With The Bell Boys	7" EP	Mercury	MEP9508	1956	**£15**	
Rock With The Bell Boys Vol.2	7" EP	Mercury	MEP9512	1957	**£15**	

BELL, GRAHAM

Graham Bell	LP	Charisma	CAS1061	1972	**£15**	
How Can You Say I Don't Love You	7"	Polydor	56067	1966	**£8**	
Sixty Minute Man	7"	Charisma	CB209	1973	**£4**	

BELL, MADELINE

Because You Didn't Care	7"	HMV	POP1215	1963	**£4**	
Bells A-Poppin'	LP	Philips	SBL7818	1967	**£12**	
Comin' Atcha	LP	RCA	SF8393	1974	**£10**	
Daytime	7"	Columbia	DB7512	1965	**£4**	
Doin' Things	LP	Philips	SBL7865	1969	**£10**	
I'm Gonna Make You Love Me	7"	Philips	BF1656	1968	**£4**	
Picture Me Gone	7"	Philips	BF1611	1967	**£8**	

BELL, MAGGIE

Oh My My	7"	Polydor	2058447	1974	**£4**	
Queen Of The Night	LP	Polydor	2383239	1973	**£12**	
Suicide Sal	LP	Polydor	2383313	1975	**£12**	

BELL, WILLIAM

Eloise	7"	Stax	601019	1967	**£4**	
Every Day Will Be Like A Holiday	7"	Atlantic	584259	1969	**£4**	
Never Like This Before	7"	Atlantic	584076	1967	**£4**	
Tribute To A King	7"	Stax	601038	1968	**£4**	chart single

BELLAMY, GEORGE

Where I'm Bound	7"	Parlophone	R5282	1965	**£4**	

BELLAMY, PETER

Oak,Ash & Thorn	LP	Argo	ZFB11	1970	**£10**	

BELLAMY, PETER & LOUIS KILLEN

Won't You Go My Way	LP	Argo	ZFB37	1970	**£10**	

BELLES

Don't Pretend	7"	President	PT311	1970	**£4**	

BELLNOTES

I've Had It	7"	Top Rank	JAR102	1959	**£4**	
She Went Thataway	7"	Top Rank	JAR147	1959	**£4**	

BELLUS, TONY

Robbing The Cradle	7"	London	HL8933	1959	**£10**	
Robbing The Cradle	LP	NRC	LPA8	1960	**£50**	US

BELMONTS

Carnival Of Hits	LP	Sabina	SALP5001	1962	**£75**	US
Come On Little Angel	7"	Stateside	SS128	1962	**£4**	
Tell Me Why	7"	Pye	7N25094	1961	**£6**	

BELTONES

Broken Heart	7"	High Note	HS023	196-	**£8**	
Home Without You	7"	Duke	DU17	196-	**£8**	
Mary Mary	7"	High Note	HS017	196-	**£8**	
No More Heartaches	7"	Blue Cat	BS142	196-	**£10**	
No More Heartaches	7"	Trojan	TR628	1969	**£6**	
Wailing Festival	7"	High Note	HS024	196-	**£8**	

BELVIN, JESSE

Funny	7"	RCA	RCA1119	1959	**£4**	
Just Jesse Belvin	LP	RCA	LPM2089	1959	**£20**	US

Title	Format	Label	Cat. No.	Year	Price	Notes
Mr.Easy	LP	RCA	LPM2105	1960	**£20**	US

BEN

Title	Format	Label	Cat. No.	Year	Price	Notes
Ben	LP	Vertigo	6360052	1971	**£150**	spiral label

BENATAR, PAT

Title	Format	Label	Cat. No.	Year	Price	Notes
Fire And Ice	7"	Chrysalis	CHS2529	1981	**£6**	clear vinyl
Fire And Ice	7"	Chrysalis	CHSP2529	1981	**£5**	pic disc
Get Nervous	LP	Chrysalis	PCHR1396	1982	**£10**	pic disc
Hit Me With Your Best Shot	7"	Chrysalis	CHS2474	1980	**£4**	red vinyl
If You Think You Know How To Love Me	7"	Chrysalis	CHS2373	1979	**£6**	
In The Heat Of The Night	LP	Mobile Fid.	MFSL1057	1981	**£15**	US audiophile
Live From Earth	LP	Chrysalis	CHRP1451	1984	**£10**	pic disc
Love Is A Battlefield	7"	Chrysalis	CHS2747	1984	**£4**	chart single
Love Is A Battlefield	7"	Chrysalis	CHSP2747	1984	**£5**	pic disc
Shadows Of The Night	7"	Chrysalis	CHS2662	1983	**£4**	
Shadows Of The Night	7"	Chrysalis	PATP2	1985	**£6**	shaped pic disc, plinth
Shadows Of The Night	12"	Chrysalis	PATX2	1985	**£6**	blue vinyl
Treat Me Right	7"	Chrysalis	CHS2511	1981	**£4**	
Treat Me Right	7"	Chrysalis	CHS2511	1981	**£6**	clear vinyl
We Belong	7"	Chrysalis	CHSP2821	1984	**£4**	pic disc

BENATAR, PAT & MICHAEL SCHENKER GROUP

Title	Format	Label	Cat. No.	Year	Price	Notes
Promises In The Dark	7"	Sounds		1981	**£4**	flexi

BENBOW, STEVE

Title	Format	Label	Cat. No.	Year	Price	Notes
Of Situations And Predicaments	LP	Decca	LK4881	1967	**£10**	

BENNETT, BOBBY

Title	Format	Label	Cat. No.	Year	Price	Notes
All My Life Is You	7"	Columbia	DB8435	1968	**£5**	
You're Ready Now	7"	Columbia	DB8532	1969	**£20**	

BENNETT, BOBBY (2)

Title	Format	Label	Cat. No.	Year	Price	Notes
Big New York	7"	London	HLZ10274	1960	**£5**	
Just Say Goodbye	7"	CBS	202511	1967	**£5**	

BENNETT, BOYD & BIG MOE

Title	Format	Label	Cat. No.	Year	Price	Notes
Hi That Jive Jack	7"	Parlophone	R4214	1956	**£30**	
Rocking Up A Storm	7"	Parlophone	R4252	1957	**£40**	

BENNETT, BOYD & HIS ROCKETS

Title	Format	Label	Cat. No.	Year	Price	Notes
Banjo Rock And Roll	7"	Parlophone	MSP6203	1956	**£40**	
Blue Suede Shoes	7"	Parlophone	MSP6233	1956	**£30**	
Boogie At Midnight	7"	Parlophone	MSP6161	1955	**£40**	
Boyd Bennett	LP	King	594	1957	**£600**	US
Move	7"	Parlophone	R4423	1958	**£30**	
Seventeen	7"	Parlophone	MSP6180	1955	**£40**	chart single
Tight Tights	7"	Mercury	AMT1031	1959	**£12**	

BENNETT, BRIAN

Title	Format	Label	Cat. No.	Year	Price	Notes
Canvas	7"	Columbia	DB8294	1967	**£12**	
Change Of Direction	LP	Columbia	SCX6144	1968	**£30**	
Chase Side Shoot Up	7"	Fontana	6007040	1974	**£5**	
Girls Back Home	7"	DJM	DJS10791	1977	**£4**	
Illustrated London Noise	LP	Studio Two	TWO268	1969	**£50**	
Melissa	7"	EMI	EMI2253	1974	**£5**	
Pendulum Force	7"	DJM	DJS10843	1978	**£4**	
Riding	7"	Columbia	DB8706	1970	**£8**	
Rock Dreams	LP	DJM	20499	1977	**£10**	
Saturday Night Special	7"	DJM	DJS10756	1977	**£5**	
Thunderbolt	7"	DJM	DJS10714	1976	**£5**	
Voyage	LP	DJM	20532	1978	**£10**	

BENNETT, CLIFF

Title	Format	Label	Cat. No.	Year	Price	Notes
Back In The USSR	7"	Parlophone	R5749	1968	**£4**	
Branches Out	LP	Parlophone	PCS7054	1968	**£20**	
Good Times	7"	Parlophone	R5711	1968	**£4**	
House Of A Thousand Dolls	7"	Parlophone	R5666	1968	**£4**	
Memphis Streets	7"	Parlophone	R5792	1969	**£4**	
Nobody Runs Forever	7"	Parlophone	R5728	1968	**£4**	
Rebellion	LP	CBS	64487	1971	**£10**	
You're Breaking Me Up	7"	Parlophone	R5691	1968	**£4**	

BENNETT, CLIFF & REBEL ROUSERS

Title	Format	Label	Cat. No.	Year	Price	Notes
Cliff Bennett & The Rebel Rousers	LP	Parlophone	PMC1242	1964	**£20**	
Cliff Bennett & The Rebel Rousers	7" EP	Parlophone	GEP8923	1964	**£8**	
Don't Help Me Out	7"	Parlophone	R5534	1966	**£4**	
Driving You Wild	LP	MFP	1121	1966	**£10**	chart LP
Driving You Wild	LP	Regal Z.	REG1035	1966	**£20**	
Everybody Loves A Lover	7"	Parlophone	R5046	1963	**£5**	
Got My Mojo Working	7"	Parlophone	R5119	1964	**£5**	
Got To Get You into My Life	7"	Parlophone	R5489	1966	**£4**	chart single
Got To Get You Into Our Lives	LP	Parlophone	PCS7017	1967	**£20**	
Hold On I'm Coming	7"	Parlophone	R5466	1966	**£4**	
I Have Cried My Last Tear	7"	Parlophone	R5317	1965	**£4**	
I'll Take Good Care Of You	7"	Parlophone	R5565	1967	**£4**	
I'll Take You Home	7"	Parlophone	R5229	1965	**£4**	chart single
One Way Love	7"	Parlophone	R5173	1964	**£4**	chart single
Poor Joe	7"	Parlophone	R4895	1962	**£10**	
Three Rooms With Running Water	7"	Parlophone	R5259	1965	**£5**	
Try It Baby	7" EP	Parlophone	GEP8936	1965	**£8**	
Use Me	7"	Parlophone	R5598	1967	**£4**	
We're Gonna Make It	7" EP	Parlophone	GEP8955	1966	**£8**	
When I Get Paid	7"	Parlophone	R4836	1961	**£10**	
You Can't Love 'Em All	7"	Parlophone	R5406	1966	**£4**	
You Got What I Like	7"	Parlophone	R4793	1961	**£10**	
You Really Got A Hold On Me	7"	Parlophone	R5080	1963	**£4**	

BENNETT, DUSTER

Using his nickname to avoid an obvious confusion, Tony Bennett was a one man band who played the blues, and played it rather well. Although a few supporting musicians are used in places on his records, what one hears is essentially Duster Bennett's voice and harmonica, his guitar, and his bass drum. If the format sounds limited, then Bennett proves that it need not be. He was an unlikely addition to John Mayall's band in the early seventies, but this facet of his career was never recorded.

Title	Format	Label	Cat. No.	Year	Price	Notes
12 dBs	LP	Blue Horizon	763868	1970	**£30**	
Act Nice And Gentle	7"	Blue Horizon	573179	1970	**£8**	
Bright Lights	LP	Blue Horizon	763221	1969	**£25**	
Bright Lights, Big City	7"	Blue Horizon	573154	1969	**£8**	
Comin' Home	7"	RAK	RAK177	1974	**£4**	
I Chose To Sing The Blues	7"	Blue Horizon	573173	1970	**£8**	
I'm Gonna Wind Up Endin' Up	7"	Blue Horizon	573164	1969	**£8**	
It's A Man Down There	7"	Blue Horizon	573141	1967	**£8**	
Raining In My Heart	7"	Blue Horizon	573148	1967	**£8**	
Smiling Like I'm Happy	LP	Blue Horizon	763208	1968	**£30**	

BENNETT, JOE & THE SPARKLETONES

Title	Format	Label	Cat. No.	Year	Price	Notes
Black Slacks	7"	HMV	POP399	1957	**£15**	
Rocket	7"	HMV	POP445	1958	**£20**	

BENNETT, LEE

Title	Format	Label	Cat. No.	Year	Price	Notes
Poor Bachelor Boy	7"	Decca	F12024	1964	**£5**	

BENNETT, PETER E.

Title	Format	Label	Cat. No.	Year	Price	Notes
Ballad Of Goldwain	LP	RCA	SF8190	1971	**£12**	

BENNETT, VAL

Title	Format	Label	Cat. No.	Year	Price	Notes
All In The Game	7"	Trojan	TR625	1969	**£6**	
Any More	7"	Fab	FAB131	196-	**£8**	
Baby Baby	7"	Trojan	TR640	1969	**£6**	
Demonstration	7"	Trojan	TR649	1969	**£6**	
Jumping With Mr.Lee	7"	Island	WI3113	1967	**£8**	
Reggae City	7"	Crab	CRAB6	196-	**£8**	
Russians Are Coming	7"	Island	WI3146	1968	**£8**	
Soul Survivor	7"	Island	WI3116	1967	**£8**	
South Parkway Rock	7"	Trojan	TR626	1969	**£6**	
Spanish Harlem	7"	Trojan	TR611	1968	**£8**	

BENNO, MARC

Title	Format	Label	Cat. No.	Year	Price	Notes
Ambush	LP	A&M	AMLS64634	1972	**£10**	
Marc Benno	LP	A&M	SP4273	1970	**£10**	US
Minnows	LP	A&M	AMLS64303	1971	**£10**	

BENSON, BARRY

Title	Format	Label	Cat. No.	Year	Price	Notes
Always Waitin'	7"	Parlophone	R5544	1966	**£4**	
Cousin Jane	7"	Parlophone	R5578	1967	**£4**	

Title	Format	Label	Number	Year	Price	Notes
I Can't Wait	7"	Page One	POF034	1967	**£5**	
Stay A Little While	7"	Parlophone	R5446	1966	**£15**	
Sunshine Child	7"	Parlophone	R5484	1966	**£4**	

BENSON, HOAGY

Title	Format	Label	Number	Year	Price	Notes
Kangaroo	7"	Ember	CBM003	196-	**£4**	

BENT WIND

Title	Format	Label	Number	Year	Price	Notes
Sussex	LP	Trend		1972	**£1000**	Canadian

BENTINE, MICHAEL

Title	Format	Label	Number	Year	Price	Notes
It's A Square World	LP	Parlophone	PMC1179	1962	**£12**	
Square Bashing	LP	RCA	RD7885	1967	**£10**	

BENTON, BROOK

Title	Format	Label	Number	Year	Price	Notes
Rainy Night In Georgia	7"	Atlantic	584315	1970	**£4**	
Rockin' Good Way	7"	Mercury	MF1100	1969	**£4**	

BENTON, BROOK & DINAH WASHINGTON

Title	Format	Label	Number	Year	Price	Notes
Rockin' Good Way	7" EP	Mercury	SEZ19022	1961	**£8**	stereo
Rockin' Good Way	7" EP	Mercury	ZEP10120	1961	**£5**	

BERKELEY KITES

Title	Format	Label	Number	Year	Price	Notes
Alice In Wonderland	7"	Polydor	56770	1969	**£5**	
Hang Up City	7"	Polydor	56742	1968	**£4**	

BERMUDAS

Title	Format	Label	Number	Year	Price	Notes
Donnie	7"	London	HLN9894	1964	**£4**	

BERNARD, KENNY

Title	Format	Label	Number	Year	Price	Notes
Ain't No Sole Left In These Old Shoes	7"	Pye	7N17233	1967	**£10**	
Nothing Can Change That Love	7"	Pye	7N17131	1966	**£12**	
Somebody	7"	CBS	2936	1967	**£8**	

BERNARD, ROD

Title	Format	Label	Number	Year	Price	Notes
This Should Go On Forever	7"	London	HLM8849	1959	**£10**	

BERNIE & THE BUZZ BAND

Title	Format	Label	Number	Year	Price	Notes
House That Jack Built	7"	Decca	F22829	1968	**£4**	
When Something's Wrong With My Baby	7"	Deram	DM181	1968	**£5**	

BERNSTEIN, ELMER

Title	Format	Label	Number	Year	Price	Notes
Rat Race	7"	MGM	MGM1238	1963	**£5**	
Staccato's Theme	7"	Capitol	CL15101	1960	**£4**	chart single
Walk On The Wild Side	7"	MGM	MGM1164	1962	**£4**	

BERRY, CHUCK

Title	Format	Label	Number	Year	Price	Notes
After School Session	LP	Chess	LP1426	1958	**£40**	US
Back To Memphis	7"	Mercury	MF994	1967	**£4**	
Beautiful Delilah	7"	London	HL8677	1958	**£8**	
Berry Is On Top	LP	Chess	LP1435	1959	**£35**	US
Best Of Chuck Berry	7" EP	Pye	NEP44018	1964	**£6**	
Blue Mood	7" EP	Pye	NEP44033	1964	**£6**	
Bye Bye Johnny	7"	London	HLM9159	1960	**£8**	
Carol	7"	London	HL8712	1958	**£8**	
Chuck Berry	LP	Golden Guin.	GGL0352	1965	**£10**	
Chuck Berry	LP	Pye	NPL28024	1963	**£10**	chart LP
Chuck Berry	7" EP	Pye	NEP44011	1963	**£6**	
Chuck Berry Hits	7" EP	Pye	NEP44028	1964	**£6**	
Chuck In London	LP	Chess	CRL4005	1965	**£10**	
Club Nitty Gritty	7"	Mercury	MF958	1966	**£4**	
Come On	7" EP	Chess	CRE6005	1965	**£5**	
Dear Dad	7"	Chess	CRS8012	1965	**£4**	
Fresh Berrys	LP	Chess	CRL4506	1965	**£10**	
Go Go Go	7"	Pye	7N25209	1963	**£4**	chart single
I Got A Booking	7" EP	Chess	CRE6012	1966	**£5**	
I'm Talking About You	7"	Pye	7N25100	1961	**£4**	
It Wasn't Me	7"	Chess	CRS8022	1965	**£4**	
Johnny B Goode	7"	London	HLM8629	1958	**£8**	
Johnny B.Goode	7"	Chess	CRS8075	1968	**£4**	
Latest And Greatest	LP	Pye	NPL28031	1964	**£10**	chart LP
Let It Rock	7"	London	HLM9069	1960	**£6**	

Title	Format	Label	Number	Year	Price	Notes
Little Marie	7"	Pye	7N25271	1964	**£4**	
Little Queenie	7"	London	HLM8853	1959	**£8**	
Lonely School Days	7"	Chess	CRS8006	1965	**£4**	
Memphis Tennessee	7"	London	HLM8921	1959	**£8**	
Memphis Tennessee	7"	Pye	7N25218	1963	**£4**	chart single
More Chuck Berry	LP	Pye	NPL28028	1963	**£10**	chart LP
Nadine	7"	Pye	7N25236	1964	**£4**	chart single
New Juke Box Hits	LP	Pye	NPL28019	1962	**£10**	
No Money Down	7"	London	HLU8275	1956	**£30**	
No Particular Place To Go	7"	Chess	CRS8089	1969	**£4**	
No Particular Place To Go	7"	Pye	7N25242	1964	**£4**	chart single
On Stage	LP	Pye	NPL28027	1963	**£10**	chart LP
One Dozen Berrys	LP	London	HAM2132	1958	**£40**	
Promised Land	7" EP	Chess	CRE6002	1965	**£5**	
Promised Land	7"	Pye	7N25285	1965	**£4**	chart single
Ramona Say Yes	7"	Chess	CRS8037	1966	**£4**	
Reeling And Rocking	7" EP	London	REM1188	1959	**£30**	gold label
Reeling And Rocking	7" EP	London	REM1188	1960	**£15**	
Rhythm And Blues With..	7" EP	London	REU1053	1956	**£15**	
Rhythm And Blues With..	7" EP	London	REU1053	1956	**£30**	gold label
Rock & Roll Music	7"	London	HLM8531	1957	**£8**	
Rockin' At The Hops	LP	Chess	LP1448	1960	**£35**	US
Roll Over Beethoven	7"	London	HLU8428	1957	**£10**	
Roll Over Beethoven	7"	Mercury	MF1102	1969	**£4**	
Run Rudolph Run	7"	Pye	7N25228	1963	**£5**	chart single
Saint Louis To Frisco	7"	Mercury	MF1057	1968	**£4**	
Schooldays	7"	Columbia	DB3951	1957	**£20**	chart single
Sweet Little Rock and Roller	7"	London	HLM8767	1958	**£8**	
Sweet Little Sixteen	7"	London	HLM8585	1958	**£8**	chart single
This Is Chuck Berry	7" EP	Pye	NEP44013	1963	**£6**	
You Came A Long Way From St Louis	7" EP	Chess	CRE6016	1966	**£5**	
You Can't Catch Me	7"	London	HLN8375	1957	**£30**	
You Never Can Tell	LP	Marble Arch	MALS702	1967	**£10**	stereo, 12 tracks
You Never Can Tell	LP	Pye	NPL28039	1964	**£10**	chart LP
You Never Can Tell	7"	Pye	7N25257	1964	**£4**	chart single

BERRY, CHUCK, & BO DIDDLEY

Title	Format	Label	Number	Year	Price	Notes
Chuck And Bo Vol.1	7" EP	Pye	NEP44009	1963	**£6**	
Chuck And Bo Vol.2	7" EP	Pye	NEP44012	1963	**£6**	
Chuck And Bo Vol.3	7" EP	Pye	NEP44017	1964	**£6**	
Two Great Guitars	LP	Pye	NPL28047	1964	**£12**	

BERRY, DAVE

Title	Format	Label	Number	Year	Price	Notes
Baby It's You	7"	Decca	F11876	1964	**£4**	chart single
Can I Get It From You	7" EP	Decca	DFE8625	1965	**£6**	
Chaplin House	7"	Decca	F13080	1970	**£5**	
Crying Game	7"	Decca	F11937	1964	**£4**	chart single
Dave Berry 68	LP	Decca	LK4932	1968	**£12**	
Dave Berry	LP	Decca	LK4653	1964	**£20**	
Dave Berry	7" EP	Decca	DFE8601	1964	**£6**	
Dozen Berrys	LP	Ace Of Clubs	ACL1218	1966	**£12**	
Forever	7"	Decca	F12651	1967	**£4**	
Huma Luma	7"	Decca	F12905	1969	**£4**	
I'm Gonna Take You There	7"	Decca	F12258	1965	**£4**	
If You Wait For Love	7"	Decca	F12337	1966	**£4**	
In Your Life	7"	Decca	F12771	1968	**£4**	
Just As Much As Ever	7"	Decca	F12739	1968	**£4**	
Little Things	7"	Decca	F12103	1965	**£4**	chart single
Mama	7"	Decca	F12435	1966	**£4**	chart single
Memphis Tennessee	7"	Decca	F11734	1963	**£4**	chart single
My Baby Left Me	7"	Decca	F11803	1963	**£4**	chart single
One Heart Between Two	7"	Decca	F12020	1964	**£4**	chart single
Picture Me Gone	7"	Decca	F12513	1966	**£4**	
Special Sound Of...	LP	Decca	LK4823	1966	**£15**	
Stranger	7"	Decca	F12579	1967	**£4**	
This Strange Effect	7"	Decca	F12188	1965	**£4**	chart single

BERRY, MIKE

Title	Format	Label	Number	Year	Price	Notes
Don't Try To Stand In My Way	7"	HMV	POP1362	1964	**£4**	
Don't You Think It's Time	7"	HMV	POP1105	1962	**£4**	chart single
Every Little Kiss	7"	HMV	POP1042	1962	**£4**	

It Comes And Goes	7"	HMV	POP1494	1965	**£4**	
It Really Doesn't Matter	7"	HMV	POP1194	1963	**£4**	
It's Just A Matter Of Time	7"	HMV	POP979	1962	**£4**	
It's Time For Mike Berry	7" EP	HMV	7EG8793	1963	**£10**	
Lovesick	7"	HMV	POP1284	1964	**£4**	
My Little Baby	7"	HMV	POP1142	1963	**£4**	chart single
Raining In My Heart	7"	Polydor	56182	1967	**£4**	
Talk	7"	HMV	POP1314	1964	**£4**	
That's All I Ever Want From You	7"	HMV	POP1449	1965	**£4**	
This Little Girl	7"	HMV	POP1257	1964	**£4**	
Tribute To Buddy Holly	7"	HMV	POP912	1961	**£4**	chart single
Tribute To Buddy Holly	7" EP	HMV	7EG8808	1963	**£10**	
Warm Baby	7"	HMV	POP1530	1966	**£4**	
Will You Love Me Tomorrow	7"	Decca	F11314	1961	**£8**	

BERRY, RICHARD

Live At The Century Club	LP	Pam	1001		**£20**	US
Rhythm And Blues Vol.3	7" EP	Ember	EMB4527	1962	**£50**	
Richard Berry And The Dreamers	LP	Crown	CLP5371	1963	**£12**	US
Wild Berry	LP	Pam	1002		**£20**	US

BEST, JON

Young Boy Blues	7"	Decca	F12077	1965	**£4**	

BEST, PETE

Pete Best was the original drummer with the Beatles, who is still understandably bitter at the way he was sacked to make way for Ringo Starr just as the group was about to make its first record for Parlophone. The American LP was given a deliberately misleading title - these are not Beatles recordings.

Best Of The Beatles	LP	Savage	BM71	1965	**£75**	US
I'm Gonna Knock On Your Door	7"	Decca	F11929	1964	**£20**	

BETTER DAYS

Don't Want That	7"	Polydor	56024	1965	**£30**	

BETTERS, HAROLD

Do Anything You Wanna	7"	Sue	WI378	1965	**£10**	

BEVAN, BEV

Let There Be Drums	7"	Jet	777	1976	**£4**	

BEVERLEY

Beverley became Beverley Martyn when she married John Martyn. The pair recorded two fine albums together.

Happy New Year	7"	Deram	DM101	1966	**£6**	
Museum	7"	Deram	DM137	1967	**£5**	

BEVERLEY ALLSTARS

Busy Bee	7"	Trojan	TR7714	1970	**£5**	
Easy Come Easy Go	7"	Pyramid	PYR6062	1969	**£8**	

BEVIS FROND

Nick Salomon knows about record collecting from two different sides. As a dealer, he is able to put his love and knowlege of psychedelic music to good use. As an artist, demonstrating that love by playing the same style himself,under the name of The Bevis Frond, he has seen his limited edition record releases aquiring a cult reputation and hence an increase in value. It is Salomon's good fortune that the sixties-derived music he would have been playing anyway happens to slot neatly into the growing climate of appreciation for the sixties that has made groups like the Stone Roses so popular.

Bevis Through The Looking Glass	LP	Woronzow	WOO51/2	1987	**£75**	double, booklet
Inner Marshland	LP	Woronzow	WOO4	1987	**£10**	
Miasma	LP	Woronzow	WOO3	1987	**£12**	

BIDDU

Daughter Of Love	7"	Regal Z.	RZ3002	1967	**£4**	

BIFF BANG POW!

Fifty Years Of Fun	7"	Creation	CRE003	1984	**£10**	
There Must Be A Better Life	7"	Creation	CRE007	1984	**£15**	
Wouldn't You	7"	Lyntone	LYN12903	1983	**£4**	flexi, B Side Pastels

BIG BERTHA

This group was formed by the original Move bass-player, Ace Kefford, as the Ace Kefford Stand, becoming Big Bertha when Kefford himself left. The drummer for a short while was Cozy Powell. The single would appear to have been withdrawn - or else never given a full release in the first place.

World's An Apple	7"	Atlantic	584298	1969	**£15**	

BIG BLACK

Headache	7"	Blast First	BFFP14	1987	**£40**	red vinyl
Sound Of Impact	LP		NOT2(BUT1)	1986	**£50**	

BIG BOB

Your Line Was Busy	7"	Top Rank	JAR185	1959	**£8**	

BIG BOPPER

Big Bopper	7" EP	Mercury	ZEP10004	1959	**£25**	
Big Bopper's Wedding	7"	Mercury	AMT1017	1958	**£8**	
Chantilly Lace	LP	Contour	6870531	1974	**£10**	
Chantilly Lace	LP	Mercury	MMC14008	1958	**£150**	
Chantilly Lace	7"	Mercury	AMT1002	1958	**£8**	chart single
It's The Truth Ruth	7"	Mercury	AMT1046	1959	**£12**	
Pink Petticoats	7" EP	Mercury	ZEP10027	1959	**£25**	

BIG BOY PETE

Cold Turkey	7"	Camp	602005	1968	**£40**	

BIG BOYS

Frat Cars	7"	Big Boys	BB42480	1980	**£70**	

BIG BROTHER

Confusion	LP	All American	5770	1970	**£50**	US

BIG BROTHER & THE HOLDING CO.

Big Brother & The Holding Co. had Janis Joplin as their lead singer, but were far from being just her backing group. The first LP, recorded before Cream toured America with their amplifiers turned up to maximum, sounds weak. The partly live "Cheap Thrills", however, is an exciting and vital recording. Janis Joplin without the Holding Co. failed to achieve this power, but equally, the Holding Co. without Janis Joplin (as on the 1971 recordings) lacked distinction.

Be A Brother	LP	CBS	64118	1971	**£10**	
Big Brother & The Holding Co.	LP	Fontana	TL5457	1967	**£20**	
Big Brother & The Holding Co.	LP	London	HAT8377	1968	**£15**	
Bye Bye Baby	7"	Fontana	TF881	1967	**£12**	
Cheap Thrills	LP	CBS	63392	1968	**£10**	
Down On Me	7"	London	HLT10226	1969	**£8**	
How Hard It Is	LP	CBS	30738	1971	**£12**	US
Piece Of My Heart	7"	CBS	3683	1968	**£5**	

BIG CARROT

Blackjack	7"	EMI	EMI2047	1973	**£15**	

BIG COUNTRY

Chance	12"	Mercury	COUP4	1983	**£12**	pic disc
Fields Of Fire	7"	Mercury	COUP2	1983	**£6**	pic disc
In A Big Country	12"	Mercury	COUNT313	1983	**£10**	red sleeve
Look Away (Outlaw Mix)	12"	Mercury	BIGCX11	1986	**£6**	
Look Away	7"	Mercury	BIGCP1	1986	**£6**	shaped pic disc
Where The Rose Is Sown	7"	Mercury	MERD185	1984	**£10**	double
Wonderland	7"	Mercury	COUNT55	1984	**£5**	double
Wonderland	12"	Mercury	COUNX5	1984	**£8**	clear vinyl

BIG FLAME

Sink	7"	Plaque	001	1984	**£5**	
Two Kan Guru	10"	RJ Records	RERON8	1986	**£6**	

BIG GROUP

Big Hammer	LP	Pill		1970	**£100**	

BIG IN JAPAN

Various people passing through the ranks of Big In Japan went on to be fairly big in lots of places - most notably Budgie (Siouxsie and the Banshees) and David Balfe (Teardrop Explodes). The main reason for the collectability of the group's singles, however, is the presence of Holly Johnson on bass, some time before emerging as front man with Frankie Goes To Hollywood.

Big In Japan	7"	Erics	ERICS001	1977	**£10**	
From Y To Z And Never Again	7"	Zoo	CAGE001	1978	**£10**	

BIG L

Family Man	7"	Attack	ATT8003	1974	**£5**	
Music Box	7"	Attack	ATT8001	1974	**£5**	
Soulful	7"	Attack	ATT8000	1974	**£5**	

BIG MAYBELLE

Title	Format	Label	Number	Year	Price	Notes
All Of Me	7"	London	HLC8447	1957	**£6**	
Baby Won't You Please Come Home	7"	London	HLC8854	1959	**£4**	
Careless Love	7"	London	HL9941	1965	**£5**	
Mama	7"	CBS	2926	1967	**£4**	
Quittin' Time	7"	Direction	583312	1968	**£5**	
Turn The World Around	7"	CBS	2735	1967	**£5**	

BIG SLEEP

Title	Format	Label	Number	Year	Price	Notes
Bluebell Wood	LP	Pegasus	PEG4	1971	**£20**	

BIG STAR

Big Star, the group led by Alex Chilton following the disbanding of the Box Tops, has aquired a formidable cult reputation wholly unjustified by the actual music to be found on the records. The songs are rather ordinary and Big Star's lack of success is not at all surprising.

Title	Format	Label	Number	Year	Price	Notes
Big Star	LP	Ardent	ADS1501	1971	**£15**	US
Big Star/Isaac Hayes Sampler	LP	Stax		1978	**£25**	promo
Jesus Christ	7"	Aura	AUS107	1978	**£4**	
Kizza Me	7"	Aura	AUS103	1978	**£4**	
Radio City	LP	Ardent	ADS2803	1971	**£15**	US
September Gurls	7"	Stax	STAX504	1978	**£4**	

BIG THREE

By all accounts, the Big Three were, on stage, the most impressive Liverpool group of them all. Their records, however, never did them justice - even with the live "At The Cavern" EP, it is clearly a case of "you had to be there". Bass player Johnny Gustafson has been ubiquitous ever since, however, playing, among others, with Quatermass, Hard Stuff, Gillan, and Roxy Music.

Title	Format	Label	Number	Year	Price	Notes
At The Cavern	7" EP	Decca	DFE8552	1963	**£15**	
By The Way	7"	Decca	F11689	1963	**£6**	chart single
I'm With You	7"	Decca	F11752	1963	**£5**	
If You Ever Change Your Mind	7"	Decca	F11927	1964	**£8**	
Resurrection	LP	Polydor	2383199	1973	**£10**	
Some Other Guy	7"	Decca	F11614	1963	**£8**	chart single
Some Other Guy	7"	Polydor	2058343	1973	**£4**	
Big Three	LP	FM	307	1963	**£12**	US
Big Three Featuring Cass Elliott	LP	Roulette	R42000	1967	**£10**	US
Live At The Recording Studio	LP	FM	311	1964	**£12**	US

BIG YOUTH

Of the many toasting DJs to emerge in the wake of U Roy's first successes, Big Youth was the most idiosyncratic and the most spectacular. His "Ace 90 Skank" set the pattern - a roaring motor bike engine is overlaid by thickly accented Jamaican voices; then a lanky bass guitar begins its deep descent as Big Youth unleashes a stream of words that manage to sound lazy even while tumbling over each other.

Title	Format	Label	Number	Year	Price	Notes
Ace 90 Skank	7"	Downtown	DT492	1972	**£5**	
Foreman v. Frazier	7"	Grape	GR3040	197-	**£4**	

BIGGUN, IVOR

Title	Format	Label	Number	Year	Price	Notes
Winker's Song (Misprint)	7"	Beggars B.	BOP1	1978	**£4**	chart single

BILLIE & LILLIE

Title	Format	Label	Number	Year	Price	Notes
Creeping Crawling Crying	7"	London	HLU8630	1958	**£4**	
Hanging On To You	7"	London	HLU8689	1958	**£4**	
Lucky Ladybug	7"	London	HLU8795	1959	**£4**	
Monster	7"	London	HLU8564	1958	**£4**	

BILLIE & THE ESSENTIALS

Title	Format	Label	Number	Year	Price	Notes
Maybe You'll Be There	7"	London	HLW9657	1963	**£8**	

BILLMUSS, TREVOR

Title	Format	Label	Number	Year	Price	Notes
Family Apology	LP	Charisma	CAS1017	1970	**£15**	

BIM & BAM

Title	Format	Label	Number	Year	Price	Notes
Fatty	7"	Gayfeet	GS201	1973	**£8**	

BINNS, SONNY & THE RUDIES

Title	Format	Label	Number	Year	Price	Notes
Untouchables	7"	Downtown	DT420	196-	**£8**	
Wheels	7"	Downtown	DT424	196-	**£8**	

BINTANGS

Title	Format	Label	Number	Year	Price	Notes
Ridin' On The L&N	7"	Decca	F22995	1970	**£4**	

BIRD'S BIRDS

Say Those Magic Words	7"	Reaction	591005	1966	**£60**	

BIRD, IVOR

Over The Wall We Go	7"	RSO	2090270	1978	**£4**	

BIRDLAND

Hollow Heart	7"	Lazy	LAZY13	1989	**£6**	
Hollow Heart	12"	Lazy	LAZY13T	1989	**£6**	
Paradise	12"	Lazy	LAZY14T	1989	**£6**	4 tracks

BIRDLEGS & PAULINE

Spring	7"	Sue	WI4014	1966	**£8**	

BIRDS

Leavin' Here	7"	Decca	F12140	1965	**£20**	chart single
No Good Without You Baby	7"	Decca	F12257	1965	**£20**	
You're On My Mind	7"	Decca	F12031	1964	**£25**	

BIRDS OF A FEATHER

All God's Children	7"	Page One	POF179	1970	**£4**	
Birds Of A Feather	LP	Page One		196-	**£30**	
Blacksmith Blues	7"	Page One	POF156	1969	**£4**	

BIRKIN, JANE & SERGE GAINSBOURG

Je T'Aime...Moi Non Plus	7"	Fontana	TF1042	1969	**£4**	chart single
Je T'Aime...Moi Non Plus	7"	Major Minor	MM645	1969	**£4**	chart single

BIRMINGHAM

Birmingham	LP	Grosvenor			**£120**	

BIRTH CONTROL

Birth Control	LP	Charisma	CAS1036	1971	**£15**	
Hoodoo Man	LP	CBS	65316	1972	**£10**	German
Live	LP	CBS	88088	1974	**£15**	German, double
Operation	LP	Ohr	OMM556015	1971	**£12**	German
Plastic People	LP	CBS	80921	1975	**£10**	German
Re-birth	LP	CBS	65963	1974	**£10**	German

BIRTHA

Birtha	LP	Probe	SPBA6267	1972	**£12**	
Can't Stop The Madness	LP	Probe	SPBA6272	1973	**£12**	

BIRTHDAY PARTY

Bad Seed	12"	4AD	BAD301	1983	**£6**	
Dead Joe	7"	Masterbag	BAG005	1982	**£5**	flexi
Friend Catcher	7"	4AD	AD12	1980	**£8**	
Mr.Clarinet	7"	4AD	AD114	1981	**£8**	
Mutiny	12"	Mute	12MUTE29	1983	**£6**	with insert
Release The Bats	7"	4AD	AD111	1981	**£8**	

BISHOP, DICKIE & HIS SIDEKICKS

Cumberland Gap	7"	Decca	F10869	1957	**£5**	
Jumping Judy	7"	Decca	F11028	1958	**£4**	
No Other Baby	7"	Decca	F10981	1958	**£4**	
Prisoners Song	7"	Decca	F10959	1957	**£4**	

BISHOP, TOMMY RICOCHETS

I Should Have Known	7"	Decca	F12238	1965	**£5**	

BISHOPS

Baby You're Wrong	7"	Chiswick	NS12	1977	**£4**	
Count Bishops	LP	Chiswick	CWK3006	1978	**£10**	
Count Bishops	LP	Chiswick	WIK1	1977	**£12**	
Crosscuts	LP	Chiswick	CWK3009	1979	**£12**	
I Take What I Want	7"	Chiswick	NS33	1978	**£4**	
I Want Candy	7"	Chiswick	CHIS101	1978	**£4**	
I Want Candy	6'	Chiswick	NS376	1978	**£6**	
I Want Candy	10"	Chiswick	CHIS101	1978	**£6**	
Live At The Roundhouse	12"	Chiswick	CHT7	1978	**£8**	
Live At The Roundhouse	12"	Chiswick	CWM2001	1979	**£6**	

Live At The Roundhouse	10"	Chiswick	10CWM2001	1979	**£6**	
Live At The Roundhouse	10"	Chiswick	CH7	1978	**£8**	
Mr.Jones	7"	Chiswick	CHIS111	1979	**£4**	
Sometimes Good Guys Don't Wear White	7"	Chiswick	PROMO4	1978	**£6**	
Speedball	7"	Chiswick	SW1	1976	**£6**	
Train Train	7"	Chiswick	NS5	1976	**£4**	

BITTER ALMOND

In The Morning	7"	W. Bros	WB8008	1970	**£5**	

BITTER END SINGERS

Taste Of Your Love	7"	Atlantic	584075	1967	**£4**	

BLACK

Human Features	7"	Rox	ROX17	1981	**£25**	
More Than The Sun	7"	Wond. W. Of	WW3	1982	**£4**	

BLACK ABBOTTS

Love Is Alive	7"	Evolution	E3004	1971	**£10**	

BLACK ACE

Black Ace	7" EP	XX	MIN701		**£5**	

BLACK CAT BONES

Barbed Wire Sandwich	LP	Nova	SDN15	1970	**£30**	

BLACK DYKE MILLS BAND

Thingumybob	7"	Apple	4	1968	**£10**	

BLACK DYNAMITES

Brush Those Tears	7"	Top Rank	JAR319	1960	**£6**	

BLACK FAITH

It's Alright By Me	7"	Fontana	6007018	1970	**£4**	

BLACK FLAG

Six Pack	7"	Alt. Tentacles	VIRUS9	1981	**£4**	

BLACK KNIGHTS

I Got A Woman	7"	Columbia	DB7443	1965	**£6**	

BLACK MARKET BABY

Potential Suicide	7"	Limp		1981	**£20**	

BLACK OAK ARKANSAS

Black Oak Arkansas	LP	Atlantic	2400180	1971	**£10**	
High On A Hog	LP	Atlantic	K40538	1974	**£10**	
If An Angel Came To See You	LP	Atco	7008	1972	**£10**	US
Keep The Faith	LP	Atco	SD33381	1972	**£10**	US
Raunch And Roll	LP	Atlantic	K40451	1973	**£10**	
Street Party	LP	Atlantic	K50057	1974	**£10**	

BLACK SABBATH

Black Sabbath were hated by the critics in the early days, who were discomfitted to see the group's first LP release climb high into the album charts. The achievement was based on the group's sheer hard work in building up a large and loyal following through live performance. Essentially, the group also invented the heavy metal genre, or at any rate solidified the style into the riff-based music that it has remained ever since.

Am I Going Insane?	7"	NEMS	6165300	1976	**£6**	
Black Sabbath 1	LP	Vertigo	VO6	1970	**£10**	spiral label, chart LP
Black Sabbath 4	LP	Vertigo	6360071	1972	**£10**	spiral label, booklet, chart LP
Children Of The Grave	7"	Phonogram	DJ005	1974	**£25**	promo, Status Quo B side
Die Young	12"	Vertigo	SAB412	1980	**£6**	
Evil Woman	7"	Fontana	TF1067	1970	**£30**	
Evil Woman	7"	Vertigo	V2	1970	**£15**	
Hard Road	7"	Vertigo	SAB002	1978	**£4**	purple vinyl
Master Of Reality	LP	Vertigo	6360050	1971	**£10**	spiral label, poster
Mob Rules	12"	Vertigo	SAB512	1981	**£6**	
Never Say Die	7"	Vertigo	SAB001	1978	**£4**	chart single

Paranoid	7"	NEMS	NEP1	1982	**£5**	pic disc
Paranoid	LP	Nems	NEP6003	1977	**£10**	pic disc
Paranoid	LP	Vertigo	6360011	1970	**£10**	spiral label, chart LP
Paranoid	7"	Vertigo	6059010	1970	**£4**	chart single
Paranoid	LP	W. Bros	K3104	1970	**£15**	US quad
Sabbath Bloody Sabbath	7"	WWA	WWS002	1973	**£6**	
Tomorrow's Dream	7"	Vertigo	6059061	1972	**£8**	
Turn Up The Night	7"	Vertigo	SABP6	1982	**£5**	pic disc
Turn Up The Night	12"	Vertigo	SABP612	1982	**£8**	pic disc

BLACK WIDOW

Black Widow	LP	CBS	64133	1970	**£20**	
Sacrifice	LP	CBS	63948	1970	**£20**	chart LP
Three	LP	CBS	64562	1971	**£20**	

BLACK, BILL COMBO

Bill Black's Combo	7" EP	London	REU1277	1960	**£6**	
Don't Be Cruel	7"	London	HLU9212	1960	**£4**	chart single
Greatest Hits	LP	London	HAU8113	1963	**£10**	
Let's Twist	LP	London	HAU2427	1962	**£12**	
Little Queenie	7"	London	HLU9925	1964	**£8**	
Movin'	LP	London	HAU2433	1962	**£12**	
Moving	7"	London	HLU9436	1961	**£5**	
Plays Chuck Berry	LP	London	HAU8187	1964	**£15**	
Smokie	7"	Felsted	AF129	1959	**£8**	
Solid & Raunchy	LP	London	HAU2310	1962	**£15**	
Untouchable Sound	7" EP	London	REU1369	1963	**£5**	
Untouchable Sound Of...	LP	London	HAU8080	1963	**£12**	

BLACK, CILLA

Nothing detracts from an artist's collectability as much as their becoming a popular entertainer and interest in Cilla Black's recordings has plummeted since her emergence as a television personality. She was, however, an integral part of the Merseybeat phenomenon and her first LP, in particular, stands up well.

Anyone Who Had A Heart	7" EP	Parlophone	GEP8901	1964	**£4**	
Cilla	LP	Parlophone	PCS3063	1965	**£15**	stereo, chart LP
Cilla	LP	Parlophone	PMC1243	1965	**£10**	mono, chart LP
Cilla Sings A Rainbow	LP	Parlophone	PMC7004	1966	**£10**	chart LP
Cilla's Hits	7" EP	Parlophone	GEP8954	1966	**£4**	
It's For You	7" EP	Parlophone	GEP8916	1964	**£4**	
Love Of The Loved	7"	Parlophone	R5065	1963	**£4**	chart single
Sheroo!	LP	Parlophone	PMC7041	1968	**£10**	chart LP
Time For Cilla	7" EP	Parlophone	GEP8967	1967	**£4**	

BLACKBIRDS

No Destination	LP	Saga	FID2113	1968	**£40**	

BLACKBURN, TONY

Don't Get Off That Train	7"	Fontana	TF562	1965	**£4**	
It's Only Love	7"	MGM	MGM1467	1969	**£4**	chart single
So Much Love	7"	MGM	MGM1375	1968	**£4**	chart single

BLACKBYRDS

Blackbyrds	LP	Fantasy	FT9444	1975	**£10**	
Flying Start	LP	Fantasy	FT522	1974	**£10**	

BLACKFOOT SUE

Gun Running	LP	DJM	DJLPS455	1975	**£10**	
Nothing To Hide	LP	JAM	JAL104	1973	**£10**	

BLACKFOOT, J.D.

Song Of Crazy Horse	LP	Fantasy	9468	1974	**£15**	US
Southbound And Gone	LP	Fantasy	9487	1975	**£12**	US
Ultimate Prophecy	LP	Mercury	6338031	1970	**£20**	

BLACKJACKS

Woo Hoo	7"	Pye	7N15586	1963	**£4**	

BLACKMORE, RITCHIE

Getaway	7"	Oriole	CB314	1965	**£150**	

BLACKWELL, CHARLES

Freight Train	7"	Columbia	DB4919	1962	**£4**	

Supercar	7"	Columbia	DB4839	1962	**£4**	
Taboo	7"	HMV	POP977	1962	**£5**	

BLACKWELL, FRANCES SCRAPPER

Longtime Blues	7" EP	Collector	JEN7	196-	**£4**	

BLACKWELL, OTIS

Make Ready For Love	7"	London	HLE8616	1958	**£15**	
Singin' The Blues	LP	Davis	109	1956	**£70**	US

BLACKWELL, RORY & THE BLACKJACKS

Bye Bye love	7"	Parlophone	R4326	1957	**£6**	

BLACKWELLS

Love Or Money	7"	London	HLW9334	1961	**£4**	
Why Don't You Love Me	7"	Columbia	DB7442	1965	**£20**	

BLADES OF GRASS

Charlie And Fred	7"	Stateside	SS2101	1968	**£4**	
Happy	7"	Stateside	SS2040	1967	**£4**	

BLAINE, HAL

Gear Stripper	7"	RCA	RCA1379	1963	**£6**	

BLAKE, KARL

New Pollution	cass	Daark Inc.		1979	**£10**	
Prehensile Tapes	LP	Glass	013	1982	**£10**	
Prehensile Tapes	LP	Normal	NOR131	1983	**£10**	
Tank Death	cass	Daark Inc.		1979	**£10**	

BLAKE, KEITH

Musically	7"	Blue Cat	BS102	196-	**£10**	
Woo Oh Oh	7"	Amalgam.	AMG809	196-	**£10**	

BLAKE, RALPH

High Blood Pressure	7"	Coxsone	CS7063	196-	**£10**	

BLAKE, TIM

Blake's New Jerusalem	LP	Barclay	CLAY7005	1978	**£15**	
Crystal Machine	LP	Egg	900545	1979	**£15**	French

BLANCA, BURT

Texas Rider	7"	Zodiac	ZR004	196-	**£4**	

BLANCMANGE

Irene And Mavis	7"	Blahh	no number	1979	**£8**	
Living On The Ceiling	7"	London	BLANCDJ3	1982	**£4**	1 sided promo

BLAND, BILLY

Let The Little Girl Dance	7"	London	HL9096	1960	**£6**	chart single

BLAND, BOBBY

Ain't Doing Too Bad	7" EP	Vocalion	VEP170157	1964	**£8**	
Ain't No Love In The Heart Of The City	7"	ABC	4014	1974	**£6**	
Ain't Nothin' You Can Do	LP	Vocalion	VAP8027	1964	**£20**	
Blue Moon	7"	Vogue	V9192	1962	**£5**	
Call On Me	LP	Vocalion	VAP8034	1965	**£20**	
Chains Of Love	7"	Action	ACT4553	1969	**£4**	
Chains Of Love	7"	Action	ACT4553	1969	**£10**	demo
Cry Cry Cry	7"	Vogue	V9178	1961	**£5**	
Don't Cry No More	7"	Vogue	V9188	1961	**£6**	
Good Time Charlie	7"	Vocalion	VP9273	1966	**£4**	
Gotta Get To Know You	7"	Action	ACT4538	1969	**£4**	
Gotta Get To Know You	7"	Action	ACT4538	1969	**£10**	demo
Here's The Man	LP	Vocalion	VAP8041	1962	**£20**	
Honey Child	7"	Vocalion	V9222	1964	**£4**	
I'm Too Far Gone	7"	Vocalion	VP9262	1966	**£4**	
Lead Me On	7"	Vogue	V9182	1961	**£6**	
Piece Of Gold	LP	Action	ACLP6006	1969	**£15**	
Rockin' In The Same Old Boat	7"	Action	ACT4524	1969	**£4**	
Rockin' In The Same Old Boat	7"	Action	ACT4524	1969	**£12**	demo
Share Your Love With Me	7"	Action	ACT4548	1969	**£4**	

Share Your Love With Me	7"	Action	ACT4548	1969	**£10**	demo
Share Your Love With Me	7"	Vocalion	V9229	1964	**£4**	
Soul Of The Man	LP	Duke	DLP79	1966	**£15**	US
These Hands	7"	Vocalion	VP9251	1965	**£4**	
Touch Of The Blues	LP	Island	ILP974	1968	**£20**	
Touch Of The Blues	7"	Sue	WI4044	1968	**£8**	
Two Steps From The Blues	LP	Duke	DLP74	1961	**£20**	US
Yield Not To Temptation	7"	Vocalion	VP9232	1965	**£8**	
Yield Not To Temptation	7" EP	Vocalion	VEP170153	1963	**£8**	
You're The One That I Need	7"	Vogue	V9190	1962	**£6**	

BLANE, MARCIE

Bobby's Girl	7"	London	HLU9599	1962	**£4**	
How Can I Tell Him	7"	London	HLU9673	1963	£4	
Marcie Blane	7" EP	London	REU1413	1964	**£5**	

BLEECHERS

Come Into My Parlour	7"	Upsetter	US314	1969	**£6**	
Ease Up	7"	Trojan	TR679	1969	**£6**	
Send Me The Pillow	7"	Columbia	DB118	1970	**£8**	

BLENDELLS

Dance With Me	7"	Reprise	R20340	1964	**£4**	
Lalalalalala	7"	Reprise	R20291	1964	**£5**	

BLEY, CARLA

Carla Bley's "Escalator Over The Hill" is a jazz opera, covering a range of musical styles, and bringing together some unlikely combinations of musicians. Linda Ronstadt and John McLaughlin, Don Cherry and Jack Bruce, Paul Jones and Gato Barbieri all have key roles in a work that continues to grow in stature. Carla Bley has never achieved this greatness again, and few other composers have either.

Escalator Over The Hill	LP	JCOA	EOTH3	1972	**£20**	triple, boxed

BLIND FAITH

Blind Faith	LP	Polydor	583059	1969	**£10**	chart LP
Untitled Instrumental	7"	Island	Unknown	1969	**£30**	promo

BLIND JAKE & RAMBLING THOMAS

Male Blues Vol.3	7" EP	Collector	JE14	196-	**£4**	

BLISS

Castles In Castille	7"	Chapter One	CH107	1969	**£4**	

BLITZKRIEG BOP

Let's Go	7"	Lightning	GIL504	1977	**£4**	
Let's Go	7"	Mortonsound	MTN3172/3	1977	**£15**	
U.F.O.	7"	Lightning	GTL543	1978	**£4**	

BLODWYN PIG

The natural successor to the bluesy, jazzy music to be found on Jethro Tull's first LP, "This Was", is Blodwyn Pig's "Ahead Rings Out", rather than the later recordings of Ian Anderson and his cohorts. The common factor, of course, is guitarist Mick Abrahams, whose distinctive playing style dominates both records. For Blodwyn Pig, he found an ideal foil in Jack Lancaster, whose fluent work on saxophones and flute is far more noteworthy than Ian Anderson's flautistry!

Ahead Rings Out	LP	Island	ILPS9101	1969	**£15**	chart LP
Dear Jill	7"	Island	WIP6059	1969	**£6**	
Getting To This	LP	Chrysalis	ILPS9122	1970	**£15**	chart LP
Same Old Story	7"	Island	WIP6078	1969	**£5**	
Walk On The Water	7"	Island	WIP6069	1969	**£5**	

BLOND

Wake Up And Call	7"	Fontana	TF1040	1969	**£5**	

BLONDE ON BLONDE

All Day All Night	7"	Pye	7N17637	1968	**£6**	
Blonde On Blonde	LP	Ember	NR50--	1972	**£12**	
Castles In The Sky	7"	Ember	EMBS279	1970	**£6**	
Contrasts	LP	Pye	NSPL18288	1969	**£15**	
Rebirth	LP	Ember	NR5049	1970	**£12**	
Reflections On A Life	LP	Ember	NR5058	1971	**£12**	

BLONDIE

Call Me ('88 Remix)	12"	Chrysalis	CHSP123342	1988	**£6**	pic disc
Denis ('88 Remix)	12"	Chrysalis	CHSP123328	1988	**£6**	pic disc

Title	Format	Label	Cat. No.	Year	Price	Notes
Fan Club Flexi	7"	Fan Club	FLX146	1980	**£6**	flexi
Hunter	LP	Chrysalis	PCDL1384	1982	**£10**	pic disc
In The Flesh	7"	Private Stock	PVT105	1977	**£8**	no PS
Island Of Lost Souls	7"	Chrysalis	CHSP2608	1982	**£4**	pic disc
Parallel Lines	LP	Chrysalis	CHP5001	1978	**£10**	US pic disc
Parallel Lines	LP	Mobile Fid.	MFSL1050	1981	**£15**	US audiophile
Picture This	7"	Chrysalis	CHS2242	1978	**£6**	yellow vinyl
Rapture (long)	7"	Chrysalis	BLODJ1	1981	**£6**	promo, no PS
Rip Her To Shreds	7"	Chrysalis	CHS2180	1977	**£6**	
Tide Is High	12"	Chrysalis	DH201	1981	**£6**	1 sided promo
War Child	7"	Chrysalis	CHSP2624	1982	**£4**	pic disc
Yuletide Throwdown	7"	Lyntone	LYN10840	1982	**£4**	Flexipop flexi

BLOOD, SWEAT & TEARS

Title	Format	Label	Cat. No.	Year	Price	Notes
Blood, Sweat, & Tears	LP	Columbia	CQ30994	1973	**£12**	US quad
Child Is Father To The Man	LP	CBS	63296	1968	**£10**	chart LP
Child Is Father To The Man	LP	Columbia	HC49619	1981	**£12**	US audiophile
Greatest Hits	LP	Columbia	CQ31170	1973	**£10**	US quad
I Can't Quit Her	7"	CBS	3563	1968	**£4**	
Mirror Image	LP	Columbia	PCQ32929	1974	**£10**	US quad

BLOOM, ROGER HAMMER

Title	Format	Label	Cat. No.	Year	Price	Notes
Out Of The Blue	7"	CBS	202654	1967	**£4**	
Polly Pan	7"	CBS	2848	1967	**£5**	

BLOOMFIELD, MIKE

Title	Format	Label	Cat. No.	Year	Price	Notes
It's Not Killing Me	LP	CBS	63652	1969	**£10**	
Live At Bill Graham's Fillmore West	LP	CBS	63816	1969	**£10**	

BLOOMFIELD, MIKE & AL KOOPER

Title	Format	Label	Cat. No.	Year	Price	Notes
Live Adventures	LP	CBS	66216	1969	**£15**	double
Weight	7"	CBS	4094	1969	**£8**	

BLOOMFIELD, MIKE / AL KOOPER & STEVE STILLS

Title	Format	Label	Cat. No.	Year	Price	Notes
Super Session	LP	CBS	63396	1968	**£12**	
Super Session	LP	Columbia	30991	1973	**£15**	US quad
Super Session	LP	Mobile Fid.	MFSL1178	1984	**£12**	US audiophile

BLOOMFIELD, MIKE, DR.JOHN, JOHN HAMMOND

Title	Format	Label	Cat. No.	Year	Price	Notes
Triumvirate	LP	CBS	65659	1973	**£10**	

BLOSSOM TOES

Blossom Toes were one of the most interesting groups to emerge out of the psychedelic period, but failed to find the success they deserved. All the members managed to sustain subsequent careers, however, especially guitarists Jim Cregan and Brian Godding - the former playing for Family and Rod Stewart amongst others, while the latter has placed his increasingly finely honed technique and imagination at the disposal of such diverse employers as Keith Tippett, Mike Westbrook, and Kevin Coyne, before recording an impressive solo album in 1988. What is in effect a third Blossom Toes LP, incidentally, was issued under the name of BB Blunder in 1971.

Title	Format	Label	Cat. No.	Year	Price	Notes
I'll Be Your Baby Tonight	7"	Marmalade	598009	1968	**£15**	
If Only For A Moment	LP	Marmalade	608010	1969	**£40**	
New Day	7"	Marmalade	598022	1969	**£10**	
Peace Loving Man	7"	Marmalade	598014	1969	**£10**	
Postcard	7"	Marmalade	598012	1969	**£10**	
We Are Ever So Clean	LP	Marmalade	607001	1967	**£40**	
What On Earth	7"	Marmalade	598002	1967	**£10**	

BLOSSOMS

Title	Format	Label	Cat. No.	Year	Price	Notes
Baby Daddy-O	7"	Capitol	CL14947	1958	**£4**	
Little Louie	7"	Capitol	CL14856	1958	**£4**	
Move On	7"	Capitol	CL14833	1958	**£4**	

BLOUNT, MICHAEL

Title	Format	Label	Cat. No.	Year	Price	Notes
Patchwork	LP	CBS		1970	**£15**	
Souvenirs	LP	York		1972	**£20**	

BLUE

Title	Format	Label	Cat. No.	Year	Price	Notes
Blue	LP	RSO	2394105	1973	**£10**	
Life In The Navy	LP	RSO	2394133	1974	**£10**	

BLUE & FERRIS

Title	Format	Label	Cat. No.	Year	Price	Notes
You Stole My Money	7"	Blue Cat	BS147	196-	**£10**	

BLUE ACES

All I Want	7"	Columbia	DB7755	1965	**£4**	
Land Of Love	7"	Pye	7N15672	1964	**£4**	
That's All I Want	7"	Columbia	DB7954	1966	**£4**	
You Don't Care	7"	Pye	7N15821	1965	**£4**	

BLUE CHEER

Blue Cheer	LP	Philips	6336001	1969	**£15**	
Feathers From Your Tree	7"	Philips	BF1711	1968	**£5**	
Just A Little Bit	7"	Philips	BF1684	1968	**£5**	
New Improved	LP	Philips	SBL7896	1969	**£15**	
Oh Pleasant Hope	LP	Philips	PHS600350	1971	**£20**	US
Original Human Being	LP	Philips	6336004	1970	**£20**	
Outside Inside	LP	Philips	SBL7860	1968	**£15**	
Pilot	7"	Philips	6051010	1971	**£4**	
Summertime Blues	7"	Philips	BF1646	1968	**£5**	
Vincebus Eruptum	LP	Philips	SBL7839	1967	**£15**	
West Coast Child Of Sunshine	7"	Philips	BF1778	1969	**£6**	
I'm On The Right Side	7"	Pye	7N15970	1965	**£5**	
Some Kind Of Lovin'	7"	Pye	7N17111	1966	**£5**	
Tell Her	7"	Pye	7N17155	1966	**£10**	

BLUE EPITAPH

Ode	LP	Holyground		1974	**£350**	

BLUE FLAMES

The two singles issued by the Blue Flames are often assumed to be by Georgie Fame, whose backing group had the same name. Without having heard the records in question, it does not actually seem likely that this is the case. R&B Records was a specialist ska label, which would be unlikely to have been interested in signing a white group; not only that, but if Georgie Fame had just released two singles, then surely at least one of the songs would have featured in the live set issued as "R & B At The Flamingo". If, however, any collector owns one of these singles and can be positive about the presence or otherwise of Georgie Fame, then the author would be grateful for the information!

J.A.Blues	7"	R&B	JB114	1963	**£10**	
Stop Right Here	7"	R&B	JB126	1963	**£10**	

BLUE JEANS

Hey Mrs.Housewife	7"	Columbia	DB8555	1969	**£4**	

BLUE MEN

I Hear A New World	LP	Triumph	TRXST9000	1960	**£600**	
I Hear A New World	7" EP	Triumph	RGXST5000	1960	**£100**	

BLUE OYSTER CULT

Live Bootleg	10"	Columbia	AS40	1973	**£15**	US promo
Secret Treaties	LP	CBS	PCQ32858	1974	**£12**	US quad
Tyranny and Mutation	LP	CBS	PCQ32017	1973	**£12**	US quad

BLUE PHANTOM

Distortions	LP	Kaleidoscope	KAL101	1972	**£60**	

BLUE RONDOS

Don't Want Your Lovin'	7"	Pye	7N15833	1965	**£12**	
Little Baby	7"	Pye	7N15734	1964	**£10**	

BLUE SKIES

Happy	7"	Fontana	6007026	1970	**£4**	

BLUE STARS

I Can Take It	7"	Decca	F12303	1965	**£20**	

BLUE VELVET BAND

Hitch Hiker	7"	W. Bros	WB7320	1969	**£4**	
Don't Hurt Me	7"	Decca	F12149	1965	**£4**	
Don't Make Me	7"	Decca	F12053	1965	**£4**	chart single

BLUE, DAVID

23 Days In September	LP	Reprise	RS6293	1968	**£12**	US
Comin' Back For More	LP	Asylum	SYL9025	1975	**£10**	
Cupid's Arrow	LP	Asylum	K53056	1976	**£10**	
David Blue	LP	Elektra	EKS74003	1966	**£12**	US

Me	LP	Reprise	RS6375	1970	**£12**	US
Nice Baby And The Angel	LP	Asylum	SYL9009	1973	**£10**	
Stories	LP	Asylum	SYL9001	1972	**£10**	

BLUE, PAMELA

My Friend Bobby	7"	Decca	F11761	1963	**£5**	

BLUE, TIMOTHY

She Won't See The Light	7"	Spark	SRL1014	1970	**£4**	

BLUEBERRIES

It's Gonna Work Out Fine	7"	Mercury	MF894	1965	**£6**	

BLUES BAND

Official Bootleg Album	LP	Arista	BBBP101	1980	**£12**	autographed

BLUES BLENDERS

Girl Next Door	7"	Rio	R93	196-	**£8**	

BLUES BUSTERS

Behold!	LP	Island	ILP923	1965	**£60**	
How Sweet It Is	7"	Island	WI214	1965	**£10**	
I've Been Trying	7"	Doctor Bird	DB1030	1966	**£10**	
Oh Baby	7"	Island	WI023	1962	**£5**	
Spiritual	7"	Starlite	ST45031	1961	**£8**	
There's Always A Sunshine	7"	Doctor Bird	DB1078	1967	**£10**	
Wings Of A Dove	7"	Island	WI222	1965	**£10**	
Your Love	7"	Starlite	ST45072	1962	**£8**	

BLUES BY FIVE

Boom Boom	7"	Decca	F12029	1964	**£8**	

BLUES COUNCIL

Baby Don't Look Down	7"	Parlophone	R5264	1965	**£30**	

BLUES IMAGE

Blues Image	LP	Atco	33300	1969	**£12**	US
Open	LP	Atco	33317	1970	**£12**	US
Red,White,& Blues Image	LP	Atlantic	2400120	1971	**£12**	
Ride Captain Ride	7"	Atlantic	2091009	1970	**£4**	

BLUES MAGOOS

Basic Blues Magoos	LP	Mercury	SR61167	1968	**£15**	US
Blues Magoos	LP	Fontana	STL5402	1966	**£20**	
Electric Comic Book	LP	Mercury	SR61104	1967	**£25**	US, with comic
Gulf Coast Bound	LP	ABC	ABCS710	1970	**£15**	US
Never Going Back To Georgia	LP	ABC	ABCS697	1969	**£15**	US
One By One	7"	Fontana	TF848	1967	**£6**	
Psychedelic Lollipop	LP	Mercury	SR61096	1966	**£20**	US
We Ain't Got Nothin' Yet	7"	Mercury	MF954	1966	**£8**	

BLUES PROJECT

The Blues Project had an important role within the growing maturity of rock music during the sixties, which the loss of credibility of leading member Al Kooper in the succeeding years should do nothing to diminish. The group had a loose, improvisational approach to the blues, in which Andy Kulberg's flute playing was an effective element. "Lazarus" and "Blues Project" represent an attempt to revive the group in the seventies, but by then the spark had inevitably gone.

Blues Project	LP	Capitol	EST11017	1972	**£12**	US
I Can't Keep From Crying	7"	Verve	VS1505	1967	**£6**	
Lazarus	LP	Capitol	ST872	1971	**£12**	US
Live At The Cafe Au Go-Go	LP	Verve	FT3000	1966	**£20**	US
Live At Town Hall	LP	Verve	FTS3025	1967	**£20**	US
Planned Obsolescence	LP	Verve	FTS3046	1968	**£20**	US
Projections	LP	Verve	SVLP6009	1967	**£20**	

BLUESBREAKERS

Curly	7"	Decca	F12588	1967	**£8**	

BLUESOLOGY

Bluesology worked as the backing group for Long John Baldry when the singer was still performing rhythm and blues. The group's pianist was Reg Dwight - or rather Elton John, as he subsequently chose to be known.

Come Back Baby	7"	Fontana	TF594	1965	**£100**	
Mr.Frantic	7"	Fontana	TF668	1966	**£100**	

Since I Found You Baby	7"	Polydor	56195	1967	**£100**	

BLUNSTONE, COLIN

Ennismore	LP	Epic	65278	1973	**£10**	
One Year	LP	Epic	64557	1971	**£10**	

BLUNT INSTRUMENT

No Excuse	7"	Diesel	DCL01	1978	**£4**	

BO & PEEP

Young Love	7"	Decca	F11968	1964	**£10**	

BO STREET RUNNERS

When the cult TV show "Ready Steady Go" organised a beat group talent contest in 1964, the Bo Street Runners were the winners. (The various artists' LP "Ready Steady Win" documents the affair). As is usually the case with talent contests, however, the win yielded nothing in terms of subsequent success for the Bo Street Runners. The group was led by organist Tim Hinkley, while both Mick Fleetwood and Mike Patto were members for a time.

	7" EP	Oak		196-	**£120**	
Baby Never Say Goodbye	7"	Columbia	DB7640	1965	**£20**	
Bo Street Runner	7"	Decca	F11986	1964	**£20**	
Drive My Car	7"	Columbia	DB7901	1966	**£20**	
Tell Me What You're Gonna Do	7"	Columbia	DB7488	1965	**£20**	

BOB & EARL

Baby I'm Satisfied	7"	Sue	WI393	1965	**£8**	
Don't Ever Leave Me	7"	Sue	WI4030	1967	**£8**	
Everybody Jerk	7"	W. Bros	WB6059	1969	**£4**	
Harlem Shuffle	7"	Island	WIP6053	1969	**£4**	chart single
Harlem Shuffle	LP	Sue	ILP951	1967	**£20**	
Harlem Shuffle	7"	Sue	WI374	1965	**£10**	

BOB & JERRY

Ghost Satellite	7"	Pye	7N25003	1958	**£4**	

BOB & TIE

Little Green Apples	7"	Coxsone	CS7086	196-	**£10**	

BOBBETTES

Come A Come A Come A	7"	London	HLE8597	1958	**£20**	
Have Mercy Baby	7"	London	HLU9248	1960	**£15**	
I Shot Mr.Lee	7"	London	HLK9173	1960	**£15**	
I Shot Mr.Lee	7"	Pye	7N25060	1960	**£12**	
Mr.Lee	7"	London	HLE8477	1957	**£20**	

BOBBSEY TWINS

Change Of Heart	7"	London	HLA8474	1957	**£4**	

BOBBY & LAURIE

Hitch Hiker	7"	Parlophone	R5480	1966	**£4**	

BOBCATS

Can't See For Looking	7"	Pye	7N17242	1967	**£4**	

BOCKY & THE VISIONS

I Go Crazy	7"	Atlantic	AT4049	1965	**£6**	

BODACIOUS

Bodacious was one of the many recreational groups put together by a member of Jefferson Airplane - in this case, Marty Balin.

Bodacious D F	LP	RCA	SF8391	1974	**£10**	

BODINES

God Bless	7"	Creation	CRE016	1985	**£6**	
Heard It All	7"	Creation	CRE030	1986	**£6**	
Heard It All	12"	Creation	CRET030	1986	**£8**	
Therese	7"	Creation	CRE028	1986	**£6**	
Therese	12"	Creation	CREY028	1986	**£8**	

BODKIN

Bodkin	LP	West		1972	**£200**	

BOFFALONGO

Beyond Your Head	LP	United Artists	UAG29130	1970	**£15**	

Title	Format	Label	Number	Year	Price	Notes
Boffalongo	LP	United Artists	6726	1969	**£15**	US

BOHEMIAN VENDETTA

Title	Format	Label	Number	Year	Price	Notes
Bohemian Vendetta	LP	Mainstream	56106	1968	**£20**	US

BOINES, HOUSTON

Title	Format	Label	Number	Year	Price	Notes
Superintendant Blues	7"	Blue Horizon	451006	1966	**£15**	

BOLAN, MARC

For an artist with an essentially rather limited talent, Marc Bolan has managed to attract an extraordinarily devoted following. Part of this is no doubt the direct consequence of Bolan's premature death. In any event, there are a number of quite valuable recordings to be found scattered through Bolan's catalogue. These include the original issue of his "Zinc Alloy" LP, which has an individually numbered poster sleeve, and the early solo singles (whose lack of chart success is not hard to understand once they are heard; they are somewhat less than inspiring). Records made with John's Children and Tyrannosaurus Rex are listed under those headings.

Title	Format	Label	Number	Year	Price	Notes
Hippy Gumbo	7"	Parlophone	R5539	1966	**£120**	
Jasper C.Debussy	7"	Track	2094013	1974	**£12**	PS
Third Degree	7"	Decca	F12413	1966	**£120**	
Wizard	7"	Decca	F12288	1965	**£100**	

BOLAN, MARC & GLORIA JONES

Title	Format	Label	Number	Year	Price	Notes
To Know Him Is To Love Him	7"	EMI	EMI2572	1977	**£5**	

BOLAN, MARC & T REX

Title	Format	Label	Number	Year	Price	Notes
Beginning Of Doves	LP	Track	2410201	1974	**£20**	
Celebrate Summer	7"	EMI	MARC18	1977	**£6**	
Chariot Choogle	7"	EMI	SPSR346	1972	**£100**	promo
Christmas Bop	7"	Marc	SBOLAN12P	1982	**£4**	pic disc
Christmas Time	7"	Fan Club		1972	**£35**	flexi
Dandy In The Underworld	7"	EMI	MARC17	1977	**£4**	
Deep Summer	12"	Rarn	MBFSRAP2	1982	**£6**	blue vinyl
Electric Warrior	LP	Fly	HIFLY6	1971	**£12**	with poster, chart LP
Electric Warrior	LP	Marc	ABOLAN3P	1982	**£10**	pic disc
Futuristic Dragon	LP	EMI	BLN5004	1976	**£10**	with inner, chart LP
Get It On	7"	Fly	BUG10	1971	**£4**	chart single
Get It On	7"	Fly	BUG10	1971	**£12**	silver fly on label, handwritten credits
Get It On	CD-s	Marc On Wax	MARCD10	1987	**£6**	
Great Hits	LP	EMI	BLN5003	1972	**£10**	with poster
Hard On Love	LP	Track	2406101	1972	**£150**	test pressing
History Of T Rex	LP	Marc On Wax	WARRIOR1-4	1986	**£20**	4 pic discs, boxed
Hot Love	7"	Cube	ANT2	1978	**£4**	
Hot Love	7"	Fly	BUG6	1971	**£4**	fly label, chart single
Hot Love	7"	Fly	BUG6	1971	**£6**	mustard label
Jeepster	7"	Fly	BUG16(GRUB1A)	1971	**£4**	chart single
Jeepster	7"	Fly	BUG16	1971	**£5**	
Jeepster	7"	Fly	GRUB1	1971	**£40**	promo
Life's A Gas	12"	Cube	ANTS001	1979	**£10**	
Life's A Gas	12"	Rarn	MBFSRAP1	1982	**£6**	
Megarex 2	7"	Marc	PTANX1	1985	**£4**	shaped pic disc
Ride A White Swan	7"	Fly	BUG1	1970	**£8**	PS, mustard label
Ride A White Swan	7"	Fly	BUG1	1970	**£15**	PS, purple label
Ride A White Swan	7"	Octopus	OCTO1	1970	**£300**	test pressing
Sing Me A Song	12"	Rarn	MBFS001C	1981	**£6**	clear vinyl
Sing Me A Song	12"	Rarn	MBFS001P	1981	**£12**	pic disc, black rim
Sing Me A Song	12"	Rarn	MBFS001P	1981	**£6**	pic disc, white rim
Soul Of My Suit	7"	EMI	MARC16	1977	**£4**	chart single
Steve Dixon Interview	7"	Cube	BINT1	1978	**£6**	
T Rex In Concert	LP	Marc	ABOLAN1	1981	**£12**	promo, no applause
T Rex In Concert	LP	Marc	ABOLAN1P	1981	**£10**	pic disc (2 designs)
Tanx	LP	EMI	BLN5002	1972	**£12**	with inner & poster, chart LP
Teenage Dream	7"	EMI	MARC7	1974	**£5**	Marc Bolan & T Rex' credit, chart single
Telegram Sam	7"	EMI	TREX101	1972	**£4**	chart single
Think Zinc	7"	Marc	SBOLAN14PD	1983	**£4**	pic disc
You Scare Me To Death	7"	Cherry Red	CHERRY29	1981	**£5**	with flexi (LYN10086)
You Scare Me To Death	7"	Cherry Red	CHERRYP29	1981	**£4**	pic disc
Zinc Alloy & Hidden Riders Of Tomorrow	LP	EMI	BLNA7751	1974	**£12**	with inner, chart LP
Zinc Alloy & Hidden Riders Of Tomorrow	LP	T Rex Wax Co	BLNA7751	1974	**£100**	promo fold-out sleeve

Zip Gun	LP	EMI	BLN7752	1975	**£15**	diamond cut sleeve, inner
Zip Gun Boogie	7"	EMI	MARC9	1974	**£4**	chart single

BON BONS

Circle	7"	London	HLU8262	1956	**£10**	
That's The Way Love Goes	7"	London	HL8139	1955	**£10**	

BON JOVI

Bad Medicine	7"	Vertigo	JOVS3	1988	**£4**	with 8 photos
Bad Medicine	12"	Vertigo	JOVR312	1988	**£12**	embossed sleeve
Born To Be My Baby	12"	Vertigo	JOVDJ412	1988	**£6**	promo
Born To Be My Baby	12"	Vertigo	JOVR412	1988	**£8**	pic disc
Hardest Part Is The Night	7"	Vertigo	VER22	1985	**£10**	chart single
Hardest Part Is The Night	7"	Vertigo	VERDP22	1985	**£20**	double
Hardest Part Is The Night	12"	Vertigo	BONDJ312	1985	**£15**	promo
Hardest Part Is The Night	12"	Vertigo	VERX22	1985	**£20**	
Hardest Part Is The Night	12"	Vertigo	VERXR22	1985	**£35**	red vinyl
In And Out Of Love	7"	Vertigo	VER19	1985	**£20**	
In And Out Of Love	7"	Vertigo	VERP19	1985	**£30**	pic disc
In And Out Of Love	7"	Vertigo	VERR19	1985	**£20**	promo
In And Out Of Love	12"	Vertigo	BONDJ19	1985	**£25**	promo
In And Out Of Love	12"	Vertigo	VERX19	1985	**£20**	
Lay Your Hands On Me	12"	Vertigo	JOVG612	1989	**£6**	gatefold sleeve
Let It Rock	12"	Vertigo	BONDJ412	1986	**£12**	promo
Living In Sin	12"	Vertigo	JOVR712	1990	**£6**	white vinyl
Living On A Prayer	7"	Vertigo	VERDJ28	1986	**£8**	promo
Living On A Prayer	7"	Vertigo	VERP28	1986	**£20**	pic disc
Living On A Prayer	7"	Vertigo	VERPA28	1986	**£6**	with patch
Living On A Prayer	12"	Vertigo	BONDJ512	1986	**£10**	1 sided promo
Living On A Prayer	12"	Vertigo	VERX28	1986	**£6**	
Living On A Prayer	12"	Vertigo	VERXG28	1986	**£12**	double
Living On A Prayer	12"	Vertigo	VERXR28	1986	**£20**	green vinyl
Never Say Goodbye	12"	Vertigo	JOV212	1987	**£6**	
Never Say Goodbye	12"	Vertigo	JOVR212	1987	**£10**	yellow vinyl
Never Say Goodbye	10"	Vertigo	JOVDJ210	1987	**£12**	1 sided promo
Runaway	7"	Vertigo	VER14	1984	**£20**	
Runaway	12"	Vertigo	BONDJ12	1984	**£25**	promo
Runaway	12"	Vertigo	VERX14	1984	**£20**	
She Don't Know Me	7"	Vertigo	VER11	1984	**£20**	
She Don't Know Me	7"	Vertigo	VERDJ11	1984	**£20**	
She Don't Know Me	12"	Vertigo	VERDJ11	1984	**£30**	promo
She Don't Know Me	12"	Vertigo	VERX11	1984	**£20**	
Slippery When Wet	LP	Vertigo	VERHP38	1988	**£12**	pic disc, poster
Wanted Dead Or Alive	CD-s	Vertigo	JOVCD1	1987	**£12**	
Wanted Dead Or Alive	CD-s	Vertigo	JOVCD1	1987	**£25**	promo
Wanted Dead Or Alive	7"	Vertigo	JOVDJ1	1987	**£6**	promo
Wanted Dead Or Alive	7"	Vertigo	JOVS1	1987	**£5**	with metal stickers
Wanted Dead Or Alive	12"	Vertigo	JOV112	1987	**£6**	
Wanted Dead Or Alive	12"	Vertigo	JOVPB112	1987	**£8**	poster sleeve
Wanted Dead Or Alive	12"	Vertigo	JOVR112	1987	**£12**	silver vinyl
Wanted Dead Or Alive	12"	Vertigo	JOVR112	1987	**£20**	silver vinyl, 1 sided
You Give Love A Bad Name	12"	Vertigo	VERX26	1986	**£6**	
You Give Love A Bad Name	12"	Vertigo	VERXR26	1986	**£15**	blue vinyl
You Give Love A Bad Name	10"	Vertigo	VERP26	1986	**£20**	shaped pic disc

BOND, BOBBY

One More Mile One More Town	7"	W. Bros	WB7292	1969	**£4**	
Sweet Love	7"	Pye	7N25081	1961	**£5**	

BOND, EDDIE

Greatest Country Gospel Hits	LP	Philips	1980	1961	**£50**	US

BOND, GRAHAM

Although he was undoubtedly a major influence within the development of sixties rock, Bond's tragedy was to see his ideas developed more successfully by others. Few of his records really do justice to his undoubted talents, partly because despite being a good alto sax jazz player (as his work on both the Don Rendell Quintet LP of 1962 and on the early Organisation tracks included on "Solid Bond" prove), he constantly compromised his art in a desperate search for commercial success. He never did find it, however, and yet all his sixties sidemen managed to - Ginger Baker and Jack Bruce with Cream; Jon Hiseman and Dick Heckstall-Smith with Colosseum; and John McLaughlin with Mahavishnu Orchestra. Bond himself stumbled through increasingly marginal musical projects, in which personal and drug problems did not help, until he fell under a train in 1974.

Bond In America	LP	Mercury	6499200/1	1971	**£30**	double

Title	Format	Label	Cat. No.	Year	Price	Notes
Holy Magick	LP	Vertigo	6360021	1971	**£20**	spiral label
Lease On Love	7"	Columbia	DB7647	1965	**£20**	
Long Tall Shorty	7"	Decca	F11909	1964	**£20**	
Love Is The Law	LP	Pulsar	AR10604	1968	**£20**	US
Mighty Graham Bond	LP	Pulsar	AR10606	1968	**£20**	US
Solid Bond	LP	W. Bros	WS3001	1970	**£25**	double, chart LP
Sound Of '65	LP	Columbia	33SX1711	1965	**£60**	
St.James Infirmary	7"	Columbia	DB7838	1966	**£15**	
Tammy	7"	Columbia	DB7471	1965	**£15**	
Tell Me	7"	Columbia	DB7528	1965	**£20**	
There's A Bond Between Us	LP	Columbia	33SX1750	1966	**£60**	
This Is Graham Bond	LP	Philips	6382010	1972	**£15**	
Walking In The Park	7"	W. Bros	WB8004	1970	**£10**	
We Put Our Magick On You	LP	Vertigo	6360042	1971	**£20**	spiral label
You've Gotta Have Love Babe	7"	Page One	POF014	1967	**£30**	

BOND, GRAHAM & PETE BROWN

Title	Format	Label	Cat. No.	Year	Price	Notes
Lost Tribe	7"	Greenwich	GSS104	1972	**£15**	
Two Heads Are Better Than One	LP	Chapter One	CHSR813	1972	**£60**	

BOND, JACKI

Title	Format	Label	Cat. No.	Year	Price	Notes
He Say	7"	Strike	JH320	1966	**£4**	
Now I Know	7"	Columbia	DB7719	1965	**£4**	
Tell Him To Go Away	7"	Strike	JH302	1966	**£4**	

BOND, JOHNNY

Title	Format	Label	Cat. No.	Year	Price	Notes
Hot Rod Jalopy	7"	London	HLU9189	1960	**£5**	
Songs That Made Him Famous	LP	London	HAB8228	1965	**£12**	
Ten Little Bottles	7"	London	HLB9957	1965	**£4**	

BOND, JOYCE

Title	Format	Label	Cat. No.	Year	Price	Notes
Back To School	7"	Pama	PM718	196-	**£8**	
Do The Teasy	7"	Island	WIP6010	1967	**£8**	
It's Alright	7"	Airborne	NPB0011	196-	**£8**	
Mr.Pitiful	7"	Pama	PM770	196-	**£8**	
Ob La Di Ob La Da	7"	Island	WIP6051	1968	**£8**	
Soul And Ska	LP	Island	ILP968	1968	**£60**	
Tell Me What It's All About	7"	Island	WI3019	1966	**£8**	
This Train	7"	Island	WIP6018	1967	**£8**	

BOND, OLIVER

Title	Format	Label	Cat. No.	Year	Price	Notes
Knock On Wood	7"	Parlophone	R5527	1966	**£4**	
Let Me Love You	7"	Parlophone	R5476	1966	**£4**	

BOND, RONNIE

Title	Format	Label	Cat. No.	Year	Price	Notes
Anything For You	7"	Page One	POF123	1969	**£12**	

BONDS, GARY (U.S.)

Title	Format	Label	Cat. No.	Year	Price	Notes
Dance Till Quarter To Three	LP	Legrand	LLP3001	1961	**£50**	US
Dear Lady Twist	7"	Top Rank	JAR602	1962	**£4**	
Greatest Hits	LP	Legrand	LLP3003	1962	**£40**	US
New Orleans	7"	Top Rank	JAR527	1961	**£4**	chart single
Not Me	7"	Top Rank	JAR566	1961	**£4**	
Quarter To Three	7"	Top Rank	JAR575	1961	**£4**	chart single
School Is In	7"	Top Rank	JAR595	1961	**£4**	
School Is Out	7"	Top Rank	JAR581	1961	**£4**	
Send Her To Me	7"	Stateside	SS2025	1967	**£4**	
Seven Day Weekend	7"	Stateside	SS111	1962	**£4**	
Twist Twist Senora	7"	Top Rank	JAR615	1962	**£4**	
Twist Up Calypso	LP	Legrand	LLP3002	1962	**£40**	US
Twist Up Calypso	LP	Stateside	SL10001	1962	**£10**	

BONNER, JUKE BOY

Title	Format	Label	Cat. No.	Year	Price	Notes
Runnin' Shoes	7"	Blue Horizon	573163	1969	**£8**	

BONNEY, GRAHAM

Title	Format	Label	Cat. No.	Year	Price	Notes
Baby's Gone	7"	Columbia	DB7934	1966	**£4**	
Devil's Child	7"	Columbia	DB8338	1968	**£4**	
Frenzy	7"	Columbia	DB8464	1968	**£4**	
Get Ready	7"	Columbia	DB8531	1969	**£6**	
Happy Together	7"	Columbia	DB8142	1967	**£4**	
I'll Be Your Baby Tonight	7"	Columbia	DB8382	1968	**£4**	

Leander Angeline	7"	Columbia	DB8592	1969	**£4**	
My Little World Is Blue	7"	Columbia	DB7773	1965	**£4**	
No One Knows	7"	Columbia	DB8005	1966	**£4**	
Poppa Joe	7"	Columbia	DB8283	1967	**£4**	
Sign On The Dotted Line	7"	Columbia	DB8648	1970	**£5**	
Super Girl	7"	Columbia	DB7843	1966	**£4**	chart single
Thank You Baby	7"	Columbia	DB8111	1967	**£4**	
When Evelyn Was Mine	7"	Columbia	DB8687	1970	**£4**	

BONNIE

Did You Get The Message	7"	Ska Beat	JB270	1967	**£10**	
Lovin' You	7"	Jolly	JY014	196-	**£8**	

BONNIE & THE TREASURES

Home Of The Brave	7"	London	HLU9998	1965	**£12**	

BONNIWELL, T.S.

Close	LP	Capitol	ST277	1969	**£30**	US

BONZO DOG (DOO-DAH) BAND

Alley Oop	7"	Parlophone	R5499	1966	**£15**	
Beast Of The Bonzos	LP	Liberty	LBS83332	1970	**£12**	
Doughnut In Granny's Greenhouse	LP	Liberty	LBL83158	1968	**£15**	with booklet, chart LP
Equestrian Statue	7"	Liberty	LBF15040	1967	**£6**	
Gorilla	LP	Liberty	LBL83056	1967	**£15**	with booklet
History Of The Bonzos	LP	United Artists	UAD60071/2	1974	**£20**	double
I Want To Be With You	7"	Liberty	LBF15273	1969	**£4**	
Keynsham	LP	Liberty	LBS83290	1969	**£15**	
Let's Make Up & Be Friendly	LP	United Artists	UAS29288	1972	**£15**	
Mr.Apollo	7"	Liberty	LBF15201	1969	**£5**	
My Brother Makes The Noises For The Talkies	7"	Parlophone	R5430	1966	**£12**	
Tadpoles	LP	Liberty	LBS83257	1969	**£10**	chart LP
Urban Spaceman	7"	Liberty	LBF15144	1968	**£4**	2 versions of B-side, chart single
You Done My Brain In	7"	Liberty	LBF15314	1970	**£5**	

BONZO DOG (DOO-DAH) BAND & OTHERS

Alberts,The Bonzo Dog Band & The Temperance Seven	LP	Starline	SRS5151	1973	**£10**	

BOOKER T & THE MG'S

And Now	LP	Stax	589002	1966	**£10**	
Best Of	LP	Atlantic	228015	1968	**£10**	
Booker T Set	LP	Stax	SXATS1015	1970	**£10**	
Bootleg	7"	Atlantic	AT4033	1965	**£5**	
Chinese Checkers	7"	London	HLK9784	1963	**£4**	
Chinese Checkers	7"	Stax	601026	1967	**£4**	
Doing Our Thing	LP	Atlantic	2464011	1970	**£10**	
Green Onions	LP	Atlantic	587033	1966	**£10**	
Green Onions	7"	Atlantic	584088	1967	**£4**	
Green Onions	LP	London	HAK8182	1964	**£15**	chart LP
Green Onions	7"	London	HLK9595	1962	**£6**	
Hip Hugger	7"	Stax	601009	1967	**£4**	
Jelly Bread	7"	London	HLK9670	1963	**£4**	
Jingle Bells	7"	Atlantic	584060	1966	**£4**	
McLemore Ave.	LP	Stax	SXATS1031	1970	**£10**	chart LP
My Sweet Potato	7"	Atlantic	584044	1966	**£4**	
R&B With Booker T Vol.1	7" EP	London	REK1367	1963	**£10**	
R&B With Booker T Vol.2	7" EP	Atlantic	AET6002	1964	**£10**	
Red Beans And Rice	7"	Atlantic	AT4063	1966	**£4**	
Slim Jenkins' Place	7"	Stax	601018	1967	**£4**	
Soul Clap '69	7"	Stax	STAX127	1969	**£4**	chart single
Soul Limbo	LP	Stax	SXATS1001	1968	**£10**	
Soul Limbo	7"	Stax	STAX102	1968	**£4**	chart single
Time Is Tight	7"	Stax	STAX119	1969	**£4**	chart single
Uptight	LP	Stax	SXATS1005	1968	**£10**	

BOOKER, JAMES

Cool Turkey	7"	Vogue	V9177	1961	**£6**	
Gonzo	7" EP	Vocalion	VEP170154	1963	**£12**	

BOOMERANGS

Another Tear Falls	7"	Fontana	TF555	1965	**£12**	
Dream World	7"	Pye	7N17049	1966	**£12**	
Rockin' Robin	7"	Fontana	TF507	1964	**£20**	

BOOMTOWN RATS

Rat Pack	7"	Ensign		1978	**£12**	6 singles in plastic wallet
Rat Trap	7"	Ensign	ENY16DJ	1978	**£5**	1 sided promo

BOONE, PAT

Ain't That A Shame	7"	London	HLD8172	1955	**£10**	chart single
April Love	7"	London	HLD8512	1957	**£4**	chart single
Big Hits Vol.2	LP	London	HAD2098	1958	**£10**	
Don't Forbid Me	7"	London	HLD8370	1957	**£5**	chart single
Four By Pat	7" EP	London	RED1109	1957	**£4**	
Friendly Persuasion	7"	London	HLD8346	1956	**£5**	chart single
Gee Whittakers	7"	London	HLD8233	1956	**£6**	
Golden Hits	LP	London	HAD8031	1962	**£10**	
Good Rockin' Tonight	7"	London	HLD8824	1959	**£4**	chart single
Howdy	LP	London	HAD2030	1957	**£12**	
Howdy Part 1	7" EP	London	RED1081	1957	**£4**	
Howdy Part 2	7" EP	London	RED1082	1957	**£4**	
Howdy Part 3	7" EP	London	RED1119	1958	**£4**	
I Almost Lost My Mind	7"	London	HLD8303	1956	**£6**	chart single
I'll Be Home	7"	London	HLD8253	1956	**£6**	chart single
Johnny Will	7"	London	HLD9461	1961	**£4**	chart single
Just A Closer Walk With Thee	7" EP	London	RED1095	1957	**£4**	
Latest And Greatest	7" EP	London	RED1281	1961	**£4**	
Latest And Greatest No.2	7" EP	London	RED1335	1962	**£4**	
Long Tall Sally	7"	London	HLD8291	1956	**£6**	chart single
Love Letters In The Sand	7"	London	HLD8445	1957	**£4**	chart single
Moody River	7"	London	HLD9350	1961	**£4**	chart single
No Arms Could Ever Hold You	7"	London	HLD8197	1955	**£10**	
On Mike	7" EP	London	RED1069	1957	**£4**	
Pat Boone Sings The Hits	7" EP	London	RED1063	1956	**£4**	
Pat Boone Sings The Hits No.2	7" EP	London	RED1086	1957	**£4**	
Pat Boone Sings The Hits No.3	7" EP	London	RED1112	1958	**£4**	
Pat Part 1	7" EP	London	RED1132	1958	**£4**	
Pat Part 2	7" EP	London	RED1133	1958	**£4**	
Pat Sings	LP	London	HAD2161	1959	**£10**	
Pat!	LP	London	HAD2049	1957	**£12**	
Pat's Big Hits	LP	London	HAD2024	1957	**£12**	
Pat's Big Hits	7" EP	London	RED1118	1958	**£4**	
Remember You're Mine	7"	London	HLD8479	1957	**£4**	chart single
Rich In Love	7"	London	HLD8316	1956	**£6**	
Songs From Friendly Persuasion	7" EP	London	RED1068	1957	**£4**	
Speedy Gonzales	7"	London	HLD9573	1962	**£4**	chart single
Stardust	LP	London	HAD2127	1958/59	**£10**	mono, chart LP
Stardust	LP	London	SHAD6001	1958/59	**£10**	stereo, chart LP
Stardust Part 1	7" EP	London	RED1177	1959	**£4**	
Stardust Part 2	7" EP	London	RED1178	1959	**£4**	
Stardust Part 3	7" EP	London	RED1179	1959	**£4**	
Twixt Twelve And Twenty	7"	London	HLD8910	1959	**£4**	chart single
White Christmas	7"	London	HLD8520	1957	**£4**	chart single
Why Baby Why	7"	London	HLD8404	1957	**£5**	chart single
Yes Indeed	LP	London	HAD2144	1959	**£10**	mono
Yes Indeed	LP	London	SHAD6010	1959	**£10**	stereo
Yes Indeed Part 1	7" EP	London	RED1190	1959	**£4**	
Yes Indeed Part 2	7" EP	London	RED1191	1959	**£4**	
Yes Indeed Part 3	7" EP	London	RED1192	1959	**£4**	

BOONE, PAT (& OTHERS)

April Love	LP	London	HAD2078	1958	**£10**	

BOOTH, ANTHONY

Till Death Do Us Part	7"	Tangerine	DP0008	196-	**£4**	

BOOTHE, KEN

Everybody Knows	7"	Coxsone	CS7041	196-	**£10**	
Everyone Got To Be There	7"	Studio One	SO2036	196-	**£10**	
Fat Girl	7"	Studio One	SO2014	196-	**£10**	

Feel Good	7"	Studio One	SO2000	196-	**£10**	
Home Home Home	7"	Coxsone	CS7020	196-	**£10**	
I Remember Someone	7"	Fab	FAB63	196-	**£8**	
Lady With The Starlight	7"	High Note	HS003	196-	**£8**	
Live And Learn	7"	Studio One	SO2037	196-	**£10**	
Live And Learn	7"	Studio One	SO2038	196-	**£10**	
Lonely Teardrops	7"	Coxsone	CS7006	196-	**£10**	
One I Love	7"	Caltone	TONE107	196-	**£8**	
Pleading	7"	Bamboo	BAM4	196-	**£8**	
Puppet On A String	7"	Studio One	SO2012	196-	**£10**	
Say You	7"	Doctor Bird	DB1110	1967	**£10**	
Sherry	7"	Coxsone	CS7094	196-	**£10**	
Tomorrow	7"	Studio One	SO2053	196-	**£10**	
Train Is Coming	7"	Island	WI3020	1966	**£8**	
Why Baby Why	7"	Trojan	TR7716	1970	**£5**	
Why Did You Leave	7"	Studio One	SO2026	196-	**£10**	
You Keep Me Hanging On	7"	Coxsone	CS7043	196-	**£10**	
You're On My Mind	7"	Studio One	SO2073	196-	**£10**	

BOOTHE, MILTON

Lonely And Blue	7"	Gas	GAS106	196-	**£8**	

BOOTLES

I'll Let You Hold My Hand	7"	Vocalion	VN9216	1964	**£4**	

BOOTS

Animal In Me	7"	CBS	3550	1968	**£8**	
Keep Your Lovelight Burning	7"	CBS	3833	1968	**£12**	

BOP & THE BELTONES

Smile Like An Angel	7"	Coxsone	CS7007	196-	**£10**	

BOSS GUITARS

Play The Winners	LP	London	SHR8237	1965	**£10**	

BOSTIC, EARL

Alto Magic In Hi-fi	LP	King	597	1958	**£20**	US
Alto-Tude	LP	King	515	195-	**£20**	US
Best Of Bostic	LP	King	500	195-	**£20**	US
Beyond The Blue Horizon	7"	Parlophone	R4232	1956	**£4**	
Blue Skies	7"	Parlophone	MSP6119	1954	**£5**	
Bo Do Rock	7"	Parlophone	R4208	1956	**£4**	
Bostic Rocks	LP	King	571	1958	**£20**	US
Bostic Showcase Of Swinging Dance	LP	King	583	1958	**£20**	US
Bostic Workshop	LP	King	613	1959	**£20**	US
Bubbin's Rock	7"	Parlophone	R4278	1957	**£4**	
C'mon Dance With Earl Bostic	LP	King	558	1958	**£20**	US
Dance Time	LP	King	525	195-	**£20**	US
Deep Purple	7"	Parlophone	MSP6089	1954	**£5**	
Don't You Do It	7"	Parlophone	MSP6105	1954	**£5**	
Earl Bostic	7" EP	Parlophone	GEP8520	1955	**£5**	
Earl Bostic	7" EP	Vogue	EPV1010	1955	**£6**	
Flamingo	7" EP	Parlophone	GEP8506	1954	**£5**	
Flamingo	7"	Vogue	V2145	1969	**£4**	
For You	LP	King	503	195-	**£20**	US
Harlem Nocturne	7"	Parlophone	R4263	1957	**£4**	
Honeymoon Night	7"	Island	WI271	1966	**£8**	
Invitation To Dance	LP	King	547	1957	**£20**	US
Jungle Drums	7"	Parlophone	MSP6110	1954	**£5**	
Let's Dance With Earl Bostic	LP	King	529	195-	**£20**	US
Linger Awhile	7" EP	Parlophone	GEP8513	1955	**£5**	
Mambostic	7"	Parlophone	MSP6131	1954	**£5**	
Melody Of love	7"	Parlophone	MSP6162	1955	**£5**	
Music A La Bostic No.2	7" EP	Parlophone	GEP8574	1956	**£5**	
Music A La Bostic No.3	7" EP	Parlophone	GEP8603	1957	**£5**	
Off Shore	7"	Parlophone	MSP6075	1954	**£5**	
Over The Waves Rock	7"	Parlophone	R4460	1958	**£4**	
Plays The Sweet Side Of The Fantastic 50's	LP	King	602	1959	**£20**	US
Rocking With Bostic	7" EP	Parlophone	GEP8741	1958	**£5**	
Tuxedo Junction	7"	Ember	JBS708	1962	**£4**	
Wrap It Up	7" EP	Parlophone	GEP8539	1955	**£5**	

BOSTON

Title	Format	Label	Cat. No.	Year	Price	Notes
Boston	LP	Epic	E99-34188	1978	**£12**	US pic disc
Boston	LP	Epic	EPCH81611		**£10**	audiophile
Don't Look Back	LP	Epic	HE45050	1981	**£10**	US audiophile
Don't Look Back	LP	Epic	PAL35050	1979	**£10**	US pic disc

BOSTON CRABS

In an effort to make themselves stand out from the mass of mid-sixties British beat groups, the Boston Crabs favoured an intriguing assortment of stage costumes - the lead guitarist dressed as a country bumpkin, the drummer wore an asbestos fire-fighting suit, and the lead singer posed as a blind man in a wheel chair! Uniform red shirts and blue jeans for the second half proved the last to be indeed a pose. Not that any of this did the group much good, for even substantial airplay on pirate radio for their cover of the Lovin' Spoonful's "You Didn't Have To Be So Nice" failed to give the Boston Crabs the success they sought.

Title	Format	Label	Cat. No.	Year	Price	Notes
As Long As I Have You	7"	Columbia	DB7679	1965	**£8**	
Down In Mexico	7"	Columbia	DB7586	1965	**£6**	
You Didn't Have To Be So Nice	7"	Columbia	DB7830	1966	**£8**	

BOSTON DEXTERS

Title	Format	Label	Cat. No.	Year	Price	Notes
I've Got Something To Tell You	7"	Columbia	DB7498	1965	**£15**	
I've Got Troubles Of My Own	7"	Contemp.	CR103	1964	**£20**	
La Bamba	7"	Contemp.	CR101	1964	**£25**	
Try Hard	7"	Columbia	DB7641	1965	**£12**	
You've Been Talking About Me	7"	Contemp.	CR102	1964	**£20**	

BOSWELL, ERIC

Title	Format	Label	Cat. No.	Year	Price	Notes
Little Donkey	7"	Gayfeet	GS204	1973	**£8**	

BOSWELL, SIMON

Title	Format	Label	Cat. No.	Year	Price	Notes
Mind Parasites	LP	Transatlantic	TRA307	1975	**£10**	

BOW BELLS

Title	Format	Label	Cat. No.	Year	Price	Notes
Belinda	7"	Parlophone	R5520	1966	**£5**	
Not To Be Taken	7"	Polydor	56030	1965	**£5**	

BOW STREET RUNNERS

Title	Format	Label	Cat. No.	Year	Price	Notes
Bow Street Runners	LP	B.T.Puppy	BTPS1026	1969	**£90**	US

BOW WOW WOW

Title	Format	Label	Cat. No.	Year	Price	Notes
Mile High Club	7"	Tour D'Eiffel		1981	**£4**	

BOWEN, JIMMY

Title	Format	Label	Cat. No.	Year	Price	Notes
Crossover	7"	Columbia	DB4027	1957	**£10**	
I'm Sticking With You	7"	Columbia	DB3915	1957	**£12**	
Jimmy Bowen	LP	Roulette	R25004	1957	**£50**	US
Meet Jimmy Bowen	7" EP	Columbia	SEG7757	1958	**£20**	
Meet Jimmy Bowen No.2	7" EP	Columbia	SEG7793	1958	**£20**	
Sunday Morning With The Comics	LP	Reprise	R6210	1966	**£12**	US
Two Step	7"	Columbia	DB4184	1958	**£6**	
Warm Up To Me Baby	7"	Columbia	DB3984	1957	**£10**	

BOWIE, DAVID

David Bowie achieved popularity a fairly long time after starting to make records, so that there are a considerable number of rare and expensive records from the early years of his career for the Bowie completist to obtain. Perhaps the most famous of these is the original cover of the LP "The Man Who Sold The World", which portrays Bowie casually attired in a dress - "It's a man's dress," he explained at the time. The uncensored cover of "Diamond Dogs", on which Bowie is painted as a creature half man and half dog, has the dog's genitalia intact - these were airbrushed out on all but the first issues. More recently, Bowie's RCA albums were issued on compact disc and then speedily withdrawn due to a royalty dispute. These have become, in consequence, among the first CDs to aquire collectors' values.

Title	Format	Label	Cat. No.	Year	Price	Notes
1980 All Clear	LP	RCA	DJL13545	1980	**£20**	US promo
Alabama Song	7"	RCA	BOW5	1980	**£4**	PS
Aladdin Sane	LP	RCA	BOPIC1	1984	**£12**	pic disc
Aladdin Sane	CD	RCA	PD83890	1985	**£30**	
Baal's Hymn	7"	RCA	BOW11	1982	**£4**	PS
Be My Wife	7"	RCA	PB1017	1977	**£4**	
Beauty And The Beast	7"	RCA	PB1190	1978	**£4**	PS
Bowie's Greatest Hits	7"	Lyntone	LYN2929	1974	**£5**	flexi
Boys Keep Swinging	7"	RCA	BOW2	1979	**£4**	PS
Breaking Glass	7"	RCA	BOW1	1978	**£4**	PS
Can't Help Thinking About Me	7"	Pye	7N17020	1966	**£70**	
Changes	7"	RCA	RCA2160	1972	**£5**	
ChangesOneBowie	LP	RCA	RS1055	1976	**£20**	with sax version of 'John'

ChangesOneBowie	CD	RCA	PD81732	1985	**£30**	
ChangesTwoBowie	LP	RCA	BOWLP3	1981	**£25**	promo with press kit
ChangesTwoBowie	LP/Cass	RCA	DF1	1983	**£15**	LP & cassette in holder
ChangesTwoBowie	CD	RCA	PD84202	1985	**£30**	
China Girl	7"	EMI	EAP157	1983	**£4**	pic disc
David Bowie	LP	Deram	DML1007	1967	**£100**	mono
David Bowie	LP	Deram	SML1007	1967	**£120**	stereo
David Bowie	LP	Philips	SBL7912	1969	**£120**	
David Bowie Now	LP	RCA	DJL12697	1977	**£25**	US promo
David Bowie Radio Special Vol.1	LP	RCA	DJL13829	1980	**£25**	US promo
David Live	CD	RCA	PD80771	1985	**£30**	
Diamond Dogs	LP	RCA		1974	**£100**	uncensored cover
Diamond Dogs	LP	RCA	BOPIC5	1984	**£12**	pic disc
Diamond Dogs	CD	RCA	PD83859	1985	**£30**	
Diamond Dogs	7"	RCA	APBO0293	1974	**£4**	chart single
DJ	7"	RCA	BOW3	1979	**£4**	PS
DJ	7"	RCA	BOW3	1979	**£6**	PS, green vinyl
Do Anything You Say	7"	Pye	7N17079	1966	**£70**	
Do Anything You Say	7"	Pye	7NX8002	1972	**£15**	PS
Drive-In Saturday	7"	RCA	RCA2352	1973	**£4**	chart single
Evening With David Bowie	LP	RCA	DJL13036	1977	**£25**	US promo
Fame	7"	RCA	RCA2579	1975	**£4**	chart single
Fame And Fashion	CD	RCA	PD84919	1985	**£15**	
Fashions	7"	RCA	BOW100	1982	**£40**	set of 10 pic discs in folder
Golden Years	CD	RCA	PD84792	1985	**£20**	
Golden Years	7"	RCA	RCA2640	1975	**£4**	chart single
Helden	7"	RCA	PB9168	1978	**£5**	sung in German
Heroes	CD	RCA	PD83857	1985	**£15**	
Heros	7"	RCA	PB9167	1978	**£5**	sung in French
Holy Holy	7"	Mercury	6052049	1971	**£80**	
Hunky Dory	LP	RCA	BOPIC2	1984	**£12**	pic disc
Hunky Dory	CD	RCA	PD84623	1985	**£30**	
I Dig Everything	7"	Pye	7N17157	1966	**£70**	
Jean Genie	7"	RCA	RCA2302	1972	**£4**	chart single
John I'm Only Dancing	7"	RCA	RCA2263	1972	**£4**	chart single
John I'm Only Dancing	7"	RCA	RCA2263	1973	**£6**	Mainman publishing credit
John,I'm Only Dancing (Again)	7"	RCA	BOW4	1979	**£4**	PS
John,I'm Only Dancing (Again)	12"	RCA	BOW12-4	1979	**£6**	
Knock On Wood	7"	RCA	RCA2466	1974	**£4**	chart single
Laughing Gnome	7"	Deram	DM123	1967	**£20**	matrix no. inverted on label
Let's Dance	LP	Mobile Fid.	MFSL1083	1982	**£15**	US audiophile
Let's Dance	LP	RCA	UK83	1983	**£200**	numbered promo
Let's Talk	LP	EMI	SPRO9960/1	1983	**£25**	US promo
Life On Mars	7"	RCA	RCA2316	1973	**£4**	chart single
Life On Mars	7"	RCA	RCA2316	1973	**£10**	PS
Lifetimes	LP	RCA	LIFETIMES1	1983	**£25**	promo
Live	LP	RCA	APL20771	1974	**£60**	test pressing
Lodger	LP	RCA	BOWLP1	1979	**£40**	test pressing
Lodger	CD	RCA	PD84234	1985	**£20**	
London Boys	7"	Decca	F13579	1975	**£5**	
Love You Till Tuesday	7"	Deram	DM135	1967	**£50**	
Loving The Alien	12"	EMI	12EAP195	1984	**£6**	shaped pic disc
Low	CD	RCA	PD83856	1985	**£25**	
Man Of Words, Man Of Music	LP	Mercury	SR61246	1969	**£90**	US
Man Who Sold The World	LP	Mercury	61325	1971	**£25**	US, cartoon cover, stamped matrix no.
Man Who Sold The World	LP	Mercury	6338041	1971	**£150**	dress cover
Man Who Sold The World	LP	RCA	LSP4816	1971	**£10**	with inner and poster
Man Who Sold The World	CD	RCA	PD84654	1985	**£30**	
Memory Of A Free Festival	7"	Mercury	6052026	1970	**£80**	
Narrates Peter And The Wolf	LP	RCA	ARLI2743	1978	**£10**	US green vinyl
Narrates Peter And The Wolf	CD	RCA	PD82743	1985	**£30**	
Pin-Ups	LP	RCA	BOPIC4	1984	**£12**	pic disc
Pin-Ups	CD	RCA	PD84653	1985	**£15**	
Prettiest Star	7"	Mercury	MF1135	1970	**£80**	
Ragazza Sola, Ragazza Solo	7"	Philips	BW704208	1969	**£100**	sung in Italian
Ragazza Sola, Ragazza Solo	7"	Philips	BW704208	1969	**£150**	sung in Italian, PS, black label
Ragazza Sola, Ragazza Solo	7"	Philips	BW704208	1969	**£120**	sung in Italian, PS, blue label

Title	Format	Label	Cat. No.	Year	Price	Notes
Rare Bowie	LP	RCA	PL45406	1982	**£20**	hand stamped edition
Rebel Rebel	7"	RCA	APBO0287	1974	**£10**	
Rebel Rebel	7"	RCA	LPBO5009	1974	**£4**	chart single
Rock'n'Roll Suicide	7"	RCA	LPBO5021	1974	**£4**	chart single
Rubber Band	7"	Deram	DM107	1966	**£50**	
Scary Monsters	CD	RCA	PD83647	1985	**£15**	
Scary Monsters	cass-s	RCA	BOWC8	1981	**£5**	
Scary Monsters	7"	RCA	BOW8	1981	**£4**	PS
Scary Monsters Interview	LP	RCA	DJL13840	1980	**£25**	US promo
Sorrow	7"	RCA	RCA2424	1973	**£4**	chart single
Space Oddity	7"	Philips	BF1801	1969	**£10**	chart single
Space Oddity	7"	Philips	BF1801	1969	**£30**	demo
Space Oddity	7"	Philips	BF1801	1969	**£20**	stereo
Space Oddity	CD	RCA	PD84813	1985	**£30**	
Space Oddity	7"	RCA	RCA2593	1975	**£8**	PS
Stage	LP	RCA	PL02913	1978	**£20**	double, green vinyl
Stage	LP	RCA	PL02913	1978	**£20**	double, yellow vinyl
Stage	CD	RCA	PD89002	1985	**£30**	
Starman	7"	RCA	RCA2199	1972	**£4**	chart single
Starman	7"	RCA	RCA2199	1972	**£25**	PS
Station To Station	LP	RCA	APL11327	1976	**£50**	test pressing
Station To Station	LP	RCA	APLI1327	1976	**£200**	US multicoloured vinyl
Station To Station	CD	RCA	PD81327	1985	**£30**	
Suffragette City	7"	RCA	RCA2726	1976	**£4**	
Suffragette City	7"	RCA	RCA2726	1976	**£12**	PS
TVC15	7"	RCA	RCA2682	1976	**£4**	chart single
Up The Hill Backwards	cass-s	RCA	BOWC9	1981	**£5**	
Up The Hill Backwards	7"	RCA	BOW9	1981	**£4**	PS
Wild Is The Wind	7"	RCA	BOW10	1981	**£4**	PS
World Of...	LP	Decca	PA58	1970	**£15**	mono
World Of...	LP	Decca	SPA58	1970	**£10**	pre-Ziggy cover
Young Americans	CD	RCA	PD80998	1985	**£30**	
Young Americans	7"	RCA	RCA2523	1975	**£4**	chart single
Ziggy Stardust	LP	Mobile Fid.	MFSL1064	1982	**£20**	US audiophile
Ziggy Stardust	LP	RCA	BOPIC3	1984	**£12**	pic disc
Ziggy Stardust	CD	RCA	PD84702	1985	**£30**	
Ziggy Stardust: The Motion Picture	CD	RCA	PD84862	1985	**£20**	
Ziggy Stardust: The Motion Picture	LP	RCA	CPL24862	1983	**£60**	US clear vinyl

BOWIE, DAVID (DAVIE JONES & LOWER THIRD)

Title	Format	Label	Cat. No.	Year	Price	Notes
You've Got A Habit Of Leaving	7"	Parlophone	R5315	1965	**£200**	

BOWIE, DAVID (KING BEES)

Title	Format	Label	Cat. No.	Year	Price	Notes
Liza Jane	7"	Vocalion	V9221	1964	**£250**	

BOWIE, DAVID (MANISH BOYS)

Title	Format	Label	Cat. No.	Year	Price	Notes
I Pity The Fool	7"	Parlophone	R5250	1965	**£160**	

BOWIE, DAVID (MANISH BOYS/LOWER THIRD)

Title	Format	Label	Cat. No.	Year	Price	Notes
I Pity The Fool	7"	EMI	EMI2925	1979	**£5**	

BOWN, ALAN

Title	Format	Label	Cat. No.	Year	Price	Notes
Alan Bown	LP	Deram	SML1049	1969	**£12**	
Baby Don't Push Me	7"	Pye	7N17084	1966	**£6**	
Can't Let Her Go	7"	Pye	7N15934	1965	**£6**	
Emergency	7"	Pye	7N17192	1966	**£10**	
Gonna Fix You Good	7"	Pye	7N17256	1967	**£12**	
Gypsy Girl	7"	Deram	DM278	1969	**£5**	
Headline News	7"	Pye	7N17148	1966	**£5**	
Listen	LP	Island	ILPS9131	1970	**£10**	
Outward Bown	LP	Contemp.	MF12000	1967	**£20**	
Pyramid	7"	Island	WIP6091	1970	**£5**	
Still As Stone	7"	Deram	DM259	1969	**£5**	
Story Book	7"	MGM	MGM1387	1968	**£5**	
Stretchin' Out	LP	Island	ILPS9163	1971	**£10**	
Toyland	7"	MGM	MGM1355	1967	**£5**	
We Can Help You	7"	Contemp.	CUB1	196-	**£6**	

BOWN, ALAN & JIMMY JAMES

Title	Format	Label	Cat. No.	Year	Price	Notes
London Swings	LP	Pye	NPL18156	1966	**£20**	1 side each

BOWN, ANDREW

Title	Format	Label	Cat. No.	Year	Price	Notes
Lulli Rides Again	7"	Parlophone	R5856	1970	**£4**	

BOWN, ANDY

Title	Format	Label	Cat. No.	Year	Price	Notes
Gone To My Head	LP	Mercury	6310002	1972	**£10**	
Sweet William	LP	GM	GML1001	1973	**£10**	

BOX TOPS

Title	Format	Label	Cat. No.	Year	Price	Notes
Choo Choo Train	7"	Bell	BLL1017	1968	**£4**	
Cry Like A Baby	7"	Bell	BLL1001	1968	**£4**	chart single
Cry Like A Baby	LP	Stateside		1968	**£12**	
I Met Her In Church	7"	Bell	BLL1035	1968	**£4**	
I Shall Be Released	7"	Bell	BLL1063	1969	**£4**	
Letter	7"	Stateside	SS2044	1967	**£5**	chart single
Letter/Neon Rainbow	LP	Stateside	SSL10218	1968	**£12**	
Mi Sento Felice	7"		SIR20072	1967	**£10**	sung in Italian
Neon Rainbow	7"	Stateside	SS2070	1967	**£4**	
Soul Deep	7"	Bell	BLL1068	1969	**£4**	chart single
Sweet Cream Ladies Forward March	7"	Bell	BLL1045	1968	**£4**	
Turn On A Dream	7"	Bell	BLL1084	1969	**£4**	

BOXER

Title	Format	Label	Cat. No.	Year	Price	Notes
Bloodletting	LP	Virgin	V2073	1976	**£50**	demo only

BOYCE, TOMMY

Title	Format	Label	Cat. No.	Year	Price	Notes
Pretty Thing	7"	MGM	MGM1287	1965	**£4**	

BOYCE, TOMMY & BOBBY HART

Title	Format	Label	Cat. No.	Year	Price	Notes
Alice Long	7"	A&M	AMS729	1968	**£4**	
Goodbye Baby	7"	A&M	AMS722	1968	**£4**	
I Wonder What She's Doing Tonight	7"	A&M	AMS714	1968	**£4**	
Out And About	7"	A&M	AMS705	1967	**£4**	
Sometimes She's A Little Girl	7"	A&M	AMS710	1967	**£4**	

BOYD, EDDIE

Title	Format	Label	Cat. No.	Year	Price	Notes
...& His Blues Band	LP	Decca	SKL4872	1967	**£40**	
7936 South Rhodes	LP	Blue Horizon	763202	1968	**£40**	
Big Boat	7"	Blue Horizon	573137	1967	**£12**	
Boyd's Blues	7" EP	Esquire	EP247	196-	**£5**	
Five Long Years	LP	Fontana	STJL905	1965	**£20**	
It's So Miserable To Be Alone	7"	Blue Horizon	451009	1966	**£25**	

BOYD, EDDIE & BUDDY GUY

Title	Format	Label	Cat. No.	Year	Price	Notes
With the Blues	7" EP	Chess	CRE6009	1966	**£5**	

BOYLE, BILLY

Title	Format	Label	Cat. No.	Year	Price	Notes
My Baby's Crazy About Elvis	7"	Decca	F11503	1962	**£8**	
Walk Walk Walkin'	7"	Columbia	DB7294	1964	**£6**	

BOYLES BROTHERS

Title	Format	Label	Cat. No.	Year	Price	Notes
Introducing...	LP	Int. Artists	6801	1968	**£20**	US

BOYS

The Boys, who released "It Ain't Fair" in 1964, became the Action shortly afterwards.

Title	Format	Label	Cat. No.	Year	Price	Notes
It Ain't Fair	7"	Pye	7N15726	1964	**£20**	

BOYS (2)

Title	Format	Label	Cat. No.	Year	Price	Notes
Boys	LP	NEMS	NEL6001	1977	**£12**	chart LP
Brickfield Nights	7"	NEMS	NES116	1978	**£5**	
First Time	7"	NEMS	NES111	1977	**£5**	
I Don't Care	7"	NEMS	1	1977	**£5**	
Kamikaze	7"	Safari	SAFE21	1979	**£6**	with booklet
Let It Rain	7"	Safari	SAFE33	1980	**£4**	
Terminal Love	7"	Safari	SAFE23	1980	**£4**	
To Hell With The Boys	LP	Safari	1-2BOYS	1979	**£12**	
Weekend	7"	Safari	SAFE31	1980	**£4**	
Woeh, Woeh, Woeh	7"	Parole		1981	**£4**	
You Better Move On	7"	Safari	SAFE27	1980	**£4**	

BOYS (3)

Title	Format	Label	Cat. No.	Year	Price	Notes
Polaris	7"	Parlophone	R5027	1963	**£20**	

BOYS BLUE
Take A Heart .... 7" .... HMV .... POP1427 .... 1965 ...... **£15** ....

BOZ
Baby Song .... 7" .... Columbia .... DB7972 .... 1966 .... **£5** ....
I Shall Be Released .... 7" .... Columbia .... DB8406 .... 1968 .... **£5** ....
Isn't That So .... 7" .... Columbia .... DB7832 .... 1966 .... **£6** ....
Light My Fire .... 7" .... Columbia .... DB8468 .... 1968 .... **£5** ....
Meeting Time .... 7" .... Columbia .... DB7889 .... 1966 .... **£8** ....
Pinnochio .... 7" .... Columbia .... DB7941 .... 1966 .... **£5** ....

BRACEY, ISHMAN
RCA Victor Race Series Vol.1 .... 7" EP .... RCA .... RCX7167 .... 1964 .... **£4** ....

BRADFORD, PROFESSOR ALEX SINGERS
Too Close To Heaven .... 7" EP .... London .... REU1357 .... 1963 .... **£4** ....

BRADLEY, JAN
Mama Didn't Lie .... 7" .... Pye .... 7N25182 .... 1963 .... **£8** ....

BRADLEY, OWEN QUINTET
Big Guitar .... 7" .... Brunswick .... 05736 .... 1958 .... **£4** ....

BRADSHAW, TINY
Great Composer .... LP .... King .... 653 .... 1959 ...... **£20** .... US
Off And On .... LP-10" .. King .... 29574 .... **£100** .... US
Overflow .... 7" .... Parlaphone ..... MSP6145 .... 1955 .... **£8** ....
Pompton Turnpike .... 7" EP .... Parlophone ..... GEP8552 .... 1956 .... **£8** ....
Selections .... LP .... King .... 395501 .... 195- ...... **£40** .... US
Spider Web .... 7" .... Parlaphone ..... MSP6118 .... 1954 .... **£6** ....
Train Kept A Rolling .... 7" EP .... Parlophone ..... GEP8507 .... 1954 ...... **£10** ....
Twenty-Four Great Songs .... LP .... King .... 953 .... 1966 ...... **£12** .... US

BRADY, BOB & THE CONCHORDS
Everybody Goin' To A Love-In .... 7" .... Bell .... BLL1025 .... 1968 .... **£5** ....

BRAGGS, AL TNT
Al TNT Braggs .... 7" EP .... Vocalion .... VEP170163 .... 1965 ...... **£12** ....
Earthquake .... 7" .... Action .... ACT4506 .... 1968 .... **£5** ....
Earthquake .... 7" .... Action .... ACT4506 .... 1968 ...... **£12** .... demo
Earthquake .... 7" .... Vocalion .... VP9278 .... 1966 .... **£8** ....
I'm A Good Man .... 7" .... Action .... ACT4526 .... 1969 .... **£4** ....
I'm A Good Man .... 7" .... Action .... ACT4526 .... 1969 ...... **£10** .... demo

BRAIN
Nightmares In Red .... 7" .... Parlophone ..... R5595 .... 1967 ...... **£20** ....

BRAINBOX
Brainbox .... LP .... Parlophone ..... PCS7094 .... 1970 ...... **£10** ....
Down Man .... 7" .... Parlophone ..... R5775 .... 1969 .... **£8** ....
To You .... 7" .... Parlophone ..... R5842 .... 1970 .... **£5** ....

BRAINCHILD
Healing Of The Lunatic Owl .... LP .... A&M .... NL979 .... 1970 ...... **£20** ....

BRAM STOKER
Hard Rock Spectacular .... LP .... Windmill .... WMD117 .... 1972 ...... **£35** ....

BRAMLETT, DELANEY
Liverpool Lou .... 7" .... Vocalion .... VN9237 .... 1965 ...... **£12** ....

BRAND
I'm A Lover Not A Fighter .... 7" .... Piccadilly .... 7N35216 .... 1965 ...... **£25** ....

BRANDON, JOHNNY
Glendora .... 7" .... Decca .... F10778 .... 1956 .... **£4** ....
Rock A Bye Baby .... 7" .... Parlophone ..... MSP6238 .... 1956 .... **£5** ....
Shim Sham Shuffle .... 7" .... Parlophone ..... R4207 .... 1956 .... **£5** ....
Sort Of Feeling .... 7" .... Decca .... F10858 .... 1957 .... **£4** ....

BRANDON, TONY
Candy Kisses .... 7" .... MGM .... MGM1401 .... 1968 .... **£4** ....

BRANDY BOYS

Gale Winds	7"	Columbia	DB7507	1965	**£6**	

BRANTLEY, JOHNNY

Place	7"	London	HLU8606	1958	**£8**	

BRASS TACKS

I'll Keep Holding On	7"	Transatlantic	BIG110	1968	**£4**	

BRASSEUR, ANDRE

Early Birds	7"	Pye	7N25332	1965	**£5**	
Holiday	7"	CBS	202557	1967	**£5**	

BRAUTIGAN, RICHARD

Richard Brautigan is an American writer whose whimsically poetic prose-style struck something of a chord in the late sixties and early seventies. "Trout Fishing In America" is perhaps his best known book, but his reading of extracts from it failed to achieve the release on Apple that was intended.

Listening To Richard Brautigan	LP	Straight	ST424	1969	**£12**	US
Trout Fishing In America	LP	Apple	ZAPPLE03	1969	**£220**	withdrawn

BRAVE NEW WORLD

Brave New World	LP	Vertigo			**£25**	

BRAVO, CEDRIC

Merry Christmas	7"	Ska Beat	JB229	1965	**£10**	

BREAD & BEER BAND

The high value of the Bread and Beer Band's single derives from the fact that the band's pianist was one Reg Dwight (who was shortly to adopt the stage name Elton John). There is an LP by the band, but it is believed that only one copy of this exists. It came up for sale at one of the London rock auctions at the end of the eighties and fetched £1700.

Dick Barton Theme	7"	Decca	F12891	1969	**£40**	
Dick Barton Theme	7"	Decca	F13354	1973	**£10**	

BREAD, LOVE & DREAMS

Bread, Love and Dreams were a folk trio - a man and two women - whose self-composed acoustic songs are pretty enough without being particularly memorable. The group's name is a good one, however - the perfect ingredients for a happy life.

Amarylis	LP	Decca	SKL5081	1971	**£50**	
Bread, Love & Dreams	LP	Decca	SKL5008	1969	**£30**	
Strange Tale Of Captain Shannon	LP	Decca	SKL5048	1970	**£40**	
Switch Out The Sun	7"	Decca	F12958	1969	**£6**	

BREAKTHRU

Ice Cream Tree	7"	Mercury	MF1066	1968	**£8**	

BREEDLOVE, JIMMY

Over Somebody Else's Shoulder	7"	London	HLE8490	1957	**£20**	
You're Following Me	7"	Pye	7N25121	1962	**£4**	

BREMERS, BEVERLY

Get Smart Girl	7"	Wand	WN18	1972	**£8**	

BRENDA & THE TABULATIONS

Baby You're So Right For Me	7"	Direction	583678	1968	**£4**	
Dry Your Eyes	LP	Action	ACLP6003	1969	**£15**	
Dry Your Eyes	7"	London	HL10127	1967	**£8**	
That's In The Past	7"	Action	ACT4541	1969	**£4**	
That's In The Past	7"	Action	ACT4541	1969	**£15**	demo
When You're Gone	7"	London	HL10174	1967	**£6**	

BRETT, PAUL

Clocks	LP	Bradleys	BRAD1004	1974	**£10**	
Good Old Fashioned Funky Music	7"	Dawn	DNS1010	1970	**£4**	
Jubilation Foundry	LP	Dawn	DNLS3021	1971	**£12**	
Paul Brett	LP	Bradleys	BRAD1001	1973	**£10**	
Paul Brett Sage	LP	Pye	NSPL18347	1970	**£15**	
Phoenix Future	LP	Phoenix F.	PF001	1975	**£15**	
Reason For Your Askin'	7"	Dawn	DNX2508	1971	**£4**	PS
Schizophrenia	LP	Dawn	DNLS3032	1972	**£12**	

BRETT, STEVE & THE MAVERICKS

Chains On My Heart	7"	Columbia	DB7794	1965	**£50**	

Sad Lonely And Blue	7"	Columbia	DB7581	1965	**£30**	
Wishing	7"	Columbia	DB7470	1965	**£30**	

BREVETT, LLOYD

Wayward Ska	7"	Ska Beat	JB213	1965	**£10**	

BREWER & SHIPLEY

Down In L.A.	LP	A&M	SP4154	1968	**£10**	US
Tarkio Road	LP	Kama Sutra	2316001	1970	**£10**	
Weeds	LP	Kama Sutra	2361005	1969	**£10**	

BREWERS DROOP

Opening Time	LP	RCA	SF8301	1972	**£15**	

BRIDGES

Fakkeltog	LP	Vakenatt	VN01	1980	**£20**	Norwegian

BRIERLEY, MARC

Autograph Of Time	7"	CBS	3857	1968	**£6**	
Be My Brother	7"	CBS	5266	1970	**£4**	
Hello	LP	CBS	63835	1969	**£15**	
Lady Of The Light	7"	CBS	4632	1969	**£5**	
Stay A Little Longer	7"	CBS	4191	1969	**£5**	
Welcome To The Citadel	LP	CBS	63478	1967	**£20**	

BRIGGS, ANNE

Anne Briggs	LP	Topic	12TS207	1971	**£30**	
Hazards Of Love	7" EP	Topic	TOP94	1963	**£20**	
Time Has Come	LP	CBS	64612	1971	**£60**	

BRILLIANT CORNERS

My Baby's In Black	12"	SS20	SS23T	1984	**£8**	
She's Got Fever	7"	SS20	SS21	1984	**£20**	

BRILLIANT, ASHLEIGH

In The Haight-Ashbury	LP	Dorash	1001	1967	**£30**	US

BRINSLEY SCHWARZ

Brinsley Schwarz	LP	United Artists	UAS29111	1970	**£12**	
Country Girl	7"	Liberty	LBY15419	1970	**£5**	
Country Girl	7"	United Artists	UP35312	1972	**£5**	
Despite It All	LP	Liberty	LBG83427	1970	**£10**	
Everybody	7"	United Artists	UP35768	1975	**£5**	
I've Cried My Last Tear	7"	United Artists	UP35642	1974	**£5**	
Nervous On The Road	LP	United Artists	UAS29374	1972	**£10**	
New Favourites	LP	United Artists	UAS29641	1974	**£10**	
Peace, Love, And Understanding	7"	United Artists	UP35700	1974	**£5**	
Please Don't Ever Change	LP	United Artists	UAS29489	1973	**£10**	
Shining Brightly	7"	United Artists	UP35118	1970	**£5**	
Silver Pistol	LP	United Artists	UAS29217	1972	**£10**	
Speedoo	7"	United Artists	UP35588	1973	**£5**	
There's A Cloud In My Heart	7"	United Artists	UP35812	1975	**£5**	

BRISTOL, JOHNNY

Leave My World	7"	MGM	2006505	1975	**£5**	

BRITISH WALKERS

I Found You	7"	Pye	7N25298	1965	**£5**	

BRITT

Leave My Baby Alone	7"	Piccadilly	7N35273	1966	**£8**	

BRITT, ELTON

Wandering Cowboy	LP	ABC-Para.	293	1959	**£10**	US
Yodel Songs	LP	RCA	LPM1288	1956	**£15**	US
Yodel Songs	LP-10"	RCA	LPM3222	1954	**£25**	US

BRITT, TINA

Real Thing	7"	London	HLC9974	1965	**£15**	

BRITTEN, BUDDY & THE REGENTS

Don't Spread It Around	7"	Decca	F11435	1962	**£4**	

Hey There	7"	Oriole	CB1839	1963	**£5**	
I Guess I'm In The Way	7"	Oriole	CB1911	1964	**£5**	
If You've Gotta Make A Fool...	7"	Oriole	CB1827	1963	**£6**	
Money	7"	Oriole	CB1889	1963	**£6**	
My Pride And Joy	7"	Piccadilly	7N35075	1962	**£5**	
My Resistance Is Low	7"	Oriole	CB1859	1963	**£5**	
Right Now	7"	Piccadilly	7N35257	1965	**£5**	
She's About A Mover	7"	Piccadilly	7N35241	1965	**£6**	

BRITTON, CHRIS

As I Am	LP	Page One	POLS022	1969	**£40**	

BROCK, DAVE

Social Alliance	7"	Flicknife	FLS024P	1983	**£4**	pic disc

BROMLEY, JOHN

And The Feeling Goes	7"	Polydor	56287	1968	**£5**	
Hold Me Woman	7"	Polydor	56340	1969	**£4**	
Kick A Tin Can	7"	Atlantic	584289	1969	**£5**	
Melody Fayre	7"	Polydor	56305	1969	**£4**	
What A Woman Does	7"	Polydor	56244	1968	**£5**	

BRONCO

Jess Roden, former singer with Alan Bown, hit on the idea of a group that could rock hard on acoustic guitars. Live, Bronco played sitting down, which was certainly a novelty, and their records, particularly "Country Home", still have a remarkable freshness. Guitarist Robbie Blunt is also an impressive electric player, as he later proved as a member of the Robert Plant band.

Ace Of Sunlight	LP	Island	ILPS9161	1971	**£12**	
Country Home	LP	Island	ILPS9124	1970	**£15**	
Lazy Now	7"	Chrysalis	WIP6096	1971	**£4**	
Smokin' Mixture	LP	Polydor	2383215	1973	**£10**	
Traveller	7"	Polydor	2058395	1973	**£4**	

BRONSKI BEAT

Smalltown Boy	7"	Forbidden F.	BITPD1	1984	**£5**	shaped pic disc

BRONX CHEER

Barrel House Player	7"	Dawn	DNX2522	1971	**£5**	
Drive My Car	7"	Parlophone	R5865	1970	**£5**	
Greatest Hits	LP	Dawn	DNLS3034	1972	**£10**	
Hold On To Me	7"	Dawn	DNS1019	1972	**£4**	

BROOK BROTHERS

Ain't Gonna Wash For A Week	7"	Pye	7N15369	1961	**£4**	chart single
Brook Brothers	LP	Pye		1961	**£30**	
Brook Brothers	7" EP	Pye	NEP24155	1962	**£5**	
Hit Parade	7" EP	Pye	NEP24140	1961	**£5**	
Hit Parade Vol.2	7" EP	Pye	NEP24148	1961	**£5**	
Warpaint	7"	Pye	7N15333	1961	**£4**	chart single

BROOKLYN BRIDGE

Little Red Boat By The River	7"	Pye	7N25473	1968	**£4**	
Worst That Could Happen	7"	Buddah	201029	1969	**£4**	

BROOKS & JERRY

I Got What It Takes	7"	Direction	583267	1968	**£4**	

BROOKS, BABA

Baby Elephant Walk	7"	Black Swan	WI466	1965	**£10**	
Clock	7"	Doctor Bird	DB1042	1966	**£10**	
Duck Soup	7"	Island	WI235	1965	**£10**	
Eighth Games	7"	Doctor Bird	DB1043	1966	**£10**	
Faberge	7"	Doctor Bird	DB1081	1967	**£10**	
First Session	7"	Doctor Bird	DB1001	1966	**£10**	
Girls Town Ska	7"	Ska Beat	JB218	1965	**£10**	
Guns Fever	7"	Island	WI229	1965	**£10**	
Independence Ska	7"	Island	WI233	1965	**£10**	
Ki Salaboca	7"	Gayfeet	GS202	1973	**£8**	
King Size	7"	Doctor Bird	DB1009	1966	**£10**	
Let Me Go	7"	Ska Beat	JB195	1965	**£10**	
Mattie Rag	7"	Ska Beat	JB217	1965	**£10**	
One Eyed Giant	7"	Ska Beat	JB220	1965	**£10**	

Title	Format	Label	Cat. No.	Year	Price	Notes
One Eyed Giant	7"	Ska Beat	JB268	1967	**£10**	
Open The Door	7"	Doctor Bird	DB1067	1966	**£10**	
Our Man Flint	7"	High Note	HS030	196-	**£8**	
Party Time	7"	Doctor Bird	DB1064	1966	**£10**	
Roll Call	7"	Doctor Bird	DB1062	1966	**£10**	
Scratch	7"	Doctor Bird	DB1065	1966	**£10**	
Teenage Ska	7"	Island	WI241	1965	**£10**	
Virginia Ska	7"	Island	WI247	1965	**£10**	

BROOKS, CHUCK

Title	Format	Label	Cat. No.	Year	Price	Notes
Black Sheep	7"	Soul City	SC116		**£4**	
Black Sheep	7"	Soul City	SC116		**£10**	demo

BROOKS, DALE

Title	Format	Label	Cat. No.	Year	Price	Notes
I Wanna Be Your Girl	7"	Stateside	SS553	1966	**£4**	

BROOKS, DONNIE

Title	Format	Label	Cat. No.	Year	Price	Notes
Doll House	7"	London	HLN9253	1960	**£4**	
Donnie Brooks	LP	London	HAN2391	1961	**£12**	
Happiest	LP	Era	EL105	1961	**£20**	US
Mission Bell	7"	London	HLN9168	1960	**£4**	
Oh You Beautiful Doll	7"	London	HLN9572	1962	**£4**	
That's Why	7"	London	HLN9361	1961	**£4**	
All Of My Life	7"	HMV	POP1480	1965	**£8**	
Baby Let Me Love You	7"	HMV	POP1512	1966	**£8**	
Come September	7"	Nems	564136	1969	**£6**	
He's Gotta Love Me	7"	HMV	POP1431	1965	**£8**	
Nothing Left To Do But Cry	7"	Decca	F11983	1964	**£8**	
Something's Got A Hold On Me	7"	Decca	F11928	1964	**£8**	
Way You Do The Things You do	7"	Decca	F12061	1965	**£8**	

BROOKS, JOEY

Title	Format	Label	Cat. No.	Year	Price	Notes
I Ain't Blamin' You	7"	Decca	F12328	1966	**£4**	

BROOKS, NORMAN

Title	Format	Label	Cat. No.	Year	Price	Notes
Back In Circulation	7"	London	HL8115	1955	**£8**	
Hello Sunshine	7"	London	L1166	1954	**£12**	
I Can't Give You Anything But Love	7"	London	HL8041	1954	**£8**	
I'd Like To Be In Your Shoes Baby	7"	London	HL8015	1954	**£10**	
My Three D Sweetie	7"	London	HL8051	1954	**£8**	
Skyblue Shirt & A Rainbow Tie	7"	London	L1228	1954	**£10**	chart single
You Shouldn't Have Kissed Me	7"	London	L1202	1954	**£10**	

BROOKS, TONY & THE BREAKERS

Title	Format	Label	Cat. No.	Year	Price	Notes
Meanie Greenie	7"	Columbia	DB7279	1964	**£6**	

BROONZY, BIG BILL

Title	Format	Label	Cat. No.	Year	Price	Notes
Big Bill Broonzy & Washboard Sam	LP	Chess	LP1468	1962	**£20**	US
Big Bill Broonzy	7" EP	Columbia	SEG7674	1957	**£6**	
Big Bill Broonzy No.2	7" EP	Columbia	SEG7790	1958	**£6**	
Big Bill Broonzy Sings	LP-10"	Period	1114	195-	**£20**	US
Big Bill Broonzy, Sonny Terry & Brownie McGhee	LP	Folkways	FA3817	1959	**£12**	US
Big Bill's Blues	LP	Columbia	WL111	1958	**£20**	US
Bill Bailey Won't You Please Come Home	7" EP	Tempo	EXA61	195-	**£6**	
Blues Anthology Vol.3	7" EP	Storyville	SEP383		**£5**	
Blues By Broonzy	LP	EmArcy	MG26137	1957	**£20**	US
Country Blues	LP	Folkways	FA2326	195-	**£10**	US
Do You Remember...	7" EP	Emarcy	YEP9508	1959	**£6**	
Folk Blues	LP	EmArcy	MG26034	1957	**£20**	US
Guitar Shuffle	7"	Vogue	V2351	1970	**£5**	
Guitar Shuffle	7" EP	Vogue	EPV1107	195-	**£6**	
Hey Bud Blues	7" EP	Vogue	EPV1024	1955	**£6**	
His Songs And Story	LP	Folkways	FA3586	195-	**£10**	US
Hollering Blues	7" EP	Mercury	ZEP10093	1960	**£6**	
In Paris	LP	Vogue	LO60530	1956	**£20**	US
Keep Your Hands Off	7" EP	Melodisc	EPM765	195-	**£5**	
Last Session Part 1	LP	HMV	CLP1544	1961	**£12**	
Last Session Part 2	LP	HMV	CLP1551	1961	**£12**	
Last Session Part 3	LP	HMV	CLP1562	1961	**£12**	
Memorial	LP	Mercury	MG20822	1963	**£10**	US
Midnight Special	7"	Storyville	A45053	195-	**£4**	

Mississippi Blues Vol.1	7" EP	Pye	NJE1005	1956	**£6**	
Mississippi Blues Vol.2	7" EP	Pye	NJE1015	1956	**£6**	
Remembering Big Bill Broonzy	LP	Mercury	MG20905	1964	**£10**	US
South Bound Train	7"	Pye	7NJ2016	1957	**£4**	
Southern Saga	7" EP	Pye	NJE1047	1957	**£6**	
Walking Down A Lonesome Road	7" EP	Mercury	10003MCE	1964	**£5**	
Walking Down A Lonesome Road	7" EP	Mercury	ZEP10065	1960	**£6**	
When Do I Get To Be Called A Man	7"	Pye	7NJ2012	1957	**£4**	

BROONZY, BIG BILL & JOSH WHITE

Blues	7" EP	Pieces Of 8	PEP605	1961	**£5**	

BROS

Chocolate Box (Justin Strauss Mixes)	LP	CBS	XPR1457	1989	**£15**	promo
Chocolate Box	7"	CBS	ATOMB8	1989	**£5**	postcard pack
Drop The Boy (Art Mix)	12"	CBS	ATOMQT3	1988	**£20**	
Drop The Boy	7"	CBS	ATOMB3	1988	**£4**	badge pack
Drop The Boy	7"	CBS	ATOMW3	1988	**£5**	3-fold shaped disc
I Owe You Nothing (Club Mix)	12"	CBS	ATOMQT4	1988	**£15**	
I Owe You Nothing	7"	CBS	ATOM1	1987	**£6**	2 sleeves
I Owe You Nothing	7"	CBS	ATOMQ1	1987	**£10**	poster sleeve
I Owe You Nothing	12"	CBS	ATOMT1	1987	**£20**	
I Owe You Nothing	12"	CBS	XPR1358	1988	**£10**	
I Quit	7"	CBS	ATOMP5	1988	**£5**	square pic disc
Too Much (Wembley Mix)	12"	CBS	ATOMW7	1989	**£10**	
When Will I Be Famous	7"	CBS	ATOMP2	1987	**£5**	picture disc
When Will I Be Famous	7"	CBS	ATOMQ2	1987	**£12**	poster sleeve, calendar
When Will I Be Famous	12"	CBS	ATOMQT2	1987	**£12**	poster sleeve, calendar

BROTH

Broth	LP	Mercury	6338032	1970	**£20**	

BROTHER DAN ALL STARS

Another Saturday Night	7"	Trojan	TR608	1968	**£8**	
Donkey Returns	7"	Trojan	TR601	1968	**£8**	
Eastern Organ	7"	Trojan	TR602	1968	**£8**	
Hold Pon Them	7"	Trojan	TR603	1968	**£8**	
Lovely Lady	7"	Downtown	DT405	196-	**£8**	
Read Up	7"	Trojan	TR607	1968	**£8**	

BROTHERHOOD

Paper Man	7"	Philips	BF1766	1969	**£6**	

BROTHERHOOD OF BREATH

Brotherhood Of Breath was a big band formed by South African exile Chris McGregor, in which the cream of British jazz musicians (including McGregor's contingent of mixed race compatriots) could be heard playing together. The music is an exciting blend of swing and kwela and the Neon LP in particular is something of a landmark recording.

Brotherhood	LP	RCA	SF8269	1972	**£30**	
Brotherhood Of Breath	LP	Neon	NE2	1971	**£40**	
Live At Willisau	LP	Ogun	OG100	1974	**£20**	

BROTHERS

Love Story	7"	London	HLU10158	1967	**£4**	

BROTHERS TWO

Here I Am In Love Again	7"	Action	ACT4513	1968	**£4**	
Here I Am In Love Again	7"	Action	ACT4513	1968	**£15**	demo

BROTHERS WILLIAM

Honey Love	7"	Parlophone	R5293	1965	**£5**	

BROUCHARD, J.C. & BIFF BANG POW!

Someone Stole My Wheels	7"	Creation	CRE034	1985	**£8**	

BROUGHTON, EDGAR BAND

The Edgar Broughton Band were a staple feature of the open-air festivals and free concerts of 1969-70. They were supremely good at giving an audience a good time, but on record their musical limitations become rather glaringly obvious. The crowd-pleasing chant, "Out Demons Out", with which they always ended their stage act, sounds rather weak on cold vinyl, while the fusion of Captain Beefheart with the Shadows on "Apache Drop Out" sounds silly. Nevertheless, the track "Love In The Rain", on the first LP, provides for an exhilarating three minutes or so, and would do Motorhead proud.

Apache Drop Out	7"	Harvest	HAR5032	1970	**£4**	chart single
Bandages	LP	Nems	NEL6006	1975	**£12**	

Title	Format	Label	Cat. No.	Year	Price	Notes
Call Me A Liar	7"	Harvest	HAR5040	1971	**£4**	
Edgar Broughton Band	LP	Harvest	SHVL791	1971	**£15**	chart LP
Evil	7"	Harvest	HAR5001	1969	**£6**	
Gone Blue	7"	Harvest	HAR5049	1972	**£4**	
Inside Out	LP	Harvest	SHTC252	1972	**£15**	
Oora	LP	Harvest	SHVL810	1973	**£15**	
Out Demons Out	7"	Harvest	HAR5015	1970	**£4**	chart single
Sing Brother Sing	LP	Harvest	SHVL772	1970	**£15**	chart LP
Up Yours!	7"	Harvest	HAR5021	1970	**£10**	
Wasa Wasa	LP	Harvest	SHVL757	1969	**£15**	

BROWN, ARTHUR

Arthur Brown's stage act, which began with his being lowered on to the stage with his head-dress on fire, was legendary during 1967-8. His album, "The Crazy World Of Arthur Brown" (which was actually the name of his group) easily matches the visual bombast, emerging as one of the classic recordings of the period. The music is guitar-free, which is often a recipe for dullness, but Vincent Crane's organ playing is so full of imagination, and Arthur Brown's singing so powerful, that guitars are not missed. The non-album "Devil's Grip" is in the same league, although the jokey B-side, "Give Him A Flower", is a bit of a throwaway.

Title	Format	Label	Cat. No.	Year	Price	Notes
Chisholm In My Bosom	LP	Gull	GULP1023	1978	**£10**	
Crazy World Of Arthur Brown	LP	Track	613005	1968	**£15**	chart LP
Devil's Grip	7"	Track	604008	1967	**£6**	
Fire	7"	Track	604022	1968	**£4**	chart single
Nightmare	7"	Track	604026	1968	**£5**	

BROWN, ARTHUR & THE DIAMONDS

Title	Format	Label	Cat. No.	Year	Price	Notes
You Don't Know	7"	Reading R.R.	LYN770	1965	**£30**	flexi

BROWN, B. & BUSTER

Title	Format	Label	Cat. No.	Year	Price	Notes
B. & Buster Brown	7" EP	XX	MIN713		**£5**	

BROWN, BEN

Title	Format	Label	Cat. No.	Year	Price	Notes
Ask The Lonely	7"	Polydor	56198	1967	**£4**	

BROWN, BOOTS

Title	Format	Label	Cat. No.	Year	Price	Notes
Cerveza	7"	RCA	RCA1078	1958	**£4**	
Jim Twangy	7"	RCA	RCA1102	1959	**£4**	
Rock That Beat	LP	RCA	LG1000	1958	**£20**	US

BROWN, BUSTER

Title	Format	Label	Cat. No.	Year	Price	Notes
Fannie Mae	7"	Melodisc	MEL1559	1960	**£6**	
Fannie Mae	7"	Sue	WI368	1965	**£10**	
My Blue Heaven	7"	Island	WI3031	1967	**£10**	
New King Of The Blues	LP	Fire	FLP102	1960	**£75**	US
Sugar Babe	7"	Blue Horizon	573147	1969	**£12**	

BROWN, BUSTY

Title	Format	Label	Cat. No.	Year	Price	Notes
I Can't See Myself Cry	7"	Upsetter	US320	1970	**£5**	
To Love Somebody	7"	Upsetter	US308	1969	**£5**	
What A Price	7"	Upsetter	US304	1969	**£5**	

BROWN, CHARLES

Title	Format	Label	Cat. No.	Year	Price	Notes
Ballads My Way	LP	Mainstream	6035	1965	**£10**	US
Christmas Question	7"	Parlophone	R4848	1961	**£6**	
Confidential	7"	Vogue	V9065	1957	**£25**	
Driftin' Blues	LP	Score	SLP4011	1957	**£50**	US
Great Charles Brown	LP	King	878	1963	**£20**	US
Let The Good Times Roll	7"	Vogue	V9131	1959	**£25**	
Million Sellers	LP	Imperial	A9178	1961	**£35**	US
Mood Music	LP	Aladdin	809	1956	**£100**	US
Mood Music	LP-10"	Aladdin	702	1954	**£150**	US
Mood Music	LP-10"	Aladdin	702	1954	**£300**	US, red vinyl
Sings Christmas Songs	LP	King	775	1961	**£30**	US
Soothe Me	7"	Vogue	V9061	1956	**£12**	

BROWN, CLARENCE GATEMOUTH

Title	Format	Label	Cat. No.	Year	Price	Notes
Clarence Gatemouth Brown	7" EP	Vocalion	VE170161	1965	**£10**	

BROWN, DAVID

Title	Format	Label	Cat. No.	Year	Price	Notes
All My Life	7"	Island	WI3112	1967	**£8**	

BROWN, DUSTY

Title	Format	Label	Cat. No.	Year	Price	Notes
Please Don't Go	7"	Starlite	ST45058	1961	**£6**	

BROWN, FRANK

Title	Format	Label	Number	Year	Price	Notes
Some Come Some Go	7"	Island	WI3103	1967	**£8**	

BROWN, GLEN, JOE WHITE & TREVOR

Title	Format	Label	Number	Year	Price	Notes
Way Of Life	7"	Blue Cat	BS131	1968	**£10**	

BROWN, JAMES

Title	Format	Label	Number	Year	Price	Notes
Ain't It Funky	LP	Polydor	2343010	1970	**£12**	
Ain't It Funky Now	7"	Polydor	56793	1970	**£4**	
Ain't That A Groove	7"	Pye	7N25367	1966	**£5**	
Always Amazing James Brown	LP	King	LP743	1961	**£20**	US
At The Apollo	LP	London	HA8184	1964	**£20**	
At The Apollo	LP	Polydor	582703	1967	**£15**	
At The Apollo Vol.2	LP	Polydor	583729/730	1969	**£15**	
Black Caesar	LP	Polydor	2490117	1974	**£10**	
Bring It Up	7"	Pye	7N25411	1967	**£4**	
Bring It Up	7" EP	Pye	NEP44088	1967	**£6**	
Christmas Album	LP	Pye	NPL28097	1966	**£15**	
Cold Sweat	7"	Pye	7N25430	1967	**£5**	
Don't Be A Drop-Out	7"	Pye	7N25394	1966	**£4**	
Exciting James Brown	LP	King	LP780	1962	**£20**	US
Get Involved	7"	Polydor	2001190	1971	**£4**	
Get It Together	7"	Pye	7N25441	1967	**£4**	
Get On The Good Foot	LP	Polydor	2659018	1973	**£15**	double
Gettin' Down To It	LP	Polydor	583742	1970	**£12**	
Grits And Soul	LP	Philips	BL7664	1965	**£20**	
Handful Of Soul	LP	Philips	SBL7761	1967	**£15**	
Have Mercy Baby	7"	London	HL9945	1965	**£8**	
Hell	LP	Polydor	2659036	1974	**£15**	double
Hot Pants	LP	Polydor	2425086	1971	**£10**	
How Long Darling	7" EP	Pye	NEP44076	1967	**£6**	
I Can't Stand Myself	LP	Polydor	184136	1968	**£15**	
I Can't Stand Myself	7"	Polydor	56787	1970	**£4**	
I Do Just What I Want	7" EP	Ember	EP4549	1964	**£4**	
I Got A Feeling	7"	Polydor	56743	1968	**£8**	
I Got You (I Feel Good)	LP	Pye	NPL28074	1966	**£15**	
I Got You	7"	Pye	7N25350	1966	**£5**	chart single
I Got You	7" EP	Pye	NEP44059	1966	**£6**	
I'll Go Crazy	7" EP	Pye	NEP44068	1966	**£6**	
It's A Man's Man's Man's World	LP	Pye	NPL28079	1966	**£15**	
It's A Man's Man's Man's World	7"	Pye	7N25371	1966	**£5**	chart single
It's A Mother	LP	Polydor	583768	1969	**£12**	
It's A New Day	7"	Polydor	2001018	1970	**£4**	
It's Hell	7"	Polydor	2066513	1974	**£4**	
Jump Around	LP	King	LP771	1962	**£20**	US
Kansas City	7"	Pye	7N25418	1967	**£4**	
King Of Soul	LP	Polydor	184159	1969	**£12**	
Let A Man Come In	7"	Polydor	56783	1969	**£4**	
Let Yourself Go	7"	Pye	7N25423	1967	**£4**	
Licking Stick	7"	Polydor	56744	1968	**£4**	
Live At The Garden	LP	Pye	NPL28104	1967	**£12**	
Mighty Instrumentals	LP	Pye	NPL28093	1967	**£12**	
Money Won't Change You	7"	Pye	7N25379	1966	**£4**	
Mother Popcorn	7"	Polydor	56776	1969	**£4**	
Mr.Dynamite	LP	Polydor	623032	1968	**£12**	
Mr.Excitement	LP	Pye	NPL28100	1967	**£12**	
Mr.Soul	LP	Polydor	184100	1968	**£12**	
New Breed	7"	Philips	BF1481	1966	**£5**	
Night Train	7"	Parlophone	R4922	1962	**£8**	
Night Train	7"	Sue	WI360	1964	**£8**	
Out Of Sight	LP	Mercury	SMCL20133	1969	**£15**	
Out Of Sight	7"	Philips	BF1368	1964	**£5**	
Papa's Got A Brand New Bag	LP	London	HA8262	1966	**£20**	
Papa's Got A Brand New Bag	7"	London	HL9990	1965	**£5**	chart single
Papa's Got A Brand New Bag	LP	Pye	NPL28099	1967	**£15**	
Payback	LP	Polydor	2659030	1974	**£10**	
Plays New Breed	LP	Philips	BL7718	1966	**£15**	
Plays The Real Thing	LP	Philips	SBL7823	1967	**£15**	
Plays...Today & Yesterday	LP	Philips	BL7697	1966	**£15**	
Please Please Please	LP	King	395610	1959	**£50**	US
Please Please Please	LP	London	HA8231	1965	**£20**	

Title	Format	Label	Cat. No.	Year	Price	Notes
Popcorn	LP	Polydor	184319	1970	**£12**	
Prisoner Of Love	LP	King	LP851	1963	**£20**	US
Prisoner Of Love	7"	London	HL9730	1963	**£8**	
Prisoner Of Love	7" EP	London	RE1410	1964	**£8**	
Prisoner Of Love	7" EP	Pye	NEP44072	1967	**£6**	
Pure Dynamite	LP	London	HA8177	1964	**£20**	
Raw Soul	LP	Pye	NPL28103	1967	**£12**	
Revolution Of The Mind	LP	Polydor	2659011	1972	**£15**	double
Say It Loud I'm Black & I'm Proud	LP	Polydor	583741	1969	**£12**	
Say It Loud I'm Black & I'm Proud	7"	Polydor	56541	1968	**£4**	
Say It Loud I'm Black & I'm Proud	7"	Polydor	56752	1968	**£4**	
Sex Machine	LP	Polydor	2625004	1971	**£15**	double
Sex Machine	7"	Polydor	2001071	1970	**£4**	chart single
Shout And Shimmy	7"	Parlophone	R4952	1962	**£6**	
Showtime	LP	Philips	BL7630	1964	**£20**	
Slaughter's Big Rip-Off	LP	Polydor	2391084	1973	**£10**	
Soul Brother No.1	LP	Polydor	2343036	1971	**£10**	
Soul Fire	LP	Polydor	184148	1969	**£12**	
Soul Power	7"	Polydor	2001163	1971	**£4**	
Super Bad	LP	Polydor	2310089	1971	**£12**	
Super Bad	7"	Polydor	2001097	1970	**£4**	
Tell Me What You're Gonna Do	LP	Ember	EMB3357	1964	**£20**	
Tell Me What You're Gonna Do	7"	Ember	EMBS216	1965	**£6**	
That's Life	7"	Polydor	56540	1968	**£4**	
There It Is	LP	Polydor	2391033	1972	**£10**	
There Was A Time	7"	Polydor	56740	1968	**£4**	
These Foolish Things	7"	London	HL9775	1963	**£6**	
Think	LP	King	LP683	1960	**£35**	US
Think	7"	Parlophone	R4667	1960	**£10**	
This Old Heart	7"	Fontana	H273	1960	**£15**	
Tours The USA	LP	London	HA8240	1965	**£20**	
Try Me	LP	King	395635	1959	**£50**	US
Try Me	7"	Philips	BF1458	1965	**£6**	
Turn It Loose	LP	Polydor	580701	1970	**£12**	
Unbeatable...	LP	London	HA8203	1965	**£20**	
World	7"	Polydor	56780	1969	**£4**	

BROWN, JIM EDWARD & MAXINE

Title	Format	Label	Cat. No.	Year	Price	Notes
Country Songs	7" EP	London	REP1024	1955	**£6**	
Country Songs Vol.3	7" EP	London	REU1044	1955	**£6**	
Here Today And Gone Tomorrow	7"	London	HLU8200	1955	**£6**	
Itsy Witsy Bitsy Me	7"	London	HL8123	1955	**£8**	
Your Love Is Wild As The West Wind	7"	London	HLU8166	1955	**£8**	

BROWN, JOE

As the guitarist on Billy Fury's highly regarded "Sound Of Fury" album, Joe Brown had considerable credibility, yet his own records are wildly variable in quality. The problem was that Brown seemed to be determined to prove his versatility, but when this included the performance of old music hall songs and an instrumental version of "All Things Bright And Beautiful", then the effort did not seem to be particularly worthwhile. At his best, however, such as on the succession of hit singles begun with "A Picture Of You", Brown created an effective form of robust pop-country that could, perhaps, have become a significant influence if only he had developed it further.

Title	Format	Label	Cat. No.	Year	Price	Notes
All Things Bright And Beautiful	7" EP	Piccadilly	NEP34026	1962	**£4**	
Crazy Mixed-Up Kid	7"	Piccadilly	7N35000	1961	**£4**	
Darktown Strutters Ball	7"	Decca	F11207	1960	**£4**	chart single
Here Comes Joe Brown	LP	Golden Guin.	GGL0231	1962	**£10**	
Hit Parade	7" EP	Piccadilly	NEP34025	1962	**£5**	
I'm Henry The Eighth I Am	7"	Piccadilly	7N35005	1961	**£4**	
It Only Took A Minute	7"	Piccadilly	7N35082	1962	**£4**	chart single
Jellied Eels	7"	Decca	F11246	1960	**£4**	
Live	LP	Piccadilly	NPL38006	1963	**£12**	chart LP
Nature's Time For Love	7"	Piccadilly	7N35129	1963	**£4**	chart single
People Gotta Talk	7"	Decca	F11185	1959	**£4**	
Picture Of Joe Brown	7" EP	Decca	DFE8500	1962	**£5**	
Picture Of You	LP	Ace Of Clubs	ACL1127	1962	**£10**	
Picture Of You	LP	Golden Guin.	GGL0146	1962	**£10**	chart LP
Picture Of You	7"	Piccadilly	7N35047	1962	**£4**	chart single
Sally Ann	7"	Piccadilly	7N35138	1963	**£4**	chart single
Shine	7"	Pye	7N15322	1960	**£4**	chart single
That's What Love Will Do	7"	Piccadilly	7N35106	1963	**£4**	chart single
What A Crazy World	7"	Piccadilly	7N35024	1962	**£4**	chart single
Your Tender Look	7"	Piccadilly	7N35058	1962	**£4**	chart single

BROWN, JOE & MARK WYNTER

Title	Format	Label	Cat. No.	Year	Price	
Big Hits	7" EP	Golden Guin.	WO1	1962	**£4**	
Joe Brown Mark Wynter	LP	Golden Guin.	GGL0179	1962	**£10**	

BROWN, KENT & THE RAINBOWS

Title	Format	Label	Cat. No.	Year	Price	
Come Ya Come Ya	7"	Fab	FAB53	196-	**£8**	

BROWN, MARK

Title	Format	Label	Cat. No.	Year	Price	
Brown Low Special	7"	Island	WI3097	1967	**£8**	

BROWN, MAXINE

Title	Format	Label	Cat. No.	Year	Price	
All In My Mind	7"	London	HLU9286	1961	**£5**	
Fabulous Sound Of...	LP	Wand	WD656	1963	**£12**	US
Greatest Hits	LP	Wand	WD684	1967	**£10**	US
I've Got A Lot Of Love Left In Me	7"	Pye	7N25410	1967	**£4**	
It's Gonna Be Alright	7"	Pye	7N25299	1965	**£8**	
Oh No Not My Baby	7"	Pye	7N25272	1964	**£6**	
One Step At A Time	7"	Pye	7N25317	1965	**£5**	
Promise Me Anything	7"	HMV	POP1102	1962	**£4**	
Since I Found You	7"	Pye	7N25434	1967	**£4**	
Spotlight On...	LP	Wand	WD663	1965	**£10**	US

BROWN, NAPPY

Title	Format	Label	Cat. No.	Year	Price	
Don't Be Angry	7"	London	HL8145	1955	**£30**	
It Don't Hurt No More	7"	London	HLC8760	1958	**£15**	
Little By Little	7"	London	HLC8384	1957	**£25**	
Nappy Brown Sings	LP	Savoy	MG14002	1958	**£40**	US
Pitter Patter	7"	London	HLC8182	1955	**£40**	
Right Time	LP	Savoy	MG14025	1960	**£35**	US

BROWN, NOEL

Title	Format	Label	Cat. No.	Year	Price	
Man's Temptation	7"	Island	WI3149	1968	**£8**	
Phoenix	7"	Songbird	SB1012	196-	**£8**	

BROWN, PETE

Pete Brown was one of the first poets to attempt to make a living by giving performances of his work, but achieved his greatest success as lyricist for Cream and for Jack Bruce solo. His own rock groups - Battered Ornaments and Piblokto - were interesting and featured strong contributions from musicians with their feet in both the jazz and rock camps, such as Chris Spedding, Jim Mullen, and George Khan. They were ultimately handicapped, however, by their vocalist's (Brown himself) inability to sing.

Title	Format	Label	Cat. No.	Year	Price	
Art School Dance...	LP	Harvest	SHVL768	1970	**£40**	
Can't Get Off The Planet	7"	Harvest	HAR5023	1970	**£10**	
Flying Hero Sandwich	7"	Harvest	HAR5028	1970	**£10**	
Living Life Backwards	7"	Harvest	HAR5008	1970	**£10**	
Meal You Can Shake Hands With	LP	Harvest	SHVL752	1969	**£45**	
My Last Band	LP	Harvest	SHSM2017	1977	**£20**	
Not Forgotten Association	LP	Deram	SML1103	1973	**£40**	
Thousands On A Raft	LP	Harvest	SHVL782	1970	**£40**	
Week Looked Good On Paper	7"	Parlophone	R5767	1969	**£15**	

BROWN, ROY

Title	Format	Label	Cat. No.	Year	Price	
Party Doll	7"	London	HLP8398	1957	**£60**	
Saturday Night	7"	London	HLP8448	1957	**£80**	
Sings 24 Hits	LP	King	956	1966	**£20**	US

BROWN, ROY & WYNONIE HARRIS

Title	Format	Label	Cat. No.	Year	Price	
Battle Of The Blues Vol.1	LP	King	607	1958	**£150**	US
Battle Of The Blues Vol.2	LP	King	627	1959	**£150**	US

BROWN, ROY / WYNONIE HARRIS & EDDIE VINSON

Title	Format	Label	Cat. No.	Year	Price	
Battle Of The Blues Vol.4	LP	King	668	1960	**£300**	US

BROWN, RUTH

Title	Format	Label	Cat. No.	Year	Price	
Along Comes Ruth	LP	Philips	652012BL	1962	**£15**	
As Long As I'm Moving	7"	London	HLE8210	1955	**£30**	
Best Of..	LP	Atlantic	ATL5007	1964	**£12**	
Don't Deceive Me	7"	London	HLE9093	1960	**£10**	
Gospel Time	LP	Philips	652020BL	1963	**£15**	
Gospel Time	7" EP	Philips	BE12537	1963	**£10**	
I Don't Know	7"	London	HLE8946	1959	**£12**	
I Want To Do More	7"	London	HLE8310	1956	**£30**	
Jack Of Diamonds	7"	London	HLE8887	1959	**£12**	

Just Too Much	7"	London	HLE8645	1958	**£12**	
Late Date	LP	Atlantic	1308	1959	**£35**	US
Lucky Lips	7"	Columbia	DB3913	1957	**£20**	
Mambo Baby	7"	London	HL8153	1955	**£30**	
Miss Rhythm	LP	Atlantic	8026	1959	**£35**	US
Mom Oh Mom	7"	London	HLE8401	1957	**£20**	
New Love	7"	London	HLE8552	1958	**£12**	
One More Time	7"	London	HLE8483	1957	**£15**	
Queen Of R&B	7" EP	London	REE1038	1955	**£20**	
Ruth Brown '65	LP	Mainstream	16044	1965	**£10**	US
Ruth Brown	LP	Atlantic	8004	1957	**£40**	US
Ruth Brown Sings	LP-10"	Atlantic	115	1956	**£600**	US
Sure Nuff	7"	London	HLK9304	1961	**£10**	
This Little Girl's Gone Rocking	7"	London	HLE8757	1958	**£15**	
Yes Sir That's My Baby	7"	Brunswick	05904	1964	**£6**	

BROWN, RUTH & JOE TURNER

King And Queen Of R&B	7" EP	London	REE1047	1956	**£20**	

BROWNE, DUNCAN

Duncan Browne	LP	Rak	SRKA6754	1973	**£15**	
Give Me Take You	LP	Immediate	IMSP018	1968	**£25**	
Journey	7"	RAK	RAK135	1972	**£4**	chart single
On The Bombsite	7"	Immediate	IM070	1968	**£8**	
Wild Places	7"	Logo	GO329	1978	**£4**	pic disc

BROWNE, FRIDAY

Getting Nowhere	7"	Parlophone	R5396	1966	**£4**	

BROWNE, JACKSON

Late For The Sky	LP	Asylum	K243007	1974	**£15**	quad
Pretender	LP	Mobile Fid.	MFSL1055	1981	**£15**	US audiophile

BROWNE, SANDRA

Johnny Boy	7"	Columbia	DB4998	1963	**£4**	
Knock On Any Door	7"	Columbia	DB7465	1965	**£5**	

BROWNE, THOMAS F.

Tuesday's Child	LP	Vertigo	6343700	1972	**£20**	spiral label

BROWNE, WATSON T.

Some Lovin'	7"	President	PT207	1968	**£4**	

BROWNHILL'S STAMP DUTY

Maxwell's Silver Hammer	7"	Columbia	DB8625	1969	**£5**	

BROWNS

In The Country	7" EP	RCA	RCX187	1960	**£5**	
Sweet Sounds By The Browns	LP	RCA	LPM2144	1959	**£10**	US
Three Bells	7"	RCA	RCA1140	1959	**£4**	chart single

BROX, VICTOR & ANNETTE

Rollin' Back	LP	Sonet	SNTF663	1974	**£15**	

BROX, VICTOR & ANNETTE REIS

Wake Me And Shake Me	7"	Fontana	TF536	1965	**£6**	

BRUCE, JACK

Consul At Sunset	7"	Polydor	2058153	1971	**£4**	
Harmony Row	LP	Polydor	2310107	1971	**£10**	
I'm Gettin' Tired	7"	Polydor	56036	1965	**£20**	
Keep It Down	7"	RSO	2090141	1974	**£4**	
Out Of The Storm	LP	Polydor	2394143	1974	**£10**	
Songs For A Tailor	LP	Polydor	583058	1969	**£10**	chart single
Things We Like	LP	Polydor	2343033	1970	**£12**	

BRUCE, LENNY

Berkeley Concert	LP	Transatlantic	TRA195	1969	**£25**	double
Best Of	LP	Fantasy	7012	1962	**£10**	US
Essential Lenny Bruce	LP	Douglas	SD788	1968	**£10**	US
I Am Not A Nut, Elect Me	LP	Fantasy	7007	1960	**£10**	US
Interviews Of Our Times	LP	Fantasy	7001	1959	**£10**	US

Title	Format	Label	Cat. No.	Year	Price	Notes
Lenny Bruce	LP	United Artists	UAL3580	1967	**£10**	US
Lenny Bruce Is Out Again	LP	Philles	PHLP4010	1966	**£12**	US
Lenny Bruce, American	LP	Fantasy	7011	1962	**£10**	US
Live At The Curran Theatre	LP	Fantasy	34201	1972	**£10**	US
Midnight Concert	LP	United Artists	UAS6794	197-	**£10**	US
Sick Humor Of Lenny Bruce	LP	Fantasy	7003	1959	**£10**	US
Thank You, Masked Man	LP	Fantasy	7017	1972	**£10**	US

BRUCE, TOMMY

Title	Format	Label	Cat. No.	Year	Price	Notes
Ain't Misbehaving	7"	Columbia	DB4453	1960	**£4**	chart single
Boom Boom	7"	Polydor	56006	1965	**£4**	
Broken Doll	7"	Columbia	DB4498	1960	**£4**	chart single
Knockout	7" EP	Columbia	SEG8077	1961	**£6**	

BRUISERS

Title	Format	Label	Cat. No.	Year	Price	Notes
Blue Girl	7"	Parlophone	R5042	1963	**£4**	chart single
Your Turn To Cry	7"	Parlophone	R5092	1963	**£4**	

BRUMBEATS

Title	Format	Label	Cat. No.	Year	Price	Notes
Cry Little Girl, Cry	7"	Decca	F11834	1964	**£8**	

BRUMMELL, BEAU

Title	Format	Label	Cat. No.	Year	Price	Notes
Better Man Than I	7"	Columbia	DB7675	1965	**£8**	
I Know Know Know	7"	Columbia	DB7447	1965	**£8**	
Next Kiss	7"	Columbia	DB7538	1965	**£8**	
Take Me Like I Am	7"	Columbia	DB7878	1966	**£5**	

BRUNNING HALL SUNFLOWER BLUES BAND

Saga was a bargain-priced label, specialising in cheaply produced cash-ins of BAND the prevailing trends. The Brunning Hall Band was Saga's blues band, and by having their records released on the label, the group was fighting a losing battle from the outset with regard to being taken as serious rivals for the likes of Fleetwood Mac or Savoy Brown. In fact, Bob Brunning had been the original bass player with Fleetwood Mac (and plays on one track on the group's debut LP), while Bob Hall played piano on all Savoy Brown's early records, albeit without ever being counted as a member of the group.

Title	Format	Label	Cat. No.	Year	Price	Notes
Bullen Street Blues	LP	Saga	FID2118	1968	**£15**	
Sunflower Blues Band	LP	Gemini	GM2010	1969	**£15**	
Trackside Blues	LP	Saga	EROS8132	1969	**£25**	

BRUTE FORCE

Title	Format	Label	Cat. No.	Year	Price	Notes
King Of Fuh	7"	Apple	8	1969	**£200**	

BRYAN & THE BRUNELLES

Title	Format	Label	Cat. No.	Year	Price	Notes
Jacqueline	7"	HMV	POP1394	1965	**£6**	

BRYAN, CANNONBALL

Title	Format	Label	Cat. No.	Year	Price	Notes
Man About The Town	7"	Amalgam.	AMG829	196-	**£10**	
Red Ash	7"	Trojan	TR673	1969	**£6**	

BRYAN, DORA

Title	Format	Label	Cat. No.	Year	Price	Notes
All I Want For Christmas Is A Beatle	7"	Fontana	TF427	1963	**£4**	chart single

BRYAN, WES

Title	Format	Label	Cat. No.	Year	Price	Notes
Honey Baby	7"	London	HLU8978	1959	**£12**	
Lonesome Lover	7"	London	HLU8607	1958	**£6**	

BRYANT, ANITA

Title	Format	Label	Cat. No.	Year	Price	Notes
My Little Corner Of The World	7"	London	HLL9171	1960	**£4**	chart single
Paper Roses	7"	London	HLL9144	1960	**£4**	chart single

BRYANT, DENIS

Title	Format	Label	Cat. No.	Year	Price	Notes
Soul Man	7"	Discreet	K19204	1975	**£4**	

BRYANT, SANDRA

Title	Format	Label	Cat. No.	Year	Price	Notes
Girl With Money	7"	Major Minor	MM523	1967	**£4**	
Out To Get You	7"	Major Minor	MM553	1968	**£8**	

BRYARS, GAVIN

Title	Format	Label	Cat. No.	Year	Price	Notes
Sinking Of The Titanic	7"	Island	OBSCU1	1975	**£4**	

BRYDEN, BERYL

Title	Format	Label	Cat. No.	Year	Price	Notes
Casey Jones	7"	Decca	F10823	1956	**£4**	
I'm Movin' On	7"	Columbia	DB4860	1962	**£4**	
I've Been Living With The Blues	7"	Columbia	DB7010	1963	**£4**	

BUBBLE PUPPY

Title	Format	Label	Cat. No.	Year	Price	Notes
Gathering Of Promises	LP	Int. Artists	IALP10	1969	**£30**	US

BUBBLEGUM

Title	Format	Label	Cat. No.	Year	Price	Notes
Little Red Bucket	7"	Philips	BF1677	1968	**£5**	

BUCKINGHAM-NICKS

Lindsey Buckingham and Stevie Nicks achieved little success with their LP, yet its sound is almost exactly that of the LPs "Fleetwood Mac" and "Rumours", with which the Buckingham-Nicks team managed so spectacularly to restore Fleetwood Mac's fortunes. The earlier LP was reissued in 1981, when it might have been expected to do very well, and yet once again the record sank without a trace.

Title	Format	Label	Cat. No.	Year	Price	Notes
Buckingham-Nicks	LP	Polydor	2391093	1973	**£30**	
Buckingham-Nicks	LP	Polydor	2482378	1981	**£15**	
Don't Let Me Down Again	7"	Polydor	2066398	1974	**£6**	
Don't Let Me Down Again	7"	Polydor	2066700	1976	**£4**	

BUCKINGHAMS

Title	Format	Label	Cat. No.	Year	Price	Notes
Back In Love Again	7"	CBS	3559	1968	**£4**	
Don't You Care	7"	CBS	2640	1968	**£6**	
Hey Baby	7"	CBS	2995	1967	**£4**	
I Call Your Name	7"	Stateside	SS529	1966	**£4**	
I'll Never Hurt You No More	7"	Pye	7N15848	1965	**£6**	
In One Ear And Gone Tomorrow	LP	Columbia	CS9703	1968	**£10**	US
Kind Of A Drag	7"	Stateside	SS588	1967	**£4**	
Kind Of A Drag	LP	USA	107	1967	**£12**	US
Kind Of A Drag	LP	USA	107	1967	**£20**	US, with 'I'm A Man'
Making Up And Breaking Up	7"	Stateside	SS2011	1967	**£4**	
Mercy Mercy Mercy	7"	CBS	2859	1967	**£5**	
Portraits	LP	Columbia	CL2798	1968	**£10**	US
Susan	7"	CBS	3195	1967	**£4**	
Time And Charges	LP	Columbia	CL2669	1967	**£10**	US
To Be Or Not To Be	7"	Pye	7N15921	1965	**£6**	

BUCKLEY, SEAN & THE BREADCRUMBS

Title	Format	Label	Cat. No.	Year	Price	Notes
It Hurts Me When I Cry	7"	Stateside	SS421	1965	**£4**	

BUCKLEY, TIM

Title	Format	Label	Cat. No.	Year	Price	Notes
Aren't You The Girl	7"	Elektra	EKSN45008	1967	**£5**	
Blue Afternoon	LP	Straight	STS1060	1969	**£25**	
Goodbye And Hello	LP	Elektra	EKL318	1967	**£12**	
Happy Sad	LP	Elektra	EKS74045	1968	**£12**	
Happy Time	7"	Straight	4799	1970	**£4**	
Lorca	LP	Elektra	2410005	1970	**£12**	
Morning Glory	7"	Elektra	EKSN45018	1967	**£5**	
Once I Was	7"	Elektra	EKSN45023	1968	**£5**	
Pleasant Street	7"	Elektra	EKSN45041	1968	**£5**	
Starsailor	LP	Straight	STS1064	1970	**£12**	
Tim Buckley	LP	Elektra	EKL4004	1966	**£15**	
Wings	7"	Elektra	EKSN45031	1968	**£5**	

BUDD, ROY

Title	Format	Label	Cat. No.	Year	Price	Notes
Birth Of The Budd	7"	Pye	7N15807	1965	**£4**	

BUDGIE

Title	Format	Label	Cat. No.	Year	Price	Notes
Bandolier	LP	MCA	MCF2723	1975	**£10**	chart LP
Bored With Russia	7"	RCA	RCAP271	1982	**£4**	pic disc
Budgie	LP	MCA	MKPS2018	1971	**£25**	
Crash Course In Brain Surgery	7"	MCA	MK5072	1971	**£4**	
I Ain't No Mountain	7"	MCA	MCA175	1975	**£4**	
If I Was Britannia...	LP	A&M	AMLH68377	1976	**£10**	
Impeckable	LP	A&M	AMLH64675	1978	**£10**	
In For The Kill	LP	MCA	MCF2546	1974	**£10**	chart LP
Keeping A Rendezvous	7"	RCA	BUDGE3	1981	**£4**	pic disc
Squawk	LP	MCA	MKPS2023	1972	**£15**	
Whisky River	7"	MCA	MK5085	1972	**£4**	
Zoom Club	7"	MCA	MCA133	1974	**£4**	

BUENA VISTAS

Title	Format	Label	Cat. No.	Year	Price	Notes
Hot Shot	7"	Stateside	SS525	1966	**£12**	

BUFFALO

Title	Format	Label	Cat. No.	Year	Price	Notes
Dead Forever	LP	Vertigo		1974	**£60**	
Mother's Choice	LP	Vertigo		197-	**£60**	
Only Want You For Your Body	LP			197-	**£60**	
Volcanic Rock	LP			197-	**£60**	

BUFFALO SPRINGFIELD

Title	Format	Label	Cat. No.	Year	Price	Notes
Beginning	LP	Atlantic	K30028	1973	**£10**	
Best Of/Retrospective	LP	Atlantic	K40071	1972	**£10**	
Bluebird	7"	Atlantic	K10237	1972	**£4**	PS
Buffalo Springfield	LP	Atlantic	587070	1967	**£25**	
Buffalo Springfield	LP	Atlantic	587070	1967	**£40**	with 'Baby Don't Scold Me'
Buffalo Springfield	LP	Atlantic	K70001	1973	**£15**	double
Buffalo Springfield Again	LP	Atlantic	587091	1968	**£15**	
Expecting To Fly	LP	Atlantic	2462012	1970	**£10**	
Expecting To Fly	7"	Atlantic	584165	1968	**£5**	
For What It's Worth	7"	Atlantic	584077	1967	**£5**	
Last Time Around	LP	Atlantic	K40077	1971	**£20**	
Pretty Girl Why	7"	Atco	226006	1969	**£5**	
Rock'n'Roll Woman	7"	Atlantic	584145	1967	**£5**	
Uno Mundo	7"	Atlantic	584189	1968	**£5**	

BUFFOONS

Title	Format	Label	Cat. No.	Year	Price	Notes
My World Fell Down	7"	Columbia	DB8317	1967	**£6**	

BUGGLES

Title	Format	Label	Cat. No.	Year	Price	Notes
Age Of Plastic	LP	Island	RSS18	1980	**£10**	1 sided promo

BULL, SANDY

Like a one-man Incredible String Band, Sandy Bull gathers together an impressive collection of exotic instruments for his records. He then proceeds, however, to make some rather prosaic music with them - very simple and very long blues-based instrumentals. They are pleasant enough, but the lack of imagination displayed, given the potential of the resources, is frustrating.

Title	Format	Label	Cat. No.	Year	Price	Notes
E Pluribus Unum	LP	Vanguard	VSD6513	1969	**£10**	
Inventions	LP	Vanguard	VSD79191	1965	**£12**	US

BULLDOG BREED

Title	Format	Label	Cat. No.	Year	Price	Notes
Made In England	LP	Nova	SDN5	1970	**£25**	
Portcullis Gate	7"	Deram	DM270	1969	**£20**	

BULLDOGS

Title	Format	Label	Cat. No.	Year	Price	Notes
John, Paul, George, and Ringo	7"	Mercury	MF808	1964	**£8**	

BULLET

Title	Format	Label	Cat. No.	Year	Price	Notes
Hobo	7"	Purple	PUR101	1971	**£4**	

BUMBLE, B. & THE STINGERS

Title	Format	Label	Cat. No.	Year	Price	Notes
Apple Knocker	7"	Stateside	SS113	1962	**£4**	
Baby Mash	7"	Stateside	SS192	1963	**£4**	
Bumble Boogie	7"	Top Rank	JAR561	1961	**£4**	
Dawn Cracker	7"	Stateside	SS131	1962	**£4**	
Nut Rocker	7"	Top Rank	JAR611	1962	**£4**	chart single
Piano Stylings Of B.Bumble	7" EP	Stateside	SE1001	1962	**£8**	
Silent Movies	7"	Mercury	MF977	1967	**£5**	

BUNCH

The Bunch was not a real group as such, but rather members and friends of Fairport Convention on holiday. "Rock On" contains their versions of a number of rock'n'roll classics - and it has to be admitted that once the novelty of hearing these particular musicians tackling this kind of material has worn off, the results are not especially impressive.

Title	Format	Label	Cat. No.	Year	Price	Notes
Rock On	LP	Island	ILPS9189	1972	**£15**	with flexi
When Will I Be Loved	7"	Island	WIP6130	1972	**£4**	

BUNCH OF FIVES

Title	Format	Label	Cat. No.	Year	Price	Notes
Go Home Baby	7"	Parlophone	R5494	1966	**£10**	

BUNN, ROGER

Title	Format	Label	Cat. No.	Year	Price	Notes
Piece Of Mind	LP	Major Minor	SMLP70	1971	**£15**	

BUNNIES

Title	Format	Label	Cat. No.	Year	Price	Notes
Thumper	7"	Decca	F12350	1966	**£6**	

BUNNY & RUDDY

On The Town	7"	New Beat	NB011	1968	**£8**	
Rhythm And Soul	7"	New Beat	NB007	1968	**£8**	

BUNTING, BOB

You've Got To Go Down This Way	LP	Transatlantic	TRA166	1968	**£40**	

BUNYAN, VASHTI

Diamond Day	LP	Philips		1971	**£70**	

BURDON, ERIC

Guilty	LP	United Artists	UAG29251	1971	**£12**	
Stop	LP	Capitol	EST11426	1975	**£10**	
Sun Secrets	LP	Capitol	EST11359	1974	**£10**	

BURDON, ERIC & THE ANIMALS

Best Of The Animals	LP	MGM	SE4324	1966	**£15**	US
Best Of The Animals Vol.2	LP	MGM	SE4454	1967	**£15**	US
Eric Is Here	LP	MGM	SE4433	1967	**£20**	US
Everyone Of Us	LP	MGM	SE4553	1968	**£15**	US
Good Times	7"	MGM	MGM1344	1967	**£4**	chart single
Love Is	LP	MGM	CS8104	1968	**£12**	
Love Is	LP	MGM	SE4591/2	1968	**£20**	US double
Monterey	7"	MGM	MGM1412	1968	**£4**	
Ring Of Fire	7"	MGM	MGM1461	1969	**£4**	chart single
River Deep Mountain High	7"	MGM	MGM1481	1969	**£4**	
San Franciscan Nights	7"	MGM	MGM1359	1967	**£4**	chart single
Sky Pilot	7"	MGM	MGM1373	1968	**£4**	chart single
Twain Shall Meet	LP	MGM	CS8074	1968	**£15**	
When I Was Young	7"	MGM	MGM1340	1967	**£4**	chart single
Wind Of Change	LP	MGM	CS8052	1967	**£15**	

BURGESS, DAVE

I Love Paris	7"	London	HLB8175	1955	**£8**	

BURGESS, SONNY

Sadie's Back In Town	7"	London	HLS9064	1960	**£25**	

BURKE, SOLOMON

Baby Come On Home	7"	Atlantic	AT4073	1966	**£5**	
Best Of	LP	Atlantic	587016	1966	**£10**	
Can't Nobody Love You	7"	London	HLK9763	1963	**£5**	
Cry To Me	7"	London	HLK9512	1962	**£5**	
Down In The Valley	7"	London	HLK9560	1962	**£5**	
Everybody Needs Somebody To Love	7"	Atlantic	AT4004	1964	**£6**	
Get Out Of My Mind	7"	Atlantic	AT4022	1965	**£5**	
Greatest	LP	London	HAK8018	1963	**£15**	
He'll Have To Go	7"	London	HLK9849	1964	**£5**	
I Feel A Sin Comin' On	7"	Atlantic	584005	1966	**£4**	
I Wish I Knew	LP	Atlantic	587117	1968	**£10**	
I Wish I Knew	7"	Atlantic	584191	1968	**£4**	
If You Need Me	7"	London	HLK9715	1963	**£5**	
Just Out Of Reach	7"	London	HLK9454	1961	**£10**	
Keep A Light In The Window	7"	Atlantic	584100	1967	**£4**	
Keep Lookin'	7"	Atlantic	584026	1966	**£4**	
King Of Rock'n'Soul	LP	Atlantic	590004	1966	**£15**	
King Solomon	LP	Atlantic	587105	1968	**£10**	
Maggie's Farm	7"	Atlantic	AT4030	1965	**£5**	
More Rocking Soul	7"	Atlantic	AT4014	1964	**£6**	
Only Love	7"	Atlantic	AT4061	1965	**£5**	
Proud Mary	LP	Bell	SBLL118	1969	**£10**	
Proud Mary	7"	Bell	BLL1062	1969	**£4**	
Rock'n'Soul	7" EP	Atlantic	AET6008	1965	**£6**	
Rock'n'Soul	LP	Atlantic	ATL5009	1964	**£15**	
Save It	7"	Atlantic	584204	1968	**£4**	
Solomon Burke	LP	Apollo	ALP498	1962	**£35**	US
Someone Is Watching	7"	Atlantic	AT4044	1965	**£6**	
Someone To Love	7"	London	HLK9887	1964	**£5**	
Take Me	7"	Atlantic	584122	1967	**£4**	
Tonight My Heart She Is Crying	7" EP	London	REK1379	1963	**£8**	
Uptight Good Woman	7"	Bell	BLL1047	1968	**£4**	

BURKE, SONNY

Title	Format	Label	Number	Year	Price	Notes
All You	7"	Instant	IN3	1969	**£4**	
Auntie Mame Theme	7"	Brunswick	05781	1959	**£4**	
Blue Island	7"	Blue Beat	BB363	1965	**£10**	
Choo Choo Train	7"	Island	WI3082	1967	**£8**	
Dance With Me	7"	Black Swan	WI470	1965	**£10**	
Glad	7"	Black Swan	WI469	1965	**£10**	
Grandpa	7"	Island	WI221	1965	**£10**	
Have Faith	7"	Ska Beat	JB272	1967	**£10**	
Life Without Fun	7"	Island	WI134	1963	**£10**	
Phffft Mambo	7"	Brunswick	05361	1955	**£4**	
Pride And The Passion	7"	Brunswick	05706	1957	**£4**	
Rudy Girl	7"	Island	WI3040	1967	**£8**	
Sounds Of Sonny Burke	LP	Island	ILP972	1968	**£30**	
Wicked People	7"	Black Swan	WI471	1965	**£10**	
You Rule My Heart	7"	Island	WI3022	1966	**£8**	

BURNEL, J.J.

Title	Format	Label	Number	Year	Price	Notes
Freddie Laker	7"	United Artists	UP36500	1979	**£5**	
Girl From The Snow Country	7"	United Artists	BP361	1980	**£150**	

BURNETTE, DORSEY

Title	Format	Label	Number	Year	Price	Notes
Dorsey Burnette	LP	London	HAD8050	1963	**£15**	
Dorsey Burnette Sings	7" EP	London	RED1402	1963	**£8**	
Greatest Hits	LP	Era	ES800	1969	**£10**	US
Greatest Love	7"	Liberty	LIB15190	1969	**£6**	
Hey Little One	7"	London	HLN9160	1960	**£4**	
It's No Sin	7"	London	HLN9365	1961	**£4**	
Jimmy Brown	7"	T. Motown	TMG534	1965	**£25**	
Jimmy Brown	7"	T. Motown	TMG534	1965	**£60**	demo
Tall Oak Tree	LP	Era	EL102	1960	**£75**	US
Tall Oak Tree	7"	London	HLN9047	1960	**£4**	

BURNETTE, JOHNNY

Johnny Burnette's original rock'n'roll trio played rockabilly to rival that of Elvis Presley's. Like Presley, however, Burnette rapidly descended into trite pop music - there is simply no comparison between "You're Sixteen" and "Train Kept A-Rollin'". Not for nothing has the latter song inspired furious cover versions by the Yardbirds and Motorhead.

Title	Format	Label	Number	Year	Price	Notes
10th Anniversary Album	LP	United Artists	UAS29643	1974	**£10**	
All Week Long	7"	Capitol	CL15322	1963	**£4**	
Big Big World	7" EP	London	REG1309	1961	**£8**	
Clown Shoes	7"	Liberty	LIB55416	1962	**£4**	chart single
Damn The Defiant	7"	Liberty	LIB55489	1962	**£4**	
Dreamin'	7"	Liberty	LIB10235	1966	**£4**	
Dreamin'	LP	London	HAG2306	1961	**£20**	
Dreamin'	7"	London	HLG9172	1960	**£4**	chart single
Dreamin'	7" EP	London	REG1263	1960	**£8**	
Eager Beaver Baby	7"	Vogue Coral	Q72283	1957	**£100**	
Fool	7"	London	HLG9473	1961	**£4**	
Four By Johnny Burnette	7" EP	Capitol	EAP120645	1964	**£6**	
Girls	7"	London	HLG9388	1961	**£4**	chart single
God,Country And My Baby	7"	London	HLG9453	1961	**£4**	
Hit After Hit	7" EP	Liberty	LEP2091	1963	**£6**	
Hits And Other Favourites	LP	Liberty	LBY1006	1961	**£20**	
I Wanna Thank Your Folks	7"	Pye	7N25158	1962	**£4**	
I'm The One Who Loves You	7"	Pye	7N25187	1963	**£4**	
Johnny Burnette	7" EP	London	REG1327	1961	**£8**	
Johnny Burnette Sings	LP	London	HAG2375	1961	**£20**	
Johnny Burnette Sings	LP	London	SHAG6175	1961	**£20**	
Johnny Burnette Story	LP	Liberty	LRP3389	1964	**£20**	US
Johnny Burnette/You're 16	LP	London	HAG2349	1961	**£20**	
Little Boy Sad	7"	London	HLG9315	1961	**£4**	chart single
Little Boy Sad	7" EP	London	REG1291	1961	**£8**	
Lonesome Train	7"	Vogue Coral	Q72227	1957	**£100**	
Rock'n'Roll Trio	LP	Ace Of H.	AH120	1966	**£15**	
Rock'n'Roll Trio	LP	Coral	CP61	1971	**£12**	
Rock'n'Roll Trio	LP	Coral	CRL57080	1956	**£600**	US
Rock'n'Roll Trio	LP-10"	Coral	LVC10041	1956	**£200**	
Roses Are Red	LP	Liberty	LRP3255	1962	**£20**	US
Setting The Woods On Fire	7"	London	HLG9458	1961	**£4**	
Tear It Up	LP	Coral	CP15	1969	**£12**	
Tear It Up	7"	Vogue Coral	Q72177	1956	**£100**	

Walking Talking Doll	7"	Capitol	CL15347	1964	**£4**	
You're Sixteen	7"	London	HLG9254	1960	**£4**	chart single

BURNETTE, JOHNNY & DORSEY

Hey Sue	7"	Reprise	R20153	1963	**£15**	

BURNETTE, SMILEY

Chugging On Down Sixty-Six	7"	London	HL8085	1954	**£20**	
Lazy Locomotive	7"	London	HL8071	1954	**£20**	

BURNIN' RED IVANHOE

Burnin' Red Ivanhoe	LP	W. Bros	K44062	1970	**£10**	
WWW	LP	Dandelion	2310145	1971	**£10**	

BURNS, RANDY

Evening Of The Magician	LP	Fontana		1968	**£10**	

BURNS, RAY

Ray Burns	7" EP	Columbia	SEG7594	1956	**£6**	

BURNT SUITE

Burnt Suite	LP	B.J.W.	9	1967	**£40**	US

BURRAGE, HAROLD

I'll Take One	7"	Sue	WI353	1965	**£8**	
You Made Me So Happy	7"	President	PT130	1968	**£4**	

BURROUGHS, WILLIAM

Call Me Burroughs	LP	ESP	1050	196-	**£20**	US

BURTON, JAMES

James Burton's legendary reputation as an ace guitarist is entirely justified by his playing on record. Largely content to work for others - most notably Rick Nelson and Elvis Presley - his two solo LPs are quite scarce (and undervalued).

Corn Pickin' And Slick Slidin'	LP	Capitol	ST2822	1968	**£20**	US
Guitar Sounds Of...	LP	A&M	AMLS64293	1971	**£20**	

BURTON, TREVOR

Fight For My Country	7"	Wizard	WIZ103	1971	**£4**	

BUSCH, LOU

Wild Ones	7"	Capitol	CL14730	1957	**£4**	
Zambesi	7"	Capitol	CL14504	1956	**£5**	

BUSH

Bush	LP	Probe	SPB1012	1970	**£12**	

BUSH, KATE

When Kate Bush first appeared on TV's "Top Of The Pops" wailing to Heathcliffe in that extraordinary high voice, it seemed impossible that she could ever turn out to be more than a one-hit-wonder novelty act. Instead, of course, it turned out that she was possessed of a rare talent - as a singer, as a dancer, as a performance artist, and above all as a composer and musician. Each of her album releases has been more impressive than the one before it and she is without doubt one of the most important rock artists of the eighties - and no doubt of the nineties too. Many of her records have become collectable, with picture sleeve copies of all her early singles rising steadily in value. The sought after picture disc version of Kate Bush's first LP exists in two closely similar pressings. The second can be identified by looking at the copyright clause on side two: it has the words "manufactured in the UK by EMI Records Ltd.". These are not to be found on the original pressing.

Army Dreamers	7"	EMI	EMI5106	1980	**£5**	
Babooshka	7"	EMI	EMI5085	1980	**£5**	PS
Big Sky	7"	EMI	KB4P	1986	**£15**	pic disc
Breathing	7"	EMI	EMI5058	1980	**£5**	PS
Cloudbusting	12"	EMI	12KB2	1985	**£6**	
December Will Be Magic Again	7"	EMI	EMI5121	1980	**£4**	chart single
Dreaming	7"	EMI	EMI5296	1982	**£5**	chart single
Hammer Horror	7"	EMI	EMI2887	1978	**£8**	PS
Interview With Kate Bush	LP				**£200**	Canadian promo
Kick Inside	LP	EMI/ Harvest	EMC3223/SW11751	1978	**£10**	different US sleeve on UK record
Kick Inside	LP	EMI	EMC3223	1978	**£30**	test pressing
Kick Inside	LP	EMI	EMC3223	1978	**£75**	test pressing with press kit
Kick Inside	LP	EMI	EMPC3223	1979	**£50**	pic disc
Kick Inside	LP	EMI	EMPC3223	1979	**£40**	pic disc, 2nd pressing
Lionheart	LP	EMI	EMA787	1978	**£30**	test pressing

Title	Format	Label	Cat. No.	Year	Price	Notes
Man With The Child In His Eyes	7"	EMI	EMI2806	1978	**£12**	PS
Man With The Child In His Eyes	7"	EMI	EMI2806	1978	**£20**	test pressing
Ne T'En Fui Pas	7"	EMI	PM102	1983	**£10**	sung in French
Never For Ever	7"	EMI	SFI562	1980	**£15**	promo, flexi
On Stage	7"	EMI	MIEP2991	1979	**£35**	double
On Stage	7"	EMI	PSR442/443	1979	**£50**	promo, double
On Stage	7" EP	EMI	MIEP2991	1979	**£12**	gatefold PS
On Stage	7" EP	EMI	MIEP2991	1979	**£5**	single PS
Running Up That Hill	7"	EMI	KB1	1985	**£6**	gatefold PS
Running Up That Hill	12"	EMI	12KB1	1985	**£6**	
Sat In Your Lap	7"	EMI	EMI5201	1981	**£4**	chart single
Self Portrait	LP	EMI	SSA3020	1979	**£125**	US promo
Sensual World	Spec	EMI		1989	**£75**	promo kit, CD & Cass
single File	7"	EMI	KBS1	1984	**£80**	boxed with booklet
There Goes A Tenner	7"	EMI	EMI5350	1982	**£6**	
This Woman's Work	7"	EMI	EMD119	1989	**£4**	pic disc
This Woman's Work	12"	EMI	12EMI119	1989	**£6**	with poster
Wow	7"	EMI	EMI2911	1979	**£6**	PS
Wuthering Heights	7"	EMI	EMI2719	1978	**£25**	PS

BUSHIDO

Title	Format	Label	Cat. No.	Year	Price	Notes
Among The Ruins	7"	Third Mind	TMS02	1984	**£5**	

BUSTERS

Title	Format	Label	Cat. No.	Year	Price	Notes
Bust Out	7"	Stateside	SS231	1963	**£5**	

BUTERA, SAM & THE WITNESSES

Title	Format	Label	Cat. No.	Year	Price	Notes
Bim Bam	7"	Capitol	CL14913	1958	**£15**	
Good Gracious Baby	7"	HMV	POP476	1958	**£6**	
Handle With Care	7"	Capitol	CL14988	1959	**£4**	
Rat Race	LP	London	HAD2288	1960	**£12**	

BUTLER, BILLY

Title	Format	Label	Cat. No.	Year	Price	Notes
Right Track	7"	Soul City	SC113		**£5**	
Right Track	7"	Soul City	SC113		**£15**	demo

BUTLER, JERRY

Title	Format	Label	Cat. No.	Year	Price	Notes
Are You Happy	7"	Mercury	MF1078	1969	**£4**	
Aware Of Love	LP	Vee Jay	LP1038	1961	**£15**	US
Best Of...	LP	Vee Jay	LP1048	1962	**£12**	US
Brand New Me	7"	Mercury	MF1132	1969	**£4**	
Folk Songs	LP	Stateside	SL10050	1963	**£15**	
For Your Precious Love	7"	London	HL8697	1958	**£20**	
For Your Precious Love	LP	Vee Jay	LP1075	1963	**£12**	US
Give Me Your Love	7"	Stateside	SS252	1964	**£4**	
Giving Up On Love	LP	Vee Jay	LP1076	1963	**£12**	US
Good Times	7"	Fontana	TF553	1965	**£6**	
He Will Break Your Heart	LP	Stateside	SL10032	1963	**£20**	
He Will Break Your Heart	7"	Top Rank	JAR531	1961	**£10**	
Hey Mr.Western Union Man	7"	Mercury	MF1058	1968	**£4**	
I Can't Stand To See You Cry	7"	Fontana	TF588	1965	**£5**	
I Dig You Baby	7"	Mercury	MF964	1967	**£5**	
I Found A Love	7"	Top Rank	JAR389	1960	**£8**	
I Stand Accused	7"	Sue	WI4003	1966	**£10**	
I've Been Trying	7"	Stateside	SS300	1964	**£5**	
Jerry Butler Esquire	LP	Abner	R2001	1959	**£75**	US
Jerry Butler Esquire	LP	Vee Jay	LP1027	1961	**£25**	US
Just For You	7"	Sue	WI4009	1966	**£10**	
Love	7"	Mercury	MF932	1965	**£4**	
Love Me	LP	Fontana	TL5264	1968	**£12**	
Make It Easy On Yourself	7"	Stateside	SS121	1962	**£6**	
Moody Woman	7"	Mercury	MF1122	1969	**£4**	
Moon River	7"	Columbia	DB4743	1961	**£4**	
Moon River	LP	Vee Jay	LP1046	1962	**£15**	US
More Of The Best Of...	LP	Vee Jay	1119	1965	**£10**	US
Mr.Dream Merchant	7"	Mercury	MF1005	1967	**£4**	
Never Give You up	7"	Mercury	MF1035	1968	**£4**	
Only The Strong Survive	7"	Mercury	MF1094	1969	**£4**	
Spice Of Life	LP	Mercury	6338102	1972	**£10**	
When Trouble Calls	7"	Top Rank	JAR562	1961	**£6**	

Title	Format	Label	Number	Year	Price	Notes
You Can Run	7"	Stateside	SS158	1963	**£5**	
You Go Right Through Me	7"	Stateside	SS170	1963	**£4**	
You Won't Be Sorry	7"	Stateside	SS195	1963	**£4**	

BUTLER, LESLIE

Title	Format	Label	Number	Year	Price	Notes
Ramona	7"	Doctor Bird	DB1083	1967	**£10**	
Revival	7"	High Note	HS009	196-	**£8**	
Soul Drums	7"	High Note	HS001	196-	**£8**	
Top Cat	7"	High Note	HS008	196-	**£8**	
You Don't Have To Say You Love Me	7"	Island	WI3069	1967	**£8**	

BUTTERCUPS

Title	Format	Label	Number	Year	Price	Notes
Come Put My Life In Order	7"	Pama	PM760	196-	**£8**	
If I Love You	7"	Pama	PM742	196-	**£8**	

BUTTERFIELD, BILLY

Title	Format	Label	Number	Year	Price	Notes
Magnificent Matador	7"	London	HLF8181	1955	**£8**	

BUTTERFIELD, PAUL BLUES BAND

Title	Format	Label	Number	Year	Price	Notes
All These Blues	7"	Elektra	EKSN45007	1967	**£5**	
Better Days	LP	Bearsville	K45515	1973	**£10**	
Butterfield Blues Band	LP	Elektra	EKL294	1965	**£15**	
Butterfield Blues Band	LP	Elektra	K42004	1971	**£10**	
Come On In	7"	London	HLZ10100	1966	**£10**	
East West	LP	Elektra	EKL315	1966	**£15**	
East West	LP	Elektra	K42006	1971	**£10**	
Get Yourself Together	7"	Elektra	EKSN45047	1968	**£5**	
Golden Butter	LP	Elektra	K62011	1972	**£12**	double
In My Own Dream	LP	Elektra	EKL4025	1968	**£12**	
In My Own Dream	LP	Elektra	K42042	1971	**£10**	
It All Comes Back	LP	Bearsville	K45517	1974	**£10**	
Keep On Moving	LP	Elektra	EKS74053	1969	**£12**	
Keep On Moving	LP	Elektra	K42033	1971	**£10**	
Live	LP	Elektra	EKS2001	1970	**£15**	
Live	LP	Elektra	K62001	1971	**£12**	
Put It In Your Ear	LP	Bearsville	K55509	1976	**£10**	
Resurrection Of Pigboy Crabshaw	LP	Elektra	EKL4015	1967	**£12**	
Resurrection Of Pigboy Crabshaw	LP	Elektra	K42017	1971	**£10**	
Run Out Of Time	7"	Elektra	EKSN45020	1967	**£5**	
Sometimes I Just Feel Like Smilin'	LP	Elektra	K42095	1971	**£10**	
Where Did My Baby Go	7"	Elektra	EKSN45069	1968	**£5**	

BUTTERFLYS

Title	Format	Label	Number	Year	Price	Notes
Goodnight Baby	7"	Red Bird	RB10009	1964	**£5**	

BUTTHOLE SURFERS

Title	Format	Label	Number	Year	Price	Notes
Butthole Surfers	mini LP	Alt. Tentacles	VIRUS32	1984	**£8**	black & white sleeve

BUZZ

Title	Format	Label	Number	Year	Price	Notes
You're Holding Me Down	7"	Columbia	DB7887	1966	**£50**	

BUZZ & BUCKY

Title	Format	Label	Number	Year	Price	Notes
Tiger A-Go-Go	7"	Stateside	SS428	1965	**£6**	

BUZZCOCKS

The Buzzcocks' "Spiral Scratch" EP was the first self-produced record to emerge out of punk and was an early collectors' item. A reissue brought the record's value down to its current level, although the two issues are easily distinguished by the original making no specific reference to Howard Devoto on the front cover.

Title	Format	Label	Number	Year	Price	Notes
Another Music In A Different Kitchen	LP	United Artists	UAG30159	1978	**£10**	with printed carrier bag
Moving Away From The Pulsebeat	12"	United Artists	UALP15	1978	**£15**	1 sided promo
Orgasm Addict	7"	United Artists	UP36316	1977	**£4**	
Spiral Scratch	7" EP	N. Hormones	ORG1	1977	**£15**	no Devoto reference on sleeve
Spiral Scratch	7" EP	N. Hormones	ORG1	1979	**£5**	Devoto reference on sleeve
What Do I Get	7"	United Artists	UP36348DJ	1978	**£6**	1 sided promo
Whatever Happened To	7"	United Artists	UP36316DJ	1978	**£6**	1 sided promo

BYE LAWS

Title	Format	Label	Number	Year	Price	Notes
Run Baby Run	7"	Pye	7N17701	1969	**£5**	

Then You Tell Me Goodbye	7"	Pye	7N17481	1968	**£5**	

BYRD, BOBBY

I Know You Got Soul	7"	Mojo	2027003	1971	**£4**	
I Need Help	LP	King	KS1118	1970	**£15**	US
I Need Help	7"	Polydor	2001118	1971	**£4**	

BYRD, DONALD

Black Byrd	7"	United Artists	UP35564	1973	**£4**	
Boom Boom	7"	Verve	VS532	1966	**£5**	

BYRD, JOE & THE FIELD HIPPIES

"American Metaphysical Circus" is, in effect, the follow-up to the innovative LP made by The United States Of America. With only Joe Byrd remaining from the original line-up, however, a change of name was clearly appropriate.

American Metaphysical Circus	LP	CBS	7317	1969	**£15**	US

BYRD, RUSSELL

Hitch Hike	7"	Sue	WI305	1964	**£10**	

BYRDS

All I Really Want To Do	7"	CBS	201796	1965	**£4**	chart single
Bad Night At The Whisky	7"	CBS	4055	1969	**£4**	
Ballad Of Easy Rider	LP	CBS	63795	1970	**£10**	chart LP
Byrdmaniax	LP	CBS	64389	1971	**£10**	
Byrds	LP	Asylum	SYLA8754	1973	**£10**	chart LP
Chestnut Mare	7"	CBS	5322	1971	**£4**	chart single
Dr.Byrds & Mr.Hyde	LP	CBS	63545	1969	**£10**	
Early Flight	LP	Together	ST1014	1969	**£20**	US
Eight Miles High	7"	CBS	202067	1966	**£5**	chart single
Eight Miles High	7" EP	CBS	EP6077	1966	**£6**	
Farther Along	LP	CBS	64676	1972	**£10**	
Fifth Dimension	LP	CBS	62783	1966	**£15**	chart LP
Fifth Dimension	7"	CBS	202259	1966	**£4**	
Goin' Back	7"	CBS	3093	1967	**£4**	
I Am A Pilgrim	7"	CBS	3752	1968	**£4**	
Jesus Is Just Alright	7"	CBS	4753	1970	**£4**	
Lady Friend	7"	CBS	2924	1967	**£10**	
Lay Lady Lay	7"	CBS	4284	1969	**£4**	
Mr.Spaceman	7"	CBS	202295	1966	**£5**	
Mr.Tambourine Man	LP	CBS	62571	1965	**£15**	chart LP
Mr.Tambourine Man	7"	CBS	201765	1965	**£4**	chart single
My Back Pages	7"	CBS	2648	1967	**£4**	
Notorious Byrd Brothers	LP	CBS	63169	1968	**£15**	chart LP
Preflyte	LP	Bumble	GEXP8001	196-	**£20**	US
Preflyte	LP	CBS	KC32183		**£20**	US
Preflyte	LP	Together	ST1001	1969	**£20**	US
Set You Free This Time	7"	CBS	202037	1966	**£8**	
So You Want To Be A Rock'n'Roll Star	7"	CBS	202559	1967	**£4**	
Sweetheart Of The Rodeo	LP	CBS	63353	1968	**£15**	
Times They Are A Changing	7" EP	CBS	EP6069	1966	**£6**	
Turn Turn Turn	LP	CBS	62652	1966	**£15**	chart LP
Turn Turn Turn	7"	CBS	202008	1965	**£4**	chart single
Untitled	LP	CBS	66253	1970	**£15**	double, chart LP
Wasn't Born To Follow	7"	CBS	4572	1969	**£4**	
You Ain't Goin' Nowhere	7"	CBS	3411	1968	**£4**	chart single
Younger Than Yesterday	LP	CBS	62988	1967	**£15**	chart LP

BYRNE, JERRY

Lights Out	7"	Speciality	SON5011	1976	**£5**	

BYRNES, EDDIE

Kookie	LP	W. Bros	W1309	1959	**£15**	US
Kookie	7" EP	W. Bros	WEP6010	1960	**£5**	
Kookie Vol.2	7" EP	W. Bros	WEP6108	1963	**£5**	
Kookie, Kookie, Lend Me Your Comb	7"	W. Bros	WB5	1960	**£4**	chart single

BYSTANDERS

There were a number of sixties groups who eventually achieved some measure of success in the seventies by effecting a dramatic change of style. Status Quo are the obvious example, yet the Bystanders are another good one. In their case, the change from their original harmony vocal approach was so great that they found it necessary to change their name too - to Man.

98.6	7"	Piccadilly	7N35363	1967	**£8**	chart single
My Love Come Home	7"	Piccadilly	7N35351	1966	**£8**	
Pattern People	7"	Piccadilly	7N35399	1967	**£10**	
Royal Blue Summer Sunshine Day	7"	Piccadilly	7N35382	1967	**£8**	
That's The End	7"	Pylot	501	1965	**£30**	
This World Is My World	7"	Pye	7N17540	1968	**£8**	
When Jezamine Goes	7"	Pye	7N17476	1968	**£8**	
You're Gonna Hurt Yourself	7"	Piccadilly	7N35330	1966	**£10**	

BYZANTIUM

Byzantium	LP	A&M	AMLS68104	1972	**£15**	
Live and Studio	LP	private		1972	**£50**	
Seasons Changing	LP	A&M	AMLH68163	1972	**£15**	
What A Coincidence	7"	A&M	AMS7064	1973	**£6**	

C

C & THE SHELLS
Good Morning Starshine .... 7" .... Atlantic .... 584271 .... 1969 .... **£4**

C JAM BLUES
Candy .... 7" .... Columbia .... DB8064 .... 1966 .... **£8**

C, FANTASTIC JOHNNY
Boogaloo Down Broadway .... LP .... Action .... ACLP6001 .... 1969 .... **£15**
Boogaloo Down Broadway .... 7" .... London .... HL10169 .... 1967 .... **£6**
Hitch It To The Horse .... 7" .... London .... HL10212 .... 1968 .... **£6**
New Love .... 7" .... Action .... ACT4543 .... 1969 .... **£4**
New Love .... 7" .... Action .... ACT4543 .... 1969 .... **£10** .... demo

C, FANTASTIC JOHNNY & GEORGE CLINTON
Don't Depend On Me .... 7" .... H. Of Snds .... HOS100 .... **£5**

C, ROY
Shotgun Wedding .... 7" .... Island .... WI273 .... 1966 .... **£5** .... chart single
Shotgun Wedding .... 7" .... UK .... UK19 .... 1972 .... **£4** .... chart single
Twistin' Pneumonia .... 7" .... Ember .... EMBS230 .... 1967 .... **£6**

C.A.QUINTET
Trip Through Hell .... LP .... Candy Floss .... 7764 .... 1969 .... **£300** .... US

C.O.D.'S
Michael .... 7" .... Stateside .... SS489 .... 1966 .... **£12**

CABAL, BRELLO
Margarine Flavoured Pineapple Chunk .... 7" .... CBS .... 3214 .... 1967 .... **£4**

CABARET VOLTAIRE
Do The Mussolini .... 7" .... Rough Trade .... RT003 .... 1978 .... **£4**
Eddie's Out .... 12" .... Rough Trade .... RT096T .... 1981 .... **£8** .... with pink vinyl 7" (RT095)
Nag Nag Nag .... 7" .... Rough Trade .... RT018 .... 1979 .... **£4**
Seconds Too Late .... 7" .... Rough Trade .... RT060 .... 1980 .... **£4**
Silent Command .... 7" .... Rough Trade .... RT035 .... 1980 .... **£4**
Three Mantras .... 12" .... Rough Trade .... RT038 .... 1980 .... **£6**

CABLES
Be A Man .... 7" .... Studio One .... SO2060 .... 196- **£10**
Got To Find Someone .... 7" .... Studio One .... SO2085 .... 196- **£10**
Love Is A Pleasure .... 7" .... Studio One .... SO2071 .... 196- **£10**
So Long .... 7" .... Bamboo .... BAM12 .... 196- **£8**
Soul Power .... 7" .... Coxsone .... CS7082 .... 196- **£10**
What Kind Of World .... 7" .... Coxsone .... CS7072 .... 196- **£10**

CACTUS
'Ot And Sweaty .... LP .... Atlantic .... K50013 .... 1972 .... **£10**
Cactus .... LP .... Atlantic .... 2400020 .... 1970 .... **£12**
One Way Or Another .... LP .... Atlantic .... 2460114 .... 1971 .... **£10**
Restrictions .... LP .... Atlantic .... K40307 .... 1972 .... **£10**

CADDY, ALAN
Workout .... 7" .... HMV .... POP1286 .... 1964 .... **£5**

CADETS
Cadets .... LP .... Crown .... CLP5370 .... 1963 .... **£20** .... US
Rockin' 'N' Reelin' .... LP .... Crown .... CLP5015 .... 1957 .... **£50** .... US
Stranded In The Jungle .... 7" .... London .... HLU8313 .... 1956 .... **£70**

CADILLACS
Cadillacs Meet The Orioles .... LP .... Jubilee .... JGM1117 .... 1961 .... **£50** .... US
Crazy Cadillacs .... LP .... Jubilee .... JGM1089 .... 1959 .... **£75** .... US

Fabulous Cadillacs	LP	Jubilee	JGM1045	1957	**£100**	US
Peek A Boo	7"	London	HLJ8786	1959	**£10**	
Twisting With The Cadillacs	LP	Jubilee	JGM5009	1962	**£50**	US

CAESAR & CLEO

Letter	7"	Vocalion	VL9247	1965	**£5**	
Love Is Strange	7"	Reprise	R20419	1965	**£5**	

CAESARS

Five In The Morning	7"	Decca	F12462	1966	**£12**	
On The Outside Looking In	7"	Decca	F12251	1965	**£10**	

CAFE SOCIETY

Cafe Society included Tom Robinson in its line-up, but the collectability of the group's records has more to do with the fact that they were among the few releases on the label founded by the Kinks' Ray Davies.

Cafe Society	LP	Konk	KONK102	1975	**£20**	
Whitby Two-Step	7"	Konk	KOS5	1975	**£5**	

CAGE, JOHN

Cartridge Music	LP	Deutsche G.	137009	1969	**£10**	
Concerto For Piano & Orchestra	LP	EMI	C165289547		**£10**	
Concerto For Prepared Piano & Orch.	LP	Nonesuch	H71202	1968	**£10**	B Side Lukas Foss
Fontana Mix	LP	Turnabout	TV34046	196-	**£10**	
HPSCHD	LP	Nonesuch	H71224	1970	**£10**	B Side With Ben Johnston
Sonatas & Int. For Prepared Piano	LP	Decca	HEAD9	1976	**£10**	
Variations	LP	Everest	3132		**£10**	
Variations II	LP	Columbia	MS7051		**£10**	US

CAGLE, AUBREY

Come Along Little Girl	7"	Starlite	ST45082	1962	**£20**	

CAIN

Her Emotion	7"	Page One	POF054	1968	**£5**	

CAKE

Cake	LP	MCA	MUPS303	1968	**£15**	
Slice Of Cake	LP	MCA	MUPS390	1969	**£15**	

CALE, J.J.

After Midnight	7"	A&M	AMS7022	1972	**£4**	
Cajun Moon	7"	A&M	AMS7018	1972	**£4**	
J.J.Cale	LP	Shelter	ISADJ1	1976	**£10**	promo
Katy Cool Lady	7"	Shelter	JJ1	1979	**£4**	
Mama Don't	7"	Shelter	WIP6697DJ	1981	**£4**	1 sided promo
Outside Looking In	7"	Liberty	LBY55881	1966	**£8**	

CALE, JOHN

Animal Justice	12"	Illegal	IL003	1977	**£6**	
Hear Fear	LP	Island	IXP2	1976	**£12**	US promo
Jack The Ripper	7"	Illegal	IL006	1977	**£10**	demo
Man Who Couldn't Afford To	7"	Island	WIP6202	1974	**£4**	
Sabotage	LP	Spy-IRS	SP004	1980	**£10**	US

CALE, JOHN & TERRY RILEY

Church Of Anthrax	LP	CBS	64259	1971	**£20**	

CALEB

Woman Of Distinction	7"	Philips	BF1588	1967	**£12**	

CALIFORNIA IN CROWD

Questions And Answers	7"	Fontana	TF779	1966	**£15**	

CALIFORNIA, RANDY

All Along The Watchtower	7"	Beggars B.	BEG82	1982	**£5**	
Jack Rabbit	7"	Vertigo	VER21	1985	**£4**	
Kaptain Kopter & The Twirly Birds	LP	Epic	EPC65381	1972	**£10**	

CALIFORNIANS

Congratulations	7"	Decca	F12758	1968	**£4**	
Cooks Of Cake And Kindness	7"	Fontana	TF991	1969	**£8**	
Follow Me	7"	Decca	F12678	1967	**£8**	
Golden Apples	7"	CBS	2263	1967	**£6**	

Out In The Sun	7"	Decca	F12802	1968	**£5**	
Sad Old Song	7"	Fontana	TF1052	1969	**£6**	
Sunday Will Never Be The Same	7"	Decca	F12712	1967	**£5**	

CALLAN & JOHN

House Of Delight	7"	CBS	4447	1969	**£5**	

CALLICOT, MISSISSIPPI JOE

Presenting The Country Blues	LP	Blue Horizon	763227	1968	**£30**	

CALLINAN FLYNN

Callinan Flynn	LP	Mushroom		197-	**£80**	

CALLIOPE

Wiser	7"	UNI	UNS514	1970	**£4**	

CALLOWAY, CAB

Cab Calloway	7" EP	Fontana	TFE17216	1960	**£12**	
Cabulous Calloway	7" EP	Vintage Jazz	VEP22		**£6**	
Cabulous Calloway Vol.2	7" EP	Vintage Jazz	VEP35		**£6**	

CALVERT, ROBERT

Captain Lockheed & The Starfighters	LP	United Artists	UAG29507	1974	**£30**	
Catch A Falling Starfighter	7"	United Artists		1974	**£10**	
Hype	LP	A Side	IF0311	1980	**£10**	
Lucky Leif & The Longships	LP	United Artists	UAG29852	1975	**£40**	

CAMEL

Never Let Go	7"	MCA	MU1177	1973	**£4**	

CAMEL DRIVERS

Sunday Morning Six O'Clock	7"	Pye	7N25471	1968	**£4**	

CAMEOS

My Baby's Coming Home	7"	Columbia	DB7201	1964	**£10**	
On The Good Ship Lollipop	7"	Toast	TT508	196-	**£8**	
Powercut	7"	Columbia	DB7092	1963	**£15**	
Pretty Shade Of Blue	7"	Toast	TT503	196-	**£10**	

CAMERON, DION

Get Ready	7"	Rio	R111	1967	**£8**	
Miserable Friday	7"	Doctor Bird	DB1101	1967	**£10**	

CAMERON, G.C.

Me And My Life	7"	T. Motown	TMG1033	1976	**£4**	

CAMERON, ISLA, GUY CARAWAN, PEGGY SEEGER

Origins Of Skiffle	7" EP	Pye	NJE1043	1957	**£6**	

CAMERON, JOHN

Cover Lover	LP	Columbia	SCX6116	1967	**£15**	
Off Centre	LP	Deram	SML1044	1969	**£15**	
Troublemaker	7"	Deram	DM256	1969	**£5**	
Walk Small	7"	Columbia	DB8120	1967	**£5**	

CAMERON, RAY

Doin' My Time	7"	Island	WIP6003	1967	**£5**	

CAMERON, TED & THE DEEJAYS

Early In The Morning	7"	Pye	7N15292	1960	**£6**	

CAMPBELL, AL & THE THRILLERS

Heart For Sale	7"	Blue Cat	BS118	1968	**£10**	

CAMPBELL, ALEX

...And Friends	LP	Saga	EROS8021	1967	**£30**	with Sandy Denny
Been On The Road So Long	7"	Transatlantic	TRASP4	1965	**£4**	
Victoria Dines Alone	7"	Saga	OPP2	196-	**£4**	

CAMPBELL, CHOKER

Hits Of The Sixties	LP	T. Motown	TML11011	1965	**£100**	
Mickey's Monkey	7"	T. Motown	TMG517	1965	**£30**	
Mickey's Monkey	7"	T. Motown	TMG517	1965	**£75**	demo

CAMPBELL, DOREEN

Title	Format	Label	Cat. No.	Year	Price	Notes
Rude Girls	7"	Rainbow	RAI117	196-	**£8**	

CAMPBELL, ETHNA

Title	Format	Label	Cat. No.	Year	Price	Notes
What's Easy For Two	7"	Mercury	MF804	1964	**£10**	

CAMPBELL, IAN

Title	Format	Label	Cat. No.	Year	Price	Notes
Break My Mind	7"	Major Minor	MM639	1969	**£5**	
Coaldust Ballads	LP	Transatlantic		1965	**£20**	
Come Kiss Me	7"	Transatlantic	TRASP6	1966	**£4**	
Contemporary Campbells	LP	Transatlantic		1965	**£20**	
Guantanamera	7"	Transatlantic	TRASP7	1966	**£4**	
Kelly From Killane	7"	Transatlantic	TRASP2	1965	**£4**	
Lover Let Me In	7"	Transatlantic	BIG103	1968	**£5**	
Marilyn Monroe	7"	Decca	F11802	1964	**£5**	
One Eyed Reilly	7"	Transatlantic	TRASP10	1966	**£4**	
Sun Is Burning	LP	Argo		1970	**£20**	
This Is The Ian Campbell Folk Group	LP	Transatlantic		1963	**£15**	
Times They Are A-Changin'	7"	Transatlantic	TRASP5	1965	**£5**	chart single

CAMPBELL, JIMMY

Title	Format	Label	Cat. No.	Year	Price	Notes
Album	LP	Philips		1972	**£12**	
Don't Leave Me Now	7"	Fontana	6007025	1970	**£4**	
Half Baked	LP	Vertigo	6360010	1970	**£12**	with Merseybeats
Lyanna	7"	Fontana	TF1076	1970	**£4**	
On A Monday	7"	Fontana	TF1009	1969	**£4**	
Son Of Anastasia	LP	Fontana		1969	**£10**	

CAMPBELL, JO ANN

Title	Format	Label	Cat. No.	Year	Price	Notes
Motorcycle Michael	7"	HMV	POP873	1961	**£4**	chart single
Wait A Minute	7"	London	HLU8536	1958	**£12**	

CAMPBELL, NOLA

Title	Format	Label	Cat. No.	Year	Price	Notes
Pictures Of You	7"	Gas	GAS107	196-	**£8**	

CAMPBELL, ROY

Title	Format	Label	Cat. No.	Year	Price	Notes
Another Saturday Night	7"	Giant	GN41	196-	**£8**	
Engine Number Nine	7"	Jolly	JY003	196-	**£8**	

CAMPBELL-LYONS, PATRICK

Title	Format	Label	Cat. No.	Year	Price	Notes
Everybody Should Fly A Kite	7"	Sovereign	SOV115	1973	**£5**	
Guru Song	7"	Electric	WOT12	1977	**£4**	
Me And My Friend	LP	Sovereign	SVNA7258	1973	**£20**	
Out On The Road	7"	Sovereign	SOV119	1973	**£5**	

CAN

Title	Format	Label	Cat. No.	Year	Price	Notes
Cannibalisms	LP	United Artists	UDM105/6	1978	**£12**	double
Deep End (Soundtracks)	LP	United Artists	UAS29283	1970	**£15**	
Dizzy Dizzy	7"	United Artists	UP35749	1974	**£4**	
Ege Bamyasi	LP	United Artists	UAS29414	1972	**£15**	
Flow Motion	LP	Virgin	V2071	1976	**£10**	
Future Days	LP	United Artists	UAS29505	1973	**£15**	
Landed	LP	Virgin	V2041	1975	**£12**	
Monster Movie	LP	United Artists	UAS29094	1969	**£15**	
Moonshake	7"	United Artists	UP35596	1973	**£4**	
Onlyou	cass	Pure Freude	PF23	1982	**£30**	tin container
Saw Delight	LP	Virgin	V2079	1977	**£10**	
Soon Over Babaluma	LP	United Artists	UAG29673	1974	**£15**	
Spoon	7"	United Artists	UP35506	1973	**£4**	
Tago Mago	LP	United Artists	UAD60009/10	1971	**£20**	double
Unlimited Edition	LP	Caroline	CAD3001	1976	**£15**	double

CANAAN

Title	Format	Label	Cat. No.	Year	Price	Notes
Canaan	LP	Dovetail		1973	**£50**	

CANARIES

Title	Format	Label	Cat. No.	Year	Price	Notes
Flying High	LP	B.T.Puppy	BTPS1007	1970	**£15**	US

CANDY & THE KISSES

Title	Format	Label	Cat. No.	Year	Price	Notes
Do The 81	7"	Cameo Park	C336	1965	**£20**	

CANDY CHOIR

Alexander's Ragtime Band	7"	CBS	3305	1968	**£4**	
Children And Flowers	7"	CBS	3061	1967	**£4**	
Shake Hands And Come Out Crying	7"	Parlophone	R5472	1966	**£4**	

CANDYMEN

Georgia Pines	7"	HMV	POP1612	1967	**£5**	

CANNED HEAT

At their best ("Boogie With Canned Heat"), Canned Heat were one of the most convincing white blues groups. Bob Hite and Henry Vestine had a collection of blues records of legendary proportions, so they were not short of good examples to follow. They did have a liking, however, for what they called "boogie", by which they meant a string of extremely long and extremely tedious instrumental solos played over an elemental riff. Both extremes can be found on the double "Living The Blues" : a boogie of record-breaking length, but also some short experimental tracks that take interesting liberties with the blues format. The record made with John Lee Hooker also shows Canned Heat's abilities well. They let Hooker run the show, but by virtue of their telling support, they push him into making one of his very best records.

Boogie With Canned Heat	LP	Liberty	LBL83103	1968	**£12**	chart LP
Canned Heat	LP	Liberty	LBL83059	1967	**£15**	
Christmas Blues	7"	Liberty	LBF15429	1970	**£4**	
Cookbook	LP	Liberty	LBS83303	1970	**£10**	chart LP
Future Blues	7"	Liberty	LBF15395	1970	**£4**	
Future Blues	LP	Liberty	LBS83364	1970	**£12**	chart LP
Going Up The Country	7"	Liberty	LBF15169	1968	**£4**	chart single
Hallelujah	LP	Liberty	LBS83239	1969	**£12**	
Historical Figures	LP	United Artists	UAG29304	1972	**£10**	
Let's Work Together	7"	Liberty	LBF15302	1969	**£4**	chart single
Live At Topanga Canyon	LP	Wand	WDS693	1970	**£15**	US
Live In Europe	LP	Liberty	LBS83333	1970	**£12**	chart LP
Living The Blues	LP	Liberty	LDS84001	1969	**£20**	double
New Age	LP	United Artists	UAS29455	1973	**£10**	
On The Road Again	7"	Liberty	LBS15090	1968	**£4**	chart single
One More River To Cross	LP	Atlantic	K50026	1974	**£10**	
Poor Moon	7"	Liberty	LBF15255	1969	**£4**	
Rockin' With The King	7"	United Artists	UP35248	1972	**£4**	
Spoonful	7"	Pye	7N25513	1970	**£4**	
Sugar Bee	7"	Liberty	LBF15350	1970	**£4**	chart single
Time Was	7"	Liberty	LBF15200	1969	**£4**	
Wooly Bully	7"	Liberty	LBF15439	1971	**£4**	

CANNED ROCK

Kinetic Energy	LP	Canned Rock	CAN002	1978	**£60**	
Live	LP	Canned Rock	CAN003	1979	**£30**	

CANNIBAL & THE HEADHUNTERS

Land Of 1000 Dances	LP	Date	TEM3001	1966	**£12**	US
Land Of 1000 Dances	LP	Rampart	RM3302	1966	**£15**	US
Land Of 1000 Dances	7"	Stateside	SS403	1965	**£6**	

CANNON BROTHERS

Turn Your Eyes To Me	7"	Brit	WI1003	1965	**£8**	

CANNON, FREDDIE

Bang On	LP	Stateside	SL10013	1963	**£10**	
Blast Off	7" EP	Stateside	SE1002	1962	**£5**	
Buzz Buzz A Diddle It	7"	Top Rank	JAR568	1961	**£4**	
Explosive Freddie Cannon	LP	Top Rank	25018	1960	**£15**	
Explosive Freddie Cannon	7" EP	Top Rank	JKP2058	1960	**£5**	
Four Direct Hits	7" EP	Top Rank	JKP2066	1960	**£5**	
Freddie Cannon Favourites	LP	Top Rank	25113	1961	**£15**	
Happy Shades Of Blue	LP	Top Rank	35106	1962	**£12**	
Muskrat Ramble	7"	Top Rank	JAR548	1961	**£4**	chart single
On Target	7" EP	Top Rank	JKP3010	1961	**£6**	
Palisades Park	7"	Stateside	SS101	1962	**£4**	chart single
Steps Out	LP	Stateside	SL10062	1964	**£10**	
Tallahassee Lassie	7"	Top Rank	JAR135	1959	**£4**	chart single
Way Down Yonder In New Orleans	7"	Top Rank	JAR247	1959	**£4**	chart single

CANNON, JUDY

Very First Day I Met You	7"	Pye	7N15900	1965	**£15**	

CANNON, KING

Title	Format	Label	Number	Year	Price	Notes
Soul Pipe	7"	Duke	DU13	196-	**£8**	

CANNONBALL & JOHNNY MELODY

Title	Format	Label	Number	Year	Price	Notes
Cool Hand Luke	7"	Big Shot	BI518	1973	**£5**	

CANNONBALLS

Title	Format	Label	Number	Year	Price	Notes
Calliope Boogie	7"	Coral	Q72431	1961	**£4**	
New Orleans Beat	7"	Coral	Q72428	1961	**£4**	

CANNONS

Title	Format	Label	Number	Year	Price	Notes
Bush Fire	7"	Columbia	DB4724	1961	**£4**	

CAPABILITY BROWN

Title	Format	Label	Number	Year	Price	Notes
From Scratch	LP	Charisma	CAS1056	1972	**£10**	
Voice	LP	Charisma	CAS1068	1973	**£10**	

CAPE KENNEDY CONSTRUCTION CO.

Title	Format	Label	Number	Year	Price	Notes
First Step On The Moon	7"	President	PT265	1969	**£4**	

CAPITOLS

Title	Format	Label	Number	Year	Price	Notes
Cool Jerk	7"	Atlantic	584004	1966	**£4**	
Dance The Cool Jerk	LP	Atco	33190	1966	**£12**	US

CAPP, ANDY

Title	Format	Label	Number	Year	Price	Notes
Pop A Top	7"	Treasure Isle	TI7052	196-	**£8**	

CAPRIS

Title	Format	Label	Number	Year	Price	Notes
There's A Moon Out Tonight	7"	Columbia	DB4605	1961	**£10**	

CAPT.NOAH & HIS FLOATING ZOO

Title	Format	Label	Number	Year	Price	Notes
Capt.Noah & His Floating Zoo	LP	Argo		1972	**£15**	
Holy Moses	LP	Argo		1972	**£15**	

CAPTAIN BEEFHEART

Title	Format	Label	Number	Year	Price	Notes
Bluejeans And Moonbeams	LP	Virgin	V2123	1974	**£10**	
Clear Spot	LP	Reprise	K54007	1972	**£10**	
Diddy Wah Diddy	7" EP	A&M	AME600	1971	**£80**	
Ice Cream For Crow	7"	Virgin	VS534	1982	**£4**	
Legendary A&M Sessions	12"	A&M	AMY226	1984	**£6**	
Lick My Decals Off	LP	Straight	STS1063	1970	**£15**	chart LP
Light Reflected Off The Oceans Of Moon	12"	Virgin	VS53412	1982	**£6**	
Mirror Man	LP	Buddah	2365002	1971	**£10**	chart LP
Moonchild	7"	A&M	AMS726	1968	**£15**	
Safe As Milk	LP	Buddah	623171	1969	**£10**	
Safe As Milk	LP	Marble Arch	MAL1117	1969	**£10**	
Safe As Milk	LP	Pye	NPL28110	1968	**£20**	
Sampler EP	7"	Virgin	SIXPACK1	1978	**£10**	promo pic disc
Sixpack	7"	Virgin	SIXPACK1	1979	**£15**	pic disc
Spotlight Kid	LP	Reprise	K44162	1972	**£10**	chart LP
Strictly Personal	LP	Liberty	LBR1006	1968	**£20**	
Sue 'Nuff 'N Yes I Do	7"	Buddah	BDS466	1978	**£4**	
Too Much Time	7"	Reprise	K14233	1973	**£6**	
Trout Mask Replica	LP	Straight	STS1053	1969	**£20**	double, chart LP
Unconditionally Guaranteed	LP	Virgin	V2015	1974	**£10**	
Upon The My-Oh-My	7"	Virgin	VS110	1974	**£6**	
Yellow Brick Road	7"	Pye	7N25443	1968	**£15**	

CAPTAIN BEYOND

Title	Format	Label	Number	Year	Price	Notes
Captain Beyond	LP	Capricorn	K47503	1972	**£10**	3-D cover

CAPTAIN SCARLET

Title	Format	Label	Number	Year	Price	Notes
Captain Scarlet & The Mysterons	7" EP	Century 21	MA132	1967	**£10**	
Captain Scarlet Is Indestructable	7" EP	Century 21	MA133	1967	**£10**	
Captain Scarlet Of Spectrum	7" EP	Century 21	MA134	1967	**£10**	
Captain Scarlet Vs Captain Black	7" EP	Century 21	MA135	1967	**£10**	
Introducing Captain Scarlet	7" EP	Century 21	MA131	1967	**£10**	

CAPTAIN SENSIBLE

Title	Format	Label	Number	Year	Price	Notes
Croydon	7"	A&M	CAPP3	1982	**£4**	pic disc

CARAVAN

Title	Format	Label	Number	Year	Price	Notes
All The Way	7"	BTM	SBT104	1976	**£5**	PS
And The New Symphonia	LP	Deram	SML1110	1974	**£10**	
Better By Far	LP	Arista	SPARTY1008	1977	**£10**	
Blind Dog At St.Dunstan's	LP	BTM	BTM1007	1976	**£10**	chart LP
Canterbury Tales	LP	Decca	DKLR81/82	1976	**£12**	double
Caravan	LP	Polydor	2353058	1972	**£10**	
Caravan	LP	Verve	SVLP6011	1968	**£25**	
Cunning Stunts	LP	Decca	SKL5210	1975	**£10**	chart LP
For Girls Who Grow Plump In The Night	LP	Deram	SDL12	1973	**£10**	
If I Could Do It All Over Again	7"	Decca	F13063	1970	**£8**	
If I Could Do It All Over Again...	LP	Decca	SKL5052	1970	**£10**	
In The Land Of Grey & Pink	LP	Deram	SDL1	1971	**£10**	
Love To Love You	7"	Decca	F23125	1971	**£6**	
Place Of My Own	7"	Verve	VS1518	1968	**£15**	
Stuck In A Hole	7"	Decca	FR13599	1975	**£4**	
Waterloo Lily	LP	Deram	SDL8	1972	**£10**	

CARAVELLES

Title	Format	Label	Number	Year	Price	Notes
You Don't Have To Be A Baby To Cry	LP	Smash	MGS27044	1963	**£15**	US
You Don't Have To Be A Baby To Cry	7"	Decca	F11697	1963	**£4**	chart LP

CAREFREES

Title	Format	Label	Number	Year	Price	Notes
We Love You Beatles	7"	Oriole	CB1916	1964	**£8**	

CARGO

Title	Format	Label	Number	Year	Price	Notes
Cargo	LP	Harvest		1971	**£120**	

CARIBEATS

Title	Format	Label	Number	Year	Price	Notes
Bells Of Saint Mary's Ska	7"	Ska Beat	JB246	1966	**£10**	

CARL & THE CHEETAHS

Title	Format	Label	Number	Year	Price	Notes
Beg Borrow And Steal	7"	Columbia	DB7162	1963	**£4**	

CARL & THE COMMANDERS

Title	Format	Label	Number	Year	Price	Notes
Farmer John	7"	Columbia	DB4719	1961	**£6**	

CARLEW CHOIR

Title	Format	Label	Number	Year	Price	Notes
Huma Lama	7"	Spark	SRL1028	1971	**£4**	

CARLISLE BROTHERS

Title	Format	Label	Number	Year	Price	Notes
Fresh From The Country	7" EP	Parlophone	GEP8799	1959	**£8**	

CARLISLE, BILLY

Title	Format	Label	Number	Year	Price	Notes
Down Boy	7"	Mercury	AMT1063	1959	**£8**	

CARLTON & HIS SHOES

Title	Format	Label	Number	Year	Price	Notes
Love Me Forever	7"	Coxsone	CS7065	196-	**£10**	
This Feeling	7"	Studio One	SO2062	196-	**£10**	

CARLTON, EDDIE

Title	Format	Label	Number	Year	Price	Notes
It Will Be Done	7"	Cream	5001	1976	**£4**	

CARLTON, LITTLE CARL

Title	Format	Label	Number	Year	Price	Notes
46 Drums 1 Guitar	7"	Action	ACT4514	1968	**£4**	
46 Drums 1 Guitar	7"	Action	ACT4514	1968	**£10**	demo
Competition Ain't Nothing	7"	Action	ACT4501	1968	**£10**	
Competition Ain't Nothing	7"	Action	ACT4501	1968	**£30**	demo
Look At Mary Wonder	7"	Action	ACT4537	1969	**£4**	
Look At Mary Wonder	7"	Action	ACT4537	1969	**£10**	demo

CARMEN

Title	Format	Label	Number	Year	Price	Notes
Bulerias	7"	Regal Z.	RZ3090	1974	**£8**	
Dancing On A Cold Wind	LP	Regal Z.	SLRZ1040	1975	**£20**	
Fandangos In Space	LP	Regal Z.	SRZA8518	1973	**£20**	
Flamenco Viva	7"	Regal Z.	RZ3086	1974	**£8**	

CARNABY

Title	Format	Label	Number	Year	Price	Notes
Jump And Dance	7"	Piccadilly	7N35272	1965	**£15**	

CARNATIONS

Title	Format	Label	Number	Year	Price	Notes
Mighty Man	7"	Blue Beat	BB285	1964	**£10**	

CARNE, JUDY
Sock It To Me .... 7" .... Reprise .... RS20680 .... 1968 .... **£4** ....

CARNEGIE HALL
Bells Of San Francisco .... 7" .... Polydor .... 56224 .... 1968 .... **£5** ....

CARNES, KIM
Mistaken Identity .... LP .... Mobile Fid. .... MFSL1073 .... 1982 .... **£12** .... US audiophile

CARNIVAL
Big Bright Green Pleasure Machine .... 7" .... Columbia .... DB8255 .... 1967 .... **£5** ....
Son Of A Preacher Man .... 7" .... Liberty .... LBF15252 .... 1969 .... **£4** ....

CAROL & THE MEMORIES
Tears On My Pillow .... 7" .... CBS .... 202086 .... 1966 .... **£5** ....

CAROLINES
Love Made A Fool Of Me .... 7" .... Polydor .... 56027 .... 1965 .... **£4** ....

CARPENTERS
Carpenters .... LP .... A&M .... QU53502 .... 1971 .... **£10** .... US quad
Close To You .... LP .... A&M .... QU54271 .... 1970 .... **£10** .... US quad
Horizon .... LP .... A&M .... QU54530 .... 1975 .... **£10** .... US quad
Now And Then .... LP .... A&M .... QU53519 .... 1973 .... **£10** .... US quad
Singles 1969-1973 .... LP .... A&M .... QU53601 .... 1973 .... **£10** .... US quad
Song For You .... LP .... A&M .... QU53511 .... 1972 .... **£10** .... US quad

CARR, CATHY
Ivory Tower .... 7" .... London .... HLH8274 .... 1956 .... **£8** ....

CARR, JAMES
Baby You've Got My Mind Messed Up ... 7" .... Stateside .... SS507 .... 1966 .... **£15** ....
Dark End Of The Street .... 7" .... Stateside .... SS2001 .... 1967 .... **£4** ....
I'm A Fool For You .... 7" .... Stateside .... SS2052 .... 1967 .... **£4** ....
Let It Happen .... 7" .... Stateside .... SS2038 .... 1967 .... **£4** ....
Love Attack .... 7" .... Stateside .... SS535 .... 1966 .... **£5** ....
Man Needs A Woman .... 7" .... Bell .... BLL1004 .... 1968 .... **£4** ....
Pouring Water On A Drowned Man .... 7" .... Stateside .... SS545 .... 1966 .... **£4** ....
You Got My Mind Messed Up .... LP .... Stateside .... 1967 .... **£40** ....

CARR, JOHNNY
Do You Love That Girl .... 7" .... Fontana .... TF600 .... 1965 .... **£6** ....
Things Get Better .... 7" .... Fontana .... TF823 .... 1967 .... **£6** ....

CARR, JOHNNY & THE CADILLACS
Respectable .... 7" .... Decca .... F11854 .... 1964 .... **£8** ....
Then So Do I .... 7" .... Fontana .... TF681 .... 1966 .... **£5** ....

CARR, LEROY
RCA Victor Race Series Vol.2 .... 7" EP .... RCA .... RCX7168 .... 1964 .... **£5** ....
Treasures Of N. American Negro Music 7" EP .... Fontana .... TFE17051 .... 1958 .... **£5** ....

CARR, LINDA
Everytime .... 7" .... Stateside .... SS2058 .... 1967 .... **£6** ....

CARR, ROMEY
These Things Will Keep Me Loving You 7" .... Columbia .... DB8710 .... 1970 .... **£6** ....

CARROLL, BOB
Hi Ho Silver .... 7" .... London .... HLT8724 .... 1958 .... **£4** ....
I Can't Get You Out Of My Life .... 7" .... London .... HLT8888 .... 1959 .... **£4** ....
Red Confetti,Pink Balloons & Tam. .... 7" .... London .... HLU8299 .... 1956 .... **£5** ....

CARROLL, JOHNNY & THE HOT ROCKS
Hot Rock .... 7" .... Brunswick .... 05603 .... 1956 .... **£80** ....
Wild Wild Women .... 7" .... Brunswick .... 05580 .... 1956 .... **£80** ....

CARROLL, PAT
To The Sun .... 7" .... Pye .... 7N25592 .... 1972 .... **£6** ....

CARRUTHERS, BEN & THE DEEP
Jack O'Diamonds .... 7" .... Parlophone .... R5295 .... 1965 .... **£20** ....

CARS

Title	Format	Label	Cat. No.	Year	Price	Notes
Candy O	LP	Elektra	K52148	1979	**£10**	no title on cover, sticker on shrink-wrap
Candy O	LP	Nautilus		1981	**£15**	US audiophile
Cars	LP	Nautilus		1981	**£15**	US audiophile
Double Life	7"	Elektra	K12385P	1979	**£6**	pic disc
Just What I Needed	7"	Elektra	K12301	1978	**£8**	
Just What I Needed	7"	Elektra	K12312P	1979	**£4**	pic disc
My Best Friend's Girl	7"	Elektra	K12301P	1978	**£4**	pic disc

CARSON, CHAD

Title	Format	Label	Cat. No.	Year	Price	Notes
Don't Pick On Me	7"	HMV	POP1156	1963	**£6**	

CARSON, KEN

Title	Format	Label	Cat. No.	Year	Price	Notes
Daniel Boone	7"	London	HLF8237	1956	**£6**	
Hawkeye	7"	London	HLF8213	1955	**£6**	

CARSON, KIT

Title	Format	Label	Cat. No.	Year	Price	Notes
Band Of Gold	7"	Capitol	CL14524	1956	**£4**	

CARTER FAMILY

Title	Format	Label	Cat. No.	Year	Price	Notes
Mean As Hell	7" EP	CBS	EP6073	1966	**£5**	
Mountain Music Vol.2	7" EP	Brunswick	OE9168	1955	**£5**	
Original And Great Carter Family Vol.1	7" EP	RCA	RCX7100	1962	**£5**	
Original And Great Carter Family Vol.2	7" EP	RCA	RCX7101	1962	**£5**	
Original And Great Carter Family Vol.3	7" EP	RCA	RCX7102	1962	**£5**	
Original And Great Carter Family Vol.4	7" EP	RCA	RCX7109	1963	**£5**	
Original And Great Carter Family Vol.5	7" EP	RCA	RCX7110	1963	**£5**	
Original And Great Carter Family Vol.6	7" EP	RCA	RCX7111	1963	**£5**	

CARTER LEWIS & THE SOUTHERNERS

Title	Format	Label	Cat. No.	Year	Price	Notes
Poor Joe	7"	Piccadilly	7N35085	1962	**£8**	
Skinnie Minnie	7"	Oriole	CB1919	1964	**£10**	
So Much in Love	7"	Piccadilly	7N35004	1961	**£8**	
Sweet And Tender Romance	7"	Oriole	CB1835	1963	**£8**	
Tell Me	7"	Ember	EMBS165	1962	**£15**	
Two Timing Baby	7"	Ember	EMBS145	1961	**£12**	
Your Mama's Out Of Town	7"	Oriole	CB1868	1963	**£10**	

CARTER, BETTY

Title	Format	Label	Cat. No.	Year	Price	Notes
Good Life	7"	London	HLK9748	1963	**£4**	

CARTER, CAROLYN

Title	Format	Label	Cat. No.	Year	Price	Notes
I'm Thru	7"	London	HL9959	1965	**£10**	

CARTER, CLARENCE

Title	Format	Label	Cat. No.	Year	Price	Notes
Feeling Is Right	7"	Atlantic	584272	1969	**£4**	
Looking For A Fox	7"	Atlantic	584176	1968	**£4**	
Patches	7"	Atlantic	2091030	1970	**£4**	chart single
Slip Away	7"	Atlantic	584187	1968	**£4**	
Snatchin' It Back	7"	Atlantic	584248	1969	**£4**	
Take It Off Him And Put It On Me	7"	Atlantic	584309	1970	**£4**	
This Is Clarence Carter	LP	Atlantic	SD8192	1968	**£12**	US
Thread The Needle	7"	Atlantic	584154	1968	**£4**	
Too Weak To Fight	7"	Atlantic	584223	1968	**£4**	

CARTER, HERBIE

Title	Format	Label	Cat. No.	Year	Price	Notes
Happy Time	7"	Duke	DU4	196-	**£8**	

CARTER, MARTIN

Title	Format	Label	Cat. No.	Year	Price	Notes
Ups And Downs	LP	Tradition		1972	**£10**	

CARTER, MEL

Title	Format	Label	Cat. No.	Year	Price	Notes
When A Boy Falls In Love	LP	Derby	LPM702	1963	**£50**	US
When A Boy Falls In Love	7"	Pye	7N25212	1963	**£4**	

CARTHY, MARTIN

Title	Format	Label	Cat. No.	Year	Price	Notes
But Two Came By	LP	Fontana	STL5477	1968	**£10**	
Byker Hill	LP	Fontana	STL5434	1967	**£10**	
Landfall	LP	Philips	6309049	1971	**£10**	
Martin Carthy	LP	Fontana	STL5269	1965	**£10**	
Prince Heathen	LP	Fontana	STL5529	1969	**£10**	

Second Album	LP	Fontana	STL5362	1966	**£10**	

CARTOONE

Cartoone	LP	Atlantic	588174	1969	**£30**	
Penny for The Sun	7"	Atlantic	584240	1969	**£8**	

CARTWRIGHT, DAVE

Back To The Garden	LP	Transatlantic	TRA267	1973	**£10**	
Don't Let Your Family Down	LP	Transatlantic	TRA284	1975	**£10**	
Little Bit Of Glory	LP	Transatlantic	TRA255	1972	**£10**	
Masquerade	LP	DJM	DJF20489	1976	**£10**	

CASCADES

Cheryl's Going Home	7"	Stateside	SS515	1966	**£4**	
Cinderella	7"	RCA	RCA1358	1963	**£4**	
I Bet You Won't Stay	7"	Liberty	LIB55822	1965	**£4**	
I Wanna Be Your Lover	7"	W. Bros	WB103	1963	**£4**	
Jeannie	7"	RCA	RCA1378	1964	**£4**	
Rhythm Of The Rain	LP	W. Bros	WM8127	1963	**£20**	
Rhythm Of The Rain	7" EP	W. Bros	WEP6106	1963	**£6**	
Rhythm Of The Rain	7"	W. Bros	WB88	1963	**£4**	chart single
Shy Girl	7"	W. Bros	WB98	1963	**£4**	

CASEY, HOWIE & THE SENIORS

Bony Moronie	7"	Fontana	TF403	1963	**£6**	
Double Twist	7"	Fontana	H364	1962	**£10**	
I Ain't Mad At You	7"	Fontana	H381	1962	**£8**	
Let's Twist	LP	Wing	WL1022	1965	**£20**	
Twist At The Top	LP	Fontana	TFL5180	1962	**£40**	

CASH, ALVIN

Alvin's Boogaloo	7"	President	PT119	1968	**£6**	
Charge	7"	President	PT147	1968	**£4**	
Doin' The Ali Shuffle	7"	President	PT129	1968	**£4**	
Philly Freeze	7"	President	PT115	1968	**£6**	
Philly Freeze	7"	Stateside	SS543	1966	**£10**	
Twine Time	7"	Stateside	SS386	1965	**£10**	

CASH, JOHNNY

All Aboard the Blue Train	LP	Sun	1270	1963	**£12**	US
All Over Again	7"	Philips	PB874	1958	**£4**	
Ballad Of A Teenage Queen	7"	London	HLS8586	1958	**£8**	
Country Boy	7" EP	London	RES1212	1959	**£6**	
Don't Take Your Guns To Town	7"	Philips	PB897	1959	**£5**	
Down The Street To 301	7"	London	HLS9182	1960	**£4**	
Fabulous Johnny Cash	LP	Philips	BBL7298	1960	**£10**	
Folsom Prison Blues	7" EP	CBS	EP6601	1969	**£4**	
Forty Shades Of Green	7" EP	CBS	AGG20050	1964	**£4**	
Going To Memphis	7"	Philips	PB1075	1960	**£4**	
Guess Things Happen That Way	7"	London	HLS8656	1958	**£6**	
Holy Land	LP	Columbia	CS9726	1969	**£10**	US, 3D cover
Home Of The Blues	7"	London	HLS8514	1957	**£15**	
Hymns By Johnny Cash	LP	Philips	BBL7373	1960	**£10**	
I Walk The Line	7"	London	HL8358	1957	**£20**	
It Ain't Me Babe	7" EP	CBS	EP6061	1965	**£4**	
It's Just About Time	7"	London	HLS8789	1959	**£4**	
Johnny Cash	7" EP	London	RES1120	1958	**£10**	
Johnny Cash No.2	7" EP	London	RES1230	1959	**£6**	
Johnny Cash Sings Hank Williams	7" EP	London	RES1193	1959	**£6**	
Johnny Cash Sings Hank Williams	LP	Sun	1245	1960	**£20**	US
Johnny Cash With His Hot & Blue Guitar	LP	Sun	1220	1956	**£25**	US
Johnny Cash's Greatest	LP	Sun	1240	1959	**£20**	US
Katy Too	7"	London	HLS8928	1959	**£6**	
Lonesome Me	LP	London	HAS8253	1966	**£10**	
Lure Of The Grand Canyon	LP	Columbia	CL1622	1961	**£10**	US
Luther Played The Boogie	7"	London	HLS8847	1959	**£6**	
Next In Line	7"	London	HLS8461	1957	**£20**	
Now Here's Johnny Cash	LP	Sun	1255	1961	**£15**	US
Now There Was A Song	LP	Philips	BBL7358	1960	**£10**	
Oh Lonesome Me	7"	London	HLS9314	1961	**£4**	
Original Sun Sound Of...	LP	London	HAS8220	1965	**£10**	
Original Sun Sound Of...	LP	Sun	1275	1965	**£12**	US

Title	Format	Label	Number	Year	Price	Notes
Rock Island Line	LP	London	HAS2179	1959	**£12**	
Songs Of Our Soil	LP	Philips	BBL7353	1960	**£10**	
Songs Of Our Soil	7" EP	Philips	BBE12395	1960	**£4**	
Songs That Made Him Famous	LP	London	HAS2157	1959	**£12**	
Songs That Made Him Famous	LP	Sun	1235	1958	**£20**	US
Straight A's In Love	7"	London	HLS9070	1960	**£5**	
Strictly Cash	7" EP	Philips	BBE12494	1961	**£4**	
Train Of Love	7"	London	HLS8427	1957	**£20**	
Troubadour	7" EP	Philips	BBE12377	1960	**£4**	
Ways Of A Woman In Love	7"	London	HLS8709	1958	**£6**	
You Tell Me	7"	London	HLS8979	1959	**£5**	

CASHMAN & WEST

Title	Format	Label	Number	Year	Price	Notes
Lifesong	LP	ABC	ABCL5058	1973	**£10**	
Moondog Serenade	LP	Probe	SPBA6226	1973	**£10**	
Song Or Two	LP	Probe	SPBA6270	1972	**£10**	

CASHMAN, PISTILL & WEST

Title	Format	Label	Number	Year	Price	Notes
Cashman,Pistill & West	LP	Capitol	EST211	1969	**£10**	

CASINO ROYALES

Title	Format	Label	Number	Year	Price	Notes
When I Tell You That I Love You	7"	London	HLU10122	1967	**£4**	

CASINOS

Title	Format	Label	Number	Year	Price	Notes
That's The Way	7"	Ember	EMBS241	1967	**£4**	
Then You Can Tell Me Goodbye	7"	President	PT123	1968	**£4**	chart single
To Be Loved	7"	President	PT140	1968	**£4**	
When I Stop Dreaming	7"	President	PT156	1968	**£4**	

CAST OF THOUSANDS

Title	Format	Label	Number	Year	Price	Notes
My Jeannie Wears A Mini	7"	Stateside	SS546	1966	**£4**	

CASTAWAYS

Title	Format	Label	Number	Year	Price	Notes
Liar Liar	7"	London	HL10003	1965	**£10**	

CASTE

Title	Format	Label	Number	Year	Price	Notes
Don't Cast Aside	7"	President	PT211	1968	**£5**	

CASTELL, JOEY

Title	Format	Label	Number	Year	Price	Notes
I'm Left,You're Right,She's Gone	7"	Decca	F10966	1957	**£8**	

CASTELLS

Title	Format	Label	Number	Year	Price	Notes
Sacred	7"	London	HLN9392	1961	**£4**	
So This Is Love	LP	Era	EL109	1962	**£40**	US
So This Is Love	7"	London	HLN9551	1962	**£4**	
Two Lovers	7"	Masquerade	MA5000	196-	**£4**	

CASTLE SISTERS

Title	Format	Label	Number	Year	Price	Notes
Stop Your Lying	7"	Ska Beat	JB257	1966	**£10**	

CASTLE, LEE & THE BARONS

Title	Format	Label	Number	Year	Price	Notes
Love She Can Count On	7"	Parlophone	R5151	1964	**£6**	

CASTOR, JIMMY

Title	Format	Label	Number	Year	Price	Notes
Magic Saxophone	7"	Philips	BF1590	1967	**£8**	

CASUALS

Title	Format	Label	Number	Year	Price	Notes
Adios Amor	7"	Decca	F12737	1968	**£4**	
Caroline	7"	Decca	F22969	1969	**£4**	
Hour World	LP	Decca	SKL5001	1969	**£15**	
If You Walk Out	7"	Fontana	TF635	1965	**£4**	
Jesamine	7"	Decca	F22784	1968	**£4**	chart single
Sunflower Eyes	7"	Decca	F22943	1969	**£4**	
Toy	7"	Decca	F22852	1968	**£4**	chart single

CAT MOTHER & ALL NIGHT NEWSBOYS

The first LP by Cat Mother And The All Night Newsboys was produced by Jimi Hendrix, a fact which once gave the record a higher collectors' value than it now has. The problem is that the group sound extremely ordinary. Hendrix does not play on the record and the production wizardry that he brought to his own records is nowhere in evidence.

Title	Format	Label	Number	Year	Price	Notes
Albion Doowah	LP	Polydor	2425021	1970	**£10**	
Good Old Rock'n'Roll	7"	Polydor	56543	1970	**£4**	
Street Giveth	LP	Polydor	184300	1969	**£10**	

CATAPILLA

Catapilla	LP	Vertigo	6360029	1971	**£40**	spiral label
Changes	LP	Vertigo	6360074	1972	**£120**	spiral label

CATCH

Borderline	7"	Logo	GO103	1977	**£30**	

CATFISH

Get Down	LP	Epic	EPC64006	1970	**£12**	
Live Catfish	LP	Epic	EPC64408	1971	**£12**	

CATHODE, RAY

Time Beat	7"	Parlophone	R4901	1962	**£4**	

CATHY JEAN & THE ROOMATES

At The Hop!	LP	Valmor	789	1961	**£75**	US

CATS

Dance Dance Dance	7"	Columbia	DB8850	1972	**£4**	
I Gotta Know What's Going On	7"	Columbia	DB8524	1969	**£4**	
I Love You, I Do	7"	Columbia	DB8748	1971	**£4**	
Let's Dance	7"	Columbia	DB8909	1972	**£4**	
Marian	7"	Columbia	DB8655	1970	**£4**	
One Way Wind	7"	Columbia	DB8816	1971	**£4**	
What A Crazy Life	7"	Parlophone	R5558	1967	**£4**	
What Is The World Coming To	7"	Parlophone	R5663	1968	**£4**	
Why	7"	Columbia	DB8571	1969	**£4**	

CATS EYES

Come Away Melinda	7"	MCA	MK5043	1970	**£4**	
I Thank You Marianne	7"	Deram	DM209	1968	**£4**	
Loser	7"	MCA	MK5028	1970	**£4**	
Smile Girl For Me	7"	Deram	DM190	1968	**£4**	
Where Is She Now	7"	Deram	DM251	1969	**£5**	
Wizard	7"	MCA	MK5056	1970	**£4**	

CATS PYJAMAS

Camera Man	7"	Direction	583482	1968	**£8**	
Virginia Waters	7"	Direction	583235	1968	**£8**	

CATTINI, CLEM

No Time To Think	7"	Decca	F12135	1965	**£10**	

CATTOUSE, NADIA

Beautiful Barbados	7"	Reality	RE503	1966	**£6**	
Earth Mother	LP	RCA	SF8070	1969	**£12**	
Port Mahon	7"	Parlophone	R5240	1965	**£5**	

CAVE, EDDIE & THE FIX

Fresh Out Of Tears	7"	Pye	7N17161	1966	**£5**	

CAVELL, ANDY

Always On Saturday	7"	HMV	POP1080	1962	**£5**	
Andy	7"	Pye	7N15539	1963	**£4**	
Hey There Cruel Heart	7"	HMV	POP1024	1962	**£5**	
Tell The Truth	7"	Pye	7N15610	1964	**£4**	

CAVELLO, JIMMY & THE HOUSE ROCKERS

Footstomping	7"	Vogue Coral	Q72240	1957	**£50**	
Rock Rock Rock	7"	Vogue Coral	Q72226	1957	**£25**	

CAZAZZA, MONTE

Live At Leeds Fan Club	cass	Industrial	IRL28		**£10**	
Something For Nobody	7"	Industrial	IR0010	1980	**£8**	
To Mom On Mother's Day	7"	Industrial	IR0005	1979	**£10**	

CCS

CCS was a big band assembled round Alexis Korner, in which some impressive musicians, including Korner himself, woefully under-used their talents. The band's version of "Whole Lotta Love" was adopted as the theme tune for TV's "Top Of The Pops", a somewhat ironical development in view of the fact that the song's originator, Led Zeppelin, refused to issue singles.

Best Band In The Land	LP	RAK	SRAK504	1973	**£10**	
Best Of...	LP	RAK	SRAK527	1977	**£10**	

CCS 1	LP	RAK	SRKA6751	1970	**£10**	
CCS 2	LP	RAK	SRAK503	1972	**£10**	chart LP

CEDARS

For Your Information	7"	Decca	F22720	1968	**£8**	
I Like The Way	7"	Decca	F22772	1968	**£8**	

CELIA & THE MUTATIONS

Mony Mony	7"	United Artists	UP36262	1977	**£8**	
You Better Believe Me	7"	United Artists	UP36318	1977	**£8**	

CELTIC FISHERMAN

Celtic Fisherman	LP	Mushroom		197-	**£40**	

CENTIPEDE

Centipede was so named because of its huge line-up - fifty-five people play on the record, not including Robert Fripp, who played guitar with the band on stage, but who remains in the producer's chair here. Centipede was the inspiration of jazz pianist Keith Tippett, as a piece of mad indulgence that would be unlikely to make anyone's fortune. "Septober Energy" is a single piece of music spread over four sides of vinyl, but it falls naturally into sections, which enable different combinations of musicians to be highlighted.

Septober Energy	LP	Neon	NE9	1971	**£50**	double
Septober Energy	LP	RCA	DPS2054	1974	**£40**	different cover

CHAFFIN, ERNIE

Lonesome For My Baby	7"	London	HLS8409	1957	**£20**	

CHAIRMEN OF THE BOARD

Give Me Just A Little More Time	7"	Invictus	INV501	1970	**£4**	chart single
Greatest Hits	LP	Invictus	SVT1009	1972	**£10**	
Greatest Hits	LP	Invictus	SVT1009	1973	**£10**	

CHAKARIS, GEORGE

I'm Always Chasing Rainbows	7"	Triumph	RGM1010	1960	**£6**	

CHALLENGERS

At The Teenage Fair	LP	GNP-Cres.	2010	1965	**£10**	US
Billy Strange And The Challengers	LP	GNP-Cres.	2030	1966	**£10**	US
Bulldog	7"	Stateside	SS177	1963	**£5**	
California Kicks	LP	GNP-Cres.	2025	1966	**£10**	US
Challengers Au Go-Go	LP	Vault	LP110	1966	**£20**	US
Cry Of The Wild Goose	7"	Parlophone	R4773	1961	**£5**	
Greatest Hits	LP	Vault	LP111	1967	**£15**	US
K-39	LP	Vault	LP107	1964	**£25**	US
Man From UNCLE	LP	GNP-Cres.	2018	1965	**£10**	US
Man From UNCLE	7"	Vocalion	VN9253	1965	**£5**	
On The Move	LP	Vault	LP102	1963	**£20**	US
Sidewalk Surfing	LP	Triumph	100	1965	**£15**	US
Surf's Up	LP	Vault	LP109	1965	**£20**	US
Surfbeat	LP	Stateside	SL10030	1963	**£20**	
Surfing	LP	Vault	LP101	1963	**£20**	US
Twenty-Five Great Instrumental Hits	LP	GNP-Cres.	609	1967	**£10**	US
Walk With Me	7"	Vocalion	VN9270	1966	**£5**	
Wipe Out	LP	Vocalion	SAVN8069	1967	**£20**	

CHALMERS, LLOYD

Duckey Luckey	7"	Songbird	SB1007	196-	**£8**	
Five To Five	7"	Duke	DU25	196-	**£8**	
For The Good Times	7"	Duke	DU162	1973	**£4**	
I'm Gonna Love You Just A Little	7"	Trojan	MJ6662	1974	**£4**	
Safari	7"	Duke	DU36	196-	**£8**	
Save The People	7"	Green Door	GD4064	1973	**£4**	
Time Is Getting Hard	7"	Coxsone	CS7023	196-	**£10**	
White Rum And Salvation	7"	Big Shot	BI624	1973	**£4**	
Why Baby	7"	Gas	GAS114	196-	**£8**	

CHAMBER POP ENSEMBLE

Chamber Pop Ensemble	LP	Decca		1968	**£15**	

CHAMBERLAIN, RICHARD

Love Me Tender	7"	MGM	MGM1173	1962	**£4**	chart single
Richard Chamberlain Hits	7" EP	MGM	MGMEP776	1963	**£5**	
Richard Chamberlain Sings	LP	MGM	C923	1963	**£12**	chart LP

Theme From Dr.Kildare	7"	MGM	MGM1160	1962	**£4**	chart single

CHAMBERS BROTHERS

Love Me Like The Rain	7"	Vocalion	VL9267	1966	**£5**	

CHAMELEONS

As High As You Can Go	7"	Statik	STAT30	1983	**£8**	
As High As You Can Go	12"	Statik	STAT3012	1983	**£12**	
In Shreds	7"	Epic	EPCA2210	1982	**£15**	
In Shreds	7"	Statik	TAK29	1985	**£8**	double
In Shreds	12"	Statik	TAK2912	1985	**£12**	double
Person Isn't Safe Anywhere These Days	7"	Statik	TAK6	1983	**£8**	
Person Isn't Safe Anywhere These Days	12"	Statik	TAK612	1983	**£12**	
Script Of The Bridge	LP	Statik	STATP17	1985	**£15**	pic disc
Singing Rule Britannia	7"	Statik	TAK35	1985	**£4**	
Singing Rule Britannia	12"	Statik	TAK1235	1985	**£6**	
Up The Down Escalator	7"	Statik	TAK11	1984	**£6**	
Up The Down Escalator	12"	Statik	TAK1112	1984	**£10**	

CHAMPS

All American Music	LP	Challenge	CHL614	1962	**£20**	US
Another Four By The Champs	7" EP	London	REH1209	1959	**£10**	
Beatnick	7"	London	HLH8811	1959	**£4**	
Cantina	7"	London	HLH9430	1961	**£4**	
Caramba	7"	London	HLH8864	1959	**£5**	
Chariot Rock	7"	London	HL8715	1958	**£5**	
El Rancho Rock	7"	London	HL8655	1958	**£6**	
Everybody's Rockin'	LP	London	HAH2184	1959	**£20**	
Experiment In Terror	7"	London	HLH9539	1962	**£4**	
Four By The Champs	7" EP	London	RE1176	1959	**£10**	
Go Champs Go	LP	London	HAH2152	1958	**£20**	
Great Dance Hits	LP	London	HAH2451	1962	**£15**	
Knockouts	7" EP	London	REH1250	1961	**£10**	
Latin Limbo	7"	London	HLH9604	1962	**£4**	
Limbo Rock	7"	London	HLH9506	1962	**£4**	
Still More By The Champs	7" EP	London	REH1223	1959	**£10**	
Tequila	7"	London	HLU8580	1958	**£4**	chart single
Too Much Tequila	7"	London	HL9052	1960	**£4**	chart single

CHANCES ARE

Fragile Child	7"	Columbia	DB8144	1967	**£12**	

CHANDLER, GENE

Bless Our Love	7"	Stateside	SS364	1964	**£4**	
Duke Of Earl	7"	Columbia	DB4793	1962	**£10**	
Duke Of Earl	LP	Fontana	TL5247	1962	**£20**	
Duke Of Earl	7"	President	PT234	1969	**£4**	
Fool For You	7"	Stateside	SS500	1966	**£6**	
Girl Don't Care	7"	Coral	Q72490	1967	**£8**	
Good Times	7"	Stateside	SS458	1965	**£5**	
Greatest Hits	LP	Constellation	LP1421	1964	**£12**	US
I Can't Save It	7"	Action	ACT4551	1969	**£12**	
Just Be True	LP	Constellation	LP1423	1964	**£12**	US
Live On Stage	LP	Action	ACLP6010	1969	**£15**	
Nothing Can Stop Me	7"	Stateside	SS425	1965	**£15**	
Nothing can Stop Me	7"	Soul City	SC102	1968	**£6**	chart single
Nothing can Stop Me	7"	Soul City	SC102	1968	**£15**	demo
Song Called Soul	7"	Stateside	SS331	1964	**£4**	
Such A Pretty Thing	7"	Chess	CRS8047	1966	**£15**	
What Now	7"	Stateside	SS388	1965	**£6**	
You Can't Hurt Me No More	7"	Stateside	SS401	1965	**£6**	
You Threw A Lucky Punch	7"	Stateside	SS185	1963	**£4**	
You're A Lady	7"	Mercury	6052098	1971	**£4**	

CHANDLER, JEFF

Half Of My Heart	7"	London	HLU8484	1957	**£4**	

CHANDLER, KENNY

Beyond Love	7"	Stateside	SS2110	1968	**£8**	

CHANDONS

Timber	7"	RCA	RCA1704	1968	**£4**	

CHANNEL, BRUCE

Going Back To Louisiana	7"	London	HLU9841	1964	£4	
Hey Baby	7"	Mercury	AMT1171	1962	£4	chart single
Hey Baby	LP	Smash	MGS27008	1962	£30	US
Keep On	7"	Bell	BLL1010	1968	£4	chart single
Number One Man	7"	Mercury	AMT1177	1962	£4	

CHANTAYS

Beyond	7"	King	KG1018	1964	£5	
Pipeline	7"	Dot	DS26757	1967	£4	
Pipeline	LP	Downey	DLP1002	1963	£75	US
Pipeline	LP	London	HA8087	1963	£20	
Pipeline	7" EP	London	RED1397	1963	£8	
Pipeline	7"	London	HLD9696	1963	£5	chart single
Two Sides Of The Chantays	LP	Dot	DLP3771	1966	£12	US

CHANTELLES

Blue Mood	7"	CBS	2777	1967	£5	
Gonna Get Burned	7"	Parlophone	R5350	1965	£4	
I Think Of You	7"	Parlophone	R5431	1966	£4	
I Want That Boy	7"	Parlophone	R5271	1965	£4	
Secret Of Success	7"	Parlophone	R5303	1965	£4	
There's Something About You	7"	Polydor	56119	1966	£6	

CHANTELS

Look In My Eyes	7"	London	HLL9428	1961	£4	
Maybe	7"	London	HLU8561	1958	£20	
Maybe	7"	Roulette	RO514	1969	£4	
On Tour	LP	Carlton	LP144	1961	£50	US
Still	7"	London	HLL9480	1962	£4	
Summertime	7"	London	HLL9532	1962	£4	
There's Our Song Again	LP	End	LP312	1962	£20	US
We're The Chantels	LP	End	LP301	1958	£300	US, group photo cover
We're The Chantels	LP	End	LP301	1959	£100	US, jukebox cover

CHANTER SISTERS

Birds Of A Feather	LP	Page One	POLS027	1970	£10	

CHANTER, IRENE

Make Me Happy	7"	Polydor	2058608	1975	£5	

CHANTERS

Every Night I Sit And Cry	7"	CBS	202454	1966	£5	
My Love Is For You	7"	CBS	3668	1968	£8	
What's Wrong With You	7"	CBS	3400	1968	£5	
You Can't Fool Me	7"	CBS	202616	1967	£4	

CHANTS

Ain't Nobody Home	7"	Page One	POF016	1967	£6	
Come Back & Get This Loving Boy	7"	Fontana	TF716	1966	£5	
I Could Write A Book	7"	Pye	7N15591	1964	£6	
I Don't Care	7"	Pye	7N15557	1963	£8	
I Get The Sweetest Feeling	7"	RCA	RCA1823	1969	£10	
Lover's Story	7"	Decca	F12650	1967	£5	
Man Without A Face	7"	RCA	RCA1754	1968	£8	
She's Mine	7"	Pye	7N15643	1964	£6	
Sweet Was The Wine	7"	Pye	7N15691	1964	£8	

CHANTS (2)

Close Friends	7"	Capitol	CL14876	1958	£4	

CHAOS UK

Four Minute Warning	7"	Riot City	RIOT6	1982	£4	
No Security	7"	Riot City	RIOT12	1982	£4	

CHAPIN, HARRY

Dance Band On The Titanic	LP	Elektra	K62021	1977	£10	
Greatest Stories Live	LP	Elektra	K62017	1976	£10	
Heads And Tales	LP	Elektra	K42107	1971	£10	
Legends Of The Lost And Found	LP	Elektra	K62026	1979	£10	
Living Room Suite	LP	Elektra	K52089	1978	£10	
On The Road To Kingdom Come	LP	Elektra	K52040	1976	£10	

Portrait Gallery .... LP .... Elektra .... K52023 .... 1975 ...... **£10** ....
Sequel .... LP .... CBS .... 84996 .... 1980 ...... **£10** ....
Short Stories .... LP .... Elektra .... K42155 .... 1973 ...... **£10** ....
Sniper And Other Love Songs .... LP .... Elektra .... K42125 .... 1972 ...... **£10** ....
Verities And Balderdash .... LP .... Elektra .... K52007 .... 1974 ...... **£10** ....

CHAPLAIN, PAUL & THE EMERALDS

Shortning Bread .... 7" .... London .... HLU9205 .... 1960 ...... **£6** ....

CHAPMAN, GENE

Oklahoma Blues .... 7" .... Starlite .... ST45102 .... 1963 ...... **£20** ....

CHAPMAN, MICHAEL

Banjo Song .... 7" .... Deram .... DM407 .... 1974 ...... **£4** ....
Deal Gone Down .... LP .... Deram .... SML1114 .... 1974 ...... **£15** ....
Fully Qualified Survivor .... LP .... Harvest .... SHVL764 .... 1969 ...... **£20** .... chart LP
It Didn't Work Out .... 7" .... Harvest .... HAR5002 .... 1969 ...... **£4** ....
Man Who Hated Mornings .... LP .... Decca .... SKLR5290 .... 1977 ...... **£10** ....
Millstone Grit .... LP .... Deram .... SML1105 .... 1973 ...... **£15** ....
Pleasures Of The Street .... LP .... Nova .... 622321 .... 1975 ...... **£15** .... German
Rainmaker .... LP .... Harvest .... SHVL755 .... 1969 ...... **£20** ....
Savage Amusement .... LP .... Decca .... SKLR5242 .... 1976 ...... **£12** ....
Window .... LP .... Harvest .... SHVL786 .... 1971 ...... **£20** ....
Wrecked Again .... LP .... Harvest .... SHVL798 .... 1971 ...... **£20** ....

CHAPS

Popping Medley .... 7" .... Parlophone .... R4979 .... 1962 ...... **£10** ....

CHAPTER FIVE

Anything That You Do .... 7" .... CBS .... 202395 .... 1966 ...... **£30** ....
One In A Million .... 7" .... CBS .... 202622 .... 1967 ...... **£45** ....

CHAPTER FOUR

In My Life .... 7" .... United Artists .... UP1143 .... 1966 ...... **£12** ....

CHAPTER ONE

Hang On .... 7" .... Chapter One .... CH136 .... 1970 ...... **£4** ....

CHAPTERS

Can't Stop Thinking About Her .... 7" .... Pye .... 7N15815 .... 1965 ...... **£4** ....

CHARLATANS

Charlatans .... LP .... Philips .... SBL7903 .... 1969 ...... **£30** ....

CHARLES, BOBBY

Bobby Charles .... LP .... Bearsville .... K45516 .... 1972 ...... **£10** ....
See You Later Alligator .... 7" .... Chess .... 6145024 .... 1973 ...... **£4** ....
See You Later Alligator .... 7" .... London .... HLU8247 .... 1956 ...... **£150** ....

CHARLES, DON

Angel Of Love .... 7" .... Decca .... F11602 .... 1963 ...... **£4** ....
Don Charles .... 7" EP .... Decca .... DFE8530 .... 1963 ...... **£8** ....
Heart's Ice Cold .... 7" .... Decca .... F11645 .... 1963 ...... **£4** ....
Hermit Of Misty Mountain .... 7" .... Decca .... F11464 .... 1962 ...... **£5** ....
It's My Way Of Loving You .... 7" .... Decca .... F11528 .... 1962 ...... **£4** ....
Walk With Me My Angel .... 7" .... Decca .... F11424 .... 1962 ...... **£5** .... chart single

CHARLES, RAY

Baby Don't You Cry .... 7" .... HMV .... POP1272 .... 1964 ...... **£4** ....
Baby It's Cold Outside .... 7" EP .... HMV .... 7EG8807 .... 1963 ...... **£5** ....
Ballad Style Of Ray Charles .... 7" EP .... HMV .... 7EG8783 .... 1963 ...... **£5** ....
Busted .... 7" EP .... HMV .... 7EG8841 .... 1964 ...... **£5** ....
Busted .... 7" .... HMV .... POP1221 .... 1963 ...... **£4** .... chart single
C&W Meets R&B .... LP .... HMV .... CLP1914 .... 1965 ...... **£10** .... mono
C&W Meets R&B .... LP .... HMV .... CSD1630 .... 1965 ...... **£10** .... stereo
Cincinnati Kid .... 7" .... HMV .... POP1484 .... 1965 ...... **£4** ....
Come Rain Or Come Shine .... 7" .... London .... HLK9251 .... 1960 ...... **£5** ....
Cry .... 7" .... HMV .... POP1392 .... 1965 ...... **£4** ....
Cryin' Time .... 7" .... HMV .... POP1502 .... 1966 ...... **£4** .... chart single
Dedicated To You .... LP .... HMV .... CSD1362 .... 1961 ...... **£12** .... stereo
Dedicated To You .... LP .... HMV .... CLP1449 .... 1961 ...... **£12** .... mono
Don't Set Me Free .... 7" .... HMV .... POP1133 .... 1963 ...... **£4** .... chart single

Title	Format	Label	Cat. No.	Year	Price	Notes
Early In The Mornin'	7"	London	HLK9364	1961	**£4**	
Eleanor Rigby	7"	Stateside	SS2120	1968	**£4**	chart single
Genius After Hours	LP	London	HAK8035	1963	**£12**	
Genius Hits The Road	LP	HMV	CLP1387	1960	**£12**	stereo
Genius Hits The Road	LP	HMV	CSD1320	1960	**£12**	mono
Genius Of Ray Charles	LP	London	LJZ-K15190	1960	**£15**	
Genius Sings The Blues	LP	London	LJZ-K15238	1960	**£15**	
Genius+Soul=Jazz	LP	HMV	CLP1475	1961	**£12**	mono
Genius+Soul=Jazz	LP	HMV	CSD1384	1961	**£12**	stereo
Georgia On My Mind	7"	HMV	POP792	1960	**£4**	chart single
Great Ray Charles	LP	London	LJZ-K15134	1958	**£15**	
Great Ray Charles	7" EP	London	EZK19043	1959	**£6**	
Greatest Hits	LP	HMV	CLP1626	1962	**£10**	chart LP, mono
Greatest Hits	LP	HMV	CSD1482	1962	**£10**	chart LP, stereo
Have A Smile With Me	LP	HMV	CLP1795	1964	**£10**	mono
Have A Smile With Me	LP	HMV	CSD1566	1964	**£10**	stereo
Here We Go Again	7"	HMV	POP1595	1967	**£4**	chart single
Hide Nor Hair	7"	HMV	POP1017	1962	**£4**	
Hit The Road Jack	7"	HMV	POP935	1961	**£5**	chart single
Hit the Road Jack	7" EP	HMV	7EG8729	1962	**£6**	
I Can't Stop Loving You	7" EP	HMV	7EG8781	1962	**£5**	
I Can't Stop Loving You	7"	HMV	POP1034	1962	**£4**	chart single
I Chose To Sing The Blues	7"	HMV	POP1551	1966	**£4**	
I Gotta Woman	7"	HMV	POP1437	1965	**£5**	
I Wonder Who	7"	London	HLK9435	1961	**£4**	
I'm Movin' On	7"	London	HLE9009	1959	**£5**	
In Person	LP	London	HAK2284	1960	**£15**	
In The Heat Of The Night	7"	HMV	POP1607	1967	**£4**	
Let The Good Times Roll	7"	London	HLE9058	1960	**£5**	
Let's Go Get Stoned	7"	HMV	POP1537	1966	**£4**	
Light Out Of Darkness POP1414	7"	HMV		1965	**£4**	
Live In Concert	LP	HMV	CLP1872	1965	**£10**	
Live In Concert	LP	HMV	CSD1606	1965	**£10**	
Love's Gonna Live Here	7"	HMV	POP1457	1965	**£4**	
Makin' Whoopee	7"	HMV	POP1383	1965	**£4**	chart single
Modern Sounds In C&W	LP	HMV	CLP1580	1961	**£12**	chart LP, mono
Modern Sounds In C&W CSD1451	LP	HMV		1961	**£12**	chart LP, stereo
Modern Sounds In C&W 2	LP	HMV	CLP1613	1962	**£12**	chart LP, mono
Modern Sounds In C&W 2	LP	HMV	CSD1477	1962	**£12**	chart LP, stereo
My Baby Don't Dig Me	7"	HMV	POP1315	1964	**£4**	
No One	7"	HMV	POP1202	1963	**£4**	chart single
No One To Cry To	7"	HMV	POP1333	1964	**£4**	chart single
One Mint Julep	7"	HMV	POP862	1961	**£4**	
Original Ray Charles	LP	London	HAK8022	1962	**£15**	
Original Ray Charles Vol.1	7" EP	London	REB1407	1963	**£5**	
Original Ray Charles Vol.2	7" EP	London	REB1408	1963	**£5**	
Original Ray Charles Vol.3	7" EP	London	REB1409	1963	**£5**	
Please Say You're Fooling	7"	HMV	POP1566	1966	**£5**	
Ray Charles & Betty Carter	LP	HMV	CLP1520	1961	**£12**	mono
Ray Charles & Betty Carter	LP	HMV	CSD1414	1961	**£12**	stereo
Ray Charles At Newport	LP	London	LJZ-K15149	1958	**£15**	mono
Ray Charles At Newport	LP	London	SAHK6008	1958	**£15**	stereo
Ray Charles At Newport	7" EP	London	REK1317	1961	**£5**	
Ray Charles Live	7" EP	HMV	7EG8932	1966	**£4**	
Ray Charles Sextet	LP	London	LJZ-K15178	1960	**£15**	
Ray Charles Sings	7" EP	HMV	7EG8861	1964	**£5**	
Ray Charles Story Vol.1	LP	London	HAK8023	1962	**£10**	
Ray Charles Story Vol.2	LP	London	HAK8024	1962	**£10**	
Ray Charles/Rock And Roll	LP	Atlantic	8006	1957	**£20**	US
Recipe For Soul	LP	HMV	CLP1678	1963	**£10**	
Rockhouse	7"	London	HLE8768	1958	**£10**	
Ruby	7"	HMV	POP825	1961	**£4**	
Sings Songs Of Buck Owens	7" EP	HMV	7EG8951	1966	**£4**	
Smack Dab In The Middle	7"	HMV	POP1350	1964	**£4**	
Soul Brothers	LP	London	LJZ-K15146	1959	**£15**	mono
Soul Brothers	LP	London	SAHK6030	1959	**£15**	stereo
Soul Brothers	7" EP	London	EZK19048	1959	**£6**	
Sticks And Stones	7"	HMV	POP774	1960	**£4**	
Sweet & Sour Tears	LP	HMV	CLP1728	1963	**£10**	mono
Sweet & Sour Tears	LP	HMV	CSD1537	1963	**£10**	stereo
Swinging Style Of Ray Charles	7" EP	HMV	7EG8801	1963	**£5**	

Title	Format	Label	Cat. No.	Year	Price	Notes
Take These Chains From My Heart	7" EP	HMV	7EG8812	1963	**£5**	
Take These Chains From My Heart	7"	HMV	POP1161	1963	**£4**	chart single
Tell The Truth	7"	London	HLK9181	1960	**£4**	
That Lucky Old Sun	7"	HMV	POP1251	1964	**£4**	
Them That Got	7"	HMV	POP838	1961	**£4**	
Together Again	7"	HMV	POP1519	1966	**£4**	chart single
Unchain My Heart	7"	HMV	POP969	1962	**£4**	
What I Say	7"	Atlantic	584093	1967	**£4**	
What I Say	7"	London	HLE8917	1959	**£6**	
What'd I Say	LP	London	HAK2226	1959	**£15**	
What'd I Say	7" EP	London	REK1306	1961	**£6**	
Yes Indeed	LP	London	HAE2168	1958	**£15**	
Yesterday	7"	Stateside	SS2071	1967	**£4**	chart single
You Don't Know Me	7"	HMV	POP1064	1962	**£4**	chart single
You Win Again	7"	HMV	POP1589	1967	**£4**	
Young Ray Charles	7" EP	Realm	REP4001	1964	**£5**	
Your Cheating Heart	7"	HMV	POP1099	1962	**£4**	chart single

CHARLES, RAY WITH MILT JACKSON

Title	Format	Label	Cat. No.	Year	Price	Notes
Soul Meeting	LP	London	HAK8045	1963	**£12**	

CHARLES, SONNY

Title	Format	Label	Cat. No.	Year	Price	Notes
Black Pearl	7"	A&M	AMS752	1969	**£5**	
Mastered The Art Of Love	7"	Ember	EMBS240	1967	**£4**	

CHARMERS

Title	Format	Label	Cat. No.	Year	Price	Notes
Oh Yes	7"	Vogue	V9095	1958	**£20**	
Rasta Never Fails	7"	Green Door	GD4000	1971	**£6**	

CHARMERS (2)

Title	Format	Label	Cat. No.	Year	Price	Notes
Back To Back	7"	Melodisc	CAL9	196-	**£8**	
Best Friend	7"	Ska Beat	JB237	1966	**£10**	
Dig Then Prince	7"	Blue Beat	BB251	1964	**£8**	
Stone Cold Man	7"	Melodisc	CAL8	196-	**£8**	

CHARMS

Title	Format	Label	Cat. No.	Year	Price	Notes
Everybody Say Yeah	7"	Rio	R98	196-	**£8**	

CHARMS, TEDDY

Title	Format	Label	Cat. No.	Year	Price	Notes
I Want It Girl	7"	Blue Cat	BS141	196-	**£10**	

CHASE

Title	Format	Label	Cat. No.	Year	Price	Notes
Chase	LP	Epic	64544	1971	**£10**	
Ennea	LP	Epic	64710	1972	**£10**	
Pure Music	LP	Epic	80017	1974	**£10**	

CHASERS

Title	Format	Label	Cat. No.	Year	Price	Notes
Hey Little Girl	7"	Decca	F12302	1965	**£8**	
Inspiration	7"	Parlophone	R5451	1966	**£6**	
Ways Of A Man	7"	Philips	BF1546	1967	**£8**	

CHEAP TRICK

Title	Format	Label	Cat. No.	Year	Price	Notes
Dream Police sampler	7"	Epic		1980	**£5**	promo
I Want You To Want Me	7"	Epic	EPC7258DJ	1979	**£5**	promo
Live At Budokan	LP	Epic	EPC86083	1978	**£10**	yellow vinyl, booklet
So Good To See You	7"	Epic	EPC6199	1978	**£4**	promo

CHEATIN' HEARTS

Title	Format	Label	Cat. No.	Year	Price	Notes
Bad Kind	7"	Columbia	DB8048	1966	**£8**	

CHECKER, CHUBBY

Title	Format	Label	Cat. No.	Year	Price	Notes
All The Hits	LP	Cameo Park	P7014	1963	**£10**	
Chubby Checker	LP	Cameo Park	P7036	1963	**£10**	
Class	7"	Top Rank	JAR154	1959	**£8**	
Dancing Party	7" EP	Cameo Park	CPE550	1963	**£5**	
Dancing Party	7"	Columbia	DB4876	1962	**£4**	chart single
Discotheque	7"	Cameo Park	P949	1965	**£20**	
Everything's Wrong	7"	Cameo Park	P959	1965	**£8**	
Fly	7"	Columbia	DB4728	1961	**£4**	
For Twisters Only	LP	Columbia	33SX1341	1961	**£10**	chart LP
Good Good Loving	7"	Columbia	DB4652	1961	**£4**	
Gotta Get Myself Together	7"	Pye	7N25160	1962	**£4**	

Hey You Little Boogaloo	7"	Cameo Park.	P989	1965	**£4**	
Hucklebuck	7"	Columbia	DB4541	1960	**£4**	
It's Pony Time	LP	Columbia	33SX1365	1961	**£10**	
King Of The Twist	7" EP	Columbia	SEG8155	1962	**£5**	
Let's Twist Again	7"	Cameo Park.	P824	1961	**£4**	
Let's Twist Again	7"	Columbia	DB4691	1961	**£4**	chart single
Limbo Party	LP	Cameo Park.	P7020	1963	**£10**	
Lovely Lovely	7"	Cameo Park.	P936	1965	**£4**	
Pony Time	7"	Columbia	DB4591	1961	**£4**	chart single
Slow Twisting	7"	Columbia	DB4808	1962	**£4**	chart single
Twist	7"	Columbia	DB4503	1960	**£5**	chart single
Twist Along With...	LP	Columbia	33SX1445	1962	**£10**	
Twist With...	LP	Columbia	33SX1315	1961	**£12**	chart LP
Twistin' Around The World	LP	Golden Guin.	GGL0236	1962	**£10**	
Two Hearts Make One Love	7"	Cameo Park.	P965	1965	**£25**	

CHECKER, CHUBBY & BOBBY RYDELL

Bobby Rydell/Chubby Checker	LP	Cameo	C1013	1961	**£12**	US
Chubby Checker & Bobby R. In London	7" EP	Cameo Park.	CPE554	1964	**£5**	
Jingle Bell Rock	7"	Cameo Park.	C205	1962	**£4**	chart single
Teach Me To Twist	7"	Columbia	DB4802	1962	**£4**	chart single

CHECKER, CHUBBY & DEE DEE SHARP

Down To Earth	LP	Cameo Park.	C1029	1963	**£10**	

CHECKMATES

Around	7"	Decca	F12114	1965	**£10**	
Every Day Is Just The Same	7"	Parlophone	R5495	1966	**£15**	
Rocking Minstrel	7"	Piccadilly	7N35010	1961	**£8**	
Sticks And Stones	7"	Decca	F11844	1964	**£6**	
Stop That Music	7"	Parlophone	R5337	1965	**£12**	
You Got The Gamma Goochie	7"	Parlophone	R5402	1966	**£20**	
You've Gotta Have A Gimick Today	7"	Decca	F11603	1963	**£8**	

CHECKMATES (2)

Invisible Ska	7"	Ska Beat	JB225	1965	**£10**	

CHECKMATES LTD.

Do The Walk	7"	Ember	EMBS235	1967	**£4**	
I Keep Forgettin'	7"	A&M	AMS780	1970	**£4**	
Love Is All I Have To Give	LP	A&M	AMLS943	1969	**£15**	
Love Is All I Have To Give	7"	A&M	AMS747	1969	**£4**	
Proud Mary	7"	A&M	AMS769	1969	**£4**	chart single

CHEECH & CHONG

Big Bambu	LP	A&M	AMLH67014	1972	**£10**	
Cheech & Chong	LP	A&M	AMLS67010	1971	**£10**	
Lets Make A New Dope Deal	LP	W. Bros	K56809	1977	**£10**	
Los Cochinos	LP	Ode	ODE77019	1973	**£10**	
Sleeping Beauty	LP	Ode	ODE77040	1976	**£10**	
Wedding Album	LP	Ode	ODE77025	1974	**£10**	

CHEERS

Bazoom I Need Your Loving	7"	Capitol	CL14189	1954	**£15**	
Black Denim Trousers	7"	Capitol	CL14377	1955	**£15**	
Blueberries	7"	Capitol	CL14280	1955	**£12**	
Cheers	7" EP	Capitol	EAP1584	1956	**£15**	
Chicken	7"	Capitol	CL14561	1956	**£12**	
I Must Be Dreaming	7"	Capitol	CL14337	1955	**£12**	
Que Pasa Muchacha	7"	Capitol	CL14601	1956	**£4**	
Whadya Want	7"	Capitol	CL14248	1955	**£12**	

CHEETAHS

Goodbye Baby	7"	Philips	BF1412	1965	**£8**	
Mecca	7"	Philips	BF1362	1964	**£8**	chart single
Russian Boat Song	7"	Philips	BF1499	1966	**£8**	
Soldier Boy	7"	Philips	BF1383	1965	**£8**	chart single
Whole Lotta Love	7"	Philips	BF1453	1965	**£5**	

CHELSEA

Alternative Hits	LP	Step Forward	SFLP5	1981	**£15**	
Chelsea	LP	Step Forward	SFLP2	1979	**£15**	

Title	Format	Label	Cat. No.	Year	Price	Notes
Evacuate	7"	Step Forward	SF20	1981	**£4**	
Freemans	7"	Step Forward	SF18	1981	**£4**	
High Rise Living	7"	Step Forward	SF5	1977	**£5**	
Look At The Outside	7"	Step Forward	SF15	1980	**£4**	
No Escape	7"	Step Forward	SF16	1980	**£4**	
No One's Coming Outside	7"	Step Forward	SF14	1980	**£4**	
Right To Work	7"	Step Forward	SF2	1977	**£5**	
Rocking House	7"	Step Forward	SF17	1981	**£4**	
Urban Kids	7"	Step Forward	SF8	1978	**£4**	

CHENIER, CLIFTON

Title	Format	Label	Cat. No.	Year	Price	Notes
Black Girl	7"	Action	ACT4550	1969	**£4**	

CHER

Title	Format	Label	Cat. No.	Year	Price	Notes
3614 Jackson Highway	LP	Atlantic	226026	1969	**£10**	
All I Really Want To Do	LP	Liberty	LBY3058	1965	**£10**	chart LP
All I Really Want To Do	7"	Liberty	LIB66114	1965	**£4**	chart single
Backstage	LP	Liberty	LBL83156	1968	**£10**	
Bang Bang	7"	Liberty	LIB66160	1966	**£4**	chart single
Cher	LP	Liberty	LBY3081	1967	**£10**	
Hits Of Cher	7" EP	Liberty	LEP4047	1966	**£5**	
Sonny Side Of Cher	LP	Liberty	LBY3072	1966	**£10**	chart LP
Sunny	7"	Liberty	LIB12083	1966	**£4**	chart single
Take Me Home	LP	Casablanca	NBPIX7133	1979	**£10**	pic disc
Walk On Gilded Splinters	7"	Atlantic	584278	1969	**£4**	
Where Do You Go	7"	Liberty	LIB66136	1966	**£4**	
With Love	LP	Liberty	LBL83051	1967	**£10**	

CHEROKEES

Title	Format	Label	Cat. No.	Year	Price	Notes
Dig A Little Deeper	7"	Columbia	DB7704	1965	**£5**	
Land Of A Thousand Dances	7"	Columbia	DB7822	1966	**£5**	
Seven Daffodils	7"	Columbia	DB7341	1964	**£5**	chart single
Wondrous Place	7"	Columbia	DB7473	1965	**£5**	
You've Done It Again Little Girl	7"	Decca	F11915	1964	**£6**	

CHEROKEES (2)

Title	Format	Label	Cat. No.	Year	Price	Notes
Cherokee	7"	Pye	7N25066	1961	**£4**	

CHERRY PEOPLE

Title	Format	Label	Cat. No.	Year	Price	Notes
And Suddenly	7"	MGM	MGM1438	1968	**£15**	
Gotta Get Back	7"	MGM	MGM1472	1969	**£6**	
Light Of Love	7"	MGM	MGM1489	1969	**£6**	

CHERRY SMASH

Title	Format	Label	Cat. No.	Year	Price	Notes
Fade Away Maureen	7"	Decca	F12884	1969	**£8**	
Goodtime Sunshine	7"	Decca	F12838	1968	**£5**	
Sing Songs Of Love	7"	Track	604017	1967	**£8**	

CHESTER, PETE

Title	Format	Label	Cat. No.	Year	Price	Notes
Forest Fire	7"	Pye	7N25074	1961	**£5**	
Ten Swinging Bottles	7"	Pye	7N15305	1960	**£8**	

CHESTER, VIC

Title	Format	Label	Cat. No.	Year	Price	Notes
Rock A Billy	7"	Decca	F10882	1957	**£4**	

CHESTERFIELDS

Title	Format	Label	Cat. No.	Year	Price	Notes
A Guitar In Your Bath	7"	Subway	SUBWAY3	1986	**£5**	

CHEVLONS

Title	Format	Label	Cat. No.	Year	Price	Notes
Too Long Alone	7"	Pye	7N17145	1966	**£4**	
Lullaby	7"	Top Rank	JAR308	1960	**£4**	

CHEVRONS

Title	Format	Label	Cat. No.	Year	Price	Notes
Sing Along Rock And Roll	LP	Time	T10008	1961	**£20**	US

CHEYNES

A well respected, but ultimately unsuccessful R&B group, the Cheynes included Peter Bardens and Mick Fleetwood, whose next project was the Peter B's, and Phil Sawyer, who later turned up as a member of the second Spencer Davis Group.

Title	Format	Label	Cat. No.	Year	Price	Notes
Down And Out	7"	Columbia	DB7464	1965	**£30**	
Going To The River	7"	Columbia	DB7368	1964	**£30**	
Respectable	7"	Columbia	DB7153	1963	**£30**	

CHI-LITES

Title	Format	Label	Number	Year	Price	Notes
Pretty Girl	7"	Beacon	BEA119	1968	**£5**	

CHICAGO

Chicago have fallen into almost as much disfavour as have Blood,Sweat,and Tears, but many of their records are actually rather fine. The presence of brass instruments, however, does not make the group's music jazz-rock. The primary function of the brass is to give the music power, in the manner of the Atlantic recordings by Otis Redding and Wilson Pickett. Meanwhile, the most dominant solo voice is that of Terry Kath's guitar, which is fluent and exciting, though without, perhaps, being particularly individual.

Title	Format	Label	Number	Year	Price	Notes
25 Or 6 To 4	7"	CBS	5076	1970	**£4**	chart single
Chicago At Carnegie Hall	LP	Columbia	CQ30865	1974	**£25**	US quad, 4 LPs
Chicago II	LP	Columbia	GQ33258	1975	**£15**	US quad, double
Chicago III	LP	Columbia	C2Q30110	1974	**£15**	US quad, double
Chicago IX (Greatest Hits)	LP	Columbia	HC43900	1981	**£10**	US audiophile
Chicago IX (Greatest Hits)	LP	Columbia	PCQ33900	1975	**£10**	US quad
Chicago Transit Authority	LP	Columbia	GQ33255	1975	**£15**	US quad, double
Chicago Transit Authority	LP	Mobile Fid.	MFSL2218	1983	**£15**	US audiophile, double
Chicago V	LP	Columbia	CQ31102	1974	**£10**	US quad
Chicago VI	LP	Columbia	CQ32400	1974	**£10**	US quad
Chicago VII	LP	Columbia	C2Q32810	1974	**£15**	US quad, double
Chicago VIII	LP	Columbia	PCQ33100	1975	**£10**	US quad
Chicago X	LP	Columbia	HC44200	1981	**£10**	US audiophile
Chicago X	LP	Columbia	PCQ34200	1976	**£10**	US quad
I'm A Man	7"	CBS	4503	1969	**£8**	
I'm A Man	7"	CBS	4715	1969	**£4**	chart single
IV (At Carnegie Hall)	LP	CBS	66405	1971	**£20**	4 LPs
Live In Japan 1972	LP	CBS/Sony	SCPS31	1975	**£12**	Japanese

CHICAGO LINE

Title	Format	Label	Number	Year	Price	Notes
Shimmy Shimmy Ko Ko Bop	7"	Philips	BF1488	1966	**£4**	

CHICAGO LOOP

Title	Format	Label	Number	Year	Price	Notes
She Comes To Me	7"	Stateside	SS564	1966	**£4**	

CHICKEN BONES

Title	Format	Label	Number	Year	Price	Notes
Hard Rock In Concert	LP	Procom		1973	**£200**	

CHICKEN SHACK

As the second most successful group signed to Blue Horizon (behind Fleetwood Mac), Chicken Shack relied heavily on the blues guitar of Stan Webb. He was not, however, as talented as he thought he was, as his embarrassing attempts to prove his versatility via live versions of Davey Graham's tricky instrumental, "Angie", showed only too clearly. The real talent in the group was singer and pianist Christine Perfect (later Christine McVie), but she defected to Fleetwood Mac after the first two LPs.

Title	Format	Label	Number	Year	Price	Notes
100 Ton Chicken	LP	Blue Horizon	763218	1969	**£20**	
40 Blue Fingers....	LP	Blue Horizon	763203	1968	**£20**	chart LP
Accept	LP	Blue Horizon	763861	1970	**£20**	
Goodbye (Live)	LP	Nova	621579	1974	**£12**	
I'd Rather Go Blind	7"	Blue Horizon	573153	1969	**£5**	chart single
I'd Rather Go Blind	7"	CBS	1832	1974	**£4**	
Imagination Lady	LP	Deram	SDL5	1971	**£15**	
It's OK WIth Me Baby	7"	Blue Horizon	573135	1967	**£8**	
Maudie	7"	Blue Horizon	573168	1970	**£6**	
O.K. Ken?	LP	Blue Horizon	763209	1968	**£20**	chart LP
Sad Clown	7"	Blue Horizon	573176	1970	**£6**	
Tears In The Wind	7"	Blue Horizon	573160	1969	**£6**	chart single
Unlucky Boy	LP	Deram	SML1100	1973	**£12**	
When The Train Comes Back	7"	Blue Horizon	573146	1968	**£6**	
Worried About My Woman	7"	Blue Horizon	573143	1968	**£6**	

CHIEFS

Title	Format	Label	Number	Year	Price	Notes
Apache	7"	London	HLU8624	1958	**£5**	
Enchiladas	7"	London	HLU8720	1958	**£4**	

CHIFFONS

Title	Format	Label	Number	Year	Price	Notes
Chiffons	LP	Stateside	SL10040	1963	**£15**	
He's So Fine	LP	Laurie	LLP2018	1963	**£20**	US
He's So Fine	7"	Stateside	SS172	1963	**£4**	chart single
I Have A Boyfriend	7"	Stateside	SS254	1964	**£4**	
Love So Fine	7"	Stateside	SS230	1963	**£4**	
My Boyfriend's Back	7"	Stateside	SS578	1967	**£4**	
My Secret Love	LP	B.T.Puppy	S1011	1970	**£20**	US
Nobody Knows What's Goin' On	7"	Stateside	SS437	1965	**£8**	

Awopbopalubop Awopbamboom!

Tell Me What I Say

C'mon Everybody

C'mon Everybody II

One, Two, Three O' Clock, Four O' Clock Rock!

Roll Over Beethoven (And Tell Tchaikovsky The News)

Rock Island Line

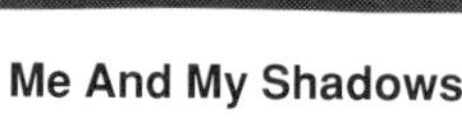
Me And My Shadows

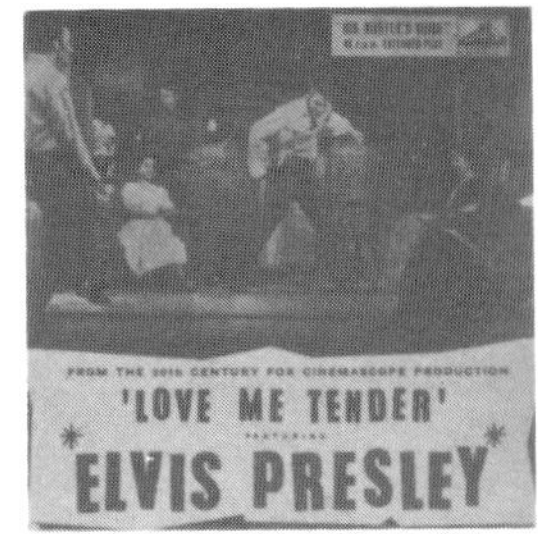

Heard The News, There's Good Rockin' Tonight

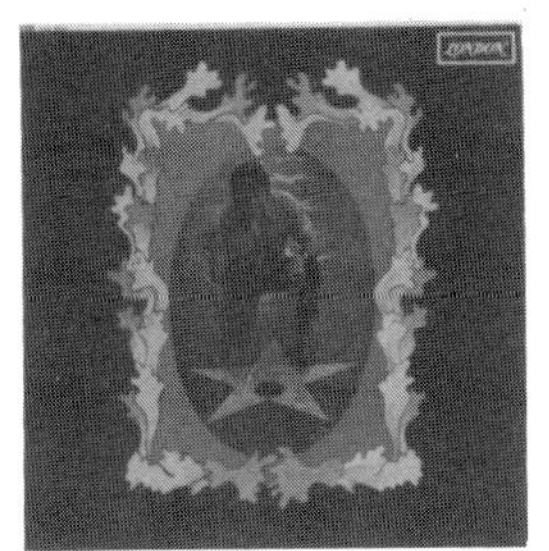

Flaming Star

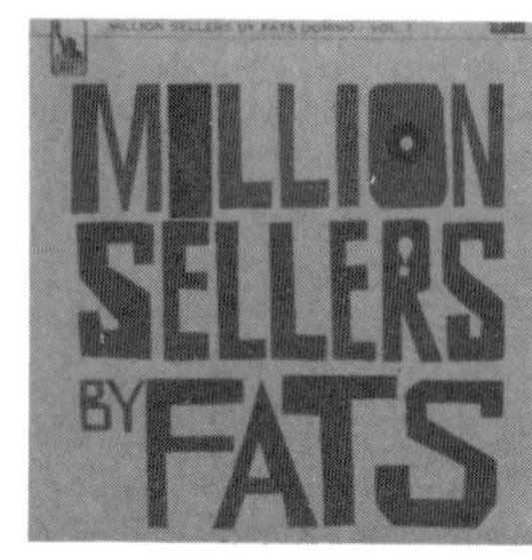

Let The Good Times Roll

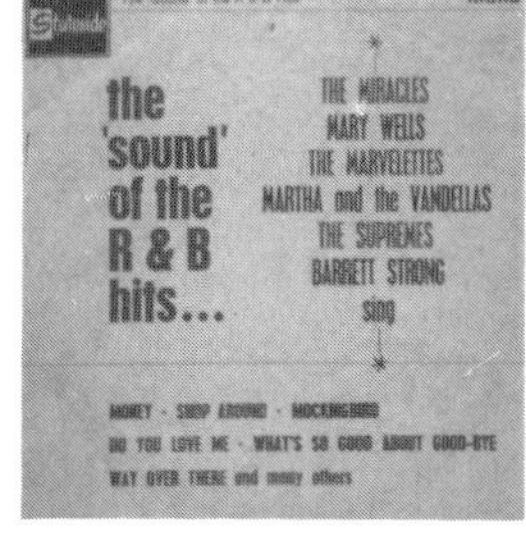

That Motown Sound

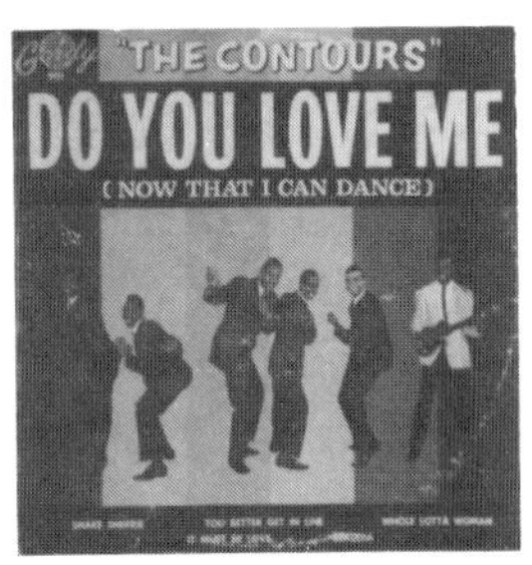

Soul Sounds

The Sound Of Young America

In The Groove

The Way You Do The Things You Do

How Sweet It Is

Dancing In The Street

Hold On, I'm Comin'

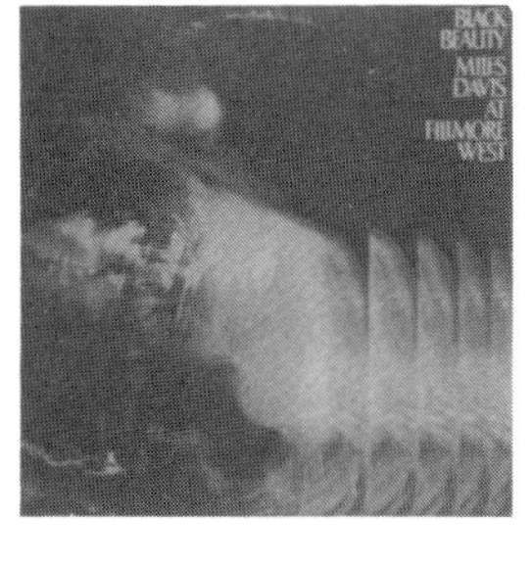

Say It Loud, I'm Black And I'm Proud

This Is Where The Story Really Starts

Peppermint Twist

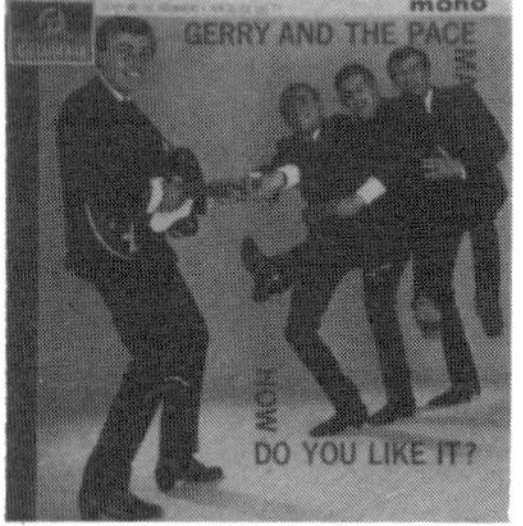

Cavern Stomp

Do You Love Me?

Got My Mojo Workin'

I'm A King Bee

Circles

Circles II

Bring It On Home To Me

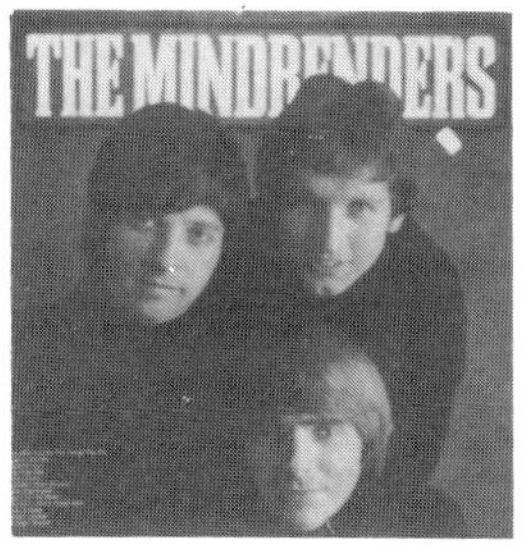

You Make It Move

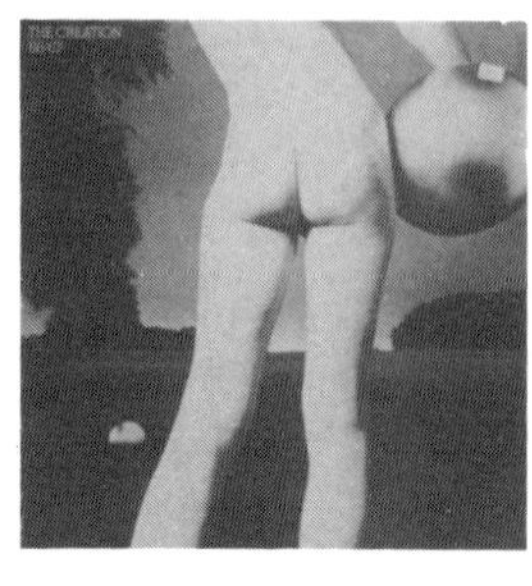

My Generation

Make It Easy On Yourself

One Fine Day	LP	Laurie	LLP2020	1963	**£20**	US
One Fine Day	7"	Stateside	SS202	1963	**£4**	chart single
Out Of This World	7"	Stateside	SS533	1966	**£4**	
Sailor Boy	7"	Stateside	SS332	1964	**£4**	
Stop,Look,& Listen	7"	Stateside	SS559	1966	**£4**	
Sweet Talkin' Guy	LP	Stateside	SL10190	1966	**£12**	
Sweet Talkin' Guy	7"	Stateside	SS512	1966	**£4**	chart single
They're So Fine	7" EP	Stateside	SE1012	1964	**£10**	

CHILDE, SONNY

Giving Up On Love	7"	Decca	F12218	1965	**£8**	
Heartbreak	7"	Polydor	56141	1966	**£5**	
Two Lovers	7"	Polydor	56108	1966	**£12**	

CHILLI WILLI & RED HOT PEPPERS

Bongos Over Balham	LP	Mooncrest	CREST21	1974	**£10**	
Kings Of The Robot Rhythm	LP	Revelation	REV002	1972	**£10**	

CHILLIWACK

All Over You	LP	A&M	4375	1972	**£15**	US
Chilliwack	LP	London	SHU8418	1971	**£20**	
Chilliwack	LP	Sire	7506	1974	**£10**	US

CHILLUM

Chillum	LP	Mushroom	100MR11	197-	**£25**	

CHILTON, ALEX

No Sex	7"	New Rose	NEW69	1986	**£5**	double

CHIMES

Once In A While	7"	London	HLU9283	1961	**£4**	

CHIPMUNKS

All My Loving	7"	Liberty	LIB10170	1964	**£4**	

CHOCOLATE FROG

Butchers And Bakers	7"	Atlantic	584207	1968	**£5**	

CHOCOLATE WATCH BAND

Inner Mystique	LP	Tower	ST5106	1968	**£50**	US
No Way Out	LP	Tower	ST5096	1967	**£50**	US
One Step Beyond	LP	Tower	ST5153	1969	**£40**	US
Requiem	7"	Decca	F12704	1967	**£15**	
Sound Of The Summer	7"	Decca	F12649	1967	**£15**	

CHOIR

It's Cold Outside	7"	Major Minor	MM537	1968	**£10**	
When You Were With Me	7"	Major Minor	MM557	1968	**£8**	

CHOPYN

Grand Slam	LP	Jet	LP08	1975	**£15**	
In The Midnight Hour	7"	Jet	751	1975	**£4**	
Wasting Time	7"	Jet	752	1975	**£4**	

CHORDETTES

Baby Of Mine	7"	London	HLA8566	1958	**£4**	
Born To Be With You	7"	London	HLA8302	1956	**£10**	chart single
Chordettes	LP	London	HAA2088	1958	**£25**	
Chordettes	7" EP	London	REA1228	1960	**£12**	
Close Harmony	LP	Cadence	CLP3002	1957	**£15**	US
Duddlesack Polka	7"	London	HLU8217	1956	**£6**	
Girl's Work Is Never Done	7"	London	HLA8926	1959	**£4**	
Harmony Encores	LP-10"	Columbia	CL6218	1953	**£15**	US
Harmony Time	LP-10"	Columbia	CL6111	1950	**£15**	US
Harmony Time Vol.2	LP-10"	Columbia	CL6170	1951	**£15**	US
Hummingbird	7"	London	HLA8169	1955	**£10**	
Just Between You And Me	7"	London	HLA8473	1957	**£6**	
Lay Down Your Arms	7"	London	HLA8323	1956	**£8**	
Like A Baby	7"	London	HLA8497	1957	**£4**	
Listen	LP	Columbia	CL956	1954	**£15**	US
Lollipop	7"	London	HLA8584	1958	**£4**	chart single
Love Is A Two Way Street	7"	London	HLA8654	1958	**£4**	

Mister Sandman	7"	Columbia	SCM5158	1954	**£15**	chart single
Never On Sunday	LP	Cadence	CLP3062	1962	**£10**	US
No Other Arms No Other Lips	7"	London	HLA8809	1959	**£4**	
Our Melody	7"	London	HLA8264	1956	**£8**	
Your Requests	LP-10"	Columbia	CL6285	1953	**£15**	US

CHORDS

British Way Of Life	7"	Polydor	2059258	1980	**£4**	chart single
In My Street	7"	Polydor	POSP185	1980	**£4**	chart single
Maybe Tomorrow	7"	Polydor	POSP101	1980	**£4**	chart single
Now It's Gone	7"	Polydor	2059141	1979	**£5**	chart single
One More Minute	7"	Polydor	POSP270	1981	**£4**	
So Far Away	LP	Polydor	POLS1019	1980	**£10**	with single (KRODS1)
Something's Missing	7"	Polydor	POSP146	1980	**£4**	chart single
Turn Away Again	7"	Polydor	POSP288	1981	**£4**	

CHORDS (2)

Sh'boom	7"	Columbia	SCM5133	1954	**£100**	

CHORDS FIVE

I'm Only Dreaming	7"	Island	WI3044	1967	**£10**	
Same Old Fat Man	7"	Polydor	56261	1968	**£15**	

CHORDS FIVE (2)

Some People	7"	Jayboy	BOY6	1968	**£10**	

CHRIS & STUDENTS

Lass Of Richmond Hill	7"	Parlophone	R4806	1961	**£5**	

CHRIS, PETER & THE OUTCASTS

Over The Hill	7"	Columbia	DB7923	1966	**£8**	

CHRISTIAN DEATH

Official Anthology Of Live Bootlegs	LP	Jungle		1986	**£30**	black & yellow cover
Only Theatre Of Pain	LP	Future		1983	**£25**	

CHRISTIAN, HANS

Mississippi Hobo	7"	Parlophone	R5698	1968	**£20**	
Never My Love	7"	Parlophone	R5676	1968	**£20**	

CHRISTIAN, LIZ

Suddenly You Find Love	7"	CBS	202520	1967	**£25**	

CHRISTIAN, NEIL

All Things Bright And Beautiful	7"	Pye	7N17372	1967	**£6**	
Little Bit Of Something Else	7" EP	Columbia	SEG8492	1966	**£20**	
Oops	7"	Strike	JH313	1966	**£8**	
That's Nice	7"	Strike	JH301	1966	**£8**	chart single
Two At A Time	7"	Strike	JH319	1966	**£8**	

CHRISTIAN, NEIL & THE CRUSADERS

Lead guitarist with this group for a time was the young Jimmy Page, although he does not play on many of the singles.

Big Beat Drum	7"	Columbia	DB4938	1962	**£10**	
Get A Load Of This	7"	Columbia	DB7075	1963	**£10**	
Honey Hush	7"	Columbia	DB7289	1964	**£10**	

CHRISTIE, LOU

All That Glitters Isn't Gold	7"	King	KG1036	196-	**£4**	
Lightnin' Strikes	7"	MGM	MGM1297	1966	**£4**	chart single
Lightnin' Strikes	LP	MGM	E4360	1966	**£10**	US
Lou Christie	LP	Roulette	R25208	1963	**£15**	US
Lou Christie Strikes Again	LP	Colpix	CP4001	1966	**£10**	US
Lou Christie Strikes Again	LP	Roulette	R25332	1966	**£10**	US
Lou Christie Strikes Back	LP	Co & Ce	LP1231	1966	**£15**	US
Painter Of Hits	LP	MGM	E4394	1966	**£10**	US

CHRISTMAS, KEITH

Brighter Day	LP	Manticore	K53503	1974	**£10**	
Fable Of The Wings	LP	B&C	CAS1015	1971	**£10**	
Pigmy	LP	B&C	CAS1041	1971	**£10**	
Stimulus	LP	RCA	SF8059	1969	**£15**	
Stories From A Human Zoo	LP	Atlantic	K53509	1976	**£10**	

CHROME

Title	Format	Label	Number	Year	Price	Notes
Alien Soundtracks	LP	Siren	DE2100	1978	**£15**	
Half Lip Machine Moves	LP	Beggars B.	BEGA18	1980	**£10**	
Inworlds	12"	Don't Fall Off	Y3	1981	**£12**	
No Humans Allowed	LP	Siren		1981	**£15**	US
Read Only Memory	12"	Siren	RS12007	1980	**£15**	with poster
Red Exposure	LP	Beggars B.	BEGA15	1980	**£10**	
Visitation	LP	Siren	DE1000	1977	**£15**	

CHRYSTAL BAND

Title	Format	Label	Number	Year	Price	Notes
Chrystal Band	LP	Carole			**£40**	

CHUCK & BETTY

Title	Format	Label	Number	Year	Price	Notes
Sissy Britches	7"	Brunswick	05815	1959	**£10**	

CHUCK & DOBBY

Title	Format	Label	Number	Year	Price	Notes
Cool School	7"	Blue Beat	BB23	1961	**£10**	
Do Du Wap	7"	Blue Beat	BB39	1961	**£10**	
Lovey Dovey	7"	Starlite	ST45044	1961	**£5**	
Sweeter Than Honey	7"	Starlite	ST45043	1961	**£5**	

CHUCK & GARY

Title	Format	Label	Number	Year	Price	Notes
Teenie Weenie Jeannie	7"	HMV	POP466	1958	**£6**	

CHUCKS

Title	Format	Label	Number	Year	Price	Notes
Chucks	7" EP	Decca	DFE8562	1964	**£6**	
Hitch Hiker	7"	Decca	F11777	1963	**£4**	
Loo Be Loo	7"	Decca	F11569	1963	**£4**	chart single
Mulberry Bush	7"	Decca	F11617	1963	**£4**	

CHURCH, EUGENE

Title	Format	Label	Number	Year	Price	Notes
Miami	7"	London	HL8940	1959	**£8**	

CHURCHILL, CHICK

Title	Format	Label	Number	Year	Price	Notes
You And Me	LP	Chrysalis	CHR1051	1973	**£10**	

CIGARETTES

Title	Format	Label	Number	Year	Price	Notes
Can't Sleep At Night	7"	Dead Good	DEAD10	1980	**£6**	
They're Back Again, Here They Come	7"	Company	CIGCO008	1979	**£10**	

CINDERELLAS

Title	Format	Label	Number	Year	Price	Notes
Baby Baby	7"	Colpix	PX11126	1964	**£12**	
Mr.Dee-Jay	7"	Brunswick	05794	1959	**£4**	
Trouble With Boys	7"	Philips	PB1012	1960	**£4**	

CIRCLES

Title	Format	Label	Number	Year	Price	Notes
Take Your Time	7"	Island	WI279	1966	**£10**	

CIRCUS

Circus played a serviceable rock style with jazz overtones and were chiefly notable for launcing the career of Mel Collins, whose saxophone and flute have been used to spice literally dozens of records since.

Title	Format	Label	Number	Year	Price	Notes
Circus	LP	Transatlantic	TRA207	1969	**£30**	
Do You Dream	7"	Parlophone	R5672	1968	**£8**	
Sink Or Swim	7"	Parlophone	R5633	1967	**£8**	

CIRCUS 2000

Title	Format	Label	Number	Year	Price	Notes
Circus 2000	LP	Rifi		1969	**£150**	
Escape From A Box	LP	Rifi		1970	**£100**	

CIRCUS MAXIMUS

Title	Format	Label	Number	Year	Price	Notes
Circus Maximus	LP	Vanguard	VSD79260	1967	**£20**	US
Neverland Revisited	LP	Vanguard	VSD79274	1968	**£20**	US

CIRKUS

Title	Format	Label	Number	Year	Price	Notes
One	LP	RCB	RCB1	1971	**£100**	

CITATIONS

Title	Format	Label	Number	Year	Price	Notes
Moon Race	7"	Columbia	DB7068	1963	**£10**	

CITY

Carole King's first LP was issued under the name of a group, City, but the sound is the same as on its successors. Following her success with "Tapestry", the City album was counterfeited - copies with black and white covers are the unofficial ones.

Title	Format	Label	Cat. No.	Year	Price	Notes
Now That Everything's Been Said	LP	Ode	Z1244012	1969	**£20**	colour cover

CITY OF WESTMINSTER STRING BAND

Title	Format	Label	Cat. No.	Year	Price	Notes
Touch Of Velvet A Sting Of Brass	7"	Pye	7N17620	1968	**£5**	

CITY RAMBLERS SKIFFLE GROUP

Title	Format	Label	Cat. No.	Year	Price	Notes
Delia's Gone	7" EP	Tempo	EXA77	195-	**£4**	
Good Morning Blues	7" EP	Tempo	EXA71	195-	**£4**	
I Shall Not Be Moved	7" EP	Storyville	SEP345		**£4**	
I Want A Girl	7" EP	Storyville	SEP327		**£4**	
I Want A Girl	7" EP	Tempo	EXA59	195-	**£4**	

CITY SMOKE

Title	Format	Label	Cat. No.	Year	Price	Notes
Sunday Morning	7"	Mercury	MF971	1967	**£4**	

CITY WAITES

Title	Format	Label	Cat. No.	Year	Price	Notes
Gorgeous Gallery Of Gallant Inventions	LP	EMI	EMC3017	1974	**£50**	

CLANTON, JIMMY

Title	Format	Label	Cat. No.	Year	Price	Notes
Another Sleepless Night	7"	Top Rank	JAR382	1960	**£4**	chart single
Best Of...	LP	Philips	PHM200154	1964	**£10**	US
Come Back	7"	Top Rank	JAR509	1960	**£4**	
Darkest Street In Town	7"	Stateside	SS159	1963	**£4**	
Go Jimmy Go	7"	Top Rank	JAR269	1960	**£4**	
Hurting Each Other	7"	Stateside	SS410	1965	**£4**	
Jimmy's Blue	LP	Ace	1008	1960	**£15**	US
Jimmy's Blue	LP	Ace	1008	1960	**£35**	US, blue vinyl
Jimmy's Happy	LP	Ace	1007	1960	**£15**	US
Jimmy's Happy	LP	Ace	1007	1960	**£35**	US, red vinyl
Just A Dream	LP	Ace	1001	1959	**£20**	US
Just A Dream	7"	London	HLS8699	1958	**£4**	
Just A Dream	7" EP	London	RES1224	1959	**£8**	
Letter To An Angel	7"	London	HLS8779	1959	**£4**	
My Best To You	LP	Ace	1011	1961	**£30**	US
My Own True Love	7"	Top Rank	JAR189	1959	**£4**	
Teenage Millionaire	LP	Ace	1014	1961	**£30**	US
Venus In Blue Jeans	LP	Ace	1026	1962	**£30**	US
Venus In Blue Jeans	7"	Stateside	SS120	1962	**£4**	
What Am I Gonna Do	7"	Top Rank	JAR544	1961	**£4**	

CLAP

Title	Format	Label	Cat. No.	Year	Price	Notes
Have You Reached Yet?	LP	Nova Sol	1001		**£100**	US

CLAPHAM SOUTH ESCALATORS

Title	Format	Label	Cat. No.	Year	Price	Notes
Leave Me Alone	7"	Upright	UPYOUR1	198-	**£5**	

CLAPTON, ERIC

Anyone attempting to collect a complete set of the records with which Eric Clapton has been involved is facing an extremely difficult task. For Clapton probably holds the prize for the highest number of guest appearances, including some on records that have become extremely rare. The rarest Clapton record of all, however, is a compilation that was due to be issued in 1978 (it was given a title, "Clapton", and even a catalogue number, RSO 2479702). This was scrapped at the last minute and apparently only four copies were left undestroyed.

Title	Format	Label	Cat. No.	Year	Price	Notes
461 Ocean Boulevard	LP	RSO	QD4801	1974	**£15**	US quad
After Midnight	7"	Polydor	2001096	1970	**£4**	
Just One Night	LP	Nautilus		1981	**£15**	US audiophile
Shape You're In	7"	Duck	W9701	1983	**£4**	pic disc
Slowhand	LP	Mobile Fid.	MFSL1030	1980	**£15**	US audiophile
There's One In Every Crowd	LP	RSO	QD4806	1974	**£15**	US quad
Wonderful Tonight	12"	RSO	JONX001	1979	**£10**	promo

CLARENDONIANS

Title	Format	Label	Cat. No.	Year	Price	Notes
Baby Baby	7"	Caltone	TONE114	196-	**£8**	
Be Bop Boy	7"	Rio	R112	1967	**£8**	
Goodbye Forever	7"	Island	WI3041	1967	**£8**	
He Who Laughs Last	7"	Studio One	SO2007	196-	**£10**	
I Can't Go On	7"	Studio One	SO2004	196-	**£10**	
I'll Never Change	7"	Island	WI3005	1966	**£8**	
Jerk	7"	Ska Beat	JB261	1966	**£10**	
Love Me With All Your Heart	7"	Studio One	SO2017	196-	**£10**	
Ma Bien	7"	Ska Beat	JB219	1965	**£10**	
Musical Train	7"	Rio	R115	1967	**£8**	
Rude Boy Gone Jail	7"	Island	WI295	1966	**£10**	

Title	Format	Label	Cat. No.	Year	Price	Notes
Sweetheart Of Beauty	7"	Island	WI3032	1967	**£8**	
Try Me One More Time	7"	Island	WI284	1966	**£10**	

CLARK SISTERS

Title	Format	Label	Cat. No.	Year	Price	Notes
Sing Sing Sing	7" EP	London	RED1198	1959	**£5**	

CLARK, ALICE

Title	Format	Label	Cat. No.	Year	Price	Notes
You Got A Deal	7"	Action	ACT4520	1969	**£4**	
You Got A Deal	7"	Action	ACT4520	1969	**£12**	demo

CLARK, CHRIS

Title	Format	Label	Cat. No.	Year	Price	Notes
C C Rides Again	LP	Weed	WS801		**£25**	US
From Head To Toe	7"	T. Motown	TMG624	1967	**£10**	
From Head To Toe	7"	T. Motown	TMG624	1967	**£40**	demo
Loves Gone Bad	7"	T. Motown	TMG591	1967	**£10**	
Loves Gone Bad	7"	T. Motown	TMG591	1967	**£40**	demo
I Want To Go Back There Again	7"	T. Motown	TMG638	1968	**£5**	
I Want To Go Back There Again	7"	T. Motown	TMG638	1968	**£20**	demo
Soul Sounds	LP	T. Motown	STML11069	1968	**£25**	

CLARK, CLAUDINE

Title	Format	Label	Cat. No.	Year	Price	Notes
Party Lights	LP	Chancellor	CHL5029	1962	**£30**	US
Party Lights	7"	Pye	7N25157	1962	**£5**	
Strength To Be Strong	7"	Sue	WI4039	1967	**£10**	
Walk Me Home From The Party	7"	Pye	7N25186	1963	**£4**	

CLARK, DAVE

Title	Format	Label	Cat. No.	Year	Price	Notes
Draggin' The Line	7"	Columbia	DB8834	1971	**£4**	
Rub It In	7"	Columbia	DB8907	1972	**£4**	
Sha-Na-Na-Na	7"	EMI	EMI2082	1973	**£4**	
Sweet City Woman	7"	EMI	EMI2013	1973	**£4**	
Think Of Me	7"	Columbia	DB8862	1972	**£4**	

CLARK, DAVE FIVE

Title	Format	Label	Cat. No.	Year	Price	Notes
14 Titles By Dave Clark	LP	Columbia	SCX6309	1968	**£20**	
5 By 5 - Go!	LP	Epic	BN26236	1967	**£20**	US
All Time Greats	7"	Columbia	DB8963	1972	**£4**	PS
American Tour	LP	Epic	LN24117	1964	**£20**	US
Anyway You Want It	7"	Columbia	DB7377	1964	**£4**	chart single
Bits And Pieces	7"	Columbia	DB7210	1964	**£4**	chart single
Can't You See That She's Mine	7"	Columbia	DB7291	1964	**£4**	chart single
Catch Us If You Can	LP	Columbia	SX1756	1965	**£20**	chart LP
Catch Us If You Can	7"	Columbia	DB7625	1965	**£4**	chart single
Chaquita	7"	Ember	EMBS156	1962	**£8**	
Coast To Coast	LP	Epic	LN24128	1965	**£20**	US
Come Home	7"	Columbia	DB7580	1965	**£4**	chart single
Dave Clark 5 & Washington DCs	LP	Ember	FA2003	1965	**£25**	
Dave Clark Five	7" EP	Columbia	SEG8289	1964	**£6**	
Dave Clark Five	LP	Epic	EG30434	1971	**£20**	US double
Do You Love Me	7"	Columbia	DB7112	1963	**£4**	chart single
Everybody Get Together	7"	Columbia	DB8660	1970	**£4**	chart single
Everybody Knows	LP	Columbia	SX6207	1968	**£20**	
Everybody Knows	7"	Columbia	DB7453	1965	**£4**	chart single
Everybody Knows	7"	Columbia	DB8286	1967	**£4**	chart single
First Love	7"	Piccadilly	7N35088	1962	**£6**	
Glad All Over	7"	Columbia	DB7154	1963	**£4**	chart single
Glad All Over	LP	Epic	LN24093	1964	**£20**	US
Good Old Rock'n'Roll	7"	Columbia	DB8638	1969	**£4**	PS, Chart Single
Greatest Hits	LP	Columbia	SX6105	1966	**£15**	
Having A Wild Weekend	LP	Epic	LN24162	1965	**£20**	US
Here Comes Summer	7"	Columbia	DB8689	1970	**£4**	chart single
Hits Of The Dave Clark Five	7" EP	Columbia	SEG8381	1965	**£5**	
I Knew It All The Time	7"	Piccadilly	7N35500	1962	**£6**	
I Like It Like That	LP	Epic	LN24178	1966	**£20**	US
If Somebody Loves You	LP	Columbia	SCX6437	1971	**£15**	
Julia	7"	Columbia	DB8681	1970	**£4**	
Live In The Sky	7"	Columbia	DB8505	1968	**£4**	chart single
Look Before You Leap	7"	Columbia	DB7909	1966	**£4**	chart single
More Good Old Rock'n'Roll	7"	Columbia	DB8724	1970	**£4**	chart single
More Greatest Hits	LP	Epic	LN24221	1966	**£15**	US
Mulberry Bush	7"	Columbia	DB7011	1963	**£5**	
Mulberry Tree	7"	Columbia	DB8545	1969	**£4**	

Title	Format	Label	Cat. No.	Year	Price	Notes
Nineteen Days	7"	Columbia	DB8028	1966	**£4**	
No One Can Break A Heart Like You	7"	Columbia	DB8342	1968	**£4**	chart single
Over And Over	7"	Columbia	DB7744	1965	**£4**	chart single
Put A Little Love In Your Heart	7"	Columbia	DB8624	1969	**£4**	chart single
Red Balloon	7"	Columbia	DB8465	1968	**£4**	chart single
Reelin' And Rockin'	7"	Columbia	DB7503	1965	**£4**	chart single
Return	LP	Epic	LN24104	1964	**£20**	US
Satisfied With You	LP	Epic	LN24212	1966	**£20**	US
Session With...	LP	Columbia	33SX1598	1964	**£20**	chart LP
Session With...	LP	MFP	1260	1968	**£10**	
Southern Man	7"	Columbia	DB8749	1971	**£4**	
Tabatha Twitchit	7"	Columbia	DB8194	1967	**£4**	
Thinking Of You Baby	7"	Columbia	DB7335	1964	**£4**	chart single
Try Too Hard	7"	Columbia	DB7863	1966	**£4**	
Try Too Hard	LP	Epic	LN24198	1966	**£20**	US
Weekend In London	LP	Epic	LN24139	1965	**£20**	US
Wild Weekend	7" EP	Columbia	SEG8447	1965	**£6**	
Won't You Be My Lady	7"	Columbia	DB8791	1971	**£4**	
You Got What It Takes	LP	Epic	BN26312	1967	**£20**	US
You've Got What It Takes	7"	Columbia	DB8152	1967	**£4**	chart single

CLARK, DEE

Title	Format	Label	Cat. No.	Year	Price	Notes
At My Front Door	7"	Top Rank	JAR373	1960	**£5**	
Best Of...	LP	Vee Jay	LP1047	1964	**£10**	US
Dee Clark	LP	Abner	LP2000	1959	**£15**	US
Dee Clark	LP	Vee Jay	LP1028	1961	**£12**	US
Don't Walk Away From Me	7"	Columbia	DB4768	1962	**£5**	
Heartbreak	7"	Stateside	SS355	1964	**£4**	
Hey Little Girl	7"	Top Rank	JAR196	1959	**£5**	
Hold On, It's Dee Clark	LP	Vee Jay	LP1037	1961	**£10**	US
How About That	LP	Top Rank	25044	1960	**£10**	
How About That	7"	Top Rank	JAR284	1960	**£6**	
I'm A Soldier Boy	7"	Stateside	SS180	1963	**£5**	
Just Keep It Up	7"	London	HL8915	1959	**£5**	chart single
Raindrops	7"	Top Rank	JAR570	1961	**£4**	
T.C.B.	7"	Stateside	SS400	1965	**£8**	
When I Call On You	7"	London	HL8802	1959	**£5**	
You're Looking Good	7"	Top Rank	JAR501	1960	**£5**	
You're Looking Good	LP	Vee Jay	LP1019	1960	**£12**	US
Your Friends	7"	Top Rank	JAR551	1961	**£4**	

CLARK, GENE

Title	Format	Label	Cat. No.	Year	Price	Notes
...& The Gosdin Brothers	LP	CBS	62934	1967	**£15**	
Early L.A. Sessions	LP	CBS	31123	1972	**£15**	US
Echoes	7"	CBS	202523	1967	**£6**	
No Other	LP	Asylum	SYL9020	1974	**£10**	
Road Master	LP	Ariola	87584	1973	**£15**	Dutch
White Light	LP	A&M	AMLS64297	1972	**£12**	

CLARK, MICHAEL

Title	Format	Label	Cat. No.	Year	Price	Notes
None Of These Girls	7"	Liberty	LIB5893	1966	**£4**	

CLARK, PETULA

Title	Format	Label	Cat. No.	Year	Price	Notes
A Date With Pet	LP-10"	Pye	NPT19014	1956	**£20**	
C'Est Ma Chanson	7" EP	Pye-Vogue	VRE5025	1967	**£4**	
Children's Choice	7" EP	Pye	NEP24006	1956	**£4**	
Downtown	7" EP	Pye	NEP24206	1965	**£4**	
En Francais	7" EP	Pye	NEP24182	1963	**£4**	
Encore En Francais	7" EP	Pye	NEP24189	1964	**£4**	
Hello Mr.Brown	7" EP	Pye-Vogue	VRE5023	1966	**£4**	
Hello Paris Vol.1	LP	Pye-Vogue	VRL3016	1966	**£10**	
Hello Paris Vol.2	LP	Pye-Vogue	VRL3019	1966	**£10**	
I Couldn't Live Without Your Love	7" EP	Pye	NEP24266	1966	**£4**	
L'Agent Secret	7" EP	Pye-Vogue	VRE5019	1966	**£4**	
Les James Dean	LP	Pye-Vogue	VRL3001	1964	**£10**	
Many Faces	7" EP	Pye	NEP24280	1967	**£4**	
Petula '65	LP	Pye-Vogue	VRL3010	1965	**£10**	
Petula '66	LP	Pye-Vogue	VRL3022	1966	**£10**	
Petula Clark Hit Parade	7" EP	Pye	NEP24016	1956	**£4**	
Petula Clark Hit Parade No.2	7" EP	Pye	NEP24056	1957	**£4**	
Petula Clark Hit Parade No.3	7" EP	Pye	NEP24080	1958	**£4**	

Title	Format	Label	Cat. No.	Year	Price	Notes
Petula Clark In Hollywood	LP	Pye	NPL18039	1959	**£15**	
Petula Clark Sings	LP-10"	Pye	NPT19002	1956	**£20**	
This Is My Song	7" EP	Pye	NEP24279	1967	**£4**	
You Are My Lucky Star	LP	Pye	NPL18007	1957	**£20**	
You Are My Lucky Star Part 1	7" EP	Pye	NEP24060	1957	**£4**	
You Are My Lucky Star Part 2	7" EP	Pye	NEP24061	1957	**£4**	
You Are My Lucky Star Part 3	7" EP	Pye	NEP24062	1957	**£4**	
You're the One	7" EP	Pye	NEP24233	1965	**£4**	

CLARK, ROY

Title	Format	Label	Cat. No.	Year	Price	Notes
Please Mr.Mayor	7"	HMV	POP581	1959	**£20**	
Texas Twist	7"	Capitol	CL15288	1963	**£4**	
Tips Of My Fingers	7"	Capitol	CL15317	1963	**£4**	

CLARK, SANFORD

Title	Format	Label	Cat. No.	Year	Price	Notes
Fool	7"	London	HLD8320	1956	**£25**	
Lowdown Blues	7" EP	London	REW1256	1960	**£20**	
Pledging My Love	7"	London	HLW9095	1960	**£4**	
Presenting Sanford Clark	7" EP	London	RED1105	1957	**£25**	
Run Boy Run	7"	London	HLW8959	1959	**£8**	
Shades	7"	Ember	EMBS250	1968	**£5**	
Son Of A Gun	7"	London	HLW9026	1960	**£5**	

CLARK, TREVOR

Title	Format	Label	Cat. No.	Year	Price	Notes
Sufferer	7"	Studio One	SO2082	196-	**£10**	

CLARK-HUTCHINSON

The Clark-Hutchinson LP, "A=MH2", was probably the best selling record on Deram's progressive offshoot, Nova, although as most of the records on the label sank without trace, this is not saying very much. The duo turned themselves into a group by extensive multi-tracking, concentrating on Mick Hutchinson's guitar playing to provide a focus of interest. In truth, he was not that remarkable a player and although Clark-Hutchinson got to make two more LPs, they have not been heard from since.

Title	Format	Label	Cat. No.	Year	Price	Notes
A=MH2	LP	Nova	SDNR2	1970	**£15**	
Gestalt	LP	Deram	SML1090	1971	**£15**	
Retribution	LP	Deram	SML1076	1970	**£15**	

CLARKE, ALLAN

Title	Format	Label	Cat. No.	Year	Price	Notes
Allan Clarke	LP	EMI	EMC3041	1974	**£10**	
Headroom	LP	EMI	EMA752	1973	**£10**	
My Real Name Is 'Arold	LP	RCA	SF8283	1972	**£10**	

CLARKE, JOHN COOPER

Title	Format	Label	Cat. No.	Year	Price	Notes
Disguise In Love	LP	CBS	83132	1978	**£10**	
Gimmix	7"	Epic	EPC127009	1978	**£5**	orange vinyl, plectrum SD
Live	LP	CBS	JCC1		**£10**	
Me And My Big Mouth	LP	Epic	EPC84979	1981	**£10**	
Ou Est La Maison Du Frommage	LP	Rabid	NOZE1	1980	**£10**	
Post-War Glamour Girls	7"	CBS	6541	1978	**£4**	
Snap Crackle & Bop	LP	Epic	EPC84083	1980	**£15**	with book
Splat/Twat	7"	Epic	7982	1979	**£8**	
Suspended Sentence	7"	Rabid	TOSH103	1977	**£4**	

CLARKE, LLOYD

Title	Format	Label	Cat. No.	Year	Price	Notes
Love Is Strange	7"	Blue Beat	BB371	1965	**£10**	
Parapinto Boogie	7"	Blue Beat	BB25	1961	**£10**	
Young Love	7"	Blue Cat	BS136	196-	**£10**	

CLARKE, TONY

Title	Format	Label	Cat. No.	Year	Price	Notes
Ain't Love Good Ain't Love Proud	7"	Pye	7N25251	1964	**£5**	
Entertainer	7"	Chess	CRS8011	1965	**£15**	
Entertainer	7"	Chess	CRS8091	1969	**£4**	
Entertainer	7"	Janus	6146030	1974	**£5**	

CLASH

Title	Format	Label	Cat. No.	Year	Price	Notes
Bank Robber	7"	CBS	8323	1980	**£4**	chart single
Call-Up	7"	CBS	9339	1980	**£4**	chart single
Capital Radio	7"	CBS	CL1	1977	**£40**	
Clash City Rockers	7"	CBS	5834	1978	**£4**	chart single
Combat Rock	LP	Epic	FE37689	1982	**£30**	US promo camoflague
Combat Rock	LP	Epic	AS991592	1982	**£40**	US promo pic disc
Complete Control	7"	CBS	5664	1977	**£4**	chart single
Cost Of Living	7"	CBS	7324	1979	**£6**	chart single
English Civil War	7"	CBS	7082	1979	**£4**	chart single

Title	Format	Label	Number	Year	Price	Notes
Give 'Em Enough Rope	LP	CBS	82431	1978	**£12**	promo with poster
Hitsville UK	7"	CBS	9480	1981	**£4**	chart single
I Fought The Law	7"	CBS	7324DJ	1979	**£10**	promo
If Music Could Talk	LP	Epic	AS952	1981	**£20**	US promo
London Calling	12"	CBS	128087	1979	**£6**	
London Calling	7"	CBS	8087	1979	**£4**	chart single
Magnificent Seven	12"	CBS	A121133	1981	**£6**	
Magnificent Seven	7"	CBS	A1133	1981	**£4**	chart single
Remote Control	7"	CBS	5293	1977	**£4**	
Remote Control	12"	CBS	125293	1978	**£20**	promo
Rock The Casbah	7"	CBS	A112479	1982	**£6**	pic disc
Sandinista Now!	LP	Epic	AS913	1980	**£25**	US single LP promo
Should I Stay Or Should I Go	7"	CBS	A2646	1982	**£5**	laser etched
Should I Stay Or Should I Go	7"	CBS	A112646	1982	**£6**	pic disc
Take A Gamble	12"	CBS		1980	**£10**	promo
This Is Radio Clash	12"	CBS	A131797	1981	**£6**	
This Is Radio Clash	7"	CBS	A1797	1981	**£4**	chart single
Tommy Gun	7"	CBS	6788	1978	**£4**	chart single
White Man In Hammersmith Palais	7"	CBS	6383	1978	**£4**	chart single
White Riot	7"	CBS	5058	1977	**£4**	chart single
World According To The Clash	LP	Epic	AS1574	1982	**£50**	US promo

CLASH & FUTURA 2000

Title	Format	Label	Number	Year	Price	Notes
Escapades Of Futura 2000	7"	Celluloid	CYZ104	1983	**£4**	
Escapades Of Futura 2000	12"	Celluloid	CYZ104	1983	**£6**	

CLASSICS

Title	Format	Label	Number	Year	Price	Notes
Life Is But A Dream	7"	Mercury	AMT1152	1961	**£10**	
Pollyanna	7"	Capitol	CL15470	1966	**£8**	
Till Then	7"	Stateside	SS215	1963	**£8**	

CLASSICS IV

Title	Format	Label	Number	Year	Price	Notes
Everyday With You Girl	7"	Liberty	LBF15231	1969	**£5**	
Spooky	7"	Liberty	LBF15051	1968	**£5**	chart single
Stormy	7"	Liberty	LBF15177	1969	**£4**	
Traces	7"	Liberty	LBF15196	1969	**£4**	

CLAY, CASSIUS

If the idea of Cassius Clay (or Mohammed Ali as he became better known) wailing "Stand By Me" seems hard to take, then the single's B side may be more to the point - "I Am The Greatest", it is called.

Title	Format	Label	Number	Year	Price	Notes
I Am The Greatest!	LP	Columbia	CL2093	1963	**£20**	US
Stand By Me	7"	CBS	202190	1966	**£8**	
Stand By Me	7"	CBS	AAG190	1964	**£10**	

CLAY, JUDY

Title	Format	Label	Number	Year	Price	Notes
You Can't Run Away From Your Heart	7"	Stax	601022	1967	**£6**	

CLAY, JUDY & WILLIAM BELL

Title	Format	Label	Number	Year	Price	Notes
Private Number	7"	Stax	STAX101	1968	**£4**	chart single

CLAY, OTIS

Title	Format	Label	Number	Year	Price	Notes
Baby Jane	7"	Atlantic	584282	1969	**£4**	

CLAY, TOM

Title	Format	Label	Number	Year	Price	Notes
What The World Needs Now	7"	T. Motown	TMG801	1972	**£6**	
What The World Needs Now	7"	T. Motown	TMG801	1972	**£15**	demo

CLAYRE, ALASDAIR

Title	Format	Label	Number	Year	Price	Notes
Alasdair Clayre	LP	Elektra		1967	**£50**	

CLAYTON SQUARES

Title	Format	Label	Number	Year	Price	Notes
Come And Get It	7"	Decca	F12250	1965	**£8**	
There She Is	7"	Decca	F12456	1966	**£8**	

CLAYTON, PAUL

Title	Format	Label	Number	Year	Price	Notes
Paul Clayton	7" EP	London	REU1276	1960	**£5**	

CLEANLINESS & GODLINESS SKIFFLE BAND

Title	Format	Label	Number	Year	Price	Notes
Greatest Hits	LP	Vanguard	SVRL19043	1968	**£12**	

CLEAR BLUE SKY

Title	Format	Label	Number	Year	Price	Notes
Clear Blue Sky	LP	Vertigo	6360013	1971	**£60**	spiral label

CLEAR LIGHT

Title	Format	Label	Number	Year	Price	Notes
Black Roses	7"	Elektra	EKSN45019	1967	**£6**	
Clear Light	LP	Elektra	EKL4011	1967	**£20**	
Night Sounds Loud	7"	Elektra	EKSN45027	1968	**£5**	

CLEARLIGHT

Title	Format	Label	Number	Year	Price	Notes
Clearlight Symphony	LP	Virgin	V2029	1975	**£15**	
Forever Blowing Bubbles	LP	Virgin	V2039	1975	**£15**	

CLEARWAYS

Title	Format	Label	Number	Year	Price	Notes
I'll Be Here	7"	Columbia	DB7333	1964	**£5**	

CLEESE, JOHN & THE 1948 CHOIR

Title	Format	Label	Number	Year	Price	Notes
Ferret Song	7"	Pye	7N17336	1967	**£4**	

CLEFS

Title	Format	Label	Number	Year	Price	Notes
Dream Train Special	7"	Salvo	SLO1810	1962	**£4**	

CLEFTONES

Title	Format	Label	Number	Year	Price	Notes
For Sentimental Reasons	LP	Gee	GLP707	1962	**£65**	US
Heart And Soul	7"	Columbia	DB4678	1961	**£8**	
Heart And Soul	LP	Gee	GLP705	1961	**£65**	US
I Love You For Sentimental Reasons	7"	Columbia	DB4720	1961	**£6**	
Little Girl Of Mine	7"	Columbia	DB3801	1956	**£15**	
Lover Come Back To Me	7"	Columbia	DB4988	1963	**£4**	

CLEMENT, JACK

Title	Format	Label	Number	Year	Price	Notes
Ten Years	7"	London	HLS8691	1958	**£20**	

CLEMENTS, SOUL JOE

Title	Format	Label	Number	Year	Price	Notes
Smoke And Ashes	7"	Plexium	PXM10	196-	**£10**	

CLIFF DWELLERS

Title	Format	Label	Number	Year	Price	Notes
Hang On Stupid	7"	Polydor	56707	1966	**£4**	

CLIFF, JIMMY

Title	Format	Label	Number	Year	Price	Notes
Aim And Ambition	7"	Island	WIP6004	1967	**£8**	
Another Cycle	LP	Island	ILPS9159	1971	**£12**	
Goodbye Yesterday	7"	Chrysalis	WIP6103	1971	**£4**	
Hard Road To Travel	LP	Island	ILPS9062	1968	**£50**	
Harder They Come	7"	Island	WIP6139	1972	**£4**	
I Got A Feeling	7"	Island	WIP6011	1967	**£8**	
Miss Jamaica	7"	Island	WI016	1962	**£10**	
One Eyed Jacks	7"	Stateside	SS342	1964	**£5**	
Pride And Passion	7"	Fontana	TF641	1966	**£5**	
Sitting In Limbo	7"	Island	WIP6110	1971	**£4**	
Struggling Man	LP	Island	ILPS9235	1974	**£10**	
Synthetic World	7"	Chrysalis	WIP6097	1971	**£4**	
That's The Way Life Goes	7"	Island	WIP6024	1967	**£6**	
Trapped	7"	Island	WIP6132	1972	**£4**	
Vietnam	7"	Trojan	TR7722	1970	**£5**	chart single
Waterfall	7"	Island	WIP6039	1968	**£8**	
Wild World	7"	Island	WIP6087	1970	**£4**	chart single
Wonderful World Beautiful People	7"	Trojan	TR690	1969	**£5**	chart single

CLIFFORD, BUZZ

Title	Format	Label	Number	Year	Price	Notes
Baby Sittin' Boogie	7"	Fontana	H297	1961	**£4**	chart single
Baby Sittin' With Buzz	LP	Columbia	CL1616	1961	**£15**	US

CLIFFORD, LINDA

Title	Format	Label	Number	Year	Price	Notes
After Loving You	7"	Paramount	3051	1974	**£4**	

CLIFTON, BILL

Title	Format	Label	Number	Year	Price	Notes
Beatle Crazy	7"	Decca	F11793	1963	**£8**	

CLIFTON, BILL & GEORGE JONES

Title	Format	Label	Number	Year	Price	Notes
Country & Western Trailblazers No.2	7" EP	Mercury	ZEP10052	1960	**£4**	

CLIFTON, BILL & JIM EANES

Title	Format	Label	Number	Year	Price	Notes
Blue River Hoedown	7" EP	Melodisc	EPM7102	196-	**£6**	

CLIMAX BLUES BAND

Title	Format	Label	Cat. No.	Year	Price	Notes
1969/72	LP	Harvest	SHSM2003	1975	**£10**	
Climax Chicago Blues Band	LP	Parlophone	PCS7069	1969	**£15**	
FM/Live	LP	Polydor	2383259	1974	**£10**	
Like Uncle Charlie	7"	Parlophone	R5809	1969	**£5**	
Lot Of Bottle	LP	Harvest	SHSP4009	1970	**£12**	
Plays On	LP	Parlophone	PCS7084	1969	**£15**	
Reap What I've Sowed	7"	Harvest	HAR5029	1970	**£4**	
Rich Man	LP	Harvest	SHSP4024	1972	**£12**	
Sense Of Direction	LP	Polydor	2883291	1974	**£10**	
Stamp Album	LP	BTM	BTM1004	1975	**£10**	
Tightly Knit	LP	Harvest	SHSP4015	1971	**£12**	
Towards The Sun	7"	Harvest	HAR5041	1971	**£4**	

CLINE, PATSY

Title	Format	Label	Cat. No.	Year	Price	Notes
Crazy	7"	Brunswick	05861	1961	**£4**	
Heartaches	7"	Brunswick	05878	1962	**£4**	chart single
I Fall To Pieces	7"	Brunswick	05855	1961	**£4**	
Leaving On Your Mind	7"	Brunswick	05883	1963	**£4**	
Patsy Cline	LP	Decca	DL8611	1957	**£25**	US
Patsy Cline Showcase	LP	Brunswick	LAT8344	1959	**£10**	
Patsy Cline Story	LP	Decca	DXB176	1963	**£15**	US, with booklet
Portrait Of Patsy Cline	LP	Brunswick	LAT8589	1964	**£10**	
Sentimentally Yours	LP	Brunswick	LAT8510	1962	**£10**	
She's Got You	7"	Brunswick	05866	1962	**£4**	chart single
So Wrong	7"	Brunswick	05874	1962	**£4**	
Sweet Dreams	7"	Brunswick	05888	1963	**£4**	
Sweet Dreams	7" EP	Brunswick	OE9490	1962	**£5**	
That's How A Heartache Begins	LP	Decca	DL4586	1964	**£12**	US
Walkin' After Midnight	7"	Brunswick	05660	1957	**£4**	
When I Get Through With You	7"	Brunswick	05869	1962	**£4**	

CLINTON, GEORGE

Title	Format	Label	Cat. No.	Year	Price	Notes
Please Don't Run From Me	7"	ABC	4053	1975	**£4**	

CLIQUE

Title	Format	Label	Cat. No.	Year	Price	Notes
She Ain't No Good	7"	Pye	7N15786	1965	**£30**	
Sugar On Sunday	7"	London	HLU10286	1969	**£30**	
We Didn't Kiss	7"	Pye	7N15853	1965	**£30**	

CLIQUE (2)

Title	Format	Label	Cat. No.	Year	Price	Notes
Love Can Be Wonderful	7"	Unity	UN505	1969	**£6**	

CLIVE ALL STARS

Title	Format	Label	Cat. No.	Year	Price	Notes
Donkey Trot	7"	Big Shot	BI501	1973	**£5**	

CLOCKWORK ORANGES

Title	Format	Label	Cat. No.	Year	Price	Notes
Ready Steady	7"	Ember	EMBS227	1966	**£6**	

CLOUDS

Clouds were an organ trio whose ultimate lack of success had much to do with the fact that, with the spotlight cast directly on to him, organist Billy Ritchie failed to reveal any of the imagination and showmanship of a Keith Emerson or a Rick Wakeman. The climax of Clouds' stage-act came when the bass player lifted his instrument into the air and the drummer tapped the strings with his sticks. It was not the same.

Title	Format	Label	Cat. No.	Year	Price	Notes
Make No Bones About It	7"	Island	WIP6055	1969	**£6**	
Scrapbook	LP	Island	ILPS9100	1969	**£15**	
Scrapbook	7"	Island	WIP6067	1969	**£6**	
Watercolour Days	LP	Island	ILPS9151	1971	**£15**	

CLOVER

Title	Format	Label	Cat. No.	Year	Price	Notes
Clover	LP	Liberty	LBS83340	1970	**£10**	
Forty-Niner	LP	Liberty	LBS83487	1971	**£10**	

CLOVERS

Title	Format	Label	Cat. No.	Year	Price	Notes
Clovers	LP	Atlantic	LP1248	1956	**£150**	US
Clovers	LP	Atlantic	LP8009	1957	**£100**	US
Dance Party	LP	Atlantic	LP8034	1959	**£50**	US
Easy Loving	7"	London	HLT9154	1960	**£15**	
From The Bottom Of My Heart	7"	London	HLE8334	1956	**£50**	
Honey Dripper	7"	HMV	POP883	1961	**£10**	
In Clover	LP	Poplar	1001	1958	**£50**	US

In Clover	LP	United Artists	UAL3033	1959	**£50**	US
In The Good Old Summertime	7"	HMV	POP542	1958	**£10**	
Love Bug	LP	Atlantic	587162	1969	**£15**	
Love Love Love	7"	London	HLE8314	1956	**£50**	
Love Potion No.9	7"	London	HLT8949	1959	**£15**	
Love Potion No.9	LP	United Artists	UAL3099	1960	**£50**	US
Nip Sip	7"	London	HLE8229	1956	**£75**	
One Mint Julep	7"	London	HLT9122	1960	**£15**	
Your Cash Ain't Nothin' But Trash	7"	Atlantic	584160	1968	**£6**	

CLYNE, JEFF & OTHERS

Springboard	LP	Polydor	545007	1966	**£40**	

CMU

Heart Of The Sun	7"	Transatlantic	BIG508	1972	**£10**	
Open Spaces	LP	Transatlantic	TRA237	1971	**£30**	
Space Cabaret	LP	Transatlantic	TRA259	1972	**£30**	

COACHMEN

Seasons In The Sun	7"	Columbia	DB8057	1966	**£5**	

COAST ROAD DRIVE

Delicious And Refreshing	LP	Deram	SML1113	1974	**£30**	

COASTERS

Ain't That Just Like Me	7"	London	HLK9493	1962	**£4**	
Along Came Jones	7"	London	HLE8882	1959	**£6**	
Besame Mucho	7"	London	HLK9111	1960	**£4**	
Charlie Brown	7"	London	HLE8819	1959	**£5**	chart single
Coast Along	LP	London	HAK8033	1963	**£15**	
Coasters	LP	Atco	33101	1958	**£100**	US
Coasters	7" EP	London	REE1203	1959	**£15**	
Coastin' Along	LP	Atlantic	587134	1968	**£10**	
Girls Girls Girls	7"	London	HLK9413	1961	**£4**	
Greatest Hits	LP	Atco	33111	1959	**£50**	US
Greatest Hits	LP	London	HAE2237	1960	**£15**	
Little Egypt	7"	London	HLK9349	1961	**£5**	
One By One	LP	Atco	33123	1960	**£20**	US
Poison Ivy	7"	London	HLE8938	1959	**£5**	chart single
Searching	7"	Atlantic	584087	1967	**£4**	
Searching	7"	London	HLE8450	1957	**£10**	chart single
Shadow Knows	7"	London	HLE8729	1958	**£8**	
She's A Yum Yum	7"	Atlantic	584033	1966	**£4**	
Shopping For Clothes	7"	London	HLK9208	1960	**£5**	
Stewball	7"	London	HLK9151	1960	**£5**	
T'ain't Nothing To Me	7"	London	HLK9863	1964	**£4**	
Wait A Minute	7"	London	HLK9293	1961	**£4**	
What About Us	7"	London	HLE9020	1960	**£5**	
Yakety Yak	7"	London	HLE8665	1958	**£5**	chart single

COB (CLIVE'S OWN BAND)

Singer and banjo-player Clive Palmer seemed to be a man who was scared of success. As a founder member of the Incredible String Band, he played on their first album, yet left just as they began to gain a following. He then formed the Famous Jug Band, recorded a promising LP, but again left when it began to seem as though the band might actually live up to its name. Finally, he formed COB, and was no doubt highly gratified when neither of the group's albums sold more than a handful of copies.

Blue Morning	7"	Polydor	2058260	1972	**£20**	
Moyshe McStiff	LP	Polydor	2383161	1972	**£150**	
Spirit Of Love	LP	CBS	69010	1971	**£60**	

COBBS

Hot Buttered Corn	7"	Amalgamated	AMG845	196-	**£10**	
Space Doctor	7"	Amalgamated	AMG849	196-	**£10**	

COCHISE

Cochise	LP	United Artists	UAS29117	1970	**£10**	
So Far	LP	United Artists	UAS29286	1972	**£10**	
Swallow Tales	LP	Liberty	LBG83428	1971	**£10**	

COCHRAN, DIB & THE EARWIGS

Oh Baby	7"	Bell	BLL1121	1970	**£80**	

COCHRAN, EDDIE

Title	Format	Label	Cat. No.	Year	Price	Notes
C'mon Again	7" EP	Liberty	LEP2165	1964	**£15**	
C'mon Everybody	7"	Liberty	LBF15366	1970	**£4**	
C'mon Everybody	7"	Liberty	LIB10233	1966	**£4**	
C'mon Everybody	7" EP	Liberty	LEP2111	1963	**£15**	
C'mon Everybody	7" EP	London	REU1214	1959	**£20**	
C'mon Everybody	7"	London	HLU8792	1959	**£8**	chart single
Cherished Memories	LP	Liberty	LBY1109	1962	**£15**	chart LP
Cherished Memories Of Eddie Cochran	7" EP	Liberty	LEP2123	1963	**£12**	
Cherished Memories Of Eddie Cochran	7" EP	London	REG1301	1961	**£20**	
Cherished Memories Vol.1	7" EP	Liberty	LEP2090	1963	**£12**	
Drive In Show	7"	Liberty	LIB10108	1963	**£8**	
Eddie's Hits	7" EP	Liberty	LEP2124	1963	**£12**	
Eddie's Hits	7" EP	London	REG1262	1960	**£20**	
Hallelujah I Love Her So	7"	London	HLW9022	1960	**£8**	chart single
Jeannie Jeannie Jeannie	7"	London	HLG9460	1961	**£12**	chart single
Memorial Album	LP	Liberty	LBY1127	1963	**£12**	chart LP
Memorial Album	LP	Liberty	LRP3172	1960	**£40**	US
Memorial Album	LP	London	HAG2267	1960	**£30**	chart LP
My Way	LP	Liberty	LBY1205	1964	**£12**	
My Way	7"	Liberty	LIB10088	1963	**£8**	chart single
Never To Be Forgotten	7" EP	Liberty	LEP2052	1962	**£15**	
Never To Be Forgotten	LP	Liberty	LRP3220	1962	**£30**	US
Pretty Girl	7"	London	HLG9464	1961	**£8**	
Singing To My Baby	LP	Liberty	LBL83152	1968	**£10**	
Singing To My Baby	LP	Liberty	LBY1158	1963	**£15**	chart LP
Singing To My Baby	LP	Liberty	LRP3061	1958	**£100**	US
Singing To My Baby	LP	London	HAG2093	1958	**£30**	chart LP
Sitting In The Balcony	7"	London	HLU8433	1957	**£70**	
Skinnie Jim	7"	Liberty	LIB10151	1964	**£12**	
Somethin' Else	7"	Liberty	LBF15109	1968	**£4**	
Somethin' Else	7" EP	Liberty	LEP2122	1963	**£12**	
Somethin' Else	7"	London	HLU8944	1959	**£10**	chart single
Somethin' Else	7" EP	London	REU1239	1960	**£20**	
Stockings And Shoes	7" EP	Liberty	LEP2180	1964	**£15**	
Stockings And Shoes	7"	London	HLG9467	1961	**£8**	
Summertime Blues	7"	Liberty	LBF15071	1968	**£4**	chart single
Summertime Blues	7"	London	HLU8702	1958	**£10**	chart single
Sweetie Pie	7"	London	HLG9196	1960	**£10**	chart single
Teenage Heaven	7"	London	HLU8880	1959	**£12**	
Think Of Me	7"	Liberty	LIB10049	1962	**£8**	
Three Stars	7"	Liberty	LIB10249	1966	**£12**	
Three Steps To Heaven	7"	Liberty	LIB10276	1967	**£8**	
Three Steps To Heaven	7"	London	HLG9115	1960	**£8**	chart single
Twenty Flight Rock	7"	London	HLU8386	1957	**£25**	
Weekend	7"	London	HLG9362	1961	**£8**	chart single

COCHRAN, JACKIE LEE

Title	Format	Label	Cat. No.	Year	Price	Notes
Mama Don't You Think I Know	7"	Brunswick	05669	1957	**£140**	

COCK SPARRER

Title	Format	Label	Cat. No.	Year	Price	Notes
Running Riot	7"	Decca	FR13710	1977	**£15**	
Running Riot	12"	Decca	FR13710	1977	**£15**	
We Love You	7"	Decca	FR13732	1977	**£5**	
We Love You	12"	Decca	FR13732	1977	**£8**	

COCKBURN, BRUCE

Bruce Cockburn is a Canadian singer-songwriter who, since first issuing LPs on his own True North label at the start of the seventies, seems to have grown in stature with each passing year. His most impressive recordings are the most recent ones, the earliest records being interesting mainly for the glimpses they afford of a great artist in the making. This, of course, is the exact reverse of the usual state of affairs where rock performers are concerned.

Title	Format	Label	Cat. No.	Year	Price	Notes
Bruce Cockburn	LP	True North	TN1	1970	**£12**	Canadian
Circles In The Stream	LP	Island	ILTA9475	1977	**£15**	US double
Further Adventures	LP	True North	TN33	1976	**£12**	Canadian
Hand Dancing	LP	True North	TN13	1974	**£12**	Canadian
High Winds White Sky	LP	True North	TN3	1971	**£12**	Canadian
In The Falling Dark	LP	True North	TN26	1976	**£12**	Canadian
Joy Will Find A Way	LP	True North	TN23	1975	**£12**	Canadian
Night Vision	LP	True North	TN11	1973	**£12**	Canadian
Salt, Sun And Time	LP	True North	TN16	1974	**£12**	Canadian
Sunwheel Dance	LP	Epic	65187	1972	**£15**	

COCKER, JOE

Title	Format	Label	Cat. No.	Year	Price	Notes
Cry Me A River	7"	Fly	BUG3	1970	**£5**	PS
Delta Lady	7"	Regal Z.	RZ3024	1969	**£4**	chart single
I'll Cry Instead	7"	Decca	F11974	1964	**£20**	
Joe Cocker	LP	Regal Z.	SLRZ1011	1969	**£12**	
Letter	7"	Regal Z.	RZ3027	1970	**£4**	chart single
Luxury You Can Afford	LP	Asylum	DP400	1978	**£15**	US promo pic disc
Marjorine	7"	Regal Z.	RZ3006	1968	**£5**	chart single
With A Little Help From My Friends	7"	MagniFly	ECHO103	1972	**£6**	PS
With A Little Help From My Friends	LP	Regal Z.	SLRZ1006	1969	**£15**	
With A Little Help From My Friends	7"	Regal Z.	RZ3013	1968	**£4**	

COCKER, JOE & OTHERS

Title	Format	Label	Cat. No.	Year	Price	Notes
Rag Goes Mad At The Mojo	7"	Action	ACT002	1967	**£20**	chart single

COCKNEY REBEL

Title	Format	Label	Cat. No.	Year	Price	Notes
Judy Teen	7"	EMI	EMI2128	1974	**£4**	chart single
Sebastian	7"	EMI	EMI2051	1973	**£6**	

COCKNEYS

Title	Format	Label	Cat. No.	Year	Price	Notes
After Tomorrow	7"	Philips	BF1338	1964	**£10**	
I Know You're Gonna Be Mine	7"	Philips	BF1360	1964	**£10**	

COCTEAU TWINS

Title	Format	Label	Cat. No.	Year	Price	Notes
Blue Bell Knoll	LP	4AD	CAD807	1988	**£10**	fold-out sleeve
Pearly Dewdrops Drop	12"	4AD	BAD405	1984	**£6**	embossed sleeve
Peppermint Pig	7"	4AD	AD303	1983	**£12**	
Pink Opaque	LP	4AD	CAD513	1985	**£10**	

COE, JAMIE

Title	Format	Label	Cat. No.	Year	Price	Notes
Fool	7"	London	HLX9713	1963	**£4**	
How Low Is Low	7"	HMV	POP991	1961	**£4**	
Schoolday Blues	7"	Parlophone	R4621	1960	**£8**	
Summertime Symphony	7"	Parlophone	R4600	1959	**£10**	

COE, TONY

Title	Format	Label	Cat. No.	Year	Price	Notes
Tony Coe	LP	77		1971	**£30**	

COFFEE SET

Title	Format	Label	Cat. No.	Year	Price	Notes
Dicky Boy	7"	Mercury	MF1076	1969	**£4**	
Happy Birthday	7"	Mercury	MF1113	1969	**£4**	

COHEN, LEONARD

Title	Format	Label	Cat. No.	Year	Price	Notes
Bird On The Wire	7"	CBS	4245	1969	**£5**	
Joan Of Arc	7"	CBS	7292	1971	**£4**	
McCabe & Mrs.Miller	7" EP	CBS	7684	1972	**£5**	
Songs From A Room	LP	CBS	63587	1968	**£10**	chart LP
Songs Of Love And Hate	LP	CBS	69004	1970	**£10**	with booklet, chart LP
Songs Of...	LP	CBS	63241	1968	**£10**	chart LP
Suzanne	7"	CBS	3337	1968	**£5**	
Suzanne	7"	CBS	8353	1973	**£5**	

COHEN, LEONARD & OTHERS

Title	Format	Label	Cat. No.	Year	Price	Notes
Canadian Poets 1	LP	CBC		1966	**£15**	Canadian
Six Montreal Poets	LP	Folkways	FL9805	1957	**£25**	US

COIL

Title	Format	Label	Cat. No.	Year	Price	Notes
Wrong Eye	7"	Shock	SX002	198-	**£20**	individually lettered
Wrong Eye	7"	Shock	SX002	198-	**£5**	individually numbered

COKER, ALVADEAN

Title	Format	Label	Cat. No.	Year	Price	Notes
We're Gonna Bop	7"	London	HLU8191	1955	**£100**	

COKER, SANDY

Title	Format	Label	Cat. No.	Year	Price	Notes
Meadowlark Melody	7"	London	HL8109	1954	**£10**	

COLD BLOOD

Title	Format	Label	Cat. No.	Year	Price	Notes
First Blood	LP	Atlantic	588218	1970	**£10**	
Sisyphus	LP	Atlantic	2400102	1971	**£12**	
You Got Me Hummin'	7"	Atlantic	584319	1970	**£4**	

COLDER, BEN

Make The World Go Away	7" EP	MGM	MGMEP791	1964	£4	

COLE, B.J.

New Hovering Dog	LP	United Artists	UAS29418	1972	£15	

COLE, BILLY

Extra Careful	7"	P. Exchange	PX104	1975	£4	

COLE, CINDY

Just Being Your Baby	7"	Columbia	DB7973	1966	£4	
Love Like Yours	7"	Columbia	DB7519	1965	£4	

COLE, CLAY

Twist Around The Clock	7"	London	HLP9499	1962	£4	

COLE, COZY

Cozy Cole All Stars	7" EP	MGM	MGMEP622	1957	£5	
Topsy	7"	London	HL8750	1958	£4	chart single
Turvy	7"	London	HL8843	1959	£4	

COLE, STRANGER

All Your Friends (with Ken)	7"	R&B	JB120	1963	£10	
Conqueror (with Gladys)	7"	Dragon	DRA1014	1973	£4	
Cow In A Pasture	7"	Island	WI169	1965	£10	
Darling Please	7"	Songbird	SB1008	196-	£8	
Down The Train Line (with Patsy)	7"	Doctor Bird	DB1087	1967	£10	
Drop The Rachet	7"	Doctor Bird	DB1040	1966	£10	
Give Me One More Chance (with Patsy)	7"	Rio	R81	196-	£10	
Give Me The Right (with Patsy)	7"	Doctor Bird	DB1050	1966	£10	
Glad You're Living	7"	Duke	DU27	196-	£8	
Hey Little Girl (with Patsy)	7"	Black Swan	WI462	1965	£10	
I Want To Go Home	7"	Black Swan	WI465	1965	£10	
If We Should Ever Meet	7"	Unity	UN502	1969	£6	
Jeboza Macod	7"	Island	WI3154	1968	£8	
Just Like A River (with Gladys)	7"	Amalgamated	AMG801	196-	£10	
Night After Night	7"	Black Swan	WI461	1965	£10	
Over And Over Again	7"	Island	WI3128	1967	£8	
Pussy Cat	7"	Ska Beat	JB192	1965	£10	
Run Joe	7"	Island	WI177	1965	£10	
Seeing Is Knowing (with Gladys)	7"	Amalgamatod	AMG806	196-	£10	
Senor Senorita (with Patsy)	7"	Island	WI113	1963	£10	
Tell It To Me (with Patsy)	7"	Doctor Bird	DB1084	1967	£10	
Things Come To Those (with Patsy)	7"	Island	WI160	1964	£10	
Tom Dick And Harry (with Patsy)	7"	Island	WI144	1964	£10	
Uno-Dos-Tres	7"	Black Swan	WI413	1964	£10	
We Shall Overcome (with Seraphines)	7"	Doctor Bird	DB1025	1966	£10	
What Moma No Want She Get	7"	Amalgamated	AMG838	196-	£10	
When I Get My Freedom	7"	Unity	UN514	1969	£6	
When The Party Is Over	7"	Blue Beat	BB345	1965	£10	
Yea Yea Baby (with Patsy)	7"	Island	WI152	1964	£10	
You Took My Love	7"	Doctor Bird	DB1066	1966	£10	

COLEMAN, BOBBY

You Don't Have To Tell Me	7"	Pye	7N25365	1966	£20	

COLEMAN, LONNIE & JESSE ROBERTSON

Dolores Diana	7"	London	HLU8335	1956	£5	

COLETTE & THE BANDITS

Ladies Man	7"	Stateside	SS416	1965	£4	

COLLAGE

Misty	LP	Columbia		1973	£12	

COLLECTORS

Collectors	LP	W. Bros	WS1746	1968	£12	
Grass And Wild Strawberries	LP	W. Bros	WS1774	1968	£15	
I Must Have Been Blind	7"	London	HLU10304	1970	£4	

COLLIER, GRAHAM

Deep Dark Blue Centre	LP	Deram	DML1005	1967	£30	

Title	Format	Label	Cat. No.	Year	Price	Notes
Down Another Road	LP	Fontana	SFJL922	1969	**£30**	
Mosaics	LP	Philips	6308051	1971	**£30**	
Portraits	LP	Saydisc	SDL244	1972	**£30**	
Songs For My Father	LP	Polydor	6309006	1970	**£30**	

COLLIER, MITTY

Title	Format	Label	Cat. No.	Year	Price	Notes
I Had A Talk With My Man	7"	Pye	7N25275	1964	**£5**	

COLLINS, ALBERT

Title	Format	Label	Cat. No.	Year	Price	Notes
Compleat Albert Collins	LP	Imperial	12445	1969	**£20**	US
Cool Sound Of...	LP	TCF Hall	8002	1965	**£20**	US
Love Can Be Found	LP	Liberty	LBS83238	1969	**£20**	
There's Gotta Be A Change	LP	Tumbleweed	TW3501	1971	**£20**	
Trash Talkin'	LP	Imperial	12438	1969	**£20**	US
Truckin'	LP	Blue Thumb	8758	197-	**£20**	US

COLLINS, ANSEL

Title	Format	Label	Cat. No.	Year	Price	Notes
Night Of Love	7"	Trojan	TR699	1969	**£6**	

COLLINS, DAVE & ANSEL

Title	Format	Label	Cat. No.	Year	Price	Notes
Double Barrel	7"	Technique	TE901	1971	**£4**	chart single
Double Barrel	LP	Trojan	TBL162	1971	**£15**	
Monkey Spanner	7"	Technique	TE914	1971	**£4**	chart single

COLLINS, DONNIE SHOW BAND

Title	Format	Label	Cat. No.	Year	Price	Notes
Get Down With It	7"	Pye	7N17628	1968	**£8**	

COLLINS, DOROTHY

Title	Format	Label	Cat. No.	Year	Price	Notes
Dorothy Collins Sings	7" EP	London	REP1025	1955	**£5**	

COLLINS, GLENDA

Title	Format	Label	Cat. No.	Year	Price	Notes
Baby It Hurts	7"	HMV	POP1283	1964	**£10**	
I Lost My Heart In The Fairground	7"	HMV	POP1163	1963	**£5**	
If You've Got To Pick A Baby	7"	HMV	POP1233	1963	**£5**	
It's Hard To Believe It	7"	Pye	7N17150	1966	**£4**	
Johnny Loves Me	7"	HMV	POP1439	1965	**£5**	
Lollipop	7"	HMV	POP1323	1964	**£5**	
Something I've Got To Tell You	7"	Pye	7N17044	1966	**£4**	
Thou Shalt Not Steal	7"	HMV	POP1475	1965	**£5**	

COLLINS, JUDY

Title	Format	Label	Cat. No.	Year	Price	Notes
Both Sides Now	7"	Elektra	EKSN45043	1970	**£4**	chart single
Concert	LP	Elektra	EKS7280	1964	**£10**	
Fifth Album	LP	Elektra	EKS7300	1965	**£10**	
Golden Apples Of The Sun	LP	Elektra	EKS7222	1962	**£10**	
I'll Keep It With Mine	7"	London	HLZ10029	1966	**£4**	
In My Life	LP	Elektra	EKS7320	1967	**£10**	
In My Life	7"	Elektra	EKSN45011	1967	**£4**	
Maid Of Constant Sorrow	LP	Elektra	EKS7209	1962	**£10**	
Pretty Polly	7"	Elektra	EKSN45073	1969	**£4**	
Someday Soon	7"	Elektra	EKSN45053	1969	**£4**	
Third Album	LP	Elektra	EKS7243	1964	**£10**	
Turn Turn Turn	7"	Elektra	EKSN45077	1969	**£4**	
Who Knows Where The Time Goes	LP	Elektra	EKS74033	1969	**£10**	
Wild Flowers	LP	Elektra	EKS74012	1968	**£10**	

COLLINS, LYN

Title	Format	Label	Cat. No.	Year	Price	Notes
Rock Me Again And Again	7"	Polydor	2066490	1974	**£8**	
Rock Me Again And Again And Again	7"	Polydor	2066520	1975	**£4**	
Think	7"	Mojo	2093029	1974	**£4**	

COLLINS, PHIL

Title	Format	Label	Cat. No.	Year	Price	Notes
Against All Odds	7"	Virgin	VSY674	1984	**£5**	pic disc
In The Air Tonight	7"	Virgin	VSDJ102	1981	**£5**	1 sided promo
In The Air Tonight	7"	Virgin	VSK102	1981	**£6**	with booklet
One More Night	7"	Virgin	VSS755	1985	**£8**	shaped pic disc
Separate Lives	7"	Virgin	VSSD818	1985	**£10**	2 pic discs
Separate Lives	7"	Virgin	VSS818	1985	**£5**	white vinyl, with poster
Sussudio	12"	Virgin	VSY73612	1985	**£8**	shaped pic disc
Take Me Home	12"	Virgin	VS77712	1985	**£6**	with map
Thru' These Walls	7"	Virgin	VSY524	1982	**£5**	pic disc
You Can't Hurry Love	7"	Virgin	VSY531	1982	**£6**	pic disc

COLLINS, ROGER

She's Looking Good	7"	Vocalion	VF9285	1967	**£8**	

COLLINS, SHIRLEY

Adieu To Old England	LP	Topic	12T238	1974	**£20**	
Amaranth	LP	Harvest	SHSM2008	1976	**£15**	
Anthems In Eden	LP	Harvest	SHVL754	1969	**£40**	
False True Lovers	LP	Folkways	FG3564	1959	**£30**	
Favourite Garland	LP	Deram	SML1117	1975	**£20**	
For As Many As Will	LP	Topic	12T380	1978	**£10**	
Love,Death And The Lady	LP	Harvest	SHVL771	1970	**£40**	
No Roses	LP	Mooncrest	CREST11	1974	**£15**	
No Roses	LP	Pegasus	PEG7	1971	**£20**	
Power Of The True Love Knot	LP	Polydor	583025	1968	**£40**	
Sweet Primroses	LP	Topic	12TS170	1967	**£25**	

COLLINS, TOMMY

Dynamic...	LP	Columbia	CL2510	1966	**£20**	US
Let Down	7"	Capitol	CL14894	1958	**£4**	
Let's Live A Little	LP	Tower	T5021	1966	**£10**	US
Light Of The Lord	LP	Capitol	T1125	1959	**£25**	US
Little June	7"	Capitol	CL15076	1959	**£4**	
On Tour	LP	Columbia	CL2778	1968	**£20**	US
Shindig	LP	Tower	T5107	1968	**£10**	US
Songs I Love To Sing	LP	Capitol	T1436	1961	**£20**	US
Think It Over Boys	7"	Capitol	CL14838	1958	**£4**	
This Is Tommy Collins	LP	Capitol	T1196	1959	**£25**	US
Words And Music Country Style	LP	Capitol	T776	1957	**£30**	US
Wreck Of The Old '97	7"	Capitol	CL15118	1960	**£4**	

COLONEL

Too Many Cooks In The Kitchen	7"	Virgin	VS380	1980	**£5**	

COLONNA, JERRY

Chicago Style	7"	London	HL8143	1955	**£8**	
Ebb Tide	7"	Brunswick	05243	1954	**£6**	
It Might As Well Be Spring	7"	Brunswick	05342	1954	**£4**	
Let Me Go Lover	7"	Parlophone	MSP6165	1955	**£4**	
Let's All Sing	LP	London	HAU2190	1959	**£10**	
Shifting Whispering Sands	7"	HMV	7M369	1956	**£4**	

COLORADOS

Lips Are Redder On You	7"	Oriole	CB1972	1964	**£6**	

COLOSSEUM

Collectors' Colosseum	LP	Bronze	ILPS9173	1971	**£10**	
Daughter Of Time	LP	Vertigo	6360017	1970	**£15**	spiral label, chart LP
Live	LP	Bronze	ICD1	1971	**£15**	double, chart LP
Those About To Die...	LP	Fontana	STL5510	1969	**£15**	chart LP
Those Who Are About To Die	7"	Fontana	TF1029	1969	**£6**	
Valentyne Suite	LP	Bronze	HELP4	1972	**£10**	
Valentyne Suite	LP	Vertigo	VO1	1969	**£12**	spiral label, chart LP

COLOSSEUM II

Strange New Flesh	LP	Bronze	ILPS9356	1976	**£10**	

COLOURBOX

Breakdown (Version Two)	7"	4AD	AD304	1983	**£4**	
Breakdown	7"	4AD	AD215	1982	**£8**	
Breakdown	12"	4AD	BAD215	1982	**£12**	
Say You	12"	4AD	BAD403	1984	**£6**	

COLOURED RAISINS

One Way Love	7"	Trojan	TR7700	1970	**£6**	

COLOURFUL SEASONS

Out Of The Blue	7"	MGM	MGM1433	1968	**£4**	

COLOURS

Wake Up Wake Up	7"	Parlophone	R5940	1972	**£4**	

COLOURS OF LOVE

I'm A Train	7"	Page One	POF060	1968	**£4**	
Just Another Fly	7"	Page One	POF086	1968	**£4**	
Mother Of Convention	7"	Page One	POF124	1969	**£4**	

COLTON, TONY

I Stand Accused	7"	Pye	7N15886	1965	**£4**	
I've Laid Some Down In My Time	7"	Pye	7N17117	1966	**£4**	
In The World Of Marnie Dreaming	7"	Columbia	DB8385	1968	**£4**	
You're Wrong There Baby	7"	Pye	7N17046	1966	**£4**	

COLUMBIA BOYS

Baby Come Back	7"	Pye	7N17513	1968	**£4**	
That's My Pa	7"	Pye	7N17763	1969	**£4**	

COLUMBUS

Everybody Loves The US Marshall	7"	Deram	DM294	1970	**£6**	

COLYER, KEN SKIFFLE GROUP

Downbound Train	7"	Decca	FJ10751	1956	**£4**	
Ella Speed	7"	Decca	FJ10972	1958	**£4**	
Green Corn	7" EP	KC	KCS11EP	195-	**£5**	
Grey Goose	7"	Decca	FJ10889	1957	**£4**	
House Rent Stomp	7"	Decca	FJ10926	1957	**£4**	
Ken Colyer's Skiffle Group In Hamburg	7" EP	Decca	DFE6563	1959	**£5**	
Ken Colyer's Skiffle Group	7" EP	Decca	DFE6286	1956	**£5**	
Ken Colyer's Skiffle Group No.2	7" EP	Decca	DFE6444	1957	**£5**	
Ole Riley	7"	Decca	FJ10772	1956	**£4**	
Streamline Train	7"	Decca	F10711	1956	**£4**	
Take This Hammer	7"	Decca	F10631	1955	**£4**	

COME 1

Come Sunday	7"	Come 1	WDC88001	1979	**£25**	
Rampton	LP	Come 1	WDC88002	1979	**£20**	

COMIC ROMANCE

Cry Myself To Sleep	7"	WEA	K17418	1978	**£5**	

COMICS, ARTHUR

Isgodaman?	7"	XS		1977	**£10**	

COMMODORES

Keep On Dancing	7"	Atlantic	584273	1969	**£4**	
The Zoo (The Human Zoo)	7"	T. Motown	TMG924	1974	**£4**	
The Zoo (The Human Zoo)	7"	T. Motown	TMG924	1974	**£10**	demo

COMMODORES (2)

Riding On A Train	7"	London	HLD8209	1955	**£80**	
Speedo	7"	London	HLD8251	1956	**£120**	

COMMUNARDS

Don't Leave Me This Way	7"	London	LONXP103	1986	**£5**	shaped pic disc
Tomorrow (Remix)	7"	London	LONR143	1987	**£4**	
You Are My World	7"	London	LONDP77	1985	**£5**	double

COMPLEX

Complex	LP	Halpix		1970	**£1000**	
Way We Feel	LP	Halpix		1971	**£1000**	

COMSAT ANGELS

Red Planet	7"	Junta	JUNTA1	1979	**£5**	
Red Planet	7"	Junta	JUNTA1	1979	**£8**	red vinyl

COMSTOCK, BOBBY

I'm A Man	7"	United Artists	UP1086	1965	**£4**	
Jambalaya	7"	London	HLE9080	1960	**£4**	
Let's Stomp	7"	Stateside	SS163	1963	**£4**	
Out Of Sight	LP	Ascot	ALM13026	1966	**£10**	US
Susie Baby	7"	Stateside	SS221	1963	**£4**	
Tennessee Waltz	7"	Top Rank	JAR223	1959	**£4**	

COMUS

Comus are like a folky version of Family, with the group's singer adopting the same gargling tones as Roger Chapman. The largely acoustic instrumentation, however, gives the vocals a considerable dramatic emphasis, especially when underscored by a female singer. "First Utterance" is not exactly a classic, but it is certainly interesting.

Title	Format	Label	Cat. No.	Year	Price	Notes
First Utterance	LP	Dawn	DNLS3019	1971	**£60**	
To Keep From Crying	LP	Virgin	V2018	1974	**£15**	

CONCLUSION IS

Title	Format	Label	Cat. No.	Year	Price	Notes
This Is Not My Country	7"	Parlophone	R5823	1970	**£4**	

CONCORDS

Title	Format	Label	Cat. No.	Year	Price	Notes
I Need Your Loving	7"	Blue Cat	BS170	196-	**£10**	

CONDOR, HOWIE G.

Title	Format	Label	Cat. No.	Year	Price	Notes
Big Noise From Winnetka	7"	Fontana	TF613	1965	**£5**	

CONEY ISLAND KIDS

Title	Format	Label	Cat. No.	Year	Price	Notes
Baby Baby You	7"	London	HLJ8207	1955	**£10**	

CONLEY, ARTHUR

Title	Format	Label	Cat. No.	Year	Price	Notes
All Day Singing	7"	Atlantic	2091025	1970	**£4**	
Aunt Dora's Love Soul Shack	7"	Atlantic	584224	1968	**£4**	
Funky Street	7"	Atlantic	584175	1968	**£4**	chart single
More Sweet Soul	LP	Atco	SD33276	1969	**£10**	US
People Sure Act Funny	7"	Atlantic	584197	1968	**£4**	
Shake Rattle And Roll	7"	Atlantic	584121	1967	**£4**	
Shake, Rattle And Roll	LP	Atlantic	587084	1967	**£12**	
Soul Directions	LP	Atco	SD33243	1968	**£10**	US
Star Revue	7"	Atco	226004	1969	**£4**	
Sweet Soul Music	LP	Atco	33215	1967	**£15**	US
Sweet Soul Music	7"	Atlantic	584083	1967	**£4**	chart single
They Call The Wind Maria	7"	Atco	226011	1970	**£4**	
Whole Lotta Woman	7"	Atlantic	584143	1967	**£4**	

CONNELL, BRIAN & THE ROUND SOUND

Brian Connell was Brian Connolly, later a member of the Sweet.

Title	Format	Label	Cat. No.	Year	Price	Notes
I Know	7"	Philips	BF1718	1968	**£8**	
Just My Kind Of Loving	7"	Mercury	MF956	1966	**£8**	
Same Thing Happened To Me	7"	Mercury	MF991	1966	**£10**	
What Good Am I	7"	Philips	BF1661	1968	**£10**	

CONNIFF, RAY & HIS ROCKING RHYTHM BOYS

Title	Format	Label	Cat. No.	Year	Price	Notes
Piggy Bank Boogie	7"	Vogue Coral	QW5001	1955	**£6**	

CONNOLLY, BRIAN

Title	Format	Label	Cat. No.	Year	Price	Notes
Hypnotised	7"	Polydor		1981	**£4**	

CONQUERORS

Title	Format	Label	Cat. No.	Year	Price	Notes
If You Can't Beat Them Join Them	7"	High Note	HS016	196-	**£8**	
Jumpy Jumpy Girl	7"	Amalgamated	AMG832	196-	**£10**	
Mr.D.J.	7"	High Note	HS025	196-	**£8**	
What A Agony	7"	Doctor Bird	DB1046	1966	**£10**	

CONRAD, JESS

Title	Format	Label	Cat. No.	Year	Price	Notes
Cherry Pie	7"	Decca	F11236	1960	**£4**	chart single
Hey Little Girl	7"	Decca	F11412	1961	**£4**	
Human Jungle	7" EP	Decca	DFE8524	1963	**£5**	
Hurt Me	7"	Pye	7N15849	1965	**£5**	
Jess Conrad	7" EP	Decca	DFE6666	1960	**£5**	
Mystery Girl	7"	Decca	F11315	1961	**£4**	chart single
Pretty Jenny	7"	Decca	F11511	1962	**£4**	chart single
Pussycat	7"	Columbia	DB7223	1964	**£4**	
Things I'd Like To Say	7"	Columbia	DB7561	1965	**£4**	
Twist My Wrist	7" EP	Decca	DFE6702	1962	**£5**	
Walkaway	7"	Decca	F11394	1961	**£4**	

CONRAD, TONY & FAUST

Title	Format	Label	Cat. No.	Year	Price	Notes
Outside The Dream Syndicate	LP	Caroline	C1501	1972	**£15**	

CONROY

The high value reached by the "London Underground" LP is rather mysterious. The full title of the record - "Conroy Recorded

Music Library: London's Underground" is an exact description, not a metaphorical one. It does not refer to the "underground" music scene, but to the railway. The recording is of buskers playing outside a London tube station.

Title	Format	Label	Cat. No.	Year	Price	Notes
London's Underground	LP	Berry M. Co.		1972	**£600**	

CONSUMATES

Title	Format	Label	Cat. No.	Year	Price	Notes
What Is It	7"	Coxsone	CS7054	196-	**£10**	

CONTINUUM

Title	Format	Label	Cat. No.	Year	Price	Notes
Autumn Grass	LP	RCA	SF8196	1971	**£15**	
Continuum	LP	RCA	SF8157	1970	**£15**	

CONTOURS

Title	Format	Label	Cat. No.	Year	Price	Notes
Baby Hit And Run	7"	T. Motown	TMG886	1974	**£4**	
Baby Hit And Run	7"	T. Motown	TMG886	1974	**£10**	demo
Can You Do It	7"	Stateside	SS299	1964	**£20**	
Can You Jerk Like Me	7"	Stateside	SS381	1965	**£20**	
Contours	7" EP	T. Motown	TME2002	1965	**£30**	
Determination	7"	T. Motown	TMG564	1966	**£15**	
Determination	7"	T. Motown	TMG564	1966	**£50**	demo
Do You Love Me	LP	Oriole	PS40043	1963	**£40**	
Do You Love Me	7"	Oriole	CBA1763	1962	**£20**	
Do You Love Me	7"	T. Motown	TMG899	1974	**£4**	
Don't Let Her Be Your Baby	7"	Oriole	CBA1831	1963	**£20**	
First I Look At The Purse	7"	T. Motown	TMG531	1965	**£12**	
First I Look At The Purse	7"	T. Motown	TMG531	1965	**£50**	demo
First I Look At The Purse	7"	T. Motown	TMG723	1970	**£10**	demo
It's So Hard Being A Loser	7"	T. Motown	TMG605	1967	**£6**	
It's So Hard Being A Loser	7"	T. Motown	TMG605	1967	**£50**	demo
Just A Little Misunderstanding	7"	T. Motown	TMG723	1970	**£4**	chart single
Shake Sherry	7"	Oriole	CBA1799	1963	**£20**	

CONTRASTS

Title	Format	Label	Cat. No.	Year	Price	Notes
What A Day	7"	Monument	MON1018	1968	**£4**	

CONVAIRS

Title	Format	Label	Cat. No.	Year	Price	Notes
Mignight Mary	7"	HMV	POP1549	1966	**£8**	

CONVY, BERT & THE THUNDERBIRDS

Title	Format	Label	Cat. No.	Year	Price	Notes
Come On Back	7"	London	HLB8190	1955	**£15**	

CONWAY, MIKE

Title	Format	Label	Cat. No.	Year	Price	Notes
I'm Gonna Get Me A Woman	7"	Plexium	PXM1	196-	**£4**	

COODER, RY

Title	Format	Label	Cat. No.	Year	Price	Notes
Borderlive	LP	W. Bros		1981	**£20**	US promo
Chicken Skin Music	7"	Reprise	PRO644	1977	**£8**	promo
Crazy 'Bout An Automobile	12"	W. Bros	PROA943	1980	**£8**	promo
How Can A Poor Man...	7"	Reprise	RE23497	1971	**£4**	
Jazz	LP	Mobile Fid.	MFSL1085	1982	**£15**	US audiophile
Money Honey	7"	Reprise	K14151	1972	**£4**	
Money Honey	7"	Reprise	PRO514	1973	**£4**	promo
Ry Cooder Radio Show	LP	Reprise	PRO558	1976	**£20**	US promo
Teardrops Will Fall	7"	W. Bros	SAM149	1982	**£4**	

COOK, LITTLE JOE

Title	Format	Label	Cat. No.	Year	Price	Notes
Don't You Have Feelings	7"	Sonet	SON2002	1973	**£6**	

COOK, LITTLE JOE (CHRIS FARLOWE)

Title	Format	Label	Cat. No.	Year	Price	Notes
Stormy Monday Blues	7"	Sue	WI385	1965	**£25**	

COOK, PETER

Title	Format	Label	Cat. No.	Year	Price	Notes
Ballad Of Spotty Muldoon	7"	Decca	F12182	1965	**£4**	chart single
Georgia	7"	Pye	7N15847	1965	**£8**	

COOK, PETER & DUDLEY MOORE

Title	Format	Label	Cat. No.	Year	Price	Notes
Bedazzled	7"	Decca	F12710	1967	**£4**	
By Appointment	7" EP	Decca	DFE8644	1965	**£5**	
Goodbye-ee	7"	Decca	F12158	1965	**£4**	chart single
Isn't She A Sweetie	7"	Decca	F12380	1966	**£4**	
L.S.Bumble Bee	7"	Decca	F12551	1967	**£6**	
Not Only...But Also	LP	Decca	LK4703	1965	**£10**	
Once Moore With Cook	LP	Decca	LK4785	1966	**£10**	chart LP

Peter Cook & Dudley Moore	7" EP	Parlophone	GEP8940	1965	**£5**	

COOK, PETER & OTHERS

Beyond The Fringe	LP	Parlophone	PMC1145	1961	**£12**	chart LP
Bridge On The River Wye	LP	Parlophone	PMC1190	1962	**£10**	
Peter Cook Presents The Establishment	LP	Parlophone	PMC1198	1963	**£12**	
Private Eye's Blue Record	LP	Transatlantic	TRA131	1965	**£15**	

COOKE, SAM

Ain't That Good News	LP	RCA	RD7635	1964	**£15**	
Another Saturday Night	7"	RCA	RCA1341	1963	**£4**	chart single
At The Copa	LP	RCA	RD7674	1965	**£15**	
Best Of...	LP	RCA	LPM2625	1962	**£10**	US
Best Of...Vol.2	LP	RCA	LPM3373	1965	**£10**	US
Bring It On Home To Me	7"	RCA	RCA1296	1962	**£4**	
Chain Gang	7"	RCA	RCA1202	1960	**£4**	chart single
Cooke's Tour	LP	RCA	RD27190, SF5076	1961	**£20**	
Cousin Of Mine	7"	RCA	RCA1420	1964	**£4**	
Cupid	7"	RCA	RCA1242	1961	**£4**	chart single
Encore	LP	HMV	CLP1273	1959	**£25**	
Feel It	7"	RCA	RCA1260	1961	**£4**	
Frankie And Johnny	7"	RCA	RCA1361	1963	**£4**	chart single
Good News	7"	RCA	RCA1386	1964	**£4**	
Good Times	7"	RCA	RCA1405	1964	**£4**	
Heart And Soul	7" EP	RCA	RCX7117	1963	**£8**	
Hit Kit	LP	Keen	86101	1959	**£20**	US
Hits Of The Fifties	LP	RCA	RD27215, SF5098	1961	**£20**	
I Need You Now	7"	London	HLU9046	1960	**£5**	
I Thank God	LP	Keen	86103	1960	**£15**	US
I'll Come Running Back To You	7"	Speciality	SON5010	1976	**£5**	
It's Got The Whole World Shakin'	7"	RCA	RCA1452	1965	**£4**	
Little Red Rooster	7"	RCA	RCA1367	1963	**£4**	
Little Things You Do	7"	HMV	POP610	1959	**£5**	
Love Me	7"	RCA	RCA1221	1961	**£5**	
Love You Most Of All	7"	HMV	POP568	1958	**£6**	
Man Who Invented Soul	LP	RCA	LSP3991	1968	**£10**	US
Mr.Soul	LP	RCA	RD7539	1963	**£15**	
My Kind Of Blues	LP	RCA	RD27245, SF5120	1962	**£20**	
Night Beat	LP	RCA	RD7583	1963	**£15**	
Nothing Can Change This Love	7"	RCA	RCA1310	1962	**£4**	
One Hour Ahead	7"	HMV	POP675	1959	**£4**	
Only Sixteen	7"	HMV	POP642	1959	**£4**	chart single
Sam Cooke	LP	Keen	A2001	1958	**£25**	US
Send Me Some Loving	7"	RCA	RCA1327	1963	**£4**	
Shake	LP	RCA	RD7730	1965	**£15**	
Shake	7"	RCA	RCA1436	1965	**£5**	
Sugar Dumpling	7"	RCA	RCA1476	1965	**£4**	
Swing Low	LP	RCA	LPM2293	1960	**£15**	US
Swing Sweetly	7" EP	RCA	RCX7128	1964	**£8**	
Teenage Sonata	7"	RCA	RCA1184	1960	**£5**	
That's All I Need To Know	7"	London	HLU8615	1958	**£8**	
That's Heaven To Me	7"	Immediate		1966	**£20**	demo only
That's It I Quit, I'm Moving On	7"	RCA	RCA1230	1961	**£4**	
Tribute To The Lady	LP	Keen	2004	1959	**£20**	US
Try A Little Love	LP	RCA	RD7764	1966	**£12**	
Twistin' The Night Away	LP	RCA	RD27263, SF5133	1962	**£15**	
Twistin' The Night Away	7"	RCA	RCA1277	1962	**£4**	chart single
Unforgettable Sam Cooke	LP	RCA	LPM3517	1966	**£10**	US
Wonderful World	7"	HMV	POP754	1960	**£4**	chart single
Wonderful World Of...	LP	Immediate	IMLP002	1966	**£15**	
You Send Me	7"	London	HLU8506	1957	**£12**	chart single

COOKIES

Chains	7"	London	HLU9634	1962	**£5**	chart single
Don't Say Nothing Bad About My Baby	7"	London	HLU9704	1963	**£4**	
Girls Grow Up Faster Than Boys	7"	Colpix	PX11020	1964	**£4**	
Willpower	7"	Colpix	PX11012	1963	**£4**	

COOL BREEZE

People Ask What Love Is	7"	Patheway	103		**£10**	

COOL CATS

Title	Format	Label	Number	Year	Price	Notes
Hold Your Love	7"	Jolly	JY009	196-	**£8**	
What Kind Of Man	7"	Jolly	JY007	196-	**£8**	

COOL MEN

Title	Format	Label	Number	Year	Price	Notes
Cool For Cats No.1	7" EP	Parlophone	GEP8739	1958	**£8**	
Cool For Cats No.2	7" EP	Parlophone	GEP8752	1958	**£8**	

COOL SPOON

Title	Format	Label	Number	Year	Price	Notes
Yakety Yak	7"	Coxsone	CS7032	196-	**£10**	

COOL STICKY

Title	Format	Label	Number	Year	Price	Notes
Train To Soulville	7"	Amalgamated	AMG825	196-	**£10**	

COOLEY, EDDIE & THE DIMPLES

Title	Format	Label	Number	Year	Price	Notes
Got A Little Woman	7"	Columbia	DB3873	1957	**£12**	

COOPER, ALICE

Title	Format	Label	Number	Year	Price	Notes
Be My Lover	7"	W. Bros	K16154	1972	**£5**	
Billion Dollar Babies	LP	W. Bros	BS42685	1973	**£12**	US quad
Billion Dollar Babies	LP	W. Bros	K56013	1973	**£10**	with var. inserts, chart LP
Clones	7"	W. Bros	K17598	1980	**£4**	
Department Of Youth	7"	Anchor	1012	1975	**£5**	PS
Easy Action	LP	Straight	STS1061	1969	**£20**	
Eighteen	7"	Straight	S7209	1971	**£8**	
Elected	7"	W. Bros	K16214	1972	**£8**	PS
For Britain Only	7"	W. Bros	K17940M	1982	**£5**	pic disc
Greatest Hits	LP	W. Bros	W42803	1974	**£12**	US quad
I Never Cry	7"	W. Bros	K16792	1976	**£4**	PS
Love At Your Convenience	7"	W. Bros	K16935	1977	**£4**	chart single
Love It To Death	LP	Straight	STS1065	1971	**£20**	
Muscle Of Love	LP	W. Bros	K56018	1974	**£10**	in cardboard box, chart LP
Muscle Of Love	LP	W. Bros	BS42748	1974	**£12**	US quad
Pretties For You	LP	Straight	STS1051	1969	**£20**	
School's Out	7"	W. Bros	K16409	1974	**£6**	
School's Out	7"	W. Bros	K17287	1979	**£4**	
School's Out	7"	W. Bros	K16188	1972	**£8**	PS
School's Out	LP	W. Bros	K56007	1972	**£10**	with panties
Schooldays	LP	W. Bros	K66021	1973	**£15**	double
Seven And Seven Is	7"	W. Bros	K17924	1982	**£4**	gatefold PS
Slick Black Limousine	7"	Lyntone	LYN2585/6	1973	**£4**	NME flexi
Under My Wheels	7"	W. Bros	K16127	1971	**£5**	
Welcome To My Nightmare	7"	Anchor	ANE7001	1975	**£4**	
Welcome To My Nightmare	12"	Anchor	ANE12001	1977	**£6**	
Welcome To My Nightmare	LP	Mobile Fid.	MFSL1063	1980	**£15**	US audiophile

COOPER, GARNELL & KINFOLK

Title	Format	Label	Number	Year	Price	Notes
Green Monkey	7"	London	HL9757	1963	**£4**	

COOPER, MIKE

Title	Format	Label	Number	Year	Price	Notes
Do I Know You	LP	Dawn	DNLS3005	1970	**£12**	
Life & Death In Paradise	LP	Fresh Air	6370500	1974	**£12**	
Machine Gun Company	LP	Dawn	DNLS3031	1972	**£12**	
Oh Really	LP	Pye	NSPL18281	1969	**£15**	
Places I Know	LP	Dawn	DNLS3026	1971	**£12**	
Time In Hand	7"	Dawn	DNS1022	1972	**£4**	
Too Late Now	7"	Dawn	DNX2511	1971	**£4**	
Trout Steel	LP	Dawn	DNLS3011	1970	**£12**	
Your Lovely Ways	7"	Dawn	DNX2501	1970	**£4**	

COPAS, COWBOY

Title	Format	Label	Number	Year	Price	Notes
Alabam	7"	Melodisc	MEL1566	196-	**£4**	
Country Entertainer No.1	LP	London	HAB8088	1963	**£10**	
Country Hits	7" EP	Stateside	SE1003	1963	**£4**	
Country Music	7" EP	Top Rank	JKP3014	1962	**£4**	
Favourite Cowboy Songs	7" EP	Parlophone	GEP8527	1955	**£5**	
Heartbreak Ago	7"	Parlophone	MSP6109	1954	**£8**	
Return To Sender	7"	Parlophone	MSP6164	1955	**£8**	
Star Of The Grand Ole Opry	LP	London	HAB8180	1964	**£10**	
Tennessee Senorita	7"	Parlophone	MSP6079	1954	**£8**	
Unforgettable...Vol.1	7" EP	London	REB1418	1964	**£4**	

Unforgettable...Vol.2	7" EP	London	REB1419	1964	£4	
Unforgettable...Vol.3	7" EP	London	REB1420	1964	£4	
Western Style	7" EP	Parlophone	GEP8575	1956	£5	

COPELAND, ALAN

Feeling Happy	7"	Vogue Coral	Q72237	1957	£6	

COPELAND, KEN

Pledge Of Love	7"	London	HLP8423	1957	£40	

COPPERFIELD

Any Old Time	7"	Instant	IN004	1969	£6	
I'll Hold Out My Hand	7"	Parlophone	R5818	1969	£4	

COPS & ROBBERS

I Could Have Danced All Night	7"	Pye	7N15870	1965	£6	
It's All Over Now Baby Blue	7"	Pye	7N15928	1965	£6	
St.James Infirmary	7"	Decca	F12019	1964	£8	

CORBETT, HARRY H. & WILFRED BRAMBELL

Steptoe And Son	LP	Pye	NPL18081	1962	£10	

CORBETT, RONNIE

Big Man	7"	Columbia	DB8512	1968	£4	

CORBY & THE CHAMPAGNE

Time Marches On	7"	Pye	7N17203	1966	£4	

CORDELL, PHIL

Chevy Van	7"	Mowest	MW3026	1975	£8	demo

CORDES

Give Her Time	7"	Cavern Sound	IMSTL1	1965	£12	

CORDET, LOUISE

Don't Let The Sun Catch You Crying	7"	Decca	F11824	1964	£4	
Don't Make Me Over	7"	Decca	F11875	1964	£4	
I'm Just A Baby	7"	Decca	F11476	1962	£4	chart single
Sweet Beat Of Louise Cordet	7" EP	Decca	DFE8515	1962	£6	
Sweet Enough	7"	Decca	F11524	1962	£4	
Which Way The Wind Blows	7"	Decca	F11673	1963	£4	

CORDUROYS

Tick Tock	7"	Planet	PLF122	1966	£10	

CORN DOLLIES

Forever Steven	7"	Farm	FARM1	1987	£5	

CORNELL, JERRY

Please Don't Talk About Me...	7"	London	HL8157	1955	£10	

CORNS, ARNOLD

Hang On To Yourself	7"	B&C	CB189	1971	£15	
Hang On To Yourself	7"	Mooncrest	MOON25	1974	£8	
Moonage Daydream	7"	B&C	CB149	1971	£15	

CORNWELL, HUGH & ROBERT WILLIAMS

White Room	7"	United Artists	BP320	1979	£5	

CORONADOS

Johnny B Goode	7"	Stateside	SS2043	1967	£4	

CORSAIRS

I'll Take You Home	7"	Pye	7N25142	1962	£6	
I'm Gonna Shut You Down	7"	CBS	202624	1967	£8	

CORT, BOB SKIFFLE GROUP

Don't You Rock Me Daddy-O	7"	Decca	FJ10831	1957	£8	
On Top Of Old Smokey	7"	Decca	F11109	1959	£4	
Schoolday	7"	Decca	F10905	1957	£5	
Six Five Special	7"	Decca	F10892	1957	£6	
Skiffle Party	7"	Decca	F10951	1957	£4	

CORTEZ, DAVE BABY

Title	Format	Label	Number	Year	Price	Notes
And His Happy Organ	LP	RCA	LPM2099	1959	**£12**	US
Countdown	7"	Roulette	RK7001	1966	**£4**	
Dave Baby Cortez	LP	Clock	C331	1960	**£12**	US
Dave Baby Cortez	7" EP	London	REU1233	1960	**£10**	
Deep In The Heart Of Texas	7"	London	HLU9126	1960	**£5**	
Golden Hits	LP	London	HAU8142	1964	**£12**	
Happy Organ	7"	London	HLU8852	1959	**£5**	
Piano Shuffle	7"	Columbia	DB4404	1960	**£6**	
Rinky Dink	LP	Chess	LP1473	1962	**£12**	US
Rinky Dink	7"	Pye	7N25159	1962	**£5**	
Whistling Organ	7"	London	HLU8919	1959	**£4**	

CORTINAS

Title	Format	Label	Number	Year	Price	Notes
Defiant Pose	7"	Step Forward	SF6	1978	**£5**	
Defiant Pose	12"	Step Forward	SF6	1978	**£8**	
Fascist Dictator	7"	Step Forward	SF1	1977	**£8**	
Heartache	7"	CBS		1978	**£4**	
True Romances	LP	CBS	82831	1978	**£10**	

CORTINAS (2)

Title	Format	Label	Number	Year	Price	Notes
Phoebe's Flower Shop	7"	Polydor	56255	1968	**£5**	

CORYELL, LARRY

Larry Coryell caused much comment as the first guitarist in a jazz group to employ feedback, but the offending track, Gary Burton's "General Mojo Cuts Up", is actually a very mild-mannered affair. Ever since, Coryell has languished in the shade of John McLaughlin, who is the real innovator where the use of a highly amplified guitar in jazz is concerned. There is a reasonable sampler of his work - the double "Essential Larry Coryell" on Vanguard. Otherwise, he has made a great many records, of which the scarcer, earlier ones listed here are just the start.

Title	Format	Label	Number	Year	Price	Notes
Barefoot Boy	LP	F. Dutchman	10139	1972	**£12**	
Coryell	LP	Vanguard	VSD6547	1969	**£15**	
Fairyland	LP	F. Dutchman	51500	1971	**£12**	
Introducing The Eleventh House	LP	Vanguard	VSD79342	1974	**£10**	
Introducing The Eleventh House	LP	Vanguard	VSD79342	1974	**£12**	quad
Lady Coryell	LP	Vanguard	VSD6509	1969	**£15**	
Live At The Village Gate	LP	Vanguard	VSD6573	1971	**£12**	
Live At The Village Gate	LP	Vanguard	VSD6573	1971	**£15**	quad
Offering	LP	Vanguard	VSD79319	1972	**£10**	
Offering	LP	Vanguard	VSD79319	1972	**£12**	quad
Real Great Escape	LP	Vanguard	VSD79329	1973	**£10**	
Restful Mind	LP	Vanguard	VSD79353	1975	**£10**	
Spaces	LP	Vanguard	VSD6558	1970	**£10**	

COSBY, BILL

Title	Format	Label	Number	Year	Price	Notes
Little Ole Man	7"	W. Bros	WB7072	1967	**£5**	

COSMIC DEALER

Title	Format	Label	Number	Year	Price	Notes
Crystallization	LP	Negram		1970	**£120**	

COSMIC EYE

Cosmic Eye represented an attempt on the part of some of the second division of British jazz musicians - basically John Mayer's Indo-jazz group - to break directly into the progressive rock market.

Title	Format	Label	Number	Year	Price	Notes
Dream Sequence	LP	Regal Z.	SLRZ1030	1972	**£100**	

COSMIC SOUNDS

"The Zodiac" was the first electronic rock record and featured spoken verses, one for each Zodiacal sign, behind which Paul Beaver put his new synthesizer through its paces.

Title	Format	Label	Number	Year	Price	Notes
Zodiac	LP	Elektra	EKS74009	1967	**£20**	

COSMO & DENZIL

Title	Format	Label	Number	Year	Price	Notes
Come On Come On	7"	Blue Beat	BB312	1964	**£10**	
Sweet Rosemarie	7"	Blue Beat	BB296	1964	**£10**	

COSTELLO, DAY

Title	Format	Label	Number	Year	Price	Notes
Long And Winding Road	7"	Spark	SRL1042	1970	**£6**	

COSTELLO, ELVIS

Two of Elvis Costello's limited edition releases are vital additions to any collection of his work. "A Conversation With Elvis Costello" spreads the contents of his "Imperial Bedroom" LP over two records, adding a substantial amount of interview material in which Costello explains the genesis of each of the songs, prior to each one being heard. (The promo version of "Almost Blue" gives the same treatment to that album, but the interview segments are much shorter and much less interesting). "Live

At The El Mocambo", meanwhile, contains a brilliant live reworking of some of the songs from Costello's first two LPs. Most copies that appear on the market are actually counterfeits, although this has little effect on their value. (As usual, the counterfeits are readily identified by their hand-written matrix numbers).

Title	Format	Label	Number	Year	Price	Notes
Alison	7"	Columbia	310641	1977	**£5**	US
Alison	7"	Columbia	310705	1978	**£5**	US
Alison	7"	Stiff	BUY14	1977	**£5**	PS
Armed Forces	LP	CBS	JC35709	1979	**£15**	Canadian, yellow vinyl
Big Sister	7"	F-Beat		1982	**£10**	1 sided promo
Blood And Chocolate	cass	Imp	FIEND80	1986	**£20**	Cadburys package
Conversation With Elvis Costello	LP	F-Beat	ECCHAT2	1982	**£50**	double promo
Don't Let Me Be Misunderstood (Live)	12"	Columbia	CAS2310	1986	**£15**	US promo
Excerpts from Almost Blue	7"	F-Beat	EC1	1981	**£25**	promo
Excerpts from Trust	12"	F-Beat	EL2	1981	**£35**	promo
Get Happy	LP	F-Beat	XXPROMO1	1980	**£40**	double 12" promo
Good Year For The Roses	7"	F-Beat	XX17	1981	**£30**	PS
High Fidelity	7"	F-Beat	XX3	1980	**£12**	promo
Highlights From Blood And Chocolate	7"	Imp	CHOC1	1986	**£10**	red vinyl promo
I Can't Stand Up For Falling Down	7"	2-Tone	CHSTT7	1980	**£12**	matrix no. XX1
I Can't Stand Up For Falling Down	7"	2-Tone	CHSTT7	1980	**£25**	paper label
I Wanna Be Loved (Radio Version)	7"	F-Beat	XX35DJ	1984	**£10**	promo
I Wanna Be Loved (Radio Version)	12"	F-Beat	XX35Z	1984	**£20**	promo
Imperial Bedroom	LP	Columbia	HC48157	1982	**£20**	US audiophile
Intro. The Tracks From Almost Blue	LP	F-Beat	ECCHAT1	1981	**£50**	promo
Less Than Zero	7"	Stiff	BUY11	1977	**£5**	PS
Live At Hollywood High	12"	Columbia	AS529	1979	**£25**	US promo
Live At Hollywood High	7"	Radar	SAM90	1979	**£4**	
Live At The El Mocambo	LP	Columbia	CDN10	1978	**£50**	Canadian promo
Man Out Of Time (DJ Edit)	7"	F-Beat	XX28DJ	1982	**£15**	promo
Man Out Of Time	12"	Columbia	AS1510	1982	**£15**	US promo
My Aim Is True/This Year's Model	LP	Columbia	no number	1978	**£150**	US promo pic disc
My Funny Valentine	7"	Columbia	AE71172	1979	**£15**	US promo, red vinyl
Neat Neat Neat	7"	Radar	SAM83	1978	**£4**	
New Amsterdam	7"	F-Beat	XX5E	1980	**£5**	4 tracks
New Amsterdam	7"	F-Beat	XX5P	1980	**£15**	pic disc, black rim
New Amsterdam	7"	F-Beat	XX5P	1980	**£8**	pic disc, white rim
Party Party	7"	A&M	PARTY5	1982	**£4**	promo,Bananarama B-side
Punch The Clock	7"	F-Beat		1983	**£40**	2x 7"in plastic wallet,promo
Radio Radio	12"	Radar	ADA24	1978	**£25**	promo
Radio Radio	7"	Radar	ADA24	1978	**£4**	PS
Red Shoes	7"	Stiff	BUY15	1977	**£8**	Max Wall mispress B side
Red Shoes	7"	Stiff	BUY15	1977	**£5**	PS
Sweet Dreams	7"	F-Beat	XX19	1981	**£4**	mispressed with 2 A sides
Taking Liberties	LP	Columbia	JC36939	1980	**£12**	US
Taking Liberties	12"	Columbia	AS847	1980	**£20**	US promo, Costello label
Talking In The Dark	7"	Radar	RG1	1978	**£15**	
Tom Snyder Interview	12"	Columbia	AS958	1980	**£15**	US promo
Watching The Detectives	7"	Stiff	BUY20DJ	1977	**£8**	promo
Watching The Detectives	7"	Stiff	BUY20	1977	**£4**	PS
Watching The Detectives	7"	Stiff	BUY20	1977	**£6**	telephone directory sleeve

COSTELLO, ELVIS & OTHERS

Title	Format	Label	Number	Year	Price	Notes
Radio Radio	12"	Columbia	AS443	1978	**£20**	US promo, orange vinyl

COTTON, JIMMY

Title	Format	Label	Number	Year	Price	Notes
Chris Barber Presents Jimmy Cotton	7" EP	Columbia	SEG8141	1962	**£5**	
Chris Barber Presents Jimmy Cotton No.2	7" EP	Columbia	SEG8189	1962	**£5**	

COTTON, MIKE JAZZMEN

Title	Format	Label	Number	Year	Price	Notes
Ain't Misbehavin'	7"	Columbia	DB4779	1962	**£4**	
Cobbler's Song	7"	Columbia	DB4821	1962	**£4**	
Senora	7"	Columbia	DB4697	1961	**£4**	
Swing That Hammer	7"	Columbia	DB7029	1963	**£4**	chart single
Zulu Warrior	7"	Columbia	DB4910	1962	**£4**	

COTTON, MIKE SOUND

Title	Format	Label	Number	Year	Price	Notes
Harlem Shuffle	7"	Polydor	56096	1966	**£8**	
I Don't Wanna Know	7"	Columbia	DB7267	1964	**£8**	
Make Up Your Mind	7"	Columbia	DB7623	1965	**£8**	
Midnight Flyer	7"	Columbia	DB7134	1963	**£8**	
Mike Cotton Sound	LP	Columbia		1964	**£70**	
Round And Round	7"	Columbia	DB7382	1964	**£8**	

Title	Format	Label	Cat. No.	Year	Price	Notes
Step Out Of Line	7"	Pye	7N17313	1967	**£8**	
Swing That Hammer	7"	Columbia	DB7029	1963	**£8**	

COUGAR, JOHN

Title	Format	Label	Cat. No.	Year	Price	Notes
Chestnut Street Incident	LP	MCA	2225	1977	**£10**	US
Miami	7"	Riva	20P	1979	**£4**	pic disc

COUGARS

Title	Format	Label	Cat. No.	Year	Price	Notes
Caviare And Chips	7"	Parlophone	R5115	1964	**£4**	
Red Square	7"	Parlophone	R5038	1963	**£4**	
Saturday Night At The Duckpond	7"	Parlophone	R4989	1963	**£5**	chart single
Saturday Night With The Cougars	7" EP	Parlophone	GEP8886	1963	**£8**	

COULSON, DEAN, MCGUINNESS, FLINT

Title	Format	Label	Cat. No.	Year	Price	Notes
Lo And Behold	LP	DJM	DJLPS424	1972	**£10**	

COUNT DOWN & THE ZEROS

Title	Format	Label	Cat. No.	Year	Price	Notes
Hello My Girl	7"	Ember	EMBS189	1964	**£10**	

COUNT FIVE

Title	Format	Label	Cat. No.	Year	Price	Notes
Psychotic Reaction	LP	Double Shot	DSM1001	1966	**£30**	US
Psychotic Reaction	7"	Pye	7N25393	1900	**£15**	

COUNT OSSIE

Title	Format	Label	Cat. No.	Year	Price	Notes
Grounation	LP	Ashanti	NTI301	1973	**£20**	triple
Man Is Two Faced	7"	Doctor Bird	DB1113	1967	**£10**	
Nyiah Bongo	7"	Doctor Bird	DB1086	1967	**£10**	

COUNT STICKY

Title	Format	Label	Cat. No.	Year	Price	Notes
Chico Chico	7"	Kalypso	XX18	196-	**£6**	

COUNT ZEBRA

Title	Format	Label	Cat. No.	Year	Price	Notes
Bedbug	7"	Kalypso	XX23	196-	**£8**	

COUNTRY GAZETTE

Title	Format	Label	Cat. No.	Year	Price	Notes
Don't Give Up Your Day Job	LP	United Artists	UAS29491	1973	**£10**	
Traitor In Our Midst	LP	United Artists	UAG29404	1972	**£10**	

COUNTRY HAMS

Title	Format	Label	Cat. No.	Year	Price	Notes
Walking In The Park With Eloise	7"	EMI	EMI2220	1974	**£25**	red & brown label
Walking In The Park With Eloise	7"	EMI	EMI2220	1982	**£8**	straw label

COUNTRY JOE & THE FISH

Title	Format	Label	Cat. No.	Year	Price	Notes
C.J.Fish	LP	Vanguard	6369002	1970	**£10**	
Electric Music For The Mind & Body	LP	Fontana	STFL6081	1967	**£20**	
Electric Music For The Mind & Body	LP	Vanguard	SVRL19026	1967	**£15**	
Here I Go Again	7"	Vanguard	VA3	1969	**£8**	
Here We Are Again	LP	Vanguard	SVRL19048	1969	**£15**	
I Feel Like I'm Fixin' To Die	7"	Vanguard	6076250	1970	**£8**	
I Feel Like I'm Fixing To Die	LP	Fontana	STFL6087	1967	**£20**	
I Feel Like I'm Fixing To Die	LP	Vanguard	SVRL19029	1967	**£15**	
Life And Times Of...	LP	Vanguard	VSD27/28	1973	**£20**	double
Life And Times Of...	LP	Vanguard	VSD27/28	1973	**£25**	quad, double
Not So Sweet Martha Lorraine	7"	Fontana	TF882	1967	**£10**	
Together	LP	Vanguard	SVRL19006	1968	**£15**	

COUNTRY LANE

Title	Format	Label	Cat. No.	Year	Price	Notes
Substratum	LP	Splendid		1973	**£200**	

COUNTY, WAYNE & THE ELECTRIC CHAIRS

Title	Format	Label	Cat. No.	Year	Price	Notes
Berlin	7"	Safari	SAFE13	1978	**£4**	
Berlin	12"	Safari	SARELS13	1978	**£6**	pink vinyl
Blatantly Offensive	7"	Attic	LAT1056	1977	**£5**	red vinyl
Blatantly Offensive	7"	Safari	WC2	1977	**£6**	yellow vinyl
Eddie And Sheena	7"	Safari	SAFE7	1978	**£4**	
Electric Chairs	LP	Safari	LONG1	1978	**£10**	
Fuck Off	7"	Sweet fa	WC1A	1977	**£5**	
I Had Too Much To Dream	7"	Safari	SAFE6	1978	**£4**	
Man Enough To Be A Woman	LP	Safari	GOOD3	197-	**£10**	
Rock And Roll Resurrection	LP	Safari	LIVE1	1980	**£10**	
So Many Ways	7"	Safari	SAFE18	1979	**£4**	
Storm The Gates Of Heaven	LP	Safari	GOOD1	1978	**£12**	multi-coloured vinyl

Stuck On You	7"	Illegal	IL002	1977	**£5**	
Thunder When She Walks	7"	Illegal	IL005	1977	**£5**	
Trying To Get On The Radio	7"	Safari	SAFE9	1978	**£4**	

COURTNEY, DEAN

I'll Always Need You	7"	RCA	RCA2534	1975	**£4**	

COUSIN EMMY & HER KINFOLK

Kentucky Mountain Ballads Vol.1	7" EP	Brunswick	OE9258	1956	**£4**	
Kentucky Mountain Ballads Vol.2	7" EP	Brunswick	OE9259	1956	**£4**	

COUSINS

Buddah	7"	Palette	KG9017	1961	**£4**	
Kili Watch	7"	Palette	KG9011	1961	**£4**	
Yes Sir That's My Baby	7"	Decca	F11924	1964	**£4**	

COUSINS, DAVE

Going Home	7"	A&M	AMS7032	1972	**£5**	
Old School Songs	LP	Slurp	1	1980	**£15**	
Two Weeks Last Summer	LP	A&M	AMLS68118	1972	**£15**	

COVAY, DON

Different Strokes	LP	Janus	3038	1970	**£10**	US
Everything I Do Goin' Be Funky	7"	Atlantic	2091018	1970	**£4**	
Forty Days - Forty Nights	7"	Atlantic	584114	1967	**£4**	
House Of Blue Light	LP	Atlantic	K50225	1969	**£15**	
Mercy	LP	Atlantic	8104	1965	**£15**	US
Mercy Mercy	7"	Atlantic	584094	1967	**£4**	
Mercy Mercy	7"	Atlantic	AT4006	1964	**£6**	
Pony Time	7"	Pye	7N25075	1961	**£5**	
Popeye Waddle	7"	Cameo Park.	C239	1962	**£10**	
See Saw	7"	Atlantic	584059	1966	**£4**	
See Saw	7"	Atlantic	AT4056	1965	**£4**	
See Saw	LP	Atlantic	8120	1966	**£15**	US
Shake Wid The Shake	7"	Philips	PB1140	1961	**£6**	
Shing-A-Ling '67	7"	Atlantic	584082	1967	**£4**	
Sookie Sookie	7"	Atlantic	AT4078	1966	**£5**	
Superdude	LP	Mercury	6338211	1973	**£10**	
Take This Hurt Off Me	7"	Atlantic	AT4016	1965	**£6**	
You Put Something On Me	7"	Atlantic	584025	1966	**£4**	

COVEN

Blood In The Snow	LP	Buddah	BDLH5011	1974	**£10**	

COVEY, JULIAN

Little Bit Hurt	7"	Island	WIP6009	1967	**£10**	

COVINGTON, JULIE

Beautiful Changes	LP	Columbia	SCX6466	1971	**£50**	
Magic Wasn't There	7"	Columbia	DB8649	1970	**£4**	
Tonight Your Love Is Over	7"	Columbia	DB8705	1970	**£4**	

COWSILLS

Captain Sad And His Ship Of Fools	LP	MGM	SE4554	1968	**£10**	US
Cowsills	LP	MGM	E4498	1967	**£10**	US
Cowsills Plus The Lincoln Park Zoo	LP	Wing	SRW16354	1968	**£10**	US
Hair	7"	MGM	MGM1469	1969	**£4**	
In Concert	LP	MGM	SE4619	1969	**£10**	US
In Need Of A Friend	7"	MGM	MGM1400	1968	**£4**	
Love American Style	7"	MGM	MGM1490	1969	**£4**	
Newspaper Blanket	7"	MGM	MGM1424	1968	**£4**	
On My Side	LP	London	587	1971	**£10**	US
Prophecy Of Daniel & John Devine	7"	MGM	MGM1484	1969	**£5**	
Rain, The Park And Other Things	7"	MGM	MGM1353	1967	**£5**	
Two By Two	LP	MGM	SE4639	1970	**£10**	US
We Can Fly	7"	MGM	MGM1383	1968	**£4**	
We Can Fly	LP	MGM	SE4534	1968	**£10**	US

COX, BILLY

Immediately after the death of his employer, Jimi Hendrix, bassist Billy Cox recorded what amounts to a tribute LP before effectively vanishing from the music scene. For "Nitro Function", he recruited a rather fine lady guitarist, who manages to convey the spirit of Jimi Hendrix rather better than most, although she too subsequently disappeared. The record cover, incidentally, is a creation by the same man who was responsible for the series of distinctive Yes sleeves - Roger Dean.

Nitro Function .... LP .... Pye .... NSPL25158 .... 1971 .... **£20** ....

COX, IDA

Ida Cox .... 7" EP .... Fontana .... TFE17136 .... 1959 .... **£5** ....

COX, IDA & MA RAINEY

Female Blues Vol.1 .... 7" EP .... Collector .... JE112 .... 196- .... **£5** ....

COX, MICHAEL

Along Came Caroline .... 7" .... HMV .... POP789 .... 1960 .... **£4** .... chart single
Angela Jones .... 7" .... Triumph .... RGM1011 .... 1960 .... **£4** .... chart single
Boy Meets Girl .... 7" .... Decca .... F11166 .... 1959 .... **£4** ....
Don't You Break My Heart .... 7" .... HMV .... POP1137 .... 1963 .... **£5** ....
Gee What A Party .... 7" .... HMV .... POP1220 .... 1963 .... **£4** ....
Gypsy .... 7" .... HMV .... POP1417 .... 1965 .... **£4** ....
I Hate Getting Up In The Morning .... 7" .... Parlophone .... R5436 .... 1966 .... **£4** ....
I'll Always Love You .... 7" .... Parlophone .... R5580 .... 1967 .... **£4** ....
Rave On .... 7" .... HMV .... POP1293 .... 1964 .... **£5** ....
Stand Up .... 7" .... HMV .... POP1065 .... 1962 .... **£5** ....
Sweet Little Sixteen .... 7" .... HMV .... POP905 .... 1961 .... **£5** ....
Teenage Love .... 7" .... HMV .... POP830 .... 1961 .... **£4** ....
Too Hot To Handle .... 7" .... Decca .... F11182 .... 1959 .... **£4** ....
Young Only Once .... 7" .... HMV .... POP972 .... 1962 .... **£4** ....

COX, MICK

Mick Cox Band .... LP .... Capitol .... ST11175 .... 1973 .... **£12** ....

COX, WALLY

I Can't Help It .... 7" .... Vogue .... V9175 .... 1961 .... **£8** ....

COXHILL, LOL

Lol Coxhill is as great an eccentric as he is a saxophone player - and his work on that instrument is very fine indeed! The Dandelion double album "Ear Of The Beholder" is the ideal introduction to both the man and the musician. It contains free group improvisation; recordings of Coxhill busking on the streets of London (he is supposed to be the inspiration behind Joni Mitchell's "For Free", although he was apparently mildly insulted by this); Victorian music-hall songs interpreted by the Coxhill-Bedford duo; and a group of school children singing "I Am The Walrus". The later "Murder In The Air" consists of a radio play with all the parts interpreted by a saxophone.

Ear Of The Beholder .... LP .... Dandelion .... 69001 .... 1971 .... **£30** .... double
Fleas In The Custard .... LP .... Caroline .... C1515 .... 1975 .... **£15** ....
Lol Coxhill & Welfare State .... LP .... Caroline .... C1514 .... 1975 .... **£15** ....
Murder In The Air .... 12" .... Chiltern Snd .... CS100 .... 1978 .... **£10** ....
Story So Far .... LP .... Caroline .... C1507 .... 1974 .... **£15** ....
Toverbal Sweet .... LP .... Mushroom .... 150MR23 .... 1972 .... **£80** ....

COXHILL, LOL & DAVID BEDFORD

Pretty Little Girl .... 7" .... Polydor .... 2001253 .... 1971 .... **£5** ....

COXHILL, LOL & STEPHEN MILLER

Coxhill Miller .... LP .... Caroline .... C1503 .... 1973 .... **£15** ....

COXSONE, LLOYD

Cruising .... 7" .... Pyramid .... PYR7003 .... 1973 .... **£4** ....

COYNE, KEVIN

Babble (with Dagmar Krause) .... LP .... Virgin .... V2128 .... 1979 .... **£10** ....
Beautiful Extremes .... LP .... Virgin .... V2527 .... 1978 .... **£10** ....
Blame It On The Night .... LP .... Virgin .... V2012 .... 1974 .... **£15** ....
Bursting Bubbles .... LP .... Virgin .... V2151 .... 1980 .... **£10** ....
Case History .... LP .... Dandelion .... 2310228 .... 1972 .... **£30** ....
Cheat Me .... 7" .... Polydor .... 2001357 .... 1972 .... **£4** ....
Don't Make Waves .... 7" .... Virgin .... VS136 .... 1976 .... **£4** ....
Dynamite Daze .... LP .... Virgin .... V2095 .... 1978 .... **£10** ....
Fever .... 7" .... Virgin .... VS160 .... 1976 .... **£4** ....
Heartburn .... LP .... Virgin .... V2047 .... 1976 .... **£12** ....
I Believe In Love .... 7" .... Virgin .... VS107 .... 1974 .... **£4** ....
In Living Black And White .... LP .... Virgin .... VD2505 .... 1976 .... **£15** .... double
Lorna .... 7" .... Virgin .... VS126 .... 1975 .... **£4** ....
Lovesick Fool .... 7" .... Virgin .... VS104 .... 1973 .... **£4** ....
Marjory Razorblade .... LP .... Virgin .... VD2501 .... 1973 .... **£15** .... double
Marlene .... 7" .... Virgin .... VS102 .... 1973 .... **£4** ....

Title	Format	Label	Number	Year	Price	Notes
Matching Head And Feet	LP	Virgin	V2033	1975	**£15**	
Millionaires And Teddy Bears	LP	Virgin	V2110	1978	**£10**	
Rock'n'Roll Hymn	7"	Virgin	VS119	1975	**£4**	
Sanity Stomp	LP	Virgin	V3504	1980	**£10**	
Walk On By	7"	Virgin	VS148	1976	**£4**	

COYNE-CLAGUE

Title	Format	Label	Number	Year	Price	Notes
Bottle Up And Go	7"	Dandelion	4493	1969	**£5**	
Stride	7"	Dandelion	4494	1969	**£6**	

CRABBY APPLETON

Title	Format	Label	Number	Year	Price	Notes
Crabby Appleton	LP	Elektra	EKS74067	1970	**£10**	
Rotten To The Core	LP	Elektra	EKS74106	1971	**£12**	

CRACKERS

Title	Format	Label	Number	Year	Price	Notes
Honey Do	7"	Fontana	TF995	1969	**£5**	

CRADDOCK, BILLY 'CRASH'

Title	Format	Label	Number	Year	Price	Notes
Boom Boom Baby	7"	Philips	PB966	1959	**£8**	
Goodtime Billy	7"	Philips	PB1092	1961	**£5**	
I'm Tore Up	LP	King	912	1964	**£20**	US
Since She Turned Seventeen	7"	Philips	PB1006	1960	**£8**	

CRAIG

Title	Format	Label	Number	Year	Price	Notes
Ain't That A Shame	7"	King	KG1022	196-	**£10**	
I Must Be Mad	7"	Fontana	TF715	1966	**£80**	
Little Bit Of Soap	7"	Fontana	TF665	1966	**£30**	

CRAMER, FLOYD

Title	Format	Label	Number	Year	Price	Notes
Fancy Pants	7"	London	HL8012	1954	**£12**	
Flip Flop And Bop	7"	RCA	RCA1050	1958	**£8**	
Jolly Cholly	7"	London	HL8062	1954	**£10**	
Last Date	7"	RCA	RCA1211	1960	**£4**	
On The Rebound	7"	RCA	RCA1231	1961	**£4**	chart single
Piano Hayride	7" EP	London	REP1023	1955	**£20**	
Rag A Tag	7"	London	HLU8195	1955	**£10**	
San Antonio Rose	7"	RCA	RCA1241	1961	**£4**	chart single
That Handsome Piano	7" EP	RCA	RCX7120	1963	**£6**	

CRAMPS

Title	Format	Label	Number	Year	Price	Notes
Can Your Pussy Do The Dog	7"	Big Beat	NS110	1985	**£4**	orange vinyl
Crusher	7"	IRS	PFS1008	1981	**£8**	
Crusher	12"	IRS	PFSX1008	1981	**£20**	
Drug Train	7"	Illegal	ILS021	1980	**£15**	
Faster Pussycat	7"	New Rose	NEW28	1984	**£5**	pic disc
Faster Pussycat	7"	New Rose	NEW28P	1983	**£5**	pic disc
Fever	7"	Illegal	ILS017	1980	**£15**	
Garbageman/Mystery Plane	7"	Illegal	ILS017	1980	**£30**	demo
Goo Goo Muck	7"	IRS	PFS1003	1981	**£10**	
Goo Goo Muck	7"	IRS	PFS1003	1981	**£15**	yellow vinyl
Gorehound	7"	New Rose	NEW33	1983	**£5**	blue vinyl
Gravest Hits	12"	Illegal	ILS12013	1979	**£6**	
Gravest Hits	12"	Illegal	ILS12013	1979	**£15**	blue vinyl
Human Fly	7"	Vengeance	668	1978	**£35**	US
Off The Bone	LP	Illegal	ILP012	1983	**£12**	pic disc
Smell Of Female	LP	Big Beat	BEDP6	1984	**£12**	pic disc
Smell Of Female	LP	Big Beat	NED6	1983	**£10**	red vinyl
Smell Of Female	7"	New Rose	CRAMPS1	1984	**£10**	4x7", coloured vinyl
Songs The Lord Taught Us	LP	Illegal	ILP005	1980	**£100**	test pressing 'Drug Train'
Way I Walk	7"	Vengeance	666	1978	**£35**	US

CRANE, DON & THE NEW DOWNLINERS SECT

Title	Format	Label	Number	Year	Price	Notes
I Can't Get Away From You	7"	Pye	7N17261	1967	**£25**	

CRANE, VINCENT & CHRIS FARLOWE

Title	Format	Label	Number	Year	Price	Notes
Can't Find A Reason	7"	Dawn	DNS1034	1972	**£5**	

CRASHERS

Title	Format	Label	Number	Year	Price	Notes
Off Track	7"	Amalgamated	AMG834	196-	**£10**	

CRASS

Title	Format	Label	Number	Year	Price	Notes
Feeding Of The Five Thousand	12"	Small Wond.	WEENY2	1978	**£20**	

Nagasaki Nightmare ... 7" ... Crass ... 421984/5 ... 1980 ... **£4** ... with patch
Our Wedding ... 7" ... Crass ... no number ... 1981 ... **£15** ... white flexi
Reality Asylum ... 7" ... Crass ... CRASS1 ... 1979 ... **£5** ...
Rival Tribal Rebel Revel ... 7" ... Crass ... 421984/6 ... 1981 ... **£4** ... flexi
Stations Of The Crass ... LP ... Crass ... 521984 ... 1979 ... **£12** ... double, patch

CRAWFORD BROTHERS

I Ain't Guilty ... 7" ... Vogue ... V9140 ... 1959 ... **£20** ...
Midnight Mover Groover ... 7" ... Vogue ... V9077 ... 1957 ... **£15** ...

CRAWFORD, CAROLYN

When Someone's Good To You ... 7" ... Stateside ... SS384 ... 1965 ... **£80** ...

CRAWFORD, GLORIA

Sad Movies ... 7" ... Doctor Bird ... DB1057 ... 1966 ... **£10** ...

CRAWFORD, JIMMY

Long Stringy Baby ... 7" ... Columbia ... DB4525 ... 1960 ... **£4** ...

CRAWFORD, JOHNNY

Captivating Johnny Crawford ... LP ... Del-Fi ... LP1220 ... 1962 ... **£15** ... US
Greatest Hits ... LP ... Del-Fi ... LP1229 ... 1963 ... **£10** ... US
Greatest Hits Vol.2 ... LP ... Del-Fi ... LP1248 ... 1964 ... **£10** ... US
Johnny Crawford ... 7" EP ... London ... RE1343 ... 1962 ... **£6** ...
Rumors ... LP ... London ... HA8060 ... 1963 ... **£10** ...
When I Fall In Love ... 7" EP ... London ... RE1416 ... 1964 ... **£5** ...
Young Man's Fancy ... LP ... Del-Fi ... LP1223 ... 1963 ... **£10** ... US

CRAWLER

Crawler ... LP ... Epic ... PAL34900 ... 1978 ... **£10** ... US pic disc

CRAZY ELEPHANT

Crazy Elephant ... LP ... Bell ... 6034 ... 1969 ... **£10** ... US
Gimme Gimme Good Lovin' ... 7" ... Major Minor ... MM609 ... 1969 ... **£4** ... chart single
Space Buggy ... 7" ... Major Minor ... MM672 ... 1970 ... **£4** ...
Sunshine Red Wine ... 7" ... Major Minor ... MM623 ... 1969 ... **£4** ...

CRAZY FEELINGS

Please Lie ... 7" ... Polydor ... 56723 ... 1967 ... **£4** ...

CRAZY HORSE

At Crooked Creek ... LP ... Epic ... EPC65223 ... 1973 ... **£10** ...
Crazy Horse ... LP ... Reprise ... RSLP6438 ... 1971 ... **£10** ...
Loose ... LP ... Reprise ... K44171 ... 1972 ... **£10** ...

CREACH, PAPA JOHN

Filthy ... LP ... Grunt ... FTR1009 ... 1972 ... **£10** ...
Papa John Creach ... LP ... Grunt ... FTR1003 ... 1971 ... **£10** ...
Zulu ... LP ... Grunt ... BFLI0418 ... 1974 ... **£10** ... US

CREAM

Cream are not highly regarded by those who feel that improvisation has no place in rock music, but on a good night the interplay between the three virtuoso musicians, each trying to outplay the others, was thrilling. Of course this approach does not always work, but when it does, the risks are entirely justified. "Crossroads" is an electric blues masterpiece, while the long modal improvisation on "Spoonful" (also included on "Wheels Of Fire") is as inspirational as the lengthy drum solo on "Toad" is tedious. The other side of Cream was their ability to create intelligent pop music with an attractive blues edge - "Disraeli Gears" was quite rightly hailed as one of the most impressive recordings in a year when the competition was extremely stiff - 1967.

Anyone For Tennis ... 7" ... Polydor ... 56258 ... 1968 ... **£5** ... chart single
Badge ... 7" ... Polydor ... 56315 ... 1969 ... **£4** ... chart single
Disraeli Gears ... LP ... Reaction ... 593003 ... 1967 ... **£15** ... mono, chart LP
Disraeli Gears ... LP ... Reaction ... 594003 ... 1967 ... **£12** ... stereo, chart LP
Fresh Cream ... LP ... Reaction ... 593001 ... 1966 ... **£15** ... mono, chart LP
Fresh Cream ... LP ... Reaction ... 594001 ... 1966 ... **£12** ... stereo, chart LP
Goodbye ... LP ... Polydor ... 583053 ... 1969 ... **£10** ... chart LP
I Feel Free ... 7" ... Reaction ... 591011 ... 1966 ... **£4** ... chart single
On Top ... LP ... Polydor ... 2855002 ... 1969 ... **£20** ...
Strange Brew ... 7" ... Reaction ... 591015 ... 1967 ... **£4** ... chart single
Sunshine Of Your Love ... 7" ... Polydor ... 56286 ... 1968 ... **£4** ... chart single
Wheels Of Fire ... LP ... Mobile Fid. ... MFSL2066 ... 1982 ... **£20** ... US audiophile
Wheels Of Fire ... LP ... Polydor ... 582031/2 ... 1968 ... **£20** ... double, mono, chart LP
Wheels Of Fire ... LP ... Polydor ... 583031/2 ... 1968 ... **£15** ... double, stereo, chart LP
Wheels Of Fire In The Studio ... LP ... Polydor ... 582033 ... 1968 ... **£12** ... mono, chart LP

Wheels Of Fire In The Studio	LP	Polydor	583033	1968	**£10**	stereo, chart LP
Wheels Of Fire Live At Fillmore	LP	Polydor	582040	1968	**£12**	mono
Wheels Of Fire Live At Fillmore	LP	Polydor	583040	1968	**£10**	stereo
White Room	7"	Polydor	56300	1968	**£4**	chart single
Wrapping Paper	7"	Reaction	591007	1966	**£5**	chart single

CREARY SISTERS

Oh What A Glory	7"	High Note	HS020	196-	**£8**	

CREATION

The Creation have aquired the status of one of the great groups of the sixties, with guitarist Eddie Phillips being a pioneer in the use of feedback and violin bow techniques. The group failed to find much success, however, and in all honesty they are not well served by their records, which are much less impressive than those of their rivals, the Who.

1966-67	LP	Charisma	CS8	1973	**£20**	
Best Of...	LP	Pop Schall.	ZS10168	1968	**£40**	German
How Does It Feel To Feel	7"	Polydor	56230	1968	**£12**	
If I Stay Too Long	7"	Polydor	56177	1967	**£15**	
Making Time	7"	Charisma	CB213	1973	**£5**	
Making Time	7"	Planet	PLF116	1966	**£15**	chart single
Making Time	7"	Raw	RAW4	1977	**£4**	
Midway Down	7"	Polydor	56246	1968	**£15**	
Painter Man	7"	Planet	PLF119	1966	**£12**	chart single
Through My Eyes	7"	Polydor	56207	1967	**£15**	
We Are The Paintermen	LP	Hitton	340037	1967	**£100**	German
We Are The Paintermen	LP	Sonet	SLPS1251	1967	**£100**	Danish

CREATION (2)

I Got The Fever	7"	Stateside	SS2205	1972	**£4**	

CREATION OF SUNLIGHT

Creation Of Sunlight	LP	Windi	1001	1969	**£60**	US

CREATIONS

Get On Up	7"	Amalgamated	AMG818	196-	**£10**	
Meet Me At Eight	7"	Rio	R133	196-	**£8**	

CREATIVE SOURCE

Don't Be Afraid	7"	Polydor	2066680	1976	**£4**	

CREATURES

Mad Eyed Screamers	7"	Polydor	PODJ354	1981	**£8**	promo
Right Now	12"	Wonderland	SHEX2	1983	**£6**	
Right Now	7"	Wonderland	SHE2	1983	**£6**	gatefold PS
Wild Things	7"	Polydor	POSPG354	1981	**£8**	double, gatefold PS
Wild Things	7"	Polydor	POSPD354	1981	**£5**	double, single PS

CREEDENCE CLEARWATER REVIVAL

Bad Moon Rising	7"	Liberty	LBF15230	1969	**£4**	chart single
Bayou Country	LP	Liberty	LBS83261	1969	**£10**	chart LP
Cosmo's Factory	LP	Liberty	LBS83388	1970	**£10**	chart LP
Cosmo's Factory	LP	Mobile Fid.	MFSL1037	1979	**£15**	US audiophile
Creedence Clearwater Revival	LP	Liberty	LBS83259	1969	**£10**	
Down On The Corner	7"	Liberty	LBF15283	1970	**£4**	chart single
Green River	LP	Liberty	LBS83273	1969	**£10**	chart LP
Green River	7"	Liberty	LBF15250	1969	**£4**	chart single
Have You Ever Seen The Rain	7"	Liberty	LBF15440	1971	**£4**	chart single
Long As I Can See The Light	7"	Liberty	LBF15384	1970	**£4**	chart single
Mardi Gras	LP	Fantasy	FAN9404	1972	**£10**	
Pendulum	LP	Liberty	LBS83400	1971	**£10**	chart LP
Proud Mary	7"	Liberty	LBF15223	1969	**£4**	chart single
Proud Mary/I Put A Spell On You	7"	Liberty	LBF15223	1969	**£12**	
Sweet Hitch-Hiker	7"	United Artists	UP35261	1971	**£4**	chart single
Travellin' Band	7"	Liberty	LBF15310	1970	**£4**	chart single
Up Around The Bend	7"	Liberty	LBF15354	1970	**£4**	chart single
Willie & The Poor Boys	LP	Liberty	LBS83338	1970	**£10**	chart LP

CREME CARAMEL

Crying Eyes	7"	Pye	7N25521	1970	**£4**	
My Idea	7"	Pye	7N25495	1969	**£4**	
Your Heart's Not In Your Love	7"	Pye	7N25529	1970	**£4**	

CREME SODA

Tricky Zingers	LP	Trinity	CST11	1968	**£35**	US

CRESCENDOES

Oh Julie	7"	London	HLU8563	1958	**£12**	

CRESCENTS

Baby Baby Baby	7"	Columbia	DB4093	1958	**£6**	
Pink Dominoes	7"	London	HLN9851	1964	**£4**	

CRESSIDA

Asylum	LP	Vertigo	6360025	1971	**£60**	spiral label
Cressida	LP	Vertigo	VO7	1970	**£40**	spiral label

CRESTAS

I Want To Be Loved	7"	Fontana	TF551	1965	**£20**	

CRESTERS

I Just Don't Understand	7"	HMV	POP1249	1964	**£5**	
Put Your Arms Around Me	7"	HMV	POP1296	1964	**£5**	

CRESTS

Angels Listened In	7"	London	HL8954	1959	**£8**	
Best Of...	LP	Coed	LPC904	1961	**£80**	US
Crests Sing All The Biggies	LP	Coed	LPC901	1960	**£100**	US
Flower Of Love	7"	Top Rank	JAR150	1959	**£5**	
Gee	7"	Top Rank	JAR372	1960	**£5**	
Guilty	7"	London	HLU9671	1963	**£5**	
Isn't It Amazing	7"	HMV	POP808	1960	**£5**	
Little Miracles	7"	HMV	POP976	1962	**£5**	
Model Girl	7"	HMV	POP848	1961	**£5**	
Paper Crown	7"	Top Rank	JAR302	1960	**£5**	
Six Nights A Week	7"	Top Rank	JAR168	1959	**£5**	
Sixteen Candles	7"	London	HL8794	1959	**£12**	
Trouble in Paradise	7"	HMV	POP768	1960	**£6**	
Cecilia	7"	Decca	F13000	1970	**£4**	
Marty	7"	Plexium	PXM12	196-	**£5**	

CREWCUTS

Crewcut Capers	LP	Mercury	MG20143	1954	**£20**	US
Crewcuts	7" EP	Mercury	MEP9002	1956	**£25**	
Crewcuts	LP	Wing	MGW12177	1959	**£12**	US
Crewcuts Go Longhair	LP	Mercury	MG20067	1954	**£20**	US
Crewcuts On The Campus	LP	Mercury	MG20140	1954	**£20**	US
Crewcuts Sing	LP	RCA	LPM2037	1959	**£12**	US
Crewcuts Sing Folk	LP	Camay	CA1002	196-	**£12**	US
Earth Angel	78	Mercury	MB3202	1955	**£5**	chart single
Hey Stella	7"	RCA	RCA1075	1958	**£15**	
High School Favorites	LP	Wing	MGW12180	1959	**£12**	US
Music A La Carte	LP	Mercury	MG20199	1955	**£20**	US
Rock And Roll Bash	LP	Mercury	MG21044	1955	**£25**	US
Sh-Boom	78	Mercury	MB3140	1954	**£5**	chart single
Surprise Package	LP	RCA	LPM1933	1958	**£12**	US
You Must Have Been A Beautiful Baby	LP	RCA	LPM2067	1960	**£12**	US

CRIBBINS, BERNARD

Hole In The Ground	7"	Parlophone	R4869	1962	**£4**	chart single
Hole In The Ground	7" EP	Parlophone	GEP8859	1962	**£5**	
Right Said Fred	7"	Parlophone	R4923	1962	**£4**	chart single

CRICKETS

April Avenue	7"	Liberty	LIB55603	1966	**£4**	
Baby My Heart	7"	Coral	Q72395	1960	**£4**	chart single
Bubblegum,Pop,Ballads,& Boogies	LP	Philips		1973	**£10**	
Collection	LP	Liberty	LBY1258	1965	**£15**	
Come On	7" EP	Liberty	LEP2173	1964	**£8**	
Crickets	7" EP	Coral	FEP2053	1960	**£6**	
Crickets Don't Ever Change	7" EP	Coral	FEP2064	1961	**£8**	
Don't Ever Change	7"	Liberty	LIB55441	1962	**£4**	chart single
Don't Try To Change Me	7"	Liberty	LIB10092	1963	**£4**	chart single
He's Old Enough To Know Better	7"	London	HLG9486	1961	**£4**	
I Fought The Law	7"	Coral	Q72440	1961	**£4**	

I Think I've Got The Blues .... 7" .... Liberty .... LIB10174 .... 1964 .... **£4** ....
In Style With .... LP .... Coral .... LVA9142 .... 1959 .... **£20** .... chart LP
La Bamba .... 7" .... Liberty .... LIB55696 .... 1964 .... **£4** .... chart single
Little Hollywood Girl .... 7" .... Liberty .... LIB55495 .... 1962 .... **£4** ....
Long Way From Lubbock .... LP .... Mercury .... 6310007 .... 1974 .... **£10** ....
Love's Made A Fool Of You .... 7" .... Coral .... Q72365 .... 1959 .... **£4** .... chart single
My Little Girl .... 7" .... Liberty .... LIB10067 .... 1963 .... **£4** .... chart single
Now Hear This .... 7" .... Liberty .... LIB10196 .... 1965 .... **£4** ....
Peggy Sue Got Married .... 7" .... Coral .... Q72417 .... 1961 .... **£4** ....
Rockin' Fifties Rock'n'Roll .... LP .... CBS .... 64301 .... 1971 .... **£10** ....
Something Old Something New .... LP .... Liberty .... LBY1120 .... 1962 .... **£15** ....
Straight No Strings .... 7" EP .... Liberty .... LEP2094 .... 1963 .... **£6** ....
Straight No Strings .... 7" EP .... Liberty .... SLEP2094 .... 1963 .... **£8** .... stereo
When You Ask About Love .... 7" .... Coral .... Q72382 .... 1959 .... **£4** .... chart single

CRICKETS & BOBBY VEE

Bobby Vee Meets The Crickets .... 7" EP .... Liberty .... LEP2116 .... 1963 .... **£6** ....
Bobby Vee Meets The Crickets .... 7" EP .... Liberty .... SLEP2116 .... 1963 .... **£8** .... stereo
Bobby Vee Meets The Crickets Vol.2 .... 7" EP .... Liberty .... LEP2149 .... 1963 .... **£6** ....
Just For Fun (with The Crickets) .... 7" EP .... Liberty .... LEP2084 .... 1963 .... **£6** ....

CRIMSON BRIDGE

Crimson Bridge .... LP .... Myrrh .... MST6503 .... 1972 .... **£15** ....

CRISIS

Alienation .... 7" .... Ardkor .... CRI004 .... 1981 .... **£8** ....
Holocaust .... 12" .... Dead Russian .... 1982 .... **£12** ....
Hymns Of Faith .... 12" .... Ardkor .... CRI003 .... 1980 .... **£8** ....
No Town Hall (Southwark) .... 7" .... Peckham A.G. NOTH1 .... **£6** ....
UK '79 .... 7" .... Ardkor .... CRI002 .... 1979 .... **£10** ....

CRISPY AMBULANCE

Four Minutes From The Frontline .... 7" .... Aural Assault .. AAR001 .... 1976 .... **£6** ....

CRISS, PETER

Out Of Control .... LP .... Casablanca .... NBLP7240 .... 1980 .... **£10** .... US

CRISTO, BOBBY & THE REBELS

Other Side Of The Track .... 7" .... Decca .... F11913 .... 1964 .... **£10** ....

CRITTERS

Bad Misunderstanding .... 7" .... London .... HLR10101 .... 1966 .... **£5** ....
Don't Let The Rain Fall Down On Me .... 7" .... London .... HLR10149 .... 1967 .... **£4** ....
Marrying Kind Of Love .... 7" .... London .... HLR10119 .... 1967 .... **£4** ....
Mr.Dieingly Sad .... 7" .... London .... HLR10071 .... 1966 .... **£4** ....
Younger Girl .... LP .... London .... HAR8302 .... 1966 .... **£15** ....
Younger Girl .... 7" .... London .... HLR10047 .... 1966 .... **£5** .... chart single

CROCE, JIM

Croce (with Ingrid Croce) .... LP .... Capitol .... ST315 .... 1969 .... **£20** .... US
I Got A Name .... LP .... ABC .... CQ40008 .... 1974 .... **£10** .... US quad
Life And Times .... LP .... ABC .... CQ40007 .... 1974 .... **£10** .... US quad
Photographs And Memories .... LP .... ABC .... CQ40020 .... 1974 .... **£10** .... US quad
You Don't Mess Around With Jim .... LP .... ABC .... CQ40006 .... 1974 .... **£10** .... US quad
You Don't Mess Around With Jim .... LP .... Mobile Fid. .... MFSL1079 .... 1980 .... **£10** .... US audiophile
You Don't Mess Around With Jim .... LP .... Vertigo .... 6360700 .... 1971 .... **£12** .... spiral label

CROCHETED DOUGHNUT RING

Havana Anna .... 7" .... Deram .... DM169 .... 1967 .... **£15** ....
Maxine's Parlour .... 7" .... Deram .... DM180 .... 1968 .... **£15** ....
Two Little Ladies .... 7" .... Polydor .... 56204 .... 1967 .... **£15** ....

CROMBIE, TONY

Brighton Rock .... 7" .... Columbia .... DB3921 .... 1957 .... **£8** ....
Drums! Drums! Drums! .... LP .... Top Rank .... BUY027 .... 1960 .... **£12** ....
Let's You And I Rock .... 7" .... Columbia .... DB3859 .... 1956 .... **£8** ....
Let's You And I Rock .... 7" EP .... Columbia .... SEG7686 .... 1957 .... **£15** ....
Presenting Tony Crombie No.1 .... 7" EP .... Decca .... DFE6247 .... 1956 .... **£5** ....
Presenting Tony Crombie No.2 .... 7" EP .... Decca .... DFE6281 .... 1956 .... **£5** ....
Rock Rock Rock .... 7" EP .... Columbia .... SEG7676 .... 1957 .... **£15** ....
Rockin' With The Rockets .... LP-10" .. Columbia .... 33S1108 .... 195- .... **£50** ....
Teach You To Rock .... 7" .... Columbia .... DB3822 .... 1956 .... **£10** .... chart single

CROMWELL

Cromwell	LP	Private		1975	**£150**	Irish

CROMWELL, LINK

Crazy Like A Fox	7"	London	HLB10040	1966	**£8**	

CROPPER, STEVE

Funky Braodway	7"	Stax	STAX147	1970	**£4**	

CROSBY & NASH

Crosby And Nash	LP	Atlantic	K50011	1972	**£10**	

CROSBY, DAVID

If I Could Only Remember My Name	LP	Atlantic	2401005	1971	**£10**	chart LP

CROSBY, GARY

Judy Judy	7"	HMV	POP550	1958	**£12**	

CROSBY, STILLS & NASH

Crosby,Stills,and Nash	LP	Atlantic	588189	1969	**£10**	chart LP
CSN	LP	Nautilus		1982	**£10**	US audiophile
Marrakesh Express	7"	Atlantic	584283	1969	**£4**	chart single
Suite: Judy Blue Eyes	7"	Atlantic	584304	1969	**£4**	

CROSBY, STILLS, NASH & YOUNG

Celebration Record	LP	Atlantic	PR165	1971	**£40**	US promo
Deja Vu	LP	Atlantic	2401001	1970	**£10**	chart LP
Deja Vu	LP	Mobile Fid.	MFSL1088	1982	**£12**	US audiophile
Four Way Street	LP	Atlantic	2400132/3	1972	**£12**	double, chart LP
Ohio	7"	Atlantic	2091023	1970	**£4**	
Our House	7"	Atlantic	2091039	1970	**£4**	
Rap With...	LP	Atlantic	18102	1973	**£30**	US promo
Teach Your Children	7"	Atlantic	2091002	1970	**£4**	
Woodstock	7"	Atlantic	2091010	1970	**£4**	

CROSS, JIMMIE

Super Duper Man	7"	Red Bird	RB10042	1966	**£8**	

CROSS, KEITH & PETER ROSS

Bored Civilians	LP	Decca	SKL5129	1972	**£20**	

CROW

Crow By Crow	LP	Stateside	SSL10310	1970	**£10**	
Crow Music	LP	Stateside	SSL10301	1969	**£10**	

CROWFOOT

Crowfoot	LP	Paramount	265	1970	**£10**	US
Find The Sun	LP	Probe	SPB1042	1971	**£10**	

CROWNS

I Know It's Alright	7"	Pama	PM725	196-	**£8**	
Jerking The Dog	7"	Pama	PM736	196-	**£8**	
She Ain't Gonna Do Right	7"	Pama	PM745	196-	**£8**	
Since You Been Gone	7"	Pama	PM759	196-	**£8**	

CROWS

Gee	7"	Columbia	SCM5119	1954	**£120**	

CRUDUP, ARTHUR

Father Of Rock'n'Roll	LP	RCA	RD8224	1971	**£12**	
Mean Ole Frisco	LP	Blue Horizon	763855	1969	**£40**	
My Baby Left Me	7"	RCA	RCA1401	1964	**£8**	
Rhythm And Blues Vol.4	7" EP	RCA	RCX7161	1964	**£6**	

CRUISERS

It Ain't Me Babe	7"	Decca	F12098	1965	**£8**	

CRUM, SIMON

Stand Up Sit Down	7"	Capitol	CL14965	1958	**£10**	

CRYAN SHAMES

Nobody Waved Goodbye	7"	Decca	F12425	1966	**£10**	

Title	Format	Label	Cat. No.	Year	Price	Notes
Please Stay	7"	Decca	F12340	1966	**£6**	chart single
Scratch In The Sky	LP	CBS	CS9586	1967	**£30**	US
Sugar And Spice	7"	CBS	202344	1966	**£10**	
Sugar And Spice	LP	CBS	CS9389	1966	**£30**	US
Synthesis	LP	CBS	CS9719	1968	**£30**	US

CRYSTAL MANSION

Title	Format	Label	Cat. No.	Year	Price	Notes
Carolina In My Mind	7"	Polydor	2058070	1970	**£4**	
Thought Of Loving You	7"	Capitol	CL15577	1969	**£4**	

CRYSTALITES

Title	Format	Label	Cat. No.	Year	Price	Notes
Biafra	7"	Big Shot	BI510	1973	**£5**	
Bombshell	7"	Explosion	EX2005	1973	**£5**	
Fistful Of Dollars	7"	Explosion	EX2006	1973	**£5**	
Ilya Kuryakin	7"	Island	WI3134	1968	**£8**	
James Ray	7"	Island	WI3153	1968	**£8**	
Splashdown	7"	New Beat	NB036	1968	**£8**	

CRYSTALS

Title	Format	Label	Cat. No.	Year	Price	Notes
All Grown Up	7"	London	HLU9909	1964	**£6**	
Da Doo Ron Ron	7"	London	HLU9732	1963	**£5**	chart single
Da Doo Ron Ron	7" EP	London	REU1381	1963	**£15**	
Greatest Hits	LP	Philles	PHLP4003	1963	**£80**	US
He Sure Is The Boy I Love	7"	London	HLU9661	1963	**£6**	
He's A Rebel	LP	London	HAU8120	1963	**£30**	
He's A Rebel	7"	London	HLU9611	1962	**£5**	chart single
He's A Rebel	LP	Philles	PHLP4001	1963	**£80**	US
I Wonder	7"	London	HLU9852	1964	**£5**	chart single
Little Boy	7"	London	HLU9837	1964	**£15**	
My Place	7"	United Artists	UP1110	1965	**£4**	
Then He Kissed Me	7"	London	HLU9773	1963	**£5**	chart single
There's No Other	7"	Parlophone	R4867	1962	**£15**	
Twist Uptown	LP	Philles	PHLP4000	1962	**£80**	US

CUBY & THE BLIZZARDS

Title	Format	Label	Cat. No.	Year	Price	Notes
Appleknockers Flophouse	LP	Philips	SBL7918	1969	**£15**	
Appleknockers Flophouse	7"	Philips	BF1827	1969	**£6**	
Desolation	LP	Philips	SBL7874	1968	**£15**	
Distant Smile	7"	Philips	BF1638	1968	**£8**	
Windows Of My Eyes	7"	Philips	BF1719	1968	**£6**	

CUD

Title	Format	Label	Cat. No.	Year	Price	Notes
You're The Boss	12"	Reception	REC007	1987	**£8**	

CUDDLY TOYS

Title	Format	Label	Cat. No.	Year	Price	Notes
Astral Joe	7"	Fresh	FRESH20	1980	**£4**	
Guillotine Theatre	LP	Fresh	FLP1	1980	**£10**	
It's A Shame	7"	Fresh	FRESH39	1982	**£4**	
Madman	7"	Fresh	FRESH10	1980	**£4**	
Madman	7"	Fresh	PURL7	1980	**£4**	
Someone's Crying	7"	Fresh	FRESH25	1981	**£4**	
Someone's Crying	12"	Fresh	FRESH2512	1981	**£6**	
Trials And Crosses	LP	Fresh	FLP6	1982	**£10**	

CUES

Title	Format	Label	Cat. No.	Year	Price	Notes
Burn That Candle	7"	Capitol	CL14501	1956	**£12**	
Crackerjack	7"	Capitol	CL14651	1956	**£12**	
Prince Or Pauper	7"	Capitol	CL14682	1957	**£15**	

CULPEPPER'S ORCHARD

Title	Format	Label	Cat. No.	Year	Price	Notes
Culpepper's Orchard	LP	Polydor	2380006	1971	**£90**	
Second Sight	LP	Polydor		1972	**£60**	

CULT

Title	Format	Label	Cat. No.	Year	Price	Notes
Dreamtime	LP	Beggars B.	BEGA57P	1984	**£15**	pic disc
Dreamtime	LP	Beggars B.	BEGA57	1984	**£15**	with live LP
Electric	LP	Beggars B.	BEGA80	1987	**£15**	gold vinyl
Electric	LP	Beggars B.	CULTLP12	1987	**£20**	interview & music promo
Li'l Devil	CD-s	Beggars B.	BEG188CD	1987	**£8**	
Love Removal Machine (Radio Edit)	7"	Beggars B.	BEG182R	1987	**£12**	promo
Love Removal Machine	7"	Beggars B.	BEG182D	1987	**£10**	double PS, Rick Rubin producer credit

Revolution	7"	Beggars B.	BEG152D	1985	**£5**	double
Wildflower	CD-s	Beggars B.		1987	**£6**	

CULT HERO

I'm A Cult Hero	7"	Fiction	FICS006	1979	**£30**	

CULVER STREET PLAYGROUND

Alley Pond Park	7"	President	PT145	1968	**£5**	

CUMBERLAND THREE

Prior to joining the Kingston Trio, John Stewart was a member of a rather less well-known folk trio, the Cumberland Three.

Civil War Almanac - The Rebels	LP	Roulette	R25133	1960	**£10**	US
Civil War Almanac - The Yankees	LP	Roulette	R25132	1960	**£10**	US
Cumberland Crow	7"	Parlophone	R5113	1964	**£4**	
Folk Scene USA	LP	Roulette	R25121	1960	**£10**	US
Johnny Reb	7"	Columbia	DB4460	1960	**£4**	

CUMMINGS, BARBARA

She's The Woman	7"	London	HLU10110	1967	**£4**	

CUPID'S INSPIRATION

My World	7"	Nems	563702	1968	**£4**	chart single
Yesterday Has Gone	7"	Nems	563500	1968	**£4**	chart single
Yesterday Has Gone	LP	Nems	63553	1968	**£10**	

CUPIDS

Lillie Mae	7"	Vogue	V9102	1958	**£30**	

CUPOL

Like This For Ages	12"	4AD	BAD9	1980	**£8**	

CUPPA T

Miss Pinkerton	7"	Deram	DM144	1967	**£12**	
Streatham Hippodrome	7"	Deram	DM185	1968	**£10**	

CUPS

Good As Gold	7"	Polydor	56777	1968	**£10**	

CURE

Boys Don't Cry	7"	Fiction	FICS002	1979	**£12**	
Catch	7"	Fiction	FICSC26	1987	**£6**	clear vinyl
Caterpillar	7"	Fiction	FICS20	1984	**£4**	chart single
Caterpillar	12"	Fiction	FICSX20	1984	**£6**	
Caterpillar	7"	Fiction	FICSP20	1984	**£12**	pic disc
Charlotte Sometimes	7"	Fiction	FICS14	1981	**£10**	chart single
Charlotte Sometimes	12"	Fiction	FICSX14	1981	**£15**	
Close To Me	12"	Fiction	FICSX23	1985	**£6**	
Close To Me	10"	Fiction	FICST23	1985	**£8**	
Close To Me	7"	Fiction	FICSP23	1985	**£8**	poster sleeve
Faith	cass	Fiction	FIXC6	1981	**£10**	double play
Forest	12"	Fiction	FICSX10	1980	**£15**	
Forest	7"	Fiction	FICS10	1980	**£12**	PS,blue label,or rad. sleeve silver label, chart single
Grinding Halt	7"	Fiction	CUR1	1979	**£25**	promo
Hanging Garden	7"	Fiction	FICS15	1982	**£8**	chart single
Hanging Garden	7"	Fiction	FICS15	1982	**£15**	double
Hot! Hot! Hot!	CD-s	Fiction	FIXCD28	1988	**£6**	
In-Between Days	7"	Fiction	FICS22	1985	**£4**	chart single
In-Between Days	12"	Fiction	FICSX22	1985	**£6**	
Jumping Someone Else's Train	7"	Fiction	FICS005	1979	**£15**	
Just Like Heaven	7"	Fiction	FICSP27	1987	**£10**	pic disc
Just Like Heaven	7"	Fiction	FICSW27	1987	**£4**	white vinyl
Killing An Arab	7"	Fiction	FICS001	1979	**£12**	
Killing An Arab	7"	Small Wond.	SMALL11	1978	**£15**	
Lament	7"	Lyntone	LYN12011	1982	**£8**	Flexipop green flexi
Lament	7"	Lyntone	LYN12011	1982	**£12**	Flexipop red flexi
Let's Go To Bed	7"	Fiction	FICS17	1982	**£4**	chart single
Let's Go To Bed	12"	Fiction	FICSX17	1982	**£6**	
Love Cats	7"	Fiction	FICS19	1983	**£4**	chart single
Love Cats	12"	Fiction	FICSX19	1983	**£6**	
Love Cats	7"	Fiction	FICSP19	1983	**£25**	pic disc
Lovesong	7"	Fiction	FICSB30	1989	**£5**	boxed, with linen print

Title	Format	Label	Cat. No.	Year	Price	Notes
Lullaby	7"	Fiction	FICSP29	1989	**£10**	clear vinyl
Lullaby	7"	Fiction	FICSG29	1989	**£5**	gatefold PS
Lullaby	12"	Fiction	FICVX29	1989	**£6**	pink vinyl
One Hundred Years	12"	Fiction	CURE1	1982	**£30**	promo
Primary	7"	Fiction	FICS12	1981	**£8**	chart single
Primary	12"	Fiction	FICSX12	1981	**£12**	
Walk	7"	Fiction	FICS18	1983	**£4**	chart single
Walk	12"	Fiction	FICSX18	1983	**£6**	
Walk	7"	Fiction	FICSP18	1983	**£30**	pic disc
Walk	7"	Fiction	FICS18	1983	**£10**	poster sleeve
Why Can't I Be You	7"	Fiction	FICSG25	1987	**£10**	double

CURE, MARTIN & THE PEEPS

Title	Format	Label	Cat. No.	Year	Price	Notes
It's All Over Now	7"	Philips	BF1605	1967	**£12**	

CURIOSITY SHOPPE

Title	Format	Label	Cat. No.	Year	Price	Notes
Baby I Need You	7"	Deram	DM220	1968	**£12**	

CURLY CURVE

Title	Format	Label	Cat. No.	Year	Price	Notes
Curly Curve	LP	Brain	1040	1974	**£30**	

CURRANT KRAZE

Title	Format	Label	Cat. No.	Year	Price	Notes
Lady Pearl	7"	Deram	DM292	1970	**£4**	

CURRENT 93

Title	Format	Label	Cat. No.	Year	Price	Notes
She Is Dead And All Fall Down	7"	Shock	SX003	198-	**£8**	
She Is Dead And All Fall Down	7"	Shock	SX003	198-	**£20**	individually lettered

CURRY, CLIFFORD

Title	Format	Label	Cat. No.	Year	Price	Notes
I Can't Get A Hold Of Myself	7"	Pama	PM797	196-	**£4**	
She Shot A Hole In My Soul	7"	Action	ACT4549	1969	**£4**	

CURTIS, CHRIS

Title	Format	Label	Cat. No.	Year	Price	Notes
Aggravation	7"	Pye	7N17132	1966	**£15**	

CURTIS, DAVE & THE TREMORS

Title	Format	Label	Cat. No.	Year	Price	Notes
Summertime Blues	7"	Philips	BF1330	1964	**£8**	
Sweet Girl Of Mine	7"	Philips	BF1257	1963	**£4**	
What Kind Of Girl Are You	7"	Philips	BF1285	1963	**£4**	
What Kind of Girl Are You	7"	Philips	BF1285	1963	**£8**	
You Don't Love Me	7"	Philips	BF1257	1963	**£6**	

CURTIS, KING

Title	Format	Label	Cat. No.	Year	Price	Notes
Azure	LP	Everest	DBR1121	1961	**£12**	US
Best Of	LP	Atlantic	228002	1968	**£10**	
Doin' The Dixie Twist	LP	Tru-Sound	TS15009	1962	**£10**	US
Good To Me	7"	Atlantic	584109	1967	**£4**	
Have Tenor Sax Will Blow	7" EP	London	REK1307	1961	**£8**	
Have Tenor Sax, Will Blow	LP	London	HAK2247	1960	**£15**	
Hits Made Famous By Sam Cooke	LP	Capitol	T2341	1965	**£10**	US
Instant Groove	LP	Atlantic	228027	1968	**£10**	
It's Party Time	LP	Tru-Sound	TS15008	1962	**£10**	US
Kingsize Soul	LP	Atlantic	587043	1967	**£10**	
La Jeanne	7"	Atlantic	584287	1969	**£4**	
Live At Small's Paradise	LP	Atco	33198	1966	**£10**	US
Memphis Soul Stew	7"	Atlantic	584134	1967	**£4**	
New Scene	LP	New Jazz	8237	1960	**£12**	US
Plays Great Memphis Hits	LP	Atlantic	587067	1967	**£10**	
Soul Serenade	7"	Capitol	CL15346	1964	**£5**	
Soul Serenade	LP	Capitol	T2095	1964	**£10**	US
Soul Twist	7"	London	HLU9547	1962	**£4**	
Sweet Soul	LP	Atlantic	587115	1968	**£10**	
Teasin'	7"	Atlantic	2091012	1970	**£5**	
That Lovin' Feeling	LP	Atco	33189	1966	**£10**	US
Whole Lotta Love	7"	Atlantic	2091158	1971	**£4**	
Wiggle Wobble	7"	Speciality	SPE1000		**£4**	

CURTIS, LEE & THE ALL STARS

Title	Format	Label	Cat. No.	Year	Price	Notes
Ecstasy	7"	Philips	BF1385	1964	**£10**	
Let's Stomp	7"	Decca	F11690	1963	**£8**	
Little Girl	7"	Decca	F11622	1963	**£8**	
What About Me	7"	Decca	F11830	1964	**£8**	

CURTIS, MAC

Title	Format	Label	Number	Year	Price	Notes
You Ain't Treating Me Right	7"	Parlophone	R4279	1957	**£140**	

CURTIS, SONNY

Title	Format	Label	Number	Year	Price	Notes
Beatle Hits Flamenco Guitar Style	LP	Imperial	LP9276	1964	**£12**	US
Beatle I Want To Be	7"	Colpix	PX11024	1964	**£4**	
Red Headed Stranger	7"	Coral	Q72400	1960	**£5**	

CURTOLA, BOBBY

Title	Format	Label	Number	Year	Price	Notes
Aladdin	7"	London	HL9639	1962	**£4**	
Fortune Teller	7"	London	HL9577	1962	**£4**	

CURVED AIR

Curved Air (named after the Terry Riley piece) were more successful than most at integrating elements of classical music within a rock format and both Francis Monkman and Darryl Way have worked extensively with the same approach ever since the group's first release. The first LP, "Air Conditioning", was issued as a limited edition picture disc - probably the first rock record to be released in this form. Its value has been kept low, however, by the fact that a small number of playings causes a drastic deterioration in sound quality.

Title	Format	Label	Number	Year	Price	Notes
Air Conditioning	LP	W. Bros	WSX3012	1970	**£15**	pic disc
Air Cut	LP	W. Bros	K46224	1973	**£10**	
Back street Luv	7"	W. Bros	WB8029	1971	**£4**	chart single
It Happened Today	7"	W. Bros	WB8023	1971	**£4**	
Live	LP	Deram	SML119	1975	**£10**	
Phantasmagoria	LP	W. Bros	K46158	1972	**£10**	chart LP
Sarah's Concern	7"	W. Bros	K16164	1972	**£4**	
Second Album	LP	W. Bros	K46092	1971	**£12**	chart LP

CUSHING, JOHN

Title	Format	Label	Number	Year	Price	Notes
She's Independent	7"	Carnaby	CNS4002	1969	**£4**	

CUTLER, IVOR

Title	Format	Label	Number	Year	Price	Notes
Get Away From The Wall	7" EP	Decca	DFE6677	1961	**£15**	
Great Grey Grasshopper	7"	Parlophone	R5624	1967	**£5**	
Ludo	LP	Decca			**£30**	
Of Y'hup	7" EP	Fontana	TFE17144	1959	**£20**	
Who Tore Your Trousers	LP	Decca	LK4405	1961	**£30**	

CYAN THREE

Title	Format	Label	Number	Year	Price	Notes
Since I Lost My Baby	7"	Decca	F12371	1966	**£6**	

CYCLONES

Title	Format	Label	Number	Year	Price	Notes
Nobody	7"	Oriole	CB1898	1964	**£12**	

CYKLE

Title	Format	Label	Number	Year	Price	Notes
Cykle	LP	Label	9261	1969	**£180**	US

CYMBAL, JOHNNY

Title	Format	Label	Number	Year	Price	Notes
Cymbal Smashes	7" EP	London	RER1406	1963	**£8**	
Dum Dum De Dum	7"	London	HLR9762	1963	**£4**	chart single
Go VW Go	7"	United Artists	UP1093	1965	**£10**	
It'll Be Me	7"	MGM	MGM1106	1960	**£4**	
Mister Bass Man	LP	Kapp	KL1324	1963	**£15**	US
Mister Bass Man	7"	London	HLR9682	1963	**£5**	
Mister Bass Man	7" EP	London	RER1375	1963	**£8**	
Teenage Heaven	7"	London	HLR9731	1963	**£5**	

CYMBALINE

Title	Format	Label	Number	Year	Price	Notes
Down By The Seaside	7"	Philips	BF1681	1968	**£4**	
I Don't Want It	7"	Mercury	MF961	1967	**£6**	
Matrimonial Fears	7"	Philips	BF1624	1967	**£8**	
Peanuts And Chewy Macs	7"	Mercury	MF975	1967	**£5**	
Please Little Girl	7"	Pye	7N15916	1965	**£4**	
Top Girl	7"	Mercury	MF918	1965	**£6**	
Turn Around	7"	Philips	BF1749	1969	**£5**	

CYMERONS

Title	Format	Label	Number	Year	Price	Notes
Everyday	7"	Polydor	56098	1966	**£8**	
I'll Be There	7"	Decca	F11976	1964	**£8**	

CYRKLE

Title	Format	Label	Number	Year	Price	Notes
I Wish You Could Be There	7"	CBS	202577	1967	**£5**	
Neon	LP	CBS	62977	1967	**£15**	

Penny Arcade	7"	CBS	2917	1967	**£4**	
Please Don't Leave Me	7"	CBS	202516	1967	**£4**	
Red Rubber Ball	7"	CBS	202064	1966	**£4**	
Red Rubber Ball	LP	CBS	CS9344	1966	**£15**	US
Turn Down Day	7"	CBS	202246	1966	**£4**	
We Had A Good Thing Going	7"	CBS	2790	1967	**£4**	

CZAR

Oh Lord I'm Getting Heavy	7"	Philips	6006071	1970	**£15**	
Tread Softly On My Dreams	LP	Fontana	6309009	1970	**£120**	

CZUKAY, HOLGER & ROLF DAMMERS

Canaxis 5	LP	Music Factory	SRS002	1969	**£150**	

D

D JUNIOR, DON

Dirty Dozen	7"	Caltone	TONE124	196-	**£8**	

D'ABO, MICHAEL

Broken Rainbows	LP	A&M	AMLH63634	1974	**£10**	
D'Abo	LP	MCA	MAPS2040	1970	**£10**	
Down At Rachel's Place	LP	A&M	AMLH68097	1972	**£10**	
Gulliver's Travels	7"	Immediate	IM075	1969	**£10**	
Gulliver's Travels	LP	Instant	INLP003	1968	**£20**	
Let It Roar	7"	UNI	UNS525	1970	**£5**	

D'ALBUQUERQUE, MICHAEL

Stalking The Sleeper	LP	W. Bros	K56270	1976	**£10**	
We May Be Cattle...	LP	RCA	SF8383	1974	**£12**	

D'ARBY, TERENCE TRENT

If You Let Me Stay	12"	CBS	XPR1338	1987	**£12**	promo
Introducing The Hardline	LP	CBS	4509110	1987	**£10**	pic disc
Introducing The Hardline	CD	CBS	4509119	1987	**£15**	pic disc

D'ELL, DENNIS

It Breaks My Heart In Two	7"	CBS	202605	1967	**£30**	

D'ELL, DENNY

Woman Called Sorrow	7"	Decca	F12647	1967	**£4**	

D'SILVA, AMANCIO

Integration	LP	Columbia	SX6322	1969	**£30**	
Reflections	LP	Columbia	SCX6465	1970	**£25**	

D, KIM

Real Thing	7"	Pye	7N15953	1965	**£4**	

D, TONY & THE SHAKEDOWNS

Is It True	7"	Piccadilly	7N35168	1964	**£4**	

D.O.A.

Disco Sucks	7"	Quintessence	QEP002	1979	**£20**	
Disco Sucks	7"	Sudden D.	3097	1978	**£25**	
Hardcore '81	LP	Friends	FR010	1981	**£60**	
Positively D.O.A.	7"	Alt. Tentacles	VIRUS7	1981	**£5**	
Something Better Change	LP	Friends	FR003	1980	**£40**	
Triumph Of The Ignoroids	12"	Friends			**£40**	

DACOSTA, RITA

Don't Bring Me Down	7"	Contempo	CS2061	1975	**£8**	

DADA

Dada was an ambitious big band that unfortunately found the costs of maintaining a large line-up too great to continue when their LP failed to set the country alight. A slimmed down version of the group continued as Vinegar Joe.

Dada	LP	Atco	2400030	1970	**£15**	

DADDY LONGLEGS

Daddy Longlegs	LP	W. Bros	WS3004	1970	**£15**	
High Again	7"	W. Bros	WB8012	1970	**£6**	
Oakdown Farm	LP	Vertigo	6360038	1971	**£20**	spiral label
Shifting Sands	LP	Polydor	2371323	1972	**£15**	
Three Musicians	LP	Polydor	2371261	1972	**£15**	

DADDY'S ACT

Eight Days A Week	7"	Columbia	DB8242	1967	**£10**	

DADDY-O'S

Got A Match?	7"	Oriole	CB1454	1958	**£4**	

DAFOS, CALVIL

Title	Format	Label	Number	Year	Price	Notes
Brown Sugar	7"	Blue Beat	BB347	1965	**£10**	

DAISY CLAN

Title	Format	Label	Number	Year	Price	Notes
Bonnie Bonnie Bonnie	7"	MCA	MU1057	1969	**£4**	
Love Needs Love	7"	Pye	7N25532	1970	**£4**	
Mr.Walkie Talkie Man	7"	Major Minor	MM671	1970	**£4**	
San Francisco China Town	7"	Decca	F23168	1971	**£4**	

DAKOTA'S ALL STARS

Title	Format	Label	Number	Year	Price	Notes
Call Me Master	7"	Blue Beat	BB358	1965	**£10**	

DAKOTAS

Title	Format	Label	Number	Year	Price	Notes
Cruel Sea	7"	Parlophone	R5044	1963	**£4**	chart single
I Can't Break The News To Myself	7"	Philips	BF1645	1968	**£15**	
I'm An 'Ardworkin' Barrow Boy	7"	Page One	POF018	1967	**£12**	
Magic Carpet	7"	Parlophone	R5064	1963	**£6**	
Meet The Dakotas	7" EP	Parlophone	GEP8888	1963	**£12**	
Oyeh	7"	Parlophone	R5203	1964	**£8**	

DALE & GRACE

Title	Format	Label	Number	Year	Price	Notes
Dale And Grace No.1	7" EP	London	RE1428	1964	**£5**	
Dale And Grace No.2	7" EP	London	RE1429	1964	**£5**	
Dale And Grace No.3	7" EP	London	RE1430	1964	**£5**	
I'm Leaving It Up To You	7"	London	HL9807	1963	**£4**	chart single
I'm Leaving It Up To You	LP	Montel	LP100	1964	**£35**	US
Stop And Think It Over	7"	London	HL9857	1964	**£4**	

DALE, ALAN

Title	Format	Label	Number	Year	Price	Notes
Don't Knock The Rock	7"	Vogue Coral	Q72225	1957	**£6**	
Lonesome Road	7"	Vogue Coral	Q72231	1957	**£5**	

DALE, DICK & THE DELTONES

Title	Format	Label	Number	Year	Price	Notes
Checkered Flag	LP	Capitol	T2002	1963	**£15**	US
King Of The Surf Guitar	LP	Capitol	T1930	1963	**£20**	US
Mr.Eliminator	LP	Capitol	T2053	1964	**£15**	US
Peppermint Man	7"	Capitol	CL15296	1963	**£6**	
Rock Out	LP	Capitol	T2293	1965	**£15**	US
Scavenger	7"	Capitol	CL15320	1963	**£6**	
Summer Surf	LP	Capitol	T2111	1964	**£15**	US
Surfer's Choice	LP	Capitol	T1886	1963	**£20**	

DALE, GLEN

Title	Format	Label	Number	Year	Price	Notes
Good Day Sunshine	7"	Decca	F12475	1966	**£4**	

DALE, JIM

Title	Format	Label	Number	Year	Price	Notes
Be My Girl	7"	Parlophone	R4343	1957	**£4**	chart single
Gotta Find A Girl	7"	Parlophone	R4522	1959	**£4**	
Jane Belinda	7"	Parlophone	R4424	1958	**£4**	
Jim Dale	7" EP	Parlophone	GEP8656	1957	**£6**	
Just Born	7"	Parlophone	R4376	1957	**£4**	chart single
Piccadilly Line	7"	Parlophone	R4329	1957	**£5**	
Sugartime	7"	Parlophone	R4402	1958	**£4**	chart single

DALE, JIM VIPERS & KING BROTHERS

Title	Format	Label	Number	Year	Price	Notes
Top Ten Special	7"	Parlophone	R4356	1957	**£6**	

DALEY, BASIL

Title	Format	Label	Number	Year	Price	Notes
Born To Love	7"	Studio One	SO2054	196-	**£10**	

DALEY, JIM & THE DING A LINGS

Title	Format	Label	Number	Year	Price	Notes
Rock Pretty Baby	7"	Brunswick	05648	1957	**£25**	

DALLON, MIKI

Title	Format	Label	Number	Year	Price	Notes
Do You Call That Love?	7"	RCA	RCA1438	1965	**£4**	
I Care About You	7"	RCA	RCA1478	1965	**£4**	
I'm Gonna Find A Cave	7"	Strike	JH306	1966	**£5**	
What Will Your Mama Say	7"	Strike	JH318	1966	**£6**	

DALTON'S & BUSTER'S ALL STARS

Title	Format	Label	Number	Year	Price	Notes
Never Kiss You Again	7"	Fab	FAB30	196-	**£10**	

DALTON, KATHY

Title	Format	Label	Cat. No.	Year	Price	Notes
Amazing	LP	Discreet	K59202	1973	**£10**	
Boogie Bands & One Night Stands	LP	Discreet	DS2208	1974	**£10**	US

DALTREY, ROGER

Title	Format	Label	Cat. No.	Year	Price	Notes
I'm Free	7"	Ode	ODS66302	1972	**£5**	PS
McVicar On Record	LP	Polydor	SA038	1980	**£15**	US promo
Say It Ain't So/Satin And Lace	7"	Polydor	2058948	1976	**£5**	

DAMNED

Title	Format	Label	Cat. No.	Year	Price	Notes
Alone Again Or	CD-s	MCA	DGRIM7	1987	**£6**	
Best Of The Damned	LP	Big Beat	DAM1	1981	**£10**	red or blue vinyl
Black Album	LP	Chiswick	CWK3015	1980	**£15**	double, chart LP
Damned Damned Damned	LP	Stiff	SEEZ1	1977	**£10**	chart LP
Damned Damned Damned	LP	Stiff	SEEZ1	1977	**£50**	Eddie & Hot Rods photo
Damned Damned Damned/M.F.P.	LP	Stiff	MAIL2	1983	**£12**	double
Don't Cry Wolf	7"	Stiff	BUY24	1977	**£5**	
Don't Cry Wolf	7"	Stiff	BUY24	1977	**£6**	pink vinyl
Dozen Girls	7"	Bronze	BRODJ156	1982	**£5**	promo
Eloise (Extravagant Mix)	12"	MCA	GRIMX4	1986	**£6**	
Eloise	12"	MCA	GRIMT4	1986	**£6**	blue vinyl
Four Pack	7"	Stiff	GRAB2	1981	**£15**	BUY6,10,18,24 in wallet
Friday The 13th	7"	NEMS	TRY1	1981	**£8**	chart single
Generals	7"	Bronze	BRO159	1982	**£6**	
Grimly Fiendish	7"	MCA	GRIM1	1985	**£6**	gatefold PS, autographed
Grimly Fiendish	7"	MCA	GRIMP1	1985	**£5**	pic disc
Grimly Fiendish	12"	MCA	GRIMT1	1985	**£8**	autographed
Grimly Fiendish	12"	MCA	GRIMX1	1985	**£8**	white vinyl
History Of The World Part 1	7"	Chiswick	CHIS135	1980	**£4**	chart single
History Of The World Part 1	12"	Chiswick	CHIS12135	1980	**£6**	
I Just Can't Be Happy Today	7"	Chiswick	CHIS120	1979	**£4**	chart single
Is It A Dream	7"	MCA	GRIM3	1985	**£4**	5 badges
Is It A Dream	12"	MCA	GRIMT3	1985	**£6**	5 badges
Live In Newcastle	LP	Damned	DAMU2	1983	**£25**	
Live In Newcastle	LP	Damned	PDAMU2	1983	**£20**	pic disc
Lively Arts	7"	Big Beat	NS80	1982	**£5**	green vinyl
Lively Arts	10"	Big Beat	NST80	1982	**£5**	
Love Song	7"	Big Beat	NS75	1982	**£4**	blue vinyl, 3 PS's
Love Song	7"	Chiswick	CHIS112	1979	**£4**	chart single
Love Song	7"	Chiswick	CHIS112	1979	**£5**	red vinyl, 4 PS's
Love Song	7"	Dodgy Demo		1978	**£20**	
Lovely Money	7"	Bronze	BRODJ149	1982	**£8**	promo
Lovely Money	7"	Bronze	BROP149	1982	**£6**	pic disc
Machine Gun Etiquette	LP	Big Beat	DAM2	1982	**£10**	blue or white vinyl
Music For Pleasure	LP	Stiff	SEEZ5	1977	**£10**	
Neat Neat Neat	7"	Stiff	BUY10	1977	**£8**	
New Rose	7"	Stiff	BUY6	1976	**£10**	
New Rose	7"	Stiff	BUY6	1986	**£4**	red vinyl, insert
New Rose	7"	Stiff	BUY6	1986	**£4**	white vinyl
New Rose	7"	Stiff	DBUY6	1986	**£6**	white vinyl, insert, double
New Rose	12"	Stiff	BUYIT6	1986	**£6**	white vinyl
Phantasmagoria	LP	MCA	MCF3275	1985	**£10**	white vinyl
Phantasmagoria	LP	MCA	MCFP3275	1985	**£10**	pic disc
Problem Child	7"	Stiff	BUY18	1977	**£6**	
Shadow Of Love	7"	MCA	GRIM2	1985	**£8**	gatefold PS+7"(GRIMY2)
Smash It Up	7"	Big Beat	NS76	1982	**£4**	red vinyl
Smash It Up	7"	Chiswick	CHIS116	1979	**£4**	chart single
Stretcher Case Baby	7"	Stiff	DAMNED1	1977	**£40**	
Thanks For The Night	7"	Plus One	DAMNED1	1985	**£5**	red, white, or blue vinyl
Thanks For The Night	7"	Plus One	DAMNED1P	1984	**£5**	pic disc
Thanks For The Night	7"	Plus One	DAMNED1P	1986	**£20**	shaped pic disc, plinth
Thanks For The Night	12"	Plus One	DAMNED1T	1985	**£12**	multi-coloured vinyl
Thanks For The Night	12"	Plus One	DAMNED1T	1984	**£6**	marble vinyl
Thanks For The Night	12"	Plus One	DAMNEDP1	1986	**£6**	pic disc
There Ain't No Sanity Claus	7"	Chiswick	CHIS139	1980	**£4**	
There Ain't No Sanity Clause	7"	Chiswick	CHIS139DJ	1980	**£8**	promo
Wait For The Blackout	7"	Big Beat	NSP77	1982	**£6**	pic disc

DANCE CHAPTER

Title	Format	Label	Cat. No.	Year	Price	Notes
Anonymity	7"	4AD	AD18	1980	**£4**	
Chapter 11	12"	4AD	BAD115	1981	**£6**	

DANDO SHAFT

Dando Shaft	LP	Neon	NE5	1971	**£35**
Evening With...	LP	Youngblood	SSYB6	1970	**£25**
Kingdom	LP	Rubber	RUB034	1977	**£10**
Lantaloon	LP	RCA	SF8256	1972	**£35**
Sun Clog Dance	7"	RCA	RCA2246	1972	**£8**

DANDY

Be Natural Be Proud	7"	Downtown	DT434	196-	**£8**
Come On Home	7"	Downtown	DT437	196-	**£8**
East Of Suez	7"	Giant	GN3	196-	**£8**
Everybody Loves A Winner	7"	Downtown	DT442	196-	**£8**
Fight	7"	Ska Beat	JB247	1966	**£10**
Games People Play	7"	Downtown	DT421	196-	**£8**
Groovin' At The Cue	7"	Giant	GN20	1967	**£8**
Hey Boy Hey Girl	7"	Blue Beat	BB319	1964	**£10**
I Found Love	7"	Blue Beat	BB336	1965	**£10**
I'm Back with A Bang Bang	7"	Giant	GN36	196-	**£8**
I'm Looking For Love	7"	Blue Beat	BB308	1964	**£10**
I'm Your Puppet	7"	Downtown	DT416	196-	**£8**
In The Mood	7"	Caltone	TONE103	1967	**£8**
Let's Go Rocksteady	7"	Giant	GN7	196-	**£8**
Little More Ska	7"	Dice	CC29	1964	**£8**
Move Your Mule	7"	Downtown	DT401	196-	**£8**
My Babe	7"	Blue Beat	BB327	1965	**£10**
Now I Have You	7"	Dice	CC24	1964	**£8**
One Scotch	7"	Ska Beat	JB269	1967	**£10**
People Get Ready	7"	Downtown	DT429	196-	**£8**
Play It Cool	7"	Columbia	DB112	1969	**£8**
Propogandist	7"	Giant	GN23	1967	**£8**
Puppet On A String	7"	Giant	GN5	196-	**£8**
Reggae In Your Jeggae	7"	Downtown	DT410	196-	**£8**
Rudy A Message To You	7"	Ska Beat	JB273	1967	**£10**
Shake Me Wake Me	7"	Downtown	DT402	196-	**£8**
Somewhere My Love	7"	Giant	GN10	1967	**£8**
Sweet Ride	7"	Giant	GN27	1967	**£8**
Tears On My Pillow	7"	Giant	GN30	1967	**£8**
Tell Me Darling	7"	Downtown	DT404	196-	**£8**
There Is A Mountain	7"	Giant	GN15	1967	**£8**
Toast	7"	Trojan	TR618	1968	**£8**
Trier	7"	Downtown	DT411	196-	**£8**
Vipers	7"	Carnival	CV7020	1965	**£8**
Won't You Come Home	7"	Downtown	DT453	196-	**£8**
You're No Hustler	7"	Ska Beat	JB279	1967	**£10**

DANE, CHRIS

Cynthia's In Love	7"	London	HLA8165	1955	**£5**

DANGERFIELD, A.P.

Conversations	7"	Fontana	TF935	1968	**£12**

DANGERFIELD, KEITH

The Keith Dangerfield single owes its high value to the once-held belief that the Dangerfield name was a pseudonym for the Yardbirds' vocalist, Keith Relf. This was very much a case of wishful thinking, however, Relf did attempt a solo career while still with the Yardbirds, but his singles have the obvious credit - Keith Relf.

No Life Child	7"	Plexium	P1237	196-	**£120**

DANGERFIELD, TONY

She's Too Way Out	7"	Pye	7N15695	1964	**£25**

DANIELS, BILLY

That Old Black Magic	7" EP	Mercury	MEP9001	1956	**£5**

DANIELS, JULIUS

RCA Victor Race Series Vol.4	7" EP	RCA	RCX7175	1965	**£4**

DANLEERS

One Summer Night	7"	Mercury	AMT1003	1958	**£15**

DANNY & LEE

Sentence	7"	Trojan	TR629	1969	**£6**

DANNY & THE JUNIORS

Title	Format	Label	Number	Year	Price	Notes
At The Hop	7"	HMV	POP436	1958	**£10**	chart single
Back To The Hop	7"	Top Rank	JAR587	1961	**£5**	
Dottie	7"	HMV	POP504	1958	**£8**	
Oo-La-La-Limbo	7"	London	HL9666	1963	**£4**	
Pony Express	7"	Top Rank	JAR552	1961	**£5**	
Rock And Roll Is Here To Stay	7"	HMV	POP467	1958	**£12**	
Twisting All Night Long	7"	Top Rank	JAR604	1962	**£4**	
Twisting USA	7"	Top Rank	JAR510	1960	**£5**	

DANSE SOCIETY

Title	Format	Label	Number	Year	Price	Notes
Clock	7"	North	SOC381	1981	**£8**	

DANTALIAN'S CHARIOT

With the arrival of psychedelia, Zoot Money was able to indulge his penchant for onstage flamboyance and, with the aid of his latest re-named version of the Big Roll Band, recorded one of the classic singles of the genre. The drummer, Colin Allen, subsequently played with John Mayall and Stone The Crows; bassist Pat Donaldson joined Fotheringay and has been a busy session musician ever since; while guitarist Andy Summers eventually found mega-stardom as a member of the Police.

Title	Format	Label	Number	Year	Price	Notes
Madman Running Through The Fields	7"	Columbia	DB8260	1967	**£30**	

DANTE & THE EVERGREENS

Title	Format	Label	Number	Year	Price	Notes
Alley Oop	7"	Top Rank	JAR402	1960	**£5**	
Dante & The Evergreens	LP	Madison	MA1002	1961	**£150**	US

DARIEN SPIRIT

Title	Format	Label	Number	Year	Price	Notes
Elegy To Marilyn	LP	Charisma	CAS1065	1973	**£10**	
Magic Morning	7"	Charisma	CB216	1973	**£4**	
Magic Morning Sun	7"	Charisma	CB222	1974	**£4**	
Rock Your Soul	7"	Charisma	CB235	1974	**£4**	

DARIN, BOBBY

Title	Format	Label	Number	Year	Price	Notes
25th Day Of December	7" EP	London	REK1321	1961	**£4**	
At The Copa	LP	London	HAK2291	1960	**£10**	Mono
At The Copa	LP	London	SAHK6103	1960	**£10**	Stereo
Baby Face	7"	London	HLK9624	1962	**£4**	chart single
Bobby Darin	LP	London	HAE2140	1958	**£15**	
Bobby Darin	7" EP	London	REE1173	1959	**£10**	
Bobby Darin No.2	7" EP	London	REE1225	1959	**£10**	
Bobby Darin Story	LP	London	HAK2372	1961	**£12**	
Dream Lover	7"	London	HLE8867	1959	**£4**	chart single
For Teenagers Only	LP	London	HAK2311	1960	**£12**	
For Teenagers Only	7" EP	London	REK1286	1961	**£6**	
Hear Them Bells	7"	Brunswick	05831	1960	**£4**	
It's You Or No One	LP	London	HAK8102	1963	**£10**	
Keep A Walking	7"	London	HLK9663	1963	**£4**	
Lazy River	7"	London	HLK9303	1961	**£4**	chart single
Love Swings	LP	London	HAK2394	1961	**£10**	Mono
Love Swings	LP	London	SAHK6193	1961	**£10**	Stereo
Love Swings	7" EP	London	REK1334	1961	**£5**	
Mack The Knife	7"	London	HLE8939	1959	**£4**	chart single
Mighty Mighty Man	7"	London	HLE8793	1959	**£8**	
Milord	7"	Atlantic	AT4002	1964	**£4**	
Multiplication	7"	London	HLK9474	1961	**£4**	chart single
Plain Jane	7"	London	HLE8815	1959	**£6**	
Queen Of The Hop	7"	London	HLE8737	1958	**£8**	chart single
Rock Island Line	7"	Brunswick	05561	1956	**£8**	
Sings Ray Charles	LP	London	HAK2456	1962	**£10**	Mono
Sings Ray Charles	LP	London	SAHK6243	1962	**£10**	Stereo
Splish Splash	7"	London	HLE8666	1958	**£8**	chart single
Story	LP	Atlantic	587065	1967	**£10**	
That's All	LP	London	HAE2172	1959	**£12**	chart LP
That's All	7" EP	London	REK1243	1960	**£5**	
Things	7"	London	HLK9575	1962	**£4**	chart single
Things	7" EP	London	REK1342	1962	**£5**	
Things And Other Things	LP	London	HAK8030	1962	**£10**	
This Is Bobby Darin	LP	London	HAK2235	1959	**£10**	Mono, chart LP
This Is Bobby Darin	LP	London	SAH6067	1959	**£10**	Stereo, chart LP
Twist With Bobby Darin	7" EP	London	REK1338	1962	**£5**	
Up A Lazy River	7" EP	London	REK1290	1961	**£5**	
What'd I Say	7"	London	HLK9540	1962	**£4**	
You Must Have Been A Beautiful Baby	7"	London	HLK9429	1961	**£4**	chart single

DARIN, BOBBY & JOHNNY MERCER

Two Of A Kind	LP	London	HAK2363	1961	**£10**	Mono
Two Of A Kind	LP	London	SAHK6164	1961	**£10**	Stereo
Two Of A Kind	7" EP	London	REK1310	1961	**£5**	

DARK

The high value attaching to privately pressed progressive albums by groups like the Dark, Forever Amber, and Complex depends in part on the mystique woven around them by collectors and dealers alike. The records are certainly rare and when so few people have actually heard them, it is difficult to gainsay claims that they are masterpieces. Now these records are being reissued, but in tiny limited editions and at prices that are themselves well into the realm of serious collecting (75-90). Thus the mystique continues.

Round The Edges	LP	private		1971	**£1000**	

DARLING BUDS

Spin	7"			198-	**£8**	flexi

DARNELL, BILL

Guilty Lips	7"	London	HLU8267	1956	**£6**	
Last Frontier	7"	London	HLU8234	1956	**£8**	
My Little Mother	7"	London	HLU8204	1955	**£8**	
Tell Me More	7"	London	HLU8292	1956	**£6**	

DARRELL, GUY

Crystal Ball	7"	CBS	202642	1967	**£4**	
Go Home Girl	7"	Oriole	CB1932	1964	**£5**	
Hard Lovin'	7"	CBS	202510	1967	**£4**	
I've Been Hurt	7"	CBS	202082	1966	**£8**	
My Way Of Thinking	7"	CBS	202296	1966	**£4**	
Somewhere They Can't Find Me	7"	CBS	202033	1966	**£4**	
Sorry	7"	Oriole	CB1964	1964	**£4**	
Stupidity	7"	CBS	201806	1965	**£4**	

DARREN, JAMES

Angel Face	7"	Pye	7N25034	1959	**£4**	
Because They're Young	7"	Pye	7N25059	1960	**£4**	chart single
Conscience	7"	Pye	7N25138	1962	**£4**	chart single
Gidget	7"	Pye	7N25019	1959	**£4**	
Goodbye Cruel World	7"	Pye	7N25116	1961	**£4**	chart single
Hail To The Conquering Hero	7"	Pye	7N25168	1962	**£4**	
Her Royal Majesty	7"	Pye	7N25125	1962	**£4**	chart single
James Darren Hit Parade	7" EP	Pye	NEP44008	1962	**£5**	
Love Among The Young	LP	Pye	NPL28021	1963	**£10**	
Mary's Little Lamb	7"	Pye	7N25155	1962	**£4**	
P.S. I Love You	7" EP	Pye	NEP44004	1959	**£5**	
Pin A Medal On Joey	7"	Pye	7N25170	1963	**£4**	

DARREN, JENNIE

River Deep Mountain High	7"	Major Minor	MM611	1969	**£4**	

DARROW, CHRIS

Chris Darrow was a member of Kaleidoscope, the remarkable American group. His solo career, however, has been relatively unspectacular.

Chris Darrow	LP	United Artists	UAG29453	1973	**£15**	
Under My Own Disguise	LP	United Artists	UAG29634	1974	**£15**	

DARTELLS

Dartell Stomp	7"	London	HLD9719	1963	**£5**	
Hot Pastrami	LP	Dot	DLP3522	1963	**£12**	US

DARVELL, BARRY

How Will It End	7"	London	HL9191	1960	**£12**	

DARWIN'S THEORY

Daytime	7"	Major Minor	MM503	1967	**£5**	

DASGUPTA, NATAI

Songs Of India	LP	Mushroom		1972	**£20**	

DAUGHTERS OF THE ALBION

Daughters Of The Albion	LP	Fontana	STL5486	1968	**£20**	

DAVANI, DAVE

Don't Fool Around	7"	Columbia	DB7125	1963	**£8**	
Four Faced	LP	Parlophone		1962	**£20**	
Midnight Special	7"	Decca	F11896	1964	**£10**	
One Track Mind	7"	Parlophone	R5525	1966	**£6**	
Top Of The Pops	7"	Parlophone	R5329	1965	**£8**	
Tossin' And Turnin'	7"	Parlophone	R5490	1966	**£8**	

DAVE & THE DIAMONDS

I Walk The Lonely Night	7"	Columbia	DB7692	1965	**£5**	

DAVE DEE, DOZY, BEAKY, MICK & TICH

All I Want	7"	Fontana	TF586	1965	**£4**	
Bend It	7"	Fontana	TF746	1966	**£4**	chart single
Dave Dee, Dozy, Beaky, Mick & Tich	LP	Fontana	STL5350	1966	**£10**	chart LP
DDDBMT	LP	Fontana	SFL13002	1968	**£10**	
Don Juan	7"	Fontana	TF1000	1969	**£4**	chart single
Golden Hits	LP	Fontana	STL5441	1967	**£10**	
Hideaway	7"	Fontana	TF711	1966	**£4**	chart single
Hold Tight	7"	Fontana	TF671	1966	**£4**	chart single
If Music Be The Food Of Love	LP	Fontana	STL5388	1968	**£10**	chart LP
If No One Sang	LP	Fontana	STL5471	1968	**£10**	
Last Night In Soho	7"	Fontana	TF953	1968	**£4**	chart single
Legend Of	LP	Fontana	SFL13063	1969	**£10**	
Legend Of Xanadu	7"	Fontana	TF903	1968	**£4**	chart single
Loos Of England	7" EP	Fontana	TE17488	1967	**£5**	
No Time	7"	Fontana	TF531	1965	**£4**	
Okay	7"	Fontana	TF830	1967	**£4**	chart single
Save Me	7"	Fontana	TF775	1966	**£4**	chart single
Snake In The Grass	7"	Fontana	TF1020	1969	**£4**	chart single
Together	LP	Fontana	SFL13173	1969	**£10**	
Touch Me Touch Me	7"	Fontana	TF798	1967	**£4**	chart single
Wreck Of The Antoinette	7"	Fontana	TF971	1968	**£4**	chart single
You Make It Move	7"	Fontana	TF630	1965	**£4**	chart single
Zabadak	7"	Fontana	TF873	1967	**£4**	chart single

DAVEY & MORRIS

Davey & Morris	LP	York		1973	**£25**	

DAVEY & THE BADMEN

Wanted	LP	KRW	WA63054		**£35**	US

DAVID & JONATHAN

David & Jonathan	LP	Columbia	SCX6031	1967	**£12**	
Laughing Fit To Cry	7"	Columbia	DB7717	1965	**£4**	
Lovers Of The World Unite	7"	Columbia	DB7950	1966	**£4**	chart single
Michelle	7"	Columbia	DB7800	1966	**£4**	chart single
She's Leaving Home	7"	Columbia	DB8208	1967	**£4**	
Softly Whispering I Love You	7"	Columbia	DB8287	1967	**£4**	
Speak Her Name	7"	Columbia	DB7873	1966	**£4**	
Ten Storeys High	7"	Columbia	DB8035	1966	**£4**	
You Ought To Meet My Baby	7"	Columbia	DB8428	1968	**£4**	

DAVIDSON, DIANE

Ain't Gonna Be Treated This Way	7"	Janus	6146021	1974	**£4**	
Sympathy	7"	Janus	6146019	1974	**£4**	
Sympathy	7"	Janus	no number	1972	**£10**	demo, + 2 tracks by other artists

DAVIDSON, FRANKIE & THE HI MARKS

You're Driving Me Crazy	7"	Starlite	ST45037	1961	**£6**	

DAVIDSON, TOMMY

Half Past Kissing Time	7"	London	HLU8219	1956	**£8**	

DAVIE, HUTCH & HIS HONKY TONKERS

At The Woodchoppers' Ball	7"	London	HLE8667	1958	**£6**	

DAVIES, ALUN

Daydo	LP	CBS	65108	1972	**£12**	

DAVIES, BOB

Rock And Roll Show	7"	London	HLU9767	1963	**£5**	

DAVIES, CYRIL

Country Line Special	7"	Pye	7N17663	1969	**£5**	
Country Line Special	7"	Pye	7N25194	1963	**£10**	
Legendary Cyril Davies	LP	Folklore	FLEAT9	1970	**£30**	
Legendary Cyril Davies	LP-10"	Private	77LP2	1957	**£60**	
Preaching The Blues	7"	Pye	7N25221	1963	**£10**	
Sound Of Davies	7" EP	Pye	NEP44025	1964	**£15**	

DAVIES, DAVE

Dave Davies Hits	7" EP	Pye	NEP24289	1968	**£100**	
Death Of A Clown	7"	Pye	7N17356	1967	**£4**	chart single
Hold My Hand	7"	Pye	7N17678	1969	**£8**	
Lincoln County	7"	Pye	7N17514	1968	**£6**	
Susannah's Still Alive	7"	Pye	7N17429	1967	**£4**	chart single

DAVIES, IRVING

Method	7"	Decca	F11456	1962	**£4**	

DAVIES, RON

Silent Song Through The Land	LP	A&M	AMLS933	1970	**£10**	

DAVIS JR., SAMMY

Something For Everyone	LP	T. Motown	STML11160	1970	**£10**	

DAVIS, BILLIE

He's The One	7"	Decca	F11658	1963	**£4**	chart single
Heart And Soul	7"	Piccadilly	7N35308	1966	**£4**	
Just Walk In My Shoes	7"	Piccadilly	7N35350	1966	**£4**	
Last One To Be Loved	7"	Piccadilly	7N35227	1965	**£4**	
Make The Feeling Go Away	7"	Decca	F12870	1969	**£4**	
No Other Baby	7"	Piccadilly	7N35266	1965	**£4**	
Say Nothing	7"	Columbia	DB7195	1964	**£4**	
School Is Over	7"	Columbia	DB7246	1964	**£4**	
Tell Him	7"	Decca	F11572	1963	**£4**	chart single
Whatcha Gonna Do	7"	Columbia	DB7346	1964	**£4**	
You And I	7"	Columbia	DB7115	1963	**£4**	

DAVIS, BOBBY

Hype You Into Selling Your Head	7"	Starlite	ST45056	1961	**£4**	

DAVIS, BONNIE

Pepperhot Baby	7"	Brunswick	05507	1955	**£8**	

DAVIS, CLIFFORD

Before the Beginning	7"	Reprise	RS27003	1969	**£6**	
Come On Down And Follow Me	7"	Reprise	RS25008	1970	**£6**	
Man Of The World	7"	Reprise	K14282	1973	**£6**	

DAVIS, DANNY

Love Me	7"	Parlophone	R4657	1960	**£4**	

DAVIS, JACKIE

Land Of Make Believe	7"	Pye			**£8**	

DAVIS, JESSE ED

Every Night Is Saturday Night	7"	Atlantic	2091076	1971	**£4**	
Jesse Ed Davis	LP	Atco	2400106	1971	**£12**	
Keep On Coming	LP	CBS	65649	1973	**£12**	
Ululu	LP	Atlantic	K40329	1972	**£12**	

DAVIS, MELVIN

Save It	7"	Action	ACT4531	1969	**£5**	
Save It	7"	Action	ACT4531	1969	**£12**	demo

DAVIS, MILES

From the late sixties until a serious car crash put a temporary halt to his career in 1975, Miles Davis maintained a remarkable creative run in which he not only invented the fusion genre, but also began to explore most of the possibilities inherent in it. He released an unusually large number of records during this period, and every one is different. Of the rarities listed here, the quadrophonic mix of "Bitches Brew" is significantly different from the stereo, with extra percussion and a frequent doubling up of melodic phrases to create an echo effect. The Japanese double albums are all live recordings - "Black Beauty", with Chick Corea, Jack DeJohnette, and Steve Grossman, is close to the jazz avant-garde in places; "Dark Magus" is a densely rhythmic work-out from a 1974 Carnegie Hall concert; while "Pangaea" is a companion set to the UK released "Agharta" - the second set from the same evening's performance. It is magnificent, powerful music, though not for the faint-hearted. The Session Disc LP, a poorly recorded set from 1971, would qualify as a bootleg if it was a rock album - in the jazz world, however, such live recordings have always been accepted as part of the natural scheme of things.

Title	Format	Label	Number	Year	Price	Notes
Bitches Brew	LP	CBS	QBL30998/9	1971	**£15**	quad double
Black Beauty	LP	CBS-Sony	SOPJ39/40	1973	**£25**	Japanese double
Dark Magus	LP	CBS-Sony	40AP741/2	1977	**£25**	Japanese double
Hooray For...	LP	Session Disc	123	1972	**£15**	
Pangaea	LP	CBS-Sony	36AP1789/90	1975	**£25**	Japanese double

DAVIS, SKEETER

Title	Format	Label	Number	Year	Price	Notes
End Of The World	LP	RCA	LPM2699	1962	**£10**	US
End Of The World	7"	RCA	RCA1328	1963	**£4**	chart single
Here's The Answer	LP	RCA	LPM2327	1961	**£12**	US
I'll Sing You A Song And Harmonize Too	LP	RCA	LPM2197	1960	**£12**	US
Silver Threads And Golden Needles	7" EP	RCA	RCX7153	1964	**£4**	

DAVIS, SKEETER & PORTER WAGONER

Title	Format	Label	Number	Year	Price	Notes
Duets	LP	RCA	LPM2529	1962	**£10**	US

DAVIS, SPENCER

Title	Format	Label	Number	Year	Price	Notes
Mousetrap	LP	United Artists	UAS29361	1972	**£12**	

DAVIS, SPENCER GROUP

Spencer Davis had no dominant role within the group that bore his name, which is probably why his solo career in the seventies and eighties has been such a low-key affair. Originally, the Spencer Davis Group focussed on its dynamic young singer, Stevie Winwood, who was also a talented guitarist and keyboard player. Winwood shines throughout the group's sturdy R&B material and in particular on the impressive series of singles, which include some real classics. Remarkably, when Winwood left to form Traffic, Spencer Davis was able to find a replacement, Eddie Hardin, whose singing and keyboard playing was almost as fine. "Time Seller" and "Mr.Second Class" are a worthy continuation of the singles series, being soulful performances tinged with psychedelia. They are included on the album "With Their New Face On", which is itself a very under-rated recording.

Title	Format	Label	Number	Year	Price	Notes
After Tea	7"	United Artists	UP2213	1968	**£4**	
Autumn 66	LP	Fontana	STL5359	1966	**£20**	chart LP
Best Of...	LP	Island	ILPS9070	1968	**£12**	
Dimples	7"	Fontana	TF471	1964	**£10**	
Every Little Bit Hurts	7"	Fontana	TF530	1965	**£8**	chart single
Every Little Bit Hurts	7" EP	Fontana	TE17450	1965	**£8**	
Gimme Some Lovin'	7"	Fontana	TF762	1966	**£4**	chart single
Gimme Some Lovin'	LP	United Artists	UAL3578	1967	**£15**	US
Gluggo	LP	Vertigo	6360088	1973	**£10**	
Hits Of...	cass	Philips	MCF5003	1968	**£10**	
I Can't Stand It	7"	Fontana	TF499	1964	**£8**	chart single
I'm A Man	7"	Fontana	TF785	1967	**£4**	chart single
I'm A Man	LP	United Artists	UAL3589	1967	**£15**	US
It's Been So Long	LP	United Artists	UAS29177	1971	**£12**	
Keep On Running	7"	Fontana	TF632	1965	**£4**	chart single
Letters From Edith	LP	CBS	63842	1969	**£60**	test pressing
Living On A Back Street	LP	Vertigo	6360105	1974	**£10**	
Mr.Second Class	7"	United Artists	UP1203	1967	**£4**	chart single
Second Album	LP	Fontana	TL5295	1966	**£20**	chart LP
Short Change	7"	United Artists	UP2226	1968	**£4**	
Sitting And Thinking	7" EP	Fontana	TE17463	1966	**£8**	
Somebody Help Me	7"	Fontana	TF679	1966	**£4**	chart single
Strong Love	7"	Fontana	TF571	1965	**£6**	chart single
Their First Album	LP	Wing	WL1165	1968	**£10**	
Their First LP	LP	Fontana	TL5242	1965	**£20**	chart LP
Time Seller	7"	Fontana	TF854	1967	**£4**	chart single
When I Come Home	7"	Fontana	TF739	1966	**£4**	chart single
With Their New Face On	LP	United Artists	SULP1192	1968	**£20**	
You Put The Hurt On Me	7" EP	Fontana	TE17444	1965	**£8**	

DAVIS, SPENCER GROUP & TRAFFIC

Title	Format	Label	Number	Year	Price	Notes
Here We Go Round The Mulberry Bush	LP	United Artists	SULP1186	1968	**£15**	

DAVIS, STEVE

Title	Format	Label	Number	Year	Price	Notes
Takes Time To Know Her	7"	Fontana	TF922	1968	**£4**	

DAVIS, TYRONE

Title	Format	Label	Number	Year	Price	Notes
Can I Change My Mind	7"	Atlantic	584253	1969	**£4**	

Could I Forget You	7"	Atlantic	2091078	1971	**£4**	
If This World Were Mine	7"	Trojan	TR677	1969	**£6**	
Is It Something You've Got	7"	Atlantic	584265	1969	**£4**	
Need Your Lovin' Every Day	7"	Atlantic	584288	1969	**£4**	
Turn Back The Hands Of Time	7"	Atlantic	2091003	1970	**£4**	
What If A Man	7"	Stateside	SS2092	1968	**£5**	

DAVIS, WALTER

RCA Victor Race Series Vol.3	7" EP	RCA	RCX7169	1964	**£4**	

DAVIS, WARREN MONDAY BAND

Love Is A Hurting Thing	7"	Columbia	DB8270	1967	**£8**	
Wait For Me	7"	Columbia	DB8190	1967	**£6**	

DAVISON, BRIAN

Brian Davison, previously the drummer with the Nice, formed Every Which Way after that group split up - and probably watched with envy the rise to international stardom of Emerson, Lake and Palmer.

Every Which Way	LP	Charisma	CAS1021	1970	**£15**	
Go Placidly	7"	Charisma	BD1	197-	**£5**	

DAWE, TIM

Penrod	LP	Straight	ST1058	1969	**£15**	US

DAWKINS, CARL

Baby I Love You	7"	Rio	R137	196-	**£8**	
Hot And Sticky	7"	Rio	R138	196-	**£8**	
One Dollar Of Music	7"	Duke	DU3	196-	**£8**	
Rodney's History	7"	New Beat	NB030	1968	**£8**	

DAWKINS, HORELL

Butterfly	7"	Ska Beat	JB240	1966	**£10**	

DAWKINS, RUSS & THE WAILERS

Picture On The Wall	7"	Upsetter	US368	1971	**£12**	

DAWN & THE DEEJAYS

These Are The Things About You	7"	RCA	RCA1470	1965	**£4**	

DAWNBREAKERS

Let's Live	7"	Decca	F12110	1965	**£4**	

DAWSON, LESLEY

Run For Shelter	7"	Mercury	MF965	1967	**£5**	

DAX, DANIELLE

Pop-Eyes	LP	Initial	IRC009	1983	**£20**	

DAY BLINDNESS

Day Blindness	LP	Studio 10	DBX101	1968	**£25**	

DAY OF THE PHOENIX

Neighbour's Son	LP	Chapter One	CNSR812	1972	**£30**	
Wide Open N Way	LP	Greenwich	GSLPR1002	1970	**£30**	

DAY, BING

I Can't Help It	7"	Mercury	AMT1047	1959	**£15**	

DAY, BOBBY

Bluebird Buzzard And Oriole	7"	London	HL8800	1959	**£12**	
Little Bitty Pretty One	7"	HMV	POP425	1957	**£15**	
Love Is A One Time Affair	7"	London	HL8964	1959	**£8**	
My Blue Heaven	7"	London	HLY9044	1960	**£5**	
Over And Over	7"	Top Rank	JAR538	1961	**£8**	
Rockin' Robin	7"	London	HL8726	1958	**£10**	chart single
Rockin' Robin	7"	Sue	WI388	1965	**£8**	
Rockin' With Robin	LP	Class	LP5002	1959	**£75**	US

DAY, JACKIE

Before It's Too Late	7"	Sue	WI4040	1967	**£15**	

DAY, JILL

I Hear You Knocking	7"	HMV	7M362	1956	**£4**	

Tear Fell	7"	HMV	7M391	1956	**£4**	

DAY, MURIEL

Nine Times Out Of Ten	7"	Page One	POF151	1969	**£12**	

DAY, TERRY

That's All I Want	7"	CBS	AAG104	1962	**£4**	

DAYLIGHT

Daylight	LP	RCA	SF8194	1971	**£25**	

DAYLIGHTERS

Oh Mom Teach Me How	7"	Sue	WI343	1964	**£10**	

DE BURGH, CHRIS

Broken Wings	7"	A&M	AMS7320	1977	**£5**	
Discovery	7"	A&M	AMS7336	1978	**£5**	
Don't Pay The Ferryman	7"	A&M	AMS8256	1982	**£4**	chart single
Flying	7"	A&M	AMS7185	1975	**£4**	
Hold On	7"	A&M	AMS7148	1975	**£4**	

DE CASTRO SISTERS

Boom Boom Boomerang	7"	London	HL8137	1955	**£8**	
Christmas Is Coming	7"	London	HLU8212	1955	**£8**	
Give Me Time	7"	London	HLU8228	1956	**£6**	
I'm Bewildered	7"	London	HL8158	1955	**£8**	
If I Ever Fall In Love	7"	London	HLU8189	1955	**£8**	
No One To Blame But You	7"	London	HLU8296	1956	**£6**	
Teach Me Tonight	7"	London	HL8104	1954	**£8**	chart single

DE DANANN

De Danann	LP	Decca	SKL5287	1977	**£20**	

DE GALLIER, ZION

Dream Dream Dream	7"	Parlophone	R5710	1968	**£5**	
Winter Will Be Cold	7"	Parlophone	R5686	1968	**£6**	

DE LORY, AL

Yesterday	7"	London	HLU9999	1965	**£8**	

DE SHANNON, JACKIE

Breakin' It Up On The Beatles Tour	LP	Liberty	LRP3390	1964	**£20**	US
C'Mon Let's Live A Little	LP	Liberty	LRP3430	1966	**£10**	US
Come On Down	7"	Liberty	LIB66224	1966	**£10**	
Dancing Silhouettes	7"	Liberty	LIB10165	1964	**£4**	
Don't Turn Your Back On Me	LP	Liberty	LBY1245	1965	**£12**	
Don't Turn Your Back On Me	7"	Liberty	LIB10175	1964	**£4**	
In The Wind	LP	Imperial	LP9296	1965	**£10**	US
Jackie	7" EP	Liberty	LEP2233	1965	**£5**	
Jackie DeShannon	LP	Liberty	LRP3320	1963	**£15**	US
Needles And Pins	7"	Liberty	LIB55563	1963	**£5**	
She Don't Understand Him Like I Do	7"	Liberty	LIB10192	1965	**£4**	
This Is Jackie DeShannon	LP	Imperial	LP9286	1965	**£10**	US
What The World Needs Now	7"	Liberty	LIB10202	1965	**£4**	
When You Walk In The Room	7"	Liberty	LIB55645	1964	**£5**	
You Won't Forget Me	LP	Imperial	LP9294	1965	**£10**	US
You Won't Forget Me	7"	Liberty	LIB55497	1962	**£4**	

DE VORZON, BARRY

Barbara Jean	7"	RCA	RCA1066	1958	**£20**	B side by Jimmy Bell

DEACON BLUE

Chocolate Girl (US Remix)	7"	CBS	DEACEP6	1988	**£5**	
Chocolate Girl	CD-s	CBS	CDDEAC6	1988	**£6**	
Chocolate Girl	12"	CBS	DEACT6	1988	**£6**	
Dignity	CD-s	CBS	CDDEAC4	1988	**£6**	
Dignity	7"	CBS	DEAC1	1987	**£4**	
Dignity	7"	CBS	DEAC1	1987	**£6**	with cassette XPC4011
Dignity	12"	CBS	DEACT1	1987	**£8**	
Dignity	12"	CBS	DEACT4	1988	**£6**	
Dignity	10"	CBS	DEACQ4	1988	**£10**	
Fergus Sings The Blues	7"	CBS	DEACB9	1989	**£5**	boxed set

Loaded	7"	CBS	DEAC2	1987	**£4**	
Loaded	12"	CBS	DEACT2	1987	**£6**	
Raintown/Riches	LP	CBS	4505491/XPR1361	1988	**£30**	double
When Will You	7"	CBS	DEAC3	1987	**£4**	
When Will You	12"	CBS	DEACT3	1987	**£8**	
When Will You Make My Telephone Ring	CD-s	CBS	CPDEAC5	1988	**£6**	pic disc
When Will You Make My Telephone Ring	7"	CBS	DEAC5	1988	**£4**	
When Will You Make My Telephone Ring	7"	CBS	DEACB5	1988	**£10**	boxed set
When Will You Make My Telephone Ring	12"	CBS	DEACT5	1988	**£6**	

DEAD BOYS

Sonic Reducer	7"	Sire	SRE1004	1977	**£5**	no PS
Sonic Reducer	12"	Sire	6078609	1977	**£15**	
Tell Me	7"	Sire	SRE1029	1978	**£8**	
We Have Come For Your Children	LP	Sire	SRK6054	1978	**£12**	
Young Loud And Snotty	LP	Sire	9103329	1977	**£12**	

DEAD KENNEDYS

Kill The Poor	7"	Cherry Red	CHERRY16	1980	**£4**	with badge

DEAD OR ALIVE

I'd Do Anything	10"	Epic	QA4069	1984	**£5**	
I'm Falling	7"	Inevitable	INEV005	1980	**£20**	
Misty Circles	7"	Epic	A3399	1983	**£8**	
Misty Circles	7"	Epic	WA3399	1983	**£10**	pic disc
Nowhere To Nowhere	12"	Black Eyes	BE1	1982	**£15**	
Number Eleven	7"	Inevitable	INEV008	1981	**£8**	
Stranger	7"	Black Eyes	BE2	1982	**£12**	

DEAD SEA FRUIT

Dead Sea Fruit	LP	Camp	603001	1967	**£40**	
Kensington High Street	7"	Camp	602001	1967	**£8**	
Love At The Hippiedrome	7"	Camp	602004	1968	**£15**	

DEAL, BILL & THE RHONDELLS

I've Been Hurt	7"	MGM	MGM1479	1969	**£6**	

DEAN & JEAN

I Wanna Be Loved	7"	Stateside	SS313	1964	**£5**	

DEAN, ALAN & THE PROBLEMS

Thunder And Rain	7"	Pye	7N15749	1965	**£10**	
Time It Takes	7"	Decca	F11947	1964	**£12**	

DEAN, ELTON

Elton Dean (from whom Reg Dwight pinched half of his stage name) was the saxophonist with Soft Machine during the early seventies. His solo LP is very much a continuation of the same style of music.

Elton Dean	LP	CBS	64539	1971	**£20**	

DEAN, JIMMY

Best Of Jimmy Dean	7" EP	CBS	EP6075	1966	**£5**	
Big Bad John	LP	Columbia	CL1735	1962	**£15**	US
Big Bad John	7"	Philips	PB1187	1961	**£4**	chart single
Cajun Queen	7"	Philips	PB1210	1961	**£4**	
Hour Of Prayer	LP	Columbia	CL1025	1957	**£12**	US
Jimmy Dean	7" EP	Philips	BBE12501	1961	**£5**	
Little Bitty Big John	7"	CBS	AAG107	1962	**£4**	
Little Black Book	7"	CBS	AAG122	1962	**£4**	chart single
Smoke Smoke That Cigarette	7"	Philips	PB1223	1962	**£4**	
There's Still Time Brother	7"	Philips	PB984	1960	**£4**	
Weekend Blues	7"	Philips	PB940	1959	**£4**	

DEAN, PAUL & THE SOUL SAVAGES

She Can Build A Mountain	7"	Reaction	591002	1966	**£10**	

DEAN, PAUL & THE THOUGHTS

You Don't Own Me	7"	Decca	F12136	1965	**£10**	

DEARIE, BLOSSOM

I'm Hip	7"	Fontana	TF719	1966	**£4**	
Sweet Georgie Fame	7"	Fontana	TF788	1967	**£4**	

DEATH IN JUNE

Title	Format	Label	Cat. No.	Year	Price	Notes
And Murder Love	7"	New Euro	BADVC73	1985	**£12**	
And Murder Love	12"	New Euro	BADVC73T	1985	**£15**	
Born Again	12"	New Euro	BADVC69	1985	**£12**	
Heaven Street	7"	New Euro	SA29634	1984	**£20**	
Heaven Street	12"	New Euro	SA29634	1984	**£25**	
Heaven Street	12"	3 Circles		1982	**£40**	
Holy Water	7"	New Euro	SA30634	1982	**£20**	
She Said Destroy	7"	New Euro	BADVC6	1984	**£15**	
She Said Destroy	12"	New Euro	BADVC6T	1984	**£20**	
To Drown A Rose	10"	New Euro	BADVC10	1987	**£12**	

DEBONAIRES

Title	Format	Label	Cat. No.	Year	Price	Notes
Crying Behind Your Smile	7"	Pye	7N17204	1966	**£4**	
Love Of Our Own	7"	Pye	7N17151	1966	**£4**	

DEBONAIRES (2)

Title	Format	Label	Cat. No.	Year	Price	Notes
I'm In Love Again	7"	Track	604035	1970	**£4**	

DEBS

Title	Format	Label	Cat. No.	Year	Price	Notes
Sloopy's Gonna Hang On	7"	Mercury	MF888	1965	**£4**	

DECAMERON

Title	Format	Label	Cat. No.	Year	Price	Notes
Beyond The Light	LP	Mooncrest	CREST28	1975	**£10**	
Decameron	LP	Vertigo	6360097	1973	**£10**	
Mammoth Special	LP	Mooncrest	CREST19	1974	**£10**	
Third Light	LP	Transatlantic	TRA304	1975	**£10**	
Tomorrow's Pantomime	LP	Transatlantic	TRA325	1976	**£10**	

DEDICATED MEN'S JUG BAND

Title	Format	Label	Cat. No.	Year	Price	Notes
Boodle Am Shake	7"	Piccadilly	7N35245	1965	**£4**	
Don't Come Knocking	7"	Piccadilly	7N35283	1966	**£4**	

DEE DEE

Title	Format	Label	Cat. No.	Year	Price	Notes
Love Is Always	7"	Palette	PB25579	1968	**£20**	

DEE SET

Title	Format	Label	Cat. No.	Year	Price	Notes
I Know A Place	7"	Blue Cat	BS146	196-	**£10**	

DEE, JEANNIE

Title	Format	Label	Cat. No.	Year	Price	Notes
Don't Come Home My Little Darling	7"	Beacon	BEA142	1969	**£5**	

DEE, JOEY & THE STARLIGHTERS

Title	Format	Label	Cat. No.	Year	Price	Notes
All The World Is Twistin'	LP	Roulette	R25171	1962	**£12**	US
Back To The Peppermint Lounge Twistin'	LP	Roulette	R25173	1962	**£12**	US
Dance Dance Dance	7"	Columbia	DB7102	1963	**£4**	
Dance, Dance, Dance	LP	Roulette	R25221	1963	**£10**	US
Doin' The Twist	LP	Columbia	33SX1406	1961	**£15**	
Fannie Mae	7"	Columbia	DB4862	1962	**£4**	
Hey Let's Twist	7"	Columbia	DB4803	1962	**£4**	
Hey Let's Twist	LP	Roulette	R25168	1962	**£12**	US
Hot Pastrami	7"	Columbia	DB7055	1963	**£4**	
I Lost My Baby	7"	Columbia	DB4955	1963	**£4**	
Joey Dee	LP	Roulette	R25197	1963	**£10**	US
Peppermint Twist	7"	Columbia	DB4758	1962	**£4**	chart single
Shout	7"	Columbia	DB4842	1962	**£4**	
Two Tickets To Paris	LP	Roulette	R25182	1962	**£10**	US
What Kind Of Love Is This	7"	Columbia	DB4905	1962	**£4**	

DEE, JOHNNIE

Title	Format	Label	Cat. No.	Year	Price	Notes
Frankie's Angel	7"	Columbia	DB7612	1965	**£4**	

DEE, JOHNNY

Title	Format	Label	Cat. No.	Year	Price	Notes
Sitting In The Balcony	7"	Oriole	CB1367	1957	**£15**	

DEE, KIKI

Title	Format	Label	Cat. No.	Year	Price	Notes
Baby I Don't Care	7"	Fontana	TF490	1964	**£4**	
Can't Take My Eyes Off You	7"	Fontana	TF926	1968	**£4**	
Early Night	7"	Fontana	TF394	1963	**£5**	
Excuse Me	7"	Fontana	TF870	1967	**£4**	
Great Expectations	LP	T. Motown	STML11158	1970	**£25**	

I	7"	Fontana	TF833	1967	**£4**	
I Was Only Kidding	7"	Fontana	TF414	1963	**£4**	
I'm Going Out	7"	Fontana	TF792	1967	**£4**	
I'm Kiki Dee	LP	Fontana	STL5455	1968	**£10**	
Kiki Dee	7" EP	Fontana	TE17443	1965	**£5**	
Kiki Dee In Clover	7" EP	Fontana	TE17470	1966	**£5**	
Now The Flowers Cry	7"	Fontana	TF983	1968	**£15**	
Our Day Will Come Between Mon & Sun	7"	T. Motown	TMG739	1970	**£6**	
Our Day Will Come Between Mon & Sun	7"	T. Motown	TMG739	1970	**£15**	demo
Running Out Of Fools	7"	Fontana	TF596	1965	**£4**	
That's Right Walk On By	7"	Fontana	TF443	1964	**£4**	
Why Don't I Run Away From You	7"	Fontana	TF669	1966	**£5**	

DEE, SIMON

Julie	7"	Chapter One	CH105	1969	**£4**	

DEE, TOMMY & THE TEEN TONES

Three Stars	7"	Melodisc	MEL1516	195-	**£15**	

DEEJAYS

Dimples	7"	Polydor	56034	1965	**£12**	

DEELEY, ANTHONY

Anytime Man	7"	Pama	PM728	196-	**£8**	

DEENE, CAROL

James	7"	HMV	POP1086	1962	**£4**	
Johnny Get Angry	7"	HMV	POP1027	1962	**£4**	chart single
Norman	7"	HMV	POP973	1962	**£4**	chart single
Sad Movies	7"	HMV	POP922	1961	**£4**	chart single
Some People	7"	HMV	POP1058	1962	**£4**	chart single

DEEP

Psychedelic Moods	LP	Parkway	7051	1966	**£30**	US

DEEP FEELING

Country Heir	7"	DJM	DJS10257	1972	**£4**	
Deep Feeling	LP	DJM	DJLPS419	1971	**£12**	
Do You Love Me	7"	Page One	POF23165	1970	**£4**	chart single
Do You Wanna Dance	7"	DJM	DJS10231	1971	**£4**	
Skyline Pigeon	7"	Page One	POF23177	1970	**£4**	
Sweat, Dust And Red Wine	7"	DJM	DJS10237	1972	**£4**	

DEEP FREEZE MICE

My Geraniums Are Bulletproof	LP	Mole Emb.	MOLE1	1979	**£40**	
Teenage Head In My Refrigerator	LP	Mole Emb.	MOLE2	1981	**£40**	

DEEP PURPLE

Black Night	7"	Harvest	HAR5020	1970	**£4**	chart single
Black Night	7"	Purple	PUR135	1977	**£5**	purple vinyl
Burn	7"	Purple	PUR137	1978	**£4**	chart single
Concerto For Group And Orchestra	7"	Harvest	PSR325	1970	**£10**	promo
Deep Purple Mark 2 Singles	LP	Purple	TPS3514	1979	**£12**	purple vinyl
Emmaretta	7"	Parlophone	R5763	1969	**£8**	
Fireball	LP	EMI	EJ2603440	198-	**£10**	pic disc with poster
Fireball	7"	Harvest	HAR5045	1971	**£4**	chart single
Hallelujah	7"	Harvest	HAR5006	1969	**£5**	
Hallelujah	7"	Harvest	HAR5006	1969	**£20**	promo, PS
Hush	7"	Parlophone	7XE21158	1968	**£20**	promo, PS
Hush	7"	Parlophone	R5708	1968	**£8**	
In Rock	LP	EMI	EJ2603430	198-	**£10**	pic disc with poster
Kentucky Woman	7"	Parlophone	R5745	1968	**£10**	
Machine Head	LP	EMI	EJ2603450	198-	**£10**	pic disc with poster
Machine Head	LP	Harvest	Q4SHVL7504	1974	**£15**	quad
Might Just Take Your Life	7"	Purple	PUR117	1974	**£4**	
Never Before	7"	Purple	PUR102	1972	**£4**	chart single
Shades Of Deep Purple	LP	Parlophone	PCS7055	1968	**£15**	
Shades Of Deep Purple	LP	Parlophone	PMC7055	1968	**£30**	mono
Smoke On The Water	7"	Purple	PUR132	1977	**£4**	chart single
Stormbringer	LP	W. Bros	PR42832	1975	**£15**	US quad
Strange Kind Of Woman	7"	Harvest	HAR5033	1971	**£4**	chart single
Woman From Tokyo	7"	Purple	PUR112	1973	**£4**	

Title	Format	Label	Cat. No.	Year	Price	Notes
You Keep On Moving	7"	Purple	PUR130	1976	**£4**	

DEEP RIVER BOYS

Title	Format	Label	Cat. No.	Year	Price	Notes
Deep River Boys	7" EP	HMV	7EG8133	195-	**£5**	
Deep River Boys	LP	Vik	LXA1019	1956	**£50**	US
Ezikiel Saw The Wheel	7" EP	Nixa	45EP131	1955	**£5**	
Go On Board Little Children	7" EP	Nixa	45EP113	1955	**£5**	
Itchy Twitchy Feeling	7"	HMV	POP537	1958	**£6**	
Midnight Magic	LP	Que	FLS104	1957	**£35**	US
Negro Spirituals	7" EP	HMV	7EG8445	1957	**£5**	
Not Too Old To Rock And Roll	7"	HMV	POP449	1958	**£8**	
Presenting The Deep River Boys	LP	Camden	CAL303	1956	**£35**	US
Presenting The Deep River Boys	LP	Capitol	T6050	195-	**£20**	US
Rock A Beating Boogie	7"	HMV	7M361	1956	**£8**	
Romance A La Mode	7" EP	HMV	7EG8321	1957	**£5**	
Shake Rattle And Roll	7"	HMV	7M280	1954	**£10**	
Spirituals	LP-10"	Waldorf	120	1956	**£50**	US
Spirituals And Jubilees	LP-10"	Waldorf	108	1956	**£50**	US
Sweet Mama Tree Top Tall	7"	HMV	7M174	1954	**£8**	
Swing Low Sweet Chariot	7" EP	Nixa	45EP114	1955	**£5**	
That's Right	7"	HMV	POP263	1956	**£8**	chart single
Walk Together Children	7" EP	Nixa	45EP130	1955	**£5**	
Whole Lotta Shaking Going On	7"	HMV	POP395	1957	**£10**	

DEEP SET

Title	Format	Label	Cat. No.	Year	Price	Notes
I Started A Joke	7"	Major Minor	MM607	1969	**£8**	
That's The Way Life Goes	7"	Pye	7N17594	1968	**£5**	

DEEP SIX

Title	Format	Label	Cat. No.	Year	Price	Notes
Counting	7"	Liberty	LIB55882	1966	**£4**	

DEERFIELD

Title	Format	Label	Cat. No.	Year	Price	Notes
Nil Desperandum	LP	Flat Rock			**£75**	US

DEF LEPPARD

It would be nice to think that the rise to megastardom of Def Leppard had at least something to do with the public's appreciation of the way the group stood by their drummer, Rick Allen, when he lost an arm in an accident. In any event, as with other rock stars of the eighties, Def Leppard have released a multitude of picture discs and special packages geared directly at the collector. There is also a genuine rarity (i.e. one not expressly created by the record company) in the first single, "Getcha Rocks Off", which was a private pressing running to three separate issues.

Title	Format	Label	Cat. No.	Year	Price	Notes
Animal	CD-s	Phonogram	LEPCD1	1987	**£6**	
Animal	12"	Vertigo	LEPC1	1987	**£15**	red vinyl
Armageddon It	7"	Phonogram	LEPP4	1988	**£4**	poster sleeve
Armageddon It	12"	Phonogram	LEPXB4	1988	**£6**	box, poster, bdge, 5 cards
Armageddon It	CD-s	Phonogram	LEPCD4	1988	**£6**	
Bringin' On The Heartbreak	7"	Vertigo	LEPP3	1982	**£25**	
Bringin' On The Heartbreak	12"	Vertigo	LEPP312	1982	**£15**	
Getcha Rocks Off	7"	Bludgeon R.	MSB001	1979	**£20**	no PS
Getcha Rocks Off	7"	Bludgeon R.	SRTS78CUS232	1979	**£100**	lyric insert
Getcha Rocks Off	7"	Bludgeon R.	SRTS78CUS232	1979	**£70**	without PS
Getcha Rocks Off	7"	Vertigo	6059240	1979	**£8**	no PS
Hello America	7"	Vertigo	LEPP1	1980	**£10**	
Hysteria	LP	Phonogram	HYSPD1	1987	**£15**	pic disc
Hysteria	CD-s	Phonogram	LEPCD3	1987	**£6**	numbered edition
Hysteria	7"	Phonogram	LEPS3	1987	**£4**	with patch
Hysteria	12"	Phonogram	LEPX313	1987	**£6**	envelope sleeve, poster
Let It Go	7"	Vertigo	LEPP2	1981	**£8**	
Let It Go	7"	Vertigo	LEPP2	1981	**£12**	with patch
Loves Bites	7"	Phonogram	LEPDJ5	1988	**£4**	promo
Loves Bites	7"	Phonogram	LEPG5	1988	**£4**	gatefold sleeve,8 pg insert
Loves Bites	12"	Phonogram	LEPXB5	1988	**£6**	boxed, 4 cards
Photograph	7"	Vertigo	VER5	1983	**£10**	
Photograph	7"	Vertigo	VER9	1984	**£10**	wallet PS
Photograph	7"	Vertigo	VERG9	1984	**£35**	gatefold wallet PS
Photograph	7"	Vertigo	VERP5	1983	**£20**	3-D sleeve
Photograph	7"	Vertigo	VERQ5	1983	**£20**	3-D sleeve
Photograph	12"	Vertigo	VERX5	1983	**£20**	
Photograph	12"	Vertigo	VERX9	1984	**£20**	same sleeve as VERX5
Pour Some Sugar On Me	7"	Phonogram	LEPS2	1987	**£12**	shaped pic disc
Release Me (Stumpus Maximus)	12"	Phonogram	LEPDK6	1989	**£12**	promo
Rock Of Ages	7"	Vertigo	VER6	1983	**£8**	

Title	Format	Label	Cat. No.	Year	Price	Notes
Rock Of Ages	7"	Vertigo	VERP6	1983	**£15**	shaped pic disc
Rock Of Ages	7"	Vertigo	VERQ6	1983	**£20**	cube sleeve
Rock Of Ages	12"	Vertigo	VERX6	1983	**£20**	
Rocket	7"	Phonogram	LEPC6	1989	**£5**	envelope sleeve,6 factfiles
Rocket	12"	Phonogram	LEPXP6	1989	**£6**	pic disc
Too Late For Love	7"	Vertigo	VER8	1983	**£10**	
Too Late For Love	7"	Vertigo	VER8	1983	**£35**	soccer strip PS
Too Late For Love	7"	Vertigo	VERDJ8	1983	**£6**	no PS
Too Late For Love	12"	Vertigo	VERX8	1983	**£15**	
Wasted	7"	Vertigo	6059247	1979	**£8**	
Wasted	7"	Vertigo	6059247	1979	**£5**	without PS

DEFENDERS

Title	Format	Label	Cat. No.	Year	Price	Notes
Set Them Free	7"	Doctor Bird	DB1104	1967	**£10**	
World Goes Ska	7"	Doctor Bird	DB1103	1967	**£10**	

DEKKER, DESMOND

Title	Format	Label	Cat. No.	Year	Price	Notes
007	7"	Pyramid	PYR6004	1967	**£6**	chart single
Beautiful And Dangerous	7"	Pyramid	PYR6031	1969	**£8**	
Beware	7"	Rhino	RNO107	1972	**£4**	
Busted Lad	7"	Rhino	RNO125	1974	**£4**	
Double Dekker	LP	Trojan	TRLD401	1973	**£15**	double
Everybody Join Hands	7"	Rhino	RNO121	1973	**£4**	
Get Up Edina	7"	Island	WI181	1965	**£10**	
Israelites	LP	Cactus	CTLP111	1975	**£10**	
Israelites	7"	Cactus	CT57	1975	**£4**	chart single
Israelites	7"	Pyramid	PYR6058	1969	**£5**	chart single
It Mek	7"	Pyramid	PYR6068	1969	**£5**	chart single
It Pays	7"	Pyramid	PYR6026	1969	**£8**	
Mother's Young Gal	7"	Pyramid	PYR6012	1967	**£8**	
Pickney Girl	7"	Pyramid	PYR6078	1970	**£5**	chart single
Pickney Girl	7"	Trojan	TRM9009	1973	**£4**	
Sabotage	7"	Pyramid	PYR6020	1967	**£8**	
Sing A Little Song	7"	Rhino	RNO115	1973	**£4**	
This Is Desmond Dekker	LP	Trojan	TTL4	1969	**£15**	chart LP
This Woman	7"	Island	WI202	1965	**£10**	
Unity	7"	Pyramid	PYR6017	1967	**£8**	
You Can Get It	LP	Trojan	TRL146	1970	**£15**	
You Can Get It If You Really Want	7"	Trojan	TR7777	1970	**£4**	chart single

DEKKER, DESMOND & DON DRUMMOND

Title	Format	Label	Cat. No.	Year	Price	Notes
Dracula	7"	Black Swan	WI455	1965	**£10**	

DEL AMITRI

Title	Format	Label	Cat. No.	Year	Price	Notes
Sense Sickness	7"	No Strings	NOSP1	1983	**£15**	

DEL CANTOS

Title	Format	Label	Cat. No.	Year	Price	Notes
Feel Alright	7"	R&B	MRB5003	1965	**£4**	

DEL SATINS

Title	Format	Label	Cat. No.	Year	Price	Notes
Out To Lunch	LP	B.T.Puppy	BTPS1019	1972	**£20**	US

DEL VIKINGS

Title	Format	Label	Cat. No.	Year	Price	Notes
Angel Up In Heaven	7"	HMV	POP1145	1963	**£4**	
Come Go With Me	LP	Contour	2870388	197-	**£10**	
Come Go With Me	LP	Dot	DLP3695	1966	**£75**	US
Come Go With Me	7"	London	HLD8405	1957	**£15**	
Come Go With The Del Vikings	LP	Luniverse	LP1000	1957	**£180**	US
Confession Of Love	7"	HMV	POP1072	1962	**£4**	
Del Vikings And The Sonnets	LP	Crown	CLP5368	1963	**£20**	US
Flat Tyre	7"	Mercury	AMT1027	1959	**£8**	
Swinging, Singing Record Session	LP	Mercury	MG20353	1958	**£100**	US
They Sing They Swing	LP	Mercury	MG20314	1957	**£100**	US
Voodoo Man	7"	Mercury	7MT199	1958	**£10**	
Whispering Bells	7"	London	HLD8464	1957	**£10**	

DELACARDOS

Title	Format	Label	Cat. No.	Year	Price	Notes
Mister Dillon	7"	HMV	POP890	1961	**£8**	

DELANEY & BONNIE

The sense of well-being and fun that spills over from Delaney and Bonnie's records attracted some famous names to their cause - George Harrison, Dave Mason, and Eric Clapton were all perfectly content to play as sidemen within the band for a while. The LP "Accept No Substitute" was to have appeared on the Apple label, but was released on Elektra in ther end. Apple test pressings exist, but no cover has ever been found. Meanwhile, Eric Clapton's thrilling contributions to the Delaney and Bonnie sound can be sampled on the LP "On Tour".

Title	Format	Label	Cat. No.	Year	Price	Notes
Accept No Substitute	LP	Apple	SAPCOR7	1969	**£400**	test pressing, no sleeve
Accept No Substitute	LP	Elektra	K42024	1971	**£12**	
Comin' Home	7"	Atlantic	584308	1969	**£4**	chart single
Country Life	LP	Atco	33383	1971	**£10**	US
Free The People	7"	Atlantic	2091016	1970	**£4**	
Genesis	LP	London	ZGL113	1971	**£10**	
Get Ourselves Together	7"	Elektra	EKSN45072	1969	**£5**	
Home	LP	Stax	2362001	1974	**£12**	
Motel Shot	LP	Atco	33358	1971	**£10**	US
On Tour	LP	Atlantic	2400013	1970	**£15**	chart LP
Someday	7"	Elektra	EKSN45078	1969	**£4**	
To Bonnie From Delaney	LP	Atlantic	2400029	1970	**£10**	
Together	LP	CBS	64959	1972	**£10**	

DELFONICS

Title	Format	Label	Cat. No.	Year	Price	Notes
Didn't I (Blow Your Mind This Time)	7"	Bell	BLL1099	1970	**£4**	chart single
La La Means I Love You	LP	Bell	SBLL106	1968	**£10**	
La-La Means I Love You	7"	Bell	BLL1005	1968	**£5**	
La-La Means I Love You	7"	Bell	BLL1165	1971	**£4**	chart single
Ready or Not (Here I Come)	7"	Bell	BLL1042	1968	**£4**	

DELICATES

Title	Format	Label	Cat. No.	Year	Price	Notes
Ronnie Is My Lover	7"	London	HLT8953	1959	**£15**	
Too Young To Date	7"	London	HLT9176	1960	**£10**	

DELICATESSEN

Title	Format	Label	Cat. No.	Year	Price	Notes
Red Baron's Revenge	7"	Vocalion	VN9286	1967	**£4**	

DELL, JIMMY

Title	Format	Label	Cat. No.	Year	Price	Notes
Teenage Tops	7" EP	RCA	RCX111	1958	**£12**	

DELLO, PETE

Title	Format	Label	Cat. No.	Year	Price	Notes
Into Your Ears	LP	Nepentha	6437001	1971	**£40**	

DELLOS & OTHERS

Title	Format	Label	Cat. No.	Year	Price	Notes
Twist Off	7" EP	Starlite	STEP31	196-	**£30**	

DELLS

Title	Format	Label	Cat. No.	Year	Price	Notes
Always Together	7"	Chess	CRS8084	1969	**£4**	
Bossa Nova Bird	7"	Pye	7N25178	1963	**£5**	
Dock Of The Bay	7"	Chess	CRS8105	1970	**£4**	
It's Not Unusual	7"	President	PT223	1968	**£4**	
It's Not Unusual	LP	Vee Jay	LP1141	1965	**£12**	US
Oh What A Day	7"	Chess	CRS8107	1970	**£4**	
Oh What A Night	7"	Chess	CRS8102	1970	**£4**	
Oh What A Night	7"	President	PT270	1969	**£5**	
Oh What A Nite	LP	Vee Jay	VJLP1010	1959	**£100**	US
Oo I Love You	7"	Chess	CRS8066	1967	**£4**	
Sing A Rainbow/Love Is Blue	7"	Chess	CRS8099	1969	**£4**	chart single
Stay In My Corner	7"	Chess	CRS8079	1968	**£6**	
Wear It On Our Face	7"	Chess	CRS8071	1968	**£6**	

DELMORE BROTHERS

Title	Format	Label	Cat. No.	Year	Price	Notes
Country And Western	7" EP	Parlophone	GEP8728	1958	**£12**	
In Memory	LP	King	910	1964	**£15**	US
In Memory Vol.2	LP	King	920	1964	**£15**	US
Songs By The Delmore Brothers	LP	King	589	1958	**£30**	US
Thirtieth Anniversary Album	LP	King	785	1962	**£25**	US
Twenty-Four Great Country Songs	LP	King	983	1966	**£15**	US

DELTA CATS

Title	Format	Label	Cat. No.	Year	Price	Notes
Unworthy Baby	7"	Blue Cat	BS128	1968	**£10**	

DELTA KINGS

Title	Format	Label	Cat. No.	Year	Price	Notes
At Sundown	7" EP	London	RER1318	1961	**£5**	

DELTA RHYTHM BOYS

Title	Format	Label	Cat. No.	Year	Price	Notes
Mood Indigo	7"	Brunswick	05353	1954	**£5**	

DELTA SKIFFLE GROUP

Title	Format	Label	Cat. No.	Year	Price	Notes
Delta Skiffle Group	7" EP	Esquire	EP162	195-	**£5**	

DELTAS

Title	Format	Label	Cat. No.	Year	Price	Notes
Visitor	7"	Blue Beat	BB275	1964	**£10**	

DELTONES

Title	Format	Label	Cat. No.	Year	Price	Notes
Rocking Blues	7"	Top Rank	JAR171	1959	**£15**	

DEMENSIONS

Title	Format	Label	Cat. No.	Year	Price	Notes
Count Your Blessings Instead Of Sheep	7"	Coral	Q72437	1961	**£4**	
Over The Rainbow	7"	Top Rank	JAR505	1960	**£4**	

DEMIAN (BUBBLE PUPPY)

Title	Format	Label	Cat. No.	Year	Price	Notes
Demian	LP	ABC	S718	1971	**£15**	

DEMICK & ARMSTRONG

Title	Format	Label	Cat. No.	Year	Price	Notes
Little Willie Ramble	LP	MAM	MAM1001	1971	**£10**	
Looking Through	LP	A&M	AMLH68098	1972	**£10**	

DEMON FUZZ

Title	Format	Label	Cat. No.	Year	Price	Notes
Afreaka	LP	Dawn	DNLS3013	1971	**£15**	
I Put A Spell On You	7"	Dawn	DNX2504	1970	**£5**	

DEMON PREACHER

Title	Format	Label	Cat. No.	Year	Price	Notes
Little Miss Perfect	7"	Small Wond.	SMALL10	1978	**£6**	
Royal Northern	7"	Illegal	SRTS78110	1978	**£8**	

DEMONS

Title	Format	Label	Cat. No.	Year	Price	Notes
Bless You	7"	Big Shot	BI523	1973	**£5**	

DENE, TERRY

Title	Format	Label	Cat. No.	Year	Price	Notes
Bimbombey	7"	Decca	F11100	1959	**£4**	
Come And Get It	7"	Decca	F10938	1957	**£6**	
Come In And Be Loved	7"	Decca	F10977	1958	**£5**	
Feminine Look	7"	Aral	PS107	1963	**£4**	
Feminine Look	7"	Aral	PS107	1963	**£8**	PS
Geraldine	7"	Oriole	CB1562	1960	**£4**	
Golden Disc	7" EP	Decca	DFE6459	1958	**£10**	
I Thought Terry Dene Was Dead	LP	Decca	SPA368	1974	**£10**	
I've Come Of Age	7"	Decca	F11136	1959	**£4**	
Like A Baby	7"	Oriole	CB1594	1961	**£5**	
Lucky Lucky Bobby	7"	Decca	F10964	1957	**£6**	
Pretty Little Pearly	7"	Decca	F11076	1958	**£4**	
Seven Steps To Love	7"	Decca	F11037	1958	**£4**	
Stairway Of Love	7"	Decca	F11016	1958	**£5**	chart single
Start Moving	7"	Decca	F10914	1957	**£6**	chart single
Terry Dene No.1	7" EP	Decca	DFE6507	1958	**£8**	
Terry Dene Now	7" EP	Herald	ELR107	1966	**£5**	
Thank You Pretty Baby	7"	Decca	F11154	1959	**£4**	
White Sports Coat	7"	Decca	F10895	1957	**£6**	chart single

DENIMS

Title	Format	Label	Cat. No.	Year	Price	Notes
I'm Your Man	7"	CBS	201807	1965	**£8**	

DENISON, ROGER

Title	Format	Label	Cat. No.	Year	Price	Notes
I'm On An Island	7"	Parlophone	R5545	1966	**£10**	
She Wanders Through My Mind	7"	Parlophone	R5566	1967	**£8**	

DENIZ, HERMANOS

Title	Format	Label	Cat. No.	Year	Price	Notes
Mambo Hoo	7"	Melodisc	CAL13	196-	**£6**	

DENNIS, DENZIL

Title	Format	Label	Cat. No.	Year	Price	Notes
Donkey Train	7"	Trojan	TR614	1968	**£8**	
Hush Don't You Cry	7"	Trojan	TR615	1968	**£8**	
Oh Carol	7"	Jolly	JY011	196-	**£8**	

DENNIS, JACKIE

Title	Format	Label	Cat. No.	Year	Price	Notes
Gingerbread	7"	Decca	F11090	1958	**£4**	
Jackie Dennis No.1	7" EP	Decca	DFE6513	1958	**£6**	
La Dee Dah	7"	Decca	F10992	1958	**£5**	chart single
Miss Valerie	7"	Decca	F11011	1958	**£4**	

More Than Ever	7"	Decca	F11060	1958	**£4**	
Purple People Eater	7"	Decca	F11033	1958	**£5**	chart single

DENNISONS

Be My Girl	7"	Decca	F11691	1963	**£8**	chart single
Nobody Like My Babe	7"	Decca	F11990	1964	**£6**	
Walking The Dog	7"	Decca	F11880	1964	**£6**	chart single

DENNY, SANDY

Sandy Denny was something of a limited singer: hopeless on uptempo rock material, she nevertheless sounded gorgeous on a slow ballad - as her recording of "The Sea" with Fotheringay proves at a stroke. The small number of early, pre-Fairport Convention tracks are spread somewhat thinly over various LPs. The album with Johnny Silvo, for example, is not a collaboration, but merely includes songs recorded by each separately. The Strawbs LP, however, is a true joint effort.

Like An Old Fashioned Waltz	LP	Island	ILPS9258	1973	**£20**	
Listen Listen	7"	Island	WIP6142	1972	**£4**	
Make Me A Pallet On Your Floor	7"	Mooncrest	MOON54	1976	**£4**	
Northstar Grass Man & The Ravens	LP	Island	ILPS9165	1971	**£20**	chart LP
Pass Of Arms EP	7"	Island	WIP6141	1972	**£15**	PS
Rendezvous	LP	Island	ILPS9433	1977	**£12**	
Sandy	LP	Island	ILPS9207	1972	**£20**	
Sandy Denny	LP	Mooncrest	CREST28	1978	**£20**	1 extra track
Sandy Denny	LP	Saga	EROS8153	1970	**£30**	
Whispering Grass	7"	Island	WIP6176	1973	**£6**	PS

DENNY, SANDY & JOHNNY SILVO

Sandy And Johnny	LP	Saga	EROS8041	1967	**£30**	

DENNY, SANDY & STRAWBS

All Our Own Work	LP	Pickwick	SHM813	1968	**£12**	

DENVER, KARL

By A Sleepy Lagoon	7" EP	Decca	DFE8501	1962	**£4**	
Karl Denver Hits	7" EP	Decca	DFE8504	1962	**£4**	
Wimoweh	LP	Decca	ACL1098	1961	**£15**	chart LP
Wimoweh	7"	Decca	F11420	1962	**£4**	chart single

DENVER, NIGEL

Folk, Old And New	LP	Decca	SKL4943	1968	**£10**	
Rebellion	LP	Decca	SKL4844	1967	**£10**	

DENZIL & PAT

Dream	7"	Downtown	DT403	196-	**£8**	

DEPECHE MODE

Behind The Wheel (Beatmasters Mix)	12"	Mute	L12BONG15	1988	**£6**	
Dreaming Of Me	7"	Mute	MUTE013	1981	**£4**	chart single
Enjoy The Silence	12"	Mute	P12BONG18	1990	**£6**	promo
Enjoy The Silence	12"	Mute	XL12BONG18	1990	**£6**	1 sided
Everything Counts (Absolute Mix)	10"	Mute	10BONG16	1989	**£6**	
Everything Counts (Bomb The Bass Mix)	12"	Mute	L12BONG16	1989	**£6**	
Everything Counts	12"	Mute	L12BONG3	1983	**£8**	
Get The Balance Right	12"	Mute	L12BONG2	1983	**£8**	
It's Called A Heart	12"	Mute	D12BONG9	1985	**£6**	double
Little 15	12"	Mute	12LITTLE15	1988	**£8**	
Love In Itself	12"	Mute	L12BONG4	1983	**£8**	
Master And Servant	12"	Mute	L12BONG6	1984	**£8**	
Music For The Masses	LP	Mute	STUMM47	1987	**£10**	clear vinyl
Music For The Masses	LP	Mute	STUMM47	1987	**£12**	HMV Ltd.ed. with 12"
Never Let Me Down...(Tsangarides Mix)	12"	Mute	L12BONG14	1987	**£6**	
Never Let Me Down Again	CD-s	Mute	CDBONG14	1987	**£6**	
Never Let Me Down Again	cass-s	Mute	CBONG14	1987	**£6**	
People Are People (On U Sound Mix)	12"	Mute	L12BONG5	1984	**£8**	
Personal Jesus (Pump Mix)	12"	Mute	L12BONG17	1989	**£6**	
Personal Jesus	cass-s	Mute	PCBONG17	1989	**£12**	4 track promo
Personal Jesus	7"	Mute	7GBONG17	1989	**£4**	3 tracks
Personal Jesus	12"	Mute	P12BONG17	1989	**£8**	promo
Question Of Lust	cass-s	Mute	CBONG11	1986	**£5**	with book & badge
Question Of Time (New Town Mix)	12"	Mute	L12BONG12	1986	**£6**	
Shake The Disease (Edit The Shake)	12"	Mute	L12BONG8	1985	**£8**	
Sometimes I Wish I Was Dead	7"	Lyntone	LYN10209	1981	**£8**	Flexipop flexi
Strangelove (Blind Mix)	12"	Mute	L12BONG13	1987	**£6**	
Stripped	12"	Mute	12BONG10	1986	**£8**	promo

DEPUTIES

Title	Format	Label	Number	Year	Price	Notes
Given Half A Chance	7"	Strike	JH305	1966	**£5**	

DEREK & THE DOMINOES

Title	Format	Label	Number	Year	Price	Notes
Layla	7"	Polydor	2058130	1971	**£4**	chart single
Tell The Truth	7"	Polydor	2058057	1970	**£25**	
Why Does Love Got To Be So Sad	7"	RSO	2090104	1974	**£4**	

DEREK & THE FRESHMEN

Title	Format	Label	Number	Year	Price	Notes
Gone Away	7"	Oriole	CB305	1965	**£5**	

DERRICK & THE SOUNDS

Title	Format	Label	Number	Year	Price	Notes
Morning Papers	7"	Pye	7N17801	1969	**£5**	
My Guitar	7"	Hit	HIT10		**£4**	
My Sly Sadie	7"	Pye	7N17709	1969	**£5**	
Power Of Love	7"	Pye	7N17601	1968	**£5**	

DESANTO, SUGAR PIE

Title	Format	Label	Number	Year	Price	Notes
I Don't Wanna Fuss	7"	Pye	7N25267	1964	**£8**	
Soulful Dress	7"	Chess	CRS8093	1969	**£4**	
Soulful Dress	7"	Pye	7N25249	1964	**£8**	
Sugar Pie	LP	Checker	LP2979	1961	**£25**	US
There's Gonna Be Trouble	7"	Chess	CRS8034	1966	**£6**	

DESIGN

Title	Format	Label	Number	Year	Price	Notes
Colour All The World	7"	Regal Z.	RZ3044	1972	**£4**	
Day Of The Fox	LP	Regal Z.	SLRZ1037	1973	**£10**	
End Of The Party	7"	Regal Z.	RZ3082	1973	**£4**	
Mayday	7"	Regal Z.	RZ3060	1972	**£4**	

DESMOND, ANDY

Title	Format	Label	Number	Year	Price	Notes
Beware	7"	Konk	KOS4	1975	**£4**	
Living On A Shoe String	LP	Konk	KONK103	1975	**£15**	
So It Goes	7"	Konk	KOS2	1975	**£4**	

DESPERATE BICYCLES

Title	Format	Label	Number	Year	Price	Notes
Medium Was Tedium	7"	Refill	RR2	1978	**£4**	
New Cross New Cross	7"	Refill	RR3	1978	**£4**	
Occupied Territory	7"	Refill	RR4	1978	**£4**	
Remorse Code	LP	Refill	RR6	1980	**£15**	
Smokescreen	7"	Refill	RR1	1977	**£4**	

DESSIE & JOHN

Title	Format	Label	Number	Year	Price	Notes
Boss Sound	7"	Downtown	DT440	196-	**£8**	

DESTROY ALL MONSTERS

Title	Format	Label	Number	Year	Price	Notes
Bored	7"	Cherry Red	CHERRY3	1979	**£4**	
Bored	7"	Cherry Red	CHERRY3	1979	**£5**	red vinyl
Meet The Creeper	7"	Cherry Red	CHERRY7	1979	**£4**	
What Do I Get?	7"	Cherry Red	CHERRY9	1979	**£4**	

DETERGENTS

Title	Format	Label	Number	Year	Price	Notes
I Don't Know	7"	Columbia	DB7591	1965	**£6**	
Leader Of The Laundromat	7"	Columbia	DB7513	1965	**£8**	
Many Faces Of The Detergents	LP	Roulette	R25308	1965	**£15**	US

DETOURS

Title	Format	Label	Number	Year	Price	Notes
Run To Me Baby	7"	CBS	3213	1968	**£4**	
Whole Lotta Lovin'	7"	CBS	3401	1968	**£4**	

DETROIT SPINNERS

Title	Format	Label	Number	Year	Price	Notes
Detroit Spinners	LP	T. Motown	STML11060	1968	**£20**	
For All We Know	7"	T. Motown	TMG627	1967	**£6**	
For All We Know	7"	T. Motown	TMG627	1967	**£40**	demo
I'll Always Love You	7"	T. Motown	TMG523	1965	**£15**	
I'll Always Love You	7"	T. Motown	TMG523	1965	**£50**	demo
Sweet Thing	7"	T. Motown	TMG514	1965	**£20**	
Sweet Thing	7"	T. Motown	TMG514	1965	**£50**	demo
Together We Can Make Sweet Music	7"	T. Motown	TMG871	1973	**£8**	demo

DEUCE COUP

Title	Format	Label	Number	Year	Price	Notes
Clown In Town	7"	Mercury	MF1013	1967	**£4**	

DEUCE OF HEARTS

Closer Together	7"	CBS	202345	1966	**£4**	

DEVIANTS

The Deviants, masterminded (if the word is appropriate to such a chaotic organisation) by Mick Farren, were more about social revolution than about music. Pieces like "Let's Loot The Supermarket" describe the group's stance, although they were too disorganised and too full of drugs and alcohol to have ever achieved even this much of a blow against society. Amazingly, many of the original group members managed to continue with some kind of career in rock music - Farren with new versions of the Deviants (and he also became a successful writer) and Duncan Sanderson, Russ Hunter, and Paul Rudolph with the Pink Fairies.

Deviants	LP	Transatlantic	TRA204	1969	**£30**	
Disposable	LP	Stable	SLP7001	1968	**£30**	
Ptooff	LP	Decca	SKLR4993	1969	**£30**	
Ptooff	LP	U. Impress.	IMP1	1967	**£60**	
Screwed Up	7"	Stiff	LAST4	197-	**£4**	
You've Got To Hold On	7"	Stable	STA5601	1968	**£15**	

DEVO

Be Stiff	7"	Booji Boy	BOY2	1978	**£4**	
Be Stiff	7"	Booji Boy	BOY2	1978	**£5**	clear or yellow vinyl
Be Stiff	12"	Stiff	ODD1	1978	**£8**	white vinyl
Jocko Homo	7"	Booji Boy	DEV1	1978	**£6**	
Q:Are We Not Men?	LP	Virgin	VP2106	1978	**£10**	pic disc
Satisfaction	7"	Booji Boy	BOY1	1977	**£5**	
Satisfaction	12"	Booji Boy	BOY1	1977	**£8**	white sleeve with sticker

DEVON

Making Love	7"	New Beat	NB021	1968	**£8**	
What A Sin Thing	7"	Blue Cat	BS158	196-	**£10**	

DEVONNES

I'm Gonna Pick Up My Toys	7"	UK	USA5	1975	**£5**	

DEVOTED

I Love George Best	7"	Page One	POF076	1968	**£4**	

DEVOTIONS

For Sentimental Reasons	7"	Columbia	DB7256	1964	**£4**	

DEW DROPS

Somebody Is Knocking	7"	Blue Beat	BB381	1965	**£10**	

DEXTER, DANNY

Sweet Mama	7"	London	HLU9690	1963	**£4**	

DEXTER, RAY & THE LAYABOUTS

Coalman's Lament	7"	Decca	F11538	1962	**£5**	

DEXY'S MIDNIGHT RUNNERS

Celtic Soul Brothers	7"	Mercury	DEXYSDJ8	1981	**£4**	1 sided promo
Come On Eileen	7"	Mercury	DEXYSDJ9	1982	**£4**	1 sided promo
Dance Stance	7"	Parlophone	R6028	1979	**£4**	chart single
Dance Stance	7"	Parlophone	R6028DJ	1979	**£10**	promo
Keep It Part Two	7"	Parlophone	R6042	1980	**£4**	
Plan B	7"	Parlophone	R6046	1981	**£4**	chart single

DHARMA BLUES

The music of the Dharma Blues is a reasonably faithful copy of the country blues - piano and harmonica to the fore - but suffers badly from the perennial problem of white blues records; the vocals are totally unconvincing. The sleeve notes go on at length about how exciting the music is and how relevant it is to the present age, but in truth these versions of some well-known traditional songs are a bit boring. That anyone should be willing to pay a substantial collectors' price for the record, when for a fraction of the price they could buy a good compilation of music by the likes of Memphis Slim or Sonny Terry & Brownie McGhee, is one of the mysteries of record collecting.

Dharma Blues	LP	Major Minor	SMCP5017	1969	**£60**	

DIALOGUE

Dialogue	LP	Cold Studio		1968	**£130**	
Dialogue	LP	Cold Studio		1974	**£90**	

DIALS

Love Is A Treasure	7"	Duke	DU49	196-	**£8**	

DIAMOND HEAD

Title	Format	Label	Cat. No.	Year	Price	Notes
Diamond Lights	12"	Windsong	DHM005	1981	**£6**	
Kingmaker	7"	MCA	DHMP104	1983	**£4**	pic disc
Lightning To The Nations	LP			1981	**£25**	white label
Living On Borrowed Time	LP	MCA	DH1001	1981	**£15**	
Shoot Out the Lights	7"	Happy Face	MMDH120	1980	**£5**	

DIAMOND, BRIAN & THE CUTTERS

Title	Format	Label	Cat. No.	Year	Price	Notes
Big Bad Wolf	7"	Pye	7N15779	1965	**£8**	
Bone Idol	7"	Pye	7N15952	1965	**£6**	
Jealousy Will Get You Nowhere	7"	Decca	F11724	1963	**£8**	
Shake Shout And Go	7"	Fontana	TF452	1964	**£8**	

DIAMOND, NEIL

Title	Format	Label	Cat. No.	Year	Price	Notes
Beautiful Noise	LP	CBS	Q86004	1976	**£10**	quad
Brother Love's Travelling Salvation Show	LP	Uni	UNLS107	1969	**£10**	
Cherry Cherry	7"	London	HLZ10072	1966	**£4**	
Feel Of Neil Diamond	LP	London	HAZ8307	1966	**£10**	
Girl You'll Be A Woman Soon	7"	London	HLZ10126	1967	**£4**	
Heartlight	12"	Columbia	AS991586	1982	**£10**	US 1 sided promo pic disc
Hot August Night	LP	Mobile Fid.	MFSL2024	1980	**£15**	US audiophile
I Got The Feelin'	7"	London	HLZ10092	1966	**£4**	
Jazz Singer	LP	Mobile Fid.	MFSL2071	1982	**£10**	US audiophile
Jonathan Livingstone Seagull	LP	Columbia	HC42550	1981	**£10**	US audiophile
Just For You	LP	London		1967	**£10**	
Kentucky Woman	7"	London	HLZ10161	1967	**£4**	
New Orleans	7"	London	HLZ10177	1968	**£4**	
Open Ended Interview	LP	Uni	LP1913	1968	**£20**	US promo
Red Red Wine	7"	London	HLZ10187	1968	**£4**	
Serenade	LP	CBS	Q69067	1974	**£10**	quad
Solitary Man	7"	London	HLZ10049	1966	**£4**	
Thank The Lord For The Night Time	7"	London	HLZ10151	1967	**£4**	
Touching Me Touching You	LP	Uni	UNLS110	1969	**£10**	
Twenty Golden Greats Sampler	7"	MCA	PSR434	1978	**£5**	promo
Velvet Gloves And Spit	LP	Uni	UNLS106	1968	**£10**	
You Don't Bring Me Flowers	LP	Columbia	HC45625	1980	**£10**	US audiophile
You Got To Me	7"	London	HLZ10111	1967	**£4**	

DIAMONDS

Title	Format	Label	Cat. No.	Year	Price	Notes
Black Denim Trousers & Motorcycle Boots	7"	Vogue Coral	Q72109	1955	**£20**	
Collection Of Golden Hits	LP	Mercury	MG20213	1956	**£25**	US
Diamonds	LP	Mercury	MG20309	1958	**£20**	US
Diamonds	LP	Wing	MGW12114	1958	**£15**	US
Diamonds Are Trumps	7" EP	Mercury	ZEP10026	1959	**£10**	
Diamonds Meet Pete Rugulo	LP	Mercury	MG20368	1958	**£15**	US
Diamonds Meet Pete Rugulo	7" EP	Mercury	ZEP10020	1959	**£8**	
Diamonds Vol.1	7" EP	Mercury	MEP9523	1957	**£15**	
Diamonds Vol.2	7" EP	Mercury	MEP9527	1958	**£15**	
Diamonds Vol.3	7" EP	Mercury	MEP9530	1958	**£15**	
Dig The Diamonds	7" EP	Mercury	ZEP10003	1959	**£12**	
Eternal Lovers	7"	Mercury	AMT1004	1958	**£8**	
High Sign	7"	Mercury	7MT207	1958	**£12**	
Kathy O	7"	Mercury	7MT233	1958	**£8**	
Little Darlin'	78	Mercury	7MT148	1957	**£5**	chart single
One Summer Night	7"	Mercury	AMT1156	1961	**£8**	
Pop Hits By The Diamonds	LP	Wing	MGW12178	1959	**£15**	US
Presenting The Diamonds	7" EP	Mercury	MEP9515	1957	**£15**	
She Say Oom Dooby Oom	7"	Mercury	AMT1024	1959	**£8**	
Silhouettes	7"	Mercury	7MT187	1958	**£15**	
Star Studded Diamonds	7" EP	Mercury	ZEP10053	1960	**£12**	
Straight Skirts	7"	Mercury	7MT208	1958	**£12**	
Stroll	7"	Mercury	7MT195	1958	**£12**	
Tell The Truth	7"	Mercury	AMT1086	1960	**£8**	

DIAMONDS (2)

Title	Format	Label	Cat. No.	Year	Price	Notes
Lost City	7"	Philips	BF1264	1963	**£4**	

DIAMONDS & BEN HEWITT

Title	Format	Label	Cat. No.	Year	Price	Notes
Surprise Package	7" EP	Mercury	ZEP10088	1960	**£12**	

DIANE & THE JAVELINS

Title	Format	Label	Number	Year	Price	Notes
Heart And Soul	7"	Columbia	DB7819	1966	**£6**	

DICE THE BOSS

Title	Format	Label	Number	Year	Price	Notes
But Officer	7"	Duke	DU52	196-	**£8**	
Gun The Man Down	7"	Duke	DU51	196-	**£8**	

DICKENS

Title	Format	Label	Number	Year	Price	Notes
Standing Out	LP	Hawkmoon		197-	**£40**	

DICKENS, CHARLES

Title	Format	Label	Number	Year	Price	Notes
I Stand Alone	7"	Pye	7N15938	1965	**£5**	
So Much In Love	7"	Immediate	IM025	1966	**£8**	
That's The Way Love Goes	7"	Pye	7N15887	1965	**£5**	chart single

DICKENS, LITTLE JIMMY

Title	Format	Label	Number	Year	Price	Notes
May The Bird Of Paradise...	7"	CBS	201969	1965	**£4**	

DICKIES

The Dickies are an American group, famous for their plethora of coloured vinyl releases and famous too for their irreverent cover versions. Their supercharged interpretations of "Paranoid", "Eve Of Destruction", "Sound Of Silence", and "Silent Night" are great fun, but best of all is the headlong reading of "Nights In White Satin", where the guitar solo is actually (more or less) the same as the flute solo on the original, but played several times faster!

Title	Format	Label	Number	Year	Price	Notes
Banana Splits	7"	A&M	AMS7431	1979	**£5**	yellow vinyl (2 kinds)
Dawn Of The Dickies	LP	A&M	AMLH68510	1979	**£10**	blue and yellow vinyls
Eve Of Destruction	7"	A&M	AMS7373	1978	**£5**	pink vinyl
Fan Mail	7"	A&M	AMS7504	1980	**£6**	red vinyl, poster sleeve
Gigantor	7"	A&M	AMS7544	1980	**£6**	yellow vinyl
Give It Back	7"	A&M	AMS7391	1978	**£5**	white vinyl
Incredible Shrinking Dickies	LP	A&M	AMLH64742	1979	**£10**	blue vinyl
Manny, Moe And Jack	7"	A&M	AMS7491	1979	**£5**	black vinyl
Nights In White Satin	7"	A&M	AMS7469	1979	**£5**	white vinyl
Paranoid	7"	A&M	AMS7368	1978	**£5**	clear vinyl
Paranoid	10"	A&M	12008	1978	**£12**	promo, white vinyl
Silent Night	7"	A&M	AMS7403	1978	**£5**	white vinyl

DICKSON, BARBARA

Title	Format	Label	Number	Year	Price	Notes
John, Paul, George, Ringo & Bert	LP	RSO	2394167	1975	**£10**	

DIDDLEY, BO

Title	Format	Label	Number	Year	Price	Notes
16 All Time Hits	LP	Pye	NPL28049	1964	**£12**	
500 Per Cent More Man	7"	Chess	CRS8026	1966	**£4**	
Another Sugar Daddy	7"	Chess	CRS8078	1968	**£4**	
Beach Party	LP	Checker	LP2988	1963	**£30**	US
Beach Party	LP	Pye	NPL28032	1963	**£15**	chart LP
Bo Diddley 1969	7"	Chess	CRS8088	1969	**£4**	
Bo Diddley	LP	Checker	LP2984	1962	**£20**	US
Bo Diddley	LP	Chess	LP1431	1957	**£35**	US
Bo Diddley	LP	Pye	NPL28026	1963	**£15**	chart LP
Bo Diddley	7"	Pye	7N25210	1963	**£4**	
Bo Diddley And Company	LP	Checker	LP2985	1963	**£35**	US
Bo Diddley Is A Gunslinger	LP	Checker	LP2977	1961	**£40**	US
Bo Diddley Is A Gunslinger	LP	Pye	NJL33	1963	**£20**	chart LP
Bo Diddley Is A Lover	LP	Checker	LP2980	1961	**£30**	US
Bo Diddley Is A Lover	7"	Pye	7N25227	1963	**£4**	
Bo Diddley Is A Twister	LP	Checker	LP2982	1962	**£20**	US
Bo Diddley Rides Again	LP	Pye	NPL28029	1963	**£15**	chart LP
Bo's A Lumberjack	7" EP	Pye	NEP44031	1964	**£6**	
Boss Man	LP	Checker	LP3007	1967	**£35**	US
Diddling	7" EP	Pye	NEP44036	1964	**£6**	
Go Bo Diddley	LP	London	HAM2230	1959	**£30**	
Great Grandfather	7"	London	HLM8913	1959	**£30**	
Have Guitar, Will Travel	LP	Checker	LP2974	1959	**£25**	US
Hey Bo Diddley	LP	Golden Guin.	GGL0358	1966	**£10**	
Hey Bo Diddley	LP	Pye	NPL28025	1963	**£15**	
Hey Bo Diddley	7" EP	Pye	NEP44014	1963	**£6**	
Hey Good Looking	7"	Chess	CRS8000	1965	**£6**	chart single
Hey Good Looking	LP	Chess	CRL4002	1964	**£15**	
I'm A Man	7" EP	Chess	CRE6008	1966	**£6**	
In The Spotlight	LP	Checker	LP2976	1960	**£20**	US
In The Spotlight	LP	Pye	NPL28034	1964	**£15**	

Let Me Pass	LP	Chess	CRL4507	1965	**£15**	
Let The Kids Dance	7"	Chess	CRS8021	1965	**£4**	
Mama Keep Your Big Mouth Shut	7"	Pye	7N25258	1964	**£4**	
Memphis	7"	Pye	7N25235	1964	**£4**	
Mona	7"	Pye	7N25243	1964	**£4**	
Ooh Baby	7"	Chess	CRS8053	1967	**£4**	
Originator	LP	Chess	CRL4526	1967	**£15**	
Rhythm And Blues With Bo Diddley	7" EP	London	REU1054	1956	**£30**	
Road Runner	LP	Checker	LP2982	1962	**£30**	US
Road Runner	7"	London	HLM9112	1960	**£25**	
Road Runner	7"	Pye	7N25217	1963	**£5**	chart single
Rooster Stew	7" EP	Chess	CRE6023	1966	**£6**	
Say Man	7"	London	HLM8975	1959	**£15**	
Say Man Back Again	7"	London	HLM9035	1960	**£15**	
Somebody Beat Me	7"	Chess	CRS8014	1965	**£4**	
Story Of Bo Diddley	7" EP	Pye	NEP44019	1964	**£6**	
Surfin' With Bo Diddley	LP	Checker	LP2987	1963	**£20**	US
We're Gonna Get Married	7"	Chess	CRS8036	1966	**£4**	
Who Do You Love	7"	Pye	7N25193	1963	**£5**	
Wrecking My Love Life	7"	Chess	CRS8057	1967	**£4**	
You Can't Judge A Book By Its Cover	7"	Pye	7N25165	1962	**£6**	

DIF JUZ

Huremics	12"	4AD	BAD109	1981	**£10**	
Vibrating Air	12"	4AD	BAD116	1981	**£15**	

DIGA RHYTHM BAND

Diga Rhythm Band	LP	United Artists	UAG29975	1976	**£10**	

DILLARD & CLARK

Fantastic Expedition Of...	LP	A&M	AMLS939	1969	**£15**	
Gene Clark & Doug Dillard	LP	Ariola	86027	1975	**£10**	Dutch
Kansas City Southern	LP	Ariola	86436	1975	**£15**	Dutch
Radio Song	7"	A&M	AMS764	1969	**£5**	
Through The Morning	LP	A&M	AMLS966	1969	**£15**	

DILLARD, MOSES & JOSHUA

My Elusive Dreams	7"	Stateside	SS2059	1967	**£4**	

DILLARDS

Back Porch Blue Grass	LP	Elektra	EKS7232	1963	**£15**	US
Copperfields	LP	Elektra	EKS74054	1970	**£12**	
Live Almost	LP	Elektra	EKS7265	1964	**£15**	US
Nobody Knows	7"	Capitol	CL15420	1965	**£4**	
Pickin' And Fiddlin'	LP	Elektra	EKS7285	1965	**£15**	US
Rain Maker	7"	Elektra	EKSN45081	1970	**£5**	
Reason To Believe	7"	Elektra	EKSN45048	1968	**£5**	
Roots And Branches	LP	United Artists	UAS29366	1972	**£10**	
She Sang Hymns Out Of Tune	7"	Elektra	EKSN45062	1969	**£4**	
Tribute To The American Duck	LP	United Artists	UAS29516	1973	**£10**	
Wheatsheaf Suite	LP	Elektra	EKS74035	1968	**£12**	

DILLON, PHYLLIS

Don't Stay Away	7"	Doctor Bird	DB1061	1966	**£10**	
Get On The Right Track	7"	Trojan	TR671	1969	**£6**	
It's Rocking Time	7"	Treasure Isle	TI7015	1967	**£8**	
Lipstick On Your Collar	7"	Trojan	TR686	1969	**£6**	
Love Is All I Had	7"	Trojan	TR651	1969	**£6**	
Things Of The Past	7"	Treasure Isle	TI7003	196-	**£8**	

DILS

198 Seconds Of The Dils	7"	Dangerhouse	SLA268	1977	**£20**	

DIMENSIONS

Tears On My Pillow	7"	Parlophone	R5294	1965	**£8**	

DIMPLES

Love Of A Lifetime	7"	Decca	F12537	1966	**£6**	

DINGER

Air Of Mystery	7"	Face Value	FVRA221	1985	**£40**	
Air Of Mystery	7"	SRT	SRT394	1985	**£40**	

DINGLE BROTHERS

Tank De Lard	7"	Doctor Bird	DB1026	1966	**£10**	

DINNING SISTERS

Drifting And Dreaming	7"	London	HLF8179	1955	**£8**	
Hold Me Tight	7"	London	HLF8218	1956	**£6**	

DINNING, MARK

Mark Dinning is responsible for what is undoubtedly the worst record ever released. Forget all the other candidates for the accolade - "Teen Angel" is the one! The song has one of those lyrics that deal with death - on this occasion, the singer's girlfriend has apparently rushed back into a burning building in order to save a ring that the singer had bought her. The symbol of the romance was more important than the romance itself! Meanwhile, the singer laments: "I'll never kiss your lips again, they buried you today". The epitome of bad taste - and all delivered in a thin, quavery voice so as to pile the pathos on really thick. Needless to say, the record was an American number one!

Teen Angel	LP	MGM	E3828	1960	**£30**	US
Teen Angel	7"	MGM	MGM1053	1960	**£4**	chart single
Wanderin'	LP	MGM	E3855	1960	**£20**	US
You Win Again	7"	MGM	MGM1069	1960	**£4**	

DINO & DEL

Hey Little Girl Hey Little Boy	7"	Carnival	CV7026	1965	**£8**	

DION

Alone With Dion	LP	Laurie	LLP2004	1960	**£20**	US
Baby Let's Stick Together	7"	Phil Spector	2010018	1976	**£4**	
Be Careful Of The Stones That You	7"	CBS	AAG161	1963	**£5**	
Berimbau	7"	HMV	POP1565	1966	**£4**	
Born To Be With You	7"	Phil Spector	2010012	1976	**£4**	
By Special Request	LP	Laurie	LLP2016	1963	**£20**	US
Come Go With Me	7"	Stateside	SS209	1963	**£5**	
Dion	LP	Laurie	SLP2047	1968	**£10**	US
Dion Sings The Fifteen Million Sellers	LP	Laurie	LLP2019	1963	**£15**	US
Dion Sings To Sandy & All Other Girls	LP	Laurie	LLP2017	1963	**£15**	US
Dion's Hits	7" EP	Stateside	SE1006	1963	**£12**	
Don't Pity Me	7"	London	HL8799	1959	**£10**	
Donna La Prima Donna	7"	CBS	121053	1963	**£8**	sung in Italian
Donna The Prima Donna	7"	CBS	AAG169	1963	**£5**	
Donna The Prima Donna	LP	CBS	SBPG62203	1964	**£10**	
Drip Drop	7"	CBS	AAG177	1963	**£5**	
Greatest Hits	LP	Laurie	LLP2013	1962	**£15**	US
Having Fun	7"	Top Rank	JAR545	1961	**£5**	
I Can't Go On	7"	London	HL8718	1958	**£10**	
I Wonder Why	7"	London	HLH8646	1958	**£12**	
I'm Your Hoochie Coochie Man	7"	CBS	AAG188	1964	**£5**	
In The Still Of The Night	7"	Top Rank	JAR503	1960	**£4**	
Johnny B.Goode	7"	CBS	AAG224	1964	**£4**	
Little Diane	7"	Stateside	SS115	1962	**£5**	
Lonely Teenager	7"	Top Rank	JAR521	1960	**£5**	chart single
Love Came To Me	LP	Laurie	LLP2015	1963	**£15**	US
Love Came To Me	7"	Stateside	SS139	1962	**£5**	
Lover's Prayer	7"	Pye	7N25038	1959	**£5**	
Lovers Who Wander	7"	HMV	POP1020	1962	**£5**	
Lovers Who Wander	LP	Stateside	SL10034	1962	**£12**	
Make The Woman Love Me	7"	Phil Spector	2010005	1975	**£4**	
More Greatest Hits	LP	Laurie	LLP2022	1963	**£12**	US
Movin' Man	7"	HMV	POP1586	1967	**£4**	
Presenting Dion And The Belmonts	LP	Laurie	LLP2002	1959	**£35**	US
Presenting Dion And The Belmonts	LP	London	HAU2194	1959	**£20**	
Ruby Baby	LP	CBS	BPG62137	1963	**£12**	
Ruby Baby	7"	CBS	AAG133	1963	**£5**	
Runaround Sue	LP	HMV	CLP1539	1961	**£15**	
Runaround Sue	LP	Laurie	LLP2009	1961	**£50**	US, blue vinyl
Runaround Sue	7"	Top Rank	JAR586	1961	**£5**	chart single
Sandy	7"	Stateside	SS161	1963	**£5**	
Spoonful	7"	CBS	201780	1965	**£4**	
Sweet Sweet Baby	7"	CBS	201728	1965	**£5**	
Swing Along With Dion	7" EP	HMV	7EG8745	1962	**£10**	
Teenager In Love	7"	London	HLU8874	1959	**£12**	chart single
This Little Girl	7"	CBS	AAG145	1963	**£5**	
Together Again	LP	HMV	CSD3618	1967	**£10**	
Toppermost Vol.1	LP	Top Rank	25027	1960	**£20**	

Wanderer	7"	HMV	POP971	1962	**£5**	chart single
When You Wish Upon A Star	7"	Top Rank	JAR368	1960	**£4**	
Where Or When	7"	London	HLU9030	1960	**£8**	
Wish Upon A Star	LP	Laurie	LLP2006	1960	**£20**	US

DIPLOMATS

I Can Give You Love	7"	Direction	583899	1968	**£6**	
Strong Man	7"	Caltone	TONE112	196-	**£8**	

DIRE STRAITS

Brothers In Arms Special Edition	CD	Vertigo	8842852	1985	**£90**	promo
Dire Straits	LP	Vertigo	HS9102021	1982	**£10**	audiophile
Dire Straits Live	LP	W. Bros	WBMS109	1980	**£25**	US promo
Lady Writer	7"	Vertigo	6059230	1979	**£4**	chart single
Love Over Gold	10"	Vertigo	DSTR610	1984	**£6**	
Makin' Movies	LP	Vertigo	HS6359034	1982	**£10**	audiophile
Money For Nothing	7"	Vertigo	DSPIC10	1985	**£6**	shaped pic disc
Money For Nothing	10"	Vertigo	DSTR1010	1985	**£6**	
Private Investigations	10"	Vertigo	DSTR101	1982	**£6**	
Romeo And Juliet	7"	Vertigo	MOVIEDJ1	1981	**£5**	1 sided promo
Skateaway	7"	Vertigo	MOVIE2	1981	**£4**	chart single
Skateaway	7"	Vertigo	MOVIEDJ2	1981	**£5**	1 sided promo
Sultans Of Swing	7"	Vertigo	6059206	1979	**£4**	chart single
Telegraph Road	12"	Vertigo		1982	**£12**	promo
Tunnel Of Love	7"	Vertigo	MOVIE3	1981	**£4**	chart single
Twistin' By The Pool	7"	Vertigo	DSDJ2	1983	**£5**	promo
Walk Of Life	7"	Vertigo	DSTRD12	1986	**£5**	double

DIRECT HITS

Modesty Blaise	7"	Whaam!	WHAAM7	1982	**£6**	

DIRECTIONS

Three Bands Tonite	7"	Tortch	TOR004	1979	**£30**	

DIRK & STIG (RUTLES)

Ging Gang Goolie	7"	EMI	EMI2852	1979	**£4**	khaki vinyl
Ging Gang Goolie	7"	Ring O	DIB1	1978	**£4**	

DIRTY BLUES BAND

Dirty Blues Band	LP	Stateside	SSL10234	1967	**£15**	
Stone Dirt	LP	Stateside	SSL10268	1969	**£15**	

DISCHARGE

Decontrol	7"	Clay	CLAY5	1980	**£4**	
Fight Back	7"	Clay	CLAY3	1980	**£4**	
Never Again	7"	Clay	CLAY6	1981	**£4**	
Realities Of War	7"	Clay	CLAY1	1980	**£4**	
Why	12"	Clay	PLATE2	198-	**£6**	

DISCO 2000

I Gotta CD	7"	KLF	D2001	1987	**£10**	white label

DISCO ZOMBIES

Drums Over London	7"	S. Circular	SGS106	1979	**£6**	

DISCS

Not Meant To Be	7"	Columbia	DB7477	1965	**£6**	

DIVINE

Walk Like A Man	7"	Proto	ENAP125	1985	**£5**	shaped pic disc

DIXIE BELLES

Dixie Belles	7" EP	London	REU1434	1964	**£5**	
Down At Papa Joe's	LP	London	HAU8152	1964	**£12**	
Down At Papa Joe's	7"	London	HLU9797	1963	**£4**	
Southtown USA	7"	London	HLU9842	1964	**£4**	

DIXIE CUPS

Chapel Of Love	7"	Pye	7N25245	1964	**£5**	chart single
Chapel Of Love	LP	Red Bird	RB20100	1964	**£20**	US
Gee The Moon Is Shining Bright	7"	Red Bird	RB10032	1965	**£5**	
Iko Iko	LP	Red Bird	RB20103	1965	**£20**	US

Title	Format	Label	Cat. No.	Year	Price	Notes
Iko Iko	7"	Red Bird	RB10024	1965	**£5**	chart single
Little Bell	7"	Red Bird	RB10017	1964	**£5**	
Love Ain't So Bad	7"	HMV	POP1557	1966	**£4**	
People Say	7"	Red Bird	RB10006	1964	**£5**	
Riding High	LP	ABC-Para.	525	1965	**£15**	US
Two Way Poc-A-Way	7"	HMV	POP1453	1965	**£4**	
What Kind Of Fool	7"	HMV	POP1524	1966	**£4**	
You Should Have Seen The Way...	7"	Red Bird	RB10012	1964	**£5**	

DIXON, ERROL

Title	Format	Label	Cat. No.	Year	Price	Notes
Back To The Chicken Shack	7"	Decca	F12826	1968	**£10**	
Blues In A Pot	LP	Decca			**£50**	
Errol Sings Fats	7" EP	Decca	DFE8626	1965	**£6**	
Gloria	7"	Blue Beat	BB337	1965	**£10**	
Hoop	7"	Direct	DS5002	196-	**£8**	
I Need Someone To Love Me	7"	Rainbow	RAI104	196-	**£8**	
Midnight Party	7"	Ska Beat	JB271	1967	**£10**	
Oo Wee Baby	7"	Carnival	CV7001	1963	**£8**	
Rocks In My Pillow	7"	Oriole	CB1914	1964	**£6**	
Six Questions	7"	Decca	F12613	1967	**£8**	
True Love Never Runs Smooth	7"	Decca	F12717	1967	**£8**	
You're No Good	7"	Blue Beat	BB344	1965	**£10**	

DIXON, JEFF

Title	Format	Label	Cat. No.	Year	Price	Notes
Rock	7"	Coxsone	CS7015	196-	**£10**	
Tickle Me	7"	Studio One	SO2051	196-	**£10**	

DIXON, WILLIE

Title	Format	Label	Cat. No.	Year	Price	Notes
I Am The Blues	LP	Columbia	CS9987	1970	**£10**	US
Walking The Blues	7"	London	HLU8297	1956	**£120**	
Walking The Blues	7"	Pye	7N25270	1964	**£8**	

DIXON, WILLIE & MEMPHIS SLIM

Title	Format	Label	Cat. No.	Year	Price	Notes
Blues Every Which Way	LP	Verve	V3007	1961	**£15**	US
In Paris	LP	Battle	BV6122	1963	**£15**	US
Willie's Blues	LP	Bluesville	BV1003	1960	**£20**	US

DIZZY MAN'S BAND

Title	Format	Label	Cat. No.	Year	Price	Notes
Tickatoo	7"	W. Bros	WB8015	1970	**£4**	

DIZZY, JOHNNY

Title	Format	Label	Cat. No.	Year	Price	Notes
Sudden Destruction	7"	Ska Beat	JB204	1965	**£10**	

DNV

Title	Format	Label	Cat. No.	Year	Price	Notes
Mafia	7"	N. Pleasures	Z2	1979	**£30**	

DOBKINS JR., CARL

Title	Format	Label	Cat. No.	Year	Price	Notes
Carl Dobkins Jr.	LP	Decca	DL8938	1959	**£25**	US

DOBSON, BOBBY

Title	Format	Label	Cat. No.	Year	Price	Notes
Seems To Me I'm Losing You	7"	Coxsone	CS7058	196-	**£10**	
Sir Don	7"	Trojan	TR011	196-	**£8**	
Strange	7"	Blue Cat	BS171	196-	**£10**	

DOBSON, LYN

Lyn Dobson played saxophone with Manfred Mann and Soft Machine, but never managed to find a steady niche for himself. His solo LP attempts to show how ecelectic Dobson can be, but ends up simply sounding bitty.

Title	Format	Label	Cat. No.	Year	Price	Notes
Jam Sandwich	LP	Fresh Air	6370501	1974	**£10**	

DOCKER, ROY

Title	Format	Label	Cat. No.	Year	Price	Notes
I'm An Outcast	7"	Pama	PM756	196-	**£8**	
Mellow Moonlight	7"	Domain	D3	1968	**£6**	
When	7"	Pama	PM750	196-	**£8**	

DOCTOR & THE MEDICS

Title	Format	Label	Cat. No.	Year	Price	Notes
Druids Are Here	7"	Whaam!	WHAAM6	1982	**£8**	

DODD ALL STARS

Title	Format	Label	Cat. No.	Year	Price	Notes
Hip Shuffle	7"	Coxsone	CS7076	196-	**£10**	
Mother Aitken	7"	Coxsone	CS7096	196-	**£10**	

DODDS, NELLA

Come See About Me	7"	Pye	7N25281	1965	**£15**	
Finders Keepers Losers Weepers	7"	Pye	7N25291	1965	**£15**	

DODGERS

Let's Make A Whole...	7"	Downbeat	CHA2	1960	**£8**	

DODOS

I Made Up My Mind	7"	Polydor	56153	1967	**£10**	

DOE, ERNIE K

Certain Girl	7"	London	HLP9487	1962	**£6**	
Dancing Man	7"	Action	ACT4502	1968	**£4**	
Dancing Man	7"	Action	ACT4502	1968	**£10**	demo
Gotta Pack My Bags	7"	Action	ACT4512	1968	**£4**	
Gotta Pack My Bags	7"	Action	ACT4512	1968	**£15**	demo
Mother In Law	7"	London	HLU9330	1961	**£6**	chart single
Mother In Law	LP	Minit	LP0002	1961	**£40**	US
Mother In Law	7"	Vocalion	VP9233	1965	**£6**	
Te Ta Te Ta Ta	7"	London	HLU9390	1961	**£5**	

DOG THAT BIT PEOPLE

Dog That Bit People	LP	Parlophone	PCS7125	1971	**£100**	
Lovely Lady	7"	Parlophone	R5880	1971	**£12**	

DOGFEET

Dogfeet	LP	Reflection	REFL8	1970	**£250**	
Sad Story	7"	Reflection	RS7	1970	**£15**	

DOGGEREL BANK

Mister Skillcorn Dances	LP	Charisma	CAS1102	1975	**£10**	
Silver Faces	LP	Charisma	CAS1079	1973	**£10**	

DOGGETT, BILL

As You Desire Me	LP	King	523	195-	**£30**	US
Dame Dreaming	LP	King	532	195-	**£30**	US
Doggett Beat	LP	King	557	1958	**£30**	US
Honky Tonk	7"	Parlophone	R4231	1956	**£15**	
Honky Tonk	7" EP	Parlophone	GEP8644	1957	**£10**	
Hot Ginger	7"	Parlophone	R4379	1957	**£8**	
Hully Gully Twist	7"	W. Bros	WB32	1961	**£4**	
Leaps And Bounds	7"	Parlophone	R4413	1958	**£8**	
Ram Bunk Shush	7"	Parlophone	R4306	1957	**£10**	
Slow Walk	7"	Parlophone	R4265	1957	**£10**	
Smoke	7"	Parlophone	R4629	1960	**£5**	
Wow	LP	HMV	CLP1884	1965	**£15**	
You Can't Sit Down	7"	W. Bros	WB46	1961	**£4**	

DOGS D'AMOUR

(Un)authorised Bootleg	LP	China	WOL7	1988	**£50**	
How Come It Never Rains	7"	China	CHINA1	1988	**£5**	
How Come It Never Rains	12"	China	CHINX1	1988	**£8**	
How Come It Never Rains	7"	Supertrack	DOGS1	1987	**£40**	
How Do You Fall In Love	7"	Kumibeat	JOM3	1984	**£40**	Finnish
I Don't Want You To Go	12"	China	CHIXP10	1988	**£6**	pink vinyl
Kid From Kensington	12"	China	CHIXP5	1988	**£6**	yellow vinyl
State We're In	LP	Kumibeat		1984	**£60**	Finnish

DOLENZ, JONES, BOYCE & HART

Dolenz, Jones, Boyce & Hart	LP	Capitol	ST11513	1976	**£15**	US

DOLENZ, MICKEY

Don't Do It	7"	London	HLH10117	1967	**£6**	
Huff Puff	7"	London	HLH10152	1967	**£6**	

DOLL, LINDA & THE SUNDOWNERS

He Don't Want Your Love Any More	7"	Piccadilly	7N35166	1964	**£4**	

DOLPHIN

Goodbye	LP	P. Stock	PVLP1055	1977	**£20**	
Molecules	LP	Gale	LP02	1980	**£30**	

DOLPHINS

Title	Format	Label	Cat. No.	Year	Price	Notes
Hey Da Da Dow	7"	Stateside	SS375	1965	**£4**	

DOLTON, BILLY

Title	Format	Label	Cat. No.	Year	Price	Notes
Winkie Doll	7"	Parlophone	R4733	1961	**£4**	

DOME

Title	Format	Label	Cat. No.	Year	Price	Notes
3R4	12"	4AD	CAD16	1980	**£6**	

DOMINO, FATS

Title	Format	Label	Cat. No.	Year	Price	Notes
Ain't That A Shame	7"	London	HLU8173	1955	**£10**	chart single
Ain't That A Shame	7"	London	HLU8173	1955	**£20**	gold label
Ain't That Just Like A Woman	7"	London	HLP9301	1961	**£6**	
Be My Guest	7"	London	HLP9005	1959	**£5**	chart single
Be My Guest	7" EP	London	REP1261	1960	**£6**	
Big Beat	7"	London	HL7058	1958	**£30**	export
Big Beat	7"	London	HLP8575	1958	**£10**	chart single
Blue Monday	7"	London	HLP8377	1957	**£10**	
Blue Monday	7"	London	HLP8377	1957	**£20**	gold label, chart single
Blueberry Hill	7"	London	HLU8330	1956	**£10**	
Blueberry Hill	7"	London	HLU8330	1956	**£20**	gold label
Blues For Love Vol.1	7" EP	London	REP1022	1955	**£12**	
Blues For Love Vol.2	7" EP	London	REP1062	1956	**£10**	
Blues For Love Vol.3	7" EP	London	REP1117	1958	**£8**	
Blues For Love Vol.4	7" EP	London	REP1121	1958	**£8**	
Bo Weevil	7"	London	HLU8256	1956	**£10**	
Bo Weevil	7"	London	HLU8256	1956	**£20**	gold label
Carry On Rocking	LP	London	HAU2041	1956	**£25**	
Carry On Rocking part 1	7" EP	London	REP1115	1958	**£8**	
Carry On Rocking part 2	7" EP	London	REP1116	1958	**£8**	
Country Boy	7"	London	HLP9073	1960	**£5**	chart single
Don't Leave Me This Way	78	London	HL8096	1954	**£15**	
Everybody's Got Something To Hide...	7"	Reprise	RS20810	1969	**£4**	
Fabulous Mr.D	LP	London	HAP2135	1958	**£20**	
Fats	7" EP	London	REP1073	1957	**£12**	
Fats	LP	Reprise	RS6439	1971	**£300**	US
Fats Domino	LP	Imperial	LP9009	1956	**£50**	US
Fats Domino Swings	LP	Imperial	LP9062	1959	**£20**	US
Fats On Fire	LP	HMV	CLP1740	1963	**£10**	mono
Fats On Fire	LP	HMV	CSD1543	1963	**£10**	stereo
Here Comes Fats	LP	HMV	CLP1690	1963	**£10**	mono
Here Comes Fats	LP	HMV	CSD1520	1963	**£10**	stereo
Here Comes Fats Vol.1	7" EP	London	REP1079	1957	**£10**	
Here Comes Fats Vol.2	7" EP	London	REP1080	1957	**£10**	
Here Comes Fats Vol.3	7" EP	London	REP1138	1958	**£8**	
Here He Comes Again	LP	Imperial	LP9248	1963	**£15**	US
Here Stands Fats Domino	LP	Imperial	LP9038	1957	**£50**	US
Here Stands Fats Domino	LP	London	HAU2052	1957	**£20**	
Honest Mamas Love Their Papas	7"	Reprise	R20696	1968	**£12**	
Honey Chile	7"	London	HLU8356	1957	**£10**	
Honey Chile	7"	London	HLU8356	1957	**£20**	gold label, chart single
I Know	7"	London	HL8133	1955	**£15**	
I Know	7"	London	HL8133	1955	**£30**	gold label
I Left My Heart In San Francisco	7"	Mercury	MF869	1965	**£4**	
I Miss You So	LP	London	HAP2364	1961	**£20**	
I Want To Walk You Home	7"	London	HLP8942	1959	**£8**	chart single
I'm Livin' Right	7"	HMV	POP1582	1967	**£8**	
I'm Ready	7"	Liberty	LIB15274	1969	**£10**	
I'm Walking	7"	London	HLP8407	1957	**£8**	
I'm Walking	7"	London	HLP8407	1957	**£15**	gold label, chart single
It Keeps Raining	7"	Liberty	LIB12055	1967	**£6**	
It Keeps Raining	7"	London	HLP9374	1961	**£8**	chart single
Jambalaya	7"	London	HLP9520	1962	**£5**	chart single
Just Domino	LP	London	HAP8039	1963	**£20**	
Lady Madonna	7"	Reprise	RS20763	1968	**£4**	
Let The Four Winds Blow	LP	London	HAP2420	1961	**£20**	
Let The Four Winds Blow	7"	London	HLP9415	1961	**£5**	
Let's Dance With Domino	LP	Imperial	LP9239	1963	**£15**	US
Let's Play Fats Domino	LP	London	HAP2223	1959	**£20**	
Little Mary	7"	London	HLP8663	1958	**£10**	
Lot Of Domino's	LP	London	HAP2312	1960	**£20**	

Title	Format	Label	Number	Year	Price	Notes
Love Me	7"	London	HL8124	1955	**£25**	
Love Me	7"	London	HL8124	1955	**£50**	gold label
Margie	7"	London	HLP8865	1959	**£8**	chart single
Million Record Hits	LP	Imperial	LP9103	1960	**£20**	US
Million Sellers Vol.1	LP	Liberty	LBY3033	1965	**£10**	
Million Sellers Vol.2	LP	Liberty	LBY3046	1965	**£10**	
My Blue Heaven	7" EP	Liberty	LEP4026	1965	**£5**	
My Blue Heaven	7"	London	HLU8280	1956	**£10**	
My Blue Heaven	7"	London	HLU8280	1956	**£20**	gold label, chart single
My Girl Josephine	7"	London	HLP9244	1960	**£4**	chart single
My Real Name	7"	London	HLP9557	1962	**£4**	
Nothing New	7"	London	HLP9590	1962	**£4**	
Red Sails In The Sunset	7"	HMV	POP1219	1963	**£4**	chart single
Red Sails In The Sunset	7" EP	HMV	7EG8862	1964	**£5**	
Rock And Rollin'	LP	Imperial	LP9004	1956	**£50**	US
Rock And Rollin'	LP	London	HAU2028	1956	**£25**	
Rocking Mister D	7" EP	London	REP1265	1960	**£6**	
Rocking Mister D Vol.1	7" EP	London	REP1206	1959	**£8**	
Rocking Mister D Vol.2	7" EP	London	REP1207	1959	**£8**	
Rolling	7" EP	Liberty	LEP4045	1966	**£5**	
Shurah	7"	London	HLP9327	1961	**£5**	
Sick And Tired	7"	London	HL7040	1958	**£30**	export
Sick And Tired	7"	London	HLP8628	1958	**£10**	chart single
Stop The Clock	7"	London	HLP9616	1962	**£5**	
Tell Me That You Love Me	7"	London	HLP9133	1960	**£8**	
This Is Fats	LP	Imperial	LP9040	1957	**£50**	US
This Is Fats	LP	London	HAP2087	1958	**£20**	
This Is Fats Domino	LP	Imperial	LP9028	1957	**£50**	US
This Is Fats Domino	LP	London	HAP2073	1956	**£20**	
Three Nights A Week	7"	London	HLP9198	1960	**£4**	chart single
Twistin' The Stomp	LP	London	HAP2447	1962	**£20**	
Valley Of Tears	7"	London	HLP8449	1957	**£10**	chart single
Wait And See	7"	London	HLP8519	1957	**£10**	
Walking To New Orleans	7"	Liberty	LIB15098	1968	**£8**	
Walking To New Orleans	LP	London	HAP8084	1963	**£20**	
Walking To New Orleans	7"	London	HLP9163	1960	**£5**	chart single
What A Party	LP	London	HAP2426	1961	**£20**	
What A Party	7"	London	HLP9456	1961	**£5**	chart single
What A Party	7" EP	London	REP1340	1962	**£6**	
What's That You Got	7"	Mercury	MF1104	1969	**£4**	
What's That You Got	7"	Mercury	MF873	1965	**£5**	
When I See You	7"	London	HLP8471	1957	**£10**	
When My Dreamboat Comes Along	7"	London	HLU8309	1956	**£10**	
When My Dreamboat Comes Along	7"	London	HLU8309	1956	**£20**	gold label
When The Saints...	7"	London	HLP8822	1959	**£8**	
Whole Lotta Loving	7"	London	HLP8759	1958	**£8**	
Why Don't You Do Right	7"	HMV	POP1421	1965	**£5**	
You Always Hurt The One You Love	7"	London	HLP9738	1963	**£5**	
You Done Me Wrong	78	London	HL8063	1954	**£20**	
You Said You Loved Me	78	London	HL8007	1954	**£25**	
Young School Girl	7"	London	HLP8727	1958	**£10**	

DOMINOES & SWALLOWS

Title	Format	Label	Number	Year	Price	Notes
Rhythm And Blues	7" EP	Vogue	EPV1113	195-	**£30**	

DON & DEWEY

Title	Format	Label	Number	Year	Price	Notes
Get Your Hat	7"	London	HL9897	1964	**£4**	
Soul Motion	7"	Cameo Park.	CP750	1966	**£6**	
Soul Motion	7"	Sue	WI4032	1967	**£8**	

DON & JUAN

Title	Format	Label	Number	Year	Price	Notes
What's Your Name	7"	London	HLX9529	1962	**£4**	

DON & THE GOODTIMES

Title	Format	Label	Number	Year	Price	Notes
Greatest Hits	LP	Burdette	300	1966	**£20**	US
Happy To Me	7"	Columbia	DB8266	1967	**£4**	
I Could Be So Good	7"	Columbia	DB8199	1967	**£4**	
Where The Action Is	LP	Wand	WDS679	1969	**£12**	US

DON, DICK & JIMMY

Title	Format	Label	Number	Year	Price	Notes
Don, Dick & Jimmy	7" EP	London	REU1043	1955	**£10**	

Title	Format	Label	Cat. No.	Year	Price	Notes
Make Yourself Comfortable	7"	London	HL8144	1955	**£10**	
Spring Fever	LP	Modern	LMP1205	1956	**£20**	US
That's The Way I Feel	7"	HMV	POP280	1956	**£4**	
You Can't Have Your Cake & Eat It Too	7"	London	HL8117	1955	**£10**	

DONAHUE, JERRY

Title	Format	Label	Cat. No.	Year	Price	Notes
Theme From Catlow	7"	Philips	6006219	1972	**£4**	

DONAYS

Title	Format	Label	Cat. No.	Year	Price	Notes
Devil In His Heart	7"	Oriole	CBA1770	1962	**£8**	

DONEGAN, LONNIE

Title	Format	Label	Cat. No.	Year	Price	Notes
Backstairs Session	7" EP	Polygon	JTE107	1956	**£12**	
Backstairs Session	7" EP	Pye	NJE1014	1956	**£5**	
Battle Of New Orleans	7"	Pye	7N15206	1959	**£4**	chart single
Bring A Little Water Sylvie	78	Pye	N15071	1956	**£4**	chart single
Comancheros	7"	Pye	7N15410	1962	**£4**	chart single
Cumberland Gap	78	Pye	N15087	1957	**£4**	chart single
Digging My Potatoes	7"	Decca	FJ10695	1956	**£8**	
Does Your Chewing Gum Lose Its....	7"	Pye	7N15181	1959	**£4**	chart single
Don't You Rock Me, Daddy-O	78	Pye	N15080	1957	**£4**	chart single
Folk Album	LP	Pye	NPL18126	1965	**£10**	
Fort Worth Jail	7"	Pye	7N15198	1959	**£4**	chart single
Golden Age Of Donegan	LP	Golden Guin.	GGL0135	1962	**£10**	chart LP
Golden Age Of Donegan Vol.2	LP	Golden Guin.	GGL0170	1962	**£10**	chart LP
Grand Coulee Dam	7"	Pye	7N15129	1958	**£4**	chart single
Have A Drink On Me	7"	Pye	7N15354	1961	**£4**	chart single
I Wanna Go Home	7"	Pye	7N15267	1960	**£4**	chart single
Jack O'Diamonds	7"	Pye	7N15116	1957	**£4**	chart single
Lively	7"	Pye	7N15312	1960	**£4**	chart single
Lonesome Traveller	7"	Pye	7N15158	1958	**£4**	chart single
Lonnie	LP-10"	Pye	NPT19027	1957	**£12**	
Lonnie Donegan Hit Parade	7" EP	Pye	NEP24031	1957	**£5**	
Lonnie Donegan Hit Parade Vol.2	7" EP	Pye	NEP24040	1957	**£5**	
Lonnie Donegan Hit Parade Vol.3	7" EP	Pye	NEP24067	1958	**£5**	
Lonnie Donegan Hit Parade Vol.4	7" EP	Pye	NEP24081	1958	**£5**	
Lonnie Donegan Hit Parade Vol.5	7" EP	Pye	NEP24104	1959	**£5**	
Lonnie Donegan Hit Parade Vol.6	7" EP	Pye	NEP24114	1959	**£5**	
Lonnie Donegan Hit Parade Vol.7	7" EP	Pye	NEP24134	1961	**£5**	
Lonnie Donegan Hit Parade Vol.8	7" EP	Pye	NEP24149	1961	**£5**	
Lonnie Donegan On Stage	7" EP	Pye	NEP24075	1958	**£6**	
Lonnie Donegan Skiffle Group	7" EP	Decca	DFE6345	1956	**£6**	
Lonnie Pops	LP	Decca	SKL5068	1970	**£10**	
Lonnie's Skiffle Party	7"	Pye	7N15165	1958	**£4**	chart single
Lorelei	7"	Pye	7N15275	1960	**£4**	chart single
Lost John	78	Pye	N15036	1956	**£4**	chart single
Michael Row The Boat	7"	Pye	7N15371	1961	**£4**	chart single
Midnight Special	78	Pye	NJS2006	1956	**£4**	
Midnight Special	7"	Pye	7NJ2006	1958	**£6**	
More Tops With Lonnie	LP	Pye	NPL18063	1961	**£10**	
My Dixie Darling	78	Pye	N15108	1957	**£4**	chart single
My Old Man's A Dustman	7"	Pye	7N15256	1960	**£4**	chart single
Party's Over	7"	Pye	7N15424	1962	**£4**	chart single
Pick A Bale Of Cotton	7"	Pye	7N15455	1962	**£4**	chart single
Putting On The Style	78	Pye	N15093	1957	**£4**	chart single
Relax With Lonnie	7" EP	Pye	NEP24107	1959	**£5**	
Rides Again	LP	Pye	NPL18043	1959	**£10**	
Rock Island Line	7"	Decca	FJ10647	1955	**£6**	chart single
Sal's Got A Sugar Lip	7"	Pye	7N15223	1959	**£4**	chart single
Sally Don't You Grieve	7"	Pye	7N15148	1958	**£4**	chart single
San Miguel	7"	Pye	7N15237	1959	**£4**	chart single
Showcase	LP-10"	Pye	NPT19012	1956	**£12**	chart single
Sing Hallelujah	LP	Pye	NPL18073	1962	**£10**	
Skiffle Session	7" EP	Pye	NJE1017	1956	**£5**	chart single
Take My Hand	7"	Columbia	DB3850	1956	**£8**	
Tom Dooley	7"	Pye	7N15172	1958	**£4**	chart single
Tops With Lonnie	LP	Pye	NPL18034	1958	**£10**	
Virgin Mary	7"	Pye	7N15315	1960	**£4**	chart single
Yankee Doodle Donegan	7" EP	Pye	NEP24127	1960	**£5**	

DONEGAN, LONNIE & TOMMY REILLY

Passing Stranger	7"	Oriole	CB1329	1956	**£5**	

DONLEY, JIMMY

Shape You Left Me In	7"	Brunswick	05807	1959	**£15**	
South Of The Border	7"	Brunswick	05715	1957	**£4**	

DONNER, RAL

I Don't Need You	7"	Parlophone	R4889	1962	**£4**	
I Got Burned	7"	Reprise	R20141	1963	**£10**	
Please Don't Go	7"	Parlophone	R4859	1961	**£4**	
Takin' Care Of Business	LP	Gone	LP5012	1961	**£75**	US
You Don't Know What You Got	7"	Parlophone	R4820	1961	**£4**	chart single

DONNIE & THE DREAMERS

Count Every Star	7"	Top Rank	JAR571	1961	**£4**	

DONOVAN

Donovan is often viewed as a bit of a joke these days, seeming to epitomise all the more pretentious, self-conscious aspects of hippy culture. His achievement in moving onwards from being a pale shadow of Bob Dylan into creating music of genuine invention and charm is considerable, however. The UK album, "Sunshine Superman", which combines the best tracks of two albums issued in America, is like a folk version of "Sgt.Pepper", while the double "Gift From A Flower To A Garden", despite being inevitably too long, is almost as good. This latter album, which was issued as a boxed set, is becoming increasingly scarce, especially with its numerous poetic inserts intact.

Atlantis	7"	Pye	7N17660	1968	**£4**	chart single
Barabajagal	LP	Epic	BN26481	1968	**£12**	US
Brother Sun, Sister Moon	LP	HMV	3C06493393	1970	**£20**	German
Catch The Wind	7"	Pye	7N15801	1965	**£4**	chart single
Catch The Wind	7" EP	Pye	NEP24287	1968	**£5**	
Colours	7"	Pye	7N15866	1965	**£4**	chart single
Colours	7" EP	Pye	NEP24229	1965	**£5**	
Cosmic Wheels	LP	Epic	65450	1973	**£10**	chart LP
Donovan	LP	World Recs	ST951	1965	**£10**	
Donovan Vol.1	7" EP	Pye	NEP24239	1966	**£5**	
Fairytale	LP	Pye	NPL18128	1965	**£10**	chart LP
For Little Ones	LP	Epic	BN26350	1967	**£12**	US
Gift From A Flower To A Garden	LP	Pye	NSPL20000	1968	**£20**	double, boxed, chart LP
Greatest Hits	LP	Pye	NSPL18283	1969	**£12**	
HMS Donovan	LP	Dawn	DNLD4001	1971	**£30**	double
Hurdy Gurdy Donovan	7" EP	Pye	NEP24299	1968	**£8**	
Hurdy Gurdy Man	LP	Epic	BN26420	1968	**£12**	US
Hurdy Gurdy Man	7"	Pye	7N17537	1968	**£4**	chart single
In Concert	LP	Pye	NSPL18237	1968	**£10**	
Jennifer Juniper	7"	Epic		1967	**£10**	sung in Italian
Jennifer Juniper	7"	Pye	7N17457	1968	**£4**	chart single
Josie	7"	Pye	7N17067	1966	**£4**	
Live In Japan, Spring Tour 1973	LP	Epic	ECPM25	1973	**£20**	Japanese
Mellow Yellow	LP	Epic	BN26239	1967	**£15**	US
Mellow Yellow	7"	Pye	7N17267	1967	**£4**	chart single
Open Road	LP	Dawn	DNLS3009	1970	**£15**	chart LP
Remember The Alamo	7"	Pye	7N17088	1966	**£8**	
Sunshine Superman	LP	Epic	LN26217	1966	**£15**	US, different tracks
Sunshine Superman	LP	Pye	NPL18181	1967	**£15**	chart LP
Sunshine Superman	7"	Pye	7N17241	1966	**£4**	chart single
There Is A Mountain	7"	Pye	7N17403	1967	**£4**	chart single
To Susan On The West Coast Waiting	7"	Pye	7N17660	1968	**£12**	
Turquoise	7"	Pye	7N15894	1965	**£4**	chart single
Universal Soldier	7" EP	Pye	NEP24219	1965	**£5**	
Wear Your Love Like Heaven	LP	Epic	BN26349	1967	**£12**	US
What's Bin Did And What's Bin Hid	LP	Pye	NPL18117	1965	**£10**	chart LP

DONOVAN & DANNY THOMPSON

Celia Of The Sands	7"	Dawn	DNS1007	1970	**£5**	

DONOVAN & JEFF BECK GROUP

Goo Goo Barabajagal	7"	Pye	7N17778	1969	**£5**	chart single
Goo Goo Barabajagal	7"	Pye	7N17778	1969	**£6**	'Bed With Me' B side

DONOVAN & THE OPEN ROAD

Riki Tiki Tavi	7"	Dawn	DNS1006	1970	**£5**	

DONTELLS

In Your Heart	7"	Fontana	TF566	1965	**£8**	

DOO, DICKIE & THE DON'TS

Click Clack	7"	London	HLU8589	1958	**£5**	
Leave Me Alone	7"	London	HLU8754	1958	**£6**	
Madison	LP	United Artists	UAL3094	1960	**£12**	US
Teen Scene	LP	United Artists	UAL3097	1960	**£12**	US
Wabash Cannonball	7"	Top Rank	JAR318	1960	**£4**	

DOOBIE BROTHERS

Captain And Me	LP	Nautilus	NR 5	1980	**£10**	US audiophile
Captain And Me	LP	W. Bros	BS42694	1974	**£10**	US quad
Stampede	LP	W. Bros	BS42835	1975	**£10**	US quad
Takin' It To The Streets	LP	Mobile Fid.	MFSL1122	1984	**£10**	US audiophile
Toulouse Street	LP	W. Bros	BS42634	1974	**£10**	US quad
What Were Once Vices Are Now Habits	LP	W. Bros	WS42750	1974	**£10**	US quad

DOOLEY SISTERS

Ko Ko Mo	7"	London	HL8128	1955	**£8**	

DOORS

Absolutely Live	LP	Elektra	2665002	1970	**£15**	double, chart LP
Alabama Song	7"	Elektra	EKSN45012	1967	**£6**	
Best Of...	LP	Elektra	K242143	1974	**£12**	quad
Break On Through	7"	Elektra	EKSN45009	1967	**£6**	
Doors	LP	Elektra	EKL4007	1967	**£20**	mono
Doors	LP	Elektra	EKS74007	1967	**£15**	stereo
Doors	LP	Mobile Fid.	MFSL1051	1980	**£15**	US audiophile
Hello I Love You	7"	Elektra	EKSN45037	1968	**£4**	chart single
LA Woman	LP	Elektra	K42090	1971	**£10**	clear window sleeve, chart LP
Light My Fire	7"	Elektra	EKSN45014	1967	**£5**	chart single
Love Her Madly	7"	Elektra	EK45726	1971	**£4**	
Love Me Two Times	7"	Elektra	EKSN45022	1967	**£6**	
Morrison Hotel	LP	Elektra	EKS75007	1970	**£10**	chart LP
People Are Strange	7"	Elektra	EKSN45017	1967	**£6**	
Roadhouse Blues	7"	Elektra	2101008	1970	**£5**	
Soft Parade	LP	Elektra	EKS75005	1969	**£10**	
Strange Days	LP	Elektra	EKL4014	1968	**£20**	mono
Strange Days	LP	Elektra	EKS74014	1968	**£15**	stereo
Tell All The People	7"	Elektra	EKSN45065	1969	**£6**	
Touch Me	7"	Elektra	EKSN45050	1969	**£5**	
Unknown Soldier	7"	Elektra	EKSN45030	1968	**£5**	
Waiting For The Sun	LP	Elektra	EKL4024	1968	**£15**	mono, chart LP
Waiting For The Sun	LP	Elektra	EKS74024	1968	**£10**	stereo, chart LP
Wishful Sinful	7"	Elektra	EKSN45059	1969	**£5**	
You Make Me Real	7"	Elektra	2101004	1970	**£6**	

DOREEN & JACKIE

Welcome Home	7"	Ska Beat	JB208	1965	**£10**	

DORMAN, HAROLD

Mountain Of Love	7"	Top Rank	JAR357	1960	**£5**	
There They Go	7"	London	HLS9386	1961	**£5**	

DOROTHY

I Confess	7"	Industrial	IR0014	1980	**£6**	

DORSETS

Pork Chops	7"	Sue	WI391	1965	**£8**	

DORSEY, LEE

Best Of...	LP	Sue	ILP924	1965	**£20**	
Confusion	7"	Stateside	SS506	1966	**£5**	chart single
Do Re Mi	7"	Top Rank	JAR606	1962	**£6**	
Everything I Do Gonna Be Funky	7"	Bell	BLL1074	1969	**£4**	
Get Out Of My Life Woman	7"	Stateside	SS485	1966	**£5**	chart single
Go Go Girl	7"	Stateside	SS2055	1967	**£4**	
Holy Cow	7"	Stateside	SS552	1966	**£5**	chart single
Lee Dorsey	LP	Stateside	SL10177	1966	**£12**	
Messed Around	7"	Sue	WI399	1966	**£10**	

Title	Format	Label	Cat. No.	Year	Price	Notes
My Old Car	7"	Stateside	SS2017	1967	**£4**	
New Lee Dorsey	LP	Stateside	SL10192	1966	**£12**	chart LP
Rain Rain Go Away	7"	Stateside	SS593	1967	**£4**	
Ride Your Pony	7"	Stateside	SS441	1965	**£5**	
Ride Your Pony	7" EP	Stateside	SE1038	1966	**£8**	
Work Work Work	7"	Stateside	SS465	1965	**£5**	
Working In A Coalmine	7"	Stateside	SS528	1966	**£5**	chart single
Ya Ya	LP	Fury	1002	1962	**£25**	US
Ya Ya	7"	Sue	WI367	1965	**£10**	
You're Breaking Me Up	7" EP	Stateside	SE1043	1966	**£8**	

DORSEY, LEE & BETTY HARRIS

Title	Format	Label	Cat. No.	Year	Price	Notes
Love Lots Of Lovin'	7"	Buffalo	BFS1002	1982	**£5**	

DOTTIE & BONNIE

Title	Format	Label	Cat. No.	Year	Price	Notes
I'll Know	7"	Ska Beat	JB274	1967	**£10**	

DOUBLE FEATURE

Title	Format	Label	Cat. No.	Year	Price	Notes
Baby Get Your Head Screwed On	7"	Deram	DM115	1967	**£5**	
Handbags And Gladrags	7"	Deram	DM165	1967	**£6**	

DOUBLES

Title	Format	Label	Cat. No.	Year	Price	Notes
Hey Girl	7"	HMV	POP613	1959	**£8**	

DOUGHNUT RING

Title	Format	Label	Cat. No.	Year	Price	Notes
Dance Around Julie	7"	Deram	DM215	1968	**£15**	

DOUGLAS, CARL

Title	Format	Label	Cat. No.	Year	Price	Notes
Crazy Feeling	7"	Go	AJ401	196-	**£4**	
Let The Birds Sing	7"	Go	AJ408	196-	**£5**	
Nobody Cries	7"	United Artists	UP1206	1967	**£20**	

DOUGLAS, CRAIG

Title	Format	Label	Cat. No.	Year	Price	Notes
Across The Street	7"	Fontana	TF525	1965	**£4**	
Come Softly To Me	7"	Top Rank	JAR110	1959	**£4**	
Craig	7" EP	Decca	DFE6633	1960	**£5**	
Craig Douglas	LP	Top Rank	BUY049	1960	**£15**	chart LP
Craig Sings For Roxy	7" EP	Top Rank	JKR8033	1959	**£5**	
Craig's Movie Songs	7" EP	Columbia	SEG8219	1963	**£5**	
Cuddle Up With Craig	7" EP	Decca	DFE8509	1962	**£5**	
Girl Next Door	7"	Top Rank	JAR543	1961	**£4**	
Heart Of A Teenage Girl	7"	Top Rank	JAR340	1960	**£4**	chart single
Hundred Pounds Of Clay	7"	Top Rank	JAR555	1961	**£4**	chart single
Oh Lonesome Me	7"	Decca	F11523	1962	**£4**	chart single
Oh What A Day	7"	Top Rank	JAR406	1960	**£4**	chart single
Only Sixteen	7"	Top Rank	JAR159	1959	**£4**	chart single
Our Favourite Melodies	7"	Columbia	DB4854	1962	**£4**	chart single
Pretty Blue Eyes	7"	Top Rank	JAR268	1960	**£4**	chart single
Riddle Of Love	7"	Top Rank	JAR204	1959	**£4**	
Teenager In Love	7"	Top Rank	JAR133	1959	**£4**	chart single
Time	7"	Top Rank	JAR569	1961	**£4**	chart single
Town Crier	7"	Decca	F11575	1963	**£4**	chart single
When My Little Girl Is Smiling	7"	Top Rank	JAR610	1962	**£4**	chart single
Where's The Girl	7"	Top Rank	JAR515	1960	**£4**	

DOUGLAS, MARK

Title	Format	Label	Cat. No.	Year	Price	Notes
It Matters Not	7"	Ember	EMBS166	1962	**£5**	

DOUGLAS, NORMA

Title	Format	Label	Cat. No.	Year	Price	Notes
Be It Resolved	7"	London	HLZ8475	1957	**£4**	

DOUGLAS, ROBB & DEAN

Title	Format	Label	Cat. No.	Year	Price	Notes
I Can Make It With You	7"	Deram	DM132	1967	**£4**	
Rose Growing In The Ruins	7"	Deram	DM148	1967	**£4**	

DOVELLS

Title	Format	Label	Cat. No.	Year	Price	Notes
All The Hits Of The Teen Groups	LP	Parkway	P7010	1962	**£20**	US
Biggest Hits	LP	Wyncote	9114	1965	**£10**	US
Bristol Stomp	7"	Columbia	DB4718	1961	**£4**	
Bristol Stomp	LP	Parkway	P7006	1961	**£25**	US
Bristol Twistin' Annie	7"	Columbia	DB4877	1962	**£4**	
Discotheque	LP	Wyncote	W9052	1965	**£10**	US

Doin' The New Continental	7"	Columbia	DB4810	1962	**£4**	
Don't Knock The Twist	LP	Parkway	P7011	1962	**£20**	US
Dragster On The Prowl	7"	Cameo Park	P901	1963	**£4**	
For Your Hully Gully Party	LP	Parkway	P7021	1963	**£20**	US
Hully Gully Baby	7"	Cameo Park	P845	1962	**£4**	
You Can't Run Away From Yourself	7"	Cameo Park	P861	1963	**£4**	
You Can't Sit Down	7"	Cameo Park	P867	1963	**£4**	

DOWLANDS

All My Loving	7"	Oriole	CB1897	1964	**£6**	chart single
Breakups	7"	Oriole	CB1815	1963	**£8**	
Don't Ever Change	7"	Oriole	CB1781	1962	**£15**	
Don't Make Me Over	7"	Columbia	DB7547	1965	**£10**	
I Walk The Line	7"	Oriole	CB1926	1964	**£8**	
Julie	7"	Oriole	CB1748	1962	**£12**	
Lucky Johnny	7"	Oriole	CB1892	1963	**£200**	
Wishing And Hoping	7"	Oriole	CB1947	1964	**£20**	

DOWNBEATS

Thinking Of You	7"	Starlite	ST45051	1961	**£6**	

DOWNES, BOB

Bob Downes was an averagely talented flautist who attempted to haul himself into the first division by surrounding himself with the best British jazz musicians of the time and adopting a suitably "progressive" image. So far, so good, but he also frequently insisted on opening his mouth to sing. Bob Downes has a terrible voice!

Deep Down Heavy	LP	MFP	1412	1970	**£10**	
Diversions	LP	Ophenian	BDOM001	1973	**£20**	
Electric City	LP	Vertigo	6360005	1970	**£15**	spiral label
Episodes At 4am	LP	Ophenian	BDOM002	197-	**£20**	
Hell's Angels	LP	Ophenian	BDOM003	197-	**£20**	
No Time Like The Present	7"	Vertigo	6059011	1970	**£4**	
Open Music - Dream Journey	LP	Philips	SBL7922	1970	**£30**	

DOWNING, AL

Yes I'm Loving You	7"	Sue	WI341	1964	**£10**	

DOWNLINERS SECT

All Night Worker	7"	Columbia	DB7817	1966	**£12**	
Baby What's Wrong	7"	Columbia	DB7300	1964	**£10**	
Bad Storm Coming	7"	Columbia	DB7712	1965	**£12**	
Cost Of Living	7"	Columbia	DB8008	1966	**£10**	
Country Sect	LP	Columbia	33SX1745	1965	**£30**	
Find Out What's Happening	7"	Columbia	DB7415	1964	**£10**	
Glendora	7"	Columbia	DB7939	1966	**£15**	
I Got Mine	7"	Columbia	DB7597	1965	**£10**	
Little Egypt	7"	Columbia	DB7347	1964	**£10**	
Nite In Great Newport Street	7" EP	Contrast	RBCSP001	1964	**£80**	
Rock Sects In	LP	Columbia	SCX6028	1966	**£30**	
Sect	LP	Columbia	33SX1658	1964	**£30**	
Sect Sing Sick Songs	7" EP	Columbia	SEG8438	1965	**£50**	
Wreck Of The Old '97	7"	Columbia	DB7509	1965	**£12**	

DOWNTOWN ALL STARS

Downtown Jump	7"	Downtown	DT426	196-	**£8**	

DR.FEELGOOD & THE INTERNS

Blang Dong	7"	Columbia	DB7228	1964	**£10**	
Doctor Feelgood	LP	OKeh	M12101	1962	**£20**	US
Don't Tell Me No Dirty	7"	CBS	202099	1966	**£12**	
Dr.Feelgood & The Interns	7" EP	Columbia	SEG8310	1964	**£12**	
Dr.Feelgood	7"	Columbia	DB4838	1962	**£10**	
Sugar Bee	7"	Capitol	CL15569	1968	**£15**	

DR.HOOK

Cover Of Radio Times	7"	CBS	1037	1973	**£10**	1 sided promo

DR.JOHN

Mac Rebennack achieved early notoriety as the only white musician to break into the tough New Orleans R&B session world. With the advent of flower power, he reinvented himself as the voodoo magician, Dr.John, and recorded the weirdly mystical "Gris Gris" album. Three other LPs followed in similar style, before Rebennack reverted back to R&B, while still retaining the Dr.John pseudonym. He continues to be a prolific maker of records, both his own and other people's, for which he is an in-demand session pianist.

Babylon	LP	Atlantic	228018	1969	**£15**	
Desitively Bonaroo	LP	Atlantic	K50035	1974	**£10**	
Gris Gris	LP	Atlantic	587147	1968	**£20**	
Gumbo	LP	Atlantic	K40384	1972	**£15**	
Iko Iko	7"	Atlantic	K10158	1972	**£4**	
In The Right Place	LP	Atlantic	K50017	1973	**£12**	
Remedies	LP	Atlantic	2400015	1970	**£15**	
Right Place Wrong Time	7"	Atlantic	K10291	1973	**£4**	
Such A Night	7"	Atlantic	K10329	1973	**£4**	
Sun, Moon, & Herbs	LP	Atlantic	2400161	1971	**£15**	
Wang Dang Doodle	7"	Atlantic	K10214	1972	**£4**	
Wash Mama Wash	7"	Atlantic	2091019	1970	**£6**	

DR.K'S BLUES BAND

Dr.K's Blues Band	LP	Spark	UK101	1968	**£25**	

DR.MARIGOLD'S PRESCRIPTION

Hello Girl	LP	Pye	PNL501	1973	**£12**	
My Old Man Is A Groovy Old Man	7"	Pye	7N17493	1968	**£5**	
Pictures Of Life	LP	Marble Arch	MALS1222	1969	**£15**	
You've Got To Build Your Love	7"	Pye	7N17832	1969	**£5**	

DR.STRANGELY STRANGE

Dr.Strangely Strange attempted to play the same kind of eccentrically pitched folk music as the Incredible String Band, but found that the market was only big enough for one. "Kip Of The Serenes" is one of the rarest rock releases on the Island label, although one track is well known to the many people who bought the "Nice Enough To Eat" sampler LP.

Heavy Petting	LP	Vertigo	6360009	1970	**£50**	spiral label
Kip Of The Serenes	LP	Island	ILPS9106	1969	**£75**	

DR.WEST'S MEDICINE SHOW & JUNK BAND

Bullets La Verne	7"	Page One	POF23061	1968	**£4**	
Eggplant That Ate Chicago	7"	CBS	202492	1967	**£4**	
Eggplant That Ate Chicago	LP	Page One	POLS17	1968	**£15**	
Gondoliers, Shakespeares, Overseers	7"	CBS	202658	1967	**£4**	

DR.Z

Lady Ladybird	7"	Fontana	6007023	1970	**£20**	
Three Parts To My Soul	LP	Vertigo	6360048	1971	**£150**	spiral label

DRAG SET

Day And Night	7"	Go	AJ11405	1966	**£15**	

DRAGON

Dragon	LP	Acorn		1976	**£40**	

DRAGONFLY

Almost Abandoned	LP	Retreat	6002	1974	**£20**	

DRAGONFLY (2)

Dragonfly	LP	Megaphone	MS1202	1968	**£30**	US

DRAKE, CHARLIE

Hello My Darlings	7" EP	Parlophone	GEP8720	1958	**£5**	
Mr.Custer	7"	Parlophone	R4701	1960	**£4**	chart single
My Boomerang Won't Come Back	7"	Parlophone	R4824	1961	**£4**	chart single
Sea Cruise	7"	Parlophone	R4552	1959	**£4**	
Splish Splash	7"	Parlophone	R4461	1958	**£4**	chart single
Volare	7"	Parlophone	R4478	1958	**£4**	chart single
You Never Know	7"	Charisma	CB270	1975	**£8**	

DRAKE, NICK

Bryter Layter	LP	Island	ILPS9134	1970	**£15**	
Five Leaves Left	LP	Island	ILPS9105	1969	**£15**	
Fruit Tree	LP	Island	NDSP100	1979	**£25**	triple, boxed
Island LP Sampler	LP	Island	NDSP100	1979	**£20**	promo
Pink Moon	LP	Island	ILPS9184	1972	**£20**	

DRAMATIS

Shame	12"	Rocket	XPRES7912	1982	**£6**	with poster

DRANSFIELD, BARRY

Barry Dransfield	LP	Polydor	2383160	1972	**£40**	

DRANSFIELD, ROBIN & BARRY

Lord Of All I Behold	LP	Trailer	LER2026	1971	**£10**	

DRANSFIELDS

Fiddler's Dream	LP	Transatlantic	TRA322	1976	**£15**	
Rout Of The Blues	LP	Trailer	LER2011	1970	**£12**	

DRAPER, RUSTY

Chicken Picking Hawk	7"	Mercury	7MT229	1958	**£5**	
Folsom Prison Blues	7"	London	HLU9989	1965	**£5**	
Gambling Gal	7"	Mercury	7MT211	1958	**£5**	
Mule Skinner Blues	7"	Mercury	AMT1101	1960	**£4**	chart single
Mule Skinner Blues	7" EP	Mercury	ZEP10095	1960	**£6**	
Presenting Rusty Draper	7" EP	Mercury	MEP9506	1956	**£5**	
Rusty Draper	7" EP	Mercury	ZEP10016	1959	**£5**	
Rusty Draper No.1	7" EP	London	REU1431	1964	**£5**	
Rusty Draper No.2	7" EP	London	REU1432	1964	**£5**	
Rusty In Gambling Mood	7" EP	Mercury	ZEP10059	1960	**£5**	
Shopping Around	7"	Mercury	AMT1019	1959	**£5**	
Sun Will Always Shine	7"	Mercury	AMT1033	1959	**£4**	

DREAM

	LP	Polydor			**£70**	

DREAM POLICE

I've Got No Choice	7"	Decca	F13105	1970	**£5**	
Living Is Easy	7"	Decca	F12998	1970	**£8**	
Our Song	7"	Decca	F13078	1970	**£5**	

DREAMERS

Maybe Song	7"	Columbia	DB8340	1968	**£4**	

DREAMERS (2)

Dear Love	7"	Downtown	DT408	196-	**£8**	
Sweet Chariot	7"	Downtown	DT407	196-	**£8**	

DREAMLETS

Really Now	7"	Ska Beat	JB182	1965	**£10**	

DREAMLOVERS

Bird	LP	Columbia	CL2020	1963	**£12**	US
When We Get Married	7"	Columbia	DB4711	1961	**£6**	

DREAMS

Dreams included some talented jazz musicians - Billy Cobham, the Brecker Brothers, and John Abercrombie - but its music is disappointingly prosaic. These LPs are not vital links in the development of jazz-rock, but more like an attempt to make a quick fortune. In this, however, they were not particularly successful either.

Dreams	LP	CBS	64203	1970	**£12**	
Imagine My Surprise	LP	CBS	64597	1971	**£12**	

DREAMWEAVERS

It's Almost Tomorrow	7"	Brunswick	05515	1956	**£5**	chart single
Little Love Can Go A Long Long Way	7"	Brunswick	05568	1956	**£4**	
You're Mine	7"	Brunswick	05607	1956	**£4**	

DREVAR, JOHN EXPRESSION

Closer She Gets	7"	MGM	MGM1367	1967	**£25**	

DRIFTERS

At The Club	7"	Atlantic	AT4019	1965	**£5**	chart single
Clyde McPhatter & The Drifters	LP	Atlantic	8003	1956	**£100**	US
Come On Over To My Place	7"	Atlantic	AT4023	1965	**£5**	chart single
Dance With Me	7"	London	HLE8988	1959	**£5**	chart single
Drifters	LP	Clarion	608	1964	**£10**	US
Drifters	7" EP	London	REK1355	1963	**£6**	
Drifting	7" EP	London	REK1385	1963	**£5**	
Drifting Vol.2	7" EP	Atlantic	AET6003	1964	**£5**	
Good Gravy	LP	Atlantic	587144	1968	**£12**	
Good Life	LP	Atlantic	ATL5023	1965	**£12**	
Greatest Hits	LP	Atlantic	8041	1960	**£30**	US
Greatest Hits	LP	London	HAK2318	1960	**£15**	
I Count The Tears	7"	London	HLK9287	1961	**£5**	chart single

Title	Format	Label	Cat. No.	Year	Price	Notes
I'll Take You Home	7"	London	HLK9785	1963	**£4**	chart single
I'll Take You Where The Music's Playing	LP	Atlantic	587061	1967	**£10**	
I'll Take You Where The Music's Playing	LP	Atlantic	ATL5039	1966	**£12**	
I'll Take You Where The Music's Playing	7"	Atlantic	AT4040	1965	**£5**	
I've Got Sand In My Shoes	7"	Atlantic	AT4008	1964	**£5**	
In The Land Of Make Believe	7"	London	HLK9848	1964	**£4**	
Lonely Winds	7"	London	HLK9145	1960	**£4**	
Memories Are Made Of This	7"	Atlantic	AT4084	1966	**£5**	
Moonlight Bay	7"	London	HLE8686	1958	**£15**	
On Broadway	7"	London	HLK9699	1963	**£5**	
One Way Love	7"	London	HLK9886	1964	**£4**	
Our Biggest Hits	LP	Atlantic	587038	1966	**£10**	
Our Biggest Hits	LP	Atlantic	8093	1964	**£20**	US
Our Biggest Hits	LP	Atlantic	ATL5015	1965	**£10**	
Outside World	7"	Atlantic	AT4034	1965	**£4**	
Please Stay	7"	London	HLK9382	1961	**£4**	
Rat Race	7"	London	HLK9750	1963	**£4**	
Rockin' And Driftin'	LP	Atlantic	587123	1968	**£12**	
Rockin' And Driftin'	LP	Atlantic	8022	1958	**£100**	US
Room Full Of Tears	7"	London	HLK9500	1962	**£5**	
Saturday Night At The Movies	7"	Atlantic	AT4012	1964	**£5**	
Save The Last Dance For Me	LP	Atlantic	587063	1967	**£10**	
Save The Last Dance For Me	LP	Atlantic	8059	1962	**£30**	US
Save The Last Dance For Me	LP	London	HAK2450	1962	**£15**	
Save The Last Dance For Me	7"	London	HLK9201	1960	**£5**	chart single
Save The Last Dance For Me	7" EP	London	REK1282	1961	**£6**	
Soldier Of Fortune	7"	London	HLE8344	1956	**£25**	
Some Kind Of Wonderful	7"	London	HLK9326	1961	**£5**	
Souvenirs	LP	Atlantic	590010	1966	**£10**	
Stranger On The Shore	7"	London	HLK9554	1962	**£4**	
Sweets For My Sweet	7"	London	HLK9427	1961	**£4**	
There Goes My Baby	7"	London	HLE8892	1959	**£10**	
This Magic Moment	7"	London	HLE9081	1960	**£5**	
Tonight	7" EP	Atlantic	AET6012	1965	**£5**	
Under The Boardwalk	LP	Atlantic	8099	1964	**£25**	US
Under The Boardwalk	7"	Atlantic	AT4001	1964	**£5**	chart single
Up In The Streets Of Harlem	7"	Atlantic	584020	1966	**£4**	
Up On The Roof	LP	Atlantic	587160	1969	**£10**	
Up On The Roof	LP	Atlantic	8073	1963	**£25**	US
Up On The Roof	7"	London	HLK9626	1962	**£5**	
We Gotta Sing	7"	Atlantic	AT4062	1966	**£4**	
When My Little Girl Is Smiling	7"	London	HLK9522	1962	**£4**	chart single

DRIFTERS (UK)

Cliff Richard's backing group was originally called the Drifters, and they released two singles under that name in their own right, before changing names to the Shadows, in order to avoid confusion with the more famous American Drifters. In America, a change was made for them for the single "Jet Black", as this was credited to the Four Jets.

Title	Format	Label	Cat. No.	Year	Price	Notes
Drifting	7"	Columbia	DB4325	1959	**£25**	
Feeling Fine	7"	Columbia	DB4263	1959	**£30**	

DRIFTING SLIM

Title	Format	Label	Cat. No.	Year	Price	Notes
Good Morning Baby	7"	Blue Horizon	451005	1966	**£20**	

DRIFTWOOD

Title	Format	Label	Cat. No.	Year	Price	Notes
Driftwood	LP	Decca	SKL5069	1970	**£15**	
Say The Right Things	7"	Decca	F13139	1971	**£4**	
Shylock Bay	7"	Decca	F13084	1970	**£4**	

DRIFTWOOD, JIMMY

Title	Format	Label	Cat. No.	Year	Price	Notes
Country Guitar Vol.13	7" EP	RCA	RCX191	1960	**£4**	

DRISCOLL, JULIE

As far as the general public is concerned, Julie Driscoll is something of a one-hit wonder, having topped the charts with a superb version of Bob Dylan's "This Wheel's On Fire" and then having apparently dropped from sight. In fact, she married jazz pianist Keith Tippett, and as Julie Tippett has appeared on a number of jazz records by her husband and by others. "This Wheels's On Fire" was the most visible product of a profitable association with the Brian Auger Trinity, documented by the various Marmalade recordings credited to one or both of them, and going back, through their membership of Steampacket, to the single "Don't Do It No More".

Title	Format	Label	Cat. No.	Year	Price	Notes
Don't Do It No More	7"	Parlophone	R5296	1965	**£6**	
I Didn't Want To Have To Do It	7"	Parlophone	R5444	1966	**£6**	
I Know You Love Me Not	7"	Parlophone	R5588	1967	**£6**	

Title	Format	Label	Cat. No.	Year	Price	Notes
Julie Driscoll	LP	Polydor	2480074	1971	**£20**	
Save Me	7"	Marmalade	598004	1967	**£6**	
Sunset Glow	LP	Utopia	UTS601	1976	**£15**	
Take Me By The Hand	7"	Columbia	DB7118	1963	**£8**	

DRISCOLL, JULIE & BRIAN AUGER

Title	Format	Label	Cat. No.	Year	Price	Notes
Julie Driscoll And Brian Auger	LP	MFP	1265	1968	**£10**	
Open	LP	Marmalade	607002	1967	**£20**	chart LP
Road To Cairo	7"	Marmalade	598011	1969	**£5**	
Streetnoise	LP	Marmalade	608005/6	1968	**£30**	double
Take Me To The Water	7"	Marmalade	598018	1969	**£5**	
This Wheel's On Fire	7"	Marmalade	598006	1968	**£5**	chart single

DRIVE

Title	Format	Label	Cat. No.	Year	Price	Notes
Jerkin'	7"	NRG	RE46	1978	**£5**	no PS

DRONES

Title	Format	Label	Cat. No.	Year	Price	Notes
Be My Baby	12"	Valer		197-	**£30**	test pressing
Bone Idol	7"	Valer	VRS1	1977	**£5**	
Can't See	7"	Fabulous	JC4	1980	**£6**	
Further Temptations	LP	Valer	VRLP1	1977	**£15**	
Temptations Of A White Collar Worker	7"	Ohms	GOODMIX1	1977	**£5**	PS in plastic bag

DRUID

Title	Format	Label	Cat. No.	Year	Price	Notes
Fluid Druid	LP	EMI	EMC3128	1976	**£10**	
Towards The Sun	LP	EMI	EMC3081	1975	**£10**	

DRUID CHASE

Title	Format	Label	Cat. No.	Year	Price	Notes
Take Me In Your Garden	7"	CBS	3053	1967	**£8**	

DRUIDS

Title	Format	Label	Cat. No.	Year	Price	Notes
It's Just A Little Bit Too Late	7"	Parlophone	R5134	1964	**£6**	
Long Tall Texan	7"	Parlophone	R5097	1964	**£8**	

DRUIDS (2)

Title	Format	Label	Cat. No.	Year	Price	Notes
Burnt Offering	LP	Argo		1970	**£60**	
Pastime With Good Company	LP	Argo		1972	**£60**	

DRUMBAGO

Title	Format	Label	Cat. No.	Year	Price	Notes
Dulcimania	7"	Trojan	TR638	1969	**£6**	
Reggae Jeggae	7"	Blue Cat	BS145	196-	**£10**	

DRUMMOND, DON

Title	Format	Label	Cat. No.	Year	Price	Notes
Allepon	7"	Ska Beat	JB187	1965	**£10**	
Best Of...	LP	Studio One	SOL9008	196-	**£80**	
Cool Smoke	7"	Island	WI231	1965	**£10**	
Coolie Boy	7"	Island	WI204	1965	**£10**	
Doctor Dekker	7"	Ska Beat	JB189	1965	**£10**	
Don De Lion	7"	Ska Beat	JB191	1965	**£10**	
Everybody Bawlin'	7"	Duke	DU37	196-	**£8**	
Looking Through The Window	7"	Island	WI294	1966	**£10**	
Man In The Street	7"	Island	WI208	1965	**£10**	
Memory Of Don	7"	Trojan	TR678	1969	**£6**	
Musical Storeroom	7"	Island	WI153	1964	**£10**	
Ska Town	7"	Blue Beat	BB298	1964	**£10**	
Stampede	7"	Island	WI192	1965	**£10**	
Treasure Island	7"	Island	WI195	1965	**£10**	
University Goes Ska	7"	Island	WI242	1965	**£10**	

DRUSKY, ROY

Title	Format	Label	Cat. No.	Year	Price	Notes
Just About That Time	7"	Brunswick	05785	1959	**£4**	

DRY ICE

Title	Format	Label	Cat. No.	Year	Price	Notes
Running To The Convent	7"	B&C	CB115	1970	**£8**	

DUALS

Title	Format	Label	Cat. No.	Year	Price	Notes
Stick Shift	7"	London	HL9450	1961	**£8**	
Stick Shift	LP	Sue	LP2002	1961	**£50**	US

DUBS

Title	Format	Label	Cat. No.	Year	Price	Notes
Could This Be Magic	7"	London	HLU8526	1957	**£30**	
Dubs Meet The Shells	LP	Josie	JM4001	195-	**£30**	US

Title	Format	Label	Cat. No.	Year	Price	Notes
Gonna Make A Change	7"	London	HL8684	1958	**£20**	

DUCKS DELUXE

Ducks Deluxe was one of the better "pub rock" bands to emerge during the seventies. The group included Martin Belmont, Sean Tyla, and Andy McMaster, all of whom found a little success in subsequent years.

Title	Format	Label	Cat. No.	Year	Price	Notes
Coast To Coast	7"	RCA	RCA2438	1973	**£5**	
Ducks Deluxe	LP	RCA	PL5008	1974	**£15**	
Fireball	7"	RCA	LPBO5019	1974	**£5**	
I Fought The Law	7"	RCA	RCA2531	1975	**£5**	
Love's Melody	7"	RCA	RCA2477	1974	**£5**	
Taxi To The Terminal Zone	LP	RCA	SF8402	1974	**£15**	

DUDDLEY, CUDDLY

Title	Format	Label	Cat. No.	Year	Price	Notes
Later	7"	HMV	POP586	1959	**£4**	
Too Pooped To Pop	7"	HMV	POP725	1960	**£4**	

DUDLEY, DAVE

Title	Format	Label	Cat. No.	Year	Price	Notes
Six Days On The Road	7"	United Artists	UP1029	1963	**£4**	

DUFFAS, SHENLEY

Title	Format	Label	Cat. No.	Year	Price	Notes
La La La La	7"	Island	WI182	1965	**£10**	
Rukembine	7"	Island	WI186	1965	**£10**	
You Are Mine	7"	Island	WI184	1965	**£10**	

DUFFY'S NUCLEUS

Title	Format	Label	Cat. No.	Year	Price	Notes
Hound Dog	7"	Decca	F22547	1967	**£8**	

DUKE & DUCHESS

Title	Format	Label	Cat. No.	Year	Price	Notes
Get Ready For Love	7"	London	HLU8206	1955	**£8**	

DUKE ALL STARS

Title	Format	Label	Cat. No.	Year	Price	Notes
Letter To Mummy And Daddy	7"	Blue Cat	BS111	1968	**£10**	

DUKE'S NOBLEMEN

Title	Format	Label	Cat. No.	Year	Price	Notes
City Of Windows	7"	Philips	BF1691	1968	**£5**	

DUKE, BILLY

Title	Format	Label	Cat. No.	Year	Price	Notes
Sugar 'n' Spice	7"	London	HLU9960	1965	**£4**	

DUKE, DENVER & JEFFREY NULL BLUEGRASS BOYS

Title	Format	Label	Cat. No.	Year	Price	Notes
Denver Duke & Jeffrey Null Bluegrass Boys	7" EP	Starlite	STEP33	196-	**£6**	

DUKE, DORIS

Title	Format	Label	Cat. No.	Year	Price	Notes
I'm A Loser	LP	Mojo	2916001	1971	**£10**	

DUKES OF STRATOSPHEAR

Title	Format	Label	Cat. No.	Year	Price	Notes
Psonic Psunspot	LP	Virgin	VP2440	1987	**£10**	multi-coloured vinyl
You're A Good Man Albert Brown	7"	Virgin	VSY982	1987	**£4**	multi-coloured vinyl

DUKES, AGGIE

Title	Format	Label	Cat. No.	Year	Price	Notes
John John	7"	Vogue	V9090	1957	**£12**	

DULCIMER

Title	Format	Label	Cat. No.	Year	Price	Notes
And I Turned As I Had Turned As A Boy	LP	Nepentha	6437003	1971	**£35**	

DUM

Title	Format	Label	Cat. No.	Year	Price	Notes
In The Mood	7"	RAK	RAK179	1974	**£4**	

DUMBELLES (ROXY MUSIC)

Title	Format	Label	Cat. No.	Year	Price	Notes
Giddy Up	7"	EG		1976	**£8**	

DUMMER, JOHN

Title	Format	Label	Cat. No.	Year	Price	Notes
Blue	LP	Vertigo	6360055	1972	**£50**	spiral label
Cabal	LP	Mercury	SMCL20136	1969	**£50**	
Famous Music Band	LP	Fontana	6309008	1970	**£40**	
John Dummer's Blues Band	LP	Mercury	SMCL20167	1969	**£60**	
Medicine Weasel	7"	Philips	6006176	1971	**£6**	
Nine By Nine	7"	Fontana	6007027	1970	**£10**	
Oobleedooblee Jubilee	LP	Vertigo	6360083	1973	**£30**	spiral label
Oobleedooblee Jubilee	7"	Vertigo	6059074	1972	**£6**	
This Is...	LP	Philips	6382039	1972	**£25**	
Travelling Man	7"	Mercury	MF1040	1968	**£10**	

Try Me One More Time	7"	Mercury	MF1119	1969	**£10**	
Try Me One More Time	LP	Philips	6382040	1973	**£25**	

DUMMIES

Desperate for some more chart success, Slade tried the strategem of issuing singles under the name of the Dummies. They hoped that radio programmers who responded with disinterest to the name of Slade would hear the music of the Dummies with unprejudiced ears. They may have done just that, but unfortunately they still did not appear to like what they heard.

Didn't You Used To Be You	7"	Cheapskate	CHEAP3	1980	**£4**	
Maybe Tonite	7"	Cheapskate	CHEAP14	1981	**£4**	
When The Lights Are Out	7"	Cheapskate	FWL001	1979	**£4**	

DUNBAR, AYNSLEY

Frank Zappa once described Aynsley Dunbar as the only drummer capable of playing the complicated rhythms some of his pieces contained. A graduate of the John Mayall blues school, Dunbar tried for a couple of years to make his own group a success, before accepting that he could do very well playing drums for other people (Zappa, Jefferson Starship, and Journey). The Aynsley Dunbar Retaliation was a fairly routine blues group, but Blue Whale was a more ambitious affair, being a big band with an open, improvisational approach.

Aynsley Dunbar Retaliation	LP	Liberty	LBL83154	1968	**£20**	
Blue Whale	LP	W. Bros	K46062	1970	**£15**	
Doctor Dunbar's Prescription	LP	Liberty	LBL83177	1968	**£20**	
Remains To Be Heard	LP	Liberty	LBS83316	1970	**£20**	
To Mum From Aynsley & The Boys	LP	Liberty	LBS83223	1969	**£20**	
Warning	7"	Blue Horizon	453109	1967	**£15**	
Watch 'n' Chain	7"	Liberty	LBF15132	1968	**£8**	

DUNCAN, JOHNNY

All Of The Monkeys Ain't In The Zoo	7"	Columbia	DB4167	1958	**£4**	
Anytime	7"	Columbia	DB4415	1960	**£4**	
Beyond The Sunset	LP	Columbia	33SX1328	1961	**£12**	
Blue Blue Heartaches	7"	Columbia	DB3996	1957	**£5**	chart single
Footprints In The Snow	7"	Columbia	DB4029	1957	**£5**	chart single
Footprints In The Snow	7" EP	Columbia	SEG7753	1958	**£6**	
Goodnight Irene	7"	Columbia	DB4074	1958	**£6**	
Itching For My Baby	7"	Columbia	DB4118	1958	**£4**	
Johnny Duncan & His Blue Grass Boys	7" EP	Columbia	SEG7708	1957	**£6**	
Johnny Duncan & His Blue Grass Boys 2	7" EP	Columbia	SEG7733	1957	**£6**	
Kansas City	7"	Columbia	DB4311	1959	**£4**	
Kawliga	7"	Columbia	DB3925	1957	**£6**	
Last Train To San Fernando	7"	Columbia	DB3959	1957	**£6**	chart single
Legend Of Gunga Din	7"	Pye	7N15380	1961	**£4**	
Long Time Gone	7"	Pye	7N15420	1962	**£4**	
My Little Baby	7"	Columbia	DB7833	1966	**£4**	
My Lucky Love	7"	Columbia	DB4179	1958	**£4**	
Rosalie	7"	Columbia	DB4282	1959	**£4**	
Salute To Hank Williams	LP	Encore	ENC190	1959	**£15**	
Salutes Hank Williams	LP-10"	Columbia	33S1129	1958	**£15**	
Tennessee Sing Song	7" EP	Columbia	SEG7850	1958	**£6**	
Tennessee Song Bag	LP-10"	Columbia	33S1122	1957	**£15**	
Tobacco Road	7"	Pye	7N15358	1961	**£4**	

DUNCAN, LESLEY

Earth Mother	LP	CBS	64807	1972	**£10**	
Exactly Who You Are	7"	CBS	4585	1969	**£4**	
Hey Boy	7"	Mercury	MF939	1965	**£4**	
I Want A Steady Guy	7"	Parlophone	R5034	1963	**£4**	
Just For The Boy	7"	Mercury	MF847	1965	**£4**	
Lullaby	7"	RCA	RCA1746	1968	**£4**	
Road To Nowhere	7"	RCA	RCA1783	1969	**£4**	
Run To Love	7"	Mercury	MF876	1965	**£4**	
Sing Children Sing	LP	CBS	64202	1971	**£10**	
Sing Children Sing	7"	CBS	8061	1979	**£5**	
Tell Him	7"	Parlophone	R5106	1964	**£4**	
When My Baby Cries	7"	Mercury	MF830	1964	**£4**	

DUNCAN, TOMMY

Dance Dance Dance	7"	Sue	WI4002	1966	**£8**	

DUNKLEY, ERROL

Having A Party	7"	Jackpot	JP702	196-	**£8**	
I Am Not Your Man	7"	Amalgam.	AMG805	196-	**£10**	
I Am Not Your Man	7"	Island	WI3150	1968	**£8**	

I Spy	7"	Amalgam.	AMG820	196-	**£10**	
Love Me Forever	7"	Rio	R109	1967	**£8**	
Please Stop Your Lying	7"	Amalgam.	AMG800	196-	**£10**	
Scorcher	7"	Amalgam.	AMG807	196-	**£10**	
You're Gonna Need Me	7"	Rio	R131	196-	**£8**	

DUPREE, CHAMPION JACK

...And His Blues Band	LP	Decca	SKL4871	1967	**£25**	
Ba-La Fouche	7"	Blue Horizon	573152	1969	**£8**	
Barrelhouse Woman	7"	Decca	F12611	1967	**£4**	
Blues Anthology Vol.1	7" EP	Storyville	SEP381		**£5**	
Blues From The Gutter	LP	Atlantic	8019	1959	**£30**	US
Cabbage Greens	LP	OKeh	OKM12103	1963	**£12**	US
Champion Jack Dupree	7" EP	XX	MIN716		**£5**	
Champion Of The Blues	LP	Atlantic	8056	1961	**£15**	US
From New Orleans To Chicago	LP	Decca	LK4747	1966	**£25**	
I Haven't Done No One No Harm	7"	Blue Horizon	573140	1968	**£10**	
I Want To Be A Hippy	7"	Blue Horizon	573158	1968	**£10**	
London Special	7" EP	Decca	DFE8586	1964	**£4**	
Natural And Soulful Blues	LP	Atlantic	8045	1961	**£15**	US
Rhythm And Blues Vol.1	7" EP	RCA	RCX7137	1964	**£5**	
Scooby Dooby Doo	LP	Blue Horizon	763214	1969	**£30**	
Sings The Blues	LP	King	735	1961	**£25**	US
When You Feel The Feeling	LP	Blue Horizon	763206	1968	**£30**	
Whiskey Head Woman	7"	Storyville	A45051	195-	**£5**	
Women Blues	LP	Folkways	FS3825	1961	**£12**	US

DUPREE, CHAMPION JACK & TONY MCPHEE

Get Your Head Happy	7"	Blue Horizon	451007	1966	**£20**	

DUPREE, SIMON & THE BIG SOUND

Broken Hearted Pirates	7"	Parlophone	R5757	1969	**£6**	
Day Time, Night Time	7"	Parlophone	R5594	1967	**£6**	
Eagle Flies Tonight	7"	Parlophone	R5816	1969	**£8**	
For Whom The Bell Tolls	7"	Parlophone	R5670	1968	**£5**	chart single
I See The Light	7"	Parlophone	R5542	1966	**£8**	
Kites	7"	Parlophone	R5646	1967	**£6**	chart single
Part Of My Past	7"	Parlophone	R5697	1968	**£6**	
Reservations	7"	Parlophone	R5574	1967	**£8**	
Simon Dupree & The Big Sound	7" EP	EMI	EMI2893	1978	**£4**	
Thinking About My Life	7"	Parlophone	R5727	1968	**£8**	
Without Reservations	LP	Parlophone	PCS7029	1967	**£12**	chart LP

DUPREES

Check Yourself	7"	Polydor	2058077	1970	**£4**	
Gone With the Wind	7"	London	HLU9709	1963	**£4**	
Have You Heard	LP	Coed	LPC906	1963	**£30**	US
Have You Heard	7"	London	HLU9813	1963	**£4**	
I'd Rather Be Here In Your Arms	7"	London	HLU9678	1963	**£4**	
It's No Sin	7"	London	HLU9843	1964	**£4**	
My Special Angel	7"	MGM	MGM1460	1968	**£4**	
Why Don't You Believe Me	7"	London	HLU9774	1963	**£4**	
You Belong To Me	LP	Coed	LPC905	1962	**£30**	US
You Belong To Me	7"	HMV	POP1073	1962	**£5**	

DURAN DURAN

Big Thing	Box	EMI		1988	**£40**	promo box set, LP cass & CD
Careless Memories	12"	EMI		1981	**£8**	1 sided promo
Duran Duran	12"	EMI	PSLP344	1981	**£8**	promo sampler
Hungry Like The Wolf	12"	EMI		1982	**£6**	promo
I Don't Want Your Love	12"	EMI	12YOURDJ1	1988	**£6**	promo
I Don't Want Your Love	12"	EMI	12YOURS1	1988	**£6**	1 sided etched pic disc
My Own Way (3 versions)	12"	EMI		1982	**£10**	promo
Notorious (Latin Rascals mix)	12"	EMI	12DDN45	1986	**£10**	
Notorious	LP	EMI	DDN331	1986	**£20**	with press kit
Planet Earth	7"	EMI	EMI5137	1981	**£6**	1 sided promo
Planet Earth	12"	EMI	PSLP331	1981	**£8**	1 sided promo
Reflex	7"	EMI	DURANP2	1984	**£6**	poster sleeve
Reflex	12"	EMI	12DURANP2	1984	**£10**	pic disc
Rio	7"	EMI	EMI5346	1982	**£6**	1 sided promo

Title	Format	Label	Cat. No.	Year	Price	Notes
Skin Trade	7"	EMI	TRADEX1	1987	**£5**	
Skin Trade	12"	EMI		1987	**£6**	5 track promo
View To A Kill	7"	EMI	DURANG007	1985	**£4**	white vinyl, gatefold sleeve

DURHAM, JUDITH

Title	Format	Label	Cat. No.	Year	Price	Notes
Again And Again	7"	Columbia	DB8290	1967	**£8**	

DURHAM, TERRY

Title	Format	Label	Cat. No.	Year	Price	Notes
Crystal Telephone	LP	Deram	SML1042	1969	**£15**	

DURUTTI COLUMN

Title	Format	Label	Cat. No.	Year	Price	Notes
Enigma	7"	Sordide S.	SS45005	1981	**£15**	French
Live At The Venue London	LP	VU	VINI1	1983	**£12**	
Return Of The Durutti Column	LP	Factory	FACT14	1980	**£15**	sandpaper sleeve, with flexi (FACT14C)
Say What You Mean	7"	Factory	FAC114	1985	**£4**	

DURY, IAN

Title	Format	Label	Cat. No.	Year	Price	Notes
Sex & Drugs & Rock'n'Roll	7"	Stiff	BUY17	1977	**£5**	PS, orange vinyl
Sex & Drugs & Rock'n'Roll	7"	Stiff	FREEBIE1	1978	**£15**	flexi
What A Waste	12"	Stiff	BUY2712	1978	**£10**	

DUSTY, SLIM

Title	Format	Label	Cat. No.	Year	Price	Notes
Pub With No Beer	7"	Columbia	DB4212	1958	**£4**	chart single
Slim Dusty And His Country Rockers	7" EP	Columbia	SEG8009	1960	**£6**	

DUTCH

Title	Format	Label	Cat. No.	Year	Price	Notes
What Is Soul	7"	Philips	BF1673	1968	**£4**	

DUVEEN, BOEING & THE BEAUTIFUL SOUP

Title	Format	Label	Cat. No.	Year	Price	Notes
Jabberwock	7"	Parlophone	R5696	1968	**£4**	

DYKE & THE BLAZERS

Title	Format	Label	Cat. No.	Year	Price	Notes
Funky Broadway	LP	Original Snd	LP8876	1967	**£20**	US
Funky Broadway	7"	Pye	7N25413	1967	**£4**	
Greatest Hits	LP	Original Snd	LPS8877	1969	**£15**	US

DYLAN, BOB

Bob Dylan has recorded so prolifically over the years that collecting him consists to a large extent of trying to obtain some of the large number of bootleg LPs that have been issued. Apart from documenting some crucially important live performances (such as the famous Albert Hall concert with the Band, albums of which probably have total sales to rival those of Dylan's CBS recordings), these also allow Dylan's many studio out-takes to be heard. Many of these are arguably better than the tracks that were released. A few out-takes are also officially available on scarce promotional releases and on the very first American issue of "Freewheelin'", which included four songs that are not on any of the subsequent releases of the record. These are "Rocks And Gravel" (called "Solid Gravel" on some pressings), "Let Me Die In My Footsteps", "Gamblin' Willie's Dead Man's Hand", and "Talkin' John Birch Society Blues".

Title	Format	Label	Cat. No.	Year	Price	Notes
Another Side Of...	LP	CBS	BPG62429	1964	**£10**	chart LP
Blonde On Blonde	LP	CBS	66012	1966	**£20**	double, mono, chart LP
Blonde On Blonde	LP	CBS	66012	1966	**£12**	double, stereo, chart LP
Bob Dylan	LP	CBS	BPG62022	1962	**£12**	chart LP
Bob Dylan	7" EP	CBS	EP6051	1965	**£15**	
Bob Dylan	LP	Columbia	CL1779	1962	**£75**	US mono, 6 eye logos on label
Bob Dylan	LP	Columbia	CS8579	1962	**£100**	US stereo, 6 eye logos on label
Bob Dylan In Concerto	12"	Gong	5A/6B	1976	**£50**	Italian
Bringing It All Back Home	LP	CBS	BPG62515	1965	**£10**	chart LP
Can You Please Crawl Out Your Window	7"	CBS	201900	1965	**£8**	chart single
Changing Of The Guard (2 versions)	7"	CBS	6895DJ	1978	**£6**	promo
Corrina Corrina	7"	Columbia	442656	1963	**£50**	US
Desire	LP	CBS	Q86003	1976	**£15**	quad
Fool Such As I	7"	CBS	2006	1974	**£4**	
Forever Young (2 versions)	7"	CBS	7473DJ	1980	**£6**	promo
Four Songs From Renaldo And Clara	12"	Columbia	AS422	1978	**£40**	US promo
Freewheelin'	LP	CBS	BPG62193	1963	**£10**	chart LP
Freewheelin'	LP	Columbia	CL1986	1963	**£2000**	US, 4 different tracks
George Jackson	7"	CBS	7688	1971	**£6**	
Highway 61 Revisited	LP	CBS	BPG62572	1965	**£12**	mono, chart LP
Highway 61 Revisited	LP	CBS	SBPG62572	1965	**£10**	stereo, chart LP
Highway 61 Revisited	LP	Columbia	CS9189	1965	**£75**	US, alternate take of 'From A Buick 6'
Hurricane	7"	CBS	3878	1976	**£4**	chart single

Title	Format	Label	Number	Year	Price	Notes
Hurricane	7"	CBS	3878	1976	**£6**	PS
Hurricane	7"	CBS	3878DJ	1975	**£6**	edited promo
I Threw It All Away	7"	CBS	4219	1969	**£4**	chart single
I Want You	7"	CBS	202258	1966	**£8**	chart single
If Not For You	7"	CBS	7092	1971	**£4**	
John Wesley Harding	LP	CBS	63252	1968	**£10**	mono, chart LP
Jokerman (2 versions)	7"	CBS	A4055DJ	1983	**£6**	promo
Leopardskin Pillbox Hat	7"	CBS	202700	1967	**£6**	
Leopardskin Pillbox Hat	7"	CBS	202700	1967	**£20**	PS
Like A Rolling Stone	7"	CBS	201811	1965	**£5**	chart single
Maggie's Farm	7"	CBS	201781	1965	**£5**	chart single
Million Dollar Bash	7"	CBS	3665	1975	**£4**	
Mr.Tambourine Man	7" EP	CBS	EP6078	1966	**£15**	
Nashville Skyline	LP	CBS	63601	1969	**£12**	mono, chart LP
Nashville Skyline	LP	CBS	CQ32872	1974	**£20**	US quad
Nashville Skyline	LP	Columbia	HC49825	1981	**£20**	US audiophile
Nine Song Publisher's Sampler	LP	W. Bros	XTD221567	1963	**£600**	US promo
On A Night Like This	7"	Island	WIP6168	1974	**£4**	
One Of Us Must Know	7"	CBS	202053	1966	**£6**	chart single
One Too Many Mornings	7" EP	CBS	EP6070	1966	**£15**	
Planet Waves	LP	Ashes & S.	7E501	1973	**£50**	US own label
Planet Waves	LP	Asylum	EQ1003	1974	**£25**	US quad
Positively Fourth Street	7"	CBS	201824	1965	**£5**	chart single
Rainy Day Women	7"	CBS	202307	1966	**£5**	chart single
Rita May	7"	CBS	4859	1977	**£4**	
Rita May	7"	CBS	4859	1977	**£6**	PS
Subterranean Homesick Blues	7"	CBS	201753	1965	**£5**	chart single
Tangled Up In Blue	7"	CBS	3160	1975	**£4**	
Times They Are A-Changin'	LP	CBS	BPG62251	1964	**£10**	chart LP
Times They Are A-Changin'	7"	CBS	201751	1965	**£5**	chart single
Times They Are A-Changin'	LP	Mobile Fid.	MFSL1114	1984	**£15**	US audiophile
Tonight I'll Be Staying Here With You	7"	CBS	4611	1969	**£4**	
Vs.A.J.Weberman	LP	Folkways	FB5322	1971	**£80**	US
Watching The River Flow	7"	CBS	7329	1971	**£6**	chart single
Wigwam	7"	CBS	5122	1970	**£5**	

DYLAN, BOB, & OTHERS

Title	Format	Label	Number	Year	Price	Notes
World Of Folk Music	LP	W. Bros	XGPB508	1964	**£200**	US promo

DYNAMICS

Title	Format	Label	Number	Year	Price	Notes
Dynamics With Jimmy Hannah	LP	Bolo	BLP8001	1962	**£20**	US
Ice Cream Song	7"	Atlantic	584270	1969	**£5**	
Misery	7"	London	HLX9809	1963	**£5**	
My Friends	7"	Blue Cat	BS104	196-	**£10**	
So In Love With Me	7"	King	KG1007	196-	**£6**	

DYNAMITES

Title	Format	Label	Number	Year	Price	Notes
John Public	7"	Duke	DU30	196-	**£8**	
Mr.Midnight	7"	Clandisc	CLA200	1966	**£8**	
Rahtid	7"	Trojan	TR647	1969	**£6**	

DYNATONES

Title	Format	Label	Number	Year	Price	Notes
Fife Piper	7"	Pye	7N25389	1966	**£15**	
Steel Guitar Rag	7"	Top Rank	JAR149	1959	**£4**	

DYSON, RONNIE

Title	Format	Label	Number	Year	Price	Notes
We Can Make It Last Forever	7"	CBS	2430	1974	**£6**	

E

EAGER, VINCE

Title	Format	Label	Cat. No.	Year	Price	Notes
Any Time Is The Right Time	7"	Piccadilly	7N35110	1963	**£4**	
Five Days Five Days	7"	Parlophone	R4482	1958	**£8**	
Lonely Blue Boy	7"	Top Rank	JAR307	1960	**£4**	
Love My Life Away	7"	Top Rank	JAR539	1961	**£4**	
Making Love	7"	Top Rank	JAR191	1959	**£4**	
No Other Arms, No Other Lips	7"	Parlophone	R4550	1959	**£4**	
Vince Eager & The Vagabonds No.1	7" EP	Decca	DFE6504	1958	**£8**	
When's Your Birthday Baby	7"	Parlophone	R4531	1959	**£4**	
Why	7"	Top Rank	JAR275	1960	**£4**	
World's Loneliest Man	7"	Top Rank	JAR593	1961	**£4**	

EAGLE

Title	Format	Label	Cat. No.	Year	Price	Notes
Come Under Nancy's Tent	LP	Pye		1969	**£12**	
Kickin' It Back To You	7"	Pye	7N25530	1970	**£5**	

EAGLES

Title	Format	Label	Cat. No.	Year	Price	Notes
Desperado	LP	Asylum	K53003	1982	**£10**	audiophile
Hotel California	LP	Mobile Fid.	MFSL1126	1981	**£12**	US audiophile
On The Border	LP	Asylum	EQ1004	1975	**£10**	US quad
One Of These Nights	LP	Asylum	EQ1039	1975	**£10**	US quad

EAGLES (2)

Title	Format	Label	Cat. No.	Year	Price	Notes
Andorra	7"	Pye	7N15613	1964	**£4**	
Bristol Express	7"	Pye	7N15451	1962	**£4**	
Come On Baby	7"	Pye	7N15550	1963	**£4**	
Desperadoes	7"	Pye	7N15503	1962	**£4**	
Eagles Nest	7"	Pye	7N15571	1963	**£4**	
Exodus	7"	Pye	7N15473	1962	**£4**	
New Sound TV Themes	7" EP	Pye	NEP24166	1962	**£6**	
Smash Hits	LP	Pye	NPL18084	1963	**£20**	
Wishing And Hoping	7"	Pye	7N15650	1964	**£4**	

EAGLES & VALERIE MOUNTAIN

Title	Format	Label	Cat. No.	Year	Price	Notes
Some People	7" EP	Pye	NEP24158	1962	**£5**	

EAGLIN, SNOOKS

Title	Format	Label	Cat. No.	Year	Price	Notes
Blues Anthology Vol.6	7" EP	Storyville	SEP386		**£5**	
Country Boy	7"	Storyville	A45056	196-	**£5**	
New Orleans Street Singer	LP	Storyville	SLP119	196-	**£12**	
Vol.2 - Blues From New Orleans	LP	Storyville	SLP140	196-	**£12**	

EARL & DEAN

Title	Format	Label	Cat. No.	Year	Price	Notes
Slowly Going Out Of My Head	7"	Strike	JH323	1966	**£4**	

EARLS

Title	Format	Label	Cat. No.	Year	Price	Notes
Never	7"	London	HL9702	1963	**£8**	
Remember Me Baby	LP	Old Town	LP104	1963	**£50**	US
Remember Then	7"	Stateside	SS153	1963	**£8**	

EARTH

Title	Format	Label	Cat. No.	Year	Price	Notes
Resurrection City	7"	CBS	4671	1969	**£12**	
Stranger Of Fortune	7"	Decca	F22908	1969	**£10**	

EARTH & FIRE

Title	Format	Label	Cat. No.	Year	Price	Notes
Atlantis	LP	Polydor	2925013	1973	**£10**	
Earth And Fire	LP	Nepentha	6437004	1971	**£100**	
Song Of Marching Children	LP	Polydor	2925003	197-	**£15**	Dutch
To The World A Future	LP	Polydor	2925033	1975	**£10**	

EARTH OPERA

Title	Format	Label	Cat. No.	Year	Price	Notes
Alfie Finney	7"	Elektra	EKSN45061	1969	**£4**	
American Eagle Tragedy	7"	Elektra	EKSN45049	1968	**£4**	

Title	Format	Label	Number	Year	Price	Notes
Close Your Eyes And Shut The Door	7"	Elektra	EKSN45035	1968	**£5**	
Earth Opera	LP	Elektra	EKS74016	1968	**£15**	
Great American Eagle Tragedy	LP	Elektra	EKS74038	1969	**£10**	

EARTH QUAKERS

Title	Format	Label	Number	Year	Price	Notes
Whistling In The Sunshine	7"	Stateside	SS2050	1967	**£6**	

EARTH QUAKES

Title	Format	Label	Number	Year	Price	Notes
Brother Moses	7"	Duke	DU55	196-	**£8**	
Earth Quake	7"	Duke	DU56	196-	**£8**	
I Can't Stop Loving You	7"	Duke	DU54	196-	**£8**	

EARTH, WIND & FIRE

Title	Format	Label	Number	Year	Price	Notes
Best Of	LP	Columbia	HC45647	1981	**£10**	US audiophile
Head To The Sky	LP	Columbia	CQ32194	1974	**£10**	US quad
Open Our Eyes	LP	Columbia	CQ32712	1974	**£10**	US quad
Raise	LP	Columbia	HC47548	1982	**£10**	US audiophile
That's The Way Of The World	LP	Mobile Fid.	MFSL1159	1984	**£10**	US audiophile

EARTHLINGS

Title	Format	Label	Number	Year	Price	Notes
Landing Of The Daleks	7"	Parlophone	R5242	1965	**£10**	

EASLEY, TIM

Title	Format	Label	Number	Year	Price	Notes
Susie Q	7"	Bell	BLL1036	1968	**£4**	

EAST MAIN ST.EXPLOSION

Title	Format	Label	Number	Year	Price	Notes
Hop, Skip and Jump	7"	Fontana	TF1039	1969	**£4**	

EAST OF EDEN

East Of Eden were virtually two separate groups, with only violinist Dave Arbus being a member of both. The Harvest recordings, made after the group gained a chart hit with the atypical "Jig A Jig", are routine seventies rock. The Deram LPs, on the other hand, contain fiercely experimental music in which Don Drummond rubs shoulders with Charles Mingus and saxophones, flutes, and violins jostle with each other for supremacy.

Title	Format	Label	Number	Year	Price	Notes
Boogie Woogie Flu	7"	Harvest	HAR5055	1972	**£4**	
East Of Eden	LP	Harvest	SHVL792	1971	**£10**	
Jig A Jig	7"	Deram	DM297	1970	**£4**	chart single
King Of Siam	7"	Atlantic	584198	1968	**£8**	
New Leaf	LP	Harvest	SHVL796	1971	**£10**	
Northern Hemisphere	7"	Deram	DM242	1969	**£10**	
Ramadhan	7"	Deram	DM338	1971	**£8**	
Sin City Girls	7"	United Artists	UP35567	1973	**£4**	
Snafu	LP	Deram	SML1050	1970	**£15**	chart LP

EASTERHOUSE

Title	Format	Label	Number	Year	Price	Notes
Get Back To Russia	7"	Rough Trade	RDJ94	1986	**£4**	

EASTWOOD, CLINT

Title	Format	Label	Number	Year	Price	Notes
Cowboy Favorites	LP	Cameo	C1056	1963	**£15**	US
I Talk To The Trees	7"	Paramount	PARA3004	1970	**£4**	chart single

EASYBEATS

Title	Format	Label	Number	Year	Price	Notes
Come And See Her	7"	United Artists	UP1144	1966	**£5**	
Friday On My Mind	7"	United Artists	UP1157	1966	**£5**	chart single
Friends	LP	Polydor	2482010	1970	**£30**	
Friends	7"	Polydor	2001028	1970	**£8**	
Good Friday	LP	United Artists	SULP1167	1967	**£30**	
Good Times	7"	United Artists	UP2243	1969	**£5**	
Heaven And Hell	7"	United Artists	UP1183	1967	**£6**	
Hello How Are You	7"	United Artists	UP2209	1968	**£5**	chart single
I Love Marie	7"	Polydor	56357	1969	**£5**	
Land Of Make Believe	7"	United Artists	UP2219	1968	**£5**	
Music Goes Round My Head	7"	United Artists	UP1201	1967	**£8**	
St.Louis	7"	Polydor	56335	1969	**£6**	
Vigil	LP	United Artists	SULP1193	1968	**£30**	
Who'll Be The One	7"	United Artists	UP1175	1966	**£5**	

EATER

Title	Format	Label	Number	Year	Price	Notes
Album	LP	The Label	TLRLP001	1978	**£20**	
Get Your Yo-Yo's Out	7"	The Label	TLR007	1978	**£4**	white vinyl, 4 PS's
Get Your Yo-Yo's Out	12"	The Label	TLR007	1978	**£6**	white vinyl, 4 PS's
Lock It Up	7"	The Label	TLR004	1977	**£4**	
Lock It Up	12"	The Label	TLR004	1977	**£6**	

Title	Format	Label	Cat. No.	Year	Price	Notes
Outside View	7"	The Label	TLR001	1977	**£5**	
Thinking Of The USA	7"	The Label	TLR003	1977	**£4**	
What She Wants She Needs	7"	The Label	TLR009	1978	**£5**	

EBONIES

Title	Format	Label	Cat. No.	Year	Price	Notes
Never Gonna Break Your Heart Again	7"	Philips	BF1648	1968	**£4**	

ECCENTRICS

Title	Format	Label	Cat. No.	Year	Price	Notes
What You Got	7"	Pye	7N15850	1965	**£4**	

ECCLES

Title	Format	Label	Cat. No.	Year	Price	Notes
My September Love	7"	Parlophone	R4251	1956	**£4**	

ECCLES, CLANCY

Title	Format	Label	Cat. No.	Year	Price	Notes
Beat Dance	7"	Clandisc	CLA206	1966	**£8**	
Brighter Days Will Be Coming	7"	Harry J	HJ6664	1974	**£4**	
C.N.Express	7"	Pama	PM722	196-	**£8**	
Constantinople	7"	Trojan	TR648	1969	**£6**	
Fattie Fattie	7"	Trojan	TR658	1969	**£6**	
Festival '68	7"	New Beat	NB006	1968	**£8**	
Fight	7"	Pama	PM712	196-	**£8**	
Generation Gap	7"	Opal	PAL9	1976	**£4**	
Miss Ida	7"	Ska Beat	JB198	1965	**£10**	
Mother's Advice	7"	Pama	PM703	196-	**£8**	
Sammy No Dead	7"	Ska Beat	JB194	1965	**£10**	
Shu Be Do	7"	Duke	DU31	196-	**£8**	
Sweet Africa	7"	Trojan	TR639	1969	**£6**	
What Will Your Mama Say	7"	Pama	PM701	196-	**£8**	

ECHO & THE BUNNYMEN

Title	Format	Label	Cat. No.	Year	Price	Notes
Back Of Love	12"	Korova	KOW24T	1982	**£6**	
Bring On The Dancing Horses	7"	Korova	KOW43	1988	**£8**	shaped pic disc
Crocodiles	7"	Korova	ECHO1	1981	**£6**	promo
Cutter	cass-s	Korova	KOW26C	1983	**£6**	
Cutter	12"	Korova	KOW26T	1983	**£6**	
Do It Clean	7"	Korova	SAM128	1980	**£6**	freebie
Killing Moon	7"	Korova	KOW32/SAM202	1984	**£6**	double
Pictures On My Wall	7"	Zoo	CAGE004	1979	**£10**	
Promise	7"	Korova	KOW15	1981	**£4**	chart single
Promise	12"	Korova	KOW15T	1981	**£6**	
Puppet	7"	Korova	KOW11	1980	**£10**	
Rescue	7"	Korova	KOW1	1980	**£4**	chart single
Rescue	12"	Korova	KOW1T	1980	**£12**	
Shine So Hard	12"	Korova	ECHOZ1	1981	**£6**	
Songs To Learn And Sing	LP	Korova	KODE13P	1985	**£10**	pic disc

ECHOES

Title	Format	Label	Cat. No.	Year	Price	Notes
Baby Blue	7"	Top Rank	JAR553	1961	**£4**	
Born To Be With You	7"	Top Rank	JAR399	1960	**£5**	

ECKSTINE, BILLY

Title	Format	Label	Cat. No.	Year	Price	Notes
Gentle On My Mind	LP	T. Motown	STML11101	1969	**£20**	
Had You Been Around	7"	T. Motown	TMG533	1965	**£25**	
Had You Been Around	7"	T. Motown	TMG533	1965	**£60**	demo
My Way	LP	T. Motown	STML11046	1967	**£30**	
Prime Of My Life	LP	T. Motown	TML11025	1966	**£40**	

ECKSTINE, BILLY & SARAH VAUGHAN

Title	Format	Label	Cat. No.	Year	Price	Notes
Passing Strangers	7"	Mercury	MF1082	1969	**£4**	chart single
Passing Strangers	7"	Mercury	MT164	1957	**£4**	chart single

ECLECTION

Eclection had a very similar sound to the early Fairport Convention and two of its members - Trevor Lucas and Gerry Conway - both played with the more famous group in later years. When singer Kerilee Male left in October 1968, the group took the unusual step of re-recording their current single with Male's replacement, Doris Henderson. Despite this, however, neither version sold particularly well.

Title	Format	Label	Cat. No.	Year	Price	Notes
Another Time Another Place	7"	Elektra	EKSN45040	1968	**£6**	
Eclection	LP	Elektra	EKS74023	1968	**£40**	
Nevertheless	7"	Elektra	EKSN45033	1968	**£8**	
Nevertheless	7"	Elektra	K12196	1976	**£4**	
Please	7"	Elektra	EKSN45042	1968	**£6**	
Please	7"	Elektra	EKSN45046	1968	**£6**	

ED & ALTON & THE SOUL VENDORS

Title	Format	Label	Number	Year	Price	Notes
Whipping The Prince	7"	Coxsone	CS7038	196-	**£10**	

EDDIE & THE HOT RODS

Title	Format	Label	Number	Year	Price	Notes
At The Speed Of Sound	12"	Island	IEP5	1977	**£6**	
Do Anything You Wanna Do	7"	Island	WIP6401	1977	**£4**	chart single
Life On The Line	12"	Island	12WIP6438	1977	**£6**	
Live At the Marquee	7"	Island	IEP2	1976	**£4**	chart single
Wooly Bully	7"	Island	WIP6306	1976	**£4**	

EDDIE, JASON

Title	Format	Label	Number	Year	Price	Notes
Heart And Soul	7"	Tangerine	DP0010	196-	**£6**	
Singing The Blues	7"	Parlophone	R5473	1966	**£15**	
Whatcha Gonna Do Baby	7"	Parlophone	R5388	1965	**£12**	

EDDY & TEDDY

Title	Format	Label	Number	Year	Price	Notes
Bye Bye Butterfly	7"	London	HLU9367	1961	**£4**	

EDDY, DUANE

Title	Format	Label	Number	Year	Price	Notes
1,000,000 Dollars Of Twang	LP	London	HAW2325	1961	**£10**	chart LP
1,000,000 Dollars Of Twang Vol.2	LP	London	HAW2435	1964	**£10**	chart LP
Avenger	7"	London	HLW9477	1961	**£4**	
Ballad Of Paladin	7"	RCA	RCA1300	1962	**£4**	chart single
Because They're Young	7"	London	HLW9162	1960	**£4**	chart single
Because They're Young	7" EP	London	REW1252	1960	**£5**	
Biggest Twang Of All	LP	Reprise	R6218	1966	**£10**	
Biggest Twang Of All	LP	Reprise	RS6218	1967	**£12**	stereo
Bonnie Came Back	7"	London	HLW9050	1960	**£4**	chart single
Boss Guitar	7"	RCA	RCA1329	1963	**£4**	chart single
Break My Mind	7"	CBS	3962	1969	**£6**	
Cannonball	7"	London	HL8764	1958	**£4**	chart single
Caravan	7"	Parlophone	R4826	1961	**£4**	chart single
Cottonmouth	7" EP	Colpix	PXE304	1965	**£10**	
Country Twang	7" EP	RCA	RCX7115	1963	**£8**	
Dance With The Guitar Man	LP	RCA	RD7545	1963	**£10**	chart LP
Dance With The Guitar Man	LP	RCA	SF7545	1963	**£12**	stereo, chart LP
Dance With The Guitar Man	7"	RCA	RCA1316	1962	**£4**	stereo, chart single
Daydream	7"	Reprise	R20504	1966	**£4**	
Deep In The Heart Of Texas	7"	RCA	RCA1288	1962	**£4**	chart single
Drivin' Home	7"	London	HLW9406	1961	**£4**	chart single
Duane A Go Go	LP	Colpix	PXL490	1965	**£10**	
Duane Does Dylan	LP	Colpix	PXL494	1965	**£10**	
Duane Does Dylan	LP	Golden Guin.	GGL10337	1968	**£10**	
Duane Does Dylan	LP	Golden Guin.	GGSL10337	1968	**£12**	stereo
Especially For You	LP	London	HAW2191	1959	**£10**	chart LP
Especially For You	LP	London	SAHW6045	1959	**£12**	stereo
Forty Miles Of Bad Road	7"	London	HLW8929	1959	**£4**	chart single
Girls Girls Girls	LP	London	HAW2373	1961	**£10**	
Girls Girls Girls	LP	London	SAHW6173	1961	**£12**	stereo
Guitar Star	7"	RCA	RCA1425	1964	**£4**	
Guitared And Feathered	7"	RCA	RCA1369	1963	**£4**	
Have Twangy Guitar Will Travel	LP	London	HAW2160	1958	**£15**	chart LP
House Of The Rising Sun	7"	Colpix	PX788	1964	**£4**	
Kommotion	7"	London	HLW9225	1960	**£4**	chart single
Lonely Boy Lonely Guitar	7"	RCA	RCA1344	1963	**£4**	chart single
Lonely Guitar	LP	RCA	RD7621	1964	**£10**	
Lonely Guitar	LP	RCA	SF7621	1964	**£12**	stereo
Lonely One	7"	London	HLW8821	1959	**£4**	
Lonely One	7" EP	London	REW1216	1959	**£5**	
Mister Twang	7" EP	RCA	RCX7129	1963	**£8**	
Monsoon	7"	Reprise	R20557	1967	**£4**	
Movie Themes	7" EP	London	REW1303	1961	**£5**	
Niki Hoeky	7"	Reprise	R20690	1968	**£4**	
Pepe	7"	London	HLW9257	1961	**£4**	chart single
Pepe	7" EP	London	REW1287	1961	**£5**	
Peter Gunn	7"	London	HLW8879	1959	**£4**	chart single
Peter Gunn	7"	London	SLW4001	1959	**£6**	stereo
Ramrod	7"	London	HL8723	1958	**£4**	
Rebel Rouser	7"	London	HL8669	1958	**£5**	chart single
Rebel Rouser	7" EP	London	RE1175	1958	**£6**	
Ring Of Fire	7"	London	HLW9370	1961	**£4**	chart single

Title	Format	Label	Cat. No.	Year	Price	Notes
Roarin' Twangies	LP	Reprise	R6240	1968	**£10**	
Shazam!	7"	London	HLW9104	1960	**£4**	chart single
Some Kinda Earthquake	7"	London	HLW9007	1959	**£4**	chart single
Son Of Rebel Rouser	7"	RCA	RCA1389	1964	**£4**	
Songs Of Our Heritage	LP	London	HAW2285	1960	**£10**	chart LP
Songs Of Our Heritage	LP	London	SAHW6119	1960	**£12**	stereo
Theme From Dixie	7"	London	HLW9324	1961	**£4**	chart single
Trash	7"	Colpix	PX779	1964	**£4**	
Twang A Country Song	LP	RCA	SF7560	1963	**£12**	stereo
Twang's The Thang	LP	London	HAW2236	1960	**£10**	chart LP
Twang's The Thang	LP	London	SAHW6068	1960	**£12**	stereo
Twangin' Golden Hits	LP	RCA	RD7689	1964	**£10**	
Twangin' Golden Hits	LP	RCA	SF7689	1965	**£12**	stereo
Twangin' Up A Storm	LP	RCA	RD7568	1963	**£10**	
Twangin' Up A Storm	LP	RCA	SF7568	1963	**£12**	stereo
Twangin' Up A Small Storm	7" EP	RCA	RCX7146	1964	**£8**	
Twangs A Country Song	LP	RCA	RD7560	1963	**£10**	
Twangsville	LP	RCA	RD7754	1965	**£10**	
Twangsville	LP	RCA	SF7754	1965	**£12**	stereo
Twangy	7" EP	London	REW1257	1960	**£5**	
Twangy Guitar Silky Strings	LP	RCA	RD7510	1962	**£10**	chart LP
Twangy Guitar Silky Strings	LP	RCA	SF7510	1962	**£12**	stereo, chart LP
Twangy No.2	7" EP	London	REW1341	1961	**£5**	
Twistin' And Twangin'	LP	RCA	RD27264	1962	**£10**	chart LP
Twistin' And Twangin'	LP	RCA	SF5134	1962	**£12**	stereo
Water Skiing	LP	RCA	SF7656	1964	**£12**	stereo
Water Skiing	LP	RCA	RD7656	1964	**£10**	
Yep	7" EP	London	REW1217	1959	**£5**	
Your Baby's Gone Surfin'	7"	RCA	RCA1357	1963	**£4**	chart single

EDEN ROSE

Title	Format	Label	Cat. No.	Year	Price	Notes
On The Way To Eden	LP	Metema		1971	**£200**	

EDEN'S CHILDREN

Title	Format	Label	Cat. No.	Year	Price	Notes
Eden's Children	LP	Stateside	SSL10235	1968	**£20**	
Sure Looks Real	LP	ABC	ABCS652	1969	**£20**	US

EDGE

Title	Format	Label	Cat. No.	Year	Price	Notes
Downhill	7"	Hurricane	FIRE3	1979	**£4**	
Downhill	7"	Hurricane	FIRE3	1979	**£5**	white vinyl
Macho Man	7"	Albion	ION4	1978	**£4**	
Watching You	7"	Hurricane	FIRE6	1979	**£4**	

EDMUND JR., LADA

Title	Format	Label	Cat. No.	Year	Price	Notes
The Larue	7"	MCA	MCA172	1975	**£4**	

EDMUNDS, DAVE

Title	Format	Label	Cat. No.	Year	Price	Notes
Blue Monday	7"	Regal Z.	RZ3037	1971	**£4**	
College Radio Network Presents..	LP	Swan Song	PR320	1978	**£20**	US promo
Down Down Down	7"	Regal Z.	RZ3059	1972	**£4**	
Girls Talk	7"	Swan Song	SSK19418	1979	**£4**	clear vinyl
I Ain't Never	7"	Rockfield	ROC6	1975	**£4**	
I'm Coming Home	7"	Regal Z.	RZ3032	1971	**£4**	
Information	12"	Columbia	AS991725	1983	**£20**	US promo pic disc
Need A Shot Of Rhythm And Blues	7"	Rockfield	ROC4	1974	**£4**	
Rockpile	LP	Regal Z.	SLRZ1026	1971	**£25**	
Rockpile Collection	LP	Regal Z.	SRZA8503	1971	**£40**	
Subtle As A Flying Mallet	LP	Rockfield	RRL101	1975	**£10**	

EDSELS

Title	Format	Label	Cat. No.	Year	Price	Notes
Rama Lama Ding Dong	7"	Pye	7N25086	1961	**£10**	

EDWARD BEAR

Title	Format	Label	Cat. No.	Year	Price	Notes
Bearings	LP	Capitol	ST426	1969	**£10**	
Last Song	7"	P. Farthing	PEN801	1973	**£4**	
You, Me And Mexico	7"	Capitol	CL15637	1970	**£4**	

EDWARDS HAND

Title	Format	Label	Cat. No.	Year	Price	Notes
Edwards Hand	LP	GRT	10005	1969	**£15**	US
Rainshine	LP	Regal Z.	SRZA8513	1973	**£15**	
Stranded	LP	RCA	SF8154	1971	**£15**	

EDWARDS, BOBBY

Title	Format	Label	Cat. No.	Year	Price	Notes
You're The Reason	7"	Top Rank	JAR584	1961	£4	

EDWARDS, CHUCK

Title	Format	Label	Cat. No.	Year	Price	Notes
Downtown Soulville	7"	Soul City	SC104		£4	
Downtown Soulville	7"	Soul City	SC104		£20	demo

EDWARDS, JACKIE

Title	Format	Label	Cat. No.	Year	Price	Notes
All My Days	7"	Island	WI008	1962	£12	
Best Of	LP	Island	ILP936	1966	£60	
By Demand	LP	Island	ILP940	1966	£60	
Come Back Girl	7"	Island	WIP6008	1967	£8	
Come On Home	LP	Island	ILP931	1966	£60	
He'll Have To Go	7"	Aladdin	WI601	1965	£10	
Heaven Just Knows	7"	Starlite	ST45046	1961	£12	
Hush	7"	Aladdin	WI605	1965	£10	
Hush	7" EP	Island	IEP708	1966	£15	
I Feel So Bad	7"	Island	WI3006	1966	£10	
I Must Go Back	7"	Horse	HOSS1	197-	£4	
Julie On My Mind	7"	Island	WIP6026	1968	£8	
L-O-V-E	7"	Island	WI274	1966	£10	
Let It Be Me	LP	Direction	63977	1970	£10	
Lonely Game	7"	Decca	F11547	1962	£6	
More Than Words Can Say	7"	Starlite	ST45062	1961	£10	
Most Of Wilfred Jackie Edwards	LP	Island	ILP906	1964	£60	
Never Go Away	7"	Starlite	ST45076	1962	£10	
Oh Manio	7"	Direction	584630	1969	£5	
One More Week	7"	Island	WI019	1962	£12	
Only A Fool Breaks His Own Heart	7"	Island	WI3030	1967	£8	
Premature Golden Sands	LP	Island	ILPS9060	1967	£50	
Put Your Tears Away	LP	Island	IWPS4	1969	£10	
Royal Telephone	7"	Island	WI3018	1966	£8	
Sacred Songs Vol.1	7" EP	Island	IEP701	1966	£10	
Sacred Songs Vol.2	7" EP	Island	IEP702	1966	£10	
Same One	7"	Aladdin	WI611	1965	£10	
Sea Cruise	7"	Fontana	TF465	1964	£10	
Sometimes	7"	Island	WI270	1966	£10	
Stagger Lee	7"	Sue	WI329	1964	£10	
Stand Up For Jesus	LP	Island	ILP912	1964	£40	
Tell Me Why You Say Goodbye	7"	CBS	5147	1970	£5	
Things You Do	7"	Black Swan	WI416	1964	£10	
Think Twice	7"	Island	WI287	1966	£10	
Too Experienced	7"	Direction	584402	1969	£5	
White Christmas	7"	Island	WI255	1965	£10	
White Christmas	7"	Trojan	TR7883	1973	£4	
Why Must I Be Alone	7"	Direction	584096	1969	£5	
You're My Future Wife	7"	Trojan	TR7918	1974	£4	
You're My Girl	7"	Island	WI3157	1968	£8	
You're My Girl	7"	Island	WIP6042	1968	£8	

EDWARDS, JACKIE & JIMMY CLIFF

Title	Format	Label	Cat. No.	Year	Price	Notes
Set Me Free	7"	Island	WIP6036	1968	£6	

EDWARDS, JACKIE & MILLIE

Title	Format	Label	Cat. No.	Year	Price	Notes
Best Of Jackie And Millie	LP	Island	ILP963	1968	£40	
Pledging My Love (Jackie And Millie)	LP	Island	ILP941	1966	£50	

EDWARDS, JIMMY

Title	Format	Label	Cat. No.	Year	Price	Notes
Love Bug Crawl	7"	Mercury	7MT193	1958	£50	

EDWARDS, SAMUEL

Title	Format	Label	Cat. No.	Year	Price	Notes
Israel	7"	Blue Cat	BS159	196-	£10	

EDWARDS, TOMMY

Title	Format	Label	Cat. No.	Year	Price	Notes
For Young Lovers	LP	MGM	E3760	1959	£10	US
I've Been There	7" EP	MGM	MGMEP707	1959	£5	
It's All In The Game	LP	MGM	E3732	1959	£12	US
It's All In The Game	7"	MGM	MGM989	1958	£4	chart single
My Melancholy Baby	7"	MGM	MGM1020	1959	£4	chart single
Tommy Edwards	LP	Lion	70120	195-	£15	US
Tommy Edwards Sings	LP	Regent	MG6096	195-	£15	US

EDWARDS, VINCE

Title	Format	Label	Number	Year	Price	Notes
Aquarius	7"	United Artists	UP2236	1968	**£4**	
County Durham Dream	7"	United Artists	UP2230	1968	**£5**	
I Can't Turn Back Time	7"	United Artists	UP1179	1967	**£5**	
I Like It	7"	United Artists	UP1166	1966	**£4**	

EDWARDS, WILFRED & THE CARIBS

Title	Format	Label	Number	Year	Price	Notes
Tell Me Darling	7"	Starlite	ST45026	1960	**£12**	
We're Gonna Love	7"	Starlite	ST45016	1960	**£12**	

EDWICK RUMBOLD

Title	Format	Label	Number	Year	Price	Notes
Shades Of Grey	7"	Parlophone	R5622	1967	**£15**	

EFFIGIES

Title	Format	Label	Number	Year	Price	Notes
Haunted Town	12"	Autumn	AU3	1981	**£15**	

EGANS, WILLIE

Title	Format	Label	Number	Year	Price	Notes
Willie Egans	7" EP	XX	MIN714		**£5**	

EGG

The records made by Egg contain the most impressive music of any made by those groups whose dominant voice is that of the keyboards. Organist Dave Stewart has been making records ever since, with Hatfield and the North and other related groups (he's even been in the charts a few times, but not as a member of the Eurythmics!), but he has arguably never bettered the youthful enthusiasm of his work with Egg. The group's music is difficult in places, but only in the same way that Soft Machine's music is. It utilises awkward time signatures and convoluted melody lines, but never forgets its essential function of communicating with an audience.

Title	Format	Label	Number	Year	Price	Notes
Civil Surface	LP	Caroline	C1510	1974	**£12**	
Egg	LP	Nova	SDN14	1970	**£15**	
Polite Force	LP	Deram	SML1074	1970	**£15**	
Seven Is A Jolly Good Time	7"	Deram	DM269	1969	**£8**	

EGGY

Title	Format	Label	Number	Year	Price	Notes
You're Still Mine	7"	Spark	SRL1024	1970	**£10**	

EIGHT-EYED SPY

Title	Format	Label	Number	Year	Price	Notes
Diddy Wah Diddy	7"	Fetish	FE19	1982	**£6**	
Eight-Eyed Spy	LP	Fetish	FR2003	1981	**£10**	

EIGHTH WONDER

Title	Format	Label	Number	Year	Price	Notes
I'm Not Scared	10"	CBS	SCAREX1	1988	**£8**	

EIRE APPARENT

Title	Format	Label	Number	Year	Price	Notes
Follow Me	7"	Track	604019	1967	**£10**	
Rock'n'Roll Band	7"	Buddah	201039	1969	**£10**	
Rock'n'Roll Band	7"	Buddah	2011117	1972	**£6**	
Sunrise	LP	Buddah	203021	1969	**£40**	

EKSEPTION

Title	Format	Label	Number	Year	Price	Notes
3	LP	Philips	6423005	1971	**£12**	Dutch
4	LP	Philips	6423019	1972	**£12**	Dutch
5	LP	Philips	6423042	1972	**£12**	Dutch
Air	7"	Philips	6318990	1972	**£4**	
Beggar Julia's Time Trip	LP	Philips	6314001	1969	**£15**	
Best Of	LP	Philips	6423053	1973	**£10**	Dutch
Classics In Pop	LP	Philips	6423079	1974	**£10**	Dutch
Ekseption	LP	Philips	6314005	1970	**£15**	
Mind Mirror	LP	Philips	6423082	1975	**£10**	Dutch
Trinity	LP	Philips	6423056	1973	**£10**	Dutch

ELASTIC BAND

Title	Format	Label	Number	Year	Price	Notes
Do Unto Others	7"	Decca	F12815	1968	**£20**	
Expansions On Life	LP	Nova	SND6	1969	**£20**	
Thinking Of You Baby	7"	Decca	F12763	1968	**£20**	

ELBERT, DONNIE

Title	Format	Label	Number	Year	Price	Notes
Get Ready	7"	CBS	2807	1967	**£5**	
In Between The Heartaches	7"	Polydor	56234	1968	**£4**	
Let's Do The Stroll	7"	Parlophone	R4403	1958	**£4**	
Little Piece Of Leather	7"	Sue	WI377	1965	**£10**	
Sensational Donnie Elbert Sings	LP	King	629	1959	**£60**	US
This Old Heart Of Mine	7"	Polydor	56265	1968	**£4**	
Without You	7"	Deram	DM235	1969	**£4**	

You Can Push It Or Pull It	7"	Sue	WI396	1965	**£8**	

ELDORADOS

Crazy Little Mama	LP	Vee Jay	VJLP1001	1959	**£150**	US
Eldorados	7" EP	Decca	DFE8543	1963	**£8**	

ELECTRIC BANANA

Another Time	LP	W. Bros	2798	1972	**£15**	US
Electric Banana	LP	De Wolfe	3040	1967	**£20**	
Hot Licks	LP	De Wolfe	3284	1973	**£15**	
More Electric Banana	LP	De Wolfe	3069	1968	**£20**	
Return Of...	LP	De Wolfe	3381	1979	**£15**	

ELECTRIC FLAG

At its best, Mike Bloomfield's big band sound marvellous - the driving "Killing Floor" or the long, crafted "Another Country" (both on "A Long Time Comin') - but the Electric Flag's music was extremely uneven. Calling itself An American Music Band, the Electric Flag really wanted to play everything. It would probably have been better, however, if it had not tried to cast its net so wide. As it is, the band seems to lack focus. "Electric Flag" was recorded after many of the original members, including Bloomfield, had left. "The Trip" is a film soundtrack and contains a large number of very short tracks - frustrating.

Best Of...	LP	CBS	64337	1971	**£10**	
Electric Flag	LP	CBS	63462	1969	**£12**	
Groovin' Is Easy	7"	CBS	3584	1968	**£8**	
Long Time Comin'	LP	CBS	63294	1968	**£15**	
Sunny	7"	CBS	4066	1969	**£8**	
Trip	LP	Sidewalk	ST5908	1967	**£20**	US

ELECTRIC JOHNNY

Black Eyes Rock	7"	London	HLU9384	1961	**£8**	

ELECTRIC LIGHT ORCHESTRA

All Over The World	7"	Jet	195	1979	**£4**	blue vinyl
All Over The World	10"	Jet	10195	1980	**£6**	blue vinyl
Can't Get It Out Of My Head	7"	Jet	ELO1JB	1977	**£10**	juke box issue
Discovery	LP	Jet	HZ45769	1981	**£12**	US audiophile
Eldorado	LP	Jet		1981	**£12**	US audiophile
Eldorado	LP	Jet	LP203	1978	**£10**	yellow vinyl
Electric Light Orchestra	LP	Harvest	Q4SHVL797	1974	**£12**	quad
Face The Music	LP	Jet	LP201	1978	**£10**	green vinyl
Greatest Hits	LP	Jet	HZ46310	1981	**£12**	US audiophile
Livin' Thing	7"	United Artists	UP36184	1976	**£5**	blue vinyl
Mr.Blue Sky	7"	Jet	104	1978	**£4**	blue vinyl
Night The Light Went Out In Long Beach	LP	W. Bros	WBK56058	1974	**£12**	German
Ole Elo	LP	Jet/United Art	SP123	1976	**£15**	US promo, gold vinyl
On The Third Day	LP	Jet	LP202	1978	**£10**	clear vinyl
Out Of The Blue	LP	Jet	DP400	1978	**£10**	blue vinyl
Roll Over Beethoven	12"	Harvest	PSLP213	1977	**£6**	promo
Secret Messages	LP	Jet	HZ48490	1983	**£12**	US audiophile
Shine A Little Love	7"	Jet	144	1979	**£4**	white vinyl
Shine A Little Love	12"	Jet	12144	1979	**£6**	white vinyl
Strange Magic	7"	Jet	ELO2JB	1977	**£10**	juke box issue
Sweet Talking Woman	7"	Jet	121	1978	**£4**	mauve vinyl
Sweet Talking Woman	12"	Jet	12121	1978	**£6**	mauve vinyl
Ticket To The Moon	12"	Jet	127018	1981	**£6**	pic disc
Time	LP	Jet	HZ47371	1981	**£12**	US audiophile
Wild West Hero	7"	Jet	109	1978	**£4**	yellow vinyl
Wild West Hero	12"	Jet	12109	1978	**£6**	yellow vinyl

ELECTRIC PRUNES

The Electric Prunes were two groups, both in style and in personnel, for sometime during the recording of "Mass In F Minor" there was a complete change in membership. The 1966-7 releases contain many prime examples of psychedelia, most notably the quartet of singles. "Mass In F Minor", on the other hand, is exactly what it says it is - a rock mass. The album is an interesting and reasonably successful experiment, but it is very short on playing time.

Everybody Knows	7"	Reprise	RS20652	1968	**£12**	
Get Me To The World On Time	7"	Reprise	RS20564	1967	**£8**	chart single
Great Banana Hoax	7"	Reprise	RS20607	1967	**£10**	
I Had Too Much To Dream	7"	Radar	ADA16	1979	**£4**	
I Had Too Much To Dream	7"	Reprise	RS20532	1966	**£10**	chart single
I Had Too Much To Dream...	LP	Reprise	RLP6248	1967	**£20**	US
Just Good Old Rock'n'Roll	LP	Reprise	RSLP6342	1969	**£20**	US
Long Day's Flight	7"	Reprise	RS23212	1967	**£10**	
Mass In F Minor	LP	Reprise	RLP6275	1968	**£15**	

Release Of An Oath	LP	Reprise	RLP6316	1968	**£15**	
Underground	LP	Reprise	RS6262	1967	**£30**	US

ELECTRIC TOILET

In The Hands Of Karma	LP	Nasco	9004	1970	**£40**	US

ELEGANTS

Little Star	7"	HMV	POP520	1958	**£5**	chart single
Please Believe Me	7"	HMV	POP551	1958	**£6**	

ELEPHANT'S MEMORY

Crossroads Of The Stepping Stones	7"	Buddah	201055	1969	**£4**	
Elephant's Memory	LP	Apple	SAPCOR22	1972	**£15**	
Elephant's Memory	LP	Buddah	BDS5033	1969	**£15**	
Mongoose	7"	CBS	5207	1970	**£4**	
Old Man Willow	7"	Buddah	201067	1969	**£4**	
Power Boogie	7"	Apple	45	1972	**£6**	
Take It To The Streets	LP	Metronome	MD1052	1971	**£10**	

ELF

Carolina Country Ball	LP	Purple	TPSA3506	1974	**£15**	
Elf	LP	Epic	KE31789	1972	**£15**	
L.A. '59	7"	Purple	PUR118	1974	**£5**	

ELGINS

Darling Baby	LP	T. Motown	STML11081	1968	**£20**	
Heaven Must Have Sent You	7"	T. Motown	TMG583	1966	**£15**	
Heaven Must Have Sent You	7"	T. Motown	TMG583	1966	**£50**	demo
Heaven Must Have Sent You	7"	T. Motown	TMG771	1971	**£4**	chart single
Heaven Must Have Sent You	7"	T. Motown	TMG771	1971	**£10**	demo
It's Been A Long Time	7"	T. Motown	TMG615	1967	**£6**	
It's Been A Long Time	7"	T. Motown	TMG615	1967	**£40**	demo
Put Yourself In My Place	7"	T. Motown	TMG551	1966	**£12**	
Put Yourself In My Place	7"	T. Motown	TMG551	1966	**£60**	demo
Put Yourself In My Place	7"	T. Motown	TMG642	1968	**£5**	
Put Yourself In My Place	7"	T. Motown	TMG642	1968	**£20**	demo
Put Yourself In My Place	7"	T. Motown	TMG787	1971	**£4**	chart single
Put Yourself In My Place	7"	T. Motown	TMG787	1971	**£15**	demo

ELIAS & HIS ZIG ZAG JIVE FLUTES

Tom Hark	7"	Columbia	DB4109	1958	**£4**	chart single

ELIAS HULK

Elias Hulk Unchained	LP	Youngblood	SSYB8	1970	**£250**	

ELIZABETH

Elizabeth	LP	Vanguard	SVRL19010	1968	**£15**	
Stop Killing Me With Kindness	7"	Paramount	PARA3032	1973	**£4**	

ELLEDGE, JIMMY

Swanee River Rocket	7"	RCA	RCA1274	1962	**£6**	

ELLIMAN, YVONNE

I Don't Know How To Love Him	7"	MCA	MK5063	1971	**£4**	

ELLINGTON, MARC

Did You Give The World Some Love	7"	Philips	BF1742	1969	**£4**	
Four In The Morning	7"	Philips	BF1779	1969	**£4**	
I Shall Be Released	7"	Philips	BF1665	1968	**£5**	
Marc Ellington	LP	Philips	SBL7883	1969	**£10**	
Marc Time	LP	Xtra	XTRA1154	1972	**£10**	
Question Of Roads	LP	Philips	6308120	1972	**£10**	
Rains/Reins Of Change	LP	B&C	CAS193	1971	**£10**	
Restoration	LP	Philips	6308143	1972	**£10**	

ELLIOT, MAMA CASS

Dream A Little Dream	LP	Stateside	SSL5004	1968	**£10**	

ELLIOTT, BERN

Guess Who	7"	Decca	F12051	1965	**£6**	
Voodoo Woman	7"	Decca	F12171	1965	**£5**	

ELLIOTT, BERN & THE CLAN

Good Times	7"	Decca	F11970	1964	£5	

ELLIOTT, BERN & THE FENMEN

Bern Elliott And The Fenmen Play	7" EP	Decca	DFE8561	1964	£15	
Money	7"	Decca	F11770	1963	£5	chart single
New Orleans	7"	Decca	F11852	1964	£5	chart single

ELLIOTT, BILL & ELASTIC OZ BAND

God Save Us	7"	Apple	36	1971	£6	
God Save Us	7"	Apple	36	1971	£12	PS

ELLIOTT, RAMBLING JACK

Sings The Songs Of Woody Guthrie	LP	Vanguard		196-	£12	US
Blues And Country	7" EP	Collector	JEA6	1964	£6	
In London	LP	Encore	ENC194	1959	£20	
More Pretty Girls	7"	Fontana	TF575	1965	£4	
Rambling Jack Elliott	7" EP	Collector	JEA5	196-	£6	
Rambling Jack Elliott	LP	Vanguard		1964	£12	US
Rusty Jigs And Sandy Sam	7"	Columbia	DB7593	1965	£4	

ELLIS

Riding On The Crest Of A Slump	LP	Epic	64878	1972	£10	
Why Not?	LP	Epic	65650	1973	£10	

ELLIS, ALTON

Ain't That Loving You	7"	Treasure Isle	TI7016	196-	£8	
Change Of Plans	7"	Studio One	SO2084	196-	£10	
Comet Rock Steady	7"	Trojan	TR004	196-	£10	
Cry Tough	7"	Island	WI3046	1967	£8	
Deliver Us To Africa	7"	Harry J	HJ6653	1973	£4	
Diana	7"	Gas	GAS105	196-	£8	
Duke Of Earl	7"	Treasure Isle	TI7010	196-	£8	
Easy Squeeze	7"	Studio One	SO2003	196-	£10	
Fool	7"	Coxsone	CS7071	196-	£10	
Girl I've Got A Date	7"	Doctor Bird	DB1059	1966	£10	
I Am Just A Guy	7"	Studio One	SO2028	196-	£10	
I Am Still In Love	7"	Studio One	SO2020	196-	£10	
I Can't Stand It	7"	New Beat	NB010	1968	£8	
La-La Means I Love You	7"	New Beat	NB014	1968	£8	
Laba Laba Reggae	7"	Trojan	TR634	1969	£6	
Message	7"	Pama	PM707	196-	£8	
Mr. Soul Of Jamaica	LP	Treasure Isle	013	196-	£60	
My Time Is The Right Time	7"	Pama	PM717	196-	£8	
Only Sixteen	7"	Studio One	SO2033	196-	£10	
Rock Steady	7"	Treasure Isle	TI7004	196-	£8	
Sings Rock And Soul	LP	Coxsone	CSL8008	196-	£80	
Truly	7"	Pyramid	PYR7003	1973	£4	
Wise Birds Follow Spring	7"	Trojan	TR009	196-	£10	

ELLIS, BOBBY

Dollar A Head	7"	Island	WI3136	1968	£8	
Emperor	7"	Island	WI3089	1967	£8	
Feeling Peckish	7"	Island	WI3091	1967	£8	
Now We Know	7"	Island	WI3092	1967	£8	
Shuntin'	7"	Island	WI3135	1968	£8	

ELLIS, DON

Autumn	LP	CBS	63503	1968	£10	
Electric Bath	LP	CBS	63230	1968	£10	
Goes Underground	LP	CBS	63680	1969	£10	
Live At The Fillmore	LP	CBS		1969	£15	double
Shock Treatment	LP	CBS	63356	1968	£10	

ELLIS, HORTENSE

Groovy Kind Of Love	7"	Coxsone	CS7033	196-	£10	
I've Been A Fool	7"	Blue Beat	BB295	1964	£10	

ELLIS, JIMMY

Ellis Sings Elvis By Request	LP	Boblo	78829		£20	US

ELLIS, LARRY

Nothing You Can Do	7"	Felsted	AF110	1958	**£4**	

ELLIS, MATTHEW

Am I	LP	Regal Z.	SRZA8505	1971	**£10**	
Avalon	7"	Regal Z.	RZ3033	1971	**£4**	
Birthday Song	7"	Regal Z.	RZ3039	1971	**£4**	
Matthew Ellis	LP	Regal Z.	SRZA8501	1971	**£10**	
Palace Of Plenty	7"	Regal Z.	RZ3045	1972	**£4**	

ELLIS, SHIRLEY

Clapping Song	7"	London	HLR9961	1965	**£5**	chart single
Ever See A Diver Kiss His Wife?	7"	London	HLR10021	1966	**£4**	
In Action	LP	Congress	CGL3002	1964	**£10**	US
Name Game	LP	Congress	CGL3003	1965	**£10**	US
Name Game	7"	London	HLR9946	1965	**£4**	
Puzzle Song	7"	London	HLR9973	1965	**£4**	
Soul Time	7"	CBS	202606	1967	**£4**	
Sugar, Let's Shing A Ling	7"	CBS	2817	1967	**£4**	
Sugar, Let's Shing A Ling	LP	Columbia	CL2679	1967	**£10**	US

ELLISON, ANDY

Been A Long Time	7"	Track	604018	1967	**£30**	
Fool From Upper Eden	7"	CBS	3357	1968	**£40**	
You Can't Do That	7"	SNB	553308	1968	**£40**	

ELLISON, LORRAINE

Stay With Me	7"	W. Bros	WB5850	1966	**£4**	
Try A Little Bit Harder	7"	W. Bros	WB2094	1968	**£6**	
You've Really Got A Hold On Me	7"	W. Bros	WB7394	1970	**£4**	

ELMER GANTRY'S VELVET OPERA

Elmer Gantry's Velvet Opera	LP	Direction	863300	1968	**£40**	
Flames	7"	Direction	583083	1967	**£6**	
Mary Jane	7"	Direction	583481	1968	**£6**	
Volcano	7"	Direction	583924	1969	**£6**	

ELMOND, SIMSE

Tit For Tat	7"	Coxsone	CS7095	196-	**£10**	

ELOY

Eloy	LP	Philips		1971	**£120**	bin cover

ELROY, JEFF & THE BLUE BOYS

Honey Machine	7"	Philips	BF1533	1966	**£4**	

ELVES

Amber Velvet	7"	MCA	MU1114	1970	**£8**	

EMBERS

Chelsea Boots	7"	Decca	F11625	1963	**£4**	

EMBERS (2)

Rock And Roll Eleven	LP	JCP Rec.	2006		**£75**	US

EMERALDS

Don't Listen To Your Friends	7"	Decca	F12096	1965	**£4**	
King Lonely The Blue	7"	Decca	F12304	1965	**£4**	

EMERSON LAKE & PALMER

Brain Salad Surgery	7"	Lyntone	LYN2762	1974	**£4**	flexi
Pictures At An Exhibition	LP	Mobile Fid.	MFSL1031	1980	**£15**	US audiophile
Works Volume One	LP	Atlantic		1976	**£12**	promo

EMMET SPICELAND

Emmet Spiceland	LP	Page One		1968	**£25**	
So Long Marianne	7"	Page One	POF143	1969	**£8**	

EMMETT

Baby Ain't No Lie	7"	Columbia	DB7582	1965	**£5**	
Nancy	7"	Columbia	DB7695	1965	**£5**	

EMOTIONS

Somebody New	7"	Deep Soul	DS9104	1970	**£6**	
Story Untold	7"	Stateside	SS237	1963	**£5**	

EMOTIONS (2)

Careless Hands	7"	Caltone	TONE120	196-	**£8**	
Rainbow	7"	Caltone	TONE100	196-	**£8**	
Rudeboy Confession	7"	Ska Beat	JB263	1966	**£10**	
Rumbay	7"	High Note	HS026	196-	**£8**	
Soulful Music	7"	Caltone	TONE118	196-	**£8**	
Storm	7"	High Note	HS018	196-	**£8**	

EMPERORS

Karate	7"	Stateside	SS565	1966	**£5**	

ENCHANTED FOREST

You're Never Gonna Get My Lovin'	7"	Stateside	SS2080	1968	**£4**	

ENCHANTERS

We Got Love	7"	W. Bros	WB2054	1967	**£4**	

END

The End were managed and produced by Bill Wyman, but his patronage brought them little success. A change of name to Tucky Buzzard brought more recordings in the seventies, but only a small increase in sales.

I Can't Get Any Joy	7"	Philips	BF1444	1965	**£8**	
Introspection	LP	Decca	SKL5015	1969	**£20**	
Shades Of Orange	7"	Decca	F12750	1968	**£10**	

ENDEVERS

Remember When We Were Young	7"	Decca	F12817	1968	**£4**	
She's My Girl	7"	Decca	F12859	1968	**£4**	
Sunny And Me	7"	Decca	F12939	1969	**£4**	

ENDLE ST.CLOUD

Thank You All Very Much	LP	Int. Artists	IALP12	1970	**£25**	

ENDSLEY, MELVIN

I Got A Feeling	7"	RCA	RCA1051	1958	**£5**	
I Like Your Kind Of Love	7"	RCA	RCA1004	1957	**£6**	

ENFORCERS

Musical Fever	7"	Blue Cat	BS120	1968	**£10**	

ENGEL, SCOTT

Charlie Bop	7"	Vogue	V9150	1959	**£50**	
Living End	7"	Vogue	V9145	1959	**£50**	
Paper Doll	7"	Vogue	V9125	1958	**£35**	
Scott Engel	7" EP	Liberty	LEP2261	1966	**£15**	

ENGEL, SCOTT & JOHN STEWART

I Only Came To Dance With You	7"	Capitol	CL15440	1966	**£6**	
I Only Came To Dance With You	LP	Tower	ST5026	1965	**£20**	US

ENGLAND

England	LP	Deroy		1976	**£200**	
Garden Shed	LP	Arista	ARTY153	1977	**£30**	

ENGLISH, JOE

Lay Lady Lay	7"	Fontana	TF1034	1969	**£4**	

ENID

The Enid have never been either the most popular of the progressive bands or the most arty, yet they have managed to attract a highly devoted following. The rarest Enid records are an obvious manifestation of this devotion, the very limited edition releases issued by "The Stand" fetching increasingly high prices from the many fans who have never even seen copies, still less heard them.

And Then There Were None	12"	EMI	12EMI5505	1984	**£6**	
Dambusters March	7"	Pye	7P106	1979	**£10**	
Enid	LP	The Stand	THESTAND2	1984	**£100**	
Fool	7"	Pye	7P187	1980	**£8**	
Golden Earrings	7"	EMI	EMI5109	1980	**£8**	
Golden Earrings	7"	EMI	INTS540	1977	**£10**	
Heigh Ho	7"	Bronze	BRO134	1981	**£8**	

Itchycoo Park	7"	Sedition	EDIT3314	1986	**£6**	
Itchycoo Park	12"	Sedition	EDITL3314	1986	**£6**	
Jubilee	7"	EMI	INT534	1977	**£10**	
Liverpool Album	LP		LE1	1987	**£100**	
Lovers	7"	Buk	BUK3002	1976	**£10**	
The Stand	LP	The Stand	THESTAND1	1983	**£150**	
Then There Were None	7"	Rak	RAK349	1982	**£8**	
When You Wish Upon A Star	7"	Bronze	BRO127	1981	**£8**	

ENJAYS

All My Love All My Life	7"	Top Rank	JAR145	1959	**£4**	

ENNIS, RAY & THE BLUE JEANS

What Have They Done To Hazel?	7"	Columbia	DB8431	1968	**£15**	

ENO, BRIAN

When his task was to make some sense of the controls of a distinctly non-user-friendly synthesizer, as a member of Roxy Music, Brian Eno always used to describe himself as a non-musician. If this was in any way an accurate description, then the lack of preconceptions has clearly been an advantage for Eno, for his solo career has been distinguished by some very interesting ideas. The novelty of his approach is typified by his experiments with creative musak - what he calls "ambient" music - where the listener is not intended to listen at all closely. Eno's career has thrown up one ultra-rarity: an early, alternative version of his "Music For Films" LP, which was limited to around a hundred copies.

Before And After Science	LP	Polydor	2302071	1977	**£10**	with 4 prints
Lion Sleeps Tonight	7"	Island	WIP6233	1975	**£4**	
Music For Films	LP	Editions EG	EGM1	1976	**£500**	diff. tracks to '78 issue
Seven Deadly Finns	7"	Island	WIP6178	1974	**£4**	

ENOS & SHEILA

La La Bamba	7"	Blue Cat	BS135	196-	**£10**	
Tonight You're Mine	7"	Blue Cat	BS138	196-	**£10**	

ENTWISTLE, JOHN

Backtrack 14 (The Ox)	LP	Track	2407014	1971	**£15**	
I Believe In Everything	7"	Track	2094008	1971	**£4**	
I Wonder	7"	Track	2094107	1973	**£6**	
Mad Dog	LP	Track	TX5114	1975	**£10**	
Made In Japan	7"	Track	2094017	1973	**£4**	
Rigor Mortis Sets In	LP	Track	2406106	1973	**£10**	
Smash Your Head ...	LP	Track	2406005	1971	**£10**	
Too Late The Hero	7"	WEA	K79249P	1981	**£10**	autographed pic disc
Whistle Rhymes	LP	Track	2406104	1972	**£10**	

EPICS

Henry Long	7"	CBS	3564	1968	**£6**	
How Wrong Can You Be	7"	Pye	7N17053	1966	**£5**	
There's No Pleasing You	7"	Pye	7N15829	1965	**£5**	

EPISODE SIX

Episode Six's pleasant but undistinguished harmony music would be very much less collectable were it not for the fact that the group's vocalist was Ian Gillan (and the bass player was Roger Glover), although the likes of "Here There And Everywhere" are light years away from the dynamism of Deep Purple's "Sweet Child In Time" and "Speed King".

Here, There And Everywhere	7"	Pye	7N17147	1966	**£8**	
I Can See Through You	7"	Pye	7N17376	1967	**£10**	
I Hear Trumpets Blow	7"	Pye	7N17110	1966	**£10**	
I Will Warm Your Heart	7"	Pye	7N17194	1966	**£12**	
Little One	7"	MGM	MGM1409	1968	**£15**	
Love, Hate, Revenge	7"	Pye	7N17244	1967	**£10**	
Lucky Sunday	7"	Chapter One	CH103	1968	**£12**	
Morning Dew	7"	Pye	7N17330	1967	**£8**	
Mozart Vs. The Rest	7"	Chapter One	CH104	1969	**£12**	
Put Yourself In My Place	7"	Pye	7N17018	1966	**£12**	

EPPERSON, MINNIE

Grab Your Clothes	7"	Action	ACT4503	1968	**£4**	
Grab Your Clothes	7"	Action	ACT4503	1968	**£10**	demo

EPPS, PRESTON

Bongo Bongo Bongo	LP	Original Snd	8851	1960	**£10**	US
Surfin' Bongos	LP	Original Snd	8872	1963	**£10**	US

EPPS, PRESTON & SANDY NELSON

Title	Format	Label	Cat. No.	Year	Price	Notes
Rushing For Percussion	7" EP	Top Rank	JKP2060	1960	**£12**	

EQUALS

Title	Format	Label	Cat. No.	Year	Price	Notes
Baby Come Back	7"	President	PT135	1968	**£4**	chart single
Baby Come Back	7" EP	President	PTE1	1968	**£5**	
Baby Come Back	LP	RCA	LSP4078	1968	**£10**	US
Black Skin Blue Eyed Boys	7"	President	PT325	1970	**£4**	chart single
Unequalled	LP	President	PTL1006	1967	**£10**	chart LP
Viva Bobby Joe	7"	President	PT260	1969	**£4**	chart single

EQUATIONS

Title	Format	Label	Cat. No.	Year	Price	Notes
Waiting On The Shores Of Nowhere	7"	Fontana	TF1035	1969	**£4**	

EQUINOX

Title	Format	Label	Cat. No.	Year	Price	Notes
Hard Rock	LP	Boulevard	4118	1973	**£10**	

EQUIPPE 84

Title	Format	Label	Cat. No.	Year	Price	Notes
Auschwitz	7"	Major Minor	MM517	1967	**£15**	

ERASURE

Title	Format	Label	Cat. No.	Year	Price	Notes
Chains Of Love (Marx Brothers Mix)	12"	Mute	L12MUTE83	1988	**£6**	
Crackers International Part II: Stop(Rem)	CD-s	Mute	LCDMUTE93	1988	**£8**	with card & gift label
Crackers International Part II: Stop(Rem)	12"	Mute	L12MUTE93	1988	**£6**	
Heavenly Action (Yellow Brick Mix)	12"	Mute	L12MUTE42	1985	**£50**	
Heavenly Action	12"	Mute	D12MUTE42	1985	**£50**	double
It Doesn't Have To Be (Cement Mix)	12"	Mute	L12MUTE56	1987	**£8**	
It Doesn't Have To Be	7"	Mute	DMUTE56	1987	**£5**	double
It Doesn't Have To Be	CD-s	Mute	CDMUTE56	1987	**£10**	
Little Respect (Big Train Mix)	12"	Mute	L12MUTE85	1988	**£6**	
Oh L'Amour (Funky Sisters Mix)	12"	Mute	L12MUTE45	1986	**£15**	
Oh L'Amour (remix)	12"	Mute	12MUTE45	1986	**£20**	Thomas Tank Engine PS
Oh L'Amour	7"	Mute	7MUTE45	1986	**£10**	Thomas Tank Engine PS
Ship Of Fools (Rico Conning Mix)	12"	Mute	L12MUTE74	1988	**£6**	
Sometimes (Shiver Mix)	12"	Mute	L12MUTE51	1986	**£10**	
Sometimes	cass-s	Mute	CMUTE51	1986	**£5**	
Sometimes	7"	Mute	DMUTE51	1986	**£6**	double
Supernature (Dan Miller & Phil Legg Mix)	12"	Mute	XL12MUTE99	1990	**£6**	with outer envelope
Victim Of Love (Vixen Vitesse Mix)	12"	Mute	L12MUTE61	1987	**£8**	
Victim Of Love	CD-s	Mute	CDMUTE61	1987	**£6**	
Who Needs Love Like That (Mexican Mix)	12"	Mute	L12MUTE40	1985	**£30**	
Wild!	Spec	Mute	STUMM75	1989	**£90**	promo box set LP, MC, CD

ERROL & HIS GROUP

Title	Format	Label	Cat. No.	Year	Price	Notes
Gypsy	7"	Blue Beat	BB284	1964	**£10**	

ESCORTS

Title	Format	Label	Cat. No.	Year	Price	Notes
C'mon Home Baby	7"	Fontana	TF570	1965	**£10**	
Dizzie Miss Lizzie	7"	Fontana	TF453	1964	**£8**	
From Head To Toe	7"	Columbia	DB8061	1966	**£20**	
I Don't Want To Go On Without You	7"	Fontana	TF516	1964	**£8**	
Let It Be Me	7"	Fontana	TF651	1966	**£10**	
One To Cry	7"	Fontana	TF474	1964	**£6**	chart single

ESPERANTO ROCK ORCHESTRA

Title	Format	Label	Cat. No.	Year	Price	Notes
Danse Macabre	LP	A&M	AMLH63624	1974	**£10**	
Esperanto Rock Orchestra	LP	A&M	AMLH68175	1973	**£10**	

ESQUERITA

Title	Format	Label	Cat. No.	Year	Price	Notes
Esquerita	LP	Capitol	T1186	1959	**£180**	US
Rocking The Joint	7"	Capitol	CL14938	1958	**£25**	
Wildcat Shakeout	LP	Ember	SPE6603	196-	**£15**	

ESQUIRES

Title	Format	Label	Cat. No.	Year	Price	Notes
And Get Away	7"	Stateside	SS2077	1968	**£6**	
Get On Up	7"	Stateside	SS2048	1967	**£8**	

ESSENTIAL LOGIC

Title	Format	Label	Cat. No.	Year	Price	Notes
Aerosol Burns	7"	Cells	SELL1	1978	**£4**	
Wake Up	7"	Virgin	VS261	1979	**£4**	
Wake Up	12"	Virgin	VS26112	1979	**£6**	

ESSEX

Title	Format	Label	Number	Year	Price	Notes
Easier Said Than Done	7"	Columbia	DB7077	1963	**£6**	chart single
Easier Said Than Done	LP	Roulette	R25234	1963	**£20**	US
She's Got Everything	7"	Columbia	DB7178	1963	**£6**	
Walkin' Miracle	7"	Columbia	DB7122	1963	**£6**	
Walkin' Miracle	LP	Roulette	R25235	1963	**£12**	US
Young And Lively	LP	Roulette	R25246	1964	**£12**	US

ESSEX, DAVID

Title	Format	Label	Number	Year	Price	Notes
And The Tears Came Tumbling Down	7"	Fontana	TF559	1965	**£8**	
Can't Nobody Love You	7"	Fontana	TF620	1965	**£8**	
Day The Earth Stood Still	7"	Decca	F12967	1969	**£6**	
Just For Tonight	7"	Pye	7N17621	1968	**£6**	
Love Story	7"	UNI	UN502	1968	**£6**	
That Takes Me Back	7"	Decca	F12935	1969	**£6**	
Thigh High	7"	Fontana	TF733	1966	**£8**	
This Little Girl Of Mine	7"	Fontana	TF680	1966	**£8**	
World	7"	United Artists	UP605	1979	**£5**	

ESTEFAN, GLORIA

Title	Format	Label	Number	Year	Price	Notes
1-2-3	7"	Epic	6529580	1988	**£4**	poster sleeve
Betcha Say That	7"	Epic	6511257	1987	**£4**	
Betcha Say That	12"	Epic	65112589	1987	**£6**	7 tracks
Betcha Say That	12"	Epic	6511258	1987	**£6**	3 tracks
Can't Stay Away From You	7"	Epic	6514440	1988	**£4**	poster sleeve
Can't Stay Away From You	7"	Epic	6531957	1989	**£6**	shaped pic disc

ESTES, SLEEPY JOHN

Title	Format	Label	Number	Year	Price	Notes
Sleepy John's Got The Blues	7" EP	Delmark	DJB3	1966	**£4**	

ESTREK, JACKIE

Title	Format	Label	Number	Year	Price	Notes
Ska	7"	Ska Beat	JB256	1966	**£10**	

ETERNAL TRIANGLE

Title	Format	Label	Number	Year	Price	Notes
I Guess The Lord Must Be In New York	7"	Decca	F12979	1969	**£4**	
Windows	7"	Decca	F12954	1969	**£4**	

ETERNALS

Title	Format	Label	Number	Year	Price	Notes
Rocking In The Jungle	7"	London	HL8995	1959	**£8**	

ETERNALS (2)

Title	Format	Label	Number	Year	Price	Notes
Queen Of The Minstrels	7"	Coxsone	CS7091	196-	**£10**	

ETERNITY'S CHILDREN

Title	Format	Label	Number	Year	Price	Notes
Mrs.Bluebird	7"	Capitol	CL15558	1968	**£4**	

ETHERIDGE, CHRIS

Title	Format	Label	Number	Year	Price	Notes
L.A. Getaway	LP	Atlantic	K40310	1971	**£10**	

ETHIOPIANS

Title	Format	Label	Number	Year	Price	Notes
Buy You A Ring	7"	Harry J	HJ6663	1974	**£4**	
Do It Sweet	7"	Doctor Bird	DB1092	1967	**£10**	
Fire A Muss Muss Tail	7"	Crab	CRAB2	196-	**£8**	
I Am Free	7"	Island	WI3015	1966	**£8**	
I'm A King	7"	Crab	CRAB7	196-	**£8**	
I'm Gonna Take Over Now	7"	Rio	R114	1967	**£8**	
J.F.K.	7"	Trojan	TR697	1969	**£6**	
Leave Me Business Alone	7"	Studio One	SO2035	196-	**£10**	
Let's Get Together	7"	Coxsone	CS7022	196-	**£10**	
Live Good	7"	Ska Beat	JB260	1966	**£10**	
Owe Me No Pay Me	7"	Rio	R110	1967	**£8**	
Reggae Hit The Town	7"	Crab	CRAB4	196-	**£8**	
Sound Pressure	7"	Island	WI3036	1967	**£8**	
Train To Skaville	7"	Rio	R130	1967	**£8**	chart single
What To Do	7"	Rio	R123	196-	**£8**	
Whip	7"	Doctor Bird	DB1096	1967	**£10**	
Woman Capture Man	7"	Trojan	TR666	1969	**£6**	

ETTA & HARVEY

Title	Format	Label	Number	Year	Price	Notes
If I Can't Have You	7"	London	HLM9180	1960	**£5**	

EUBANKS, JACK

Title	Format	Label	Cat. No.	Year	Price	Notes
Searchin'	7"	London	HLU9501	1962	**£4**	
What'd I Say	7"	London	HLU9312	1961	**£4**	

EUPHORIA

Title	Format	Label	Cat. No.	Year	Price	Notes
Euphoria	LP	Heritage	HTS35005	1969	**£25**	US

EUPHORIA (2)

Title	Format	Label	Cat. No.	Year	Price	Notes
Gift From Euphoria	LP	Capitol	SKAO363	1969	**£40**	US

EURYTHMICS

Title	Format	Label	Cat. No.	Year	Price	Notes
Belinda	7"	RCA	RCA115	1981	**£10**	
Belinda	12"	RCA	RCAT115	1981	**£15**	
Here Comes The Rain Again	7"	RCA	DAP5	1984	**£5**	pic disc
I'm Never Gonna Cry Again	7"	RCA	RCA68	1981	**£10**	chart single
I'm Never Gonna Cry Again	12"	RCA	RCAT68	1981	**£12**	
Julia	7"	Virgin	VSY734	1985	**£4**	pic disc
Love Is A Stranger	7"	RCA	DAP1	1982	**£6**	pic disc
Miracle Of Love	7"	RCA	DA9P	1986	**£4**	pic disc
Rough And Tough	CD	RCA	CP353016	1987	**£60**	US live promo
Sex Crime 1984	12"	Virgin	VSY72812	1984	**£6**	pic disc
Sweet Dreams	LP	RCA	RCALP6063	1983	**£15**	pic disc
Sweet Dreams	7"	RCA	DAP2	1983	**£10**	pic disc
This Is The House	7"	RCA	RCA199	1982	**£10**	
This Is The House	12"	RCA	RCAT199	1982	**£15**	
Touch	LP	RCA	PL70109	1983	**£10**	pic disc

EVANS, CHRISTINE

Title	Format	Label	Cat. No.	Year	Price	Notes
Somewhere There's Love	7"	Philips	BF1496	1966	**£8**	

EVANS, DAVE

Title	Format	Label	Cat. No.	Year	Price	Notes
Elephantasia	LP	Village Thing	VTS14	1972	**£12**	
Words In Between	LP	Village Thing	VTS6	1971	**£12**	

EVANS, LARRY

Title	Format	Label	Cat. No.	Year	Price	Notes
Crazy About My Baby	7"	London	HLU8269	1956	**£15**	

EVANS, MAUREEN

Title	Format	Label	Cat. No.	Year	Price	Notes
Big Hurt	7"	Oriole	CB1533	1960	**£4**	chart single
Don't Want The Moonlight	7"	Oriole	CB1517	1959	**£4**	
I Love How You love Me	7"	Oriole	CB1906	1964	**£4**	chart single
Like I Do	LP	Oriole	PS40046	1963	**£12**	
Like I Do	7"	Oriole	CB1763	1962	**£4**	chart single
Love, Kisses & Heartaches	7"	Oriole	CB1540	1960	**£4**	chart single
Melancholy Me	7" EP	Oriole	EP7076	1963	**£5**	
Paper Roses	7"	Oriole	CB1550	1960	**£4**	chart single

EVANS, PAUL

Title	Format	Label	Cat. No.	Year	Price	Notes
21 Years In A Tennessee Jail	LP	Kapp	KL1346	1964	**£10**	US
Another Town, Another Jail	LP	Kapp	KL1475	1966	**£10**	US
Folk Songs Of Many Lands	LP	Carlton	130	1961	**£12**	US
Hear Paul Evans In Your Home Tonight	LP	Carlton	129	1961	**£12**	US
Midnight Special	7"	London	HLL9045	1960	**£5**	chart single
Paul Evans	7" EP	London	RER1349	1962	**£5**	
Seven Little Girls Sitting In The Back Seat	7"	London	HLL8968	1959	**£4**	chart single
Sings The Fabulous Teens	LP	London	HAL2248	1960	**£15**	

EVANS, RUSSELL & THE NITEHAWKS

Title	Format	Label	Cat. No.	Year	Price	Notes
Send Me Some Cornbread	7"	Atlantic	584010	1966	**£4**	

EVEN DOZEN JUG BAND

The Even Dozen Jug Band, while in itself having little to distinguish it from the many other folk groups playing in America during the early sixties, was nevertheless a remarkably effective training school for some later well-known musicians. Playing in the group were John Sebastian (soon to form the Lovin' Spoonful), Maria D'Amato (famous later under her married name, Maria Muldaur), Steve Katz (guitarist with the Blues Project and Blood,Sweat,and Tears), guitarist Stefan Grossman, and Joshua Rifkin (later responsible for bringing the works of Scott Joplin to public notice).

Title	Format	Label	Cat. No.	Year	Price	Notes
Even Dozen Jug Band	LP	Elektra	EKS7246	1964	**£20**	US

EVERETT, BETTY

Title	Format	Label	Cat. No.	Year	Price	Notes
Getting Mighty Crowded	7"	Fontana	TF520	1964	**£4**	chart single
I Can't Hear You	7"	Stateside	SS321	1964	**£6**	
I've Got A Claim On You	7"	Sue	WI352	1965	**£10**	

It's In His Kiss	LP	Fontana	TL5136	1965	**£25**	
It's In His Kiss	7"	President	PT215	1968	**£4**	chart single
It's In His Kiss	7"	Stateside	SS280	1964	**£5**	
There'll Come A Time	7"	MCA	MU1055	1969	**£4**	
Very Best Of...	LP	Vee Jay	VJLP1122	1965	**£10**	US
What A Sad Feeling	7"	Stateside	SS475	1965	**£4**	
You're No Good	7"	President	PT251	1969	**£4**	
You're No Good	7"	Stateside	SS259	1964	**£5**	
Your Loving Arms	7"	King	KG1002	196-	**£5**	

EVERETT, BETTY & JERRY BUTLER

Delicious Together	LP	Vee Jay	LP1099	1964	**£12**	US
Let It Be Me	7"	Stateside	SS339	1964	**£4**	
Smile	7"	Fontana	TF528	1965	**£4**	

EVERETT, KENNY

It's Been So Long	7"	MGM	MGM1421	1968	**£4**	
Nice Time	7"	Deram	DM245	1969	**£4**	

EVERETT, VINCE

Endlessly	7"	Fontana	TF818	1967	**£4**	
Every Now And Then	7"	Fontana	TF915	1968	**£8**	
Till I Lost You	7"	Fontana	TF606	1965	**£4**	

EVERGREEN BLUES

Laura	7"	Mercury	MF1025	1968	**£6**	
Midnight Confessions	7"	Mercury	MF1012	1967	**£6**	

EVERGREEN BLUESHOES

Ballad Of...	LP	London	SHU8399	1969	**£12**	

EVERLY BROTHERS

Ain't That Lovin' You Baby	7"	W. Bros	WB129	1964	**£4**	
Ain't That Lovin' You Baby	7"	W. Bros	WB129	1964	**£10**	demo
All I Have To Do Is Dream	7"	London	HLA8618	1958	**£4**	chart single
All I Have To Do Is Dream	7"	London	HLA8618	1958	**£30**	demo
Beat & Soul	LP	W. Bros	W1605	1965	**£12**	
Bird Dog	7"	London	HLA8685	1958	**£4**	chart single
Bird Dog	7"	London	HLA8685	1958	**£20**	demo
Both Sides Of An Evening	LP	W. Bros	WM4052	1961	**£15**	
Both Sides Of An Evening Vol.1	7" EP	W. Bros	WEP6115	1963	**£8**	
Both Sides Of An Evening Vol.1	7" EP	W. Bros	WSE6115	1963	**£12**	stereo
Both Sides Of An Evening Vol.2	7" EP	W. Bros	WEP6117	1964	**£8**	
Both Sides Of An Evening Vol.2	7" EP	W. Bros	WSE6117	1964	**£12**	stereo
Both Sides Of An Evening Vol.3	7" EP	W. Bros	WEP6138	1965	**£8**	
Bowling Green	7"	W. Bros	WB7020	1967	**£4**	
Bowling Green	7"	W. Bros	WB7020	1967	**£10**	demo
Bye Bye Love	7"	London	HLA8440	1957	**£6**	chart single
Bye Bye Love	7"	London	HLA8440	1957	**£40**	demo
Cathy's Clown	7"	W. Bros	WB1	1960	**£4**	chart single
Cathy's Clown	7"	W. Bros	WB1	1960	**£15**	demo
Christmas With...	LP	W. Bros	WM8116	1962	**£20**	
Crying In The Rain	7"	W. Bros	WB56	1962	**£4**	chart single
Crying In The Rain	7"	W. Bros	WB56	1962	**£12**	demo
Date With The Everly Brothers Vol.1	7" EP	W. Bros	WEP6107	1963	**£8**	
Date With The Everly Brothers Vol.1	7" EP	W. Bros	WSE6107	1963	**£12**	stereo
Date With The Everly Brothers Vol.2	7" EP	W. Bros	WEP6109	1963	**£8**	
Date With The Everly Brothers Vol.2	7" EP	W. Bros	WSE6109	1963	**£12**	stereo
Date With...	LP	W. Bros	WM4028	1960	**£20**	chart LP
End Of An Era	LP	CBS	66259	1970	**£12**	double
Especially For You	7" EP	W. Bros	WEP6034	1961	**£8**	
Especially For You	7" EP	W. Bros	WSEP2034	1961	**£12**	stereo
Everly Brothers	LP	Cadence	CLP3003	1958	**£25**	US
Everly Brothers	LP	London	HAA2081	1958	**£15**	
Everly Brothers	7" EP	London	REA1113	1958	**£8**	
Everly Brothers No.2	7" EP	London	REA1148	1958	**£8**	
Everly Brothers No.3	7" EP	London	REA1149	1958	**£8**	
Everly Brothers No.4	7" EP	London	REA1174	1959	**£8**	
Everly Brothers No.5	7" EP	London	REA1229	1960	**£8**	
Everly Brothers No.6	7" EP	London	REA1311	1961	**£8**	
Everly Brothers Show	LP	W. Bros	WS1858	1970	**£12**	
Everly Brothers Sing	LP	W. Bros	W1708	1967	**£12**	

Title	Format	Label	Cat. No.	Year	Price	Notes
Everly Brothers Single Set	7"	Lightning	SET1	1980	**£25**	15 x 7", boxed + book
Everly Brothers' Best	LP	Cadence	CLP3025	1959	**£25**	US
Fabulous Style Of...	LP	Cadence	CLP3040	1960	**£25**	US
Fabulous Style Of...	LP	London	HAA2266	1960	**£12**	chart LP
Ferris Wheel	7"	W. Bros	WB135	1964	**£4**	chart single
Ferris Wheel	7"	W. Bros	WB135	1964	**£10**	demo
Fifteen Everly Hits Fifteen	LP	Cadence	CLP3062	1963	**£25**	US
Folk Songs Of The Everly Brothers	LP	Cadence	CLP3059	1962	**£25**	US
Foreverly Yours	7" EP	W. Bros	WEP6049	1962	**£8**	
Foreverly Yours	7" EP	W. Bros	WSEP2049	1962	**£12**	stereo
Girl Sang The Blues	7"	W. Bros	WB109	1963	**£4**	chart single
Girl Sang The Blues	7"	W. Bros	WB109	1963	**£12**	demo
Golden Hits	LP	W. Bros	WM8108	1962	**£10**	
Gone Gone Gone	LP	W. Bros	WM8169	1965	**£12**	
Gone Gone Gone	7"	W. Bros	WB146	1964	**£4**	chart single
Gone Gone Gone	7"	W. Bros	WB146	1964	**£10**	demo
Hit Sound Of...	LP	W. Bros	W1676	1967	**£10**	
How Can I Meet Her	7"	W. Bros	WB67	1962	**£4**	chart single
How Can I Meet Her	7"	W. Bros	WB67	1962	**£10**	demo
I'll Never Get Over You	7"	W. Bros	WB5639	1965	**£4**	chart single
I've Been Wrong Before	7"	W. Bros	WB5754	1966	**£4**	
In Our Image	LP	W. Bros	W1620	1965	**£12**	
Instant Party	LP	W. Bros	WM4061	1962	**£12**	chart LP
Instant Party	7" EP	W. Bros	WEP6111	1963	**£8**	
Instant Party	7" EP	W. Bros	WSE6111	1963	**£12**	stereo
Instant Party Vol.2	7" EP	W. Bros	WEP6113	1963	**£8**	
Instant Party Vol.2	7" EP	W. Bros	WSE6113	1963	**£12**	stereo
It's Been Nice	7"	W. Bros	WB99	1963	**£4**	chart single
It's Been Nice	7"	W. Bros	WB99	1963	**£12**	demo
It's Everly Time	LP	W. Bros	WM4012	1960	**£15**	chart LP
It's Everly Time	7" EP	W. Bros	WEP6056	1962	**£8**	
It's Everly Time	7" EP	W. Bros	WSEP2056	1962	**£12**	stereo
It's My Time	7"	W. Bros	WB7192	1968	**£4**	chart single
It's My Time	7"	W. Bros	WB7192	1968	**£10**	demo
Leave My Girl Alone	7" EP	W. Bros	WEP622	1967	**£8**	
Let It Be Me	7"	London	HLA9039	1960	**£4**	chart single
Let It Be Me	7"	London	HLA9039	1960	**£20**	demo
Lightning Express	7"	London		1962	**£50**	test pressing
Like Strangers	7"	London	HLA9250	1960	**£4**	chart single
Like Strangers	7"	London	HLA9250	1960	**£15**	demo
Love Is Strange	7"	W. Bros	WB5649	1965	**£4**	chart single
Love Is Strange	7" EP	W. Bros	WEP610	1966	**£8**	
Love Of The Common People	7"	W. Bros	WB7088	1967	**£4**	
Love Of The Common People	7"	W. Bros	WB7088	1967	**£12**	demo
Mary Jane	7"	W. Bros	WB7062	1967	**£4**	
Mary Jane	7"	W. Bros	WB7062	1967	**£10**	demo
Milk Train	7"	W. Bros	WB7226	1968	**£4**	
Milk Train	7"	W. Bros	WB7226	1968	**£10**	demo
Muskrat	7"	W. Bros	WB50	1961	**£4**	chart single
Muskrat	7"	W. Bros	WB50	1961	**£12**	demo
No One Can Make My Sunshine Smile	7"	W. Bros	WB79	1962	**£4**	chart single
No One Can Make My Sunshine Smile	7"	W. Bros	WB79	1962	**£10**	demo
Not Fade Away	7"	RCA	RCA2286	1972	**£4**	
Oh Boy	7"	W. Bros	WB6074	1967	**£4**	
People Get Ready	7" EP	W. Bros	WEP612	1966	**£8**	
Poor Jenny	7"	London	HLA8863	1959	**£4**	chart single
Poor Jenny	7"	London	HLA8863	1959	**£20**	demo
Power Of Love	7"	W. Bros	WB5743	1966	**£4**	
Price Of Love	7"	W. Bros	WB161	1965	**£4**	chart single
Price Of Love	7"	W. Bros	WB161	1965	**£10**	demo
Price Of Love	7"	W. Bros	WB5628	1965	**£4**	
Price Of Love	7" EP	W. Bros	WEP604	1965	**£8**	
Problems	7"	London	HLA8781	1958	**£4**	chart single
Problems	7"	London	HLA8781	1958	**£20**	demo
Ridin' High	7"	RCA	RCA2232	1972	**£4**	
Rock 'N' Soul	7" EP	W. Bros	WEP608	1965	**£8**	
Rock 'N' Soul Vol.2	7" EP	W. Bros	WEP609	1965	**£8**	
Rock'n'Soul	LP	W. Bros	WM8171	1965	**£12**	
Roots	LP	W. Bros	K46128	1971	**£10**	
Roots	LP	W. Bros	W1752	1968	**£20**	
See See Rider	7" EP	W. Bros	WEP618	1966	**£8**	

Title	Format	Label	Cat. No.	Year	Price	Notes
Sing Great Country Hits	LP	W. Bros	WM8138	1963	**£15**	
Sing Great Country Hits Vol.1	7" EP	W. Bros	WEP6128	1964	**£8**	
Sing Great Country Hits Vol.2	7" EP	W. Bros	WEP6131	1964	**£8**	
Sing Great Country Hits Vol.3	7" EP	W. Bros	WEP6132	1964	**£8**	
So It Will Always Be	7"	W. Bros	WB94	1963	**£4**	chart single
So It Will Always Be	7"	W. Bros	WB94	1963	**£12**	demo
So Sad	7"	W. Bros	WB19	1960	**£4**	chart single
So Sad	7"	W. Bros	WB19	1960	**£10**	demo
Somebody Help Me	7" EP	W. Bros	WEP623	1967	**£8**	
Songs Our Daddy Taught Us	LP	Cadence	CLP3006	1958	**£25**	US
Songs Our Daddy Taught Us	LP	London	HAA2150	1958	**£20**	
Songs Our Daddy Taught Us Part 1	7" EP	London	REA1195	1959	**£10**	
Songs Our Daddy Taught Us Part 2	7" EP	London	REA1196	1959	**£10**	
Songs Our Daddy Taught Us Part 3	7" EP	London	REA1197	1959	**£10**	
Temptation	7"	W. Bros	WB42	1961	**£4**	chart single
Temptation	7"	W. Bros	WB42	1961	**£10**	demo
That'll Be The Day	7"	W. Bros	WB158	1965	**£4**	chart single
That'll Be The Day	7"	W. Bros	WB158	1965	**£10**	demo
This Little Girl Of Mine	7"	London	HLA8554	1958	**£8**	
This Little Girl Of Mine	7"	London	HLA8554	1958	**£30**	demo
Till I Kissed You	7"	London	HLA8934	1959	**£4**	chart single
Till I Kissed You	7"	London	HLA8934	1959	**£20**	demo
Two Yanks In England	LP	W. Bros	W1646	1965	**£12**	with the Hollies
Very Best Of...	LP	W. Bros	WM8163	1965	**£10**	
Wake Up Little Suzie	7"	London	HLA8498	1957	**£5**	chart single
Wake Up Little Suzie	7"	London	HLA8498	1957	**£30**	demo
Walk Right Back	7"	W. Bros	WB33	1961	**£4**	chart single
Walk Right Back	7"	W. Bros	WB33	1961	**£10**	demo
When Will I Be Loved	7"	London	HLA9157	1960	**£4**	chart single
When Will I Be Loved	7"	London	HLA9157	1960	**£15**	demo
You're My Girl	7"	W. Bros	WB154	1965	**£4**	
You're My Girl	7"	W. Bros	WB154	1965	**£10**	demo
You're The One I Love	7"	W. Bros	WB143	1964	**£4**	
You're The One I Love	7"	W. Bros	WB143	1964	**£10**	demo
Yves	7"	W. Bros	WB7425	1970	**£4**	
Yves	7"	W. Bros	WB7425	1970	**£12**	demo

EVERLY, DON

Title	Format	Label	Cat. No.	Year	Price	Notes
Don Everly	LP	A&M	AMLH2007	1971	**£20**	
Sunset Towers	LP	Ode	77023	1974	**£15**	US
Yesterday Just Passed My Way Again	7"	DJM	DJS10692	1976	**£4**	

EVERLY, PHIL

Title	Format	Label	Cat. No.	Year	Price	Notes
Air That I Breathe	7"	RCA	RCA2409	1973	**£4**	
Better Than Now	7"	Pye	7N45544	1975	**£4**	
Ich Bin Dein	7"	Elektra	ELK12381	1977	**£5**	sung in German
Invisible Man	7"	Pye	7N45398	1974	**£4**	
Mystic Line	LP	Pye	NSPL18473	1975	**£15**	
Nothing's Too Good For My Baby	LP	Pye	NSPL18448	1974	**£15**	
Star Spangled Springer	LP	RCA	SF8370	1973	**£15**	

EVERY MOTHER'S SON

Title	Format	Label	Cat. No.	Year	Price	Notes
Come And Take A Ride In My Boat	7"	MGM	MGM1341	1967	**£6**	
Pony With The Golden Mane	7"	MGM	MGM1372	1967	**£4**	
Put Your Mind At Ease	7"	MGM	MGM1350	1967	**£5**	

EVERYBODY

Title	Format	Label	Cat. No.	Year	Price	Notes
Shape Of Things To Come	7"	Page One	POF23163	1970	**£4**	

EVERYBODY'S CHILDREN

Title	Format	Label	Cat. No.	Year	Price	Notes
Time Is Now	7"	Fontana	TF1070	1970	**£4**	

EVERYONE

Title	Format	Label	Cat. No.	Year	Price	Notes
Everyone	LP	B&C	CAS1028	1971	**£12**	
Trouble At The Mill	7"	B&C	CB146	1971	**£4**	

EVERYONE INVOLVED

Title	Format	Label	Cat. No.	Year	Price	Notes
Circus Keeps On Turning	7"	Arcturus	ARC3		**£20**	
Everyone Involved	LP	Arcturus		1972	**£200**	

EVERYTHING IS EVERYTHING

Title	Format	Label	Cat. No.	Year	Price	Notes
Everything Is Everything	LP	Vanguard	VSD6512	1969	**£15**	US

Oooh Baby	7"	Vanguard	VA1	1969	**£5**	

EWAN & DENVER

I Want You So Bad	7"	Giant	GN17	1967	**£8**	

EWAN & GERRY

Oh Babe	7"	Blue Beat	BB385	1965	**£10**	
Right Track	7"	Giant	GN4	196-	**£8**	
Rock Steady Train	7"	Giant	GN9	1967	**£8**	
Tennessee Waltz	7"	Giant	GN14	1967	**£8**	

EX PISTOLS

The single by the Ex Pistols was strongly implied to be an early out-take by the Sex Pistols. The group name, the sleeve design, and even the record company name all suggested as much. In fact, the whole exercise was a strategem on the part of Dave Goodman. The single has still acquired a modest collectors' value, however, just in case...

Land Of Hope And Glory	7"	Virginia	PISTOL76P	1985	**£6**	pic disc

EXCELS

California On My Mind	7"	Atlantic	584133	1967	**£4**	

EXCELSIOR SPRING

Happy Miranda	7"	Instant	IN002	1968	**£8**	

EXCEPTIONS

Eagle Flies On Sunday	7"	CBS	202632	1967	**£15**	
Gaberdine Saturday Night	7"	CBS	2830	1967	**£20**	
Helicopter	7"	President	PT205	1968	**£4**	
Jack Rabbit	7"	President	PT236	1969	**£5**	
Pendulum	7"	President	PT271	1969	**£4**	
Rub It Down	7"	President	PT181	1968	**£4**	
Tailor Made Babe	7"	President	PT218	1968	**£5**	
What More Do You Want	7"	Decca	F12100	1965	**£8**	

EXCHECKERS

All The World Is Mine	7"	Decca	F11871	1964	**£8**	

EXCITERS

Doo Wah Diddy Diddy	7"	United Artists	UP1041	1964	**£5**	
Doo Wah Diddy Diddy	7" EP	United Artists	UEP1005	1965	**£12**	
Exciters	LP	Roulette	R25326	1966	**£10**	US
He's Got The Power	7"	United Artists	UP1017	1963	**£5**	
I Want You To Be My Boy	7"	Columbia	DB7479	1965	**£5**	
It's So Exciting	7"	United Artists	UP1026	1963	**£5**	
Just Not Ready	7"	Columbia	DB7544	1965	**£8**	
Little Bit Of Soap	7"	London	HLZ10018	1966	**£4**	
Run Mascara	7"	Columbia	DB7606	1965	**£5**	
Tell Him	LP	United Artists	UAL3264	1963	**£20**	US
Tell Him	7"	United Artists	UP1011	1963	**£5**	chart single
Weddings Make Me Cry	7"	London	HLZ10038	1966	**£4**	

EXECUTIVES

Ginza Strip	7"	CBS	3067	1967	**£8**	
I Ain't Got Nobody	7"	CBS	4013	1969	**£8**	
It's Been So Long	7"	Columbia	DB7573	1965	**£6**	
Lock Your Door	7"	Columbia	DB7919	1966	**£6**	
March Of The Mods	7"	Columbia	DB7323	1964	**£8**	
Return Of The Mods	7"	Columbia	DB7770	1965	**£8**	
Smokey Atmosphere	7"	CBS	202652	1967	**£8**	
Strictly For The Beat	7"	Columbia	DB7393	1964	**£6**	
Tracy Took A Trip	7"	CBS	3431	1968	**£10**	

EXITS

Yodelling	7" EP	Way Out	WOO1		**£20**	

EXITS (2)

Fashion Plague	7"	Lightning	GIL519	1978	**£4**	

EXOTICS

Don't Lead Me On	7"	Columbia	DB8418	1968	**£4**	

EXPLOSIVE

Cities Make The Country Colder	7"	President	PT244	1969	**£5**	

Crying All Night	7"	President	PT221	1968	**£4**
Who Planted Thorns In Alice's Garden	7"	President	PT262	1969	**£5**

EXTREEM

On The Beach	7"	Strike	JH326	1966	**£5**

EXUMA

Exuma	LP	Mercury	6338018	1970	**£15**

EYE FULL TOWER

How About Me	7"	Polydor	56734	1967	**£6**

EYES

Arrival Of The Eyes	7" EP	Mercury	MCE10035	1966	**£100**
Good Day Sunshine	7"	Mercury	MF934	1965	**£30**
Man With Money	7"	Mercury	MF910	1966	**£30**
My Immediate Pleasure	7"	Mercury	MF897	1966	**£35**
When The Night Falls	7"	Mercury	MF881	1965	**£30**

EYES OF BLUE

Crossroads Of Time	LP	Mercury	SMCL20134	1968	**£25**
In Fields Of Ardath	LP	Mercury	SMCL20164	1969	**£25**
Largo	7"	Mercury	MF1049	1968	**£8**
Supermarket Full Of Cans	7"	Deram	DM114	1967	**£10**
Up And Down	7"	Deram	DM106	1966	**£8**

F

FABARES, SHELLEY

Title	Format	Label	Cat. No.	Year	Price	Notes
Johnny Angel	7"	Pye	7N25132	1962	**£5**	chart single
Johnny Loves Me	7"	Pye	7N25151	1962	**£4**	
Shelley	LP	Colpix	CLP426	1962	**£20**	US
Things We Did Last Summer	LP	Colpix	CLP431	1962	**£20**	US
Things We Did Last Summer	7"	Pye	7N25166	1962	**£4**	

FABIAN

Title	Format	Label	Cat. No.	Year	Price	Notes
Fabulous Fabian	LP	Chancellor	CHL5005	1959	**£20**	US
Good Old Summertime	LP	Chancellor	CHL5012	1960	**£15**	US
Got The Feeling	7"	HMV	POP659	1959	**£5**	
Grapevine	7"	HMV	POP869	1961	**£4**	
High Time	LP	RCA	LPM2314	1960	**£10**	US
Hold That Tiger	LP	Chancellor	CHL5003	1959	**£20**	US
Hound Dog Man	7"	HMV	POP695	1960	**£5**	chart single
I'm A Man	7"	HMV	POP587	1959	**£8**	
I'm Gonna Sit Right Down...	7"	HMV	POP778	1960	**£4**	
Kissin' And Twistin'	7"	HMV	POP810	1960	**£4**	
Rockin' Hot	LP	Chancellor	CHL5019	1961	**£25**	US
Sixteen Fabulous Hits	LP	Chancellor	CHL5024	1962	**£20**	US
String Along	7"	HMV	POP724	1960	**£4**	
Tiger	7"	HMV	POP643	1959	**£8**	
Tomorrow	7"	HMV	POP800	1960	**£4**	
Turn Me Loose	7"	HMV	POP612	1959	**£8**	
You Know You Belong To Somebody	7"	HMV	POP829	1961	**£4**	
You're Only Young Once	7"	HMV	POP934	1961	**£4**	

FABIAN & FRANKIE AVALON

Title	Format	Label	Cat. No.	Year	Price	Notes
Hit Makers	LP	Chancellor	CHL5009	1960	**£20**	US

FABULOUS DIALS

Title	Format	Label	Cat. No.	Year	Price	Notes
Bossa Nova Stomp	7"	Pye	7N25200	1963	**£4**	

FABULOUS POODLES

Title	Format	Label	Cat. No.	Year	Price	Notes
Workshy	7"	Pye	7NPX46188	1978	**£4**	pic disc

FACELLS

Title	Format	Label	Cat. No.	Year	Price	Notes
So Fine	7"	Kalypso	AB116	196-	**£6**	

FACES

Title	Format	Label	Cat. No.	Year	Price	Notes
Borstal Boys	7"	W. Bros	K16281	1973	**£10**	
Dishevelment Blues	7"	NME	SFI139	1973	**£4**	flexi disc
First Step	LP	W. Bros	WS3000	1970	**£10**	chart LP
Flying	7"	W. Bros	WB8005	1970	**£4**	
Had Me A Real Good Time	7"	W. Bros	WB8018	1970	**£4**	
Long Player	LP	W. Bros	W3011	1971	**£10**	chart LP
Ooh La La	LP	W. Bros	K56011	1973	**£10**	chart LP

FACTORY

Title	Format	Label	Cat. No.	Year	Price	Notes
Path Through the Forest	7"	MGM	MGM1444	1968	**£60**	
Try A Little Sunshine	7"	CBS	4540	1969	**£60**	

FACTOTUMS

Title	Format	Label	Cat. No.	Year	Price	Notes
Cloudy	7"	Pye	7N17402	1967	**£6**	
Here Today	7"	Piccadilly	7N35333	1966	**£5**	
I Can't Give You Anything	7"	Piccadilly	7N35355	1966	**£5**	
In My Lonely Room	7"	Immediate	IM009	1965	**£8**	
Mr.And Mrs.Regards	7"	CBS	4140	1969	**£6**	
You're So Good To Be	7"	Immediate	IM022	1965	**£10**	

FAD GADGET

Title	Format	Label	Cat. No.	Year	Price	Notes
Back To Nature	7"	Mute	MUTE002	1979	**£4**	
Fireside Favourite	7"	Mute	MUTE009	1980	**£4**	

Ricky's Hand .... 7" .... Mute .... MUTE006 .... 1980 .... **£4** ....

FADING COLOURS

Just Like Romeo And Juliet .... 7" .... Ember .... EMBS229 .... 1966 .... **£6** ....

FAGEN, DONALD

Nightfly .... LP .... Mobile Fid. .... MFSL1120 .... 1984 .... **£10** .... US audiophile

FAHEY, BRIAN ORCHESTRA

"At The Sign Of The Swinging Cymbal" is the theme tune of radio's "Pick Of The Pops", although it inevitably sounds incomplete without Alan Freeman's perfectly timed interjections.

At The Sign Of The Swinging Cymbal .... 7" .... Parlophone .... R4686 .... 1960 .... **£4** ....

FAHEY, JOHN

America .... LP .... Sonet .... SNTF628 .... 1972 .... **£10** ....
Death Chants & Breakdowns .... LP .... Sonet .... SNTF608 .... 1969 .... **£12** ....
Essential... .... LP .... Vanguard .... VSD55/56 .... 1974 .... **£15** .... double
Requia .... LP .... Vanguard .... SVRL19055 .... 1968 .... **£10** ....
Transfiguration Of Blind Joe Death .... LP .... Sonet .... SNTF607 .... 1967 .... **£12** ....
Transfiguration Of Blind Joe Death .... LP .... Transatlantic .... TRA173 .... 1967 .... **£10** ....
Transfiguration Of Blind Joe Death .... LP .... Transatlantic .... TRA173 .... 1967 .... **£15** .... with booklet
Yellow Princess .... LP .... Vanguard .... SVRL19033 .... 1968 .... **£10** ....

FAINE JADE

Introspection: A Faine Jade Recital .... LP .... R.S.V.P. .... 8002 .... 1968 .... **£60** .... US

FAIRBURN, WERLY

All The Time .... 7" .... London .... HLC8349 .... 1956 .... **£100** ....

FAIRE, JOHNNY

Bertha Lou .... 7" .... London .... HLU8569 .... 1958 .... **£30** ....

FAIRFIELD PARLOUR

"From Home To Home" is the third LP by the English Kaleidoscope. The change of name to Fairfield Parlour brought no more than a marginal improvement to the group's fortunes, however, and the record today is almost as scarce as the first two.

Bordeaux Rose .... 7" .... Prism .... PRI1 .... 1976 .... **£8** ....
Bordeaux Rose .... 7" .... Vertigo .... 6059003 .... 1970 .... **£6** ....
From Home To Home .... LP .... Vertigo .... 6360001 .... 1970 .... **£50** .... spiral label
Just Another Day .... 7" .... Vertigo .... 6059008 .... 1970 .... **£15** ....

FAIRIES

Don't Mind .... 7" .... HMV .... POP1445 .... 1965 .... **£50** ....
Don't Think Twice It's Alright .... 7" .... Decca .... F11943 .... 1964 .... **£50** ....
Get Yourself Home .... 7" .... HMV .... POP1404 .... 1965 .... **£50** ....

FAIRPORT CONVENTION

On their first LP Fairport Convention sound like an English Jefferson Airplane. The folk music influence begins to be felt on "What We Did On Our Holidays" and takes over altogether on "Liege and Lief". Thus over the course of four LPs, recorded in a period of not much more than a year, it is possible to hear the genesis of a new kind of rock music. The personnel changes in the group became rather complicated after this, but the various editions of Fairport Convention - and indeed the many groups derived from it - were able to explore the possibilities of the folk-rock fusion in many fruitful ways.

Angel Delight .... LP .... Island .... ILPS9162 .... 1971 .... **£10** .... chart LP
AT2 .... LP .... Woodworm .... WR1 .... 1984 .... **£15** ....
Babbacombe Lee .... LP .... Island .... ILPS9176 .... 1971 .... **£10** ....
Bonny Bunch Of Roses .... LP .... Vertigo .... 9102015 .... 1977 .... **£15** ....
Fairport Convention .... LP .... Polydor .... 583035 .... 1968 .... **£15** ....
Fairport Nine .... LP .... Island .... ILPS9246 .... 1973 .... **£10** ....
Farewell Farewell .... LP .... Simons .... GAMA1 .... 1979 .... **£15** ....
Full House .... LP .... Island .... ILPS9130 .... 1970 .... **£12** .... chart LP
Gottle O'Geer .... LP .... Island .... ILPS9389 .... 1976 .... **£15** ....
History Of... .... LP .... Island .... ICD4 .... 1972 .... **£20** .... blue ribbon on seal
If I Had A Ribbon Bow .... 7" .... Track .... 604020 .... 1967 .... **£12** ....
If (Stomp) .... 7" .... Polydor .... 2058014 .... 1970 .... **£5** ....
John Lee .... 7" .... Island .... WIP6128 .... 1971 .... **£4** ....
Liege And Lief .... LP .... Island .... ILPS9115 .... 1969 .... **£15** .... chart LP
Live A Movable Feast .... LP .... Island .... ILPS9285 .... 1974 .... **£15** ....
Live At L.A. Troubadour .... LP .... Island .... HELP28 .... 1976 .... **£15** ....
Meet On The Ledge .... 7" .... Island .... WIP6047 .... 1968 .... **£8** ....
Moat On The Ledge .... LP .... Woodworm .... WR001 .... 1982 .... **£15** ....
Now Be Thankful .... 7" .... Island .... WIP6089 .... 1970 .... **£5** ....
Rising For The Moon .... LP .... Island .... ILPS9313 .... 1975 .... **£15** .... chart LP

Title	Format	Label	Number	Year	Price	Notes
Rosie	LP	Island	ILPS9208	1973	**£15**	
Rosie	7"	Island	WIP6155	1973	**£4**	
Rubber Band	7"	Simons	PMW1	1979	**£4**	
Si Tu Dois Partir	7"	Island	WIP6064	1969	**£4**	chart single
Tippler's Tales	LP	Vertigo	9102022	1978	**£15**	
Unhalfbricking	LP	Island	ILPS9102	1969	**£15**	chart LP
What We Did On Our Holidays	LP	Island	ILPS9092	1969	**£15**	
White Dress	7"	Island	WIP6241	1975	**£4**	

FAIRWAYS

Title	Format	Label	Number	Year	Price	Notes
Yoko Ono	7"	Mercury	MF1116	1969	**£6**	

FAIRWEATHER

Named after lead singer Andy Fairweather-Low, Fairweather were essentially a slimmed down version of Amen Corner. Seeing the way that rock music was going, the group attempted to put their pop past behind it by signing to RCA's new progressive label, Neon. They blew it, however, by gaining a hit single!

Title	Format	Label	Number	Year	Price	Notes
Beginning From An End	LP	Neon	NE1	1971	**£15**	
Lay It On Me	7"	Neon	NE1000	1971	**£5**	
Natural Sinner	7"	RCA	RCA1977	1970	**£4**	chart single
Road To Freedom	7"	RCA	RCA2040	1971	**£4**	

FAIRYTALE

Title	Format	Label	Number	Year	Price	Notes
Guess I Was Dreaming	7"	Decca	F12644	1967	**£20**	
Lovely People	7"	Decca	F12665	1967	**£20**	

FAITH, ADAM

Title	Format	Label	Number	Year	Price	Notes
Adam	LP	Parlophone	PCS3010	1960	**£12**	stereo, chart LP
Adam	LP	Parlophone	PMC1128	1960	**£10**	mono, chart LP
Adam	7" EP	Parlophone	GEP8824	1960	**£4**	
Adam	7" EP	Parlophone	SGE2014	1960	**£6**	stereo
Adam Faith	LP	Amy	8005	1965	**£12**	US
Adam Faith	LP	Parlophone	PCS3025	1961	**£12**	stereo, chart LP
Adam Faith	LP	Parlophone	PMC1162	1961	**£10**	mono, chart LP
Adam No.2	7" EP	Parlophone	GEP8826	1960	**£4**	
Adam No.2	7" EP	Parlophone	SGE2015	1960	**£6**	stereo
Adam No.3	7" EP	Parlophone	GEP8831	1960	**£4**	
Adam No.3	7" EP	Parlophone	SGE2018	1960	**£6**	stereo
Adam's Hit Parade	7" EP	Parlophone	GEP8811	1960	**£4**	
Adam's Hit Parade Vol.2	7" EP	Parlophone	GEP8841	1961	**£4**	
Adam's Hit Parade Vol.3	7" EP	Parlophone	GEP8862	1962	**£4**	
Adam's Latest Hits	7" EP	Parlophone	GEP8877	1963	**£4**	
All These Things	7" EP	Parlophone	GEP8852	1961	**£4**	
Baby Take A Bow	7"	Parlophone	R4964	1962	**£4**	chart single
Cheryl's Going Home	7"	Parlophone	R5516	1966	**£4**	chart single
Daddy What'll Happen To Me	7"	Parlophone	R5635	1967	**£4**	
Don't You Know It	7"	Parlophone	R4807	1961	**£4**	chart single
Easy Going Me	7"	Parlophone	R4766	1961	**£4**	chart single
England's Top Singer	LP	MGM	E3591	1961	**£15**	US
Faith Alive	LP	Parlophone	PMC1249	1965	**£10**	chart LP
First Time	7"	Parlophone	R5061	1963	**£4**	chart single
For You - Adam	7" EP	Parlophone	GEP8904	1964	**£4**	
For You	LP	Parlophone	PMC1213	1963	**£10**	
From Adam With Love	LP	Parlophone	PCS3038	1962	**£12**	stereo
From Adam With Love	LP	Parlophone	PMC1192	1962	**£10**	mono
Hand Me Down Things	7"	Parlophone	R5260	1965	**£4**	
Heartsick Feeling	7"	HMV	POP438	1958	**£15**	
Hey Little Lovin' Girl	7"	Parlophone	R5673	1968	**£4**	
High School Confidential	7"	HMV	POP557	1958	**£15**	
I Don't Need That Kind Of Love	7"	Parlophone	R5349	1965	**£4**	
I Just Don't Know	7"	Parlophone	R5174	1964	**£4**	
I Love Being In Love With You	7"	Parlophone	R5138	1964	**£4**	chart single
Idle Gossip	7"	Parlophone	R5398	1966	**£4**	
If He Tells You	7"	Parlophone	R5109	1964	**£4**	chart single
Lonesome	7"	Parlophone	R4864	1962	**£4**	chart single
Message To Martha - From Adam	7" EP	Parlophone	GEP8929	1965	**£4**	
On The Move	LP	Parlophone	PMC1228	1964	**£10**	
Runk Dunk	7"	Top Rank	JAR126	1959	**£8**	
Someone's Taken Maria Away	7"	Parlophone	R5289	1965	**£4**	chart single
Songs And Things	7" EP	Parlophone	GEP8939	1965	**£4**	
Stop Feeling Sorry For Yourself	7"	Parlophone	R5235	1965	**£4**	chart single
Sure Know A Lot About Love	7" EP	Parlophone	GEP8854	1961	**£4**	

Title	Format	Label	Cat. No.	Year	Price	Notes
Time Has Come	7" EP	Parlophone	GEP8851	1961	**£4**	
To Hell With Love	7"	Parlophone	R5649	1967	**£4**	
To Make A Big Man Cry	7"	Parlophone	R5412	1966	**£4**	
Top Of The Pops	7" EP	Parlophone	GEP8893	1964	**£4**	
Walkin' Tall	7"	Parlophone	R5039	1963	**£4**	chart single
We Are In Love	7"	Parlophone	R5091	1963	**£4**	chart single
What More Can Anyone Do	7"	Parlophone	R5556	1967	**£4**	
What Now	7"	Parlophone	R4990	1963	**£4**	chart single

FAITH, ADAM & JOHN BARRY

Title	Format	Label	Cat. No.	Year	Price	Notes
Beat Girl	LP	Columbia	33SX1225	1960	**£12**	chart LP
Beat Girl	7" EP	Columbia	SEG8138	1962	**£6**	

FAITH, HOPE & CHARITY

Title	Format	Label	Cat. No.	Year	Price	Notes
So Much Love	7"	Crewe	CRW3	1970	**£4**	

FAITH, HORACE

Title	Format	Label	Cat. No.	Year	Price	Notes
Black Pearl	7"	Trojan	TR7790	1970	**£4**	chart single
Daddy's Home	7"	Downtown	DT446	196-	**£8**	
Spinning Wheel	7"	B&C	CB104	1969	**£5**	

FAITHFULL, AUSTIN

Title	Format	Label	Cat. No.	Year	Price	Notes
Eternal Love	7"	Pyramid	PYR6028	1969	**£8**	
Uncle Joe	7"	Blue Cat	BS140	196-	**£10**	

FAITHFULL, MARIANNE

Title	Format	Label	Cat. No.	Year	Price	Notes
As Tears Go By	7"	Decca	F11923	1964	**£4**	chart single
Blowing In The Wind	7"	Decca	F12007	1964	**£4**	
Come And Stay With Me	7"	Decca	F12075	1965	**£4**	chart single
Come My Way	LP	Decca	LK4688	1965	**£20**	chart LP
Counting	7"	Decca	F12443	1966	**£4**	
Is This What I Get For Loving You	7"	Decca	F12524	1966	**£4**	chart single
Love In A Mist	LP	Decca	LK4854	1967	**£20**	
Marianne Faithfull	LP	Decca	LK4689	1965	**£20**	chart LP
Marianne Faithfull	7" EP	Decca	DFE8624	1965	**£5**	
North Country Maid	LP	Decca	LK4778	1966	**£20**	
Sister Morphine	7"	Decca	F12889	1969	**£8**	
Summer Nights	7"	Decca	F12193	1965	**£4**	chart single
This Little Bird	7"	Decca	F12162	1965	**£4**	chart single
Tomorrow's Calling	7"	Decca	F12408	1966	**£4**	
Yesterday	7"	Decca	F12268	1965	**£4**	chart single

FALCONS

Title	Format	Label	Cat. No.	Year	Price	Notes
Billy The Kid	7"	London	HLU10146	1967	**£5**	
I Found A Love	7"	London	HLK9565	1962	**£8**	
Stampede	7"	Philips	BF1297	1964	**£4**	
You're So Fine	7"	London	HLT8876	1959	**£8**	

FALL

Title	Format	Label	Cat. No.	Year	Price	Notes
Bingo Masters Breakout	7"	Step Forward	SF7	1978	**£8**	
C.R.E.E.P.	7"	Beggars B.	BEG116	1984	**£4**	
C.R.E.E.P.	12"	Beggars B.	BEG116T	1984	**£6**	green vinyl
Cruiser's Creek	7"	Beggars B.	BEG150	1985	**£4**	
Fiery Jack	7"	Step Forward	SF13	1980	**£6**	2 PS's
Hit The North	7"	Beggars B.	BEG200P	1987	**£5**	PD, clear printed sleeve
How I Wrote Elastic Man	7"	Rough Trade	RT048	1980	**£6**	
It's The New Thing	7"	Step Forward	SF9	1978	**£6**	
Kicker Conspiracy	7"	Rough Trade	RT143	1983	**£6**	double PS
Lie, Dream Of A Casino Soul	7"	Kamera	ERA001	1981	**£5**	
Live In London	cass	Chaos	LIVE006	1982	**£10**	
Living Too Late	7"	Beggars B.	BEG165	1986	**£4**	
Look, Know	7"	Kamera	ERA004	1982	**£5**	
Man Whose Head Expanded	7"	Rough Trade	RT133	1982	**£5**	
Marquis Cha Cha	7"	Kamera	ERA014	1982	**£10**	
Oh Brother	7"	Beggars B.	BEG10	1984	**£4**	
Rollin' Danny	7"	Beggars B.	BEG134	1985	**£4**	
Rowche Rumble	7"	Step Forward	SF11	1979	**£6**	
Slates	10"	Rough Trade	RT071	1981	**£8**	
There's A Ghost In My House	7"	Beggars B.	BEG187H	1987	**£5**	hologram sleeve
Totally Wired	7"	Rough Trade	RT056	1980	**£6**	
Victoria	7"	Beggars B.	BEG206	1987	**£5**	boxed

FALLEN ANGELS

Title	Format	Label	Cat. No.	Year	Price	Notes
I Don't Want To Fall	7"	London	HL10166	1967	**£4**	

FALLIN, JOHNNY

Title	Format	Label	Cat. No.	Year	Price	Notes
Party Kiss	7"	Capitol	CL15043	1959	**£6**	
Wild Streak	7"	Capitol	CL15091	1959	**£6**	

FALLING LEAVES

Title	Format	Label	Cat. No.	Year	Price	Notes
Beggar's Parade	7"	Decca	F12420	1966	**£10**	
She Loves To Be Loved	7"	Parlophone	R5233	1965	**£8**	

FALTSKOG, AGNETHA

Title	Format	Label	Cat. No.	Year	Price	Notes
Agnetha	LP	Cupol		1968	**£15**	Swedish
Agnetha Faltskog	LP	Cupol		1972	**£12**	Swedish
Agnetha Vol.2	LP	Cupol		1969	**£15**	Swedish
Basta	LP	Cupol	CLP1023	1973	**£12**	Swedish
Elva Kvinnor I Ett Hus	LP	Cupol	CLPS531	1975	**£12**	Swedish
Som Jag Ar	LP	Cupol	CLP1016	1970	**£12**	Swedish
Tio Ar Med	LP	Cupol	CLPS352	1970	**£10**	Swedish

FAME, GEORGIE

Title	Format	Label	Cat. No.	Year	Price	Notes
Ballad Of Bonnie And Clyde	7"	CBS	3124	1967	**£4**	chart single
Because I Love You	7"	CBS	202587	1967	**£4**	chart single
Bend A Little	7"	Columbia	DB7328	1964	**£5**	
By The Time I Get To Phoenix	7"	CBS	3526	1968	**£4**	
Do Re Mi	7"	Columbia	DB7255	1964	**£6**	
Fame At Last	LP	Columbia	33SX1638	1964	**£15**	chart LP
Fame At Last	7" EP	Columbia	SEG8393	1964	**£6**	
Fats For Fame	7" EP	Columbia	SEG8406	1965	**£10**	
Get Away	7"	208 Luxem		1964	**£8**	1 sided promo
Get Away	7"	Columbia	DB7946	1966	**£4**	chart single
Get Away	7" EP	Columbia	SEG8518	1966	**£6**	
Hall Of Fame	LP	Columbia	SX6120	1967	**£12**	chart LP
In The Meantime	7"	Columbia	DB7494	1965	**£4**	chart single
Knock On Wood	7" EP	CBS	EP6363	1967	**£5**	
Like We Used To Be	7"	Columbia	DB7633	1965	**£4**	chart single
Move It On Over	7" EP	Columbia	SEG8454	1965	**£8**	
Peaceful	7"	CBS	4295	1969	**£4**	chart single
R&B At The Flamingo	LP	Columbia	SX1599	1964	**£25**	
R&B At The Flamingo	7" EP	Columbia	SEG8382	1964	**£12**	
Rhythm And Blue Beat	7" EP	Columbia	SEG8334	1964	**£12**	
Seventh Son	LP	CBS	63786	1969	**£10**	
Seventh Son	7"	CBS	4659	1969	**£4**	chart single
Shop Around	7"	Columbia	DB7193	1964	**£8**	
Sitting In The Park	7"	Columbia	DB8096	1966	**£4**	chart single
Something	7"	Columbia	DB7727	1965	**£4**	chart single
Sound Venture	LP	Columbia	SX6076	1966	**£12**	chart LP
Sunny	7"	Columbia	DB8015	1966	**£4**	chart single
Sweet Things	LP	Columbia	SX6043	1966	**£12**	chart LP
Third Face Of Fame	LP	CBS	63293	1968	**£10**	
Try My World	7"	CBS	2945	1967	**£4**	chart single
Two Faces Of Fame	LP	CBS	63018	1967	**£10**	chart LP
Yeah Yeah	7"	Columbia	DB7428	1964	**£4**	chart single

FAMILY

Family's first single, "Scene Thru The Eye Of A Lens", is something of a psychedelic classic, and has not been reissued. "Music In A Doll's House" was to some extent taken over by Dave Mason, who produced the record and played on it. It is a wonderful LP, however, and proof that the real sixties gems have already been discovered, and do not cost a fortune. Subsequent Family records are increasingly ordinary, although each undoubtedly has its moments, and they are all highlighted by the extraordinary Roger Chapman voice.

Title	Format	Label	Cat. No.	Year	Price	Notes
Anyway	LP	Reprise	RSX9005	1970	**£10**	chart LP
Bandstand	LP	Reprise	K54006	1972	**£10**	chart LP
Boom Bang	7"	Raft	RA18501	1973	**£4**	
Burlesque	7"	Reprise	K14196	1972	**£4**	chart single
Family Entertainment	LP	Reprise	RSLP6340	1969	**£15**	with poster, chart LP
Fearless	LP	Reprise	K54003	1971	**£10**	chart LP
In My Own Time	7"	Reprise	K14090	1971	**£4**	chart single
It's Only A Movie	LP	Raft	RA58501	1973	**£10**	chart LP
Me My Friend	7"	Reprise	RS23270	1968	**£6**	
Music In A Doll's House	LP	Reprise	RLP6312	1968	**£20**	mono, chart LP
Music In A Doll's House	LP	Reprise	RSLP6312	1968	**£15**	+ poster, stereo, chart LP

My Friend The Sun	7"	Reprise	K14218	1973	**£4**	
No Mule's Fool	7"	Reprise	RS27001	1969	**£4**	chart single
No Mule's Fool	7"	Reprise	RS27001	1969	**£10**	PS
Scene Thru The Eye Of A Lens	7"	Liberty	LBF15031	1967	**£40**	
Second Generation Woman	7"	Reprise	RS23315	1968	**£6**	
Song For Me	LP	Reprise	RSLP9001	1970	**£12**	chart LP
Strange Band	7"	Reprise	RS27009	1970	**£4**	chart single
Strange Band	7"	Reprise	RS27009	1970	**£6**	PS
Sweet Desiree	7"	Raft	RA18503	1973	**£4**	
Today	7"	Reprise	RS27005	1970	**£4**	
Today	7"	Reprise	RS27005	1970	**£10**	PS

FAMILY AFFAIR

Family Affair	LP	Saga			**£30**	

FAMILY CIRCLE

Reggae Hare Krishna	7"	Attack	ATT8002	1974	**£5**	

FAMILY DOGG

Arizona	7"	Bell	BLL1077	1969	**£4**	
Brown Eyed Girl	7"	Fontana	TF968	1968	**£5**	
Family Dogg	7"	MGM	MGM1360	1967	**£8**	
I Wear A Silly Grin	7"	Fontana	TF921	1968	**£4**	
View From Rowland's Head	LP	Polydor	2318061	1972	**£10**	
Way Of Life	LP	Bell	SP22122	1969	**£12**	
Way Of Life	7"	Bell	BLL1055	1969	**£4**	chart single

FAMILY PLANN

Sexy Summer	7"	President	PT441	1975	**£4**	

FAMOUS JUG BAND

Chameleon	LP	Liberty	LBS83355	1970	**£15**	
Only Friend I Own	7"	Liberty	LBF15224	1969	**£8**	
Sunshine Possibilities	LP	Liberty	LBS83263	1969	**£25**	

FAMOUS WARD SINGERS

I Knew It Was The Lord	78	London	HL8065	1954	**£20**	

FAN CLUB

Avenue	7"	M&S	SJP791	1978	**£10**	

FANDANGO

Last Kiss	LP	RCA	AFL12696	1978	**£10**	US, pic disc

FANKHAUSER, MERRELL

Merrell Fankhauser & His HMS Bounty	LP	Shamley	SS701	197-	**£15**	US
Merrell Fankhauser	LP	Maui	101	1976	**£20**	US

FANNY

Charity Ball	LP	Reprise	K44144	1971	**£10**	
Fanny	LP	Reprise	RSLP6416	1970	**£10**	

FANTASTIC BAGGIES

Summer Means Fun	7"	United Artists	UP36142	1976	**£4**	
Tell 'Em I'm Surfin'	LP	Imperial	LP9270	1964	**£40**	US

FANTASTIC FOUR

Fantastic Four	LP	T. Motown	STML11105	1969	**£20**	
I Love You Madly	7"	T. Motown	TMG678	1968	**£10**	
I Love You Madly	7"	T. Motown	TMG678	1968	**£30**	demo

FANTASTICS

Baby Make Your Own Sweet Music	7"	MGM	MGM1434	1968	**£5**	
Face To Face With Heartache	7"	Deram	DM264	1969	**£4**	

FANTASY

Paint A Picture	LP	Polydor	2383246	1973	**£350**	
Politely Insane	7"	Polydor	2058405	1973	**£20**	

FANTONI, BARRY

Little Man In A Little Box	7"	Fontana	TF707	1966	**£5**	
Nothing Today	7"	Columbia	DB8238	1967	**£5**	

FAPARDOKLY

Fapardokly	LP	V.I.P.	250	1966	**£250**	US

FAR CRY

Far Cry	LP	Vanguard	SVRL19041	1969	**£12**	

FAR EAST FAMILY BAND

Cave Down To Earth	LP	Muland	CD7139M	1975	**£20**	Japanese
Far Out	LP	Denon		1975	**£20**	Japanese
Nepporjin	LP	Vertigo	6370850	1975	**£15**	
Parallel World	LP	Muland	LQ7002M	1976	**£20**	Japanese
Tenkeyin	LP	All Ears	114797	1977	**£15**	US
Torn Hatano	LP	Muland		1977	**£20**	Japanese

FARAWAY FOLK

Seasonal Man	LP	RA		1975	**£100**	

FARDON, DON

Good Lovin'	7"	Pye	7N25486	1969	**£4**	
I've Paid My Dues	LP	Decca	75225	1970	**£10**	US
Indian Reservation	7"	Pye	7N25437	1967	**£5**	
Indian Reservation	7"	Pye	7N25475	1968	**£4**	
Indian Reservation	7"	Young Blood	YB1015	1970	**£4**	chart single
Lament Of The Cherokee	LP	GNP	2044	1968	**£10**	US
Released	LP	Young Blood	SSYB13	1970	**£10**	
We Can Make It Together	7"	Pye	7N25483	1969	**£4**	

FAREWELL NANCY

Sea Songs And Shanties	LP	Topic		1964	**£20**	

FARINA, RICHARD & MIMI

Richard and Mimi Farina were a folk duo typical of the many folk acts that were a dominant strain within the American music of the early sixties. Most managed to come up with a significant song or two - the Farinas' included "Pack Up All Your Sorrows" and "Hard Lovin' Loser", which were recorded byJudy Collins. Richard Farina was killed in a motorcycle accident in 1966, but his wife Mimi, who is Joan Baez' sister, has managed to follow a reasonably successful career since as a musician and actress.

Best Of...	LP	Vanguard	VSD21/22	1973	**£15**	double
Celebrations For A Grey Day	LP	Fontana	6060	1965	**£15**	
Memories	LP	Vanguard	VSD79263	1968	**£15**	US
Refelections In A Crystal Wind	LP	Fontana	6075	1965	**£15**	
Richard And Mimi Farina	LP	Vanguard	VSD79174	1965	**£15**	US
Richard Farina	LP	Vanguard	VSD79281	1968	**£15**	US

FARINAS

The Farinas were a blues and soul group from Leicester, but as soon as they began to write their own material, they changed their name - to Family.

I Like It Like That	7"	Fontana	TF493	1964	**£30**	

FARLOWE, CHRIS

... And The Thunderbirds	LP	Columbia	SCX6034	1966	**£30**	
14 Things To Think About	LP	Immediate	IMLP005	1966	**£25**	chart LP
Air Travel	7"	Decca	F11536	1962	**£20**	
Art Of...	LP	Immediate	IMLP006	1966	**£25**	chart LP
Best Of...	LP	Immediate	IMLP010	1968	**£15**	
Black Sheep Of The Family	7"	Polydor	2066017	1971	**£5**	
Buzz With The Fuzz	7"	Columbia	DB7614	1965	**£25**	
Chris Farlowe	7" EP	Decca	DFE8665	1965	**£15**	
Dawn	7"	Immediate	IM074	1969	**£8**	
Fool	7"	Immediate	IM016	1965	**£8**	
From Here To Mama Rosa	LP	Polydor	2425029	1970	**£10**	
Girl Trouble	7"	Columbia	DB7237	1964	**£10**	
Handbags And Gladrags	7"	Immediate	IM065	1967	**£4**	chart single
Hits	7" EP	Immediate	IMEP004	1966	**£10**	
Hound Dog	7"	Columbia	DB7379	1964	**£8**	
I Remember	7"	Columbia	DB7120	1963	**£8**	
In The Midnight Hour	7" EP	Immediate	IMEP001	1965	**£12**	
Just A Dream	7"	Columbia	DB7311	1964	**£5**	
Just A Dream	7"	Columbia	DB7983	1966	**£6**	
Last Goodbye	LP	Immediate	IMLP021	1969	**£25**	
Moanin'	7"	Immediate	IM056	1967	**£5**	chart single
My Way Of Giving	7"	Immediate	IM041	1967	**£8**	chart single
Out Of Time	7"	Immediate	IM035	1966	**£5**	chart single

Out Of Time	7"	Immediate	IM078	1969	**£4**	
Paint It Black	7"	Immediate	IM071	1968	**£6**	
Paperman Fly In The Sky	7"	Immediate	IM066	1968	**£10**	
Put Out The Light	7"	Polydor	2066046	1971	**£5**	
Ride On Baby	7"	Immediate	IM038	1966	**£5**	chart single
Stormy Monday	7" EP	Island	IEP709	1966	**£20**	
Think	7"	Immediate	IM023	1966	**£5**	chart single
We Can Work It Out	7"	Polydor	2058650	1975	**£4**	
Yesterday's Papers	7"	Immediate	IM049	1967	**£5**	

FARNABY, GILES

	LP	Argo			**£40**	

FARNER, MARK & DON BREWER

Monumental Funk	LP	Quadico	Q7401	1974	**£12**	US
Monumental Funk	LP	Quadico	Q7401	1974	**£20**	US pic disc

FARO, WAYNE SCHMALTZ BAND

There's Still Time	7"	Deram	DM222	1969	**£8**	

FARON'S FLAMINGOES

See If She Cares	7"	Oriole	CB1834	1963	**£8**	
Shake Sherry	7"	Oriole	CB1867	1963	**£10**	

FARQUAHR

Farquahr	LP	Elektra	EKS74083	1970	**£10**	
Hanging On By A Thread	7"	Elektra	EK45713	1970	**£4**	

FARR, GARY

Addressed To The Censors Of Love	LP	Atco	SD7034	1973	**£10**	US
Hey Daddy	7"	Marmalade	598017	1969	**£10**	
Revolution Of The Season	7"	CBS	5430	1971	**£5**	
Strange Fruit	LP	CBS	64138	1971	**£15**	
Take Something With You	LP	Marmalade	608013	1969	**£40**	

FARR, GARY & KEVIN WESTLAKE

Everyday	7"	Marmalade	598007	1968	**£6**	

FARR, GARY & THE T-BONES

Dem Bones Dem Bones Dem T-Bones	7" EP	Columbia	SEG8414	1965	**£50**	
Give All She's Got	7"	Columbia	DB7608	1965	**£10**	

FARREN, MICK

Carnivorous Circus (Mona)	LP	Transatlantic	TRA212	1970	**£30**	

FASCINATIONS

Girls Are Out To Get You	7"	Mojo	2092004	1971	**£4**	chart single
Girls Are Out To Get You	7"	Stateside	SS594	1967	**£15**	
Girls Are Out To Get You	7"	Sue	WI4049	1968	**£12**	

FASCINATORS

Chapel Bells	7"	Capitol	CL14942	1958	**£6**	
Oh Rose Marie	7"	Capitol	CL15062	1959	**£6**	

FASHIONS

I.O.U.	7"	Evolution	E2444	1969	**£6**	
I.O.U.	7"	Stateside	SS2115	1968	**£4**	

FAST SET

Junction One	7"	Axis	AXIS1	1980	**£12**	

FAT

Fat	LP	RCA	LPS4368	1970	**£15**	

FAT MATTRESS

Even while still a member of the Jimi Hendrix Experience, bassist Noel Redding began playing with his own group in order to switch back to the guitar he had always really preferred. Fat Mattress inevitably attracted attention simply because of Redding's presence, but the sad fact was that the most interesting aspect of the group was the cover of the first LP, which opens out into a two-foot square sheet of card.

Fat Mattress 1	LP	Polydor	583056	1969	**£10**	
Fat Mattress 2	LP	Polydor	2383025	1970	**£10**	
Highway	7"	Polydor	2058053	1970	**£6**	

Title	Format	Label	Cat. No.	Year	Price	Notes
Magic Forest	7"	Polydor	56367	1969	**£8**	
Naturally	7"	Polydor	56352	1969	**£8**	

FATAL MICROBES & POISON GIRLS

Title	Format	Label	Cat. No.	Year	Price	Notes
Violence Grows/Closed Shop	12"	Small Wond.	WEENY3	1978	**£6**	

FATBACK BAND

Title	Format	Label	Cat. No.	Year	Price	Notes
Par-r-rty Time	7"	Polydor	2066682	1976	**£4**	

FATHER YOD

Title	Format	Label	Cat. No.	Year	Price	Notes
All Or Nothing At All	LP	Higher Key	3304	1974	**£50**	US
Kahoutek	LP	Higher Key	3301	1973	**£50**	US

FATHERS ANGELS

Title	Format	Label	Cat. No.	Year	Price	Notes
Back To Bach	7"	MGM	MGM1459	1968	**£50**	

FATS & THE CHESSMEN

Title	Format	Label	Cat. No.	Year	Price	Notes
Big Ben Twist	7"	Pye	7N25122	1962	**£4**	
Let's Twist	LP	Golden Guin.	GGL0117	1961	**£10**	
Let's Twist To The Oldies	LP	Golden Guin.	GGL0125	1962	**£10**	

FAUN

Title	Format	Label	Cat. No.	Year	Price	Notes
Faun	LP	Gregar	GG70000	1969	**£20**	US

FAUST

Title	Format	Label	Cat. No.	Year	Price	Notes
Faust 4	LP	Virgin	V2004	1973	**£12**	
Faust	LP	Polydor	2310142	1971	**£15**	
Faust	LP	Polydor	2310142	1971	**£20**	clear vinyl
So Far	LP	Polydor	2310196	1972	**£12**	

FAVOURITE SONS

Title	Format	Label	Cat. No.	Year	Price	Notes
That Driving Beat	7"	Mercury	MF911	1965	**£8**	

FAY, BILL

Title	Format	Label	Cat. No.	Year	Price	Notes
Bill Fay	LP	Nova	SDN12	1970	**£25**	
Some Good Advice	7"	Deram	DM143	1967	**£20**	
Time Of Last Persecution	LP	Deram	SML1079	1971	**£40**	

FEAR

Title	Format	Label	Cat. No.	Year	Price	Notes
Fear	LP	Slash	SR111	1982	**£20**	

FEARNS BRASS FOUNDRY

Title	Format	Label	Cat. No.	Year	Price	Notes
Don't Change It	7"	Decca	F12721	1968	**£5**	
Love, Sink And Drown	7"	Decca	F12835	1968	**£4**	

FEATHERS, CHARLIE & MAC CURTIS

Title	Format	Label	Cat. No.	Year	Price	Notes
Rockabilly Kings	LP	Polydor	2310293	1974	**£10**	

FEDERALMEN

Title	Format	Label	Cat. No.	Year	Price	Notes
Soul Serenade	7"	London	HLJ10303	1970	**£4**	

FEDERALS

Title	Format	Label	Cat. No.	Year	Price	Notes
Boot Hill	7"	Parlophone	R5013	1963	**£4**	
Brazil	7"	Parlophone	R4988	1963	**£4**	
Bucket Full Of Love	7"	Parlophone	R5320	1965	**£4**	
Climb	7"	Parlophone	R5100	1964	**£4**	
Marlena	7"	Parlophone	R5139	1964	**£4**	
Twilight Time	7"	Parlophone	R5193	1964	**£4**	

FEDERALS (2)

Title	Format	Label	Cat. No.	Year	Price	Notes
I've Passed This Way Before	7"	Island	WI3126	1967	**£8**	
Shocking Love	7"	Island	WI3152	1968	**£8**	

FEDERATION

Title	Format	Label	Cat. No.	Year	Price	Notes
Two Minutes To Love	7"	20th Century	1023	1976	**£4**	

FELDER'S ORIOLES

Title	Format	Label	Cat. No.	Year	Price	Notes
Backstreet	7"	Piccadilly	7N35332	1966	**£5**	
Down Home Girl	7"	Piccadilly	7N35247	1965	**£8**	
I Know You Don't Love Me No More	7"	Piccadilly	7N35311	1966	**£5**	
Sweet Tasting Wine	7"	Piccadilly	7N35269	1965	**£6**	

FELDMAN, MARTY

Title	Format	Label	Cat. No.	Year	Price	Notes
Funny He Never Married	7"	Pye	7N17643	1968	**£4**	
I Feel A Song Going Off	LP	Decca	SKL4983	1969	**£10**	
Joyous Time Of Year	7"	Decca	F12857	1968	**£4**	
Marty	LP	Pye	NPL18258	1968	**£10**	

FELDMAN, MARTY / JOHN CLEESE & OTHERS

Title	Format	Label	Cat. No.	Year	Price	Notes
At Last The 1948 Show	LP	Pye	NPL18198	1967	**£10**	

FELIUS ANDROMEDA

Title	Format	Label	Cat. No.	Year	Price	Notes
Meditations	7"	Decca	F12694	1967	**£15**	

FELIX, JULIE

Title	Format	Label	Cat. No.	Year	Price	Notes
Changes	LP	Fontana	TL5368	1966	**£10**	chart LP
Flowers	LP	Fontana	TL5437	1967	**£10**	
Julie Felix	LP	Decca	LK4626	1964	**£10**	
Second Album	LP	Decca	LK4724	1965	**£10**	
Sings Dylan And Guthrie	LP	Decca	LK4683	1965	**£10**	
Third Album	LP	Decca	LK4820	1966	**£10**	

FELIX, MIKE

Title	Format	Label	Cat. No.	Year	Price	Notes
Blueberry Hill	7"	Decca	F12701	1967	**£4**	
You Belong To Me	7"	Pye	7N17058	1966	**£4**	

FELT

Title	Format	Label	Cat. No.	Year	Price	Notes
Ballad Of The Band	7"	Creation	CRE027	1986	**£6**	
Ballad Of The Band	12"	Creation	CRET027	1986	**£8**	
Final Resting Of The Ark	12"	Creation	CRET048	1987	**£8**	
Index	7"	Shanghai	CUS321	1979	**£20**	
My Face Is On Fire	7"	Cherry Red	CHERRY45	1982	**£5**	
Penelope Tree	7"	Cherry Red	CHERRY59	1983	**£4**	
Rain Of Crystal Spires	7"	Creation	CRE032	1986	**£6**	
Rain Of Crystal Spires	12"	Creation	CRET032	1986	**£8**	
Something Sends Me To Sleep	7"	Cherry Red	CHERRY26	1981	**£6**	

FEMININE TOUCH

Title	Format	Label	Cat. No.	Year	Price	Notes
You Make Me Come Alive	7"	Paladin	PAL11	1976	**£4**	

FENDER, JAN & BUSTER

Title	Format	Label	Cat. No.	Year	Price	Notes
Sweet Pea	7"	Fab	FAB164	196-	**£8**	

FENDERMEN

Title	Format	Label	Cat. No.	Year	Price	Notes
Don't You Just Know It	7"	Top Rank	JAR513	1960	**£4**	
Mule Skinner Blues	LP	Soma	MG1240	1960	**£400**	US
Mule Skinner Blues	7"	Top Rank	JAR395	1960	**£4**	chart single

FENMEN

Title	Format	Label	Cat. No.	Year	Price	Notes
Be My Girl	7"	Decca	F11955	1964	**£8**	
California Dreamin'	7"	CBS	202075	1966	**£8**	
I've Got Everything You Need	7"	Decca	F12269	1965	**£8**	
Rejected	7"	CBS	202236	1966	**£6**	

FENTON, PETER

Title	Format	Label	Cat. No.	Year	Price	Notes
I Was Lord Kitchener's Valet	7"	Fontana	TF789	1967	**£4**	
Marble Breaks Iron Bends	7"	Fontana	TF748	1966	**£4**	chart single

FENTON, SHANE & THE FENTONES

Bernard Jewry has had two separate singing careers. Best known as Alvin Stardust in the seventies, he was also Shane Fenton in the early sixties, achieving a few minor successes in a style which owed everything to Cliff Richard and Billy Fury.

Title	Format	Label	Cat. No.	Year	Price	Notes
Don't Do That	7"	Parlophone	R5047	1963	**£5**	
Fool's Paradise	7"	Parlophone	R5020	1963	**£5**	
Hey Lulu	7"	Parlophone	R5131	1964	**£5**	
I Ain't Got Nobody	7"	Parlophone	R4982	1963	**£6**	
I'm A Moody Guy	7"	Parlophone	R4827	1961	**£6**	chart single
It's All Over Now	7"	Parlophone	R4883	1962	**£5**	chart single
It's Gonna Take Magic	7"	Parlophone	R4921	1962	**£6**	chart single
Too Young For Sad Memories	7"	Parlophone	R4951	1962	**£5**	
Walk Away	7"	Parlophone	R4866	1962	**£5**	chart single

FENTONES

Title	Format	Label	Cat. No.	Year	Price	Notes
Breeze And I	7"	Parlophone	R4937	1962	**£5**	chart single
Mexican	7"	Parlophone	R4899	1962	**£5**	chart single

FENWAYS

Walk .... 7" .... Liberty .... LIB66082 .... 1965 .... **£8**

FENWICK, RAY

Keep America Beautiful .... LP .... Decca .... SKL5090 .... 1971 .... **£10**

FERGUSON, HELENA

Where Is The Party .... 7" .... London .... HLZ10164 .... 1967 .... **£8**

FERGUSON, JESSIE LEE & THE OUTER LIMITS

New Shoes .... 7" .... Pye .... 7N25492 .... 1969 .... **£6**

FERGUSON, JOHNNY

Angela Jones .... 7" .... MGM .... MGM1059 .... 1960 .... **£4**

FERLINGHETTI, LAWRENCE

Impeachment Of President Eisenhower . LP .... Fantasy .... 7004 .... 1958 .... **£25** .... US, red vinyl
Poetry Readings In The Cellar .... LP .... Fantasy .... 7002 .... 1957 .... **£25** .... US, red vinyl

FERNBACH, ANDY

If You Miss Your Connection .... LP .... Liberty .... LBS83233 .... 1969 .... **£50**

FERRIS WHEEL

Can't Break The Habit .... LP .... Pye .... NPL18203 .... 1967 .... **£15**
Can't Stop Now .... 7" .... Polydor .... 56366 .... 1969 .... **£5**
Ferris Wheel .... LP .... Polydor .... 588066 .... 1970 .... **£10**
Let It Be Me .... 7" .... Pye .... 7N17538 .... 1968 .... **£5**
Na Na Song .... 7" .... Pye .... 7N17631 .... 1968 .... **£6**
Number One Guy .... 7" .... Pye .... 7N17387 .... 1967 .... **£8**

FERRIS, EUGENE

There Was A Smile In Your Eyes .... 7" .... Planet .... PLF112 .... 1966 .... **£5**

FERRY, BRYAN

Extended Play .... 7" EP .... Island .... 1EP1 .... 1976 .... **£4**
Hard Rain's Gonna Fall .... 7" .... Island .... WIP6170DJ .... 1973 .... **£6** .... 1 sided promo
Hold On I'm Coming .... 12" .... Polydor .... PPSP10 .... 1978 .... **£6** .... promo
Price Of Love .... 7" .... Island .... 1976 .... **£4** .... promo/ juke box issue
Price Of Love .... 7" .... Island .... IEP1DJ .... 1976 .... **£5** .... 1 sided promo
These Foolish Things .... 7" .... Island .... 1973 .... **£10** .... promo sampler

FEVER TREE

Fever Tree were one of the many San Francisco groups who got to make a few records, but never managed to consolidate them into a long-term career. The group was responsible for a terrific single, "San Francisco Girls", which was something of a Haight-Asbury response to the Beach Boys, with gritty vocals and a keening guitar reclaiming the California girls as their own. In general, however, Fever Tree did not feature the guitar playing enough, preferring a pseudo-classical approach which squandered the group's real strengths without replacing them with anything that was not done better by others.

Another Time Another Place .... LP .... MCA .... MUPS347 .... 1968 .... **£15**
Creation .... LP .... Uni .... 73067 .... 1969 .... **£20** .... US
Fever Tree .... LP .... Uni .... UNLS102 .... 1968 .... **£15**
For Sale .... LP .... Ampex .... A10113 .... 1970 .... **£15** .... US
San Francisco Girls .... 7" .... MCA .... MU1043 .... 1968 .... **£8**

FICKLE FINGER

Fickle Lizzie Anne .... 7" .... Page One .... POF150 .... 1969 .... **£4**

FICKLE PICKLE

American Pie .... 7" .... B&C .... CB177 .... 1972 .... **£6**
California Calling .... 7" .... B&C .... CB178 .... 1972 .... **£6**
Millionaire .... 7" .... Fontana .... TF1069 .... 1970 .... **£8**
Sinful Skinful .... LP .... Explosion .... 1970 .... **£100**

FIELDING, JERRY

When I Grow Too Old To Dream .... 7" .... London .... HL8017 .... 1954 .... **£8**

FIELDS

Fields .... LP .... CBS .... 69009 .... 1971 .... **£15**
Friends Of Mine .... 7" .... CBS .... 7555 .... 1971 .... **£4**

FIELDS OF THE NEPHILIM

Blue Water .... 7" .... Situation .... SIT48 .... 1987 .... **£10**
Blue Water .... 12" .... Situation .... SIT48T .... 1987 .... **£10** .... with poster

Burning The Fields	12"	Tower	N1	1984	**£40**	red sleeve
Burning The Fields	12"	Tower	N1	1985	**£20**	green sleeve + band pics
Preacher Man	7"	Situation	SIT46	1987	**£12**	
Psychonaut	7"	Situation	SIT57	1989	**£4**	
Psychonaut	7"	Situation	SIT57	1989	**£8**	green vinyl

FIELDS OF THE NEPHILIM & OTHERS

Dawnrazor	7"	H. Of Dolls		1987	**£6**	flexi

FIELDS, ERNIE

Saxy	7" EP	London	RE1260	1960	**£6**	

FIELDS, KANSAS & MILTON SEALEY

Kansas Fields And Milton Sealey	7" EP	Ducretet	DEP95017	1956	**£4**	

FIESTAS

So Fine	7"	London	HL8870	1959	**£5**	

FIFTH AVENUE

Bells Of Rhymney	7"	Immediate	IM002	1965	**£15**	

FIFTH COLUMN

Benjamin Day	7"	Columbia	DB8068	1966	**£5**	

FIFTH DIMENSION

I'll Be Loving You For Ever	7"	Liberty	LIB15356	1970	**£5**	

FIFTH ESTATE

Coney Island Sally	7"	Stateside	SS2125	1969	**£4**	
Ding Dong The Witch Is Dead	LP	Jubilee	JGM8005	1967	**£10**	US
Ding Dong The Witch Is Dead	7"	Stateside	SS2034	1967	**£5**	
Do Drop In	7"	Stateside	SS2105	1968	**£4**	
Heigh Ho	7"	Stateside	SS2068	1967	**£5**	

FIFTY FOOT HOSE

Cauldron	LP	Limelight	86062	1969	**£30**	US

FINCHLEY BOYS

Everlasting Tribute	LP	Gold. Throat	20019	1968	**£70**	US

FINDERS KEEPERS

Light	7"	CBS	202249	1966	**£8**	
On The Beach	7"	Fontana	TF892	1967	**£8**	
Sadie The Cleaning Lady	7"	Fontana	TF938	1968	**£6**	

FINE YOUNG CANNIBALS

Funny How Love Is	7"	London	LONP88	1986	**£5**	pic disc
Good Thing	7"	London	LONB218	1989	**£6**	tin box
Johnny Come Home	7"	London	LONP68	1985	**£5**	pic disc
She Drives Me Crazy	7"	London	LON199	1988	**£6**	marbled yellow vinyl in tin box
Suspicious Minds	7"	London	LONP82	1986	**£4**	pic disc

FINGERS

All Kinds Of People	7"	Columbia	DB8112	1967	**£8**	
I'll Take You Where The Music's...	7"	Columbia	DB8026	1966	**£5**	

FINN Mc COOL

Finn McCool	LP	RCA	SF8112	1970	**£30**	

FINN, LEE & THE RHYTHM MEN

High Class Feeling	7"	Starlite	ST45103	1963	**£20**	

FINN, MICKEY

Garden Of My Mind	7"	Direction	583086	1967	**£20**	
If I Had You Baby	7"	Polydor	56719	1966	**£30**	
Sporting Life	7"	Columbia	DB7510	1965	**£30**	

FINN, MICKEY & THE BLUE MEN

Pills	7"	Oriole	CB1927	1964	**£20**	
Reeling And Rocking	7"	Oriole	CB1940	1964	**£15**	

FINN, SIMON

Pass The Distance	LP	Mushroom	100MR2	1970	**£60**	

FINNEGAN, LARRY

Dear One	7"	HMV	POP1022	1962	**£4**	
Other Ringo	7"	Ember	EMBS207	1965	**£6**	

FIRE

Father's Name Is Dad	7"	Decca	F12753	1968	**£40**	
Magic Shoemaker	LP	Pye	NSPL18343	1970	**£200**	
Round The Gum Tree	7"	Decca	F12856	1968	**£20**	

FIRE ENGINES

Aufgeladen Und Bereit Fur Action...	LP	Fast	FPA002	1981	**£10**	
Big Gold Dream	7"	Pop:Aural	POP013	1981	**£6**	
Big Gold Dream	12"	Pop:Aural	POP013	1981	**£6**	
Candyskin	7"	Pop:Aural	POP010	1981	**£6**	
Get Up And Use Me	7"	Codex	CDX01	1980	**£5**	
Lubricate Your Living Room	LP	Accessory	ACC001	1981	**£10**	

FIRE ESCAPE

Psychotic Reaction	LP	GNP-Cres.	2034	1966	**£20**	US

FIREBALL XL5 CAST

Journey To The Moon	7" EP	Century 21	MA100	1966	**£10**	
Marina Speaks	7" EP	Century 21	MA104	1966	**£10**	

FIREBALLS

Baby What's Wrong	7"	Stateside	SS417	1965	**£4**	
Bottle Of Wine	LP	Stateside	SL10237	1968	**£10**	
Bottle Of Wine	7"	Stateside	SS2095	1967	**£4**	
Bulldog	7"	Top Rank	JAR276	1960	**£4**	
Carioca	7"	Stateside	SS151	1963	**£4**	
Come On, React	LP	London	STHA8396	1969	**£10**	
Come On, React	7"	Stateside	SS2134	1969	**£4**	
Fireballs	LP	Top Rank	RM324	1960	**£30**	US
Foot Patter	7"	Top Rank	JAR354	1960	**£4**	
Goin' Away	7"	Stateside	SS2106	1968	**£4**	
Here Are The Fireballs	LP	Warwick	W2042	1961	**£25**	US
Long Green	7"	London	HLZ10260	1969	**£4**	
Quite A Party	7"	Pye	7N25092	1961	**£4**	chart single
Rik-A-Tik	7"	Stateside	SS106	1962	**£4**	
Torquay	7"	Top Rank	JAR218	1959	**£5**	
Vaquero	LP	Top Rank	25105	1961	**£15**	
Vaquero	7"	Top Rank	JAR507	1960	**£4**	

FIREFLIES

I Can't Say Goodbye	7"	London	HLU9057	1960	**£4**	
You Were Mine	LP	Taurus	1002	1961	**£50**	US
You Were Mine	7"	Top Rank	JAR198	1959	**£4**	

FIRESIGN THEATRE

Dear Friends	LP	CBS	31099	1972	**£15**	US, double
Don't Crush That Dwarf...	LP	CBS	30102	1972	**£10**	US
Everything You Know Is Wrong	LP	CBS	33141	1975	**£10**	US
Forward Into The Past	LP	CBS	34391	1977	**£10**	US
How To Be In Two Places At Once	LP	CBS	65130	1968	**£20**	
I Think We're All Bozos...	LP	CBS	30737	1972	**£10**	US
In The Next World ...	LP	CBS	31383	1972	**£10**	US
Not Insane Or Anything You Want	LP	CBS	31585	1972	**£10**	US
Tale Of The Giant Rat...	LP	CBS	32370	1974	**£10**	US
TV Or Not TV	LP	CBS	32199	1973	**£10**	US
Waiting For The Electrician...	LP	CBS	65129	1968	**£20**	

FIRING SQUAD

Little Bit More	7"	Parlophone	R5152	1964	**£8**	

FIRM

Radioactive	7"	Atlantic	A9586P	1985	**£6**	shaped pic disc

FIRST AID

Nostradamus	LP	Decca	TXS117	1977	**£12**	

FIRST EDITION
Just Dropped In .... 7" .... Reprise .... RS20655 .... 1968 .... **£4**

FIRST GEAR
Certain Girl .... 7" .... Pye .... 7N15703 .... 1964 .... **£20**
In Crowd .... 7" .... Pye .... 7N15763 .... 1965 .... **£12**

FIRST IMPRESSION
Beat Club .... LP .... Saga .... SOC1045 .... 1967 .... **£12**

FIRST IMPRESSION/GOOD EARTH
Swinging London .... LP .... Saga .... FID2117 .... 1968 .... **£12**

FIRST STEPS
Beat Is Back .... 7" .... English Rose .. ER1 .... 1980 .... **£4**

FISCHER, WILD MAN
Evening With... .... LP .... Reprise .... RSLP6332 .... 1970 .... **£35**

FISCHER-Z
Worker .... 7" .... United Artists .. UP36509 .... 1979 .... **£4** .... pic disc

FISH
State Of Mind .... 12" .... EMI .... 12EMPD109 .... 1989 .... **£6** .... pic disc

FISHBAUGH FISHBAUGH ZORN
Fishbaugh Fishbaugh Zorn .... LP .... CBS .... 64783 .... 1972 .... **£10**

FISHER, CHIP
At The Sugar Bowl .... 7" EP .... RCA .... RCX143 .... 1959 .... **£8**

FISHER, MATTHEW
I'll Be There .... LP .... RCA .... APLI0325 .... 1974 .... **£10** .... US
Journey's End .... LP .... RCA .... SF8380 .... 1973 .... **£10**

FISHER, RAY
Bonny Birdy .... LP .... Trailer .... 1972 .... **£15**

FISHER, TONI
Big Hurt .... 7" .... Top Rank .... JAR261 .... 1960 .... **£4** .... chart single

FITS
Bored Of Education .... 7" .... Stagefright .... 1979 .... **£4**
You Said We'd Never Make it .... 7" .... Lightbeat .... FIT1 .... 198- **£5**

FITZ & COOZERS
Cover Me .... 7" .... New Beat .... NB003 .... 1968 .... **£8**

FITZGERALD, ELLA
Get Ready .... 7" .... Reprise .... R20850 .... 1969 .... **£4**

FITZGERALD, G.F.
Mouseproof .... LP .... Uni .... UNLS115 .... 1970 .... **£10**

FITZGERALD, PATRICK
Backstreet Boys .... 7" .... Small Wond. ... SMALL6 .... 1978 .... **£4**
Paranoid Ward .... 7" .... Small Wond. ... WEENY1 .... 1978 .... **£4**
Safety Pin Stuck In My Heart .... 7" .... Small Wond. ... SMALL4 .... 1977 .... **£4**

FIVE & A PENNY
You Don't Know Where Your Interest... .. 7" .... Polydor .... 56282 .... 1968 .... **£12**

FIVE A.M. EVENT
Hungry .... 7" .... Pye .... 7N17154 .... 1966 .... **£12**

FIVE AMERICANS
7.30 Guided Tour .... 7" .... Stateside .... SS2097 .... 1968 .... **£5**
Evil, Not Love .... 7" .... Pye .... 7N25373 .... 1966 .... **£5**
I See The Light .... LP .... H. Barbera .... LP8503 .... 1966 .... **£10** .... US
I See The Light .... 7" .... Pye .... 7N25354 .... 1966 .... **£6**
Now And Then .... LP .... Abnak .... ABST2071 .... 1968 .... **£10** .... US
Progressions .... LP .... Abnak .... AB2069 .... 1967 .... **£10** .... US
Sound Of Love .... 7" .... Stateside .... SS2036 .... 1967 .... **£5**

Western Union	LP	Abnak	AB2067	1967	**£10**	US
Western Union	7"	Stateside	SS2012	1967	**£5**	

FIVE BLIND BOYS

Five Blind Boys	7" EP	Vocalion	EPVP1282	1964	**£4**	

FIVE BLIND BOYS & SPIRITS OF MEMPHIS

Negro Spirituals	7" EP	Vocalion	EPVP1276	1964	**£4**	

FIVE BY FIVE

Fire	7"	Pye	7N25477	1968	**£15**	

FIVE CHESTERNUTS

Jean Dorothy	7"	Columbia	DB4165	1958	**£30**	

FIVE DALLAS BOYS

Five Dallas Boys	7" EP	Columbia	SEG8035	1960	**£5**	

FIVE DAY WEEK STRAW PEOPLE

Five Day Week Straw People	LP	Saga	FID2123	1968	**£60**	

FIVE DU TONES

Shake A Tail Feather	7"	Stateside	SS206	1963	**£8**	

FIVE EMPREES

Five Emprees	LP	Freeport	FR3001	1965	**£30**	US
Little Miss Sad	LP	Freeport	FR3002	1966	**£15**	US
Little Miss Sad	7"	Stateside	SS470	1965	**£4**	

FIVE FLEETS

Oh What A Feeling	7"	Felsted	AF103	1958	**£25**	

FIVE KEYS

Best Of...	LP	Aladdin	806	1956	**£300**	US
Blues Don't Care	7"	Capitol	CL14756	1957	**£15**	
Cos' You're My Love	7"	Capitol	CL14545	1956	**£25**	
Doggone It	7"	Capitol	CL14325	1955	**£30**	
Fantastic Five Keys	LP	Capitol	T1769	1962	**£90**	US
Five Keys	LP	King	688	1960	**£150**	US
Five Keys On Stage	LP	Capitol	T828	1957	**£60**	US
Five Keys On The Town	LP	Score	LP4003	1957	**£240**	US
Four Walls	7"	Capitol	CL14736	1957	**£15**	
From Me To You	7"	Capitol	CL14829	1958	**£15**	
Really O Truly Oh	7"	Capitol	CL14967	1958	**£15**	
Rhythm & Blues Hits Past And Present	LP	King	692	1960	**£150**	US
She's The Most	7"	Capitol	CL14582	1956	**£20**	
That's Right	7"	Capitol	CL14639	1956	**£20**	
Verdict	7"	Capitol	CL14313	1955	**£40**	
Wisdom Of A Fool	7"	Capitol	CL14686	1957	**£20**	

FIVE ROYALES

Dedicated To The One I Love	7"	Ember	EMBS124	1960	**£10**	
Dedicated To You	LP	King	580	1957	**£100**	US
Five Royales	LP	King	678	1960	**£75**	US
Five Royales Sing For You	LP	King	616	1959	**£75**	US
Rockin' Five Royales	LP	Apollo	LP488	1956	**£240**	US
Twenty-Four All Time Hits	LP	King	955	1966	**£20**	US

FIVE SATINS

Encore	LP	Ember	ELP401	1960	**£25**	US
Five Satins Sing	LP	Ember	ELP100	1957	**£75**	US
Five Satins Sing	LP	Ember	ELP100	1957	**£400**	US, blue vinyl
Five Satins Sing	LP	Mnt. Vernon	108	196-	**£15**	US
Shadows	7"	Top Rank	JAR239	1959	**£10**	
To The Aisle	7"	London	HL8501	1957	**£80**	
Wonderful Girl	7"	Top Rank	JAR199	1959	**£15**	
Your Memory	7"	MGM	MGM1087	1960	**£6**	

FIVE SMITH BROTHERS

ABC Boogie	7"	Decca	F10403	1954	**£6**	

FIVE STAIRSTEPS & CUBIE

Title	Format	Label	Cat. No.	Year	Price	Notes
Five Stairsteps	LP	Windy	C6000	1967	**£10**	US
Million To One	7"	Pye	7N25448	1968	**£6**	
Stay Close To Me	7"	Buddah	201026	1968	**£4**	
We Must Be In Love	7"	Buddah	201070	1969	**£4**	

FIVE STAR

Title	Format	Label	Cat. No.	Year	Price	Notes
Crazy	12"	Tent	RCAT451	1984	**£6**	
Crunchie Live Tour	12"			1986	**£8**	pic disc
Hide And Seek	12"	Tent	RCAT399	1984	**£6**	
Problematic	7"	Tent	TENT4	1983	**£5**	
Problematic	12"	Tent	TENTT4	1983	**£6**	
Slightest Touch	7"	Tent	PT41265B	1987	**£5**	2 singles, 5 photos, boxed
Stay Out Of My Life	7"	Tent	PB41131	1987	**£4**	with badges

FIVE TOWNS

Title	Format	Label	Cat. No.	Year	Price	Notes
It Isn't What You've Got	7"	Direction	583115	1967	**£4**	

FIVE'S COMPANY

Title	Format	Label	Cat. No.	Year	Price	Notes
Ballad Of Fred The Pixie	LP	Saga	FID2151	1969	**£15**	
Session Man	7"	Pye	7N17199	1966	**£8**	
Some Girls	7"	Pye	7N17162	1966	**£6**	
Sunday For Seven Days	7"	Pye	7N17118	1966	**£8**	

FLAG OF CONVENIENCE

Title	Format	Label	Cat. No.	Year	Price	Notes
Life On The Telephone	7"	Sire	SIR4057	1982	**£4**	

FLAIRS

Title	Format	Label	Cat. No.	Year	Price	Notes
Flairs	LP	Crown	CLP5356	1963	**£25**	US
Swing Pretty Mama	7"	Oriole	CB1392	1957	**£70**	

FLAME

Title	Format	Label	Cat. No.	Year	Price	Notes
See The Light	7"	Stateside	SS2183	1970	**£4**	

FLAMES

Title	Format	Label	Cat. No.	Year	Price	Notes
Broadway Jungle	7"	Island	WI139	1964	**£10**	
It Takes Time	7"	Blue Beat	BB300	1964	**£10**	
You've Lost Your Date	7"	New Beat	NB028	1968	**£8**	

FLAMIN' GROOVIES

Title	Format	Label	Cat. No.	Year	Price	Notes
Absolutely Sweet Marie	7"	Sire	SIR4018	1979	**£8**	PS
Don't You Lie To Me	7"	Sire	6198086	1976	**£5**	PS
Feel A Whole Lot Better	7"	Sire	6078619	1978	**£8**	PS
Feel A Whole Lot Better	12"	Sire	6078619	1978	**£8**	PS
Flamingo	LP	Kama Sutra	KSBS2021	1971	**£10**	US
Gonna Rock Tonight	7"	Kama Sutra		197-	**£5**	
Married Woman	7"	United Artists	UP35464	1972	**£6**	
Move It	7"	Sire	SIR4002	1978	**£6**	
Shake Some Action	LP	Sire	9103251	1977	**£12**	
Shake Some Action	7"	Sire	6078602	1976	**£4**	
Slow Death	7"	United Artists	REM406	1976	**£8**	
Slow Death	7"	United Artists	UP35392	1972	**£6**	
Sneekers	LP-10"	Snazz	R2371	1969	**£20**	US
Supersnazz	LP	Epic	BN26487	1969	**£12**	US
Teenage Head	LP	Kama Sutra	KSBS2031	1971	**£10**	US
Teenage Head	7"	Kama Sutra	2013031	1971	**£6**	
Teenage Head	7"	Kama Sutra	KSS707	1976	**£5**	

FLAMING EMBER

Title	Format	Label	Cat. No.	Year	Price	Notes
Westbound No.9	LP	Hot Wax	SHW5001	1970	**£10**	

FLAMING YOUTH

Flaming Youth's "Ark II" was a Melody Maker album of the month, but its remarkable lack of commercial success probably goes to show that the music press is very much less influential than it would like to believe. The group's drummer, however, has done very well subsequently - he is Phil Collins, albeit almost unrecogniseable from the picture on the LP cover!

Title	Format	Label	Cat. No.	Year	Price	Notes
Ark 2	LP	Fontana	STL5533	1969	**£20**	
From Now On	7"	Fontana	6001003	1970	**£10**	
Guide Me Orion	7"	Fontana	TF1057	1969	**£15**	PS
Man, Woman And Child	7"	Fontana	6001002	1970	**£10**	

FLAMINGO, JOHNNY

My Teenage Girl	7"	Vogue	V9089	1957	**£8**	
So Long	7"	Vogue	V9100	1958	**£8**	

FLAMINGOS

At Night	7"	Top Rank	JAR519	1960	**£5**	
Boogaloo Party	7"	Philips	BF1483	1966	**£4**	
Favorites	LP	End	LP307	1960	**£15**	US
Flamingos	LP	Checker	LP1433	1959	**£75**	US
Flamingos	LP	Constellation	CS3	1964	**£10**	US
Flamingos Meet The Moonglows	LP	Vee Jay	LP1052	1962	**£20**	US
I Only Have Eyes For You	7"	Top Rank	JAR263	1960	**£8**	
Just For A Kick	7"	London	HLN8373	1957	**£90**	
Ladder Of Love	7"	Brunswick	05696	1957	**£70**	
Love Walked In	7"	Top Rank	JAR213	1959	**£8**	
Nobody Loves Me Like You	7"	Top Rank	JAR367	1960	**£6**	
Requestfully Yours	LP	End	LP308	1960	**£15**	US
Serenade	LP	End	LP304	1959	**£25**	US
Sound Of The Flamingos	LP	End	LP316	1962	**£15**	US
Their Hits - Then And Now	LP	Philips	200206	1966	**£10**	US

FLANAGAN BROTHERS

Salton City	7"	Coral	Q72342	1958	**£6**	

FLANDERS, MICHAEL & DONALD SWANN

At The Drop Of A Hat	LP	Parlophone	PMC1033	1957	**£10**	chart LP
At The Drop Of Another Hat	LP	Parlophone	PMC1216	1964	**£10**	chart LP
Bestiary Of Flanders And Swann	LP	Parlophone	PMC1164	1961	**£10**	
Gnu	7"	Parlophone	R4354	1957	**£4**	

FLANDERS, TOMMY

Moonstone	LP	Verve	SVLP6020	1969	**£15**	

FLARES

Foot Stompin' Hits	LP	London	HAU8034	1963	**£15**	
Foot Stomping	7"	London	HLU9441	1961	**£4**	

FLASH

Flash	LP	Sovereign	SVNA7251	1972	**£10**	
Flash In The Can	LP	Sovereign	SVNA7255	1972	**£10**	
Out Of Our Hands	LP	Sovereign	SVNA7260	1973	**£10**	
Small Beginnings	7"	Sovereign	SOV105	1972	**£4**	
Watch Your Step	7"	Sovereign	SOV116	1973	**£4**	

FLASH & THE BOARD OF DIRECTORS

Busy Signal	7"	Bell	BLL1007	1968	**£4**	

FLAT EARTH SOCIETY

Waleeco	LP	Fleetwood	3027	1968	**£100**	US

FLAVOUR

Sally Had A Party	7"	Direction	583597	1968	**£4**	

FLAX

One	LP	Vertigo		1976	**£150**	

FLEE REKKERS

Blue Tango	7"	Pye	7N15326	1960	**£4**	
Fabulous Flee Rekkers	7" EP	Pye	NEP24141	1961	**£10**	
Fireball	7"	Piccadilly	7N35109	1963	**£5**	
Green Jeans	7"	Top Rank	JAR431	1960	**£6**	
Green Jeans	7"	Triumph	RGM1008	1960	**£20**	chart single
Lone Rider	7"	Piccadilly	7N35006	1961	**£6**	
Stage To Cimmaron	7"	Piccadilly	7N35048	1962	**£5**	
Sunburst	7"	Piccadilly	7N35081	1962	**£5**	
Sunday Date	7"	Pye	7N15288	1960	**£4**	

FLEETWOOD MAC

Most of the collectable Fleetwood Mac records come from the first part of the group's career, when its sound was very different to the commercial pop style that is now its forte. The Blue Horizon recordings - and especially the eponymous first LP - are probably the most authentic blues recordings to have been made by white, English musicians. Remarkably, that first LP climbed to number four in the album charts, although mint copies of the record have become surprisingly scarce these days.

Title	Format	Label	Cat. No.	Year	Price	Notes
Albatross	7"	Blue Horizon	573145	1968	**£4**	chart single
Bare Trees	LP	Reprise	K44181	1972	**£10**	
Big Love	12"	W. Bros	W8398TP	1987	**£6**	pic disc
Black Magic Woman	7"	Blue Horizon	573138	1968	**£5**	chart single
Blues Jam At Chess	LP	Blue Horizon	766227	1969	**£30**	double
Did You Ever Love Me	7"	Reprise	K14280	1973	**£4**	
Dragonfly	7"	Reprise	RS27010	1971	**£4**	
Family Man	7"	W. Bros	W8114B	1987	**£5**	boxed, 2 prints
Fleetwood Mac	LP	Blue Horizon	763200	1968	**£20**	chart LP
Fleetwood Mac	LP	Mobile Fid.	MFSL1012	1978	**£15**	US audiophile
Fleetwood Mac	LP	Reprise	K54043	1975	**£10**	white vinyl
For Your Love	7"	Reprise	K14315	1974	**£4**	
Future Games	LP	Reprise	K44153	1971	**£10**	
Green Manalishi	7"	Reprise	RS27007	1970	**£4**	chart single
Green Manalishi	7"	Reprise	RS27007	1970	**£8**	PS
Heroes Are Hard To Find	LP	Reprise	K54026	1974	**£10**	
Heroes Are Hard To Find	7"	Reprise	K14388	1975	**£4**	
I Believe My Time Ain't Long	7"	Blue Horizon	3051	1967	**£10**	
Kiln House	LP	Reprise	RSLP9004	1970	**£10**	chart LP
Little Lies	12"	W. Bros	W8291TP	1987	**£6**	pic disc
Man Of The World	7"	Immediate	IM080	1969	**£4**	chart single
Mirage	LP	Mobile Fid.	MFSL1119	1984	**£10**	US audiophile
Mr.Wonderful	LP	Blue Horizon	763205	1968	**£25**	chart LP
Need Your Love So Bad	7"	Blue Horizon	573139	1968	**£6**	chart single
Need Your Love So Bad	7"	Blue Horizon	573157	1969	**£5**	chart single
Oh Diane	7"	W. Bros	FLEET1P	1982	**£5**	pic disc
Oh Well	7"	Reprise	RS27000	1969	**£4**	chart single
Original Fleetwood Mac	LP	Blue Horizon	763875	1971	**£12**	
Penguin	LP	Reprise	K44235	1973	**£10**	
Pious Bird Of Good Omen	LP	Blue Horizon	763215	1969	**£15**	chart LP
Rumours	LP	Nautilus	NR 8	1981	**£15**	US audiophile
Seven Wonders	12"	W. Bros	W8317TP	1987	**£6**	pic disc
Sunny Side Of Heaven	7"	Reprise	K14194	1972	**£4**	
Then Play On	LP	Reprise	RSLP9000	1969	**£10**	chart LP
Tusk	LP	W. Bros	PROA866	1979	**£10**	US promo sampler

FLEETWOODS

Title	Format	Label	Cat. No.	Year	Price	Notes
Almost There	7"	Liberty	LIB10191	1965	**£5**	
Before And After	LP	Dolton	BLP2030	1965	**£12**	US
Best Of The Oldies	LP	Dolton	BLP2011	1962	**£12**	US
Come Softly To Me	7"	London	HLU8841	1959	**£5**	chart single
Deep In A Dream	LP	Dolton	BLP2007	1961	**£12**	US
Fleetwoods	LP	Dolton	BLP2002	1960	**£15**	US
Fleetwoods Sing For Lovers By Night	LP	Dolton	BLP2020	1963	**£12**	US
Folk Rock	LP	Dolton	BLP2039	1965	**£12**	US
Goodnight My Love	LP	Dolton	BLP2025	1963	**£12**	US
Goodnight My Love	7"	Liberty	LIB75	1964	**£4**	
Graduation's Here	7"	London	HLU8895	1959	**£4**	
Greatest Hits	LP	Dolton	BLP2018	1962	**£12**	US
He's The Great Imposter	7"	London	HLG9426	1961	**£4**	
Mister Blue	7"	Top Rank	JAR202	1959	**£4**	
Mr.Blue	LP	Top Rank	BUY028	1960	**£20**	
Outside My Window	7"	Top Rank	JAR294	1960	**£4**	
Ruby Red Baby Blue	7"	Liberty	LIB93	1964	**£4**	
Runaround	7"	Top Rank	JAR383	1960	**£4**	
Softly	LP	Dolton	BLP2005	1961	**£12**	US
They Tell Me It's Summer	7"	Liberty	LIB62	1964	**£4**	
Tragedy	7"	London	HLG9341	1961	**£4**	

FLEMING, HELEN

Title	Format	Label	Cat. No.	Year	Price	Notes
Eve's Ten Commandments	7"	Blue Beat	BB341	1965	**£10**	

FLEMONS, WADE

Title	Format	Label	Cat. No.	Year	Price	Notes
Easy Loving	7"	Top Rank	JAR371	1960	**£4**	
Slow Motion	7"	Top Rank	JAR206	1959	**£4**	
Wade Flemons	LP	Vee Jay	LP1011	1959	**£30**	US
What's Happening	7"	Top Rank	JAR327	1960	**£4**	

FLETCHER, DARROW

Title	Format	Label	Cat. No.	Year	Price	Notes
Pain Gets A LIttle Deeper	7"	London	HLU10024	1966	**£10**	

FLETCHER, DON

Two Wrongs Don't Make A Right .... 7" .... Vocalion......... VP9271 .... 1966........ **£5**..

FLEUR DE LYS

A legendary psychedelic group, the Fleur De Lys recorded both under their own name and as backing group to singer Sharon Tandy. They produced a number of striking singles, but with little commercial impact. Bryn Haworth, however, began a solo career during the seventies, while Pete Sears ended up as a member of Jefferson Starship.

Circles .... 7" .... Immediate....... IM032................... 1966...... **£50**..
Dong With A Luminous Nose .... 7" .... Polydor .... 56251 .... 1968...... **£30**..
I Can See A Light .... 7" .... Polydor .... 56200................... 1967...... **£25**..
Moondreams .... 7" .... Immediate....... IM020................... 1965...... **£40**..
Mud In Your Eye .... 7" .... Polydor .... 56124................... 1966...... **£50**..
Stop Crossing The Bridge .... 7" .... Atlantic........... 584193................. 1968...... **£30**..
You're Just A Liar .... 7" .... Atlantic........... 584243................. 1969...... **£30**..

FLIED EGG

Goodbye .... LP .... Vertigo .... 1972.... **£150**......................... Japanese

FLIES

House Of Love .... 7" .... Decca .... F12594................. 1967...... **£15**..
I'm Not Your Stepping Stone .... 7" .... Decca .... F12533................. 1966...... **£20**..
Magic Train .... 7" .... RCA............... RCA1757 .... 1968...... **£15**..

FLINTLOCK

Tears'n'Cheers .... LP .... Pinnacle.. 1976...... **£30**..

FLINTLOCKS

What Goes On .... 7" .... Decca .... F12412................. 1966........ **£4**..

FLINTSTONES

Workout .... 7" .... HMV.............. POP1266 .... 1964........ **£4**..

FLIP & THE DATELINERS

My Johnny Doesn't Come Around... ...... 7" .... HMV.............. POP1359 .... 1964........ **£8**..

FLIPS

Rockin' Twist .... 7" .... London........... HLU9490.............. 1962........ **£4**..

FLIRTATIONS

Can't Stop Loving You .... 7" .... Deram............ DM295 .... 1970........ **£4**..
Give Me Love .... 7" .... Deram............ DM329 .... 1971........ **£4**..
Keep On Searchin' .... 7" .... Deram............ DM281 .... 1970........ **£4**..
Need Your Loving .... 7" .... Deram............ DM351 .... 1972........ **£4**..
Nothing But A Heartache .... LP .... Deram............ DES18028 .... 1969...... **£12**.. US
Nothing But A Heartache .... 7" .... Deram............ DM216 .... 1968........ **£4**..
Someone Out There .... 7" .... Deram............ DM195 .... 1968........ **£4**..
Take Me In Your Arms And Love Me ..... 7" .... Polydor .... 2058167............... 1971........ **£4**..
What's Good About Goodbye My Love? 7" .... Deram............ DM252 .... 1969........ **£4**..

FLO & EDDIE

Afterglow .... 7" .... Reprise .... K14261................. 1973........ **£4**..
Flo And Eddie .... LP .... Reprise .... K44234................. 1973...... **£15**..
Flo And Eddie Interview Barry Mann ...... LP .... RCA............... DJL11162 .... 1973...... **£15**......................... US promo
Immoral, Illegal And Fattening .... LP .... CBS .... 33554................... 1974...... **£12**.. US
Let Me Make Love To You .... 7" .... CBS .... 2753..................... 1974........ **£4**..
Moving Targets .... LP .... CBS .... 81509................... 1976...... **£10**..
Phlorescent Leech And Eddie .... LP .... Reprise .... K44201................. 1972...... **£15**..
Rebecca .... 7" .... CBS .... 3972..................... 1976........ **£4**..

FLOATING BRIDGE

Floating Bridge .... LP .... Liberty............ LBS83271 .... 1969...... **£15**..

FLOCK

The Flock were one of the crop of rock big bands to emerge at the end of the sixties. They were made distinctive by the presence of a violin as a lead instrument; its wielder, Jerry Goodman, later finding a context in which he could shine even brighter, as a member of John McLaughlin's Mahavishnu Orchestra.

Dinosaur Swamps .... LP .... CBS .... 64055................... 1971...... **£10**..
Flock .... LP .... CBS .... 63733................... 1969...... **£15**......................... chart LP
Tired Of Waiting For You .... 7" .... CBS .... 4932..................... 1970........ **£5**..

FLOOD, DICK

Title	Format	Label	Cat. No.	Year	Price	Notes
Three Bells	7"	Felsted	AF125	1959	**£4**	

FLOWER TRAVELLING BAND

Title	Format	Label	Cat. No.	Year	Price	Notes
Satori	7"	Atlantic	2091128	1971	**£4**	

FLOWERPOT MEN

Title	Format	Label	Cat. No.	Year	Price	Notes
In A Moment Of Madness	7"	Deram	DM248	1969	**£4**	
Let's Go To San Francisco	7"	Deram	DM142	1967	**£4**	chart single
Man Without A Woman	7"	Deram	DM183	1968	**£4**	
Walk In The Sky	7"	Deram	DM160	1967	**£6**	

FLOWERS, PHIL

Title	Format	Label	Cat. No.	Year	Price	Notes
Like A Rolling Stone	7"	A&M	AMS766	1969	**£4**	

FLOYD, EDDIE

Title	Format	Label	Cat. No.	Year	Price	Notes
Big Bird	7"	Stax	601035	1968	**£4**	
Bye Bye Baby	7"	Speciality	SPE1001		**£6**	
I've Never Found A Girl	LP	Stax	STS2002	1968	**£12**	US
Knock On Wood	7"	Atlantic	584041	1966	**£6**	chart single
Knock On Wood	LP	Stax	589006	1967	**£15**	chart LP
On A Saturday Night	7"	Stax	601024	1967	**£4**	
Raise Your Hand	7"	Stax	601001	1967	**£5**	chart single
Rare Stamps	LP	Stax	STS2011	1969	**£10**	US
Set My Soul On Fire	7"	London	HL10129	1967	**£5**	
Things Get Better	7"	Stax	601016	1967	**£6**	chart single
You've Got To Have Eddie	LP	Stax	STS2017	1969	**£10**	US

FLOYD, KING

Title	Format	Label	Cat. No.	Year	Price	Notes
Baby Let Me Kiss You	7"	Atlantic	2091079	1971	**£4**	
Groove Me	7"	Atlantic	2091051	1971	**£4**	

FLYING BURRITO BROTHERS

Title	Format	Label	Cat. No.	Year	Price	Notes
Burrito Deluxe	LP	A&M	983	1970	**£10**	
Gilded Palace Of Sin	LP	A&M	931	1969	**£10**	
Train Song	7"	A&M	AMS756	1969	**£5**	

FLYING CIRCUS

Title	Format	Label	Cat. No.	Year	Price	Notes
Prepared In Peace	LP	Harvest	SHSP4010	1970	**£15**	

FLYING MACHINE

Title	Format	Label	Cat. No.	Year	Price	Notes
Devil Has Possession Of Your Mind	7"	Pye	7N45001	1970	**£4**	
Down To Earth	LP	Pye	NSPL18328	1970	**£15**	
Send My Baby Home Again	7"	Pye	7N17811	1969	**£5**	
Smile A Little Smile For Me	7"	Pye	7N17722	1969	**£5**	
Yes I Understand	7"	Pye	7N45093	1970	**£4**	

FLYNN, STEVE

Title	Format	Label	Cat. No.	Year	Price	Notes
Mr.Rainbow	7"	Parlophone	R5625	1967	**£5**	
Your Life And My Life	7"	Parlophone	R5689	1968	**£6**	

FLYS

Title	Format	Label	Cat. No.	Year	Price	Notes
Bunch Of Five	7"	Zama	ZA10	1977	**£6**	
Love And A Molotov Cocktail	7"	EMI	EMI2747	1978	**£4**	

FOCAL POINT

Title	Format	Label	Cat. No.	Year	Price	Notes
Love You Forever	7"	Deram	DM186	1968	**£25**	

FOCUS

Title	Format	Label	Cat. No.	Year	Price	Notes
Hocus Pocus	7"	Blue Horizon	2096004	1971	**£4**	
Tommy	7"	Blue Horizon	2096008	1972	**£5**	

FOCUS THREE

Title	Format	Label	Cat. No.	Year	Price	Notes
Ten Thousand Years Behind My Mind	7"	Columbia	DB8279	1967	**£15**	

FOETUS

Title	Format	Label	Cat. No.	Year	Price	Notes
Ache	LP	S. Immolation	WOMBOYBL2	1982	**£50**	
Deaf	LP	S. Immolation	WOMBOYBL1	1981	**£50**	
Finely Honed Machine	12"	S. Immolation	OMBUNC712	1985	**£30**	
OKFM	7"	S. Immolation	WOMBS201	1981	**£25**	
Tell Me, What Is The Bane Of Your Life	7"	S. Immolation	WOMBKX07	1982	**£25**	
Wash It All Off	7"	S. Immolation	WOMBALL007	1981	**£25**	

FOGCUTTERS

Title	Format	Label	Cat. No.	Year	Price	Notes
Cry Cry Cry	7"	Liberty	LIB55793	1964	**£8**	

FOGERTY, JOHN

Title	Format	Label	Cat. No.	Year	Price	Notes
Almost Saturday Night	7"	Fantasy	FTC120	1975	**£4**	
Blue Ridge Rangers	LP	Fantasy	FT511	1973	**£10**	
Comin' Down The Road	7"	Fantasy	FTC111	1974	**£4**	
Hearts Of Stone (Blue Ridge Rangers)	7"	Fantasy	FTC105	1973	**£4**	
John Fogerty	LP	Fantasy	FT526	1975	**£10**	
Rockin' All Over The World	7"	Fantasy	FTC119	1975	**£4**	
You Don't Owe... (Blue Ridge Rangers)	7"	Fantasy	FTC110	1974	**£4**	
You Got The Magic	7"	Fantasy	FTC133	1976	**£4**	

FOGERTY, TOM

Title	Format	Label	Cat. No.	Year	Price	Notes
Cast The First Stone	7"	Fantasy	F680	1972	**£4**	
Excalibur	LP	Fantasy	9413	1973	**£10**	US
Goodbye Media Man	7"	United Artists	UP35264	1971	**£4**	
Joyful Resurrection	7"	Fantasy	FTC109	1973	**£4**	
Myopia	LP	Fantasy	9469	1975	**£10**	US
Tom Fogerty	LP	Fantasy	FAN9407	1972	**£10**	
Zephyr National	LP	Fantasy	9448	1974	**£10**	US

FOGGY

Title	Format	Label	Cat. No.	Year	Price	Notes
Simple Gifts	LP	York		1972	**£20**	

FOGGY DEW-O

Title	Format	Label	Cat. No.	Year	Price	Notes
Born To Take The Highway	LP	Decca		1969	**£12**	
Foggy Dew-O	LP	Decca		1968	**£15**	

FOLEY, RED

Title	Format	Label	Cat. No.	Year	Price	Notes
Beyond The Sunset	LP	Decca	DL8296	1958	**£15**	US
Company's Comin'	LP	Decca	DL4140	1961	**£12**	US
Country Double Date	7" EP	Brunswick	OE9148	1955	**£4**	
Dear Hearts And Gentle People	LP	Decca	DL4290	1962	**£10**	US
Golden Favorites	LP	Decca	DL4107	1961	**£12**	US
He Walks With Thee	LP	Decca	DL8767	1958	**£15**	US
Let's All Sing To Him	LP	Decca	DL8903	1959	**£10**	US
Let's All Sing With Red Foley	LP	Decca	DL8847	1959	**£15**	US
Lift Up Your Voice	LP-10"	Decca	DL5338	1954	**£30**	US
My Keepsake Album	LP	Decca	DL8806	1958	**£15**	US
Red And Ernie	LP	Decca	DL8298	1956	**£25**	US
Skinnie Minnie Fishtail	7"	Brunswick	05321	1954	**£4**	
Songs Of Devotion	LP	Decca	DL4198	1961	**£10**	US
Souvenir Album	LP	Decca	DL8294	1958	**£20**	US
Souvenir Album	LP-10"	Decca	DL5303	1951	**£30**	US

FOLEY, RED & BETTY

Title	Format	Label	Cat. No.	Year	Price	Notes
Hearts Of Stone	7"	Brunswick	05363	1955	**£8**	
Night Watch	7"	Brunswick	05508	1955	**£4**	

FONTAINE, EDDIE

Title	Format	Label	Cat. No.	Year	Price	Notes
Cool It Baby	7"	Brunswick	05624	1956	**£20**	
Nothing Shaking	7"	London	HLM8711	1958	**£15**	
Rock Love	7"	HMV	7M304	1955	**£20**	

FONTANA, WAYNE

Title	Format	Label	Cat. No.	Year	Price	Notes
24 Sycamore	7"	Fontana	TF827	1967	**£4**	
Come On Home	7"	Fontana	TF684	1966	**£4**	chart single
Dayton Ohio 1903	7"	Fontana	TF1008	1969	**£4**	
Gina	7"	Fontana	TF889	1967	**£4**	
Give Me Just A Little More Time	7"	Philips	6006035	1970	**£20**	
Goodbye Bluebird	7"	Fontana	TF737	1966	**£4**	chart single
Impossible Years	7"	Fontana	TF866	1967	**£4**	
It Was Easier To Hurt Her	7"	Fontana	TF642	1965	**£4**	chart single
Never An Everyday Thing	7"	Fontana	TF976	1968	**£4**	
Pamela Pamela	7"	Fontana	TF770	1966	**£4**	
Storybook Children	7"	Fontana	TF911	1968	**£4**	
Wayne One	LP	Fontana	SFL13144	1969	**£10**	
Wayne One	LP	Fontana	STL5351	1966	**£12**	
We're Building A Love	7"	Fontana	TF1054	1969	**£4**	
Words Of Bartholomew	7"	Fontana	TF933	1968	**£4**	

FONTANA, WAYNE & THE MINDBENDERS

Title	Format	Label	Number	Year	Price	Notes
Eric, Rick, Wayne & Bob	LP	Fontana	TL5257	1966	**£35**	
For You, For You	7"	Fontana	TF418	1963	**£6**	
Game Of Love	7"	Fontana	TF535	1965	**£4**	chart single
Game Of Love	7" EP	Fontana	TE17449	1965	**£5**	
Hello Josephine	7"	Fontana	TF404	1963	**£6**	chart single
Just A Little Bit Too Late	7"	Fontana	TF579	1965	**£4**	chart single
Little Darling	7"	Fontana	TF436	1964	**£6**	
Road Runner	7" EP	Fontana	TE17421	1964	**£8**	
She Needs Love	7"	Fontana	TF611	1965	**£4**	chart single
Stop Look And Listen	7"	Fontana	TF451	1964	**£6**	chart single
Um Um Um Um Um	7"	Fontana	TF497	1964	**£4**	chart single
Um Um Um Um Um	7" EP	Fontana	TE17435	1964	**£5**	
Walking On Air	7" EP	Fontana	TE17453	1965	**£5**	
Wayne Fontana & The Mindbenders	LP	Fontana	SFL13106	1969	**£10**	chart LP
Wayne Fontana & The Mindbenders	LP	Fontana	TL5230	1965	**£20**	
Wayne Fontana & The Mindbenders	LP	Wing	WL1166	1967	**£10**	

FONTANE SISTERS

Title	Format	Label	Number	Year	Price	Notes
Adorable	7"	London	HLD8225	1956	**£8**	
Banana Boat Song	7"	London	HLD8378	1957	**£6**	
Billy Boy	7"	London	HLD8861	1959	**£4**	
Chanson D'Amour	7"	London	HLD8621	1958	**£4**	
Eddie My Love	7"	London	HLD8265	1956	**£12**	
Fontane Sisters	LP	Dot	DLP3004	1956	**£12**	US
Fontane Sisters No.1	7" EP	London	RED1029	1955	**£10**	
Fontane Sisters No.2	7" EP	London	RED1037	1955	**£10**	
Fontanes Sing	LP	London	HAD2053	1957	**£12**	
Fool Around	7"	London	HLD8488	1957	**£4**	
Happy Days And Lonely Nights	7"	London	HLD8099	1954	**£8**	
Hearts Of Stone	7"	London	HL8113	1955	**£15**	
I'm In Love Again	7"	London	HLD8289	1956	**£12**	
Listen To Your Heart	7"	London	HLD9037	1960	**£4**	
Please Don't Leave Me	7"	London	HLD8415	1957	**£6**	
Rock Love	7"	London	HL8126	1955	**£10**	
Rolling Stone	7"	London	HLD8211	1955	**£12**	
Seventeen	7"	London	HLD8177	1955	**£15**	
Silver Bells	7"	London	HLD8343	1956	**£6**	
Theme From A Summer Place	7"	London	HLD9078	1960	**£4**	
Tips Of My Fingers	LP	Dot	DLP3531	1963	**£10**	US
Voices	7"	London	HLD8318	1956	**£8**	

FOOL

Simon and Marijke of the Fool were a design team (the Beatles' shop mural; Eric Clapton's guitar; the Incredible String Band's second LP cover), rather than musicians, but they nevertheless recorded two interesting and eclectic LPs (the second was credited to "Simon and Marijke"), the first being produced by the Hollies' Graham Nash.

Title	Format	Label	Number	Year	Price	Notes
Fool	LP	Mercury	SMCL20138	1969	**£30**	

FOOT IN COLD WATER

Title	Format	Label	Number	Year	Price	Notes
Breaking Through	LP	Anthem	11008	1976	**£12**	Canadian
Foot In Cold Water	LP	Elektra	K52011	1974	**£12**	
In My Life	7"	Island	WIP6162	1973	**£4**	
Or All Around Us	LP	Elektra	71025	1974	**£12**	US
Second Foot In Cold Water	LP	Daffodil	16028	1973	**£15**	Canadian

FORBES, BILL

Title	Format	Label	Number	Year	Price	Notes
Once More	7"	Columbia	DB4269	1959	**£4**	

FORCE FIVE

Title	Format	Label	Number	Year	Price	Notes
Baby Don't Care	7"	United Artists	UP1102	1965	**£20**	
Don't Know Which Way To Turn	7"	United Artists	UP1141	1966	**£20**	
Don't Make My Baby Blue	7"	United Artists	UP1051	1964	**£15**	
I Want You Babe	7"	United Artists	UP1118	1965	**£15**	
Yeah I'm Waiting	7"	United Artists	UP1089	1965	**£15**	

FORCE WEST

Title	Format	Label	Number	Year	Price	Notes
All The Children Sleep	7"	Columbia	DB8174	1967	**£8**	
Gotta Find Another Baby	7"	Columbia	DB7908	1966	**£10**	
I Can't Give What I Haven't Got	7"	Decca	F12223	1965	**£8**	
I'll Be Moving On	7"	CBS	3798	1968	**£6**	
I'll Walk In The Rain	7"	CBS	3632	1968	**£6**	

Sherry	7"	CBS	4385	1969	**£8**	
When the Sun Comes Out	7"	Columbia	DB7963	1966	**£10**	

FORD, DEAN & THE GAYLORDS

Mr. Heartbreak's Here Instead	7"	Columbia	DB7402	1964	**£8**	
Name Game	7"	Columbia	DB7610	1965	**£10**	
Twenty Miles	7"	Columbia	DB7264	1964	**£8**	

FORD, EMILE

Emile	7" EP	Pye	NEP24119	1959	**£4**	
Emile Ford Hit Parade	7" EP	Pye	NEP24124	1960	**£4**	
Emile Ford Hit Parade Vol.2	7" EP	Pye	NEP24133	1960	**£4**	
New Tracks With Emile	LP	Pye	NPL18049	1959	**£10**	
What Do You Want To Make...	7"	Pye	7N15225	1959	**£4**	chart LP

FORD, FRANKIE

Alimony	7"	Top Rank	JAR186	1959	**£5**	
Cheating Woman	7"	Top Rank	JAR282	1960	**£5**	
Let's Take A Sea Cruise	LP	Ace	LP1005	1959	**£75**	US
Sea Cruise	7"	London	HL8850	1959	**£12**	
Sea Cruise	7"	Sue	WI366	1965	**£8**	
Time After Time	7"	Top Rank	JAR299	1960	**£5**	
What's Going On	7"	Sue	WI369	1965	**£8**	
You Talk Too Much	7"	London	HLP9222	1960	**£6**	

FORD, JON

You Got Me Where You Want Me	7"	Philips	6006030	1970	**£35**	

FORD, TENNESSEE ERNIE

Anticipation Blues	7" EP	Capitol	EAP120067	1961	**£10**	
Ballad Of Davy Crockett	7"	Capitol	CL14506	1956	**£5**	chart single
Catfish Boogie	7"	Capitol	CL14006	1953	**£15**	
First Born	7"	Capitol	CL14657	1956	**£4**	
Gather Round	7" EP	Capitol	EAP11227	1960	**£5**	
Give Me Your Word	7"	Capitol	CL14005	1953	**£8**	chart single
His Hands	7"	Capitol	CL14261	1955	**£4**	
Little Red Rocking Hood	7"	Capitol	CL15210	1961	**£5**	
Lonely Man	7"	Capitol	CL14734	1957	**£4**	
Sixteen Tons	7"	Capitol	CL14500	1956	**£6**	chart single
Sixteen Tons	7"	Capitol	CL15403	1965	**£4**	
Sixteen Tons	7" EP	Capitol	EAP1014	1956	**£10**	
Sunday Barbecue	7"	Capitol	CL14896	1958	**£4**	
That's All	7"	Capitol	CL14557	1956	**£4**	
There Is Beauty In Everything	7"	Capitol	CL14273	1955	**£4**	
Watermelon Song	7"	Capitol	CL14691	1957	**£4**	
Who Will Shoe Your Pretty Little Foot	7"	Capitol	CL14616	1956	**£4**	

FORD, TENNESSEE ERNIE & BETTY HUTTON

This Must Be The Place	7"	Capitol	CL14133	1954	**£5**	

FOREHAND, EDDIE BUSTER

Young Boy Blues	7"	Action	ACT4519	1969	**£4**	
Young Boy Blues	7"	Action	ACT4519	1969	**£15**	demo

FOREIGNER

Blue Morning, Blue Day	7"	Atlantic	K11236	1979	**£4**	pic disc
Double Vision	LP	Mobile Fid.	MFSL1052	1982	**£12**	US audiophile
Hot Blooded	7"	Atlantic	K11167	1978	**£4**	red vinyl, clear sleeve
I Want To Know What Love Is	7"	Atlantic	A9596	1984	**£6**	F shaped disc

FOREST

Forest	LP	Harvest	SHVL760	1969	**£60**	
Full Circle	LP	Harvest	SHVL784	1970	**£70**	
Searching For Shadows	7"	Harvest	HAR5007	1969	**£8**	

FORESTERS

Broken Hearted Clown	7"	Polydor	56038	1965	**£8**	
Comin' Home In The Evening	7"	Columbia	DB8176	1967	**£5**	
Early Morning Hours	7"	Polydor	56104	1966	**£8**	
How Can I Tell Her	7"	Polydor	56057	1965	**£8**	
Mr.Smith	7"	Columbia	DB8086	1966	**£5**	
Sometimes When You're Lonely	7"	Columbia	DB8040	1966	**£6**	

FOREVER AMBER
Love Cycle .... LP .... Advance .... 1969 .. **£1000** ....

FOREVER MORE
Words On Black Plastic .... LP .... RCA .... 3015 .... 1971 ...... **£12** ....
Yours Forever More .... LP .... RCA .... 1970 ...... **£12** ....

FORMAT
Maxwell's Silver Hammer .... 7" .... CBS .... 4600 .... 1969 .... **£4** ....

FORMATIONS
At The Top Of The Stairs .... 7" .... MGM .... MGM1399 .... 1968 ...... **£25** ....
At The Top Of The Stairs .... 7" .... Mojo .... 2027001 .... 1971 .... **£5** .... chart single

FORMERLY FAT HARRY
Formerly Fat Harry .... LP .... Harvest .... SHSP4016 .... 1971 ...... **£15** ....

FORMULA
Close To Me .... 7" .... HMV .... POP1438 .... 1965 .... **£4** ....

FORMULA ONE
I Just Can't Go To Sleep .... 7" .... W. Bros .... WB155 .... 1965 .... **£5** ....

FORRAY, ANDY
Dream With Me .... 7" .... Decca .... F12733 .... 1968 .... **£8** ....
Let The Sunshine In .... 7" .... Fontana .... TF999 .... 1969 .... **£5** ....
Proud One .... 7" .... Parlophone ..... R5729 .... 1968 .... **£6** ....
Sarah Jane .... 7" .... Parlophone ..... R5715 .... 1968 .... **£6** ....

FORTES MENTUM
Gotta Go .... 7" .... Parlophone ..... R5768 .... 1969 .... **£6** ....
I Can't Go On .... 7" .... Parlophone ..... R5726 .... 1968 .... **£5** ....
Saga Of A Wrinkled Man .... 7" .... Parlophone ..... R5684 .... 1968 .... **£8** ....

FORTUNES
Caroline .... 7" .... Decca .... F11809 .... 1964 .... **£4** ....
Fortunes .... LP .... Decca .... LK4736 .... 1965 ...... **£20** ....
Here It Comes Again .... 7" .... Decca .... F12243 .... 1965 .... **£4** .... chart single
I Like The Look Of You .... 7" .... Decca .... F11912 .... 1964 .... **£4** ....
Idol .... 7" .... United Artists .. UP1188 .... 1967 .... **£4** ....
Is It Really Worth Your While .... 7" .... Decca .... F12485 .... 1966 .... **£4** ....
Look Homeward Angel .... 7" .... Decca .... F11985 .... 1964 .... **£4** ....
Our Love Has Gone .... 7" .... Decca .... F12612 .... 1967 .... **£4** ....
Our Love Has Gone .... 7" .... Decca .... F12874 .... 1969 .... **£4** ....
Silent Street .... 7" .... Decca .... F12429 .... 1966 .... **£4** ....
Summertime Summertime .... 7" .... Decca .... F11718 .... 1963 .... **£5** ....
This Golden Ring .... 7" .... Decca .... F12321 .... 1966 .... **£4** .... chart single
You've Got Your Troubles .... 7" .... Decca .... F12173 .... 1965 .... **£4** .... chart single

FORTY NINE AMERICANS
E Pluribus Unum .... LP .... C.C. Train .... CHUG1 .... 1980 ...... **£15** ....
Too Young To Be Ideal .... 12" .... C.C. Train .... CHUG2 .... 1980 ...... **£10** ....
14 Track Single .... 7" .... NB .... NB4 .... 1980 .... **£4** ....

FORTY NINTH PARALLEL
Forty-Ninth Parallel .... LP .... Maverick .... MAS7001 .... 1969 ...... **£50** .... US

FORWOOD, SHIRLEY
Two Hearts .... 7" .... London .... HLD8402 .... 1957 .... **£8** ....

FOSTER, JOHN
John Foster Sings .... LP .... Island .... ILP939 .... 1966 ...... **£60** ....

FOSTER, LES
Do It Nice .... 7" .... Big Shot .... BI529 .... 1973 .... **£5** ....
Muriel .... 7" .... Jolly .... JY022 .... 196- .... **£8** ....

FOTHERINGAY
Fotheringay .... LP .... Island .... ILPS9125 .... 1970 ...... **£20** .... chart LP
Peace In The End .... 7" .... Island .... WIP6085 .... 1970 .... **£6** ....

FOUNDATIONS

Any Old Time	7"	Pye	7N17503	1968	**£4**	chart single
Baby Now That I've Found You	7"	Pye	7N17366	1967	**£4**	chart single
Back On My Feet Again	7"	Pye	7N17417	1968	**£4**	chart single
Born To Live And Born To Die	7"	Pye	7N17809	1969	**£4**	chart single
Build Me Up Buttercup	7"	Pye	7N17638	1968	**£4**	chart single
Digging The Foundations	LP	Pye	NPL18290	1969	**£10**	
From The Foundations	LP	Pye	NPL18206	1967	**£10**	
In The Bad Bad Old Days	7"	Pye	7N17702	1969	**£4**	chart single
It's All Right	7" EP	Pye	NEP24297	1968	**£5**	
Rocking The Foundations	LP	Pye	NPL18227	1968	**£10**	
Stoney Ground	7"	MCA	MK5075	1971	**£5**	

FOUNTAIN, JAMES

Seven Day Lover	7"	Cream	5002	1976	**£4**	

FOUR

It's Alright	7"	Decca	F11999	1964	**£5**	

FOUR ACES

Bahama Mama	7"	Brunswick	05663	1957	**£4**	
Beyond The Blue Horizon	LP	Decca	DL8944	1959	**£12**	US
Dreamer	7"	Brunswick	05601	1956	**£4**	
Four Aces	LP-10"	Decca	DL5429	195-	**£20**	US
Friendly Persuasion	7"	Brunswick	05623	1956	**£4**	chart single
Gal With The Yaller Shoes	7"	Brunswick	05566	1956	**£4**	
Gang That Sang	7"	Brunswick	05256	1954	**£4**	
Golden Hits	LP	Decca	DL4013	1960	**£10**	US
Half Of My Heart	7"	Brunswick	05712	1957	**£4**	
Hanging Up A Horseshoe	7"	Brunswick	05758	1958	**£4**	
Heart	7"	Brunswick	05651	1957	**£4**	
Heart And Soul	LP	Decca	DL8228	1956	**£15**	US
Hits From Broadway	LP	Decca	DL8855	1959	**£12**	US
Hits From Hollywood	LP	Decca	DL8693	1958	**£15**	US
If You Can Dream	7"	Brunswick	05573	1956	**£4**	
It Shall Come To Pass	7"	Brunswick	05322	1954	**£4**	
It's A Woman's World	7"	Brunswick	05348	1954	**£4**	
Jingle Bells	7"	Brunswick	05504	1955	**£4**	
Love Is A Many Splendoured Thing	7"	Brunswick	05480	1955	**£6**	chart single
Melody Of Love	7"	Brunswick	05379	1955	**£4**	
Mood For Love	LP	Decca	DL8122	1956	**£15**	US
Mr.Sandman	7"	Brunswick	05355	1954	**£6**	chart single
Rock And Roll Rhapsody	7"	Brunswick	05743	1958	**£4**	
Sentimental Souvenirs	LP	Decca	DL8191	1956	**£15**	US
She Sees All The Hollywood Hits	LP	Decca	DL8312	1957	**£15**	US
Shuffling Along	LP	Decca	DL8567	1958	**£15**	US
Slewfoot	7"	Brunswick	05429	1955	**£4**	
Stranger In Paradise	7"	Brunswick	05418	1955	**£5**	chart single
Swingin' Aces	LP	Decca	DL8766	1958	**£12**	US
There Goes My Heart	7"	Brunswick	05401	1955	**£4**	
Three Coins In The Fountain	7"	Brunswick	05308	1954	**£5**	chart single
Three Sheets To The Wind	7"	Brunswick	05695	1957	**£4**	
To Love Again	7"	Brunswick	05562	1956	**£4**	
Woman In Love	7"	Brunswick	05589	1956	**£4**	chart single
World Outside	7"	Brunswick	05767	1958	**£5**	chart single
World Outside	7"	Brunswick	05773	1959	**£4**	
Written On The Wind	LP	Decca	DL8424	1957	**£20**	US
You Can't Run Away From It	7"	Brunswick	05613	1956	**£4**	

FOUR ACES (2)

Little Girl	7"	Island	WI180	1965	**£10**	
River Bank Coberley Again	7"	Island	WI178	1965	**£10**	
Sweet Chariot	7"	Island	WI179	1965	**£10**	

FOUR ESQUIRES

Adorable	7"	London	HLA8224	1956	**£5**	
Always And Forever	7"	London	HLO8579	1958	**£4**	
Hideaway	7"	London	HL8746	1958	**£4**	
Look Homeward Angel	7"	London	HL8376	1957	**£6**	
Love Me Forever	7"	London	HLO8533	1958	**£4**	chart single
Sphinx Won't Tell	7"	London	HL8152	1955	**£8**	

FOUR FRESHMEN

Title	Format	Label	Number	Year	Price	Notes
Four Freshmen And Five Saxes	LP	Capitol	T844	1957	**£12**	US
Four Freshmen And Five Trombones	LP	Capitol	T683	1956	**£12**	US
Four Freshmen And Five Trumpets	LP	Capitol	T763	1957	**£12**	US
Freshmen Favorites	LP	Capitol	T743	1956	**£12**	US
Graduation Day	7"	Capitol	CL14610	1956	**£4**	
Voices In Latin	LP	Capitol	T992	1958	**£12**	US
Voices In Modern	LP	Capitol	T522	1955	**£12**	US

FOUR JONES BOYS

Title	Format	Label	Number	Year	Price	Notes
Tutti Frutti	7"	Decca	F10717	1956	**£4**	

FOUR KINSMEN

Title	Format	Label	Number	Year	Price	Notes
It Looks Like The Daybreak	7"	Decca	F22671	1967	**£6**	

FOUR KNIGHTS

Title	Format	Label	Number	Year	Price	Notes
Four Knights	7" EP	Capitol	EAP1506	1955	**£5**	
Four Knights	LP	Coral	CRL52221	195-	**£20**	US
Four Knights	LP	Coral	CRL52221	195-	**£20**	US
In The Chapel In The Moonlight	7"	Capitol	CL14154	1954	**£4**	
Million Dollar Baby	LP	Coral	CRL57309	1960	**£15**	US
Million Dollar Baby	LP	Coral	CRL57309	1960	**£15**	US
Spotlight Songs	LP	Capitol	T345	1956	**£30**	US
Spotlight Songs	LP-10"	Capitol	H345	1953	**£75**	US
Till Then	7"	Capitol	CL14076	1954	**£6**	chart single

FOUR LADS

Title	Format	Label	Number	Year	Price	Notes
Standing On The Corner	7"	Philips	PB1000	1960	**£4**	chart single

FOUR LOVERS

Title	Format	Label	Number	Year	Price	Notes
Joyride	LP	RCA	LPM1317	1956	**£300**	US

FOUR MATADORS

Title	Format	Label	Number	Year	Price	Notes
Man's Gotta Stand Tall	7"	Columbia	DB7806	1966	**£12**	

FOUR PALMS

Title	Format	Label	Number	Year	Price	Notes
Jeannie, Joanie, Shirley And Tony	7"	Vogue	V9116	1958	**£12**	

FOUR PENNIES

Title	Format	Label	Number	Year	Price	Notes
Black Girl	7"	Philips	BF1366	1964	**£4**	chart single
Do You Want Me To	7"	Philips	BF1296	1964	**£6**	chart single
Four Pennies	7" EP	Philips	BE12561	1964	**£5**	
I Found Out the Hard Way	7"	Philips	BF1349	1964	**£4**	chart single
Juliet	7"	Philips	BF1322	1964	**£4**	
Juliet	LP	Wing	WL1146	1967	**£10**	chart single
Keep The Freeway Open	7"	Philips	BF1491	1966	**£6**	
Mixed Bag	LP	Philips	BL7734	1966	**£30**	
No Sad Songs For Me	7"	Philips	BF1519	1966	**£6**	
Smooth Side Of The Four Pennies	7" EP	Philips	BE12571	1964	**£5**	
Spin With The Four Pennies	7" EP	Philips	BE12562	1964	**£5**	
Swinging Side Of The Four Pennies	7" EP	Philips	BE12570	1964	**£5**	
Trouble Is My Middle Name	7"	Philips	BF1469	1966	**£5**	chart single
Two Sides Of The Four Pennies	LP	Philips	BL7642	1964	**£15**	chart LP
Until It's Time For You To Go	7"	Philips	BF1435	1965	**£4**	chart single
Way Of Love	7"	Philips	BF1398	1965	**£5**	

FOUR PENNIES (USA)

Title	Format	Label	Number	Year	Price	Notes
My Block	7"	Stateside	SS198	1963	**£5**	
When The Boys Are Happy	7"	Stateside	SS244	1963	**£5**	

FOUR PLUS ONE

The group that issued its first single under the name Four Plus One, issued its second as The In Crowd, and eventually, after a few changes in personnel, got round to making an LP - as Tomorrow.

Title	Format	Label	Number	Year	Price	Notes
Time Is On My Side	7"	Parlophone	R5221	1965	**£15**	

FOUR PREPS

Title	Format	Label	Number	Year	Price	Notes
Big Man	7"	Capitol	CL14873	1958	**£4**	chart single
Big Man	7" EP	Capitol	EAP11064	1959	**£5**	
Campus Encores	7" EP	Capitol	EAP11647	1961	**£5**	
Dreamy Eyes	7" EP	Capitol	EAP1862	1957	**£5**	
Four Preps	LP	Capitol	T994	1958	**£12**	US

Got A Girl	7"	Capitol	CL15128	1960	**£4**	chart single
Lazy Summer Nights	7" EP	Capitol	EAP11139	1959	**£5**	
More Money For You And Me	7"	Capitol	CL15217	1961	**£4**	chart single
Things We Did Last Summer	LP	Capitol	T1090	1958	**£10**	US
Twenty Six Miles	7"	Capitol	CL14815	1957	**£4**	
Twenty Six Miles	7" EP	Capitol	EAP11015	1958	**£5**	

FOUR SEASONS

Ain't That A Shame	LP	Stateside	SL10042	1963	**£15**	
Ain't That A Shame	7"	Stateside	SS194	1963	**£4**	chart single
All The Song Hits	LP	Philips	200150	1964	**£10**	US
Alone	7"	Stateside	SS315	1964	**£4**	
Beggin'	7"	Philips	BF1556	1967	**£4**	
Big Girls Don't Cry	7"	Stateside	SS145	1963	**£4**	
Big Girls Don't Cry	LP	Vee Jay	LP1056	1963	**£15**	US
Big Man In Town	7"	Philips	BF1372	1965	**£4**	chart single
Born To Wander	LP	Philips	BL7611	1964	**£15**	
Bye Bye Baby	7"	Philips	BF1395	1965	**£4**	
C'mon Marianne	7"	Philips	BF1584	1967	**£4**	
Candy Girl	7"	Stateside	SS216	1963	**£4**	
Christmas Album	LP	Philips	BL7753	1966	**£10**	
Dawn	LP	Philips	BL7621	1964	**£12**	
Dawn	7"	Philips	BF1317	1964	**£4**	
Electric Stories	7"	Philips	BF1743	1969	**£4**	
Entertain You	LP	Philips	BL7663	1965	**£12**	
Extracts From The Four Seasons Story	7"	P. Stock	PVT50DJ	1976	**£4**	promo
Folk-Nanny	LP	Vee Jay	LP1082	1964	**£12**	US
Four Seasons Sing	7" EP	Stateside	SE1011	1964	**£6**	
Girl Come Running	7"	Philips	BF1420	1965	**£4**	
Golden Hits	LP	Vee Jay	LP1065	1963	**£10**	US
Greetings	LP	Stateside	SL10051	1963	**£15**	
Hits Of The Four Seasons	cass-s	Philips	MCP1000	1968	**£6**	
I've Got You Under My Skin	7"	Philips	BF1511	1966	**£4**	chart single
Let's Hang On	7"	Philips	BF1439	1965	**£4**	chart single
Looking Back	LP	Philips	BL7752	1966	**£10**	
More Golden Hits	LP	Vee Jay	LP1088	1964	**£10**	US
More Great Hits Of 1964	LP	Vee Jay	LP1136	1965	**£12**	US
Opus 17	7"	Philips	BF1493	1966	**£4**	chart single
Peanuts	7"	Stateside	SS262	1964	**£4**	
Rag Doll	LP	Philips	BL7643	1964	**£12**	
Rag Doll	7"	Philips	BF1347	1964	**£4**	chart single
Rag Doll	7"	Philips	BF1763	1969	**£4**	PS
Recorded Live On Stage	LP	Vee Jay	LP1154	1965	**£12**	US
Ronnie	7"	Philips	BF1334	1964	**£4**	
Santa Claus Is Coming To Town	7"	Stateside	SS241	1963	**£4**	
Saturday's Father	7"	Philips	BF1685	1968	**£4**	
Save It For Me	7"	Philips	BF1364	1965	**£4**	
Seasoned Hits	LP	Fontana	SFJL952	1968	**£10**	
Sherry	LP	Stateside	SL10033	1963	**£15**	chart LP
Sherry	7"	Stateside	SS122	1962	**£4**	chart single
Since I Don't Have You	7"	Stateside	SS343	1964	**£4**	
Sing Big Hits	LP	Philips	BL7687	1965	**£10**	
Stay	LP	Vee Jay	LP1082	1964	**£10**	US
Tell It To The Rain	7"	Philips	BF1538	1967	**£4**	chart single
Toy Soldier	7"	Philips	BF1411	1965	**£4**	
Walk Like a Man	7"	Stateside	SS169	1963	**£4**	chart single
Watch The Flowers Grow	7"	Philips	BF1621	1967	**£4**	
We Love Girls	LP	Vee Jay	LP1121	1965	**£12**	US
Will You Love Me Tomorrow	7"	Philips	BF1651	1968	**£4**	
Working My Way Back To You	LP	Philips	BL7699	1965	**£10**	
Working My Way Back To You	7"	Philips	BF1474	1966	**£4**	chart single

FOUR SIGHTS

But I Can Tell	7"	Columbia	DB7227	1964	**£4**	

FOUR SKINS

Low Life	7"	Secret	SHH141	1982	**£4**	
One Law For Them	7"	Clockwork Fun	CF101	1981	**£4**	
Yesterday's Heroes	7"	Secret	SHH125	1981	**£4**	

FOUR TOPHATTERS

Title	Format	Label	Cat. No.	Year	Price	Notes
Go Baby Go	7"	London	HLA8163	1955	**£15**	
Wild Rosie	7"	London	HLA8198	1955	**£15**	

FOUR TOPS

Title	Format	Label	Cat. No.	Year	Price	Notes
Ask The Lonely	7"	T. Motown	TMG507	1965	**£12**	
Ask The Lonely	7"	T. Motown	TMG507	1965	**£50**	demo
Baby I Need Your Loving	7"	Stateside	SS336	1964	**£15**	
Baby I Need Your Loving	7"	Stateside	SS336	1964	**£50**	demo
Bernadette	7"	T. Motown	TMG601	1967	**£6**	chart single
Bernadette	7"	T. Motown	TMG601	1967	**£35**	demo
Bernadette	7"	T. Motown	TMG803	1972	**£4**	chart single
Bernadette	7"	T. Motown	TMG803	1972	**£10**	demo
Do What You Gotta Do	7"	T. Motown	TMG710	1969	**£6**	chart single
Do What You Gotta Do	7"	T. Motown	TMG710	1969	**£20**	demo
Four Tops	LP	T. Motown	TML11010	1965	**£20**	
Four Tops	7" EP	T. Motown	TME2012	1966	**£8**	
Four Tops Hits	7" EP	T. Motown	TME2018	1967	**£8**	
I Can't Help Myself	7"	T. Motown	TMG515	1965	**£8**	chart single
I Can't Help Myself	7"	T. Motown	TMG515	1965	**£50**	demo
I Can't Help Myself	7"	T. Motown	TMG732	1970	**£4**	chart single
I Can't Help Myself	7"	T. Motown	TMG732	1970	**£10**	demo
I Can't Quit Your Love	7"	T. Motown	TMG858	1973	**£4**	
I Can't Quit Your Love	7"	T. Motown	TMG858	1973	**£10**	demo
I'll Turn To Stone	7"	T. Motown	TMG829	1972	**£4**	
I'll Turn To Stone	7"	T. Motown	TMG829	1972	**£10**	demo
I'm In A Different World	7"	T. Motown	TMG675	1968	**£4**	chart single
I'm In A Different World	7"	T. Motown	TMG675	1968	**£20**	demo
If I Were A Carpenter	7"	T. Motown	TMG647	1968	**£4**	chart single
If I Were A Carpenter	7"	T. Motown	TMG647	1968	**£15**	demo
It's All In The Game	7"	T. Motown	TMG736	1970	**£4**	chart single
It's All In The Game	7"	T. Motown	TMG736	1970	**£10**	demo
It's The Same Old Song	7"	T. Motown	TMG528	1965	**£10**	chart single
It's The Same Old Song	7"	T. Motown	TMG528	1965	**£50**	demo
Jazz Impressions	LP	Workshop	217	1962	**£300**	US
Just Seven Numbers	7"	T. Motown	TMG770	1971	**£4**	chart single
Just Seven Numbers	7"	T. Motown	TMG770	1971	**£10**	demo
Live	LP	T. Motown	STML11041	1967	**£10**	chart LP
Loving You Is Sweeter Than Ever	7"	T. Motown	TMG568	1966	**£6**	chart single
Loving You Is Sweeter Than Ever	7"	T. Motown	TMG568	1966	**£50**	demo
On Broadway	LP	Motown	657	1967	**£10**	US
On Top	LP	T. Motown	STML11037	1966	**£12**	chart LP
Reach Out And I'll Be There	7"	T. Motown	TMG579	1966	**£4**	chart single
Reach Out And I'll Be There	7"	T. Motown	TMG579	1966	**£40**	demo
Reach Out	LP	T. Motown	STML11056	1967	**£10**	chart LP
Second Album	LP	T. Motown	TML11021	1966	**£10**	
Seven Rooms Of Gloom	7"	T. Motown	TMG612	1967	**£4**	chart single
Seven Rooms Of Gloom	7"	T. Motown	TMG612	1967	**£35**	demo
Shake Me Wake Me	7"	T. Motown	TMG553	1966	**£10**	
Shake Me Wake Me	7"	T. Motown	TMG553	1966	**£50**	demo
Simple Game	7"	T. Motown	TMG785	1971	**£4**	chart single
Simple Game	7"	T. Motown	TMG785	1971	**£10**	demo
So Deep Within You	7"	T. Motown	TMG850	1973	**£4**	
So Deep Within You	7"	T. Motown	TMG850	1973	**£10**	demo
Something About You	7"	T. Motown	TMG542	1965	**£12**	
Something About You	7"	T. Motown	TMG542	1965	**£50**	demo
Standing In The Shadows Of Love	7"	T. Motown	TMG589	1967	**£6**	chart single
Standing In The Shadows Of Love	7"	T. Motown	TMG589	1967	**£40**	demo
Still Water	7"	T. Motown	TMG752	1970	**£4**	chart single
Still Water	7"	T. Motown	TMG752	1970	**£12**	demo
Walk Away Renee	7"	T. Motown	TMG634	1967	**£4**	chart single
Walk Away Renee	7"	T. Motown	TMG634	1967	**£25**	demo
Walk With Me Talk With Me	7"	T. Motown	TMG823	1972	**£4**	chart single
Walk With Me Talk With Me	7"	T. Motown	TMG823	1972	**£10**	demo
What Is A Man	7"	T. Motown	TMG698	1969	**£4**	chart single
What Is A Man	7"	T. Motown	TMG698	1969	**£15**	demo
Without The One You Love	7"	Stateside	SS371	1965	**£20**	
Without The One You Love	7"	Stateside	SS371	1965	**£50**	demo
Yesterday's Dreams	7"	T. Motown	TMG665	1968	**£4**	chart single
Yesterday's Dreams	7"	T. Motown	TMG665	1968	**£20**	demo
You Keep Running Away	7"	T. Motown	TMG623	1967	**£6**	chart single

You Keep Running Away	7"	T. Motown	TMG623	1967	**£30**	demo

FOUR TUNES

12 X 4	LP	Jubilee	LP1039	195-	**£40**	US
I Sold My Heart To The Junkman	7"	London	HL8151	1955	**£25**	
Tired Of Waiting	7"	London	HLJ8164	1955	**£15**	

FOUR WINDS

Short Shorts	7"	London	HLU8556	1958	**£8**	

FOURMOST

Apples,Peaches,Pumpkin Pie	7"	CBS	3814	1968	**£12**	
Auntie Maggie's Remedy	7"	Parlophone	R5528	1966	**£10**	
Baby I Need Your Lovin'	7"	Parlophone	R5194	1964	**£5**	chart single
Easy Squeezy	7"	CBS	4461	1969	**£15**	
Everything In The Garden	7"	Parlophone	R5304	1965	**£6**	
First And Fourmost	LP	Parlophone	PMC1259	1965	**£70**	
Fourmost Sound	7" EP	Parlophone	GEP8892	1964	**£20**	
Girls Girls Girls	7"	Parlophone	R5379	1965	**£5**	chart single
Hello Little Girl	7"	Parlophone	R5056	1963	**£4**	chart single
Here There And Everywhere	7"	Parlophone	R5491	1966	**£8**	
How Can I Tell Her	7"	Parlophone	R5157	1964	**£5**	chart single
How Can I Tell Her	7" EP	Parlophone	GEP8917	1964	**£20**	
I'm In Love	7"	Parlophone	R5078	1963	**£4**	chart single
Little Lovin'	7"	Parlophone	R5128	1964	**£4**	chart single
Rosetta	7"	CBS	4041	1969	**£12**	

FOURMYULA

Honey Chile	7"	Columbia	DB8549	1969	**£6**	

FOURTH WAY

Fourth Way	LP	Capitol	ST317	1970	**£12**	US
Sun And Moon Have Come Together	LP	Harvest	SKAO423	1970	**£12**	US

FOWLEY, KIM

Born To Be Wild	LP	Imperial	LP12413	1968	**£20**	US
Good Clean Fun	LP	Imperial	LP12443	1969	**£20**	US
I'm Bad	LP	Capitol	ST11075	1972	**£15**	US
International Heroes	LP	Capitol	ST11159	1973	**£15**	US
Lights	7"	Parlophone	R5521	1966	**£12**	
Lights The Blind Can See	7"	CBS	202338	1966	**£8**	
Love Is Alive And Well	LP	Tower	ST5080	1967	**£20**	US
Outrageous	LP	Imperial	LP12423	1969	**£20**	US
They're Coming To Take Me Away	7"	CBS	202243	1966	**£8**	
Trip	7"	Island	WI278	1966	**£10**	

FOX

Blue Hotel	LP	GTO	GTLP020	1977	**£15**	
Fox	LP	GTO	GTLP001	1975	**£10**	chart LP
Tales Of Illusion	LP	GTO	GTLP006	1975	**£10**	

FOX (2)

For Fox Sake	LP	Fontana	6309007	1970	**£60**	
Second Hand Love	7"	Fontana	6007016	1970	**£5**	

FOX (3)

Mr.Carpenter	7"	CBS	3381	1968	**£8**	

FOX, DON

Be My Girl	7"	Decca	F10927	1957	**£4**	
Party Time	7"	Decca	F10955	1957	**£4**	
T'Ain't What You Do	7"	Triumph	RGM1022	1960	**£5**	

FOXX

Revolt Of Emily Young	LP	MCA	MUPS419	1971	**£12**	

FOXX, INEZ & CHARLIE

Baby Give It To Me	7"	Direction	584042	1969	**£5**	
Come By Here	LP	Direction	863085	1968	**£10**	
Come On In	7"	Direction	583816	1968	**£5**	
Here We Go Round	7"	Sue	WI307	1964	**£10**	
Hi Diddle Diddle	7"	Sue	WI314	1964	**£10**	

Title	Format	Label	Cat. No.	Year	Value	Notes
Hummingbird	7"	London	HLC10009	1965	**£5**	
Hurt By Love	7"	Sue	WI323	1964	**£10**	chart single
Inez And Charles Foxx	LP	London	SHA8241	1965	**£10**	
Jaybirds	7"	Sue	WI304	1964	**£10**	
La De Dah I Love You	7"	Sue	WI356	1964	**£10**	
Mockingbird	LP	Sue	ILP911	1964	**£20**	
Mockingbird	7"	Sue	WI301	1963	**£10**	
Mockingbird	7"	United Artists	UP2269	1969	**£4**	chart single
My Momma Told Me	7"	London	HLC9971	1965	**£6**	
No Stranger To Love	7"	Stateside	SS556	1966	**£6**	
Tightrope	7"	Pye	7N25561	1971	**£5**	
Tightrope	7"	Stateside	SS586	1967	**£12**	

FRABJOY & RUNCIBLE SPOON

The tracks credited to Graham Gouldman and Kevin Godley on the Marmalade label sampler LP were actually by Frabjoy and the Runcible Spoon. The group also included Lol Creme in its line-up and can be viewed, therefore, as a first dry-run for Ten cc. An album was apparently recorded, but was lost when the Marmalade label folded.

Title	Format	Label	Cat. No.	Year	Value	Notes
I'm Beside Myself	7"	Marmalade	598019	1969	**£10**	

FRACTION

Title	Format	Label	Cat. No.	Year	Value	Notes
	LP	Angelias		197-	**£400**	

FRAME

Title	Format	Label	Cat. No.	Year	Value	Notes
Doctor Doctor	7"	RCA	RCA1571	1967	**£6**	
My Feet Don't Fit His Shoes	7"	RCA	RCA1556	1966	**£6**	

FRAMPTON, PETER

Title	Format	Label	Cat. No.	Year	Value	Notes
Frampton Comes Alive (edited)	LP	A&M	PR3703	1978	**£12**	US pic disc

FRANCIS & THE SWINGERS

Title	Format	Label	Cat. No.	Year	Value	Notes
Warn The People	7"	Blue Beat	BB379	1965	**£10**	

FRANCIS, B.

Title	Format	Label	Cat. No.	Year	Value	Notes
Judy Dronned	7"	Ska Beat	JB193	1965	**£10**	

FRANCIS, CONNIE

Title	Format	Label	Cat. No.	Year	Value	Notes
All Time International Hits	LP	MGM	C1012, CS6083	1965	**£10**	
Among My Souvenirs	7"	MGM	MGM1046	1959	**£4**	chart single
Another Page	7"	MGM	MGM1334	1967	**£4**	
At The Copa	LP	MGM	C861, CS6035	1961	**£12**	
Award-Winning Motion Picture Hits	LP	MGM	C940, CS6070	1963	**£10**	
Baby's First Christmas	7"	MGM	MGM1145	1961	**£4**	chart single
Be Anything	7"	MGM	MGM1236	1963	**£4**	
Best Of Connie Francis	LP	MGM	C8041	1967	**£10**	
Blue Winter	7"	MGM	MGM1224	1963	**£4**	
Breakin' In A Brand New Broken Heart	7"	MGM	MGM1136	1961	**£4**	chart single
Christmas With Connie	LP	MGM	C797	1959	**£12**	
Connie And Clyde	LP	MGM	C8086	1968	**£10**	
Connie Francis	7" EP	MGM	MGMEP686	1958	**£8**	
Connie Francis	7" EP	MGM	MGMEP792	1965	**£8**	
Connie Francis Favourites	7" EP	MGM	MGMEP759	1961	**£8**	
Connie Sings For Mama	7" EP	MGM	MGMEP789	1964	**£8**	
Connie's American hits	7" EP	MGM	MGMEP769	1963	**£8**	
Connie's Greatest Hits	LP	MGM	C831	1960	**£10**	chart LP
Country And Western Golden Hits	LP	MGM	C812	1960	**£10**	
Country Music Connie Style	LP	MGM	C916, CS6062	1962	**£10**	
Do The Twist	LP	MGM	C897	1962	**£12**	
Don't Break The Heart That Loves You	7"	MGM	MGM1157	1962	**£4**	chart single
Don't Ever Leave Me	7"	MGM	MGM1253	1964	**£4**	
Drowning My Sorrows	7"	MGM	MGM1207	1963	**£4**	
Everybody's Somebody's Fool	7"	MGM	MGM1086	1960	**£4**	chart single
Exciting...	LP	MGM	C786	1959	**£15**	
Faded Orchid	7"	MGM	MGM962	1957	**£6**	
First Lady Of Record	7" EP	MGM	MGMEP742	1960	**£8**	
Folk Song Favourites	LP	MGM	C883, CS6054	1961	**£10**	
Follow The Boys	LP	MGM	C931, CS6068	1963	**£10**	
Follow The Boys	7"	MGM	MGM1193	1962	**£4**	
For Mama	LP	MGM	C1006, CS6082	1965	**£10**	
Forget Domani	7"	MGM	MGM1265	1965	**£4**	
From Italy With Love	7" EP	MGM	MGMEP783	1963	**£8**	
Fun Songs For Children	LP	MGM	C819	1960	**£10**	

Title	Format	Label	Cat. No.	Year	Price	Notes
Girl In Love	7" EP	MGM	MGMEP568	1956	**£8**	
Great American Waltzes	LP	MGM	C958, CS6075	1964	**£10**	
Heartaches	7" EP	MGM	MGMEP677	1958	**£8**	
Hey Ring A Ding	7" EP	MGM	MGMEP773	1963	**£8**	
I Never Had A Sweetheart	7"	MGM	MGM945	1957	**£8**	
I Was Such A Fool	7"	MGM	MGM1171	1956	**£4**	
I'll Get By	7"	MGM	MGM993	1958	**£4**	chart single
I'm Gonna Be Warm This Winter	7"	MGM	MGM1185	1962	**£4**	chart single
I'm Sorry I Made You Cry	7"	MGM	MGM982	1958	**£4**	chart single
If I Didn't Care	7" EP	MGM	MGMEP697	1959	**£8**	
If My Pillow Could Talk	7"	MGM	MGM1202	1963	**£4**	
Irish Favourites	LP	MGM	C898, CS6056	1962	**£10**	
Italian Favourites	LP	MGM	C821, CS6020	1960	**£10**	
Italian Favourites	7" EP	MGM	MGMEP760	1961	**£8**	
Jealous Heart	LP	MGM	C8009	1966	**£10**	
Jealous Heart	7"	MGM	MGM1293	1966	**£4**	chart single
Jewish Favourites	LP	MGM	C845, CS6021	1961	**£10**	
Lipstick On Your Collar	7"	MGM	MGM1018	1959	**£4**	chart single
Live At Sahara In Las Vegas	LP	MGM	C8036	1967	**£10**	
Looking For Love	LP	MGM	C983, CS6079	1965	**£10**	
Love Is Me, Love Is You	7"	MGM	MGM1305	1966	**£4**	
Love Italian Style	LP	MGM	C8050	1968	**£10**	
Majesty Of Love	7"	MGM	MGM969	1957	**£6**	
Mala Femmena	7" EP	MGM	MGMEP780	1963	**£8**	
Mama	7"	MGM	MGM1076	1960	**£4**	chart single
Many Tears Ago	7"	MGM	MGM1111	1960	**£4**	chart single
More Italian Favourites	LP	MGM	C854, CS6029	1961	**£10**	
More Italian Hits	LP	MGM	C930, CS6067	1963	**£10**	
Movie Greats Of The Sixties	LP	MGM	C8027	1966	**£10**	
Mr.Twister	7"	MGM	MGM1151	1962	**£4**	
My Child	7"	MGM	MGM1271	1965	**£4**	chart single
My First Real Love	7"	MGM	SP1169	1956	**£15**	
My Happiness	7"	MGM	MGM1001	1959	**£4**	chart single
My Heart Cries For You	LP	MGM	C8054	1968	**£10**	
My Heart Cries For You	7"	MGM	MGM1347	1967	**£4**	
My Heart Has A Mind Of Its Own	7"	MGM	MGM1100	1960	**£4**	chart single
My Sailor Boy	7"	MGM	MGM932	1956	**£8**	
My Thanks To You	LP	MGM	C782	1959	**£15**	
My World Is Slipping Away	7"	MGM	MGM1381	1968	**£4**	
Never On Sunday	LP	MGM	C875, CS6047	1961	**£10**	
New Kind Of Connie	LP	MGM	C998, CS6080	1965	**£10**	
Phoenix Love Theme	7"	MGM	MGM1295	1966	**£4**	
Plenty Good Lovin'	7"	MGM	MGM1036	1959	**£4**	chart single
Rock And Roll Million Sellers	7" EP	MGM	MGMEP717	1960	**£8**	
Rock And Roll Million Sellers	LP	MGM	C804	1960	**£15**	chart LP
Rock And Roll Million Sellers No.2	7" EP	MGM	MGMEP720	1960	**£8**	
Rock And Roll Million Sellers No.3	7" EP	MGM	MGMEP731	1960	**£8**	
Roundabout	7"	MGM	MGM1282	1965	**£4**	
Sixteen Of Connie's Greatest Hits	LP	MGM	C970	1964	**£10**	
Somewhere My Love	7"	MGM	MGM1320	1966	**£4**	
Songs Of Les Reed	LP	MGM	CS8117	1969	**£10**	
Songs To A Swinging Band	LP	MGM	C870, CS6044	1961	**£10**	
Spanish And Latin American Favourites	LP	MGM	C836, CS6012	1960	**£10**	
Spanish Nights And You	7"	MGM	MGM1327	1966	**£4**	
Stupid Cupid	7"	MGM	MGM985	1958	**£4**	chart single
Summer Of His Years	7"	MGM	MGM1220	1963	**£4**	
Time Alone Will Tell	7"	MGM	MGM1336	1967	**£4**	
Together	7"	MGM	MGM1138	1961	**£4**	chart single
Toward The End Of The Day	7"	MGM	MGM1012	1959	**£4**	
Vacation	7"	MGM	MGM1165	1962	**£4**	chart single
Valentino	7"	MGM	MGM1060	1960	**£4**	chart single
What Kind Of Fool Am I	7" EP	MGM	MGMEP775	1963	**£8**	
Whatever Happened To Rosemary	7"	MGM	MGM1212	1963	**£4**	
Where The Boys Are	7"	MGM	MGM1121	1961	**£4**	chart single
Where The Boys Are	7" EP	MGM	MGMEP756	1961	**£8**	
Who's Sorry Now	LP-10"	MGM	153	1958	**£30**	
Who's Sorry Now	7"	MGM	MGM975	1958	**£4**	chart single
You Always Hurt The One You Love	7"	MGM	MGM998	1958	**£4**	chart single
You're My Everything	7" EP	MGM	MGMEP711	1960	**£8**	

FRANCIS, CONNIE & HANK WILLIAMS JR.

Title	Format	Label	Cat. No.	Year	Value	Notes
Great Country Favourites	LP	MGM	C1003	1965	**£10**	

FRANCIS, JOE 'KING'

Title	Format	Label	Cat. No.	Year	Value	Notes
Have Me Baby	7"	Rio	R90	196-	**£8**	
I Don't Want You No More	7"	Ska Beat	JB184	1965	**£10**	
I Got A Ska	7"	Ska Beat	JB262	1966	**£10**	
My Baby	7"	Rio	R94	196-	**£8**	
Pull It Out	7"	Rainbow	RAI114	196-	**£8**	
Wicked Woman	7"	Blue Beat	BB323	1964	**£10**	

FRANCIS, NAT

Title	Format	Label	Cat. No.	Year	Value	Notes
Three Nights Of Love	7"	Blue Beat	BB376	1965	**£10**	
You Only Want My Money	7"	Blue Beat	BB361	1965	**£10**	

FRANCIS, RITCHIE

Title	Format	Label	Cat. No.	Year	Value	Notes
Songbird	LP	Pegasus	PEG10	1971	**£10**	

FRANCIS, WILBERT

Title	Format	Label	Cat. No.	Year	Value	Notes
Memories Of You	7"	Ska Beat	JB267	1966	**£10**	

FRANCIS, WINSTON

Title	Format	Label	Cat. No.	Year	Value	Notes
If Your Heart Be Lonely	7"	Coxsone	CS7087	196-	**£10**	
Reggae And Cry	7"	Coxsone	CS7089	196-	**£10**	

FRANK, JACKSON C.

Title	Format	Label	Cat. No.	Year	Value	Notes
Blues Run The Game	7"	Columbia	DB7795	1965	**£5**	
Jackson C. Frank	LP	Columbia	33SX1788	1965	**£15**	

FRANKIE & JOHNNY

Title	Format	Label	Cat. No.	Year	Value	Notes
Climb Every Mountain	7"	Parlophone	R5518	1966	**£8**	
I'll Hold You	7"	Decca	F22376	1966	**£30**	

FRANKIE & THE CLASSICALS

Title	Format	Label	Cat. No.	Year	Value	Notes
I Only Have Eyes For You	7"	Philips	BF1586	1967	**£20**	

FRANKIE GOES TO HOLLYWOOD

As record companies became aware of the collectors' market during the eighties, they realised that it was possible to create instant collectors' items by issuing various limited edition versions of each potential hit record. Arguably the most thorough exploration of the possibilities of this tactic was carried out by ZTT records and Frankie Goes To Hollywood. Each single by the group comes in a bewildering variety of alternative mixes, and different shaped picture discs, with a correspondingly wide range of values. In fact, due to Trevor Horn's skill as a producer, the different mixes make sense on musical grounds, but this is very much a happy accident!

Title	Format	Label	Cat. No.	Year	Value	Notes
Liverpool	cass	ZTT	ZCIQ8	1986	**£15**	remix 'Wildlife' + new inlay
Pleasurefix/Starfix	12"	ZTT	FGTH1	1985	**£15**	red label promo
Power Of Love	cass-s	ZTT	CTIS105	1984	**£8**	
Power Of Love	7"	ZTT	PZTAS5	1984	**£5**	pic disc
Power Of Love	12"	ZTT	12PZTAS5	1984	**£8**	pic disc
Power Of Love	12"	ZTT	12XZTAS5	1984	**£8**	gatefold sleeve, 5 photos
Rage Hard (++ Mix)	12"	ZTT	12ZTAX22	1986	**£6**	
Rage Hard (++ Mix)	12"	ZTT	12ZTAXB22	1986	**£8**	boxed with list
Rage Hard (Stamped)	7"	ZTT	ZTAX22	1986	**£5**	
Rage Hard	various	ZTT	ZTAB22	1986	**£30**	2x7", 3x12", CD, boxed
Rage Hard	CD-s	ZTT	ZCID22	1986	**£10**	
Rage Hard	7"	ZTT	ZTD22	1986	**£4**	gatefold PS
Rage Hard	12"	ZTT	12ZTAQ22	1986	**£6**	with poster
Relax (Original Mix)	12"	ZTT	12ZTAS1 (1A1U)	1983	**£30**	33rpm
Relax (Original Mix)	12"	ZTT	12ZTAS1 (1A5)	1984	**£15**	
Relax (Sex Mix)	12"	ZTT	12PZTAS1	1983	**£12**	pic disc
Relax (Sex Mix)	12"	ZTT	12ZTAS1 (1A2U)	1983	**£15**	
Relax (Sex Mix)	12"	ZTT	12ZTAS1 (1A5U)	1983	**£10**	'US' PS
Relax (The Last Seven Inches)	7"	ZTT	ZTAS1DJ	1983	**£6**	promo
Relax (The Last Seven Inches)	7"	ZTT	ZTAS1DJ	1983	**£8**	PM, Mis-Press B-side plays 'Ferry (Go)'
Relax (US Mix)/Two Tribes (Carnage)	12"	ZTT	XZTAS3DJ	1984	**£15**	promo, grey ZTT sleeve
Relax (Warp Mix)	7"	ZTT	ZTAS1	1983	**£10**	white label promo
Relax	cass-s	ZTT	CTIS102	1984	**£10**	
Relax	7"	ZTT	PZTAS1	1983	**£8**	pic disc
Two Tribes (Annihilation)	12"	ZTT	12ZTAS3	1984	**£8**	with poster
Two Tribes (Carnage)	12"	ZTT	XZTAS3	1984	**£6**	
Two Tribes (Carnage)/War (Hidden)	12"	ZTT	WARTZ3	1984	**£6**	

Title	Format	Label	Cat. No.	Year	Price	Notes
Two Tribes (Carnage)/War (Hidden)	12"	ZTT	WARTZ3	1984	**£10**	pic disc
Two Tribes (Hibakusha)	12"	ZTT	XZIP1	1984	**£20**	ZTT sleeve
Two Tribes	cass-s	ZTT	CTIS103	1984	**£8**	
Two Tribes	7"	ZTT	PZTAS3	1984	**£5**	pic disc
Warriors (Attack Mix)	12"	ZTT	12ZTAK25	1986	**£10**	white label promo
Warriors (Turn Of The Knife Mix)	12"	ZTT	12ZTAK25	1986	**£6**	
Warriors	CD-s	ZTT	ZCID25	1986	**£10**	
Warriors	cass-s	ZTT	CTIS25	1986	**£8**	
Watching The Wildlife (Die Letzen...Mix)	12"	ZTT	ZTE26	1987	**£8**	
Watching The Wildlife (Movement 2)	12"	ZTT	12ZTAX26	1987	**£6**	
Watching The Wildlife	CD-s	ZTT	ZCID26	1987	**£10**	
Watching The Wildlife	cass-s	ZTT	CTIS26	1987	**£10**	
Welcome To The Pleasure...(Alt. Mix)	12"	ZTT	XZTAS7	1985	**£6**	
Welcome To The Pleasure...(Tribal Mix)	12"	ZTT	12ZTAJ7	1985	**£25**	promo
Welcome To The Pleasure Dome	LP	ZTT	NEAT1	1984	**£20**	double pic disc
Welcome To The Pleasure Dome	CD	ZTT	CID101	1984	**£50**	same tracks as cassette
Welcome To The Pleasure Dome	7"	ZTT	PZTAS7	1985	**£8**	shaped pic disc
Welcome To The Pleasure Dome	7"	ZTT	ZTAS7 (7A7U)	1985	**£20**	different mix, blue label
Welcome To The Pleasure Dome	cass-s	ZTT	CTIS107	1985	**£6**	

FRANKLIN, ARETHA

Title	Format	Label	Cat. No.	Year	Price	Notes
Amazing Grace	LP	Atlantic	K60023	1972	**£15**	double
Angel	7"	Atlantic	K10346	1973	**£4**	chart single
Aretha	LP	Fontana	TFL5173	1961	**£15**	
Aretha Arrives	LP	Atlantic	587085	1967	**£15**	
Aretha Arrives	LP	Atlantic	K40157	1972	**£10**	
Aretha Gold	LP	Atlantic	588192	1969	**£10**	
Aretha Now	LP	Atlantic	587114	1968	**£12**	chart LP
Baby I Love You	7"	Atlantic	584127	1967	**£5**	chart single
Best Of...	LP	Atlantic	QD8295	1971	**£12**	US quad
Brand New Me	7"	Atlantic	2091127	1971	**£4**	
Bridge Over Troubled Water	7"	Atlantic	2091090	1971	**£4**	
Call Me	7"	Atlantic	584322	1970	**£4**	
Can't You See Me	7"	CBS	201732	1965	**£5**	
Cry Like A Baby	7"	CBS	202468	1967	**£5**	
Don't Play That Song	LP	Atlantic	2400021	1970	**£12**	
Don't Play That Song	7"	Atlantic	2091027	1970	**£4**	chart single
Eleanor Rigby	7"	Atlantic	584306	1969	**£4**	
Electrifying Aretha Franklin	LP	Columbia	CL1761	1962	**£12**	US
Greatest Hits	LP	CBS	64536	1971	**£10**	
Hey Now Hey	LP	Atlantic	K40504	1973	**£10**	
House That Jack Built	7"	Atlantic	584239	1969	**£4**	
I Never Loved A Man	LP	Atlantic	587066	1967	**£15**	chart LP
I Never Loved A Man	LP	Atlantic	K40134	1972	**£10**	
I Never Loved A Man	7"	Atlantic	584084	1967	**£5**	
I Say A Little Prayer	LP	Atlantic	2464007	1970	**£12**	
I Say A Little Prayer	7"	Atlantic	584206	1968	**£4**	chart single
Lady Soul	LP	Atlantic	587099	1968	**£12**	chart LP
Lady Soul	LP	Atlantic	K40016	1972	**£10**	
Laughing On The Outside	LP	Columbia	CL2079	1963	**£12**	US
Lee Cross	LP	CBS	63160	1967	**£10**	
Lee Cross	7"	CBS	3059	1967	**£5**	
Let It Be Me	7"	Atlantic	2091008	1970	**£4**	
Live At Paris Olympia	LP	Atlantic	587149	1968	**£15**	
Live At The Fillmore West	LP	Atlantic	2400136	1971	**£12**	
Live At The Fillmore West	LP	Atlantic	K40222	1972	**£10**	
Live At The Fillmore West	LP	Atlantic	QD7205	1971	**£12**	US quad
Love Is The Only Thing	7"	Fontana	H271	1961	**£10**	
Natural Woman	7"	Atlantic	584141	1967	**£5**	
Oh No Not My Baby	7"	Atlantic	2091044	1971	**£4**	
Operation Heartbreak	7"	Fontana	H343	1961	**£5**	
Queen Of Soul	LP	CBS	52562	1968	**£10**	
Respect	7"	Atlantic	584115	1967	**£5**	chart single
Rock Steady	7"	Atlantic	2091168	1971	**£4**	
Runnin' Out Of Fools	LP	Columbia	CL2281	1964	**£12**	US
Satisfaction/Chain Of Fools	7"	Atlantic	584157	1967	**£5**	chart single
Satisfaction/Night Life	7"	Atlantic	584157	1967	**£6**	
Share Your Love With Me	7"	Atlantic	584285	1969	**£4**	
Since You've Been Gone	7"	Atlantic	584172	1968	**£4**	chart single
Songs Of Faith	LP	Chess	CRL54550	1967	**£10**	
Soul '69	LP	Atlantic	588163	1969	**£12**	

Title	Format	Label	Number	Year	Price	Notes
Soul Sister	LP	CBS	BPG62744	1966	**£10**	
Spanish Harlem	7"	Atlantic	2091138	1971	**£4**	chart single
Take A Look	LP	CBS	63269	1967	**£10**	
Take It Like You Give It	LP	CBS	BPG62969	1967	**£12**	
Tender...Swinging Aretha Franklin	LP	Columbia	CL1876	1962	**£12**	US
Think	7"	Atlantic	584186	1968	**£4**	chart single
This Girl's In Love With You	LP	Atlantic	2400004	1969	**£10**	
Today I Sing The Blues	7" EP	Fontana	TE467217	1962	**£6**	
Unforgettable	LP	Columbia	CL2163	1964	**£12**	US
Until You Come Back To Me	7"	Atlantic	K10399	1974	**£4**	chart single
Weight	7"	Atlantic	584252	1969	**£4**	
Yeah/In Person	LP	CBS	BPG62556	1965	**£10**	
You're All I Need To Get By	7"	Atlantic	2091063	1971	**£4**	
Young Gifted And Black	LP	Atlantic	K40323	1972	**£10**	
Young Gifted And Black	LP	Atlantic	2400188	1971	**£10**	

FRANKLIN, ERMA

Title	Format	Label	Number	Year	Price	Notes
Gotta Find Me A Lover	7"	MCA	MU1073	1969	**£4**	
Her Name Is Erma	LP	Epic	LN3824	1962	**£10**	US
Open Up Your Soul	7"	London	HLZ10201	1968	**£6**	
Piece Of My Heart	7"	London	HLZ10170	1967	**£8**	
Right To Cry	7"	London	HLZ10220	1968	**£6**	
Time After Time	7"	Soul City	SC118		**£5**	
Time After Time	7"	Soul City	SC118		**£15**	demo

FRANKLIN, MARIE

Title	Format	Label	Number	Year	Price	Notes
You Ain't Changed	7"	MGM	MGM1455	1968	**£4**	

FRANKSON, BONNIE

Title	Format	Label	Number	Year	Price	Notes
Dearest	7"	Columbia	DB114	1969	**£8**	
Dearest	7"	Jolly	JY021	196-	**£8**	

FRANTIC ELEVATORS

Mick Hucknall was the leader of the Frantic Elevators, who began as a punk group, but who had anticipated the smooth soul sound of Hucknall's Simply Red by the end of their career. The song "Holding Back The Years" was, in fact, recorded by both groups.

Title	Format	Label	Number	Year	Price	Notes
Hunchback Of Notre Dame	7"	TJM	TJM6	1980	**£4**	
Searching For The Only One	7"	Crackin'	CRAK1	1980	**£4**	
Voice In The Dark	7"	TJM	TJM5	1980	**£4**	
You Know What You Told Me	7"	Erics	006	1980	**£4**	

FRASER, ANDY

Title	Format	Label	Number	Year	Price	Notes
Andy Fraser Band	LP	CBS	80731	1975	**£10**	
In Your Eyes	LP	CBS	81027	1975	**£10**	

FRASER, NORMA

Title	Format	Label	Number	Year	Price	Notes
Everybody Loves A Lover	7"	Ska Beat	JB223	1965	**£10**	
First Cut Is The Deepest	7"	Coxsone	CS7017	196-	**£10**	
Heartaches	7"	Coxsone	CS7049	196-	**£10**	
Heartaches	7"	Doctor Bird	DB1032	1966	**£10**	
Respect	7"	Coxsone	CS7060	196-	**£10**	
Telling Me Lies	7"	Studio One	SO2025	196-	**£10**	

FRATERNITY OF MAN

Title	Format	Label	Number	Year	Price	Notes
Don't Bogart Me	7"	Stateside	SS2166	1970	**£4**	
Fraternity Of Man	LP	ABC	S647	1968	**£10**	US
Get It On	LP	Dot	DLP25955	1969	**£10**	US

FRAYS

Title	Format	Label	Number	Year	Price	Notes
For Your Precious Love	7"	Decca	F12229	1965	**£25**	
Walk On	7"	Decca	F12153	1965	**£20**	

FREAKS OF NATURE

Title	Format	Label	Number	Year	Price	Notes
People, Let's Freak Out!	7"	Island	WI3017	1966	**£20**	

FREBERG, STAN

Title	Format	Label	Number	Year	Price	Notes
Banana Boat Song	7"	Capitol	CL14712	1957	**£6**	
Best Of The Stan Freberg Show	LP	Capitol	WBO1035	1958	**£12**	US
Best Of...	LP	Capitol	T2020	1964	**£12**	US
Child's Garden Of Freberg	LP	Capitol	T777	1957	**£15**	US
Comedy Caravan	LP	Capitol	T732	1956	**£15**	US
Face The Funnies	LP	Capitol	T1694	1962	**£12**	US

Title	Format	Label	Number	Year	Price	Notes
Great Pretender	7"	Capitol	CL14571	1956	**£8**	
Great Pretender	7" EP	Capitol	EAP120050	1961	**£6**	
Green Christmas	7"	Capitol	CL14966	1958	**£5**	
Heartbreak Hotel	7"	Capitol	CL14608	1956	**£10**	chart single
Lone Psychiatrist	7"	Capitol	CL14316	1955	**£8**	
Madison Avenue Werewolf	LP	Capitol	T1816	1962	**£12**	US
Mickey Mouse's Birthday Party	LP	Capitol	J3264	1963	**£15**	US
Old Payola Roll Blues	7"	Capitol	CL15122	1960	**£10**	chart single
Real Saint George	7" EP	Capitol	EAP1628	1956	**£6**	
Sh'boom	7"	Capitol	CL14187	1954	**£15**	chart single
Stan Freberg With The Original Cast	LP	Capitol	T1242	1959	**£12**	US
Underground Show Number One	LP	Capitol	T2551	1966	**£10**	US
United States Of America	LP	Capitol	W1573	1961	**£10**	US
Yellow Rose Of Texas	7"	Capitol	CL14509	1956	**£6**	

FRED, JOHN & HIS PLAYBOY BAND

Title	Format	Label	Number	Year	Price	Notes
34:40 Of John Fred	LP	Paula	LP2193	1967	**£15**	US
Agnes English	LP	Paula	LP2197	1967	**£15**	US
Agnes English	7"	Pye	7N25433	1967	**£4**	
Hey Hey Bunny	7"	Pye	7N25453	1968	**£4**	
John Fred And His Playboys	LP	Paula	LP2191	1966	**£15**	US
Judy In Disguise	LP	Paula	LPS2197	1968	**£15**	US
Judy In Disguise	7"	Pye	7N25442	1967	**£4**	chart single
Little Dum Dum	7"	Pye	7N25470	1968	**£4**	
Permanently Stated	LP	Paula	LPS2201	1968	**£15**	US
Shirley	7"	CBS	3475	1968	**£6**	
Silly Sarah Carter	7"	MCA	MU1088	1969	**£4**	
We Played Games	7"	Pye	7N25462	1968	**£4**	

FREDDIE & THE DREAMERS

Title	Format	Label	Number	Year	Price	Notes
Brown And Porters	7"	Columbia	DB8200	1967	**£4**	
Freddie And The Dreamers	LP	Columbia	33SX1577	1963	**£12**	chart LP
Freddie And The Dreamers	7" EP	Columbia	SEG8323	1964	**£5**	
Freddie And The Dreamers	7" EP	Columbia	SEG8457	1965	**£5**	
Freddie Sings Just For You	7" EP	Columbia	SEG8349	1964	**£5**	
Gabardine Mac	7"	Columbia	DB8517	1968	**£4**	
Get Around Downtown Girl	7"	Columbia	DB8606	1969	**£4**	
Hello Hello	7"	Columbia	DB8137	1967	**£4**	
I Love You Baby	7"	Columbia	DB7286	1964	**£4**	chart single
I Understand	7"	Columbia	DB7381	1964	**£4**	chart single
I'm Telling You Now	7"	Columbia	DB7086	1963	**£4**	chart single
If You Gotta Make A Fool Of Somebody	7"	Columbia	DB7032	1963	**£4**	chart single
If You Gotta Make A Fool Of Somebody	7" EP	Columbia	SEG8275	1963	**£5**	
If You've Gotta Minute Baby	7"	Columbia	DB7857	1966	**£4**	
In Disneyland	LP	Columbia	SCX6069	1966	**£10**	
Just For You	7"	Columbia	DB7322	1964	**£4**	chart single
King Freddie And Dreaming Knights	LP	Columbia	SX6177	1967	**£10**	
Little You	7"	Columbia	DB7526	1965	**£4**	chart single
Over You	7"	Columbia	DB7214	1964	**£4**	chart single
Playboy	7"	Columbia	DB7929	1966	**£4**	
Ready Freddie Go	7" EP	Columbia	SEG8403	1965	**£5**	
Sing Along	LP	Columbia	SX1785	1965	**£10**	
Songs From What A Crazy World	7" EP	Columbia	SEG8287	1963	**£5**	
Thou Shalt Not Steal	7"	Columbia	DB7720	1965	**£4**	chart single
Turn Around	7"	Columbia	DB8033	1966	**£4**	
You Belong To Me	7"	Columbia	DB8496	1968	**£4**	
You Were Made For Me	LP	Columbia	33SX1663	1964	**£10**	
You Were Made For Me	7"	Columbia	DB7147	1963	**£4**	chart single
You Were Made For Me	7" EP	Columbia	SEG8302	1964	**£5**	

FREDDIE & THE DREAMERS / PETER & GORDON

Title	Format	Label	Number	Year	Price	Notes
Just For You	7" EP	Columbia	SEG8337	1964	**£5**	

FREDDIE & THE RUDIES

Title	Format	Label	Number	Year	Price	Notes
I Don't Want To Lose That Girl	7"	Downtown	DT427	196-	**£8**	

FREDDY & FITZY

Title	Format	Label	Number	Year	Price	Notes
Do Good	7"	Doctor Bird	DB1033	1966	**£10**	

FREDERICKS, DOLORES

Title	Format	Label	Number	Year	Price	Notes
Cha Cha Joe	7"	Brunswick	05540	1956	**£8**	

FREDERICKS, DOTTY

Just Wait .... 7" .... Top Rank .... JAR106 .... 1959 .... **£4** ....

FREDERICKS, MARC

Mystic Midnight .... 7" .... London .... HLD8281 .... 1956 .... **£4** ....

FREDERICKS, TOMMY

Prince Of Players .... 7" .... London .... HLU8555 .... 1958 .... **£6** ....

FREDRIC

Phases And Faces .... LP .... Forte .... 301 .... 1968 .... **£250** .... US

FREE

With an average age of around eighteen, the members of the newly-formed Free had amazingly still managed to acquire some professional experience - most notably in the case of Andy Fraser, who had played bass (albeit briefly) with John Mayall. They could have been enormous (and the classic "All Right Now" - included in extended form on "Fire And Water" - was indeed a considerable hit), but dissipated their momentum in a welter of petty disputes, leading to members leaving and returning in a quite bewildering manner. The most collectable record remaining from all this is "Kossoff, Kirke, Tetsu And Rabbit", which is prevented from being a Free LP only by the absence of singer Paul Rodgers.

All Right Now .... 7" .... Island .... WIP6082 .... 1970 .... **£5** .... chart single
All Right Now .... 12" .... Island .... 12PIEP6 .... 1982 .... **£6** .... pic disc
Broad Daylight .... 7" .... Island .... WIP6054 .... 1969 .... **£20** ....
Fire And Water .... LP .... Island .... ILPS9120 .... 1970 .... **£10** .... chart LP
Free .... LP .... Island .... ILPS9104 .... 1969 .... **£10** ....
Free Story .... LP .... Island .... ISLD4 .... 1973 .... **£20** .... double, chart LP
Highway .... LP .... Island .... ILPS9138 .... 1970 .... **£10** .... chart LP
Hunter .... 7" .... Island .... WIP6351 .... 1976 .... **£4** ....
I'll Be Creepin' .... 7" .... Island .... WIP6062 .... 1969 .... **£20** ....
Little Bit Of Love .... 7" .... Island .... WIP6129 .... 1972 .... **£4** .... chart single
Live .... LP .... Island .... ILPS9160 .... 1971 .... **£12** .... chart LP
My Brother Jake .... 7" .... Island .... WIP6100 .... 1971 .... **£4** .... chart single
Stealer .... 7" .... Island .... WIP6093 .... 1970 .... **£5** ....
Tons Of Sobs .... LP .... Island .... ILPS9089 .... 1969 .... **£12** ....
Travellin' In Style .... 7" .... Island .... WIP6160 .... 1973 .... **£5** ....
Wishing Well .... 7" .... Island .... WIP6146 .... 1972 .... **£4** ....

FREE (2)

Keep In Touch .... 7" .... Philips .... BF1754 .... 1969 .... **£15** ....

FREE FERRY

Mary What Have You Become .... 7" .... CBS .... 4456 .... 1969 .... **£8** ....

FREEBORNE

Peak Impressions .... LP .... Monitor .... MPS607 .... 1967 .... **£40** .... US

FREED, ALAN

Right Now Right Now .... 7" .... Vogue Coral .... Q72219 .... 1957 .... **£25** ....
Rock 'n' Roll Boogie .... 7" .... Vogue Coral .... Q72230 .... 1957 .... **£25** ....
Rock 'n'Roll Dance Party .... LP .... Coral .... CRL57063 .... 1957 .... **£20** .... US

FREEDOM

At Last .... LP .... Metronome .... MLP15371 .... 1970 .... **£25** ....
Escape While You Can .... 7" .... Plexium .... PXM3 .... 196- .... **£6** ....
Freedom .... LP .... Probe .... SPBA6252 .... 1970 .... **£20** ....
Is More Than A Word .... LP .... Vertigo .... 6360072 .... 1972 .... **£25** .... spiral label
Through The Years .... LP .... Vertigo .... 6360049 .... 1971 .... **£20** .... spiral label
Where Will You Be Tonight .... 7" .... Mercury .... MF1033 .... 1968 .... **£5** ....

FREEDOM CRY

In Disneyland .... LP .... Columbia .... 1966 .... **£25** ....

FREEDOM SINGERS

I Want Money .... 7" .... Coxsone .... CS7016 .... 196- .... **£10** ....
Work Crazy .... 7" .... Studio One .... SO2010 .... 196- .... **£10** ....

FREEMAN, ART

Slipping Around .... 7" .... Atlantic .... 584053 .... 1966 .... **£15** ....

FREEMAN, BOBBY

Betty Lou Got A New Pair Of Shoes .... 7" .... London .... HLJ8721 .... 1958 .... **£10** ....
C'Mon And Swim .... LP .... Autumn .... LP102 .... 1964 .... **£15** .... US
C'Mon And Swim .... 7" .... Pye .... 7N25260 .... 1964 .... **£8** ....

Do You Wanna Dance	LP	Jubilee	JLP1086	1959	**£25**	US
Do You Wanna Dance	7"	London	HLJ8644	1958	**£8**	
Duck	7"	Pye	7N25347	1966	**£6**	
Ebb Tide	7"	London	HLJ9031	1960	**£6**	
Get In The Swim	LP	Josie	JM4007	1965	**£15**	US
Lovable Style Of...	LP	King	930	1965	**£20**	US
Mary Ann Thomas	7"	London	HLJ8898	1959	**£6**	
Need Your Love	7"	London	HLJ8782	1959	**£10**	
Shimmy Shimmy	7"	Parlophone	R4684	1960	**£6**	
Swim	7"	Pye	7N25280	1964	**£6**	
Twist With Bobby Freeman	LP	Jubilee	JGM5010	1962	**£15**	US

FREEMAN, ERNIE

Big River	7"	London	HLP9041	1960	**£4**	
Dumplings	7"	London	HLP8558	1958	**£6**	
Ernie Freeman And His Rhythm Guitar	7" EP	London	REU1059	1956	**£12**	
Ernie Freeman Vol.2	7" EP	London	REP1210	1959	**£8**	
Indian Love Call	7"	London	HLP8660	1958	**£4**	
Raunchy '65	7"	London	HLA9944	1965	**£4**	
Raunchy	7"	London	HLP8523	1957	**£8**	

FREEMAN, EVELYN

I Heard The Voice	7"	London	HLU10287	1969	**£5**	

FREEWHEELERS

Why Do You Treat Me Like A Fool?	7"	HMV	POP1406	1965	**£8**	

FRENCH REVOLUTION

Nine Till Five	7"	Decca	F22898	1969	**£8**	

FRENCH, DON

Goldilocks	7"	London	HLW8884	1959	**£30**	
Little Blond Girl	7"	London	HLW8989	1959	**£25**	

FRESH

Fresh Out Of Borstal	LP	RCA	SF8122	1970	**£15**	
Fresh Today	LP	RCA	3027	1971	**£12**	US
Stoned In Saigon	7"	RCA	RCA2003	1970	**£4**	

FRESH AIR

Running Wild	7"	Pye	7N17736	1969	**£50**	

FRESH MAGGOTS

Fresh Maggots	LP	RCA	SF8205	1971	**£60**	

FRESH WINDOWS

Fashion Conscious	7"	Fontana	TF839	1967	**£35**	

FRESHIES

I'm In Love With The Girl...	7"	Razz	RAZZ11	1980	**£5**	lyric booklet
I'm In Love With The Girl...	7"	Razz	RAZZ12	1980	**£10**	promo
Men From Banana Island...	7"	Razz	RAZZ3	1979	**£10**	
My Tape's Gone	7"	Razz	RAZZ4	1980	**£8**	with magazine
No Money	7"	Razz	RAZZ7	1980	**£6**	
Straight In At No.2	7"	Razz	RAZZEP2	1979	**£8**	

FRIDAY, CAROL

Everybody I Know	7"	Parlophone	R5369	1965	**£5**	

FRIEDMAN, DEAN

Dean Friedman	LP	Lifesong	LSLP6008	1977	**£10**	
'Well, Well,' Said The Rocking Chair	LP	Lifesong	LSLP6019	1978	**£10**	chart LP

FRIEDMAN, KINKY

Lasso From El Paso	LP	Epic	81640	1976	**£10**	

FRIEL, BRIAN

Arrivederci Adrossan	LP	Dawn	DNLS3064	1975	**£12**	
Brian Joseph Friel	LP	Dawn	DNLS3054	1974	**£12**	

FRIEND & LOVER

Reach Out Of The Darkness	7"	Verve	VS1515	1968	**£4**	

FRIENDS

Title	Format	Label	Number	Year	Price	Notes
Piccolo Man	7"	Deram	DM198	1968	**£15**	

FRIJID PINK

Title	Format	Label	Number	Year	Price	Notes
Defrosted	LP	Deram	SML1077	1970	**£15**	
Frijid Pink	LP	Deram	SML1062	1970	**£15**	
Heartbreak Hotel	7"	Deram	DM321	1970	**£5**	
House Of The Rising Sun	7"	Deram	DM288	1970	**£5**	chart single
Lost Son	7"	Deram	DM347	1971	**£5**	
Music For The People	7"	Deram	DM332	1971	**£5**	
Sing A Song Of Freedom	7"	Deram	DM309	1970	**£5**	
We're Gonna Be There	7"	Deram	DM336	1971	**£4**	

FRITCHIE, VONNIE

Title	Format	Label	Number	Year	Price	Notes
Sugar Booger Avenue	7"	London	HLU8178	1955	**£15**	

FRITH, FRED

Title	Format	Label	Number	Year	Price	Notes
Guitar Solos 1	LP	Caroline	C1508	1974	**£10**	
Guitar Solos 2	LP	Caroline	C1518	1976	**£10**	

FRIZZELL, LEFTY

Title	Format	Label	Number	Year	Price	Notes
Greatest Hits	LP	Columbia	CL2488	1966	**£15**	US
Listen To Lefty	LP-10"	Columbia	HL9021	1952	**£30**	US
One And Only	LP	Columbia	CL1342	1959	**£25**	US
Puttin' On	LP	Columbia	CL2772	1967	**£15**	US
Sad Side Of Love	LP	Columbia	CL2386	1965	**£15**	US
Saginaw, Michigan	LP	Columbia	CL2169	1964	**£15**	US
Songs Of Jimmie Rodgers	LP-10"	Columbia	HL9019	1951	**£30**	US

FRIZZLE, REV. DWIGHT

Title	Format	Label	Number	Year	Price	Notes
Beyond The Black Crack	LP				**£40**	US

FROG, WYNDER K.

Title	Format	Label	Number	Year	Price	Notes
Green Door	7"	Island	WIP6006	1967	**£6**	
I'm A Man	7"	Island	WIP6014	1967	**£8**	
Jumping Jack Flash	7"	Island	WIP6044	1968	**£6**	
Out Of The Frying Pan	LP	Island	ILPS9082	1968	**£15**	
Sunshine Super Frog	LP	Island	ILPS9044	1967	**£20**	
Sunshine Superman	7"	Island	WI3011	1966	**£5**	
Turn On Your Lovelight	7"	Island	WI280	1966	**£8**	

FROGGATT, RAYMOND

Title	Format	Label	Number	Year	Price	Notes
Bleach	LP	Bell	BELLS207	1972	**£25**	
Callow La Vita	7"	Polydor	56249	1968	**£4**	
Lazy Jack	7"	Polydor	56358	1969	**£4**	
Little Bit Of Love	7"	Polydor	56274	1968	**£4**	
Movin' Down South	7"	Polydor	56334	1969	**£4**	
Red Balloon	7"	Polydor	56284	1968	**£4**	
Ring Ting A Ling	7"	Polydor	56314	1969	**£4**	
Rogues And Thieves	LP	Reprise	K44257	1974	**£15**	
Rosalind	7"	Polydor	56294	1968	**£4**	
Time Goes By	7"	Polydor	56294	1968	**£4**	
Voice And Writing Of...	LP	Polydor	583044	1969	**£25**	

FROGMEN

Title	Format	Label	Number	Year	Price	Notes
Underwater	7"	Oriole	CB1617	1961	**£6**	

FROGMORTON

Title	Format	Label	Number	Year	Price	Notes
At Last	LP	Philips	6308261	1976	**£12**	
White Swans	7"	Philips	6006506	1976	**£4**	

FRONT LINE

Title	Format	Label	Number	Year	Price	Notes
Got Love	7"	Atlantic	AT4057	1965	**£10**	

FROST

Title	Format	Label	Number	Year	Price	Notes
Frost Music	LP	Vanguard	VSD6520	1969	**£15**	US
Rock and Roll Music	LP	Vanguard	VSD6541	1969	**£15**	US
Through The Eyes Of Love	LP	Vanguard	VSD6556	1970	**£15**	US

FROST, DAVID

Title	Format	Label	Number	Year	Price	Notes
Deck Of Cards	7"	Parlophone	R5441	1966	**£4**	
Frost Report On Britain	LP	Parlophone	PMC7005	1966	**£10**	

Title	Format	Label	Number	Year	Price	Notes
Frost Report On Everything	LP	Pye	NPL18199	1967	£10	

FROST, DAVID & OTHERS

Title	Format	Label	Number	Year	Price	Notes
That Was The Week That Was	LP	Parlophone	PMC1197	1963	£10	chart LP

FROST, FRANK & THE NIGHTHAWKS

Title	Format	Label	Number	Year	Price	Notes
Hey Boss Man!	LP	Philips	1975	1961	£400	US

FROST, MAX & THE TROOPERS

Title	Format	Label	Number	Year	Price	Notes
Shape Of Things To Come	7"	Capitol	CL15565	1968	£5	

FROSTY LANE

Title	Format	Label	Number	Year	Price	Notes
Frosty Lane	LP	Cully Wren		1971	£50	

FRUGAL SOUND

Title	Format	Label	Number	Year	Price	Notes
Abilene	7"	RCA	RCA1595	1967	£4	
All Strung Out	7"	RCA	RCA1659	1968	£4	
Backstreet Girl	7"	RCA	RCA1566	1967	£5	
Just Outside The Door	7"	Pye	7N17129	1966	£4	
Norwegian Wood	7"	Pye	7N17062	1966	£5	

FRUIT MACHINE

Title	Format	Label	Number	Year	Price	Notes
Follow Me	7"	Spark	SRL1003	1969	£30	
I'm Alone Today	7"	Spark	SRL1027	1970	£60	

FRUMPY

Title	Format	Label	Number	Year	Price	Notes
All Will Be Changed	LP	Philips	6305067	1971	£15	
Frump 2	LP	Philips	6305098	1972	£20	blue & black vinyl

FRUUPP

Title	Format	Label	Number	Year	Price	Notes
Future Legends	LP	Dawn	DNLS3053	1973	£25	
Modern Masquerades	LP	Dawn	DNLS3070	1975	£25	
Prince Of Heaven	7"	Dawn	DNS1087	1974	£8	
Prince Of Heaven's Eyes	LP	Dawn	DNLH2	1974	£25	
Seven Secrets	LP	Dawn	DNLS3058	1974	£25	

FUCHSIA

Title	Format	Label	Number	Year	Price	Notes
Fuchsia	LP	Pegasus	PEG8	1971	£50	

FUGI

Title	Format	Label	Number	Year	Price	Notes
Red Moon	7"	Blue Horizon	2096005	1971	£5	

FUGITIVES

Title	Format	Label	Number	Year	Price	Notes
Fugitive	7"	Vogue	V9176	1961	£8	

FUGITIVES (2)

Title	Format	Label	Number	Year	Price	Notes
Lecture	7"	Doctor Bird	DB1097	1967	£10	
Musical Pressure	7"	Doctor Bird	DB1082	1967	£10	
Real Gone Loser	7"	Doctor Bird	DB1116	1967	£10	

FUGITIVES (3)

Title	Format	Label	Number	Year	Price	Notes
Fugitives Said Goodbye	LP	Westchester	1005	1969	£40	US

FUGITIVES (4)

Title	Format	Label	Number	Year	Price	Notes
Fugitives At Dave's Hideout	LP	Hideout	1001	1968	£180	US

FUGS

Title	Format	Label	Number	Year	Price	Notes
Ballads Of Contemporary Protest	LP	Broadside	304	1966	£40	US
Belle Of Avenue A	LP	Reprise	RS6359	1969	£12	US
Crystal Liaison	7"	Transatlantic	BIG115	1968	£10	
First Album	LP	Fontana	STL5513	1965	£20	
Fugs 4 Rounders Score	LP	ESP	2018	1967	£20	US
Fugs II	LP	Fontana	STL5524	1966	£20	
Golden Filth	LP	Reprise	RS6396	1970	£12	US
It Crawled Into My Hand Honest	LP	Transatlantic	TRA181	1968	£15	
Tenderness Junction	LP	Transatlantic	TRA180	1968	£15	
Virgin Fugs	LP	Fontana	STL5501	1967	£20	

FULLER, BOBBY

Title	Format	Label	Number	Year	Price	Notes
I Fought The Law	7"	London	HLU10030	1966	£6	chart single
I Fought The Law	LP	Mustang	M901	1966	£25	US
KRLA King Of The Wheels	LP	Mustang	M900	1966	£30	US
Love's Made A Fool Of You	7"	London	HLU10041	1966	£8	

Memorial Album	LP	President	PTL1003	1967	**£15**	

FULLER, JERRY

Teenage Love	LP	Lin	LP100	1960	**£12**	US
Tennessee Waltz	7"	London	HLH8982	1959	**£4**	

FULLER, JESSE

Frisco Bound	LP	Cavalier	6009	195-	**£30**	US
Frisco Bound	LP-10"	Cavalier	5006	195-	**£40**	US
Going Back To My Old Used To Be	7"	Fontana	TF821	1967	**£5**	
Jesse Fuller	LP	G.T. Jazz	LAG12159	1958	**£15**	
Lone Cat	LP	G.T. Jazz	LAG12279	1960	**£15**	
San Francisco Bay Blues	LP	G.T. Jazz	LAG574	1963	**£15**	
San Francisco Bay Blues	7"	G.T. Jazz	GV2426	1965	**£5**	

FULLER, RANDY

It's Love Come What May	7"	President	PTL111	1967	**£8**	

FULSON, LOWELL

Black Nights	7"	Polydor	56515	1970	**£4**	
Hung Down Head	LP	Chess	408	196-	**£15**	US
I Love My Baby	78	London	L1199	1953	**£10**	
Lowell Fulson	LP	Kent	KLP5016	1965	**£15**	US
Lowell Fulson Now	LP	Kent	KST531	1969	**£12**	US
Talking Woman	7"	Sue	WI4023	1966	**£10**	
Too Many Drivers	7"	Sue	WI375	1965	**£10**	
Tramp	7"	Fontana	TF795	1967	**£12**	
Tramp	LP	Kent	KLP520	1967	**£15**	US

FULSON, LOWELL & LEON BLUE

Stop And Think	7"	Outasite	45502	1966	**£20**	

FUMBLE

Alexandra Park	7"	Sovereign	SOV121	1973	**£4**	
Don't Take Love	7"	RCA	RCA2512	1975	**£4**	
Fumble	LP	Sovereign	SVNA7254	1972	**£12**	
Million Seller	7"	Sovereign	SOV118	1973	**£4**	
Not Fade Away	7"	RCA	RCA2479	1974	**£4**	
One Last Dance	7"	RCA	RCA2628	1975	**£4**	
Poetry In Lotion	LP	RCA	SF8403	1974	**£12**	

FUN FOUR

Singing In The Showers	7"	NMC	NMC010		**£4**	

FUNHOUSE

Out Of Control	7"	Ensign	ENY22	1982	**£20**	
Out Of Control	12"	Ensign	ENY22	1982	**£20**	

FUNKADELIC

America Eats Its Young	LP	Westbound	2WB2020	1972	**£30**	US
Cosmic Slop	LP	Westbound	WB2022	1973	**£20**	US
Free Your Mind & Your Ass Will Follow	LP	Pye	NSPL28144	1971	**£20**	
Funkadelic	LP	Pye	NSPL28137	1970	**£20**	
Greatest Hits	LP	Westbound	1004	1975	**£10**	US
I Got A Thing, You Got A Thing...	7"	Pye	7N25519	1970	**£4**	
Let's Take It To The Stage	LP	20th Century	W215	1975	**£10**	
Maggot Brain	LP	Westbound	6310200	1971	**£20**	
Standing On The Verge Of Getting It On	LP	Westbound	1001	1974	**£20**	US
Tales Of Kidd Funkadelic	LP	Westbound	227	1976	**£20**	US
You And Your Folks, Me And Mine	7"	Pye	7N25548	1971	**£4**	

FUNKY JUNCTION

Records like that of Funky Junction's "Tribute To Deep Purple" are essentially exploitative in nature. At least on this occasion the group's name is written clearly enough, although the record company was no doubt still rather hoping that potential customers would think the music really was by Deep Purple. According to rumour, members of Thin Lizzy are actually involved, although if they were, it was not one of their better days. The vocalist is definitely not Phil Lynott.

Tribute To Deep Purple	LP	Gold Award	MER373	1973	**£15**	

FURTADO, TOMMY

Sun Tan Sam	7"	London	HLA8418	1957	**£6**	

FURY, BILLY

Billy Fury is held in high regard as one of the most convincing British rock'n'rollers and yet the proportion of rock to ballads in his output is far too small for the reputation to be sustained by deep enquiry. "The Sound Of Fury" is certainly a competent slice of rockabilly, and Fury wrote much of the material himself, but to release an album in this style in 1960 was to indulge in a piece of historical re-creation rather than to be part of the development of something new. Cliff Richard's exploration of the Buddy Holly style was much more to the point, and it is significant that he survived the onslaught of the Beatles, whereas Billy Fury did not.

All The Way To The USA	7"	Parlophone	R5819	1969	**£12**	
Am I Blue	7" EP	Decca	DFE8558	1963	**£20**	
Angel Face	78	Decca	F11158	1959	**£30**	
Angel Face	7"	Decca	F11158	1959	**£8**	
Because Of Love	7"	Decca	F11508	1962	**£4**	chart single
Best Of...	LP	Ace Of Clubs	ACL1229	1967	**£15**	
Beyond The Shadow Of A Doubt	7"	Parlophone	R5658	1967	**£8**	
Billy	LP	Decca	LK4533	1963	**£25**	chart LP
Billy Fury	LP	Ace Of Clubs	ACL1047	1960	**£20**	
Billy Fury	7" EP	Decca	DFE6694	1961	**£15**	
Billy Fury And The Gamblers	7" EP	Decca	DFE8641	1965	**£30**	
Billy Fury And The Tornadoes	7" EP	Decca	DFE8525	1963	**£12**	
Billy Fury Hits	7" EP	Decca	DFE8505	1962	**£10**	
Billy Fury No.2	7" EP	Decca	DFE6699	1962	**£20**	
Colette	7"	Decca	F11200	1960	**£6**	chart single
Devil Or Angel	7"	Lyntone	BF001	1983	**£5**	flexi
Do You Really Love Me Too	7"	Decca	F11792	1963	**£4**	chart single
Don't Let A Little Pride	7"	Decca	F12409	1966	**£6**	
Don't Worry	7"	Decca	F11334	1961	**£5**	chart single
Give Me Your Word	7"	Decca	F12459	1966	**£5**	chart single
Halfway To Paradise	LP	Ace Of Clubs	ACL1083	1961	**£20**	chart LP
Halfway To Paradise	7"	Decca	F11349	1961	**£4**	chart single
Halfway To Paradise	7"	NEMS	NES018	1976	**£4**	
Hippy Hippy Shake	7"	Decca	F40719	1964	**£15**	export
Hurtin' Is Lovin'	7"	Parlophone	R5560	1967	**£8**	
I Call For My Rose	7"	Parlophone	R5788	1969	**£8**	
I Will	7"	Decca	F11888	1964	**£6**	chart single
I'd Never Find Another You	7"	Decca	F11409	1961	**£4**	chart single
I'll Be Your Sweetheart	7"	W. Bros	WB16402	1974	**£4**	
I'll Never Quite Get Over You	7"	Decca	F12325	1966	**£5**	chart single
I'm Lost Without You	7"	Decca	F12048	1965	**£4**	chart single
I've Got A Horse	LP	Decca	LK4677	1965	**£30**	
In Summer	7"	Decca	F11701	1963	**£4**	chart single
In Thoughts Of You	7"	Decca	F12178	1965	**£4**	chart single
Interview With Stuart Colman	LP-10"	Polydor		1982	**£15**	promo
It's Only Make Believe	7"	Decca	F11939	1964	**£4**	chart single
Jealousy	7"	Decca	F11384	1961	**£4**	chart single
Lady	7"	Parlophone	R5747	1968	**£8**	
Last Night Was Made For Love	7"	Decca	F11458	1962	**£4**	chart single
Letter Full Of Tears	7"	Decca	F11437	1962	**£5**	chart single
Like I've Never Been Gone	7"	Decca	F11582	1963	**£4**	chart single
Loving You	7"	Parlophone	R5605	1967	**£10**	
Margo	78	Decca	F11128	1959	**£20**	
Margo	7"	Decca	F11128	1959	**£8**	chart single
Maybe Tomorrow	78	Decca	F11102	1959	**£20**	
Maybe Tomorrow	7"	Decca	F11102	1959	**£8**	round centre
Maybe Tomorrow	7"	Decca	F11102	1959	**£12**	tri-centre, chart single
Maybe Tomorrow	7" EP	Decca	DFE6597	1959	**£20**	
My Christmas Prayer	78	Decca	F11189	1959	**£35**	
My Christmas Prayer	7"	Decca	F11189	1959	**£20**	
My Christmas Prayer	7" EP	Decca	DFE8686	1983	**£4**	
Once Upon A Dream	7"	Decca	F11485	1962	**£4**	chart single
Paradise Alley	7"	Parlophone	R5874	1970	**£20**	
Phone Box	7"	Parlophone	R5723	1968	**£8**	
Play It Cool	7" EP	Decca	DFE6708	1962	**£10**	
Run To My Lovin' Arms	7"	Decca	F12230	1965	**£5**	chart single
Silly Boy Blue	7"	Parlophone	R5681	1968	**£12**	
Somebody Else's Girl	7"	Decca	F11744	1963	**£4**	chart single
Sound Of Fury	LP-10"	Decca	LF1329	1960	**£35**	chart LP
Suzanne In The Mirror	7"	Parlophone	R5634	1967	**£8**	
That's Love	7"	Decca	F11237	1960	**£6**	chart single
Thousand Stars	7"	Decca	F11311	1960	**£6**	chart single
We Want Billy	LP	Decca	LK4548	1963	**£25**	chart LP

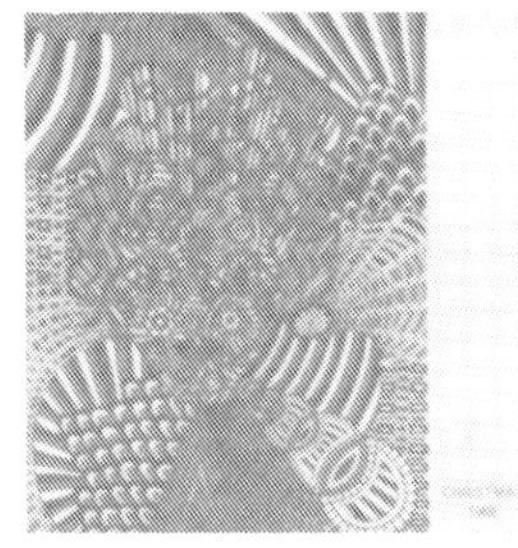

Magical Mystery Tour

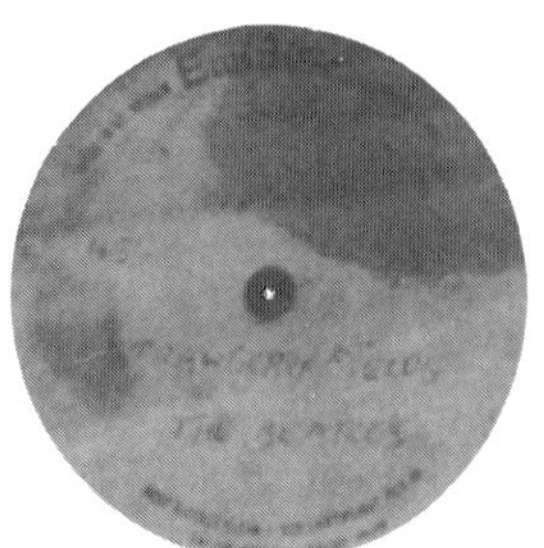

Magical Mystery Tour II

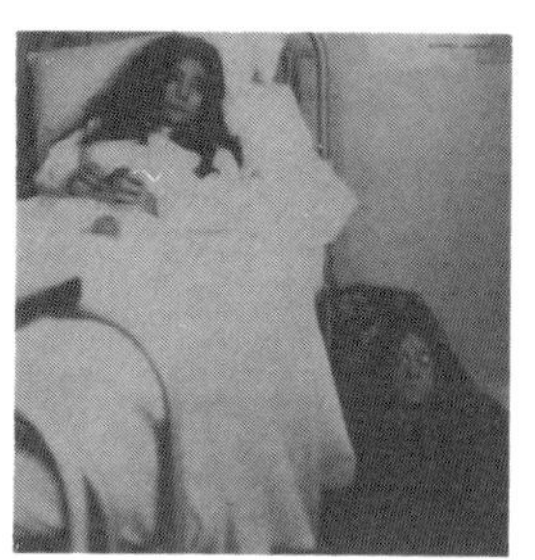

The Long And Winding Road

Come And Get It

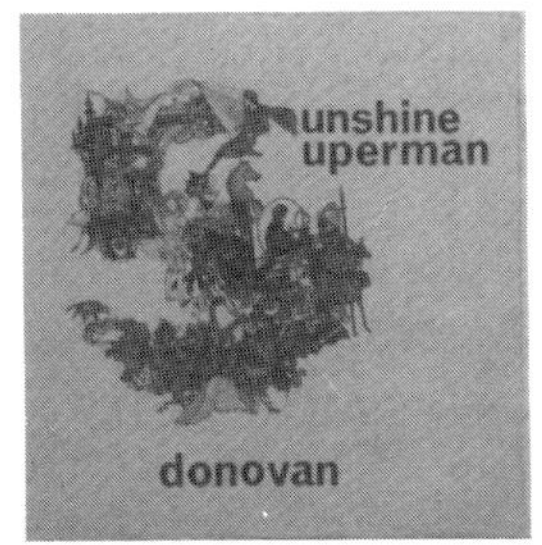

We're Sgt. Pepper's Lonely Hearts Club Band

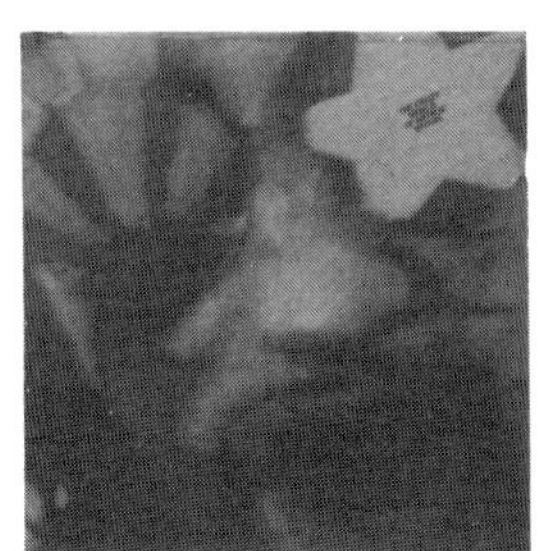

Dear Mr. Fantasy

Winds Of Change

With Their New Face On

We Shall Overcome

Pack Up Your Sorrows

Because They're Young

American Pie

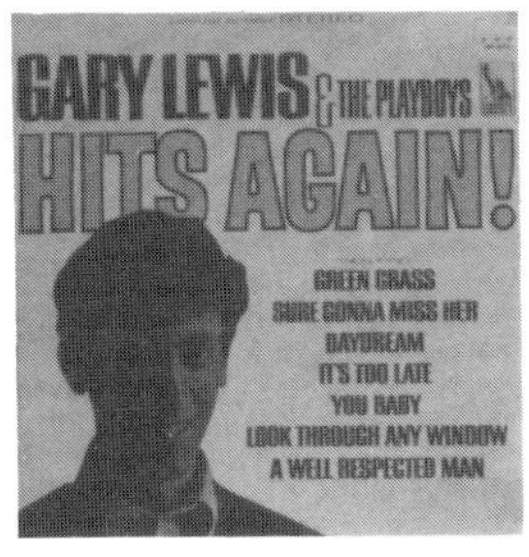

Summer In The City

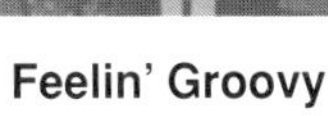
Feelin' Groovy

The Faster We Go, The Rounder We Get

Electric Music For The Mind And Body

The Beauty Of Time Is That It's Snowing

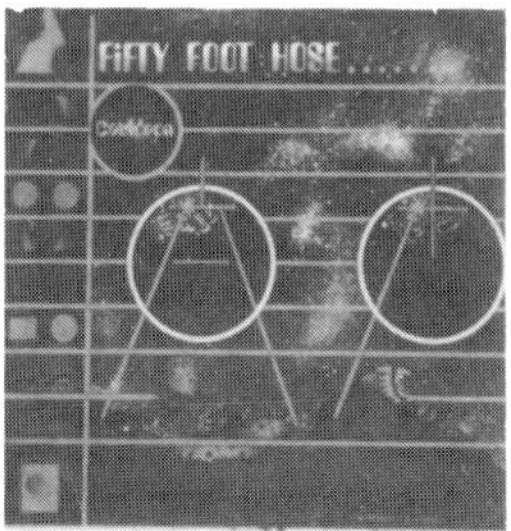

Ultimate Spinach

Pushin' Too Hard

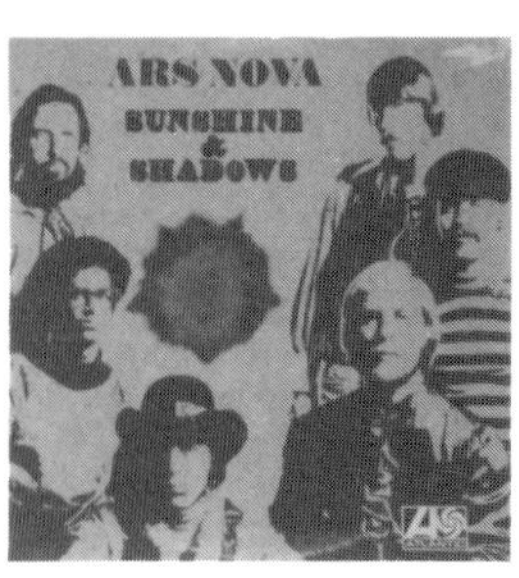

Sunshine And Shadows

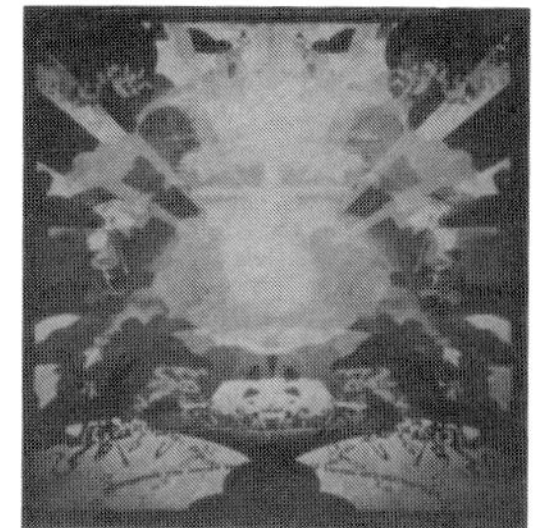

I Had Too Much To Dream

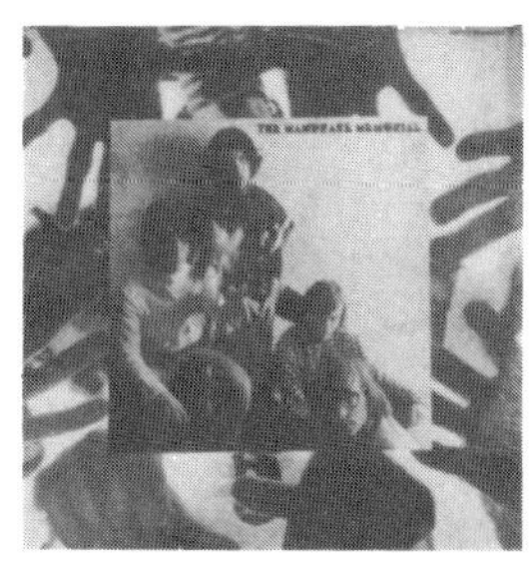

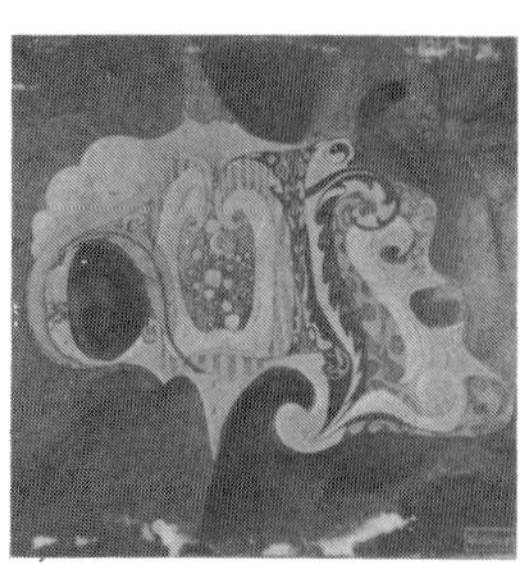

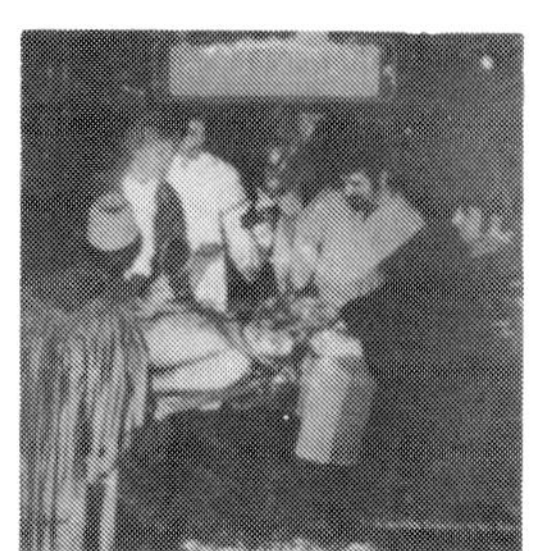

Serpent Power

So You Want To Be A Rock 'n' Roll Star

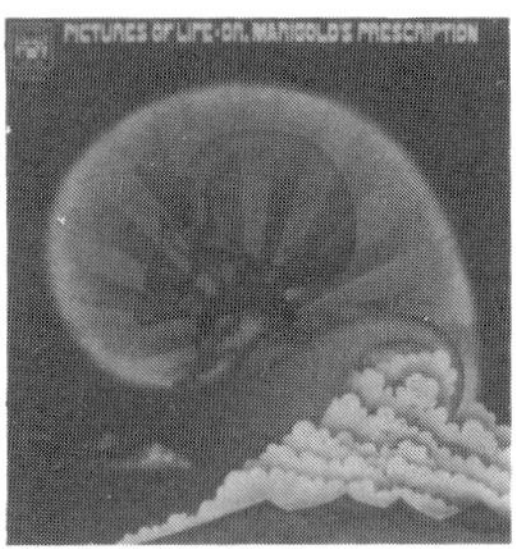

One Wheel On My Wagon

Fattening Frogs For Snakes

Rebel Music

Honky - Tonkin'

Sweetheart Of The Rodeo

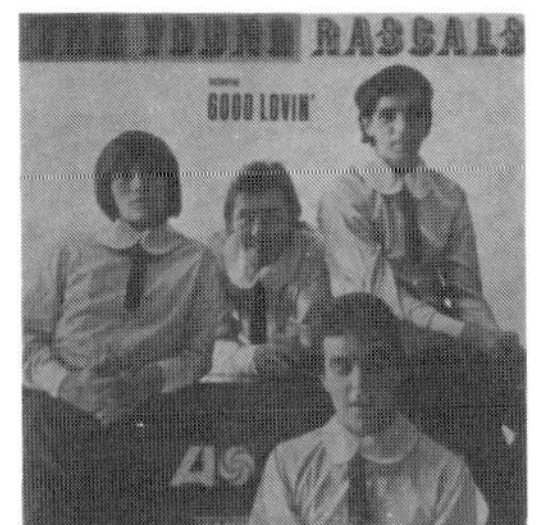

Groovin'

Pure Pop For Now People

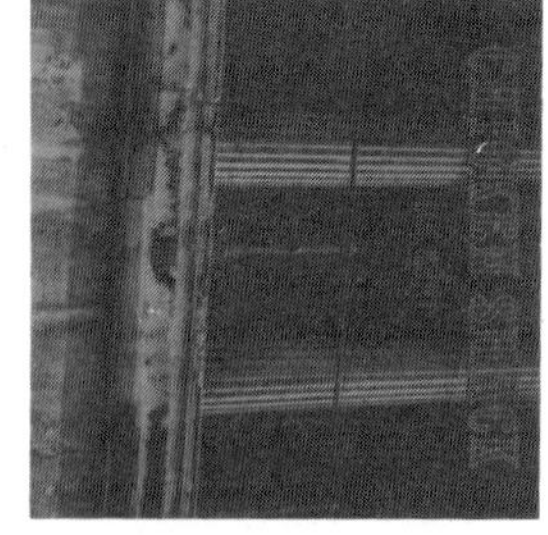

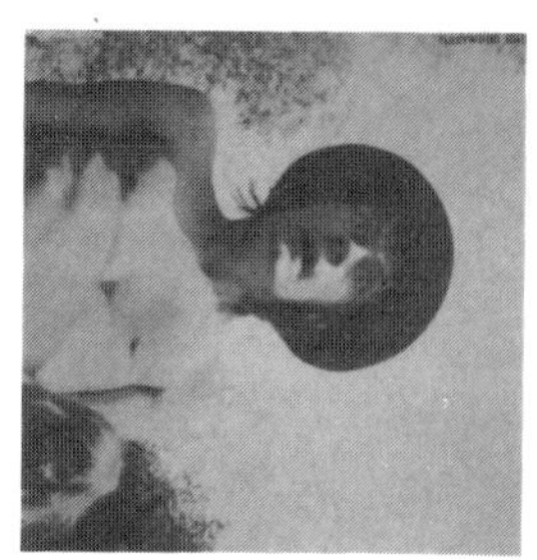

Dust My Blues

Woke Up This Morning

We Want Billy .... LP .... Decca .... SKL4548 .... 1963 .... **£30** .... stereo, chart LP
We Want Billy .... 12" .... Decca .... 1983 .... **£6** .... promo sampler
When Will You Say I Love You .... 7" .... Decca .... F11655 .... 1963 .... **£4** .... chart single
Why Are You Leaving? .... 7" .... Parlophone .... R5845 .... 1970 .... **£15** ....
Will The Real Man Stand Up .... 7" .... Fury .... FY301 .... 1972 .... **£8** ....
Wondrous Place .... 7" .... Decca .... F11267 .... 1960 .... **£6** .... chart single

FURY, BILLY & OTHERS

Long Live Rock .... 7" EP .... Ronco .... MREP001 .... 1973 .... **£15** ....

FURYS

I'm Satisfied With You .... 7" .... Jayboy .... BOY68 .... 1973 .... **£5** ....
Zing Went The Strings Of My Heart .... 7" .... Stateside .... SS182 .... 1963 .... **£5** ....

FUSION

Cold Outside .... 12" .... Plastic F. .... PFUL1104 .... 1979 .... **£10** ....
Till I Hear from You .... LP .... Telephone .... TEL101 .... 1980 .... **£25** .... blue vinyl

FUSION ORCHESTRA

Skeleton In Armour .... LP .... EMI .... EMA758 .... 1973 .... **£40** ....
When My Mama's Not At Home .... 7" .... EMI .... EMI2056 .... 1973 .... **£6** ....

FUT

Desperate to believe in the existence of rare Beatles out-takes, collectors seized on "Have You Heard The Word" as being one such. Unless, of course, it was really the Bee Gees - or, again, perhaps it was actually the Bee Gees and the Beatles singing together? Actually, it was the Fut (whoever they were), just as the label said.

Have You Heard The Word .... 7" .... Beacon .... BEA160 .... 1971 .... **£10** ....

FUTURES

You Better Be Certain .... 7" .... Buddah .... BDS430 .... 1975 .... **£5** ....

FUZZ FACE

Mighty Quinn .... 7" .... Page One .... POF065 .... 1968 .... **£4** ....

FUZZY DUCK

Big Brass Band .... 7" .... Mam .... MAM51 .... 1971 .... **£20** ....
Double Time Woman .... 7" .... Mam .... MAM37 .... 1971 .... **£20** ....
Fuzzy Duck .... LP .... Mam .... MAM1005 .... 1971 .... **£100** ....

FYNN McCOOL

US Thumbstyle .... 7" .... RCA .... RCA1956 .... 1970 .... **£8** ....

G

G, WINSTON

Title	Format	Label	Cat. No.	Year	Price	Notes
Cloud Nine	7"	Decca	F12444	1966	**£10**	
Mother Ferguson's Love Dust	7"	Decca	F12559	1967	**£12**	
Riding With The Milkman	7"	Decca	F12623	1967	**£10**	

G, WINSTON & THE WICKED

Title	Format	Label	Cat. No.	Year	Price	Notes
Like A Baby	7"	Parlophone	R5266	1965	**£12**	
Until You Were Gone	7"	Parlophone	R5330	1966	**£8**	

G-CLEFS

Title	Format	Label	Cat. No.	Year	Price	Notes
Girl Has To Know	7"	London	HLU9530	1962	**£4**	
I Understand	7"	London	HLU9433	1961	**£4**	chart single
Ka Ding Dong	7"	Columbia	DB3851	1956	**£20**	
Make Up Your Mind	7"	London	HLU9563	1962	**£4**	

G-FORCE

Title	Format	Label	Cat. No.	Year	Price	Notes
G-Force	LP	Jet	JETLP229	1980	**£10**	pic disc

G-NOTES

Title	Format	Label	Cat. No.	Year	Price	Notes
Ronnie	7"	Oriole	CB1456	1958	**£4**	

GABRIEL & THE ANGELS

Title	Format	Label	Cat. No.	Year	Price	Notes
Don't Wanna Twist No More	7"	Stateside	SS150	1963	**£4**	

GABRIEL, PETER

Title	Format	Label	Cat. No.	Year	Price	Notes
Big Time	CDV	Virgin	VVD241	1988	**£10**	
Big Time	CD-s	Virgin	GAIL312	1987	**£10**	
Big Time	cass-s	Virgin	PGT312	1987	**£8**	
Big Time	12"	Virgin	PGS312DJ	1987	**£8**	promo
Biko (edited version)	7"	Charisma	CBDJ370	1980	**£10**	promo
Biko (Live)	cass-s	Virgin	PGSC612	1987	**£8**	
Biko	7"	Charisma	CB370	1980	**£10**	chart single
Biko	12"	Charisma	CB37012	1980	**£12**	
Biko	CD-s	Virgin	CDPGS612	1987	**£6**	
D.I.Y. (remix)	7"	Charisma	CB319	1978	**£30**	
D.I.Y.	7"	Charisma	CB311	1978	**£8**	
Deutsches Album	LP	Charisma	6302221	1982	**£10**	4th LP in German
Don't Give Up	7"	Virgin	PGSDJ2	1986	**£8**	promo
Don't Give Up	7"	Virgin	PGSP2	1986	**£6**	poster sleeve
Ein Deutsches Album	LP	Charisma	6302035	1980	**£10**	3rd LP in German
Games Without Frontiers (live)	12"	Virgin	GAB122	1983	**£15**	
Games Without Frontiers	7"	Charisma	CB354	1980	**£4**	chart single
I Don't Remember	7"	Virgin	GAB1	1983	**£4**	chart single
Modern Love	7"	Charisma	CB302	1977	**£5**	
Modern Love	7"	Charisma	CB302	1977	**£12**	pic label
Out Out	12"	Geffen	A124953	1984	**£12**	
Peter Gabriel 4	LP	Charisma		1982	**£15**	audiophile
Peter Gabriel Plays Live	LP	Charisma		1983	**£50**	double TP, orig. mixes
Plays Live DJ Sampler	12"	Charisma	RAD10	1983	**£12**	Promo
Plays Live Shop Sampler	12"	Charisma	REP1420	1983	**£12**	Promo
Plays Live/The Fugitive (Tony Banks)	LP	Charisma	REP1	1983	**£15**	promo sampler
Red Rain	cass-s	Virgin	PGSC120	1987	**£8**	
Schock Den Affen	7"	Charisma	60000876	1982	**£15**	German
Shock The Monkey	7"	Charisma	SHOCK122	1982	**£10**	pic disc
Shock The Monkey	7"	Charisma	SHOCK350DJ	1982	**£6**	promo
Shock The Monkey/instrumental	7"	Charisma	SHOCK1	1982	**£12**	chart single
Shock The Monkey/instrumental	12"	Charisma	SHOCK343	1982	**£12**	
Shock The Monkey/Soft Dog	7"	Charisma	SHOCK1	1982	**£4**	
Shock The Monkey/Soft Dog	12"	Charisma	SHOCK12	1982	**£6**	
Sledgehammer (dance mix)	12"	Virgin	PGS113	1986	**£10**	
Sledgehammer	cass-s	Virgin	PGT112	1986	**£8**	
Solsbury Hill	7"	Charisma	CB301	1977	**£10**	PS

Solsbury Hill	7"	Charisma	CB301DJ	1977	**£12**	demo
Solsbury Hill	7"	Snd For Ind.	SFI381	1978	**£8**	flexi
Spiel Ohne Grenzen	7"	Charisma	6000448	1980	**£15**	German
Walk Through The Fire	7"	Virgin	VS689	1984	**£4**	chart single

GABRIELLI BRASS

Ride Your Pony	7"	Polydor	56047	1965	**£4**	

GADGETS

The Gadgets performed improvised industrial music which was released on three limited edition albums. One of the trio was Matt Johnson, subsequently the central pillar of The The.

Blue Album	LP	Glass	GLALP006	1983	**£15**	
Gadgetree	LP	Final Solution	FSLP001	1979	**£20**	blue/brown cover + insert
Love, Curiosity, Freckles & Doubt	LP	Final Solution	FSLP002	1980	**£15**	

GAINORS

Secret	7"	London	HLU8734	1958	**£20**	

GALACTIC FEDERATION

March Of The Sky People	7"	Polydor	56093	1966	**£15**	

GALE, SUNNY

Certain Smile	7"	Brunswick	05753	1958	**£4**	
Come Go With Me	7"	Brunswick	05661	1957	**£5**	
Please Love Me Forever	7"	London	HLU9322	1961	**£4**	
Sunny And Blue	LP	RCA	LPM1277	1956	**£15**	US
Two Hearts	7"	Brunswick	05659	1957	**£5**	

GALLAHADS

Ooh-Ah	7"	Capitol	CL15366	1964	**£4**	

GALLIARD

I Wrapped Her In Ribbons	7"	Deram	DM306	1970	**£8**	
New Dawn	LP	Deram	SML1075	1970	**£40**	
Strange Pleasure	LP	Nova	SDN4	1969	**£20**	

GAMBLERS

Cry Me A River	7"	Parlophone	R5557	1967	**£10**	
Dr.Goldfoot	7"	Decca	F12399	1966	**£10**	
Nobody But Me	7"	Decca	F11872	1964	**£10**	
Now I'm All Alone	7"	Decca	F12060	1965	**£8**	
You've Really Got A Hold On Me	7"	Decca	F11780	1963	**£8**	

GAME

Addicted Man	7"	Parlophone	R5553	1967	**£35**	
But I Do	7"	Pye	7N15889	1965	**£30**	
Gonna Get Me Someone	7"	Decca	F12469	1966	**£30**	
It's Shocking What They Call Me	7"	Parlophone	R5569	1967	**£30**	

GANDALF

Gandalf	LP	Capitol	ST121	1969	**£30**	US

GANDALF THE GREY

Grey Wizard Am I	LP	G.W.R.	7	196-	**£75**	US

GANDERTON, RON WARREN

Guitar Star	LP	S. Ceremony		1973	**£120**	

GANT, CECIL

Cecil Gant	LP	King	671	1960	**£35**	US
Incomparable...	LP	Sound	601	1957	**£30**	US

GANTS

Gants Again	LP	Liberty	LRP3473	1966	**£10**	US
Gants Galore	LP	Liberty	LRP3455	1966	**£10**	US
Greener Days	7"	Liberty	LIB55940	1967	**£5**	
Road Runner	LP	Liberty	LRP3432	1965	**£12**	US
Road Runner	7"	Liberty	LIB55829	1965	**£8**	

GARCIA, JERRY

Garcia	LP	Round	RX59301	1974	**£10**	
Garcia	LP	W. Bros	K46139	1972	**£12**	

Hooteroll	LP	CBS	69013	1972	**£12**	
Live At The Keystone	LP	Fantasy	F79002	1973	**£12**	
Reflections	LP	United Artists	UAG29921	1976	**£10**	

GARDEN ODYSSEY ENTERPRISE

Sad And Lonely	7"	Deram	DM267	1969	**£8**	

GARDINER, PAUL

Stormtrooper In Drag	12"	Beggars B.	BEG61T	1981	**£60**	promo

GARDNER, DAVE

All By Myself	7"	Brunswick	05740	1958	**£12**	

GARDNER, DON & DEE DEE FORD

Don't You Worry	7"	Soul City	SC101	1968	**£5**	
Don't You Worry	7"	Soul City	SC101	1968	**£12**	demo
I Need Your Loving	7"	Stateside	SS114	1962	**£6**	
I'm Coming Home To Stay	7"	Stateside	SS130	1962	**£5**	
In Sweden	LP	Sue	LP1044	1965	**£20**	US
Need Your Lovin'	LP	Fire	LP105	1962	**£50**	US

GARFIELD, JOHNNY

Stranger In Paradise	7"	Pye	7N15758	1965	**£5**	

GARFUNKEL, ART

Angel Clair	LP	CBS	Q69021	1974	**£10**	quad

GARNETT, COL

With A Girl Like You	7"	Page One	POF002	1966	**£6**	

GARRETT, VERNON

If I Could Turn Back The Hands Of Time	7"	Stateside	SS2006	1967	**£8**	
Shine It On	7"	Action	ACT4508	1968	**£4**	
Shine It On	7"	Action	ACT4508	1968	**£15**	demo
Shine It On	7"	Stateside	SS2026	1967	**£4**	

GARRICK, DAVID

A Boy Called David	LP	Pye		1967	**£12**	
Dear Mrs.Applebee	7"	Piccadilly	7N35335	1966	**£4**	chart single
Lady Jane	7"	Piccadilly	7N35317	1966	**£4**	chart single

GARRICK, MICHAEL

Anthem	LP	Argo	ZFA92	1965	**£40**	
Before Night/Day	LP	Argo	EAF115	1966	**£40**	
Black Marigolds	LP	Argo	ZDA88	1966	**£40**	
Case Of Jazz	LP	Airborne		1963	**£50**	
Cold Mountain	LP	Argo	ZDA153	1972	**£40**	
Epiphany	7"	Argo	AFW105	1971	**£8**	
Home Stretch Blues	LP	Argo	ZDA154	1972	**£40**	
Jazz Praises At St.Pauls	LP	Airborne	NBP0021	1968	**£40**	
Moonscape	LP	Airborne		1964	**£50**	
Mr.Smith's Apocalypse	LP	Argo	ZAGF1	1971	**£40**	
October Woman	LP	Argo	ZDA33	1964	**£40**	
Poetry And Jazz In Concert 250	LP	Argo	ZPR264/5	1969	**£50**	double
Promises	LP	Argo	ZDA36	1965	**£40**	

GARRICK, MICHAEL & NORMA WINSTONE

Heart Is A Lotus	LP	Argo	ZDA135	1970	**£40**	
Poetry And Jazz In Concert	LP	Argo	ZDA26/27	1964	**£60**	double

GARRITY, FREDDIE

Little Red Donkey	7"	Columbia	DB8348	1968	**£4**	

GARVIN, REX & THE MIGHTY CRAVERS

I Gotta Go Now	7"	Atlantic	584097	1967	**£5**	
Sock It To Them JB	7"	Atlantic	584028	1966	**£5**	

GARY & THE ARIELS

Say You Love Me	7"	Fontana	TF476	1964	**£8**	

GARYBALDI

Title	Format	Label	Cat. No.	Year	Price	Notes
Astrolabia	LP	Fonit		1973	**£120**	
Nuda	LP	CGD		1972	**£75**	

GAS WORKS

Title	Format	Label	Cat. No.	Year	Price	Notes
Cider With Rosie	7"	Regal Z.	RZ3080	1973	**£4**	
Gas Works	LP	Regal Z.	SLRZ1036	1973	**£12**	
Standing Stiff	7"	Regal Z.	RZ3075	1973	**£4**	

GASOLINE BAND

Title	Format	Label	Cat. No.	Year	Price	Notes
Gasoline Band	LP	Cube	HIFLY9	1972	**£10**	

GASS

Title	Format	Label	Cat. No.	Year	Price	Notes
Dream Baby	7"	CBS	202647	1967	**£5**	
Gass	LP	Polydor	2383022	1970	**£12**	
New Breed	7"	Parlophone	R5456	1966	**£5**	
One Of These Days	7"	Parlophone	R5344	1965	**£5**	

GATES OF EDEN

Title	Format	Label	Cat. No.	Year	Price	Notes
In Your Love	7"	Pye	7N17252	1967	**£10**	
One To Seven	7"	Pye	7N17278	1967	**£8**	
Too Much On My Mind	7"	Pye	7N17195	1966	**£10**	

GATES, DAVID

Title	Format	Label	Cat. No.	Year	Price	Notes
Happiest Man Alive	7"	Top Rank	JAR504	1960	**£10**	

GATOR CREEK

Title	Format	Label	Cat. No.	Year	Price	Notes
Danny's Song	7"	Mercury	6052058	1971	**£4**	
Gator Creek	LP	Mercury	6338035	1970	**£15**	

GAVIN, JIMMY

Title	Format	Label	Cat. No.	Year	Price	Notes
I Sit In My Window	7"	London	HLU8478	1957	**£10**	

GAYDEN, MAC

Title	Format	Label	Cat. No.	Year	Price	Notes
McGavock Gayden	LP	EMI	EMA760	1973	**£20**	

GAYE, MARVIN

Title	Format	Label	Cat. No.	Year	Price	Notes
Abraham, Martin And John	7"	T. Motown	TMG734	1970	**£4**	chart single
Abraham, Martin And John	7"	T. Motown	TMG734	1970	**£10**	demo
Ain't That Peculiar	7"	T. Motown	TMG539	1965	**£10**	
Ain't That Peculiar	7"	T. Motown	TMG539	1965	**£50**	demo
Can I Get A Witness	7"	Stateside	SS243	1963	**£20**	
Can I Get A Witness	7"	Stateside	SS243	1963	**£50**	demo
Chained	7"	T. Motown	TMG676	1968	**£4**	
Chained	7"	T. Motown	TMG676	1968	**£10**	demo
Greatest Hits	LP	T. Motown	STML11065	1968	**£10**	chart LP
Hello Broadway	LP	T. Motown	TML11015	1965	**£30**	
How Sweet It Is	7"	Stateside	SS360	1964	**£20**	chart single
How Sweet It Is	7"	Stateside	SS360	1964	**£50**	demo
How Sweet It Is	LP	T. Motown	TML11004	1965	**£20**	
I Heard It Through The Grapevine	7"	T. Motown	TMG686	1969	**£4**	chart single
I Heard It Through The Grapevine	7"	T. Motown	TMG686	1969	**£15**	demo
I Heard It Through The Grapevine	7"	T. Motown	TMG923	1974	**£4**	
I'll Be Doggone	7"	T. Motown	TMG510	1965	**£12**	
I'll Be Doggone	7"	T. Motown	TMG510	1965	**£50**	demo
In The Groove	LP	T. Motown	STML11091	1969	**£15**	
Inner City Blues	7"	T. Motown	TMG817	1972	**£4**	
Inner City Blues	7"	T. Motown	TMG817	1972	**£10**	demo
Let's Get It On	7"	T. Motown	TMG868	1973	**£4**	chart single
Let's Get It On	7"	T. Motown	TMG868	1973	**£10**	demo
Let's Get It On	7"	T. Motown	TMG868	1973	**£15**	demo, PS
Little Darling	7"	T. Motown	TMG574	1966	**£10**	chart single
Little Darling	7"	T. Motown	TMG574	1966	**£50**	demo
Marvin Gaye And His Girls	LP	T. Motown	STML11123	1969	**£12**	
Marvin Gaye	LP	Stateside	SL10100	1964	**£40**	
Marvin Gaye	7" EP	T. Motown	TME2016	1966	**£15**	
Mercy Mercy Me	7"	T. Motown	TMG802	1972	**£4**	
Mercy Mercy Me	7"	T. Motown	TMG802	1972	**£10**	demo
Moods Of Marvin Gaye	LP	T. Motown	STML11033	1966	**£15**	
MPG	LP	T. Motown	STML11119	1969	**£15**	
On Stage Recorded Live	LP	Tamla	242	1963	**£30**	US
One More Heartache	7"	T. Motown	TMG552	1966	**£10**	

Title	Format	Label	Cat. No.	Year	Price	Notes
One More Heartache	7"	T. Motown	TMG552	1966	**£50**	demo
Originals From Marvin Gaye	7" EP	T. Motown	TME2019	1967	**£15**	
Pretty Little Baby	7"	T. Motown	TMG524	1965	**£12**	
Pretty Little Baby	7"	T. Motown	TMG524	1965	**£50**	demo
Pride And Joy	7"	Oriole	CBA1846	1963	**£40**	
Save The Children	7"	T. Motown	TMG796	1971	**£4**	
Save The Children	7"	T. Motown	TMG796	1971	**£10**	demo
Soulful Moods Of Marvin Gaye	LP	Tamla	221	1961	**£60**	US
Stubborn Kind Of Fellow	7"	Oriole	CBA1803	1963	**£40**	
Take This Heart Of Mine	7"	T. Motown	TMG563	1966	**£12**	
Take This Heart Of Mine	7"	T. Motown	TMG563	1966	**£50**	demo
That Stubborn Kind Of Fella	LP	Tamla	239	1963	**£60**	US
That's The Way Love Is	LP	T. Motown	STML11136	1970	**£15**	
That's The Way Love Is	7"	T. Motown	TMG718	1969	**£4**	
That's The Way Love Is	7"	T. Motown	TMG718	1969	**£10**	demo
Too Busy Thinking About My Baby	7"	T. Motown	TMG705	1969	**£4**	chart single
Too Busy Thinking About My Baby	7"	T. Motown	TMG705	1969	**£15**	demo
Tribute To Nat King Cole	LP	T. Motown	TML11022	1966	**£25**	
Trouble Man	7"	T. Motown	TMG846	1973	**£4**	
Trouble Man	7"	T. Motown	TMG846	1973	**£10**	demo
Try It Baby	7"	Stateside	SS326	1964	**£20**	
Try It Baby	7"	Stateside	SS326	1964	**£50**	demo
What's Going On	7"	T. Motown	TMG775	1971	**£4**	
What's Going On	7"	T. Motown	TMG775	1971	**£10**	demo
When I'm Alone I Cry	LP	Tamla	251	1964	**£30**	US
You	7"	T. Motown	TMG640	1968	**£5**	
You	7"	T. Motown	TMG640	1968	**£20**	demo
You're A Wonderful One	7"	Stateside	SS284	1964	**£20**	
You're A Wonderful One	7"	Stateside	SS284	1964	**£50**	demo
Your Unchanged Love	7"	T. Motown	TMG618	1967	**£4**	
Your Unchanged Love	7"	T. Motown	TMG618	1967	**£30**	demo

GAYE, MARVIN & KIM WESTON

Title	Format	Label	Cat. No.	Year	Price	Notes
It Takes Two	7"	T. Motown	TMG590	1967	**£8**	chart single
It Takes Two	7"	T. Motown	TMG590	1967	**£50**	demo
Take Two	LP	T. Motown	STML11049	1967	**£15**	
What Good Am I Without You	7"	Stateside	SS363	1964	**£20**	
What Good Am I Without You	7"	Stateside	SS363	1964	**£50**	demo

GAYE, MARVIN & MARY WELLS

Title	Format	Label	Cat. No.	Year	Price	Notes
Once Upon A Time	7"	Stateside	SS316	1964	**£20**	chart single
Once Upon A Time	7"	Stateside	SS316	1964	**£50**	demo
Together	LP	Stateside	SL10097	1964	**£30**	

GAYE, MARVIN & TAMMI TERRELL

Title	Format	Label	Cat. No.	Year	Price	Notes
Ain't No Mountain High Enough	7"	T. Motown	TMG611	1967	**£4**	
Ain't No Mountain High Enough	7"	T. Motown	TMG611	1967	**£30**	demo
Ain't Nothing Like The Real Thing	7"	T. Motown	TMG655	1968	**£5**	chart single
Ain't Nothing Like The Real Thing	7"	T. Motown	TMG655	1968	**£20**	demo
Easy	LP	T. Motown	STML11132	1970	**£10**	
Good Lovin' Ain't Easy To Come By	7"	T. Motown	TMG697	1969	**£20**	demo
Good Lovin' Ain't Easy To Come by	7"	T. Motown	TMG697	1969	**£4**	chart single
If I Could Build My Whole World	7"	T. Motown	TMG635	1967	**£5**	chart single
If I Could Build My Whole World	7"	T. Motown	TMG635	1967	**£25**	demo
Onion Song	7"	T. Motown	TMG715	1969	**£4**	chart single
Onion Song	7"	T. Motown	TMG715	1969	**£12**	demo
United	LP	T. Motown	STML11062	1968	**£12**	
You Ain't Livin' Till You're Lovin'	7"	T. Motown	TMG681	1969	**£4**	chart single
You Ain't Livin' Till You're Lovin'	7"	T. Motown	TMG681	1969	**£15**	demo
You're All I Need To Get By	LP	T. Motown	STML11084	1968	**£10**	
You're All I Need To Get By	7"	T. Motown	TMG668	1968	**£4**	chart single
You're All I Need To Get By	7"	T. Motown	TMG668	1968	**£30**	demo
Your Precious Love	7"	T. Motown	TMG625	1967	**£4**	
Your Precious Love	7"	T. Motown	TMG625	1967	**£25**	demo

GAYLADS

Title	Format	Label	Cat. No.	Year	Price	Notes
Rock Steady	LP	Coxsone	CSL8005	196-	**£80**	
Stop Making Love	7"	Island	WI3002	1966	**£10**	
Sunshine Golden 18	LP	Coxsone	CSL8006	196-	**£80**	

GAYLETTS

Son Of A Preacher Man	7"	London	HLJ10302	1970	**£4**	

GAYLORDS

He's A Good Face	7"	Columbia	DB7805	1966	**£20**	

GAYTEN, PAUL

Hunch	7"	London	HLM8998	1959	**£15**	

GBH

Give Me Fire	7"	Clay	CLAY16P	1982	**£4**	pic disc

GEESIN, RON

As He Stands	LP	Ron	RON28	1973	**£15**	
Patrons	LP	Ron	RON31	1975	**£15**	
Raise Of The Eyebrows	LP	Transatlantic	TRA161	1967	**£20**	
Right Through	LP	Ron	RON323	197-	**£15**	

GEESIN, RON & ROGER WATERS

Body	LP	Harvest	SHSP4008	1970	**£10**	

GEILS, J. BAND

Bloodshot	LP	Atlantic	QD7260	1973	**£10**	US quad
Bloodshot	LP	Atlantic	SD7260	1973	**£10**	US red vinyl
Ladies Invited	LP	Atlantic	QD7286	1973	**£10**	US quad
Love Stinks	LP	Nautilus	NR25	1981	**£10**	US audiophile
Nightmares	LP	Atlantic	QD18107	1974	**£10**	US quad

GEMINI

Space Walk	7"	Columbia	DB7638	1965	**£12**	

GENE & EUNICE

Bom Bom Lulu	7"	Vogue	V9136	1959	**£12**	
Doodle Doodle Do	7"	Vogue	V9083	1957	**£12**	
I Gotta Go Home	7"	Vogue	V9062	1956	**£12**	
I Mean Love	7"	Vogue	V9106	1958	**£8**	
Let's Get Together	7"	Vogue	V9071	1957	**£12**	
Poco Loco	7"	London	HL8956	1959	**£8**	
This Is My Story	7"	Vogue	V9066	1957	**£15**	
Vow	7"	Vogue	V9126	1958	**£8**	

GENE LOVES JEZEBEL

Bruises	7"	Situation 2	SIT24	1983	**£10**	
Bruises	12"	Situation 2	SIT24T	1983	**£12**	
Cow	7"	Situation 2	SIT36	1985	**£5**	
Cow	12"	Situation 2	SIT36T	1985	**£6**	
Desire (US Club Mix)	12"	Beggars B.	BEG173TC	1986	**£10**	
Desire	12"	Beggars B.	BEG173TP	1986	**£6**	with poster
Desire	12"	Situation 2	SIT41T	1985	**£6**	
Flame	7"	Situation 2	SIT41	1985	**£5**	
Gorgeous	7"	Beggars B.	BEG202S	1987	**£5**	gatefold PS, 2 cards
Heartache	cass-s	Beggars B.	BEG161C	1986	**£6**	
Heartache	12"	Beggars B.	BEG161TP	1986	**£6**	with poster
Influenza	7"	Situation 2	SIT31	1984	**£4**	
Influenza	12"	Situation 2	SIT31T	1984	**£6**	
Promise	LP	Situation 2	SITU7	1983	**£12**	'Wraps & Arms' vocal
Screaming	7"	Situation 2	SIT20	1982	**£8**	
Screaming	12"	Situation 2	SIT20T	1982	**£12**	
Shame	7"	Situation 2	SIT35	1984	**£5**	
Shame	12"	Situation 2	SIT35T	1984	**£6**	
Shaving My Neck	12"	Situation 2	SIT18T	1982	**£50**	
Sweetest Thing	7"	Beggars B.	BEG156	1986	**£4**	chart single
Sweetest Thing	7"	Beggars B.	BEG156	1986	**£6**	with cassette (161F)
Sweetest Thing	12"	Beggars B.	BEG156TP	1986	**£6**	with poster

GENERATION X

Dancing With Myself	7"	Chrysalis	CHS2488	1981	**£4**	clear vinyl
Dancing With Myself	7"	Chrysalis	GENDX1	1980	**£5**	promo
Friday's Angels	7"	Chrysalis	CHS2330	1979	**£4**	pink vinyl
King Rocker	7"	Chrysalis	CHS2261	1979	**£5**	pink, red, yellow or orange vinyl
Ready Steady Go	7"	Chrysalis	CHS2207	1978	**£5**	chart single

Title	Format	Label	Cat. No.	Year	Price	Notes
Valley Of The Dolls	7"	Chrysalis	CHS2310	1979	**£5**	black vinyl
Valley Of The Dolls	7"	Chrysalis	CHS2310	1979	**£4**	brown(ish) vinyl
Wild Youth	7"	Chrysalis	CHS2189	1977	**£5**	
Wild Youth	7"	Chrysalis	CHS2189	1977	**£20**	MP B-side, 'No No No '
Your Generation	7"	Chrysalis	CHS2165	1977	**£5**	chart single

GENESIS

Genesis' first LP was produced by Jonathan King - an unlikely choice for a determinedly progressive group, except that King and Genesis were all ex-pupils of Charterhouse. The record has been reissued several times - the first being as early as 1973 - but the original "From Genesis To Revelation" is quite scarce. Even more so are the early singles, of which "Happy The Man", "I Know What I Like", and "The Carpet Crawlers" all have non-album B sides. The albums "Trespass" and "Nursery Cryme" are still available, of course, but their inclusion here refers to the original pressings with their deep pink Charisma labels.

Title	Format	Label	Cat. No.	Year	Price	Notes
Abacab	7"	Charisma	CB388	1981	**£4**	juke box iss. Genesis logo
And Then There Were Three	LP	Charisma	CDS4010	1978	**£20**	test pressing
Carpet Crawlers	7"	Charisma	CB251	1975	**£15**	
Counting Out Time	7"	Charisma	CB238	1974	**£15**	
Duke	LP	Charisma	CBR101	1983	**£20**	test pressing
Firth Of Fifth	7"	Genesis Inf	GI01	1983	**£8**	flexi
Follow You Follow Me	7"	Charisma	CB309	1978	**£4**	PS
Foxtrot/Selling England...	LP	Charisma	CGS103	1975	**£75**	boxed, poster
From Genesis To Revelation	LP	Decca	LK4990	1969	**£70**	
Genesis	LP	Charisma	GENLP1	1983	**£20**	test pressing
Happy The Man	7"	Charisma	CB181	1972	**£100**	PS
I Know What I Like	7"	Charisma	CB224	1974	**£8**	chart single
Illegal Alien	7"	Charis/Vir	DJAL1	1984	**£4**	promo
In The Beginning	LP	Decca	SKL4990	1974	**£20**	
It's Gonna Get Better	7"	Charis/Vir	MAMA1	1983	**£12**	1 sided test pressing
Knife	7"	Charisma	CB152	1971	**£100**	PS
Lady Lies	7"	Lyntone	LYN11806	1982	**£4**	Flexipop flexi
Lady Lies	7"	Lyntone	LYN11806	1982	**£10**	hard vinyl promo
Lamb Lies Down On Broadway	LP	Charisma	CGS101	1974	**£30**	double test pressing
Land Of Confusion	CD-s	Virgin	SNEG312	1986	**£6**	
Looking For Someone	7"	Charisma	GS1	1970	**£150**	
Mama	7"	Charis/Vir	DJMAMA1	1983	**£4**	promo
Mama	7"	Charis/Vir	MAMA1	1983	**£12**	1 sided test pressing
Man On The Corner	7"	Charisma	CB393	1982	**£10**	PS
Many Too Many	7"	Charisma	CB315	1978	**£4**	PS
Nursery Cryme	LP	Charisma	CAS1052	1971	**£15**	
Paperlate	7"	Charisma	JBGEN1	1982	**£4**	juke box issue
Seconds Out	LP	Charisma	GE2001	1977	**£30**	double test pressing
Silent Sun	7"	Decca	F12735	1968	**£50**	
Spot The Pigeon	7"	Charisma	GEN001	1977	**£6**	PS
Taking It All Too Hard	7"	Charis/Vir	TATA1	1983	**£12**	1 sided test pressing
That's All	7"	Charis/Vir	TATA1	1983	**£12**	1 sided test pressing
That's All	7"	Charis/Vir	TATA1	1983	**£4**	pic disc
That's All	7"	Charis/Vir	TATA1	1983	**£20**	white test pressing
Tonight Tonight Tonight	CD-s	Virgin	DRAW412	1987	**£6**	
Trespass	LP	Charisma	CAS1020	1970	**£15**	
Trespass/Nursery Cryme	LP	Charisma	CGS102	1975	**£75**	boxed, poster
Trick Of The Tail	7"	Charisma	CB277	1976	**£4**	
Trick Of The Tail	7"	Charisma	CB277	1976	**£6**	juke box issue purple label
Trick Of The Tail	LP	Mobile Fid.	MFSL1062	1981	**£20**	US audiophile
Twilight Alehouse	7"	Charisma		1975	**£30**	flexi
Where The Sour Turns To Sweet	7"	Decca	F12949	1969	**£50**	
Wind And Wuthering	LP	Charisma	CDS4005	1977	**£20**	test pressing
Winter's Tale	7"	Decca	F12775	1968	**£60**	
Your Own Special Way	7"	Charisma	CB300	1977	**£4**	chart single

GENESIS (2)

Title	Format	Label	Cat. No.	Year	Price	Notes
In The Beginning	LP	Mercury	SR61175	1968	**£10**	US

GENTILES

Title	Format	Label	Cat. No.	Year	Price	Notes
Goodbye Baby	7"	Pye	7N17530	1968	**£8**	

GENTLE GIANT

Gentle Giant's intricately constructed and faultlessly performed music seems to epitomise what the Vertigo label was all about. The album "Octopus", in particular, stands as something of a landmark within the progressive rock genre. One can hear the band, on successive albums, learning how to create music that requires a high degree of skill for its execution and an even higher degree of inventiveness for its original creation. At the same time, the music is perfectly accessible, if a little hard to dance to! Gentle Giant's ancestor, by the way, was Simon Dupree and the Big Sound, both groups revolving around the Shulman brothers, although they have little in common musically.

Title	Format	Label	Cat. No.	Year	Price	Notes
Acquiring The Taste	LP	Vertigo	6360041	1971	**£20**	spiral label
Free Hand	LP	Chrysalis	1093	1975	**£10**	
Gentle Giant	LP	Vertigo	6360020	1970	**£20**	spiral label
Giant Step	LP	Vertigo	6641334	1975	**£12**	double
In A Glass House	LP	WWA	WWA002	1973	**£15**	
In A Glass House	7"	WWA	WWP1001	1974	**£5**	
Octopus	LP	Vertigo	6360080	1973	**£15**	spiral label
Power And Glory	7"	WWA	WWS17	1974	**£5**	
Power And The Glory	LP	WWA	WWA010	1974	**£15**	
Three Friends	LP	Vertigo	6360070	1972	**£20**	spiral label

GENTLE PEOPLE

Title	Format	Label	Cat. No.	Year	Price	Notes
It's Too Late	7"	Columbia	DB8276	1967	**£4**	

GENTLE, JOHNNY

Title	Format	Label	Cat. No.	Year	Price	Notes
Gentle Touch	7" EP	Philips	BBE12345	1959	**£5**	

GENTLE, TIM & THE GENTLEMEN

Title	Format	Label	Cat. No.	Year	Price	Notes
Without You	7"	Oriole	CB1988	1965	**£8**	

GENTRY, BOBBIE

Title	Format	Label	Cat. No.	Year	Price	Notes
Ode To Billy Joe	LP	Capitol		1967	**£10**	
Ode To Billy Joe	7"	Capitol	CL15511	1967	**£4**	chart single

GENTRYS

Title	Format	Label	Cat. No.	Year	Price	Notes
Brown Paper Sack	7"	MGM	MGM1296	1966	**£5**	
Everyday I Have To Cry	7"	MGM	MGM1312	1966	**£5**	
Gentrys	LP	MGM	GAS127	1966	**£10**	US
Gentrys	LP	Sun	117	1970	**£12**	US
Keep On Dancing	LP	MGM	E4336	1965	**£10**	US
Keep On Dancing	7"	MGM	MGM1284	1965	**£5**	
Time	LP	MGM	E4346	1966	**£10**	US

GEORDIE

Title	Format	Label	Cat. No.	Year	Price	Notes
All Because Of You	7"	EMI	EMI2008	1973	**£4**	chart single
Can You Do It	7"	EMI	EMI2031	1973	**£4**	chart single
Don't Be Fooled By The Name	LP	EMI	EMA764	1974	**£15**	
Don't Do That	7"	Regal Z.	RZ3067	1972	**£4**	chart single
Electric Lady	7"	EMI	EMI2048	1973	**£4**	chart single
Hope You Like It	LP	EMI	EMC3001	1973	**£12**	
Save The World	LP	EMI	EMC3134	1976	**£20**	

GEORGE & BEN

Title	Format	Label	Cat. No.	Year	Price	Notes
Boa Constrictions Natural Vine	LP	Vanguard		1968	**£15**	

GEORGE, BARBARA

Title	Format	Label	Cat. No.	Year	Price	Notes
I Know	7"	London	HL9513	1962	**£5**	
I Know You Don't Love Me Anymore	LP	A.F.O.	5001	1962	**£50**	US
Send For Me	7"	Sue	WI316	1964	**£10**	

GEORGE, LLOYD

Title	Format	Label	Cat. No.	Year	Price	Notes
Sing Real Loud	7"	London	HLP9562	1962	**£4**	

GEORGETTES

Title	Format	Label	Cat. No.	Year	Price	Notes
Love Like A Fool	7"	London	HL8548	1958	**£4**	

GERMS

Title	Format	Label	Cat. No.	Year	Price	Notes
Lexicon Devil	7"	Slash		1978	**£70**	various different sleeves
What We Do Is Secret	12"	Slash	SREP108	1981	**£20**	

GERONIMO BLACK

Title	Format	Label	Cat. No.	Year	Price	Notes
Geronimo Black	LP	MCA	MCF2683	1974	**£12**	

GERRARD, DENNY (& HIGH TIDE)

Title	Format	Label	Cat. No.	Year	Price	Notes
Gerrard	LP	Nova	SND10	1970	**£30**	

GERRY & THE HOLOGRAMS

Title	Format	Label	Cat. No.	Year	Price	Notes
Emperor's New Music	7"	Absurd	A5	1980	**£8**	

GERRY & THE PACEMAKERS

Title	Format	Label	Cat. No.	Year	Price	Notes
Don't Let The Sun Catch You Crying	7"	Columbia	DB7268	1964	**£4**	chart single

Title	Format	Label	Number	Year	Price	Notes
Don't Let The Sun Catch You Crying	7" EP	Columbia	SEG8346	1964	**£5**	
Don't Let The Sun Catch You Crying	LP	Laurie	LLP2024	1964	**£15**	US
Ferry Cross The Mersey	LP	Columbia	33SX1693	1965	**£20**	mono, chart LP
Ferry Cross The Mersey	LP	Columbia	SCX3544	1965	**£20**	stereo, chart LP
Ferry Cross The Mersey	7"	Columbia	DB7437	1964	**£4**	chart single
Gerry In California	7" EP	Columbia	SEG8388	1965	**£8**	
Girl On A Swing	LP	Laurie	LLP2037	1965	**£15**	US
Girl On A Swing	7"	Columbia	DB8044	1966	**£5**	
Greatest Hits	LP	Laurie	LLP2031	1965	**£12**	US
Hits From Ferry Cross The Mersey	7" EP	Columbia	SEG8397	1965	**£6**	
How Do You Do It	7"	Columbia	DB4987	1963	**£4**	chart single
How Do You Do It	7" EP	Columbia	SEG8257	1963	**£5**	
How Do You Like It	LP	Columbia	33SX1546	1963	**£20**	mono, chart LP
How Do You Like It	LP	Columbia	SCX3492	1963	**£20**	stereo, chart LP
I Like It	7"	Columbia	DB7041	1963	**£4**	chart single
I'll Be There	7"	Columbia	DB7504	1965	**£4**	chart single
I'll Be There	LP	Laurie	LLP2030	1964	**£15**	US
I'm The One	7"	Columbia	DB7189	1964	**£4**	chart single
I'm The One	7" EP	Columbia	SEG8311	1964	**£5**	
It's Gonna Be Alright	7"	Columbia	DB7353	1964	**£4**	chart single
It's Gonna Be Alright	7" EP	Columbia	SEG8367	1964	**£6**	
La La La	7"	Columbia	DB7835	1966	**£5**	
Remember	7"	DJM	DJS298	1974	**£5**	
Rip It Up	7" EP	Columbia	SEG8426	1965	**£8**	
Second Album	LP	Laurie	LLP2027	1964	**£15**	US
Walk Hand In Hand	7"	Columbia	DB7738	1965	**£4**	chart single
You'll Never Walk Alone	7"	Columbia	DB7126	1963	**£4**	chart single
You'll Never Walk Alone	7" EP	Columbia	SEG8295	1963	**£6**	
You'll Never Walk Alone	LP	MFP	1153	1966	**£10**	

GESTURES

Title	Format	Label	Number	Year	Price	Notes
Run Run Run	7"	Stateside	SS379	1965	**£8**	

GEZA-X

Title	Format	Label	Number	Year	Price	Notes
We Need More Power	7"	Alt. Tentacles	VIRUS20	1982	**£4**	

GHERKIN, AMOS QUARTET

Title	Format	Label	Number	Year	Price	Notes
Theme From An Unmade Silent Movie	7"	Parlophone	R5872	1970	**£4**	

GHOST

Title	Format	Label	Number	Year	Price	Notes
I've Got To Get To Know You	7"	Gemini	GMS014	1970	**£15**	
When You're Dead	7"	Gemini	GMS007	1969	**£20**	
When You're Dead-One Second	LP	Gemini	GME1004	1970	**£40**	

GHOST DANCE

Title	Format	Label	Number	Year	Price	Notes
Gathering Dust	LP	Karbon	KARXL303		**£15**	
Grip Of Love	7"	Karbon	KAR604	1986	**£12**	
Grip Of Love	12"	Karbon	KAR604T	1986	**£12**	
Heart Full Of Soul	7"	Karbon	KAR606	1986	**£10**	promo
Heart Full of Soul	12"	Karbon	KAR606T	1986	**£12**	
River Of No Return	12"	Karbon	KAR602T	1986	**£12**	
Word To The Wise	12"	Karbon	KAR608T	1987	**£10**	

GIANT CRAB

Title	Format	Label	Number	Year	Price	Notes
Cool It Helios	LP	Uni	73057	1969	**£15**	
Giant Crab Comes Forth	LP	Uni	73037	1968	**£15**	US
Hot Line Conversation	7"	Uni	UN509	1968	**£4**	

GIANT SUNFLOWER

Title	Format	Label	Number	Year	Price	Notes
Big Apple	7"	CBS	2805	1967	**£8**	
Mark Twain	7"	CBS	3033	1967	**£10**	

GIBB, BARRY

Title	Format	Label	Number	Year	Price	Notes
I'll Kiss Your Memory	7"	Polydor	2058030	1970	**£4**	

GIBB, MAURICE

Title	Format	Label	Number	Year	Price	Notes
Railroad	7"	Polydor	2058013	1970	**£4**	
Sing A Rude Song	LP	Polydor		1970	**£20**	

GIBB, ROBIN

Title	Format	Label	Number	Year	Price	Notes
August October	7"	Polydor	56371	1970	**£4**	chart single
One Million Years	7"	Polydor	56368	1969	**£4**	

Robin's Reign	LP	Polydor	583085	1970	**£10**	
Saved By The Bell	7"	Polydor	56337	1969	**£4**	chart single

GIBBONS, STEVE

Short Stories	LP	Wizard	SWZA5501	1971	**£30**	

GIBBS, GEORGIA

Balling The Jack	7"	Vogue Coral	Q72088	1955	**£4**	
Great Balls Of Fire	7"	RCA	RCA1029	1958	**£4**	

GIBBS, MICHAEL

Just Ahead	LP	Polydor	2683011	1972	**£30**	double
Michael Gibbs	LP	Deram	SML1063	1970	**£50**	
Nairam	7"	Bronze	BRO21	1975	**£4**	
Tanglewood '63	LP	Deram	SML1087	1971	**£30**	

GIBBS, MIKE

Only Chrome-Waterfall Orchestra	LP	Bronze	ILPS9353	1975	**£10**	

GIBBS, MIKE & GARY BURTON

In The Public Interest	LP	Polydor	2383252	1974	**£10**	

GIBSON, BOB

Where I'm Bound	LP	Elektra		1966	**£10**	

GIBSON, DON

Blue And Lonesome	7" EP	RCA	RCX1050	1960	**£5**	
Lonesome Number One	7"	RCA	RCA1272	1962	**£4**	chart single
Look Who's Blue	LP	RCA	LPM2184	1960	**£10**	US
Look Who's Blue	7" EP	RCA	RCX213	1962	**£5**	
May You Never Be Alone	7" EP	RCA	RCX7122	1963	**£5**	
No One Stands Alone	LP	RCA	LPM1918	1959	**£10**	US
Oh Lonesome Me	LP	RCA	LPM1743	1958	**£15**	US
Oh Lonesome Me	7"	RCA	RCA1056	1958	**£4**	
Sea Of Heartbreak	7"	RCA	RCA1243	1961	**£4**	chart single
Songs By Don Gibson	LP	Lion	70069	1958	**£25**	US
Sweet Dreams	7"	MGM	SP1177	1956	**£6**	
Sweet Dreams	LP	RCA	LPM2269	1960	**£10**	US
That Gibson Boy	LP	RCA	LPM2038	1959	**£10**	US
That Gibson Boy	7" EP	RCA	RCX214	1962	**£5**	

GIBSON, STEVE & THE RED CAPS

Silhouettes	7"	HMV	POP417	1957	**£6**	
Steve Gibson And The Red Caps	LP-10"	Mercury	MG25116	195-	**£100**	US

GIBSON, WAYNE

Come On Let's Go	7"	Decca	F11800	1964	**£10**	
Ding Dong The Witch Is Dead	7"	Parlophone	R5357	1965	**£8**	
For No One	7"	Columbia	DB7998	1966	**£6**	
Kelly	7"	Pye	7N15680	1964	**£6**	chart single
Linda Lu	7"	Decca	F11713	1963	**£10**	
One Little Smile	7"	Columbia	DB7683	1965	**£8**	
Portland Town	7"	Pye	7N15798	1965	**£8**	
Under My Thumb	7"	Columbia	DB7911	1966	**£10**	

GIBSONS

Any Time	7"	CBS	202015	1965	**£4**	
Come Summertime	7"	CBS	202063	1966	**£4**	
Magic Book	7"	Deram	DM119	1967	**£4**	
Ode To A Doll's House	7"	Major Minor	MM547	1968	**£5**	
Two Kinds Of Lovers	7"	Deram	DM103	1966	**£4**	

GIDIAN

Feeling	7"	Columbia	DB8041	1966	**£8**	
Fight For Your Love	7"	Columbia	DB7916	1966	**£6**	
Try Me Out	7"	Columbia	DB7826	1966	**£6**	

GIFTED CHILDREN

Painting By Numbers	7"	Whaam!	WHAAM001	1981	**£20**	

GIGUERE, RUSS

Hexagram II	LP	W. Bros	WS1910	1971	**£15**	US

GILBERT & LEWIS

Title	Format	Label	Cat. No.	Year	Price	Notes
Drop	7"	Dome	DOM45	1980	**£4**	
Ends With The Sea	7"	4AD	AD106	1981	**£4**	

GILES,GILES & FRIPP

Although this is the group that evolved into King Crimson, little of the music on "Cheerful Insanity" sounds much like that produced by any King Crimson line-up. Instead, much of it is of the novelty-song variety, with flat "English" vocals conveying lyrics that aim to be whimsical, but which mostly sound embarassing. The record is certainly distinctive, however, and in places Robert Fripp does reveal himself to be a highly talented guitarist, even if conveying no hint that he would ever become a major influence within seventies rock.

Title	Format	Label	Cat. No.	Year	Price	Notes
Cheerful Insanity Of...	LP	Deram	DML1022	1968	**£40**	
One In A Million	7"	Deram	DM188	1968	**£30**	
Thursday Morning	7"	Deram	DM210	1968	**£30**	

GILGAMESH

Title	Format	Label	Cat. No.	Year	Price	Notes
Gilgamesh	LP	Caroline	CA2007	1975	**£12**	

GILKYSON, TERRY & THE EASYRIDERS

Title	Format	Label	Cat. No.	Year	Price	Notes
Lonesome Rider	7" EP	Fontana	TFE17327	1960	**£5**	
Marianne	7"	Philips	JK1007	1958	**£8**	
Remember The Alamo	LP	London	HAR2323	1961	**£12**	
Rolling	LP	London	HAR2301	1961	**£12**	mono
Rolling	LP	London	SAHR6111	1961	**£12**	stereo
Rolling	7" EP	London	RER1333	1961	**£6**	
Strolling Blues	7" EP	Fontana	TFE17326	1960	**£5**	

GILLAN, IAN

Title	Format	Label	Cat. No.	Year	Price	Notes
Child In Time	LP	Oyster	2490136	1976	**£10**	
Magic	LP	Virgin	VP2238	1982	**£10**	pic disc
Restless	7"	Virgin	VSY465	1982	**£4**	pic disc

GILLESPIE, DANA

Title	Format	Label	Cat. No.	Year	Price	Notes
Ain't Gonna Play No Second Fiddle	LP	RCA	APLI0682	1974	**£10**	
Andy Warhol	7"	RCA	RCA2446	1974	**£8**	
Box Of Surprises	LP	Decca	SKL5012	1969	**£15**	
Donna Donna	7"	Pye	7N15872	1965	**£6**	
Pay You Back With Interest	7"	Pye	7N17280	1967	**£6**	
Thank You Boy	7"	Pye	7N15962	1965	**£6**	
Weren't Born A Man	LP	RCA	APLI0354	1973	**£10**	
You Gotta Know My Mind	7"	Decca	F12847	1968	**£5**	

GILLEY, MICKEY

Title	Format	Label	Cat. No.	Year	Price	Notes
Lonely Wine	LP	Astro	101	1964	**£180**	US

GILMER, JIMMY

Title	Format	Label	Cat. No.	Year	Price	Notes
Ain't Gonna Tell Nobody	7"	London	HLD9872	1964	**£4**	
Buddy's Buddy	LP	Dot	DLP3577	1964	**£20**	US
Campusology	LP	Dot	DLP3709	1966	**£12**	US
Daisy Petal Picking	7"	London	HLD9827	1964	**£4**	
Firewater	LP	Dot	DLP25856	1968	**£12**	US
Folkbeat	LP	Dot	DLP3668	1965	**£12**	US
I'm Gonna Go Walkin'	7"	London	HLD9632	1962	**£4**	
Look At Me	7"	London	HLD9898	1964	**£4**	
Lucky 'Leven	LP	Dot	DLP3643	1965	**£12**	US
She Belongs To Me	7"	Stateside	SS472	1965	**£4**	
Sugar Shack	LP	London	HAD8150	1964	**£15**	
Sugar Shack	7"	London	HLD9789	1963	**£4**	chart single
Thunder 'N' Lightnin'	7"	Stateside	SS418	1965	**£4**	
Torquay	LP	Dot	DLP3512	1963	**£15**	US

GILMOUR, DAVID

Title	Format	Label	Cat. No.	Year	Price	Notes
Love On The Air	12"	Harvest	HARP5229	1984	**£6**	pic disc

GILTRAP, GORDON

Title	Format	Label	Cat. No.	Year	Price	Notes
Giltrap	LP	Philips	6308175	1973	**£20**	
Portrait	LP	Transatlantic	TRA202	1969	**£15**	
Testament Of Time	LP	MCA	MKPS2020	1971	**£20**	

GINGER JUG BAND

Title	Format	Label	Cat. No.	Year	Price	Notes
Ginger Jug Band	LP	private			**£40**	

GINHOUSE

Title	Format	Label	Cat. No.	Year	Price	Notes
Ginhouse	LP	B&C	CAS1031	1971	**£30**	

GINO & GINA

Title	Format	Label	Cat. No.	Year	Price	Notes
Pretty Baby	7"	Mercury	7MT230	1958	**£6**	

GINSBERG, ALLEN

Title	Format	Label	Cat. No.	Year	Price	Notes
Allen Ginsberg Reads Kaddish	LP	Atlantic	4001	1966	**£15**	US
At The ICA	LP	Saga		1967	**£20**	
G Thing	LP	Douglas		1968	**£20**	US
Howl And Other Poems	LP	Fantasy	7006	1959	**£25**	US, red vinyl
Songs Of Innocence And Experience	LP	Forecast	FVS3083	1969	**£15**	US

GIRL

Title	Format	Label	Cat. No.	Year	Price	Notes
My Number	7"	Jet	159	1979	**£8**	clear vinyl & sleeve
Thru The Twilite	7"	Jet	JETP7014	1981	**£5**	pic disc

GIRLS TOGETHER OUTRAGEOUSLY

Title	Format	Label	Cat. No.	Year	Price	Notes
Permanent Damage	LP	Straight	STS1059	1969	**£40**	

GIRLSCHOOL

Title	Format	Label	Cat. No.	Year	Price	Notes
Take It All Away	7"	City	NIK6	1979	**£6**	

GLADIATORS

Title	Format	Label	Cat. No.	Year	Price	Notes
Bleak House	7"	HMV	POP1134	1963	**£8**	

GLADIATORS (2)

Title	Format	Label	Cat. No.	Year	Price	Notes
Girl Don't Make Me Wait	7"	Direction	583854	1968	**£4**	

GLADIOLAS

Title	Format	Label	Cat. No.	Year	Price	Notes
Little Darling	7"	London	HLO8435	1957	**£20**	

GLADSTONE

Title	Format	Label	Cat. No.	Year	Price	Notes
Gladstone	LP	Probe	SPBA6264	1972	**£10**	

GLASER, TOMPALL

Title	Format	Label	Cat. No.	Year	Price	Notes
Land - Folk Songs	LP	Decca	DL4041	1960	**£10**	US

GLASS HARP

Title	Format	Label	Cat. No.	Year	Price	Notes
Glass Harp	LP	MCA	MUPS431	1972	**£12**	
It Makes Me Glad	LP	MCA	MUPS470	1973	**£10**	
Synergy	LP	MCA	MUPS449	1972	**£12**	

GLASS MENAGERIE

Title	Format	Label	Cat. No.	Year	Price	Notes
Do My Thing Myself	7"	Polydor	56341	1969	**£6**	
Frederick Jordan	7"	Pye	7N17615	1968	**£8**	
Have You Forgotten Who You Are	7"	Polydor	56318	1969	**£6**	
She's A Rainbow	7"	Pye	7N17518	1968	**£6**	
You Didn't Have To Be So Nice	7"	Pye	7N17568	1968	**£6**	

GLASS, PHILIP

Title	Format	Label	Cat. No.	Year	Price	Notes
Music In Fifths/Music In Similar Motion	LP	Chatham Sq.	LP1003		**£20**	
Music With Changing Parts	LP	Chatham Sq.	LP1001/2		**£30**	double
Two Pages	LP	Folkways	FTS33902		**£10**	
Two Pages	LP	Shandar	83515		**£10**	

GLENCOE

Title	Format	Label	Cat. No.	Year	Price	Notes
Glencoe	LP	Epic	65207	1972	**£10**	
Spirit Of Glencoe	LP	Epic	65717	1973	**£10**	

GLENN, LLOYD

Title	Format	Label	Cat. No.	Year	Price	Notes
Chica Boo	LP	Aladdin	808	1956	**£30**	US
Chica Boo	LP	Aladdin	808	1956	**£100**	US, red vinyl

GLITTER, GARY

Title	Format	Label	Cat. No.	Year	Price	Notes
Another Rock'n'Roll Christmas	7"	Arista	ARISD592	1984	**£4**	shaped pic disc, plinth
Dance Me Up	7"	Arista	ARISD570	1984	**£4**	pic disc
Love Comes	7"	Arista	ARISD615	1985	**£4**	pic disc
Shout! Shout! Shout!	7"	Arista	ARICV586	1984	**£4**	mirror disc

GLOBAL VILLAGE TRUCKING CO.

Title	Format	Label	Cat. No.	Year	Price	Notes
Global Village Trucking Co.	LP	Caroline	C1516	1976	**£10**	

GLOBE SHOW

Title	Format	Label	Cat. No.	Year	Price	Notes
Yes Or No	7"	Page One	POF128	1969	**£4**	

GLOOMYS

Title	Format	Label	Cat. No.	Year	Price	Notes
Daybreak	7"	Columbia	DB8391	1968	**£8**	

GLORIES

Title	Format	Label	Cat. No.	Year	Price	Notes
I Love You But Give Me My Freedom	7"	Direction	583084	1967	**£4**	
I Stand Accused	7"	CBS	2736	1967	**£8**	
My Sweet Sweet Baby	7"	Direction	583646	1968	**£4**	
Sing Me A Love Song	7"	Direction	583300	1968	**£4**	

GLOVE

Title	Format	Label	Cat. No.	Year	Price	Notes
Blue Sunshine	LP	Wonderland	SHELP2	1983	**£12**	chart LP
Like An Animal	7"	Wonderland	SHE3	1983	**£12**	chart single
Like An Animal	12"	Wonderland	SHEX3	1983	**£15**	
Punish Me With Kisses	7"	Wonderland	SHE5	1983	**£15**	

GLOVER, ROGER

Title	Format	Label	Cat. No.	Year	Price	Notes
Butterfly Ball	LP	Purple	TPSA7514	1974	**£10**	
Love Is All	7"	Purple	PUR125	1974	**£4**	

GNIDROLOG

Title	Format	Label	Cat. No.	Year	Price	Notes
In Spite Of Harry's Toenail	LP	RCA	SF8261	1971	**£25**	
Lady Lake	LP	RCA	SF8322	1972	**£60**	

GNOMES OF ZURICH

Title	Format	Label	Cat. No.	Year	Price	Notes
Hang On Baby	7"	CBS	202556	1967	**£5**	
High Hopes	7"	CBS	2694	1967	**£4**	
Please Mr.Sun	7"	Planet	PLF121	1966	**£8**	
Second Fiddle	7"	RCA	RCA1606	1967	**£6**	

GO-BETWEENS

Title	Format	Label	Cat. No.	Year	Price	Notes
I Need Two Heads	7"	Postcard	80-4	1980	**£8**	white or brown sleeves

GO-GO'S

Title	Format	Label	Cat. No.	Year	Price	Notes
Automatic	7"	Initial	IRS101	1981	**£5**	pic disc
Our Lips Are Sealed	7"	IRS	PFP1007	1981	**£6**	pink vinyl
Our Lips Are Sealed	7"	IRS	PFP1007	1981	**£5**	pink vinyl
We Got The Beat	7"	IRS	PFP1010	1981	**£4**	
We Got The Beat	7"	Stiff	BUY78	1980	**£6**	

GOBBLEDEGOOKS

Title	Format	Label	Cat. No.	Year	Price	Notes
Where Have You been	7"	Decca	F12023	1964	**£10**	

GOBLIN

Title	Format	Label	Cat. No.	Year	Price	Notes
Suspiria	LP	EMI	EMC3222	1977	**£10**	

GODARD, VIC & SUBWAY SECT

Title	Format	Label	Cat. No.	Year	Price	Notes
Ambition	7"	Rough Trade	RT007	1979	**£5**	
Nobody's Scared	7"	Braik	BRS01	1978	**£5**	
Stop That Girl	7"	Rough Trade	RT068	1981	**£4**	

GODCHAUX, KEITH & DONNA

Title	Format	Label	Cat. No.	Year	Price	Notes
Keith And Donna Godchaux	LP	Round	RX104	1975	**£10**	

GODDARD, GEOFF

Title	Format	Label	Cat. No.	Year	Price	Notes
Girl Bride	7"	HMV	POP938	1961	**£8**	
My Little Girl's Come Home	7"	HMV	POP1068	1962	**£8**	
Saturday Dance	7"	HMV	POP1160	1963	**£8**	
Sky Man	7"	HMV	POP1213	1963	**£30**	

GODFREY, ROBERT JOHN

To all intents and purposes, Robert John Godfrey is the Enid. His solo album is effectively the first Enid album, therefore, and the hardest to find of the fully released series as it has not been reissued.

Title	Format	Label	Cat. No.	Year	Price	Notes
Fall Of Hyperion	LP	Charisma	CAS1084	1974	**£20**	

GODLEY & CREME

Title	Format	Label	Cat. No.	Year	Price	Notes
Consequences	LP	Mercury	CONS017	1977	**£15**	triple, boxed
Consequences	LP	Mercury	LKP1001	1977	**£15**	promo
Consequences	7"	Mercury	SAMP017	1977	**£6**	promo dble

GODS

Ken Hensley, the leader of Uriah Heep, began his career as a member of The Gods. The original line-up also included guitarist Mick Taylor, although no records were made (unless the Polydor single, listed as being by a different Gods, is in fact this group?). The 1976 release is a compilation LP - the Gods broke up in 1969.

Baby's Rich	7"	Columbia	DB8486	1968	**£8**	
Genesis	LP	Columbia	SCX6286	1968	**£40**	
Gods	LP	Harvest	SHSM2011	1976	**£10**	
Hey Bulldog	7"	Columbia	DB8544	1969	**£10**	
Maria	7"	Columbia	DB8572	1969	**£8**	
To Samuel A Son	LP	Columbia	SCX6372	1970	**£40**	

GODS (2)

Come On Down To My Boat Baby	7"	Polydor	56168	1967	**£10**	

GODZ

Contact High	LP	Fontana	STL5500	1967	**£15**	
Godz 2	LP	Fontana	STL5512	1969	**£15**	
Godzundheit	LP	ESP	2017	1970	**£15**	US
Third Testament	LP	ESP	1077	1969	**£15**	US

GOINS, HERBIE & NIGHT-TIMERS

Incredible Miss Brown	7"	Parlophone	R5533	1966	**£8**	
Number One In Your Heart	LP	Parlophone	PMC7026	1967	**£30**	
Number One in Your Heart	7"	Parlophone	R5478	1966	**£15**	

GOLDBERG, BARRY

Another Day	7"	Pye	7N25465	1968	**£4**	
Blast From My Past	LP	Polydor	2318938	1974	**£10**	
Blowing My Mind	LP	Epic	LN24199	1966	**£15**	US
Reunion	LP	Pye	NSPL28116	1968	**£15**	
Two Jews Blues	LP	Buddah	203020	1969	**£12**	

GOLDEN APPLES OF THE SUN

Monkey Time	7"	Decca	F12194	1965	**£12**	
Monkey Time	7"	Immediate	IM010	1965	**£15**	

GOLDEN CRUSADERS

Hey Good Looking	7"	Columbia	DB7357	1964	**£8**	
I Don't Care	7"	Columbia	DB7485	1965	**£8**	
I'm In Love With You	7"	Columbia	DB7232	1964	**£10**	

GOLDEN DAWN

Power Plant	LP	Int. Artists	IA4	1967	**£35**	US

GOLDEN EARRING

Another Forty-Five Miles	7"	Major Minor	MM679	1970	**£8**	
Candy's Going Bad	7"	Track	2094126	1974	**£5**	
Ce Soir	7"	Track	2094130	1975	**£4**	
Eight Miles High	LP	Major Minor	SM65	1969	**£20**	
Eight Miles High	LP	Polydor	658900	1969	**£15**	
Golden Earring	LP	Polydor	2482329	197-	**£15**	
Hearing Earring	LP	Track	2406109	1973	**£12**	
Instant Poetry	7"	Track	2094121	1974	**£5**	
It's Alright But It Could Be Better	7"	Major Minor	MM633	1969	**£8**	
Just A Little Bit Of Peace	7"	Major Minor	MM601	1969	**£8**	
Just Earring	LP	Polydor	736007	1964	**£25**	Dutch
Miracle Mirror	LP	Polydor	1236283		**£20**	Dutch
Moontan	LP	Track	2406112	1973	**£10**	chart LP
On The Double	LP	Polydor	2653001		**£35**	Dutch double
Radar Love	12"	Polydor	2121335	1977	**£6**	
Radar Love	7"	Track	2094116	1973	**£4**	chart single
Seven Tears	LP	Polydor	2310135	1971	**£15**	
That Day	7"	Polydor	56514	1970	**£10**	
Together	LP	Polydor	2310210	1972	**£15**	
Winter Harvest	LP	Polydor	736068	196-	**£25**	Dutch

GOLDEN FLEECE

Athens 6a.m.	7"	Decca	F12669	1967	**£4**	

GOLDENROD

Goldenrod	LP	Chartmaker	CSG1101	1968	**£70**	US

GOLDIE

Title	Format	Label	Cat. No.	Year	Price	Notes
Going Back	7"	Immediate	IM026	1966	**£12**	
I Do	7"	Fontana	TF693	1966	**£8**	

GOLDIE & THE GINGERBREADS

Title	Format	Label	Cat. No.	Year	Price	Notes
Can't You Hear My Heartbeat	7"	Decca	F12070	1965	**£6**	chart single
Sailor Boy	7"	Decca	F12199	1965	**£4**	
That's Why I Love You	7"	Decca	F12126	1965	**£6**	

GOLDSBORO, BOBBY

Title	Format	Label	Cat. No.	Year	Price	Notes
Autumn Of My Life	7"	United Artists	UP2223	1968	**£4**	
Bobby Goldsboro Album	LP	United Artists	UAL3358	1964	**£10**	US
I Can't Stop Loving You	LP	United Artists	UAL3381	1964	**£10**	US
Little Things	LP	United Artists	UAL3425	1965	**£10**	US
Little Things	7" EP	United Artists	UEP1006	1965	**£5**	
Take Your Love	7"	United Artists	UP1146	1966	**£10**	
Talented Bobby Goldsboro	7" EP	United Artists	UEP1016	1966	**£5**	
Too Many People	7"	United Artists	UP1177	1967	**£8**	

GOLIATH

Title	Format	Label	Cat. No.	Year	Price	Notes
Goliath	LP	CBS	64229	1970	**£20**	
Port And Lemon Lady	7"	CBS	5312	1971	**£6**	

GOLLIWOGS

Title	Format	Label	Cat. No.	Year	Price	Notes
Brown-Eyed Girl	7"	Vocalion	VF9266	1966	**£20**	
Fight Fire	7"	Vocalion	VF9283	1967	**£20**	
Golliwogs	LP	Fantasy	FAN5996	1975	**£10**	

GONG

Title	Format	Label	Cat. No.	Year	Price	Notes
Angel's Egg	LP	Virgin	V2007	1973	**£30**	with book
Camembert Electrique	LP	Byg	529353	1971	**£20**	French, with insert
Continental Circus	LP	Philips	6332033	1971	**£20**	
Flying Teapot	LP	Virgin	V2002	1973	**£10**	
Magick Brother	LP	Byg	529029	1970	**£30**	French
Magick Brother	LP	Byg	5293305	1970	**£25**	French

GONKS

Title	Format	Label	Cat. No.	Year	Price	Notes
That's All Right Mama	7"	Decca	F11984	1964	**£4**	

GONZALEZ, BELLE

Title	Format	Label	Cat. No.	Year	Price	Notes
Belle	LP	Columbia		1971	**£15**	

GOOD EARTH

Title	Format	Label	Cat. No.	Year	Price	Notes
It's Hard Rock And All That	LP	Saga	FID2112	1968	**£12**	

GOOD MISSIONARIES

Title	Format	Label	Cat. No.	Year	Price	Notes
Fire From Heaven	LP	Deptford F. C.	DLP04	1979	**£12**	

GOOD RATS

Title	Format	Label	Cat. No.	Year	Price	Notes
Hobo	7"	London	HLR10237	1969	**£4**	

GOOD SHIP LOLLIPOP

Title	Format	Label	Cat. No.	Year	Price	Notes
Maxwell's Silver Hammer	7"	Ember	EMBS276	1970	**£6**	

GOOD THUNDER

Title	Format	Label	Cat. No.	Year	Price	Notes
Good Thunder	LP	Elektra	K42123	1972	**£10**	

GOOD TIME LOVERS

Title	Format	Label	Cat. No.	Year	Price	Notes
Trafalgar Square	7"	Fontana	TF791	1967	**£5**	

GOODHAND-TAIT, PHILIP

Title	Format	Label	Cat. No.	Year	Price	Notes
Good Old Phil's	LP	Gundog	GUNLP1	1980	**£10**	
I'll Write A Song	LP	DJM	DJLPS416	1971	**£15**	
I'm Gonna Put Some Hurt On You	7"	Parlophone	R5448	1966	**£8**	
Jingle Jangle Man	LP	DJM	DJLPS453	1975	**£12**	
Love Has Got A Hold On Me	7"	Decca	F12868	1969	**£6**	
No Problem	7"	Parlophone	R5498	1966	**£8**	
Oceans Away	LP	Chrysalis	CHR1113	1976	**£10**	
Philip Goodhand-Tait	LP	DJM	DJLPS432	1973	**£12**	
Rehearsal	LP	DJM	DJLPS411	1971	**£15**	
Songfall	LP	DJM	DJLPS425	1972	**£15**	
Teaching An Old Dog	LP	Chrysalis	CHR1146	1977	**£10**	

Title	Format	Label	Number	Year	Price	Notes
You Can't Take Love	7"	Parlophone	R5547	1966	**£8**	

GOODISON, JOHNNY

Title	Format	Label	Number	Year	Price	Notes
Little Understanding	7"	Deram	DM319	1970	**£4**	

GOODMAN, DAVE

Title	Format	Label	Number	Year	Price	Notes
Justifiable Homicide	7"	The Label	TLR008	1978	**£4**	red vinyl
Justifiable Homicide	7"	The Label	TLR008	1978	**£30**	Steve & Paul Jones credit

GOODMAN, STEVE

Title	Format	Label	Number	Year	Price	Notes
Somebody Else's Trouble	LP	Buddah	BDLP4019	1973	**£10**	
Steve Goodman	LP	Buddah	BDLH5007	1972	**£10**	

GOOFERS

Title	Format	Label	Number	Year	Price	Notes
Dipsy Doodle	7"	Vogue Coral	Q72289	1957	**£8**	
Flip Flop And Fly	7"	Vogue Coral	Q72074	1955	**£15**	
Goofie Dry Bones	7"	Vogue Coral	Q72094	1955	**£6**	
Hearts Of Stone	7"	Vogue Coral	Q72051	1955	**£15**	
Push Push Push Cart	7"	Vogue Coral	Q72267	1957	**£6**	
Sick Sick Sick	7"	Vogue Coral	Q72124	1956	**£8**	
Tennessee Rock And Roll	7"	Vogue Coral	Q72171	1956	**£8**	

GOONS

Title	Format	Label	Number	Year	Price	Notes
Best Of The Goon Shows	LP	Parlophone	PMC1108	1959	**£10**	chart LP
Best Of The Goon Shows No.2	LP	Parlophone	PMC1129	1960	**£10**	chart LP
Eeh Ah Oh Oooh	7"	Decca	F10885	1957	**£5**	
Goons	7" EP	Decca	DFE6396	1956	**£6**	
I'm Walking Backwards For Christmas	7"	Decca	F10756	1956	**£5**	chart single
Russian Love Song	7"	Decca	F10945	1957	**£5**	
Unchained Melodies	LP-10"	Decca	LF1332	1964	**£15**	
Ying Tong Song	7"	Decca	F10780	1956	**£5**	chart single

GOPAL, SAM

Title	Format	Label	Number	Year	Price	Notes
Sam Gopal	LP	Stable	SLE8001	1969	**£60**	

GORDAN, RABBI JOSEPH (JULIAN COPE)

Title	Format	Label	Number	Year	Price	Notes
Competition	7"	Bam Caruso	NRICO30	1984	**£8**	

GORDON, ROSCOE

Title	Format	Label	Number	Year	Price	Notes
Just A Little Bit	7"	Stateside	SS204	1963	**£6**	
Just A Little Bit	7"	Top Rank	JAR332	1960	**£8**	
Keep On Doggin'	7"	Vocalion	VP9245	1965	**£8**	
No More Doggin'	7"	Island	WI272	1966	**£8**	
Surely I Love You	7"	Island	WI256	1965	**£8**	

GORE, LESLEY

Title	Format	Label	Number	Year	Price	Notes
All About Love	LP	Mercury	20076MCL	1965	**£12**	
Boys Boys Boys	LP	Mercury	20020MCL	1964	**£12**	
California Nights	LP	Mercury	MG21120	1967	**£12**	US
Girl Talk	LP	Mercury	20033MCL	1964	**£12**	
Golden Hits	LP	Mercury	MG21024	1965	**£10**	US
Golden Hits Vol.2	LP	Mercury	SR61185	1968	**£12**	US
I Don't Wanna Be A Loser	7"	Mercury	MF821	1964	**£4**	
I Won't Love You Any More	7"	Mercury	MF889	1965	**£4**	
I'll Cry If I Want To	LP	Mercury	MMC14127	1963	**£15**	
It's My Party	7"	Mercury	AMT1205	1963	**£4**	chart single
Judy's Turn To Cry	7"	Mercury	AMT1210	1963	**£4**	
Lesley Gore	7" EP	Mercury	10017MCE	1964	**£6**	
Look Of Love	7"	Mercury	MF846	1965	**£4**	
Maybe I Know	7"	Mercury	MF829	1964	**£4**	chart single
My Town, My Guy And Me	7"	Mercury	MF872	1965	**£10**	
My Town, My Guy And Me	LP	Mercury	20071MCL	1965	**£12**	
She's A Fool	7"	Mercury	AMT1213	1963	**£4**	
Sings Of Mixed-Up Hearts	LP	Mercury	20001MCL	1963	**£12**	
Sometimes I Wish I Were A Boy	7"	Mercury	MF837	1964	**£4**	
Sunshine, Lollipops And Rainbows	7"	Mercury	MF862	1965	**£4**	
That's The Way Boys Are	7"	Mercury	MF810	1964	**£4**	
You Don't Own Me	7"	Mercury	MF803	1964	**£4**	
Young Love	7"	Mercury	MF902	1966	**£4**	

GORME, EYDIE

Title	Format	Label	Number	Year	Price	Notes
Blame It On The Bossa Nova	7"	CBS	AAG131	1963	**£4**	chart single

Everybody Go Home	7"	CBS	202470	1967	**£4**	
Love Me Forever	7"	HMV	POP432	1958	**£4**	chart single
Yes My Darling Daughter	7"	CBS	AAG105	1962	**£4**	chart single

GOSPEL GARDEN

Finders Keepers	7"	Camp	602006	1968	**£8**	

GOSPEL OAK

Brown Haired Girl	7"	UNI	UNS527	1970	**£5**	
Gospel Oak	LP	Uni	UNLS113	1970	**£15**	

GOTHENBURG, FREDA

Like A Dream	7"	GHM	GHM1	1979	**£4**	plays from centre out!

GOTHIC HORIZON

Jason Lodge Poetry Book	LP	Argo	ZFB26	1970	**£40**	
Tomorrow Is Another Day	LP	Argo	ZDA150	1972	**£30**	

GOULDMAN, GRAHAM

Graham Gouldman Thing	LP	RCA	LPS3954	1968	**£20**	US
Nowhere To Go	7"	CBS	7739	1972	**£6**	
Stop Stop Stop	7"	Decca	F12334	1966	**£15**	
Upstairs Downstairs	7"	RCA	RCA1667	1968	**£12**	
Windmills Of Your Mind	7"	Spark	SRL1026	1969	**£8**	

GOVE

Dead Letter Blues	7"	London	HLE10295	1969	**£8**	

GRABHAM, MICK

Mick The Lad	LP	United Artists	UAS29341	1972	**£20**	

GRACIE, CHARLIE

Angel Of Love	7"	Coral	Q72373	1959	**£6**	
Butterfly	7"	Parlophone	R4290	1957	**£12**	chart single
Cool Baby	7"	London	HLU8521	1957	**£8**	chart single
Crazy Girl	7"	London	HLU8596	1958	**£8**	
Doodlebug	7"	Coral	Q72362	1959	**£6**	
Fabulous	7"	Parlophone	R4313	1957	**£15**	chart single
Fabulous Charlie Gracie	7" EP	Parlophone	GEP8630	1957	**£20**	
He'll Never Love You Like I Do	7"	Stateside	SS402	1965	**£20**	
Night And Day USA	7"	London	HLU9603	1962	**£4**	
Oh Well-a	7"	Coral	Q72381	1959	**£6**	
Race	7"	Columbia	DB4477	1960	**£6**	
Wandering Eyes	7"	London	HL8467	1957	**£10**	chart single

GRACIOUS

Gracious	LP	Vertigo	6360002	1970	**£50**	spiral label
Once On A Windy Day	7"	Polydor	56333	1968	**£25**	
This Is...	LP	Philips	6382004	1972	**£60**	

GRADUATE

Rock musicians whose respected careers start from shakey beginnings have difficulty forgetting the fact when they are unwise enough to commit them to vinyl. Two of the grinning mod revivalists on the cover of the Graduate LP are Roland Orzabel and Curt Smith, later of Tears For Fears. The extraordinary perfectionism applied to the recording of the "Seeds Of Love" album shows how these two like to be taken seriously. With Graduate's forgettable music in their past, however, it is hard.

Acting My Age	LP	Precision	PART1	1980	**£10**	
Ambition	7"	Precision	PAR111	1980	**£6**	
Elvis Should Play Ska	7"	Precision	PAR100	1980	**£6**	no PS
Ever Met A Day	7"	Precision	PAR104	1980	**£6**	
Shut Up	7"	Precision	PAR117	1981	**£6**	no PS
Troubled Son	7"	Graduate	GRAD1	1981	**£6**	

GRAHAM, BILLY & THE ESCALATORS

Ooh-Poo-Pah-Doo	7"	Atlantic	584073	1967	**£4**	

GRAHAM, BOBBY

The two singles released by drummer Bobby Graham were actually co-recordings with guitarist Jimmy Page, which explains their high value.

Skin Deep	7"	Fontana	TF521	1965	**£60**	
Teensville	7"	Fontana	TF667	1966	**£60**	

GRAHAM, CHICK & THE COASTERS

Title	Format	Label	Cat. No.	Year	Price	Notes
Dance Baby Dance	7"	Decca	F11932	1964	**£8**	
Education	7"	Decca	F11859	1964	**£8**	

GRAHAM, DAVEY

Title	Format	Label	Cat. No.	Year	Price	Notes
All That Moody	LP	Eron		1976	**£30**	
Both Sides Now	7"	Decca	F12841	1968	**£6**	
Complete Guitarist	LP	Kicking Mule	SNKF138	1978	**£10**	
Dance For Two People	LP	Kicking Mule	SNKF158	1979	**£10**	
Folk Blues And Beyond	LP	Decca	LK4649	1964	**£35**	
Folk Roots New Routes	LP	Decca	LK4652	1964	**£30**	
From A London Hootenanny	7" EP	Decca	DFE8538	1963	**£8**	
Godington Boundary	LP	President	PTLS1039	1970	**£20**	
Guitar Player	LP	Golden Guin	GGL0224	1962	**£25**	
Hat	LP	Decca	SKL5011	1969	**£20**	
Holly Kaleidoscope	LP	Decca	SKL5056	1970	**£20**	
Large As Life And Twice As Natural	LP	Decca	SKL4969	1968	**£20**	
Midnight Man	LP	Decca	LK4780	1966	**£25**	

GRAHAM, DAVEY & ALEXIS KORNER

Title	Format	Label	Cat. No.	Year	Price	Notes
3/4 AD	7" EP	Topic	TOP70		**£30**	

GRAHAM, ERNIE

Title	Format	Label	Cat. No.	Year	Price	Notes
Ernie Graham	LP	Liberty	LBS83485	1971	**£30**	

GRAHAM, LOU

Title	Format	Label	Cat. No.	Year	Price	Notes
Wee Willie Brown	7"	Coral	Q72322	1958	**£20**	

GRAMMER, BILLY

Title	Format	Label	Cat. No.	Year	Price	Notes
Billy Grammer Hits	7" EP	Felsted	GEP1005	1959	**£8**	
Gotta Travel On	7"	London	HLU8752	1958	**£4**	
Kissing Tree	7"	Felsted	AF121	1959	**£4**	
Rainbow Round My Shoulder	7"	Brunswick	05851	1961	**£4**	
Travellin' On	LP	Monument	MLP4000	1961	**£15**	US
Willy, Quit Your Playing	7"	Felsted	AF128	1959	**£4**	

GRANAHAN, GERRY

Title	Format	Label	Cat. No.	Year	Price	Notes
It Hurts	7"	Top Rank	JAR262	1960	**£4**	
No Chemise Please	7"	London	HL8668	1958	**£8**	

GRAND FUNK RAILROAD

Following in the footsteps of such American groups as Iron Butterfly and Blue Cheer, Grand Funk Railroad presented a form of heavy metal in which loud excess took precedence over everything - certainly over genuine instrumental skill. The group's approach must have appealed to Frank Zappa's sense of kitsch, however, for he produced an album for them, calling it "Good Singing, Good Playing" - and he played guitar on the record as well.

Title	Format	Label	Cat. No.	Year	Price	Notes
All The Girls In The World Beware	LP	Capitol	11356	1975	**£15**	
Bad Time	7"	Capitol	CL15816	1975	**£4**	
Born To Die	LP	Capitol	11482	1976	**£15**	
Can You Do It	7"	EMI	EMI523	1976	**£4**	
Caught In The Act	LP	Capitol	ESTSP15	1975	**£20**	double
Closer To Home	LP	Capitol	EST471	1970	**£15**	
Closer To Home	7"	Capitol	CL15661	1970	**£4**	
E Pluribus Funk	LP	Capitol	EAS853	1972	**£15**	
Feelin' Alright	7"	Capitol	CL15683	1971	**£4**	
Footstompin' Music	7"	Capitol	CL15709	1972	**£4**	
Gimme Shelter	7"	Capitol	CL15694	1971	**£4**	
Good Singing,Good Playing	LP	EMI	1503	1976	**£15**	
Grand Funk	LP	Capitol	EST406	1970	**£15**	
Heartbreaker	7"	Capitol	CL15632	1970	**£4**	
Hits	LP	Capitol	11579	1977	**£12**	
I Can Feel Him In The Morning	7"	Capitol	CL15689	1971	**£4**	
Inside Looking Out	7"	Capitol	CL15668	1971	**£4**	chart single
Live	LP	Capitol	EST633	1971	**£20**	double
Loco-motion	7"	Capitol	CL15780	1974	**£4**	
Mark,Don,& Mel 1969-71	LP	Capitol	ESTSP10	1972	**£15**	double
On Time	LP	Capitol	EST307	1969	**£15**	
People Let's Stop The War	7"	Capitol	CL15705	1971	**£4**	
Phoenix	LP	Capitol	11099	1973	**£15**	
Rock'n'Roll Soul	7"	Capitol	CL15738	1972	**£4**	
Shinin' On	LP	Capitol	11278	1974	**£15**	
Shinin' On	7"	Capitol	CL15789	1974	**£4**	

Some Kind Of Wonderful	7"	Capitol	CL15805	1975	**£4**	
Survival	LP	Capitol	ESW764	1971	**£15**	
Upsetter	7"	Capitol	CL15720	1972	**£4**	
Walk Like A Man	7"	Capitol	CL15771	1973	**£4**	
We're An American Band	LP	Capitol	SMAS11207	1973	**£15**	
We're An American Band	LP	Capitol	SMAS11207	1973	**£20**	US, yellow vinyl
We're An American Band	7"	Capitol	CL15760	1973	**£4**	

GRANDFATHER

Dear Mr.Time	LP	Square		1970	**£55**	

GRANDMA'S ROCKERS

Homemade Apple Pie	LP	Fredlo	6727	1967	**£240**	US

GRANNY'S INTENTIONS

Hilda The Builder	7"	Deram	DM214	1968	**£10**	
Honest Injun	LP	Deram	SML1060	1970	**£25**	
Julie Don't Love Me Anymore	7"	Deram	DM184	1968	**£10**	
Story Of David	7"	Deram	DM158	1967	**£12**	
Take Me Back	7"	Deram	DM293	1970	**£8**	

GRANT, EARL

Earl Grant	7" EP	Brunswick	OE9460	1960	**£6**	
Stand By Me	7"	Brunswick	05945	1965	**£5**	

GRANT, ERKEY & THE EARWIGS

I'm A Hog For You	7"	Pye	7N15521	1963	**£15**	

GRANT, GOGI

If You Want To Get To Heaven - Shout!	LP	London	HAG2242	1960	**£12**	mono
If You Want To Get To Heaven - Shout!	LP	London	SAHG6072	1960	**£12**	stereo
Suddenly There's A Valley	7"	London	HLB8192	1955	**£8**	
Suddenly There's Gogi Grant	LP	London	HAB2032	1957	**£12**	
Wayward Wind	7"	London	HLB8282	1956	**£6**	chart single
We Believe In Love	7"	London	HLB8257	1956	**£6**	
You're In Love	7"	London	HLB8364	1957	**£6**	

GRANT, JULIE

Baby Baby	7"	Pye	7N15756	1965	**£4**	
Come To Me	7"	Pye	7N15684	1964	**£4**	chart single
Count On Me	7"	Pye	7N15508	1963	**£4**	chart single
This Is Julie Grant	7" EP	Pye	NEP24171	1962	**£5**	
Up On The Roof	7"	Pye	7N15483	1962	**£4**	chart single

GRANT, LEE & THE CAPITOLS

Breaking Point	7"	Parlophone	R5531	1966	**£8**	

GRANT, TOP

Suzie	7"	Island	WI052	1962	**£4**	

GRAPEFRUIT

Around Grapefruit	LP	Stateside	SSL5008	1969	**£15**	
C'mon Marianne	7"	RCA	RCA1716	1968	**£4**	chart single
Dear Delilah	7"	RCA	RCA1656	1968	**£4**	chart single
Deep Water	LP	RCA	SF8030	1969	**£15**	
Deep Water	7"	RCA	RCA1855	1969	**£6**	
Elevator	7"	RCA	RCA1677	1968	**£5**	
Lady Godiva	7"	RCA	RCA1907	1969	**£5**	
Round Going Round	7"	Stateside	SS8011	1969	**£6**	
Sha Sha	7"	Deram	DM343	1971	**£4**	
Someday Soon	7"	Stateside	SS8005	1968	**£6**	

GRASS ROOTS

All Good Things Come To An End	7"	Stateside	SS8012	1969	**£4**	
Bella Linda	7"	Stateside	SS8006	1969	**£5**	
Heaven Knows	7"	Stateside	SS8033	1969	**£4**	
I'd Wait A Million Years	7"	Stateside	SS8029	1969	**£4**	
Leaving It Behind	LP	Stateside	SSL5012	1969	**£12**	
Let's Live For Today	LP	Dunhill	D50020	1967	**£12**	US
Let's Live For Today	7"	Pye	7N25422	1967	**£6**	
Melody For You	7"	RCA	RCA1682	1968	**£4**	
Midnight Confessions	7"	RCA	RCA1737	1968	**£8**	

Title	Format	Label	Cat. No.	Year	Price	Notes
River Is Wide	7"	Stateside	SS8018	1969	**£4**	
Their Sixteen Greatest Hits	LP	ABC	QD40013	1974	**£10**	US quad
Things I Should Have Said	7"	Pye	7N25431	1967	**£6**	
Where Were You When I Needed You	7"	RCA	RCA1532	1966	**£5**	
Where Were You When I Needed You	LP	Dunhill	D50011	1966	**£12**	US
Who Will You Be Tomorrow	7"	Stateside	SS8023	1969	**£4**	

GRATEFUL DEAD

Title	Format	Label	Cat. No.	Year	Price	Notes
American Beauty	LP	Mobile Fid.	MFSL1014	1978	**£15**	US audiophile
American Beauty	LP	W. Bros	WS1893	1971	**£10**	
Anthem For The Sun	LP	W. Bros	WS1749	1968	**£12**	
Aoxomoxoa	LP	W. Bros	WS1790	1969	**£12**	
Born Cross-Eyed	7"	W. Bros	WB7186	1967	**£15**	
Dancing In The Streets	12"	Arista	DEAD1	1977	**£6**	
Dark Star	7"	W. Bros	SAM79	1977	**£6**	promo
Dead Zone	CD			198-	**£100**	6 discs, booklet, poster
Europe '72	LP	W. Bros	K66019	1972	**£20**	triple
From The Mars Hotel	LP	Mobile Fid.	MFSL1172	1980	**£20**	US audiophile
Good Lovin'	7"	Arista	ARIST236	1978	**£4**	
Grateful Dead	LP	W. Bros	WS1689	1967	**£12**	
Grateful Dead Live	LP	W. Bros	K66009	1971	**£12**	double
Historic Dead	LP	Polydor	2310171	1971	**£15**	
Historic Dead	LP	Sunflower	SNF5004	1971	**£20**	US
History Of...(Bear's Choice)	LP	W. Bros	K46246	1973	**£12**	
Let Me Sing Your Blues Away	7"	W. Bros	K19301	1973	**£5**	
Live Dead	LP	W. Bros	WS1830	1970	**£15**	double
One More Saturday Night	7"	W. Bros	K16167	1972	**£6**	
Steal Your Face	LP	United Artists	UAD60131/2	1976	**£20**	double + bonus LP
Stealin'	7"	Scorpio	003201	1966	**£20**	US
Terrapin Station	LP	Direct Disk	SD16619	1979	**£30**	US audiophile
U.S. Blues	7"	United Artists	UP36030	1974	**£5**	
Uncle John's Band	7"	W. Bros	WB7410	1970	**£8**	
Vintage Dead	LP	Polydor	2310172	1970	**£15**	
Vintage Dead	LP	Sunflower	SNF5001	1970	**£20**	US
Workingman's Dead	LP	W. Bros	WS1869	1970	**£10**	chart LP

GRAVENITES, NICK

Title	Format	Label	Cat. No.	Year	Price	Notes
My Labours	LP	CBS	63818	1969	**£15**	
Steelyard Blues	LP	Liberty	352662	1973	**£12**	US

GRAVES, CARL

Title	Format	Label	Cat. No.	Year	Price	Notes
Baby Hang Up The Phone	7"	A&M	AMS7151	1975	**£4**	

GRAVY TRAIN

Title	Format	Label	Cat. No.	Year	Price	Notes
Ballad Of A Peaceful Man	LP	Vertigo	6360051	1971	**£80**	spiral label
Climb Aboard The Gravy Train	7"	Dawn	DNS1115	1975	**£8**	
Gravy Train	LP	Vertigo	6360023	1970	**£30**	spiral label
Second Birth	LP	Dawn	DNLS3046	1973	**£20**	
Staircase To The Day	LP	Dawn	DNLH1	1974	**£20**	
Starbright Starlight	7"	Dawn	DNS1058	1974	**£8**	
Strength Of A Dream	7"	Dawn	DNS1036	1973	**£8**	

GRAY, BARRY

Title	Format	Label	Cat. No.	Year	Price	Notes
Fireball XL5	7"	Melodisc	MEL1591	1964	**£10**	
Great Themes From Thunderbirds	7" EP	Century 21	MA116	1966	**£10**	
Lady Penelope And Other TV Themes	7" EP	Century 21	MA111	1966	**£10**	
TV Themes	7" EP	Century 21	MA136	1967	**£6**	

GRAY, CLAUDE

Title	Format	Label	Cat. No.	Year	Price	Notes
Country And Western Aces	7" EP	Mercury	10012MCE	1964	**£4**	

GRAY, DOBIE

Title	Format	Label	Cat. No.	Year	Price	Notes
Dobie Gray Sings For In Crowders	LP	Charger	CHRM2002	1965	**£15**	US
In Crowd	7"	London	HL9953	1965	**£8**	chart single
See You At The Go-Go	7"	Pye	7N25307	1965	**£8**	

GRAY, DOLORES

Title	Format	Label	Cat. No.	Year	Price	Notes
Rock Love	7"	Brunswick	05407	1955	**£4**	

GRAY, OWEN

Title	Format	Label	Cat. No.	Year	Price	Notes
Best Twist	7"	Blue Beat	BB113	1962	**£10**	
Come On Baby	7"	Chek	TD101	1962	**£5**	

Title	Format	Label	Cat. No.	Year	Price	Notes
Cutest Little Woman	7"	Blue Beat	BB8	1961	**£10**	
Do You Want To Jump	7"	Blue Beat	BB108	1962	**£10**	
Dolly Baby	7"	Island	WI020	1962	**£6**	
Get Drunk	7"	Blue Beat	BB43	1961	**£10**	
I Feel Good	7"	Starlite	ST45078	1962	**£5**	
I'm Still Waiting	7"	Island	WI048	1962	**£5**	
In My Dreams	7"	Starlite	ST45088	1962	**£5**	
Jenny Lee	7"	Starlite	ST45019	1960	**£5**	
Mash It	7"	Starlite	ST45032	1961	**£5**	
Midnight Track	7"	Island	WI030	1962	**£5**	
No Good Woman	7"	Blue Beat	BB103	1962	**£10**	
Please Let Me Go	7"	Starlite	ST45015	1960	**£5**	
Twist Baby	7"	Island	WI002	1962	**£5**	

GRAYZELL, RUDY

Title	Format	Label	Cat. No.	Year	Price	Notes
Looking At The Moon	7"	London	HL8094	1954	**£8**	

GRAZINA

Title	Format	Label	Cat. No.	Year	Price	Notes
Be My Baby	7"	HMV	POP1212	1963	**£4**	
Don't Be Shy	7"	HMV	POP1149	1963	**£4**	
Lover Please Believe Me	7"	HMV	POP1094	1962	**£6**	

GREASE BAND

Title	Format	Label	Cat. No.	Year	Price	Notes
Grease Band	LP	Harvest	SHVL790	1971	**£10**	
Laughed At The Judge	7"	Harvest	HAR5052	1972	**£4**	

GREAT AWAKENING

Title	Format	Label	Cat. No.	Year	Price	Notes
Amazing Grace	7"	London	HLU10284	1969	**£8**	

GREAT BEAR

Title	Format	Label	Cat. No.	Year	Price	Notes
Great Bear	LP	Wand	WNS8	1971	**£15**	

GREAT METROPOLITAN STEAM BAND

Title	Format	Label	Cat. No.	Year	Price	Notes
Great Metropolitan Steam Band	LP	MCA	MUPS403	1969	**£10**	

GREAT SOCIETY

Title	Format	Label	Cat. No.	Year	Price	Notes
Conspicuous Only In Its Absence	LP	CBS	63476	1968	**£12**	
How It Was	LP	CBS	CS9702	1968	**£15**	US

GREATEST SHOW ON EARTH

Title	Format	Label	Cat. No.	Year	Price	Notes
Going's Easy	LP	Harvest	SHVL783	1970	**£25**	
Greatest Show On Earth	LP	Harvest	SHSM2004	1975	**£20**	double
Horizons	LP	Harvest	SHVL769	1970	**£25**	
Real Cool World	7"	Harvest	HAR5012	1970	**£4**	
Tell The Story	7"	Harvest	HAR5026	1970	**£4**	

GRECH, RICK

Title	Format	Label	Cat. No.	Year	Price	Notes
Last Five Years	LP	RSO	2394111	1973	**£10**	

GREEK FOUNTAIN RIVER FRONT BAND

Title	Format	Label	Cat. No.	Year	Price	Notes
Takes Requests	LP	Montel	LLP110	1965	**£50**	US

GREEN ANGELS

Title	Format	Label	Cat. No.	Year	Price	Notes
Exile's Dream	7"	Parlophone	R5512	1966	**£5**	
Let It Happen	7"	Parlophone	R5390	1965	**£8**	

GREEN BEAN

Title	Format	Label	Cat. No.	Year	Price	Notes
Garden's Lovely	7"	Regal Z.	RZ3017	1969	**£5**	

GREEN BULLFROG

Title	Format	Label	Cat. No.	Year	Price	Notes
Green Bullfrog	LP	MCA	MKPS2021	1972	**£20**	

GREEN RIVER BOYS

Title	Format	Label	Cat. No.	Year	Price	Notes
Big Bluegrass Special	LP	Capitol	T1810	1962	**£25**	US

GREEN, AL

Title	Format	Label	Cat. No.	Year	Price	Notes
Back Up Train	LP	Action	ACLP6008	1969	**£15**	
Back Up Train	7"	Stateside	SS2079	1968	**£6**	
Call Me	7"	London	HLU10406	1973	**£4**	
Don't Hurt Me No More	7"	Action	ACT4540	1969	**£4**	
Don't Hurt Me No More	7"	Action	ACT4540	1969	**£15**	demo
Full Of Fire (extended)	7"	London	HLU10511	1975	**£5**	promo only

Here I Am	7"	London	HLU10426	1973	**£4**	
I Can't Get Next To You	7"	London	HLU10324	1971	**£4**	
I'm Still In Love With You	7"	London	HLU10382	1972	**£4**	chart single
Keep Me Crying	7"	London	HLU10542	1976	**£4**	
L-O-V-E	7"	London	HLU10482	1975	**£4**	chart single
Let It Shine	7"	London	HLU10527	1976	**£4**	
Let's Get Married	7"	London	HLU10452	1974	**£4**	
Let's Stay Together	7"	London	HLU10348	1971	**£4**	chart single
Livin' For You	7"	London	HLU10443	1974	**£4**	
Look What You Done For Me	7"	London	HLU10369	1972	**£4**	chart single
Love And Happiness	7"	London	HLU10419	1973	**£4**	
Oh Me Oh My	7"	London	HLU10493	1975	**£4**	
Sha-La-La	7"	London	HLU10470	1974	**£4**	chart single
Tired Of Being Alone	7"	London	HLU10337	1971	**£4**	chart single
You Ought To Be With Me	7"	London	HLU10393	1972	**£4**	
You Say It	7"	London	HLU10300	1970	**£4**	

GREEN, HUGHIE & MONICA ROSE

Cuddle Up	7"	Columbia	DB8085	1966	**£4**	

GREEN, IAN

Last Pink Rose	7"	Polydor	56194	1967	**£8**	
Revelation	LP	CBS	63840	1970	**£15**	
Revelation	7"	CBS	4623	1969	**£5**	
When You Love A Man	7"	CBS	3997	1969	**£5**	

GREEN, KATHE

Run The Length Of Your Wildness	LP	Deram		1969	**£15**	

GREEN, PETER

Like B.B.King before him, Peter Green discovered the knack of playing a single note on the guitar with real soul. Performances like "The Supernatural", with John Mayall, or "I Loved Another Woman" and "Love That Burns" with Fleetwood Mac are testimony and tribute to an outstanding blues guitar voice. "The End Of The Game" is a different kind of guitar playing. In place of soul and beauty, there is anger and anguish, burning out of every twisted note of these largely improvised instrumentals. It is no wonder that Green's next act was to quit the music business, give away all his money, and embark on a life of withdrawn paranoia from which he has never really recovered, despite the occasional foray back into the recording studio.

Apostle	7"	PVK	PV16	1978	**£4**	
Beast Of Burden	7"	Reprise	K14141	1972	**£5**	
Blue Guitar	LP	Creole	CRX5	1981	**£10**	blue vinyl
Clown	7"	Headline	LIN2	1982	**£4**	
End Of The Game	LP	Reprise	RSLP9006	1970	**£12**	
Give Me Back My Freedom	7"	PVK	PV103	1981	**£4**	
Heavy Heart	7"	Reprise	K14092	1971	**£4**	
Heavy Heart	7"	Reprise	RS27012	1971	**£5**	
In The Skies	LP	PVK	PVLS101	1979	**£10**	green vinyl
In The Skies	7"	PVK	PV24	1980	**£4**	
Promised Land	7"	PVK	PV112	1981	**£4**	
Walking In The Road	7"	PVK	PV36	1980	**£4**	

GREENBAUM, NORMAN

Back Home Again	LP	Reprise	6422	1972	**£10**	US
Petaluma	LP	Reprise	2084	1973	**£10**	US
Spirit In The Sky	LP	Reprise	6365	1969	**£12**	US

GREENE, LORNE

Ringo	7"	RCA	RCA1428	1964	**£4**	chart single

GREENSLADE, DAVE

"The Pentateuch" is not so much a double LP that includes a book, as a book that just happens to have a couple of records tucked into pockets in its cover. The illustrations, packed with a wealth of often disturbing detail, are the essence of "The Pentateuch" - Dave Greenslade's rather simple keyboard music just cannot match their impact. Now if only Patrick Woodruffe, or some other talented illustrator, would get together with Vangelis, or, better still, Tomita...

Pentateuch	LP	EMI	EMC3321/2	1979	**£15**	double with book

GREENWICH, ELLIE

Composes, Produces And Sings	LP	United Artists	UAS6648	1968	**£12**	US
I Want You To Be My Baby	7"	United Artists	UP1180	1967	**£4**	
Sunshine After The Rain	7"	United Artists	UP2214	1968	**£4**	

GREENWOOD, MICK

Living Game	LP	MCA	8003	1971	**£10**	

Midnight Dreamer	LP	W. Bros	K56059	1974	**£10**	
To Friends	LP	MCA	2026	1972	**£10**	

GREENWOOD, NICK

Although Vincent Crane was perfectly capable of supplying a bass line with his organ pedals, Arthur Brown's management insisted on adding a bass player to the Crazy World. This was Nick Greenwood - later a member of Khan. Kingdom records issued his solo LP in 1972, which is now extremely scarce.

Cold Cuts	LP	Kingdom	KVLP9002	1972	**£120**	

GREGORY, GLENN & CLAUDIA BRUCKEN

When Your Heart Runs Out Of Time	7"	ZTT	PZTAS15	1985	**£5**	shaped pic disc
When Your Heart Runs Out Of Time	12"	ZTT	12ZTAS15	1985	**£6**	

GREGORY, IAN

Can't You Hear The Beat	7"	Pye	7N15397	1961	**£5**	chart single
Mr. Lovebug	7"	Pye	7N15435	1962	**£5**	
Time Will Tell	7"	Pye	7N15295	1960	**£5**	

GREMLINS

Coming Generation	7"	Mercury	MF981	1966	**£8**	
You Gotta Believe It	7"	Mercury	MF1004	1967	**£6**	

GREY, RONNIE & THE JETS

Run Manny Run	7"	Capitol	CL14329	1955	**£4**	

GRIER, ROOSEVELT

C'mon Cupid	7"	Pama	PM784	196-	**£5**	
People Make The World	7"	Action	ACT4515	1968	**£10**	demo

GRIFFIN

I Am The Noise In Your Head	7"	Bell	BLL1075	1969	**£8**	

GRIFFITHS, ANDY

Andy Griffiths	7" EP	Capitol	EAP1630	1956	**£4**	

GRIMES, CAROL

Carol Grimes	LP	Decca	SKLR5258	1976	**£10**	
Dynamite	7"	Goodear	EAR605	1975	**£4**	
Fools Meeting (with Delivery)	LP	B&C	CAS1023	1970	**£20**	
Give It Everything You've Got	7"	Goodear	EAR105	1974	**£4**	
Harry Lucky (with Delivery)	7"	B&C	CB129	1970	**£6**	
Warm Blood	LP	Caroline	CA2001	1974	**£12**	

GRIMMS

As the loose association of Liverpool poets and musicians, formerly trading as the Liverpool Scene and Scaffold, moved into the seventies, they collected a few musicians of like mind (such as Neil Innes and Zoot Money) and issued a trio of albums under the name of Grimms. The democratic nature of the proceedings means that the quality varies considerably from track to track, but the best material (which includes everything in which Roger McGough has a hand) is the equal of its predecessors from the sixties.

Grimms	LP	Island	HELP11	1973	**£10**	
Rocking Duck	LP	Island	ILPS9248	1973	**£10**	
Sleepers	LP	DJM	DJLPS470	1976	**£10**	

GRIN

Ain't Love Nice	7"	Epic	EPC1463	1973	**£4**	
All Out	LP	Epic	65166	1972	**£12**	
Everybody's Missin' The Sun	7"	CBS	7405	1971	**£4**	
Grin	LP	Epic	64272	1971	**£12**	
One Plus One	LP	Epic	64652	1972	**£12**	
We All Sung Together	7"	CBS	5239	1970	**£4**	

GRINGO

Gringo	LP	MCA	MKPS2017	1971	**£12**	
I'm Another Man	7"	MCA	MK5067	1971	**£4**	

GRISBY DYKE

Adventures Of Miss Rosemary La Page	7"	Deram	DM232	1969	**£6**	

GRODECK WHIPPERJENNY

Grodeck Whipperjenny	LP	People	3000	196-	**£20**	US

GROOM, DEWEY

Title	Format	Label	Cat. No.	Year	Price	Notes
Butane Blues	7"	Starlite	ST45085	1962	**£4**	

GROOVE

Title	Format	Label	Cat. No.	Year	Price	Notes
Wind	7"	Parlophone	R5783	1969	**£8**	

GROSSMAN, STEFAN

Title	Format	Label	Cat. No.	Year	Price	Notes
Ann Molly Murray's Farm	LP	Sonet	SNTF640	1973	**£10**	
Gramercy Park Sheik	LP	Sonet	SNTF627	1972	**£10**	
Hot Dogs	LP	Transatlantic	TRA257	1972	**£10**	
Live	LP	Transatlantic	TRA264	1973	**£15**	double
Memphis Jellyroll	LP	Transatlantic	TRA274	1973	**£10**	
Ragtime Cowboy Jew	LP	Transatlantic	TRA223	1970	**£10**	
Those Pleasant Days	LP	Transatlantic	TRA246	1971	**£10**	
Yazoo Basin Boogie	LP	Transatlantic	TRA217	1970	**£10**	

GROSVENOR, LUTHER

Title	Format	Label	Cat. No.	Year	Price	Notes
All The People	7"	Island	WIP6124	1972	**£5**	
Here Comes The Queen	7"	Island	WIP6109	1971	**£5**	
Under Open Skies	LP	Island	ILPS9168	1971	**£15**	

GROUNDHOGS

Tony McPhee is a guitarist with a particularly good understanding of the blues, as his numerous session appearances on records by people like John Lee Hooker and Champion Jack Dupree testify. He was also one of the first musicians involved in the British blues boom of the late sixties to realise that it would not be possible to keep recycling the same twelve bar repertoire indefinitely without the public losing interest. "Blues Obituary" announced the end of an era with music that while obviously inspired by a love of the blues, nevertheless ranged very much more widely. Subsequently, McPhee became a little too convinced that he could play like Jimi Hendrix, but each Groundhogs LP still has its moments, with "Split" being something of a minor classic.

Title	Format	Label	Cat. No.	Year	Price	Notes
BDD	7"	Liberty	LBF15263	1969	**£10**	
Best Of 1969-72	LP	United Artists	600063/4	1974	**£15**	double
Blues Obituary	LP	Liberty	LBS83253	1969	**£40**	
Eccentric Man	7"	Liberty	LBF15346	1970	**£10**	
Hogwash	LP	United Artists	UAG29419	1972	**£10**	
I'll Never Fall In Love Again	7"	Planet	PLF104	1966	**£25**	
Live A Little Lady	7"	United Artists	UP36095	1976	**£4**	
Pastoral Future	7"	United Artists	UP36177	1976	**£4**	
Plea Sing, Plea Song	7"	W.W. Artists	WWS012	1974	**£5**	
Sad Go Round	7"	W.W. Artists	WWS006	1973	**£5**	
Scratching The Surface	LP	Liberty	LBL83199	1968	**£40**	
Split	LP	Liberty	LBS83401	1971	**£10**	chart LP
Thank Christ For The Bomb	LP	Liberty	LBS83295	1970	**£10**	chart LP
Who Will Save The World	LP	United Artists	UAG29237	1972	**£10**	chart LP
You Don't Love Me	7"	Liberty	LBF15174	1968	**£10**	

GROUP 1850

Title	Format	Label	Cat. No.	Year	Price	Notes
Agemos Trip To Mother Earth	LP	Philips		1968	**£70**	
Live 2	LP	Rubber		1974	**£12**	
Live	LP	Orange		1975	**£10**	
Live On Tour	LP	Rubber		1973	**£12**	
Paradise Now	LP	Discotoon		1969	**£70**	
Polyandri	LP	Rubber		1974	**£12**	

GROUP B

Title	Format	Label	Cat. No.	Year	Price	Notes
I Know Your Name Girl	7"	Vocalion	VF9284	1967	**£4**	

GROUP IMAGE

Title	Format	Label	Cat. No.	Year	Price	Notes
Mouth In The Clouds	LP	Stable	SLE8005	1969	**£20**	

GROUP SIX

Title	Format	Label	Cat. No.	Year	Price	Notes
Rock A Boogie	7"	Oriole	CB1488	1959	**£4**	

GROUP TWO

Title	Format	Label	Cat. No.	Year	Price	Notes
It's Raining Outside	7"	Columbia	DB8374	1968	**£4**	

GROUP X

Title	Format	Label	Cat. No.	Year	Price	Notes
Roti Calliope	7"	Fontana	TF417	1963	**£4**	
There Are 8 Million Cossack Melodies	7"	Fontana	267274	1963	**£4**	

GRUNT FUTTOCK

Title	Format	Label	Cat. No.	Year	Price	Notes
Rock 'N' Roll Christian	7"	Regal Z.	RZ3042	1972	**£10**	

GRYPHON

The growing influence of folk music during the early seventies led a few groups to try the integration of medieval instruments into a folk-rock setting. The most successful of these was Gryphon, whose "Midnight Mushrumps" in particular is something of a landmark. Later albums found the group retreating to a more ordinary rock sound, but Richard Harvey subsequently made much use of his love for medieval music in his solo career.

Title	Format	Label	Cat. No.	Year	Price	Notes
Gryphon	LP	Transatlantic	TRA262	1973	**£15**	
Midnight Mushrumps	LP	Transatlantic	TRA282	1974	**£15**	
Raindance	LP	Transatlantic	TRA302	1975	**£15**	
Red Queen To Gryphon 3	LP	Transatlantic	TRA287	1974	**£15**	
Treason	LP	Harvest	SHSP4063	1977	**£12**	

GTO'S

Title	Format	Label	Cat. No.	Year	Price	Notes
She Rides With Me	7"	Polydor	56721	1967	**£8**	

GUESS WHO

Title	Format	Label	Cat. No.	Year	Price	Notes
American Woman	LP	RCA	SF8107	1970	**£10**	
American Woman	7"	RCA	RCA1943	1970	**£4**	chart single
Artificial Paradise	LP	RCA	SF8349	1973	**£10**	
Best Of...	LP	RCA	AFLI2594	1971	**£10**	
Born In Canada	LP	Wand	WDS691	1969	**£10**	US
Canned Wheat	LP	RCA	LSP4157	1969	**£10**	US
Guess Who	LP	MGM	SE4645	1969	**£10**	US
His Girl	7"	King	KG1044	1967	**£6**	chart single
Laughing	7"	RCA	RCA1870	1969	**£4**	
Live At The Paramount	LP	RCA	SF8329	1972	**£10**	
Miss Felicity Grey	7"	Fontana	TF861	1967	**£8**	
Rockin'	LP	RCA	SF8269	1972	**£10**	
Shakin' All Over	7"	Pye	7N25305	1965	**£8**	
Share The Land	LP	RCA	SF8153	1970	**£10**	
So Long Bannatyne	LP	RCA	SF8216	1971	**£10**	
These Eyes	7"	RCA	RCA1832	1969	**£4**	
This Time Long Ago	7"	Fontana	TF831	1967	**£6**	
Wheatfield Soul	LP	RCA	SF8037	1969	**£10**	

GUEST, EARL

Title	Format	Label	Cat. No.	Year	Price	Notes
Foxy	7"	Columbia	DB7212	1964	**£4**	

GUILLOTEENS

Title	Format	Label	Cat. No.	Year	Price	Notes
I Don't Believe	7"	Pye	7N25324	1965	**£4**	

GUITAR CRUSHER WITH JIMMY SPRUILL

Title	Format	Label	Cat. No.	Year	Price	Notes
Since My Baby Hit The Numbers	7"	Blue Horizon	573149	1969	**£12**	

GUITAR NUBBIT

Title	Format	Label	Cat. No.	Year	Price	Notes
Guitar Nubbit	7" EP	XX	MIN705		**£4**	

GUITAR RED

Title	Format	Label	Cat. No.	Year	Price	Notes
Just You And I	7"	Pye	7N25219	1963	**£6**	

GUITAR, BONNIE

Title	Format	Label	Cat. No.	Year	Price	Notes
Dark Moon	LP	Dot	DLP3335	1962	**£10**	US
Moonlight And Shadows	LP	London	HAD2122	1958	**£15**	
Whispering Hope	LP	Dot	DLP3151	1959	**£10**	US

GULLIVER

Title	Format	Label	Cat. No.	Year	Price	Notes
Gulliver	LP	Elektra	2410006	1969	**£15**	

GULLIVER'S PEOPLE

Title	Format	Label	Cat. No.	Year	Price	Notes
Fi Fo Fum	7"	Parlophone	R5464	1966	**£4**	
On A Day Like This	7"	Parlophone	R5709	1968	**£4**	
Somehow Somewhere	7"	Columbia	DB8588	1969	**£4**	
Splendour in The Grass	7"	Parlophone	R5435	1966	**£5**	
Gulliver's Travels	LP	Instant		1968	**£12**	

GUN

The Gun were a guitar trio fronted by Adrian Gurvitz, who has popped up periodically ever since. "Race With The Devil" was the Gun's calling card, a classic piece of hard rock, powered by one of those simple guitar riffs that seems to have been waiting around for ever for someone to just come along and play it. Not much of the rest of the Gun's material is in the same class, unfortunately.

Title	Format	Label	Cat. No.	Year	Price	Notes
Drives You Mad	7"	CBS	4052	1969	**£4**	
Gun	LP	CBS	63552	1968	**£12**	

Title	Format	Label	Number	Year	Price	Notes
Gunsight	LP	CBS	63683	1969	**£25**	
Hobo	7"	CBS	4443	1969	**£5**	
Race With The Devil	7"	CBS	3764	1968	**£4**	chart single
Running Wild	7"	CBS	4952	1970	**£5**	

GUN CLUB

Title	Format	Label	Number	Year	Price	Notes
Fire Of Love	7"	Animal	CHCAT2636	1982	**£4**	
Fire Of Love	LP	New Rose	GUN1	1986	**£10**	blue vinyl
Ghost On The Highway	7"	Beggars B.	BEG80	1982	**£4**	
House On Highland Avenue	7"	Animal	GUN1	1983	**£4**	

GUNN, JON

Title	Format	Label	Number	Year	Price	Notes
I've Just Made My Mind Up	7"	Deram	DM133	1967	**£8**	
If You Wish It	7"	Deram	DM166	1967	**£5**	

GUNS 'N' ROSES

Title	Format	Label	Number	Year	Price	Notes
It's So Easy	12"	Geffen	GEF22TP	1987	**£10**	pic disc
Paradise City	7"	Geffen	GEF50P	1989	**£6**	SPD, clear background
Paradise City	7"	Geffen	GEF50P	1989	**£10**	SPD, white background
Paradise City	7"	Geffen	GEF50X	1989	**£5**	holster pack
Sweet Child Of Mine	7"	Geffen	GEF55P	1989	**£10**	shaped pic disc
Sweet Child Of Mine	12"	Geffen	GEF43TV	1988	**£6**	metallic sleeve
Sweet Child Of Mine	10"	Geffen	GEF43TE	1988	**£10**	
Welcome To The Jungle	12"	Geffen	GEF30TP	1987	**£8**	pic disc
Welcome To The Jungle	12"	Geffen	GEF30TW	1987	**£6**	poster sleeve
Welcome To The Jungle	12"	Geffen	GEF47TP	1988	**£6**	pic disc

GUNTER, ARTHUR

Title	Format	Label	Number	Year	Price	Notes
Black And Blues	LP	Excello	8017	1970	**£75**	US
Blues After Hours	LP	Blue Horizon	2431012	1971	**£25**	

GUNTHER, HARDROCK

Title	Format	Label	Number	Year	Price	Notes
Mountain Music	7" EP	Brunswick	OE9167	1955	**£6**	

GURU GURU

Title	Format	Label	Number	Year	Price	Notes
Dance Of The Flames	LP	Atlantic	K50044	1974	**£10**	
Der Elektrolurch	LP	Brain	21057	1974	**£15**	German double
Don't Call Us We'll Call You	LP	Atlantic	K50022	1973	**£10**	
Guru Guru	LP	Brain	1025	1973	**£12**	German
Hinten	LP	Ohr	556027	1971	**£15**	German
Kan Guru	LP	Brain	1007	1972	**£12**	German
This Is...	LP	Brain	200145	1973	**£10**	German
UFO	LP	Ohr	556005	1970	**£15**	German

GURUS

Title	Format	Label	Number	Year	Price	Notes
Blue Snow Night	7"	United Artists	UP1160	1966	**£8**	

GUSTAFSON, JOHNNY

Title	Format	Label	Number	Year	Price	Notes
Just To Be With You	7"	Polydor	56022	1965	**£8**	
Take Me For A Little While	7"	Polydor	56043	1965	**£8**	

GUTHRIE, ARLO

Title	Format	Label	Number	Year	Price	Notes
Alice's Restaurant	LP	Reprise	RLP6267	1967	**£12**	chart LP
Alice's Restaurant Soundtrack	LP	United Artists	UAS29061	1969	**£10**	
Alice's Rock'n'Roll Restaurant	7"	Reprise	RS20877	1970	**£5**	
Arlo	LP	Reprise	RSLP6299	1968	**£10**	
Running Down The Road	LP	Reprise	RSLP6346	1969	**£10**	
Washington County	LP	Reprise	RSLP6411	1970	**£10**	

GUTHRIE, WOODY

Title	Format	Label	Number	Year	Price	Notes
Hard It Ain't Hard	7" EP	Melodisc	EPM784	195-	**£8**	
Hey Lolly Lolly	7" EP	Melodisc	EPM791	195-	**£8**	
Worried Man Blues	7" EP	Melodisc	EPM785	195-	**£8**	

GUY, BUDDY

Title	Format	Label	Number	Year	Price	Notes
...And Junior Wells Play The Blues	LP	Atlantic	K40240	1972	**£12**	
Blues Today	LP	Vanguard		1968	**£15**	
Buddy And The Juniors	LP	Blue Thumb	20	1970	**£10**	US
Buddy And The Juniors	LP	Blue Thumb	20	1970	**£15**	US, coloured vinyl
Coming At You	LP	Vanguard	SVRL19001	1968	**£15**	
Crazy Music	7" EP	Chess	CRE6004	1965	**£6**	
Honey Dripper	7"	Atlantic	K10195	1972	**£4**	

I Was Walking Through The Woods	LP	Chess	LP409	196-	**£15**	US
Left My Blues In San Francisco	LP	Chess	LPS1527	1969	**£10**	US
Let Me Love You Baby	7"	Chess	CRS8004	1965	**£6**	
Man And His Blues	LP	Vanguard	SVRL19002	1968	**£15**	
Mary Had A Little Lamb	7"	Fontana	TF951	1968	**£5**	
This Is Buddy Guy	LP	Vanguard	SVRL19008	1969	**£15**	

GYGAFO

Legend Of The Kingfisher	LP	Holyground		1973	**£100**	

GYPSIES

Jerk it	7"	CBS	2785	1967	**£15**	

GYPSY

Brand New Car	7"	United Artists	UP35462	1972	**£4**	
Brenda And The Rattlesnake	LP	United Artists	UAS29420	1972	**£10**	
Changes Coming	7"	United Artists	UP35272	1971	**£4**	
Gypsy	LP	United Artists	UAS29155	1971	**£12**	
Let's Roll	7"	United Artists	UP35546	1973	**£4**	
What Makes A Man A Man	7"	United Artists	UP35202	1971	**£4**	

H

H.P.LOVECRAFT

Title	Format	Label	Cat. No.	Year	Price	Notes
H.P.Lovecraft	LP	Philips	BL7830	1967	**£25**	
H.P.Lovecraft 2	LP	Philips	SBL7872	1968	**£25**	
Wayfarin' Stranger	7"	Philips	BF1620	1967	**£8**	
White Ship	LP	Philips	6336210	1970	**£20**	
White Ship	7"	Philips	BF1639	1968	**£8**	

HA'PENNYS

Title	Format	Label	Cat. No.	Year	Price	Notes
Love Is Not The Same	LP	Fersch	1110	1968	**£150**	US

HABIBIYYA

Title	Format	Label	Cat. No.	Year	Price	Notes
If Man But Knew	LP	Island	HELP7	1972	**£10**	

HABITS

Title	Format	Label	Cat. No.	Year	Price	Notes
Elbow Baby	7"	Decca	F12348	1966	**£12**	

HACKENSACK

Title	Format	Label	Cat. No.	Year	Price	Notes
Moving On	7"	Island	WIP6149	1972	**£20**	
Up The Hardway	LP	Polydor	2383263	1974	**£60**	

HACKETT, STEVE

Title	Format	Label	Cat. No.	Year	Price	Notes
Cell 151	7"	Charisma	CELL1	1983	**£4**	PS, chart single
Cell 151	12"	Charisma	CELL12	1983	**£6**	
Clocks - The Angel Of Mons	7"	Charisma	CB341	1979	**£4**	
Clocks - The Angel Of Mons	12"	Charisma	CB34112	1979	**£8**	
Clocks - The Angel Of Mons	12"	Charisma	CELL13	1983	**£6**	white label
Every Day	7"	Charisma	CB334	1979	**£4**	
Hope I Don't Wake	7"	Charisma	CB385	1981	**£4**	PS
How Can I	7"	Charisma	CB312	1978	**£6**	
Narnia	7"	Charisma	CB318	1978	**£4**	
Picture Postcard	7"	Charisma	CB390	1981	**£4**	
Sentimental Institution	7"	Charisma	CB368	1980	**£4**	PS
Show	7"	Charisma	CB357	1980	**£4**	PS

HAFFY'S WHISKEY SOUR

Title	Format	Label	Cat. No.	Year	Price	Notes
Shot In The Head	7"	Deram	DM345	1971	**£5**	

HAGAR, SAMMY

Title	Format	Label	Cat. No.	Year	Price	Notes
Sammy Hagar	LP	Capitol	EST11599	1977	**£10**	red vinyl

HAHN, JERRY BROTHERHOOD

Title	Format	Label	Cat. No.	Year	Price	Notes
Jerry Hahn Brotherhood	LP	Columbia	CS1044	1970	**£12**	US

HAIG, PAUL

Title	Format	Label	Cat. No.	Year	Price	Notes
Heaven Sent	7"	Crepuscule	IS111	1983	**£4**	
Justice	7"	Crepuscule	IS138	1983	**£4**	
Running Away	7"	Twilight	OPT03	1982	**£4**	
Uncle Sam	7"	Rhythm O.L.	RATE7	1981	**£4**	

HAINES, NORMAN

Title	Format	Label	Cat. No.	Year	Price	Notes
Daffodil	7"	Parlophone	R5871	1970	**£20**	
Den Of Iniquity	LP	Parlophone		1971	**£400**	
Give To You Girl	7"	Parlophone	R5960	1972	**£20**	

HAIR

Title	Format	Label	Cat. No.	Year	Price	Notes
Hair Piece	LP	Columbia	SCX6452	1970	**£100**	

HAIRBAND

Title	Format	Label	Cat. No.	Year	Price	Notes
Band On The Wagon	LP	Bell		1969	**£25**	
Big Louis	7"	Bell	BLL1076	1969	**£10**	

HAIRCUT 100

Title	Format	Label	Cat. No.	Year	Price	Notes
Blue Hat For A Blue Day	LP	Arista	HCC101	1982	**£20**	test pressing only

Fantastic Day	7"	Arista	CLIPD3	1982	£4	pic disc
Pelican Dance King Size	12"	Arista	TERRY1	1982	£6	promo sampler
Whistle Down The Wind	7"	Arista	CLIP5	1983	£8	

HAL HOPPERS

Baby I've Had It	7"	London	HL8129	1955	£8	
Do Nothing Blues	7"	London	HL8107	1954	£8	

HALEY, BILL

Bill Haley And His Comets	7" EP	Brunswick	OE9459	1959	£12	
Bill Haley And His Comets	7" EP	W. Bros	WEP6001	1960	£8	
Bill Haley And The Comets	LP	W. Bros	W1738	1960	£15	US
Bill Haley Vol.1	7" EP	W. Bros	WEP6133	1964	£8	
Bill Haley Vol.2	7" EP	W. Bros	WEP6136	1964	£8	
Bill Haley's Chicks	LP	Ace O.H.	AH66	1964	£10	
Bill Haley's Chicks	LP	Brunswick	LAT8295	1959	£15	
Bill Haley's Chicks	LP	Brunswick	STA3011	1959	£20	stereo
Bill Haley's Chicks	LP	Decca	DL8821	1959	£35	US
Bill Haley's Juke Box	7" EP	W. Bros	WEP6025	1961	£8	
Billy Goat	7"	Brunswick	05688	1957	£10	
Birth Of The Boogie	7"	Brunswick	05910	1964	£6	
Caldonia	7"	Brunswick	05805	1959	£6	
Candy Kisses	7"	W. Bros	WB6	1960	£4	
Crazy Man Crazy	78	London	L1190	1953	£10	
Dim Dim The Lights	7"	Brunswick	05373	1955	£12	gold label
Dim Dim The Lights	7"	Brunswick	05373	1955	£8	silver label
Dim Dim The Lights	7" EP	Brunswick	OE9129	1955	£20	
Dipsy Doodle	7"	Brunswick	05719	1957	£8	
Don't Knock The Rock	7"	Brunswick	05640	1957	£12	chart single
Farewell So Long Goodbye	7"	London	HLF8161	1955	£40	
Forty Cups Of Coffee	7"	Brunswick	05658	1957	£12	
Goofing Around	7"	Brunswick	05641	1957	£10	
Green Door	7"	Brunswick	05917	1964	£4	
Greentree Boogie	7"	London	HL8142	1955	£50	
Haley's Juke Box	LP	W. Bros	W1391	1960	£12	
He Digs Rock And Roll	LP	Decca	DL8315	1956	£75	US
I Got A Woman	7"	Brunswick	05788	1959	£4	
I'm Gonna Dry Every Little Tear	78	Melodisc	1376	1956	£15	
Lean Jean	7"	Brunswick	05752	1958	£6	
Live It Up	LP-10'	London	HAPB1042	1955	£40	
Live It Up Pt.1	7" EP	London	REF1049	1956	£15	
Live It Up Pt.2	7" EP	London	REF1050	1956	£15	
Live It Up Pt.3	7" EP	London	REF1058	1956	£20	
Mambo Rock	7"	Brunswick	05405	1955	£12	gold label, chart single
Mambo Rock	7"	Brunswick	05405	1955	£6	silver label
Mary Mary Lou	7"	Brunswick	05735	1958	£6	
Ooh Looka There Ain't She Pretty	7"	Brunswick	05810	1959	£4	
Pat-A-Cake	78	London	L1216	1953	£10	
Razzle Dazzle	7"	Brunswick	05453	1955	£12	gold label
Razzle Dazzle	7"	Brunswick	05453	1955	£6	silver label, chart single
Rip It Up	7"	Brunswick	05615	1956	£10	chart single
Rock 'n' Roll	7" EP	Brunswick	OE9214	1956	£12	
Rock 'n' Roll	7" EP	London	REF1031	1955	£20	
Rock 'n' Roll Stage Show	LP	Decca	DL8345	1956	£75	US
Rock 'n' Roll Stage Show	LP	Brunswick	LAT8139	1956	£20	chart single
Rock 'n' Roll Stage Show Pt.1	7" EP	Brunswick	OE9278	1956	£12	
Rock 'n' Roll Stage Show Pt.2	7" EP	Brunswick	OE9279	1956	£12	
Rock 'n' Roll Stage Show Pt.3	7" EP	Brunswick	OE9280	1956	£12	
Rock A Beatin' Boogie	7"	Brunswick	05509	1955	£12	gold label, chart LP
Rock-A-Beatin' Boogie	7"	Brunswick	05509	1955	£8	silver label
Rock Around The Clock	LP	Ace O.H.	AH13	1961	£10	chart LP
Rock Around The Clock	LP	Brunswick	LAT8117	1956	£20	
Rock Around The Clock	7"	Brunswick	05317	1954	£20	gold label, chart single
Rock Around The Clock	7"	Brunswick	05317	1954	£12	silver label, chart single
Rock Around The Clock	7" EP	Brunswick	OE9250	1956	£12	2 covers
Rock Around The Clock	LP	Decca	DL8225	1955	£100	US
Rock Around The Clock	7"	W. Bros	WB133	1964	£4	
Rock The Joint	LP	Golden Guin.	GGL0282	1963	£10	
Rock The Joint	LP	London	HAF2037	1957	£25	
Rock The Joint	7"	London	HLF8371	1957	£30	chart single
Rock With Bill Haley And The Comets	LP	Essex	LP202	1956	£100	US

Title	Format	Label	Number	Year	Price	Notes
Rock With Bill Haley And The Comets	LP	Somerset	P4600	1956	**£25**	US
Rock With Bill Haley And The Comets	LP	Trans World	202	1956	**£40**	US
Rockin' Around The World	7" EP	Brunswick	OE9446	1959	**£12**	
Rockin' Around The World	LP	Decca	DL8692	1957	**£40**	US
Rockin' Chair On The Moon	7"	London	HLF8194	1955	**£30**	
Rockin' The Joint	LP	Brunswick	LAT8268	1957	**£20**	
Rockin' The Joint	LP	Decca	DL8775	1958	**£40**	US
Rockin' The Oldies	LP	Ace O.H.	AH35	1962	**£10**	
Rockin' The Oldies	LP	Brunswick	LAT8219	1957	**£15**	
Rockin' The Oldies	LP	Decca	DL8569	1957	**£40**	US
Rockin' The Oldies Pt.1	7" EP	Brunswick	OE9349	1958	**£12**	
Rockin' The Oldies Pt.2	7" EP	Brunswick	OE9350	1958	**£12**	
Rockin' The Oldies Pt.3	7" EP	Brunswick	OE9351	1958	**£12**	
Rockin' Through The Rye	7"	Brunswick	05582	1956	**£12**	chart single
Rudy's Rock	7"	Brunswick	05616	1956	**£10**	chart single
Saints Rock 'n' Roll	7"	Brunswick	05565	1956	**£12**	chart single
See You Later Alligator	7"	Brunswick	05530	1956	**£12**	gold label, chart single
See You Later Alligator	7"	Brunswick	05530	1956	**£8**	silver label, chart single
Shake, Rattle And Roll	7"	Brunswick	05338	1954	**£12**	gold label, chart single
Shake, Rattle And Roll	7"	Brunswick	05338	1954	**£8**	silver label
Shake, Rattle And Roll	LP-10"	Decca	DL5560	1954	**£300**	US
Skinnie Minnie	7"	Brunswick	05742	1958	**£5**	
Skokiaan	7"	Brunswick	05818	1960	**£4**	
Spanish Twist	7"	London	HLU9471	1961	**£4**	
Strictly Instrumental	LP	Brunswick	LAT8326	1960	**£15**	
Strictly Instrumental	LP	Decca	DL8964	1959	**£35**	US
Tenor Man	7"	Stateside	SS196	1963	**£4**	
Twisting Knights At The Round Table	LP	Columbia	33SX1460	1962	**£12**	
Whoa Mabel	7"	Brunswick	05766	1958	**£5**	

HALEY, BILL & FOUR ACES

Title	Format	Label	Number	Year	Price	Notes
They Sold A Million No.15	7" EP	Brunswick	OE9431	1959	**£8**	

HALF NELSON (SPARKS)

Half Nelson was the name originally used by Sparks. The one LP made under this name was reissued as "Sparks" a year later.

Title	Format	Label	Number	Year	Price	Notes
Half Nelson	LP	Bearsville	BV2048	1972	**£20**	US

HALL & OATES

Title	Format	Label	Number	Year	Price	Notes
Abandoned Luncheonette	LP	Mobile Fid.	MFSL1069	1980	**£10**	US audiophile
Private Eyes	LP	RCA		1983	**£10**	plus cassette
Your Imagination	7"	RCA	RCA239	1982	**£4**	promo

HALL, DICKSON

Title	Format	Label	Number	Year	Price	Notes
Fabulous Country Hits Way Out West	LP	Kapp	KL1067	1957	**£10**	US
Outlaws Of The Old West	LP	MGM	E3263	1956	**£10**	US
Outlaws Of The Old West	LP-10"	MGM	E329	1954	**£12**	US
Outlaws Of The Old West	7" EP	MGM	MGMEP626	1957	**£6**	
Twenty-Five All-Time Country	LP	Epic	LN3427	1958	**£10**	US

HALL, GERRI

Title	Format	Label	Number	Year	Price	Notes
Who Can I Run To	7"	Sue	WI4026	1966	**£25**	demo only

HALL, JIMMY GRAY

Title	Format	Label	Number	Year	Price	Notes
Be That Way	7"	Epic	2312	197-	**£8**	

HALL, JUANITA

Title	Format	Label	Number	Year	Price	Notes
Storyville Blues Anthology Vol.2	7" EP	Storyville	SEP382		**£4**	

HALL, RENE

Title	Format	Label	Number	Year	Price	Notes
Twitchy	7"	London	HLU8581	1958	**£10**	

HALL, RONNIE

Title	Format	Label	Number	Year	Price	Notes
I'll Stand Aside	7"	Fontana	TF569	1965	**£8**	

HALL, ROY

Title	Format	Label	Number	Year	Price	Notes
Blue Suede Shoes	7"	Brunswick	05555	1956	**£80**	
See You Later Alligator	7"	Brunswick	05531	1956	**£100**	
Three Alley Cats	7"	Brunswick	05627	1956	**£100**	

HALLYDAY, JOHNNY

Title	Format	Label	Number	Year	Price	Notes
America's Rockin' Hits	LP	Philips	BBL7556	1961	**£60**	
Hey Little Girl	7"	Philips	373012BF	1963	**£4**	

Pour Moi Tu Es La Seule	7"	Philips	BF1449	1965	**£4**	
Rocking	7" EP	Philips	432813BE	1962	**£40**	
Shake The Hand Of A Fool	7"	Philips	PB1238	1962	**£4**	

HALOS

Halos	LP	Warwick	W2046	1962	**£60**	US
Nag	7"	London	HLU9424	1961	**£4**	

HAMILL, CLAIRE

Abracadabra	LP	Konk	KONK104	1975	**£15**	
Baseball Blues	7"	Island	WIP6133	1972	**£4**	
October	LP	Island	ILPS9225	1973	**£10**	
One House Left Standing	LP	Island	ILPS9182	1971	**£10**	
Rory	7"	Konk	KOS3	1975	**£4**	
Speedbreaker	7"	Island	WIP6154	1973	**£4**	
Stage Door Johnnies	LP	Konk	KONK101	1974	**£15**	
When I Was A Child	7"	Island	WIP6122	1972	**£4**	

HAMILTON & THE MOVEMENT

I'm Not the Marrying Kind	7"	CBS	202573	1967	**£8**	

HAMILTON FACE BAND

Ain't Got No Time	LP	Bell	SBLL132	1970	**£12**	

HAMILTON IV, GEORGE

I Know Where I'm Going	7"	HMV	POP505	1958	**£4**	chart single
On Campus	LP	ABC-Para.	220	1958	**£12**	US
Rose And A Candy Bar	7"	London	HL8361	1957	**£20**	
Sing Me A Sad Song	LP	ABC-Para.	251	1958	**£12**	US
Why Don't They Understand	7"	HMV	POP429	1957	**£4**	chart single

HAMILTON, ROY

Crazy Feeling	7"	Fontana	H143	1958	**£5**	
Dark End Of The Street	7"	Deep Soul	DS9106	1970	**£8**	
I Need Your Loving	7"	Fontana	H193	1959	**£5**	
Pledging My Love	7"	Fontana	H180	1959	**£5**	
There She Is	7"	MGM	MGM1251	1964	**£8**	
Thousand Years Ago	7"	MGM	MGM1268	1965	**£6**	
You Can Have Her	7"	Fontana	H298	1961	**£5**	
You're Gonna Need Magic	7"	Fontana	H320	1961	**£5**	

HAMILTON, RUSS

Rainbow	LP	Kapp	KL1076	1957	**£30**	US

HAMILTON, SCOTT

Good Day Sunshine	7"	Parlophone	R5492	1966	**£4**	

HAMMER, JACK

Thanks	7"	Polydor	56091	1966	**£5**	
What Greater Love	7"	United Artists	UP35029	1969	**£10**	

HAMMERS

Baby And Me	7"	President	PT247	1969	**£5**	
Sugar Baby	7"	President	PT276	1969	**£5**	

HAMMILL, PETER

Birthday Special	7"	Charisma	CB245	1975	**£5**	
Chameleon In The Shadow Of	LP	Charisma	CAS1067	1973	**£20**	
Film Noir	7"	Naive	NAV8	1983	**£5**	
Fool's Mate	LP	Charisma	CAS1037	1971	**£15**	
Future Now	LP	Charisma	CAS1137	1978	**£10**	
In Camera	LP	Charisma	CAS1089	1974	**£15**	
My Experience	7"	Virgin	VS424	1981	**£4**	
Nadir's Last Chance	LP	Charisma	CAS1099	1975	**£15**	
Over	LP	Charisma	CAS1125	1977	**£20**	
Paradox Drive	7"	Naive	NAV3	1982	**£5**	
PH7	LP	Charisma	CAS1146	1979	**£20**	
Silent Corner Of The Empty Stage	LP	Charisma	CAS1083	1974	**£20**	
Vision	LP	GIR	92111016	1978	**£10**	US compilation

HAMMILL, PETER (AS RIKKI NADIR)

Polaroid	7"	Charisma	CB339	1979	**£10**	

HAMMOND, ALBERT

Title	Format	Label	Number	Year	Price	Notes
Albert Hammond	LP	Mum	80026	1974	**£10**	
Free Electric Band	LP	Mum	65554	1973	**£10**	
It Never Rains In Southern California	LP	Mum	65320	1973	**£10**	

HAMMOND, JOHN

Title	Format	Label	Number	Year	Price	Notes
Best Of (Southern Fried)	LP	Vanguard	VSD11/12	1974	**£15**	double
Big City Blues	LP	Fontana	TFL6046	1964	**£20**	
Brown Eyed Handsome Man	7"	Atlantic	584190	1968	**£8**	
Country Blues	LP	Vanguard	VSD79198	1965	**£20**	US
I Can Tell	LP	Atlantic	SD8152	1968	**£20**	US
I Live The Life I Love	7"	Fontana	TF560	1965	**£15**	
I'm Satisfied	LP	CBS	65051	1972	**£15**	
John Hammond	LP	Vanguard	VRS9132	1963	**£20**	US
Little Big Man	LP	CBS	30545	1971	**£15**	US
Mirrors	LP	Vanguard	VSD79245	1968	**£20**	US
So Many Roads	LP	Fontana	TFL6059	1965	**£20**	
Sooner Or Later	LP	Atlantic	SD8206	1968	**£20**	US
Source Point	LP	CBS	64365	1971	**£15**	
Southern Fried	LP	Atlantic	SD8251	1970	**£15**	US
When I Need	LP	CBS	30549	1971	**£15**	US

HAMPSHIRE, SUSAN

Title	Format	Label	Number	Year	Price	Notes
When Love Is True	7"	Decca	F12185	1965	**£4**	

HANCOCK, HERBIE

Jazz pianist Herbie Hancock has tried his hand at a particularly wide range of styles over the years, from straightforward "modern" jazz to hiphop. The trilogy of early seventies recordings, "Mwandishi", "Crossings", and "Sextant" find him entering the composed electric jazz world defined by Weather Report. Typically, they are amongst the most impressive jazz recordings of the period, and arguably they are Hancock's personal best. "Crossings" is especially fine. "Treasure Chest" is an anthology of music taken from these electric jazz recordings and from Hancock's sixties work. It also includes a short track whose music is taken from "Crossings", but in a remixed form not otherwise available.

Title	Format	Label	Number	Year	Price	Notes
Crossings	LP	W. Bros.	K46164	1972	**£10**	
Direct Step	LP	CBS Sony	30AP1032	1979	**£15**	Japanese
Live In Japan	LP	CBS Sony	98/99	1975	**£25**	Japanese double
Live Under The Sky	LP	CBS Sony	1037875	1976	**£15**	Japanese
Mwandishi	LP	W. Bros	K46077	1971	**£10**	
Sextant	LP	CBS	65582	1972	**£10**	
Treasure Chest	LP	W. Bros	2WS2807	1974	**£15**	US double

HANCOCK, TONY

Title	Format	Label	Number	Year	Price	Notes
Blood Donor And The Radio Ham	LP	Pye	NPL18068	1961	**£10**	chart LP
Pieces Of Hancock	LP	Pye	NPL18054	1960	**£12**	chart LP
This Is Hancock	LP	Pye	NPL18045	1960	**£12**	chart LP

HANDY, WAYNE

Title	Format	Label	Number	Year	Price	Notes
Say Yeah	7"	London	HL8547	1958	**£20**	

HANNA, BOBBY

Title	Format	Label	Number	Year	Price	Notes
Blame It On Me	7"	Decca	F12695	1967	**£6**	
Thanks To You	7"	Decca	F12604	1967	**£4**	
To Wait For Love	7"	Decca	F12833	1968	**£4**	
Too Much Love	7"	Decca	F12738	1968	**£4**	
Winter Love	7"	Decca	F22917	1969	**£4**	
Written On The Wind	7"	Decca	F12783	1968	**£6**	

HANNETT, MARTIN

Title	Format	Label	Number	Year	Price	Notes
First Aspect Of The Same Thing	7"	Factory	FACT14C	1980	**£4**	flexi

HANNIBAL

Hannibal's only album is definitely a neglected gem from the progressive era. Occasionally let down a little by the lyrics, the music is nevertheless sparkling and inventive, these qualities being enhanced by fluent jazz-rock playing from all concerned. The keyboard player turned up on a few Roy Wood records, but remarkably none of the members of Hannibal were able to sustain a career in music.

Title	Format	Label	Number	Year	Price	Notes
Hannibal	LP	B&C	CAS1022	1970	**£25**	
Winds Of Change	7"	B&C	HB1	1974	**£10**	

HANOI ROCKS

Title	Format	Label	Number	Year	Price	Notes
Don't You Ever Leave Me	12"	CBS	WA4885	1984	**£10**	pic disc
Malibu Beach	7"	Lick	LIX1	1983	**£5**	
Malibu Beach	7"	Lick	LIXPD1	1983	**£6**	pic disc

Title	Format	Label	Cat. No.	Year	Price	Notes
Underwater World	12"	CBS	WA4732	1984	**£10**	pic disc

HANSSON & KARLSSON

Title	Format	Label	Cat. No.	Year	Price	Notes
Monument	LP	Polydor	46260	1969	**£15**	
Swedish Underground	LP	Polydor	184196	1967	**£20**	

HANSSON, BO

Title	Format	Label	Cat. No.	Year	Price	Notes
Black Riders Flight To The Ford	7"	Charisma	CB230	1974	**£4**	

HAPPENINGS

Title	Format	Label	Cat. No.	Year	Price	Notes
Breaking Up Is Hard To Do	7"	B.T.Puppy	BTS45543	1968	**£4**	
Crazy Rhythm	7"	B.T.Puppy	BTS45545	1969	**£4**	
Go Away Little Girl	7"	Fontana	TF766	1966	**£4**	
Golden Hits	LP	B.T.Puppy	BTLPS1004	1968	**£20**	US
Goodnight My Love	7"	Stateside	SS587	1967	**£4**	
Greatest Hits	LP	Jubilee	JGS8030	1969	**£12**	US
Happenings	LP	B.T.Puppy	BTLP1001	1966	**£15**	US
I Got Rhythm	7"	Stateside	SS2013	1967	**£4**	chart single
Music Music Music	7"	B.T.Puppy	BTS45538	1968	**£4**	
My Mammy	7"	B.T.Puppy	BTS45530	1967	**£4**	chart single
My Mammy	7"	Pye	7N25501	1967	**£4**	chart single
New Day Comin'	7"	B.T.Puppy	BTS45546	1969	**£4**	
Piece Of Mind	LP	Jubilee	JGS8028	1969	**£12**	US
Psycle	LP	B.T.Puppy	BTLP1003	1967	**£15**	US
Randy	7"	B.T.Puppy	BTS45540	1968	**£4**	
See You In September	7"	Fontana	TF735	1966	**£4**	
Why Do Fools Fall In Love	7"	B.T.Puppy	BTS45532	1967	**£4**	

HAPPENINGS & TOKENS

Title	Format	Label	Cat. No.	Year	Price	Notes
Back To Back	LP	B.T.Puppy	BTLP1002	1967	**£10**	US

HAPPY CONFUSION

Title	Format	Label	Cat. No.	Year	Price	Notes
Yes Sir	7"	P. Farthing	PEN706	1970	**£4**	

HAPPY FAMILY

Title	Format	Label	Cat. No.	Year	Price	Notes
Puritans	7"	4AD	AD204	1982	**£5**	

HAPPY MAGAZINE

Title	Format	Label	Cat. No.	Year	Price	Notes
Satisfied Street	7"	Polydor	56233	1968	**£6**	
Who Belongs To You	7"	Polydor	56307	1968	**£5**	

HAPPY MONDAYS

Title	Format	Label	Cat. No.	Year	Price	Notes
24 Hour Party People	7"	Factory	FAC192/7	1987	**£4**	
Madchester Rave On	7"	Factory	FAC242/7	1989	**£4**	
Step On (Melon Mix)	7"	Factory	FAC272	1990	**£15**	1 sided promo

HAPSHASH & THE COLOURED COAT

Title	Format	Label	Cat. No.	Year	Price	Notes
Colinda	7"	Liberty	LBF15188	1969	**£10**	
Human Host And Heavy Metal Kids	LP	Minit	MLL40001E	1967	**£30**	
Western Flyer	LP	Liberty	LBL83212	1969	**£20**	

HARBOUR LITES

Title	Format	Label	Cat. No.	Year	Price	Notes
Run For Your Life	7"	Fontana	TF682	1966	**£4**	

HARD MEAT

Title	Format	Label	Cat. No.	Year	Price	Notes
Ballad Of Marmalade Emma And	7"	W. Bros	WB8010	1970	**£6**	
Hard Meat	LP	W. Bros	WS1852	1970	**£15**	
Rain	7"	Island	WIP6066	1969	**£10**	
Through A Window	LP	W. Bros	WS1879	1970	**£15**	

HARD STUFF

Title	Format	Label	Cat. No.	Year	Price	Notes
Bolex Dementia	LP	Purple	TPSA7507	1973	**£15**	
Bullet Proof	LP	Purple	TPSA7505	1972	**£15**	
Inside Your Life	7"	Purple	PUR116	1973	**£4**	
Orchestrator	7"	Purple	PUR103	1972	**£4**	

HARDIN & YORK

Title	Format	Label	Cat. No.	Year	Price	Notes
For The World	LP	Decca	SKL5095	1971	**£10**	
Tomorrow Today	LP	Bell	SBLL125	1969	**£15**	
World's Smallest Big Band	LP	Bell	SBLL136	1970	**£15**	

HARDIN, EDDIE

Title	Format	Label	Cat. No.	Year	Price	Notes
Driving	7"	Decca	F13252	1971	**£4**	
Home Is Where You Find It	LP	Decca	TXS106	1972	**£10**	
Why Does Everybody Put Me Down	7"	Decca	F13307	1972	**£4**	
Wizard's Convention	LP	RCA	RS1085	1976	**£10**	

HARDIN, TIM

Tim Hardin's fragile voice made his own interpretations of his best material the most versions of all - and he wrote some classic songs; "Hang On To A Dream", "If I Were A Carpenter", and "Reason To Believe" among them. Particularly moving is his "Suite For Susan Moore and Damian", which is a kind of stream-of-consciousness tribute to his wife and child. It was a real tragedy when this precious talent succumbed to heroin addiction in 1980.

Title	Format	Label	Cat. No.	Year	Price	Notes
Archetypes	LP	MGM	4952	1973	**£12**	US
Best Of...	LP	Verve	2317003	1970	**£10**	
Bird On A Wire	LP	CBS	64335	1970	**£15**	
Don't Make Promises	7"	Verve	VS1516	1968	**£5**	
Hang On To a Dream	7"	Verve	VS1504	1966	**£4**	chart single
Lady Came From Baltimore	7"	Verve	VS1511	1967	**£5**	
Live In Concert	LP	Verve	6010	1968	**£15**	
Nine	LP	GM	1004	1974	**£12**	
Painted Head	LP	CBS	65209	1973	**£12**	
Simple Song Of Freedom	7"	CBS	4441	1969	**£4**	
Suite For Susan Moore And Damian	LP	CBS	63571	1970	**£15**	
This Is Tim Hardin	LP	Atco	588082	1967	**£15**	
Tim Hardin 1	LP	Verve	5018	1966	**£15**	
Tim Hardin 1/Tim Hardin 2	LP	Verve	2683048	1974	**£20**	double
Tim Hardin 2	LP	Verve	6002	1967	**£15**	
Tim Hardin 4	LP	Verve	6016	1969	**£15**	

HARDY, FRANCOISE

As one of France's top sixties pop music stars, Francoise Hardy also gained a considerable following in Britain. The EPs "C'Est Fab" and "C'Est Francoise" in particular sold well enough to enter the lower reaches of the charts - a rare feat for records sung in a language other than English.

Title	Format	Label	Cat. No.	Year	Price	Notes
All Because Of You	7"	United Artists	UP35070	1969	**£4**	
All Over The World	7"	Pye	7N15802	1965	**£5**	chart single
Autumn Rendezvous	7"	Vogue	VRS7014	1966	**£4**	
C'Est Fab	7" EP	Pye	NEP24188	1964	**£5**	
C'Est Francoise	7" EP	Pye	NEP24193	1964	**£5**	
Catch A Falling Star	7"	Pye	7N15612	1964	**£4**	
Comment Te Dire Adieu	7"	United Artists	UP35011	1969	**£4**	chart single
Et Meme	7"	Pye	7N15740	1964	**£4**	
Francoise Hardy	LP	Pye	NPL18094	1964	**£12**	
Francoise Hardy	LP	Vogue	VRL3000	1965	**£12**	
Francoise Hardy	LP	Vogue	VRL3021	1966	**£12**	
Francoise Hardy Sings In English	LP	Vogue	VRL3025	1966	**£12**	
Francoise Sings In English	7" EP	Pye	NEP24192	1964	**£5**	
In Vogue	LP	Pye	NPL18099	1964	**£12**	
Just Call And I'll Be There	7"	Vogue	VRS7001	1966	**£4**	
La Maison Ou J'Ai Grandi	7"	Vogue	VRS7011	1966	**£4**	
Le Meilleur De Francoise Hardy	LP	Vogue	VRL3023	1966	**£10**	
Now You Want To Be Loved	7"	United Artists	UP1208	1968	**£4**	
On Se Quitte Toujours	7"	Vogue	VRS7026	1967	**£4**	
Pourtant Tu M'Aimes	7"	Pye	7N15696	1964	**£4**	
Si C'Est Ca	7"	Vogue	VRS7020	1966	**£4**	
So Many Friends	7"	Vogue	VRS7004	1966	**£4**	
Soon Is Slipping Away	7"	United Artists	UP35105	1970	**£4**	
This Little Heart	7"	Vogue	VRS7010	1966	**£4**	
Tous Les Garcons Et Les Filles	7"	Pye	7N15653	1964	**£4**	chart single
Voila	7"	Vogue	VRS7025	1966	**£4**	
Will You Love Me Tomorrow	7"	United Artists	UP2253	1968	**£4**	

HARE, COLIN

Title	Format	Label	Cat. No.	Year	Price	Notes
Didn't I Tell You	7"	W. Bros	K16203	1972	**£8**	
March Hare	LP	P. Farthing	PELS516	1971	**£30**	

HARGRAVE, RON

Title	Format	Label	Cat. No.	Year	Price	Notes
Latch On	7"	MGM	MGM956	1957	**£75**	

HARLAN COUNTY

Title	Format	Label	Cat. No.	Year	Price	Notes
Harlan County	LP	Nashville		1970	**£12**	

HARMONICA FATS

Tore Up	7"	Action	ACT4507	1968	**£8**	
Tore Up	7"	Action	ACT4507	1968	**£20**	demo
Tore Up	7"	Stateside	SS184	1963	**£6**	

HARMONY GRASS

Cecilia	7"	RCA	RCA1932	1970	**£4**	
First Time Loving	7"	RCA	RCA1828	1969	**£4**	
I Remember	7"	RCA	RCA1885	1969	**£4**	
Move In A Little Bit Closer Baby	7"	RCA	RCA1772	1968	**£4**	chart single
This Is Us	LP	RCA		1968	**£15**	

HARNER, BILLY

What About The Music	7"	Kama Sutra	2013029	1971	**£5**	
What About The Music	7"	Kama Sutra	2013029	1971	**£50**	demo

HARPER, BUD

Mr. Soul	7"	Vocalion	VP9252	1965	**£15**	

HARPER, LEE POPCORN

Love Is Coming	7"	Page One	POF053	1968	**£4**	

HARPER, ROY

Bank Of The Dead	7"	Harvest	HAR5059	1972	**£4**	
Bullinamingvase	LP	Harvest	SHSP4060	1977	**£15**	+ 'Watford Gap', chart LP
Bullinamingvase	LP	Harvest	SHSP4060	1977	**£20**	with 7" (PSR407)
Come Out Fighting Ghengis Smith	LP	CBS	63184	1967	**£20**	
Commercial Break	LP	Harvest	SHSP4077	1977	**£100**	test pressing only
Flashes From The Archives...	LP	Harvest	SHDW405	1974	**£20**	double
Flat Baroque And Beserk	LP	Harvest	SHVL776	1970	**£10**	
Folkjokeopus	LP	Liberty	LBS83231	1969	**£15**	
Forever	7"	Harvest	HAR5080	1974	**£4**	
Grown-Ups Are Just Silly Children	7"	Harvest	HAR5102	1975	**£4**	
Home	7"	Harvest	HAR5089	1974	**£4**	
Introducing Roy Harper	LP	Chrysalis	PRO620	1977	**£30**	US promo
Life Goes By	7"	CBS	3371	1968	**£15**	
Life Mask	LP	Harvest	SHVL808	1973	**£10**	
Midspring Dithering	7"	CBS	203001	1967	**£20**	
Mrs. Space	7"	Harvest	PSR408	1977	**£6**	promo
One Of Those Days In England	7"	Harvest	HAR5120	1977	**£5**	
Playing Games	7"	Harvest	HAR5203	1980	**£4**	
Sail Away	7"	Harvest	HAR5140	1977	**£4**	
Sail Away	7"	Harvest	HAR5140S	1977	**£5**	promo
Sophisticated Beggar	LP	Birth	RAB3	1972	**£10**	
Sophisticated Beggar	LP	Strike	JHL105	1967	**£40**	
Sophisticated Beggar	LP	Youngblood	SYB7	1970	**£15**	
Stormcock	LP	Harvest	SHVL789	1971	**£10**	
Take Me In Your Eyes	7"	Strike	JH304	1966	**£20**	PS
Valentine	LP	Harvest	SHSP4027	1974	**£10**	chart LP
When An Old Cricketer Leaves The ...	7"	Harvest	HAR5096	1975	**£5**	
When An Old Cricketer Leaves The ...	7"	Harvest	HAR5160	1978	**£5**	PS

HARPERS BIZARRE

59th Street Bridge Song	7"	W. Bros	WB5890	1967	**£5**	chart single
Anything Goes	LP	W. Bros	WS1716	1967	**£15**	US
Anything Goes	7"	W. Bros	WB7063	1967	**£5**	chart single
Anything Goes	7"	W. Bros	WB7388	1970	**£4**	
As Time Goes By	LP	Forest Bay Co.	7545	1976	**£10**	US
Battle Of New Orleans	7"	W. Bros	WB7223	1968	**£4**	
Best Of	LP	W. Bros	K56044	1974	**£10**	
Come To The Sunshine	7"	W. Bros	WB7528	1967	**£4**	
Cotton Candy Sandman	7"	W. Bros	WB7172	1968	**£4**	
Feelin' Groovy	LP	W. Bros	WS1693	1967	**£15**	US
Harpers Bizarre 4	LP	W. Bros	WS1784	1969	**£15**	US
I Love You Alice B.Toklas	7"	W. Bros	WB7238	1969	**£4**	
Secret Life Of...	LP	W. Bros	WS1739	1968	**£15**	

HARPO, SLIM

Baby Scratch My Back	LP	Excello	LP8005	1966	**£25**	US
Baby Scratch My Back	7"	Stateside	SS491	1966	**£5**	
Best Of...	LP	Excello	LP8010	1969	**£15**	US

Title	Format	Label	Cat. No.	Year	Price	Notes
Folsom Prison Blues	7"	Blue Horizon	573175	1970	**£8**	
He Knew The Blues	LP	Blue Horizon	763854	1970	**£30**	
I'm A King Bee	7"	Stateside	SS557	1966	**£5**	
I'm Your Breadmaker Baby	7"	Stateside	SS581	1967	**£4**	
Long Drink Of The Blues	LP	Stateside	SL10135	1965	**£20**	
Raining In My Heart	LP	Excello	LP8003	1961	**£40**	US
Raining In My Heart	7"	Pye	7N25098	1961	**£6**	
Raining In My Heart	7"	Pye	7N25220	1963	**£6**	
Shake Your Hips	7"	Stateside	SS527	1966	**£5**	
Slim Harpo Knew The Blues	LP	Excello	LP8013	1970	**£12**	US
Tip On In	LP	Excello	LP8008	1968	**£15**	US
Tip On In	LP	President	PTL1017	196-	**£10**	
Trigger Finger	LP	Blue Horizon	2431013	1971	**£25**	

HARRIOTT, DERRICK

Title	Format	Label	Cat. No.	Year	Price	Notes
Best Of Vol.1	LP	Island	ILP928	1965	**£60**	
Give You My Love	7"	New Beat	NB027	1968	**£8**	
I'm Only Human	7"	Island	WI170	1965	**£12**	
Rock Steady Party	LP	Island	ILP955	1967	**£60**	
Two Of A Kind	7"	Island	WI193	1965	**£10**	
You Never Miss The Water	7"	Pyramid	PYR6027	1969	**£8**	

HARRIOTT, DERRICK & THE CRYSTALITES

Title	Format	Label	Cat. No.	Year	Price	Notes
Best Of	LP	Island	ILP983	1968	**£50**	

HARRIOTT, JOE

Title	Format	Label	Cat. No.	Year	Price	Notes
Abstract	LP	Columbia	33SX1477	1962	**£50**	
Free Form	LP	Jazzland	JLP49	1960	**£50**	
High Spirits	LP	Columbia	33SX1692	1964	**£50**	
Hum-Dono	LP	Columbia	SCX6354	1969	**£40**	
Indo-Jazz Suite	LP			1965	**£50**	
Movement	LP	Columbia	33SX1627	1963	**£50**	
Swings High	LP	Melodisc	SLP12150	1967	**£50**	

HARRIS SISTERS

Title	Format	Label	Cat. No.	Year	Price	Notes
Kissing Bug	7"	Capitol	CL14232	1955	**£4**	

HARRIS, BETTY

Title	Format	Label	Cat. No.	Year	Price	Notes
Cry To Me	7"	London	HL9796	1963	**£6**	
Nearer To You	7"	Stateside	SS2045	1967	**£8**	
Ride Your Pony	7"	Action	ACT4535	1969	**£6**	
Ride Your Pony	7"	Action	ACT4535	1969	**£15**	demo
Soul Perfection	LP	Action	ACLP6007	1969	**£15**	

HARRIS, DON 'SUGARCANE'

Title	Format	Label	Cat. No.	Year	Price	Notes
Cupful Of Dreams	LP	BASF	MPS68030	1973	**£12**	
Don 'Sugarcane' Harris	LP	Epic	26286	1970	**£12**	US
Fiddler On The Rock	LP	BASF	MPS68028	1970	**£12**	
Got The Blues	LP	BASF	MPS68029	1972	**£10**	
I'm On Your Case	LP	BASF	BFL3093	1974	**£10**	
Keep On Driving	LP	BASF	MPS68027	1970	**£12**	
Sugarcane	LP	Epic	30027	1971	**£12**	

HARRIS, EDDIE

Title	Format	Label	Cat. No.	Year	Price	Notes
Listen Here	7"	Atlantic	584218	1969	**£4**	

HARRIS, EMMYLOU

Title	Format	Label	Cat. No.	Year	Price	Notes
Gliding Bird	LP	Jubilee	JGS8031	1969	**£50**	US, colour cover
Quarter Moon In A Ten Cent Town	LP	Mobile Fid.	MFSL1015	1978	**£10**	US audiophile

HARRIS, JET

Title	Format	Label	Cat. No.	Year	Price	Notes
Besame Mucho	7"	Decca	F11466	1962	**£4**	chart single
Big Bad Bass	7"	Decca	F11841	1964	**£4**	
Jet Harris	7" EP	Decca	DFE8502	1962	**£10**	
Man With The Golden Arm	7"	Decca	F11488	1962	**£4**	chart single
My Lady	7"	Fontana	TF849	1967	**£6**	
Theme For A Fallen Idol	7"	SRT	SRTS75355	1975	**£4**	

HARRIS, JET & TONY MEEHAN

Title	Format	Label	Cat. No.	Year	Price	Notes
Applejack	7"	Decca	F11710	1963	**£4**	chart single
Diamonds	7"	Decca	F11563	1963	**£4**	chart single
Jet And Tony	7" EP	Decca	DFE8528	1963	**£8**	

Scarlet O'Hara .... 7" .... Decca .... F11644 .... 1963 .... **£4** .... chart single

HARRIS, JOHNNY

Johnny Harris is a light orchestral arranger and conductor, whose records one would not normally expect to be particularly collectable. "All To Bring You Morning", however, includes guest appearances by Yes-men Jon Anderson and Steve Howe.

All To Bring You Morning .... LP .... W. Bros .... K56185 .... 1973 .... **£10** ....

HARRIS, OSCAR

I Don't Wanna Listen .... 7" .... Upfront .... UP6 .... 197- .... **£4** ....

HARRIS, PAT

Hippy Hippy Shake .... 7" .... Pye .... 7N15567 .... 1963 .... **£8** ....

HARRIS, ROLF

Ringo For President .... 7" .... Columbia .... DB7349 .... 1964 .... **£4** ....
Sun Arise .... 7" .... Columbia .... DB4888 .... 1962 .... **£4** .... chart single
Tie Me Kangaroo Down Sport .... 7" .... Columbia .... DB4483 .... 1960 .... **£4** .... chart single

HARRIS, SHAKEY JAKE

Devil's Harmonica .... LP .... Polydor .... 2391015 .... 1972 .... **£15** ....
Further On Up The Road .... LP .... Liberty .... 83217 .... 1969 .... **£15** ....

HARRIS, THURSTON

Be Baba Leba .... 7" .... Vogue .... V9108 .... 1958 .... **£30** ....
Do What You Did .... 7" .... Vogue .... V9098 .... 1958 .... **£30** ....
Hey Little Girl .... 7" .... Vogue .... V9146 .... 1959 .... **£15** ....
In The Bottom Of My Heart .... 7" .... Vogue .... V9144 .... 1959 .... **£15** ....
Little Bitty Pretty One .... 7" .... Sue .... WI4016 .... 1966 .... **£8** ....
Little Bitty Pretty One .... 7" .... Vogue .... V9092 .... 1957 .... **£15** ....
Purple Stew .... 7" .... Vogue .... V9139 .... 1959 .... **£12** ....
Runk Bunk .... 7" .... Vogue .... V9149 .... 1959 .... **£30** ....
Slip Slop .... 7" .... Vogue .... V9151 .... 1959 .... **£12** ....
Smokey Joes .... 7" .... Vogue .... V9122 .... 1958 .... **£12** ....
Tears From My Heart .... 7" .... Vogue .... V9127 .... 1958 .... **£12** ....

HARRIS, WEE WILLIE

Love Bug Crawl .... 7" .... Decca .... F10980 .... 1958 .... **£10** ....
No Chemise Please .... 7" .... Decca .... F11044 .... 1958 .... **£6** ....
Rocking At The Two I's .... 7" .... Decca .... F10970 .... 1957 .... **£10** ....
Rocking With Wee Willie .... 7" EP .... Decca .... DFE6465 .... 1958 .... **£20** ....
Someone's In The Kitchen With Dinah .. 7" .... Parlophone .... R5504 .... 1966 .... **£4** ....
Wild One .... 7" .... Decca .... F11217 .... 1960 .... **£5** ....

HARRIS, WYNONIE

Battle Of The Blues .... 7" EP .... Bluebeat .... BBEP301 .... 1961 .... **£20** ....
Bloodshot Eyes .... 7" .... Vogue .... V2127 .... 1969 .... **£4** ....
Drinkin' Wine Spo Dee O Dee .... 7" .... Vogue .... V2006 .... 1968 .... **£4** ....
Good Rockin' Blues .... LP .... King .... KS1086 .... 1970 .... **£12** .... US
Wynonie Mister Blues Harris .... 7" EP .... Vogue .... EPV1103 .... 195- .... **£40** ....

HARRIS, WYNONIE / AMOS MILBURN & PRINCE WATERFORD

Party After Hours .... LP-10' .. Aladdin .... 703 .... 1956 .... **£150** .... US
Party After Hours .... LP-10' .. Aladdin .... 703 .... 1956 .... **£250** .... US, red vinyl

HARRISON, DANNY

I'm A Rolling Stone .... 7" .... Coral .... Q72479 .... 1965 .... **£15** ....
Introducing Danny Harrison .... 7" EP .... Starlite .... STEP23 .... 196- .... **£5** ....

HARRISON, EARL

Humphrey Stomp .... 7" .... London .... HL10121 .... 1967 .... **£6** ....

HARRISON, GEORGE

"Songs By George Harrison" consists of three out-takes from "Somewhere In England" together with a live version of "For You Blue". It is available as either a CD or a vinyl single, but in either case only as a bonus within a deluxe, partly hand-made, edition of a book of George Harrison's lyrics. £245 was the new selling price of the set in 1990, and it was produced as a limited edition of 2,500 copies. The price is likely to rise once all the new copies are sold (as of August 1990 there were still some copies remaining), although despite a return to the charts, George Harrison is not the subject of extreme collectors' interest that he once was.

All Things Must Pass .... LP .... Apple .... STCH639 .... 1971 .... **£20**.3 LP box, poster, chart LP
All Those Years Ago .... 7" .... Dark Horse .... K17807 .... 1981 .... **£8** .... demo
Bangla Desh .... 7" .... Apple .... R5912 .... 1971 .... **£6** .... PS
Blow Away .... 7" .... Dark Horse .... K17327 .... 1979 .... **£4** .... chart single

Blow Away	7"	Dark Horse	K17327	1979	**£10**	demo
Dark Horse	7"	Apple	R6001	1975	**£6**	PS
Dark Horse Radio Special	LP	Dark Horse	SP22002	1974	**£30**	US promo
Ding Dong	7"	Apple	R6002	1974	**£12**	demo
Electronic Sounds	LP	Apple	ZAPPLE2	1969	**£50**	
Faster	7"	Dark Horse	K17423	1979	**£10**	demo
Faster	7"	Dark Horse	K17423	1979	**£6**	pic disc
Give Me Love	7"	Apple	R5988	1973	**£12**	demo
Gone Troppo	LP	Dark Horse	9237341	1982	**£20**	US audiophile promo
It's What You Value	7"	Dark Horse	K16967	1977	**£4**	
It's What You Value	7"	Dark Horse	K16967	1977	**£10**	demo
Love Comes To Everyone	7"	Dark Horse	K17384	1979	**£10**	demo
My Sweet Lord	7"	Apple	R5884	1971	**£10**	PS
My Sweet Lord	7"	Apple	R5884	1976	**£4**	different PS
Somewhere In England	LP	Dark Horse	DHK3472	1980	**£30**	US orig. issue + four different tracks
Songs By George Harrison	CD	Genesis pub.	SGHCD777	1988	**£245**	issued with ltd.ed. book
Songs By George Harrison	7"	Genesis pub.	SGH777	1988	**£245**	issued with ltd.ed. book
Teardrops	7"	Dark Horse	K17837	1981	**£8**	demo
Thirty-Three And A Third Dialogue	LP	Dark Horse	PRO649	1976	**£30**	US promo
This Guitar	7"	Apple	R6012	1976	**£4**	
This Guitar	7"	Apple	R6012	1976	**£12**	demo
This Song	7"	Dark Horse	K16856	1976	**£4**	
This Song	7"	Dark Horse	K16856	1976	**£10**	demo
True Love	7"	Dark Horse	K16896	1977	**£4**	
True Love	7"	Dark Horse	K16896	1977	**£10**	demo
Wonderwall	LP	Apple	APCOR1	1968	**£35**	mono
Wonderwall	LP	Apple	SAPCOR1	1968	**£25**	
You	7"	Apple	R6007	1975	**£6**	PS

HARRISON, GEORGE & OTHERS

Concert For Bangla Desh	LP	Apple	STCX3385	1972	**£25**	box set, booklet, Chart LP

HARRISON, MIKE

Mike Harrison	LP	Island	ILPS9170	1971	**£10**	
Smokestack Lightning	LP	Island	ILPS9209	1972	**£10**	

HARRISON, NOEL

It's All Over Now Baby Blue	7"	Decca	F12345	1966	**£4**	
Love Minus Zero/No Limit	7"	Decca	F12918	1969	**£4**	
Noel Harrison	7" EP	Decca	DFE8616	1965	**£5**	
Noel Harrison	7" EP	HMV	7EG8383	1957	**£5**	
To Ramona	7" EP	Decca	DFE8639	1965	**£5**	
Trees	7"	Decca	F12201	1965	**£4**	
Windmills Of Your Mind	7"	Reprise	RS20758	1969	**£4**	chart single
Young Girl Of Sixteen	7"	Decca	F12314	1966	**£4**	

HARRISON, WILBERT

I'm Broke	7"	Island	WI031	1962	**£4**	
Kansas City	LP	Sphere Sound	SR7000	1964	**£25**	US
Kansas City	7"	Top Rank	JAR132	1959	**£5**	
Let's Stick Together	7"	Sue	WI363	1965	**£8**	
Let's Work Together	LP	London	SH8415	1969	**£12**	
Let's Work Together	7"	London	HL10307	1970	**£4**	

HARSH REALITY

Heaven And Hell	LP	Philips	SBL7891	1969	**£50**	
Heaven And Hell	7"	Philips	PB1769	1969	**£10**	
Tobacco Ash Sunday	7"	Philips	PB1710	1968	**£8**	

HART, CAJUN

Got To Find A Way	7"	W. Bros	WB7258	1969	**£15**	

HART, DERRY & THE HARTBEATS

Come On Baby	7"	Decca	F11138	1959	**£5**	

HART, MICKEY

Rolling Thunder	LP	W. Bros	K46182	1972	**£15**	

HART, MIKE

Basher, Chalky, Pongo And Me	LP	Polydor	2310211	1972	**£10**	
Mike Hart Bleeds	LP	Dandelion	63756	1970	**£12**	

Title	Format	Label	Cat. No.	Year	Price	Notes
Son Son	7"	Deram	DM409	1974	**£4**	
Yawney Morning Song	7"	Dandelion	4781	1970	**£5**	

HART, TIM & MADDY PRIOR

Title	Format	Label	Cat. No.	Year	Price	Notes
Folk Songs Of Olde England 1	LP	Tepee	TEPEE105	1968	**£12**	
Folk Songs Of Olde England 2	LP	Tepee	TRPM105	1968	**£12**	
Summer Solstice	LP	B&C	CAS1035	1972	**£12**	

HARTLEY, KEEF

The Keef Hartley Band was one of the many groups to emerge from the John Mayall school of blues, and one of the best. They favoured a tough, riff-based approach to blues-rock, and by gradually adding brass instruments the group became a key element within the growth of jazz-rock. The first two albums are the best - after that Miller Anderson, who was both the lead singer and the lead guitarist, became a little too fond of writing sensitive, reflective material, which did not really suit the band. "Little Big Band", however, which presents the group's most exciting music re-arranged for a much bigger unit, is a splendid return to form.

Title	Format	Label	Cat. No.	Year	Price	Notes
Battle Of NW6	LP	Deram	SML1054	1970	**£12**	
Best Of...	LP	Deram	DPA3011/2	1974	**£15**	double
Dance To The Music	7"	Deram	DM380	1973	**£5**	
Halfbreed	LP	Deram	SML1037	1969	**£12**	
Lancashire Hustler	LP	Deram	SDL13	1973	**£12**	
Leave It Till The Morning	7"	Deram	DM250	1969	**£8**	
Little Big Band	LP	Deram	SDL4	1971	**£20**	
Overdog	LP	Deram	SDL2	1971	**£12**	
Roundabout	7"	Deram	DM316	1970	**£5**	
Seventy Second Brave	LP	Deram	SDL9	1972	**£12**	
Time Is Near	LP	Deram	SML1071	1970	**£12**	chart LP
Waiting Around	7"	Deram	DM273	1969	**£6**	

HARVEY & THE MOONGLOWS

Title	Format	Label	Cat. No.	Year	Price	Notes
Ten Commandments Of Love	7"	London	HLM8730	1958	**£40**	

HARVEY BOYS

Title	Format	Label	Cat. No.	Year	Price	Notes
Nothing Is Too Good For You	7"	London	HLA8397	1957	**£6**	

HARVEY, ALEX

Title	Format	Label	Cat. No.	Year	Price	Notes
Agent OO Soul	7"	Fontana	TF610	1965	**£15**	
Ain't That Just Too Bad	7"	Polydor	56017	1965	**£30**	
Alex Harvey Soul Band	LP	Polydor	SLPH237624	1964	**£25**	
Blues	LP	Polydor	SLPH237641	1964	**£50**	
Framed	LP	Vertigo	6360081	1972	**£40**	spiral label
Got My Mojo Working	7"	Polydor	NH52907	1964	**£20**	
I Just Wanna Make Love To You	7"	Polydor	NH52264	1964	**£20**	
Mafia Stole My Guitar	LP	RCA	PL25257	1979	**£10**	
Maybe Someday	7"	Decca	F12660	1967	**£25**	
Midnight Moses	7"	Fontana	TF1063	1969	**£15**	
Penthouse Tapes	LP	Vertigo	9102007	1975	**£10**	chart LP
Roman Wall Blues	LP	Fontana	STL5534	1969	**£30**	
Sunday Song	7"	Decca	F12640	1967	**£25**	
Work Song	7"	Fontana	TF764	1966	**£20**	

HARVEY, JANICE

Title	Format	Label	Cat. No.	Year	Price	Notes
Portrait Of...	LP	Westwood		1976	**£30**	

HARVEY, RICHARD

Richard Harvey was the dominant influence within Gryphon and his interest, knowledge, and skill with medieval instruments has kept him busy as a session musician and soundtrack composer ever since. "A New Way Of Seeing" was produced specially for a new equipment launch by the computer company ICL and has never been issued commercially.

Title	Format	Label	Cat. No.	Year	Price	Notes
Division On The Ground	LP	Transatlantic	TRA292	1975	**£60**	
New Way Of Seeing	LP	ICL	ICL001	1979	**£100**	

HARWOOD, CHRISTINE

Title	Format	Label	Cat. No.	Year	Price	Notes
Nice To Meet Miss Christine	LP	Birth		1970	**£30**	

HASKELL, GORDON

Title	Format	Label	Cat. No.	Year	Price	Notes
It Is And It Isn't	LP	Atlantic	K40311	1972	**£20**	
Sailin' My Boat	LP	CBS	63741	1969	**£60**	

HASSLES

The first recordings by Billy Joel (apart from a little unspecified session work) were with the Hassles, whose only claim to fame this is.

Title	Format	Label	Cat. No.	Year	Price	Notes
Hassles	LP	United Artists	UAS6631	1968	**£20**	US

Hour Of The Wolf	LP	United Artists	UAS6699	1969	**£20**	US
You Got Me Humming	7"	United Artists	UP1199	1967	**£8**	

HATCH, TONY ORCHESTRA

Crossroads	7"	Pye	7N15754	1965	**£5**	PS

HATE

Hate Kills	LP	Famous	SFMA5752	1970	**£15**	

HATFIELD & THE NORTH

Afters	LP	Virgin	VR5	1980	**£25**	
Hatfield And The North	LP	Virgin	V2008	1974	**£10**	
Let's Eat	7"	Virgin	VS116	1975	**£4**	
Rotters Club	LP	Virgin	V2030	1975	**£10**	chart LP

HATHAWAY, DONNY

Donny Hathaway	LP	Atlantic	503068	1970	**£10**	
Everything Is Everything	LP	Atlantic	2465019	1970	**£10**	
Ghetto	7"	Atco	226010	1970	**£5**	
Live	LP	Atlantic	K40369	1972	**£10**	

HAVEN, ALAN

Image	7"	Fontana	TF542	1965	**£6**	

HAVENS, RICHIE

1983	LP	Verve	2620001	1969	**£15**	double
Alarm Clock	LP	Polydor	2310080	1971	**£10**	
Electric Havens	LP	Transatlantic	TRA187	1966	**£12**	
Great Blind Degree	LP	Polydor	2480049	1972	**£10**	
Handsome Johnny	7"	Verve	VS1524	1969	**£4**	
Here Comes The Sun	7"	Polydor	2001162	1971	**£4**	
Lady Madonna	7"	Verve	VS1519	1969	**£4**	
Live On Stage	LP	Polydor	2659015	1972	**£12**	double
Mixed Bag	LP	Verve	2317002	1967	**£12**	
Mixed Bag 2	LP	Polydor	2310356	1974	**£10**	
Oxford Town	7"	Transatlantic	BIG119	1969	**£4**	
Portfolio	LP	Polydor	2480166	1973	**£10**	
Richie Havens' Record	LP	Transatlantic	TRA199	1965	**£12**	
Rocky Raccoon	7"	Verve	VS1521	1969	**£4**	
Something Else Again	LP	Verve	2317030	1968	**£12**	
State Of Mind	LP	Verve	2304050	1971	**£10**	
Stonehenge	LP	Polydor	2371004	1970	**£10**	
There's A Hole In The Future	7"	Verve	VS1523	1969	**£4**	
Three Day Eternity	7"	Verve	VS1512	1968	**£4**	

HAWKES, CHIP

Nashville Album	LP	RCA		1977	**£25**	

HAWKINS, DALE

Hot Dog	7"	London	HLM9060	1960	**£10**	
La Do Da Da	7"	London	HLM8728	1958	**£20**	
LA, Memphis And Tyler, Texas	LP	Bell	SBLL127	1970	**£15**	
Let's All Twist	LP	Roulette	R25175	1962	**£40**	US
Liza Jane	7"	London	HLM9016	1959	**£12**	
Susie Q	7"	Janus	no number	1971	**£20**	DJ promo, + extra tracks
Susie Q	7"	London	HL8482	1957	**£40**	
Suzie Q	LP	Chess	1429	1958	**£200**	US
Yea Yea Classcutter	7"	London	HLM8842	1959	**£15**	

HAWKINS, HAWKSHAW

All New Hawkshaw Hawkins	LP	King	808	1963	**£12**	US
Country And Western	7" EP	Parlophone	GEP8742	1958	**£12**	
Country And Western	7" EP	Vogue	VE170117	195-	**£15**	
Grand Ole Opry Favorites	LP	King	592	1958	**£20**	US
Hawkshaw Hawkins	LP	King	587	1958	**£20**	US
Hawkshaw Hawkins	LP	King	599	1959	**£20**	US
Lonesome 7-7203	7"	London	HL9737	1963	**£4**	
Taken From Our Vaults Vol.1	LP	King	858	1963	**£10**	US
Taken From Our Vaults Vol.2	LP	King	870	1963	**£10**	US
Taken From Our Vaults Vol.3	LP	King	873	1963	**£10**	US

HAWKINS, RONNIE

Title	Format	Label	Number	Year	Price	Notes
Arkansas Rockpile	LP	Roulette	RCP1003		**£10**	
Best Of Ronnie Hawkins And His Band	LP	Roulette	SR42045	1970	**£15**	US
Bitter Green	7"	Atlantic	2091007	1970	**£5**	
Clara	7"	Columbia	DB4442	1960	**£12**	
Down In The Alley	7"	Atlantic	584320	1970	**£5**	
Folk Ballads	LP	Columbia	33SX1295	1960	**£25**	mono
Folk Ballads	LP	Columbia	SCX3358	1960	**£40**	stereo
Forty Days	7"	Columbia	DB4319	1959	**£15**	
Mary Lou	7"	Columbia	DB4345	1959	**£15**	
Mr. Dynamo	LP	Columbia	33SX1238	1960	**£40**	mono
Mr. Dynamo	LP	Columbia	SCX3315	1960	**£80**	stereo
Mr. Dynamo	LP	Roulette	SR25102	1960	**£150**	US, red vinyl
Rocking With Ronnie	7" EP	Columbia	ESG7792	1960	**£25**	stereo
Rocking With Ronnie	7" EP	Columbia	SEG7983	1960	**£20**	
Rocking With Ronnie No.2	7" EP	Columbia	ESG7795	1960	**£25**	stereo
Rocking With Ronnie No.2	7" EP	Columbia	SEG7988	1960	**£20**	
Ronnie Hawkins	LP	Roulette	R25078	1959	**£40**	US
Ronnie Hawkins	LP	Roulette	SR25078	1959	**£150**	US, red vinyl
Songs Of Hank Williams	LP	Roulette	R25137	1960	**£20**	US
Southern Love	7"	Columbia	DB4412	1960	**£12**	
Who Do You Love	7"	Columbia	DB7036	1963	**£8**	
Who Do You Love	7"	Roulette	RO512	1969	**£4**	

HAWKINS, SCREAMING JAY

Title	Format	Label	Number	Year	Price	Notes
At Home	LP	Epic	LN3448	1956	**£180**	US
I Hear Voices	7"	Sue	WI379	1965	**£10**	
I Put A Spell On You	LP	Direction	863481	1969	**£20**	
I Put A Spell On You	7"	Direction	584097	1969	**£5**	
I Put A Spell On You	LP	Epic	LN3457	1957	**£100**	US
I Put A Spell On You	78	Fontana	H107	1958	**£20**	
Night At Forbidden City	LP	S.O. Hawaii	5015	196-	**£25**	US
Screaming Jay Hawkins	LP	Philips	PHS600336	1970	**£15**	US
Whammy	7"	Columbia	DB7460	1965	**£12**	
What That Is	LP	Mercury	SMCL20178	1969	**£15**	

HAWKWIND

By overlaying simple riff music with electronic noise Hawkwind succeeded in creating the perfect backdrop for Michael Moorcock's science fiction and sword and sorcery novels. The link was cemented by Moorcock himself contributing to many of the group's records; by Hawkwind returning the favour in supplying the music for Moorcock's own "New World's Fair" LP; and by Moorcock inspiring the creation of a science fiction novel in which the members of Hawkwind were the main characters. Here is the origin of the close inter-relation between fantasy and heavy metal music. The perfect artefact to summarise all this is the Hawkwind LP "Warrior On The Edge Of Time", whose cover showing a mounted hero waiting on the edge of a precipice opens out into a cardboard shield.

Title	Format	Label	Number	Year	Price	Notes
Psi Power	7"	Charisma	CB323	1978	**£5**	
25 Years	7"	Charisma	CB332	1979	**£4**	
25 Years	12"	Charisma	CB33212	1979	**£6**	
Angel Of Death	7"	RCA	RCA137	1981	**£4**	
Back On The Streets	7"	Charisma	CB299	1977	**£5**	
Church Of Hawkwind	LP	RCA	RCALP9004	1982	**£12**	with booklet
Doremi Fasolatido	LP	United Artists	UAG29364	1972	**£12**	with poster, chart LP
Hall Of The Mountain Grill	LP	United Artists	UAG29672	1974	**£10**	chart LP
Hawkwind	LP	Liberty	LBA83348	1970	**£15**	
Hurry On Hawkwind	7"	United Artists	US4501/2	197-	**£60**	double
Hurry On Hawkwind	7" EP	United Artists	USEP1	1973	**£50**	
Hurry On Sundown	7"	Flicknife	SLEP101	1981	**£4**	
Hurry On Sundown	12"	Flicknife	FLEP100	1982	**£6**	pic disc
Hurry On Sundown	12"	Flicknife	SLEP101	1981	**£6**	
Hurry On Sundown	7"	Liberty	LBF15382	1970	**£30**	
In Search Of Space	LP	United Artists	UAG29202	1971	**£12**	chart LP
Kerb Crawler	7"	Charisma	CB289	1976	**£4**	PS
Kings Of Speed	7"	United Artists	UP35808	1975	**£4**	
Levitation	LP	Bronze	BRON530	1980	**£12**	blue vinyl
Official Picture Log Book	LP	Flicknife			**£25**	3 pic discs, boxed
Over The Top	12"	Flicknife	FLEP101	1981	**£6**	
Psychedelic Warlords	7"	United Artists	UP35715	1974	**£5**	
PXR5	LP	Charisma	CDS4016	1979	**£10**	
Quark Strangeness And Charm	7"	Charisma	CB305	1977	**£4**	
Shot Down In The Night	7"	Bronze	BRO98	1980	**£4**	chart single
Silver Machine	7"	RCA	RCAP267	1982	**£5**	pic disc
Silver Machine	7"	United Artists	UP35381	1972	**£4**	chart single

Title	Format	Label	Cat. No.	Year	Price	Notes
Silver Machine	7"	United Artists	UP35381	1972	**£6**	PS
Silver Machine	7"	United Artists	UPP35381	1982	**£5**	pic disc
Sonic Attack	7"	United Artists		1972	**£100**	PS, 1 sided promo
Space Ritual	LP	United Artists	UAD60037/8	1973	**£15**	double, chart LP
Urban Guerilla	7"	United Artists	UP35566	1973	**£8**	chart single
Warrior On The Edge Of Time	LP	United Artists	UAG29766	1975	**£12**	shield cover, chart LP
Who's Gonna Win The War	7"	Bronze	BRO109	1980	**£4**	
Who's Gonna Win The War	7"	Flicknife	FLS209	1982	**£4**	

HAWKWIND/BEATLES

Title	Format	Label	Cat. No.	Year	Price	Notes
Silver Machine	7"	United Artists	UPP35381	1982	**£10**	Mis-press - B side plays 'Ask Me Why'

HAYDOCK'S ROCKHOUSE

Title	Format	Label	Cat. No.	Year	Price	Notes
Cupid	7"	Columbia	DB8050	1966	**£12**	
Lovin' You	7"	Columbia	DB8135	1967	**£12**	

HAYES, BILL

Title	Format	Label	Cat. No.	Year	Price	Notes
Ballad Of Davy Crockett	7"	London	HLA8220	1956	**£10**	chart single
Berry Tree	7"	London	HL8149	1955	**£6**	
Das Ist Musik	7"	London	HLA8300	1956	**£6**	
Great Pioneers Of The West	7" EP	London	REA1051	1956	**£6**	
Kwela Kwela	7"	London	HLA8239	1956	**£6**	
Legend Of Wyatt Earp	7"	London	HLA8325	1956	**£8**	
Wimoweh	7"	London	HLR8833	1959	**£4**	
Wringle Wrangle	7"	London	HL8430	1957	**£4**	

HAYES, ISAAC

Title	Format	Label	Cat. No.	Year	Price	Notes
Hot Buttered Soul	LP	Stax	2325011	1969	**£10**	
I Stand Accused	7"	Stax	STAX154	1970	**£4**	
Isaac Hayes Movement	LP	Stax		1970	**£10**	
Presenting Isaac Hayes	LP	Stax		1967	**£10**	
To Be Continued	LP	Stax	2325026	1971	**£10**	
Walk On By	7"	Stax	STAX133	1969	**£4**	

HAYES, LINDA

Title	Format	Label	Cat. No.	Year	Price	Notes
Oochi Pachi	7"	Parlophone	MSP6174	1955	**£30**	

HAYMARKET SQUARE

Title	Format	Label	Cat. No.	Year	Price	Notes
Magic Lantern	LP	Chaparral	201	1968	**£150**	US

HAYWARD, JUSTIN

Title	Format	Label	Cat. No.	Year	Price	Notes
Eve Of The War	12"	CBS	117731	1980	**£8**	pic disc
I Can't Face The World Without You	7"	Parlophone	R5496	1966	**£10**	
London Is Behind Me	7"	Pye	7N17014	1965	**£10**	

HAYWARD, RICK

Title	Format	Label	Cat. No.	Year	Price	Notes
Rick Hayward	LP	Blue Horizon	2431006	1971	**£20**	

HAZELWOOD, LEE

Title	Format	Label	Cat. No.	Year	Price	Notes
Words Mean Nothing	7"	London	HLW9223	1960	**£8**	

HAZZARD, TONY

Title	Format	Label	Cat. No.	Year	Price	Notes
Loudwater House	LP	Bronze	ILPS9174	1971	**£12**	
Sound Of The Candyman's Trumpet	7"	CBS	3452	1968	**£5**	
Tony Hazzard Sings	LP	CBS	63608	1969	**£12**	
Was That Alright Then	LP	Bronze	ILPS9222	1973	**£10**	
You'll Never Put Shackles On Me	7"	Columbia	DB7927	1966	**£5**	

HEAD MACHINE

Title	Format	Label	Cat. No.	Year	Price	Notes
Orgasm	LP	Major Minor	SMLP79	1970	**£60**	

HEAD SHOP

Title	Format	Label	Cat. No.	Year	Price	Notes
Head Shop	LP	Epic	BN26476	1969	**£20**	US

HEAD, MURRAY

Title	Format	Label	Cat. No.	Year	Price	Notes
Alberta	7"	Columbia	DB7635	1965	**£4**	
Bells Of Rhymney	7"	Columbia	DB7771	1965	**£4**	
Nigel Lived	LP	CBS	65503	1973	**£10**	
Say It Ain't So	LP	Island	ILPS9347	1975	**£12**	
She Was Perfection	7"	Immediate	IM053	1967	**£8**	
Someday Soon	7"	Columbia	DB8102	1967	**£4**	

HEAD, ROY

Title	Format	Label	Number	Year	Price	Notes
Apple Of My Eye	7"	Vocalion	VP9254	1966	**£4**	
Just A Little Bit	7"	Pye	7N25340	1965	**£4**	
Just A Little Bit Of Roy Head	7" EP	Pye	NEP44053	1966	**£5**	
Most Wanted Man In Town	7"	London	HLD10487	1975	**£4**	
My Babe	7"	Vocalion	VP9269	1966	**£4**	
Roy Head And The Traits	LP	TNT	101	1965	**£50**	US
To Make A Big Man Cry	7"	London	HLZ10097	1966	**£4**	
Treat Her Right	7"	Vocalion	VP9248	1965	**£5**	chart single
Treat Me Right	LP	Scepter	S532	1965	**£15**	US
Wigglin' And Gigglin'	7"	Vocalion	VP9274	1966	**£4**	

HEADLINERS

Title	Format	Label	Number	Year	Price	Notes
That's The Way I Must Go	7"	Decca	F12209	1965	**£4**	
What Became Of Love	7"	Decca	F12279	1965	**£4**	

HEADS, HANDS & FEET

Title	Format	Label	Number	Year	Price	Notes
Heads, Hands And Feet	LP	Island	ILPS9149	1971	**£15**	
Just Another Ambush	7"	Atlantic	K10312	1973	**£4**	
Old Soldiers Never Die	LP	Atlantic	K40465	1973	**£15**	
One Woman	7"	Atlantic	K10292	1973	**£4**	
Tracks	LP	Island	ILPS9185	1972	**£15**	
Warming Up The Band	7"	Island	WIP6115	1971	**£5**	

HEART

Title	Format	Label	Number	Year	Price	Notes
Dreamboat Annie	LP	Mushroom	MRS5005	1976	**£25**	US pic disc
Dreamboat Annie	LP	Nautilus	NR 3	1979	**£15**	US audiophile
Little Queen	LP	Portrait	HR44799	1981	**£15**	US audiophile
Magazine	LP	Mushroom	MRS1SP	1978	**£20**	US, pic disc
Nothin' At All	7"	Capitol	CL406	1986	**£5**	heart shaped pic disc

HEARTBEATS

Title	Format	Label	Number	Year	Price	Notes
Thousand Miles Away	LP	Roulette	R25107	1960	**£50**	US

HEARTBREAKERS

Title	Format	Label	Number	Year	Price	Notes
Chinese Rocks	7"	Track	2094135	1977	**£4**	
Get Off The Phone	7"	Beggars B.	BEG21	1979	**£4**	
It's Not Enough	7"	Track	2094142	1977	**£60**	
LAMF	LP	Track	2409218	1977	**£12**	chart LP
Live at Max's Kansas City	LP	Beggars B.	BEGA9	1979	**£10**	
One Track Mind	7"	Track	2094137	1977	**£4**	

HEARTS & FLOWERS

Title	Format	Label	Number	Year	Price	Notes
Now Is The Time	LP	Capitol	ST2762	1967	**£40**	US
Of Horses, Kids And Forgotten Women	LP	Capitol	ST2868	1968	**£40**	US
Rock'n'Roll Gypsies	7"	Capitol	CL15492	1967	**£8**	
She Sang Hymns Out Of Tune	7"	Capitol	CL15549	1968	**£8**	

HEARTS OF STONE

Title	Format	Label	Number	Year	Price	Notes
We Wanna Get On	LP	VIP	VS404	1970	**£15**	US

HEATHER BLACK

Title	Format	Label	Number	Year	Price	Notes
Heather Black	LP	American P.	1001	196-	**£50**	US

HEAVEN

Title	Format	Label	Number	Year	Price	Notes
Brass Rock	LP	CBS	66293	1971	**£15**	double

HEAVY JELLY

Title	Format	Label	Number	Year	Price	Notes
I Keep Singing The Same Old Song	7"	Island	WIP6049	1968	**£10**	
Take Me Down	LP	Island		1969	**£50**	demo

HEAVY JELLY (2)

Title	Format	Label	Number	Year	Price	Notes
Chewn In	7"	Head	HEAD4001	1969	**£15**	

HEAVY METAL KIDS

Title	Format	Label	Number	Year	Price	Notes
Anvil Chorus	LP	Atlantic	K50143	1975	**£10**	
Heavy Metal Kids	LP	Atlantic	K50047	1974	**£10**	
Kitsch	LP	RAK	SRAK523	1977	**£10**	

HEBB, BOBBY

Title	Format	Label	Number	Year	Price	Notes
Satisfied Mind	7"	Philips	BF1522	1966	**£5**	
Sunny	LP	Philips	200212	1966	**£15**	US

Sunny	7"	Philips	BF1503	1966	**£4**	

HECKSTALL-SMITH, DICK

Colosseum broke apart during the extensive rehearsals of the difficult "Pirate's Dream", but the piece was rescued for Dick Heckstall-Smith's solo LP. This is close enough to the sound of Colosseum to make it the legitimate follow-up to "Colosseum Live" and is something of an odd record for a saxophonist to have made, as Heckstall-Smith's own contributions do not exactly dominate the centre stage. The record is, however, a fine addition to the small body of adventurous song-writing otherwise largely occupied by the works of Jack Bruce. Meanwhile the very scarce Heckstall-Smith EP provides a kind of glimpse of an alternative world; the start of the career of a straight-ahead jazz saxophonist, that never actually came to be.

Story Ended	LP	Bronze	ILPS9196	1972	**£20**	chart single
Very Special Old Jazz	7" EP	Pye	NJE1037	1957	**£20**	

HEDAYAT, DASHIELL (DAEVID ALLEN)

Melmoth La Devanture...	LP	Arion	30T079	1969	**£30**	French
Obsolete	LP	Shandar	SR83512	1971	**£20**	

HEDGEHOG PIE

Green Lady	LP	Rubber	RUB014	1975	**£10**	
Hedgehog Pie	LP	Rubber	RUB009	1975	**£10**	
His Round	LP	Rubber	RUB002	1972	**£12**	

HEDGEHOPPERS ANONYMOUS

Baby	7"	Decca	F12400	1966	**£4**	
Daytime	7"	Decca	F12479	1966	**£4**	
Don't Push Me	7"	Decca	F12298	1965	**£4**	
It's Good News Week	7"	Decca	F12241	1965	**£4**	chart single
Stop Press	7"	Decca	F12530	1966	**£4**	

HEIGHT, DONALD

365 Days	7"	London	HLZ10116	1967	**£6**	
Rags To Riches	7"	Avco	6105005	1971	**£6**	
Talk Of The Grapevine	7"	London	HLZ10062	1966	**£12**	

HEINZ

Country Boy	7"	Decca	F11768	1963	**£4**	chart single
Diggin' My Potatoes	7"	Columbia	DB7482	1965	**£8**	chart single
Don't Think Twice It's Alright	7"	Columbia	DB7559	1965	**£8**	
Dreams Do Come True	7"	Decca	F11652	1963	**£5**	
End Of The World	7"	Columbia	DB7656	1965	**£8**	
Heart Full Of Sorrow	7"	Columbia	DB7779	1965	**£8**	
Heinz	7" EP	Decca	DFE8545	1963	**£8**	
Just Like Eddie	7"	Decca	F11693	1963	**£4**	chart single
Live It Up	7" EP	Decca	DFE8559	1963	**£8**	
Movin' In	7"	Columbia	DB7942	1966	**£8**	
Please Little Girl	7"	Decca	F11920	1964	**£5**	
Questions I Can't Answer	7"	Columbia	DB7374	1964	**£5**	chart single
Tribute To Eddie	LP	Decca	LK4599	1964	**£25**	
You Were There	7"	Decca	F11831	1964	**£4**	chart single

HEIR

Pollution	LP	Capitol	EST205	1969	**£15**	

HELL PREACHERS INC.

Supreme Psychedelic Underground	LP	Marble Arch	MALS1169	1969	**£30**	

HELL, RICHARD

It was the American Richard Hell who invented the punk style. The ripped clothing comes from him, as does the nihilist attitude - Richard Hell's theme song is "Blank Generation". He was originally the bass player for Television, which is presumably why that group tend to be classed as punk/new wave, despite a fascination with long guitar solos.

Blank Generation	7"	Ork	81976	1976	**£12**	US
Blank Generation	LP	Sire	SR6037	1977	**£15**	
Blank Generation	7"	Sire	6078608	1977	**£10**	
Blank Generation	12"	Sire	6078608	1977	**£10**	
I Could Live With You In Another World	7"	Stiff	BUY7	1976	**£8**	
Kid With The Replaceable Head	7"	Radar	ADA30	1979	**£5**	

HELLING, DAVE

Christine	7"	Planet	PLF101	1966	**£8**	
It Ain't Me Babe	7"	Stateside	SS409	1965	**£5**	

HELLIONS

Three singles, but all of them unsuccessful, for a group that included two future members of Traffic (Dave Mason and Jim

Capaldi) and one future member of Spooky Tooth and Mott The Hoople (Luther Grosvenor/Ariel Bender).

Title	Format	Label	Cat. No.	Year	Price	Notes
Daydreaming Of You	7"	Piccadilly	7N35213	1965	**£15**	
Little Lovin'	7"	Piccadilly	7N35265	1965	**£15**	
Tomorrow Never Comes	7"	Piccadilly	7N35232	1965	**£15**	

HELLMET

Title	Format	Label	Cat. No.	Year	Price	Notes
Hellmet	LP	Deram			**£25**	

HELLO

Title	Format	Label	Cat. No.	Year	Price	Notes
Another School Day	7"	Bell	BLL1333	1973	**£4**	
Bend Me Shape Me	7"	Bell	BLL1424	1975	**£4**	
Game's Up	7"	Bell	BLL1406	1974	**£4**	
Love Stealer	7"	Bell	BLL1482	1976	**£4**	
Star Studded Sham	7"	Bell	BLL1470	1976	**£4**	

HELMS, BOBBY

Title	Format	Label	Cat. No.	Year	Price	Notes
Best Of...	LP	Columbia	CL2060	1963	**£10**	US
Bobby Helms	7" EP	Brunswick	OE9461	1960	**£6**	
Fraulein	7"	Brunswick	05711	1957	**£4**	
I Guess I'll Miss The Prom	7"	Brunswick	05801	1959	**£4**	
Jacqueline	7"	Brunswick	05748	1958	**£4**	chart single
Jingle Bell Rock	7"	Brunswick	05765	1958	**£4**	
Love My Lady	7"	Brunswick	05741	1958	**£4**	
My Lucky Day	7"	Brunswick	05813	1959	**£4**	
My Special Agent	7"	Brunswick	05721	1957	**£4**	chart single
New River Train	7"	Brunswick	05786	1959	**£4**	
No Other Baby	7"	Brunswick	05730	1958	**£4**	chart single
Sad Eyed Baby	7"	Brunswick	05852	1961	**£4**	
Schoolboy Crush	7"	Brunswick	05754	1958	**£4**	
To My Special Angel	LP	Decca	DL8638	1957	**£30**	US

HELMS, JIMMY

Title	Format	Label	Cat. No.	Year	Price	Notes
Magnificent Sanctuary Band	7"	Capitol	CL15762	1973	**£4**	

HELP YOURSELF

Title	Format	Label	Cat. No.	Year	Price	Notes
Beware Of The Shadow	LP	United Artists	UAS29413	1972	**£15**	
Heaven Row	7"	United Artists	UP35355	1972	**£4**	
Help Yourself	LP	Liberty	LIBS83484	1971	**£30**	
Mummy Won't Be Home For Christmas	7"	United Artists	UP35466	1972	**£4**	
Return Of Ken Whaley	LP	United Artists	UAS29487	1973	**£15**	
Return Of Ken Whaley/Happy Days	LP	United Artists	UDG4001	1973	**£25**	double
Running Down Deep	7"	Liberty	LBF15459	1971	**£8**	
Strange Affair	LP	United Artists	UAS29287	1972	**£15**	

HEMLOCK

Title	Format	Label	Cat. No.	Year	Price	Notes
Hemlock	LP	Deram	SML1102	1973	**£30**	
Mr. Horizontal	7"	Deram	DM379	1973	**£8**	

HENDERSON, BERTHA & ROSA HENDERSON

Title	Format	Label	Cat. No.	Year	Price	Notes
Female Blues Vol.2	7" EP	Collector	JE114	196-	**£5**	

HENDERSON, BILL

Title	Format	Label	Cat. No.	Year	Price	Notes
Sweet Pumpkin	7"	Top Rank	JAR412	1960	**£6**	

HENDERSON, DORIS

Doris Henderson was the second female lead singer to be employed by folk-rock pioneers, The Eclection. She had earlier made two very scarce folk LPs on which she is backed by John Renbourn and Danny Thompson.

Title	Format	Label	Cat. No.	Year	Price	Notes
Hangman	7"	Columbia	DB7567	1965	**£8**	
Message To Pretty	7"	Fontana	TF811	1967	**£6**	
There You Go	LP	Columbia	SX6001	1965	**£150**	
Watch The Stars	LP	Fontana	STL5385	1967	**£150**	

HENDERSON, JOE

Title	Format	Label	Cat. No.	Year	Price	Notes
Big Love	7"	London	HLU9615	1962	**£4**	
Joe Henderson	7" EP	London	REU1376	1963	**£6**	
Snap Your Fingers	7"	London	HLU9553	1962	**£4**	

HENDRICKS, BOBBY

Title	Format	Label	Cat. No.	Year	Price	Notes
Itchy Twitchy Feeling	7"	London	HL8714	1958	**£10**	
Itchy Twitchy Feeling	7"	Sue	WI315	1964	**£10**	

HENDRIX, JIMI

Collecting Jimi Hendrix begins with a copy of "Electric Ladyland", which is as good a demonstration of the power and potential of rock music as one is likely to find anywhere. There are any number of examples of Hendrix' genius as a guitarist to be found amongst the double album's tracks, while for those who still believe that Hendrix was all about noise and bombast, there is "1983..A Mermaid I Should Turn To Be", an extended composition in which the resources of the recording studio are tested to the limit, yet to a largely gentle and subtle effect. With regard to actual collectors' items, there is the original "puppet" cover for "Band Of Gypsies"; the scarce red vinyl edition of "The Cry Of Love"; and the even scarcer record club compilation "Electric Hendrix". None, however, can give the excitement and emotional impact of an hour and a half spent in "Electric Ladyland".

Title	Format	Label	Number	Year	Price	Notes
All Along The Watchtower	7"	Polydor	POSPX401	1981	**£4**	
All Along The Watchtower	7"	Track	604025	1968	**£5**	chart single
Angel	7"	Track	2094007	1971	**£4**	
Are You Experienced	LP	Track	612001	1967	**£15**	mono, chart LP
Are You Experienced	LP	Track	613001	1967	**£12**	stereo, chart LP
Axis: Bold As Love	LP	Reprise	R6281	1968	**£150**	US mono
Axis: Bold As Love	LP	Track	612003	1967	**£15**	mono, chart LP
Axis: Bold As Love	LP	Track	613003	1967	**£12**	stereo, chart LP
Band Of Gypsys	LP	Track	2406002	1970	**£12**	kaftan g-fold, chart LP
Band Of Gypsys	LP	Track	2406002	1970	**£20**	puppet cover, chart LP
Burning Of The Midnight Lamp	7"	Track	604007	1967	**£6**	chart single
Crosstown Traffic	7"	Track	604029	1969	**£6**	chart single
Cry Of Love	LP	Track	2408101	1971	**£10**	chart LP
Cry Of Love	LP	Track	2408101	1971	**£180**	red vinyl
Electric Hendrix	LP	Track	2856002	1968	**£280**	
Electric Ladyland	LP	Track	613008/9	1968	**£20**	double, chart LP
Fire	7"	Track	604033	1969	**£6**	
Gloria	7"	Polydor	JIMI1	1978	**£4**	1 sided
Gypsy Eyes	7"	Track	2094010	1971	**£8**	PS, chart single
Hear My Train A-Comin'	7"	Reprise	K14286	1973	**£5**	
Hey Joe	7"	Polydor	56139	1966	**£6**	chart single
Jimi Hendrix	LP	St.Michael		1978	**£45**	
Johnny B Goode	7"	Polydor	2001277	1972	**£5**	chart single
Little Drummer Boy	7"	Reprise	PRO595	1975	**£20**	US promo
Little Drummer Boy	12"	Reprise	PROA840	1979	**£40**	US promo
Live And Unreleased - The Radio Show	LP	Castle	HBCD100	1989	**£40**	3 CD set
Live And Unreleased - The Radio Show	LP	Castle	HBLP100	1989	**£40**	5 LP set
Purple Haze	7"	Track	604001	1967	**£6**	chart single
Singles Boxed Set	7"	Polydor	2608001	1980	**£12**	6 x 7"
Smash Hits	LP	Polydor	ACB00219	1973	**£12**	
Smash Hits	LP	Reprise	MS2025	1969	**£40**	US, with poster
Smash Hits	LP	Track	612004	1968	**£12**	mono, chart LP
Smash Hits	LP	Track	613004	1968	**£10**	stereo, chart LP
Voodoo Chile	7"	Track	2095001	1970	**£6**	chart single
Wind Cries Mary	7"	Track	604004	1967	**£6**	chart single

HENDRIX, JIMI & CURTIS KNIGHT

Title	Format	Label	Number	Year	Price	Notes
Ballad Of Jimi	7"	London	HL10321	1970	**£5**	
Get That Feeling	LP	London	SHU8349	1968	**£12**	chart LP
How Would You Feel	7"	Track	604009	1967	**£5**	
Hush Now	7"	London	HL10160	1967	**£5**	
No Such Animal	7"	RCA	RCA2033	1970	**£5**	
Strange Thing	LP	London	SHU8369	1968	**£12**	

HENDRIX, MARGIE

Title	Format	Label	Number	Year	Price	Notes
Restless	7"	Mercury	MF1001	1967	**£6**	

HENRY COW

Title	Format	Label	Number	Year	Price	Notes
Leg End	LP	Virgin	V2005	1973	**£10**	
Unrest	LP	Virgin	V2011	1974	**£10**	

HENRY, CLARENCE 'FROGMAN'

Title	Format	Label	Number	Year	Price	Notes
Ain't Got No Home	7"	London	HLN8389	1957	**£20**	
Ain't Got No Home	7"	London	HLU10025	1966	**£5**	
Alive & Well And Living In New Orleans	LP	Roulette	SR42039	1969	**£12**	US
But I Do	7"	Pye	7N25078	1961	**£4**	chart single
Clarence Henry Hit Parade	7" EP	Pye	NEP44007	1961	**£15**	
Dream Myself A Sweetheart	7"	Pye	7N25141	1962	**£4**	
Jealous Kind	7"	Pye	7N25169	1962	**£4**	
Little Green Frog	7"	London	HLU9936	1964	**£5**	
Little Too Much	7"	Pye	7N25123	1962	**£4**	
Lonely Street	7"	Pye	7N25108	1961	**£4**	chart single
Standing In The Need Of Love	7"	Pye	7N25115	1961	**£4**	

You Always Hurt The One You Love	LP	Argo	LP4009	1961	**£50**	US
You Always Hurt The One You Love	7"	Pye	7N25089	1961	**£5**	chart single

HENRY, HOUND HEAD & FRANKIE JAXON

Male Blues Vol.6	7" EP	Collector	JE110	196-	**£5**	

HENRY, RICHARD

Oh Girl	7"	Regal Z.	RZ3014	1968	**£5**	

HENSKE, JUDY

Death Defying	LP	Reprise	RS6203	1965	**£15**	
High Flying Bird	LP	Elektra	EKS7241	1964	**£15**	US
Judy Henske	LP	Elektra	EKS7231	1963	**£15**	US
Little Bit Of Sunshine	LP	Mercury	SR61010	1965	**£15**	US

HENSKE, JUDY & JERRY YESTER

Farewell Aldebaran	LP	Straight	STS1052	1969	**£25**	
Road To Nowhere	7"	Reprise	RS20485	1966	**£6**	
Rosebud	LP	Reprise	RS6426	1971	**£20**	US

HENSLEY, KEN

Eager To Please	LP	Bronze	ILPS9307	1975	**£10**	
Proud Words On A Dusty Shelf	LP	Bronze	ILPS9223	1973	**£10**	

HENTSCHEL, DAVID

Oh My My	7"	Ring'O	2017101	1975	**£4**	
Sta*rtling Music	LP	Ring'O	2320101	197-	**£10**	

HEP STARS

Hep Stars	LP	Olga	LP004	196-	**£12**	Swedish
Sunny Girl	7"	Decca	F22446	1966	**£15**	

HERBAL MIXTURE

Love That's Died	7"	Columbia	DB8021	1966	**£12**	
Machines	7"	Columbia	DB8083	1966	**£20**	

HERBIE & THE ROYALISTS

Soul Of The Matter	LP	Saga	FID2121	1968	**£15**	

HERBIE'S PEOPLE

One Little Smile	7"	CBS	202058	1966	**£8**	
Residential Area	7"	CBS	202584	1967	**£8**	
Sweet And Tender Romance	7"	CBS	202005	1965	**£6**	

HERD

From The Underworld	7"	Fontana	TF856	1967	**£4**	chart single
Game	7"	Fontana	TF1011	1969	**£6**	
Goodbye Baby Goodbye	7"	Parlophone	R5284	1965	**£8**	
I Can Fly	7"	Fontana	TF819	1967	**£6**	
I Don't Want Our Loving To Die	7"	Fontana	TF925	1968	**£4**	chart single
Paradise Lost	LP	Fontana	STL5458	1968	**£20**	chart LP
Paradise Lost	7"	Fontana	TF887	1967	**£4**	chart single
She Was Really Saying Something	7"	Parlophone	R5353	1965	**£8**	
So Much In Love	7"	Parlophone	R5413	1966	**£8**	
Sunshine Cottage	7"	Fontana	TF975	1968	**£6**	

HERMAN'S HERMITS

Bet Yer Life I Do	7"	RAK	RAK102	1970	**£4**	chart single
Both Sides Of...	LP	Columbia	SX6084	1966	**£10**	
Dandy	7" EP	Columbia	SEG8520	1967	**£6**	
East West	7"	Columbia	DB8076	1966	**£4**	chart single
Here Comes The Star	7"	Columbia	DB8626	1969	**£4**	chart single
Herman's Hermits	LP	Columbia	33SX1727	1965	**£10**	chart LP
Herman's Hermits' Hits	7" EP	Columbia	SEG8442	1965	**£5**	
Hermania	7" EP	Columbia	SEG8380	1965	**£5**	
Hold On - Soundtrack Songs	7" EP	Columbia	SEG8503	1966	**£6**	
I Can Take Or Leave Your Loving	7"	Columbia	DB8327	1968	**£4**	chart single
I'm Into Something Good	7"	Columbia	DB7338	1964	**£4**	chart single
Just A Little Bit Better	7"	Columbia	DB7670	1965	**£4**	chart single
Lady Barbara	7"	RAK	RAK106	1970	**£4**	chart single
Mrs.Brown	LP	Columbia	SCX6303	1968	**£10**	
Mrs.Brown You've Got A Lovely ...	7" EP	Columbia	SEG8440	1965	**£5**	

Must To Avoid	7"	Columbia	DB7791	1965	**£4**	chart single
Must To Avoid	7" EP	Columbia	SEG8477	1966	**£6**	
My Sentimental Friend	7"	Columbia	DB8563	1969	**£4**	chart single
No Milk Today	7"	Columbia	DB8012	1966	**£4**	chart single
Show Me Girl	7"	Columbia	DB7408	1964	**£4**	chart single
Silhouettes	7"	Columbia	DB7475	1965	**£4**	chart single
Sleepy Joe	7"	Columbia	DB8404	1968	**£4**	chart single
Something's Happening	7"	Columbia	DB8504	1968	**£4**	chart single
Sunshine Girl	7"	Columbia	DB8446	1968	**£4**	chart single
There's A Kind Of Hush	LP	Columbia	SCX6174	1967	**£10**	
There's A Kind Of Hush	7"	Columbia	DB8123	1967	**£4**	chart single
This Door Swings Both Ways	7"	Columbia	DB7947	1966	**£4**	chart single
Wonderful World	7"	Columbia	DB7546	1965	**£4**	chart single
Years May Come, Years May Go	7"	Columbia	DB8656	1970	**£4**	chart single
You Won't Be Leaving	7"	Columbia	DB7861	1966	**£4**	chart single

HERMAN, WOODY

Hush	7"	Chess	CRS8095	1969	**£4**	

HERON

Bye And Bye	7"	Dawn	DNX2509	1971	**£10**	
Heron	LP	Dawn	DNLS3010	1970	**£40**	
Take Me Back Home	7"	Dawn	DNS1015	1970	**£10**	
Twice As Nice	LP	Dawn	DNLS3025	1972	**£40**	double

HERON, MIKE

Diamond Of Dream	LP	Bronze	ILPS9460	1977	**£10**	
Evie	7"	Neighborhood	NBH3109	1975	**£4**	
Lady Wonder	7"	Chrysalis	WIP6101	1971	**£4**	
Mike Heron	LP	Casablanca	NBLP7186	1980	**£10**	US
Mike Heron's Reputation	LP	Neighborhood	NBH80637	1975	**£10**	
Smiling Men With Bad Reputations	LP	Island	ILPS9146	1971	**£12**	
Sold On Your Love	7"	Zoom	ZUM5	1978	**£4**	

HESTER, CAROLYN

Ain't That Rain	7"	Dot	DS16750	1965	**£5**	
At The Town Hall	LP	Dot	DLP3649	1965	**£10**	US
Carolyn Hester	LP	Columbia	CL1796	1962	**£12**	US
Playboys And Playgirls	7"	Dot	DS16751	1965	**£4**	
Reason To Believe	7"	CBS	202409	1966	**£5**	
That's My Song	LP	Dot	DLP3604	1964	**£10**	US
This Is My Living	LP	Columbia	CL2031	1963	**£10**	US

HEWITT, BEN

Break It Up	7" EP	Mercury	ZEP10035	1959	**£15**	
For Quite A While	7"	Mercury	AMT1055	1959	**£10**	
I Want A Girl	7"	Mercury	AMT1084	1960	**£10**	
You Break Me Up	7"	Mercury	AMT1041	1959	**£12**	

HEYWOOD, EDDIE

Soft Summer Breeze	7"	Mercury	7MT131	1957	**£4**	

HI FI FOUR

Davy You Upset My Life	7"	Parlophone	MSP6210	1956	**£8**	

HI FI'S

Baby's In Black	7"	Pye	7N15788	1965	**£8**	
I Keep Forgettin'	7"	Pye	7N15710	1964	**£8**	
It's Gonna Be Morning	7"	Alp	595010	1966	**£8**	

HI LITERS

Dance Me To Death	7"	Mercury	AMT1011	1958	**£20**	

HI NUMBERS

Heart Belongs To You	7"	Decca	F12233	1965	**£8**	

HICKEY, ERSEL

Don't Be Afraid Of Love	7"	Fontana	H198	1959	**£10**	

HICKS, COLIN & THE CABIN BOYS

La Dee Dah	7"	Pye	7N15125	1958	**£5**	
Little Boy Blue	7"	Pye	7N15163	1958	**£5**	

Wild Eyes And Tender Lips	7"	Pye	7N15114	1957	**£6**	

HICKS, DAN & HIS HOT LICKS

Striking It Rich	LP	Blue Thumb	ILPS9204	1972	**£10**	

HIDEAWAYS

Hideout	7"	Action	ACT4544	1969	**£10**	demo

HIGGINS, CHUCK

Pachuko Hop	LP	Combo	LP300	1960	**£40**	US, Higgins cover
Pachuko Hop	LP	Combo	LP300	1960	**£100**	US, nude cover

HIGGS & WILSON

Come On Home	7"	Starlite	ST45042	1961	**£5**	
It Is The Day	7"	Starlite	ST45036	1961	**£5**	
Pretty Baby	7"	Starlite	ST45035	1961	**£5**	
Sha Ba Ba	7"	Starlite	ST45053	1961	**£5**	
When You Tell Me	7"	Blue Beat	BB3	1960	**£10**	

HIGH

Long Live The High	7"	CBS	4164	1969	**£8**	

HIGH & MIGHTY

Tryin' To Stop Cryin'	7"	HMV	POP1548	1966	**£15**	

HIGH BROOM

Dancing In The Moonlight	7"	Island	WIP6088	1970	**£6**	

HIGH KEYS

Que Sera Sera	7"	London	HLK9768	1963	**£6**	

HIGH NUMBERS

"I'm The Face" is one of the most celebrated single rarities. The High Numbers was, of course, the original name of the Who. The group also recorded a version of "The Kids Are Alright" before the name change, but this was not given a full release.

I'm The Face	7"	Back Door	BACK1	1980	**£10**	PS
I'm The Face	7"	Back Door	DOOR4	1980	**£8**	chart single
I'm The Face	7"	Fontana	TF480	1964	**£200**	
Kids Are Alright	7"	Fontana		1964	**£400**	demo

HIGH SOCIETY

People Passing By	7"	Fontana	TF771	1966	**£10**	

HIGH TIDE

High Tide were a heavy group from the time when the heavy metal style was not so rigidly set as to preclude a more experimental approach like this. A heavily distorted guitar is here partnered by an electric violin (courtesy of Simon House, who was later to join Hawkwind) and the two instruments manage to create an extraordinary maelstrom of sound. The singer, meanwhile, is a Jim Morrison sound-alike, the slightly doom-laden voice sounding very effective in this context.

High Tide	LP	Liberty	LBS83294	1970	**£25**	
Sea Shanties	LP	Liberty	LBS83264	1969	**£20**	

HIGHWAY

Highway	LP	EMI	EMA3019	1974	**£12**	
Smoking At The Edge	LP	EMI	EMA770	1975	**£12**	

HILL, BENNY

Benny Hill	7" EP	Pye	NEP24144	1961	**£4**	
Harvest Of Love	7" EP	Pye	NEP24174	1962	**£4**	

HILL, BUNKER

Hide And Go Seek	7"	Stateside	SS135	1962	**£5**	

HILL, JESSE

Jesse Hill	7" EP	Liberty	LEP4036	1965	**£8**	
Ooh Poo Pah Doo	7"	London	HLU9117	1960	**£6**	

HILL, Z.Z.

Gimme Gimme	7" EP	Sue	IEP711	1966	**£30**	
I Keep On Loving You	7"	United Artists	UP35727	1975	**£4**	
Make Me Yours	7"	Action	ACT4532	1969	**£5**	
Make Me Yours	7"	Action	ACT4532	1969	**£15**	demo
Someone To Love	7"	R&B	MRB5005	1965	**£10**	
Whole Lot Of Soul	LP	Action	ACLP6004	1969	**£15**	

HILLAGE, STEVE

Title	Format	Label	Cat. No.	Year	Price	Notes
Green	LP	Virgin	V2098	1978	**£10**	green vinyl
Rainbow Dome Musick	LP	Virgin	VR1	1979	**£10**	clear vinyl
Salmon Song	7"	Virgin	SIXPACK2	1979	**£5**	pic disc

HILLOW HAMMET

Title	Format	Label	Cat. No.	Year	Price	Notes
Hammer	LP	House Of Fox	2	196-	**£20**	US

HILLTOPPERS

Title	Format	Label	Cat. No.	Year	Price	Notes
Alone	7"	London	HLD9038	1960	**£4**	
Do The Bop	7"	London	HLD8278	1956	**£10**	
Fallen Star	7"	London	HLD8455	1957	**£4**	
From The Vine Came The Grape	7"	London	HL8026	1954	**£8**	
Hilltoppers	LP	Dot	DLP3073	1958	**£15**	US
Hilltoppers Vol.2	7" EP	London	RED1030	1955	**£10**	
Hilltoppers Vol.3	7" EP	London	RED1099	1957	**£10**	
I'm Serious	7"	London	HLD8441	1957	**£5**	
If I Didn't Care	7"	London	HL8092	1954	**£8**	
Joker	7"	London	HLD8528	1957	**£6**	
Kentuckian Song	7"	London	HLD8168	1955	**£6**	
Marianne	7"	London	HLD8381	1957	**£6**	chart single
My Treasure	7"	London	HLD8255	1956	**£6**	
Only You	7"	London	HLD8221	1956	**£8**	chart single
Poor Butterfly	7"	London	HL8070	1954	**£6**	
Presenting The Hilltoppers	7" EP	London	RED1012	1955	**£10**	
Searching	7"	London	HLD8208	1955	**£6**	
So Tired	7"	London	HLD8333	1956	**£6**	
Tops In Pops	LP	London	HAD2071	1957	**£15**	
Towering Hilltoppers	LP	Dot	DLP3029	1957	**£15**	US
Towering Hilltoppers	LP	London	HAD2029	1957	**£15**	
Tryin'	7"	London	HLD8298	1956	**£8**	chart single
Will You Remember	7"	London	HL8081	1954	**£8**	
You Sure Look Good To Me	7"	London	HLD8603	1958	**£4**	
You Try Somebody Else	7"	London	HL8116	1955	**£8**	

HILTONAIRES

Title	Format	Label	Cat. No.	Year	Price	Notes
Best Of...	LP	Coxsone	CSL8004	196-	**£80**	

HIM & OTHERS

Title	Format	Label	Cat. No.	Year	Price	Notes
I Mean It	7"	Parlophone	R5510	1966	**£25**	

HINES, JUSTIN & THE DOMINOES

Title	Format	Label	Cat. No.	Year	Price	Notes
Rub Up, Push Up	7"	Island	WI194	1965	**£10**	

HINGE

Title	Format	Label	Cat. No.	Year	Price	Notes
Village Postman	7"	RCA	RCA1721	1968	**£15**	

HINTON, JOE

Title	Format	Label	Cat. No.	Year	Price	Notes
Funny How Time Slips Away	LP	Backbeat	B60	1965	**£12**	US
Funny How Time Slips Away	7"	Vocalion	VP9224	1964	**£8**	
Just A Kid Named Joe	7"	Vocalion	VP9258	1966	**£5**	

HIPSTER IMAGE

Title	Format	Label	Cat. No.	Year	Price	Notes
Can't Let You Go	7"	Decca	F12137	1965	**£10**	

HIT PACK

Title	Format	Label	Cat. No.	Year	Price	Notes
Never Say No To Your Baby	7"	Tamla Motown	TMG513	1965	**£20**	
Never Say No To Your Baby	7"	Tamla Motown	TMG513	1965	**£60**	demo

HITCHCOCK, ROBYN

Title	Format	Label	Cat. No.	Year	Price	Notes
America	7"	Albion	ION103	1982	**£5**	
Eaten By Her Own Dinner	7"	Midnight Mus.	DING2	1982	**£6**	
Man Who Invented Himself	7"	Armageddon	AS008	1981	**£8**	
Man Who Invented Himself	7"	Armageddon	AS008	1981	**£12**	with flexi (4SPURT1)

HITTERS (BRINSLEY SCHWARZ)

Title	Format	Label	Cat. No.	Year	Price	Notes
Hypocrite	7"	United Artists	UP35530	1973	**£6**	

HOBBITS

Title	Format	Label	Cat. No.	Year	Price	Notes
Daffodil Days	7"	MCA	MU1002	1968	**£4**	
Down To Middle Earth	LP	MCA	MUP301	1967	**£20**	
Men And Doors	LP	Decca	DL75009	1968	**£12**	US

HOBBY SHOP

Why Must It Be This Way	7"	Columbia	DB8395	1968	**£5**	

HODGE, CHRIS

We're On Our Way	7"	Apple	43	1972	**£4**	
We're On Our Way	7"	Apple	43	1972	**£8**	PS

HODGE, MARVA

Ghetto	7"	Polydor	56792	1970	**£4**	

HODGE, RALPH & JACK CHAMBERS

Country And Western Express No.2	7" EP	Top Rank	JKP2056	1960	**£5**	

HODGES, CHARLES

Try A Little Love	7"	Major Minor	MM654	1969	**£12**	
Eddie Hodges	7" EP	London	REA1353	1963	**£10**	
I'm Gonna Knock On Your Door	7"	London	HLA9369	1961	**£5**	chart single
Love Minus Zero: No Limit	7"	Stateside	SS469	1965	**£4**	
Made To Love	7"	London	HLA9576	1962	**£4**	chart single
New Orleans	7"	Stateside	SS442	1965	**£4**	

HOGAN, SILAS

Trouble At Home	LP	Blue Horizon	2431008	1971	**£25**	

HOGARTH

Suzie's Getting Married	7"	Liberty	LBF15156	1968	**£5**	

HOGSNORT RUPERT'S ORIGINAL FLAGON BAND

Pretty Girl	7"	Columbia	DB8711	1970	**£4**	

HOKUS POKE

Earth Harmony	LP	Vertigo	6360064	1972	**£30**	spiral label

HOLDEN, RANDY

Population II	LP	Hobbit	5002	1968	**£50**	US

HOLDEN, RON

I Love You So	LP	Donna	DLP2111	1960	**£30**	US
I Love You So	7"	London	HLU9116	1960	**£8**	

HOLDER, RAM BROTHERS

Ramblues	7"	Parlophone	R5471	1966	**£4**	

HOLDER, RAM JAM

Black London Blues	LP	Beacon	BEA2	1974	**£12**	
Bootleg Blues	LP	Beacon	BEA17	1974	**£12**	
You Simply Are	LP	Fresh Air	9299470	1975	**£10**	
I Need Somebody	7"	Columbia	DB8157	1967	**£4**	
It Won't Be Long Before I Love You	7"	Columbia	DB8262	1967	**£4**	

HOLIDAY, BILLIE

Last Live Recording	LP	Island	ILP929	1966	**£15**	

HOLIDAY, CHICO

Chico Holiday	7" EP	RCA	RCX171	1959	**£10**	

HOLIDAY, JIMMY

Baby I Love You	7"	Liberty	LIB12040	1966	**£4**	
Give Me Your Love	7"	Liberty	LIB12048	1967	**£5**	
Give Me Your Love	7"	Minit	MLF11008	1968	**£4**	
How Can I Forget	7"	Vocalion	V9206	1963	**£10**	

HOLIDAY, JIMMY & CLYDIE KING

Oh Darling How I Miss You	7"	Polydor	56035	1965	**£8**	
One Man In My Life	7"	Polydor	56166	1967	**£4**	
Ready Willing And Able	7"	Liberty	LIB12058	1967	**£10**	

HOLIDAYS

I'll Love You Forever	7"	Polydor	56720	1966	**£15**	

HOLLAND, EDDIE

Eddie Holland	LP	Motown	604	1963	**£40**	US

If It's Love	7"	Oriole	CBA1808	1963	**£80**	
Jamie	7"	Fontana	H387	1962	**£80**	

HOLLIDAY, BRENDA

Hurt A Little Everyday	7"	Tamla Motown	TMG581	1966	**£60**	demo only

HOLLIDAY, SUSAN

Sometimes	7"	Columbia	DB7616	1965	**£5**	

HOLLIER, TIM

Sky Sail	LP	Philips		1971	**£20**	

HOLLIES

The Hollies were easily one of the most successful of the first wave of British beat groups to emerge in the sixties and yet they seldom seem to receive much credit for the fact. Inevitably they tended to labour in the shadow of the Beatles and their records show a similar pattern of development. "Evolution" is a kind of Lance Corporal Pepper - it uses the same kind of inventive arranging and is one of the more interesting albums of the period. Dare one say that it is actually much more of a psychedelic classic than celebrated rarities like those of Kaleidoscope?

Ain't That Just Like Me	7"	Parlophone	R5030	1963	**£5**	chart single
Air That I Breathe	7"	Polydor	2058435	1974	**£4**	chart single
Baby	7"	Polydor	2058199	1972	**£4**	chart single
Boulder To Birmingham	7"	Polydor	2058694	1976	**£4**	
Bus Stop	LP	Imperial	LP9330	1966	**£12**	US
Bus Stop	7"	Parlophone	R5469	1966	**£4**	chart single
Butterfly	LP	Parlophone	PCS7039	1967	**£20**	
Carrie-Anne	7"	Parlophone	R5602	1967	**£4**	chart single
Confessions Of The Mind	LP	Parlophone	PCS7116	1970	**£10**	chart LP
Day That Curly Billy Shot...	7"	Polydor	2058403	1973	**£4**	chart single
Distant Light	LP	Parlophone	PCS10005	1971	**£10**	
Everything You Wanted To Hear	LP	Epic	AS138	1972	**£25**	US promo
Evolution	LP	Parlophone	PCS7022	1967	**£20**	chart LP
For Certain Because	LP	Parlophone	PCS7011	1966	**£25**	chart LP
Gasoline Alley Bred	7"	Parlophone	R5862	1970	**£4**	chart single
Greatest Hits Vol.2	LP	Parlophone	PCS7148	1972	**£10**	
He Ain't Heavy He's My Brother	7"	Parlophone	R5806	1969	**£4**	chart single
Hear! Here!	LP	Imperial	LP9299	1965	**£25**	US
Here I Go Again	LP	Imperial	LP9265	1964	**£30**	US
Here I Go Again	7"	Parlophone	R5137	1964	**£4**	chart single
Here I Go Again	7" EP	Parlophone	GEP8915	1964	**£25**	
Hey Willy	7"	Parlophone	R5905	1971	**£4**	chart single
Hollies - Beat Group	LP	Imperial	LP9312	1966	**£15**	US
Hollies	LP	Parlophone	PMC1261	1965	**£30**	chart LP
Hollies	7" EP	Parlophone	GEP8909	1964	**£20**	
Hollies Greatest	LP	Parlophone	PCS7057	1968	**£10**	chart LP
I Can't Let Go	7"	Parlophone	R5409	1966	**£4**	chart single
I Can't Let Go	7" EP	Parlophone	GEP8951	1966	**£30**	
I Can't Tell The Bottom From The Top	7"	Parlophone	R5837	1970	**£4**	chart single
I'm Alive	7"	Parlophone	R5287	1965	**£4**	chart single
I'm Alive	7" EP	Parlophone	GEP8942	1965	**£30**	
I'm Down	7"	Polydor	2058533	1974	**£4**	
If I Needed Someone	7"	Parlophone	R5392	1965	**£4**	chart single
In The Hollies Style	LP	Parlophone	PMC1235	1965	**£40**	
In The Hollies Style	7" EP	Parlophone	GEP8934	1965	**£25**	
Jennifer Eccles	7"	Parlophone	R5680	1968	**£4**	chart single
Jesus Was A Crossmaker	7"	Epic	510989	1973	**£8**	US
Just One Look	7"	Parlophone	R5104	1964	**£4**	chart single
Just One Look	7" EP	Parlophone	GEP8911	1964	**£20**	
Kill Me Quick	7"	Parlophon	QMSP16410	1967	**£30**	Italian
King Midas In Reverse	7"	Parlophone	R5637	1967	**£4**	chart single
Like Every Time Before	7"	Hansa	14093	1968	**£10**	German
Listen To Me	7"	Parlophone	R5733	1968	**£4**	chart single
Long Cool Woman In A Black Dress	7"	Parlophone	R5939	1972	**£4**	chart single
Look Through Any Window	7"	Parlophone	R5322	1965	**£4**	chart single
Magic Woman Touch	7"	Polydor	2058289	1972	**£4**	
Non Prego Per Me	7"	Parlophon	QMSP16402	1967	**£30**	Italian
On A Carousel	7"	Parlophone	R5562	1967	**£4**	chart single
Out On The Road	LP	Hansa	87119	1973	**£20**	German
Romany	LP	Polydor	2383144	1972	**£10**	
Sandy	7"	Polydor	2058595	1975	**£4**	
Searchin'	7"	Parlophone	R5052	1963	**£4**	chart single
Sing Dylan	LP	Parlophone	PCS7078	1969	**£10**	chart LP

Sing Hollies	LP	Parlophone	PCS7092	1969	**£10**	
Son Of A Rotten Gambler	7"	Polydor	2058476	1974	**£4**	
Sorry Suzanne	7"	Parlophone	R5765	1969	**£4**	chart single
Star	7"	Polydor	2058719	1976	**£4**	
Stay	7"	Parlophone	R5077	1963	**£4**	chart single
Stay With The Hollies	LP	Parlophone	PMC1220	1964	**£30**	chart LP
Stay With The Hollies	LP	World Records	ST1035	1968	**£15**	
Stop Stop Stop	LP	Imperial	LP9339	1967	**£12**	US
Stop Stop Stop	7"	Parlophone	R5508	1966	**£4**	chart single
Vintage Hollies	LP	World Records	ST979	1967	**£15**	
We're Through	7"	Parlophone	R5178	1964	**£4**	chart single
We're Through	7" EP	Parlophone	GEP8927	1964	**£25**	
Would You Believe	LP	Parlophone	PCS7008	1966	**£25**	chart LP
Yes I Will	7"	Parlophone	R5232	1965	**£4**	chart single

HOLLIES & OTHERS

Music For 5am	7"	Mercury	YARD002	1978	**£10**	

HOLLIES & PETER SELLERS

After The Fox	7"	United Artists	UP1152	1966	**£12**	

HOLLOWAY, BRENDA

Artistry Of...	LP	Tamla Motown	STML11083	1968	**£30**	
Every Little Bit Hurts	7"	Stateside	SS307	1964	**£20**	
Every Little Bit Hurts	7"	Stateside	SS307	1964	**£50**	demo
Every Little Bit Hurts	LP	Tamla	257	1965	**£30**	US
Hurt A Little Everyday	7"	Tamla Motown	TMG581	1966	**£12**	
Hurt A Little Everyday	7"	Tamla Motown	TMG581	1966	**£50**	demo
Just Look What I've Done	7"	Tamla Motown	TMG608	1967	**£10**	
Just Look What I've Done	7"	Tamla Motown	TMG608	1967	**£50**	demo
Just Look What You've Done	7"	Tamla Motown	TMG700	1969	**£5**	
Just Look What You've Done	7"	Tamla Motown	TMG700	1969	**£15**	demo
Operator	7"	Tamla Motown	TMG519	1965	**£20**	
Operator	7"	Tamla Motown	TMG519	1965	**£60**	demo
Together Till The End Of Time	7"	Tamla Motown	TMG556	1966	**£12**	
Together Till The End Of Time	7"	Tamla Motown	TMG556	1966	**£60**	demo
When I'm Gone	7"	Tamla Motown	TMG508	1965	**£20**	
When I'm Gone	7"	Tamla Motown	TMG508	1965	**£50**	demo
You've Made Me So Very Happy	7"	Tamla Motown	TMG622	1967	**£10**	
You've Made Me So Very Happy	7"	Tamla Motown	TMG622	1967	**£30**	demo

HOLLOWAY, PATRICE

Love And Desire	7"	Capitol	CL15484	1966	**£10**	

HOLLY

Hobo Joe	7"	Erics	ERICS007	1979	**£12**	
Yankee Rose	7"	Erics	ERICS003	1979	**£12**	

HOLLY & JOEY

I Got You Babe	7"	Virgin	VS478	1982	**£6**	

HOLLY, BUDDY

Considering Buddy Holly's crucial importance within the development of rock music, the values of his original record releases are quite modest. It was Buddy Holly and the Crickets who set the pattern for the line-up that is still considered as the classic one for a rock group - lead and rhythm guitars, bass guitar and drums. His songs too, based on blues chord progressions but with bright, major tonalities, defined a style that has been revisited by song-writers from Lennon and McCartney to Costello and all points in between.

Baby I Don't Care	7"	Coral	Q72432	1961	**£4**	chart single
Best Of...	LP	Coral	CXB8	1966	**£20**	US
Blue Days Black Nights	78	Brunswick	05581	1956	**£30**	
Blue Days Black Nights	7"	Brunswick	05581	1956	**£75**	
Bo Diddley	7"	Coral	Q72463	1963	**£4**	chart single
Brown Eyed Handsome Man	7"	Coral	Q72459	1963	**£4**	chart single
Buddy By Request	7" EP	Coral	FEP2065	1964	**£12**	
Buddy Holly	LP	Coral	CRL57210	1958	**£150**	US
Buddy Holly	LP	Coral	LVA9085	1958	**£20**	
Buddy Holly	7" EP	Coral	FEP2002	1958	**£20**	no glasses cover
Buddy Holly	7" EP	Coral	FEP2002	1958	**£12**	tri-centre
Buddy Holly	7" EP	Coral	FEP2002	1960	**£8**	round centre
Buddy Holly And The Crickets	LP	Coral	CRL57405	1962	**£35**	US
Buddy Holly No.1	7" EP	Brunswick	OE9456	1959	**£15**	tri-centre

Buddy Holly No.1	7" EP	Brunswick	OE9456	1960	**£10**	round centre
Buddy Holly No.2	7" EP	Brunswick	OE9457	1959	**£15**	tri-centre
Buddy Holly No.2	7" EP	Brunswick	OE9457	1960	**£10**	round centre
Buddy Holly Sings	7" EP	Coral	FEP2070	1965	**£10**	
Buddy Holly Story 2	LP	Coral	LVA9127	1960	**£12**	chart LP
Buddy Holly Story	LP	Coral	CRL57279	1959	**£60**	US
Buddy Holly Story	LP	Coral	LVA9105	1959	**£10**	chart LP
Buddy Holly Story	7" EP	Coral	FEP2032	1959	**£10**	tri-centre
Buddy Holly Story	7" EP	Coral	FEP2032	1960	**£8**	round centre
Buddy Holly Story	LP	World Records	SM301-5	1975	**£25**	5 LPs, boxed
Buddy Holly Story Vol.2	LP	Coral	CRL57326	1959	**£50**	US
Chirping Crickets	LP	Brunswick	BL54038	1957	**£180**	US
Chirping Crickets	LP	Coral	LVA9081	1958	**£15**	
Complete Buddy Holly	LP	MCA	CDMSP807	1978	**£30**	6 LPs, book, boxed
Early In The Morning	78	Coral	Q72333	1958	**£6**	
Early In The Morning	7"	Coral	Q72333	1958	**£6**	tri-centre, chart single
Early In The Morning	7"	Coral	Q72333	1960	**£4**	round centre
Four More	7" EP	Coral	FEP2060	1960	**£10**	
Giant	LP	Coral	CRL757504	1969	**£15**	US
Good Rockin'	LP	Vocalion	VL73923	1971	**£50**	US
Great Buddy Holly	LP	Vocalion	VL3811	1967	**£20**	US
Greatest Hits	LP	Coral	CRL57492	1967	**£20**	US
Heartbeat	78	Coral	Q72346	1958	**£4**	
Heartbeat	78	Coral	Q72392	1960	**£12**	
Heartbeat	7"	Coral	Q72346	1958	**£4**	tri-centre, chart single
Heartbeat	7"	Coral	Q72392	1960	**£4**	chart single
Heartbeat	7" EP	Coral	FEP2015	1959	**£10**	tri-centre
Heartbeat	7" EP	Coral	FEP2015	1960	**£8**	round centre
Heartbeat	LP	Marks & Spen.	IMP114	1980	**£10**	
Holly In The Hills	LP	Coral	CRL57463	1965	**£35**	US
Holly In The Hills	LP	Coral	LVA9227	1965	**£15**	plus 'Reminiscing' chart LP
Holly In The Hills	LP	Coral	LVA9227	1965	**£20**	with 'Wishing'
It Doesn't Matter Anymore	78	Coral	Q72360	1959	**£4**	
It Doesn't Matter Anymore	7"	Coral	Q72360	1959	**£6**	tri-centre, chart single
It Doesn't Matter Anymore	7"	Coral	Q72360	1960	**£4**	round centre
It's So Easy	78	Coral	Q72345	1958	**£4**	
It's So Easy	7"	Coral	Q72343	1958	**£6**	tri-centre
It's So Easy	7"	Coral	Q72343	1960	**£4**	round centre
It's So Easy	7" EP	Coral	FEP2014	1959	**£10**	
Late Great Buddy Holly	7" EP	Coral	FEP2044	1960	**£8**	
Learning The Game	7"	Coral	Q72411	1960	**£4**	chart single
Listen To Me	78	Coral	Q72288	1958	**£6**	
Listen To Me	7"	Coral	Q72288	1958	**£6**	tri-centre, chart single
Listen To Me	7"	Coral	Q72288	1960	**£4**	round centre
Listen To Me	7"	Coral	Q72449	1962	**£4**	chart single
Look At Me	7"	Coral	Q72445	1961	**£4**	
Love's Made A Fool Of You	7"	Coral	Q72475	1964	**£4**	chart single
Maybe Baby	78	Coral	Q72307	1958	**£6**	
Maybe Baby	7"	Coral	Q72307	1958	**£5**	tri-centre, chart single
Maybe Baby	7"	Coral	Q72483	1966	**£4**	
Midnight Shift	78	Brunswick	05800	1959	**£8**	
Midnight Shift	7"	Brunswick	05800	1959	**£10**	
Oh Boy	78	Coral	Q72298	1957	**£6**	
Oh Boy	7"	Coral	Q72298	1957	**£5**	tri-centre, chart single
Peggy Sue	7"	Coral	Q72293	1958	**£5**	chart single
Peggy Sue	78	Vogue Coral	Q72293	1957	**£8**	
Peggy Sue	7"	Vogue Coral	Q72293	1957	**£12**	
Peggy Sue Got Married	78	Coral	Q72376	1959	**£10**	
Peggy Sue Got Married	7"	Coral	Q72376	1959	**£6**	tri-centre, chart single
Peggy Sue Got Married	7"	Coral	Q72376	1960	**£4**	round centre
Rave On	78	Coral	Q72325	1958	**£6**	
Rave On	7"	Coral	Q72325	1958	**£6**	tri-centre, chart single
Rave On	7"	Coral	Q72325	1960	**£4**	round centre
Rave On	7" EP	Coral	FEP2005	1958	**£10**	tri-centre
Rave On	7" EP	Coral	FEP2005	1960	**£8**	round centre
Reminiscing	LP	Coral	CRL57426	1963	**£30**	US
Reminiscing	LP	Coral	LVA9212	1963	**£12**	chart LP
Reminiscing	7"	Coral	Q72455	1962	**£4**	chart single
Rock And Roll Collection	LP	Decca	DXSE7207	1972	**£10**	US
Showcase	LP	Coral	CRL57450	1964	**£30**	US

Showcase	LP	Coral	LVA9222	1964	**£10**	chart LP
Showcase Vol.1	7" EP	Coral	FEP2068	1964	**£12**	
Showcase Vol.2	7" EP	Coral	FEP2069	1964	**£12**	
Sound Of The Crickets	7" EP	Coral	FEP2003	1958	**£8**	
That Tex Mex Sound	7" EP	Coral	FEP2066	1964	**£12**	
That'll Be The Day	LP	Ace Of H.	AH3	1961	**£12**	chart LP
That'll Be The Day	7"	Coral	Q72279	1957	**£4**	tri-centre, chart single
That'll Be The Day	7" EP	Coral	FEP2062	1960	**£10**	
That'll Be The Day	LP	Decca	DL8707	1958	**£300**	US
That'll Be The Day	78	Vogue Coral	Q72279	1957	**£10**	
That'll Be The Day	7"	Vogue Coral	Q72279	1957	**£10**	
Think It Over	78	Coral	Q72329	1958	**£6**	
Think It Over	7"	Coral	Q72329	1958	**£6**	tri-centre, chart single
Think It Over	7"	Coral	Q72329	1960	**£4**	round centre
True Love Ways	7"	Coral	Q72397	1960	**£4**	chart single
What To Do	7"	Coral	Q72469	1963	**£4**	chart single
What To Do	7"	Coral	Q72419	1961	**£4**	chart single
Wishing	7"	Coral	Q72466	1963	**£4**	chart single
Wishing	7" EP	Coral	FEP2067	1964	**£12**	
You've Got Love..	7"	Coral	Q72472	1964	**£4**	

HOLLY, STEVE

Strange World	7"	Planet	PLF107	1966	**£8**	

HOLLYWOOD ARGYLES

Alley Oop	7"	London	HLU9146	1960	**£6**	chart single
Alley Oop	LP	Lute	L9001	1960	**£150**	US
Bugeye	7"	Top Rank	JAR530	1961	**£4**	

HOLLYWOOD BRATS

Then He Kissed Me	7"	Cherry Red	CHERRY6	1979	**£4**	

HOLLYWOOD FLAMES

Buzz Buzz Buzz	7"	London	HL8545	1958	**£15**	
If I Thought You Needed Me	7"	London	HLE9071	1960	**£8**	
Much Too Much	7"	London	HLW8955	1959	**£8**	

HOLLYWOOD VINES

When Johnny Comes Sliding Home	7"	Capitol	CL15191	1961	**£5**	

HOLLYWOOD, KENNY

Magic Star	7"	Decca	F11546	1962	**£4**	

HOLM, MIKE

Mendocino	7"	Major Minor	MM659	1969	**£5**	

HOLMAN, EDDIE

This Can't Be True	7"	Cameo Park.	P960	1965	**£25**	
I Surrender	7"	Action	ACT4547	1969	**£15**	

HOLMES, JAKE

How Are You	7"	Polydor	56547	1970	**£4**	
How Much Time	LP	CBS	64905	1972	**£10**	
Jake Holmes	LP	Polydor	583578	1969	**£10**	
Saturday Night	7"	Ember	EMB269	1969	**£4**	
So Close So Very Far To Go	LP	Polydor	2425036	1970	**£10**	

HOLTS, ROOSEVELT

Presenting The Country Blues	LP	Blue Horizon	763201	1968	**£35**	

HOLY MACKEREL

Ballad Of Joe McCann	7"	Santa Ponsa	PNS18	1974	**£4**	
Holy Mackerel	LP	CBS	65297	1972	**£15**	
Rock'N'Bye	7"	CBS	8447	1972	**£4**	
Tennessee Waltz	7"	Santa Ponsa	PNS11	1974	**£4**	
We Got It Nailed Down	7"	Santa Ponsa	PNS6	1973	**£4**	
Jason Crest	LP	CBS			**£15**	

HOLY MODAL ROUNDERS

Alleged In Their Own Time	LP	Rounder	3004	1972	**£15**	US

Good Taste Is Timeless	LP	Metromedia	MD1039	1967	**£15**	US
Holy Modal Rounders 2	LP	Prestige	PRS7451	1967	**£15**	US
Holy Modal Rounders	LP	Prestige	PR7410	1965	**£15**	US
Holy Modal Rounders	LP	Transatlantic	TRA7451	1970	**£15**	
Indian War Whoop	LP	ESP	1068	1969	**£15**	US
Moray Eels Eat The...	LP	Elektra	EKL4026	1968	**£15**	
Stampfel And Weber	LP	Fantasy	F24711	1972	**£20**	US double

HOLY MOSES

Holy Moses	LP	RCA	SF8204	1971	**£10**	

HOMBRES

Let It All Hang Out	7"	Verve	VS1510	1967	**£12**	

HOME

Alchemist	LP	CBS	65550	1973	**£10**	
Fancy Lady, Hollywood Child	7"	CBS	7809	1972	**£4**	
Home	LP	CBS	64752	1972	**£12**	
Pause For A Hoarse Horse	LP	Epic	64365	1971	**£15**	

HOMER & JETHRO

Barefoot Ballads	LP	RCA	LPM1412	1957	**£12**	US
Battle Of Kookamonga	7"	RCA	RCA1148	1959	**£4**	
Homer & Jethro Fracture Frank Loesser	LP-10"	RCA	LPM3112	1953	**£25**	US
Life Can Be Miserable	LP	RCA	LPM1880	1958	**£10**	US
Musical Madness	LP	Audio Lab	AL1513	1958	**£25**	US
Swappin' Partners	7"	HMV	7M211	1954	**£4**	
They Sure Are Corny	LP	King	639	1959	**£15**	US
Worst Of...	LP	RCA	LPM1560	1957	**£12**	US

HONDELLS

Cheryl's Going Home	7"	Mercury	MF967	1967	**£8**	
Go Little Honda	LP	Mercury	MG20940	1964	**£15**	US
Hondells	LP	Mercury	MG20982	1965	**£15**	US
Little Honda	7"	Mercury	MF834	1964	**£8**	
Younger Girl	7"	Mercury	MF925	1965	**£6**	

HONEST MEN

Cherie	7"	Tamla Motown	TMG706	1969	**£10**	
Cherie	7"	Tamla Motown	TMG706	1969	**£30**	demo

HONEYBUS

Delighted To See You	7"	Deram	DM131	1967	**£5**	
Do I Still Figure In Your Life	7"	Deram	DM152	1967	**£6**	
For You Baby	7"	W. Bros	K16250	1973	**£4**	
Girl Of Independent Means	7"	Deram	DM207	1968	**£5**	
I Can't Let Maggie Go	7"	Deram	DM182	1968	**£4**	chart single
Recital	LP	W. Bros	K46248	1973	**£100**	
She Is The Female To My Soul	7"	Bell	BLL1205	1972	**£4**	
She Sold Blackpool Rock	7"	Deram	DM254	1969	**£5**	
Story	LP	Deram	SML1056	1970	**£35**	
Story	7"	Deram	DM289	1970	**£6**	

HONEYCOMBS

All Systems Go	LP	Pye	NPL18132	1965	**£50**	
Don't Love You No More	7"	Pye	7N15781	1965	**£6**	
Eyes	7"	Pye	7N15736	1964	**£5**	
Have I The Right	7"	Pye	7N15664	1964	**£4**	chart single
Honeycombs	LP	Golden Guin.	GGL0350	1965	**£20**	
Honeycombs	LP	Pye	NPL18097	1964	**£40**	
Is It Because	7"	Pye	7N15705	1964	**£4**	chart single
It's So Hard	7"	Pye	7N17138	1966	**£8**	
Something Better Beginning	7"	Pye	7N15827	1965	**£5**	chart single
That Loving Feeling	7"	Pye	7N17173	1966	**£8**	
That's The Way	7"	Pye	7N15890	1965	**£4**	chart single
That's The Way	7" EP	Pye	NEP24230	1965	**£15**	
This Year Next Year	7"	Pye	7N15979	1965	**£5**	
Who Is Sylvia	7"	Pye	7N17059	1966	**£6**	

HONEYDRIPPERS

Sea Of Love	7"	Es Paranza	SAM220	1984	**£4**	radio promo

HONEYS

Title	Format	Label	Cat. No.	Year	Price	Notes
Surfing Down The Swanee River	7"	Capitol	CL15299	1963	**£12**	

HONEYTONES

Title	Format	Label	Cat. No.	Year	Price	Notes
Don't Look Now But	7"	London	HLX8671	1958	**£15**	

HOOK

Title	Format	Label	Cat. No.	Year	Price	Notes
Show You The Way	7"	UNI	UN507	1969	**£4**	

HOOKER, EARL

Title	Format	Label	Cat. No.	Year	Price	Notes
Boogie Don't Blot	7"	Blue Horizon	573166	1969	**£10**	
Don't Have To Worry	LP	Stateside	SSL10298	1969	**£20**	
Sweet Black Angel	LP	Blue Horizon	763850	1970	**£30**	

HOOKER, JOHN LEE

Title	Format	Label	Cat. No.	Year	Price	Notes
Alone	LP	Speciality	SNTF5005	1974	**£10**	
Best Of	LP	Joy	JOYS156	196-	**£12**	
Big Maceo Merriweather And Hooker	LP	Fortune	3002	196-	**£20**	US
Big Soul	LP	Joy	JOYS147	196-	**£15**	
Blues Of John Lee Hooker	7" EP	Stateside	SE1019	1964	**£6**	
Boom Boom	7"	Stateside	SS203	1963	**£6**	
Burnin'	LP	Joy	JOYS124	196-	**£15**	
Concert At Newport	LP	Joy	JOYS142	196-	**£15**	
Democrat Man	7" EP	Riverside	REP3207	1960	**£6**	
Detroit Special	LP	Atlantic	K40405	1972	**£10**	
Dimples	7"	President	PT295	1970	**£4**	
Dimples	7"	Stateside	SS297	1964	**£6**	chart single
Don't Turn Me From Your Door	LP	Atlantic	K40507	1974	**£10**	
Don't Turn Me From Your Door	LP	London	HAK8097	1963	**£25**	
Down At The Landing	7" EP	Chess	CRE6000	1965	**£6**	
Driftin' Blues	LP	Polydor	590003		**£15**	
Endless Boogie	LP	Probe	SPB1034	1971	**£12**	
Folk Blues	LP	Riverside	12838	196-	**£10**	US
Folklore	LP	Joy	JOYS133	196-	**£15**	
Folklore Of...	LP	Stateside	SL10014	1962	**£25**	
Free Beer And Chicken	LP	ABC	ABCL5059	1974	**£10**	
High Priced Woman	7"	Pye	7N25255	1964	**£5**	
House Of The Blues	LP	Chess	LP1438	1960	**£20**	US
I Love You Honey	7"	Stateside	SS341	1964	**£5**	
I Want To Shout The Blues	LP	Stateside	SL10074	1964	**£20**	
I'm In The Mood	7"	Sue	WI361	1965	**£10**	
I'm John Lee Hooker	LP	Joy	JOYS101	196-	**£15**	
I'm John Lee Hooker	7" EP	Stateside	SE1023	1964	**£6**	
I'm John Lee Hooker	LP	Vee Jay	LP1007	1959	**£30**	US
In Person	LP	Joy	JOYS152	196-	**£15**	
It Serves You Right	LP	HMV	CSD3542	1966	**£20**	
John Lee Hooker	7" EP	Atlantic	AET6010	1965	**£6**	
John Lee Hooker	LP	XTRA	XTRA114	1971	**£15**	
John Lee Hooker Sings The Blues	LP	King	727	1961	**£35**	US
Journey	7" EP	Chess	CRE6014	1966	**£6**	
Let's Go Out Tonight	7"	Chess	CRS8039	1966	**£6**	
Life At Cafe Au Go-Go	LP	HMV	CSD3612	1966	**£20**	
Live At Soledad Prison	LP	ABC	716	1972	**£12**	
Love Blues	7" EP	Pye	NEP44034	1964	**£6**	
Mai Lee	7"	Planet	PLF114	1966	**£6**	
Need Somebody	78	London	HL8037	1954	**£20**	
On Campus	LP	Vee Jay	LP1066	1963	**£10**	US
Plays & Sings The Blues	LP	Chess	CRL4500	196-	**£15**	
Preachin' The Blues	LP	Stateside	SL10053	1964	**£25**	
Real Folk Blues	LP	Chess	LP1508	1966	**£10**	US
Real Folk Blues Vol.3	7" EP	Chess	CRE6021	1966	**£6**	
Shake It Baby	7"	Polydor	NH52930	1964	**£5**	
Simply The Truth	LP	Stateside	SL10280	1969	**£15**	
Slim's Stomp	LP	Polydor	2310256	1973	**£10**	
That's Where It's At	LP	Stax	SXATS1025	1970	**£15**	
Thinking Blues	7" EP	Ember	EP4561	1964	**£6**	
Travellin'	LP	Joy	JOYS129	196-	**£15**	
Tupelo Blues	LP	Storyville	673020	1962	**£15**	
Urban Blues	LP	Stateside	SL10246	1968	**£15**	
Walking The Boogie	7" EP	Chess	CRE6007	1966	**£6**	
Wednesday Evening	7" EP	Riverside	REP3202	1960	**£6**	

You're Leavin' Me Baby	LP	Storyville	673005		**£15**	

HOOKER, JOHN LEE & CANNED HEAT

Hooker And Heat	LP	Liberty	LPS103/4	1971	**£20**	double

HOOKER, JOHN LEE & JIMMY REED

Rhythm And Blues	7" EP	Stateside	SE1008	1962	**£6**	

HOOKFOOT

Communications	LP	DJM	DJLPS428	1973	**£12**	
Good Times A Comin'	LP	DJM	DJLPS422	1972	**£10**	
Hookfoot	LP	DJM	DJLPS413	1971	**£10**	
Way Of The Musician	7"	Page One	POF144	1969	**£5**	

HOOTENANNY SINGERS

Basta	LP	Polar	POLL101	196-	**£12**	Swedish
Bellman Pa Vart Satt	LP	Polar	POLS214	196-	**£12**	Swedish
Civila	LP	Polar	POLS211	196-	**£12**	Swedish
Dan Andersson Pa Van Satt	LP	Polar	POLS249	197-	**£12**	Swedish
Evert Taube	LP	Polar	POLS204	196-	**£12**	Swedish
Evert Taube Pa Van Satt	LP	Polar	POLS260	197-	**£12**	Swedish
Gabriella	7"	United Artists	UP1082	1965	**£15**	
Hootenanny Singers	LP	Polar	POLS201	196-	**£12**	Swedish
Skillingtryck	LP	Polar	POLS225	1970	**£12**	Swedish
Vara Vackraste Visor	LP	Polar	POLS229	197-	**£12**	Swedish

HOPE, LYNN

Blue Moon	7"	Vogue	V9081	1957	**£10**	
Eleven Till Two	7"	Vogue	V9082	1957	**£10**	
Lynn Hope And His Tenor Sax	7" EP	Vogue	VE170103	195-	**£30**	
Lynn Hope And His Tenor Sax	7" EP	Vogue	VE170146	196-	**£30**	
Lynn Hope And His Tenor Sax	LP-10"	Aladdin	707	195-	**£75**	US
Lynn Hope	LP	Aladdin	820	195-	**£50**	US
Shocking	7"	Blue Beat	BB21	1961	**£10**	
Temptation	7"	Vogue	V9115	1958	**£10**	
Tenderly	LP	Score	LP4015	1957	**£35**	US

HOPESTREET

Iron Sky	7"	Parlophone	R5943	1972	**£4**	
Wait Until Tomorrow	7"	Parlophone	R5982	1973	**£4**	

HOPKIN, MARY

Earth Song	LP	Apple	SAPCOR21	1971	**£15**	
Knock Knock Who's There	7"	Apple	26	1970	**£5**	PS
Let My Name Be Sorrow	7"	Apple	34	1971	**£8**	PS
Llais Swynol Mary Hopkin	7" EP	Cambrian	CEP414	1968	**£6**	
Mary Ac Edward	7" EP	Cambrian	CEP420	1969	**£6**	
Postcard	LP	Apple	APCOR5	1969	**£15**	mono
Postcard	LP	Apple	SAPCOR5	1969	**£10**	chart LP
Temma Harbour	7"	Apple	22	1970	**£6**	PS
Think About Your Children	7"	Apple	30	1970	**£8**	PS
Those Were The Days	LP	Apple	SAPCOR23	1972	**£50**	
Water, Paper And Clay	7"	Apple	39	1971	**£4**	
Water, Paper And Clay	7"	Apple	39	1971	**£10**	PS

HOPKINS, LIGHTNIN'

Autobiography In Blues	LP	Tradition	TLP1040	1960	**£20**	US
Blues Hoot	LP	Stateside	SL10076	1964	**£20**	
Blues In The Bottle	LP	XTRA	XTRA5036	196-	**£15**	
Blues/Folk	LP	Time	1	1962	**£10**	US
Blues/Folk Vol.2	LP	Time	3	1962	**£10**	US
Country Blues	LP	Tradition	TLP1035	1960	**£20**	US
Down Home Blues	LP	Stateside	SL10155	1965	**£20**	
Earth Blues	LP	Liberty	MLS40006	196-	**£15**	
Fast Life Woman	LP	Verve	V8453	1962	**£15**	US
Goin' Away	LP	Bluesville	BV1073	1964	**£12**	US
Got To Move Your Baby	LP	XTRA	XTRA5044	196-	**£15**	
His Greatest Hits	LP	Bluesville	BV1084	1964	**£12**	US
Hootin' The Blues	LP	Stateside	SL10110	1965	**£20**	
Last Night Blues	LP	Bluesville	BV1029	1961	**£15**	US
Last Of The Great Blues Singers	LP	Time	70004	1960	**£15**	US
Let's Work Awhile	LP	Blue Horizon	2431 005	1971	**£20**	

Title	Format	Label	Number	Year	Price	Notes
Lightnin'	LP	Bluesville	BV1019	1961	**£15**	US
Lightnin' And The Blues	LP	Herald	1012	1960	**£150**	US
Lightnin' Hopkins	LP	Vee Jay	LP1044	1962	**£20**	US
Lightnin' Hopkins And The Blues	LP	Imperial	LP9211	1962	**£15**	US
Lightnin' Hopkins On Stage	LP	Imperial	LP9180	1962	**£15**	US
Lightnin' Hopkins Strums The Blues	LP	Score	4022	1960	**£75**	US
Lightnin' Strikes	LP	Stateside	SL10031	1963	**£20**	
Mojo Hand	LP	Fire	104	1962	**£50**	US
My Life In The Blues	LP	Prestige	PR7370	1965	**£12**	US
Nothin' But The Blues	LP	Mount Vernon	104	196-	**£10**	US
Roots Of...	LP	XTRA	XTRA1127	1971	**£15**	
Smokes Like Lightnin'	LP	Bluesville	BV1070	1963	**£12**	US
Walkin' This Road By Myself	LP	Bluesville	BV1057	1961	**£15**	US

HOPKINS, LINDA

Title	Format	Label	Number	Year	Price	Notes
I Diddle Dum Dum	7"	Coral	Q72423	1961	**£4**	
Mama Doing The Twist	7"	Coral	Q72448	1962	**£4**	

HOPKINS, NICKY

Title	Format	Label	Number	Year	Price	Notes
High On A Hill	7"	Fontana	TF906	1968	**£8**	
Mr. Big	7"	CBS	202055	1966	**£10**	
Mr. Pleasant	7"	Polydor	56175	1967	**£12**	
No More Changes	LP	Mercury	SRMI1028	1975	**£10**	US
Revolutionary Piano	LP	CBS	62679	1966	**£20**	
Tin Man Was A Dreamer	LP	CBS	65416	1973	**£10**	

HOPPER, HUGH

Title	Format	Label	Number	Year	Price	Notes
1984	LP	CBS	65466	1973	**£10**	
Cruel But Fair	LP	Compendium	FIDARDO4	1976	**£12**	
Hopper Tunity Box	LP	Compendium	FIDARDO7	1977	**£12**	
Rogue Element	LP	Ogun	OG527	197-	**£10**	

HOPSON, WASH SINGERS

Title	Format	Label	Number	Year	Price	Notes
He's Got A Blessing	7"	Action	ACT4546	1969	**£10**	demo

HORIZON

Title	Format	Label	Number	Year	Price	Notes
She's A Rainbow	7"	Parlophone	R5947	1972	**£4**	

HORNE, KENNETH & OTHERS

Title	Format	Label	Number	Year	Price	Notes
Beyond Our Ken	LP	Parlophone	PMC1238	1964	**£10**	

HORSE

Title	Format	Label	Number	Year	Price	Notes
Horse	LP	RCA	SF8109	1970	**£50**	

HORSLIPS

Horslips were employing traditional musical elements from their native Ireland long before the Pogues and the Waterboys made it fashionable. Their first LP, "Happy To Meet", comes within an intricate package that is designed to look like a concertina and which is not often found in mint condition.

Title	Format	Label	Number	Year	Price	Notes
Dearg Doom	7"	Oats	OAT2	1973	**£4**	
Drive The Cold Winter Away	LP	Oats	MOO9	1976	**£12**	
Fairy King	7"	Oats	MOO2	1973	**£4**	
Happy To Meet	LP	Oats	MOO3	1972	**£20**	octagonal cover
High Reel	7"	Oats	OAT1	1973	**£4**	
Loneliness	7"	DJM	DJT15001	1979	**£4**	shamrock shaped disc- green vinyl
More Than You Can Chew	7"	Oats	OAT3	1974	**£4**	
Tain	LP	Oats	MOO5	1973	**£10**	

HORTON, JOHNNY

Title	Format	Label	Number	Year	Price	Notes
All Grown Up	7"	CBS	AAG132	1963	**£4**	
Battle Of New Orleans	7"	Philips	PB932	1959	**£5**	chart single
Country And Western Aces	7" EP	Mercury	10008MCE	1964	**£12**	
Done Rovin'	LP	Briar	104	195-	**£50**	US
Done Rovin'	LP	London	HAU8096	1963	**£12**	
Fantastic ...	LP	Mercury	MG20478	1959	**£20**	US
Fantastic Johnny Horton	7" EP	Mercury	ZEP10074	1960	**£12**	
Free And Easy Songs	LP	SESAC	1201	1959	**£75**	US
Greatest Hits	LP	Columbia	CL1596	1961	**£12**	US
Honky Tonk Man	LP	Columbia	CL1721	1962	**£12**	US
I Can't Forget You	LP	Columbia	CL2299	1965	**£10**	US
Johnny Horton	LP	Dot	DLP3221	1962	**£15**	US
Johnny Horton Makes History	LP	Columbia	CL1478	1960	**£10**	US

Johnny Reb	7"	Philips	PB951	1959	**£4**	
Mr. Moonlight	7"	Philips	PB1130	1961	**£4**	
North to Alaska	7"	Philips	PB1062	1960	**£4**	chart single
Ole Slew Foot	7"	Philips	PB1170	1961	**£4**	
Sink The Bismarck	7"	Philips	PB995	1960	**£4**	
Sleepy Eyed John	7"	Philips	PB1132	1961	**£4**	
Spectacular...	LP	Philips	BBL7464	1960	**£15**	
Take Me Like I Am	7"	Philips	PB976	1959	**£4**	
Words	7"	Philips	PB1226	1962	**£4**	

HORTON, SHAKEY

Soul Of Blues Harmonica	LP	Argo	4037	1964	**£40**	US

HOT BUTTER

Popcorn	LP	Pye	NSPL28169	1972	**£10**	

HOT CHOCOLATE BAND

Give Peace A Chance	7"	Apple	18	1969	**£15**	

HOT DOGGERS

Surfin' USA	LP	Epic	LN24054	1963	**£30**	US

HOT TODDYS

Shakin' And Stompin'	7"	Pye	7N25020	1959	**£8**	

HOT TUNA

America's Choice	LP	Grunt	BFD10820	1975	**£12**	US quad
America's Choice	LP	Grunt	FTR2003	1975	**£10**	
Burgers	LP	Grunt	1004	1972	**£10**	
Double Dose	LP	Grunt	FL02545	1977	**£15**	double
Final Vinyl	LP	Grunt	FLI3357	1979	**£10**	
First Pull Up	LP	RCA	LSP4550	1971	**£10**	US
Hoppkorv	LP	Grunt	FTR2006	1976	**£10**	
Hot Tuna	LP	RCA	SF8125	1970	**£10**	
Keep On Truckin'	7"	Grunt	650502	1972	**£4**	
Phosphorescent Rat	LP	RCA	BFLI0348	1973	**£10**	
Yellow Fever	LP	Grunt	BFD11238	1975	**£12**	US quad
Yellow Fever	LP	Grunt	BFLI1238	1975	**£10**	US

HOTLEGS

Hotlegs were not the one-hit wonders they might appear to be. The group who scored with a novelty recording, "Neanderthal Man", were only waiting for successful song-writer Graham Gouldman to join them before starting to make records as Ten cc.

Lady Sadie	7"	Philips	6006140	1971	**£4**	
Neanderthal Man	7"	Fontana	6007019	1970	**£4**	chart single
Songs	LP	Philips	6308080	1971	**£10**	
Thinks School Stinks	LP	Philips	6308057	1971	**£10**	

HOTRODS

I Don't Love You No More	7"	Columbia	DB7693	1965	**£20**	

HOURGLASS

Hourglass	LP	Liberty	LBL83219	1968	**£15**	
Power Of Love	LP	Liberty	LST7555	1968	**£15**	US

HOUSE OF LORDS

In The Land Of Dreams	7"	B&C	CB112	1969	**£8**	

HOUSE OF LOVE

Christine	7"	Creation	CRE053	1988	**£8**	
Christine	7"	Creation	CREFRE01	1988	**£8**	
Christine	12"	Creation	CRE053T	1988	**£15**	
Destroy The Heart	7"	Creation	CRE057	1988	**£8**	
Real Animal	12"	Creation	CRE044T	1987	**£35**	
Shine On	7"	Creation	CREFRE5	1988	**£8**	flexi
Shine On	12"	Creation	CRE043T	1987	**£35**	

HOUSEMARTINS

Caravan Of Love	7"	Go Discs	GOD16	1986	**£5**	rectangular pic disc
Happy Hour	7"	Go Discs	GOD11	1986	**£5**	shaped pic disc
Sheep	7"	Go Discs	GOD9	1986	**£4**	pic disc
Think For A Minute	7"	Go Discs	GOD13	1986	**£5**	shaped pic disc

HOUSTON, CISSY

Cissy Houston	LP	Janus	6310205	1971	**£10**	
Presenting...	LP	Major Minor	SMLP80	1970	**£12**	

HOUSTON, DAVID

Blue Prelude	7"	London	HL8147	1955	**£8**	

HOUSTON, JOE

Joe Houston Blows All Night Long	LP	Modern	LMP1206	1956	**£20**	US
Rockin' At The Drive-In	LP	Combo	LP400	1960	**£50**	US
Where Is Joe?	LP	Combo	LP100	1960	**£50**	US

HOUSTON, THELMA

Black California	7"	Mowest	MW3004	1973	**£20**	demo
I Want To Go Back There Again	7"	Tamla Motown	TMG799	1972	**£4**	
I Want To Go Back There Again	7"	Tamla Motown	TMG799	1972	**£15**	demo
I've Got The Music In Me	LP	Sheffield Lab	2	1974	**£12**	US audiophile
Jumpin' Jack Flash	7"	Stateside	SS8026	1969	**£4**	
Save The Country	7"	Stateside	SS8036	1970	**£4**	
Sunshower	LP	Stateside	SSL5010	1969	**£10**	

HOWARD, BRIAN & THE SILHOUETTES

Back In The USA	7"	Fontana	TF464	1964	**£12**	
Somebody Help Me	7"	Columbia	DB4914	1962	**£15**	
Worrying Kind	7"	Columbia	DB7067	1963	**£12**	

HOWARD, HARLAN

All-Time Favorite Country Songwriter	LP	Monument	MLP8038	1965	**£10**	US
Harlan Howard Sings Harlan Howard	LP	Capitol	T1631	1961	**£12**	US

HOWARD, JOHNNY

Mind Reader	7"	Decca	F11423	1962	**£4**	
Orbit	7"	Decca	F11298	1960	**£4**	
Rinky Dink	7"	Decca	F11925	1964	**£4**	

HOWE, CATHERINE

What A Beautiful Place	LP	Reflection		1971	**£10**	

HOWELL, EDDIE & QUEEN

Man From Manhattan	7"	W. Bros	K16701	1976	**£5**	

HOWERD, FRANKIE

At The Establishment	LP	Decca	LK4556	1963	**£12**	

HOWLIN' WOLF

AKA Chester Burnett	LP	Chess	60016	1972	**£12**	US
Back Door Wolf	LP	Chess	CH50045	1974	**£12**	US
Big City Blues	LP	Ember	3370	1966	**£15**	
Down In The Bottom	7"	Pye	7N25101	1961	**£6**	
Evil	LP	Chess	LP1540	1969	**£15**	US
Evil	7"	Chess	CRS8097	1969	**£4**	
Howlin' Wolf	LP	Chess	LP1469	1962	**£35**	US
Howlin' Wolf Album	LP	Chess	CRLS4543	1969	**£12**	
Just Like I Treat You	7"	Pye	7N25192	1963	**£6**	
Killing Floor	7"	Chess	CRS8010	1965	**£8**	
Little Girl	7"	Pye	7N25269	1964	**£5**	
London Sessions	LP	Rolling Stones	49101	1971	**£10**	
Love Me Darling	7"	Pye	7N25283	1964	**£5**	
Message To The Young	LP	Chess	6310108	1971	**£10**	
Moanin' In The Moonlight	LP	Chess	LP1434	1958	**£40**	US
Moaning In The Moonlight	LP	Chess	CRL4006	1964	**£20**	
Moaning In The Moonlight	LP	Marble Arch	MAL665	1967	**£10**	
More Real Folk Blues	LP	Chess	LP1512	1966	**£20**	US
Ooh Baby	7"	Chess	CRS8016	1965	**£6**	
Poor Boy	LP	Chess	CRL4508	1965	**£20**	
Real Folk Blues	LP	Chess	LP1502	1966	**£20**	US
Real Folk Blues Vol.1	7" EP	Chess	CRE6017	1966	**£10**	
Rhythm And Blues With Howlin' Wolf	7" EP	London	REU1072	1956	**£40**	
Smokestack Lightning	7"	Pye	7N25244	1964	**£6**	chart single
Smokestack Lightning	7" EP	Pye	NEP44015	1963	**£10**	
Tell Me	7" EP	Pye	NEP44032	1964	**£8**	
This Is Howlin' Wolf's New Album	LP	Cadet	319	1969	**£15**	US

HOYLE, LINDA

Linda Hoyle was the singer with Affinity and her jazz-inflected tones on that group's album suggested that she could make a good jazz record. Her solo LP, recorded with members of Nucleus, is exactly that.

Pieces Of Me	LP	Vertigo	6360060	1971	**£100**	spiral label

HRATCH

Beautiful Bare Back Rider	7"	Decca	F13007	1970	**£4**	

HUCKNALL, MICK

Early Years	mini LP	TJM	TJM101		**£10**	

HUG

Neon Dream	LP	Polydor	2383330	1975	**£12**	

HUGG, MIKE

Blue Suede Shoes Again	7"	Polydor	2058265	1972	**£4**	
Somewhere	LP	Polydor	2383140	1972	**£12**	
Stress And Strain	LP	Polydor	2383213	1973	**£12**	

HUGHES, FRED

Oo Wee Baby I Love You	7"	Fontana	TF583	1965	**£10**	
Send My Baby Back	LP	Wand	WD664	1965	**£10**	US

HUGHES, JIMMY

Goodbye My Love	7"	Sue	WI4006	1966	**£10**	
Hi Heel Sneakers	7"	Atlantic	584135	1967	**£4**	
I'm Qualified	7"	London	HL9680	1963	**£10**	
Neighbour Neighbour	7"	Atlantic	584017	1966	**£6**	
Steal Away	7"	Pye	7N25254	1964	**£5**	
Steal Away	LP	Vee Jay	1102	1965	**£10**	US
Why Not Tonight	LP	Atco	33209	1967	**£10**	US

HUGO & LUIGI

La Plume De Ma Tante	7"	RCA	RCA1127	1959	**£4**	chart single
Shenandoah Rose	7"	Columbia	DB3978	1957	**£6**	
Twilight In Tennessee	7"	Columbia	DB4156	1958	**£5**	

HULL, ALAN

We Can Sing Together	7"	Transatlantic	BIG129	1970	**£10**	

HULLABALOOS

Don't Stomp	7"	Columbia	DB7626	1965	**£5**	
England's Newest Singing Sensations	LP	Roulette	R25297	1965	**£12**	US
Hullabaloos On Hullabaloo	LP	Roulette	R25310	1965	**£12**	US
I'll Show You How To Love	7"	Columbia	DB7558	1965	**£5**	
I'm Gonna Love You Too	7"	Columbia	DB7392	1964	**£6**	

HULTGREEN, GEORG

Say Hello	7"	W. Bros	WB8017	1970	**£5**	

HUMAN BEANS

Morning Dew	7"	Columbia	DB8230	1967	**£50**	

HUMAN BEAST

Human Beast Vol.1	LP	Decca	SKL5053	1970	**£80**	

HUMAN BEINZ

Evolutions	LP	Capitol	ST2926	1968	**£12**	US
Nobody But Me	LP	Capitol	ST2906	1968	**£12**	US
Nobody But Me	LP	Capitol	CL15529	1968	**£12**	
Nobody But Me	LP	Gateway	GLP3012	1968	**£15**	US
Turn On Your Lovelight	7"	Capitol	CL15542	1968	**£15**	

HUMAN INSTINCT

Can't Stop Loving You	7"	Mercury	MF951	1965	**£10**	
Day In My Mind's Mind	7"	Deram	DM167	1967	**£15**	
Go Go	7"	Mercury	MF990	1966	**£15**	
Renaissance Fair	7"	Deram	DM177	1968	**£12**	
Rich Man	7"	Mercury	MF927	1966	**£15**	

HUMAN LEAGUE

Dare	LP	Virgin	VP2192	1981	**£10**	pic disc, black sleeve

Dignity Of Labour	12"	Fast	FASTVF1	1979	**£6**	with flexi (F10X)
Empire State Human	7"	Virgin	VS351	1980	**£5**	double
Empire State Human	12"	Virgin	VS35112	1980	**£6**	
Holidays '80	7"	Virgin	VS105	1980	**£4**	gatefold PS
Love Action	12"	Virgin	VS43512	1981	**£6**	with flexi
Sound Of The Crowd	12"	Virgin	VS41612	1981	**£6**	

HUMAN ZOO

Human Zoo	LP	Accent	5055	1969	**£20**	US

HUMBLE PIE

As Safe As Yesterday Is	LP	Immediate	IMSP025	1969	**£15**	chart LP
Eat It	LP	A&M	AMLS6004	1973	**£12**	double, chart LP
Humble Pie	LP	A&M	AMLS986	1970	**£10**	
Natural Born Bugie	7"	Immediate	IM082	1969	**£4**	
Rock On	LP	A&M	AMLS2013	1971	**£10**	
Smokin'	LP	A&M	AMLS64342	1972	**£10**	chart LP
Street Rats	LP	A&M	AMLS68282	1975	**£10**	
Thunderbox	LP	A&M	AMLH63611	1974	**£10**	
Town And Country	LP	Immediate	IMSP027	1969	**£15**	

HUMBLEBUMS

"He's humble..," Billy Connolly used to quip when explaining the origin of his group's name. Originally a folk duo featuring Connolly and fellow Glaswegian Tam Harvey, the Humblebums broadened their appeal a little when Harvey was replaced by singer-songwriter Gerry Rafferty. Some of Rafferty's songs with the group are amongst the best that Paul McCartney never wrote, although both Rafferty and Connolly have become rather more famous since.

First Collection	LP	Transatlantic	TRA186	1969	**£12**	
Humblebums	LP	Transatlantic	TRA201	1969	**£10**	
Open Up The Door	LP	Transatlantic	TRA218	1970	**£10**	
Saturday Roundabout Sunday	7"	Transatlantic	BIG122	1969	**£4**	
Shoeshine Boy	7"	Transatlantic	BIG130	1970	**£4**	

HUMES, HELEN & JIMMY WITHERSPOON

Rhythm And Blues Concert	7" EP	Vogue	EPV1198	195-	**£15**	

HUMPHREY, DELLA

Don't Make The Good Girls So Bad	7"	Action	ACT4525	1969	**£12**	demo

HUMPY BONG

Don't You Be Too Long	7"	Parlophone	R5859	1970	**£5**	

HUNGER

Strickly From Hunger	LP	Public	1006	1969	**£50**	US

HUNGRY WOLF

Hungry Wolf	LP	Philips	6308009	1970	**£50**	

HUNT, GERALDINE

Never Never Leave Me	7"	Roulette	RO515	1969	**£4**	

HUNT, MARSHA

Desdemona	7"	Track	604034	1969	**£12**	
Keep The Customer Satisfied	7"	Track	604037	1970	**£5**	chart single
Walk On Gilded Splinters	7"	Track	604030	1969	**£6**	chart single
Woman Child	LP	Track	2410101	1971	**£15**	

HUNT, TOMMY

Greatest Hits	LP	Dynamo	8001	1967	**£10**	US
I Just Don't Know What To Do With...	LP	Scepter	S506	1962	**£15**	US
I'm Wondering	7"	Top Rank	JAR605	1962	**£6**	

HUNT, WILLIE AMOS

Would You Believe	7"	Camp	602003	1967	**£20**	

HUNTER MUSKETT

Everytime You Move	LP	Nova	SND20	1970	**£20**	
Hunter Muskett	LP	Bradley	1003	1969	**£20**	US
John Blair	7"	Bradley	BRAD303	1973	**£6**	

HUNTER, DAVE

Don't Throw Your Love To The Wind	7"	RCA	RCA1841	1969	**£4**	
She's A Heartbreaker	7"	RCA	RCA1766	1968	**£6**	

HUNTER, IAN

Title	Format	Label	Cat. No.	Year	Price	Notes
All American Alien Boy	LP	CBS	81310	1976	**£10**	
Ian Hunter	LP	CBS	80710	1975	**£10**	chart LP

HUNTER, IVORY JOE

Title	Format	Label	Cat. No.	Year	Price	Notes
Fabulous Ivory Joe Hunter	LP	Goldisc	403	1961	**£20**	US
Golden Hits	LP	Smash	MGS27037	1963	**£12**	US
I Get That Lonesome Feeling	LP	MGM	E3488	1957	**£50**	US
I'm Hooked	7"	Capitol	CL15220	1961	**£6**	
Ivory Joe Hunter	LP	Atlantic	8008	1958	**£50**	US
Ivory Joe Hunter	LP	Sage	603	1959	**£30**	US
Ivory Joe Hunter	LP	Sound	603	1957	**£50**	US
Love's A Hurting Game	7"	London	HLE8486	1957	**£20**	
May The Best Man Win	7"	Capitol	CL15226	1961	**£4**	
Since I Met You Baby	7"	Columbia	DB3872	1957	**£40**	
Sings The Old And The New	LP	Atlantic	8015	1958	**£50**	US
Sixteen Of His Greatest Hits	LP	King	605	1958	**£75**	US
Tear Fell	7"	London	HLE8261	1956	**£30**	
This Is Ivory Joe Hunter	LP	Dot	DLP3569	1964	**£12**	US
Tales Of Great Rum Runners	LP	Round	RX101	1974	**£12**	
Tiger Rose	LP	Round	RX105	1975	**£12**	

HUNTER, TAB

Title	Format	Label	Cat. No.	Year	Price	Notes
Don't Let It Get Around	7"	London	HLD8535	1958	**£4**	
I Can't Stop Loving You	7"	London	HLD9559	1962	**£4**	
Ninety-Nine Ways	7"	London	HLD8410	1957	**£4**	chart single
R.F.D. Tab Hunter	LP	W. Bros	W1367	1960	**£12**	US
Tab Hunter	LP	W. Bros	W1221	1958	**£12**	US
Tab Hunter	7" EP	W. Bros	WEP6023	1961	**£5**	
When I Fall In Love	LP	W. Bros	W1292	1959	**£12**	US
Wild Side Of Life	7"	London	HLD9381	1961	**£4**	
Young Love	LP	Dot	DLP3370	1961	**£10**	US
Young Love	7"	London	HLD8380	1957	**£8**	chart single
Young Love	7" EP	London	RED1134	1958	**£10**	

HUNTERS

Title	Format	Label	Cat. No.	Year	Price	Notes
Golden Earrings	7"	Fontana	H303	1961	**£5**	
Hits From The Hunters	LP	Fontana	STFL572	1962	**£25**	
Storm	7"	Fontana	H323	1961	**£5**	
Teen Scene	LP	Fontana	TFL5140	1961	**£25**	mono
Teen Scene	LP	Fontana	STFL561	1961	**£25**	stereo
Teen Scene	7"	Fontana	H276	1960	**£6**	
Teen Scene	7"	Fontana	TF514	1964	**£4**	

HURDY GURDY

Title	Format	Label	Cat. No.	Year	Price	Notes
Hurdy Gurdy	LP	CBS		1971	**£200**	

HURT, MISSISSIPPI JOHN

Title	Format	Label	Cat. No.	Year	Price	Notes
Blues At Newport	LP	Vanguard	VRS9145	1965	**£12**	US
Immortal Mississippi John Hurt	LP	Vanguard	VRS9248	1967	**£12**	US
Mississippi John Hurt Today	LP	Vanguard	VRS9220	1966	**£12**	US

HUSH

Title	Format	Label	Cat. No.	Year	Price	Notes
Grey	7"	Fontana	TF944	1968	**£40**	

HUSKER DU

Title	Format	Label	Cat. No.	Year	Price	Notes
Amusement	7"	Reflex	38285	1980	**£40**	
In A Free Land	7"	New Alliance		1982	**£40**	
Sorry Somehow	7"	WEA	W8612	1986	**£10**	double

HUSKY, FERLIN

Title	Format	Label	Cat. No.	Year	Price	Notes
Black Sheep	7"	Capitol	CL15094	1959	**£4**	
Born To Lose	LP	Capitol	T1204	1959	**£12**	US
Boulevard Of Broken Dreams	LP	Capitol	T880	1957	**£15**	US
Country Music Holiday	7" EP	Capitol	EAP1921	1957	**£6**	
Country Round Up	7" EP	Parlophone	GEP8795	1959	**£12**	
Country Tunes Sung From The Heart	LP	King	647	1959	**£15**	US
Draggin' The River	7"	Capitol	CL15027	1959	**£4**	
Easy Livin'	LP	King	728	1960	**£15**	US
Fallen Star	7"	Capitol	CL14753	1957	**£4**	
Ferlin Husky Hits	7" EP	Capitol	EAP1837	1957	**£5**	

Ferlin's Favorites	LP	Capitol	T1280	1960	**£12**	US
Ferlin's Favourites Part 1	7" EP	Capitol	EAP11280	1960	**£5**	
Ferlin's Favourites Part 2	7" EP	Capitol	EAP21280	1960	**£5**	
Ferlin's Favourites Part 3	7" EP	Capitol	EAP31280	1960	**£5**	
Gone	LP	Capi tol	T1383	1960	**£10**	US
Gone	7"	Capitol	CL14702	1957	**£5**	
I Feel That Old Heartache Again	7"	Capitol	CL14916	1958	**£4**	
I Will	7"	Capitol	CL14954	1958	**£4**	
Kingdom Of Love	7"	Capitol	CL14922	1958	**£4**	
Make Me Live Again	7"	Capitol	CL14785	1957	**£4**	
My Reason For Living	7"	Capitol	CL14995	1959	**£4**	
Sittin' On A Rainbow	LP	Capitol	T976	1959	**£15**	US
Slow Down Brother	7"	Capitol	CL14883	1958	**£5**	
Songs Of The Home And Heart	LP	Capitol	T718	1956	**£20**	US
Songs Of The Home And Heart	7" EP	Capitol	EAP1718	1957	**£6**	
Wang Dang Do	7"	Capitol	CL14824	1958	**£6**	
Wings Of A Dove	7"	Capitol	CL15160	1960	**£4**	

HUSTLERS

Gimme What I Want	7"	Philips	BF1275	1963	**£6**	
Sick Of Giving	7"	Mercury	MF817	1964	**£10**	

HUTCH, WILLIE

Brothers Gonna Work It Out	7"	Tamla Motown	TMG862	1973	**£4**	
Brothers Gonna Work It Out	7"	Tamla Motown	TMG862	1973	**£10**	demo
Tell Me Why Our Love Has Turned Cold	7"	Tamla Motown	TMG885	1974	**£50**	demo

HUTCHINGS, ASHLEY

Compleat Dancing Master	LP	Island	HELP17	1974	**£10**	
Kickin' Up The Sawdust	LP	Harvest	SHSP4073	1977	**£10**	
Rattlebone And Ploughjack	LP	Island	HELP24	1976	**£10**	
Son Of Morris On	LP	Harvest	SHSM2012	1976	**£10**	

HUTTON SISTERS

Ko Ko Mo	7"	Capitol	CL14250	1955	**£10**	

HUTTON, DANNY

Funny How Love Can Be	7"	MGM	MGM1314	1966	**£4**	

HYATT, CHARLIE

Kiss Me Neck	LP	Island	ILP932	1966	**£60**	

HYGRADES

She Cared	7"	Columbia	DB7734	1965	**£4**	

HYLAND, BRIAN

Bashful Blonde	LP	London	HAR2289	1961	**£15**	
Country Meets Folk	LP	ABC-Para.	463	1964	**£10**	US
Four Little Heels	7"	London	HLR9203	1960	**£4**	chart single
Ginny Come Lately	7"	HMV	POP1013	1962	**£4**	chart single
Here's To Our Love	LP	Philips	PHM200136	1964	**£10**	US
I Gotta Go	7"	London	HLR9262	1961	**£4**	
Itsy Bitsy Teeny Weeny...	7"	London	HLR9161	1960	**£4**	chart single
Joker Went Wild	LP	Philips	PHM200217	1966	**£10**	US
Joker Went Wild	7"	Philips	BF1508	1966	**£4**	
Let Me Belong To You	LP	ABC-Para.	400	1961	**£10**	US
Rockin' Folk	LP	Philips	PHM200158	1965	**£10**	US
Sealed With A Kiss	LP	ABC-Para.	431	1962	**£12**	US
Sealed With A Kiss	7"	HMV	POP1051	1962	**£4**	chart single
Sealed With A Kiss	7" EP	HMV	7EG8780	1962	**£6**	
Warmed Over Kisses	7"	HMV	POP1079	1962	**£4**	chart single

HYMAN, DICK

Electrics	LP	Command		1968	**£50**	US

I

I LUV WIGHT
Let The World Wash In ... 7" ... Philips ... 6006043 ... 1970 ... **£35**

I-JOG & THE TRACKSUITS
Red Box ... 7" ... Tyger ... TYG1 ... 1978 ... **£6**

IAN & SYLVIA
Best Of... ... LP ... Vanguard ... SVRL19004 ... 1968 ... **£10**
Early Morning Rain ... LP ... Fontana ... TF6053 ... 1965 ... **£10**
Four Strong Winds ... 7" ... Fontana ... TF426 ... 1963 ... **£4**
Four Strong Winds ... LP ... Vanguard ... VSD2149 ... 1964 ... **£10** ... US
Full Circle ... LP ... MGM ... 4550 ... 1968 ... **£10** ... US
Greatest Hits ... LP ... Vanguard ... VSD5/6 ... 1973 ... **£15** ... double
Greatest Hits Vol.2 ... LP ... Vanguard ... VSD23/24 ... 1974 ... **£15** ... double
Ian And Sylvia ... LP ... Vanguard ... VSD2113 ... 1962 ... **£10** ... US
Nashville ... LP ... Vanguard ... VSD79284 ... 1968 ... **£10** ... US
Northern Journey ... LP ... Vanguard ... VSD79154 ... 1964 ... **£10** ... US
Play One More ... LP ... Vanguard ... VSD79215 ... 1966 ... **£10** ... US
So Much Dreaming ... LP ... Vanguard ... VSD79241 ... 1967 ... **£10** ... US

IAN & THE ZODIACS
Beechwood 45789 ... 7" ... Oriole ... CB1849 ... 1963 ... **£12**
Gear Again - 12 Hits ... LP ... Wing ... WL1074 ... 1965 ... **£75**
Just The Little Things I Like ... 7" ... Fontana ... TF548 ... 1965 ... **£10**
No Money, No Honey ... 7" ... Fontana ... TF708 ... 1966 ... **£10**
Wade In The Water ... 7" ... Fontana ... TF753 ... 1966 ... **£10**

IAN, JANIS
For All The Seasons ... LP ... Verve ... FTS3024 ... 1968 ... **£10** ... US
Janis Ian ... LP ... Verve ... VLP6001 ... 1967 ... **£12**
Present Company ... LP ... Capitol ... SM683 ... 1971 ... **£10**
Secret Life Of Eddie Fink ... LP ... Verve ... FTS3048 ... 1968 ... **£10** ... US
Society's Child ... 7" ... Verve ... VS1503 ... 1967 ... **£5**
Society's Child ... 7" ... Verve ... VS1506 ... 1967 ... **£5**
Sunflakes Fall, Snowrays Call ... 7" ... Verve ... VS1513 ... 1968 ... **£6**
Who Really Cares ... LP ... Verve ... FTS3063 ... 1969 ... **£10** ... US

ICARUS
Devil Rides Out ... 7" ... Spark ... SRL1012 ... 1969 ... **£12**
Marvel World ... LP ... Pye ... 1971 ... **£100**

ICE
Anniversary Of Love ... 7" ... Decca ... F12680 ... 1967 ... **£20**
Ice Man ... 7" ... Decca ... F12749 ... 1968 ... **£20**
Saga Of The Ice King ... LP ... Storm ... 1979 ... **£150**

ICICLE WORKS
Here Comes Trouble ... 12" ... Beggars B. ... BEG220T ... 1988 ... **£8** ... boxed
Kiss Off ... 12" ... Beggars B. ... BEG208TX ... 1988 ... **£6** ... promo
Little Girl Lost ... CD-s ... Beggars B. ... BEG215 ... 1988 ... **£12** ... pic disc
Love Is A Wonderful Colour ... 7" ... Beggars B. ... BEG99 ... 1983 ... **£6** ... double
Love Is A Wonderful Colour ... 7" ... Beggars B. ... BEG99P ... 1983 ... **£6** ... pic disc
Love Is A Wonderful Colour ... 12" ... Beggars B. ... BEG99PT ... 1983 ... **£6** ... pic disc
Nirvana ... 7" ... Troll Kitch. ... WORKS1 ... 1983 ... **£15**
Seven Horses ... 7" ... Beggars B. ... BEG142 ... 1985 ... **£5** ... double

IDEALS
Knee Socks ... 7" ... Pye ... 7N25103 ... 1961 ... **£4**

IDES OF MARCH
Hole In My Soul ... 7" ... London ... HLU10183 ... 1968 ... **£4**
Melody ... 7" ... W. Bros ... WB7426 ... 1970 ... **£4**

Superman	7"	W. Bros	WB7403	1970	**£4**	
Vehicle	7"	W. Bros	WB7378	1970	**£4**	chart single
You Wouldn't Listen	7"	London	HLU10058	1966	**£4**	

IDLE RACE

The Idle Race produced intelligent pop music with occasional touches of psychedelia (most notably in the single "Imposters Of Life's Magazine"). The group's records displayed a degree of production skill and craftsmanship unusual in a little-known pop act of the time, but then the group's leader was Jeff Lynne.

Birthday Party	LP	Liberty	LBL83132	1968	**£30**	
Birthday Party	LP	Sunset	SLS50381	1976	**£12**	
Come With Me	7"	Liberty	LBF15242	1969	**£10**	
Dancing Flower	7"	Regal Z.	RZ3036	1971	**£6**	
Days Of Broken Arrows	7"	Liberty	LBF15218	1969	**£10**	
End Of The Road	7"	Liberty	LBF15101	1968	**£10**	
I Like My Toys	7"	Liberty	LBF15129	1968	**£12**	
Idle Race	LP	Liberty	LBS83211	1969	**£25**	
Imposters Of Life's Magazine	7"	Liberty	LBF15026	1967	**£12**	
On With The Show	LP	Sunset	SLS50354	1973	**£12**	
Skeleton And The Roundabout	7"	Liberty	LBF15054	1968	**£10**	
Skeleton And The Roundabout	7"	United Artists	UP36060	1976	**£4**	
Time Is	LP	Regal Z.	SLRZ1017	1971	**£40**	

IDOL, BILLY

Don't Need A Gun	12"	Chrysalis	IDOLP9	1987	**£6**	pic disc
Eyes Without A Face	12"	Chrysalis	IDOLP3	1984	**£10**	pic disc
Eyes Without A Face	7"	Chrysalis	IDOLD3	1984	**£5**	double
Flesh For Fantasy	7"	Chrysalis	IDOLDJ4	1984	**£5**	promo
Flesh For Fantasy	12"	Chrysalis	IDOLP4	1984	**£8**	pic disc
Hot In The City	7"	Chrysalis	CHS2625	1982	**£5**	pic disc
Mony Mony	12"	Chrysalis	CHS122543	1981	**£6**	
Rebel Yell	7"	Chrysalis	IDOLD2	1984	**£5**	double
Rebel Yell	7"	Chrysalis	IDOLP2	1984	**£6**	square pic disc
Rebel Yell	12"	Chrysalis	IDOLP6	1985	**£6**	pic disc
Sweet 16	12"	Chrysalis	IDOLP10	1987	**£6**	pic disc
To Be A Lover	12"	Chrysalis	IDOLP8	1986	**£6**	pic disc
White Wedding	7"	Chrysalis	CHS2656	1982	**£5**	white vinyl
White Wedding	12"	Chrysalis	IDOLP5	1985	**£8**	pic disc

IDOLS

You	7"	ORK	NYC2	1979	**£4**	

IF

If was a jazz-rock group formed by the previously mainstream jazz players Dick Morrissey and Terry Smith (saxophone and guitar respectively). It was interesting as a group formed from the jazz side of the jazz-rock divide, but was ultimately less convincing than the likes of Colosseum or Manfred Mann Chapter Three. Morrissey reappeared later as co-leader of the successful fusion group, Morrissey-Mullen.

Far Beyond	7"	United Artists	UP35263	1971	**£5**	
I Believe In Rock & Roll	7"	Gull	GULS5	1974	**£4**	
If	LP	Island	ILPS9129	1970	**£15**	
If 2	LP	Island	ILPS9137	1970	**£15**	
If 3	LP	United Artists	UAG29158	1971	**£15**	
If 4	LP	United Artists	UAG29315	1972	**£15**	
Not Just A Bunch Of Pretty Faces	LP	Gull	GULP1004	1974	**£10**	
Raise The Level Of Your Conscious	7"	Island	WIP6083	1970	**£6**	
Tea Break Is Over	LP	Gull	GULP1007	1975	**£10**	

IFE, KRIS

Haven't We Had A Good Time	7"	Parlophone	R5770	1969	**£4**	
Hush	7"	MGM	MGM1369	1967	**£4**	
Imagination	7"	Parlophone	R5741	1968	**£5**	
Sands Of Time	7"	Music Factory	CUB3	196-	**£6**	
This Woman's Love	7"	MGM	MGM1390	1968	**£4**	

IGGINBOTTOM'S WRENCH

The LP by Igginbottom's Wrench marks the recording debut of the guitarists' guitarist, Allan Holdsworth, in a surprisingly understated context.

Igginbottom's Wrench	LP	Deram	SML1051	1969	**£100**	

IGNERENTS

Radio Interference	7"	Rundown	ACE008	1979	**£4**	

IGUANA

Iguana	LP	Polydor	2383108	1972	**£25**	

IKETTES

Fine Fine Fine	7" EP	Stateside	SE1033	1965	**£10**	
Fine Fine Fine	7"	Stateside	SS434	1965	**£4**	
I'm Blue	7"	London	HLK9508	1962	**£5**	
I'm So Thankful	7"	Polydor	56506	1970	**£4**	
Never More Lonely For You	7"	Polydor	56516	1970	**£4**	
Peaches 'n' Cream	7"	Stateside	SS407	1965	**£5**	
Prisoner Of Love	7"	Sue	WI389	1965	**£8**	
Soul Hits	LP	Modern	M102	1965	**£10**	US
Whatcha Gonna Do	7"	London	HLU10081	1966	**£4**	

ILL WIND

Flashes	LP	ABC	S641	1968	**£30**	US

ILLINOIS SPEED PRESS

Duet	LP	CBS	9976	1970	**£15**	US
Illinois Speed Press	LP	CBS	63691	1969	**£20**	

ILLUSION

Did You See Her Eyes	7"	Dot	122	1969	**£8**	
Let's Make Each Other Happy	7"	Paramount	PARA3007	1970	**£5**	
Together	7"	Dot	DOT133	1970	**£5**	

ILLUSIVE DREAM

Electric Garden	7"	RCA	RCA1791	1969	**£6**	

ILLUSTRATION

Illustration	LP	Pye	NSPL28140	1970	**£10**	

IMAGE

Come To The Party	7"	Parlophone	R5281	1965	**£25**	
Home Is Anywhere	7"	Parlophone	R5352	1965	**£20**	
I Can't Stop Myself	7"	Parlophone	R5442	1966	**£20**	

IMPAC

Too Far Out	7"	CBS	202402	1966	**£15**	

IMPACS

Impact!	LP	King	886	1964	**£20**	US
Weekend With The Impacs	LP	King	916	1964	**£20**	US

IMPACTS

Wipe Out	LP	Del-Fi	DFLP1234	1963	**£15**	US

IMPALAS

Oh What A Fool	7"	MGM	MGM1031	1959	**£4**	
Sorry	7" EP	MGM	MGMEP696	1959	**£10**	
Sorry	7"	MGM	MGM1015	1959	**£4**	chart single
Sorry I Ran All The Way Home	LP	Cub	8003	1959	**£75**	US

IMPRESSIONS

Ain't Got Time	7"	Buddah	2011068	1971	**£4**	
Amen	LP	Buddah	2359009	1970	**£10**	
Amen	7"	HMV	POP1492	1965	**£6**	
Big 16	LP	HMV	CLP1935	1965	**£15**	mono
Big 16	LP	HMV	CSD1642	1965	**£15**	stereo
Big 16 Vol.2	LP	Stateside	SSL10279	1969	**£10**	
Can't Satisfy	7"	HMV	POP1545	1966	**£8**	
Can't Satisfy	7"	Stateside	SS2139	1969	**£4**	
Check Out Your Mind	LP	Buddah	2318017	1971	**£10**	
Check Out Your Mind	7"	Buddah	2011030	1970	**£4**	
Fabulous Impressions	LP	HMV	CLP3631	1967	**£12**	
Fool For You	7"	Buddah	201021	1968	**£4**	
Gypsy Woman	7"	HMV	POP961	1961	**£8**	
I Need You	7"	HMV	POP1472	1965	**£6**	
I'm So Proud	7"	HMV	POP1295	1964	**£6**	
I'm The One Who Loves You	7"	HMV	POP1129	1963	**£6**	
Impressions	LP	ABC-Para.	450	1963	**£20**	US
It's All Right	7" EP	HMV	7EG8896	1965	**£8**	

It's All Right	7"	HMV	POP1226	1963	**£6**	
Keep On Pushing	LP	ABC-Para.	493	1964	**£15**	US
Keep On Pushing	7"	HMV	POP1317	1964	**£6**	
Love Me	7"	Buddah	2011087	1971	**£4**	
Meeting Over Yonder	7"	HMV	POP1446	1965	**£6**	
Mighty Mighty Spade And Whitey	7"	Buddah	201062	1969	**£4**	
Never Ending Impressions	LP	HMV	CLP1743	1964	**£20**	
One By One	LP	ABC-Para.	523	1965	**£15**	US
People Get Ready	LP	ABC-Para.	505	1965	**£15**	US
People Get Ready	7"	HMV	POP1408	1965	**£8**	
Ridin' High	LP	HMV	CLP3548	1966	**£15**	
Since I Lost The One I Love	7"	HMV	POP1516	1966	**£5**	
Soulfully	7" EP	HMV	7EG8954	1966	**£8**	
Talking About My Baby	7"	HMV	POP1262	1964	**£6**	
This Is My Country	LP	Buddah	203012	1969	**£10**	
Too Slow	7"	HMV	POP1526	1966	**£5**	
Turn On To Me	7"	Buddah	2011045	1970	**£4**	
We're A Winner	LP	Stateside	SSL10239	1968	**£10**	
We're A Winner	7"	Stateside	SS2083	1968	**£4**	
Woman's Got Soul	7"	HMV	POP1429	1965	**£6**	
You Always Hurt Me	7"	HMV	POP1581	1967	**£5**	
You Must Believe Me	7"	HMV	POP1343	1964	**£6**	
You've Been Cheating	7"	HMV	POP1498	1966	**£8**	
Young Mod's Forgotten Story	LP	Buddah	2359003	1970	**£12**	

IN CAMERA

Die Laughing	7"	4AD	AD8	1980	**£4**	
Fin	12"	4AD	BAD205	1982	**£6**	
IV Songs	12"	4AD	BAD19	1980	**£6**	

IN CROWD

The soul singles of the In Crowd gave no indication that the group would ever evolve into that cornerstone of psychedelia, Tomorrow. "That's How Strong My Love Is" was recorded before Steve Howe joined the group, but the other singles all feature his guitar playing, in behind Keith West's singing.

Stop! Wait A Minute	7"	Parlophone	R5328	1965	**£15**	
That's How Strong My Love Is	7"	Parlophone	R5276	1965	**£15**	chart single
Where In The World	7"	Deram	DM272	1969	**£15**	
Why Must They Criticise	7"	Parlophone	R5364	1965	**£15**	

INADEQUATES

Audie	7"	Capitol	CL15051	1959	**£4**	

INCAS

I'll Keep Holding On	7"	Parlophone	R5551	1966	**£10**	

INCREDIBLE BONGO BAND

Bongo Rock	LP	DJM	20452	1976	**£20**	
Bongo Rock	7"	MGM	2006161	1973	**£4**	

INCREDIBLE HOG

Volume One	LP	Dart	65372	1973	**£50**	

INCREDIBLE STRING BAND

5000 Spirits...	LP	Elektra	EUKS7257	1967	**£10**	chart LP
At The Lighthouse Dance	7"	Island	WIP6158	1973	**£4**	
Be Glad For The Song....	LP	Island	ILPS9140	1970	**£10**	
Big Huge	LP	Elektra	EKS74037	1968	**£12**	
Big Ted	7"	Elektra	EKSN45074	1969	**£6**	
Black Jack Diamond	7"	Island	WIP6145	1972	**£4**	
Changing Horses	LP	Elektra	EKS74057	1969	**£10**	chart LP
Earth Span	LP	Island	ILPS9211	1972	**£10**	
Hangman's Beautiful Daughter	LP	Elektra	EKS74021	1968	**£10**	chart LP
Hard Rope & Silken Twine	LP	Island	ILPS9270	1974	**£10**	
I Looked Up	LP	Elektra	EKS74061	1970	**£10**	chart LP
Incredible String Band	LP	Elektra	EKL322	1966	**£12**	
Incredible String Band	LP	Elektra	EUK254	1966	**£15**	chart LP
Liquid Acrobat	LP	Island	ILPS9172	1971	**£10**	chart LP
No Ruinous Feud	LP	Island	ILPS9229	1973	**£10**	
Painting Box	7"	Elektra	EKSN45028	1968	**£6**	
This Moment	7"	Elektra	2101003	1970	**£4**	
U	LP	Elektra	2665001	1970	**£15**	double, chart LP

Title	Format	Label	Cat. No.	Year	Price	Notes
Wee Tam	LP	Elektra	EKS74036	1968	**£12**	
Wee Tam/The Big Huge	LP	Elektra	EKS74036/7	1968	**£20**	double

INCREDIBLES

Title	Format	Label	Cat. No.	Year	Price	Notes
There's Nothing Else To Say	7"	Stateside	SS2053	1967	**£30**	

INDEX

Title	Format	Label	Cat. No.	Year	Price	Notes
Index	LP			1969	**£200**	US

INDIAN SUMMER

Title	Format	Label	Cat. No.	Year	Price	Notes
Indian Summer	LP	Neon	NE3	1971	**£30**	

INDIANS IN MOSCOW

Title	Format	Label	Cat. No.	Year	Price	Notes
Chicken	7"	Kennick	KNK1004	1984	**£4**	white vinyl

INDO JAZZMEN

Title	Format	Label	Cat. No.	Year	Price	Notes
Ragas And Reflections	LP	Saga	FID2145	1968	**£15**	

INFA RIOT

Title	Format	Label	Cat. No.	Year	Price	Notes
Kids Of The Eighties	7"	Secret	SHH117	1981	**£5**	
Winner	7"	Secret	SHH133	1982	**£5**	

INFANTS JUBILATE

Title	Format	Label	Cat. No.	Year	Price	Notes
Exploding Galaxy	7"	Music Factory	CUB5	196-	**£20**	

INFAS

Title	Format	Label	Cat. No.	Year	Price	Notes
Sound And Fury	7"	Panache	PAN101	1984	**£4**	

INFESTED

Title	Format	Label	Cat. No.	Year	Price	Notes
Flies	7"	Dead City		197-	**£100**	existence doubtful
No But I've Got A Dark Brown Overcoat	7"	Great Disaster		197-	**£100**	existence doubtful

INFORMATION

Title	Format	Label	Cat. No.	Year	Price	Notes
Face To The Sun	7"	Evolution	E2461S	1970	**£8**	
Orphan	7"	Beacon	BEA3121	1968	**£6**	

INGLE, RED

Title	Format	Label	Cat. No.	Year	Price	Notes
Cigareets, Whuskey & Wild Wild Women	7" EP	Capitol	EAP20052	1959	**£8**	

INGMANN, JORGEN

Title	Format	Label	Cat. No.	Year	Price	Notes
Africa	7"	Fontana	267237	1962	**£4**	
Apache	LP	Atco	33130	1961	**£15**	US
Cherokee	7"	Fontana	H311	1961	**£4**	
Drina	7" EP	Columbia	SEG8340	1964	**£6**	
Many Guitars Of...	LP	Atco	33139	1962	**£12**	US
Milord	7"	Fontana	H333	1961	**£4**	
Swinging Guitar	LP	Mercury	MG20200	1956	**£15**	US
Violetta	7"	Fontana	267184	1962	**£4**	
Violetta	7"	Fontana	H353	1961	**£4**	

INGRAM, LUTHER

Title	Format	Label	Cat. No.	Year	Price	Notes
Home Don't Seem Like A Home	7"	Stax	STAX148	1970	**£4**	

INKSPOTS

Title	Format	Label	Cat. No.	Year	Price	Notes
Charlie Fuqua's Inkspots	7" EP	HMV	7EG8410	1957	**£6**	
Ebb Tide	7"	Parlophone	MSP6074	1954	**£12**	
Here In My Lonely Room	7"	Parlophone	MSP6063	1954	**£12**	
Melody Of Love	7"	Parlophone	MSP6152	1955	**£12**	chart single
Swing High Swing Low Vol.1	7" EP	Brunswick	OE9158	1955	**£6**	
Yesterdays	7"	Parlophone	MSP6126	1954	**£12**	
Yesterdays	7" EP	Parlophone	GEP8673	1957	**£6**	

INNES, NEIL

Title	Format	Label	Cat. No.	Year	Price	Notes
How Sweet To Be An Idiot	LP	United Artists	UAG29492	1973	**£15**	
Lie Down And Be Counted	7"	United Artists	UP35745	1975	**£4**	
Momma B	7"	United Artists	UP35639	1974	**£4**	
Recycled Vinyl Blues	7"	United Artists	UP35676	1974	**£4**	
Rutland Times	LP	BBC	REB233	1976	**£10**	
What Noise Annoys A Noisy Oyster	7"	United Artists	UP35772	1975	**£4**	

INNOCENCE

Title	Format	Label	Cat. No.	Year	Price	Notes
Lifetime Loving You	7"	Kama Sutra	KAS206	1967	**£4**	
There's Got To Be A Word	7"	Kama Sutra	KAS203	1966	**£4**	

INNOCENTS

Gee Whiz	7"	Top Rank	JAR541	1961	**£5**	
Honest I Do	7"	Top Rank	JAR508	1960	**£10**	

INNOCENTS (2)

Fine Fine Bird	7"	Columbia	DB7173	1963	**£6**	
Stepping Stones	7"	Columbia	DB7098	1963	**£8**	
Stick With Me Baby	7"	Columbia	DB7314	1964	**£6**	

INSECT TRUST

At a time when rock was blossoming with new approaches and unusual instruments, the Insect Trust still managed to sound unique. They are like a folk group, with a strong female lead singer, into which a couple of avant garde jazz saxophonists have unaccountably wandered. The combination still sounds fresh today.

Hoboken Saturday Night	LP	Atco	SD33313	1970	**£20**	US
Insect Trust	LP	Capitol	EST109	1968	**£20**	

INSPIRAL CARPETS

Garage Full Of Flowers	7"	Debris	DEB06	1987	**£10**	flexi
Keep The Circle Around	12"	Cow	MOO1	1989	**£15**	test pressing only
Keep The Circle Around	7"	Playtime	AMUSE2	1988	**£40**	
Keep The Circle Around	12"	Playtime	AMUSE2T	1988	**£40**	

INSPIRATIONS

Touch Me, Hold Me, Kiss Me	7"	Polydor	56730	1967	**£30**	

INTERNATIONAL SUBMARINE BAND

The International Submarine Band, led by Gram Parsons, is often credited with making the first country-rock LP, for "Safe At Home" pre-dates the Byrds' "Sweetheart Of The Rodeo", in which Parsons was also involved.

Safe At Home	LP	LHI	LHI12001	1968	**£60**	US
Safe At Home	LP	Shiloh	RI4088	1979	**£10**	US

INTERNS

Cry To Me	7"	Philips	BF1345	1964	**£10**	
Don't You Dare	7"	Philips	BF1320	1964	**£8**	
Is It Really What You Want	7"	Parlophone	R5479	1966	**£8**	
Please Say Something Nice	7"	Parlophone	R5586	1967	**£6**	

INTRIGUES

In A Moment	7"	London	HL10293	1969	**£4**	
In A Moment	LP	Yew	YS777	1970	**£15**	US

INTRUDERS

Cowboys To Girls	7"	Ember	EMB254	1969	**£5**	
Cowboys To Girls	LP	Gamble	KZ5004	1968	**£10**	US
Intruders Are Together	LP	Gamble	5001	1967	**£10**	US
Slow Drag	7"	Action	ACT4523	1969	**£15**	demo
Slow Drag	7"	Action	ACT4523	1969	**£6**	
United	7"	London	HL10069	1966	**£15**	

INVADERS

Limbo Girl	7"	Blue Beat	BB105	1962	**£10**	
Limbo Girl	7"	Columbia	DB105	1967	**£8**	
Stop Teasing	7"	Blue Beat	BB109	1962	**£10**	
Stop Teasing	7"	Columbia	DB109	1968	**£8**	

INVADERS (2)

On The Right Track	LP	Justice	JLP125	1967	**£150**	US

INVITATIONS

Hallelujah	7"	Stateside	SS453	1965	**£6**	
What's Wrong With Me Baby	7"	Stateside	SS478	1965	**£25**	
What's Wrong With My Baby	7"	Mojo	2092055	1972	**£4**	Mis-press 'Me' with 'My'

INXS

Don't Change	12"	Mercury	INXS121	1983	**£10**	
Don't Change	7"	Mercury	INXS1	1983	**£6**	
I Send A Message	7"	Philips	PH2	1984	**£5**	with postcard, biography
I Send A Message	12"	Philips	PH212	1984	**£8**	
Just Keep Walking	7"	RCA	89	1981	**£25**	
Kiss The Dirt	7"	Mercury	INXSD7	1986	**£5**	double
Listen Like Thieves	7"	Mercury	INXSP6	1986	**£5**	shaped pic disc

Listen Like Thieves	7"	Mercury	INXSSD6	1986	**£5**	double
Listen Like Thieves	12"	Mercury	INXS612	1986	**£6**	with poster
New Sensation	12"	Mercury	INXSP912	1987	**£6**	poster sleeve
One Thing	12"	Mercury	INXS212	1983	**£15**	2 tracks
One Thing	7"	Mercury	INXS2	1983	**£6**	
One Thing	12"	Mercury	INXS222	1983	**£8**	3 tracks
Original Sin	7"	Mercury	INXS3	1984	**£5**	
Original Sin	12"	Mercury	INXS312	1984	**£8**	
This Time	cass	Mercury	INXSC5	1986	**£6**	promo
This Time	7"	Mercury	INXSD4	1986	**£6**	double
What You Need	12"	Mercury	INXSD512	1986	**£6**	double
What You Need	7"	Mercury	INXSC5	1986	**£8**	with cassette

IPSISSIMUS

Hold On	7"	Parlophone	R5774	1969	**£20**	

IQ

It All Stops Here	7"	Samurai	IQSD1	1986	**£4**	shaped pic disc

IRON BUTTERFLY

Ball	LP	Atlantic	228011	1969	**£12**	
Evolution (Best Of)	LP	Atlantic	K40298	1972	**£10**	
Heavy	LP	Atco	2465015	1967	**£15**	
In-A-Gadda-Da-Vida	LP	Atco	588166	1968	**£12**	
In-A-Gadda-Da-Vida	7"	Atlantic	2091024	1970	**£4**	
Live	LP	Atlantic	2400014	1970	**£15**	
Metamorphosis	LP	Atlantic	2401003	1970	**£10**	
Possession	7"	Atlantic	584188	1968	**£5**	
Scorching Beauty	LP	MCA	MCF2694	1975	**£10**	
Soul Experience	7"	Atlantic	584254	1969	**£5**	
Sun And Steel	LP	MCA	MCF2738	1975	**£10**	

IRON MAIDEN

Iron Maiden's striking death mascot has found particularly effective use as a recurring theme on the group's record covers and picture discs. Many of these are now very collectable, as befits a group that is probably the most successful of the New Wave of British Heavy Metal (though Def Leppard might argue the point).

Aces High	12"	EMI	12EMIP5502	1984	**£15**	pic disc
Aces High	7"	EMI	EMI5502	1984	**£4**	chart single
Can I Play With Madness	7"	EMI	EMP49	1988	**£8**	shaped pic disc
Evil That Men Do	7"	EMI	EMP64	1988	**£8**	shaped pic disc
Flight Of Icarus	12"	EMI	12EMIP5378	1983	**£15**	pic disc
Flight Of Icarus	7"	EMI	EMI5378	1983	**£4**	chart single
Maiden Japan	12"	EMI	12EMI5219	1981	**£15**	
Maiden Japan	7"	EMI	EMI5219	1981	**£8**	chart single
Number Of The Beast	LP	EMI	EMCP3400	1982	**£30**	pic disc
Number Of The Beast	7"	EMI	EMI5287	1982	**£4**	chart single
Number Of The Beast	7"	EMI	EMI5287	1982	**£8**	red vinyl
Powerslave	LP	EMI	POWERP1	1984	**£25**	pic disc
Purgatory	7"	EMI	EMI5184	1981	**£30**	chart single
Run To The Hills	7"	EMI	EMIP5263	1982	**£10**	pic disc
Run To The Hills	12"	EMI	12EMIP5542	1985	**£12**	pic disc
Run To The Hills	7"	EMI	EMI5263	1982	**£4**	chart single
Running Free	12"	EMI	12EMIP5532	1985	**£12**	pic disc
Running Free	7"	EMI	EMI5032	1980	**£25**	chart single
Running Free	7"	EMI	EMI5532	1985	**£4**	poster sleeve
Sanctuary	7"	EMI	EMI5065	1980	**£15**	chart single
Seventh Son Of A Seventh Son	LP	EMI	EMDP1006	1988	**£15**	pic disc with banner
Soundhouse Tapes	7" EP	Rock Hard	ROK1	1979	**£50**	
Stranger In A Strange Land	12"	EMI	12EMIP5589	1986	**£12**	pic disc
Stranger In A Strange Land	7"	EMI	EMI5589	1986	**£4**	poster sleeve
Trooper	7"	EMI	EMIP5397	1983	**£20**	shaped pic disc
Trooper	7"	EMI	EMI5397	1983	**£4**	chart single
Twilight Zone	7"	EMI	EMI5145	1981	**£12**	chart single
Twilight Zone	7"	EMI	EMI5145	1981	**£20**	red or clear vinyl
Twilight Zone	cass-s	EMI	EMI5145	1981	**£5**	
Two Minutes To Midnight	12"	EMI	12EMIP5489	1984	**£15**	pic disc
Two Minutes To Midnight	7"	EMI	EMI5489	1984	**£4**	chart single
Wasted Years	7"	EMI	EMIP5583	1986	**£10**	shaped pic disc
Women In Uniform	12"	EMI	12EMI5105	1980	**£10**	
Women In Uniform	7"	EMI	EMI5105	1980	**£15**	Thatcher PS, chart single
Women In Uniform	7"	EMI	EMI5105	1980	**£8**	

IRVING, LONNIE

Title	Format	Label	Cat. No.	Year	Price	Notes
Pinball Machine	7"	Melodisc	MEL1546	1960	**£5**	

IRWIN, BIG DEE

Title	Format	Label	Cat. No.	Year	Price	Notes
Donkey Walk	7"	Stateside	SS261	1964	**£4**	
Heigh Ho	7"	Colpix	PX11040	1964	**£4**	
Personality	7"	Colpix	PX11050	1964	**£4**	
You Satisfy My Needs	7"	Stateside	SS450	1965	**£4**	

IRWIN, BIG DEE & LITTLE EVA

Title	Format	Label	Cat. No.	Year	Price	Notes
I Wish You A Merry Christmas	7"	Colpix	PX11021	1964	**£4**	
Swinging On A Star	7"	Colpix	PX11010	1963	**£4**	chart single
Swinging On A Star	7" EP	Colpix	PXE301	1963	**£6**	

ISHERWOOD, JON

Title	Format	Label	Cat. No.	Year	Price	Notes
A Laughing Cry	LP	Decca	SKL5051	1970	**£10**	

ISLE, JIMMY

Title	Format	Label	Cat. No.	Year	Price	Notes
Billy Boy	7"	Top Rank	JAR274	1960	**£4**	
Diamond Ring	7"	London	HLS8832	1959	**£6**	

ISLEY BROTHERS

Title	Format	Label	Cat. No.	Year	Price	Notes
Behind A Painted Smile	LP	T. Motown	STML11112	1969	**£20**	
Behind A Painted Smile	7"	T. Motown	TMG693	1969	**£20**	demo
Behind A Painted Smile	7"	T. Motown	TMG693	1969	**£4**	chart single
Brothers Isley	LP	Stateside	SSL10300	1970	**£12**	
Got To Have You Back	7"	T. Motown	TMG606	1967	**£35**	demo
Got To Have You Back	7"	T. Motown	TMG606	1967	**£8**	
How Deep Is The Ocean	7"	RCA	RCA1190	1960	**£6**	
I Guess I'll Always Love You	7"	T. Motown	TMG572	1966	**£12**	chart single
I Guess I'll Always Love You	7"	T. Motown	TMG683	1969	**£12**	demo
I Guess I'll Always Love You	7"	T. Motown	TMG683	1969	**£4**	chart single
I Guess I'll Always Love You	7"	T. Motown	TMG572	1966	**£50**	demo
I Turned You On	7"	Major Minor	MM631	1969	**£4**	
Isley Brothers	7" EP	RCA	RCX7149	1964	**£10**	
It's Our Thing	LP	Major Minor	SMLP59	1969	**£12**	
It's Your Thing	7"	Major Minor	MM621	1969	**£4**	chart single
Last Lost Girl	7"	Atlantic	AT4010	1964	**£6**	
Love The One You're With	7"	Stateside	SS2193	1971	**£4**	
Nobody But Me	7"	Stateside	SS218	1963	**£8**	
Put Yourself In My Place	7"	T. Motown	TMG708	1969	**£15**	demo
Put Yourself In My Place	7"	T. Motown	TMG708	1969	**£4**	chart single
Respectable	7"	RCA	RCA1172	1960	**£8**	
Shake It With Me Baby	7"	United Artists	UP1050	1964	**£6**	
Shout	7"	RCA	RCA1149	1959	**£10**	
Shout	LP	RCA	RD27165, SF7055	1960	**£20**	
Soul On The Rocks	LP	T. Motown	STML11066	1968	**£15**	
Take Me In Your Arms	7"	T. Motown	TMG652	1968	**£10**	
Take Me In Your Arms	7"	T. Motown	TMG652	1968	**£40**	demo
Take Some Time Out	LP	Scepter	SC552	1966	**£10**	US
Take Some Time Out For Love	7"	T. Motown	TMG719	1969	**£10**	demo
Take Some Time Out For Love	7"	T. Motown	TMG566	1966	**£12**	
Take Some Time Out For Love	7"	T. Motown	TMG719	1969	**£4**	
Take Some Time Out For Love	7"	T. Motown	TMG566	1966	**£50**	demo
Tango	7"	United Artists	UP1034	1963	**£5**	
Tell Me It's Just A Rumour Baby	7"	T. Motown	TMG877	1973	**£10**	demo
Tell Me It's Just A Rumour Baby	7"	T. Motown	TMG877	1973	**£4**	
Tell Me Who	7"	RCA	RCA1213	1960	**£6**	
This Old Heart Of Mine	LP	T. Motown	STML11034	1966	**£10**	chart LP
This Old Heart Of Mine	7"	T. Motown	TMG555	1966	**£50**	demo
This Old Heart Of Mine	7"	T. Motown	TMG555	1966	**£5**	chart single
Twist And Shout	7"	Stateside	SS112	1962	**£5**	chart single
Twist And Shout	LP	Wand	WD653	1962	**£15**	US
Twisting And Shouting	LP	United Artists	ULP1064	1964	**£15**	
Twisting With Linda	7"	Stateside	SS132	1962	**£5**	
Warpath	7"	Stateside	SS2188	1971	**£4**	
Was It Good To You	7"	Stateside	SS2162	1970	**£4**	

IT BITES

Title	Format	Label	Cat. No.	Year	Price	Notes
All In Red	7"	Virgin	VS839	1986	**£4**	
All In Red	12"	Virgin	VS83912	1986	**£6**	

Calling All The Heroes	7"	Virgin	VSD872	1986	**£8**	double
Calling All The Heroes	7"	Virgin	VSY872	1986	**£8**	pic disc
Midnight	7"	Virgin	VSS1085	1988	**£4**	square pic disc

IT'S A BEAUTIFUL DAY

1001 Nights	LP	CBS	65812	1974	**£10**	
Choice Quality Stuff	LP	CBS	64314	1971	**£10**	
It's A Beautiful Day	LP	CBS	63722	1968	**£12**	chart LP
It's A Beautiful Day	LP	Columbia	CS9768	1969	**£40**	US, topless girl on cover
It's A Beautiful Day	LP	S. F. Sound	11790	1985	**£15**	US audiophile
Live At Carnegie Hall	LP	CBS	64929	1972	**£10**	
Marrying Maiden	LP	CBS	64065	1970	**£12**	chart LP
Soapstone Mountain	7"	CBS	4933	1970	**£6**	
Today	LP	CBS	65483	1973	**£10**	
White Bird	7"	CBS	4457	1969	**£8**	

IT'S IMMATERIAL

Gigantic Raft In The Philipinnes	7"	Inevitable	INEV009	1982	**£4**	
Young Man	7"	Hit Machine	HIT001	1980	**£4**	

ITHACA

Game For All Who Know	LP	Merlin	6	1973	**£1000**	

IVAN

Real Wild Child	7"	Coral	Q72341	1958	**£30**	

IVAN'S MEADS

Sins Of A Family	7"	Parlophone	R5342	1965	**£10**	
We'll Talk About It Tomorrow	7"	Parlophone	R5503	1966	**£12**	

IVES, BURL

Australian Folk Songs	LP-10"	Brunswick	LA8739	195-	**£12**	
Ballads And Folk Songs Vol.1	LP-10"	Brunswick		1956	**£12**	
Ballads And Folk Songs Vol.2	LP-10"	Brunswick		1956	**£12**	
Down To The Sea In Ships	LP	Brunswick		1956	**£12**	
I Know An Old Lady	78	Brunswick	05148	1953	**£4**	
Woman	LP-10"	Brunswick		1954	**£12**	

IVEYS

The Iveys was the original name for the group Badfinger. The album "Maybe Tomorrow" was planned to be given a full Apple release, but in the event the UK issue never happened, while the American issue was withdrawn on the first day. Counterfeits exist, but they are easily identified by their black labels.

Maybe Tomorrow	7"	Apple	5	1968	**£15**	
Maybe Tomorrow	LP	Apple	SAPCOR8	1968	**£250**	US
Maybe Tomorrow	LP	Apple	SAPCOR8	1969	**£50**	European

IVORY, JACK

Hi Heeled Sneakers	7"	Atlantic	AT4075	1966	**£8**	
Soul Discovery	LP	Atco	33178	1965	**£12**	US

IVY LEAGUE

Four And Twenty Hours	7"	Piccadilly	7N35365	1967	**£4**	
Funny How Love Can Be	7"	Piccadilly	7N35222	1965	**£4**	chart single
Funny How Love Can Be	7" EP	Piccadilly	NEP34038	1965	**£5**	
Holly And The Ivy League	7" EP	Piccadilly	NEP34046	1965	**£5**	
My World Fell Down	7"	Piccadilly	7N35348	1966	**£4**	
Our Love Is Slipping Away	7"	Piccadilly	7N35267	1965	**£4**	
Our Love Is Slipping Away	7" EP	Piccadilly	NEP34048	1966	**£5**	
Running Around In Circles	7"	Piccadilly	7N35294	1966	**£4**	
Sounds Of...	LP	Marble Arch		1965	**£15**	
Suddenly Things	7"	Piccadilly	7N35397	1967	**£4**	
Thank You For Loving Me	7"	Pye	7N17386	1967	**£4**	
That's Why I'm Crying	7"	Piccadilly	7N35228	1965	**£4**	chart single
This Is The Ivy League	LP	Piccadilly	NPL38015	1965	**£20**	
Tomorrow Is Another Day	LP	Marble Arch	MAL821	1968	**£10**	
Tossing And Turning	7"	Piccadilly	7N35251	1965	**£4**	chart single
Tossing And Turning	7" EP	Piccadilly	NEP34042	1965	**£5**	
What More Do You Want	7"	Piccadilly	7N35200	1964	**£5**	
Willow Tree	7"	Piccadilly	7N35326	1966	**£4**	chart single

IVY THREE

Yogi	7"	London	HLW9178	1960	**£4**	

J, DAVID

Promised Land	7"	Glass	GLASS031	1983	**£4**	

J, HARRY ALL STARS

Liquidator	7"	Trojan	TR675	1969	**£4**	chart single

JACK THE LAD

Jack The Lad	LP	Charisma	CAS1085	1974	**£10**	
Old Straight Track	LP	Charisma	CAS1094	1974	**£10**	
Rough Diamonds	LP	Charisma	CAS1110	1975	**£10**	

JACKIE & DOREEN (JACKIE OPEL)

Adorable You	7"	Ska Beat	JB209	1965	**£5**	

JACKIE & MILLIE

In A Dream	7"	Island	WIP6012	1967	**£6**	

JACKLIN

Jacklin	LP	Stable		1969	**£150**	

JACKPOTS

Jack In The Box	LP	Sonet		1968	**£25**	

JACKS

Jacks	LP	Crown	CLP5021	1957	**£20**	US
Jumpin' With The Jacks	LP	RPM	LRP3006	195-	**£75**	US

JACKSON BROTHERS

Tell Him No	7"	London	HLX8845	1959	**£4**	

JACKSON FIVE

ABC	7"	T. Motown	TMG738	1970	**£4**	chart single
ABC	7"	T. Motown	TMG738	1970	**£10**	demo
Christmas Album	LP	T. Motown	STML11168	1970	**£10**	
Diana Ross Presents...	LP	T. Motown	STML11142	1970	**£10**	chart LP
Doctor My Eyes	7"	T. Motown	TMG842	1973	**£4**	chart single
Doctor My Eyes	7"	T. Motown	TMG842	1973	**£10**	demo
Goin' Places	LP	Epic	PAL348351G	1978	**£10**	US pic disc
Hallelujah Day	7"	T. Motown	TMG856	1973	**£4**	chart single
Hallelujah Day	7"	T. Motown	TMG856	1973	**£10**	demo
I Want You Back	7"	T. Motown	TMG724	1970	**£4**	chart single
I Want You Back	7"	T. Motown	TMG724	1970	**£12**	demo
I'll Be There	7"	T. Motown	TMG758	1970	**£4**	chart single
I'll Be There	7"	T. Motown	TMG758	1970	**£10**	demo
Jacksons	LP	CBS	AL34229	1977	**£10**	US pic disc
Little Bitty Pretty One	7"	T. Motown	TMG825	1972	**£4**	
Little Bitty Pretty One	7"	T. Motown	TMG825	1972	**£10**	demo
Looking Through The Windows	7"	T. Motown	TMG833	1972	**£4**	chart single
Looking Through The Windows	7"	T. Motown	TMG833	1972	**£10**	demo
Looking Through The Windows	7"	T. Motown	TMG833	1972	**£15**	demo, PS
Love You Save	7"	T. Motown	TMG746	1970	**£4**	chart single
Love You Save	7"	T. Motown	TMG746	1970	**£10**	demo
Mama's Pearl	7"	T. Motown	TMG769	1971	**£4**	chart single
Mama's Pearl	7"	T. Motown	TMG769	1971	**£10**	demo
Never Can Say Goodbye	7"	T. Motown	TMG778	1971	**£4**	chart single
Never Can Say Goodbye	7"	T. Motown	TMG778	1971	**£10**	demo
Santa Claus Is Coming To Town	7"	T. Motown	TMG837	1972	**£4**	chart single
Santa Claus Is Coming To Town	7"	T. Motown	TMG837	1972	**£10**	demo
Skywriter	7"	T. Motown	TMG865	1973	**£4**	chart single
Skywriter	7"	T. Motown	TMG865	1973	**£10**	demo
Skywriter	7"	T. Motown	TMG865	1973	**£15**	demo, PS
Sugar Daddy	7"	T. Motown	TMG809	1972	**£4**	

Sugar Daddy .... 7" .... T. Motown .... TMG809 .... 1972 .... **£10** .... demo

JACKSON HEIGHTS

Bump And Grind .... LP .... Vertigo .... 6360092 .... 1973 .... **£15** ....
Doubting Thomas .... 7" .... Charisma .... JH1 .... 197- .... **£4** ....
Fifth Avenue Bus .... LP .... Vertigo .... 6360067 .... 1972 .... **£20** .... spiral label
King Progress .... LP .... Charisma .... CAS1018 .... 1970 .... **£12** ....
Ragamuffin's Fool .... LP .... Vertigo .... 6360077 .... 1973 .... **£20** .... spiral label

JACKSON SISTERS

I Believe In Miracles .... 7" .... Mums .... MUM1829 .... 1973 .... **£20** ....

JACKSON, ALEXANDER & THE TURNKEYS

Whip .... 7" .... Sue .... WI386 .... 1965 .... **£8** ....

JACKSON, BULL MOOSE

Bull Moose Jackson .... LP .... Audio Lab .... AL1524 .... 1959 .... **£50** .... US

JACKSON, CHRIS

I'll Never Forget You .... 7" .... Soul City .... SC112 .... **£8** ....
I'll Never Forget You .... 7" .... Soul City .... SC112 .... **£20** .... demo
Since There's No Doubt .... 7" .... Soul City .... SC120 .... **£50** .... demo

JACKSON, CHUCK

Any Day Now .... 7" .... Pye .... 7N25276 .... 1964 .... **£4** ....
Any Day Now .... 7" .... Stateside .... SS102 .... 1962 .... **£5** ....
Any Day Now .... LP .... Wand .... LP654 .... 1962 .... **£12** .... US
Beg Me .... 7" .... Pye .... 7N25247 .... 1964 .... **£6** ....
Breaking Point .... 7" .... Top Rank .... JAR607 .... 1962 .... **£6** ....
Chains Of Love .... 7" .... Pye .... 7N25384 .... 1966 .... **£15** ....
Chuck Jackson Arrives .... LP .... T. Motown .... STML11071 .... 1968 .... **£15** ....
Dedicated To The King .... LP .... Wand .... LP680 .... 1966 .... **£12** .... US
Encore .... LP .... Wand .... LP655 .... 1963 .... **£12** .... US
Girls Girls Girls .... 7" .... T. Motown .... TMG651 .... 1968 .... **£5** ....
Girls Girls Girls .... 7" .... T. Motown .... TMG651 .... 1968 .... **£20** .... demo
Goin' Back To... .... LP .... T. Motown .... STML11117 .... 1969 .... **£12** ....
Greatest Hits .... LP .... Wand .... LP683 .... 1967 .... **£10** .... US
Honey Come Back .... 7" .... T. Motown .... TMG729 .... 1970 .... **£5** ....
Honey Come Back .... 7" .... T. Motown .... TMG729 .... 1970 .... **£12** .... demo
I Don't Want To Cry .... 7" .... Top Rank .... JAR564 .... 1961 .... **£10** ....
I Don't Want To Cry .... LP .... Wand .... LP650 .... 1961 .... **£12** .... US
I Keep Forgettin' .... 7" .... Stateside .... SS127 .... 1962 .... **£4** ....
I Need You .... 7" .... Pye .... 7N25301 .... 1965 .... **£4** ....
If I Didn't Love You .... 7" .... Pye .... 7N25321 .... 1965 .... **£5** ....
Mr.Everything .... LP .... Wand .... LP667 .... 1965 .... **£10** .... US
On Tour .... LP .... Wand .... LP658 .... 1964 .... **£10** .... US
Shame On Me .... 7" .... Pye .... 7N25439 .... 1967 .... **£4** ....
Since I Don't Have You .... 7" .... Pye .... 7N25287 .... 1965 .... **£12** ....
Tell Him I'm Not Home .... 7" .... Stateside .... SS171 .... 1963 .... **£4** ....
Tribute To Rhythm And Blues .... LP .... Wand .... LP673 .... 1966 .... **£10** .... US
Tribute To Rhythm And Blues Vol.2 .... LP .... Wand .... LP676 .... 1966 .... **£10** .... US

JACKSON, CHUCK & MAXINE BROWN

Hold On, We're Coming .... LP .... Wand .... WD678 .... 1966 .... **£10** .... US
Saying Something .... LP .... Wand .... WD669 .... 1965 .... **£10** .... US
Something You Got .... 7" .... Pye .... 7N25308 .... 1965 .... **£4** ....

JACKSON, CHUCK & TAMMI TERRELL

Early Show .... LP .... Wand .... LP682 .... 1967 .... **£10** .... US

JACKSON, DEON

Love Makes The World Go Round .... 7" .... Atlantic .... AT4070 .... 1966 .... **£6** ....
Love Makes The World Go Round .... LP .... Atco .... 33188 .... 1966 .... **£12** .... US
Love Takes A Long Time Growing .... 7" .... Atlantic .... 584012 .... 1966 .... **£5** ....
Ooh Baby .... 7" .... Atlantic .... 584159 .... 1968 .... **£4** ....

JACKSON, GORDON

Me And My Zoo .... 7" .... Marmalade .... 598010 .... 1969 .... **£5** ....
Song For Freedom .... 7" .... Marmalade .... 598021 .... 1969 .... **£5** ....
Thinking Back .... LP .... Marmalade .... 608012 .... 1969 .... **£20** ....

JACKSON, HAROLD TORNADOES

Move It On Down The Line	7"	Vogue	V9105	1958	**£20**	

JACKSON, J.J.

Although he called his group "The Greatest Little Soul Band", the music that J.J.Jackson played was actually jazz-rock. Indeed, the soul band description was probably a marketing mistake. Fans of Colosseum and Manfred Mann Chapter Three would have loved this, but they looked no further than the cover. More precise is the comparison with the group If, whose leaders Dick Morrissey and Terry Smith both played with Jackson. The sleeve notes to the MCA album end with the words: "go and see the band and you'll realise that if they aren't the biggest thing in the country in six months, there's no justice". Sadly, there was none.

And Proud Of It	LP	Perception	PLP12		**£15**	US
But It's Alright	LP	Calla	C1101	1967	**£15**	US
But It's Alright	7"	W. Bros	WB7276	1969	**£4**	
Courage Ain't Strength	7"	W. Bros	WB6029	1968	**£4**	
Do The Boogaloo	7"	Polydor	56718	1966	**£4**	
Down But Not Out	7"	W. Bros	WB2090	1968	**£4**	
Great J.J.Jackson	LP	W. Bros	WS1797	1969	**£15**	US
Greatest Little Soul Band	LP	MCA	SKA100	1969	**£15**	
J.J.Jackson's Dilemma	LP	RCA	SF8093	1971	**£15**	
Sho Nuff	7"	W. Bros	WB2082	1967	**£4**	
Something For My People	7"	MCA/Soul Bag	BAG6	1969	**£4**	
Tenement Halls	7"	MCA/Soul Bag	BAG4	1969	**£4**	
With The Greatest Little Soul Band	LP	Strike	104	1967	**£15**	

JACKSON, JERMAINE

Daddy's Home	7"	T. Motown	TMG851	1973	**£4**	
Daddy's Home	7"	T. Motown	TMG851	1973	**£10**	demo
That's How Love Goes	7"	T. Motown	TMG838	1973	**£4**	
That's How Love Goes	7"	T. Motown	TMG838	1973	**£10**	demo

JACKSON, JERRY

Gypsy Eyes	7"	London	HLR9689	1963	**£4**	
It's Rough Out There	7"	Cameo Park.	P100	1962	**£15**	

JACKSON, JIM

RCA Victor Race Series Vol.7	7" EP	RCA	RCX7182	1966	**£5**	

JACKSON, JIMMY

Country And Blues	7" EP	Columbia	SEG7768	1958	**£6**	
I Shall Not Be Moved	7"	Columbia	DB3898	1957	**£4**	
Love A Love A Love A	7"	Columbia	DB4085	1958	**£4**	
River Line	7"	Columbia	DB3957	1957	**£4**	
Rock 'N' Skiffle	7" EP	Columbia	SEG7750	1958	**£8**	
Sitting In The Balcony	7"	Columbia	DB3937	1957	**£6**	
This Little Light Of Mine	7"	Columbia	DB4153	1958	**£4**	
White Silver Sands	7"	Columbia	DB3988	1957	**£4**	

JACKSON, JOE

I'm The Man	7"	A&M	SP1800	1980	**£12**	US 5 x 7", poster, boxed
Is She Really Going Out With Him	7"	A&M	AMS7392	1978	**£4**	
Look Sharp!	LP	A&M	AMLH64743	1979	**£10**	white vinyl
Look Sharp!	LP-10"	A&M	SP3666	1979	**£10**	US double, poster
Night And Day	LP	Mobile Fid.	MFSL1050	1980	**£10**	US audiophile
One More Time	10'	A&M	AMSP7433	1979	**£6**	white vinyl, badge
Real Men	7"	A&M	AMS8231	1982	**£5**	pic disc

JACKSON, LEVI

This Beautiful Day	7"	Columbia	DB8807	1971	**£25**	

JACKSON, LIL' SON

Rockin' And Rollin'	LP	Imperial	9142	1961	**£60**	US

JACKSON, MICHAEL

Michael Jackson has made the two biggest selling albums ever, but the range of available collectors' items by him is comparatively modest. There are few of the picture discs and limited editions associated with other major artists in the eighties - presumably Epic records felt that he would sell quite well enough without them. There is, however, a scarce 12" megamix of several of his hits with a price tag matching its rarity.

Ain't No Sunshine	7"	T. Motown	TMG826	1972	**£4**	chart single
Ain't No Sunshine	7"	T. Motown	TMG826	1972	**£10**	demo
Bad	7"	Epic	EPCMJ5	1988	**£15**	5 pic discs
Ben	7"	T. Motown	TMG834	1972	**£4**	chart single

Ben	7"	T. Motown	TMG834	1972	**£15**	demo
Billie Jean (Meanjean Mix)	CD-s	Epic		198-	**£40**	
ET	cass	MCA		1983	**£15**	with book & poster, boxed
Girl Is Mine	7"	Epic	A2729	1982	**£8**	pic disc
Got To Be There	7"	T. Motown	TMG797	1972	**£4**	chart single
Got To Be There	7"	T. Motown	TMG797	1972	**£10**	demo
Happy	7"	T. Motown	TMG986	1983	**£5**	pic disc
Man In The Mirror	7"	Epic	EPC6513889	1988	**£5**	shaped pic disc
Megamix	12"	Epic		198-	**£150**	
Morning Glow	7"	T. Motown	TMG863	1973	**£4**	
Morning Glow	7"	T. Motown	TMG863	1973	**£10**	demo
Off The Wall	LP	Epic	HE47545	1980	**£12**	US audiophile
Rockin' Robin	7"	T. Motown	TMG816	1972	**£4**	chart single
Rockin' Robin	7"	T. Motown	TMG816	1972	**£12**	demo
Singles Pack	7"	Epic	MJ1	1983	**£25**	9 x red vinyl
Smooth Criminal (Funkin' Smooth Mix)	12"	Epic		1988	**£30**	
Smooth Criminal (Smokin' Gun Mix)	12"	Epic		1988	**£40**	
Smooth Criminal (Vancouver Feetbeat)	12"	Epic		1988	**£35**	
Thriller	LP	Epic	EPC1185930	1982	**£12**	pic disc
Thriller	LP	Epic	HE48112	1982	**£20**	US audiophile
You Can't Win	7"	Epic	EPC7135	1979	**£8**	pic disc

JACKSON, MICHAEL & PAUL MCCARTNEY

Girl Is Mine	7"	Epic	EPCA112729	1982	**£6**	pic disc

JACKSON, MILLIE

If Loving You Is Wrong	7"	Polydor	2066536	1975	**£4**	
Loving Arms	7"	Polydor	2066612	1975	**£5**	
My Man's A Sweet Man	7"	Mojo	2093022	1972	**£4**	chart single

JACKSON, STONEWALL

Dynamic Stonewall Jackson	LP	Columbia	CL1391	1959	**£10**	US
Sadness In A Song	LP	Columbia	CL1770	1962	**£10**	US

JACKSON, TONY & THE VIBRATIONS

It must have seemed a good idea to Tony Jackson, as the lead singer of the Searchers, to strike out on his own. Unfortunately, it turned out that his personal following was only a fraction of the following enjoyed by the Searchers as a group. None of Tony Jackson's singles got anywhere at all, while the remaining Searchers gained an immediate number one, with "Needles And Pins".

Anything Else You Want	7"	CBS	202408	1966	**£15**	
Bye Bye Baby	7"	Pye	7N15685	1964	**£10**	chart single
Follow Me	7"	CBS	202297	1966	**£15**	
Love Potion No.9	7"	Pye	7N15766	1965	**£15**	
Never Leave Your Baby's Side	7"	CBS	202069	1966	**£20**	
Stage Door	7"	Pye	7N15876	1965	**£15**	
This Little Girl Of Mine	7"	Pye	7N15745	1964	**£15**	
You're My Number One	7"	CBS	202039	1966	**£15**	

JACKSON, WALTER

Corner In The Sun	7"	Columbia	DB8054	1966	**£5**	
It's An Uphill Climb To The Bottom	7"	Columbia	DB7949	1966	**£5**	
Speak Her Name	7"	Columbia	DB8154	1967	**£5**	
Welcome Home	7"	Columbia	DB7620	1965	**£5**	

JACKSON, WANDA

Wanda Jackson was one of the best female rock'n'roll singers, although her competition was rather limited. Adopting the same rasping tones as Brenda Lee on her uptempo material, Wanda Jackson's older voice had a greater depth and hence rather more power. In common with most of the American singers of her generation, she took the country route once the initial rock'n'roll years were over.

Blues In My Heart	LP	Capitol	T2306	1964	**£10**	
If I Cried Every Time You Hurt Me	7"	Capitol	CL15249	1962	**£5**	
In The Middle Of A Heartache	7"	Capitol	CL15234	1962	**£5**	
Let's Have A Party	7"	Capitol	CL15147	1960	**£8**	chart single
Let's Have A Party	7" EP	Capitol	EAP11041	1959	**£20**	
Little Bitty Tear	7" EP	Capitol	EAP120353	1962	**£10**	
Love Me Forever	LP	Capitol	T1911	1963	**£10**	US
Lovin' Country Style	LP	Decca	DL4224	1962	**£20**	US
Mean Mean Man	7"	Capitol	CL15176	1961	**£8**	chart single
Reaching	7"	Capitol	CL15090	1959	**£6**	
Right Or Wrong	LP	Capitol	T1596	1961	**£15**	
Right Or Wrong	7"	Capitol	CL15223	1961	**£6**	

Rockin' With Wanda	LP	Capitol	T1384	1960	**£20**	
Rockin' With Wanda	LP	Capitol	T1384	1960	**£50**	US
There's A Party Goin' On	LP	Capitol	T1511	1961	**£50**	US
There's A Party Goin' On	LP	Capitol	T1511	1961	**£15**	
Two Sides Of...	LP	Capitol	T2030	1964	**£15**	US
Wanda Jackson	LP	Capitol	T1041	1958	**£50**	US
Wonderful Wanda	LP	Capitol	T1776	1962	**£12**	
You're The One For Me	7"	Capitol	CL15033	1959	**£6**	

JACKSONS

Triumph	LP	Epic	HE46424	1981	**£10**	US audiophile

JACKY

White Horses	7"	Philips	BF1674	1968	**£4**	chart single

JACOBITES

Like Now	7"	Pye	7N17852	1969	**£6**	

JACOBS, HANK

Monkey Hips And Rice	7"	Sue	WI313	1964	**£8**	

JADE WARRIOR

Jade Warrior are essentially a duo - Tony Duhig and Jon Field - whose music is perfectly described by their album covers. Mostly instrumental, with a hint of the orient and an emphasis on a gentle textural beauty, Jade Warrior's music laid down the ground rules for much of what is defined as "new age".

Demon Trucker	7"	Vertigo	6059069	1972	**£10**	
Eclipse	LP	Vertigo			**£200**	promo only
Floating World	LP	Island	ILPS9290	1974	**£10**	
Jade Warrior	LP	Vertigo	6360033	1971	**£30**	spiral label
Kites	LP	Island	ILPS9393	1976	**£10**	
Last Autumn's Dream	LP	Vertigo	6360079	1972	**£30**	spiral label
Released	LP	Vertigo	6360062	1971	**£30**	spiral label
Waves	LP	Island	ILPS9318	1975	**£10**	
Way Of The Sun	LP	Island	ILPS9552	1978	**£10**	
Way Of The Sun	7"	Island	JAD1	1978	**£4**	

JAGGER, MICK

Memo From Turner	7"	Decca	F13067	1970	**£6**	chart single
Mick Jagger Tells All	CD	RCA		198-	**£130**	US promo

JAGGER, MICK & OTHERS

Ned Kelly	LP	United Artists	UAS5213	1970	**£20**	
Ned Kelly	7"	United Artists	UP29108	1970	**£10**	
Performance	LP	W. Bros	WS2554	1970	**£10**	

JAGS

Cry Wolf	7"	Decca	F11397	1961	**£4**	

JAIM

Prophesy Fulfilled	LP	Ethereal	1001	1970	**£20**	US

JAKE & THE FAMILY JEWELS

Jake & The Family Jewels	LP	Polydor	2425027	1970	**£15**	

JAM

Beat Surrender	7"	Polydor	PODJ540	1982	**£125**	autographed double, handwritten lyrics
Beat Surrender	7"	Polydor	PODJ540	1982	**£6**	promo, censored version
Beat Surrender	7"	Polydor	POSPJ540/JAM1	1982	**£6**	double
Beat Surrender	12"	Polydor	POSP540X	1982	**£15**	promo
David Watts	7"	Polydor	2059054DJ	1978	**£30**	promo
Funeral Pyre	7"	Fan Club		198-	**£15**	flexi
Going Underground	7"	Polydor	POSPJ113	1980	**£8**	double
Going Underground	7"	Polydor	2816024	1980	**£8**	double
In The City	7"	Polydor	2058866	1977	**£4**	chart single
Move On Up	7"	Polydor	PAULO100	1982	**£5**	flexi
Pop Art Poem	7"	Lyntone	LYN9048	1980	**£5**	Flexipop flexi
Precious	7"	Polydor	PODJ400	1980	**£8**	1 sided promo
Snap!	LP	Polydor	SNAP1	1983	**£10**	with 7" (SNAP45)
Snap!	cass	Polydor	SNAPC1	1983	**£10**	with bonus 7" material
Snap! Medley	7"	Polydor	LEE1	1983	**£15**	promo
Tales From The Riverbank	7"	Fan Club	no number	1982	**£15**	flexi

Town Called Malice	12"	Polydor	POSP400X	1980	**£15**	promo
When You're Young	7"	Fan Club		1981	**£15**	flexi

JAMES GANG

Bang	LP	Atlantic	K50028	1973	**£10**	
Funk No.48	7"	Stateside	SS2158	1970	**£4**	
Live In Concert	LP	Probe	1045	1971	**£10**	
Miami	LP	Atco	QD36102	1974	**£12**	US quad
Miami	LP	Atlantic	K50068	1974	**£10**	
Passin' Thru	LP	Probe	1065	1972	**£10**	
Rides Again	LP	Probe	6253	1970	**£10**	
Stop	7"	Stateside	SS2173	1970	**£4**	
Straight Shooter	LP	Probe	1056	1972	**£10**	
Thirds	LP	Probe	038	1971	**£10**	
Yer Album	LP	Stateside	10295	1969	**£10**	

JAMES, BRIAN

Ain't That A Shame	7"	BJ	BJ1	1979	**£4**	
Ain't That A Shame	12"	BJ	BJLP1	1979	**£6**	
Why Why Why	7"	Illegal	ILS0026	1982	**£4**	green vinyl

JAMES, DICK

Garden Of Eden	7"	Parlophone	R4255	1957	**£4**	chart single
Robin Hood	7"	Parlophone	MSP6199	1956	**£4**	chart single
Sing A Song Of Beatles	7"	Parlophone	R5212	1964	**£5**	

JAMES, ELMORE

Anthology Of The Blues Legend	LP	Kent	KLP9001	196-	**£12**	US
Best Of...	LP	Sue	ILP918	1965	**£20**	
Blues After Hours	LP	Crown	CLP5168	1961	**£25**	US
Calling The Blues	7"	Sue	WI392	1965	**£10**	
Dust My Blues	7"	Sue	WI335	1964	**£10**	
I Need You	LP	Sphere Snd	7008	1964	**£15**	US
I Need You	7"	Sue	WI4007	1966	**£10**	
It Hurts Me Too	7"	Sue	WI383	1965	**£10**	
Late Fantastically Great...	LP	Ember	EMB3397	1968	**£10**	
Legend Of...	LP	United Artists	UAS29109	1970	**£15**	
Memorial Album	LP	Sue	ILP927	1965	**£20**	
Original Folk Blues	LP	Kent	KLP5022	1964	**£20**	US
Resurrection Of Elmore James	LP	Kent	KLP9010	196-	**£12**	US
Sky Is Crying	LP	Sphere Snd	7002	1964	**£15**	US
Something Inside Of Me	LP	Bell	MBLL104	1968	**£15**	
To Know A Man	LP	Blue Horizon	766230	1969	**£40**	double
Whose Muddy Shoes	LP	Chess	1537	1969	**£12**	US

JAMES, ELMORE & JOHN BRIM

Tough	LP	Blue Horizon	763204	1968	**£30**	

JAMES, ETTA

All I Could Do Was Cry	7"	London	HLM9139	1960	**£10**	
Anything To Say You're Mine	7"	Pye	7N25080	1961	**£5**	
At Last	LP	Argo	4003	1961	**£15**	US
At Last	7"	Pye	7N25079	1961	**£5**	
Etta James	LP	Argo	4013	1962	**£15**	US
Etta James Sings For Lovers	LP	Argo	4018	1962	**£15**	US
Fool That I Am	7"	Pye	7N25113	1961	**£5**	
I Got You Babe	7"	Chess	CRS8076	1968	**£4**	
I Prefer You	7"	Chess	CRS8052	1967	**£4**	
Miss Etta James	LP	Kent	3002	196-	**£10**	US
Miss Etta James	LP	Kent	3002	196-	**£15**	US, red vinyl
My Dearest Darling	7"	London	HLM9234	1960	**£6**	
Pushover	7"	Pye	7N25205	1963	**£5**	
Queen Of Soul	LP	Argo	4040	1965	**£12**	US
Rock With Me Henry	7"	Sue	WI359	1965	**£15**	
Rocks The House	LP	Chess	CRL4502	1963	**£12**	
Second Time Around	LP	Argo	4011	1961	**£15**	US
Security	7"	Chess	CRS8069	1967	**£4**	
Something's Got A Hold Of Me	7"	Pye	7N25131	1962	**£8**	
Soul Of...	LP	Ember	EMB3390	1968	**£12**	
Stop The Wedding	7"	Pye	7N25162	1962	**£5**	
Tell Mama	LP	Chess	CRL4536	1969	**£12**	
Tell Mama	7"	Chess	CRS8063	1967	**£5**	

Top Ten	LP	Argo	4025	1963	**£12**	US
You Got It	7"	Chess	CRS8082	1968	**£4**	

JAMES, ETTA & SUGAR PIE DESANTO

Do I Make Myself Clear	7"	Chess	CRS8025	1965	**£5**	

JAMES, HOMESICK

Crossroads	7"	Sue	WI319	1964	**£10**	
Set A Date	7"	Sue	WI330	1965	**£10**	

JAMES, JASON

Miss Pilkington's Maid	7"	CBS	2705	1967	**£8**	

JAMES, JIMMY & THE VAGABONDS

Ain't Love Good	7"	Piccadilly	7N35349	1966	**£4**	
Help Yourself	7"	Trojan	TR7806	197-	**£4**	
Hi Diddley Dee Dum Dum	7"	Piccadilly	7N35320	1966	**£4**	
I Can't Get Back Home To My Baby	7"	Piccadilly	7N35360	1967	**£4**	
I Feel Alright	7"	Piccadilly	7N35298	1966	**£4**	
Jimmy James & The Vagabonds	7" EP	Piccadilly	NEP34053	1966	**£6**	
New Religion	LP	Piccadilly	NPL38027	1966	**£15**	
No Good To Cry	7"	Piccadilly	7N35374	1967	**£6**	
Open Up Your Soul	LP	Pye	NSPL18231	1968	**£15**	
Red Red Wine	7"	Pye	7N17579	1968	**£4**	chart single
Shoo Be Doo You're Mine	7"	Columbia	DB7653	1965	**£6**	
This Heart Of Mine	7"	Piccadilly	7N35331	1966	**£5**	
This Is Jimmy James	LP	Marble Arch	MAL823	1968	**£10**	

JAMES, JOHN

Head In The Clouds	LP	Transatlantic	TRA305	1975	**£10**	
John James	LP	Transatlantic	TRA242	1971	**£10**	
Morning Brings The Light	LP	Transatlantic	TRA219	1970	**£10**	
Sky In My Pie	LP	Transatlantic	TRA250	1972	**£10**	

JAMES, JONI

After Hours	LP	MGM	E4088	1962	**£10**	US
At Carnegie Hall	LP	MGM	E3800	1959	**£10**	US
Award Winning Album	LP	MGM	E3346	1956	**£15**	US
Award Winning Album	LP-10"	MGM	E234	195-	**£20**	US
Country Girl Style	LP	MGM	E4101	1962	**£10**	US
Give Us This Day	LP	MGM	E3528	1958	**£15**	US
Hundred Strings And Joni	LP	MGM	E3755	1959	**£10**	US
I Feel A Song Comin' On	LP	MGM	E4053	1962	**£10**	US
I'm Your Girl	LP	MGM	E4054	1962	**£10**	US
In The Still Of The Night	LP	MGM	E3328	1956	**£15**	US
Irish Favorites	LP	MGM	E3749	1959	**£10**	US
Joni James	7" EP	MGM	MGMEP504	1954	**£6**	
Joni James Sings Sweet	LP	MGM	E3772	1959	**£10**	US
Joni James Sings To You	7" EP	MGM	MGMEP518	1955	**£4**	
Little Girl Blue	7" EP	MGM	MGMEP530	1956	**£4**	
Merry Christmas From Joni	LP	MGM	E3468	1957	**£15**	US
Mood Is Blue	LP	MGM	E3991	1961	**£10**	US
Mood Is Romance	LP	MGM	E3990	1961	**£10**	US
Mood Is Swinging	LP	MGM	E3987	1961	**£10**	US
Songs Of Hank Williams	LP	MGM	E3739	1959	**£12**	US
Songs Of Hank Williams	7" EP	MGM	MGMEP728	1960	**£4**	
Songs Of Hank Williams	7" EP	MGM	MGMES3501	1960	**£6**	stereo

JAMES, LEONARD

Boppin' And A-Strollin'	LP	Decca	DL8772	1958	**£20**	US

JAMES, NICKY

Every Home Should Have One	LP	Threshold	THS10	1973	**£10**	
Maggie	7"	Threshold	TH25	1976	**£4**	
My Style	7"	Threshold	TH17	1973	**£4**	
Nicky James	LP	Philips	6308069	1971	**£10**	
She Came To Me	7"	Threshold	TH16	1973	**£4**	
Thunderthroat	LP	Threshold	THS19	1976	**£10**	
Why	7"	Threshold	TH12	1972	**£4**	

JAMES, NICKY MOVEMENT

Title	Format	Label	Number	Year	Price	Notes
Stagger Lee	7"	Columbia	DB7747	1965	**£8**	

JAMES, RICKY

Title	Format	Label	Number	Year	Price	Notes
Knee Deep In The Blues	7"	HMV	POP306	1957	**£6**	
Party Doll	7"	HMV	POP334	1957	**£6**	

JAMES, ROGER FOUR

Title	Format	Label	Number	Year	Price	Notes
Better Than Here	7"	Columbia	DB7813	1966	**£4**	
Better Than Here	7"	Columbia	DB7829	1966	**£4**	

JAMES, SKIP

Title	Format	Label	Number	Year	Price	Notes
Devil Got My Woman	LP	Vanguard	VSD79273	1968	**£15**	
Greatest Of The Delta Blues Singers	LP	Storyville	670185		**£15**	
Skip James Today	LP	Vanguard	VSD79219	1965	**£15**	

JAMES, SONNY

Title	Format	Label	Number	Year	Price	Notes
Cat Came Back	7"	Capitol	CL14635	1956	**£5**	chart single
Honey	LP	Capitol	T988	1958	**£12**	US
Mighty Lovable Man	7"	Capitol	CL14788	1957	**£4**	
Sonny	LP	Capitol	T867	1957	**£12**	US
Southern Gentleman	LP	Capitol	T779	1957	**£15**	US
This Is Sonny James	LP	Capitol	T1178	1959	**£12**	US
Uh Uh Umm	7"	Capitol	CL14814	1957	**£4**	
You're The Only World I Know	7" EP	Capitol	EAP120654	1964	**£4**	
Young Love	7"	Capitol	CL14683	1957	**£4**	chart single
Young Love	7" EP	Capitol	EAP1827	1957	**£6**	

JAMES, STU

Title	Format	Label	Number	Year	Price	Notes
Beth	7"	Philips	6006611	1979	**£4**	
I Only Wish I Had The Time	7"	Bradleys	BRAD7406	1974	**£4**	
I'm In The Mood	7"	Bradleys	BRAD7614	1976	**£4**	

JAMES, SULLIVAN BAND

Title	Format	Label	Number	Year	Price	Notes
Goodbye Mr.Heartache	7"	Parlophone	R5465	1966	**£8**	

JAMES, TOMMY & THE SHONDELLS

Tommy James and the Shondells produced a kind of basic guitar pop whose closest British equivalent was perhaps the Troggs. Records like "Hanky Panky", "Mony Mony", and "I Think We're Alone Now" were enormous American hits and have proved to be a considerable influence on the kind of straight-forward teenage rock typified by the likes of the Ramones and the Runaways.

Title	Format	Label	Number	Year	Price	Notes
Ball And Chain	7"	Roulette	RO518	1969	**£4**	
Ball Of Fire	7"	Roulette	RO511	1969	**£4**	
Best Of...	LP	Roulette	SR42040	1970	**£12**	US
Cellophane Symphony	LP	Roulette	SR42030	1969	**£15**	US
Crimson And Clover	LP	Roulette	SR42023	1968	**£15**	US
Crimson And Clover	7"	Roulette	RO502	1968	**£5**	
Crystal Blue Persuasion	7"	Roulette	RO507	1969	**£5**	
Do Something To Me	7"	Roulette	RO500	1967	**£5**	
Getting Together	LP	Roulette	SR25357	1968	**£15**	US
Hanky Panky	LP	Roulette	R25336	1966	**£15**	US
Hanky Panky	7"	Roulette	RK7000	1966	**£5**	chart single
I Think We're Alone Now	7"	Major Minor	MM511	1967	**£4**	
I Think We're Alone Now	LP	Roulette	R25353	1967	**£15**	US
It's Only Love	7"	Pye	7N25398	1966	**£4**	
It's Only Love	LP	Roulette	R25344	1967	**£15**	US
Mony Mony	7"	Major Minor	MM567	1968	**£4**	
Mony Mony	LP	Roulette	SR42012	1968	**£15**	US
Out Of The Blue	7"	Major Minor	MM548	1967	**£4**	
She	7"	Roulette	RO513	1969	**£4**	
Something Special	LP	Roulette	SR25355	1968	**£15**	US
Sweet Cherry Wine	7"	Roulette	RO506	1969	**£4**	
Wish It Were You	7"	Major Minor	MM558	1968	**£4**	

JAMESON, BOBBY

Title	Format	Label	Number	Year	Price	Notes
All I Want Is My Baby	7"	Decca	F12032	1964	**£20**	
Rum-Pum	7"	Brit	WI1001	1965	**£10**	

JAMIES

Title	Format	Label	Number	Year	Price	Notes
Summertime Summertime	7"	Columbia	DB4885	1962	**£4**	
Summertime Summertime	7"	Fontana	H153	1958	**£6**	

JAMMER, JOE

Bad News	LP	Regal Z.	SRZA8515	1973	**£10**	

JAN & ARNIE

Jennie Lee	7"	London	HL8653	1958	**£15**	

JAN & DEAN

Baby Talk	7"	London	HLN8936	1959	**£10**	
Batman	7"	Liberty	LIB55860	1966	**£5**	
Clementine	7"	London	HLU9063	1960	**£8**	
Command Performance	LP	Liberty	LRP3403	1965	**£12**	US
Dead Man's Curve	7"	Liberty	LIB55672	1964	**£5**	
Dead Man's Curve/New Girl In School	LP	Liberty	LBY1220	1964	**£15**	
Drag City	LP	Liberty	LRP3339	1963	**£12**	US
Drag City	7"	Liberty	LIB55641	1964	**£5**	
Filet Of Soul	LP	Liberty	LBY1339	1966	**£15**	
Folk And Roll	LP	Liberty	LBY1304	1965	**£15**	
From All Over The World	7"	Liberty	LIB55766	1965	**£4**	
Golden Hits	LP	Liberty	LBY1279	1962	**£15**	
Golden Hits Vol.2	LP	Liberty	LRP3417	1965	**£10**	US
Golden Hits Vol.3	LP	Liberty	LRP3460	1966	**£12**	US
Heart And Soul	7"	London	HLH9395	1961	**£8**	chart single
Honolulu Lulu	7"	Liberty	LIB55613	1963	**£5**	
I Found A Girl	7"	Liberty	LIB55833	1965	**£4**	
Jan & Dean	LP	Dore	101	1960	**£75**	US with photo
Linda	7"	Liberty	LIB55531	1963	**£5**	
Little Old Lady From Pasadena	LP	Liberty	LRP3377	1964	**£12**	US
Little Old Lady From Pasadena	7"	Liberty	LIB55704	1964	**£5**	
Meet Batman	LP	Liberty	LBY1309	1966	**£20**	
Norwegian Wood	7"	Liberty	LIB10225	1966	**£6**	
Pop Symphony No.1	LP	Liberty	LRP3414	1965	**£15**	US
Popsicle	LP	Liberty	LRP3458	1966	**£15**	US
Popsicle	7"	Liberty	LIB10244	1966	**£5**	
Remember Jan And Dean	7" EP	United Artists	REM402		**£4**	
Ride The Wild Surf	LP	Liberty	LBY1229	1964	**£15**	
Ride The Wild Surf	7"	Liberty	LIB55724	1964	**£5**	
Save For A Rainy Day	LP	J&D	101	1967	**£75**	US
Sidewalk Surfin'	7"	Liberty	LIB55727	1965	**£5**	
Sunday Kind Of Love	7"	Liberty	LIB55397	1962	**£5**	
Surf 'N' Drag Hits	7" EP	Liberty	LEP2213	1965	**£8**	
Surf City	LP	Liberty	LBY1163	1963	**£15**	
Surf City	7"	Liberty	LIB55580	1963	**£5**	chart single
Take Linda Surfing	LP	Liberty	LRP3294	1963	**£15**	US, with Beach Boys
Tennessee	7"	Liberty	LIB10252	1966	**£5**	
There's A Girl	7"	London	HLU8990	1959	**£10**	
Titanic Twosome	7" EP	Liberty	LEP2258	1966	**£8**	
Yellow Balloon	7"	CBS	202630	1967	**£6**	
You Really Know How To Hurt A Guy	7"	Liberty	LIB55792	1964	**£4**	

JAN & KELLY

Time For A Laugh	7" EP	Philips	BE12536	1963	**£4**	

JAN DUKES DE GREY

Mice & Rats In The Loft	LP	Transatlantic	TRA234	1971	**£20**	
Sorcerers	LP	Nova	SDN8	1970	**£20**	

JANIS, JOHNNY

Better To Love You	7"	London	HLU8650	1958	**£4**	

JANSCH, BERT

With Davy Graham maintaining a deliberately low profile, it was left to Bert Jansch to define the sound and style of folk guitar playing. His serviceable folk-singer's voice gives added interest to his records, but the guitar is the real focus - beginning with a faultless version of Graham's difficult "Angie" and moving onwards from there.

Bert Jansch	LP	Transatlantic	TRA125	1965	**£12**	
Bert Jansch	7" EP	Transatlantic	EP145	1966	**£5**	
Birthday Blues	LP	Transatlantic	TRA179	1968	**£10**	
It Don't Bother Me	LP	Transatlantic	TRA132	1965	**£12**	
Jack Orion	LP	Transatlantic	TRA143	1966	**£12**	
Life Depends On Love	7"	Transatlantic	BIG102	1968	**£4**	
Nicola	LP	Transatlantic	TRA157	1967	**£10**	
Rosemary Lane	LP	Transatlantic	TRA235	1971	**£10**	

JANSCH, BERT & JOHN RENBOURN

Title	Format	Label	Cat. No.	Year	Price	Notes
Bert & John	LP	Transatlantic	TRA144	1966	**£12**	

JAPAN

The pretty-boy posing of Japan was an unlikely environment for intelligent, questing music to be produced, and yet with each record release, the group became more and more of a vital force. Peaking with the refreshingly innovative "Ghosts", it was perhaps inevitable that David Sylvian would then wish to continue the quest on his own.

Title	Format	Label	Cat. No.	Year	Price	Notes
Art Of Parties	7"	Virgin	VS409	1981	**£5**	gatefold PS
Don't Rain On My Parade	7"	Ariola	AHA510	1978	**£15**	
Gentlemen Take Polaroids	7"	Virgin	VS379	1980	**£4**	chart single
Gentlemen Take Polaroids	7"	Virgin	VS379	1980	**£8**	double
Ghosts	7"	Virgin	VSY472	1982	**£5**	pic disc
I Second That Emotion	7"	Ariola	AHA559	1980	**£6**	
I Second That Emotion	7"	Ariola	AHA559	1980	**£10**	red vinyl
Interview Album	LP	Ariola		1979	**£20**	US promo
Life In Tokyo	7"	Ariola	AHA540	1979	**£8**	red vinyl
Life In Tokyo	12"	Ariola	AHAD540	1979	**£10**	red vinyl
Life In Tokyo	7"	Hansa	HANSA4	1981	**£5**	
Life In Tokyo	12"	Hansa	HANSA124	1981	**£6**	
Nightporter	7"	Virgin	VSDJ552	1982	**£6**	1 sided promo
Sometimes I Feel So Low	7"	Ariola	AHA529	1978	**£8**	
Sometimes I Feel So Low	7"	Ariola	AHA529	1978	**£12**	blue vinyl
Unconventional	7"	Ariola	AHA525	1978	**£15**	

JARMELS

Title	Format	Label	Cat. No.	Year	Price	Notes
Little Bit Of Soap	7"	Top Rank	JAR580	1961	**£4**	
She Loves To Dance	7"	Top Rank	JAR560	1961	**£5**	

JARRE, JEAN MICHEL

There is no rarer record than Jean Michel Jarre's "Music For Supermarkets" - the LP was issued in a limited edition of just one copy and auctioned for charity in 1983. If the record were ever to be auctioned again, it would no doubt fetch a four figure sum. Meanwhile, there are a number of other Jarre albums which the keen collector does stand a reasonable chance of obtaining, although at a considerable price nonetheless, for the series of soundtracks begun with "Des Garcons Et Des Filles" has never been issued outside France and are scarce even in that country.

Title	Format	Label	Cat. No.	Year	Price	Notes
Deserted Palace	LP		SF1029	1972	**£200**	US promo
Equinoxe 4 (remix)	12"	Polydor	JM1	1979	**£15**	promo
Equinoxe 5	7"	Polydor	JARRE1	1979	**£10**	1 sided promo
Equinoxe 7 (live)	7"	Polydor	2001968	1980	**£10**	
Les Granges Brulees	LP			1973	**£200**	French
Magnetic Fields 4 (remix)	7"	Polydor	POSP363	1981	**£10**	
Orient Express	7"	Polydor	POSP430	1982	**£10**	
Orient Express	12"	Polydor	POSPX430DJ	1982	**£12**	promo
Rendezvous 4 (remix)	12"	Polydor	POSPX788	1986	**£10**	2 different sleeves
Zoolook (remix)	12"	Polydor	POSPX718	1984	**£8**	
Zoolookologie (remix)	7"	Polydor	POSP740	1985	**£5**	
Zoolookologie (remix)	7"	Polydor	POSPG740	1985	**£10**	double
Zoolookologie (remix)	12"	Polydor	POSPX740	1985	**£10**	

JARVIS STREET REVUE

Title	Format	Label	Cat. No.	Year	Price	Notes
Mr.Oil Man	LP	Columbia			**£125**	Canadian

JARVIS, MARIAN

Title	Format	Label	Cat. No.	Year	Price	Notes
Penny For Your Thoughts	7"	Chelsea	2005038	1975	**£5**	

JASMINE MINKS

Title	Format	Label	Cat. No.	Year	Price	Notes
Think	7"	Creation	CRE004	1984	**£15**	
What's Happening	7"	Creation	CRE018	1985	**£8**	
Where The Traffic Goes	7"	Creation	CRE008	1984	**£15**	

JASON CREST

Title	Format	Label	Cat. No.	Year	Price	Notes
Black Mass	7"	Philips	BF1809	1969	**£15**	
Juliano The Bull	7"	Philips	BF1650	1968	**£15**	
Lemon Tree	7"	Philips	BF1687	1968	**£15**	
Turquoise Tandem Cycle	7"	Philips	BF1633	1968	**£20**	
Waterloo Road	7"	Philips	BF1752	1969	**£10**	

JASPER

Title	Format	Label	Cat. No.	Year	Price	Notes
Liberation	LP	Spark	SRLP103	1969	**£200**	

JASPER WRAITH

Title	Format	Label	Cat. No.	Year	Price	Notes
Jasper Wraith	LP	Sunflower	SNF5003	1971	**£15**	US

JAWBONE

Gotta Go	7"	B&C	CB190	1972	**£8**	
How's Ya Pa	7"	Carnaby	CNS4007	1970	**£10**	
Jawbone	LP	Carnaby		1970	**£40**	
Way Way Down	7"	Carnaby	CNS4020	1971	**£10**	

JAXON, BOB

Ali Baba	7"	London	HL8156	1955	**£10**	
Beach Party	7"	RCA	RCA1019	1957	**£12**	

JAY & THE AMERICANS

At The Cafe Wha	LP	United Artists	UAL3300	1963	**£12**	US
Capture The Moment	LP	United Artists	UAS6762	1971	**£10**	US
Cara Mia	7"	United Artists	UP1094	1965	**£4**	
Come A Little Bit Closer	7" EP	United Artists	UEP1003	1965	**£5**	
Come A Little Bit Closer	7"	United Artists	UP1069	1964	**£4**	
Come Dance With Me	7"	United Artists	UP1039	1964	**£4**	
Crying	7"	United Artists	UP1132	1966	**£4**	
Got Hung Up Along The Way	7"	United Artists	UP1191	1967	**£20**	
Let's Lock The Door	7"	United Artists	UP1075	1965	**£4**	
Living Above Your Head	7"	United Artists	UP1142	1966	**£6**	
Living With Jay & The Americans	7" EP	United Artists	UEP1017	1966	**£5**	
Raining In My Sunshine	7"	United Artists	UP1162	1966	**£4**	
She Cried	7"	HMV	POP1009	1962	**£5**	
She Cried	LP	United Artists	UAL3222	1962	**£12**	US
Some Enchanted Evening	7"	United Artists	UP1108	1965	**£4**	
Strangers Tomorrow	7"	United Artists	UP1018	1963	**£4**	
Sunday Alone	7"	United Artists	UP1128	1966	**£4**	
Think Of The Good Times	7"	United Artists	UP1088	1965	**£4**	
This Is It	7"	United Artists	UP1002	1964	**£4**	
This Magic Moment	7"	United Artists	UP2268	1969	**£4**	
Why Can't You Bring Me Home	7"	United Artists	UP1129	1966	**£4**	

JAY & THE TECHNIQUES

Apples, Peaches, Pumpkin Pie	LP	Philips	BL7834	1967	**£10**	
Apples, Peaches, Pumpkin Pie	7"	Philips	BF1597	1967	**£4**	
Baby Make Your Own Sweet Music	7"	Mercury	MF1034	1968	**£4**	
I Feel Love Comin' On	7"	Polydor	2066473	1975	**£5**	
Keep The Ball Rolling	7"	Philips	PB1618	1967	**£4**	
Strawberry Shortcake	7"	Philips	BF1644	1968	**£4**	

JAY, DAVID & RENE HALKETT

Nothing	7"	4AD	AD112	1981	**£10**	with lyric sheet

JAY, PETER & THE BLUEMEN

Just Too Late	7"	Triumph	RGM1000	1960	**£8**	

JAY, PETER & THE JAYWALKERS

Before The Beginning	7"	Piccadilly	7N35325	1966	**£5**	
Can Can '62	7"	Decca	F11531	1962	**£4**	chart single
Parade Of Tin Soldiers	7"	Decca	F11757	1963	**£4**	
Paradise Garden	7"	Pye	7N15290	1960	**£6**	
Parchman Farm	7"	Piccadilly	7N35220	1965	**£5**	
Poet And Peasant	7"	Decca	F11659	1963	**£4**	
Tonight You're Gonna Fall	7"	Piccadilly	7N35212	1964	**£5**	
Totem Pole	7"	Decca	F11593	1963	**£4**	
Where Did Our Love Go	7"	Piccadilly	7N35199	1964	**£5**	
You Girl	7"	Decca	F11840	1964	**£4**	

JAYBIRDS

Somebody Help Me	7"	Sue	WI4013	1966	**£10**	

JAYE SISTERS

Sure Fire Love	7"	London	HLT9011	1959	**£4**	

JAYHAWKS

Stranded In The Jungle	7"	Parlophone	R4228	1956	**£70**	

JAYNETTS

Sally Go Round The Roses	7"	Stateside	SS227	1963	**£4**	
Sally Go Round The Roses	LP	Tuff	LP13	1963	**£50**	US

JAYWALKERS

Title	Format	Label	Number	Year	Price	Notes
Can't Live Without You	7"	Cream	5003	1976	**£4**	

JAZZ ROCK EXPERIENCE

Title	Format	Label	Number	Year	Price	Notes
Jazz Rock Experience	LP	Nova	SDN19	1970	**£20**	

JB'S

Title	Format	Label	Number	Year	Price	Notes
Damn Right I Am Somebody	LP	Polydor	2391125	1974	**£15**	
Doing It To Death	LP	Polydor	2391087	1974	**£15**	
Food For Thought	LP	Polydor	2391034	1972	**£15**	
Gimme Some More	7"	Mojo	2093007	1974	**£4**	
Givin' Up Food For Funk	7"	Mojo	2093021	1974	**£4**	
Givin' Up Food For Funk	LP	Polydor	2391204	1976	**£10**	
Grunt	7"	Mojo	2027002	1971	**£4**	
Hot Pants Road	7"	Mojo	2093016	1974	**£4**	
Hustle With Speed	LP	Polydor	2391194	1975	**£15**	
Pass The Peas	LP	Polydor	2918004	1972	**£15**	
There Are The JB's	7"	Polydor	2001115	1971	**£4**	

JEAN & THE STATESIDERS

Title	Format	Label	Number	Year	Price	Notes
Putty In Your Hands	7"	Columbia	DB7287	1964	**£4**	
You Won't Forget Me	7"	Columbia	DB7439	1965	**£4**	
Mama Didn't Lie	7"	Columbia	DB7651	1965	**£4**	

JEAN, EARL

Title	Format	Label	Number	Year	Price	Notes
I'm Into Something Good	7"	Colpix	PX729	1964	**£10**	
Randy	7"	Colpix	PX748	1964	**£8**	

JEANNIE & THE BIG GUYS

Title	Format	Label	Number	Year	Price	Notes
Don't Lie To Me	7"	Piccadilly	7N35147	1963	**£6**	
I Want You	7"	Piccadilly	7N35164	1964	**£8**	

JEEPS

Title	Format	Label	Number	Year	Price	Notes
Ain't It A Great Big Laugh	7"	Strike	JH315	1966	**£4**	
He Saw Eesaw	7"	Strike	JH308	1966	**£4**	

JEFFERSON

Title	Format	Label	Number	Year	Price	Notes
Colour Of My Love	LP	Pye	NSPL18316	1969	**£10**	

JEFFERSON AIRPLANE

Title	Format	Label	Number	Year	Price	Notes
30 Seconds Over Winterland	LP	Grunt	FTR0147	1973	**£10**	
After Bathing At Baxters	LP	RCA	RD7926	1967	**£12**	mono
After Bathing At Baxters	LP	RCA	SF7926	1967	**£10**	stereo
Ballad Of You And Me And Pooneil	7"	RCA	RCA1647	1967	**£8**	
Bark	LP	Grunt	FTR1001	1971	**£10**	bag sleeve, chart LP
Bless Its Pointed Little Head	LP	RCA		1969	**£35**	US interview promo
Bless Its Pointed Little Head	LP	RCA	SF8019	1969	**£10**	chart LP
Crown Of Creation	LP	RCA	SF7976	1968	**£10**	
Greasy Heart	7"	RCA	RCA1711	1968	**£8**	
If You Feel Like China Breaking	7"	RCA	RCA1736	1968	**£8**	
Long John Silver	LP	Grunt	FTR1007	1972	**£10**	open-out cover, chart LP
Long John Silver	7"	Grunt	650506	1972	**£4**	
Mexico	7"	RCA	RCA1989	1970	**£6**	
Pretty As You Feel	7"	Grunt	650500	1971	**£4**	
Somebody To Love	7"	RCA	RCA1594	1967	**£5**	
Surrealistic Pillow	LP	RCA	LSP3766	1967	**£15**	US
Surrealistic Pillow	LP	RCA	RD7889	1967	**£12**	mono
Surrealistic Pillow	LP	RCA	SF7889	1967	**£10**	stereo
Takes Off	LP	RCA	INT1476	1974	**£10**	
Takes Off	LP	RCA	LPM3584	1966	**£15**	US
Takes Off	LP	RCA	LPM3584	1966	**£100**	US with 'Runnin' Round The World'
Takes Off	LP	RCA	SF8195	1971	**£12**	
Trial By Fire	7"	Grunt	65511	1972	**£4**	
Volunteers	LP	RCA	APDI0320	1973	**£15**	US quad
Volunteers	LP	RCA	SF8076	1969	**£10**	chart LP
Volunteers	7"	RCA	RCA1933	1970	**£5**	
White Rabbit	7"	RCA	RCA1631	1967	**£5**	
White Rabbit	7"	RCA	RCA1964	1970	**£4**	
Wild Turkey	7"	Grunt	65500	1972	**£4**	

JEFFERSON STARSHIP

Title	Format	Label	Number	Year	Price	Notes
Dragonfly	LP	Grunt	BFD10717	1974	**£15**	US quad
Gold	LP	Grunt	DJL13363	1978	**£15**	US promo pic disc
Red Octopus	LP	Grunt	BFD10999	1975	**£15**	US quad
Spitfire	LP	Grunt	BFD11557	1976	**£15**	US quad

JEFFERSON, BLIND LEMON & BUDDY BOY HAWKINS

Title	Format	Label	Number	Year	Price	Notes
	7" EP	Collector	JE18	196-	**£6**	

JEFFERSON, BLIND LEMON & ED BELL

Title	Format	Label	Number	Year	Price	Notes
Male Blues Vol.7	7" EP	Collector	JE113	196-	**£5**	

JEFFERSON, BLIND LEMON & LEADBELLY

Title	Format	Label	Number	Year	Price	Notes
Male Blues Vol.8	7" EP	Collector	JE124	196-	**£5**	

JEFFERSON, EDDIE

Title	Format	Label	Number	Year	Price	Notes
Some Other Time	7"	Stateside	SS591	1967	**£4**	

JELLY BEANS

Title	Format	Label	Number	Year	Price	Notes
Baby Be Mine	7"	Red Bird	RB10011	1964	**£6**	
I Wanna Love Him So Bad	7"	Pye	7N25252	1964	**£8**	
You Don't Mean Me No Good	7"	Right On	102	1975	**£4**	

JELLYBREAD

Title	Format	Label	Number	Year	Price	Notes
65 Parkway	LP	Blue Horizon	2431002	1970	**£20**	
65 Parkway	LP	Blue Horizon	763866	1970	**£25**	
Back To Begin Again	LP	Blue Horizon	2931004	1972	**£50**	
Chairman Mao's Boogaloo	7"	Blue Horizon	573162	1969	**£6**	
Comment	7"	Blue Horizon	573169	1970	**£5**	
Creepin' And Crawlin'	7"	Blue Horizon	2096001	1971	**£5**	
Down Along The Cove	7"	Blue Horizon	2096006	1971	**£5**	
First Slice	LP	Blue Horizon	763853	1969	**£25**	
Old Man Hank	7"	Blue Horizon	573180	1970	**£5**	
Rockin' Pneumonia	7"	Blue Horizon	573174	1970	**£5**	

JELLYROLL

Title	Format	Label	Number	Year	Price	Notes
Jellyroll	LP	MCA	MUPS420	1971	**£10**	

JENKINS, JOHNNY

Title	Format	Label	Number	Year	Price	Notes
Ton Ton Macoute	LP	Atlantic	2400033	1970	**£12**	
Ton Ton Macoute	LP	Atlantic	K40105	1972	**£10**	
Voodoo In You	7"	Atco	226009	1969	**£4**	

JENNINGS, WAYLON

Title	Format	Label	Number	Year	Price	Notes
At JD's	LP	Sounds	1001	1964	**£75**	US
Folk Country	LP	RCA	LPM3523	1966	**£10**	US
Leavin' Town	LP	RCA	LPM3620	1966	**£10**	US
Waylon Sings Ol' Harlan	LP	RCA	LPM3660	1967	**£12**	US

JENSEN, KRIS

Title	Format	Label	Number	Year	Price	Notes
Claudette	7"	Fontana	267267TF	1963	**£5**	
Come Back To Me	7"	Hickory	451256	1964	**£4**	
Donna Donna	7"	Hickory	451224	1964	**£4**	
Looking For Love	7"	Hickory	451243	1964	**£4**	
Somebody's Smiling	7"	Hickory	451285	1965	**£4**	
That's A Whole Lotta Love	7"	Hickory	451311	1965	**£4**	
Torture	LP	Hickory	MH110	1962	**£20**	US

JENSEN, KRIS & SUE THOMPSON

Title	Format	Label	Number	Year	Price	Notes
Introducing...	7" EP	Hickory	LPE1507	1965	**£10**	

JEREMY & THE SATYRS

Jeremy and The Satyrs, led by flautist Jeremy Steig, were one of the first American groups to bring jazz skills and sounds to rock. This was fledgling jazz-rock, with the two halves meeting on equal terms (unlike Blood,Sweat,and Tears, for example, where the jazz content was no more than superficial). The Satyrs' experiment only lasted for one album, but each member has been a familiar session name ever since - Eddie Gomez, Donald McDonald, Warren Bernhardt, and Adrian Guillory.

Title	Format	Label	Number	Year	Price	Notes
Jeremy & The Satyrs	LP	Reprise	RS6282	1968	**£15**	US

JERICHO

Title	Format	Label	Number	Year	Price	Notes
Jericho	LP	A&M	AMLS68079	1972	**£60**	
Mama's Gonna Take You Home	7"	A&M	AMS7037	1972	**£20**	

JERICHO JONES

Title	Format	Label	Cat. No.	Year	Price	Notes
Junkies, Monkeys & Donkeys	LP	A&M	AMLH68050	1971	**£70**	

JERUSALEM

Title	Format	Label	Cat. No.	Year	Price	Notes
Jerusalem	LP	Deram	SDL6	1972	**£40**	
Kamakazi Moth	7"	Deram	DMS358	1972	**£10**	

JESSE & JAMES

Title	Format	Label	Cat. No.	Year	Price	Notes
Something For Nothing	7"	MGM	MGM1420	1968	**£4**	

JESUS & MARY CHAIN

Title	Format	Label	Cat. No.	Year	Price	Notes
April Skies	7"	Blanco Y.N.	NEGF024	1987	**£6**	double
April Skies	7"	Blanco Y.N.	SAM360	1987	**£6**	double
Happy When It Rains	7"	Blanco Y.N.	NEGB025	1987	**£5**	boxed, cards
Just Like Honey	7"	Blanco Y.N.	NEGF017	1985	**£10**	double
Just Like Honey	7"	Blanco Y.N.	SAM259	1985	**£10**	double
Just Like Honey	12"	Blanco Y.N.	NEGT017	1985	**£6**	
Never Understand	7"	Blanco Y.N.	NEG008	1985	**£4**	chart single
Never Understand	12"	Blanco Y.N.	NEGT008	1985	**£6**	
Some Candy Talking	7"	Blanco Y.N.	NEGF019	1986	**£10**	double
Some Candy Talking	7"	Blanco Y.N.	SAM291	1986	**£10**	double
Upside Down	7"	Creation	CRE012	1984	**£10**	
Upside Down	7"	Creation	CRE012	1984	**£15**	fold-out sleeve
Upside Down	12"	Creation	CRE012T	1984	**£80**	demo only
You Trip Me Up	12"	Blanco Y.N.	NEGT013	1985	**£6**	

JET

Title	Format	Label	Cat. No.	Year	Price	Notes
Jet	LP	CBS	80699	1975	**£12**	
My River	7"	CBS	3143	1975	**£5**	
Nothing To Do With Us	7"	CBS	3317	1975	**£4**	

JETHRO TOE (JETHRO TULL)

Title	Format	Label	Cat. No.	Year	Price	Notes
Sunshine Day	7"	MGM	MGM1384	1968	**£70**	credited to 'Jethro Toe'

JETHRO TULL

The first record made by Jethro Tull, the MGM single "Sunshine Day", was mistakenly credited to "Jethro Toe" (See above). Both sides of the record - less bluesy than the music on "This Was", but easily recogniseable as the same group - were subsequently made available on the Polydor compilation "Rare Tracks", but the single itself hardly sold at all and is extremely scarce. Copies that correct the spelling of the group's name on the label are counterfeits, this being emphasized by their having American-style large centre holes on what is supposed to be a UK release.

Title	Format	Label	Cat. No.	Year	Price	Notes
1982 Tour Sampler	LP	Chrysalis	47PDJ	1982	**£12**	US promo
Aqualung	LP	Chrysalis	CH41044	1973	**£15**	US quad
Aqualung	LP	Island	ILPS9145	1971	**£10**	chart LP
Aqualung	LP	Mobile Fid.	MFSL1061	1980	**£30**	US audiophile
Benefit	LP	Island	ILPS9123	1970	**£10**	chart LP
Broadsword & The Beast	LP	Mobile Fid.	MFSL1092	1982	**£15**	US audiophile
Broadsword	7"	Chrysalis	CHSP2619	1982	**£6**	pic disc
Bungle In The Jungle	7"	Chrysalis	CHS2054	1974	**£4**	
Inside	7"	Chrysalis	WIP6081	1970	**£4**	
Jethro Tull Radio Show	LP	Chrysalis	PRO622	1976	**£20**	US promo
Life's A Long Song	7"	Chrysalis	WIP6106	1971	**£4**	PS
Living In The Past	LP	Chrysalis	CJT1	1972	**£200**	double, leather cover
Living In The Past	LP	Chrysalis	CJT1	1972	**£12**	hard cover double, chart LP
Living In The Past	7"	Island	WIP6056	1969	**£4**	chart single
Love Story	7"	Island	WIP6048	1968	**£6**	chart single
Minstrel In The Gallery	7"	Chrysalis	CHS2075	1975	**£4**	
Ring Out Solstice Bells	7"	Chrysalis	CXP2	1976	**£4**	PS
Song For Jeffrey	7"	Island	WIP6043	1968	**£20**	
Stand Up	LP	Island	ILPS9103	1969	**£15**	
Stitch In Time	7"	Chrysalis	CHS2260	1978	**£5**	white vinyl
Sweet Dream	7"	Chrysalis	WIP6070	1969	**£4**	chart single
Thick As A Brick	LP	Chrysalis	CHR1003	1972	**£15**	newspaper sleeve
This Was	LP	Island	ILP985	1968	**£25**	mono
This Was	LP	Island	ILPS9085	1968	**£20**	chart LP
War Child	LP	Chrysalis	CH41067	1974	**£15**	US quad
Witch's Promise	7"	Chrysalis	WIP6077	1970	**£4**	PS

JETSTREAMS

Title	Format	Label	Cat. No.	Year	Price	Notes
Bongo Rock	7"	Decca	F11149	1959	**£8**	

JEWELS

But I Do	7"	Colpix	PX11048	1965	**£10**	
Opportunity	7"	Colpix	PX11034	1964	**£8**	

JIGSAW

Aurora Borealis	LP	Philips	6308072	1971	**£40**	
Broken Hearted	LP	BASF		1973	**£20**	
I've Seen The Film	LP	BASF		1974	**£20**	
I've Seen The Film	7"	BASF	BA1002	1974	**£6**	
Jesu Joy Of Man's Desiring	7"	Philips	6006131	1971	**£10**	
Keeping My Head Above Water	7"	Philips	6006182	1971	**£10**	
Leatherslade Farm	LP	Philips	6308033	1970	**£50**	
Lollipop And Goody Man	7"	Fontana	6007017	1970	**£10**	
One Way Street	7"	Philips	6006112	1970	**£15**	
You're Not The Only Girl	7"	BASF	BA1010	1974	**£6**	

JILTED JOHN

Jilted John	7"	Rabid	TOSH105	1978	**£4**	PS

JIM & JOE

Fireball Mail	7"	London	HL9831	1964	**£4**	

JIM & MONICA

Slippin' And Slidin'	7"	Stateside	SS266	1964	**£4**	

JIMMIE & THE NIGHT HOPPERS

Night Hop	7"	London	HLP8830	1959	**£12**	

JIV-A-TONES

Flirty Gertie	7"	Felsted	AF101	1958	**£25**	

JIVE FIVE

Jive Five	LP	United Artists	UAL3455	1965	**£15**	US
My True Story	7"	Parlophone	R4822	1961	**£20**	
What Time Is It	7"	Stateside	SS133	1962	**£10**	

JIVERS

Little Mama	7"	Vogue	V9060	1956	**£20**	
Ray Pearl	7"	Vogue	V9068	1957	**£20**	

JIVING JUNIORS

Don't Leave Me	7"	Island	WI027	1962	**£5**	
Lollipop Girl	7"	Blue Beat	BB4	1960	**£10**	
My Heart's Desire	7"	Blue Beat	BB5	1960	**£10**	
Slop And Mash	7"	Starlite	ST45049	1961	**£5**	
Tu Woo Up Tu Woo	7"	Starlite	ST45028	1960	**£5**	

JO JO GUNNE

Bite Down Hard	LP	Asylum	SYL9005	1973	**£10**	
Jo Jo Gunne	LP	Asylum	SYLA8752	1972	**£10**	
Jumpin' The Gunne	LP	Asylum	SYL9015	1973	**£10**	
So...Where's The Show	LP	Asylum	SYL9019	1974	**£10**	

JO MAMA

J Is For Jump	LP	Atlantic	2400174	1971	**£10**	
Jo Mama	LP	Atlantic	2400129	1971	**£10**	

JO, DAMITA

I'll Save The Last Dance For You	7" EP	Mercury	ZEP10118	1961	**£8**	

JOBRIATH

Creatures Of The Street	LP	Elektra	K42163	1974	**£15**	
Jobriath	LP	Elektra	EKS75070	1973	**£15**	
Oo La La	7"	Elektra	K12156	1974	**£4**	
Street Corner Love	7"	Elektra	K12146	1974	**£4**	
Take Me I'm Yours	7"	Elektra	K12129	1973	**£4**	

JODIMARS

Cloud Ninety-nine	7"	Capitol	CL14700	1957	**£12**	
Dance To The Bop	7"	Capitol	CL14642	1956	**£15**	
Lotsa Love	7"	Capitol	CL14627	1956	**£15**	
Midnight	7"	Capitol	CL14663	1956	**£15**	

Title	Format	Label	Cat. No.	Year	Price	Notes
Rattle Shaking Daddy	7"	Capitol	CL14641	1956	**£15**	
Well Now Dig This	7"	Capitol	CL14518	1956	**£15**	

JODY GRIND

Title	Format	Label	Cat. No.	Year	Price	Notes
Far Canal	LP	Transatlantic	TRA221	1970	**£20**	
One Step On	LP	Transatlantic	TRA210	1969	**£20**	

JOE SOAP

Title	Format	Label	Cat. No.	Year	Price	Notes
Keep It Clean	LP	Polydor	2383233	1973	**£15**	

JOEL, BILLY

Title	Format	Label	Cat. No.	Year	Price	Notes
52nd Street	LP	Columbia	HC45609	1981	**£10**	US audiophile
Ballad Of Billy The Kid	7"	Philips	6078018	1973	**£10**	
Billy Joel	LP	Columbia	ABS1	1978	**£75**	US promo, 5 LPs, boxed
Cold Spring Harbour	LP	Philips	6369150	1972	**£12**	recorded too fast
Entertainer	7"	Philips		1973	**£25**	
Interchords	LP	Columbia	AS402	1976	**£15**	US interview promo
Now Playing	LP	CBS	BJ1	1978	**£15**	promo
Piano Man	LP	Columbia	CQ32544	1974	**£10**	US quad
Piano Man	LP	Philips	6369160	1973	**£25**	
She's Got A Way	7"	Philips	6078001	1972	**£5**	
Songs From The Attic	LP	Columbia	AS1343	1981	**£20**	US sampler & interview (promo)
Souvenir	LP	Columbia	AS326	1974	**£20**	US 1 sided live promo
Stranger	LP	Columbia	HC34987	1980	**£10**	US audiophile
Streetlife Serenade	LP	Columbia	PCQ33146	1974	**£10**	US quad
Turnstiles	LP	Columbia	PCQ33848	1976	**£10**	US quad

JOEY & THE CONTINENTALS

Title	Format	Label	Cat. No.	Year	Price	Notes
Like I Love You	7"	Fontana	TF444	1964	**£8**	
She Rides With Me	7"	Polydor	56520	1970	**£6**	

JOEY, SHADE & THE NIGHT OWLS

Title	Format	Label	Cat. No.	Year	Price	Notes
Bluebirds Over The Mountain	7"	Parlophone	R5180	1964	**£5**	

JOHN & JOHNNY

Title	Format	Label	Cat. No.	Year	Price	Notes
Bumper To Bumper	7"	Polydor	56087	1966	**£8**	

JOHN & PAUL

Title	Format	Label	Cat. No.	Year	Price	Notes
People Say	7"	London	HLU9997	1965	**£6**	

JOHN BULL BREED

Title	Format	Label	Cat. No.	Year	Price	Notes
I'm A Man	7"	Polydor	56065	1966	**£20**	

JOHN'S CHILDREN

The collectability of John's Children derives mainly from the fact that Marc Bolan played with the group for a short time. "Desdemona" is a Bolan song, as is the withdrawn and extremely scarce "Midsummer Night's Scene". (Other unreleased Marc Bolan contributions were included on his LP "Beginning Of Doves"). Many of the other John's Children recordings were actually made by session musicians (including Jeff Beck on the B side of "Just What You Want"), as the group was too incompetent to do the job themselves.

Title	Format	Label	Cat. No.	Year	Price	Notes
Come And Play With Me In The Garden	7"	Track	604005	1967	**£20**	
Come And Play With Me In The Garden	7"	Track	604005	1967	**£60**	PS
Desdemona	7"	Track	604003	1967	**£15**	
Desdemona	7"	Track	604003	1967	**£50**	PS
Go Go Girl	7"	Track	604010	1967	**£30**	
Just What You Want	7"	Columbia	DB8124	1967	**£35**	
Love I Thought I'd Found	7"	Columbia	DB8030	1966	**£35**	
Midsummer Night's Scene	7"	Track	604005	1967	**£600**	test pressing
Orgasm	LP	White Whale	WW7128	1967	**£60**	US

JOHN, CLIVE

Title	Format	Label	Cat. No.	Year	Price	Notes
You Always Know Where You Stand...	LP	United Artists	UAS29733	1975	**£12**	

JOHN, DAVID & THE MOOD

Title	Format	Label	Cat. No.	Year	Price	Notes
Bring It To Jerome	7"	Parlophone	R5255	1965	**£60**	
Diggin' For Gold	7"	Parlophone	R5301	1965	**£50**	
Pretty Thing	7"	Vocalion	V9220	1964	**£80**	

JOHN, ELTON

Title	Format	Label	Cat. No.	Year	Price	Notes
All Quiet On The Western Front	7"	Rocket	XPRPO88	1982	**£4**	poster sleeve
Bite Your Lip	12"	Rocket	PSLP206(GUAD1)	1977	**£8**	1 sided promo
Border Song	7"	DJM	DJS217	1970	**£4**	

Title	Format	Label	Cat. No.	Year	Price	Notes
Candle In The Wind	LP	St.Michael	20940102	1978	**£15**	
Captain Fantastic	LP	DJM	DJLPX1	1975	**£20**	brown vinyl
Captain Fantastic	LP	DJM	DJLPX1	1975	**£70**	brown vinyl,signed cover
Captain Fantastic	LP	DJM	DJV2300	1978	**£12**	pic disc
Dear God	7"	Rocket	XPRES45	1981	**£5**	double
Dear God	7"	Rocket	ELTON1	1981	**£5**	double
Elton John	LP	DJM	DJM14512	1978	**£40**	5 LPs, boxed
Empty Garden (2 versions)	7"	Rocket	ZPRESDJ77	1982	**£5**	promo
Empty Garden	7"	Rocket	XPPIC77	1982	**£4**	pic disc
Empty Sky	LP	DJM	DJLPM403	1969	**£10**	mono
Friends (mono/stereo)	7"	DJM	DJS244	1971	**£8**	promo
Friends	7"	DJM	DJS244	1971	**£4**	
Gli Opera	7"	Rocket		1977	**£8**	sung in Italian
Goaldigger Song	7"	Rocket	GOALD1	1977	**£40**	
Goodbye Yellow Brick Road	LP	DJM	DJE29001	1976	**£12**	yellow vinyl
Goodbye Yellow Brick Road	LP	Nautilus	10003	1980	**£25**	US audiophile
Goodbye Yellow Brick Road	LP	Superdisk	SD216614	1982	**£15**	audiophile
Greatest Hits Volume One	LP	Nautilus		1981	**£12**	US audiophile
I Guess That's Why They Call It	7"	Rocket	XPRES91	1983	**£4**	embossed sleeve
I'm Still Standing	7"	Rocket	EJPIC1	1983	**£8**	shaped pic disc
I've Been Loving You	7"	Philips	BF1643	1968	**£30**	
It's Me That You Need	7"	DJM	DJS205	1969	**£35**	PS
Je Veux De La Tendresse	7"	Rocket	6000675	1980	**£6**	sung in French
Jump Up	12"	Rocket		1982	**£10**	promo sampler
Lady Samantha	7"	Philips	BF1739	1969	**£20**	
Mama Can't Buy You Love	7"	Rocket	XPRESS20	1979	**£20**	
Rock And Roll Madonna	7"	DJM	DJS222	1970	**£6**	
Rocket Man	7"	DJM	DJX501	1972	**£12**	gatefold PS
Sad Songs	7"	Rocket	PHPIC7	1984	**£4**	shaped pic disc
Single Man	LP	MCA	MCAP14591	1979	**£10**	US pic disc
Singles Collection	7"	DJM	EJBOX12	1978	**£40**	12 singles, boxed
Superior Sound Of...	CD	DJM	8100622	1983	**£20**	remix compilation
Wrap Her Up	7"	Rocket	EJPIC10	1985	**£4**	shaped pic disc

JOHN, ELTON & FRANCE GALL

Title	Format	Label	Cat. No.	Year	Price	Notes
Les Areuse	cass-s			1981	**£5**	sung in French
Les Areuse	7"			1981	**£4**	sung in French
Les Areuse	12"			1981	**£6**	sung in French

JOHN, ELTON & OTHERS

Title	Format	Label	Cat. No.	Year	Price	Notes
Games	LP	Viking	105	1970	**£75**	US

JOHN, LITTLE WILLIE

Title	Format	Label	Cat. No.	Year	Price	Notes
Action	LP	King	691	1960	**£30**	US
Come On And Join Little Willie John	LP	London	HA8126	1964	**£25**	
Fever	LP	King	395564	1956	**£50**	US
Fever	7"	Parlophone	R4209	1956	**£15**	
Free At Last	LP	King	KS1081	1970	**£20**	US
Heartbreak	7"	Parlophone	R4674	1960	**£10**	
Leave My Kitten Alone	7"	Parlophone	R4571	1959	**£12**	
Let's Rock While The Rocking's Good	7"	Parlophone	R4472	1958	**£15**	
Little Willie Sings All Originals	LP	King	K949	1966	**£20**	US
Mr.Little Willie John	LP	King	603	1958	**£40**	US
Sleep	7"	Parlophone	R4699	1960	**£8**	
Sure Things	LP	King	739	1961	**£25**	US
Sweet, The Hot, The Teenage Beat	LP	King	767	1961	**£25**	US
Talk To Me	LP	King	395596	1958	**£40**	US
Talk To Me	7"	Parlophone	R4432	1958	**£15**	
These Are My Favorite Songs	LP	King	895	1964	**£25**	US
Uh Uh Baby	7"	Parlophone	R4396	1958	**£12**	

JOHN, MABLE

Title	Format	Label	Cat. No.	Year	Price	Notes
Able Mable	7"	Stax	601034	1968	**£4**	
It's Catching	7"	Atlantic	584022	1966	**£5**	
Same Time Same Place	7"	Stax	601010	1967	**£4**	

JOHN, ROBERT

Title	Format	Label	Cat. No.	Year	Price	Notes
Don't Leave Me	7"	CBS	3730	1968	**£4**	
If You Don't Want My Love	7"	CBS	3436	1968	**£4**	

JOHNNIE & JOE

Title	Format	Label	Cat. No.	Year	Price	Notes
Over the Mountain Across The Sea	7"	London	HLM8682	1958	**£20**	

JOHNNY & CHAS & THE GUNNERS

Title	Format	Label	Cat. No.	Year	Price	Notes
Bobby	7"	Decca	F11365	1961	**£5**	

JOHNNY & JACK

Title	Format	Label	Cat. No.	Year	Price	Notes
Hits	LP	RCA	LPM2017	1959	**£12**	US
Tennessee Mountain Boys	LP	RCA	LPM1587	1957	**£12**	US

JOHNNY & JUDY

Title	Format	Label	Cat. No.	Year	Price	Notes
Bother Me Baby	7"	Vogue	V9128	1959	**£4**	

JOHNNY & THE COPYCATS

Title	Format	Label	Cat. No.	Year	Price	Notes
I'm A Hog For You Baby	7"	Narco	AB102		**£25**	

JOHNNY & THE HURRICANES

Title	Format	Label	Cat. No.	Year	Price	Notes
Beatnik Fly	7"	London	HLI9072	1960	**£4**	chart single
Big Sound	LP	London	HAX2322	1960	**£15**	chart LP
Big Sound Of...	LP	Big Top	121302	1960	**£30**	US
Crossfire	7"	London	HL8899	1959	**£5**	
Down Yonder	7"	London	HLX9134	1960	**£4**	chart single
Greens And Jeans	7"	London	HLX9660	1963	**£5**	
Ja-Da	7"	London	HLX9289	1961	**£4**	chart single
Johnny & The Hurricanes	LP	Warwick	W2007	1959	**£40**	US
Johnny & The Hurricanes	7" EP	London	REX1347	1962	**£8**	
Johnny & The Hurricanes Vol.2	7" EP	London	REX1414	1964	**£8**	
Live At The Star Club	LP	Atila	1030	1962	**£35**	US
Minnesota Fats	7"	London	HLX9617	1962	**£5**	
Money Honey	7"	Stateside	SS347	1964	**£5**	
Old Smokey	7"	London	HLX9378	1961	**£4**	chart single
Red River Rock	LP	London	HA2227	1960	**£20**	
Red River Rock	7"	London	HL8948	1959	**£4**	chart single
Remember Johnny & The Hurricanes	7" EP	United Artists	REM401		**£4**	
Reveille Rock	7"	London	HL9017	1959	**£4**	chart single
Rocking Goose	7"	London	HLX9190	1960	**£4**	chart single
Rocking Goose	7" EP	London	REX1284	1961	**£8**	
Salvation	7"	London	HLX9536	1962	**£5**	
Stormsville	LP	London	HAI2269	1960	**£15**	chart LP
Stormsville	LP	Warwick	W2010	1960	**£30**	US
Traffic Jam	7"	London	HLX9491	1962	**£5**	

JOHNNY & THE SELF ABUSERS

It is unlikely that Johnny & The Self Abusers would have become international stars if they had retained that name. Fortunately they decided to change it to Simple Minds...

Title	Format	Label	Cat. No.	Year	Price	Notes
Saints And Sinners	7"	Chiswick	NS22	1977	**£12**	

JOHNNY'S BOYS

Title	Format	Label	Cat. No.	Year	Price	Notes
Sleepwalk	7"	Decca	F11156	1959	**£4**	

JOHNS, GLYN

Title	Format	Label	Cat. No.	Year	Price	Notes
I'll Follow The Sun	7"	Pye	7N15818	1965	**£6**	
January Blues	7"	Decca	F11478	1962	**£4**	
Mary Anne	7"	Immediate	IM013	1965	**£10**	

JOHNSON, BETTY

Title	Format	Label	Cat. No.	Year	Price	Notes
1492	7"	London	HLU8432	1957	**£8**	
Betty Johnson	LP	Atlantic	8017	1958	**£12**	US
Does Your Heart Beat For Me	7"	London	HLE8839	1959	**£8**	
Dream	7"	London	HLE8678	1958	**£6**	
Dream	7" EP	London	REE1221	1959	**£15**	
Honky Tonk Rock	7"	London	HLU8326	1956	**£15**	
Hoopa Hula	7"	London	HLE8725	1958	**£8**	
I Dreamed	7"	London	HLU8365	1957	**£12**	
I'll Wait	7"	London	HLU8307	1956	**£10**	
Little Blue Man	7"	London	HLE8557	1958	**£8**	
Songs You Heard When You Fell In	LP	Atlantic	8027	1959	**£12**	US
There's Never Been A Night	7"	London	HLE8701	1958	**£12**	

JOHNSON, BLIND WILLIE

Title	Format	Label	Cat. No.	Year	Price	Notes
Treasures Of Nth. American Negro..#2	7" EP	Fontana	TFE17052	1958	**£5**	

JOHNSON, BOB & PETE KNIGHT

Title	Format	Label	Cat. No.	Year	Price	Notes
The King Of Elfland's Daughter	LP	Chrysalis	CHR1137	1977	**£10**	

JOHNSON, BUBBER

Come Home	LP	King	395569	1957	**£40**	US
Confidential	7"	Parlophone	R4259	1957	**£6**	
Sings Sweet Love Songs	LP	King	624	1959	**£30**	US

JOHNSON, BUDDY

Buddy Johnson Wails	LP	Mercury	MG20072	1958	**£15**	US
Buddy Johnson Wails	7" EP	Mercury	ZEP10009	1959	**£5**	
Rock'N'Roll	LP	Mercury	MG20209	1956	**£20**	US
Rock'N'Roll Stage Show	LP	Wing	MGW12005	1956	**£20**	US
Walkin'	LP	Mercury	MG20322	1958	**£15**	US

JOHNSON, BUDDY & ELLA

Go Ahead And Rock And Roll	LP	Roulette	R25085	1959	**£15**	US
Swing Me	LP	Mercury	MG20347	1958	**£12**	US

JOHNSON, GENERAL

All In The Family	7"	Arista	ARIST45	1976	**£5**	

JOHNSON, JAMES P. & FATS WALLER

Louisiana Sugar Babies	7" EP	HMV	7EG8215	1957	**£8**	

JOHNSON, JIMMY

Don't Answer The Door	7"	Sue	WI387	1965	**£8**	

JOHNSON, JOHNNY & BANDWAGON

Breaking Down The Walls Of Heartache	7"	Direction	583670	1968	**£4**	chart single

JOHNSON, LARRY

Presenting The Country Blues	LP	Blue Horizon	763851	1970	**£30**	

JOHNSON, LONNIE

Another Night To Cry	LP	Bluesville	BV1062	1963	**£15**	US
Blues And Ballads	LP	Bluesville	BV1011	1960	**£20**	US
Blues By Lonnie Johnson	LP	Bluesville	BV1007	1960	**£20**	US
Idle Hours	LP	Bluesville	BV1044	1961	**£20**	US
Lonesome Road	LP	King	395520	195-	**£60**	US
Lonesome Road	7" EP	Parlophone	GEP8635	1957	**£6**	
Lonnie's Blues	7" EP	Parlophone	GEP8663	1957	**£6**	
Lonnie's Blues No.2	7" EP	Parlophone	GEP8693	1958	**£6**	
Losing Game	LP	Bluesville	BV1024	1961	**£20**	US
Sings 24 Twelve Bar Blues	LP	King	K958	1966	**£12**	US
Woman Blues	LP	Bluesville	BV1054	1963	**£15**	US

JOHNSON, LOU

Always Something There To ...	7"	London	HLX9917	1964	**£4**	
Magic Potion	7"	London	HLX9805	1963	**£12**	
Magic Potion Of Lou Johnson	7" EP	London	REX1438	1964	**£10**	
Message To Martha	7"	London	HLX9929	1964	**£4**	chart single
Please Stop The Wedding	7"	London	HLX9965	1965	**£5**	
Unsatisfied	7"	London	HLX9994	1965	**£15**	

JOHNSON, MARV

Ain't Gonna Be That Way	7"	London	HLT9165	1960	**£4**	chart single
Come To Me	7"	London	HLT8856	1959	**£8**	
Happy Days	7"	London	HLT9265	1961	**£4**	
I Believe	LP	United Artists	UAL3187	1962	**£15**	US
I Love The Way You Love Me	7"	London	HLT9109	1960	**£4**	chart single
I Miss You Baby	7"	T. Motown	TMG713	1969	**£4**	chart single
I Miss You Baby	7"	T. Motown	TMG713	1969	**£20**	demo
I'll Pick A Rose For My Rose	LP	T. Motown	STML11111	1969	**£15**	
I'll Pick A Rose For My Rose	7"	T. Motown	TMG680	1969	**£5**	chart single
I'll Pick A Rose For My Rose	7"	T. Motown	TMG680	1969	**£20**	demo
Marvellous Marv	LP	London	HAT2271	1960	**£20**	
Merry-Go-Round	7"	London	HLT9311	1961	**£4**	
More Marv Johnson	LP	United Artists	UAL3118	1960	**£15**	US
Move Two Mountains	7"	London	HLT9187	1960	**£4**	
So Glad You Chose Me	7"	T. Motown	TMG737	1970	**£4**	
So Glad You Chose Me	7"	T. Motown	TMG737	1970	**£10**	demo
Why Do You Want To Let Me Go	7"	T. Motown	TMG525	1965	**£10**	
Why Do You Want To Let Me Go	7"	T. Motown	TMG525	1965	**£100**	demo
You Got What It Takes	7"	London	HLT9013	1959	**£5**	chart single

JOHNSON, MATT

Title	Format	Label	Number	Year	Price	Notes
Burning Blue Soul	LP	4AD	CAD113	1981	**£25**	psychedelic eye sleeve

JOHNSON, MIRRIAM

Title	Format	Label	Number	Year	Price	Notes
Lonesome Road	7"	London	HLW9337	1961	**£6**	

JOHNSON, NORMAN

Title	Format	Label	Number	Year	Price	Notes
Take It Baby	7"	Action	ACT4545	1969	**£10**	demo
You're Everything	7"	Action	ACT4601	1971	**£5**	

JOHNSON, NORMAN & THE SHOWMEN

Title	Format	Label	Number	Year	Price	Notes
You're Everything	7"	Action	ACT4529	1969	**£6**	
You're Everything	7"	Action	ACT4529	1969	**£20**	demo

JOHNSON, PETE

Title	Format	Label	Number	Year	Price	Notes
J.J.Boogie	7"	Vogue	V2007	1968	**£8**	
Pete Johnson	7" EP	Vogue	EPV1039	1955	**£10**	
Pete's Blues	LP	Savoy	MG14018	195-	**£15**	US
Roll Em Boy	7" EP	Top Rank	JKR8009	1959	**£10**	
Swanee River Boogie	7"	Vogue	V2008	1968	**£8**	

JOHNSON, PLAS

Title	Format	Label	Number	Year	Price	Notes
Big Twist	7"	Capitol	CL14772	1957	**£4**	
Dinah	7"	Capitol	CL14903	1958	**£4**	
Popcorn	7"	Capitol	CL14836	1958	**£4**	
Robbins Nest Cha Cha	7"	Capitol	CL14973	1959	**£4**	
You Send Me	7"	Capitol	CL14816	1957	**£5**	

JOHNSON, RAY

Title	Format	Label	Number	Year	Price	Notes
If You Don't Want Me Baby	7"	Vogue	V9073	1957	**£8**	

JOHNSON, ROY LEE

Title	Format	Label	Number	Year	Price	Notes
So Anna Just Love Me	7"	Action	ACT4518	1969	**£4**	
So Anna Just Love Me	7"	Action	ACT4518	1969	**£15**	demo

JOHNSON, RUBY

Title	Format	Label	Number	Year	Price	Notes
If I Ever Needed Love	7"	Stax	601020	1967	**£5**	

JOHNSTON BROTHERS

Title	Format	Label	Number	Year	Price	Notes
In The Middle Of The House	7"	Decca	F10781	1956	**£5**	chart single
Sh'boom	7"	Decca	F10364	1954	**£4**	

JOHNSTON, BRUCE

Title	Format	Label	Number	Year	Price	Notes
Original Surfer Stomp	7"	London	HL9780	1963	**£15**	
Surfer's Pajama Party	LP	Del-Fi	DFLP1228	1963	**£30**	US
Surfin' Round The World	LP	Columbia	CL2057	1963	**£40**	US

JOHNSTONE, DAVEY

Title	Format	Label	Number	Year	Price	Notes
Smiling Face	LP	Rocket	ROLA2	1973	**£10**	

JOHNSTONS

Title	Format	Label	Number	Year	Price	Notes
Give A Damn	LP	Transatlantic	TRA184	1968	**£10**	

JOKERS

Title	Format	Label	Number	Year	Price	Notes
Dogfight	7"	Salvo	SLO1806	1962	**£8**	

JOKERS WILD

The ultra-collectability of the Jokers Wild's privately pressed record derives not so much from the fact that the drummer, Willie Wilson, was later in Quiver, nor from the fact that the bassist, Ricky Wills, was later in Cochise and the re-formed Small Faces, but from the presence of the lead guitarist, who is David Gilmour - subsequently to be found playing within the ranks of Pink Floyd.

Title	Format	Label	Number	Year	Price	Notes
Don't Ask Me Why	7"	private		1966	**£250**	
Jokers Wild	LP	private		1966	**£600**	1 sided

JOLLIVER ARKANSAW

Title	Format	Label	Number	Year	Price	Notes
Home	LP	Bell	SBLL119	1969	**£20**	US

JOLT

Title	Format	Label	Number	Year	Price	Notes
I Can't Explain	7"			1978	**£4**	
Jolt	7"	Polydor	2383504	1978	**£4**	
Maybe Tonight	7"	Polydor	2229215	1979	**£4**	
Route 66	7"	Polydor	2059039	1978	**£4**	

Title	Format	Label	Catalogue No.	Year	Price	Notes
What'cha Gonna Do About It	7"	Polydor	2059008	1978	**£4**	
You're Cold	7"	Polydor	2058936	1977	**£4**	

JON / ROBIN & THE IN CROWD

Title	Format	Label	Catalogue No.	Year	Price	Notes
Do It Again A Little Bit Slower	7"	Stateside	SS2027	1967	**£5**	

JON & VANGELIS

Title	Format	Label	Catalogue No.	Year	Price	Notes
Friends Of Mr.Cairo	12"	Polydor	POSPX258	1981	**£10**	blue metal can

JONES, AL

Title	Format	Label	Catalogue No.	Year	Price	Notes
Mad Mad World	7"	HMV	POP451	1958	**£8**	

JONES, BEVERLY

Title	Format	Label	Catalogue No.	Year	Price	Notes
Heatwave	7"	Parlophone	R5189	1964	**£4**	
Wait Until My Bobby Gets Home	7"	HMV	POP1201	1963	**£4**	
Why Do Lovers Break Each Others' ...	7"	HMV	POP1140	1963	**£4**	

JONES, BRIAN

Title	Format	Label	Catalogue No.	Year	Price	Notes
Pipes Of Pan At Joujouka	LP	R. Stones	COC49100	1971	**£30**	

JONES, CAROL

Title	Format	Label	Catalogue No.	Year	Price	Notes
Boys With Eyes Of Blue	7"	Triumph	RGM1012	1960	**£6**	

JONES, CASEY & THE ENGINEERS

Title	Format	Label	Catalogue No.	Year	Price	Notes
One Way Ticket	7"	Columbia	DB7083	1963	**£12**	

JONES, CURTIS

Title	Format	Label	Catalogue No.	Year	Price	Notes
Now Resident In Europe	LP	Blue Horizon	763207	1968	**£30**	
RCA Victor Race Series Vol.9	7" EP	RCA	RCX7184	1966	**£8**	

JONES, DAVY

Title	Format	Label	Catalogue No.	Year	Price	Notes
Davy Jones	LP	Bell	6067	1971	**£10**	US
Davy Jones	LP	Pye	NPL18178	1967	**£20**	
It Ain't Me Babe	7"	Pye	7N17302	1967	**£4**	
Theme For A New Love	7"	Pye	7N17380	1967	**£4**	

JONES, GEORGE

Title	Format	Label	Catalogue No.	Year	Price	Notes
Accidentally On Purpose	7"	Mercury	AMT1100	1960	**£6**	
Ballad Side Of George Jones	LP	Mercury	MG20836	1963	**£10**	US
Best Of American Country Music Vol.4	7" EP	Ember	EMB4548	1964	**£4**	
Big Harlen Taylor	7"	Mercury	AMT1078	1959	**£4**	
Blue And Lonesome	LP	Mercury	MG20906	1964	**£10**	US
C & W Aces	7" EP	Mercury	10009MCE	1964	**£6**	
Candy Hearts	7"	Mercury	AMT1124	1961	**£4**	
Country & Western #1 Male Singer	LP	Mercury	MG20937	1964	**£10**	US
Country And Western Hits	LP	Mercury	MG20624	1961	**£10**	US
Country Church Time	LP	Mercury	MG20462	1959	**£20**	US
Country Heart	LP	Musicor	P25094	1966	**£10**	US
Country Song Hits	7" EP	Melodisc	EPM7109	196-	**£10**	
Crown Prince Of Country Music	LP	Starday	SLP125	1960	**£15**	US
Fabulous Country Music Sound	LP	Starday	SLP151	1962	**£15**	US
Fourteen Country Favourites	LP	Mercury	MG20306	1958	**£20**	US
From The Heart	LP	Mercury	MG20694	1962	**£10**	US
George Jones	7" EP	Mercury	ZEP10036	1959	**£10**	
George Jones Salutes Hank Williams	LP	Mercury	MG20257	1958	**£12**	US
George Jones Sings Like The Dickens	LP	United Artists	UAL3364	1964	**£10**	US
George Jones Story	LP	Starday	SLP366	1966	**£15**	US
Grand Ole Opry's New Star	LP	Starday	SLP101	1958	**£50**	US
Greatest Hits	LP	London	HAB8125	1964	**£12**	
Heartaches And Tears	LP	Mercury	MG20990	1965	**£10**	US
Musical Loves, Life And Sorrows...	LP	Musicor	MS3159	1968	**£10**	US
Novelty Side Of George Jones	LP	Mercury	MG20793	1963	**£15**	US
Race Is On	7"	United Artists	UP1080	1965	**£4**	
She Thinks I Still Care	7"	HMV	POP1037	1962	**£4**	
Singing The Blues	LP	Mercury	MG21029	1965	**£10**	US
Song Book And Picture Album	LP	Starday	SLP401	1967	**£15**	US
Treasure Of Love	7"	Mercury	AMT1021	1959	**£4**	
White Lightning	7"	Mercury	AMT1036	1959	**£8**	
White Lightning And Other Favorites	LP	Mercury	MG20477	1959	**£20**	US
Who Shot Sam	7"	Mercury	AMT1058	1959	**£8**	

JONES, GEORGE & JIMMIE SKINNER

Title	Format	Label	Cat. No.	Year	Price	Notes
Country And Western	7" EP	Mercury	ZEP10012	1959	**£10**	

JONES, GEORGE & MARGIE SINGLETON

Title	Format	Label	Cat. No.	Year	Price	Notes
Duets Country Style	LP	Mercury	MG20747	1962	**£10**	US

JONES, GLORIA

Title	Format	Label	Cat. No.	Year	Price	Notes
Finders Keepers	7"	Stateside	SS555	1966	**£8**	
Get It On	7"	EMI	EMI2437	1976	**£4**	
Heartbeat	7"	Capitol	CL15429	1966	**£8**	
Tin Can People	7"	T. Motown	TMG910	1974	**£5**	

JONES, GRACE

Title	Format	Label	Cat. No.	Year	Price	Notes
I Need A Man	7"	Polydor	2058898	1977	**£4**	
La Vie En Rose	12"	Island	IPR2004	1986	**£8**	
My Jamaican Guy	7"	Island	ISP103	1983	**£5**	pic disc
Party Girl	7"	Manhattan	MTP20	1987	**£5**	shaped pic disc
Slave To The Rhythm	7"	ZTT	ISP206	1985	**£4**	pic disc
Slave To The Rhythm	12"	ZTT	12IS206	1985	**£6**	with poster
Slave To The Rhythm	12"	ZTT	12ISP206	1985	**£6**	pic disc
That's The Trouble	7"	Polydor	2058856	1977	**£4**	

JONES, GRANDPA

Title	Format	Label	Cat. No.	Year	Price	Notes
Country And Western	7" EP	Parlophone	GEP8766	1958	**£10**	
Country Round Up	7" EP	Parlophone	GEP8781	1959	**£8**	
Dark As A Dungeon	7"	Brunswick	05676	1957	**£6**	
Do You Remember?	LP	King	845	1963	**£15**	US
Evening With...	LP	Decca	DL4364	1963	**£10**	US
Grandpa Sings Jimmie Rodgers	7" EP	London	REU1417	1964	**£8**	
Greatest Hits	LP	King	554	1958	**£15**	US
Make The Rafters Ring	LP	London	HAU8010	1962	**£10**	
Meet Grandpa Jones	7" EP	Parlophone	GEP8666	1957	**£8**	
Mountain Music Vol.3	7" EP	Brunswick	OE9455	1959	**£8**	
Other Side Of...	LP	King	888	1964	**£12**	US
Rollin' Along	LP	King	809	1963	**£15**	US
Sixteen Sacred Gospel Songs	LP	King	822	1963	**£15**	US
Strictly Country Tunes	LP	King	625	1959	**£15**	US
Yodelling Hits	LP	London	HAU8119	1964	**£10**	

JONES, JANIE

Title	Format	Label	Cat. No.	Year	Price	Notes
Gunning For You	7"	HMV	POP1514	1966	**£4**	
Tickle Me Tootsie Wootsies	7"	Columbia	DB8173	1967	**£4**	
Witches Brew	7"	HMV	POP1495	1965	**£4**	chart single

JONES, JIMMY

Title	Format	Label	Cat. No.	Year	Price	Notes
39-21-46	7"	Stateside	SS2041	1967	**£4**	
Good Timin'	LP	MGM	C832	1960	**£15**	
Good Timin'	7"	MGM	MGM1078	1960	**£4**	chart single
Handy Man	7"	MGM	MGM1051	1960	**£4**	chart single
I Just Go For You	7"	MGM	MGM1091	1960	**£4**	chart single
I Told You So	7"	MGM	MGM1123	1961	**£4**	chart single
Jimmy Handyman Jones	7" EP	MGM	MGMEP745	1960	**£10**	
Ready For Love	7"	MGM	MGM1103	1960	**£4**	chart single

JONES, JOE

Title	Format	Label	Cat. No.	Year	Price	Notes
You Talk Too Much	7"	Columbia	DB4533	1960	**£4**	
You Talk Too Much	LP	Roulette	R25143	1961	**£15**	US

JONES, JOHN PAUL

Title	Format	Label	Cat. No.	Year	Price	Notes
Baja	7"	Pye	7N15637	1964	**£50**	

JONES, KEN

Title	Format	Label	Cat. No.	Year	Price	Notes
Joxsville	7"	Parlophone	R4788	1961	**£4**	
On The Rebound	7"	Parlophone	R4763	1961	**£4**	

JONES, LINDA

Title	Format	Label	Cat. No.	Year	Price	Notes
Hypnotised	LP	Loma	5907	1967	**£12**	US
Hypnotised	7"	W. Bros	WB2070	1967	**£20**	
I Just Can't Live My Life	7"	W. Bros	K16621	1975	**£5**	
Your Precious Love	LP	Turbo	7007	196-	**£12**	US

JONES, NIGEL MAZLYN

Breaking Cover	LP	Isle Of L.	IOL0230	1982	**£20**	
Sentinel	LP	Avada	AVA105	1978	**£25**	
Ship To Shore	LP	Isle Of L.	IOL666/1	1976	**£40**	

JONES, PAUL

And The Sun Will Shine	7"	Columbia	DB8379	1968	**£5**	
Aquarius	7"	Columbia	DB8514	1969	**£4**	chart single
Come Into My Music Box	LP	Columbia		1969	**£25**	
Crucifix In A Horseshoe	LP	Vertigo	6360059	1971	**£20**	spiral label
High Time	7"	HMV	POP1554	1966	**£4**	chart single
I've Been A Bad Bad Boy	7"	HMV	POP1576	1967	**£4**	chart single
It's Getting Better	7"	Columbia	DB8567	1969	**£4**	
Love Me Love My Friends	LP	HMV	CSD3602	1967	**£20**	
My Way	LP	HMV	CLP3586	1966	**£20**	
Privilege	LP	HMV	CLP3523	1966	**£20**	
Privilege	7" EP	HMV	7EG8974	1966	**£5**	
Sheena Is A Punk Rocker	7"	RSO	RSO003	1978	**£4**	
Sons And Lovers	7"	Columbia	DB8303	1967	**£4**	
Thinkin' Ain't For Me POP1602	7"	HMV		1967	**£4**	chart single
When I Was Six Years Old	7"	Columbia	DB8417	1968	**£4**	

JONES, RONNIE

I Need Your Loving	7"	Decca	F12012	1964	**£5**	

JONES, RONNIE & THE BLUEJAYS

I'm So Clean	7"	Parlophone	R5326	1965	**£4**	

JONES, SAMANTHA

And Suddenly	7"	United Artists	UP2258	1968	**£20**	
Surrounded By A Ray Of Sunshine	7"	United Artists	UP1185	1967	**£15**	

JONES, THELMA

House That Jack Built	7"	Soul City	SC110		**£5**	
House That Jack Built	7"	Soul City	SC110		**£12**	demo
Stranger	7"	Sue	WI4047	1968	**£8**	

JONES, TOM

Chills And Fever	7"	Decca	F11966	1964	**£4**	
It's Not Unusual	7"	Decca	F12062	1965	**£4**	chart single
Little Lonely One	7"	Columbia	DB7566	1965	**£4**	
Lonely Joe	7"	Columbia	DB7733	1965	**£4**	
Tom Jones	7" EP	Columbia	SEG8464	1965	**£5**	

JONES, U.K.

Let Me Tell Ya	7"	Deram	DM231	1969	**£5**	

JONES, WIZZ

Legendary Me	LP	Village Thing		1970	**£15**	
Right Now	LP	CBS		1971	**£25**	
Sixteen Tones Of Bluegrass	LP	Columbia		1966	**£30**	US
When I Leave Berlin	LP	Village Thing		1974	**£15**	

JONESY

Growing	LP	Dawn	DNLS3055	1973	**£20**	
Keeping Up	LP	Dawn	DNLS3048	1973	**£20**	
No Alternative	LP	Dawn	DNLS3042	1972	**£25**	
Ricochet	7"	Dawn	DNS1030	1972	**£6**	

JONNS, HARLEM RESHUFFLE

Everything Under The Sun	7"	Fontana	TF1004	1969	**£5**	
You Are The One I Love	7"	Fontana	TF970	1968	**£5**	

JONSTON MCPHILBRY

She's Gone	7"	Fontana	TF663	1966	**£5**	

JOOK

Alright With Me	7"	RCA	RCA2279	1972	**£5**	
Bish Bash Bosh	7"	RCA	RCA5024	1974	**£4**	
Oo Oo Rudi	7"	RCA	RCA2368	1973	**£4**	
Shame	7"	RCA	RCA2344	1973	**£4**	
Watch Your Step	7"	Chiswick	SW30	1978	**£4**	

JOPLIN, JANIS

Title	Format	Label	Cat. No.	Year	Price	Notes
Cry Baby	7"	CBS	7217	1971	**£4**	
Down On Me	7"	CBS	8241	1972	**£4**	
Me And Bobby McGhee	7"	CBS	7019	1971	**£4**	
Move Over	7"	CBS	9136	1971	**£5**	
Piece Of My Heart	7"	CBS	3960	1976	**£4**	PS

JORDAN BROTHERS

Title	Format	Label	Cat. No.	Year	Price	Notes
Never Never	7"	London	HLW8908	1959	**£4**	
No Wings On My Angel	7"	London	HLW9308	1961	**£4**	
Things I Didn't Say	7"	London	HLW9235	1960	**£4**	

JORDAN, LOUIS

Title	Format	Label	Cat. No.	Year	Price	Notes
Go Blow Your Horn	LP	Score	4007	195-	**£50**	US
Greatest Hits	LP	Decca	DL5035	1967	**£12**	US
Let The Good Times Roll	LP	Ace Of H.	AH85	1965	**£15**	
Let The Good Times Roll	LP	Coral	CP59	1970	**£10**	
Let The Good Times Roll	LP	Decca	DL8551	1958	**£20**	US
Louis Jordan	7" EP	Melodisc	EPM766	195-	**£20**	
Man, We're Wailin'	LP	Mercury	MG20331	1958	**£20**	US
Ooo Wee	7"	Downbeat	CHA3	1960	**£8**	
Somebody Up There Digs Me	LP	Mercury	MG20242	1957	**£20**	US

JORDANAIRES

Title	Format	Label	Cat. No.	Year	Price	Notes
Beautiful City	LP-10"	RCA	LPM3081	1953	**£20**	US
Don't Be Cruel	7"	Capitol	CL15281	1963	**£8**	
Gloryland	LP	Capitol	T1167	1959	**£10**	US
Heavenly Spirit	LP	Capitol	T1011	1958	**£10**	US
Little Miss Ruby	7"	Capitol	CL14921	1958	**£6**	
Peace In The Valley	LP	Decca	DL8681	1957	**£15**	US
Sugaree	7"	Capitol	CL14687	1957	**£12**	
Summer Vacation	7"	Capitol	CL14773	1957	**£6**	

JOSEF K

Title	Format	Label	Cat. No.	Year	Price	Notes
Chance Meeting	7"	Absolute	ABS1	1980	**£20**	
Chance Meeting	7"	Postcard	81-5	1981	**£8**	
Chance Meeting	7"	Postcard	81-5	1981	**£10**	lyric postcard
It's Kinda Funny	7"	Postcard	80-5	1980	**£8**	
It's Kinda Funny	7"	Postcard	80-5	1980	**£20**	colour insert in bag
Missionary	7"	Crepuscule	TWI053	1982	**£8**	
Only Fun In Town	LP	Postcard	81-7	1981	**£15**	
Radio Drill Time	7"	Postcard	80-3	1980	**£8**	
Radio Drill Time	7"	Postcard	80-3	1980	**£20**	poster sleeve
Radio Drill Time	7"	Postcard	80-3	1980	**£25**	with poster
Sorry For Laughing	7"	Crepuscule	TWI023	1981	**£8**	
Sorry For Laughing	LP	Postcard	81-1	1981	**£150**	test pressing
Sorry For Laughing	LP	Postcard	81-1	1981	**£300**	unfinished sleeve

JOSEFUS

Title	Format	Label	Cat. No.	Year	Price	Notes
Dead Man	LP	Hookah	330	1969	**£75**	US
Josefus	LP	Mainstream	6127	1970	**£20**	US

JOURNEY

Title	Format	Label	Cat. No.	Year	Price	Notes
Departure	LP	Columbia	HC46339	1981	**£12**	US audiophile
Don't Stop Believing	12"	CBS	12A1728	1982	**£6**	pic disc
Dream After Dream	LP	Columbia	HC47998	1982	**£12**	US audiophile
Escape	LP	Columbia	HC47408	1981	**£15**	US audiophile
Escape	LP	Mobile Fid.	MFSL1144	1981	**£50**	US audiophile
Infinity	LP	Columbia	HC4912	1981	**£12**	US audiophile
Look Into The Future	LP	Columbia	PCQ33904	1976	**£10**	US quad

JOURNEYMEN

Title	Format	Label	Cat. No.	Year	Price	Notes
Introducing The...	LP	Ember	EMB3382	1967	**£15**	
Journeymen	LP	Capitol	T1629	1961	**£15**	US
Live	LP	Capitol		1962	**£25**	US
New Directions In Folk Music	LP	Capitol	T1951	1963	**£15**	US

JOY & DAVID

Title	Format	Label	Cat. No.	Year	Price	Notes
Joe's Been A Gitting There	7"	Parlophone	R4855	1961	**£5**	
Let's Go See Grandma	7"	Triumph	RGM1002	1960	**£6**	
My Very Good Friend The Milkman	7"	Decca	F11291	1960	**£6**	

Title	Format	Label	Number	Year	Price	Notes
Rocking Away The Blues	7"	Decca	F11123	1959	**£4**	
Whoopee	7"	Parlophone	R4477	1958	**£4**	

JOY DIVISION

Title	Format	Label	Number	Year	Price	Notes
Atmosphere	7"	Sordide S.	SS33002	1980	**£100**	A4 folder
Ideal Beginning	7"	Enigma	PSS138	1981	**£15**	
Ideal For Living	12"	Anonymous	ANON1	1978	**£60**	
Ideal For Living	7"	Enigma	PSS139	1978	**£100**	
Komakino	7"	Factory	FAC28	1980	**£4**	flexi
Still	LP	Factory	FACT40	1981	**£15**	double, hard cloth cover

JOY DIVISION & OTHERS

Title	Format	Label	Number	Year	Price	Notes
Earcom 2	12"	Fast Prod.	FAST9	1979	**£12**	
Factory Sample	7" EP	Factory	FAC2	1979	**£35**	double, 5 stickers

JOY UNLIMITED

Title	Format	Label	Number	Year	Price	Notes
Daytime Night Time	7"	Page One	POF23147	1969	**£5**	
Oh Darlin'	7"	Page One	POF23160	1969	**£5**	
Turbulence	LP	Page One	POLS028	1970	**£15**	

JOY, CARL & THE JOYBOYS

Title	Format	Label	Number	Year	Price	Notes
Be My Girl	7"	Top Rank	JAR529	1961	**£4**	
Bye Bye Baby Goodbye	7"	Brunswick	05806	1959	**£4**	

JSD BAND

Title	Format	Label	Number	Year	Price	Notes
Country Of The Blind	LP	Regal Z.	SLRZ1018	1971	**£15**	
JSD Band	LP	Fly	HIFLY11	1972	**£10**	
Travelling Days	LP	Cube	HIFLY14	1973	**£10**	

JUDAS JUMP

Title	Format	Label	Number	Year	Price	Notes
Beer Drinking Woman	7"	Parlophone	R5873	1970	**£5**	
Run For Your Life	7"	Parlophone	R5828	1970	**£5**	
Scorch	LP	Parlophone	PAS10001	1970	**£12**	
This Feelin' We Feel	7"	Parlophone	R5838	1970	**£6**	

JUDAS PRIEST

Title	Format	Label	Number	Year	Price	Notes
Best Of...	LP	Gull	PGULP1026	1978	**£10**	pic disc
Evening Star	12"	CBS	127312	1979	**£6**	clear vinyl fake pic disc
Love Bites	12"	Atlantic		1988	**£15**	pic disc
Ripper	7"	Gull	GULS31	1976	**£4**	
Rocka Rolla	7"	Gull	GUL86	1974	**£4**	
You've Got Another Thing Comin'	7"	CBS	A112611	1982	**£4**	pic disc

JUDD

Title	Format	Label	Number	Year	Price	Notes
Judd	LP	P. Farthing	PEL504	1969	**£12**	
Snarlin' Mama Lion	7"	P. Farthing	PEN709	1970	**£4**	

JUDGE, TERRY & THE BARRISTERS

Title	Format	Label	Number	Year	Price	Notes
Come With Me And Love Me	7"	Fontana	TF599	1965	**£8**	
Hey Look At Her	7"	Oriole	CB1896	1963	**£4**	
I Don't Care	7"	Oriole	CB1938	1964	**£4**	

JUG TRUST

Title	Format	Label	Number	Year	Price	Notes
Cat And Mouse	7"	Parlophone	R5825	1970	**£4**	

JUICE ON THE LOOSE

Title	Format	Label	Number	Year	Price	Notes
Juice On The Loose	LP	Juice	JJOS1	1981	**£15**	

JUICY LUCY

Title	Format	Label	Number	Year	Price	Notes
Get A Whiff Of This	LP	Bronze	ILPS9157	1971	**£15**	
Juicy Lucy	LP	Vertigo	VO2	1969	**£20**	spiral label, chart LP
Lie Back & Enjoy It	LP	Vertigo	6360014	1970	**£20**	spiral label, chart LP
Pieces	LP	Polydor	2310160	1972	**£12**	
Who Do You Love	7"	Vertigo	V1	1970	**£4**	chart single
Pretty Woman	7"	Vertigo	6059015	1970	**£4**	chart single

JULIAN

Title	Format	Label	Number	Year	Price	Notes
Sue Saturday	7"	Pye	7N15236	1959	**£4**	

JULIAN'S TREATMENT

Title	Format	Label	Number	Year	Price	Notes
Phantom City	7"	Youngblood	YB1009	1972	**£8**	
Time Before This	LP	Youngblood	SYB2	1972	**£70**	double

JULY

The LP by July is a typical piece of psychedelia from 1968 - full of interesting ideas and sounds, but definitely a formative record for the musicians involved. These include Tony Duhig and Jon Field, who went on to form Jade Warrior, and Tom Newman, later a solo artist and also studio engineer for Virgin records.

Hello Who's There	7"	Major Minor	MM580	1968	**£20**	
July	LP	Major Minor	SMLP29	1968	**£200**	
My Clown	7"	Major Minor	MM568	1968	**£20**	

JUMBLE LANE

Jumble Lane	LP	Holyground		1971	**£150**	

JUMBO

Jumbo	LP	Philips			**£50**	

JUMPING JACKS

Lady Play Your Mandolin	7"	Capitol	CL14597	1956	**£4**	
Tried And Tested	7"	HMV	POP440	1958	**£5**	

JUNCO PARTNERS

As Long As I Have You	7"	Columbia	DB7665	1965	**£12**	
Junco Partners	LP	Philips	6308032	1971	**£30**	

JUNE, ROSANNE

Charge Of The Light Brigade	7"	London	HLU8352	1956	**£6**	

JUNIOR'S EYES

Battersea Power Station	LP	Regal Z.	SLRZ1008	1969	**£30**	
Mr.Golden Trumpet Player	7"	Regal Z.	RZ3009	1968	**£12**	
Star Child	7"	Regal Z.	RZ3023	1969	**£10**	
Woman Love	7"	Regal Z.	RZ3018	1969	**£10**	

JUNIORS

There's A Pretty Girl	7"	Columbia	DB7339	1964	**£6**	

JUNOFF, LENA

Yesterday Has Gone	7"	Olga	008		**£15**	

JUPITER

Life Is Getting Better All The Time	7"	Parlophone	R5967	1972	**£4**	

JUPP, ERIC ORCHESTRA

Eric Jupp & His Orchestra	7" EP	Columbia	SEG7589	1956	**£8**	
Perfect Combination	7" EP	Columbia	SEG7621	1956	**£6**	
Rhythm And Blues	7" EP	Columbia	SEG7603	1956	**£8**	

JUPP, MICKY

Nature's Radio	7"	Stiff	UPP1	197-	**£8**	promo

JUST FOUR MEN

Don't Come Any Closer	7"	Parlophone	R5241	1965	**£10**	
That's My Baby	7"	Parlophone	R5208	1964	**£8**	

JUSTICE, JIMMY

Ain't That Funny	7"	Pye	7N15443	1962	**£4**	chart single
I'm Past Forgetting	7"	RCA	RCA1681	1968	**£15**	
Jimmy Justice Hit Parade	7" EP	Pye	NEP24159	1962	**£6**	
Smash Hits	LP	Pye	NPL18085	1962	**£10**	
Spanish Harlem	7"	Pye	7N15457	1962	**£4**	chart single
Two Sides Of	LP	Pye	NPL18080	1962	**£10**	
When My Little Girl Is Smiling	7"	Pye	7N15421	1962	**£4**	chart single

JUSTIFIED ANCIENTS OF MU MU

"1987" is an entirely brilliant example of the art of disc jockey-as-producer, consisting of a kaleidoscope of bits of other people's records welded together into an inspired whole. Unfortunately, some of these other people - Benny Andersson and Bjorn Ulvaeus of Abba to be precise - took exception to their music being used in this way and obtained a court order for the recall of all remaining copies of the record. In a way, the JAMMS were able to have the last laugh, for they later successfully advertised "the last remaining five copies" of the record at 1000 each.

1987	LP	KLF	JAMSLP1	1987	**£40**	
All You Need Is Love	7"	KLF	JAMS23	1987	**£12**	
All You Need Is Love	12"	KLF	JAMS23T	1987	**£15**	
Deep Shit	7"	KLF	DS1	1987	**£10**	flexi

JUSTINE

Title	Format	Label	Cat. No.	Year	Price	Notes
Justine	LP	Uni	UNLS111	1970	**£10**	
Right Now	7"	Buffalo	BFS1001	1982	**£4**	
She Brings Back The Morning With Her	7"	Uni	UNS528	1970	**£4**	

JUSTIS, BILL

Title	Format	Label	Cat. No.	Year	Price	Notes
Cloud Nine	LP	Philips	1950	1959	**£100**	US
College Man	7"	London	HLS8614	1958	**£5**	
Raunchy	7"	London	HLS8517	1957	**£5**	chart single

JUVENILES

Title	Format	Label	Cat. No.	Year	Price	Notes
Bo Diddley	7"	Pye	7N25349	1966	**£50**	

K, MOSES & THE PROPHETS

Title	Format	Label	Number	Year	Price	Notes
I Went Out With My Baby Tonight	7"	Decca	F12244	1965	**£4**	

KAK

Title	Format	Label	Number	Year	Price	Notes
Kak	LP	Epic	BN26429	1969	**£40**	US

KALA

Title	Format	Label	Number	Year	Price	Notes
Kala	LP	Bradleys	BRADL1002	1973	**£10**	

KALEIDOSCOPE

The two LPs made by Kaleidoscope were among the first of the more obscure psychedelic records to attract the attention of collectors. Accordingly, they reached the hundred pound mark some time before other similar records, but have stayed there while more recent "discoveries" have leap frogged ahead. In truth, the records are interesting, but lack the finesse of the established classics of the period (like "Music From A Doll's House" or "Dear Mr.Fantasy"). They have the kudos of rarity, but, as is usually the case, their lack of renown is not without reason.

Title	Format	Label	Number	Year	Price	Notes
Balloon	7"	Fontana	TF1048	1969	**£25**	
Do It Again For Jeffrey	7"	Fontana	TF1002	1969	**£20**	
Dream For Julie	7"	Fontana	TF895	1968	**£20**	
Faintly Blowing	LP	Fontana	STL5491	1969	**£100**	
Flight From Ashiya	7"	Fontana	TF863	1967	**£25**	PS
Jenny Artichoke	7"	Fontana	TF964	1968	**£20**	
Tangerine Dream	LP	Fontana	TL5448	1967	**£100**	

KALEIDOSCOPE (US)

The American Kaleidoscope had a sound like no other group of the time. Over the course of three LPs ("Bernice" is an unfortunate fall from grace; "When Scopes Collide is a later attempt at a reunion) and culminating with the magnificent "Incredible", which entirely lives up to its name, the group maintained a questing, innovative approach. A key factor was their fascination with Middle Eastern music, which gives some of Kaleidoscope's material a world music flavour very much ahead of its time. Both Chris Darrow and David Lindley have recorded much music since Kaleidoscope's demise, although little of it has been in the same league.

Title	Format	Label	Number	Year	Price	Notes
Beacon From Mars	LP	Epic	BN26333	1968	**£40**	US
Bernice	LP	CBS	64005	1970	**£10**	
Incredible	LP	Epic	BN26467	1969	**£20**	US
Side Trips	LP	Epic	BN26305	1967	**£30**	US
When Scopes Collide	LP	Island	ILPS9462	1976	**£10**	

KALEN, KITTY

Title	Format	Label	Number	Year	Price	Notes
It's A Lonesome Old Town	LP	Decca	DL8397	1958	**£15**	US
Little Things Mean A Lot	LP	Vocalion	VL3679	1959	**£12**	US
Pretty Kitty Kalen Sings	LP-10"	Mercury	MG25206	195-	**£20**	US

KALIN TWINS

Title	Format	Label	Number	Year	Price	Notes
Chicken Thief	7"	Brunswick	05826	1960	**£4**	
Cool	7"	Brunswick	05797	1959	**£4**	
Forget Me Not	7"	Brunswick	05759	1958	**£4**	
Kalin Twins	7" EP	Brunswick	OE9449	1959	**£10**	
Kalin Twins	LP	Decca	DL8812	1958	**£30**	US
Meaning Of The Blues	7"	Brunswick	05814	1959	**£4**	
Momma Poppa	7"	Brunswick	05848	1961	**£4**	
Oh My Goodness	7"	Brunswick	05775	1959	**£4**	
One More Time	7"	Brunswick	05862	1961	**£4**	
Sweet Sugar Lips	7"	Brunswick	05803	1959	**£4**	
When	7"	Brunswick	05751	1958	**£5**	chart single
When	7" EP	Brunswick	OE9383	1958	**£10**	
Zing Went The Strings Of My Heart	7"	Brunswick	05844	1960	**£4**	

KANE GANG

Title	Format	Label	Number	Year	Price	Notes
Motor Town	CDV			198-	**£20**	promo CD video

KANE, AMORY

Title	Format	Label	Number	Year	Price	Notes
Him Or Me	7"	CBS	5111	1970	**£4**	
Just To Be There	LP	CBS	63849	1970	**£12**	

Title	Format	Label	Number	Year	Price	Notes
Memories Of Time Unwound	LP	MCA	MUPS348	1968	**£12**	
Reflections Of Your Face	7"	MCA	MU1036	1968	**£5**	
You Were On My Mind	7"	UNI	UNS518	1970	**£4**	

KANE, EDEN

Title	Format	Label	Number	Year	Price	Notes
Boys Cry	7"	Fontana	TF438	1964	**£4**	chart single
Come Back	7"	Fontana	TF413	1963	**£4**	
Eden Kane	LP	Ace Of Clubs	ACL1133	1962	**£30**	
Eden Kane Hits	7" EP	Decca	DFE8503	1962	**£5**	
Forget Me Not	7"	Decca	F11418	1962	**£4**	chart single
Get Lost	7"	Decca	F11381	1961	**£4**	chart single
Hangin' Around	7"	Fontana	TF508	1964	**£4**	
Hot Chocolate Crazy	7"	Pye	7N15284	1960	**£4**	
House To Let	7"	Decca	F11504	1962	**£4**	
I Don't Know Why	7"	Decca	F11460	1962	**£4**	chart single
If You Want This Love	7"	Fontana	TF582	1965	**£4**	
It's Eden	LP	Fontana	TL5211	1964	**£40**	
It's Eden	7" EP	Fontana	TFE17424	1964	**£6**	
Magic Town	7"	Decca	F12342	1966	**£4**	
Rain Rain Go Away	7"	Fontana	TF462	1964	**£4**	
Six Great New Swingers	7" EP	Decca	DFE8567	1964	**£6**	
Smoke Gets In Your Eyes	LP	Wing		1966	**£20**	
Sounds Funny To Me	7"	Decca	F11568	1963	**£4**	
Tomorrow Night	7"	Fontana	TF398	1963	**£4**	
Well I Ask You	7"	Decca	F11353	1961	**£4**	chart single
Well I Ask You	7" EP	Decca	DFE6696	1962	**£6**	

KANSAS

Strange how all the groups called after place names seem to have the same sound! Regardless of the musical content, however, the LP "Point Of Know Return" by Kansas has a particularly striking cover, showing a galleon in full sail, just about to fall over the edge of the world. The record is available as a picture disc, which shows off the artwork even more dramatically, but this was unfortunately issued as an American promotional release only and is scarce.

Title	Format	Label	Number	Year	Price	Notes
Leftoverture	LP	Kirshner	HZ44224	1981	**£15**	US audiophile
Point Of Know Return	LP	Kirshner	HZ44929	1981	**£15**	US audiophile
Point Of Know Return	LP	Kirshner	JZ34929	1977	**£30**	US promo pic disc
Vinyl Confessions	LP	Kirshner	HZ48002	1982	**£15**	US audiophile

KANTNER, PAUL

Title	Format	Label	Number	Year	Price	Notes
Baron Von Tollbooth...	LP	Grunt	BFL10148	1973	**£10**	
Blows Against The Empire	LP	RCA	LSP4448	1970	**£60**	US clear vinyl
Blows Against The Empire	LP	RCA	SF8163	1970	**£10**	
Planet Earth Rock'n'Roll Orchestra	LP	RCA	4320	1983	**£12**	US clear vinyl
Sunfighter	LP	Grunt	FTR1002	1971	**£10**	with booklet

KAPLAN

Title	Format	Label	Number	Year	Price	Notes
Do You Believe In Magic	7"	Philips	BF1636	1968	**£5**	
I Love It	7"	Philips	BF1699	1968	**£4**	

KARMEN, STEVE & JIMMY RADCLIFFE

Title	Format	Label	Number	Year	Price	Notes
Breakaway	7"	United Artists	UP35770	1975	**£4**	

KASENETZ-KATZ SINGING ORCHESTRAL CIRCUS

Title	Format	Label	Number	Year	Price	Notes
Down In Tennessee	7"	Pye	7N25472	1968	**£4**	
Quick Joey Small	7"	Buddah	201022	1968	**£4**	chart single
We Can Work It Out	7"	Pye	7N25480	1969	**£4**	

KATCH 22

Title	Format	Label	Number	Year	Price	Notes
100,000 Years	7"	Fontana	TF984	1968	**£5**	
Major Catastrophe	7"	Fontana	TF768	1966	**£6**	
Makin' Up My Mind	7"	Fontana	TF874	1967	**£5**	
Mrs.Jones	7"	CBS	4644	1969	**£5**	
Out Of My Life	7"	Fontana	TF1005	1969	**£5**	
Soft Rock And Allsorts	LP	Saga	EROS8047	1968	**£12**	
World's Getting Smaller	7"	Fontana	TF930	1968	**£4**	

KATE

Title	Format	Label	Number	Year	Price	Notes
Shout It	7"	CBS	4123	1969	**£5**	

KAUFMANN, BOB

Title	Format	Label	Number	Year	Price	Notes
Trip Through A Blown Mind	LP	LHI	12002	1967	**£20**	US

KAUKONEN, JORMA

Quah	LP	Grunt	BFL10209	1975	**£15**	US

KAUKONEN, PETER

Black Kangaroo	LP	Grunt	FTR1006	1971	**£10**	US

KAY, JOHN

Forgotten Songs And Unsung Heroes	LP	Probe	1054	1972	**£10**	
John Kay And The Sparrows	LP	Columbia	CS9758	1970	**£12**	US
My Sporting Life	LP	Probe	8011	1973	**£10**	

KAYAK

Kayak	LP	Harvest	SHSP4036	1974	**£10**	
Royal Bed Bouncer	LP	Vertigo	6360530	1975	**£10**	
See See The Sun	LP	Harvest	SHSP4033	1973	**£10**	
Starlight Dancer	LP	Vertigo	6360856	1977	**£10**	

KAYE, DAVE & THE DYKONS

Yesterday When I Was Young	7"	Major Minor	MM641	1969	**£6**	

KAYE, DAVY

Fool Such As I	7"	Decca	F11866	1964	**£4**	
In My Way	7"	Decca	F12073	1965	**£5**	

KAYE, LINDA

I Can't Stop Thinking About You	7"	Columbia	DB7915	1966	**£8**	

KAYE, THOMAS JEFFERSON

First Grade	LP	ABC	ABCL5048	1974	**£10**	
Thomas Jefferson Kaye	LP	Probe	SPB1074	1973	**£10**	

KAYE, TONY & THE HEARTBEATS

Dream World	7"	Pye	7N25412	1967	**£4**	

KEANE, SHAKE

That's The Voice	LP	Ace Of Clubs	ACL1219	1967	**£10**	

KEFFORD, ACE STAND

For Your Love	7"	Atlantic	584260	1969	**£10**	

KEITH

98.6	LP	Mercury		1967	**£10**	
98.6	7"	Mercury	MF955	1967	**£5**	chart single
Adventures Of Keith	LP	RCA	LSP4143	1969	**£10**	US
Ain't Gonna Lie	7"	Mercury	MF940	1966	**£5**	
Daylight Saving Time	7"	Mercury	MF989	1966	**£5**	
Sugar Man	7"	Mercury	MF1002	1967	**£5**	
Tell Me To My Face	7"	Mercury	MF968	1967	**£4**	chart single

KEITH & ENID

Keith And Enid Sing	LP	Island	ILP901	1963	**£50**	

KEITH, BRIAN

Mean Mama	7"	London	HLU9707	1963	**£4**	

KELLER, JERRY

Here Comes Jerry Keller	LP	London	HAR2261	1960	**£12**	mono
Here Comes Jerry Keller	LP	London	SAHR6083	1960	**£12**	stereo
Here Comes Summer	7"	London	HLR8890	1959	**£4**	chart single
If I Had A Girl	7"	London	HLR8980	1959	**£4**	
Now Now Now	7"	London	HLR9106	1960	**£4**	

KELLUM, MURRAY

Long Tall Texan	7"	London	HLU9830	1964	**£4**	

KELLY BROTHERS

Falling In Love Again	7"	Sue	WI4034	1967	**£15**	
That's What You Mean To Me	7"	Blue Horizon	573177	1970	**£6**	

KELLY, DAVE

Black Blue Kelly	LP	Mercury	6310001	1971	**£60**	
Keeps It In The Family	LP	Mercury	SMCL20151	1969	**£60**	

KELLY, JO ANN

Do It	LP	Red Rag	RRR006	1976	**£25**	
Jo Ann Kelly	LP	CBS	63841	1969	**£40**	
With Fahey, Mann And Miller	LP	Blue Goose	2009	1972	**£15**	US

KELLY, JO ANN & TONY MCPHEE

Same Thing On Their Minds	LP	Sunset	SLS50209	1971	**£30**	

KELLY, JONATHAN

Denver	7"	Parlophone	R5805	1969	**£5**	
Don't You Believe It	7"	Parlophone	R5851	1970	**£8**	
Jonathan Kelly	LP	Parlophone	PCS7114	1970	**£15**	
Make A Stranger Your Friend	7"	Parlophone	R5830	1970	**£5**	
Twice Around The Houses	LP	RCA	SF8262	1972	**£10**	
Two Days In Winter	LP	RCA	SF8415	1975	**£10**	
Wail Till They Change The Backdrop	LP	RCA	SF8353	1973	**£10**	
Waiting On You	LP	RCA	LPL15022	1974	**£10**	

KELLY, PAUL

Chills And Fever	7"	Atlantic	AT4053	1965	**£8**	
Sweet Sweet Lovin'	7"	Philips	BF1591	1967	**£5**	

KEMP, WAYNE

Watch Your Step	7"	Atlantic	584006	1966	**£4**	

KEN, ROD & THE CAVALIERS

Magic Wheel	7"	Triumph	RGM1001	1960	**£20**	

KENDALL SISTERS

Won't You Be My Baby	7"	London	HLM8622	1958	**£8**	

KENDRICK, GRAHAM

Bright Side Up	LP	Key		1973	**£20**	
Footsteps	LP	Key	KL101	1973	**£20**	

KENDRICK, NAT & THE SWANS

Dish Rag	7"	Top Rank	JAR387	1960	**£4**	
Mashed Potato	7"	Top Rank	JAR351	1960	**£4**	

KENDRICKS, EDDIE

Girl You Need A Change Of Mind	7"	T. Motown	TMG916	1974	**£4**	
If You Let Me	7"	T. Motown	TMG845	1973	**£4**	
If You Let Me	7"	T. Motown	TMG845	1973	**£10**	demo
Keep On Truckin'	7"	T. Motown	TMG873	1973	**£8**	demo

KENNEDY, JERRY

Dancing Guitars Rock Elvis' Hits	LP	Smash	MGS27004	1962	**£10**	US

KENNER, CHRIS

I Like It Like That	7"	London	HLU9410	1961	**£5**	
Land Of 1000 Dances	7"	Sue	WI351	1965	**£15**	

KENNY & CASH

Knees	7"	Decca	F12283	1965	**£8**	

KENNY & THE KASUALS

Garage Kings	LP	Mark	7000	1969	**£25**	US
Impact Sound	LP	Mark	5000	1966	**£240**	US
Teen Dreams	LP	Mark	6000	1968	**£100**	US, red vinyl

KENT, AL

You Got To Pay The Price	7"	Mojo	2092015	1971	**£15**	
You Gotta Pay The Price	7"	Track	604016	1967	**£15**	

KENT, KLARK

According to legend, the first Police LP was to have contained a mixture of routine R&B covers and dull Stewart Copeland songs. That was before the others realised that Sting could write... So Copeland issued his songs under the name of Klark Kent. Suffice to say that the Police would have been unlikely to have achieved megastar status with these.

Don't Care	7"	Kryptone	KK1	1978	**£5**	green vinyl
Too Kool To Kalypso	7"	Kryptone	KMS7390	1978	**£5**	green vinyl

KENT, PAUL

Title	Format	Label	Cat. No.	Year	Price	Notes
P.C.Kent	LP	RCA	SF8083	1970	**£15**	
Paul Kent	LP	B&C	CAS1044	1971	**£10**	

KENT, RICHARD STYLE

Title	Format	Label	Cat. No.	Year	Price	Notes
Crocodile Tears	7"	MCA	MU1032	1968	**£10**	
Little Bit O' Soul	7"	Mercury	MF1090	1969	**£6**	
Marching Off To War	7"	Columbia	DB8182	1967	**£8**	
No Matter What You Do	7"	Columbia	DB7964	1966	**£8**	
You Can't Put Me Down	7"	Columbia	DB8051	1966	**£8**	

KENT, SHIRLEY

Title	Format	Label	Cat. No.	Year	Price	Notes
My Dad	7"	Tadpole	TAD001	1980	**£5**	
Sings For Charec 67	7"	Keele Univ.	103	1966	**£20**	

KENTUCKY COLONELS

Title	Format	Label	Cat. No.	Year	Price	Notes
Appalachian Swing	LP	World Pacific	T1821	1964	**£20**	US
Kentucky Colonels	LP	United Artists	UAS29514	1974	**£10**	
New Sound Of Bluegrass	LP	Briar	M109	1963	**£20**	US

KERN, WOODY

Title	Format	Label	Cat. No.	Year	Price	Notes
Awful Disclosures Of Maria Monk	LP	Pye	NSPL18273	1967	**£20**	
Biography	7"	Pye	7N17672	1969	**£6**	

KEROUAC, JACK

Title	Format	Label	Cat. No.	Year	Price	Notes
Blues And Haikus	LP	Hanover	HML5006	1959	**£50**	US
Poetry For The Beat Generation	LP	Dot	DLP3154	1959	**£75**	US
Poetry For The Beat Generation	LP	Hanover	HML5000	1959	**£50**	US
Readings On The Beat Generation	LP	Verve	MGV15005	1959	**£50**	US

KERR, PATRICK

Title	Format	Label	Cat. No.	Year	Price	Notes
Magic Potion	7"	Decca	F12069	1965	**£10**	

KERR, RICHARD

Title	Format	Label	Cat. No.	Year	Price	Notes
Happy Birthday Blues	7"	Deram	DM138	1967	**£4**	

KESEY, KEN & THE GRATEFUL DEAD

Title	Format	Label	Cat. No.	Year	Price	Notes
Acid Test	LP	Sound City	EX27690	1967	**£100**	US

KESTREL

Title	Format	Label	Cat. No.	Year	Price	Notes
Kestrel	LP	Cube	HIFLY19	1975	**£125**	
All These Things	7"	Decca	F11391	1961	**£4**	
Don't Want To Cry	7"	Piccadilly	7N35079	1962	**£4**	
I Can't Say Goodbye	7"	Pye	7N15248	1960	**£4**	
Love Me With All Your Heart	7"	Piccadilly	7N35144	1963	**£4**	
Smash Hits	LP	Piccadilly	NPL38009	1963	**£12**	
There Comes A Time	7"	Pye	7N15234	1959	**£4**	
There's A Place	7"	Piccadilly	7N35126	1963	**£4**	
Walk Right In	7"	Piccadilly	7N35104	1963	**£4**	
Wolverton Mountain	7"	Piccadilly	7N35056	1962	**£4**	

KEY LARGO

Title	Format	Label	Cat. No.	Year	Price	Notes
Key Largo	LP	Blue Horizon	763859	1970	**£20**	
Voodoo Rhythm	7"	Blue Horizon	573178	1971	**£5**	

KEYES, KAROL

Title	Format	Label	Cat. No.	Year	Price	Notes
One In A Million	7"	Columbia	DB8001	1966	**£12**	
You Beat Me To The Punch	7"	Fontana	TF517	1964	**£4**	

KEYES, TROY

Title	Format	Label	Cat. No.	Year	Price	Notes
Love Explosions	7"	Stateside	SS2087	1968	**£5**	

KEYS, BOBBY

Title	Format	Label	Cat. No.	Year	Price	Notes
Bobby Keys	LP	W. Brothers	K46141	1972	**£10**	

KGB

Title	Format	Label	Cat. No.	Year	Price	Notes
KGB	LP	MCA	MCF2749	1976	**£10**	

KHAN

Title	Format	Label	Cat. No.	Year	Price	Notes
Space Shanty	LP	Deram	SDLR11	1972	**£20**	

KHAN, USTAD VILAYET

Ustad Vilayet Khan	LP	Track		1971	**£15**	

KHANS

New Orleans 2am	7"	London	HLU9555	1962	**£4**	

KHAZAD-DOOM

Level Six And A Half	LP	LPL			**£60**	US

KIDD, JOHNNY & THE PIRATES

Always And Ever	7"	HMV	POP1269	1964	**£4**	chart single
Birds And The Bees	7"	HMV	POP1397	1965	**£5**	
Hungry For Love	7"	HMV	POP1228	1963	**£4**	chart single
Hurry On Back To Love	7"	HMV	POP978	1962	**£6**	
I'll Never Get Over You	7"	HMV	POP1173	1963	**£4**	chart single
If You Were The Only Girl	7"	HMV	POP674	1959	**£8**	
It's Got To Be You	7"	HMV	POP1520	1965	**£5**	
Jealous Girl	7"	HMV	POP1309	1964	**£4**	
Johnny Kidd And The Pirates	7" EP	HMV	7EG8834	1964	**£8**	
Linda Lu	7"	HMV	POP853	1961	**£6**	chart single
Please Don't Bring Me Down	7"	HMV	POP919	1961	**£6**	
Please Don't Touch	7"	HMV	POP615	1959	**£8**	chart single
Restless	7"	HMV	POP790	1960	**£5**	chart single
Send For That Girl	7"	HMV	POP1559	1966	**£5**	
Shaking All Over '65	7"	HMV	POP1424	1965	**£5**	
Shaking All Over	7"	HMV	POP753	1960	**£5**	chart single
Shaking All Over	7" EP	HMV	7EG8628	1960	**£12**	
Shot Of Rhythm And Blues	7"	HMV	POP1088	1962	**£5**	chart single
Whole Lotta Woman	7"	HMV	POP1353	1964	**£4**	
You've Got What It Takes	7"	HMV	POP698	1960	**£5**	chart single

KILBURN & THE HIGH ROADS

Crippled With Nerves	7"	Dawn	DNS1102	1975	**£4**	

KILEEN, JUDY

Just Walking In The Rain	7"	London	HLU8328	1956	**£15**	

KILGORE, MERLE

Ernie	7"	London	HLP8392	1957	**£8**	
It Can't Rain All The Time	7"	London	HL8103	1954	**£8**	

KILGORE, THEOLA

I'll Keep Trying	7"	Sue	WI4035	1967	**£10**	

KILLERMETERS

Twisted Wheel	7"	Gem	GEMS22	1980	**£10**	
Why Should It Happen To Me	7"	Psycho	P2620	1979	**£30**	PS
Why Should It Happen To Me	7"	Psycho	P2620	1979	**£15**	without PS

KILLIGREW

Killigrew	LP	P. Farthing		1971	**£12**	

KILLING FLOOR

Call For The Politicians	7"	P. Farthing	PEN745	1970	**£20**	
Killing Floor	LP	Spark	SRLM2004	1973	**£35**	
Killing Floor	LP	Spark	SRLP102	1970	**£80**	
Out Of Uranus	LP	P. Farthing	PELS511	1970	**£60**	

KILLING JOKE

Birds Of A Feather	7"	EG	EGO10	1982	**£4**	chart single
Chop-Chop	7"	Malicious D.	EGO7	1982	**£4**	
Empire Song	7"	Malicious D.	EG04	1982	**£4**	chart single
Follow The Leaders	7"	Malicious D.	EGMDS101	1981	**£4**	chart single
Follow The Leaders	10"	Malicious D.	EGMDX101	1981	**£6**	
Me Or You	7"	EG	KILL1/2	1983	**£5**	double
Nervous System	7"	Island	WIP6550	1980	**£4**	
Nervous System	12"	Island	WIP6550	1981	**£8**	
Nervous System	10"	Malicious D.	MD410	1979	**£12**	with 5 inserts
New Day	7"	EG	EGO17	1984	**£4**	
Requiem	7"	Malicious D.	EGMD100	1980	**£5**	
Requiem	12"	Malicious D.	EGMDX100	1980	**£8**	
Wardance	7"	Malicious D.	MD540	1980	**£4**	with insert

KILLJOYS

Johnny Won't Get To Heaven	7"	Raw	RAW3	1977	**£6**	

KIMBLE, STEVIE

Some Things Take A Little Time	7"	Decca	F12378	1966	**£6**	

KING BROTHERS

76 Trombones	7"	Parlophone	R4737	1961	**£4**	chart single
Doll House	7"	Parlophone	R4715	1960	**£4**	chart single
Harmony Kings	7" EP	Parlophone	GEP8638	1957	**£5**	
In The Middle Of An Island	7"	Parlophone	R4338	1957	**£4**	chart single
Little By Little	7"	Parlophone	R4288	1957	**£4**	
Mais Oui	7"	Parlophone	R4672	1960	**£4**	chart single
Making Love	7"	Parlophone	R4577	1959	**£4**	
Put A Light In The Window	7"	Parlophone	R4389	1958	**£4**	chart single
Sitting In A Tree House	7"	Parlophone	R4469	1958	**£4**	
Six Five Jive	7"	Parlophone	R4410	1958	**£4**	
Standing On The Corner	7"	Parlophone	R4639	1960	**£4**	chart single
Wake Up Little Susie	7"	Parlophone	R4367	1957	**£4**	chart single
White Sports Coat	7"	Parlophone	R4310	1957	**£4**	chart single

KING CRIMSON

Cat Food	7"	Island	WIP6080	1970	**£8**	PS
Court Of The Crimson King	7"	Island	WIP6071	1969	**£6**	
In The Court Of The Crimson King	LP	Island	ILPS9111	1969	**£15**	chart LP
In The Court Of The Crimson King	LP	Mobile Fid.	MFSL1075	1980	**£25**	US audiophile
In The Wake Of Poseidon	LP	Island	ILPS9127	1970	**£15**	chart LP
Islands	LP	Island	ILPS9175	1971	**£10**	chart LP
Lizard	LP	Island	ILPS9141	1970	**£10**	chart LP
Night Watch	7"	Island	WIP6189	1974	**£4**	
Return Of KIng Crimson	LP	EG		1981	**£15**	interview promo
Thela Hun Ginjeet	12"	EG	KCX001	1981	**£6**	promo

KING EARL BOOGIE BAND

Trouble At Mill	LP	Dawn	DNLS3040	1972	**£10**	

KING GEORGE

I'm Gonna Be Somebody	7"	RCA	RCA1573	1967	**£6**	

KING HARVEST

Dancing In The Moonlight	LP	Pye	NSPL28174	1973	**£10**	

KING KURT

America	7"	Polydor	KURTP1	1986	**£5**	shaped pic disc
Banana Banana	7"	Stiff	BUY206	1984	**£4**	
Banana Banana	7"	Stiff	BUY206	1984	**£5**	scratch 'n' sniff sleeve
Banana Banana	7"	Stiff	BUY206	1984	**£8**	shaped pic disc
Destination Zululand	7"	Stiff	BUY189	1983	**£8**	shaped pic disc
Mack The Knife	7"	Stiff	BUY199	1984	**£8**	shaped pic disc
Mack The Knife	7"	Stiff	BUY199	1984	**£5**	with flexi
Mack The Knife	7"	Stiff	PBUY199	1984	**£4**	pic disc
Zulu Beat	7"	Thin Sliced	TSR2	1982	**£10**	60+ coloured vinyl/ sleeve combinations!

KING SPORTY

Girl I've Got A Date	7"	Harry J	HJ6660	1973	**£4**	
Thinking Of You	7"	Attack	ATT8061	1973	**£4**	
Year Of Sundays	7"	Green Door	GD4063	1974	**£4**	

KING, AL

Think Twice Before You Speak	7"	Sue	WI4045	1968	**£12**	

KING, ALBERT

Big Blues	LP	King	852	1962	**£40**	US
Born Under A Bad Sign	LP	Stax	723	1967	**£15**	US
Born Under A Bad Sign	7"	Stax	601015	1967	**£4**	
Breaking Up Somebody's Home	7"	Stax	2025162	1973	**£4**	
Cold Feet	7"	Stax	601029	1968	**£4**	
Crosscut Saw	7"	Atlantic	584099	1967	**£5**	
Does The King Thing	LP	Stax	1017	1968	**£12**	
I Wanna Get Funky	LP	Stax	1003	1974	**£10**	
I'll Play The Blues For You	LP	Stax	1019	1972	**£10**	

King Of The Blues Guitar	LP	Atlantic	588173	1969	**£12**	
Live Wire Blues Power	LP	Stax	1002	1968	**£12**	
Lovejoy	LP	Stax	2325	1971	**£10**	
Lucy	7"	Stax	601042	1968	**£4**	
Travelling To California	LP	Polydor	2343026	1967	**£15**	
Years Gone By	LP	Stax	1022	1969	**£10**	

KING, ALBERT & OTIS RUSH

Door To Door	LP	Chess	1538	1969	**£10**	US

KING, ANNA & BOBBY BYRD

Baby Baby Baby	7"	Philips	BF1402	1965	**£6**	

KING, B.B.

B.B.King	LP	Crown	CLP5359	1963	**£10**	US
B.B.King Sings Spirituals	LP	Crown	CLP5119	1960	**£10**	US
B.B.King Sings Spirituals	LP	Crown	CLP5119	1960	**£15**	US, red vinyl
B.B.King Story Vol.1	LP	Blue Horizon	763216	1968	**£20**	
B.B.King Story Vol.2	LP	Blue Horizon	763226	1969	**£20**	
B.B.King Wails	LP	Crown	CLP5115	1960	**£10**	US
B.B.King Wails	LP	Crown	CLP5115	1960	**£15**	US, red vinyl
Best Of...	LP	Galaxy	202	1963	**£10**	US
Best Of...	LP	Probe	SPB1069	1973	**£10**	
Blues	LP	Crown	CLP5063	1960	**£10**	US
Blues In My Heart	LP	Crown	CLP5309	1962	**£10**	US
Blues Is King	LP	HMV	CLP3608	1967	**£20**	
Blues On Top Of Blues	LP	Stateside	SSL10238	1968	**£20**	
Completely Well	LP	Stateside	SSL10299	1970	**£20**	
Confessin' The Blues	LP	HMV	CLP3514	1966	**£20**	
Don't Answer The Door	7"	HMV	POP1568	1966	**£8**	
Don't Waste My Time	7"	Stateside	SS2141	1969	**£4**	
Easy Listening Blues	LP	Crown	CLP5286	1962	**£10**	US
Electric B.B.King	LP	Stateside	SSL10284	1969	**£20**	
Every Day I Have The Blues	7"	Blue Horizon	573161	1969	**£6**	
Friends	LP	ABC	ABCL5051	1974	**£10**	
Great B.B.King	LP	Crown	CLP5143	1961	**£10**	US
Guess Who	LP	Probe	SPB1063	1973	**£12**	
Hummingbird	7"	Stateside	SS2176	1970	**£4**	
In London	LP	ABC	ABCL5015	1974	**£10**	
In London	LP	Probe	SPB1041	1971	**£15**	
Indianola Mississippi Seed	LP	Probe	SPBA6255	1970	**£15**	
Jungle	7"	Polydor	56735	1967	**£5**	
King Of The Blues	LP	Crown	CLP5167	1961	**£10**	US
King Of The Blues	LP	Crown	CLP5167	1961	**£15**	US, red vinyl
L.A. Midnight	LP	Probe	SPB1051	1972	**£12**	
Live And Well	LP	Stateside	SSL10297	1970	**£20**	
Live At Cook County Jail	LP	Probe	SPB1032	1971	**£15**	
Live At The Regal	LP	HMV	CLP1870	1965	**£20**	
Lucille	LP	Stateside	SSL10272	1969	**£20**	
Lucille Talks Back	LP	ABC	ABCL5149	1975	**£10**	
Mr.Blues	LP	ABC-Para.	456	1963	**£10**	US
My Kind Of Blues	LP	Crown	CLP5188	1961	**£10**	US
Night Life	7"	HMV	POP1580	1967	**£5**	
Paying The Cost To Be The Boss	7"	Stateside	SS2112	1968	**£4**	
R&B And Soul	LP	Ember	EMB3379	1967	**£15**	
Rock Me Baby	7"	Ember	EMBS196	1964	**£8**	
So Excited	7"	Stateside	SS2169	1970	**£4**	
Take A Swing With Me	LP	Blue Horizon	2431004	1970	**£20**	
Think It Over	7"	HMV	POP1594	1967	**£4**	
Thrill Is Gone	7"	Stateside	SS2161	1970	**£4**	
To Know You Is To Love You	LP	Probe	SPB1083	1973	**£12**	
Tomorrow Night	7"	HMV	POP1101	1962	**£5**	
Twist With B.B.King	LP	Crown	CLP5248	1962	**£10**	US
Woman I Love	7"	Blue Horizon	573144	1968	**£6**	
You Never Know	7"	Sue	WI358	1965	**£8**	

KING, B.B. & BOBBY BLAND

Together Again	LP	Impulse	IMPL8027	1976	**£10**	
Together For The First Time	LP	ABC	ABCD695	1974	**£15**	double

KING, BEN E.

Title	Format	Label	Cat. No.	Year	Price	Notes
Amor Amor	7"	London	HLK9416	1961	**£4**	chart single
Cry No More	7"	Atlantic	AT4043	1965	**£4**	
Don't Play That Song	7"	London	HLK9544	1962	**£4**	
Don't Play That Song	LP	London	HAK8012	1962	**£15**	
Goodbye My Old Gal	7"	Crewe	CRW2	1970	**£4**	
Goodnight My Love, Pleasant Dreams	7"	Atlantic	AT4065	1966	**£4**	
Greatest Hits	LP	Atco	SD33165	1964	**£12**	US
Grooving	7"	London	HLK9840	1964	**£4**	
Here Comes The Night	7"	London	HLK9457	1961	**£4**	
How Can I Forget	7"	London	HLK9691	1963	**£4**	
How Can I Forget	7" EP	London	REK1361	1963	**£5**	
I (Who Have Nothing)	7"	London	HLK9778	1963	**£4**	
I Could Have Danced All Night	7"	London	HLK9819	1963	**£4**	
I Swear By The Stars Above	7"	Atlantic	584046	1966	**£4**	
I'm Standing By	7"	London	HLK9631	1962	**£4**	
I'm Standing By	7" EP	London	REK1386	1963	**£5**	
Let The Water Run Down	7"	Atlantic	AT4007	1964	**£4**	
Record	7"	Atlantic	AT4025	1965	**£4**	
Save The Last Dance For Me	7"	Atlantic	584090	1967	**£4**	
Seven Letters	LP	Atco	SD33174	1965	**£12**	US
Seven Letters	7"	Atlantic	AT4018	1965	**£4**	
Sings For Soulful Lovers	LP	London	HAK8026	1963	**£15**	
So Much Love	7"	Atlantic	584008	1966	**£4**	
Spanish Harlem	LP	Atco	SD33133	1961	**£15**	US
Spanish Harlem	LP	Atlantic	590001	1967	**£10**	chart LP
Spanish Harlem	7"	London	HLK9258	1961	**£5**	chart single
Stand By Me	7"	London	HLK9358	1961	**£5**	chart single
Too Bad	7"	London	HLK9586	1962	**£4**	
What Is Soul?	7"	Atlantic	584069	1967	**£4**	
What Is Soul?	LP	Atlantic	587072	1967	**£15**	
What Now My Love	7" EP	Atlantic	AET6004	1964	**£5**	
Yes	7"	London	HLK9517	1962	**£4**	

KING, BOB

Title	Format	Label	Cat. No.	Year	Price	Notes
Hey Honey	7"	Oriole	CB1497	1959	**£15**	

KING, CAROLE

Title	Format	Label	Cat. No.	Year	Price	Notes
It Might As Well Rain Until September	7"	London	HLU9591	1962	**£4**	chart single
Music	LP	Ode	SQ88013	1971	**£10**	US quad
Road To Nowhere	7"	London	HLU10036	1966	**£5**	
Tapestry	LP	Epic/Ode	HE44946	1980	**£15**	US audiophile

KING, CLYDIE

Title	Format	Label	Cat. No.	Year	Price	Notes
One Part Two Part	7"	Minit	MLF11014	1969	**£4**	

KING, DANNY & MAYFAIR SET

Title	Format	Label	Cat. No.	Year	Price	Notes
Amen	7"	Columbia	DB7792	1965	**£12**	
Pretty Things	7"	Columbia	DB7456	1965	**£25**	
Tossing And Turning	7"	Columbia	DB7276	1964	**£15**	

KING, FREDDIE

Title	Format	Label	Cat. No.	Year	Price	Notes
...Is A Blues Master	LP	Atlantic	588186	1969	**£12**	
...Is A Blues Master	LP	Atlantic	K40496	1973	**£10**	
Bonanza Of Instrumentals	LP	King	928	1965	**£12**	US
Bossa Nova And Blues	LP	King	821	1962	**£25**	US
Boy-Girl-Boy	LP	King	777	1962	**£25**	US
Burglar	LP	RSO	2394140	1974	**£10**	
Driving Sideways	7"	Sue	WI349	1965	**£12**	
Freddie King Goes Surfin'	LP	King	856	1963	**£20**	US
Freddie King Sings The Blues	LP	King	762	1961	**£30**	US
Getting Ready	LP	A&M	AMLS65004	1971	**£10**	
Hideaway	LP	King	KS1059	1969	**£10**	US
Hideaway	7"	Parlophone	R4777	1961	**£6**	
His Early Years	LP	Polydor	2343047	1971	**£10**	
King Of R&B Vol.2	LP	Polydor	2343009	1969	**£12**	
Larger Than Life	LP	RSO	2394163	1975	**£10**	
Let's Hide Away And Dance Away	LP	King	773	1961	**£30**	US
My Feeling For The Blues	LP	Atlantic	K40947	1975	**£10**	
Play It Cool	7"	Atlantic	584235	1969	**£4**	
Texas Cannonball	LP	A&M	AMLS68113	1972	**£10**	

Title	Format	Label	Number	Year	Price	Notes
Twenty-Four Vocals And Instrumentals	LP	King	964	1966	£12	US
Woman Across The Water	LP	A&M	AMLS68919	1973	£10	

KING, HANK

Title	Format	Label	Number	Year	Price	Notes
Country And Western	7" EP	Starlite	STEP41	196-	£4	

KING, JAY W.

Title	Format	Label	Number	Year	Price	Notes
I'm So Afraid	7"	Stateside	SS505	1966	£10	

KING, JONATHAN

Title	Format	Label	Number	Year	Price	Notes
Everyone's Gone To The Moon	7"	Decca	F12187	1965	£4	chart single
Or Then Again	LP	Parrot	PA61013	1967	£12	US

KING, MARTIN LUTHER

Title	Format	Label	Number	Year	Price	Notes
Great March To Freedom	LP	T. Motown	TML11076	1968	£100	

KING, PAUL

Title	Format	Label	Number	Year	Price	Notes
Been In The Pen Too Long	LP	Dawn	DNLS3035	1972	£10	

KING, RAMONA

Title	Format	Label	Number	Year	Price	Notes
It's In His Kiss	7"	W. Brothers	WB125	1964	£4	

KING, REG

Title	Format	Label	Number	Year	Price	Notes
Reg King	LP	United Artists	UAS29157	1971	£30	

KING, SAMMY

Title	Format	Label	Number	Year	Price	Notes
Great Balls Of Fire	7"	HMV	POP1285	1964	£8	
Rag Doll	7"	HMV	POP1330	1964	£5	

KING, SAMMY & THE VOLTAIRES

Title	Format	Label	Number	Year	Price	Notes
Only You	7"	HMV	POP1384	1965	£4	
Past Caring	7"	HMV	POP1540	1966	£4	

KING, SOLOMON

Title	Format	Label	Number	Year	Price	Notes
Say A Prayer	7"	Columbia	DB8676	1970	£20	
She Wears My Ring	7"	Columbia	DB8325	1967	£4	chart single

KINGDOM

Title	Format	Label	Number	Year	Price	Notes
Kingdom	LP	Speciality	2135	1970	£25	US

KINGDOM COME

Title	Format	Label	Number	Year	Price	Notes
Galactic Zoo Dossier	LP	Polydor	2310130	1972	£15	
General Messenger	7"	Polydor	2001234	1971	£5	
Journey	LP	Polydor	2310254	1973	£15	
Kingdom Come	LP	Polydor	2310178	1973	£15	
Spirit Of Joy	7"	Polydor	2001416	1972	£5	

KINGDOMS

Title	Format	Label	Number	Year	Price	Notes
Heartland	7"	Regard	RG114	1984	£30	
Heartland	7"	Regard	RGT114	1984	£35	

KINGPINS

Title	Format	Label	Number	Year	Price	Notes
It Won't Be This Way Always	LP	King	865	1963	£20	US
Ungaua	7"	London	HLU8658	1958	£5	

KINGS HENCHMEN

Title	Format	Label	Number	Year	Price	Notes
Alan Freed Presents Vol.1	7" EP	Coral	FEP2025	1959	£15	

KINGS IV

Title	Format	Label	Number	Year	Price	Notes
Some Like It Hot	7"	London	HLT8914	1959	£4	

KINGSLEY, CHARLES CREATION

Title	Format	Label	Number	Year	Price	Notes
Summer Without Sun	7"	Columbia	DB7758	1965	£12	

KINGSMEN

Title	Format	Label	Number	Year	Price	Notes
15 Great Hits	LP	Wand	WD674	1966	£10	US
Annie Fanny	7"	Pye	7N25322	1965	£6	
Climb	7"	Pye	7N25311	1965	£8	
Daytime Shadows	7"	Pye	7N25406	1967	£10	
Death Of An Angel	7"	Pye	7N25273	1964	£8	
Fever	7" EP	Pye	NEP44063	1966	£8	
In Person	LP	Wand	WD657	1964	£12	US
Jolly Green Giant	7"	Pye	7N25292	1965	£8	

Killer Joe	7"	Pye	7N25370	1966	**£10**	
Kingsmen	7" EP	Pye	NEP44023	1964	**£8**	
Little Latin Lupe Lu	7"	Pye	7N25262	1964	**£8**	
Louie Louie	7"	Pye	7N25231	1963	**£6**	chart single
Louie Louie	7"	Pye	7N25366	1966	**£5**	
Mojo Workout	7" EP	Pye	NEP44040	1965	**£8**	
On Campus	LP	Wand	WD670	1965	**£10**	US
Volume II	LP	Pye	NPL28054	1964	**£15**	
Volume III	LP	Wand	WD662	1965	**£10**	US

KINGSMEN (2)

Better Believe It	7"	London	HLE8735	1958	**£15**	
Conga Rock	7"	London	HLE8812	1959	**£12**	
Weekend	7" EP	London	REE1211	1959	**£15**	

KINGSTON TRIO

The Kingston Trio were enormously popular in America, their harmonised approach to folk music inspiring many future rock stars to begin their careers in music. The line of influence leads from the Kingston Trio to Haight-Asbury, to the music of Jefferson Airplane and the Grateful Dead, and from there to the entire sound of modern AOR. John Stewart was a member of the Kingston Trio on the later releases.

Aspen Gold	LP	Nautilus	NR2	1979	**£15**	US audiophile
At Large	LP	Capitol	T1199	1959	**£10**	
Back In Town	LP	Capitol	T2081	1964	**£10**	
Best Of...	LP	Capitol	T1705	1962	**£10**	
Best Of...Vol.2	LP	Capitol	T2280	1965	**£10**	
Best Of...Vol.3	LP	Capitol	T2614	1966	**£10**	
Children In The Morning	LP	Decca	DL4758	1966	**£10**	US
Close Up	LP	Capitol	T1642	1961	**£10**	
College Concert	LP	Capitol	T1658	1962	**£10**	
Encores	LP	Capitol	DT1612	1961	**£12**	
Folk Era	LP	Capitol	TCL2180	1964	**£15**	
From The Hungry	LP	Capitol	T1107	1959	**£12**	
Goin' Places	LP	Capitol	T1564	1961	**£10**	
Greenback Dollar	7"	Capitol	CL15287	1963	**£4**	
Greenback Dollar	7" EP	Capitol	EAP120460	1963	**£4**	
Here We Go Again	LP	Capitol	T1258	1959	**£10**	
Here We Go Again Part 1	7" EP	Capitol	EAP11258	1960	**£4**	
Here We Go Again Part 2	7" EP	Capitol	EAP21258	1960	**£4**	
Here We Go Again Part 3	7" EP	Capitol	EAP31258	1960	**£4**	
Kingston Trio	7" EP	Brunswick	OE9511	1965	**£5**	
Kingston Trio	LP	Capitol	T996	1958	**£15**	
Last Month Of The Year	LP	Capitol	T1446	1960	**£10**	US
Lemon Tree	7" EP	Capitol	EAP120655	1964	**£4**	
M.T.A.	7" EP	Capitol	EAP11119	1959	**£4**	
Make Way!	LP	Capitol	T1474	1961	**£10**	
New Frontier	LP	Capitol	T1809	1962	**£10**	
Nick-Bob-John	LP	Decca	DL4613	1965	**£10**	US
Number Sixteen	LP	Capitol	T1871	1963	**£10**	
Once Upon A Time	LP	Tetragramm.	5101	1969	**£10**	US
Raspberries Strawberries	7" EP	Capitol	EAP11182	1959	**£4**	
Scarlet Ribbons	7"	Capitol	CL14918	1958	**£4**	
Sold Out	LP	Capitol	T1352	1960	**£10**	
Somethin' Else	LP	Decca	DL4694	1965	**£10**	US
Something Special	LP	Capitol	T1747	1962	**£10**	
Stay Awhile	LP	Decca	DL4656	1965	**£10**	US
Stereo Concert	LP	Capitol	ST1183	1959	**£15**	
String Along	LP	Capitol	T1397	1960	**£10**	
Sunny Side	LP	Capitol	T1935	1963	**£10**	
Time To Think	LP	Capitol	T2011	1963	**£10**	
Time To Think	7" EP	Capitol	EAP42011	1962	**£4**	
Tom Dooley	7"	Capitol	CL14951	1958	**£4**	chart single
Tom Dooley	7" EP	Capitol	EAP11136	1959	**£4**	
Where Have All The Flowers Gone	7"	Capitol	CL15242	1962	**£4**	
Worried Man	7" EP	Capitol	EAP11322	1960	**£4**	

KINKS

The Kinks' long career is shot through with many collectors' items, although the majority of these come from the early, hit-making years. All the original Pye albums are becoming increasingly scarce, although their value is held down by the Kinks being seemingly irredeemably out of fashion. The original pressing of "Village Green Preservation Society" was withdrawn and replaced with a version containing more tracks, but the shorter album does contain one or two different mixes. The American compilations, "Kink Kronikles" and "The Great Lost Kinks Album", are highly sought after in the UK as they contain many tracks that are not otherwise available. Meanwhile, no Kinks records have sold as few copies as the first two singles, "Long Tall Sally" and "You Still Want Me" - most copies appearing on the market are likely, therefore, to be demos.

Title	Format	Label	Cat. No.	Year	Price	Notes
All Day And All Of The Night	7"	Pye	7N15714	1964	**£4**	chart single
All Day And All Of The Night	7"	Pye	7N15714	1964	**£60**	demo
All The Good Times	LP	Pye	IIPP100	1973	**£40**	4 LPs, boxed
Apeman	7"	Pye	7N45016	1970	**£4**	chart single
Apeman	7"	Pye	7N45016	1970	**£25**	demo
Arthur	LP	Pye	NSPL18317	1969	**£15**	
Autumn Almanac	7"	Pye	7N17400	1967	**£4**	chart single
Autumn Almanac	7"	Pye	7N17400	1967	**£25**	demo
Celluloid Heroes	LP	RCA	RS1059	1976	**£10**	
Celluloid Heroes	7"	RCA	RCA2299	1972	**£4**	
Celluloid Heroes	7"	RCA	RCA2299DJ	1973	**£12**	1 sided promo
Days	7"	Pye	7N17573	1968	**£4**	chart single
Days	7"	Pye	7N17573	1968	**£25**	demo
Dead End Street	7"	Pye	7N17222	1966	**£4**	chart single
Dead End Street	7"	Pye	7N17222	1966	**£30**	demo
Dedicated Follower Of Fashion	7"	Pye	7N17064	1966	**£4**	chart single
Dedicated Follower Of Fashion	7"	Pye	7N17064	1966	**£30**	demo
Dedicated Kinks	7" EP	Pye	NEP24258	1966	**£8**	
Don't Forget To Dance	7"	Arista	ARISTDJ524	1983	**£6**	1 sided promo
Drivin'	7"	Pye	7N17776	1969	**£4**	
Drivin'	7"	Pye	7N17776	1969	**£25**	demo
Ducks On The Wall	7"	RCA	RCA2546	1975	**£4**	
Everybody's Gonna Be Happy	7"	Pye	7N15813	1965	**£4**	chart single
Everybody's Gonna Be Happy	7"	Pye	7N15813	1965	**£40**	demo
Everybody's In Showbiz	LP	RCA	DPS2035	1972	**£15**	double
Face To Face	LP	Pye	NPL18149	1966	**£15**	chart LP
Give The People What They Want	LP	Arista	AL9567	1981	**£10**	US, different mixes
Give The People What They Want	LP	Arista	SPART1171	1981	**£20**	test pressing, US mix
Give The People What They Want	12"	Konk	STORE4	1981	**£12**	promo sampler
Great Lost Kinks Album	LP	Reprise	MS2172	1973	**£30**	US
Greatest Hits	LP	PRT	KINK1	1983	**£12**	with 10" LP (Dead End Street)
Greatest Hits	LP	Reprise	R6217	1966	**£12**	US
Holiday Romance (mono/stereo)	7"	RCA	RCA2478DJ	1974	**£12**	promo
Holiday Romance	7"	RCA	RCA2478	1974	**£4**	
Kinda Kinks	LP	Pye	NPL18112	1965	**£15**	chart LP
Kinda Kinks	LP	Reprise	R6173	1965	**£15**	US
Kink Kronikles	LP	Reprise	RS6454	1972	**£30**	US
Kinks	LP	Golden Guin.	GGL0357	1966	**£10**	
Kinks	LP	Pye	NPL18096	1964	**£15**	chart LP
Kinks	LP	Pye	NPL18326	1970	**£20**	double
Kinks	7" EP	Pye	AMEP1001	1975	**£10**	export, red or blue vinyl
Kinks Kontroversy	LP	Pye	NPL18131	1966	**£15**	chart LP
Kinks' Kinkdom	LP	Reprise	R6185	1965	**£15**	US
Kinksize	LP	Reprise	R6158	1965	**£15**	US
Kinksize Hits	7" EP	Pye	NEP24203	1964	**£8**	
Kinksize Session	7" EP	Pye	NEP24200	1964	**£8**	
Kwyet Kinks	7" EP	Pye	NEP24221	1965	**£8**	
Live At Kelvin Hall	LP	Pye	NPL18191	1967	**£15**	
Lola	7"	Pye	7N17961	1970	**£4**	chart single
Lola	7"	Pye	7N17961	1970	**£25**	demo
Lola Vs Powerman	LP	Pye	NSPL18359	1970	**£10**	
Long Tall Sally	7"	Pye	7N15611	1964	**£35**	
Long Tall Sally	7"	Pye	7N15611	1964	**£80**	demo
Low Budget Interview	LP	Arista	SP69	1979	**£20**	US promo
Mirror Of Love	7"	RCA	RCA5015	1974	**£4**	
Mirror Of Love	7"	RCA	RCA5042	1974	**£4**	
Misfits	LP	Mobile Fid.	MFSL1070	1981	**£10**	US audiophile
Mr.Pleasant	7"	Pye	7N17314	1967	**£25**	export
Muswell Hillbillies	LP	RCA	SF8423	1971	**£12**	
No More Looking Back	7"	RCA	RCM1	1976	**£4**	
Percy	LP	Pye	NSPL18365	1971	**£12**	
Percy	7"	Pye	7NX8001	1971	**£4**	
Percy	7"	Pye	7NX8001	1971	**£5**	PS
Plastic Man	7"	Pye	7N17724	1969	**£4**	chart single
Plastic Man	7"	Pye	7N17724	1969	**£25**	demo
Predictable	7"	Arista	ARIPD426	1981	**£4**	pic disc
Preservation Act 1	LP	RCA	SF8392	1973	**£10**	
Preservation Act 2	LP	RCA	5040	1974	**£15**	double

Title	Format	Label	Cat. No.	Year	Price	Notes
Rock'n'Roll Fantasy (2 versions)	7"	Arista	189DJ	1977	**£6**	promo
Schoolboys In Disgrace	LP	RCA	RS1028	1976	**£10**	
See My Friend	7"	Pye	7N15919	1965	**£4**	chart single
See My Friend	7"	Pye	7N15919	1965	**£40**	demo
Set Me Free	7"	Pye	7N15854	1965	**£4**	chart single
Set Me Free	7"	Pye	7N15854	1965	**£40**	demo
Shangri-La	7"	Pye	7N17812	1969	**£4**	
Shangri-La	7"	Pye	7N17812	1969	**£25**	demo
Sitting In The Midday Sun	7"	RCA	RCA2387	1973	**£4**	
Soap Opera	LP	RCA	SF8411	1975	**£10**	
Something Else	LP	Pye	NSPL18193	1967	**£15**	chart LP
Something Else	7" EP	Pye	NEP24296	1968	**£80**	
Sunny Afternoon	7"	Pye	7N17125	1966	**£4**	chart single
Sunny Afternoon	7"	Pye	7N17125	1966	**£30**	demo
Supersonic Rocket Ship	7"	RCA	RCA2211	1972	**£4**	chart single
Sweet Lady Genevieve	7"	RCA	RCA2418	1973	**£4**	
Then, Now And In Between	LP	Reprise	PRO328	1969	**£200**	US, boxed with various items of memorabilia
Till The End Of The Day	7"	Pye	7N15981	1965	**£4**	chart single
Till The End Of The Day	7"	Pye	7N15981	1965	**£40**	demo
Tired Of Waiting For You	7"	Pye	7N15759	1965	**£4**	chart single
Tired Of Waiting For You	7"	Pye	7N15759	1965	**£50**	demo
Victoria	7"	Pye	7N17865	1969	**£4**	chart single
Victoria	7"	Pye	7N17865	1969	**£25**	demo
Village Green Preservation Society	LP	Pye	NSPL18233	1967	**£100**	12 tracks
Village Green Preservation Society	LP	Pye	NSPL18233	1968	**£15**	
Waterloo Sunset	7"	Pye	7N17321	1967	**£4**	chart single
Waterloo Sunset	7"	Pye	7N17321	1967	**£30**	demo
Well Respected Man	7"	Pye	7N17100	1966	**£25**	export
Wonderboy	7"	Pye	7N17468	1968	**£4**	chart single
Wonderboy	7"	Pye	7N17468	1968	**£25**	demo
You Can't Stop The Music	7"	RCA	RCA2567	1975	**£4**	
You Really Got Me	7"	Pye	7N15673	1964	**£4**	chart single
You Really Got Me	7"	Pye	7N15673	1964	**£80**	demo
You Really Got Me	LP	Reprise	R6143	1965	**£15**	US
You Still Want Me	7"	Pye	7N15636	1964	**£75**	
You Still Want Me	7"	Pye	7N15636	1964	**£80**	demo

KINSMEN

Title	Format	Label	Cat. No.	Year	Price	Notes
Glasshouse Green Splinter Red	7"	Decca	F22724	1968	**£10**	
It's Good To See You	7"	Decca	F22777	1968	**£8**	

KIPPINGTON LODGE

There was a time when Nick Lowe was not a feature of the rock music scene, although it does not seem like it! His career actually begins here, as singer and bass player for the group that was later renamed after the guitarist, Brinsley Schwarz.

Title	Format	Label	Cat. No.	Year	Price	Notes
In My Life	7"	Parlophone	R5776	1969	**£20**	
Rumours	7"	Parlophone	R5677	1968	**£15**	
Shy Boy	7"	Parlophone	R5645	1967	**£15**	
Tell Me A Story	7"	Parlophone	R5717	1968	**£15**	
Tomorrow Today	7"	Parlophone	R5750	1968	**£20**	

KIRBY

Title	Format	Label	Cat. No.	Year	Price	Notes
Composition	LP	Hot Wax	HW2	1978	**£50**	

KIRBY, KATHY

Title	Format	Label	Cat. No.	Year	Price	Notes
Big Man	7"	Decca	F11506	1962	**£4**	
Dance On	7"	Decca	F11682	1963	**£4**	chart single
Kathy Kirby	7" EP	Decca	DFE8547	1963	**£4**	
Kathy Kirby Vol.2	7" EP	Decca	DFE8596	1965	**£4**	
Let Me Go Lover	7"	Decca	F11832	1964	**£4**	chart single
Secret Love	7"	Decca	F11759	1963	**£4**	chart single
Song For Europe	7" EP	Decca	DFE8611	1965	**£4**	
You're The One	7"	Decca	F11892	1964	**£4**	chart single

KIRBY, LARRY & THE ENCORES

Title	Format	Label	Cat. No.	Year	Price	Notes
My Baby Don't Love Me	7"	Top Rank	JAR143	1959	**£4**	

KIRCHIN BAND

Title	Format	Label	Cat. No.	Year	Price	Notes
Ivor And Basil Kirchin Band	7" EP	Parlophone	GEP8569	1956	**£6**	
Kirchin Bandbox	7" EP	Parlophone	GEP8531	1955	**£5**	

KIRKPATRICK, JOHN & SUE HARRIS

Jump At The Sun	LP	Trailer	LER2033	1972	**£10**	

KIRSCH, JULIAN

Clever Little Man	7"	Columbia	DB8541	1969	**£10**	

KISS

2000 Man	7"	Casablanca	NB1001	1980	**£5**	
Beth	7"	Casablanca	CBX519	1976	**£6**	
Crazy Crazy Nights	12"	Vertigo	KISSP7	1987	**£8**	pic disc
Creatures Of The Night	12"	Casablanca	KISS4	1983	**£15**	1 sided, double groove, etched autographs
Creatures Of The Night	7"	Casablanca	KISS4	1983	**£4**	chart single
Hard Luck Woman	7"	Casablanca	CAN102	1977	**£6**	
I Was Made For Lovin' You	7"	Casablanca	CAN152	1979	**£4**	chart single
Killer	7"	Casablanca	KISS3	1982	**£4**	
Lick It Up	7"	Vertigo	KISS5	1983	**£20**	shaped pic disc
Nothin' To Lose	7"	Casablanca	CBX503	1975	**£6**	
Originals	LP	Casablanca	NBLP7032	1976	**£20**	US, with inserts
Reason To Love	CD-s	Vertigo	KISCD8	1987	**£6**	
Rock And Roll All Nite	7"	Casablanca	CAN126	1978	**£5**	
Rock And Roll All Nite	7"	Casablanca	CBX510	1975	**£6**	
Rocker Ride	7"	Casablanca	CAN117	1978	**£5**	
Shout It Out Loud	7"	Casablanca	CBX516	1976	**£6**	
Sure Know Something	7"	Casablanca	CAN163	1979	**£5**	
Talk To Me	7"	Mercury	MER19	1980	**£5**	
Then She Kissed Me	7"	Casablanca	CANL110	1977	**£6**	
What Makes The World Go Round	7"	Mercury	KISS1	1980	**£5**	
World Without Heroes	7"	Casablanca	KISS2	1982	**£10**	pic disc

KISS - ACE FREHLEY

Ace Frehley	LP	Casablanca	NBPIX7121	1978	**£15**	pic disc
New York Groove	7"	Casablanca	CAN135	1979	**£20**	with mask

KISS - GENE SIMMONS

Radioactive	7"	Casablanca	CAN134	1979	**£15**	with mask
To Ace, Paul And Peter	LP	Casablanca	NBPIX7120	1978	**£15**	pic disc

KISS - PAUL STANLEY

Hold Me, Touch Me	7"	Casablanca	CAN140	1979	**£15**	with mask
To Ace, Gene And Peter	LP	Casablanca	NBPIX7123	1978	**£15**	pic disc

KISS - PETER CRISS

To Ace, Paul And Gene	LP	Casablanca	NBPIX7122	1978	**£15**	pic disc
You Matter To Me	7"	Casablanca	CAN139	1979	**£15**	with mask

KLEIN, ALAN

Age Of Corruption	7"	Parlophone	R5370	1965	**£5**	
Honey Pie	7"	Page One	POF119	1969	**£6**	
It Ain't Worth The Lonely Road	7"	Parlophone	R5292	1965	**£5**	
Striped Purple Shirt	7"	Oriole	CB1719	1962	**£10**	
Three Coins In The Sewer	7"	Oriole	CB1737	1962	**£10**	

KLEINOW, SNEAKY PETE

Sneaky Pete	LP	Shiloh	SLP4086	1970	**£12**	US

KLOOGER, ANNETTE

Why Do Fools Fall In Love?	7"	Decca	F10738	1956	**£4**	

KNACK

Did You Ever Have To Make Up Your Mind?	7"	Piccadilly	7N35315	1966	**£6**	
It's Love Baby	7"	Decca	F12278	1965	**£6**	
Marriage Guidance And Advice Bureau	7"	Piccadilly	7N35367	1967	**£5**	
Save All My Love For Joey	7"	Piccadilly	7N35347	1966	**£5**	
Stop!	7"	Piccadilly	7N35322	1966	**£5**	
Who'll Be The Next In Line	7"	Decca	F12234	1965	**£8**	

KNEES (BRINSLEY SCHWARZ)

Daytripper	7"	United Artists	UP35773	1974	**£6**	

KNICKERBOCKERS

Title	Format	Label	Number	Year	Price	Notes
Can You Help Me	7"	London	HLH10102	1967	**£10**	
High On Love	7"	London	HLH10061	1966	**£12**	
Jerk And Twine Time	LP	Challenge	LP621	1965	**£30**	US
Lies	7"	Elektra	K12102	1973	**£5**	B side by The Electric Prunes
Lies	LP	London	HA8294	1966	**£20**	
Lies	7"	London	HLH10013	1966	**£12**	
Lloyd Thaxton Presents	LP	Challenge	LP12664	1965	**£30**	US
One Track Mind	7"	London	HLH10035	1966	**£10**	
Rumours, Gossip, Words Untrue	7"	London	HLH10093	1966	**£10**	

KNIGHT BROTHERS

Title	Format	Label	Number	Year	Price	Notes
Temptation 'Bout To Get Me	7"	Chess	CRS8015	1965	**£5**	

KNIGHT, GLADYS & THE PIPS

Title	Format	Label	Number	Year	Price	Notes
Didn't You Know	7"	T. Motown	TMG728	1970	**£4**	
Didn't You Know	7"	T. Motown	TMG728	1970	**£10**	demo
Didn't You Know	7"	T. Motown	TMG903	1974	**£4**	
End Of Our Road	7"	T. Motown	TMG645	1968	**£6**	
End Of Our Road	7"	T. Motown	TMG645	1968	**£20**	demo
Everybody Needs Love	LP	T. Motown	STML11058	1968	**£12**	
Everybody Needs Love	7"	T. Motown	TMG619	1967	**£6**	
Everybody Needs Love	7"	T. Motown	TMG619	1967	**£30**	demo
Feelin' Bluesy	LP	T. Motown	STML11080	1968	**£12**	
Friendship Train	7"	T. Motown	TMG756	1970	**£4**	
Friendship Train	7"	T. Motown	TMG756	1970	**£10**	demo
Giving Up	7"	Stateside	SS318	1964	**£12**	
Gladys Knight And The Pips	LP	Maxx	3000	1964	**£20**	US
Gladys Knight And The Pips	LP	Sphere Sound	7006	1964	**£20**	US
Help Me Make It Through The Night	7"	T. Motown	TMG830	1972	**£4**	chart single
Help Me Make It Through The Night	7"	T. Motown	TMG830	1972	**£10**	demo
I Heard It Through The Grapevine	7"	T. Motown	TMG629	1967	**£8**	chart single
I Heard It Through The Grapevine	7"	T. Motown	TMG629	1967	**£35**	demo
I Wish It Would Rain	7"	T. Motown	TMG674	1968	**£5**	
I Wish It Would Rain	7"	T. Motown	TMG674	1968	**£20**	demo
If I Were Your Woman	7"	T. Motown	TMG765	1971	**£4**	
If I Were Your Woman	7"	T. Motown	TMG765	1971	**£10**	demo
It Should Have Been Me	7"	T. Motown	TMG660	1968	**£5**	
It Should Have Been Me	7"	T. Motown	TMG660	1968	**£20**	demo
Just Walk In My Shoes	7"	T. Motown	TMG576	1966	**£12**	
Just Walk In My Shoes	7"	T. Motown	TMG576	1966	**£50**	demo
Just Walk In My Shoes	7"	T. Motown	TMG813	1972	**£4**	chart single
Just Walk In My Shoes	7"	T. Motown	TMG813	1972	**£12**	demo
Letter Full Of Tears	LP	Fury	1003	1962	**£50**	US
Letter Full Of Tears	7"	Sue	WI394	1965	**£12**	
Look Of Love	7"	T. Motown	TMG844	1973	**£4**	chart single
Look Of Love	7"	T. Motown	TMG844	1973	**£10**	demo
Lovers Always Forgive	7"	Stateside	SS352	1964	**£12**	
Make Me The Woman You Go Home To	7"	T. Motown	TMG805	1972	**£4**	
Make Me The Woman You Go Home To	7"	T. Motown	TMG805	1972	**£10**	demo
Neither One Of Us	7"	T. Motown	TMG855	1973	**£8**	demo
Nitty Gritty	7"	T. Motown	TMG714	1969	**£5**	
Nitty Gritty	7"	T. Motown	TMG714	1969	**£15**	demo
Take Me In Your Arms And Love Me	7"	T. Motown	TMG604	1967	**£5**	chart single
Take Me In Your Arms And Love Me	7"	T. Motown	TMG604	1967	**£35**	demo
Take Me In Your Arms And Love Me	7"	T. Motown	TMG864	1973	**£4**	
Take Me In Your Arms And Love Me	7"	T. Motown	TMG864	1973	**£10**	demo
Why Don't You Leave Me	7"	Contempo	CS2021	1974	**£4**	

KNIGHT, JASON

Title	Format	Label	Number	Year	Price	Notes
Our Love Is Getting Stronger	7"	Pye	7N17399	1967	**£15**	

KNIGHT, MARIE

Title	Format	Label	Number	Year	Price	Notes
Come Tomorrow	7"	Fontana	H354	1962	**£4**	
Cry Me A River	7"	Stateside	SS419	1965	**£4**	

KNIGHT, ROBERT

Title	Format	Label	Number	Year	Price	Notes
Blessed Are The Lonely	7"	Monument	MON1016	1968	**£4**	
Everlasting Love	7"	Monument	MON1008	1968	**£4**	chart single
Love On A Mountain Top	7"	Monument	MON1017	1968	**£5**	

KNIGHT, SONNY

Title	Format	Label	Cat. No.	Year	Price	Notes
But Officer	7"	Vogue	V9134	1959	**£15**	
Confidential	7"	London	HLD8362	1957	**£20**	
If You Want This Love	LP	Aura	AR3001	1964	**£10**	US

KNIGHT, TERRY & THE PACK

Title	Format	Label	Cat. No.	Year	Price	Notes
I (Who Have Nothing)	7"	Cameo Park.	C102	1962	**£8**	
Reflections	LP	Cameo	C2007	1967	**£10**	US
Terry Knight And The Pack	LP	Lucky Eleven	8000	1966	**£10**	US

KNIGHT, TONY & THE LIVE WIRES

Title	Format	Label	Cat. No.	Year	Price	Notes
Did You Ever Hear The Sound?	7"	Decca	F11989	1964	**£5**	

KNIGHT, TONY CHESSMEN

Title	Format	Label	Cat. No.	Year	Price	Notes
How Sweet	7"	Decca	F12109	1965	**£8**	

KNIGHTS

Title	Format	Label	Cat. No.	Year	Price	Notes
Hot Rod High	LP	Capitol	T2189	1964	**£25**	US

KNIGHTS (2)

Title	Format	Label	Cat. No.	Year	Price	Notes
Across The Road	LP	Ace	MG200854	1966	**£75**	US
Knights 1967	LP	Ace	MG201303	1967	**£65**	US

KNOCKOUTS

Title	Format	Label	Cat. No.	Year	Price	Notes
Darling Lorraine	7"	Top Rank	JAR279	1960	**£4**	
Go Ape With The Knockouts	LP	Tribute	1202	1964	**£20**	US

KNOPFLER, MARK

Arguably, the instantly memorable theme that he wrote for the film "Local Hero" is the best piece of music that Mark Knopfler has ever produced.

Title	Format	Label	Cat. No.	Year	Price	Notes
Going Home	12"	Vertigo	DSTR412	1983	**£6**	

KNOPOV

Title	Format	Label	Cat. No.	Year	Price	Notes
Misadventure	7"			1980	**£6**	

KNOX, BUDDY

Title	Format	Label	Cat. No.	Year	Price	Notes
All Time Loser	7"	Liberty	LIB55694	1964	**£4**	
Buddy Knox	LP	Roulette	R25003	1957	**£50**	US
C'mon Baby	7"	Columbia	DB4180	1958	**£10**	
Chi-Hua-Hua	7"	Liberty	LIB55411	1962	**£4**	
Devil Woman	7"	Columbia	DB4014	1957	**£15**	
Golden Hits	LP	Liberty	LRP3251	1962	**£15**	US
Gypsy Man	LP	United Artists	UAS6689	1969	**£10**	US
I Think I'm Gonna Kill Myself	7"	Columbia	DB4302	1959	**£10**	
Ling Ting Tong	7"	London	HLG9331	1961	**£5**	
Lovey Dovey	7"	London	HLG9268	1961	**£6**	
Party Doll	7"	Columbia	DB3914	1957	**£20**	chart single
Rock A Buddy Knox	7" EP	Columbia	SEG7732	1957	**£30**	
Rock Your Little Baby To Sleep	7"	Columbia	DB3952	1957	**£20**	
Shadaroom	7"	Liberty	LIB55592	1963	**£4**	
She's Gone	7"	Liberty	LIB55473	1962	**£4**	chart single
Swinging Daddy	7"	Columbia	DB4077	1958	**£15**	
Three Eyed Man	7"	London	HLG9472	1961	**£5**	

KNOX, BUDDY & JIMMY BOWEN

Title	Format	Label	Cat. No.	Year	Price	Notes
Buddy Knox And Jimmy Bowen	LP	Roulette	R25048	1957	**£75**	US

KOCJAN, KRYSIA

Title	Format	Label	Cat. No.	Year	Price	Notes
Krysia	LP	RCA	LPL15052	1974	**£10**	

KODAKS

Title	Format	Label	Cat. No.	Year	Price	Notes
Kodaks Vs. The Starlites	LP	Sphere Sound	LP7005	1964	**£50**	US
Tell Me Rhonda	7"	Decca	F12942	1969	**£6**	

KOERNER, SPIDER JOHN

Title	Format	Label	Cat. No.	Year	Price	Notes
Won't You Give Me Some Love	7"	Elektra	EKSN45005	1967	**£8**	

KOERNER, SPIDER JOHN & WILLIE MURPHY

Title	Format	Label	Cat. No.	Year	Price	Notes
Friends And Lovers	7"	Elektra	EKSN45063	1969	**£8**	
Running Jumping Standing Still	LP	Elektra	EKS74041	1968	**£20**	
Running Jumping Standing Still	LP	Elektra	K42026	1971	**£15**	

KOFFMAN, MOE

Title	Format	Label	Cat. No.	Year	Price	Notes
Little Pixie	7" EP	London	REJ1163	1958	**£5**	
Swingin' Shepherd Blues	7"	London	HLJ8549	1958	**£4**	chart single

KOKOMO

Title	Format	Label	Cat. No.	Year	Price	Notes
Asia Minor	7"	London	HLU9305	1961	**£4**	chart single
Journey Home	7"	London	HLU9497	1962	**£4**	

KOLETTES

Title	Format	Label	Cat. No.	Year	Price	Notes
Who's That Guy?	7"	Pye	7N25278	1964	**£8**	

KONGOS, JOHN

Title	Format	Label	Cat. No.	Year	Price	Notes
Confusions About Goldfish	LP	Dawn	DNLS3002	1969	**£10**	
He's Gonna Step On You Again	7"	Fly	BUG8	1971	**£4**	PS
John Kongos	LP	Fly	HIFLY7	1971	**£10**	chart LP

KOOBAS

Title	Format	Label	Cat. No.	Year	Price	Notes
First Cut Is The Deepest	7"	Columbia	DB8419	1968	**£10**	
Gypsy Fred	7"	Columbia	DB8187	1967	**£10**	
Koobas	LP	Columbia	SCX6271	1969	**£220**	
Sally	7"	Columbia	DB8103	1967	**£10**	
Sweet Music	7"	Columbia	DB7988	1966	**£12**	
Take Me For A Little While	7"	Pye	7N17012	1965	**£10**	
You'd Better Make Up Your Mind	7"	Pye	7N17087	1966	**£10**	

KOOL

Title	Format	Label	Cat. No.	Year	Price	Notes
Look At Me, Look At Me	7"	CBS	203003	1967	**£4**	
Lovin'	7"	MCA	MU1085	1969	**£4**	
Step Out Of Your Mind	7"	CBS	2865	1967	**£5**	

KOOPER, AL

Title	Format	Label	Cat. No.	Year	Price	Notes
Hey Western Union Man	7"	CBS	4160	1969	**£10**	
I Stand Alone	LP	CBS	63538	1969	**£10**	
Kooper Sessions	LP	CBS	63797	1970	**£10**	
Parchman Farm	7"	Mercury	MF885	1965	**£12**	
You Never Know Who Your Friends Are	LP	CBS	63651	1969	**£10**	
You Never Know Who Your Friends Are	7"	CBS	4011	1969	**£8**	

KOOPER, AL & STEPHEN STILLS

Title	Format	Label	Cat. No.	Year	Price	Notes
Season Of The Witch	7"	CBS	3770	1968	**£8**	

KORDA, PAUL

Title	Format	Label	Cat. No.	Year	Price	Notes
Go On Home	7"	Columbia	DB7994	1966	**£12**	
Passing Strangers	LP	MAM	MAM1003	1971	**£12**	
Seagull	7"	Parlophone	R5778	1969	**£5**	

KORNER, ALEXIS

Somewhat like John Mayall, Alexis Korner's importance within the development of rock music had more to do with the musicians he managed to discover than with what he actually played himself. "R & B From The Marquee", viewed as being of crucial significance at the time, today sounds rather thin and ineffectual, and an unlikely base from which to begin a rock revolution. In truth, musicians like Charlie Watts, Jack Bruce, and Robert Plant achieved far more after they left Korner than they ever did with him. Nevertheless, Alexis Korner was an important catalyst - a position best demonstrated on the double LP "Bootleg Him" , which provides a useful survey of his career via a well chosen selection of out-takes and otherwise unreleased tracks.

Title	Format	Label	Cat. No.	Year	Price	Notes
Accidentally Born In New Orleans	LP	Transatlantic	TRA269	1973	**£20**	
Ain't That Peculiar	7"	CBS	3877	1976	**£4**	
Alexis	LP	RAK	SRAK501	1971	**£25**	
Alexis Korner	LP	Polydor	2374109	1974	**£20**	German
Alexis Korner Blues Incorporated	7" EP	Tempo	EXA102	1958	**£25**	
Alexis Korner Skiffle Group	7" EP	Tempo	EXA76	1957	**£25**	
All Stars Blues Inc	LP	Transatlantic	TRASAM7	1969	**£15**	
At The Cavern	LP	Oriole		1964	**£75**	
Blues At The Roundhouse	LP	77		1957	**£200**	
Blues Inc	LP	Ace Of Clubs	ACL1187	1965	**£50**	
Blues Incorporated	LP	Polydor	236206	1967	**£50**	
Bootleg Him	LP	RAK	SRAKSP51	1972	**£30**	double
Both Sides	LP	Metronome	MLP15364	1969	**£30**	German
C.C.Rider	7"	King	KG1017	1964	**£15**	
County Jail	7"	Tempo	A166	1957	**£20**	
Get Off My Cloud	LP	CBS	69155	1975	**£15**	
Get Off My Cloud	7"	CBS	3520	1975	**£4**	
I Need Your Loving	7"	Parlophone	R5206	1963	**£15**	

I Wonder Who	LP	Fontana	STL5381	1967	**£40**	
Just Easy	LP	Intercord	INT60099	1978	**£15**	German
Little Baby	7"	Parlophone	R5247	1965	**£15**	
Me	LP	Jeton	1003305	1979	**£15**	German
Mr. Blues	LP	Mushroom	35434	1974	**£20**	German
New Church	LP	Metronome		1970	**£30**	German
New Generation Of Blues	LP	Liberty	LBL83147	1968	**£30**	
Party LP	LP	Intercord	170000	1980	**£15**	German
R&B At The Marquee	LP	Ace Of Clubs	ACL1130	1962	**£30**	
Red Hot From Alex	LP	Transatlantic	TRA117	1964	**£75**	
River's Invitation	7"	Fontana	TF706	1966	**£12**	
Rocket 88	LP	Atlantic	50776	1981	**£10**	
Rosie	7"	Fontana	TF817	1967	**£12**	
Sky High	LP	Spot	JW551	1965	**£160**	
Snape Live On Tour	LP	Brain	21039	1974	**£20**	German
What's That Sound I Hear	LP	Sunset	SLS50245	1971	**£15**	

KORNFELD, ARTIE

Island Song	7"	Neighborhood	NBH3	1972	**£4**	

KORNFELD, ARTIE TREE

Time To Remember	LP	Probe	SPB1022	1970	**£12**	

KOSSOFF, KIRKE, TETSU & RABBIT

Kossoff, Kirke, Tetsu And Rabbit	LP	Island	ILPS9188	1971	**£30**	

KOSSOFF, PAUL

Croydon June 15th 1975	LP	Street Tones	STLP1002	1983	**£20**	double
Hunter	LP	Street Tones	STLP001	1981	**£10**	
Leaves In The Wind	LP	Street Tones	STLP002	1982	**£10**	
Mr.Big/Blue Soul	LP	Street Tones	SDLP0012PD	1983	**£15**	pic disc

KOTHARI, CHIM

Sitar And Spice	7"	Deram	DM108	1966	**£6**	
Sound Of Sitar	LP	Deram	DML1002	1966	**£12**	

KOTTKE, LEO

Circle Around The Sun	LP	Symposium	2001	1970	**£15**	

KRAAN

Andy Nogger	LP	Gull	GULP1009	1975	**£10**	
Kraan	LP	Speigelei	28778/9	1973	**£20**	German
Kraan Live	LP	Gull	G2001/2	1975	**£12**	double
Let It Out	LP	Gull	GULP1013	1975	**£10**	
Winthrup	LP	Speigelei	28523/9	1972	**£20**	German

KRAFTWERK

Comet Melody 2	7"	Vertigo	6147015	1975	**£4**	
Computer Welt	LP	Kling Klang		1981	**£15**	sung in German
Kraftwerk	LP	Vertigo	6641077	1973	**£15**	spiral label double
Man Machine	LP	Kling Klang		1977	**£15**	sung in German
Neon Lights	12"	Capitol	CL15998	1978	**£6**	luminous vinyl
Pocket Calculator	7"	EMI		1981	**£4**	promo, English/ German versions
Radioactivity	7"	Capitol	CL15853	1976	**£4**	
Radioactivity	LP	Kling Klang		1975	**£15**	sung in German
Ralf And Florian	LP	Vertigo	6360616	1973	**£20**	
Robots	7"	Capitol	CL15981	1978	**£4**	
Showroom Dummies	7"	Capitol	CL104	1977	**£4**	
Showroom Dummies	12"	Capitol	CL16098	1979	**£6**	
Showroom Dummies	12"	Capitol	CLX104	1977	**£6**	
Technopop	LP	EMI	EMC3407	1983	**£20**	
Trans-Europe Express	7"	Capitol	CL15917	1977	**£4**	

KRAMER, BILLY J.

1941	7"	NEMS	563396	1968	**£4**	
Colour Of My Love	7"	MGM	MGM1474	1969	**£4**	
Town Of Tuxley Toymaker	7"	Reaction	591014	1967	**£4**	
World Without Love	7"	NEMS	563635	1968	**£4**	

KRAMER, BILLY J. & THE DAKOTAS

Bad To Me	7"	Parlophone	R5049	1963	**£4**	chart single

Title	Format	Label	Cat. No.	Year	Price	Notes
Billy J Plays The States	7" EP	Parlophone	GEP8928	1965	**£8**	
Do You Want To Know A Secret	7"	Parlophone	R5023	1963	**£4**	chart single
From A Window	7"	Parlophone	R5156	1964	**£4**	chart single
From A Window	7" EP	Parlophone	GEP8921	1964	**£6**	
I'll Keep You Satisfied	LP	Imperial	LP9273	1964	**£12**	US
I'll Keep You Satisfied	7"	Parlophone	R5073	1963	**£4**	chart single
I'll Keep You Satisfied	7" EP	Parlophone	GEP8895	1964	**£6**	
It's Gotta Last Forever	7"	Parlophone	R5234	1965	**£4**	
Kramer Hits	7" EP	Parlophone	GEP8885	1963	**£6**	
Listen To...	LP	Parlophone	PMC1209	1963	**£12**	chart LP
Little Children	LP	Imperial	LP9267	1964	**£15**	US
Little Children	7"	Parlophone	R5105	1964	**£4**	chart single
Little Children	7" EP	Parlophone	GEP8907	1964	**£6**	
Neon City	7"	Parlophone	R5362	1965	**£4**	
Trains And Boats And Planes	LP	Imperial	LP9291	1965	**£12**	US
Trains And Boats And Planes	7"	Parlophone	R5285	1965	**£4**	chart single
We're Doing Fine	7"	Parlophone	R5408	1966	**£4**	
You Make Me Feel Like Someone	7"	Parlophone	R5482	1966	**£4**	

KRAMER, WAYNE

Title	Format	Label	Cat. No.	Year	Price	Notes
Harder They Come	7"	Radar	ADA41	1979	**£4**	
Ramblin' Rose	7"	Stiffwick	DEA/SUK1	1978	**£4**	

KRAUT

Title	Format	Label	Cat. No.	Year	Price	Notes
Kill For Cash	7"	Cabbage		198-	**£20**	
Unemployed	7"	Cabbage	K0002	1982	**£15**	

KRAZY KATS

Title	Format	Label	Cat. No.	Year	Price	Notes
Movin' Out	LP	Damon	12478		**£20**	US

KRENZ, BILL RAGTIMERS

Title	Format	Label	Cat. No.	Year	Price	Notes
Goofus	7"	London	HLU8258	1956	**£6**	

KREW KATS

Title	Format	Label	Cat. No.	Year	Price	Notes
Samovar	7"	HMV	POP894	1961	**£6**	
Trambone	7"	HMV	POP840	1961	**£6**	chart single

KRIMSON KAKE

Title	Format	Label	Cat. No.	Year	Price	Notes
Feelin' Better	7"	P. Farthing	PEN707	1970	**£5**	

KRISTINA, SONJA

Title	Format	Label	Cat. No.	Year	Price	Notes
Let The Sunshine In	7"	Polydor	56299	1968	**£8**	
Sonja Kristina	LP	Chopper	CHOPE5	1980	**£20**	

KROKODIL

Title	Format	Label	Cat. No.	Year	Price	Notes
Krokodil	LP	Liberty	LBS83306	1969	**£15**	
Swamp	LP	Liberty	LBS83417	1970	**£15**	

KUBAN, BOB & THE IN MEN

Title	Format	Label	Cat. No.	Year	Price	Notes
Cheater	7"	Stateside	SS488	1966	**£12**	
Look Out For The Cheater	LP	Musicland	3500	1966	**£10**	US
Teaser	7"	Stateside	SS514	1966	**£4**	

KUBAS

Title	Format	Label	Cat. No.	Year	Price	Notes
I Love Her	7"	Columbia	DB7451	1965	**£12**	

KUFF LINX

Title	Format	Label	Cat. No.	Year	Price	Notes
So Tough	7"	London	HLU8583	1958	**£15**	

KULT

Title	Format	Label	Cat. No.	Year	Price	Notes
No Home Today	7"	CBS	4276	1969	**£30**	

KUPFERBERG, TULI

Title	Format	Label	Cat. No.	Year	Price	Notes
No Deposit No Return	LP	ESP	1035	196-	**£12**	US
No Deposit No Return	LP	ESP	1035	196-	**£20**	US, gold vinyl

KURSAAL FLYERS

Title	Format	Label	Cat. No.	Year	Price	Notes
Great Artiste	LP	UK	UKAL1018	1975	**£10**	

KUSTOM KINGS

Title	Format	Label	Cat. No.	Year	Price	Notes
Kustom City, USA	LP	Smash	MGS27051	1964	**£20**	US

KWESKIN, JIM JUG BAND

Title	Format	Label	Number	Year	Price	Notes
Garden Of Joy	LP	Reprise	RS6266	1967	**£10**	US
Greatest Hits	LP	Vanguard	VSD13/14	1973	**£15**	double
Jim Kweskin Jug Band	LP	Fontana	TFL6036	1964	**£12**	
Jug Band Music	LP	Vanguard	VRS9163	1966	**£10**	US
See Reverse Side For Title	LP	Fontana	TL6080	1967	**£10**	

KWIL

Title	Format	Label	Number	Year	Price	Notes
Every Little Thing	7"	Parlophone	R5969	1972	**£4**	

KYDDS

Title	Format	Label	Number	Year	Price	Notes
Sun Is A Laughing Child	7"	NEMS	564095	1969	**£4**	

L

LA DE DA BAND

Come Together	7"	Parlophone	R5810	1969	£8	

LA PESTE

Better Off Dead	7"	Backlash	CB711	1978	£20	

LA ROSA, JULIUS

Domani	7"	London	HLA8170	1955	£6	
Jingle Bells	7"	London	HLA8353	1956	£4	
Julius La Rosa Sings	7" EP	London	REP1005	1954	£15	
Mobile	7"	London	HL8154	1955	£8	
No Other Love	7"	London	HLA8272	1956	£6	
Suddenly There's A Valley	7"	London	HLA8193	1955	£6	

LABELLE, PATTI & THE BLUEBELLES

All Or Nothing	7"	Atlantic	AT4055	1965	£4	
Apollo Presents...	LP	Newtown	631	1963	£25	US
Danny Boy	7"	Cameo Park	P935	1965	£4	
Down The Aisle	7"	Sue	WI324	1964	£10	
Dreamer	LP	Atlantic	8101	1965	£12	US
Groovy Kind Of Love	7"	Atlantic	AT4064	1966	£4	
I Sold My Heart To The Junkman	7"	HMV	POP1029	1962	£4	
On Stage	LP	Parkway	7043	1965	£20	US
Over The Rainbow	LP	Atlantic	8119	1966	£12	US
Patti's Prayer	7"	Atlantic	584007	1966	£4	
Sleigh Bells, Jingle Bells And Bluebelles	LP	Newtown	632	1963	£20	US
Take Me For A Little While	7"	Atlantic	584072	1967	£4	

LACE

I'm A Gambler	7"	Page One	POF135	1969	£6	
People People	7"	Columbia	DB8499	1968	£8	

LACKEY & SWEENEY

Junk Store Songs For Sale	LP	Village Thing	VTS23	1973	£15	

LADY JUNE

Linguistic Leprosy	LP	Caroline	C1509	1974	£15	

LADY PENELOPE

Perils Of Penelope	7" EP	Century 21	MA114	1966	£10	
Stately Home Robberies	7" EP	Century 21	MA110	1966	£10	

LAINE, DENNY

The singles released by Denny Laine on the Deram label represented a bold experiment by the former Moody Blue and future Wing. Abandoning the usual rock group line-up, Laine surrounded himself with a small group of amplified violins and cellos - the Electric String Band - and thereby anticipated some of what was later achieved by the Electric Light Orchestra. Sadly, Laine's innovations found little public support and he never again attempted anything similar.

Aah Laine	LP	Wizard	SWZ2001	1971	£10	
Caroline	7"	Paladin	PAL5014	1973	£4	
Find A Way Somehow	7"	Wizard	WIZ104	1971	£4	
Holly Days	LP	Capitol	EMI781	1976	£10	
Say You Don't Mind	7"	Deram	DM122	1967	£6	
Say You Don't Mind	7"	Deram	DM227	1971	£4	
Too Much In Love	7"	Deram	DM171	1968	£10	

LAINE, LINDA & THE SINNERS

Don't Do It Baby	7"	Columbia	DB7549	1965	£10	
Doncha Know	7"	Columbia	DB7204	1964	£8	
Low Grades And High Fever	7"	Columbia	DB7370	1964	£8	

LAKE, BONNIE & HER BEAUX

Miracle Of Love	7"	Brunswick	05622	1956	£6	

LAMAR, LEE

Title	Format	Label	Cat. No.	Year	Price	Notes
Sophia	7"	London	HLB8508	1957	**£6**	

LAMB, CHRIS & THE UNIVERSALS

Title	Format	Label	Cat. No.	Year	Price	Notes
Mysterious Land	7"	Decca	F12176	1965	**£5**	

LAMB, KEVIN

Title	Format	Label	Cat. No.	Year	Price	Notes
Who Is The Hero?	LP	Birth	RAB4	1972	**£12**	
Who Is The Hero?	7"	Birth	RAB1004	1973	**£4**	
Who Is The Hero?	7"	Concord	CON23	1970	**£5**	

LAMBRETTAS

Title	Format	Label	Cat. No.	Year	Price	Notes
Da-a-a-ance	7"	Rocket	XPRES333	1980	**£4**	pic disc
Go Steady	7"	Rocket	XPRES23	1979	**£4**	1st PS
Poison Ivy	7"	Two Stroke	XPRES25	1980	**£5**	

LAMEGO, DANNY & HIS JUMPIN' JACKS

Title	Format	Label	Cat. No.	Year	Price	Notes
Big Weekend	LP	For.-Me-Not	105A	1964	**£20**	US

LAMP SISTERS

Title	Format	Label	Cat. No.	Year	Price	Notes
Woman With The Blues	7"	Sue	WI4048	1968	**£10**	

LANCASTRIANS

Title	Format	Label	Cat. No.	Year	Price	Notes
Ballad Of The Green Berets	7"	Pye	7N17072	1966	**£5**	
Let's Lock The Door	7"	Pye	7N15791	1965	**£6**	
Lonely Man	7"	Pye	7N15927	1965	**£6**	
There'll Be No More Goodbyes	7"	Pye	7N15846	1965	**£6**	
This World Keeps Going Round	7"	Pye	7N17043	1966	**£6**	
We'll Sing In The Sunshine	7"	Pye	7N15732	1964	**£6**	chart single

LANCE, MAJOR

Title	Format	Label	Cat. No.	Year	Price	Notes
Ain't No Soul	7"	Columbia	DB8122	1967	**£15**	
Ain't No Soul	7"	Contempo	C9	1973	**£4**	
Beat	7"	Soul City	SC114		**£6**	
Beat	7"	Soul City	SC114		**£20**	demo
Best Of Major Lance	LP	Epic		1976	**£10**	
Come See	7"	Columbia	DB7527	1965	**£10**	
Everybody Loves A Good Time	7"	Columbia	DB7787	1965	**£10**	
Follow The Leader	7"	Atlantic	584277	1969	**£5**	
Gimme Little Sign	7"	Contempo	CS2017	1974	**£4**	
Greatest Hits	LP	OKeh	OKM12110	1965	**£12**	US
Hey Little Girl	7"	Columbia	DB7168	1963	**£10**	
I'm So Lost	7"	Columbia	DB7463	1965	**£10**	
Investigate	7"	Columbia	DB7967	1966	**£12**	
Live At The Torch	LP	Contempo	COLP1001	1973	**£10**	
Matador	7"	Columbia	DB7271	1964	**£10**	
Monkey Time	7"	Columbia	DB7099	1963	**£12**	
Monkey Time	LP	OKeh	OKM12105	1963	**£15**	US
Pride And Joy	7"	Columbia	DB7609	1965	**£10**	
Rhythm	7"	Columbia	DB7365	1964	**£10**	
Rhythm Of Major Lance	LP	Columbia	33SX1728	1965	**£25**	
Right Track	7"	Contempo	C1	1973	**£4**	
Sweeter As The Days Go By	7"	Atlantic	584302	1969	**£5**	
Too Hot To Hold	7"	Columbia	DB7688	1965	**£10**	
Um Um Um Um Um Um	7"	Columbia	DB7205	1964	**£10**	chart single
Um Um Um Um Um Um	7" EP	Columbia	SEG8318	1964	**£20**	
Um Um Um Um Um Um	LP	OKeh	OKM12106	1964	**£15**	US

LANCERS

Title	Format	Label	Cat. No.	Year	Price	Notes
Alphabet Rock	7"	Vogue Coral	Q72128	1956	**£4**	
Get Out Of The Car	7"	Vogue Coral	Q72081	1955	**£4**	
Mister Sandman	7"	Vogue Coral	Q2038	1954	**£4**	
Presenting The Lancers	7" EP	London	REP1027	1955	**£10**	
So High So Low So Wide	7"	London	HL8079	1954	**£8**	
Stop Chasing Me Baby	7"	London	HL8027	1954	**£8**	

LANDER, BOB & THE SPOTNIKS

Title	Format	Label	Cat. No.	Year	Price	Notes
Midnight Special	7"	Oriole	CB1784	1962	**£5**	
My Old Kentucky Home	7"	Oriole	CB1756	1962	**£5**	

LANDIS, JERRY

Jerry Landis was one of the many pseudonyms adopted by Paul Simon in the years before he discovered folk music. In America, the "Carlos Diminquez" single was issued under the name Paul Kane.

Carlos Diminquez	7"	Oriole	CB1390	1962	**£20**	

LANDS, HOAGY

I'm Yours	7"	Stateside	SS2085	1968	**£4**	
Next In Line	7"	Stateside	SS2030	1967	**£35**	
Next In Line	7"	UK	USA14	1975	**£4**	

LANE BROTHERS

Mimi	7"	London	HLR9150	1960	**£4**	

LANE, MICKEY LEE

Hey Sah-lo-ney	7"	Stateside	SS456	1965	**£20**	
Shaggy Dog	7"	Stateside	SS354	1964	**£5**	

LANE, RONNIE

Anymore For Anymore	LP	GM	1024	1974	**£10**	chart LP
How Come	7"	GM	GMS011	1973	**£4**	PS
One For The Road	LP	Island	ILPS9366	1976	**£10**	
Ronnie Lane's Slim Chance	LP	Island	ILPS9321	1975	**£10**	
See Me	LP	Gem	GEM107	1979	**£10**	

LANG, DON

Cloudburst	78	HMV	POP115	1955	**£5**	chart single
Come Go With Me	7"	HMV	POP335	1957	**£10**	
Don't Open That Door	7"	HMV	POP805	1960	**£4**	
Four Brothers	7"	HMV	7M354	1956	**£10**	
Hand Jive	LP	HMV	DLP		**£25**	
Hey Daddy	7"	HMV	POP510	1958	**£5**	
Hoot And A Holler	7"	HMV	POP649	1959	**£5**	
Percy Green	7"	HMV	POP623	1959	**£4**	
Queen Of The Hop	7"	HMV	POP547	1958	**£8**	
Red Planet Rock	7"	HMV	POP414	1957	**£12**	
Reveille Rock	7"	HMV	POP682	1959	**£6**	
Rock 'N' Roll	7" EP	HMV	7EG8208	1957	**£25**	
Rock 'N' Blues	7"	HMV	7M416	1956	**£12**	
Rock Around The Islands	7"	HMV	7M381	1956	**£12**	
Rock Mister Piper	7"	HMV	POP289	1957	**£12**	
Sink The Bismarck	7"	HMV	POP714	1960	**£8**	chart single
Six Five Hand Jive	7"	HMV	POP434	1958	**£10**	
Six Five Special	7"	HMV	POP350	1957	**£8**	chart single
Sweet Sue	7"	HMV	POP260	1956	**£6**	
Tequila	7"	HMV	POP465	1958	**£8**	
White Silver Sands	7"	HMV	POP382	1957	**£6**	
Wiggle Wiggle	7"	HMV	POP585	1959	**£6**	
Witch Doctor	7"	HMV	POP488	1958	**£6**	chart single

LANG, RAY

Last Train	7"	Brunswick	05683	1957	**£4**	

LANGLEY, PERPETUAL

So Sad	7"	Planet	PLF110	1966	**£8**	
Surrender	7"	Planet	PLF115	1966	**£6**	

LANSON, SNOOKY

It's Almost Tomorrow	7"	London	HLD8223	1956	**£10**	
Last Minute Love	7"	London	HLD8236	1956	**£15**	
Seven Days	7"	London	HLD8249	1956	**£10**	

LARKS

Jerk	LP	Money	LP1102	1965	**£20**	US
Jerk	7"	Pye	7N25284	1964	**£10**	
Soul Kaleidoscope	LP	Money	LP1107	1966	**£12**	US
Superslick	LP	Money	MY1110	1967	**£12**	US

LARO

Jamaican Referendum Calypso	7"	Kalypso	XX21	196-	**£6**	

LARRY & JOHNNY

Beatle Time	7"	Outasite	45501	1965	**£20**	

LAST EXIT

Last Exit was a rock group formed from within the ranks of the Newcastle Big Band, and like its parent organisation, played in pubs and clubs around Newcastle. The singer/bass player was Gordon Sumner - better known as Sting - and it is he that can be heard on the group's locally produced single.

Title	Format	Label	Number	Year	Price	Notes
Whispering Voices	7"	Wudwink	WUD01	1975	**£20**	

LAST POETS

The sound of Black Power. The Last Poets deliver their angry, razor-sharp rants over a percussion backing - and if that sounds like a description of rap music, then that is exactly what it is. The rhythms are 1971 rhythms (no drum machines), but the style and the stance is the same.

Title	Format	Label	Number	Year	Price	Notes
Chastisement	LP	Blue Thumb	539	1972	**£15**	US
Last Poets	LP	Douglas	Z30811	1971	**£12**	US
Right On	LP	Juggernaut	8802	1971	**£12**	US
This Is Madness	LP	Douglas	DGL69012	1971	**£12**	

LAST RITUAL

Title	Format	Label	Number	Year	Price	Notes
Last Ritual	LP	Capitol		1969	**£15**	US

LATTER, GENE

Title	Format	Label	Number	Year	Price	Notes
Always	7"	CBS	202655	1967	**£4**	
Help Me Judy, Help Me	7"	Parlophone	R5800	1969	**£4**	
Just A Minute Or Two	7"	Decca	F12364	1966	**£4**	
Little Piece Of Leather	7"	CBS	2843	1967	**£6**	
Mother's Little Helper	7"	Decca	F12397	1966	**£6**	
My Life Ain't Easy	7"	Spark	SRL1015	1970	**£4**	
Old Iron Bell	7"	Spark	SRL1031	1971	**£4**	
Sign On The Dotted Line	7"	Spark	SRL1022	1970	**£5**	
Something Inside Me Died	7"	CBS	202483	1967	**£5**	
Tiger Bay	7"	Parlophone	R5815	1969	**£4**	
Too Busy Thinkin' 'Bout My Baby	7"	Parlophone	R5913	1971	**£4**	
Tribute To Otis	7"	Direction	583245	1968	**£4**	
With A Child's Heart	7"	CBS	2986	1967	**£4**	

LAUGHING APPLE

Title	Format	Label	Number	Year	Price	Notes
Ha-Ha He-He	7"	Autonomy	AUT001	1981	**£8**	
Participate	7"	Autonomy	AUT002	1981	**£8**	
Precious Feeling	7"	Essential	ESS001	1982	**£12**	

LAUGHING WIND

Title	Format	Label	Number	Year	Price	Notes
Laughing Wind	LP	Tower		1967	**£25**	US

LAUPER, CYNDI

Title	Format	Label	Number	Year	Price	Notes
Change Of Heart	7"	Portrait	CYNDI1	1986	**£4**	spinning wheel PS
She Bop	7"	Portrait	WA4620	1984	**£4**	pic disc
Time After Time	7"	Portrait	WA4290	1984	**£4**	pic disc

LAUREL & OWEN

Title	Format	Label	Number	Year	Price	Notes
She's Gone To Napoli	7"	Blue Beat	BB149	1962	**£10**	

LAURENCE, ZACK

Title	Format	Label	Number	Year	Price	Notes
Beatle Concerto	7" EP	HMV	7EG8968	1966	**£4**	

LAURENZ, JOHN

Title	Format	Label	Number	Year	Price	Notes
Goodbye Stranger Goodbye	7"	London	HL8138	1955	**£8**	

LAURIE

Title	Format	Label	Number	Year	Price	Notes
I Love Onions	7"	Decca	F12424	1966	**£4**	

LAVERN, ROGER & THE MICRONS

Title	Format	Label	Number	Year	Price	Notes
Christmas Stocking	7"	Decca	F11791	1963	**£8**	

LAVETTE, BETTY

Title	Format	Label	Number	Year	Price	Notes
He Made A Woman Out Of Me	7"	Polydor	56786	1969	**£4**	
I Feel Good All Over	7"	Stateside	SS2015	1967	**£5**	
Only Your Love	7"	Pama	PM748	196-	**£4**	

LAWRENCE, STEVE

Title	Format	Label	Number	Year	Price	Notes
Fabulous	7"	Vogue Coral	Q72264	1957	**£5**	
Footsteps	7"	HMV	POP726	1960	**£4**	chart single
Girls Girls Girls	7"	London	HLT9166	1960	**£4**	chart single
I Only Have Eyes For You	7"	Coral	Q72353	1959	**£4**	

Party Doll	7"	Vogue Coral	Q72243	1957	**£5**	
Pretty Blue Eyes	7"	HMV	POP689	1960	**£4**	
Speedo	7"	Vogue Coral	Q72133	1956	**£5**	

LAWRIE, BILLY

Rock And Roller	7"	RCA	RCA2439	1973	**£4**	

LAWRIE, BILLY M.

Roll Over Beethoven	7"	Polydor	56363	1969	**£6**	

LAWSON, JULIET

Boo	LP	Sovereign		1972	**£25**	

LAWSON, SHIRLEY

Star	7"	Soul City	SC108		**£8**	
Star	7"	Soul City	SC108		**£20**	demo

LAWSON-HAGGART ROCKING BAND

Bopping At The Hop	7" EP	Brunswick	OE9451	1959	**£12**	

LAWTON, LOU

Doin' The Philly Dog	7"	Ember	EMBS232	1967	**£5**	
I'm Just A Fool	7"	Speciality	SPE1005		**£15**	

LAZARUS, KEN & THE CREW

Monkey Man	7"	London	HLJ10301	1970	**£4**	

LAZY LESTER

I'm A Lover Not A Fighter	7"	Stateside	SS277	1964	**£5**	
Made Up My Mind	LP	Blue Horizon	2431007	1971	**£20**	

LAZY SMOKE

Corridor Of Faces	LP	Heyoka		1972	**£150**	

LE ORME

Felona And Serona	LP	Charisma	CAS1072	1973	**£10**	

LEA VALLEY SKIFFLE GROUP

Lea Valley Skiffle Group	7" EP	Esquire	EP163	195-	**£6**	

LEADBELLY

Backwater Blues	78	Capitol	CL13282	1950	**£8**	
From The Last Sessions	LP	Folkways	3019	1967	**£10**	US
How Long Blues	7" EP	Melodisc	EPM763	195-	**£5**	
Huddie Ledbetter	LP-10"	Folkways	2013	1960	**£20**	US
Keep Your Hands Off Her	LP	Folkways	FV9021	1965	**£10**	US
Last Sessions Part 2	LP	Folkways	2941	1963	**£10**	US
Leadbelly 2	LP	Storyville	SLP139	196-	**£12**	
Leadbelly	LP-10"	Capitol	H369	195-	**£75**	US
Leadbelly	7" EP	Capitol	EAP120111	1961	**£5**	
Leadbelly	LP-10"	Folkways	14	1960	**£10**	US
Leadbelly	LP-10"	Folkways	24	1960	**£10**	US
Leadbelly	LP-10"	Folkways	43	1960	**£10**	US
Leadbelly	LP-10"	Folkways	4	1960	**£10**	US
Leadbelly	7" EP	Melodisc	EPM777	195-	**£5**	
Leadbelly	LP	Storyville			**£12**	
Leadbelly	7" EP	Storyville	SEP337		**£5**	
Ledbetter's Best	7" EP	Capitol	EAP11821	1961	**£5**	
Ledbetter's Best	7" EP	Capitol	EAP41821	1961	**£5**	
Library Of Congress Recordings	LP	Elektra	EKL3012	1966	**£12**	US
Memorial Vol.3	LP	Stinson	SLP48	1962	**£15**	US, red vinyl
Midnight Special	LP	RCA	LPV505	1964	**£12**	US
Party Plays And Songs	7" EP	Melodisc	EPM787	195-	**£5**	
Rock Island Line	LP-10"	Folkways	2014	1960	**£20**	US
Rock Island Line	7" EP	RCA	RCX146	1959	**£5**	
See See Rider	7" EP	Melodisc	EPM782	195-	**£5**	
Sinful Songs	LP-10"	Allegro	4027	195-	**£30**	US
Storyville Blues Anthology Vol.7	7" EP	Storyville	SEP387		**£5**	
Take This Hammer	LP	Folkways	FV9001	1965	**£10**	US

LEADERS

Night People	7"	Fontana	TF602	1965	**£4**	

LEADING FIGURES

Oscillation '67 .... LP .... Deram .... DML1006 .... 1967 ...... **£15** ....
Sound And Movement .... LP .... Ace Of Clubs .. SCL1225 .... 1967 ...... **£15** ....

LEAFHOUND

Some records gain a reputation within the collectors' market out of all proportion to their musical worth. The Leafhound LP is very much a case in point - the cover and its title imply some kind of psychedelic masterpiece, whereas the music is actually rather ordinary hard rock, with a singer who would love to be Robert Plant, but who sadly is not. The lead guitarist manages the odd nice phrase or two, though...

Growers Of Mushrooms .... LP .... Decca .... SKLR5094 .... 1971 .... **£700** ....
Leafhound .... LP .... Telefunken ...... 14604 .... 1971 ...... **£40** .... German

LEAGUE OF GENTLEMEN

Each Little Falling Tear .... 7" .... Columbia .... DB7666 .... 1965 .... **£5** ....
How Can You Tell .... 7" .... Planet .... PLF109 .... 1966 .... **£8** ....

LEANDER, MIKE

Heroes .... 7" .... Decca .... F11849 .... 1964 .... **£4** ....

LEARY, TIMOTHY

L.S.D. .... LP .... Pixie .... CA1069 .... 1966 ...... **£30** .... US
Turn On, Tune In, Drop Out .... LP .... ESP .... 1027 .... 1966 ...... **£20** .... US
Turn On, Tune In, Drop Out .... LP .... Mercury .... MG21131 .... 1967 ...... **£15** .... US
You Can Be Anyone This Time Around . LP .... Douglas .... 1 .... 196- ...... **£25** .... US

LEATHER COATED MINDS

The album by the Leathercoated Minds contains the recording debut of J.J.Cale, although those seeking the roots of his inimitable sleepy guitar and singing style will be disappointed. Instead the music is exactly the kind of fare that bad sixties films included in their soundtracks whenever a party was shown. As is often the case in the record collectors' market, a high price tag is no guarantee of musical quality!

Trip Down Sunset Strip .... LP .... Fontana .... STL5412 .... 1967 ...... **£60** ....

LEATHER NUN

Slow Death .... 7" .... Industrial .... IR006 .... 1979 ...... **£12** ....

LEAVES

All The Good That's Happening .... LP .... Capitol .... T2638 .... 1967 ...... **£25** .... US
Hey Joe .... 7" .... Fontana .... TF713 .... 1966 ...... **£15** ....
Hey Joe .... LP .... Mire .... 3005 .... 1966 ...... **£25** .... US

LED ZEPPELIN

Original pressings of the Led Zeppelin LPs I - IV are easily identified by their purple and red Atlantic labels and pre-Kinney catalogue numbers, but for the very first LP, it is possible to identify which copies were issued during the few weeks following its release. These all have covers on which the title and company name are printed in turquoise, instead of the orange which has been used on every copy since. The rarest Led Zeppelin records, however, are the UK singles, all of which exist in demonstration form only due to the group's constant refusal to allow their full commercial release.

Communication Breakdown .... 7" .... Atlantic .... 584269 .... 1969 .... **£100** .... demo
D'Yer Maker .... 7" .... Atlantic .... K10296 .... 1973 ...... **£50** .... demo
In Through The Out Door .... LP .... Swan Song ..... SSK59410 .... 1979 ...... **£50** ..... set of 6 LPs in different sleeves A-F
In Through The Out Door .... LP .... Swan Song ..... SSK59410 .... 1979 ...... **£25** .... test pressing
Led Zeppelin 2 .... LP .... Atlantic .... 588198 .... 1969 ...... **£10** .... chart LP
Led Zeppelin 2 .... LP .... Mobile Fid. ...... MFSL1065 .... 1980 ...... **£25** .... US audiophile
Led Zeppelin 3 .... LP .... Atlantic .... 2401002 .... 1970 ...... **£10** .... chart LP
Led Zeppelin 3 .... LP .... Atlantic .... SD7201 .... 1971 ...... **£30** .... US mono promo
Led Zeppelin 4 .... LP .... Atlantic .... 2401012 .... 1971 ...... **£10** .... chart LP
Led Zeppelin 4 .... LP .... Atlantic .... K50008 .... 1978 ...... **£20** .... purple vinyl
Led Zeppelin .... LP .... Atlantic .... 588171 .... 1969 ...... **£10** .... chart LP
Led Zeppelin .... LP .... Atlantic .... 588171 .... 1969 ...... **£20** .... turquoise lettering on cover
Trampled Underfoot .... 7" .... Swan Song ..... DC1 .... 1979 ...... **£10** .... demo
Whole Lotta Love .... 7" .... Atlantic .... 584309 .... 1969 .... **£100** .... demo

LED ZEPPELIN & DUSTY SPRINGFIELD

Climb Aboard Led Zeppelin/
Dusty In Memphis .... LP .... Atlantic .... TLST135 .... 1969 ...... **£40** .... US promo

LEE, ALVIN

Road To Freedom .... LP .... Chrysalis .... 1054 .... 1973 ...... **£10** ....

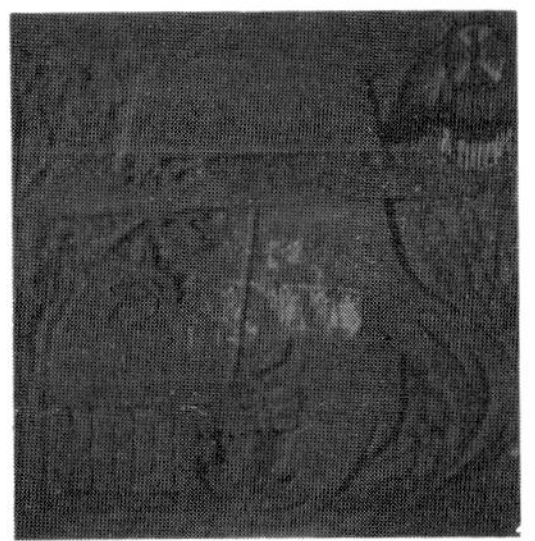

Blues Breakers

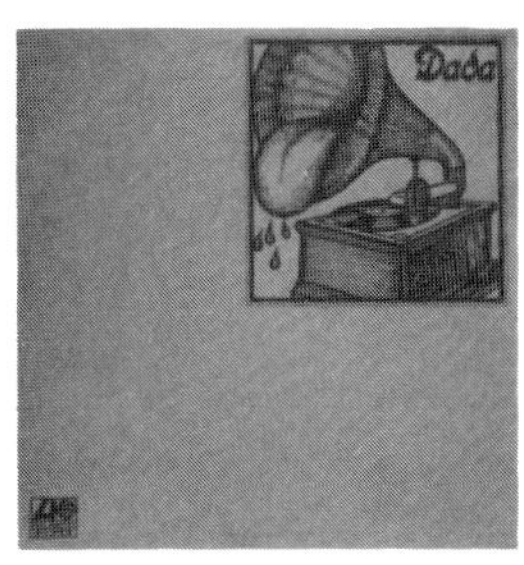

Fancy Colours

I've Got This Guitar And I've Learned How To Make It Talk

All Bold As Love

Distortions

Forms And Feelings

I Wanna Be Bobby's Girl

Fiends And Angels

Like A Circle Round The Sun

Anthems In Eden

Electric Muse

Liege And Lief

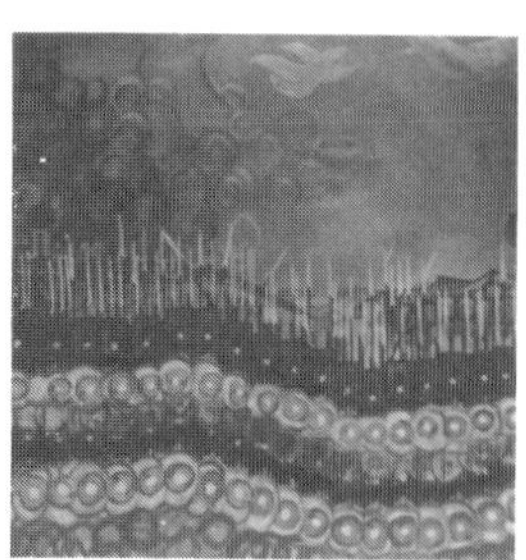

Sunshine Possibilities

Writer Of Songs

Bread, Love And Dreams

Children Of The Sun

Back To The Garden

Divisions On A Crowd

Happy Sad

Under My Own Disguise

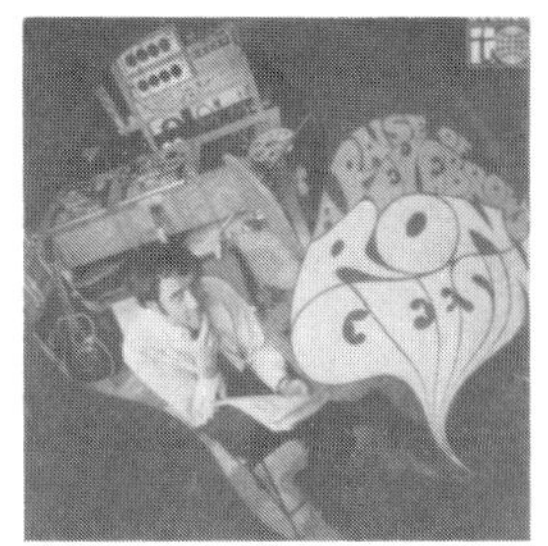

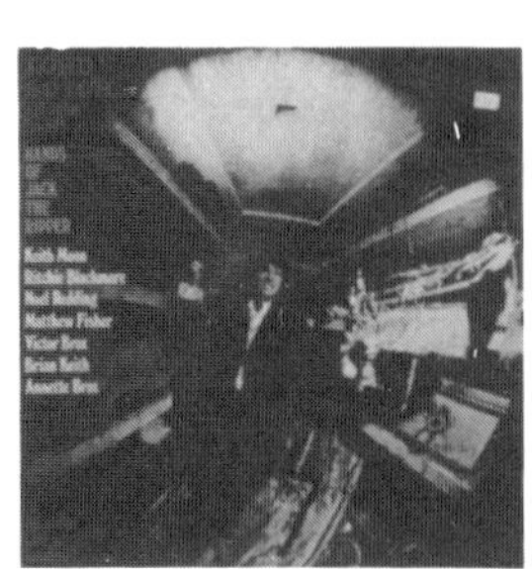

Certainly Random

You're Driving Me Crazy

Naval Aviation In Art

Strictly Personal

Package Tour

All Together Now

They're Gonna Put Me In The Movies

Tonight At Noon

The Rock Machine Turns You On

Strange Pleasure

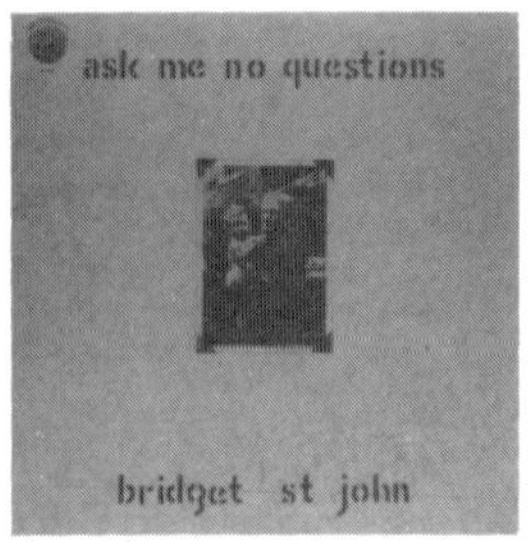

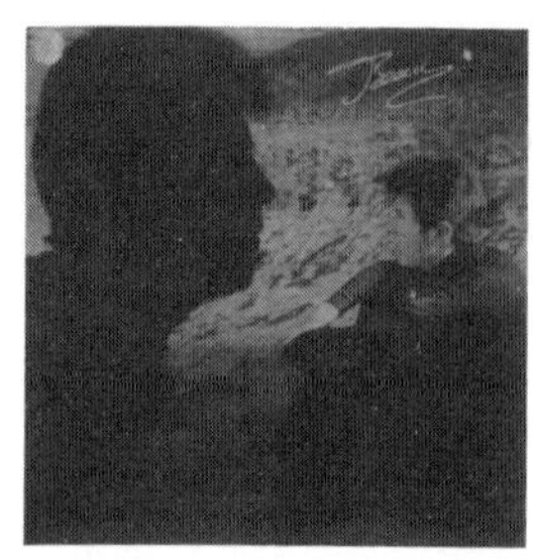

The Perfumed Garden

The Dawn Take-Away Concert

LEE, ARTHUR

Title	Format	Label	Cat. No.	Year	Price	Notes
Sad Song	7"	A&M		1972	**£5**	
Vindicator	LP	A&M	AMLS64356	1972	**£15**	

LEE, BRENDA

Title	Format	Label	Cat. No.	Year	Price	Notes
Ain't Gonna Cry No More	7"	Brunswick	05963	1966	**£4**	
Ain't That Love	7"	Brunswick	05720	1957	**£20**	
All Alone Am I	LP	Brunswick	LAT8530	1962	**£12**	chart LP
All Alone Am I	7"	Brunswick	05882	1963	**£4**	chart single
All Alone Am i	7" EP	Brunswick	OE9492	1963	**£6**	
All The Way	LP	Brunswick	LAT8383	1961	**£10**	mono, chart LP
All The Way	LP	Brunswick	STA3048	1961	**£10**	stereo, chart LP
Alone With You	7"	Brunswick	05911	1964	**£4**	
As Usual	7"	Brunswick	05899	1964	**£4**	chart single
Bill Bailey	7"	Brunswick	05780	1959	**£6**	
Break It To Me Gently	7"	Brunswick	05864	1962	**£4**	chart single
By Request	LP	Brunswick	LAT8576	1964	**£10**	
Bye Bye Blues	LP	Brunswick	LAT8649	1966	**£10**	chart LP
Christmas Will Be Just Another Lonely Day	7"	Brunswick	05921	1964	**£4**	chart single
Coming On Strong	LP	Brunswick	LAT8672	1967	**£10**	
Coming On Strong	7"	Brunswick	05967	1966	**£4**	
Dum Dum	7"	Brunswick	05854	1961	**£4**	chart single
Emotions	LP	Brunswick	LAT8376	1961	**£12**	mono
Emotions	LP	Brunswick	STA3044	1961	**£12**	stereo
Emotions	7"	Brunswick	05847	1961	**£4**	chart single
Fool Number One	7"	Brunswick	05860	1961	**£4**	chart single
Four From Sixty Four	7" EP	Brunswick	OE9510	1965	**£6**	
Grandma What Great Songs	LP	Brunswick	LAT8319	1958	**£15**	
Here Comes That Feeling	7"	Brunswick	05871	1962	**£4**	chart single
I Want To Be Wanted	7"	Brunswick	05839	1960	**£4**	chart single
I Wonder	7"	Brunswick	05891	1963	**£4**	chart single
I'm Gonna Lassoo Santa Claus	7"	Brunswick	05628	1956	**£30**	
I'm Sorry	7"	Brunswick	05833	1960	**£4**	chart single
Is It True	7"	Brunswick	05915	1964	**£4**	chart single
It Started All Over Again	7"	Brunswick	05876	1962	**£4**	chart single
Let Me Sing	LP	Brunswick	LAT8548	1963	**£10**	
Let's Jump The Broomstick	7"	Brunswick	05823	1960	**£5**	chart single
Losing You	7"	Brunswick	05886	1963	**£4**	chart single
Love You	LP	Ace Of H.	AH59	1963	**£15**	
Love You Till I Die	7"	Brunswick	05685	1957	**£25**	
Love You Till I Die	7" EP	Brunswick	OE9462	1961	**£12**	
Merry Christmas From Brenda	LP	Brunswick	LAT8590	1964	**£10**	
Miss Dynamite	LP	Brunswick	LAT8347	1959	**£15**	
Pretend	7" EP	Brunswick	OE9482	1962	**£8**	
Ride Ride Ride	7"	Brunswick	05970	1967	**£4**	
Ring A My Phone	7"	Brunswick	05755	1958	**£20**	
Rockin' Around The Christmas Tree	7"	Brunswick	05880	1962	**£4**	chart single
Rusty Bells	7"	Brunswick	05943	1965	**£4**	
Show For Christmas Seals	LP	Decca	MG9226	1962	**£12**	US
Sincerely	LP	Brunswick	LAT8396	1961	**£10**	mono
Sincerely	LP	Brunswick	STA3056	1961	**£10**	stereo
Speak To Me Pretty	7"	Brunswick	05867	1962	**£4**	chart single
Speak To Me Pretty	7" EP	Brunswick	OE9488	1962	**£6**	
Sweet Impossible You	7"	Brunswick	05896	1963	**£4**	chart single
Sweet Nothings	7"	Brunswick	05819	1960	**£4**	chart single
Ten Golden Years	LP	Decca	DL4757	1966	**£10**	US, gatefold
Thanks A Lot	7"	Brunswick	05927	1965	**£4**	chart single
That's All	LP	Brunswick	LAT8516	1962	**£10**	chart LP
Think	7"	Brunswick	05903	1964	**£4**	chart single
This Is Brenda Lee	LP	Brunswick	LAT8360	1960	**£12**	
Too Little Time	7"	Brunswick	05957	1966	**£4**	
Too Many Rivers	LP	Brunswick	LAT8622	1965	**£10**	
Too Many Rivers	7"	Brunswick	05936	1965	**£4**	chart single
Top Teen Hits	LP	Brunswick	LAT8603	1965	**£10**	
Tribute To Al Jolson	7" EP	Brunswick	OE9499	1964	**£6**	
Truly Truly True	7"	Brunswick	05933	1965	**£4**	
Versatile Brenda Lee	LP	Brunswick	LAT8614	1965	**£10**	
Where's The Melody	7"	Brunswick	05976	1967	**£5**	
You Can Depend On Me	7"	Brunswick	05849	1961	**£4**	

LEE, BUNNY ALL STARS

Leaping With Mr.Lee	LP	Island	ILP986	1968	**£50**	

LEE, BYRON

Caribbean Jungle	LP	Island	ILP905	1964	**£40**	
Dumplings	7"	Blue Beat	BB2	1960	**£10**	
Every Day Will Be Like A Holiday	7"	Major Minor	MM615	1969	**£5**	
In The Mood	7"	Dragon	DRA1008	1973	**£4**	
Jamaica Ska	7"	Parlophone	R5182	1964	**£6**	
Joy Ride	7"	Starlite	ST45045	1961	**£6**	
Make It Reggae	7"	Dynamic	DYN435	197-	**£4**	
Mash Mr.Lee	7"	Blue Beat	BB28	1961	**£10**	
My Sweet Lord	7"	Dynamic	DYN409	197-	**£4**	
Night Train From Jamaica	7"	MGM	MGM1256	1964	**£6**	
River Bank	7"	Parlophone	R5124	1964	**£6**	
Say Bye Bye	7"	Parlophone	R5140	1964	**£6**	
Ska Time	7" EP	Atlantic	AET6014	1965	**£8**	
Sour Apples	7"	Parlophone	R5125	1964	**£6**	
Too Late	7"	Parlophone	R5177	1964	**£6**	
Way Back Home	7"	Dynamic	DYN414	197-	**£4**	

LEE, CURTIS

Get My Bag	7"	CBS	2717	1967	**£4**	
Night At Daddy Gees	7"	London	HLX9533	1962	**£4**	
Pledge Of Love	7"	London	HLX9313	1961	**£6**	
Pretty Little Angel Eyes	7"	London	HLX9397	1961	**£6**	chart single
Under The Moon Of Love	7"	London	HLX9445	1961	**£6**	
With All My Heart	7"	Top Rank	JAR317	1960	**£8**	

LEE, DEREK

Girl	7"	Parlophone	R5468	1966	**£4**	

LEE, DINAH

I Can't Believe What You Say	7"	Aladdin	WI608	1965	**£8**	
I'll Forgive You Then Forget You	7"	Aladdin	WI606	1965	**£8**	

LEE, FREDDIE FINGERS

Friendly Undertaker	7"	Fontana	TF619	1965	**£5**	
I'm Gonna Buy Me A Dog	7"	Fontana	TF655	1966	**£8**	
Bossy Boss	7"	Columbia	DB8002	1966	**£5**	

LEE, JACKIE

Duck	7"	Fontana	TF646	1965	**£6**	
Duck	7"	London	HLM10233	1968	**£4**	
Oh My Darling	7"	Jayboy	BOY66	1972	**£5**	
Would You Believe	7"	Jayboy	BOY28	1970	**£5**	

LEE, JAMIE & THE ATLANTICS

In The Night	7"	Decca	F11571	1963	**£20**	

LEE, JIMMY

All My Life	7"	Starlite	ST45059	1961	**£5**	

LEE, JOHNNY

Cindy Lou	7"	Fontana	H257	1960	**£4**	
Lonely Joe	7"	Fontana	H306	1961	**£4**	
Poetry In Motion	7"	Fontana	H280	1960	**£4**	

LEE, LADY

When Love Comes Along	7"	Decca	F11961	1964	**£4**	

LEE, LAURA

As Long As I Got You	7"	Chess	CRS8070	1968	**£4**	
Dirty Man	7"	Chess	CRS8062	1967	**£4**	
Rip Off	7"	Hot Wax	HWX115	1972	**£4**	
To Win Your Heart	7"	T. Motown	TMG831	1972	**£4**	
To Win Your Heart	7"	T. Motown	TMG831	1972	**£20**	demo
Two Sides Of Laura Lee	LP	Hot Wax		197-	**£12**	

Wedlock Is A Padlock	7"	Hot Wax	HWX118	1973	**£4**	
Women's Love Rights	LP	Hot Wax		197-	**£12**	
You've Got The Love To Save Me	7"	Hot Wax	HWX119	1973	**£4**	

LEE, LAURA (2)

Tell Tommy I Miss Him	7"	Triumph	RGM1030	1960	**£8**	

LEE, LEAPY

Little Arrows	7"	MCA	MU1028	1968	**£4**	chart single

LEE, NICKIE

And Black Is Beautiful	7"	Deep Soul	DS9103	1970	**£4**	

LEE, ROY

Two Initials	7"	Decca	F11406	1961	**£4**	

LEEMAN, MARK FIVE

Blow My Blues Away	7"	Columbia	DB7648	1965	**£10**	
Follow Me	7"	Columbia	DB7955	1966	**£10**	
Forbidden Fruit	7"	Columbia	DB7812	1966	**£10**	
Portland Town	7"	Columbia	DB7452	1965	**£10**	

LEER, THOMAS

Private Plane	7"	Oblique	ER101	1978	**£8**	

LEES, JOHN

Best Of My Love	7"	Polydor	2058513	1974	**£6**	
Child Of The Universe	7"	Harvest	HAR5132	1977	**£5**	
Major Fancy	LP	Harvest	SHVL811	1973	**£10**	

LEFEVRE, MYLON

Mylon	LP	Atlantic	2400104	1971	**£10**	
Over The Influence	LP	CBS	31472	1972	**£10**	US
Pierce And Mylon Lefevre	LP	Canaan	CAS7673	1972	**£10**	
Road To Freedom	LP	Chrysalis	CHR1054	1973	**£10**	

LEFEVRE, RAYMOND

Soul Coaxing	7"	Major Minor	MM559	1968	**£4**	chart single

LEFT BANKE

Desiree	7"	Philips	BF1614	1967	**£8**	
Ivy Ivy	7"	Philips	BF1575	1967	**£6**	
Pretty Ballerina	7"	Philips	BF1540	1967	**£6**	
Too	LP	Smash	SRS67113	1968	**£30**	US
Walk Away Renee	LP	Philips	SBL7773	1967	**£30**	
Walk Away Renee	7"	Philips	BF1517	1966	**£8**	

LEGAY

No One	7"	Fontana	TF904	1969	**£15**	

LEGEND

Don't You Know	7"	Vertigo	6059036	1971	**£10**	
Georgia George	7"	Bell	BLL1082	1970	**£10**	
Legend	LP	Bell	SBLL115	1969	**£50**	
Moonshine	LP	Vertigo	6360063	1972	**£50**	spiral label
National Gas	7"	Bell	BLL1048	1969	**£8**	
Red Boot Album	LP	Vertigo	6360019	1971	**£50**	spiral label

LEGEND (2)

Destroys The Blues	7"	Creation	CRE010	1984	**£15**	

LEGEND (3)

Legend	LP	Megaphone	101	1970	**£20**	US

LEGENDARY PINK DOTS

Tower	LP	Inphaze	IPNER1	1982	**£15**	

LEGENDS

Let Loose	LP	Capitol	T1925	1963	**£20**	US
Let Loose	LP	Ermine	101	1963	**£30**	US
Tomorrows's Gonna Be Another Day	7"	Parlophone	R5581	1967	**£4**	
Under The Sky	7"	Parlophone	R5613	1967	**£4**	

LEGRAND, MICHEL & GIL ASKEY
Love Theme From Lady Sings The Blues 7" .... T. Motown....... TMG848 .... 1973........ £4 ....
Love Theme From Lady Sings The Blues 7" .... T. Motown....... TMG848 .... 1973...... £10 .... demo
Love Theme From Lady Sings The Blues 7" .... T. Motown....... TMG848 .... 1973...... £15 .... demo, PS

LEHRER, TOM
Evening Wasted .... LP .... Decca .... LK4332 .... 1960...... £10 .... chart LP
More Songs By Tom Lehrer .... LP .... Lehrer .... 102 .... 1959...... £10 .... US
Songs By Tom Lehrer .... LP-10".. Decca .... LF1311 .... 1958...... £15 .... chart LP
Songs By Tom Lehrer .... LP .... Lehrer .... 101 .... 1958...... £10 .... US

LEIBER STOLLER BIG BAND
Yakety Yak .... LP .... Atlantic........... 847 .... 1960...... £15 .... US

LEIBER STOLLER ORCHESTRA
Blue Baion .... 7" .... HMV............... POP1050 .... 1962........ £6 ....

LEIBER, JERRY
Scooby-Doo .... LP .... Kapp .... KL1127................... 1959...... £25 .... US

LEIBSTANDARTE SS
Triumph Of The Will .... LP .... Come .... 1981...... £60 ....
Weltanschauung .... LP .... Come .... 198- ...... £60 ....

LEIGH, ANDY
Magician .... LP .... Polydor .... 2343034 .... 1970...... £15 ....

LEMER, PETE
Local Colour .... LP .... ESP .... 1057 .... 1966...... £60 ....

LEMMINGS
Out Of My Mind .... 7" .... Pye .... 7N15837 .... 1965........ £8 ....
You Can't Blame Me For Trying .... 7" .... Pye .... 7N15899 .... 1965........ £8 ....

LEMON KITTENS
Big Dentist .... LP .... Illuminated ...... JAM10 .... 1982...... £60 ....
Cake Beast .... 12" .... United Dairies. UD07 .... 1981...... £30 ....
Spoonfed And Writhing .... 7" .... Step Forward .. SF10 .... 1979...... £15 ....
We Buy A Hammer For Daddy .... LP .... United Dairies. UD02 .... 1980...... £60 ....

LEMON LINE
For Your Precious Love .... 7" .... Decca .... F12688 .... 1967........ £4 ....

LEMON MEN
I've Seen You Cut Lemons .... 7" .... Polydor .... 56365 .... 1969........ £5 ....

LEMON PIPERS
Green Tambourine .... LP .... Buddah .... 2349006 .... 1968...... £10 ....
Green Tambourine .... 7" .... Pye .... 7N25444 .... 1968........ £4 .... chart single
Jelly Jungle .... 7" .... Pye .... 7N25464 .... 1968........ £5 ....
Rice Is Nice .... 7" .... Pye .... 7N25454 .... 1968........ £4 .... chart single

LEMON PIPERS & NINETEEN TEN FRUITGUM COMPANY
Presenting .... 7" EP.... Pye .... NEP44091 .... 1968........ £5 ....

LEMON TREE
It's So Nice To Come Home .... 7" .... Parlophone..... R5739 .... 1968...... £10 ....
William Chalker's Time Machine .... 7" .... Parlophone..... R5671 .... 1968...... £12 ....

LENNON, FREDDIE
John Lennon's father was one of the many people who tried to divert a little piece of Beatlemania in his own direction, but with no more success than most of the others.

That's My Life .... 7" .... Piccadilly .... 7N35290 .... 1966...... £15 ....

LENNON, JIMMY & THE ATLANTICS
I Learned To Yodel .... 7" .... Decca .... F11825 .... 1964........ £8 ....

LENNON, JOHN
The expensive albums recorded by John Lennon and Yoko Ono together are rare because, at the height of the Beatles influence and popularity, even John Lennon could not sell records of a foetal heartbeat, inconsequential chatter, ambient noises, and the like. Later Lennon-Ono collaborations include some excellent and underrated pieces of rock avant garde, such as the superbly cathartic "Open Your Box", but the early records are strictly for the completist. The American "Roots" album is not a

bootleg (although bootleg copies of the Adam VIII original do exist). The owner of the label claimed that Lennon had assigned the album to him and began an intensive TV advertising campaign for it. Lennon disagreed, however, and won a court injunction for the record's withdrawal. "Roots" is of particular interest to collectors, however, because it consists of the original version of the LP that became "Rock'n'Roll" - all the tracks are Phil Spector productions and the selection of songs is slightly different.

Borrowed Time	7"	Polydor	PODJ701	1984	**£6**	promo
Borrowed Time	7"	Polydor	POSPG701	1984	**£6**	poster sleeve
Borrowed Time	12"	Polydor	POSPX701	1984	**£6**	
Cold Turkey	7"	Apple	1001	1969	**£12**	PS
Give Peace A Chance	7"	Apple	13	1969	**£25**	demo, PS
Give Peace A Chance	7"	Apple	13	1969	**£10**	PS
Give Peace A Chance	7"	Apple	R5795	1969	**£20**	
Happy First Birthday Capital Radio	7"	W. Bros	SAM20	1974	**£20**	promo
I'm Stepping Out	7"	Polydor	POSP702	1984	**£4**	
I'm Stepping Out	12"	Polydor	POSPX702	1984	**£6**	
Imagine	LP	Apple	PAS10004	1971	**£25**	demo
Imagine	LP	Apple	PAS10004	1971	**£10**	inner, postcard, chart LP
Imagine	LP	Apple	Q4PAS10004	1974	**£20**	quad
Imagine	7"	Apple	R6009	1975	**£15**	demo, PS
Imagine	7"	Apple	R6009	1975	**£8**	PS
Imagine	LP	Mobile Fid.	MFSL1153	1984	**£15**	US audiophile
Instant Karma	7"	Apple	1003	1970	**£12**	PS
John Lennon Collection	LP	Geffen	LS2023	1982	**£15**	US audiophile promo
Long Rap/ The Short Rap	7"	Cotillion	PR104/5	1972	**£20**	US promo for Ronnie Hawkins LP
Milk And Honey	LP	Polydor	POLHP5	1984	**£15**	pic disc
Mind Games	7"	Apple	R5994	1973	**£15**	demo, PS
Mind Games	7"	Apple	R5994	1973	**£6**	PS
Number Nine Dream (2 versions)	7"	Apple	R6003DJ	1974	**£20**	promo
Number Nine Dream	7"	Apple	R6003	1975	**£15**	demo
Plastic Ono Band	LP	Apple	PCS7124	1970	**£10**	chart LP
Plastic Ono Band	LP	Apple	PCS7124	1970	**£30**	demo
Power To The People	7"	Apple	R5892	1971	**£20**	demo, PS
Power To The People	7"	Apple	R5892	1971	**£15**	halved apple label on side 1
Power To The People	7"	Apple	R5892	1971	**£8**	PS
Roots	LP	Adam VIII	LP8018	1975	**£200**	US
Stand By Me	7"	Apple	R6005	1975	**£4**	
Stand By Me	7"	Apple	R6005	1975	**£15**	demo
Starting Over	7"	Geffen		1980	**£25**	promo
Whatever Gets You Thru' The Night	7"	Apple	R5998	1974	**£15**	demo
Whatever Gets You Thru' The Night	7"	EMI	PSR369	1974	**£20**	interview promo
Woman Is The Nigger Of The World	7"	Apple	R5953	1972	**£100**	demo only
You Know My Name	7"	Apple	1002	1969	**£300**	demo

LENNON, JOHN & ELTON JOHN

I Saw Her Standing There	7"	DJM	DJS10965	1981	**£4**	
I Saw Her Standing There	7"	DJM	DJS354	1975	**£5**	PS

LENNON, JOHN & YOKO ONO

Double Fantasy	LP	Nautilus	NR47	1980	**£25**	US audiophile, poster
Happy Xmas (War Is Over)	7"	Apple	R5970	1972	**£20**	demo, PS
Happy Xmas (War Is Over)	7"	Apple	R5970	1972	**£12**	PS, green vinyl
KYA Peace Talk	LP	Capitol	KYA1969	1969	**£30**	US promo
Life With The Lions	LP	Apple	ZAPPLE1	1969	**£50**	
Live Peace In Toronto	LP	Apple	CORE2001	1969	**£40**	with calendar
Two Virgins	LP	Apple	APCOR2	1968	**£100**	mono
Two Virgins	LP	Apple	SAPCOR2	1968	**£50**	stereo
Wedding Album	LP	Apple	SAPCOR11	1969	**£100**	boxed, inserts

LENNON, JULIAN

Too Late For Goodbyes	7"	Charisma	JLY1	1984	**£6**	pic disc
Valotte	7"	Charisma	JLS2	1984	**£6**	shaped pic disc

LENOIR, J.B.

Crusade	LP	Polydor	2482014	1970	**£10**	
I Sing The Way I Feel	7"	Sue	WI339	1965	**£12**	
Mojo Boogie	7"	Blue Horizon	451004	1966	**£20**	
Natural Man	LP	Chess	1410	195-	**£20**	US

LENT, ROBIN

Scarecrow's Journey	LP	Nepentha	6437002	1971	**£20**	

LENTILMAS

The Lentilmas flexi-disc was a promotional release given away to journalists as a 1977 Christmas present. The record is supposed to contain Christmas carols sung by the Sex Pistols.

	7"	Virgin		1977	**£125**	flexi

LENTON, VAL

You Don't Care	7"	Immediate	IM008	1965	**£15**	

LEONARD, DEKE

Diamond Road	7"	United Artists	UP35494	1973	**£4**	
Hard Way To Live	7"	United Artists	UP35556	1973	**£4**	
Iceberg	LP	United Artists	UAG29646	1973	**£10**	
Kamikaze	LP	United Artists	UAG29544	1974	**£10**	chart LP
Louisiana Hoedown	7"	United Artists	UP35668	1974	**£4**	

LEROYS

California GL903	7"	HMV	POP1368	1964	**£4**	
Chills	7"	HMV	POP1312	1964	**£8**	
Don't Cry Baby	7"	HMV	POP1274	1964	**£6**	
Money	7"	Lyntone	LYN504	1963	**£8**	flexi

LES HOBEAUX

Dynamo	7"	HMV	POP444	1958	**£4**	
Mama Don't Allow	7"	HMV	POP403	1957	**£4**	
Oh Mary Don't You Weep	7"	HMV	POP377	1957	**£4**	
Soho Skiffle	7" EP	HMV	7EG8297	1957	**£10**	

LESTER, KETTY

But Not For Me	7"	London	HLN9574	1962	**£4**	chart single
Ketty Lester	7" EP	London	REN1348	1962	**£10**	
Love Letters	LP	Era	EL108	1963	**£20**	US
Love Letters	7"	London	HLN9527	1962	**£5**	chart single
West Coast	7"	Capitol	CL15427	1965	**£5**	

LETTERMEN

Lettermen	7" EP	Capitol	EAP41669	1961	**£4**	

LEVEE BREAKERS

Baby I'm Leaving You	7"	Parlophone	R5291	1965	**£8**	

LEVEE CAMP MOAN

Levee Camp Moan	LP	private		1969	**£180**	

LEVEL 42

Are You Hearing	12"	Polydor	POSPX396	1982	**£6**	
Hot Water	12"	Polydor	PODJX697	1984	**£6**	promo
Level 42	7"	Polydor		1981	**£6**	promo sampler
Love Games	12"	Polydor	POSPX234	1981	**£8**	
Love Meeting Love	7"	Elite	DAZZ5	1980	**£6**	
Love Meeting Love	12"	Elite	DAZZ5	1980	**£15**	
Love Meeting Love	12"	Polydor	POSPX170	1980	**£10**	
Out Of Sight Out Of Mind	7"	Polydor	POSPP570	1983	**£4**	pic disc
Running In The Family	12"	Polydor	PODJX842	1987	**£6**	promo
Running In The Family	12"	Polydor	POSPXX842	1987	**£6**	double
Starchild	12"	Polydor	POSPX343	1981	**£6**	
To Be With You Again	7"	Polydor	POSPP855	1987	**£4**	pic disc
Turn It On	12"	Polydor	POSPX286	1981	**£8**	
Wings Of Love (Remix)	12"	Polydor	POSPX200	1980	**£8**	
Wings Of Love	7"	Polydor	POSP200	1980	**£4**	
Wings Of Love	12"	Polydor	POSPX200	1980	**£10**	
World Machine	12"	Polydor		1985	**£6**	promo sampler

LEVENE, GERRY & THE AVENGERS

Doctor Feelgood	7"	Decca	F11815	1964	**£10**	

LEVIATHAN

Flames	7"	Elektra	EKSN45075	1969	**£6**	
Remember The Times	7"	Elektra	EKSN45052	1968	**£8**	
War Machine	7"	Elektra	EKSN45057	1969	**£8**	

LEVON & THE HAWKS

Stones I Throw	7"	Atlantic	AT4054	1965	**£12**	

LEWIE, JONA

On The Other Hand There's A Fist	LP	Stiff	SEEZ8	1978	**£12**	
On The Other Hand There's A Fist	LP	Stiff	SEEZ8	1978	**£12**	pic disc

LEWIS SISTERS

You Need Me	7"	T. Motown	TMG536	1965	**£25**	
You Need Me	7"	T. Motown	TMG536	1965	**£60**	demo

LEWIS, BARBARA

Baby I'm Yours	LP	Atlantic	8110	1965	**£15**	US
Baby I'm Yours	7"	Atlantic	AT4031	1965	**£6**	
Baby What You Do To Me	7"	Atlantic	584061	1967	**£5**	
Don't Forget About Me	7"	Atlantic	AT4068	1966	**£6**	
Hello Stranger	LP	Atlantic	8086	1963	**£15**	US
Hello Stranger	7"	Atlantic	584153	1968	**£5**	
Hello Stranger	7"	London	HLK9724	1963	**£6**	
It's Magic	LP	Atlantic	8118	1966	**£12**	US
Make Me Belong To You	7"	Atlantic	584037	1966	**£5**	
Make Me Your Baby	7"	Atlantic	AT4041	1965	**£6**	
Pushing A Good Thing Too Far	7"	Atlantic	AT4013	1964	**£6**	
Sho-Nuff	7"	Atlantic	584174	1968	**£5**	
Snap Your Fingers	LP	Atlantic	8090	1964	**£15**	US
Snap Your Fingers	7" EP	Atlantic	AET6015	1965	**£10**	
Snap Your Fingers	7"	London	HLK9832	1964	**£6**	
Some Day We're Gonna Love Again	7"	Atlantic	2091143	1971	**£4**	
Straighten Up Your Heart	7"	London	HLK9779	1963	**£6**	
Workin' On A Groovy Thing	LP	Atlantic	SD8173	1968	**£12**	US

LEWIS, BOBBY

I'm Tossing And Turning Again	7"	Stateside	SS126	1962	**£5**	
One Track Mind	7"	Parlophone	R4831	1961	**£5**	
Tossing And Turning	LP	Beltone	4000	1961	**£50**	US
Tossing And Turning	7"	Parlophone	R4794	1961	**£5**	

LEWIS, FURRY

Back On My Feet Again	LP	Bluesville	BV1036	1961	**£20**	US
Presenting The Country Blues	LP	Blue Horizon	763228	1969	**£30**	

LEWIS, GARY & THE PLAYBOYS

Count Me In	7"	Liberty	LIB55778	1965	**£4**	
Everybody Loves A Clown	LP	Liberty	LRP3428	1965	**£10**	US
Everybody Loves A Clown	7"	Liberty	LIB55818	1965	**£4**	
Girls In Love	7"	Liberty	LIB55971	1967	**£4**	
Golden Greats	LP	Liberty	LRP3468	1966	**£10**	US
Green Grass	7"	Liberty	LIB55880	1966	**£4**	
Hits Again	LP	Liberty	LRP3452	1966	**£10**	US
Jill	7"	Liberty	LBF15025	1967	**£4**	
Listen	LP	Liberty	LRP3524	1967	**£10**	US
Loser	7"	Liberty	LIB55949	1967	**£4**	
My Heart's Symphony	7"	Liberty	LIB55898	1966	**£8**	
New Directions	LP	Liberty	LRP3519	1967	**£10**	US
Orangutan	7"	Liberty	LBF15335	1970	**£4**	
Out Of Sight	LP	Decca	DL4751	1966	**£10**	US
Paint Me A Picture	7"	Liberty	LIB55914	1966	**£4**	
Save Your Heart For Me	7"	Liberty	LIB55809	1965	**£4**	
Sealed With A Kiss	7"	Liberty	LBF15131	1968	**£4**	
Session With...	LP	Liberty	LRP3419	1965	**£10**	US
She's Just My Style	LP	Liberty	LRP3435	1966	**£10**	US
She's Just My Style	7"	Liberty	LIB55846	1966	**£4**	
Sure Gonna Miss Her	7"	Liberty	LIB55865	1966	**£4**	
This Diamond Ring	LP	Liberty	LRP3408	1965	**£10**	US
This Diamond Ring	7"	Liberty	LIB10187	1965	**£4**	
Where Will The Words Come From	7"	Liberty	LIB55933	1967	**£4**	
You Don't Have To Paint...	LP	Liberty	LRP3487	1967	**£10**	US

LEWIS, HOPETON

Take It Easy	LP	Island	ILP957	1967	**£60**	

LEWIS, HUEY & THE NEWS

Tattoo	7"	Chrysalis	CHS2620	1982	**£5**	newspaper sleeve
Tattoo	7"	Chrysalis	CHSP2620	1982	**£5**	pic disc

LEWIS, JENNIFER

Bring It To Me	7"	Columbia	DB7662	1965	**£4**	

LEWIS, JERRY LEE

Baby Baby Bye Bye	7"	London	HLS9131	1960	**£6**	chart single
Baby Hold Me Close	7"	Philips	BF1407	1965	**£4**	
Break Up	7"	London	HLS8700	1958	**£8**	
Breathless	LP	London	HAS8323	1966	**£20**	
Breathless	7"	London	HLS8592	1958	**£6**	chart single
By Request	LP	Philips	BL7746	1966	**£10**	
Carry Me Back To Old Virginia	7"	London	HLS9980	1965	**£4**	
Country Songs For City Folks	LP	Philips	BL7688	1965	**£10**	
Country Style	7" EP	Philips	BE12599	1966	**£6**	
Four More From Jerry Lee Lewis	7" EP	London	RES1378	1963	**£6**	
Golden Hits	LP	Smash	MGS27040	1964	**£10**	US
Good Golly Miss Molly	7"	London	HLS9688	1963	**£4**	chart single
Great Balls Of Fire	7"	London	HLS8529	1957	**£8**	chart single
Greatest Live Show On Earth	LP	Philips	SBL7650	1964	**£10**	
Hang Up My Rock 'N' Roll Shoes	7"	London	HLS9202	1960	**£5**	
Hi Heel Sneakers	7"	Philips	BF1371	1965	**£4**	
High School Confidential	7"	London	HLS8780	1959	**£8**	chart single
Hit The Road Jack	7"	Mercury	AMT1216	1963	**£4**	
I'll Sail My Ship Alone	7"	London	HLS9083	1960	**£4**	
I'm On Fire	7"	Philips	BF1324	1964	**£4**	
It Won't Happen With Me	7"	London	HLS9414	1961	**£4**	
It's A Hang Up Baby	7"	Philips	BF1594	1967	**£4**	
Jerry Lee Lewis	LP	London	HAS2138	1959	**£20**	
Jerry Lee Lewis	LP	Sun	SLP1230	1958	**£60**	US
Jerry Lee Lewis No.1	7" EP	London	RES1140	1958	**£10**	
Jerry Lee Lewis No.2	7" EP	London	RES1186	1959	**£10**	
Jerry Lee Lewis No.3	7" EP	London	RES1187	1959	**£10**	
Jerry Lee Lewis No.4	7" EP	London	RES1296	1961	**£10**	
Jerry Lee Lewis No.5	7" EP	London	RES1336	1962	**£10**	
Jerry Lee Lewis No.6	7" EP	London	RES1351	1963	**£8**	
Jerry Lee Lewis Vol.2	LP	London	HAS2440	1962	**£20**	chart LP
Jerry Lee's Greatest	LP	Sun	SLP1265	1961	**£75**	US
Let's Talk About Us	7"	London	HLS8941	1959	**£4**	
Lewis Boogie	7"	London	HLS9867	1964	**£4**	
Little Queenie	7"	London	HLS8993	1959	**£4**	
Loving Up A Storm	7"	London	HLS8840	1959	**£6**	chart single
Memphis Beat	LP	Philips	SBL7706	1967	**£10**	
Memphis Beat	7"	Philips	BF1521	1966	**£4**	
Rambling Rose	7"	London	HLS9526	1962	**£4**	
Return Of Rock	LP	Philips	SBL7668	1967	**£10**	
Rocking Pneumonia	7"	Philips	BF1425	1965	**£4**	
Shotgun Man	7"	Philips	BF1615	1967	**£4**	
Soul My Way	LP	Philips	BL20117	196-	**£10**	
Sweet Little Sixteen	7"	London	HLS9584	1962	**£4**	chart single
Teenage Letter	7"	London	HLS9722	1963	**£4**	
What'd I Say	7"	London	HLS10193	1968	**£4**	
What'd I Say	7"	London	HLS9335	1961	**£4**	chart single
When I Get Paid	7"	London	HLS9446	1961	**£4**	
Whole Lotta Shaking Going On	LP	London	HAS8251	1965	**£20**	
Whole Lotta Shaking Going On	7"	London	HLS8457	1957	**£10**	chart single
You Win Again	7"	London	HLS8559	1958	**£12**	

LEWIS, JERRY LEE & NASHVILLE TEENS

Live At The Star Club Hamburg	LP	Philips	BL7646	1965	**£10**	

LEWIS, JIMMY

Girl From Texas	7"	Minit	MLF11002	1968	**£4**	

LEWIS, LINDA

Fathoms Deep	LP	Raft	48501	1973	**£10**	
Hacienda View	LP	Ariola	ARL5033	1970	**£10**	
Lark	LP	Reprise	K44208	1972	**£10**	
Say No More	LP	Reprise	K44130	1971	**£10**	
You Turn My Bitter Into Sweet	7"	Polydor	56173	1967	**£12**	

LEWIS, MARGARET

Something's Wrong Baby	7"	Starlite	ST45081	1962	**£4**	

LEWIS, MEADE LUX

Title	Format	Label	Cat. No.	Year	Price	Notes
Barrel House Piano	LP	Tops	L1533		**£20**	US
Blues Piano Artistry	LP	Riverside	9402		**£20**	US
Boogie Woogie And Blues	7" EP	Melodisc	EPM7107	196-	**£10**	
Boogie Woogie Piano And Drums No.1	7" EP	Columbia	SEB10030	1956	**£5**	
Boogie Woogie Piano And Drums No.2	7" EP	Columbia	SEB10052	1957	**£5**	
Meade Lux Lewis	7" EP	Vogue	EPV1065	195-	**£10**	
Out Of The Roaring '20s	LP	ABC-Para.	164	1957	**£10**	US

LEWIS, MIA

Title	Format	Label	Cat. No.	Year	Price	Notes
Nothing Lasts Forever	7"	Parlophone	R5526	1966	**£10**	

LEWIS, RAMSEY

Title	Format	Label	Cat. No.	Year	Price	Notes
1-2-3	7"	Chess	CRS8055	1967	**£4**	
At The Bohemian Caverns	LP	Pye	NJL55	1965	**£12**	
Cry Baby Cry	7"	Chess	CRS8096	1969	**£4**	
Dancin' In The Street	LP	Chess	CRL4533	1968	**£10**	
Function At The Junction	7"	Chess	CRS8058	1967	**£4**	
Girl Talk	7"	Chess	CRS8061	1967	**£4**	
Hang On Ramsey	LP	Chess	CRL4517	1966	**£15**	chart LP
Hang On Sloopy	7"	Chess	CRS8024	1965	**£5**	
Hard Day's Night	7"	Chess	CRS8029	1966	**£4**	
Hard Day's Night	7" EP	Chess	CRE6019	1966	**£5**	
Hi Heel Sneakers	7"	Chess	CRS8031	1966	**£4**	
In Crowd	7"	Chess	CRS8020	1965	**£5**	
In Crowd	LP	Chess	CRL4511	1965	**£15**	
Julia	7"	Chess	CRS8104	1970	**£4**	
Saturday Night After The Movies	7"	Chess	CRS8060	1967	**£4**	
Soul Man	7"	Chess	CRS8064	1967	**£4**	
Uptight	7"	Chess	CRS8044	1966	**£5**	
Wade In The Water	LP	Chess	CRL4522	1966	**£15**	
Wade In The Water	7"	Chess	CRS8041	1966	**£4**	

LEWIS, RICHARD

Title	Format	Label	Cat. No.	Year	Price	Notes
Hey Little Girl	7"	Downbeat	CHA1	1960	**£8**	

LEWIS, SMILEY

Title	Format	Label	Cat. No.	Year	Price	Notes
Big Mamou	78	London	L1189	1953	**£20**	
Don't Be That Way	7"	London	HLU8337	1956	**£100**	
I Hear You Knocking	LP	Imperial	LP9141	1961	**£100**	US
One Night	7"	London	HLU8312	1956	**£100**	
Shame Shame Shame	7"	London	HLP8367	1957	**£75**	

LEWIS, STEVIE

Title	Format	Label	Cat. No.	Year	Price	Notes
Take Me For A Little While	7"	Mercury	MF871	1965	**£5**	

LEWIS, TINY

Title	Format	Label	Cat. No.	Year	Price	Notes
Too Much Rocking	7"	Parlophone	R4617	1959	**£40**	

LEYTON, JOHN

Title	Format	Label	Cat. No.	Year	Price	Notes
Always Yours	LP	HMV	CLP1664	1962	**£25**	
Beautiful Dreamer	7"	HMV	POP1230	1963	**£4**	
Beautiful Dreamer	7" EP	HMV	7EG8843	1964	**£10**	
Cupboard Love	7"	HMV	POP1122	1963	**£4**	chart single
Don't Let Her Go Away	7"	HMV	POP1338	1964	**£4**	
Down The River Nile	7"	HMV	POP1054	1962	**£4**	chart single
Girl On The Floor Above	7"	HMV	POP798	1960	**£4**	
I'll Cut Your Tail Off	7"	HMV	POP1175	1963	**£4**	chart single
John Leyton	7" EP	Top Rank	JKP3016	1962	**£15**	
John Leyton Hit Parade	7" EP	HMV	7EG8747	1962	**£10**	
Johnny Remember Me	7"	Top Rank	JAR577	1961	**£4**	chart single
Lone Rider	7"	HMV	POP992	1962	**£4**	chart single
Lonely City	7"	HMV	POP1014	1962	**£4**	chart single
Lonely Johnny	7"	HMV	POP1076	1962	**£4**	
Make Love To Me	7"	HMV	POP1264	1964	**£4**	chart single
On Lovers' Hill	7"	HMV	POP1204	1963	**£4**	
Son This Is She	7"	HMV	POP956	1961	**£4**	chart single
Tell Laura I Love Her	7" EP	HMV	7EG8854	1964	**£15**	
Tell Laura I Love Her	7"	Top Rank	JAR426	1960	**£6**	
Two Sides Of...	LP	HMV	CLP1497	1961	**£25**	
Wild Wind	7"	Top Rank	JAR585	1961	**£4**	chart single

LEYTON, JOHN & MIKE SARNE

All I Want Is You	7"	HMV	POP1374	1964	**£4**	

LIAR

Set The World On Fire	LP	Bearsville	K55524	1978	**£12**	pic disc

LIBERMAN, JEFFREY

Jeffrey Liberman	LP	Librah	1545	1975	**£40**	US
Solitude Within	LP	Librah	6969	1975	**£40**	US

LIEUTENANT PIGEON

Mouldy Old Music	LP	Decca	SKL5154	1973	**£10**	

LIFE

Hands Of The Clock	7"	Polydor	56778	1969	**£6**	
Life After Death	LP	Polydor	2383295	1974	**£40**	
Woman	7"	Polydor	2058500	1974	**£10**	

LIFE 'N' SOUL

Here Comes Yesterday Again	7"	Decca	F12851	1968	**£8**	
Peacefully Asleep	7"	Decca	F12659	1967	**£8**	

LIFETIME

"Emergency" and "Turn It Over" are densely electric albums like no other. Tony Williams, the group's leader, was the drummer with Miles Davis during the sixties. Lifetime was his idea of a rock group, but filtered through his jazz background, it did not sound very much like anyone else's. Larry Young makes the organ sound like a banshee, pressing adjacent treble keys down all at the same time; John McLaughlin, who has just discovered the delights of high amplification, employs a ferocious fuzz-tone; while Tony Williams plays his customary churning, multi-layered rhythms. Unfortunately, the group was plagued by management problems and when Jack Bruce joined during the recording of "Turn It Over" these only became worse. Later Lifetime recordings are much more routine affairs, although "Believe It", with Allan Holdsworth in fine form on guitar, has its moments.

Believe It	LP	CBS	69201	1976	**£10**	
Emergency	LP	Polydor	583574	1969	**£30**	double
Million Dollar Legs	LP	CBS	81510	1976	**£10**	
One Word	7"	Polydor		1970	**£5**	
Turn It Over	LP	Polydor	2425019	1970	**£12**	

LIGHTCRUST DOUGHBOYS

Lightcrust Doughboys	LP	Audio Lab	AL1525	1959	**£30**	US

LIGHTFOOT, GORDON

Back Here On Earth	LP	United Artists	SULP1239	1969	**£10**	
Bitter Green	7"	United Artists	UP35020	1969	**£4**	
Black Day In July	7"	United Artists	UP2216	1968	**£4**	
Circle Is Small	7"	United Artists	UP2272	1969	**£4**	
Cold On The Shoulder	LP	Reprise	MS42206	1975	**£10**	US quad
Day Before Yesterday	7"	Fontana	TF405	1963	**£6**	
Did She Mention My Name	LP	United Artists	SULP1199	1968	**£10**	
Early Lightfoot	LP	United Artists	UAS29012	1969	**£10**	
Early Morning Rain	7"	United Artists	UP35036	1969	**£4**	
I'm Not Sayin'	7"	W. Bros	WB5621	1966	**£4**	
I'm The One	7"	Decca	F11527	1962	**£6**	
If You Could Read My Mind	7"	Reprise	R20974	1970	**£4**	chart single
Just Like Tom Thumb's Blues	7"	United Artists	UP1109	1965	**£5**	
Lightfoot	LP	United Artists	UAL3487	1965	**£10**	US
Negotiations	7"	Fontana	267275	1963	**£6**	
Sunday Concert	LP	United Artists	UAS29040	1969	**£10**	
Sundown	LP	Mobile Fid.	MFSL1018	1978	**£10**	US audiophile
Sundown	LP	Reprise	MS42177	1974	**£10**	US quad
Way I Feel	LP	United Artists	UAL3587	1967	**£10**	US

LIGHTFOOT, PAPA

Wine Women Whiskey	7"	Liberty	LBF15176	1969	**£4**	

LIGHTFOOT, PAPA GEORGE

Natchez Trace	LP	Liberty	LBS83353	1969	**£12**	

LIGHTHOUSE

Eight Miles High	7"	RCA	RCA1884	1969	**£5**	
Lighthouse	LP	RCA	LSP4173	1969	**£15**	US
One Fine Morning	7"	Philips	6073152	1972	**£4**	
One Fine Morning	LP	Vertigo	6342010	1971	**£20**	spiral label

Title	Format	Label	Cat. No.	Year	Price	Notes
Peacing It All Together	LP	RCA	SF8121	1970	**£15**	
Suite Feeling	LP	RCA	SF8103	1970	**£15**	
Sunny Days	LP	Mooncrest	CREST2	1972	**£10**	
Take It Slow	7"	Philips	6073153	1972	**£4**	
Thoughts Of Moving On	LP	Vertigo	6342011	1971	**£20**	spiral label

LIGHTNIN' ROD & JIMI HENDRIX

Title	Format	Label	Cat. No.	Year	Price	Notes
Doriella Du Fontane	12"	Celluloid	CRT332	1984	**£6**	

LIGHTNIN' SLIM

Title	Format	Label	Cat. No.	Year	Price	Notes
Bell Ringer	LP	Excello	8004	1965	**£20**	US
High And Low Down	LP	Excello	8018	1971	**£10**	US
Just A Little Bit	7"	Blue Horizon	2096013	1972	**£6**	
London Gumbo	LP	Blue Horizon	2931005	1972	**£25**	
Rooster Blues	LP	Blue Horizon	763863	1970	**£30**	
Rooster Blues	LP	Excello	8000	1960	**£35**	US

LIMELIGHT

Title	Format	Label	Cat. No.	Year	Price	Notes
Limelight	LP	Avatar		1981	**£35**	with 7"
Limelight	LP	Future Earth	FER008	1980	**£25**	
Metal Man	7"	Future Earth	FER006	1980	**£8**	

LIMELIGHT (BRINSLEY SCHWARZ)

Title	Format	Label	Cat. No.	Year	Price	Notes
I Should Have Known Better	7"	United Artists	UP35779	1975	**£6**	

LIMEYS

Title	Format	Label	Cat. No.	Year	Price	Notes
Cara Lin	7"	Decca	F12382	1966	**£5**	
I Can't Find My Way Through	7"	Pye	7N15820	1965	**£4**	
Mountain's High	7"	Decca	F12466	1966	**£4**	
Some Tears Fall Dry	7"	Pye	7N15909	1965	**£4**	

LINCOLN, PHILAMORE

Title	Format	Label	Cat. No.	Year	Price	Notes
North Wind Blew South	LP	Epic	BN26497	1967	**£15**	US
Running By The River	7"	Nems	3711	1968	**£5**	

LIND, BOB

Title	Format	Label	Cat. No.	Year	Price	Notes
Don't Be Concerned	LP	Fontana	TL5340	1966	**£10**	
Elusive Butterfly	7"	Fontana	TF670	1966	**£4**	chart single
Hey Nellie Nellie	7"	Verve	VS1501	1967	**£4**	
Photographs Of Feelings	LP	World Pacific		1967	**£10**	US
Remember The Rain	7"	Fontana	TF702	1966	**£4**	chart single
San Francisco Woman	7"	Fontana	TF750	1966	**£4**	
The Elusive Bob Lind	LP	Verve	FT3005	1967	**£10**	US

LINDEN, KATHY

Title	Format	Label	Cat. No.	Year	Price	Notes
Billy	7"	Felsted	AF102	1958	**£4**	
Goodbye Jimmy, Goodbye	7"	Felsted	AF122	1959	**£4**	
Kathy	7" EP	Felsted	GEP1001	1959	**£5**	
Kathy In Love Vol.1	7" EP	Felsted	GEP1002	1959	**£5**	
Kathy In Love Vol.2	7" EP	Felsted	GEP1004	1959	**£5**	
Kissin' Conversation	7"	Felsted	AF111	1958	**£4**	
Mary Lou Wilson And Johnny Brown	7"	Felsted	AF130	1960	**£4**	
Oh Johnny Oh Johnny Oh	7"	Felsted	AF108	1958	**£4**	
That Certain Boy	LP	Felsted	7501	195-	**£20**	US
You Don't Know Girls	7"	Felsted	AF124	1959	**£4**	
You'd Be Surprised	7"	Felsted	AF105	1958	**£4**	

LINDISFARNE

Title	Format	Label	Cat. No.	Year	Price	Notes
Clear White Light	7"	Charisma	CB137	1970	**£10**	
Lady Eleanor	7"	Charisma	CB153	1971	**£4**	PS

LINDYS

Title	Format	Label	Cat. No.	Year	Price	Notes
Train Of Love	7"	Decca	F11253	1960	**£5**	

LINHART, BUZZY

Title	Format	Label	Cat. No.	Year	Price	Notes
Buzzy	LP	Kama Sutra	2319024	1972	**£10**	
Buzzy	LP	Philips	SBL7885	1969	**£10**	
Music	LP	Buddah	2318028	1971	**£10**	
Time To Live Is Now	LP	Kama Sutra	2319011	1971	**£10**	

LINN COUNTY

Title	Format	Label	Cat. No.	Year	Price	Notes
Fever Shot	LP	Mercury	SMCL20165	1969	**£20**	

Proud Flesh Soothseer	LP	Mercury	SMCL20142	1968	**£20**	
Till The Break Of Dawn	LP	Philips	SBL7923	1970	**£20**	

LIONS OF JUDAH

Our Love's A Growin' Thing	7"	Fontana	TF1016	1969	**£8**	

LIPSCOMB, MANCE

Trouble In Mind	LP	Reprise	R2012	1961	**£12**	US

LIQUID SMOKE

Liquid Smoke	LP	Avco	33005	1969	**£35**	

LISTEN

The lead singer of Listen was Robert Plant and he is, in fact, the only member of the group to appear on the single credited to them.

You Better Run	7"	CBS	202456	1965	**£100**	

LITTER

$100 Fine	LP	Hexagon	HX681	1969	**£100**	US
Distortions	LP	Warwick	UR5M1940	1968	**£200**	US
Emerge	LP	Probe	CLPS4504	1969	**£20**	

LITTLE ANTHONY & THE IMPERIALS

Bayou Bayou Baby	7"	Top Rank	JAR366	1960	**£6**	
Best Of...	LP	DCP	DC3809	1966	**£10**	US
Better Use Your Head	7"	United Artists	UP1137	1966	**£12**	
Goin' Out Of My Head	LP	DCP	DC3808	1965	**£10**	US
Goin' Out Of My Head	7"	United Artists	UP1073	1964	**£4**	
Gonna Fix You Good	7"	United Artists	UP1151	1966	**£10**	
Hurt	7"	United Artists	UP1126	1966	**£4**	
Hurt So Bad	7"	United Artists	UP1083	1965	**£5**	
I Miss You	7"	United Artists	UP1112	1965	**£4**	
I'm On The Outside	7"	United Artists	UP1065	1964	**£4**	
I'm On The Outside Lookin' In	LP	United Artists	ULP1089	1964	**£15**	
Little Anthony And The Imperials	7" EP	United Artists	REM405		**£4**	
Little Anthony And The Imperials	7" EP	United Artists	UEP1004	1965	**£5**	
My Love Is A Rainbow	7"	United Artists	UP1189	1967	**£4**	
Oh Yeah	7"	London	HL8848	1959	**£10**	
Shades Of The 40s	LP	End	311	1960	**£35**	US
Shimmy Shimmy Ko Ko Bop	7"	Top Rank	JAR256	1959	**£5**	
Take Me Back	7"	United Artists	UP1098	1965	**£4**	
Tears On My Pillow	7"	London	HLH8704	1958	**£15**	
We Are Little Anthony & The Imperials	LP	End	303	1960	**£50**	US

LITTLE ARCHIE

I Need You	7"	Atlantic	584209	1968	**£4**	

LITTLE BEVERLEY

What A Guy	7"	Pama	PM731	196-	**£8**	

LITTLE BOY BLUE

Dark End Of The Street	7"	Jackpot	JP701	196-	**£8**	
Since You Are Gone	7"	Jackpot	JP705	196-	**£8**	

LITTLE BOY BLUES

In The Woodland Of Weir	LP	Fontana	MGF27578	1967	**£20**	US

LITTLE DARLINGS

Little Bit Of Soul	7"	Fontana	TF539	1965	**£4**	

LITTLE ESTHER

Chains	7"	Sue	WI395	1965	**£8**	

LITTLE EVA

Keep Your Hands Off My Baby	7"	London	HLU9633	1962	**£4**	chart single
Let's Turkey Trot	7"	London	HLU9687	1963	**£4**	chart single
Lllocomotion	LP	London	HAU8036	1963	**£25**	
Locomotion	7"	London	HL9581	1962	**£5**	chart single
Please Hurt Me	7"	Colpix	PX11019	1963	**£4**	
Run To Her	7"	Colpix	PX11035	1964	**£4**	
Stand By Me	7"	Stateside	SS477	1965	**£4**	
Trouble With Boys	7"	Colpix	PX11013	1963	**£4**	

LITTLE FEAT

Title	Format	Label	Number	Year	Price	Notes
Waiting For Columbus	LP	Mobile Fid.	MFSL2013	1978	**£20**	US audiophile double

LITTLE FREE ROCK

Title	Format	Label	Number	Year	Price	Notes
Little Free Rock	LP	Transatlantic	TRA608	1969	**£35**	

LITTLE HANK

Title	Format	Label	Number	Year	Price	Notes
Mr.Bang Bang Man	7"	London	HLU10090	1966	**£12**	
Mr.Bang Bang Man	7"	Monument	MON1045	1970	**£5**	

LITTLE LUTHER

Title	Format	Label	Number	Year	Price	Notes
Eenie Meenie Minie Mo	7"	Pye	7N25266	1964	**£5**	

LITTLE MAC & THE BOSS SOUNDS

Title	Format	Label	Number	Year	Price	Notes
In The Midnight Hour	7"	Atlantic	584031	1966	**£5**	

LITTLE MILTON

Little Milton is a fine blues singer and an even finer blues guitarist - very much in the manner of B.B.King on both counts - but most of his releases are soul records, where he is rather more ordinary. The "Grits And Groceries" LP provides a reasonable balance between the styles, with the outstanding track being a smouldering version of "I Can't Quit You Baby" (also the B side of the "Grits Ain't Groceries" single).

Title	Format	Label	Number	Year	Price	Notes
Blindman	7"	Pye	7N25289	1965	**£5**	
Early In The Morning	7"	Sue	WI4021	1966	**£12**	
Grits Ain't Groceries	LP	Chess	CRLS4552	1969	**£12**	
Grits Ain't Groceries	7"	Chess	CRS8087	1969	**£4**	
If Walls Could Talk	LP	Checker	3012	1970	**£10**	US
Let's Get Together	7"	Chess	CRS8101	1969	**£4**	
Little Milton Sings Big Blues	LP	Checker	3002	1966	**£20**	US
We're Gonna Make It	LP	Checker	2995	1965	**£20**	US
We're Gonna Make It	7"	Chess	CRS8013	1965	**£4**	
Who's Cheating Who?	7"	Chess	CRS8018	1965	**£4**	

LITTLE MR.LEE & THE CHEROKEES

Title	Format	Label	Number	Year	Price	Notes
Young Lover	7"	Vocalion	VP9268	1966	**£10**	

LITTLE RICHARD

Title	Format	Label	Number	Year	Price	Notes
Baby Face	7"	London	HLU8770	1958	**£4**	chart single
Baby What You Want Me To Do	7"	Action	ACT4528	1969	**£4**	
Bama Lama Bama Loo	7"	London	HL9896	1964	**£4**	chart single
Blueberry Hill	7"	Fontana	TF519	1964	**£5**	
By The Light Of The Silvery Moon	7"	London	HLU8831	1959	**£6**	chart single
Coming Home	LP	Coral	LVA9220	1964	**£10**	
Crying In The Chapel	7"	London	HLK9708	1963	**£4**	
Do You Feel It	7" EP	Stateside	SE1042	1966	**£6**	
Explosive Little Richard	LP	Columbia	SCX6136	1967	**£12**	
Fabulous Little Richard	LP	London	HAU2193	1959	**£20**	
Fabulous Little Richard	LP	Speciality	SP2104	1958	**£30**	US
Get Down And Get With It	7"	Columbia	DB8116	1967	**£8**	
Girl Can't Help It	7"	London	HLO8382	1957	**£20**	chart single
Good Golly Miss Molly	7"	London	HLU8560	1958	**£8**	chart single
Great Hits	LP	Fontana	TL5314	1966	**£10**	
He Got What He Wanted	7"	Mercury	AMT1189	1962	**£4**	chart single
He's Back	7" EP	London	REK1400	1963	**£6**	
Here's Little Richard	LP	London	HAO2055	1957	**£20**	
Here's Little Richard	LP	Speciality	100	1957	**£150**	US
Here's Little Richard	LP	Speciality	2100	1957	**£30**	US
I Don't Know What You've Got	7"	Fontana	TF652	1966	**£6**	
I Don't Wanna Discuss It	7"	Columbia	DB8263	1967	**£10**	
I Got It	7"	London	HLU9065	1960	**£6**	
I Need Love	7"	Columbia	DB8058	1966	**£5**	
It Ain't What You Do...	7"	Sue	WI4015	1966	**£8**	
It's Real	LP	Mercury	MCL20036	1965	**£10**	
It's Real	LP	Mercury	MG20656	1961	**£20**	US
Jenny Jenny	7"	London	HLO8470	1957	**£10**	chart single
Joy Joy Joy	7"	Mercury	AMT1165	1961	**£6**	
Kansas City	7"	London	HLU8868	1959	**£4**	chart single
Keep A Knocking	7"	London	HLO8509	1957	**£8**	chart single
King Of The Gospel Singers	LP	Fontana	SFL13010	1968	**£10**	
Little Bit Of Something	7"	Columbia	DB8240	1967	**£12**	
Little Richard And His Band Vol.1	7" EP	London	REO1071	1957	**£10**	
Little Richard And His Band Vol.2	7" EP	London	REO1074	1957	**£10**	

Little Richard And His Band Vol.3	7" EP	London	REO1103	1957	**£10**	
Little Richard And His Band Vol.4	7" EP	London	REO1106	1957	**£10**	
Little Richard And His Band Vol.5	7" EP	London	REU1208	1959	**£10**	
Little Richard And His Band Vol.6	7" EP	London	REU1234	1960	**£10**	
Little Richard And His Band Vol.7	7" EP	London	REU1235	1960	**£10**	
Little Richard 2	LP	London	HAU2126	1958	**£20**	
Little Richard	LP	Camden	CAL420	1956	**£50**	US
Little Richard	LP	Camden	CDN125	1959	**£20**	
Little Richard	LP	Mercury	MCL20019	196-	**£10**	
Little Richard	LP	Speciality	SP2103	1957	**£30**	US
Little Richard Is Back	LP	Fontana	TL5235	1965	**£10**	
Little Richard Sings Freedom Songs	LP	Egmont	EGM9207	1963	**£15**	
Little Richard Sings Gospel	LP	Fidelio	ATL4124	1964	**£10**	
Long Tall Sally	7"	London	HLO8366	1957	**£20**	chart single
Lucille	7"	London	HLO8446	1957	**£12**	chart single
Ooh My Soul	7"	London	HLO8647	1958	**£8**	chart single
Peace In The Valley	7"	Mercury	MF841	1964	**£4**	
Poor Dog	7"	Columbia	DB7974	1966	**£5**	
Pray Along With...	LP	Egmont	EGM9270	196-	**£10**	
Pray Along With...Vol.1	LP	Top Rank	25025	1960	**£15**	
Pray Along With...Vol.2	LP	Top Rank	25026	1960	**£20**	
Rip It Up	7"	London	HLO8336	1956	**£20**	chart single
Sings Gospel	LP	Stateside	SL10054	1964	**£12**	
Travelling Shoes	7"	London	HLK9756	1963	**£4**	
Whole Lotta Shaking Going On	7"	Stateside	SS340	1964	**£6**	
Without Love	7"	Sue	WI4001	1966	**£8**	

LITTLE RICHARD & BROCK PETERS

Little Richard And Brock Peters	7" EP	Summit	LSE2049	1963	**£10**	

LITTLE RICHARD & MEMPHIS SLIM

Little Richard/Memphis Slim	7" EP	Vocalion	VEP170155	1964	**£15**	

LITTLE TONY & THE BROTHERS

Presenting Little Tony	7" EP	Durium	U20058	1958	**£10**	
Teddy Girl	7"	Decca	F21247	1960	**£4**	
Too Good	7"	Decca	F11190	1959	**£4**	chart single
Who's That Knocking	7"	Durium	DC16639	1959	**£8**	

LITTLE WALTER

Best Of...	LP	Chess	LP1428	1958	**£30**	US
Little Walter And His Jukes	7" EP	London	REU1061	1956	**£30**	
Little Walter	LP	Pye	NPL28043	1964	**£20**	
My Babe	7"	London	HLM9175	1960	**£15**	
My Babe	7"	Pye	7N25263	1964	**£4**	

LITTLE, BIG TINY

School Day	7"	Vogue Coral	Q72263	1957	**£4**	

LIVELY ONES

Great Surf Hits	LP	Del-Fi	DFLP1238	1963	**£12**	US
Surf Drums	LP	London	HA8082	1963	**£12**	
Surf Rider	LP	London	HA8107	1963	**£12**	
Surfin' South Of The Border	LP	Del-Fi	DFLP1240	1964	**£12**	US
This Is Surf City	LP	Del-Fi	DFLP1237	1963	**£12**	US

LIVERPOOL BEATS

New Merseyside Sound	LP	Rondo	2026	1964	**£20**	US

LIVERPOOL FIVE

Arrive	LP	RCA	LPM3583	1966	**£10**	US
Out Of Sight	LP	RCA	LPM3682	1967	**£10**	US

LIVERPOOL KIDS

Beatle Mash	LP	Palace	777	1964	**£20**	US

LIVERPOOL SCENE

The first Liverpool Scene consisted of the three poets Roger McGough, Brian Patten, and Adrian Henri, with music supplied by guitarist Andy Roberts. The group that performs on the RCA records is more of a regular rock group, although it is still one that tends to act as an umbrella for the individual talents beneath - Henri and Roberts as before, with poet/saxophonist Mike Evans and singer/guitarist Mike Hart also making telling contributions. Each LP is tremendously varied, encompassing rock, jazz, and folk; poetry, comedy and drama - a real pot pourri, in fact, but it worked.

Amazing Adventures Of	LP	RCA	SF7995	1968	**£15**	
Bread On The Night	LP	RCA	SF8057	1969	**£15**	
Heirloon	LP	RCA	SF8134	1970	**£15**	
Incredible New Liverpool Scene	LP	CBS	63045	1967	**£25**	
Recollections	LP	Charisma	CS3	1972	**£10**	
Son Son	7"	RCA	RCA1762	1968	**£4**	
St.Adrian And Co.	LP	RCA	SF8100	1970	**£15**	
Woo Woo	7"	RCA	RCA1816	1969	**£4**	

LIVERPOOLS

Beatle-Mania In The USA	LP	Wyncote	9001	1964	**£20**	US
Hit Sounds From England	LP	Wyncote	9061	1965	**£20**	US

LIVING DAYLIGHTS

Always With Him	7"	Philips	BF1613	1967	**£8**	
Let's Live For Today	7"	Philips	BF1561	1967	**£8**	

LLAN

Realise	7"	CBS	202405	1966	**£8**	

LLOYD, CHARLES

Dream Weaver	LP	Atlantic	SD1459	1966	**£10**	US
Forest Flower	LP	Atlantic	SD1473	1967	**£10**	US
In Europe	LP	Atlantic	SD1500	1968	**£10**	US
Journey Within	LP	Atlantic	587101	1968	**£10**	
Love-In	LP	Atlantic	SD1481	1967	**£10**	US
Soundtrack	LP	Atlantic	SD1519	1969	**£10**	US
Waves	LP	A&M	SP3044	1972	**£10**	US

LLOYD, KATHY

Our Future Has Only Just Begun	7"	Decca	F10464	1955	**£4**	
Teach Me Tonight	7"	Decca	F10418	1954	**£4**	
Tomorrow Night	7"	Decca	F10386	1954	**£4**	

LLOYD, MARK

Everybody Tries	7"	Parlophone	R5332	1965	**£4**	
I Keep Thinking About You	7"	Parlophone	R5277	1965	**£5**	

LLOYD, PEGGY

Dixieland Honky Tonk	7" EP	London	REP1017	1955	**£4**	

LLOYD-WEBBER, ANDREW

Joseph And The Amazing Technicolour Dreamcoat	LP	Decca		1968	**£10**	

LLOYDIE & THE LOWBITES

Censored	LP	Lowbite	001		**£20**	

LLYGOD FFYRNIG

N.C.B.	7"	Pwdwr	PWDWR1	1978	**£12**	

LOADING ZONE

Loading Zone	LP	RCA	LSP3959	1968	**£15**	US
One For All	LP	Umbrella	US101	1968	**£30**	US

LOCKJAW

Journalist Jive	7"	Raw	RAW19	1978	**£4**	
Radio Call Sign	7"	Raw	RAW8	1977	**£4**	

LOCKLIN, HANK

Best Of...	LP	King	672	1961	**£15**	US
Country Guitar Vol.3	7" EP	RCA	RCX115	1958	**£5**	
Encores	LP	King	738	1961	**£15**	US
Encores	7" EP	Parlophone	GEP8875	1963	**£6**	
Foreign Love	LP	RCA	LPM1673	1958	**£15**	US
Happy Journey	LP	RCA	LPM2464	1962	**£10**	US
Irish Songs Country Style	7" EP	RCA	RCX7150	1964	**£4**	
Please Help Me, I'm Falling	7"	RCA	RCA1188	1960	**£4**	
Please Help Me, I'm Falling	LP	RCA	LPM2291	1960	**£10**	US
Seven Days	7" EP	RCA	RCX217	1962	**£5**	
Tribute To Roy Acuff	LP	RCA	LPM2597	1962	**£10**	US

Waltz Of The Wind	7" EP	RCA	RCX7116	1963	**£5**	
Ways Of Love	LP	RCA	LPM2680	1963	**£10**	US

LOCKRAN, GERRY

Blues At Sunrise	LP	Saga	FID2165	1969	**£15**	
Essential	LP	Spark	SRLP104	1969	**£15**	
Hey Jude	7"	Decca	F12873	1969	**£4**	
Hold On I'm Coming	LP	Planet	PLL1002	1967	**£30**	
Standing On Your Own	7"	Decca	F12919	1969	**£4**	
Wun	LP	Polydor	2383122	1972	**£10**	

LOCOMOTIVE

Mr.Armageddon	7"	Parlophone	R5758	1969	**£10**	
Roll Over Mary	7"	Parlophone	R5835	1970	**£8**	
Rudi's In Love	7"	Parlophone	R5718	1968	**£5**	
Rudi's In Love	7"	Parlophone	R5915	1971	**£4**	
Rudy, A Message To You	7"	Direction	583114	1967	**£5**	
We Are Everything You See	LP	Parlophone	PCS7093	1969	**£100**	
You Must Be Joking	7"	Parlophone	R5801	1969	**£10**	

LOFT

Up The Hill And Down The Slope	7"	Creation	CRE015	1985	**£10**	
Why Does The Rain Fall	7"	Creation	CRE009	1984	**£15**	

LOFTON, CRIPPLE CLARENCE

Cripple Clarence Lofton	7" EP	Vogue	EPV1209	195-	**£12**	

LOGUE, CHRISTOPHER & TONY KINSEY

Red Bird Jazz And Poetry	7" EP	Parlophone	GEP8765	1958	**£5**	

LOLLIPOP SHOPPE

Lollipop Shoppe	LP	Uni	73019	1968	**£20**	US

LOMAN, LAURIE

Whither Thou Goest	7"	London	HL8101	1954	**£5**	

LOMAX ALLIANCE

Try As You May	7"	CBS	2729	1967	**£8**	

LOMAX, ALAN

Alan Lomax Sings	7" EP	Pye	NJE1055	1957	**£5**	
Dirty Old Town	7"	Decca	F10787	1956	**£4**	
Oh Lula	7" EP	Decca	DFE6367	1956	**£5**	
Songs From Texas	7" EP	Melodisc	EPM788	195-	**£5**	

LOMAX, JACKIE

Genuine Imitation Life	7"	CBS	2554	1968	**£6**	
Home Is In My Head	LP	W. Bros	K46091	1971	**£10**	
How The Web Was Woven	7"	Apple	23	1970	**£5**	
How The Web Was Woven	7"	Apple	23	1970	**£15**	PS
Interview With...	LP	W. Bros	PRO520	1972	**£25**	US promo
Is This What You Want	LP	Apple	APCOR6	1969	**£20**	mono
Is This What You Want	LP	Apple	SAPCOR6	1969	**£15**	stereo
New Day	7"	Apple	11	1969	**£5**	
New Day	7"	Apple	11	1969	**£15**	PS
Sour Milk Sea	7"	Apple	3	1968	**£15**	
Three	LP	W. Bros	K46151	1972	**£10**	

LOMBARDY, AL

Blues	7"	London	HL8076	1954	**£12**	
In A Little Spanish Town	7"	London	HL8127	1955	**£8**	

LONDON

Animal Games	LP	MCA	MCF2823	1978	**£10**	
Animal Games	7"	MCA	MCA336	1977	**£4**	
Everyone's A Winner	7"	MCA	MCA305	1977	**£4**	
Summer Of Love	7"	MCA	MCA319	1977	**£5**	
Summer Of Love	12"	MCA	12MCA319	1977	**£8**	

LONDON WAITS

Serenadio	7"	Immediate	IM030	1966	**£15**	

LONDON, LAURIE

Basin Street Blues	7"	Parlophone	R4450	1958	**£4**	
Gospel Train	7"	Parlophone	R4408	1958	**£4**	
Handed Down	7"	Parlophone	R4388	1958	**£4**	
He's Got The Whole World In His Hands	7"	Parlophone	R4359	1957	**£4**	chart single
I Gotta Robe	7"	Parlophone	R4426	1958	**£4**	
I'm Afraid	7"	Parlophone	R4635	1960	**£4**	
Laurie London	LP	Capitol	T1016	1958	**£15**	US
Laurie London	7" EP	Parlophone	GEP8664	1957	**£5**	
Little Laurie London No.2	7" EP	Parlophone	GEP8689	1958	**£5**	
My Mother	7"	Parlophone	R4474	1958	**£4**	
Old Time Religion	7"	Parlophone	R4601	1959	**£4**	
Pretty-Eyed Baby	7"	Parlophone	R4557	1959	**£4**	
Up Above My Head	7"	Parlophone	R4499	1958	**£4**	

LONDON, PETER

Bless You	7"	Pye	7N15957	1965	**£10**	

LONESOME STONE

Lonesome Stone	LP	Reflection		1973	**£25**	

LONESOME SUNDOWN

Lonesome Lonely Blues	LP	Blue Horizon	763864	1970	**£30**	

LONG & THE SHORT

Choc Ice	7"	Decca	F12043	1964	**£5**	chart single
Letter	7"	Decca	F11964	1964	**£8**	chart single

LONG, SHORTY

Chantilly Lace	7"	T. Motown	TMG600	1967	**£6**	
Chantilly Lace	7"	T. Motown	TMG600	1967	**£35**	demo
Function At The Junction	7"	T. Motown	TMG573	1966	**£10**	
Function At The Junction	7"	T. Motown	TMG573	1966	**£50**	demo
Here Comes The Judge	LP	T. Motown	STML11086	1968	**£15**	
Here Comes The Judge	7"	T. Motown	TMG663	1968	**£4**	chart single
Here Comes The Judge	7"	T. Motown	TMG663	1968	**£20**	demo
Night Fo' Last	7"	T. Motown	TMG644	1968	**£8**	
Night Fo' Last	7"	T. Motown	TMG644	1968	**£20**	demo
Out To Get You	7"	T. Motown	TMG512	1965	**£15**	
Out To Get You	7"	T. Motown	TMG512	1965	**£50**	demo
Prime Of Shorty Long	LP	T. Motown	STML11144	1970	**£15**	

LONGBOATMEN

Take Her Any Time	7"	Polydor	56115	1966	**£30**	

LONGBRANCH PENNYWHISTLE

Longbranch Pennywhistle was a duo comprising J.D.Souther and Glenn Frey, both of whom have been familiar faces within the American country-rock scene ever since - Frey being a member of the Eagles.

Longbranch Pennywhistle	LP	Amos	AAS7007	1969	**£20**	US

LONGDANCER

Which is the "other" Dave Stewart depends on whether one is a fan of the Eurythmics or a follower of Hatfield and the North and its many offshoots. It is the future Eurythmic, in unfamiliar hippy guise, who is to be found as a member of the otherwise undistinguished Longdancer.

If It Was So Simple	LP	Rocket	PIGL1	1973	**£10**	
If It Was So Simple	7"	Rocket	PIG1	1973	**£4**	
Puppet Man	7"	Rocket	PIG11	1974	**£4**	
Trailer For A Good Life	LP	Rocket	PIGL6	1974	**£10**	

LOOP

Collision	7"	Chapter 22	CHAP27	1988	**£4**	
Collision	12"	Chapter 22	12CHAP27	1988	**£6**	
Keep On Movin'	12"	Rock T.House	T001	1987	**£10**	
Spinning	7"	Head	HEADL7	1987	**£8**	
Spinning	12"	Head	HEAD7	1987	**£15**	

LOOSE ENDS

Send The People Away	7"	Decca	F12437	1966	**£5**	
Taxman	7"	Decca	F12476	1966	**£6**	

LOOT

Title	Format	Label	Cat. No.	Year	Price	Notes
Baby Come Closer	7"	Page One	POF013	1966	**£6**	
Don't Turn Around	7"	CBS	3231	1968	**£8**	
I've Just Gotta Love You	7"	Page One	POF026	1967	**£8**	
She's A Winner	7"	Page One	POF095	1968	**£8**	
Try To Keep It Secret	7"	Page One	POF115	1969	**£8**	
Whenever You're Ready	7"	CBS	2938	1967	**£6**	

LOPEZ, TRINI

Title	Format	Label	Cat. No.	Year	Price	Notes
Gonna Get Along Without Ya Now	7"	Reprise	R20547	1967	**£4**	chart single
I'm Coming Home Cindy	7"	Reprise	R20455	1966	**£4**	chart single
If I Had A Hammer	7"	Reprise	R20198	1963	**£4**	chart single
Kansas City	7"	Reprise	R20236	1963	**£4**	chart single
La Bamba	7"	Reprise	R20480	1966	**£4**	
Lemon Tree	7"	Reprise	R20336	1964	**£4**	

LORD BEGINNER

Title	Format	Label	Cat. No.	Year	Price	Notes
Black Market	78	Brunswick	04720	1951	**£5**	
Victory Test Match	7"	Melodisc	CAL1	196-	**£8**	

LORD BRISCOE

Title	Format	Label	Cat. No.	Year	Price	Notes
Jonah	7"	Island	WI187	1965	**£10**	

LORD BRYNNER

Title	Format	Label	Cat. No.	Year	Price	Notes
Congo War	7"	Island	WI266	1966	**£10**	

LORD BUCKLEY

Title	Format	Label	Cat. No.	Year	Price	Notes
Bad Rapping The Marquis De Sade	LP	World Pacific	WPS21889	1969	**£15**	US
Best Of...	LP	Crestview	CRV801	1963	**£15**	US
Best Of...	LP	Elektra	EKS74047	1969	**£10**	US
Blowing His Mind And Yours Too	LP	World Pacific	WP1849	1966	**£15**	US
Buckley's Best	LP	World Pacific	WPS21879	1968	**£15**	US
Hipsters, Flipsters And Finger Poppin' Daddies	LP-10"	RCA	LPM3246	195-	**£50**	US
In Concert	LP	World Pacific	WP1815	1964	**£15**	US
Lord Buckley	LP	Bizarre	RS6389	1970	**£15**	US
Most Immaculately Hip Autocrat	LP	Straight	STS1054	1970	**£15**	US
Way Out Humor Of...	LP	World Pacific	WP1279	1959	**£20**	US

LORD CREATOR

Title	Format	Label	Cat. No.	Year	Price	Notes
Big Bamboo	7"	Jump Up	JU524	196-	**£8**	
Drive With Care	7"	N. Calypso	NC2001	196-	**£8**	
Evening News	7"	Blue Beat	BB292	1964	**£10**	
Jamaica Jump Up	7"	Jump Up	JU503	196-	**£8**	
Obeah Wedding	7"	Doctor Bird	DB1029	1966	**£10**	
Peeping Tom	7"	Kalypso	XX24	196-	**£8**	
Wicked Lady	7"	Black Swan	WI463	1965	**£10**	

LORD CRISTO

Title	Format	Label	Cat. No.	Year	Price	Notes
Dumb Boy And The Parrot	7"	Jump Up	JU515	196-	**£8**	
Election War Zone	7"	Jump Up	JU517	196-	**£8**	

LORD DANIEL

Title	Format	Label	Cat. No.	Year	Price	Notes
Small Island Gal	7"	Kalypso	XX26	196-	**£6**	

LORD KITCHENER

Title	Format	Label	Cat. No.	Year	Price	Notes
Black Pudding	7"	Melodisc	1498	196-	**£6**	
Black Pudding	7"	Melodisc	CAL19	196-	**£6**	
Carnival	7"	Melodisc	CAL23	196-	**£6**	
Come Back In The Morning	7"	Melodisc	CAL21	196-	**£6**	
Drink A Rum	7"	Melodisc	CAL5	196-	**£6**	
Federation	7"	Melodisc	CAL14	196-	**£6**	
If You're Brown	7"	Melodisc	1531	196-	**£6**	
Jamaica Turkey	7"	Melodisc	1577	196-	**£6**	
Jamaica Turkey	7"	Melodisc	CAL22	196-	**£6**	
Kitch	7"	Melodisc	CAL2	196-	**£6**	
Kitch Take It Easy	7"	Melodisc	CAL4	196-	**£6**	
Life Begins At Forty	7"	Melodisc	CAL11	196-	**£6**	
Mitch Mambo Calypso	7"	Melodisc	CAL10	196-	**£6**	
Muriel And The Bug	7"	Melodisc	CAL3	196-	**£6**	
Romeo	7"	Melodisc	CAL12	196-	**£6**	
Too Late Kitch	7"	Melodisc	CAL6	196-	**£6**	

Wife And Mother	7"	Melodisc	CAL7	196-	**£6**	

LORD LEBBY

Caledonia	7"	Starlite	ST45018	1960	**£12**	

LORD NELSON

I Got A Itch	7"	Stateside	SS189	1963	**£4**	
It's Delinquency	7"	Stateside	SS281	1964	**£4**	
Proud West Indian	7" EP	Stateside	SE1024	1964	**£5**	

LORD ROCKINGHAM'S XI

Hoots Mon	7"	Decca	F11059	1958	**£4**	chart single
Oh Boy	7" EP	Decca	DFE6555	1958	**£6**	
Ra Ra Rockingham	7"	Decca	F11139	1959	**£4**	
Rockingham Twist	7"	Decca	F11426	1962	**£4**	
Squelch	7"	Decca	F11024	1958	**£5**	
Wee Tom	7"	Decca	F11104	1959	**£4**	chart single

LORD SITAR

Lord Sitar	LP	Capitol	ST3916	1968	**£12**	US

LORD TANAMO

I'm In The Mood For Ska	7"	Ska Beat	JB224	1965	**£10**	

LORD, JON

Bouree	7"	Purple	PUR131	1976	**£4**	
Gemini Suite	LP	Purple	TPSA7501	1971	**£10**	
Windows	LP	Purple	TPSA7513	1974	**£10**	

LORD, TONY

World's Champion	7"	Planet	PLF102	1966	**£6**	

LORDAN, JERRY

I'll Stay Single	7"	Parlophone	R4588	1959	**£4**	chart single
Let's Try Again	7"	Parlophone	R4748	1961	**£4**	
Ring, Write Or Call	7"	Parlophone	R4695	1960	**£4**	
Sing Like An Angel	7"	Parlophone	R4653	1960	**£4**	chart single
Who Could Be Bluer?	7"	Parlophone	R4627	1960	**£5**	chart single

LORDS

Don't Mince Matters	7"	Columbia	DB8121	1967	**£6**	
Gloryland	7"	Columbia	DB8367	1968	**£6**	

LORDS OF THE NEW CHURCH

New Church	7"	Illegal	ILS0028	1982	**£5**	
Russian Roulette	7"	Illegal	ILSP0033	1983	**£5**	pic disc

LORRIE, MYRNA

Life's Changing Scene	7"	London	HLU8294	1956	**£5**	

LORRIE, MYRNA & BUDDY DEVAL

Underway	7"	London	HLU8187	1955	**£10**	

LORY, DICK

Cool It Baby	7"	London	HLD8348	1956	**£60**	
I Got Over You	7"	Liberty	LIB55529	1963	**£4**	
My Last Date	7"	London	HLG9284	1961	**£4**	
Pain Is Here	7"	Liberty	LIB55415	1962	**£4**	

LOS BRAVOS

Black Is Black	7"	Decca	F22419	1966	**£4**	chart single
Black Is Black	LP	Press	PR73003	1966	**£12**	US
Bring A Little Lovin'	7"	Decca	F22765	1968	**£4**	
Bring A Little Lovin'	LP	Parrot	PAS71021	1968	**£10**	US
Going Nowhere	7"	Decca	F22529	1966	**£4**	
I Don't Care	7"	Decca	F22484	1966	**£4**	chart single
I'm All Ears	7"	Decca	F22615	1967	**£4**	
Like Nobody Else	7"	Decca	F22682	1967	**£4**	
Save Me Save Me	7"	Decca	F22853	1968	**£4**	

LOS BRINCOS

Lola	7"	Page One	POF023	1967	**£5**	

Nobody Wants You Now	7"	Page One	POF031	1967	**£6**	

LOS CANARIOS

Get On Your Knees	7"	Major Minor	MM532	1967	**£10**	
Three Two One Ah	7"	Major Minor	MM502	1967	**£5**	

LOS CINCOS

Most Exclusive Residence For Sale	7"	Philips	BF1525	1966	**£5**	

LOS LOBOS

Just Another Band From East LA	LP	New Vista	1001	1978	**£75**	US
Si Se Puede!	LP	Pan American	101	1976	**£50**	US

LOST & FOUND

Everybody's Here	LP	Int. Artists	IALP3	1967	**£25**	US

LOTHAR & THE HAND PEOPLE

Presenting...	LP	Capitol	ST2997	1968	**£25**	US
Sdrawkcab	7"	Capitol	CL15610	1969	**£10**	
Space Hymn	LP	Capitol	ST247	1969	**£30**	US

LOUDERMILK, JOHN D.

Angela Jones	7"	RCA	RCA1323	1962	**£4**	
Country Love Songs	LP	RCA	LSP4040	1968	**£10**	US
Elloree Vol.1	LP	W. Bros	K46124	1971	**£10**	
Language Of Love	LP	RCA	LPM2434	1961	**£10**	US
Language Of Love	7"	RCA	RCA1269	1962	**£4**	chart single
Open Mind Of...	LP	RCA	LSP4097	1969	**£10**	US
Sings A Bizarre Collection	LP	RCA	LPM3497	1965	**£10**	US
Suburban Attitudes...	LP	RCA	LPM3807	1967	**£10**	US
Thou Shalt Not Steal	7"	RCA	RCA1287	1962	**£4**	
Twelve Sides Of...	LP	RCA	LPM2539	1962	**£10**	US

LOUDEST WHISPER

Children Of Lir	LP	Polydor			**£250**	Irish

LOUISIANA RED

I Done Woke Up	7"	Sue	WI337	1964	**£10**	
Keep Your Hands Of My Woman	7"	Columbia	DB7270	1964	**£6**	
Lowdown Back Porch Blues	LP	Roulette	R25200	1963	**£20**	US

LOUSSIER, JACQUES

Air On A G String	7"	Decca	F22383	1966	**£4**	
Air On A G String	7"	Decca	F22876	1969	**£4**	

LOUVIN BROTHERS

Country Christmas	LP	Capitol	T1616	1961	**£10**	US
Country Love Ballads	LP	Capitol	T1106	1959	**£25**	US
Country Love Ballads	7" EP	Capitol	EAP11106	1959	**£4**	
Encore	LP	Capitol	T1547	1961	**£12**	US
Family Who Prays	LP	Capitol	T1061	1958	**£25**	US
Ira And Charlie	LP	Capitol	T910	1958	**£40**	US
Ira And Charlie	7" EP	Capitol	EAP1910	1957	**£5**	
Keep Your Eyes On Jesus	LP	Capitol	T1834	1963	**£10**	US
Knoxville Girl	7"	Capitol	CL14989	1959	**£4**	
Louvin Brothers	LP	MGM	E3426	1956	**£100**	US
My Baby's Gone	LP	Capitol	T1385	1960	**£25**	US
Nearer My God To Thee	LP	Capitol	T825	1957	**£40**	US
Satan Is Real	LP	Capitol	T1277	1960	**£25**	US
Sing And Play Their Current Hits	LP	Capitol	T2091	1964	**£10**	US
Tragic Songs Of Life	LP	Capitol	T769	1956	**£50**	US
Tragic Songs Of Life	7" EP	Capitol	EAP1769	1957	**£5**	
Tribute To The Delmore Brothers	LP	Capitol	T1449	1960	**£20**	US
Weapon Of Prayer	LP	Capitol	T1721	1962	**£10**	US
You're Learning	7"	Capitol	CL15078	1959	**£4**	

LOUVIN, CHARLIE

I Forgot To Cry	LP	Capitol	T2787	1967	**£10**	US
I'll Remember Always	LP	Capitol	T2689	1967	**£10**	US
Less And Less	LP	Capitol	T2208	1965	**£10**	US
Lonesome Is Me	LP	Capitol	T2482	1966	**£10**	US
Many Moods Of...	LP	Capitol	T2437	1966	**£10**	US

Title	Format	Label	Number	Year	Price	Notes
Will You Visit Me On Sundays?	LP	Capitol	T2958	1968	**£10**	US

LOUVIN, IRA

Title	Format	Label	Number	Year	Price	Notes
Unforgettable...	LP	Capitol	T2413	1965	**£10**	US

LOVE

The personnel of Love varies from album to album, but the group always revolves around the singing and writing talents of Arthur Lee. His was an inconsistent talent, but at his best he was little short of brilliant. All of Love's albums (except perhaps the first, on which the group have barely emerged from their garage punk beginnings) contain moments of pure magic, although none is entirely flawless. The critics' favourite is "Forever Changes", whose largely gentle sound is enhanced by modest orchestration, but the heavier, guitar-centred "Four Sail" actually has songs of greater distinction. It is a very fine, and very underrated record. The first side of "Da Capo" has some excellent songs too, but the album as a whole is let down by the extended jam on side two, which does not really work. "Out Here" and "False Start" are similar in sound to "Four Sail", though overall neither is in the same league. Each contains one masterpiece, however - "The Everlasting First" is a collaboration with Jimi Hendrix, who makes a typically fine contribution to an unusually structured song; while "Love Is More Than Words" is dominated by a long, highly charged guitar solo that turns the track into one of the classic pieces of rock improvisation.

Title	Format	Label	Number	Year	Price	Notes
7 And 7 Is	7"	London	HLZ10073	1966	**£10**	
Alone Again Or	7"	Elektra	2101019	1971	**£4**	
Alone Again Or	7"	Elektra	EKSN45024	1968	**£5**	
Alone Again Or	7"	Elektra	K12231	1976	**£4**	
Andmoreagain	7"	Elektra	EKSN45026	1968	**£8**	
Da Capo	LP	Elektra	EKS74005	1967	**£15**	
Everlasting First	7"	Harvest	HAR5030	1970	**£10**	
False Start	LP	Harvest	SHVL787	1970	**£15**	
Forever Changes	LP	Elektra	EKS74013	1967	**£15**	chart LP
Four Sail	LP	Elektra	EKS74049	1969	**£20**	
Four Sail	LP	Elektra	K42030	1976	**£12**	
I'm With You	7"	Elektra	EKSN45086	1970	**£5**	
Laughing Stock	7"	Elektra	EKSN45038	1968	**£10**	
Love	LP	Elektra	EKS74001	1966	**£25**	
Love Masters	LP	Elektra	K32002	1972	**£10**	
Love Revisited	LP	Elektra	EKS74058	1970	**£12**	
My Little Red Book	7"	London	HLZ10053	1966	**£12**	
Out Here	LP	Harvest	SHDW3/4	1970	**£25**	double, chart LP
Reel To Real	LP	RSO	2394145	1974	**£12**	
She Comes In Colours	7"	Elektra	EKSN45010	1967	**£8**	
Softly To Me	7"	Elektra	EKSN45016	1967	**£6**	
Stand Out	7"	Harvest	HAR5014	1970	**£8**	
Time Is Like A River	7"	RSO	2090151	1975	**£5**	

LOVE AFFAIR

Title	Format	Label	Number	Year	Price	Notes
Bring On Back The Good Times	7"	CBS	4300	1969	**£4**	chart single
Day Without Love	7"	CBS	3674	1968	**£4**	chart single
Everlasting Love	7"	CBS	3125	1967	**£4**	chart single
Everlasting Love Affair	LP	CBS		1968	**£12**	
New Day	LP	CBS	64109	1970	**£12**	
One Road	7"	CBS	3994	1969	**£4**	chart single
Rainbow Valley	7"	CBS	3366	1968	**£4**	chart single

LOVE CHILDREN

Title	Format	Label	Number	Year	Price	Notes
Easy Squeezy	7"	Deram	DM268	1969	**£4**	
Paper Chase	7"	Deram	DM303	1970	**£5**	

LOVE GENERATION

Title	Format	Label	Number	Year	Price	Notes
She Touched Me	7"	Liberty	LBF15018	1967	**£5**	

LOVE SCULPTURE

Love Sculpture evolved from the Human Beans as a blues group and showcase for the flashy guitar playing of Dave Edmunds. The success of their version of Khachaturian's "Sabre Dance" led them to try another classical reworking, but due to copyright problems, "Mars" was only made available on the US version of "Forms And Feelings" and has not been reissued since.

Title	Format	Label	Number	Year	Price	Notes
Blues Helping	LP	Parlophone	PCS7059	1968	**£25**	
Forms And Feelings	LP	Parlophone	PCS7090	1969	**£25**	
Forms And Feelings	LP	Parrot	PAS71035	1969	**£30**	US
In The Land Of The Few	7"	Parlophone	R5831	1970	**£8**	
River To Another Day	7"	Parlophone	R5664	1968	**£10**	
Sabre Dance	7"	Parlophone	R5744	1968	**£4**	chart single
Wang Dang Doodle	7"	Parlophone	R5731	1968	**£12**	

LOVE, CHRISTOPHER

Title	Format	Label	Number	Year	Price	Notes
Curse Goes On	7"	London	HLU10263	1969	**£8**	

LOVE, DARLENE

Boy I'm Gonna Marry .... 7" .... London .... HLU9725 .... 1963 .... **£8**
Fine Fine Boy .... 7" .... London .... HLU9815 .... 1963 .... **£8**
Lord If You're A Woman .... 7" .... Phil Spector .... 2010019 .... 1977 .... **£4**
Wait Till My Bobby Gets Home .... 7" .... London .... HLU9765 .... 1963 .... **£8**
Wait Till My Bobby Gets Home .... 7" EP .... London .... REU1411 .... 1964 .... **£50**

LOVE, GARFIELD & JIMMY SPRUILL

Next Time You See Me .... 7" .... Blue Horizon .... 573150 .... 1969 .... **£10**

LOVE, MARY

Hurt Is Just Beginning .... 7" .... Stateside .... SS2135 .... 1969 .... **£5**
Lay This Burden Down .... 7" .... Stateside .... SS2009 .... 1967 .... **£12**
You Turned My Bitter Into Sweet .... 7" .... King .... KG1024 .... 196- **£25**

LOVE, RONNIE

Chills And Fever .... 7" .... London .... HLD9272 .... 1961 .... **£4**

LOVECRAFT

Valley Of The Moon .... LP .... Reprise .... RS6419 .... 1970 .... **£15** .... US
We Love You Whoever You Are .... LP .... Mercury .... SRM11031 .... 1976 .... **£10** .... US

LOVEJOY, JOY

In Orbit .... 7" .... Chess .... 6145010 .... 1972 .... **£4**

LOVERS

Let's Elope .... 7" .... Vogue .... V9111 .... 1958 .... **£15**

LOVICH, LENE

I Saw Mommy Kissing Santa Claus .... 7" .... Polydor .... 2058812 .... 1976 .... **£15**
I Think We're Alone Now (Japanese) .... 7" .... Stiff .... BUYJ32 .... 1978 .... **£12**

LOVIN'

All You've Got .... 7" .... Page One .... POF041 .... 1967 .... **£6**
Keep On Believing .... 7" .... Page One .... POF035 .... 1967 .... **£5**

LOVIN' SPOONFUL

Darling Be Home Soon .... 7" .... Kama Sutra .... KAS207 .... 1967 .... **£4** .... chart single
Day Blues .... 7" EP .... Kama Sutra .... KEP303 .... 1967 .... **£5**
Daydream .... LP .... Pye .... NPL28078 .... 1966 .... **£12** .... chart LP
Daydream .... 7" .... Pye .... 7N25361 .... 1966 .... **£4** .... chart single
Did You Ever Have To Make Up Your Mind .... 7" .... Kama Sutra .... KAS209 .... 1967 .... **£4**
Did You Ever Have To Make Up Your Mind .... 7" EP .... Kama Sutra .... KEP300 .... 1966 .... **£5**
Do You Believe In Magic? .... 7" EP .... Kama Sutra .... KEP306 .... 1967 .... **£5**
Do You Believe In Magic? .... LP .... Pye .... NPL28069 .... 1965 .... **£12**
Do You Believe In Magic? .... 7" .... Pye .... 7N25327 .... 1965 .... **£4**
Everything Playing .... LP .... Kama Sutra .... KLP404 .... 1968 .... **£10**
Hums Of The... .... LP .... Kama Sutra .... KLP401 .... 1967 .... **£10**
Jug Band Music .... 7" EP .... Kama Sutra .... KEP301 .... 1966 .... **£5**
Loving You .... 7" EP .... Kama Sutra .... KEP305 .... 1967 .... **£5**
Money .... 7" .... Kama Sutra .... KAS211 .... 1967 .... **£4**
Nashville Cats .... 7" .... Kama Sutra .... KAS204 .... 1967 .... **£4** .... chart single
Nashville Cats .... 7" EP .... Kama Sutra .... KEP304 .... 1967 .... **£5**
Never Going Back .... 7" .... Kama Sutra .... KAS213 .... 1967 .... **£4**
Rain On The Roof .... 7" .... Kama Sutra .... KAS201 .... 1966 .... **£4**
Revelation Revolution '69 .... LP .... Kama Sutra .... KLP406 .... 1969 .... **£10**
She Is Still A Mystery .... 7" .... Kama Sutra .... KAS210 .... 1967 .... **£4**
Six O'Clock .... 7" .... Kama Sutra .... KAS208 .... 1967 .... **£4**
Summer In The City .... 7" .... Kama Sutra .... KAS200 .... 1966 .... **£4** .... chart single
Summer In The City .... 7" EP .... Kama Sutra .... KEP302 .... 1966 .... **£5**
You Didn't Have To Be So Nice .... 7" .... Kama Sutra .... KAS205 .... 1967 .... **£4**
You Didn't Have To Be So Nice .... 7" .... Pye .... 7N25344 .... 1966 .... **£4**
You're A Big Boy Now .... LP .... Kama Sutra .... KLP402 .... 1967 .... **£10**

LOVING AWARENESS

Loving Awareness .... LP .... More Love .... ML001 .... 1976 .... **£10**

LOVING KIND

Accidental Love .... 7" .... Piccadilly .... 7N35299 .... 1966 .... **£10**
Ain't That Peculiar .... 7" .... Piccadilly .... 7N35342 .... 1966 .... **£12**
I Love The Things You Do .... 7" .... Piccadilly .... 7N35318 .... 1966 .... **£10**

LOWE, JIM

Blue Suede Shoes	7"	London	HLD8276	1956	**£25**	
By You By You By You	7"	London	HLD8368	1957	**£10**	
Close The Door	7"	London	HLD8171	1955	**£15**	
Door Of Fame	LP	Mercury	MG20246	1957	**£20**	US
Four Walls	7"	London	HLD8431	1957	**£10**	
Green Door	7"	London	HLD8317	1956	**£15**	chart single
He'll Have To Go	7"	London	HLD9043	1960	**£4**	
Love Is A $64,000 Question	7"	London	HLD8288	1956	**£10**	
Rock A Chicka	7"	London	HLD8538	1958	**£15**	
Songs They Sing Behind The Green Door	LP	Dot	DLP3051	1957	**£50**	US
Songs They Sing Behind The Green Door	LP	London	HAD2108	1958	**£30**	
Wicked Women	LP	Dot	DLP3114	1958	**£40**	US
Wicked Women	LP	London	HAD2146	1959	**£20**	

LOWE, NICK

American Squirm	7"	Radar	ADA26	1978	**£4**	
Bowi	7"	Stiff	LAST1	1977	**£4**	
Bowi	12"	Stiff	LAST1	1977	**£10**	promo
Live At The El Mocambo	7"	Columbia		1978	**£20**	Canadian promo
So It Goes	7"	Stiff	BUY1	1976	**£5**	

LOWTHER, HENRY

Henry Lowther is a classically trained violinist who took up the trumpet in order to play jazz and plays both instruments as a session musician on numerous LP releases. He played on the fringes of jazz as a member of Manfred Mann, John Mayall's Bluesbreakers, and the Keef Hartley Band, and he is featured on several of the British jazz albums to be made during the late sixties and early seventies. His own moment came with the LP "Child Song", which is as fresh and sparkling as British jazz gets. The record is also, unfortunately, as rare as British jazz gets, and commands a correspondingly high price.

Child Song	LP	Deram	SML1070	1970	**£100**	

LUCAS & THE MIKE COTTON SOUND

Mother In Law	7"	MGM	MGM1427	1968	**£4**	
Soul Serenade	7"	MGM	MGM1398	1968	**£10**	
Step Out Of Line	7"	Pye	7N17313	1967	**£8**	

LUCAS, TREVOR

Overlander	LP	Reality	RY1002	1966	**£100**	
Waltzing Matilda	7"	Reality	RE505	1966	**£20**	

LUCIFER

Big Gun	LP	private	LLP1	1972	**£40**	
Exit	LP	private		1972	**£50**	

LUKE, ROBIN

Chicka Chicka Honey	7"	London	HLD8771	1958	**£5**	
Robin Luke	7" EP	London	RED1222	1959	**£15**	
Susie Darling	7"	London	HLD8676	1958	**£4**	chart single

LULU

Boat That I Row	7"	Columbia	DB8169	1967	**£4**	chart single
Boy	7"	Columbia	DB8425	1968	**£4**	chart single
Call Me	7"	Decca	F12326	1966	**£4**	
Can't Hear You No More	7"	Decca	F11965	1964	**£4**	
Here Comes The Night	7"	Decca	F12017	1964	**£4**	chart single
I'm A Tiger	7"	Columbia	DB8500	1968	**£4**	chart single
Leave A Little Love	7"	Decca	F12169	1965	**£4**	chart single
Love Loves To Love Love	7"	Columbia	DB8295	1967	**£4**	chart single
Love Loves To Love Lulu	LP	Columbia	SCX6201	1968	**£10**	
Lulu	LP	Ace Of Clubs	ACL1232	1967	**£10**	
Lulu	7" EP	Decca	DFE8597	1965	**£5**	
Lulu's Album	LP	Columbia	SCX6365	1969	**£10**	
Me The Peaceful Heart	7"	Columbia	DB8358	1968	**£4**	chart single
Satisfied	7"	Decca	F12128	1965	**£4**	
Shout	7"	Decca	F11884	1964	**£4**	chart single
Something To Shout About	LP	Decca	LK4719	1965	**£12**	
Tell It Like It Is	7"	Decca	F12254	1965	**£4**	
To Sir With Love	7"	Columbia	DB8221	1967	**£4**	chart single
Try To Understand	7"	Decca	F12214	1965	**£4**	chart single
What A Wonderful Feelin'	7"	Decca	F12491	1966	**£4**	

LULU & THE MINDBENDERS

Title	Format	Label	Cat. No.	Year	Price	Notes
To Sir With Love	LP	Fontana	STL5446	1967	**£12**	

LUMAN, BOB

Title	Format	Label	Cat. No.	Year	Price	Notes
Bad Bad Day	7"	Hickory	451289	1965	**£4**	
Bigger Men Than I	7"	Hickory	451238	1964	**£4**	
Come On And Sing	7"	Hickory	451410	1965	**£4**	
Dreamy Doll	7"	W. Bros	WB12	1960	**£4**	
Great Snowman	7"	W. Bros	WB37	1961	**£4**	chart single
Hey Joe	7"	W. Bros	WB75	1962	**£4**	
I Like Your Kind Of Love	7"	Hickory	451221	1964	**£4**	
Let's Think About Living	LP	W. Bros	W1396	1960	**£15**	US
Let's Think About Living	LP	W. Bros	WM4025	1960	**£15**	chart LP
Let's Think About Living	7"	W. Bros	WB18	1960	**£5**	chart single
Let's Think About Living	7" EP	W. Bros	WEP6046	1961	**£8**	
Let's Think About Living	7" EP	W. Bros	WSEP2046	1961	**£12**	stereo
Let's Think About Living No.2	7" EP	W. Bros	WEP6055	1962	**£8**	
Let's Think About Living No.2	7" EP	W. Bros	WSEP2055	1962	**£12**	stereo
Let's Think About Living No.3	7" EP	W. Bros	WEP6102	1962	**£8**	
Let's Think About Living No.3	7" EP	W. Bros	WSE6102	1962	**£12**	stereo
Old George Dickie	7"	Hickory	451277	1964	**£4**	
Private Eye	7"	W. Bros	WB49	1961	**£4**	
Run On Home Baby Brother	7"	Hickory	451266	1964	**£4**	
Why Why Bye Bye	7"	W. Bros	WB28	1960	**£4**	chart single

LUMAN, BOB & BOBBY LORD

Title	Format	Label	Cat. No.	Year	Price	Notes
	7" EP	Hickory	LPE1504	1964	**£6**	
Hickory Showcase Vol.2	7" EP	Hickory	LPE1501	1964	**£6**	

LUMLEY, RUFUS

Title	Format	Label	Cat. No.	Year	Price	Notes
I'm Standing	7"	Stateside	SS516	1966	**£25**	

LUREX, LARRY

Larry Lurex is Freddie Mercury, and his single, issued just before the start of Queen's career is sought after in both its UK and US incarnations (the latter being on the Anthem label).

Title	Format	Label	Cat. No.	Year	Price	Notes
I Can Hear Music	7"	EMI	EMI2030	1973	**£30**	

LURKERS

Title	Format	Label	Cat. No.	Year	Price	Notes
Ain't Got A Clue	7"	Beggars B.	BEG6	1978	**£4**	with clear flexi
Ain't Got A Clue	7"	Beggars B.	BEG6	1978	**£5**	with gold flexi
Freak Show	7"	Beggars B.	BEG2	1977	**£4**	
Fulham Fallout	LP	Beggars B.	BEGA2	1978	**£10**	chart LP
Shadow	7"	Beggars B.	BEG1	1977	**£5**	
Shadow	7"	Beggars B.	BEG1	1978	**£8**	red, blue, or white vinyl

LUTCHER, NELLIE

Title	Format	Label	Cat. No.	Year	Price	Notes
Blues In The Night	7"	Brunswick	05352	1954	**£4**	
It's Been Said	7"	Brunswick	05437	1955	**£4**	
Nellie Lutcher	7" EP	Philips	BBE12045	1956	**£6**	
Our New Nellie	LP	London	HAU2036	1957	**£12**	
Real Gone	LP	Capitol	T232	195-	**£20**	US
Real Gone	LP-10"	Capitol	H232		**£25**	US
Real Gone	7" EP	Capitol	EAP20066	1959	**£6**	
Whee! Nellie	LP-10"	Epic	1108		**£25**	US
Whose Honey Are You?	7"	Brunswick	05497	1955	**£4**	

LUTHER

Title	Format	Label	Cat. No.	Year	Price	Notes
It's Good For The Soul	7"	Atlantic	K10781	1976	**£20**	

LUTHER & LITTLE EVA

Title	Format	Label	Cat. No.	Year	Price	Notes
Ain't Got No Home	7"	Parlophone	R4292	1957	**£15**	

LUTHER, FRANK

Title	Format	Label	Cat. No.	Year	Price	Notes
Three Billygoats Gruff	7"	Decca	F9051	1954	**£5**	

LUV MACHINE

Title	Format	Label	Cat. No.	Year	Price	Notes
Luv Machine	LP	Polydor		1971	**£70**	

LUVVERS

Title	Format	Label	Cat. No.	Year	Price	Notes
House On The Hill	7"	Parlophone	R5459	1966	**£6**	

LYMON, FRANKIE & THE TEENAGERS

...In London	LP	Columbia	33SX1127	1958	**£40**	
ABC's In Love	7"	Columbia	DB3858	1956	**£12**	
Frankie Lymon And The Teenagers	7" EP	Columbia	SEG7734	1957	**£15**	
Goody Goody	7"	Columbia	DB3983	1957	**£8**	chart single
I Promise To Remember	7"	Columbia	DB3819	1956	**£15**	
I Want You To Be My Girl	7"	Columbia	SCM5285	1956	**£15**	
I'm Not A Juvenile Delinquent	7"	Columbia	DB3878	1957	**£15**	chart single
I'm Not A Juvenile Delinquent	7" EP	Columbia	SEG7694	1957	**£15**	
Jerry Blavatt Presents The Teenagers	LP	Roulette	R25250	1964	**£50**	US
Little Bitty Pretty One	7"	Columbia	DB4499	1960	**£6**	
Mama Don't Allow It	7"	Columbia	DB4134	1958	**£6**	
My Girl	7"	Columbia	DB4028	1957	**£6**	
No Matter What You've Done	7"	Columbia	DB4295	1959	**£6**	
Only Way To Love	7"	Columbia	DB4245	1959	**£5**	
Out In The Cold Again	7"	Columbia	DB3942	1957	**£10**	
Rock And Roll	LP	Roulette	R25036	1958	**£100**	US
Rockin'	LP-10"	Columbia		1957	**£40**	
Teenage Love	7"	Columbia	DB3910	1957	**£12**	
Teenage Rock	7" EP	Columbia	SEG7662	1957	**£15**	
Teenagers	LP	Gee	GLP701	1957	**£180**	US
Teenagers At The London Palladium	LP	Roulette	R25013	1958	**£100**	US
Thumb Thumb	7"	Columbia	DB4073	1958	**£5**	
Why Do Fools Fall In Love?	LP	Columbia		1956	**£50**	
Why Do Fools Fall In Love?	7"	Columbia	SCM5265	1956	**£20**	chart single

LYMON, LEWIS

Too Young	7"	Oriole	CB1419	1958	**£15**	

LYNCH, KENNY

I'll Stay By You	7"	HMV	POP1430	1965	**£4**	chart single
It's Too Late	7"	HMV	POP1577	1967	**£4**	
Misery	7"	HMV	POP1136	1963	**£4**	
Mountain Of Love	7"	HMV	POP751	1960	**£4**	chart single
Puff	7"	HMV	POP1057	1962	**£4**	chart single
Stand By Me	7"	HMV	POP1280	1964	**£4**	chart single
Up On The Roof	7"	HMV	POP1090	1962	**£4**	chart single
What Am I To Do?	7"	HMV	POP1321	1964	**£4**	chart single
You Can Never Stop Me Loving You	7"	HMV	POP1165	1963	**£4**	chart single

LYNCH, LEE & THE BLUE ANGELS

You Won't See Me	7"	Decca	F12375	1966	**£4**	

LYNDELL, LINDA

Bring Your Love Back To Me	7"	Stax	601041	1968	**£6**	

LYNGSTAD, ANNI-FRID

Anni-Frid Lyngstad	LP	Columbia	04851017	197-	**£12**	Swedish
Frida	LP	Columbia	E05434549	1971	**£12**	Swedish
Frida	LP	Columbia	06234380	197-	**£12**	Swedish
Frida Ensam	LP	Polar	POLS265	1976	**£12**	Swedish

LYNN, BARBARA

Barbara Lynn Story	LP	Sue	ILP949	1967	**£20**	
Here Is Barbara Lynn	LP	Atlantic	SD8171	1968	**£12**	US
Letter To Mommy And Daddy	7"	Sue	WI4028	1967	**£10**	
Oh Baby	7"	London	HLW9918	1964	**£4**	
Sister Of Soul	LP	Jamie	JLP3026	1964	**£12**	US
Until Then I Suffer	7"	Atlantic	2091133	1971	**£5**	
You Can't Buy Me Love	7"	Immediate	IM011	1965	**£12**	
You Left The Water Running	7"	London	HLU10094	1966	**£4**	
You'll Lose A Good Thing	LP	Jamie	JLP3023	1962	**£15**	US
You'll Miss A Good Thing	7"	Sue	WI4038	1967	**£10**	

LYNN, BOBBI

Earthquake	7"	Stateside	SS2088	1968	**£10**	

LYNN, LORETTA

Before I'm Over You	LP	Decca	DL4541	1964	**£15**	US
Blue Kentucky Girl	LP	Decca	DL4665	1965	**£15**	US
Country Christmas	LP	Decca	DL4817	1966	**£10**	US

Hymns	LP	Decca	DL4695	1965	**£10**	US
I Like 'Em Country	LP	Decca	DL4744	1966	**£10**	US
Loretta Lynn Sings	LP	Decca	DL4457	1963	**£20**	US
Songs From My Heart	LP	Decca	DL4620	1965	**£15**	US
You Ain't Woman Enough	LP	Decca	DL4783	1966	**£10**	US

LYNN, LORETTA & ERNEST TUBB

Mr. & Mrs.Used To Be	LP	Decca	DL4639	1965	**£12**	US

LYNN, PATTI

Johnny Angel	7"	Fontana	H391	1962	**£4**	chart single
Patti	7" EP	Fontana	TFE17392	1962	**£5**	
Tell Me Telstar	7"	Fontana	267247TF	1962	**£4**	

LYNN, TAMMI

I'm Gonna Run Away From You	7"	Atlantic	AT4071	1966	**£12**	
I'm Gonna Run Away From You	7"	Mojo	2092001	1971	**£4**	chart single

LYNNE, GLORIA

I Should Care	7"	London	HLY9888	1964	**£4**	
I Wish You Love	7"	London	HLY9846	1964	**£4**	

LYNNE, SUE

Don't Pity Me	7"	RCA	RCA1822	1969	**£20**	

LYNOTT, PHIL

Solo In Soho	LP	Vertigo	PHIL1	1980	**£10**	pic disc

LYNTON, JACKIE

The backing group on the A side of "All Of Me" is called The Jury. The bass player is Pat Donaldson - kept busy on a variety of sessions following his stints with Zoot Money and with Fotheringay - while the guitarist is Albert Lee, here making his first recording.

All Of Me	7"	Piccadilly	7N35064	1962	**£10**	
I'm Talkin' About You	7"	Piccadilly	7N35156	1963	**£4**	
Jackie Lynton Album	LP	WWA	WWA012	1974	**£10**	
Little Child	7"	Piccadilly	7N35177	1964	**£4**	

LYNYRD SKYNYRD

Freebird	12"	MCA	MCATP251	1982	**£6**	pic disc
Street Survivors	LP	MCA	3029	1977	**£10**	US, amended sleeve

LYON, BARBARA

My Four Friends	7" EP	Columbia	SEG7640	1956	**£4**	
Tell Me	7"	Triumph	RGM1027	1960	**£10**	

LYTELL, JIMMY

Hot Cargo	7"	London	HL8873	1959	**£4**	

M

Moderne Man	7"	Do It	640147	1978	**£5**	

M.I.FIVE

You'll Never Stop Me Loving You	7"	Parlophone	R5486	1966	**£15**	

MABEL JOY

Mabel Joy	LP	Real		1975	**£15**	

MABON, WILLIE

Got To Have Some	7"	Sue	WI320	1964	**£8**	
I'm The Fixer	7"	Sue	WI382	1965	**£10**	
Just Got Some	7"	Sue	WI331	1965	**£10**	
Willie Mabon	LP	Chess	1439	195-	**£40**	US

MACC LADS

Beer & Sex & Chips 'n' Gravy	LP	FM	WKFMLP56	1985	**£10**	white vinyl

MacCOLL, EWAN

Big Hewer	LP	Argo	DA140	1967	**£25**	

MacCOLL, EWAN & CHARLES PARKER

Ballad Of John Axon	LP	Argo	RG474	1965	**£25**	

MacCOLL, EWAN & PEGGY SEEGER

Amorous Muse	LP	Argo		196-	**£12**	
Wanton Muse	LP	Argo		196-	**£12**	

MacCOLL,EWAN/PEGGY SEEGER & CHARLES PARKER

Travelling People	LP	Argo	DA133	1969	**£20**	

MACEO & ALL THE KING'S MEN

It is extraordinary how the same musicians as formed James Brown's band in the late sixties lack a significant percentage of their drive and rhythmic power when Brown is not there. Here is the proof that James Brown is indeed the master of his own music.

Got To Get 'Cha	7"	Pye	7N25571	1972	**£5**	
Us	LP	Polydor	2391122	1974	**£15**	

MACK SISTERS

Long Range Love	7"	London	HLU8331	1956	**£8**	

MACK, JOHNNY

Reggae All Night Long	7"	Columbia	DB116	1970	**£8**	

MACK, LONNIE

For Collectors Only	LP	Elektra	2410007	1970	**£15**	
Glad I'm In The Band	LP	Elektra	EKS74040	1969	**£15**	
Hills Of Indiana	LP	Elektra	K42097	1972	**£12**	
Lonnie On The Move	7"	Stateside	SS312	1964	**£5**	
Memphis	7"	Elektra	EKSN45044	1969	**£5**	
Memphis	7"	Stateside	SS207	1963	**£6**	
Sa-Ba-Hoola	7"	Stateside	SS393	1965	**£5**	
Save Your Money	7"	Elektra	EKSN45060	1969	**£4**	
Wham	7"	Stateside	SS226	1963	**£5**	
Wham Of The Memphis Man	LP	President	PTL1004	1967	**£20**	
Whatever's Right	LP	Elektra	EKS74050	1969	**£15**	

MACK, WARNER

Country Touch	LP	Brunswick	LAT8658	1966	**£15**	
Drifting Apart	LP	Brunswick	LAT8684	1967	**£12**	
Golden Country Hits	LP	London	HAR8002	1962	**£10**	
Golden Country Hits Vol.2	LP	London	HAR8025	1963	**£10**	
Rock A Chicka	7"	Brunswick	05728	1958	**£50**	

MacKAY, ANDY

Title	Format	Label	Number	Year	Price	Notes
In Search Of Eddie Riff	LP	Island	ILPS9278	1974	**£10**	

MacKAY, RABBIT

Title	Format	Label	Number	Year	Price	Notes
Bug Cloth	LP	MCS	MUPS351	1968	**£15**	
Hard Time Woman	7"	MCA	MU1041	1968	**£4**	

MACKERAL

Title	Format	Label	Number	Year	Price	Notes
Trying Again	7"	Columbia	DB8388	1968	**£4**	

MacKINTOSH, KEN

Title	Format	Label	Number	Year	Price	Notes
Applejack	7"	HMV	POP300	1957	**£4**	
Big Guitar	7"	HMV	POP464	1958	**£4**	
Creeping Tom	7"	HMV	7M343	1955	**£4**	
Dizzy Fingers	7"	HMV	7M417	1956	**£4**	
Highway Patrol	7"	HMV	POP270	1956	**£4**	
Keep It Moving	7"	HMV	POP358	1957	**£4**	
No Hiding Place	7"	HMV	POP713	1960	**£4**	
Raunchy	7"	HMV	POP426	1957	**£4**	
Regimental Rock	7"	HMV	POP287	1957	**£4**	
Rock Man Rock	7"	HMV	POP327	1957	**£4**	
Six Five Blues	7"	HMV	POP396	1957	**£4**	
Swinging Shepherd Blues	7"	HMV	POP441	1958	**£4**	
Teenager's Special	7" EP	HMV	7EG8170	195-	**£8**	

MacNEE, PATRICK & HONOR BLACKMAN

Title	Format	Label	Number	Year	Price	Notes
Kinky Boots	7"	Decca	F11843	1964	**£4**	

MACON, UNCLE DAVE

Title	Format	Label	Number	Year	Price	Notes
Uncle Dave Macon No.1	7" EP	RCA	RCX7112	1963	**£6**	
Uncle Dave Macon No.2	7" EP	RCA	RCX7113	1963	**£6**	

MacRAE, JOSH

Title	Format	Label	Number	Year	Price	Notes
Messing About On The River	LP	Golden Guin.	GGL0355	1965	**£10**	
Messing About On The River	7"	Pye	7N15319	1960	**£4**	chart single
Walking Talking Singing	7" EP	Pye	NEP24131	1960	**£4**	

MAD LADS

Title	Format	Label	Number	Year	Price	Notes
Don't Have To Shop Around	7"	Atlantic	AT4051	1965	**£4**	
I Want Someone	7"	Atlantic	AT4083	1966	**£4**	
Mad Lads In Action	LP	Volt	414	1966	**£10**	US
Sugar Sugar	7"	Atlantic	584038	1966	**£4**	
Sugar Sugar	7"	Atlantic	584038	1966	**£10**	demo

MAD RIVER

Title	Format	Label	Number	Year	Price	Notes
Mad River	LP	Capitol	ST2985	1968	**£20**	US
Paradise Bar And Grill	LP	Capitol	ST185	1969	**£15**	US

MADARA, JOHNNY

Title	Format	Label	Number	Year	Price	Notes
Be My Girl	7"	HMV	POP389	1957	**£4**	

MADDOX BROTHERS & ROSE

Title	Format	Label	Number	Year	Price	Notes
Collection Of Standard Sacred Songs	LP	King	669	1960	**£30**	US
I'll Write Your Name In The Sand	LP	King	752	1961	**£25**	US
Maddox Brothers And Rose	LP	King	677	1961	**£25**	US

MADDOX, JOHNNY

Title	Format	Label	Number	Year	Price	Notes
Crazy Otto Medley	7"	London	HL8134	1955	**£6**	
Dixieland Band	7"	London	HLD8347	1956	**£6**	
Do Do Do	7"	London	HLD8203	1955	**£6**	
Hands Off	7"	London	HLD8277	1956	**£8**	
Honky Tonk Jazz	7" EP	London	RED1150	1958	**£5**	
Old Fashioned Love	7" EP	London	RED1270	1961	**£4**	
Presenting...	7" EP	London	REP1020	1955	**£8**	
Presenting... No.2	7" EP	London	REP1040	1955	**£8**	
Yellow Dog Blues	7"	London	HLD8540	1958	**£4**	

MADDOX, ROSE

Title	Format	Label	Number	Year	Price	Notes
Alone With You	LP	Capitol	T1993	1963	**£10**	US
Big Bouquet Of Roses	LP	Capitol	T1548	1961	**£10**	US
Gambler's Love	7"	Capitol	CL15023	1959	**£4**	
Glorybound Train	LP	Capitol	T1437	1960	**£10**	US

One Rose	LP	Capitol	T1312	1960	**£10**	US
Precious Memories	LP	Columbia	CL1159	1958	**£20**	US
Rose Maddox Sings Bluegrass	LP	Capitol	T1779	1962	**£12**	US

MADE IN SHEFFIELD

Amelia Jane	7"	Fontana	TF871	1967	**£6**	

MADE IN SWEDEN

Live At The Golden Circle	LP	Sonet	SLP2506	1970	**£12**	
Mad River	LP	Sonet	SNTF621	1971	**£12**	
Made In England	LP	Sonet	SLP2512	1970	**£12**	
Made In Sweden	LP	Sonet	SLP71	1969	**£12**	
Snakes In A Hole	LP	Sonet	SLP2504	1969	**£12**	
Where Do We Begin	LP	Polydor	2480358	1976	**£10**	

MADNESS

Madness Pack	7"	Stiff	GRAB1	1982	**£20**	6 x 7" in plastic wallet
Never Ask Twice	7"	Stiff		1982	**£5**	1 sided promo
Night Boat To Cairo	7"	Stiff	BUYJB71	1980	**£4**	juke box issue
Our House	7"	Stiff	BUYJB163	1982	**£5**	1 sided promo
Swan Lake	12"	Stiff	MAD1	1979	**£6**	promo
Uno Paso Adalante	7"	Stiff	MO1922	1980	**£6**	sung in Spanish
Waiting For The Ghost Train	7"	Zarjazz	JAZZ9	1986	**£4**	shaped pic disc
Yesterday's Men/Uncle Sam	7"	Zarjazz	JAZZ5	1985	**£5**	double with square shaped pic disc

MADONNA

Astute marketing has kept Madonna at the top for far longer than seemed likely when her pictures first started to appear on teenage bedroom walls. Virtually everything she has released is now a collectors' item of some kind, with particular interest being generated by the series of picture disc releases. The value of many of these is much higher than can be explained merely by their rarity, although the early "Crazy For You" is reckoned to be one of the scarcest picture discs of all.

Angel (Extended Dance Mix)	12"	Sire	W8881T	1985	**£10**	
Angel	7"	Sire	W8881	1985	**£4**	chart single
Angel	7"	Sire	W8881P	1985	**£20**	shaped pic disc, plinth
Borderline (Edit)	7"	Sire	W9260	1984	**£5**	chart single
Borderline (US Remix)	12"	Sire	W9260T	1986	**£10**	
Borderline	7"	Sire	W9260	1986	**£4**	chart single
Borderline	7"	Sire	W9260P	1986	**£20**	shaped pic disc
Borderline	12"	Sire	W9260T	1984	**£15**	2 tracks
Borderline	12"	Sire	W9260T	1986	**£10**	3 tracks
Causing A Commotion (Silver Screen Mix)	12"	Sire	W8224TP	1987	**£12**	pic disc
Causing A Commotion	7"	Sire	W8224	1987	**£10**	with badge
Cherish	12"	Sire	W2883TP	1989	**£8**	pic disc
Crazy For You	7"	Geffen	A6323	1985	**£6**	chart single
Crazy For You	7"	Geffen	WA6323P	1985	**£50**	shaped pic disc
Dear Jessie	12"	Sire	W2668T	1989	**£8**	poster sleeve
Dear Jessie	12"	Sire	W2668TP	1989	**£8**	pic disc
Dress You Up (Formal Mix)	12"	Sire	W8848T	1985	**£10**	
Dress You Up (Formal Mix)	12"	Sire	W8848T	1985	**£15**	poster sleeve
Dress You Up	7"	Sire	W8848	1985	**£4**	chart single
Dress You Up	7"	Sire	W8848P	1985	**£20**	shaped pic disc
Everybody	7"	Sire	W9899	1982	**£30**	
Everybody	12"	Sire	W9899T	1982	**£30**	
Express Yourself (Non-Stop Express Mix)	12"	Sire	W2948TP	1989	**£10**	pic disc
Express Yourself	7"	Sire	W2948W	1989	**£10**	zipper sleeve
Express Yourself	7"	Sire	W2948X	1989	**£5**	poster sleeve
Gambler	7"	Geffen	QA6585	1985	**£15**	poster sleeve
Gambler	12"	Geffen	A6585TA	1985	**£15**	
Gambler	7"	Sire	A6585	1985	**£6**	chart single
Holiday (Edit)	7"	Sire	W9405	1983	**£25**	train PS
Holiday (Full Length Version)	12"	Sire	W9405P	1985	**£20**	pic disc
Holiday (Full Length Version)	12"	Sire	W9405T	1983	**£25**	train PS
Holiday (Full Length Version)	12"	Sire	W9405T	1985	**£10**	
Holiday	7"	Sire	W9405	1985	**£4**	chart single
Into The Groove	7"	Sire	W8934	1985	**£4**	chart single
Into The Groove	7"	Sire	W8934P	1985	**£25**	shaped pic disc
Into The Groove	12"	Sire	W8934T	1985	**£10**	
Into The Groove	12"	Sire	W8934T	1985	**£15**	with poster
La Isla Bonita (Extended Remix)	12"	Sire	W8378TP	1987	**£15**	pic disc
La Isla Bonita	12"	Sire	W8378T	1987	**£6**	
Like A Prayer (3 mixes)	12"	Sire	W7539TX	1989	**£8**	

Title	Format	Label	Cat. No.	Year	Price	Notes
Like A Prayer (Extended Remix)	12"	Sire	W7539TP	1989	**£10**	pic disc
Like A Prayer	7"	Sire	W7539	1989	**£5**	poster sleeve
Like A Prayer	Spec	WEA		1989	**£100**	promo pack, CD & Cassette
Like A Virgin (US Dance Remix)	12"	Sire	W9210T	1984	**£10**	
Like A Virgin (US Dance Remix)	12"	Sire	W9210T	1984	**£15**	with poster
Like A Virgin	LP	Sire	9251571	1984	**£10**	9 tracks
Like A Virgin	LP	Sire	WX20P	1985	**£30**	pic disc
Like A Virgin	7"	Sire	W9210	1984	**£4**	chart single
Live To Tell	7"	Sire	W8717	1986	**£4**	chart single
Live To Tell	12"	Sire	W8717T	1986	**£8**	
Live To Tell	12"	Sire	W8717T	1986	**£15**	with poster
Look Of Love	12"	Sire	W8115T	1987	**£8**	with poster
Look Of Love	12"	Sire	W8115TP	1987	**£12**	pic disc
Lucky Star (full length version)	12"	Sire	W9522T	1983	**£30**	2 PS's
Lucky Star (full length version)	12"	Sire	W9522T	1983	**£30**	with poster
Lucky Star (US Remix)	12"	Sire	W9522TV	1983	**£100**	with poster
Lucky Star	7"	Sire	W9522	1983	**£8**	chart single
Madonna	LP	Sire	923867	1983	**£10**	chart LP
Material Girl (Jellybean Dance Remix)	12"	Sire	W9083T	1985	**£10**	
Material Girl (Jellybean Dance Remix)	12"	Sire	W9083T	1985	**£15**	with poster
Material Girl	7"	Sire	W9083	1985	**£25**	poster sleeve
Open Your Heart (Extended Version)	12"	Sire	W8480TP	1986	**£15**	pic disc
Open Your Heart	12"	Sire	W8480T	1986	**£6**	
Papa Don't Preach (Extended Remix)	12"	Sire	W8636TP	1986	**£15**	pic disc
Papa Don't Preach (Extended Version)	12"	Sire	W8636T	1986	**£12**	with poster
Papa Don't Preach	12"	Sire	W8636T	1986	**£8**	
True Blue (Extended Dance Version)	12"	Sire	W8550TP	1986	**£15**	pic disc
True Blue	LP	Sire	WX54	1986	**£25**	blue vinyl
True Blue	LP	Sire	WX54	1986	**£10**	with poster
True Blue	12"	Sire	W8550T	1986	**£6**	
Vogue	7"	Sire	W9851P	1990	**£6**	pic disc
Vogue	12"	Sire	W9851TP	1990	**£8**	pic disc
Vogue	12"	Sire	W9851TW	1990	**£10**	with poster
Vogue	12"	Sire	W9851TX	1990	**£15**	with poster
Who's That Girl (Extended Version)	12"	Sire	W8341TP	1987	**£20**	pic disc

MAESTRO, JOHNNY

Title	Format	Label	Cat. No.	Year	Price	Notes
Before I Loved Her	7"	United Artists	UP1004	1964	**£4**	
Johnny Maestro Story	LP	Buddah	BDS5091	1971	**£20**	US
Mr.Happiness	7"	HMV	POP909	1961	**£5**	
What A Surprise	7"	HMV	POP875	1961	**£4**	

MAGAZINE

Title	Format	Label	Cat. No.	Year	Price	Notes
About The Weather	12"	Virgin	VS41212	1981	**£6**	
Shot By Both Sides	12"	Virgin	VS59212	1983	**£6**	
Sweetheart Contract	7"	Virgin	VS365	1980	**£6**	double

MAGIC

Title	Format	Label	Cat. No.	Year	Price	Notes
Enclosed	LP	Armadillo	8031	1970	**£100**	US

MAGIC CARPET

Title	Format	Label	Cat. No.	Year	Price	Notes
Magic Carpet	LP	Mushroom		1971	**£120**	

MAGIC CHRISTIANS

Title	Format	Label	Cat. No.	Year	Price	Notes
If You Want It	7"	Major Minor	MM673	1970	**£5**	

MAGIC LANTERNS

Title	Format	Label	Cat. No.	Year	Price	Notes
Auntie Grizelda	7"	CBS	202637	1967	**£5**	
Country Woman	7"	Polydor	2058202	1972	**£4**	
Excuse Me Baby	7"	CBS	202094	1966	**£5**	chart single
Knight In Rusty Armour	7"	CBS	202459	1967	**£5**	
Let The Sunshine In	7"	Polydor	2058096	1971	**£4**	
Lit Up With...	LP	CBS	62935	1969	**£10**	
Melt All Your Troubles Away	7"	Camp	602009	1969	**£5**	
One Night Stand	LP	Polydor	24601131	1971	**£10**	
Rumplestiltskin	7"	CBS	202250	1966	**£5**	
Shame Shame	LP	Atlantic	8217	1969	**£25**	US
Shame Shame	7"	Camp	602007	1969	**£4**	
We'll Meet Again	7"	CBS	2750	1967	**£4**	

MAGIC MICHAEL

Title	Format	Label	Cat. No.	Year	Price	Notes
Millionaire	7"	Atomic	MAGIC1	1980	**£4**	

MAGIC MIXTURE

Title	Format	Label	Cat. No.	Year	Price	Notes
This Is...	LP	Saga	FID2125	1968	**£70**	

MAGIC NOTES

Title	Format	Label	Cat. No.	Year	Price	Notes
Album Of Memory	7"	Blue Beat	BB9	1961	**£10**	

MAGIC SAM

Title	Format	Label	Cat. No.	Year	Price	Notes
Magic Sam 1937-69	LP	Blue Horizon	763223	1969	**£40**	

MAGIC VALLEY

Title	Format	Label	Cat. No.	Year	Price	Notes
Taking The Heart Out Of Love	7"	P. Farthing	PEN701	1969	**£8**	

MAGICIANS

Title	Format	Label	Cat. No.	Year	Price	Notes
Liars	7"	Decca	F12374	1966	**£4**	
Painting On Wood	7"	MCA	MU1046	1968	**£4**	
Tarzan March	7"	Decca	F12602	1967	**£4**	
Wet Your Whistle	7"	Decca	F12361	1966	**£4**	

MAGMA

Title	Format	Label	Cat. No.	Year	Price	Notes
1001 Centigrade	LP	Philips	6397031	1971	**£10**	
Kohn Tarkosz	LP	A&M	AMLH68260	1974	**£10**	
Live	LP	Utopia	CYL21245	1975	**£15**	US double
Magma	LP	Philips	635951/2	1970	**£15**	double
Mekanik Destructiw Kommandoh	LP	A&M	AMLH64397	1974	**£10**	
Mekanik Machine	7"	A&M	AMS7119	1974	**£4**	

MAGNA CARTA

Title	Format	Label	Cat. No.	Year	Price	Notes
All My Life	7"	Vertigo	6059073	1972	**£4**	
Give Me Luv	7"	Vertigo	6059092	1973	**£4**	
In Concert	LP	Vertigo	6360068	1972	**£10**	spiral label
Magna Carta	LP	Mercury	SMCL20166	1969	**£20**	
Mid Winter	7"	Mercury	MF1096	1969	**£8**	
Romeo Jack	7"	Fontana	TF1060	1969	**£8**	
Seasons	LP	Vertigo	6360003	1970	**£10**	spiral label, chart LP
Songs From Wasties Orchard	LP	Vertigo	6360040	1971	**£10**	spiral label

MAGNIFICENT MEN

Title	Format	Label	Cat. No.	Year	Price	Notes
Peace Of Mind	7"	Capitol	CL15462	1966	**£5**	

MAHAL, TAJ

Taj Mahal is in some ways the black equivalent of Ry Cooder. He has an archivist's approach to his musical culture, rediscovering old songs and presenting them as fresh pieces of music in order to encourage his audience to delve further. His earliest records are exclusively concerned with the blues, but he has ranged more widely since. Interestingly, Ry Cooder is a member of the band on the first LP.

Title	Format	Label	Cat. No.	Year	Price	Notes
Everybody's Got To Change Sometime	7"	Direction	583547	1968	**£4**	
Giant Step/De Ole Folks	LP	CBS	66226	1969	**£15**	double
Give Your Woman What She Wants	7"	Direction	584586	1969	**£4**	
Natch'l Blues	LP	Direction	863397	1968	**£12**	
Real Thing	LP	CBS	66288	1971	**£12**	double
Taj Mahal	LP	Direction	863279	1967	**£12**	

MAHOGANY RUSH

Title	Format	Label	Cat. No.	Year	Price	Notes
Child Of The Novelty	LP	20th Century	S451	1973	**£12**	US
Maxoom	LP	20th Century	S463	1975	**£12**	US
Maxoom	LP	Nine	936	1972	**£25**	US
Strange Universe	LP	20th Century	S482	1975	**£10**	US

MAIL

Title	Format	Label	Cat. No.	Year	Price	Notes
Omnibus	7"	Parlophone	R5916	1971	**£4**	

MAIN ATTRACTION

Title	Format	Label	Cat. No.	Year	Price	Notes
And Now	LP	Tower	ST5177	1968	**£12**	US

MAINHORSE

Title	Format	Label	Cat. No.	Year	Price	Notes
Mainhorse	LP	Polydor	2383049	1971	**£15**	

MAJIC SHIP

Title	Format	Label	Cat. No.	Year	Price	Notes
Majic Ship	LP	Bel Ami	BA711	1968	**£150**	US

MAJOR ACCIDENT

Title	Format	Label	Cat. No.	Year	Price	Notes
Fight To Win	7"	Flicknife	FLS016	1983	**£5**	
Mr.Nobody	7"	Step Forward	SF23	1983	**£5**	
Respectable Man	7"	Flicknife	FLS026	1984	**£4**	
Tortured Tunes	LP	Syndicate	SYNLP9	1984	**£10**	
Warboots	7"	M. Melodies	MAME1001	1982	**£25**	

MAJORITY

Title	Format	Label	Cat. No.	Year	Price	Notes
All Our Christmases	7"	Decca	F12727	1968	**£4**	
I Hear A Rhapsody	7"	Decca	F12573	1967	**£4**	
Little Bit Of Sunlight	7"	Decca	F12271	1965	**£4**	
Pretty Little Girl	7"	Decca	F12186	1965	**£4**	
Running Away With My Baby	7"	Decca	F12638	1967	**£4**	
Simplified	7"	Decca	F12453	1966	**£4**	
To Make Me A Man	7"	Decca	F12504	1966	**£4**	
We Kiss In The Shadow	7"	Decca	F12313	1966	**£4**	

MAJORS

Title	Format	Label	Cat. No.	Year	Price	Notes
Meet The Majors	LP	Imperial	LP9222	1963	**£15**	US
Meet The Majors	LP	London	HAP8068	1963	**£20**	
Meet The Majors	7" EP	London	REP1358	1963	**£10**	
Ooh Wee Baby	7"	Liberty	LIB66009	1964	**£10**	
She's A Troublemaker	7"	London	HLP9627	1962	**£4**	
What In The World	7"	London	HLP9693	1963	**£4**	
Wonderful Dream	7"	London	HLP9602	1962	**£5**	

MAL & THE PRIMITIVES

Title	Format	Label	Cat. No.	Year	Price	Notes
Every Minute Of Every Day	7"	Pye	7N15915	1965	**£20**	

MALLARD

Mallard were Captain Beefheart's Magic Band after they had left Captain Befheart and their music shares many of the same characteristics - notably the fractured rhythms and the splintery guitar playing. The first LP, with its Mallard engine and ducks, is especially fine and a good companion record to Beefheart's "Clear Spot".

Title	Format	Label	Cat. No.	Year	Price	Notes
In A Different Climate	LP	Virgin	V2077	1977	**£10**	
Mallard	LP	Virgin	V2045	1975	**£10**	

MALMKVIST, SIW

Title	Format	Label	Cat. No.	Year	Price	Notes
Man Who Took The Valise...	7"	Atlantic	584229	1968	**£4**	

MALONE, CINDY

Title	Format	Label	Cat. No.	Year	Price	Notes
Weird Beard	7"	RCA	RCA1254	1961	**£4**	

MALONE, WIL

Title	Format	Label	Cat. No.	Year	Price	Notes
Wil Malone	LP	Fontana		1970	**£50**	

MALTBY, RICHARD

Title	Format	Label	Cat. No.	Year	Price	Notes
Rat Race	7"	Columbia	DB4606	1961	**£12**	

MAMA CASS

Title	Format	Label	Cat. No.	Year	Price	Notes
Dream A Little Dream Of Me	7"	RCA	RCA1726	1968	**£4**	chart single
It's Getting Better	7"	Stateside	SS8021	1969	**£4**	

MAMA LION

Title	Format	Label	Cat. No.	Year	Price	Notes
Give It Everything I've Got	LP	Philips		1973	**£10**	
Mama Lion	LP	Philips	6369153	1972	**£12**	

MAMAS & PAPAS

Title	Format	Label	Cat. No.	Year	Price	Notes
California Dreaming	7"	RCA	RCA1503	1966	**£4**	chart single
Cass, John, Michelle & Denny	LP	RCA	SF7834	1966	**£12**	chart LP
Creeque Alley	7"	RCA	RCA1613	1967	**£4**	chart single
Dedicated To The One I Love	7"	RCA	RCA1576	1967	**£4**	chart single
Deliver	LP	RCA	SF7880	1967	**£12**	chart LP
For The Love Of Ivy	7"	RCA	RCA1744	1968	**£4**	
Gathering Of Flowers	LP	Probe	1003/4	1970	**£12**	double
Glad To Be Unhappy	7"	RCA	RCA1649	1967	**£4**	
I Saw Her Again	7"	RCA	RCA1533	1966	**£4**	chart single
If You Can Believe Your Eyes And Ears	LP	RCA	RD7803	1966	**£12**	chart LP
Look Through My Window	7"	RCA	RCA1551	1966	**£4**	
Monday Monday	7"	RCA	RCA1516	1966	**£4**	chart single
Monterey Pop Festival	LP	Dunhill	DS50100	1971	**£15**	US
Papas And Mamas	LP	RCA	SF7960	1968	**£10**	

Title	Format	Label	Number	Year	Price	Notes
People Like Us	LP	Probe	SPB1048	1972	**£10**	
Safe In My Garden	7"	RCA	RCA1710	1968	**£4**	
Twelve Thirty	7"	RCA	RCA1630	1967	**£4**	
Words Of Love	7"	RCA	RCA1564	1967	**£4**	chart single

MAMMUT

Title	Format	Label	Number	Year	Price	Notes
Mammut	LP	Mouse			**£120**	

MAN

Title	Format	Label	Number	Year	Price	Notes
2oz Of Plastic With A Hole...	LP	Dawn	DNLS3003	1969	**£15**	
Bananas	7"	United Artists	UPS408	1976	**£4**	
Be Good To Yourself	LP	United Artists	UAG29417	1972	**£10**	Map of Wales cover
Christmas At The Patti	LP-10"	United Artists	UDX205/6	1973	**£15**	double
Daughter Of The Fireplace	7"	Liberty	LBF15448	1971	**£12**	
Day And Night	7"	United Artists	UP35739	1974	**£4**	
Do You Like It Here	LP	United Artists	UAG29236	1971	**£10**	
Don't Go Away	7"	United Artists	UP35643	1974	**£5**	
Live At The Padget Rooms	LP	United Artists	USP100	1972	**£20**	
Man	LP	Liberty	LBS83464	1970	**£12**	
Out Of Your Head	7"	MCA	MCA236	1976	**£4**	
Revelation	LP	Pye	NSPL18275	1969	**£15**	
Sudden Life	7"	Pye	7N17684	1969	**£10**	
Taking The Easy Way Out Again	7"	United Artists	UP35703	1974	**£4**	

MANASSAS

Manassas was the group formed by Steve Stills in the wake of the first disbanding of Crosby, Stills, & Nash. It was something of a supergroup itself, with various ex-members of the CSN rhythm section and of the Flying Burrito Brothers being involved. Steve Stills, however, remains firmly in control and the Manassas albums are very much a showcase for his talents. They include some of Stills' best songs.

Title	Format	Label	Number	Year	Price	Notes
Down The Road	LP	Atlantic	K40440	1973	**£10**	chart LP
Manassas	LP	Atlantic	K60021	1972	**£15**	double, chart LP

MANCHESTER MEKON

Title	Format	Label	Number	Year	Price	Notes
No Forgetting	7"	Newmarket	NEW102	1979	**£5**	

MANCHESTER MOB

Title	Format	Label	Number	Year	Price	Notes
Bony Maronie At The Hop	7"	Parlophone	R5552	1967	**£10**	

MANCHESTER'S PLAYBOYS

Title	Format	Label	Number	Year	Price	Notes
I Feel So Good	7"	Fontana	TF745	1966	**£20**	

MANCHESTERS

Title	Format	Label	Number	Year	Price	Notes
Tribute To The Beatles	LP	Ember		1966	**£25**	

MANDALA BAND

Title	Format	Label	Number	Year	Price	Notes
Eye Of Wendor	LP	Chrysalis	CHR1181	1978	**£10**	
Mandala Band	LP	Chrysalis	CHR1095	1975	**£10**	

MANDEL, HARVEY

Title	Format	Label	Number	Year	Price	Notes
Baby Batter	LP	Dawn	DNLS3015	1971	**£12**	
Best Of...	LP	Janus	7014	1975	**£10**	US
Cristo Redentor	LP	Philips	SBL7873	1968	**£15**	
Feel The Sound Of	LP	Janus	3067	1974	**£12**	US
Games Guitars Play	LP	Philips	SBL7915	1970	**£15**	
Get Off In Chicago	LP	London	SHO8426	1972	**£12**	
Righteous	LP	Philips	SBL7904	1969	**£15**	
Shangrenade	LP	Janus	6499831	1973	**£12**	
Snake	LP	Janus	6310210	1972	**£12**	
Uno Ino	7"	Janus	6146024	1974	**£4**	

MANDRAKE MEMORIAL

Title	Format	Label	Number	Year	Price	Notes
Mandrake Memorial	LP	Poppy	PYS40002	1968	**£15**	US
Medium	LP	RCA	SF8028	1969	**£30**	
Puzzle	LP	Poppy	11003	1970	**£20**	

MANDRAKE PADDLE STEAMER

Title	Format	Label	Number	Year	Price	Notes
Strange Walking Man	7"	Parlophone	R5780	1969	**£8**	

MANDRILL

Title	Format	Label	Number	Year	Price	Notes
Best Of	LP	Polydor	2391186	1975	**£10**	
Composite Truth	LP	Polydor	2391061	1973	**£12**	
Fencewalk	7"	Polydor	2066357	1973	**£4**	

Just Outside Of Town	LP	Polydor	2391092	1973	**£12**	
Mandrill	LP	Polydor	2489028	1970	**£12**	
Mandrill	7"	Polydor	2066320	1973	**£4**	
Mandrill Is	LP	Polydor	2391030	1972	**£12**	

MANEATERS

Nine To Five	7"	Editions EG	EGO8	1982	**£8**	

MANHATTANS

I Wanna Be Your Everything	7"	Sue	WI384	1965	**£8**	

MANIACS

Chelsea 1977	7"	United Artists	UP36327	1977	**£5**	

MANN, BARRY

Bless You	7"	HMV	POP1108	1963	**£4**	
Hey Baby I'm Dancing	7"	HMV	POP1084	1962	**£4**	
Little Miss USA	7"	HMV	POP949	1961	**£4**	
Talk To Me Baby	7"	Colpix	PX776	1964	**£4**	
Who Put The Bomp	LP	ABC-Para.	399	1963	**£20**	US
Who Put The Bomp	7"	HMV	POP911	1961	**£5**	

MANN, CARL

Like Mann	LP	London	HAS2277	1960	**£25**	
Like Mann	LP	Philips	PLP1960	1960	**£300**	US
Mona Lisa	7"	London	HLS8935	1959	**£10**	
Pretend	7"	London	HLS9006	1959	**£10**	
South Of The Border	7"	London	HLS9170	1960	**£6**	

MANN, GLORIA

It Happened Again	7"	Brunswick	05610	1956	**£4**	
Why Do Fools Fall In Love	7"	Brunswick	05569	1956	**£6**	

MANN, HERBIE

Philly Dog	7"	Atlantic	584052	1966	**£8**	

MANN, MANFRED

When Manfred Mann decided to call a halt to his pop career, the result was one of the best albums of all to emerge from the interface between jazz and rock. Essentially the work of a big band, "Manfred Mann Chapter Three" showcased some fine playing - most notably from saxophonist Bernie Living, formerly with the Mike Westbrook band - and also demonstrated the excellence of the Mann-Hugg writing team. "Travelling Lady" was an update of "A B Side" - to be found on the reverse of the single "Ragamuffin Man" and itself the same piece of music as that used in a TV advert. The powerful brass riff that drives "Time", meanwhile, was adopted as the theme tune for a radio jazz programme. Manfred Mann had earlier indicated that he might have something like this up his sleeve when he released the "Instrumental Asylum" EP (whose tracks are also to be found on the LP "Soul Of Mann"). Paul Jones had just left the group, so the others took advantage of their singerless condition to make a record of sparkling jazz versions of a few well-known rock tunes. The presence of Jack Bruce on bass, together with trumpeter Henry Lowther and saxophonist Lyn Dobson, was a distinct bonus. "Instrumental Assassination" attempted to repeat the formula, but somewhat less successfully, as new member Klaus Voorman was no substitute, in this kind of music, for the three jazzers he replaced.

5-4-3-2-1	7"	HMV	POP1252	1964	**£4**	chart single
As Is	LP	Fontana	STL5377	1966	**£15**	chart LP
As Was	7" EP	HMV	7EG8962	1966	**£8**	
Chapter Three	LP	Vertigo	VO3	1969	**£20**	spiral label
Chapter Three Vol.2	LP	Vertigo	6360012	1970	**£20**	spiral label
Cock A Hoop	7"	HMV	POP1225	1963	**£6**	
Come Tomorrow	7"	HMV		1965	**£10**	sung in German
Come Tomorrow	7"	HMV	POP1381	1965	**£4**	chart single
Do Wah Diddy Diddy	7"	HMV	POP1320	1964	**£4**	chart single
Don't Kill It Carol	7"	Bronze	BROP77	1979	**£4**	pic disc
Five Faces Of Manfred Mann	LP	Ascot	ALM13018	1965	**£15**	US
Five Faces Of...	LP	HMV	CLP1731	1964	**£15**	chart LP
Fox On The Run	7"	Fontana	TF985	1968	**£4**	chart single
Greatest Hits	LP	United Artists	UAL3551	1966	**£12**	US
Grooving With Manfred Mann	7" EP	HMV	7EG8876	1965	**£6**	
Ha Ha Said The Clown	7"	Fontana	TF812	1967	**£4**	chart single
Happy Being Me	7"	Vertigo	6059012	1970	**£4**	
Hits Of Manfred Mann & DDDBM&T	cass-s	Philips	MCF5005	1968	**£10**	
Hits Of Manfred Mann	cass-s	Philips	MCF5002	1968	**£10**	
Hubble Bubble	7"	HMV	POP1282	1964	**£4**	chart single
If You Gotta Go, Go Now	7"	HMV	POP1466	1965	**£4**	chart single
Instrumental Assassination	7" EP	Fontana	TE17483	1966	**£5**	
Instrumental Asylum	7" EP	HMV	7EG8949	1966	**£8**	

Just Like A Woman	7"	Fontana	TF730	1966	**£4**	chart single
Living Without You	7"	Philips	6006122	1971	**£4**	
Machines	7" EP	HMV	7EG8942	1966	**£8**	
Manfred Mann	7" EP	HMV	7EG8848	1964	**£6**	
Manfred Mann Album	LP	Ascot	ALM13015	1964	**£15**	US
Mann Made	LP	Ascot	ALM13024	1966	**£15**	US
Mann Made	LP	HMV	CLP1911	1964	**£15**	chart LP, mono
Mann Made	LP	HMV	CSD1628	1964	**£15**	chart LP, stereo
Mann Made Hits	LP	HMV	CLP3559	1966	**£15**	chart LP
Messin'	LP	Vertigo	6360087	1973	**£10**	
Michelin Theme	7"	Michelin	MIC1	1971	**£8**	gatefold sleeve
Mighty Garvey	LP	Fontana	STL5470	1968	**£15**	
Mighty Quinn	7"	Fontana	TF897	1968	**£4**	chart single
Mighty Quinn	LP	Mercury	SR61168	1968	**£12**	US
My Little Red Book Of Winners	LP	Ascot	ALM13021	1965	**£30**	US
My Name Is Jack	7"	Fontana	TF943	1968	**£4**	chart single
No Living Without Loving	7" EP	HMV	7EG8922	1965	**£6**	
Oh No Not My Baby	7"	HMV	POP1413	1965	**£4**	chart single
One In The Middle	7" EP	HMV	7EG8908	1965	**£6**	
Please Mrs.Henry	7"	Philips	6006159	1971	**£4**	
Pretty Flamingo	7"	HMV	POP1523	1966	**£4**	chart single
Pretty Flamingo	LP	United Artists	UAL3549	1966	**£12**	US
Ragamuffin Man	7"	Fontana	TF1013	1969	**£4**	chart single
Roaring Silence	12"	Bronze		1976	**£10**	promo sampler
Semi-Detached Suburban Mr.James	7"	Fontana	TF757	1966	**£4**	chart single
Sha La La	7"	HMV	POP1346	1964	**£4**	chart single
Ski, The Full Of Fitness Food	7"	Ski Yoghurt	SKI01	1971	**£8**	
So Long Dad	7"	Fontana	TF862	1967	**£5**	
Soul Of Mann	LP	HMV	CLP3594	1967	**£15**	chart LP
Sweet Pea	7"	Fontana	TF828	1967	**£4**	chart single
Up The Junction	LP	Fontana	STL5460	1968	**£15**	
Up The Junction	7"	Fontana	TF908	1968	**£5**	
What A Man	LP	Fontana	SFL13003	1968	**£15**	
Why Should We Not	7"	HMV	POP1189	1963	**£6**	
You Gave Me Somebody To Love	7"	HMV	POP1541	1966	**£5**	chart single

MANN, SHADOW

Come Live With Me	7"	Roulette	RO504	1968	**£4**	

MANONE, WINGY

Party Doll	7"	Brunswick	05655	1957	**£5**	

MANSON, CHARLES

Lie	LP	Awareness	22145	1970	**£50**	US

MANTELL, JOHN

Remember Child	7"	CBS	201783	1965	**£4**	

MANTLER, MIKE

Jazz Composers' Orchestra	LP	Virgin	JD3001	1974	**£15**	double

MAPHIS, JOE

Fire On The Strings	LP	Columbia	CL1005	1957	**£25**	US

MAPHIS, JOE & ROSE LEE

Mr.And Mrs.Country Music	LP	Starday	SLP286	1964	**£10**	US
With The Blue Ridge Mountain Boys	LP	Capitol	T1778	1962	**£10**	US

MAPLE OAK

Maple Oak	LP	Decca		1971	**£150**	
Son Of A Gun	7"	Decca	F13008	1970	**£4**	

MAPP, LUCILLE

Mangos	7"	Columbia	DB3916	1957	**£4**	

MARAN, MIKE

Fair Warning	LP	Bronze	ILPS9221	1972	**£15**	

MARATHONS

Peanut Butter	LP	Arvee	A428	1961	**£50**	US
Peanut Butter	7"	Pye	7N25088	1961	**£4**	
Peanut Butter	7"	Vogue	V9185	1961	**£6**	

MARAUDERS

Baby	7"	Fontana	TF609	1965	£8	
Check In	LP	no label		196-	£40	US
Heart Full Of Tears	7"	Decca	F11748	1963	£5	
Little Egypt	7"	Decca	F11836	1964	£6	
That's What I Want	7"	Decca	F11695	1963	£6	chart single

MARBLE PHROGG

Marble Phrogg	LP	Derrick	8868	1968	£300	US

MARBLE STAIRCASE

Still Dreaming	12"	Whaam	WHAAM11	1983	£6	

MARBLES

Only One Woman	7"	Polydor	56272	1968	£4	chart single
Walls Fell Down	7"	Polydor	56310	1969	£4	chart single

MARC & THE MAMBAS

Big Louise	12"	Some Bizarre	BZS1512	1982	£6	
Bite Black And Blues	LP	Gutterheart	GH1	1984	£25	fan club only
Black Heart	7"	Some Bizarre	BZS19	1983	£8	with card
Black Heart	12"	Some Bizarre	BZS1912	1983	£10	
Discipline	7"	Lyntone	LYN12505	1982	£10	flexi
Sleaze	12"	Some Bizarre	BZS512	1982	£20	fan club
Torment	12"	Some Bizarre	BZS2112	1983	£15	
Untitled	LP	Some Bizarre	BZS13	1982	£10	with 12", chart LP

MARCELLE, LYDIA

Another Kind Of Fellow	7"	Sue	WI4025	1966	£8	

MARCELLINO, MUZZY

Mary Lou	7"	London	HLU8355	1956	£6	

MARCELS

Blue Moon	LP	Colpix	CP416	1961	£50	US
Blue Moon	7"	Pye	7N25073	1961	£6	chart single
Heartaches	7"	Pye	7N25114	1961	£4	
I Wanna Be The Leader	7"	Pye	7N25201	1963	£4	
My Melancholy Baby	7"	Pye	7N25124	1962	£4	
Summertime	7"	Pye	7N25083	1961	£4	chart single
You Are My Sunshine	7"	Pye	7N25105	1961	£4	

MARCH HARE

I Could Make It There With You	7"	Deram	DM258	1969	£4	

MARCH VIOLETS

Crow Baby	7"	Rebirth	RB18	1983	£5	
Crow Baby	12"	Rebirth	REB1812	1983	£6	
Grooving In Green	7"	Merciful Rel.	MR017	1982	£12	
Religious As Hell	7"	Merciful Rel.	MR013	1982	£12	
Snake Dance	7"	Rebirth	RB21	1983	£5	
Snake Dance	12"	Rebirth	REB2112	1983	£6	
Walk Into The Sun	7"	Rebirth	VRB24	1984	£4	

MARCH, HAL

Hear Me Good	7"	London	HLD8534	1958	£10	

MARCH, PEGGY

Hello Heartache Goodbye Love	7"	RCA	RCA1362	1963	£4	
I Will Follow Him	LP	RCA	LPM2732	1963	£12	US
I Will Follow Him	7"	RCA	RCA1338	1963	£4	
If You Loved Me	7"	RCA	RCA1687	1968	£10	
In Our Fashion	LP	RCA	LPM3408	1965	£15	US
No Foolin'	LP	RCA	LSP3883	1968	£12	US

MARCHAN, BOBBY

Ain't No Reason For Girls To Be Lonely	7"	Action	ACT4533	1969	£10	demo
Get Down With It	7"	Atlantic	584155	1968	£4	
There's Something On Your Mind	LP	Sphere Snd	SSR7004	1964	£25	US

MARESCA, ERNIE

It's Their World	7"	London	HLU10008	1965	£4	

Title	Format	Label	Cat. No.	Year	Price	Notes
Love Express	7"	London	HLU9720	1963	**£4**	
Mary Jane	7"	London	HLU9579	1962	**£4**	
Rovin' Kind	7"	London	HLU9834	1964	**£4**	
Shout Shout	7"	London	HLU9531	1962	**£6**	
Shout! Shout! Knock Yourself Out	LP	Seville	SV77001	1962	**£15**	US

MARGO & THE MARVETTES

Title	Format	Label	Cat. No.	Year	Price	Notes
Cherry Pie	7"	Parlophone	R5154	1964	**£4**	
Copper Kettle	7"	Parlophone	R5227	1965	**£4**	

MARGRET, ANN

Title	Format	Label	Cat. No.	Year	Price	Notes
Gimme Love	7"	RCA	RCA1267	1961	**£4**	
I Just Don't Understand	7"	RCA	RCA1245	1961	**£4**	
Man's Favourite Sport	7"	RCA	RCA1396	1964	**£4**	
Vivacious One	7" EP	RCA	RCX7148	1964	**£8**	

MARIANNE

Title	Format	Label	Cat. No.	Year	Price	Notes
You Know My Name	7"	Columbia	DB8420	1968	**£6**	
You'd Better Change Your Evil Ways	7"	Columbia	DB8456	1968	**£4**	

MARILLION

The considerable success of an "old-fashioned" progressive group was one of the more surprising aspects of rock music in the eighties. Marillion achieved this, however, by gigging hard up and down the country and building a sizeable following before making any records at all. In common with other stars of the eighties, Marillion's recording career has been highlighted by a succession of picture disc releases, and it is these that now form the central axis of a Marillion collection.

Title	Format	Label	Cat. No.	Year	Price	Notes
Assassing	12"	EMI	12MARILP2	1984	**£25**	pic disc
Clutching At Straws	LP	EMI	EMDP1002	1987	**£10**	pic disc
Freaks	7"	EMI	MARIL9	1988	**£5**	
Freaks	7"	EMI	MARILP9	1988	**£10**	shaped pic disc
Freaks	12"	EMI	12MARILP9	1988	**£20**	pic disc
Fugazi	LP	EMI	MRLP1	1984	**£15**	pic disc
Garden Party	7"	EMI	EMIP5393	1983	**£15**	shaped pic disc
Garden Party	12"	EMI	12EMIS5393	1983	**£6**	with poster
He Knows You Know	7"	EMI	EMI5362	1983	**£4**	chart single
He Knows You Know	12"	EMI	12EMI5362	1983	**£6**	
Heart Of Lothian	12"	EMI	12MARILP5	1985	**£10**	pic disc
Incommunicado	CD-s	EMI	CDMARIL6	1987	**£8**	
Incommunicado	12"	EMI	12MARILP6	1987	**£15**	pic disc
Kayleigh	7"	EMI	MARILP3	1985	**£8**	pic disc
Kayleigh	12"	EMI	12MARILP3	1985	**£12**	pic disc
Lavender Blue	12"	EMI	12MARILP4	1985	**£10**	pic disc
Market Square Heroes	7"	EMI	EMI5351	1982	**£4**	chart single
Market Square Heroes	12"	EMI	12EMI5351	1982	**£6**	
Market Square Heroes	12"	EMI	12EMIP5351	1983	**£40**	pic disc
Misplaced Childhood	LP	EMI	MRLP2	1985	**£15**	pic disc
Punch And Judy	12"	EMI	12MARILP1	1984	**£15**	pic disc
Real To Reel	LP	EMI	JESTP1	1984	**£10**	pic disc
Script For A Jester's Tear	LP	EMI	EMCP3429	1984	**£30**	pic disc
Sugar Mice (Radio Edit)	CD-s	EMI	CDMARIL7	1987	**£20**	
Sugar Mice	7"	EMI	MARILP7	1987	**£5**	pic disc with poster
Sugar Mice	12"	EMI	12MARIL7	1987	**£8**	
Warm Wet Circles	CD-s	EMI	CDMARIL8	1987	**£6**	
Warm Wet Circles	12"	EMI	12MARILP8	1987	**£8**	pic disc

MARINERS

Title	Format	Label	Cat. No.	Year	Price	Notes
I Love You Fair Dinkum	7"	London	HLA8201	1955	**£6**	

MARIONETTES

Title	Format	Label	Cat. No.	Year	Price	Notes
At The End Of The Day	7"	Parlophone	R5374	1965	**£4**	
Like A Man	7"	Parlophone	R5416	1966	**£4**	
Was It Me?	7"	Parlophone	R5300	1965	**£4**	
Whirlpool Of Love	7"	Decca	F12056	1965	**£4**	

MARK & JOHN

Title	Format	Label	Cat. No.	Year	Price	Notes
Walk Right Back	7"	Decca	F12044	1964	**£5**	

MARK-ALMOND

Title	Format	Label	Cat. No.	Year	Price	Notes
City	7"	Harvest	HAR5044	1971	**£4**	
Mark Almond	LP	Harvest	SHSP4011	1971	**£10**	
Mark Almond 2	LP	Blue Thumb	BT32	1972	**£10**	US
Mark Almond '73	LP	CBS	32486	1973	**£10**	US
Other People's Rooms	LP	Horizon	AMLJ730	1978	**£10**	

Rising	LP	Harvest	SHVL809	1972	**£10**	
To The Heart	LP	ABC	ABCL5183	1976	**£10**	

MARK FIVE

Baby What's Wrong	7"	Fontana	TF513	1964	**£30**	

MARK FOUR

The Mark Four who recorded singles for Decca and Fontana were an early line-up of the Creation. The bass player was John Dalton, later a member of the Kinks.

Hurt Me If You Will	7"	Decca	F12204	1965	**£20**	
Work All Day	7"	Fontana	TF664	1966	**£20**	

MARK IV

Crazy Country Hop	7"	Mercury	MF825	1964	**£15**	
I Got A Wife	7"	Mercury	AMT1025	1959	**£15**	
Move Over Rover	7"	Mercury	AMT1045	1959	**£15**	
Rock Around The Clock	7"	Mercury	MF815	1964	**£15**	

MARK, JON

All Neat In Black Stockings	7"	Philips	BF1772	1969	**£4**	
Baby I Got A Long Way To Go	7"	Brunswick	05929	1965	**£4**	
Paris Bells	7"	Brunswick	05952	1966	**£4**	
Songs For A Friend	LP	CBS	33339	1975	**£10**	US

MARKETTS

Balbao Blue	7"	Liberty	LIB55443	1962	**£4**	
Batman Theme	LP	W. Bros	T1642	1966	**£10**	US
Batman Theme	7"	W. Bros	WB5696	1966	**£5**	
Out Of Limits	LP	W. Bros	T1537	1964	**£10**	US
Out Of Limits	7"	W. Bros	WB120	1964	**£5**	
Surfer Stomp	7"	Liberty	LIB55401	1962	**£4**	
Surfer Stomp	LP	Liberty	LRP3226	1962	**£15**	US
Surfing Scene	LP	Liberty	LRP3326	1963	**£12**	US
Take To Wheels	LP	W. Bros	T1509	1963	**£10**	US
Tarzan	7"	W. Bros	WB5847	1967	**£15**	
Vanishing Point	7"	W. Bros	WB130	1964	**£4**	

MARKEYS

Do The Pop-Eye	LP	London	HAK8011	1962	**£12**	
Foxy	7"	London	HLK9510	1962	**£4**	
Great Memphis Sound	LP	Atlantic	587024	1965	**£15**	
Last Night	LP	Atlantic	8055	1961	**£12**	US
Last Night	7"	Atlantic	584074	1967	**£4**	
Last Night	7"	London	HLK9399	1961	**£5**	
Mellow Jelly	LP	Atlantic	587135	1968	**£15**	
Morning After	7"	London	HLK9449	1961	**£4**	
Philly Dog	7"	Atlantic	AT4079	1966	**£5**	

MARKHAM, PIGMEAT

Pigmeat Markham was a black American comedian who might well be described as the James Brown of comedy for the way in which he kept his art in the ghetto, even when he himself had moved out of it. Markham invented the "Here Comes The Judge" by-line which featured on the TV show "Rowan And Martin's Laugh-In", although the song built around it was commandeered by Shorty Long for Tamla Motown.

Here Comes The Judge	LP	Chess	LPS1523	1968	**£15**	US
Here Comes The Judge	7"	Chess	CRS8077	1968	**£5**	chart single
Sock It To 'Em Judge	7"	Chess	CRS8085	1968	**£4**	

MARKLEY

Markely: A Group	LP	Forward	STF1007	1969	**£20**	US

MARKSMEN

Smersh	7"	Parlophone	R5075	1963	**£8**	

MARLEY, BOB

African Herbsman	LP	Trojan	TRL62	1973	**£10**	
African Herbsman	7"	Upsetter	US392	1972	**£5**	
Baby We've Got A Date	7"	Blue Mount.	1021	1973	**£5**	
Catch A Fire	LP	Island	ILPS9241	1972	**£10**	lighter cover
Duppy Conqueror	7"	Upsetter	US348	1971	**£10**	
Get Up Stand Up	7"	Island		1973	**£5**	1 sided promo
Guava Jelly	7"	Green Door	GD4025	1972	**£8**	

I Like It Like This	7"	Supreme	SUP216	196-	**£30**	
I Shot The Sheriff	7"	Island	IDJ2	1974	**£6**	promo
Jah Live	7"	Island	WIP6265	1974	**£4**	
Johnny Was	7"	Island	WIP6296	1975	**£4**	
Judge Not	7"	Island	WI088	1963	**£70**	
Kaya	7"	Upsetter	US356	1971	**£10**	
Let Him Go	7"	Island	WI3009	1966	**£30**	instrumental B side
Lick Samba	7"	Bullet	BU493	1971	**£8**	
Lively Up Yourself	7"	Green Door	GD4002	1971	**£8**	
Lively Up Yourself	7"	Punch	PH102	1973	**£5**	
More Axe	7"	Upsetter	US369	1971	**£10**	
More Axe	7"	Upsetter	US372	1971	**£10**	
Mr.Brown	7"	Upsetter	US354	1971	**£10**	
My Cup	7"	Upsetter	US340	1970	**£12**	
Natty Dread	7"	Island	WIP6212	1974	**£4**	
One Cup Of Coffee	7"	Island	WI128	1963	**£50**	
One Love	12"	Island	12ISP169	1984	**£6**	pic disc
Rasta Revolution	LP	Trojan	TRLS89	1974	**£10**	
Run For Cover	7"	Escort	ERT842	1970	**£12**	
Screw Face	7"	Punch	PH101	1973	**£5**	
Small Axe	7"	Punch	PH69	1971	**£8**	
Small Axe	7"	Upsetter	US357	1971	**£10**	
Soul Rebel	LP	Trojan	TBL126	1971	**£10**	
Soul Shake Down Party	7"	Trojan	TR7759	1970	**£12**	
Soul Shake Down Party	7"	Trojan	TR7911	1974	**£4**	
Soultown	7"	Bullet	BU464	1971	**£8**	
Stir It Up	7"	Trojan	TR617	1968	**£10**	
Trenchtown Rock	7"	Green Door	GD4005	1971	**£8**	
Trenchtown Rock	7"	Island	IDJ7	1974	**£6**	promo

MARLEY, BOB & ROBERT PALMER

Record Shop Sampler	LP	Island	RSS1		**£15**	promo

MARLEY, RITA

Pied Piper	7"	Rio	R108	1967	**£10**	

MARLO, MICKI

Prize Of Gold	7"	Capitol	CL14271	1955	**£4**	

MARLO, MICKI & PAUL ANKA

That's Right	7"	London	HL8481	1957	**£10**	

MARLOWE, MARION

Hands Of Time	7"	London	HLA8306	1956	**£20**	

MARMALADE

There's A Lot Of It About	LP	CBS	63414	1968	**£10**	

MARQUIS OF KENSINGTON

Changing Of The Guards	7"	Immediate	IM052	1967	**£10**	

MARR, HANK

Tonk Game	7"	Blue Beat	BB26	1961	**£10**	

MARRIOTT, STEVE

Give Her My Regards	7"	Decca	F11619	1963	**£15**	
Marriott	LP	A&M	AMLH64572	1976	**£10**	

MARS, JOHNNY

Blues From Mars	LP	Polydor	2460168	1972	**£12**	

MARSDEN, BERYL

I Know	7"	Decca	F11707	1963	**£6**	
Music Talk	7"	Columbia	DB7797	1965	**£8**	
What's She Got	7"	Columbia	DB7888	1966	**£8**	
When The Lovelight Starts	7"	Decca	F11819	1964	**£8**	
Who You Gonna Hurt	7"	Columbia	DB7718	1965	**£6**	

MARSDEN, GERRY

Gilbert Green	7"	CBS	2946	1967	**£4**	
Please Let Them Be	7"	CBS	2784	1967	**£4**	

MARSHALL HOOKS & CO.

I Want The Same Thing Tomorrow .... 7" .... Blue Horizon ... 2096002 .... 1971 .... **£5** ....
Marshall Hooks And Co. .... LP .... Blue Horizon ... 2431003 .... 1971 .... **£20** ....

MARSHMALLOW HIGHWAY

I Don't Wanna Live This Way .... 7" .... London .... HLR10204 .... 1968 .... **£4** ....

MARSUPILAMI

Arena .... LP .... Transatlantic ... TRA230 .... 1971 .... **£30** ....
Marsupilami .... LP .... Transatlantic ... TRA213 .... 1970 .... **£30** ....

MARTHA & THE VANDELLAS

Bless You .... 7" .... T. Motown .... TMG794 .... 1971 .... **£4** .... chart single
Bless You .... 7" .... T. Motown .... TMG794 .... 1971 .... **£15** .... demo
Come And Get These Memories .... LP .... Oriole .... PS40052 .... 1963 .... **£40** ....
Come And Get These Memories .... 7" .... Oriole .... CBA1819 .... 1963 .... **£40** ....
Dance Party .... LP .... T. Motown .... TML11013 .... 1965 .... **£30** ....
Dancing In The Street .... 7" .... Stateside .... SS345 .... 1964 .... **£12** .... chart single
Dancing In The Street .... 7" .... Stateside .... SS345 .... 1964 .... **£50** .... demo
Dancing In The Street .... LP .... T. Motown .... STML11099 .... 1969 .... **£12** ....
Dancing In The Street .... 7" .... T. Motown .... TMG684 .... 1969 .... **£4** .... chart single
Dancing In The Street .... 7" .... T. Motown .... TMG684 .... 1969 .... **£15** .... demo
Forget Me Not .... 7" .... T. Motown .... TMG762 .... 1971 .... **£4** .... chart single
Forget Me Not .... 7" .... T. Motown .... TMG762 .... 1971 .... **£15** .... demo
Greatest Hits .... LP .... T. Motown .... STML11040 .... 1967 .... **£10** ....
Heatwave .... 7" .... Stateside .... SS228 .... 1963 .... **£15** ....
Heatwave .... 7" .... Stateside .... SS228 .... 1963 .... **£50** .... demo
Heatwave .... LP .... T. Motown .... TML11005 .... 1965 .... **£20** ....
Hitting .... 7" EP .... T. Motown .... TME2017 .... 1966 .... **£15** ....
Honey Chile .... 7" .... T. Motown .... TMG636 .... 1968 .... **£4** .... chart single
Honey Chile .... 7" .... T. Motown .... TMG636 .... 1968 .... **£20** .... demo
I Can't Dance To The Music You're Playing .... 7" .... T. Motown .... TMG669 .... 1968 .... **£5** ....
I Can't Dance To The Music You're Playing .... 7" .... T. Motown .... TMG669 .... 1968 .... **£20** .... demo
I Promise To Wait My Love .... 7" .... T. Motown .... TMG657 .... 1968 .... **£5** ....
I Promise To Wait My Love .... 7" .... T. Motown .... TMG657 .... 1968 .... **£20** .... demo
I'll Have To Let Him Go .... 7" .... Oriole .... CBA1814 .... 1963 .... **£40** ....
I'm Ready For Love .... 7" .... T. Motown .... TMG582 .... 1966 .... **£6** .... chart single
I'm Ready For Love .... 7" .... T. Motown .... TMG582 .... 1966 .... **£40** .... demo
In My Lonely Room .... 7" .... Stateside .... SS305 .... 1964 .... **£15** ....
In My Lonely Room .... 7" .... Stateside .... SS305 .... 1964 .... **£50** .... demo
Jimmy Mack .... 7" .... T. Motown .... TMG599 .... 1967 .... **£5** .... chart single
Jimmy Mack .... 7" .... T. Motown .... TMG599 .... 1967 .... **£50** .... demo
Live .... LP .... Gordy .... 925 .... 1967 .... **£12** .... US
Live Wire .... 7" .... Stateside .... SS272 .... 1964 .... **£15** ....
Live Wire .... 7" .... Stateside .... SS272 .... 1964 .... **£50** .... demo
Love Bug Leave My Heart Alone .... 7" .... T. Motown .... TMG621 .... 1967 .... **£8** ....
Love Bug Leave My Heart Alone .... 7" .... T. Motown .... TMG621 .... 1967 .... **£30** .... demo
Martha & The Vandellas .... 7" EP .... T. Motown .... TME2009 .... 1965 .... **£15** ....
My Baby Loves Me .... 7" .... T. Motown .... TMG549 .... 1966 .... **£10** ....
My Baby Loves Me .... 7" .... T. Motown .... TMG549 .... 1966 .... **£50** .... demo
No One There .... 7" .... T. Motown .... TMG843 .... 1973 .... **£4** ....
No One There .... 7" .... T. Motown .... TMG843 .... 1973 .... **£10** .... demo
Nowhere To Run .... 7" .... T. Motown .... TMG694 .... 1969 .... **£4** .... chart single
Nowhere To Run .... 7" .... T. Motown .... TMG694 .... 1969 .... **£15** .... demo
Nowhere To Run .... 7" .... T. Motown .... TMG502 .... 1965 .... **£8** .... chart single
Nowhere To Run .... 7" .... T. Motown .... TMG502 .... 1965 .... **£50** .... demo
Quicksand .... 7" .... Stateside .... SS250 .... 1964 .... **£12** ....
Quicksand .... 7" .... Stateside .... SS250 .... 1964 .... **£50** .... demo
Ridin' High .... LP .... T. Motown .... STML11078 .... 1968 .... **£12** ....
Watch Out .... LP .... T. Motown .... STML11051 .... 1967 .... **£12** ....
What Am I Going To Do .... 7" .... T. Motown .... TMG567 .... 1966 .... **£8** ....
What Am I Going To Do .... 7" .... T. Motown .... TMG567 .... 1966 .... **£50** .... demo
Wild One .... 7" .... Stateside .... SS383 .... 1965 .... **£15** ....
Wild One .... 7" .... Stateside .... SS383 .... 1965 .... **£50** .... demo
You've Been In Love Too Long .... 7" .... T. Motown .... TMG530 .... 1965 .... **£15** ....
You've Been In Love Too Long .... 7" .... T. Motown .... TMG530 .... 1965 .... **£60** .... demo

MARTIN & FINLEY

It's Another Sunday .... 7" .... T. Motown .... TMG867 .... 1973 .... **£40** .... demo

MARTIN & THE BROWNSHIRTS

Taxi Driver	7"	Lightning	GIL507	1978	**£4**	

MARTIN'S MAGIC SOUNDS

Martin's Magic Sounds	LP	Deram		1968	**£15**	

MARTIN, DERAK

Daddy Rolling Stone	7"	Sue	WI308	1964	**£12**	

MARTIN, DEREK

Soul Power	7"	Stax	601039	1968	**£8**	
You Better Go	7"	Columbia	DB7694	1965	**£10**	

MARTIN, DEWEY

...And Medicine Ball	LP	Uni	73088		**£15**	US

MARTIN, GEORGE ORCHESTRA

All My Loving	7"	Parlophone	R5135	1964	**£5**	
All Quiet On The Mersey Front	7"	Parlophone	R5222	1965	**£5**	
And I Love Her	LP	Studio Two	TWO141	1966	**£12**	
I Feel Fine	7"	Parlophone	R5256	1965	**£5**	
Instrumentally Salutes Beatles Girls	LP	United Artists	ULP1157	1966	**£15**	
Love In The Open Air	7"	United Artists	UP1165	1966	**£20**	
Music From A Hard Day's Night	7" EP	Parlophone	GEP8930	1965	**£12**	
Off The Beatles Track	LP	Parlophone	PMC1227	1964	**£20**	
Plays Help	LP	Columbia	SX1775	1965	**£15**	
Plays Help	LP	Studio Two	TWO102	1965	**£15**	
Ringo's Theme	7"	Parlophone	R5166	1964	**£6**	
Yesterday	7"	Parlophone	R5375	1965	**£5**	

MARTIN, GRADY SLEW FOOT FIVE

Nashville	7"	Brunswick	05535	1956	**£4**	

MARTIN, JANIS

Here Today & Gone Tomorrow Love	7"	Palette	PG9000	1960	**£12**	

MARTIN, JEAN

Ain't Gonna Kiss Ya	7"	Decca	F11751	1963	**£4**	
Will You Still Love Me Tomorrow	7"	Decca	F11897	1964	**£4**	

MARTIN, PAUL

Snake In The Grass	7"	Sue	WI4041	1967	**£10**	

MARTIN, SHANE

You're So Young	7"	CBS	3894	1969	**£50**	

MARTIN, TONY

Bigger Your Heart Is	7"	T. Motown	TMG537	1965	**£25**	
Bigger Your Heart Is	7"	T. Motown	TMG537	1965	**£50**	demo
Talkin' To Your Picture	7"	Stateside	SS394	1965	**£15**	

MARTIN, TRADE

Hula Hula Dancin' Doll	7"	London	HL9662	1963	**£4**	

MARTIN, VINCE & THE TARRIERS

Cindy Oh Cindy	7"	London	HLN8340	1956	**£15**	

MARTINDALE, WINK

Black Land Farmer	7"	London	HLD9419	1961	**£4**	
Deck Of Cards	7" EP	Dot	DEP20000	1965	**£4**	
Deck Of Cards	7"	London	HLD8962	1959	**£4**	chart single
Deck Of Cards	7" EP	London	RED1370	1963	**£6**	
Life Gets Teejus Don't It?	7"	London	HLD9042	1960	**£4**	
Wink Martindale	LP	London	HAD2240	1960	**£12**	

MARTYN, JOHN

John Martyn's first two albums are fairly conventional folk affairs, but his marriage to singer Beverley seemed to make him decide to experiment a little. The two LPs recorded by John and Beverley together are wonderful pieces of folk-rock with the strongly melodic, distinctive songs being enhanced by sympathetic playing from some well-known session names. Thereafter, John Martyn began to explore the sonic possibilities of the amplified guitar, coaxing a range of exciting and unusual sounds from his effects pedals, but without ever abandoning his love of melody. In live performance he was particularly impressive, as a dense wash of echoplexed sound would fill the hall - emanating from a man apparently playing nothing more than an acoustic guitar! This is brilliantly captured on the mock- bootleg "Live At Leeds", which was available in some European record shops, but could only be obtained by mail order from John Martyn himself in the UK.

Title	Format	Label	Cat. No.	Year	Price	Notes
Classic John Martyn	CD-s	Island	CID265	1986	**£8**	
Live At Leeds	LP	Island	ILPS9343	1975	**£20**	
Live At Leeds	LP	Island	ILPS9343	1975	**£25**	autographed
London Conversation	LP	Island	ILP952	1967	**£12**	
May You Never	7"	Island	WIP6116	1971	**£4**	
Tumbler	LP	Island	ILPS9091	1968	**£10**	

MARTYN, JOHN & BEVERLEY

Title	Format	Label	Cat. No.	Year	Price	Notes
John The Baptist	7"	Island	WIP6076	1969	**£5**	
Road To Ruin	LP	Island	ILPS9133	1970	**£10**	
Stormbringer	LP	Island	ILPS9113	1970	**£10**	

MARVELETTES

Title	Format	Label	Cat. No.	Year	Price	Notes
As Long As I Know He's Mine	7"	Stateside	SS251	1964	**£20**	
As Long As I Know He's Mine	7"	Stateside	SS251	1964	**£50**	demo
Beechwood 45789	7"	Oriole	CBA1764	1962	**£30**	
Danger Heartbreak Dead Ahead	7"	T. Motown	TMG535	1965	**£15**	
Danger Heartbreak Dead Ahead	7"	T. Motown	TMG535	1965	**£60**	demo
Don't Mess With Bill	7"	T. Motown	TMG546	1966	**£10**	
Don't Mess With Bill	7"	T. Motown	TMG546	1966	**£50**	demo
He's A Good Guy	7"	Stateside	SS273	1964	**£20**	
He's A Good Guy	7"	Stateside	SS273	1964	**£50**	demo
Here I Am Baby	7"	T. Motown	TMG659	1968	**£6**	
Here I Am Baby	7"	T. Motown	TMG659	1968	**£20**	demo
Hunter Gets Captured By The Game	7"	T. Motown	TMG594	1967	**£10**	
Hunter Gets Captured By The Game	7"	T. Motown	TMG594	1967	**£40**	demo
I'll Keep Holding On	7"	T. Motown	TMG518	1965	**£15**	
I'll Keep Holding On	7"	T. Motown	TMG518	1965	**£60**	demo
In Full Bloom	LP	T. Motown	STML11145	1970	**£12**	
Locking Up My Heart	7"	Oriole	CBA1817	1963	**£30**	
Marvelettes	LP	T. Motown	STML11052	1967	**£25**	
Marvelettes	7" EP	T. Motown	TME2003	1965	**£30**	
Marvellous Marvelettes	LP	T. Motown	TML11008	1965	**£60**	
My Baby Must Be A Magician	7"	T. Motown	TMG639	1968	**£4**	
My Baby Must Be A Magician	7"	T. Motown	TMG639	1968	**£30**	demo
Please Mr.Postman	7"	Fontana	H355	1961	**£30**	
R&B Chartmakers No.2	7" EP	Stateside	SE1018	1964	**£20**	
Reaching For Something I Can't Have	7"	T. Motown	TMG701	1969	**£4**	
Reaching For Something I Can't Have	7"	T. Motown	TMG701	1969	**£12**	demo
Reaching For Something I Can't Have	7"	T. Motown	TMG860	1973	**£4**	
Reaching For Something I Can't Have	7"	T. Motown	TMG860	1973	**£10**	demo
Reaching For Something I Can't Have/Magician	7"	T. Motown	TMG860	1973	**£25**	demo
Sophisticated Soul	LP	T. Motown	STML11090	1969	**£12**	
Too Many Fish In The Sea	7"	Stateside	SS369	1965	**£20**	
Too Many Fish In The Sea	7"	Stateside	SS369	1965	**£50**	demo
Twisting Postman	7"	Fontana	H386	1962	**£30**	
When You're Young And In Love	7"	T. Motown	TMG609	1967	**£4**	chart single
When You're Young And In Love	7"	T. Motown	TMG609	1967	**£30**	demo
You're My Remedy	7"	Stateside	SS334	1964	**£20**	
You're My Remedy	7"	Stateside	SS334	1964	**£50**	demo
You're The One	7"	T. Motown	TMG562	1966	**£12**	
You're The One	7"	T. Motown	TMG562	1966	**£50**	demo

MARVELOWS

Title	Format	Label	Cat. No.	Year	Price	Notes
I Do	7"	HMV	POP1433	1965	**£10**	

MARVELS

Title	Format	Label	Cat. No.	Year	Price	Notes
Keep On Searching	7"	Columbia	DB8341	1968	**£8**	

MARVELS FIVE

Title	Format	Label	Cat. No.	Year	Price	Notes
Don't Play That Song	7"	HMV	POP1452	1965	**£4**	

MARVETTES

Title	Format	Label	Cat. No.	Year	Price	Notes
It's Revival Time	LP	Coxsone	TLP1002	196-	**£80**	

MARVIN & FARRAR

Title	Format	Label	Cat. No.	Year	Price	Notes
Marvin And Farrar	LP	EMI	EMA755	1973	**£12**	
Music Makes My Day	7"	EMI	EMI2044	1973	**£4**	

Title	Format	Label	Cat. No.	Year	Price	Notes
Small And Lonely Light	7"	EMI	EMI2335	1975	**£4**	

MARVIN & JOHNNY

Title	Format	Label	Cat. No.	Year	Price	Notes
Cherry Pie	7"	Black Swan	WI467	1965	**£8**	
Smack Smack	7"	Vogue	V9099	1958	**£40**	
Yak Yak	7"	Vogue	V9074	1957	**£50**	

MARVIN, BRETT & THE THUNDERBOLTS

Title	Format	Label	Cat. No.	Year	Price	Notes
Alias Terry Dactyl And The Dinosaurs	LP	Sonet	SNTF630	1972	**£10**	
Best Of Friends	LP	Sonet	SNTF620	1971	**£10**	
Brett Marvin And The Thunderbolts	LP	Sonet	SNTF616	1970	**£10**	
Ten Legged Friend	LP	Sonet	SNTF651	1973	**£10**	
Twelve Inches Of...	LP	Sonet	SNTF619	1971	**£10**	

MARVIN, HANK

Title	Format	Label	Cat. No.	Year	Price	Notes
Break Another Dawn	7"	Columbia	DB8693	1970	**£5**	
Goodnight Dick	7"	Columbia	DB8552	1969	**£5**	
Hank Marvin	LP	Columbia	SCX6352	1969	**£15**	chart LP
London's Not Too Far	7"	Columbia	DB8326	1968	**£5**	
Sacha	7"	Columbia	DB8601	1969	**£5**	
Slaughter On Tenth Avenue	7"	Columbia	DB8628	1969	**£5**	

MARVIN, WELCH & FARRAR

Title	Format	Label	Cat. No.	Year	Price	Notes
Faithful	7"	Regal Z.	RZ3030	1971	**£5**	
Lady Of The Morning	7"	Regal Z.	RZ3035	1971	**£5**	
Marmaduke	7"	Regal Z.	RZ3048	1972	**£5**	
Marvin, Welch And Farrar	LP	Regal Z.	SRZA8502	1971	**£12**	chart LP
Second Opinion	LP	Regal Z.	4SRZA8504	1971	**£20**	quad
Second Opinion	LP	Regal Z.	SRZA8504	1971	**£15**	

MARY BUTTERWORTH

Title	Format	Label	Cat. No.	Year	Price	Notes
Mary Butterworth	LP	Breeder			**£200**	US

MASCOTS

Title	Format	Label	Cat. No.	Year	Price	Notes
Hey Little Angel	7"	Pye	7N25189	1963	**£4**	

MASEKELA, HUGH

Title	Format	Label	Cat. No.	Year	Price	Notes
And The Union Of South Africa	LP	Rare Earth	SRE3002	1971	**£10**	

MASKED MARAUDERS

Title	Format	Label	Cat. No.	Year	Price	Notes
Masked Marauders	LP	Reprise	RS6378	1969	**£15**	US

MASKED PHANTOM

Title	Format	Label	Cat. No.	Year	Price	Notes
These Clogs Are Made For Waltzing	7"	Parlophone	R5437	1966	**£4**	

MASON, BARBARA

Title	Format	Label	Cat. No.	Year	Price	Notes
Keep Him	7"	London	HL9977	1965	**£6**	
Oh How It Hurts	LP	Action	ACLP6002	1969	**£15**	
Oh How It Hurts	7"	Direction	583382	1968	**£4**	
Slipping Away	7"	Action	ACT4542	1969	**£6**	
Slipping Away	7"	Action	ACT4542	1969	**£20**	demo

MASON, BARRY

Title	Format	Label	Cat. No.	Year	Price	Notes
Over The Hills And Far Away	7"	Deram	DM104	1966	**£25**	

MASON, CURTISS

Title	Format	Label	Cat. No.	Year	Price	Notes
Monkberry Moon Delight	7"	Columbia	DB8800	1971	**£4**	

MASON, DAVE

Title	Format	Label	Cat. No.	Year	Price	Notes
Alone Together	LP	Blue Thumb	BTS19	1970	**£12**	US, marbled vinyl
Alone Together	LP	Harvest	SHTC251	1970	**£10**	
Headkeeper	LP	Island	ILPS9203	1972	**£10**	
Little Woman	7"	Island	WIP6032	1968	**£12**	
Only You Know And I Know	7"	Harvest	HAR5024	1970	**£4**	
World In Changes	7"	Harvest	HAR5017	1970	**£4**	

MASON, GLEN

Title	Format	Label	Cat. No.	Year	Price	Notes
Battle Of New Orleans	7"	Parlophone	R4562	1959	**£4**	
Don't Forbid Me	7"	Parlophone	R4271	1957	**£4**	
End	7"	Parlophone	R4485	1958	**£4**	
Glendora	7"	Parlophone	R4203	1956	**£4**	chart single
Green Door	7"	Parlophone	R4244	1956	**£5**	chart single

Hot Diggity	7"	Parlophone	MSP6240	1956	**£5**	
Round And Round	7"	Parlophone	R4291	1957	**£4**	
That's What I Want	7"	Parlophone	R4723	1960	**£4**	
Why Don't They Understand?	7"	Parlophone	R4334	1957	**£4**	
You Got What It Takes	7"	Parlophone	R4626	1960	**£4**	

MASS

Labour Of Love	LP	4AD	CAD107	1981	**£10**	
You And I	7"	4AD	AD14	1980	**£5**	with poster

MASSED ALBERTS

Goodbye Dolly	7"	Parlophone	R5159	1964	**£4**	

MASTER'S APPRENTICES

Choice Cuts	LP	Columbia	SCX07903	1971	**£50**	
I'm Your Satisfier	7"	Regal Z.	RZ3031	1971	**£20**	
Master's Apprentices	LP	Regal Z.	SLRZ1016	1970	**£50**	
Masterpiece	LP	Columbia	SCX07915	1972	**£50**	
Nickelodeon	LP	Regal Z.			**£120**	
Toast To Panama Red	LP	Regal Z.	SLRZ1022	1971	**£50**	

MASTERMINDS

She Belongs To Me	7"	Immediate	IM005	1965	**£12**	

MASTERS, SAMMY

Big Man Cried	7"	London	HLR9949	1965	**£5**	
Rocking Red Wing	7"	W. Bros	WB10	1960	**£15**	chart single

MASTERS, VALERIE

Christmas Calling	7"	Columbia	DB7426	1964	**£6**	

MATCHING MOLE

Little Red Record	LP	CBS	65260	1973	**£12**	
Matching Mole	LP	CBS	64850	1972	**£10**	
O Caroline	7"	CBS	8101	1972	**£6**	

MATHEWS, JOE

Sorry Ain't Good Enough	7"	Sue	WI4046	1968	**£8**	

MATTHEWS SOUTHERN COMFORT

Ballad Of Obray Ramsey	7"	Uni	UNS521	1970	**£4**	
Colorado Springs Eternal	7"	Uni	UNS513	1970	**£4**	
Later That Same Year	LP	MCA	MKPS2015	1970	**£10**	
Second Spring	LP	Uni	UNLS112	1970	**£12**	chart LP
Woodstock	7"	Uni	UNS526	1970	**£4**	chart single

MATTHEWS, IAN

Da Doo Ron Ron	7"	Philips	6006197	1972	**£4**	
Hearts	7"	Vertigo	6059041	1971	**£4**	
If You Saw Through My Eyes	LP	Vertigo	6360034	1971	**£12**	spiral label
Journeys From Gospel Oak	LP	Mooncrest	CREST18	1974	**£10**	
Matthews Southern Comfort	LP	Uni	UNLS108	1970	**£15**	
Some Days You Eat The Bear...	LP	Elektra	K42160	1974	**£10**	
Stealin' Home	LP	Mushroom		1979	**£10**	US pic disc
Tigers Will Survive	LP	Vertigo	6360056	1972	**£12**	spiral label
Valley Hi	LP	Elektra	K42144	1973	**£10**	

MATUSOV'S JEWS HARP BAND

War Between The Fats And The Thins	LP	Head		1969	**£25**	

MAU MAUS

Facts Of War	7"	Paragon	PAX12	1983	**£4**	
No Concern	7"	Pax	PAX8	1982	**£4**	
Society's Rejects	7"	Pax	PAX6	1982	**£4**	

MAUDS

Hold On	LP	Mercury	MG21135	1967	**£10**	US
Hold On	7"	Mercury	MF1000	1967	**£5**	

MAUGHAN, SUSAN

Bobby's Girl	7"	Philips	326544BF	1962	**£4**	chart single
Bobby's Girl	LP	Wing	WL1105	1965	**£10**	

Effervescent Miss Maughan	7" EP	Philips	433621BE	1962	**£5**	
Four Beaux And A Belle	7" EP	Philips	BE12549	1963	**£5**	
Hand A Handkerchief To Helen	7"	Philips	326562BF	1963	**£4**	chart single
Hey Lover	7"	Philips	BF1301	1964	**£4**	
Hi I'm Susan Maughan & I Sing	7" EP	Philips	BBE12525	1962	**£6**	
I Didn't Mean What I Said	7"	Philips	326533BF	1962	**£4**	
Kiss Me Sailor	7"	Philips	BF1336	1964	**£4**	
Mama Do The Twist	7"	Philips	PB1216	1961	**£4**	
More Of Susan Maughan	7" EP	Philips	433641BE	1963	**£6**	
She's New To You	7"	Philips	326586BF	1963	**£4**	
Some Of These Days	7"	Philips	PB1236	1962	**£4**	
Verdict Is Guilty	7"	Philips	BF1266	1963	**£4**	

MAUGHAN, SUSAN & DAVID KOSSOFF

Oliver	7" EP	Oriole	EP7039	196-	**£4**	

MAUREENY WISHFUL

Maureeny Wishful	LP	Moonshine	WO2388	196-	**£100**	

MAURICE & MAC

Why Don't You Try Me	7"	Chess	CRS8081	1968	**£4**	
You Left The Water Running	7"	Chess	CRS8074	1968	**£4**	

MAX CREEK

Drink The Stars	LP	Wranger			**£30**	US double

MAXIMILIAN

Snake	7"	London	HLX9356	1961	**£5**	

MAY BLITZ

May Blitz	LP	Vertigo	6360007	1970	**£30**	spiral label
Second Of May	LP	Vertigo	6360037	1971	**£60**	spiral label

MAY, PHIL

...And The Fallen Angels	LP	Philips	6410969	1978	**£10**	Dutch

MAYALL, JOHN

The various editions of the Bluesbreakers that John Mayall led during the sixties were an extraordinary training-ground for many of the more influential musicians of that time. Cream, Fleetwood Mac, the Aynsley Dunbar Retaliation, the Keef Hartley Band, Colosseum, Free, Mark-Almond, Stone The Crows, and even the Rolling Stones were all staffed by Mayall alumni. By placing a premium on instrumental prowess, but at the same time managing to place many of his albums among the best-sellers, John Mayall was of crucial importance in the growing maturity of rock music generally. He was never really a singles artist, however, and his original 45rpm releases have become quite scarce. All the songs are actually available on LP, except that the version of "Double Trouble" included on "Looking Back" lacks the echo that helps to make the lead guitar part on the single into one of Peter Green's finest performances.

Back To The Roots	LP	Polydor	2657005	1971	**£15**	double, chart LP
Banquet In Blues	LP	ABC	ABCL5187	1976	**£10**	
Bare Wires	LP	Decca	SKL4945	1968	**£15**	chart LP
Bear	7"	Decca	F12846	1968	**£5**	
Blues Alone	LP	Ace Of Clubs	ACL1243	1967	**£15**	chart LP
Blues From Laurel Canyon	LP	Decca	SKL4972	1969	**£15**	chart LP
Bluesbreakers	LP	Decca	LK4804	1966	**£15**	chart LP
Bottom Line	LP	DJM	DJF20556	1979	**£10**	
Crawling Up A Hill	7"	Decca	F11900	1964	**£15**	
Crocodile Walk	7"	Decca	F12120	1965	**£15**	
Crusade	LP	Decca	LK4890	1967	**£15**	chart LP
Diary Of A Band Vol.1	LP	Decca	LK4918	1968	**£15**	chart LP
Diary Of A Band Vol.2	LP	Decca	LK4919	1968	**£15**	chart LP
Don't Waste My Time	7"	Polydor	56544	1969	**£5**	
Double Trouble	7"	Decca	F12621	1967	**£10**	
Empty Rooms	LP	Polydor	583580	1970	**£12**	chart LP
Hard Core Package	LP	ABC	ABCD1039	1977	**£10**	US
Hard Road	LP	Decca	LK4853	1967	**£15**	chart LP
I'm Your Witchdoctor	7"	Immediate	IM012	1965	**£20**	
I'm Your Witchdoctor	7"	Immediate	IM051	1967	**£8**	
Jazz Blues Fusion	LP	Polydor	2425103	1972	**£12**	
Jenny	7"	Decca	F12732	1968	**£8**	
John Mayall Plays John Mayall	LP	Decca	LK4680	1965	**£25**	
Last Of The British Blues	LP	MCA	MCL1643	1978	**£10**	
Latest Edition	LP	Polydor	2391141	1975	**£10**	
Lonely Years	7"	Purdah	453502	1966	**£35**	
Looking Back	LP	Decca	SKL5010	1970	**£12**	chart LP

Looking Back	7"	Decca	F12506	1966	**£8**	
Lots Of People	LP	ABC	ABCL5126	1977	**£10**	
Memories	LP	Polydor	2425085	1971	**£12**	
Moving On	LP	Polydor	2391047	1973	**£10**	
New Year, New Band, New Company	LP	ABC	ABCL5115	1975	**£10**	
No More Interviews	LP	DJM	DJF20564	1979	**£10**	
No Reply	7"	Decca	F12792	1968	**£5**	
Notice To Appear	LP	ABC	ABCL5142	1975	**£10**	
Parchman Farm	7"	Decca	F12490	1966	**£8**	
Road Show Blues	LP	DJM	64231	1981	**£10**	German
Sitting In The Rain	7"	Decca	F12545	1967	**£8**	
Suspicions	7"	Decca	F12684	1967	**£8**	
Ten Years Are Gone	LP	Polydor	2683036	1973	**£10**	
Thinking Of My Woman	7"	Polydor	2066021	1970	**£5**	
Through The Years	LP	Decca	SKL5086	1971	**£12**	
Turning Point	LP	Polydor	583571	1970	**£12**	chart LP
USA Union	LP	Polydor	2425020	1970	**£12**	chart LP

MAYALL, JOHN & OTHERS

Raw Blues	LP	Ace Of Clubs	ACL1220	1967	**£15**	

MAYALL, JOHN & PAUL BUTTERFIELD

John Mayall's Bluesbreakers With Paul Butterfield	7" EP	Decca	DFER8673	1967	**£10**	

MAYER, JOHN

Etudes	LP	Sonet		1969	**£20**	
Indo-Jazz Fusions	LP	Columbia	SX6122	1967	**£30**	
Indo-Jazz Fusions II	LP	Columbia	SCX6215	1968	**£30**	
Radha Krishna	LP	Columbia		1971	**£30**	

MAYER, JOHN INDO-JAZZ 7

Acka Raga	7"	Columbia	DB8037	1966	**£8**	

MAYER, NATHANIEL

Going Back To The Village Of Love	LP	Fortune	8014	1964	**£15**	US
Village Of Love	7"	HMV	POP1041	1962	**£6**	

MAYFIELD'S MULE

Mayfield's Mule included Andy Scott who was later a member of the Sweet.

Double Dealing Woman	7"	Parlophone	R5817	1969	**£8**	
I See A River	7"	Parlophone	R5843	1970	**£8**	
We Go Rollin'	7"	Parlophone	R5858	1970	**£8**	

MAYFIELD, CURTIS

Back To The World	LP	Buddah	2318085	1973	**£10**	
Curtis	LP	Buddah	2318015	1971	**£10**	
Curtis In Chicago	LP	Buddah	2318091	1974	**£10**	
Curtis Live	LP	Buddah	2659004	1971	**£15**	double
Early Years	LP	Probe	GTSP201	1973	**£10**	
If There's A Hell Below	7"	Buddah	2011055	1970	**£4**	
Move On Up	LP	Buddah	BDLP4015	1974	**£10**	
Move On Up	7"	Buddah	2011080	1971	**£5**	multi-coloured label, chart single
Roots	LP	Buddah	2318045	1972	**£10**	
Superfly	LP	Buddah	2318065	1972	**£10**	chart LP
Sweet Exorcist	LP	Buddah	2318099	1974	**£10**	
We Got To Have Peace	7"	Buddah	2011101	1971	**£4**	

MAYFIELD, PERCY

River's Invitation	7"	HMV	POP1185	1963	**£4**	

MAYPOLE

Maypole	LP	Colossus		1970	**£20**	US

MAYTALS

5446 Was My Number	7"	Pyramid	PYR6030	1969	**£8**	
Christmas Feelings	7"	Ska Beat	JB174	1964	**£10**	
Country Road	7"	Dragon	DRA1013	1973	**£5**	
Do The Reggay	7"	Pyramid	PYR6057	1968	**£10**	
Fever	7"	Dragon	DRA1021	1974	**£5**	
Funky Kingston	LP	Dragon	DRLS5002	1973	**£10**	

Title	Format	Label	Number	Year	Price	Notes
Give Me Your Love	7"	R&B	JB153	1964	**£10**	
Hallelujah	7"	Blue Beat	BB176	1963	**£10**	
He Is Real	7"	Blue Beat	BB215	1963	**£10**	
Hurry Up	7"	R&B	JB130	1963	**£10**	
I've Got A Pain	7"	Blue Beat	BB220	1963	**£10**	
In The Dark	LP	Dragon	DRLS5004	1974	**£10**	
In The Dark	7"	Dragon	DRA1016	1973	**£5**	
John And James	7"	Black Swan	WI464	1965	**£8**	
Judgement Day	7"	Blue Beat	BB255	1964	**£10**	
Light Of The World	7"	Blue Beat	BB299	1964	**£10**	
Little Slea	7"	Blue Beat	BB245	1963	**£10**	
Looking Down The Street	7"	Blue Beat	BB281	1964	**£10**	
Monkey Man	LP	Trojan	TBL107	1970	**£15**	
Monkey Man	7"	Trojan	TR7711	1970	**£6**	chart single
My New Name	7"	Island	WI213	1965	**£10**	
Never Grow Old	LP	R&B	JBL1113	196-	**£100**	
Never You Change	7"	Island	WI200	1965	**£10**	
Pressure Drop	7"	Trojan	TR7709	1970	**£6**	
Redemption Song	7"	Dynamic	DYN438	197-	**£6**	
Sailing On	7"	Dragon	DRA1026	1974	**£5**	
Sit Right Down	7"	Dragon	DRA1007	1973	**£5**	
Ska War	7"	Blue Beat	BB306	1964	**£10**	
Time Tough	7"	Dragon	DRA1024	1974	**£5**	
You Got Me Spinning	7"	Blue Beat	BB270	1964	**£10**	

MAYTONES

Title	Format	Label	Number	Year	Price	Notes
Billy Goat	7"	Blue Cat	BS149	196-	**£10**	
Black And White	7"		GG4522	1971	**£6**	
Copper Girl	7"	Blue Cat	BS166	196-	**£10**	
Mi Nah Tek You Lick	7"	Blue Cat	BS173	196-	**£10**	
TNT	7"	Blue Cat	BS165	196-	**£10**	

MAZE

Ian Paice and Roger Evans of Maze were soon to experience a considerable change of fortune (albeit short-lived in the case of Evans), as they were recruited by Ritchie Blackmore as founder members of Deep Purple.

Title	Format	Label	Number	Year	Price	Notes
Armageddon	LP	MTA	5012	1971	**£30**	US
Catari Catari	7"	MGM	MGM1368	1967	**£8**	
Hello Stranger	7"	Reaction	591009	1966	**£10**	

MC5

Title	Format	Label	Number	Year	Price	Notes
Back In The USA	LP	Atlantic	2400016	1970	**£20**	
High Time	LP	Atlantic	K40223	1971	**£20**	
Kick Out The Jams	LP	Elektra	EKS74042	1969	**£20**	
Kick Out The Jams	7"	Elektra	EKSN45036	1968	**£12**	
Ramblin' Rose	7"	Elektra	EKSN45067	1969	**£10**	

McARTHUR, NEIL

Immediately after the demise of the Zombies, lead singer Colin Blunstone adopted a new stage name, Neil McArthur, and recorded a new version of the Zombies best known song, "She's Not There". The new interpretation is dramatically different from the original, even while keeping the same tempo. Few people were fooled by the name change, however, for Blunstone's breathy singing voice is very distinctive. Before long he was back using his own name.

Title	Format	Label	Number	Year	Price	Notes
Don't Try To Explain	7"	Deram	DM262	1969	**£5**	
It's Not Easy	7"	Deram	DM275	1969	**£5**	
She's Not There	7"	Deram	DM225	1969	**£5**	chart single

McAULEY, JACKIE

Title	Format	Label	Number	Year	Price	Notes
Jackie McAuley	LP	Dawn	DNLS3023	1971	**£25**	
Rocking Shoes	7"	Dawn	DNS1020	1971	**£5**	

McCAFFERTY, DAN

Title	Format	Label	Number	Year	Price	Notes
Dan McCafferty	LP	Mountain	TOPS108	1975	**£10**	

McCALL, CASH

Title	Format	Label	Number	Year	Price	Notes
Anytime	7"	Ember	EMBS173	1963	**£4**	
It's Wonderful	7"	Chess	CRS8056	1967	**£6**	

McCALL, TOUSSAINT

Title	Format	Label	Number	Year	Price	Notes
Nothing Takes The Place Of You	7"	Pye	7N25420	1967	**£4**	

McCALLUM, DAVID

Title	Format	Label	Number	Year	Price	Notes
Communication	7"	Capitol	CL15439	1966	**£6**	chart single

In The Garden	7"	Capitol	CL15474	1966	**£4**	
Music A Bit More Of Me	LP	Capitol		1966	**£20**	
Music...A Part Of Me	LP	Capitol	T2432	1966	**£20**	

McCARTNEY, CECIL

Om	LP	Columbia		1968	**£12**	

McCARTNEY, PAUL

Some of Paul McCartney's more unusual records were released under pseudonyms - The Country Hams, Suzy & The Redstripes, and Percy "Thrills" Thrillington. Rarities issued under his own name include a series of lavish packages promoting various of his album releases. Most collectable of these is the picture disc version of "Back To The Egg", which has aquired legendary status. The rare version of the Apple single R5999, it should be mentioned, has "Sally G" as the A side; copies with "Junior's Farm" on the A side are common.

Another Day	7"	Apple	R5889	1971	**£10**	demo
Back Seat Of My Car	7"	Apple	R5914	1971	**£10**	demo
Back To The Egg	LP	Parlophone	PCTC257	1979	**£30**	promo, boxed
Back To The Egg	LP	Parlophone	PCTCP257	1979	**£500**	promo, pic disc
Band On The Run	LP	Apple	PAS10007	1973	**£20**	demo
Band On The Run	7"	Apple	R5997DJ	1974	**£8**	promo
Band On The Run	LP	Capitol	SEAX11901	1978	**£25**	US pic disc
Band On The Run	LP	Columbia	HC36482	1981	**£20**	US audiophile
Band On The Run Interview Album	LP	Apple	SPRO2955/6	1974	**£40**	US promo
Boxed Set Of 9 Promo Singles	7"	Parlophone	PMBOX1	1986	**£150**	numbered and signed
Brung To Ewe By Ram	LP	Apple	SPRO6210	1971	**£35**	US 1 sided interview promo
CHOBA B CCCP	LP	Melodia	A6000415006	1988	**£25**	Russian, 11 tracks
CHOBA B CCCP	LP	Melodia	A6000415006	1988	**£10**	Russian, 13 tracks
Coming Up	7"	Parlophone	R6035	1980	**£6**	demo
Getting Closer	7"	Parlophone	R6027	1979	**£5**	demo
Give Ireland Back To The Irish	7"	Apple	R5936	1972	**£5**	shamrock sleeve
Give My Regards To Broad Street	LP	Parlophone	EL2602781	1984	**£40**	promo, press pack
Goodnight Tonight	7"	Parlophone	R6023	1979	**£8**	demo
Goodnight Tonight	12"	Parlophone	12R6023	1979	**£6**	
Helen Wheels	7"	Apple	R5993	1973	**£8**	demo
Hi Hi Hi	7"	Apple	R5973	1972	**£4**	Wings sleeve
I've Had Enough	7"	Parlophone	R6020	1978	**£5**	demo
Jet	7"	Apple	R5996	1974	**£8**	demo
Junior's Farm	7"	Apple	R5999DJ	1974	**£10**	promo
Let 'Em In	7"	Capitol	R6015DJ	1976	**£8**	promo
Letting Go	7"	Capitol	R6008	1975	**£8**	demo
Listen To What The Man Said	7"	Capitol	R6006	1975	**£4**	PS
Live And Let Die	7"	Apple	R5987	1973	**£8**	demo
London Town	LP	Parlophone	PAS10012	1978	**£20**	demo
London Town	7"	Parlophone	R6021	1978	**£8**	demo
Mary Had A Little Lamb	7"	Apple	R5949	1972	**£5**	PS
Maybe I'm Amazed	7"	Capitol	R6017	1977	**£8**	demo
McCartney	r-reel	Apple	TAPMC7102	1970	**£40**	mono
McCartney	r-reel	Apple	TDPCS7102	1970	**£20**	stereo
McCartney	LP	Apple	PCS7102	1970	**£40**	promo + interview sheets
McCartney II	LP	Parlophone	PCTC258	1980	**£20**	demo
McCartney Interview	LP	Columbia	A2S821	1980	**£100**	US promo double with book
Mull Of Kintyre	7"	Capitol	R6018	1977	**£8**	blue vinyl test pressing
Mull Of Kintyre	7"	Capitol	R6018DJ	1977	**£6**	promo
My Love	7"	Apple	R5985	1973	**£8**	demo
No More Lonely Nights (Mole Mix)	12"	Parlophone	12R6080DJ	1984	**£200**	1 sided promo
No More Lonely Nights	12"	Parlophone	12PR6080	1984	**£6**	pic disc
Old Siam Sir	7"	Parlophone	R6026	1979	**£5**	demo
Once Upon A Long Ago	CD	Parlophone		1987	**£100**	promo, different sleeve
Once Upon A Long Ago	CD-s	Parlophone	CDR6170	1987	**£6**	
Paul McCartney And Bob Harris Talk About Buddy Holly	LP	MCA	BH1	1983	**£25**	US promo
Pipes Of Peace	LP	Parlophone	PCTC1652301	1983	**£30**	promo, press pack
Press	10"	Parlophone	10R6133	1986	**£8**	round sleeve
Pretty Little Head	cass-s	Parlophone	TCR6145	1987	**£6**	
Ram	LP	Apple	PAS10003	1971	**£20**	demo
Red Rose Speedway	LP	Apple	PCTC251	1973	**£20**	demo
Sally G	7"	Apple	R5999	1975	**£10**	
Silly Love Songs	7"	Capitol	R6014DJ	1976	**£8**	promo
Spies Like Us	7"	Parlophone	RP6118	1985	**£4**	pic disc
Spies Like Us	12"	Parlophone	12RP6118	1985	**£6**	pic disc
Temporary Secretary	7"	Parlophone	R6039DJ	1980	**£10**	1 sided promo

Title	Format	Label	Cat. No.	Year	Price	Notes
Temporary Secretary	12"	Parlophone	12R6039	1980	**£6**	
Tug Of War	LP	Parlophone	PCTC259	1982	**£30**	promo, press pack, cassette interview
Venus And Mars	LP	Capitol	PCTC254	1975	**£20**	demo
Venus And Mars	7"	Capitol	R6010	1975	**£8**	demo
Waterfalls	7"	Parlophone	R6037	1980	**£5**	demo
Waterfalls	7"	Parlophone	R6037DJ	1980	**£8**	promo
We All Stand Together	7"	Parlophone	RP6086	1984	**£5**	pic disc
Wild Life	LP	Apple	PCS7142	1971	**£20**	demo
Wings At The Speed Of Sound	LP	Capitol	PAS10010	1976	**£20**	demo
Wings Greatest	LP	Parlophone	PCTC256	1978	**£20**	demo
Wings Over America	LP	Capitol	PCSP720	1976	**£30**	triple, demo
Wings Over America	LP	Capitol	SWCO11593	1977	**£30**	US promo, red white and blue vinyl
With A Little Luck	7"	Parlophone	R6019DJ	1978	**£8**	promo
Wonderful Christmas Time	7"	Parlophone	R6029	1979	**£6**	demo

McCARTNEY, PAUL & GEORGE MARTIN

Title	Format	Label	Cat. No.	Year	Price	Notes
Family Way	LP	Decca	LK4847	1966	**£60**	

McCARTNEY, PAUL & MICHAEL JACKSON

Title	Format	Label	Cat. No.	Year	Price	Notes
Say Say Say	12"	Parlophone		1983	**£10**	1 sided promo

McCLAINE, PETE & CLAN

Title	Format	Label	Cat. No.	Year	Price	Notes
U.S. Mail	7"	Decca	F11699	1963	**£5**	

McCLINTON, DELBERT

Title	Format	Label	Cat. No.	Year	Price	Notes
Hully Gully	7"	Decca	F11541	1962	**£4**	

McCLURE, BOBBY

Title	Format	Label	Cat. No.	Year	Price	Notes
Peak Of Love	7"	Chess	CRS8048	1966	**£12**	

McCLURE, CHRIS

Title	Format	Label	Cat. No.	Year	Price	Notes
Answer To Everything	7"	Polydor	56259	1968	**£5**	
Dying Swan	7"	Decca	F12346	1966	**£4**	
Hazy People	7"	Polydor	56227	1968	**£8**	
Our Song Of Love	7"	RCA	RCA1849	1969	**£4**	

McCOLL, KIRSTY

Title	Format	Label	Cat. No.	Year	Price	Notes
They Don't Know	7"	Stiff	PBUY47	1979	**£4**	pic disc

McCOOK, TOMMY

Title	Format	Label	Cat. No.	Year	Price	Notes
Buck And The Preacher	7"	Pyramid	PYR7002	1973	**£5**	
Love Is A Treasure	7"	Duke	DU161	1973	**£5**	
Rub It Down	7"	Technique	TE927	1973	**£5**	

McCORMACK BROTHERS

Title	Format	Label	Cat. No.	Year	Price	Notes
Authentic Bluegrass Hits	7" EP	Hickory	LPE1509	1966	**£4**	
Red Hen Boogie	7"	Polydor	NH66986	1963	**£15**	

McCOY, VAN

Title	Format	Label	Cat. No.	Year	Price	Notes
Hustle	7"	Avco	6105037	1975	**£6**	

McCOYS

Title	Format	Label	Cat. No.	Year	Price	Notes
Don't Worry Mother	7"	Immediate	IM028	1966	**£5**	
Fever	7"	Immediate	IM021	1965	**£5**	chart single
Hang On Sloopy	LP	Immediate	IMLP001	1965	**£20**	
Hang On Sloopy	7"	Immediate	IM001	1965	**£5**	chart single
Hang On Sloopy	7"	Immediate	IM076	1969	**£4**	
Human Ball	LP	Mercury	SR61207	1969	**£15**	US
I Got To Go Back	7"	Immediate	IM046	1967	**£5**	
Infinite McCoys	LP	Mercury	SR61163	1968	**£15**	US
Jesse Brady	7"	Mercury	MF1067	1968	**£5**	
McCoys Vol.1	7" EP	Immediate	IMEP002	1966	**£8**	
McCoys Vol.2	7" EP	Immediate	IMEP003	1966	**£8**	
Runaway	7"	Immediate	IM034	1966	**£5**	
Say Those Magic Words	7"	London	HLZ10154	1967	**£5**	
So Good	7"	Immediate	IM037	1966	**£5**	
Up And Down	7"	Immediate	IM029	1966	**£5**	
You Make Me Feel So Good	LP	Bang	BLP213	1966	**£15**	US

McCRACKLIN, JIMMY

Title	Format	Label	Number	Year	Price	Notes
Best Of...	LP	Minit	LP4009	1967	**£10**	US
Christmas Time	7"	Outasite	45120	1966	**£25**	
Every Night, Every Day	7"	Liberty	LIB66094	1965	**£5**	
Every Night, Every Day	LP	Imperial	LP9285	1965	**£12**	US
How Do You Like Your Love	7"	Minit	MLF11003	1968	**£5**	
I Got Eyes For You	7"	R&B	MRB5001	1965	**£10**	
I Just Gotta Know	LP	Stax	8506	1963	**£20**	US
Jimmy McCracklin	7" EP	Vocalion	VEP170160	1965	**£15**	
Jimmy McCracklin Sings	LP	Chess	1464	1961	**£25**	US
Just Got To Know	7"	Top Rank	JAR617	1962	**£10**	
Let's Get Together	LP	Minit	LP24011	1968	**£10**	US
My Answer	LP	Imperial	LP9306	1966	**£12**	US
New Soul	LP	Imperial	LP9316	1966	**£12**	US
Stinger Man	LP	Minit	LP24017	1969	**£10**	US
Think	LP	Imperial	LP9297	1965	**£12**	US
Think	7"	Liberty	LIB66129	1966	**£4**	
Walk	7"	London	HLM8598	1958	**£15**	

McCULLOCH, DANNY

Title	Format	Label	Number	Year	Price	Notes
Blackbird	7"	Capitol	CL15607	1969	**£4**	

McCULLOUGH, HENRY

Title	Format	Label	Number	Year	Price	Notes
Mind Your Own Business	LP	Dark Horse	AMLH22005	1975	**£10**	

McDANIELS, GENE

Title	Format	Label	Number	Year	Price	Notes
Change Of Mood	7" EP	Liberty	LEP2054	1962	**£5**	
Chip Chip	7"	Liberty	LIB55405	1962	**£4**	
Cry Baby Cry	7"	Liberty	LIB55541	1963	**£4**	
Gene McDaniels	7" EP	London	REG1298	1961	**£8**	
Gene McDaniels Sings Movie Memories	LP	Liberty	LRP3204	1962	**£10**	US
Hit After Hit	LP	Liberty	LRP3258	1962	**£10**	US
Hundred Pounds Of Clay	LP	London	HAG2384	1961	**£12**	mono
Hundred Pounds Of Clay	LP	London	SAHG6184	1961	**£12**	stereo
Hundred Pounds Of Clay	7"	London	HLG9319	1961	**£4**	
In Times Like These	LP	Liberty	LRP3146	1960	**£12**	US
In Times Like These	7"	Liberty	LIB55723	1964	**£4**	
It's A Lonely Town	7"	Liberty	LIB55597	1963	**£4**	
Make Me A Present Of You	7"	Liberty	LIB55923	1964	**£4**	
Point Of No Return	7"	Liberty	LIB55480	1962	**£4**	
Sometimes I'm Happy	LP	Liberty	LRP3175	1960	**£12**	US
Spanish Lace	LP	Liberty	LRP3275	1963	**£12**	US
Spanish Lace	7"	Liberty	LIB55510	1963	**£4**	
Tear	7"	London	HLG9396	1961	**£4**	
Tower Of Strength	LP	Liberty	LRP3215	1962	**£12**	US
Tower Of Strength	7"	London	HLG9448	1961	**£4**	chart single
Walk With A Winner	7"	Liberty	LIB55805	1965	**£15**	
Wonderful World Of...	LP	Liberty	LRP3311	1963	**£10**	US

McDEVITT, CHAS

Title	Format	Label	Number	Year	Price	Notes
Across The Bridge	7"	Oriole	CB1465	1958	**£4**	
Face In The Rain	7"	Oriole	CB1386	1957	**£4**	
Forever	7"	Top Rank	JAR338	1960	**£4**	
I've Got A Thing About You	7"	HMV	POP928	1961	**£4**	
It Takes A Worried Man	7"	Oriole	CB1357	1957	**£4**	
Johnny O	7"	Oriole	CB1403	1958	**£4**	
Juke Box Jumble	7"	Oriole	CB1457	1958	**£4**	
One Love	7"	HMV	POP845	1961	**£4**	
Sing Sing Sing	7"	Oriole	CB1395	1957	**£4**	
Teenage Letter	7"	Oriole	CB1511	1959	**£4**	
Throwing Pebbles In A Pool	7"	HMV	POP999	1962	**£4**	

McDEVITT, CHAS & NANCY WHISKEY

Title	Format	Label	Number	Year	Price	Notes
Chas And Nancy	7" EP	Oriole	EP7002	1957	**£12**	
Freight Train	7"	Oriole	CB1352	1957	**£6**	chart single
Greenback Dollar	7"	Oriole	CB1371	1957	**£4**	chart single

McDONALD & GILES

Title	Format	Label	Number	Year	Price	Notes
McDonald And Giles	LP	Island	ILPS9126	1970	**£15**	

McDONALD, COUNTRY JOE

Title	Format	Label	Number	Year	Price	Notes
Essential	LP	Vanguard	VSD85/86	1976	**£15**	double
Hold On Its Coming	LP	Vanguard	VSD79314	1971	**£10**	
Incredible Live	LP	Vanguard	VSD79316	1972	**£10**	
Paradise With An Ocean View	LP	Mobile Fid	MFSL1056	1980	**£10**	US audiophile
Paris Sessions	LP	Vanguard	VSD79328	1973	**£10**	
Quiet Day In Clichy	LP	Sonet	SNTF622	1971	**£10**	
Thinking Of Woody Guthrie	LP	Vanguard	VRL19057	1970	**£10**	
Tonight I'm Singing For You	LP	Vanguard	6359004	1970	**£10**	
War War War	LP	Vanguard	VSD79315	1971	**£10**	

McDONALD, MICHAEL

Title	Format	Label	Number	Year	Price	Notes
If That's What It Takes	LP	Mobile Fid	MFSL1149	1984	**£10**	US audiophile

McDONALD, SHELAGH

Title	Format	Label	Number	Year	Price	Notes
Shelagh McDonald	LP	B&C	CAS1019	1970	**£10**	
Stargazer	LP	B&C	CAS1043	1971	**£10**	

McDONALD, SKEETS

Title	Format	Label	Number	Year	Price	Notes
Country's Best	LP	Capitol	T1179	1959	**£15**	US
Fallen Angel	7"	Capitol	CL14566	1956	**£15**	
Going Steady With The Blues	LP	Capitol	T1040	1958	**£20**	US
Going Steady With The Blues	7" EP	Capitol	EAP11040	1959	**£15**	

McDOWELL, MISSISSIPPI FRED

Title	Format	Label	Number	Year	Price	Notes
I Do Not Play No Rock'N'Roll	LP	Capitol	409	1969	**£12**	US
London 1	LP	Transatlantic	TRA194	1970	**£10**	
London 2	LP	Transatlantic	TRA203	1969	**£10**	
Mississippi Delta Blues	LP	Polydor	2460193	1972	**£10**	

McDUFF, BROTHER JACK

Title	Format	Label	Number	Year	Price	Notes
Carpetbaggers	7"	Stateside	SS328	1964	**£4**	
Change Is Gonna Come	LP	Atlantic	587030	1966	**£10**	
Down In The Valley	7"	Atlantic	584036	1966	**£5**	
Rock Candy	7"	Stateside	SS302	1964	**£4**	
Sanctified Samba	7"	Stateside	SS275	1964	**£4**	

McEVOY, JOHNNY

Title	Format	Label	Number	Year	Price	Notes
Sounds Like...	LP	Halpix	117	197-	**£20**	

McFADDEN, BOB

Title	Format	Label	Number	Year	Price	Notes
Beat Generation	7"	Coral	Q72378	1959	**£4**	

McGARRIGLE, KATE & ANNA

Title	Format	Label	Number	Year	Price	Notes
Complainte Pour Sainte Catherine	7"	W. Bros	K16710	1976	**£4**	

McGEAR, MIKE

After various jokey performances as a member of the Scaffold and of Grimms, the solo recordings by Mike McGear find him in a relatively serious singer-songwriting mode. "McGear" is of considerable interest to Paul McCartney collectors as the album is virtually a Wings album with Mike McGear as guest star. McGear and McCartney are, of course, brothers.

Title	Format	Label	Number	Year	Price	Notes
Dance The Do	7"	W. Bros	K16573	1975	**£4**	
Leave It	7"	W. Bros	K16446	1974	**£4**	chart single
McGear	LP	Centre Labs			**£30**	6 tracks, numbered & autographed
McGear	LP	W. Bros	K56051	1974	**£10**	
Sea Breezes	7"	W. Bros	K16520	1975	**£4**	
Simply Love You	7"	W. Bros	K16658	1975	**£4**	
Woman	LP	Island	ILPS9191	1972	**£12**	
Woman	7"	Island	WIP6131	1972	**£4**	

McGHEE, BROWNIE

Title	Format	Label	Number	Year	Price	Notes
At The Bunkhouse	LP	Smash	MGS27067	1965	**£12**	US
Blues	LP-10"	Folkways	2030		**£15**	US
Brownie McGhee	LP	Sharp	2003		**£25**	US

McGHEE, BROWNIE & DAVE LEE

Title	Format	Label	Number	Year	Price	Notes
Bluest	7" EP	Pye	NJE1060	1957	**£5**	

McGHEE, BROWNIE & SONNY TERRY

Title	Format	Label	Number	Year	Price	Notes
Me And Sonny	7" EP	Melodisc	EPM783	195-	**£5**	
Pawn Shop Blues	7" EP	Realm	REP4002	1964	**£4**	
Sonny Terry And Brownie McGhee	7" EP	Vocalion	EPV1274	1963	**£5**	

Sonny Terry And Brownie McGhee	7" EP	Vocalion	EPVF1279	1964	**£5**	
Work-Play-Faith-Fun Songs	7" EP	Top Rank	JKP3007	1961	**£5**	

McGHEE, STICKS & JOHN LEE HOOKER

Highway Of Blues	LP	Audio Lab	AL1520	1959	**£35**	US

McGOUGH & McGEAR

It would be pleasing to imagine that the high value of the album recorded by two-thirds of the Scaffold was in some way a tribute to the song writing of Mike McGear or the inimitable poetic talents of Roger McGough. Sadly, the value has more to do with the cast of supporting musicians used on this poor-selling album, which includes Jimi Hendrix.

McGough & McGear	LP	Parlophone	PCS7047	1968	**£200**	

McGOUGH, ROGER

Summer With Monika	LP	Island	ILPS9551	1978	**£10**	

McGOUGH, ROGER & BRIAN PATTEN

British Poets Of Our Time	LP	Argo	ZPL1190	1975	**£12**	

McGREGOR, CHRIS

African Sound	LP	Gallojazz		1963	**£100**	
Kwela	LP	77		1968	**£80**	
Up To Earth	LP	Polydor	583072	1968	**£200**	test pressing
Very Urgent	LP	Polydor	184137	1968	**£50**	

McGREGOR, CHRIS & OTHERS

Cold Castle Jazz Festival	LP	Gallojazz		1963	**£100**	

McGRIFF, JIMMY

All About My Girl	7"	Sue	WI303	1963	**£8**	
Blues For Mr.Jimmy	LP	London	HAC8247	1966	**£20**	
Gospel Time	LP	Sue	ILP908	1964	**£20**	
I've Got A Woman	LP	Sue	ILP907	1964	**£20**	
I've Got A Woman	7"	Sue	WI317	1964	**£8**	
Last Minute	7"	Sue	WI310	1964	**£8**	
Round Midnight	7"	Sue	WI333	1964	**£15**	
See See Rider	7"	United Artists	UP1170	1966	**£4**	
Worm	7"	United Artists	UP35025	1969	**£4**	

McGUINN, ROGER

Airplay Anthology	LP	Columbia	AS353	1975	**£20**	US promo
Peace On You	LP	CBS	80171	1974	**£10**	
Roger McGuinn	LP	CBS	65214	1973	**£10**	

McGUINNESS FLINT

C'est La Vie	LP	Bronze	ILPS9302	1974	**£10**	
Happy Birthday Ruthie Baby	LP	Capitol	ST22794	1971	**£10**	
Happy Birthday Ruthy Baby	7"	Capitol	CL15691	1971	**£4**	
Malt And Barley Blues	7"	Capitol	CL15682	1971	**£4**	chart single
McGuiness Flint	LP	Capitol	EST22625	1971	**£10**	chart LP
Rainbow	LP	Bronze	ILPS9244	1973	**£10**	
When I'm Dead And Gone	7"	Capitol	CL15662	1970	**£4**	chart single

McGUIRE SISTERS

By Request	LP-10"	Coral	CRL56123	1955	**£12**	US
Children's Holiday	LP	Coral	CRL57097	1956	**£10**	US
Delilah Jones	7"	Vogue Coral	Q72161	1956	**£4**	chart single
Do You Remember When?	LP	Coral	CRL57026	195-	**£10**	US
Greetings	LP	Coral	CRL57225	1958	**£10**	US
He	LP	Coral	CRL57033	195-	**£10**	US
Lonesome Polecat	7"	Vogue Coral	Q2028	1954	**£5**	
May You Always	7"	Coral	Q72356	1959	**£4**	chart single
May You Always	7" EP	Coral	FEP2033	1959	**£8**	
McGuire Sisters	7" EP	Coral	FEP2001	1958	**£8**	
Musical Magic	LP	Coral	CRL57180	1957	**£10**	US
No More	7"	Vogue Coral	Q72050	1955	**£5**	chart single
Our Golden Favorites	LP	Coral	CRL57349	1960	**£10**	US
Sincerely	LP	Coral	CRL57052	195-	**£10**	US
Sugartime	LP	Coral	CRL57217	1958	**£10**	US
Sugartime	7"	Coral	Q72305	1958	**£4**	chart single
Teenage Party	LP	Coral	CRL57134	1957	**£10**	US
Volare	7" EP	Coral	FEP2006	1958	**£8**	
When The Lights Are Low	LP	Coral	CRL57145	1957	**£10**	US

McGUIRE, BARRY

Barry McGuire And The Doctor	LP	A&M	AMLS2008	1971	**£12**	
Cloudy Summer Afternoon	7"	RCA	RCA1525	1966	**£4**	
Eve Of Destruction	LP	ABC	ABCL5110	1965	**£15**	
Eve Of Destruction	LP	RCA	RD7751	1965	**£15**	
Eve Of Destruction	7"	RCA	RCA1469	1965	**£5**	chart single
Eve Of Destruction	LP	Ember	EMB3362	1965	**£10**	
Masters Of War	7"	RCA	RCA1638	1967	**£4**	
So Long Stay Well	7"	Ember	EMBS208	1965	**£4**	
This Precious Time	LP	Dunhill	D50005	1966	**£12**	US
This Precious Time	7"	RCA	RCA1497	1966	**£4**	
Upon A Painted Ocean	7"	RCA	RCA1493	1965	**£4**	
Walking My Cat Named Dog	7"	RCA	RCA1508	1966	**£4**	
World's Last Private Citizen	LP	Dunhill	D50033	1968	**£12**	US

McKAY, SCOTT

Cold Cold Heart	7"	London	HLU9885	1964	**£4**	

McKEE, LONETTE

Save It	7"	Sussex	SXX4	1975	**£4**	

McKENDREE SPRING

Get Me To The Country	LP	Dawn	DNLS3076	1975	**£10**	
McKendree Spring	LP	MCA	277	1969	**£10**	
Second Thoughts	LP	MCA	MUPS433	1971	**£10**	
Spring Suite	LP	MCA	370	1973	**£10**	US
Three	LP	MCA	MUPS454	1972	**£10**	
Too Young To Feel This Old	LP	Pye	12124	1976	**£10**	US
Tracks	LP	MCA	MUPS476	1973	**£10**	

McKENNA MENDELSON MAINLINE

Don't Give Me No Goose For Christmas	7"	Liberty	LBF15276	1969	**£5**	
Stink	LP	Liberty	LBS83251	1969	**£15**	
You Better Watch Out	7"	Liberty	LBF15235	1969	**£6**	

McKENNA, VAL

Mixed Up Shook Up Girl	7"	Piccadilly	7N35256	1965	**£6**	

McKENZIE, JUDY

Judy	LP	Key		1970	**£30**	

McKENZIE, SCOTT

San Francisco	7"	CBS	2816	1967	**£4**	chart single
Stained Glass Morning	LP	Ode	77007	1970	**£10**	US
Voice Of...	LP	CBS	63157	1967	**£10**	

McKINLEYS

Give Him My Love	7"	Columbia	DB7583	1965	**£6**	

McKUEN, ROD

Happy Is A Boy Named Me	7"	London	HLU8390	1957	**£10**	

McLAIN, TOMMY

Sweet Dreams	7"	London	HL10065	1966	**£4**	chart single
Think It Over	7"	London	HL10091	1966	**£4**	

McLAUGHLIN, JOHN

John McLaughlin apparently spent much of the sixties driving a van for an amplification company, while playing his guitar where-ever and whenever he could. He was given the chance to make an album for the Marmalade label, but while "Extrapolation" is an above-average British jazz record of the period, it was almost immediately eclipsed by McLaughlin's good fortune in being invited with Miles Davis. As a player on the key albums to start electric jazz, it was therefore John McLaughlin who made highly amplified guitar respectable in jazz (although he had to work up to it - the tone on both "In A Silent Way" and "Bitches Brew" is quite mild).

Devotion	LP	Douglas	DGL65075	1972	**£10**	
Extrapolation	LP	Marmalade	2343012	1970	**£12**	
Extrapolation	LP	Marmalade	608007	1969	**£15**	
My Goal's Beyond	LP	Douglas	DGL69014	1972	**£10**	

McLAUGHLIN, JOHN & OTHERS

Where Fortune Smiles	LP	Dawn	DNLS3018	1971	**£15**	

McLOLLIE, OSCAR HONEYJUMPERS

Title	Format	Label	Cat. No.	Year	Price	Notes
Love Me Tonight	7"	London	HL8130	1955	**£20**	

McLUHAN, MARSHALL

Title	Format	Label	Cat. No.	Year	Price	Notes
Medium Is The Message	LP	Columbia	CL2701	1967	**£12**	US

McMANUS, ROSS

Title	Format	Label	Cat. No.	Year	Price	Notes
I'm The Greatest	7"	HMV	POP1279	1964	**£4**	
Stop Your Playing Around	7"	HMV	POP1543	1966	**£4**	

McNAIR, BARBARA

Title	Format	Label	Cat. No.	Year	Price	Notes
Here I Am	LP	Motown	644	1966	**£15**	US
I Enjoy Being A Girl	LP	W. Bros	W1541	1964	**£12**	US
Livin' End	LP	W. Bros	W1570	1964	**£12**	US
Real Barbara McNair	LP	Motown	S680	1969	**£15**	US
You're Gonna Love My Baby	7"	T. Motown	TMG544	1966	**£60**	
You're Gonna Love My Baby	7"	T. Motown	TMG544	1966	**£100**	demo

McNAIR, HAROLD

Title	Format	Label	Cat. No.	Year	Price	Notes
Affectionate Funk	LP	Island	ILP926	1965	**£30**	
Fence	LP	B&C	CAS1016	1970	**£20**	
Harold McNair	LP	B&C	CAS1045	1971	**£20**	
Harold McNair	LP	RCA	SF7969	1968	**£25**	

McNEELY, BIG JAY

Title	Format	Label	Cat. No.	Year	Price	Notes
Big Jay McNeely	LP-10"	Federal	29596	1954	**£100**	US
Big Jay McNeely	LP	W. Bros	W1523	1963	**£15**	US
Big Jay McNeely In 3-D	LP	Federal	395530	1956	**£75**	US
Big Jay McNeely In 3-D	LP	King	650	1959	**£35**	US
Rhythm And Blues Concert	LP-10"	Savoy	MG15045	1955	**£75**	US
Something On Your Mind	7"	Sue	WI373	1965	**£8**	
Something On Your Mind	7"	Top Rank	JAR169	1959	**£8**	

McNEIL, PAUL

Title	Format	Label	Cat. No.	Year	Price	Notes
Traditionally At The Troubadour	LP	Decca	LK4803	1966	**£12**	

McNEIL, PAUL & LINDA PETERS

Title	Format	Label	Cat. No.	Year	Price	Notes
You Ain't Goin' Nowhere	7"	MGM	MGM1408	1968	**£5**	

McPHATTER, CLYDE

Title	Format	Label	Cat. No.	Year	Price	Notes
Baby You Got It	7"	Deram	DM223	1969	**£4**	
Best Of...	LP	Atlantic	ATL5001	1964	**£15**	
Clyde	LP	Atlantic	8031	1959	**£50**	US
Clyde McPhatter	7" EP	London	REE1202	1959	**£20**	
Come What May	7"	London	HLE8707	1958	**£15**	
Denver	7"	B&C	CB106	1969	**£4**	
Everybody's Somebody's Fool	7"	Stateside	SS487	1966	**£4**	
Golden Blues Hits	LP	Mercury	MG20655	1962	**£12**	US
Greatest Hits	LP	Mercury	MG20783	1963	**£12**	US
Greatest Hits	LP	MGM	E3866	1960	**£20**	US
Just Give Me A Ring	7"	London	HLE9079	1960	**£10**	
Just To Hold Your Hand	7"	London	HLE8462	1957	**£20**	
Lavender Lace	7"	Stateside	SS592	1967	**£4**	
Let's Start Over Again	LP	MGM	E3775	1959	**£20**	US
Let's Try Again	7"	MGM	MGM1048	1959	**£4**	
Little Bitty Pretty One	7"	Mercury	AMT1181	1962	**£4**	
Live At The Apollo	LP	Mercury	MG20915	1964	**£12**	US
Long Lonely Nights	7"	London	HLE8476	1957	**£20**	
Love Ballads	LP	Atlantic	8024	1958	**£75**	US
Lover Please	LP	Mercury	MG20711	1962	**£12**	US
Lover Please	7"	Mercury	AMT1174	1962	**£4**	
Lover's Question	7"	London	HLE8755	1958	**£10**	
Lovey Dovey	7"	London	HLE8878	1959	**£10**	
Masquerade Is Over	7"	MGM	MGM1014	1959	**£5**	
Only A Fool	7"	Deram	DM202	1968	**£4**	
Rhythm And Soul	LP	Mercury	MG20750	1962	**£12**	US
Rock And Cry	7"	London	HLE8525	1957	**£15**	
Seven Days	7"	London	HLE8250	1956	**£40**	
Shot Of Rhythm And Blues	7"	Pama	PM775	196-	**£4**	
Shot Of Rhythm And Blues	7"	Stateside	SS567	1966	**£4**	
Since You've Been Gone	7"	London	HLE8906	1959	**£10**	

Songs Of The Big City	LP	Mercury	MG20902	1964	**£12**	US
Ta Ta	LP	Mercury	MG20597	1960	**£12**	US
Ta Ta	7"	Mercury	AMT1108	1960	**£4**	
Think Me A Kiss	7"	MGM	MGM1061	1960	**£4**	
This Is Not Goodbye	7" EP	MGM	MGMEP739	1960	**£10**	
Tomorrow Is A-Comin'	7"	Mercury	AMT1136	1961	**£4**	
Treasure Of Love	7"	London	HLE8293	1956	**£30**	chart single
Twice As Nice	7"	MGM	MGM1040	1959	**£4**	
Twice As Nice	7" EP	MGM	MGMEP705	1959	**£10**	
You Went Back On Your Word	7"	London	HLE9000	1959	**£12**	
You're For Me	7"	Mercury	AMT1120	1960	**£4**	

McPHEE, TONY

Me And The Devil	LP	Liberty	LBL83190	1968	**£35**	
Pastoral Future	7"	United Artists	UP36177	1976	**£4**	
Someone To Love Me	7"	Purdah	453501	1966	**£25**	
Two Sides Of	LP	WWA	WWA001	1973	**£20**	

McPHEE, TONY & JO ANN KELLY

Same Thing On Their Minds	LP	Sunset	SLS50209	1971	**£30**	

McPHEE, TONY & OTHERS

I Asked For Water...	LP	Liberty	LBS83252	1969	**£50**	

McPHERSON, GILLIAN

Poets And Painters And Performers Of Blues	LP	RCA		1971	**£10**	

McTELL, RALPH

8 Frames A Second	LP	Transatlantic	TRA165	1968	**£10**	
First And Last Man	7"	Famous	FAM105	1971	**£4**	
Kew Gardens	7"	Transatlantic	BIG131	1970	**£4**	
My Side Of Your Window	LP	Transatlantic	TRA209	1969	**£10**	
Spiral Staircase	LP	Transatlantic	TRA177	1969	**£10**	
Summer Comes Along	7"	Transatlantic	BIG125	1969	**£4**	
Teacher Teacher	7"	Famous	FAM111	1971	**£4**	
You Well Meaning Brought Me Here	LP	Famous	5753	1971	**£10**	

McVAY, RAY

Kinda Kinky	7"	Pye	7N15816	1965	**£8**	
Revenge	7"	Pye	7N15777	1965	**£6**	

McVOY, CARL

Tootsie	7"	London	HLU8617	1958	**£20**	

McWILLIAMS, DAVID

"The Days Of Pearly Spencer" by David McWilliams, with its megaphone vocals and fountaining strings, was heavily promoted by the pirate radio stations and is, in consequence, particularly redolent of that era. The song is something of an oddity within McWilliams' recordings, however, as none of his other, folky material makes any attempt to match the inventiveness of Pearly Spencer's arrangement.

Beggar And The Priest	LP	Dawn	DNLS3047	1973	**£10**	
David McWilliams Vol. 2	LP	Major Minor	MMLP10	1967	**£10**	chart LP
David McWilliams Vol. 3	LP	Major Minor	MMLP11	1968	**£10**	chart LP
Days Of Pearly Spencer	7"	Major Minor	MM533	1968	**£5**	
Days Of Pearly Spencer	7"	Parlophone	R5886	1971	**£4**	
Living Just A State Of Mind	LP	Dawn	DNLS3059	1974	**£10**	
Lord Offaly	LP	Dawn	DNLS3039	1972	**£10**	
Mama Are You My Friend?	7"	Major Minor	MM616	1969	**£5**	
Singing Songs By...	LP	Major Minor	MMLP2	1967	**£10**	chart LP
Stranger	7"	Major Minor	MM592	1969	**£6**	
This Side Of Heaven	7"	Major Minor	MM561	1968	**£5**	

ME & THEM

Everything I Do Is Wrong	7"	Pye	7N15631	1964	**£8**	
Feel So Good	7"	Pye	7N15596	1964	**£8**	
Getaway	7"	Pye	7N15683	1964	**£6**	

MEASLES

Casting My Spell	7"	Columbia	DB7531	1965	**£12**	
Kicks	7"	Columbia	DB7875	1966	**£12**	
Night People	7"	Columbia	DB7673	1965	**£10**	
Walking In	7"	Columbia	DB8029	1966	**£15**	

MEATLOAF

Bat Out Of Hell	LP	Epic	82419	1979	**£30**	pic disc
Bat Out Of Hell	LP	Epic	HE44974	1981	**£10**	US audiophile
Bat Out Of Hell	7"	Epic	EPC7018DJ	1978	**£8**	promo
Bat Out Of Hell	12"	Epic	SEPC127018	1978	**£10**	red vinyl
Dead Ringer	LP	Epic	EPC1183645	1981	**£10**	pic disc
Dead Ringer	7"	Epic		1981	**£6**	promo sampler
Getting Away With Murder	7"	Arista	ARIST683P	1986	**£4**	shaped pic disc
Live At Father's Place	LP	Epic	AS409	1978	**£25**	US promo
Live At The El Mocambo	LP	CBS	CDN9	1978	**£20**	Canadian promo
Modern Girl	7"	Arista	ARISD585	1984	**£4**	shaped pic disc
Rock'n'Roll Mercenaries	7"	Arista	ARIST666P	1986	**£4**	shaped pic disc
Rock'n'Roll Mercenaries	12"	Arista	ARIST666XP	1986	**£6**	shaped pic disc
Stoney And Meatloaf	LP	Rare Earth	SRE3005	1973	**£10**	
What You See Is What You Get	7"	Rare Earth	RES103	1973	**£5**	
You Took The Words Right Out...	7"	Epic	EPC5980DJ	1978	**£6**	promo

MEATMEN

Blood Sausage	7"	Touch & Go		198-	**£30**	
Crippled Children Suck	7"	Touch & Go		198-	**£30**	

MEDDY EVILS

Find Somebody To Love	7"	Pye	7N15941	1965	**£8**	
Ma's Place	7"	Pye	7N17091	1966	**£6**	

MEDICINE HEAD

Dark Side Of The Moon	LP	Polydor	2310166	1971	**£10**	
Heavy On The Drum	LP	Dandelion	K49005	1971	**£15**	
His Guiding Hand	7"	Dandelion	4461	1969	**£8**	
Kum On	7"	Polydor	2001276	1972	**£6**	
New Bottles Old Medicine	LP	Dandelion	63757	1970	**£15**	
Pictures In The Sky	7"	Dandelion	DAN7003	1971	**£5**	chart single

MEDIUM

Medium	LP	Gamma	GS503		**£15**	

MEDLEY, BILL

100% Bill Medley	LP	MGM	C8091	1968	**£10**	
Gone	LP	MGM	4741	1970	**£10**	US
Nobody Knows	LP	MGM	4702	1970	**£10**	US
Soft And Soulful	LP	MGM	4603	1969	**£10**	US
Someone Is Standing Outside	LP	MGM	4640	1970	**£10**	US

MEDLIN, JOE

I Kneel At Your Throne	7"	Mercury	AMT1032	1959	**£4**	

MEEHAN, KEITH

Darkness Of My Life	7"	Marmalade	598016	1969	**£8**	

MEEHAN, TONY

Song Of Mexico	7"	Decca	F11801	1964	**£4**	chart single

MEEK, JOE ORCHESTRA

Kennedy March	7"	Decca	F11796	1963	**£12**	

MEGADETH

Anarchy In The UK	7"	Capitol	CLP480	1988	**£5**	pic disc
Mary Jane	7"	Capitol	CLP489	1988	**£5**	pic disc
Wake Up Dead	7"	Capitol	CLP476	1987	**£6**	pic disc

MEGATON

Megaton	LP	Deram	SMLR1086	1971	**£170**	
Out Of Your Own Little World	7"	Deram	DM331	1971	**£5**	

MEGATRONS

Velvet Waters	7"	Top Rank	JAR146	1959	**£4**	
Whispering Winds	7"	Top Rank	JAR236	1959	**£4**	

MEKONS

Beaten And Broken	12"	Sin	SIN2	1986	**£6**	
Crime And Punishment	12"	Sin	SIN1	1986	**£6**	

Title	Format	Label	Cat. No.	Year	Price	Notes
Edge Of The World	7"	Sin	SIN4	1986	**£4**	
Fear And Whisky	7"	Sin	SIN6	1986	**£4**	
Hole In The Ground	12"	Cooking Vinyl	SINT7	1985	**£6**	
Never Been In A Riot	7"	Fast Product	FAST1	1978	**£8**	
Quality Of Mercy Is Not Strnen	LP	Virgin	V2143	1979	**£10**	
Slightly South Of The Border	10"	Sin	SIN5	1986	**£6**	
Snow	7"	Red Rhino	RED7	1980	**£4**	
Teeth	7"	Virgin	SV101	1980	**£5**	double
This Sporting Life	7"	CNT	001	1981	**£4**	
This Sporting Life	7"	CNT	008	1984	**£4**	
This Sporting Life	12"	Pure Freude	PF12	1981	**£6**	
Where Were You	7"	Fast Product	FAST7	1978	**£4**	
Work All Week	7"	Virgin	VS300	1979	**£4**	

MEL & TIM

Title	Format	Label	Cat. No.	Year	Price	Notes
Backfield In Motion	7"	Concord	CON004	1974	**£4**	

MELANIE

Title	Format	Label	Cat. No.	Year	Price	Notes
Affectionately	LP	Buddah	203028	1969	**£10**	
All The Right Noises	LP	Buddah	2318034	1971	**£10**	
Beautiful People	7"	Buddah	201066	1969	**£4**	
Bo Bo's Party	7"	Buddah	201028	1969	**£4**	
Born To Be	LP	Buddah	203019	1969	**£10**	
Candles In The Rain	LP	Buddah	2318009	1970	**£10**	chart LP
Christopher Robin	7"	Buddah	201027	1968	**£4**	
Four Sides Of Melanie	LP	Buddah	26590013	1974	**£15**	double, chart LP
Gather Me	LP	Buddah	2322002	1971	**£10**	chart LP
Gift From Honey	7"	Lyntone	2673/4	1973	**£4**	flexi
Good Book	LP	Buddah	2322001	1971	**£10**	chart LP
Leftover Wine	LP	Buddah	2318011	1970	**£10**	chart LP
Stoneground Words	LP	Neighborhood	NHTC251	1972	**£10**	
Tuning My Guitar	7"	Buddah	201063	1969	**£10**	
What Have They Done To My Song Ma	7"	Buddah	2011038	1970	**£4**	chart single

MELCHER, TERRY

Title	Format	Label	Cat. No.	Year	Price	Notes
Royal Flush	LP	RCA	0948	1976	**£10**	US
Terry Melcher	LP	Reprise	K54016	1974	**£10**	

MELLOKINGS

Title	Format	Label	Cat. No.	Year	Price	Notes
Tonight Tonight	LP	Herald	H1013	1960	**£100**	US

MELLOW CANDLE

Title	Format	Label	Cat. No.	Year	Price	Notes
Dan The Wing	7"	Deram	DM357	1972	**£12**	
Feeling High	7"	SNB	553645	1968	**£20**	
Swaddling Songs	LP	Deram	SDL7	1972	**£300**	

MELLOW LARKS & CLUE J. & HIS BLUES BLASTERS

Title	Format	Label	Cat. No.	Year	Price	Notes
Love You Baby	7"	Blue Beat	BB16	1961	**£10**	

MELLY, GEORGE

Title	Format	Label	Cat. No.	Year	Price	Notes
Black Bottom	7"	Decca	F10840	1957	**£4**	
Cemetery Blues	7"	Tempo	A147	1956	**£4**	
Frankie And Johnny	7"	Decca	F10457	1955	**£4**	
Heebie Jeebies	7"	Decca	FJ10806	1956	**£4**	
Kingdom Come	7"	Decca	F10763	1956	**£4**	
Waiting For A Train	7"	Decca	FJ10779	1956	**£4**	

MELODIANS

Title	Format	Label	Cat. No.	Year	Price	Notes
Sweet Sensation	7"	Trojan	TR695	1969	**£5**	chart single

MELODIC ENERGY COMMISSION

Title	Format	Label	Cat. No.	Year	Price	Notes
Migration Of The Snails	LP	Energy			**£12**	
Stranger In Mystery	LP	Energy			**£15**	

MELSON, JOE

Title	Format	Label	Cat. No.	Year	Price	Notes
Hey Mister Cupid	7"	Polydor	NH66961	1961	**£4**	
Oh Yeah	7"	Polydor	NH66959	1961	**£8**	

MELTON, BARRY

Title	Format	Label	Cat. No.	Year	Price	Notes
Bright Sun Is Shining	LP	Vanguard	VSD6551	1970	**£10**	US
Melton, Levy And The Dey Brothers	LP	CBS	31279	1972	**£10**	US
We Are Like The Ocean	LP	Music Is M.	MIM9007	1977	**£30**	US

MELTZER, TINA & DAVID

Title	Format	Label	Cat. No.	Year	Price	Notes
Poet Song	LP	Vanguard		196-	**£25**	US

MEMBERS

Title	Format	Label	Cat. No.	Year	Price	Notes
1980, The Choice Is Yours	LP	Virgin	V2153	1980	**£10**	
At The Chelsea Nightclub	LP	Virgin	V2120	1979	**£10**	chart LP
Fear On The Streets	7"	XS		1977	**£10**	
Flying Again	7"	Virgin	VS352	1980	**£4**	
Killing Time	7"	Virgin	VS292	1979	**£4**	
Offshore Banking Business	7"	Stiff	OFF3	1978	**£10**	
Offshore Banking Business	7"	Virgin	VS248	1979	**£4**	chart single
Offshore Banking Business	12"	Virgin	VS24812	1979	**£6**	
Radio	7"	Island	WIP6773	1982	**£4**	
Radio	12"	Island	12WIP6773	1982	**£6**	
Romance	7"	Virgin	VS333	1980	**£4**	
Sound Of The Suburbs	7"	Virgin	VS242	1979	**£4**	chart single
Sound Of The Suburbs	7"	Virgin	VS242	1979	**£6**	windowed PS, clear vinyl
Working Girl	7"	Albion	ION1012	1981	**£4**	
Working Girl	12"	Albion	12ION1012	1981	**£6**	

MEMBRANES

Title	Format	Label	Cat. No.	Year	Price	Notes
Fashionable Junkies	7"	Vinyl Drip	VD005	1980	**£5**	
Muscles	7"	Rondelet	ROUND19	1982	**£4**	
Pinstripe Hype	7"	Rondelet	ROUND28	1982	**£4**	
Spike Milligan's Tape Recorder	7"	Criminal D		1984	**£4**	

MEMOS

Title	Format	Label	Cat. No.	Year	Price	Notes
My Type Of Girl	7"	Parlophone	R4616	1959	**£12**	

MEMPHIS HORNS

Title	Format	Label	Cat. No.	Year	Price	Notes
Get Up And Dance	7"	RCA	PB0836	1977	**£5**	
Wooly Bully	7"	Atlantic	2091080	1971	**£4**	

MEMPHIS SLIM

Title	Format	Label	Cat. No.	Year	Price	Notes
All Kinds Of Blues	LP	Bluesville	BV1053	1963	**£12**	US
Alone With My Friends	LP	Battle	BM6118	1963	**£12**	US
At The Gate Of Horn	LP	Joy	JOYS143	196-	**£10**	
At The Gate Of Horn	LP	Vee Jay	VJLP1012	1959	**£30**	US
Big City Girl	7"	Storyville	A45055	196-	**£5**	
Blue Memphis	LP	W. Bros	WS1899	1971	**£10**	US
Blues In Europe	LP	Storyville	SLP188	196-	**£10**	
Boogie Woogie And The Blues	7" EP	Storyville	SEP385		**£5**	
Broken Soul Blues	LP	United Artists	UAL3137	1961	**£12**	US
Chicago Blues	LP	XTRA	XTRA1085		**£10**	
Frisco Bay Blues	LP	Fontana	688315	1960	**£15**	
Going To Kansas City	7" EP	Collector	JEN5	196-	**£6**	
Just Blues	LP	Bluesville	BV1018	1961	**£12**	US
Legend Of The Blues	LP	Jubilee	JGM8003	1967	**£10**	US
Memphis Slim	LP	Chess	LP1455	1961	**£25**	US
Memphis Slim	LP	Everest	215	1968	**£10**	US
Memphis Slim	LP	King	LP885	1964	**£12**	US
Memphis Slim, USA	LP	Candid	9024	1962	**£20**	US
Messin' Around With The Blues	LP	King	KS1082	1970	**£10**	US
Mother Earth	LP	Buddah	BDS7505	1969	**£10**	US
No Strain	LP	Bluesville	BV1031	1962	**£12**	US
Pinetop Blues	7"	Collector	JDN102	1960	**£4**	
Real Folk Blues	LP	Chess	1510	1966	**£20**	US
Self Portrait	LP	Scepter	SM535	1966	**£12**	US
Steady Rollin' Blues	LP	Bluesville	BV1075	1964	**£12**	US
Tribute To Big Bill Broonzy	LP	Candid	9023	1961	**£20**	US
World's Foremost Blues Singer	LP	Strand	SLS1046	1960	**£12**	US
World's Foremost Blues Singer	7" EP	Summit	LSE2041	196-	**£4**	

MEMPHIS THREE

Title	Format	Label	Cat. No.	Year	Price	Notes
Wild Thing	7"	Page One	POF070	1968	**£4**	

MEN

One of the Men was thinking of growing his hair long on one side only; the others were still working out how to get the best out of their new synthesizers. This was, in fact, the Human League.MI5Deep Purple's drummer, Ian Paice, first appeared on record with MI5, as did the original singer with the more famous group, Rod Evans.

Title	Format	Label	Cat. No.	Year	Price	Notes
I Don't Depend On You	12"	Virgin	VS26912	1979	**£6**	

MEN AT WORK

Title	Format	Label	Cat. No.	Year	Price	Notes
Down Under	7"	Epic	EPCA1980	1983	**£8**	shaped pic disc

MENACE

Title	Format	Label	Cat. No.	Year	Price	Notes
G.L.C.	7"	Small Wonder	SMALL5	1978	**£4**	
I Need Nothing	7"	Illegal	IL008	1978	**£4**	
Last Year's Youth	7"	Small Wonder	SMALL16	1979	**£4**	
Screwed Up	7"	Illegal	IL004	1977	**£5**	
Screwed Up	12"	Illegal	IL004	1977	**£6**	
Young Ones	7"	Fresh	FRESH14	1978	**£4**	

MERCER, MARY MAE

Title	Format	Label	Cat. No.	Year	Price	Notes
Mary Mae Mercer	7" EP	Decca	DFE8599	1965	**£5**	

MERCURY, FREDDIE

Title	Format	Label	Cat. No.	Year	Price	Notes
Great Pretender	7"	Parlophone	RP6151	1987	**£10**	shaped pic disc & plinth
Great Pretender	10"	Parlophone		1987	**£10**	promo
I Was Born To Love You	7"	CBS	DA6019	1985	**£6**	double
Love Kills	7"	CBS	WA4735	1984	**£5**	pic disc
Made In Heaven	7"	CBS	WA6413	1985	**£5**	shaped pic disc

MERKIN

Title	Format	Label	Cat. No.	Year	Price	Notes
Music From Merkin Manor	LP	Windi	1004	1969	**£200**	US

MERRICK, TONY

Title	Format	Label	Cat. No.	Year	Price	Notes
Lady Jane	7"	Columbia	DB7913	1966	**£5**	chart single
Wake Up	7"	Columbia	DB7995	1966	**£5**	

MERRILL, BOB

Title	Format	Label	Cat. No.	Year	Price	Notes
Nairobi	7"	Columbia	DB4086	1958	**£4**	

MERRYMEN

Title	Format	Label	Cat. No.	Year	Price	Notes
Caribbean Treasure Chest	LP	Island	ILP984	1968	**£50**	

MERRYWEATHER, NEIL

Title	Format	Label	Cat. No.	Year	Price	Notes
Ivar Avenue Reunion	LP	RCA	LSP4442	1970	**£10**	US
Merryweather	LP	Capitol	SKAO220	1969	**£10**	US
Neil Merryweather And The Boers	LP	Kent	KST546	1972	**£10**	US
Vacuum Cleaner	LP	RCA	SF8210	1971	**£10**	
Word Of Mouth	LP	Capitol	STBB278	1969	**£15**	double

MERSEY BOYS

Title	Format	Label	Cat. No.	Year	Price	Notes
15 Great Songs Composed By Beatles	LP	Ace Of Clubs		196-	**£15**	

MERSEYBEATS

Title	Format	Label	Cat. No.	Year	Price	Notes
Don't Let It Happen To Us	7"	Fontana	TF568	1965	**£6**	
Don't Turn Around	7"	Fontana	TF459	1964	**£4**	chart single
I Love You, Yes I Do	7"	Fontana	TF607	1965	**£4**	chart single
I Stand Accused	7"	Fontana	TF645	1965	**£4**	chart single
I Think Of You	7"	Fontana	TF431	1963	**£4**	chart single
I Think Of You	7" EP	Fontana	TE17423	1964	**£6**	
It's Love That Really Counts	7"	Fontana	TF412	1963	**£4**	chart single
Last Night	7"	Fontana	TF504	1964	**£4**	chart single
Merseybeats	LP	Fontana	TL5210	1964	**£60**	chart LP
Merseybeats	LP	Wing	WL1163	1965	**£30**	
Merseybeats On Stage	7" EP	Fontana	TE17422	1964	**£8**	
Wishin' And Hopin'	7"	Fontana	TF482	1964	**£4**	chart single
Wishin' And Hopin'	7" EP	Fontana	TE17432	1964	**£6**	

MERSEYBOYS

Title	Format	Label	Cat. No.	Year	Price	Notes
Fifteen Greatest Songs Of The Beatles	LP	Vee Jay	VJ1101	1964	**£20**	US

MERSEYS

Title	Format	Label	Cat. No.	Year	Price	Notes
Cat	7"	Fontana	TF845	1967	**£6**	
Lovely Loretta	7"	Fontana	TF955	1968	**£5**	
Penny In My Pocket	7"	Fontana	TF916	1968	**£5**	
Rhythm Of Love	7"	Fontana	TF776	1966	**£4**	
So Sad About Us	7"	Fontana	TF732	1966	**£6**	
Sorrow	7"	Fontana	TF694	1966	**£4**	chart single

MERTON PARKAS

Title	Format	Label	Cat. No.	Year	Price	Notes
Face In The Crowd	LP	Beggars B.	BEGA11	1979	**£10**	

Flat Nineteen	7"	Well Suspect	BLAM002	1983	**£4**	
Give It To Me Now	7"	Beggars B.	BEG30	1979	**£4**	
Plastic Smile	7"	Beggars B.	BEG25	1979	**£4**	
Put Me In The Picture	7"	Beggars B.	BEG43	1980	**£4**	
You Need Wheels	7"	Beggars B.	BEG22	1979	**£4**	chart single
You Need Wheels	7"	Beggars B.	BEG93E	1983	**£5**	

MESMERIZING EYE

Psychedelia	LP	Smash	MGS27090	1967	**£20**	US

MESSENGER

Oy I Value Elation	7"	Anagram	A001	1967	**£4**	

MESSENGERS

I'm Stealing Back	7"	Columbia	DB7344	1964	**£5**	
More Pretty Girls Than One	7"	Columbia	DB7495	1965	**£4**	

MESSINA, JIM

Dragsters	LP	Audio Fid.	DF7037	1964	**£15**	US
Jim Messina And The Jesters	LP	Thimble	3	196-	**£12**	US

METAL URBAIN

Panik	7"	Cobra	COB47004	1977	**£5**	
Paris Maquis	7"	Rough Trade	RT001	1978	**£4**	

METALLICA

Creeping Death	12"	Music For N.	CV12KUT112	1987	**£6**	blue vinyl
Creeping Death	12"	Music For N.	GV12KUT112	1987	**£8**	gold vinyl
Creeping Death	12"	Music For N.	P12KUT112	1984	**£6**	pic disc
Harvester Of Sorrow	7"	Vertigo	METAL2	1988	**£15**	promo, special sleeve
Harvester Of Sorrow	12"	Vertigo	METAL212	1988	**£15**	promo, special sleeve
Jump In The Fire	12"	Music For N.	12KUT105	1984	**£10**	gold vinyl
Jump In The Fire	12"	Music For N.	12KUT105	1984	**£6**	red vinyl
Jump In The Fire	7"	Music For N.	PKUT105	1986	**£10**	shaped pic disc
Kill 'em All	LP	Music For N.	MFN7	1983	**£10**	pic disc
One	7"	Vertigo	MET5	1989	**£15**	promo, special sleeve
One	12"	Vertigo	MET512	1989	**£10**	gatefold PS
One	10"	Vertigo	METPD510	1989	**£8**	pic disc
Ride The Lightning	LP	Music For N.	MFN27	1984	**£10**	pic disc

METEORS

Johnny Remember Me	7"	ID	EYE1	1982	**£4**	
Johnny Remember Me	7"	ID	EYE1	1983	**£6**	pic disc
Johnny Remember Me	7"	ID	EYE1P	1982	**£6**	pic disc
Meteor Madness	7"	Ace	SW65	1981	**£8**	blue vinyl
Mutant Rock	7"	WXYZ	ABCD5	1982	**£4**	
Radioactive Kid	7"	Ace	NS74	1981	**£6**	clear vinyl
Wreckin' Crew	12"	ABC	EYE10	1986	**£6**	blue vinyl

METEORS (2)

Get A Load Of This	7"	Polydor	NH52263	1964	**£4**	

METHUSELAH

Matthew, Mark, Luke And John	LP	Elektra	EKS74052	1969	**£60**	

METROPHASE

In Black	7"	Fresh	FRESH6	1981	**£6**	
In Black	7"	Neo London	MS01	1979	**£6**	

METROTONES

Tops In Rock And Roll	LP-10"	Columbia	6341	1955	**£100**	US

MEV

Musica Elettronica Viva	LP	Polydor	583769	1969	**£20**	

MEZA, LEE

If It Happens	7"	Stateside	SS589	1967	**£25**	

MIAMI SOUND MACHINE

Conga	7"	Epic	A6661	1985	**£4**	
Conga	12"	Epic	TA6661	1985	**£6**	
Falling In Love	12"	Epic	6502516	1986	**£6**	

Prisoner Of Love	7"	Epic	A4800	1984	**£4**	
Prisoner Of Love	12"	Epic	TX4800	1984	**£6**	

MICHAEL, GEORGE

Careless Whisper (Wexler mix)	7"	Epic	WA4603	1984	**£20**	shaped pic disc
Careless Whisper (Wexler mix)	12"	Epic	QTA4603	1984	**£20**	
Different Corner	12"	Epic	GTA7033	1986	**£6**	gatefold sleeve
Faith	7"	Epic	EMUP3	1987	**£5**	shaped pic disc
I Want Your Sex	7"	Epic	LUSTP1	1987	**£4**	poster sleeve
One More Try	7"	Epic	EMUB5	1988	**£4**	with badge

MICHAEL, GEORGE & ELTON JOHN

Wrap Her Up	7"	Rocket	EJSC10	1985	**£4**	cube bag sleeve
Wrap Her Up	7"	Rocket	EJSP10	1985	**£5**	shaped pic disc

MICHAELS, LEE

Barrel	LP	A&M	AMLS991	1970	**£10**	
Carnival Of Life	LP	A&M	4140	1968	**£10**	US
Fifth	LP	A&M	AMLS64302	1971	**£10**	
Heighty Hi	7"	A&M	AMS763	1968	**£4**	
Lee Michaels	LP	A&M	AMLS956	1969	**£10**	
Live	LP	Ariola	86725	1972	**£10**	
Recital	LP	A&M	AMLS928	1969	**£10**	
Space And First Takes	LP	A&M	AMLS64336	1972	**£10**	

MICHIGAN RAG

Don't Run Away	7"	Blue Horizon	2096009	1972	**£5**	

MICKEY & KITTY

Buttercup	7"	London	HLE9054	1960	**£4**	

MICKEY & SYLVIA

Bewildered	7"	RCA	RCA1064	1958	**£12**	
Love Is Strange	LP	Camden	CAL863	1965	**£25**	US
Love Is Strange	7"	HMV	POP331	1957	**£25**	
New Sounds	LP	Vik	LX1102	1958	**£75**	US
Sweeter As The Day Goes By	7"	RCA	RCA1206	1960	**£8**	

MIDDLETON, TONY

Don't Ever Leave Me	7"	Polydor	56704	1966	**£20**	
My Little Red Book	7"	London	HLR9983	1965	**£15**	

MIDNIGHT SHIFT

Saturday Jump	7"	Decca	F12487	1966	**£8**	

MIDNIGHT SUN

Midnight Dream	LP	Sonet	SLPS1547	1974	**£15**	
Midnight Sun	LP	MCA	MKPS2019	1972	**£15**	
Nickels And Dimes	7"	MCA	MK5081	1971	**£4**	
Rainbow Band	LP	Sonet	SLPS1523	1970	**£15**	
Rainbow Band	LP	Sonet	SLPS1523A	1971	**£15**	different vocals
Walking Circles	LP	MCA	MKPS2024	1972	**£15**	
Walking Circles	LP	Sonet	SLPS1536	1972	**£15**	

MIDNIGHTS

Show Me Around	7"	Ember	EMBS220	1966	**£5**	

MIGHTY AVENGERS

Blue Turns To Grey	7"	Decca	F12085	1965	**£6**	
Hide Your Pride	7"	Decca	F11891	1964	**£6**	
Sleepy City	7"	Decca	F12198	1965	**£8**	
So Much In Love	7"	Decca	F11962	1964	**£6**	chart single

MIGHTY BABY

Devil's Whisper	7"	Blue Horizon	2096003	1971	**£15**	
Jug Of Love	LP	Blue Horizon	2931001	1971	**£40**	
Mighty Baby	LP	Head	HDLS6002	1969	**£40**	

MIGHTY MEN

No Way Out	7"	Salvo	SLO1804	1962	**£4**	

MIGHTY MO

Title	Format	Label	Cat. No.	Year	Price	Notes
Ape Call	7"	Columbia	DB8851	1972	**£4**	

MIGHTY SAM

Title	Format	Label	Cat. No.	Year	Price	Notes
Fannie Mae	7"	Stateside	SS544	1966	**£5**	
Papa True Love	7"	Soul City	SC115		**£4**	
Papa True Love	7"	Soul City	SC115		**£10**	demo
Sweet Dreams	7"	Stateside	SS534	1966	**£4**	

MIGHTY SPARROW

Title	Format	Label	Cat. No.	Year	Price	Notes
Mr.Herbert	7"	Kalypso	XX22	196-	**£6**	
Mr.Walker	7"	Nems	3558	196-	**£6**	
Slave	LP	Island	ILP902	1963	**£40**	

MIGHTY SPARROW & BYRON LEE

Title	Format	Label	Cat. No.	Year	Price	Notes
Sparrow Meets The Dragon	LP	Trojan	TRLS8	196-	**£10**	

MIGIL FIVE

Title	Format	Label	Cat. No.	Year	Price	Notes
Boys And Girls	7"	Pye	7N15677	1964	**£4**	
If I Had My Way	7"	Jayboy	BOY4	1969	**£5**	
Just Behind The Rainbow	7"	Pye	7N15757	1965	**£4**	
Meet The Migil Five	7" EP	Pye	NEP24191	1964	**£5**	
Mockingbird Hill	7"	Pye	7N15597	1964	**£4**	chart single
Mockingbird Hill	LP	Pye	NPL18093	1964	**£15**	
Near You	7"	Pye	7N15645	1964	**£4**	chart single
One Hundred Years	7"	Pye	7N15874	1965	**£4**	
Pencil And Paper	7"	Pye	7N17023	1966	**£4**	
Together	7"	Columbia	DB8196	1967	**£5**	

MIGIL FOUR

Title	Format	Label	Cat. No.	Year	Price	Notes
Maybe	7"	Pye	7N15572	1963	**£4**	

MIKE & THE MODIFIERS

Title	Format	Label	Cat. No.	Year	Price	Notes
I Found Myself A Brand New Baby	7"	Oriole	CB1775	1962	**£120**	

MILBURN JR., AMOS

Title	Format	Label	Cat. No.	Year	Price	Notes
Gloria	7"	London	HLU9795	1963	**£4**	

MILBURN, AMOS

Title	Format	Label	Cat. No.	Year	Price	Notes
Blues Boss	LP	Motown	608	1963	**£120**	US
Every Day Of The Week	7"	Vogue	V9064	1957	**£15**	
Let's Have A Party	LP	Score	LP4012	1957	**£75**	US
Million Sellers	LP	Imperial	A9176	1962	**£40**	US
One Scotch One Bourbon One Beer	7"	Vogue	V9163	1960	**£15**	
Rock And Roll	7" EP	Vogue	VE170102	195-	**£30**	
Rockin' The Boogie	LP	Aladdin	810	1958	**£100**	US
Rockin' The Boogie	LP-10"	Aladdin	704	1956	**£180**	US
Rockin' The Boogie	LP-10"	Aladdin	704	1956	**£250**	US, red vinyl
Rum And Coca Cola	7"	Vogue	V9069	1957	**£15**	
Thinking Of You Baby	7"	Vogue	V9080	1957	**£15**	

MILES, BUDDY

"Expressway To Your Skull" is exciting and dynamic big-band jazz-rock and it deserves to be very much more widely appreciated than it seems to be. This is the music that the Electric Flag were trying to create, without ever quite getting there - here Buddy Miles manages it without guitarist Mike Bloomfield's help. The sleeve notes to the album are by Jimi Hendrix, who knew a good thing when he heard it, although he does not play on the record. It is possible that he does play on the follow-up, "Electric Church", but in a surprisingly understated manner, if it is he.

Title	Format	Label	Cat. No.	Year	Price	Notes
Electric Church	LP	Mercury	SMCL20163	1969	**£12**	
Expressway To Your Skull	LP	Mercury	SMCL20137	1969	**£15**	
Live	LP	Mercury	6641033	1971	**£10**	
Message To The People	LP	Mercury	6338048	1970	**£10**	
Miss Lady	7"	Mercury	MF1098	1969	**£4**	
Them Changes	LP	Mercury	6338016	1970	**£10**	
Them Changes	7"	Mercury	6052036	1971	**£4**	
Train	7"	Mercury	MF1065	1968	**£4**	
We Got To Live Together	LP	Mercury	6338028	1970	**£10**	

MILES, GARRY

Title	Format	Label	Cat. No.	Year	Price	Notes
Look For A Star	7"	London	HLG9155	1960	**£4**	
Looking For A Star	7" EP	London	REG1264	1960	**£5**	

MILES, LENNY

Don't Believe Him Donna	7"	Top Rank	JAR546	1961	**£8**	

MILES, LIZZIE

Clambake On Bourbon Street	LP	Cook	1185	1957	**£15**	US
Hot Songs	LP	Cook	1183	1956	**£15**	US
Lizzie Miles New Orleans Boys	7" EP	Melodisc	EPM755	195-	**£4**	
Moans And Blues	LP	Cook	1182	1956	**£15**	US
Torchy Lullabies	LP	Cook	1184	1956	**£15**	US

MILES, LIZZIE & BILLY YOUNG

Blues They Sang	7" EP	HMV	7EG8178	195-	**£8**	

MILK'N'COOKIES

Milk'n'Cookies	LP	Island	ILPS9320	1977	**£10**	

MILKSHAKES

Please Don't Tell My Baby	7"	Bilko	BILK0	1982	**£4**	

MILKWOOD

Many of the groups to emerge as "new wave" at the end of the seventies were not as new as all that. The Cars evolved from a group called Milkwood, who released a (fairly) hard rock LP as early as 1973.

How's The Weather	LP	Paramount	PAS6046	1973	**£30**	US
I'm A Song	7"	W. Bros	K16283	1973	**£5**	
Watching You Go	7"	W. Bros	K16141	1972	**£5**	
What Can I Do To Make You Love Me	7"	W. Bros	K16418	1974	**£5**	

MILLER

Baby I Got News For You	7"	Columbia	DB7735	1965	**£20**	

MILLER, BETTY

Jack O'Diamonds	7"	Top Rank	JAR127	1959	**£4**	

MILLER, BOBBIE

Every Beat Of My Heart	7"	Decca	F12252	1965	**£5**	
Everywhere I Go	7"	Decca	F12354	1966	**£10**	
What A Guy	7"	Decca	F12064	1965	**£4**	

MILLER, CHUCK

Auctioneer	7"	Mercury	AMT1026	1959	**£5**	
Down The Road Apiece	7"	Mercury	7MT215	1958	**£15**	
Going Going Gone	7" EP	Mercury	ZEP10058	1960	**£10**	
No Baby Like You	7"	Capitol	CL14543	1956	**£4**	

MILLER, FRANKIE

Country Music	7" EP	Top Rank	JKP3013	1962	**£10**	
Popping Johnnie	7"	Melodisc	MEL1529	195-	**£8**	
Rain Rain	7"	Melodisc	MEL1552	1960	**£6**	
True Blue	7"	Melodisc	MEL1519	195-	**£8**	

MILLER, GARY

Gary Miller Hit Parade Vol.1	7" EP	Pye	NEP24047	1957	**£8**	
Lollipop	7"	Pye	7N15136	1958	**£4**	
Stingray	7"	Pye	7N15698	1964	**£4**	
Story Of My Life	7"	Pye	7N15120	1958	**£4**	chart single
Yellow Rose Of Texas	7" EP	Pye	NEP24013	1956	**£8**	

MILLER, JIMMY BARBECUES

Jelly Baby	7"	Columbia	DB4081	1958	**£6**	
Sizzling Hot	7"	Columbia	DB4006	1957	**£6**	

MILLER, JODY

Home Of The Brave	7"	Capitol	CL15415	1965	**£4**	chart single
If You Were A Carpenter	7"	Capitol	CL15482	1966	**£4**	

MILLER, KENNY

Take My Tip	7"	Stateside	SS405	1965	**£10**	

MILLER, MANDY

Children's Choice	7" EP	Parlophone	GEP8776	1958	**£5**	

MILLER, NED

Title	Format	Label	Cat. No.	Year	Price	Notes
Do What You Do Do Well	7"	London	HL9937	1964	£4	chart single
From A Jack To A King	LP	Fabor	FLP1001	1963	£40	US, coloured vinyl
From A Jack To A King	LP	London	HA8072	1963	£12	
From A Jack To a King	7"	London	HL9648	1963	£4	chart single
Go On Back, You Fool	7"	Capitol	CL15301	1963	£4	
Just Before Dawn	7"	London	HL9728	1963	£4	
Ned Miller	7" EP	Capitol	EAP120492	1963	£5	
Ned Miller	7" EP	London	RE1382	1963	£5	

MILLER, ROGER

Title	Format	Label	Cat. No.	Year	Price	Notes
Dang Me	7"	Philips	BF1354	1964	£4	
King Of The Road	7"	Philips	BF1397	1965	£4	chart single
King Of The Road	7" EP	Philips	BE12578	1965	£5	

MILLER, RUSS

Title	Format	Label	Cat. No.	Year	Price	Notes
I Sit In My Window	7"	HMV	POP391	1957	£8	

MILLER, STEPHEN

Title	Format	Label	Cat. No.	Year	Price	Notes
Story So Far	LP	Caroline	C1507	1974	£15	

MILLER, STEVE BAND

Title	Format	Label	Cat. No.	Year	Price	Notes
Anthology	LP	Capitol	ESTSP12	1972	£15	double
Brave New World	LP	Capitol	EST184	1969	£10	
Children Of The Future	LP	Capitol	ST2920	1968	£10	
Fly Like An Eagle	LP	Mobile Fid	MFSL1021	1978	£12	US audiophile
Going To The Country	7"	Capitol	CL15656	1970	£4	
Greatest Hits 1974-78	LP	Mercury	HS9919916	1982	£10	audiophile
Joker	LP	Capitol	EAST11235	1973	£10	
Little Girl	7"	Capitol	CL15618	1969	£5	
Living In The USA	7"	Capitol	CL15564	1968	£5	
Macho City	12"	Mercury	STEVE12	1981	£6	promo
My Dark Hour	7"	Capitol	CL15604	1969	£5	
Number Five	LP	Capitol	EAST436	1970	£10	
Recall The Beginning	LP	Capitol	EAST11022	1972	£10	
Rock Love	LP	Capitol	ESW748	1971	£10	
Sailor	LP	Capitol	ST2984	1969	£10	
Sittin' In Circles	7"	Capitol	CL15539	1968	£6	
Your Saving Grace	LP	Capitol	EST331	1970	£10	

MILLER, STEVE BAND & OTHERS

Title	Format	Label	Cat. No.	Year	Price	Notes
Revolution	LP	United Artists	UAS5185	1968	£12	US

MILLER, SUZI

Title	Format	Label	Cat. No.	Year	Price	Notes
Dance With Me Henry	7"	Decca	F10512	1955	£4	
Tweedle Dee	7"	Decca	F10475	1955	£4	

MILLER, SUZI & JOHNSTON BROTHERS

Title	Format	Label	Cat. No.	Year	Price	Notes
Happy Days And Lonely Nights	7"	Decca	F10389	1954	£6	chart single

MILLIE

Title	Format	Label	Cat. No.	Year	Price	Notes
Best Of Jackie And Millie Vol.2	LP	Trojan	TTL52	197-	£20	
Best Of Millie Small	LP	Island	ILP953	1967	£40	
Best Of Millie Small	LP	Trojan	TTL49	197-	£20	
Bloodshot Eyes	7"	Fontana	TF617	1965	£5	chart single
Chicken Feed	7"	Fontana	TF796	1967	£5	
Don't You Know	7"	Fontana	TF525	1963	£5	
I Love The Way You Love	7"	Fontana	TF502	1964	£5	
I've Fallen In Love With A Snowman	7"	Fontana	TF515	1965	£5	
Killer Joe	7"	Fontana	TF740	1966	£5	
Millie	7" EP	Bluebeat	BBEP302	1961	£12	
Millie And Her Boyfriends	7" EP	Island	IEP705	1966	£12	
Millie And Her Boyfriends	LP	Trojan	TTL17	1969	£20	
More Millie	LP	Fontana		196-	£25	
My Boy Lollipop	7"	Fontana	TF449	1964	£5	chart single
My Boy Lollipop	7" EP	Fontana	TE17425	1964	£8	
My Boy Lollipop	LP	Smash	MGS27055	1964	£20	US
My Desire (Millie And Jackie)	7"	Island	WI265	1966	£10	
My Love And I	7"	Pyramid	PYR6080	1970	£6	
My Street	7"	Brit	WI1002	1965	£10	
My Street	7"	Fontana	TF591	1965	£5	

Pledging My Love (Jackie And Millie)	LP	Trojan	TTL47	197-	**£20**	
Readin' Writin' Arithmetic	7"	Decca	F12948	1969	**£6**	
See You Later Alligator	7"	Fontana	TF529	1965	**£5**	
Stop Baby (Millie And Winston)	7"	Big Shot	BI623	1973	**£4**	
Sugar Plum (Owen And Millie)	7"	Island	WI014	1962	**£10**	
Sweet William	7"	Fontana	TF479	1964	**£5**	chart single
This Is My Story (Millie And Jackie)	7"	Island	WI253	1965	**£10**	
This World (Roy And Millie)	7"	Island	WI050	1962	**£10**	
Time Will Tell	LP	Trojan	TBL108	1970	**£15**	
We'll Meet (Roy And Millie)	7"	Island	WI005	1962	**£10**	
When I Dance With You	7"	Fontana	TF948	1968	**£5**	
You Better Forget	7"	Island	WIP6021	1967	**£8**	

MILLIGAN, SPIKE

Milligan Preserved	LP	Parlophone	PMC1148	1961	**£12**	chart LP
World Of Beachcomber	LP	Pye	NPL18271	1969	**£10**	

MILLIONAIRES

Chatterbox	7"	Decca	F12468	1966	**£8**	

MILLS, BARBARA

Queen Of Fools	7"	Hickory	451323	1965	**£40**	
Try	7"	Hickory	451392	1965	**£5**	

MILLS, GARY

Bless You	7"	Decca	F11383	1961	**£4**	
Comin' Down With Love	7"	Top Rank	JAR393	1960	**£4**	
Hey Baby	7"	Top Rank	JAR119	1959	**£4**	
I'll Step Down	7"	Decca	F11358	1961	**£4**	chart single
Look For A Star	7"	Top Rank	JAR336	1960	**£4**	chart single
Looking For A Star	7" EP	Top Rank	JKP3001	1961	**£6**	
Running Bear	7"	Top Rank	JAR301	1960	**£4**	
Sad Little Girl	7"	Decca	F11415	1961	**£4**	
Seven Little Girls Sitting In The Back Seat	7"	Top Rank	JAR219	1959	**£4**	
Top Teen Baby	7"	Top Rank	JAR500	1960	**£4**	chart single
Who's Gonna Take You Home Tonight	7"	Top Rank	JAR542	1961	**£4**	

MILLS, HAYLEY

Let's Get Together	7"	Decca	F21396	1961	**£4**	chart single

MILLS, MAUDE

Maude Mills	7" EP	Vintage Jazz	VEP34		**£8**	

MILLS, RUDY

Reggae Hits	LP	Pama	SECO12	1969	**£20**	

MILLS, STEPHANIE

This Empty Place/ I See You For The First Time	7"	T. Motown	TMG1020	1976	**£30**	demo

MILSAP, RONNIE

Ain't No Sole Left In These Ole Shoes	7"	Pye	7N25392	1966	**£6**	

MILSAP, RONNIE & ROSCOE ROBINSON

Soul Sensations	7" EP	Pye	NEP44078	1966	**£6**	

MILTON, JOHNNY & THE CONDORS

Cry Baby	7"	Fontana	TF488	1964	**£5**	
Somethin' Else	7"	Decca	F11862	1964	**£5**	

MILTON, ROY

Great Roy Milton	LP	Kent	554	1963	**£25**	US

MILTON, ROY & CHUCK HIGGINS

Rock'N'Roll Versus Rhythm And Blues	LP	Dooto	DL223	1959	**£50**	US

MIMMS, GARNETT

As Long As I Have You	LP	United Artists	UAL3396	1965	**£10**	US
As Long As I Love You	7"	United Artists	UP1186	1967	**£4**	
Cry Baby	LP	United Artists	UAL3305	1963	**£12**	US
Cry Baby	7"	United Artists	UP1033	1963	**£4**	

For Your Precious Love	7"	United Artists	UP1038	1963	**£4**	
I Can Hear My Baby Crying	7"	Verve	VS569	1968	**£5**	
I'll Take Good Care Of You	LP	United Artists	UAL3498	1965	**£10**	US
I'll Take Good Care Of You	7"	United Artists	UP1130	1966	**£20**	
It Was Easier To Hurt Her	7"	United Artists	UP1090	1965	**£6**	
It's Been Such A Long Time	7"	United Artists	UP1147	1966	**£4**	
My Baby	7"	United Artists	UP1153	1966	**£4**	
Remember Garnett Mimms	7" EP	United Artists	REM403		**£4**	
Roll With The Punches	7"	United Artists	UP1181	1967	**£4**	
Tell Me Baby	7"	United Artists	UP1048	1964	**£4**	
We Can Find That Love	7"	Verve	VS574	1968	**£4**	

MIND EXPANDERS

What's Happening	LP	Dot	DLP25773	1967	**£20**	US, stereo
What's Happening	LP	Dot	DLP3773	1967	**£60**	US, mono

MINDBENDERS

Ashes To Ashes	7"	Fontana	TF731	1966	**£4**	chart single
Blessed Are The Lonely	7"	Fontana	TF910	1968	**£6**	
Can't Live With You	7"	Fontana	TF697	1966	**£4**	chart single
Groovy Kind Of Love	LP	Fontana	MGF27554	1966	**£15**	US
Groovy Kind Of Love	7"	Fontana	TF644	1966	**£4**	chart single
I Want Her, She Wants Me	7"	Fontana	TF780	1966	**£4**	
Letter	7"	Fontana	TF869	1967	**£4**	chart single
Mindbenders	LP	Fontana	SFL13045	1968	**£20**	
Mindbenders	LP	Fontana	TL5324	1966	**£20**	chart LP
Schoolgirl	7"	Fontana	TF877	1967	**£6**	
Uncle Joe The Ice Cream Man	7"	Fontana	TF961	1968	**£8**	
We'll Talk About It Tomorrow	7"	Fontana	TF806	1967	**£4**	
With Woman In Mind	LP	Fontana	STL5403	1967	**£20**	

MINEO, SAL

Aladdin	LP	Columbia	CL1117	1958	**£35**	US
Cutting In	7"	Fontana	H118	1958	**£5**	
Sal	LP	Epic	LN3405	1958	**£30**	US
Seven Steps To Love	7"	Fontana	H135	1958	**£5**	
Start Moving	7"	Philips	JK1024	1958	**£10**	chart single

MINIM

Wrapped In A Union Jack	LP	Polydor		1967	**£20**	

MINISTRY OF SOUND

White Collar Worker	7"	Decca	F12449	1966	**£8**	

MINOR THREAT

Filler	7"	Dischord	3	1981	**£60**	with insert
In My Eyes	7"	Dischord	5	1981	**£60**	red vinyl, with insert
Out Of Step	LP	Dischord		198-	**£30**	US

MINORBOPS

Need You Tonight	7"	Vogue	V9110	1958	**£30**	

MINOTAURUS

Fly Away	LP	private		1971	**£50**	
Rain Over Thessalia	LP	Thorofon		1970	**£50**	

MINT TATTOO

Mint Tattoo	LP	Dot	DLP25918	1969	**£12**	US

MIRACLES

Ain't It Baby	7"	London	HL9366	1961	**£40**	
Away We A Go Go	LP	T. Motown	STML11044	1967	**£25**	
Christmas With The Miracles	LP	Tamla	236	1963	**£100**	US
Come On Do The Jerk	7"	Stateside	SS377	1965	**£50**	demo
Come On Do The Jerk	7"	Stateside	SS377	1965	**£20**	
Cookin' With The Miracles	LP	Tamla	223	1962	**£100**	US
Doin' Mickey's Monkey	LP	Tamla	245	1963	**£50**	US, mono
Doin' Mickey's Monkey	LP	Tamla	T2245	1963	**£80**	US, stereo
Fabulous Miracles	LP	Stateside	SL10099	1964	**£40**	
From The Beginning	LP	T. Motown	TML11031	1966	**£25**	
Going To A Go-Go	LP	T. Motown	TML11024	1966	**£25**	
Going To A Go-Go	7"	T. Motown	TMG547	1966	**£8**	chart single

Title	Format	Label	Cat. No.	Year	Price	Notes
Going To A Go-Go	7"	T. Motown	TMG547	1966	**£50**	demo
Hi We're The Miracles	LP	Oriole	PS40044	1963	**£40**	
Hi We're The Miracles	LP	Tamla	220	1961	**£120**	US
I Gotta Dance To Keep From Crying	7"	Stateside	SS263	1964	**£20**	
I Gotta Dance To Keep From Crying	7"	Stateside	SS263	1964	**£50**	demo
I Like It Like That	7"	Stateside	SS324	1964	**£20**	
I Like It Like That	7"	Stateside	SS324	1964	**£50**	demo
I Like It Like That	LP	T. Motown	TML11003	1965	**£30**	
I'll Try Something New	LP	Tamla	230	1962	**£100**	US
I'm The One You Need	7"	T. Motown	TMG584	1966	**£6**	chart single
I'm The One You Need	7"	T. Motown	TMG584	1966	**£40**	demo
Man In You	7"	Stateside	SS282	1964	**£20**	
Man In You	7"	Stateside	SS282	1964	**£50**	demo
Mickey's Monkey	7"	Oriole	CBA1863	1963	**£40**	
My Girl Has Gone	7"	T. Motown	TMG540	1965	**£12**	
My Girl Has Gone	7"	T. Motown	TMG540	1965	**£60**	demo
On Stage	LP	Tamla	241	1963	**£50**	US
Ooh Baby Baby	7"	T. Motown	TMG503	1965	**£12**	
Ooh Baby Baby	7"	T. Motown	TMG503	1965	**£50**	demo
Shop Around	7"	London	HL9276	1961	**£40**	
Shop Around	7" EP	London	RE1295	1961	**£30**	
Shop Around	LP	Tamla	224	1962	**£100**	US
That's What Love Is Made Of	7"	Stateside	SS353	1964	**£20**	
That's What Love Is Made Of	7"	Stateside	SS353	1964	**£50**	demo
Tracks Of My Tears	7"	T. Motown	TMG522	1965	**£12**	
Tracks Of My Tears	7"	T. Motown	TMG522	1965	**£50**	demo
What's So Good About Goodbye	7"	Fontana	H384	1962	**£40**	
Whole Lotta Shakin' In My Heart	7"	T. Motown	TMG569	1966	**£10**	
Whole Lotta Shakin' In My Heart	7"	T. Motown	TMG569	1966	**£50**	demo
You've Really Got A Hold On Me	7"	Oriole	CBA1795	1963	**£40**	

MIRACLES & OTHERS

Title	Format	Label	Cat. No.	Year	Price	Notes
Nothing But A Man	LP	Motown	MT630	1965	**£15**	US

MIRAGE

Title	Format	Label	Cat. No.	Year	Price	Notes
Carolyn	7"	Page One	POF111	1969	**£4**	
Go Away	7"	CBS	202007	1965	**£4**	
Hold On	7"	Philips	BF1554	1967	**£5**	
It's In Her Kiss	7"	CBS	201772	1965	**£4**	
Mystery Lady	7"	Page One	POF078	1968	**£4**	
Tomorrow Never Knows	7"	Philips	BF1534	1966	**£5**	
Wedding Of Ramona Blair	7"	Philips	BF1571	1967	**£8**	

MIRAGE (2)

Title	Format	Label	Cat. No.	Year	Price	Notes
Mirage	LP	Compendium	FIDARDO9	1977	**£10**	

MIRETTES

Title	Format	Label	Cat. No.	Year	Price	Notes
Real Thing	7"	UNI	UN505	1968	**£4**	
To Love Somebody	7"	UNI	UN501	1968	**£4**	

MIRKWOOD

Title	Format	Label	Cat. No.	Year	Price	Notes
Mirkwood	LP	Flams Ltd		1971	**£800**	

MIRROR

Title	Format	Label	Cat. No.	Year	Price	Notes
Faster Than Light	7"	Philips	BF1666	1968	**£10**	

MISFITS

Title	Format	Label	Cat. No.	Year	Price	Notes
Beware	12"	Cherry Red	PLP9	1981	**£60**	
Horror Business	7"	Plan 9	PL1009	198-	**£60**	
Night Of The Living Dead	7"	Plan 9		1980	**£60**	

MISS LAVELL

Title	Format	Label	Cat. No.	Year	Price	Notes
Everybody's Got Somebody	7"	Vocalion	VP9236	1965	**£6**	

MISS X

Title	Format	Label	Cat. No.	Year	Price	Notes
Christine	7"	Ember	EMB175	1963	**£4**	chart single

MISSING SCIENTISTS

Title	Format	Label	Cat. No.	Year	Price	Notes
Big City Bright Lights	7"	Rough Trade	RT057	1980	**£10**	

MISSION

Title	Format	Label	Cat. No.	Year	Price	Notes
Garden Of Delight	12"	Chapter 22		1986	**£20**	promo

Title	Format	Label	Cat. No.	Year	Price	Notes
God's Own Medicine	LP	Mercury	MERH102	1986	£10	gatefold sleeve
Like A Hurricane	7"	Chapter 22	CHAP7	1986	£6	chart single
Like A Hurricane	12"	Chapter 22	12CHAP7	1986	£8	
Like A Hurricane	12"	Chapter 22	L12CHAP7	1986	£25	autographed
Serpents Kiss	7"	Chapter 22	CHAP6	1986	£6	chart single
Serpents Kiss	12"	Chapter 22	12CHAP6	1986	£8	
Severina	7"	Mercury	MYTHP3	1987	£5	with poster
Severina	12"	Mercury	MYTHL3	1987	£8	with poster
Severina	12"	Mercury	MYTHX3DJ	1987	£10	promo
Stay With Me (2 versions)	7"	Mercury	MYDJ1	1986	£6	promo
Stay With Me	7"	Mercury	MYSG1	1986	£8	autographed single, gatefold PS
Stay With Me	12"	Mercury	MYXDJ1	1986	£8	1 sided promo
Wasteland (Anniversay Mix)	12"	Mercury	MYTHX22	1987	£10	
Wasteland	7"	Mercury	MYTHB22	1987	£10	2 singles, 5 photos, boxed
Wasteland	12"	Mercury	MYTHX22DJ	1987	£10	promo with poster

MISUNDERSTOOD

Title	Format	Label	Cat. No.	Year	Price	Notes
Children Of The Sun	7"	Fontana	TF998	1969	£12	
I Can Take You To The Sun	7"	Fontana	TF777	1966	£15	
Never Had A Girl Like You	7"	Fontana	TF1041	1969	£20	
You're Tough Enough	7"	Fontana	TF1028	1969	£15	

MITCHELL, JONI

Title	Format	Label	Cat. No.	Year	Price	Notes
Chelsea Morning	7"	Reprise	RS23402	1969	£4	
Chinese Cafe	7"	Geffen	DA3122	1983	£4	with interview 7"
Clouds	LP	Reprise	RSLP6341	1969	£10	
Court And Spark	LP	Asylum	EQ10001	1974	£12	US quad
Court And Spark	LP	Nautilus	NR11	1981	£12	US audiophile
Hissing Of Summer Lawns	LP	Nimbus/Asylum	K53018	1982	£12	audiophile
Ladies Of The Canyon	LP	Reprise	RSLP6376	1970	£10	chart LP
Night In The City	7"	Reprise	RS20694	1968	£4	
Song To A Seagull	LP	Reprise	RSLP6293	1968	£10	
Wild Things Run Fast	LP	Geffen	GHS2019	1982	£25	US audiophile promo
You Turn Me On I'm A Radio	7"	Asylum	AYM511	1972	£6	

MITCHELL, PHILLIP

Title	Format	Label	Cat. No.	Year	Price	Notes
Free For All	7"	Jayboy	BOY57	1972	£5	

MITCHELL, WARREN & OTHERS

Title	Format	Label	Cat. No.	Year	Price	Notes
Till Death Us Do Part	LP	Pye	NPL18154	1966	£10	

MITCHELL, WILLIE

Title	Format	Label	Cat. No.	Year	Price	Notes
20-75	7"	London	HLU9926	1964	£5	
Bad Eye	7"	London	HLU10039	1966	£4	
Driving Beat	LP	Hi	HL32029	1966	£10	US
Everything Is Gonna Be Alright	7"	London	HLU10004	1965	£4	
Hit Sound Of Willie Mitchell	LP	Hi	HL32034	1967	£10	US
Hold It	LP	Hi	HL32021	1964	£10	US
It's Dance Time	LP	Hi	HL32026	1965	£10	US
Live	LP	London	SHU8368	1968	£10	
Mercy	7"	London	HLU10085	1966	£4	
On Top	LP	London	SHU8388	1969	£10	
Ooh Baby, You Turn Me On	LP	Hi	HL32039	1967	£10	US
Prayer Meetin'	7"	London	HLU10215	1968	£4	
Robin's Nest	7"	London	HLU10313	1970	£4	
Solid Soul	LP	London	SHU8372	1969	£10	
Soul Bag	LP	London	SHU8408	1970	£10	
Soul Serenade	LP	London	SHU8365	1968	£10	
Soul Serenade	7"	London	HLU10186	1968	£4	chart single
Sunrise Serenade	LP	Hi	HL32010	1963	£10	US
Up Hard	7"	London	HLU10224	1968	£4	
Young People	7"	London	HLU10282	1969	£4	

MITHRANDIR

Title	Format	Label	Cat. No.	Year	Price	Notes
For You The Old Women	LP	private		1976	£40	US

MITTOO, JACKIE

Title	Format	Label	Cat. No.	Year	Price	Notes
Ba Ba Boom	7"	Coxsone	CS7009	196-	£10	
Evening Time	LP	Coxsone	CSL8014	196-	£80	
In London	LP	Coxsone	CSL8009	196-	£80	
Keep On Dancing	LP	Coxsone	CSL8020	196-	£80	

Man Pon Spot	7"	Coxsone	CS7046	196-	**£10**	
Mission Impossible	7"	Coxsone	CS7075	196-	**£10**	
Napoleon Solo	7"	Coxsone	CS7050	196-	**£10**	
Norwegian Wood	7"	Coxsone	CS7040	196-	**£10**	
Ram Jam	7"	Coxsone	CS7019	196-	**£10**	
Somebody Help Me	7"	Coxsone	CS7002	196-	**£10**	
Somethin' Stupid	7"	Coxsone	CS7026	196-	**£10**	
Sure Shot	7"	Coxsone	CS7042	196-	**£10**	

MIXED BAG

Potiphar	7"	Decca	F12880	1969	**£4**	
Round And Round	7"	Decca	F12907	1969	**£4**	

MIXTURE

One By One	7"	Fontana	TF640	1965	**£4**	

MIXTURES

Stompin' At The Rainbow	LP	Linda	3301	1962	**£20**	US

MIXTURES (2)

Mixtures	LP	Polydor		1971	**£10**	

MJ6

Private Eye	7"	Decca	F11212	1960	**£4**	

MO-DETTES

Paint It Black	7"	Deram	DETR1	1980	**£4**	with flexi & photo
White Mice	7"	Mode	MODE1	1979	**£4**	

MOB

Mirror Breaks	7"	All T.Madmen	MAD6	1981	**£4**	
Witch Hunt	7"	All T.Madmen	MAD2	1980	**£4**	

MOBY GRAPE

When Columbia records in America decided to try the marketing device of simultaneously releasing every track from Moby Grape's first LP as a single, this was certainly recognition of the fact that every track is distinctive enough to withstand the treatment. The LP is frequently held up as San Francisco's best, an assessment that is not far from the truth. Thereafter, Moby Grape's career was one of decline, although "Wow" has its moments. The "Grape Jam" record that accompanied the US release is a wasted opportunity, however. Acquiring the services of a master guitarist like Mike Bloomfield and then sitting him in front of a piano is simply daft.

20 Granite Creek	LP	Reprise	K44152	1972	**£10**	
Can't Be So Bad	7"	CBS	3555	1968	**£6**	
Great Grape	LP	CBS	64743	1974	**£10**	
Moby Grape	LP	CBS	63090	1967	**£15**	
Moby Grape	LP	S.F. Sound	04805	1983	**£12**	US audiophile
Moby Grape '69	LP	CBS	63430	1969	**£10**	
Omaha	7"	CBS	2935	1967	**£10**	
Trucking Man	7"	CBS	3945	1969	**£8**	
Truly Fine Citizen	LP	CBS	63698	1970	**£10**	
Wow	LP	CBS	63271	1968	**£12**	
Wow/Grape Jam	LP	Columbia	CS9613	1968	**£20**	US double
Wow/Grape Jam	LP	S.F. Sound	04801	1983	**£20**	US audiophile double

MOCKINGBIRDS

How To Find A Lover	7"	Decca	F12510	1966	**£10**	
I Can Feel We're Parting	7"	Columbia	DB7565	1965	**£12**	
One By One	7"	Decca	F12434	1966	**£10**	
That's How It's Gonna Stay	7"	Columbia	DB7480	1965	**£12**	
You Stole My Love	7"	Immediate	IM015	1965	**£20**	

MODELS

Freeze	7"	Step Forward	SF3	1977	**£5**	

MODERN ENGLISH

Chapter Twelve	7"	4AD	AD401	1984	**£4**	
Drowning Man	7"	Limp	LMP2	1979	**£15**	
Gathering Dust	7"	4AD	AD15	1980	**£6**	
I Melt With You	7"	4AD	AD212	1982	**£5**	
Life In The Gladhouse	7"	4AD	AD208	1982	**£5**	
Smiles And Laughter	7"	4AD	AD110	1981	**£6**	
Someone's Calling	7"	4AD	AD309	1983	**£4**	
Swans On Glass	7"	4AD	AD6	1980	**£8**	

MODERN EON

Child's Play	7"	Dindisc	DIN31	1981	**£4**	
Euthenics	7"	Dindisc	DIN30	1981	**£4**	
Euthenics	7"	Inevitable	INEV003	1981	**£8**	
Fiction Tales	LP	Dindisc	DID11	1981	**£10**	
Mechanic	7"	Dindisc	DIN35	1981	**£4**	
Pieces	7"	Modern Eon	EON001	1980	**£20**	

MODERN FOLK QUARTET

Changes	LP	W. Bros	W1546	1964	**£10**	US
Love Of A Clown	7"	W. Bros	WB147	1964	**£4**	
MFQ	LP	W. Bros	W1511	1963	**£10**	US
Night Time Girl	7"	RCA	RCA1514	1966	**£4**	

MODERN FOLK QUARTET & CONNIE STEVENS

Palm Springs Weekend	LP	W. Bros	W1519	1963	**£12**	US

MODERN JAZZ QUARTET

Space	LP	Apple	SAPCOR10	1969	**£25**	
Under The Jasmine Tree	LP	Apple	APCOR4	1968	**£35**	mono
Under The Jasmine Tree	LP	Apple	SAPCOR4	1968	**£20**	stereo

MODS

Something On My Mind	7"	RCA	RCA1399	1964	**£4**	

MOGUL THRASH

Mogul Thrash	LP	RCA	SF8156	1971	**£15**	
Sleeping In The Kitchen	7"	RCA	RCA2030	1970	**£5**	

MOHAWKS

The Champ	7"	Pama	PM719	196-	**£8**	

MOJO HANNAH

Six Days On The Road	LP	Kingdom	KVL9001	1972	**£10**	

MOJO MEN

Dance With Me	7"	Pye	7N25336	1965	**£8**	
Hanky Panky	7"	Reprise	RS20486	1966	**£8**	
Me About You	7"	Reprise	RS20580	1967	**£8**	
Sit Down I Think I Love You	7"	Reprise	RS20539	1967	**£8**	

MOJOS

Comin' On To Cry	7"	Decca	F12127	1965	**£8**	
Everything's Alright	7"	Decca	F11853	1964	**£4**	chart single
Forever	7"	Decca	F11732	1963	**£6**	
Goodbye Dolly Gray	7"	Decca	F12557	1967	**£10**	
Mojos	7" EP	Decca	DFE8591	1964	**£15**	
Seven Daffodils	7"	Decca	F11959	1964	**£5**	chart single
Until My Baby Comes Home	7"	Liberty	LBF15097	1968	**£10**	
Wait A Minute	7"	Decca	F12231	1965	**£15**	
Why Not Tonight	7"	Decca	F11918	1964	**£5**	chart single

MOLES

Noting that the Moles' single was on the Parlophone label, and that it had moreover been produced by George Martin, many observers concluded that it must be a Beatles performance. In fact, "the Moles" was indeed a pseudonym, but for the rather less exciting Simon Dupree And The Big Sound.

We Are The Moles	7"	Parlophone	R5743	1968	**£20**	

MOLLY HATCHET

Flirtin' With Disaster	LP	CBS	AL36110	1979	**£25**	US pic disc
Molly Hatchet	LP	Epic	35347	1978	**£25**	US pic disc

MOLOCH

Moloch	LP	Enterprise	ENS1002		**£25**	US

MOM'S APPLE PIE

Mom's Apple Pie	LP	Brown Bag	14200	1973	**£12**	US, vagina in pie on cover

MOMENTS

Sexy Mama	7"	London	HLU10449	1974	**£5**	

MONARCHS

Look Homeward Angel	7"	London	HLU9862	1964	**£4**	

MONDAY, PAUL

Here Comes The Sun	7"	MCA	MK5008	1969	**£8**	

MONEY

Breaking Of Her Heart	7"	Major Minor	MM669	1970	**£4**	
Come Laughing Home	7"	Major Minor	MM620	1969	**£5**	
First Investment	LP	Gull	GULP1031	1979	**£10**	

MONEY, ZOOT

Big Time Operator	7"	Columbia	DB7975	1966	**£8**	chart single
Big Time Operator	7" EP	Columbia	SEG8519	1966	**£20**	
Good	7"	Columbia	DB7518	1965	**£15**	
It Should Have Been Me	LP	Columbia	SX1734	1965	**£40**	
Let's Run For Cover	7"	Columbia	DB7876	1966	**£10**	
Nick Nack	7"	Columbia	DB8172	1967	**£12**	
No One But You	7"	Polydor	2058020	1970	**£6**	
Please Stay	7"	Columbia	DB7600	1965	**£10**	
Something Is Worrying Me	7"	Columbia	DB7697	1965	**£12**	
Star Of the Show	7"	Columbia	DB8090	1966	**£12**	
Transition	LP	Direction	863231	1968	**£20**	
Uncle Willie	7"	Decca	F11954	1964	**£12**	
Welcome To My Head	LP	Capitol	318	1969	**£15**	US
Zoot	LP	Columbia	SCX6075	1966	**£25**	chart LP
Zoot Money	LP	Polydor	2482019	1970	**£15**	

MONGREL

Get Your Teeth Into This	LP	Polydor	2383182	1973	**£10**	

MONGRELS

I Long To Hear	7"	Decca	F12003	1964	**£15**	
My Love For You	7"	Decca	F12086	1965	**£15**	

MONITORS

Greetings We're The Monitors	LP	T. Motown	STML11108	1969	**£40**	

MONKEES

Alternate Title	7"	RCA	RCA1604	1967	**£4**	chart single
Barrel Full Of Monkees	LP	Colgems	SCOS1001	1971	**£15**	US
Birds, The Bees And The Monkees	LP	RCA	RD7948	1968	**£10**	
Changes	LP	Colgems	COS119	1970	**£20**	US
D.W.Washburn	7"	RCA	RCA1706	1968	**£4**	chart single
Daydream Believer	7"	RCA	RCA1645	1967	**£4**	chart single
Golden Hits	LP	RCA	PRS329	1972	**£10**	US
Good Clean Fun	7"	RCA	RCA1887	1969	**£6**	
Greatest Hits	LP	Colgems	COS115	1969	**£15**	US
Head	LP	RCA	SF8015	1969	**£30**	
Headquarters	LP	Colgems	COM103	1967	**£15**	US, photo of 2 bearded Monkees
Headquarters	LP	RCA	RD7886	1967	**£10**	chart LP
I'm A Believer	7"	RCA	RCA1560	1966	**£4**	chart single
Instant Replay	LP	RCA	SF8016	1969	**£15**	
Last Train To Clarksville	7"	RCA	RCA1547	1966	**£4**	chart single
Listen To The Band	7"	RCA	RCA1824	1969	**£4**	
Little Bit Me, A Little Bit You	7"	RCA	RCA1580	1967	**£4**	chart single
Monkees	LP	RCA	RD7844	1967	**£10**	chart LP
Monkees Present	LP	Colgems	COS117	1969	**£20**	US
More Of The Monkees	LP	RCA	RD7868	1967	**£10**	chart LP
Oh My My	7"	RCA	RCA1958	1970	**£6**	
Pisces, Aquarius, Capricorn And Jones	LP	RCA	RD7912	1967	**£10**	chart LP
Pleasant Valley Sunday	7"	RCA	RCA1620	1967	**£4**	chart single
Porpoise Song	7"	RCA	RCA1862	1969	**£6**	
Re-Focus	LP	Bell	6081	1973	**£10**	US
Teardrop City	7"	RCA	RCA1802	1969	**£4**	chart single
Tema Dei Monkees	7"	RCA	1546	1967	**£15**	sung in Italian
Valleri	7"	RCA	RCA1679	1968	**£4**	chart single

MONOCHROME SET

Eine Symphonie Des Grauens	7"	Rough Trade	RT019	1979	**£4**	

He's Frank (Slight Return)	7"	Disque Bleu	BL1	1979	**£4**	
He's Frank	7"	Rough Trade	RT005	1979	**£4**	
Monochrome Set	7"	Rough Trade	RT028	1979	**£4**	

MONOPOLY

House Of Lords	7"	Polydor	56164	1967	**£5**	
We're All Going To The Seaside	7"	Polydor	56188	1967	**£5**	

MONOTONES

Book Of Love	7"	London	HLM8625	1958	**£20**	
It's Great	7"	Pye	7N15640	1964	**£5**	
No Waiting	7"	Pye	7N15761	1965	**£5**	
Something's Hurting Me	7"	Pye	7N15814	1965	**£5**	
What Would I Do	7"	Pye	7N15608	1964	**£5**	

MONROE BROTHERS

Country Guitar Vol.14	7" EP	RCA	RCX7103	1963	**£5**	
Country Guitar Vol.15	7" EP	RCA	RCX7104	1963	**£5**	

MONROE BROTHERS & BILL MONROE

Country Guitar Vol.16	7" EP	RCA	RCX7105	1963	**£5**	

MONROE, BILL

Blue Ridge Mountain Blues	7"	Brunswick	05960	1966	**£4**	
Bluegrass Ramble	LP	Decca	DL4266	1962	**£10**	US
Bluegrass Special	LP	Decca	DL4382	1963	**£10**	US
Country Date	7" EP	Brunswick	OE9160	1955	**£5**	
Country Waltz	7" EP	Brunswick	OE9195	1955	**£5**	
Early Bluegrass	LP	Camden	CAL774	1963	**£10**	US
Father Of Bluegrass Music	LP	Camden	CAL719	1962	**£10**	US
Four Walls	7"	Brunswick	05681	1957	**£4**	
Gotta Travel On	7"	Brunswick	05776	1959	**£4**	
Great Bill Monroe	LP	Harmony	HL7290	1961	**£10**	US
I Saw The Light	LP	Decca	DL8769	1959	**£15**	US
Knee Deep In Bluegrass	LP	Decca	DL8731	1958	**£15**	US
Mr.Bluegrass	LP	Decca	DL4080	1960	**£15**	US
My All Time Country Favorites	LP	Decca	DL4327	1962	**£10**	US
New John Henry Blues	7"	Brunswick	05567	1956	**£4**	

MONTCLAIRS

Hung Up On Your Love	7"	Contempo	CS2036	1975	**£8**	

MONTE CAZZA

Something For Nobody	7"	Industrial	IR0010	1980	**£10**	
To Mom On Mothers Day	7"	Industrial	IR0005	1979	**£20**	

MONTE, LOU

Lazy Mary	7"	RCA	RCA1048	1958	**£4**	

MONTE, VINNIE

Summer Spree	7"	London	HL8947	1959	**£4**	

MONTEZ, CHRIS

Foolin' Around	LP	A&M	AML906	1967	**£10**	
Let's Dance	LP	London	HAU8079	1963	**£15**	
Let's Dance	7"	London	HLU9596	1962	**£5**	chart single
Let's Dance	7" EP	London	REU1392	1963	**£8**	
Let's Dance And Have Some Kinda Fun!	LP	Monogram	M100	1963	**£35**	US
More I See You	LP	Pye	NPL23080	1966	**£10**	
More I See You	7"	Pye	7N25369	1966	**£4**	chart single
More I See You	7" EP	Pye	NEP44071	1966	**£5**	
My Baby Loves To Dance	7"	London	HLU9764	1963	**£4**	
Some Kinda Fun	7"	London	HLU9650	1963	**£4**	chart single
Time After Time	LP	Pye	NSPL28187	1967	**£10**	
Watch What Happens	LP	A&M	AML925	1968	**£10**	

MONTGOMERY, LITTLE BROTHER

Little Brother Montgomery	LP	Columbia	33SX1289	1960	**£20**	
Little Brother Montgomery	LP	Decca	LK4664	1965	**£15**	
Pinetop's Boogie Woogie	7"	Columbia	DB4595	1961	**£6**	

MONTY & ROY & DRUMBAGO ORCHESTRA

Tra La La Boogie	7"	Blue Beat	BB61	1961	**£10**	

MONTY PYTHON

Brian	7"	W. Bros	K17495PRO	1980	**£6**	bleeped promo
Contractual Obligations Album	LP	Charisma	CAS1152	1981	**£10**	with 'Farewell To John Denver'
Live At The City Center, April 1976	LP	Arista	AL4073	1976	**£10**	US
Python On Song	7"	Charisma	MP001	1975	**£6**	double

MONUMENT

First Monument	LP	Beacon	BEAS15	1971	**£50**	

MOOCHE

Hot Smoke And Sasafrass	7"	Pye	7N17735	1969	**£20**	

MOOD MOSAIC

Chinese Chequers	7"	Columbia	DB8149	1967	**£4**	
Touch Of Velvet	7"	Columbia	DB7801	1966	**£4**	
Touch Of Velvet, A Sting Of Brass	7"	Columbia	DB8618	1969	**£4**	
Yellow Spotted Capricorn	7"	Parlophone	R5716	1968	**£4**	

MOODS

Duckwalk	7"	Starlite	ST45098	1963	**£6**	

MOODY BLUES

Boulevard De La Madelaine	7"	Decca	F12498	1966	**£4**	
Days Of Future Passed	LP	Deram	DML707	1968	**£10**	mono, chart LP
Days Of Future Passed	LP	Mobile Fid	MFSL1042	1980	**£15**	US audiophile
Everyday	7"	Decca	F12266	1965	**£4**	chart single
Fly Me High	7"	Decca	F12607	1967	**£10**	
From The Bottom Of My Heart	7"	Decca	F12166	1965	**£4**	chart single
Go Now	7"	Decca	F12022	1964	**£4**	chart single
I Don't Want To Go On Without You	7"	Decca	F12095	1965	**£4**	chart single
In Search Of The Lost Chord	LP	Deram	DML717	1968	**£10**	mono, chart LP
Life's Not Life	7"	Decca	F12543	1967	**£30**	
Lose Your Money	7"	Decca	F11971	1964	**£6**	
Love And Beauty	7"	Decca	F12670	1967	**£10**	
Magnificent Moodies	LP	Decca	LK4711	1966	**£10**	
Moody Blues	7" EP	Decca	DFE8622	1965	**£10**	
Never Comes The Day	7"	Deram	DM247	1969	**£4**	
On The Threshold Of A Dream	LP	Deram	DML1035	1968	**£10**	mono, chart LP
On The Threshold Of A Dream	LP	Nautilus	NR21	1981	**£15**	US audiophile
Ride My See-Saw	7"	Deram	DM213	1968	**£4**	chart single
Seventh Sojourn	LP	Mobile Fid	MFSL1151	1984	**£12**	US audiophile
Talking Out Of Turn	7"	Threshold	THPD29	1981	**£5**	pic disc
To Our Children's Children's Children	LP	Threshold	THM1	1969	**£12**	mono, chart LP
Voices In The Sky	7"	Deram	DM196	1968	**£4**	chart single
Watching And Waiting	7"	Threshold	TH1	1969	**£4**	

MOON

Pirate	7"	Liberty	LBF15333	1970	**£4**	
Someday Girl	7"	Liberty	LIB15076	1968	**£5**	
Without Earth	LP	Liberty	LBL83146	1968	**£12**	

MOON'S TRAIN

Deed I Do	7"	MGM	MGM1333	1967	**£8**	

MOON, KEITH

Don't Worry Baby	7"	Polydor	2058584	1975	**£4**	
Two Sides Of The Moon	LP	Polydor	2442134	1975	**£15**	

MOONDOG

H'art Songs	LP	Kopf	RRF33016		**£15**	German
Moondog	LP	CBS	63906	1969	**£20**	
Moondog 2	LP	CBS	30897	1971	**£20**	US
Moondog In Europe	LP	Kopf	RRF33014		**£15**	German
On The Streets Of New York	7" EP	London	REP1010	1954	**£15**	

MOONDOGS

Ya Don't Do Ya	7"	Good Vibs	GOT10	1979	**£5**	

MOONGLOWS

Title	Format	Label	Number	Year	Price	Notes
Best Of Bobby Lester & The Moonglows	LP	Chess	LP1471	1962	**£50**	US
Collectors Showcase	LP	Constellation	CS2	1964	**£15**	US
I Knew From The Start	7"	London	HLN8374	1957	**£100**	
Look It's The Moonglows	LP	Chess	LP1430	1958	**£75**	US
Return Of The Moonglows	LP	RCA	LSP4722	1972	**£10**	US

MOONKYTE

Title	Format	Label	Number	Year	Price	Notes
Count Me Out	LP	Mother	SMOT1	1971	**£80**	

MOONSHINE, MICKEY

Title	Format	Label	Number	Year	Price	Notes
Baby Blue	7"	Decca	F13555	1974	**£4**	

MOONTREKKERS

Title	Format	Label	Number	Year	Price	Notes
Moondust	7"	Decca	F11714	1963	**£5**	
Night Of The Vampire	7"	Parlophone	R4814	1961	**£5**	chart single
There's Something At The Bottom	7"	Parlophone	R4888	1962	**£5**	

MOORCOCK, MICHAEL

Title	Format	Label	Number	Year	Price	Notes
Dodgem Dude	7"	Flicknife	FLEP200	1982	**£4**	

MOORCOCK, MICHAEL & DEEP FIX

Title	Format	Label	Number	Year	Price	Notes
New World's Fair	LP	United Artists	UAG29732	1975	**£40**	

MOORE, ADA & JIMMY RUSHING

Title	Format	Label	Number	Year	Price	Notes
Cat Meets Chick	7" EP	Philips	BBE12150	1957	**£5**	

MOORE, ANTHONY

Title	Format	Label	Number	Year	Price	Notes
Pieces From The Cloudland Ballroom	LP	Polydor	2310162	1971	**£20**	
Secrets Of The Blue Bag	LP	Polydor	2310179	1972	**£20**	

MOORE, BOB

Title	Format	Label	Number	Year	Price	Notes
Viva	LP	Hickory		1968	**£40**	US

MOORE, BOBBY

Title	Format	Label	Number	Year	Price	Notes
Searching For My Love	7"	Chess	CRS8033	1966	**£5**	

MOORE, GARY

Title	Format	Label	Number	Year	Price	Notes
Always Gonna Love You	7"	Virgin	VSY528	1982	**£4**	pic disc
Empty Rooms	12"	10	TEN2512	1984	**£6**	double
Falling In Love With You	7"	Virgin	VSY564	1983	**£4**	pic disc
Friday On My Mind	7"	10	TENP164	1987	**£4**	pic disc
G-Force	LP	Jet	JETLP229	1980	**£10**	pic disc
Grinding Stone	LP	Columbia	65527	1973	**£10**	
Hold On To Your Love	7"	10	TENS13	1984	**£10**	shaped pic disc
Over The Hills And Far Away	7"	10	TENS134	1986	**£6**	shaped pic disc
Run For Cover	LP	10	DIXP16	1985	**£10**	pic disc
Shapes Of Things	7"	10	TENS19	1984	**£10**	shaped pic disc

MOORE, GARY & PHIL LYNOTT

Title	Format	Label	Number	Year	Price	Notes
Out In The Fields	7"	10	TENS49	1985	**£15**	shaped pic disc
Out In The Fields	12"	10		1985	**£8**	1 sided promo

MOORE, GATEMOUTH

Title	Format	Label	Number	Year	Price	Notes
I'm A Fool To Care	LP	King	684	1960	**£300**	US

MOORE, MERRILL

Title	Format	Label	Number	Year	Price	Notes
Hard Top Race	7"	Capitol	CL14369	1955	**£50**	
Sweet Mama	7"	B&C	CB100	1969	**£5**	
Tree Top Tall	LP	B&C	CAS1001	1969	**£10**	

MOORE, R.STEVIE

R.Stevie Moore is one of rock music's eccentrics, preferring to issue his records through his own mail order scheme than to tangle with record companies who would doubtless attempt to compromise Moore's quirky approach. The original issue of his first album, "Phonography", was produced in an edition of just ninety-nine copies and long ago sold out. Frank Zappa has one, and so does UK collector Michael Gerzon, whose copy is likely to be the only one in the country.

Title	Format	Label	Number	Year	Price	Notes
Phonography	LP	private	US0001	1976	**£200**	US

MOORE, SCOTTY

Title	Format	Label	Number	Year	Price	Notes
Guitar That Changed The World	LP	Epic	LN24103	1964	**£30**	US

MOORE, SHELLEY

Where Is The Bluebird	7"	Starlite	ST45003	1958	**£4**	
You've Tied Me Up	7"	Starlite	ST45002	1958	**£4**	

MOORS MURDERERS

The Moors Murderers, a punk group of which Steve Strange And Chrissie Hynde were both members, were supposed to have released a single called "Free Myra Hindley". Although acetates have turned up, however, it seems unlikely that regular vinyl copies exist.

Free Myra Hindley	7"	Pop Corn		1978	**£1000**	existence doubtful

MOPED, JOHNNY

Basically The Original Johnny Moped	7"	Chiswick	PROMO3	1976	**£12**	promo
Darling Let's Have Another Baby	7"	Chiswick	NS27	1978	**£4**	
Little Queenie	7"	Chiswick	NS41	1978	**£4**	
No One	7"	Chiswick	S15	1977	**£5**	

MOPEDS

Whiskey And Soda	7"	Columbia	DB108	1968	**£8**	

MOQUETTES

Right String But Wrong Yo Yo	7"	Columbia	DB7315	1964	**£8**	

MORECAMBE & WISE

Bring Me Sunshine	7"	Columbia	DB8646	1969	**£4**	
Bring Me Sunshine	7"	Columbia	DB8753	1971	**£4**	

MORGAN

Nova Solis	LP	RCA		1972	**£25**	

MORGAN TWINS

Let's Get Going	7"	RCA	RCA1083	1958	**£12**	

MORGAN, DAVY

Tomorrow I'll Be Gone	7"	Columbia	DB7624	1965	**£8**	
True To Life	7"	Parlophone	R5692	1968	**£10**	

MORGAN, DERRICK

...And His Friends	LP	Island	ILP990	1969	**£50**	
Amelita	7"	Island	WI289	1966	**£10**	
Angel With Blue Eyes	7"	Island	WI080	1963	**£10**	
Are You Going To Marry Me? (Derrick And Patsy)	7"	Blue Beat	BB110	1962	**£10**	
Baby Please Don't Leave Me (Derrick And Patsy)	7"	Blue Beat	BB65	1961	**£10**	
Be Still	7"	Blue Beat	BB76	1961	**£10**	
Blazing Fire	7"	Island	WI051	1962	**£10**	
Call My Name (Derrick And Patsy)	7"	Blue Beat	BB171	1963	**£10**	
Cherry Home	7"	Island	WI013	1962	**£10**	
Cherry Pie	7"	Black Swan	WI425	1964	**£10**	
Come Back My Love	7"	Blue Beat	BB121	1962	**£10**	
Come On Over	7"	Blue Beat	BB85	1961	**£10**	
Conquering Ruler	7"	Island	WI3094	1967	**£10**	
Contented Wife	7"	Blue Beat	BB261	1964	**£10**	
Do The Beng Beng	7"	Pyramid	PYR6025	1968	**£10**	
Don't Cry	7"	Blue Beat	BB12	1961	**£10**	
Don't You Know Little Girl (Derrick & Basil)	7"	Blue Beat	BB82	1961	**£10**	
Eternity (Derrick And Patsy)	7"	Blue Beat	BB318	1964	**£10**	
Fat Man	7"	Blue Beat	BB7	1961	**£10**	
Feel So Fine (Derrick And Patsy And Drumbago)	7"	Blue Beat	BB57	1961	**£10**	
Forward March	LP	Island	ILP903	1963	**£60**	
Forward March	LP	Trojan	TTL38	197-	**£10**	
Gather Together	7"	Island	WI3010	1966	**£10**	
Gimme Back	7"	Island	WI3101	1967	**£10**	
Heart Of Stone (With Naomi And Baba Brooks)	7"	Ska Beat	JB185	1965	**£10**	
Hey Little Girl	7"	Downtown	DTS520	1973	**£4**	
Hold You Jack	7"	Island	WI3159	1968	**£10**	
Hop	7"	Island	WI006	1962	**£10**	
Housewive's Choice (Derrick & Patsy)	7"	Island	WI018	1962	**£10**	
I Found A Queen	7"	Island	WI288	1966	**£10**	

I Who Have Nothing	7"	Bread	BR1119	1973	**£4**	
I Wish I Were An Apple (With Naomi)	7"	Ska Beat	JB188	1965	**£10**	
In London	LP	Pama	ECO10	1969	**£20**	
In My Heart	7"	Blue Beat	BB100	1962	**£10**	
It's Alright	7"	Island	WI277	1966	**£10**	
Jezebel	7"	Blue Beat	BB148	1962	**£10**	
Johnny Grove	7"	Blue Beat	BB283	1964	**£10**	
Joybells (With Duke Reid)	7"	Blue Beat	BB141	1962	**£10**	
Katy Katy	7"	Blue Beat	BB268	1964	**£10**	
Kill Me Dead	7"	Pyramid		196-	**£8**	
Leave Earth	7"	Blue Beat	BB35	1961	**£10**	
Leave Her Alone	7"	Island	WI037	1962	**£10**	
Little Brown Jug (Derrick And Patsy)	7"	Blue Beat	BB152	1962	**£10**	
Look Before You Leap (Derrick & Patsy)	7"	Island	WI055	1962	**£10**	
Love And Leave Me (Derrick And Lloyd Clarke)	7"	Blue Beat	BB135	1962	**£10**	
Love Not To Brag (Derrick And Patsy And Drumbago)	7"	Blue Beat	BB97	1962	**£10**	
Lover Boy (Derrick And Patsy)	7"	Blue Beat	BB207	1963	**£10**	
Lover Man	7"	Blue Beat	BB18	1961	**£10**	
Meekly Wait (Derrick And Yvonne)	7"	Blue Beat	BB94	1961	**£10**	
Millie Girl	7"	Blue Beat	BB91	1961	**£10**	
Miss Lulu (Derrick And Patsy)	7"	Blue Beat	BB239	1963	**£10**	
Moon Hop	7"	Crab	21	1970	**£4**	chart single
National Dance (Derrick And Patsy)	7"	Island	WI224	1965	**£10**	
No Raise, No Praise	7"	Island	WI053	1962	**£10**	
Now We Know	7"	Blue Beat	BB31	1961	**£10**	
Oh My Love (Derrick And Patsy)	7"	Blue Beat	BB123	1962	**£10**	
Oh Shirley (Derrick & Patsy & Basil)	7"	Blue Beat	BB106	1962	**£10**	
Patricia My Dear	7"	Blue Beat	BB177	1963	**£10**	
Please Don't Talk About Me (with Eric Morris)	7"	Island	WI011	1962	**£10**	
Shake A Leg (Derrick And Drumbago)	7"	Blue Beat	BB62	1961	**£10**	
Should Be Ashamed	7"	Blue Beat	BB130	1962	**£10**	
Someone	7"	Island	WI3079	1967	**£10**	
Steal Away (Derrick And Patsy)	7"	Blue Beat	BB224	1963	**£10**	
Street Girl	7"	Black Swan	WI402	1964	**£10**	
Sweeter Than Honey	7"	Blue Beat	BB329	1965	**£10**	
Tears On My Pillow	7"	Blue Beat	BB187	1963	**£10**	
Telephone	7"	Blue Beat	BB196	1963	**£10**	
Throw Them Away	7"	Blue Beat	BB311	1964	**£10**	
Times Are Going (Martin And Derrick)	7"	Blue Beat	BB48	1961	**£10**	
Travel On	7"	Island	WI004	1962	**£10**	
Troubles (Derrick And Patsy)	7"	Blue Beat	BB247	1964	**£10**	
Trying To Make You Mine	7"	Blue Beat	BB160	1962	**£10**	
Weep No More	7"	Blue Beat	BB276	1964	**£10**	
You I Love (Derrick And Patsy)	7"	Blue Beat	BB291	1964	**£10**	

MORGAN, JANE

All The Way Part 1	7" EP	London	RER1161	1958	**£5**	
All The Way Part 2	7" EP	London	RER1162	1958	**£5**	
Around The World	7"	London	HLR8436	1957	**£4**	
Day The Rains Came	LP	Kapp	KL1105	1958	**£10**	US
Day The Rains Came	7" EP	London	RER1204	1959	**£5**	
Day The Rains Came	7"	London	HLR8751	1958	**£4**	chart single
Fascination	LP	Kapp	KL1066	1957	**£10**	US
Fascination	7"	London	HLR8468	1957	**£4**	
From The First Hello	7"	London	HLR8395	1957	**£6**	
Jane In Spain	LP	Kapp	KL1129	1959	**£10**	US
Jane Morgan	LP	Kapp	KL1023	195-	**£10**	US
Jane Morgan	LP	Kapp	KL1098	1958	**£10**	US
Jane Morgan	7" EP	London	RER1331	1961	**£4**	
Why Oh Why	7"	London	HL8148	1955	**£8**	

MORGAN, JAYE P.

Have You Ever Been Lonely	7"	Brunswick	05519	1956	**£4**	
Jaye P Sings	7" EP	London	REP1013	1954	**£8**	

MORGAN, MACE THUNDERBIRDS

Shake And Swing	7" EP	Starlite	STEP36	196-	**£8**	

MORGEN

Morgen	LP	Probe	CPLP4507	1969	**£30**	US

MORIN, RON PAUL

Peaceful Company	LP	Sovereign	SVNA7252	1972	**£25**	

MORLY GREY

Only Truth	LP	Starshine		1969	**£40**	US

MORMOS

Mormos	LP	CBS			**£25**	

MORNETTE, JOHNNY

Meet Me At The Twisting Place	7"	Stateside	SS107	1962	**£4**	

MORNING

Morning	LP	Liberty	LBS83463	1970	**£12**	
Struck Like Silver	LP	United Artists	UAS29337	1974	**£10**	

MORNING DEW

Morning Dew	LP	Roulette	R41045	1967	**£20**	US

MORNING GLORY

Morning Glory	LP	Island	ILPS9237	1973	**£15**	

MORRIS & MITCH

Cumberland Gap	7"	Decca	F10900	1957	**£4**	
Highway Patrol	7"	Decca	F11086	1958	**£4**	
Six Five Nothing Special	7" EP	Decca	DFE6486	1958	**£8**	
What Is A Skiffler?	7"	Decca	F10929	1957	**£4**	

MORRIS, ERIC

Children Of Today	7"	Island	WI234	1965	**£10**	
Fast Mouth	7"	Island	WI199	1965	**£10**	
G.I. Lady	7"	Blue Beat	BB115	1962	**£10**	
Home Sweet Home	7"	Black Swan	WI445	1965	**£10**	
Humpty Dumpty	7"	Blue Beat	BB53	1961	**£10**	
Lonely Blue Boy	7"	Blue Beat	BB153	1962	**£10**	
Love Can Make A Mansion	7"	Island	WI183	1965	**£10**	
Mama No Fret	7"	Island	WI147	1964	**£10**	
Miss Peggy's Grandmother	7"	Blue Beat	BB137	1962	**£10**	
Money Can't Buy Life	7"	Blue Beat	BB83	1961	**£10**	
My Forty-Five	7"	Blue Beat	BB74	1961	**£10**	
Over The Hills	7"	Blue Beat	BB128	1962	**£10**	
Penny Reel	7"	Island	WI142	1964	**£10**	
River Come Down	7"	Black Swan	WI439	1964	**£10**	
Search The World	7"	Starlite	ST45052	1961	**£10**	
Seven Long Years	7"	Blue Beat	BB140	1962	**£10**	
Sinners Repent And Pray	7"	Blue Beat	BB81	1961	**£10**	
So You Shot Reds	7"	Blue Beat	BB193	1963	**£10**	
Solomon Grundie	7"	Black Swan	WI414	1964	**£10**	
Stitch In Time	7"	Blue Beat	BB273	1964	**£10**	
Supper In The Gutter	7"	Black Swan	WI433	1964	**£10**	
What A Man Doeth	7"	Island	WI151	1964	**£10**	

MORRIS, HEMLEY

Little Things	7"	Jolly	JY7	196-	**£8**	

MORRIS, ROGER

First Album	LP	Regal Z.	SRZA8509	1972	**£10**	

MORRISON, CURLEY JIM

Air Force Blues	7"	Starlite	ST45065	1961	**£15**	

MORRISON, VAN

Astral Weeks	LP	W. Bros	WS1768	1968	**£10**	
Blowin' Your Mind	LP	London	HA8346	1967	**£15**	
Blowin' Your Mind	LP	London	HAZ8346	1967	**£12**	
Brown Eyed Girl	7"	London	HLM10453	1974	**£4**	
Brown Eyed Girl	7"	London	HLZ10150	1967	**£8**	
Caldonia	7"	W. Bros	K16392	1974	**£6**	
Come Running	7"	W. Bros	WB7383	1970	**£4**	

Domino	7"	W. Bros	WB7434	1970	**£4**	
Dweller On The Threshold	7"	Mercury	MERDJ99	1982	**£4**	promo
His Band And Street Choir	LP	W. Bros	WS1884	1970	**£10**	
Jackie Wilson Said	7"	W. Bros	K16210	1972	**£6**	
Joyous Sound	7"	W. Bros	K16986	1977	**£6**	
Live At The Roxy	LP	W. Bros	WBMS102	1978	**£30**	US promo
Moondance	LP	Nautilus	SD110	1981	**£12**	US audiophile
Moondance	LP	W. Bros	WS1835	1970	**£10**	chart LP

MORSE, ELLA MAE

Barrelhouse Boogie And The Blues	LP	Capitol	T513	1956	**£25**	US
Barrelhouse Boogie And The Blues	LP-10"	Capitol	H513	195-	**£50**	US
Barrelhouse Boogie And The Blues	7" EP	Capitol	EAP1513	1955	**£15**	
Birmingham	7"	Capitol	CL14376	1955	**£4**	
Bring Back My Baby To Me	7"	Capitol	CL14223	1955	**£15**	
Down In Mexico	7"	Capitol	CL14572	1956	**£8**	
Heart Full Of Hope	7"	Capitol	CL14332	1955	**£12**	
Hits Of Ella Mae Morse & Freddie Slack	LP	Capitol	T1802	1962	**£20**	US
I'm Gone	7"	Capitol	CL14760	1957	**£4**	
Morse Code	LP	Capitol	T898	1957	**£20**	US
Razzle Dazzle	7"	Capitol	CL14341	1955	**£20**	
Seventeen	7"	Capitol	CL14362	1955	**£10**	
Smack Dab In The Middle	7"	Capitol	CL14303	1955	**£10**	
What Good'll It Do Me	7"	Capitol	CL14726	1957	**£4**	
When Boy Kiss Girl	7"	Capitol	CL14508	1956	**£4**	

MORSE, ELLA MAE & FREDDIE SLACK

Rockin' Brew	LP	Ember	SPE6605	196-	**£15**	

MOSAICS

Let's Go Drag Racing	7"	Columbia	DB7990	1966	**£12**	

MOSES & JOSHUA

Get Out Of My Heart	7"	Bell	BLL1018	1968	**£4**	

MOSS, JENNY

Hobbies	7"	Columbia	DB7061	1963	**£6**	

MOST BROTHERS

Dottie	7"	Decca	F11040	1958	**£5**	
Teen Angel	7"	Decca	F10998	1958	**£5**	
Whistle Bait	7"	Decca	F10968	1957	**£6**	

MOST, ABE OCTET

Presenting...	7" EP	London	REP1028	1955	**£6**	

MOST, MICKIE

Feminine Look	7"	Columbia	DB7117	1963	**£10**	
Money Honey	7"	Columbia	DB7245	1964	**£8**	
Sea Cruise	7"	Columbia	DB7180	1963	**£8**	
Yes Indeed I Do	7"	Decca	F11664	1963	**£8**	

MOTHER EARTH

Bring Me Home	LP	Reprise	K44133	1971	**£12**	
I Did My Part	7"	Mercury	MF1081	1969	**£6**	
Living With The Animals	LP	Mercury	SR61194	1968	**£15**	US
Make A Joyful Noise	LP	Mercury	SMCL20173	1969	**£15**	
Revolution	LP	United Artists	51185	1968	**£15**	US
Satisfied	LP	Mercury	6338023	1970	**£15**	
Temptation Took Control	7"	Reprise	K14089	1972	**£4**	
Tracy Nelson Country	LP	Mercury	SMCL20179	1969	**£15**	

MOTHER TUCKER'S YELLOW DUCK

Home Grown Stuff	LP	Capitol		197-	**£40**	Canadian
Starting A New Day	LP	Capitol		197-	**£40**	Canadian

MOTHERLIGHT

Bobak Jons Malone	LP	Morgan B.T.	BT5003	1969	**£100**	

MOTHERLODE

Motherlode	LP	Buddah	5108	1973	**£15**	US

MOTHMEN

Title	Format	Label	Cat. No.	Year	Price	Notes
Does It Matter Irene	7"	Absurd	ABSURD6	1979	**£5**	
Pay Attention	LP	On-U Sounds	ONULP2	1981	**£12**	
Show Me Your House And Car	7"	Do It	DUN12	1981	**£10**	
Show Me Your House And Car	12"	Do It	DUNIT12	1981	**£12**	
Temptation	7"	Do It	DUN14	1981	**£4**	
Wadada	7"	Do It	DUN19	1982	**£4**	

MOTIONS

Title	Format	Label	Cat. No.	Year	Price	Notes
Every Step I Take	7"	Pye	7N25390	1966	**£4**	

MOTLEY CRUE

Title	Format	Label	Cat. No.	Year	Price	Notes
Dr.Feelgood	7"	Elektra	EKR97P	1989	**£6**	shaped pic disc
Helter Skelter	12"	Elektra			**£25**	US promo pic disc, with poster
Smokin' In The Boys' Room	7"	Elektra	EKR33P	1986	**£30**	interlocking shaped pic disc
Smokin' In The Boys' Room	7"	Elektra	EKR33P	1986	**£15**	mask shaped pic disc
Smokin' In The Boys' Room	12"	Elektra	EKR33T	1986	**£8**	with patch & poster
You're All I Need	12"	Elektra	EKR65TB	1988	**£8**	with patch & poster, boxed
You're All I Need	12"	Elektra	EKR65TP	1988	**£8**	pic disc

MOTORHEAD

When Lemmy left Hawkwind, he covered over the psychedelic designs on his equipment with black paint and thereby defined the image for his new group. Motorhead managed to become popular among fans of punk at a time when heavy metal was distinctly out of fashion. Of course, the group's approach to heavy metal was a bit different - short pieces played very fast, the emphasis being on energy rather than on displays of vituosity - and they very much anticipated the thrash metal style of the late eighties. Motorhead's collectable records consist of the usual assortment of limited edition coloured vinyl and picture discs. No value is given, however, for the white vinyl pressing of the "Motorhead" single on Big Beat, as this was limited to ten copies only.

Title	Format	Label	Cat. No.	Year	Price	Notes
Ace Of Spades	LP	Bronze	BRON531	1980	**£10**	gold vinyl
Ace Of Spades	12"	Bronze	12BRO106	1980	**£8**	
Beerdrinkers And Hellraisers	7"	Big Beat	NS61	1980	**£8**	promo
Beerdrinkers And Hellraisers	12"	Big Beat	SWT61	1980	**£6**	pink or blue vinyl
Bomber	LP	Bronze	BRON523	1979	**£10**	blue vinyl
Bomber	7"	Bronze	BRO85	1979	**£4**	chart single
Bomber	7"	Bronze	BRO85	1979	**£5**	blue vinyl
Golden Years	12"	Bronze	12BRO92	1980	**£6**	
I Got Mine	12"	Bronze	12BRO165	1983	**£6**	
Iron Fist	7"	Bronze	BRO146	1982	**£5**	blue or red vinyl
Killed By Death	7"	Bronze	BROP185	1984	**£15**	shaped pic disc
Killed By Death	12"	Bronze	12BRO185	1984	**£6**	with poster
Leavin' Here	7"	Stiff	BUY9	1977	**£15**	
Louie Louie	7"	Bronze	BRO60	1978	**£4**	chart single
Motorhead	7"	Big Beat	NS13	1980	**£4**	orange or pink marbled vinyl
Motorhead	7"	Big Beat	NSP13	1980	**£5**	pic disc
Motorhead	LP	Chiswick	WIK2	1977	**£10**	red, white, or clear vinyl
Motorhead	12"	Chiswick	NS13	1977	**£6**	
No Class	7"	Bronze	BRO78	1979	**£6**	3 PS's, chart single
No Remorse	LP	Bronze	PROLP5	1984	**£15**	double, 'leather' sleeve
No Sleep Till Hammersmith	LP	Bronze	BRON535	1981	**£12**	gold vinyl
Overkill	LP	Bronze	BRON515	1979	**£10**	green vinyl
Overkill	7"	Bronze	BRO67	1979	**£4**	chart single
Train Kept A-Rollin'	7"	Flexipop	007	1981	**£4**	flexi

MOTOWN SPINNERS

Title	Format	Label	Cat. No.	Year	Price	Notes
It's A Shame	7"	T. Motown	TMG755	1970	**£4**	chart single
It's A Shame	7"	T. Motown	TMG755	1970	**£10**	demo
Together We Can Make Such Sweet Music	7"	T. Motown	TMG766	1971	**£4**	
Together We Can Make Such Sweet Music	7"	T. Motown	TMG766	1971	**£10**	demo

MOTT THE HOOPLE

Title	Format	Label	Cat. No.	Year	Price	Notes
All The Young Dudes	LP	CBS	65184	1972	**£10**	chart LP
All The Young Dudes	7"	CBS	8271	1972	**£4**	chart single
Brain Capers	LP	Island	ILPS9178	1971	**£12**	
Downtown	7"	Island	WIP6112	1971	**£8**	
Mad Shadows	LP	Island	ILPS9119	1970	**£12**	chart LP
Midnight Lady	7"	Island	WIP6105	1971	**£8**	
Mott The Hoople	LP	Island	ILPS9108	1969	**£15**	chart LP
Mott The Hoople	LP	Island	ILPS9108	1969	**£30**	+ 'Road To Birmingham'

Rock And Roll Queen	7"	Island	WIP6072	1969	**£12**	
Roll Away The Stone	7"	CBS	1895DJ	1973	**£20**	1 sided promo
The Hoople	LP	Columbia	PCQ32871	1974	**£12**	US quad
Wild Life	LP	Island	ILPS9144	1971	**£12**	chart LP

MOULTRIE, MATTIE

That's How Strong My Love Is	7"	CBS	202547	1967	**£5**	

MOUNT RUSHMORE

Stone Free	7"	Dot	115	1968	**£5**	

MOUNTAIN

Mountain was formed by Felix Pappalardi in a deliberate attempt to capture some of the market that had been opened up by Cream. Pappalardi had, of course, worked with Cream on both "Disraeli Gears" and "Wheels Of Fire". Guitarist Leslie West was not in Eric Clapton's league, but Mountain nevertheless had its momemts - most notably on "Nantucket Sleighride", a section of which was made familiar to Sunday TV viewers in the London area as the theme tune to "Weekend World".

Avalanche	LP	Columbia	CQ33088	1974	**£12**	US quad
Avalanche	LP	Epic	80492	1974	**£10**	
Best Of...	LP	Columbia	CQ32079	1973	**£12**	US quad
Dreams Of Milk And Honey	7"	Bell	BLL1078	1970	**£8**	
Flowers Of Evil	LP	Island	ILPS9179	1971	**£12**	
Mississippi Queen	7"	Bell	BLL1112	1970	**£5**	
Mountain Climbing	LP	Bell	SBLL133	1970	**£12**	
Nantucket Sleighride	LP	Island	ILPS9148	1971	**£12**	chart LP
Road Goes On Forever	LP	Island	ILPS9199	1972	**£12**	chart LP
Roll Over Beethoven	7"	Island	WIP6119	1972	**£4**	
Sittin' On A Rainbow	7"	Bell	BLL1125	1970	**£5**	
Twin Peaks	LP	CBS	88095	1974	**£15**	double

MOUNTAIN BUS

Sundance	LP	Good	101	1971	**£50**	US

MOUNTAIN, VALERIE

Some People	7"	Pye	7N15450	1962	**£4**	

MOUSE

All The Fallen Teen Angels	7"	Sovereign	SOV127	1974	**£20**	
Lady Killer	LP	Sovereign	SVNA7262	1974	**£100**	
We Can Make It	7"	Sovereign	SOV122	1973	**£20**	

MOUSE & THE TRAPS

L.O.V.E.	7"	President	PT174	1968	**£8**	
Sometimes You Just Can't Win	7"	President	PT210	1968	**£6**	

MOVE

The Move could never quite decide whether they wished to become part of the burgeoning progressive rock scene or whether they just wanted to be a pop group. In the event, much of the group's music is an uneasy compromise between the two, with the series of hit singles receiving the most care and invention in their construction. The most interesting Move release is possibly the live EP "Something Else", where the group powers its way through an assortment of dynamic cover versions. They turn Spooky Tooth's "Sunshine Help Me" into something of a showcase for Roy Wood's squally lead guitar, but the fact that the melodic bass playing is given at least as much prominence in the mix makes the music sound remarkably fresh.

Blackberry Way	7"	Regal Z.	RZ3015	1969	**£4**	chart single
Brontosaurus	7"	Regal Z.	RZ3026	1970	**£4**	chart single
California Man	LP	Harvest	SHSP4035	1972	**£10**	
California Man	7"	Harvest	HAR5050	1972	**£4**	chart single
Cherry Blossom Clinic	7"	Regal Z.		1968	**£50**	
Chinatown	7"	Harvest	HAR5043	1971	**£4**	chart single
Curly	7"	Regal Z.	RZ3021	1969	**£4**	chart single
Do Ya	7"	Harvest	HAR5086	1974	**£4**	
Fire Brigade	7"	MagniFly	ECHO104	1972	**£6**	PS
Fire Brigade	7"	Regal Z.	RZ3005	1968	**£4**	chart single
Flowers In The Rain	7"	Regal Z.	RZ3001	1967	**£4**	chart single
I Can Hear The Grass Grow	7"	Deram	DM117	1967	**£4**	chart single
Looking On	LP	Fly	FLY1	1971	**£10**	
Message From The Country	LP	Harvest	SHSP4013	1971	**£10**	
Move	LP	Regal Z.	SLRZ1002	1968	**£15**	chart LP
Move/Shazam	LP	Cube	TOOFA5/6	1972	**£15**	double
Night Of Fear	7"	Deram	DM109	1966	**£4**	chart single
Shazam	LP	Regal Z.	SLRZ1012	1970	**£15**	
Something Else	7" EP	Regal Z.	TRZ2001	1968	**£20**	
Something Else From The Move	7"	EMI	PSRS315	1968	**£30**	1 sided promo sampler

Tonight	7"	Harvest	HAR5038	1971	**£4**	chart single
When Alice Comes Back To The Farm	7"	Fly	BUG2	1970	**£4**	
Wild Tiger Woman	7"	Regal Z.	RZ3012	1968	**£5**	

MOVEMENT

Head For The Sun	7"	Transatlantic	BIG112	1968	**£6**	
Something You've Got	7"	Pye	7N17443	1968	**£8**	

MOVING FINGER

Higher And Higher	7"	Mercury	MF1077	1969	**£8**	
Jeremy The Lamp	7"	Mercury	MF1051	1968	**£10**	
So Many People	7"	Decca	F13406	1973	**£8**	

MOVING GELATINE PLATES

Moving Gelatine Plates	LP	CBS	64399	1971	**£70**	
World Of Genius Hans	LP	CBS	64146	1971	**£70**	

MOVING SIDEWALKS

Flash	LP	Tantara	TYS6919	1968	**£75**	US

MR.DYNAMITE

Sh'mon	7"	Sue	WI4027	1967	**£8**	

MR.FLOOD'S PARTY

Compared To What	7"	Ember	EMBS312	197-	**£5**	
Mr.Flood's Party	LP	Cotillion	9003	1969	**£15**	US

MR.FOUNDATION

See Them Come	7"	Studio One	SO2001	196-	**£10**	
Time-oh	7"	Studio One	SO2061	196-	**£10**	

MR.FOX

Complete Mr.Fox	LP	Transatlantic	TRA303	1975	**£25**	double
Gypsy	LP	Transatlantic	TRA236	1971	**£25**	
Little Woman	7"	Transatlantic	BIG135	1970	**£5**	
Mr.Fox	LP	Transatlantic	TRA226	1970	**£25**	

MR.GASSER & THE WEIRDOS

Hot Rod Hootenanny	LP	Capitol	T2010	1963	**£15**	US
Rods 'N' Ratfinks	LP	Capitol	T2057	1963	**£15**	US
Surfink!	LP	Capitol	T2114	1964	**£20**	US

MR.MO'S MESSENGERS

Feelin' Good	7"	Columbia	DB8133	1967	**£6**	

MU

Lemurian Music	LP	United Artists		1974	**£20**	
Mu	LP	RTV	300	1972	**£40**	US
Mu	LP	United Artists	UAG29709	1975	**£15**	

MUCKY DUCK

Jefferson	7"	Deram	DM314	1970	**£4**	

MUDLARKS

Book Of Love	7"	Columbia	DB4133	1958	**£4**	chart single
Lollipop	7"	Columbia	DB4099	1958	**£4**	chart single
Love Game	7"	Columbia	DB4250	1959	**£4**	chart single
Mudlarks	7" EP	Columbia	SEG7854	1958	**£6**	
New Love	7"	Columbia	DB4064	1958	**£4**	
There's Never Been A Night	7"	Columbia	DB4190	1958	**£4**	
Which Witch Doctor	7"	Columbia	DB4210	1958	**£4**	

MUGWUMPS

Historical Recordings	LP	Valiant	VS134		**£10**	
I Don't Wanna Know	7"	W. Bros	WB144	1964	**£6**	

MULCAYS

Harbour Lights	7"	London	HLF8188	1955	**£15**	
Harmonics By The Mulcays	7" EP	London	REF1046	1956	**£12**	
Merry Christmas	7" EP	London	REP1016	1954	**£6**	

MULDAUR, GEOFF

Geoff Muldaur	LP	Prestige	14004	1964	**£15**	US

Is Having A Wonderful Time	LP	Reprise	K54046	1975	**£10**	
Sleepy Man Blues	LP	Prestige	7727	1965	**£15**	US

MULDAUR, GEOFF & MARIA

Pottery Pie	LP	Reprise	RS6350	1970	**£12**	US
Sweet Potatoes	LP	W. Bros	MS2073	1972	**£12**	US

MULESKINNER

Muleskinner	LP	W. Bros	2787	1973	**£12**	US

MULESKINNERS

Back Door Man	7"	Fontana	TF527	1965	**£15**	

MULL, MARTIN

Martin Mull	LP	Capricorn	K47506	1973	**£10**	

MULLICAN, MOON

Cherokee Boogie	78	Vogue	V9013	1951	**£8**	
Country Round Up	7" EP	Parlophone	GEP8794	1959	**£10**	
His All-Time Greatest Hits	LP	King	555	1958	**£40**	US
I'll Sail My Ship Alone	LP	Sterling	ST601	196-	**£25**	US
Instrumentals	LP	Audio Lab	AL1568	1962	**£40**	US
Many Moods Of...	LP	King	681	1960	**£40**	US
Moon Over Mullican	LP	Coral	CRL57235	1958	**£150**	US
Mr.Piano Man	LP	Starday	SLP267	1964	**£12**	US
Sixteen Of His Favorite Tunes	LP	King	628	1959	**£40**	US
Twenty-Four Of His Favorite Tunes	LP	KIng	937	1965	**£12**	US
Unforgettable...	LP	Starday	SLP398	1967	**£10**	US

MULLICAN, MOON / BOYD BENNETT & ROCKETS

Seven Nights To Rock	7"	Parlophone	MSP6254	1956	**£80**	

MUNGO JERRY

Mungo Jerry	LP	Dawn	DNLS3008	1970	**£10**	chart LP

MURE, BILLY

Supersonics In Flight	7" EP	RCA	RCX158	1959	**£8**	
Versatile Billy Mure	7" EP	Felsted	GEP1006	1959	**£5**	

MURMAIDS

Popsicles And Icicles	7"	Stateside	SS247	1963	**£4**	

MURPHEY, MICHAEL

Boy From The Country	7"	Regal Z.	RZ3062	1972	**£4**	
Geronimo's Cadillac	LP	Regal Z.	ZONO8512	1972	**£10**	

MURPHY, ELLIOTT

Aquashow	LP	Polydor	2391100	1974	**£10**	

MURPHY, MARK

Who Can I Turn To	LP	Immediate	IMSP004	1966	**£30**	

MURRAT, ALEX

Teen Angel	7"	Decca	F11203	1960	**£4**	

MURRAY, LARRY

Sweet Country Suite	LP	Verve		1969	**£20**	US

MUSHROOM

Devil Among The Tailors	7"	Hawk	HASP320	1975	**£40**	
Early One Morning	LP	Halpix	116	197-	**£300**	

MUSHROOM SOUP

The Mushroom Soup album "And Other Recipes" on the Roll and Butter label, catalogue number PAT1, is such a delightful concept that one longs for it to be real. There exists the suspicion, however, that the record is no more than the invention of a dealer with a lively sense of humour. Has any collector actually seen a copy?

And Other Recipes	LP	Roll & Butt.	PAT1	1968	**£40**	

MUSIC BOX

Songs Of Sunshine	LP	Westwood	MRS013	1972	**£20**	

MUSIC EMPORIUM

Music Emporium	LP	Sentinel	1000	1969	**£500**	US

MUSIC EXPLOSION

Little Bit O'Soul	LP	Laurie	LLP2040	1967	**£12**	US
Little Bit O'Soul	7"	Stateside	SS2028	1967	**£6**	
Little Black Egg	7"	Philips	BF1547	1967	**£6**	
Sunshine Games	7"	Stateside	SS2054	1967	**£5**	

MUSIC MACHINE

Bonniwell Music Machine	LP	W. Bros	WS1732	1968	**£20**	US
People In Me	7"	Pye	7N25414	1967	**£6**	
Talk Talk	7"	Pye	7N25407	1967	**£6**	
Turn On The Music Machine	LP	Original Snd	5015, 8875	1966	**£30**	US

MUSICAL THEATRE

Revolutionary Revelation	LP	Pye		1970	**£12**	

MUSKETEER GRIPWEED

How I Won The War	7"	United Artists	UP1196	1966	**£25**	

MUSSELWHITE, CHARLIE

Charlie Musselwhite	LP	Vanguard	VSD79287	1968	**£15**	US
Stand Back, Here Comes...	LP	Vanguard	VSD79232	1967	**£15**	US
Stone Blues	LP	Vanguard	SVRL19012	1968	**£15**	
Tennessee Woman	LP	Vanguard	VSD6528	1969	**£12**	US

MUSTANG

Why	7"	Parlophone	R5579	1967	**£5**	

MUSTANGS

Dartell Stomp	LP	Providence	PLP001	1963	**£20**	US

MUSTWANGS

Rock Lomond	7"	Mercury	AMT1140	1961	**£4**	

MUTANTS

Boss Man	7"	Rox	ROX002	1978	**£4**	
Hard Times	7"	Rox	ROX005	1979	**£4**	
Hard Times	7"	Rox	ROX005	1979	**£5**	red vinyl

MUTT'N'JEFF

Don't Nag Me Ma	7"	Decca	F12335	1966	**£8**	

MY BLOODY VALENTINE

Ecstasy	mini LP	Lazy	LAZY08	1987	**£35**	
Feed Me With Your Kiss	7"	Creation	CRE061	1988	**£4**	
Geek!	12"	Fever	FEV5	1986	**£20**	
Instrumental	7"	Creation	CREFRE4	1988	**£6**	
New Record By My Bloody Valentine	12"	Kaleid. Snd	KS101	1986	**£20**	
No Place To Go	7"	Fever	FEV5X	1986	**£10**	
Strawberry Wine	12"	Lazy	LAZY07T	1987	**£20**	
Sunny Sundae Smile	7"	Lazy	LAZY04	1987	**£15**	
Sunny Sundae Smile	12"	Lazy	LAZY04T	1987	**£20**	
This Is Your Bloody Valentine	mini LP	Tycoon	ST7501	1985	**£50**	German
You Made Me Realise	7"	Creation	CRE055	1988	**£4**	

MY CAPTAINS

My Captains	7"	4AD	AD103	1981	**£4**	

MY DEAR WATSON

Elusive Face	7"	Parlophone	R5687	1968	**£15**	
Have You Seen Your Saviour	7"	DJM	DJS224	1970	**£8**	
Stop Stop I'll Be There	7"	Parlophone	R5737	1968	**£15**	

MY SOLID GROUND

My Solid Ground	LP	Bacillus		1971	**£50**	

MYERS, DAVE

Greatest Racing Themes	LP	Carole	CAR8002	1967	**£12**	US
Hangin' Twenty	LP	Del-Fi	DFLP1239	1963	**£15**	US

MYHILL, RICHARD

Richard Myhill's single, "It Takes Two To Tango" has the distinction of being the first record ever to have been issued in a shape other than round. In 1978, exotically shaped picture discs were still a little time away - this single was black and square.

It Takes Two To Tango .... 7" .... Mercury ....TANGO1 .... 1978........ **£4**....................... square disc

MYLES, BILLY

Joker .... 7" .... HMV...............POP423 .... 1957........ **£6**..

MYSTERIES

Give Me Rhythm And Blues .... 7" .... Decca ....F11919................. 1964...... **£25**..

MYSTIC ASTROLOGICAL CRYSTAL BAND

Clip Out, Put On Book .... LP .... Carole............S8003.................. 1968...... **£15**....................................US
Mystic Astrological Crystal Band .... LP .... Carole............S8001.................. 1967...... **£15**....................................US

MYSTIC MOODS ORCHESTRA

Cosmic Force .... LP .... Mobile Fid.......1002....................... 1981...... **£20**.................. US audiophile
Emotions .... LP .... Mobile Fid.......1001....................... 1981...... **£20**.................. US audiophile
Stormy Weekend .... LP .... Mobile Fid.......1003....................... 1981...... **£20**.................. US audiophile

MYSTIC NUMBER NATIONAL BANK

Mystic Number National Bank .... LP .... Probe.............CPLPS4501 .... 1969...... **£12**..

MYSTIC SIVA

Mystic Siva .... LP .... Vo ....19713.................. 1970.... **£100**..................................US

MYSTICS

Adam And Eve .... 7" .... HMV...............POP646 .... 1959........ **£6**..
Don't Take The Stars .... 7" .... Top Rank........JAR243 .... 1959........ **£4**..

N BETWEENS

The N Betweens' sole single, a version of the Young Rascals' American hit, "You Better Run", was produced by the legendary Kim Fowley. Success did not come to the group until a few years later, however, when it had changed its name to Slade.

Title	Format	Label	Cat. No.	Year	Price	Notes
Take A Heart	7" EP	Barclay	2017	1966	**£120**	French
You Better Run	7"	Columbia	DB8080	1966	**£120**	

N BETWEENS & HILLS

Title	Format	Label	Cat. No.	Year	Price	Notes
Take A Heart	7" EP	Barclay	70987	1965	**£100**	French

NAGLE, RON

Title	Format	Label	Cat. No.	Year	Price	Notes
Bad Rice	LP	W. Bros	WS1902	1970	**£12**	US

NAKED TRUTH

Title	Format	Label	Cat. No.	Year	Price	Notes
Two Little Rooms	7"	Deram	DM287	1970	**£5**	

NANTOS, NICK

Title	Format	Label	Cat. No.	Year	Price	Notes
Guitars On Fire	LP	Summit		1964	**£20**	

NAPOLEON XIV

Title	Format	Label	Cat. No.	Year	Price	Notes
I'm In Love With My Little Red Tricycle	7"	W. Bros	WB5853	1966	**£5**	
They're Coming To Take Me Away	LP	W. Bros	W1661	1966	**£50**	US
They're Coming To Take Me Away	7"	W. Bros	WB5831	1966	**£5**	chart single

NARIZ, WAZMO

Title	Format	Label	Cat. No.	Year	Price	Notes
Tele Tele Telephone	12"	Stiff	NAZZ1	1978	**£8**	promo

NARNIA

Title	Format	Label	Cat. No.	Year	Price	Notes
Narnia	LP	Myrrh		1974	**£40**	

NASH, BILLY

Title	Format	Label	Cat. No.	Year	Price	Notes
Madison Step	7"	Philips	370406BF	1963	**£4**	
Sunset	7"	Philips	PB1181	1961	**£4**	

NASH, GENE

Title	Format	Label	Cat. No.	Year	Price	Notes
Ja Ja Ja	7"	Capitol	CL15042	1959	**£4**	

NASH, GRAHAM

Title	Format	Label	Cat. No.	Year	Price	Notes
Chicago	7"	Atlantic	2091096	1971	**£4**	
Military Madness	7"	Atlantic	2091135	1971	**£4**	
Songs For Beginners	LP	Atlantic	2401011	1971	**£10**	chart LP

NASH, JOHNNY

Title	Format	Label	Cat. No.	Year	Price	Notes
As Time Goes By	7"	HMV	POP620	1959	**£4**	
Baby Baby Baby	7"	HMV	POP651	1959	**£4**	
Cigareets, Whiskey & Wild Wild Women	7"	W. Bros	WB93	1963	**£4**	
Cupid	7"	Major Minor	MM603	1969	**£4**	chart single
Don't Take Away Your Love	7"	W. Bros	WB65	1962	**£4**	
Glad You're My Baby	7"	MGM	MGM1480	1969	**£5**	
Goodbye	7"	HMV	POP746	1960	**£4**	
Groovy Feeling	7"	Major Minor	MM701	1970	**£4**	
Hold Me Tight	7"	Regal Z.	RZ3010	1968	**£4**	chart single
Imagination	7"	HMV	POP673	1959	**£4**	
Ladder Of Love	7"	HMV	POP402	1957	**£4**	
Let's Move And Groove	7"	Pye	7N25353	1966	**£4**	
Love Ain't Nothing	7"	Pye	7N25250	1964	**£4**	
Love And Peace	7"	Major Minor	MM630	1969	**£4**	
Love Me Tender	7"	Major Minor	MM646	1969	**£4**	
Midnight Moonlight	7"	HMV	POP553	1958	**£4**	
My Pledge To You	7"	HMV	POP475	1958	**£4**	
Ol' Man River	7"	W. Bros	WB76	1962	**£4**	
One More Time	7"	Pye	7N25363	1966	**£4**	
Presenting Johnny Nash	7" EP	RCA	RCX7163	1964	**£5**	

Roots Of Heaven	7"	HMV	POP597	1959	**£4**	
Somebody	7"	HMV	POP822	1960	**£4**	
Stir It Up	7"	CBS	7800	1972	**£4**	chart single
Strange Feeling	7"	Chess	CRS8005	1965	**£6**	
Very Special Love	7"	HMV	POP435	1958	**£4**	
You Got Soul	7"	Major Minor	MM586	1969	**£4**	chart single

NASHVILLE FIVE

Brainwave	7"	Decca	F11484	1962	**£5**	
Like Nashville	7" EP	Decca	DFE6706	1962	**£10**	
Stand Up And Say That	7"	Decca	F11427	1962	**£5**	

NASHVILLE TEENS

All Along The Watchtower	7"	Decca	F12754	1968	**£8**	
Biggest Night Of Her Life	7"	Decca	F12657	1967	**£8**	
Cherokee Reservation	7"	Major Minor	MM599	1969	**£10**	
Ella James	7"	Parlophone	R5925	1971	**£10**	
Find My Way Back Home	7"	Decca	F12089	1965	**£4**	chart single
Forbidden Fruit	7"	Decca	F12458	1966	**£5**	
Google Eye	7"	Decca	F12000	1964	**£4**	chart single
Hard Way	7"	Decca	F12316	1966	**£4**	chart single
I'm Coming Home	7"	Decca	F12580	1967	**£6**	
Lawdy Miss Clawdy	7"	Enterprise	ENT001	1972	**£4**	
Nashville Teens	7" EP	Decca	DFE8600	1965	**£12**	
Nashville Teens	LP	New World	AW6002	1974	**£10**	
Soon Forgotten	7"	Decca	F12255	1965	**£5**	
That's My Woman	7"	Decca	F12542	1966	**£5**	
This Little Bird	7"	Decca	F12143	1965	**£4**	chart single
Tobacco Road	7"	Decca	F11930	1964	**£4**	chart single
Tobacco Road	LP	London	LL3407	1964	**£40**	US

NATIONAL HEAD BAND

Albert One	LP	W. Bros	K46094	1971	**£15**	

NATIONAL LAMPOON

Cold Turkey	LP	Epic	33410	1975	**£10**	US
Goodbye Pop	LP	Epic	33956	1976	**£10**	US
Lemmings	LP	Blue Thumb	BTS6006	1973	**£10**	US
Missing White House Tapes	LP	Blue Thumb	BTS6008	1974	**£10**	US
Radio Dinner	LP	Island	HELP8	1972	**£10**	

NATIONAL PINION POLE

Make Your Mark Little Mark	7"	Planet	PLF111	1966	**£10**	

NATURAL ACOUSTIC BAND

Branching In	LP	RCA	SF8314	1974	**£12**	
Echoes	7"	RCA	RCA2324	1973	**£4**	
Learning To Live	LP	RCA	SF8272	1972	**£12**	

NATURAL BRIDGE BUNCH

Pig Snoots	7"	Atlantic	584231	1969	**£4**	

NATURALS

Blue Roses	7"	Parlophone	R5257	1965	**£4**	
Daisy Chain	7"	Parlophone	R5116	1964	**£4**	
I Should Have Known Better	7"	Parlophone	R5165	1964	**£4**	chart single
It Was You	7"	Parlophone	R5202	1964	**£4**	

NAYLOR, SHEL

How Deep Is The Ocean	7"	Decca	F11776	1963	**£15**	
One Fine Day	7"	Decca	F11856	1964	**£40**	

NAZ NOMAD & THE NIGHTMARES

Give Daddy The Knife Cindy	LP	Big Beat	WIK21	1984	**£10**	purple vinyl

NAZARETH

Morning Dew	7"	Pegasus	PEG6	1972	**£4**	

NAZZ

Hello It's Me	7"	SGC	219002	1969	**£10**	
Nazz	LP	Screen Gems	SGC22001	1968	**£25**	
Nazz 3	LP	Screen Gems	SGC22004	1969	**£25**	

Title	Format	Label	Number	Year	Price	Notes
Nazz 3	LP	Screen Gems	SGC22004	1969	**£30**	green vinyl
Nazz Nazz	LP	Screen Gems	SGC22002	1969	**£25**	
Nazz Nazz	LP	Screen Gems	SGC22002	1969	**£30**	red vinyl
Not Wrong Long	7"	Atco		1969	**£25**	
Not Wrong Long	7"	SGC	219003	1969	**£12**	
Open My Eyes	7"	Atlantic	584224	1968	**£30**	
Open My Eyes	7"	SGC	219001	1968	**£8**	

NEAL, CHRIS

Title	Format	Label	Number	Year	Price	Notes
Blame It All On Eve	7"	Fly	BUG15	1971	**£5**	PS

NEAL, JOHNNY & THE STARLINERS

Title	Format	Label	Number	Year	Price	Notes
And I Will Love You	7"	Pye	7N15388	1961	**£15**	

NEAL, TOMMY

Title	Format	Label	Number	Year	Price	Notes
Goin' To A Happening	7"	Vocalion	VL9290	1968	**£5**	

NECROMONICON

Title	Format	Label	Number	Year	Price	Notes
Tips Zum Selbsmord	LP	Private		1972	**£700**	

NECROS

Title	Format	Label	Number	Year	Price	Notes
I.Q.32	7"	Dischord	4	1981	**£35**	with insert
Sex Drive	7"	Touch & Go		1981	**£40**	

NEE, BERNIE

Title	Format	Label	Number	Year	Price	Notes
Medal Of Honour	7"	Philips	PB794	1958	**£4**	

NEIGHBORHOOD CHILDREN

Title	Format	Label	Number	Year	Price	Notes
Neighborhood Children	LP	Acta	38005	1968	**£20**	US

NEIL, FRED

Title	Format	Label	Number	Year	Price	Notes
Bleecker & MacDonald	LP	Elektra	EKS7293	1965	**£15**	US
Candy Man	7"	Elektra	EKSN45036	1968	**£4**	
Everybody's Talkin'	LP	Capitol	ST2665	1969	**£15**	US
Everybody's Talkin'	7"	Capitol	CL15616	1969	**£4**	
Hootenanny Live At The Bitter End	LP	FM	FM309	1964	**£15**	US
Little Bit Of Rain	LP	Elektra	EKS74073	1970	**£12**	US
Other Side Of This Life	LP	Capitol	ST657	1971	**£12**	US
Sessions	LP	Capitol	ST2862	1971	**£12**	US
Tear Down The Walls	LP	Elektra	EKS7248	1964	**£15**	US
World Of Folk Music	LP	FM	FM319	1964	**£15**	US

NEKTAR

Title	Format	Label	Number	Year	Price	Notes
Astral Man	7"	United Artists	UP35853	1975	**£4**	
Down To Earth	LP	United Artists	UAG29680	1974	**£10**	
Fidgety Queen	7"	United Artists	UP35706	1974	**£4**	
Journey To The Centre Of The Eye	LP	Bellaphon	BLPS19064	1972	**£10**	German
Live At The Roundhouse	LP	Bellaphon	BLPS19182	1974	**£10**	German
Live In New York	LP	Bellaphon	BAC2004	1977	**£10**	German
Magic Is A Child	LP	Bellaphon	BAC2050	1977	**£10**	German
More Live In New York	LP	Bellaphon	BAC2058	1978	**£10**	German
Nektar	LP	Bellaphon	BLPS19224	1976	**£10**	German
Recycled	LP	Decca	SKLR5250	1976	**£10**	
Remember The Future	LP	United Artists	UAS29545	1973	**£10**	
Sounds Like This	LP	United Artists	UAD60041/2	1973	**£12**	double
Tab In The Ocean	LP	United Artists	UAS29499	1972	**£10**	

NELSON, BILL

Title	Format	Label	Number	Year	Price	Notes
Northern Dream	LP	Smile	LAF2182	1971	**£20**	

NELSON, EARL

Title	Format	Label	Number	Year	Price	Notes
No Time To Cry	7"	London	HLW8950	1959	**£4**	

NELSON, OZZIE & HARRIET

Title	Format	Label	Number	Year	Price	Notes
Ozzie And Harriet Nelson	LP	London	HAP2145	1959	**£20**	

NELSON, RICK

Title	Format	Label	Number	Year	Price	Notes
Album Seven	LP	London	HAP2445	1962	**£15**	mono
Album Seven	LP	London	SAHP6236	1962	**£20**	stereo
Another Side Of Rick	LP	MCA	MUPS302	1968	**£10**	
Be Bop Baby	7"	London	HLP8499	1957	**£10**	
Believe What You Say	7"	London	HLP8594	1958	**£6**	

Title	Format	Label	Number	Year	Price	Notes
Best Always	LP	Brunswick	LAT8615	1965	**£10**	
Bright Lights, Country Music	LP	Brunswick	LAT8657	1966	**£10**	
Come Out Dancin'	7"	Brunswick	05939	1965	**£4**	
Country Fever	LP	Brunswick	LAT8680	1967	**£10**	
Everlovin'	7"	London	HLP9440	1961	**£4**	chart single
Fools Rush In	7"	Brunswick	05895	1963	**£4**	chart single
For You	7"	Brunswick	05900	1964	**£4**	chart single
For Your Sweet Love	LP	Brunswick	LAT8545	1963	**£12**	mono
For Your Sweet Love	LP	Brunswick	STA8545	1963	**£15**	stereo
Happy Guy	7"	Brunswick	05924	1964	**£4**	
Happy Guy	7" EP	Brunswick	OE9512	1965	**£8**	
Hello Mary Lou	7"	London	HLP9347	1961	**£4**	chart single
I Got A Feeling	7" EP	London	REP1238	1960	**£10**	
I Got A Woman	7"	Brunswick	05885	1963	**£4**	
I Need You	7"	Liberty	LIB12033	1966	**£4**	
I Wanna Be Loved	7"	London	HLP9021	1960	**£4**	chart single
I'm In Love Again	7" EP	Liberty	LEP4028	1965	**£6**	
I'm Walking	7"	HMV	POP355	1957	**£25**	
It's A Young World	7" EP	London	REP1339	1962	**£8**	
It's Up To You	LP	London	HAP8066	1963	**£15**	
It's Up To You	7"	London	HLP9648	1963	**£4**	chart single
It's Up To You	7" EP	London	REP1362	1963	**£8**	
Just A Little Too Much	7"	London	HLP8927	1959	**£4**	chart single
Lonely Corner	7"	Brunswick	05918	1964	**£4**	
Long Vacation	LP	Imperial	LP9244	1963	**£15**	US
Love And Kisses	LP	Brunswick	LAT8630	1965	**£10**	
Milkcow Blues	7"	London	HLP9260	1961	**£5**	
Million Sellers	LP	Liberty	LBY3027	1963	**£10**	
More Songs By Ricky	LP	Imperial	LP12059	1960	**£150**	US, blue vinyl
More Songs By Ricky	LP	London	HAP2290	1960	**£15**	mono
More Songs By Ricky	LP	London	SAHP6102	1960	**£20**	stereo
My Babe	7"	London	HLP8738	1958	**£5**	
Nelson Sings For You	7" EP	Liberty	LEP4001	1964	**£6**	
Never Be Anyone Else But You	7"	London	HLP8817	1959	**£4**	
One Boy Too Late	7" EP	Brunswick	OE9502	1963	**£8**	
Perspective	LP	Decca	DL75014	1968	**£10**	US
Poor Little Fool	7"	London	HLP8670	1958	**£5**	chart single
Rick Is 21	LP	London	HAP2379	1961	**£15**	mono
Rick Is 21	LP	London	SAHP6179	1961	**£20**	stereo
Rick Nelson Country	LP	MCA	24004	1973	**£10**	US
Rick Sings Nelson	LP	MCA	MUPS422	1970	**£10**	
Ricky	LP	London	HAP2080	1957	**£25**	
Ricky Nelson	LP	London	HAP2119	1958	**£20**	
Ricky Nelson No.1	7" EP	London	REP1168	1959	**£10**	
Ricky Nelson No.2	7" EP	London	REP1169	1959	**£10**	
Ricky Nelson No.3	7" EP	London	REP1170	1959	**£10**	
Ricky Nelson No.4	7" EP	London	REP1300	1961	**£8**	
Ricky No.1	7" EP	London	REP1141	1958	**£10**	
Ricky No.2	7" EP	London	REP1142	1958	**£10**	
Ricky No.3	7" EP	London	REP1143	1958	**£10**	
Ricky No.4	7" EP	London	REP1144	1958	**£10**	
Ricky Sings Again	LP	London	HAP2159	1959	**£20**	
Ricky Sings Again Pt.1	7" EP	London	REP1200	1959	**£10**	
Ricky Sings Again Pt.2	7" EP	London	REP1201	1959	**£10**	
Ricky Sings Spirituals	7" EP	London	REP1249	1960	**£8**	
Rudy The Fifth	LP	MCA	MUPS440	1971	**£10**	
Sings For You	LP	Brunswick	LAT8562	1964	**£12**	mono
Sings For You	LP	Brunswick	STA8562	1964	**£15**	stereo
Someday	7"	London	HLP8732	1958	**£4**	chart single
Songs By Ricky	LP	London	HAP2206	1959	**£20**	
Spotlight On Rick	LP	Brunswick	LAT8596	1964	**£12**	mono
Spotlight On Rick	LP	Brunswick	STA8596	1964	**£12**	stereo
Stood Up	7"	London	HLP8542	1958	**£6**	chart single
String Along	7"	Brunswick	05889	1963	**£4**	
Teen Time	LP	Verve	V2083	1957	**£100**	US
Teenage Idol	7"	London	HLP9583	1962	**£4**	chart single
That's All	7" EP	Liberty	LEP4019	1964	**£6**	
Today's Teardrops	7"	Liberty	LIB66004	1964	**£4**	
Very Thought Of You	LP	Brunswick	LAT8581	1964	**£10**	mono
Very Thought Of You	LP	Brunswick	STA8581	1964	**£12**	stereo
Very Thought Of You	7"	Brunswick	05908	1964	**£4**	

Yes Sir That's My Baby	7"	London	HLP9188	1960	**£4**	
You Are My One And Only Love	7"	HMV	POP390	1957	**£20**	
You Can't Just Quit	7"	Brunswick	05964	1966	**£4**	
Young Emotions	7"	London	HLP9121	1960	**£4**	chart single
Young World	7"	London	HLP9524	1962	**£4**	chart single

NELSON, RICK & JOANIE SOMMERS

On The Flip Side	LP	Decca	DL4836	1967	**£10**	US

NELSON, SANDY

And Then There Were Drums	7"	London	HLP9612	1962	**£4**	
Beat Goes On	LP	Liberty	LBL83043	1967	**£10**	
Boogaloo Beat	LP	Liberty	LBL83110	1968	**£10**	
Bouncy	7"	London	HLP9214	1960	**£4**	
Compelling Percussion	LP	London	HAP8029	1963	**£12**	
Drum Party	7"	London	HLP9015	1959	**£4**	
Drummin' Up A Storm	LP	London	HAP8009	1962	**£12**	
Drummin' Up A Storm	7"	London	HLP9558	1962	**£4**	chart single
Drums A Go-go	LP	Liberty	LBY3061	1965	**£10**	
Drums Are My Beat	7"	London	HLP9521	1962	**£4**	
Get With It	7"	London	HLP9377	1961	**£4**	
In The Mood	7" EP	London	REP1371	1963	**£8**	
Let There Be Drums	LP	London	HAP2425	1961	**£15**	
Let There Be Drums	7"	London	HLP9466	1961	**£4**	chart single
Let There Be Drums	7" EP	London	REP1337	1962	**£8**	
Live In Las Vegas	LP	Liberty	LBY3035	1965	**£10**	
Ooh Poo Pah Doo	7"	London	HLP9717	1963	**£4**	
Sandy Nelson Plays	LP	Liberty	LBY3007	1964	**£10**	
Sandy Nelson Plays	7" EP	Liberty	LEP4033	1965	**£6**	
Soul Beat	LP	Liberty	LBL83094	1968	**£10**	
Superdrums	LP	Liberty	LBY3080	1967	**£10**	
Teen Beat	LP	London	HAP2260	1960	**£15**	mono
Teen Beat	LP	London	SAHP6082	1960	**£15**	stereo
Teen Beat	7"	Top Rank	JAR197	1959	**£5**	chart single
Teen Beat '65	7"	Liberty	LIB66060	1964	**£4**	
Teenage House Party	LP	London	HAP8051	1963	**£12**	

NELSON, WILLIE

And Then I Wrote	LP	Liberty	LRP3238	1962	**£15**	US
Country Willie	LP	RCA	RD7749	1965	**£10**	
Half A Man	7"	Liberty	LIB55532	1963	**£4**	
Here's Willie Nelson	LP	Liberty	LRP3308	1963	**£15**	US
River Boy	7"	Liberty	LIB55697	1964	**£4**	
Texas In My Soul	LP	RCA	RD7997	1969	**£10**	

NEO MAYA

I Won't Hurt You	7"	Pye	7N17371	1967	**£20**	

NEOGY, CHIITRA

Perfumed Garden	LP	Gemini	GMX5030	1968	**£20**	

NEPTUNE'S EMPIRE

Neptune's Empire	LP	Private	PXX01	1971	**£80**	

NERO & THE GLADIATORS

Czardas	7"	Decca	F11413	1961	**£10**	
Entry Of The Gladiators	7"	Decca	F11329	1961	**£10**	chart single
In The Hall Of The Mountain King	7"	Decca	F11367	1961	**£10**	chart single

NERVE

It Is	7"	Page One	POF081	1968	**£8**	
Magic Spectacles	7"	Page One	POF055	1968	**£8**	
Piece By Piece	7"	Page One	POF097	1968	**£8**	
Ten Downing Street	7"	Page One	POF019	1967	**£6**	

NERVOUS NORVUS

Ape Call	7"	London	HLD8338	1956	**£20**	
Bullfrog	7"	London	HLD8383	1957	**£20**	
Does A Chinese Chicken Have A Pigtail	7"	Salvo	SLO1812	1962	**£8**	

NESMITH, MICHAEL

...& First National Band	7" EP	Island	IEP4	1976	**£5**	

Title	Format	Label	Cat. No.	Year	Price	Notes
And The Hits Just Keep On Coming	LP	RCA	LSP4695	1972	**£10**	US
Best Of...	LP	RCA	RS1064	1976	**£10**	US
Compilation	LP	Island	ILPS9425	1977	**£10**	
From A Radio Engine To The Photon Wing	LP	Island	ILPS9486	1977	**£10**	
Infinite Rider On The Big Dogma	LP	Pacific Arts	PAC7130	1979	**£10**	US
Joanne	7"	RCA	RCA2001	1970	**£4**	
Lady Of The Valley	7"	RCA	RCA2053	1971	**£4**	
Live At The Palais	LP	Pacific Arts	PAC7118	1978	**£10**	US
Loose Salute	LP	RCA	LSP4415	1970	**£10**	US
Magnetic South	LP	RCA	SF8136	1970	**£10**	
Mike Nesmith Radio Special	LP	Pacific Arts	PAC71300	1976	**£15**	US promo
Nevada Fighter	LP	RCA	SF8209	1971	**£10**	
Pretty Much Your Standard Ranch Stash	LP	RCA	APL10164	1973	**£10**	US
Prison	LP	Island	ILPS9428	1975	**£10**	
Prison	LP	Pacific Arts	7101	1978	**£20**	US, boxed with booklet
Rio	7"	Island	WIP6373	1977	**£4**	chart single
Tantamount To Treason	LP	RCA	SF8276	1972	**£10**	
Wichita Train Whistle Sings	LP	Dot	SLDP516	1968	**£20**	

NEU

Title	Format	Label	Cat. No.	Year	Price	Notes
Isi	7"	United Artists	UP35874	1975	**£4**	
Neu	LP	United Artists	UAS29396	1972	**£10**	
Neu 2	LP	United Artists	UAS29500	1973	**£10**	
Neu '75	LP	United Artists	UAS29782	1975	**£10**	
Super	7"	United Artists	UP35485	1973	**£4**	

NEUTRONS

Title	Format	Label	Cat. No.	Year	Price	Notes
Black Hole Star	LP	United Artists	UAG29652	1974	**£10**	
Dance Of The Psychedelic Lounge Lizard	7"	United Artists	UP35704	1974	**£4**	
Tales From The Blue Cocoons	LP	United Artists	UAG29726	1975	**£10**	

NEVILLE, AARON

Title	Format	Label	Cat. No.	Year	Price	Notes
Like It Is	LP	Minit	LP40007	1967	**£12**	US
Tell It Like It Is	LP	Par-Lo	LP1	1967	**£15**	US
Tell It Like It Is	7"	Stateside	SS584	1967	**£4**	

NEW AGE STEPPERS

Title	Format	Label	Cat. No.	Year	Price	Notes
Fade Away	7"	ONU Sound	ONU1	1980	**£6**	B side by The London Underground
New Age Steppers	LP	ONU Sound	ONULP1	1980	**£12**	

NEW CHRISTS

Title	Format	Label	Cat. No.	Year	Price	Notes
Face A New God	7"	Green	LRS076	1981	**£60**	
Living Eyes	LP	Trafalgar		1981	**£15**	

NEW COLONY SIX

Title	Format	Label	Cat. No.	Year	Price	Notes
At The River's Edge	7"	Stateside	SS522	1966	**£8**	
Breakthrough	LP	Sentar	LP101	1966	**£150**	US
Colonization	LP	Sentar	ST3001	1967	**£12**	US
I Confess	7"	London	HLZ10033	1966	**£8**	
I Will Always	7"	Mercury	MF1030	1968	**£5**	
Things I'd Like To Say	7"	Mercury	MF1086	1969	**£5**	

NEW DREAM

Title	Format	Label	Cat. No.	Year	Price	Notes
Turn 21	7"	Parlophone	R5946	1972	**£4**	

NEW GENERATION

Title	Format	Label	Cat. No.	Year	Price	Notes
Police Is Here	7"	Spark	SRL1019	1970	**£4**	
Sadie And Her Magic Mr.Garland	7"	Spark	SRL1000	1969	**£5**	
Smokey Blues Away	7"	Spark	SRL1007	1969	**£5**	chart single

NEW HEAVENLY BLUE

Title	Format	Label	Cat. No.	Year	Price	Notes
Educated Homegrown	LP	RCA	SF8189	1971	**£10**	

NEW JUMP BAND

Title	Format	Label	Cat. No.	Year	Price	Notes
Only Kind Of Girl	7"	Domain	D1	1968	**£5**	

NEW MODEL ARMY

Title	Format	Label	Cat. No.	Year	Price	Notes
Better Than Them	7"	EMI	NMA2	1985	**£5**	chart single
Better Than Them	7"	EMI	NMAD2	1985	**£8**	double
Better Than Them	12"	EMI	12NMA2	1985	**£8**	
Bittersweet	7"	Shout	QS002	1983	**£15**	with flexi

Bittersweet	7"	Shout	QS002	1986	**£5**	
Brave New World	7"	EMI	NMA3	1986	**£5**	chart single
Brave New World	12"	EMI	12NMA3	1985	**£8**	
Brave New World	12"	EMI	12NMAD3	1985	**£12**	double
Fifty-First State	12"	EMI	12NMAD4	1986	**£12**	double
Fifty-First State	7"	EMI	NMA4	1986	**£5**	chart single
Fifty-First State	12"	EMI	12NMA4	1986	**£8**	
Great Expectations	7"	Abstract	ABS0020	1983	**£15**	
Green And Grey	7"	EMI	NMAP9	1989	**£4**	pic disc
No Rest	cass-s	EMI	TCNMA1	1985	**£6**	
No Rest	7"	EMI	NMA1	1985	**£4**	chart single
No Rest	12"	EMI	12NMA1	1985	**£12**	double
Poison Street	12"	EMI	12NMA5	1987	**£8**	
Poison Street	12"	EMI	12NMAD5	1987	**£12**	double
Price	7"	Abstract	ABS0028	1984	**£12**	
Stupid Questions	7"	EMI	NMAG7	1989	**£4**	gatefold PS
Vagabonds	7"	EMI	NMAG8	1989	**£4**	gatefold PS, badge
Vagabonds	7"	EMI	NMAP8	1989	**£4**	pic disc
White Coats	7"	EMI	NMA6	1987	**£8**	red vinyl
White Coats	12"	EMI	12NMA6	1987	**£6**	

NEW ORDER

Blue Monday	CDV-s	Factory	FACDV73R	1988	**£6**	
Ceremony (new version)	12"	Factory	FAC3312	1981	**£6**	cream/blue sleeve
Confusion (radio edit)	7"	Factory	FAC93	1983	**£12**	promo
Everything's Gone Green	12"	Factory	FBN8	1981	**£6**	Belgian
Hacienda Christmas Flexi	7"	Factory	FAC51B	1982	**£10**	flexi
Run 2 (radio edit)	7"	Factory	FAC273	1989	**£10**	promo
Substance 1987	CD	Factory	FACD200	1987	**£25**	
Thieves Like Us (radio edit)	7"	Factory	FAC103	1984	**£15**	promo
Touched By The Hand Of God	CD-s	Factory	FACD193	1987	**£6**	

NEW RIDERS OF THE PURPLE SAGE

Adventures Of Panama Red	LP	CBS	65687	1973	**£10**	
Brujo	LP	CBS	80405	1975	**£10**	
Gypsy Cowboy	LP	CBS	65008	1973	**£10**	
Home Home On The Road	LP	CBS	80060	1974	**£10**	
New Riders Of The Purple Sage	LP	CBS	64557	1971	**£10**	
Oh What A Mighty Time	LP	CBS	69182	1975	**£10**	
Powerglide	LP	CBS	64843	1972	**£10**	

NEW TWEEDY BROTHERS

New Tweedy Brothers	LP	Ridon	234		**£300**	US

NEW VAUDEVILLE BAND

Finchley Central	7"	Fontana	TF824	1967	**£4**	chart single
Green Street Green	7"	Fontana	TF853	1967	**£4**	chart single
New Vaudeville Band	7" EP	Fontana	TFE17497	1968	**£5**	
Peek-A-Boo	7"	Fontana	TF784	1967	**£4**	chart single
Winchester Cathedral	LP	Fontana	886408TY	1966	**£10**	
Winchester Cathedral	7"	Fontana	TF741	1966	**£4**	chart single

NEW YORK BLONDES

The "Madam X" featured on the New York Blondes' single is Debbie Harry, who was highly annoyed at the record's release. She had in fact recorded her vocal part purely as a demo for US DJ Rodney Bigenheimer to follow when making his own record (and the single's B side is indeed by him).

Little GTO	7"	London	HL10574	1979	**£5**	PS

NEW YORK DOLLS

Jet Boy	7"	Mercury	6052402	1973	**£5**	
Jet Boy	7"	Mercury	6160008	1977	**£4**	
Looking For A Kiss	7"	Kamera	ERA13	1986	**£4**	pic disc
Looking For A Kiss	12"	Kamera	ERA1312	1986	**£6**	pic disc
New York Dolls	LP	Mercury	6338270	1973	**£10**	
Too Much Too Soon	LP	Mercury	6338498	1974	**£10**	

NEW YORK PUBLIC LIBRARY

Got To Get Away	7"	MCA	MU1025	1968	**£6**	
I Ain't Gonna Eat Out My Heart Anymore	7"	Columbia	DB7948	1966	**£8**	
Love Me Two Times	7"	MCA	MU1045	1968	**£5**	

NEW YORK ROCK & ROLL ENSEMBLE

Faithful Friends	LP	Atco	228932	1969	**£20**	
Freedomburger	LP	CBS	64324	1972	**£15**	
New York Rock & Roll Ensemble	LP	Atco	33240	1968	**£20**	US
Reflections	LP	Atco	33312	1970	**£20**	US
Roll Over	LP	CBS	64126	1971	**£15**	
Running Down The Highway	7"	CBS	5292	1971	**£4**	

NEWBEATS

Ain't That Lovin' You Baby	7" EP	Hickory	LPE1506	1965	**£6**	
Big Beat Sounds	LP	Hickory	LP122	1965	**£15**	US
Birds Are For The Bees	7"	Hickory	451305	1965	**£4**	
Bread And Butter	LP	Hickory	LP120	1964	**£20**	US
Bread And Butter	7"	Hickory	451269	1964	**£5**	chart single
Crying My Heart Out	7"	Hickory	451387	1965	**£12**	
Newbeats	7" EP	Hickory	LPE1503	1964	**£6**	
Oh Girls Girls	7" EP	Hickory	LPE1510	1966	**£6**	
Run Baby Run	LP	Hickory	LP128	1965	**£15**	US
Run Baby Run	7"	Hickory	451332	1965	**£10**	
Run Baby Run	7"	London	HL10341	1971	**£4**	chart single
Too Sweet To Be Forgotten	7"	Hickory	451366	1965	**£6**	

NEWCASTLE BIG BAND

The Newcastle Big Band was a semi-professional sixteen-piece jazz band whose privately produced LP would mean little to anyone who had not actually seen the band live, were it not for the fact that the bass player just happened to go by the name of Sting.

Newcastle Big Band	LP	Impulse	ISSNBB106	1972	**£50**	

NEWEY, DENNIS

Border Patrol	7"	Philips	PB1198	1961	**£4**	
Checkpoint	7"	Philips	PB1134	1961	**£4**	

NEWLEY, ANTHONY

And The Heavens Cried	7"	Decca	F11331	1961	**£4**	chart single
Do You Mind	7"	Decca	F11220	1960	**£4**	chart single
I've Waited So Long	7"	Decca	F11127	1959	**£4**	chart single
Idle On Parade	7"	Decca	F11137	1959	**£4**	
Idle On Parade	7" EP	Decca	DFE6566	1959	**£10**	chart single
If She Should Come To You	7"	Decca	F11254	1960	**£4**	chart single
Love Is A Now And Then Thing	LP	Decca	LK4343	1960	**£10**	chart LP
More Hits From Tony	7" EP	Decca	DFE6655	1960	**£6**	
Personality	7"	Decca	F11142	1959	**£4**	chart single
Pop Goes the Weasel	7"	Decca	F11362	1961	**£4**	chart single
Someone To Love	7"	Decca	F11163	1959	**£4**	
Strawberry Fair	7"	Decca	F11295	1960	**£4**	chart single
This Time The Dream's On Me	7" EP	Decca	DFE6687	1961	**£5**	
Tony	LP	Decca	LK4406	1961	**£10**	chart LP
Tony's Hits	7" EP	Decca	DFE6629	1960	**£8**	
What Kind Of Fool Am I	7"	Decca	F11376	1961	**£4**	chart single
Why	7"	Decca	F11194	1960	**£4**	chart single

NEWLEY, ANTHONY, PETER SELLERS & JOAN COLLINS

Fool Britannia	LP	Ember	CEL902	1963	**£10**	chart LP

NEWMAN, ANDY

Rainbow	LP	Track	2406103	1971	**£12**	

NEWMAN, BRAD

Somebody To Love	7"	Fontana	H357	1962	**£4**	chart single

NEWMAN, COLIN

Not To	LP	4AD	CAD201	1982	**£10**	
Provisionally Entitled The Singing Fish	LP	4AD	CAD108	1981	**£10**	
We Means We Starts	7"	4AD	AD209	1982	**£5**	

NEWMAN, JIMMY

Fallen Star	7"	London	HLD8460	1957	**£10**	
Grin And Bear It	7"	MGM	MGM1037	1959	**£4**	
Grin And Bear It	7" EP	MGM	MGMEP706	1959	**£6**	
What About Me	7"	MGM	MGM1085	1960	**£4**	
Whatcha Gonna Do	7"	MGM	MGM1009	1959	**£4**	

NEWMAN, RANDY

Title	Format	Label	Cat. No.	Year	Price	Notes
12 Songs	LP	Reprise	K44084	1970	**£10**	
Blues (with Paul Simon)	7"	W. Bros	W9803	1983	**£6**	promo
Creates Something New Under The Sun	LP	Reprise	RS6286	1968	**£15**	
Gone Dead Train	7"	Reprise	RS20945	1970	**£4**	
Good Old Boys	LP	Reprise	MS42193	1974	**£10**	US quad
Live	LP	Reprise	K44151	1971	**£10**	
Lonely At The Top	7"	Reprise	K14155	1972	**£4**	
Love Story	7"	Reprise	RS20692	1968	**£4**	
Randy Newman	LP	Reprise	RS6286	1968	**£15**	
Sail Away	7"	Reprise	K14190	1972	**£4**	

NEWMAN, TOM

Title	Format	Label	Cat. No.	Year	Price	Notes
Don't Treat Your Woman Bad	7"	Virgin	VS130	1975	**£5**	
Ebony Eyes	7"	Virgin	VS141	1976	**£5**	
Faerie Symphony	LP	Decca	TXS123	1977	**£20**	
Fine Old Tom	LP	Virgin	V2022	1975	**£20**	
Live At The Argonaut	LP	Virgin	V2042	1975	**£80**	test pressing only
Sad Sing	7"	Virgin	VS120	1975	**£5**	
Sleep	7"	Virgin	VS133	1976	**£5**	
Soul Thing	7"	Decca	F12795	1968	**£8**	
Soul Thing	7"	Decca	F13041	1970	**£4**	

NEWS

Title	Format	Label	Cat. No.	Year	Price	Notes
Entertainer	7"	Decca	F12356	1966	**£6**	
This Is The Moment	7"	Decca	F12477	1966	**£6**	

NEWTON, WAYNE

Title	Format	Label	Cat. No.	Year	Price	Notes
Summer Wind	7"	Capitol	CL15410	1965	**£4**	

NEWTON-JOHN, OLIVIA

Title	Format	Label	Cat. No.	Year	Price	Notes
Deeper Than The Night	12"	EMI	12EMI2954	1979	**£6**	
Don't Stop Believin'	7"	EMI	EMI2519	1976	**£6**	PS
If Not For You	LP	Uni	73117	1971	**£15**	US
Magic	7"	Jet	P196	1980	**£6**	pic disc
Music Makes My Day	LP	Pye	NSPL28185	1974	**£10**	chart LP
Olivia	LP	Pye	NSPL28168	1972	**£10**	
Olivia Newton-John	LP	Pye	NSPL28155	1971	**£10**	
Sam	7"	EMI	EMI2616	1977	**£6**	PS
Till You Say You'll Be Mine	7"	Decca	F12396	1966	**£20**	
Totally Hot	LP	EMI	EMAP789	1978	**£12**	pic disc
Totally Hot	LP	Mobile Fid.	MFSL1040	1981	**£10**	US audiophile

NEWTON-JOHN, OLIVIA & E.L.O.

Title	Format	Label	Cat. No.	Year	Price	Notes
Xanadu	7"	Jet	185	1980	**£4**	pink vinyl
Xanadu	10"	Jet	10185	1980	**£6**	pink vinyl

NICE

Title	Format	Label	Cat. No.	Year	Price	Notes
America	7"	Immediate	IM068	1968	**£4**	chart single
Ars Longa Vita Brevis	LP	Immediate	IMSP020	1968	**£10**	
Brandenburger	7"	Immediate	IM072	1968	**£5**	
Country Pie	7"	Charisma	CB132	1971	**£4**	
Nice	LP	Immediate	IMSP026	1969	**£10**	chart LP
She Belongs To Me	7"	Immediate	AS4	1969	**£4**	
Thoughts Of Emerlist Davjack	LP	Immediate	IMSP016	1967	**£12**	
Thoughts Of Emerlist Davjack	7"	Immediate	AS2	1967	**£30**	sampler & John Peel interview
Thoughts Of Emerlist Davjack	7"	Immediate	IM059	1967	**£5**	

NICHOLLS, BILLY

Title	Format	Label	Cat. No.	Year	Price	Notes
Would You Believe	LP	Immediate	IMLP009	1967	**£30**	
Would You Believe	7"	Immediate	IM063	1968	**£10**	

NICHOLLS, JANICE

Title	Format	Label	Cat. No.	Year	Price	Notes
Oi'll Give It Five	7"	Decca	F11586	1963	**£5**	

NICKS, STEVIE

Title	Format	Label	Cat. No.	Year	Price	Notes
Bella Donna	LP	Mobile Fid.	MFSL1121	1982	**£12**	US audiophile

NICO

Title	Format	Label	Cat. No.	Year	Price	Notes
Chelsea Girl	LP	MGM	2353025	1968	**£15**	
Desert Shore	LP	Reprise	RSLP6424	1971	**£15**	

Title	Format	Label	Cat. No.	Year	Price	Notes
End	LP	Island	ILPS9311	1974	**£10**	
I'm Not Saying	7"	Immediate	IM003	1965	**£25**	
Marble Index	LP	Elektra	EKL4029	1968	**£20**	mono
Marble Index	LP	Elektra	EKS74029	1968	**£15**	stereo
Vegas	7"	Flicknife	FLS206	1981	**£5**	

NICOL, JIMMY

Title	Format	Label	Cat. No.	Year	Price	Notes
Baby Please Don't Go	7"	Pye	7N15699	1964	**£10**	
Clementine	7"	Decca	F12107	1965	**£10**	
Humpty Dumpty	7"	Pye	7N15623	1964	**£12**	
Husky	7"	Pye	7N15666	1964	**£10**	

NIGHT OWLS

Title	Format	Label	Cat. No.	Year	Price	Notes
Twisting The Oldies	LP	Valmor	79	1962	**£20**	US

NIGHT SHADES

Title	Format	Label	Cat. No.	Year	Price	Notes
Be My Guest	7"	CBS	201763	1965	**£4**	
Fell So Fast	7"	CBS	201817	1965	**£4**	

NIGHT SHADOWS

Title	Format	Label	Cat. No.	Year	Price	Notes
Square Root Of Two	LP	Hottrax	1414	1968	**£100**	US

NIGHT-TIMERS

Title	Format	Label	Cat. No.	Year	Price	Notes
Music Played On	7"	Parlophone	R5355	1965	**£8**	

NIGHTCAPS

Title	Format	Label	Cat. No.	Year	Price	Notes
Wine Wine Wine	LP	Vandan	VRLP8124	1961	**£40**	US

NIGHTCRAWLERS

Title	Format	Label	Cat. No.	Year	Price	Notes
Little Black Egg	LP	Kapp	KL1520	1967	**£25**	US
Little Black Egg	7"	London	HLR10109	1967	**£12**	

NIGHTHAWK, ROBERT

Title	Format	Label	Cat. No.	Year	Price	Notes
Robert Nighthawk	7" EP	XX	MIN718		**£4**	

NIGHTHAWKS

Title	Format	Label	Cat. No.	Year	Price	Notes
Rock And Roll	LP	Aladdin	101	195-	**£75**	US

NIGHTMARES IN WAX

Title	Format	Label	Cat. No.	Year	Price	Notes
Birth Of A Nation	7"	Inevitable	INEV0002	1980	**£15**	

NIGHTRIDERS

Title	Format	Label	Cat. No.	Year	Price	Notes
It's Only The Dog	7"	Polydor	56116	1966	**£15**	

NIGHTSHIFT

Title	Format	Label	Cat. No.	Year	Price	Notes
Corrine Corrina	7"	Piccadilly	7N35243	1965	**£10**	
That's My Story	7"	Piccadilly	7N35264	1965	**£8**	

NILE, BILL & HIS GOODTIME BAND

Title	Format	Label	Cat. No.	Year	Price	Notes
I Try Not To Laugh	7"	Deram	DM290	1970	**£5**	

NILSSON, HARRY

Title	Format	Label	Cat. No.	Year	Price	Notes
Aerial Pandemonium Ballet	LP	RCA	SF8326	1972	**£10**	
Duit On Mon Dei	LP	RCA	APD10817	1974	**£10**	US quad
Nilsson Schmilsson	LP	RCA	APD10319	1974	**£10**	US quad
Point	LP	RCA	LPSX1004	1972	**£12**	US, with book
Sandman	LP	RCA	APD11031	1975	**£10**	US quad
Scatalogue	LP	RCA	SP33567	1974	**£20**	US promo compilation
Son Of Dracula	LP	Rapple	APL10220	1974	**£10**	
Spotlight On...	LP	Tower	ST5095	1967	**£15**	US

NILSSON, HARRY & JOHN LENNON

Title	Format	Label	Cat. No.	Year	Price	Notes
Pussy Cats	LP	RCA	APD10570	1974	**£12**	US quad

NIMOY, LEONARD

Title	Format	Label	Cat. No.	Year	Price	Notes
Mr.Spock's Music From Outer Space	LP	Dot	DLP3794	1967	**£20**	US
New World Of...	LP	Dot	DLP25966	1969	**£12**	US
Outer Space/Inner Mind	LP	Paramount	1030	197-	**£15**	US
Touch Of...	LP	Dot	DLP25910	1969	**£12**	US
Two Sides Of...	LP	Dot	DLP25835	1968	**£12**	US
Way I Feel	LP	Dot	DLP25883	1968	**£12**	US

NINE DAYS WONDER

Title	Format	Label	Cat. No.	Year	Price	Notes
Nine Days Wonder	LP	Harvest	SHSP4014	1971	**£12**	

NINE NINE NINE

Title	Format	Label	Cat. No.	Year	Price	Notes
Action	12"	Labritian		1978	**£6**	
Homicide	7"	United Artists	UP36467	1978	**£4**	green vinyl
I'm Alive	7"	Labritian	LAB999	1977	**£12**	
Nasty Nasty	78	United Artists	FREE7	1977	**£25**	promo
Nasty Nasty	7"	United Artists	UP36299	1977	**£5**	green vinyl
Titanic	12"	Wizard	ZS12309	197-	**£6**	

NINE-THIRTY FLY

Title	Format	Label	Cat. No.	Year	Price	Notes
Nine-Thirty Fly	LP	Ember		1972	**£50**	

NINETEEN TEN FRUITGUM COMPANY

Title	Format	Label	Cat. No.	Year	Price	Notes
1,2,3, Red Light	7"	Pye	7N25468	1968	**£4**	
Goody Goody Gum Drops	LP	Buddah	BDS5027	1968	**£10**	US
Hard Rode	LP	Buddah	BDS5043	1969	**£10**	US
Indian Giver	LP	Buddah	BDS5036	1969	**£10**	US
Juiciest Fruitgum	LP	Buddah	BDS5057	1969	**£10**	US
May I Take A Giant Step	7"	Pye	7N25458	1968	**£4**	
Pop Goes The Weasel	7"	Pye	7N25478	1968	**£4**	
Red Light	LP	Buddah	BDS5022	1968	**£10**	US
Simon Says	LP	Buddah	BDS5010	1968	**£10**	US
Simon Says	7"	Pye	7N25447	1968	**£4**	chart single

NING

Title	Format	Label	Cat. No.	Year	Price	Notes
Machine	7"	Decca	F23114	1971	**£6**	

NINO & THE EBBTIDES

Title	Format	Label	Cat. No.	Year	Price	Notes
Those Oldies But Goodies	7"	Top Rank	JAR572	1961	**£6**	

NIPPLE ERECTORS

The Pogues' Shane MacGowan began his recording career with the punk Nipple Erectors, later abbreviated to the less controversial Nips (See below).

Title	Format	Label	Cat. No.	Year	Price	Notes
King Of The Bop	7"	Soho	SH1	1978	**£10**	

NIPS

Title	Format	Label	Cat. No.	Year	Price	Notes
All The Time In The World	7"	Soho	SH4	1978	**£4**	
Gabrielle	7"	Soho	SH9	1980	**£4**	
Happy Song	7"	Burning Rome	TP5	1981	**£5**	
Only At The End Of The Beginning	LP	Soho	HOHO1	1980	**£10**	

NIRVANA

Title	Format	Label	Cat. No.	Year	Price	Notes
All Of Us	LP	Island	ILPS9087	1968	**£30**	
All Of Us	7"	Island	WIP6045	1968	**£8**	
Dedicated To Markos III	LP	Pye	NSPL28132	1970	**£40**	
Girl In The Park	7"	Island	WIP6038	1968	**£10**	
Local Anaesthetic	LP	Vertigo	6360031	1971	**£20**	spiral label
Nirvana	LP	Metromedia	1018	1970	**£20**	US
Oh! What A Performance	7"	Island	WIP6057	1969	**£8**	
Pentecost Hotel	7"	Island	WIP6020	1967	**£8**	
Pentecost Hotel	7"	Philips	6006127	1971	**£5**	
Rainbow Chaser	7"	Island	WIP6029	1968	**£8**	chart single
Rainbow Chaser	7"	Island	WIP6180	1976	**£4**	
Rainbow Chaser	7"	Philips	6006129	1972	**£5**	
Saddest Day Of My Life	7"	Vertigo	6059035	1970	**£10**	
Simon Simopath	LP	Island	ILPS9059	1967	**£30**	
Songs Of Love And Praise	LP	Philips	6308089	1972	**£30**	
Stadium	7"	Philips	6006166	1972	**£5**	
Tiny Goddess	7"	Island	WIP6016	1967	**£8**	
Wings Of Love	7"	Island	WIP6052	1968	**£10**	
World Is Cold Without You	7"	Pye	7N25525	1970	**£10**	

NITE PEOPLE

Title	Format	Label	Cat. No.	Year	Price	Notes
Is This A Dream	7"	Page One	POF159	1969	**£6**	
Love, Love, Love	7"	Page One	POF149	1969	**£10**	
Morning Sun	7"	Fontana	TF919	1968	**£10**	
Nite People	LP	Page One		1968	**£90**	
Season Of The Rain	7"	Page One	POF174	1970	**£6**	
Summertime Blues	7"	Fontana	TF885	1967	**£8**	

Title	Format	Label	Cat. No.	Year	Price	Notes
Sweet Tasting Wine	7"	Fontana	TF747	1966	**£6**	

NITE ROCKERS

Title	Format	Label	Cat. No.	Year	Price	Notes
Ooh Bay	7"	RCA	RCA1079	1958	**£20**	

NITTY GRITTY DIRT BAND

Title	Format	Label	Cat. No.	Year	Price	Notes
Alive	LP	Liberty	LST7615	1969	**£12**	US
All The Good Times	LP	United Artists	UAS29284	1972	**£10**	
Dead And Alive	LP	Liberty	LBS83286	1969	**£10**	
Dirt, Silver & Gold	LP	United Artists	UAT9802	1976	**£15**	US triple
Dreams	LP	United Artists	SP469	1979	**£15**	US promo sampler
Interview	LP	United Artists	SP117	1975	**£15**	US promo
Jambalaya	7"	United Artists	UP35357	1972	**£4**	
Nitty Gritty Dirt Band	LP	Liberty	LST7501	1967	**£12**	US
Pure Dirt	LP	Liberty	LBL83122	1968	**£12**	
Rare Junk	LP	Liberty	LST7611	1967	**£12**	US
Rave On	7"	Liberty	LBF15358	1970	**£4**	
Ricochet	LP	Liberty	LST7516	1967	**£12**	US
Some Of Shelley's Blues	7"	United Artists	UP35282	1971	**£4**	
Some Of Shelley's Blues	7"	United Artists	UP35500	1973	**£4**	
Stars And Stripes Forever	LP	United Artists	UAS29570	1974	**£12**	double
Symphonion Dream	LP	United Artists	UAS29850	1975	**£10**	
Uncle Charlie And His Dog Teddy	LP	Liberty	LBG83345	1970	**£12**	
Will The Circle Be Unbroken	LP	United Artists	UAT9801	1973	**£25**	US triple

NITZSCHE, JACK

Jack Nitzsche was Phil Spector's arranger during the sixties and hence due to as much credit as Spector himself for the invention of the "wall of sound" that is so characteristic of Spector's productions. Nitzsche made a number of instrumental records in a series of attempts to take advantage of contemporary music fads, but his masterpiece is "St.Giles Cripplegate", recorded in 1972. This is a suite of short pieces scored for a small group of strings and is essentially a classical work made contemporary by its use of acid harmonies.

Title	Format	Label	Cat. No.	Year	Price	Notes
Chopin '66	LP	Reprise	R6200	1966	**£15**	US
Hits Of The Beatles	LP	Reprise	R6115	1964	**£20**	US
Lonely Surfer	LP	Reprise	R6101	1963	**£20**	US
Lonely Surfer	7"	Reprise	R20202	1963	**£10**	
Night Walker	7"	Reprise	R20337	1964	**£8**	
St.Giles Cripplegate	LP	Reprise	MS2092	1972	**£15**	US

NIX NOMADS

Title	Format	Label	Cat. No.	Year	Price	Notes
You're Nobody Till Somebody Loves You	7"	HMV	POP1354	1964	**£40**	

NNB

Title	Format	Label	Cat. No.	Year	Price	Notes
Slack	7"	Wave Seven	WSNNB	1978	**£30**	

NO INTRODUCTION

Title	Format	Label	Cat. No.	Year	Price	Notes
No Introduction	LP	Spark		1968	**£20**	

NOAKES, RAB

Title	Format	Label	Cat. No.	Year	Price	Notes
Do You See The Light	LP	Decca	SKL5061	1970	**£15**	
Never Too Late	LP	W. Bros	K56114	1975	**£10**	
Rab Noakes	LP	A&M	AMLS68119	1972	**£12**	
Red Pump Special	LP	W. Bros	K46284	1974	**£10**	
Restless	LP	Ring O	2339201	1978	**£10**	

NOBLE, LISA

Title	Format	Label	Cat. No.	Year	Price	Notes
It's A Boy	7"	Decca	F11051	1958	**£4**	
Maggie	7"	Decca	F11006	1958	**£4**	

NOBLEMEN

Title	Format	Label	Cat. No.	Year	Price	Notes
Thunder Wagon	7"	Top Rank	JAR155	1959	**£4**	

NOCTURNES

Title	Format	Label	Cat. No.	Year	Price	Notes
Troika	7"	Solar	SRP102	1964	**£6**	

NOCTURNS

Title	Format	Label	Cat. No.	Year	Price	Notes
Carpet Man	7"	Columbia	DB8453	1968	**£4**	
Carrying On	7"	Decca	F12002	1964	**£6**	
I Wish You Would Show Me Your Mind	7"	Columbia	DB8158	1967	**£4**	
Montage	7"	Columbia	DB8493	1968	**£4**	
New Man	7"	Columbia	DB8332	1968	**£4**	
Wanted Alive	LP	Columbia	SCX6315	1968	**£15**	
Why	7"	Columbia	DB8219	1967	**£5**	

NODE, PROF. ERNEST
Egg Plant That Ate Chicago 7" Columbia DB8100 1967 **£4**

NOEL
Is There More To Life (With Sparks) LP Virgin 1980 **£10** pic disc

NOEL, DICK
Birds And The Bees 7" London HLH8295 1956 **£8**

NOIR
We Had To Let You Have It LP Dawn DNLS3029 1971 **£20**

NOLAND, TERRY
Oh Baby Look At Me 7" Coral Q72311 1958 **£20**
Terry Noland LP Brunswick BL54041 1958 **£100** US

NOONE, PETER
Oh You Pretty Thing 7" RAK RAK114 1971 **£4** chart single
Right On Mother 7" RAK RAK121 1971 **£6**

NORDINE, KEN
Classic Collection LP Dot DLP25880 1968 **£12** US
Colors LP Philips 200224 196- **£10** US
Concert In The Sky LP Decca DL8550 1957 **£20** US
Ken Nordine Reads 7" EP London RED1091 1957 **£6**
Love Words LP Dot DLP3115 1958 **£12** US
My Baby LP Dot DLP3142 1958 **£12** US
Next! LP Dot DLP3196 1959 **£12** US
Shifting Whispering Sands 7" London HLD8205 1955 **£10**
Son Of Word Jazz LP Dot DLP3096 1958 **£15** US
Twink LP Philips 200258 196- **£10** US
Word Jazz 7" EP London EZD19040 1959 **£5**
Word Jazz LP Dot DLP3075 1958 **£15** US
Word Jazz Vol.2 LP Dot DLP3301 1960 **£12** US

NORMAL
T.V.O.D. 7" Mute MUTE001 1978 **£4**

NORMAN & THE INVADERS
Night Train To Surbiton 7" United Artists UP1077 1965 **£12**

NORMAN CONQUEST
Two People 7" MGM MGM1376 1968 **£5**

NORMAN, LARRY
Bootleg LP One Way JC900 1971 **£12** US
In Another Land LP Solid Rock SRA2001 **£10** US
Only Visiting This Planet LP Street Level 8885 1974 **£10** US
So Long Ago/The Garden LP MGM SE4942 1973 **£10** US
Streams Of White Light LP Sunrise AB777 **£10** US
Street Level LP One Way JC7937 1970 **£12** US
Upon This Rock LP Impac HWS3121 **£10** US
Upon This Rock LP Key DOVE6 1969 **£12**

NORMAN, MONTY
Garden Of Eden 7" HMV POP281 1957 **£4**

NORMAN, OLIVER
Down In The Basement 7" Polydor 56176 1967 **£4**

NORTHERN LIGHTS
No Time 7" United Artists UP1123 1966 **£15**
Through Darkness Light 7" United Artists UP1161 1966 **£15**

NORTHWIND
Sister Brother Lover LP Regal Z. SLRZ1020 1971 **£70**

NOSEBLEEDS
Ain't Bin To No Music School 7" Rabid TOSH12 1977 **£5**

NOTATIONS
Need Your Love 7" Chapter One **£5**

NOTES, FREDDIE & THE RUDIES

Title	Format	Label	Number	Year	Price	Notes
It Came Out Of The Sky	7"	B&C	CB125	1970	**£4**	
Montego Bay	7"	Trojan	TR7791	1970	**£4**	chart single
Unity	LP	Trojan	TBL109	1970	**£15**	

NOVA LOCAL

Title	Format	Label	Number	Year	Price	Notes
Nova 1	LP	MCA	MUPS377	1968	**£10**	

NOVAS

Title	Format	Label	Number	Year	Price	Notes
Crusher	7"	London	HLU9940	1965	**£4**	
Push A Little Harder	7"	RCA	RCA1360	1963	**£4**	

NRBQ

Title	Format	Label	Number	Year	Price	Notes
NRBQ	LP	CBS	63653	1969	**£10**	
Scraps	LP	Polydor	2329018	1971	**£10**	
Workshop	LP	Kama Sutra	KSBS2065	1973	**£10**	US

NSU

Title	Format	Label	Number	Year	Price	Notes
Turn On Or Turn Me Down	LP	Stable	SLE8002	1969	**£60**	

NU NOTES

Title	Format	Label	Number	Year	Price	Notes
Hall Of Mirrors	7"	HMV	POP1232	1963	**£5**	
Kathy	7"	HMV	POP1311	1964	**£4**	

NU TORNADOS

Title	Format	Label	Number	Year	Price	Notes
Philadelphia USA	7"	London	HLU8756	1958	**£4**	

NUCLEUS

Title	Format	Label	Number	Year	Price	Notes
Alley Cat	LP	Vertigo	6360124	1975	**£10**	
Awakening	LP	Mood	24000	1980	**£10**	
Belladonna	LP	Vertigo	6360076	1972	**£20**	spiral label
Direct Hits	LP	Vertigo	9286019	1976	**£10**	
Elastic Rock	LP	Vertigo	6360008	1970	**£15**	spiral label, chart LP
In Flagrante Delicto	LP	Capitol	11771	1977	**£10**	
Labyrinth	LP	Vertigo	6360091	1973	**£15**	
Out Of The Long dark	LP	Capitol	11916	1979	**£10**	
Roots	LP	Vertigo	6360100	1973	**£10**	
Snake Hips Etcetera	LP	Vertigo	6360119	1975	**£10**	
Solar Plexus	LP	Vertigo	6360039	1971	**£15**	spiral label
Under The Sun	LP	Vertigo	6360110	1974	**£10**	
We'll Talk About It Later	LP	Vertigo	6360027	1970	**£15**	spiral label

NUCLEUS (2)

Title	Format	Label	Number	Year	Price	Notes
Nucleus	LP	Mainstream	6120	1967	**£15**	US

NUGENT, TED

Title	Format	Label	Number	Year	Price	Notes
State Of Shock	LP	Epic	AS99607	1979	**£10**	US pic disc
Sweet Revenge	7"	Discreet	K19200	1973	**£5**	

NUGGETS

Title	Format	Label	Number	Year	Price	Notes
Quirl Up In My Arms	7"	Capitol	CL14216	1955	**£5**	
Shtiggy Boom	7"	Capitol	CL14267	1955	**£5**	

NUMAN, GARY

Title	Format	Label	Number	Year	Price	Notes
Beserker	7"	Numa	NUP4	1984	**£4**	shaped pic disc
Cars (E Reg Model)	7"	Beggars B.	BEG199P	1987	**£4**	pic disc
Cars	12"	Intercord	INT126502	1979	**£12**	German
Complex	12"	Beggars B.	BEG29T	1979	**£6**	
Fury	LP	Numa	NUMAZ1003	1985	**£10**	pic disc
I Die: You Die	7"	Beggars B.	BEG46A1	1980	**£15**	test pressing, different mix
Images Five And Six	7"	Fan Club	GNFCDA3		**£10**	
Images Nine And Ten	7"	Fan Club	GNFCDA5		**£10**	
Images One And Two	7"	Fan Club	GNFCDA1		**£10**	
Images Seven And Eight	7"	Fan Club	GNFCDA4		**£10**	
Images Three And Four	7"	Fan Club	GNFCDA2		**£10**	
Love Needs No Disguise	12"	Beggars B.	BEG68T	1981	**£6**	
Miracles	12"	Numa	NUM13	1985	**£6**	white vinyl
Photograph	LP	Intercord	INT146606		**£75**	German
Remember I Was Vapour	12"	Intercord	INT126600	1980	**£12**	German
Sister Surprise	12"	Beggars B.	BEG101T	1983	**£6**	
This Is Love	12"	Numa	NUMX16	1986	**£6**	double
Warriors	7"	Beggars B.	BEG95P	1983	**£15**	shaped pic disc

Photograph	LP	Intercord	INT146606		**£75**	German
Remember I Was Vapour	12"	Intercord	INT126600	1980	**£12**	German
Sister Surprise	12"	Beggars B.	BEG101T	1983	**£6**	
This Is Love	12"	Numa	NUMX16	1986	**£6**	double
Warriors	7"	Beggars B.	BEG95P	1983	**£15**	shaped pic disc
Your Fascination	7"	Numa	NUP9	1985	**£5**	pic disc
Your Fascination	12"	Numa	NUMP9	1985	**£8**	pic disc

NUMBER NINE BREAD STREET

	LP	Holyground			**£100**	

NURSE WITH WOUND

Chance Meeting On A Dissecting Table.	LP	United Dairies	UD01	1979	**£80**	
Insect And Individual Silenced	LP	United Dairies	UD08	1981	**£50**	
Merzbild Schwet	LP	United Dairies	UD04	1980	**£80**	
Ostranenie 1913	LP	Third Mind		1982	**£40**	
To The Quiet Man From A Tiny Girl	LP	United Dairies	UD03	1980	**£80**	

NUTTER, MAYF

Head Shrinker	7"	Vocalion	VL9282	1966	**£4**	

NYRO, LAURA

Laura Nyro is a singer-songwriter with soul - and it is that quality that makes her records so distinctive. The trilogy begun by "Eli And The Thirteenth Confession" represents her best work, with "Eli" perhaps having the edge. Any album that can take the listener from the bleakest despair ("Poverty Train"), through the wistfully romantic ("Emmie"), to uplifting joy ("Eli's Comin'") can only be described as special.

Christmas & The Beads Of Sweat	LP	CBS	64157	1970	**£12**	
Eli & The 13th Confession	LP	CBS	63346	1968	**£12**	
Eli's Coming	7"	CBS	3604	1968	**£4**	
First Songs	LP	CBS	64991	1973	**£10**	
Gonna Take A Miracle	LP	CBS	64770	1971	**£10**	
More Than A New Discovery	LP	Verve	FTS3020	1966	**£15**	
New York Tendaberry	LP	CBS	63510	1969	**£12**	
Up On The Roof	7"	CBS	5218	1970	**£4**	
Wedding Bell Blues	7"	Verve	VS1502	1967	**£4**	
When I Was A Freeport	7"	CBS	7028	1971	**£4**	

O

O LEVEL

East Sheen	7"	Psycho	PSYCHO1	1978	**£20**	2 PS's
Malcolm McLaren	7"	King's Road	KR002	197-	**£10**	2 PS's

O'HARA'S PLAYBOYS

Ballad Of The Soon Departed	7"	Fontana	TF872	1967	**£4**	
I Started A Joke	7"	Fontana	TF974	1968	**£4**	
In The Shelter Of My Heart	7"	Fontana	TF924	1968	**£4**	
Island In The Sun	7"	Fontana	TF893	1967	**£4**	
Spicks And Specks	7"	Fontana	TF793	1967	**£4**	
Start All Over	7"	Fontana	TF763	1966	**£4**	
Voices	7"	Fontana	TF949	1968	**£4**	

O'JAYS

Back On Top	LP	Bell	6014	1968	**£10**	US
Comin' Through	LP	Imperial	LP9290	1965	**£10**	US
I'll Be Sweeter Tomorrow	7"	Stateside	SS2073	1967	**£15**	
Lipstick Traces	7"	Liberty	LIB66102	1965	**£20**	
Soul Sounds	LP	Minit	LP40008	1967	**£10**	US
Stand In For Love	7"	Liberty	LIB66197	1966	**£8**	

O'KEEFE, JOHNNY

Real Wild Child	7"	Coral	Q72330	1958	**£25**	
Tell The Blues So Long	7"	Zodiac	ZR0016	196-	**£4**	

O'NEIL, MATTY

Don't Sell Daddy Any More Whisky	7"	London	L1037	1954	**£8**	

O.M.D.

The rarest Orchestral Manoeuvres In The Dark record is not one that a collector of the group's music is ever likely to find. As a mispressing, however, it is arguably only of interest to the completist in any case - the song "Souvenir" replaces "Love Action" as the A side on forty copies of the Human League single. Thirty-five of these were destroyed, which leaves a grand total of five copies available for collectors. In the circumstances, it is not realistic to quote a price for these.

Constructive Conversation With OMD	LP	Epic	AS1408	198-	**£15**	US promo
Dreaming	CD-s	Virgin	VSCD987	1988	**£20**	promo
Electricity	7"	Factory	FAC6	1979	**£10**	
Forever Live And Die	7"	Virgin	VSY888	1986	**£4**	pic disc
Genetic Engineering	7"	Virgin	VSY527	1983	**£4**	pic disc
La Femme Accident	7"	Virgin	VSS811	1985	**£4**	square pic disc
Locomotion	7"	Virgin	VSY660	1984	**£4**	pic disc
Never Turn Away	7"	Virgin	VSY727	1984	**£4**	pic disc
Telegraph	7"	Virgin	VSY580	1983	**£4**	pic disc

OCCASIONAL WORD ENSEMBLE

Year Of The Great Leap Sideways	LP	Dandelion	63753	1970	**£20**	

OCHS, PHIL

All The News That's Fit To Sing	LP	Elektra	EKL269	1964	**£20**	
Chords Of Fame	LP	A&M	AMLM64599	1974	**£15**	double
Greatest Hits	LP	A&M	AMLS973	1970	**£15**	
Gunfight At Carnegie Hall	LP	A&M	SP9010	1971	**£20**	Canadian
I Ain't Marchin' Anymore	LP	Elektra	EKL287	1965	**£20**	
I Ain't Marchin' Anymore	7"	Elektra	EKSN45002	1965	**£5**	
In Concert	LP	Elektra	EKL310	1966	**£20**	
Interviews With Phil Ochs	LP	Folkways	FB5321	1971	**£20**	US
Pleasure Of The Harbour	LP	A&M	AML913	1967	**£15**	
Rehearsals For Retirement	LP	A&M	AMLS934	1969	**£15**	
Small Circle Of Friends	7"	A&M	AMS716	1968	**£5**	
Tape From California	LP	A&M	AMLS919	1968	**£15**	

OCTOPUS

Laugh At The Poor Man	7"	P. Farthing	PEN705	1970	**£10**	

Restless Nights	LP	P. Farthing	PELS508	1969	**£120**	
River	7"	P. Farthing	PEN716	1970	**£10**	

OCTOPUS (2)

Octopus	LP	ESP	2000	1969	**£15**	US

ODDSOCKS

Men Of The Moment	LP	Sweet Folk	SFA030	1975	**£10**	

ODELL, ANN

A Little Taste	LP	DJM	DJLPS434	1973	**£15**	

ODIN

Odin	LP	Vertigo	6360608	1972	**£12**	

ODYSSEY

How Long Is Time	7"	Strike	JH312	1966	**£8**	
Odyssey	LP	Private			**£600**	US

OHIO EXPRESS

Beg Borrow And Steal	LP	Cameo	CS20000	1968	**£12**	US
Chewy Chewy	LP	Buddah	203015	1968	**£10**	
Down At Lulu's	7"	Pye	7N25469	1968	**£4**	
Mercy	LP	Buddah	BDS5037	1969	**£10**	US
Ohio Express	LP	Pye	NSPL28117	1968	**£10**	
Salt Water Taffy	LP	Buddah	BDS5021	1968	**£10**	US
Very Best Of...	LP	Buddah	BDS5058	1969	**£10**	US
Yummy Yummy Yummy	7"	Pye	7N25459	1968	**£4**	chart single

OHIO KNOX

Ohio Knox	LP	Reprise	RSLP6435	1971	**£10**	

OHO

Okinawa	LP	Private			**£35**	US

OKAYSIONS

Girl Watcher	7"	Stateside	SS2126	1969	**£12**	

OLA & THE JANGLERS

I Can Wait	7"	Decca	F12646	1967	**£5**	
What A Way To Die	7"	Transatlantic	BIG108	1968	**£6**	

OLD & IN THE WAY

Old And In The Way	LP	Round	RX103	1975	**£12**	

OLD MAN & THE SEA

Old Man And The Sea	LP	Sonet		1972	**£200**	

OLDFIELD, MIKE

Interesting variations exist with regard to the quadraphonic version of Mike Oldfield's "Tubular Bells". All copies of the picture disc are a stereo remix of the quadraphonic version, the same as first appeared in the four album "Boxed" compilation. The first forty thousand copies of the black vinyl edition are not a true quadraphonic recording at all, but merely a doctored version of the stereo issue. Thereafter, the records are a true quadraphonic mix, but there is no indication on the cover or label of the record that the substitution has been made.

Blue Peter	7"	Virgin	VSDJ317	1979	**£6**	1 sided promo
Cuckoo Song	7"	Virgin	VS198	1977	**£4**	PS
Don Alfonso	7"	Virgin	VS117	1975	**£8**	
Family Man	7"	Virgin	VSY489	1982	**£5**	pic disc
Five Miles Out	7"	Virgin	VSY464	1982	**£5**	pic disc
Guilty	12"	Virgin	VS24512	1979	**£6**	blue vinyl
Hergest Ridge	7"	Virgin		1974	**£10**	1 sided promo sampler
Impressions	LP	Tellydisc	TEL4	1979	**£20**	
In Dulce Jubilo	7"	Virgin	VS131	1975	**£4**	PS
Mike Oldfield's Single	7"	Virgin	VS101	1974	**£6**	PS
Mistake	7"	Virgin	VSY541	1982	**£5**	pic disc
Moonlight Shadow	7"	Virgin	VSY586	1983	**£4**	pic disc
Ommadawn	LP	Virgin	QV2043	1976	**£15**	quad
Ommadawn	12"	Virgin	VDJ9	1975	**£12**	promo sampler
Orchestral Tubular Bells	7"	Virgin	VDJ1	1975	**£8**	promo sampler
Portsmouth	7"	Virgin	VS163	1976	**£4**	PS
Shine	7"	Virgin	VSS863	1986	**£5**	shaped pic disc
Spanish Tune	7"	Virgin	VS112	1974	**£20**	promo

Tubular Bells	LP	Virgin	QV2001	1974	**£15**	quad
Tubular Bells	LP	Virgin	VP2001	1978	**£10**	pic disc
William Tell Overture	7"	Virgin	VS167	1977	**£4**	PS

OLDHAM, ANDREW ORCHESTRA

16 Hip Hits	LP	Ace Of Clubs	ACL1180	1964	**£35**	
365 Rolling Stones	7"	Decca	F11878	1964	**£15**	
East Meets West	LP	Parrot	PA61003	1965	**£20**	US
Funky And Fleopatra	7"	Decca	F11829	1964	**£15**	B side plays Jeannie & Her Redheads
Maggie May	LP	Decca	LK4636	1964	**£20**	
Right Of Way	7"	Decca	F11987	1964	**£15**	
Rolling Stones Songbook	LP	Decca	LK4796	1966	**£30**	
There Are But Five Rolling Stones	7"	Decca	F11817	1964	**£20**	

OLENN, JOHNNY

Born Reckless	7"	Mercury	AMT1050	1959	**£15**	
Just Rollin'	LP	Liberty	LRP3029	1958	**£75**	US
My Idea Of Love	7"	London	HLU8388	1957	**£30**	

OLIVER

Good Morning Starshine	7"	CBS	4435	1969	**£4**	chart single
Standing Stone	LP	Private		1974	**£250**	

OLIVER, JOHNNY

Chain Gang	7"	MGM	SP1165	1956	**£4**	

OLSSON, NIGEL

Alabama	7"	DJM	DJS10266	1972	**£4**	
Drum Orchestra	LP	DJM	DJLPS417	1972	**£12**	
Girl We've Got To Keep On	7"	Rocket	ROKN506	1976	**£4**	
Nature's Way	7"	DJM	DJS10239	1972	**£4**	
Nigel Olsson	LP	Rocket	ROLL2	1975	**£10**	
Only One Woman	7"	Rocket	PIG13	1974	**£4**	
Something Lacking In Me	7"	Rocket	ROKN502	1975	**£4**	

OLYMPICS

Baby Do The Philly Dog	7"	Action	ACT4539	1969	**£5**	
Baby Do The Philly Dog	7"	Action	ACT4539	1969	**£20**	demo
Baby Do The Philly Dog	7"	Fontana	TF778	1966	**£4**	
Baby It's Hot	7"	Vogue	V9204	1962	**£4**	
Dance By The Light Of The Moon	LP	Arvee	A424	1961	**£40**	US
Dance With A Dolly	7"	Vogue	V9181	1961	**£4**	
Dance With The Teacher	7"	HMV	POP564	1958	**£6**	
Do The Bounce	LP	Tri-Disc	1001	1963	**£20**	US
Doin' The Hully Gully	LP	Arvee	A423	1960	**£50**	US
Good Lovin'	7"	W. Bros	WB157	1965	**£12**	
I Wish I Could Shimmy	7"	Vogue	V9174	1960	**£5**	chart single
I'll Do A Little Bit More	7"	Action	ACT4556	1969	**£6**	demo
Little Pedro	7"	Vogue	V9184	1961	**£6**	B side Cappy Lewis
Party Time	LP	Arvee	A429	1961	**£40**	US
Private Eye	7"	Columbia	DB4346	1959	**£5**	
Something Old, Something New	LP	Mirwood	M7003	1966	**£15**	US
Stomp	7"	Vogue	V9198	1962	**£5**	
The Bounce	7"	Sue	WI348	1964	**£8**	
Twist	7"	Vogue	V9196	1962	**£5**	
We Go Together	7"	Fontana	TF678	1966	**£5**	
Western Movies	7"	HMV	POP528	1958	**£10**	chart single

ONE

One	LP	Fontana	STL5539	1969	**£20**	

ONE (2)

One	LP	Grunt	FTR1008	1972	**£10**	US

ONE-O-ONERS

Elgin Avenue Breakdown	LP	Andalucia	AND101	1981	**£10**	
Key To Your Heart	7"	Chiswick	NS3	1976	**£6**	PS
Sweet Revenge	7"	Chiswick	NS63	1981	**£4**	

ONES

The lead guitarist with The Ones was Edgar Froese, later to play in an entirely different style as leader of Tangerine Dream.

Lady Greengrass	7"	Star Club	148593STF	1966	**£50**	German

ONES (2)

Ones	LP	Ashwood Hse	1105	1966	**£120**	US

ONLY ONES

Many of the punk musicians to emerge in the late seventies were far from being the brash youngsters they were painted. Skulking at the back of the Only Ones' line-up was the familiar face of Mike Kellie, formerly the drummer with Spooky Tooth. The pedigree of the group's bass player went back even further - he was a member of Scottish beat group, the Beatstalkers. This experience was no doubt the reason the Only Ones were able to deliver such convincing interpretations of Peter Perrett's material. "Another Girl, Another Planet" in particular is a classic rock recording by any standard.

Another Girl, Another Planet	7"	CBS	6228	1978	**£8**	
Another Girl, Another Planet	7"	CBS	6576	1978	**£12**	promo only
Another Girl, Another Planet	12"	CBS	126576	1978	**£8**	
Baby's Got A Gun	7"	Vengeance	VEN002	1983	**£4**	
Fools	7"	CBS	8535	1980	**£5**	
Lovers Of Today	7"	Vengeance	VEN001	1977	**£15**	
Lovers Of Today	12"	Vengeance	VEN001	1977	**£15**	
Out There In The Night	12"	CBS	127285	1979	**£6**	blue vinyl
Trouble In The World	7"	CBS	7963	1979	**£5**	
Trouble In The World	7"	CBS	7963	1979	**£50**	black & red PS
You've Got To Pay	7"	CBS	7086	1979	**£4**	

ONO, YOKO

Approximately Infinite Universe	LP	Apple	SAPDO1001	1973	**£30**	double
Death Of Samantha	7"	Apple	47	1973	**£8**	
Feeling The Space	LP	Apple	SAPCOR26	1973	**£30**	
Fly	LP	Apple	SPTU101/2	1971	**£30**	double
Mind Train	7"	Apple	41	1972	**£4**	
Mind Train	7"	Apple	41	1972	**£10**	PS
Mrs.Lennon	7"	Apple	38	1971	**£6**	
Plastic Ono Band	LP	Apple	SAPCOR17	1970	**£30**	
Run Run Run	7"	Apple	48	1973	**£8**	
Walking On Thin Ice	12"	WEA	PROA934	1981	**£15**	promo
Welcome (Many Sides Of Yoko Ono)	LP	Apple	PRP18026	1974	**£50**	Japanese promo

ONYX

Air	7"	Parlophone	R5888	1971	**£4**	
Next Stop Is Mine	7"	Parlophone	R5906	1971	**£4**	

OPAL BUTTERFLY

Beautiful Beige	7"	CBS	3576	1968	**£15**	
Mary Anne With The Shakey Hand	7"	CBS	3921	1969	**£20**	

OPEL, JACKIE

Cry Me A River	7"	King	KG1011	196-	**£10**	
Done With A Friend	7"	Ska Beat	JB190	1965	**£10**	
Go Whey	7"	Island	WI209	1965	**£10**	
Little More	7"	Ska Beat	JB227	1965	**£10**	
Pity The Fool	7"	R&B	JB160	1964	**£10**	
Solid Rock	7"	R&B	JB138	1964	**£10**	
Wipe Those Tears	7"	Island	WI203	1965	**£10**	

OPEN MIND

Magic Potion	7"	Philips		1969	**£50**	
Open Mind	LP	Philips	SBL7893	1969	**£170**	

OPEN ROAD

Swamp Fever	7"	Greenwich	GSS102	1972	**£8**	
Windy Daze	LP	Greenwich	GSLP1001	1971	**£25**	

OPUS

Baby Come On	7"	Columbia	DB8675	1970	**£15**	

ORA

Ora	LP	Tangerine		1969	**£150**	

ORANGE BICYCLE

Carry That Weight	7"	Parlophone	R5811	1969	**£10**	
Early Pearly Morning	7"	Columbia	DB8352	1968	**£10**	
Goodbye Stranger	7"	Regal Z.	RZ3029	1971	**£10**	
Hyacinth Threads	7"	Columbia	DB8259	1967	**£10**	

Jelly On The Bread	7"	Parlophone	R5854	1970	**£10**	
Jenskadajka	7"	Columbia	DB8413	1968	**£10**	
Laura's Garden	7"	Columbia	DB8311	1967	**£10**	
Orange Bicycle	LP	Parlophone	PCS7108	1970	**£40**	
Sing This All Together	7"	Columbia	DB8483	1968	**£10**	
Take Me To The Pilot	7"	Parlophone	R5827	1970	**£10**	
Tonight I'll Be Staying Here	7"	Parlophone	R5789	1969	**£10**	

ORANGE JUICE

One feature of the punk explosion was the emergence of a number of independently run record labels. Only a lucky few have survived, but one of the most fondly regarded of those that have not is Postcard records. Much of this regard has to do with the label's sponsoring of Orange Juice. The group's series of sparkling singles are amongst the delights of the immediate post-punk years and they possess a drive and a liveliness somewhat lacking in the new versions of the same songs recorded for the first Polydor LP. These singles are rightly highly prized.

Blue Boy	7"	Postcard	80-2	1980	**£20**	hand coloured sleeve
Blue Boy	7"	Postcard	80-2	1980	**£8**	white or brown sleeve
Falling And Laughing	7"	Postcard	80-0	1980	**£40**	pic in bag
Falling And Laughing	7"	Postcard	80-0	1980	**£60**	pic in bag, Felicity flexi
Falling And Laughing	7"	Postcard	80-0	1980	**£75**	pic in bag, Felicity flexi, postcard
Poor Old Soul	7"	Postcard	81-2	1981	**£8**	
Poor Old Soul	7"	Postcard	81-2	1981	**£10**	lyric postcard
Simply Thrilled Honey	7"	Postcard	80-6	1980	**£8**	
Simply Thrilled Honey	7"	Postcard	80-6	1980	**£20**	colour insert in bag

ORANGE MACHINE

Three Jolly Little Dwarfs	7"	Pye	7N17559	1968	**£20**	
You Can All Join In	7"	Pye	7N17680	1969	**£15**	

ORANGE PEEL

I Got No Time	7"	Reflection	R55	1970	**£8**	

ORANGE SEAWEED

Stay Awhile	7"	Pye	7N17515	1968	**£8**	

ORBISON, ROY

At The Rockhouse	LP	Sun	LP1260	1961	**£100**	US
Big O	LP	London	HAU8406	1970	**£15**	
Blue Angel	7"	London	HLU9207	1960	**£4**	chart single
Blue Bayou	7"	London	HLU9777	1963	**£4**	chart single
Born To Be Loved By You	7"	London	HLU10176	1968	**£4**	
Borne On The Wind	7"	London	HLU9845	1964	**£4**	chart single
Break My Mind	7"	London	HLU10294	1969	**£4**	
Breakin' Up Is Breakin' My Heart	7"	London	HLU10015	1966	**£4**	chart single
Classic	LP	London	HAU8297	1966	**£12**	chart LP
Crawling Back	7"	London	HLU10000	1965	**£4**	chart single
Crowd	7"	London	HLU9561	1962	**£4**	chart single
Cry Softly Lonely One	7"	London	HLU10143	1967	**£4**	
Cry Softly Lonely One	LP	London	HAU8357	1968	**£15**	
Crying	7"	London	HLU9405	1961	**£4**	
Crying	LP	London	HAU2437	1962	**£15**	chart LP, mono
Crying	LP	London	SHU6229	1962	**£15**	chart LP, stereo
Crying	LP	Monument	M4007	1962	**£40**	US
Devil Doll	7" EP	Ember	EP4570	1965	**£8**	
Dream Baby	7"	London	HLU9511	1962	**£4**	chart single
Early Orbison	LP	Monument	LMO5013	1967	**£10**	
Exciting Sounds	LP	Ember	NR5013	1964	**£10**	chart LP
Falling	7"	London	HLU9727	1963	**£4**	chart single
Fastest Guitar Alive	LP	London	HAU8358	1968	**£20**	
God Loves You	7"	London	HLU10358	1972	**£4**	
Goodnight	7"	London	HLU9951	1965	**£4**	chart single
Greatest Hits	LP	Monument	M4009	1962	**£15**	US
Hank Williams The Roy Orbison Way	LP	MGM	SE4683	1970	**£10**	US
Heartache	7"	London	HLU10222	1968	**£4**	chart single
Hillbilly Rock	7" EP	London	RES1089	1957	**£40**	
I'm Hurtin'	7"	London	HLU7108	1961	**£6**	export
I'm Hurtin'	7"	London	HLU9307	1961	**£4**	
In Dreams	LP	London	HAU8108	1963	**£15**	chart LP
In Dreams	7"	London	HLU9676	1963	**£4**	chart single
In Dreams	7" EP	London	REU1373	1963	**£6**	
It's Over	7"	London	HLU9882	1964	**£4**	chart single

Title	Format	Label	Cat. No.	Year	Price	Notes
It's Over	7" EP	London	REU1435	1964	**£6**	
Lana	7"	London	HLU10051	1966	**£4**	chart single
Last Night	7"	London	HLU10339	1971	**£4**	
Lonely And Blue	LP	London	HAU2342	1961	**£15**	chart LP
Lonely And Blue	LP	Monument	M4002	1961	**£40**	US
Love Hurts	7" EP	London	REU1440	1965	**£6**	
Memphis	LP	London	SHU8445	1973	**£12**	
Memphis Tennessee	7"	London	HLU10388	1972	**£4**	
More Greatest Hits	LP	Monument	MLP8024	1962	**£12**	US
My Friend	7"	London	HLU10261	1969	**£4**	chart single
Oh Pretty Woman	LP	London	HAU8207	1964	**£15**	chart LP
Oh Pretty Woman	7"	London	HLU9919	1964	**£4**	chart single
Oh Pretty Woman	7" EP	London	REU1437	1964	**£6**	
Only The Lonely	7"	London	HLU9149	1960	**£4**	chart single
Only The Lonely	7" EP	London	REU1274	1960	**£8**	
Ooby Dooby	7"	Sun	6094001	197-	**£4**	
Orbison Way	LP	London	HAU8279	1966	**£15**	chart LP
Orbisongs	LP	Monument	LMO5004	1966	**£10**	chart LP
Penny Arcade	7"	London	HLU10285	1969	**£4**	chart single
Pretty Paper	7"	London	HLU9930	1964	**£4**	chart single
Ride Away	7"	London	HLU9986	1965	**£4**	chart single
Roy Orbison And Others	LP	Ember	FA2005	1966	**£10**	
Roy Orbison Sings	LP	London	SHU8435	1972	**£10**	
Roy Orbison's Stage Show Hits	7" EP	London	REU1439	1965	**£6**	
Runnin' Scared	7"	London	HLU9342	1961	**£4**	chart single
She	7"	London	HLU10159	1967	**£4**	
Sings Don Gibson	LP	London	HAU8318	1967	**£15**	
So Good	7"	London	HLU10113	1967	**£4**	chart single
So Young	7"	London	HLU10310	1970	**£4**	
Special Delivery	LP	Camden	CAL820	1964	**£12**	US
Sweet And Easy To Love	7"	Ember	EMBS209	1965	**£4**	
Sweet And Easy To Love	7"	Ember	EMBS209	1965	**£8**	PS
Sweet And Easy To Love	7" EP	Ember	EP4546	1964	**£8**	
There Is Only One	LP	London	HAU8252	1965	**£15**	chart LP
There Won't Be Many Coming Home	7"	London	HLU10096	1966	**£4**	chart single
This Kind Of Love	7"	Ember	EMBS200	1964	**£4**	
Too Soon To Know	7"	London	HLU10067	1966	**£4**	chart single
Trying To Get To You	7" EP	Ember	EP4563	1964	**£8**	
Twinkle Toes	7"	London	HLU10034	1966	**£4**	chart single
Uptown	7" EP	London	REU1354	1963	**£6**	
Walk On	7"	London	HLU10206	1968	**£4**	chart single
Wild Hearts	7"	ZTT	DZTAS9	1985	**£5**	double
Workin' For The Man	7"	London	HLU9607	1962	**£4**	chart single
You're My Baby	7"	Ember	EMBS197	1964	**£4**	
You're My Girl	7"	London	HLU9978	1965	**£4**	chart single

ORBIT FIVE

Title	Format	Label	Cat. No.	Year	Price	Notes
I Wanna Go To Heaven	7"	Decca	F12799	1968	**£10**	

ORCHESTRA LUNA

Title	Format	Label	Cat. No.	Year	Price	Notes
Orchestra Luna	LP	CBS			**£10**	

ORCHIDS

Title	Format	Label	Cat. No.	Year	Price	Notes
Gonna Make Him Mine	7"	Decca	F11743	1963	**£6**	
I've Got That Feeling	7"	Decca	F11861	1964	**£8**	
Love Hit Me	7"	Decca	F11785	1963	**£6**	

ORE

Title	Format	Label	Cat. No.	Year	Price	Notes
Halcyon Days	LP	Akashic		1979	**£30**	US pic disc

ORGANISATION

Title	Format	Label	Cat. No.	Year	Price	Notes
Tone Float	LP	RCA	SF8111	1970	**£30**	

ORIGINAL CHECKMATES

Title	Format	Label	Cat. No.	Year	Price	Notes
Checkmate Twist	7"	Pye	7N15442	1962	**£8**	
Hot Toddy	7"	Pye	7N15428	1962	**£6**	
Union Pacific	7"	Decca	F11688	1963	**£10**	

ORIGINAL DYAKS

Title	Format	Label	Cat. No.	Year	Price	Notes
Gotta Get A Good Thing Going	7"	Columbia	DB8184	1967	**£4**	

ORIGINAL TORNADOES

Title	Format	Label	Cat. No.	Year	Price	Notes
Telstar	7"	SRT	SRTS75350	1965	**£5**	

ORIGINALS

Title	Format	Label	Cat. No.	Year	Price	Notes
Baby I'm For Real	7"	T. Motown	TMG733	1970	**£5**	
Baby I'm For Real	7"	T. Motown	TMG733	1970	**£12**	demo
Down To Love Town	7"	T. Motown	TMG1038	1976	**£4**	
God Bless Whoever Sent You	7"	T. Motown	TMG822	1972	**£4**	
God Bless Whoever Sent You	7"	T. Motown	TMG822	1972	**£10**	demo
Good Night Irene	7"	T. Motown	TMG592	1967	**£15**	
Good Night Irene	7"	T. Motown	TMG592	1967	**£60**	demo
Green Grow The Lilacs	LP	T. Motown	STML11116	1969	**£12**	
Green Grow The Lilacs	7"	T. Motown	TMG702	1969	**£5**	
Green Grow The Lilacs	7"	T. Motown	TMG702	1969	**£15**	demo

ORIGINELLS

Title	Format	Label	Cat. No.	Year	Price	Notes
My Girl	7"	Columbia	DB7259	1964	**£10**	
Nights	7"	Columbia	DB7388	1964	**£8**	

ORIOLES

Title	Format	Label	Cat. No.	Year	Price	Notes
Crying In The Chapel	78	London	L1201	1953	**£20**	
Hold Me, Thrill Me, Kiss Me	78	London	L1180	1953	**£20**	
In The Mission Of St. Augustine	78	London	HL8001	1954	**£20**	

ORION, P.J. & THE MAGNATES

Title	Format	Label	Cat. No.	Year	Price	Notes
P.J. Orion And The Magnates	LP	Magnate	122459	1961	**£20**	US

ORLANDO, TONY

Title	Format	Label	Cat. No.	Year	Price	Notes
Bless You	7" EP	Columbia	SEG8238	1963	**£4**	

ORLONS

Title	Format	Label	Cat. No.	Year	Price	Notes
All The Hits	LP	Cameo Park.	C1033	1963	**£12**	
All The Hits	LP	Cameo	C1033	1962	**£15**	US
Biggest Hits	LP	Cameo Park.	C1061	1963	**£15**	
Bon Doo Wah	7"	Cameo Park.	C287	1963	**£4**	
Crossfire	7"	Cameo Park.	C273	1963	**£4**	
Don't Hang Up	7"	Cameo Park.	C231	1962	**£4**	chart single
Down Memory Lane	LP	Cameo	C1073	1963	**£15**	US
Knock Knock	7"	Cameo Park.	C332	1964	**£4**	
Not Me	7"	Cameo Park.	C257	1963	**£4**	
Not Me	LP	Cameo	C1054	1963	**£15**	US
Rules Of Love	7"	Cameo Park.	C319	1964	**£4**	
Shimmy Shimmy	7"	Cameo Park.	C295	1963	**£4**	
South Street	7"	Cameo Park.	C243	1963	**£4**	
South Street	LP	Cameo	C1041	1963	**£20**	US
Spinning Top	7"	Mojo	2092029	1972	**£4**	
Spinning Top	7"	Planet	PLF117	1966	**£25**	
Wah Watusi	LP	Cameo	C1020	1962	**£20**	US
Wah Watusi	7"	Columbia	DB4865	1962	**£4**	

ORLONS & DOVELLS

Title	Format	Label	Cat. No.	Year	Price	Notes
Golden Hits	LP	Cameo	C1067	1963	**£15**	US

ORPHEUS

Title	Format	Label	Cat. No.	Year	Price	Notes
My Life	7"	Red Bird	RB10041	1966	**£5**	

OSBORNE BROTHERS

Title	Format	Label	Cat. No.	Year	Price	Notes
Country Picking And Hillside Singing	7" EP	MGM	MGMEP691	1959	**£5**	

OSBORNE, MIKE

Title	Format	Label	Cat. No.	Year	Price	Notes
Outback	LP	Turtle	TUR300	1971	**£50**	

OSBOURNE, OZZY

Title	Format	Label	Cat. No.	Year	Price	Notes
Bark At The Moon	12"	Epic	TA3915	1983	**£30**	silver vinyl
Bark At The Moon	12"	Epic	WA3915	1983	**£12**	pic disc
Diary Of A Madman	LP	Jet		1981	**£30**	US promo pic disc
Mr.Crowley	7"	Jet	JET7003	1980	**£4**	chart single
Shot In The Dark	7"	Epic	A6859	1986	**£5**	with signature
So Tired	12"	Epic	DA4452	1984	**£6**	double
So Tired	12"	Epic	WA4452	1984	**£20**	gold vinyl
Symptom Of The Universe	7"	Jet	JETP7030	1982	**£10**	pic disc
Ultimate Sin	LP	Epic	EPC1126404	1986	**£10**	pic disc

OSCAR

Club Of Lights	7"	Reaction	591003	1966	**£12**	
Holiday	7"	Reaction	591016	1967	**£15**	
Join My Gang	7"	Reaction	591006	1966	**£15**	
Open Up The Skies	7"	Polydor	56257	1968	**£15**	
Over The Wall We Go	7"	Reaction	591012	1967	**£20**	

OSIBISA

Osibisa	LP	MCA	MDKS8001	1971	**£10**	chart LP
Woyaya	LP	MCA	MDKS8005	1971	**£10**	chart LP

OTHERS

Oh Yeah	7"	Fontana	TF501	1964	**£40**	

OTIS, JOHNNY

All I Want Is Your Love	7"	Capitol	CL14837	1958	**£4**	
Bye Bye Baby	7"	Capitol	CL14817	1958	**£4**	chart single
Casting My Spell	7"	Capitol	CL15018	1959	**£4**	
Cold Shot	LP	Sonet	SNTF613	1969	**£10**	
Crazy Country Hop	7"	Capitol	CL14941	1958	**£8**	
Cuttin' Up	LP	Epic	BN26524	1970	**£10**	US
Formidable	LP	Ember	SPE6604	196-	**£15**	
Johnny Otis	7" EP	Vocalion	VEP170162	1965	**£12**	
Johnny Otis Show	LP	Capitol	T940	1958	**£50**	US
Johnny Otis Show	7" EP	Capitol	EAP11134	1959	**£15**	
Live At Monterey	LP	Epic	66295	1971	**£12**	
Ma He's Making Eyes At Me	7"	Capitol	CL14794	1957	**£4**	chart single
Mumbling Mosie	7"	Capitol	CL15112	1960	**£5**	
Ring A Ling	7"	Capitol	CL14875	1958	**£6**	
Rock And Roll Hit Parade Vol.1	LP	Dig	104	1957	**£100**	US
Three Girls Named Molly	7"	Capitol	CL15057	1959	**£5**	
Well Well Well Well	7"	Capitol	CL14854	1958	**£4**	
You	7"	Capitol	CL15008	1959	**£4**	

OTIS, JOHNNY ORCHESTRA

Harlem Nocturne	78	Parlophone	R3291	1950	**£6**	B side Slim Gailard

OTIS, SHUGGIE

Al Kooper Introduces	LP	CBS	63797	1969	**£10**	
Here Comes Shuggie Otis	LP	CBS	63996	1970	**£10**	

OTWAY, JOHN & WILD WILLIE BARRETT

John Otway And Wild Willie Barrett	LP	Extracted	ELP1	1977	**£10**	
Louisa On A Horse	7"	Track	2094133	1976	**£4**	
Murder Man	7"	Track	2094111	1973	**£4**	
Racing Cars	7"	Polydor	2058916	1977	**£4**	
Really Free	7"	Polydor	2058951	1977	**£4**	chart single

OUR PLASTIC DREAM

Little Bit Of Shangrila	7"	Go	AJ11411	1967	**£8**	

OUT OF DARKNESS

Out Of Darkness	LP	Key	KL006	1970	**£250**	

OUTCASTS

Just Another Teenage Rebel	7"	Good Vibs	GOT3	1978	**£4**	2 different PS's
Self Conscious Over You	LP	Good Vibs	BIG1		**£10**	
Self Conscious Over You	7"	Good Vibs	GOT17	1979	**£4**	

OUTER LIMITS

Dark Side Of The Moon	7"	Decca	F13176	1971	**£8**	
Great Train Robbery	7"	Instant	IN001	1968	**£15**	
Just One More Chance	7"	Deram	DM125	1967	**£10**	

OUTLAW BLUES BAND

Breaking In	LP	Stateside	SSL10290	1969	**£12**	
Outlaw Blues Band	LP	Bluesway	BLS6021	1968	**£12**	US

OUTLAWS

The Outlaws were employed as session men by producer Joe Meek and therefore appear on records by the likes of Mike Berry, John Leyton, and Heinz. Between October 1962 and April 1964 the lead guitarist was Ritchie Blackmore. He can be heard on the four Outlaws singles issued in 1963-4, but not on the Outlaws This record, which contains cowboy-oriented instrumentals, has been highly sought after since the early days of record collecting

Title	Format	Label	Number	Year	Price	Notes
Ambush	7"	HMV	POP877	1961	**£10**	chart single
Dream Of The West	LP	HMV	CLP1484	1961	**£100**	
Keep A Knocking	7"	HMV	POP1277	1964	**£15**	
Last Stage West	7"	HMV	POP990	1962	**£10**	
Law And Order	7"	HMV	POP1241	1963	**£12**	
Return Of The Outlaws	7"	HMV	POP1124	1963	**£12**	
Sioux Serenade	7"	HMV	POP1074	1962	**£12**	
Swinging Low	7"	HMV	POP844	1961	**£10**	chart single
That Set The Wild West Free	7"	HMV	POP1195	1963	**£12**	
Valley Of The Sioux	7"	HMV	POP927	1961	**£10**	

OUTSIDERS

Title	Format	Label	Number	Year	Price	Notes
Album No.2	LP	Capitol	T2568	1966	**£12**	US
Girl In Love	7"	Capitol	CL15450	1966	**£10**	
Happening Live	LP	Capitol	T2745	1967	**£12**	US
Help Me Girl	7"	Capitol	CL15480	1966	**£8**	
I'll Give You Time	7"	Capitol	CL15495	1967	**£8**	
Keep On Doing It	7"	Decca	F12213	1965	**£4**	
Outsiders In	LP	Capitol	T2636	1967	**£12**	US
Respectable	7"	Capitol	CL15468	1966	**£8**	
Time Won't Let Me	LP	Capitol	T2501	1966	**£12**	US
Time Won't Let Me	7"	Capitol	CL15435	1966	**£12**	

OUTSIDERS (2)

Title	Format	Label	Number	Year	Price	Notes
Calling On Youth	LP	Raw Edge	RER001	1977	**£15**	
Close Up	LP	Raw Edge	RER003	1978	**£15**	
One To Infinity	7"	Raw Edge	RER002	1977	**£4**	
Vital Hours	7"	Xciting P.		1978	**£4**	

OUTSKIRTS OF INFINITY

Title	Format	Label	Number	Year	Price	Notes
Lord Of The Dark Skies	LP	Woronzow	WOO7	1987	**£12**	

OVARY LODGE

Title	Format	Label	Number	Year	Price	Notes
Ovary Lodge	LP	Ogun	OG600	1976	**£15**	
Ovary Lodge	LP	RCA	SF83724	1973	**£30**	

OVERLANDERS

Title	Format	Label	Number	Year	Price	Notes
Along Came Jones	7"	Pye	7N15804	1965	**£4**	
Michelle	LP	Pye		1966	**£15**	
Michelle	7"	Pye	7N17034	1966	**£4**	chart single
Michelle	7" EP	Pye	NEP24245	1966	**£5**	

OWEN B

Title	Format	Label	Number	Year	Price	Notes
Owen B	LP	Musicol		197-	**£80**	US

OWEN, RAY

Title	Format	Label	Number	Year	Price	Notes
Ray Owen's Moon	LP	Polydor	2325061	1971	**£12**	
Tonight I'll Be Staying Here With You	7"	Fontana	TF1045	1969	**£4**	

OWENS, BUCK

Title	Format	Label	Number	Year	Price	Notes
Act Naturally	7" EP	Capitol	EAP120602	1964	**£6**	
Buck Owens Sings Harlan Howard	LP	Capitol	T1482	1961	**£12**	US
Fabulous Country Music Sound	LP	Starday	SLP172	1962	**£10**	US
Foolin' Around	7" EP	Capitol	EAP11550	1961	**£5**	
Under Your Spell Again	LP	Capitol	T1489	1961	**£10**	US

OWENS, DONNIE

Title	Format	Label	Number	Year	Price	Notes
Need You	7"	London	HL8747	1958	**£6**	

OWL

Title	Format	Label	Number	Year	Price	Notes
Run To The Sun	7"	United Artists	UP2240	1968	**£10**	

OXLEY, TONY

Title	Format	Label	Number	Year	Price	Notes
Baptised Traveller	LP	CBS	52664	1969	**£40**	
Four Compositions For Sextet	LP	CBS	64071	1970	**£40**	
Ichnos	LP	RCA	SF8215	1971	**£40**	

OZZ II

Title	Format	Label	Number	Year	Price	Notes
Assassin	LP	Zebra	ZEB2	1984	**£20**	

P

PACIFIC DRIFT

Feelin' Free	LP	Nova	SND13	1970	**£15**	
Water Woman	7"	Deram	DM304	1970	**£5**	

PACIFIC GAS & ELECTRIC

Are You Ready	LP	CBS	64026	1970	**£10**	
Get It On	LP	B&C	CAS1003	1969	**£10**	
Hard Burn	LP	CBS	64295	1971	**£10**	
Pacific Gas And Electric	LP	CBS	63822	1969	**£10**	

PACIFIC SOUND

Forget Your Dream	LP	Splendid		1972	**£350**	

PACK

Do You Believe In Magic	7"	Columbia	DB7702	1965	**£8**	

PACK (2)

Brave New Soldiers	7"	SS	PAK1	1979	**£10**	
King Of Kings	7"	Rough Trade	RT025	1979	**£10**	
Kirk Brandon And The Pack Of Lies	7"	SS	SS1N2/SS2N1	1980	**£15**	
Live 1979	cass	Donut	DONUT2	1982	**£12**	
Long Live The Past	7"	Cyclops	CYCLOPS1	1982	**£8**	

PACKABEATS

Dream Lover	7"	Pye	7N15549	1963	**£5**	
Evening In Paris	7"	Pye	7N15480	1962	**£5**	
Gypsy Beat	7"	Parlophone	R4729	1961	**£4**	chart single

PACKERS

Hole In The Wall	7"	Pye	7N25343	1966	**£6**	
Hole In The Wall	7"	Soul City	SC111		**£4**	
Hole In The Wall	7"	Soul City	SC111		**£12**	demo

PADDY, KLAUS AND GIBSON

I Wanna Know	7"	Pye	7N15906	1965	**£6**	
No Good Without You Baby	7"	Pye	7N17060	1966	**£8**	
Teresa	7"	Pye	7N17112	1966	**£8**	

PAGE FIVE

Let Sleeping Dogs Lie	7"	Parlophone	R5426	1966	**£12**	

PAGE TEN

Boutique	7"	Decca	F12248	1965	**£10**	

PAGE, HAL & THE WHALERS

Going Back To My Home Town	7"	Melodisc	MEL1553	1960	**£4**	chart single

PAGE, JIMMY

She Just Satisfies	7"	Fontana	TF533	1965	**£200**	

PAGE, LARRY

Cool Shake	7"	Columbia	DB3965	1957	**£4**	
Kinky Music	LP	Decca	LK4692	1965	**£50**	
That'll Be The Day	7"	Columbia	DB4012	1957	**£4**	
Theme From Peyton Place	7"	Decca	F12368	1966	**£4**	
Waltzing To Jazz	7"	Decca	F12320	1966	**£5**	

PAGEBOYS

When I Meet A Girl Like You	7"	London	HLU9948	1965	**£4**	

PAICE, ASHTON & LORD

Malice In Wonderland	LP	Oyster	2391269	1977	**£10**	

PAIGE, JOEY
Cause I'm In Love With You ..... 7" ..... Fontana ..... TF554 ..... 1965 ..... **£8**

PAIGE, ROSALIND
When The Saints ..... 7" ..... London ..... HL8120 ..... 1955 ..... **£5**

PAINTBOX
Get Ready For Love ..... 7" ..... Youngblood ..... YB1013 ..... 1971 ..... **£4**

PAISLEYS
Cosmic Mind At Play ..... LP ..... Audio City ..... 70 ..... 1968 ..... **£70** ..... US

PALADIN
Anyway ..... 7" ..... Bronze ..... WIP6108 ..... 1971 ..... **£5**
Charge ..... LP ..... Bronze ..... ILPS9190 ..... 1972 ..... **£25**
Paladin ..... LP ..... Bronze ..... ILPS9150 ..... 1971 ..... **£20**
Sweet Sweet Music ..... 7" ..... Bronze ..... BRO3 ..... 1973 ..... **£5**

PALEY BROTHERS & THE RAMONES
Come On Let's Go ..... 7" ..... Sire ..... SIR4005 ..... 1978 ..... **£5**

PALMER, BRUCE
Cycle Is Complete ..... LP ..... Verve ..... VRF3086 ..... 1971 ..... **£15** ..... US

PALMER, EARL
Drum Village ..... 7" ..... Capitol ..... CL14859 ..... 1958 ..... **£5**

PALMER, EARL & BILLY MAY
Swingin' Drums ..... 7" EP ..... Capitol ..... EAP11026 ..... 1958 ..... **£5**

PALMER, ROBERT
Addicted To Love ..... 7" ..... Island ..... ISP270 ..... 1986 ..... **£4** ..... shaped pic disc
I Didn't Mean To Turn You On ..... CD-s ..... Island ..... CID283 ..... 1986 ..... **£40**
Live In Boston ..... LP ..... W. Bros ..... WBMS111 ..... 1979 ..... **£20** ..... US promo
Pride ..... 7" ..... Island ..... PWIP6833 ..... 1982 ..... **£4** ..... pic disc
Secrets ..... LP ..... Island ..... 1979 ..... **£20** ..... US promo pic disc
Some Guys Have All The Luck ..... 7" ..... Island ..... PWIP6754 ..... 1982 ..... **£4** ..... pic disc
You Can Have It ..... 7" ..... Island ..... ISP121 ..... 1983 ..... **£4** ..... pic disc

PAN
Pan ..... LP ..... Sonet ..... 1970 ..... **£200**

PAN (2)
Pan ..... LP ..... Columbia ..... 32062 ..... 1973 ..... **£15** ..... US

PANAMA LTD. JUG BAND
Indian Summer ..... LP ..... Harvest ..... SHVL779 ..... 1970 ..... **£30**
Lady Of Shallott ..... 7" ..... Harvest ..... HAR5010 ..... 1969 ..... **£8**
Panama Ltd.Jug Band ..... LP ..... Harvest ..... SHVL753 ..... 1969 ..... **£30**
Round And Round ..... 7" ..... Harvest ..... HAR5022 ..... 1970 ..... **£8**

PANDAMONIUM
Chocolate Buster Dan ..... 7" ..... CBS ..... 3451 ..... 1968 ..... **£20**
No Presents For Me ..... 7" ..... CBS ..... 2664 ..... 1967 ..... **£20**
Season Of The Witch ..... 7" ..... CBS ..... 202462 ..... 1967 ..... **£15**

PANHANDLE
Panhandle ..... LP ..... Decca ..... 1972 ..... **£15**

PANIK
It Won't Sell ..... 7" ..... Rainy City ..... SHOT1 ..... 1977 ..... **£5**

PANTA REI
..... LP ..... Harvest ..... 197- **£40**

PAPER BLITZ TISSUE
Boy Meets Girl ..... 7" ..... RCA ..... RCA1652 ..... 1967 ..... **£40**

PAPER BUBBLE
Scenery Dream ..... LP ..... Deram ..... DMLS1059 ..... 1970 ..... **£15**

PAPER GARDEN
Paper Garden ..... LP ..... Musicor ..... MS3175 ..... 1970 ..... **£20**

PAPER WINGED DREAMS

Paper Winged Dreams	LP	Brimstone		1970	**£40**	US

PARADONS

Diamonds And Pearls	7"	Top Rank	JAR514	1960	**£4**	

PARAFFIN JACK FLASH LTD.

Movers And Groovers	LP	Pye	NSPL18252	1968	**£15**	

PARAGONS

Paragons Meet The Jesters	LP	Jubilee	JLP1098	1959	**£40**	US
Paragons Meet The Jesters	LP	Jubilee	JLP1098	1959	**£100**	US, coloured vinyl
Paragons Vs.The Harptones	LP	Musicnote	M8001	1964	**£20**	US

PARAGONS (2)

Memories By The Score	7"	Island	WI3138	1968	**£10**	
So Depressed	7"	Island	WI3093	1967	**£10**	
Talking Love	7"	Island	WI3067	1967	**£10**	
Teardrops Falling	7"	Island	WI3142	1968	**£10**	

PARAMOR, NORRIE ORCHESTRA

Dance Of The Warriors	7"	Columbia	DB7446	1965	**£4**	

PARAMOUNTS

The Paramounts were yet another R&B group who gigged hard through the sixties without ever gaining very much success and who made several singles that essentially serve to emphasise why this was. Arguably, however, the group was capable of very much more, for the handful of unreleased tracks included on the Edsel compilation of the Paramounts singles are easily the most impressive. And later, the original line-up of the group made two LPs which do much more to realise its potential - but these, "Home" and "Broken Barricades", came out under a different name; that of Procol Harum.

Bad Blood	7"	Parlophone	R5187	1964	**£10**	
Blue Ribbons	7"	Parlophone	R5272	1965	**£10**	
I'm The One Who Loves You	7"	Parlophone	R5155	1964	**£15**	
Little Bitty Pretty One	7"	Parlophone	R5107	1964	**£10**	
Paramounts	7" EP	Parlophone	GEP8908	1964	**£100**	
Poison Ivy	7"	Parlophone	R5093	1963	**£10**	chart single
You've Never Had It So Good	7"	Parlophone	R5351	1965	**£12**	

PARFITT, PAULA

I'm Gonna Give Back Your Ring	7"	Beacon	BEA145	1969	**£20**	

PARIS SISTERS

Dream Lover	7"	MGM	MGM1240	1964	**£10**	
I Love How You Love Me	7"	Top Rank	JAR588	1961	**£12**	

PARIS, BOBBY

Personally	7"	Polydor	56747	1968	**£20**	

PARISH HALL

Parish Hall	LP	Liberty	LBS83374	1970	**£12**	

PARKER, BENNY & THE DYNAMICS

Boys And Girls	7"	Decca	F11944	1964	**£15**	

PARKER, BILLY

Thanks A Lot	7"	Decca	F11668	1963	**£4**	

PARKER, BOBBY

It's Hard But It's Fair	7"	Blue Horizon	573151	1969	**£10**	
Watch Your Step	7"	London	HLU9393	1961	**£5**	
Watch Your Step	7"	Sue	WI340	1964	**£8**	

PARKER, DAVID

David Parker	LP	Polydor		1971	**£60**	

PARKER, DEAN & THE REDCAPS

Stormy Evening	7"	Decca	F11555	1962	**£12**	

PARKER, GRAHAM

Live At Marble Arch	LP	Vertigo	GP1	1977	**£15**	promo
Live Sparks	LP	Arista	SP63	1979	**£20**	US promo
Pink Parker	7"	Vertigo	PARK001	1977	**£6**	pink vinyl

PARKER, JIMMY

Title	Format	Label	Cat. No.	Year	Price	Notes
We Gonna	7"	Top Rank	JAR608	1962	**£4**	

PARKER, JUNIOR

Title	Format	Label	Cat. No.	Year	Price	Notes
Annie Get Your Yo Yo	7"	Vogue	V9193	1962	**£6**	
Driving Wheel	LP	Duke	DLP76	1962	**£25**	US
Goodbye Little Girl	7"	Vocalion	VP9275	1966	**£4**	
Like It Is	LP	Mercury	SMCL20097	1967	**£10**	
Stand By Me	7"	Vogue	V9179	1961	**£8**	
These Kind Of Blues	7"	Vocalion	VP9256	1966	**£6**	

PARKER, KEN

Title	Format	Label	Cat. No.	Year	Price	Notes
Down Low	7"	Island	WI3096	1967	**£10**	
It's Alright	7"	Amalgam.	AMG847	196-	**£10**	
Jimmy Brown	7"	Duke Reid	DR2521	1971	**£6**	
Lonely Man	7"	Island	WI3105	1967	**£10**	
Only Yesterday	7"	Amalgam.	AMG853	196-	**£10**	
We Must Be In Love	7"	A&M	AMS7092	1974	**£6**	

PARKER, RAY JNR.

Title	Format	Label	Cat. No.	Year	Price	Notes
Ghostbusters	12"	Arista	ARIPD12580	1984	**£15**	luminous pic disc

PARKER, RAYMOND

Title	Format	Label	Cat. No.	Year	Price	Notes
Ring Around The Roses	7"	Sue	WI4024	1966	**£8**	

PARKER, ROBERT

Title	Format	Label	Cat. No.	Year	Price	Notes
Barefootin'	LP	Island	ILP942	1966	**£20**	
Barefootin'	7"	Island	WI286	1966	**£5**	chart single
Happy Feet	7"	Island	WI3008	1966	**£4**	

PARKER, SONNY

Title	Format	Label	Cat. No.	Year	Price	Notes
My Soul's On Fire	7"	Vogue	V2392	1970	**£20**	

PARKER, WINFIELD

Title	Format	Label	Cat. No.	Year	Price	Notes
Stop Her On Sight	7"	Mojo	2093019	1972	**£4**	

PARKING LOT

Title	Format	Label	Cat. No.	Year	Price	Notes
World Spinning Sadly	7"	Parlophone	R5779	1969	**£15**	

PARKINSON, JIMMY

Title	Format	Label	Cat. No.	Year	Price	Notes
But You	7"	Columbia	DB3876	1957	**£4**	
Great Pretender	7"	Columbia	SCM5236	1956	**£8**	chart single
In The Middle Of The House	7"	Columbia	DB3833	1956	**£4**	chart single
Lover's Quarrel	7"	Columbia	DB3808	1956	**£4**	
Walk Hand In Hand	7"	Columbia	SCM5267	1956	**£6**	chart single
Whatever Lola Wants	7"	Columbia	DB3912	1957	**£4**	

PARKS, VAN DYKE

Title	Format	Label	Cat. No.	Year	Price	Notes
Clang Of The Yankee Reaper	LP	W. Bros	BS2878	1975	**£10**	US
Discover America	LP	W. Bros	BS2589	1972	**£10**	US
Number Nine	7"	MGM	MGM1301	1966	**£5**	
Song Cycle	LP	W. Bros	WS1727	1968	**£10**	US

PARLIAMENT

Title	Format	Label	Cat. No.	Year	Price	Notes
Chocolate City	LP	Casablanca	NBLP7014	1975	**£10**	
Come In Out Of The Rain	7"	Invictus	INV522	1972	**£4**	
Gloryhallastoopid	LP	Casablanca	NBLP7195	1979	**£10**	US
Motor Booty Affair	LP	Casablanca	NBPIX7125	1978	**£10**	US pic disc
Osmium	LP	Invictus	SVT1004	1971	**£20**	
Silent Boatman	7"	Invictus	INV513	1971	**£4**	
Trombipulation	LP	Casablanca	NBLP7294	1981	**£10**	US
Up For The Down Stroke	LP	Casablanca	NBLP7002	1974	**£10**	

PARLIAMENTS

Title	Format	Label	Cat. No.	Year	Price	Notes
I Wanna Testify	7"	Track	604013	1967	**£5**	
I Wanna Testify	7"	Track	604032	1969	**£4**	

PARLOUR BAND

Title	Format	Label	Cat. No.	Year	Price	Notes
Is A Friend	LP	Deram	SDL10	1972	**£75**	

PARRISH & GURVITZ

Title	Format	Label	Cat. No.	Year	Price	Notes
Parrish And Gurvitz	LP	Regal Z.	SRZA8506	1971	**£15**	

PARRISH, DEAN

Determination	7"	Stateside	SS550	1966	**£15**	
I'm On My Way	7"	UK	USA2	1975	**£4**	
Skate	7"	Stateside	SS580	1967	**£4**	
Tell Her	7"	Stateside	SS531	1966	**£10**	

PARRY, SAM

Sam Parry	LP	Argo		1970	**£50**	

PARSONS, ALAN PROJECT

Best Of..	7"	Arista	STORE2	1983	**£5**	promo sampler
Best Of...	LP	Mobile Fid.	MFSL1175	1984	**£10**	US audiophile
Don't Answer Me	7"	Arista	ARISD553	1984	**£4**	pic disc
I, Robot	LP	Mobile Fid.	MFSL1084	1982	**£10**	US audiophile
I, Robot	LP	Mobile Fid.	MFSL1084		**£20**	US audiophile (UHQR)
Tales Of Mystery And Imagination	7"	Charisma		1976	**£5**	promo sampler
Turn Of A Friendly Card	LP	Arista		1980	**£10**	audiophile
Vulture Culture	LP	Arista		1984	**£15**	US promo pic disc

PARSONS, BILL

All American Boy	7"	London	HL8798	1959	**£8**	chart single

PARSONS, GENE

Kindling	LP	W. Bros	K46257	1974	**£10**	

PARSONS, GRAM

New Soft Shoe	7"	Reprise	K14245	1973	**£4**	

PARTON, DOLLY

Hello I'm Dolly	LP	Monument	MLP8085	1967	**£10**	US

PARTON, DOLLY & GEORGE JONES

Dolly Parton And George Jones	LP	Starday	SLP429	1968	**£10**	US

PARTRIDGE, DON

Blue Eyes	7"	Columbia	DB8416	1968	**£4**	chart single
Breakfast On Pluto	7"	Columbia	DB8538	1969	**£4**	chart single
Colour My World	7"	Columbia	DB8583	1969	**£4**	
Don Partridge	LP	Columbia		1968	**£10**	
Going To Germany	7"	Columbia	DB8617	1969	**£4**	
Rosie	7"	Columbia	DB8330	1968	**£4**	chart single
We Have Ways Of Making You Laugh	7"	Columbia	DB8484	1968	**£4**	
We're All Happy Together	7"	Columbia	DB8723	1970	**£4**	

PASSAGE

About Time	7"	Object Music	OM08	1979	**£5**	
New Love Songs	7"	Object Music	OM02	1978	**£5**	
Pindrop	LP	Object	OBJ011	1980	**£10**	

PASSING FANCY

Passing Fancy	LP	Boo	6801	196-	**£75**	US

PASSIONS

I Only Want You	7"	Top Rank	JAR313	1960	**£4**	
Jackie Brown	7"	Capitol	CL14874	1958	**£4**	
Just To Be With You	7"	Top Rank	JAR224	1959	**£4**	

PASSPORT

Doldinger	LP	Atlantic	K44243	1973	**£10**	
Doldinger Jubilee	LP	Atlantic	K60073	1973	**£20**	triple
Doldinger Jubilee Concert	LP	Atlantic	K50070	1974	**£10**	
Handmade	LP	Atlantic	K40483	1973	**£10**	
Looking Thru	LP	Atlantic	K50024	1973	**£10**	
Passport	LP	Atlantic	K40299	1971	**£10**	
Second	LP	Atlantic	K40417	1972	**£10**	

PAST SEVEN DAYS

Raindance	7"	4AD	AD102	1981	**£6**	

PASTEL SIX

Cinnamon Cinder	7"	London	HLU9651	1963	**£4**	
Cinnamon Cinder	LP	Zen	1001	1963	**£20**	US

Golden Oldies	LP	Mark 56 Recs	MLP511	1963	£15	US

PASTIES & CREAM

Pasties And Cream	LP	Sentinel		1971	£15	

PASTORAL SYMPHONY

Love Machine	7"	President	PT202	1968	£8	

PAT & MARIE

I Try Not To Tell You	7"	Ska Beat	JB234	1966	£10	
You're Really Leaving	7"	Ska Beat	JB235	1966	£10	

PATCHES

Living In America	7"	W. Bros	K16201	1972	£10	

PATHETIX

Aleister Crowley	7"	No Records	001	1978	£4	
Love In Decay	7"	TJM	TJM12	198-	£4	

PATHFINDERS

Don't You Believe It	7"	Parlophone	R5372	1965	£5	
I Love You Caroline	7"	Decca	F12038	1964	£6	

PATHWAY TO YOUR MIND

Pathway To Your Mind	LP	Major Minor			£50	

PATIENCE & PRUDENCE

Dreamers' Bay	7"	London	HLU8425	1957	£4	
Gonna Get Along Without You Now	7"	London	HLU8369	1957	£8	chart single
Smile And A Song	7" EP	London	REU1087	1957	£8	
Tonight You Belong To Me	7"	London	HLU8321	1956	£12	chart single
You Tattletale	7"	London	HLU8493	1957	£4	

PATRICK, BOBBY BIG SIX

Monkey Time	7"	Decca	F12030	1964	£10	
Shake It Easy Baby	7"	Decca	F11898	1964	£10	
Tenbeat From Star Club Hamburg	7" EP	Decca	DFE8570	1964	£8	

PATRICK, KENTRICK

Don't Stay Out Late	7"	Island	WI079	1963	£10	
End Of The World	7"	Island	WI104	1963	£10	
Golden Love	7"	Island	WI119	1963	£10	
I Am Wasting Time	7"	Island	WI140	1964	£10	
Man To Man	7"	Island	WI066	1963	£10	
Take Me To The Party	7"	Island	WI132	1963	£10	

PATRON OF THE ARTS

Eleanor Rigby	7"	Page One	POF012	1966	£15	

PATTEN, BRIAN

Brian Patten	LP	Caedmon	TC1300	1970	£20	
Sly Cormorant	LP	Argo	ZSW607	1977	£12	
Vanishing Trick	LP	Tangent	TGS116	1971	£40	

PATTERSON, BOBBY

I'm In Love With You	7"	Action	ACT4604	1971	£4	

PATTERSON, OTTILIE

3000 Years With Ottilie	LP	Marmalade	608011	1969	£10	
Baby Please Don't Go	7"	Columbia	DB7208	1964	£4	
Bitterness Of Death	7"	Marmalade	598020	1969	£4	
Blues	7" EP	Decca	DFE6303	1956	£4	
That Patterson Girl	7" EP	Polygon	JTE102	1956	£8	
That Patterson Girl	7" EP	Pye	NJE1012	1956	£4	
That Patterson Girl Vol.2	7" EP	Pye	NJE1023	1956	£4	

PATTO

Hold Your Fire	LP	Vertigo	6360032	1971	£50	spiral label
Patto	LP	Vertigo	6360016	1970	£30	spiral label
Roll Em Smoke Em	LP	Island	ILPS9210	1972	£20	

PATTO, MIKE

Can't Stop Talking About My Baby	7"	Columbia	DB8091	1966	£10	

PATTON, ALEXANDER

Title	Format	Label	Cat. No.	Year	Price	Notes
Li'l Lovin' Sometimes	7"	Capitol	CL15461	1966	**£50**	

PATTON, JIMMY

Title	Format	Label	Cat. No.	Year	Price	Notes
Blue Darlin'	LP	Sims	127	1965	**£20**	US
Make Room For The Blues	LP	Moon	101	196-	**£20**	US

PATTY & THE EMBLEMS

Title	Format	Label	Cat. No.	Year	Price	Notes
Mixed Up Shook Up Girl	7"	Stateside	SS322	1964	**£12**	

PAUL & PAULA

Title	Format	Label	Cat. No.	Year	Price	Notes
Hey Paula	7"	Philips	304012BF	1963	**£4**	chart single
Holiday For Teens	LP	Philips	PHM200101	1963	**£15**	US
Paul And Paula Sing For Young Lovers	LP	Philips	PHM200078	1963	**£15**	US
We Go Together	LP	Philips	PHM200089	1963	**£15**	US
Young Lovers	7"	Philips	304016BF	1963	**£4**	chart single
Young Lovers	7" EP	Philips	BBE12539	1963	**£10**	

PAUL & RITCHIE & THE CRYIN' SHAMES

Title	Format	Label	Cat. No.	Year	Price	Notes
C'mon Back	7"	Decca	F12483	1966	**£30**	

PAUL'S DISCIPLES

Title	Format	Label	Cat. No.	Year	Price	Notes
See That My Grave Is Kept Clean	7"	Decca	F12081	1965	**£6**	

PAUL, BUNNY

Title	Format	Label	Cat. No.	Year	Price	Notes
Please Have Mercy	7"	Capitol	CL14279	1955	**£4**	

PAUL, CLARENCE

Title	Format	Label	Cat. No.	Year	Price	Notes
I'm In Love Again	7"	London	HLU10492	1975	**£4**	

PAUL, JOHN E.

Title	Format	Label	Cat. No.	Year	Price	Notes
I Wanna Know	7"	Decca	F12685	1967	**£6**	

PAULETTE SISTERS

Title	Format	Label	Cat. No.	Year	Price	Notes
Dream Boat	7"	Capitol	CL14294	1955	**£4**	
Ring-A-Dang-A-Do	7"	Capitol	CL14310	1955	**£4**	
You Win Again	7"	Capitol	CL14347	1955	**£4**	

PAUPERS

Title	Format	Label	Cat. No.	Year	Price	Notes
Ellis Island	LP	Verve	SVLP6017	1968	**£10**	
Magic People	LP	Verve	3026	1967	**£10**	US
Southdown Road	7"	Verve	VS1520	1969	**£4**	
Think I Care	7"	Verve	VS1514	1968	**£4**	

PAVILION, PERCY (CAPTAIN SENSIBLE)

Title	Format	Label	Cat. No.	Year	Price	Notes
Cricket EP	7"	Pav In Splen	PIS1	1983	**£8**	
Gower Power	7"	Dead G.D.P.	DMS002	1984	**£4**	

PAVLOV'S DOG

Title	Format	Label	Cat. No.	Year	Price	Notes
St.Louis Hounds	LP	Private		197-	**£75**	US

PAX ETERNAL

Title	Format	Label	Cat. No.	Year	Price	Notes
Second Chance Mr.Jones	7"	Decca	F13167	1971	**£6**	

PAXTON, GARY

Title	Format	Label	Cat. No.	Year	Price	Notes
Stop Twisting Baby	7"	Liberty	LIB55485	1962	**£4**	

PAXTON, TOM

Title	Format	Label	Cat. No.	Year	Price	Notes
Ain't That News	LP	Elektra	EKL289	1965	**£10**	
Crazy John	7"	Elektra	EKSN45064	1969	**£4**	
Jennifer's Rabbit	7"	Elektra	EKSN45021	1967	**£4**	
Last Thing On My Mind	7"	Elektra	EKSN45001	1965	**£4**	
Leaving London	7"	Elektra	EKSN45006	1967	**£4**	
Morning Again	LP	Elektra	EKL4019	1968	**£10**	
Number Six	LP	Elektra	EKS74066	1970	**£10**	chart LP
One Time And One Time Only	7"	Elektra	EKSN45003	1967	**£4**	
Outward Bound	LP	Elektra	EKL317	1966	**£10**	
Ramblin' Boy	LP	Elektra	EKL277	1964	**£10**	
Things I Notice Now	LP	Elektra	EKS74043	1969	**£10**	
Tom Paxton	7" EP	Elektra	EPK802	1967	**£4**	
Victoria Dines Alone	7"	Elektra	EKSN45045	1969	**£4**	

PAYNE, FREDA

Band Of Gold	7"	Invictus	INV502	1970	**£4**	chart single
Band Of Gold	7"	Invictus	INV533	1973	**£8**	
He Who Laughs Last	7"	HMV	POP1091	1962	**£5**	

PEACE, DAVE QUARTET

Good Morning Mr.Blues	LP	Saga	FID2155	1969	**£15**	

PEACHES & HERB

For Your Love	7"	CBS	2866	1967	**£10**	
Let's Fall In Love	7"	CBS	202509	1967	**£8**	

PEACOCK, ANNETTE

I'm The One	LP	RCA	SF8255	1972	**£15**	
Live In Paris	LP	Aura		1981	**£50**	

PEACOCK, ANNETTE & PAUL BLEY

Dual Unity	LP	Freedom	2383105	1973	**£15**	
Improvisie	LP	America	30AM6121	197-	**£15**	
Revenge	LP	Polydor	2425043	1971	**£25**	

PEANUT

Peanut was a teenage American girl singer (at least she sounds like a teenager - she features in no rock reference books) whose version of "Home Of The Brave" was played on the radio a few times without becoming a chart hit. Nevertheless, her singing conveys such a sense of angst, of youthful hopes and wishes and love - and frustration in the face of blind adult unreason - that the song is an absolute classic, even if an unheralded one.

Home Of The Brave	7"	Pye	7N15963	1965	**£4**	
I Didn't Love Him Anyway	7"	Columbia	DB8104	1967	**£4**	
I'm Waiting For The Day	7"	Columbia	DB8032	1966	**£4**	
Thank You For The Rain	7"	Pye	7N15901	1965	**£4**	

PEANUT BUTTER CONSPIRACY

The Peanut Butter Conspiracy added Mamas and Papas-style harmony vocals on to the instrumental sound of Jefferson Airplane. The combination works brilliantly and the group's best songs are quite delightful, although somehow the group failed to find the success that they should have.

Back In L.A.	7"	London	HLH10290	1969	**£8**	
For Children Of All Ages	LP	Challenge	2000	1968	**£20**	US
Great Conspiracy	LP	CBS	63277	1968	**£20**	
Is Spreading	LP	Columbia	CS9495	1967	**£20**	US
It's A Happening Thing	7"	CBS	2981	1967	**£6**	
Turn On A Friend	7"	CBS	3543	1968	**£5**	

PEARCE, BOB, BLUES BAND

Blues Crusade	LP	Avenue	BEV1054	1968	**£12**	

PEARLS BEFORE SWINE

Balaklava	LP	Fontana	STL5503	1968	**£20**	
Beautiful Lies You Could Live	LP	Reprise	RSLP6467	1971	**£15**	
City Of Gold	LP	Reprise	RSLP6442	1971	**£15**	
One Nation Underground	LP	Fontana	STL5505	1967	**£20**	
These Things Too	LP	Reprise	RSLP6364	1969	**£15**	
Use Of Ashes	LP	Reprise	RSLP6405	1970	**£15**	

PEARSON, KEITH

Right Hand Band	LP	Eron	014	1976	**£20**	

PEARSON, RONNIE

Teenage Fancy	7"	HMV	POP489	1958	**£20**	

PEASANTS

Got Some Lovin' For You Baby	7"	Columbia	DB7642	1965	**£8**	

PEBBLES

First Time Loving	7"	Parlophone	R5921	1971	**£5**	
Goodnight Ma	7"	Parlophone	R5900	1971	**£6**	
Incredible George	7"	Decca	F22944	1969	**£8**	
Stand Up And Be Counted	7"	Deram	DM305	1970	**£5**	

PEDDLERS

Birthday	LP	CBS	63682	1969	**£10**	chart LP
Free Wheelers	LP	CBS	631831	1968	**£10**	chart LP

Title	Format	Label	Cat. No.	Year	Price	Notes
Live At The Pickwick	LP	Philips		1962	**£20**	
Three For All	LP	Electrola		1970	**£12**	
Three In A Cell	LP	CBS	63411	1968	**£10**	

PEDECIN, MIKE QUINTET

Title	Format	Label	Cat. No.	Year	Price	Notes
Musical Medicine	LP	Apollo	LP484	1957	**£50**	US
When The Cats Come Twistin' In	7"	HMV	POP1001	1962	**£4**	

PEDRICKS, BOBBY

Title	Format	Label	Cat. No.	Year	Price	Notes
White Bucks And Saddle Shoes	7"	London	HLX8740	1958	**£12**	

PEEBLES, ANN

Title	Format	Label	Cat. No.	Year	Price	Notes
Beware	7"	London	HLU10484	1975	**£4**	
Breaking Up Somebody's Home	7"	London	HLU10361	1972	**£4**	
Come To Mama	7"	London	HLU10508	1975	**£4**	
Do I Need You	7"	London	HLU10460	1974	**£4**	
Dr.Love Power	7"	London	HLU10517	1976	**£4**	
Hangin' On	7"	London	HLU10468	1974	**£4**	
I Can't Stand The Rain	LP	London	SHU8468	1974	**£12**	
I Can't Stand The Rain	7"	London	HLU10428	1973	**£4**	chart single
I Don't Lend My Man	7"	London	HLU10529	1976	**£4**	
I Pity The Fool	7"	London	HLU10328	1971	**£4**	
I'm Gonna Tear Your Playhouse Down	7"	London	HLU10405	1973	**£4**	
Part Time Love	LP	Hi	HL32059	1971	**£15**	US
Part Time Love	7"	London	HLU10322	1970	**£4**	
Slipped, Tripped And Fell In Love	7"	London	HLU10346	1971	**£4**	
Somebody's On Your Case	7"	London	HLU10385	1972	**£4**	
Straight From The Heart	LP	London	SHU8434	1972	**£12**	
Tellin' It	LP	London	SHU8490	1976	**£10**	
This Is	LP	Hi	HL32053	1969	**£15**	US

PEEL, DAVID & LOWER EAST SIDE

Title	Format	Label	Cat. No.	Year	Price	Notes
American Revolution	LP	Elektra	EKS74069	1970	**£15**	
Have A Marijuana	LP	Elektra	EKS74032	1968	**£15**	
Pope Smokes Dope	LP	Apple	SW3391	1972	**£20**	US

PEEL, JOHN

John Peel has made many cameo appearances on other people's records - the odd spoken line, the occasional burst of jew's harp - but "Archive Things", which is credited to him, contains not a single sound of Peel. Instead, the record is a compilation of short world music extracts that were included in John Peel's wide-ranging "Night Ride" radio programme. There are some fascinating noises to be heard here, and as a sixties artefact, the record is almost as essential as "Sgt.Pepper", if rather less celebrated.

Title	Format	Label	Cat. No.	Year	Price	Notes
Archive Things	LP	BBC	REC68M	1970	**£20**	

PEELERS

Title	Format	Label	Cat. No.	Year	Price	Notes
Banished Misfortune	LP	Polydor		1972	**£60**	

PEELS

Title	Format	Label	Cat. No.	Year	Price	Notes
Juanita Banana	LP	Karate	5402	1966	**£20**	US
Juanita Banana	7"	Stateside	SS513	1966	**£6**	
Time Marches On	7"	Audio Fid.	527	196-	**£8**	

PEEP SHOW

Title	Format	Label	Cat. No.	Year	Price	Notes
Mazy	7"	Polydor	56196	1967	**£30**	

PEEPS

Title	Format	Label	Cat. No.	Year	Price	Notes
Gotta Get A Move On	7"	Philips	BF1478	1966	**£8**	
Now Is The Time	7"	Philips	BF1421	1965	**£10**	
Tra La La	7"	Philips	BF1509	1966	**£8**	
What Can I Say	7"	Philips	BF1443	1965	**£10**	

PEGG, BOB

Title	Format	Label	Cat. No.	Year	Price	Notes
Ancient Maps	LP	Transatlantic	TRA299	1975	**£15**	
Bob Pegg And Nick Strutt	LP	Transatlantic	TRA265	1973	**£15**	
Shipbuilder	LP	Transatlantic	TRA280	1974	**£15**	

PEGG, BOB & CAROLANNE

Title	Format	Label	Cat. No.	Year	Price	Notes
He Came From The Mountain	LP	Trailer	LER3016	1971	**£20**	

PEGG, CAROLANNE

Title	Format	Label	Cat. No.	Year	Price	Notes
Carolanne Pegg	LP	Transatlantic	TRA266	1973	**£12**	

PEMBROKE, JIM

Corporal Cauliflower...	LP	Love		1977	**£20**	Swedish
Pigworm	LP	Love	LRLP103	1974	**£20**	Swedish
Wicked Ivory	LP				**£20**	

PENDARVIS, TRACY

South Bound Line	7"	London	HLS9213	1960	**£5**	
Thousand Guitars	7"	London	HLS9059	1960	**£5**	

PENETRATION

Come Into The Open	7"	Virgin	VS268	1979	**£4**	
Danger Signs	7"	Virgin	VS257	1979	**£4**	
Danger Signs	12"	Virgin	VS25712	1979	**£6**	
Don't Dictate	7"	Virgin	VS192	1977	**£6**	
Firing Squad	7"	Virgin	VS213	1978	**£5**	
Life's A Gamble	7"	Virgin	VS226	1978	**£4**	
Moving Targets	LP	Virgin	V2109	1978	**£10**	luminous vinyl
Race Against Time	LP	Clifdayn	PEN1	1979	**£10**	

PENETRATION (2)

Aquarian Symphony	LP	Higher Key	33071	1974	**£60**	US

PENGUINS

Cool Cool Penguins	LP	Dootone	DTL242	1959	**£100**	US
Earth Angel	7"	London	HL8114	1955	**£150**	

PENN, TONY

That's What I Like	7"	Starlite	ST45083	1962	**£4**	

PENNY LANE

Loving Or Losing You	7"	Columbia	DB8377	1968	**£4**	

PENNY PEEPS

Model Village	7"	Liberty	LBF15053	1968	**£20**	

PENNY, HANK

Bloodshot Eyes	7"	Parlophone	MSP6202	1956	**£6**	

PENTAD

Don't Throw It All Away	7"	Parlophone	R5368	1965	**£8**	
It Better Be Me	7"	Parlophone	R5424	1966	**£8**	
Silver Dagger	7"	Parlophone	R5288	1965	**£15**	

PENTAGONS

To Be Loved	7"	London	HLU9333	1961	**£4**	

PENTANGLE

Basket Of Light	LP	Transatlantic	TRA205	1969	**£10**	chart LP
Cruel Sister	LP	Transatlantic	TRA228	1970	**£10**	chart LP
Light Flight	7"	Transatlantic	BIG128	1970	**£4**	chart single
Once I Had A Sweetheart	7"	Transatlantic	BIG124	1969	**£4**	chart single
Pentangle	LP	Transatlantic	TRA162	1968	**£12**	chart LP
Reflections	LP	Transatlantic	TRA240	1971	**£10**	
Solomon's Seal	LP	Reprise	K44197	1972	**£10**	
Sweet Child	LP	Transatlantic	TRA178	1968	**£15**	double
Travellin' Song	7"	Transatlantic	BIG109	1968	**£5**	

PEOPLE

Both Sides Of People	LP	Capitol	ST151	1969	**£25**	US
I Love You	LP	Capitol	ST2924	1968	**£25**	US
In Ancient Times	7"	Deram	DM346	1971	**£8**	
Somebody Tell Me My Name	7"	Capitol	CL15553	1968	**£6**	
There Are People And There Are	LP	Paramount	PAS5013	1970	**£20**	US
Ulla	7"	Capitol	CL15599	1969	**£6**	

PEOPLE BAND

People Band	LP	Transatlantic	TRA214	1970	**£20**	

PEPPER

We'll Make It Together	7"	Pye	7N17569	1968	**£8**	

PEPPER POT

Title	Format	Label	Cat. No.	Year	Price	Notes
Happy Together	7"	Parlophone	R5966	1972	**£4**	

PEPPER, BILLY & THE PEPPERPOTS

Title	Format	Label	Cat. No.	Year	Price	Notes
Merseymania	LP	Hurrah	HURALL731	196-	**£10**	
More Merseymania	LP	Hurrah	HURALL699	196-	**£10**	

PEPPER, JIM

Title	Format	Label	Cat. No.	Year	Price	Notes
Pepper's Pow Wow	LP	Atlantic	2400149	1971	**£15**	

PEPPERMINT CIRCUS

Title	Format	Label	Cat. No.	Year	Price	Notes
Let Me Go	7"	A&M	AMS778	1970	**£4**	
One Thing Can Lead To Another	7"	A&M	AMS765	1969	**£5**	

PEPPERMINT RAINBOW

Title	Format	Label	Cat. No.	Year	Price	Notes
Pink Lemonade	7"	MCA	MU1034	1968	**£6**	
Rosemary	7"	MCA	MU1091	1969	**£5**	
Will You Be Staying After Sunday	7"	MCA	MU1076	1969	**£5**	

PEPPERMINT TROLLEY COMPANY

Title	Format	Label	Cat. No.	Year	Price	Notes
Peppermint Trolley Company	LP	Acta	A38007	1968	**£20**	US

PEPPERMINT, DANNY

Title	Format	Label	Cat. No.	Year	Price	Notes
Maybe Tomorrow	7"	London	HLL9614	1962	**£4**	
One More Time	7"	London	HLL9516	1962	**£4**	
Peppermint Twist	7"	London	HLL9478	1961	**£4**	chart single

PEPPI

Title	Format	Label	Cat. No.	Year	Price	Notes
I Never Danced Before	7"	Decca	F11638	1963	**£4**	
Pistol Packin' Mama	7"	Decca	F11991	1964	**£4**	

PERCIVAL, LANCE

Title	Format	Label	Cat. No.	Year	Price	Notes
Shame And Scandal In The Family	7"	Parlophone	R5335	1965	**£4**	chart single

PERE UBU

Title	Format	Label	Cat. No.	Year	Price	Notes
Art Of Walking	LP	Rough Trade	ROUGH14	1980	**£12**	with 'Miles' & 'Arabia'
Datapanik In The Year Zero	12"	Radar	RDR1	1978	**£8**	
Fabulous Sequel	7"	Chrysalis	CHS2372	1979	**£8**	
Final Solution	7"	Hearthan	HR102	1976	**£75**	US
Modern Dance	LP	Blank	001	1978	**£20**	
Modern Dance	7"	Hearthan	HR104	1977	**£30**	US
Street Waves	7"	Hearthan	HR103	1976	**£15**	US
Thirty Seconds Over Tokyo	7"	Hearthan	HR101	1975	**£50**	US
Thirty Seconds Over Tokyo	7"	Hearthan	HR101	1975	**£25**	US, without PS

PERFECT PEOPLE

Title	Format	Label	Cat. No.	Year	Price	Notes
House In The Country	7"	MCA	MU1079	1969	**£5**	

PERFECT, CHRISTINE

Christine Perfect was pianist and vocalist with Chicken Shack and since the songs that she led were always the best that the group produced, it is not surprising that her solo LP is a particularly good example of British blues. When Peter Green left Fleetwood Mac, Christine Perfect was drafted in as his replacement, when she began to use her married name, Christine McVie

Title	Format	Label	Cat. No.	Year	Price	Notes
Christine Perfect	LP	Blue Horizon	763860	1970	**£20**	
I'm Too Far Gone	7"	Blue Horizon	573172	1970	**£8**	
When You Say	7"	Blue Horizon	573165	1969	**£6**	

PERISHERS

Title	Format	Label	Cat. No.	Year	Price	Notes
How Does It Feel	7"	Fontana	TF965	1968	**£4**	

PERKINS, CARL

Title	Format	Label	Cat. No.	Year	Price	Notes
All Mama's Children	7"	CBS	4991	1970	**£4**	
Any Way The Wind Blows	7"	Philips	PB1179	1961	**£5**	
Blue Suede Shoes	LP	London	HAS2202	1969	**£10**	
Blue Suede Shoes	7"	London	HLS10192	1968	**£4**	
Blue Suede Shoes	7"	London	HLU8271	1956	**£20**	chart single
Country Boy's Dream	LP	London	SHP8366	1968	**£10**	
Country Boy's Dream	7"	Stateside	SS599	1967	**£4**	
Dance Album (Teen Beat)	LP	London	HAS2202	1959	**£40**	
Dance Album	LP	Sun	LP1225	1957	**£240**	US
Dixie Fried	7"	London	HLS10192	1968	**£60**	demo
Glad All Over	7"	London	HLS8527	1957	**£20**	

Help Me Find My Baby	7"	Brunswick	05905	1964	**£5**	
King Of Rock	LP	CBS	63309	1968	**£12**	
Lake County Cotton Country	7"	Spark	SRL1009	1968	**£6**	
Matchbox	7"	London	HLS8408	1957	**£20**	
Monkeyshine	7"	Brunswick	05923	1964	**£5**	
One Ticket To Loneliness	7"	Philips	PB983	1959	**£5**	
Restless	7"	CBS	3932	1969	**£4**	
Teen Beat	LP	Sun	LP1225	1961	**£150**	US
That's Right	7"	London	HLS8608	1958	**£20**	
Whole Lotta Carl Perkins	LP	Realm	52305	1962	**£10**	
Whole Lotta Shakin'	LP	Columbia	CL1234	1958	**£100**	US

PERKINS, CARL & NASHVILLE TEENS

Big Bad Blues	7"	Brunswick	05909	1964	**£5**	

PERKINS, CARL & NRBQ

Boppin' The Blues	LP	CBS	63826	1970	**£10**	

PERKINS, JOE

Little Eefin Annie	7"	London	HLU9794	1963	**£4**	
Wrapped Up In Your Love	7"	Mojo	2092047	1972	**£4**	

PERRINE, PEP

Live And In Person	LP	Hideout	1004	1968	**£100**	US

PERRY SISTERS

Willie Boy	7"	Brunswick	05802	1959	**£10**	

PERRY, LEE

Bad Minded People	7"	Port-O-Jam	PJ4003	196-	**£10**	
Doctor Dick	7"	Island	WI292	1966	**£12**	
Help The Weak	7"	Port-O-Jam	PJ4001	196-	**£10**	
Just Keep It Up	7"	Island	WI259	1965	**£12**	
Man And Wife	7"	R&B	JB106	1963	**£12**	
Never Get Weary	7"	Island	WI118	1963	**£15**	
Old For New	7"	R&B	JB104	1963	**£12**	
Open Up	7"	Ska Beat	JB215	1965	**£10**	
People Funny Boy	7"	Doctor Bird	DB1146	1968	**£10**	
Prince In The Dark	7"	R&B	JB102	1963	**£12**	
Roast Duck	7"	Ska Beat	JB201	1965	**£10**	
Royalty	7"	R&B	JB135	1964	**£12**	
Trial And Crosses	7"	Ska Beat	JB203	1965	**£10**	
Upsetter	7"	Amalgam.	AMG808	196-	**£10**	
Upsetter Again	LP	Trojan	TTL28	1970	**£20**	
Wishes Of The Wicked	7"	Ska Beat	JB212	1965	**£10**	
Woodman	7"	Ska Beat	JB251	1966	**£10**	

PERRY, MAL

That's When Your Heartaches Begin	7"	Fontana	H133	1958	**£4**	
Things I Didn't Say	7"	Fontana	H157	1958	**£4**	

PERRY, MARK

Whole World's Down On Me	7"	Deptford F.C.	DFC012	1979	**£4**	

PERRY, STEVE

Step By Step	7"	HMV	POP745	1960	**£4**	chart single

PERSEPHONE, BILLY

Billy Persephone	LP	Orion		1972	**£30**	US

PERSIMMON'S PECULIAR SHADES

Watchmaker	7"	Major Minor	MM554	1968	**£10**	

PERSUADERS

Surfer's Nightmare	LP	Saturn	SAT5000	1963	**£40**	US
Thin Line Between Love And Hate	7"	Atlantic	2091164	1971	**£4**	

PERSUASIONS

Acappella	LP	Straight	STS1062	1970	**£15**	
Chirpin'	LP	Elektra	7E1099	1977	**£10**	
I Just Wanna Sing	LP	A&M	SP3656	1976	**£10**	US
More Than Before	LP	A&M	AMLS63835	1974	**£10**	

Spread The Word	LP	Capitol	ST11101	1972	**£10**	
Street Corner Symphony	LP	Island	ILPS9201	1972	**£12**	
We Came To Play	LP	Capitol	ST791	1971	**£12**	US
We Still Ain't Got No Band	LP	MCA	326	197-	**£10**	

PERSUASIONS (2)

Big Brother	7"	Columbia	DB7700	1965	**£6**	
I'll Go Crazy	7"	Columbia	DB7560	1965	**£6**	
La La La La La	7"	Columbia	DB7859	1966	**£8**	

PERT, MORRIS

Book Of Love/ Fragmenti I/ Ultimate Deacy	LP	Chantry	CHT007	1982	**£50**	
Luminos/ Chromosphere/ 4 Japanese Verses	LP	Chantry	ABM21	1975	**£60**	
Luminos/ Chromosphere/ 4 Japanese Verses	LP	Chantry	CHT001		**£50**	

PESKY GEE

Exclamation Mark	LP	Pye	NSPL18293	1969	**£40**	
Where Is My Mind	7"	Pye	7N17708	1969	**£15**	

PET SHOP BOYS

Always On My Mind (Dance Mix)	12"	Parlophone	12RS6171	1987	**£6**	gatefold PS
Always On My Mind (Phil Harding Mix)	12"	Parlophone	12RX6171	1987	**£6**	
Always On My Mind	7"	Parlophone	RS6171	1987	**£4**	gatefold PS
Domino Dancing (Disco Mix)	12"	Parlophone	12RS6190	1988	**£6**	gatefold PS
Domino Dancing (Remix)	12"	Parlophone	12RX6190	1988	**£6**	
Domino Dancing	7"	Parlophone	RS6190	1988	**£4**	gatefold PS
It's A Sin (Ian Levine Remix)	12"	Parlophone	12RX6158	1987	**£6**	
It's A Sin	CD-s	Parlophone	CDR6158	1987	**£6**	
It's A Sin	cass-s	Parlophone	TCR6158	1987	**£6**	
It's A Sin	7"	Parlophone	R6158	1987	**£5**	double sleeve
It's A Sin	12"	Parlophone	12R6158	1987	**£8**	double sleeve
It's Alright	10"	Parlophone	10R6220	1989	**£5**	with poster
Love Comes Quickly (Dance Mix)	12"	Parlophone	12R6116	1986	**£8**	
Love Comes Quickly (Dance Mix)	12"	Parlophone	12R6116	1986	**£6**	cut out sleeve
Love Comes Quickly	7"	Parlophone	R6116	1986	**£4**	chart single
Love Comes Quickly	10"	Parlophone	10R6116	1986	**£15**	with poster
Opportunities	7"	Parlophone	R6097	1985	**£10**	2 different mixes
Opportunities	12"	Parlophone	12R6097	1985	**£20**	
Opportunities (Version Latina)	12"	Parlophone	12RA6097	1985	**£25**	
Rent	CD-s	Parlophone	CDR6168	1987	**£6**	
Suburbia	cass-s	Parlophone	TCR6140	1986	**£10**	2 versions
Suburbia	7"	Parlophone	RD6140	1986	**£10**	double
Suburbia	12"	Parlophone	12R6140	1986	**£10**	double sleeve
West End Girls (Dance Mix)	12"	Parlophone	12R6115	1985	**£10**	2 sleeves
West End Girls (Shep Pettibone Mix)	12"	Parlophone	12RA6115	1986	**£10**	2 sleeves
West End Girls (Untitled Remix)	10"	Parlophone	10R6115	1985	**£20**	round sleeve
West End Girls	7"	Epic	A4292	1984	**£15**	
West End Girls	12"	Epic	TA4292	1984	**£25**	
West End Girls	7"	Parlophone	RP6115	1985	**£15**	shaped pic disc
What Have I Done To Deserve This?	CD-s	Parlophone	CDR6163	1987	**£6**	

PETER & GORDON

Baby I'm Yours	7"	Columbia	DB7729	1965	**£4**	chart single
Devant Toi Je Suis Sans Voix	7" EP	Columbia	ESRF1726	1966	**£15**	sung in French
Hits Of Nashville	LP	Capitol	T2430	1966	**£10**	US
Hot, Cold And Custard	LP	Capitol	T2882	1968	**£10**	US
Hurtin' 'n' Lovin'	LP	Columbia	33SX1761	1965	**£10**	
I Can Remember	7"	Columbia	DB8585	1969	**£4**	
I Don't Want To See You Again - (Cilla Black B side)	7"	Capitol	PRO2720	1964	**£30**	US promo - John Lennon & Paul McCartney intros
I Don't Want To See You Again	LP	Capitol	T2220	1964	**£10**	US
I Don't Want To See You Again	7"	Columbia	DB7356	1964	**£4**	
I Feel Like Going Out	7"	Columbia	DB8398	1968	**£4**	
I Go To Pieces	LP	Capitol	T2324	1965	**£10**	US
I Go To Pieces	LP	Columbia	SCXC25	1965	**£15**	export
I Go To Pieces	7"	Columbia	DB7407	1964	**£4**	
In London For Tea	LP	Capitol	T2747	1967	**£10**	US
In Touch	LP	Columbia	33SX1660	1964	**£12**	

Title	Format	Label	Cat. No.	Year	Price	Notes
Jokers	7"	Columbia	DB8198	1967	**£4**	
Knight In Rusty Armour	LP	Capitol	T2729	1967	**£10**	US
Knight In Rusty Armour	7"	Columbia	DB8075	1966	**£4**	
Lady Godiva	LP	Capitol	T2664	1967	**£10**	US
Lady Godiva	LP	Columbia	SCXC33	1966	**£15**	export
Lady Godiva	7"	Columbia	DB8003	1966	**£4**	chart single
Nobody I Know	7"	Columbia	DB7292	1964	**£4**	chart single
Nobody I Know	7" EP	Columbia	SEG8348	1964	**£6**	
Peter And Gordon	LP	Columbia	33SX1630	1964	**£12**	chart LP
Peter And Gordon	LP	Columbia	SX6045	1966	**£10**	
Somewhere	LP	Columbia	SX6097	1966	**£10**	
Sunday For Tea	7"	Columbia	DB8159	1967	**£4**	
To Know You Is To Love You	7"	Columbia	DB7617	1965	**£4**	chart single
To Show I Love You	7"	Columbia	DB7951	1966	**£4**	
True Love Ways	LP	Capitol	T2368	1965	**£10**	US
True Love Ways	7"	Columbia	DB7524	1965	**£4**	chart single
Woman	LP	Capitol	T2477	1966	**£10**	US
Woman	LP	Columbia	SCXC29	1965	**£15**	export
Woman	7"	Columbia	DB7834	1966	**£4**	chart single
World Without Love	LP	Capitol	T2115	1964	**£10**	US
World Without Love	7"	Columbia	DB7225	1964	**£4**	chart single
You've Had Better Times	7"	Columbia	DB8451	1968	**£4**	

PETER & THE HEADLINES

Title	Format	Label	Cat. No.	Year	Price	Notes
Don't Cry Little Girl	7"	Decca	F11980	1964	**£8**	
I've Got My Reasons	7"	Decca	F12035	1964	**£8**	

PETER & THE WOLVES

Title	Format	Label	Cat. No.	Year	Price	Notes
Lanternlight	7"	MGM	MGM1374	1968	**£5**	
Little Girl Lost And Found	7"	MGM	MGM1352	1967	**£5**	

PETER B'S

Each member of this instrumental group went on to further success. Initially, they all formed the backing group for Shotgun Express; later bassist Dave Ambrose joined the Brian Auger Trinity, organist Peter Bardens formed Camel, while guitarist Peter Green and drummer Mick Fleetwood became half of Fleetwood Mac.

Title	Format	Label	Cat. No.	Year	Price	Notes
If You Wanna Be Happy	7"	Columbia	DB7862	1966	**£20**	

PETER'S FACES

Title	Format	Label	Cat. No.	Year	Price	Notes
De-Boom-Lay-Boom	7"	Piccadilly	7N35225	1965	**£5**	
Wait	7"	Piccadilly	7N35205	1964	**£6**	

PETER, PAUL & MARY

Title	Format	Label	Cat. No.	Year	Price	Notes
Album 1700	LP	W. Bros	W1700	1967	**£10**	
In Concert	LP	W. Bros	W21555	1964	**£15**	double, chart LP
In The Wind	LP	W. Bros	W1507	1963	**£10**	chart LP
In The Wind Vol.1	7" EP	W. Bros	WEP6135	1964	**£4**	
In The Wind Vol.2	7" EP	W. Bros	WEP6137	1964	**£4**	
Moving	LP	W. Bros	W1473	1962	**£10**	
Moving	7" EP	W. Bros	WEP6119	1964	**£4**	
Peter, Paul And Mary	LP	W. Bros	W1449	1962	**£10**	chart LP
Peter, Paul And Mary	7" EP	W. Bros	WEP6114	1963	**£4**	
Peter, Paul And Mary	7" EP	W. Bros	WEP6122	1964	**£4**	
Peter, Paul And Mary Album	LP	W. Bros	W1648	1966	**£10**	
See What Tomorrow Brings	LP	W. Bros	W1615	1965	**£10**	
Song Will Rise	LP	W. Bros	W1589	1965	**£10**	

PETERS, JANICE

Title	Format	Label	Cat. No.	Year	Price	Notes
This Little Girl's Gone Rocking	7"	Columbia	DB4222	1958	**£10**	
You're The One	7"	Columbia	DB4276	1959	**£8**	

PETERS, MARK

Title	Format	Label	Cat. No.	Year	Price	Notes
Candy's Gonna Cry	7"	Oriole	CB1909	1964	**£8**	
Don't Cry For Me	7"	Piccadilly	7N35207	1964	**£6**	
Janie	7"	Oriole	CB1836	1963	**£8**	

PETERS, WENDY

Title	Format	Label	Cat. No.	Year	Price	Notes
Morning Dew	7"	Saga	OPP1	196-	**£12**	

PETERSON, BOBBY

Title	Format	Label	Cat. No.	Year	Price	Notes
Hunch	7"	Top Rank	JAR232	1959	**£6**	
Piano Rock	7"	Sue	WI346	1965	**£8**	
Rocking Charlie	7"	Sue	WI342	1964	**£10**	

PETERSON, PAUL

Little Bit Of Sandy	7"	T. Motown	TMG670	1968	**£8**	
Little Bit Of Sandy	7"	T. Motown	TMG670	1968	**£30**	demo

PETERSON, RAY

Answer Me	7"	RCA	RCA1175	1960	**£4**	chart single
Corrine Corrina	7"	London	HLX9246	1960	**£5**	chart single
Corrine Corrina	7" EP	London	REX1293	1961	**£6**	
Give Us Your Blessing	7"	London	HLX9746	1963	**£4**	
I Could Have Loved You So Well	7"	London	HLX9489	1962	**£4**	
If You Were Here	7"	MGM	MGM1249	1964	**£4**	
Other Side Of...	LP	MGM	E4277	1965	**£12**	US
Shirley Purly	7"	RCA	RCA1154	1959	**£4**	
Sweet Little Kathy	7"	London	HLX9332	1961	**£4**	
Tell Laura I Love Her	LP	RCA	LPM2297	1960	**£30**	US
Tell Laura I Love Her	7"	RCA	RCA1195	1960	**£4**	
Very Best Of...	LP	MGM	E4250	1964	**£12**	US
Wonder Of You	7"	RCA	RCA1131	1959	**£4**	chart single
You Didn't Care	7"	London	HLX9569	1962	**£4**	
You Thrill Me	7"	London	HLX9379	1961	**£4**	

PETS

Cha Hua Hua	7"	London	HL8652	1958	**£4**	

PETTI, MARY

Hey Lawdy Lawdy	7"	RCA	RCA1239	1961	**£4**	

PETTY, NORMAN

Corsage	LP	Vik	1073	1959	**£20**	US
Mood Indigo	7"	HMV	7M274	1954	**£6**	
Moondreams	LP	Columbia	CL1092	1958	**£50**	US
Petty For Your Thoughts	LP	Top Rank	RS639	1960	**£15**	US

PETTY, TOM

Damn The Torpedoes	LP	MCA	MCA5105	1980	**£12**	Canadian audiophile
Hard Promises	LP	MCA	BSR5162	1981	**£12**	Canadian audiophile
Official Bootleg	LP	Shelter	IDJ24	1977	**£12**	promo
Straight Into Darkness	7"	MCA	MCADJ805	1983	**£4**	promo

PFM

Per Un Amico	LP	Numero Uno	ZSLN55155	1972	**£12**	Italian
Photos Of Ghosts	LP	Manticore	K43502	1973	**£10**	
Storia Di Un Minoto	LP	Numero Uno	ZSLN55055	1972	**£12**	Italian

PHANTOM

Divine Comedy	LP	Capitol	ST11313	1974	**£15**	US

PHANTOMS

Great Guitar Hits	LP	Arc		1964	**£30**	
Phantom Guitar	7"	Palette	PG9014	1961	**£4**	

PHAROAHS

Pharoahs	7" EP	Decca	DFE6522	1958	**£100**	

PHASE 4

What Do You Say About That	7"	Decca	F12327	1966	**£4**	

PHELPS, JAMES

Check Yourself	7"	Paramount	3019	1971	**£4**	

PHILIPS, CONFREY

Shotgun Rock And Roll	7"	Decca	F10866	1957	**£4**	

PHILLIPS, ANTHONY

Prelude '84	7"	RCA	RCA102	1981	**£5**	PS
Um And Aargh	7"	Arista	ARIST252	1978	**£6**	PS
We're All As We Lie	7"	Arista	ARIST192	1978	**£8**	
Wise After The Event	LP	Passport	PB9828	1978	**£10**	US pic disc

PHILLIPS, ESTHER

Am I That Easy To Forget	7"	Ember	EMBS174	1963	**£4**	
And I Love Him	LP	Atlantic	8102	1965	**£10**	US

And I Love Him	7"	Atlantic	584103	1967	**£4**	
And I Love Him	7"	Atlantic	AT4028	1965	**£4**	
Country Side Of...	LP	Atlantic	8130	1966	**£10**	US
Esther	LP	Atlantic	8122	1966	**£10**	US
Memory Lane	LP	King	LP622	1956	**£600**	US
Release Me	7"	Ember	EMBS221	1966	**£4**	
Release Me	LP	Lenox	227	1962	**£25**	US
Release Me	7"	Stateside	SS140	1962	**£5**	
Sings	LP	Atlantic	587010	1966	**£10**	
Tonight I'll Be Staying Here With You	7"	Roulette	RO508	1968	**£4**	
Too Late To Worry, Too Blue To Cry	7"	Roulette	RO505	1968	**£4**	

PHILLIPS, GLENN

Lost At Sea	LP	Caroline	C1519	1975	**£10**	
Swim In The Wind	LP	Virgin	V2087	1977	**£10**	

PHILLIPS, GREGORY

Angie	7"	Pye	7N15546	1963	**£4**	
Don't Bother Me	7"	Pye	7N15633	1964	**£4**	
Down In The Boondocks	7"	Immediate	IM004	1965	**£8**	
Everybody Knows	7"	Pye	7N15583	1963	**£4**	

PHILLIPS, JOHN

Mississippi	7"	Stateside	SS8046	1970	**£4**	
Wolfking Of L.A.	LP	Stateside	SSL5027	1970	**£12**	

PHILLIPS, PHIL

I Love To Love You	7"	Mercury	AMT1139	1961	**£6**	
Sea Of Love	7"	Mercury	AMT1059	1959	**£5**	
Take This Heart	7"	Mercury	AMT1072	1960	**£4**	
Your True Love Once More	7"	Mercury	AMT1093	1960	**£4**	

PHILLIPS, SHAWN

Bright White	LP	A&M	AMLH64402	1974	**£10**	
Collaboration	LP	A&M	AMLS64324	1972	**£10**	
Contribution	LP	A&M	AMLS978	1970	**£10**	
Do You Wonder	LP	A&M	AMLH64539	1975	**£10**	
Faces	LP	A&M	AMLS64363	1973	**£10**	
Furthermore	LP	A&M	AMLH68278	1974	**£10**	
I'm A Loner	LP	Columbia	33SX1748	1965	**£50**	
Little Tin Soldier	7"	Columbia	DB7789	1965	**£6**	
Nobody Listens	7"	Columbia	DB7699	1965	**£8**	
Rumpelstiltskin's Resolve	LP	A&M	AMLH64582	1976	**£10**	
Second Contribution	LP	A&M	AMLS2006	1971	**£10**	
Shawn	LP	Columbia	SCX6006	1966	**£50**	
Solitude	7"	Columbia	DB7611	1965	**£6**	
Spaced	LP	A&M	AMLH64650	1977	**£10**	
Stargazer	7"	Parlophone	R5606	1967	**£8**	
Summer Came	7"	Columbia	DB7956	1966	**£6**	

PHILLIPS, STU

Champlain And St.Lawrence Line	7"	London	HL8673	1958	**£4**	

PHILLIPS, TEDDY

Ridin' To Tennessee	7"	London	HL8032	1954	**£6**	

PHILLIPS, WARREN & THE ROCKETS (SAVOY BROWN)

World Of Rock'n'Roll	LP	Decca	SPA43	1969	**£20**	

PHILOSOPHERS

After Sundown	LP	PS		196-	**£30**	US

PHILPOTT, VINCE & THE DRAGS

Cramp	7"	Decca	F11997	1964	**£15**	

PHILWIT & PEGASUS

And I Try	7"	Chapter One	CH131	1970	**£5**	
Elephant Song	7"	Chapter One	CH137	1970	**£5**	
Philwit And Pegasus	LP	Chapter One		1970	**£25**	

PHLUPH

Phluph	LP	Verve	V65054	1968	**£12**	US

PIANO RED

In Concert	LP	Groove	1002	1964	**£100**	US
Jump Man Jump	LP	Groove	1001	1964	**£100**	US
Rhythm 'n' Blues Vol.2	7" EP	RCA	RCX7138	1964	**£10**	
Rocking With Red	7"	HMV	7M108	1953	**£40**	

PICCADILLY LINE

At The Third Stroke	7"	CBS	2785	1967	**£8**	
Emily Small	7"	CBS	2958	1967	**£8**	
Huge World Of Emily Small	LP	CBS	63129	1967	**£20**	

PICKETT, BOBBY & THE CRYPT KICKERS

Monster Mash	LP	Garpax	GP67001	1962	**£25**	US
Monster Mash	7"	London	HLU9597	1962	**£4**	

PICKETT, DAN

Dan Pickett	7" EP	XX	MIN710		**£4**	

PICKETT, NICK

Silversleeves	LP	W. Bros		1972	**£20**	

PICKETT, WILSON

634-5789	7"	Atlantic	AT4072	1966	**£4**	chart single
99 & A Half Won't Do	7"	Atlantic	584023	1966	**£4**	
Best Of...	LP	Atlantic	587092	1968	**£12**	
Call My Name, I'll Be There	7"	Atlantic	2091153	1971	**£4**	
Don't Fight It	7"	Atlantic	AT4052	1965	**£4**	chart single
Don't Knock My Love	7"	Atlantic	2091124	1971	**£4**	
Engine No.9	LP	Atlantic	2400026	1971	**£10**	
Engine No.9	7"	Atlantic	2091032	1970	**£4**	
Everybody Needs Somebody To Love	7"	Atlantic	584101	1967	**£4**	
Exciting...	LP	Atlantic	587029	1966	**£15**	
Fire And Water	7"	Atlantic	2091086	1971	**£4**	
Funky Broadway	7"	Atlantic	584130	1967	**£4**	chart single
Hey Joe	7"	Atlantic	584281	1969	**£4**	
Hey Jude	LP	Atlantic	588170	1969	**£12**	
Hey Jude	7"	Atlantic	584236	1969	**£4**	chart single
I Found A True Love	7"	Atlantic	584221	1968	**£4**	
I'm A Midnight Mover	7"	Atlantic	584203	1968	**£4**	chart single
I'm In Love	LP	Atlantic	587107	1968	**£12**	
In The Midnight Hour	LP	Atlantic	587032	1966	**£15**	
In The Midnight Hour	LP	Atlantic	ATL5037	1965	**£20**	
In The Midnight Hour	7"	Atlantic	584150	1968	**£4**	
In The Midnight Hour	7"	Atlantic	AT4036	1965	**£5**	chart single
It's Too Late	LP	Double-L	DL2300	1963	**£20**	US
It's Too Late	7"	Liberty	LIB10115	1963	**£6**	
Land Of 1000 Dances	7"	Atlantic	584039	1966	**£4**	chart single
Midnight Mover	LP	Atlantic	587111	1968	**£12**	
Mini-Skirt Minnie	7"	Atlantic	584261	1969	**£4**	
Mustang Sally	7"	Atlantic	584066	1966	**£4**	chart single
My Heart Belongs To You	7"	MGM	MGM1286	1965	**£8**	
New Orleans	7"	Atlantic	584107	1967	**£4**	
Right On	LP	Atlantic	2465002	1970	**£10**	
She's Looking Good	7"	Atlantic	584183	1968	**£4**	
Sound Of...	LP	Atlantic	587080	1967	**£15**	
Stag-o-lee	7"	Atlantic	584142	1967	**£4**	
Sugar Sugar	7"	Atlantic	2091005	1970	**£4**	
That Kind Of Love	7"	Atlantic	584173	1968	**£4**	
Wicked Pickett	LP	Atlantic	587057	1967	**£15**	
You Keep Me Hanging On	7"	Atlantic	584313	1970	**£4**	

PICKETTYWITCH

Pickettywitch	LP	Pye	NSPL18357	1970	**£10**	

PICKWICKS

Apple Blossom Time	7"	Decca	F11901	1964	**£8**	
Little By Little	7"	W. Bros	WB151	1965	**£12**	
You're Old Enough	7"	Decca	F11957	1964	**£8**	

PIED PIPERS

Ragamuffin	7"	Columbia	DB7883	1966	**£6**	

PIERCE, WEBB

Title	Format	Label	Cat. No.	Year	Price	Notes
Bound For The Kingdom	LP	Decca	DL8889	1959	**£10**	US
Bye Bye Love	7"	Brunswick	05682	1957	**£20**	
Country And Western Favourites Vol.1	7" EP	Ember	EMB4520	1962	**£5**	
Country Round Up	7" EP	Parlophone	GEP8792	1959	**£10**	
Drifting Texas Sands	7"	Brunswick	05842	1960	**£4**	
I Ain't Never	7"	Brunswick	05809	1959	**£8**	
Just Imagination	LP	Decca	DL8728	1957	**£20**	US
No Love Have I	7"	Brunswick	05820	1960	**£8**	
One And Only Webb Pierce	LP	King	648	1959	**£15**	US
Teenage Boogie	7"	Brunswick	05630	1956	**£40**	
That Wondering Boy	LP	Decca	DL8295	1956	**£20**	US
That Wondering Boy	LP-10"	Decca	DL5536	1953	**£25**	US
Webb	LP	Brunswick	LAT8324	1959	**£15**	
Webb Pierce	LP	Decca	DL8129	1955	**£20**	US
Webb Pierce Pt.1	7" EP	Brunswick	OE9253	1956	**£10**	
Webb Pierce Pt.2	7" EP	Brunswick	OE9254	1956	**£10**	
Webb Pierce Pt.3	7" EP	Brunswick	OE9255	1956	**£10**	
Webb Pierce Story	LP	Decca	DXB181	1964	**£10**	US, with booklet

PIGS

Title	Format	Label	Cat. No.	Year	Price	Notes
Youthanasia	7"	New Bristol	NBR01	1977	**£4**	

PIGSTY HILL LIGHT ORCHESTRA

Title	Format	Label	Cat. No.	Year	Price	Notes
Cushion Foot Stomp	LP	Village Thing	VTS1	1970	**£10**	
Piggery Jokery	LP	Village Thing	VTS8	1971	**£10**	

PILOT

Title	Format	Label	Cat. No.	Year	Price	Notes
Pilot	LP	RCA	LSP4730	1972	**£12**	US
Point Of View	LP	RCA	LSP4825	197-	**£12**	US

PILTDOWN MEN

Title	Format	Label	Cat. No.	Year	Price	Notes
Gargantua	7"	Capitol	CL15211	1961	**£4**	
Goodnight Mrs.Flintstone	7"	Capitol	CL15186	1961	**£4**	chart single
McDonald's Cave	7"	Capitol	CL15149	1960	**£4**	chart single
Piltdown Rides Again	7"	Capitol	CL15175	1961	**£4**	chart single
Piltdown Rides Again	7" EP	Capitol	EAP120155	1961	**£10**	
Pretty Girl Is Like A Melody	7"	Capitol	CL15245	1962	**£4**	

PIMM, SIR HUBERT

Title	Format	Label	Cat. No.	Year	Price	Notes
Goodnight And Cheerio	7"	London	HL8155	1955	**£15**	

PINEAPPLE CHUNKS

Title	Format	Label	Cat. No.	Year	Price	Notes
Drive My Car	7"	Mercury	MF922	1965	**£8**	

PINEWOOD TOM & TALL TOM

Title	Format	Label	Cat. No.	Year	Price	Notes
Male Blues Vol.4	7" EP	Collector	JE15	196-	**£5**	

PINK FAIRIES

Title	Format	Label	Cat. No.	Year	Price	Notes
Between The Lines	7"	Stiff	BUY2	1976	**£5**	
Kings Of Oblivion	LP	Polydor	2383212	1973	**£15**	with poster
Never Never Land	LP	Polydor	2383045	1971	**£10**	
Never Never Land	LP	Polydor	2383045	1971	**£20**	plastic cover
Pink Fairies	LP	Polydor	2384071	1975	**£10**	
Snake	7"	Polydor	2058089	1970	**£15**	
Well Well Well	7"	Polydor	2059302	1972	**£10**	
What A Bunch Of Sweeties	LP	Polydor	2383132	1972	**£10**	chart LP

PINK FLOYD

In their early days, Pink Floyd epitomised what British psychedelic music was all about and their first two albums are rightly prized as crucially important documents of the period. Like many LPs recorded in the second half of the sixties, there are many differences between the mono and stereo versions, this being particularly noticeable on the often densely arranged "Saucerful Of Secrets" record. The Columbia singles are also much in demand, especially since the only reissue of the last three consists of a German compilation LP. Promotional copies of the 1967 singles were issued in picture sleeves, which are extremely scarce today.

Title	Format	Label	Cat. No.	Year	Price	Notes
Animals	LP	Columbia	JC34474	1976	**£20**	US promo
Animals	LP	Columbia	PCQ34474	1977	**£25**	US quad
Another Brick In The Wall Pt.2 (live)	12"	EMI	12PF1	1988	**£12**	promo only
Apples And Oranges	7"	Columbia	DB8310	1967	**£10**	
Apples And Oranges	7"	Columbia	DB8310	1967	**£200**	promo, PS
Arnold Layne	7"	Columbia	DB8156	1967	**£8**	chart single

Title	Format	Label	Cat. No.	Year	Price	Notes
Arnold Layne	7"	Columbia	DB8156	1967	**£200**	promo, PS
Atom Heart Mother	LP	Harvest	Q4SHVL781	1973	**£25**	quad
Collection Of Great Dance Songs	LP	Columbia	HC47680	1983	**£20**	US audiophile
Dark Side Of The Moon (UHQR)	LP	Mobile Fid.	MFSL1017	1982	**£120**	US audiophile
Dark Side Of The Moon	LP	Capitol	SEAX11902	1978	**£20**	US pic disc
Dark Side Of The Moon	LP	Harvest	Q4SHVL804	1973	**£25**	quad
Dark Side Of The Moon	LP	Mobile Fid.	MFSL1017	1977	**£20**	US audiophile
Final Cut	LP	Columbia	QC38243	1983	**£15**	US promo
First XI	LP	Harvest	PF11	1979	**£100**	9LPs + 2pic discs, boxed
It Would Be So Nice	7"	Columbia	DB8401	1968	**£12**	
Learning To Fly	CD-s	EMI	CDEM26	1987	**£6**	
Learning To Fly	7"	EMI	EM26	1987	**£6**	pink vinyl
Money	7"	Harvest	HAR5217	1981	**£20**	1 sided demo, pink vinyl
More	LP	Columbia	SCX6346	1969	**£10**	green photo rear sleeve chart LP
Nice Pair	LP	Harvest	SHDW403	1973	**£12**	double, Mr.Phang sleeve
Not Now John	7"	Harvest	PSR533	1983	**£10**	promo
Off The Wall	LP	Columbia	AS756	1979	**£20**	US promo sampler
On The Turning Away	7"	EMI	EMP34	1987	**£5**	pink vinyl
Piper At The Gates Of Dawn	LP	Columbia	SCX6157	1967	**£15**	stereo, chart LP
Piper At The Gates Of Dawn	LP	Columbia	SX6157	1967	**£20**	mono, chart LP
Point Me At The Sky	7"	Columbia	DB8511	1968	**£12**	
Saucerful Of Secrets	LP	Columbia	SCX6258	1968	**£12**	stereo, chart LP
Saucerful Of Secrets	LP	Columbia	SX6258	1968	**£20**	mono, chart LP
See Emily Play	7"	Columbia	DB8214	1967	**£8**	chart single
See Emily Play	7"	Columbia	DB8214	1967	**£200**	promo, PS
Tour '75	LP	Capitol	SPRO8116/7	1975	**£30**	US promo compilation
Wall	LP	Columbia	H2C46183	1983	**£50**	US audiophile
Wall In Store	LP	Columbia	XDAP93012	1979	**£60**	US promo
Wish You Were Here	LP	Columbia	HC43453	1982	**£20**	US audiophile
Wish You Were Here	LP	Harvest	Q4SHVL814	1976	**£25**	quad

PINK FLOYD & OTHERS

Title	Format	Label	Cat. No.	Year	Price	Notes
Tonight Let's All Make Love...	LP	Instant	INLP002	1968	**£60**	
Zabriskie Point	LP	MGM	2315002	1970	**£10**	

PINK PEOPLE

Title	Format	Label	Cat. No.	Year	Price	Notes
Indian Hate Call	7"	Philips	BF1356	1964	**£12**	
Psychologically Unsound	7"	Philips	BF1355	1964	**£15**	

PINKERTON'S ASSORTED COLOURS

Title	Format	Label	Cat. No.	Year	Price	Notes
Don't Stop Lovin' Me Baby	7"	Decca	F12377	1966	**£4**	chart single
Magic Rocking Horse	7"	Decca	F12493	1966	**£5**	
Mirror Mirror	7"	Decca	F12307	1966	**£4**	chart single

PINNACLE

Title	Format	Label	Cat. No.	Year	Price	Notes
Assassin	LP	Stag		1974	**£100**	

PIONEERS

Title	Format	Label	Cat. No.	Year	Price	Notes
Bad To Be Good	7"	Trojan	TR7897	1973	**£4**	
Battle Of The Giants	LP	Trojan	TBL139	1970	**£12**	
Don't You Know	7"	Amalgam.	AMG833	196-	**£10**	
Freedom Feeling	LP	Trojan	TRLS64	1973	**£10**	
Give And Take	7"	Trojan	TR7846	1972	**£4**	chart single
Give It To Me	7"	Blue Cat	BS103	196-	**£10**	
Give Me A Little Loving	7"	Amalgam.	AMG811	196-	**£10**	
Greetings From The...	LP	Amalgam.	AMGLP2003	196-	**£40**	
Honey Bee	7"	Trojan	TR7923	1974	**£4**	
I Believe In Love	LP	Trojan	TRLS48	1972	**£10**	
I Love No Other Girl	7"	Caltone	TONE119	196-	**£8**	
I'm Gonna Knock On Your Door	7"	Trojan	TR7913	1974	**£4**	
Jackpot	7"	Amalgam.	AMG821	196-	**£10**	
Jamaica Jerk Off	7"	Trojan	TR7931	1974	**£4**	
Let Your Yeah Be Yeah	7"	Trojan	TR7825	1971	**£4**	chart single
Little Bit Of Soap	7"	Trojan	TR7906	1973	**£4**	
Long Shot	7"	Amalgam.	AMG814	196-	**£10**	
Long Shot Kick The Bucket	7"	Trojan	TR672	1969	**£5**	chart single
Longshot	LP	Trojan	TBL103	1970	**£12**	
Love Love Every Day	7"	Amalgam.	AMG846	196-	**£10**	
Mama Look Deh	7"	Amalgam.	AMG835	1969	**£10**	
No Dope Me Pony	7"	Amalgam.	AMG823	196-	**£10**	

Reggae Beat	7"	Blue Cat	BS139	196-	**£10**	
Shake It Up	7"	Blue Cat	BS100	196-	**£10**	
Sweet Number One	7"	Trojan	TR7939	1974	**£4**	
Tickle Me For Days	7"	Amalgam.	AMG826	196-	**£10**	
Whip Them	7"	Blue Cat	BS105	196-	**£10**	
Who The Cap Fits	7"	Amalgam.	AMG840	196-	**£10**	
Yeah	LP	Trojan	TRL24	1971	**£10**	

PIPKINS

Gimme Dat Ding	7"	Columbia	DB8662	1970	**£4**	chart single

PIPS

Every Beat Of My Heart	7"	Top Rank	JAR574	1961	**£8**	

PIRANA

Pirana	LP	Harvest	SHVL603	1972	**£10**	
Pirana II	LP	Harvest	SHVL609	1972	**£10**	

PIRANHAS

Somethin' Fishy	LP	Custom Fid.	1452	1969	**£750**	US

PIRATES

My Babe	7"	HMV	POP1250	1964	**£10**	
Shades Of Blue	7"	Polydor	56712	1966	**£8**	

PISCES

Pisces	LP	Trailer	LER2025	1971	**£20**	

PITNEY, GENE

Backstage	7" EP	Stateside	SE1040	1966	**£4**	
Every Breath I Take	7"	HMV	POP933	1961	**£6**	
Gene Italiano	7" EP	Stateside	SE1032	1965	**£4**	
Gene Pitney Sings Just For You	7" EP	Stateside	SE1036	1966	**£4**	
I Must Be Seeing Things	7" EP	Stateside	SE1030	1965	**£4**	
I Wanna Love My Life Away	7"	London	HL9270	1961	**£4**	chart single
Man Who Shot Liberty Valance	7"	HMV	POP1018	1962	**£4**	
Many Sides Of...	LP	HMV	CLP1566	1961	**£12**	
Only Love Can Break A Heart	LP	United Artists	ULP1028	196-	**£10**	
Pitney Sings Just For You	LP	United Artists	ULP1043	196-	**£10**	
San Remo Winners And Others	7" EP	Stateside	SE1041	1967	**£4**	
Something's Gotten Hold Of My Heart	7"	Stateside	SS2060	1967	**£4**	chart single
That Girl Belongs To Yesterday	7" EP	Stateside	SE1028	1965	**£4**	chart single
That Girl Belongs To Yesterday	7"	United Artists	UP1045	1964	**£4**	
That Girl Belongs To Yesterday	7" EP	United Artists	UEP1002	1964	**£4**	
There's No Living Without Your Love	7" EP	Stateside	SE1045	1967	**£4**	
Town Without Pity	7"	HMV	POP952	1962	**£4**	chart single
Town Without Pity	7" EP	HMV	7EG8832	1963	**£5**	
Twenty Four Hours From Tulsa	7" EP	Stateside	SE1027	1965	**£4**	
Twenty Four Hours From Tulsa	7"	United Artists	UP1035	1963	**£4**	chart single
Twenty Four Hours From Tulsa	7" EP	United Artists	UEP1001	1964	**£4**	

PIXIES

Live	LP	4AD		1989	**£40**	promo

PIXIES THREE

Party With The Pixies Three	LP	Mercury	MG20912	1964	**£40**	US

PLAGUE

Looking For The Sun	7"	Decca	F12730	1968	**£20**	

PLAINSONG

In Search Of Amelia Earhart	LP	Elektra	K42120	1972	**£15**	
Plainsong II	LP	Elektra		197-	**£50**	demo only

PLANETS

Chunky	7"	HMV	POP818	1960	**£4**	
Jam Roll	7"	HMV	POP832	1961	**£4**	
Jungle Street	7"	HMV	POP895	1961	**£4**	
Like Party	7"	Palette	PG9008	1960	**£4**	

PLANT, ROBERT

In The Mood	7"	Es Paranza	SAM179	1983	**£4**	promo

You Can All Join In

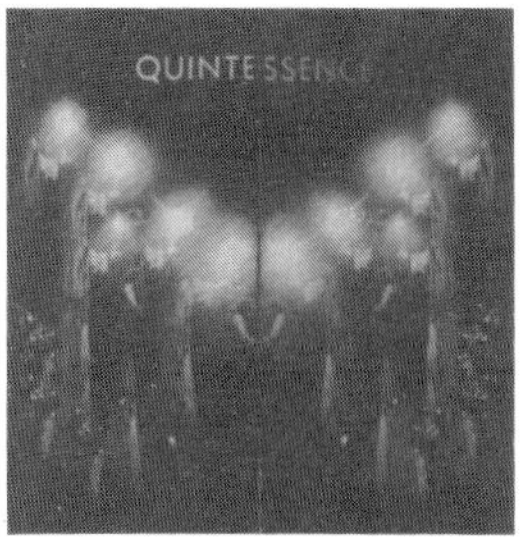

Nice Enough To Eat

Heads Together

Open Music

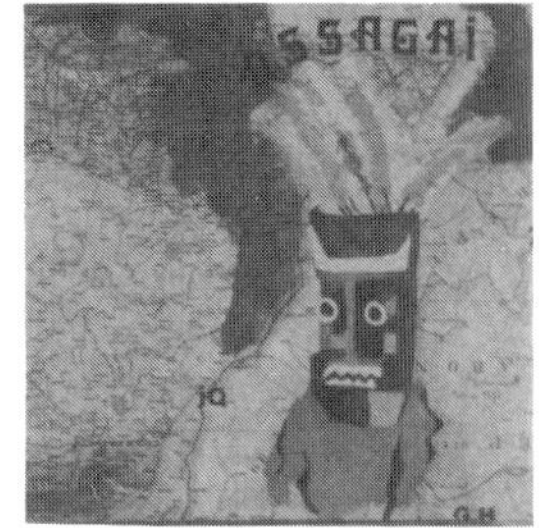

Spiral Dance

A Breath Of Fresh Air

Celebration

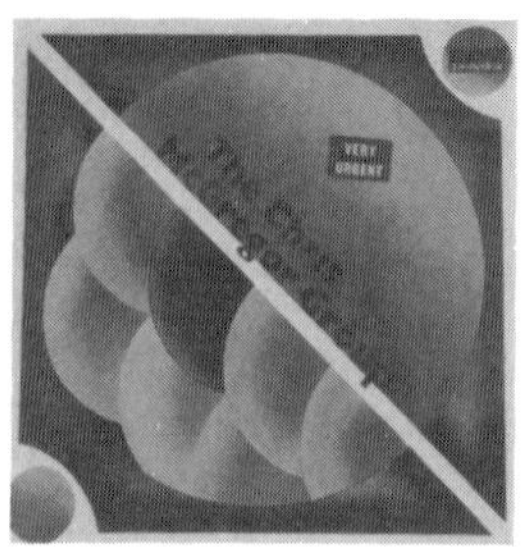

Some Echoes, Some Shadows

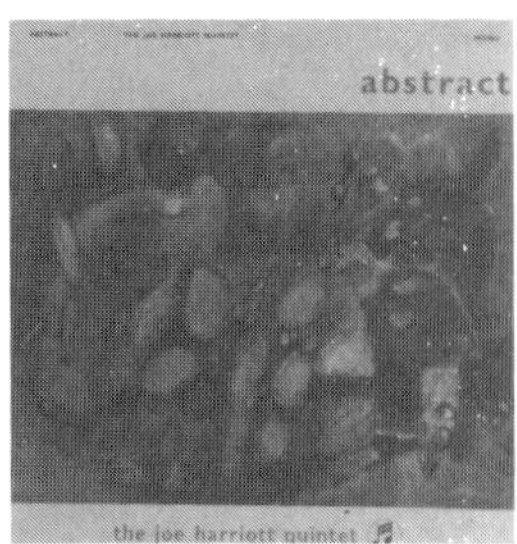

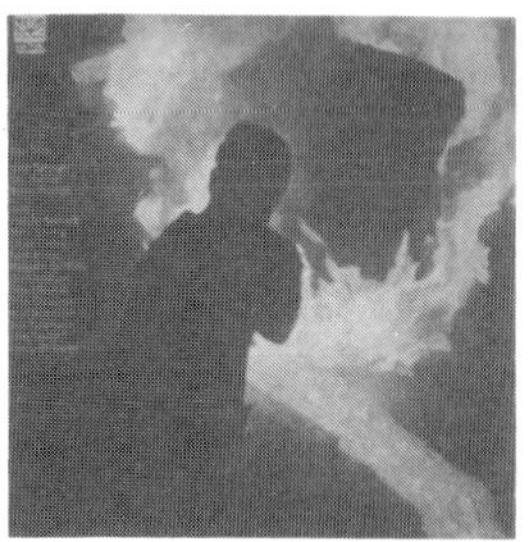

Conflagration

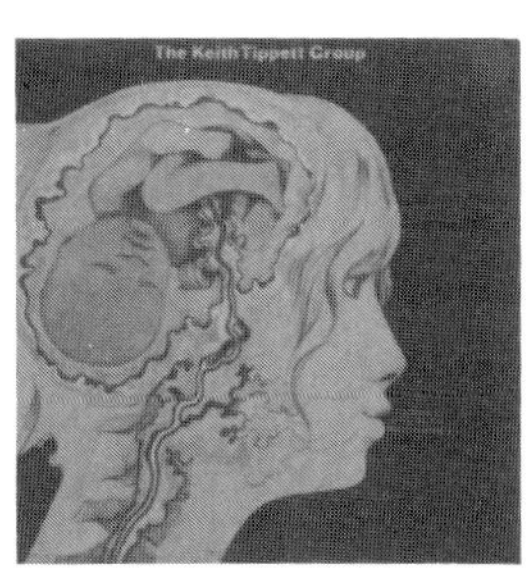

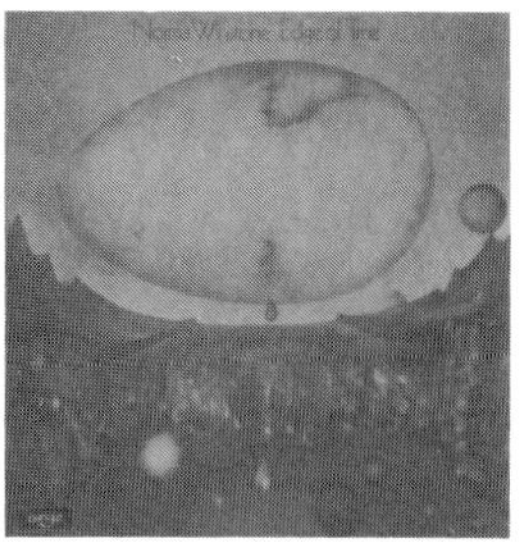

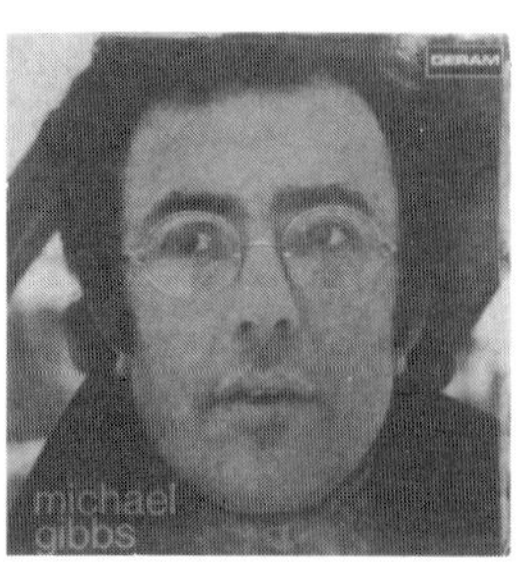

Dedicated To You But You Weren't Listening

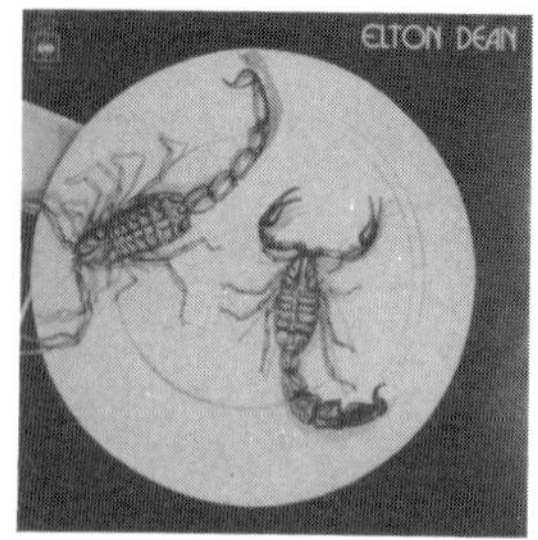

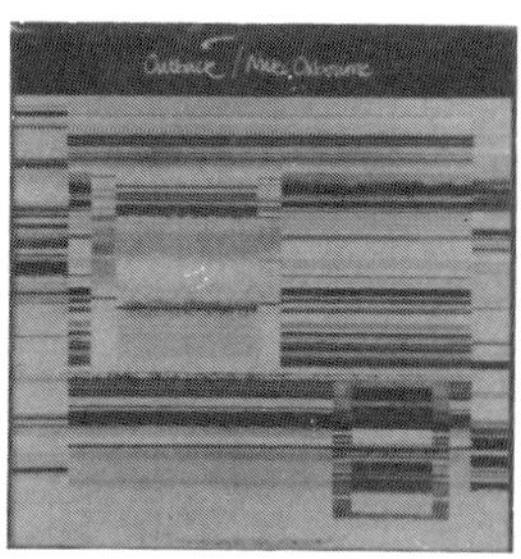

Body And Soul

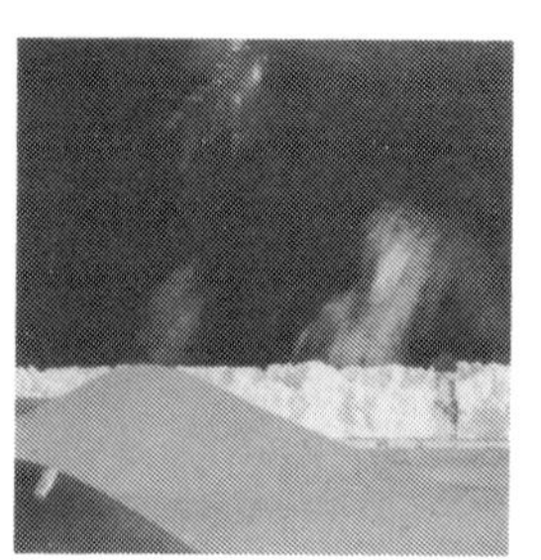

Crossings

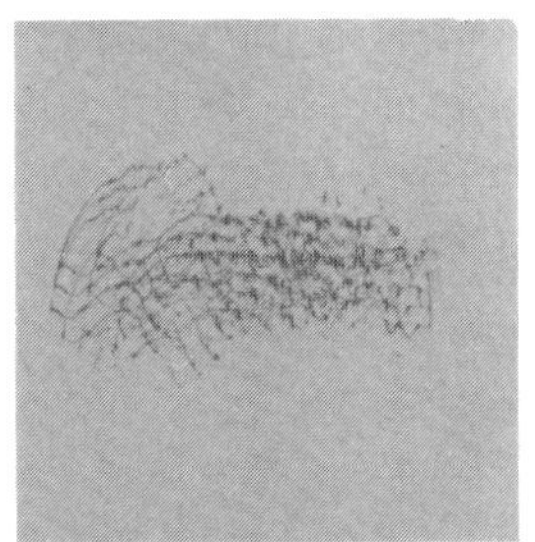

Music In Similar Motion

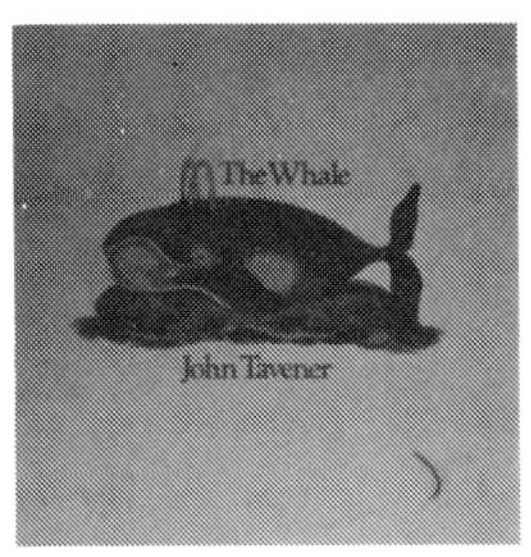

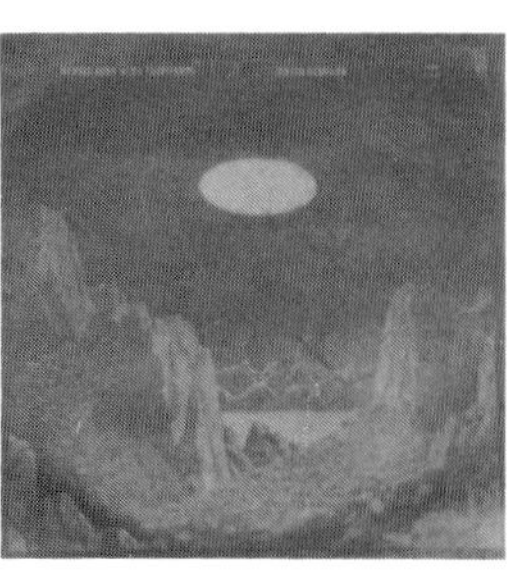

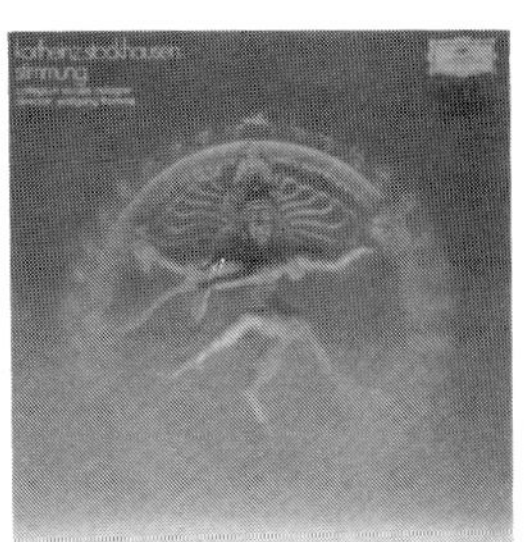

Orchestral Manoeuvres In The Dark

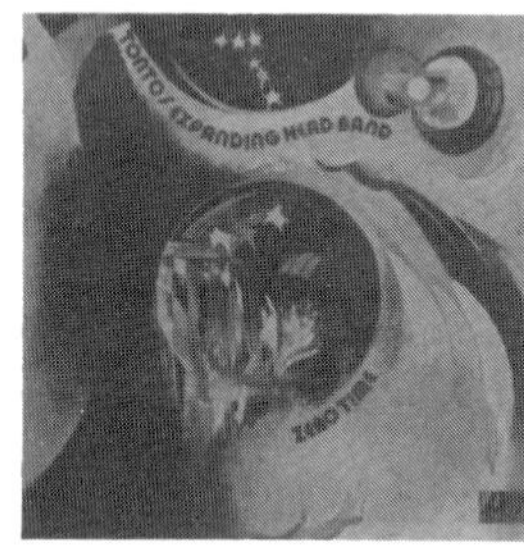

Electromagnetic Waves Descend

Wir Fahr'n Auf Der Autobahn

In The Land Of Grey And Pink

Forever Blowing Bubbles

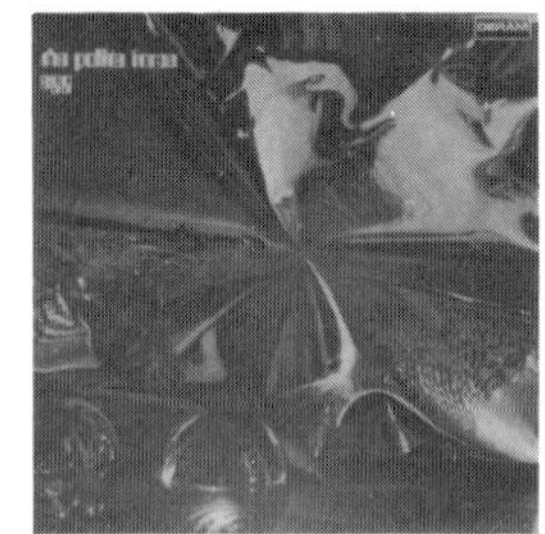

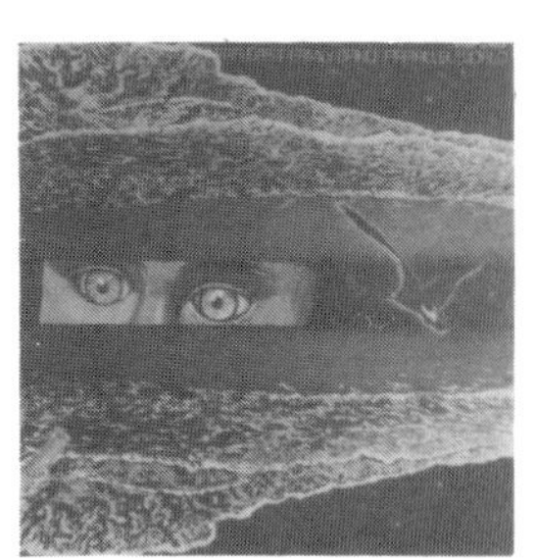

Parallel World

Ebony And Ivory

The Pattern Juggler Lifts His Hand, The Orchestra Begin

Modern Masquerades

Breathe Awhile

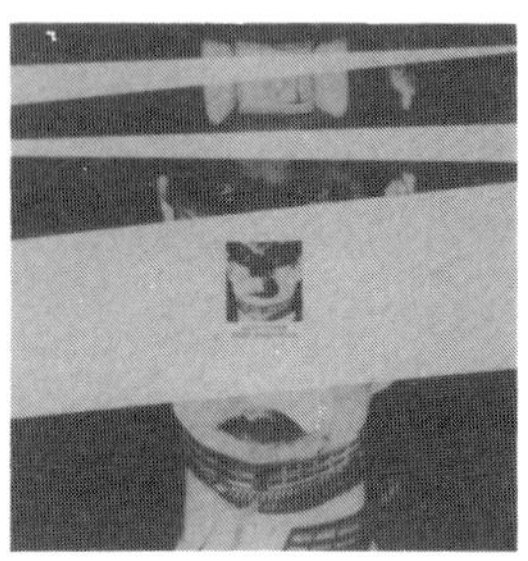

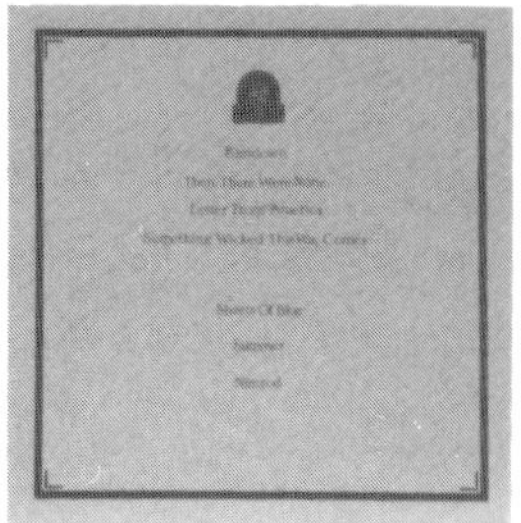

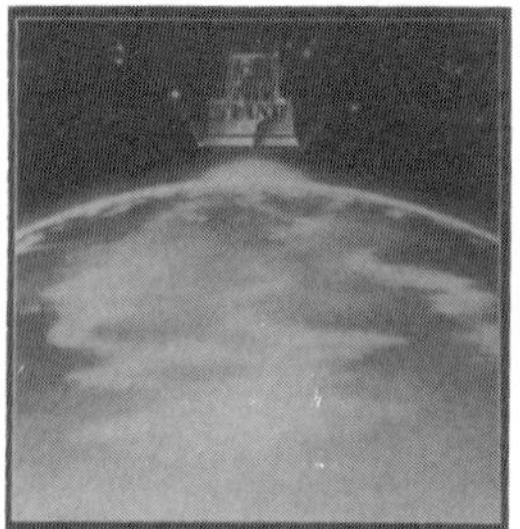

Members One Of Another

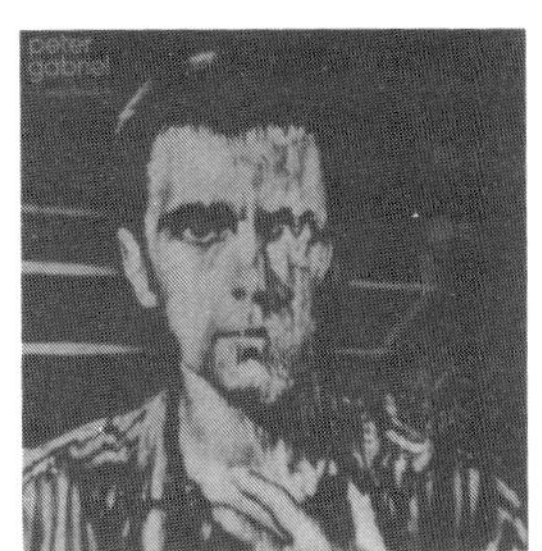

I Wish I Were In A Group Again

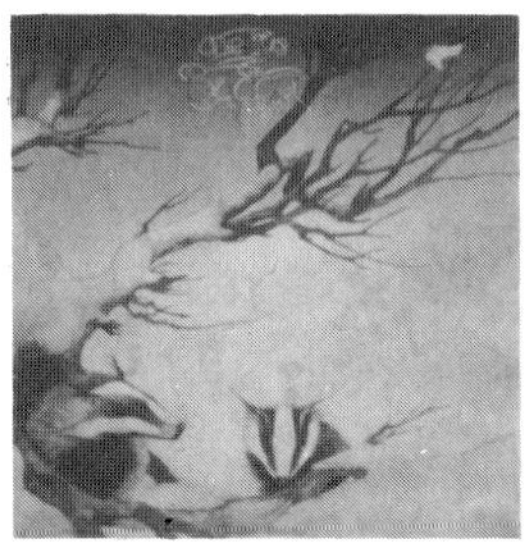

Extravaganza

In Hearing Of

Kings Of Obivion

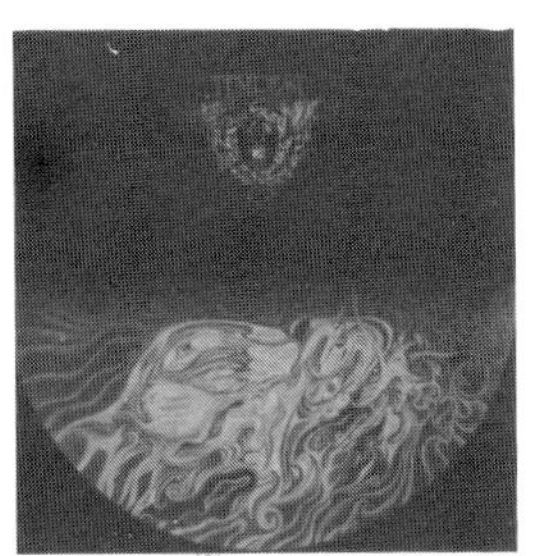

Child Of The Novelty

E Plurilous Funk

Where The Boys Are

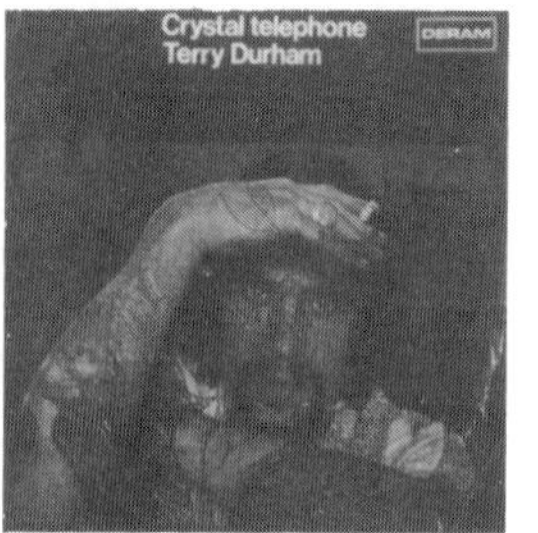

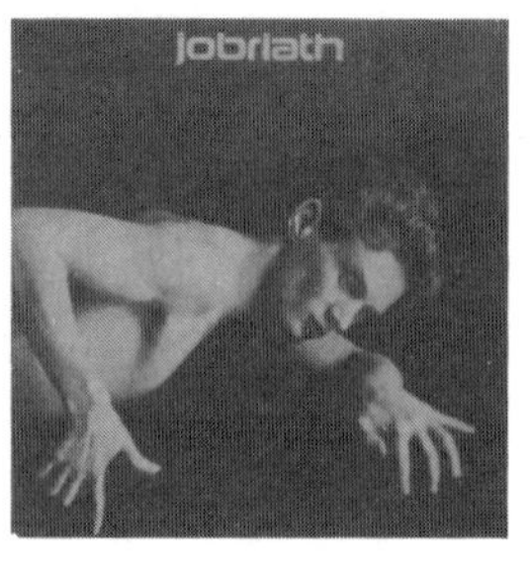

Where The Boys Are II

Interview With Andy Peebles	cass	Es Paranza	PRO654	1985	**£15**	promo
Long Time Coming	7"	CBS	202858	1966	**£100**	
Non Stop Go!	LP	Es Paranza	PR2244	1988	**£12**	double radio promo interview
Our Song	7"	CBS	202656	1966	**£100**	
Pictures At Eleven	LP	Swan Song	SAM154	1982	**£12**	interview promo
Principal Of Moments	LP	Es Paranza	SAM169	1983	**£12**	interview promo

PLANXTY

Cold Blow And Rainy Night	LP	Polydor	2383301	1974	**£10**	
Planxty	LP	Polydor	2383186	1973	**£10**	
Well Below The Valley	LP	Polydor	2383232	1973	**£10**	

PLASMATICS

Butcher Baby	7"	Stiff	BUY76	1980	**£4**	white and red vinyl

PLASTIC CLOUD

Plastic Cloud	LP	Allied		196-	**£150**	Canadian

PLASTIC PENNY

Currency	LP	Page One	POLS014	1969	**£30**	
Everything I Am	7"	Page One	POF051	1967	**£4**	chart single
Heads I Win, Tails You Lose	LP	Page One	POLS611	1970	**£30**	
Hound Dog	7"	Page One	POF107	1969	**£4**	
Nobody Knows It	7"	Page One	POF062	1968	**£4**	
She Does	7"	Page One	POF146	1969	**£4**	
Two Sides Of...	LP	Page One	POLS005	1968	**£35**	
Your Way To Tell Me Go	7"	Page One	POF079	1968	**£4**	

PLATTERS

...On Parade	LP	Mercury	MMC14010	1959	**£12**	
Are You Sincere	7"	Mercury	7MT205	1958	**£10**	
Around The World	LP	Mercury	MMC14009	1959	**£12**	
Best Of	LP	Ember	EMB3339	1962	**£10**	
Ebb Tide	7"	Mercury	AMT1098	1960	**£4**	
Enchanted	7"	Mercury	AMT1039	1959	**£4**	
Fabulous Platters	7" EP	Mercury	MEP9504	1956	**£8**	
Fabulous Platters Vol.2	7" EP	Mercury	MEP9514	1957	**£6**	
Fabulous Platters Vol.3	7" EP	Mercury	MEP9524	1957	**£6**	
Flying Platters	LP	Mercury	MG20298	1957	**£20**	US
Flying Platters	LP	Mercury	MPL6528	1957	**£12**	
Flying Platters	7" EP	Mercury	MEP9526	1958	**£5**	
Flying Platters No.2	7" EP	Mercury	MEP9528	1958	**£5**	
Golden Hits	LP	Mercury	MMC14091	1962	**£10**	
Great Pretender	78	Mercury	MT117	1956	**£4**	chart single
Harbour Lights	7"	Mercury	AMT1081	1960	**£4**	chart single
Harbour Lights	7" EP	Mercury	ZEP10112	1961	**£4**	
Helpless	7"	Mercury	7MT197	1958	**£10**	
I Love You A Thousand Times	7"	Stateside	SS511	1966	**£4**	
I Wish	7"	Mercury	AMT1001	1958	**£4**	
I'll Be Home	7"	Stateside	SS568	1966	**£4**	
I'll Never Smile	7"	Mercury	AMT1154	1961	**£4**	
I'm Sorry	78	Mercury	MT145	1957	**£4**	chart single
If I Didn't Care	7"	Mercury	AMT1128	1961	**£4**	
Life Is Just A Bowl Of Cherries	LP	Mercury	MMC14072	1961	**£10**	
My Blue Heaven	7"	Mercury	AMT1066	1959	**£4**	
My Prayer	78	Mercury	MT120	1956	**£4**	chart single
My Secret	7"	Mercury	AMT1076	1960	**£4**	
Only You	7"	Ember	JBS701	1962	**£30**	
Pick Of The Platters No.1	7" EP	Mercury	ZEP10000	1959	**£5**	
Pick Of The Platters No.2	7" EP	Mercury	ZEP10008	1959	**£5**	
Pick Of The Platters No.3	7" EP	Mercury	ZEP10025	1959	**£5**	
Pick Of The Platters No.4	7" EP	Mercury	ZEP10031	1959	**£5**	
Pick Of The Platters No.5	7" EP	Mercury	ZEP10042	1959	**£5**	
Pick Of The Platters No.6	7" EP	Mercury	ZEP10056	1960	**£5**	
Pick Of The Platters No.7	7" EP	Mercury	ZEP10070	1960	**£5**	
Platters	LP-10"			195-	**£80**	
Platters	LP	Federal	395549	1955	**£300**	US
Platters	LP	King	LP549	1956	**£180**	US
Platters	LP	Mercury	MG20146	1956	**£50**	US
Platters	LP	Mercury	MPL6504	1956	**£15**	

Title	Format	Label	Cat. No.	Year	Price	Notes
Platters	7" EP	Mercury	MEP9537	1958	**£5**	
Platters	LP	Parlophone	PMD1058	1958	**£20**	
Platters On A Platter	7" EP	Mercury	ZEP10126	1962	**£4**	
Platters Vol.2	LP	Mercury	MG20216	1956	**£30**	US
Platters Vol.2	LP	Mercury	MPL6511	1957	**£12**	
Presenting The Platters	LP	W. Rec. Club	TP233		**£10**	
Red Sails In The Sunset	7"	Mercury	AMT1106	1960	**£4**	
Reflections	LP	Mercury	MMC14045	1960	**£10**	
Remember When	LP	Mercury	MMC14014	1959	**£10**	
Remember When	7"	Mercury	AMT1053	1959	**£4**	chart single
Smoke Gets In Your Eyes	7"	Mercury	AMT1016	1958	**£4**	chart single
Sweet Sweet Lovin'	7"	Stateside	SS2067	1967	**£5**	
To Each His Own	7"	Mercury	AMT1118	1960	**£4**	
Twilight Time	7"	Mercury	7MT214	1958	**£5**	chart single
Washed Ashore	7"	Stateside	SS2042	1967	**£4**	
With This Ring	7"	Stateside	SS2007	1967	**£4**	
You'll Never Never Know	78	Mercury	MT130	1957	**£4**	chart single
You're Making A Mistake	7"	Mercury	7MT227	1958	**£5**	

PLAYBOYS

Title	Format	Label	Cat. No.	Year	Price	Notes
Over The Weekend	7"	London	HLU8681	1958	**£8**	

PLAYERS

Title	Format	Label	Cat. No.	Year	Price	Notes
Mockingbird	7"	Oriole	CB1861	1963	**£8**	

PLAYGIRLS

Title	Format	Label	Cat. No.	Year	Price	Notes
Hey Sport	7"	RCA	RCA1133	1959	**£4**	

PLAYGIRLS (2)

Title	Format	Label	Cat. No.	Year	Price	Notes
Looks Are Deceiving	7"	Black Swan	WI456	1965	**£10**	

PLAYGROUND

Title	Format	Label	Cat. No.	Year	Price	Notes
Rain, The Wind And Other Things	7"	Decca	F13011	1970	**£4**	

PLAYMATES

Title	Format	Label	Cat. No.	Year	Price	Notes
At Play With The Playmates	7" EP	Columbia	SEG7864	1958	**£5**	
Barefoot Girl	7"	Columbia	DB3941	1957	**£4**	
Beep Beep	7"	Columbia	DB4224	1958	**£4**	
Darling It's Wonderful	7"	Columbia	DB4033	1957	**£4**	
Day I Died	7"	Columbia	DB4207	1958	**£4**	
Don't Go Home	7"	Columbia	DB4151	1958	**£4**	
Jo-Ann	7"	Columbia	DB4084	1958	**£4**	
Let's Be Lovers	7"	Columbia	DB4127	1958	**£4**	
Party Playmates	7" EP	Columbia	SEG7949	1959	**£4**	
Party Playmates No.2	7" EP	Columbia	SEG7966	1960	**£4**	

PLAYTHINGS

Title	Format	Label	Cat. No.	Year	Price	Notes
Stop What You're Doing To Me	7"	Pye	7N45212	1970	**£4**	

PLEASE, BOBBY

Title	Format	Label	Cat. No.	Year	Price	Notes
Your Driver's License Please	7"	London	HLB8507	1957	**£40**	

PLEASURE FAIR

Title	Format	Label	Cat. No.	Year	Price	Notes
Morning Glory Days	7"	UNI	UN500	1968	**£4**	

PLEASURES

Title	Format	Label	Cat. No.	Year	Price	Notes
Music City	7"	Sue	WI357	1965	**£10**	

PLEBS

Title	Format	Label	Cat. No.	Year	Price	Notes
Bad Blood	7"	Decca	F12006	1964	**£15**	

PLUS

Title	Format	Label	Cat. No.	Year	Price	Notes
Seven Deadly Sins	LP	Probe		1970	**£20**	

PLUTO

Title	Format	Label	Cat. No.	Year	Price	Notes
I Really Want It	7"	Dawn	DNS1026	1972	**£20**	
Pluto	LP	Dawn	DNLS3030	1972	**£50**	
Rag A Bone Joe	7"	Dawn	DNS1017	1971	**£20**	

POCO

Title	Format	Label	Cat. No.	Year	Price	Notes
Cantamos	LP	Epic	80596	1975	**£10**	
Cantamos	LP	Epic	PEQ33192	1974	**£12**	US quad

Crazy Eyes	LP	Epic	65631	1973	**£10**	
Crazy Eyes	LP	Epic	EQ32354	1973	**£12**	US quad
Deliverin'	LP	Epic	64204	1971	**£10**	
Deliverin'	LP	Epic	EQ30209	1971	**£12**	US quad
From The Inside	LP	Epic	64543	1971	**£10**	
Good Feelin' To Know	LP	Epic	65126	1973	**£10**	
Legend	LP	Mobile Fid.	MFSL1020	1978	**£12**	US audiophile
Live	LP	Epic	80705	1975	**£10**	
Picking Up The Pieces	LP	Epic	65327	1969	**£10**	
Poco	LP	Epic	64082	1970	**£10**	
Seven	LP	Epic	80082	1974	**£10**	

POET & THE ONE MAN BAND

Poet & The One Man Band featured neither a poet nor a one man band, but instead was the home for some subsequently well known musicians - notably guitarists Albert Lee and Jerry Donahue and bass player Pat Donaldson. The group was not able to survive the collapse of its record company, but eventually metamorphosed into Heads, Hands And Feet.

Poet And The One Man Band	LP	Verve	SVLP6012	1969	**£30**	

POETS

Alone Am I	7"	Pye	7N17668	1968	**£35**	Probably different Poets
Baby Don't You Do It	7"	Immediate	IM024	1966	**£30**	
Call Again	7"	Immediate	IM006	1965	**£25**	
Heyla Hola	7"	Strike Cola		1971	**£20**	
I Am So Blue	7"	Decca	F12195	1965	**£15**	
Now We're Thru	7"	Decca	F11995	1964	**£8**	chart single
That's The Way It's Got To Be	7"	Decca	F12074	1965	**£12**	
Wooden Spoon	7"	Decca	F12569	1967	**£20**	

POGUES

Dirty Old Town	7"	Stiff	PBUY229	1985	**£5**	pic disc
Dirty Old Town	12"	Stiff	MAIL3	1985	**£6**	mail order
Pair Of Brown Eyes	7"	Stiff	DBUY220	1985	**£5**	pic disc
Poguetry In Motion	7"	Stiff	PBUY243	1986	**£6**	pic disc
Sally MacLennane	7"	Stiff	BUY224	1985	**£6**	green vinyl wrap-around PS
Sally MacLennane	7"	Stiff	PBUY224	1985	**£5**	shaped pic disc

POISON

Cry Tough	12"	Music For N.	P12KUT127	1987	**£6**	pic disc
Fallen Angel	12"	Capitol	12CLP500	1988	**£6**	pic disc
Talk Dirty To Me	12"	Music For N.	P12KUT125	1987	**£6**	pic disc

POISON GIRLS

Chappaquidick	LP	Crass	421984/2	1980	**£10**	with flexi (421984/7)
Fatal Microbes Meet...	7"	Small Wonder	WEENY3	1978	**£4**	
Hex	7"	Small Wonder	WEENY4	1978	**£4**	

POLICE

In addition to the various coloured vinyl releases, picture discs, and other limited edition rarities issued by the Police, there is an American version of "Ghost In The Machine" too rare to be given a realistic value. This is a picture disc, with red LED lights set into the vinyl, along with the (small!) batteries to operate them. Whether it was ever intended to issue this commercially is not clear, but in the event only ten copies were actually produced.

Can't Stand Losing You	7"	A&M	AMS7381	1978	**£5**	blue vinyl
Can't Stand Losing You	7"	A&M	AMS7381	1979	**£5**	dark blue, light blue yellow or red vinyl
Can't Stand Losing You	7"	A&M	AMS7381	1979	**£6**	green or white vinyl
Don't Stand So Close To Me	7"	A&M	SP3720	1981	**£10**	US star shaped pic disc
Every Breath You Take	7"	A&M	AM117	1983	**£8**	double
Every Breath You Take	7"	A&M	AMSP117	1983	**£5**	pic disc
Fall Out	7"	Illegal	IL001	1977	**£8**	black & white sleeve
Ghost In The Machine	LP	Nautilus	NR40	1982	**£15**	US audiophile
Message In A Bottle	7"	A&M	AMS7474	1979	**£5**	green vinyl
Message In A Bottle	7"	A&M	PR4400	1980	**£12**	US star shaped pic disc
Outlandos D'Amour	LP	A&M	AMLN68502	1978	**£12**	blue vinyl
Police Enquiry	LP	A&M	SAMP13	1981	**£15**	interview promo
Police Pack	7"	A&M	AMPP6001	1980	**£20**	6x7", blue vinyl
Regatta De Blanc	LP-10"	A&M	AMLT64792	1979	**£15**	double
Roxanne	7"	A&M	2096/2147	1979	**£15**	US badge shaped pic disc
Roxanne	7"	A&M	AMS7348	1978	**£15**	telephone PS
Roxanne	7"	A&M	AMS7348	1979	**£5**	blue vinyl
Roxanne	12"	A&M	AMS7348	1978	**£15**	telephone PS

Roxanne	12"	A&M	AMSP7348	1979	**£6**	
Spirits In The Material World	7"	A&M	AMS8194	1981	**£6**	poster sleeve, badge
Synchronicity 2	7"	A&M	AM153	1983	**£8**	promo with g-fold sleeve
Walking On The Moon	12"	A&M	AMSP7494	1979	**£6**	
Wrapped Around Your Finger	7"	A&M	AMP127	1983	**£6**	pic disc (Stewart or Andy)
Wrapped Around Your Finger	7"	A&M	AMP127	1983	**£4**	pic disc (Sting)
Zenyatta Mondatta	LP	Nautilus	NR19	1981	**£15**	US audiophile

POLK, FRANK

Trying To Keep Up With The Joneses	7"	Capitol	CL15389	1965	**£5**	

POLLARD, RAY

Drifter	7"	United Artists	UP1111	1965	**£20**	
It's A Sad Thing	7"	United Artists	UP1133	1966	**£6**	

POLYPHONY

Polyphony	LP	Zella		1973	**£200**	

PONI-TAILS

Born Too Late	7"	HMV	POP516	1958	**£6**	chart single
Close Friends	7"	HMV	POP558	1958	**£4**	
Early To Bed	7"	HMV	POP596	1959	**£4**	chart single
I'll Be Seeing You	7"	HMV	POP663	1959	**£4**	
Moody	7"	HMV	POP644	1959	**£4**	
Poni-tails	7" EP	HMV	7EG8427	1957	**£12**	

PONTY, JEAN-LUC

King Kong	LP	Liberty	LBS83375	1970	**£10**	

POOLE, BRIAN

Everything I Touch Turns To Tears	7"	CBS	202349	1966	**£4**	
Hey Girl	7"	Decca	F12402	1966	**£4**	
Just How Loud	7"	CBS	3005	1967	**£4**	
Send Her To Me	7"	President	PT239	1969	**£4**	
That Reminds Me Baby	7"	CBS	202661	1967	**£4**	
What Do Women Most Desire	7"	President	PT264	1969	**£4**	

POOLE, BRIAN & THE TREMELOES

After A While	7"	Decca	F12124	1965	**£4**	
Big Hits Of 1962	LP	Ace Of Clubs	ACL1146	1963	**£35**	
Brian Poole And The Tremeloes	7" EP	Decca	DFE8566	1964	**£6**	
Brian Poole And The Tremeloes Vol.2	7" EP	Decca	DFE8610	1965	**£6**	
Brian Poole Is Here	LP	Audio Fid.	2151	1966	**£15**	US
Candy Man	7"	Decca	F11823	1964	**£4**	chart single
Do You Love Me	7"	Decca	F11739	1963	**£4**	chart single
Good Lovin'	7"	Decca	F12274	1965	**£4**	
I Can Dance	7"	Decca	F11771	1963	**£4**	chart single
I Want Candy	7"	Decca	F12197	1965	**£4**	chart single
It's About Time	LP	Decca	LK4685	1965	**£20**	
Keep On Dancing	7"	Decca	F11616	1963	**£4**	
Meet Me Where We Used To Meet	7"	Decca	F11567	1963	**£4**	
Someone Someone	7"	Decca	F11893	1964	**£4**	chart single
That Ain't Right	7"	Decca	F11515	1962	**£4**	
Three Bells	7"	Decca	F12037	1964	**£4**	chart single
Tremeloes Are Here	LP	Audio Fid.	2177	1967	**£15**	US
Twelve Steps To Love	7"	Decca	F11951	1964	**£4**	chart single
Twist And Shout	LP	Decca	LK4550	1963	**£35**	
Twist And Shout	7"	Decca	F11694	1963	**£4**	chart single
Twist Little Sister	7"	Decca	F11455	1962	**£4**	

POOR SOULS

Love Me	7"	Alp	595004	1966	**£12**	
When My Baby Cries	7"	Decca	F12183	1965	**£12**	

POP GROUP

For How Much Longer...	LP	Rough Trade	ROUGH9	1980	**£12**	with 4 posters
She Is Beyond Good And Evil	7"	Radar	ADA29	1979	**£4**	
She Is Beyond Good And Evil	12"	Radar	ADA29	1979	**£6**	
We Are All Prostitutes	7"	Rough Trade	RT023	1980	**£4**	
We Are Time	LP	Rough Trade	ROUGH12	1980	**£10**	
Where There's A Will	7"	Rough Trade	RT039	1980	**£4**	other side Slits
Y	LP	Radar	RAD20	1979	**£10**	with poster

POP RIVETS

Empty Sounds From Anarchy Ranch	LP	Hipocrite	HIP0	1979	**£10**	
Greatest Hits	LP	Hipocrite	HIP007	1979	**£10**	

POP WILL EAT ITSELF

Beaver Patrol	7"	Chapter 22	LCHAP16	1987	**£5**	pink or clear vinyl
Def Con One (Doomsday Power Mix)	12"	Chapter 22	PWEIL12001	1988	**£6**	
Love Missile (Designer Grebo Mix)	12"	Chapter 22	L12CHAP13	1987	**£6**	
The Poppies Say Grrr	7"	Desperate	DAN1	1986	**£5**	orange sleeve
The Poppies Say Grrr	7"	Desperate	SRT1	1986	**£20**	brown paper sleeve
Very Metal Noise Pollution	7"	RCA	PA43022	1989	**£4**	shaped pic disc

POP WORKSHOP

Punch And Judy Man	7"	Page One	POF129	1969	**£5**	

POP, IGGY

Bang Bang	7"	Arista	ARIST407	1981	**£4**	
China Girl	7"	RCA	PB9093	1977	**£4**	
Five Foot One	7"	Arista	ARIST274	1979	**£4**	
Five Foot One	7"	Arista	ARIST274	1979	**£6**	pic disc
Gimme Danger	12"	Skydog	SGS12	1978	**£6**	
I Got A Right	7"	Siamese	PM001	1977	**£4**	
I'm Bored	7"	Arista	ARIST255	1979	**£4**	
Loco Mosquito	7"	Arista	ARIST327	1980	**£4**	
Passenger	7"	RCA	PB9160	1977	**£4**	
Sixteen	7"	RCA	PB9213	1978	**£4**	
Zombie Birdhouse	7"	Chrysalis		1983	**£4**	flexi, B/S info to comments

POP, IGGY & JAMES WILLIAMSON

Kill City	7"	Radar	ADA4	1978	**£4**	

POP, IGGY & THE STOOGES

Fun House	LP	Elektra	EKS74071	1970	**£20**	
Jesus Loves The Stooges	7"	Bomp	EP114	1977	**£5**	US
Metallic K.O.	LP	Skydog	SGIS008	1976	**£10**	Fronch
Raw Powor	LP	CBS	65586	1973	**£15**	
Sick Of You	7"	Bomp	EP113	1977	**£5**	US
Stooges	LP	Elektra	EKS74051	1969	**£20**	

POPCORNS

Zero Zero	7"	Columbia	DB4968	1963	**£4**	

POPPIES

Lullaby Of Love	7"	Columbia	DB7879	1966	**£8**	

POPULAR FIVE

I'm A Lovemaker	7"	Minit	MLF11011	1968	**£5**	

PORK DUKES

Bend And Flush	7"	Wood	WOOD9	1977	**£5**	
Making Bacon	12"	Wood	BRANCH9	1978	**£8**	
Pork Dukes	LP	Butt	PORK001	1978	**£12**	pink vinyl
Telephone Masturbator	7"	Wood	WOOD56	1978	**£5**	

PORTOBELLO EXPLOSION

We Can Fly	7"	Carnaby	CNS4001	1969	**£8**	

POSEY, SANDY

Born A Woman	7"	MGM	MGM1321	1966	**£4**	chart single
Single Girl	7"	MGM	MGM1330	1966	**£4**	chart single

POSTER, ADRIENNE

He Doesn't Love Me	7"	Decca	F12079	1965	**£4**	
Only Fifteen	7"	Decca	F11797	1963	**£4**	
Shang A Doo Lang	7"	Decca	F11864	1964	**£5**	
Something Beautiful	7"	Decca	F12329	1966	**£4**	
They Long To Be Close To You	7"	Decca	F12455	1966	**£4**	
Winds That Blow	7"	Decca	F12181	1965	**£4**	

POTATOES

Bend	7"	Fontana	TF756	1966	**£5**	

POTLIQUOR

First Taste .... LP .... Janus .... 1971 ...... £10
Levee Blues .... LP .... Janus .... 3033 .... 1972 ...... £10

POUNDS, ALAN GET RICH

Searching In The Wilderness .... 7" .... Parlophone ..... R5532 .... 1966 ...... £80

POWELL, JIMMY

I Can Go Down .... 7" .... Strike .... JH309 .... 1966 .... £5
I Just Can't Get Over You .... 7" .... Decca .... F12751 .... 1968 .... £8
Remember Then .... 7" .... Decca .... F11570 .... 1963 .... £5
Sugar Babe .... 7" .... Decca .... F11447 .... 1962 .... £5
Sugar Babe .... 7" .... Pye .... 7N15735 .... 1964 .... £5
That's Alright .... 7" .... Pye .... 7N15663 .... 1964 .... £8
Tom Hark .... 7" .... Decca .... F11544 .... 1962 .... £5
Unexpected Mirrors .... 7" .... Decca .... F12664 .... 1967 .... £8

POWELL, KEITH

Answer Is No .... 7" .... Columbia .... DB7116 .... 1963 .... £8
Goodbye Girl .... 7" .... Piccadilly .... 7N35275 .... 1966 .... £4
I Should Know Better .... 7" .... Columbia .... DB7366 .... 1964 .... £8
It Keeps Rainin' .... 7" .... Piccadilly .... 7N35353 .... 1966 .... £6
People Get Ready .... 7" .... Piccadilly .... 7N35235 .... 1965 .... £5
Swingin' Tight .... 7" .... Piccadilly .... 7N35340 .... 1966 .... £4
Tore Up .... 7" .... Columbia .... DB7229 .... 1964 .... £8
Victory .... 7" .... Piccadilly .... 7N35300 .... 1966 .... £4

POWELL, KEITH & BILLIE DAVIS

When You Move You Lose .... 7" .... Piccadilly .... 7N35288 .... 1966 .... £5
You Don't Know Like I Know .... 7" .... Piccadilly .... 7N35321 .... 1966 .... £5

POWELL, MARILYN

All My Loving .... 7" .... Fontana .... TF448 .... 1964 .... £4

POWER OF ZEUS

Gospel According To Zeus .... LP .... Rare Earth .... 1970 ...... £15 .... US

POWER STATION

Some Like It Hot .... 7" .... Parlophone ..... RP6091 .... 1985 .... £4 .... pic disc
Some Like It Hot .... 12" .... Parlophone ..... 12RP6091 .... 1985 .... £6 .... pic disc

POWER, DUFFY

Davy O'Brien .... 7" .... Parlophone ..... R5631 .... 1967 .... £4
Dream Lover .... 7" .... Fontana .... H194 .... 1959 .... £8
Duffy Power .... LP .... Spark .... SRLM2005 .... 1973 ...... £12
Hey Girl .... 7" .... Parlophone ..... R5059 .... 1963 .... £6
I Saw Her Standing There .... 7" .... Parlophone ..... R5024 .... 1963 ...... £15
I've Got Nobody .... 7" .... Fontana .... H302 .... 1961 .... £4
Innovations .... LP .... Transatlantic ... TRA229 .... 1971 ...... £15
It Ain't Necessarily So .... 7" .... Parlophone ..... R4992 .... 1963 .... £8
Kissing Time .... 7" .... Fontana .... H214 .... 1959 .... £6
No Other Love .... 7" .... Fontana .... H344 .... 1961 .... £4
Starry Eyed .... 7" .... Fontana .... H230 .... 1959 .... £5
Tired Broke And Busted .... 7" .... Parlophone ..... R5111 .... 1964 .... £8
Where Am I .... 7" .... Parlophone ..... R5169 .... 1964 .... £6
Whole Lotta Shaking Going On .... 7" .... Fontana .... H279 .... 1960 .... £8

POWERHOUSE

Chain Gang .... 7" .... Decca .... F12471 .... 1966 .... £6
Raindrops .... 7" .... Decca .... F12507 .... 1966 .... £6

POWERPACK

I'll Be Anything For You .... 7" .... CBS .... 202551 .... 1967 .... £4

PRANNATH, PANDIT

Earth Groove .... LP .... Transatlantic .... 1969 ...... £15

PRATT, ANDY

Records Are Like Life .... LP .... Polydor .... 2489003 .... 1969 ...... £10

PRAYING MANTIS

Soundhouse Tapes .... 7" EP .... Ripper .... 1980 .... £8

PREACHERS

Hole In My Soul	7"	Columbia	DB7680	1965	**£12**	

PRECIOUS FEW

Young Girl	7"	Pye	7N17510	1968	**£4**	

PRECISIONS

If This Is Love	7"	Track	604014	1967	**£5**	

PREFAB SPROUT

Johnny Johnny	7"	Kitchenware	SK24	1986	**£5**	shaped pic disc

PREGNANT INSOMNIA

Wallpaper	7"	Direction	583132	1967	**£10**	

PREMIERS

Farmer John	LP	W. Bros	W1565	1964	**£20**	US
Farmer John	7"	W. Bros	WB134	1964	**£10**	

PRESLEY, ELVIS

Elvis Presley's position as the most popular rock solo artist ever is indisputable and the list of collectable records made by him is correspondingly long. Although American singles are generally outside the scope of the present volume, Presley's Sun singles were felt to be of such historical importance that they have been included. For the same reason, the legendary "Elvis And Janis" South African release is also included. As far as Presley's earliest records in the UK are concerned, the HMV issues are not that rare: they were all enormous sellers at the time of their release. What are rare, however, are copies in anything like mint condition. The values quoted are for these rarities. For records in less than mint condition, the drop in value with deteriorating condition is dramatic - one of the hundred pound albums, with its cover torn and repaired with selotape and with its playing surface displaying an impressive network of scratches and scars, would be worth a nominal few pounds only, if anything at all. Meanwhile, it should be noted that, with the exception of the last issued records which were available by special order only, 78rpm releases are worth considerably less than their 45rpm equivalents.

Ain't That Lovin' You Baby	7"	RCA	RCA1422	1964	**£4**	chart single
Ain't That Lovin' You Baby	7"	RCA	RCA1422	1964	**£20**	demo
All Shook Up	78	HMV	POP359	1957	**£10**	
All Shook Up	7"	HMV	POP359	1957	**£150**	demo
All Shook Up	7"	HMV	POP359	1957	**£30**	gold label, chart single
All Shook Up	7"	HMV	POP359	1957	**£15**	silver label
All Shook Up	78	RCA	RCA1088	1958	**£10**	
All Shook Up	7"	RCA	RCA1088	1958	**£40**	1 sided demo
All Shook Up	7"	RCA	RCA1088	1958	**£8**	tri-centre
All Shook Up	7"	RCA	RCA1088	1960	**£5**	round centre
All That I Am	7"	RCA	RCA1545	1966	**£4**	chart single
All That I Am	7"	RCA	RCA1545	1966	**£20**	demo
Aloha From Hawaii Via Satellite	LP	RCA	VPSX6089	1973	**£750**	US, with 'Chicken of the sea' sticker
Always On My Mind	7"	RCA	RCA2304	1972	**£8**	demo
American Trilogy	7"	RCA	RCA2229	1972	**£8**	demo
Are You Lonesome Tonight	7"	RCA	RCA1216	1961	**£4**	chart single
Are You Lonesome Tonight	7"	RCA	RCA1216	1961	**£25**	demo
Baby I Don't Care	7"	RCA	RCAP332	1983	**£5**	pic disc
Best Of Elvis	LP-10"	HMV	DLP1159	1956	**£100**	
Best Of Elvis	LP-10"	HMV	DLP1159	1956	**£400**	demo
Big Boss Man	7"	RCA	RCA1642	1967	**£5**	
Big Boss Man	7"	RCA	RCA1642	1967	**£20**	demo
Big Hunk Of Love	78	RCA	RCA1136	1959	**£12**	
Big Hunk Of Love	7"	RCA	RCA1136	1959	**£30**	1 sided demo
Big Hunk Of Love	7"	RCA	RCA1136	1959	**£4**	tri-centre, chart single
Blue Christmas	7"	RCA	RCA1430	1964	**£4**	chart single
Blue Christmas	7"	RCA	RCA1430	1964	**£20**	demo
Blue Hawaii	LP	RCA	LPM2426	1961	**£20**	US, black label 'Long 33 1/3 Play'
Blue Hawaii	LP	RCA	LPM2426	1961	**£45**	US, black label, 'Long 33 1/3 Play',' Contains The Twist Special'
Blue Hawaii	LP	RCA	LSP2426	1961	**£30**	US, black label 'Living Stereo'
Blue Hawaii	LP	RCA	LSP2426	1961	**£50**	US, black label 'Living Stereo' , 'Contains The Twist Special'
Blue Hawaii	LP	RCA	RD27238	1961	**£12**	mono, chart LP
Blue Hawaii	LP	RCA	SF5115	1961	**£20**	stereo
Blue Moon	78	HMV	POP272	1956	**£10**	

Title	Format	Label	Cat. No.	Year	Price	Notes
Blue Moon	7"	HMV	POP272	1956	**£150**	demo
Blue Moon	7"	HMV	POP272	1956	**£30**	gold label, chart single
Blue Moon	7"	HMV	POP272	1956	**£20**	silver label
Blue Moon	7"	RCA	RCA2601	1975	**£8**	demo
Blue Moon	7"	RCA	RCA2601	1975	**£6**	
Blue River	7"	RCA	RCA1504	1966	**£4**	chart single
Blue River	7"	RCA	RCA1504	1966	**£20**	demo
Blue Suede Shoes	78	HMV	POP213	1956	**£10**	
Blue Suede Shoes	78	HMV	POP213	1956	**£300**	1 sided demo
Blue Suede Shoes	7"	HMV	7M405	1956	**£50**	gold label, chart single
Blue Suede Shoes	7"	HMV	7M405	1956	**£30**	silver label
Blue Suede Shoes	7"	RCA	RCA1095	1958	**£40**	1 sided demo
Bossa Nova Baby	7"	RCA	RCA1374	1963	**£4**	chart single
Bossa Nova Baby	7"	RCA	RCA1374	1963	**£20**	demo
Burning Love	7"	RCA	RCA2267	1972	**£8**	demo
Californian Holiday	LP	RCA	RD7820	1966	**£12**	mono, chart LP
Californian Holiday	LP	RCA	SF7820	1966	**£15**	stereo
Canadian Tribute	LP	RCA	KKL17065	1978	**£10**	US, yellow vinyl
Christmas Album	LP	RCA	LOC1035	1957	**£240**	US, black label 'Long 33 1/3 Play'
Christmas Album	LP	RCA	LPM1951	1958	**£50**	US, black label, 'Long 33 1/3 Play'
Christmas Album	LP	RCA	RD27052	1957	**£250**	2 1 sided demos
Christmas Album	LP	RCA	RD27052	1957	**£60**	glossy cover
Christmas Album	LP	RCA	RD27052	1958	**£40**	matt cover
Clambake	LP	RCA	LPM3893	1967	**£75**	US, black label, 'Monaural'
Clambake	LP	RCA	LPM3893	1967	**£90**	US, black label, 'Monaural' with photo
Clambake	LP	RCA	LSP3893	1967	**£20**	US, black label, 'Stereo'
Clambake	LP	RCA	LSP3893	1967	**£35**	US, black label, 'Stereo' with photo
Clambake	LP	RCA	RD7917	1967	**£12**	mono, chart LP
Clambake	LP	RCA	SF7917	1967	**£15**	stereo
Clean Up Your Own Backyard	7"	RCA	RCA1869	1969	**£10**	demo
Crying In The Chapel	7"	RCA	RCA1455	1965	**£4**	chart single
Crying In The Chapel	7"	RCA	RCA1455	1965	**£20**	demo
Date With Elvis	LP	RCA	LPM2011	1959	**£50**	US, black label 'Long 33 1/3 Play'
Date With Elvis	LP	RCA	LPM2011	1959	**£100**	US, black label, 'Long 33 1/3Play" titles on sticker
Date With Elvis	LP	RCA	RD27128	1959	**£25**	chart LP
Date With Elvis	LP	RCA	RD27128	1959	**£200**	2 1 sided demos
Devil In Disguise	7"	RCA	RCA1355	1963	**£4**	chart single
Devil In Disguise	7"	RCA	RCA1355	1963	**£20**	demo
Dixieland Rock	7"	RCA	RCA1081	1958	**£40**	1 sided demo
Do The Clam	7"	RCA	RCA1443	1965	**£4**	chart single
Do The Clam	7"	RCA	RCA1443	1965	**£20**	demo
Don't	78	RCA	RCA1043	1958	**£8**	
Don't	7"	RCA	RCA1043	1958	**£40**	1 sided demo
Don't	7"	RCA	RCA1043	1958	**£6**	tri-centre, chart single
Don't	7"	RCA	RCA1043	1960	**£4**	round centre
Don't Ask Me Why	7"	RCA	RCA1070	1958	**£40**	1 sided demo
Don't Be Cruel	7"	RCA	PB9265	1978	**£6**	demo
Don't Cry Daddy	7"	RCA	RCA1916	1970	**£10**	demo
Double Trouble	LP	RCA	LPM3787	1967	**£25**	US, black label, 'Monaural'
Double Trouble	LP	RCA	LPM3787	1967	**£40**	US, black label, 'Monaural' with photo
Double Trouble	LP	RCA	LSP3787	1967	**£20**	US, black label, 'Stereo'
Double Trouble	LP	RCA	LSP3787	1967	**£35**	US, black label, 'Stereo' with photo
Double Trouble	LP	RCA	RD7892	1967	**£12**	mono, chart LP
Double Trouble	LP	RCA	SF7892	1967	**£15**	stereo
Easy Come Easy Go	7" EP	RCA	RCX7187	1967	**£12**	
Elvis - A Golden Celebration	LP	RCA	PL85172	1985	**£30**	6 LPs, boxed
Elvis - For LP Fans Only	LP	RCA	RD27120	1959	**£25**	
Elvis	LP	RCA	LPM1382	1956	**£50**	US, black label, 'Long 33 1/3 Play'
Elvis	LP	RCA	LPM1382	1956	**£75**	US, black label, 'Long 33 1/3 Play' album ads on cover
Elvis	LP	RCA	LPM1382	1956	**£650**	US, black label, 'Long 33 1/3 Play', alternate 'Old Shep'

Title	Format	Label	Cat. No.	Year	Price	Notes
Elvis	LP	RCA	LPM1382	1956	**£150**	US, black label, 'Long 33 1/3 Play', tracks listed as 'band'..
Elvis	LP	RCA	LPM1382	1957	**£200**	US mispress, same song 6 times on one side
Elvis	LP	RCA	LPM1382	1957	**£200**	US mispress - unbanded
Elvis Aron Presley	LP	RCA	CPL83699	1980	**£40**	8 LPs, booklet, boxed
Elvis Aron Presley (Radio Sampler)	LP	RCA	DJL13781	1980	**£20**	promo
Elvis Aron Presley Sampler	LP	RCA	DJL13729	1980	**£20**	promo
Elvis For Everyone	LP	RCA	LPM3450	1965	**£20**	US, black label, 'Monaural'
Elvis For Everyone	LP	RCA	LSP3450	1965	**£25**	US, black label, 'Stereo'
Elvis For Everyone	LP	RCA	RD7752	1965	**£12**	mono, chart LP
Elvis For Everyone	LP	RCA	SF7752	1965	**£15**	stereo
Elvis For You Vol.1	7" EP	RCA	RCX7142	1964	**£8**	
Elvis For You Vol.2	7" EP	RCA	RCX7143	1964	**£8**	
Elvis In Tender Mood	7" EP	RCA	RCX135	1959	**£10**	
Elvis Is Back	LP	RCA	LPM2231	1960	**£40**	US, black label, 'Long 33 1/3 Play'
Elvis Is Back	LP	RCA	LPM2231	1960	**£60**	US, black label 'Long 33 1/3 Play' titles on sticker
Elvis Is Back	LP	RCA	LSP2231	1960	**£50**	US, black label 'Living Stereo'
Elvis Is Back	LP	RCA	LSP2231	1960	**£75**	US, black label, 'Living 'Stereo' song titles on sticker
Elvis Is Back	LP	RCA	RD27171	1960	**£15**	gatefold mono, chart LP
Elvis Is Back	LP	RCA	SF5060	1960	**£20**	gatefold stereo
Elvis Presley	LP	RCA	LPM1254	1956	**£50**	US, black label 'Long 33 1/3 Play' dark pink 'Elvis' on cover
Elvis Presley	LP	RCA	LPM1254	1956	**£75**	US, black label, 'Long 33 1/3 Play, light pink 'Elvis' on cover
Elvis Presley	LP	St.Michael	IMP113	1978	**£30**	
Elvis Presley Interview Record	LP	RCA	PL80835		**£20**	promo
Elvis Presley Story	LP	Watermark Inc	EPS1A13B	1977	**£500**	promo 13 LP boxed set
Elvis Sails	7" EP	RCA	RCX131	1959	**£15**	
Elvis Sings Christmas Songs	7" EP	RCA	RCX121	1958	**£12**	
Elvis Sings Christmas Songs	7" EP	RCA	RCX121	1958	**£20**	book cover
Elvis Sings Christmas Songs	7" EP	RCA	RCX121	1958	**£40**	demo
Elvis Today	LP	RCA	APD11039	1975	**£40**	US quad (black label)
Elvis Today	LP	RCA	APD11039	1975	**£80**	US quad (orange label)
EP Collection	7" EP	RCA	, RCX1	1982	**£30**	(RCX7188-7197) 11 discs booklet in wallet
EP Collection Vol.2	7" EP	RCA	RCX2-3	1983	**£30**	(RCX7198-7206) 11 discs, booklet
Fame And Fortune	7"	RCA	RCA1187	1960	**£30**	1 sided demo
Flaming Star & Summer Kisses	LP	RCA	RD7723	1965	**£20**	mono, chart LP
Follow That Dream (Side 1 -Della Reece side 2)	7" EP	RCA	RCX211	1962	**£30**	mispress
Follow That Dream	7" EP	RCA	RCX211	1962	**£6**	chart single
Fool	7"	RCA	RCA2393	1973	**£8**	demo
Fool Such As I	78	RCA	RCA1113	1959	**£10**	
Fool Such As I	7"	RCA	RCA1113	1959	**£30**	demo
Fool Such As I	7"	RCA	RCA1113	1959	**£4**	tri-centre, chart single
For LP Fans Only	LP	RCA	LPM1990	1959	**£75**	US, black label 'Long 33 1/3 Play'
Frankie And Johnny	LP	RCA	LPM3553	1966	**£20**	US, black label, 'Monaural'
Frankie And Johnny	LP	RCA	LPM3553	1966	**£35**	US, black label 'Monaural', with photo
Frankie And Johnny	LP	RCA	LSP3553	1966	**£20**	US, black label, 'Stereo'
Frankie And Johnny	LP	RCA	LSP3553	1966	**£35**	US, black label 'Stereo', with photo
Frankie And Johnny	LP	RCA	RD7793	1966	**£12**	mono, chart LP
Frankie And Johnny	LP	RCA	SF7793	1966	**£15**	stereo
Frankie And Johnny	7"	RCA	RCA1509	1966	**£4**	chart single
Frankie And Johnny	7"	RCA	RCA1509	1966	**£20**	demo
From Elvis In Memphis	LP	Mobile Fid.	MFSL1059	1980	**£12**	US audiophile
From Elvis In Memphis	LP	RCA	RD8029	1969	**£15**	mono
Fun In Acapulco	LP	RCA	LPM2756	1963	**£20**	US, black label, 'Mono'
Fun In Acapulco	LP	RCA	LSP2756	1963	**£25**	US, black label 'Living Stereo'
Fun In Acapulco	LP	RCA	RD7609	1963	**£10**	mono, chart LP

Title	Format	Label	Cat. No.	Year	Price	Notes
Fun In Acapulco	LP	RCA	SF7609	1963	**£15**	stereo
GI Blues	LP	RCA	LPM2256	1960	**£20**	US, black label 'Long 33 1/3 Play'
GI Blues	LP	RCA	LSP2256	1960	**£30**	US, black label 'Living Stereo'
GI Blues	LP	RCA	RD27192	1960	**£12**	mono, chart LP
GI Blues	LP	RCA	SF5078	1960	**£15**	stereo
Girl Happy	LP	RCA	LPM3338	1965	**£20**	US, black label, 'Monaural'
Girl Happy	LP	RCA	LSP3338	1965	**£25**	US, black label, 'Stereo'
Girl Happy	LP	RCA	RD7714	1965	**£10**	mono, chart LP
Girl Happy	LP	RCA	SF7714	1965	**£15**	stereo
Girl Of My Best Friend	78	RCA	RCA1194	1960	**£100**	
Girl Of My Best Friend	7"	RCA	RCA1194	1960	**£4**	chart single
Girl Of My Best Friend	7"	RCA	RCA1194	1960	**£25**	1 sided demo
Girl Of My Best Friend	7"	RCA	RCA2729	1976	**£8**	demo
Girls Girls Girls	LP	RCA	LPM2621	1962	**£20**	US, black label 'Long 33 1/3 Play'
Girls Girls Girls	LP	RCA	LPM2621	1962	**£60**	US, black label 'Long 33 1/3 Play' with calendar
Girls Girls Girls	LP	RCA	LSP2621	1962	**£30**	US, black label 'Living Stereo'
Girls Girls Girls	LP	RCA	LSP2621	1962	**£70**	US, black label 'Living Stereo' with calendar
Girls Girls Girls	LP	RCA	SF7534	1963	**£15**	stereo
Girls Girls Girls	LP	RCA	RD7534	1963	**£10**	mono, chart LP
Gold 16 Series	7"	RCA	RCA2694-2709	1977	**£40**	16 x 7" in cardboard carrier
Gold 16 Series	7"	RCA	RCA2694-2709	1977	**£60**	16 x demo 7" in cardboard carrier
Golden Records	LP	RCA	LPM1707	1958	**£60**	US, black label 'Long 33 1/3 Play' title in blue print
Golden Records Vol.1	LP	RCA	RD16069	1958	**£25**	gatefold sleeve, chart LP
Golden Records Vol.1	LP	RCA	RD16069	1958	**£15**	single sleeve, chart LP
Golden Records Vol.1	LP	RCA	SF8129	1963	**£12**	stereo
Golden Records Vol.2	LP	RCA	LPM2075	1960	**£50**	US, black label 'Long 33 1/3 Play'
Golden Records Vol.2	LP	RCA	RD27159	1959	**£15**	chart LP
Golden Records Vol.3	LP	RCA	LPM2765	1963	**£20**	US, black label, 'Mono'
Golden Records Vol.3	LP	RCA	LPM2765	1963	**£45**	US, black label 'Mono', with book
Golden Records Vol.3	LP	RCA	LSP2765	1963	**£25**	US, black label 'Living Stereo'
Golden Records Vol.3	LP	RCA	LSP2765	1963	**£50**	US, black label 'Living Stereo', with book
Golden Records Vol.3	LP	RCA	RD7630	1964	**£10**	mono, chart LP
Golden Records Vol.3	LP	RCA	SF7630	1964	**£15**	stereo
Golden Records Vol.4	LP	RCA	LPM3921	1968	**£300**	US, black label 'Monaural'
Golden Records Vol.4	LP	RCA	LPM3921	1968	**£350**	US, black label 'Monaural', with photo
Golden Records Vol.4	LP	RCA	LSP3921	1968	**£20**	US, black label, 'Stereo'
Golden Records Vol.4	LP	RCA	LSP3921	1968	**£70**	US, black label 'Stereo', with photo
Golden Records Vol.4	LP	RCA	RD7924	1968	**£10**	mono
Golden Records Vol.4	LP	RCA	SF7924	1968	**£12**	stereo
Good Luck Charm	7"	RCA	RCA1280	1962	**£4**	chart single
Good Luck Charm	7"	RCA	RCA1280	1962	**£20**	demo
Good Rockin' Tonight	7" EP	HMV	7EG8256	1957	**£40**	
Good Rockin' Tonight	7" EP	HMV	7EG8256	1957	**£150**	demo
Good Rockin' Tonight	78	Sun	210	1954	**£150**	US
Good Rockin' Tonight	7"	Sun	210	1954	**£260**	US
Got A Lot Of Living To Do	78	RCA	RCA1020	1957	**£8**	
Got A Lot Of Living To Do	7"	RCA	RCA1020	1957	**£50**	1 sided demo
Got A Lot Of Living To Do	7"	RCA	RCA1020	1957	**£6**	tri-centre, chart single
Got A Lot Of Living To Do	7"	RCA	RCA1020	1960	**£4**	round centre
Green Green Grass Of Home	7"	RCA	RCA2635	1975	**£8**	demo
Guitar Man	7"	RCA	RCA1663	1968	**£4**	chart single
Guitar Man	7"	RCA	RCA1663	1968	**£20**	demo
Guitar Man	7"	RCA	RCA43	1981	**£5**	demo sleeve
Hard Headed Woman	78	RCA	RCA1070	1958	**£8**	

Title	Format	Label	Cat. No.	Year	Price	Notes
Hard Headed Woman	7"	RCA	RCA1070	1958	**£40**	1 sided demo
Hard Headed Woman	7"	RCA	RCA1070	1958	**£6**	tri-centre, chart single
Hard Headed Woman	7"	RCA	RCA1070	1960	**£4**	round centre
Harem Holiday	LP	RCA	RD7767	1965	**£200**	2 1 sided demos
Harem Holiday	LP	RCA	RD7767	1965	**£10**	mono, chart LP
Harem Holiday	LP	RCA	SF7767	1965	**£15**	stereo
Harum Scarum	LP	RCA	LPM3468	1965	**£20**	US, black label, 'Monaural'
Harum Scarum	LP	RCA	LPM3468	1965	**£35**	US, black label 'Monaural', with photo
Harum Scarum	LP	RCA	LSP3468	1965	**£20**	US, black label, 'Stereo'
Harum Scarum	LP	RCA	LSP3468	1965	**£35**	US, black label 'Stereo', with photo
Having Fun On Stage	LP	Boxcar		1974	**£75**	US
Having Fun On Stage	LP	RCA	APM10818	1974	**£10**	
Heartbreak Hotel	78	HMV	POP182	1956	**£10**	
Heartbreak Hotel	78	HMV	POP182	1956	**£300**	1 sided demo
Heartbreak Hotel	7"	HMV	7M385	1956	**£40**	gold label, chart single
Heartbreak Hotel	7"	HMV	7M385	1956	**£25**	silver label, chart single
Heartbreak Hotel	7"	RCA	RCA1088	1958	**£40**	1 sided demo
Heartbreak Hotel	7"	RCA	RCAMAXI2104	1971	**£5**	
His Hand In Mine	LP	RCA	LPM2328	1961	**£25**	US, black label 'Long 33 1/3 Play'
His Hand In Mine	LP	RCA	LSP2328	1961	**£35**	US, black label 'Living Stereo'
His Hand In Mine	LP	RCA	RD27211	1960	**£15**	mono, chart LP
His Hand In Mine	LP	RCA	SF5094	1960	**£20**	stereo
His Latest Flame	7"	RCA	RCA1258	1961	**£4**	chart single
His Latest Flame	7"	RCA	RCA1258	1961	**£20**	demo
Hound Dog	78	HMV	POP249	1956	**£10**	
Hound Dog	7"	HMV	POP249	1956	**£40**	gold label, chart single
Hound Dog	7"	HMV	POP249	1956	**£20**	silver label
Hound Dog	78	RCA	RCA1095	1958	**£10**	
Hound Dog	7"	RCA	RCA1095	1958	**£40**	1 sided demo
Hound Dog	7"	RCA	RCA1095	1958	**£8**	tri-centre
Hound Dog	7"	RCA	RCA1095	1960	**£5**	round centre
How Great Thou Art	LP	RCA	LPM3758	1967	**£25**	US, black label, 'Monaural'
How Great Thou Art	LP	RCA	LSP3758	1967	**£20**	US, black label, 'Stereo'
How Great Thou Art	LP	RCA	RD7867	1967	**£12**	mono, chart LP
How Great Thou Art	LP	RCA	SF7867	1967	**£15**	stereo
Hurt	7"	RCA	RCA2674	1976	**£8**	demo
I Beg Of You	7"	RCA	RCA1043	1958	**£40**	1 sided demo
I Can Help (2 versions)	7"	RCA	PRO369	1983	**£8**	promo
I Can Help	10"	RCA	RCAP369	1983	**£6**	pic disc
I Got Stung	7"	RCA	RCA1100	1959	**£35**	1 sided demo
I Just Can't Help Believing	7"	RCA	RCA2158	1971	**£10**	demo
I Need You So	7" EP	RCA	RCX104	1957	**£10**	
I Want You I Need You I Love You	78	HMV	POP235	1956	**£10**	
I Want You I Need You I Love You	7"	HMV	7M424	1956	**£30**	gold label, chart single
I Want You I Need You I Love You	7"	HMV	7M424	1956	**£25**	silver label
I'm Leavin'	7"	RCA	RCA2125	1971	**£10**	demo
I'm Left You're Right She's Gone	78	HMV	POP428	1958	**£10**	
I'm Left You're Right She's Gone	7"	HMV	POP428	1957	**£20**	chart single
I'm Left You're Right She's Gone	7"	HMV	POP428	1957	**£125**	demo
I'm Left You're Right She's Gone	78	Sun	217	1955	**£160**	US
I'm Left You're Right She's Gone	7"	Sun	217	1955	**£275**	US
I've Got A Thing About You Baby	7"	RCA	APBO0196	1974	**£8**	demo
I've Lost You	7"	RCA	RCA1999	1970	**£10**	demo
If Every Day Was Like Christmas	7"	RCA	RCA1557	1966	**£4**	chart single
If Every Day Was Like Christmas	7"	RCA	RCA1557	1966	**£20**	demo
If I Can Dream	7"	RCA	RCA1795	1969	**£10**	demo
If You Talk In Your Sleep	7"	RCA	APBO0280	1974	**£8**	demo
In The Ghetto	7"	RCA	RCA1831	1969	**£10**	demo
Indescribably Blue	7"	RCA	RCA1565	1967	**£4**	chart single
Indescribably Blue	7"	RCA	RCA1565	1967	**£20**	demo
International Hotel, Las Vegas	LP	RCA	LSP6020	1970	**£500**	US double LP 7", various inserts, boxed
It Happened At The World's Fair	LP	RCA	LPM2697	1963	**£25**	US, black label 'Long 33 1/3 Play'
It Happened At The World's Fair	LP	RCA	LPM2697	1963	**£100**	US, black label 'Long 33 1/3 Play' plus photo

Title	Format	Label	Cat. No.	Year	Price	Notes
It Happened At The World's Fair	LP	RCA	LSP2697	1963	**£30**	US, black label 'Living Stereo'
It Happened At The World's Fair	LP	RCA	LSP2697	1963	**£105**	US, black label 'Living Stereo', with photo
It Happened At The World's Fair	LP	RCA	RD7565	1963	**£10**	mono, chart LP
It Happened At The World's Fair	LP	RCA	SF7565	1963	**£15**	stereo
It Won't Seem Like Christmas	7"	RCA	PB9464	1979	**£6**	demo
It's Now Or Never	7"	RCA	RCA1207	1960	**£4**	chart single
It's Now Or Never	7"	RCA	RCA1207	1960	**£25**	demo
It's Only Love	7"	RCA	RCA4	1980	**£5**	demo sleeve
Jailhouse Rock (B side not Elvis)	78	Decca		1958	**£70**	promo
Jailhouse Rock (Side One)	7" EP	RCA	RCX106	1958	**£50**	demo
Jailhouse Rock (Side Two)	7" EP	RCA	RCX106	1958	**£50**	demo
Jailhouse Rock	LP	MGM		1957	**£100**	US red vinyl promo with Leiber & Stoller interview
Jailhouse Rock	78	RCA	RCA1028	1958	**£8**	
Jailhouse Rock	7"	RCA	RCA1028	1958	**£50**	1 sided demo
Jailhouse Rock	7"	RCA	RCA1028	1958	**£6**	tri-centre, chart single
Jailhouse Rock	7"	RCA	RCA1028	1960	**£4**	round centre
Jailhouse Rock	7"	RCA	RCA2153	1971	**£6**	chart single
Jailhouse Rock	7"	RCA	RCAP1028	1983	**£8**	B side credits 'Hound Dog'
Jailhouse Rock	7"	RCA	RCAP1028	1983	**£6**	pic disc
Jailhouse Rock	7" EP	RCA	RCX106	1958	**£10**	chart single
Kentucky Rain	7"	RCA	RCA1949	1970	**£10**	demo
Kid Galahad	7" EP	RCA	RCX7106	1963	**£6**	
King Creole	LP	RCA	LPM1884	1958	**£60**	US, black label 'Long 33 1/3 Play'
King Creole	LP	RCA	LPM1884	1958	**£120**	US, black label 'Long 33 1/3 Play', with bonus photo
King Creole	LP	RCA	RD27088	1958	**£25**	mono, chart LP
King Creole	LP	RCA	SF8231	1963	**£20**	stereo
King Creole	78	RCA	RCA1081	1958	**£8**	
King Creole	7"	RCA	RCA1081	1958	**£40**	1 sided demo
King Creole	7"	RCA	RCA1081	1958	**£6**	tri-centre, chart single
King Creole	7"	RCA	RCA1081	1960	**£4**	round centre
King Creole Vol.1	7" EP	RCA	RCX117	1958	**£10**	black label
King Creole Vol.1	7" EP	RCA	RCX117		**£8**	orange label
King Creole Vol.2	7" EP	RCA	RCX118	1958	**£10**	
Kiss Me Quick	7"	RCA	RCA1375	1963	**£4**	chart single
Kiss Me Quick	7"	RCA	RCA1375	1963	**£20**	demo
Kissin' Cousins	LP	RCA	LPM2894	1964	**£45**	US, black label, 'Mono' no photo on cover
Kissin' Cousins	LP	RCA	LPM2894	1964	**£20**	US, black label, 'Mono' with photo on cover
Kissin' Cousins	LP	RCA	LSP2894	1964	**£50**	US, black label, 'Living Stereo' no photo on cover
Kissin' Cousins	LP	RCA	LSP2894	1964	**£25**	US, black label, 'Living Stereo' photo on cover
Kissin' Cousins	LP	RCA	RD7645	1964	**£10**	mono, chart LP
Kissin' Cousins	LP	RCA	SF7645	1964	**£15**	stereo
Kissin' Cousins	7"	RCA	RCA1404	1964	**£4**	chart single
Kissin' Cousins	7"	RCA	RCA1404	1964	**£20**	demo
Lawdy Miss Clawdy	78	HMV	POP408	1957	**£10**	
Lawdy Miss Clawdy	78	HMV	POP408	1957	**£100**	demo
Lawdy Miss Clawdy	7"	HMV	POP408	1957	**£25**	chart single
Lawdy Miss Clawdy	7"	HMV	POP408	1957	**£125**	demo
Legend	CD	RCA	PD89000	1983	**£75**	gold box
Legend	CD	RCA	PD89000	1984	**£35**	silver box
Legend	CD	RCA	PD8900		**£180**	3 gold discs, boxed
Little Less Conversation	7"	RCA	RCA1768	1968	**£6**	
Little Less Conversation	7"	RCA	RCA1768	1968	**£20**	demo
Live In Memphis	LP	RCA	APD10606	1973	**£120**	US quad
Long Legged Girl	7"	RCA	RCA1616	1967	**£6**	chart single
Long Legged Girl	7"	RCA	RCA1616	1967	**£20**	demo
Love In Las Vegas	7" EP	RCA	RCX7141	1964	**£8**	
Love Letters	7"	RCA	RCA1526	1966	**£4**	chart single
Love Letters	7"	RCA	RCA1526	1966	**£20**	demo
Love Machine	7"	RCA	RCA1593	1967	**£5**	chart single
Love Machine	7"	RCA	RCA1593	1967	**£20**	demo
Love Me Tender	78	HMV	POP253	1956	**£10**	
Love Me Tender	7"	HMV	POP253	1956	**£30**	gold label, chart single

Title	Format	Label	Cat. No.	Year	Price	Notes
Love Me Tender	7"	HMV	POP253	1956	**£20**	silver label
Love Me Tender	7" EP	HMV	7EG8199	1957	**£30**	
Loving Arms	7"	RCA	RCA48	1981	**£5**	demo sleeve
Loving You	LP	RCA	LPM1515	1957	**£60**	US, black label 'Long 33 1/3 Play'
Loving You	LP-10"	RCA	RC24001	1957	**£40**	
Loving You	78	RCA	RCA1013	1957	**£8**	
Loving You	7"	RCA	RCA1013	1957	**£50**	1 sided demo
Loving You	7"	RCA	RCA1013	1957	**£6**	tri-centre, chart single
Loving You	7"	RCA	RCA1013	1960	**£4**	round centre
Mess Of Blues	7"	RCA	RCA1194	1960	**£25**	1 sided demo
Milkcow Blues Boogie	78	Sun	215	1955	**£150**	US
Milkcow Blues Boogie	7"	Sun	215	1955	**£225**	US
Moody Blue	LP	RCA	AFL12428	1977	**£100**	US, black vinyl
Moody Blue	7"	RCA	PB0857	1977	**£6**	demo
My Boy	7"	RCA	RCA2458	1974	**£8**	demo
My Way	7"	RCA	PB1165	1977	**£6**	demo
My Wish Came True	7"	RCA	RCA1136	1959	**£30**	1 sided demo
Mystery Train	78	HMV	POP295	1957	**£12**	
Mystery Train	78	HMV	POP295	1957	**£120**	demo
Mystery Train	7"	HMV	7MC42	1957	**£75**	export
Mystery Train	7"	HMV	POP295	1957	**£50**	gold label, chart single
Mystery Train	7"	HMV	POP295	1957	**£30**	silver label
Mystery Train	78	Sun	223	1955	**£150**	US
Mystery Train	7"	Sun	223	1955	**£225**	US
NBC Special	LP	RCA	RD8011	1968	**£10**	mono, chart LP
O Sole Mio	7"	RCA	479314	1961	**£10**	sung in Italian
Old Shep	7"	RCA	PB9334	1979	**£6**	demo
One Broken Heart For Sale	7"	RCA	RCA1337	1963	**£4**	chart single
One Broken Heart For Sale	7"	RCA	RCA1337	1963	**£20**	demo
One Night	78	RCA	RCA1100	1959	**£10**	
One Night	7"	RCA	RCA1100	1959	**£35**	1 sided demo
One Night	7"	RCA	RCA1100	1959	**£35**	demo
One Night	7"	RCA	RCA1100	1959	**£6**	tri-centre, chart single
One Night	7"	RCA	RCA1100	1960	**£4**	round centre
Paradise Hawaiian Style	LP	RCA	LPM3643	1966	**£20**	US, black label, 'Monaural'
Paradise Hawaiian Style	LP	RCA	LSP3643	1966	**£20**	US, black label, 'Stereo'
Paradise Hawaiian Style	LP	RCA	RD7810	1966	**£12**	mono, chart LP
Paradise Hawaiian Style	LP	RCA	SF7810	1966	**£15**	stereo
Paralyzed	78	HMV	POP378	1957	**£10**	
Paralyzed	7"	HMV	POP378	1957	**£130**	1 sided demo
Paralyzed	7"	HMV	POP378	1957	**£30**	gold label, chart single
Paralyzed	7"	HMV	POP378	1957	**£20**	silver label
Party	7"	RCA	RCA1020	1957	**£50**	1 sided demo
Peace In The Valley	7" EP	RCA	RCX101	1957	**£10**	
Peace In The Valley	7" EP	RCA	RCX101	1957	**£50**	demo
Polk Salad Annie	7"	RCA	RCA2359	1973	**£8**	demo
Pot Luck	LP	RCA	RD27265	1962	**£12**	mono, chart LP
Pot Luck	LP	RCA	SF5135	1962	**£20**	stereo
Pot Luck With Elvis	LP	RCA	LSP2523	1962	**£40**	US, black label 'Living Stereo'
Pot Luck with Elvis	LP	RCA	LPM2523	1962	**£30**	US, black label 'Long 33 1/3 Play'
Promised Land	LP	RCA	APD10873	1974	**£40**	US quad (black label)
Promised Land	LP	RCA	APD10873	1974	**£80**	US quad (orange label)
Promised Land	7"	RCA	PB10074	1975	**£8**	demo
Pure Elvis	LP	RCA	DJL13455	1980	**£200**	US promo
Rags To Riches	7"	RCA	RCA2084	1971	**£10**	demo
Raised On Rock	7"	RCA	RCA2435	1973	**£8**	demo
Return To Sender	7"	RCA	RCA1320	1962	**£4**	chart single
Return To Sender	7"	RCA	RCA1320	1962	**£20**	demo
Rip It Up	78	HMV	POP305	1957	**£12**	
Rip It Up	7"	HMV	POP305	1957	**£50**	gold label, chart single
Rip It Up	7"	HMV	POP305	1957	**£30**	silver label
Rock'n'Roll	LP	HMV	CLP1093	1956	**£100**	chart LP
Rock'n'Roll	LP	HMV	CLP1093	1956	**£400**	demo
Rock'n'Roll No.2	LP	HMV	CLP1105	1956	**£110**	
Rock'n'Roll No.2	LP	HMV	CLP1105	1956	**£400**	demo
Rock'n'Roll No.2	LP	RCA	RD7528	1962	**£15**	mono, chart LP
Rock'n'Roll No.2	LP	RCA	SF7528	1962	**£20**	stereo
Rock-A-Hula Baby	7"	RCA	RCA1270	1962	**£4**	chart single

Title	Format	Label	Cat. No.	Year	Price	Notes
Rock-A-Hula Baby	7"	RCA	RCA1270	1962	**£20**	demo
Roustabout	LP	RCA	LPM2999	1964	**£25**	US, black label, 'Mono'
Roustabout	LP	RCA	LSP2999	1964	**£240**	US, black label 'Living Stereo'
Roustabout	LP	RCA	LSP2999	1964	**£25**	US, black label, 'Stereo'
Roustabout	LP	RCA	RD7678	1965	**£10**	mono, chart LP
Roustabout	LP	RCA	SF7678	1965	**£15**	stereo
Santa Bring My Baby Back	78	RCA	RCA1025	1957	**£10**	
Santa Bring My Baby Back	7"	RCA	RCA1025	1957	**£50**	1 sided demo
Santa Bring My Baby Back	7"	RCA	RCA1025	1957	**£6**	tri-centre, chart single
Santa Bring My Baby Back	7"	RCA	RCA1025	1960	**£4**	round centre
Santa Claus Is Back In Town	7"	RCA	RCA1025	1957	**£50**	1 sided demo
Santa Claus Is Back In Town	7"	RCA	RCA16	1980	**£5**	demo sleeve
She's Not You	7"	RCA	RCA1303	1962	**£4**	chart single
She's Not You	7"	RCA	RCA1303	1962	**£20**	demo
Singer Presents Elvis	LP	RCA	PRS279	1968	**£10**	US
Singer Presents Elvis	LP	RCA	PRS279	1968	**£20**	US, with photo
Sings The Wonderful World Of Xmas	LP	RCA	PL42371	1978	**£10**	'Vol.1' on cover
Something For Everybody	LP	RCA	LPM2370	1961	**£25**	US, black label 'Long 33 1/3 Play'
Something For Everybody	LP	RCA	LSP2370	1961	**£35**	US, black label 'Living Stereo'
Something For Everybody	LP	RCA	RD27244	1961	**£15**	mono, chart LP
Something For Everybody	LP	RCA	SF5106	1961	**£20**	stereo
Sound Of Your Cry	7"	RCA	RCAP232	1982	**£5**	pic disc
Special Palm Sunday Programme	LP	RCA	SP33461	1967	**£600**	US promo
Speedway	LP	RCA	LPM3989	1968	**£400**	US, black label, Monaural
Speedway	LP	RCA	LPM3989	1968	**£425**	US, black label, Monaural with photo
Speedway	LP	RCA	LSP3989	1968	**£20**	US, black label, 'Stereo'
Speedway	LP	RCA	LSP3989	1968	**£45**	US, black label, 'Stereo' with photo
Speedway	LP	RCA	RD7957	1968	**£10**	mono
Speedway	LP	RCA	SF7957	1968	**£12**	stereo
Spinout	LP	RCA	LPM3702	1966	**£20**	US, black label, 'Monaural'
Spinout	LP	RCA	LPM3702	1966	**£35**	US, black label, 'Monaural' with photo
Spinout	LP	RCA	LSP3702	1966	**£20**	US, black label, 'Stereo'
Spinout	LP	RCA	LSP3702	1966	**£35**	US, black label 'Stereo', with photo
Strictly Elvis	7" EP	RCA	RCX175	1959	**£10**	chart single
Stuck On You	78	RCA	RCA1187	1960	**£30**	
Stuck On You	7"	RCA	RCA1187	1960	**£4**	chart single
Stuck On You	7"	RCA	RCA1187	1960	**£30**	1 sided demo
Such A Night	7"	RCA	RCA1411	1964	**£4**	chart single
Such A Night	7"	RCA	RCA1411	1964	**£20**	demo
Such A Night	7" EP	RCA	RCX190	1960	**£10**	
Surrender	7"	RCA	RCA1227	1961	**£4**	chart single
Surrender	7"	RCA	RCA1227	1961	**£20**	demo
Suspicion	7"	RCA	RCA2768	1976	**£8**	demo
Suspicious Minds	7"	RCA	RCA1900	1969	**£10**	demo
T.R.O.U.B.L.E.	7"	RCA	RCA2562	1975	**£8**	demo
Teddy Bear	7"	RCA	RCA1013	1957	**£50**	1 sided demo
Tell Me Why	7"	RCA	RCA1489	1965	**£4**	chart single
Tell Me Why	7"	RCA	RCA1489	1965	**£20**	demo
That's All Right	78	Sun	209	1954	**£200**	US
That's All Right	7"	Sun	209	1954	**£300**	US
There Goes My Everything	7"	RCA	RCA2060	1971	**£10**	demo
There's Always Me	7"	RCA	RCA1628	1967	**£6**	
There's Always Me	7"	RCA	RCA1628	1967	**£20**	demo
Tickle Me Vol.1	7" EP	RCA	RCX7173	1965	**£10**	
Tickle Me Vol.2	7" EP	RCA	RCX7174	1965	**£12**	
Too Much	78	HMV	POP330	1957	**£10**	
Too Much	7"	HMV	POP330	1957	**£35**	gold label
Too Much	7"	HMV	POP330	1957	**£20**	silver label
Torna A Surrento	7"	RCA	1160	1960	**£10**	sung in Italian
Touch Of Gold	7" EP	RCA	RCX1045	1959	**£10**	
Touch Of Gold Vol.2	7" EP	RCA	RCX1048	1960	**£10**	
Treat Me Nice	7"	RCA	RCA1028	1958	**£50**	1 sided demo
Truth About Me	78	Weekend Mail		1957	**£100**	cardboard folder
TV Guide Presents Elvis Presley	7"	RCA	GBMW8705	1956	**£3500**	promo

U.S. Male	7"	RCA	RCA1688	1968	**£4**	chart single
U.S. Male	7"	RCA	RCA1688	1968	**£20**	demo
Until It's Time For You To Go	7"	RCA	RCA2188	1972	**£8**	demo
Viva Las Vegas	7"	RCA	RCA1390	1964	**£4**	chart single
Viva Las Vegas	7"	RCA	RCA1390	1964	**£20**	demo
Way Down	7"	RCA	PB0998	1977	**£6**	demo
Wear My Ring Around Your Neck	78	RCA	RCA1058	1958	**£8**	
Wear My Ring Around Your Neck	7"	RCA	RCA1058	1958	**£40**	1 sided demo
Wear My Ring Around Your Neck	7"	RCA	RCA1058	1958	**£40**	demo
Wear My Ring Around Your Neck	7"	RCA	RCA1058	1958	**£6**	tri-centre, chart single
Wear My Ring Around Your Neck	7"	RCA	RCA1058	1960	**£4**	round centre
Wild In The Country	7"	RCA	RCA1244	1961	**£4**	chart single
Wild In The Country	7"	RCA	RCA1244	1961	**£20**	demo
Wonder Of You (B side not Elvis)	7"	RCA	LB1	1979	**£5**	intro by Noel Edmonds
Wonder Of You	7"	RCA	RCA1974	1970	**£10**	demo
Wonderful World Of Elvis Presley	LP	St.Michael	IMP204	1978	**£50**	
Wooden Heart	7"	RCA	RCA1226	1961	**£4**	chart single
Wooden Heart	7"	RCA	RCA1226	1961	**£20**	demo
World 50 Gold Hits Vol.1	LP	RCA	LPM6401	1970	**£20**	4 LPs, booklet, boxed chart LP
World 50 Gold Hits Vol.2	LP	RCA	LPM6402	1971	**£25**	4 LPs, piece of cloth boxed
You Don't Have To Say You Love Me	7"	RCA	RCA2046	1970	**£10**	demo
You'll Never Walk Alone	7"	RCA	RCA1747	1968	**£5**	chart single
You'll Never Walk Alone	7"	RCA	RCA1747	1968	**£20**	demo
Your Time Hasn't Come Yet Baby	7"	RCA	RCA1714	1968	**£4**	chart single
Your Time Hasn't Come Yet Baby	7"	RCA	RCA1714	1968	**£20**	demo

PRESLEY, ELVIS & JANIS MARTIN

Elvis And Janis	LP-10"	RCA		1958	**£800**	South African

PRESLEY, REG

It's Down To You Marianne	7"	CBS	1478	1973	**£4**	
Lucinda Lee	7"	Page One	POF131	1969	**£4**	

PRESTON, BILLY

All That I've Got	7"	Apple	21	1970	**£4**	
All That I've Got	7"	Apple	21	1970	**£10**	PS
Billy's Bag	7"	Sue	WI4012	1966	**£8**	
Encouraging Words	LP	Apple	SAPCOR14	1969	**£15**	
Everything's Alright	7"	Apple	19	1969	**£5**	
Greazee	7"	Soul City	SC107		**£4**	
Greazee	7"	Soul City	SC107		**£12**	demo
I Wrote A Simple Song	LP	A&M	AMLH63507	1971	**£10**	
In The Midnight Hour	7"	Capitol	CL15458	1966	**£4**	
It's My Pleasure	LP	A&M	AMLH64532	1975	**£10**	
Most Exciting Organ Ever	LP	Sue	ILP935	1966	**£20**	
Sunny	7"	Capitol	CL15471	1966	**£4**	
That's The Way God Planned It	LP	Apple	SAPCOR9	1969	**£15**	
That's The Way God Planned It	LP	Apple	ST3359	1969	**£25**	US, face close-up on cover
That's The Way God Planned It	LP	Apple	ST3359	1969	**£12**	US, multiple face cover
That's The Way God Planned It	7"	Apple	12	1969	**£4**	chart single
That's The Way God Planned It	7"	Apple	12	1969	**£10**	PS
Wildest Organ In Town	LP	Capitol	ST2532	1966	**£10**	

PRESTON, EARL

That's For Sure	7"	Fontana	TF481	1964	**£8**	
Watch Your Step	7"	Fontana	TF406	1963	**£10**	

PRESTON, JOHNNY

Big Chief Heartache	7"	Mercury	AMT1145	1961	**£4**	
Charming Billy	7"	Mercury	AMT1114	1960	**£4**	chart single
Come Rock With Me	LP	Mercury	MG20609	1961	**£20**	US
Cradle Of Love	7"	Mercury	AMT1092	1960	**£4**	chart single
Free Me	7"	Mercury	AMT1167	1961	**£4**	
I'm Starting To Go Steady	7"	Mercury	AMT1104	1960	**£4**	chart single
Leave My Kitten Alone	7"	Mercury	AMT1129	1961	**£6**	
Ring Tail Tooter	7" EP	Mercury	ZEP10098	1960	**£10**	
Rock And Roll Guitar	7"	Mercury	AMT1164	1961	**£4**	
Running Bear	LP	Mercury	MG20592	1960	**£25**	US

Title	Format	Label	Cat. No.	Year	Price	Notes
Running Bear	7"	Mercury	AMT1079	1960	**£5**	chart single
Running Bear	7" EP	Mercury	ZEP10078	1960	**£10**	
Token Of Love	7" EP	Mercury	ZEP10116	1961	**£10**	

PRESTON, MIKE

Title	Format	Label	Cat. No.	Year	Price	Notes
Four Songs By Ray Noble	7" EP	Decca	DFE6635	1960	**£5**	
I'd Do Anything	7"	Decca	F11255	1960	**£4**	chart single
Marry Me	7"	Decca	F11335	1961	**£4**	chart single
Marry Me	7" EP	Decca	DFE6679	1961	**£5**	
Mr.Blue	7"	Decca	F11167	1959	**£4**	chart single
Togetherness	7"	Decca	F11287	1960	**£4**	chart single

PRETENDERS

Title	Format	Label	Cat. No.	Year	Price	Notes
Adultress	7"	Real		1981	**£5**	promo only
I Go To Sleep	7"	Real		1981	**£5**	33rpm promo
I Go To Sleep	7"	Real	ARE18S	1981	**£4**	3 track version
Kid	cass-s	Real		1981	**£5**	
Pretenders	LP	Nautilus	NR38	1981	**£15**	US audiophile
Pretenders	LP	Real	RAL3	1980	**£15**	autographed
Pretenders	7"	Real	SAM117	1980	**£8**	promo sampler, signed
Talk Of The Town	cass-s	Real		1981	**£5**	
Talk Of The Town	7"	Real	ARE12	1980	**£5**	MP Detroit Spinners B side

PRETTY THINGS

The Pretty Things always seemed to suffer from too much labouring in the shadow of the Rolling Stones (Dick Taylor had, of course, been an early member of the Stones), but they nevertheless achieved a fair degree of success and, despite numerous comings and goings on the part of various of the group's members, they are still around and playing. "S.F.Sorrow" has received a fair amount of acclaim for being a kind of rock opera pre-dating the Who's "Tommy", but the group's best work has always been their singles. The early Fontana singles are tough, gritty R&B that easily stand comparison with the likes of Them, or even the Rolling Stones. Later, the Columbia singles "Defecting Grey" and "Talkin' About The Good Times" are superb pieces of psychedelia and should definitely be included on any list of the essential recordings of the period.

Title	Format	Label	Cat. No.	Year	Price	Notes
Children	7"	Fontana	TF829	1967	**£10**	
Come See Me	7"	Fontana	TF688	1966	**£5**	chart single
Cry To Me	7"	Fontana	TF585	1965	**£5**	chart single
Defecting Grey	7"	Columbia	DB8300	1967	**£8**	
Don't Bring Me Down	7"	Fontana	TF503	1964	**£5**	chart single
Emotions	LP	Fontana	TL5425	1967	**£25**	
Freeway Madness	LP	W. Bros	K46190	1972	**£12**	
Get The Picture	LP	Fontana	TL5280	1965	**£25**	
Good Mr.Square	7"	Harvest	HAR5016	1970	**£8**	
Honey I Need	7"	Fontana	TF537	1965	**£5**	chart single
House In The Country	7"	Fontana	TF722	1966	**£5**	chart single
Midnight To Six Man	7"	Fontana	TF647	1965	**£6**	chart single
October 26	7"	Harvest	HAR5031	1970	**£6**	
On Film	7" EP	Fontana	TE17472	1966	**£40**	
Parachute	LP	GI Records	WAX6	1982	**£10**	
Parachute	LP	Harvest	SHVL774	1970	**£15**	chart LP
Pretty Things	LP	Fontana	TL5239	1965	**£30**	chart LP
Pretty Things	7" EP	Fontana	TE17434	1964	**£15**	
Pretty Things	LP	Wing	WL1167	1967	**£15**	
Private Sorrow	7"	Columbia	DB8494	1968	**£8**	
Progress	7"	Fontana	TF773	1966	**£8**	
Raining In My Heart	7" EP	Fontana	TE17442	1965	**£15**	
Rosalyn	7"	Fontana	TF1024	1969	**£4**	chart single
Rosalyn	7"	Fontana	TF469	1964	**£5**	
S.F.Sorrow	LP	Columbia	SCX6306	1968	**£25**	
S.F.Sorrow/Parachute	LP	Harvest	SHDW406	1975	**£20**	double
Savage Eye	LP	Swansong	SSK59401	1975	**£10**	
Silk Torpedo	LP	Swansong	SSK59400	1974	**£10**	
Stone Hearted Mama	7"	Harvest	HAR5037	1971	**£6**	
Talkin' About The Good Times	7"	Columbia	DB8353	1968	**£8**	

PREVIN, DORY

Title	Format	Label	Cat. No.	Year	Price	Notes
Dory Previn	LP	W. Bros	K56066	1974	**£10**	
Live At Carnegie Hall	LP	United Artists	UAD60045	1973	**£15**	double
Mary C Brown And The Hollywood Sign	7"	United Artists	UP35353	1972	**£4**	
Mary C Brown And The Hollywood Sign	LP	United Artists	UAG29435	1972	**£10**	
Mythical Kings And Iguanas	7"	United Artists	UP35309	1971	**£4**	
On My Way To Where	LP	United Artists	UAG29176	1973	**£10**	
Reflections In A Mud Puddle	LP	United Artists	UAG29346	1972	**£10**	
We're Children Of Coincidence	LP	W. Bros	K56213	1976	**£10**	

PRICE, ALAN

Title	Format	Label	Number	Year	Price	Notes
Amazing Alan Price	7" EP	Decca	DFE8677	1967	**£5**	
Any Day Now	7"	Decca	F12217	1965	**£4**	
Baby Of Mine	7"	Jet	12135	1978	**£4**	red vinyl, heart shaped
Don't Stop The Carnival	7"	Decca	F12731	1968	**£4**	chart single
Hi Lili Hi Lo	7"	Decca	F12442	1966	**£4**	chart single
House That Jack Built	7"	Decca	F12641	1967	**£4**	chart single
I Put A Spell On You	7"	Decca	F12367	1966	**£4**	chart single
Love Story	7"	Decca	F12808	1968	**£4**	
Price On His Head	LP	Decca	LK4907	1967	**£15**	
Price To Pay	LP	Decca	LK4839	1966	**£20**	
Shame	7"	Decca	F12691	1967	**£4**	chart single
Simon Smith And His Amazing Dancing	7"	Decca	F12570	1967	**£4**	chart single
Trimdon Grange Explosion	7"	Deram	DM263	1969	**£4**	
When I Was A Cowboy	7"	Decca	F12774	1968	**£4**	
Willow Weep For Me	7"	Decca	F12518	1966	**£4**	

PRICE, LLOYD

Title	Format	Label	Number	Year	Price	Notes
Another Fairy Tale	7"	HMV	POP983	1962	**£4**	
Boo-Hoo	7"	HMV	POP926	1961	**£4**	
Come Into My Heart	7"	HMV	POP672	1959	**£4**	
Cookin' With Lloyd Price	LP	ABC-Para.	382	1961	**£12**	US
Exciting Lloyd Price	LP	HMV	CLP1285	1959	**£25**	
Exciting Lloyd Price	7" EP	HMV	7EG8538	1959	**£15**	
Exciting Lloyd Price	7" EP	HMV	GES5784	1959	**£20**	stereo
Fantastic Lloyd Price	LP	ABC-Para.	346	1960	**£15**	US
Fantastic Lloyd Price	LP	HMV	CLP1393	1960	**£20**	mono
Fantastic Lloyd Price	LP	HMV	CSD1323	1960	**£20**	stereo
I'm Gonna Get Married	7"	HMV	POP650	1959	**£4**	chart single
Just Because	7"	London	HL8438	1957	**£15**	
Just Call Me	7"	HMV	POP799	1960	**£4**	
Know What You're Doing	7"	HMV	POP826	1961	**£4**	
Lady Luck	7"	HMV	POP712	1960	**£4**	chart single
Lloyd Price	LP	London	HAU2213	1960	**£25**	
Lloyd Price Orchestra	LP	Double-L	D2301	1963	**£10**	US
Lloyd Price Sings The Million Sellers	LP	ABC-Para.	366	1961	**£12**	US
Lloyd Swings For Sammy	LP	Monument	MLP8032	1965	**£10**	US
Love Music	7"	GSF	5	1973	**£6**	
Misty	LP	Double-L	D2303	1963	**£10**	US
Mr.Personality	LP	ABC-Para.	297	1959	**£15**	US
Mr.Personality Sings The Blues	LP	ABC-Para.	315	1960	**£15**	US
Mr.Personality's Big 15	LP	ABC-Para.	324	1960	**£15**	US
No Ifs No Ands	7"	HMV	POP741	1960	**£4**	
Personality	7"	HMV	POP626	1959	**£4**	chart single
Question	7"	HMV	POP772	1960	**£4**	
Stagger Lee	7"	HMV	POP580	1959	**£6**	chart single
Under Your Spell Again	7"	HMV	POP1100	1962	**£4**	
Where Were You On Our Wedding Day	7"	HMV	POP598	1959	**£4**	chart single

PRICE, MALCOLM

Title	Format	Label	Number	Year	Price	Notes
His Songs, His Guitars	LP	Saga		1969	**£10**	

PRICE, RAY

Title	Format	Label	Number	Year	Price	Notes
Greatest Hits	LP	Columbia	CL1566	1961	**£10**	US
Ray Price	7" EP	Philips	BBE12137	1957	**£5**	
Ray Price Sings Heart Songs	LP	Columbia	CL1015	1957	**£15**	US
Talk To Your Heart	LP	Columbia	CL1148	1958	**£12**	US

PRICE, RICK

Title	Format	Label	Number	Year	Price	Notes
Talking To The Flowers	LP	Gemini	GME1017	1971	**£15**	

PRICE, RIKKI

Title	Format	Label	Number	Year	Price	Notes
Rikki Price	7" EP	Fontana	TFE17100	1958	**£5**	

PRICE, SAMMY

Title	Format	Label	Number	Year	Price	Notes
Boogieing With Big Sid	7"	Storyville	A45068	196-	**£8**	
Original Sammy Blues	7" EP	Columbia	SEG7679	1957	**£5**	
Sammy Price	7" EP	Vogue	EPV1146	195-	**£5**	
Sammy Price's Bluesicians	7" EP	Vogue	EPV1151	195-	**£5**	

PRIDE, DICKIE

Title	Format	Label	Cat. No.	Year	Price	Notes
Betty Betty	7"	Columbia	DB4403	1960	**£6**	
Midnight Oil	7"	Columbia	DB4296	1959	**£6**	
Pride Without Prejudice	LP	Columbia	33SX1307	1960	**£15**	
Primrose Lane	7"	Columbia	DB4340	1959	**£10**	chart single
Sheik Of Shake	7" EP	Columbia	SEG7937	1959	**£20**	
Slipping And Sliding	7"	Columbia	DB4283	1959	**£12**	
You're Singing Our Love Song	7"	Columbia	DB4451	1960	**£4**	

PRIMAL SCREAM

Title	Format	Label	Cat. No.	Year	Price	Notes
All Fall Down	7"	Creation	CRE17	1985	**£20**	
Crystal Crescent	7"	Creation	CRE26	1986	**£10**	
Crystal Crescent	12"	Creation	CRET26	1986	**£10**	
Gentle Tuesday	7"	Elevation	ACID3	1987	**£6**	
Gentle Tuesday	12"	Elevation	ACIDT3	1987	**£8**	
Gentle Tuesday/Imperial	7"	Elevation		1987	**£8**	promo
Imperial	7"	Elevation	ACID5	1987	**£6**	
Imperial	12"	Elevation	ACIDT5	1987	**£8**	

PRIMATES

Title	Format	Label	Cat. No.	Year	Price	Notes
Hot Tamalas	7"	Action	ACT4530	1969	**£4**	
Hot Tamalas	7"	Action	ACT4530	1969	**£12**	demo

PRIMETTES

"Looking Back With The Primettes" consists of early material recorded by the Supremes under their original name. Only one US single ("Tears Of Sorrow"/"Pretty Baby") was actually released prior to the group signing with Motown records

Title	Format	Label	Cat. No.	Year	Price	Notes
Looking Back With The Primettes	LP	Ember	EMBS3398	1968	**£20**	
Looking Back With The Primettes	LP	Windmill		197-	**£12**	

PRIMITIVES

Title	Format	Label	Cat. No.	Year	Price	Notes
Blow Up	LP	Arc		1967	**£70**	Italian
Help Me	7"	Pye	7N15721	1964	**£100**	
You Said	7"	Pye	7N15755	1965	**£100**	

PRIMITIVES (2)

Title	Format	Label	Cat. No.	Year	Price	Notes
Crash	7"	RCA	PB41761E	1988	**£8**	
Crash	10"	RCA	PB4176X	1988	**£10**	signed
New Year's Card	78	Lazy	LAZY9	1987	**£10**	
Ocean Blue	7"	Lazy	LAZY5	1987	**£20**	
Really Stupid	7"	Lazy	LAZY2	1986	**£20**	
Really Stupid	12"	Lazy	LAZYT2	1986	**£25**	
Stop Killing Me	7"	Lazy	LAZY3	1986	**£20**	
Stop Killing Me	12"	Lazy	LAZYT3	1986	**£25**	
Thru The Flowers	7"	Lazy	LAZY6	1987	**£10**	
Thru The Flowers	12"	Lazy	LAZY1	1986	**£30**	
Thru The Flowers	12"	Lazy	LAZYT6	1987	**£15**	

PRIMROSE CIRCUS

Title	Format	Label	Cat. No.	Year	Price	Notes
P.S. Call Me Lulu	7"	President	PT314	1970	**£5**	

PRINCE

All the major stars of the eighties have had their recording careers boostedby a proliferation of picture disc and other limited edition releases, and Prince is no exception. Whether the legendary "Black Album" should be counted as one of these is not clear. The record was not supposed to have been released, yet there have been reports of the existence of a very limited number of copies on Warner Brothers. Whatever the truth of this, all the copies in common circulation are bootlegs.

Title	Format	Label	Cat. No.	Year	Price	Notes
1999	7"	WEA	W9896	1983	**£8**	chart single
1999	7"	WEA	W9896C	1983	**£15**	with cassette
1999	12"	WEA	K1999T	1985	**£6**	
1999	12"	WEA	W9896T	1983	**£15**	
Anotherloverholenyohead	12"	WEA	W8521T	1986	**£6**	
Anotherloverholenyohead	12"	WEA	W8521TP	1986	**£10**	pic disc
Batdance	CD-s	WEA	W2924CDX	1989	**£20**	batpack box
Batdance	12"	WEA	W2924TP	1989	**£10**	pic disc
Batdance(Batmix)	12"	WEA	W2924TX	1989	**£10**	
Black Album	LP	Paisley Park	WX147	1988	**£500**	promo only
Controversy	7"	WEA	K17866	1981	**£20**	
Controversy	12"	WEA	K17866T	1981	**£20**	
Do It All Night	7"	WEA	K17768	1981	**£8**	no PS
Do It All Night	12"	WEA	K17768T	1981	**£15**	no PS
For You	LP	WEA	BSK3150	1978	**£12**	US
Girls And Boys	7"	WEA	W8586P	1986	**£20**	shaped pic disc

Title	Format	Label	Cat. No.	Year	Price	Notes
Girls And Boys	12"	WEA	W8586T	1986	**£8**	
Girls And Boys	12"	WEA	W8586T	1986	**£12**	with poster
Gotta Stop	7"	WEA	K17819	1981	**£55**	2 different B sides
Gotta Stop	12"	WEA	LV47	1981	**£55**	2 different B sides
I Could Never Take The Place Of	12"	WEA	W8288T	1987	**£6**	
I Could Never Take The Place Of	12"	WEA	W8288TP	1987	**£10**	pic disc
I Wanna Be Your Lover	7"	WEA	K17537	1979	**£8**	no PS, chart single
I Wanna Be Your Lover	12"	WEA	K17527T	1979	**£12**	no PS
I Wish U Heaven	7"	WEA	W7745	1988	**£4**	poster sleeve
I Would Die 4 U	12"	WEA	W9121T	1984	**£6**	
If I Was Your Girlfriend	7"	WEA	W8334E	1987	**£8**	peach vinyl, cards & stickers
If I Was Your Girlfriend	7"	WEA	W8334W	1987	**£6**	poster sleeve
If I Was Your Girlfriend	12"	WEA	W8334T	1987	**£6**	
If I Was Your Girlfriend	12"	WEA	W8334TP	1987	**£10**	pic disc
Kiss	7"	WEA	W8751P	1986	**£20**	pic disc
Kiss	7"	WEA	W8751P	1986	**£25**	pic disc, stand
Kiss	12"	WEA	W8751T	1986	**£8**	
Kiss	12"	WEA	W8751T	1986	**£12**	with poster
Let's Go Crazy	12"	WEA	W2000T	1985	**£6**	with poster & sticker
Let's Work	7"	WEA	K17922	1982	**£20**	
Let's Work	12"	WEA	K17922T	1982	**£35**	
Little Red Corvette	7"	WEA	W9436	1983	**£15**	chart single
Little Red Corvette	7"	WEA	W9436	1983	**£25**	poster sleeve
Little Red Corvette	7"	WEA	W9688	1983	**£6**	chart single
Little Red Corvette	12"	WEA	W9436T	1983	**£20**	
Little Red Corvette	12"	WEA	W9436T	1983	**£40**	with poster
Little Red Corvette	12"	WEA	W9888T	1983	**£20**	with poster & sticker
Mountains	12"	WEA	W8711T	1986	**£8**	
Mountains	12"	WEA	W8711T	1986	**£12**	with poster
Mountains	10"	WEA	W8711TW	1986	**£20**	white vinyl
Paisley Park	7"	WEA	W9052P	1985	**£15**	shaped pic disc
Paisley Park	12"	WEA	W9052T	1985	**£10**	
Parade	LP	WEA	WX39P	1986	**£30**	pic disc
Partyman	CD-s	WEA	W2814CDX	1989	**£8**	hex pack with film stills
Partyman	12"	WEA	W2814TP	1989	**£8**	pic disc
Pop Life	12"	WEA	W8858T	1985	**£6**	
Purple Rain	LP	WEA	9251101	1984	**£25**	purple vinyl, poster
Purple Rain	7"	WEA	W9174P	1984	**£30**	shaped pic disc
Purple Rain	12"	WEA	W9174T	1984	**£15**	with poster
Raspberry Beret	12"	WEA	W8929T	1985	**£6**	
Sexy Dancer	7"	WEA	K17590	1980	**£10**	no PS
Sexy Dancer	12"	WEA	K17590T	1980	**£30**	no PS
Sign O The Times	12"	WEA	W8399T	1987	**£6**	
Sign O The Times	12"	WEA	W8399TP	1987	**£10**	pic disc
U Got The Look	12"	WEA	W8289T	1987	**£6**	
U Got The Look	12"	WEA	W8289TP	1987	**£10**	pic disc
When Doves Cry	cass-s	WEA	W9296C	1984	**£5**	
When Doves Cry	7"	WEA	W9296	1984	**£4**	chart single
When Doves Cry	12"	WEA	W9296T	1984	**£6**	
When Doves Cry/1999	12"	WEA	W9296T	1984	**£25**	shrinkwrapped double

PRINCE BUSTER

Title	Format	Label	Cat. No.	Year	Price	Notes
Aguar Fumar	7"	Blue Beat	BB293	1964	**£10**	
Al Capone	7"	Blue Beat	BB324	1964	**£10**	chart single
All My Loving	7"	Fab	FAB35	196-	**£8**	
All On My Mind	7"	Blue Beat	BB400	1965	**£10**	
Ambition	7"	Blue Beat	BB328	1965	**£10**	
Big Fight	7"	Blue Beat	BB282	1964	**£12**	
Big Fight	7"	Blue Beat	BB338	1965	**£10**	
Big Five	7"	Fab	FAB150	196-	**£8**	
Big Five	LP	Melodisc	MLP12157	1972	**£10**	
Big Five	7"	Pr. Buster	PB1		**£6**	
Black Organ	7"	Fab	FAB141	196-	**£8**	
Blackhead Chinaman	7"	Dice	CC11	1963	**£10**	
Blood Pressure	7"	Blue Beat	BB278	1964	**£12**	
Blue Beat Spirit	7"	Blue Beat	BB211	1963	**£12**	
Bonanza	7"	Blue Beat	BB307	1964	**£10**	
Bull Buck	7"	Fab	FAB118	196-	**£8**	
Burning Creation	7"	Blue Beat	BB173	1963	**£15**	
Buster's Shack	7"	Starlite	ST45023	1960	**£15**	
Bye Bye Baby	7"	Fab	FAB16	196-	**£8**	

Title	Format	Label	Cat. No.	Year	Price
Captain Burke	7"	Blue Beat	BB333	1965	**£10**
Cincinatti Kid	7"	Blue Beat	BB342	1965	**£10**
Come And Do It With Me	7"	Fab	FAB32	196-	**£8**
Come Home	7"	Blue Beat	BB317	1964	**£10**
Congo Revolution	7"	Blue Beat	BB325	1965	**£10**
Dallas Texas	7"	Fab	FAB37	196-	**£8**
Dance Cleopatra	7"	Blue Beat	BB388	1965	**£10**
Dark End Of The Street	7"	Blue Beat	BB377	1965	**£10**
Doctor Rodney	7"	Fab	FAB82	196-	**£8**
Don't Throw Stones	7"	Blue Beat	BB343	1965	**£10**
Drunkard's Psalm	7"	Blue Beat	BB378	1965	**£10**
Everybody Ska	7"	Stateside	SS335	1964	**£10**
Eye For An Eye	7"	Blue Beat	BB294	1964	**£10**
Fabulous Greatest Hits	LP	Melodisc	MS1	1968	**£12**
Fishey	7"	Pr. Buster	PB4		**£6**
Float Like A Butterfly	7"	Blue Beat	BB314	1964	**£10**
Fowl Thief	7"	Blue Beat	BB186	1963	**£12**
Ganja Plant	7"	Fab	FAB132	196-	**£8**
Glory Of Love	7"	Fab	FAB36	196-	**£8**
Glory Of Love	7"	Fab	FAB49	196-	**£8**
Going To The River	7"	Fab	FAB26	196-	**£8**
Going West	7"	Blue Beat	BB277	1964	**£12**
Green Green Grass Of Home	7"	Fab	FAB57	196-	**£8**
Here Comes The Bride	7"	Blue Beat	BB309	1964	**£10**
Hey Jude	7"	Fab	FAB94	196-	**£8**
Hit Me Back	7"	Fab	FAB140	196-	**£8**
Hypocrite	7"	Fab	FAB80	196-	**£8**
I Feel The Spirit	LP	Blue Beat	BBLP802	196-	**£50**
I Feel The Spirit	LP	Fab	MS2		**£10**
I May Never Love You Again	7"	Blue Beat	BB274	1964	**£12**
I Wish Your Picture Was You	7"	Pr. Buster	PB7		**£6**
I Won't Let You Cry	7"	Blue Beat	BB357	1965	**£10**
Independence Day	7"	Blue Beat	BB116	1962	**£15**
Intensified Dirt	7"	Fab	FAB56	196-	**£8**
It's Burke's Law	LP	Blue Beat	BBLP806	196-	**£50**
It's Too Late	7"	Blue Beat	BB352	1965	**£10**
Jealous	7"	Blue Beat	BB243	1963	**£12**
Johnny Cool	7"	Fab	FAB11	196-	**£10**
Johnny Dark	7"	Blue Beat	BB290	1964	**£10**
Johnny Dollar	7"	Blue Beat	BB326	1965	**£10**
Judge Dread	LP	Blue Beat	BBLP809	196-	**£50**
Judge Dread	7"	Blue Beat	BB387	1965	**£10**
King Duke Sir	7"	Blue Beat	BB163	1962	**£15**
Kings Of Old	7"	Fab	FAB31	196-	**£8**
Knock On Wood	7"	Blue Beat	BB373	1965	**£10**
Land Of Imagination	7"	Blue Beat	BB391	1965	**£10**
Ling Ting Tang	7"	Blue Beat	BB302	1964	**£10**
Little Boy's Blues	7"	Blue Beat	BB162	1962	**£15**
Love Each Other	7"	Rainbow	RAI110	196-	**£10**
Madness	7"	Blue Beat	BB170	1963	**£15**
Medley	7"	Pr. Buster	PB19		**£6**
Mules Mules Mules	7"	Blue Beat	BB279	1964	**£12**
My Girl	7"	Blue Beat	BB321	1964	**£10**
My Happiness	7"	Pr. Buster	PB9		**£6**
My Heart Is Gone	7"	Pr. Buster	PB16		**£6**
Nice Nice	7"	Fab	FAB64	196-	**£8**
No Knowledge In College	7"	Blue Beat	BB271	1964	**£12**
Now You Want To Cry	7"	Blue Beat	BB114	1962	**£15**
Ob La Di Ob La Da	7"	Fab	FAB93	196-	**£8**
Oh Lady Oh	7"	Blue Beat	BB262	1964	**£12**
One Hand Washes The Other	7"	Blue Beat	BB138	1962	**£15**
Open Up Bartender	7"	Blue Beat	BB158	1962	**£15**
Original Golden Oldies Vol.1	LP	Pr. Buster	PB9		**£10**
Pharaoh House Crash	7"	Fab	FAB92	196-	**£8**
Picket Line	7"	Blue Beat	BB349	1965	**£10**
Police Trim Rasta	7"	Fab	FAB176	196-	**£8**
Prince Buster On Tour	LP	Blue Beat	BBLP808	1967	**£50**
Prophet	7"	Blue Beat	BB359	1965	**£10**
Pum Pum A Go Kill You	7"	Fab	FAB101	196-	**£8**
Queen Of The Outlaws	LP	Blue Beat	BBLP822	196-	**£50**
Quiet Place	7"	Blue Beat	BB393	1965	**£10**

Title	Format	Label	Number	Year	Price	Note
Rat Trap	7"	Fab	FAB142	196-	**£8**	
Rat Trap	7"	Pr. Buster	PB2		**£6**	
Rebel	7"	Fab	FAB124	196-	**£8**	
Repect	7"	Blue Beat	BB335	1965	**£10**	
Rock And Shake	7"	Fab	FAB20	196-	**£8**	
Rolling Stones	7"	Blue Beat	BB192	1963	**£12**	
Rough Rider	7"	Fab	FAB40	196-	**£8**	
Rum And Coca Cola	7"	Blue Beat	BB330	1965	**£10**	
Run Man Run	7"	Blue Beat	BB150	1962	**£15**	
Shakin' Up Orange Street	7"	Fab	FAB10	196-	**£10**	
Shanty Town Get Scanty	7"	Blue Beat	BB370	1965	**£10**	
She Loves You	7"	Blue Beat	BB234	1963	**£12**	
She Pon Top	7"	Blue Beat	BB232	1963	**£12**	
She Was A Rough Rider	LP	Blue Beat	BBLP820	196-	**£50**	
Shepherd Beng (with Teddy King)	7"	Fab	FAB41	1968	**£15**	
Sister's Big Stuff	LP	Melodisc	MLP12156		**£10**	
Sit And Wonder	7"	Blue Beat	BB382	1965	**£10**	
Sit Down And Cry	7"	Blue Beat	BB389	1965	**£10**	
Ska-Lip-Soul	LP	Blue Beat	BBLP805	196-	**£50**	
Soul Dance	7"	Blue Beat	BB398	1965	**£10**	
Soul Serenade	7"	Blue Beat	BB390	1965	**£10**	
Sounds And Pressure	7"	Blue Beat	BB372	1965	**£10**	
Spider And The Fly	7"	Blue Beat	BB199	1963	**£12**	
Stand Up	7"	Fab	FAB122	196-	**£8**	
Still	7"	Pr. Buster	PB32		**£6**	
Sugar Pop	7"	Blue Beat	BB316	1964	**£10**	
Take It Easy	7"	Blue Beat	BB384	1965	**£10**	
Talkin' 'Bout My Girl	7"	Blue Beat	BB355	1965	**£10**	
Ten Commandments	7"	Blue Beat	BB167	1963	**£15**	
Ten Commandments	7"	Blue Beat	BB334	1965	**£10**	
Ten Commandments	7"	Philips	BF1552	1967	**£8**	
Ten Commandments	LP	RCA	LPM3792	1967	**£15**	US
They To Come	7"	Dice	CC6	1962	**£10**	
Thirty Pieces Of Silver	7"	Blue Beat	BB248	1964	**£12**	
Thirty Pieces Of Silver	7"	Unity	UN522	1969	**£6**	
This Gun For Hire	7"	Blue Beat	BB395	1965	**£10**	
Three Blind Mice	7"	Blue Beat	BB225	1963	**£12**	
Three More Rivers To Cross	7"	Blue Beat	BB180	1963	**£12**	
Tie The Donkey's Tail	7"	Fab	FAB119	196-	**£8**	
Time Longer Than Rope	7"	Blue Beat	BB133	1962	**£15**	
To Be Loved	7"	Blue Beat	BB362	1965	**£10**	
Tra La La	7"	Blue Beat	BB346	1965	**£10**	
Train To Girls Town	7"	Fab	FAB25	196-	**£8**	
Tutti Frutti	LP	Fab	MS6		**£10**	
Under Arrest - But Officer	7"	Blue Beat	BB339	1965	**£10**	
Vagabond	7"	Blue Beat	BB402	1965	**£10**	
Wash All Your Troubles Away	7"	Blue Beat	BB210	1963	**£12**	
Watch It Blackhead	7"	Blue Beat	BB189	1963	**£12**	
We Shall Overcome	7"	Fab	FAB58	196-	**£8**	
Welcome To Jamaica	LP	Blue Beat	BBLP821	196-	**£50**	
What A Hard Man Fe Dead	LP	Blue Beat	BBLP807	196-	**£50**	
Window Shopping	7"	Blue Beat	BB197	1963	**£12**	
Wine And Grind	7"	Fab	FAB108	196-	**£8**	
Wine And Grind	7"	Fab	FAB81	196-	**£8**	
Wings Of A Dove	7"	Blue Beat	BB254	1964	**£12**	
World Peace	7"	Dice	CC18	1963	**£10**	
You'll Be Lonely And Blue	7"	Blue Beat	BB383	1965	**£10**	
You're Mine	7"	Blue Beat	BB216	1963	**£12**	
Young Gifted And Black	7"	Fab	FAB127	196-	**£8**	
Your Turn	7"	Rainbow	RAI107	196-	**£10**	

PRINCE CHARLIE

Title	Format	Label	Number	Year	Price
Hit And Run	7"	Coxsone	CS7101	196-	**£10**

PRINCE HAROLD

Title	Format	Label	Number	Year	Price
Forget About Me	7"	Mercury	MF952	1966	**£4**

PRINCE, VIV

Title	Format	Label	Number	Year	Price
Light Of The Charge Brigade	7"	Columbia	DB7960	1966	**£15**

PRINCIPAL EDWARD'S MAGIC THEATRE

Principal Edward's Magic Theatre were the first, and perhaps the only group THEATRE ever to receive an Arts Council Grant. They were a large organisation, incorporating dancers and light-show operators as well as musicians, so that their records do not entirely succeed in conveying what they did. "Soundtrack", however, is an interesting record, crossing folk with rock and poetry so well that one is never quite sure what is coming next. The music also features a cameo appearance from John Peel, who delivers one spoken line (in the role of a child!).

Title	Format	Label	Cat. No.	Year	Price	Notes
Asmoto Running Band	LP	Dandelion	DAN8002	1971	**£15**	
Captain Lifeboy	7"	Deram	DM391	1973	**£4**	
Round One	LP	Deram	SML1108	1974	**£15**	
Soundtrack	LP	Dandelion	63752	1969	**£20**	
Weekdaze	7"	Deram	DM398	1973	**£4**	
Ballad	7"	Dandelion	4405	1969	**£6**	

PRINE, JOHN

Title	Format	Label	Cat. No.	Year	Price	Notes
Bruised Orange	LP	Asylum	K53084	1978	**£10**	
Common Sense	LP	Atlantic	K50137	1975	**£10**	
Diamonds In The Rough	LP	Atlantic	K40427	1973	**£10**	
John Prine	LP	Atlantic	K40357	1972	**£10**	
Pink Cadillac	LP	Asylum	K52164	1979	**£10**	
Prime Prine	LP	Atlantic	SD18202	1976	**£10**	US
Storm Windows	LP	Asylum	6E280	1980	**£10**	US
Sweet Revenge	LP	Atlantic	K40524	1974	**£10**	

PROBY, P.J.

Title	Format	Label	Cat. No.	Year	Price	Notes
Believe It Or Not	LP	Liberty	LBL83087	1968	**£20**	
Christmas With P.J.Proby	7" EP	Liberty	LEP2239	1965	**£6**	
Day That Lorraine Came Down	7"	Liberty	LIB15152	1968	**£6**	
Enigma	LP	Liberty	LBL83032	1967	**£10**	
Enigma	LP	Liberty	LBY1361	1966	**£15**	
Go Go P.J.Proby	LP	Liberty	LRP3406	1965	**£15**	US
Hanging From Your Loving Tree	7"	Liberty	LIB15245	1969	**£6**	
Hold Me	7"	Decca	F11904	1964	**£4**	chart single
I Am P.J.Proby	LP	Liberty	LBY1235	1964	**£15**	chart LP
I Apologise	7"	Liberty	LIB10188	1965	**£4**	chart single
I Can't Make It Alone	7"	Liberty	LIB10250	1966	**£4**	chart single
I'm Yours	LP	Ember	NR5069	1973	**£12**	
It's Goodbye	7"	Liberty	LIB15386	1970	**£6**	
It's Your Day Today	7"	Liberty	LIB15046	1968	**£4**	chart single
Let The Water Run Down	7"	Liberty	LIB10206	1965	**£4**	chart single
Maria	7"	Liberty	LIB10218	1965	**£4**	chart single
Niki Hoeky	7"	Liberty	LIB55936	1967	**£4**	
P.J.Proby	LP	Liberty	LBY1264	1965	**£15**	
P.J.Proby	7" EP	Liberty	LEP2192	1965	**£6**	
P.J.Proby Again	7" EP	Liberty	LEP2267	1966	**£6**	
P.J.Proby Hits	7" EP	Liberty	LEP2251	1966	**£6**	
P.J.Proby's In Town	LP	Liberty	LBL83018	1967	**£10**	
P.J.Proby's In Town	LP	Liberty	LBY1291	1965	**£15**	
Phenomenon	LP	Liberty	LBL83045	1967	**£20**	
Somewhere	7"	Liberty	LIB10182	1964	**£4**	chart single
Somewhere	7" EP	Liberty	LEP2229	1965	**£5**	
That Means A Lot	7"	Liberty	LIB10215	1965	**£5**	chart single
Three Week Hero	LP	Liberty	LBS83219	1969	**£40**	
To Make A Big Man Cry	7"	Liberty	LIB10236	1966	**£4**	chart single
Today I Killed A Man	7"	Liberty	LIB15280	1970	**£6**	
Together	7"	Decca	F11967	1964	**£4**	chart single
Try To Forget Her	7"	Liberty	LIB55367	1964	**£5**	
We'll Meet Again	7"	Columbia	DB8874	1972	**£4**	
What's Wrong With My World	LP	Liberty	LST7561	1968	**£12**	US
What's Wrong With My World	7"	Liberty	LIB15085	1968	**£4**	
Work With Me Annie	7"	Liberty	LIB55974	1967	**£6**	
You Got Me Cryin'	7"	Melodisc	FAB3879	1967	**£5**	
You've Come Back	7"	Liberty	LIB10223	1966	**£4**	chart single

PROBY, P.J. & OTHERS

Title	Format	Label	Cat. No.	Year	Price	Notes
Elvis	LP	Astoria	1	1978	**£15**	
Hero	LP	Palm	7007	1981	**£15**	

PROBY, P.J. (AS JET POWERS)

Title	Format	Label	Cat. No.	Year	Price	Notes
California License	LP	Liberty	LBL83320	1969	**£60**	

PROCOL HARUM

Title	Format	Label	Number	Year	Price	Notes
Broken Barricades	LP	Chrysalis	ILPS9158	1971	£15	chart LP
Exotic Birds And Fruit	LP	Chrysalis	CHR1058	1974	£10	
Grand Hotel	LP	Chrysalis	CHR1037	1973	£10	
Homburg	7"	Regal Z.	RZ3003	1967	£4	chart single
Home	LP	Regal Z.	SLRZ1014	1970	£15	chart LP
Il Tuo Diamente	7"	IL	IL9005	1969	£10	sung in Italian
Lives	LP	A&M	SP8053	1972	£30	US interview promo
Procol Harum	LP	Regal Z.	LRZ1001	1967	£15	
Procul's Ninth	LP	Chrysalis	CHR1080	1975	£10	chart LP
Quite Rightly So	7"	Regal Z.	RZ3007	1968	£4	chart single
Salty Dog	LP	Regal Z.	SLRZ1009	1969	£15	chart LP
Salty Dog	7"	Regal Z.	RZ3019	1969	£4	chart single
Shine On Brightly	LP	Regal Z.	SLRZ1004	1969	£15	
Shine On Brightly/Home	LP	Cube	TOOFA10	1972	£15	double
Something Magic	LP	Chrysalis	CHR1130	1977	£10	
Whiter Shade Of Pale	12"	Cube	HBUG77	1979	£6	white vinyl
Whiter Shade Of Pale	7"	Deram	DM126	1967	£4	chart single
Whiter Shade Of Pale	7"	MagniFly	ECHO10	1972	£5	PS
Whiter Shade/A Salty Dog	LP	Cube	TOOFA7/8	1972	£15	double, chart LP

PROFESSOR LONGHAIR

Title	Format	Label	Number	Year	Price	Notes
Baby Let Me Hold Your Hand	7"	Sue	WI397	1965	£10	
Professor Longhair	7" EP	XX	MIN708		£6	

PROFILE

Title	Format	Label	Number	Year	Price	Notes
Haven't They Got Better Things To Do	7"	Mercury	MF875	1965	£6	

PROPAGANDA

Title	Format	Label	Number	Year	Price	Notes
13th Life Of Dr.Mabuse	12"	ZTT	12ZTAS2 (2A2U)	1985	£15	
Bejewelled Duel	12"	ZTT	12ZTAS8	1985	£8	white label promo
Complete Machinery	cass-s	ZTT	CTIS12	1985	£15	
Das Testaments Des Mabuse	cass-s	ZTT	CTIS101	1985	£8	
Das Testaments Des Mabuse	12"	ZTT	12ZTAS2	1985	£12	dark PS
Das Testaments Des Mabuse	12"	ZTT	12ZTAS2	1985	£15	white PS
Do Well	cass-s	ZTT	CTIS108	1985	£8	
Dr.Mabuse (Remix)	12"	ZTT	12ZTAS2DJ	1985	£12	promo
Dr.Mabuse	7"	ZTT	ZTAS2	1985	£5	white PS
Duel	7"	ZTT	DUAL1	1985	£5	double
Duel	7"	ZTT	PZTAS8	1985	£5	shaped pic disc
Duel	7"	ZTT	ZTAS8DJ	1985	£6	white label promo
P Machinery (Beta Wrap Around Of)	12"	ZTT	12ZTAS21	1985	£6	
P Machinery (Beta)	12"	ZTT	12XZTAS12	1985	£10	
P Machinery (Beta)	12"	ZTT	12ZTAST12	1985	£15	double, poster
P Machinery (Polish)	12"	ZTT	12PZTAS12	1985	£10	clear vinyl
P Machinery (Polish)	12"	ZTT	12ZTAS12	1985	£6	
P Machinery	7"	ZTT	PZTAS12	1985	£6	clear vinyl
P Machinery	7"	ZTT	ZTAS12	1985	£4	

PROPHET, ORVAL

Title	Format	Label	Number	Year	Price	Notes
Run Run Run	7"	London	HLL9729	1963	£4	

PROPHET, REX

Title	Format	Label	Number	Year	Price	Notes
Canadian Plowboy	7" EP	Brunswick	OE9144	1955	£4	

PROPHETS

Title	Format	Label	Number	Year	Price	Notes
I Got The Fever	7"	Mercury	MF1097	1969	£15	

PROTEX

Title	Format	Label	Number	Year	Price	Notes
Don't Ring Me Up	7"	Good Vibs	GOT6	1978	£4	
I Can Only Dream	7"	Polydor	2059167	1979	£4	
I Can't Cope	7"	Polydor	2059124	1979	£4	
Strange Obsessions	LP	Polydor		1980	£10	

PROVIDENCE

Title	Format	Label	Number	Year	Price	Notes
Ever Sense The Dawn	LP	Threshold	THS9	1972	£15	
Fantasy Fugue	7"	Threshold	TH14	1973	£5	

PRYSOCK, ARTHUR

Title	Format	Label	Number	Year	Price	Notes
Again	7" EP	CBS	EP6076	1966	£10	
I Worry About You	LP	Old Town	LP102	1962	£12	US
It's Too Late Baby, Too Late	7"	CBS	201820	1965	£4	

PRYSOCK, RED

Title	Format	Label	Cat. No.	Year	Price	Notes
Battle Royal	LP	Mercury	MG20106	1956	**£20**	US
Beat	LP	Mercury	MG20307	1958	**£12**	US
Chop Suey	7"	Mercury	AMT1028	1959	**£4**	
Fruit Boots	LP	Mercury	MG20211	1957	**£20**	US
Rock'N'Roll	LP	Mercury	MG20086	1955	**£25**	US
Swing Softly Red	LP	Mercury	MG20188	1956	**£20**	US
Teen Age Rock	7"	Mercury	AMT154	1957	**£4**	

PSYCHEDELIC FURS

Title	Format	Label	Cat. No.	Year	Price	Notes
Dumb Waiters	7"	CBS	A1166	1981	**£4**	playable sleeve
Interchords	LP	Columbia	AS1296	1981	**£40**	US interview promo
Sister Europe (2 versions)	7"	Epic	8179DJ	1979	**£6**	promo
We Love You	7"	Epic	8005DJ	1979	**£6**	censored promo

PSYCHIC TV

When Throbbing Gristle split apart, the pieces flew off into three directions, one of which led to the group Psychic TV. Genesis P.Orridge retained a similar record release policy to that of Throbbing Gristle, with a plethora of limited edition issues that were inevitably destined to rise in value. The music is considerably more commercial on the whole, but with a sardonic streak reminiscent of Frank Zappa's irreverent approach.

Title	Format	Label	Cat. No.	Year	Price	Notes
Album Ten	LP	Temple	TOPY032	1988	**£20**	pic disc
Face The Hand Of Chance	LP	Some Bizarre	PSY1	1982	**£20**	double, with poster
Godstar	12"	Temple	TOPIC009	1986	**£6**	pic disc
Jack The Tab	12"	DC	DC23	1988	**£6**	
Pagan Day	LP	Temple	TOPY003	1984	**£20**	pic disc
Rev.Jim Jones	LP				**£35**	US pic disc
Roman P	7"	Sordide S.	SS33009	1984	**£15**	
Those Who Do Not	LP	Gramm/Temp	GRAMM23	1984	**£20**	double

PUBLIC FOOT THE ROMAN

Title	Format	Label	Cat. No.	Year	Price	Notes
Public Foot The Roman	LP	Sovereign	SVNA7259	1973	**£25**	

PUBLIC IMAGE LTD.

Title	Format	Label	Cat. No.	Year	Price	Notes
Commercial Zone	LP	XYZ	007	1984	**£10**	US
Metal Box	LP	Virgin	METAL1	1979	**£15**	3x12" in can
Public Image	7"	Virgin	VS228	1978	**£5**	newspaper sleeve
Seattle	7"	Virgin	VS988	1987	**£4**	boxed, + badge, card, patch

PUCKETT, GARY & UNION GAP

Title	Format	Label	Cat. No.	Year	Price	Notes
Incredible	LP	CBS	63429	1968	**£10**	
New Album	LP	CBS	63794	1970	**£10**	
Woman Woman	LP	Columbia	9612	1968	**£10**	US
Young Girl	LP	CBS	63342	1968	**£10**	chart LP

PUDDING

Title	Format	Label	Cat. No.	Year	Price	Notes
Magic Bus	7"	Decca	F12603	1967	**£15**	

PUDDLETOWN EXPRESS

Title	Format	Label	Cat. No.	Year	Price	Notes
Lost Ears	LP	Gull	G2003/4	1976	**£10**	

PUGSLEY MUNION

Title	Format	Label	Cat. No.	Year	Price	Notes
Just Like You	LP	J&S	SLP0001		**£35**	US

PULSAR

Title	Format	Label	Cat. No.	Year	Price	Notes
Pollen	LP	Decca	SKLR5228	1976	**£20**	
Strands Of The Future	LP	Decca	TXS119	1976	**£20**	

PULSE

Title	Format	Label	Cat. No.	Year	Price	Notes
Pulse	LP	Major Minor	SMLP64	1970	**£12**	

PUPILS

Title	Format	Label	Cat. No.	Year	Price	Notes
Tribute To The Rolling Stones	LP	Wing	WL1150	1966	**£80**	

PUPPETS

Title	Format	Label	Cat. No.	Year	Price	Notes
Baby Don't Cry	7"	Pye	7N15634	1964	**£12**	
Everybody's Talking	7"	Pye	7N15556	1963	**£12**	
Shake With Me	7"	Pye	7N15625	1964	**£12**	

PURDIE, BERNARD

Title	Format	Label	Cat. No.	Year	Price	Notes
Soul Drums	LP	Direction	863290	1968	**£10**	

PURIFY, JAMES & BOBBY

Title	Format	Label	Cat. No.	Year	Price	Notes
Do Unto Me	7"	Stateside	SS2093	1968	**£5**	
I Can't Remember	7"	Bell	BLL1008	1968	**£4**	
I'm Your Puppet	7"	Stateside	SS547	1966	**£4**	
Let Love Come Between Us	7"	Stateside	SS2049	1967	**£4**	
Pure Sound Of...	LP	Bell	SBLL101	1967	**£15**	
Shake A Tail Feather	7"	Stateside	SS2016	1967	**£5**	
Wish You Didn't Have To Go	7"	Stateside	SS595	1967	**£4**	

PURPLE FOX

Title	Format	Label	Cat. No.	Year	Price	Notes
Tribute To Jimi Hendrix	LP	Saga		1973	**£20**	

PURPLE GANG

Title	Format	Label	Cat. No.	Year	Price	Notes
Granny Takes A Trip	7"	Transatlantic	BIG101	1967	**£8**	
Kiss Me Goodnight Sally Green	7"	Transatlantic	BIG111	1968	**£5**	
Purple Gang Strikes	LP	Transatlantic		1968	**£20**	

PURPLE HEARTS

Title	Format	Label	Cat. No.	Year	Price	Notes
Frustration	7"	Fiction	FICS007	1979	**£4**	
Jimmy	7"	Fiction	FICS9	1980	**£4**	chart single
Millions Like Us	7"	Fiction	FICS003	1979	**£5**	chart single
My Life's A Jigsaw	7"	Safari	SAFE30	1980	**£4**	

PURSEY, JIMMY

Title	Format	Label	Cat. No.	Year	Price	Notes
Animals Have More Fun	7"			1981	**£8**	

PUSSY

Title	Format	Label	Cat. No.	Year	Price	Notes
Feline Woman	7"	Deram	DM368	1972	**£20**	
Plays	LP	Morgan B.T.	5002	1969	**£200**	

PUSSYFOOT

Title	Format	Label	Cat. No.	Year	Price	Notes
Freeloader	7"	Decca	F12474	1966	**£4**	
Mr.Hyde	7"	Decca	F12561	1967	**£4**	

PUZZLE

Title	Format	Label	Cat. No.	Year	Price	Notes
Puzzle	LP	Motown	768	1973	**£12**	US

PVC2

Title	Format	Label	Cat. No.	Year	Price	Notes
Put You In The Picture	7"	Zoom	ZUM2	1977	**£4**	

PYRAMID

The lead singer on the Pyramid's impressive Deram single was Ian Matthews, subsequently a member of Fairport Convention before embarking on a solo career.

Title	Format	Label	Cat. No.	Year	Price	Notes
Pyramid	LP	President		1968	**£20**	
Summer Of Last Year	7"	Deram	DM111	1967	**£15**	

PYRAMIDS

Title	Format	Label	Cat. No.	Year	Price	Notes
Penetration	LP	Best	LPM1001	1964	**£40**	US
Penetration	7"	London	HLU9847	1964	**£4**	
Train Tour To Rainbow City	7"	President	PT161	1967	**£4**	chart single

Q65

Title	Format	Label	Cat. No.	Year	Price	Notes
Revolution	LP	Decca	6440675	1966	**£60**	Dutch

QUAKERS

Title	Format	Label	Cat. No.	Year	Price	Notes
I'm Ready	7"	Oriole	CB1992	1965	**£10**	

QUARTET

Title	Format	Label	Cat. No.	Year	Price	Notes
Now	7"	Decca	F12974	1969	**£4**	

QUARTZ

Title	Format	Label	Cat. No.	Year	Price	Notes
Deleted	LP	Jet	JETLP223	1979	**£10**	
Live Count Dracula	LP	Reddington	001	1980	**£12**	
Quartz	LP	Pye	NSPL28261	1978	**£10**	
Quartz	LP	United Artists	UAG30081	1977	**£10**	

QUATERMASS

Title	Format	Label	Cat. No.	Year	Price	Notes
Quatermass	LP	Harvest	SHVL775	1970	**£35**	

QUATRAIN

Title	Format	Label	Cat. No.	Year	Price	Notes
Quatrain	LP	Polydor	583743	1969	**£12**	

QUATRO, SUZI

Title	Format	Label	Cat. No.	Year	Price	Notes
Rolling Stone	7"	Rak	RAK134	1972	**£4**	

QUEEN

Title	Format	Label	Cat. No.	Year	Price	Notes
Back Chat	12"	EMI	12EMI5325	1982	**£6**	
Bicycle Race	7"	EMI	EMI2870	1978	**£4**	chart single
Bohemian Rhapsody	7"	EMI	EMI2375	1975	**£200**	blue vinyl
Bohemian Rhapsody	7"	EMI	EMI2375	1975	**£10**	demo
Bohemian Rhapsody	7"	EMI	EMI2375	1975	**£15**	PS
Friends Will Be Friends	7"	EMI	QUEENP8	1986	**£4**	pic disc
It's A Hard Life	12"	EMI	12QUEENP3	1984	**£6**	pic disc
Jealousy	7"	EMI		1979	**£8**	promo
Keep Yourself Alive	7"	EMI	EMI2036	1973	**£8**	
Killer Queen	7"	EMI	EMI2229	1974	**£4**	chart single
Killer Queen	7"	EMI	EMI2229	1974	**£10**	demo
Kind Of Magic	12"	EMI	12QUEENP7	1986	**£10**	pic disc
Las Palabras De Amor	7"	EMI	EMI5316	1982	**£10**	mispressed demo
Man On The Prowl	7"	EMI		1984	**£10**	test pressing
News Of The World	LP	EMI	EMA784	1977	**£100**	promo, boxed
Night At The Opera	LP	Mobile Fid.	MFSL1067	1980	**£15**	US audiophile
Now I'm Here	7"	EMI	EMI2256	1975	**£4**	chart single
Play The Game	7"	EMI	EMI5076	1980	**£4**	PS, chart single
Queen	LP	Elektra	EQ5064	1973	**£15**	US quad
Queen	LP	EMI	EMC3006	1973	**£25**	EMI conference copy unfinished sleeve
Queen's First EP	7" EP	EMI	EMI2623	1977	**£4**	chart single
Radio Ga Ga	7"	EMI	QUEEN1	1984	**£8**	demo
Save Me	7"	EMI	EMI5022	1980	**£4**	PS, chart single
Seven Seas Of Rhye	7"	EMI	EMI2121	1974	**£5**	chart single
Seven Seas Of Rhye	7"	EMI	EMI2121	1974	**£20**	demo
Somebody To Love	7"	EMI	EMI2565	1976	**£10**	demo
Somebody To Love	7"	EMI	EMI2565	1976	**£8**	PS
Spread Your Wings	7"	EMI	EMI2757	1978	**£4**	PS, chart single
Under Pressure (Live)	7"	EMI		1986	**£20**	promo
We Are The Champions	7"	EMI	EMI2708	1977	**£4**	PS, chart single
Works	LP	EMI	WORK1	1984	**£20**	promo
Works	7"	EMI		1984	**£5**	promo flexi

QUESTION MARK & THE MYSTERIANS

Title	Format	Label	Cat. No.	Year	Price	Notes
96 Tears	7"	Cameo Park.	C428	1966	**£8**	chart single
96 Tears	LP	Cameo	C2004	1966	**£30**	US

Action .... LP .... Cameo .... C2006 .... 1966 .... **£30** .... US
Do Something To Me .... 7" .... Cameo Park .... C496 .... 1967 .... **£10**
I Need Somebody .... 7" .... Cameo Park .... C441 .... 1966 .... **£10**
You Captivate Me .... 7" .... Cameo Park .... C479 .... 1967 .... **£10**

QUESTIONS

We Got Love .... 7" .... Decca .... F22740 .... 1968 .... **£8**

QUICKLY, TOMMY

Humpty Dumpty .... 7" .... Pye .... 7N15748 .... 1964 .... **£5**
Kiss Me Now .... 7" .... Piccadilly .... 7N35151 .... 1963 .... **£6**
Prove It .... 7" .... Piccadilly .... 7N35167 .... 1964 .... **£5**
Tip Of My Tongue .... 7" .... Piccadilly .... 7N35137 .... 1963 .... **£35**
Wild Side Of Life .... 7" .... Pye .... 7N15708 .... 1964 .... **£4** .... chart single
You Might As Well Forget Him .... 7" .... Piccadilly .... 7N35183 .... 1964 .... **£5**

QUICKSAND

Home Is Where I Belong .... LP .... Dawn .... DNLS3056 .... 1974 .... **£30**
Passing By .... 7" .... Carnaby .... CNS4015 .... 1970 .... **£8**
Time To Live .... 7" .... Dawn .... DNS1046 .... 1973 .... **£8**

QUICKSILVER MESSENGER SERVICE

Anthology .... LP .... Capitol .... ESTSP13 .... 1978 .... **£12** .... double
Comin' Thru' .... LP .... Capitol .... ST11002 .... 1972 .... **£12**
Gypsy Lights .... 7" .... Capitol .... CL15859 .... 1976 .... **£4**
Happy Trails .... LP .... Capitol .... EST120 .... 1969 .... **£15**
Just For Love .... LP .... Capitol .... EAST498 .... 1970 .... **£15**
Quicksilver .... LP .... Capitol .... SW819 .... 1972 .... **£12**
Quicksilver Messenger Service .... LP .... Capitol .... ST2904 .... 1968 .... **£25**
Shady Grove .... LP .... Capitol .... EST391 .... 1969 .... **£15**
Solid Silver .... LP .... Capitol .... ST11462 .... 1975 .... **£10**
What About Me .... LP .... Capitol .... EAST630 .... 1971 .... **£15**

QUIET FIVE

Homeward Bound .... 7" .... Parlophone .... R5421 .... 1966 .... **£5** .... chart single
Honeysuckle Rose .... 7" .... Parlophone .... R5302 .... 1965 .... **£6**
I Am Waiting .... 7" .... Parlophone .... R5470 .... 1966 .... **£5**
When Morning Sun Dries The Dew .... 7" .... Parlophone .... R5273 .... 1965 .... **£5** .... chart single

QUIET WORLD

Love Is Walking .... 7" .... Dawn .... DNS1005 .... 1970 .... **£20**
Rest Comfortably .... 7" .... Pye .... 7N45005 .... 1970 .... **£15**
Road .... LP .... Dawn .... DNLS3007 .... 1970 .... **£40**

QUIK

I Can't Sleep .... 7" .... Deram .... DM155 .... 1967 .... **£10**
King Of The World .... 7" .... Deram .... DM139 .... 1967 .... **£8**
Love Is A Beautiful Thing .... 7" .... Deram .... DM121 .... 1967 .... **£6**

QUILL

Quill .... LP .... Cotillion .... SD9017 .... 1970 .... **£10** .... US

QUINN, MIKE

Someone Slipping Into My Mind .... 7" .... Fontana .... TF761 .... 1966 .... **£5**

QUINTESSENCE

Quintessence seem to epitomise hippiedom - living communally, radiating peace and love, and above all being obsessed with Eastern religion and music. The group's albums are a smooth blend of Indian chanting and English electric guitar, the two being held together by Raja Ram's fluid, melodic flute playing. They are among the most successful attempts to fuse Eastern and Western musics, although the hippy context will inevitably make the music sound rather dated to modern listeners.

Dive Deep .... LP .... Island .... ILPS9143 .... 1970 .... **£15** .... chart LP
In Blissful Company .... LP .... Island .... ILPS9110 .... 1969 .... **£15**
Indweller .... LP .... RCA .... SF8317 .... 1972 .... **£12**
Notting Hill Gate .... 7" .... Island .... WIP6075 .... 1970 .... **£5**
Quintessence .... LP .... Island .... ILPS9128 .... 1970 .... **£15** .... chart LP
Self .... LP .... RCA .... SF8273 .... 1971 .... **£12** .... chart LP
Sweet Jesus .... 7" .... Neon .... NE1003 .... 197- **£5**

QUIST, DARYL

Above And Beyond .... 7" .... Pye .... 7N15605 .... 1964 .... **£8**
Goodbye To You .... 7" .... Pye .... 7N15563 .... 1963 .... **£5**
Keep Moving .... 7" .... Pye .... 7N15538 .... 1963 .... **£5**

Put Away Your Teardrops .... 7" .... Decca .... F12058 .... 1965 .... **£4** ....
When She Comes To You .... 7" .... Pye .... 7N15656 .... 1964 .... **£5** ....

QUIVER

Quiver was quite brilliant live, playing tight, melodic rock music with a fire and a joy that easily communicated itself to the audiences. On record, however, the group sounded more like a poor man's Neil Young. Part of the band eventually amlgamated with the Sutherland Brothers, and all the members have been busy since - especially guitarist Tim Renwick, who is a familiar session name, and bass player Bruce Thomas, who became one of Elvis Costello's Attractions.

Gone In The Morning .... LP .... W. Bros .... K46153 .... 1972 ..... **£10** ....
Quiver .... LP .... W. Bros .... K46089 .... 1971 ..... **£10** ....

QUOTATIONS (UK)

Alright Baby .... 7" .... Decca .... F11907 .... 1964 ..... **£10** ....

QUOTATIONS (USA)

Imagination .... 7" .... HMV .... POP975 .... 1962 ..... **£10** ....

R

R.E.M.

Title	Format	Label	Cat. No.	Year	Price	Notes
Can't Get There From Here	12"	IRS	IRT102	1985	**£6**	
Chronic Town	mini LP	IRS		1982	**£12**	US, label with cover art
Femme Fatale	7"	The Bob		198-	**£15**	US, flexi, PS
It's The End Of The World As We	CD-s	IRS		1987	**£15**	promo
One I Love	CD-s	IRS	DIRM146	1987	**£6**	
Orange Crush	7"		W2960B	1989	**£5**	boxed with poster
Radio Free Europe	7"	Hib-Tone		1981	**£25**	US
Radio Free Europe	7"	IRS	PFD1017	1983	**£25**	
Rockville	7"	IRS	IRS107	1984	**£10**	
Rockville	12"	IRS	IRSX107	1984	**£10**	
So. Central Rain	7"	IRS	IRS105	1984	**£10**	
So. Central Rain	12"	IRS	IRSX105	1984	**£10**	
Talk About The Passion	7"	IRS	PFB1026	1983	**£10**	promo only
Talk About The Passion	12"	IRS	PFSX1026	1983	**£12**	
Tighten Up	7"	B. Of Brains	BOB5	1985	**£15**	flexi
Tighten Up	7"	B. Of Brains	BOB5	1985	**£50**	promo
Wendell Gee	7"	IRS	IRMD105	1985	**£8**	double
Wolves, Lower	7"	Trouser Press		1982	**£25**	US, flexi

RABBIT

Title	Format	Label	Cat. No.	Year	Price	Notes
Broken Arrows	LP	Island	ILPS9238	1973	**£10**	
Broken Arrows	7"	Island	WIP6161	1973	**£4**	
Dark Saloon	LP	Island	ILPS9289	1974	**£10**	

RABBLE

Title	Format	Label	Cat. No.	Year	Price	Notes
Rabble	LP	Roulette		1969	**£30**	US
Rabble Album	LP	Transworld	6700	1966	**£30**	US

RABIN, MIKE & THE DEMONS

Title	Format	Label	Cat. No.	Year	Price	Notes
Head Over Heels	7"	Columbia	DB7350	1964	**£8**	

RADCLIFFE, JIMMY

Title	Format	Label	Cat. No.	Year	Price	Notes
Long After Tonight Is All Over	7"	Stateside	SS374	1965	**£15**	chart single

RADHA KRISHNA TEMPLE

Title	Format	Label	Cat. No.	Year	Price	Notes
Govinda	7"	Apple	25	1970	**£6**	chart single
Govinda	7"	Apple	25	1970	**£15**	PS
Hare Krishna Mantra	7"	Apple	15	1969	**£4**	chart single
Hare Krishna Mantra	7"	Apple	15	1969	**£10**	PS
Radha Krishna Temple	LP	Apple	SAPCOR18	1971	**£20**	

RADIANTS

Title	Format	Label	Cat. No.	Year	Price	Notes
Hold On	7"	Chess	CRS8073	1968	**£4**	
Voice Your Choice	7"	Chess	CRS8002	1965	**£4**	

RADIATORS FROM SPACE

Title	Format	Label	Cat. No.	Year	Price	Notes
Dancing Years	7"	Chiswick	CHIS133	1980	**£4**	
Enemies	7"	Chiswick	NS19	1977	**£6**	
Enemies	7"	Chiswick	SW57	1979	**£5**	
Ghostown	LP	Chiswick	CWK3003	1979	**£10**	
Kitty Ricketts	7"	Chiswick	CHIS115	1979	**£4**	
Let's Talk About The Weather	7"	Chiswick	CHIS113/NS45	1979	**£4**	
Million Dollar Hero	7"	Chiswick	CHIS106/NS29	1978	**£5**	
Stranger Than Fiction	7"	Chiswick	CHIS126	1980	**£4**	
Teenager In Love	7"	Chiswick	NS24	1978	**£5**	
Television Screen	7"	Chiswick	NS10	1977	**£6**	
TV Tube Heart	LP	Chiswick	WIK4	1977	**£12**	

RADIO BIRDMAN

Title	Format	Label	Cat. No.	Year	Price	Notes
Aloha Steve And Danno	7"	Trafalgar	TRS12	1978	**£10**	
Alone In The Endzone	7"	WEA	100160	1981	**£50**	

Burn My Eye	7"	Trafalgar	ME109	1976	**£100**	
Living Eyes	LP	WEA	600085	1981	**£15**	
New Race	7"	Trafalgar	TRS11	1977	**£50**	
Radios Appear	LP	Sire	9103332	1978	**£20**	
Radios Appear (Second Version)	LP	Sire	6050	1978	**£20**	
What Gives?	7"	Sire	6078617	1978	**£10**	

RADIO HEART

London Times	7"	GFM	GFMP112	1987	**£4**	pic disc
London Times	7"	GFM	GFMX112	1987	**£4**	shaped pic disc
Radio Heart	7"	GFM	GFMP109	1987	**£4**	pic disc
Radio Heart	7"	GFM	GFMR109	1987	**£4**	3 tracks
Radio Heart	7"	GFM	GFMX109	1987	**£5**	shaped pic disc
Radio Heart	LP	NBR	NBRLPX1	1987	**£10**	pic disc

RADIO STARS

Dirty Pictures	7"	Chiswick	NS9	1977	**£12**	
From A Rabbit	7"	Chiswick	NS36	1978	**£4**	
From A Rabbit	6'	Chiswick	NS366	1978	**£5**	
Holiday Album	LP	Chiswick	CWK3001	1978	**£12**	
Nervous Wreck	7"	Chiswick	NS23	1977	**£4**	
Nervous Wreck	12"	Chiswick	NS23	1977	**£6**	
No Russians In Russia	7"	Chiswick	PROMO2	1977	**£4**	
Radio Stars	7"	Chiswick	CHIS103	1978	**£4**	
Real Me	7"	Chiswick	CHIS109	1979	**£4**	
Songs For Swinging Lovers	LP	Chiswick	CWK3005	1978	**£10**	
Songs For Swinging Lovers	LP	Chiswick	WIK5	1977	**£12**	
Stop It!	7"	Chiswick	SW17	1977	**£4**	

RAEBURN, BOYD

Teen Rock	LP	Columbia	CL1073	1957	**£20**	US

RAELETS

One Hurt Deserves Another	7"	HMV	POP1591	1967	**£4**	

RAFFERTY, GERRY

City To City	LP	Mobile Fid.	MFSL1058	1980	**£10**	US audiophile

RAGING STORMS

Dribble	7"	London	HLU9556	1962	**£4**	

RAGLAND, LOU

Since You Said You'd Be Mine	7"	W. Bros	K16312	1973	**£4**	

RAINBOW

Can't Let You Go	7"	Polydor	POSPP654	1983	**£5**	shaped pic disc
Down To Earth	LP	Polydor	POLD5023	1979	**£10**	clear vinyl
Kill The King	7"	Oyster	2066845	1977	**£4**	chart single
L.A.Connection	7"	Polydor	2066968	1978	**£5**	red vinyl
Long Live Rock'n'Roll	7"	Polydor	2066913	1978	**£4**	chart single
Man On The Silver Mountain	7"	Oyster	OYR103	1974	**£4**	
Street Of Dreams	7"	Polydor	POSPP631	1983	**£8**	pic disc
Street Of Dreams	12"	Polydor	POSPX631	1983	**£6**	

RAINBOW FFOLLY

Drive My Car	7"	Parlophone	R5701	1968	**£20**	
Sallies Forth	LP	Parlophone	PCS7050	1967	**£100**	

RAINBOW PEOPLE

Living In A Dream World	7"	Pye	7N17582	1968	**£10**	

RAINCHECKS

How Are You Baby	7"	R&B	MRB5002	1965	**£15**	

RAINCOATS

Fairytale In The Supermarket	7"	Rough Trade	RT013	1979	**£4**	
Raincoats	LP	Rough Trade	ROUGH3	1979	**£10**	

RAINDROPS

Kind Of Boy You Can't Forget	7"	London	HL9769	1963	**£5**	
Raindrops	LP	London	HA8140	1964	**£20**	
That Boy John	7"	London	HL9825	1964	**£5**	

What A Guy	7"	London	HL9718	1963	**£5**	
What A Guy	7" EP	London	RE1415	1964	**£10**	

RAINDROPS (2)

Along Came Jones	7"	Parlophone	R4559	1959	**£4**	
Banjo Boy	7"	Oriole	CB1555	1960	**£4**	
Book Of Love	7"	Fontana	TF463	1964	**£4**	
If I Had My Life To Live Over	7"	Oriole	CB1544	1960	**£4**	
Will You Love Me Tomorrow	7"	Oriole	CB1595	1961	**£4**	

RAINE, LORRY

Love Me Tonight	7"	London	HL8132	1955	**£8**	
You Broke My Broken Heart	7"	London	HL8043	1954	**£8**	

RAINEY, MA & TRIXIE SMITH

Female Blues Vol.3	7" EP	Collector	JE122	196-	**£5**	

RAINWATER, MARVIN

Country And Western Favourites Vol.2	7" EP	Ember	EMB4521	1962	**£5**	
Dance Me Daddy	7"	MGM	MGM988	1958	**£4**	
Gonna Find Me A Bluebird	LP	MGM	E4046	1962	**£25**	US
Gonna Find Me A Bluebird	7"	MGM	MGM961	1957	**£10**	
Half Breed	7"	MGM	MGM1030	1959	**£4**	
I Can't Forget	7"	London	HLU9447	1961	**£15**	
I Dig You Baby	7"	MGM	MGM980	1958	**£4**	chart single
Marvin Rainwater	7" EP	MGM	MGMEP685	1958	**£8**	
Meet Marvin Rainwater	7" EP	MGM	MGMEP647	1958	**£10**	
Nothin' Needs Nothin'	7"	MGM	MGM1052	1960	**£4**	
Songs By Marvin Rainwater	LP	MGM	E3534	1957	**£30**	US
Songs By Marvin Rainwater...	LP-10"	MGM	D152	1957	**£15**	
Tennessee Hound Dog Yodel	7"	MGM	SP1150	1955	**£15**	
What Am I Supposed To Do	7"	MGM	MGM929	1956	**£8**	
Whole Lotta Marvin	7" EP	MGM	MGMEP662	1958	**£8**	
Whole Lotta Woman	7"	MGM	MGM974	1958	**£6**	chart single
With A Heart, With A Beat	LP	MGM	E3721	1958	**£30**	US

RAINWATER, MARVIN & CONNIE FRANCIS

Majesty Of Love	7"	MGM	MGM969	1957	**£6**	

RAINY DAZE

Autumn Leaves	7"	CBS	3200	1967	**£10**	
That Acapulco Gold	7"	Polydor	56731	1968	**£8**	

RAISINS

Ain't That Lovin' You Baby	7"	Major Minor	MM540	1968	**£15**	
I Thank You	7"	Major Minor	MM602	1969	**£10**	

RAM

Where? In Conclusion	LP	Polydor		1972	**£20**	US

RAM JAM BAND

Shake Shake Senora	7"	Columbia	DB7621	1965	**£8**	

RAM, BUCK

Magic Touch	LP	Mercury	MG20392	1960	**£10**	US

RAMASES

Glass Top Coffin	LP	Vertigo	6360115	1975	**£12**	
Space Hymns	LP	Vertigo	6360046	1971	**£20**	spiral label

RAMATAM

Ramatam represented a rare attempt on the part of Mitch Mitchell to continue a career in rock music after the death of his former employer, Jimi Hendrix. The group also included Mike Pinera, from Iron Butterfly, and a rather fine lady guitarist called April Lawton. Unfortunately, the group's music was worthy but rather unspectacular, and Ramatam folded after just two albums.

In April Came The Dawning	LP	Atlantic	SD7261	1973	**£10**	US
Ramatam	LP	Atlantic	K40415	1972	**£10**	

RAMBLERS

Dodge City	7"	Decca	F11775	1963	**£10**	

RAMONES

Baby I Love You	cass-s	Sire		1981	**£5**	

Title	Format	Label	Number	Year	Price	Notes
Blitzkrieg Bop	7"	Sire	6078601	1976	**£50**	picture sleeve
Do You Wanna Dance?	7"	Sire	6078615	1978	**£5**	
Don't Come Close	7"	Sire	SRE1031	1978	**£6**	yellow vinyl
Don't Come Close	12"	Sire	SRE1031	1978	**£6**	yellow & red vinyl
I Remember You	7"	Sire	6078603	1977	**£8**	
Ramones Leave Home	LP	Sire	9103254	1977	**£10**	with 'Carbona Not Glue'
Road To Ruin	7"	Sire	PROMO1	1978	**£8**	promo sampler
Rockaway Beach	7"	Sire	6078611	1977	**£6**	
Rockaway Beach	12"	Sire	6078611	1977	**£6**	with poster
Sheena Is A Punk Rocker	7"	Sire	6078606	1977	**£6**	
Sheena Is A Punk Rocker	12"	Sire	6078606	1977	**£8**	
Swallow My Pride	7"	Sire	6078607	1977	**£6**	
Time Has Come Today	7"	Sire	W9606	1983	**£12**	
Time Has Come Today	12"	Sire	WT9606	1983	**£12**	

RAMRODS

Title	Format	Label	Number	Year	Price	Notes
Loch Lomond Rock	7"	London	HLU9355	1961	**£4**	
Overdrive	7"	United Artists	UP1113	1965	**£4**	
Riders In The Sky	7"	London	HLU9282	1961	**£4**	chart single
Riders In The Sky	7" EP	London	REU1292	1961	**£8**	

RANCHERS

Title	Format	Label	Number	Year	Price	Notes
American Sailor At The Cavern	7"	Cavern Sound	IMSTL2	1965	**£8**	

RANDALL, ELLIOTT

Title	Format	Label	Number	Year	Price	Notes
Randall's Island	LP	Polydor	2489004	1970	**£10**	

RANDELL, LYNNE

Title	Format	Label	Number	Year	Price	Notes
Ciao Baby	7"	CBS	2847	1967	**£60**	

RANDELLS

Title	Format	Label	Number	Year	Price	Notes
Martian Hop	7"	London	HLU9760	1963	**£6**	

RANDOLPH, BARBARA

Title	Format	Label	Number	Year	Price	Notes
I Got A Feeling	7"	T. Motown	TMG628	1967	**£8**	
I Got A Feeling	7"	T. Motown	TMG628	1967	**£40**	demo
I Got A Feeling	7"	T. Motown	TMG788	1971	**£4**	
I Got A Feeling	7"	T. Motown	TMG788	1971	**£10**	demo

RANDOLPH, BOOTS

Title	Format	Label	Number	Year	Price	Notes
Boots With Strings	LP	Monument	5003	1966	**£10**	
Fantastic Boots Randolph	LP	Monument	5012	1966	**£10**	
Hey Mr.Sax Man	7"	London	HLU9891	1964	**£4**	
Hip Boots	LP	Monument	5002	1966	**£10**	
More Yakety Sax	LP	Monument	18037	1965	**£10**	US
Saxsational	LP	Monument	5022	1967	**£10**	
Shadow Of Your Smile	7"	Monument	MON1001	1967	**£4**	
These Boots Were Made For Walking	7"	London	HLU10028	1966	**£4**	
Yakety Sax	LP	London	HAU8106	1963	**£10**	
Yakety Sax	7"	London	HLU9685	1963	**£4**	
Yakety Sax Of Boots Randolph	7" EP	London	REU1365	1963	**£5**	

RANDY & THE RAINBOWS

Title	Format	Label	Number	Year	Price	Notes
Denise	7"	Stateside	SS214	1963	**£10**	

RANDY PIE

Title	Format	Label	Number	Year	Price	Notes
Sightseeing Tour	LP	Polydor	2349491	1974	**£10**	

RANEY, WAYNE

Title	Format	Label	Number	Year	Price	Notes
Country And Western	7" EP	Parlophone	GEP8746	1958	**£6**	

RANGLIN, ERNEST

Title	Format	Label	Number	Year	Price	Notes
Reflections	LP	Island	ILP915	1964	**£40**	
Soho	7" EP	Black Swan	IEP704	1966	**£10**	
Wranglin'	LP	Island	ILP909	1964	**£40**	

RANSOME, PETER

Title	Format	Label	Number	Year	Price	Notes
Peter Ransome	LP	York		1972	**£12**	

RAPED

Title	Format	Label	Number	Year	Price	Notes
Cheap Night Out	7"	Parole	PURL1	1978	**£4**	
Raped	7"	Parole	KNIT1	1978	**£6**	

RAPKIN, BRIAN & KELVIN JONES

Title	Format	Label	Number	Year	Price	Notes
Dreams Of The Blue Beast	LP	MSR		197-	**£30**	

RAPP, TOM

Title	Format	Label	Number	Year	Price	Notes
Stardancer	LP	Blue Thumb	BTS44	1972	**£15**	US
Sunforest	LP	Blue Thumb	BTS56	1973	**£15**	US
Tom Rapp	LP	Reprise	MS2069	1972	**£15**	US

RARE AMBER

Title	Format	Label	Number	Year	Price	Notes
Malfunction Of The Engine	7"	Polydor	56309	1969	**£8**	
Rare Amber	LP	Polydor	583046	1969	**£50**	

RARE BIRD

Title	Format	Label	Number	Year	Price	Notes
As Your Mind Flies By	LP	Charisma	CAS1011	1970	**£15**	
Body And Soul	7"	Polydor	2058471	1974	**£4**	
Born Again	LP	Polydor	2383274	1974	**£10**	
Don't Be Afraid	7"	Polydor	2058591	1975	**£4**	
Epic Forest	LP	Polydor	2442101	1972	**£20**	with 7"
Rare Bird	LP	Charisma	CAS1005	1969	**£15**	
Rare Bird	LP	Polygram	9299008	1975	**£10**	
Roadside Welcome	7"	Polydor	2814011	197-	**£4**	
Somebody's Watching	LP	Polydor	2383211	1973	**£10**	
Sympathy	7"	Charisma	CB120	1970	**£4**	chart single
Sympathy	7"	Charisma	CB179	1972	**£4**	PS
Virginia	7"	Polydor	2058402	1973	**£4**	
What You Want To Know	7"	Charisma	CB138	1971	**£6**	

RARE BREED

Title	Format	Label	Number	Year	Price	Notes
Beg Borrow And Steal	7"	Strike	JH316	1966	**£10**	

RARE EARTH

Title	Format	Label	Number	Year	Price	Notes
Dream Answers	LP	Verve	5056	1968	**£10**	US
Ecology	LP	T. Motown	STML11180	1971	**£10**	
Get Ready	LP	T. Motown	STML11165	1970	**£10**	
Get Ready	7"	T. Motown	TMG742	1970	**£6**	
Get Ready	7"	T. Motown	TMG742	1970	**£15**	demo
In Concert	LP	Rare Earth	301	1972	**£10**	
In Concert	LP	Rare Earth	SRESP301	1972	**£10**	
Ma	LP	Rare Earth	3010	1973	**£10**	
One World	LP	Rare Earth	4001	1971	**£10**	
Willie Remembers	LP	Rare Earth	3008	1973	**£10**	

RASCALS

Title	Format	Label	Number	Year	Price	Notes
Beautiful Morning	7"	Atlantic	584182	1968	**£4**	
Carry Me Back	7"	Atlantic	584292	1969	**£4**	
Collection	LP	Atlantic	587060	1967	**£12**	
Come On Up	7"	Atlantic	584050	1966	**£4**	
Freedom Suite	LP	Atlantic	588183	1969	**£10**	
Freedom Suite Narration	LP	Atlantic		1969	**£15**	US promo
Girl Like You	7"	Atlantic	584128	1967	**£4**	chart single
Glory Glory	7"	Atlantic	2091029	1970	**£4**	
Good Lovin'	7"	Atlantic	AT4082	1966	**£5**	
Greatest Hits	LP	Atlantic	587120	1968	**£10**	
Groovin'	LP	Atlantic	587074	1967	**£12**	
Groovin'	7"	Atlantic	584111	1967	**£4**	chart single
Heaven	7"	Atlantic	584255	1969	**£4**	
Hold On	7"	Atlantic	584307	1970	**£4**	
How Can I Be Sure	7"	Atlantic	584138	1967	**£4**	
I Ain't Gonna Eat Out My Heart	7"	Atlantic	584085	1967	**£4**	
I Ain't Gonna Eat Out My Heart	7"	Atlantic	AT4059	1965	**£5**	
I've Been Lonely Too Long	7"	Atlantic	584081	1967	**£4**	
Island Of Real	LP	CBS	64756	1972	**£10**	
It's Wonderful	7"	Atlantic	584161	1968	**£4**	
Love Is A Beautiful Thing	7"	Atlantic	584024	1966	**£4**	
Once Upon A Dream	LP	Atlantic	587098	1968	**£10**	
Peaceful World	LP	CBS	66292	1971	**£10**	
People Got To Be Free	7"	Atlantic	584210	1968	**£4**	
Search And Nearness	LP	Atlantic	2400113	1971	**£10**	
See	LP	Atlantic	588210	1969	**£10**	
See	7"	Atlantic	584274	1969	**£4**	
Sentirai La Pioggla	7"	Atlantic	NP3124	1968	**£8**	sung in Italian

Too Many Fish In The Sea	7"	Atlantic	584067	1966	**£4**	
Young Rascals	LP	Atlantic	587012	1966	**£12**	

RASPBERRIES

Fresh	LP	Capitol	ST11123	1972	**£12**	US
Go All The Way	7"	Capitol	CL15730	1972	**£4**	
I Don't Want To Say Goodbye	7"	Capitol	CL15718	1972	**£4**	
I Wanna Be With You	7"	Capitol	CL15740	1973	**£4**	
Overnight Sensation	7"	Capitol	CL15801	1974	**£4**	
Raspberries	LP	Capitol	ST11036	1972	**£12**	US
Side Three	LP	Capitol	SMAS11220	1973	**£12**	US
Starting Over	LP	Capitol	ST11329	1974	**£10**	US

RAT & THE WHALE

Wheels On Fire	7"	Rewind	REWIND5	1980	**£4**	

RATIP, ARMAN

Spy From Istanbul	LP	Regal Z.		1973	**£10**	

RATS

The Rats, whose recording career had begun and ended a little earlier, were the group taken on by David Bowie and renamed The Spiders From Mars. Both Mick Ronson and Woody Woodmansey play on the singles.

Every Day I Have The Blues	7"	Oriole	CB1967	1964	**£35**	
I Gotta See My Baby	7"	Columbia	DB7607	1965	**£30**	
Sack Of Woe	7"	CBS	201740	1965	**£25**	
Spoonful	7"	Columbia	DB7483	1965	**£25**	

RATTLES

Bye Bye Johnny	7"	Decca	F11873	1964	**£8**	
Come On And Sing	7"	Fontana	TF618	1965	**£6**	
Greatest Hits	LP	Mercury	MG21127	1967	**£30**	US
Rattles	LP	Decca	SKL5080	1971	**£20**	
Say All Right	7"	Fontana	TF724	1966	**£6**	
Stomp	7"	Philips	BF1277	1963	**£6**	
Teenbeat From the Star Club Hamburg	7" EP	Decca	DFE8568	1964	**£8**	
Tell Me What Can I Do	7"	Decca	F11936	1964	**£8**	
Twist At The Star Club	LP	Philips	BL7614	1964	**£75**	
Witch	7"	Decca	F23058	1970	**£4**	chart single
You Can't Have Sunshine Every Day	7"	Decca	F23119	1971	**£4**	

RAVAN, GENYA

Genya Ravan With Baby	LP	CBS	64872	1972	**£10**	

RAVEL, CHRIS & THE RAVERS

Chris Ravel was Chris Andrews, later a moderately successful solo artist and a more successful songwriter and producer - most notably for Sandie Shaw.

Don't You Dig This Kind Of Beat	7"	Decca	F11696	1963	**£8**	

RAVEN

Children At Our Feet	7"	CBS	5043	1970	**£5**	
Live At The Inferno	LP	Discovery	36133	196-	**£15**	US
Raven	LP	Columbia	9903	1969	**£15**	US

RAVEN, MIKE

Mike Raven was a disc jockey on pirate radio and then on Radio One. He used to present a specialist programme of soul and blues and the two LPs listed here are to some extent re-creations of the blues part. The "Blues Show" provides a necessarily brief, but effective history of the blues. Mike Raven introduces each track and his comments are relevant enough - and his voice soothing enough - to prevent the introductions becoming irritating on successive hearings. The "Blues Sampler" is similar, but attempts to show the range of blues styles rather than following a historical approach.

Mike Raven Blues Sampler	LP	Transatlantic	TRASAM5	1969	**£10**	
Mike Raven Blues Show	LP	XTRA	XTRA1047	1966	**£10**	

RAVEN, PAUL

Musical Man	7"	MCA	MU1024	1968	**£10**	
Paul Raven	7" EP	EMI	NUT2855	1978	**£4**	
Soul Thing	7"	MCA	MU1035	1968	**£10**	
Stand	7"	MCA	MKS5053	1970	**£8**	
Too Proud	7"	Decca	F11202	1960	**£20**	
Tower Of Strength	7"	Parlophone	R4842	1961	**£12**	
Walk On Boy	7"	Parlophone	R4812	1961	**£12**	

RAVENS

Title	Format	Label	Number	Year	Price	Notes
Career Girl	7"	Pye	7N25077	1961	**£4**	
I Just Wanna Hear You Say	7"	Oriole	CB1910	1964	**£4**	
Write Me A Letter	LP	Regent	MG6062	195-	**£50**	US

RAW HOLLY

Title	Format	Label	Number	Year	Price	Notes
Raw Holly	LP	Coral	757515	1971	**£15**	US

RAW MATERIAL

Title	Format	Label	Number	Year	Price	Notes
Raw Material Album	LP	Evolution	Z1006	1970	**£150**	
Time And Illusion	7"	Evolution	E2441	1969	**£30**	
Time Is	LP	Neon	NE8	1971	**£100**	

RAWLS, LOU

Title	Format	Label	Number	Year	Price	Notes
I Don't Love You Anymore	7"	Capitol	CL15515	1967	**£4**	
Lost And Looking	7" EP	Capitol	EAP120646	1964	**£5**	
Soul Serenade	7"	Capitol	CL15548	1968	**£4**	
Yes It Hurts Doesn't It	7"	Capitol	CL15499	1967	**£4**	

RAY, JAMES

Title	Format	Label	Number	Year	Price	Notes
If You Gotta Make A Fool...	LP	Caprice	LP1002	1962	**£15**	US
If You Gotta Make A Fool...	7"	Pye	7N25126	1962	**£5**	
Itty Bitty Pieces	7"	Pye	7N25147	1962	**£4**	

RAY, RICARDO

Title	Format	Label	Number	Year	Price	Notes
Nitty Gritty	7"	Roulette	RO501	1967	**£5**	

RAY, WADE

Title	Format	Label	Number	Year	Price	Notes
Burning Desire	7"	London	HL9700	1963	**£4**	

RAYBURN, MARGIE

Title	Format	Label	Number	Year	Price	Notes
I Would	7"	London	HLU8648	1958	**£4**	
I'm Available	7"	London	HLU8515	1957	**£4**	

RAYE, SOL

Title	Format	Label	Number	Year	Price	Notes
While I'm Here	7"	Deram	DM154	1967	**£4**	

RAYNOR, MARTIN & THE SECRETS

Title	Format	Label	Number	Year	Price	Notes
Candy To Me	7"	Columbia	DB7563	1965	**£8**	

RAYNOR, MIKE

Title	Format	Label	Number	Year	Price	Notes
Is She A Woman Now	7"	Decca	F22690	1967	**£4**	
Ob La Di Ob La Da	7"	Decca	F22864	1969	**£4**	
Turn Your Head	7"	Decca	F12605	1967	**£5**	
Wonderful Day	7"	Decca	F22790	1968	**£4**	

RAYS

Title	Format	Label	Number	Year	Price	Notes
Silhouettes	7"	London	HLU8505	1957	**£15**	

RAZOR'S EDGE

Title	Format	Label	Number	Year	Price	Notes
Let's Call It A Day Girl	7"	Stateside	SS532	1966	**£5**	

REA, CHRIS

Title	Format	Label	Number	Year	Price	Notes
Excerpts From Bombollini	7"	Magnet	CHRIS2DJ	1984	**£6**	promo
Fool If You Think It's Over	7"	Magnet	CHRIS1DJ	1984	**£8**	promo
It's All Gone	cass-s	Magnet	ZCMAG283	1986	**£5**	
Josephine	7"	Magnet	MAG280AA	1985	**£8**	promo
So Much Love	7"	Magnet	MAG10	1974	**£4**	
Stainsby Girls	cass-s	Magnet	ZCMAG276	1985	**£5**	

REACTION

Title	Format	Label	Number	Year	Price	Notes
Oh Me Oh My	7"	Columbia	DB119	1970	**£8**	

READ, JILL

Title	Format	Label	Number	Year	Price	Notes
Maybe	7"	Parlophone		1969	**£10**	

READER, PAT

Title	Format	Label	Number	Year	Price	Notes
Ricky	7"	Triumph	RGM1024	1960	**£10**	

READING, BEATRICE

Title	Format	Label	Number	Year	Price	Notes
Rock Baby Rock	7"	Parlophone	R4462	1958	**£8**	

REALLY RED

Title	Format	Label	Cat. No.	Year	Price	Notes
Crowd Control	7"	CIA	CIA001	1979	**£40**	
Despise Moral Majority	7"	CIA	CIA003	1981	**£40**	
Modern Needs	7"	CIA	CIA002	1980	**£40**	
Teaching You The Fear	LP	CIA	CIA006	1981	**£50**	

REALM

Title	Format	Label	Cat. No.	Year	Price	Notes
Hard Time Loving You	7"	CBS	202044	1966	**£15**	

REBEL ROUSERS

Title	Format	Label	Cat. No.	Year	Price	Notes
Should I	7"	Fontana	TF973	1968	**£5**	

REBIRTH

Title	Format	Label	Cat. No.	Year	Price	Notes
Rebirth	LP	Avantgarde		1968	**£40**	US

REBOUNDS

Title	Format	Label	Cat. No.	Year	Price	Notes
Help Me	7"	Fontana	TF461	1964	**£10**	

REBS

Title	Format	Label	Cat. No.	Year	Price	Notes
Bunky	7"	Capitol	CL14932	1958	**£4**	

RECO, EZO & THE LAUNCHERS

Title	Format	Label	Cat. No.	Year	Price	Notes
Jamaica Blue Beat	7" EP	Columbia	SEG8326	1964	**£6**	
King Of Kings	7"	Columbia	DB7217	1964	**£8**	chart single
Little Girl	7"	Columbia	DB7222	1964	**£6**	
Please Come Back	7"	Columbia	DB7290	1964	**£10**	

RED CRAYOLA

Title	Format	Label	Cat. No.	Year	Price	Notes
God Bless The Red Crayola	LP	Int. Artists	IALP7	1968	**£20**	US
Hurricane Fighter Plane	7"	Zigzag		197-	**£4**	flexi, B side by 13th Floor Elevators
Parable Of Arable Land	LP	Int. Artists	IALP2	1967	**£45**	US mono
Parable Of Arable Land	LP	Int. Artists	IALP2	1967	**£25**	US stereo
Wives In Orbit	7"	Radar	ADA22	1978	**£5**	red vinyl

RED DIRT

Title	Format	Label	Cat. No.	Year	Price	Notes
Red Dirt	LP	Fontana		1970	**£250**	

RED HOT CHILI PEPPERS

Title	Format	Label	Cat. No.	Year	Price	Notes
Fight Like A Brave	12"	EMI	12EA241	1988	**£6**	
Fight Like A Brave	12"	EMI	12EAP241	1988	**£15**	pic disc
Hollywood (Africa)	7"	EMI	EA205	1985	**£6**	
Hollywood (Africa)	12"	EMI	12EA205	1985	**£10**	
Knock Me Down	7"	EMI	MTPD70	1989	**£8**	pic disc

RED SQUARES

Title	Format	Label	Cat. No.	Year	Price	Notes
Mountain's High	7"	Columbia	DB8160	1967	**£8**	
True Love Story	7"	Columbia	DB8247	1967	**£6**	

RED TELEVISION

Title	Format	Label	Cat. No.	Year	Price	Notes
Red Television	LP	Brecht Times			**£220**	

REDBONE

Title	Format	Label	Cat. No.	Year	Price	Notes
Potlatch	LP	CBS	64198	1971	**£10**	
Redbone	LP	CBS	64069	1970	**£10**	
Witch Queen Of New Orleans	LP	Epic	64709	1971	**£10**	

REDCAPS

Title	Format	Label	Cat. No.	Year	Price	Notes
Mighty Fine Girl	7"	Decca	F11903	1964	**£8**	
Shout	7"	Decca	F11716	1963	**£8**	
Talking About You	7"	Decca	F11789	1963	**£10**	

REDDING, OTIS

Title	Format	Label	Cat. No.	Year	Price	Notes
Champagne And Wine	7"	Atlantic	584220	1968	**£4**	
Come To Me	7"	London	HLK9876	1964	**£8**	
Daytripper	7"	Stax	601005	1967	**£4**	chart single
Dictionary Of Soul	LP	Atlantic	587050	1967	**£20**	chart LP
Dock Of The Bay	LP	Atco	228022	1969	**£12**	
Dock Of The Bay	LP	Stax	231001	1968	**£15**	chart LP
Dock Of The Bay	7"	Stax	601031	1968	**£4**	chart single
Early Otis Redding	7" EP	Sue	IEP710	1966	**£20**	
Fa Fa Fa Fa Fa Song	7"	Atlantic	584049	1966	**£5**	chart single

Title	Format	Label	Number	Year	Price	Notes
Free Me	7"	Atco	226002	1969	**£4**	
Gettin' Hip	7"	Evolution	E2442	1969	**£5**	
Glory Of Love	7"	Stax	601017	1967	**£5**	
Happy Song	7"	Stax	601040	1968	**£4**	chart single
Hard To Handle	7"	Atlantic	584199	1968	**£4**	chart single
History Of Otis Redding	LP	Atco	228001	1969	**£12**	
History Of Otis Redding	LP	Volt	418	1968	**£15**	chart LP
I Can't Turn You Loose	7"	Atlantic	584030	1966	**£5**	chart single
I've Been Loving You Too Long	7"	Atlantic	AT4029	1965	**£30**	demo only
Immortal Otis Redding	LP	Atlantic	587113	1968	**£15**	chart LP
In Person At The Whiskey	LP	Atlantic	587148	1968	**£15**	
Let Me Come On Home	7"	Stax	601007	1967	**£4**	chart single
Live In Europe	LP	Atco	228017	1969	**£12**	
Live In Europe	LP	Stax	589016	1968	**£15**	chart LP
Look At The Girl	7"	Atco	226012	1970	**£4**	
Love Man	LP	Atco	228025	1969	**£15**	
Love Man	7"	Atco	226001	1969	**£4**	chart single
Lover's Question	7"	Atlantic	584249	1969	**£4**	
Mr.Pitiful	7"	Atlantic	AT4024	1965	**£8**	
My Girl	7"	Atlantic	584092	1967	**£4**	chart single
My Girl	7"	Atlantic	AT4050	1965	**£5**	chart single
My Lover's Prayer	7"	Atlantic	584019	1966	**£5**	chart single
Otis Blue	LP	Atlantic	587036	1966	**£15**	chart LP
Otis Blue	LP	Atlantic	ATL5041	1966	**£20**	chart LP
Pain In My Heart	LP	Atco	SD33161	1964	**£20**	US
Pain In My Heart	LP	Atlantic	587042	1967	**£20**	chart LP
Pain In My Heart	7"	London	HLK9833	1964	**£8**	
Papa's Got A Brand New Bag	7"	Atlantic	584234	1968	**£4**	
Remembering	LP	Atlantic	2464003	1970	**£10**	
Respect	7"	Atlantic	584091	1967	**£4**	
Respect	7"	Atlantic	AT4039	1965	**£5**	
Satisfaction	7"	Atlantic	AT4080	1966	**£5**	chart single
Satisfaction	7"	Stax	601027	1967	**£4**	
Shake	7"	Stax	601011	1967	**£5**	chart single
She's Alright	7"	Pye	7N25463	1968	**£5**	
Shout Bamalama	7"	Sue	WI362	1965	**£15**	
Sings Soul Ballads	LP	Atlantic	587035	1966	**£15**	
Sings Soul Ballads	LP	Atlantic	ATL5029	1965	**£20**	chart LP
Soul Album	LP	Atlantic	587011	1966	**£15**	chart LP
Tell The Truth	LP	Atco	2400018	1971	**£15**	
Try A Little Tenderness	7"	Atlantic	584070	1967	**£5**	chart single
Wonderful World	7"	Atlantic	2091020	1970	**£4**	

REDDING, OTIS & CARLA THOMAS

Title	Format	Label	Number	Year	Price	Notes
King And Queen	LP	Atlantic	589007	1967	**£20**	chart LP
Knock On Wood	7"	Stax	601021	1967	**£4**	chart single
Lovey Dovey	7"	Stax	601033	1968	**£4**	
Tramp	7"	Stax	601012	1967	**£4**	chart single

REDELL, TEDDY

Title	Format	Label	Number	Year	Price	Notes
Judy	7"	London	HLK9140	1960	**£8**	

REDMOND, ROY

Title	Format	Label	Number	Year	Price	Notes
Good Day Sunshine	7"	W. Bros	WB2075	1967	**£4**	

REDWING

Title	Format	Label	Number	Year	Price	Notes
Redwing	LP	United Artists	UAS29188	1971	**£10**	

REDWOODS

Title	Format	Label	Number	Year	Price	Notes
Please Mister Scientist	7"	Columbia	DB4859	1962	**£8**	

REED, CHUCK

Title	Format	Label	Number	Year	Price	Notes
Let's Put Our Hearts Together	7"	Columbia	DB4113	1958	**£5**	

REED, DENNY

Title	Format	Label	Number	Year	Price	Notes
Teenager Feels It Too	7"	London	HLK9274	1961	**£4**	

REED, JERRY

Title	Format	Label	Number	Year	Price	Notes
Bessie Baby	7"	Capitol	CL14851	1958	**£25**	

REED, JIMMY

Title	Format	Label	Number	Year	Price	Notes
At Carnegie Hall	LP	Stateside	SL10012	1962	**£20**	

Title	Format	Label	Cat. No.	Year	Price	Notes
At Soul City	LP	Vee Jay	LP1095	1964	**£15**	US
Baby What You Want Me To Do	7"	Top Rank	JAR333	1960	**£6**	
Best Of...	LP	Vee Jay	LP1039	1962	**£15**	US
Big Boss Man	LP	BluesWay	BLS6013	1968	**£12**	US
Blues Of Jimmy Reed	7" EP	Stateside	SE1016	1964	**£8**	
Boss Man Of The Blues	LP	Stateside	SL10091	1964	**£15**	
Down In Virginia	LP	Action	ACLP6011	1969	**£15**	
Found Love	7"	Top Rank	JAR394	1960	**£4**	
Found Love	LP	Vee Jay	LP1022	1960	**£20**	US
Hush Hush	7"	Top Rank	JAR533	1961	**£5**	
I'm Jimmy Reed	7" EP	Stateside	SE1026	1964	**£8**	
I'm Jimmy Reed	LP	Vee Jay	LP1004	1958	**£50**	US
Just Jimmy Reed	LP	Stateside	SL10055	1964	**£20**	
Legend, The Man	LP	Vee Jay	VJ8501	1965	**£15**	US
More Of The Best Of...	LP	Vee Jay	LP1080	1964	**£15**	US
New Jimmy Reed	LP	HMV	CLP3611		**£15**	
Now Appearing	LP	Vee Jay	LP1025	1960	**£20**	US
Odds And Ends	7"	Sue	WI4004	1966	**£8**	
Plays 12 String Guitar Blues	LP	Stateside	SL10086	1964	**£15**	
Rockin' With Reed	LP	Vee Jay	LP1008	1959	**£40**	US
Shame Shame Shame	7"	Stateside	SS205	1963	**£5**	
Shame Shame Shame	7"	Stateside	SS330	1964	**£4**	chart single
Sings The Best Of The Blues	LP	Stateside	SL10069	1964	**£15**	
Soulin'	LP	Stateside	SL10221	1968	**£15**	
T'Ain't No Big Thing	LP	Vee Jay	LP1067	1963	**£15**	US
Two Ways To Skin A Cat	7"	HMV	POP1579	1967	**£8**	

REED, JIMMY & EDDIE TAYLOR

Title	Format	Label	Cat. No.	Year	Price	Notes
Jimmy Reed & Eddie Taylor	7" EP	XX	MIN704		**£4**	

REED, LOU

Title	Format	Label	Cat. No.	Year	Price	Notes
Blue Mask	LP	RCA	DJL14266	1981	**£12**	US interview promo
Caroline Says	7"	RCA	APBO221	1974	**£4**	
Lou Reed	LP	RCA	SF8281	1972	**£10**	
Metal Machine Music	LP	RCA	CPD21101	1975	**£35**	US quad
Metal Machine Music	LP	RCA	CPL21101	1975	**£30**	
No Money Down	12"	RCA		1986	**£10**	promo, green vinyl
Nowhere At All	7"	RCA	PB9135		**£10**	French, 1 sided
Sally Can't Dance	7"	RCA	RCA2467	1974	**£4**	
Sweet Jane	7"	RCA	APBO238	1974	**£4**	
Vicious	7"	RCA	RCA2318	1973	**£4**	
Walk And Talk It	7"	RCA	RCA2240	1972	**£4**	
Walk On The Wild Side	7"	RCA	RCA2303	1972	**£5**	demo

REED, LULU

Title	Format	Label	Cat. No.	Year	Price	Notes
Blue And Moody	LP	King	604	1959	**£180**	US

REED, LULU & FREDDY KING

Title	Format	Label	Cat. No.	Year	Price	Notes
Lulu Reed And Freddy King	7" EP	Ember	EMB4536	1963	**£10**	

REED, LULU & SYL JOHNSON

Title	Format	Label	Cat. No.	Year	Price	Notes
Lulu Reed And Syl Johnson	7" EP	Ember	EMB4535	1963	**£10**	

REED, MARTIN WYNDHAM

Title	Format	Label	Cat. No.	Year	Price	Notes
Harry The Hawker Is Dead	LP	Argo		1972	**£30**	
Ned Kelly And That Gang	LP	Trailer		1970	**£15**	

REED, TAWNY

Title	Format	Label	Cat. No.	Year	Price	Notes
Needle In A Haystack	7"	Pye	7N15935	1965	**£4**	
You Can't Take It Away	7"	Pye	7N17078	1966	**£5**	

REESE, DELLA

Title	Format	Label	Cat. No.	Year	Price	Notes
Home	7"	HMV	POP1504	1966	**£6**	
It Wasn't A Very Good Year	7"	HMV	POP1553	1966	**£5**	

REEVES, EDDIE

Title	Format	Label	Cat. No.	Year	Price	Notes
Cry Baby	7"	London	HL9548	1962	**£4**	

REEVES, JIM

Title	Format	Label	Cat. No.	Year	Price	Notes
Bimbo	LP	London	HAU8015	1962	**£15**	
Bimbo	7"	London	HL8014	1954	**£20**	
Bimbo Boy	7" EP	London	REP1015	1954	**£25**	

Title	Format	Label	Cat. No.	Year	Price	Notes
Bimbo Vol.2	7" EP	London	REP1033	1955	**£20**	
Butterfly Love	7"	London	HL8055	1954	**£20**	
Drinking Tequila	7"	London	HL8159	1955	**£15**	
Echo Bonita	7"	London	HL8064	1954	**£20**	
Four Walls	7"	RCA	RCA1005	1957	**£4**	
Girls I Have Known	LP	RCA	LPM1685	1958	**£20**	US
God Be With You	LP	RCA	LPM1950	1958	**£15**	US
He'll Have To Go	LP	RCA	LPM2223	1960	**£10**	US
Intimate Jim Reeves	LP	RCA	LPM2216	1960	**£10**	US
Jim Reeves	LP	RCA	LPM1576	1957	**£25**	US
Jim Reeves Sings	LP	Abbott	LP5001	1956	**£350**	US
Jimbo	LP	RCA	LPM1410	1957	**£30**	US
Mexican Joe	7"	London	HL8030	1954	**£20**	
Padre Of Old San Antone	7"	London	HL8105	1954	**£15**	
Penny Candy	7"	London	HL8118	1955	**£12**	
Singing Down The Lane	LP	RCA	LPM1256	1956	**£50**	US
Songs To Warm Your Heart	LP	RCA	LPM2001	1959	**£15**	US
Tahiti	7"	London	HLU8185	1955	**£10**	
Talkin' To Your Heart	LP	RCA	LPM2339	1961	**£10**	US
Tall Tales And Short Tempers	LP	RCA	LPM2284	1961	**£10**	US
Wilder Your Heart Beats	7"	London	HLU8351	1956	**£15**	

REFLECTION

Title	Format	Label	Cat. No.	Year	Price	Notes
Present Tense	LP	Reflection	RL3015	1968	**£25**	

REFLECTIONS

Title	Format	Label	Cat. No.	Year	Price	Notes
Just Like Romeo And Juliet	LP	Golden World	300	1964	**£40**	US
Just Like Romeo And Juliet	7"	T. Motown	TMG907	1974	**£4**	
Just Like Romeo And Juliet	7"	T. Motown	TMG907	1974	**£10**	demo
Poor Man's Son	7"	Stateside	SS406	1965	**£8**	
Poor Man's Son	7" EP	Stateside	SE1034	1965	**£15**	
Romeo And Juliet	7"	Stateside	SS294	1964	**£10**	

REFUGEE

Title	Format	Label	Cat. No.	Year	Price	Notes
Refugee	LP	Charisma	CAS1087	1974	**£10**	

REGAN, JOAN

Title	Format	Label	Cat. No.	Year	Price	Notes
Don't Talk To Me About Love	7"	CBS	202100	1966	**£15**	
No One Beside You	7"	CBS	2657	1967	**£10**	

REGAN, VALA & THE VALARONS

Title	Format	Label	Cat. No.	Year	Price	Notes
Fireman	7"	Atlantic	584009	1966	**£60**	

REGENTS

Title	Format	Label	Cat. No.	Year	Price	Notes
Barbara Ann	7"	Columbia	DB4666	1961	**£8**	
Barbara Ann	LP	Gee	GLP708	1961	**£40**	US
Live At The Am/Pm Discotheque	LP	Capitol	KAO2153	1964	**£20**	US
Runaround	7"	Columbia	DB4694	1961	**£6**	

REGENTS (2)

Title	Format	Label	Cat. No.	Year	Price	Notes
Bye Bye Johnny	7"	Oriole	CB1912	1964	**£4**	

REGGAE BOYS

Title	Format	Label	Cat. No.	Year	Price	Notes
Me No Born Ya	7"	Amalgam.	AMG841	196-	**£10**	
Reggae Train	7"	Amalgam.	AMG843	196-	**£10**	
Walk By Day, Fly By Night	7"	Press. Beat	PB5503		**£6**	

REICH, STEVE

Title	Format	Label	Cat. No.	Year	Price	Notes
Come Out	LP	Odyssey	32160160		**£10**	
Four Organs	LP	Angel	S36059		**£10**	
Four Organs	LP	Shandar	83511		**£10**	
It's Gonna Rain	LP	Columbia	MS7265		**£10**	US

REID, AL

Title	Format	Label	Cat. No.	Year	Price	Notes
Vietcong	7"	Blue Cat	BS161	196-	**£10**	

REID, BERYL

Title	Format	Label	Cat. No.	Year	Price	Notes
Love Makes The World Go Around	7"	HMV	POP1489	1965	**£5**	

REID, CARLTON

Title	Format	Label	Cat. No.	Year	Price	Notes
Leave Me To Cry	7"	Blue Cat	BS162	196-	**£10**	
Turn On The Lights	7"	Ska Beat	JB254	1966	**£10**	

REID, DUKE

Duke's Cookies	7"	Blue Beat	BB24	1961	**£10**	
Hurt	7"	Duke Reid	DR2522	1971	**£6**	
Mood I Am In	7"	Blue Beat	BB165	1963	**£10**	

REID, LEROY

Fiddler	7"	Blue Cat	BS125	1968	**£10**	

REID, P.

Redeemed	7"	Ska Beat	JB197	1965	**£10**	

REID, TERRY

Bang Bang, You're Terry Reid	LP	Epic	26427	1968	**£15**	US
Better By Far	7"	Columbia	DB8409	1968	**£8**	
Hand Don't Fit The Glove	7"	Columbia	DB8166	1967	**£10**	
Move Over For Terry Reid	LP	Columbia	SCX6370	1969	**£15**	
River	LP	W. Bros	K40340	1973	**£12**	
Seeds Of Memory	LP	ABC	ABCL5162	1976	**£10**	

REIGN

Line Of Least Resistance	7"	Regal Z.	RZ3028	1970	**£15**	

REIGN GHOST

Allied	LP				**£200**	Canadian

REINCARNATION

Fat City	LP	Probe		1969	**£15**	

REJOICE

November Snow	7"	Stateside	SS8010	1969	**£4**	
Rejoice	LP	Stateside	SSL5009	1968	**£10**	

RELF, JANE

Without A Song From You	7"	Decca	F13231	1971	**£5**	

RELF, KEITH

Mr.Zero	7"	Columbia	DB7920	1966	**£15**	chart single
Shapes In My Mind	7"	Columbia	DB8084	1966	**£20**	

REMA REMA

Wheel In The Roses	12"	4AD	BAD5	1980	**£8**	blue label

REMAINS

Remains	LP	Epic	LN24214	1966	**£50**	US

REMO FOUR

Attention	LP	Phonogram	6434158	1973	**£10**	German
Live Like A Lady	7"	Fontana	TF787	1967	**£8**	
Peter Gunn	7"	Piccadilly	7N35175	1964	**£8**	
Sally Go Round The Roses	7"	Piccadilly	7N35186	1964	**£8**	
Smile	LP	Starclub	158034	1967	**£20**	German

RENAISSANCE

The history of Renaissance is complicated by the fact that the name covers what, in effect, are two entirely different groups. The first eponymous LP was made by ex-Yardbirds Keith Relf and Jim McCarty and represented the results of a conscious attempt to broaden their music beyond the Yardbirds' blues-based material. It is Beethoven, rather than Jimmy Reed, who is the major influence here. While making the second LP, however (eventually given a limited release as "Illusion"), the group fell apart, with only pianist John Hawken prepared to carry on. He found a new group of musicians to complete the line-up, then decided to leave himself! The immediate result was a stage set consisting of songs from the first LP played by a set of musicians, none of whom had played on the record! Somewhat later, most of the original members got back together, but now had to issue their records under the name Illusion, as the second Renaissance had become quite successful in their own right during the intervening years.

Illusion	LP	Island	6339017	1972	**£20**	European
Illusion	LP	Island	HELP27	1971	**£40**	test pressing only
Jekyll And Hyde	7"	Sire	SIR4019	1979	**£10**	
Northern Lights	7"	Sire	SRE1022	1978	**£15**	export pic disc
Prologue	LP	Sovereign	SVNA7253	1972	**£10**	
Prologue/Ashes Are Burning	LP	Sovereign	CAPACK3	1979	**£15**	double
Renaissance	LP	Island	ILPS9114	1969	**£15**	chart LP
Scheherazade	LP	Mobile Fid.	MFSL1099	1982	**£12**	US audiophile
Sea	7"	Island	WIP6079	1970	**£6**	
Some Love	7"	Sovereign	SOV113	1972	**£4**	

RENALDO & THE LOAF

Songs For Swinging Larvae	LP	Do It	RIDE6	1981	**£10**	

RENAY, DIANE

Kiss Me Sailor	7"	Stateside	SS290	1964	**£4**	
Navy Blue	LP	20th Century	TF3133	1964	**£15**	US
Unbelievable Guy	7"	Stateside	SS270	1964	**£4**	

RENBOURN, JOHN

Another Monday	LP	Transatlantic	TRA149	1967	**£12**	
Faro Annie	LP	Transatlantic	TRA247	1971	**£10**	
John Renbourn	LP	Transatlantic	TRA135	1965	**£12**	
Lady & The Unicorn	LP	Transatlantic	TRA224	1970	**£10**	
Sir John Alot Of Merrie England	LP	Transatlantic	TRA167	1968	**£12**	

RENDELL, DON

As one of the British jazz musicians to emerge after the War, saxophonist Don Rendell's earliest records are nothing remarkable. Unlike the majority of his contemporaries, however, Rendell was interested in the way jazz in America was moving forwards. "Roarin'" is a good hard bop recording which stands up well against the American competition. It also features the playing of a young Graham Bond on alto saxophone. Later Don Rendell formed a quintet with trumpeter Ian Carr and the pair proceeded to create an English version of what Miles Davis was doing in America. When Davis went electric, Ian Carr did the same, founding the group Nucleus. For Rendell, however, this was a step too far. His contribution to rock-influenced jazz is limited to membership of the jazz orchestra used on Neil Ardley's "Symphony Of Amaranths".

Spacewalk	LP	Columbia	SCX6491	1971	**£40**	

RENDELL, DON & IAN CARR QUINTET

Change Is	LP	Columbia	SCX6368	1969	**£40**	
Dusk Fire	LP	Columbia	SX6064	1966	**£40**	
Live	LP	Columbia	SCX6316	1969	**£40**	
Phase III	LP	Columbia	SCX6214	1968	**£40**	
Shades Of Blue	LP	Columbia	33SX1733	1965	**£40**	

RENDELL, DON NEW JAZZ QUINTET

Roarin'	LP	Jazzland	JLP51	1962	**£60**	

RENE & THE ALLIGATORS

She Broke My Heart	7"	Decca	F22324	1966	**£6**	

RENE, GOOGIE

Forever	7"	London	HLY9056	1960	**£4**	
Smokey Joe's Lala	7"	Atlantic	AT4076	1966	**£6**	

RENEGADES

Cadillac	7"	Polydor	56508	1970	**£12**	
No Man's Land	7"	Columbia	DB8383	1968	**£15**	
Take A Message	7"	Parlophone	R5592	1967	**£15**	
Thirteen Women	7"	President	PT106	1968	**£12**	

RENIA

First Offenders	LP	Transatlantic	TRA261	1973	**£20**	

RENO, DON & RED SMILEY

Country And Western	7" EP	Parlophone	GEP8777	1958	**£6**	

RENO, GERRY

Don't Ever Change	7"	Decca	F11477	1962	**£4**	

RENTAL, ROBERT

Double Heart	7"	Mute	MUTE010	1980	**£4**	
Live	12"	Rough Trade	ROUGH17	1980	**£6**	1 sided
Paralysis	7"	Regular	ER102	1978	**£4**	

RENTAL, ROBERT & THOMAS LEER

Bridge	LP	Industrial	IR0007	1979	**£10**	

REO SPEEDWAGON

You Can Tune A Piano	LP	Epic	HE45082	1982	**£10**	US audiophile

REPARATA & THE DELRONS

Captain Of Your Ship	7"	Bell	BLL1002	1968	**£4**	chart single
Saturday Night It Didn't Happen	7"	Bell	BLL1014	1968	**£10**	
Tommy	7"	Stateside	SS414	1965	**£6**	

Whenever A Teenager Cries	7"	Stateside	SS382	1965	**£4**	
Whenever A Teenager Cries	LP	W. Artists	2006	1965	**£15**	US

RESIDENTS

The Residents' gimmick of keeping the individual members' identities completely secret has, amazingly, been successfully maintained since the early seventies. Their music is extremely eccentric, a quality that is emphasised by their record release policy. The proliferation of limited edition cover designs, coloured vinyls, and so forth, listed here does not include such ultra-rarities as a one-sided clear vinyl 12" of "Duck Stab", of which just six copies were made.

Babyfingers	7"	Ralph	RR0377	1977	**£200**	US
Babyfingers	7"	W.E.I.R.D.	1	1979	**£30**	US
Big Bubble	LP	Ralph	RZ8552	198-	**£50**	US pink marbled vinyl
Blorp Esette	LP	LAFMS	005	1975	**£50**	US
Census Taker	LP	Episode	ED21	1985	**£30**	US
Commercial Album	LP	Ralph	RZ8052	1980	**£15**	US
Diskomo	12"	Ralph	RZ8006D	1980	**£15**	US
Duck Stab	7"	Ralph	RR1177	1978	**£5**	US
Duck Stab/Buster And Glen	LP	Ralph	RR0278	1978	**£10**	US
Earth Vs. The Flying Saucers	7"	Ralph	SP1		**£20**	US green vinyl, 1 sided
Eskimo	LP	Ralph	ESK7906	1979	**£15**	US
Eskimo	LP	Ralph	ESK7906	1979	**£25**	US, white vinyl
Eskimo	LP	Ralph	ESK7906	1983	**£20**	US, pic disc
Fingerprince	LP	Ralph	RR1276	1977	**£50**	US, brown sleeve
Fingerprince	LP	Ralph	RR1276	1978	**£15**	US, black & pink sleeve
Fingerprince	LP	Ralph	RR1276	1978	**£20**	US, sienna sleeve
George And James	LP	Ralph	RZ8402	1984	**£30**	US
George And James	LP	Ralph	RZ8402	1984	**£50**	US, clear vinyl
Hit The Road Jack	7"	Torso	70032	1987	**£4**	pic disc
Hit The Road Jack	12"	Torso	TORSO120032	1987	**£6**	
Intermission	LP	Ralph	RZ8522	1982	**£15**	US
It's A Man's Man's Man's World	7"	Korova	KOW36	1984	**£4**	
It's A Man's Man's Man's World	7"	Ralph	RZ8422		**£10**	US pic disc
Kaw-Liga	7"	Ralph	RZ8621		**£10**	US pic disc
Mark Of The Mole	LP	Ralph	RZ8152	1981	**£15**	US
Mark Of The Mole	LP	Ralph	RZ8152	1981	**£25**	US, brown vinyl
Meet The Residents (excerpts)	7"	Lyntone		1974	**£15**	US clear vinyl flexi, square
Meet The Residents (remixed)	LP	Ralph	RR0677	1977	**£10**	US
Meet The Residents	LP	Ralph	RR0274	1974	**£80**	US
Meet The Residents	LP	Ralph	RR0677	1985	**£20**	US, pic disc
Mole Show	LP	Ralph	RZ0001	1983	**£20**	US
Mole Show	LP	Ralph	RZ0001	1983	**£25**	US, pic disc
Nibbles	LP	Virgin	VR3	1979	**£10**	
Not Available	LP	Ralph	RR1174	1978	**£10**	US
Not Available	LP	Ralph	RR1174	1978	**£50**	US, purple label
Pal TV LP	LP	Doublevision	DVR17		**£10**	red vinyl
Please Do Not Steal It	LP	Ralph	DJ7901	1979	**£20**	US
Residents Play The Beatles	7"	Ralph	RR0577	1977	**£100**	US
Residents Radio Special	LP	Ralph	173	1977	**£25**	US promo
Santa Dog 78	7"	Ralph	RR7812	1978	**£40**	US
Santa Dog	7"	Ralph	RR1272	1972	**£100**	US double
Satisfaction	7"	Ralph	RR0776	1976	**£150**	US
Satisfaction	7"	Ralph	RR7803	1978	**£5**	US, yellow vinyl
Stars And Hank Forever	LP	Ralph			**£50**	US green vinyl
Subterranean Modern	LP	Ralph	SM7908	1979	**£15**	US
Ten Years In Twenty Minutes	LP	Ralph	RR8205D	198-	**£50**	US clear vinyl, 1 sided no sleeve
Third Reich And Roll	LP	Ralph	RR1075	1976	**£50**	US, orange & green carrot on sleeve
Third Reich And Roll	LP	Ralph	RR1075	1978	**£10**	US
Third Reich And Roll	LP	Ralph	RR1075	1978	**£20**	US, censored sleeve
Thirteenth Anniversary Edition	LP	Ralph			**£20**	US pic disc
Tunes Of Two Cities	LP	Ralph	RR8202	1982	**£15**	US
Vileness Fats	LP	Ralph	RZ8452	1984	**£50**	US, red vinyl

RESTIVO, JOHNNY

I Like Girls	7"	RCA	RCA1159	1959	**£5**	
Oh Johnny	LP	RCA	LPM2149	1959	**£20**	US
Shape I'm In	7"	RCA	RCA1143	1959	**£10**	

REVELL, DIGGER & THE DENVER MEN

Surfside	7"	Decca	F11657	1963	**£5**	

REVELLS

Title	Format	Label	Number	Year	Price	Notes
Mind Party	7"	CBS	7050	1971	**£8**	

REVELS

Title	Format	Label	Number	Year	Price	Notes
Midnight Stroll	7"	Top Rank	JAR235	1959	**£4**	

REVELS (2)

Title	Format	Label	Number	Year	Price	Notes
Revels On A Rampage	LP	Impact	LPM1	1964	**£50**	US

REVERE, PAUL & THE RAIDERS

Title	Format	Label	Number	Year	Price	Notes
Alias Pink Puzz	LP	Columbia	CS9905	1969	**£10**	US
Christmas Past And Present	LP	Columbia	CL2755	1967	**£10**	US
Cinderella Sunshine	7"	CBS	3757	1968	**£5**	
Collage	LP	CBS	63973	1970	**£10**	
Don't Take It So Hard	7"	CBS	3586	1968	**£6**	
Goin' To Memphis	LP	CBS	63265	1968	**£10**	
Good Thing	LP	CBS	62963	1969	**£12**	
Good Thing	7"	CBS	202502	1967	**£8**	
Great Airplane Strike	7"	CBS	202411	1966	**£8**	
Greatest Hits	LP	Columbia	KCL2662	1967	**£10**	
Hard 'n' Heavy	LP	Columbia	CS9753	1969	**£10**	US
Here They Come	LP	Columbia	CL2307	1965	**£15**	US
Him Or Me - Who's It Gonna Be?	7"	CBS	2737	1967	**£8**	
Hungry	7"	CBS	202253	1966	**£8**	
In The Beginning	LP	Jerden	JRS7004	1966	**£15**	US
Indian Reservation	LP	CBS	64471	1971	**£10**	
Indian Reservation	LP	Columbia	CQ30768	1973	**£12**	US quad
Just Like Us	LP	CBS	62406	1966	**£12**	
Kicks	7"	CBS	202205	1966	**£8**	
Let Me	7"	CBS	4260	1969	**£6**	
Like Long Hair	LP	Gardena	G1000	1961	**£150**	US
Like Long Hair	7"	Sue	WI344	1966	**£10**	
Like Long Hair	7"	Top Rank	JAR557	1961	**£12**	
Midnight Ride	LP	CBS	62397	1966	**£12**	
Moreen	7"	CBS	3186	1967	**£6**	
Paul Revere & The Raiders	LP	Sande	1001	1962	**£200**	US
Paul Revere & The Raiders	LP	Sears	SPS439	1970	**£50**	US
Revolution	LP	CBS	63095	1967	**£10**	
Something Happening	LP	Columbia	CS9665	1968	**£10**	US
Spirit Of '67	LP	Columbia	CL2595	1967	**£12**	US
Ups And Downs	7"	CBS	202610	1967	**£8**	

REVEREND BLACK & THE ROCKIN' VICARS

Title	Format	Label	Number	Year	Price	Notes
Zing Went The Strings Of My Heart	7"	Decca		1963	**£30**	Irish

REVILLOS

Title	Format	Label	Number	Year	Price	Notes
Tell Him	7"	Aura	AUS135	1982	**£4**	

REVOLUTION

Title	Format	Label	Number	Year	Price	Notes
Hallelujah	7"	Piccadilly	7N35289	1966	**£15**	

REVOLUTIONARY BLUES BAND

Title	Format	Label	Number	Year	Price	Notes
Revolutionary Blues Band	LP	MCA	MUPS402	1970	**£15**	

REVOLVING PAINT DREAM

Title	Format	Label	Number	Year	Price	Notes
Flowers In The Sky	7"	Creation	CRE2	1984	**£20**	

REX & THE MINORS

Title	Format	Label	Number	Year	Price	Notes
Chicken Sax	7"	Triumph	RGM1023	1960	**£10**	

REYNOLDS, JODY

Title	Format	Label	Number	Year	Price	Notes
Endless Sleep	7"	London	HL8651	1958	**£10**	

REZILLOS

Title	Format	Label	Number	Year	Price	Notes
Can't Stand My Baby	7"	Sensible	FAB1(MARK2)	1979	**£4**	
Can't Stand My Baby	7"	Sensible	FAB1	1977	**£8**	chart single
Can't Stand My Baby/Good Sculptures	7"	Sensible	FAB1(MARK2)	1979	**£6**	
Can't Stand The Rezillos	LP	Sire	K56530	1978	**£10**	chart LP
Cold Wars	7"	Sire	SIR4014	1979	**£8**	
Destination Venus	7"	Sire	SIR4008	1978	**£6**	chart single
Flying Saucer Attack	7"	Sensible	FAB2	1977	**£25**	
Flying Saucer Attack	7"	Sire	6078612	1977	**£8**	

Mission Accomplished	LP	Sire	SRK6069	1979	**£10**	chart LP
Top Of The Pops	cass-s	Sire	SPC3	1981	**£5**	
Top Of The Pops	7"	Sire	SIR4001	1978	**£8**	chart single

RHINO 39

Xerox	7"	Dangerhouse	RH39	1979	**£30**	

RHINOCEROS

Apricot Brandy	7"	Elektra	EKSN45051	1968	**£4**	
Back Door	7"	Elektra	EKSN45080	1969	**£5**	
Better Times Are Coming	LP	Elektra	EKS74075	1970	**£10**	
I Will Serenade You	7"	Elektra	EKSN45058	1969	**£5**	
Rhinoceros	LP	Elektra	EKS74030	1969	**£10**	
Satin Chicken	LP	Elektra	EKS74056	1969	**£10**	

RHODES, EMITT

American Dream	LP	A&M	AMLS64254	1971	**£12**	
Emitt Rhodes	LP	Probe	SPBA6256	1971	**£12**	
Farewell To Paradise	LP	Probe	SPBA6266	1972	**£10**	
Mirror	LP	Probe	SPBA6262	1971	**£10**	

RHUBARB RHUBARB

Rainmaker	7"	President	PT229	1968	**£8**	

RHYTHM & BLUES INC.

Honey Don't	7"	Fontana	TF524	1965	**£10**	

RHYTHM ACES

Christmas	7"	Island	WI032	1962	**£10**	
I'll Be There	7"	Blue Beat	BB134	1962	**£10**	
Please Don't Go Away	7"	Starlite	ST45066	1961	**£10**	
Thousand Teardrops	7"	Starlite	ST45061	1961	**£10**	

RIBA, PAU

Jo, La Donya I El Gripau	LP	Edigsa		1971	**£60**	US

RICE, MACK

Love's A Mother Brother	7"	Atlantic	584250	1969	**£4**	

RICH KIDS

Rich Kids	7"	EMI	EMI2738	1978	**£4**	red vinyl

RICH MOUNTAIN TOWER

Rich Mountain Tower	LP	Ovation		1972	**£15**	

RICH, CHARLIE

Big Boss Man	LP	RCA	LPM3537	1966	**£10**	US
Charlie Rich	LP	Groove	G1000	1964	**£12**	US
Just A Little Bit Sweet	7"	London	HLS9482	1962	**£5**	
Lonely Weekends	7"	London	HLU9107	1960	**£6**	
Lonely Weekends	LP	Philips	1970	1960	**£240**	US
Love Is After Me	7"	London	HLU10104	1967	**£5**	
Many New Sides Of...	LP	Philips	BL7695	1966	**£10**	
Mohair Sam	7"	Mercury	MF1109	1969	**£4**	
Mohair Sam	7"	Philips	BF1432	1965	**£4**	
That's Rich	LP	RCA	RD7719	1965	**£12**	
Too Many Teardrops	7"	RCA	RCA1433	1965	**£4**	

RICH, DAVE

City Lights	7"	RCA	RCA1092	1958	**£4**	

RICH, LEWIS

I Don't Want To Hear It Anymore	7"	Parlophone	R5434	1966	**£4**	

RICHARD, CLIFF

Cliff Richard's first two LPs were issued in mono only and yet stereo mixes of some the tracks can be found on EPs. These are consequently much sought after. Cliff's 78rpm releases are also scarce and break the usual maxim that 78's are much less valuable than their 45rpm equivalents. Few of the religious records he has made over the years have sold particularly well and many of these now fetch quite high prices. The most desirable Cliff Richard collectors' item of all, however (apart from unreleased acetates which are too scarce to be a realistic collectors' goal for most people), is likely to be one of the complete film soundtrack albums that were presented to all the people involved in the making of "Summer Holiday" and "Wonderful Life".

21 Today	LP	Columbia	33SX1368	1961	**£20**	mono, chart LP

Title	Format	Label	Number	Year	Price	Notes
21 Today	LP	Columbia	SCX3409	1961	**£25**	stereo
31st Of February Street	LP	EMI	EMC3048	1974	**£10**	
32 Minutes 17 Seconds	LP	Columbia	33SX1431	1962	**£12**	mono, chart LP
32 Minutes 17 Seconds	LP	Columbia	SCX3436	1962	**£20**	stereo
About That Man	LP	Columbia	SCX6408	1970	**£50**	
Aladdin And His Wonderful Lamp	LP	Columbia	33SX1676	1964	**£12**	mono, chart LP
Aladdin And His Wonderful Lamp	LP	Columbia	SCX3522	1964	**£15**	stereo
All My Love	7"	Columbia	DB8293	1967	**£4**	chart single
All My Love	7"	Columbia	DB8293	1967	**£12**	demo
Always Guaranteed	LP	EMI	EMDB1004	1987	**£10**	boxed set
Angel	7"	Columbia	DC762	1965	**£15**	export
Angel	7" EP	Columbia	SEG8444	1965	**£10**	
Best Of	LP	Columbia	SCX6343	1969	**£10**	chart LP
Best Of Cliff Volume 2	LP	Columbia	SCX6519	1972	**£10**	chart LP
Big Ship	7"	Columbia	DB8581	1969	**£4**	chart single
Big Ship	7"	Columbia	DB8581	1969	**£10**	demo
Blue Turns To Grey	7"	Columbia	DB7866	1966	**£4**	chart single
Blue Turns To Grey	7"	Columbia	DB7866	1966	**£15**	demo
Boyfriend flexi	7"	Boyfriend			**£12**	flexi
Brand New Song	7"	Columbia	DB8957	1972	**£4**	
Brand New Song	7"	Columbia	DB8957	1972	**£10**	demo
Can't Take The Hurt Anymore	7"	EMI	EMI2885	1978	**£6**	demo
Carol Singers	7" EP	Columbia	SEG8533	1967	**£20**	
Carrie	7"	EMI	EMI5006	1980	**£5**	demo
Cinderella	LP	Columbia	SX6103	1967	**£20**	chart LP
Cinderella	7" EP	Columbia	SEG8527	1967	**£12**	
Cliff	LP	Columbia	33SX1147	1959	**£25**	chart LP
Cliff En Espania	7" EP	HMV		196-	**£12**	sung in Spanish
Cliff In Japan	LP	Columbia	SCX6244	1968	**£15**	stereo, chart LP
Cliff In Japan	LP	Columbia	SX6244	1968	**£20**	mono
Cliff No.1	7" EP	Columbia	ESG7754	1959	**£25**	stereo
Cliff No.1	7" EP	Columbia	SEG7903	1959	**£10**	
Cliff No.2	7" EP	Columbia	ESG7769	1959	**£25**	stereo
Cliff No.2	7" EP	Columbia	SEG7910	1959	**£10**	
Cliff Richard	LP	Columbia	33SX1709	1965	**£15**	mono, chart LP
Cliff Richard	LP	Columbia	SCX3546	1965	**£20**	stereo
Cliff Richard	7" EP	Columbia	SEG8151	1962	**£8**	
Cliff Richard	LP	W. Rec. Club	STP1051	1966	**£25**	
Cliff Richard In Spain	LP	Epic	LN24115	1964	**£15**	US
Cliff Richard No.2	7" EP	Columbia	SEG8168	1962	**£8**	
Cliff Richard Songbook	LP	W. Rec. Club	ALBUM26	1980	**£30**	6 LPs, boxed
Cliff Richard Story	7"	Lyntone	LYNSF1218	1973	**£6**	sampler flexi with interview
Cliff Richard Story	LP	W. Rec. Club	SM255-260	1972	**£30**	6 LPs, boxed
Cliff Sings	LP	ABC-Para.	321	1960	**£20**	US
Cliff Sings	LP	Columbia	33SX1192	1959	**£25**	chart LP
Cliff Sings No.1	7" EP	Columbia	ESG7788	1960	**£20**	stereo
Cliff Sings No.1	7" EP	Columbia	SEG7979	1960	**£10**	
Cliff Sings No.2	7" EP	Columbia	ESG7794	1960	**£20**	stereo
Cliff Sings No.2	7" EP	Columbia	SEG7987	1960	**£10**	
Cliff Sings No.3	7" EP	Columbia	ESG7808	1960	**£20**	stereo
Cliff Sings No.3	7" EP	Columbia	SEG8005	1960	**£8**	
Cliff Sings No.4	7" EP	Columbia	ESG7816	1960	**£20**	stereo
Cliff Sings No.4	7" EP	Columbia	SEG8021	1960	**£8**	
Cliff's Hit Parade	7" EP	Columbia	SEG8133	1962	**£10**	
Cliff's Hits	7" EP	Columbia	SEG8203	1962	**£6**	
Cliff's Hits From Aladdin	7" EP	Columbia	SEG8395	1965	**£8**	
Cliff's Lucky Lips	7" EP	Columbia	SEG8269	1963	**£6**	
Cliff's Palladium Successes	7" EP	Columbia	SEG8320	1964	**£10**	
Cliff's Silver Discs	7" EP	Columbia	SEG8050	1960	**£6**	
Congratulations	7"	Columbia	DB8376	1968	**£10**	demo
Congratulations	7" EP	Columbia	SEG8540	1968	**£12**	
Constantly	7"	Columbia	DB7272	1964	**£4**	chart single
Constantly	7"	Columbia	DB7272	1964	**£15**	demo
Day I Met Marie	7"	Columbia	DB8245	1967	**£4**	chart single
Day I Met Marie	7"	Columbia	DB8245	1967	**£12**	demo
Devil Woman	7"	EMI	EMI2458	1976	**£6**	demo
Don't Forget To Catch Me	7"	Columbia	DB8503	1968	**£4**	chart single
Don't Forget To Catch Me	7"	Columbia	DB8503	1968	**£10**	demo
Don't Stop Me Now	LP	Columbia	SX6133	1967	**£12**	chart LP
Don't Talk To Him	7"	Columbia	DB7150	1963	**£4**	chart single
Don't Talk To Him	7"	Columbia	DB7150	1963	**£20**	demo

Title	Format	Label	Cat. No.	Year	Price	Notes
Don't Talk To Him	7" EP	Columbia	SEG8299	1964	**£8**	
Dream	7" EP	Columbia	ESG7867	1961	**£20**	stereo
Dream	7" EP	Columbia	SEG8119	1961	**£8**	
Dreamin'	7"	EMI	EMI5095	1980	**£5**	demo
Dressed For The Occasion	LP	EMI	PSLP372	1983	**£12**	promo
Du Bist Mein Erster Gedanke	7"	Columbia		196-	**£10**	sung in German
Ein Girl Wiedu	7"	Columbia	C23510	196-	**£10**	sung in German
Established 1958	LP	Columbia	SCX6282	1968	**£12**	chart LP
Every Face Tells A Story	7"	EMI	PSR410	1977	**£20**	promo sampler
Expresso Bongo	7" EP	Columbia	ESG7783	1960	**£25**	stereo
Expresso Bongo	7" EP	Columbia	SEG7971	1960	**£10**	chart single
Fall In Love With You	7"	Columbia	DB4431	1960	**£4**	chart single
Fall In Love With You	7"	Columbia	DB4431	1960	**£25**	demo
Finders Keepers	LP	Columbia	SX6079	1966	**£12**	chart LP
Finders Keepers	7"	EMI	PSR304	1967	**£12**	1 sided promo
Flying Machine	7"	Columbia	DB8797	1971	**£4**	chart single
Flying Machine	7"	Columbia	DB8797	1971	**£10**	demo
Forever Kind Of Love	7" EP	Columbia	SEG8347	1964	**£8**	
Forty Greatest Hits	7"	EMI	PSR414/5	1977	**£15**	double promo sampler
Gee Whiz It's You	7"	Columbia	DC756	1961	**£4**	export, chart single
Girl Like You	7"	Columbia	DB4667	1961	**£4**	chart single
Girl Like You	7"	Columbia	DB4667	1961	**£25**	demo
Good News	LP	Columbia	JSX6167	1967	**£35**	export
Good News	LP	Columbia	SX6167	1967	**£20**	chart LP
Good Times (Better Times)	7"	Columbia	DB8548	1969	**£4**	chart single
Good Times (Better Times)	7"	Columbia	DB8548	1969	**£10**	demo
Goodbye Sam Hello Samantha	7"	Columbia	DB8685	1970	**£4**	chart single
Goodbye Sam Hello Samantha	7"	Columbia	DB8685	1970	**£10**	demo
Green Light	7"	EMI	EMI2920	1979	**£6**	demo
Gut Dasses Freunde Gibt	7"	Electrola		196-	**£10**	sung in German
Hangin' On	7"	EMI	EMI2150	1974	**£8**	demo
Help It Along	LP	EMI	EMA768	1974	**£10**	
Help It Along	7"	EMI	EMI2022	1973	**£4**	chart single
Hey Mr.Dream Maker	7"	EMI	EMI2559	1976	**£6**	demo
High Class Baby	78	Columbia	DB4203	1958	**£15**	
High Class Baby	7"	Columbia	DB4203	1958	**£6**	chart single
High Class Baby	7"	Columbia	DB4203	1958	**£30**	demo
His Land	LP	Columbia	SCX6443	1970	**£50**	
Hit Album	LP	Columbia	33SX1512	1963	**£10**	mono, chart LP
Hits From Summer Holiday	7" EP	Columbia	ESG7896	1963	**£20**	stereo
Hits From Summer Holiday	7" EP	Columbia	SEG8250	1963	**£6**	
Hits From The Young Ones	7" EP	Columbia	SEG8159	1962	**£12**	different mixes
Hits From When In Rome	7" EP	Columbia	SEG8478	1966	**£10**	
Hits From Wonderful Life	7" EP	Columbia	ESG7906	1964	**£20**	stereo
Hits From Wonderful Life	7" EP	Columbia	SEG8376	1964	**£6**	
Holiday Carnival	7" EP	Columbia	ESG7892	1963	**£20**	stereo
Holiday Carnival	7" EP	Columbia	SEG8246	1963	**£10**	
Honky Tonk Angel	7"	EMI	EMI2344	1975	**£4**	
Hot Shot	7"	EMI	EMI5003	1979	**£5**	demo
How Wonderful To Know	LP	W. Rec. Club	ST643	1964	**£20**	
I Ain't Got Time Anymore	7"	Columbia	DB8708	1970	**£4**	chart single
I Ain't Got Time Anymore	7"	Columbia	DB8708	1970	**£10**	demo
I Can't Ask For Anymore Than You	7"	EMI	EMI2499	1976	**£6**	demo
I Could Easily Fall	7"	Columbia	DB7420	1964	**£4**	chart single
I Could Easily Fall	7"	Columbia	DB7420	1964	**£15**	demo
I Love You	7"	Columbia	DB4547	1960	**£4**	chart single
I Love You	7"	Columbia	DB4547	1960	**£25**	demo
I'll Come Running	7"	Columbia	DB8210	1967	**£4**	chart single
I'll Come Running	7"	Columbia	DB8210	1967	**£12**	demo
I'll Love You Forever Today	7"	Columbia	DB8437	1968	**£4**	chart single
I'll Love You Forever Today	7"	Columbia	DB8437	1968	**£10**	demo
I'm Looking Out The Window	7"	Columbia	DB4828	1962	**£4**	chart single
I'm Looking Out The Window	7"	Columbia	DB4828	1962	**£20**	demo
I'm The Lonely One	7"	Columbia	DB7203	1964	**£4**	chart single
I'm The Lonely One	7"	Columbia	DB7203	1964	**£15**	demo
Ich Traume Deine Traume	7"	Columbia		196-	**£10**	sung in German
In The Country	7"	Columbia	DB8094	1966	**£4**	chart single
In The Country	7"	Columbia	DB8094	1966	**£15**	demo
It'll Be Me	7"	Columbia	DB4886	1962	**£4**	chart single
It'll Be Me	7"	Columbia	DB4886	1962	**£20**	demo
It's All In The Game	7"	Columbia	DB7089	1963	**£4**	chart single

It's All In The Game	7"	Columbia	DB7089	1963	**£20**	demo
It's All In The Game	LP	Epic	LN24089	1964	**£15**	US
It's All Over	7"	Columbia	DB8150	1967	**£4**	chart single
It's All Over	7"	Columbia	DB8150	1967	**£12**	demo
It's Only Me You've Left Behind	7"	EMI	EMI2279	1975	**£4**	
Japan Tour 1974	LP	EMI	EMS67037	1975	**£40**	Japanese
Jesus	7"	Columbia	DB8864	1972	**£4**	chart single
Jesus	7"	Columbia	DB8864	1972	**£10**	demo
Joy Of Living	7"	Columbia	DB8657	1970	**£4**	chart single
Joy Of Living	7"	Columbia	DB8657	1970	**£10**	demo
Kinda Latin	LP	Columbia	SCX6039	1966	**£15**	stereo
Kinda Latin	LP	Columbia	SX6039	1966	**£12**	mono, chart LP
La La La La La	7" EP	Columbia	SEG8517	1966	**£12**	
Listen To Cliff	LP	ABC-Para.	391	1961	**£20**	US
Listen To Cliff	LP	Columbia	33SX1320	1961	**£15**	mono, chart LP
Listen To Cliff	LP	Columbia	SCX3375	1961	**£25**	stereo
Listen To Cliff No.1	7" EP	Columbia	ESG7858	1961	**£20**	stereo
Listen To Cliff No.1	7" EP	Columbia	SEG8105	1961	**£8**	
Listen To Cliff No.2	7" EP	Columbia	ESG7870	1961	**£20**	stereo
Listen To Cliff No.2	7" EP	Columbia	SEG8126	1961	**£8**	
Little Town	7"	EMI	EMIP5348	1982	**£5**	pic disc
Living Doll	78	Columbia	DB4306	1959	**£6**	
Living Doll	7"	Columbia	DB4306	1959	**£4**	chart single
Living Doll	7"	Columbia	DB4306	1959	**£30**	demo
Living In Harmony	7"	Columbia	DB8917	1972	**£4**	chart single
Living In Harmony	7"	Columbia	DB8917	1972	**£10**	demo
Living Loving Doll	78	Columbia	DB4249	1959	**£20**	
Living Loving Doll	7"	Columbia	DB4249	1959	**£8**	chart single
Living Loving Doll	7"	Columbia	DB4249	1959	**£30**	demo
Look In My Eyes Maria	7" EP	Columbia	SEG8405	1965	**£12**	
Love Is Forever	LP	Columbia	SCX3569	1965	**£15**	stereo
Love Is Forever	LP	Columbia	SX1769	1965	**£12**	mono, chart LP
Love Is Forever	7" EP	Columbia	SEG8488	1966	**£10**	
Love Songs	7" EP	Columbia	ESG7900	1963	**£20**	stereo
Love Songs	7" EP	Columbia	SEG8272	1963	**£8**	
Lucky Lips	7"	Columbia	DB7034	1963	**£4**	chart single
Lucky Lips	7"	Columbia	DB7034	1963	**£20**	demo
Man Gratuliert Mir	7"	Columbia		196-	**£10**	sung in German
Maria No Mas	7"	Columbia		196-	**£10**	sung in Spanish
Marianne	7"	Columbia	DB8476	1968	**£4**	chart single
Marianne	7"	Columbia	DB8476	1968	**£10**	demo
Me And My Shadows	LP	Columbia	33SX1261	1960	**£15**	mono, chart LP
Me And My Shadows	LP	Columbia	SCX3330	1960	**£30**	stereo
Me And My Shadows No.1	7" EP	Columbia	ESG7837	1961	**£20**	stereo
Me And My Shadows No.1	7" EP	Columbia	SEG8065	1961	**£10**	
Me And My Shadows No.2	7" EP	Columbia	ESG7841	1961	**£20**	stereo
Me And My Shadows No.2	7" EP	Columbia	SEG8071	1961	**£10**	
Me And My Shadows No.3	7" EP	Columbia	ESG7843	1961	**£20**	stereo
Me And My Shadows No.3	7" EP	Columbia	SEG8078	1961	**£10**	
Mean Streak	78	Columbia	DB4290	1959	**£15**	
Mean Streak	7"	Columbia	DB4290	1959	**£6**	chart single
Mean Streak	7"	Columbia	DB4290	1959	**£30**	demo
Minute You're Gone	7"	Columbia	DB7496	1965	**£4**	chart single
Minute You're Gone	7"	Columbia	DB7496	1965	**£15**	demo
Miss You Nights	7"	EMI	EMI2376	1976	**£8**	demo
More Hits	LP	Columbia	SCX3555	1965	**£15**	stereo
More Hits	LP	Columbia	SX1737	1965	**£10**	mono, chart LP
More Hits From Summer Holiday	7" EP	Columbia	ESG7898	1963	**£20**	stereo
More Hits From Summer Holiday	7" EP	Columbia	SEG8263	1963	**£8**	
Move It	78	Columbia	DB4178	1958	**£15**	
Move It	7"	Columbia	DB4178	1958	**£6**	chart single
Move It	7"	Columbia	DB4178	1958	**£50**	demo
Music And Life Of Cliff Richard	cass	EMI	TCEXSP1601	1974	**£30**	6 tapes, boxed
Music From America	7"	Rainbow			**£12**	flexi
My Italian Friends	LP	Columbia	CCMQ8024	196-	**£20**	sung in Italian
My Kinda Life	7"	EMI	EMI2584	1977	**£6**	demo
Next Time	7"	Columbia	DB4950	1962	**£4**	chart single
Next Time	7"	Columbia	DB4950	1962	**£20**	demo
Nine Times Out Of Ten	7"	Columbia	DB4506	1960	**£4**	chart single
Nine Times Out Of Ten	7"	Columbia	DB4506	1960	**£25**	demo
Non Dimenti Care Chitiama	7"	HMV		196-	**£10**	sung in Italian

Title	Format	Label	Cat. No.	Year	Price	Notes
Non L'Ascoltare	7"	Columbia	SCMQ1860	196-	**£10**	sung in Italian
Nothing To Remind Me	7"	EMI		1967	**£15**	promo
O Mio Signore	7" EP	Columbia	2221	196-	**£12**	sung in Italian
On My Word	7"	Columbia	DB7596	1965	**£4**	chart single
On My Word	7"	Columbia	DB7596	1965	**£15**	demo
On The Beach	7"	Columbia	DB7305	1964	**£4**	chart single
On The Beach	7"	Columbia	DB7305	1964	**£15**	demo
Per Un Bacio Diamour	LP	Columbia	CCMQ8081	196-	**£20**	sung in Italian
Personal Message To You	7"	Serenade		1960	**£20**	blue flexi
Please Don't Tease	7"	Columbia	DB4479	1960	**£4**	chart single
Please Don't Tease	7"	Columbia	DB4479	1960	**£25**	demo
Please Remember Me	7"	EMI	EMI2832	1978	**£6**	demo
Pote Lippen Soll Man Kussen	7"	Columbia	C22503	196-	**£10**	sung in German
Power To All Our Friends	7"	EMI		196-	**£10**	sung in Spanish
Power To All Our Friends	7"	EMI	EMI2012	1973	**£8**	demo
Schon Wie Ein Traume	7"	Columbia	C21843	196-	**£10**	sung in German
Serious Charge	7" EP	Columbia	SEG7895	1959	**£15**	
Shooting From The Heart	7"	EMI	RICHP1	1984	**£5**	shaped pic disc
Silver	LP	EMI	EMC1077873	1983	**£12**	boxed double
Silvery Rain	7"	Columbia	DB8774	1971	**£4**	chart single
Silvery Rain	7"	Columbia	DB8774	1971	**£10**	demo
Sincerely	LP	Columbia	SCX6537	1969	**£10**	stereo, chart LP
Sincerely	LP	Columbia	SX6537	1969	**£12**	mono
Sing A Song Of Freedom	7"	Columbia	DB8836	1971	**£4**	chart single
Sing A Song Of Freedom	7"	Columbia	DB8836	1971	**£10**	demo
Singles Sampler	12"	EMI	PSLP350	1981	**£10**	promo
Some People	7"	EMI	EMP18	1987	**£4**	shaped pic disc
Summer Holiday	LP	Columbia	33SX1472	1963	**£12**	mono, chart LP
Summer Holiday	LP	Columbia	SCX3462	1963	**£20**	stereo
Summer Holiday	7"	Columbia	DB4977	1963	**£4**	chart single
Summer Holiday	7"	Columbia	DB4977	1963	**£20**	demo
Summer Holiday	LP	Elstree S.		1962	**£300**	Original film soundtrack double
Summer Holiday	LP	Epic	LN24063	1963	**£15**	US
Sunny Honey Girl	7"	Columbia	DB8747	1971	**£4**	chart single
Sunny Honey Girl	7"	Columbia	DB8747	1971	**£10**	demo
Swinger's Paradise	LP	Epic	LN24145	1965	**£12**	US
Take Four	7" EP	Columbia	SEG8450	1965	**£12**	
Take Me High	LP	EMI	EMC3016	1973	**£10**	chart LP
Take Me High	7"	EMI	EMI2088	1973	**£4**	chart single
Theme For A Dream	7"	Columbia	DB4593	1961	**£25**	demo
Theme for A Dream	7"	Columbia	DB4593	1961	**£4**	chart single
This Was My Special Day	7"	Columbia	DB7435	1964	**£25**	demo only
Throw Down A Line	7"	Columbia	DB8615	1969	**£4**	chart single
Throw Down A Line	7"	Columbia	DB8615	1969	**£10**	demo
Thunderbirds Are Go	7" EP	Columbia	SEG8510	1966	**£20**	
Time Drags By	7"	Columbia	DB8017	1966	**£4**	chart single
Time Drags By	7"	Columbia	DB8017	1966	**£15**	demo
Time For Cliff And The Shadows	7" EP	Columbia	ESG7887	1963	**£20**	stereo
Time For Cliff And The Shadows	7" EP	Columbia	SEG8228	1963	**£10**	
Time In Between	7"	Columbia	DB7660	1965	**£4**	chart single
Time In Between	7"	Columbia	DB7660	1965	**£15**	demo
Tracks And Grooves	LP	Columbia	SCX6435	1970	**£10**	chart LP
Travelling Light	78	Columbia	DB4351	1959	**£20**	
Travelling Light	7"	Columbia	DB4351	1959	**£4**	chart single
Travelling Light	7"	Columbia	DB4351	1959	**£25**	demo
Twelfth Of Never	7"	Columbia	DB7372	1964	**£4**	chart single
Twelfth Of Never	7"	Columbia	DB7372	1964	**£15**	demo
Two A Penny	LP	Columbia	SCX6262	1968	**£15**	stereo
Two A Penny	LP	Columbia	SX6262	1968	**£20**	mono
Un Saludo De Cliff	7" EP	HMV	13955	196-	**£12**	sung in Spanish
Visions	7"	Columbia	DB7968	1966	**£4**	chart single
Visions	7"	Columbia	DB7968	1966	**£15**	demo
Voice In The Wilderness	78	Columbia	DB4398	1960	**£30**	
Voice In The Wilderness	7"	Columbia	DB4398	1960	**£4**	chart single
Voice In The Wilderness	7"	Columbia	DB4398	1960	**£25**	demo
We Don't Talk Anymore (2 versions)	12"	EMI	SPRO9252	1979	**£10**	US promo
We Don't Talk Anymore	7"	EMI	EMI2975	1979	**£5**	demo
What'd I Say	7"	Columbia	DC758	1963	**£15**	export
When In France	7" EP	Columbia	SEG8290	1964	**£12**	
When In Rome	LP	Columbia	SX1762	1965	**£20**	

Title	Format	Label	Cat. No.	Year	Price	Notes
When In Spain	LP	Columbia	33SX1541	1963	**£15**	mono, chart LP
When In Spain	LP	Columbia	SCX3488	1963	**£20**	stereo
When The Girl In Your Arms	7"	Columbia	DB4716	1961	**£4**	chart single
When The Girl In Your Arms	7"	Columbia	DB4716	1961	**£25**	demo
When Two Worlds Drift Apart	7"	EMI	EMI2633	1977	**£6**	demo
Why Don't They Understand	7" EP	Columbia	SEG8384	1965	**£8**	
Wind Me Up	7"	Columbia	DB7745	1965	**£4**	chart single
Wind Me Up	7"	Columbia	DB7745	1965	**£15**	demo
Wind Me Up	7" EP	Columbia	SEG8474	1966	**£10**	
With The Eyes Of A Child	7"	Columbia	DB8641	1969	**£4**	chart single
With The Eyes Of A Child	7"	Columbia	DB8641	1969	**£10**	demo
Wonderful Life	LP	Columbia	33SX1628	1964	**£12**	mono, chart LP
Wonderful Life	LP	Columbia	SCX3515	1964	**£15**	stereo
Wonderful Life	LP	Elstree S.		1963	**£300**	Original film soundtrack double
Wonderful Life No.1	7" EP	Columbia	ESG7902	1964	**£20**	stereo
Wonderful Life No.1	7" EP	Columbia	SEG8338	1964	**£8**	
Wonderful Life No.2	7" EP	Columbia	ESG7903	1964	**£20**	stereo
Wonderful Life No.2	7" EP	Columbia	SEG8354	1964	**£8**	
Wonderful To Be Young	LP	Dot	DLP3474	1962	**£12**	US
Yes He Lives	7"	EMI	EMI2730	1978	**£4**	
Young Ones	LP	Columbia	33SX1384	1961	**£10**	mono, chart LP
Young Ones	LP	Columbia	SCX3397	1961	**£20**	stereo
Young Ones	7"	Columbia	DB4761	1962	**£4**	chart single
Young Ones	7"	Columbia	DB4761	1962	**£20**	demo

RICHARD, CLIFF & SHEILA WALSH

Title	Format	Label	Cat. No.	Year	Price	Notes
Drifting	7"	DJM	SHEILP1	1983	**£4**	pic disc

RICHARDS, KEITH

Title	Format	Label	Cat. No.	Year	Price	Notes
Before They Make Me Run	7"	R. Stones		1979	**£12**	promo

RICHARDS, LISA

Title	Format	Label	Cat. No.	Year	Price	Notes
Mean Old World	7"	Vocalion	VP9244	1965	**£10**	

RICHARDS, LLOYD

Title	Format	Label	Cat. No.	Year	Price	Notes
Be Good	7"	Port-O-Jam	PJ4004	196-	**£10**	

RICHARDS, ROY

Title	Format	Label	Cat. No.	Year	Price	Notes
Contact	7"	Doctor Bird	DB1012	1966	**£10**	
Double Trouble	7"	Island	WI283	1966	**£10**	
Rub-A-Dub	7"	Island	WI3027	1967	**£10**	
South Vietnam	7"	Island	WI3000	1966	**£10**	
Ungrateful Baby	7"	Island	WI3037	1967	**£10**	
Western Standard Time	7"	Island	WI299	1966	**£10**	

RICHARDS, WENDY & DIANA BERRY

Title	Format	Label	Cat. No.	Year	Price	Notes
We Had A Dream	7"	Decca	F11680	1963	**£4**	

RICHARDS, WINSTON

Title	Format	Label	Cat. No.	Year	Price	Notes
Green Coolie	7"	Island	WI297	1966	**£10**	

RICHMAN, JONATHAN

Title	Format	Label	Cat. No.	Year	Price	Notes
Modern Lovers	LP	H. Of Hits	1910	1975	**£20**	US
Road Runner	7"	United Artists	UP36006	1975	**£5**	

RICHMOND

Title	Format	Label	Cat. No.	Year	Price	Notes
Frightened	LP	CBS		1973	**£20**	

RICK & THE KEENS

Title	Format	Label	Cat. No.	Year	Price	Notes
Peanuts	7"	Mercury	AMT1150	1961	**£5**	

RICOTTI & ALBUQUERQUE

Title	Format	Label	Cat. No.	Year	Price	Notes
First Wind	LP	Pegasus	PEG2	1971	**£15**	

RICOTTI, FRANK

Title	Format	Label	Cat. No.	Year	Price	Notes
Our Point Of View	LP	CBS	52668	1969	**£20**	

RIDDLERS

Title	Format	Label	Cat. No.	Year	Price	Notes
Batman Theme	7"	Polydor	56716	1966	**£4**	

RIFF RAFF

Original Man .... LP .... RCA .... LPL15023 .... 1974 .... **£10**
Riff Raff .... LP .... RCA .... SF8351 .... 1973 .... **£10**

RIFFS

Oh What A Feeling .... 7" .... Blue Beat .... BB242 .... 1963 .... **£10**

RIFKIN, JOSHUA

Baroque Beatles .... LP .... Elektra .... 1968 .... **£25** .... US

RIGGS, JACKIE

Great Pretender .... 7" .... London .... HLF8244 .... 1956 .... **£10**

RIGHTEOUS BROTHERS

Back To Back .... LP .... London .... HA8278 .... 1966 .... **£20**
Bring Your Love To Me .... 7" .... Pye .... 7N25297 .... 1965 .... **£4**
Ebb Tide .... 7" .... London .... HL10011 .... 1965 .... **£4** .... chart single
For Your Love .... 7" .... Pye .... 7N25334 .... 1965 .... **£4**
Georgia On My Mind .... 7" .... Pye .... 7N25358 .... 1966 .... **£4**
Go Ahead And Cry .... LP .... Verve .... SVLP9140 .... 1966 .... **£10**
Go Ahead And Cry .... 7" .... Verve .... VS542 .... 1966 .... **£4**
He .... 7" .... Verve .... VS537 .... 1966 .... **£4**
In Action .... LP .... Sue .... ILP937 .... 1966 .... **£20**
Island In The Sun .... 7" .... Verve .... VS547 .... 1966 .... **£4** .... chart single
Just Once In My Life .... LP .... London .... HA8245 .... 1965 .... **£20**
Just Once In My Life .... 7" .... London .... HL9962 .... 1965 .... **£25** .... demo only
Just Once In My Life .... 7" .... London .... HLU10066 .... 1966 .... **£4**
Let The Good Times Roll .... 7" .... Pye .... 7N25253 .... 1964 .... **£4**
Let The Good Times Roll .... 7" .... Pye .... 7N25323 .... 1965 .... **£4**
Little Latin Lupe Lu .... 7" .... London .... HL9743 .... 1963 .... **£4**
My Babe .... 7" .... London .... HL9814 .... 1963 .... **£4**
One For The Road .... LP .... Verve .... SVLP9228 .... 1968 .... **£15**
Rebirth .... LP .... Verve .... SVLP9249 .... 1970 .... **£10**
Right Now .... LP .... Pye .... NPL28059 .... 1965 .... **£20**
Righteous Brothers .... 7" EP .... Pye .... NEP44043 .... 1965 .... **£5**
Righteous Brothers .... 7" EP .... Verve .... VEP5024 .... 1966 .... **£5**
Sayin' Somethin' .... LP .... Verve .... SVLP9168 .... 1967 .... **£10**
Some Blue Eyed Soul .... LP .... Pye .... NPL28056 .... 1965 .... **£20**
Something's Got A Hold On Me .... 7" .... Pye .... 7N25304 .... 1965 .... **£4**
Soul And Inspiration .... LP .... Verve .... SVLP9131 .... 1966 .... **£12**
Soul And Inspiration .... 7" .... Verve .... VS535 .... 1966 .... **£4** .... chart single
Souled Out .... LP .... Verve .... SVLP9190 .... 1967 .... **£10**
Standards .... LP .... Verve .... SVLP9204 .... 1967 .... **£10**
Unchained Melody .... 7" .... London .... HL9975 .... 1965 .... **£4** .... chart single
White Cliffs Of Dover .... 7" .... London .... HL10086 .... 1966 .... **£4** .... chart single
You Can Have Her .... 7" .... Sue .... WI4018 .... 1966 .... **£8**
You've Lost That Lovin' Feelin' .... LP .... London .... HA8226 .... 1965 .... **£20**
You've Lost That Lovin' Feelin' .... 7" .... London .... HL9943 .... 1965 .... **£5** .... chart single

RIGHTEOUS TWINS

If I Could Hear My Master .... 7" .... Blue Cat .... BS174 .... 196- **£10**

RILEY, BILLY LEE

Harmonica Beatlemania .... LP .... Mercury .... SR60974 .... 1964 .... **£12** .... US
I've Been Searchin' .... 7" .... King .... 1965 .... **£8**

RILEY, BOB

Midnight Line .... 7" .... MGM .... MGM977 .... 1958 .... **£15**

RILEY, HOWARD

Angle .... LP .... CBS .... 52669 .... 1969 .... **£25**
Day Will Come .... LP .... CBS .... 64077 .... 1970 .... **£15**
Discussions .... LP .... Opportunity .... 2500 .... 1967 .... **£40**
Flight .... LP .... Turtle .... 301 .... 1970 .... **£30**

RILEY, TERRY

Composer Terry Riley pioneered the use of tape-loops to create a dense, meditational sound and was a direct influence on the Soft Machine school of rock music. His "Church Of Anthrax" is co-credited to John Cale, and the well-known ex-member of the Velvet Underground gets the star billing. Really, however, the music is all Riley's, with Cale essentially sitting at the feet of the master and following as best as he can.

Happy Ending .... LP .... W. Bros .... 46125 .... 1972 .... **£15**

Title	Format	Label	Number	Year	Price	Notes
In 'C'	LP	CBS	64565	1970	**£10**	
Keyboards Studies	LP	Byg		1969	**£30**	French
Le Secret De La Vie	LP	Philips	9120037	1975	**£10**	
Persian Surgery Dervishes	LP	Shandar	83501	1972	**£25**	double
Reed Streams	LP	Mass Art Inc.	M131	1967	**£30**	US

RINGS & THINGS

Title	Format	Label	Number	Year	Price	Notes
Strange Things Are Happening	7"	Fontana	TF987	1968	**£4**	

RINKY DINKS

Title	Format	Label	Number	Year	Price	Notes
Choo Choo Cha Cha	7"	Capitol	CL14999	1959	**£4**	

RINKY DINKS & BOBBY DARIN

Title	Format	Label	Number	Year	Price	Notes
Early In The Morning	7"	London	HLE8679	1958	**£10**	

RIO, BOBBY

Title	Format	Label	Number	Year	Price	Notes
Boy Meets Girl	7"	Pye	7N15790	1965	**£10**	
Don Diddly	7"	Stateside	SS211	1963	**£4**	
Everything In The Garden	7"	Pye	7N15897	1965	**£12**	
Value For Love	7"	Pye	7N15958	1965	**£10**	

RIOT SQUAD

Title	Format	Label	Number	Year	Price	Notes
Any Time	7"	Pye	7N15752	1965	**£12**	
Cry Cry Cry	7"	Pye	7N17041	1966	**£12**	
Gotta Be A First Time	7"	Pye	7N17237	1967	**£12**	
I Take It We're Through	7"	Pye	7N17092	1966	**£12**	
I Wanna Talk About My Baby	7"	Pye	7N15817	1965	**£12**	
It's Never Too Late to Forgive	7"	Pye	7N17130	1966	**£12**	
Not A Great Talker	7"	Pye	7N15869	1965	**£12**	

RIOTS

Title	Format	Label	Number	Year	Price	Notes
I Am In Love	7"	Island	WI197	1965	**£10**	
You Don't Know	7"	Island	WI195	1965	**£10**	

RIPCHORDS

Title	Format	Label	Number	Year	Price	Notes
Gone	7"	CBS	AAG162	1963	**£5**	
Here I Stand	7"	CBS	AAG143	1963	**£5**	
Hey Little Cobra	LP	CBS	BPG62228	1964	**£25**	
Hey Little Cobra	7"	CBS	AAG181	1964	**£8**	
Three Window Coupe	LP	CBS	9016	1965	**£25**	
Three Window Coupe	7"	CBS	AAG202	1964	**£8**	

RIPPERS

Title	Format	Label	Number	Year	Price	Notes
Honestly	LP	Saga		1968	**£12**	

RISING MOON

Title	Format	Label	Number	Year	Price	Notes
Rising Moon	LP	Theatre Pros		197-	**£30**	

RISING SONS

Title	Format	Label	Number	Year	Price	Notes
You're My Girl	7"	Stateside	SS426	1965	**£8**	

RISING STORM

Title	Format	Label	Number	Year	Price	Notes
Calm Before The Rising Storm	LP	Remnant	BBA3571	1968	**£1000**	US

RITTER, TEX

Title	Format	Label	Number	Year	Price	Notes
Blood On The Saddle	LP	Capitol	T1292	1960	**£10**	US
Cowboy Favorites	LP-10"	Capitol	H4004	195-	**£30**	US
Deck Of Cards	7" EP	Capitol	EAP11323	1960	**£4**	
Hillbilly Heaven	LP	Capitol	T1623	1961	**£10**	US
Lincoln Hymns	LP	Capitol	W1562	1961	**£10**	US
Psalms	LP	Capitol	T1100	1959	**£15**	US
Songs From The Western Screen	LP	Capitol	T971	1958	**£25**	US

RIVERS, BLUE & THE MAROONS

Title	Format	Label	Number	Year	Price	Notes
Witchcraft Man	7"	Columbia	DB103	1967	**£8**	

RIVERS, BOYD & CLIFF AUNGIER

Title	Format	Label	Number	Year	Price	Notes
Wanderin'	LP	Decca		1965	**£20**	

RIVERS, DANNY

Title	Format	Label	Number	Year	Price	Notes
Can't You Hear My Heart	7"	Decca	F11294	1960	**£8**	chart single
Hawk	7"	Top Rank	JAR408	1960	**£4**	

Moving In	7"	HMV	POP1000	1962	**£8**	
My Baby's Gone Away	7"	Decca	F11357	1961	**£8**	
There Will Never Be Anyone	7"	Decca	F11865	1964	**£4**	

RIVERS, JOHNNY

And I Know You Wanna Dance	LP	Imperial	LP9307	1966	**£10**	US
At The Whisky A Go Go	LP	Liberty	LBY3031	1964	**£12**	
Back At The Whisky	LP	Imperial	LP9284	1965	**£12**	US
Changes	LP	Liberty	LBY3087	1967	**£10**	
Go Johnny Go	LP	United Artists	UAL3386	1964	**£12**	US
Golden Hits	LP	Imperial	LP9324	1966	**£10**	US
He Don't Love You	7"	Liberty	LIB12021	1965	**£4**	
Here We Go Go Again	LP	Liberty	LBY3036	1964	**£12**	
I Washed My Hands In Muddy Water	7"	Liberty	LIB66175	1966	**£4**	
In Action	LP	Imperial	LP9280	1965	**£12**	US
Maybellene	7"	Liberty	LIB66056	1964	**£4**	
Memphis	7"	Liberty	LIB66032	1964	**£4**	
Midnight Special	7"	Liberty	LIB66087	1965	**£4**	
More Johnny Rivers	7" EP	Liberty	LEP4049	1966	**£5**	
Mountain Of Love	7"	Liberty	LIB66075	1964	**£4**	
Realization	LP	Imperial	LP12372	1968	**£10**	US
Rewind	LP	Imperial	LP9341	1967	**£10**	US
Rocks The Folk	LP	Liberty	LBY3064	1965	**£10**	
Sensational Johnny Rivers	LP	Capitol	T2161	1964	**£12**	US
Seventh Son	7"	Liberty	LIB66112	1965	**£4**	
Tom Dooley	7"	Liberty	LIB12023	1965	**£4**	
Touch Of Gold	LP	Liberty	LBL83141	1968	**£10**	
Tracks Of My Tears	7"	Liberty	LIB66244	1966	**£4**	
Under Your Spell Again	7"	Liberty	LIB66155	1966	**£4**	

RIVERS, TONY & THE CASTAWAYS

Come Back	7"	Columbia	DB7536	1965	**£5**	
Girl Don't Tell Me	7"	Immediate	IM027	1966	**£8**	
God Only Knows	7"	Columbia	DB7971	1966	**£5**	
I Can Guarantee Your Love	7"	Polydor	56245	1968	**£6**	
I Love The Way You Walk	7"	Columbia	DB7224	1964	**£8**	
Life's Too Short	7"	Columbia	DB7336	1964	**£6**	
Nowhere Man	7"	Parlophone	R5400	1966	**£6**	
Shake Shake Shake	7"	Columbia	DB7135	1963	**£6**	
She	7"	Columbia	DB7448	1965	**£5**	

RIVIERAS

California Sun	7"	Pye	7N25237	1964	**£12**	
Campus Party	LP	Riviera	701	1964	**£20**	US
Let's Have A Party	LP	USA	102	1964	**£20**	US

RIVIERAS (2)

Blessings Of Love	7"	HMV	POP773	1960	**£6**	

RIVINGTONS

Bird's The Word	7"	Liberty	LIB55553	1963	**£4**	
Doin' The Bird	LP	Liberty	LRP3282	1963	**£25**	US
Pappa Oom Mow Mow	7"	Liberty	LIB55427	1962	**£5**	

RO RO

Blackbird	7"	Regal Z.	RZ3076	1973	**£8**	
Down On The Road	7"	Regal Z.	RZ3056	1972	**£8**	
Here I Go Again	7"	Parlophone	R5920	1971	**£8**	
Meet At The Water	LP	Regal Z.	SRZA8510	1972	**£30**	

ROAD

Road	LP	Rare Earth	3006	1972	**£10**	

ROADRUNNERS

Pantomania	7" EP	Cavern Sound	2BSNL7	1965	**£15**	

ROADSTERS

Joy Ride	7"	Stateside	SS293	1964	**£8**	

ROARING SIXTIES

The group who made a single in defence of the pirate radio stations were actually the Farinas - later to evolve into Family.

We Love The Pirates	7"	Marmalade	598001	1966	**£25**	

ROBAN'S SKIFFLE GROUP

Title	Format	Label	Cat. No.	Year	Price	Notes
Roban's Skiffle Group	7" EP	Storyville	SEP507		**£6**	
Roban's Skiffle Group	7" EP	Storyville	SEP509		**£6**	
Roban's Skiffle Group	7" EP	Storyville	SEP511		**£6**	

ROBBINS, MARTY

Title	Format	Label	Cat. No.	Year	Price	Notes
By The Time I Get To Phoenix	LP	Columbia	CL2817	1968	**£10**	US
Carl, Lefty And Marty	LP-10"	Columbia	CL2544	1956	**£100**	US
Devil Woman	7"	CBS	AAG114	1962	**£4**	chart single
Greatest Hits	LP	Columbia	CL1325	1959	**£15**	US
Gunfighter	7" EP	Fontana	TFE17224	1960	**£5**	
Gunfighter Ballads And Trail Songs	LP	Columbia	CL1358	1959	**£10**	US
Hawaii's Calling Me	LP	Columbia	CL2040	1963	**£10**	US
Heart Of Marty Robbins	LP	Columbia	STS2016	1969	**£15**	US
Island Woman	LP	Columbia	CL2176	1964	**£10**	US
Just A Little Sentimental	LP	Columbia	CL1666	1961	**£10**	US
Marty After Midnight	LP	Columbia	CL1801	1962	**£10**	US
Marty Robbins	LP	Columbia	CL1189	1958	**£20**	US
Marty's Big Hits	7" EP	Fontana	TFE17161	1959	**£6**	
More Greatest Hits	LP	Columbia	CL1635	1961	**£10**	US
More Gunfighter Ballads & Trail Songs	LP	Columbia	CL1472	1960	**£10**	US
Portrait Of Marty	LP	Columbia	CL1855	1962	**£12**	US
Rock'N'Roll'N'Robbins	LP-10"	Columbia	CL2601	1956	**£350**	US
Song Of Robbins	LP	Columbia	CL2621	1967	**£10**	US
Song Of Robbins	LP	Columbia	CL976	1957	**£25**	US
Song Of The Islands	LP	Columbia	CL1087	1957	**£25**	US
Song Of The Islands	LP	Columbia	CL2625	1967	**£10**	US
Wedding Bells	7" EP	Fontana	TFE17168	1959	**£5**	

ROBBINS, MEL

Title	Format	Label	Cat. No.	Year	Price	Notes
Save It	7"	London	HLM8966	1959	**£40**	

ROBBS

Title	Format	Label	Cat. No.	Year	Price	Notes
Robbs	LP	Mercury	21130	1966	**£15**	US

ROBERTS, ANDY

Title	Format	Label	Cat. No.	Year	Price	Notes
...And The Great Stampede	LP	Elektra	K42151	1973	**£10**	
Home Grown	LP	RCA	SF8086	1971	**£10**	
Nina And The Dream Tree	LP	Pegasus	PEG5	1971	**£10**	
Urban Cowboy	LP	Elektra	K42139	1973	**£10**	

ROBERTS, JOHN

Title	Format	Label	Cat. No.	Year	Price	Notes
I'll Forget About You	7"	Action	ACT4511	1968	**£5**	
I'll Forget About You	7"	Action	ACT4511	1968	**£15**	demo
Sockin' 1,2,3,4	7"	Sue	WI4042	1968	**£8**	

ROBERTS, KENNY

Title	Format	Label	Cat. No.	Year	Price	Notes
Run Like The Devil	7"	Pye	7N17054	1966	**£18**	

ROBERTS, KIM

Title	Format	Label	Cat. No.	Year	Price	Notes
I'll Prove It	7"	Decca	F11813	1964	**£8**	

ROBERTS, RICK

Title	Format	Label	Cat. No.	Year	Price	Notes
She Is A Song	LP	A&M	SP4404	1973	**£10**	US
Windfalls	LP	A&M	AMLH64372	1972	**£10**	

ROBERTSON, B.A.

Title	Format	Label	Cat. No.	Year	Price	Notes
Wringing Applause	LP	Ardent	ADS2804	1973	**£15**	US

ROBIN, TINA

Title	Format	Label	Cat. No.	Year	Price	Notes
Everyday	7"	Vogue Coral	Q72309	1958	**£4**	
Get Out Of My Life	7"	Mercury	AMT1199	1962	**£4**	
Lady Fair	7"	Vogue Coral	Q72284	1957	**£8**	
Never In A Million Years	7"	Vogue Coral	Q72294	1957	**£5**	
No School Tomorrow	7"	Coral	Q72323	1958	**£4**	

ROBINS

Title	Format	Label	Cat. No.	Year	Price	Notes
Cherry Lips	7"	Vogue	V9168	1960	**£25**	
Just Like That	7"	Vogue	V9173	1960	**£25**	
Rock'N'Roll With The Robins	LP	Whippet	WLP703	195-	**£150**	US

ROBINSON, ALVIN

Down Home Girl	7"	Red Bird	RB10010	1964	**£12**	
Something You Got	7"	Pye	7N25248	1964	**£5**	
You Brought My Heart Right Down	7"	Strike	JH307	1966	**£5**	

ROBINSON, HARRY, XV

Heavy Date	7"	Decca	F11319	1961	**£4**	

ROBINSON, JACKIE

Let The Little Girl Dance	7"	Amalgam.	AMG824	196-	**£10**	
Over And Over	7"	Amalgam.	AMG819	196-	**£10**	

ROBINSON, LLOYD

You Told Me	7"	Blue Beat	BB159	1962	**£10**	

ROBINSON, ROSCOE

That's Enough	7"	Pye	7N25385	1966	**£8**	
That's Enough	7"	Wand	WN27	1972	**£5**	

ROBINSON, SMOKEY & THE MIRACLES

Baby Baby Don't Cry	7"	T. Motown	TMG687	1969	**£4**	
Baby Baby Don't Cry	7"	T. Motown	TMG687	1969	**£15**	demo
Four In Blue	LP	T. Motown	STML11151	1970	**£10**	
Going To A Go-Go	7"	T. Motown	TMG853	1973	**£8**	demo
I Don't Blame You At All	7"	T. Motown	TMG774	1971	**£4**	chart single
I Don't Blame You At All	7"	T. Motown	TMG774	1971	**£10**	demo
I Second That Emotion	7"	T. Motown	TMG631	1967	**£5**	chart single
I Second That Emotion	7"	T. Motown	TMG631	1967	**£30**	demo
I'm The One You Need	7"	T. Motown	TMG761	1971	**£4**	chart single
I'm The One You Need	7"	T. Motown	TMG761	1971	**£10**	demo
If You Can Want	7"	T. Motown	TMG648	1968	**£5**	chart single
If You Can Want	7"	T. Motown	TMG648	1968	**£15**	demo
Live	LP	T. Motown	STML11107	1969	**£10**	
Love I Saw In You Was Just A Mirage	7"	T. Motown	TMG598	1967	**£5**	
Love I Saw In You Was Just A Mirage	7"	T. Motown	TMG598	1967	**£40**	demo
Make It Happen	LP	T. Motown	STML11067	1968	**£10**	
More Love/Come Spy With Me	7"	T. Motown	TMG614	1967	**£8**	
More Love/Come Spy With Me	7"	T. Motown	TMG614	1967	**£50**	demo
More Love/Swept For You Baby	7"	T. Motown	TMG614	1967	**£4**	
More Love/Swept For You Baby	7"	T. Motown	TMG614	1967	**£35**	demo
My Girl Has Gone	7"	T. Motown	TMG811	1972	**£10**	
My Girl Has Gone	7"	T. Motown	TMG811	1972	**£40**	demo
Smokey And The Miracles	LP	T. Motown	STML11172	1971	**£10**	
Special Occasion	LP	T. Motown	STML11089	1969	**£10**	
Special Occasion	7"	T. Motown	TMG673	1968	**£5**	chart single
Special Occasion	7"	T. Motown	TMG673	1968	**£15**	demo
Tears Of A Clown	7"	T. Motown	TMG745	1970	**£4**	
Tears Of A Clown/Who's Gonna Take	7"	T. Motown	TMG745	1970	**£10**	demo
Tears Of A Clown/You Must Be Love	7"	T. Motown	TMG745	1970	**£35**	demo
Time Out	LP	T. Motown	STML11129	1970	**£10**	
Tracks Of My Tears	7"	T. Motown	TMG696	1969	**£15**	demo
Tracks Of My tears	7"	T. Motown	TMG696	1969	**£4**	chart single
Yester-Love	7"	T. Motown	TMG661	1968	**£6**	
Yester-love	7"	T. Motown	TMG661	1968	**£20**	demo

ROBINSON, TOM

All Right All Night	7"	EMI	EMI2946	1978	**£5**	
Bully For You	7"	EMI	EMI2916	1979	**£4**	chart single
Don't Take No For An Answer	7"	EMI		1978	**£4**	juke box issue
Live In Hamburg	7"	Panic		1982	**£4**	flexi
Pre-Album Sampler	LP	Harvest	SPRO8791	1978	**£20**	US
Too Good To Be True	7"	EMI	EMI2847DJ	1978	**£5**	promo

ROBISON, CARSON

Jitterbug	7"	MGM	SP1024	1953	**£6**	
Lady Round	7"	MGM	SP1004	1953	**£4**	
Life Gets Teejus	7" EP	MGM	MGMEP669	1958	**£6**	
Square Dance - With Calls	7" EP	MGM	MGMEP755	1961	**£5**	

ROCK BROTHERS

Dungaree Doll	7"	Parlophone	MSP6201	1956	**£8**	

ROCK SHOP

Title	Format	Label	Number	Year	Price	Notes
Rock Shop	LP	Lee		1969	**£60**	US

ROCK WORKSHOP

Title	Format	Label	Number	Year	Price	Notes
Rock Workshop	LP	CBS	64075	1970	**£20**	
Very Last Time	LP	CBS	64394	1971	**£20**	
You To Lose	7"	CBS	5046	1970	**£5**	

ROCK, DICKIE

Title	Format	Label	Number	Year	Price	Notes
Boys	7"	Piccadilly	7N35154	1963	**£4**	
Twenty Flight Rock	7"	Piccadilly	7N35202	1964	**£4**	

ROCK, JOHNNY

Title	Format	Label	Number	Year	Price	Notes
Johnny Rock	7" EP	Vogue	VE170112	195-	**£5**	

ROCK-A-TEENS

Title	Format	Label	Number	Year	Price	Notes
Woo Hoo	7"	Columbia	DB4361	1959	**£8**	
Woo Hoo	LP	Roulette	R25109	1960	**£40**	US

ROCKADROME

Title	Format	Label	Number	Year	Price	Notes
Rockadrome	LP	private			**£75**	Canadian

ROCKERS

Title	Format	Label	Number	Year	Price	Notes
Get Cracking	7"	Oriole	CB1501	1959	**£4**	

ROCKETS

Title	Format	Label	Number	Year	Price	Notes
Gibraltar Rock	7"	Philips	PB982	1959	**£5**	
Warrior	7"	Zodiac	ZR0010	196-	**£5**	

ROCKETS (2)

Neil Young became friendly with The Rockets while still a member of Buffalo Springfield. When later he was looking for a permanent backing band, the Rockets were an obvious choice. Young renamed the group Crazy Horse, recording a "Requiem For The Rockets" on the first album they made together ("Everybody Knows This Is Nowhere").

Title	Format	Label	Number	Year	Price	Notes
Rockets	LP	White Whale	S7116	1968	**£20**	US

ROCKIN' BERRIES

Title	Format	Label	Number	Year	Price	Notes
Black Gold	LP	Satril	SATL4002	1976	**£12**	
Dawn Go Away	7"	Pye	7N17411	1967	**£6**	
Happy To Be Blue	7" EP	Piccadilly	NEP34045	1965	**£8**	
He's In Town	7"	Piccadilly	7N35203	1964	**£4**	chart single
I Could Make You Fall In Love	7"	Piccadilly	7N35304	1966	**£5**	
I Didn't Mean To Hurt You	7"	Piccadilly	7N35197	1964	**£5**	chart single
I Didn't Mean To Hurt You	7" EP	Piccadilly	NEP34039	1965	**£8**	
In Town	LP	Piccadilly	NPL38013	1964	**£50**	chart LP
Itty Bitty Pieces	7"	Decca	F11760	1963	**£6**	
Life Is Just A Bowl Of Berries	LP	Piccadilly	NPL38022	1964	**£50**	
Midnight Mary	7"	Piccadilly	7N35327	1966	**£6**	
New From The Berries	7" EP	Piccadilly	NEP34043	1965	**£8**	
Poor Man's Son	7"	Piccadilly	7N35236	1965	**£4**	chart single
Smiles	7"	Piccadilly	7N35400	1967	**£5**	
Sometimes	7"	Piccadilly	7N35373	1967	**£5**	
Wah Wah Woo	7"	Decca	F11698	1963	**£8**	
Water Is Over My Head	7"	Piccadilly	7N35270	1965	**£4**	chart single
What In The World's Come Over You	7"	Piccadilly	7N35217	1965	**£4**	chart single
You're My Girl	7"	Piccadilly	7N35254	1965	**£4**	chart single

ROCKIN' FOO

Title	Format	Label	Number	Year	Price	Notes
Rockin' Foo	LP	Hobbit	5001	1971	**£12**	US

ROCKIN' HORSE

Title	Format	Label	Number	Year	Price	Notes
Yes It Is	LP	Philips		1970	**£30**	

ROCKIN' R'S

Title	Format	Label	Number	Year	Price	Notes
Crazy Baby	7"	London	HL8872	1959	**£15**	

ROCKIN' RAMRODS

Title	Format	Label	Number	Year	Price	Notes
Don't Fool With Fu Manchu	7"	Polydor	56512	1970	**£8**	

ROCKIN' REBELS

Title	Format	Label	Number	Year	Price	Notes
Rockin' Crickets	7"	Stateside	SS187	1963	**£4**	
Wild Weekend	7"	Stateside	SS162	1963	**£4**	
Wild Weekend	LP	Swan	SLP509	1962	**£50**	US

ROCKIN' SAINTS

Title	Format	Label	Cat. No.	Year	Price	Notes
Cheat On Me Baby	7"	Brunswick	05843	1960	**£15**	

ROCKIN' STRINGS

Title	Format	Label	Cat. No.	Year	Price	Notes
Red Sails In The Sunset	7"	Columbia	DB4349	1959	**£5**	

ROCKIN' VICKERS

Title	Format	Label	Cat. No.	Year	Price	Notes
Dandy	7"	CBS	202241	1966	**£20**	
I Go Ape	7"	Decca	F11993	1964	**£15**	
It's Alright	7"	CBS	202051	1966	**£15**	

ROCKSTEADYS

Title	Format	Label	Cat. No.	Year	Price	Notes
Squeeze And Freeze	7"	Giant	GN2	196-	**£10**	

ROCKYFELLERS

Title	Format	Label	Cat. No.	Year	Price	Notes
Killer Joe	LP	Scepter	SP512	1963	**£10**	US
Killer Joe	7"	Stateside	SS175	1963	**£4**	
Like The Big Guys Do	7"	Stateside	SS212	1963	**£4**	

ROCOMARS

Title	Format	Label	Cat. No.	Year	Price	Notes
All In Black Woman	7"	King	KG1031	1966	**£30**	

RODGERS, EILEEN

Title	Format	Label	Cat. No.	Year	Price	Notes
Sailor	7"	London	HLR9271	1961	**£10**	

RODGERS, JIMMIE (1)

Title	Format	Label	Cat. No.	Year	Price	Notes
Best Of...	LP	RCA	LPM3315	1965	**£12**	US
Country Music Hall Of Fame	LP	RCA	LPM2531	1962	**£12**	US
Jimmie Rodgers	7" EP	HMV	7EG8163	195-	**£10**	
Jimmie The Kid	LP	RCA	LPM2213	1961	**£12**	US
Legendary Jimmie Rodgers	7" EP	RCA	RCX1058	1960	**£8**	
Memorial Album Vol.1	LP-10"	RCA	LPT3037	1952	**£25**	US
Memorial Album Vol.2	LP-10"	RCA	LPT3038	1952	**£25**	US
Memorial Album Vol.3	LP-10"	RCA	LPT3039	1952	**£25**	US
My Rough And Rowdy Ways	LP	RCA	LPM2112	1960	**£12**	US
My Time Ain't Long	LP	RCA	LPM2865	1964	**£12**	US
Never No Mo' Blues	LP	RCA	LPM1232	1955	**£15**	US
Short But Brilliant Life Of...	LP	RCA	LPM2634	1963	**£12**	US
Train Whistle Blues	LP	RCA	LPM1640	1957	**£15**	US
Travellin' Blues	LP-10"	RCA	LPT3073	1952	**£25**	US

RODGERS, JIMMIE (2)

Title	Format	Label	Cat. No.	Year	Price	Notes
English Country Garden	7"	Columbia	DB4847	1962	**£4**	chart single
English Country Garden	7" EP	Columbia	SEG8253	1963	**£4**	
English Country Garden	7" EP	Dot	DEP20002	1965	**£4**	
Folk Songs And Readings	LP	Roulette	R25020	1958	**£10**	US
His Golden Year	LP	Roulette	R25057	1959	**£10**	US
Honeycomb	7"	Columbia	DB3986	1957	**£8**	chart single
Jimmie Rodgers	7" EP	Columbia	SEG7770	1958	**£6**	
Jimmie Rodgers Favourites	7" EP	Dot	DEP20007	1965	**£5**	
Jimmie Rodgers No.2	7" EP	Columbia	SEG7911	1959	**£4**	
Jimmie Rodgers Sings	7" EP	Columbia	SEG7811	1958	**£5**	
Jimmie Rodgers Sings Folk Songs	LP	Roulette	R25042	1958	**£10**	US
Kisses Sweeter Than Wine	7"	Columbia	DB4052	1957	**£4**	chart single
Long Hot Summer	LP	Roulette	R25026	1958	**£15**	US
Number One Ballads	LP	Roulette	R25033	1958	**£10**	US
Oh Oh, I'm Falling In Love Again	7"	Columbia	DB4078	1958	**£4**	chart single
Woman From Liberia	7"	Columbia	DB4206	1958	**£4**	chart single

RODRIGUEZ, RICO

Title	Format	Label	Cat. No.	Year	Price	Notes
Luke Lane Shuffle	7"	Blue Beat	BB56	1961	**£10**	

ROE, TOMMY

Title	Format	Label	Cat. No.	Year	Price	Notes
Dizzy	LP	ABC	S683	1969	**£10**	US
Don't Cry Donna	7"	HMV	POP1117	1963	**£4**	
Everybody	7"	HMV	POP1207	1963	**£4**	chart single
Everybody Likes Tommy Roe	LP	HMV	CLP1074	1965	**£10**	
Folk Singer	7"	HMV	POP1138	1963	**£4**	chart single
Folk Singer	7" EP	HMV	7EG8806	1963	**£5**	
It's Now Winter's Day	LP	ABC	594	1967	**£10**	US
Kiss And Run	7"	HMV	POP1174	1963	**£4**	
Phantasy	LP	ABC	610	1967	**£10**	US

Title	Format	Label	Number	Year	Price	Notes
Sheila	LP	ABC	432	1962	**£12**	US
Sheila	7"	HMV	POP1060	1962	**£5**	chart single
Something For Everybody	LP	ABC	467	1964	**£10**	US
Susie Darlin'	7"	HMV	POP1092	1962	**£4**	chart single
Sweet Pea	LP	ABC	575	1966	**£10**	US

ROGERS, DEAN

Title	Format	Label	Number	Year	Price	Notes
Keep The Miracle Going	7"	Parlophone	R4732	1961	**£4**	
Timber	7"	Parlophone	R4835	1961	**£4**	

ROGERS, JULIE

Title	Format	Label	Number	Year	Price	Notes
Julie Rogers	7" EP	Mercury	10023MCE	1964	**£4**	
Sound Of Julie	7" EP	Mercury	10028MCE	1965	**£4**	

ROGERS, MARK & THE MARKSMEN

Title	Format	Label	Number	Year	Price	Notes
Hold It	7"	Parlophone	R5045	1963	**£10**	

ROGERS, ROY

Title	Format	Label	Number	Year	Price	Notes
Bible Tells Me So	LP	Capitol	T1745	1962	**£12**	US
Christmas Is Always	LP	Capitol	T2818	1967	**£10**	US
Happy Trails	7" EP	HMV	7EG8182	195-	**£8**	
Hymns Of Faith	LP-10"	RCA	LPT3168	1954	**£20**	US
Jesus Loves Me	LP	Bluebird	LBY1022	1959	**£12**	US
Roy Rogers	7" EP	HMV	7EG8145	195-	**£6**	
Souvenir Album	LP-10"	RCA	LPT3041	1952	**£25**	US
Sweet Hour Of Prayer	LP	RCA	LPM1439	1957	**£15**	US

ROGERS, TIMMIE

Title	Format	Label	Number	Year	Price	Notes
Back To School Again	7"	London	HLU8510	1957	**£12**	
Take Me To Your Leader	7"	London	HLU8601	1958	**£25**	

ROGUES

Title	Format	Label	Number	Year	Price	Notes
Memories Of Missy	7"	Decca	F12718	1967	**£6**	
Rogers Reef	7"	CBS	201731	1965	**£8**	

ROKES

Title	Format	Label	Number	Year	Price	Notes
Hold My Hand	7"	RCA	RCA1646	1967	**£8**	

ROLAND, CHERRY

Title	Format	Label	Number	Year	Price	Notes
Boys	7"	Fontana	TF420	1963	**£4**	
Handy Sandy	7"	Decca	F11579	1963	**£4**	
What A Guy	7"	Decca	F11648	1963	**£4**	

ROLAND, WALTER & GEORGIA SLIM

Title	Format	Label	Number	Year	Price	Notes
Male Blues Vol.1	7" EP	Collector	JE12	196-	**£5**	

ROLLERS

Title	Format	Label	Number	Year	Price	Notes
Continental Walk	7"	London	HLG9340	1961	**£4**	

ROLLING STONES

It is easily forgotten how the Rolling Stones had some of the role of tougher alter egoes for the Beatles during the sixties. As the Beatles started to become more and more experimental in their approach, so the Rolling Stones did the same. When eventually the Beatles came up with "Sgt.Pepper" and "Strawberry Fields For Ever", the Rolling Stones responded with "Their Satanic Majesties Request" and "We Love You". Critics do not like these records very much, seeing them as being apart from what the Rolling Stones are all about, but they quite clearly achieve everything that psychedelic music tried to do. The death of Brian Jones, who loved to experiment with different instruments, apparently robbed the Rolling Stones of their ambition, for little of what the group has played since has extended much beyond a diet of the blues and Chuck Berry.

Title	Format	Label	Number	Year	Price	Notes
12 X 5	LP	London	LL3402	1964	**£20**	US
12 X 5	LP	London	LL3402	1964	**£1000**	US, blue vinyl
19th Nervous Breakdown	7"	Decca	F12331	1966	**£4**	chart single
19th Nervous Breakdown	7"	Decca	F12331	1966	**£60**	demo
19th Nervous Breakdown	7"	Decca	F12331	1966	**£12**	export, PS
19th Nervous Breakdown	7"	Decca	STONE8	1981	**£8**	demo
2000 Light Years From Home	7"	Decca	F22706	1967	**£20**	export
Aftermath	LP	Decca	LK4786	1966	**£20**	chart LP
Aftermath	LP	London	LL3476	1966	**£20**	US
Angie	7"	R. Stones	RS19105	1973	**£4**	chart single
Angie	7"	R. Stones	RS19105	1973	**£12**	demo
Beggar's Banquet	LP	Decca	SKL4955	1968	**£12**	chart LP
Between The Buttons	LP	Decca	LK4852	1967	**£20**	chart LP
Between The Buttons	LP	London	LL499	1967	**£20**	US
Brown Sugar	7"	Atlantic	K19107	1974	**£15**	

Title	Format	Label	Number	Year	Price	Notes
Brown Sugar	7"	R. Stones	RS19100	1971	**£4**	chart single
Brown Sugar	7"	R. Stones	RS19100	1971	**£15**	demo
Brown Sugar	7"	R. Stones	RS19100	1971	**£12**	PS
Brown Sugar	7"	R. Stones	SUGARP1	1984	**£6**	shaped pic disc
Come On	7"	Decca	F11675	1963	**£5**	chart single
Come On	7"	Decca	F11675	1963	**£125**	demo
Come On	7"	Decca	STONE1	1981	**£8**	demo
Con Le Mie La Crime	7"	Decca	F22270	1965	**£20**	sung in Italian
Could You Walk On The Waters	LP	Decca		1966	**£200**	
December's Children	LP	London	LL4451	1965	**£20**	US
Ed Rudy Interview Album	LP	INS Radio	1003	1965	**£50**	US
Emotional Rescue (2 versions)	7"	R. Stones	RSR105DJ	1981	**£6**	promo
Emotional Rescue	LP	R. Stones	CUN39111	1980	**£25**	test pressing
Emotional Rescue	7"	R. Stones		1980	**£5**	interview promo, blue flexi
Emotional Rescue	7"	R. Stones	RSR105	1980	**£5**	demo
Empty Heart	7"	Decca	AT15035	1964	**£20**	export
Exile On Main Street	LP	R. Stones	COC69100	1972	**£12**	double, with postcards chart LP
Exile On Main Street Excerpts	7"	NME	SFI107	1972	**£4**	flexi
Fan Club Single	7"	R. Stones	R8370/1	1983	**£10**	interview disc
First Eight Studio Albums	LP	Decca	ROLL1	1983	**£60**	8 LPs, book, boxed
Five By Five	7" EP	Decca	DFE8590	1964	**£5**	
Five By Five	7" EP	Decca	DFE8590	1964	**£75**	demo
Flowers	LP	Decca	LK4888	1967	**£50**	export
Flowers	LP	London	LL509	1967	**£20**	US
Fool To Cry	7"	R. Stones	RS19121	1976	**£10**	demo
Get Off My Cloud	7"	Decca	F12263	1965	**£4**	chart single
Get Off My Cloud	7"	Decca	F12263	1965	**£70**	demo
Get Off My Cloud	7"	Decca	F22265	1965	**£20**	export
Get Off My Cloud	7"	Decca	STONE6	1981	**£8**	demo
Going To A Go-Go	7"	R. Stones	RSR110	1982	**£5**	demo
Got Live If You Want It	7" EP	Decca	DFE8620	1965	**£5**	
Got Live If You Want It	7" EP	Decca	DFE8620	1965	**£70**	demo
Got Live If You Want It	7" EP	Decca	DFE8620	1965	**£20**	export, red label
Got Live If You Want It	7" EP	Decca	SDE7502	1965	**£20**	export
Got Live If You Want It	LP	London	LL4493	1966	**£20**	US
Great Years	LP	Reader's Dig		1983	**£25**	5 LPs, boxed
Greatest Hits	LP	RCA	SP0268	1972	**£30**	US
Happy	7"	R. Stones	SAM4	1971	**£20**	promo
Have You Seen Your Mother Baby?	7"	Decca	F12497	1966	**£4**	chart single
Have You Seen Your Mother Baby?	7"	Decca	F12497	1966	**£60**	demo
Heart Of Stone	7"	Decca	F22180	1965	**£20**	export
Hightide And Green Grass	LP	Decca	TXL101	1966	**£15**	chart LP
Hightide And Green Grass	LP	London	NP1	1966	**£20**	US
Honky Tonk Women	7"	Decca	F12952	1969	**£4**	chart single
Honky Tonk Women	7"	Decca	F12952	1969	**£30**	demo
Honky Tonk Women	7"	Decca	F13635	1976	**£12**	demo
Honky Tonk Women	7"	Decca	STONE10	1981	**£8**	demo
Hot Stuff	12"	R. Stones		1976	**£20**	promo, black & blue vinyl
Hot Stuff	12"	R. Stones		1976	**£25**	promo, clear vinyl
I Don't Know Why	7"	Decca	F13584	1975	**£8**	
I Don't Know Why	7"	Decca	F13584	1975	**£15**	demo
I Don't Know Why	7"	Decca	F13584	1975	**£12**	Jagger/Richards writing credit
I Wanna Be Your Man	7"	Decca	AT15005	1963	**£20**	export
I Wanna Be Your Man	7"	Decca	F11764	1963	**£4**	chart single
I Wanna Be Your Man	7"	Decca	F11764	1963	**£100**	demo
I Wanna Be Your Man/Stones	7"	Decca	F11764	1963	**£12**	
Interview With Mick Jagger	LP	R. Stones	PR164	1971	**£30**	Tom Donahue - US promo
It's All Over Now	7"	Decca	F11934	1964	**£4**	chart single
It's All Over Now	7"	Decca	F11934	1964	**£90**	demo
It's All Over Now	7"	Decca	F13517	1974	**£40**	
It's All Over Now	7"	Decca	STONE2	1981	**£8**	demo
It's Only Rock'n'Roll	7"	R. Stones	RS19114	1974	**£4**	chart single
It's Only Rock'n'Roll	7"	R. Stones	RS19114	1974	**£12**	demo
It's Only Rock'n'Roll	7"	R. Stones	RS19114DJ	1974	**£15**	promo
Jumpin' Jack Flash	7"	Decca	F12782	1968	**£4**	chart single
Jumpin' Jack Flash	7"	Decca	F12782	1968	**£40**	demo
Jumpin' Jack Flash	7"	Decca	STONE7	1981	**£8**	demo
Last Time	7"	Decca	F12104	1965	**£4**	chart single
Last Time	7"	Decca	F12104	1965	**£80**	demo

Last Time	7"	Decca	F12104	1965	**£12**	export, PS
Last Time	7"	Decca	STONE5	1981	**£8**	demo
Let It Bleed	LP	Decca	SKL5025	1969	**£12**	chart LP
Let's Spend The Night Together	7"	Decca	F12546	1967	**£4**	chart single
Let's Spend The Night Together	7"	Decca	F12546	1967	**£50**	demo
Let's Spend The Night Together	7"	Decca	STONE9	1981	**£8**	demo
Let's Spend The Night Together	7"	R. Stones	RSR112DJ	1982	**£6**	promo
Let's Spend The Night Together	12"	R. Stones	RSR112	1983	**£5**	demo
Little Queenie	7"	Decca	F13126	1971	**£20**	export
Little Red Rooster	7"	Decca	AT15040	1965	**£20**	export
Little Red Rooster	7"	Decca	F12014	1964	**£4**	chart single
Little Red Rooster	7"	Decca	F12014	1964	**£80**	demo
Miss You	7"	R. Stones	EMI2802	1978	**£8**	demo
Miss You	12"	R. Stones	12EMI2802	1978	**£6**	pink vinyl
Miss You	12"	R. Stones		1978	**£15**	1 sided promo
Not Fade Away	7"	Decca	AT15008	1964	**£20**	export
Not Fade Away	7"	Decca	F11845	1964	**£4**	chart single
Not Fade Away	7"	Decca	F11845	1964	**£90**	demo
Not Fade Away	7"	Decca	STONE4	1981	**£8**	demo
Out Of Our Heads	LP	Decca	LK4725	1965	**£70**	export
Out Of Our Heads	LP	Decca	LK4733	1965	**£20**	chart LP
Out Of Our Heads	LP	London	LL3429	1965	**£20**	US
Out Of Time	7"	Decca	F13597	1975	**£4**	chart single
Out Of Time	7"	Decca	F13597	1975	**£15**	demo
Paint It Black	7"	Decca	F12395	1966	**£4**	chart single
Paint It Black	7"	Decca	F12395	1966	**£60**	demo
Poison Ivy	7"	Decca	F11742	1963	**£175**	
Promotional LP	LP	Decca	RSM1	1969	**£300**	promo compilation
Respectable	7"	R. Stones	EMI2861	1978	**£8**	demo
Rest Of The Best Of...	LP	Teldec	630125FX	1984	**£60**	4 LPs, boxed, with 7" German
Rewind 1971-1984	LP	R. Stones	CUN1	1984	**£20**	test pressing
Rocks Off	7"	R. Stones	SAM3	1971	**£20**	promo
Rolling Stones	LP	Decca	LK4605	1964	**£20**	chart LP
Rolling Stones	7" EP	Decca	DFE8560	1964	**£5**	
Rolling Stones	7" EP	Decca	DFE8560	1964	**£80**	demo
Rolling Stones	7" EP	Decca	SDE7503	1966	**£20**	export
Rolling Stones	LP	London	LL3375	1964	**£20**	US
Rolling Stones	LP	London	LL3375	1964	**£100**	US, maroon label, London/ffrr' inbox, bonus photo advertised
Rolling Stones No.2	LP	Decca	LK4661	1965	**£20**	chart LP
Rolling Stones Now!	LP	London	LL3420	1965	**£20**	US
Rolling Stones Vol.2	7" EP	Decca	SDE7501	1964	**£20**	export
Sad Day	7"	Decca	F13404	1973	**£5**	
Sad Day	7"	Decca	F13404	1973	**£20**	demo
Satisfaction	7"	Decca	F12220	1965	**£4**	chart single
Satisfaction	7"	Decca	F12220	1965	**£80**	demo
Satisfaction	7"	Decca	STONE3	1981	**£8**	demo
Satisfaction/Under Assistant W. Coast...	7"	Decca	F12220	1965	**£125**	
Satisfaction/Under Assistant W. Coast...	7"	Decca	F12220	1965	**£10**	export
She Was Hot	7"	R. Stones	RSRP114	1984	**£6**	shaped pic disc
She's So Cold	7"	R. Stones	RSR106	1980	**£5**	demo
Single Stones	7"	Decca	STONE1-12	1981	**£30**	mail order box set with poster & badge
Some Girls	LP	Mobile Fid.	MFSL1087	1982	**£15**	US audiophile
Songs Of The Rolling Stones	LP	ABKCO	MPD1	1973	**£90**	US promo
Songs Of The Rolling Stones Vol.2	LP	ABKCO		197-	**£90**	US promo
Start Me Up	7"	R. Stones	RSR108	1981	**£5**	demo
Sticky Fingers	LP	Mobile Fid.	MFSL1060	1980	**£20**	US audiophile
Sticky Fingers	LP	R. Stones	COC59100	1971	**£10**	insert, chart LP
Still Life	LP	R. Stones	CUNP39115	1982	**£10**	pic disc
Stones On CD	CD	CBS	SAMP1103	198-	**£80**	promo
Street Fighting Man	7"	Decca	F13195	1971	**£4**	chart single
Street Fighting Man	7"	Decca	F13195	1971	**£20**	demo
Street Fighting Man	7"	Decca	F13203	1971	**£10**	
Street Fighting Man	7"	Decca	F13203	1971	**£20**	demo
Street Fighting Man	7"	Decca	F13204	1971	**£20**	export
Street Fighting Man	7"	Decca	F22825	1968	**£25**	export
Street Fighting Man	7"	Decca	STONE11	1981	**£8**	demo
Suckin' In The Seventies	LP	R. Stones	CUN39112	1981	**£20**	test pressing

Title	Format	Label	Cat. No.	Year	Price	Notes
Sympathy For The Devil	7"	Decca	STONE12	1981	**£8**	demo
Tell Me	7"	Decca	AT15032	1964	**£20**	export
Their Satanic Majesties Request	LP	Decca	TXS103	1967	**£25**	3D Cover, chart LP
Their Satanic Majesties Request	LP	London	NP2	1967	**£75**	US, mono
Through The Past Darkly	LP	Decca	SKL5019	1969	**£15**	Octagonal cover, chart LP
Time Is On My Side	7"	Decca	AT15039	1965	**£20**	export
Time Is On My Side	7"	R. Stones	RSR111	1982	**£5**	demo
Time Is On My Side	12"	R. Stones	12RSR111	1982	**£8**	demo
Trident Mixes	LP	ABKCO	PR164	197-	**£400**	US promo double
Tumbling Dice	7"	R. Stones	RS19103	1972	**£4**	chart single
Tumbling Dice	7"	R. Stones	RS19103	1972	**£15**	demo
Under Cover	LP	R. Stones	CUN1654361	1983	**£10**	stickers on cover
Under Cover Of The Night	7"	R. Stones	RSR113DJ	1983	**£6**	1 sided promo
Waiting On A Friend	7"	R. Stones	RSR109	1981	**£5**	demo
Waiting On A Friend	7"	R. Stones	RSR109DJ	1982	**£6**	promo
We Love You	7"	Decca	F12654	1967	**£4**	chart single
We Love You	7"	Decca	F12654	1967	**£50**	demo

ROLLING STONES & OTHERS

Title	Format	Label	Cat. No.	Year	Price	Notes
Jamming With Edward	LP	R. Stones	COC39100	1972	**£10**	

ROMAN, MARK

Title	Format	Label	Cat. No.	Year	Price	Notes
Cuddly Toy	7"	Columbia	DB8360	1968	**£4**	

ROMAN, MURRAY

Title	Format	Label	Cat. No.	Year	Price	Notes
Blind Man's Movie	LP	Track	613015	1969	**£15**	
You Can't Beat People Up	LP	Track	2407013	1970	**£12**	
You Can't Beat People Up...	LP	Track	613007	1969	**£15**	

ROMEO, MAX

Title	Format	Label	Cat. No.	Year	Price	Notes
A Dream	LP	Pama	PMLP11		**£20**	
Clap Clap	7"	Unity	UN545	1969	**£6**	
Don't Want To Let You Go	7"	Caltone	TONE106	196-	**£8**	
It's Not The Way	7"	Blue Cat	BS163	196-	**£10**	
My Jamaican Collie	7"	Ackee	ACK523	1973	**£4**	
No Joshua No	7"	Dragon	DRA1028	1974	**£4**	
Sixpence	7"	Ackee	ACK529	1974	**£4**	
Twelfth Of Never	7"	Island	WI3124	1967	**£10**	
War In A Babylon	7"	Island	WIP6283	1976	**£4**	
Wet Dream	7"	Unity	UN503	1969	**£4**	chart single
Wine Her Goosie	7"	Unity	UN516	1969	**£6**	

ROMERO, CHAN

Title	Format	Label	Cat. No.	Year	Price	Notes
Hippy Hippy Shake	7"	Columbia	DB4341	1959	**£15**	
My Little Ruby	7"	Columbia	DB4405	1960	**£15**	

ROMNEY, HUGH 'WAVY GRAVY'

Title	Format	Label	Cat. No.	Year	Price	Notes
Third Stream Humor	LP	W. Pacific	WP1805	1962	**£15**	US

RONALD & RUBY

Title	Format	Label	Cat. No.	Year	Price	Notes
Lollipop	7"	RCA	RCA1053	1958	**£4**	

RONDELLS

Title	Format	Label	Cat. No.	Year	Price	Notes
Backbeat Number One	7"	London	HLU9404	1961	**£6**	
Good Good	7"	London	HLU8716	1958	**£10**	

RONDO, DON

Title	Format	Label	Cat. No.	Year	Price	Notes
Don't	7"	Columbia	DB3909	1957	**£4**	
Rondo Part One	7" EP	London	REJ1154	1958	**£4**	
Rondo Part Two	7" EP	London	REJ1155	1958	**£4**	
Two Different Worlds	7"	Columbia	DB3854	1956	**£4**	
What A Shame	7"	London	HLJ8567	1958	**£4**	
White Silver Sands	7"	London	HLJ8466	1957	**£4**	

RONETTES

Title	Format	Label	Cat. No.	Year	Price	Notes
Baby I Love You	7"	London	HLU9826	1964	**£5**	chart single
Be My Baby	7"	London	HLU9793	1963	**£5**	chart single
Best Part Of Breaking Up	7"	London	HLU9905	1964	**£6**	chart single
Born To Be Together	7"	London	HLU9952	1965	**£6**	
Do I Love You	7"	London	HLU9922	1964	**£5**	chart single
Fabulous Ronettes	LP	London	HAU8212	1964	**£50**	
I Can Hear Music	7"	London	HLU10087	1966	**£6**	

Is This What I Get For Loving You?	7"	London	HLU9976	1965	**£6**	
Presenting The Fabulous Ronettes	LP	Philles	PHLP4006	1964	**£70**	US, mono
Presenting The Fabulous Ronettes	LP	Philles	PHLPST4006	1964	**£100**	US, stereo
Ronettes	LP	Colpix	PXL486	1965	**£30**	
Walking In The Rain	7"	London	HLU9931	1964	**£5**	
You Came You Saw You Conquered	7"	A&M	AMS748	1969	**£4**	

RONNIE & ROY

Big Fat Sally	7"	Capitol	CL15028	1959	**£15**	

RONNIE & THE DEL AIRES

Drag	7"	Coral	Q72473	1964	**£4**	

RONNIE & THE HI-LITES

Twistin' And Kissin'	7"	Pye	7N25140	1962	**£4**	

RONNIE & THE RAINBOWS

Loose Ends	7"	London	HL9345	1961	**£4**	

RONNO

Fourth Hour Of My Sleep	7"	Vertigo	6059029	1970	**£15**	

RONNY & THE DAYTONAS

Beach Boy	7"	Stateside	SS432	1965	**£6**	
Bucket T	7"	Stateside	SS391	1965	**£8**	
California Bound	7"	Stateside	SS367	1964	**£6**	
GTO	LP	Mala	4001	1964	**£20**	US
GTO	7"	Stateside	SS333	1964	**£6**	
Sandy	LP	Mala	4002	1964	**£20**	US
Sandy	7"	Stateside	SS484	1966	**£6**	

RONSON, MICK

Love Me Tender	7"	RCA	APBO212	1974	**£4**	
Play Don't Worry	LP	RCA	APL10681	1975	**£10**	chart LP
Slaughter On Tenth Avenue	LP	RCA	APL10353	1974	**£10**	chart LP

RONSTADT, LINDA

What's New?	LP	Mobile Fid.	MFSL1158	1984	**£10**	US audiophile

ROOFTOP SINGERS

Walk Right In	7"	Fontana	271700TF	1963	**£4**	chart single
Walk Right In	LP	Vanguard	VRS2136	1963	**£10**	US

ROOGALATOR

Play It By Ear	LP	Do It	RIDE1	1977	**£12**	

ROOM

Pre-Flight	LP	Deram	SML1073	1970	**£120**	

ROOM 13

Murder Mystery	12"	Woronzow	WOO2	1982	**£25**	

ROOM TEN

I Love My Love	7"	Decca	F12249	1965	**£4**	

ROOT BOYS

Please Don't Stop The Wedding	7"	Columbia	DB115	1970	**£8**	

ROSE GARDEN

Next Plane To London	7"	Atlantic	584163	1968	**£4**	

ROSE, ANDY

Just Young	7"	London	HLU8761	1958	**£8**	

ROSE, DAVID ORCHESTRA

Stripper	7"	MGM	MGM1158	1962	**£4**	

ROSE, DUSTY

Birds And The Bees	7"	London	HLU8162	1955	**£20**	
Country Songs	7" EP	London	REU1078	1957	**£10**	

ROSE, TIM

Hide Your Love Away	7"	Dawn	DNS1085	1974	**£4**	

I Guess It's Over	7"	CBS	3478	1968	**£4**	
I've Gotta Get A Message To You	7"	Capitol	CL15664	1970	**£4**	
Love - A Kind Of Hate Story	LP	Capitol	673	1970	**£15**	US
Morning Dew	7"	CBS	202631	1967	**£6**	
Musician	LP	Atlantic	K50183	1975	**£12**	
Musician	7"	Atlantic	K10667	1975	**£4**	
Roanoke	7"	CBS	4209	1969	**£4**	
Through Rose Coloured Glasses	LP	CBS	63636	1969	**£15**	
Tim Rose	LP	CBS	63168	1967	**£20**	
Tim Rose	LP	Dawn	DNLS3062	1974	**£12**	
Tim Rose	LP	Playboy	101	1972	**£15**	US

ROSENMAN, LEONARD

Lord Of The Rings	LP	Fantasy	LORPD2	1978	**£20**	US double pic disc

ROSIE

Lonely Blue Nights	7"	Coral	Q72426	1961	**£4**	

ROSIE & THE ORIGINALS

Angel Baby	7"	London	HLU9266	1961	**£10**	

ROSS, DIANA

Ain't No Mountain High Enough	7"	T. Motown	TMG751	1970	**£4**	chart single
Ain't No Mountain High Enough	7"	T. Motown	TMG751	1970	**£10**	demo
Doobodoodbe N'Doobe	7"	T. Motown	TMG812	1972	**£4**	chart single
Doobodoodbe N'Doobe	7"	T. Motown	TMG812	1972	**£10**	demo
Good Morning Heartache	7"	T. Motown	TMG849	1973	**£4**	
Good Morning Heartache	7"	T. Motown	TMG849	1973	**£10**	demo
I'm Still Waiting	7"	T. Motown	TMG781	1971	**£4**	chart single
I'm Still Waiting	7"	T. Motown	TMG781	1971	**£10**	demo
Reach Out And Touch Somebody's	7"	T. Motown	TMG743	1970	**£4**	chart single
Reach Out And Touch Somebody's	7"	T. Motown	TMG743	1970	**£10**	demo
Remember Me	7"	T. Motown	TMG768	1971	**£4**	chart single
Remember Me	7"	T. Motown	TMG768	1971	**£12**	demo
Surrender	7"	T. Motown	TMG792	1971	**£4**	chart single
Surrender	7"	T. Motown	TMG792	1971	**£10**	demo
Theme From Mahogany	7"	T. Motown	TMG1010	1976	**£8**	demo, PS
Touch Me In The Morning	7"	T. Motown	TMG861	1973	**£4**	chart single
Touch Me In The Morning	7"	T. Motown	TMG861	1973	**£10**	demo

ROSS, DIANA & MARVIN GAYE

You Are Everything	7"	T. Motown	TMG890	1974	**£8**	demo

ROSS, DIANA & SUPREMES & TEMPTATIONS

I Second That Emotion	7"	T. Motown	TMG709	1969	**£4**	chart single
I Second That Emotion	7"	T. Motown	TMG709	1969	**£15**	demo
I'm Gonna Make You Love Me	7"	T. Motown	TMG685	1969	**£4**	chart single
I'm Gonna Make You Love Me	7"	T. Motown	TMG685	1969	**£12**	demo
We Must Fall In Love	7"	T. Motown	TMG730	1970	**£4**	
We Must Fall In Love	7"	T. Motown	TMG730	1970	**£10**	demo

ROSS, DIANA & THE SUPREMES

Forever Came Today	7"	T. Motown	TMG650	1968	**£5**	chart single
Forever Came Today	7"	T. Motown	TMG650	1968	**£15**	demo
Greatest Hits	LP	T. Motown	STML11063	1968	**£10**	chart LP
I'm Living In Shame	7"	T. Motown	TMG695	1969	**£5**	chart single
I'm Living In Shame	7"	T. Motown	TMG695	1969	**£15**	demo
In And Out Of Love	7"	T. Motown	TMG632	1967	**£30**	demo
In And Out of Love	7"	T. Motown	TMG632	1967	**£5**	chart single
Live At The Talk Of The Town	LP	T. Motown	STML11070	1968	**£12**	chart LP
Love Child	LP	T. Motown	STML11095	1969	**£10**	chart LP
Love Child	7"	T. Motown	TMG677	1968	**£4**	chart single
Love Child	7"	T. Motown	TMG677	1968	**£20**	demo
No Matter What Sign You Are	7"	T. Motown	TMG704	1969	**£4**	chart single
No Matter What Sign You Are	7"	T. Motown	TMG704	1969	**£15**	demo
Reflections	LP	T. Motown	STML11073	1968	**£12**	chart LP
Sing And Perform Funny Girl	LP	T. Motown	STML11088	1969	**£12**	
Some Day We'll Be Together	7"	T. Motown	TMG721	1969	**£10**	demo
Some Things You Never Get Used To	7"	T. Motown	TMG662	1968	**£4**	chart single
Some Things You Never Get Used To	7"	T. Motown	TMG662	1968	**£20**	demo
Someday We'll Be Together	7"	T. Motown	TMG721	1969	**£4**	chart single

ROSS, DR. ISAIAH

Title	Format	Label	Cat. No.	Year	Price	Notes
Flying Eagle	LP	Blue Horizon	LP1	1966	**£40**	

ROSS, GENE

Title	Format	Label	Cat. No.	Year	Price	Notes
Endless Sleep	7"	Parlophone	R4434	1958	**£8**	

ROSS, JACKIE

Title	Format	Label	Cat. No.	Year	Price	Notes
Jerk And Twine	7"	Chess	CRS8003	1965	**£10**	
Selfish One	7"	Pye	7N25259	1964	**£15**	

ROSSI, NITA

Title	Format	Label	Cat. No.	Year	Price	Notes
Here I Go Again	7"	Piccadilly	7N35307	1966	**£12**	
Untrue Unfaithful	7"	Piccadilly	7N35258	1965	**£4**	

ROSSO, NINI

Title	Format	Label	Cat. No.	Year	Price	Notes
Il Silenzio	7"	Durium	DRS54000	1965	**£4**	chart single

ROSTILL, JOHN

Title	Format	Label	Cat. No.	Year	Price	Notes
Funny old World	7"	Columbia	DB8794	1971	**£5**	

ROTARY CONNECTION

Title	Format	Label	Cat. No.	Year	Price	Notes
Aladdin	LP	Cadet	LPS317	1968	**£10**	US
Dinner Music	LP	Cadet	LPS328	1970	**£10**	US
Hey Love	LP	Cadet	50006	1971	**£10**	US
Peace At Last	LP	Cadet	LPS318	1969	**£10**	US
Rotary Connection	LP	Chess	CRL4538	1968	**£10**	
Songs	LP	Cadet	LPS322	1969	**£10**	US

ROTH, DAVE LEE

Title	Format	Label	Cat. No.	Year	Price	Notes
Yankee Rose	7"	W. Bros	W8656	1986	**£5**	shaped pic disc

ROTHCHILDS

Title	Format	Label	Cat. No.	Year	Price	Notes
Artificial City	7"	Decca	F12488	1966	**£10**	
You've Made Your Choice	7"	Decca	F12411	1966	**£8**	

ROULETTES

The Roulettes were formed as a backing group for Adam Faith, when the singer attempted to meet the challenge of the Beatles head-on by adopting the same style himself. The Roulettes tried very hard to establish an independent career for themselves as well, but little of the group's material was sufficiently distinctive. The closest they came to a hit was with "Long Cigarette", which is a memorable song for all that it is closely modelled on a John Lennon performance, but a BBC ban put a stop to its progress up the charts.

Title	Format	Label	Cat. No.	Year	Price	Notes
Bad Time	7"	Parlophone	R5110	1964	**£6**	
Help Me Help Myself	7"	Fontana	TF876	1967	**£10**	
Hully Gully Slip And Slide	7"	Pye	7N15467	1962	**£10**	
I Can't Stop	7"	Parlophone	R5461	1966	**£8**	
I Hope He Breaks Your Heart	7"	Parlophone	R5278	1965	**£6**	
I'll Remember Tonight	7"	Parlophone	R5148	1964	**£6**	
Long Cigarette	7"	Parlophone	R5382	1965	**£6**	
Rhyme Boy Rhyme	7"	Fontana	TF822	1967	**£10**	
Soon You'll Be Leaving	7"	Parlophone	R5072	1963	**£8**	
Stakes 'n' Chips	LP	Parlophone	PMC1257	1965	**£200**	
Stubborn Kind Of Fellow	7"	Parlophone	R5218	1964	**£6**	
Tracks Of My Tears	7"	Parlophone	R5419	1966	**£8**	

ROUND ROBIN

Title	Format	Label	Cat. No.	Year	Price	Notes
Kick That Little Foot Sally Ann	7"	London	HLU9908	1964	**£12**	

ROUTERS

Title	Format	Label	Cat. No.	Year	Price	Notes
A Ooga	7"	W. Bros	WB108	1963	**£4**	
Let's Go	7"	W. Bros	WB77	1962	**£4**	chart single
Make It Snappy	7"	W. Bros	WB91	1963	**£4**	
Stamp And Shake	7"	W. Bros	WB139	1964	**£4**	
Stingray	7"	W. Bros	WB97	1963	**£4**	

ROWELY, MAJOR

Title	Format	Label	Cat. No.	Year	Price	Notes
There's A Riot Going On	7"	Stateside	SS438	1965	**£4**	

ROXY MUSIC

Title	Format	Label	Cat. No.	Year	Price	Notes
Manifesto	LP	EG	EGPD001	1983	**£10**	pic disc
Oh Yeah	7"	Polydor		1980	**£5**	1 sided promo
Over You/Eight Miles High	12"	Polydor	POSPX93	1980	**£8**	promo
Trash	12"	Polydor	POSPX32	1978	**£8**	promo

Virginia Plain	7"	Island	WIP6144	1972	**£4**	chart single
Virginia Plain	7"	Island	WIP6144	1972	**£12**	PS

ROY & ANNETTE

My Baby	7"	R&B	JB107	1963	**£10**	

ROY & ENID

He'll Have To Go	7"	Coxsone	CS7069	196-	**£10**	
Reggae For Days	7"	Coxsone	CS7088	196-	**£10**	

ROY & ENID

Rockin' Time	7"	Coxsone	CS7063	196-	**£10**	

ROY & MILLIE

Cherry I Love You	7"	Black Swan	WI409	1964	**£10**	
I'll Go	7"	Blue Beat	BB154	1962	**£10**	
Oh Merna	7"	Black Swan	WI410	1964	**£10**	
Oh Shirley	7"	Black Swan	WI427	1964	**£10**	
There'll Come A Day	7"	Island	WI090	1963	**£10**	

ROY & PATSY

In Your Arms Dear	7"	Blue Beat	BB118	1962	**£10**	

ROY & PAULINE

Have You Seen My Baby	7"	Island	WI067	1963	**£10**	

ROY & THE DUKE ALL STARS

Pretty Blue Eyes	7"	Blue Cat	BS113	1968	**£10**	
Train	7"	Blue Cat	BS117	1968	**£10**	

ROY & YVONNE

Little Girl	7"	Blue Beat	BB258	1964	**£10**	
Two Roads	7"	Black Swan	WI436	1964	**£10**	

ROY, I

Blackman Time	7"	Downtown	DT503	1973	**£5**	
Monkey Fashion	7"	Technique	TE930	1973	**£4**	
Musical Drum Sound	7"	Harry J	HJ6655	1973	**£4**	
Outformer Parker	7"	Attack	ATT8102	1975	**£4**	
Welding	7"	Philips	6006479	1975	**£4**	
Yaha Ma Ride	7"	Atra	ATRA17	1974	**£4**	

ROY, LEE

Oh Ee Baby	7"	Island	WI251	1965	**£10**	

ROY, U

U Roy is the major pioneer where the art of Jamaican DJ music is concerned. It was U Roy who first scored a series of successes with singles that used the stripped down backing tracks from other people's hits as a springboard for his spoken rants. This "toasting" style rapidly became all-pervasive in reggae and was undoubtedly a significant influence on the later American rapping scene.

Festival Wise	7"	Dynamic	DYN448	197-	**£6**	
Flashing My Whip	7"	Duke Reid	DR2519	1971	**£8**	
Hard Feeling	7"	Gay Feet	GS210	1973	**£4**	
Rule The Nation	7"	Duke Reid	DR2510	1970	**£8**	
Tom Drunk	7"	Duke Reid	DR2517	1971	**£8**	
True True	7"	Duke Reid	DR2518	1971	**£8**	
Version Galore	7"	Duke Reid	DR2515	1970	**£8**	
Wake The Town	7"	Duke Reid	DR2509	1970	**£8**	
Wear You To The Ball	7"	Duke Reid	DR2513	1970	**£8**	
You'll Never Get Away	7"	Duke Reid	DR2514	1970	**£8**	

ROYAL GUARDSMEN

Baby Let's Wait	7"	London	HLP10235	1968	**£4**	
I Say Love	7"	London	HLP10182	1968	**£4**	
Return Of The Red Baron	LP	Laurie	LLP2039	1967	**£15**	US
Return Of The Red Baron	7"	Stateside	SS2010	1967	**£4**	chart single
Snoopy And His Friends	LP	Laurie	LLP2042	1967	**£15**	US
Snoopy For President	LP	Laurie	SLLP2046	1968	**£15**	US
Snoopy For President	7"	London	HLP10211	1968	**£4**	
Snoopy Vs. The Red Baron	7"	Stateside	SS574	1967	**£4**	chart single
Snoopy Vs.The Red Baron	LP	Laurie	LLP2038	1967	**£15**	US
Snoopy's Christmas	7"	London	HLP10171	1967	**£4**	

Wednesday .... 7" .... Stateside .... SS2051 .... 1967 .... **£10**

ROYAL HOLIDAYS

Margaret .... 7" .... London .... HLU8722 .... 1958 .... **£8**

ROYAL JOKERS

Rock And Roll Spectacular .... LP .... Dawn .... 1119 .... **£20** .... US
Jet II .... 7" .... Top Rank .... JAR329 .... 1960 .... **£4**

ROYAL TEENS

Little Cricket .... 7" .... Capitol .... CL15068 .... 1959 .... **£5**
Short Shorts .... 7" .... HMV .... POP454 .... 1958 .... **£10**

ROYAL, BILLY JOE

Billy Joe Royal .... LP .... Columbia .... CL2781 .... 1967 .... **£10** .... US
Cherry Hill Park .... LP .... Columbia .... CS9974 .... 1969 .... **£10** .... US
Down In The Boondocks .... 7" .... CBS .... 201802 .... 1965 .... **£4** .... chart single
Down In The Boondocks .... LP .... Columbia .... CL2403 .... 1965 .... **£10** .... US
Heart's Desire .... 7" .... CBS .... 202087 .... 1966 .... **£30**
Introducing .... LP .... CBS .... 1966 .... **£12**
Never In A Hundred Years .... 7" .... Atlantic .... 584002 .... 1966 .... **£4**
Never In A Hundred Years .... 7" .... Oriole .... CB1751 .... 1962 .... **£4**
Yo Yo .... 7" .... CBS .... 202548 .... 1967 .... **£4**

ROYAL, JAMES

Call My Name .... 7" .... CBS .... 202525 .... 1967 .... **£4**
Hey Little Girl .... 7" .... CBS .... 3450 .... 1968 .... **£10**
Send Out Love .... 7" .... CBS .... 4463 .... 1969 .... **£8**
She's About A Mover .... 7" .... Parlophone .... R5290 .... 1965 .... **£5**
Work Song .... 7" .... Parlophone .... R5383 .... 1965 .... **£4**

ROYALETTES

Elegant Sound Of... .... LP .... MGM .... E4366 .... 1966 .... **£10** .... US
It's Gonna Take A Miracle .... LP .... MGM .... E4332 .... 1965 .... **£10** .... US
It's Gonna Take A Miracle .... 7" .... MGM .... MGM1279 .... 1965 .... **£6**
Poor Boy .... 7" .... MGM .... MGM1272 .... 1965 .... **£10**

ROYALS

Never See Come See .... 7" .... Amalgam. .... AMG831 .... 196- **£10**
Save Mama .... 7" .... Blue Beat .... BB259 .... 1964 .... **£10**

ROYALTONES

Flamingo Express .... 7" .... London .... HLU9296 .... 1961 .... **£5**
Holy Smokes .... 7" .... Stateside .... SS309 .... 1964 .... **£5**
Poor Boy .... 7" .... London .... HLJ8744 .... 1958 .... **£8**

ROYCE, EARL & THE OLYMPICS

Guess Things Happen That Way .... 7" .... Parlophone .... R5261 .... 1965 .... **£10**
Que Sera Sera .... 7" .... Columbia .... DB7433 .... 1964 .... **£10**

RUB-A-DUBS

Without Love .... 7" .... Blue Beat .... BB304 .... 1964 .... **£10**

RUBBER BAND

Cream Song Book .... LP .... Major Minor .... SMLP5045 .... 1969 .... **£15**
Hendrix Song Book .... LP .... Major Minor .... 1969 .... **£20**
Moonwalker .... 7" .... Youngblood .... YB1052 .... 1973 .... **£4**

RUBBER BOOTZ

Joy Ride .... 7" .... Deram .... DM134 .... 1967 .... **£4**

RUBBER BUCKET

We Are Living In One Place .... 7" .... MCA .... MK5006 .... 1969 .... **£12**

RUBBER MEMORY

Welcome .... LP .... RPC .... 69401 .... 1966 .... **£25** .... US

RUBEN & THE JETS

Con Safos .... LP .... Mercury .... SRM1694 .... 1973 .... **£12** .... US
For Real .... LP .... Mercury .... SRM1659 .... 1973 .... **£15** .... US

RUBIAYATS

Omar Khayam .... 7" .... Action .... ACT4516 .... 1968 .... **£10** .... demo

RUBIN

You've Been Away	7"	MCA	MCA196	1975	**£5**	

RUBY & THE ROMANTICS

Baby Come Home	7"	London	HLR9916	1964	**£4**	
Greatest Hits	LP	London	HAR8282	1966	**£12**	
Hey There Lonely Boy	7"	London	HLR9771	1963	**£4**	
Hey There Lonely Boy	7" EP	London	RER1427	1964	**£8**	
More Than Yesterday	LP	ABC	S638	1968	**£10**	US
My Summer Love	7"	London	HLR9734	1963	**£4**	
Our Day Will Come	LP	London	HAR8078	1963	**£12**	
Our Day Will Come	7"	London	HLR9679	1963	**£4**	chart single
Our Day Will Come	7" EP	London	RER1389	1963	**£8**	
Our Everlasting Love	7"	London	HLR9881	1964	**£4**	
Ruby And The Romantics	LP	Kapp	KL1526	1967	**£10**	US
Till Then	LP	Kapp	KL1341	1963	**£10**	US
When You're Young And In Love	7"	London	HLR9935	1964	**£5**	
Young Wings Can Fly	7"	London	HLR9801	1963	**£4**	
Your Baby Doesn't Love You Anymore	7"	London	HLR9972	1965	**£4**	

RUDE BOYS

Rock Steady Massachusetts	7"	Island	WI3088	1967	**£10**	

RUDI

Big Time	7"	Good Vibs	GOT1	1978	**£4**	
Big Time	7"	Good Vibs	GOT1	1978	**£5**	folded paper 'Mummy' PS
I Spy	7"	Good Vibs	GOT12	1979	**£4**	

RUDIES

7-11	7"	Blue Cat	BS107	196-	**£10**	
Cupid	7"	Blue Cat	BS109	1968	**£10**	

RUDY & SKETTO

ABC Boogie	7"	Dice	CC2	1962	**£10**	
Hold The Fire	7"	Dice	CC16	1963	**£10**	
Little Schoolgirl	7"	Dice	CC7	1962	**£10**	
Minna	7"	Blue Beat	BB252	1964	**£10**	
Mr.Postman	7"	Dice	CC10	1963	**£10**	
Never Set You Free	7"	Dice	CC19	1963	**£10**	
Oh Dolly	7"	Blue Beat	BB310	1964	**£10**	
See What You Done	7"	Blue Beat	BB297	1964	**£10**	
Show Me The Way To Go Home	7"	Blue Beat	BB208	1963	**£10**	
Summer Is Just Around The Corner	7"	Dice	CC5	1962	**£10**	
Ten Thousand Miles From Home	7"	Blue Beat	BB230	1963	**£10**	
Was It Me	7"	Blue Beat	BB198	1963	**£10**	

RUFF, RAY & THE CHECKMATES

I Took A Liking To You	7"	London	HLU9889	1964	**£10**	

RUFFIN, DAVID

Feelin' Good	LP	T. Motown	STML11139	1970	**£12**	
Heavy Love	7"	T. Motown	TMG1022	1976	**£4**	
I've Lost Everything I Ever Loved	7"	T. Motown	TMG711	1969	**£4**	
I've Lost Everything I Ever Loved	7"	T. Motown	TMG711	1969	**£12**	demo
My Whole World Ended	LP	T. Motown	STML11118	1969	**£10**	
Whole World Ended	7"	T. Motown	TMG689	1969	**£4**	
Whole World Ended	7"	T. Motown	TMG689	1969	**£10**	demo

RUFFIN, DAVID & JIMMY

I Am My Brother's Keeper	LP	T. Motown	STML11176	1971	**£10**	

RUFFIN, JIMMY

Don't Let Him Take Your Love From Me	7"	T. Motown	TMG664	1968	**£5**	
Don't Let Him Take Your Love From Me	7"	T. Motown	TMG664	1968	**£20**	demo
Don't You Miss Me A Little Bit Baby	7"	T. Motown	TMG617	1967	**£6**	
Don't You Miss Me A Little Bit Baby	7"	T. Motown	TMG617	1967	**£30**	demo
Farewell Is A Lonely Sound	7"	T. Motown	TMG726	1970	**£4**	chart single
Farewell Is A Lonely Sound	7"	T. Motown	TMG726	1970	**£10**	demo
Gonna Give Her All The Love I Got	7"	T. Motown	TMG603	1967	**£6**	chart single
Gonna Give Her All The Love I Got	7"	T. Motown	TMG603	1967	**£35**	demo
I'll Say Forever My Love	7"	T. Motown	TMG649	1968	**£5**	
I'll Say Forever My Love	7"	T. Motown	TMG649	1968	**£15**	demo

Title	Format	Label	Cat. No.	Year	Price	Notes
I'll Say Forever My Love	7"	T. Motown	TMG740	1970	**£4**	chart single
I'll Say Forever My Love	7"	T. Motown	TMG740	1970	**£10**	demo
I've Passed This Way Before	7"	T. Motown	TMG593	1967	**£6**	chart single
I've Passed This Way Before	7"	T. Motown	TMG593	1967	**£40**	demo
I've Passed This Way Before	7"	T. Motown	TMG703	1969	**£4**	chart single
I've Passed This Way Before	7"	T. Motown	TMG703	1969	**£15**	demo
It's Wonderful	7"	T. Motown	TMG753	1970	**£4**	chart single
It's Wonderful	7"	T. Motown	TMG753	1970	**£10**	demo
Jimmy Ruffin	LP	Polydor	2383240	1973	**£10**	
Jimmy Ruffin Way	LP	T. Motown	STML11048	1967	**£15**	chart LP
Let's Say Goodbye Tomorrow	7"	T. Motown	TMG767	1971	**£4**	
Let's Say Goodbye Tomorrow	7"	T. Motown	TMG767	1971	**£10**	demo
On The Way Out	7"	T. Motown	TMG784	1971	**£4**	
On The Way Out	7"	T. Motown	TMG784	1971	**£10**	demo
Ruff 'N' Ready	LP	T. Motown	STML11106	1969	**£15**	
What Becomes Of The Broken Hearted	7"	T. Motown	TMG577	1966	**£5**	chart single
What Becomes Of The Broken Hearted	7"	T. Motown	TMG577	1966	**£40**	demo

RULERS

Title	Format	Label	Cat. No.	Year	Price	Notes
Copasetic	7"	Rio	R107	1967	**£10**	
Don't Be A Rude Boy	7"	Rio	R105	1966	**£10**	

RUMBLE

Title	Format	Label	Cat. No.	Year	Price	Notes
Rich Man Poor Man	7"	W. Bros	WB8011	1970	**£4**	

RUMBLERS

Title	Format	Label	Cat. No.	Year	Price	Notes
Boss	LP	London	HAD8081	1963	**£12**	
Boss	7"	London	HLD9684	1963	**£5**	
Bossounds	7" EP	London	RED1396	1963	**£8**	

RUMOUR

Title	Format	Label	Cat. No.	Year	Price	Notes
Emotional Traffic	7"	Stiff	BUY45DJ	1979	**£6**	black or blue vinyl
Frozen Years	7"	Stiff	RUM1	1979	**£6**	promo

RUMPELSTILTSKIN

Title	Format	Label	Cat. No.	Year	Price	Notes
Rumpelstiltskin	LP	Bell	6047	1969	**£15**	US

RUNAWAYS

Title	Format	Label	Cat. No.	Year	Price	Notes
Little Lost Girls	12"	Rhino		1981	**£8**	US pic disc

RUNDGREN, TODD

Title	Format	Label	Cat. No.	Year	Price	Notes
Ballad Of Todd Rundgren	LP	Bearsville	K45506	1971	**£12**	
Dream Goes On Forever	7"	Bearsville	K15515	1974	**£4**	
Good Vibrations	7"	Bearsville	K15524	1976	**£4**	
Healing	LP	Bearsville	ILPS9657	1981	**£10**	with 7" (PSR455)
Hello It's Me	7"	Bearsville	K15513	1974	**£4**	
I Saw The Light	7"	Bearsville	K15506	1972	**£4**	chart single
Real Man	7"	Bearsville	K15521	1975	**£4**	
Runt	LP	Bearsville	K45505	1970	**£12**	
Something Anything	LP	Bearsville	2BR2066	1972	**£80**	US double promo 1 red, 1 blue vinyl
Something Anything	LP	Bearsville	K65501	1972	**£12**	double
Time Heals	7"	Avatar	AVAB1	1982	**£4**	pic disc
Todd	LP	Bearsville	K85501	1974	**£12**	double
Todd Rundgren Radio Show	LP	Bearsville	PRO524	1972	**£30**	US promo
Todd Rundgren Radio Show	LP	Bearsville	PRO597	1974	**£25**	US promo
We Gotta Get You A Woman	7"	Bearsville	K15509	1973	**£4**	
Wizard A True Star	LP	Bearsville	K45513	1973	**£10**	
Wolfman Jack	7"	Bearsville	K15519	1974	**£4**	

RUNDGREN, TODD & PATTI SMITH

Title	Format	Label	Cat. No.	Year	Price	Notes
Back To The Bars	LP	Bearsville	PROA788	1978	**£25**	US promo

RUNDGREN, TODD & UTOPIA

Title	Format	Label	Cat. No.	Year	Price	Notes
I Just Want To Touch You	7"	Bearsville	IEP12DJ	1980	**£4**	1 sided promo
Utopia	LP	Epic	25207	1982	**£10**	with 7" (XPS166)

RUNNING MAN

Title	Format	Label	Cat. No.	Year	Price	Notes
Running Man	LP	Neon	NE11	1972	**£60**	

RUNNING, JUMPING & STANDING STILL

Title	Format	Label	Cat. No.	Year	Price	Notes
Aye O	7"	Liberty	LBF15209	1969	**£5**	

RUPERT & DAVID

Title	Format	Label	Cat. No.	Year	Price	Notes
Sound Of Silence	7"	Decca	F12306	1965	**£4**	

RUPERT'S PEOPLE

Title	Format	Label	Cat. No.	Year	Price	Notes
I Can Show You	7"	Columbia	DB8362	1968	**£12**	
Prologue To A Magic World	7"	Columbia	DB8278	1967	**£15**	
Reflections Of Charles Brown	7"	Columbia	DB8226	1967	**£10**	

RUSH

Title	Format	Label	Cat. No.	Year	Price	Notes
Big Money	7"	Vertigo	RUSHDJ12	1985	**£4**	promo
Big Money	12"	Vertigo	RUSH1212	1985	**£6**	double
Body Electric	10"	Mercury	RUSH1110	1984	**£6**	red vinyl
Closer To The Heart	7"	Mercury	RUSH7	1981	**£4**	chart single
Closer To The Heart	12"	Mercury	RUSH12	1978	**£6**	
Everything You Always Wanted To Hear	LP	Mercury	MK32	1975	**£25**	US promo
Hemispheres	LP	Mercury	9100059	1978	**£12**	pic disc
Power Windows	LP				**£10**	pic disc
Rush Through Time	LP	Mercury	001	1978	**£25**	US promo pic disc
Rush'n'Roulette	12"	Mercury		1982	**£15**	US promo, 6 tracks running simultaneously
Spirit Of Radio	7"	Mercury	RADIO7	1980	**£4**	chart single
Spirit Of Radio	12"	Mercury	RADIO12	1980	**£6**	
Subdivisions	7"	Mercury	RUSHP9	1982	**£4**	pic disc
Time Stand Still	12"	Vertigo	RUSHP1312	1986	**£6**	pic disc
Vital Signs	7"	Mercury	VITAL7	1981	**£4**	chart single
Vital Signs	7"	Mercury	VITAL7DJ1	1980	**£5**	1 sided promo
Vital Signs	12"	Mercury	VITAL12	1981	**£6**	

RUSH (2)

Title	Format	Label	Cat. No.	Year	Price	Notes
Happy	7"	Decca	F12614	1967	**£5**	
Make Mine Music	7"	Decca	F12635	1967	**£5**	

RUSH, OTIS

Title	Format	Label	Cat. No.	Year	Price	Notes
All Your Love	7"	Blue Horizon	573159	1969	**£10**	
Chicago Blues Today Vol.2	LP	Vanguard	VSD79217	1966	**£15**	
Homework	7"	Vocalion	VP9260	1966	**£4**	
Mourning In The Morning	LP	Atco	K40495	1969	**£15**	
This One's A Good Un	LP	Blue Horizon	763222	1968	**£40**	

RUSH, TOM

Title	Format	Label	Cat. No.	Year	Price	Notes
Blues And Folk	LP	XTRA	XTRA5024	1965	**£15**	
Circle Game	LP	Elektra	EKS74018	1968	**£15**	
I Got A Mind To Ramble	LP	XTRA	XTRA5053	1968	**£15**	
Merrimack County	LP	CBS	64887	1972	**£10**	
Mind Ramblin'	LP	Prestige	14003	1963	**£15**	US
No Regrets	7"	Elektra	EKSN45025	1968	**£4**	
On The Road Again	7"	Elektra	EKSN45015	1967	**£5**	
Something In The Way She Moves Me	7"	Elektra	EK45718	1970	**£4**	
Something In The Way She Moves Me	7"	Elektra	EKSN45032	1968	**£4**	
Take A Little Walk With Me	LP	Elektra	EKL308	1966	**£15**	
Tom Rush	LP	CBS	63940	1970	**£10**	
Tom Rush	LP	Elektra	EKL288	1965	**£15**	
Wrong End Of A Rainbow	LP	CBS	64268	1970	**£10**	

RUSHENT, MARTIN

Title	Format	Label	Cat. No.	Year	Price	Notes
Give It All You've Got	7"	Albion	DEL1	1979	**£4**	

RUSSAL, THANE

Title	Format	Label	Cat. No.	Year	Price	Notes
Drop Everything And Run	7"	CBS	202403	1966	**£10**	
Security	7"	CBS	202049	1966	**£8**	

RUSSELL, DOROTHY

Title	Format	Label	Cat. No.	Year	Price	Notes
You're The One I Love	7"	Duke Reid	DR2524	1971	**£6**	

RUSSELL, LEON

Title	Format	Label	Cat. No.	Year	Price	Notes
And The Shelter People	LP	A&M	AMLS65003	1971	**£10**	chart LP
Asylum Choir II	LP	A&M	AMLS68089	1971	**£10**	
Everybody's Talkin' 'Bout The Young	7"	Pye	7N16771	1965	**£5**	
Leon Russell	LP	A&M	AMLS982	1970	**£10**	
Leon Russell	LP	Shelter	SHE1001	1968	**£12**	US, extra track
Looking Inside The Asylum Choir	LP	Mercury	SMCL21041	1968	**£10**	

RUSSELL, RAY

Dragon Hill	LP	CBS	52663	1969	**£25**	
June 11th 1971	LP	RCA	SF8214	1971	**£20**	
Rites And Rituals	LP	CBS	64271	1971	**£25**	
Secret Asylum	LP	Black Lion	BLP12100	1973	**£20**	
Turn Circle	LP	CBS	52586	1968	**£25**	

RUSSO, WILLIAM

Three Pieces For Blues Band And Symphony Orchestra	LP	Deutsche Gra.	2530309	197-	**£10**	with Siegel-Schwall Band

RUSTIKS

I'm Not The Loving Kind	7"	Decca	F12059	1965	**£5**	
What A Memory Can Do	7"	Decca	F11960	1964	**£8**	

RUSTY & DOUG

Hey Mae	7"	Oriole	CB1510	1959	**£15**	
Hey Mae	7"	Polydor	NH66970	1962	**£8**	

RUTHERFORD, MIKE

Time And Time Again/End Of The Day	7"	Charisma	CB364	1980	**£8**	PS
Time And Time Again/Overnight Job	7"	Charisma	CB364	1980	**£8**	PS
Time And Time Again/Overnight Job	7"	Charisma	CB364	1980	**£4**	PS, B side labelled 'End Of The Day'
Working In Line	7"	Charisma	CB353	1980	**£4**	

RUTLES

The Rutles album and its accompanying television program is an affectionate parody by Neil Innes and Eric Idle of the career of the Beatles. The cover of the LP is almost better than the music inside - it displays numerous photographs of album sleeves and group portraits that exactly mirror originals featuring the Beatles. The music is cleverly constructed to be reminiscent of key songs by the Beatles, although ultimately Neil Innes' recreations are rather less skillful than those put together by XTC on their Dukes Of Stratosfear albums.

I Must Be In Love	7"	W. Bros	K17125	1978	**£4**	chart single
Let's Be Natural	7"	W. Bros	K17180	1978	**£4**	
Rutles	LP	W. Bros	K56459	1978	**£10**	chart LP
Rutles Sampler	12"	W. Bros	PROA723	1978	**£12**	US promo, yellow vinyl

RYAN, BARRY

Eloise	7"	MGM	MGM1442	1968	**£4**	chart single

RYAN, CHARLIE

Hot Rod	LP	King	751	1961	**£20**	US

RYAN, KRIS & THE QUESTIONS

On THe Right Track	7" EP	Mercury	10024MCE	1965	**£8**	

RYAN, PAUL & BARRY

Claire	7"	Decca	F12633	1967	**£4**	chart single
Don't Bring Me Your Heartaches	7"	Decca	F12260	1965	**£4**	chart single
Have Pity On The Boy	7"	Decca	F12319	1966	**£4**	chart single
Have You Ever Loved Somebody	7"	Decca	F12494	1966	**£4**	chart single
I Love Her	7"	Decca	F12391	1966	**£4**	chart single
I Love How You Love Me	7"	Decca	F12445	1966	**£4**	chart single
Keep It Out Of Sight	7"	Decca	F12567	1967	**£4**	chart single
Missy Missy	7"	Decca	F12520	1966	**£4**	chart single
Two Of A Kind	LP	Decca	LK4878	1967	**£10**	

RYAN, PHIL & THE CRESCENTS

Gypsy Woman	7"	Columbia	DB7574	1965	**£6**	
Mary Don't You Weep	7"	Columbia	DB7406	1964	**£5**	

RYDELL, BOBBY

All The Hits	LP	Cameo Park	C1019	1962	**£10**	
All The Hits Vol.2	LP	Cameo Park	C1040	1963	**£10**	
At The Copa	LP	Cameo	C1011	1961	**£10**	US
Best Of Bobby Rydell	7" EP	Summit	LSE2036	196-	**£4**	
Biggest Hits	LP	Cameo	C1009	1961	**£15**	US, gatefold
Biggest Hits Vol.2	LP	Cameo	C1028	1962	**£10**	US
Bobby Rydell	7" EP	Cameo Park	CPE553	1963	**£6**	
Bobby Rydell Salutes The Great Ones	LP	Cameo	C1010	1961	**£12**	US
Bobby Sings	LP	Cameo	C1007	1960	**£15**	US
Bye Bye Birdie	LP	Cameo Park	C1043	1963	**£10**	

Fish	7"	Columbia	DB4690	1961	**£4**	
Forget Him	7"	Cameo Park.	C108	1963	**£4**	chart single
Good Time Baby	7"	Columbia	DB4600	1961	**£4**	chart single
I Wanna Thank You	7"	Columbia	DB4731	1961	**£4**	
I'll Never Dance Again	7"	Columbia	DB4858	1962	**£4**	
I've Got Bonnie	7"	Columbia	DB4785	1962	**£4**	
It's Time We Parted	7"	Cameo Park.	C129	1962	**£4**	
Kissin' Time	7"	Top Rank	JAR181	1959	**£4**	
Lovingest	7" EP	Top Rank	JKP2059	1960	**£8**	
Sings And Swings	LP	Columbia	33SX1308	1960	**£12**	
Sway	7"	Columbia	DB4545	1960	**£4**	chart single
Sway With Bobby Rydell	7" EP	Cameo Park.	CPE551	1963	**£6**	
Swinging School	7"	Columbia	DB4471	1960	**£4**	chart single
That Old Black Magic	7"	Columbia	DB4651	1961	**£4**	
Volare	7"	Columbia	DB4495	1960	**£4**	chart single
We Got Love	LP	Cameo	C1006	1959	**£15**	US
We Got Love	7"	Top Rank	JAR227	1959	**£4**	
Wild (Wood) Days	LP	Cameo	C1055	1963	**£10**	US
Wild One	7"	Columbia	DB4429	1960	**£4**	chart single

RYDER, MAL

Cry Baby	7"	Decca	F11669	1963	**£10**	
Lonely Room	7"	Piccadilly	7N35234	1965	**£12**	
See The Funny Little Clown	7"	Vocalion	V9219	1964	**£10**	
Your Friend	7"	Piccadilly	7N35209	1964	**£10**	

RYDER, MITCH

All Mitch Ryder Hits!	LP	New Voice	2004	1967	**£10**	US
Breakout	LP	Stateside	SL10189	1967	**£12**	
Breakout	7"	Stateside	SS521	1966	**£15**	
Devil With A Blue Dress On	7"	Stateside	SS549	1966	**£6**	
Jenny Take A Ride	7"	Stateside	SS481	1966	**£5**	chart single
Joy	7"	Stateside	SS2037	1967	**£5**	
Little Latin Lupe Lu	7"	Stateside	SS498	1966	**£6**	
Mitch Ryder Sings The Hits	LP	New Voice	S2005	1968	**£10**	US
Personality	7"	Stateside	SS2096	1968	**£5**	
Ridin'	7" EP	Stateside	SE1039	1966	**£8**	
Sock It To Me Baby	7"	Stateside	SS596	1967	**£6**	
Sock It To Me!	LP	New Voice	2003	1967	**£12**	US
Take A Ride	LP	Stateside	SL10178	1966	**£15**	
Too Many Fish In The Sea	7"	Stateside	SS2023	1967	**£5**	
What Now My Love	LP	Stateside	SL10229	1967	**£10**	
What Now My Love	7"	Stateside	SS2063	1967	**£5**	
You Are My Sunshine	7"	Stateside	SS2075	1968	**£5**	

S

S.O.A.

Title	Format	Label	Cat. No.	Year	Price	Notes
No Policy	7"	Dischord	2 (NR12554)	1981	**£30**	with insert
No Policy	7"	Dischord	2 (NR12554)	1981	**£70**	with insert, green vinyl

SABLE, PAUL & THE JUNGLE 'N' BEATS

Title	Format	Label	Cat. No.	Year	Price	Notes
Rave On	7"	Fontana	TF457	1964	**£4**	

SABRES

Title	Format	Label	Cat. No.	Year	Price	Notes
Roly Poly	7"	Decca	F12528	1966	**£8**	

SACRED MUSHROOM

Title	Format	Label	Cat. No.	Year	Price	Notes
Sacred Mushroom	LP	Parallax	P4001	1969	**£40**	US

SAFARIS

Title	Format	Label	Cat. No.	Year	Price	Notes
Image Of A Girl	7"	Top Rank	JAR424	1960	**£4**	
Summer Nights	7"	Top Rank	JAR528	1961	**£4**	

SAGITTARIUS

Title	Format	Label	Cat. No.	Year	Price	Notes
Blue Marble	LP	Together	STT1002	1969	**£25**	US
My World Fell Down	7"	CBS	2867	1967	**£8**	
Present Tense	LP	Columbia	CS9644	1968	**£20**	US

SAGRAM

Title	Format	Label	Cat. No.	Year	Price	Notes
Pop Explosion Sitar Style	LP	Windmill	WMD118	1972	**£40**	
Sunrise	LP	Dawn	DNLS3068	1975	**£10**	

SAINT STEVEN

Title	Format	Label	Cat. No.	Year	Price	Notes
Saint Steven	LP	Probe		1968	**£20**	

SAINTE MARIE, BUFFY

Title	Format	Label	Cat. No.	Year	Price	Notes
Best Of...	LP	Vanguard	VSD3/4	1973	**£12**	double
Best Of...Vol.2	LP	Vanguard	VSD33/34	1974	**£12**	double
Fire,Fleet & Candle Light	LP	Vanguard	VSD79250	1967	**£10**	
I'm Gonna Be A Country Girl Again	LP	Vanguard	VSD79280	1968	**£10**	
It's My Way	LP	Fontana	TFL6040	1964	**£10**	
Little Wheel Spin	LP	Fontana	TFL6071	1966	**£10**	
Many A Mile	LP	Fontana	TFL6047	1965	**£10**	
Soldier Blue	7"	RCA	RCA2081	1971	**£4**	chart single
Universal Soldier	7"	Fontana	TF614	1965	**£4**	
Until It's Time For You To Go	7"	Fontana	TF574	1965	**£4**	

SAINTS

Title	Format	Label	Cat. No.	Year	Price	Notes
Always	7"	Larrikin	RISS003	1980	**£5**	
Always	7"	New Rose	NEW3	1981	**£4**	
Erotic Neurotic	7"	Harvest	HAR5123	1977	**£5**	
Eternally Yours	LP	Harvest	SHSP4078	1978	**£10**	
I'm Stranded	7"	Fatal	MA7158	1976	**£12**	Australian
I'm Stranded	LP	Harvest	SHSP4065	1977	**£12**	
I'm Stranded	7"	P. Exchange	PX242	1976	**£6**	
I'm Stranded	7"	P. Exchange	PXE101	1977	**£4**	
Know Your Product	7"	EMI	EMI11673	1978	**£4**	
Know Your Product	7"	Harvest	HAR5148	1978	**£4**	
Let's Pretend	7"	Lost	13093	1981	**£4**	
Paralytic Tonight	7"	Lost	PRS2773	1980	**£4**	
Paralytic Tonight	12"	New Rose	NEW1	1981	**£6**	
Prehistoric Sounds	LP	Harvest	SHSP4094	1978	**£10**	
River Deep Mountain High	7"	EMI	EMI11597	1978	**£4**	
River Deep Mountain High	7"	Harvest	HAR5137	1977	**£5**	double
Security	7"	Harvest	11795	1978	**£4**	
Security	7"	Harvest	HAR5166	1978	**£4**	
This Perfect Day	7"	Harvest	HAR5130	1977	**£4**	chart single
This Perfect Day	12"	Harvest	HAR5130	1977	**£8**	

SAINTS (2)

Husky Team .... 7" .... Pye .... 7N15582 .... 1963 .... **£6** ....
Wipe Out .... 7" .... Pye .... 7N15548 .... 1963 .... **£8** ....

SAINTS (3)

Alive .... LP .... **£140** ....

SAINTY, RUSS

Don't Believe Him Donna .... 7" .... Decca .... F11325 .... 1961 .... **£4** ....
Race With The Devil .... 7" .... Decca .... F11270 .... 1960 .... **£4** ....

SAITHESWAITE, SIR SIDNEY

Our Mabel .... 7" .... Parlophone .... R5636 .... 1967 .... **£4** ....
Tea Lovely Tea .... 7" .... Parlophone .... R5591 .... 1967 .... **£4** ....

SAKAMOTO, KYU

Sukiyaki .... LP .... Capitol .... T10349 .... 1963 .... **£12** .... US

SAKER

Even Though We Ain't Got Money .... 7" .... CBS .... 7399 .... 1971 .... **£5** ....
Foggy Tuesday .... 7" .... Parlophone .... R5740 .... 1968 .... **£8** ....
Hey Joe .... 7" .... Parlophone .... R5752 .... 1969 .... **£8** ....
What A Beautiful World .... 7" .... CBS .... 7010 .... 1971 .... **£5** ....

SALAMANDER

Crystal Ball .... 7" .... CBS .... 5102 .... 1970 .... **£5** ....
Ten Commandments .... LP .... Youngblood .... SSYB14 .... 1970 .... **£100** ....

SALLY & THE ALLEYCATS

Is It Something I Said .... 7" .... Parlophone .... R5183 .... 1964 .... **£6** ....

SALLYANGIE

The Sallyangie was a folky duo comprising Sally Oldfield and her young brother Michael. Their one LP was re-released in the seventies, in a vain attempt on the part of Transatlantic records to gain some spin-off benefit from the success of "Tubular Bells" and its successors. The new cover, however, is completely different to the original, which shows a close-up of the two Oldfields, so distinguishing the two versions is no problem.

Child Of Allah .... 7" .... Philips .... 6006259 .... 1972 .... **£10** ....
Children Of The Sun .... LP .... Transatlantic .... TRA176 .... 1968 .... **£15** ....
Children Of The Sun .... LP .... Transatlantic .... TRA176 .... 197- .... **£10** .... reissue, different sleeve
Two Ships .... 7" .... Transatlantic .... BIG126 .... 1969 .... **£10** ....

SALVATION

Cinderella .... 7" .... United Artists .... UP35048 .... 1969 .... **£4** ....
Salvation .... LP .... United Artists .... UAS29062 .... 1969 .... **£15** ....

SALVO, SAMMY

Say Yeah .... 7" .... RCA .... RCA1032 .... 1958 .... **£6** ....

SAM & BILL

I Feel Like Tryin' .... 7" .... Brunswick .... 05973 .... 1967 .... **£5** ....

SAM & DAVE

Baby Baby Don't Stop Now .... 7" .... Atlantic .... 584324 .... 1970 .... **£4** ....
Best Of... .... LP .... Atlantic .... 587155 .... 1969 .... **£10** ....
Can't You Find Another Way .... 7" .... Atlantic .... 584211 .... 1968 .... **£4** ....
Double Dynamite .... LP .... Atlantic .... 588181 .... 1969 .... **£15** ....
Double Dynamite .... LP .... Stax .... 589003 .... 1967 .... **£20** .... chart LP
Everybody Got To Believe .... 7" .... Atlantic .... 584228 .... 1968 .... **£4** ....
Hold On I'm Coming .... LP .... Atlantic .... 587045 .... 1966 .... **£20** .... US, chart LP
Hold On I'm Coming .... 7" .... Atlantic .... 584003 .... 1966 .... **£5** ....
I Thank You .... LP .... Atlantic .... 587154 .... 1968 .... **£15** ....
I Thank You .... 7" .... Stax .... 601030 .... 1968 .... **£4** .... chart single
If You Got The Loving .... 7" .... Atlantic .... 584047 .... 1966 .... **£4** ....
No More Pain .... 7" .... King .... KG1041 .... 196- .... **£5** ....
Ooh Ooh Ooh .... 7" .... Atlantic .... 584303 .... 1969 .... **£4** ....
Sam And Dave .... LP .... Roulette .... R25323 .... 1966 .... **£15** .... US
Soothe Me .... 7" .... Stax .... 601004 .... 1967 .... **£4** .... chart single
Soul Man .... 7" .... Stax .... 601023 .... 1967 .... **£5** .... chart single
Soul Men .... LP .... Atlantic .... 588185 .... 1969 .... **£15** ....
Soul Men .... LP .... Stax .... 589015 .... 1967 .... **£20** .... chart LP
Soul Sister Brown Sugar .... 7" .... Atlantic .... 584237 .... 1969 .... **£4** .... chart single
When Something Is Wrong With My Baby .... 7" .... Stax .... 601006 .... 1967 .... **£4** ....

You Don't Know Like I Know	7"	Atlantic	584086	1967	**£4**	
You Don't Know Like I Know	7"	Atlantic	584247	1969	**£4**	
You Don't Know Like I Know	7"	Atlantic	AT4066	1966	**£5**	
You Don't Know What You Mean	7"	Atlantic	584192	1968	**£4**	
You Got Me Hummin'	7"	Atlantic	584064	1967	**£4**	

SAM APPLE PIE

Call Me Boss	7"	DJM	DJS274	1973	**£5**	
East 17	LP	DJM	DJLPS429	1973	**£15**	
Sam Apple Pie	LP	Decca	SKLR5005	1969	**£30**	
Sometime Girl	7"	Decca	F22932	1969	**£5**	

SAM THE SHAM & THE PHARAOHS

Best Of...	LP	MGM	E4422	1967	**£10**	US
Hair On My Chinny Chin Chin	7"	MGM	MGM1326	1966	**£4**	
How Do You Catch A Girl	7"	MGM	MGM1331	1966	**£4**	
Ju Ju Hand	7"	MGM	MGM1278	1965	**£6**	
Li'l Red Riding Hood	LP	MGM	C8032	1966	**£12**	
Li'l Red Riding Hood	7"	MGM	MGM1315	1966	**£6**	chart single
Nefertiti	LP	MGM	E4479	1967	**£10**	US
Oh That's Bad No That's Good	7"	MGM	MGM1337	1967	**£4**	
On Tour	LP	MGM	E4347	1966	**£12**	US
Red Hot	7"	MGM	MGM1298	1966	**£6**	
Red Hot	7" EP	MGM	MGMEP794	1966	**£8**	
Ring Dang Doo	7"	MGM	MGM1285	1965	**£6**	
Sam, Hard And Heavy	LP	Atlantic	SD8271	1970	**£10**	US
Ten Of Pentacles	LP	MGM	SE4526	1968	**£10**	US
Their Second Album	LP	MGM	E4314	1965	**£12**	US
Wooly Bully	LP	MGM	E4297	1965	**£15**	US
Wooly Bully	7"	MGM	MGM1269	1965	**£8**	chart single
Wooly Bully	7"	MGM	MGM1473	1969	**£4**	
Yakety Yak	7"	MGM	MGM1379	1968	**£4**	

SAM, ERV & TOM

Soul Teacher	7"	Direction	583339	1968	**£4**	

SAMAIN

Vibrations Of Doom	LP	Roadrunner			**£70**	Canada

SAMPSON, DAVE & THE HUNTERS

Dave	7" EP	Columbia	ESG7853	1961	**£30**	stereo
Dave	7" EP	Columbia	SEG8095	1961	**£25**	
Easy To Dream	7"	Columbia	DB4625	1961	**£4**	
If You Need Me	7"	Columbia	DB4502	1960	**£8**	
Sweet Dreams	7"	Columbia	DB4449	1960	**£4**	chart single
Why The Chicken	7"	Columbia	DB4597	1961	**£4**	
Wide Wide World	7"	Fontana	H361	1962	**£4**	

SAMSON

Are You Samson	LP	Instant	INSP004	1968	**£30**	

SAMSON (2)

Head On	LP	Gem	GEMLP108	1980	**£10**	
Mr.Rock'N'Roll	7"	Laser	LAS6	1979	**£4**	
Samson	LP	Gem	GEMLP113	1981	**£10**	
Shock Tactics	LP	RCA	LP5031	1981	**£10**	
Survivors	LP	Laser	LAP1	1979	**£10**	
Telephone	7"	Lightning	GIL547	1978	**£4**	
Venus	7"	Parlophone	R5867	1970	**£8**	

SAMUELS, FUZZY

Fuzzy Samuels	LP	Caroline	CA2002	1974	**£10**	

SAMUELS, JERRY

Puppy Love	7"	HMV	7M411	1956	**£4**	

SAMUELS, WINSTON

Be Prepared	7"	Ska Beat	JB196	1965	**£10**	
Follow	7"	Rio	R26	196-	**£10**	
Greatest	7"	Island	WI3051	1967	**£10**	
I Won't Be Discouraged	7"	Island	WI3053	1967	**£10**	
Luck Will Come My Way	7"	Black Swan	WI419	1964	**£10**	

Title	Format	Label	Number	Year	Price	Notes
My Angel	7"	Ska Beat	JB214	1965	**£10**	
Time Will Tell	7"	Ska Beat	JB244	1966	**£10**	
Up And Down	7"	Ska Beat	JB241	1966	**£10**	
What Have I Done	7"	Ska Beat	JB238	1966	**£10**	
You Are The One	7"	Black Swan	WI426	1964	**£10**	
You Are The One	7"	Columbia	DB7405	1964	**£6**	

SAMURAI

Title	Format	Label	Number	Year	Price	Notes
Samurai	LP	Greenwich	GSLP1003	1971	**£40**	

SAN FRANCISCO EARTHQUAKE

Title	Format	Label	Number	Year	Price	Notes
Fairy Tales Can Come True	7"	Mercury	MF1036	1968	**£8**	

SAN REMO STRINGS

Title	Format	Label	Number	Year	Price	Notes
Festival Time	7"	T. Motown	TMG795	1971	**£4**	chart single
Festival Time	7"	T. Motown	TMG795	1971	**£25**	demo
Reach Out And I'll Be There	7"	T. Motown	TMG807	1972	**£4**	
Reach Out And I'll Be There	7"	T. Motown	TMG807	1972	**£12**	demo
San Remo Strings Swing	LP	T. Motown	STML11216	1973	**£10**	

SAND

Title	Format	Label	Number	Year	Price	Notes
Sand	LP	Barnaby	BR15006	1973	**£20**	US double

SAND PEBBLES

Title	Format	Label	Number	Year	Price	Notes
Love Power	7"	Track	604015	1967	**£4**	
Love Power	7"	Track	604028	1967	**£4**	
Love Power	7"	Track	604028	1969	**£4**	

SANDERS, ALEX

Title	Format	Label	Number	Year	Price	Notes
Witch Is Born	LP	A&M	AMLS984	1970	**£30**	

SANDERS, CAROL

Title	Format	Label	Number	Year	Price	Notes
Ain't No Beatle	7"	W. Bros	WB5676	1966	**£8**	

SANDERS, ED

Title	Format	Label	Number	Year	Price	Notes
Beer Cans On The Moon	LP	Reprise	MS2105	1973	**£12**	US
Sanders' Truckstop	LP	Reprise	RS6374	1969	**£12**	US

SANDERS, GARY

Title	Format	Label	Number	Year	Price	Notes
Ain't No Beatle	7"	W. Bros	WB5676	1966	**£4**	

SANDFORD, CHRIS

Title	Format	Label	Number	Year	Price	Notes
I Wish They Wouldn't Always Say...	7"	Fontana	TF633	1965	**£4**	
Not Too Little Not Too Much	7"	Decca	F11778	1963	**£4**	chart single
You're Gonna Be My Girl	7"	Decca	F11842	1964	**£4**	

SANDON, JOHNNY

Title	Format	Label	Number	Year	Price	Notes
Blizzard	7"	Pye	7N15717	1964	**£8**	
Donna Means Heartbreak	7"	Pye	7N15665	1964	**£8**	
Lies	7"	Pye	7N15542	1963	**£8**	
Magic Potion	7"	Pye	7N15559	1963	**£8**	
Sixteen Tons	7"	Pye	7N15602	1964	**£8**	

SANDPIPERS

Title	Format	Label	Number	Year	Price	Notes
Guantanamera	7"	Pye	7N25380	1966	**£4**	chart single
Guantanamera	7" EP	Pye	NEP44081	1966	**£4**	
Louie Louie	7"	Pye	7N25396	1966	**£4**	

SANDROSE

Title	Format	Label	Number	Year	Price	Notes
Sandrose	LP	Polydor	2480137	1972	**£120**	

SANDS

Title	Format	Label	Number	Year	Price	Notes
Mrs.Gillespie's Refrigerator	7"	Reaction	591017	1967	**£10**	
Venus	7"	Major Minor	MM681	1970	**£8**	

SANDS, CLIVE

Title	Format	Label	Number	Year	Price	Notes
Hooked On A Feeling	7"	SNB	554058	1969	**£6**	
Witchi Rai Yo	7"	SNB	554431	1969	**£10**	

SANDS, DAVEY & THE ESSEX

Title	Format	Label	Number	Year	Price	Notes
Please Be Mine	7"	Decca	F12170	1965	**£4**	

SANDS, EVIE

Title	Format	Label	Number	Year	Price	Notes
Picture Me Gone	7"	Cameo Park	C413	1966	**£20**	
Take Me For A Little While	7"	Red Bird	RB10118	196-	**£8**	

SANDS, TOMMY

Title	Format	Label	Number	Year	Price	Notes
Big Date	7"	Capitol	CL14889	1958	**£4**	
Blue Ribbon Baby	7"	Capitol	CL14925	1958	**£4**	
Dream With Me	LP	Capitol	T1426	1961	**£10**	US
Going Steady	7"	Capitol	CL14745	1957	**£4**	
Hawaiian Rock	7"	Capitol	CL14872	1958	**£4**	
Is It Ever Gonna Happen	7"	Capitol	CL15013	1959	**£5**	
Let Me Be Loved	7"	Capitol	CL14781	1957	**£4**	
Man Like Wow	7"	Capitol	CL14811	1957	**£6**	
Old Oaken Bucket	7"	Capitol	CL15143	1960	**£4**	chart single
Ring A Ding Ding	7"	Capitol	CL14724	1957	**£5**	
Sands At The Sands	LP	Capitol	T1364	1960	**£10**	US
Sands Storm	LP	Capitol	T1081	1959	**£12**	US
Sands Storm Part 1	7" EP	Capitol	EAP11081	1959	**£10**	
Sands Storm Part 2	7" EP	Capitol	EAP21081	1959	**£10**	
Sands Storm Part 3	7" EP	Capitol	EAP31081	1959	**£10**	
Sing Boy Sing	LP	Capitol	T929	1958	**£20**	
Sing Boy Sing	7"	Capitol	CL14834	1958	**£5**	
Sinner Man	7"	Capitol	CL15047	1959	**£4**	
Statue	7"	Liberty	LIB55842	1966	**£12**	
Steady Date	LP	Capitol	T848	1957	**£20**	US
Teenage Crush	7"	Capitol	CL14695	1957	**£6**	
Teenage Crush	7" EP	Capitol	EAP1851	1957	**£10**	
Teenage Rock	LP	Capitol	T1109	1959	**£15**	US
That's The Way I Am	7"	Capitol	CL15071	1959	**£4**	
This Thing Called Love	LP	Capitol	T1123	1959	**£10**	US
This Thing Called Love	7" EP	Capitol	EAP11123	1959	**£5**	
When I'm Thinking Of You	LP	Capitol	T1239	1960	**£10**	US
Worrying Kind	7"	Capitol	CL14971	1959	**£5**	
You Hold The Future	7"	Capitol	CL15109	1960	**£4**	

SANDS, WES

Title	Format	Label	Number	Year	Price	Notes
There's Lots More	7"	Columbia	DB4996	1963	**£8**	

SANDY

Title	Format	Label	Number	Year	Price	Notes
Solitary Man	7"	Columbia	DB7938	1966	**£4**	

SANDY COAST

Title	Format	Label	Number	Year	Price	Notes
Blackboard Jungle Lady	7"	Polydor	2001457	1973	**£20**	
From The Stereo Workshop	LP	Page One		196-	**£120**	
Shipwreck	LP	Page One			**£100**	

SANSOM, BOBBY

Title	Format	Label	Number	Year	Price	Notes
There's A Place	7"	Oriole	CB1837	1963	**£4**	
Where Have You Been	7"	Oriole	CB1888	1963	**£4**	

SANSON, VERONIQUE

French singer-songwriter Veronique Sanson composed "Amoureuse", which was a big hit for Kiki Dee. Her own version is the lead track of an excellent album which was released in two versions, one with French lyrics and one with English. One would not have thought that it would make much difference, but the French version is far superior. The way in which Ms.Sanson's voice takes on an attractive soft vibrato at the end of the lines is ideally matched to the soft endings of the French words. In English she sounds a little ordinary, but in French the record stands revealed as a superb example of the singer-songwriting genre.

Title	Format	Label	Number	Year	Price	Notes
Amoureuse	LP	Elektra	K42106	1972	**£10**	English vocals
Veronique Sanson	LP	Elektra	K42106	1972	**£10**	French, English Vocals

SANTAMARIA, MONGO

Title	Format	Label	Number	Year	Price	Notes
25 Miles	7"	Direction	584430	1969	**£4**	
Black Eyed Peas	7"	CBS	201766	1965	**£4**	
Cloud Nine	7"	Direction	584086	1969	**£4**	
El Pussycat	7"	CBS	201766	1965	**£4**	
Watermelon Man	7"	Riverside	RIF106909	1963	**£5**	

SANTANA

Title	Format	Label	Number	Year	Price	Notes
Abraxas	LP	CBS	Q64087	1974	**£12**	quad
Abraxas	LP	Columbia	HC40130	1981	**£12**	US audiophile
Amigos	LP	Columbia	PCQ33576	1975	**£12**	US quad

Title	Format	Label	Cat. No.	Year	Price	Notes
Barboletta	LP	CBS	Q69084	1974	**£12**	quad
Caravanserai	LP	CBS	Q65299	1974	**£12**	quad
Festival	LP	Columbia	PCQ34423	1977	**£12**	US quad
Greatest Hits	LP	CBS	Q69081	1974	**£12**	quad
Illuminations	LP	Columbia	PCQ32900	1974	**£12**	US quad
Samba Pa Ti (2 versions)	7"	CBS	2561DJ	1973	**£6**	promo
Santana	LP	Columbia	PCQ32964	1974	**£12**	US quad
Santana III	LP	CBS	Q69015	1974	**£12**	quad
Solo Guitar Of Devadip Carlos Santana	LP	Columbia	AS573	1979	**£20**	US promo
Welcome	LP	CBS	Q69040	1974	**£12**	quad
Zebop	LP	Columbia	HC47158	1981	**£12**	US audiophile

SANTANA, CARLOS & BUDDY MILES

Title	Format	Label	Cat. No.	Year	Price	Notes
Live	LP	Columbia	CAQ31308	1974	**£12**	US quad

SANTELLS

Title	Format	Label	Cat. No.	Year	Price	Notes
So Fine	7"	Sue	WI4020	1966	**£8**	

SANTO & JOHNNY

Title	Format	Label	Cat. No.	Year	Price	Notes
Beatles' Greatest Hits	LP	Canadian Am.	1017	1964	**£20**	US
Birmingham	7"	Parlophone	R4865	1962	**£4**	
Brilliant Guitar Sounds	LP	Imperial	LP9363	1967	**£10**	US
Bullseye	7"	Parlophone	R4844	1961	**£4**	
Caravan	7"	Parlophone	R4644	1960	**£4**	
Come On In	LP	Canadian Am.	1006	1962	**£15**	US
Come September	7"	Pye	7N25111	1961	**£4**	
Encore	LP	Canadian Am.	1002	1960	**£15**	US
Golden Guitars	LP	Imperial	LP12366	1968	**£10**	US
Hawaii	LP	Canadian Am.	1004	1961	**£15**	US
In THe Still Of The Night	LP	Canadian Am.	1014	1963	**£15**	US
In The Still Of The Night	7"	Stateside	SS292	1964	**£4**	
Mucho	LP	Canadian Am.	1018	1965	**£12**	US
Off Shore	LP	Canadian Am.	1011	1963	**£15**	US
On The Road Again	LP	Imperial	LP12418	1968	**£10**	US
Santo & Johnny No.1	7" EP	Parlophone	GEP8806	1960	**£8**	
Santo & Johnny No.2	7" EP	Parlophone	GEP8813	1960	**£8**	
Santo And Johnny	LP	Canadian Am.	1001	1959	**£20**	US
Sleepwalk	7"	Pye	7N25037	1959	**£4**	chart single
Spanish Harlem	7"	Stateside	SS110	1962	**£4**	
Teardrop	7"	Parlophone	R4619	1960	**£4**	chart single
Three Caballeros	7"	Stateside	SS253	1964	**£4**	
Wish You Were Here	LP	Canadian Am.	1016	1964	**£15**	US

SAPPHIRES

Title	Format	Label	Cat. No.	Year	Price	Notes
Evil One	7"	HMV	POP1461	1965	**£20**	
Gotta Have Your Love	7"	HMV	POP1441	1965	**£25**	
Who Do You Love	7"	Stateside	SS267	1964	**£5**	
Who Do You Love	LP	Swan	LP513	1964	**£40**	US
Your True Love	7"	Stateside	SS223	1963	**£6**	

SARGENT, DON

Title	Format	Label	Cat. No.	Year	Price	Notes
Gypsy Boots	7"	Vogue	V9160	1960	**£12**	

SARI & THE SHALIMARS

Title	Format	Label	Cat. No.	Year	Price	Notes
It's So Lonely Being Together	7"	United Artists	UP2235	1968	**£8**	

SARNE, MIKE

Title	Format	Label	Cat. No.	Year	Price	Notes
Code Of Love	7"	Parlophone	R5010	1963	**£4**	chart single
Come Outside	LP	Parlophone	PMC1187	1962	**£12**	
Come Outside	7"	Parlophone	R4902	1962	**£4**	chart single
Hello Lover Boy	7"	Parlophone	R5090	1963	**£4**	
Just For Kicks	7"	Parlophone	R4974	1962	**£4**	chart single
Love Me Please	7"	Parlophone	R5170	1964	**£4**	
Mike Sarne Hit Parade	7" EP	Parlophone	GEP8879	1963	**£8**	
Out And About	7"	Parlophone	R5129	1964	**£4**	
Please Don't Say	7"	Parlophone	R5060	1963	**£4**	
Will I What	7"	Parlophone	R4932	1962	**£4**	chart single

SAROFEEN & SMOKE

Title	Format	Label	Cat. No.	Year	Price	Notes
Do It	LP	Pye	NSPL28153	1971	**£10**	
Susan Jane	7"	Pye	7N25556	1971	**£4**	

SAROLTA

Title	Format	Label	Cat. No.	Year	Price	Notes
Open Your Hands	7"	Island	WIP6035	1968	**£5**	

SARSTEDT BROTHERS

Title	Format	Label	Cat. No.	Year	Price	Notes
Worlds Apart Together	LP	Regal Z.		1973	**£10**	

SARSTEDT, PETER

Title	Format	Label	Cat. No.	Year	Price	Notes
Peter Sarstedt	LP	United Artists	ULP1219	1969	**£10**	chart LP
Where Do You Go To	7"	United Artists	UP2262	1968	**£4**	chart single

SASPARELLA

Title	Format	Label	Cat. No.	Year	Price	Notes
Spooky	7"	Decca	F12892	1969	**£5**	

SASSAFRAS

Title	Format	Label	Cat. No.	Year	Price	Notes
Expecting Company	LP	Polydor	2383245	1973	**£12**	

SASSENACHS

Title	Format	Label	Cat. No.	Year	Price	Notes
That Don't Worry Me	7"	Fontana	TF518	1964	**£8**	

SATAN & THE DE-CIPLES

Title	Format	Label	Cat. No.	Year	Price	Notes
Underground	LP	Goldband	7750	1969	**£100**	US

SATAN'S RATS

Title	Format	Label	Cat. No.	Year	Price	Notes
Year Of The Rats	7"	DJM	DJS10821	1978	**£10**	
You Make Me Sick	7"	DJM	DJS10840	1978	**£10**	

SATIN BELLS

Title	Format	Label	Cat. No.	Year	Price	Notes
I Stand Accused	7"	Decca	F22937	1969	**£4**	

SATISFACTION

Title	Format	Label	Cat. No.	Year	Price	Notes
Satisfaction	LP	Decca	SKL5075	1971	**£15**	

SATTIN, LONNIE

Title	Format	Label	Cat. No.	Year	Price	Notes
High Steel	7"	Capitol	CL14638	1956	**£4**	
I'll Never Stop Loving You	7"	Capitol	CL14771	1957	**£4**	
Ring Around The Moon	7"	Capitol	CL14831	1958	**£4**	
Trapped	7"	Capitol	CL14552	1956	**£4**	

SATURNALIA

Like the other early rock LP picture disc (Curved Air's "Airconditioning"), "Magical Love" looks rather better than it sounds, for only a few playings are enough to make the sound quality begin to seriously deteriorate. And unlike the situation with Curved Air, Saturnalia's record was never issued in the more conventional form. As a result, it is hard to be fair to the music: It sounds like third division progressive fare - a bit like Principal Edward's Magic Theatre on an off day - but listening through the welter of background hiss one cannot be sure. To be complete, by the way, the record should come with a booklet, although few copies of this seem to have survived.

Title	Format	Label	Cat. No.	Year	Price	Notes
Magical Love	LP	Matrix		1980	**£10**	pic disc
Magical Love	LP	Matrix	TRIX1	1969	**£25**	pic disc

SAUNDERS, MERL

Title	Format	Label	Cat. No.	Year	Price	Notes
Fire Up	LP	Fantasy	FT514	1973	**£12**	
Heavy Turbulence	LP			1971	**£12**	

SAVAGE RESURRECTION

Title	Format	Label	Cat. No.	Year	Price	Notes
Savage Resurrection	LP	Mercury	SMCL20123	1968	**£25**	
Thing In E	7"	Mercury	MF1027	1968	**£8**	

SAVAGE ROSE

Title	Format	Label	Cat. No.	Year	Price	Notes
Babylon	LP	Polydor	2380019	1973	**£10**	
Dodens Truimf	LP	Polydor	2380016	1973	**£10**	
In The Plain	LP	Polydor	46292	1968	**£12**	
Refugee	LP	RCA	SF8250	1972	**£10**	
Savage Rose	LP	Polydor	184144	1968	**£12**	
Travellin'	LP	Polydor	184316	1969	**£12**	
Wild Child	LP	Polydor	2380021	1973	**£10**	
Your Daily Gift	LP	RCA	SF8169	1971	**£10**	

SAVAGE, JOAN

Title	Format	Label	Cat. No.	Year	Price	Notes
Five Oranges, Four Apples	7"	Columbia	DB3929	1957	**£4**	
Left Right Out Of My Heart	7"	Columbia	DB4159	1958	**£4**	
Love Letters In The Sand	7"	Columbia	DB3968	1957	**£4**	
Shake Me I Rattle	7"	Columbia	DB4039	1957	**£4**	

SAVAGE, ROBERT

Adventures Of...	LP	Paramount			**£20**	US

SAVAGES

Everybody Surf	7" EP	Decca	DFE8546	1963	**£8**	
Live And Wild	LP	Drone		196-	**£100**	US

SAVARIN, JULIAN JAY

Waiters On The Dance	LP	Birth		1969	**£100**	

SAVILLE, JIMMY

Ahab The Arab	7"	Decca	F11493	1962	**£4**	
Bossa Nova	7"	Decca	F11576	1963	**£4**	

SAVOY BROWN

Savoy Brown passed through numerous line-ups, in which the presence of guitarist Kim Simmonds was the only constant factor. Simmonds and his companions lacked the imagination to break very far out of the constraints of playing the blues, although they tried hardest on "Blue Matter", which includes the memorable "Train To Nowhere".

Blue Matter	LP	Decca	SKL4994	1968	**£20**	
Boogie Brothers	LP	Decca	SKL5186	1974	**£10**	
Coming Down Your Way	7"	Decca	F13431	1973	**£4**	
Getting To The Point	LP	Decca	SKL4925	1968	**£20**	
Hard Way To Go	7"	Decca	F13019	1970	**£4**	
Hellbound Train	LP	Decca	TXS107	1972	**£10**	
I Tried	7"	Purdah	453503	1966	**£30**	
I'm Tired	7"	Decca	F12978	1969	**£5**	
Jack The Toad	LP	Decca	TXS112	1973	**£10**	
Lion's Share	LP	Decca	SKL5152	1973	**£10**	
Looking In	LP	Decca	SKL5066	1970	**£12**	chart LP
Poor Girl	7"	Decca	F13098	1970	**£4**	
Raw Sienna	LP	Decca	SKL5030	1970	**£12**	
Shake Down	LP	Decca	SKL4883	1967	**£20**	
Skin 'n' Bone	LP	London	PS670	1976	**£10**	US
So Tired	7"	Decca	F13372	1973	**£4**	
Step Further	LP	Decca	SKL5013	1969	**£15**	
Street Corner Talking	LP	Decca	TXS104	1970	**£10**	
Taste And Try Before You Buy	7"	Decca	F12702	1967	**£6**	
Tell Mama	7"	Decca	F13247	1971	**£4**	
Train To Nowhere	7"	Decca	F12843	1969	**£5**	
Walking By Myself	7"	Decca	F12797	1968	**£6**	
Wire Fire	LP	London	PS659	1975	**£10**	US

SAXON

And The Bands Played On	7"	Carrere	CAR180P	1981	**£4**	pic disc
Back On The Streets	7"	Parlophone	RP6103	1985	**£5**	shaped pic disc
Innocence Is No Excuse	LP	Parlophone	SAXONP2	1985	**£10**	pic disc
Nightmare	7"	Carrere	CARP284	1983	**£4**	pic disc
Power And The Glory	7"	RCA	SAXONP1	1983	**£4**	pic disc
Rock The Nations	12"	EMI	12EMIP5587	1986	**£6**	pic disc
Meet The Saxons	LP	Ace Of Clubs	ACL1173	1963	**£50**	
Saxon War Cry	7"	Decca	F12179	1965	**£10**	

SAXONS (2)

Love Minus Zero	LP	Mirrosonic	AS1017	1966	**£20**	US
Love Minus Zero	LP	Mirrosonic	AS1017	1966	**£30**	US

SAYLE, ALEXEI

Ullo John Got A New Motor	7"	Springtime	IST162	1984	**£4**	shaped pic disc

SAYLES, JOHNNY

Deep Down In Your Heart	7"	Liberty	LIB12042	1966	**£4**	

SCABIES, RAT

Let There Be Rats	7"	Parta. M.	HIT1	1984	**£4**	

SCAFFOLD

1-2-3	7"	Parlophone	R5703	1968	**£4**	
All The Way Up	7"	Parlophone	R5847	1970	**£4**	
Busdreams	7"	Parlophone	R5866	1970	**£4**	
Charity Bubbles	7"	Parlophone	R5784	1969	**£4**	
Do The Albert	7"	Parlophone	R5922	1971	**£4**	

Do You Remember?	7"	Parlophone	R5679	1968	**£4**	chart single
Evening With...	LP	Parlophone	PCS7051	1968	**£15**	
Fresh Liver	LP	Island	ILPS9234	1973	**£10**	
Gin Gan Goolie	7"	Parlophone	R5812	1969	**£4**	chart single
Goodbat Nightman	7"	Parlophone	R5548	1966	**£8**	
L The P	LP	Parlophone	PCS7077	1969	**£12**	
Lily The Pink	7"	Parlophone	R5734	1968	**£4**	chart single
Sold Out	LP	W. Bros	K56097	1975	**£10**	
Thank U Very Much	7"	Parlophone	R5643	1967	**£4**	chart single
Today's Monday	7"	Parlophone	R5443	1966	**£4**	

SCAGGS, BOZ

Boz	LP	Polydor	LPHM46253	1965	**£40**	
Boz Scaggs	LP	Atlantic	588205	1969	**£10**	
Boz Scaggs	LP	Columbia	AS203	1974	**£20**	US promo sampler
Silk Degrees	LP	Columbia	HC43920	1980	**£12**	US audiophile
Simone	7"	CBS	XPS107	1978	**£4**	promo
Still Falling For You	LP	Columbia		1978	**£20**	US early version of 'Two Down Then Left'

SCALES, HARVEY & THE SOUND

Get Down	7"	Atlantic	584146	1967	**£4**	

SCAMPS

Teen Dance	LP	Ace Of Clubs	ACL1116	1962	**£10**	

SCARECROW

Live At The Brecknock	LP	Spilt Milk		1977	**£60**	
Live At The Marquee	LP	Spilt Milk		1978	**£100**	
Scarecrow	LP	Spilt Milk	SMFM11278	1978	**£60**	

SCARLETS

Let's Go	7"	Philips	BF1376	1965	**£4**	

SCHAUBROECK, ARMAND

I Came To Visit	LP	Mirror		1977	**£15**	US
Rat Fucker	LP	Mirror	7	1978	**£10**	US
Shakin' Shakin'	LP	Mirror	5	1978	**£20**	US

SCHENKER, MICHAEL GROUP

Dancer	7"	Chrysalis	CHSP2636	1982	**£4**	pic disc

SCHMIDT, IRMIN

Film Musik Vols 3 & 4	LP	Spoon	SPOON018/019	1984	**£12**	double

SCHMITT, OLIVER LINDSEY

Graffenstadden	LP	private		1972	**£45**	

SCHOLARS

Versatility Of...	LP	Unicorn	254	1972	**£10**	

SCHOOL BOYS

Beatle Mania	LP	Palace	778	1964	**£20**	US
Dream Lover	7"	Port-O-Jam	PJ4000	196-	**£8**	
Little Dilly	7"	Blue Beat	BB174	1963	**£10**	

SCHOOL GIRLS

Last Time	7"	Blue Beat	BB214	1963	**£10**	
Live Up To Justice	7"	Blue Beat	BB185	1963	**£10**	
Love Another Love	7"	Blue Beat	BB168	1963	**£10**	
Never Let You Go	7"	Blue Beat	BB263	1964	**£10**	

SCHROEDER, JOHN ORCHESTRA

Agent OO Soul	7"	Piccadilly	7N35271	1965	**£6**	
Hungry For Love	7"	Piccadilly	7N35285	1966	**£8**	
The Virgin Soldiers March	7"	Pye	7N17862	1969	**£8**	
You've Lost That Loving Feeling	7"	Piccadilly	7N35362	1967	**£6**	

SCHULMAN, IVY & THE BOWTIES

Rock Pretty Baby	7"	London	HLN8372	1957	**£20**	

SCHUNGE

Ballad Of A Simple Love	LP	Regal Z.	SLRZ1033	1972	**£20**	
Ballad Of A Simple Love	7"	Regal Z.	RZ3077	1973	**£6**	
Misty	7"	Regal Z.	RZ3066	1972	**£6**	

SCIENCE POPTION

You've Got Me High	7"	Columbia	DB8106	1967	**£8**	

SCIENTIST

Professor In Action	7"	Amalgamated	AMG848	196-	**£10**	

SCORCHERS

Ugly Man	7"	Doctor Bird	DB1170	196-	**£10**	

SCORE

Please Please Me	7"	Decca	F12527	1966	**£15**	

SCORPION

Deadly Sting	7"	Dragon	DRA1002	1973	**£4**	

SCORPIONS

Big City Nights	12"	Harvest	12HARP5231	1984	**£6**	pic disc
Lonesome Crow	LP	Heavy Metal	MHIPD2	1982	**£15**	pic disc
No One Like You	7"	Harvest	HARP5219	1982	**£4**	pic disc

SCORPIONS (2)

Riders In The Sky	7"	Parlophone	R4740	1961	**£4**	
Scorpio	7"	Parlophone	R4768	1961	**£4**	

SCOT, COLIN

Colin Scot With Friends	LP	United Artists	UAG29154	1971	**£15**	
Hey Sandy	7"	United Artists	UP35216	1971	**£4**	

SCOTT, ANDY

Krugerrands	12"	Statik	TAK1012	1983	**£6**	
Lady Starlight	7"	RCA	RCA2629	1975	**£4**	

SCOTT, BILLY

You're The Greatest	7"	London	HLU8565	1958	**£4**	

SCOTT, BOBBY

Bobby Scott And Two Horns	LP	ABC-Para.	148	1957	**£12**	US
Bobby Scott Trio	7" EP	London	EZC19008	1956	**£10**	
Chain Gang	7"	London	HL8254	1956	**£10**	
Complete Musician	LP	Atlantic	1341	1960	**£10**	US
Compositions	LP	Bethlehem	8	1955	**£20**	US
Compositions Vol.1	LP-10"	Bethlehem	1009	1954	**£20**	US
Compositions Vol.2	LP-10"	Bethlehem	1029	1954	**£20**	US
Great Scott	LP-10"	Bethlehem	1004	1954	**£20**	US
Scott Free	LP	ABC-Para.	102	1956	**£12**	US
Taste Of Honey	LP	Atlantic	1355	1960	**£10**	US
When The Feeling Hits You	LP	Mercury	MG20767	1963	**£10**	US

SCOTT, FREDDIE

Am I Grooving You?	7"	London	HLZ10139	1967	**£5**	
Are You Lonely For Me	7"	London	HLZ10103	1967	**£8**	
Are You Lonely For Me	LP	Shout	SLP501	1967	**£10**	US
Cry To Me	7"	London	HLZ10123	1967	**£8**	
Everything I Have Is Yours	LP	Columbia	CL2258	1964	**£10**	US
Freddie Scott Sings	LP	Colpix	CP461	1964	**£10**	US
Great If	7"	Upfront	UP1	197-	**£4**	
He Ain't Gonna Give You None	7"	London	HLZ10172	1967	**£4**	
Hey Girl	7"	Colpix	PX692	1963	**£8**	
I Got A Woman	7"	Colpix	PX709	1963	**£4**	
Lonely Man	LP	Columbia	CL2660	1967	**£10**	US
Sugar Sunday	7"	Roulette	RO509	1969	**£5**	

SCOTT, JACK

All I See Is Blue	7"	Capitol	CL15302	1963	**£4**	
Burning Bridges	LP	Capitol	T2035	1964	**£40**	US
Burning Bridges	7" EP	Capitol	EAP20035	1959	**£12**	
Burning Bridges	7"	Top Rank	JAR375	1960	**£4**	chart single

Goodbye Baby	7"	London	HLU8804	1959	**£8**	
I Can't Hold Your Letters In My Arms	7"	Capitol	CL15261	1962	**£4**	
I Never Felt Like This	7"	London	HLL8851	1959	**£6**	
I Remember Hank Williams	LP	Top Rank	BUY034	1960	**£25**	chart LP
I Remember Hank Williams	LP	Top Rank	RM319	1960	**£50**	US
I Remember Hank Williams	7" EP	Top Rank	JKP3011	1961	**£8**	
Is There Something On Your Mind	7"	Top Rank	JAR547	1961	**£4**	
Jack Scott	LP	Carlton	LP12107	1958	**£50**	US
Jack Scott	LP	London	HAL2156	1958	**£40**	
Little Feeling	7"	Capitol	CL15200	1961	**£4**	
My Dream Come True	7"	Capitol	CL15216	1961	**£4**	
My True Love	7"	London	HLU8626	1958	**£8**	chart single
My True Love	7" EP	London	REI1205	1959	**£15**	
Patsy	7"	Top Rank	JAR524	1960	**£4**	
Spirit Moves Me	LP	Top Rank	35109	1961	**£25**	
Spirit Moves Me	LP	Top Rank	RM348	1961	**£50**	US
Steps One And Two	7"	Capitol	CL15236	1962	**£4**	
There Comes A Time	7"	London	HLL8970	1959	**£5**	
Way I Walk	7"	London	HLL8912	1959	**£8**	chart single
What Am I Living For	LP	Carlton	LP12122	1958	**£50**	US
What In The World's Come Over You	LP	Top Rank	25024	1960	**£25**	chart LP
What In The World's Come Over You	7"	Top Rank	JAR280	1960	**£5**	chart single
What In The World's Come Over You	7" EP	Top Rank	JKP3002	1961	**£10**	
With Your Love	7"	London	HLU8765	1958	**£8**	

SCOTT, JOHN

Hi-Fluting Boogie	7"	Parlophone	R4697	1960	**£4**	

SCOTT, JUDI

Billy Sunshine	7"	Page One	POF066	1968	**£8**	

SCOTT, LINDA

Count Every Star	7"	Parlophone	R4829	1961	**£4**	
Don't Bet Money Honey	7"	Parlophone	R4692	1961	**£4**	chart single
Greatest Hits	LP	Canadian Am.	1007	1962	**£20**	US
Hey Look At Me Now	LP	Kapp	KL1424	1965	**£12**	US
I've Told Every Little Star	7"	Parlophone	R4638	1960	**£4**	chart single
It's All Because	7"	Parlophone	R4748	1961	**£4**	
Let's Fall In Love	7"	London	HLR9802	1963	**£4**	
Linda	LP	Congress	3001	1962	**£15**	US
Never In A Million Years	7"	Pye	7N25146	1962	**£4**	
Starlight, Starbright	LP	Canadian Am.	1005	1961	**£20**	US

SCOTT, MARSHALL ETC.

Goin' Where The Lovin' Is	7"	HMV	POP1585	1967	**£4**	
Same Old Feeling	7"	HMV	POP1536	1966	**£4**	

SCOTT, NICKY

Back Street Girl	7"	Immediate	IM045	1967	**£8**	
Big City	7"	Immediate	IM044	1967	**£8**	

SCOTT, ROBIN

Sailor	7"	Head	HEAD4003	1969	**£8**	
Woman From The Warm Grass	LP	Head		1969	**£50**	

SCOTT, SIMON & THE LEROYS

Move It Baby	7"	Parlophone	R5164	1964	**£8**	chart single
My Baby's Got Soul	7"	Parlophone	R5207	1964	**£5**	
Tell Him I'm Not Home	7"	Parlophone	R5298	1965	**£6**	

SCOTT, TOMMY

Who Will It Be?	7"	Decca	F11839	1964	**£4**	
Wrap Your Troubles In Dreams	7"	Decca	F11942	1964	**£4**	

SCOTT-HERON, GIL

B Movie	7"	Arista	ARIST452	1981	**£4**	
B Movie	7"	Arista	ARIST573	1984	**£4**	
B Movie	12"	Arista	ARIST573	1984	**£6**	
B Movie	10"	Arista	ARIST10643	1985	**£6**	
Bottle	7"	Arista	ARIST169	1978	**£4**	
Bottle	12"	Arista	ARIST169	1978	**£6**	
Bottle	LP	Audio Fid.	1017	197-	**£12**	US

Title	Format	Label	Cat. No.	Year	Price	Notes
Bottle	7"	Inferno	HEAT23	1979	**£4**	
Bridges	LP	Arista	SPARTY1031	1977	**£12**	
First Minute Of A New Day	LP	Arista	ARTY106	1975	**£15**	
Free Will	LP	F. Dutchman	10153	1972	**£20**	US
From South Africa To South Carolina	LP	Arista	ARTY121	1976	**£12**	
It's Your World	LP	Arista	DARTY1	1976	**£12**	
Lady Day And John Coltrane	7"	Philips	6073705	1971	**£4**	
Pieces Of a Man	LP	Philips	6369415	1973	**£20**	
Real Eyes	LP	Arista	9540	1980	**£12**	US
Revolution Will Not Be Televised	LP	RCA	SF8428	1975	**£15**	
Secrets	LP	Arista	SPARTY1073	1978	**£12**	
Small Talk At 125th And Lennox	LP	F. Dutchman		1972	**£20**	US
Winter In America	LP	Strata East	19742	1975	**£15**	US

SCRAMBLERS

Title	Format	Label	Cat. No.	Year	Price	Notes
Cycle Psychos	LP	Crown	384	1964	**£20**	US

SCRATCH & THE UPSETTERS (LEE PERRY)

Title	Format	Label	Cat. No.	Year	Price	Notes
Three In One	7"	Island	WIP6328	1976	**£10**	

SCREAMING GYPSY BANDITS

Title	Format	Label	Cat. No.	Year	Price	Notes
Screaming Gypsy Bandits	LP	BRBQ		1973	**£50**	US

SCRITTI POLITTI

Title	Format	Label	Cat. No.	Year	Price	Notes
4 A-Sides	12"	Rough Trade	RT027	1979	**£6**	
Absolute	12"	Virgin	VSY68012	1984	**£6**	pic disc
Asylums In Jerusalem	7"	Rough Trade	RT111P	1982	**£4**	pic disc
Doubt Beat	12"	Rough Trade	RT027T	1979	**£6**	
Skank Bloc	7"	St.Pancras	SCRIT1	1978	**£6**	
Word Girl	7"	Virgin	VSS747	1985	**£4**	shaped pic disc
Work In Progress	7"	Rough Trade	RT034	1979	**£6**	

SCRUFFY DUFFY

Title	Format	Label	Cat. No.	Year	Price	Notes
Scruffy Duffy	LP	Chapter One	CHSR814	1970	**£30**	

SEA-DERS

Title	Format	Label	Cat. No.	Year	Price	Notes
Thanks A Lot	7"	Decca	F22576	1967	**£6**	

SEAMAN, PHIL

Title	Format	Label	Cat. No.	Year	Price	Notes
Phil Seaman Now	LP	Verve	SVLP9220	1968	**£30**	

SEARCHERS

Title	Format	Label	Cat. No.	Year	Price	Notes
Ain't Gonna Kiss Ya	7" EP	Pye	NEP24177	1963	**£5**	
Bumble Bee	7" EP	Pye	NEP24218	1965	**£5**	
Desdemona	7"	RCA	RCA2057	1971	**£5**	
Don't Make Promises	7"	private		197-	**£10**	
Don't Throw Your Love Away	7"	Pye	7N15630	1964	**£4**	chart single
Don't Throw Your Love Away	7"	Pye	7N15630	1964	**£12**	demo
Four By Four	7" EP	Pye	NEP24228	1965	**£6**	
Four Strong Winds	7"	private		197-	**£10**	
Goodbye My Love	7"	Pye	7N15794	1965	**£4**	chart single
Goodbye My Love	7"	Pye	7N15794	1965	**£12**	demo
Have You Ever Loved Somebody	7"	Pye	7N17170	1966	**£4**	chart single
Have You Ever Loved Somebody	7"	Pye	7N17170	1966	**£10**	demo
He's Got No Love	7"	Pye	7N15878	1965	**£4**	chart single
He's Got No Love	7"	Pye	7N15878	1965	**£10**	demo
Hear Hear	LP	Mercury	MG20914	1964	**£25**	US
Hungry For Love	7" EP	Pye	NEP24184	1964	**£5**	
It's The Searchers	LP	Pye	NPL18092	1964	**£20**	chart LP
Kinky Kathy Abernathy	7"	Liberty	LBF15340	1969	**£5**	
Les Searchers Chantent En Francais	7" EP	Vogue	PNV24121	196-	**£100**	sung in French
Love Is Everywhere	7"	RCA	RCA2139	1971	**£5**	
Meet The Searchers	LP	Golden Guin.	GGL0349	1965	**£10**	
Meet The Searchers	LP	Kapp	KL1363	1964	**£15**	US
Meet The Searchers	LP	Pye	NPL18086	1963	**£20**	chart LP
Needles And Pins	7"	Ariola		1964	**£20**	sung in German
Needles And Pins	7"	Pye	7N15594	1964	**£4**	chart single
Needles And Pins	7"	Pye	7N15594	1964	**£15**	demo
Needles And Pins	7"	Pye		1964	**£20**	sung in French
Needles And Pins	7"	RCA	RCA2248	1972	**£5**	
New Searchers LP	LP	Kapp	KL1412	1965	**£15**	US
Play The System	7" EP	Pye	NEP24201	1964	**£8**	

Title	Format	Label	Cat. No.	Year	Price	Notes
Popcorn Double Feature	7"	Pye	7N17225	1967	**£5**	
Searchers '65	7" EP	Pye	NEP24222	1965	**£6**	
Searchers	LP	private		1962	**£150**	
Searchers Meet The Rattles	LP	Mercury	MG20994	1965	**£30**	US
Searchers No.4	LP	Kapp	KL1449	1965	**£15**	US
Second Take	LP	RCA	SF8289	1972	**£10**	
Secondhand Dealer	7"	Pye	7N17424	1967	**£5**	
Sing Singer Sing	7"	RCA	RCA2231	1972	**£5**	
Solitaire	7"	RCA	RCA2330	1973	**£5**	
Some Day We're Gonna Love Again	7"	Pye	7N15670	1964	**£4**	chart single
Some Day We're Gonna Love Again	7"	Pye	7N15670	1964	**£12**	demo
Sounds Like The Searchers	LP	Pye	NPL18111	1964	**£20**	chart LP
Sub Ist Sie	7"	Vogue	14116	1963	**£20**	sung in German
Sugar And Spice	LP	Pye	NPL18089	1963	**£20**	chart LP
Sugar And Spice	7"	Pye	7N15566	1963	**£4**	chart single
Sugar And Spice	7"	Pye	7N15566	1963	**£15**	demo
Sweet Nothings	7"	Philips	BF1274	1963	**£6**	chart single
Sweet Nothings	7"	Philips	BF1274	1963	**£15**	demo
Sweets For My Sweet	7"	Pye	7N15533	1963	**£4**	chart single
Sweets For My Sweet	7"	Pye	7N15533	1963	**£15**	demo
Sweets For My Sweet	7" EP	Pye	NEP24183	1963	**£5**	
Take It Or Leave It	7"	Pye	7N17094	1966	**£4**	chart single
Take It Or Leave It	7"	Pye	7N17094	1966	**£10**	demo
Take Me For What I'm Worth	LP	Kapp	KL1477	1966	**£15**	US
Take Me For What I'm Worth	LP	Pye	NPL18120	1965	**£20**	
Take Me For What I'm Worth	7"	Pye	7N15992	1965	**£4**	chart single
Take Me For What I'm Worth	7"	Pye	7N15992	1965	**£10**	demo
Take Me For What I'm Worth	7" EP	Pye	NEP24263	1966	**£6**	
Tausend Nadelstiche	7"	Vogue	14130	1963	**£20**	sung in German
This Is Us	LP	Kapp	KL1409	1964	**£15**	US
Umbrella Man	7"	Liberty	LBF15159	1968	**£5**	
Vahevala	7"	RCA	RCA2288	1972	**£5**	
Verzeih My Love	7"	Vogue	14338	1965	**£20**	sung in German
Western Union	7"	Pye	7N17308	1967	**£5**	
What Have They Done To The Rain	7"	Pye	7N15739	1964	**£4**	chart single
What Have They Done To The Rain	7"	Pye	7N15739	1964	**£12**	demo
When I Get Home	7"	Pye	7N15950	1965	**£4**	chart single
When I Get Home	7"	Pye	7N15950	1965	**£10**	demo
When You Walk In The Room	7"	Pye	7N15694	1964	**£4**	chart single
When You Walk In The Room	7"	Pye	7N15694	1964	**£12**	demo
When You Walk In The Room	7" EP	Pye	NEP24204	1964	**£6**	

SEASTONE

Title	Format	Label	Cat. No.	Year	Price	Notes
Mirrored Image	LP	Plankton		1978	**£75**	

SEASTONES

Title	Format	Label	Cat. No.	Year	Price	Notes
Seastones	LP	Round	RX106	1975	**£20**	US

SEATHROUGH

Title	Format	Label	Cat. No.	Year	Price	Notes
Lala Lapla	LP	private		197-	**£50**	

SEATON, B.B.

Title	Format	Label	Cat. No.	Year	Price	Notes
Hold On	7"	R&B	JB143	1964	**£10**	
Rub It Down	7"	Blue Beat	BB289	1964	**£10**	
Thin Line Between Love And Hate	LP	Trojan	TRLS59	1973	**£10**	

SEATRAIN

Seatrain evolved out of The Blues Project, following the departure of founder members Danny Kalb, Steve Katz, and Al Kooper. The new sounds of violin and saxophone aquired a dominant role and for the first Seatrain LP the musicians are clearly inspired by the novelty of their new line-up. Unfortunately, this inspiration was short lived and the two LPs that followed are rather ordinary.

Title	Format	Label	Cat. No.	Year	Price	Notes
Marblehead Messenger	LP	Capitol	EAST829	1972	**£10**	
Marblehead Messenger	7"	Capitol	CL15697	1971	**£4**	
Seatrain	LP	A&M	AMLS941	1969	**£15**	
Seatrain	LP	Capitol	EAST659	1971	**£10**	
Thirteen Questions	7"	Capitol	CL15680	1971	**£4**	

SEBASTIAN, JOHN

Title	Format	Label	Cat. No.	Year	Price	Notes
Cheapo Cheapo Productions Presents	LP	Reprise	K44127	1971	**£10**	
John B.Sebastian	LP	Reprise	K44086	1970	**£10**	
Live	LP	MGM	SE4720	1970	**£20**	US

SEBASTIAN, JOHN (2)

Title	Format	Label	Cat. No.	Year	Price	Notes
Inca Dance	7"	London	HL8029	1954	**£6**	
Stranger In Paradise	7"	London	HL8131	1955	**£6**	

SECOND CITY SOUND

Title	Format	Label	Cat. No.	Year	Price	Notes
Tchaikovsky One	7"	Decca	F12310	1965	**£4**	chart single

SECOND COMING

Title	Format	Label	Cat. No.	Year	Price	Notes
Second Coming	LP	Mercury	6338030	1970	**£15**	

SECOND HAND

Second Hand revolved around keyboard virtuoso Ken Elliott and drummer Kieran O'Connor, who subsequently recorded as Seventh Wave. Their music is an interesting blend of classical and avant garde influences within a sound that is nevertheless rock based - rather like the better-known Egg, in fact. "Death May Be Your Santa Claus" is that rare thing, an expensive progressive album that is actually something of a forgotten masterpiece.

Title	Format	Label	Cat. No.	Year	Price	Notes
Death May Be Your Santa Claus	LP	Mushroom	200MR6	1972	**£100**	
Reality (Moving Fingers)	LP	Polydor	583045	1969	**£60**	
Thomopoulos-Tears Of The Sun	LP	Mushroom		197-	**£50**	

SECRET AFFAIR

Title	Format	Label	Cat. No.	Year	Price	Notes
Lost In The Night	7"	I Spy	SEE11	1982	**£4**	

SECRETS

Title	Format	Label	Cat. No.	Year	Price	Notes
Boy Next Door	7"	Philips	BF1298	1964	**£4**	
Other Side Of Town	7"	Philips	BF1318	1964	**£4**	
Such A Pity	7"	CBS	202466	1967	**£4**	

SEDAKA, NEIL

Title	Format	Label	Cat. No.	Year	Price	Notes
Bad Blood	7"	Polydor	2058532	1974	**£4**	
Bad Girl	7"	RCA	RCA1368	1963	**£4**	
Breaking Up Is Hard To Do	7"	RCA	RCA1298	1962	**£4**	chart single
Calendar Girl	7"	RCA	RCA1220	1961	**£4**	chart single
Circulate	LP	RCA	RD27207, SF5090	1960	**£20**	
Circulate	7"	RCA	RCA1331	1963	**£4**	
Dreamer	7"	RCA	RCA1359	1963	**£4**	
Happy Birthday Sweet Sixteen	7"	RCA	RCA1266	1961	**£4**	chart single
I Go Ape	7"	RCA	RCA1115	1959	**£6**	chart single
King Of Clowns	7"	RCA	RCA1282	1962	**£4**	chart single
Let's Go Steady Again	7"	RCA	RCA1343	1963	**£4**	chart single
Little Devil	7"	RCA	RCA1236	1961	**£4**	chart single
Neil Sedaka	LP	RCA	RD27140	1959	**£20**	
Neil Sedaka	7" EP	RCA	RCX166	1959	**£10**	
Neil Sedaka No.2	7" EP	RCA	RCX186	1960	**£8**	
Neil Sedaka No.3	7" EP	RCA	RCX212	1962	**£8**	
Next Door To An Angel	7"	RCA	RCA1319	1962	**£4**	chart single
No Vacancy	7"	RCA	RCA1099	1959	**£4**	
Oh Carol	7"	RCA	RCA1152	1959	**£4**	chart single
Oh Delilah	7"	Stateside	SS105	1962	**£6**	
Ring A Rocking	7"	London	HLW8961	1959	**£15**	
Stairway To Heaven	7"	RCA	RCA1178	1960	**£4**	chart single
Sweet Little You	7"	RCA	RCA1250	1961	**£4**	
World Through A Tear	7"	RCA	RCA1475	1965	**£4**	
You Mean Everything To Me	7"	RCA	RCA1198	1960	**£4**	chart single
You've Got To Learn Your R&B	7"	RCA	RCA1130	1959	**£6**	

SEEDORF, RUDY

Title	Format	Label	Cat. No.	Year	Price	Notes
One Million Stars	7"	Island	WI189	1965	**£10**	

SEEDS

Title	Format	Label	Cat. No.	Year	Price	Notes
Can't Seem To Make You Mine	7"	Vocalion	VN9287	1967	**£15**	
Full Spoon Of Seedy Blues	LP	GNP-Cres.	2040	1967	**£20**	US red label
Future	LP	Vocalion	VAN8070	1967	**£20**	
Merlin's Music Box	LP	GNP-Cres.	2043	1967	**£20**	US red label
Pushin' Too Hard	7"	Vocalion	VN9277	1966	**£12**	
Seeds	LP	GNP-Cres.	2023	1966	**£20**	US red label
Web Of Sound	LP	Vocalion	VAN8062	1966	**£20**	

SEEDS & OTHERS

Title	Format	Label	Cat. No.	Year	Price	Notes
Psych-Out	LP	Sidewalk	ST5913	1968	**£15**	US

SEEGER, PETE

Broadsides	LP	Transatlantic		1964	**£10**	
I Can See A New Day	LP	CBS		1964	**£10**	
In Person	LP	Verve	VLP5004	1965	**£10**	
Little Boxes	7"	CBS	201743	1965	**£4**	
We Shall Overcome	LP	CBS	BPG62209	1963	**£15**	

SEEMON & MARIJKE

Son Of America	LP	A&M	SP4309	1970	**£15**	US

SEGER, BOB

Against The Wind	LP	Mobile Fid.	MFSL1127	1983	**£10**	US audiophile
Back In '72	LP	Reprise	K44227	1973	**£10**	
Bob Seger Story	LP	Capitol		1981	**£15**	US promo
Brand New Morning	LP	Capitol	ST731	1971	**£15**	US
Get Out Of Denver	7"	Reprise	K14364	1974	**£4**	
Hollywood Nights	7"	Capitol	CL16004	1978	**£4**	silver vinyl
If I Were A Carpenter	7"	Reprise	K14208	1972	**£4**	
Lucifer	7"	Capitol	CL15642	1970	**£8**	
Main Street	12"	Capitol	PSLP193	1976	**£8**	promo
Mongrel	LP	Capitol	SKAO499	1970	**£10**	US gatefold
Night Moves	LP	Mobile Fid.	MFSL1034	1980	**£15**	US audiophile
Noah	LP	Capitol	ST236	1969	**£15**	US
Ramblin' Gamblin' Man	LP	Capitol	ST172	1969	**£10**	US
Ramblin' Gamblin' Man	7"	Capitol	CL15574	1968	**£8**	
Rosalie	7"	Reprise	K14243	1973	**£4**	
Seger Classics	LP	Capitol	PSLP271/2	1977	**£25**	promo double
Smokin' O.P.'s	LP	Palladium	P1006	1972	**£15**	US
Smokin' OPs	LP	Reprise	K44214	1972	**£10**	
Stranger In Town	LP	Capitol	EAST11698	1978	**£12**	grey vinyl
Stranger In Town	LP	Capitol	SEAX11904	1978	**£10**	US pic disc

SELF, FREDDIE

Don't Cry	7"	Mercury	MF839	1964	**£4**	

SELLERS, BROTHER JOHN

Big Beat Up The River	LP	Monitor	505		**£20**	US
Blues & Spirituals	7" EP	Columbia	SEG7740	1957	**£5**	
Blues & Spirituals	7" EP	Vanguard	EPP14002	1956	**£5**	
In London	7" EP	Decca	DFE6457	1957	**£5**	

SELLERS, PETER

Any Old Iron	7"	Parlophone	R4337	1957	**£4**	chart single
Best Of Sellers	LP-10"	Parlophone	PMD1069	1958	**£12**	chart LP
Drop Of The Hard Stuff	7"	Parlophone	R4491	1958	**£4**	
Hard Day's Night	7"	Parlophone	R5393	1965	**£5**	chart single
Putting on The Smile	7"	Parlophone	R4605	1959	**£4**	
Songs For Swingin' Sellers	LP	Parlophone	PMC1111	1959	**£10**	chart LP

SELLERS, PETER & SOPHIA LOREN

Bangers And Mash	7"	Parlophone	R4724	1961	**£4**	chart single
Goodness Gracious Me	7"	Parlophone	R4702	1960	**£4**	chart single
Peter And Sophia	LP	Parlophone	PMC1131	1960	**£10**	chart LP

SELLERS, PETER, SPIKE MILLIGAN & HARRY SECOMBE

How To Win An Election	LP	Philips	AL3464	1964	**£10**	chart LP

SENATE

I Can't Stop	7"	Columbia	DB8110	1967	**£4**	

SENATE (2)

Original Sin	7"	Burning Rome	BRR7	1984	**£4**	
Original Sin	7"	War	WAR1	1984	**£4**	

SENATORS

Breakdown	7"	Oriole	CB1957	1964	**£5**	
Tables Are Turning	7"	CBS	201768	1965	**£5**	

SENSATIONS

Let Me In	LP	Argo	LP4022	1963	**£30**	US
Let Me In	7"	Pye	7N25128	1962	**£8**	
Music Music Music	7"	Pye	7N25110	1961	**£8**	

SENSATIONS (2)

Born To Love You	7"	Doctor Bird	DB1102	1967	**£10**	
Look At My Baby	7"	Decca	F12392	1966	**£8**	
Right On Time	7"	Doctor Bird	DB1100	1967	**£10**	
Thing Called Soul	7"	Doctor Bird	DB1074	1967	**£10**	

SERENDIPITY

Castles	7"	CBS	4428	1969	**£8**	
Through With You	7"	CBS	3733	1968	**£12**	

SERFS

Early Bird Cafe	LP	Capitol		1969	**£15**	US

SERPENT POWER

Serpent Power	LP	Vanguard	VSD79252	1967	**£25**	US

SETTLERS

As Long As There's Love	7"	Columbia	DB8424	1968	**£4**	
Early Morning Rain	7"	Pye	7N17104	1966	**£4**	
Early Settlers	LP	Island	ILP947	1967	**£20**	
Keep Moving On	7"	Columbia	DB8750	1971	**£4**	
Lightning Tree	7"	York	SYK505	1971	**£4**	chart single
Nowhere Man	7"	Pye	7N17065	1966	**£5**	
On The Other Side	7"	Pye	7N17213	1966	**£4**	
Settle Down	7"	Decca	F11938	1964	**£5**	
Till Winter Follows Spring	7"	Pye	7N17171	1966	**£5**	
When's It Gonna Be My Turn	7"	Decca	F12123	1965	**£5**	
Woman Called Freedom	7"	Pye	7N15965	1965	**£4**	

SEVEN AGES OF MAN

Seven Ages Of Man	LP	Rediffusion		1972	**£40**	

SEVEN LETTERS

Bam Bam Baji	7"	Doctor Bird	DB1209	196-	**£10**	
Flour Dumpling	7"	Doctor Bird	DB1195	196-	**£10**	
Fung Sure	7"	Doctor Bird	DB1306	196-	**£10**	
La Bella Jig	7"	Treasure Isle	TI7055	196-	**£10**	
Mama Me Want Girl	7"	Doctor Bird	DB1206	196-	**£10**	
Parsons Corner	7"	Treasure Isle	TI7054	196-	**£10**	
Please Stay	7"	Doctor Bird	DB1194	196-	**£10**	
Skinhead Moonstomp	7"	Treasure Isle	TI7050	196-	**£10**	
Soul Crash	7"	Doctor Bird	DB1207	196-	**£10**	
There Goes My Heart	7"	Doctor Bird	DB1208	196-	**£10**	

SEVEN SECONDS

Skins,Brains And Guts	7"	Alt. Tentacles	VIRUS15	1982	**£4**	

SEVENTEEN

Don't Let Go	7"	Vendetta	VD001	1980	**£30**	

SEVENTH WAVE

Fail To See	7"	Gull	GULS10	1974	**£4**	
Manifestations	7"	Gull	GULS17	1975	**£4**	
Psi Fi	LP	Gull	GULP1010	1975	**£10**	
Things To Come	LP	Gull	GULP1001	1974	**£10**	

SEVILLE, DAVID

Armen's Theme	7"	London	HLU8359	1957	**£4**	
David Seville & His Orchestra	7" EP	London	REU1085	1957	**£5**	
Got To Get To Your House	7"	London	HLU8485	1957	**£4**	
Witch Doctor & His Friends	7" EP	London	REU1219	1959	**£5**	
Witch Doctor	LP	London	HAU2153	1959	**£10**	
Witch Doctor	7"	London	HLU8619	1958	**£4**	chart single

SEX PISTOLS

What was revolutionary about the Sex Pistols was not so much their music or their image, but the way in which they (or rather their manager, Malcolm McLaren) saw rock music as an institution out of which it was possible to make a considerable amount of money. The strategy of signing to a label for a large advance, which was retained when the record company became too outraged by the group's behaviour to honour its side of the contract, worked supremely well. The Sex Pistols found themselves wealthy almost before they had recorded anything. Curiously, when Sigue Sigue Sputnik demonstrated a similarly mercenary attitude to music making, they found themselves vilified, rather than lauded as the Sex Pistols had been. Meanwhile, the Sex Pistols' early carryings-on have left us with one of the most valuable of modern collectors' items: the version of "God Save The

Queen" that was very briefly available on the A&M label.

Title	Format	Label	Cat. No.	Year	Price	Notes
Anarchy In The UK	7"	EMI	EMI2566	1976	**£8**	chart single
Anarchy In The UK	7"	EMI	EMI2566	1976	**£75**	1 sided test pressing
Anarchy In The UK	7"	EMI	EMI2566	1976	**£15**	black PS
Anarchy In The UK	7"	Sex Pistols	640112	1977	**£5**	French, PS
Anarchy In The UK	7"	Virgin		1980	**£20**	test pressing
Biggest Blow	12"	Virgin	VS22012	1978	**£8**	with Interview
C'Mon Everybody	7"	Virgin	VS272	1979	**£15**	test pressing
Frigging In The Rigging	7"	Virgin	VS240	1979	**£15**	mispress, A side plays 'Silly Thing'
God Save The Queen	7"	A&M	AMS7284	1977	**£500**	
God Save The Queen	7"	Sex Pistols	640106	1977	**£5**	French, PS
God Save The Queen	7"	Virgin	VS181	1977	**£35**	test pressing
Great Rock'n'Roll Swindle	7"	Virgin	VS290	1979	**£5**	credit card PS
Great Rock'n'Roll Swindle	7"	Virgin	VS290	1979	**£12**	demo
Heyday	cass	Factory	FACT30	1980	**£12**	satin pouch, Xmas card
Holidays In The Sun	7"	Virgin	VS191	1977	**£5**	PS
Holidays In The Sun	7"	Virgin	VS191	1977	**£30**	test pressing
Mini Album	mini LP	Chaos	AMPL37	1986	**£8**	pic disc
My Way	7"	Virgin	VS220	1978	**£15**	mispress, other side plays The Motors
Never Mind The Bollocks	LP	Virgin	V2086	1977	**£15**	no track listing on sleeve
Never Mind The Bollocks	LP	Virgin	V2086	1977	**£25**	with poster & 1 sided 7" (VDJ24)
Never Mind The Bollocks	LP	Virgin	VP2086	1978	**£25**	pic disc
No One Is Innocent	7"	Virgin	VS220	1978	**£20**	test pressing
Pistols Pack	7"	Virgin	SEX1	1980	**£20**	6x7", plastic wallet
Pretty Vacant	7"	Sex Pistols	640109	1977	**£5**	French, PS
Pretty Vacant	7"	Virgin	VS184	1977	**£30**	test pressing
Silly Thing	7"	Virgin	VS256	1979	**£20**	test pressing
Something Else	7"	Virgin	VS240	1979	**£20**	test pressing
Stepping Stone	7"	Virgin	VS339	1980	**£12**	mispress, plays Gillan
Submission	7"	Chaos	DICK1	1985	**£6**	blue, pink, or yellow vinyl
Submission	12"	Chaos	EXPORT1	1985	**£6**	6 different coloured vinyls
The Great Rock'N'Roll Swindle	LP	Virgin	VD2510	1979	**£12**	with 'Whatcha Gonna Do About It'

SEX PISTOLS & NEW YORK DOLLS

Title	Format	Label	Cat. No.	Year	Price	Notes
After The Storm	mini LP	Receiver		1985	**£8**	

SEXY GIRLS

Title	Format	Label	Cat. No.	Year	Price	Notes
Pom-Pom Song	7"	Dice	CC100	196-	**£8**	

SEYTON, DENNY

Title	Format	Label	Cat. No.	Year	Price	Notes
Just A Kiss	7"	Parlophone	R5363	1965	**£10**	

SEYTON, DENNY & THE SABRES

Title	Format	Label	Cat. No.	Year	Price	Notes
It's The Gear (14 Hits)	LP	Wing	WL1032	1965	**£30**	
Short Fat Fanny	7"	Mercury	MF814	1964	**£12**	
Tricky Dicky	7"	Mercury	MF800	1964	**£10**	
Way You Look Tonight	7"	Mercury	MF824	1964	**£15**	chart single

SHADE JOEY & THE NIGHTOWLS

Title	Format	Label	Cat. No.	Year	Price	Notes
Blue Birds Fly Over	7"	Parlophone	R5180	1964	**£15**	

SHADES

Title	Format	Label	Cat. No.	Year	Price	Notes
Undivided Attention	7"	London	HLX8713	1958	**£8**	
Weird Walk	7"	Starlite	ST45074	1962	**£6**	

SHADES OF BLUE

Title	Format	Label	Cat. No.	Year	Price	Notes
Happiness Is The Shades Of Blue	LP	Impact	IM101	1966	**£15**	US
Oh How Happy	7"	Sue	WI4022	1966	**£10**	
Voodoo Blues	7"	Parlophone	R5270	1965	**£10**	
Where Did All The Good Times Go	7"	Pye	7N15988	1965	**£5**	

SHADES OF GREEN

Title	Format	Label	Cat. No.	Year	Price	Notes
Rockin' Poppin' Ravin'	LP	Windmill		1973	**£10**	

SHADES OF JOY

Title	Format	Label	Cat. No.	Year	Price	Notes
Shades Of Joy	LP	Fontana	STL5498	1969	**£12**	

SHADOWS

Title	Format	Label	Cat. No.	Year	Price	Notes
Alice In Sunderland	7" EP	Columbia	SEG8445	1965	**£8**	
Apache	7"	Columbia	DB4484	1960	**£4**	chart single
Atlantis	7"	Columbia	DB7047	1963	**£4**	chart single
Boys	7" EP	Columbia	ESG7881	1962	**£15**	stereo
Boys	7" EP	Columbia	SEG8193	1962	**£5**	
Chelsea Boot	7"	Columbia	PSR310	1967	**£8**	promo
Dance On	7"	Columbia	DB4948	1962	**£4**	chart single
Dance On With The Shadows	7" EP	Columbia	SEG8233	1963	**£5**	
Dance With The Shadows	LP	Columbia	33SX1619, SCX3511	1964	**£10**	chart LP
Dance With The Shadows No.1	7" EP	Columbia	SEG8342	1964	**£5**	
Dance With The Shadows No.2	7" EP	Columbia	SEG8375	1964	**£5**	
Dance With The Shadows No.3	7" EP	Columbia	SEG8408	1965	**£5**	
Dancing In The Dark	12"	Polydor	POSPX808	1986	**£6**	
Dear Old Mrs.Bell	7"	Columbia	DB8372	1968	**£5**	
Don't Make My Baby Blue	7"	Columbia	DB7650	1965	**£4**	chart single
Dreams I Dream	7"	Columbia	DB8034	1966	**£5**	chart single
F.B.I.	7"	Columbia	DB4580	1961	**£4**	chart single
Foot Tapper	7"	Columbia	DB4984	1963	**£4**	chart single
Foot Tapping With The Shadows	7" EP	Columbia	SEG8268	1963	**£5**	
Frightened City	7"	Columbia	DB4637	1961	**£4**	chart single
From Hank,Bruce,Brian,& John	LP	Columbia	SCX6199	1967	**£10**	
Genie With The Light Brown Lamp	7"	Columbia	DB7416	1964	**£4**	chart single
Geronimo	7"	Columbia	DB7163	1963	**£4**	chart single
Guitar Tango	7"	Columbia	DB4870	1962	**£4**	chart single
I Met A Girl	7"	Columbia	DB7853	1966	**£5**	chart single
It'll Be Me Babe	7"	EMI	EMI2451	1976	**£4**	
Jigsaw	LP	Columbia	SCX6148	1967	**£10**	chart LP
Kon-Tiki	7"	Columbia	DB4698	1961	**£4**	chart single
Los Shadows	7"	Columbia		1964	**£20**	export
Los Shadows	7" EP	Columbia	SEG8278	1963	**£8**	
Love De Luxe	7"	EMI	EMI2838	1978	**£4**	
Magical Mrs. Clamps	7"	EMI	PSR316	1968	**£10**	promo, B side by Cliff Richard
Man Of Mystery	7"	Columbia	DB4530	1960	**£4**	chart single
Maroc 7	7"	Columbia	DB8170	1967	**£4**	chart single
Maroc 7	7"	Columbia	PSR304	1967	**£10**	promo, spoken intro
Mary Anne	7"	Columbia	DB7476	1965	**£4**	chart single
More Hits	LP	Columbia	33SX1791, SCX3578	1965	**£10**	
Naughty Nippon Nights	7"	Columbia	PSR313	1967	**£8**	promo
On Stage And Screen	7" EP	Columbia	SEG8528	1967	**£10**	
Out Of The Shadows	LP	Columbia	33SX1458	1962	**£10**	chart LP
Out Of The Shadows	LP	Columbia	SCX3449	1962	**£10**	chart LP
Out Of The Shadows	7" EP	Columbia	ESG7883	1963	**£12**	stereo
Out Of The Shadows	7" EP	Columbia	SEG8218	1963	**£5**	
Out Of The Shadows No.2	7" EP	Columbia	ESG7895	1963	**£12**	stereo
Out Of The Shadows No.2	7" EP	Columbia	SEG8249	1963	**£5**	
Place In The Sun	7"	Columbia	DB7952	1966	**£4**	chart single
Rhythm And Greens	7"	Columbia	DB7342	1964	**£4**	chart single
Rhythm And Greens	7" EP	Columbia	ESG7904	1964	**£15**	stereo
Rhythm And Greens	7" EP	Columbia	SEG8362	1964	**£6**	
Rise And Fall Of Flingel Bunt	7"	Columbia	DB7261	1964	**£4**	chart single
Rise And Fall Of Flingel Bunt	7"	Columbia	DB7261	1964	**£10**	mispress, 2 A sides
Run Billy Run	7"	EMI	EMI2310	1975	**£4**	
Saturday Dance	7"	Columbia	DB4387	1959	**£20**	
Savage	7"	Columbia	DB4726	1961	**£4**	chart single
Shadow Music	LP	Columbia	33SX6041	1966	**£10**	chart LP
Shadows	LP	Columbia	33SX1374, SCX3414	1962	**£12**	chart LP
Shadows	7" EP	Columbia	ESG7834	1961	**£15**	stereo
Shadows	7" EP	Columbia	SEG8061	1961	**£5**	
Shadows	7"	Lyntone	LYN10099	1972	**£5**	promo flexi
Shadows	LP	MFP	1388	1970	**£10**	royal blue sleeve
Shadows	LP	W. Rec. Club	ALBUM72	1972	**£30**	6 LPs, boxed
Shadows Know	LP	Atlantic	8097	1964	**£15**	US
Shadows No.2	7" EP	Columbia	SEG8148	1962	**£5**	
Shadows No.3	7" EP	Columbia	SEG8166	1962	**£5**	
Shadows To The Fore	7" EP	Columbia	SEG8094	1961	**£5**	

Title	Format	Label	Cat. No.	Year	Price	Notes
Shindig	7"	Columbia	DB7106	1963	**£4**	chart single
Shindig With The Shadows	7" EP	Columbia	SEG8286	1963	**£5**	
Sound Of The Shadows	LP	Columbia	33SX1736	1965	**£10**	chart LP
Sound Of The Shadows	LP	Columbia	SCX3554	1965	**£10**	chart LP
Sound Of The Shadows No.1	7" EP	Columbia	SEG8459	1965	**£6**	
Sound Of The Shadows No.2	7" EP	Columbia	SEG8473	1966	**£6**	
Sound Of The Shadows No.3	7" EP	Columbia	SEG8494	1966	**£6**	
Spotlight On The Shadows	7" EP	Columbia	SEG8135	1962	**£5**	
Stingray	7"	Columbia	DB7588	1965	**£4**	chart single
Surfing With The Shadows	LP	Atlantic	8089	1963	**£15**	US
Theme For Young Lovers	7"	Columbia	DB7231	1964	**£4**	chart single
Themes From Aladdin	7" EP	Columbia	SEG8396	1965	**£5**	
Those Brilliant Shadows	7" EP	Columbia	SEG8321	1964	**£5**	
Those Talented Shadows	7" EP	Columbia	SEG8500	1966	**£6**	
Thunderbirds Are Go	7"	EMI	PSR305	1967	**£8**	1 sided promo
Tomorrow's Cancelled	7"	Columbia	DB8264	1967	**£6**	
Treat Me Nice	7"	Polydor	POSP439	1982	**£4**	
Twenty Golden Greats	LP	EMI	EMTV3	1977	**£12**	mispress, Pink Floyd on side 2
Twenty Golden Greats	7"	EMI		1977	**£5**	promo sampler
Warlord	7"	Columbia	DB7769	1965	**£4**	chart single
Wonderful Land	7"	Columbia	DB4790	1962	**£4**	chart single
Wonderful Land Of The Shadows	7" EP	Columbia	SEG8171	1962	**£5**	

SHADOWS (2)

Title	Format	Label	Cat. No.	Year	Price	Notes
Under Stars Of Love	7"	HMV	POP563	1958	**£6**	

SHADOWS OF KNIGHT

Title	Format	Label	Cat. No.	Year	Price	Notes
Back Door Men	LP	Dunwich	667	1966	**£30**	US
Bad Little Woman	7"	Atlantic	584045	1966	**£8**	
Gloria	7"	Atlantic	AT4085	1966	**£10**	
Gloria	LP	Dunwich	666	1966	**£30**	US
Oh Yeah	7"	Atlantic	584021	1966	**£8**	
Shadows Of Knight	LP	Super K	SKS6002	1969	**£15**	US
Shake	7"	Buddah	201024	1968	**£8**	
Someone Like Me	7"	Atlantic	584136	1967	**£8**	

SHADRACK CHAMELEON

Title	Format	Label	Cat. No.	Year	Price	Notes
Shadrack Chameleon	LP	Iglus		1969	**£125**	US

SHADROCKS

Title	Format	Label	Cat. No.	Year	Price	Notes
Go Go Special	7"	Island	WI3061	1967	**£10**	

SHAFTESBURY

Title	Format	Label	Cat. No.	Year	Price	Notes
Lull Before The Storm	LP	OK Records	OKA001	1980	**£50**	
We Are The Boys	LP	OK		1981	**£30**	

SHAGGS

Title	Format	Label	Cat. No.	Year	Price	Notes
Philosophy Of The World	LP	Third World	3001		**£100**	US

SHAKE

Title	Format	Label	Cat. No.	Year	Price	Notes
Culture Shock	10"	Sire	SIR401610	1979	**£5**	

SHAKEOUTS

Title	Format	Label	Cat. No.	Year	Price	Notes
Every Little Once In A While	7"	Columbia	DB7613	1965	**£20**	

SHAKERS (KINGSIZE TAYLOR & DOMINOES)

Title	Format	Label	Cat. No.	Year	Price	Notes
Hippy Hippy Shake	7"	Polydor	NH66991	1963	**£15**	
Let's Do The Slop,Twist,Madison...	LP			1963	**£30**	
Money	7"	Polydor	NH52158	1963	**£12**	
Whole Lotta Loving	7"	Polydor	NH52272	1964	**£12**	

SHAKEY JAKE

Title	Format	Label	Cat. No.	Year	Price	Notes
Further On Up The Road	LP	Liberty		1969	**£12**	

SHAKEY VICK

Title	Format	Label	Cat. No.	Year	Price	Notes
Little Woman You're So Sweet	LP	Pye	NSPL18276	1969	**£30**	

SHALIMAR

Title	Format	Label	Cat. No.	Year	Price	Notes
Kentucky River Line	7"	Pye	7N25527	1970	**£4**	

SHAM 69

Angels With Dirty Faces	7"	Polydor	2059023	1978	**£4**	chart single
Borstal Breakout	7"	Polydor	2058966	1978	**£5**	
Hersham Boys	7"	Polydor	POSP64	1979	**£4**	chart single
Hersham Boys	12"	Polydor	POSPX64	1978	**£6**	
Hurry Up Harry	7"	Polydor	POSP7	1978	**£4**	chart single
I Don't Wanna	7"	Step Forward	SF4	1977	**£5**	
I Don't Wanna	12"	Step Forward	SF4	1977	**£8**	
If The Kids Are United	7"	Polydor	2059050	1978	**£4**	chart single
Questions And Answers	7"	Polydor	POSP27	1979	**£4**	chart single
Sons Of The Streets	7"	no label	no number	1977	**£10**	1 sided
Tell The Children	7"	Polydor	POSP136	1980	**£4**	chart single
You're A Better Man Than I	7"	Polydor	POSP82	1979	**£4**	chart single
What Have We Got	7"	Polydor		1978	**£5**	1 sided promo

SHAMES

Greenburg Glickstein Charles	7"	CBS	3820	1968	**£8**	
I Wanna Meet You	7"	CBS	202450	1966	**£8**	
Mr.Unreliable	7"	CBS	2704	1967	**£8**	
Sugar And Spice	7"	CBS	202344	1966	**£5**	

SHANANETTES

Romeo And Juliet	7"	Pye	DDS114	196-	**£8**	

SHAND, WINSTON

I'll Run Away	7"	Moodisc	MU3505	197-	**£4**	

SHANE, JOHN

Cross My Palm With Silver	LP	Full Moon		1977	**£15**	

SHANES

I Don't Want Your Love	7"	Columbia	DB7601	1965	**£10**	

SHANGRI-LAS

Give Him A Great Big Kiss	7"	Red Bird	RB10018	1965	**£8**	
Give Us Your Blessings	7"	Red Bird	RB10030	1965	**£6**	
Golden Hits	LP	Mercury	MCL20096	1966	**£15**	
He Cried	7"	Red Bird	RB10053	1966	**£6**	
I Can Never Go Home Any More	7"	Red Bird	RB10043	1966	**£5**	
I Can Never Go Home Any More	7" EP	Red Bird	RB40004	1966	**£15**	
I Can Never Go Home Anymore	LP	Red Bird	RB20104	1965	**£50**	US
Leader Of The Pack	LP	Red Bird	RB20101	1964	**£50**	
Leader Of The Pack	7"	Red Bird	RB10014	1964	**£5**	chart single
Long Live Our Love	7"	Red Bird	RB10048	1966	**£6**	
Out In The Streets	7"	Red Bird	RB10025	1965	**£6**	
Past Present And Future	7"	Red Bird	RB10068	1966	**£6**	
Remember Walking In The Sand	7"	Red Bird	RB10008	1964	**£5**	chart single
Right Now And Not Later	7"	Red Bird	RB10036	1965	**£6**	
Shangri-Las '65	LP	Red Bird	RB20104	1965	**£35**	US
Shangri-Las	7" EP	Red Bird	RB40002	1965	**£15**	
Shangri-Las Sing	LP	Post	4000		**£10**	US
Sweet Sound Of Summer	7"	Mercury	MF962	1967	**£5**	
Take Your Time	7"	Mercury	MF979	1967	**£5**	

SHANKAR, ANANDA

Ananda Shankar	LP	Reprise	K44092	1970	**£10**	

SHANKAR, L.

Touch Me There	LP	Zappa	SRZ11602	1979	**£10**	US

SHANKAR, RAVI

In Concert 1972	LP	Apple	SAPDO1002	1973	**£100**	double
Joi Bangla	7"	Apple	37	1971	**£5**	
Joi Bangla	7"	Apple	37	1971	**£10**	PS
Raga	LP	Apple	SWAO3384	1971	**£15**	US

SHANNON, CHICK

Tears On The Console	LP	Holyground		1975	**£500**	

SHANNON, DEAN

Jezebel	7"	HMV	POP820	1960	**£4**	
Ubangi Stomp	7"	HMV	POP1103	1962	**£10**	

SHANNON, DEL

Title	Format	Label	Number	Year	Price	Notes
1,661 Seconds Of...	LP	Amy	S8006	1965	**£35**	US, stereo
1,661 Seconds Of...	LP	Stateside	SL10140	1965	**£20**	
Best Of	LP	Dot	DLP3834	1967	**£10**	US
Big Hurt	7"	Liberty	LIB55866	1966	**£4**	
Break Up	7"	Stateside	SS430	1965	**£4**	
Comin' Back To Me	7"	Stateside	SS8025	1969	**£4**	
Cry Myself To Sleep	7"	London	HLX9587	1962	**£4**	chart single
Del Shannon	7" EP	London	REX1332	1962	**£8**	
Del Shannon No.2	7" EP	London	REX1346	1963	**£8**	
Del Shannon's Hits	7" EP	Stateside	SE1029	1965	**£6**	
Del's Own Favourites	7" EP	London	REX1383	1963	**£8**	
Do You Want To Dance	7"	Stateside	SS349	1964	**£4**	
For A Little While	7"	Liberty	LIB55889	1966	**£4**	
From Del To You	7" EP	London	REX1387	1963	**£8**	
Further Adventures Of C.Westover	LP	Liberty	LBL83114	1968	**£10**	
Gemini	7"	Liberty	LBF15079	1968	**£4**	
Handy Man	LP	Stateside	SL10115	1965	**£15**	
Handy Man	7"	Stateside	SS317	1964	**£4**	chart single
Hats Off To Del Shannon	LP	London	HAX8071	1963	**£20**	chart LP
Hats Off To Larry	7"	London	HLX9402	1961	**£4**	chart single
Hey Little Girl	7"	London	HLX9515	1962	**£4**	chart single
I Can't Believe My Ears	7"	Stateside	SS494	1966	**£4**	
Keep Searchin'	7"	Stateside	SS368	1965	**£4**	chart single
Little Town Flirt	LP	Big Top	S121308	1963	**£50**	US, stereo
Little Town Flirt	LP	London	HAX8091	1963	**£20**	chart LP
Little Town Flirt	7"	London	HLX9653	1963	**£4**	chart single
Mary Jane	7"	Stateside	SS269	1964	**£4**	chart single
Mind Over Matter	7"	Liberty	LIB10277	1967	**£4**	
Move It On Over	7"	Stateside	SS452	1965	**£4**	
New Del Shannon	7" EP	Liberty	LEP2272	1967	**£6**	
Runaway '67	7"	Liberty	LBF15020	1967	**£4**	
Runaway	LP	Big Top	123003	1961	**£35**	US, mono
Runaway	LP	Big Top	S123003	1961	**£240**	US, stereo
Runaway	LP	London	HAX2402	1961	**£20**	
Runaway	7"	London	HLX9317	1961	**£5**	chart single
Runaway	7"	London	HLX9317	1961	**£8**	B side mispress - plays 'Snake'
She	7"	Liberty	LIB55939	1967	**£4**	
Sings Hank Williams	LP	Stateside	SL10130	1965	**£15**	
Sister Isabelle	7"	Stateside	SS8040	1970	**£4**	
So Long Baby	7"	London	HLX9462	1961	**£4**	chart single
Stranger In Town	7"	Stateside	SS395	1965	**£4**	chart single
Sue's Gonna Be Mine	7"	London	HLX9800	1963	**£4**	chart single
Swiss Maid	7"	London	HLX9609	1962	**£4**	chart single
That's The Way Love Is	7"	London	HLX9858	1964	**£4**	
Thinkin' It Over	7"	Liberty	LBF15061	1968	**£4**	
This Is My Bag	LP	Liberty	LBY1320	1966	**£10**	
Total Commitment	LP	Liberty	LBY1335	1966	**£10**	
Two Kinds Of Teardrops	7"	London	HLX9719	1963	**£4**	chart single
Two Silhouettes	7"	London	HLX9761	1963	**£4**	chart single

SHANNON, HUGH

Title	Format	Label	Number	Year	Price	Notes
Hugh Shannon Sings	LP-10"	Atlantic	406		**£20**	US

SHANNON, MIKE & THE STRANGERS

Title	Format	Label	Number	Year	Price	Notes
One And One Is Two	7"	Philips	BF1335	1964	**£35**	

SHAPE & SIZES

Title	Format	Label	Number	Year	Price	Notes
Little Lovin' Somethin'	7"	Decca	F12441	1966	**£4**	

SHAPE OF THE RAIN

Title	Format	Label	Number	Year	Price	Notes
Riley Riley	LP	Neon	NE7	1971	**£30**	

SHAPIRO, HELEN

Title	Format	Label	Number	Year	Price	Notes
Don't Treat Me Like A Child	7"	Columbia	DB4589	1961	**£4**	chart single
Even More Hits From Helen	7" EP	Columbia	SEG8209	1962	**£5**	
Fever	7"	Columbia	DB7190	1964	**£4**	chart single
Forget About The Bad Things	7"	Columbia	DB7810	1966	**£4**	
He Knows How To Love Me	7"	Columbia	DB7340	1964	**£4**	
Helen	7" EP	Columbia	ESG7872	1961	**£6**	stereo

Title	Format	Label	Cat. No.	Year	Price	Notes
Helen	7" EP	Columbia	SEG8128	1961	**£4**	
Helen Hits Out	LP	Columbia	33SX1661	1964	**£15**	
Helen In Nashville	LP	Columbia	33SX1561	1963	**£20**	
Helen's 16	LP	Columbia	33SX1494	1963	**£15**	
Helen's Hit Parade	7" EP	Columbia	SEG8136	1961	**£4**	
Here In Your Arms	7"	Columbia	DB7587	1965	**£4**	
I Wish I'd Never Loved You	7"	Columbia	DB7395	1964	**£4**	
In My Calendar	7"	Columbia	DB8073	1966	**£4**	
Keep Away From Other Girls	7"	Columbia	DB4908	1962	**£4**	chart single
Let's Talk About Love	7"	Columbia	DB4824	1962	**£4**	chart single
Little Miss Lonely	7"	Columbia	DB4869	1962	**£4**	chart single
Look Over Your Shoulder	7"	Columbia	DB7266	1964	**£4**	
Look Who It Is	7"	Columbia	DB7130	1963	**£4**	chart single
Make Me Belong To You	7"	Columbia	DB8148	1967	**£4**	
More Hits From Helen	7" EP	Columbia	SEG8174	1962	**£5**	
Not Responsible	7"	Columbia	DB7072	1963	**£4**	
Queen For Tonight	7"	Columbia	DB4966	1963	**£4**	chart single
Something Wonderful	7"	Columbia	DB7690	1965	**£4**	
Stop & You'll Become Aware	7"	Columbia	DB8256	1967	**£30**	
Teenager In Love	LP	Epic	LN24075	1963	**£12**	US
Teenager Sings The Blues	7" EP	Columbia	ESG7880	1962	**£8**	stereo
Teenager Sings The Blues	7" EP	Columbia	SEG8170	1962	**£5**	
Tell Me What He Said	7"	Columbia	DB4782	1962	**£4**	chart single
Tomorrow Is Another Day	7"	Columbia	DB7517	1965	**£4**	
Tops With Me	LP	Columbia	33SX1397	1962	**£12**	chart LP
Tops With Me No.1	7" EP	Columbia	ESG7888	1962	**£10**	stereo
Tops With Me No.1	7" EP	Columbia	SEG8229	1963	**£6**	
Tops With Me No.2	7" EP	Columbia	ESG7891	1962	**£10**	stereo
Tops With Me No.2	7" EP	Columbia	SEG8243	1963	**£6**	
Walking Back To Happiness	7"	Columbia	DB4715	1961	**£4**	chart single
Woe Is Me	7"	Columbia	DB7026	1963	**£4**	chart single
You Don't Know	7"	Columbia	DB4670	1961	**£4**	chart single
You've Guessed It	7"	Pye	7N17785	1969	**£4**	

SHARADES

Title	Format	Label	Cat. No.	Year	Price	Notes
Dumbhead	7"	Decca	F11811	1964	**£12**	

SHARKS

Title	Format	Label	Cat. No.	Year	Price	Notes
First Water	LP	Island	ILPS9233	1973	**£10**	
Jab It In Your Eye	LP	Island	ILPS9271	1974	**£10**	

SHARONS

Title	Format	Label	Cat. No.	Year	Price	Notes
Someone To Turn To	LP	Emblem		1970	**£80**	

SHARP, DEE DEE

Title	Format	Label	Cat. No.	Year	Price	Notes
All The Hits	LP	Cameo	C1032	1962	**£10**	US
Biggest Hits	LP	Cameo	C1062	1963	**£12**	US
Do The Bird	7"	Cameo Park.	C244	1963	**£4**	chart single
Do The Bird	LP	Cameo	C1050	1963	**£10**	US
Down Memory Lane	LP	Cameo	C1074	1963	**£12**	US
Eighteen Golden Hits	LP	Cameo	C2002	1966	**£10**	US
Gravy	7"	Columbia	DB4874	1962	**£5**	
I Really Love You	7"	Cameo Park.	C375	1965	**£15**	
It's A Funny Situation	7"	Cameo Park.	C382	1965	**£4**	
It's Mashed Potato Time	LP	Cameo	C1018	1962	**£15**	US
Mashed Potato Time	7"	Columbia	DB4818	1962	**£5**	
My Best Friend's Man	7"	Atlantic	584056	1966	**£4**	
Ride	7"	Cameo Park.	C230	1962	**£4**	
Rock Me In The Cradle Of Love	7"	Cameo Park.	C260	1963	**£4**	
Songs Of Faith	LP	Cameo	C1022	1962	**£12**	US
What Kinda Lady	7"	Action	ACT4522	1969	**£8**	
What Kinda Lady	7"	Action	ACT4522	1969	**£20**	demo
Wild	7"	Cameo Park.	C274	1963	**£4**	

SHARPE, BILL

Title	Format	Label	Cat. No.	Year	Price	Notes
Change Your Mind	7"	Polydor	POSPP722	1985	**£6**	pic disc
Change Your Mind	12"	Polydor	POP722	1985	**£6**	
Change Your Mind	12"	Polydor	POPX722	1985	**£10**	pic disc

SHARPE, RAY

Title	Format	Label	Cat. No.	Year	Price	Notes
Hey Little Girl	7"	United Artists	UP1032	1963	**£6**	
Linda Lu	7"	London	HLW8932	1959	**£15**	

SHARPEES

Title	Format	Label	Number	Year	Price	Notes
Tired Of Being Lonely	7"	Stateside	SS495	1966	**£8**	

SHARPS

Title	Format	Label	Number	Year	Price	Notes
Lock My Heart	7"	Vogue	V9086	1957	**£40**	
Shuffling	7"	Vogue	V9096	1958	**£30**	

SHATNER, WILLIAM

Title	Format	Label	Number	Year	Price	Notes
Transformed Man	LP	Decca	DL75043	1968	**£15**	US

SHAW, NINA

Title	Format	Label	Number	Year	Price	Notes
Woven In My Soul	7"	CBS	3239	1968	**£4**	

SHAW, SANDIE

Title	Format	Label	Number	Year	Price	Notes
Always Something There To Remind Me	7"	Pye	7N15704	1964	**£4**	chart single
Always Something There To Remind Me	7" EP	Pye	NEP24208	1964	**£5**	
As Long As You're Happy Baby	7"	Pye	7N15671	1964	**£5**	
Girl Don't Come	7"	Pye	7N15743	1964	**£4**	chart single
Golden Hits	LP	Golden Guin.	GGL0360	1966	**£10**	
How Can You Tell	7"	Pye	7N15987	1965	**£4**	chart single
I Don't Need Anything	7"	Pye	7N17239	1967	**£4**	chart single
I'll Stop At Nothing	7"	Pye	7N15783	1965	**£4**	chart single
Long Live Love	7"	Pye	7N15841	1965	**£4**	chart single
Long Live Love	7" EP	Pye	NEP24220	1965	**£5**	
Love Me, Please Love Me	LP	Pye	NSPL18205	1967	**£10**	
Me	LP	Pye	NPL18122	1965	**£12**	
Message Understood	7"	Pye	7N15940	1965	**£4**	chart single
Message Understood	7" EP	Pye	NEP24236	1966	**£5**	
Nothing Comes Easy	7"	Pye	7N17086	1966	**£4**	chart single
Nothing Comes Easy	7" EP	Pye	NEP24254	1966	**£5**	
Puppet On A String	LP	Pye	NSPL18182	1967	**£10**	
Reviewing The Situation	LP	Pye	NSPL18323	1969	**£10**	
Run	7"	Pye	7N17163	1966	**£4**	chart single
Run With Sandie Shaw	7" EP	Pye	NEP24264	1966	**£5**	
Sandie	LP	Pye	NPL18110	1965	**£12**	chart LP
Sandie	7" EP	Pye	NEP24232	1965	**£5**	
Sandie Shaw In French	7" EP	Pye	NEP24271	1967	**£6**	
Sandie Shaw In Italian	7" EP	Pye	NEP24273	1967	**£6**	
Sandie Shaw Supplement	LP	Pye	NSPL18232	1968	**£10**	
Tell The Boys	7" EP	Pye	NEP24281	1967	**£6**	
Think Sometimes About Me	7"	Pye	7N17212	1966	**£4**	chart single
Tomorrow	7"	Pye	7N17036	1966	**£4**	chart single
Tomorrow	7" EP	Pye	NEP24247	1966	**£5**	

SHAW, TIMMY & THE STERNPHONES

Title	Format	Label	Number	Year	Price	Notes
Gonna Send You Back To Georgia	7"	Pye	7N25239	1964	**£8**	

SHAYNE, LISA

Title	Format	Label	Number	Year	Price	Notes
Don't Ever Change	7"	Fontana	TF563	1965	**£4**	

SHE TRINITY

Title	Format	Label	Number	Year	Price	Notes
Have I Sinned	7"	Columbia	DB7943	1966	**£5**	
He Fought The Law	7"	Columbia	DB7874	1966	**£5**	
Wild Flower	7"	Columbia	DB7959	1966	**£5**	
Yellow Submarine	7"	Columbia	DB7992	1966	**£8**	

SHEEN, BOBBY

Title	Format	Label	Number	Year	Price	Notes
Dr.Love	7"	Capitol	CL15455	1966	**£15**	
Dr.Love	7"	Capitol	CL15713	1972	**£4**	

SHEEP

Title	Format	Label	Number	Year	Price	Notes
Hide And Seek	7"	Stateside	SS493	1966	**£12**	
Sheep	LP	Myrrh		1973	**£30**	

SHEEPS HEAD BAY

Title	Format	Label	Number	Year	Price	Notes
My Name Is The Wind	7"	Parlophone	R5897	1971	**£4**	

SHEFFIELDS

Title	Format	Label	Number	Year	Price	Notes
Bag's Groove	7"	Pye	7N15767	1965	**£50**	
Got My Mojo Working	7"	Pye	7N15627	1964	**£50**	
It Must Be Love	7"	Pye	7N15600	1964	**£50**	

SHEIKS
Missing You .... 7" .... Parlophone ..... R5500 .... 1966 .... **£8** ....
Tres Chic .... 7" .... London .... HLW9012 .... 1959 .... **£4** ....

SHELDON, DOUG
Big Big Baby .... 7" .... Decca .... F11463 .... 1962 .... **£4** ....
Book Of Love .... 7" .... Decca .... F11368 .... 1961 .... **£4** ....
Here I Stand .... 7" EP .... Decca .... DFE8527 .... 1963 .... **£6** ....
I Saw Linda Yesterday .... 7" .... Decca .... F11564 .... 1963 .... **£4** .... chart single
I Was Alone .... 7" .... Decca .... F11654 .... 1963 .... **£4** ....
It's Because Of You .... 7" .... Pye .... 7N17011 .... 1965 .... **£4** ....
Live Now Pay Later .... 7" .... Decca .... F11529 .... 1962 .... **£4** ....
Lollipops And Roses .... 7" .... Decca .... F11514 .... 1962 .... **£4** ....
Mickey's Monkey .... 7" .... Decca .... F11790 .... 1963 .... **£4** ....
Runaround Sue .... 7" .... Decca .... F11398 .... 1961 .... **£4** .... chart single
Take It Like A Man .... 7" .... Sue .... WI332 .... 1965 .... **£8** ....
You Never Had It So Good .... 7" .... Decca .... F11433 .... 1962 .... **£4** ....
Your Ma Said You Cried.... .... 7" .... Decca .... F11416 .... 1961 .... **£4** .... chart single

SHELL
Goodbye Little Girl .... 7" .... Columbia .... DB8082 .... 1966 .... **£8** ....

SHELLEY
I Will Be Wishing .... 7" .... Pye .... 7N15711 .... 1964 .... **£8** ....

SHELLS
Baby Oh Baby .... 7" .... London .... HLU9288 .... 1961 .... **£10** ....
It's A Happy Holiday .... 7" .... London .... HLU9644 .... 1962 .... **£5** ....

SHELTON, ROSCOE
Question .... 7" .... Sue .... WI354 .... 1965 .... **£8** ....
Roscoe Shelton .... LP .... Excello .... 8002 .... 1961 .... **£35** .... US

SHENLEY & ANNETTE
Million Dollar Baby .... 7" .... Blue Beat .... BB72 .... 1961 .... **£10** ....

SHENLEY & HYACINTH
World Is On A Wheel .... 7" .... Rio .... R80 .... 196- .... **£8** ....

SHEP & THE LIMELITES
Daddy's Home .... 7" .... Pye .... 7N25090 .... 1961 .... **£20** ....
Our Anniversary .... LP .... Hull .... 1001 .... 1962 .... **£180** .... US
Our Anniversary .... LP .... Roulette .... R25350 .... 1967 .... **£20** .... US
Ready For Your Love .... 7" .... Pye .... 7N25112 .... 1961 .... **£15** ....

SHEPARD, JEAN
Lonesome Love .... LP .... Capitol .... T1126 .... 1959 .... **£12** .... US
Songs Of A Love Affair .... LP .... Capitol .... T728 .... 1956 .... **£20** .... US
This Is Jean Shepard .... LP .... Capitol .... T1253 .... 1959 .... **£12** .... US

SHEPHERD BOYS
Summer Sweetheart .... 7" .... Columbia .... DB3816 .... 1956 .... **£4** ....
Teenage Love .... 7" .... Columbia .... SCM5282 .... 1956 .... **£4** ....

SHEPHERD SISTERS
Alone .... 7" .... HMV .... POP411 .... 1957 .... **£4** .... chart single

SHEPPARDS
Sheppards .... LP .... Constellation ... CS4 .... 1964 .... **£20** .... US

SHEPPERTON FLAMES
Take Me For What I Am .... 7" .... Deram .... DM257 .... 1969 .... **£10** ....

SHERIDAN, DANI
Guess I'm Dumb .... 7" .... Planet .... PLF106 .... 1966 .... **£8** ....

SHERIDAN, MIKE & THE NIGHTRIDERS
Here I Stand .... 7" .... Columbia .... DB7462 .... 1965 .... **£12** ....
No Other Guy .... 7" .... Columbia .... DB7141 .... 1963 .... **£10** ....
Please Mister Postman .... 7" .... Columbia .... DB7183 .... 1963 .... **£10** ....
What A Sweet Thing That Was .... 7" .... Columbia .... DB7302 .... 1964 .... **£12** ....

SHERIDAN, MIKE LOT

Don't Turn Your Back On Me	7"	Columbia	DB7798	1966	**£15**	
Take My Hand	7"	Columbia	DB7677	1965	**£15**	

SHERIDAN, TONY

Skinnie Minnie	7"	Polydor	NH52927	1964	**£12**	
Will You Still Love Me Tomorrow	7"	Polydor	NH52315	1964	**£12**	

SHERIDAN-PRICE

Sometimes I Wonder	7"	Gemini	GMS009	1979	**£8**	
This Is To Certify That	LP	Gemini	GME1002	1970	**£20**	

SHERMAN, ALLAN

Hello Muddah Hello Fadduh	7"	W. Bros	WB106	1963	**£4**	chart single

SHERMAN, FLAMMA

Move Me	7"	SNB	554142	1969	**£12**	

SHERRILL, BILLY

Like Making Love	7"	Mercury	AMT1131	1961	**£4**	

SHERRYS

At The Hop With The Sherrys	LP	Guyden	GLP503	1962	**£50**	US
Do The Popeye	7" EP	London	RE1363	1963	**£8**	
Pop Pop Popeye	7"	London	HLW9625	1962	**£4**	
Slop Time	7"	London	HL9686	1963	**£4**	

SHERWOOD, TONY

Piano Boogie Twist	7"	Zodiac	ZR010	196-	**£4**	

SHEVELLS

Big City Lights	7"	Polydor	56239	1968	**£5**	
Walking On The Edge	7"	United Artists	UP1076	1965	**£6**	
Watermelon Man	7"	United Artists	UP1081	1965	**£6**	

SHIELD, TREVOR

Moon is Playing A Trick	7"	Trojan	TR664	1969	**£6**	

SHIELDS

You Cheated	7"	London	HLD8706	1958	**£10**	

SHIELDS, KEITH

Hey Gyp	7"	Decca	F12572	1967	**£15**	
So Hard Living Without You	7"	Decca	F12666	1967	**£12**	
Wonder Of You	7"	Decca	F12609	1967	**£10**	

SHIFRIN, SUSAN

25 Miles	7"	Decca	F13145	1971	**£4**	

SHILOH

Shiloh	LP	Amos	AAS7015	1970	**£10**	US

SHINDIGS

Little While Back	7"	Parlophone	R5377	1965	**£8**	
One Little Letter	7"	Parlophone	R5316	1965	**£8**	
Who Do You Think You Are	7"	Fontana	TF790	1967	**£4**	

SHINES, JOHNNY

Country Blues	LP	XTRA	XTRA1142	1974	**£10**	
Last Night's Dream	LP	Blue Horizon	763212	1969	**£35**	

SHINN, DON

Departures	LP	Columbia	SCX6355	1969	**£20**	
Temples With Prophets	LP	Columbia	SCX6319	1969	**£25**	

SHIP

Ship	LP	Elektra	K42122	1972	**£10**	

SHIRALEE

I'll Stay By Your Side	7"	Fontana	TF855	1967	**£6**	

SHIRELLES

...Sing To Trumpet & Strings	LP	Top Rank	35115	1961	**£15**	

Title	Format	Label	Number	Year	Price	Notes
Are You Still My Baby	7"	Pye	7N25288	1965	**£4**	
Baby It's You	LP	Stateside	SL10006	1962	**£20**	
Baby It's You	7"	Top Rank	JAR601	1962	**£4**	
Big John	7"	Top Rank	JAR590	1961	**£4**	
Dedicated To The One I Love	7"	Top Rank	JAR549	1961	**£4**	
Don't Say Goodnight	7"	Stateside	SS213	1963	**£4**	
Everybody Loves A Lover	7"	Stateside	SS152	1963	**£4**	
Foolish Little Girl	LP	Scepter	S511	1963	**£15**	US
Foolish Little Girl	7"	Stateside	SS181	1963	**£4**	chart single
Greatest Hits	LP	Stateside	SL10041	1963	**£15**	
Greatest Hits Vol.2	LP	Scepter	S560	1967	**£10**	US
Here And Now	LP	Pricewise	P4002	197-	**£12**	US
I Met Him On A Sunday	7"	Brunswick	05746	1958	**£10**	
It's A Mad, Mad, Mad, Mad World	7"	Pye	7N25229	1963	**£4**	
It's A Mad, Mad, Mad, Mad World	LP	Scepter	S514	1963	**£12**	US
It's Love That Really Counts	7"	Stateside	SS129	1962	**£4**	
Mama Said	7"	Top Rank	JAR567	1961	**£5**	
Sha La La	7"	Pye	7N25240	1964	**£4**	
Shades of Blue	7"	Pye	7N25386	1966	**£4**	
Shirelles Sing The Golden Oldies	LP	Scepter	S516	1964	**£12**	US
Shirelles Sound	7" EP	Top Rank	JKP3012	1961	**£10**	
Soldier Boy	7"	HMV	POP1019	1962	**£4**	chart single
Spontaneous Combustion	LP	Scepter	S562	1967	**£10**	US
Swing The Most	LP	Pricewise	P4001	197-	**£12**	US
There's Gonna Be A Storm	7"	Mercury	MF1093	1969	**£8**	
Tonight You're Gonna Fall In Love	7"	Pye	7N25233	1964	**£4**	
Tonight's The Night	7"	London	HL9233	1960	**£5**	
Tonight's The Night	LP	Scepter	S501	1961	**£25**	US
Too Much Of A Good Thing	7"	Pye	7N25425	1967	**£4**	
Welcome Home Baby	7"	Stateside	SS119	1962	**£4**	
What A Difference A Day Made	7"	Top Rank	JAR578	1961	**£5**	
What Does A Girl Do	7"	Stateside	SS232	1963	**£4**	
Will You Still Love Me Tomorrow	7"	Top Rank	JAR540	1960	**£4**	chart single

SHIRELLES & KING CURTIS

Title	Format	Label	Number	Year	Price	Notes
Twist Party	LP	Scepter	S505	1962	**£20**	US

SHIRLEY & LEE

Title	Format	Label	Number	Year	Price	Notes
Come On And Have Your Fun	7"	Vogue	V9129	1959	**£15**	
Everybody's Rocking	7"	Vogue	V9118	1958	**£15**	
I Feel Good	7"	Vogue	V9063	1957	**£15**	
I Want To Dance	7"	Vogue	V9088	1957	**£15**	
I'll Do It	7"	Vogue	V9137	1959	**£15**	
I'll Thrill You	7"	Vogue	V9103	1958	**£15**	
I've Been Loved Before	7"	London	HLI9186	1960	**£10**	
Legendary Masters	LP	United Artists	LA026G2	1974	**£12**	US
Let The Good Times Roll	LP	Aladdin	807	1956	**£180**	US
Let The Good Times Roll	LP	Imperial	A9179	1962	**£40**	US
Let The Good Times Roll	7"	Island	WI257	1965	**£8**	
Let The Good Times Roll	7"	London	HLI9209	1960	**£10**	
Let The Good Times Roll	LP	Score	SLP4023	1957	**£50**	US
Let The Good Times Roll	7"	Vogue	V9059	1956	**£15**	
Let The Good Times Roll	LP	Warwick	2028	1961	**£40**	US
Little Word	7"	Vogue	V9135	1959	**£15**	
Rock 'N' Roll	7" EP	Vogue	VE170101	1957	**£50**	
Rock All Nite	7"	Vogue	V9072	1957	**£20**	
Rocking With The Clock	7"	Vogue	V9084	1957	**£20**	
Shirley And Lee	7" EP	Vogue	VE170145	196-	**£50**	
That's What I Wanna Do	7"	Vogue	V9067	1957	**£15**	
True Love	7"	Vogue	V9156	1959	**£15**	
You'd Be Thinking Of Me	7"	Vogue	V9094	1957	**£15**	

SHIRLEY & THE RUDE BOYS

Title	Format	Label	Number	Year	Price	Notes
Gently Set Me Free	7"	Blue Beat	BB375	1965	**£10**	

SHIRLEY & THE SHIRELLES

Title	Format	Label	Number	Year	Price	Notes
Look What You've Done	7"	Bell	BLL1049	1969	**£4**	

SHIRLEY, ROY

Title	Format	Label	Number	Year	Price	Notes
Dance Arena	7"	Giant	GN32	1967	**£10**	
Dance The Reggae	7"	Doctor Bird	DB1168	196-	**£10**	

Title	Format	Label	Number	Year	Price	Notes
Get On The Ball	7"	Caltone	TONE101	196-	**£10**	
Good Is Better Than Bad	7"	Island	WI3118	1967	**£10**	
Hold Them	7"	Doctor Bird	DB1068	1966	**£10**	
Hush A Bye	7"	Doctor Bird	DB1165	196-	**£10**	
I'm The Winner	7"	Doctor Bird	DB1079	1967	**£10**	
If I Did Know	7"	Island	WI3125	1967	**£10**	
Million Dollar Baby	7"	Island	WI3110	1967	**£10**	
Move All Day	7"	Island	WI3108	1967	**£10**	
Musical Field	7"	Doctor Bird	DB1093	1967	**£10**	
Musical War	7"	Island	WI3071	1967	**£10**	
Paradise	7"	Ska Beat	JB253	1966	**£10**	
Prophet	7"	Doctor Bird	DB1088	1967	**£10**	
Thank You	7"	Doctor Bird	DB1108	1967	**£10**	
Thank You	7"	Island	WI3098	1967	**£10**	
Warming Up The Scene	7"	Giant	GN33	1967	**£10**	
World Needs Love	7"	Amalgamated	AMG815	196-	**£10**	

SHIRLEY, SUSAN

Title	Format	Label	Number	Year	Price	Notes
Imagine	7"	Columbia	DB8937	1972	**£4**	
Jealous Guy	7"	Columbia	DB8835	1971	**£4**	
Really Into Something Good	7"	Philips	6006037	1970	**£12**	

SHIRTS

Title	Format	Label	Number	Year	Price	Notes
Shirts	LP	Harvest	SHSP4089	1978	**£10**	blue vinyl

SHIVA'S HEADBAND

Title	Format	Label	Number	Year	Price	Notes
Coming To A Head	LP	Armadillo	None	1969	**£30**	US
Psychedelic Yesterday	LP	Ape	1001	1981	**£15**	US
Take Me To The Mountains	LP	Capitol	ST538	1970	**£20**	US

SHIVEL, BUNNY

Title	Format	Label	Number	Year	Price	Notes
You'll Never Find Another Love Like Mine	7"	Capitol	CL15487	1967	**£5**	

SHOCK ABSORBERS

Title	Format	Label	Number	Year	Price	Notes
Guitar Party	LP	Major Minor		1969	**£10**	

SHOCK HEADED PETERS

Title	Format	Label	Number	Year	Price	Notes
I Bloodbrother Be	7"	el	1	1984	**£8**	
I Bloodbrother Be	12"	el	ONE T	1984	**£10**	
Kissing Of Gods	12"	el Benelux	ELT3	1985	**£6**	
Life Extinguisher	12"	Beach Culture	3BC	1986	**£6**	

SHOCKING BLUE

With a lead singer who sounded not unlike Grace Slick, Shocking Blue would have loved to have been taken seriously as the Dutch Jefferson Airplane. Unfortunately, their material was cast a little too firmly in the light-weight pop mould, but this stood the group in good stead in the case of their hit single "Venus", whose absurdly catchy melody and rhythm have made the song into a perennial favourite.

Title	Format	Label	Number	Year	Price	Notes
Inkpot	7"	Polydor	2001299	1972	**£4**	chart single
Mighty Joe	7"	P. Farthing	PEN713	1970	**£4**	
Never Marry A Railroad Man	7"	P. Farthing	PEN721	1970	**£4**	
Out Of Sight Out Of Mind	7"	Polydor	2001266	1972	**£4**	
Sally Was A Good Old Girl	7"	P. Farthing	PEN744	1970	**£4**	
Scorpio's Dance	LP	P. Farthing	PELS510	1970	**£12**	
Shocking Blue	LP	P. Farthing	PELS500	1969	**£12**	
Shocking You	7"	P. Farthing	PEN758	1971	**£4**	
Venus	7"	P. Farthing	PEN702	1969	**£4**	chart single

SHOES

Title	Format	Label	Number	Year	Price	Notes
Black Vinyl Shoes	LP	Black Vinyl	S51477	1978	**£30**	US
Black Vinyl Shoes	LP	Sire	SRK6075	1979	**£15**	
I Don't Miss You	7"	Elektra	46598	197-	**£5**	
Okay	7"	Bomp	BMP116	1978	**£8**	
Present Tense	LP	Elektra	K52187	1979	**£10**	
Tomorrow Nite	7"	Elektra	46571	197-	**£5**	
Tongue Twister	LP	Elektra	K52261	1980	**£10**	
Too Late	7"	Elektra	46557	197-	**£5**	
Un Dans Versailles	LP	private		1974	**£100**	US

SHOES (2)

Title	Format	Label	Number	Year	Price	Notes
Farewell In The Rain	7"	Polydor	56739	1968	**£4**	

SHONDELL, TROY

Title	Format	Label	Number	Year	Price	Notes
I Got A Woman	7"	London	HL9668	1963	**£4**	
Many Sides Of...	LP	London	HAY8128	1964	**£12**	
This Time	7"	London	HLG9432	1961	**£4**	chart single

SHONDELLS

Title	Format	Label	Number	Year	Price	Notes
At The Saturday Hop	LP	La Louisianne	109	1964	**£40**	US

SHOOT

Title	Format	Label	Number	Year	Price	Notes
On The Frontier	LP	Capitol	SMAS11229	1972	**£15**	
On The Frontier	7"	EMI	EMI2026	1973	**£4**	

SHOP ASSISTANTS

Title	Format	Label	Number	Year	Price	Notes
All Day Long	7"	Subway	SUBWAY1	1985	**£5**	

SHOP ASSISTANTS & BUBA

Title	Format	Label	Number	Year	Price	Notes
Something To Do	7"	Villa 21	002	1985	**£30**	

SHOPS AROUND

Title	Format	Label	Number	Year	Price	Notes
What Does She Do	7"	Piccadilly	7N35345	1966	**£8**	

SHORT CROSS

Title	Format	Label	Number	Year	Price	Notes
Arising	LP	Breeder			**£150**	

SHORT, BRIAN

Title	Format	Label	Number	Year	Price	Notes
Anything For A Laugh	LP	Transatlantic	TRA245	1971	**£10**	

SHORTKUTS

Title	Format	Label	Number	Year	Price	Notes
Your Eyes May Shine	7"	United Artists	UP2233	1968	**£6**	

SHORTY & THEM

Title	Format	Label	Number	Year	Price	Notes
Pills	7"	Fontana	TF460	1964	**£15**	

SHOTGUN EXPRESS

Title	Format	Label	Number	Year	Price	Notes
Funny 'Cos Neither Could I	7"	Columbia	DB8178	1967	**£20**	
I Could Feel The Whole World	7"	Columbia	DB8025	1966	**£20**	

SHOTS

Title	Format	Label	Number	Year	Price	Notes
Keep A Hold Of What You've Got	7"	Columbia	DB7713	1965	**£20**	

SHOUTS

Title	Format	Label	Number	Year	Price	Notes
She Was My Baby	7"	React	EA001		**£8**	

SHOW OF HANDS

Title	Format	Label	Number	Year	Price	Notes
Formerly Anthrax	LP	Elektra	EKS74084	1970	**£10**	

SHOWMEN

Title	Format	Label	Number	Year	Price	Notes
Action	7"	Pama	PM767	196-	**£4**	
It Will Stand	7"	London	HLP9481	1962	**£10**	
Wrong Girl	7"	London	HLP9571	1962	**£5**	

SHOWSTOPPERS

Title	Format	Label	Number	Year	Price	Notes
Ain't Nothing But A House Party	7"	Beacon	3100	1968	**£5**	chart single

SHOX

Title	Format	Label	Number	Year	Price	Notes
No Turning Back	7"	Axis	AXIS4	1980	**£10**	

SHRIEVE, MICHAEL

Title	Format	Label	Number	Year	Price	Notes
Transfer Station Blue	LP	Fortuna		1984	**£30**	US

SHUMAN, MORT

Title	Format	Label	Number	Year	Price	Notes
Cry A Little	7"	Fontana	H685	1966	**£5**	
I'm A Man	7"	Decca	F11184	1959	**£10**	
Monday Monday	7"	Immediate	IM048	1967	**£8**	

SHUSHA

Title	Format	Label	Number	Year	Price	Notes
Before The Deluge	LP	United Artists	UAS29879	1975	**£10**	
From East To West	LP	Tangent	TGS138	1978	**£12**	
Persian Love Songs And Mystic Chants	LP	Tangent	TGS108	1970	**£12**	
Shusha	LP	United Artists	UAS29575	1974	**£10**	
Song Of Long Time Lovers	LP	Tangent	TGS114	1972	**£12**	
This Is The Day	LP	United Artists	UAS29684	1974	**£10**	

SHUTDOWNS

Title	Format	Label	Cat. No.	Year	Price	Notes
Four In The Floor	7"	Colpix	PX11016	1963	**£6**	

SHY LIMBS

Title	Format	Label	Cat. No.	Year	Price	Notes
Lady In Black	7"	CBS	4624	1969	**£15**	
Reputation	7"	CBS	4190	1969	**£12**	

SHY ONES

Title	Format	Label	Cat. No.	Year	Price	Notes
La Route	7"	Oriole	CB1924	1964	**£10**	
Nightcap	7"	Oriole	CB1848	1963	**£12**	

SIBLEY, DUDLEY

Title	Format	Label	Cat. No.	Year	Price	Notes
Gun Man	7"	Island	WI3034	1967	**£10**	

SIDRAN, BEN

Title	Format	Label	Cat. No.	Year	Price	Notes
Don't Let Go	LP	Blue Thumb	BTS6012	1972	**£10**	US
Feel Your Groove	LP	Capitol	ST825	1971	**£10**	US
I Lead A Life	LP	Blue Thumb	BTS40	1972	**£10**	US
Puttin' In Time On Planet Earth	LP	Blue Thumb	BTS55	1973	**£10**	US

SIEBEL, PAUL

Title	Format	Label	Cat. No.	Year	Price	Notes
Jack-knife Gypsy	LP	Elektra	EKS74081	1971	**£10**	
Woodsmoke & Oranges	LP	Elektra	EKS74064	1970	**£10**	

SIEGEL-SCHWALL BAND

The Siegel-Schwall Band so accurately epitomise the worst aspects of the late sixties fascination with the blues on the part of white rock performers, that it is amazing how the group managed to make such a large number of albums. Each is characterised by an entirely routine approach to the blues in which the form is reproduced without any genuine understanding or feeling. Composer William Russo was able to use this to interesting effect, however, when he incorporated the group within his "Three Pieces For Blues Band And Symphony Orchestra". Here it is vital that the blues group play cliches, so that they can be subverted by the oblique lines superimposed by the orchestra. It is an unusual approach to the combination of rock and classical styles, but it works superbly well.

Title	Format	Label	Cat. No.	Year	Price	Notes
953 West	LP	Teldec	10121	1973	**£10**	German
Best Of	LP	Vanguard	VSD79336	1974	**£10**	US
Live Last Summer	LP	Teldec	624215	1974	**£10**	German
Live Last Summer	LP	Wooden N.	WNS1288	1974	**£10**	US
RIP Siegel-Schwall	LP	Teldec	624217	1974	**£10**	German
RIP Siegel-Schwall	LP	Wooden N.	WNS1554	1974	**£10**	US
Say Siegel-Schwall	LP	Vanguard	VRS9249	1967	**£12**	US
Shake	LP	Vanguard	SVRL19044	1968	**£12**	
Siegel-Schwall '70	LP	Vanguard	VSD6562	1970	**£12**	US
Siegel-Schwall Band	LP	RCA	SF8246	1971	**£10**	
Siegel-Schwall Band	LP	Vanguard	VRS9235	1966	**£12**	US
Sleepy Hollow	LP	RCA	LSP10394	1972	**£10**	

SIFFRE, LABI

Title	Format	Label	Cat. No.	Year	Price	Notes
It Must Be Love	7"	Pye	7N25572	1971	**£4**	chart single

SIGHT & SOUND

Title	Format	Label	Cat. No.	Year	Price	Notes
Alley Alley	7"	Fontana	TF982	1968	**£8**	
Our Love Is In The Pocket	7"	Fontana	TF927	1968	**£10**	

SIGLER, BUNNY

Title	Format	Label	Cat. No.	Year	Price	Notes
Let The Good Times Roll	7"	Cameo Park	P153	1962	**£10**	
Let The Good Times Roll	7"	London	HLU10518	1976	**£4**	
Let The Good Times Roll	LP	Parkway	P50000	1967	**£10**	US

SIGNS

Title	Format	Label	Cat. No.	Year	Price	Notes
Ain't You Got A Heart	7"	Decca	F12522	1966	**£10**	

SILENT PARTNER

Title	Format	Label	Cat. No.	Year	Price	Notes
Hung By A Thread	LP	Lucky Boy			**£150**	US

SILHOUETTES

Title	Format	Label	Cat. No.	Year	Price	Notes
Get A Job	LP	Goodway	GLP100	195-	**£75**	US
Get A Job	7"	Parlophone	R4407	1958	**£15**	
Heading For The Poorhouse	7"	Parlophone	R4425	1958	**£15**	

SILK

Title	Format	Label	Cat. No.	Year	Price	Notes
Smooth As Raw Silk	LP	ABC		1969	**£20**	US

SILKIE

Blood Red River	7"	Fontana	TF556	1965	**£4**	
Born To Be With You	7"	Fontana	TF709	1966	**£4**	
Keys To My Soul	7"	Fontana	TF659	1966	**£4**	
Sing Dylan	LP	Fontana		1965	**£12**	
You've Got To Hide Your Love Away	LP	Fontana	MGF27548	1965	**£20**	US
You've Got To Hide Your Love Away	7"	Fontana	TF603	1965	**£5**	chart single

SILL, JUDEE

Heart Food	LP	Asylum	SYL9006	1973	**£10**	
Jesus Was A Cross Maker	7"	Asylum	AYM502	1972	**£4**	
Judee Sill	LP	Asylum	SYLA8751	1971	**£12**	

SILLY SURFERS

Sounds Of The Silly Surfers	LP	Mercury	MG20977	1965	**£12**	US

SILVER & NOREEN

Love Me Forever	7"	Columbia	DB117	1970	**£8**	

SILVER APPLES

Contracts	LP	Kapp	3584	1969	**£25**	US
Silver Apples	LP	Kapp	3562	1968	**£15**	US

SILVER BULLITT

Willpower Weak, Temptation Strong	7"	Philips	6073808	197-	**£5**	

SILVER BYKE

Who Needs Tomorrow	7"	London	HLZ10200	1968	**£4**	

SILVER SISTERS

Waiting For The Stars To Shine	7"	Parlophone	R4669	1960	**£4**	

SILVER STARS STEEL BAND

Silver Stars Steel Band	LP	Island	ILP904	1963	**£30**	

SILVER, LORRAINE

Lost Summer Love	7"	Pye	7N15922	1965	**£6**	

SILVER, EDDIE

Rockin' Robin	7"	Parlophone	R4483	1958	**£4**	
Seven Steps To Love	7"	Parlophone	R4439	1958	**£4**	

SILVER, LORRAINE

Happy Faces	7"	Pye	7N17055	1966	**£30**	

SILVERHEAD

Ace Supreme	7"	Purple	PUR104	1972	**£4**	
Rolling With My Baby	7"	Purple	PUR110	1972	**£4**	

SILVERS

What A Way To Start A Day	7"	Polydor	56094	1966	**£5**	

SILVERSPOON, DOOLEY

Game Players	7"	Seville	SEV1022	1976	**£4**	

SILVERSTARS

Old Man Say	7"	Trojan	TR646	1969	**£6**	

SILVERSTEIN, SHEL

Boy Named Sue	LP	RCA	LSP4192	1968	**£12**	US
Crouching On The Outside	LP	Janus	2JLS3052	1970	**£12**	US
Drain My Brain	LP	Cadet	LP4054	1966	**£12**	US
Freakin' At The Freakers Ball	LP	CBS	65452	1973	**£10**	
Hairy Jazz	LP	Elektra	EKL176	1959	**£15**	US
I'm So Good, I Don't Have To Brag	LP	Cadet	LP4052	1965	**£12**	US
Inside Folk Songs	LP	Atlantic	8072	1963	**£12**	US
Inside Shel Silverstein	LP	Atlantic	8257	1969	**£12**	US

SILVERTONES

Cool Down	7"	Treasure Isle	TI7020	196-	**£10**	
It's Real	7"	Doctor Bird	DB1041	1966	**£10**	
Midnight Hour	7"	Treasure Isle	TI7027	196-	**£10**	

That's When It Hurts ..... 7" ..... Technique ..... TE924 ..... 1973 ..... **£4** .....
True Confession ..... 7" ..... Doctor Bird ..... DB1028 ..... 1966 ..... **£10** .....

SIMMONS, BEVERLY

Mr.Pitiful ..... 7" ..... Pama ..... PM716 ..... 196- ..... **£8** .....

SIMMONS, CARL

King Of Rock'n'Roll ..... 7" ..... Atlantic ..... K10421 ..... 1974 ..... **£4** .....

SIMMONS, JEFF

Lucille Has Messed Up My Mind ..... LP ..... Reprise ..... RS6391 ..... 1969 ..... **£40** .....
Lucille Has Messed Up My Mind ..... LP ..... Straight ..... STS1057 ..... 1969 ..... **£40** .....
Naked Angels Soundtrack ..... LP ..... Straight ..... STS1056 ..... 1969 ..... **£30** ..... US

SIMMONS, JUMPIN' GENE

Haunted House ..... 7" ..... London ..... HLU9913 ..... 1964 ..... **£5** .....
Jump ..... 7" ..... London ..... HLU9933 ..... 1964 ..... **£5** .....
Jumpin' Gene Simmons ..... LP ..... Hi ..... HL12018 ..... 1964 ..... **£12** ..... US

SIMMONS, LITTLE MAC

Blues From Chicago ..... 7" EP ..... Outasite ..... OSEP1 ..... 1966 ..... **£25** .....

SIMON & GARFUNKEL

At The Zoo ..... 7" ..... CBS ..... 202608 ..... 1967 ..... **£4** .....
Bridge Over Troubled Waters ..... LP ..... CBS ..... Q63699 ..... 1973 ..... **£12** ..... quad
Bridge Over Troubled Waters ..... LP ..... Columbia ..... HC49914 ..... 1981 ..... **£15** ..... US audiophile
Bridge Over Troubled Waters ..... LP ..... Mobile Fid. ..... MFSL1173 ..... 1981 ..... **£15** ..... US audiophile
Dangling Conversation ..... 7" ..... CBS ..... 202285 ..... 1966 ..... **£4** .....
Fakin' It ..... 7" ..... CBS ..... 2911 ..... 1967 ..... **£4** .....
Feelin' Groovy ..... 7" EP ..... CBS ..... EP6360 ..... 1967 ..... **£4** .....
Greatest Hits ..... LP ..... Columbia ..... HC41350 ..... 1981 ..... **£15** ..... US audiophile
Hazy Shade Of Winter ..... 7" ..... CBS ..... 202378 ..... 1966 ..... **£4** .....
Hit Sounds Of... ..... LP ..... Pickwick ..... SPC3059 ..... 1966 ..... **£15** ..... US
Homeward Bound ..... 7" ..... CBS ..... 202045 ..... 1966 ..... **£4** ..... chart single
I Am A Rock ..... 7" ..... CBS ..... 202303 ..... 1966 ..... **£4** ..... chart single
I Am A Rock ..... 7" EP ..... CBS ..... EP6074 ..... 1966 ..... **£4** .....
Mrs.Robinson ..... 7" EP ..... CBS ..... EP6400 ..... 1968 ..... **£4** ..... chart single
Simon & Garfunkel ..... LP ..... Sears ..... SP435 ..... 1969 ..... **£15** ..... US
Simon And Garfunkel ..... LP ..... Allegro ..... ALL836 ..... 1967 ..... **£15** .....
Sound Of Silence ..... 7" ..... CBS ..... 201977 ..... 1965 ..... **£4** .....
Wednesday Morning 3 a.m. ..... 7" EP ..... CBS ..... EP6053 ..... 1965 ..... **£4** .....

SIMON SISTERS

The Simon Sisters made a number of records of mainly children's songs, before sister Lucy got married and decided to leave the music business. Younger sister Carly carried on by herself and eventaully became rather successful.

Cuddlebug ..... LP ..... Kapp ..... KL1397 ..... 1964 ..... **£12** ..... US
Cuddlebug ..... 7" ..... London ..... HLR9984 ..... 1965 ..... **£4** .....
Lobster Quadrille ..... LP ..... Columbia ..... CS24506 ..... 1969 ..... **£10** ..... US
Simon Sisters ..... LP ..... Kapp ..... KL1359 ..... 1964 ..... **£12** ..... US
Winkin' Blinkin' And Nod ..... 7" ..... London ..... HLR9893 ..... 1964 ..... **£4** .....

SIMON, JOE

Get Down Get Down ..... 7" ..... Polydor ..... 2066551 ..... 1975 ..... **£4** .....
My Special Prayer ..... 7" ..... Monument ..... MON1004 ..... 1967 ..... **£4** .....
Teenager's Prayer ..... 7" ..... London ..... HLU10057 ..... 1966 ..... **£4** .....
That's The Way I Want Our Love ..... 7" ..... Monument ..... MON1051 ..... 1970 ..... **£5** .....

SIMON, PAUL

Early Songs ..... LP ..... Crest ..... EBM7172 ..... 196- ..... **£30** ..... US promo
Greatest Hits, Etc. ..... LP ..... Columbia ..... HC45032 ..... 1981 ..... **£15** ..... US audiophile
I Am A Rock ..... 7" ..... CBS ..... 201797 ..... 1965 ..... **£6** .....
Kodakchrome ..... 7" ..... CBS ..... 1545 ..... 1973 ..... **£10** .....
Paul Simon ..... LP ..... CBS ..... Q69007 ..... 1972 ..... **£12** ..... quad
Paul Simon Plus (with Neil Sedaka & Four Seasons) ..... LP ..... MCP ..... 8027 ..... 1966 ..... **£20** ..... US
Paul Simon Songbook ..... LP ..... CBS ..... 62579 ..... 1965 ..... **£10** .....
Something So Right ..... 7" ..... CBS ..... 2822DJ ..... 1976 ..... **£6** ..... promo
Sound Of Silence (2 versions) ..... 7" ..... CBS ..... 2349DJ ..... 1973 ..... **£6** ..... promo
Still Crazy After All These Years ..... LP ..... CBS ..... Q86001 ..... 1975 ..... **£12** ..... quad
Still Crazy After All These Years ..... LP ..... Columbia ..... HC43540 ..... 1981 ..... **£15** ..... US audiophile
There Goes Rhymin' Simon ..... LP ..... CBS ..... Q69035 ..... 1973 ..... **£12** ..... quad

SIMON, PLUG & GRIMES

Title	Format	Label	Cat. No.	Year	Price	Notes
Is This A Dream?	7"	Deram	DM296	1970	**£8**	

SIMON, TONY

Title	Format	Label	Cat. No.	Year	Price	Notes
Gimme A Little Sign	7"	Track	604012	1967	**£6**	

SIMONE, NINA

Title	Format	Label	Cat. No.	Year	Price	Notes
Ain't Got No - I Got Life	7"	RCA	RCA1743	1968	**£4**	chart single
At The Town Hall	LP	Pye	NPL28014	1962	**£10**	
Do I Move You?	7"	RCA	RCA1583	1967	**£4**	
Do What You Gotta Do	7"	RCA	RCA1961	1970	**£4**	
Don't Let Me Be Misunderstood	7"	Philips	BF1388	1965	**£5**	
Don't Let Me Be Misunderstood	7" EP	Philips	BE12585	1965	**£5**	
Either Way I Lose	7"	Philips	BF1465	1966	**£4**	
Exactly Like You	7"	Colpix	PX799	1964	**£5**	
Fine And Mellow	7" EP	Colpix	PXE303	1964	**£5**	
Gimme Some	7"	Philips	BF1785	1969	**£4**	
I Love To Love	7" EP	Colpix	PXE307	1966	**£5**	
I Loves You Porgy	7"	Parlophone	R4583	1959	**£4**	
I Put A Spell On You	7"	Philips	BF1415	1965	**£4**	chart single
I Put A Spell On You	LP	Philips	BL7671	1965	**£10**	chart LP
In The Morning	7"	RCA	RCA1879	1969	**£4**	
Intimate Nina Simone	7" EP	Parlophone	GEP8864	1962	**£5**	
Just Say I Love Him	7" EP	Colpix	PXE306	1966	**£5**	
Little Girl Blue	LP	Bethlehem	BCP6028	1959	**£10**	US
My Baby Just Cares For Me	7" EP	Parlophone	GEP8844	1961	**£6**	
Nuff Said	LP	RCA	SF7979	1969	**£10**	chart LP
Other Woman	7"	Pye	7N25466	1968	**£4**	
Revolutin'	7"	RCA	RCA1805	1969	**£4**	
Save Me	7"	RCA	RCA1903	1969	**£4**	
Solitaire	7"	Pye	7N25029	1959	**£4**	
Strange Fruit	7" EP	Philips	BE12589	1965	**£5**	
To Love Somebody	7"	RCA	RCA1779	1968	**£4**	chart single
Why Must Your Love Well Be So Dry	7"	RCA	RCA1968	1970	**£4**	
Why?	7"	RCA	RCA1697	1970	**£4**	
You Can Have Him	7"	Colpix	PX200	1963	**£5**	

SIMONE, SUGAR

Title	Format	Label	Cat. No.	Year	Price	Notes
Black Is Gold	7"	Doctor Bird	DB1192	196-	**£10**	
Come And Try	7"	Doctor Bird	DB1201	196-	**£10**	
Squeeze Is On	7"	Doctor Bird	DB1193	196-	**£10**	
Suddenly	7"	Sue	WI4029	1967	**£10**	

SIMPLE MINDS

Title	Format	Label	Cat. No.	Year	Price	Notes
Alive And Kicking	7"	Virgin	VS817	1985	**£6**	double
Alive And Kicking	12"	Virgin	VS81713	1985	**£6**	gold sleeve
American	7"	Virgin	VS410	1981	**£4**	
American	12"	Virgin	VS41012	1981	**£8**	
Amsterdam EP	CD-s	Virgin	SMXX6	1989	**£6**	4 tracks
Amsterdam EP	12"	Virgin	SMXTR6	1989	**£6**	gatefold sleeve, poster
Ballad Of The Streets	12"	Virgin	SMXB3	1989	**£8**	boxed with 4 photos
Celebrate	7"	Arista	ARIST394	1981	**£10**	
Celebrate	12"	Arista	ARIST12394	1981	**£15**	
Changeling	7"	Zoom	ARIST325	1980	**£10**	
Chelsea Girl	7"	Zoom	ZUM11	1979	**£8**	
Chelsea Girl	7"	Zoom	ZUM11DJ	1979	**£12**	promo
Don't You Forget About Me	7"	Virgin	VSS749	1985	**£20**	shaped pic disc
Ghostdancing	CD-s	Virgin	MIKE90712	1986	**£10**	
I Travel	7"	Arista	ARIST372	1980	**£5**	
I Travel	7"	Arista	ARIST372	1980	**£15**	with blue flexi 7"
I Travel	7"	Arista	ARIST448	1982	**£5**	
I Travel	12"	Arista	ARIST12372	1980	**£12**	
I Travel	12"	Arista	ARIST12448	1982	**£12**	
Kick It In	CD-s	Virgin	SMXCD5	1989	**£6**	
Kick It In	12"	Virgin	SMXTG5	1989	**£8**	gatefold sleeve, poster
Life In A Day	LP	Zoom	ZULP1	1979	**£12**	chart LP
Life In A Day	7"	Zoom	ZUM10	1979	**£8**	chart single
Live In The City Of Light	LP	Virgin	SMDL1	1987	**£15**	double, booklet, gold embossed sleeve
Love Song	7"	Virgin	VS434	1981	**£5**	chart single
Love Song	12"	Virgin	VS43412	1981	**£8**	

Title	Format	Label	Number	Year	Price	Notes
Once Upon A Time	LP	Virgin	V2364	1985	**£15**	pic disc
Promised You A Miracle (live)	10"	Virgin	SM210	1987	**£6**	with poster
Promised You A Miracle	cass-s	Virgin	SMC212	1987	**£6**	
Promised You A Miracle	12"	Virgin	SM212	1987	**£6**	
Promised You A Miracle	12"	Virgin	VS48812	1982	**£6**	
Real To Real Cacophony	LP	Arista	SPART1109	1980	**£12**	
Sanctify Yourself	7"	Virgin	SMP1	1986	**£8**	double
Someone Somewhere In Summertime	7"	Virgin	VS538	1982	**£10**	poster sleeve
Someone Somewhere In Summertime	7"	Virgin	VSY538	1982	**£10**	pic disc
Sons And Fascination/Sister Feelings Call	LP	Virgin	V2207	1981	**£20**	double
Sparkle In The Rain	LP	Virgin	V2300	1984	**£20**	white vinyl
Speed Your Love To Me	7"	Virgin	VSY649	1984	**£10**	pic disc
Street Fighting Years	CD	Virgin	SMBXD1	1989	**£30**	boxed with book & interview cassettes
Street Fighting Years	cass	Virgin	SMBXC1	1989	**£25**	boxed with book & interview cassettes
Sweat In Bullet	7"	Virgin	VS451	1981	**£4**	chart single
Sweat In Bullet	7"	Virgin	VS451	1981	**£8**	double
Sweat In Bullet	12"	Virgin	VS45112	1981	**£6**	
This Is Your Land	12"	Virgin	SMXTG4	1989	**£6**	gatefold sleeve
Up On The Catwalk	7"	Virgin	VSY661	1984	**£10**	pic disc

SIMPLY RED

Title	Format	Label	Number	Year	Price	Notes
Every Time We Say Goodbye	CD-s	Elektra	YZ161CD	1987	**£6**	
Every Time We Say Goodbye	12"	Elektra	YZ161TX	1987	**£6**	with sheet music & 4 postcards
Every Time We Say Goodbye	10"	Elektra	YZ161TE	1987	**£6**	
Holding Back The Years	7"	Elektra	EKR29F	1985	**£4**	poster sleeve
Holding Back The Years	7"	Elektra	EKR29P	1985	**£5**	pic disc
If You Don't Know Me By Now	10"	Elektra	YZ377TE	1989	**£6**	
Infidelity	12"	Elektra	YZ114TP	1987	**£6**	pic disc
It's Only Love (Valentine Mix)	10"	Elektra	YZ349TE	1989	**£6**	
Money's Too Tight To Mention (remix)	12"	Elektra	EKR9TX	1985	**£6**	
Money's Too Tight To Mention	7"	Elektra	EKR9P	1985	**£5**	pic disc
New Flame	7"	Elektra	SAM520	1989	**£10**	promo sampler
Picture Book	LP	Elektra	EKT27P	1985	**£10**	pic disc
Right Thing	7"	Elektra	YZ103DP	1987	**£8**	double

SIMPSON, DANNY

Title	Format	Label	Number	Year	Price	Notes
Outa Sight	7"	Trojan	TR653	1969	**£6**	

SIMPSON, JEANETTE

Title	Format	Label	Number	Year	Price	Notes
My Baby Just Cares For Me	7"	Giant	GN29	1967	**£10**	
Rain	7"	Giant	GN16	1967	**£10**	
Through Loving You	7"	Giant	GN35	196-	**£10**	

SIMPSON, LEO

Title	Format	Label	Number	Year	Price	Notes
I Love Her So	7"	Blue Beat	BB351	1965	**£10**	
Waxy Doodle	7"	Pyramid	PYR7004	1973	**£5**	

SIMPSON, LIONEL

Title	Format	Label	Number	Year	Price	Notes
Eight People	7"	Ska Beat	JB221	1965	**£10**	
Give Over	7"	Ska Beat	JB233	1966	**£10**	
Love Is A Game	7"	Ska Beat	JB205	1965	**£10**	

SIMS, CHUCK

Title	Format	Label	Number	Year	Price	Notes
Little Pigeon	7"	London	HLR8577	1958	**£60**	

SIMS, ZOOT

Title	Format	Label	Number	Year	Price	Notes
Please Don't Do It	7"	Port-O-Jam	PJ4007	196-	**£10**	
Press Along	7"	Blue Beat	BB183	1963	**£10**	
Searching (with Lloyd Robinson)	7"	Blue Beat	BB143	1962	**£10**	

SINATRA, NANCY

Title	Format	Label	Number	Year	Price	Notes
Boots	LP	Reprise	RSLP6202	1966	**£12**	chart LP
Country My Way	LP	Reprise	R6251	1967	**£10**	US
Cuff Links And A Tie Clip	7"	Reprise	R20017	1961	**£4**	
Friday's Child	7"	Reprise	RS20491	1966	**£4**	
Greatest Hits	LP	Reprise	RS6409	1970	**£10**	chart LP
Highway Song	7"	Reprise	RS20869	1969	**£4**	chart single
How Does That Grab You Darlin'	7"	Reprise	R20461	1966	**£4**	chart single

Title	Format	Label	Cat. No.	Year	Price	Notes
How Does That Grab You?	LP	Reprise	R6207	1966	**£12**	chart LP
I Move Around	7" EP	Reprise	REP30072	1966	**£6**	
In Our Time	7"	Reprise	RS20514	1966	**£4**	
Movin' With Nancy	LP	Reprise	R6277	1968	**£10**	US
Nancy	LP	Reprise	RS6333	1969	**£10**	US
Nancy In London	LP	Reprise	R6221	1966	**£12**	US
Nashville Nancy	7" EP	Reprise	REP30086	1967	**£6**	
Put Your Head On My Shoulder	7"	Reprise	R20144	1963	**£4**	
Run For Your Life	7" EP	Reprise	REP30069	1966	**£6**	
So Long Babe	7"	Reprise	R20407	1965	**£4**	
Something Stupid	7" EP	Reprise	REP30082	1967	**£4**	
Sorry 'Bout That	7" EP	Reprise	REP30080	1967	**£6**	
Sugar	LP	Reprise	R6239	1966	**£10**	US
Sugar Town	7"	Reprise	RS20527	1967	**£4**	chart single
These Boots Are Made For Walking	7"	Reprise	R20432	1966	**£4**	chart single
To Know Him Is To Love Him	7"	Reprise	R20045	1962	**£4**	
True Love	7"	Reprise	R20335	1964	**£4**	
Woman	LP	RCA	SF8331	1972	**£10**	
You Only Live Twice	7"	Reprise	RS20595	1967	**£4**	chart single

SINATRA, NANCY & LEE HAZELWOOD

Title	Format	Label	Cat. No.	Year	Price	Notes
Jackson	7" EP	Reprise	REP30083	1967	**£5**	
Ladybird	7"	Reprise	RS20629	1967	**£4**	chart single
Nancy And Lee	LP	Reprise	RS6273	1968	**£10**	chart LP
Nancy And Lee Again	LP	RCA	LSP4645	1972	**£10**	US

SINCLAIR, JIMMY

Title	Format	Label	Cat. No.	Year	Price	Notes
Verona	7"	Blue Beat	BB47	1961	**£10**	

SINDELFINGEN

Title	Format	Label	Cat. No.	Year	Price	Notes
Sindelfingen	LP	Medway		1973	**£600**	

SINFIELD, PETE

Title	Format	Label	Cat. No.	Year	Price	Notes
Still	LP	Manticore	K43501	1973	**£10**	

SINGING DOGS

Title	Format	Label	Cat. No.	Year	Price	Notes
Medley	7"	Pye	7N15009	1955	**£4**	chart single
Singing Dogs	7" EP	Pye	NEP24029	1957	**£8**	

SINGING POSTMAN

Title	Format	Label	Cat. No.	Year	Price	Notes
First Delivery	7" EP	Parlophone	GEP8956	1966	**£5**	

SINK, EARL

Title	Format	Label	Cat. No.	Year	Price	Notes
Little Suzie Parker	7"	W. Bros	WB51	1961	**£4**	
Looking For Love	7"	Capitol	CL15310	1963	**£5**	
Supermarket	7"	W. Bros	WB38	1961	**£4**	

SINNERS

Title	Format	Label	Cat. No.	Year	Price	Notes
I Can't Stand It	7"	Columbia	DB7158	1963	**£8**	
It's So Exciting	7"	Columbia	DB7295	1964	**£10**	
Sinneresmes	LP	Jupiter		1974	**£100**	Canadian
Vox Populi	LP			197-	**£40**	Canadian

SIOUXSIE & THE BANSHEES

Title	Format	Label	Cat. No.	Year	Price	Notes
Arabian Knights	12"	Polydor	POSPX309	1981	**£8**	
Candyman	7"	Wonderland	SHEDP10	1986	**£8**	double, gatefold PS
Christine	7"	Polydor	2059249	1980	**£4**	chart single
Cities In Dust	7"	Wonderland	SHE9	1985	**£4**	poster sleeve
Dear Prudence	7"	Wonderland	SHE4	1983	**£5**	fold-out PS
Fireworks	7"	Polydor	POSPG450	1982	**£5**	gatefold PS
Fireworks	12"	Polydor	POSPX450	1982	**£6**	
Happy House	7"	Polydor	POSP117	1980	**£4**	chart single
Hong Kong Garden	7"	Polydor	2059052	1978	**£4**	chart single
Hong Kong Garden	7"	Polydor	2059052	1978	**£15**	gatefold sleeve
Hyaena	7"	Wonderland		1984	**£10**	promo sampler
Israel	7"	Polydor	POSP205	1980	**£4**	chart single
Israel	12"	Polydor	POSPX205	1980	**£15**	no PS
Melt	12"	Polydor	POSPX539	1982	**£6**	
Mittageisen	7"	Polydor	2059151	1979	**£6**	chart single
Once Upon A Time - The Singles	LP	Polydor	POLS1056	1981	**£10**	with colour print
Passenger	7"	Wonderland	SHEG12	1987	**£4**	poster sleeve
Peek A Boo	7"	Wonderland	SHEG14	1988	**£4**	numbered gatefold PS

Title	Format	Label	Cat. No.	Year	Price	Notes
Peepshow	12"	Wonderland	PEEP1	1988	**£10**	promo sampler
Playground Twist	7"	Polydor	POSP59	1979	**£4**	chart single
Running Town	7"	Fan Club		1983	**£40**	
Slowdive	12"	Polydor	POSPX510	1982	**£6**	
Songs From The Edge Of The World	7"	Wonderland	SHEP13	1987	**£5**	pic disc
Spellbound	12"	Polydor	POSPX273	1981	**£8**	
Staircase (Mystery)	7"	Polydor	POSP9	1979	**£6**	chart single
This Wheel's On Fire	7"	Wonderland	SHEG11	1987	**£8**	double, gatefold PS, numbered
Thorn	12"	Wonderland	SHEEP8	1984	**£6**	
Through The Looking Glass	LP	Wonderland	SHELP4	1987	**£15**	mispress, 1 side plays Jimi Hendrix
Through The Looking Glass	7"	Wonderland		1987	**£25**	3 x 7" in plastic wallet, promo
Voices	7"	Wonderland		1984	**£5**	promo

SIR DOUGLAS QUINTET

Title	Format	Label	Cat. No.	Year	Price	Notes
1+1+1=4	LP	Philips	PHS600344	1970	**£10**	US
Best Of...	LP	London	HAU8311	1965	**£12**	
Dynamite Woman	7"	Mercury	MF1129	1969	**£5**	
Groover's Paradise	LP	W. Bros	K56067	1974	**£10**	
Honkey Blues	LP	Smash	SRS67108	1968	**£12**	US
Mendocino	LP	Mercury	SMCL20160	1969	**£10**	
Mendocino	7"	Mercury	MF1079	1969	**£5**	
Rains Came	7"	London	HLU10019	1966	**£6**	
Return Of Doug Saldana	LP	Philips	PHS600353	1971	**£12**	US
Rough Edges	LP	Mercury	SRM1655	1972	**£10**	US
She's About A Mover	7"	London	HLU10248	1969	**£5**	
She's About A Mover	7"	London	HLU9964	1965	**£6**	chart single
Story Of John Hardy	7"	London	HLU10001	1965	**£6**	
Together After Five	LP	Mercury	SMCL20186	1970	**£10**	
Tracker	7"	London	HLU9982	1965	**£8**	

SIR HENRY

Title	Format	Label	Cat. No.	Year	Price	Notes
Pretty Style	7"	Columbia	DB8497	1968	**£12**	

SIR LORD BALTIMORE

Title	Format	Label	Cat. No.	Year	Price	Notes
Kingdom Come	LP	Mercury	SR61328	1970	**£12**	US
Sir Lord Baltimore	LP	Mercury	SRM1613	1971	**£12**	US

SIR LORD COMIC

Title	Format	Label	Cat. No.	Year	Price	Notes
Great Wuga Wuga	7"	Doctor Bird	DB1070	1967	**£10**	

SIR LORD COMIC & THE COWBOYS

Title	Format	Label	Cat. No.	Year	Price	Notes
Ska-ing West	7"	Doctor Bird	DB1019	1966	**£10**	

SIREN

Originally named Coyne-Clague after the lead singer and guitarist, the group had settled on the rather more wieldy Siren by the time of their first recording for John Peel's Dandelion label. Dave Clague has since disappeared from music, but Kevin Coyne has made Siren's bluesy style into the basis of a still continuing career.

Title	Format	Label	Cat. No.	Year	Price	Notes
Siren	LP	Dandelion	62755	1969	**£15**	
Strange Locomotion	LP	Dandelion	DAN8001	1971	**£15**	
Strange Locomotion	7"	Dandelion	DAN7002	1971	**£5**	

SISTERS LOVE

Title	Format	Label	Cat. No.	Year	Price	Notes
I'm Learning To Trust My Man	7"	Mowest	MW3009	1973	**£6**	
Mr.Fix-It Man	7"	T. Motown	TMG828	1972	**£10**	demo
Mr.Fix-It Man	7"	T. Motown	TMG828	1972	**£4**	

SISTERS OF MERCY

Title	Format	Label	Cat. No.	Year	Price	Notes
Alice	7"	Merciful Rel.	MR015	1982	**£15**	white background
Body And Soul	7"	Merciful Rel.	MR029	1984	**£5**	
Body And Soul	12"	Merciful Rel.	MR029T	1984	**£8**	
Body Electric	7"	CNT	002	1982	**£50**	
Damage Done	7"	Merciful Rel.	MR007	1980	**£60**	
Dominion	CD-s	Merciful Rel.	MR043CD	1988	**£6**	
Dominion	cass-s	Merciful Rel.	MR043C	1988	**£5**	
Dominion	12"	Merciful Rel.	MR043T	1988	**£8**	boxed with poster
First And Last And Always	LP	Merciful Rel.	MR337L	1985	**£15**	gatefold sleeve
Floodland	CD	Merciful Rel.	2422462		**£20**	black promo disc
No Time To Cry	7"	Merciful Rel.	MR035	1985	**£5**	

Title	Format	Label	Cat. No.	Year	Price	Notes
No Time To Cry	12"	Merciful Rel.	MR035T	1985	**£8**	
Reptile House	12"	Merciful Rel.	MR023	1983	**£12**	with lyric sheet
Temple Of Love	7"	Merciful Rel.	MR027	1983	**£4**	
This Corrosion	CD-s	Merciful Rel.	MR039CD	1987	**£30**	
This Corrosion	cass-s	Merciful Rel.	MR039C	1987	**£5**	
This Corrosion	7"	Merciful Rel.	MR039	1987	**£20**	boxed with 3 postcards
This Corrosion	12"	Merciful Rel.	MR039T	1987	**£40**	promo with video
Walk Away	7"	Merciful Rel.	MR033	1984	**£5**	
Walk Away	7"	Merciful Rel.	MR033	1984	**£15**	with flexi
Walk Away	12"	Merciful Rel.	MR033T	1984	**£8**	
Walk Away	12"	Merciful Rel.	MR033T	1984	**£20**	with flexi
Wasteland	7"	Merciful Rel.			**£12**	2 x 7", 5 photos, boxed

SITUATION

Title	Format	Label	Cat. No.	Year	Price	Notes
Situation	7"	CBS	202392	1966	**£8**	

SIX TEENS

Title	Format	Label	Cat. No.	Year	Price	Notes
Casual Look	7"	London	HLU8345	1956	**£50**	

SKA CHAMPIONS

Title	Format	Label	Cat. No.	Year	Price	Notes
My Tears	7"	Blue Beat	BB305	1964	**£10**	

SKA KINGS

Title	Format	Label	Cat. No.	Year	Price	Notes
Oil In My Lamp	7"	Atlantic	AT4003	1964	**£6**	
Skasville	7"	Parlophone	R5338	1965	**£6**	

SKATALITES

Title	Format	Label	Cat. No.	Year	Price	Notes
Ball Of Fire	7"	Island	WI207	1965	**£10**	
Beardman Ska	7"	Island	WI228	1965	**£10**	
Confucius	7"	Doctor Bird	DLM5000	1966	**£10**	
Dick Tracy	7"	Island	WI226	1965	**£10**	
Don't Knock It	7"	Decca	F12743	1968	**£8**	
Dr.Kildare	7"	Island	WI191	1965	**£10**	
Dragon Weapon	7"	Island	WI175	1965	**£10**	
Guns Of Navarone	7"	Island	WI168	1965	**£10**	chart single
Latin Goes Ska	7"	Ska Beat	JB177	1965	**£10**	
Lucky Seven	7"	Island	WI244	1965	**£10**	
Timothy	7"	Ska Beat	JB206	1965	**£10**	

SKID ROW

Title	Format	Label	Cat. No.	Year	Price	Notes
34 Hours	LP	CBS	64411	1971	**£10**	
New Places, Old Faces	7"	Song	SO0002	1969	**£20**	Irish
Night Of The Warm Witch	7"	CBS	7181	1971	**£5**	
Sandie's Gone	7"	CBS	4893	1970	**£5**	
Saturday Morning Man	7"	Song	SO0003	1969	**£20**	Irish
Skid	LP	CBS	63965	1970	**£10**	chart LP

SKIDMORE, ALAN

Title	Format	Label	Cat. No.	Year	Price	Notes
Once Upon A Time	LP	Nova	SDN11	1969	**£40**	
TCB	LP	Philips		1970	**£40**	

SKIDMORE, ALAN & OTHERS

Title	Format	Label	Cat. No.	Year	Price	Notes
Jazz In Britain 1968-69	LP	Decca	ECS2114	1972	**£20**	

SKIDS

Title	Format	Label	Cat. No.	Year	Price	Notes
Reasons	7"	No Bad	NB1	1978	**£5**	

SKIN ALLEY

Title	Format	Label	Cat. No.	Year	Price	Notes
In The Midnight Hour	7"	Transatlantic	BIG511	1972	**£4**	
Skin Alley	LP	CBS	63847	1969	**£20**	
Skintight	LP	Transatlantic	TRA273	1973	**£15**	
To Pagham & Beyond	LP	CBS	64140	1970	**£20**	
Two Quid Deal	LP	Transatlantic	TRA260	1972	**£15**	
You Got Me Danglin'	7"	Transatlantic	BIG506	1972	**£4**	

SKIN, FLESH & BONES

Title	Format	Label	Cat. No.	Year	Price	Notes
Butter Te Fish	7"	Pyramid	PYR7014	1974	**£5**	

SKINNER, JIMMIE

Title	Format	Label	Cat. No.	Year	Price	Notes
Country Singer	LP	Decca	DL4132	1961	**£10**	US
I'm A Lot More Lonesome Now	7"	Mercury	AMT1117	1960	**£4**	
John Wesley Harding	7"	Mercury	AMT1062	1959	**£4**	

Kentucky Colonel Vol.1	7" EP	London	REB1421	1964	**£4**	
Kentucky Colonel Vol.2	7" EP	London	REB1422	1964	**£4**	
Kentucky Colonel Vol.3	7" EP	London	REB1423	1964	**£4**	
Riverboat Gambler	7"	Mercury	AMT1088	1960	**£4**	
Songs That Make The Juke Box Play	LP	Mercury	MG20352	1957	**£20**	US
Walking My Blues Away	7"	Mercury	AMT1030	1959	**£4**	

SKIP & FLIP

Cherry Pie	7"	Top Rank	JAR358	1960	**£4**	
Fancy Nancy	7"	Top Rank	JAR248	1959	**£5**	
It Was I	7"	Top Rank	JAR156	1959	**£5**	

SKIP & THE CREATIONS

Mobarn	LP	Justice		196-	**£150**	US

SKIP BIFFERTY

Happy Land	7"	RCA	RCA1648	1967	**£10**	
Man In Black	7"	RCA	RCA1720	1968	**£8**	
On Love	7"	RCA	RCA1621	1967	**£8**	
Skip Bifferty	LP	RCA	SF7941	1967	**£50**	

SKREWDRIVER

All Skrewed Up	12"	Chiswick	CH3	1977	**£10**	
All Skrewed Up	12"	Chiswick	WIK3	1977	**£6**	
Anti-Social	7"	Chiswick	NS18	1977	**£5**	
Built Up	7"	TJM	TJM4	1980	**£6**	
You're So Dumb	7"	Chiswick	S11	1977	**£5**	
You're So Dumb	7"	Chiswick	S11	1977	**£6**	orange or green vinyl

SKULLSNAPS

It's A New Day	7"	GSF	GSZ7	1973	**£10**	

SKUNKS

Gettin' Started	LP	Teen Town	101	196-	**£20**	US

SKY, PATRICK

Harvest Of A Gentle Clang	LP	Vanguard	SVRL19054	1966	**£15**	
Patrick Sky	LP	Vanguard	VSD79179	1965	**£15**	
Photographs	LP	Verve	FTS3079	1969	**£10**	US
Reality Is Bad Enough	LP	Verve	FTS3052	1968	**£12**	US

SKYBIRD

Summer Of '73	LP	Holyground	HGS118	1973	**£60**	

SKYLINERS

I'll Close My Eyes	7"	Pye	7N25091	1961	**£4**	
It Happened Today	7"	London	HLU8971	1959	**£5**	
Pennies From Heaven	7"	Polydor	NH66951	1962	**£4**	
Since I Don't Have You	7"	London	HLB8829	1959	**£10**	
Since I Don't Have You	LP	Original Snd	8873	1963	**£15**	US
Skyliners	LP	Calico	LP3000	1959	**£100**	US
This I Swear	7"	London	HLU8924	1959	**£5**	

SLACK ALICE

Slack Alice	LP	Philips	6308214	1974	**£10**	

SLACK, FREDDIE

Boogie Woogie On The 88	LP-10"	Wing	MGW60003		**£20**	US

SLADE

All Join Hands	12"	RCA	RCAT455	1984	**£10**	
Burning In The Heat Of Love	7"	Barn	2014106	1977	**£4**	
Coz I Love You	7"	Polydor	2058155	1971	**£15**	demo
Do You Believe In Miracles	7"	RCA	PB40449	1985	**£6**	double
Do You Believe In Miracles	12"	RCA	RCAPT40449D	1985	**£8**	double
Far Far Away	7"	Lyntone	LYN3157	1975	**£5**	flexi
Get Down And Get With It	7"	Polydor	2058112	1971	**£4**	chart single
Ginny Ginny	7"	Barn	002	1979	**£12**	black vinyl promo
Ginny Ginny	7"	Barn	002	1979	**£4**	yellow vinyl
Give Us A Goal	7"	Barn	2014121	1978	**£4**	
Gypsy Road Hog	7"	Barn	2014105	1977	**£4**	chart single
Hear Me Calling	7"	Polydor	2814008	1970	**£50**	promo

Hokey Cokey	7"	Speed	SPEED201	1982	**£4**	pic disc
Know Who You Are	7"	Polydor	2058054	1970	**£30**	
Lock Up Your Daughters	7"	RCA	RCA124	1981	**£8**	demo
Merry Xmas Everybody	7"	Cheapskate	CHEAP11	1980	**£4**	chart single
My Baby Left Me/That's Alright Mama	7"	Barn	2014114	1977	**£4**	chart single
Myzsterious Mizster Jones	7"	RCA	PB40027	1985	**£6**	pic disc
Nobody's Fool	7"	Polydor	2058716	1976	**£4**	
Okey Cokey	7"	Barn	011	1979	**£4**	
Play It Loud	LP	Polydor	2383026	1970	**£10**	
Rock'n'Roll	7"	Barn	2014127	1978	**£4**	
Ruby Red	7"	RCA	RCAD191	1982	**£5**	double
Shape Of Things To Come	7"	Fontana	TF1079	1970	**£40**	
Sign Of The Times	7"	Barn	010	1979	**£4**	
Six Of The Best	12"	S.O.T.B.	SUPER453	1980	**£8**	
Slade Talk To 19 Readers	7"	Lyntone	LYN2797	1973	**£5**	flexi
Slade Talk To Melanie Readers	7"	Lyntone	LYN2645	1973	**£5**	flexi
Slade Talk To Melanie/19 Readers	7"	Fan Club		197-	**£8**	flexi
Still The Same	7"	RCA	PB41147	1980	**£6**	double
Thanks For The Memory	7"	Polydor	2058585	1975	**£25**	promo, different lyrics
Whole World's Going Crazy	7"	Polydor	SFI122	1972	**£5**	flexi, Mike Hugg B side
Wild Winds Are Blowing	7"	Fontana	TF1056	1969	**£40**	

SLADE, PRENTIS

I Can Tell	7"	Parlophone	R4850	1961	**£4**	

SLAPP HAPPY

Slapp Happy	LP	Virgin	V2014	1974	**£10**	
Sort Of	LP	Polydor	2310204	1972	**£40**	with insert

SLAPP HAPPY & HENRY COW

Desperate Straights	LP	Virgin	V2024	1974	**£10**	

SLAUGHTER & THE DOGS

Bite Back	LP	DJM	DJM20566	1980	**£10**	
Build Up Not Down	12"	TJM	TJM3		**£6**	
Cranked Up Really High	7"	Rabid	TOSH101	1977	**£5**	
Dame To Blame	7"	Decca	F13743	1977	**£4**	
Do It Dog Style	LP	Damaged Goods	FNARRLP2	1989	**£10**	multi-coloured vinyl
Do It Dog Style	LP	Decca	SKL5292	1978	**£25**	
Live At The Factory	LP	Thrush	THRUSH1		**£10**	
Live Slaughter Rabid Dogs	LP	Rabid	HAT23		**£12**	
Quick Joey Small	7"	Decca	F13758	1978	**£4**	
Where Have All The Bootboys Gone	7"	Decca	F13723	1977	**£5**	
Where Have All The Bootboys Gone	12"	Decca	F13723	1977	**£6**	
You And Me	7"	Atlantic	K10967	1977	**£4**	
You're Ready Now	7"	DJM	DJMS10927	1979	**£4**	

SLAUGHTER JOE

I'll Follow You Down	7"	Creation	CRE019	1985	**£6**	
I'll Follow You Down	12"	Creation	CRET019	1985	**£8**	
She's So Out Of Touch	7"	Creation	CRE035	1986	**£6**	
She's So Out Of Touch	12"	Creation	CRET035	1986	**£8**	

SLEDGE, F.

Red Eye Girl	7"	Blue Beat	BB386	1965	**£10**	

SLEDGE, PERCY

Any Day Now	7"	Atlantic	584264	1969	**£4**	
Baby Help Me	7"	Atlantic	584080	1967	**£4**	
Best Of...	LP	Atlantic	587153	1969	**£10**	
Come Softly To Me	7"	Atlantic	584225	1968	**£4**	
Heart Of A Child	7"	Atlantic	584055	1966	**£4**	
It Tears Me Up	7"	Atlantic	584071	1967	**£4**	
Kind Woman	7"	Atlantic	584286	1969	**£4**	
Out Of Left Field	7"	Atlantic	584108	1967	**£4**	
Percy Sledge Way	LP	Atlantic	587081	1967	**£15**	
Pledging My Love	7"	Atlantic	584140	1967	**£4**	
Take Time To Know Her	LP	Atlantic	SD8180	1968	**£15**	US
Take Time To Love Her	7"	Atlantic	584177	1968	**£4**	
True Love Travels On A Gravel Road	7"	Atlantic	584300	1969	**£4**	
Warm And Tender Love	7"	Atlantic	584034	1966	**£4**	chart single
Warm And Tender Soul	LP	Atlantic	587048	1967	**£15**	

When A Man Loves A Woman	LP	Atlantic	587105	1968	**£12**	
When A Man Loves A Woman	7"	Atlantic	584001	1966	**£5**	chart single

SLEEPWALKERS

Sleepwalk	7"	Parlophone	R4580	1959	**£5**	

SLENDER PLENTY

Silver Tree Top School For Boys	7"	Polydor	56189	1967	**£15**	

SLICK, GRACE

And Through The Hoop	LP	RCA	DJL13544	1979	**£15**	US interview promo
Manhole	LP	Grunt	BFL10347	1974	**£10**	
Welcome To The Wrecking Ball	LP	RCA	DJL13922	1981	**£15**	US interview promo

SLICK, RICKY

Family Man	7"	Dynamic	DYN449	197-	**£4**	

SLICKEE BOYS

Separated Vegetables	LP	Dacoit	1001	1977	**£60**	US
Separated Vegetables	LP	Limp	10003	1980	**£50**	US

SLICKERS

Frying Pan	7"	Blue Cat	BS154	196-	**£10**	
Johnny Too Bad	7"	Dynamic	DYN406	197-	**£8**	
Man Beware	7"	Amalgamated	AMG852	196-	**£10**	
Nana	7"	Blue Cat	BS134	1968	**£10**	
Wala Wala	7"	Blue Cat	BS133	1968	**£10**	
You Can't Win	7"	Dynamic	DYN419	197-	**£6**	

SLIK

Boogiest Band In Town	7"	Bell	BLL1414	1975	**£4**	
Boogiest Band In Town	7"	Polydor	2058523	1974	**£4**	
Don't Take Your Love Away	7"	Arista	ARIST83	1976	**£4**	
Forever And Ever	7"	Bell	BLL1464	1975	**£4**	PS
Happy Together	7"	CBS	1458	1973	**£4**	
Kid's A Punk	7"	Bell	BLL1490	1976	**£4**	
Requiem	7"	Bell	BLL1478	1976	**£4**	chart single

SLITS

Cut	LP	Island	ILPS9573	1979	**£15**	chart LP
Return Of The Giant Slits	LP	CBS	85269	1981	**£10**	with 7" (XPS125)
Typical Girls	12"	Island	12WIP6505	1979	**£6**	

SLOAN, P.F.

12 More Times	LP	Dunhill	D50007	1966	**£10**	US
Measure Of Pleasure	LP	Atco	33268	1968	**£10**	US
Raised On Records	LP	Epic	65179	1972	**£10**	
Sins Of The Family	7"	RCA	RCA1482	1965	**£4**	
Songs Of Our Time	LP	Dunhill	D50004	1965	**£10**	US

SLOAN, SAMMI

Yes I Would	7"	Columbia	DB8480	1968	**£4**	

SLOW DOG

Ain't Never Going Home	7"	Parlophone	R5942	1972	**£4**	

SLY & THE FAMILY STONE

Dance To The Music	7"	Columbia	DB8369	1968	**£20**	
Dance To The Music	LP	Direction	863412	1968	**£10**	
Dance To The Music	7"	Direction	583568	1968	**£4**	chart single
Everyday People	7"	Direction	583938	1969	**£4**	chart single
Family Affair	7"	Epic	EPC7632	1971	**£4**	chart single
Greatest Hits	LP	CBS	Q69002	1973	**£15**	quad
High On You	LP	Epic	PEQ33835	1975	**£10**	US quad
Hot Fun In The Summertime	7"	Direction	584471	1969	**£4**	
Life	LP	Epic	BN26397	1968	**£10**	US
M'Lady	LP	Direction	863461	1968	**£10**	
M'Lady	7"	Direction	583707	1968	**£4**	chart single
Running Away	7"	Epic	EPC7810	1972	**£4**	chart single
Small Talk	LP	Epic	PEQ32930	1974	**£10**	US quad
Stand	7"	Direction	584279	1969	**£4**	
Stand	LP	Epic	EPC63655	1969	**£10**	

Thank You	7"	Direction	584782	1970	**£4**	
There's A Riot Going On	LP	Epic	EPC64613	1971	**£10**	chart LP
Whole New Thing	LP	Epic	LN26324	1967	**£12**	US

SMALL FACES

Afterglow Of Your Love	7"	Immediate	IM077	1969	**£5**	chart single
All Or Nothing	7"	Decca	F12470	1966	**£4**	chart single
Autumn Stone	LP	Immediate	IMA101/2	1969	**£25**	double
E To D	7"	Decca	F12619	1967	**£5**	
From The Beginning	LP	Decca	LK4879	1967	**£30**	chart LP
Here Comes The Nice	7"	Immediate	IM050	1967	**£4**	chart single
Hey Girl	7"	Decca	F12393	1966	**£4**	chart single
I Can't Make It	7"	Decca	F12565	1967	**£6**	chart single
I've Got Mine	7"	Decca	F12276	1965	**£5**	
In Memoriam	LP	Immediate	IMSP022	1970	**£10**	
Itchycoo Park	7"	Immediate	IM057	1967	**£4**	chart single
Lazy Sunday	7"	Immediate	IM064	1968	**£4**	chart single
My Mind's Eye	7"	Decca	F12500	1967	**£4**	chart single
Ogden's Nut Gone Flake	LP	Immediate	IMSP012	1967	**£15**	round cover, chart LP
Sha La La La Lee	7"	Decca	F12317	1966	**£4**	chart single
Small Faces	LP	Decca	LK4790	1966	**£25**	chart LP
Small Faces	LP	Immediate	IMSP008	1967	**£25**	chart LP
There Are But Four Small Faces	LP	Immediate	Z1252002	1968	**£15**	US
Tin Soldier	7"	Immediate	IM062	1967	**£4**	
Tin Soldier	7"	Immediate	IM062	1967	**£10**	PS, chart single
Universal	7"	Immediate	IM069	1968	**£4**	chart single
Whatcha Gonna Do About it	7"	Decca	F12208	1965	**£4**	chart single

SMILE

Smile included Brian May and Roger Taylor who, not long after the release of the group's only single, left in order to help found Queen. Red vinyl copies of the single, incidentally, are counterfeits.

Earth	7"	Mercury	72977	1969	**£40**	US

SMITH, ADAM

I Wonder Why	7"	Island	WI057	1962	**£10**	

SMITH, ARTHUR 'GUITAR BOOGIE'

...And His Crackerjacks	7" EP	MGM	MGMEP510	1954	**£8**	
...And His Crackerjacks	7" EP	MGM	MGMEP695	1959	**£10**	
Express Boogie	7"	MGM	SP1039	1953	**£15**	
Fingers On Fire	LP	MGM	E3525	1958	**£20**	US
Fingers On Fire	LP-10"	MGM	E533	195-	**£25**	US
Five String Banjo Boogie	7"	MGM	SP1021	1953	**£15**	
Foolish Questions	LP-10"	MGM	E236	195-	**£25**	US
Guitar Boogie	7"	MGM	SP1008	1953	**£15**	
Hi Lo Boogie	7"	MGM	SP1122	1955	**£15**	
I Get So Lonely	7"	MGM	SP1096	1954	**£15**	
Mister Guitar	7" EP	Stateside	SE1005	1963	**£8**	
Original Guitar Boogie	LP	Dot	DLP5600	1964	**£12**	US
Red Headed Stranger	7"	MGM	SP1110	1954	**£15**	
Specials	LP-10"	MGM	E3301	195-	**£25**	US

SMITH, BARRY

Hold On To It	7"	People	PEO114	1974	**£15**	

SMITH, BEASLEY

Goodnight Sweet Dreams	7"	London	HLD8235	1956	**£6**	
My Foolish Heart	7"	London	HLD8273	1956	**£8**	

SMITH, BETTY

Betty Smith Quintet	7" EP	Decca	DFE6446	1957	**£6**	
Betty's Blues	7"	Decca	F11031	1958	**£4**	

SMITH, BETTY SKIFFLE GROUP

Bewitched	7"	Decca	F10986	1958	**£5**	
Sweet Georgia Brown	7"	Tempo	A163	1957	**£4**	
There's A Blue Ridge Mountain	7"	Tempo	A162	1957	**£4**	

SMITH, BOB

Visit	LP	Kent	KST551	1969	**£30**	US

SMITH, BUSTER

Legendary Buster Smith	LP	Atlantic	1323	1960	**£15**	US

SMITH, CARL

Carl Smith	LP-10"	Columbia	HL2579	1956	**£15**	US
Carl Smith Touch	LP	Philips	BBL7437	1960	**£10**	
Let's Live A Little	LP	Columbia	CL1172	1958	**£10**	US
Sentimental Songs	LP-10"	Columbia	HL9023	195-	**£15**	US
Smith's The Name	LP	Columbia	CL1022	1957	**£10**	US
Softly And Tenderly	LP-10"	Columbia	HL9026	195-	**£15**	US
Sunday Down South	LP	Columbia	CL959	1957	**£10**	US
Ten Thousand Drums	7"	Philips	PB943	1959	**£4**	
Blues	7" EP	Philips	BBE12491	1961	**£6**	

SMITH, DAVE & THE ASTRONAUTS

Lover Like You	7"	Blue Beat	BB104	1962	**£10**	
Lover Like You	7"	Columbia	DB104	1967	**£8**	

SMITH, EDDIE

Silver Star Stomp	7"	Parlophone	MSP6186	1955	**£5**	
Upturn	7"	Top Rank	JAR285	1960	**£8**	

SMITH, EDGEWOOD & FABULOUS TAILFEATHERS

Ain't That Lovin' You	7"	Sue	WI4037	1967	**£8**	

SMITH, EFFIE

Dial That Phone	7"	Sue	WI4010	1966	**£8**	

SMITH, ELSON

Flip Flop	7"	Fontana	H291	1961	**£4**	

SMITH, GEORGE

Someday You're Gonna Learn	7"	Blue Horizon	573170	1970	**£10**	

SMITH, GEORGE HARMONICA

Arkansas Trap	LP	Deram	SML1082	1971	**£12**	
No Time To Jive	LP	Blue Horizon	763856	1970	**£35**	

SMITH, GORDON

Long Overdue	LP	Blue Horizon	763211	1968	**£35**	
Too Long	7"	Blue Horizon	573156	1969	**£10**	

SMITH, HUEY 'PIANO'

Don't You Know Yokomo	7"	Top Rank	JAR282	1960	**£6**	
For Dancing	LP	Ace	LP1015	1961	**£50**	US
Having A Good Time	LP	Ace	LP1004	1959	**£50**	US
High Blood Pressure	7"	Columbia	DB4138	1958	**£12**	
If It Ain't One Thing It's Another	7"	Sue	WI364	1965	**£10**	
Popeye	7"	Top Rank	JAR614	1962	**£8**	
Rock'N'Roll Revival	LP	Ace	LP2021	196-	**£40**	US
Rockin' Pneumonia	7"	Sue	WI380	1965	**£10**	
Rockin' Pneumonia...	LP	Sue	ILP917	1965	**£20**	
Twas The Night Before Christmas	LP	Ace	LP1027	1962	**£40**	US

SMITH, HURRICANE

Don't Let It Die	7"	Columbia	DB8785	1971	**£4**	chart single

SMITH, JIMMY

Cat	7"	Verve	VS523	1964	**£4**	
Cat In A Tree	7"	Verve	VS551	1967	**£4**	
Creeper	7" EP	Verve	VEP5021	1965	**£4**	
Got My Mojo Working	7"	Verve	VS536	1966	**£4**	chart single
Hobo Flats	7"	Verve	VS509	1965	**£4**	
I'm Your Hoochie Coochie Man	7"	Verve	VS540	1966	**£4**	
Mickey Mouse	7"	Verve	VS562	1967	**£4**	
Organ Grinder's Swing	7"	Verve	VS531	1965	**£4**	
Plays The Blues	7" EP	Verve	VEP5016	1965	**£4**	
Swinging With The Incredible...	7" EP	Verve	VEP5022	1965	**£4**	
Walk On The Wild Side	7"	HMV	POP1025	1962	**£5**	
Walk On The Wild Side	7" EP	Verve	VEP5008	1964	**£4**	
Where The Spies Are	7"	Verve	VS534	1966	**£4**	

SMITH, JUDI

Leaves Come Tumbling Down	7"	Decca	F12132	1965	**£10**	

SMITH, JUNIOR

Come Cure Me	7"	Giant	GN25	1967	**£10**	
Cool Down Your Temper	7"	Giant	GN1	196-	**£10**	
I'm Gonna Leave You Girl	7"	Giant	GN18	1967	**£10**	

SMITH, LITTLE GEORGIE

Blues In The Dark	7"	Blue Horizon	451002	1966	**£15**	

SMITH, LONNIE LISTON

Lonnie Liston Smith is a jazz keyboard player who was briefly a part of the Miles Davis band during the time in the early seventies when the trumpeter was engaged in some of his most experimental work with densely constructed rhythms. Smith's own records contain a very much more commercial form of jazz-funk, the track "Expansions" having aquired some of the status of a disco classic.

Chance For Peace	7"	RCA	RCA2668	1976	**£4**	
Expansions	LP	RCA	SF8434	1975	**£15**	
Expansions	7"	RCA	PB9450	1975	**£4**	
Expansions	7"	RCA	RCA2568	1975	**£5**	
Get Down Everybody	7"	RCA	RCA2727	1976	**£4**	

SMITH, LORENZO

Firewater	7"	Outasite	45503	1966	**£20**	

SMITH, MARVIN

Time Stopped	7"	Coral	Q72486	1966	**£15**	

SMITH, O.C.

Hickory Holler Revisited	LP	CBS	63362	1968	**£10**	chart LP
Son Of Hickory Holler's Tramp	7"	CBS	3343	1968	**£4**	chart single

SMITH, OCIE

Lighthouse	7"	London	HLA8480	1957	**£10**	

SMITH, PATTI

Gloria	7"	Arista	AS171	1976	**£4**	
Hey Joe	7"	Mer	601	1974	**£25**	US
Horses	LP	Arista	S4066	1975	**£20**	US grey vinyl

SMITH, PERKINS, SMITH

Smith,Perkins,Smith	LP	Island	ILPS9198	1972	**£10**	

SMITH, RAY

Best Of...	LP	T	56062	196-	**£12**	US
Greatest Hits	LP	Columbia	CL1937	1963	**£10**	US
Rocking Little Angel	7"	London	HL9051	1960	**£10**	
Travellin' With Ray	LP	Judd	JLPA701	1960	**£75**	US

SMITH, SLIM

Everybody Needs Love	LP	Pama	ECO9	1969	**£20**	
I've Got Your Number	7"	Island	WI3023	1966	**£10**	
Just a Dream	7"	Dynamic	DYN428	197-	**£4**	
Rougher Yet	7"	Coxsone	CS7034	196-	**£10**	
Watch This Sound	7"	Trojan	TR619	1968	**£6**	

SMITH, T.V., EXPLORERS

Have Fun	7"	Kaleidoscope	KRLA1359	1981	**£5**	no 'Explorers' credit
Servant	cass-s	Kaleidoscope	KRLA401162	1981	**£30**	
Tomahawk Cruise	7"	Big Beat	NS64	1980	**£25**	1 sided test pressing

SMITH, TAB

All My Life	7"	Vogue	V2299	1969	**£4**	
Jump Time	7"	Vogue	V2410	1970	**£4**	
Music Styled By Tab Smith	LP-10"	United	LP001		**£50**	US
Red Hot And Cool Blues	LP-10"	United	LP003		**£50**	US

SMITH, TERRY

Terry Smith	LP	Lambert		1977	**£25**	

SMITH, VERDELLE

I Don't Need Anything	7"	Capitol	CL15481	1966	**£5**	

Title	Format	Label	Cat. No.	Year	Price	Notes
In My Room	7"	Capitol	CL15434	1966	**£4**	
Tar And Cement	7"	Capitol	CL15456	1966	**£4**	
There's So Much Love Around Me	7"	Capitol	CL15514	1967	**£4**	

SMITH, WARREN

Title	Format	Label	Cat. No.	Year	Price	Notes
First Country Collection	LP	Liberty	LRP3199	1961	**£20**	US
Judge And Jury	7"	Liberty	LIB55699	1964	**£4**	

SMITH, WHISPERING

Title	Format	Label	Cat. No.	Year	Price	Notes
Over Easy	LP	Blue Horizon	2431015	1971	**£25**	

SMITH, WHISTLING JACK

Title	Format	Label	Cat. No.	Year	Price	Notes
I Was Kaiser Bill's Batman	7"	Deram	DM112	1967	**£4**	chart single

SMITHEREENS

Title	Format	Label	Cat. No.	Year	Price	Notes
Beauty And Sadness	LP	Little Ricky		1983	**£20**	US

SMITHS

The Smiths remained with Rough Trade for the major part of their career and saw the record company's fortunes rise along with their own, so that there are no obscure early singles for the Smiths collector to seek out. The single "This Charming Man", available in three versions, has, however, become quite scarce, despite gaining a respectable position in the lower reaches of the charts. The original cover of "What Difference Does It Make", showing a film still of Terence Stamp in "The Collector" is not particularly rare. One suspects that its withdrawal in favour of a cover with Morrisey in identical pose was designed solely to illustrate the song's title.

Title	Format	Label	Cat. No.	Year	Price	Notes
Ask	7"	Rough Trade	RT194	1986	**£10**	test pressing
Ask	12"	Rough Trade	RTT194	1986	**£10**	test pressing
Barbarism Begins At Home (2 versions)	12"	Rough Trade	RTT171	1985	**£20**	promo
Barbarism Begins At Home	12"	Rough Trade	RTT171	1985	**£20**	1 sided promo
Bigmouth Strikes Again	7"	Rough Trade	RT192	1986	**£10**	test pressing
Bigmouth Strikes Again	12"	Rough Trade	RTT192	1986	**£10**	test pressing
Boy With The Thorn In His Side	7"	Rough Trade	RT191	1985	**£10**	test pressing
Boy With The Thorn In His Side	12"	Rough Trade	RTT191	1985	**£10**	test pressing
Girlfriend In A Coma	7"	Rough Trade	RT197	1987	**£10**	test pressing
Girlfriend In A Coma	12"	Rough Trade	RTT197	1987	**£10**	test pressing
Hand In Glove	7"	Rough Trade	RT132	1983	**£5**	Rough Trade logo on label
Hand In Glove	7"	Rough Trade	RT132	1983	**£15**	test pressing
Hand In Glove	7"	Rough Trade	RT132	1987	**£40**	blue sleeve, silver photo
Heaven Knows I'm Miserable Now	7"	Rough Trade	RT156	1984	**£15**	test pressing
Heaven Knows I'm Miserable Now	12"	Rough Trade	RTT156	1984	**£15**	test pressing
How Soon Is Now?	12"	Rough Trade	RTT176	1985	**£10**	test pressing
How Soon Is Now?	7"	Rough Trade	RT176	1985	**£10**	test pressing
I Started Something	7"	Rough Trade	RT198	1987	**£10**	test pressing
I Started Something	12"	Rough Trade	RTT198	1987	**£10**	test pressing
Last Night	7"	Rough Trade	RT200	1987	**£10**	test pressing
Last Night	12"	Rough Trade	RTT200	1987	**£10**	test pressing
Panic	7"	Rough Trade	RT193	1986	**£10**	test pressing
Panic	12"	Rough Trade	RTT193	1986	**£10**	test pressing
Reel Around The Fountain	7"	Rough Trade	RT136	1983	**£75**	test pressing
Shakespeare's Sister	7"	Rough Trade	RT181	1985	**£10**	test pressing
Shakespeare's Sister	12"	Rough Trade	RTT181	1985	**£10**	test pressing
Sheila Take A Bow	7"	Rough Trade	RT196	1987	**£10**	test pressing
Sheila Take A Bow	12"	Rough Trade	RTT196	1987	**£10**	test pressing
Shoplifters Of The World Unite	7"	Rough Trade	RT195	1987	**£10**	test pressing
Shoplifters Of The World Unite	12"	Rough Trade	RTT195	1987	**£10**	test pressing
Still Ill	7"	Rough Trade	RT161DJ	1984	**£15**	promo
That Joke Isn't Funny Anymore	7"	Rough Trade	RTT186	1985	**£10**	test pressing
That Joke Isn't Funny Anymore	12"	Rough Trade	RTT186	1985	**£10**	test pressing
This Charming Man (New York remix)	12"	Rough Trade	RTT136NY	1983	**£30**	
This Charming Man	7"	Rough Trade	RT136	1983	**£15**	chart single
This Charming Man	12"	Rough Trade	RTT136	1983	**£20**	
What Difference Does It Make?	7"	Rough Trade	RT146	1984	**£15**	test pressing
What Difference Does It Make?	12"	Rough Trade	RTT146	1984	**£15**	test pressing
William It Was Really Nothing	7"	Rough Trade	RT166	1984	**£15**	test pressing
William It Was Really Nothing	12"	Rough Trade	RTT166	1984	**£15**	test pressing
You Just Haven't Earned It Yet Baby	12"	Rough Trade	RTT195	1987	**£10**	mispressing

SMOKE

The English Smoke managed to maintain a surprisingly long career (including making records under the name of Chords Five) for a group that were essentially a one-hit wonder. That one hit, however, "My Friend Jack", is something of a psychedelic classic, driven by viciously reverbed and fuzzed guitars.

Title	Format	Label	Cat. No.	Year	Price	Notes
Dreams Of Dreams	7"	Revolution	REVP1002	1970	**£10**	

If The Weather's Sunny .... 7" .... Columbia .... DB8252 .... 1967 ...... **£12** ....
It Could Be Wonderful .... 7" .... Island .... WIP6023 .... 1967 ...... **£12** ....
It's Smoke Time .... LP .... Metronome .... 1967 ...... **£40** .... German
My Friend Jack .... 7" .... Columbia .... DB8115 .... 1967 ...... **£8** .... chart single
My Lullaby .... 7" .... Decca .... FR13514 .... 1974 ...... **£5** ....
Ride Ride Ride .... 7" .... Pageant .... SAM101 .... 1971 ...... **£10** ....
Shagalagalu .... 7" .... Decca .... FR13484 .... 1974 ...... **£5** ....
Smoke .... LP .... BASF .... 1968 ...... **£25** .... German
Sugar Man .... 7" .... Regal Z. .... RZ3071 .... 1972 ...... **£10** ....
Utterly Simple .... 7" .... Island .... WIP6031 .... 1968 ...... **£40** ....

SMOKE (2)

At George's Coffee Shop .... LP .... Uni .... 73065 .... 1970 ...... **£15** .... US
Smoke .... LP .... Sidewalk .... ST5912 .... 1968 ...... **£20** .... US
Smoke .... LP .... Uni .... 73052 .... 1969 ...... **£15** .... US

SMOKESTACK LIGHTNING

Although the name would suggest a blues group, Smokestack Lightnin' actually played blue-eyed soul, though without very much ambition, or even very much soulfulness. The long version of the song after which the group was named is used as a climax to the "Off The Wall" album. The piece becomes stretched out as each member delivers a solo on his instrument - but none is in the least memorable.

Light In My Window .... 7" .... Bell .... BLL1046 .... 1969 ...... **£8** ....
Off The Wall .... LP .... Bell .... SBLL116 .... 1969 ...... **£25** ....

SMOKEY CIRCLES

Smokey Circles' Album .... LP .... Carnaby .... **£25** ....

SMOTHERS, SMOKEY

Backporch Blues .... LP .... King .... 779 .... 1962 ...... **£100** .... US

SNAFU

Dixie Queen .... 7" .... WWA .... WWS007 .... 1974 ...... **£4** ....
Situation Normal .... LP .... WWA .... 013 .... 1974 ...... **£10** ....
Snafu .... LP .... WWA .... 003 .... 1974 ...... **£10** ....

SNAPPERS

If There Were .... 7" .... Top Rank .... JAR167 .... 1959 ...... **£4** ....

SNATCH

All I Want .... 7" .... Lightning .... LIG505 .... 1978 ...... **£5** ....
IRT .... 7" .... Lightning .... LIG502 .... 1978 ...... **£5** ....
Shopping For Clothes .... 12" .... Fetish .... FET004 .... 1980 ...... **£6** ....

SNEAKERS

In The Red .... LP .... Car .... 0398 .... 1978 ...... **£20** .... US

SNEEKERS

I Just Can't Get To Sleep .... 7" .... Columbia .... DB7385 .... 1964 ...... **£15** ....

SNIVELLING SHITS

Terminal Stupid .... 7" .... Ghetto R. .... PRE2 .... 1977 ...... **£8** ....

SNOBS

Buckle Shoe Stomp .... 7" .... Decca .... F11867 .... 1964 ...... **£20** ....

SNOOKY & MOODY

Snooky And Moody's Blues .... 7" .... Blue Horizon ... 451003 .... 1966 ...... **£15** ....

SNOW, HANK

Big Country Hits .... LP .... RCA .... LPM2458 .... 1961 ...... **£15** .... US
Country & Western Jamboree .... LP .... RCA .... LPM1419 .... 1957 ...... **£25** .... US
Country Classics .... LP .... RCA .... LPM1233 .... 1955 ...... **£25** .... US
Country Classics .... LP-10" .. RCA .... LPT3026 .... 1952 ...... **£30** .... US
Country Guitar No.4 .... 7" EP .... RCA .... RCX116 .... 1958 ...... **£5** ....
Country Guitar No.7 .... 7" EP .... RCA .... RCX142 .... 1959 ...... **£5** ....
Hank Snow Salutes Jimmie Rodgers ..... LP-10" .. RCA .... LPT3131 .... 1953 ...... **£30** .... US
Hank Snow Sings .... LP-10" .. RCA .... LPT3070 .... 1952 ...... **£30** .... US
Hank Snow Sings Jimmie Rodgers Songs LP .... RCA .... LPM2043 .... 1959 ...... **£15** .... US
Hank Snow Sings Sacred Songs .... LP .... RCA .... LPM1638 .... 1958 ...... **£20** .... US
Hank Snow's Country Guitar .... LP .... RCA .... LPM1435 .... 1957 ...... **£25** .... US
Hank Snow's Country Guitar .... LP-10" .. RCA .... LPT3267 .... 1954 ...... **£30** .... US
Hits, Hits And More Hits .... LP .... RCA .... LPM3965 .... 1968 ...... **£10** .... US

I've Been Everywhere	LP	RCA	LPM2675	1963	**£12**	US
Just Keep A-Movin'	LP	RCA	LPM1113	1955	**£25**	US
Old Doc Brown	LP	RCA	LPM1156	1955	**£30**	US
Railroad Man	LP	RCA	LPM2705	1963	**£10**	US
Souvenirs	LP	RCA	LPM2285	1961	**£15**	US
That Country Gentleman	7" EP	RCA	RCX7154	1964	**£5**	
Together Again	LP	RCA	LPM2580	1962	**£12**	US
When Tragedy Struck	LP	RCA	LPM1861	1958	**£20**	US

SNYDER, BILL

Bewitched	7" EP	London	REP1011	1954	**£4**	

SOCIALITES

Jive Jimmy	7"	W. Bros	WB148	1964	**£6**	

SOCIETIE

Bird Has Flown	7"	Deram	DM162	1967	**£15**	

SOCRATES

On The Wings	LP	Peters	PILPS9002	1976	**£20**	US
Phos	LP	Peters	PILPS9013	1977	**£20**	US

SOFT BOYS

Angelepoise Lamp	7"	Radar	ADA8	1978	**£4**	
Can Of Bees	LP	Aura	AUL709	1979	**£10**	
Can Of Bees	LP	Two Crabs	CLAW1001	1977	**£25**	
Give It To The Soft Boys	7"	Raw	RAW5	1977	**£20**	
I Wanna Destroy You	7"	Armageddon	AS005	1980	**£4**	
Near The Soft Boys	7"	Armageddon	AEP002	1980	**£4**	
Only The Stones Remain	LP	Armageddon	BYE1	1981	**£10**	
Only The Stones Remain	7"	Armageddon	AS029	1981	**£4**	
Wading Through The Ventilator	LP	Delorean	SOFT1P		**£10**	pic disc
Wading Through The Ventilator	7"	Raw	RAW37	1978	**£5**	

SOFT CELL

The combination of a singer with a limited, rather tuneless voice and a keyboard player still struggling with the opening chapter of his synthesizer instruction manual was an unlikely recipe for the creation of some of the finest single releases of the eighties. Soft Cell proved that rock music's perennial reliance on the inspired amateur can sometimes strike gold.

12" Singles	12"	Some Bizarre	CELBX1	1982	**£80**	6x12", boxed
A Man Can Get Lost	7"	Some Bizarre	HARD1	1981	**£25**	
Art Of Falling Apart	LP	Some Bizarre	BIZL3	1983	**£10**	with 12"
Bedsitter	12"	Some Bizarre	BZS612	1981	**£6**	
Down In The Subway	12"	Some Bizarre	BZSR2212	1984	**£12**	
Memorabilia	12"	Some Bizarre	HARD12	1981	**£25**	
Metro Mr.X	7"	Lyntone	LYN10410	1981	**£10**	green vinyl flexi
Mutant Moments	7"	Big Frock	ABF1	1980	**£75**	with insert
Numbers	7"	Some Bizarre	BXSDJ17	1983	**£10**	1 sided promo
Numbers	12"	Some Bizarre	BZS1712	1983	**£6**	
Say Hello, Wave Goodbye	12"	Some Bizarre	BZS712	1982	**£6**	
Soul Inside	7"	Some Bizarre	BZS2020	1983	**£8**	double
Soul Inside	12"	Some Bizarre	BZS2012	1983	**£8**	
Tainted Love	12"	Some Bizarre	BZS212	1981	**£6**	
Tainted Love/Memorabilia	12"	Some Bizarre	BZS212	1981	**£12**	
Torch	12"	Some Bizarre	BZS912	1982	**£6**	
What!	12"	Some Bizarre	BZS112	1982	**£10**	
Where The Heart Is	12"	Some Bizarre	BZS1612	1982	**£6**	

SOFT MACHINE

Fourth	LP	CBS	64280	1971	**£10**	chart LP
Love Makes Sweet Music	7"	Polydor	56151	1967	**£30**	
Sixth	LP	CBS	68214	1973	**£10**	
Soft Machine	LP	Probe	4500	1968	**£20**	US, wheel cover
Third	LP	CBS	66246	1970	**£15**	double, chart LP
Triple Echo	LP	Harvest	SHTW800	1977	**£25**	triple
Volume 2	LP	Probe	SPB1002	1969	**£15**	
Volumes 1 & 2	LP	ABC	ABCL5004	1974	**£15**	double

SOFTLEY, MICK

Am I The Red One	7"	CBS	202469	1967	**£6**	
Any Mother Doesn't Grumble	LP	CBS	64841	1972	**£20**	
Can You Hear Me Now	7"	CBS	5130	1970	**£4**	
I'm So Confused	7"	Immediate	IM014	1965	**£8**	

Lady Willow	7"	CBS	8269	1972	**£4**	
Songs For Swinging Survivors	LP	Columbia		1965	**£60**	
Street Singer	LP	CBS	64395	1971	**£20**	
Sunrise	LP	CBS	64098	1970	**£15**	

SOHO SKIFFLE GROUP

Soho Skiffle Group	7" EP	Melodisc	EPM772	195-	**£8**	

SOLAR PLEXUS

Concerto Grosso(English)	LP	Odeon	34684/5	1972	**£20**	Swedish double
Concerto Grosso(Swedish)	LP	Odeon	34573/4	1972	**£20**	Swedish double
Det Er Inte Baten	LP	Harvest	06234975	1974	**£12**	European
Hellrre Gycklare An Hycklare	LP	Harvest	06235166	1975	**£12**	European
Solar Plexus 2	LP	Odeon	34797	1973	**£15**	Swedish
Solar Plexus	LP	Polydor	2383222	1973	**£15**	

SOLID GOLD CADILLAC

In common with most British jazz musicians of the time, Mike Westbrook incorporated many elements of rock music within his compositions, while many of the members of his band were equally at home whether playing jazz, rock, or somewhere in between. Solid Gold Cadillac was the closest that Westbrook came to leading a straight rock group, although the music is inevitably suffused with a jazz sensibility.

Brain Damage	LP	RCA	SF8365	1973	**£15**	
Solid Gold Cadillac	LP	RCA	SF8311	1972	**£15**	

SOLITAIRES

Walking Along	7"	London	HLM8745	1958	**£15**	

SOLO

Solo	LP			197-	**£60**	US

SOLSTICE

Silent Dance	LP	private		1984	**£25**	

SOLUTION

Divergence	LP	EMI	EMC3002	1973	**£10**	
Solution	LP	Decca	SKLR5124	1972	**£10**	

SOME CHICKEN

Arabian Daze	7"	Raw	RAW13	1978	**£50**	coloured vinyl
New Religion	7"	Raw	RAW7	1977	**£10**	

SOMEONE'S BAND

Someone's Band	LP	Deram	SML1068	1970	**£20**	
Story	7"	Deram	DM313	1970	**£4**	

SOMERS, GORDON

Sound Of The Beatles	7" EP	Top Ten	TPSX101		**£5**	

SOMMERS, JOANIE

Behind Closed Doors	LP	W. Bros	B1348	1960	**£12**	US, boxed with booklet
Come Alive	LP	Columbia	CL2495	1966	**£10**	US
For Those Who Think Young	LP	W. Bros	W1436	1962	**£10**	US
Johnny Get Angry	LP	W. Bros	W1470	1962	**£12**	US
Johnny Get Angry Vol.1	7" EP	W. Bros	WEP6121	1964	**£6**	
Johnny Get Angry Vol.1	7" EP	W. Bros	WSEP6121	1964	**£8**	stereo
Johnny Get Angry Vol.2	7" EP	W. Bros	WEP6123	1964	**£6**	
Johnny Get Angry Vol.2	7" EP	W. Bros	WSEP6123	1964	**£8**	stereo
Let's Talk About Love	LP	W. Bros	W1474	1962	**£10**	US
Lively Set	LP	Decca	DL9119	1964	**£10**	US
Positively The Most	LP	W. Bros	W1346	1960	**£10**	US
Positively The Most	7" EP	W. Bros	WEP6013	1960	**£4**	
Positively The Most	7" EP	W. Bros	WSEP2013	1960	**£6**	stereo
Softly, The Brazilian Sound	LP	W. Bros	W1575	1965	**£10**	US
Sommers' Seasons	LP	W. Bros	W1504	1964	**£10**	US
Voice Of The Sixties	LP	W. Bros	W1412	1961	**£10**	US
Voice Of The Sixties	7" EP	W. Bros	WEP6047	1961	**£4**	
Voice Of The Sixties	7" EP	W. Bros	WSEP2047	1961	**£6**	stereo

SONGSTERS

Bahama Buggy Ride	7"	London	HL8100	1954	**£8**	

SONIC ASSASSINS (HAWKWIND)

Title	Format	Label	Cat. No.	Year	Price	Notes
Motorhead	7"	Flicknife	FLS205	1981	**£4**	

SONIC YOUTH

Title	Format	Label	Cat. No.	Year	Price	Notes
Daydream Nation	LP	Blast First		1988	**£150**	promo double LP, 2 x 7", T-shirt, poster, boxed
Daydream Nation	LP	Blast First	BFFP34	1988	**£12**	double, with signed poster
Daydream Nation	LP	Blast First	BFFP34	1988	**£20**	test pressing
Death Valley '69	7"	Iridescence	112	1984	**£10**	US
Evol	LP	Blast First	BFFP4	1986	**£30**	test pressing
Flower	7"	Blast First		1985	**£25**	promo, censored version
Flower	7"	Blast First	BFFP3	1985	**£15**	
Flower	12"	Blast First	BFFP3	1986	**£10**	yellow vinyl
Making The Nature Scene	7"	F. Exposure	FE001	1985	**£30**	US
Marilyn Moore	7"	Chemical Im	CT1	1986	**£10**	US
Providence	7"	Blast First		1989	**£30**	promo
Savage Pencil	12"	Blast First	BFFP3	1986	**£10**	
Savage Pencil	12"	Blast First	BFFP3	1986	**£25**	signed by S.Pencil
Silver Rocket	7"	F. Exposure		1988	**£4**	US
Sister	LP	Blast First	BFFP20	1987	**£20**	test pressing
Sister Interview Disc	LP	Blast First	CHAT1	1987	**£10**	
Sonic Death	cass	Ecstatic P		1984	**£15**	US
Starpower	7"	Blast First	BFFP7	1986	**£5**	with badge & poster
Stick Me Donna Magick Momma	7"	Fierce		1988	**£8**	
Stick Me Donna Magick Momma	7"	Fierce	FRIGHT015/6	1988	**£20**	2 x 1 sided 7"
Walls Have Ears	LP	NOT	NOT1	1986	**£50**	double

SONIC'S RENDEZVOUS BAND

Title	Format	Label	Cat. No.	Year	Price	Notes
City Slang	7"	Orchide	OR1002	1978	**£60**	

SONICS

Title	Format	Label	Cat. No.	Year	Price	Notes
Explosives	LP	Buckshot	BSR001	1974	**£20**	US
Here Are The Sonics	LP	Etiquette	LP024	1965	**£50**	US
Introducing The Sonics	LP	Jerden	JRL7007	1967	**£40**	US
Sonics Boom	LP	Etiquette	LP027	1966	**£40**	US

SONICS & WAILERS (2)

Title	Format	Label	Cat. No.	Year	Price	Notes
Merry Christmas	LP	Etiquette	ALB02	196-	**£100**	US

SONNY

Title	Format	Label	Cat. No.	Year	Price	Notes
Inner Views	LP	Atco		1967	**£15**	US
Laugh At Me	7"	Atlantic	AT4038	1965	**£4**	chart single
Revolution Kind	7"	Atlantic	AT4060	1965	**£4**	

SONNY & CHER

Title	Format	Label	Cat. No.	Year	Price	Notes
Baby Don't Go	7"	Reprise	R20309	1964	**£4**	chart single
Beat Goes On	7"	Atlantic	584078	1967	**£4**	chart single
Best Of...	LP	Atlantic	587083	1967	**£10**	
But You're Mine	7"	Atlantic	AT4047	1965	**£4**	chart single
Circus	7"	Atlantic	584168	1968	**£4**	
Get It Together	7"	Atlantic	2091021	1970	**£4**	
Good Combination	7"	Atlantic	584162	1968	**£4**	
Good Times	LP	Atco	33214	1967	**£10**	US
Have I Stayed Too Long	7"	Atlantic	584018	1966	**£4**	chart single
I Got You Babe	7"	Atlantic	AT4035	1965	**£4**	chart single
In Case You're In Love	LP	Atlantic	587052	1967	**£12**	
It's The Little Things	7"	Atlantic	584129	1967	**£4**	
Little Man	7"	Atlantic	584040	1966	**£4**	chart single
Live	LP	MCA	MUPS435	1972	**£10**	
Living For You	7"	Atlantic	584057	1966	**£4**	chart single
Look At Us	LP	Atlantic	ATL5036	1964	**£15**	chart LP
Podunk	7"	Atlantic	584110	1967	**£4**	
Sonny And Cher And Caesar And Cleo	7" EP	Reprise	R30056	1965	**£10**	
What Now My Love	7"	Atlantic	AT4069	1966	**£4**	chart single
Wondrous World Of...	LP	Atlantic	587006	1966	**£15**	chart LP
You've Got To Have A Thing	7"	Atlantic	584215	1968	**£4**	

SONNY & THE CASCADES

Title	Format	Label	Cat. No.	Year	Price	Notes
Exciting New Liverpool Sound	LP	Columbia	CL2172	1964	**£15**	US

SONNY & THE DAFFODILS

Title	Format	Label	Number	Year	Price	Notes
Sonny And The Daffodils	7" EP	Ember	EMB4538	1963	**£8**	

SONS OF CHAMPLIN

Title	Format	Label	Number	Year	Price	Notes
Circle Filled With Love	LP	Ariola	50007	1976	**£10**	US
Follow Your Heart	LP	Capitol	ST675	1971	**£15**	US
Loosen Up Naturally	LP	Capitol	SWBB200	1969	**£25**	US double
Loving Is Why	LP	Ariola	AAS1505	1977	**£10**	
Sons	LP	Capitol	SKAO322	1969	**£15**	US
Sons Of Champlin	LP	Ariola	AAS1501	1975	**£10**	
Welcome To The Dance	LP	CBS	65663	1973	**£12**	

SONS OF FRED

Title	Format	Label	Number	Year	Price	Notes
I, I, I	7"	Parlophone	R5391	1965	**£20**	
Sweet Love	7"	Columbia	DB7605	1965	**£30**	
You Told Me	7"	Parlophone	R5415	1966	**£25**	

SONS OF PILTDOWN MEN

Title	Format	Label	Number	Year	Price	Notes
Mad Goose	7"	Pye	7N25206	1963	**£4**	

SONS OF THE PIONEERS

Title	Format	Label	Number	Year	Price	Notes
Cowboy Classics	LP-10"	RCA	LPM3032	1952	**£30**	US
Cowboy Hymns And Spirituals	LP-10"	RCA	LPM3095	1952	**£30**	US
Favorite Cowboy Songs	LP	RCA	LPM1130	1955	**£12**	US
How Great Thou Art	LP	RCA	LPM1431	1957	**£12**	US
One Man's Songs	LP	RCA	LPM1483	1957	**£12**	US
Sons Of The Pioneers	7" EP	HMV	7EG8069	195-	**£6**	
Western Classics	LP-10"	RCA	LPM3162	1953	**£30**	US

SOPHOMORES

Title	Format	Label	Number	Year	Price	Notes
Sophomores	LP	Seeco	CELP451		**£20**	US

SOPWITH CAMEL

Title	Format	Label	Number	Year	Price	Notes
Hello Hello	LP	Kama Sutra	KSBS2063	1973	**£12**	US
Hello Hello	7"	Kama Sutra	KAS205	1966	**£6**	
Miraculous Hump Returns From The Moon	LP	Reprise	K44251	1973	**£12**	
Sopwith Camel	LP	Kama Sutra	KLPS8060	1967	**£20**	US

SORROWS

Title	Format	Label	Number	Year	Price	Notes
Baby	7"	Piccadilly	7N35230	1965	**£12**	
I Don't Wanna Be Free	7"	Piccadilly	7N35219	1965	**£10**	
Let Me In	7"	Piccadilly	7N35336	1966	**£10**	
Let The Love Live	7"	Piccadilly	7N35309	1966	**£10**	
Old Songs New Songs	LP	Miura		1968	**£100**	Italian
Pink, Purple, Yellow, Red	7"	Piccadilly	7N35385	1967	**£10**	
Take A Heart	7"	Piccadilly	7N35260	1965	**£6**	chart single
Take A Heart	LP	Pye	NPL38023	1965	**£80**	
You've Got What I Want	7"	Piccadilly	7N35277	1966	**£12**	

SORT COL

Title	Format	Label	Number	Year	Price	Notes
Marble Station	7"	4AD	AD101	1981	**£6**	

SOUL AGENTS

Title	Format	Label	Number	Year	Price	Notes
Don't Break It Up	7"	Pye	7N15768	1965	**£20**	
I Just Want To Make Love To You	7"	Pye	7N15660	1964	**£20**	
Seventh Son	7"	Pye	7N15707	1964	**£20**	

SOUL BROTHERS

Title	Format	Label	Number	Year	Price	Notes
Carib Soul	LP	Coxsone	CSL8002	196-	**£80**	
Good Lovin' Never Hurt	7"	Mercury	MF916	1965	**£6**	
Hot Shot Ska	LP	Coxsone	CSL8001	196-	**£80**	
Hot Shot	LP	Studio One	112	196-	**£80**	chart single
I Can't Believe It	7"	Parlophone	R5321	1965	**£12**	
I Keep Ringing My Baby	7"	Decca	F12116	1965	**£8**	chart single

SOUL BROTHERS SIX

Title	Format	Label	Number	Year	Price	Notes
Some Kind Of Wonderful	7"	Atlantic	584118	1967	**£4**	

SOUL CITY

Title	Format	Label	Number	Year	Price	Notes
Everybody Dance Now	7"	Cameo Park.	C103	1962	**£12**	

SOUL CITY EXECUTIVES

Title	Format	Label	Cat. No.	Year	Price	Notes
Happy Chatter	7"	Soul City	SC109		**£4**	
Happy Chatter	7"	Soul City	SC109		**£12**	demo

SOUL CLAN

Title	Format	Label	Cat. No.	Year	Price	Notes
Soul Meeting	7"	Atlantic	584202	1968	**£4**	

SOUL LEADERS

Title	Format	Label	Cat. No.	Year	Price	Notes
Pour On The Sauce	7"	Rio	R134	196-	**£8**	

SOUL PURPOSE

Title	Format	Label	Cat. No.	Year	Price	Notes
Hummin'	7"	Island	WIP6040	1968	**£10**	

SOUL SISTERS

Title	Format	Label	Cat. No.	Year	Price	Notes
Good Time Tonight	7"	London	HLC9970	1965	**£12**	
I Can't Stand It	7"	Sue	WI312	1964	**£12**	
Loop De Loop	7"	Sue	WI336	1964	**£15**	
Soul Sisters	LP	Sue	ILP913	1964	**£20**	

SOUL SISTERS

Title	Format	Label	Cat. No.	Year	Price	Notes
Wreck A Buddy	7"	Amalgamated	AMG839	196-	**£10**	

SOUL SOUNDS

"Soul Survival" is an album of R&B instrumentals played by various ex-Savages and Rebel Rousers. Soul Sounds was not a working group, but the musicians could play this kind of music with one arm tied behind their backs (well, perhaps not quite!) and the record is a convincing addition to the genre, if a little out-of-date for 1967.

Title	Format	Label	Cat. No.	Year	Price	Notes
Soul Survival	LP	Columbia	SX6158	1967	**£15**	

SOUL STIRRERS

Title	Format	Label	Cat. No.	Year	Price	Notes
Soul Stirrers Featuring Sam Cooke	LP	London	HAU8232	1965	**£20**	

SOUL SURVIVORS

Title	Format	Label	Cat. No.	Year	Price	Notes
Explosion	7"	Stateside	SS2094	1968	**£4**	
Expressway To Your Heart	7"	Stateside	SS2057	1967	**£4**	
Mama Soul	7"	Atlantic	584275	1969	**£4**	

SOUL VENDORS

Title	Format	Label	Cat. No.	Year	Price	Notes
On Tour	LP	Coxsone	CSL8010	196-	**£80**	

SOUL, JIMMY

Title	Format	Label	Cat. No.	Year	Price	Notes
If You Wanna Be Happy	LP	SPQR	E16001	1963	**£20**	US
If You Wanna Be Happy	7" EP	Stateside	SE1010	1964	**£5**	
If You Wanna Be Happy	7"	Stateside	SS178	1963	**£4**	
Jimmy Soul And The Belmonts	LP	Spinorama	123	1963	**£10**	US

SOULFUL STRINGS

Title	Format	Label	Cat. No.	Year	Price	Notes
Burning Spear	7"	Chess	CRS8068	1967	**£10**	
I Wish It Would Rain	7"	Chess	CRS8094	1969	**£5**	

SOULMATES

Title	Format	Label	Cat. No.	Year	Price	Notes
Bring Your Love Back Home	7"	Parlophone	R5407	1966	**£6**	
Is That You	7"	Parlophone	R5601	1967	**£6**	
Mood Melancholy	7"	Parlophone	R5506	1966	**£8**	
Too Late To Say You're Sorry	7"	Parlophone	R5334	1965	**£6**	

SOULMATES (2)

Title	Format	Label	Cat. No.	Year	Price	Notes
On The Move	7"	Amalgamated	AMG842	196-	**£10**	
Them A Laugh And A Ki Ki	7"	Amalgamated	AMG836	196-	**£10**	

SOUND

Title	Format	Label	Cat. No.	Year	Price	Notes
Heyday	7"	Korova	KOW10	1980	**£4**	
Physical World	7"	Tortch	TOR003	1979	**£20**	
Sense Of Purpose	7"	Korova	KOW21	1981	**£4**	
Sense Of Purpose	12"	Korova	KOW21T	1981	**£6**	
Sound	LP	Tortch	TOR008		**£12**	

SOUND DIMENSION

Title	Format	Label	Cat. No.	Year	Price	Notes
More Scorcia	7"	Coxsone	CS7093	196-	**£10**	
Scorcia	7"	Coxsone	CS7083	196-	**£10**	
Soul Trombone	7"	Coxsone	CS7085	196-	**£10**	
Soulful Strut	7"	Coxsone	CS7090	196-	**£10**	
Time Is Tight	7"	Coxsone	CS7097	196-	**£10**	

SOUND SIXTY-SIX

Flight 4864	7"	Decca	F12323	1966	**£5**	

SOUND SYSTEM

You Don't Know Like I Know	7"	Island	WI258	1965	**£10**	

SOUNDS INCORPORATED

Emily	7"	Parlophone	R4815	1961	**£6**	
Go	7"	Decca	F11590	1963	**£5**	
I'm Coming Through	7"	Columbia	DB7737	1965	**£4**	
Keep Moving	7"	Decca	F11723	1963	**£6**	
My Little Red Book	7"	Columbia	DB7676	1965	**£4**	
Sounds Incorporated	LP	Columbia	SCX3531	1964	**£10**	
Sounds Incorporated	LP	Studio Two	TWO144	1966	**£10**	
Sounds Like Locomotion	7"	Decca	F11540	1962	**£4**	
Spanish Harlem	7"	Columbia	DB7321	1964	**£4**	chart single
Spartans	7"	Columbia	DB7239	1964	**£4**	chart single
Time For You	7"	Columbia	DB7545	1965	**£4**	
Top Gear	7" EP	Columbia	SEG8360	1964	**£6**	
William Tell	7"	Columbia	DB7404	1964	**£4**	

SOUNDS NICE

Love At First Sight	LP	Parlophone	PCS7089	1969	**£12**	
Love At First Sight	7"	Parlophone	R5797	1969	**£4**	chart single

SOUNDS SENSATIONAL

Love In The Open Air	7"	HMV	POP1584	1967	**£8**	

SOUP

Soup	LP	Arf Arm	1	1970	**£25**	US, insert but no cover
Soup Album	LP	Big Tree	2007	1971	**£10**	US

SOUP DRAGONS

Can't Take No More	12"	Raw TV Prod.	RTVL123	1987	**£6**	4 tracks
Deep Trash (Lovegod)	cass	Raw TV Prod.		1989	**£12**	
Hang Ten	7"	Raw TV Prod.	RTV1	1986	**£5**	red or blue vinyl
Hang Ten	12"	Raw TV Prod.	RTV121	1986	**£6**	
If You Were The Only Girl In The World	7"			1985	**£5**	flexi
Soft As Your Face/Can't Take No More	12"	Raw TV Prod.	RTV124D	1987	**£6**	double groove
Sun Is In The Sky	7"	Subway	SUBWAY2	1986	**£25**	

SOUP GREENS

Like A Rolling Stone	7"	Stateside	SS457	1965	**£15**	

SOUTH, JOE

Birds Of A Feather	7"	Capitol	CL15535	1968	**£4**	
Birds Of A Feather	7"	Capitol	CL15602	1969	**£4**	
Clock Up On The Wall	7"	Capitol	CL15636	1970	**£4**	
Concrete Jungle	7"	MGM	MGM1267	1965	**£5**	
Don't It Make You Wanna Go Home	7"	Capitol	CL15608	1969	**£6**	
Don't Throw Your Love To The Wind	7"	Capitol	CL15568	1968	**£4**	
Games People Play	7"	Capitol	CL15579	1969	**£4**	chart single
Hush	7"	Capitol	CL15666	1970	**£4**	
I Want To Be Somebody	7"	HMV	POP1474	1965	**£5**	
Introspect	LP	Capitol	EST108	1968	**£10**	
Leanin' On You	7"	Capitol	CL15594	1969	**£4**	
Masquerade	7"	Oriole	CB1752	1962	**£6**	
Walk A Mile In My Shoes	7"	Capitol	CL15625	1970	**£4**	

SOUTHERN COMFORT

Frog City	LP	Harvest	SHSP4012	1971	**£10**	
I Sure Like Your Smile	7"	Harvest	HAR5039	1971	**£4**	
Morning Has Broken	7"	Harvest	HAR5047	1971	**£4**	
Southern Comfort	LP	Harvest	SHVL799	1971	**£10**	
Stir Don't Shake	LP	Harvest	SHSP4021	1972	**£10**	
Wedding Song	7"	Harvest	HAR5054	1972	**£4**	
Willie Hurricane	7"	Harvest	HAR5035	1971	**£4**	

SOUTHERN SOUND

Just The Same As You	7"	Columbia	DB7982	1966	**£60**	

SOUTHERN, JERI

Fire Down Below	7"	Brunswick	05665	1957	**£4**	chart single
I Waited So Long	7"	Brunswick	05737	1958	**£4**	
Jeri Southern At The Crescendo	LP	Capitol	T1278	1960	**£12**	US
Jeri Southern Gently Jumps	LP	Decca	DL8472	1957	**£12**	US
Jeri Southern Meets Cole Porter	LP	Capitol	T1173	1959	**£12**	US
Man That Got Away	7"	Brunswick	05367	1955	**£4**	
Occasional Man	7"	Brunswick	05490	1955	**£4**	
Prelude To A Kiss	LP	Decca	DL8745	1958	**£12**	US
Remind Me	7"	Brunswick	05343	1954	**£4**	
Scarlet Ribbons	7"	Brunswick	05709	1957	**£4**	
Southern Hospitality	LP	Decca	DL8761	1958	**£12**	US
Warm	LP-10"	Decca	DL5331		**£15**	US
When Your Heart's On Fire	LP	Decca	DL8394	1957	**£12**	US
Where Walks My True Love	7"	Brunswick	05529	1956	**£4**	
You Better Go Now	LP	Decca	DL8214	1956	**£12**	US

SOUTHLANDERS

Ain't That A Shame	7"	Parlophone	MSP6182	1955	**£12**	
Alone	7"	Decca	F10946	1957	**£4**	chart single
Choo-Choo-Choo Cha-Cha-Cha	7"	Decca	F11067	1958	**£4**	
Down Deep	7"	Decca	F11014	1958	**£4**	
Hush A Bye Rock	7"	Parlophone	MSP6236	1956	**£6**	
Peanuts	7"	Decca	F10958	1957	**£4**	
Put A Light In The Window	7"	Decca	F10982	1958	**£4**	
Southlanders No.1	7" EP	Decca	DFE6508	1958	**£8**	
Torero	7"	Decca	F11032	1958	**£4**	

SOUTHSIDE JOHNNY & THE ASBURY DUKES

Little Girl So Fine	7"	Epic	EPC5230	1977	**£10**	
Live At The Bottom Line	LP	Epic	AS275	1976	**£15**	US promo

SOUTHWEST F.O.B.

Smell Of Incense	LP	Hip	HIS7001	1969	**£15**	US
Smell Of Incense	7"	Stax	STAX107	1968	**£4**	

SOUTHWIND

Boogie Woogie Country Girl	7"	Harvest	HAR5019	1970	**£5**	

SOVINE, RED

Country Music	7" EP	Top Rank	JKP3015	1962	**£5**	
I Didn't Jump The Fence	LP	London	HAB8343	1967	**£10**	
One And Only Red Sovine	LP	Starday	SLP132	1961	**£10**	US
Red Sovine	LP	MGM	E3465	1957	**£15**	US
Sixteen Tons	7"	Brunswick	05513	1956	**£12**	

SOXX, BOB B. & THE BLUE JEANS

Not Too Young To Get Married	7"	London	HLU9754	1963	**£5**	
Why Do Lovers Break Each Others' Hearts	7"	London	HLU9694	1963	**£6**	
Zip A Dee Doo Dah	LP	London	HAU8121	1963	**£30**	
Zip A Dee Doo Dah	7"	London	HLU9646	1963	**£4**	chart single
Zip A Dee Doo Dah	LP	Philles	PHLP4002	1963	**£80**	US

SPACE

Just Blue	LP	Pye		1979	**£20**	pic disc

SPACE (2)

Space	LP	Hand	5167	1969	**£15**	US

SPACEMEN

Clouds	7"	Top Rank	JAR228	1959	**£4**	
Music For Batman And Robin	LP	Roulette	MG25322	1966	**£12**	US
Rockin' In The 25th Century	LP	Roulette	MG25275	1964	**£10**	US

SPANDAU BALLET

Communication	7"	Chrysalis	CHSP2668	1983	**£4**	pic disc
Lifeline	7"	Chrysalis	CHSP2642	1982	**£4**	pic disc
Round And Round	12"	Chrysalis	SPAN6	1984	**£6**	gatefold, with booklet
Round And Round	12"	Chrysalis	SPAN6	1984	**£6**	with poster, sticker, postcard, 5 photos
Through The Barricades	CD-s	CBS		1986	**£15**	promo

Title	Format	Label	Cat. No.	Year	Price	Notes
True	LP	Mobile Fid.	MFSL1152	1984	**£10**	US audiophile

SPANIELS

Title	Format	Label	Cat. No.	Year	Price	Notes
Goodnite, It's Time To Go	LP	Vee Jay	LP1002	1958	**£180**	US
Spaniels	LP	Vee Jay	LP1024	1960	**£75**	US

SPANISH BOYS

Title	Format	Label	Cat. No.	Year	Price	Notes
I Am Alone	7"	Blue Beat	BB331	1965	**£10**	

SPANISHTOWN SKABEATS

Title	Format	Label	Cat. No.	Year	Price	Notes
Oh My Baby	7"	Blue Beat	BB315	1964	**£10**	
Solomon	7"	Blue Beat	BB320	1964	**£10**	

SPANKY & OUR GANG

Title	Format	Label	Cat. No.	Year	Price	Notes
Lazy Day	7"	Mercury	MF1010	1967	**£4**	
Like To Get To Know You	LP	Mercury	SMCL20121	1968	**£12**	
Like To Get To Know You	7"	Mercury	MF1023	1968	**£4**	
Live	LP	Mercury	SR61326	1970	**£12**	US
Spank's Greatest Hits	LP	Mercury	SR61227	1970	**£10**	US
Spanky & Our Gang	LP	Mercury	SMCL20114	1967	**£12**	
Sunday Morning	7"	Mercury	MF1018	1968	**£4**	
Without Rhyme Or Reason	LP	Mercury	SR61183	1968	**£12**	US

SPANN, OTIS

Title	Format	Label	Cat. No.	Year	Price	Notes
Bloody Murder	7"	Blue Horizon	573142	1968	**£10**	
Blues Are Where It's At	LP	HMV	CSD3609	1963	**£20**	
Blues Never Die	LP	Stateside	SL10169	1966	**£15**	
Blues Of Otis Spann	LP	Decca	LK4615	1964	**£15**	
Bottom Of The Blues	LP	Stateside	SL10255	1968	**£15**	
Cracked Spanner Head	LP	Deram	SML1036	1969	**£15**	
Cryin' Time	LP	Vanguard	VSD6514	1970	**£12**	
Fathers And Sons	LP	Chess	CRLS4556	1969	**£15**	
Nobody Knows My Troubles	LP	Polydor	545030	1967	**£15**	
Otis Spann Is The Blues	LP	Candid	CJS9001	1960	**£35**	US
Portrait In Blues	LP	Storyville	SLP157	1963	**£15**	
Stirs Me Up	7"	Decca	F11972	1964	**£8**	
Walking Blues	LP	Epic	64888	1972	**£12**	

SPANN, OTIS & MEMPHIS SLIM

Title	Format	Label	Cat. No.	Year	Price	Notes
Piano Blues	LP	Storyville	SLP168	196-	**£15**	

SPANN, OTIS WITH FLEETWOOD MAC

Title	Format	Label	Cat. No.	Year	Price	Notes
Biggest Thing Since Colossus	LP	Blue Horizon	763217	1969	**£40**	
Walkin'	7"	Blue Horizon	573155	1969	**£15**	

SPARKERS

Title	Format	Label	Cat. No.	Year	Price	Notes
Dip It Up	7"	Blue Cat	BS155	196-	**£10**	

SPARKS

Title	Format	Label	Cat. No.	Year	Price	Notes
Girl From Germany	7"	Bearsville	K15516	1974	**£4**	
Introducing Sparks	LP	Columbia	PC34901	1976	**£30**	US red vinyl promo
Wonder Girl	7"	Bearsville	K15505	1972	**£6**	

SPARROW

Title	Format	Label	Cat. No.	Year	Price	Notes
Carnival Boycott	7"	Kalypso	XX10	196-	**£6**	
Clara Honey Bunch	7"	Melodisc	CAL17	196-	**£6**	
Goaty	7"	Melodisc	CAL18	196-	**£6**	
Leading Calypsonians	7"	Melodisc	CAL15	196-	**£6**	
Party With The Sparrow	7" EP	Melodisc	XXEP3	196-	**£6**	
Sack	7"	Kalypso	XX17	196-	**£6**	

SPARROW (2)

Title	Format	Label	Cat. No.	Year	Price	Notes
Tomorrow's Ship	7"	CBS	202342	1966	**£10**	

SPARROW, JACK

Title	Format	Label	Cat. No.	Year	Price	Notes
Ice Water	7"	Doctor Bird	DB1005	1966	**£10**	
More Ice Water	7"	Doctor Bird	DB1027	1966	**£10**	

SPARROWS

Title	Format	Label	Cat. No.	Year	Price	Notes
Mersey Sound	LP	Elkay	3009	1964	**£15**	US

SPARTANS

Can You Waddle?	7"	Stateside	SS117	1962	**£4**	

SPEAR OF DESTINY

All My Love	12"	Epic	QTA6333	1985	**£6**	5 tracks
Come Back	12"	Epic	DTA6445	1985	**£8**	double
Flying Scotsman	7"	Epic	SPEAR1	1983	**£5**	
Flying Scotsman	12"	Epic	SPEAR131	1983	**£6**	
Flying Scotsman	12"	Epic	SPEAR131	1983	**£8**	with poster
Liberator	7"	Epic	A4310	1984	**£5**	chart single
Liberator	12"	Epic	TA4310	1984	**£8**	
Prisoner Of Love	7"	Epic	A4068	1984	**£4**	
Prisoner Of Love	7"	Epic	DA4068	1984	**£8**	double
Prisoner Of Love	7"	Epic	TA4068	1984	**£4**	chart single
So In Love With You	7"	10		1988	**£4**	boxed
Strangers In Our Town	12"	10	TENX148	1987	**£6**	double
Traveller	7"	10	TEN189	1987	**£4**	with lyrics, patch, sticker, boxed
Wheel	7"	Epic	A3372	1983	**£4**	chart single
Wheel	7"	Epic	DA3372	1983	**£10**	double
Wheel	7"	Epic	WA3372	1983	**£8**	pic disc
Wheel	12"	Epic	TA3372	1983	**£8**	

SPEAR, ROGER RUSKIN

Electric Shocks	LP	United Artists	UAS29508	1972	**£15**	
I Love To Bumpity Bump	7"	United Artists	UP35720	1974	**£4**	
On Her Doorstep Last Night	7"	United Artists	UP35683	1974	**£4**	
Rebel Trouser	7"	United Artists	UP35221	1971	**£5**	
Unusual	LP	United Artists	UAG29381	1972	**£15**	

SPECIALS

Do Nothing	7"	2-Tone	CHSTT16	1980	**£4**	paper label, chart single
Gangsters	7"	2-Tone	TT1/TT2	1979	**£4**	paper label, chart single
Message To You Rudy	7"	2-Tone	CHSTT5	1979	**£4**	paper label, chart single
Rat Race	7"	2-Tone	CHSTT11	1980	**£4**	paper label, chart single
Stereotype	7"	2-Tone	CHSTT13	1980	**£4**	paper label, chart single
Too Much Too Young	7"	2-Tone	CHSTT7	1980	**£4**	chart single

SPECKLED RED

Dirty Dozen	LP	Storyville	SLP117	196-	**£10**	
Storyville Blues Anthology Vol.4	7" EP	Storyville	SEP384		**£6**	

SPECTOR, PHIL

Despite the growing importance in the late eighties of record producers as artists, Phil Spector is still the only producer with the status of a star. His Christmas album, released a number of times over the years, is the perfect seasonal recording. Various of the artists associated with Spector are given traditional songs to peform (none of them carols, interestingly) and surrounded by dense arrangements that stay just on the right side of mawkishness.

Christmas Album	LP	Apple	APCOR24	1972	**£20**	chart LP
Christmas Gift For You	LP	London	HAU8141	1963	**£50**	
Christmas Gift For You	LP	Philles	PHLP4005	1963	**£35**	US blue label
Christmas Gift For You	LP	Philles	PHLP4005	1964	**£15**	US yellow label
Presents Today's Hits	LP	Philles	PHLP4004	1963	**£50**	US

SPECTOR, RONNIE

Try Some Buy Some	7"	Apple	33	1971	**£4**	
Try Some Buy Some	7"	Apple	33	1971	**£10**	PS

SPECTRES

The three singles recorded by the Spectres are the first releases by the group that was eventually to gain international success as Status Quo.

Hurdy Gurdy Man	7"	Piccadilly	7N35352	1966	**£120**	
I Who Have Nothing	7"	Piccadilly	7N35339	1966	**£120**	
We Ain't Got Nothin' Yet	7"	Piccadilly	7N35368	1967	**£120**	

SPECTRUM

Free	7"	RCA	RCA1853	1969	**£5**	
Glory	7"	RCA	RCA1883	1969	**£5**	
Headin' For A Heatwave	7"	RCA	RCA1651	1967	**£5**	
I'll Be Gone	7"	Parlophone	R5908	1971	**£8**	
Light Is Dark Enough	LP	RCA		1974	**£40**	
Little Girl	7"	Columbia	DB7742	1965	**£5**	

Ob La Di, Ob La Da	7"	RCA	RCA1775	1968	**£5**	
Portobello Road	7"	RCA	RCA1619	1967	**£5**	
Portobello Road	7"	RCA	RCA1976	1970	**£4**	
Saturday's Child	7"	RCA	RCA1589	1967	**£5**	
Tables And Chairs	7"	RCA	RCA1700	1968	**£5**	

SPEDDING, CHRIS

Backwoods Progression	LP	Harvest	SHSP4004	1970	**£15**	
Guitar Jamboree	7"	RAK	RAK236	1976	**£4**	
Jump In My Car	7"	RAK	RAK228	1976	**£4**	
Motor Bikin'	7"	RAK	RAK210	1975	**£4**	chart single
My Bucket's Got A Hole In It	7"	Island	WIP6225	1975	**£4**	
New Girl In The Neighbourhood	7"	RAK	RAK232	1976	**£4**	
Only Lick I Know	LP	Harvest	SHSP4017	1972	**£15**	
Pogo Dancing	7"	RAK	RAK246	1976	**£4**	
Rock'n'Roll Band	7"	Harvest	HAR5013	1970	**£5**	

SPELLBINDERS

Chain Reaction	7"	Direction	583970	1969	**£6**	
Help Me	7"	CBS	202453	1966	**£8**	
Since I Don't Have You	7"	CBS	2776	1967	**£4**	

SPELLMAN, BENNY

Lipstick Traces	7"	London	HLP9570	1962	**£12**	

SPENCE, SKIP

Oar	LP	Columbia	CS9831	1968	**£20**	US

SPENCER, DON

Busy Doing Nothing	7"	HMV	POP1186	1963	**£4**	
Fireball & Other Titles	7" EP	HMV	7EG8802	1963	**£12**	
Fireball	7"	HMV	POP1087	1962	**£8**	chart single
In My Life	7"	Fontana	TF701	1966	**£4**	
Why Don't They Understand	7"	Page One	POF006	1966	**£4**	

SPENCER, JEREMY

...And The Children	LP	CBS	65387	1973	**£15**	
Jeremy Spencer	LP	Reprise	K44105	1970	**£30**	
Linda	7"	Reprise	RS27002	1970	**£5**	

SPENCER, JO

Bed Of Roses	7"	Dynamic	DYN415	197-	**£4**	

SPENCER, SONNY

Oh Boy	7"	Parlophone	R4611	1959	**£8**	

SPERMULL

Spermull	LP	Brain		1973	**£40**	

SPHERICAL OBJECTS

Elliptical Optimism	LP	Object	OBJ004	1979	**£10**	
Further Ellipses	LP	Object	OBJ012	1980	**£10**	
Kill	7"	Object	OM01	1978	**£4**	
No Man's Land	LP	Object	OBJ016	1980	**£10**	
Past And Parcel	LP	Object	OBJ001	1978	**£10**	
Seventies Romance	7"	Object	OM04	1978	**£4**	

SPICE

What About The Music	7"	United Artists	UP2246	1968	**£10**	

SPIDELLS

Find Out What's Happening	7"	Sue	WI4019	1966	**£8**	

SPIDER

Comedown Song	7"	Decca	F12430	1966	**£8**	

SPIDERS

I Didn't Wanna Do It	LP	Imperial	LP9140	1961	**£100**	US

SPIDERS FROM MARS

Limbo	7"	Pye	7N45578	1976	**£4**	
Spiders From Mars	LP	Pye	NSPL18479	1976	**£12**	

Title	Format	Label	Cat. No.	Year	Price	Notes
White Man Black Man	7"	Pye	7N45549	1975	**£4**	

SPINNERS

Title	Format	Label	Cat. No.	Year	Price	Notes
Heebie Jeebies	7"	Columbia	DB4693	1961	**£100**	
Original Spinners	LP	Motown	639	1967	**£15**	US
Party My Pad	LP	Time	52092	1963	**£40**	US
Second Time Around	LP	VIP	405	1970	**£10**	US
Sweet Thing	7"	T. Motown	TMG514	1965	**£90**	demo only

SPIRAL STAIRCASE

Title	Format	Label	Cat. No.	Year	Price	Notes
Baby What I Mean	7"	CBS	3507	1968	**£8**	
More Today Than Yesterday	7"	CBS	4187	1969	**£15**	
No One For Me To Turn To	7"	CBS	4524	1969	**£15**	

SPIRALS

Title	Format	Label	Cat. No.	Year	Price	Notes
Rocking Cow	7"	Capitol	CL14958	1958	**£8**	

SPIRIT

Title	Format	Label	Cat. No.	Year	Price	Notes
12 Dreams Of Dr.Sardonicus	LP	Epic	64191	1970	**£10**	
1984	7"	CBS	4773	1970	**£6**	
Animal Zoo	7"	CBS	5149	1970	**£6**	
Cadillac Cowboys	7"	Epic	EPC8083	1972	**£4**	
Clear	LP	CBS	63729	1969	**£12**	
Dark Eyed Woman	7"	CBS	4511	1969	**£5**	
Dark Eyed Woman	7"	CBS	4565	1969	**£5**	
Family That Plays Together	LP	CBS	63523	1968	**£12**	
Feedback	LP	Epic	64507	1971	**£10**	
Highlights Of Spirit Of '76	LP	Mercury	001	1976	**£15**	promo
I Got A Line On You	7"	CBS	3880	1969	**£6**	
Midnight Train	7"	Illegal	SFI326	1978	**£4**	flexi
Mr.Skin	7"	Epic	EPC7082	1973	**£4**	
Potatoland	LP	Beggars B.	BEGA23	1981	**£10**	with cartoon book
Potatoland	LP	Rhino		1981	**£10**	1 sided interview promo
Spirit	LP	CBS	63278	1968	**£12**	
Spirit Of '76	LP	Mercury	6672012	1975	**£15**	double
Uncle Jack	7"	CBS	3523	1968	**£6**	

SPIRIT OF JOHN MORGAN

Title	Format	Label	Cat. No.	Year	Price	Notes
Age Machine	LP	Carnaby	CNLS6007	1970	**£50**	
Kaleidoscope	LP	Carnaby	6302010	1972	**£50**	
Spirit Of John Morgan	LP	Carnaby	CNLS6002	1969	**£50**	
Train For All Reasons	7"	Carnaby	CNS4005	1969	**£15**	

SPIROGYRA

Title	Format	Label	Cat. No.	Year	Price	Notes
Bells Boots & Shambles	LP	Polydor	2310246	1973	**£70**	
Dangerous Dave	7"	Pegasus	PGS3	1972	**£10**	
Old Boot Wine	LP	Pegasus	PEG13	1972	**£35**	
St.Radigunds	LP	B&C	CAS1042	1971	**£30**	

SPIVEY, VICTORIA

Title	Format	Label	Cat. No.	Year	Price	Notes
Treasures Of North American Negro Music No.5	7" EP	Fontana	TFE17264	1960	**£6**	
Victoria Spivey	7" EP	HMV	7EG8190	195-	**£6**	

SPIZZ ENERGI

Title	Format	Label	Cat. No.	Year	Price	Notes
Soldier Soldier	7"	Rough Trade	RTS03	1979	**£4**	
Where's Captain Kirk?	7"	Rough Trade	RTS04	1979	**£6**	

SPIZZ OIL

Title	Format	Label	Cat. No.	Year	Price	Notes
6,000 Crazy	7"	Rough Trade	RTS01	1978	**£4**	
Cold City	7"	Rough Trade	RTS02	1979	**£4**	

SPLINTER

Title	Format	Label	Cat. No.	Year	Price	Notes
Harder To Live	LP	Dark Horse	AMLH22006	1975	**£10**	
Place I Love	LP	Dark Horse	AMLH22001	1974	**£10**	

SPLIT ENZ

Title	Format	Label	Cat. No.	Year	Price	Notes
True Colours	LP	A&M	AMLH64822	1980	**£12**	laser etched

SPOELSTRA, MARK

Title	Format	Label	Cat. No.	Year	Price	Notes
5 & 20 Questions	LP	Elektra	EKL283	1965	**£15**	
Mark Spoelstra	LP	CBS	9793	1969	**£12**	

State Of Mind .... LP .... Elektra .... EKL307 .... 1966 .... **£15**

SPOKESMEN

Dawn Of Correction .... 7" .... Brunswick .... 05941 .... 1965 .... **£4**
Dawn Of Correction .... LP .... Decca .... DL4712 .... 1965 .... **£12** .... US
It Ain't Fair .... 7" .... Brunswick .... 05948 .... 1965 .... **£4**
Michelle .... 7" .... Brunswick .... 05950 .... 1966 .... **£4**
Today's The Day .... 7" .... Brunswick .... 05958 .... 1966 .... **£4**

SPONTANEOUS COMBUSTION

Gay Time Night .... 7" .... Harvest .... HAR5060 .... 1972 .... **£8**
Leaving .... 7" .... Harvest .... HAR5046 .... 1971 .... **£8**
Sabre Dance .... 7" .... Harvest .... HAR5066 .... 1973 .... **£8**
Spontaneous Combustion .... LP .... Harvest .... SHVL801 .... 1972 .... **£25**
Triad .... LP .... Harvest .... SHVL805 .... 1972 .... **£25**

SPONTANEOUS MUSIC ENSEMBLE

Birds Of A Feather .... LP .... Byg .... 529023 .... 1972 .... **£20** .... French
Bobby Bradford And The SME .... LP .... Freedom .... SLP40111 .... 1974 .... **£20**
Challenge .... LP .... Eyemark .... EMPL1002 .... 1966 .... **£50**
For CND For Peace And You To Share . LP .... A Records .... 1970 .... **£30**
Karyobin .... LP .... Island .... ILPS9079 .... 1968 .... **£30**
Oliv .... LP .... Marmalade .... 608008 .... 1969 .... **£30**
So What Do You Think .... LP .... Tangent .... TGS118 .... 1971 .... **£20**
Source From & Towards .... LP .... Tangent .... TNGS107 .... 1971 .... **£20**

SPOOKY TOOTH

It's All About .... LP .... Island .... ILPS9080 .... 1968 .... **£20**
Last Puff .... LP .... Island .... ILPS9117 .... 1970 .... **£15**
Love Really Changed Me .... 7" .... Island .... WIP6037 .... 1968 .... **£8**
Mirror .... LP .... Goodear .... EARL2001 .... 1974 .... **£10**
Son Of Your Father .... 7" .... Island .... WIP6060 .... 1969 .... **£6**
Spooky Two .... LP .... Island .... ILPS9098 .... 1969 .... **£20**
Sunshine Help Me .... 7" .... Island .... WIP6022 .... 1967 .... **£8**
Weight .... 7" .... Island .... WIP6046 .... 1968 .... **£6**
Witness .... LP .... Island .... ILPS9255 .... 1973 .... **£10**
You Broke My Heart... .... LP .... Island .... ILPS9227 .... 1973 .... **£10**

SPOOKY TOOTH & PIERRE HENRY

Ceremony .... LP .... Island .... ILPS9107 .... 1969 .... **£15**

SPORTS

Who Listens To The Radio .... 7" .... Stiff .... AUS1 .... 197- .... **£8** .... promo

SPOTLIGHTERS

Please Be My Girlfriend .... 7" .... Vogue .... V9130 .... 1959 .... **£40**

SPOTNICKS

The Spotniks were Sweden's answer to the Shadows (and are still playing in fact). The lead guitarist was impressive in a Hank Marvinish sort of way, and the two singles "Orange Blossom Special" and "Rocket Man" (which also turn up on the EP "On The Air" and on the LP "Out-a Space") are as good as anything produced by the English group. The Spotniks also had two gimmicks - they performed wearing rather unserviceable-looking space suits, and they used radio controlled guitars rather than electric leads, although the equipment tended to be somewhat temperamental!

Anna .... 7" .... Oriole .... CB1886 .... 1963 .... **£4**
Donner Wetter .... 7" .... Oriole .... CB1981 .... 1964 .... **£4**
Hava Nagila .... 7" .... Oriole .... CB1790 .... 1963 .... **£4** .... chart single
In Paris .... LP .... Oriole .... PS40040 .... 1963 .... **£12**
Just Listen To My Heart .... 7" .... Oriole .... CB1818 .... 1963 .... **£4** .... chart single
Lovesick Blues .... 7" .... Oriole .... CB1953 .... 1964 .... **£4**
On The Air .... 7" EP .... Oriole .... EP7075 .... 1963 .... **£6**
Orange Blossom Special .... 7" .... Oriole .... CB1724 .... 1962 .... **£4** .... chart single
Out-a Space/In London .... LP .... Oriole .... PS40036 .... 1962 .... **£10** .... chart LP
Rocket Man .... 7" .... Oriole .... CB1755 .... 1962 .... **£4** .... chart single
Spotnicks At The Olympia Paris .... 7" EP .... Oriole .... EP7079 .... 1964 .... **£6**
Spotnicks In Berlin .... LP .... Oriole .... PS40064 .... 1965 .... **£15**
Spotnicks In Paris .... 7" EP .... Oriole .... EP7078 .... 1964 .... **£6**
Spotnicks In Spain .... LP .... Oriole .... PS40054 .... 1964 .... **£15**
Valentina .... 7" .... Oriole .... CB1844 .... 1963 .... **£4**

SPRATT, JACK

Give Me Your Love .... 7" .... Coxsone .... CS7100 .... 196- **£10**

SPREADEAGLE

How Can We Be Lost	7"	Charisma	CB183	1972	**£4**	
Nightingale Lane	7"	Charisma	BCP7	197-	**£4**	PS
Piece Of Paper	LP	Charisma	CAS1055	1972	**£15**	

SPRIGUNS

Magic Lady	LP	Banshee	BAN1101	1979	**£15**	
Nothing Else To Do	7"	Decca	F13676	1976	**£5**	
Revel Weird And Wild	LP	Decca	SKL5262	1976	**£20**	
Time Will Pass	LP	Decca	SKL5286	1977	**£20**	
White Witch	7"	Decca	F13739	1977	**£5**	

SPRIGUNS OF TOLGUS

Jack With A Feather	LP	Alidai Star		1973	**£350**	

SPRING

Spring	LP	Neon	NE6	1971	**£100**	double

SPRINGBOARD

Springboard	LP	Polydor		1969	**£30**	

SPRINGFIELD, DUSTY

All I See Is You	7"	Philips	BF1510	1966	**£5**	PS, chart single
Am I The Same Girl	7"	Philips	BF1811	1969	**£4**	chart single
Brand New Me	7"	Philips	BF1826	1969	**£4**	
Cameo	LP	Philips	6308152	1973	**£10**	
Dusty	7" EP	Philips	BE12564	1964	**£6**	
Dusty Definitely	LP	Philips	SBL7864	1968	**£12**	chart LP
Dusty In Memphis	LP	Philips	SBL7889	1969	**£12**	
Dusty In New York	7" EP	Philips	BE12572	1965	**£6**	
Dusty Springfield	LP	W. Rec. Club	ST848	1968	**£12**	
Everything Is Coming Up Dusty	LP	Philips	SBL1002	1965	**£12**	chart LP
From Dusty With Love	LP	Philips	SBL7927	1970	**£10**	chart LP
Girl Called Dusty	LP	Philips	BL7594	1964	**£12**	chart LP
Give Me Time	7"	Philips	BF1577	1967	**£4**	chart single
Going Back	7"	Philips	BF1502	1966	**£4**	chart single
Hits Of Dusty Springfield	cass-s	Philips	MCP100	1968	**£10**	
Hits Of The Walker Brothers & Dusty Springfield	cass-s	Philips	MCP1004	1968	**£10**	
How Can I Be Sure	7"	Philips	6006045	1970	**£4**	chart single
I Close My Eyes And Count To Ten	7"	Philips	BF1682	1968	**£4**	chart single
I Just Don't Know What To Do With Myself	7"	Philips	BF1348	1964	**£4**	chart single
I Only Want To Be With You	7"	Philips	BF1292	1963	**£4**	chart single
I Only Want To Be With You	7" EP	Philips	BE12560	1964	**£6**	
I Will Come To You	7"	Philips	BF1706	1968	**£4**	
I'll Try Anything	7"	Philips	BF1553	1967	**£4**	chart single
If You Go Away	7" EP	Philips	BE12605	1968	**£6**	
In The Middle Of Nowhere	7"	Philips	BF1418	1965	**£4**	chart single
Learn To Say Goodbye	7"	Philips	6006325	1974	**£4**	
Little By Little	7"	Philips	BF1466	1966	**£4**	chart single
Losing You	7"	Philips	BF1369	1964	**£4**	chart single
Mademoiselle Dusty	7" EP	Philips	BE12579	1965	**£6**	
Oh Holy Child	7"	Philips	BF1381	1964	**£6**	PS
See All Her Faces	LP	Philips	6308117	1972	**£10**	
Sheer Magic	LP	Audio Club	6856020	1972	**£10**	
Some Of Your Loving	7"	Philips	6006151	1971	**£4**	
Some Of Your Loving	7"	Philips	BF1430	1965	**£4**	chart single
Son Of A Preacher Man	7"	Philips	BF1730	1968	**£4**	chart single
Star Dusty	LP	Audio Club	6850002	1972	**£10**	
Stay Awhile	7"	Philips	BF1313	1964	**£4**	chart single
Warten Und Hoffen	7"	Philips		1964	**£12**	German
What's It Gonna Be	7"	Philips	6006350	1974	**£4**	
What's It Gonna Be	7"	Philips	BF1608	1967	**£4**	
Where Am I Going	LP	Philips	SBL7820	1967	**£12**	chart LP
Who Gets Your Love	7"	Philips	6006295	1973	**£4**	
Yesterday When I Was Young	7"	Philips	6006214	1972	**£4**	
You Don't Have To Say You Love Me	7"	Philips	BF1482	1966	**£4**	chart single
Your Hurtin' Kind Of Love	7"	Philips	BF1396	1965	**£4**	chart single

SPRINGFIELD, DUSTY & TOM

Morning Please Don't Come	7"	Philips	BF1835	1970	**£4**	

SPRINGFIELDS

Title	Format	Label	Cat. No.	Year	Price	Notes
Bambino	7"	Philips	BF1178	1961	**£4**	chart single
Breakaway	7"	Philips	BF1168	1961	**£4**	chart single
Christmas With The Springfields	7" EP	Woman's Own	P125	1962	**£6**	
Come On Home	7"	Philips	BF1263	1963	**£4**	chart single
Dear John	7"	Philips	BF1145	1961	**£4**	
Goodnight Irene	7"	Philips	BF1220	1962	**£4**	
Hit Sounds	7" EP	Philips	BE12538	1963	**£4**	
If I Was Down And Out	7"	Philips	BF1306	1964	**£4**	
Island Of Dreams	7"	Philips	326557BF	1962	**£4**	chart single
Kinda Folksy	LP	Philips	BBL7551	1961	**£10**	
Kinda Folksy No.1	7" EP	Philips	433622BE	1962	**£4**	
Kinda Folksy No.2	7" EP	Philips	433623BE	1962	**£4**	
Kinda Folksy No.3	7" EP	Philips	433624BE	1962	**£4**	
Say I Won't Be There	7"	Philips	326577BF	1963	**£4**	chart single
Silver Threads And Golden Needles	7"	Philips	BF1241	1962	**£4**	
Springfields	7" EP	Philips	BBE12476	1961	**£5**	
Springfields	7" EP	Philips	SBBE9068	1961	**£10**	stereo
Swahili Papa	7"	Philips	326536BF	1962	**£4**	

SPRINGSTEEN, BRUCE

Title	Format	Label	Cat. No.	Year	Price	Notes
As Requested Around The World	LP	Columbia	AS978	1981	**£25**	US promo sampler
Atlantic City	7"	CBS	A2794	1982	**£8**	demo
Badlands	7"	CBS	6532	1978	**£5**	
Badlands	7"	CBS	6532	1978	**£25**	demo
Born In The USA	LP	CBS	86304	1984	**£25**	demo
Born In The USA	LP	CBS	86304	1984	**£30**	pic disc
Born In The USA	7"	CBS			**£30**	5 track promo
Born To Run	LP	CBS	69170	1975	**£100**	demo
Born To Run	CD-s	CBS	BRUCEC2	1987	**£10**	
Born To Run	7"	CBS	3661	1975	**£4**	
Born To Run	7"	CBS	3661	1975	**£20**	demo
Born To Run	7"	CBS	BRUCEB2	1987	**£12**	2 X 7", boxed
Born To Run	48'	CBS		1975	**£75**	US unplayable promo!
Born To Run	LP	Columbia	HC43795	1980	**£30**	US audiophile
Born To Run	LP	Columbia	PC33795	1975	**£200**	US, cover titles in script
Cadillac Ranch	7"	CBS	A1557	1981	**£8**	demo
Cover Me	7"	CBS	DA4662	1984	**£6**	double
Cover Me	7"	CBS	WA4662	1984	**£15**	shaped pic disc, stand
Dancing In The Dark	7"	CBS	A4436	1984	**£8**	demo
Dancing In The Dark	7"	CBS	WA4436	1984	**£20**	shaped pic disc
Darkness On The Edge Of Town	LP	CBS	86061	1978	**£40**	demo
Darkness On The Edge Of Town	LP	Columbia	HC45318	1981	**£30**	US audiophile
Darkness On The Edge Of Town	LP	Columbia	PAL35318	1978	**£125**	US promo pic disc
Greetings From Asbury Park, N.J.	LP	CBS	65480	1973	**£12**	gatefold sleeve
Greetings From Asbury Park, N.J.	LP	CBS	65480	1973	**£200**	demo
Hungry Heart	7"	CBS	9309	1980	**£25**	demo
I'm On Fire	7"	CBS	WA6342	1985	**£10**	shaped pic disc
Interviews	7"	CBS		198-	**£12**	2 X 7", boxed
Live 1975-'85	LP	CBS	SAMP1104	1986	**£25**	promo
One Step Up	CD-s	CBS	6514422	1988	**£6**	
Open All Night (2 versions)	7"	CBS	A2969	1982	**£15**	promo
Promised Land	7"	CBS	6720	1978	**£5**	
Promised Land	7"	CBS	6720	1978	**£25**	demo
Prove It All Night	7"	CBS	6424	1978	**£4**	
Prove It All Night	7"	CBS	6424	1978	**£25**	demo
River	LP	CBS	88510	1980	**£30**	demo
River	7"	CBS	A1179	1981	**£8**	demo
River	12"	CBS	A121179	1981	**£15**	demo
Sherry Darling	7"	CBS	9568	1980	**£10**	demo
Sherry Darling/Independence Day	7"	CBS	9568	1980	**£60**	promo
Sherry Darling/Independence Day	7"	CBS	9568	1980	**£140**	promo, PS
Spare Parts	CD-s	CBS	BRUCEC4	1988	**£6**	
Spare Parts	CD-s	CBS	BRUCEC4	1988	**£20**	tin can
Tenth Avenue Freeze-Out	7"	CBS	3940	1976	**£5**	
Tenth Avenue Freeze-Out	7"	CBS	3940	1976	**£25**	demo
Tougher Than The Rest	CD-s	CBS	BRUCEC3	1988	**£6**	
Tunnel Of Love	LP	CBS	4602701	1987	**£10**	pic disc
Tunnel Of Love	CD	CBS	CDCBS4602792	1987	**£15**	pic disc
Tunnel Of Love	CD-s	CBS	6512952	1987	**£15**	
Wild, The Innocent & E Street Shuffle	LP	CBS	65780	1974	**£150**	demo

Wild,Innocent & E Street Shuffle .... LP........ CBS .... 65780 .... 1973...... **£15**...... yellow sleeve lettering

SPRINGSTEEN, BRUCE & OTHERS

Blinded By The Light .... 7" EP.... Columbia .... AS45................ 1973.... **£150**... US, with special sleeve, questionaire, booklet
Circus Song .... 7" EP.... Columbia .... AS52................ 1973.... **£250**... US, with special sleeve, questionaire, booklet
Rosalita .... 7" EP.... Columbia .... AS66................ 1973.... **£150**... US, with special sleeve, questionaire, booklet

SPROUD, BILLY & THE ROCK & ROLL SIX

Rock Mister Piper .... 7"........ Columbia .... DB3893 .... 1957 ...... **£8** ....

SPROUTS

Teen Billy Baby .... 7"........ RCA .... RCA1031........... 1958 ...... **£15** ....

SPUR

Spur Of The Moment .... LP........ Cinema .... **£50** .... US

SPYROGYRA

Morning Dance .... LP........ MCA.............. INF9004 .... 1979 ...... **£15** ...... US pic disc, 2 B-side designs

SPYS (XTC)

Young Ones .... 7"........ Virgin............ NB3 .... 1979 ...... **£5** ....

SQUAD

Out For Revenge .... LP........ Harvest .... 1979 ...... **£15** ....

SQUEEZE

Another Nail In My Heart .... 5' .... A&M .... 1981 ...... **£4** ....
Bang Bang .... 7"........ A&M .... AMS7360 .... 1978 ...... **£4** .... green vinyl
Black Coffee In Bed (2 versions) .... 7"........ A&M .... AMS8219DJ......... 1982 ...... **£5** .... promo
Christmas Day .... 7"........ A&M .... AMS7495 .... 1979 ...... **£4** .... white vinyl
Cool For Cats .... 7"........ A&M .... AMS7426 .... 1979 ...... **£4** .... brilliant pink vinyl
Cool For Cats .... 7"........ A&M .... AMS7426 .... 1979 ...... **£6** .... red vinyl
Cool For Cats .... 12"...... A&M .... AMSP7426........... 1979 ...... **£6** .... pink vinyl
East Side Story .... 12"...... A&M .... SAMP9.............. 1981 ...... **£8** .... promo sampler
Goodbye Girl .... 7"........ A&M .... AMS7398 .... 1978 ...... **£15** .... 3-D PS
Packet Of Three .... 7"........ Deptford F.C. .. DFC01 .... 1977 ...... **£5** ....
Packet Of Three .... 12"...... Deptford F.C. .. 01 .... 1977 ...... **£8** .... pink sleeve
Singles 45s And Under .... 7"........ A&M .... 1982 ...... **£5** .... 1 sided promo
Six Squeeze Songs Crammed On
To One Ten Inch Record .... LP-10" .. A&M .... SP3719 .... 1980 ...... **£10** .... US
Take Me I'm Yours .... 12"...... A&M .... AMSP7335.......... 1978 ...... **£6** ....
UK Squeeze .... LP........ A&M .... SP4687 .... 1978 ...... **£10** .... US red vinyl
When The Hangover Strikes .... 7"........ A&M .... AMS8237 .... 1982 ...... **£4** .... pic disc

SQUIRES

Pop The Question .... 7"........ Decca............ F12226.............. 1965 ...... **£4** ....

SRC

Black Sheep .... 7"........ Capitol........... CL15576............ 1969 ...... **£8** ....
Milestones .... LP........ Capitol........... ST134................ 1969 ...... **£30** ....
SRC .... LP........ Capitol........... ST2991.............. 1968 ...... **£30** ....
Traveller's Tale .... LP........ Capitol........... ST273................ 1970 ...... **£30** ....

ST.JOHN, BARRY

Bread And Butter .... 7"........ Decca............ F11975.............. 1964 ...... **£6** ....
Come Away Melinda .... 7"........ Columbia .... DB7783 .... 1965 ...... **£6** .... chart single
Cry Like A Baby .... 7"........ Major Minor..... MM587 .... 1969 ...... **£6** ....
Everything I Touch Turns To Tears ...... 7"........ Columbia .... DB7868 .... 1966 ...... **£20** ....
Hey Boy .... 7"........ Decca............ F12145.............. 1965 ...... **£5** ....
Little Bit Of Soap .... 7"........ Decca............ F11933.............. 1964 ...... **£6** ....
Mind How You Go .... 7"........ Decca............ F12111.............. 1965 ...... **£5** ....

ST.JOHN, BRIDGET

Ask Me No Questions .... LP........ Dandelion .... 62750 .... 1969 ...... **£15** ....
Fly High .... 7"........ Polydor.......... 2001280 .... 1972 ...... **£4** ....
If You've Got Money .... 7"........ W. Bros .... WB8019 .... 1970 ...... **£4** ....
Jumble Queen .... LP........ Chrysalis........ CHR1062 .... 1974 ...... **£10** ....

Nice	7"	Polydor	2001361	1972	**£4**	
Passing Thru'	7"	MCA	MU1203	1973	**£4**	
Songs For A Gentle Man	LP	Dandelion	DAN8007	1971	**£15**	
Thank You For	LP	Dandelion	2310193	1972	**£15**	
To B Without A Hitch	7"	Dandelion	K4404	1970	**£5**	

ST.JOHN, TAMMY

Boys	7"	Pye	7N15682	1964	**£4**	
Nobody Knows What's Goin' On	7"	Pye	7N17042	1966	**£15**	

ST.LOUIS JIMMY

Goin' Down Slow	LP	Bluesville	BV1028	1961	**£10**	US

ST.LOUIS UNION

Behind The Door	7"	Decca	F12386	1966	**£4**	
East Side Story	7"	Decca	F12508	1966	**£4**	
Girl	7"	Decca	F12318	1966	**£4**	chart single

ST.PATRICK, OLIVER

I Want To Be Loved By You	7"	Trojan	TR005	196-	**£10**	

ST.PETERS, CRISPIAN

Almost Persuaded	7"	Decca	F12596	1967	**£4**	
Almost Persuaded	7" EP	Decca	DFE8678	1967	**£6**	
At This Moment	7"	Decca	F12080	1965	**£4**	
But She's Untrue	7"	Decca	F12525	1966	**£4**	
Carolina	7"	Decca	F12861	1968	**£4**	
Changes	7"	Decca	F12480	1966	**£4**	
Follow Me	LP	Decca	LK4805	1966	**£12**	
Free Spirit	7"	Decca	F12677	1967	**£4**	
No No No	7"	Decca	F12207	1965	**£4**	
Pied Piper	7"	Decca	F12359	1966	**£4**	chart single
Simply	LP	Square	SQA102	1970	**£12**	
That's The Time	7"	Decca	F12761	1968	**£4**	
You Were On My Mind	7"	Decca	F12287	1965	**£4**	chart single

ST.ROMAIN, KIRBY

Summer's Comin'	7"	Stateside	SS199	1963	**£4**	

ST.VALENTINE'S DAY MASSACRE

Brother Can You Spare A Dime	7"	Fontana	TF883	1967	**£25**	

STACCATOS

Butchers And Bakers	7"	Fontana	TF966	1968	**£4**	
Half Past Midnight	7"	Capitol	CL15505	1967	**£4**	
Let's Run Away	7"	Capitol	CL15478	1966	**£4**	
Main Line	7"	Parlophone	R4828	1961	**£4**	

STACEY, CLARENCE

Just Your Love	7"	Pye	7N25025	1959	**£4**	

STACKRIDGE

Anyone For Tennis	7"	MCA	MK5103	1972	**£4**	
Dangerous Bacon	7"	MCA	MCA124	1974	**£4**	
Do The Stanley	LP	MCA	MCF2747	1976	**£10**	
Do The Stanley	7"	MCA	MUS1182	1973	**£4**	
Dora The Female Explorer	7"	MCA	MK5065	1971	**£4**	
Extravaganza	LP	Rocket	PIGL11	1974	**£10**	
Friendliness	LP	MCA	MKPS2025	1972	**£15**	
Galloping Gaucho	7"	MCA	MUS1224	1973	**£4**	
Hold Me Tight	7"	Rocket	ROKN507	1976	**£4**	
Man In A Bowler Hat	LP	MCA	MCG3501	1973	**£15**	
Mr.Mick	LP	Rocket	ROLL3	1976	**£12**	
Pinafore Days	LP	Sire	7503	1974	**£15**	US
Slark	7"	MCA	MK5091	1972	**£4**	
Spin Round The Room	7"	Rocket	PIG15	1975	**£4**	
Stackridge	LP	MCA	MDKS8002	1971	**£15**	

STACKWADDY

Bugger Off	LP	Dandelion	2310231	1972	**£25**	
Roadrunner	7"	Dandelion	5119	1970	**£8**	
Stackwaddy	LP	Dandelion	2310154	1971	**£25**	

Stackwaddy	LP	Dandelion	DAN8003	1971	**£25**	
You Really Got Me	7"	Dandelion	2001331	1972	**£5**	

STAEHELY BROTHERS

Sta-Hay-Lee	LP	Epic		1973	**£15**	US

STAFFORD, TERRY

Follow The Rainbow	7"	London	HLU9923	1964	**£4**	
Heartache On The Way	7"	Stateside	SS225	1963	**£4**	
I'll Touch A Star	7"	London	HLU9902	1964	**£4**	
Suspicion	LP	Crusader	CLP1001	1964	**£20**	US
Suspicion	7"	London	HLU9871	1964	**£6**	chart single
Suspicion	7" EP	London	REU1436	1964	**£8**	

STAMP, TERRY

Eaststicks	LP	A&M	AMLH63329	1975	**£15**	

STAMPEDERS

From The Fire	LP	Regal Z.	SLRZ1039	1974	**£10**	
Me And My Stone	7"	Regal Z.	RZ3087	1974	**£4**	
Minstrel Gypsy	7"	Regal Z.	RZ3083	1973	**£4**	
No Destination	7"	Regal Z.	RZ3079	1973	**£4**	
Ride In The Wind	7"	Regal Z.	RZ3085	1974	**£4**	
Stampeders	LP	Regal Z.	SLRZ1032	1972	**£10**	
Today Is The Beginning...	7"	Regal Z.	RZ3069	1972	**£4**	

STANBACK, JEAN

I Still Love You	7"	Deep Soul	DS9101	1970	**£5**	

STANDELLS

Dirty Water	7"	Capitol	CL15446	1966	**£15**	
Dirty Water	LP	Tower	T5027	1966	**£25**	US
Help Yourself	7"	Liberty	LIB55722	1964	**£20**	
Hot Ones	LP	Tower	T5049	1966	**£20**	US
In Person At P.J.'s	LP	Liberty	LRP3384	1964	**£25**	US
Live & Out Of Sight	LP	Sunset	SUM1186	1966	**£20**	US
Try It	LP	Tower	T5098	1967	**£20**	US
Why Pick On Me	LP	Tower	T5044	1966	**£20**	US

STANLEY

I'll Go Down And Getcha	7"	Action	ACT4615	1971	**£4**	

STANSHALL, VIV

The former lead singer of the Bonzo Dog Band has made a number of eccentric records since the demise of that group. One recording not listed here is the alternative ending to Mike Oldfield's "Tubular Bells" (included in the four album boxed set of Oldfield's first Virgin recordings) in which Stanshall is the commentator for a drunken guided tour of the Manor recording studio complex. This favourite caricature of a vacuous aristocrat was the inspiration behind Stanshall's classic comedy recording "Sir Henry At Rawlinson End", versions of which were first broadcast on the radio.

Lakanga	7"	W. Bros	K16424	1974	**£4**	
Men Opening Umbrellas Ahead	LP	W. Bros	K56052	1974	**£15**	
Sir Henry At Rawlinson End	LP	Charisma	CAS1139	1978	**£10**	
Suspicion	7"	Fly	BUG4	1970	**£6**	
Teddy Boys Don't Knit	LP	Charisma	CAS1153	1981	**£10**	

STANSHALL, VIVIAN

Labio-Dental Fricative	7"	Liberty		1970	**£6**	
Question	7"	Harvest	HAR5114	1976	**£4**	

STAPLE SINGERS

For What It's Worth	7"	Columbia	DB8292	1967	**£4**	
For What It's Worth	7"	Soul City	SC117		**£5**	
For What It's Worth	7"	Soul City	SC117		**£12**	demo
Hammer And Nails	7"	Riverside	106902	1963	**£5**	

STARCASTLE

Citadel	LP	Epic	34935	1978	**£15**	US pic disc

STARCHER, BUDDY

And His Mountain Guitar Vol.1	7" EP	London	REB1424	1964	**£4**	
And His Mountain Guitar Vol.2	7" EP	London	REB1425	1964	**£4**	
And His Mountain Guitar Vol.3	7" EP	London	REB1426	1964	**£4**	

STARFIRE

Starfire	LP	Crimson	SCAREC1		**£20**	US

STARFIRES

Starfires Play	LP	Ohio Rec S.	34	1964	**£20**	US
Teenbeat A Go-Go	LP	La Brea	LS8018	1965	**£20**	US

STARGAZERS

Close The Door	7"	Decca	F10594	1955	**£4**	chart single
Happy Wanderer	7"	Decca	F10259	1954	**£4**	chart single
I See The Moon	7"	Decca	F10213	1953	**£4**	chart single
Rocking And Rolling	7" EP	Decca	DFE6362	1956	**£5**	
Rocking And Rolling	7"	Decca	F10731	1956	**£4**	
She Loves To Rock	7"	Decca	F10775	1956	**£4**	
Stargazers	7" EP	Decca	DFE6341	1956	**£6**	
Twenty Tiny Fingers	7"	Decca	F10626	1955	**£4**	chart single

STARR, CINDY & THE MOPEDS

Way I Do	7"	Columbia	DB110	1968	**£8**	

STARR, CINDY & THE RUDE BOYS

Pain Of Love	7"	Columbia	DB107	1968	**£8**	

STARR, EDWIN

25 Miles	LP	T. Motown	STML11115	1969	**£12**	
25 Miles	7"	T. Motown	TMG672	1968	**£5**	chart single
25 Miles	7"	T. Motown	TMG672	1968	**£20**	demo
Agent OO-Soul	7"	T. Motown	TMG790	1971	**£15**	demo
Agent OO-Soul	7"	T. Motown	TMG790	1971	**£4**	
Funky Music Sho' Nuff Turns Me On	7"	T. Motown	TMG810	1972	**£4**	
Funky Music Sho' Nuff Turns Me On	7"	T. Motown	TMG810	1972	**£10**	demo
Headline News	7"	Polydor	56717	1966	**£5**	chart single
I Am The Man For You Baby	7"	T. Motown	TMG646	1968	**£10**	
I Am The Man For You Baby	7"	T. Motown	TMG646	1968	**£30**	demo
I Want My Baby Back	7"	T. Motown	TMG630	1967	**£10**	
I Want My Baby Back	7"	T. Motown	TMG630	1967	**£40**	demo
It's My Turn Now	7"	Polydor	56726	1967	**£6**	
Soul Master	LP	T. Motown	STML11094	1969	**£25**	
Stop Her On Sight	7"	Polydor	56702	1966	**£5**	chart single
Stop Her On Sight	7"	Polydor	56753	1968	**£4**	chart single
Stop The War Now	7"	T. Motown	TMG764	1971	**£4**	chart single
Stop The War Now	7"	T. Motown	TMG764	1971	**£10**	demo
Time	7"	T. Motown	TMG725	1970	**£5**	
Time	7"	T. Motown	TMG725	1970	**£12**	demo
War	7"	T. Motown	TMG754	1970	**£4**	chart single
War	7"	T. Motown	TMG754	1970	**£10**	demo
Way Over There	7"	T. Motown	TMG692	1969	**£5**	
Way Over There	7"	T. Motown	TMG692	1969	**£20**	demo

STARR, EDWIN & BLINKY

Oh How Happy	7"	T. Motown	TMG720	1969	**£100**	demo only
Oh How Happy	7"	T. Motown	TMG748	1970	**£4**	
Oh How Happy	7"	T. Motown	TMG748	1970	**£10**	demo

STARR, FRANK

Little Bitty Feeling	7"	London	HLU9545	1962	**£5**	

STARR, FREDDIE

Baby Blue	7"	Decca	F11786	1963	**£8**	
Never Cry On Someone's Shoulder	7"	Decca	F12009	1964	**£8**	
Who Told You	7"	Decca	F11663	1963	**£8**	

STARR, JIMMY

It's Only Make Believe	7"	London	HL8731	1958	**£12**	

STARR, RANDY

After School	7"	London	HL8443	1957	**£5**	
Count On Me	7"	Felsted	AF106	1958	**£5**	

STARR, RINGO

The rarest Ringo Starr record typifies the variety of work that Starr has undertaken since the break-up of the Beatles. "Scouse The Mouse" is a children's story produced by Donald Pleasance and dramatised with Ringo Starr playing the title role (and singing eight songs). A projected TV version never happened so that the album failed to attract any attention at the time of its release.

Title	Format	Label	Number	Year	Price	Notes
Back Off Boogaloo	7"	Apple	R5944	1972	**£20**	demo
Back Off Boogaloo	7"	Apple	R5944	1972	**£6**	PS
Beaucoups Of Blues	LP	Apple	PAS10002	1970	**£15**	
Dose Of Rock'n'Roll	7"	Polydor	2001694	1976	**£4**	
Drowning In A Sea Of Love	7"	Polydor	2001734	1977	**£4**	
Hey Baby	7"	Polydor	2001699	1976	**£4**	
It Don't Come Easy	7"	Apple	R5898	1971	**£20**	demo
It Don't Come Easy	7"	Apple	R5898	1971	**£6**	PS
Lipstick Traces	7"	Polydor	2001782	1978	**£10**	
Oh My My	7"	Apple	R6011	1976	**£10**	
Only You	7"	Apple	R6000	1974	**£6**	PS
Only You	7"	EMI		1974	**£10**	promo
Photograph	7"	Apple	R5992	1973	**£20**	demo
Photograph	7"	Apple	R5992	1973	**£6**	PS
Ringo	LP	Apple	SWAL3413	1973	**£12**	US, with long version of 'Six O'Clock'
Sentimental Journey	r-reel	Apple	TAPMC7101	1970	**£20**	mono
Sentimental Journey	r-reel	Apple	TDPCS7101	1970	**£15**	stereo
Sentimental Journey	LP	Apple	PCS7101	1970	**£15**	chart LP
Snookeroo	7"	Apple	R6004	1975	**£4**	
Snookeroo	7"	Apple	R6004	1975	**£20**	demo
Tonight	7"	Polydor	2001795	1978	**£4**	
You're Sixteen	7"	Apple	R5995	1973	**£20**	demo
You're Sixteen	7"	Apple	R5995	1974	**£6**	PS

STARR, RINGO & OTHERS

Title	Format	Label	Number	Year	Price	Notes
Scouse The Mouse	LP	Polydor	2480429	1978	**£90**	

STARR, STELLA

Title	Format	Label	Number	Year	Price	Notes
Bring Him Back	7"	Piccadilly	7N35366	1967	**£15**	

STARR, TONY

Title	Format	Label	Number	Year	Price	Notes
Rocket To The Moon	7"	Decca	F11847	1964	**£4**	

STARRY EYED & LAUGHING

Title	Format	Label	Number	Year	Price	Notes
Starry Eyed & Laughing	LP	CBS	80450	1974	**£10**	
Thought Talk	LP	CBS	80907	1975	**£10**	

STATESMEN

Title	Format	Label	Number	Year	Price	Notes
I've Just Fallen In Love	7"	Fontana	TF432	1964	**£6**	
Look Around	7"	Decca	F11687	1963	**£6**	

STATIC

Title	Format	Label	Number	Year	Price	Notes
When You Went Away	7"	Page One	POF039	1967	**£6**	

STATION SKIFFLE GROUP

Title	Format	Label	Number	Year	Price	Notes
Station Skiffle Group	7" EP	Esquire	EP161	195-	**£10**	

STATON, CANDI

Title	Format	Label	Number	Year	Price	Notes
Love Chain	7"	United Artists	UP35823	1975	**£4**	

STATUS QUO

Status Quo are one of the more unlikely success stories of rock music, having stuck with the same Chuck Berry and boogie style ever since first deciding on it some time around 1970. The group's earlier recordings - as the Spectres and Traffic Jam before becoming Status Quo - are more varied in style, but perhaps not very expertly performed. The slightly psychedelic "Pictures Of Matchstick Men" was a considerable hit, of course, but no one bought the accompanying album, which is now extremely scarce. Its awkward title probably did not help its sales when released - "Picturesque Matchstickable Messages". The succeeding "Spare Parts" is also highly sought after today, as is the Marble Arch release "Status Quotations", even though this is only a compilation of singles and tracks from the first LP.

Title	Format	Label	Number	Year	Price	Notes
Ain't Complainin'	LP	Vertigo			**£12**	1 sided promo
Ain't Complainin'	7"	Vertigo	QUOLP99	1988	**£8**	1 sided promo sampler
Are You Growing Tired Of My Love	7"	Pye	7N17728	1969	**£12**	chart single
Back To Back	LP	Vertigo	VERH10	1983	**£15**	1 sided promo
Black Veils Of Melancholy	7"	Pye	7N17497	1968	**£10**	
Caroline	7"	Vertigo	QUOP10	1982	**£6**	pic disc
Down Down Down	7"	Lyntone	LYN3154/5	1976	**£5**	flexi
From The Makers Of	LP	Vertigo	PROBX1	1982	**£20**	3 LPs in metal box
Gerdundula	7"	Pye	7N45253	1973	**£5**	
Ice In The Sun	7"	Pye	7N17581	1968	**£5**	chart single

Title	Format	Label	Number	Year	Price	Notes
In My Chair	7"	Pye	7N17998	1970	**£8**	PS
In My Chair	7"	Pye	QUO1(SFI434)	1979	**£5**	flexi
In The Army Now	7"	Vertigo	QUODP20	1986	**£6**	double
In The Army Now	7"	Vertigo	QUOPD20	1986	**£6**	pic disc
Just For The Record	LP	Pye	NSPL18607	1979	**£10**	coloured vinyl
Make Me Stay A Bit Longer	7"	Pye	7N17665	1969	**£12**	
Marguerita Time	7"	Vertigo	QUOP1414	1983	**£8**	double Xmas gift pack
Marguerita Time	7"	Vertigo	QUOP14	1983	**£6**	pic disc
Ol' Rag Blues	7"	Vertigo	QUOB11	1983	**£4**	blue vinyl
Pictures Of Matchstick Men	7"	Pye	7N17449	1968	**£4**	chart single
Pictures Of Matchstick Men	7"	Pye	7N17449	1968	**£8**	'75cc Minimum' on label
Pictures Of Matchstick Men	7"	Pye	FBS2	1979	**£6**	yellow vinyl
Picturesque Matchstickable Messages	LP	Pye	NSPL18220	1968	**£50**	
Pile Driver	LP	Vertigo	6360082	1973	**£10**	spiral label
Price Of Love	7"	Pye	7N17825	1969	**£12**	
Red Sky	7"	Vertigo	QUOD19	1986	**£5**	double
Red Sky	12"	Vertigo	QUO1912	1986	**£6**	poster sleeve
Rock'n'Roll	7"	Vertigo	QUOJB6	1981	**£6**	jukebox issue
Rollin' Home	7"	Vertigo	QUOP18	1986	**£6**	shaped pic disc
Spare Parts	LP	Pye	NSPL18301	1968	**£50**	
Status Quotations	LP	Marble Arch	MAL1193	1969	**£50**	
Tune To The Music	7"	Pye	7N45077	1971	**£6**	
Wanderer	12"	Vertigo	QUOP16	1984	**£6**	clear vinyl, pic disc centre

STEAHMAMMER

Steamhammer arrived at the tail end of the British blues boom amidst publicity that spoke of them being a next-generation group who would find ways of going beyond the blues. For once, this was no hype, the second LP in particular being a fine example of jazz-rock in which Martin Pugh's fluid guitar playing is ably complemented by Steve Joliffe's flute and saxophone. The long "Another Travelling Tune" shows how improvised rock can be entirely successful when the musicians are as inspired as these.

Title	Format	Label	Number	Year	Price	Notes
Autumn Song	7"	CBS	4496	1969	**£8**	
Mountains	LP	B&C	CAS1024	1970	**£20**	
Speech	LP	Brain	1009	1972	**£20**	German
Steamhammer	LP	CBS	63611	1968	**£25**	
Steamhammer	LP	Reflection	REFL1	1970	**£25**	
Steamhammer Mark 2	LP	CBS	63694	1969	**£15**	

STEEL MILL

Bruce Springsteen once led a group called Steel Mill, but the hard rock group who recorded the scarce "Green Eyed God" album has no connection with this.

Title	Format	Label	Number	Year	Price	Notes
Get On The Line	7"	P. Farthing	PEN783	1971	**£20**	
Green Eyed God	LP	P. Farthing	PELS549	1975	**£100**	
Green Eyed God	7"	P. Farthing	PEN770	1971	**£20**	
Green Eyed God	7"	P. Farthing	PEN894	1975	**£8**	

STEEL RIVER

Title	Format	Label	Number	Year	Price	Notes
Better Road	LP	Evolution	3006		**£15**	
Weighing Heavy	LP	Evolution	2018		**£15**	

STEELE, BETTE ANN

Title	Format	Label	Number	Year	Price	Notes
Barricade	7"	Capitol	CL14315	1955	**£4**	

STEELE, JAN & JOHN CAGE

Title	Format	Label	Number	Year	Price	Notes
Voices & Instruments	LP	Obscure	OBS5	1976	**£15**	

STEELE, TOMMY

Title	Format	Label	Number	Year	Price	Notes
Boys And Girls	7"	Decca	F11299	1960	**£4**	
Butterfingers	7"	Decca	F10877	1957	**£4**	chart single
Butterfly	7"	Decca	F10915	1957	**£4**	
Come On Let's Go	7"	Decca	F11072	1958	**£4**	chart single
Come On Let's Go	7" EP	Decca	DFE6551	1958	**£6**	
Doomsday Rock	7"	Decca	F10808	1956	**£15**	
Drunken Guitar	7"	Decca	F11372	1961	**£4**	
Duke Wore Jeans	LP-10"	Decca	LF1308	195-	**£12**	
Duke Wore Jeans	7" EP	Decca	DFE6472	1958	**£5**	
Get Happy	LP	Decca	LK4351	195-	**£10**	
Happy Go Lucky	7"	Decca	F11275	1960	**£4**	
Happy Guitar	7"	Decca	F10976	1958	**£4**	chart single
Hey You	7"	Decca	F10941	1957	**£6**	chart single
Hit Record	7"	Decca	F11479	1962	**£4**	
It's All Happening	7"	Decca	F11026	1958	**£4**	

Knee Deep In The Blues	7"	Decca	F10849	1957	**£8**	chart single
Little White Bull	7"	Decca	F11177	1959	**£4**	
Marriage Type Love	7"	Decca	F11089	1958	**£4**	
My Big Best Shoes	7"	Decca	F11361	1961	**£4**	
Nairobi	7"	Decca	F10991	1958	**£4**	chart single
Only Man On The Island	7"	Decca	F11041	1958	**£4**	chart single
Rock With The Caveman	7"	Decca	F10795	1956	**£12**	chart single
Shiralee	7"	Decca	F10896	1957	**£8**	chart single
Singing The Blues	7"	Decca	F10819	1956	**£10**	chart single
Singing The Blues	7" EP	Decca	DFE6389	1956	**£8**	
Tallahassie Lassie	7"	Decca	F11152	1959	**£6**	chart single
Tommy Steele	7" EP	Decca	DFE6592	1959	**£5**	
Tommy Steele Stage Show	LP-10"	Decca	LF1287	195-	**£20**	
Tommy Steele Story	LP-10"	Decca	LF1288	195-	**£20**	
Tommy Steele Story Vol.1	7" EP	Decca	DFE6398	1957	**£8**	
Tommy Steele Story Vol.2	7" EP	Decca	DFE6424	1957	**£8**	
Tommy The Toreador	7" EP	Decca	DFE6607	1959	**£4**	
Trial	7"	Decca	F11117	1959	**£4**	
Water Water	7"	Decca	F10923	1957	**£5**	chart single
What A Mouth	7"	Decca	F11245	1960	**£4**	chart single
What A Mouth	7" EP	Decca	DFE6660	1960	**£4**	
Young Ideas	7"	Decca	F11162	1959	**£4**	
Young Love	7" EP	Decca	DFE6388	1956	**£8**	

STEELERS

Get It From The Bottom	7"	Direction	584675	1969	**£4**	

STEELEYE SPAN

All Around My Hat	LP	Mobile Fid.	MFSL1027	1978	**£15**	US audiophile
Hark The Village Wait	LP	RCA	SF8113	1970	**£10**	
Please To See The King	LP	B&C	CAS1029	1971	**£10**	chart LP
Rave On	7"	B&C	CB164	1971	**£4**	
Ten Man Mop	LP	Pegasus	PEG9	1971	**£10**	

STEELY DAN

Aja	LP	Mobile Fid.	MFSL1033	1979	**£10**	US audiophile
Can't Buy A Thrill	LP	Command	QD40009	1974	**£10**	US quad
Countdown To Ecstasy	LP	Command	QD40010	1974	**£10**	US quad
Dallas	7"	ABC	SD1	1978	**£5**	1 sided promo
Dallas	7"	Probe	PRO562	1972	**£5**	
Gaucho	LP	MCA	MCA6102	1980	**£10**	Canadian audiophile
Gold	LP	MCA	MCA16016	1982	**£10**	audiophile
Gold	LP	MCA	MCF3145	1982	**£10**	with 12" (MSAMT21)
Katy Lied	LP	Mobile Fid.	MFSL1007	1978	**£20**	US audiophile
Pretzel Logic	LP	Command	QD40015	1974	**£10**	US quad

STEEPLECHASE

Lady Bright	LP	Polydor		1970	**£25**	

STEGMEYER, BILL

On The Waterfront	7"	London	HL8078	1954	**£15**	

STEIN, LOU

Almost Paradise	7"	London	HLZ8419	1957	**£4**	
Who Slammed The Door	7"	Mercury	7MT226	1958	**£4**	

STEINMAN, JIM

Bad For Good	LP	Epic	EPC84361	1981	**£10**	pic disc
Rock'n'Roll Dreams	12"	Epic	EPCA131236	1981	**£6**	blue vinyl

STEPHENS, LEIGH

Cast Of Thousands	LP	Charisma	CAS1040	1971	**£15**	
Red Weather	LP	Philips	SBL7897	1969	**£20**	

STEPHENSON, MARTIN & THE DAINTEES

There Comes A Time	7"	Kitchenware	SKXDJ34	1987	**£10**	promo

STEPPENWOLF

At Your Birthday Party	LP	Stateside	SSL5011	1969	**£10**	
Born To Be Wild	7"	RCA	RCA1735	1968	**£5**	
Born To Be Wild	7"	Stateside	SS8017	1969	**£4**	chart single
Early Steppenwolf	LP	Stateside	SSL5015	1969	**£12**	

For Ladies Only	7"	Probe	PRO544	1971	**£4**	
Hey Lawdy Mama	7"	Stateside	SS8049	1970	**£4**	
Live	LP	Stateside	SSL5029	1970	**£10**	chart LP
Magic Carpet Ride	7"	Stateside	SS8003	1968	**£4**	
Magic Carpet Ride	7"	Stateside	SS8027	1969	**£4**	
Monster	LP	Stateside	SSL5021	1970	**£10**	chart LP
Monster	7"	Stateside	SS8035	1970	**£4**	
Pusher	7"	Stateside	SS8038	1970	**£5**	
Ride With Me	7"	Probe	PRO534	1971	**£4**	
Rock Me	7"	Stateside	SS8013	1969	**£4**	
Screaming Night Hog	7"	Stateside	SS8056	1970	**£4**	
Second	LP	Stateside	SSL5003	1968	**£10**	
Snowblind Friend	7"	Probe	PRO525	1970	**£4**	
Sookie Sookie	7"	RCA	RCA1679	1968	**£6**	
Steppenwolf	LP	RCA	RD7974	1968	**£12**	
Who Needs Ya	7"	Probe	PRO510	1970	**£4**	

STEREOS

Big Knock	7"	MGM	MGM1149	1961	**£4**	
Please Come Back To Me	7"	MGM	MGM1143	1961	**£4**	
Sweet Water	7"	MGM	MGM1328	1966	**£4**	

STERLING, LESTER

Air Raid Shelter	7"	R&B	JB111	1963	**£10**	
Baskin' Hop	7"	R&B	JB155	1964	**£10**	
Clean The City	7"	Island	WI121	1963	**£10**	
Hot Cargo	7"	R&B	JB150	1964	**£10**	
Indian Summer	7"	R&B	JB172	1964	**£10**	
Soul Voyage	7"	Doctor Bird	DB1107	1967	**£10**	
Zigaloo	7"	Blue Cat	BS116	1968	**£10**	

STEVENS, APRIL

Coldest Night Of The Year	7"	Atlantic	584048	1966	**£4**	
Falling In Love Again	7"	MGM	MGM1366	1967	**£30**	
How Could Red Riding Hood	7"	Parlophone	MSP6088	1954	**£4**	
Soft Warm Lips	7"	Parlophone	MSP6060	1953	**£4**	
Wanting You	7"	MGM	2006586	1976	**£4**	

STEVENS, CAT

Bad Night	7"	Deram	DM140	1967	**£4**	chart single
Buddha And The Chocolate Box	LP	A&M	QU53623	1974	**£12**	US quad
Catch Bull At Four	LP	A&M	QU54365	1972	**£12**	US quad
Cats And Dogs	LP	Deram		1967	**£30**	
Foreigner	LP	A&M	QU54391	1974	**£12**	US quad
Greatest Hits	LP	A&M	QU54519	1975	**£12**	US quad
Here Comes My Wife	7"	Deram	DM211	1968	**£4**	
I Love My Dog	7"	Deram	DM102	1966	**£4**	chart single
I'm Gonna Get Me A Gun	7"	Deram	DM118	1967	**£4**	chart single
Kitty	7"	Deram	DM156	1967	**£4**	chart single
Lady D'Arbanville	7"	Island	WIP6086	1970	**£4**	chart single
Lovely City	7"	Deram	DM178	1968	**£4**	
Matthew And Son	LP	Deram	SML1004	1967	**£12**	chart LP
Matthew And Son	7"	Deram	DM110	1966	**£4**	
Mona Bone Jakon	LP	Island	ILPS9118	1970	**£10**	chart LP
New Masters	LP	Deram	SML1018	1968	**£12**	
Saturday Night Live	LP	A&M		1975	**£15**	US promo
Tea For The Tillerman	LP	A&M	QU54280	1972	**£12**	US quad
Tea For The Tillerman	LP	Mobile Fid.	MFSL1035	1979	**£15**	US audiophile
Tea For The Tillerman	LP	Mobile Fid.	MFSL1135	1984	**£30**	US audiophile (UHQR)
Teaser And The Firecat	LP	A&M	QU54313	1972	**£12**	US quad
Where Are You	7"	Deram	DM260	1969	**£4**	

STEVENS, CHUCK

My London	7"	Columbia	DB3938	1957	**£4**	
Take A Walk	7"	Columbia	DB3883	1957	**£4**	

STEVENS, CONNIE

And This Is Mine	7"	W. Bros	WB41	1961	**£4**	
Apollo	7"	W. Bros	WB25	1960	**£4**	
Conchetta	LP	W. Bros	W1208	1958	**£12**	US
Connie	LP	W. Bros	W1432	1961	**£10**	US
Connie Stevens From Hawaiian Eye	LP	W. Bros	W1382	1960	**£10**	US

Greenwood Tree	7"	W. Bros	WB47	1961	**£4**	
Hank Williams Songbook	LP	W. Bros	W1460	1962	**£10**	US
Hawaiian Eye	LP	W. Bros	W1335	1959	**£12**	US
Just One Kiss	7"	W. Bros	WB63	1962	**£4**	
Mr.Songwriter	7"	W. Bros	WB73	1962	**£4**	
Sixteen Reasons	7"	W. Bros	WB3	1960	**£4**	chart single
They're Jealous Of Me	7"	W. Bros	WB128	1964	**£4**	
Too Young To Go Steady	7"	W. Bros	WB17	1960	**£4**	

STEVENS, DODIE

Dodie Stevens	LP	Dot	DLP3212	1960	**£10**	US
Don't Send Me Roses	7"	London	HLD9672	1963	**£4**	
I Wore Out The Record	7"	Liberty	LIB83	1964	**£4**	
No	7"	London	HLD9174	1960	**£4**	
Over The Rainbow	LP	Dot	DLP3323	1960	**£10**	US
Pink Shoe Laces	7"	London	HLD8834	1959	**£5**	
Pink Shoelaces	LP	Dot	DLP3371	1961	**£10**	US
Yes I'm Lonesome Tonight	7"	London	HLD9280	1961	**£5**	

STEVENS, JIMMY

I Love You	7"	Fontana	TF721	1966	**£4**	

STEVENS, JOHN

John Stevens, the erstwhile motivator behind the Spontaneous Music Ensemble (whose music sounds just as the name would suggest it should), began to move into more commercial areas during the seventies. He is the drummer on John Martyn's "Live At Leeds", and for the single "Anni", John Martyn returned the favour - playing guitar and singing on a version of the piece that is quite different from the one found on the LP "John Stevens' Away".

Anni	7"	Vertigo	6059140	1976	**£5**	
Can't Explain	7"	Vertigo	6059154	1976	**£4**	

STEVENS, MEIC

Ballad Of Old Joe Blind	7"	W. Bros	WB8007	1970	**£15**	
Outlander	LP	W. Bros		1970	**£80**	

STEVENS, RAY

1,837 Seconds Of Humor	LP	Mercury	MG20732	1962	**£10**	US
Ahab The Arab	7"	Mercury	AMT1184	1962	**£4**	
Crying Goodbye	7"	Capitol	CL14881	1958	**£4**	
Harry The Hairy Ape	7"	Mercury	AMT1207	1963	**£4**	
Jeremiah Peabody	7"	Mercury	AMT1158	1961	**£4**	

STEVENS, RICKY

I Cried For You	7"	Columbia	DB4739	1961	**£4**	chart single
I Cried For You	7" EP	Columbia	SEG8172	1962	**£5**	

STEVENS, SHAKIN'

Cry Just A Little Bit	7"	Epic	WA3774	1983	**£5**	pic disc
Down On The Farm	7"	Parlophone	R5860	1970	**£8**	
Frantic	7"	Magnum Force	MFEP007	1982	**£5**	
Give Me Your Heart Tonight	7"	Epic	EPCA2656	1982	**£5**	pic disc
Honey Honey	7"	Emerald	MD1176	1974	**£6**	
I'm No J.D.	LP	CBS	52901	1971	**£12**	
It's Late	7"	Epic	WA3565	1983	**£5**	shaped pic disc
It's Raining	7"	Epic	EPCA1643	1981	**£5**	pic disc
Jungle Rock	7"	Battle Of B.	BOB2	1981	**£5**	
Jungle Rock	7"	Mooncrest	MOON51	1976	**£6**	
Justine	7"	Magnum Force	MFEP010	1983	**£5**	
Justine	7"	Track	2094141	1978	**£4**	
Legend	LP	Parlophone	PCS7112	1970	**£15**	
Memphis Earthquake	7"	Magnum Force	MFEP001	1981	**£5**	
Never	7"	Track	2094134	1977	**£4**	
Somebody Touched Me	7"	Track	2094136	1977	**£4**	
Sweet Little Rock'n'Roller	7"	Polydor	2058213	1972	**£6**	
Teardrops	7"	Epic	DA4882	1984	**£5**	double

STEWART, AL

As soon as he achieved a small measure of success, Al Stewart decided that his first LP was not as he would have liked it to be, and managed to persuade CBS to issue a new version, with a slightly different track selection and with the whole album re-mixed. The original "Bed Sitter Images" is now quite scarce. As for the even scarcer "Elf" single, Al Stewart would probably prefer to forget about it altogether!

Al Stewart Concert	LP	Arista	SP40	1977	**£15**	US promo

Title	Format	Label	Cat. No.	Year	Price	Notes
Amsterdam	7"	CBS	7292	1971	**£4**	
Bedsitter Images	LP	CBS	63087	1967	**£40**	
Bedsitter Images	7"	CBS	3034	1967	**£5**	
Electric Los Angeles Sunset	7"	CBS	4843	1970	**£4**	
Elf	7"	Decca	F12467	1966	**£60**	
First Album (Bedsitter Images)	LP	CBS	64023	1970	**£10**	
Love Chronicles	LP	CBS	63460	1969	**£10**	
News From Spain	7"	CBS	5351	1971	**£4**	
On The Border	7"	RCA	PB5019DJ	1977	**£4**	promo
Orange	LP	CBS	64730	1972	**£10**	
Time Passages	LP	Mobile Fid.	MFSL1082	1981	**£10**	US audiophile
Twenty-Four Carrots	LP	Nautilus		1981	**£10**	US audiophile
Year Of The Cat (2 versions)	7"	RCA	RCA2771DJ	1976	**£5**	promo
Year Of The Cat	LP	Mobile Fid.	MFSL1009	1979	**£15**	US audiophile
You Don't Even Know Me	7"	CBS	7763	1972	**£4**	
Zero She Flies	LP	CBS	63848	1970	**£10**	chart LP

STEWART, BILLY

Title	Format	Label	Cat. No.	Year	Price	Notes
Because I Love You	7"	Chess	CRS8028	1966	**£6**	
Billy Stewart Remembered	LP	Chess	LP1547	1968	**£10**	US
I Do Love You	LP	Chess	LP1496	1965	**£12**	US
I Do Love You	7"	Chess	CRS8009	1965	**£8**	
I Do Love You	7" EP	Chess	CRE6024	1966	**£6**	
Reap What You Sow	7"	Pye	7N25164	1962	**£4**	
Sitting In The Park	7"	Chess	CRS8017	1965	**£4**	
Strange Feeling	7"	Pye	7N25222	1963	**£4**	
Summertime	7"	Chess	CRS8040	1966	**£4**	chart single
Teaches Old Standards New Tricks	LP	Chess	LP1513	1967	**£10**	US
Unbelievable	LP	Chess	LP1499	1965	**£10**	US

STEWART, DELANO

Title	Format	Label	Cat. No.	Year	Price	Notes
That's Life	7"	Doctor Bird	DB1138	196-	**£10**	

STEWART, JOHN

Title	Format	Label	Cat. No.	Year	Price	Notes
California Bloodlines	LP	Capitol	EST203	1969	**£10**	
Cannons In The Rain	LP	RCA	SF8359	1973	**£10**	
July, You're A Woman	7"	Capitol	CL15589	1969	**£4**	
Signals Through The Glass	LP	Capitol	T2975	1968	**£12**	US
Sunstorm	LP	W. Bros	BS2611	1972	**£10**	US
Until It's Time For You To Go	7"	CBS	202091	1966	**£4**	
Willard	LP	Capitol	EST540	1970	**£10**	

STEWART, ROD

The fact that Rod Stewart often performs indifferent material should not be allowed to obscure the fact that he is one of the great rock singers. His early Vertigo LPs are fine records that successfully blend acoustic and electric styles into a very satisfying whole. Even better is Stewart's powerful blues singing on Jeff Beck's two sixties albums, "Truth" and "Beckola". Before this, Rod Stewart learnt his craft as a member of Long John Baldry's Hoochie Coochie Men and of Steampacket - his first singles come from this period and still hold up well, especially a version of "Shake", backed by Brian Auger' Trinity (who were also a part of Steampacket), which is actually more dynamic than Sam Cooke's original.

Title	Format	Label	Cat. No.	Year	Price	Notes
Blondes Have More Fun	LP	Mobile Fid.	MFSL1054	1981	**£10**	US audiophile
Day Will Come	7"	Columbia	DB7766	1965	**£20**	
Do Ya Think I'm Sexy	12"	Riva	SAM92	1978	**£10**	promo
Do Ya Think I'm Sexy	12"	Riva	SAM92	1978	**£20**	promo, green or blue vinyl
Do Ya Think I'm Sexy	12"	W. Bros	WBSD8727	1978	**£8**	US
Gasoline Alley	LP	Vertigo	6360500	1970	**£10**	spiral label, chart LP
Good Morning Little Schoolgirl	7"	Decca	F11996	1964	**£25**	
Handbags And Gladrags	7"	Mercury	73031	1970	**£4**	
Infatuation	7"	W. Bros	SAM194	1984	**£15**	1 sided pic disc with interview tape
It's All Over Now	7"	Vertigo	6086002	1970	**£4**	
Little Miss Understood	7"	Immediate	IM060	1967	**£8**	
Maggie May	7"	Mercury	BRAUN3	197-	**£4**	
Old Raincoat Won't Ever...	LP	Vertigo	VO4	1970	**£10**	spiral label
Reason To Believe	7"	Mercury	6052097	1970	**£4**	Maggie May' on B side, chart single
Reason To Believe	LP	St.Michael	21020102	1978	**£15**	
Shake	7"	Columbia	DB7892	1966	**£20**	
Tonight's The Night	7"	Riva	3	1977	**£8**	
You're Insane	12"	Riva	DISCO1A	1980	**£20**	promo

STEWART, TINGA
Message .... 7" .... Dragon .... DRA1025 .... 1974 .... **£4**

STEWART, WINSTON
All Of My Life .... 7" .... Port-O-Jam .... PJ4002 .... 196- **£8**

STIFF LITTLE FINGERS
Alternative Ulster .... 7" .... Rough Trade .... RT004 .... 1978 .... **£4**
Gotta Get Away .... 7" .... Rough Trade .... RT015 .... 1979 .... **£4**
Listen (2 versions) .... 7" .... Chrysalis .... 1982 .... **£6** .... promo
Listen .... 7" .... Chrysalis .... CHSDJ2580 .... 1982 .... **£5** .... juke box issue
Suspect Device .... 7" .... Rigid Digits .... SRD1 .... 1978 .... **£10**
Suspect Device .... 7" .... Rough Trade .... RT006 .... 1978 .... **£4**

STILL LIFE
Still Life .... LP .... Vertigo .... 6360026 .... 1971 .... **£50** .... spiral label
What Did We Miss .... 7" .... Columbia .... DB8345 .... 1968 .... **£10**

STILLS, STEPHEN
Change Partners .... 7" .... Atlantic .... 2091117 .... 1971 .... **£4**
Love The One You're With .... 7" .... Atlantic .... 2091046 .... 1971 .... **£4** .... chart single
Sit Yourself Down .... 7" .... Atlantic .... 2091069 .... 1971 .... **£4**
Stephen Stills 2 .... LP .... Atlantic .... 2401013 .... 1971 .... **£10** .... chart LP
Stephen Stills .... LP .... Atlantic .... 2401004 .... 1970 .... **£10** .... chart LP

STILLS-YOUNG BAND
Long May You Run .... 7" .... Reprise .... K14446 .... 1976 .... **£4**

STING
Dream Of The Blue Turtles .... LP .... A&M .... DREAM1 .... **£10** .... pic disc
Tutti Frutti .... 7" .... A&M .... PARTY2 .... 1982 .... **£6** .... promo, Dave Edmunds B side

STITES, GARY
Lawdy Miss Clawdy .... 7" .... London .... HLL9082 .... 1960 .... **£5**
Lonely For You .... LP .... Carlton .... LP120 .... 1960 .... **£20** .... US
Lonely For You .... 7" .... London .... HLL8881 .... 1959 .... **£4**
Starry Eyed .... 7" .... London .... HLL9003 .... 1959 .... **£4**

STOCKER, GREENWOOD & FRIENDS
Billy Plus Nine .... LP .... Changes .... 1979 .... **£60**

STOCKHAUSEN, KARLHEINZ
Stockhausen has always tended to be the first port of call for those wishing to investigate the classical avant garde, and with good reason, for he pioneered most of it. Amongst his vast output are to be found purely electronic works (try "Telemusik" and "Kontakte" for starters); works that mix electronics with voices and acoustic instruments ("Gesang Der Junglinge" and "Mixtur"); works that experiment with spatial effects ("Carre"); essentially mantric exercises ("Stimmung"); orchestral freak-outs ("Trans"); and free improvisation ("Aus Den Sieben Tagen"). None of it is rock music and yet his ideas have been a considerable influence on many of the more open rock musicians.

Aus Den Sieben Tagen .... LP .... Deutsche Gram. .... 1971 .... **£10** .... 6 separate LPs - price is for each
Bird Of Passage/Ceylon .... LP .... Chrysalis .... CHR1110 .... 1976 .... **£10**
Elektronische Studie I & II .... LP .... Deutsche Gram. .... LP16133 .... **£10**
Gesang Der Junglinge/Kontakte .... LP .... Deutsche Gram. .... 138811 .... 1962 .... **£10** .... also a later remixed issue
Gruppen/Carre .... LP .... Deutsche Gram. .... 137002 .... 1968 .... **£10**
Hymnen .... LP .... Deutsche Gram. .... 2707039 .... 19769 .... **£15** .... double
Klavierstucke 8 .... LP .... Vox .... STGBY637 .... 1971 .... **£10**
Klavierstucke 9,11 .... LP .... Philips .... 6500101 .... 1971 .... **£10**
Klavierstucken .... LP .... CBS .... 72591/2 .... **£15** .... double
Kontakte (piano version)/Refrain .... LP .... Vox .... STGBY638 .... 1970 .... **£10**
Kurzwellen .... LP .... Deutsche Gram. .... 2707045 .... 1971 .... **£15** .... double
Mantra .... LP .... Deutsche Gram. .... 2530208 .... 1972 .... **£10**
Mikrophonie I and II .... LP .... Deutsche Gram. .... 2530583 .... 197- **£10**
Momente .... LP .... Deutsche Gram. .... 2709055 .... 1976 .... **£20** .... triple
Momente .... LP .... Nonesuch .... H71157 .... 196- **£10**
Opus 1970 .... LP .... Deutsche Gram. .... 139461 .... 197- **£10**
Prozession .... LP .... Deutsche Gram. .... 2530582 .... 197- **£10**
Prozession .... LP .... Vox .... STGBY615 .... 1969 .... **£10**
Solo .... LP .... Deutsche Gram. .... 137005 .... 196- **£10**
Stimmung .... LP .... Deutsche Gram. .... 2543003 .... 1970 .... **£10**
Stop/Ylem .... LP .... Deutsche Gram. .... 2530442 .... 1974 .... **£10**

Telemusik/Mixtur	LP	Deutsche Gram.	137012	1970	**£10**	
Trans	LP	Deutsche Gram.	2530726	1976	**£10**	
Zyklus	LP	Erato	STU70603		**£10**	

STOICS

Earth, Wind And Fire	7"	RCA	RCA1745	1968	**£4**	
Whipped Cream	7"	London	HLU9955	1965	**£4**	

STOLLER, RHET

Bandit	7"	Windsor	PS118	1964	**£8**	
Caravan	7"	Windsor	PS119	1964	**£8**	
Chariot	7"	Decca	F11302	1960	**£4**	chart single
Countdown	7"	Decca	F11738	1963	**£4**	
Richochet	7"	Windsor	WPS130	1964	**£6**	
Sunshine Anytime	7" EP	Mosaic	MOSAIC1		**£5**	
Treble Gold + One	7"	Melodisc	MEL1595	1964	**£5**	
Walk Don't Run	7"	Decca	F11271	1960	**£6**	

STOMPERS

Foolish Idea	7"	Fontana	H385	1962	**£4**	

STONE ANGEL

Stone Angel	LP	private			**£90**	

STONE PONEYS

Different Drum	7"	Capitol	CL15523	1967	**£4**	
Evergreen	LP	Capitol	ST2763	1967	**£10**	US
Stone Poneys & Friends	LP	Capitol	ST2863	1968	**£10**	US
Stone Poneys	LP	Capitol	ST2666	1967	**£10**	US

STONE ROSES

The keenness on the part of fans of recently successful groups to discover rare collectors items recorded by their heroes - whether or not these really exist - is well illustrated by the Stone Roses. Acquiring a considerable cult following in 1990, the group's records on Black and Silvertone were still available in ordinary record shops, yet were remarkably fetching quite high prices within the collectors' market. To be fair, tiny design differences can identify the very first pressings - the catalogue number on the back of the cover for "Elephant Stone" was originally black, but later red. There does not appear to be even that small justification on other releases, however. Meanwhile, the Thin Line release has climbed in value to an incredibly high figure for a record of such recent vintage. It remains to be seen whether this value can be sustained.

Elephant Stone	7"	Silvertone	ORE1	1988	**£15**	
Elephant Stone	12"	Silvertone	ORE1T	1988	**£25**	
Fool's Gold	7"	Silvertone	ORE13	1989	**£6**	with postcard & paper labels
Fool's Gold	7"	Silvertone	OREDJ13	1989	**£10**	promo
Fool's Gold	12"	Silvertone	ORET13	1989	**£6**	
Fool's Gold	12"	Silvertone	ORET13	1989	**£8**	with print
Fool's Gold	12"	Silvertone	ORETDJ13	1989	**£20**	1 sided promo
Made Of Stone	7"	Silvertone	ORE2	1989	**£10**	
Made Of Stone	12"	Silvertone	ORE2T	1989	**£15**	
Sally Cinnamon	7"	Black	REV36	1989	**£6**	
Sally Cinnamon	12"	Black	12REV36	1987	**£20**	
She Bangs The Drums	7"	Silvertone	OREDJ6	1989	**£15**	promo
She Bangs The Drums	7"	Silvertone	OREX6	1989	**£6**	with postcard
She Bangs The Drums	12"	Silvertone	ORET6	1989	**£6**	
She Bangs The Drums	12"	Silvertone	OREZ6	1989	**£8**	with print
So Young	12"	Thin Line	THIN001	1985	**£80**	

STONE THE CROWS

Continuous Performance	LP	Polydor	2391043	1972	**£10**	chart LP
Good Time Girl	7"	Polydor	2058301	1972	**£4**	
Mad Dogs And Englishmen	7"	Polydor	2066060	1971	**£4**	
Ode To John Law	LP	Polydor	2425042	1970	**£10**	
Stone The Crows	LP	Polydor	2425017	1970	**£10**	
Teenage Licks	LP	Polydor	2425071	1971	**£10**	

STONE'S MASONRY

Flapjacks	7"	Purdah	453504	1966	**£25**	

STONE, CLIFFIE

Cool Cowboy	LP	Capitol	T1230	1959	**£10**	US
Party's On Me	LP	Capitol	T1080	1958	**£15**	US
Popcorn Song	7"	Capitol	CL14330	1955	**£4**	

STONE, GEORGE
Title	Format	Label	Cat. No.	Year	Price	Note
Hole In The Wall	7"	Stateside	SS479	1965	**£4**	

STONE, KIRBY FOUR
Title	Format	Label	Cat. No.	Year	Price	Note
Honey Hush	7"	Vogue Coral	Q72129	1956	**£4**	

STONE, MARK
Title	Format	Label	Cat. No.	Year	Price	Note
Stroll	7"	London	HLR8543	1958	**£10**	

STONE, ROLAND
Title	Format	Label	Cat. No.	Year	Price	Note
Just A Moment	LP	Ace	LP1018	1961	**£15**	US

STONEFIELD TRAMP
Title	Format	Label	Cat. No.	Year	Price	Note
Dreaming Again	LP	Acorn		1974	**£100**	

STONEGROUND
Title	Format	Label	Cat. No.	Year	Price	Note
Family Album	LP	W. Bros	K53999	1971	**£10**	
Stoneground	LP	W. Bros	K46087	1971	**£10**	

STONEHENGE MEN
Title	Format	Label	Cat. No.	Year	Price	Note
Big Feet	7"	HMV	POP981	1962	**£8**	

STONEHOUSE
Title	Format	Label	Cat. No.	Year	Price	Note
Stonehouse Creek	LP	RCA	SF8197	1971	**£60**	

STONEPILLOW
Title	Format	Label	Cat. No.	Year	Price	Note
Eleazer's Circus	LP	Decca		1969	**£12**	

STOREY SISTERS
Title	Format	Label	Cat. No.	Year	Price	Note
Bad Motorcycle	7"	London	HLU8571	1958	**£12**	

STOREY, DAVE & THE HARLEQUINS
Title	Format	Label	Cat. No.	Year	Price	Note
Who's Sorry	7"	Parlophone	R5365	1965	**£4**	

STORM
Title	Format	Label	Cat. No.	Year	Price	Note
	LP	Vampire		197-	**£100**	

STORM, BILLY
Title	Format	Label	Cat. No.	Year	Price	Note
Billy Storm	LP	Buena Vista	BV3315	1963	**£30**	US
Sure As You're Born	7"	London	HLK9236	1960	**£4**	
This Is The Night	LP	Famous	F504	1969	**£15**	US

STORM, DANNY
Title	Format	Label	Cat. No.	Year	Price	Note
Honest I Do	7"	Piccadilly	7N35025	1962	**£8**	chart single
I Just Can't Fool My Heart	7"	Piccadilly	7N35091	1962	**£10**	
Just You	7"	Piccadilly	7N35053	1962	**£8**	

STORM, GALE
Title	Format	Label	Cat. No.	Year	Price	Note
Dark Moon	7"	London	HLD8424	1957	**£4**	
Don't Be That Way	7"	London	HLD8311	1956	**£8**	
Farewell To Arms	7"	London	HLD8570	1958	**£6**	
Gale Storm	LP	Dot	DLP3011	1956	**£12**	US
Heart Without A Sweetheart	7"	London	HLD8329	1956	**£6**	
Hits	LP	Dot	DLP3098	1958	**£10**	US
I Hear You Knocking	7"	London	HLD8222	1956	**£15**	
Ivory Tower	7"	London	HLD8283	1956	**£8**	
Lucky Lips	7"	London	HLD8393	1957	**£15**	
Memories Are Made Of This	7"	London	HLD8232	1956	**£15**	
Orange Blossoms	7"	London	HLD8413	1957	**£4**	
Sentimental Me	LP	London	HAD2104	1958	**£12**	
Why Do Fools Fall In Love	7"	London	HLD8286	1956	**£12**	

STORM, RORY & THE HURRICANES
Title	Format	Label	Cat. No.	Year	Price	Note
America	7"	Parlophone	R5197	1964	**£15**	
Doctor Feelgood	7"	Oriole	CB1858	1963	**£15**	

STORME, ROBB
Title	Format	Label	Cat. No.	Year	Price	Note
Bu Bop A Lu Bop A Lie	7"	Piccadilly	7N35160	1963	**£4**	
Earth Angel	7"	Decca	F11388	1961	**£4**	
Five Minutes More	7"	Decca	F11313	1961	**£4**	
Happens Every Day	7"	Piccadilly	7N35133	1963	**£4**	
Here Today	7"	Columbia	DB7993	1966	**£4**	

I Don't Need Your Love Anymore	7"	Decca	F11282	1960	**£4**	
Lonely Town	7"	Decca	F11364	1961	**£4**	
Pretty Hair And Angel Eyes	7"	Decca	F11432	1962	**£4**	
Sixteen Years Ago Tonight	7"	Pye	7N15515	1963	**£4**	
Wheels	7" EP	Decca	DFE6700	1962	**£10**	
Where Is My Girl	7"	Columbia	DB7756	1965	**£4**	

STORYTELLER

Storyteller's blend of poetry and folk song was greeted with ecstatic reviews and the chance of a performance at the Festival Hall while still very much an up-and-coming group. The first track on the "Storyteller" LP is a delightful piece of folk-rock, with a sparkling guitar solo from Peter Frampton, but its companion tracks are not often in the same league. Singer Caroline Attard married the group's producer, Andy Bown (who was formerly a member of the Herd), but her attractive voice has not been heard on record since the early seventies.

More Pages	LP	Transatlantic	TRA232	1971	**£12**	
Remarkable	7"	CBS	7182	1971	**£5**	
Storyteller	LP	Transatlantic	TRA220	1970	**£12**	

STOWAWAYS

Stowaways	LP	Justice		196-	**£180**	US

STRAKER, EMILE & HIS MERRYMEN

Big Bamboo	7"	Doctor Bird	DB1004	1966	**£10**	

STRANGE

Raw Power	LP	O. Galaxie	1001	1976	**£25**	US
Translucent World	LP	O. Galaxie	1000	1973	**£30**	US

STRANGE DAYS

Monday Morning	7"	Retreat	RTS263	1975	**£6**	
Nine Parts To The Wind	LP	Retreat	RTL6005	1975	**£25**	

STRANGE FOX

Rock And Roll Band	7"	Parlophone	R5978	1973	**£4**	
Time And Tide	7"	Parlophone	R5876	1970	**£4**	

STRANGE, RICHARD

International Language	7"	Cherry Red	CHERRY10	1980	**£4**	

STRANGELOVES

Cara Lin	7"	Immediate	IM007	1965	**£10**	
Hand Jive	7"	London	HLZ10063	1966	**£10**	
Honey Do	7"	London	HLK10238	1969	**£10**	
I Want Candy	LP	Bang	BLP211	1965	**£25**	US
I Want Candy	7"	London	HLM10481	1975	**£4**	
I Want Candy	7"	Stateside	SS446	1965	**£8**	
Night Time	7"	London	HLZ10020	1966	**£12**	

STRANGERS

Do You Or Don't You	7"	Philips	PB1378	1964	**£4**	

STRANGLERS

All Day And All Of The Night	CD-s	Epic	CDVICE1	1988	**£12**	
All Day And All Of The Night	7"	Epic	VICE1	1988	**£5**	Monica Couglan sleeve
All Day And All Of The Night	7"	Epic	VICEP1	1988	**£5**	shaped pic disc
Always The Sun	7"	Epic	SOLARP1	1986	**£5**	shaped pic disc
Aural Sculpture	7"	Epic	XPS167	1983	**£4**	
Bear Cage	7"	United Artists	BP344	1980	**£4**	chart single
Bear Cage	12"	United Artists	12BP344	1980	**£10**	
Big In America	7"	Epic	HUGEP1	1986	**£5**	shaped pic disc
Black And White	LP	A&M	SP4706	1978	**£15**	US, black & white vinyl
Choosey Susie	7"	United Artists	FREE3	1977	**£6**	
Don't Bring Harry	7"	United Artists	STR1	1979	**£4**	chart single
Don't Bring Harry	7"	United Artists	STR1DJ	1978	**£10**	1 sided promo
Dreamtime	LP	Epic	EPC1126648	1986	**£12**	pic disc
Duchess	7"	United Artists	BP308	1979	**£4**	chart single
European Female (2 versions)	7"	Epic	EPCA2893DJ	1982	**£8**	promo
European Female	7"	Epic	EPCA112893	1983	**£6**	pic disc
Five Minutes	7"	United Artists	UP36350	1978	**£4**	chart single
Gospel According To The Men In Black	LP	Liberty	LBG30313	1981	**£20**	test pressing
Grip '89	7"	Liberty	EMR84	1989	**£4**	red vinyl, folder, poster
Grip	7"	United Artists	UP36211	1977	**£6**	chart single
Just Like Nothing On Earth	7"	United Artists	BP393	1981	**£4**	

Title	Format	Label	Cat. No.	Year	Price	Notes
La Folie	7"	Liberty	BP410DJ	1982	**£8**	promo
N'Emmenes Pas Harry	7"	United Artists		1979	**£10**	sung in French
Nice 'N' Sleazy	7"	United Artists	UP36379	1978	**£4**	chart single
Nice 'N' Sleazy	7"	United Artists	UP36379	1978	**£6**	promo
Nice In Nice	7"	Epic	EPC6500550	1986	**£6**	shaped pic disc
No Mercy	7"	Epic	GA4921	1984	**£4**	gatefold PS
No Mercy	7"	Epic	WA4921	1984	**£6**	shaped pic disc
No More Heroes	7"	United Artists	FREE8	1977	**£20**	1 sided promo
No More Heroes	7"	United Artists	UP36300	1977	**£4**	chart single
No More Heroes	7"	United Artists	UP36300	1977	**£15**	demo
No More Heroes	7"	United Artists	UP36300	1977	**£6**	wreath on label
Nuclear Device	7"	United Artists	BP318	1979	**£4**	chart single
Peaches	7"	United Artists	FREE4	1977	**£60**	1 sided promo
Peaches	7"	United Artists	UP36248	1977	**£6**	chart single
Peaches	7"	United Artists	UP36248	1977	**£120**	PS with newspaper lettering
Peaches	7"	United Artists	UP36248	1978	**£15**	mispress, B side plays Buzzcocks
Rattus Norvegicus	LP	United Artists	UAG30045	1977	**£30**	demo
Raven	LP	United Artists	UAG30262	1979	**£12**	3-D cover
Shakin' Like A Leaf	7"	Epic	SHEIKP1	1987	**£5**	shaped pic disc
Skin Deep	7"	Epic	A4738	1983	**£4**	'skin' textured sleeve
Skin Deep	12"	Epic	TA4738	1983	**£6**	'skin' textured sleeve
Something Better Change	7"	A&M	AM1973	1977	**£5**	US, pink marbled vinyl
Something Better Change	7"	United Artists	UP36277	1977	**£4**	chart single
Something Better Change	7"	United Artists	UP36277	1977	**£15**	demo
Strange Little Girl	7"	Liberty	BP412A	1982	**£15**	demo
Stranglers Singles Collection	LP	Liberty	LBG30353	1982	**£15**	with original dark cover
Sverge	7"	United Artists	UP36459	1978	**£8**	sung in Swedish
Tomorrow Was The Hereafter	7"	Strang.Inf.S.	SIS001	1980	**£8**	
Walk On By	7"	United Artists		1978	**£15**	1 sided promo
Walk On By	7"	United Artists	FREE9	1978	**£4**	white vinyl
Walk On By	7"	United Artists	UP36429	1978	**£4**	chart single
Who Wants The World	7"	United Artists	BPX355	1980	**£4**	red corner to PS
You Better Believe It	7"	United Artists	UP36262	1977	**£15**	demo

STRAPPS

Title	Format	Label	Cat. No.	Year	Price	Notes
Secret Damage	LP	Harvest	SHSP4064	1977	**£10**	
Sharp Conversation	LP	Harvest	SHSP4088	1978	**£10**	
Strapps	LP	Harvest	SHSP4055	1976	**£10**	

STRAWBERRY ALARM CLOCK

Title	Format	Label	Cat. No.	Year	Price	Notes
Best Of...	LP	Uni	73074	1970	**£20**	US
Changes	LP	Vocalion	73915	1971	**£20**	US
Good Morning Starshine	7"	MCA	MU1080	1969	**£8**	
Good Morning Starshine	LP	Uni	73054	1969	**£25**	US
Incense & Peppermints	LP	Pye	NSPL28106	1968	**£25**	
Incense & Peppermints	7"	Pye	7N25436	1967	**£10**	
Sit With The Guru	7"	Pye	7N25456	1968	**£12**	
Tomorrow	7"	Pye	7N25446	1968	**£12**	
Wake Up It's Tomorrow	LP	Uni	73025	1967	**£25**	US
World In A Sea Shell	LP	Uni	73035	1968	**£25**	US

STRAWBERRY CHILDREN

Title	Format	Label	Cat. No.	Year	Price	Notes
Love Years Coming	7"	Liberty	LBF15012	1967	**£8**	

STRAWBERRY SWITCHBLADE

Title	Format	Label	Cat. No.	Year	Price	Notes
Jolene	7"	Korova	KOW42	1985	**£4**	shaped pic disc
Let Her Go	7"	Korova	KOW39	1985	**£4**	shaped pic disc

STRAWBS

Title	Format	Label	Cat. No.	Year	Price	Notes
Burning For You	LP	Oyster	2391287	1977	**£10**	
Bursting At The Seams	LP	A&M	AMLH68144	1973	**£10**	chart LP
Dead Lines	LP	Arista	SPART1036	1978	**£10**	
Deep Cuts	LP	Oyster	2391234	1976	**£10**	
Dragonfly	LP	A&M	AMLS970	1970	**£12**	
From The Witchwood	LP	A&M	AMLS64304	1971	**£10**	chart LP
Ghosts	LP	A&M	AMLH68277	1975	**£10**	
Grave New World	LP	A&M	AMLS68078	1972	**£10**	chart LP
Heartbreak Hill	LP	Arista		1979	**£20**	
Hero And Heroine	LP	A&M	AMLH63607	1974	**£10**	chart LP

Just A Collection Of Antiques...	LP	A&M	AMLS994	1970	**£10**	chart LP
Nomadness	LP	A&M	AMLH68331	1976	**£10**	
Strawbs	LP	A&M	AMLS936	1969	**£15**	

STRAWHEAD

Fortunes Of War	LP	Tradition		1978	**£10**	

STRAY

Hallelujah	7"	Transatlantic	BIG512	1972	**£4**	
Hearts Of Fire	LP	Pye	NSPL18512	1976	**£10**	
Houdini	LP	Pye	NSPL18482	1976	**£10**	
Move It	LP	Transatlantic	TRA281	1974	**£12**	
Move It	7"	Transatlantic	BIG516	1972	**£4**	
Mudanzas	LP	Transatlantic	TRA268	1973	**£12**	
Our Song	7"	Transatlantic	BIG141	1971	**£4**	
Saturday Morning Pictures	LP	Transatlantic	TRA248	1972	**£15**	
Stand Up & Be Counted	LP	Dawn	DNLS3066	1975	**£10**	
Stray	LP	Transatlantic	TRA216	1970	**£12**	
Suicide	LP	Transatlantic	TRA233	1971	**£12**	

STRAY CATS

She's Sexy And Seventeen	7"	Arista	SCAT6	1983	**£8**	shaped pic disc

STRAY DOG

Stray Dog	LP	Manticore	K43506	1974	**£10**	
While You're Down There	LP	Manticore	K53504	1974	**£10**	

STREET, GARY & THE FAIRWAYS

Flippedy Flop	7"	Domain	D2	1968	**£4**	

STREET, HILLARD

River Love	7"	Capitol	CL14960	1958	**£4**	

STREET, JOHN & THE INMATES OF NO.12

Keep A Little Love	7"	Deram	DM147	1967	**£4**	

STREETWALKERS

Downtown Flier	LP	Vertigo	6360123	1975	**£10**	
Red Card	LP	Vertigo	9102010	1976	**£10**	chart LP
Red Card	LP	Vertigo	9102010	1976	**£12**	red vinyl
Streetwalkers	LP	Reprise	K54017	1974	**£10**	
Streetwalkers Live	LP	Vertigo	6641703	1977	**£12**	double
Vicious But Fair	LP	Vertigo	9102012	1977	**£10**	

STREISAND, BARBRA

Barbra Joan Streisand	LP	Columbia	PCQ30792	1971	**£10**	US quad
Barbra Streisand	7" EP	CBS	AGG20054	1964	**£4**	
Butterfly	LP	Columbia	PCQ33005	1974	**£10**	US quad
Color Me Barbra	LP	Columbia	CL2478	1966	**£35**	US, red vinyl
En Francais	7" EP	CBS	EP6048	1965	**£8**	
Funny Girl	LP	Columbia	SQ30992	1972	**£10**	US quad
Funny Lady	LP	Arista	AQ9004	1975	**£10**	US quad
Greatest Hits Volume 2	LP	Columbia	HC45679	1982	**£10**	US audiophile
Guilty	LP	Columbia	HC46750	1982	**£10**	US audiophile
Lazy Afternoon	LP	Columbia	PCQ33815	1975	**£10**	US quad
Live In Concert At The Forum	LP	Columbia	PCQ31760	1972	**£10**	US quad
Lover Come Back To Me	7" EP	CBS	AGG20042	1964	**£4**	
Memories	LP	Columbia	HC47678	1982	**£10**	US audiophile
My Man	7" EP	CBS	EP6068	1966	**£4**	
Second Barbra Streisand Album	LP	Columbia	CS8854	1963	**£50**	US, blue vinyl
Second Hand Rose	7" EP	CBS	EP6150	1967	**£4**	
Stoney End	LP	Columbia	PCQ30378	1971	**£10**	US quad
Way We Were	LP	Columbia	PCQ32801	1974	**£10**	US quad

STRENGTH, TEXAS BILL

Yellow Rose Of Texas	7"	Capitol	CL14357	1955	**£10**	

STRETCH

Can't Beat Your Brain For Entertainment	LP	Anchor	ANCL2016	1976	**£12**	
Elastique	LP	Anchor	ANCL2014	1975	**£12**	
Forget The Past	LP	Hot Wax	HW1	1978	**£20**	
Life Blood	LP	Anchor	ANCL2023	1977	**£12**	

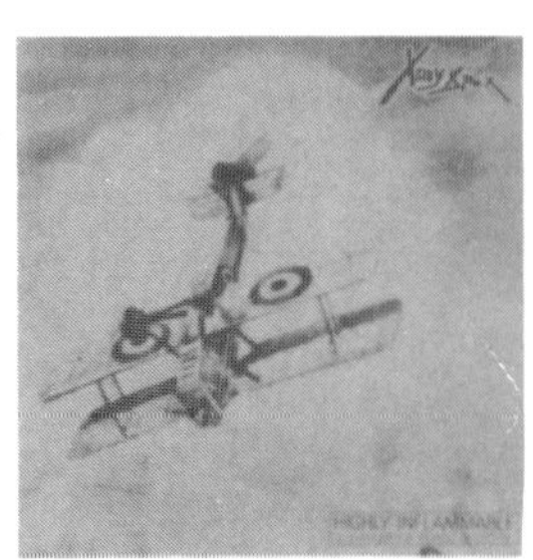

I-I-I- Don't Want To Be Like You!

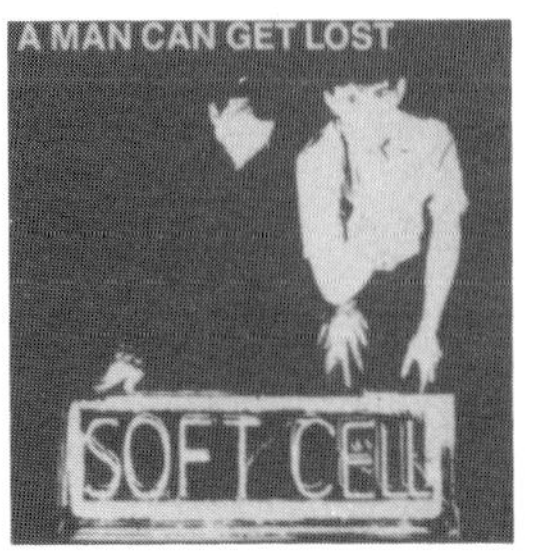

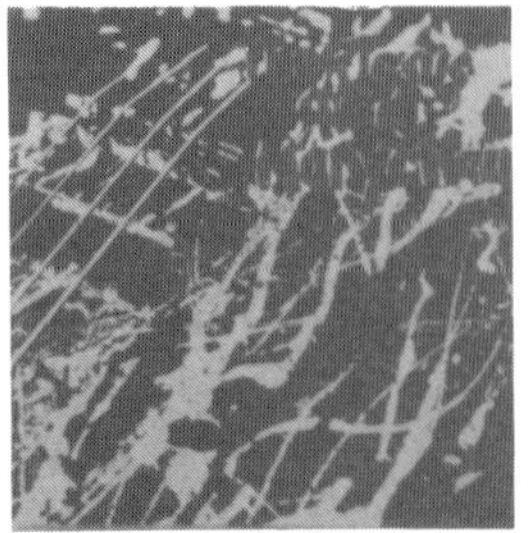

It's The New Thing

Plate 65

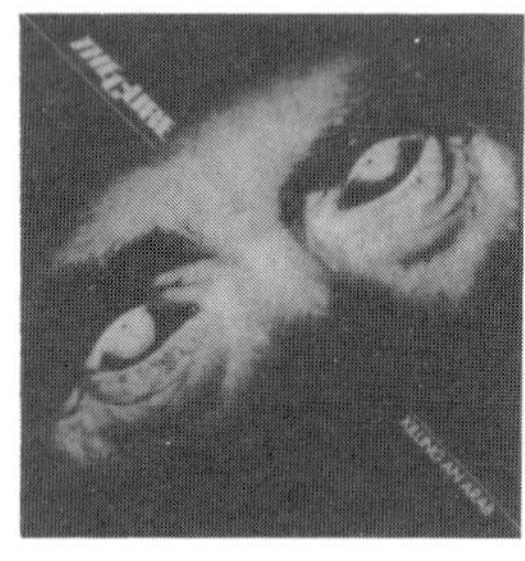

Faith

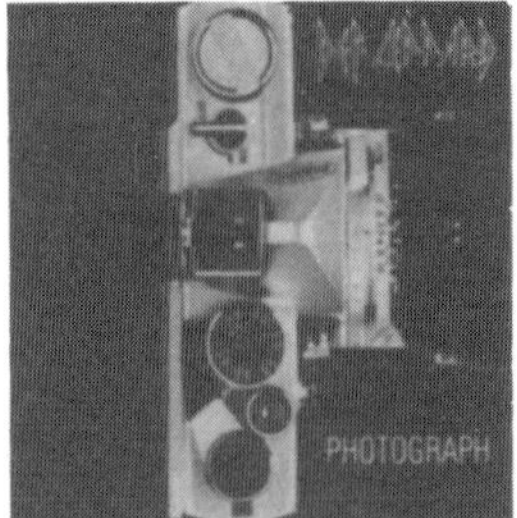

Just Like Gold

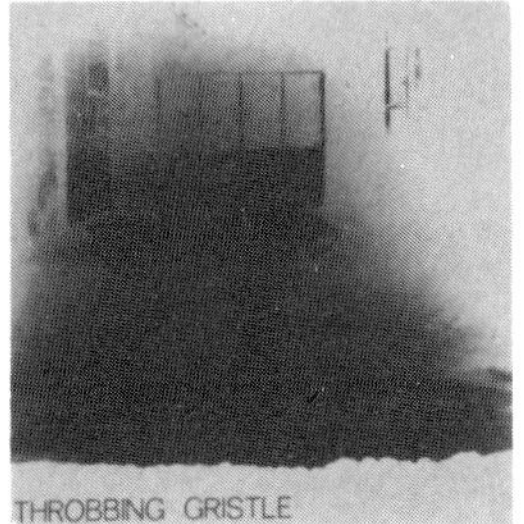

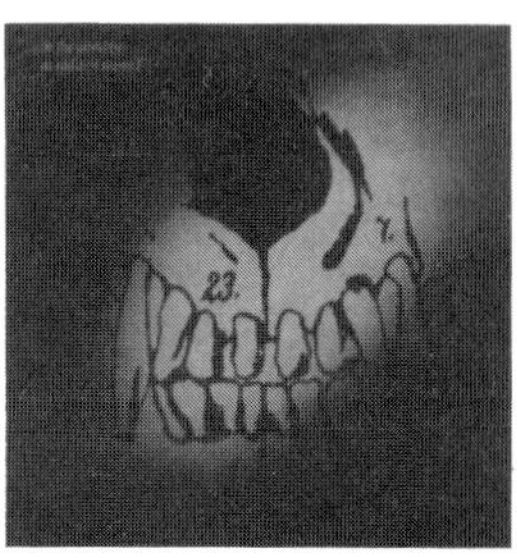

Entertainment Through Fun

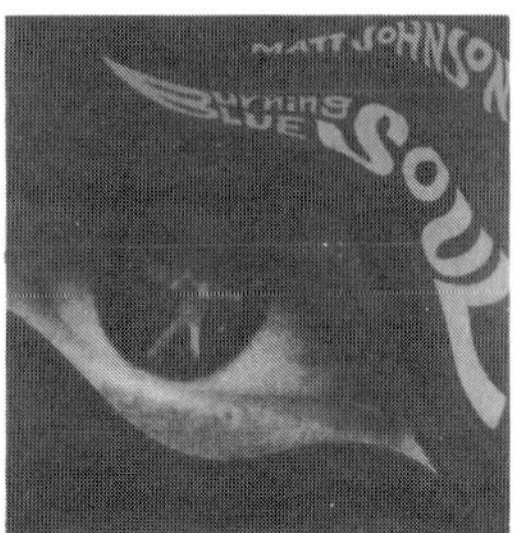

Soul Mining

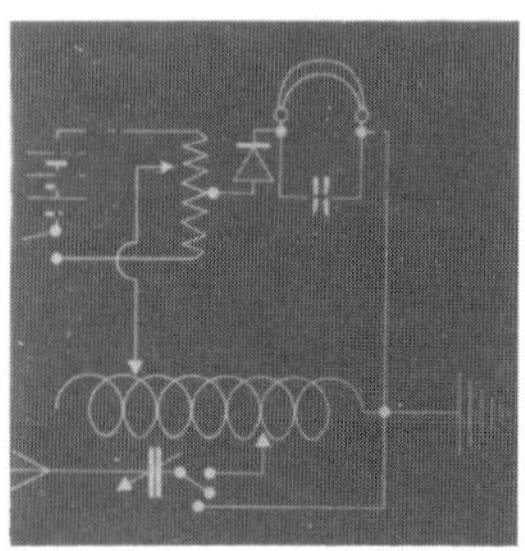

Lubricate Your Living Room

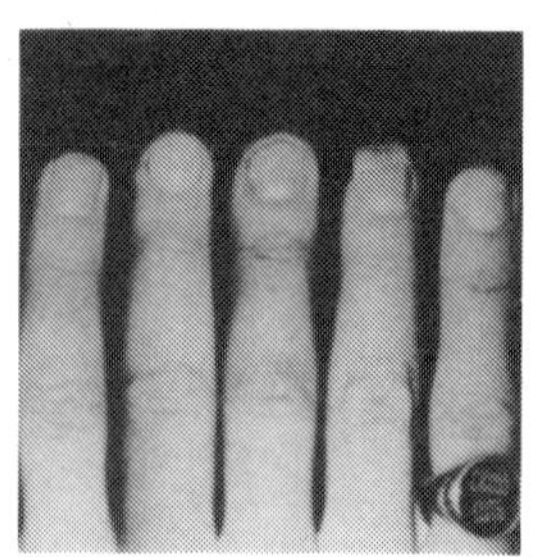

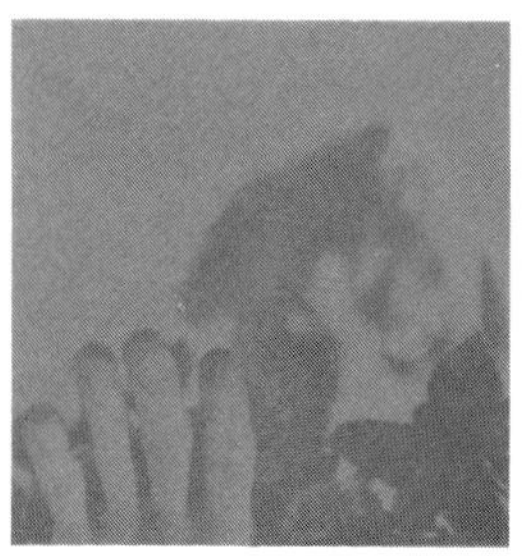

Pay Attention!

You got it all, Dad! We're gonna hit!

(SOUND OF IMPACT.)

Phonography

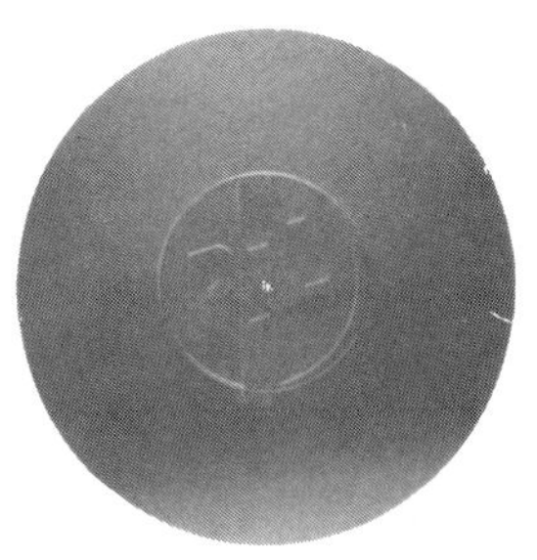

Gimmix! Play Loud

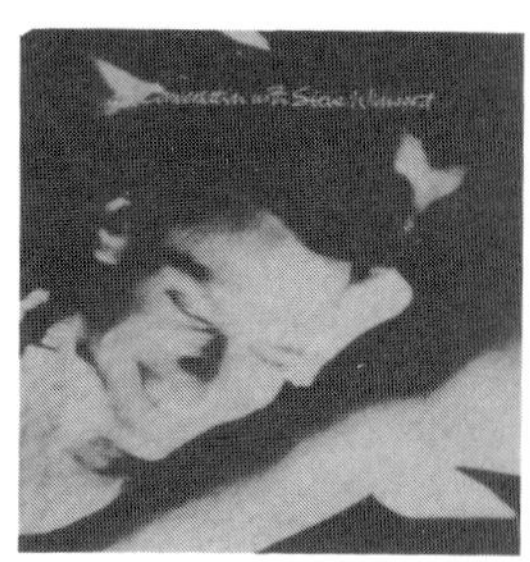

For Promotional Use Only

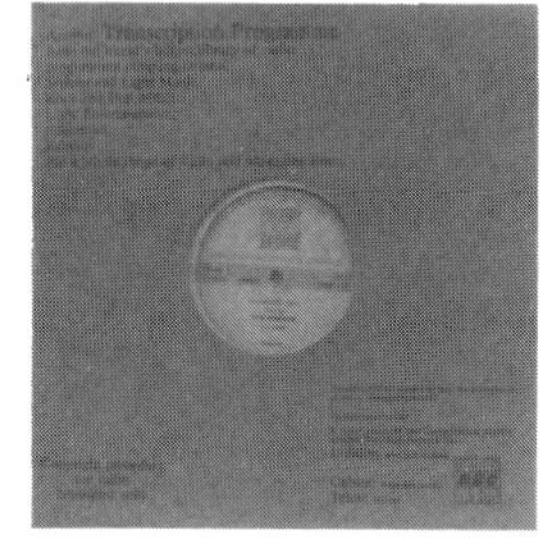

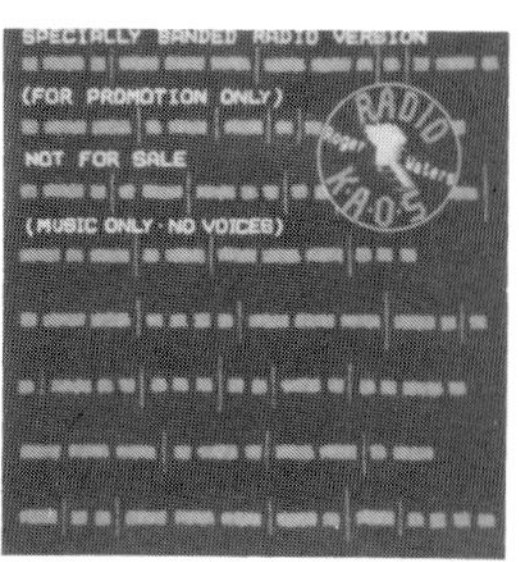

Radio Radio

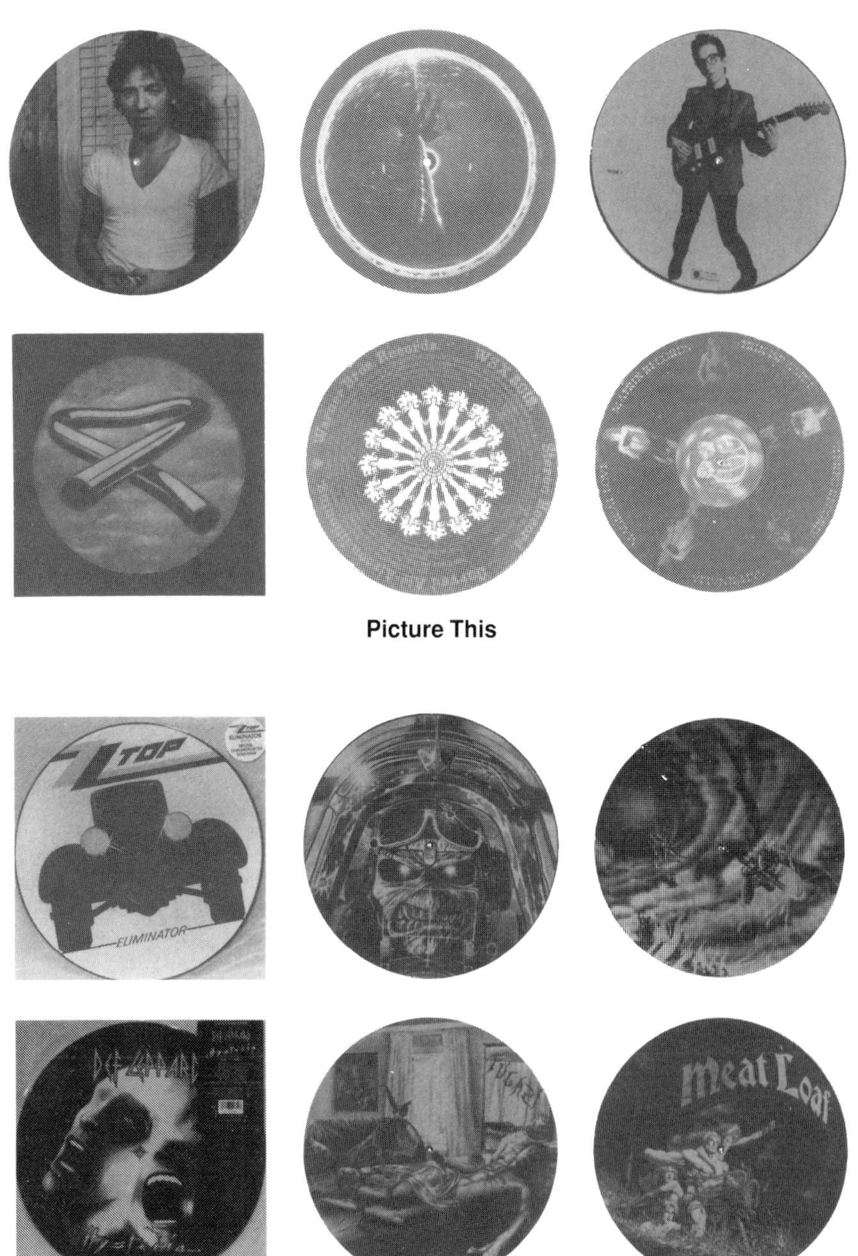

Picture This

Every Picture Tells A Story

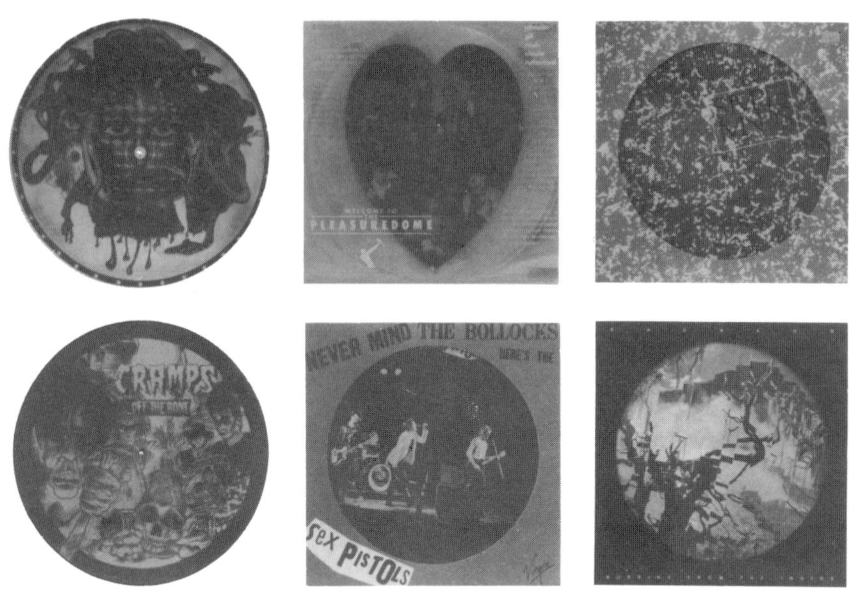

Pictures At An Exhibition

If I Had A Talking Picture Of You

Shape Of Things

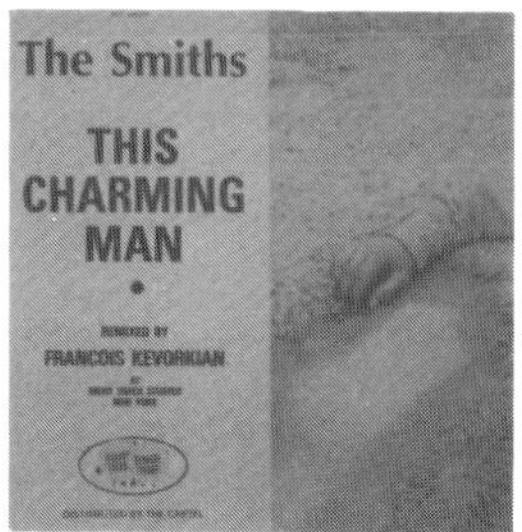

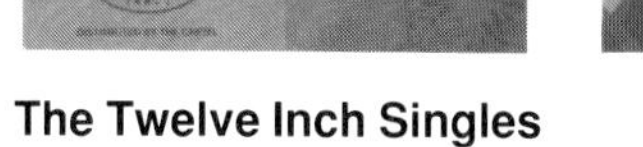

The Twelve Inch Singles

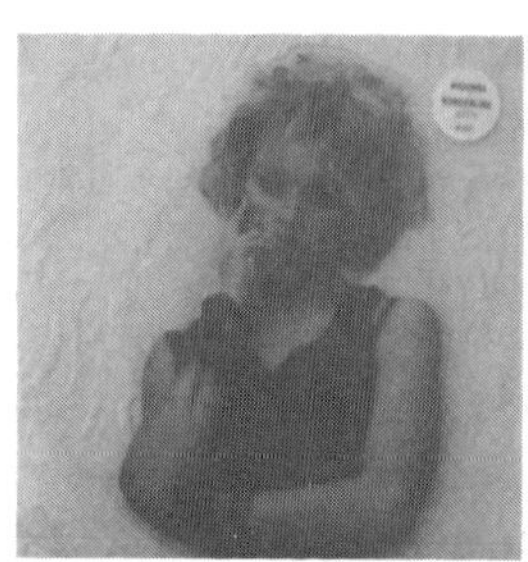

Material Girl

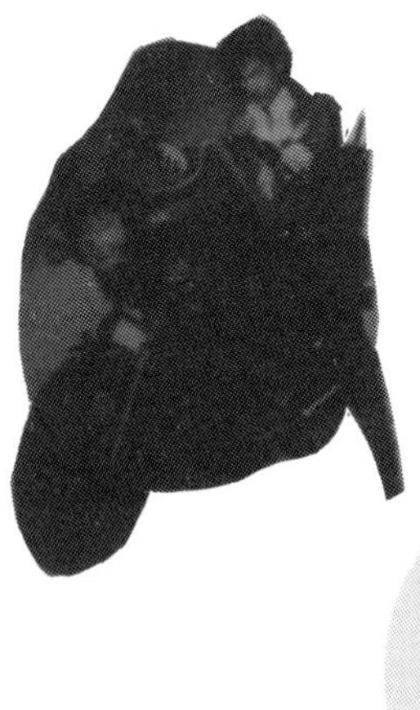

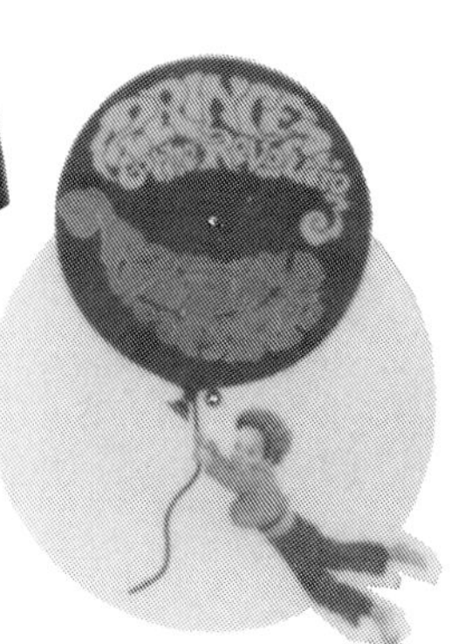

Purple Rain

Pre-Kinney LP Label Designs

EMI LP Label Designs

Plate 75

Decca LP Label Designs

Island/Immediate/Charisma LP Label Designs

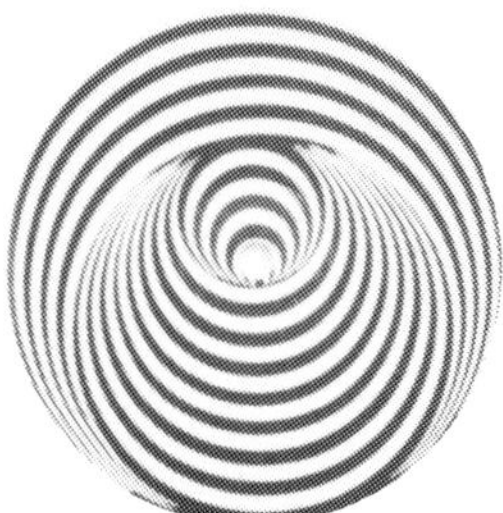

Phonogram LP Label Designs

Pye LP Label Designs

Sixties LP Label Designs

Sixties LP Label Designs

Sixties LP Label Designs

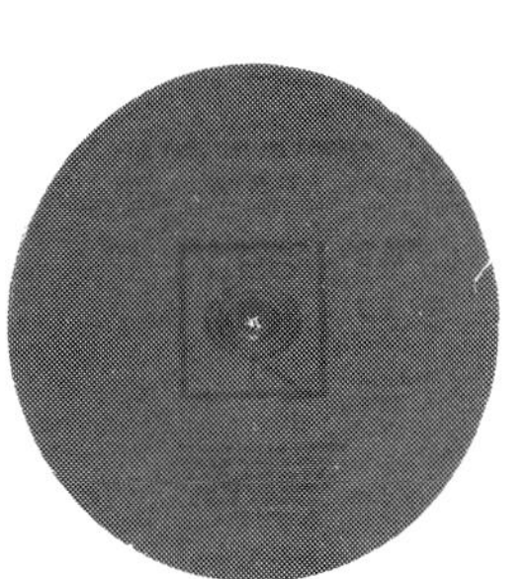

LP Label Designs

Sixties LP Label Designs

Sixties Demonstration Single Label Designs

STRICKLAND, WILLIAM R.

William Strickland was reputed to have made his songs up as he went along and certainly they sound ramshackle enough for him to have done so. At the time, the Deram label was willing to try anything, but in the end, all that can really be said about Mr.Strickland is that he is no Syd Barrett.

...Is Only The Name .... LP .... Deram .... SML1041 .... 1969 .... **£20**

STRIDER

Exposed .... LP .... GM .... GML1002 .... 1973 .... **£10**
Misunderstanding .... LP .... GM .... GML1012 .... 1974 .... **£10**

STRING CHEESE

String Cheese .... LP .... RCA .... SF8222 .... 1971 .... **£15**

STRING DRIVEN THING

Another Night .... 7" .... Concord .... CON7 .... 1970 .... **£15**
Are You A Rock And Roller .... 7" .... Charisma .... CB210 .... 1973 .... **£4**
Circus .... 7" .... Charisma .... CB203 .... 1973 .... **£4**
I'll Sing One For You .... 7" .... B&C .... CB223 .... 1974 .... **£4**
Keep Yer 'And On It .... LP .... Charisma .... CAS1112 .... 1975 .... **£10**
Machine That Cried .... LP .... Charisma .... CAS1070 .... 1973 .... **£10**
Mrs.O'Reilly .... 7" .... Charisma .... CB239 .... 1974 .... **£4**
Please Mind Your Head .... LP .... Charisma .... CAS1097 .... 1974 .... **£10**
String Driven Thing .... LP .... Charisma .... CAS1062 .... 1972 .... **£10**
String Driven Thing .... LP .... Concord .... CON1001 .... 1970 .... **£50**
Timpani For The Devil .... 7" .... Charisma .... CB247 .... 1975 .... **£4**

STRINGALONGS

Brass Buttons .... 7" .... London .... HLU9354 .... 1961 .... **£4**
Matilda .... 7" .... London .... HLD9652 .... 1963 .... **£4**
Mina Bird .... 7" .... London .... HLU9452 .... 1961 .... **£4**
Should I .... 7" .... London .... HLU9394 .... 1961 .... **£4**
Spinnin' My Wheels .... 7" .... London .... HLD9588 .... 1962 .... **£4**
Stringalong With The Stringalongs .... 7" EP .... London .... REU1398 .... 1963 .... **£8**
Stringalongs .... 7" EP .... London .... REU1322 .... 1961 .... **£8**
Stringalongs .... 7" EP .... London .... REU1350 .... 1963 .... **£8**
Twistwatch .... 7" .... London .... HLD9535 .... 1962 .... **£4**
Wheels .... 7" .... London .... HLU9278 .... 1961 .... **£4** .... chart single

STROLLERS

Come On Over .... 7" .... London .... HLL9336 .... 1961 .... **£4**
Cuckoo .... 7" .... Fontana .... TF598 .... 1965 .... **£4**
Jumping With Symphony Sid .... 7" .... Vogue .... V9113 .... 1958 .... **£4**
Little Bitty Pretty One .... 7" .... Vogue .... V9124 .... 1958 .... **£6**

STRONG, BARRETT

Money .... 7" .... London .... HLU9088 .... 1960 .... **£20**

STRONG, NOLAN & THE DIABLOS

Fortune Of Hits .... LP .... Fortune .... LP8010 .... 1961 .... **£30** .... US
Fortune Of Hits Vol.2 .... LP .... Fortune .... LP8012 .... 1962 .... **£30** .... US
Mind Over Matter .... LP .... Fortune .... LP8015 .... 1963 .... **£30** .... US

STRYPER

Yellow And Black Attack .... LP .... Music For N. ... MFN74 .... **£10** .... round sleeve, blue vinyl

STUART, CHAD & JEREMY CLYDE

Best Of .... LP .... Ember .... 5036 .... 1967 .... **£10**
Early In The Morning .... 7" .... Ember .... EMBS186 .... 1964 .... **£5**
Evil Hearted Me .... 7" .... CBS .... 201769 .... 1965 .... **£10**
I Don't Wanna Lose You Baby .... LP .... Ember .... 5031 .... 1965 .... **£10**
Yesterday's Gone .... 7" .... Ember .... EMBS180 .... 1963 .... **£4** .... chart single
Yesterday's Gone .... 7" EP .... Ember .... EMB4543 .... 1964 .... **£5**

STUART, MIKE SPAN

Come On Over To Our Place .... 7" .... Columbia .... DB8066 .... 1966 .... **£5**
Dear .... 7" .... Columbia .... DB8206 .... 1967 .... **£4**
You Can Understand Me .... 7" .... Fontana .... TF959 .... 1968 .... **£5**

STUD

Goodbye Live At Command .... LP .... BASF .... 2029117 .... 1973 .... **£20**
September .... LP .... BASF .... 2029054 .... 1972 .... **£25**

Stud	LP	Deram	SMLR1084	1971	**£20**	

STYLE COUNCIL

Cafe Bleu	12"	Polydor	CAFE1	1984	**£6**	promo sampler
It Just Came To Pieces (live)	7"	Lyntone	LYN15344/5	1984	**£10**	flexi
Long Hot Summer	7"	Polydor	TSCD3	1983	**£4**	juke box issue
Long Hot Summer	12"	Polydor	TSCDM3	1983	**£6**	promo
Money-Go-Round	12"	Polydor	TSCDM2	1983	**£6**	promo
Paris Match	7"	Polydor	TSCDJ3	1983	**£4**	1 sided promo
Solid Bond In Your Heart	7"	Polydor	TSCD4	1983	**£4**	juke box issue
Speak Like A Child	7"	Polydor	TSCDJ1	1983	**£4**	promo

STYLE SISTERS

Summer Magic	7"	London	HLU9753	1963	**£4**	

STYLOS

Head Over Heels	7"	Liberty	LIB10173	1964	**£8**	

STYRENE, POLY

Translucence	LP	United Artists	UAG30320	1980	**£10**	

STYVERS, LAURIE

Spilt Milk	LP	Chrysalis	CHR1007	1972	**£10**	

STYX

Best Of	LP	RCA	3597	1979	**£12**	Canadian blue vinyl
Blue Collar Man	LP	A&M	AMSP7388		**£10**	gatefold sleeve
Collection Of Styx	LP	A&M	SAMP3	1980	**£10**	promo sampler
Collection Of Styx	LP	A&M		1979	**£20**	promo, 3 LPs, boxed
Cornerstone	LP	A&M	SP3711	1979	**£20**	US silver vinyl
Cornerstone	LP	Nautilus		198-	**£15**	US audiophile
Don't Let Go	7"	A&M			**£4**	shaped pic disc
Don't Let It End	7"	A&M	AM120	1983	**£4**	shaped pic disc
Equinox	LP	A&M	SP4604	1975	**£10**	Canadian yellow vinyl
Grand Illusion	LP	A&M	SP4637	1977	**£12**	Canadian gold vinyl
Grand Illusion	LP	Mobile Fid.	MFSL1026	1978	**£15**	US audiophile
Lady	7"	RCA	RCA2518	1975	**£4**	
Paradise Theatre	LP	Nautilus		198-	**£15**	US audiophile
Pieces Of Eight	LP	A&M	AMLH64724	1978	**£10**	translucent vinyl
Pieces Of Eight	LP	A&M	PR4724	1978	**£12**	US, pic disc
Pieces Of Eight	LP	Nautilus		198-	**£15**	US audiophile
Styx Radio Show	LP	A&M	SP8431	1976	**£20**	US promo
Styx Radio Special	LP	A&M	SP17053	1977	**£20**	US promo

SUB

In Concert	LP	Help		197-	**£300**	

SUBHUMANS

Incorrect Thoughts	LP	Friends	FR008	1980	**£30**	
No Wishes No Prayers	LP				**£15**	Canadian

SUBOTNICK, MORTON

Silver Apples Of The Moon	LP	Nonesuch	H71174	196-	**£10**	
The Wild Bull	LP	Nonesuch	H71208	1968	**£10**	

SUBURBAN STUDS

I Hate School	7"	Pogo	POG002	1978	**£4**	
No Faith	7"	Pogo	POG001	1977	**£4**	
Slam	LP	Pogo	POW001	1978	**£10**	

SUE & SUNNY

Every Ounce Of Strength	7"	Columbia	DB7748	1965	**£4**	
I Like Your Style	7"	Columbia	DB8099	1967	**£4**	
Show Must Go On	7"	CBS	3874	1968	**£4**	
Sue & Sunny	LP	CBS	63740	1970	**£10**	

SUGAR & PEEWEE

One Two Let's Rock	7"	Vogue	V9112	1958	**£40**	

SUGAR & SPICE

Cruel War	7"	London	HLU10259	1969	**£5**	

SUGAR 'N' DANDY

Title	Format	Label	Cat. No.	Year	Price	Notes
I'm Into Something Good	7"	Carnival	CV7024	1965	**£6**	
I'm Not Crying Now	7"	Carnival	CV7016	1964	**£6**	
Let's Ska	7"	Carnival	CV7023	1965	**£6**	
Let's Ska	7"	Page One	POF23044	1967	**£6**	
Oh Dear What Can The Matter Be	7"	Carnival	CV7009	1964	**£6**	
One Man Went To Mow	7"	Carnival	CV7006	1963	**£6**	
Think Of The Good Times	7"	Carnival	CV7027	1965	**£6**	
What A Life	7"	Carnival	CV7015	1964	**£6**	

SUGAR SHOPPE

Title	Format	Label	Cat. No.	Year	Price	Notes
Skip Along Sam	7"	Capitol	CL15555	1968	**£6**	

SUGARBEATS

Title	Format	Label	Cat. No.	Year	Price	Notes
Alice Designs	7"	Polydor	56120	1966	**£6**	
I Just Stand Here	7"	Polydor	56069	1966	**£6**	

SUGARCUBES

Title	Format	Label	Cat. No.	Year	Price	Notes
12.11	12"	One L. Ind.	TPBOX1	1990	**£45**	11 x 12", boxed
7.8	7"	One L. Ind.	TPBOX2	1990	**£25**	8 x 7", boxed
Birthday	CD-s	One L. Ind.	7TP7CD	1987	**£6**	
Birthday	12"	One L. Ind.	12TP7	1987	**£6**	
CD.6	CD-s	One L. Ind.	TPBOX3	1990	**£35**	6 x CD-s, boxed
Here Today, Tomorrow, Next Week	LP	One L.Ind.	TRLP15	1989	**£10**	chart single

SUGARCUBES (SYKURMOLARNIR)

Title	Format	Label	Cat. No.	Year	Price	Notes
Einn Mol'a Mann	7"	Smekkleysa	SM3/86	1986	**£60**	Icelandic
Luftgitar	12"	Smekkleysa	SM7	1987	**£30**	Icelandic
Skytturnar	12"	Gramm	GRAMM31	1986	**£25**	Icelandic

SUGARLOAF

Title	Format	Label	Cat. No.	Year	Price	Notes
Don't Call Us, We'll Call You	LP	Polydor	2310394	1975	**£25**	
Spaceship Earth	LP	United Artists	UAS29165	1974	**£10**	
Sugarloaf	LP	Liberty	LBS83415	1970	**£10**	

SUICIDAL TENDENCIES

Title	Format	Label	Cat. No.	Year	Price	Notes
Possessed To Skate	12"	Virgin	VS96712	1987	**£10**	pic disc

SUICIDE

Title	Format	Label	Cat. No.	Year	Price	Notes
23 Minutes In Brussels	LP	Bronze	FRANKIE1	1978	**£15**	
Alan Vega - Martin Rev	LP	Ze	ILPS7007	1980	**£10**	
Cheree	7"	Bronze	BRO57	1978	**£4**	
Dream Baby Dream	12"	Ze	WIP6543	1979	**£6**	
Suicide	LP	Bronze	BRON508	1977	**£12**	

SUICIDE COMMANDOS

Title	Format	Label	Cat. No.	Year	Price	Notes
Commandos Commit Suicide Dance Concert	LP	Twintone	TTR7906	1979	**£20**	US
Make A Record	LP	Blank	002	1977	**£10**	US

SULLIVAN, BIG JIM

Title	Format	Label	Cat. No.	Year	Price	Notes
She Walks Through The Fair	7"	Mercury	MF928	1965	**£4**	
Sitar Beat	LP	Mercury	SML30001	1968	**£15**	
You Don't Know What You've Got	7"	Decca	F11387	1961	**£6**	

SUMLIN, HUBERT

Title	Format	Label	Cat. No.	Year	Price	Notes
Across The Board	7"	Blue Horizon	451000	1965	**£20**	

SUMMER SET

Title	Format	Label	Cat. No.	Year	Price	Notes
Farmer's Daughter	7"	Columbia	DB8004	1966	**£8**	
It's A Dream	7"	Columbia	DB8215	1967	**£8**	

SUMMER, DONNA

Title	Format	Label	Cat. No.	Year	Price	Notes
Dinner With Gershwin	12"	WEA	U8237P	1987	**£8**	pic disc
Hot Stuff	12"	Casablanca	CANL151	1979	**£15**	red vinyl
This Time I Know It's For Real	7"	WEA	U7780P	1989	**£4**	shaped pic disc

SUMMERFIELD, SAFFRON

Title	Format	Label	Cat. No.	Year	Price	Notes
Fancy Meeting You Here	LP	Mother Earth	MUM1202	1976	**£25**	
Salisbury Plain	LP	Mother Earth	MUM1001	1974	**£25**	

SUMMERS, BOB

Title	Format	Label	Number	Year	Price	Notes
Excitement	7"	Capitol	CL15063	1959	**£4**	

SUN ALSO RISES

Title	Format	Label	Number	Year	Price	Notes
Sun Also Rises	LP	Village Thing	VTS2	1970	**£10**	

SUNDAE TIMES

Title	Format	Label	Number	Year	Price	Notes
Baby Don't Cry	7"	President	PT203	1968	**£5**	
Jackboy	7"	President	PT219	1968	**£5**	

SUNDANCE

Title	Format	Label	Number	Year	Price	Notes
Chuffer	LP	Decca	SKL5183	1974	**£12**	
Rain Steam Speed	LP	Decca	TXS111	1973	**£12**	

SUNDOWN PLAYBOYS

Title	Format	Label	Number	Year	Price	Notes
Saturday Night Special	7"	Apple	44	1972	**£6**	
Saturday Night Special	7"	Apple	44	1972	**£12**	PS
Saturday Night Special	78	Apple	44	1972	**£30**	promo

SUNDOWNERS

Title	Format	Label	Number	Year	Price	Notes
Dr.J.Wallace-Browne	7"	Columbia	DB8339	1968	**£8**	
House Of The Rising Sun	7"	Piccadilly	7N35142	1963	**£6**	
Shot Of Rhythm And Blues	7"	Piccadilly	7N35162	1964	**£6**	
Where Am I	7"	Parlophone	R5243	1965	**£5**	

SUNDRAGON

Title	Format	Label	Number	Year	Price	Notes
Blueberry Blue	7"	MGM	MGM1391	1968	**£8**	
Five White Horses	7"	MGM	MGM1458	1968	**£8**	
Green Tambourine	7"	MGM	MGM1380	1968	**£6**	chart single

SUNFOREST

Title	Format	Label	Number	Year	Price	Notes
Sound Of Sunforest	LP	Nova	SDN7	1969	**£30**	

SUNNY & THE HI-JUMPERS

Title	Format	Label	Number	Year	Price	Notes
Going To Damascus	7"	Carnival	CV7025	1965	**£6**	
Tarry Till You're Better	7"	Carnival	CV7022	1965	**£6**	

SUNNY & THE SUNGLOWS

Title	Format	Label	Number	Year	Price	Notes
All Night Worker	LP	Tear Drop	2019	196-	**£15**	US
Peanuts	LP	Sunglow	SLP103	1965	**£15**	US
Talk To Me	7"	London	HL9792	1963	**£4**	
Talk To Me/Rags To Riches	LP	Tear Drop	2000	1963	**£15**	US

SUNNYLAND SLIM

Title	Format	Label	Number	Year	Price	Notes
Midnight Jump	LP	Blue Horizon	763213	1969	**£30**	
Slim's Got This Thing Goin' On	LP	Liberty	LBS83237	1969	**£30**	
Slim's Shout	LP	Bluesville	BV1016	1961	**£20**	US

SUNNYSIDERS

Title	Format	Label	Number	Year	Price	Notes
Banjo Woogie	7"	London	HLU8180	1955	**£8**	
Doesn't He Love Me	7"	London	HLU8246	1956	**£10**	
Hey Mister Banjo	7"	London	HL8135	1955	**£8**	
I Love You Fair Dinkum	7"	London	HLU8202	1955	**£6**	
Oh Me Oh My	7"	London	HL8160	1955	**£8**	

SUNRAYS

Title	Format	Label	Number	Year	Price	Notes
Andrea	7"	Capitol	CL15433	1966	**£5**	
Andrea	LP	Tower	T5017	1966	**£12**	US
I Live For The Sun	7"	Capitol	CL15416	1965	**£5**	

SUNSETS

Title	Format	Label	Number	Year	Price	Notes
Cry Of The Wild Goose	7"	Ember	EMBS125	1960	**£4**	
Surfing With The Sunsets	LP	Palace	752	1963	**£15**	US

SUNSHINE

Title	Format	Label	Number	Year	Price	Notes
Sunshine	LP	W. Bros	K46169	1972	**£10**	

SUNSHINE COMPANY

Title	Format	Label	Number	Year	Price	Notes
Back On The Street Again	7"	Liberty	LBF15034	1967	**£4**	
Happy Is The Sunshine Company	LP	Imperial	12359	1967	**£10**	US
Look Here Comes The Sun	7"	Liberty	LBF15060	1968	**£4**	
On A Beautiful Day	7"	Liberty	LBF15149	1968	**£4**	

Title	Format	Label	Cat. No.	Year	Price	Notes
Sunshine & Shadows	LP	Liberty	LBL83159	1968	**£10**	
Sunshine Company	LP	Imperial	12368	1968	**£10**	US

SUNTREADER

Title	Format	Label	Cat. No.	Year	Price	Notes
Zin Zin	LP	Island	HELP13	1973	**£10**	

SUPERBOYS

Title	Format	Label	Cat. No.	Year	Price	Notes
Ain't That A Shame	7"	Giant	GN22	1967	**£10**	

SUPERFINE DANDELION

Title	Format	Label	Cat. No.	Year	Price	Notes
Superfine Dandelion	LP	Mainstream	S6102	1968	**£15**	US

SUPERSISTER

Title	Format	Label	Cat. No.	Year	Price	Notes
Islander	LP	Polydor	2485134	1973	**£10**	
Present From Nancy	LP	Polydor	2419061	1972	**£12**	
Pudding And Gisteren	LP	Polydor	2419058	1972	**£10**	
Super Starshine 3	LP	Polydor	2419030	1971	**£10**	
Sweet Okay	LP	Polydor	2441048	1974	**£10**	Dutch
To The Highest Bidder	LP	Dandelion	2310146	1971	**£12**	

SUPERSONICS

Title	Format	Label	Cat. No.	Year	Price	Notes
Second Fiddle	7"	Trojan	TRL6	1968	**£10**	

SUPERSTOCKS

Title	Format	Label	Cat. No.	Year	Price	Notes
School Is A Drag	LP	Capitol	T2190	1964	**£40**	US
Surf Route 101	LP	Capitol	T2113	1964	**£40**	US
Thunder Road	LP	Capitol	T2060	1964	**£40**	US

SUPERTRAMP

Title	Format	Label	Cat. No.	Year	Price	Notes
Breakfast In America	LP	Mobile Fid.	MFSL1045	1980	**£10**	US audiophile
Crime Of The Century	LP	Mobile Fid.	MFSL1005	1978	**£12**	US audiophile
Crime Of The Century	LP	Mobile Fid.	MFSL1005		**£20**	US audiophile (UHQR)
Crisis? What Crisis	LP				**£10**	audiophile
Even In The Quietest Moments	LP				**£10**	audiophile
Famous Last Words	LP				**£10**	audiophile
Land Ho	7"	A&M	AMS7101	1974	**£4**	
Paris	LP				**£15**	audiophile double

SUPREMES

Title	Format	Label	Cat. No.	Year	Price	Notes
A Go-Go	LP	T. Motown	STML11039	1966	**£12**	chart LP
At The Copa	LP	T. Motown	TML11026	1966	**£20**	
Automatically Sunshine	7"	T. Motown	TMG821	1972	**£4**	chart single
Automatically Sunshine	7"	T. Motown	TMG821	1972	**£10**	demo
Baby Love	7"	Stateside	SS350	1964	**£5**	chart single
Baby Love	7"	Stateside	SS350	1964	**£50**	demo
Back In My Arms Again	7"	T. Motown	TMG516	1965	**£10**	chart single
Back In My Arms Again	7"	T. Motown	TMG516	1965	**£50**	demo
Bad Weather	7"	T. Motown	TMG847	1973	**£4**	chart single
Bad Weather	7"	T. Motown	TMG847	1973	**£10**	demo
Bit Of Liverpool	LP	Motown	M623	1964	**£25**	US
Come See About Me	7"	Stateside	SS376	1965	**£5**	chart single
Come See About Me	7"	Stateside	SS376	1965	**£50**	demo
Country,Western & Pop	LP	T. Motown	TML11018	1965	**£25**	
Everybody's Got The Right To Love	7"	T. Motown	TMG747	1970	**£4**	
Everybody's Got The Right To Love	7"	T. Motown	TMG747	1970	**£10**	demo
Floy Joy	7"	T. Motown	TMG804	1972	**£4**	chart single
Floy Joy	7"	T. Motown	TMG804	1972	**£12**	demo
Happening	7"	T. Motown	TMG607	1967	**£6**	chart single
Happening	7"	T. Motown	TMG607	1967	**£35**	demo
I Hear A Symphony	LP	T. Motown	TML11028	1966	**£12**	
I Hear A Symphony	7"	T. Motown	TMG543	1965	**£6**	chart single
I Hear A Symphony	7"	T. Motown	TMG543	1965	**£50**	demo
L'Amore Verra	7"	T. Motown	TM8004	1966	**£20**	sung in Italian
Love Is Here And Now You're Gone	7"	T. Motown	TMG597	1967	**£4**	chart single
Love Is Here And Now You're Gone	7"	T. Motown	TMG597	1967	**£40**	demo
Love Is Like An Itching In My Heart	7"	T. Motown	TMG560	1966	**£10**	
Love Is Like An Itching In My Heart	7"	T. Motown	TMG560	1966	**£60**	demo
Meet The Supremes	LP	Motown	M606	1964	**£150**	US, group seated on stools on cover
Meet The Supremes	LP	Stateside	SL10109	1964	**£30**	chart LP
Merry Christmas	LP	Motown	M638	1965	**£15**	US

Title	Format	Label	Number	Year	Price	Notes
Moonlight And Kisses	7"	T. Motown	GO42625	1967	**£20**	Dutch, B side sung in French
More Hits	LP	T. Motown	TML11020	1965	**£10**	
My World Is Empty Without You	7"	T. Motown	TMG548	1966	**£8**	
My World Is Empty Without You	7"	T. Motown	TMG548	1966	**£50**	demo
Nathan Jones	7"	T. Motown	TMG782	1971	**£4**	chart single
Nathan Jones	7"	T. Motown	TMG782	1971	**£15**	demo
Nothing But Heartaches	7"	T. Motown	TMG527	1965	**£10**	
Nothing But Heartaches	7"	T. Motown	TMG527	1965	**£50**	demo
Reflections	7"	T. Motown	TMG616	1967	**£6**	chart single
Reflections	7"	T. Motown	TMG616	1967	**£35**	demo
Shake	7" EP	T. Motown	TME2011	1966	**£12**	
Sing Motown	LP	T. Motown	STML11047	1967	**£15**	chart LP
Sing Rodgers & Hart	LP	T. Motown	STML11054	1967	**£12**	chart LP
Stoned Love	7"	T. Motown	TMG760	1971	**£4**	chart single
Stoned Love	7"	T. Motown	TMG760	1971	**£10**	demo
Stop In The Name Of Love	7"	T. Motown	TMG501	1965	**£5**	chart single
Stop In The Name Of Love	7"	T. Motown	TMG501	1965	**£50**	demo
Supremes Hits	7" EP	T. Motown	TME2008	1965	**£8**	
Thank You Darling	7"	T. Motown	GO42609	1967	**£20**	Dutch, B side sung in French
Tossin' And Turnin'	7"	T. Motown	TMG859	1973	**£4**	
Tossin' And Turnin'	7"	T. Motown	TMG859	1973	**£10**	demo
Up The Ladder To The Roof	7"	T. Motown	TMG735	1970	**£4**	chart single
Up The Ladder To The Roof	7"	T. Motown	TMG735	1970	**£10**	demo
We Remember Sam Cooke	LP	T. Motown	TML11012	1965	**£20**	
When The Lovelight Starts Shining	7"	Stateside	SS257	1964	**£12**	
When The Lovelight Starts Shining	7"	Stateside	SS257	1964	**£50**	demo
Where Did Our Love Go	LP	Motown	M621	1964	**£15**	US
Where Did Our Love Go	7"	Stateside	SS327	1964	**£5**	chart single
Where Did Our Love Go	7"	Stateside	SS327	1964	**£50**	demo
With Love From Us To You	LP	T. Motown	TML11002	1965	**£30**	
You Can't Hurry Love	7"	T. Motown	TMG575	1966	**£6**	chart single
You Can't Hurry Love	7"	T. Motown	TMG575	1966	**£50**	demo
You Keep Me Hanging On	7"	T. Motown	TMG585	1966	**£5**	chart single
You Keep Me Hanging On	7"	T. Motown	TMG585	1966	**£40**	demo
Your Wonderful Sweet Sweet Love	7"	T. Motown	TMG835	1972	**£4**	
Your Wonderful Sweet Sweet Love	7"	T. Motown	TMG835	1972	**£10**	demo

SUPREMES & FOUR TOPS

Title	Format	Label	Number	Year	Price	Notes
Reach Out And Touch	7"	T. Motown	TMG836	1972	**£4**	
Reach Out And Touch	7"	T. Motown	TMG836	1972	**£10**	demo
River Deep Mountain High	7"	T. Motown	TMG777	1971	**£4**	chart single
River Deep Mountain High	7"	T. Motown	TMG777	1971	**£10**	demo
Without The One You Love	7"	T. Motown	TMG815	1972	**£4**	
Without The One You Love	7"	T. Motown	TMG815	1972	**£10**	demo
You Got To Have Love in Your Hearts	7"	T. Motown	TMG793	1971	**£4**	chart single
You Got To Have Love in Your Hearts	7"	T. Motown	TMG793	1971	**£10**	demo

SURFARIS

Title	Format	Label	Number	Year	Price	Notes
Fun City	LP	Brunswick	LAT8582	1964	**£10**	
Hit City '64	LP	Brunswick	LAT8567	1964	**£10**	
Hit City '65	LP	Brunswick	LAT8605	1965	**£10**	
It Ain't Me Babe	LP	Decca	DL4683	1965	**£15**	US
Point Panic	7"	Brunswick	05894	1963	**£4**	
Scatter Shield	7"	Brunswick	05902	1964	**£4**	
Surfaris Play	LP	Brunswick	LAT8561	1963	**£10**	
Wipe Out	LP	London	HAD8110	1963	**£15**	
Wipe Out	7"	London	HLD9751	1963	**£4**	chart single
Wipe Out	7" EP	London	RED1405	1963	**£10**	

SURFRIDERS

Title	Format	Label	Number	Year	Price	Notes
Surfbeat	LP	Vault	V105	1963	**£12**	US

SURFSIDE FIVE

Title	Format	Label	Number	Year	Price	Notes
Recorded Live	LP	Intermountain	153	196-	**£75**	US

SURMAN, JOHN

Title	Format	Label	Number	Year	Price	Notes
Alors!	LP	Futura	GER12	1970	**£50**	
Conflagration	LP	Dawn	DNLS3022	1971	**£30**	
How Many Clouds Can You See?	LP	Deram	SMLR1045	1969	**£40**	

John Surman .... LP .... Deram .... DML1030 .... 1968 ...... **£40** ....
Obeah Wedding .... 7" .... Deram .... DM224 .... 1969 ...... **£8** ....
Westering Home .... LP .... Island .... HELP10 .... 1972 ...... **£20** ....

SURMAN, JOHN & JOHN WARREN

Tales Of The Algonquin .... LP .... Deram .... SML1094 .... 1971 ...... **£40** ....

SURPRISE PACKAGE

Free Up .... LP .... LHI .... S12005 .... 1968 ...... **£15** .... US

SURVIVOR

American Heartbeat .... 7" .... Scotti Bros ...... SCTA2813 .... 1984 ...... **£4** .... shaped pic disc
Eye Of The Tiger .... 7" .... Scotti Bros ...... A2411P .... 1982 ...... **£5** .... pic disc

SURVIVORS

Rawhide Ska .... 7" .... Rio .... R70 .... 196- ...... **£6** ....
Take Charge .... 7" .... Rio .... R55 .... 196- ...... **£6** ....

SUTCH, SCREAMING LORD

That a small-time rock'n'roll singer who has never had a hit record can still be a celebrity is a tribute to David Sutch's skills at self-publicity. Well known as the leader of the Monster Raving Loony Party, Sutch has also never let it be forgotten that he is also a rock performer. His concerts, however, have always been chaotic affairs. In the wake of his "Lord Sutch And Heavy Friends" LP, expectations were high that he would appear accompanied by some of those same heavy friends - Jeff Beck, Jimmy Page and the rest. People turned up in droves to watch Sutch chase members of an anonymous backing group around the stage with a mop!

Cause I Love You .... 7" .... Atlantic .... 2091006 .... 1970 ...... **£10** ....
Cause I Love You .... 7" .... Atlantic .... 584321 .... 1970 ...... **£12** ....
Cheat .... 7" .... CBS .... 202080 .... 1966 ...... **£15** ....
Dracula's Daughter .... 7" .... Oriole .... CB1962 .... 1964 ...... **£12** ....
Election Fever .... 7" .... Atlantic .... 2091017 .... 1970 ...... **£8** ....
Good Golly Miss Molly .... 7" .... HMV .... POP953 .... 1961 ...... **£12** ....
Gotta Keep A-Rockin' .... 7" .... Atlantic .... K10221 .... 1972 ...... **£8** ....
Hands Of Jack The Ripper .... LP .... Atlantic .... K40313 .... 1972 ...... **£20** ....
Honey Hush .... 7" .... CBS .... 201767 .... 1965 ...... **£15** ....
I Drink To Your Health Marie .... 7" .... SRT .... SRTS76375 .... 1976 ...... **£4** ....
I'm A Hog For You .... 7" .... Decca .... F11747 .... 1963 ...... **£10** ....
Jack The Ripper .... 7" .... Decca .... F11598 .... 1963 ...... **£8** ....
Lord Sutch & Heavy Friends .... LP .... Atlantic .... SD9015 .... 1970 ...... **£20** ....
Monster Ball .... 7" .... SRT .... SRTS76361 .... 1976 ...... **£4** ....
She's Fallen In Love With A Monster ..... 7" .... Oriole .... CB1944 .... 1964 ...... **£12** ....

SUTCH, SCREAMING LORD & THE METEORS

Screaming Lord Sutch Meets The Meteors 10" .... Ace .... MAD1 .... 1981 ...... **£20** ....

SUZY & THE RED STRIPES

Seaside Woman .... 7" .... A&M .... AMS7461 .... 1979 ...... **£6** .... special sleeve
Seaside Woman .... 7" .... A&M .... AMS7548 .... 1980 ...... **£5** ....
Seaside Woman .... 7" .... A&M .... AMSP7461 .... 1979 ...... **£20** .... yellow vinyl, boxed
Seaside Woman .... 12" .... A&M .... AMSP7548 .... 1980 ...... **£8** ....

SVANTE

Baby I Need Your Loving .... 7" .... United Artists .. UP2224 .... 1968 ...... **£10** ....

SVENSK

Dream Magazine .... 7" .... Page One .... POF036 .... 1967 ...... **£8** ....
You .... 7" .... Page One .... POF050 .... 1967 ...... **£6** ....

SWALLOW

Out Of The Nest .... LP .... W. Bros .... K56174 .... 1972 ...... **£10** ....

SWAMP DOGG

Total Destruction To Your Mind .... LP .... Canyon .... LP7706 .... **£12** .... US

SWAN ARCADE

Swan Arcade .... LP .... Trailer .... LER2032 .... 1973 ...... **£10** ....

SWANN, BETTYE

Don't Touch Me .... 7" .... Capitol .... CL15586 .... 1969 ...... **£5** ....
Make Me Yours .... 7" .... CBS .... 2942 .... 1967 ...... **£15** ....

SWANS

Boy With The Beatle Hair .... 7" .... Cameo Park .... C302 .... 1964 ...... **£4** ....

He's Mine .... 7" .... Stateside .... SS224 .... 1963 .... **£5**

SWANS (2)

Filth .... LP .... 198- **£40**

SWANSON, BERNICE

Baby I'm Yours .... 7" .... Chess .... CRS8008 .... 1965 .... **£10**

SWARBRICK, DAVE

Prince Heathen .... LP .... Fontana .... 1969 .... **£12**
Rags,Reels,& Airs .... LP .... Polydor .... 236514 .... 1967 .... **£15**
Selections .... LP .... Pegasus .... 1972 .... **£10**
Smiddy Burn .... LP .... Logo .... 1029 .... 1981 .... **£10**
Swarbrick 2 .... LP .... Transatlantic .... TRA341 .... 1977 .... **£10**
Swarbrick .... LP .... Transatlantic .... TRA337 .... 1976 .... **£10**

SWEED, ROBERTA

Words Are Impossible .... 7" .... Dragon .... DRA1034 .... 1975 .... **£4**

SWEENEY TODD

If Wishes Were Horses .... LP .... London .... 1977 .... **£15** .... Canadian

SWEENEY'S MEN

Galleries Revisited .... LP .... Transatlantic .... 1973 .... **£10**
Rattlin' & Roarin' Willy .... LP .... Transatlantic .... TRA170 .... 1968 .... **£20**
Sullivan's John .... 7" .... Transatlantic .... TRASP19 .... 1968 .... **£4**
Sweeney's Men .... LP .... Transatlantic .... TRASAM37 .... 1976 .... **£12**
Tracks Of Sweeney .... LP .... Transatlantic .... TRA200 .... 1969 .... **£20**
Tracks Of Sweeney .... LP .... Transatlantic .... TRASAM40 .... 1977 .... **£10**

SWEET

Beginning as a teeny-bopper group, the Sweet's music gradually became heavier as it progressed. At the same time, the group aligned itself with the glamour rock movement, and as the only way for anyone to adopt the kind of extravagant image favoured by the likes of Gary Glitter was with his tongue placed firmly in his cheek, so the Sweet became high princes of camp, mocking themselves and their music even while playing it. In the end, of course, this rebounded on them, and the classy "Love Is Like Oxygen" apart, the group failed to convince when they tried to become serious artists.

Action .... 7" .... RCA .... RCA2578 .... 1975 .... **£4** .... chart single
All You'll Ever Get From Me .... 7" .... Parlophone .... R5826 .... 1970 .... **£12**
All You'll Ever Get From Me .... 7" .... Parlophone .... R5902 .... 1971 .... **£10**
Ballroom Blitz .... 7" .... RCA .... RCA2403 .... 1973 .... **£4** .... chart single
Big Apple .... 7" .... Polydor .... POSP73 .... 1979 .... **£4**
Blockbuster .... 7" .... RCA .... RCA2305 .... 1973 .... **£4** .... chart single
California Nights .... 7" .... Polydor .... POSP5 .... 1978 .... **£4**
Call Me .... 7" .... Polydor .... POSP36 .... 1979 .... **£4**
Cut Above The Rest .... LP .... Polydor .... POLD5022 .... 1979 .... **£10**
Desolation Boulevard .... LP .... RCA .... LP15080 .... 1975 .... **£12**
Fever Of Love .... 7" .... RCA .... PB5001 .... 1977 .... **£4**
For AOR Radio Only .... LP .... Capitol .... 1975 .... **£20** .... US promo
Fox On The Run .... 7" .... RCA .... PE5226 .... 1980 .... **£4**
Fox On The Run .... 7" .... RCA .... RCA2524 .... 1975 .... **£4** .... chart single
Funny How Sweet Coco Can Be .... LP .... RCA .... SF8288 .... 1971 .... **£15**
Get On The Line .... 7" .... Parlophone .... R5848 .... 1970 .... **£12**
Give The Lady Some Respect .... 7" .... Polydor .... POSP131 .... 1980 .... **£4**
Give Us A Wink .... LP .... RCA .... RS1036 .... 1976 .... **£12**
Hell Raiser .... 7" .... RCA .... RCA2357 .... 1973 .... **£4** .... chart single
Identity Crisis .... LP .... Polydor .... 23111179 .... 1982 .... **£10**
Level Headed .... LP .... Polydor .... POLD5001 .... 1978 .... **£10**
Lies In Your Eyes .... 7" .... RCA .... RCA2641 .... 1976 .... **£4** .... chart single
Lollipop Man .... 7" .... Parlophone .... R5803 .... 1969 .... **£12**
Lost Angels .... 7" .... RCA .... RCA2748 .... 1976 .... **£4**
Off The Record .... LP .... RCA .... PL25072 .... 1977 .... **£10**
Six Teens .... 7" .... RCA .... LPBO5037 .... 1974 .... **£4** .... chart single
Sixties Man .... 7" .... Polydor .... POSP160 .... 1980 .... **£4**
Slow Motion .... 7" .... Fontana .... TF958 .... 1968 .... **£80**
Stairway To The Stars .... 7" .... RCA .... PB5046 .... 1977 .... **£4**
Strung Up .... LP .... RCA .... SPC0001 .... 1975 .... **£15** .... double
Sweet Fanny Adams .... LP .... RCA .... LP15039 .... 1974 .... **£12** .... chart LP
Sweet's Biggest Hits .... LP .... RCA .... SF8316 .... 1971 .... **£10**
Teenage Rampage .... 7" .... RCA .... LPBO5004 .... 1974 .... **£4** .... chart single
Teenage Rampage .... 7" .... RCA .... LPBO5004 .... 1974 .... **£10** .... pressed too fast
Turn It Down .... 7" .... RCA .... RCA2480 .... 1974 .... **£4** .... chart single

Water's Edge ... LP ... Polydor ... POLS1021 ... 1980 ... **£10** ...

SWEET & PIPKINS

Sweet And The Pipkins ... LP ... MFP ... 5248 ... 1973 ... **£10** ...

SWEET INSPIRATIONS

Brand New Lover ... 7" ... Atlantic ... 584312 ... 1970 ... **£4** ...
Evidence ... 7" ... Atlantic ... 2091073 ... 1971 ... **£4** ...
Let It Be Me ... 7" ... Atlantic ... 584132 ... 1967 ... **£4** ...
Sweet Inspiration ... 7" ... Atlantic ... 584167 ... 1968 ... **£4** ...
Sweet Inspirations ... LP ... Atlantic ... SD8155 ... 1968 ... **£10** ... US
Sweet Sweet Soul ... LP ... Atlantic ... SD8253 ... 1970 ... **£10** ... US
Sweets For My Sweet ... LP ... Atlantic ... 588194 ... 1969 ... **£10** ...
Sweets For My Sweet ... 7" ... Atlantic ... 584279 ... 1969 ... **£4** ...
What The World Needs Now Is Love ... LP ... Atlantic ... SD8201 ... 1969 ... **£10** ... US
What The World Needs Now Is Love ... 7" ... Atlantic ... 584233 ... 1968 ... **£4** ...
Why Am I Treated So Bad ... 7" ... Atlantic ... 584117 ... 1967 ... **£4** ...

SWEET PAIN

Sweet Pain ... LP ... Mercury ... SMCL20146 ... 1969 ... **£20** ...
Timber Gibbs ... 7" ... United Artists .. UP35268 ... 1971 ... **£4** ...

SWEET PLUM

Lazy Day ... 7" ... Middle Earth ... MDS103 ... 1969 ... **£8** ...
Set The Wheels In Motion ... 7" ... Middle Earth ... MDS105 ... 1969 ... **£10** ...

SWEET SAVAGE

Killing Time ... 7" ... Sweet Savage ... 1980 ... **£12** ...

SWEET SLAG

Tracking With Close Ups ... LP ... XTRA ... XTRA1112 ... 1971 ... **£30** ...
Tracking With Close-Ups ... LP ... President ... PTLS1042 ... 1971 ... **£30** ...

SWEET SMOKE

Just A Poke ... LP ... Catfish ... 1972 ... **£15** ...

SWEET THURSDAY

Sweet Thursday ... LP ... CBS ... 65573 ... 1973 ... **£15** ...
Sweet Thursday ... LP ... Polydor ... 2310051 ... 1969 ... **£20** ...

SWEETING, HARRY

From Jamaica With Love ... 7" ... Coxsone ... CS7012 ... 196- ... **£10** ...

SWEETSHOP

Barefoot And Tiptoe ... 7" ... Parlophone ... R5707 ... 1968 ... **£4** ...

SWEGAS

Child Of Light ... LP ... Trend ... 197- ... **£20** ...

SWELL MAPS

Collision Time ... LP ... Rough Trade ... ROUGH41 ... 1982 ... **£10** ...
Dresden Style ... 7" ... Rather ... GEAR3 ... 1979 ... **£4** ...
Jane From Occupied Europe ... LP ... Rough Trade ... ROUGH15 ... 1980 ... **£10** ...
Let's Build A Car ... 7" ... Rather ... GEAR7 ... 1980 ... **£4** ...
Read About Seymour ... 7" ... Rather ... GEAR1 ... 1977 ... **£6** ...
Real Shocks ... 7" ... Rather ... GEAR6 ... 1979 ... **£4** ...
Trip to Marineville ... LP ... Big Rather ... TROY1 ... 1979 ... **£12** ... with 7" (GEAR5)
Whatever Happens Next ... LP ... Rough Trade ... ROUGH21 ... 1981 ... **£12** ... double

SWINDELLS, STEVE

Messages ... LP ... RCA ... SF5057 ... 1974 ... **£10** ...

SWINGERS

Love Makes The World Go Round ... 7" ... Vogue ... V9158 ... 1960 ... **£4** ...

SWINGING BLUE JEANS

Blue Jeans A Swinging ... LP ... HMV ... CLP1802 ... 1964 ... **£50** ...
Blue Jeans A Swinging ... LP ... HMV ... CSD1570 ... 1964 ... **£50** ...
Crazy 'Bout My Baby ... 7" ... HMV ... POP1477 ... 1965 ... **£4** ...
Do You Know ... 7" ... HMV ... POP1206 ... 1963 ... **£5** ...
Don't Go Out Into The Rain ... 7" ... HMV ... POP1605 ... 1967 ... **£4** ...
Don't Make Me Over ... 7" ... HMV ... POP1501 ... 1966 ... **£4** ... chart single

Good Golly Miss Molly	7"	HMV	POP1273	1964	**£4**	chart single
Hippy Hippy Shake	7"	HMV	POP1242	1963	**£4**	chart single
Hippy Hippy Shake	LP	Imperial	LP9261	1964	**£50**	US
It Isn't There	7"	HMV	POP1375	1964	**£4**	
It's Too Late Now	7"	HMV	POP1170	1963	**£4**	chart single
Make Me Know You're Mine	7"	HMV	POP1409	1965	**£4**	
Promise You'll Tell Her	7"	HMV	POP1327	1964	**£4**	
Rumours,Gossip,Words Untrue	7"	HMV	POP1564	1966	**£4**	
Sandy	7"	HMV	POP1533	1966	**£4**	
Shake With The Swinging Blue Jeans	7" EP	HMV	7EG8850	1964	**£10**	
Swinging Blue Jeans	LP	MFP	1163	1967	**£20**	
Tremblin'	7"	HMV	POP1596	1967	**£4**	
You're No Good	7"	HMV	POP1304	1964	**£4**	chart single
You're No Good Miss Molly	7" EP	HMV	7EG8868	1964	**£10**	

SWINGING MEDALLIONS

Double Shot	LP	Smash	MGS27083	1966	**£10**	US
She Drives Me Out Of My Mind	7"	Philips	BF1500	1966	**£4**	
She Drives Me Out Of My Mind	7"	Philips	BF1515	1966	**£4**	

SWINGING SOUL MACHINE

Spooky's Day Off	7"	Polydor	56760	1969	**£4**	

SWINGTONES

Geraldine	7"	HMV	POP471	1958	**£25**	

SYKES, ERIC, & HATTIE JACQUES

Eric, Hattie And Things	LP	Decca	LK4507	1963	**£12**	

SYKES, ROOSEVELT

Back To The Blues	7" EP	Delmark	DJB2	1966	**£6**	
Big Man Of The Blues	LP	Encore	ENC183	1959	**£15**	
Blues From Bar Rooms	LP	77	77LEU1250	1967	**£15**	
Honeydripper	LP	Bluesville	BV1014	1961	**£25**	US
Return Of...	LP	Bluesville	BV1006	1960	**£25**	US
Too Hot To Hold	7"	Vogue	V2389	1970	**£10**	
Walking This Boogie	7"	Vogue	V2393	1970	**£15**	

SYKO & THE CARIBS

Do The Dog	7"	Blue Beat	BB213	1963	**£10**	
Sugar Baby	7"	Blue Beat	BB223	1963	**£10**	

SYLVAIN, SYLVAIN

Every Boy And Every Girl	7"	RCA	PB9500	1980	**£4**	

SYLVESTER, C. & THE PLANETS

Going South	7"	Blue Beat	BB206	1963	**£10**	

SYLVESTER, ROLAND

Grandfather's Clock	7"	Carnival	CV7018	1964	**£6**	

SYLVESTER, TERRY

I Believe	LP	Polydor	2383394	1976	**£10**	

SYLVIA

I Can't Help It	7"	Soul City	SC103		**£4**	
I Can't Help It	7"	Soul City	SC103		**£10**	demo

SYLVIAN, DAVID

Ink In The Well	7"	Virgin	VS700	1984	**£4**	poster sleeve
Ink In The Well	12"	Virgin	VS70012	1984	**£6**	poster sleeve
Let The Happiness In	7"	Virgin	VSDJ1001	1987	**£5**	promo
Red Guitar	7"	Virgin	VSY633	1984	**£6**	pic disc
Silver Moon	7"	Virgin	VSDJ895	1986	**£5**	promo
Silver Moon	7"	Virgin	VSP895	1986	**£4**	gatefold PS
Taking The Veil	7"	Virgin	VSDJ815	1986	**£5**	promo
Taking The Veil	7"	Virgin	VSY815	1986	**£5**	square pic disc
Weatherbox	CD	Virgin	POPCD1	1989	**£20**	promo sampler

SYLVIAN, DAVID & RYUICHI SAKAMOTO

Bamboo Houses	7"	Virgin	VS510	1982	**£5**	gatefold sleeve
Bamboo Houses	12"	Virgin	VS51012	1982	**£6**	

SYMBOLS

Best Part Of...	LP	President		1968	**£20**	
One Fine Girl	7"	Columbia	DB7459	1965	**£4**	
You're My Girl	7"	Columbia	DB7664	1965	**£4**	

SYMON & PI

Got To See The Sunrise	7"	Parlophone	R5719	1968	**£5**	
Sha La La La Lee	7"	Parlophone	R5662	1968	**£5**	

SYMPHONICS

Heaven Must Have Sent You	7"	Polydor	2058341	1972	**£5**	

SYN

The Syndicats eventually metamorphosed into the Syn, none of whose members had been in the original Syndicats line-up. The Yes connection continued, however, for the bass player and guitarist on the Syn's psychedelic singles were Chris Squire and Peter Banks.

Created By Clive	7"	Deram	DM130	1967	**£40**	
Flowerman	7"	Deram	DM145	1967	**£40**	

SYNANTHESIA

Synanthesia	LP	RCA	SF8058	1969	**£40**	

SYNDICATE OF SOUND

Little Girl	LP	Stateside	SSL10185	1966	**£15**	
Little Girl	7"	Stateside	SS523	1966	**£8**	
Rumours	7"	Stateside	SS538	1966	**£8**	

SYNDICATS

The singles made by the Syndicats are collectable on three counts. They are good examples of mid-sixties British R&B; they were produced by legendary producer Joe Meek; and the group's guitarist was Steve Howe, of later Yes fame.

Crawdaddy Simone	7"	Columbia	DB7686	1965	**£100**	
Howlin' For My Baby	7"	Columbia	DB7441	1965	**£60**	
Maybelline	7"	Columbia	DB7238	1964	**£50**	

SYRINX

Long Lost Relatives	LP	True North		1971	**£25**	Canadian
Syrinx	LP	True North		1970	**£25**	Canadian

T

T-BONES

I'm A Lover	7"	Columbia	DB7401	1964	**£25**	
Won't You Give Me One More Chance	7"	Columbia	DB7489	1965	**£15**	

T.C.ATLANTIC

T.C.Atlantic	LP	Dove	LP4459		**£50**	US

T.I.M.E.

Smooth Ball	LP	Liberty	LBS83232	1969	**£20**	
T.I.M.E.	LP	Liberty	LST7558	1968	**£20**	US

T.V. & THE TRIBESMEN

Barefootin'	7"	Pye	7N25375	1966	**£10**	

T2

It'll All Work Out In Boomland	LP	Decca	SKL5050	1970	**£50**	

TABLE

Do The Standing Still	7"	Virgin	VS176	1977	**£4**	
Sex Cells	7"	Chiswick	NS31	1978	**£4**	

TABLETOPPERS

Rocking Mountain Dew	7"	Starlite	ST45069	1962	**£4**	

TAD & THE SMALL FRY

Checkered Continental Pants	7"	London	HLU9542	1962	**£4**	

TAGES

Crazy 'Bout My Baby	7"	Columbia	DB8019	1966	**£5**	
So Many Girls	7"	HMV	POP1515	1966	**£6**	
There's A Blind Man Playing	7"	Parlophone	R5702	1968	**£5**	
Treat Me Like A Lady	7"	Parlophone	R5640	1967	**£4**	

TAITT, LYN & THE JETS

El Casino Royale	7"	Amalgam.	AMG810	196-	**£10**	
I Don't Want To Make You Cry	7"	Island	WI3075	1967	**£10**	
Napoleon Solo	7"	Island	WI3139	1968	**£10**	
Something Stupid	7"	Island	WI3066	1967	**£10**	
Sounds Rock Steady	LP	Island	ILP969	1968	**£50**	
Spanish Eyes (with Tommy McCook)	7"	Doctor Bird	DB1047	1966	**£10**	
Vilmas Jump Up	7"	Doctor Bird	DB1006	1966	**£10**	
Way Of Life	7"	Blue Cat	BS108	1968	**£10**	

TAKERS

If You Don't Come Back	7"	Pye	7N15690	1964	**£10**	

TALES OF JUSTINE

Albert	7"	HMV	POP1614	1967	**£4**	

TALISKER

Dreaming Of Glenista	LP	Caroline	CA1513	1975	**£10**	

TALISMEN

Masters Of War	7"	Stateside	SS408	1965	**£10**	

TALK TALK

Life's What You Make It	12"	EMI	EMID5540	1986	**£6**	double
Living In Another World	7"	EMI	EMIP5551	1986	**£4**	shaped pic disc

TALKING HEADS

And She Was	12"	EMI	12EMIP5543	1986	**£6**	pic disc
Cities	7"	Sire	SIR4040	1980	**£4**	
Cities	12"	Sire	SIR4040T	1980	**£6**	

Title	Format	Label	Cat. No.	Year	Price	Notes
Fear Of Music	LP	Sire	K56707	1979	**£12**	with 'Psycho Killer' 7"
Fear Of Music	LP	Sire	SRK6076	1979	**£10**	with 'Psycho Killer' 7"
I Zimbra	7"	Sire	SIR4033	1980	**£4**	
Lady Don't Mind	12"	EMI	12EMID5520	1985	**£6**	double
Life During Wartime	7"	Sire	SIR4027	1979	**£4**	
Live At The Roxy	LP	W. Bros	WBMS104	1979	**£30**	promo
Love Goes To Building On Fire	7"	Sire	6078604	1977	**£6**	
Psycho Killer	7"	Sire	6078610	1977	**£6**	
Psycho Killer	12"	Sire	6078610	1977	**£8**	
Pulled Up	7"	Sire	6078620	1978	**£6**	
Road To Nowhere	7"	EMI	EMIP5530	1985	**£6**	pic disc
Speaking In Tongues	LP	EMI	9238831	1983	**£15**	clear vinyl
Stop Making Sense	LP	EMI	TAH1	1984	**£10**	with booklet
Take Me To The River	7"	Sire	SIR4004	1979	**£4**	
Take Me To The River	7"	Sire	SIR4004	1979	**£8**	double
This Must Be The Place	12"	Sire	W9451T	1984	**£6**	double

TALL BOYS

Title	Format	Label	Cat. No.	Year	Price	Notes
Island Of Lost Souls	7"	Big Beat	NS79	1982	**£5**	

TALL, TOM

Title	Format	Label	Cat. No.	Year	Price	Notes
Are You Mine (with Ginny Wright)	7"	London	HL8150	1955	**£15**	
Country Songs Vol.2 (with Ginny Wright)	7" EP	London	REU1035	1955	**£10**	
Don't You Know (with Ruckus Taylor)	7"	London	HLU8429	1957	**£6**	
Give Me A Chance	7"	London	HLU8216	1955	**£10**	
Underway	7"	London	HLU8231	1956	**£10**	

TALMY/STONE BAND

Title	Format	Label	Cat. No.	Year	Price	Notes
Madison Time	7"	Decca	F11543	1962	**£6**	
Roses Are Red & Other Hits	LP	Ace Of Clubs	ACL1134	1962	**£12**	

TAM, TIM & THE TURN ONS

Title	Format	Label	Cat. No.	Year	Price	Notes
Wait A Minute	7"	Island	WIP6007	1967	**£8**	

TAMPA RED

Title	Format	Label	Cat. No.	Year	Price	Notes
Don't Jive With Me	LP	Bluesville	BV1043	1962	**£15**	US
Don't Tampa With The Blues	LP	Bluesville	BV1030	1961	**£15**	US
R&B Vol.3	7" EP	RCA	RCX7160	1964	**£6**	

TAMPA RED & GEORGIA TOM

Title	Format	Label	Cat. No.	Year	Price	Notes
Male Blues No.2	7" EP	Collector	JE13	196-	**£5**	

TAMS

Title	Format	Label	Cat. No.	Year	Price	Notes
Be Young,Be Foolish,Be Happy	7"	Stateside	SS2123	1969	**£6**	chart single
Concrete Jungle	7"	HMV	POP1464	1965	**£4**	
Hey Girl Don't Bother Me	LP	ABC-Para.	499	1964	**£10**	US
Hey Girl Don't Bother Me	7"	HMV	POP1331	1964	**£10**	
Hey Girl Don't Bother Me	7"	Probe	PRO532	1971	**£4**	chart single
It's All Right	7"	HMV	POP1298	1964	**£4**	
Presenting The Tams	LP	ABC-Para.	481	1964	**£12**	US
Too Much Foolin' Around	7"	Capitol	CL15650	1970	**£4**	
Untie Me	7"	Stateside	SS146	1963	**£4**	
What Kind Of Fool	7"	HMV	POP1254	1963	**£5**	

TANDY, SHARON

Title	Format	Label	Cat. No.	Year	Price	Notes
Fool On The Hill	7"	Atlantic	584166	1968	**£4**	
Gotta Get Enough Time	7"	Atlantic	584242	1969	**£4**	
Hold On	7"	Atlantic	584219	1968	**£8**	
I've Found Love	7"	Pye	7N15939	1965	**£4**	
Love Is Not A Simple Affair	7"	Atlantic	584181	1968	**£4**	
Love Makes The World Go Round	7"	Mercury	MF898	1965	**£4**	
Now That You've Gone	7"	Pye	7N15806	1965	**£4**	
Our Day Will Come	7"	Atlantic	584137	1967	**£8**	
Stay With Me	7"	Atlantic	584124	1967	**£6**	
Toe-Hold	7"	Atlantic	584098	1967	**£4**	
Way She Looks At You	7"	Atlantic	584214	1968	**£4**	
You Gotta Believe It	7"	Atlantic	584194	1968	**£4**	

TANEGA, NORMA

Title	Format	Label	Cat. No.	Year	Price	Notes
Walking My Cat Named Dog	LP	Stateside	SL10182	1966	**£12**	
Walking My Cat Named Dog	7"	Stateside	SS496	1966	**£4**	chart single

TANGERINE DREAM

Perhaps it has something to do with the German character, that the rock musicians in that country seized on the newly developed synthesizer, not as a device for creating previously unheard sounds, but as a means for performing mathematically precise patterns of notes. Such is the main approach of Tangerine Dream, as it is of Klaus Schulze and Kraftwerk. "Ultima Thule" is a particularly rare non-album track and is a typical in style.

Alpha Centauri	LP	Ohr	OMM556012	1971	**£10**	German
Das Madchen Auf Der Treppe	12"	Virgin	60065213	1982	**£6**	German
Electronic Meditation	LP	Ohr	OMM556004	1970	**£10**	German
Flashpoint	LP	Heavy Metal	HM1PD29	198-	**£10**	pic disc
Poland - The Warsaw Concert	LP	Jive Electro	HIPX22	198-	**£15**	double pic disc
Stratosfear	7"	Virgin	VDJ17	1976	**£6**	promo
Thief	LP	Elektra		1981	**£10**	US promo pic disc
Ultima Thule	7"	Ohr	OSS7006	1972	**£40**	German
Warsaw In The Sun	7"	Jive	JIVEP74	1984	**£6**	pic disc

TANGERINE PEEL

Every Christian Lion-Hearted Man	7"	United Artists	UP1193	1967	**£6**	
Move Into My World	7"	RCA	RCA1936	1970	**£5**	
Never Say Never Again	7"	MGM	MGM1470	1969	**£5**	
Play Me A Sad Song And I'll Dance	7"	MGM	MGM1487	1969	**£5**	
Soft Delights	LP	RCA	LSA3002	1970	**£20**	US
Solid Gold Mountain	7"	CBS	3402	1968	**£5**	
Talking To No One	7"	CBS	3676	1968	**£5**	
Thinking Of Me	7"	RCA	RCA1990	1970	**£5**	
What Am I To Do	7"	RCA	RCA2036	1970	**£5**	

TANGERINE ZOO

Outside Looking In	LP	Mainstream	S6116	1968	**£20**	US
Tangerine Zoo	LP	Mainstream	S6107	1968	**£20**	US

TANTONES

So Afraid	7"	Vogue	V9085	1957	**£20**	

TANZ DER YOUTH

I'm Sorry I'm Sorry	7"	Radar	ADA19	1978	**£4**	

TAOS

Taos	LP	Mercury	61257	1972	**£10**	US

TAPESTRY

Carnaby Street	7"	London	HLZ10138	1967	**£5**	

TARA

Happy	7"	Polydor	2066009	1978	**£4**	

TARBUCK, JIMMY

Someday	7"	Immediate	IM018	1965	**£5**	

TARGEL, JEM

Lucky Guy	LP	Sheany		1978	**£60**	US

TARHEEL SLIM & LITTLE ANN

You Make Me Feel So Good	7"	Sue	WI390	1965	**£8**	

TARRIERS

Banana Boat Song	7"	Columbia	DB3891	1957	**£4**	chart single
Hard Travellin'	LP	United Artists	UAL4033	1959	**£10**	US
Hard Travellin' Vol.1	7" EP	London	RET1236	1960	**£4**	
Hard Travellin' Vol.2	7" EP	London	RET1237	1960	**£4**	
Tell The World About This	LP	Atlantic	8042	1960	**£10**	US

TARTANS

Awake The Town	7"	Caltone	TONE115	196-	**£8**	
Coming On Strong	7"	Caltone	TONE117	196-	**£8**	
Dance All Night	7"	Island	WI3058	1967	**£10**	

TASAVALIAN PRESIDENTTI

Lambertland	LP	Sonet	SNTF636	1973	**£15**	
Milky Way Moses	LP	Sonet	SNTF658	1974	**£15**	
Tasavalian Presedentti	LP	Love	LRLP7	1969	**£20**	Swedish
To A Soldier Boy	7"	London	HL8885	1959	**£10**	
To A Young Lover	7"	Top Rank	JAR229	1959	**£4**	

TASTE

Guitarist Rory Gallagher began his long career with this trio. The titles issued as singles can be found on the "Taste" LP, but these are re-recordings. The Major Minor originals sound significantly different.

Title	Format	Label	Cat. No.	Year	Price	Notes
Blister On The Moon	7"	Major Minor	MM560	1968	**£6**	
Born On The Wrong Side Of Time	7"	Major Minor	MM718	197-	**£5**	
Taste	LP	Polydor	583042	1969	**£10**	

TATE, ERIC QUINCY

Title	Format	Label	Cat. No.	Year	Price	Notes
Can't Keep A Good Band Down	LP	EQT		1977	**£40**	US
Eric Quincy Tate	LP	Cotillion	9025	1971	**£10**	US

TATE, HOWARD

Title	Format	Label	Cat. No.	Year	Price	Notes
Baby I Love You	7"	Verve	VS555	1967	**£5**	
Get It While You Can	LP	Verve		1967	**£12**	

TATE, TOMMY

Title	Format	Label	Cat. No.	Year	Price	Notes
Big Blue Diamonds	7"	Columbia	DB8046	1966	**£6**	

TAUPIN, BERNIE

Title	Format	Label	Cat. No.	Year	Price	Notes
An Interview With Bernie Taupin	LP	RCA		1987	**£15**	US double promo
Taupin	LP	DJM	DJLPS415	1971	**£10**	

TAVERNER, JOHN

Of all the surprising records to have been issued on the Apple label, the pair of works composed by John Taverner are perhaps the most surprising at all. They have nothing to do with rock music at all in themselves, being prime examples of the classical avant-garde, but they were apparently included in the Beatles' release schedule because Ringo Starr liked them.

Title	Format	Label	Cat. No.	Year	Price	Notes
Celtic Requiem	LP	Apple	SAPCOR20	1971	**£75**	
Whale	LP	Apple	SAPCOR15	1970	**£40**	

TAYLES

Title	Format	Label	Cat. No.	Year	Price	Notes
Who Are These?	LP	CV		1969	**£50**	US

TAYLOR, ALLAN

Title	Format	Label	Cat. No.	Year	Price	Notes
Lady	LP	United Artists	UAS29275	1972	**£10**	
Sometimes	LP	Liberty	LBG83483	1971	**£10**	

TAYLOR, BOBBY

Title	Format	Label	Cat. No.	Year	Price	Notes
I Can't Quit Your Love	7"	Epic	EPC1720	1973	**£4**	
Taylor Made Soul	LP	T. Motown	STML11125	1970	**£10**	

TAYLOR, BOBBY, & THE VANCOUVERS

Title	Format	Label	Cat. No.	Year	Price	Notes
Bobby Taylor And The Vancouvers	LP	T. Motown	STML11093	1969	**£12**	
Does Your Mama Know About Me?	7"	T. Motown	TMG654	1968	**£12**	
Does Your Mama Know About Me?	7"	T. Motown	TMG654	1968	**£40**	demo

TAYLOR, EARL

Title	Format	Label	Cat. No.	Year	Price	Notes
Bluegrass Taylor Made	LP	Capitol	T2090	1963	**£12**	US

TAYLOR, EDDIE & FLOYD JONES

Title	Format	Label	Cat. No.	Year	Price	Notes
Eddie Taylor And Floyd Jones	7" EP	XX	MIN712		**£4**	

TAYLOR, FELICE

Title	Format	Label	Cat. No.	Year	Price	Notes
I Feel Love Comin' On	7"	President	PT155	1967	**£4**	chart single

TAYLOR, GLORIA

Title	Format	Label	Cat. No.	Year	Price	Notes
You Gotta Pay The Price	7"	Polydor	56788	1970	**£5**	

TAYLOR, HOUND DOG

Title	Format	Label	Cat. No.	Year	Price	Notes
Christine	7"	Outasite	45504	1966	**£20**	

TAYLOR, JAMES

Title	Format	Label	Cat. No.	Year	Price	Notes
Carolina In My Mind	7"	Apple	32	1970	**£5**	
Gorilla	LP	Nautilus		1980	**£10**	US audiophile
Gorilla	LP	W. Bros	BS42866	1975	**£10**	US quad
James Taylor	LP	Apple	APCOR3	1968	**£20**	mono, black letters
James Taylor	LP	Apple	SAPCOR3	1968	**£12**	orange lettering
James Taylor	LP	Apple	SAPCOR3	1968	**£15**	stereo, black letters
One Man Dog	LP	W. Bros	BS42660	1974	**£10**	US quad

TAYLOR, JEREMY

Title	Format	Label	Cat. No.	Year	Price	Notes
Jobsworth	LP	JT		197-	**£12**	
Piece Of Ground	LP	Galliard		1972	**£15**	

TAYLOR, JOHN

Pause And Think Again	LP	Turtle	TUR302	1971	**£50**	

TAYLOR, JOHNNIE

Ain't That Loving You	7"	Stax	601003	1967	**£4**	
Eargasm	LP	Columbia	PCQ33951	1976	**£10**	US quad
Philosophy Continues	LP	Stax	1024	1969	**£10**	
Rare Stamps	LP	Stax	STS2012	1969	**£10**	US
Rated Extraordinaire	LP	Columbia	PCQ34401	1977	**£10**	US quad
Raw Blues	LP	Stax	STS2008	1969	**£10**	US
Stealaway	7"	Stax	STAX150	1970	**£4**	
Wanted: One Soul Singer	LP	Stax	ST715	1967	**£12**	US
Who's Making Love?	LP	Stax	STS2005	1968	**£10**	US

TAYLOR, KINGSIZE & THE DOMINOES

Memphis Tennessee	7"	Polydor	NH66990	1963	**£12**	
Real Gonk Man	LP	Midnight	HLP2101	196-	**£25**	US
Somebody's Always Trying	7"	Decca	F11935	1964	**£12**	
Stupidity	7"	Decca	F11874	1964	**£12**	
Teenbeat 2 - Teanbeat From The Star Club Hamburg	7" EP	Decca	DFE8569	1964	**£20**	
Twist And Shake	7" EP	Polydor	EPH21628	1963	**£20**	

TAYLOR, KOKO

Koko Taylor	LP	Chess	LPS1532	1968	**£10**	US
Wang Dang Doodle	7"	Chess	CRS8035	1966	**£6**	

TAYLOR, LITTLE JOHNNY

Everybody Knows About My Good Thing	LP	Polydor	2916015		**£10**	
Little Johnny Taylor	LP	Galaxy	203	1963	**£12**	US
One More Chance	7"	Vocalion	VF9264	1966	**£4**	
Open House	LP	Contempo	1003	1973	**£10**	
Part Time Love	7"	Vocalion	VF9234	1965	**£6**	

TAYLOR, MICK

If the single by Mick Taylor has aquired any value by reason of its authorship by the future Bluesbreaker and Rolling Stone, then the justification for this is a little dubious. The Mick Taylor who joined John Mayall in 1967 was only seventeen at the time and a confirmed blues guitarist. It is not at all likely that he would have been having a single released two years earlier under the title of "London Town/Hoboin'". Unless, of course, any collector who has actually heard this undoubtedly scarce record can confirm that the two Mick Taylors are in fact the same.

London Town	7"	CBS	201770	1965	**£10**	

TAYLOR, MIKE

Mike Taylor showed every sign of developing into a major talent before his premature death in the late sixties. He co-wrote songs for Cream ("Those Were The Days", "Passing The Time") and for Colosseum ("Jumping Off The Sun") and was also a fine jazz pianist. The two rare albums he made have Jack Bruce, Tony Reeves, and Jon Hiseman among the small supporting cast.

Pendulum	LP	Columbia	SX6042	1965	**£100**	
Trio	LP	Columbia	SX6137	1966	**£100**	

TAYLOR, NEVILLE & THE CUTTERS

Baby Lay Sleeping	7"	Parlophone	R4493	1958	**£4**	
First Words Of Love	7"	Parlophone	R4524	1959	**£4**	
Mercy Mercy Percy	7"	Parlophone	R4447	1958	**£4**	
Tears On My Pillow	7"	Parlophone	R4476	1958	**£4**	

TAYLOR, R.DEAN

Ain't It A Sad Thing	7"	Rare Earth	RES101	1971	**£10**	TMG786 matrix
Ain't It A Sad Thing	7"	T. Motown	TMG786	1971	**£40**	demo only
Gotta See Jane	7"	T. Motown	TMG656	1968	**£5**	chart single
Gotta See Jane	7"	T. Motown	TMG656	1968	**£15**	demo
Indiana Wants Me	7"	T. Motown	TMG763	1971	**£4**	chart single
Indiana Wants Me	7"	T. Motown	TMG763	1971	**£10**	demo
There's A Ghost In My House	7"	T. Motown	TMG896	1974	**£4**	chart single
There's A Ghost In My House	7"	T. Motown	TMG896	1974	**£15**	demo

TAYLOR, ROGER

Future Management	7"	EMI	EMI5157	1981	**£6**	chart single
I Wanna Testify	7"	EMI	EMI2679	1977	**£8**	
My Country	7"	EMI	EMI5200	1981	**£5**	
Strange Frontier	12"	EMI	EMI5490	1984	**£6**	

TAYLOR, TED

Title	Format	Label	Cat. No.	Year	Price	Notes
Cat's Eyes	7"	Oriole	CB1628	1961	**£4**	
Jericho	7"	Oriole	CB1713	1962	**£4**	
M1	7"	Oriole	CB1573	1961	**£4**	
Son Of Honky Tonk	7"	Oriole	CB1464	1958	**£4**	
Surfrider	7"	Oriole	CB1767	1962	**£4**	

TAYLOR, VERNON

Title	Format	Label	Cat. No.	Year	Price	Notes
Mystery Train	7"	London	HLS9025	1960	**£10**	

TAYLOR, VIC

Title	Format	Label	Cat. No.	Year	Price	Notes
Heartaches	7"	Treasure Isle	TI7021	196-	**£10**	

TAYLOR, VINCE

Title	Format	Label	Cat. No.	Year	Price	Notes
Brand New Cadillac	7"	Chiswick	N2	1976	**£5**	

TAYLOR, VINCE & THE PLAYBOYS

Title	Format	Label	Cat. No.	Year	Price	Notes
Brand New Cadillac	7"	Parlophone	R4539	1959	**£12**	
Jet Black Machine	7"	Palette	PG9001	1960	**£8**	
Right Behind You Baby	7"	Parlophone	R4505	1958	**£12**	
Whatcha Gonna Do	7"	Palette	PG9020	1961	**£5**	

TEA

Title	Format	Label	Cat. No.	Year	Price	Notes
Good Times	7"	Vertigo	6147006	1974	**£4**	
Ship	LP	Philips	9118001	1975	**£10**	
Tea	LP	Philips	6305238	1975	**£10**	

TEA & SYMPHONY

Title	Format	Label	Cat. No.	Year	Price	Notes
Asylum For The Musically Insane	LP	Harvest	SHVL761	1969	**£50**	
Boredom	7"	Harvest	HAR5005	1969	**£8**	
Jo Sago	LP	Harvest	SHVL785	1970	**£50**	

TEA COMPANY

Title	Format	Label	Cat. No.	Year	Price	Notes
Come & Have Some Tea With...	LP	Mercury	SMCL20127	1968	**£20**	

TEA SET

Title	Format	Label	Cat. No.	Year	Price	Notes
Join The Tea Set	7"	King	KG1048	196-	**£8**	

TEA SET (2)

Title	Format	Label	Cat. No.	Year	Price	Notes
Cups And Saucers	7"	Waldo's	BS003	1978	**£5**	
Parry Thomas	7"	Waldo's	PS006	1980	**£4**	

TEACHO & THE STUDENTS

Title	Format	Label	Cat. No.	Year	Price	Notes
Rocket	7"	Felsted	AF104	1958	**£4**	

TEAL, J. BAND

Title	Format	Label	Cat. No.	Year	Price	Notes
Cooks	LP	Mother Cleo		1977	**£30**	US

TEAR GAS

Tear Gas was a Scottish heavy rock group, whose "Piggy Go Getter" LP received a considerable publicity campaign to little avail. The members' fortunes gained a considerable boost, however, when Tear Gas was taken on entire by singer Alex Harvey, to become The Sensational Alex Harvey Band.

Title	Format	Label	Cat. No.	Year	Price	Notes
Piggy Go Getter	LP	Famous	SFMA5751	1971	**£25**	
Tear Gas	LP	Regal Z.	SLRZ1021	1971	**£60**	

TEARDROP EXPLODES

The LP "Kilimanjaro" by Teardrop Explodes exists in two versions. The second has a cover photograph of Mount Kilimanjaro and includes the hit track "Reward". The first has a cover photograph of the group and lacks "Reward". Inevitably, it is the first version that is the collectable one.

Title	Format	Label	Cat. No.	Year	Price	Notes
Bouncing Babies	7"	Zoo	CAGE005	1979	**£10**	
Colours Fly Away	7"	Mercury	TEAR6	1981	**£4**	with lyrics
Colours Fly Away	12"	Mercury	TEAR612	1981	**£6**	
Ha Ha I'm Drowning	7"	Mercury	TEAR44	1981	**£8**	double
Ha Ha I'm Drowning	7"	Mercury	TEAR4	1981	**£5**	
Kilimanjaro	LP	Mercury	6359035	1980	**£10**	without 'Reward', chart LP
Reward	12"	Mercury	TEAR912	1985	**£6**	
Sleeping Gas	7"	Zoo	CAGE003	1979	**£12**	
Tiny Children (live)	12"	Mercury		1983	**£8**	white label
Tiny Children	7"	Mercury	TEAR7G	1982	**£4**	gatefold PS
Tiny Children	12"	Mercury	TEAR712	1982	**£6**	
Treason	12"	Mercury	TEAR312	1981	**£6**	

Treason	7"	Zoo	CAGE008	1980	**£8**	
You Disappear From View	7"	Mercury	TEAR88	1983	**£5**	double
You Disappear From View	12"	Mercury	TEAR812	1983	**£6**	

TEARDROPS

Final Vinyl	LP	Illuminated	JAMS2	1981	**£10**	
Leave Me No Choice	12"	Bent	BIGB3	198-	**£6**	
Seeing Double	7"	TJM	TJM9	198-	**£4**	

TEARS FOR FEARS

Change	7"	Mercury	IDEA4	1982	**£4**	poster sleeve
Everybody Wants To Rule The World	7"	Mercury	IDEA99	1985	**£8**	double
Everybody Wants To Rule The World	10"	Mercury	IDEA910	1985	**£6**	
Head Over Heels	7"	Mercury	IDEP10	1985	**£6**	pic disc
I Believe	7"	Mercury	IDEA1111	1985	**£6**	double
Mad World	7"	Mercury	IDEA33	1982	**£10**	double
Mother's Talk (Beat Of The Drum Mix)	12"	Mercury	IDEAR712	1984	**£6**	
Mother's Talk	7"	Mercury	IDEA7	1984	**£6**	green vinyl
Mother's Talk	7"	Mercury	IDEP7	1984	**£15**	pic disc
Pale Shelter	7"	Mercury	IDEA2	1982	**£6**	no PS
Pale Shelter	7"	Mercury	IDEA2	1982	**£8**	white vinyl
Pale Shelter	7"	Mercury	IDEAP5	1983	**£8**	pic disc
Pale Shelter	12"	Mercury	IDEA212	1982	**£10**	
Shout	7"	Mercury	IDEC8	1985	**£4**	calendar pack
Shout	10"	Mercury	IDEA810	1984	**£6**	
Suffer the Children	7"	Mercury	IDEA1	1981	**£6**	no PS
Suffer the Children	12"	Mercury	IDEA12	1981	**£10**	
Way You Are	7"	Mercury	IDEA6	1983	**£4**	
Way You Are	7"	Mercury	IDEAS6	1983	**£10**	double
Way You Are	12"	Mercury	IDEA612	1983	**£6**	

TECHNIQUES

Hey Little Girl	7"	Columbia	DB4072	1958	**£4**	

TECHNIQUES (2)

Devoted (with Tommy McCook)	7"	Treasure Isle	TI7038	196-	**£10**	
It's You I Love	7"	Treasure Isle	TI7040	196-	**£10**	
Love Is Not A Gamble	7"	Treasure Isle	TI7026	196-	**£10**	
My Girl (with Tommy McCook)	7"	Treasure Isle	TI7031	196-	**£10**	
Queen Majesty	7"	Treasure Isle	TI7019	196-	**£10**	
You Don't Care	7"	Treasure Isle	TI7001	196-	**£10**	

TEDDY & THE PANDAS

Basic Magnetism	LP	Tower	ST5125	1968	**£20**	US

TEDDY BEARS

Although Phil Spector is famous as a producer - indeed he was the first such to attain fame independently of the artists he produced - he started his career as a singer. He was one third of a group, the Teddybears, whose best known song is remembered as a particularly golden oldie - "To Know Him Is To Love Him".

If Only You Knew	7"	London	HLP8889	1959	**£8**	
Oh Why	7"	London	HLP8836	1959	**£8**	
Teddy Bears Sing	LP	Imperial	LP9067	1959	**£200**	US, mono
Teddy Bears Sing	LP	Imperial	SLP12067	1959	**£300**	US, stereo
Teddy Bears Sing	LP	London	HAP2183	1959	**£100**	
To Know Him Is To Love Him	7"	London	HLN8733	1958	**£4**	chart single

TEE SET

Ma Belle Amie	7"	Major Minor	MM666	1970	**£6**	
Morning Of My Daze	LP	Negram			**£25**	
What Can I Do	7"	Pye	7N25452	1968	**£6**	

TEE, WILLIE

Thank You John	7"	Atlantic	584116	1967	**£6**	

TEEN QUEENS

Eddie My Love	LP	Crown	CLP5022	1957	**£50**	US
Eddie My Love	7"	R&B	MRB5000	1965	**£15**	
Teen Queens	LP	Crown	CLP5373	1963	**£20**	US

TEENAGE FILMSTARS

Cloud Over Liverpool	7"	Clockwork	COR002	1979	**£10**	no PS
I Helped Patrick McGoohan Escape	7"	Fab Listening	FL1	1980	**£10**	

Title	Format	Label	Cat. No.	Year	Price	Notes
Odd Man Out	7"	Blueprint	BLU2013	1980	**£10**	
Odd Man Out	7"	Wessex	WEX275	1980	**£10**	no PS

TEENAGERS

Title	Format	Label	Cat. No.	Year	Price	Notes
Teenagers	7" EP	RCA	RCX102	1957	**£8**	
Califf Boogie	7"	Top Rank	JAR342	1960	**£5**	

TELEVISION

Title	Format	Label	Cat. No.	Year	Price	Notes
Adventure	LP	Elektra	K52072	1978	**£10**	red vinyl
Little Johnny Jewel	7"	Ork	81975	1975	**£15**	US
Little Johnny Jewel	12"	Ork	NYC1		**£15**	US

TELEVISION PERSONALITIES

Title	Format	Label	Cat. No.	Year	Price	Notes
14th Floor	7"	Overground	OVER03	1989	**£4**	white or yellow vinyl
14th Floor	7"	Teen	CUS77089	1978	**£40**	3 PS's
And Don't The Kids Just Love It	LP	Rough Trade	RT24	1981	**£30**	
Biff Bang Pow!	7"	Commu. Blur			**£20**	flexi
How I Learned To Love The Bomb	7"	Dreamworld	DREAM4	198-	**£10**	
How I Learned To Love The Bomb	12"	Dreamworld	DREAM4	198-	**£10**	
I Know Where Syd Barrett Lives	7"	Rough Trade	RT063	1981	**£15**	
Mummy You're Not Watching Me	LP	Whaam!	BIG1		**£30**	
Painted Word	LP	Illuminated	JAMS37	1984	**£25**	
Sense Of Belonging	7"	Rough Trade	RT109	1983	**£10**	
Smashing Time	7"	Rough Trade	RT051	1980	**£12**	
They Could Have Been Bigger Than The Beatles	LP	Dreamworld	BIG002	198-	**£12**	
They Could Have Been Bigger Than The Beatles	LP	Whaam!	BIG4		**£35**	
Three Wishes	7"	Whaam!	WHAAM4	1982	**£12**	
Where's Bill Grundy Now?	7"	no label	LYN5976/7ICRS	1978	**£12**	4 PS's
Where's Bill Grundy Now?	7"	Rough Trade	RT033	1979	**£10**	

TELLERS

Title	Format	Label	Cat. No.	Year	Price	Notes
A-Ya-It-Deh	7"	Dragon	DRA1031	1974	**£4**	
Innocent People Cry	7"	Pyramid	PYR7012	1974	**£5**	

TEMPERANCE SEVEN

Title	Format	Label	Cat. No.	Year	Price	Notes
Charleston	7"	Parlophone	R4851	1961	**£4**	chart single
Everybody Loves My Baby	7"	Parlophone	R4893	1962	**£4**	
Hard Hearted Hannah	7"	Parlophone	R4823	1961	**£4**	chart single
Letkiss	7"	Parlophone	R5236	1965	**£4**	
Pasadena	7"	Parlophone	R4781	1961	**£4**	chart single
Temperance Seven	LP	Parlophone	PMC1152	1961	**£10**	chart LP
Temperance Seven Plus One	LP	Argo	RG11	1961	**£10**	chart LP
You're Driving Me Crazy	7"	Parlophone	R4757	1961	**£4**	chart single

TEMPEST

Title	Format	Label	Cat. No.	Year	Price	Notes
Living In Fear	LP	Bronze	ILPS9267	1974	**£15**	
Tempest	LP	Bronze	ILPS9220	1973	**£15**	

TEMPEST, BOBBY

Title	Format	Label	Cat. No.	Year	Price	Notes
Love Or Leave	7"	Decca	F11125	1959	**£4**	

TEMPLE, GERRY

Title	Format	Label	Cat. No.	Year	Price	Notes
Angel Face	7"	HMV	POP1114	1963	**£6**	
No More Tomorrows	7"	HMV	POP823	1961	**£8**	
Seventeen Come Sunday	7"	HMV	POP939	1961	**£4**	

TEMPO, NICK

Title	Format	Label	Cat. No.	Year	Price	Notes
Rock'N'Roll Beach Party	LP	Liberty	LRP3023	1958	**£20**	US

TEMPO, NINO

Title	Format	Label	Cat. No.	Year	Price	Notes
Rock'N'Roll Beach Party	LP-10"	London	HBU1075	1958	**£20**	
Tempo's Tempo	7"	London	HLU8387	1957	**£15**	

TEMPO, NINO & APRIL STEVENS

Title	Format	Label	Cat. No.	Year	Price	Notes
Deep Purple	LP	Atco	33156	1963	**£12**	US
Deep Purple	7"	London	HLK9782	1963	**£4**	chart single
Deep Purple	7" EP	London	REK1412	1964	**£6**	
Sweet And Lovely	7"	London	HLK9580	1962	**£5**	
Whispering	7"	London	HLK9829	1964	**£4**	chart single

TEMPOS

Title	Format	Label	Cat. No.	Year	Price	Notes
See You In September	7"	Pye	7N25026	1959	**£8**	
Speaking Of The Tempos	LP	Justice	104	1966	**£200**	US

TEMPTATIONS

Title	Format	Label	Cat. No.	Year	Price	Notes
Ain't Too Proud To Beg	7"	T. Motown	TMG565	1966	**£6**	chart single
Ain't Too Proud To Beg	7"	T. Motown	TMG565	1966	**£50**	demo
Ain't Too Proud To Beg	7"	T. Motown	TMG699	1969	**£4**	
Ain't Too Proud To Beg	7"	T. Motown	TMG699	1969	**£15**	demo
All I Need	7"	T. Motown	TMG610	1967	**£5**	
All I Need	7"	T. Motown	TMG610	1967	**£30**	demo
Ball Of Confusion	7"	T. Motown	TMG749	1970	**£4**	chart single
Ball Of Confusion	7"	T. Motown	TMG749	1970	**£10**	demo
Beauty Is Only Skin Deep	7"	T. Motown	TMG578	1966	**£10**	chart single
Beauty Is Only Skin Deep	7"	T. Motown	TMG578	1966	**£50**	demo
Cloud Nine	LP	T. Motown	STML11109	1969	**£10**	chart LP
Cloud Nine	7"	T. Motown	TMG707	1969	**£4**	chart single
Cloud Nine	7"	T. Motown	TMG707	1969	**£15**	demo
Get Ready	7"	T. Motown	TMG557	1966	**£10**	
Get Ready	7"	T. Motown	TMG557	1966	**£50**	demo
Get Ready	7"	T. Motown	TMG688	1969	**£4**	chart single
Get Ready	7"	T. Motown	TMG688	1969	**£15**	demo
Gettin' Ready	LP	T. Motown	STML11035	1966	**£20**	chart LP
Greatest Hits	LP	T. Motown	STML11042	1967	**£10**	chart LP
I Can't Get Next To You	7"	T. Motown	TMG722	1970	**£4**	chart single
I Can't Get Next To You	7"	T. Motown	TMG722	1970	**£10**	demo
I Could Never Love Another	7"	T. Motown	TMG658	1968	**£5**	chart single
I Could Never Love Another	7"	T. Motown	TMG658	1968	**£20**	demo
I Wish It Would Rain	LP	T. Motown	STML11079	1968	**£12**	
I Wish It Would Rain	7"	T. Motown	TMG641	1968	**£5**	chart single
I Wish It Would Rain	7"	T. Motown	TMG641	1968	**£20**	demo
I'll Be In Trouble	7"	Stateside	SS319	1964	**£20**	
I'll Be In Trouble	7"	Stateside	SS319	1964	**£50**	demo
I'm Losing You	7"	T. Motown	TMG587	1966	**£6**	chart single
I'm Losing You	7"	T. Motown	TMG587	1966	**£40**	demo
In A Mellow Mood	LP	T. Motown	STML11068	1968	**£10**	
It's Growing	7"	T. Motown	TMG504	1965	**£12**	chart single
It's Growing	7"	T. Motown	TMG504	1965	**£50**	demo
It's The Temptations	7" EP	T. Motown	TME2010	1966	**£12**	
It's You That I Need	7"	T. Motown	TMG633	1967	**£4**	
It's You That I Need	7"	T. Motown	TMG633	1967	**£35**	demo
Just My Imagination	7"	T. Motown	TMG773	1971	**£4**	chart single
Just My Imagination	7"	T. Motown	TMG773	1971	**£10**	demo
Law Of The Land	7"	T. Motown	TMG866	1973	**£4**	chart single
Law Of The Land	7"	T. Motown	TMG866	1973	**£10**	demo
Live	LP	T. Motown	STML11053	1967	**£12**	chart LP
Live At The Copa	LP	T. Motown	STML11104	1969	**£10**	
Live At The Talk Of The Town	LP	T. Motown	STML11141	1970	**£12**	
Masterpiece	7"	T. Motown	TMG854	1973	**£4**	
Masterpiece	7"	T. Motown	TMG854	1973	**£10**	demo
Meet The Temptations	LP	T. Motown	TML11009	1965	**£20**	
Memories	7"	T. Motown	TMG948	1975	**£8**	demo, PS
Mother Nature	7"	T. Motown	TMG832	1972	**£4**	
Mother Nature	7"	T. Motown	TMG832	1972	**£10**	demo
My Baby	7"	T. Motown	TMG541	1965	**£10**	
My Baby	7"	T. Motown	TMG541	1965	**£50**	demo
My Girl	7"	Stateside	SS378	1965	**£20**	chart single
My Girl	7"	Stateside	SS378	1965	**£50**	demo
Papa Was A Rolling Stone	7"	T. Motown	TMG839	1973	**£4**	chart single
Papa Was A Rolling Stone	7"	T. Motown	TMG839	1973	**£10**	demo
Psychedelic Shack	7"	T. Motown	TMG741	1970	**£4**	chart single
Psychedelic Shack	7"	T. Motown	TMG741	1970	**£10**	demo
Runaway Child Running Wild	7"	T. Motown	TMG716	1969	**£4**	
Runaway Child Running Wild	7"	T. Motown	TMG716	1969	**£10**	demo
Since I Lost My Baby	7"	T. Motown	TMG526	1965	**£12**	
Since I Lost My Baby	7"	T. Motown	TMG526	1965	**£50**	demo
Sing Smokey	LP	T. Motown	TML11016	1965	**£15**	
Superstar	7"	T. Motown	TMG800	1972	**£4**	chart single
Superstar	7"	T. Motown	TMG800	1972	**£10**	demo
Take A Look Around	7"	T. Motown	TMG808	1972	**£4**	chart single
Take A Look Around	7"	T. Motown	TMG808	1972	**£10**	demo

Temptations .... 7" EP .... T. Motown .... TME2004 .... 1965 ...... £12 ....
Temptations Show .... LP .... Gordy .... GS933 .... 1969 ...... £10 .... US
Temptin' Temptations .... LP .... T. Motown .... TML11023 .... 1966 ...... £20 ....
Unite The World .... 7" .... T. Motown .... TMG783 .... 1971 ...... £4 ....
Unite The World .... 7" .... T. Motown .... TMG783 .... 1971 ...... £10 .... demo
Way You Do The Things You Do .... 7" .... Stateside .... SS278 .... 1964 ...... £20 ....
Way You Do The Things You Do .... 7" .... Stateside .... SS278 .... 1964 ...... £50 .... demo
Why Did You Leave Me Darling .... 7" .... T. Motown .... TMG671 .... 1968 ...... £5 ....
Why Did You Leave Me Darling .... 7" .... T. Motown .... TMG671 .... 1968 ...... £20 .... demo
Why You Wanna Make Me Blue .... 7" .... Stateside .... SS348 .... 1964 ...... £20 ....
Why You Wanna Make Me Blue .... 7" .... Stateside .... SS348 .... 1964 ...... £50 .... demo
With A Lot O'Soul .... LP .... T. Motown .... STML11057 .... 1967 ...... £15 .... chart LP
You're My Everything .... 7" .... T. Motown .... TMG620 .... 1967 ...... £5 .... chart single
You're My Everything .... 7" .... T. Motown .... TMG620 .... 1967 ...... £30 .... demo

TEMPTATIONS (2)

Barbara .... 7" .... Top Rank .... JAR384 .... 1960 ...... £5 ....

TEN CC

Greatest Hits .... LP .... Mercury .... HS9102504 .... 1982 ...... £10 .... audiophile
I'm Not In Love (2 versions) .... 7" .... Mercury .... 6008014 .... 1975 ...... £4 .... promo
Original Soundtrack .... LP .... Mercury .... HS9102500 .... 1982 ...... £10 .... audiophile
Worst Band In The World .... 7" .... UK .... UK57 .... 1974 ...... £4 .... promo - radio version

TEN FEET FIVE

Two members of Ten Feet Five left to join the Troggs soon after the release of the group's only single - guitarist Chris Britton and bass player Pete Staples.

Baby's Back In Town .... 7" .... Fontana .... TF578 .... 1965 ...... £20 ....

TEN THOUSAND MANIACS

Secrets Of The I Ching .... LP .... Private .... 198- ...... £15 .... US

TEN WHEEL DRIVE

Brief Replies .... LP .... Polydor .... 2425022 .... 1970 ...... £12 ....
Construction No.1 .... LP .... Polydor .... 583577 .... 1969 ...... £12 ....
Morning Much Better .... 7" .... Polydor .... 2066034 .... 1971 ...... £4 ....
Peculiar Friends .... LP .... Polydor .... 2425065 .... 1971 ...... £10 ....

TEN YEARS AFTER

Before Woodstock showed Alvin Lee the mileage he could get from guitar excess, Ten Years After had a light, jazzy sound that made them stand out from the mass of blues bands emerging at the time. "Undead" shows off this quality well - it even includes a lengthy jam on "Woodchopper's" ball, which succeeds in dragging the Woody Herman original into the rock age with its dignity intact. "Stonedhenge" is still impressive too as the work of a band thinking hard and imaginatively of ways in which to break free of the constraints of playing the blues, even if that imagination was largely placed on hold for subsequent recordings.

Alvin Lee And Co .... LP .... Deram .... SML1096 .... 1972 ...... £10 ....
Cricklewood Green .... LP .... Deram .... SML1065 .... 1970 ...... £10 .... chart LP
Hear Me Calling .... 7" .... Deram .... DM221 .... 1968 ...... £5 ....
Love Like A Man .... 7" .... Deram .... DM299 .... 1970 ...... £4 .... chart single
Portable People .... 7" .... Deram .... DM176 .... 1967 ...... £5 ....
Recorded Live .... LP .... Chrysalis .... CHR1049 .... 1973 ...... £10 .... chart LP
Rock'n'Roll To The World .... LP .... Chrysalis .... CHR1009 .... 1972 ...... £10 .... chart LP
Space In Time .... LP .... Chrysalis .... CHR1001 .... 1972 ...... £10 .... chart LP
Space In Time .... LP .... Columbia .... CQ30801 .... 1972 ...... £10 .... US quad
Sssssssh .... LP .... Deram .... SML1052 .... 1969 ...... £10 .... chart LP
Stonedhenge .... LP .... Deram .... SML1029 .... 1968 ...... £10 .... chart LP
Ten Years After .... LP .... Deram .... SML1015 .... 1967 ...... £15 ....
Undead .... LP .... Deram .... SML1023 .... 1968 ...... £10 .... chart LP
Watt .... LP .... Deram .... SML1078 .... 1970 ...... £10 .... chart LP

TENDER SLIM & COUSIN LEROY

Tender Slim And Cousin Leroy .... 7" EP .... XX .... MIN702 .... £4 ....

TENNENT-MORRISON

Tennent-Morrison .... LP .... Polydor .... 2383152 .... 1972 ...... £10 ....

TENNORS

Copy Me Donkey .... 7" .... Island .... WI3140 .... 1968 ...... £10 ....
Grampa .... 7" .... Island .... WI3156 .... 1968 ...... £10 ....
Hopeful Village .... 7" .... Duke Reid .... DR2502 .... 196- ...... £10 ....
Khaki .... 7" .... Blue Cat .... BS127 .... 1968 ...... £10 ....

Massie Massa	7"	Doctor Bird	DB1152	196-	**£10**	
Money Never Built A Mountain	7"	Pyramid	PYR7000	1973	**£5**	
Pressure And Slide	7"	Coxsone	CS7024	196-	**£10**	
Ride Your Donkey	7"	Island	WI3133	1968	**£10**	
Sufferer	7"	Doctor Bird	DB1175	196-	**£10**	

TERMITES

Tell Me	7"	Oriole	CB1989	1965	**£6**	

TERMITES (2)

Do It Right Now	7"	Coxsone	CS7025	196-	**£10**	
It Takes Two To Make Love	7"	Studio One	SO2029	196-	**£10**	
Mama Didn't Know	7"	Coxsone	CS7039	196-	**£10**	
Mercy Mr.Percy	7"	Studio One	SO2006	196-	**£10**	
Sign Up	7"	Coxsone	CS7008	196-	**£10**	

TERRACE, PETE

At The Party	7"	Pye	7N25427	1967	**£5**	
Shotgun Boogaloo	7"	Pye	7N25440	1967	**£10**	

TERRELL, LLOYD

Bang Bang Lulu	7"	Pama	PM710	196-	**£8**	

TERRELL, TAMMI

Come On And See Me	7"	T. Motown	TMG561	1966	**£15**	
Come On And See Me	7"	T. Motown	TMG561	1966	**£60**	demo
Irresistible Tammi Terrell	LP	T. Motown	STML11103	1969	**£20**	

TERRY & JERRY

People Are Doing It Every Day	7"	R&B	MRB5009	1965	**£8**	

TERRY, GORDON

Country Clambake	7" EP	London	REA1098	1957	**£8**	

TERRY, SONNY

Blues	LP-10"	Stinson	55		**£12**	US
Blues And Folk Songs	LP-10"	Folkways	2327		**£12**	US
Blues From Everywhere	LP	XTRA	XTRA1099		**£10**	
Folk Blues	LP-10"	Elektra	14		**£12**	US
Harmonica	LP-10"	Folkways	2035		**£12**	US
Harmonica	LP-10"	Folkways	35		**£12**	US
Harmonica Blues	LP-10"	Topic	10T30	1958	**£12**	
On The Road	LP	XTRA	XTRA1110	1971	**£10**	
Sonny Is King	LP	Bluesville	BV1059	1963	**£15**	US
Sonny Terry	LP	Everest	206	196-	**£15**	US
Sonny Terry	7" EP	Vogue	EPV1095	195-	**£5**	
Sonny Terry And His Mouth Harp	LP	Riverside	12644		**£15**	US
Sonny's Story	LP	Bluesville	BV1025	1961	**£15**	US
Talkin' 'Bout The Blues	LP	Washington	W702	1961	**£20**	US
Washboard Band	LP-10"	Folkways	2006		**£12**	US

TERRY, SONNY & BROWNIE MCGHEE

At The Second Fret	LP	Bluesville	BV1058	1962	**£15**	US
Back Country Blues	LP	Savoy	MG14019	195-	**£30**	US
Blues	LP	Folkways	F63557	1959	**£20**	US
Blues All Around My Head	LP	Bluesville	BV1020	1961	**£15**	US
Blues And Folk	LP	Bluesville	BV1005	1960	**£15**	US
Blues And Shouts	LP	Fantasy	F3317	1962	**£15**	US
Blues And Shouts	LP	Fantasy	F3317	1962	**£30**	US, red vinyl
Blues In My Soul	LP	Bluesville	BV1033	1961	**£15**	US
Blues Is A Story	LP	W. Pacific	WP1294	1960	**£15**	US
Blues Is My Companion	LP	Verve	V63008	1961	**£15**	US
Brownie's Blues	LP	Bluesville	BV1042	1962	**£12**	US
Down Home Blues	LP	Bluesville	BV1002	1960	**£15**	US
Folk Songs Of Sonny And Brownie	LP	Roulette	R25074	1959	**£20**	US
Going Down Slow	7"	Oriole	CBA1946	1964	**£5**	
Guitar Highway	LP	Folkways	FV9019	1965	**£10**	US
Hometown Blues	LP	Ace Of H.	AHT182	1969	**£10**	
Hooting Blues	7"	Parlophone	MSP6017	1953	**£15**	
Just A Closer Walk With Thee	LP	Fantasy	F3296	1962	**£15**	US
Just A Closer Walk With Thee	LP	Fantasy	F3296	1962	**£30**	US, red vinyl
Key To The Highway	LP	XTRA	XTRA1004	196-	**£10**	

Title	Format	Label	Number	Year	Price	Notes
Penetentiary Blues	LP	Fontana	688007	1960	**£10**	
Rocking And Whooping	7"	Columbia	DB4433	1960	**£6**	
Simply Heavenly	LP	Columbia	OL5240	1957	**£20**	US
Sonny & Brownie At Sugar Hill	LP	Fantasy	F8091	1962	**£15**	US
Sonny & Brownie At Sugar Hill	LP	Fantasy	F8091	1962	**£30**	US, blue vinyl
Sonny Terry & Brownie McGhee & Chris Barber	7" EP	Pye	NJE1073	1957	**£4**	
Sonny Terry & Brownie McGhee	7" EP	Ember	EP4562	1964	**£5**	
Sonny Terry & Brownie McGhee	LP	Fantasy	F3254	1961	**£15**	US
Sonny Terry & Brownie McGhee	LP	Fantasy	F3254	1961	**£30**	US, red vinyl
Terry & McGhee In London	7" EP	Pye	NJE1074	1957	**£5**	
Traditional Blues Vol.1	LP	Folkways	F2421	1961	**£15**	US
Traditional Blues Vol.2	LP	Folkways	F2422	1961	**£15**	US
Way Down South Summit Meeting	LP	W. Pacific	WP1296	1960	**£15**	US
Where The Blues Began	LP	Fontana	SFJL979	1968	**£10**	
Where The Blues Begin	LP	Fontana	SGF67599	1969	**£10**	US
Whoopin' The Blues	LP	Capitol	T20906	196-	**£10**	

TEST DEPARTMENT

Title	Format	Label	Number	Year	Price	Notes
Compulsion	12"	Test	TEST112	1983	**£6**	

TEX, JOE

Title	Format	Label	Number	Year	Price	Notes
Best Of...	LP	King	935	1965	**£12**	US
Best Of...	LP	Parrot	61002	1965	**£10**	US
Buying A Book	LP	Atlantic	SD8231	1969	**£10**	US
Go Home And Do It	7"	Atlantic	584212	1968	**£4**	
Greatest Hits	LP	Atlantic	587089	1967	**£10**	
Happy Soul	LP	Atlantic	SD8211	1969	**£10**	US
Hold On	LP	Checker	2993	1964	**£15**	US
Hold On To What You've Got	LP	Atlantic	8106	1965	**£10**	US
Hold On To What You've Got	7"	Atlantic	AT4015	1965	**£5**	
Hold On To What You've Got	7"	Atlantic	584096	1967	**£4**	
I Want To Do Everything	7"	Atlantic	AT4045	1965	**£4**	
I've Got To Do A Little Better	LP	Atlantic	8133	1966	**£10**	US
Live And Lively	LP	Atlantic	587104	1968	**£10**	
Love You Save	LP	Atlantic	8124	1966	**£10**	US
Love You Save	7"	Atlantic	AT4081	1966	**£4**	
Men Are Getting Scarce	7"	Atlantic	584171	1968	**£4**	
New Boss	LP	Atlantic	8115	1965	**£10**	US
Papa Was Too	7"	Atlantic	584068	1967	**£4**	
S.Y.S.L.J.F.M.	7"	Atlantic	584016	1966	**£4**	
Show Me	7"	Atlantic	584102	1967	**£4**	
Skinny Legs And All	7"	Atlantic	584144	1967	**£4**	
Soul Country	LP	Atlantic	587118	1968	**£10**	
Sweet Woman Like You	7"	Atlantic	AT4058	1965	**£4**	
We Can't Sit Down Now	7"	Atlantic	584296	1969	**£4**	
Woman Can Change A Man	7"	Atlantic	AT4027	1965	**£4**	
Woman Like That, Yeah	7"	Atlantic	584119	1967	**£4**	
You Better Believe It	7"	Atlantic	584035	1966	**£4**	
You Better Get It	LP	Atlantic	587130	1968	**£10**	
You Better Get It	7"	Atlantic	AT4021	1965	**£5**	
You're Alright Ray Charles	7"	Atlantic	584318	1970	**£4**	
Yum Yum Yum	7"	Sue	WI370	1965	**£10**	

TEXANS

Title	Format	Label	Number	Year	Price	Notes
Being With You	7"	Columbia	DB7242	1964	**£4**	

TEXAS RANGERS

Title	Format	Label	Number	Year	Price	Notes
Way Out West	7" EP	HMV	7EG8387	1957	**£4**	

THE THE

Title	Format	Label	Number	Year	Price	Notes
Beat(en) Generation	12"	Epic	EMUB8	1989	**£6**	boxed, poster, cards, badge
Cold Spell Ahead	7"	Some Bizarre	BZS4	1981	**£25**	
Controversial Subject	7"	4AD	AD10	1980	**£30**	
Flesh And Bones	7"	Some Bizarre		1985	**£15**	1 sided promo
Heartland	cass-s	Epic	TRUTHC2	1986	**£6**	
Heartland	12"	Epic	TRUTHD2	1986	**£8**	double
Infected	LP	Epic	26770	1986	**£10**	torture sleeve, poster
Infected	cass-s	Epic	TRUTHC3	1986	**£6**	
Infected	12"	Epic	TRUTHD3	1986	**£10**	double
Infected	12"	Epic	TRUTHQ3	1986	**£10**	uncensored PS

Title	Format	Label	Cat. No.	Year	Price	Notes
Perfect	7"	Epic	EPCA3119	1983	**£10**	
Perfect	12"	Epic	EPCA133119	1983	**£15**	
Slow Train To Dawn	7"	Epic	TENSE1	1987	**£5**	with stickers
Soul Mining	LP	Epic	25525	1983	**£25**	with 12"
Soul Mining	cass	Epic		1983	**£10**	
Sweet Bird Of Truth	cass-s	Epic	TENSEC2	1987	**£6**	
Sweet Bird Of Truth	12"	Epic	TRUTH1	1986	**£8**	
This Is The Day	7"	Epic	A3710	1983	**£10**	chart single
This Is The Day	7"	Epic	A3710	1983	**£20**	double
This Is The Day	12"	Epic	TA3710	1983	**£20**	
Uncertain Smile	7"	Epic	A3588	1983	**£10**	
Uncertain Smile	7"	Epic	EPCA2787	1982	**£10**	with insert, chart single
Uncertain Smile	12"	Epic	EPC132787	1982	**£20**	insert
Uncertain Smile	12"	Epic	EPC132787	1982	**£30**	yellow vinyl, insert
Uncertain Smile	12"	Epic	TA3588	1983	**£12**	

THEATRE OF HATE

Title	Format	Label	Cat. No.	Year	Price	Notes
Eastworld	7"	Burning Rome	BRR4	1982	**£4**	
Eastworld	12"	Burning Rome	BRR4T	1982	**£6**	
Ghost Of Love	7"	Masterbag	BAG002	1982	**£5**	flexi
He Who Dares Wins - Live At The Warehouse Leeds	LP	SS	SSSSS1P	1981	**£12**	
He Who Dares Wins - Live In Berlin	LP	SS	SSSSS2P	1982	**£10**	
Hop	7"	Burning Rome	BRR3	1982	**£4**	chart single
Live At The Lyceum	cass	Straight M.	TOH1	1981	**£12**	
Nero	12"	Burning Rome	BRR1931	1981	**£8**	
Original Sin	7"	SS	SS3	1980	**£10**	
Poppies	7"	Vinyl	V17	1982	**£6**	flexi
Rebel Without A Brain	7"	Burning Rome	BRR1	1981	**£8**	
Wake	7"	Bliss	TOH1EP	1985	**£5**	

THEE

Title	Format	Label	Cat. No.	Year	Price	Notes
Each And Every Day	7"	Decca	F12163	1965	**£10**	

THEE MIDNIGHTERS

Title	Format	Label	Cat. No.	Year	Price	Notes
Bring You Love Special Delivery	LP	Whittier	W5000	1966	**£12**	US
Giants	LP	Whittier	WS5002	1967	**£12**	US
Thee Midnighters	LP	Chatta.	CS1001	1965	**£15**	US
Unlimited	LP	Whittier	W5001	1966	**£12**	US

THELWALL, LLANS & THE CELESTIALS

Title	Format	Label	Cat. No.	Year	Price	Notes
Choo Choo Ska	7"	Island	WI262	1966	**£10**	

THEM

Despite being continually plagued by management and record company problems, Them managed to produce some of the toughest and most enduring of British R&B. Much of the credit for this inevitably goes to the group's lead singer - Van Morrison - already a distinctive and commanding vocalist.

Title	Format	Label	Cat. No.	Year	Price	Notes
Angry Young Them	LP	Decca	LK4700	1965	**£30**	
Baby Please Don't Go	7"	Decca	F12018	1964	**£5**	chart single
Belfast Gypsies	LP	Grand Prix	GP9923	1967	**£30**	Swedish
Call My Name	7"	Decca	F12355	1966	**£8**	
Don't Start Crying Now	7"	Decca	F11973	1964	**£10**	
Gloria	7"	Major Minor	MM509	1967	**£8**	
Here Comes The Night	7"	Decca	F12094	1965	**£4**	chart single
It Won't Hurt Half As Much	7"	Decca	F12215	1965	**£8**	
Mystic Eyes	7"	Decca	F12281	1965	**£8**	
Now & Them	LP	Tower	ST5104	1968	**£40**	US
One More Time	7"	Decca	F12175	1965	**£6**	
Richard Cory	7"	Decca	F12403	1966	**£8**	
Story Of Them	7"	Major Minor	MM513	1967	**£10**	
Them	7" EP	Decca	DFE8612	1965	**£20**	
Them	LP	Happy Tiger	HT1004	1970	**£20**	US
Them Again	LP	Decca	LK4751	1966	**£30**	
Them In Reality	LP	Happy Tiger	HT1012	1971	**£30**	US
Time Out,Time In For Them	LP	Tower	ST5116	1968	**£30**	US

THEN JERICHO

Title	Format	Label	Cat. No.	Year	Price	Notes
Big Sweep	12"	Immaculate	TJ1	1985	**£50**	
Fault	12"	London	LONX63	1985	**£20**	
Let Her Fall	12"	London	LONX97	1987	**£10**	
Motive	12"	London	LONX145	1987	**£15**	poster sleeve

Motive	10"	London	LONX145	1987	**£15**	
Prairie Rose	12"	London	LONX131	1987	**£15**	

THIN LIZZY

Bad Reputation	7"	Vertigo	LIZZYDJ8	1979	**£5**	promo
Chinatown (2 versions)	7"	Vertigo	LIZZYDJ6	1978	**£5**	promo
Dublin	7"	Decca	F13208	1972	**£8**	
Farmer	7"	Parlophone	DIP513	1970	**£20**	Irish
Hollywood	7"	Vertigo	LIZZYDJ10	1981	**£5**	1 sided promo
Little Darling	7"	Decca	F13507	1974	**£5**	
Philomena	7"	Vertigo	6059111	1974	**£4**	
Randolph's Tango	7"	Decca	F13402	1973	**£6**	
Rocker	7"	Decca	F13467	1973	**£5**	
Rosalie	7"	Vertigo	6059124	1975	**£4**	
Shades Of A Blue Orphanage	LP	Decca	TXS108	1972	**£12**	
Thin Lizzy	LP	Decca	SKL5082	1971	**£12**	
Thunder And Lightning	12"	Vertigo	LIZZY1212	1983	**£6**	with poster
Vagabonds Of The Western World	LP	Decca	SKL5170	1973	**£10**	
Vagabonds Of The Western World	7"	Decca		1973	**£8**	promo
Wild One	7"	Vertigo	6059129	1975	**£4**	

THIRD EAR BAND

Alchemy	LP	Harvest	SHVL756	1969	**£12**	
Macbeth	LP	Harvest	SHSP4019	1972	**£15**	
Third Ear Band	LP	Harvest	SHVL773	1970	**£15**	chart LP

THIRD QUADRANT

Seeing Yourself	LP	private		1982	**£100**	

THIRD RAIL

Id Music	LP	Epic	LN24327	1967	**£15**	US
Run Run Run	7"	Columbia	DB8274	1967	**£8**	

THIRD TIME AROUND

Soon Everything Gonna Be Alright	7"	Contempo	CS2076	1975	**£4**	

THIRD WORLD WAR

Ascension Day	7"	Fly	BUG7	1971	**£5**	PS
Little Bit Of Urban Rock	7"	Cube	BUG11	1971	**£5**	
Third World War	LP	Fly	HIFLY4	1971	**£12**	
Third World War II	LP	Track	2406108	1972	**£12**	

THIRTEENTH FLOOR ELEVATORS

Bull Of The Woods	LP	Int. Artists	IA9	1969	**£30**	US
Easter Everywhere	LP	Int. Artists	IA5	1968	**£40**	US
Easter Everywhere	LP	Radar	RAD15	1979	**£15**	
Live	LP	Int. Artists	IA8	1968	**£30**	US
Psychedelic Sounds	LP	Int. Artists	LP1	1966	**£40**	US
Psychedelic Sounds	LP	Radar	RAD13	1978	**£15**	
You're Gonna Miss Me	7"	Radar	ADA13	1978	**£4**	

THIRTY SECOND TURN OFF

Thirty Second Turn Off	LP	Jay Boy			**£30**	

THIRTY-FIRST OF FEBRUARY

Thirty-First Of February	LP	Vanguard	VSD6503	1969	**£12**	US

THIS HEAT

Deceit	LP	Rough Trade	RT26	1981	**£12**	
Health And Efficiency	12"	Piano	THIS1201	1980	**£8**	
This Heat	LP	Piano	THIS1	1979	**£15**	

THIS MORTAL COIL

Come Here My Love	10"	4AD	BAD606	1986	**£10**	
Song To The Siren	7"	4AD	AD310	1983	**£4**	chart single

THOMAS, B.J.

B.J.Thomas And The Triumphs	LP	Pacemaker	PLP3001	196-	**£20**	US
Very Best Of...	LP	Hickory	LP133	1966	**£10**	US

THOMAS, CARLA

B-a-b-y	7"	Atlantic	584042	1966	**£5**	

Best Of...	LP	Atlantic	SD8232	1969	**£10**	US
Carla	LP	Stax	709	1966	**£15**	US
Comfort Me	7"	Atlantic	AT4074	1966	**£4**	
Comfort Me	LP	Stax	ST706	1966	**£15**	US
Gee Whiz	LP	Atlantic	8057	1961	**£30**	US
Gee Whiz	7"	London	HLK9310	1961	**£5**	
I'll Bring It On Home To You	7"	London	HLK9618	1962	**£4**	
I've Got No Time To Lose	7"	Atlantic	AT4005	1964	**£4**	
Let Me Be Good To You	7"	Atlantic	584011	1966	**£4**	
Love Means...	LP	Stax	STS2044	1971	**£10**	US
Love Of My Own	7"	London	HLK9359	1961	**£4**	
Memphis Queen	LP	Stax	SXATS2019	1969	**£10**	
Pick Up The Pieces	7"	Stax	601032	1968	**£4**	
Queen Alone	LP	Stax	718	1967	**£15**	US
Something Good	7"	Stax	601002	1967	**£4**	
When Tomorrow Comes	7"	Stax	601008	1967	**£4**	

THOMAS, CLAUDETTE

Roses Are Red My Love	7"	Caltone	TONE116	196-	**£8**	

THOMAS, CREEPY JOHN

Creepy John Thomas	LP	RCA	SF8061	1969	**£40**	
Ride A Rainbow	7"	RCA	RCA1912	1970	**£10**	

THOMAS, IRMA

Don't Mess With My Man	7"	Sue	WI372	1965	**£8**	
I'm Gonna Cry Till My Tears Run Dry	7"	Liberty	LIB66106	1965	**£10**	
It's A Man's Woman's World	7"	Liberty	LIB66178	1966	**£4**	
Some Things You Never Get Used To	7"	Liberty	LIB66095	1965	**£8**	
Take A Look	7"	Liberty	LIB66137	1966	**£6**	
Take A Look	LP	Minit	40004	1966	**£12**	
Time Is On My Side	7"	Liberty	LIB66041	1964	**£12**	
Time Is On My Side	7" EP	Liberty	LEP4035	1965	**£12**	
True True Love	7"	Liberty	LIB66080	1965	**£5**	
Wish Someone Would Care	LP	Imperial	LP9266	1964	**£12**	US
Wish Someone Would Care	7"	Liberty	LIB66013	1964	**£8**	

THOMAS, JAMO

I Spy (For The FBI)	7"	Polydor	56709	1966	**£5**	
I Spy (For The FBI)	7"	Polydor	56755	1969	**£4**	chart single

THOMAS, JIMMY

This Beautiful Night	7"	Parlophone	R5773	1969	**£12**	

THOMAS, RUFUS

Can Your Monkey Do The Dog	7"	London	HLK9850	1964	**£4**	
Do The Dog	7" EP	Atlantic	AET6001	1964	**£8**	
Down To My House	7"	Stax	601028	1968	**£4**	
Greasy Spoon	7"	Stax	601013	1967	**£4**	
Jump Back	7"	Atlantic	584089	1967	**£4**	
Jump Back	7"	Atlantic	AT4009	1964	**£4**	
Jump Back With Rufus Thomas	7" EP	Atlantic	AET6011	1965	**£8**	
Memphis Train	7"	Stax	601037	1968	**£4**	
Somebody Stole My Dog	7"	London	HLK9884	1964	**£4**	
Walking The Dog	LP	London	HAK8183	1964	**£20**	
Walking The Dog	7"	London	HLK9799	1963	**£5**	
Willy Nilly	7"	Atlantic	584029	1966	**£4**	

THOMOPOULAS, ANDREAS

Born Out Of The Tears Of The Sun	LP	Mushroom		1971	**£80**	
Songs Of The Street	LP	Mushroom		1970	**£100**	

THOMPSON TWINS

Perfect Game	7"	T	TEE1	1981	**£4**	
She's In Love With Mystery	7"	Latent	LATE1	1980	**£6**	
Squares And Triangles	7"	Dirty Discs	RANK1	1980	**£8**	

THOMPSON, BOBBY

That's How Strong My Love Is	7"	Columbia	DB113	1969	**£8**	
That's How Strong My Love Is	7"	Jolly	JY001	196-	**£4**	

THOMPSON, CHRIS

Title	Format	Label	Cat. No.	Year	Price	
Chris Thompson	LP	Village Thing		1973	**£15**	

THOMPSON, HANK

Title	Format	Label	Cat. No.	Year	Price	
Anybody's Girl	7"	Capitol	CL15014	1959	**£4**	
Favourite Waltzes	LP	Capitol	T1111	1959	**£12**	US
Favourite Waltzes	7" EP	Capitol	EAP11111	1959	**£4**	
Gathering Flowers	7"	Capitol	CL14945	1958	**£4**	
Hank	LP	Capitol	T826	1957	**£15**	US
Hank	7" EP	Capitol	EAP1826	1957	**£5**	
Hank Thompson Favorites	LP	Capitol	T911	1957	**£15**	US
Hank Thompson Favorites	LP-10"	Capitol	H911	1956	**£25**	US
Hank Thompson's Dance Ranch	LP	Capitol	T975	1958	**£15**	US
Honey, Honey Bee Ball	7"	Capitol	CL14517	1956	**£4**	
I Guess I'm Getting Over You	7"	Capitol	CL15074	1959	**£4**	
I'm Not Mad, Just Hurt	7"	Capitol	CL14668	1956	**£4**	
I've Run Out Of Tomorrows	7"	Capitol	CL14961	1958	**£4**	
Li'l Liza Jane	7"	Capitol	CL14869	1958	**£4**	
Most Of All	LP	Capitol	T1360	1960	**£10**	US
New Recordings Of Hank's All-Time Hits	LP	Capitol	T729	1956	**£20**	US
New Recordings Of Hank's All-Time Hits	LP-10"	Capitol	H729	1956	**£25**	US
North Of The Rio Grande	LP	Capitol	T618	1956	**£20**	US
North Of The Rio Grande	LP-10"	Capitol	H618	1955	**£25**	US
She's Just A Whole Lot Like You	7"	Capitol	CL15156	1960	**£4**	
Six Pack To Go	7"	Capitol	CL15114	1960	**£5**	
Songs For Rounders	LP	Capitol	T1246	1959	**£10**	US
Songs Of The Brazos Valley	LP	Capitol	T418	1956	**£20**	US
Songs Of The Brazos Valley	LP-10"	Capitol	H418	1953	**£25**	US
Songs Of The Brazos Valley No.1	7" EP	Capitol	EAP1028	1956	**£5**	
This Broken Heart Of Mine	LP	Capitol	T1469	1960	**£10**	US
Wild Side Of Life	7"	Capitol	CL15247	1962	**£4**	
Will We Start It All Over	7"	Capitol	CL15177	1961	**£4**	

THOMPSON, HAYDEN

Title	Format	Label	Cat. No.	Year	Price	
Here's Hayden Thompson	LP	Kapp	KL1507	1966	**£12**	US

THOMPSON, KAY

Title	Format	Label	Cat. No.	Year	Price	
Eloise	7"	London	HLA8268	1956	**£6**	
Kay Thompson	LP	MGM	E3146	195-	**£12**	US

THOMPSON, MAYO

Title	Format	Label	Cat. No.	Year	Price	
Corky's Debt To His Father	LP	Texas Rev.	CFS2270	1970	**£25**	US

THOMPSON, PAUL & THE NINTH DEGREE

Title	Format	Label	Cat. No.	Year	Price	
For Me It's All Over	7"	Fontana	TF656	1965	**£4**	

THOMPSON, RICHARD

Since leaving Fairport Convention, Richard Thompson has matured, not only into a song-writer of particularly fine material, but also into a brilliant and highly individual guitarist. Inevitably, a man who is a major but not especially fashionable talent has had trouble in the eighties in finding suitable recording contracts. The relative scarcity of the "Strict Tempo" album is an immediate consequence of this.

Title	Format	Label	Cat. No.	Year	Price	
Henry The Human Fly	LP	Island	ILPS9197	1972	**£10**	
Strict Tempo	LP	Elixir	LP1	1981	**£12**	

THOMPSON, RICHARD & LINDA

Title	Format	Label	Cat. No.	Year	Price	
Don't Let A Thief Steal	7"	Chrysalis	CHS2278	1979	**£4**	
Georgie On A Spree	7"	Chrysalis	CHS2369	1979	**£4**	
Hokey Pokey	7"	Island	WIP6220	1975	**£4**	
I Want To See The Bright Lights Tonight	7"	Island	WIP6186	1974	**£4**	

THOMPSON, ROY

Title	Format	Label	Cat. No.	Year	Price	
Sookie Sookie	7"	Columbia	DB8108	1967	**£5**	

THOMPSON, SONNY

Title	Format	Label	Cat. No.	Year	Price	
Mellow Blues For The Late Hours	LP	King	655	1959	**£40**	US
Moody Blues	LP	King	568	1956	**£50**	US
Screaming Boogie	7"	Starlite	ST45008	1960	**£40**	

THOMPSON, SUE

Title	Format	Label	Cat. No.	Year	Price	
Bad Boy	7"	Hickory	451255	1964	**£4**	
Big Daddy	7"	Hickory	451240	1964	**£4**	

Title	Format	Label	Number	Year	Price	Notes
Have A Good Time	7"	Polydor	NH66979	1962	**£4**	
It's Break-Up Time	7"	Hickory	451328	1965	**£4**	
James	7"	Fontana	267244TF	1962	**£4**	
Just Kiss Me	7"	Hickory	451340	1965	**£4**	
Norman	7"	Polydor	NH66973	1962	**£4**	
Paper Tiger	7"	Hickory	451284	1965	**£4**	chart single
Sad Movies	7"	Polydor	NH66967	1961	**£4**	chart single
Two Of A Kind	7"	Polydor	NH66976	1962	**£4**	
What Should I Do	7"	Hickory	451381	1965	**£4**	
What's Wrong Billy	7"	Polydor	NH66987	1963	**£4**	
Willie Can	7"	Fontana	267262TF	1963	**£4**	

THOMPSON, SUE & BOB LUMAN

Title	Format	Label	Number	Year	Price	Notes
I Like Your Kind Of Love	7"	Polydor	NH66989	1963	**£4**	

THORN, GUNILLA

Title	Format	Label	Number	Year	Price	Notes
Merry Go Round	7"	HMV	POP1239	1963	**£5**	

THORNE, DAVID

Title	Format	Label	Number	Year	Price	Notes
Alley Cat Song	7"	Stateside	SS141	1962	**£4**	chart single

THORNE, WOODY

Title	Format	Label	Number	Year	Price	Notes
Sadie Lou	7"	Vogue	V9202	1962	**£15**	

THORNHILL, CLAUDE

Title	Format	Label	Number	Year	Price	Notes
Claude Thornhill Goes Modern	7" EP	London	REP1009	1954	**£8**	
Pussyfooting	7"	London	HL8042	1954	**£10**	

THORNTON, BIG MAMA

Title	Format	Label	Number	Year	Price	Notes
Stronger Than Dirt	LP	Mercury	SRM161225	1969	**£10**	US
Way It Is	LP	Mercury	SRM161249	1970	**£10**	US

THORNTON, EDDIE

Title	Format	Label	Number	Year	Price	Notes
Baby Be My Gal	7"	Instant	IN003	1969	**£8**	

THORNTON, WILLA MAE

Title	Format	Label	Number	Year	Price	Notes
Tom Cat	7"	Sue	WI345	1964	**£20**	

THORNTON, FRADKIN & UNGER

Title	Format	Label	Number	Year	Price	Notes
God Bless California	7"	ESP-Disk	4563019	1974	**£5**	
Pass On This Side	LP	ESP-Disk		1974	**£12**	

THORPE, BILLY & THE AZTECS

Title	Format	Label	Number	Year	Price	Notes
Twilight Time	7"	Parlophone	R5381	1965	**£4**	

THOUGHTS

Title	Format	Label	Number	Year	Price	Notes
All Night Stand	7"	Planet	PLF118	1966	**£15**	

THOUGHTS & WORDS

Title	Format	Label	Number	Year	Price	Notes
Thoughts & Words	LP	Liberty	LBL83224	1969	**£10**	

THREADS OF LIFE

Title	Format	Label	Number	Year	Price	Notes
Threads Of Life	LP	Atco			**£240**	

THREE BELLS

Title	Format	Label	Number	Year	Price	Notes
Cry No More	7"	Columbia	DB7980	1966	**£5**	

THREE CAPS

Title	Format	Label	Number	Year	Price	Notes
Cool Jerk	7"	Atlantic	584251	1969	**£4**	
I Got To Handle It	7"	Atlantic	584043	1966	**£4**	

THREE CHUCKLES

Title	Format	Label	Number	Year	Price	Notes
Three Chuckles	LP	Vik	LX1067	1956	**£40**	US
We're Gonna Rock Tonight	7"	HMV	POP292	1957	**£15**	

THREE CITY FOUR

Title	Format	Label	Number	Year	Price	Notes
Smoke And Dust	LP	CBS		1967	**£50**	
Three City Four	LP	Decca		1965	**£120**	

THREE DEGREES

Title	Format	Label	Number	Year	Price	Notes
Close Your Eyes	7"	Stateside	SS459	1965	**£15**	
Gee Baby I'm Sorry	7"	Stateside	SS413	1965	**£4**	
Maybe	7"	Pye	7N25671	1975	**£4**	

THREE DOG NIGHT

It Ain't Easy .... LP........ Dunhill........ DS50078........ 1970...... **£15**.. US, nude group on cover

THREE GOOD REASONS

Build Your Love .... 7"........ Mercury........ MF883........ 1965........ **£4**........
Nowhere Man .... 7"........ Mercury........ MF899........ 1966........ **£5**........ chart single

THREE MAN ARMY

Mahesha .... LP........ Polydor........ 2310241........ 1974...... **£40**........
Third Of A Lifetime .... LP........ Pegasus........ PEG3........ 1971...... **£20**........
Three Man Army 2 .... LP........ Reprise........ K54015........ 1974...... **£20**........
Three Man Army .... LP........ Reprise........ K44254........ 1973...... **£15**........
What's Your Name .... 7"........ Pegasus........ PGS1........ 1972........ **£5**........

THREE PEOPLE

Have You Ever Been There .... 7"........ Decca........ F12473........ 1966........ **£4**........
Simple Thing Would Be For You... .... 7"........ Decca........ F12581........ 1967........ **£4**........
Suspicions .... 7"........ Decca........ F12514........ 1966........ **£4**........

THREE TOPS

Do It Right .... 7"........ Treasure Isle... TI7008........ 196-....... **£10**........
It's Raining .... 7"........ Trojan........ TR003........ 196-....... **£10**........

THREE WISE MEN

Thanks For Christmas .... 7"........ Virgin........ VS642........ 1983........ **£4**........

THREE'S A CROWD

Look Around The Corner .... 7"........ Fontana........ TF673........ 1966........ **£4**........

THRILLINGTON, PERCY 'THRILLS'

Thrillington .... LP........ Regal Z. .... EMC3175........ 1975...... **£50**........
Uncle Albert,Admiral Halsey .... 7"........ EMI........ EMI2594........ 1977...... **£15**........

THRILLS

No One .... 7"........ Capitol........ CL15469........ 1966...... **£15**........

THROBBING GRISTLE

Throbbing Gristle emerged at about the same time as punk, yet their music was more profoundly revolutionary than anything produced by the Sex Pistols or their colleagues. Designed to counterpoint the squallor and cruelty that the group saw in late twentieth century city life, Throbbing Gristle's music consisted of ugly and angry sound, with none of the melodic or rhythmic landmarks that are normally taken for granted. Due to the group's habit of taping all their live performances, the amount of available Throbbing Gristle material is vast and much of it has become very collectable.

24 Hours .... cass ..... Industrial........ **£180**........ 26 tapes in case with inserts
Adrenalin .... 7"........ Industrial........ IR0015........ 1980...... **£12**........ polythene bag, PS
Assume Power Focus .... LP........ Cause For C. .. POWERFOCUS001 1982...... **£25**........
Best Of Vol.2 .... cass ..... Industrial........ IR0001........ 1975...... **£50**........
Boxed Set .... LP........ Fetish........ FX001........ 1981 .... **£100**....... 5 LPs, booklet, badge
D.O.A. The Third And Final Report .... LP........ Industrial........ IR0004........ 1978...... **£20**. with calendar and postcard
D.O.A. The Third And Final Report .... LP........ Industrial........ IR0004........ 1979...... **£20**...... 16 equal length tracks
Discipline .... 12"........ Fetish........ FET006........ 1981...... **£15**........
Editions Frankfurt - Berlin .... LP........ Svensk Illum. .. SJAMS31........ 1983...... **£20**........
Fuhrer Der Menscheit .... LP-10".. Am. Phonogram 1JAPSO36........ 1983...... **£20**........
Fuhrer Der Menscheit .... LP-10".. Bundestag. ..... 29681........ 1982...... **£25**........ some orange vinyl
Funeral In Berlin .... LP........ Zensor........ ZENSOR01........ 1981...... **£20**........
Greatest Hits - Entertainment Through Pain .... LP........ Rough Trade... ROUGHUS23........ 1981...... **£12**........
Heathen Earth .... LP........ Industrial........ IR0009........ 1980...... **£15**........
Heathen Earth .... LP........ Industrial........ IR0009........ 1980...... **£75**........ blue vinyl
In The Shadow Of The Sun .... LP........ Illuminated...... JAMS35........ 1984...... **£15**........
Journey Through A Body .... LP........ W. Ulbricht...... ST3382........ 1982...... **£25**........
Mission Is Terminated .... LP+12". Nice........ EX39LY2........ 1983...... **£20**........ with booklet
Music From The Death Factory .... LP........ Death........ 01........ 1982.... **£150**........
Music From The Death Factory .... LP........ Throbbing G.... 33033........ 1982...... **£25**........ pic disc
Once Upon A Time .... LP........ Casual Ab. ...... CAS1J........ 1984...... **£20**........
Rafters .... LP........ Italian........ EX23........ 1981...... **£15**........
Sacrifice .... LP........ Castle Commu. DOJOLP29........ 1986...... **£10**........
Second Annual Report .... LP........ Fetish........ FET2001........ 1978...... **£20**.. with questionnaire, insert
Second Annual Report .... LP........ Fetish........ FET2001........ 1979...... **£15**........ glossy sleeve
Second Annual Report .... LP........ Fetish........ FET2001........ 1981...... **£20**........ backwards version, 2 sleeves

Second Annual Report .... LP .... Industrial .... IR0002 .... 1977 ...... £75 .... with questionnaire
Special Treatment .... LP .... Mental Decay . 011 .... 1984 ...... £15 ....
Subhuman .... 7" .... Industrial .... IR0013 .... 1980 ...... £12 .... polythene bag, PS
Thee Psychick Sacrifice .... LP .... Karnage .... KILL1 .... 1982 ...... £25 .... double
Twenty Jazz Funk Greats .... LP .... Industrial .... IR0008 .... 1979 ...... £20 .... with poster
Twenty Jazz Funk Greats .... LP .... Industrial .... IR0008 .... 1979 ...... £15 .... without poster
United .... 7" .... Industrial .... IR0003 .... 1978 ...... £10 ....
United .... 7" .... Industrial .... IR0003 .... 1980 ...... £20 ..... extended B side, white or clear vinyl
We Hate You Little Girls .... 7" .... Adolescent ...... ARTT010 .... 1981 ...... £15 .... US
We Hate You Little Girls .... 7" .... Sordide S. .... SS45001 .... 1979 ...... £60 .... A4 sleeve, numbered

THUNDER COMPANY (BRIAN BENNETT)

Riding On The Gravy Train .... 7" .... Columbia .... DB8706 .... 1970 ...... £12 ....

THUNDER, JOHNNY

Dear John I'm Going To Leave You .... 7" .... Stateside .... SS454 .... 1965 .... £4 ....
Everybody Do The Sloopy .... 7" .... Stateside .... SS476 .... 1965 .... £4 ....
Hey Child .... 7" .... Stateside .... SS229 .... 1963 .... £4 ....
Jailer Bring Me Water .... 7" .... Stateside .... SS200 .... 1963 .... £4 ....
Loop De Loop .... LP .... Diamond .... D5001 .... 1963 ...... £25 .... US
Loop De Loop .... 7" .... Stateside .... SS149 .... 1963 .... £4 ....
More More More Love Love Love .... 7" .... Stateside .... SS337 .... 1964 .... £4 ....
My Prayer .... 7" .... Stateside .... SS499 .... 1966 .... £4 ....
Rock A Bye My Darling .... 7" .... Stateside .... SS168 .... 1963 .... £4 ....
Send Her To Me .... 7" .... Stateside .... SS370 .... 1965 .... £4 ....

THUNDERBIRDS

Alias Mister Hackenbacker .... 7" EP.... Century 21 ...... MA123 .... 1967 ...... £10 ....
Atlantic Inferno .... 7" EP.... Century 21 ...... MA125 .... 1967 ...... £10 ....
Brink Of Disaster .... 7" EP.... Century 21 ...... MA124 .... 1967 ...... £10 ....
Chain Chain .... 7" EP.... Century 21 ...... MA122 .... 1967 ...... £10 ....
Day Of Disaster .... 7" EP.... Century 21 ...... MA121 .... 1967 ...... £10 ....
Fab .... 7" EP.... Century 21 ...... MA107 .... 1966 ...... £10 ....
Introducing Thunderbirds .... 7" EP.... Century 21 ...... MA103 .... 1966 ...... £10 ....
Ricochet .... 7" EP.... Century 21 ...... MA126 .... 1967 ...... £10 ....
Thunderbird Four .... 7" EP.... Century 21 ...... MA113 .... 1966 ...... £10 ....
Thunderbird One .... 7" EP.... Century 21 ...... MA108 .... 1966 ...... £10 ....
Thunderbird Three .... 7" EP.... Century 21 ...... MA112 .... 1966 ...... £10 ....
Thunderbird Two .... 7" EP.... Century 21 ...... MA109 .... 1966 ...... £10 ....

THUNDERBIRDS (2)

Ayuh Ayuh .... 7" .... London .... HL8146 .... 1955 .... £8 ....
Meet The Fabulous Thunderbirds .... LP .... Red Feather ... TH1 .... 195- .... £100 .... US

THUNDERBIRDS (3)

New Orleans Beat .... 7" .... Oriole .... CB1625 .... 1961 .... £8 ....
Wild Weekend .... 7" .... Oriole .... CB1610 .... 1961 .... £8 ....

THUNDERBIRDS (4)

Your Ma Said You Cried .... 7" .... Polydor .... 56710 .... 1966 .... £5 ....

THUNDERBOLTS

Fugitive .... 7" .... Decca .... F11522 .... 1962 .... £4 ....

THUNDERCLAP NEWMAN

Accidents .... 7" .... Track .... 2094001 .... 1970 .... £4 .... chart single
Hollywood Dream .... LP .... Track .... 2406003 .... 1970 ...... £15 ....
Peter Townshend Talks To, And About, Thunderclap Newman .... LP .... Track .... PR160 .... 1969 ...... £20 .... US interview promo
Reason .... 7" .... Track .... 2094003 .... 1970 .... £4 ....
Something In The Air .... 7" .... Track .... 604031 .... 1969 .... £4 .... chart single

THUNDERMUG

Thundermug Strikes .... LP .... Axe .... AXS502 .... 1972 ...... £12 ....

THUNDERPUSSY

Documents Of Captivity .... LP .... MRT .... 1973 ...... £70 .... US

THUNDERTRAIN

Teenage Suicide .... LP .... Jelly .... JPLP1 .... 1977 ...... £20 ....

THYRDS
Hide'n'Seek	7"	Decca	F12010	1964	**£15**	

TICKAWINDA
Rosemary Lane	LP	Pennine		1975	**£200**	

TICKLE
Subway	7"	Regal Z.	RZ3004	1967	**£20**	

TIDAL WAVE
With Tears In My Eyes	7"	Decca	F22973	1969	**£8**	

TIDE
Almost Live	LP	Mouth	7237	196-	**£20**	US

TIEKIN, FREDDIE & THE ROCKERS
By Popular Demand	LP	IT	2301	1957	**£20**	US
Freddie Tiekin And The Rockers	LP	IT	2304	1958	**£20**	US

TIERNEY'S FUGITIVES
Did You Want To Run Away	7"	Decca	F12247	1965	**£8**	

TIERNEY, PETER & THE NIGHTHAWKS
Oh How I Need You	7"	Fontana	TF547	1965	**£4**	

TIFFANIES
It's Got To Be A Great Song	7"	Chess	CRS8059	1967	**£8**	

TIFFANY
I Know	7"	Parlophone	R5311	1965	**£4**	

TIFFANY SHADE
Tiffany Shade	LP	Fontana		1968	**£30**	

TIFFANY'S THOUGHTS
Find Out What's Happening	7"	Parlophone	R5439	1966	**£4**	

TIGER
Going Down Laughing	LP	EMI	EMC3153	1976	**£10**	
Tiger	LP	Retreat	RTL6006	1976	**£12**	

TIGER LILY
The single by Tiger Lily was the first release by the group that issued all its subsequent records as Ultravox.

Monkey Jive	7"	Dead Good	DEAD11	1980	**£4**	
Monkey Jive	7"	Gull	GULS54	1977	**£6**	

TIGG, JIMMY & LOUIS
Who Can I Turn To	7"	Deep Soul	DS9105	1970	**£6**	

TIK & TOK
Intolerance	LP	Survival	SURLPX8	198-	**£10**	pic disc
Summer In The City	7"	Survival	SUR007	1982	**£4**	

TILLER BOYS
Big Noise From The Jungle	7"	New Hormones	ORG3	1979	**£12**	

TILLOTSON, JOHNNY
Dreamy Eyes	7"	London	HLA9514	1962	**£4**	
Earth Angel	7"	London	HLA9101	1960	**£4**	
Funny How Time Slips Away	7"	London	HLA9811	1963	**£4**	
I Can't Help It	7"	London	HLA9642	1962	**£4**	chart single
It Keeps Right On A-Hurtin'	LP	London	HAA8019	1962	**£10**	
It Keeps Right On A-Hurtin'	7"	London	HLA9550	1962	**£4**	chart single
J.T.	7" EP	London	REA1388	1963	**£6**	
Jimmy's Girl	7"	London	HLA9275	1961	**£4**	chart single
Johnny Tillotson	7" EP	London	REA1345	1962	**£6**	
Johnny Tillotson	7" EP	MGM	MGMEP788	1963	**£5**	
Johnny Tillotson's Best	LP	London	HAA2431	1961	**£10**	
Johnny Tillotson's Hit Parade	7" EP	MGM	MGMEP790	1964	**£5**	
Out Of My Mind	7"	London	HLA9695	1963	**£4**	chart single
Poetry In Motion	7"	London	HLA9231	1960	**£4**	chart single
Send Me The Pillow You Dream On	7"	London	HLA9598	1962	**£4**	chart single

True True Happiness	7"	London	HLA8930	1959	**£4**	
Why Do I Love You So?	7"	London	HLA9048	1960	**£4**	
Without You	7"	London	HLA9412	1961	**£4**	
You Can Never Stop Me Loving You	LP	Cadence	CLP3067	1963	**£10**	US

TILSTON, STEVE

Acoustic Confusion	LP	Village Thing	VTS5	1971	**£10**	
Collection	LP	Transatlantic	TRA252	1972	**£10**	

TIMBER

Bring America Home	LP	Elektra	K42093	1971	**£10**	
Part Of What You Hear	LP	Kapp	KS3633		**£10**	US

TIME

Time	LP	Buk	BULP2005	1975	**£70**	

TIMEBOX

Timebox were an interesting soul-inflected group, several of whose songs employ touches of psychedelia to worthwhile effect. In the seventies, the group became Patto.

Baked Jam Roll In Your Eye	7"	Deram	DM246	1969	**£8**	
Beggin'	7"	Deram	DM194	1968	**£8**	chart single
Don't Make Promises	7"	Deram	DM153	1967	**£10**	
Girl Don't You Make Me Wait	7"	Deram	DM219	1968	**£8**	
I'll Always Love You	7"	Piccadilly	7N35369	1967	**£10**	
Original Moose On The Loose	LP	Cosmos	CCLPS9016	1977	**£20**	US
Soul Sauce	7"	Piccadilly	7N35379	1967	**£10**	
Yellow Van	7"	Deram	DM271	1969	**£8**	

TIMES

Blue Fire	7"	Artpop	POP45	1984	**£6**	
Boys Brigade	7"	Artpop	POP46	1984	**£6**	
Hello Europe	LP	Artpop	ART17	1984	**£10**	
Here Comes The Holidays	7"	Artpop	POP50	1982	**£12**	
I Helped Patrick McGoohan Escape	7"	Artpop	POP49	1983	**£12**	
I Helped Patrick McGoohan Escape	12"	Artpop	No1	1983	**£10**	
Pop Goes Art	LP	Artpop	ART20	1984	**£25**	
Pop Goes Art	LP	Whaam!	WHAAMLP1	1982	**£35**	
Red With Purple Flashes	7"	Whaam!	WHAAM002	1981	**£25**	

TIMES (2)

Looking Thru' The Eyes Of A Beautiful Girl	7"	Parlophone	R5855	1970	**£4**	
Love We Knew	7"	Columbia	DB7904	1966	**£4**	
Smile A Tender Smile	7"	Parlophone	R5956	1972	**£4**	
Think About The Times	7"	Columbia	DB7804	1966	**£4**	

TIMMONS, BOBBY

Moanin'	7"	Riverside	3204	196-	**£4**	

TIMON

I'm Just A Travelling Man	7"	Threshold	TH3	1970	**£4**	

TIMONEERS

Roasted Live	LP	WHM		1976	**£30**	

TIMOTHY, AL

Gruntin' Blues	7"	Decca	F10558	1955	**£4**	

TIN TIN

Astral Taxi	LP	Polydor	2382080	1972	**£10**	
Come On Over Again	7"	Polydor	2058076	1970	**£4**	
Is That The Way	7"	Polydor	2058114	1971	**£4**	
Toast And Marmalade For Tea	7"	Polydor	2058023	1970	**£5**	

TINKERBELL'S FAIRYDUST

In My Magic Garden	7"	Decca	F12705	1967	**£6**	
Sheila's Back In Town	7"	Decca	F12865	1969	**£6**	
Twenty Ten	7"	Decca	F12778	1968	**£8**	

TINKERS

Spring Rain	LP	Argo	ZFB35	1970	**£15**	

TINO, BABS

Forgive Me .... 7" EP .... London .... RER1377 .... 1963 .... **£4** ....

TINTERN ABBEY

Beeside .... 7" .... Deram .... DM164 .... 1967 .... **£70** ....

TINY ALICE

Tiny Alice .... LP .... Kama Sutra .... 1971 .... **£10** ....

TINY TIM

For All My Little Friends .... LP .... Reprise .... 6351 .... 1969 .... **£10** .... US
God Bless Tiny Tim .... LP .... Reprise .... 6292 .... 1968 .... **£12** .... US
Great Balls Of Fire .... 7" .... Reprise .... R20802 .... 1968 .... **£4** .... chart single
Hello Hello .... 7" .... Reprise .... R20769 .... 1968 .... **£4** ....
Mickey The Monkey .... 7" .... Reprise .... R20855 .... 1969 .... **£4** ....
Second Album .... LP .... Reprise .... 6323 .... 1968 .... **£10** .... US
Tip Toe Thru The Tulips .... 7" .... Reprise .... R23258 .... 1968 .... **£4** ....

TIP TOPS

Oo-Kook-A-Boo .... 7" .... Cameo Park .... P868 .... 1963 .... **£4** ....

TIPPETT, JULIE

Sunset Glow .... LP .... RCA .... 1975 .... **£10** ....

TIPPETT, KEITH

Blue Print .... LP .... RCA .... SF8290 .... 1972 .... **£30** ....
Dedicated To You... .... LP .... Vertigo .... 6360024 .... 1971 .... **£20** .... spiral label
Frames .... LP .... Ogun .... OGD003/4 .... 1978 .... **£15** .... double
Warm Spirits Cool Spirits .... LP .... Vinyl .... VS101 .... 1977 .... **£15** ....
You Are Here I Am There .... LP .... Polydor .... 2384004 .... 1969 .... **£50** ....

TIPPETT, KEITH & STAN TRACEY

T'N'T .... LP .... Steam .... SJ104 .... 1976 .... **£15** ....

TIPPI & THE CLOVERS

My Heart Said .... 7" .... Stateside .... SS160 .... 1963 .... **£4** ....

TIR NA NOG

I'm Happy To Be .... 7" .... Chrysalis .... WIP6090 .... 1970 .... **£5** ....
Strong In The Sun .... LP .... Chrysalis .... CHR1047 .... 1973 .... **£15** ....
Strong In The Sun .... 7" .... Chrysalis .... CHS2016 .... 1973 .... **£4** ....
Tear And A Smile .... LP .... Chrysalis .... CHR1006 .... 1972 .... **£15** ....
Tir Na Nog .... LP .... Chrysalis .... ILPS9153 .... 1971 .... **£15** ....

TITANS

Don't You just Know It .... 7" .... London .... HLU8609 .... 1958 .... **£15** ....
Today's Teen Beat .... LP .... MGM .... E3992 .... 1961 .... **£12** .... US

TITUS GROAN

Titus Groan .... LP .... Dawn .... DNLS3012 .... 1970 .... **£40** ....

TITUS OATS

Jungle Lady .... LP .... 1971 .... **£120** .... US

TJADER, CAL

Soul Sauce .... 7" .... Verve .... VS529 .... 1965 .... **£15** ....

TOAD

Toad .... LP .... RCA .... SF8241 .... 1972 .... **£50** ....

TOADS

Toads .... LP .... Wiggins .... 04021 .... 1964 .... **£100** .... US

TOBY JUG

.... LP .... Private .... 1969 .. **£1000** ....

TODD, NICK

At The Hop .... 7" .... London .... HLD8537 .... 1958 .... **£5** ....
Plaything .... 7" .... London .... HLD8500 .... 1957 .... **£8** ....
Tiger .... 7" .... London .... HLD8902 .... 1959 .... **£4** ....

TODD, SHARKEY & THE MONSTERS

Cool Ghoul	7"	Parlophone	R4536	1959	**£4**	

TODD, WILF

He Took Her Away	7"	Blue Beat	BB240	1963	**£10**	

TOEFAT

Toefat's LP is most notable for its unsettling cover, showing human figures with enormous toes replacing their heads. The group was one of Cliff Bennett's attempts to revive his career after the demise of the Rebel Rousers - on this occasion he effectively took over a pre-existing band, the Gods.

Bad Side Of The Road	7"	Parlophone	R5829	1970	**£5**	
Brand New Band	7"	Chapter One	CH175	1972	**£5**	
Toefat	LP	Parlophone	PCS7097	1970	**£20**	
Toefat II	LP	Regal Z.	SLRZ1015	1971	**£25**	

TOGETHER

Henry's Coming Home	7"	Columbia	DB8491	1968	**£15**	

TOGGERY FIVE

I'd Much Rather Be With The Boys	7"	Parlophone	R5249	1965	**£15**	
I'm Gonna Jump	7"	Parlophone	R5175	1964	**£15**	

TOKENS

B'wna Nina	7"	RCA	RCA1279	1962	**£4**	
December 5th	LP	B.T.Puppy	BTPS1014	1971	**£12**	US
Greatest Moments	LP	B.T.Puppy	BTPS1012	1970	**£12**	US
Green Plant	7"	Stateside	SS598	1967	**£4**	
He's In Town	7"	Fontana	TF500	1964	**£4**	
I Hear Trumpets Blow	LP	B.T.Puppy	BTLP1000	1966	**£10**	US
I Hear Trumpets Blow	7"	Fontana	TF683	1966	**£4**	
I'll Do My Crying Tomorrow	7"	RCA	RCA1313	1962	**£4**	
It's A Happening World	7"	W. Bros	WB7056	1967	**£4**	
Lion Sleeps Tonight	LP	RCA	LPM2514	1961	**£20**	US
Lion Sleeps Tonight	7"	RCA	RCA1263	1961	**£4**	chart single
Portrait Of My Love	7"	W. Bros	WB5900	1967	**£4**	
She Lets Her Hair Down	7"	Buddah	201069	1969	**£4**	
She Lets Her Hair Down	7"	Buddah	201076	1969	**£4**	
Till	7"	W. Bros	WB7169	1968	**£4**	
Tokens Again	LP	RCA	LPM3685	1966	**£12**	US
Tokens Of Gold	LP	B.T.Puppy	BTPS1006	1969	**£12**	US
Tonight I Fell In Love	7"	Parlophone	R4790	1961	**£4**	
We Sing Folk	LP	RCA	SF7535	1962	**£12**	
Wheels	LP	RCA	LPM2886	1964	**£12**	US
Wishing	7"	RCA	RCA1322	1962	**£4**	

TOLEDO, HARRY

Busted Chevrolet	7"	Spy	SPY001	1977	**£4**	

TOM & JERRY

The Tom and Jerry who made the single "Baby Talk" were Tom Graph and Jerry Landis, otherwise known (in the reverse order) as Simon and Garfunkel.

Baby Talk	7"	Gala	GSP806	196-	**£20**	
I'm Lonesome	7"	Pye	7N25202	1963	**£10**	

TOM & JERRYO

Boogaloo	7"	HMV	POP1435	1965	**£8**	

TOM CATS

Tom Tom Cat	7"	Starlite	ST45054	1961	**£5**	

TOMITA

Given the potentially infinite array of sounds at the disposal of a synthesiser player, it is surprising how unexciting most electronic music manages to be. With Tomita, however, one begins to glimpse what could be achieved - begins only, because Tomita is primarily an interpreter. He works at recasting the classics into a fairly radical modern form in which the original music is liable to become transformed into pure Tomita. In the case of his version of "The Planets", Holst's family, who still hold the copywrite, objected to the treatment (Robert Fripp and Dave Edmunds have both come up against the same problem) and the record was withdrawn.

Planets	LP	RCA	RL11919	1976	**£10**	chart LP

TOMLIN, LEE

Sweet Sweet Lovin'	7"	CBS	202455	1966	**£8**	

TOMORROW

Tomorrow are usually held up as the classic psychedelic group, but this reputation derives less from their album, which is very uneven in quality, as from the two wonderful singles, "My White Bicycle" and "Revolution". The chaotic, anarchist streak within the group (Twink) carried through into the Pink Fairies; the musically inventive part (Steve Howe) joined the group Yes.

Title	Format	Label	Cat. No.	Year	Price	Notes
Claramount Lake	7"	Parlophone	R5813	1969	**£8**	
My White Bicycle	7"	Parlophone	R5597	1967	**£12**	
Revolution	7"	Parlophone	R5627	1967	**£15**	
Tomorrow	LP	Harvest	SHSP2010	1976	**£10**	
Tomorrow	LP	Parlophone	PCS7042	1968	**£40**	

TOMORROW'S CHILDREN

Title	Format	Label	Cat. No.	Year	Price	Notes
Bang Bang Rock Steady	7"	Island	WI3073	1967	**£10**	

TONES ON TAIL

Title	Format	Label	Cat. No.	Year	Price	Notes
Lions	7"	Beggars B.	BEG109	1984	**£12**	red vinyl
Lions	12"	Beggars B.	BEGT109	1984	**£8**	red vinyl

TONETTES

Title	Format	Label	Cat. No.	Year	Price	Notes
Love That Is Real	7"	Island	WI064	1962	**£10**	

TONEY JR., OSCAR

Title	Format	Label	Cat. No.	Year	Price	Notes
For Your Precious Love	7"	Stateside	SS2033	1967	**£4**	
No Sad Songs	7"	Bell	BLL1011	1968	**£4**	
Turn On Your Lovelight	7"	Stateside	SS2046	1967	**£4**	
You Can Lead Your Woman To The Altar	7"	Stateside	SS2061	1967	**£4**	

TONGUE & GROOVE

Title	Format	Label	Cat. No.	Year	Price	Notes
Tongue And Groove	LP	Fontana		1969	**£20**	

TONTO'S EXPANDING HEADBAND

Tonto is an instrument (The Original New Timbral Orchestra) - a huge synthesizer - played by Robert Margouleff and Malcolm Cecil. These two are among the more imaginative electronic keyboard performers and the first LP in particular is a good example of what can be achieved. They take advantage of the possibilities afforded to them, by such stratagems as using a ten note, equally tempered scale (impossible on conventional instruments) and yet the music still manages to be as accessible as it is interesting. Margouleff and Cecil also worked as advisers to Stevie Wonder and their sounds can be heard on many of his records.

Title	Format	Label	Cat. No.	Year	Price	Notes
It's About Time	LP	Polydor	2383308	1974	**£10**	
Zero Time	LP	Atlantic	K40251	1971	**£12**	

TONTON MACOUTE

Title	Format	Label	Cat. No.	Year	Price	Notes
Tonton Macoute	LP	Neon	NE4	1971	**£35**	

TONY & DENNIS

Title	Format	Label	Cat. No.	Year	Price	Notes
Folk Song	7"	Trojan	TR002	196-	**£10**	

TONY & JOE

Title	Format	Label	Cat. No.	Year	Price	Notes
Freeze	7"	London	HLN8694	1958	**£8**	

TONY & LOUISE

Title	Format	Label	Cat. No.	Year	Price	Notes
Ups And Downs	7"	Island	WI059	1962	**£10**	

TONY & TANDY

Title	Format	Label	Cat. No.	Year	Price	Notes
Two Can Make It Together	7"	Atlantic	2091075	1971	**£8**	
Two Can Make It Together	7"	Atlantic	584262	1969	**£15**	

TONY'S DEFENDERS

Title	Format	Label	Cat. No.	Year	Price	Notes
Since I Lost My Baby	7"	Columbia	DB7996	1966	**£8**	
*Yes I Do	7"	Columbia	DB7850	1966	**£10**	

TOOMORROW

Toomorrow was a group put together, Monkees-style, for the purpose of making a rather silly film. This was the flop it deserved to be, but the group's lead singer, Olivia Newton-John, persevered with her musical career.

Title	Format	Label	Cat. No.	Year	Price	Notes
I Could Never Live Without Your Love	7"	Decca	F13070	1970	**£20**	
Toomorrow	LP	RCA	LSA3008	1970	**£70**	
You're My Baby Now	7"	RCA	RCA1978	1970	**£12**	

TOP DRAWER

Title	Format	Label	Cat. No.	Year	Price	Notes
Solid Oak	LP	Wishbone		1969	**£200**	US

TOPHAM, TOP

Title	Format	Label	Cat. No.	Year	Price	Notes
Ascension Heights	LP	Blue Horizon	763857	1970	**£40**	

Christmas Cracker	7"	Blue Horizon	573167	1969	**£15**	

TOPSY, TINY & THE CHARMS

After Marriage Blues	7"	Pye	7N25104	1961	**£15**	
Come On Come On Come On	7"	Parlophone	R4397	1958	**£12**	
You Shocked Me	7"	Parlophone	R4427	1958	**£12**	

TORNADOES

Bustin' Surfboards	LP	Josie	4005	1963	**£50**	US

TORNADOS

Away From It All	LP	Decca	LK4552	1963	**£20**	
Dragonfly	7"	Decca	F11745	1963	**£4**	chart single
Earlybird	7"	Columbia	DB7589	1965	**£6**	
Exodus	7"	Decca	F11946	1964	**£5**	
Globetrotter	7"	Decca	F11562	1963	**£4**	chart single
Granada	7"	Columbia	DB7455	1965	**£6**	
Hot Pot	7"	Decca	F11838	1964	**£4**	
Ice Cream Man	7"	Decca	F11662	1963	**£4**	chart single
Is That A Ship I Hear	7"	Columbia	DB7984	1966	**£6**	
Love And Fury	7"	Decca	F11449	1962	**£5**	
Monte Carlo	7"	Decca	F11889	1964	**£5**	
More Sounds From The Tornados	7" EP	Decca	DFE8521	1963	**£8**	
Pop Art Goes Mozart	7"	Columbia	DB7856	1966	**£6**	
Robot	7"	Decca	F11606	1963	**£4**	chart single
Sounds Of The Tornados	7" EP	Decca	DFE8510	1962	**£6**	
Sounds Of The Tornados	LP	London	LL3293	1963	**£15**	US
Stingray	7"	Columbia	DB7687	1965	**£6**	
Telstar	7"	Decca	F11494	1962	**£4**	chart single
Telstar	7" EP	Decca	DFE8511	1962	**£8**	
Telstar	LP	London	LL3279	1962	**£20**	US
Tornado Rock	7" EP	Decca	DFE8533	1963	**£10**	

TOROK, MITCHELL

Caribbean	7"	London	HL8004	1954	**£15**	
Haunting Waterfall	7"	London	HL8083	1954	**£10**	
Havana Huddle	7"	Brunswick	05626	1956	**£5**	
Hootchy Coochy	7"	London	HL8048	1954	**£10**	
Louisiana Hayride	7" EP	London	REP1014	1954	**£8**	

TORQUES

Live	LP	Lemco	604	196-	**£50**	US
Zoom!	LP	Wiggins	64010	1964	**£75**	US

TORRENCE, GEORGE & THE NATURALS

Lickin' Stick	7"	London	HLZ10181	1968	**£5**	

TOSH, PETER

Return Of Al Capone	7"	Unity	UN525	1969	**£6**	
Rudies Medley	7"	Punch	PH91	1972	**£6**	
Selassie Serenade	7"	Bullet	BU414	1971	**£6**	
Sun Valley	7"	Unity	UN529	1969	**£6**	
Them A Fi Get A Beatin'	7"	Press. Beat	PB5509		**£6**	

TOSH, PETER & THE WAILERS

Hoot Nanny Hoot	7"	Island	WI211	1965	**£25**	
I Am The Toughest	7"	Island	WI3042	1967	**£20**	

TOTO

Africa	7"	CBS	A2510	1982	**£6**	shaped pic disc
Rosanna	7"	CBS	A2079	1982	**£6**	shaped pic disc
Toto	LP	Epic	PJC35317	1978	**£12**	French pic disc

TOUCH

Miss Teach	7"	Deram	DM243	1969	**£8**	
This Is Touch	LP	Deram	SML1033	1969	**£25**	

TOUCHSTONE

Tarot	LP	United Artists	UAS5563	1972	**£15**	US

TOURISTS

Blind Among The Flowers	7"	Logo	GOD350	1979	**£5**	double

Loneliest Man In The World .... 7" .... Logo .... GOP360 .... 1979 .... £4 .... pic disc

TOUSSAINT, ALLEN
We The People .... 7" .... Soul City .... SC119 .... £8 .... demo
Wild Sound Of New Orleans .... LP .... RCA .... LPM1767 .... 1958 ...... £40 .... US

TOWNSEND, ED
Ed Townsend .... 7" EP .... Capitol .... EAP11091 .... 1959 .... £5 ....

TOWNSEND, HENRY
Tired Of Bein' Mistreated .... LP .... Bluesville .... BV1041 .... 1962 ...... £12 .... US

TOWNSHEND, PETE
Pete's Listening Time .... LP .... Atco .... SAM150 .... 1982 ...... £20 .... interview promo
Pete's Listening Time .... LP .... Atco .... SAM150 .... 1982 ...... £30 .... interview promo, autographed
Townshend Tapes .... LP .... Atco .... SAM121/2 .... 1980 ...... £30 ..... double interview promo
Townshend Tapes .... LP .... Atco .... SAM121/2 .... 1980 ...... £40 .... double interview promo, autographed
Uniforms .... 7" .... Atco .... K11751P .... 1982 .... £4 .... pic disc
Uniforms .... 12" .... Atco .... K11751PT .... 1982 .... £6 .... pic disc
Who Came First .... LP .... Track .... 2408201 .... 1972 ...... £10 .... chart LP

TOWNSHEND, PETE & MEHER BABA
All Time Star... .... LP .... Uni S.L. .... MBO1 .... 1975 ...... £30 .... reissue of USL001
Happy Birthday .... LP .... Uni S.L. .... USL001 .... 1970 ...... £65 ....
I Am .... LP .... Uni S.L. .... MBO2 .... 1975 ...... £30 ....
I Am .... LP .... Uni S.L. .... USL002 .... 1973 ...... £65 ....
With Love .... LP .... Uni S.L. .... USL003 .... 1974 ...... £65 ....

TOWNSHEND, PETE & JOHN WILLIAMS
Won't Get Fooled Again .... 7" .... Island .... SPB1 .... 1981 .... £8 .... 1 sided promo

TOWNSHEND, PETE & RONNIE LANE
Street In The City .... 12" .... Polydor .... 2058944 .... 1977 .... £6 ....

TOXIC REASONS
Ghost Town .... 7" .... Risky .... 1981 ...... £30 ....
War Hero .... 7" .... Banit .... 1981 ...... £30 ....

TOY DOLLS
Everybody Jitterbug .... 7" .... Zonophone ...... Z31 .... 1982 .... £4 ....
Tommy Kowie's Car .... 7" .... Grl .... 104 .... 1981 ...... £10 ....

TOY FACTORY
Toy Factory .... LP .... Avco .... £20 .... US

TOYAH
Ieya .... 12" .... Safari .... SAFE28 .... 1981 .... £6 .... white vinyl
It's A Mystery .... 7" .... Safari .... TOY1 .... 1980 .... £4 .... promo

TOYS
Attack .... 7" .... Stateside .... SS483 .... 1966 .... £4 .... chart single
Baby Toys .... 7" .... Stateside .... SS539 .... 1966 .... £4 ....
Lover's Concerto/Attack .... LP .... DynoVoice ...... 9002 .... 1966 ...... £15 .... US
Lover's Concerto .... 7" .... Stateside .... SS460 .... 1965 .... £5 .... chart single
Lover's Concerto .... 7" .... Bell .... BLL1053 .... 1969 ...... £10 ....
May My Heart Be Cast To Stone .... 7" .... Stateside .... SS502 .... 1966 .... £4 ....
My Love's Sonata .... 7" .... Philips .... BF1581 .... 1967 .... £6 ....
Silver Spoon .... 7" .... Stateside .... SS519 .... 1966 .... £4 ....

TRACE
Birds .... LP .... Vertigo .... 6413080 .... 1975 ...... £10 ....
Trace .... LP .... Vertigo .... 6360852 .... 1974 ...... £10 ....
White Ladies .... LP .... RCA .... PPL18125 .... 1976 ...... £10 .... German

TRACEY, GRANT & THE SUNSETS
Everybody Shake .... 7" .... Decca .... F11741 .... 1963 .... £4 ....

TRACEY, WENDALL
Who's To Know? .... 7" .... London .... HLM8664 .... 1958 .... £4 ....

TRACEY, ZEN

Two By Two	7"	Decca	F11492	1962	**£4**	

TRACK

Why Do Fools Fall In Love	7"	Columbia	DB7987	1966	**£4**	

TRACTOR

Stone Glory	7"	Polydor	2001282	1972	**£8**	
Tractor	LP	Dandelion	2310217	1972	**£40**	

TRADE WINDS

Crossroads	7"	RCA	RCA1141	1959	**£4**	
Excursions	LP	Kama Sutra	KLP8057	1967	**£12**	US
Mind Excursion	7"	Kama Sutra	KAS202	1966	**£4**	
New York's A Lonely Town	7"	Red Bird	RB10020	1965	**£5**	

TRADER HORNE

Trader Horne was a folky group formed by Jackie McAuley, who had played keyboards with Them for a while, and Judy Dyble, who was the original lead singer with Fairport Convention. Their one album was followed by a Jackie McAuley solo LP in a similar style, but neither was sufficiently distinctive to make much head-way in the market place.

Here Comes The Rain	7"	Dawn	DNS1003	1970	**£5**	
Morning Way	LP	Dawn	DNLS3004	1970	**£60**	
Sheena	7"	Pye	7N17846	1969	**£5**	

TRAFFIC

There are many examples of LPs issued in the middle-to-late sixties, in which the mono and stereo versions are different. The reason for this is, that with no more than four track recording available, any more than very simple overdubbing had to be carried out at the final mixing stage. With the mono and stereo mixes being prepared separately, the overdubs on these were inevitably different. Traffic's "Dear Mr.Fantasy" is a classic example of this. A track by track comparison of the mono and stereo versions reveals much of the detail to be different, while "Heaven Is In Your Mind" actually includes two entirely different guitar solos.

Best Of	LP	Island	ILPS9112	1969	**£10**	
Empty Pages	7"	Island		1974	**£4**	promo
Feelin' Alright	7"	Island	WIP6041	1968	**£4**	
Gimme Some Lovin'	7"	Island		1971	**£6**	1 sided promo
Heaven Is In Your Mind	LP	United Artists	UAS6651	1968	**£15**	US
Here We Go Round The Mulberry Bush	7"	Island	WIP6025	1967	**£5**	chart single
Here We Go Round The Mulberry Bush	7"	Island	WIP6025	1967	**£10**	PS
Hole In My Shoe	7"	Island	IEP7	1978	**£8**	pic disc
Hole In My Shoe	7"	Island	IEP7DJ	1978	**£4**	1 sided promo
Hole In My Shoe	7"	Island	WIP6017	1967	**£5**	chart single
Hole In My Shoe	7"	Island	WIP6017	1967	**£8**	PS
Hole In My Shoe/Paper Sun	7"	Island	IEP7DJ	1978	**£4**	promo
Hole In My Shoe/Paper Sun	7"	Island	IEP7JB	1978	**£4**	juke box issue
John Barleycorn Must Die	LP	Island	ILPS9116	1970	**£10**	chart LP
Last Exit	LP	Island	ILPS9097	1969	**£10**	
Live At The Fillmore	LP	Island	ILPS9124	1970	**£100**	demo only
Medicated Goo	7"	Island	WIP6050	1968	**£4**	
Mr.Fantasy	LP	Island	ILP961	1967	**£12**	mono, chart LP
Mr.Fantasy	LP	Island	ILPS9061	1967	**£10**	stereo, chart LP
No Face, No Name, No Number	7"	Island	WIP6030	1968	**£4**	
Paper Sun	7"	Island	WIP6002	1967	**£5**	
Paper Sun	7"	Island	WIP6002	1967	**£15**	PS
Traffic	LP	Island	ILP981	1968	**£15**	mono
Traffic	LP	Island	ILPS9081	1968	**£10**	stereo
Welcome To The Canteen	LP	Island	ILPS9166	1971	**£10**	
Welcome To The Canteen	7"	Island		1971	**£6**	promo sampler

TRAFFIC JAM

The Spectres changed their name to Traffic Jam for one single, before deciding that the possible confusion with Steve Winwood's new group, Traffic, was not helping their career. Accordingly, they changed names yet again, this time to Status Quo.

Almost But Not Quite There	7"	Piccadilly	7N35386	1967	**£120**	

TRAINER, PHIL

Phil Trainer	LP	BASF		197-	**£25**	

TRAITS

Harlem Shuffle	7"	Pye	7N25404	1967	**£4**	

TRAMLINE

Moves Of Vegetable Centuries	LP	Island	ILPS9095	1969	**£30**	
Somewhere Down The Line	LP	Island	ILPS9088	1968	**£30**	

TRAMMELL, BOBBY LEE

Arkansas Twist	LP	Atlantic	LPM1503	1962	**£35**	US
New Dance In France	7"	Sue	WI326	1964	**£8**	

TRAMP

Put A Record On	LP	Spark	SRLP112	1974	**£25**	
Put A Record On	7"	Spark	SRL1107	1974	**£8**	
Tramp	LP	Music Man	603	1969	**£30**	
Tramp	LP	Spark	SRLM2001	1973	**£25**	

TRANQUILITY

Silver	LP	Epic	31989	1973	**£12**	US
Tranquility	LP	Epic	64729	1972	**£10**	

TRANSVISION VAMP

Baby I Don't Care	7"	MCA	TVVG6	1989	**£4**	gatefold PS
Baby I Don't Care	12"	MCA	TVVTG6	1989	**£6**	gatefold sleeve
I Want Your Love	CD-s	MCA	DTVV3	1988	**£12**	
I Want Your Love	12"	MCA	TVVTR3	1988	**£6**	poster sleeve
Landslide Of Love	7"	MCA	TVVP8	1989	**£4**	pic disc
Pop Art	LP	MCA	MCFP3421	1988	**£15**	pic disc
Revolution Baby (Electra-Glide Mix)	12"	MCA	TVVTP4	1988	**£8**	pic disc
Revolution Baby (Remix)	7"	MCA	TVVPR4	1988	**£4**	poster insert
Revolution Baby	7"	MCA	TVV1	1987	**£4**	
Revolution Baby	12"	MCA	TVVT1	1987	**£15**	
Sister Moon	7"	MCA	TVVP5	1988	**£4**	pic disc
Sister Moon	12"	MCA	TVVTG5	1988	**£6**	gatefold sleeve
Tell That Girl To Shut Up	7"	MCA	TVVPR2	1988	**£4**	poster sleeve
Tell That Girl To Shut Up	12"	MCA	TVVT2	1988	**£6**	

TRAPEZE

Coast To Coast	7"	Threshold	TH11	1972	**£4**	
Final Swing	LP	Threshold	THS11	1974	**£12**	
Hot Wire	LP	W. Bros	K56064	1974	**£10**	
Medusa	LP	Threshold	THS4	1970	**£15**	
Send Me No More Letters	7"	Threshold	TH2	1969	**£4**	
Trapeze	LP	Threshold	THS2	1970	**£15**	
Trapeze	LP	W. Bros	K56165	1975	**£10**	
You Are The Music	LP	Threshold	THS8	1972	**£15**	

TRASH

Golden Slumbers	7"	Apple	17	1969	**£12**	chart single

TRASHMEN

Bird Dance Beat	7"	Stateside	SS276	1964	**£6**	
Surfin' Bird	LP	Garrett	GA200	1964	**£40**	US
Surfin' Bird	7"	Stateside	SS255	1964	**£8**	

TRAUM, HAPPY & ARTIE

Doubleback	LP	Capitol	ST799	1971	**£12**	
Happy And Artie Traum	LP	Capitol	ST586	1969	**£12**	
Mud Acres	LP	Matchbox	239	1972	**£10**	

TRAVIS, MERLE

Back Home	LP	Capitol	T891	1957	**£12**	
Back Home	7" EP	Capitol	EAP1891	1957	**£5**	
Merle Travis Guitar	LP	Capitol	T650	1956	**£25**	US
Merle Travis Guitar No.1	7" EP	Capitol	EAP1032	1956	**£6**	
Merle Travis Guitar No.2	7" EP	Capitol	EAP2650	1956	**£5**	
Walkin' The Strings	LP	Capitol	T1391	1960	**£15**	US
Walkin' The Strings	7" EP	Capitol	EAP41391	1960	**£5**	

TRAYLOR, JACK & STEELWIND

Child Of Nature	LP	Grunt	FTR0194	1973	**£10**	

TREASURE ISLE BOYS

Love Is A Treasure	7"	Trojan	TR010	196-	**£10**	

TREE, VIRGINIA (SHIRLEY KENT)

Fresh Out	LP	Minstrel	0001	1975	**£20**	

TREES

Garden Of Jane Delawney	LP	CBS	63837	1970	**£65**	
Nothing Special	7"	CBS	5078	1970	**£8**	
On The Shore	LP	CBS	64168	1970	**£75**	

TREETOPS

Morning To Progress	7"	Studio One	SO2023	196-	**£10**	

TREETOPS (2)

California My Way	7"	Parlophone	R5669	1968	**£8**	
Don't Worry Baby	7"	Parlophone	R5628	1967	**£8**	

TREKKAS

Please Go	7"	Planet	PLF105	1965	**£8**	

TREMELOES

58/68 World Explosion	LP	CBS	26388	1968	**£10**	US
Be Mine	7"	CBS	3043	1967	**£4**	chart single
Blessed	7"	Decca	F12423	1966	**£4**	
By The Way	7"	CBS	4815	1970	**£4**	chart single
Call Me Number One	7"	CBS	4582	1969	**£4**	chart single
Even The Bad Times Are Good	7"	CBS	2930	1967	**£4**	chart single
Good Day Sunshine	7"	CBS	202242	1966	**£4**	
Hello Buddy	7"	CBS	7294	1971	**£4**	chart single
Hello World	7"	CBS	4065	1969	**£4**	chart single
Helule Helule	7"	CBS	2889	1967	**£4**	chart single
Here Come The Tremeloes	LP	CBS	63017	1967	**£10**	chart LP
Here Comes My Baby	7"	CBS	202519	1967	**£4**	chart single
I Like It That Way	7"	CBS	8048	1972	**£4**	
I Shall Be Released	7"	CBS	3873	1968	**£4**	chart single
Live In Cabaret	LP	CBS	63547	1969	**£10**	
Master	LP	CBS	64242	1970	**£10**	
Me And My Life	7"	CBS	5139	1970	**£4**	chart single
My Little Lady	7"	CBS	3443	1968	**£4**	chart single
My Little Lady	7" EP	CBS	EP6402	1968	**£5**	
Once On A Sunday Morning	7"	CBS	4313	1969	**£4**	
Right Wheel Left Hammer Sham	7"	CBS	5429	1971	**£4**	
Silence Is Golden	7"	CBS	2723	1967	**£4**	chart single
Suddenly You Love Me	LP	CBS	63138	1967	**£10**	
Suddenly You Love Me	7"	CBS	3234	1968	**£4**	chart single
Too Late	7"	CBS	7579	1971	**£4**	

TRENDS

Shot On Sight	7"	Page One	POF004	1966	**£10**	

TRENDSETTERS LTD.

Funny Way Of Showing Your Love	7"	Parlophone	R5324	1965	**£6**	
Go Away	7"	Parlophone	R5191	1964	**£8**	
Hello Josephine	7"	Parlophone	R5161	1964	**£10**	
In A Big Way	7"	Parlophone	R5118	1964	**£8**	

TRENIERS

	LP-10"			195-	**£150**	
Go Go Go	7"	Fontana	H137	1958	**£15**	
Ooh La La	7"	Coral	Q72319	1958	**£8**	
Souvenir Album	LP	Dot	DLP3257	1960	**£20**	US
Treniers On TV	LP	Epic	LG3125	195-	**£30**	US
When Your Hair Has Turned Silver	7"	London	HLD8858	1959	**£8**	

TRENT, JACKIE

Where Are You Now?	7"	Pye	7N15776	1965	**£4**	chart single
Where Are You Now?	7" EP	Pye	NEP24225	1965	**£5**	
You Baby	7"	Pye	7N17047	1966	**£6**	

TRESPASS

Jealousy	7"	Trial	CASE2	1980	**£6**	
One Of These Days	7"	Trial	CASE1	1979	**£6**	

TREVOR

Down In Virginia	7"	Blue Beat	BB228	1963	**£10**	
Everyday Like A Holiday (with the Maytones)	7"	Blue Cat	BS153	196-	**£10**	

TRIBAN

Rainmaker	LP	Cambrian		1972	**£20**	

TRIBE

Gamma Goodi	7"	Planet	PLF108	1966	**£8**	

TRIFFIDS

Lonely Boy	7"	Columbia	DB7177	1963	**£6**	
Lookin' Around	7"	Columbia	DB7084	1963	**£8**	
So Shy	7"	Columbia	DB7251	1964	**£6**	

TRIFLE

First Meeting	LP	Dawn		1971	**£20**	
Old Fashioned Prayer Meeting	7"	Dawn	DNS1008	1970	**£6**	

TRILCHA, PANDIT KANWAR SAIN

Three Sitar Pieces	LP	Mushroom		1970	**£40**	

TRILOGY

I'm Beginning To Feel It	LP	Mercury	6338034	1970	**£20**	

TRIO

Trio	LP	Dawn	DNLS3006	1970	**£25**	

TRIP

Atlantide	LP	RCA		1972	**£50**	

TRIPPERS

Dance With Me	7"	Pye	7N25388	1966	**£4**	

TRIPSICHORD MUSIC BOX

Tripsichord Music Box	LP	Janus		1971	**£40**	US

TRIUMPH

Rock'n'Roll Machine	LP	Attic	LATX1036	1977	**£15**	Canadian, vinyl & metal

TRO, MARCUS

Tell Me	7"	Ember	S203	1965	**£5**	

TROGGS

When the Trogg's "Wild Thing", with its novelty ocarina solo offsetting the Louie Louie riff, climbed to the top of the charts, Jonathan King offered to treat the group to a slap-up meal if they were still in the charts three years later. He lost his bet - but only just. The Trogg's simple hard(ish) rock bordered on the inept, but they have managed to create a considerable affection in the minds of the record collecting public. All the Trogg's original recordings are becoming increasingly sought after, especially the LP "Mixed Bag", which includes the group's over-the-top attempts at psychedelia.

Anyway That You Want Me	7"	Page One	POF010	1966	**£4**	chart single
Best Of Vol.1	LP	Page One	FOR001	1967	**£20**	chart LP
Best Of Vol.2	LP	Page One	FOR002	1967	**£20**	
Cellophane	LP	Page One	POL003	1967	**£30**	
Contrasts	LP	DJM	DJML009	1970	**£12**	
Easy Livin'	7"	Page One	POF164	1970	**£4**	
Evil Woman	7"	Page One	POF114	1969	**£4**	
From Nowhere	LP	Fontana	TL5355	1966	**£20**	chart LP
Girl Like You	LP	DJM	DJML26047	1975	**£10**	
Give It To Me	7"	Page One	POF015	1967	**£4**	chart single
Hi Hi Hazel	7"	Page One	POF030	1967	**£4**	chart single
Hip Hip Hooray	7"	Page One	POF092	1968	**£4**	
I Can't Control Myself	7"	Page One	POF001	1966	**£4**	chart single
Lazy Weekend	7"	DJM	DJS248	1971	**£4**	
Little Girl	7"	Page One	POF056	1968	**£4**	chart single
Lost Girl	7"	CBS	202038	1966	**£6**	
Love Is All Around	7"	Page One	POF040	1967	**£4**	chart single
Lover	7"	Page One	POF171	1970	**£4**	
Mixed Bag	LP	Page One	POLS012	1968	**£80**	
My Girl	7"	Page One	POF022	1967	**£20**	demo only
Night Of The Long Grass	7"	Page One	POF022	1967	**£4**	chart single
Original Trogg Tapes	LP	DJM	DJM44314	1976	**£10**	
Raver	7"	Page One	POF182	1970	**£4**	

Surprise Surprise	7"	Page One	POF064	1968	**£4**	
Trogg Tapes	LP	P. Farthing	PELS551	1976	**£10**	
Trogg Tops Vol.1	7" EP	Page One	POE001	1967	**£8**	
Trogg Tops Vol.2	7" EP	Page One	POE002	1967	**£8**	
Trogglodynamite	LP	Page One	POL001	1966	**£20**	chart LP
Trogglomania	LP	Page One	POS602	1969	**£20**	
Troggs	LP	P. Farthing	PEN543	1975	**£10**	
Wild Thing	LP	Fontana	SRF27556	1966	**£20**	
Wild Thing	7"	Fontana	TF689	1966	**£4**	chart single
With a Girl Like You	7"	Fontana	TF717	1966	**£4**	chart single
You Can Cry If You Want To	7"	Page One	POF082	1968	**£4**	

TROIS, CHUCK & AMAZING MAZE

Call On You	7"	Action	ACT4517	1968	**£5**	
Call On You	7"	Action	ACT4517	1968	**£20**	demo

TROJANS

Man I'm Gonna Be	7"	Decca	F11065	1958	**£8**	

TROLL

Animated Music	LP	Smash		1968	**£20**	US

TRONICS

Cantina	7"	Fontana	H348	1961	**£4**	

TROOPERS

Get Out	7"	Vogue	V9087	1957	**£20**	

TROTT, ARCHIBALD

Get Together	7"	Black Swan	WI407	1964	**£10**	

TROUBADOURS

Fascination	7"	London	HLR8469	1957	**£4**	
Lights Of Paris	7"	London	HLR8541	1958	**£4**	
Troubadours	7" EP	London	RER1135	1958	**£5**	

TROUP, BOBBY

Bobby Troup	7" EP	Capitol	EAP1484	1955	**£4**	

TROW, BOB

Soft Squeeze Baby	7"	London	HL8082	1954	**£6**	

TROY & THE T-BIRDS

Twistle	7"	London	HL9476	1961	**£4**	

TROY, DORIS

Ain't That Cute	7"	Apple	24	1970	**£8**	PS
Doris Troy	LP	Apple	SAPCOR13	1970	**£15**	
Heartaches	7"	Atlantic	AT4032	1965	**£5**	
I'll Do Anything	7"	Cameo Park.	C101	1962	**£20**	
I'll Do Anything	7"	Toast	TT507	196-	**£4**	
Jacob's Ladder	7"	Apple	28	1970	**£6**	
Just One Look	LP	Atlantic	8088	1964	**£12**	US
Just One Look	7"	Atlantic	584148	1968	**£5**	
Just One Look	7"	London	HLK9749	1963	**£5**	
One More Chance	7"	Atlantic	AT4020	1965	**£5**	
Whatcha Gonna Do About It	7"	Atlantic	AT4011	1964	**£5**	chart single
Whatcha Gonna Do About It	7" EP	Atlantic	AET6007	1965	**£8**	

TROYKA

Troyka	LP	Cotillion	SD9020	1970	**£12**	US

TRUCKAWAY, WILLIAM

Breakaway	LP	Reprise	K44165	1971	**£10**	

TRUK

Truk Tracks	LP	CBS	64367	1971	**£12**	

TRUMPETEERS

Milky White Way	LP	Score	4021	1960	**£50**	US

TRUTH

Baby Don't You Know	7"	Pye	7N15923	1965	**£6**	

Title	Format	Label	Cat. No.	Year	Price	Notes
Girl	7"	Pye	7N17035	1966	**£5**	chart single
I Go To Sleep	7"	Pye	7N17095	1966	**£8**	
Jingle Jangle	7"	Deram	DM105	1966	**£8**	
Seuno	7"	Decca	F12764	1968	**£5**	
Truth	LP	People		1970	**£20**	US
Walk Away Renee	7"	Decca	F12582	1967	**£6**	
Who's Wrong	7"	Pye	7N15998	1965	**£6**	

TRUTH & JANEY

Title	Format	Label	Cat. No.	Year	Price	Notes
No Rest For The Wicked	LP	Montrose		1976	**£50**	US

TRUTH OF TRUTHS

Title	Format	Label	Cat. No.	Year	Price	Notes
Truth Of Truths	LP	Oak	OR1001	1971	**£25**	double

TU-TONES

Title	Format	Label	Cat. No.	Year	Price	Notes
Still In Love With You	7"	London	HLW8904	1959	**£10**	

TUBB, ERNEST

Title	Format	Label	Cat. No.	Year	Price	Notes
All Time Hits	LP	Decca	DL4046	1961	**£10**	US
Daddy Of 'Em All	LP	Decca	DL8553	1956	**£20**	US
Daddy Of 'Em All Pt.1	7" EP	Brunswick	OE9372	1958	**£5**	
Daddy Of 'Em All Pt.2	7" EP	Brunswick	OE9373	1958	**£5**	
Daddy Of 'Em All Pt.3	7" EP	Brunswick	OE9374	1958	**£5**	
Ernest Tubb Story	LP	Decca	DXA159	1958	**£15**	US, with booklet
Favorites	LP	Decca	DL8291	1956	**£20**	US
Favorites	LP-10"	Decca	DL5301	1951	**£25**	US
Golden Favorites	LP	Decca	DL4118	1961	**£10**	US
Importance Of Being Ernest	LP	Decca	DL8834	1959	**£12**	US
Jimmie Rodgers Songs	LP-10"	Decca	DL5336	1951	**£25**	US
Just Call Me Lonesome	LP	Decca	DL4385	1964	**£10**	US
Midnight Jamboree	LP	Decca	DL4045	1960	**£10**	US
Old Rugged Cross	LP-10"	Decca	DL5334	1951	**£25**	US
On Tour	LP	Decca	DL4321	1962	**£10**	US
Record Shop	LP	Decca	DL4042	1960	**£10**	US
Sing A Song Of Christmas	LP-10"	Decca	DL5497	1954	**£25**	US
So Doggone Lonesome	7"	Brunswick	05587	1956	**£6**	
Thirty Days	7"	Brunswick	05527	1956	**£10**	

TUBES

Title	Format	Label	Cat. No.	Year	Price	Notes
Prime Time	7"	A&M	AMS7423	1979	**£4**	7 different coloured vinyls
Prime Time	7"	A&M	AMS7423	1979	**£35**	7 x coloured vinyl 7" + pic disc, boxed, promo
Remote Control	LP	A&M	AMLH9964751	1979	**£10**	Dutch pic disc
Talk To You Later	12"	Capitol	PSLP338	1981	**£6**	promo, B side Billy Squier
Tubes First Clean Album	LP	A&M	SP17012	1978	**£15**	US promo

TUBEWAY ARMY

Title	Format	Label	Cat. No.	Year	Price	Notes
Are 'Friends' Electric?	7"	Beggars B.	BEG18P	1979	**£10**	pic disc, insert
Are 'Friends' Electric?	12"	Intercord	INT126501	1979	**£12**	German
Are 'Friends' Electric?	7"	Beggars B.	BEG18P	1979	**£6**	pic disc
Bombers	7"	Beggars B.	BEG8	1978	**£8**	
Down In The Park	12"	Beggars B.	BEG17T	1979	**£30**	
Plan	LP	Beggars B.	BEGA55P	1985	**£10**	pic disc
That's Too Bad	7"	Beggars B.	BEG5	1978	**£8**	
That's Too Bad/Bombers	7"	Beggars B.	BACK2	1979	**£5**	double
This Is My Life	7"	Beggars B.	TUB1	1985	**£15**	promo
Tubeway Army '78 Vol.1	12"	Beggars B.	BEG92E	1983	**£8**	
Tubeway Army '78 Vol.1	12"	Beggars B.	BEG92E	1983	**£6**	yellow vinyl
Tubeway Army '78-79' Vol.2	12"	Beggars B.	BEG123E	1984	**£6**	red vinyl
Tubeway Army '78-79' Vol.3	12"	Beggars B.	BEG124E	1984	**£6**	blue vinyl
Tubeway Army	LP	Beggars B.	BEGA4	1978	**£15**	blue gatefold sleeve
Tubeway Army	LP	Beggars B.	BEGA4	1978	**£35**	blue vinyl

TUCKER, BESSIE

Title	Format	Label	Cat. No.	Year	Price	Notes
Blues By Bessie	7" EP	HMV	7EG8085	195-	**£6**	

TUCKER, BILLY JOE

Title	Format	Label	Cat. No.	Year	Price	Notes
Boogie Woogie Bill	7"	London	HLD9455	1961	**£20**	

TUCKER, CY

Title	Format	Label	Cat. No.	Year	Price	Notes
I Apologise	7"	Fontana	TF470	1964	**£4**	
My Prayer	7"	Fontana	TF424	1963	**£4**	

TUCKER, MAUREEN

Playin' Possum	LP	Trash	TLP1001	1981	**£10**	US

TUCKER, TOMMY

Hi Heel Sneakers	LP	Checker	2990	1964	**£20**	US
Hi Heel Sneakers	7"	Pye	7N25238	1964	**£6**	chart single
Hi Heel Sneakers	7" EP	Pye	NEP44027	1964	**£6**	
Hi Heel Sneakers	7"	Chess	CRS8086	1969	**£6**	
Long Tall Shorty	7"	Pye	7N25246	1964	**£5**	
Oh What A Feeling	7"	London	HLU9932	1964	**£5**	

TUCKY BUZZARD

Alright On The Night	LP	Purple	TPSA7510	1973	**£10**	
Buzzard	LP	Purple	TPSA7512	1973	**£10**	
Coming On Again	LP	Capitol	864	1971	**£12**	US
Gold Medallions	7"	Purple	PUR113	1973	**£4**	
She's A Striker	7"	Capitol	CL15687	1971	**£4**	
Warm Slash	LP	Capitol	787	1969	**£12**	US

TUDOR LODGE

Lady's Changing Home	7"	Vertigo		1971	**£25**	
Tudor Lodge	LP	Vertigo	6360043	1971	**£120**	

TUDOR MINSTRELS

Family Way	7"	Decca	F12536	1966	**£8**	

TUESDAY'S CHILDREN

High On A Hill	7"	Columbia	DB8018	1966	**£10**	
When You Walk In The Sun	7"	Columbia	DB7978	1966	**£8**	

TULLY, LEE

Around The World With Elwood Pretzel	7"	London	HL8363	1957	**£10**	

TUNEROCKERS

Green Mosquito	7"	London	HLT8717	1958	**£12**	

TUNEWEAVERS

Happy Happy Birthday Baby	7"	London	HL8503	1957	**£12**	

TURNER, DENNIS

Lover Please	7"	London	HL9537	1962	**£4**	

TURNER, GORDON

Meditation	LP	Charisma	CAS1009	1969	**£10**	

TURNER, IKE

Ike Turner Rocks The Blues	LP	Ember	EMB3395	1968	**£10**	

TURNER, IKE & TINA

Anything You Wasn't Born With	7"	HMV	POP1544	1966	**£8**	
Crazy 'Bout You Baby	7"	Liberty	LIB15233	1969	**£4**	
Dance With Ike And Tina Turner	LP	Sue	LP2003	1962	**£30**	US
Don't Play Me Cheap	LP	Sue	LP2005	1963	**£30**	US
Dynamite	LP	Sue	LP2004	1963	**£30**	US
Finger Poppin'	7"	W. Bros	WB153	1965	**£4**	
Fool In Love	7"	London	HLU9226	1960	**£4**	
Goodbye So Long	7"	Stateside	SS551	1966	**£5**	
Greatest Hits	LP	London	HAC8248	1965	**£12**	
Greatest Hits	LP	Sue	LP1038	1965	**£25**	US
Hunter	LP	Harvest	SHSP4001	1970	**£10**	
Hunter	7"	Harvest	HAR5018	1970	**£4**	
I Can't Believe What You Say	7"	Sue	WI350	1964	**£8**	
I'll Never Need More Than This	7"	London	HLU10155	1967	**£4**	
I'm Gonna Do All I Can	7"	Minit	MLF11016	1969	**£5**	
I'm Hooked	7"	HMV	POP1583	1967	**£12**	
Ike And Tina Turner Revue	LP	Ember	EMB3368	1966	**£10**	
Ike And Tina Turner Show	LP	W. Bros	WM8170	1965	**£12**	
Ike And Tina Turner Show	LP	W. Bros	W1579	1966	**£10**	
Ike And Tina Turner Show II	LP	W. Bros	WB5904	1967	**£10**	
Ike And Tina Turner Show Vol.1	7" EP	W. Bros	WEP619	1965	**£10**	
In Person	LP	Minit	MLS40014	1969	**£12**	
It's Gonna Work Out Fine	7"	London	HL9451	1961	**£4**	

Title	Format	Label	Number	Year	Price	Notes
It's Gonna Work Out Fine	LP	Sue	LP2007	1963	**£30**	US
It's Gonna Work Out Fine	7"	Sue	WI306	1964	**£8**	
Love Like Yours	7"	London	HLU10083	1966	**£4**	chart single
Make Em Wait	7"	A&M	AMS783	1970	**£4**	
Please Please Please	7"	Sue	WI376	1965	**£8**	
Poor Fool	7"	Sue	WI322	1964	**£8**	
River Deep And Mountain High	LP	A&M	AMS971	1970	**£10**	
River Deep And Mountain High	LP	London	HAU8298	1966	**£15**	chart LP
River Deep And Mountain High	LP	Philles	PHLP4011	1966	**£1200**	US, no cover
River Deep Mountain High	7"	A&M	AMS829	1971	**£4**	
River Deep Mountain High	7"	London	HLU10046	1966	**£5**	chart single
So Fine	LP	London	SHU8370	1969	**£10**	
So Fine	7"	London	HLU10189	1968	**£4**	
Somebody	7"	W. Bros	WB5766	1966	**£5**	
Somebody Needs You	7" EP	W. Bros	WEP620	1966	**£10**	
Soul Of Ike And Tina Turner	7" EP	Sue	IEP706	1966	**£30**	
Sound Of Ike And Tina Turner	LP	Sue	LP2001	1961	**£30**	US
Tell Her I'm Not At Home	7"	W. Bros	WB5753	1966	**£4**	chart single
We Need An Understanding	7"	London	HLU10217	1968	**£4**	

TURNER, JESSE LEE

Title	Format	Label	Number	Year	Price	Notes
Do I Worry	7"	Top Rank	JAR516	1960	**£4**	
I'm The Little Space Girl's Father	7"	London	HLP9108	1960	**£4**	
Shake Baby Shake	7"	London	HLL8785	1959	**£20**	
Teenage Misery	7"	Top Rank	JAR303	1960	**£8**	
Voice Changing Song	7"	Vogue	V9201	1962	**£8**	

TURNER, JOE

Title	Format	Label	Number	Year	Price	Notes
Best Of...	LP	Atlantic	8081	1963	**£20**	US
Big Joe Is Here	LP	London	HAE2231	1960	**£25**	
Big Joe Rides Again	LP	London	LJZ-K15205	1960	**£30**	
Big Joe Rides Again	LP	London	SAHK6123	1960	**£35**	
Boogie Woogie Country Girl	7"	London	HLE8332	1956	**£75**	
Boss Of The Blues	LP	London	LJZ-K15053	195-	**£40**	
Boss Of The Blues	LP	London	SAHK6019	1959	**£50**	
Careless Love	LP	Savoy	MG14106	1963	**£20**	US
Corrine Corrina	7"	London	HLE8301	1956	**£50**	
Honey Hush	7"	London	HLE9055	1960	**£15**	
Joe Turner And Pete Johnson Group	7" EP	Emarcy	ERE1500	1956	**£15**	
Joe Turner And The Blues	LP	Savoy	MG14012	1962	**£20**	US
Joe Turner	LP	Atlantic	8005	1957	**£35**	US
Kansas City Jazz	LP	Atlantic	1243	1956	**£35**	US
Lipstick Powder And Paint	7"	London	HLE8357	1957	**£60**	
Midnight Cannonball	7"	Atlantic	AT4026	1965	**£8**	
My Little Honeydripper	7"	London	HLK9119	1960	**£15**	
Presenting Joe Turner	7" EP	London	REE1111	1957	**£40**	
Rockin' The Blues	LP	London	HAE2173	1959	**£30**	
Singing The Blues	LP	Stateside	SL10226	1967	**£10**	

TURNER, JOE & PETE JOHNSON

Title	Format	Label	Number	Year	Price	Notes
Joe Turner And Pete Johnson	LP	EmArcy	36014	1955	**£25**	US

TURNER, MEL

Title	Format	Label	Number	Year	Price	Notes
Doing The Ton	7"	Columbia	DB7076	1963	**£4**	
Don't Cry	7"	Columbia	DB4963	1963	**£4**	
Let Me Hold Your Hand	7"	Melodisc	MEL1580	196-	**£4**	
Swing Low Sweet Chariot	7"	Columbia	DB4791	1962	**£4**	

TURNER, NIK

Title	Format	Label	Number	Year	Price	Notes
Maximum Effect	LP	Avatar	AALP5004	1982	**£10**	
New Anatomy	LP	Demi Monde	DM001	1985	**£10**	
Pass Out	LP	Riddle	RID002	1980	**£15**	
Punkadelia	LP	Flicknife	SHARP103	1982	**£10**	
Xitintoday	LP	Charisma	CDS4011	1978	**£15**	

TURNER, SAMMY

Title	Format	Label	Number	Year	Price	Notes
Always	7"	London	HLX8963	1959	**£4**	chart single
Lavender Blue	7"	London	HLX8918	1959	**£4**	
Lavender Blue Moods	LP	London	HAX2246	1960	**£10**	
Paradise	7"	London	HLX9062	1960	**£4**	
Raincoat In The River	7"	London	HLX9488	1962	**£5**	

TURNER, SPYDER

Title	Format	Label	Cat. No.	Year	Price	Notes
Stand By Me	LP	MGM	E4450	1967	**£10**	US
Stand By Me	7"	MGM	MGM1332	1967	**£8**	

TURNER, TITUS

Title	Format	Label	Cat. No.	Year	Price	Notes
Miss Rubberneck Jones	7"	Blue Beat	BB32	1961	**£10**	
Pony Train	7"	Oriole	CB1611	1961	**£4**	
Sound Off	LP	Jamie	JLP3018	1961	**£10**	US
Sound Off	7"	Parlophone	R4746	1961	**£4**	
We Told You Not To Marry	7"	London	HLU9024	1960	**£6**	

TURNQUIST REMEDY

Title	Format	Label	Cat. No.	Year	Price	Notes
Turnquist Remedy	LP	Pentagram			**£20**	US

TURQUOISE

Title	Format	Label	Cat. No.	Year	Price	Notes
53 Summer Street	7"	Decca	F12756	1968	**£6**	
Woodstock	7"	Decca	F12842	1968	**£8**	

TURTLES

Title	Format	Label	Cat. No.	Year	Price	Notes
Battle Of The Bands	LP	London	SHU8376	1968	**£12**	
Can I Get To Know You Better	7"	London	HLU10095	1966	**£4**	
Elenore	7"	London	HLU10223	1968	**£4**	chart single
Golden Hits	LP	White Whale	WW7115	1967	**£10**	
Happy Together	LP	London	HAU8330	1967	**£15**	chart LP
Happy Together	7"	London	HLU10115	1967	**£4**	chart single
It Ain't Me Babe	7"	Pye	7N25320	1965	**£4**	
It Ain't Me Babe	7" EP	Pye	NEP44089	1967	**£6**	
It Ain't Me Babe	LP	White Whale	WW7111	1965	**£15**	US
Let Me Be	7"	Pye	7N25341	1966	**£4**	
Let Me Be	7"	Pye	7N25421	1967	**£4**	
Love In The City	7"	London	HLU10291	1969	**£4**	
More Golden Hits	LP	White Whale	WW7127	1970	**£10**	US
She'd Rather Be With Me	7"	London	HLU10135	1967	**£4**	chart single
She's My Girl	7"	London	HLU10168	1967	**£4**	
Sound Asleep	7"	London	HLU10184	1968	**£4**	
Story Of Rock And Roll	7"	London	HLU10207	1968	**£4**	
Turtle Soup	LP	White Whale	WW7124	1969	**£12**	US
Wooden Head	LP	White Whale	WW7133	1971	**£12**	US
You Baby	7"	Immediate	IM031	1966	**£5**	
You Baby	LP	White Whale	WW7112	1966	**£15**	US
You Don't Have To Walk In The Rain	7"	London	HLU10279	1969	**£4**	
You Know What I Mean	7"	London	HLU10153	1967	**£4**	
You Showed Me	7"	London	HLU10251	1969	**£4**	

TWELFTH NIGHT

Title	Format	Label	Cat. No.	Year	Price	Notes
Live At The Target	LP	Twelfth Night	TN002	1981	**£10**	

TWENTIETH CENTURY ZOO

Title	Format	Label	Cat. No.	Year	Price	Notes
Thunder On A Clear Day	LP	Vault		1965	**£20**	US

TWENTY SEVEN DOLLAR SNAP ON FACE

Title	Format	Label	Cat. No.	Year	Price	Notes
Heterodyne State Hospital	LP	Heterodyne		1977	**£30**	US, blue vinyl

TWENTY SIXTY-SIX AND THEN

Title	Format	Label	Cat. No.	Year	Price	Notes
Reflections Of The Future	LP	United Artists	UAS29314	1972	**£100**	

TWENTY-THIRD TURNOFF

Title	Format	Label	Cat. No.	Year	Price	Notes
Michael Angelo	7"	Deram	DM150	1967	**£20**	

TWICE AS MUCH

Title	Format	Label	Cat. No.	Year	Price	Notes
Crystal Ball	7"	Immediate	IM042	1967	**£8**	
Own Up	LP	Immediate	IMSP007	1966	**£15**	
Sittin' On A Fence	7"	Immediate	IM033	1966	**£5**	chart single
Step Out Of Line	7"	Immediate	IM036	1966	**£5**	
That's All	LP	Immediate	IMSP013	1968	**£15**	
True Story	7"	Immediate	IM039	1966	**£6**	

TWIGGY & ANNE

Title	Format	Label	Cat. No.	Year	Price	Notes
Some Do, Some Don't	7"	Columbia	DB7799	1966	**£4**	

TWILIGHTS

Title	Format	Label	Cat. No.	Year	Price	Notes
Cathy Come Home	7"	Columbia	DB8396	1968	**£4**	

Needle In A Haystack	7"	Columbia	DB8065	1966	**£5**	
Take What I Got	7"	London	HLU9992	1965	**£4**	

TWIN TONES

Jo Ann	7"	RCA	RCA1040	1958	**£4**	

TWINK

Do It 1977	12"	Chiswick	SWT26	1978	**£6**	
Think Pink	LP	Polydor	2343032	1970	**£45**	
Think Pink	LP	Polydor	2343032	1970	**£50**	pink vinyl

TWINKLE

End Of The World	7"	Decca	F12305	1965	**£4**	
Golden Lights	7"	Decca	F12076	1965	**£4**	chart single
Micky	7"	Instant	IN005	1969	**£6**	
Poor Old Johnny	7"	Decca	F12219	1965	**£4**	
Terry	7"	Decca	F12013	1964	**£4**	chart single
Tommy	7"	Decca	F12139	1965	**£5**	
Twinkle	7" EP	Decca	DFE8621	1965	**£6**	
What Am I Doing Here With You	7"	Decca	F12464	1966	**£4**	

TWINS

Teenagers Love The Twins	LP	RCA	LPM1708	1958	**£20**	US

TWINSET

Tremblin'	7"	Decca	F12629	1967	**£8**	

TWIRL, TOBY

Harry Faversham	7"	Decca	F12728	1968	**£10**	
Movin' In	7"	Decca	F12867	1969	**£10**	
Toffee Apple Sunday	7"	Decca	F12804	1968	**£10**	

TWISTERS

Doin' The Twist	LP	Treasure	TLP890	1962	**£15**	US

TWISTIN' KINGS

The Twistin' Kings are not a well-known name, and their music is not in the label's usual house style, but "Twistin' The World Around" just happens to be the first album release on the Motown label. As such, it is more sought after in the UK than in its native America - the value quoted here reflects the fact that it is possible to obtain copies at a lower price than that often charged by UK dealers.

Twistin' The World Around	LP	Motown	MLP601	1960	**£50**	US

TWITTY, CONWAY

C'Est Si Bon	7"	MGM	MGM1118	1961	**£4**	chart single
Comfy 'N' Cozy	7"	MGM	MGM1170	1962	**£4**	
Conway Twitty Sings	LP	MGM	C781	1959	**£15**	
Conway Twitty Sings	LP	MGM	E3744	1959	**£40**	US
Conway Twitty Touch	LP	MGM	E3943	1961	**£25**	US
Greatest Hits	LP	MGM	E3849	1960	**£25**	US
Greatest Hits	LP	MGM	E3849	1960	**£50**	US, with poster
Handy Man	7"	MGM	MGM1201	1963	**£4**	
Hey Little Lucy	7"	MGM	MGM1016	1959	**£4**	
Hey Little Lucy	7" EP	MGM	MGMEP698	1959	**£12**	
Hit The Road	LP	MGM	E4217	1964	**£12**	US
Hurt In My Heart	7"	MGM	MGM1066	1960	**£4**	
I Need Your Lovin'	7" EP	Mercury	ZEP10069	1960	**£30**	
Is A Bluebird Blue	7"	MGM	MGM1082	1960	**£4**	chart single
Is A Bluebird Blue	7" EP	MGM	MGMEP738	1960	**£12**	
It's Drivin' Me Wild	7"	MGM	MGM1137	1961	**£4**	
It's Only Make Believe	7"	MGM	MGM992	1958	**£4**	chart single
It's Only Make Believe	7" EP	MGM	MGMEP684	1958	**£15**	
Lonely Blue Boy	LP	MGM	E3818	1960	**£40**	US
Lonely Blue Boy	7"	MGM	MGM1056	1960	**£4**	
Mona Lisa	7"	MGM	MGM1029	1959	**£4**	chart single
Next Kiss	7"	MGM	MGM1129	1961	**£4**	
Pick-Up	7"	MGM	MGM1187	1962	**£4**	
Portrait Of A Fool	LP	MGM	E4019	1962	**£20**	US
R&B '63	LP	MGM	E4089	1963	**£20**	US
Rock And Roll Story	LP	MGM	E3907	1961	**£25**	US
Rock And Roll Story	7" EP	MGM	MGMEP752	1961	**£15**	
Rosaleena	7"	MGM	MGM1047	1959	**£4**	
Saturday Night With Conway	LP	MGM	C801	1959	**£15**	

Title	Format	Label	Cat. No.	Year	Price	Notes
Saturday Night With Conway	LP	MGM	E3786	1959	**£40**	US
Saturday Night With Conway	7" EP	MGM	MGMEP719	1960	**£15**	
She Ain't No Angel	7"	MGM	MGM1209	1963	**£4**	
Story Of My Love	7"	MGM	MGM1003	1959	**£4**	chart single
Tell Me One More Time	7"	MGM	MGM1095	1960	**£4**	
Tower Of Tears	7"	MGM	MGM1152	1962	**£4**	
Whole Lotta Shakin' Goin' On	7"	MGM	MGM1108	1960	**£4**	

TWO AND A HALF

Title	Format	Label	Cat. No.	Year	Price	Notes
I Don't Need To Tell You	7"	Decca	F22715	1967	**£10**	
Suburban Early Morning Station	7"	Decca	F22672	1967	**£12**	

TWO KINGS

Title	Format	Label	Cat. No.	Year	Price	Notes
Hit You Let You Feel It	7"	Island	WI249	1965	**£10**	
Rolling Stone	7"	Island	WI240	1965	**£10**	

TWO MUCH

Title	Format	Label	Cat. No.	Year	Price	Notes
It's A Hip Hip Hippy World	7"	Fontana	TF900	1968	**£4**	
Wonderland Of Love	7"	Fontana	TF858	1967	**£4**	

TWO NINETEEN SKIFFLE GROUP

Title	Format	Label	Cat. No.	Year	Price	Notes
Two Nineteen Skiffle Group	7" EP	Esquire	EP126	195-	**£6**	
Two Nineteen Skiffle Group	7" EP	Esquire	EP146	195-	**£6**	
Two Nineteen Skiffle Group	7" EP	Esquire	EP176	195-	**£6**	
Two Nineteen Skiffle Group	7" EP	Esquire	EP196	195-	**£6**	

TWO OF CLUBS

Title	Format	Label	Cat. No.	Year	Price	Notes
Angel Must Have Made You	7"	Columbia	DB7371	1964	**£4**	

TWO OF EACH

Title	Format	Label	Cat. No.	Year	Price	Notes
Every Single Day	7"	Decca	F12626	1967	**£4**	

TYE, ARLYNE

Title	Format	Label	Cat. No.	Year	Price	Notes
Universe	7"	London	HLL8825	1959	**£5**	

TYGERS OF PAN TANG

Title	Format	Label	Cat. No.	Year	Price	Notes
Don't Touch Me There	7"	Neat	03	1979	**£4**	

TYLER, BIG T

Title	Format	Label	Cat. No.	Year	Price	Notes
King Kong	7"	Vogue	V9079	1957	**£25**	

TYLER, RED & THE GYROS

Title	Format	Label	Cat. No.	Year	Price	Notes
Rockin' And Rollin'	LP	Ace	LP1006	1960	**£20**	US

TYLER, T.TEXAS

Title	Format	Label	Cat. No.	Year	Price	Notes
Country Round Up	7" EP	Parlophone	GEP8788	1959	**£6**	
Deck Of Cards	LP	Sound	607	1958	**£25**	US
Great Texan	LP	King	686	1960	**£20**	US
Songs Along The Way	LP	King	734	1961	**£20**	US
T.Texas Tyler	LP	King	664	1959	**£20**	US
T.Texas Tyler	LP	King	721	1961	**£20**	US

TYMES

Title	Format	Label	Cat. No.	Year	Price	Notes
Come With Me To The Sea	7"	Cameo Park.	P884	1963	**£4**	
Here She Comes	7"	Cameo Park.	P924	1964	**£20**	
Magic Of Our Summer Love	7"	Cameo Park.	P919	1964	**£4**	
So Much In Love	LP	Cameo Park.	P7032	1963	**£12**	
So Much In Love	7"	Cameo Park.	P871	1963	**£5**	chart single
Somewhere	7"	Cameo Park.	P891	1964	**£4**	
Somewhere	LP	Parkway	P7039	1964	**£12**	US
Sound Of Wonderful Tymes	LP	Parkway	P7038	1963	**£12**	US
To Each His Own	7"	Cameo Park.	P908	1964	**£4**	
Twelfth Of Never	7"	Cameo Park.	P933	1964	**£5**	

TYNER, ROBIN & THE RODS

Title	Format	Label	Cat. No.	Year	Price	Notes
Till The Night Is Gone	7"	Island	WIP6418	1977	**£4**	

TYRANNOSAURUS REX

Tyrannosaurus Rex was originally a duo consisting of Marc Bolan on vocals and acoustic guitar and Steve Peregrine Took on bongos - the style of their acoustic music being determined less by a burning desire to create modern folk music than by the fact that they had all their electric equipment stolen just as they were starting out. The duo did have a very distinctive sound, although this became considerably diluted once they began to expand the line-up and switched the electricity back on.

Beard Of Stars	LP	Regal Z.	SLRZ1013	1970	**£15**	with insert, chart LP
By The Light Of A Magical Moon	7"	Regal Z.	RZ3025	1970	**£20**	
Debora	7"	Magnifly	ECHO102	1972	**£6**	PS
Debora	7"	Regal Z.	RZ3008	1968	**£12**	
Debora	7"	Regal Z.	RZ3008	1968	**£65**	PS
King Of The Rumbling Spires	7"	Regal Z.	RZ3022	1969	**£20**	
King Of The Rumbling Spires	7"	Regal Z.	RZ3022	1969	**£80**	PS
My People Were Fair...	LP	Regal Z.	SLRZ1003	1968	**£25**	with insert, chart LP
My People.../Prophets...	LP	Cube	TOOFA3/4	1972	**£15**	double, chart LP
One Inch Rock	7"	Regal Z.	RZ3011	1968	**£15**	
One Inch Rock	7"	Regal Z.	RZ3011	1968	**£60**	PS
Pewter Suitor	7"	Regal Z.	RZ3016	1969	**£25**	
Prophets,Seers and Sages	LP	Regal Z.	SLRZ1005	1968	**£25**	with insert
Unicorn	LP	Regal Z.	SLRZ1007	1969	**£15**	chart LP
Unicorn/Beard Of Stars	LP	Cube	TOOFA9/10	1972	**£15**	double

TZUKE & PAXO

Tzuke and Paxo are Judie Tzuke and her writing partner, Mike Paxman. Her next attempt at a hit was as Zookie, before finally achieving success under her own full name.

These Are The Laws	7"	Good Earth	GD12	1976	**£5**	

TZUKE, JUDIE

For You (live)	7"	Chrysalis	JUD102	1982	**£4**	promo
For You (live)	12"	Chrysalis	JUD12103	1982	**£6**	promo
For You	7"	Rocket	ROKN541	1978	**£4**	
Love On The Border	7"	Chrysalis	CHS2600DJ	1982	**£4**	1 sided promo

U

U.K.'S

Title	Format	Label	Cat. No.	Year	Price	Notes
Ever Faithful Ever True	7"	HMV	POP1310	1964	£5	
I Will Never Let You Go	7"	HMV	POP1357	1964	£5	

U2

Title	Format	Label	Cat. No.	Year	Price	Notes
11 O'Clock Tick Tock	7"	CBS	8687	1980	£12	Irish
11 O'Clock Tick Tock	7"	CBS	8687	1980	£25	Irish, yellow vinyl
11 O'Clock Tick Tock	7"	Island	WIP6601	1980	£12	
4 U2 Play	7"	CBS	PAC1	1982	£20	Irish, 4-pack
4 U2 Play	7"	CBS	PAC1		£110	Irish, 4-pack coloured vinyl
Another Day	7"	CBS	8306	1980	£20	Irish
Celebration	7"	CBS	2214	1982	£10	Irish
Celebration	7"	Island	WIP6770	1982	£10	chart single
Day Without Me	7"	CBS	8905	1980	£10	Irish
Day Without Me	7"	Island	WIP6630	1980	£10	
Fire	7"	CBS	1376	1981	£8	Irish
Fire	7"	Island	UWIP6679	1981	£15	double
Fire	7"	Island	WIP6679	1981	£6	chart single
Gloria	7"	CBS	1718	1981	£8	Irish
Gloria	7"	Island	WIP6733	1981	£8	chart single
I Still Haven't Found What I'm Looking For	CD-s	Island	CID328	1987	£6	
I Will Follow	7"	CBS	9065	1980	£8	Irish
I Will Follow	7"	CBS	9065	1980	£25	Irish, yellow vinyl
I Will Follow	7"	Island	WIP6650DJ	1980	£15	1 sided promo
I Will Follow	7"	Island	WIP6656	1980	£10	
New Year's Day	7"	Island	UWIP6848	1983	£15	double
New Year's Day	7"	Island	WIP6848	1983	£4	chart single
New Year's Day	12"	Island	12WIP6848	1983	£8	
PAC2	7"	CBS	PAC2		£20	Irish, 4-pack
PAC3	7"	CBS	PAC3		£20	Irish, 4-pack
Pride	7"	CBS	A4727	1984	£4	Irish
Pride	7"	Island	ISD202	1984	£8	double
Pride	7"	Island	ISP202	1984	£20	pic disc
Pride	12"	Island	12IS202	1984	£6	4 tracks
Pride	12"	Island	ISX202	1984	£6	5 tracks
Rattle And Hum	LP	Island	U27	1988	£35	double, test pressing
Sunday Bloody Sunday	12"	Island	600820	1983	£6	
Two Hearts Beat As One	7"	Island	ISD109	1983	£10	double
Two Hearts Beat As One	12"	Island	12IS109	1983	£8	
Two Sides Live	LP	W. Bros		1981	£100	US promo
U2: 3	7"	CBS	7951	1979	£20	Irish
U2: 3	12"	CBS	127951	1979	£40	Irish, numbered
U2: 3	cass	CBS	40-7951	1985	£8	
Under A Blood Red Sky	LP	Island	US1PR	1983	£25	promo with interviews
Unforgettable Fire	7"	Island	ISD220	1985	£6	double
Unforgettable Fire	7"	Island	ISP220	1985	£12	shaped pic disc
Unforgettable Fire	12"	Island	12IS220	1985	£6	
War	LP	Island	ILPS9733	1983	£40	pic disc
Where The Streets Have No Name	CD-s	Island	CID340	1987	£6	
Wide Awake In America	12"	Island	ISSP22	1985	£6	
With Or Without You	CD-s	Island	CID319	1987	£6	

UB40

Title	Format	Label	Cat. No.	Year	Price	Notes
Cherry Oh Baby	7"	Dep Int.	DEPY10	1984	£5	pic disc
UB44	LP	Dep Int.	LPDEP3	1982	£10	hologram sleeve

UFO

Title	Format	Label	Cat. No.	Year	Price	Notes
Back Into My Life	7"	Chrysalis	CHSP2607	1982	£4	pic disc
Boogie For George	7"	Beacon	BEA172	1971	£10	
Call My Name	7"	Chrysalis	UFODJ1	1981	£4	1 sided promo
Come Away Melinda	7"	Beacon	BEA165	1971	£12	

Title	Format	Label	Number	Year	Price	Notes
Doctor Doctor	7"	Chrysalis	CHS2040	1974	**£4**	
Flying	LP	Beacon	BES19	1972	**£15**	
Prince Kajuki	7"	Beacon	BEA181	1971	**£12**	
This Time	7"	Chrysalis	UFOP1	1985	**£4**	pic disc
UFO	LP	Beacon	BEAS12	1971	**£15**	
When It's Time To Rock	7"	Chrysalis	CHSP2672	1983	**£4**	pic disc

UGLY CUSTARD

Title	Format	Label	Number	Year	Price	Notes
Ugly Custard	LP	Kaleidoscope	100	1970	**£75**	

UGLY DUCKLINGS

Title	Format	Label	Number	Year	Price	Notes
Off The Wall	LP	Razor		1968	**£15**	Canadian
Somewhere Outside	LP	Yorktown		1966	**£80**	Canadian

UGLYS

Title	Format	Label	Number	Year	Price	Notes
End Of The Season	7"	Pye	7N17178	1966	**£15**	
Good Idea	7"	Pye	7N17027	1966	**£15**	
I See The Light	7"	MGM			**£60**	
It's Alright	7"	Pye	7N15968	1965	**£12**	
Real Good Girl	7"	CBS	2933	1967	**£20**	
Wake Up My Mind	7"	Pye	7N15858	1965	**£15**	

UK BONDS

Title	Format	Label	Number	Year	Price	Notes
Anything You Do Is Alright	7"	Polydor	56112	1966	**£4**	

UK DECAY

Title	Format	Label	Number	Year	Price	Notes
Black 45	7"	Plastic	PLAS002	1981	**£8**	
For My Country	7"	Fresh	FRESH12	1981	**£5**	
Sexual	7"	Fresh	FRESH33	1981	**£5**	
UK Decay	7"	Plastic	PLAS2	1979	**£20**	B side by Pneumania
Unexpected Guest	7"	Fresh	FRESH26	1981	**£8**	with badge

UK SUBS

Title	Format	Label	Number	Year	Price	Notes
C.I.D.	7"	City	NIK5	1978	**£5**	various coloured vinyls

ULTIMATE SPINACH

Title	Format	Label	Number	Year	Price	Notes
Behold And See	LP	MGM	C8094	1968	**£20**	
Ultimate Spinach	LP	MGM	C8071	1968	**£25**	
Ultimate Spinach	LP	MGM	SE4600	1969	**£20**	US

ULTRAVOX

Title	Format	Label	Number	Year	Price	Notes
Dangerous Rhythm	7"	Island	WIP6375	1977	**£4**	
Quirks	7"	Island	WIP6417	1977	**£4**	
Systems Of Romance	12"	Island	UV1	1978	**£8**	promo sampler
Young Savage	7"	Island	WIP6392	1977	**£4**	

ULTRAVOX & MICHAEL SCHENKER GROUP

Title	Format	Label	Number	Year	Price	Notes
Ultravox/Michael Schenker Group	12"	Chrysalis		1981	**£8**	promo

ULTRAVOX & SPANDAU BALLET

Title	Format	Label	Number	Year	Price	Notes
Rage In Eden/Diamond	LP	Chrysalis		1982	**£12**	promo sampler

ULVAEUS, BJORN & BENNY ANDERSSON

Title	Format	Label	Number	Year	Price	Notes
Lycka	LP	Polar	POLL113	1970	**£15**	Swedish, mono
Lycka	LP	Polar	POLS226	1970	**£12**	Swedish, mono

UNBEATABLES

Title	Format	Label	Number	Year	Price	Notes
Live At Palisades Park	LP	Fawn	LP5050	1964	**£35**	US

UNCLE DOG

Title	Format	Label	Number	Year	Price	Notes
Old Hat	LP	Signpost	SG4253	1969	**£10**	
River Road	7"	Signpost	SGP752	1972	**£4**	

UNDERGROUND SET

Title	Format	Label	Number	Year	Price	Notes
Underground Set	LP	Pantonic		1970	**£25**	

UNDERGROUND SUNSHINE

Title	Format	Label	Number	Year	Price	Notes
Birthday	7"	Fontana	TF1049	1969	**£6**	
Let There Be Light	LP	Intrepid	IT4003	1969	**£15**	US

UNDERGROUNDS

Title	Format	Label	Number	Year	Price	Notes
Psychedelic Visions	LP	Mercury	MG16337	1967	**£15**	US

UNDERTAKERS

Title	Format	Label	Number	Year	Price	Notes
Everybody Loves A Lover	7"	Pye	7N15543	1963	**£10**	
Just A Little Bit	7"	Pye	7N15607	1964	**£10**	chart single
What About Us	7"	Pye	7N15562	1963	**£10**	

UNDERTONES

Title	Format	Label	Number	Year	Price	Notes
Get Over You	7"	Sire	SIR4010	1979	**£5**	chart single
Hypnotised Apetizer	10" LP	Sire	SAM1120	1979	**£8**	promo sampler
Jimmy Jimmy	7"	Sire	SIR4015	1979	**£5**	green vinyl, plastic sleeve
Love Parade	7"	Ardeck	ARDS11DJ	1982	**£4**	1 sided promo
My Perfect Cousin	7"	Ardeck	ARDS6	1983	**£6**	double PS
Teenage Kicks	7"	Good Vibs	GOT4	1978	**£10**	poster sleeve
Teenage Kicks	7"	Sire		1978	**£5**	promo
Teenage Kicks	7"	Sire	SIR4007	1978	**£4**	chart single
Teenage Kicks	10"	Sire		1978	**£8**	promo
Undertones	LP	Sire	SRK6071	1978	**£10**	chart LP

UNDISPUTED TRUTH

Title	Format	Label	Number	Year	Price	Notes
Save My Love For A Rainy Day	7"	T. Motown	TMG776	1971	**£4**	
Save My Love For A Rainy Day	7"	T. Motown	TMG776	1971	**£12**	demo
Smiling Face Sometimes	7"	T. Motown	TMG789	1971	**£4**	
Smiling Face Sometimes	7"	T. Motown	TMG789	1971	**£15**	demo
Superstar	7"	T. Motown	TMG818	1972	**£4**	
Superstar	7"	T. Motown	TMG818	1972	**£10**	demo

UNFOLDING

Title	Format	Label	Number	Year	Price	Notes
How To Blow Your Mind	LP	Audio Fid.	6184	196-	**£20**	US

UNFOLDING OF THE BOOK OF LIFE

Title	Format	Label	Number	Year	Price	Notes
Vol.1	LP	Island	ILPS9093	1969	**£20**	
Vol.2	LP	Island	ILPS9094	1969	**£20**	

UNICORN

Title	Format	Label	Number	Year	Price	Notes
Blue Pine Trees	LP	Charisma	CAS1092	1974	**£10**	
Cosmic Kid	7"	Transatlantic	BIG509	1972	**£4**	
P.F.Sloan	7"	Transatlantic	BIG138	1971	**£4**	
Uphill All The Way	LP	Transatlantic	TRA238	1971	**£12**	

UNIFICS

Title	Format	Label	Number	Year	Price	Notes
Court Of Love	7"	London	HLZ10231	1968	**£4**	

UNION GAP

Title	Format	Label	Number	Year	Price	Notes
Lady Willpower	7"	CBS	3551	1968	**£4**	
Woman Woman	7"	CBS	3100	1967	**£4**	
Young Girl	7"	CBS	3365	1968	**£4**	

UNIQUES

Title	Format	Label	Number	Year	Price	Notes
A-Yuh	7"	Trojan	TR645	1969	**£6**	
Absolutely The Uniques	LP	Trojan	TRL15	196-	**£20**	
Beatitude	7"	Island	WI3123	1967	**£10**	
Build My World Around You	7"	Island	WI3114	1967	**£10**	
Fast Way Of Living feat. Joe Stampley	7"	Pye	7N25303	1965	**£15**	
Girl Of My Dreams	7"	Island	WI3145	1968	**£10**	
Gypsy Woman	7"	Island	WI3084	1967	**£10**	
Lesson Of Love	7"	Island	WI3107	1967	**£10**	
Lonely For Your Love	7"	Trojan	TR7866	197-	**£4**	
More Love	7"	Island	WI3117	1967	**£10**	
Mother And Child Reunion	7"	Trojan	TR7852	197-	**£4**	
My Conversation	7"	Island	WI3122	1967	**£10**	
Never Let Me Go	7"	Island	WI3081	1967	**£10**	
People Rock Steady	7"	Island	WI3070	1967	**£10**	
Speak No Evil	7"	Island	WI3106	1967	**£10**	

UNIT FOUR PLUS TWO

Title	Format	Label	Number	Year	Price	Notes
Baby Never Say Goodbye	7"	Decca	F12333	1966	**£5**	chart single
Butterfly	7"	Fontana	TF840	1967	**£6**	
Concrete And Clay	7"	Decca	F12071	1965	**£4**	chart single
For A Moment	7"	Decca	F12398	1966	**£5**	
Green Fields	7"	Decca	F11821	1964	**£5**	chart single
Hark	7"	Decca	F12211	1965	**£5**	
I Was Only Playing Games	7"	Decca	F12509	1966	**£5**	
Loving Takes A Little Understanding	7"	Fontana	TF891	1967	**£6**	

Sorrow And Pain .... 7" .... Decca .... F11994 .... 1964 .... **£5** ....
Three Thirty .... 7" .... Fontana .... TF990 .... 1969 .... **£12** ....
Too Fast, Too Slow .... 7" .... Fontana .... TF834 .... 1967 .... **£8** ....
Unit Four Plus Two .... LP .... Decca .... LK4697 .... 1965 .... **£30** ....
Unit Four Plus Two .... 7" EP .... Decca .... DFE8619 .... 1965 .... **£6** ....
Unit Four Plus Two .... LP .... Fontana .... SFL13123 .... 1969 .... **£20** ....
Would You Believe What You Say .... 7" .... Fontana .... TF852 .... 1967 .... **£6** ....
You Ain't Goin' Nowhere .... 7" .... Fontana .... TF931 .... 1968 .... **£6** ....
You've Got To Be Cruel To Be Kind .... 7" .... Decca .... F12299 .... 1965 .... **£5** ....
You've Never Been In Love
Like This Before .... 7" .... Decca .... F12144 .... 1965 .... **£4** .... chart single

UNITED SONS OF AMERICA

Greetings From The US of A .... LP .... Mercury .... 6338036 .... 1970 .... **£12** ....

UNITED STATES DOUBLE QUARTET

Life Is Groovy .... LP .... B.T.Puppy .... BTPS1005 .... 1969 .... **£15** .... US
Life Is Groovy .... 7" .... Stateside .... SS590 .... 1967 .... **£6** ....

UNITED STATES OF AMERICA

Garden Of Earthly Delights .... 7" .... CBS .... 3745 .... 1968 .... **£8** ....
United States Of America .... LP .... CBS .... 63340 .... 1968 .... **£20** ....

UNIVERSALS

Green Veined Orchid .... 7" .... Page One .... POF049 .... 1967 .... **£6** ....
I Can't Find You .... 7" .... Page One .... POF032 .... 1967 .... **£5** ....

UNTAMED

Daddy Longlegs .... 7" .... Planet .... PLF113 .... 1966 .... **£20** ....
I'll Go Crazy .... 7" .... Stateside .... SS431 .... 1965 .... **£15** ....
It's Not True .... 7" .... Planet .... PLF103 .... 1966 .... **£20** ....
Once Upon A Time .... 7" .... Parlophone .... R5258 .... 1965 .... **£12** ....
So Long .... 7" .... Decca .... F12045 .... 1964 .... **£12** ....

UNTOUCHABLES

Prisoner In Love .... 7" .... Blue Cat .... BS137 .... 196- .... **£10** ....

UNUSUAL WE

Unusual We .... LP .... Pulsar .... 10608 .... 1969 .... **£12** .... US

UNWANTED

Memory Man .... 7" .... Raw .... RAW30 .... 1978 .... **£6** ....
Secret Police .... 7" .... Raw .... RAW15 .... 1978 .... **£6** ....
Withdrawal .... 7" .... Raw .... RAW6 .... 1977 .... **£15** .... PS
Withdrawal .... 7" .... Raw .... RAWT6 .... 1978 .... **£8** ....

UPBEATS

Keep Cool Crazy Heart .... 7" .... Pye .... 7N25016 .... 1959 .... **£4** ....
My Foolish Heart .... 7" .... London .... HLJ8688 .... 1958 .... **£6** ....
Teeny Weeny Bikini .... 7" .... Pye .... 7N25028 .... 1959 .... **£4** ....

UPCHURCH, PHIL

Darkness, Darkness .... LP .... Blue Thumb .... ILPS9219 .... 1972 .... **£10** ....
Nothing But Soul .... 7" .... Sue .... WI4017 .... 1966 .... **£8** ....
You Can't Sit Down .... 7" .... HMV .... POP899 .... 1961 .... **£12** .... chart single
You Can't Sit Down .... 7" .... Sue .... WI4005 .... 1966 .... **£10** ....

UPSETTERS

Black IPA .... 7" .... Downtown .... DT499 .... 197- .... **£5** ....
Black Man's Time .... 7" .... Upsetter .... US384 .... 1971 .... **£5** ....
Chapter Two .... 7" .... Upsetter .... US383 .... 1971 .... **£5** ....
Country Girl .... 7" .... Island .... WI223 .... 1965 .... **£10** ....
Cow Thief Skank .... 7" .... Upsetter .... US398 .... 1972 .... **£5** ....
Crummy People .... 7" .... Upsetter .... US395 .... 1972 .... **£5** ....
Freak Out Skank .... 7" .... Upsetter .... US397 .... 1972 .... **£5** ....
French Connection .... 7" .... Upsetter .... US385 .... 1971 .... **£5** ....
Hail To Power .... 7" .... Dynamic .... DYN432 .... 197- .... **£6** ....
Live Injection .... 7" .... Upsetter .... US313 .... 1969 .... **£5** ....
Mice Skank .... 7" .... Summit .... SUM8539 .... 1972 .... **£5** ....
Mighty Cloud Of Joy .... 7" .... Upsetter .... US379 .... 1971 .... **£5** ....
Nebuchadnezzar .... 7" .... Randys .... RAN523 .... **£8** ....
Peace .... 7" .... Dynamic .... DYN451 .... 197- .... **£6** ....

Public Enemy No.1	7"	Upsetter	US382	1971	**£5**	
Puss See Hole	7"	Upsetter	US396	1972	**£5**	
Rasta Dub	7"	Grape	GR3035	197-	**£6**	
Return Of Django	LP	Trojan	TRL19	1969	**£15**	
Return Of Django	7"	Upsetter	US301	1969	**£5**	chart single
Ring Of Fire	7"	Upsetter	US380	1971	**£5**	
Vampire	7"	Upsetter	US317	1969	**£5**	
Water Pump	7"	Upsetter	US394	1972	**£5**	
Wildcat	7"	Doctor Bird	DB1034	1966	**£10**	
Wonder Man	7"	Upsetter	US381	1971	**£5**	

UPTOWNERS

If'n	7"	London	HLU9877	1964	**£4**	

URIAH HEEP

Best Of	LP	Bronze	ILPS9375	1975	**£10**	chart LP
Demons And Wizards	LP	Bronze	ILPS9193	1972	**£10**	
Easy Livin'	7"	Bronze	WIP6140	1972	**£4**	
Firefly	LP	Bronze	ILPS9483	1977	**£10**	chart LP
High And Mighty	LP	Bronze	ILPS9384	1976	**£10**	
Innocent Victim	LP	Bronze	BRON504	1977	**£10**	
Lady In Black	7"	Vertigo	6059037	1971	**£6**	
Live	LP	Bronze	ISLD1	1973	**£12**	double, chart LP
Look At Yourself	LP	Bronze	ILPS9169	1971	**£10**	chart LP
Look At Yourself	7"	Bronze	WIP6111	1971	**£4**	
Magician's Birthday	LP	Bronze	ILPS9213	1972	**£10**	chart LP
Return To Fantasy	LP	Bronze	ILPS9335	1975	**£10**	chart LP
Salisbury	LP	Bronze	ILPS9152	1971	**£10**	
Salisbury	LP	Island	ILPS9152	1971	**£12**	
Salisbury	LP	Vertigo	6360028	1971	**£12**	spiral label
Sweet Freedom	LP	Bronze	ILPS9245	1973	**£10**	chart LP
Very 'Umble, Very 'Eavy	LP	Bronze	ILPS9142	1971	**£10**	
Very 'Umble, Very 'Eavy	LP	Vertigo	6360006	1970	**£12**	spiral label
Wizard	7"	Bronze	WIP6126	1972	**£4**	
Wonderworld	LP	Bronze	ILPS9280	1974	**£10**	chart LP

URSA MAJOR

Ursa Major	LP	RCA	LSP4777	1972	**£12**	US

US T-BONES

Proper Thing To Do	7"	Liberty	LIB55951	1967	**£4**	
Sippin' And Chippin'	7"	Liberty	LIB55867	1966	**£4**	

USERS

Kicks In Style	7"	Warped	WARP1	197-	**£5**	
Sick Of You	7"	Raw	RAW1	1977	**£5**	
Sick Of You	12"	Raw	RAWT1	1978	**£6**	

UTOPIA

Utopia	LP	United Artists	UAG29438	1973	**£15**	

UTOPIA (2)

Utopia	LP	Kent		1967	**£20**	US

V

V.I.P.'S

Title	Format	Label	Number	Year	Price	Notes
I Wanna Be Free	7" EP	Fontana	460982	1966	**£40**	French
I Wanna Be Free	7"	Island	WI3003	1966	**£20**	
Mercy Mercy	7"	Philips	40387	1966	**£25**	US
Stagger Lee	7" EP	Fontana	460219	1967	**£40**	French
Straight Down To The Bottom	7" EP	Fontana	460996	1967	**£40**	French
Straight Down To The Bottom	7"	Island	WIP6005	1967	**£20**	
What's That Sound	7" EP	Fontana	460238	1968	**£40**	French

V.I.P.'S (2)

Title	Format	Label	Number	Year	Price	Notes
Don't Keep Shouting At Me	7"	RCA	RCA1427	1964	**£30**	

V.I.P.'S (3)

Title	Format	Label	Number	Year	Price	Notes
Music For Funsters	7"	Bust	SOL3	1978	**£4**	

VACELS

Title	Format	Label	Number	Year	Price	Notes
Can You Please Crawl Out Of Your Window	7"	Pye	7N25330	1965	**£4**	

VAGABONDS

Title	Format	Label	Number	Year	Price	Notes
Ska Time	LP	Decca	LK4617	1964	**£20**	

VAGRANTS

Title	Format	Label	Number	Year	Price	Notes
I Can't Make A Friend	7"	Fontana	TF703	1966	**£10**	

VALADIERS

Title	Format	Label	Number	Year	Price	Notes
I Found A Girl	7"	Oriole	CBA1809	1963	**£160**	

VALANCE, RICKY

Title	Format	Label	Number	Year	Price	Notes
Bobby	7"	Columbia	DB4680	1961	**£4**	
Don't Play Number Nine	7"	Columbia	DB4864	1962	**£4**	
Jimmy's Girl	7"	Columbia	DB4586	1961	**£4**	
Lipstick On Your Lips	7"	Columbia	DB4543	1960	**£4**	
Six Boys	7"	Decca	F12129	1965	**£4**	
Tell Laura I Love Her	7"	Columbia	DB4493	1960	**£5**	chart single

VALE, RICKY & HIS SURFERS

Title	Format	Label	Number	Year	Price	Notes
Everybody's Surfin'	LP	Strand	SL1104	1963	**£10**	US

VALENS, RITCHIE

Title	Format	Label	Number	Year	Price	Notes
C'mon Let's Go	7"	Pye	7N25000	1958	**£15**	
Donna	7"	London	HL8803	1959	**£10**	chart single
Greatest Hits	LP	Del-Fi	1225	1963	**£40**	US
Greatest Hits	LP	London	HA8196	1964	**£15**	
Greatest Hits Vol.2	LP	Del-Fi	1247	1965	**£30**	US
I Remember Ritchie Valens	LP	President	PTL1001	1967	**£10**	
In Concert At Pacoima Jr.High	LP	Del-Fi	1214	1960	**£50**	US
La Bamba	7"	London	HL9494	1962	**£5**	
La Bamba	7"	Sue	WI4011	1966	**£8**	
Ritchie	LP	Del-Fi	1206	1959	**£40**	US
Ritchie	LP	London	HA2390	1961	**£25**	
Ritchie Valens	LP	Del-Fi	1201	1959	**£40**	US
Ritchie Valens	7" EP	London	RE1232	1959	**£20**	
Ritchie Valens	LP	MGM	GAS117	1970	**£10**	US
Rock Li'l Darlin'	LP	Joy	JOYS264	1973	**£10**	
That's My Little Suzie	7"	London	HL8886	1959	**£10**	

VALENTE, DINO

Title	Format	Label	Number	Year	Price	Notes
Dino	LP	CBS	65715	1968	**£15**	
Dino Valente	LP	CBS	63443	1968	**£30**	

VALENTINE, BILLY

Title	Format	Label	Number	Year	Price	Notes
It's A Sin	7"	Capitol	CL14320	1955	**£4**	

VALENTINE, HILTON

All In Your Head	LP	Capitol	ST330	1969	**£120**	US

VALENTINES

Hey Baby	7"	Ember	EMBS123	1960	**£4**	

VALENTINO

I Was Born This Way	7"	Gaiee	GAE101	1975	**£4**	

VALENTINO, ANNA

Calypso Joe	7"	London	HLD8421	1957	**£4**	

VALENTINO, DANNY

Biology	7"	MGM	MGM1067	1960	**£5**	
Stampede	7"	MGM	MGM1049	1959	**£10**	

VALENTINO, MARK

Do It	7"	Stateside	SS186	1963	**£4**	
Jiving At The Drive In	7"	Stateside	SS233	1963	**£5**	
Mark Valentino	LP	Swan	LP508	1963	**£15**	US
Push And Kick	7"	Stateside	SS148	1963	**£4**	

VALENTINOS

It's All Over Now	7"	Soul City	SC106		**£4**	
It's All Over Now	7"	Soul City	SC106		**£10**	demo
Raise Your Hand In Anger	7"	Polydor	2058090	1971	**£4**	

VALENTINOS & SIMS TWINS

Valentinos/The Sims Twins	LP	Soul City	SCM001	1968	**£15**	

VALERIE & THE ROCK 'N' ROLL YOUNGSTERS

Tonight You Belong To Me	7"	Columbia	DB3832	1956	**£4**	

VALINO, JOE

Garden Of Eden	7"	HMV	POP283	1957	**£4**	chart single
God's Little Acre	7"	London	HLT8705	1958	**£4**	

VALKYRIES

Rip It Up	7"	Parlophone	R5123	1964	**£8**	

VALLEY, JIM

Harpo	LP	Panorama	104	1969	**£20**	US

VALLI, FRANKIE

Proud One	7"	Philips	BF1529	1966	**£4**	
Solo	LP	Philips	SBL7814	1967	**£10**	
Timeless	LP	Philips	SBL7856	1969	**£10**	
You're Gonna Hurt Yourself	7"	Philips	BF1467	1966	**£5**	
You're Ready Now	7"	Philips	BF1512	1966	**£4**	

VALLI, FRANKIE & THE FOUR SEASONS

Night	7"	Mowest	MW3002	1972	**£4**	
Walk On, Don't Look Back	7"	Mowest	MW3003	1973	**£4**	
Whatever You Say	7"	W. Bros	K16107	1971	**£10**	
You're A Song	7"	T. Motown	TMG819	1972	**£4**	
You're A Song	7"	T. Motown	TMG819	1972	**£10**	demo

VALVES

Don't Mean Nothing At All	7"	Albion	DEL3	1979	**£4**	
Robot Love	7"	Zoom	ZUM1	1977	**£4**	
Tarzan Of The King's Road	7"	Zoom	ZUM3	1977	**£4**	

VAMP

Floatin'	LP	Atlantic			**£35**	
Floatin'	7"	Atlantic	584213	1968	**£8**	
Green Pea	7"	Atlantic	584263	1969	**£8**	

VAMPIRES

Do You Wanna Dance	7"	Pye	7N17553	1968	**£4**	
Swinging Ghosts	7"	Parlophone	R4599	1959	**£4**	

VAN DER GRAAF GENERATOR

Title	Format	Label	Number	Year	Price	Notes
Aerosol Grey Machine	LP	Fontana	6430083	1975	**£15**	
Aerosol Grey Machine	LP	Mercury	SR61238	1968	**£25**	US
Firebrand	7"	Polydor	56758	1968	**£120**	
Godbluff	LP	Charisma	CAS1109	1975	**£10**	
H To He Who Am The Only One	LP	Charisma	CAS1027	1970	**£12**	
Least We Can Do Is Wave	LP	Charisma	CAS1007	1969	**£20**	with poster, chart LP
Long Hello	LP	no label	no number	1973	**£50**	
Pawn Hearts	LP	Buddah		1971	**£15**	US, with 'Theme One'
Pawn Hearts	LP	Charisma	CAS1051	1971	**£12**	
Refugees	7"	Charisma	CB122	1970	**£35**	
Theme One	7"	Charisma	CB175	1972	**£25**	PS
Wondering	7"	Charisma	CB297	1976	**£8**	

VAN DYKE, EARL

Title	Format	Label	Number	Year	Price	Notes
All For You	7"	T. Motown	TMG506	1965	**£20**	
All For You	7"	T. Motown	TMG506	1965	**£50**	demo
Earl Of Funk	LP	Soul	SS715	1970	**£15**	US
I Can't Help Myself	7"	T. Motown	TMG814	1972	**£4**	
I Can't Help Myself	7"	T. Motown	TMG814	1972	**£15**	demo
Six By Six	7"	T. Motown	TMG759	1970	**£4**	
Six By Six	7"	T. Motown	TMG759	1970	**£15**	demo
Soul Stomp	7"	Stateside	SS357	1964	**£15**	
That Motown Sound	LP	T. Motown	TML11014	1965	**£25**	

VAN DYKE, LEROY

Title	Format	Label	Number	Year	Price	Notes
Big Man In A Big House	7"	Mercury	AMT1173	1962	**£4**	chart single
Broken Promise	7"	Mercury	AMT1183	1962	**£4**	
Walk On By	7"	Mercury	AMT1166	1961	**£4**	chart single

VAN DYKES

Title	Format	Label	Number	Year	Price	Notes
I've Gotta Go On Without You	7"	Stateside	SS530	1966	**£5**	
No Man Is An Island	7"	Stateside	SS504	1966	**£4**	
Tellin' It Like It Is	LP	Bell	6004	1967	**£10**	US

VAN EATON, LON & DERREK

Title	Format	Label	Number	Year	Price	Notes
Brother	LP	Apple	SAPCOR25	1973	**£15**	
Warm Woman	7"	Apple	46	1973	**£4**	
Warm Woman	7"	Apple	46	1973	**£10**	PS

VAN HALEN

Title	Format	Label	Number	Year	Price	Notes
And The Cradle Will Rock	7"	W. Bros	K17645	1980	**£4**	
Dance The Night Away	7"	W. Bros	K17371	1979	**£4**	
Dance The Night Away	7"	W. Bros	K17371	1979	**£6**	pic disc
Runnin' With The Devil	7"	W. Bros	K17162	1978	**£4**	
You Really Got Me	7"	W. Bros	K17107	1978	**£4**	

VAN RONK, DAVE

Title	Format	Label	Number	Year	Price	Notes
Ballads And Blues And Spirituals	LP	Folkways	F3818	1959	**£10**	US

VAN ZANDT, TOWNES

Title	Format	Label	Number	Year	Price	Notes
Delta Momma Blues	LP	Poppy	PYS40012	1971	**£10**	US
For The Sake Of A Song	LP	Poppy	PYS40001	1968	**£10**	US
High, Low And In Between	LP	Poppy	PYS5700	1971	**£10**	US
Late Great...	LP	United Artists	UAS29442	1973	**£10**	
Our Mother The Mountain	LP	Poppy	PYS40004	1969	**£10**	US
Townes Van Zandt	LP	Poppy	PYS40007	1970	**£10**	US

VAN, ILA

Title	Format	Label	Number	Year	Price	Notes
No Good Jim	7"	Patheway	104		**£5**	

VANCE, TOMMY

Title	Format	Label	Number	Year	Price	Notes
Off The Hook	7"	Columbia	DB8062	1966	**£8**	
You Must Be The One	7"	Columbia	DB7999	1966	**£5**	

VANILLA FUDGE

Title	Format	Label	Number	Year	Price	Notes
Beat Goes On	LP	Atlantic	587100	1968	**£10**	
Eleanor Rigby	7"	Atlantic	584139	1967	**£8**	
Near The Beginning	LP	Atlantic	228020	1969	**£10**	
Renaissance	LP	Atlantic	587110	1968	**£10**	
Rock'n'Roll	LP	Atlantic	288029	1970	**£10**	
Shotgun	7"	Atlantic	584257	1969	**£5**	

Some Velvet Morning	7"	Atlantic	584276	1969	**£4**	
Vanilla Fudge	LP	Atlantic	587086	1967	**£12**	chart LP
Where Is My Mind	7"	Atlantic	584179	1968	**£6**	
You Keep Me Hanging On	7"	Atlantic	584123	1967	**£4**	chart single

VANILLA, CHERRY

Punk	7"	RCA	PB5053	1977	**£4**	

VANITY FARE

The Sun, The Wind And Other Things	LP	Page One		1968	**£15**	

VARDIS

100 Mph	LP	Logo	MOGO4012	1980	**£10**	
All You'll Ever Need	7"	Logo	VAR4	1981	**£4**	
If I Were King	7"	Castle	QUEL2/100	1980	**£10**	
Let's Go	7"	Logo	VAR1	1980	**£4**	
Silver Machine	7"	Logo	VAR3	1981	**£4**	
Too Many People	7"	Logo	VAR2	1980	**£4**	

VARIATIONS

Man With All The Toys	7"	Immediate	IM019	1965	**£10**	

VARIOUS

Various Artist albums can become collectable for a number of reasons. Some contain tracks that are only available on that particular record. The most valuable of this sort is the "Glastonbury Fayre" triple album, which within its extravagant packing and multiple inserts contains material by artists like David Bowie, Marc Bolan, and the Grateful Dead, none of which has been released anywhere else. Other albums are on labels that are themselves collectable, like the various Tamla Motown anthologies, or the United Dairies compilation. Others simply seem to epitomise an area or era of music particularly well - the classic example here being the "Nuggets" double, which gathers together a number of the American groups whose music represents what was meant by "punk rock" in the sixties.

1968 Memphis Country Music Festival	LP	Blue Horizon	763210	1968	**£35**	
50 Minutes & 24 Seconds Of Recorded Dynamite	LP	Sue	ILP920	1965	**£20**	
Action Packed Soul	LP	Action	ACLP6005	1969	**£15**	
All For Art...And Art For All	LP	Whaam!	BIG8		**£20**	
All Good Clean Fun	LP	United Artists	UDX201/2	1971	**£12**	
All Star Hit Parade	7" EP	Pye	NEP24168	1962	**£4**	
All The Hits By All The Stars	LP	Golden Guin.	GGL0162	1962	**£10**	chart LP
All This And World War Two	LP	Riva	RVLP2	1977	**£20**	double
American Country Jubilee No.1	7" EP	Decca	DFE8571	1964	**£4**	
American Folk Blues Festival	LP	Fontana	TL5225	1965	**£15**	
Apollo Saturday Night	LP	London	HAK8174	1964	**£20**	
Astrology Album	LP	Columbia	CS2689	1967	**£15**	US
At The Cavern	LP	Decca	LK4597	1964	**£20**	
Atlantic Discotheque	LP	Atlantic	ATL5020	1965	**£12**	
Atlanticlassics	LP	Atlantic	AC3		**£40**	
Battle Of Bands	7"	Good Vibs.	GOT7	1978	**£6**	double
Be Stiff	LP	Stiff	ODD2	1978	**£12**	
Begin Here	LP	Elektra	EKS7262	1969	**£10**	
Best Of Golden Guinea	7" EP	Golden Guin.	7GG3	196-	**£4**	
Best Of Radio Luxembourg	LP	Golden Guin.	GGL0208	1962	**£10**	chart LP
Big Four	7" EP	Fontana	TE17469	1966	**£4**	
Big Four	7" EP	Philips	BBE12593	1966	**£4**	
Bitter End Years	LP	Roxbury	RX3300	1976	**£25**	US triple
Blackpool Nights	LP	Columbia	33SX1244	1960	**£15**	
Blue Beat Special	LP	Coxsone	CSP1	1968	**£80**	
Blues Anytime Vol.1	LP	Immediate	IMLP014	1968	**£12**	chart LP
Blues Anytime Vol.2	LP	Immediate	IMLP015	1968	**£12**	
Blues Anytime Vol.3	LP	Immediate	IMLP019	1968	**£12**	
Blues Came Down From Memphis	LP	London	HAS8265	1966	**£20**	
Blues Festival	7" EP	Pye	NEP44038	1964	**£6**	
Blues Leftovers	LP	Immediate	IMLP024	1969	**£10**	
Blues Like Showers Of Rain	LP	Matchbox	SDM142	196-	**£50**	
Blues Now	LP	Decca	LK4681	1965	**£25**	
Blues On Parade No.1	7" EP	Columbia	SEG8226	1963	**£5**	
Blues Vol.1	7" EP	Pye	NEP44029	1964	**£5**	
Blues Vol.1	LP	Pye	NPL28030	1964	**£12**	chart LP
Blues Vol.2	LP	Pye	NPL28035	1964	**£12**	chart LP
Blues Vol.2 Part 1	7" EP	Chess	CRE6011	1966	**£5**	
Blues Vol.3	LP	Pye	NPL28045	1964	**£12**	
Bob Dylan,Pete Seeger And Joan Baez	7" EP	Fontana	TFE18009	1965	**£40**	

Title	Format	Label	Cat. No.	Year	Price	Notes
Bob Dylan,Pete Seeger And Joan Baez	7" EP	Fontana	TFE18010	1965	**£40**	
Bob Dylan,Pete Seeger And Joan Baez	7" EP	Fontana	TFE18011	1965	**£40**	
Bristol Recorder Vol.2	LP	Bristol Rec.	BR002	1981	**£40**	
British Blue-Eyed Soul	LP	Island	ILPS9066	1968	**£20**	
Brumbeat	LP	Dial	DLP1		**£50**	
Bumpa Bundle	LP	Decca	LK4734	1965	**£15**	
Busted At Oz	LP	Autumn	AU2	1981	**£25**	
Calypso Time	7" EP	Melodisc	EPM767	195-	**£5**	
Cameo Big Four	7" EP	Cameo Park	CPE552	1963	**£5**	
Club Rock Steady '68	LP	Island	ILP965	1968	**£40**	
Club Ska '67	LP	Island	ILP948	1967	**£40**	chart LP
Club Ska '67 Vol.2	LP	Island	ILP956	1967	**£40**	
Club Soul	LP	Island	ILP964	1968	**£20**	
Collection Of 16 Big Hits Vol.6	LP	T. Motown	STML11074	1968	**£15**	chart LP
Collection Of 16 Original Big Hits Vol.4	LP	T. Motown	TML11043	1967	**£20**	chart LP
Collection Of 16 Original Big Hits Vol.5	LP	T. Motown	TML11050	1967	**£15**	chart LP
Collection Of 16 Tamla Motown Hits	LP	T. Motown	TML11001	1965	**£20**	chart LP
Collection Of Big Hits Vol.7	LP	T. Motown	STML11092	1969	**£12**	
Come Fly With Me	LP	Blue Beat	BBLP803	196-	**£50**	
Communicate!!!! Live At Thames Poly	LP	TPSU	TPSU0001	1985	**£12**	double
Country And Western Spectacular	7" EP	Philips	BBE12149	1957	**£6**	
Country And Western Trail Blazers No.1	7" EP	Mercury	ZEP10038	1959	**£4**	
Country Guitar Vol.10	7" EP	RCA	RCX176	1959	**£4**	
Country Guitar Vol.2	7" EP	RCA	RCX110	1958	**£4**	
Country Guitar Vol.9	7" EP	RCA	RCX159	1959	**£4**	
Crab - Biggest Hits	LP	Pama	ECO2	1969	**£20**	
Daleks	7" EP	Century 21	MA106	1966	**£10**	
Dark Muddy Bottom	7" EP	XX	MIN706		**£5**	
Desperate Intruder	7" EP	Century 21	MA119	1967	**£6**	
Devastate To Liberate	LP	YANGKI	1	1985	**£10**	
Dimension Of Miracles	LP	Mercury	6641006	1970	**£12**	double
Discs A Go Go	7" EP	Decca	DFE8520	1962	**£10**	
Doctor Soul	LP	Island	ILP943	1967	**£20**	
Down Home Blues - Sixties Style	7" EP	Jan & Dil	JR450		**£5**	
Downhome Harp	7" EP	XX	MIN709		**£4**	
Dr.Kitch	LP	Island	ILP954	1967	**£60**	
Drumbeat	7" EP	Fontana	TFE17146	1959	**£8**	
Drumbeat	LP	Parlophone	PMC1101	1959	**£20**	
Duke And The Peacock	LP	Island	ILP976	1968	**£50**	
Duke Reid's Rock Steady	LP	Island	ILP958	1967	**£60**	
E.S.C.A. EP	7" EP	Edinburgh S.C.	ESC02	1965	**£20**	
E.S.C.A. EP	7" EP	Edinburgh S.C.	ESC03	1966	**£20**	
Earcom 2	12"	Fast	EARCOM2	1979	**£15**	
Electric Blues	LP	Chess	109597/8/9	1969	**£25**	German, 3 LPs in metal box
Electric Muse	LP	Island/Trans	FOLK1001	1975	**£35**	4 LP set
Europe In The Year Zero	12"	Sexual Ph.	SPH1	1982	**£6**	
European Song Cup 1963	7" EP	Decca	DFE8534	1963	**£4**	
Excello Story	LP	Blue Horizon	2683007	1972	**£20**	
Extracts From Stiff's Greatest Hits	7"	Stiff	FREEBIE2	1978	**£20**	
Festival Of The Blues Vol.1	7" EP	Pye	NEP44030	1964	**£5**	
Fifty-two Stations	7"	Albion	FREEBIE	1982	**£10**	square flexi
Fillmore Last Days	LP	W. Bros	K66013	1972	**£35**	boxed set, with booklet, ticket, poster
Fillmore Last Days	LP	W. Bros	K66013	1972	**£50**	promo boxed set with interview single
Fings Ain't Wot They Used To Be	LP	HMV	CLP1358	1960	**£15**	
Firepoint	LP	Spark	SRLM2003	1969	**£20**	
First Fifteen Minutes	7"	Neutron	NT003	1980	**£5**	
Flex Your Head	LP	Alt. Tentacles	VIRUS22	1982	**£10**	
Folk Box	LP	Elektra	EUK251/2	1966	**£15**	double
Folk Festival Of The Blues	LP	Pye	NPL28033	1964	**£15**	chart LP
Fool Brittania	7" EP	Ember	EP4530	1963	**£4**	
Four Of The Tops	7" EP	Pye	NEP24300	1968	**£4**	
Fourteen	LP	Decca	LK4695	1965	**£15**	
Fresh From The Can	LP	Polydor	2675004	1970	**£25**	German, 3 LPs in metal box
Gas - Greatest Hits	LP	Pama	ECO4	1969	**£20**	
Get Ready Rock Steady	LP	Coxsone	CSL8007	196-	**£80**	
Gift From Pama	LP	Pama	SECO20	1970	**£20**	

Title	Format	Label	Cat. No.	Year	Price	Notes
Give Him My Regards	7" EP	Columbia	SEG8495	1966	**£6**	
Glastonbury Fayre	LP	Revelation	REV1	1974	**£90**	triple, 4 inserts
Go	LP	Columbia	SX6062	1966	**£12**	
Goin' Up The Country	LP	Decca	LK4931	1968	**£10**	
Gonks Go Beat	LP	Decca	LK4673	1965	**£50**	
Good Time Music	LP	Elektra	EUKS7260	1967	**£12**	
Grand Old Fifties	LP	Atlantic	ATL5004	1964	**£12**	
Greasy Truckers Live At Dingwalls	LP	G. Truckers	GT4997	1973	**£20**	double
Greasy Truckers Party	LP	United Artists	UDX203/4	1974	**£20**	double
Great Country And Western Hits	7" EP	Philips	BBE12318	1959	**£4**	
Greatest On Stage	7" EP	Pye	NEP44054	1966	**£5**	
Groovy Baby	LP	Direction	863452	1968	**£12**	
Group Beat '63	LP	Realm	RM149	1963	**£20**	
Group Of Goodies	LP	London	HAU8086	1963	**£10**	
Group Of Goodies	7" EP	London	REU1393	1963	**£5**	
Groups Galore	7" EP	Mercury	ZEP10010	1959	**£25**	
Gutbucket	LP	Liberty	LBX3	1969	**£10**	
Guy Stevens' Testament Of Rock'n'Roll	LP	Island	ILP977	1968	**£20**	
Hallucinations Off 2 - Psychedelic Underground	LP	Elektra/Met.	KMLP310	1969	**£20**	German pic disc
Headline News	LP	Polydor	582701	1966	**£15**	
Heads Together, First Round	LP	Vertigo	6360045	1971	**£10**	spiral label
Here Come The Girls	LP	Pye	NPL18121	1965	**£10**	
History Of R&B Vol.1	LP	Atlantic			**£10**	
History Of R&B Vol.2	LP	Atlantic			**£10**	
History Of R&B Vol.3	LP	Atlantic	587096	1968	**£10**	
History Of R&B Vol.4	LP	Atlantic	587097	1968	**£10**	
History Of R&B Vol.5	LP	Atlantic	587140	1968	**£10**	
History Of R&B Vol.6	LP	Atlantic	587141	1968	**£10**	
Hit Makers	7" EP	Pye	NEP24241	1966	**£4**	
Hit Parade Vol.2	7" EP	Mercury	MEP9510	1956	**£8**	
Hit The Road Stax	LP	Stax	589005	1967	**£15**	chart LP
Hitmakers	LP	Marble Arch	MAL1259	1970	**£10**	
Hitmakers No.1	7" EP	Pye	NEP24213	1965	**£4**	
Hitmakers No.2	7" EP	Pye	NEP24214	1965	**£6**	
Hitmakers No.3	7" EP	Pye	NEP24215	1965	**£4**	
Hitmakers Vol.2	7" EP	Pye	NEP24242	1966	**£4**	
Hits And Corruption	LP	Hits & Corr.	HAC1	1986	**£12**	with cassette
Hits Vol.1	7" EP	Decca	DFE8648	1965	**£4**	
Hits Vol.2	7" EP	Decca	DFE8649	1965	**£4**	
Hits Vol.3	7" EP	Decca	DFE8653	1965	**£5**	
Hits Vol.5	7" EP	Decca	DFE8663	1966	**£4**	
Hits Vol.6	7" EP	Decca	DFE8667	1966	**£4**	
Hitsville	7" EP	Mercury	ZEP10133	1962	**£8**	
Hitsville USA	LP	T. Motown	TML11019	1965	**£15**	
Hitsville USA No.1	7" EP	T. Motown	TME2001	1965	**£15**	
Hitsville Vol.1	7" EP	Coral	FEP2034	1959	**£10**	
Hitsville Vol.2	7" EP	Coral	FEP2035	1959	**£5**	
Hitsville!	LP	Golden Guin.	GGL0202	1962	**£10**	chart LP
Hoisting The Black Flag	LP	United Dairies	UD06	1981	**£60**	
Hope And Anchor Front Row Festival	LP	W. Bros	WB66077	1978	**£15**	double
House That Track Built	LP	Track	613016	1969	**£10**	
How Blue Can We Get	LP	Blue Horizon	PR45/46	1970	**£15**	double
Ideal Home Sampler	7" EP	Golden Guin.	7GG4	196-	**£4**	
Imposters	7" EP	Century 21	MA120	1967	**£6**	
In Crowd	7" EP	Chess	CRE6010	1966	**£4**	
In Loving Memory	LP	T. Motown	STML11124	1969	**£25**	
In Our Own Way/Oldies But Goodies	LP	Blue Horizon	PR37	1969	**£10**	
Industrial Records Story	LP	Illuminated	JAMS39	1984	**£25**	
Into Action With Roy Tempest	7" EP	Century 21	MA101	1966	**£4**	
Isle Of Wight/Atlanta Festival	LP	CBS	66311	1971	**£25**	triple
It's All Happening	LP	Columbia	SCX3486	1963	**£12**	
It's Cha Cha Time	7" EP	Mercury	ZEP10001	1959	**£5**	
It's Trad Dad	LP	Columbia	33SX1412	1962	**£20**	chart LP
Jack Good's Oh Boy!	LP	Parlophone	PMC1072	1958	**£30**	chart LP
Jackpot Of Hits	LP	Amalgam.	CSP3	196-	**£40**	
Jazz Explosion	LP	Columbia	SLJS1	1969	**£10**	
John Peel Presents Top Gear	LP	BBC	REC52S	1969	**£20**	
Just For Fun	LP	Decca	LK4524	1963	**£20**	chart LP
Just For Kicks	LP	CBS			**£15**	Irish
Kings Of The Blues Vol.1	7" EP	RCA	RCX202	1961	**£5**	

Title	Format	Label	Cat. No.	Year	Price	Notes
Kings Of The Blues Vol.2	7" EP	RCA	RCX203	1961	**£5**	
Kings Of The Blues Vol.3	7" EP	RCA	RCX204	1961	**£5**	
Label - Sofa	LP	The Label	TRLP002	1979	**£10**	
Label - Sofa	LP	The Label	TRLP002S	1979	**£35**	pic disc
Let Me Tell You About The Blues	LP	Blue Horizon	LP2	1966	**£30**	
Let Them Eat Jellybeans	LP	Alt. Tentacles	VIRUS4	1981	**£10**	
Let's Go	7" EP	Top Rank	JKR8008	1959	**£4**	
Let's Go Vol.2	7" EP	Top Rank	JKR8012	1959	**£4**	
Liberty/United Artists Sampler	LP	United Artists	REP102	1971	**£30**	promo
Live In The Living Room	LP	Creation	CRELP001	198-	**£12**	
Liverpool Beat	LP	Embassy	WLP6065	1964	**£15**	
London Hit Parade Vol.1	7" EP	London	RED1075	1957	**£6**	
London Hit Parade Vol.2	7" EP	London	REP1096	1957	**£12**	
London Hit Parade Vol.3	7" EP	London	RED1097	1958	**£6**	
London Hit Parade Vol.4	7" EP	London	RED1130	1958	**£4**	
London Hit Parade Vol.5	7" EP	London	RED1145	1958	**£4**	
Lonely Is An Eyesore	LP	4AD	CAD703D	1987	**£15**	cardboard package, book
Lonely Is An Eyesore	Spec.	4AD	CADX703	1987	**£150**	wooden box, etching, screen print, CD, video, cassette
Marmalade 100% Proof	LP	Marmalade	643314	1969	**£10**	
Memories Are Made Of Hits Vol.1	LP	London	HA8129	1964	**£12**	
Memories Are Made Of Hits Vol.2	LP	London	HA8130	1964	**£12**	
Memories Are Made Of Hits Vol.3	LP	London	HA8131	1964	**£12**	
Memories Are Made Of Hits Vol.4	LP	London	HA8138	1964	**£12**	
Memories Are Made Of Hits Vol.5	LP	London	HA8148	1964	**£12**	
Memories Are Made Of Hits Vol.6	LP	London	HA8171	1964	**£12**	
Memories Are Made Of Hits Vol.7	LP	London	HA8189	1964	**£10**	
Memories Are Made Of Hits Vol.8	LP	London	HA8213	1965	**£10**	
Merry Christmas From Motown	LP	T. Motown	STML11126	1969	**£10**	
MGM Evergreens	7" EP	MGM	MGMEP749	1960	**£5**	
Midnight Soul	LP	Atlantic	587021	1966	**£12**	chart LP
Mill Valley Jam Session	LP	Polydor		1972	**£15**	
Million-Airs	LP	Coral	LVA9126	1960	**£15**	
More American Graffiti	LP	MCA		1979	**£15**	US, promo pic disc, 4 different B sides
More Down Home Blues	7" EP	Jan & Dil	JR451		**£4**	
Morris On	LP	Island	HELP5	1972	**£12**	
Motortown Revue	LP	T. Motown	TML11007	1965	**£40**	
Motortown Revue Live	LP	T. Motown	STML11127	1970	**£10**	
Motortown Revue Live In Paris	LP	T. Motown	TML11027	1966	**£20**	
Motown Chartbusters Vol.9	LP	T. Motown	STML11270	1974	**£10**	lime green vinyl
Motown Magic	LP	T. Motown	TML11030	1966	**£15**	
Motown Memories	LP	T. Motown	TML11064	1968	**£25**	chart LP
Motown Memories Vol.2	LP	T. Motown	TML11077	1968	**£20**	
Motown Memories Vol.3	LP	T. Motown	STML11143	1970	**£15**	
Motown Story - The First 25 Years	LP	T. Motown	TMSP6019	1983	**£20**	boxed set
Motown Story	LP	T. Motown	TMSP1130	1972	**£20**	boxed set, chart LP
Murderer's Home	LP	Pye	NJL11	1957	**£15**	
Murderer's Home (Part 1)	7" EP	Pye	NJE1062	1957	**£5**	
Murderer's Home (Part 2)	7" EP	Pye	NJE1063	1957	**£5**	
Murderer's Home (Part 3)	7" EP	Pye	NJE1064	1957	**£5**	
Murderer's Home (Part 4)	7" EP	Pye	NJE1065	1957	**£5**	
Music And Rhythm	LP	WEA	K68045	1982	**£12**	double
Music From Free Creek	LP	Charisma	CADS101	1973	**£20**	double
Natures Mortes - Still Lives	LP	4AD	CAD117	1981	**£35**	
New Faces From Hitsville	7" EP	T. Motown	TME2014	1966	**£15**	
Newport Broadside	LP	Fontana	TFL6038	1965	**£15**	
Newport Folk Festival Evening Concert Vol.1	LP	Fontana	TFL6041	1965	**£15**	
Newport Folk Festival Vol.1	LP	Fontana	TFL6050	1965	**£15**	
Nixa Hit Parade Vol.1	7" EP	Pye	NEP24052	1957	**£4**	
Nixa Hit Parade Vol.2	7" EP	Pye	NEP24064	1958	**£4**	
Nixa Hit Parade Vol.3	7" EP	Pye	NEP24071	1958	**£4**	
No Wave	LP	A&M	PR4738	1978	**£15**	US, pic disc
No-one's Gonna Change Our World	LP	Regal S.	SRS5013	1970	**£12**	
Noise Fest	cass	ZG Music	No.5	1982	**£10**	
Nothing But The Blues	LP	CBS	66278	1971	**£15**	double
Nova Sampler	LP	Nova/Decca	SPA72	1970	**£15**	
Nubeat - Greatest Hits	LP	Pama	ECO6	1969	**£20**	

Title	Format	Label	Number	Year	Price	Notes
Nuggets	LP	Elektra	K62012	1972	**£30**	double
Oh No It's More From Raw	LP	Raw	RAWLP2	1978	**£15**	
On Stage	LP	Stateside	SL10065	1963	**£40**	
On The Scene	LP	Columbia	33SX1662	1964	**£15**	
On The Scene	7" EP	Columbia	SEG8413	1965	**£8**	
One More Chance	LP	Charisma	CLASS3	1973	**£12**	
Original Hits	LP	London	HAG2308	1960	**£10**	
Original Hits	7" EP	London	REK1390	1963	**£5**	
Original Hits	7" EP	MGM	MGMEP787	1963	**£6**	
Original Hits Vol.2	7" EP	Atlantic	AET6006	1965	**£5**	
Original Hits Vol.2	LP	London	HAG2339	1961	**£10**	
Original Rhythm And Blues Hits	7" EP	Ember	EMB4522	1962	**£6**	
Ossiach Live	LP	BASF	49211193	1971	**£25**	German
Package Tour	LP	Golden Guin.	GGL0268	1963	**£25**	
Pakistani Soul Session	LP	Island	ILP945	1967	**£20**	
Phantom Of The Opera	CD	Polydor		1987	**£20**	4 track promo
Picnic	LP	Harvest	SHSS1/2	1970	**£12**	double
Presages	mini LP	4AD	BAD11	1980	**£10**	
Pure Blues Vol.1	LP	Sue	ILP919	1965	**£20**	
Put It On, It's Rock Steady	LP	Island	ILP978	1968	**£50**	
R&B Chartmakers	7" EP	Stateside	SE1009	1964	**£20**	
R&B Chartmakers No.2	7" EP	Stateside		1964	**£20**	
R&B Chartmakers No.3	7" EP	Stateside	SE1022	1964	**£20**	
R&B Chartmakers No.4	7" EP	Stateside	SE1025	1964	**£20**	
Raindrops Pattering On Banana Leaves	LP	WOMAD	WOMAD001	1984	**£12**	
Rare Tracks	LP	Polydor	2482274	1975	**£10**	
Raw Blues	LP	Ace Of Clubs	ACL1220	1967	**£15**	
Ready Steady Go	LP	Decca	LK4577	1964	**£20**	chart LP
Ready Steady Win	LP	Decca	LK4634	1964	**£25**	
Red Bird Goldies	LP	Red Bird	RB20102	1965	**£30**	
Reggae Hits '69 Vol.1	LP	Pama	ECO3	1969	**£20**	
Reggae Hits '69 Vol.2	LP	Pama	ECO11	1969	**£20**	
Revolution	LP	United Artists	SULP1226	1967	**£10**	
Revolution	LP	United Artists	UAS29069	1969	**£15**	
Rhythm & Blues	LP	Decca	LK4616	1964	**£30**	
Rhythm & Blues	LP	Golden Guin.	GGL0351	1965	**£10**	
Rhythm & Blues	LP	Golden Guin.	GGL0280	1963	**£10**	
Rhythm & Blues All Stars	LP	Golden Guin.	GGL0293	1963	**£10**	
Rhythm & Blues Showcase Vol.1	7" EP	Pye	NEP44021	1964	**£5**	
Rhythm & Blues Showcase Vol.2	7" EP	Pye	NEP44022	1964	**£6**	
Ric Tic Relics	LP	T. Motown	STML11232	1973	**£10**	
Rock And Roll	7" EP	Vogue	VE170111	195-	**£25**	
Rock'N'Roll	LP-10"	London	HBC1067	1957	**£15**	
Rock'n'Roll Forever	LP	London	HAE2180	1959	**£20**	
Rock, Rock, Rock	LP	Chess	LP1425	1957	**£50**	US
Rock-A-Hits	LP	London	HAA2338	1961	**£10**	
Rockin' Together	LP	London	HAE2167	1959	**£15**	
Round Up	7" EP	Capitol	EAP120197	1962	**£5**	
Saturday Club	LP	Decca	LK4583	1964	**£20**	
Saturday Club	LP	Parlophone	PMC1130	1960	**£30**	
Saturday Night At The Apollo	LP	Atlantic	590007	1966	**£10**	
Scandal In A Brixton Market	LP	Pama	ECO8	1969	**£20**	
Scene '65	LP	Columbia	33SX1730	1965	**£15**	
Shades Of Gospel Soul	LP	Motown	MS701	1969	**£15**	US
Shake, Rattle And Roll	LP	Atlantic	587109	1968	**£10**	
Short Circuit - Live At The Electric Circus	LP-10"	Virgin	VCL5003	1978	**£12**	blue vinyl
Short Circuit - Live At The Electric Circus	LP-10"	Virgin	VCL5003	1978	**£50**	orange vinyl
Short Circuit - Live At The Electric Circus	LP-10"	Virgin	VCL5003	1978	**£40**	yellow vinyl
Singing The Blues	7" EP	London	REP1403	1963	**£12**	
Sire Machine Turns You Up	LP	Sire	SMP1	1978	**£10**	
Ska at The Jamaican Playboy Club	LP	Island	ILP930	1966	**£60**	
Skiffle	LP	Ace Of Clubs	ACL1250	1967	**£20**	
Solid Gold Soul	LP	Atlantic	ATL5048	1966	**£12**	chart LP
Some Bizarre Album	LP	Some Bizarre	BZLP1	1981	**£12**	
Sometimes A Great Notion	LP	EMI	TOPCAT1	1984	**£12**	
Son Of Gutbucket	LP	Liberty	LBX4	1969	**£10**	
Soul '66	LP	Sue	ILP934	1966	**£20**	
Soul Deep Vol.1	LP	Contempo	CLP526	1975	**£10**	
Sound Of The R&B Hits	LP	Stateside	SL10077	1964	**£40**	
Sound Of The Stars	7"	Lyntone	LYN995	1966	**£15**	Disc And Music Echo flexi
Southend Rock	LP	Sonet	SNTF806	1979	**£10**	

Star Souvenir Greetings	7"	208 Radio L.		196-	**£20**	flexi
Stars Of Liberty	LP	Liberty	LBY1001	1960	**£10**	
Stars Of the 6.5 Special	LP	Decca	LF1299	1958	**£20**	
Stax/Volt Tour In London Vol.1	LP	Stax	589010	1967	**£15**	
Stax/Volt Tour In London Vol.2	LP	Stax	589011	1967	**£15**	
Streets	LP	Beggars B.	BEGA1	1977	**£10**	
Sue Story	LP	Sue	ILP925	1965	**£20**	
Sue Story Vol.2	LP	Sue	ILP933	1966	**£20**	
Sue Story Vol.3	LP	Sue	ILP938	1966	**£20**	
Super Duper Blues	LP	Blue Horizon	PR31	1969	**£10**	
Swamp Blues	LP	Blue Horizon	766263	1970	**£30**	double
Take Off Your Head And Listen	LP	Rubber	LP001	1971	**£10**	
Take Six	7" EP	Oriole	EP7080	1964	**£15**	
Tartan Album	LP	REL Records	RELP466	1979	**£10**	tartan vinyl
Tear It Up	7" EP	Mercury	ZEP10015	1959	**£40**	
Teen Scene '64	7" EP	Ember	EMB4540	1964	**£8**	
Teenage Rock	LP	Capitol	T1009	1958	**£30**	
Teenage Rock	7" EP	Mercury	MEP9522	1957	**£10**	
Thank Your Lucky Stars	LP	Golden Guin.	GGL0190	1962	**£10**	
Thank Your Lucky Stars Vol.2	LP	Decca	LK4554	1963	**£20**	
That's Underground	LP	CBS	SPR23	1970	**£15**	German, multi-coloured vinyl
These Kind Of Blues Vol.1	LP	Action	ACLP6009	1969	**£15**	
They Sold A Million No.11	7" EP	Brunswick	OE9427	1959	**£8**	
This Is Blue Beat	LP	Island	ILP910	1964	**£50**	
This Is Merseybeat Vol.1	LP	Oriole	PS40047	1963	**£50**	chart LP
This Is Merseybeat Vol.2	LP	Oriole	PS40048	1963	**£50**	
Tighten Up	LP	Trojan	TBL120	1969	**£10**	
To The Shores Of Lake Placid	LP	Zoo	ZOO4	1982	**£10**	
Top 10 Hits By Original Artists	LP	Golden Guin.	GGL0277	1963	**£10**	
Top Teen Dances	7" EP	Stateside	SE1004	1963	**£5**	
Tops In Pops No.1	7" EP	Decca	DFE6411	1957	**£5**	
Tribute To Woody Guthrie pt.1	LP	CBS	64861	1972	**£10**	
Trip To Marineville	7" EP	Century 21	MA102	1966	**£10**	
Troublemakers	LP	W. Bros	PROA857	1981	**£35**	promo double
TV Themes	7" EP	Decca	DFE8585	1964	**£5**	
TV21 Themes	7" EP	Century 21	MA105	1966	**£10**	
Twist At The Star Club	LP	Philips	BL7578	1963	**£20**	
Twist On	7" EP	Starlite	STEP29	196-	**£10**	
Unity's Great Reggae Hits	LP	Pama	ECO7	1969	**£20**	
(Unknown Title)	7" EP	Mercury	MEP9003	1956	**£8**	
(Unknown Title)	7"	T. Motown	TMG956-975	1975	**£100**	demo, boxed
(Unknown Title)	7"	T. Motown	TMG1000	1975	**£100**	demo, boxed
(Unknown Title)	7" EP	Track	2094011		**£4**	
(Unknown Title)	LP	Treasure Isle	TI101	1966	**£60**	
Urban Development	cass	Pungent	PUN1		**£15**	
Vault Of Death	7" EP	Century 21	MA118	1967	**£6**	
Vertigo Annual 1970	LP	Vertigo	6499407/8	1970	**£15**	double
Walking The Blues	LP	Pye	NPL28044	1964	**£12**	
Walls Ice Cream Presents	7" EP	Apple	CT1	1969	**£40**	
We Sing The Blues	LP	London	HAP8061	1963	**£12**	
We Sing The Blues	LP	Sue	ILP921	1965	**£20**	
What's Shakin'	LP	Elektra	EUK260	1966	**£15**	
Woodstock	CD	MFSL	MFCD4816	198-	**£90**	4 discs
World Of Blues	LP	London	HAP8099	1963	**£15**	
Wowie Zowie	LP	Decca	SPA34	1969	**£10**	chart LP
Yes L.A.	LP	Dangerhouse	EW79	1979	**£30**	1 sided clear pic disc
You're Either On The Train....	LP	Stiff	DEAL1	1978	**£15**	promo
Your Chess Requests	7" EP	Chess	CRE6026	1968	**£5**	
Your Choice	7" EP	Mercury	MEP9525	1957	**£8**	

VASHTI

Some Things Just Stick In Your Mind	7"	Decca	F12157	1965	**£8**	
Train Song	7"	Columbia	DB7917	1966	**£5**	

VASSY, KIN

That's The Bag I'm In	7"	UNI	UN506	1969	**£4**	

VEDDAR, CHUCK

Spanky Boy	7"	London	HLU8951	1959	**£8**	

VEE, BOBBY

Title	Format	Label	Cat. No.	Year	Price	Notes
Bobby Tomorrow	7"	Liberty	LIB55530	1963	**£4**	chart single
Bobby Vee Meets The Ventures	7" EP	Liberty	LEP2212	1965	**£6**	
Bobby Vee No.1	7" EP	London	REG1278	1961	**£6**	
Bobby Vee No.2	7" EP	London	REG1299	1961	**£6**	
Bobby Vee No.3	7" EP	London	REG1308	1961	**£6**	
Bobby Vee No.4	7" EP	London	REG1323	1961	**£6**	
Bobby Vee's Biggest Hits	7" EP	Liberty	LEP2102	1963	**£6**	
Bobby Vee's Biggest Hits	7" EP	Liberty	SLEP2102	1963	**£8**	stereo
Buddy's Song	7"	Liberty	LIB10141	1963	**£5**	
Come Back When You Grow Up	7"	Liberty	LBF15016	1967	**£4**	
Devil Or Angel	7"	London	HLG9179	1960	**£6**	
Do What You Gotta Do	LP	Liberty	LBL83130	1968	**£10**	
Electric Trains And You	7"	Liberty	LBF15305	1970	**£4**	
Forever Kind Of Love	7"	Liberty	LIB10046	1962	**£4**	chart single
Forever Kind Of Love	7" EP	Liberty	LEP2089	1963	**£6**	
Golden Greats	LP	Liberty	LBY1112	1962	**£10**	chart LP
Hickory, Dick And Dock	7"	Liberty	LIB55700	1964	**£4**	
Hits Of The Rockin' Fifties	7" EP	London	REG1324	1961	**£8**	
Hits Of The Rockin' Fifties	LP	London	HAG2406	1961	**£15**	chart LP
How Many Tears	7"	London	HLG9389	1961	**£5**	chart single
I Remember Buddy Holly	LP	Liberty	LBY1188	1963	**£12**	
I'm Gonna Make It Up To You	7"	Liberty	LBF15234	1969	**£4**	
I'm Looking For Someone To Love	7"	Liberty	LBF15178	1969	**£4**	
Just Today	LP	Liberty	LBL83112	1968	**£10**	
Keep On Trying	7"	Liberty	LIB10197	1965	**£4**	
Like You've Never Known Before	7"	Liberty	LIB10272	1967	**£4**	
Live On Tour	LP	Liberty	LBY1263	1965	**£12**	
Look At Me Girl	LP	Liberty	LBY1341	1966	**£10**	
Look At Me Girl	7"	Liberty	LIB55877	1966	**£4**	
Love's Made A Fool Of You	7"	London	HLG9459	1961	**£5**	
Maybe Just Today	7"	Liberty	LBF15058	1968	**£4**	
Meets The Crickets	LP	Liberty	LBY1086	1962	**£12**	chart LP
Meets The Ventures	LP	Liberty	LBY1147	1963	**£15**	
Merry Christmas From Bobby Vee	LP	Liberty	LRP3267	1962	**£10**	US
More Than I Can Say	7"	London	HLG9316	1961	**£4**	chart single
New Sound From England	LP	Liberty	LRP3352	1964	**£10**	US
New Sounds	7" EP	Liberty	LEP2181	1964	**£6**	
Night Has A Thousand Eyes	LP	Liberty	LBY1139	1963	**£10**	chart LP
Night Has A Thousand Eyes	7"	Liberty	LIB10069	1963	**£4**	chart single
Nothing Like A Sunny Day	LP	United Artists	UAG29457	1973	**£10**	
Please Don't Ask About Barbara	7"	Liberty	LIB55419	1962	**£4**	chart single
Recording Session	LP	Liberty	LBY1084	1962	**£10**	chart LP
Rubber Ball	LP	London	HAG2352	1961	**£12**	
Rubber Ball	7"	London	HLG9255	1961	**£5**	chart single
Run Like The Devil	7"	Liberty	LIB55828	1965	**£4**	
Run To Him	7"	Liberty	LIB55388	1962	**£4**	
Run To Him	7"	London	HLG9470	1961	**£5**	chart single
Sharing You	7"	Liberty	LIB55451	1962	**£4**	chart single
Sincerely	7" EP	Liberty	LEP2053	1962	**£6**	
Sings Your Favourites	LP	London	HAG2320	1961	**£15**	
Stranger In Your Arms	7"	Liberty	LIB10124	1963	**£4**	
Sweet Sweetheart	7"	Liberty	LBF15420	1970	**£4**	
Take Good Care Of My Baby	LP	Liberty	LBY1004	1961	**£10**	
Take Good Care Of My Baby	7"	Liberty	LBF15096	1968	**£4**	
Take Good Care Of My Baby	LP	London	HAG2428	1961	**£12**	chart LP
Take Good Care Of My Baby	7"	London	HLG9438	1961	**£5**	
Thirty Big Hits From The 60s	LP	Liberty	LRP3385	1964	**£12**	chart single
True Love Never Runs Smooth	7"	Liberty	LIB10213	1965	**£4**	
With Strings And Things	LP	London	HAG2374	1961	**£10**	mono
With Strings And Things	LP	London	SAHG6174	1961	**£10**	stereo
Woman In My Life	7"	Liberty	LBF15370	1970	**£4**	

VEGA, SUZANNE

Title	Format	Label	Cat. No.	Year	Price	Notes
Left Of Center	CD-s	A&M	CDQ320	1986	**£15**	

VEJTABLES

Title	Format	Label	Cat. No.	Year	Price	Notes
I Still Love You	7"	Pye	7N25339	1965	**£5**	

VELEZ, MARTHA

Title	Format	Label	Cat. No.	Year	Price	Notes
Boogie Kitchen	7"	Blue Horizon	2096010	1972	**£5**	

Title	Format	Label	Number	Year	Price	Notes
Fiends And Angels	LP	London	SHK8395	1969	**£15**	
Fiends And Angels Again	LP	Blue Horizon	763867	1970	**£25**	
It Takes A Lot To Laugh	7"	London	HLK10266	1966	**£5**	
Tell Mama	7"	London	HLK10280	1969	**£5**	

VELOURS

Title	Format	Label	Number	Year	Price	Notes
I'm Gonna Change	7"	MGM	2006603	1977	**£4**	

VELVELETTES

Title	Format	Label	Number	Year	Price	Notes
He Was Really Sayin' Something	7"	Stateside	SS387	1965	**£20**	
He Was Really Sayin' Something	7"	Stateside	SS387	1965	**£50**	demo
Lonely Lonely Girl Am I	7"	T. Motown	TMG521	1965	**£20**	
Lonely Lonely Girl Am I	7"	T. Motown	TMG521	1965	**£50**	demo
Needle In A Haystack	7"	Stateside	SS361	1964	**£20**	
Needle In A Haystack	7"	Stateside	SS361	1964	**£50**	demo
Needle In A Haystack	7"	T. Motown	TMG595	1967	**£8**	
Needle In A Haystack	7"	T. Motown	TMG595	1967	**£40**	demo
Needle In A Haystack	7"	T. Motown	TMG806	1972	**£4**	
Needle In A Haystack	7"	T. Motown	TMG806	1972	**£10**	demo
These Things Keep Me Loving You	7"	T. Motown	TMG580	1966	**£12**	
These Things Keep Me Loving You	7"	T. Motown	TMG580	1966	**£50**	demo
These Things Keep Me Loving You	7"	T. Motown	TMG780	1971	**£4**	chart single
These Things Keep Me Loving You	7"	T.Motown	TMG780	1971	**£15**	demo

VELVET OPERA

Title	Format	Label	Number	Year	Price	Notes
Anna Dance Square	7"	CBS	4189	1969	**£5**	
Black Jack Davy	7"	CBS	4802	1970	**£4**	
Ride A Hustler's Dream	LP	CBS	63692	1969	**£25**	

VELVET UNDERGROUND

Title	Format	Label	Number	Year	Price	Notes
Candy Says	7"	MGM	2006283	1973	**£8**	
Loaded	LP	Atlantic	2400111	1970	**£10**	
Squeeze	LP	Polydor	2383180	1972	**£10**	
Sweet Jane	7"	Atlantic	K10339	1973	**£8**	
Velvet Underground	LP	MGM	CS8108	1969	**£15**	
Velvet Underground With Nico	LP	Verve	SVLP9184	1967	**£20**	
Velvet Underground With Nico	LP	Verve	V5008	1967	**£40**	US, peelable banana cover, male torso airbrushed out, mono
Velvet Underground With Nico	LP	Verve	V5008	1967	**£75**	US, peelable banana cover, male torso frames group photo, mono
Velvet Underground With Nico	LP	Verve	V5008	1967	**£50**	US, peelable banana cover, sticker covers group photo, mono
Velvet Underground With Nico	LP	Verve	V65008	1967	**£25**	US, peelable banana cover, male torso airbrushed out, stereo
Velvet Underground With Nico	LP	Verve	V65008	1967	**£50**	US, peelable banana cover, male torso frames group photo, stereo
Velvet Underground With Nico	LP	Verve	V65008	1967	**£35**	US, peelable banana cover, sticker covers group photo, stereo
White Light/White Heat	LP	Verve	SVLP9201	1967	**£15**	
Who Loves The Sun	7"	Atlantic	2091088	1971	**£15**	

VELVETS

Title	Format	Label	Number	Year	Price	Notes
I Got To Find Me Somebody	7"	Pye	DDS109	1974	**£4**	
Laugh	7"	London	HLU9444	1961	**£4**	
That Lucky Old Sun	7"	London	HLU9328	1961	**£4**	chart single
Tonight	7"	London	HLU9372	1961	**£4**	chart single
Velvets	7" EP	London	REU1297	1961	**£10**	

VELVETTES

Title	Format	Label	Number	Year	Price	Notes
He's The One I Want	7"	Mercury	MF802	1964	**£5**	

VENDORS

Title	Format	Label	Number	Year	Price	Notes
Peace Pipe	7"	private		1964	**£250**	demo

VENTURA, TOBY

Title	Format	Label	Cat. No.	Year	Price	Notes
If My Heart Were A Story Book	7"	Decca	F11581	1963	**£10**	

VENTURAS

Title	Format	Label	Cat. No.	Year	Price	Notes
Here They Are	LP	Drum Boy	DB1003	1964	**£25**	US

VENTURES

The Ventures are the American equivalent of the Shadows, maintaining a long and still buoyant career by playing melodic guitar instrumentals regardless of the prevailing musical fashions. The size of the Ventures' output is astonishing - they have released far more albums than are listed here, including many that have been Issued only in Japan. Despite this, the group still found it necessary to issue an album on their own label in 1964, thereby producing the only real rarity in their catalogue.

Title	Format	Label	Cat. No.	Year	Price	Notes
A Go-Go	LP	Liberty	LBY1274	1965	**£10**	
Another Smash	LP	London	HAG2376	1961	**£15**	mono
Another Smash	LP	London	SAHG6176	1961	**£15**	stereo
Another Smash	7" EP	London	REG1326	1961	**£8**	
Batman Theme	LP	Dolton	BLP2042	1966	**£12**	US
Beach Party	LP	Dolton	BLP2016	1963	**£10**	US
Blue Moon	7"	London	HLG9465	1961	**£4**	
Christmas Album	LP	Liberty	LBY1285	1965	**£12**	
Colourful Ventures	7" EP	London	REG1328	1961	**£6**	
Colourful Ventures	LP	London	HAG2409	1961	**£15**	
Dance Party	LP	Liberty	LBY1110	1962	**£10**	
Dance With The Ventures	LP	Dolton	BLP2014	1963	**£10**	US
Dance!	LP	Dolton	BLP2010	1963	**£10**	US
Diamond Head	7"	Liberty	LIB303	1965	**£4**	
El Cumbanchero	7"	Liberty	LIB68	1964	**£4**	
Fabulous Ventures	LP	Dolton	BLP2029	1964	**£10**	US
Flights Of Fantasy	LP	Liberty	LBL83138	1968	**£10**	
Flights Of Fantasy	7"	Liberty	LBF15075	1968	**£4**	
Go With...	LP	Liberty	LBY1323	1966	**£10**	
Golden Greats	LP	Liberty	LRP4053	1967	**£10**	US
Great Performances Vol.1	LP	Liberty	LBL83085	1968	**£10**	
Guitar Freakout	LP	Liberty	LBY1345	1967	**£12**	
Hawaii Five-O	LP	Liberty	LST8061	1969	**£10**	US
Horse	LP	Liberty	LBL83164	1968	**£10**	
I Like It Like That	LP	Liberty	LBL83116	1968	**£10**	
In Space	LP	Liberty	LBY1189	1964	**£12**	
Journey To The Stars	7"	Liberty	LIB91	1964	**£4**	
Knock Me Out	LP	Liberty	LBY1252	1965	**£10**	
Let's Go	LP	Liberty	LBY1169	1963	**£10**	
Lolita Ya Ya	7"	Liberty	LIB60	1964	**£4**	
Lullaby Of The Leaves	7"	London	HLG9344	1961	**£4**	chart single
Mashed Potatoes And Gravy	LP	Dolton	BLP2016	1962	**£10**	US
Million Dollar Weekend	LP	Liberty	LBL83092	1968	**£10**	
More Golden Greats	LP	Liberty	LST8060	1970	**£10**	US
Ninth Wave	7"	Liberty	LIB78	1964	**£4**	
On Stage	LP	Liberty	LBY1270	1965	**£10**	
Out Of Limits	LP	Liberty	LBL83126	1968	**£10**	
Penetration	7"	Liberty	LIB10142	1964	**£4**	
Perfidia	7"	London	HLG9232	1960	**£4**	chart single
Perfidia	7" EP	London	REG1279	1960	**£8**	
Play Guitar With The Ventures	LP	Dolton	BLP16501	1965	**£12**	US
Play Guitar With The Ventures Vol.2	LP	Dolton	BLP16502	1966	**£12**	US
Play Guitar With The Ventures Vol.3	LP	Dolton	BLP16503	1966	**£12**	US
Play Guitar With The Ventures Vol.4	LP	Dolton	BLP16504	1966	**£12**	US
Ram Bunk Shush	7"	London	HLG9292	1961	**£4**	chart single
Ram Bunk Shush	7" EP	London	REG1288	1961	**£8**	
Secret Agent Man	7"	Liberty	LIB316	1966	**£4**	
Secret Agent Man	7" EP	Liberty	LEP2250	1966	**£6**	
Slaughter On Tenth Avenue	7"	Liberty	LIB300	1965	**£4**	
Sleigh Ride	7"	Liberty	LIB10210	1965	**£4**	
Smash Hits	7" EP	Liberty	LEP2131	1963	**£5**	
Stranger	7"	Liberty	LIB308	1965	**£4**	
Strawberry Fields Forever	7"	Liberty	LIB55967	1967	**£4**	
Super Psychedelics	LP	Liberty	LBL83033	1967	**£10**	
Super Psychedelics	LP	Liberty	LBY1372	1967	**£12**	
Surfing	LP	Liberty	LBY1150	1963	**£12**	
Swamp Rock	LP	Liberty	LBS83279	1969	**£10**	
Swingin' Creeper	7"	Liberty	LIB306	1965	**£4**	
Telstar, The Lonely Bull	LP	Dolton	BLP2019	1963	**£10**	US
Tenth Anniversary Album	LP	Liberty	LST35000	1970	**£12**	US

Theme From Silver City	7"	London	HLG9411	1961	**£4**	
Theme From The Wild Angels	7"	Liberty	LIB10266	1967	**£4**	
Twist Party	LP	Liberty	LBY1072	1962	**£10**	
Twist With The Ventures	7" EP	Liberty	LEP2058	1962	**£5**	
Twist With The Ventures	LP	London	HAG2429	1962	**£12**	
Two Thousand Pound Bee	7"	Liberty	LIB67	1964	**£4**	
Underground Fire	LP	Liberty	LBL83193	1969	**£10**	
Ventures	LP	Dolton	BLP2042	1966	**£10**	US
Ventures	LP	Liberty	LBX2	1969	**£10**	
Ventures	LP	London	HAG2430	1961	**£15**	
Ventures	LP	Ventures	BG101	1964	**£50**	US
Ventures On Stage	LP	Liberty	LBL83015	1967	**£10**	
Ventures Play Country Greats	7" EP	Liberty	LEP2174	1964	**£6**	
Ventures Play Telstar And Lonely Bull	7" EP	Liberty	LEP2104	1963	**£5**	
Ventures Play The Country Classics	LP	Dolton	BLP2023	1963	**£10**	US
Versatile Ventures	LP	Liberty	SCR5	1966	**£12**	US
Walk Don't Run '64	7"	Liberty	LIB96	1964	**£4**	
Walk Don't Run	LP	Liberty	LBY1002	1960	**£10**	
Walk Don't Run	7"	Top Rank	JAR417	1960	**£5**	chart single
Walk Don't Run Vol.2	LP	Liberty	LBY1228	1964	**£10**	
Where The Action Is	LP	Liberty	LBY1297	1966	**£10**	
Wild Things	LP	Dolton	BLP2047	1966	**£10**	US

VENUS & THE RAZORBLADES

I Want To Be Where The Boys Are	7"	Spark	SRL1153	1977	**£4**	
Punk-A-Rama	7"	Spark	SRL1156	1977	**£4**	
Workin' Girl	7"	Spark	SRL1159	1978	**£4**	

VERITY, JOHN

John Verity Band	LP	Probe	SPB1087	1974	**£10**	

VERNE, LARRY

Mr.Custer	7"	London	HLN9194	1960	**£4**	
Mr.Larry Verne	LP	Era	EL104	1961	**£15**	US
Mr.Livingston	7"	London	HLN9263	1961	**£4**	

VERNON, MIKE

Although he has made the occasional record himself, both under his own name and as a member of the Olympic Runners, Mike Vernon is best known as a producer and as the proprietor of Blue Horizon records. As the producer of John Mayall's pivotal "Bluesbreakers" and "Hard Road" albums, Vernon was ideally placed to take a major role within the development of British blues, and he went on to work with most of the significant talents within the genre, including Fleetwood Mac, Chicken Shack, Savoy Brown, and the Groundhogs. Every record on his Blue Horizon label is now a collectors' item, as indeed are the handful of singles issued by the label's predecessor, Purdah.

Bring It Back Home	LP	Blue Horizon	2931003	1971	**£25**	
Let's Try It Again	7"	Blue Horizon	2096007	1971	**£8**	

VERNONS GIRLS

Do The Bird	7"	Decca	F11629	1963	**£4**	chart single
Don't Look Now	7"	Parlophone	R4596	1959	**£4**	
Funny All Over	7"	Decca	F11549	1962	**£4**	chart single
He'll Never Come Back	7"	Decca	F11685	1963	**£4**	
It's A Sin To Tell A Lie	7"	Decca	F12021	1964	**£4**	
Jealous Heart	7"	Parlophone	R4532	1959	**£4**	
Let's Get Together	7"	Parlophone	R4832	1961	**£4**	
Locomotion	7"	Decca	F11495	1962	**£4**	chart single
Lover Please	7"	Decca	F11450	1962	**£4**	chart single
Madison Time	7"	Parlophone	R4654	1960	**£4**	
Only You Can Do It	7"	Decca	F11887	1964	**£4**	
Ten Little Lonely Boys	7"	Parlophone	R4734	1961	**£4**	
Tomorrow Is Another Day	7"	Decca	F11781	1963	**£4**	
Vernons Girls	7" EP	Decca	DFE8506	1962	**£8**	
We Like Boys	7"	Parlophone	R4624	1960	**£4**	
We Love The Beatles	7"	Decca	F11807	1964	**£4**	
White Bucks And Saddle Shoes	7"	Parlophone	R4497	1958	**£4**	

VERSATILES

Just Can't Win	7"	Amalgam.	AMG802	196-	**£10**	
Lu Lu Bell	7"	Amalgam.	AMG854	196-	**£10**	

VERSATONES

Versatones	LP	RCA	LPM1538	1957	**£20**	US

VETERANS

Administration .... LP .... 1968 ..... **£25** ..... US

VIBRATIONS

Canadian Sunset .... 7" .... Columbia .... DB7895 .... 1966 .... **£5**
Greatest Hits .... LP .... OKeh .... OKS14129 .... 1969 .... **£20** .... US
Love In Them There Hills .... 7" .... Direction .... 583511 .... 1968 .... **£5**
Misty .... LP .... OKeh .... OKM4112 .... 1966 .... **£12** .... US
My Girl Sloopy .... 7" .... London .... HLK9875 .... 1964 .... **£4**
New Vibrations .... LP .... Columbia .... SX6106 .... 1966 .... **£10**
One Mint Julep .... 7" .... Columbia .... DB8319 .... 1967 .... **£4**
Pick Me .... 7" .... Columbia .... DB8175 .... 1967 .... **£4**
Shout .... LP .... OKeh .... OKM4111 .... 1965 .... **£15** .... US
Talkin' 'Bout Love .... 7" .... Columbia .... DB8318 .... 1967 .... **£4**
Watusi .... LP .... Checker .... 2978 .... 1961 .... **£20** .... US
Watusi .... 7" .... Pye .... 7N25107 .... 1961 .... **£6**

VIBRATORS

Bad Time .... 7" .... RAK .... RAK253 .... 1977 .... **£200** .... existence doubtful
We Vibrate .... 7" .... RAK .... RAK245 .... 1976 .... **£4**

VICE CREEMS

Danger Love .... 7" .... Zigzag .... ZZ22001 .... 197- **£5**
Won't You Be My Girl .... 7" .... Tiger .... GRRRR1 .... 1978 .... **£4**

VICE SQUAD

Last Rockers .... 7" .... Riot City .... RIOT1 .... 1980 .... **£4** .... with poster
Out Of Reach .... 7" .... Zonophone .... Z26 .... 1982 .... **£4**
Resurrection .... 7" .... Riot City .... RIOT2 .... 1981 .... **£4**

VICE VERSA

Music 4 .... 7" .... Neutron .... NT001 .... 1980 .... **£6**

VICE VERSA (2)

Stilyagi .... 7" .... BBR .... 003 .... 1981 .... **£4**

VICEROYS

At Granny's Pad .... LP .... Bolo .... BLP8000 .... 1963 .... **£20** .... US
Far Fish .... 7" .... Blue Cat .... BS121 .... 1968 .... **£10**
Last Night .... 7" .... Studio One .... SO2064 .... 196- **£10**
Lips And Tongue .... 7" .... Island .... WI3095 .... 1967 .... **£10**

VICKERS, MIKE

Air On A G String .... 7" .... Columbia .... DB8171 .... 1967 .... **£6**
Captain Scarlet And The Mysterons .... 7" .... Columbia .... DB8281 .... 1967 .... **£8**
Eleventy One .... 7" .... Columbia .... DB7825 .... 1966 .... **£6**
I Wish I Were A Group Again .... LP .... Columbia .... SCX6180 .... 1968 .... **£15**
Morgan .... 7" .... Columbia .... DB7906 .... 1966 .... **£6**
Puff Adder .... 7" .... Columbia .... DB7657 .... 1965 .... **£20**

VICKERS, SUE

Loving You The Way I Do .... 7" .... Threshold .... TH8 .... 1972 .... **£4**

VICTIM

Strange things By Night .... 7" .... Good Vibs. .... GOT2 .... 1978 .... **£4**
Teenage .... 7" .... Illuminated .... ILL1 .... 197- **£4**
Teenage .... 7" .... TJM .... TJM15 .... 198- **£4**
Why Are Fire Engines Red .... 7" .... TJM .... TJM14 .... 198- **£4**

VICTIMS OF CHANCE

Victims Of Chance .... LP .... Stable .... 1969 .... **£25**

VICTOR, TONY

Dear One .... 7" .... Decca .... F11459 .... 1962 .... **£5**
In The Still Of The Night .... 7" .... Decca .... F11708 .... 1963 .... **£4**

VICTORS

Things Come Up To Bump .... 7" .... Studio One .... SO2077 .... 196- **£10**

VIDELS

Mister Lonely .... 7" .... London .... HLI9153 .... 1960 .... **£4**

VIGILANTES

Eclipse	7"	Pye	7N25082	1961	**£4**	

VIKINGS

Come Into The Parlour	7"	Black Swan	WI430	1964	**£10**	
Daddy	7"	Island	WI167	1965	**£10**	
Down By The Riverside	7"	Black Swan	WI423	1964	**£10**	
Fever	7"	Island	WI117	1963	**£12**	
Hallelujah	7"	Island	WI065	1962	**£12**	
Just Got To Be	7"	Island	WI107	1963	**£12**	
Maggie Don't Leave Me	7"	Island	WI035	1962	**£12**	
Never Grown Old	7"	Island	WI101	1963	**£12**	
Six And Seven Books Of Moses	7"	Island	WI075	1963	**£12**	
Treat Me Bad	7"	Black Swan	WI428	1964	**£10**	

VIKINGS (2)

Bad News Feeling	7"	Alp	595011	1966	**£8**	

VILLAGE

Man In The Moon	LP	Head	HDS4002	1969	**£20**	
Man In The Moon	7"	Head	HEAD4002	1969	**£12**	

VILLAGE STOMPERS

Washington Square	7"	Columbia	DB7123	1963	**£5**	

VINCENT, GENE

Anna Annabelle	7"	Capitol	CL15169	1960	**£10**	
B I Bickey Bi Bo Bo Go	7"	Capitol	CL14722	1957	**£30**	
Baby Blue	7"	Capitol	CL14868	1958	**£15**	
Baby Don't Believe Him	7"	Capitol	CL15243	1962	**£10**	
Be Bop A Lula '62	7"	Capitol	CL15264	1962	**£10**	
Be Bop A Lula	7"	Capitol	CL14599	1956	**£15**	chart single
Be Bop A Lula	7"	Dandelion	4596	1969	**£4**	
Best Of...	LP	Capitol	T20957	1967	**£10**	
Best Of...Vol.2	LP	Capitol	T21144	1969	**£10**	
Bird Doggin'	LP	London	HAH8333	1967	**£15**	
Bird Doggin'	7"	London	HLH10079	1966	**£5**	
Bluejean Bop	LP	Capitol	T764	1956	**£30**	
Bluejean Bop	LP	Capitol	T764	1957	**£180**	US
Bluejean Bop	7"	Capitol	CL14637	1956	**£15**	chart single
Crazy Beat	7"	Capitol	CL15307	1963	**£8**	
Crazy Beat Of Gene Vincent	LP	Capitol	T20453	1963	**£25**	
Crazy Beat Of Gene Vincent Pt.1	7" EP	Capitol	EAP120453	1963	**£15**	
Crazy Beat Of Gene Vincent Pt.2	7" EP	Capitol	EAP220453	1964	**£15**	
Crazy Beat Of Gene Vincent Pt.3	7" EP	Capitol	EAP320453	1964	**£15**	
Crazy Legs	7"	Capitol	CL14693	1957	**£25**	
Crazy Times	LP	Capitol	ST1342	1960	**£25**	stereo
Crazy Times	LP	Capitol	T1342	1960	**£20**	chart LP
Crazy Times	LP	Capitol	T1342	1960	**£150**	US
Crazy Times	LP	MFP	1053	1965	**£12**	
Dance To The Bop	7"	Capitol	CL14808	1957	**£15**	
Day The World Turned Blue	LP	Kama Sutra	KSBS2027	1971	**£12**	
Day The World Turned Blue	7"	Kama Sutra	2013018	1971	**£4**	
Gene Vincent & The Blue Caps	LP	Capitol	T811	1957	**£180**	US
Gene Vincent & The Blue Caps	LP	Capitol	T811	1957	**£25**	
Gene Vincent	LP	Kama Sutra	KSBS2019	1970	**£12**	
Gene Vincent Record Date	LP	Capitol	T1059	1958	**£25**	
Gene Vincent Record Date	LP	Capitol	T1059	1958	**£180**	US
Gene Vincent Record Date Pt.1	7" EP	Capitol	EAP11059	1959	**£15**	
Gene Vincent Record Date Pt.2	7" EP	Capitol	EAP21059	1959	**£30**	
Gene Vincent Record Date Pt.3	7" EP	Capitol	EAP31059	1960	**£15**	
Gene Vincent Rocks & The Blue Caps Roll	LP	Capitol	T970	1958	**£180**	US
Gene Vincent Rocks & The Blue Caps Roll	LP	Capitol	T970	1958	**£25**	
Git It	7"	Capitol	CL14935	1958	**£12**	
Held For Questioning	7"	Capitol	CL15290	1963	**£8**	
Hot Rod Gang	7" EP	Capitol	EAP1985	1958	**£30**	
Humpty Dumpty	7"	Columbia	DB7218	1964	**£6**	
I Got A Baby	7"	Capitol	CL14830	1958	**£15**	
I'm Back & I'm Proud	LP	Dandelion	63754	1969	**£12**	
I'm Going Home	7"	Capitol	CL15215	1961	**£8**	chart single
If You Want My Loving	7" EP	Capitol	EAP120173	1961	**£20**	

Title	Format	Label	Cat. No.	Year	Price	Notes
If You Want My Loving	7"	Capitol	CL15185	1961	**£10**	
Jumps Giggles And Shouts	7"	Capitol	CL14681	1957	**£20**	
La Den Da Den Da Da	7"	Columbia	DB7293	1964	**£6**	
Lonely Street	7"	London	HLH10099	1966	**£5**	
Maybe	7"	Capitol	CL15179	1961	**£10**	
My Heart	7"	Capitol	CL15115	1960	**£8**	chart single
Over The Rainbow	7"	Capitol	CL15000	1959	**£10**	
Pistol Packing Mama	7"	Capitol	CL15136	1960	**£8**	chart single
Private Detective	7"	Columbia	DB7343	1964	**£6**	
Race With The Devil	7"	Capitol	CL14628	1956	**£20**	chart single
Race With The Devil	7" EP	Capitol	EAP120354	1962	**£20**	
Rainy Day Sunshine	7"	Rollin' D.	RD1	1979	**£10**	
Right Now	7"	Capitol	CL15053	1959	**£10**	
Rip It Up	7"	Capitol	CL15307	1963	**£30**	
Rocky Road Blues	7"	Capitol	CL14908	1958	**£12**	
Roll Over Beethoven	7"	BBC	BEEB001	1974	**£4**	
Say Mama	7"	Capitol	CL14974	1959	**£10**	
Say Mama	7"	Capitol	CL15546	1968	**£5**	
Say Mama	7"	Capitol	CL15906	1977	**£4**	
Shakin' Up A Storm	LP	Columbia	33SX1646	1964	**£15**	
She She Little Sheila	7"	Capitol	CL15202	1961	**£8**	chart single
Sounds Like Gene Vincent	LP	Capitol	T1207	1959	**£150**	US
Sounds Like Gene Vincent	LP	Capitol	T1207	1959	**£25**	
Summertime	7"	Capitol	CL15035	1959	**£10**	
Temptation Baby	7"	Columbia	DB7174	1963	**£6**	
True To You	7" EP	Capitol	EAP120461	1963	**£15**	
Unchained Melody	7"	Capitol	CL15231	1961	**£8**	
Wear My Ring	7"	Capitol	CL14763	1957	**£15**	
White Lightning	7"	Dandelion	4974	1970	**£4**	
Wild Cat	7"	Capitol	CL15099	1959	**£8**	chart single

VINE, JOEY

Title	Format	Label	Cat. No.	Year	Price	Notes
Down And Out	7"	Immediate	IM017	1965	**£8**	

VINEGAR JOE

Title	Format	Label	Cat. No.	Year	Price	Notes
Black Smoke From The Calumet	7"	Island	WIP6174	1973	**£4**	
Never Met A Dog	7"	Island	WIP6125	1972	**£4**	
Rock'n'Roll Gypsies	LP	Island	ILPS9214	1972	**£10**	
Rock'n'Roll Gypsies	7"	Island	WIP6148	1972	**£4**	
Six Star General	LP	Island	ILPS9262	1973	**£10**	
Vinegar Joe	LP	Island	ILPS9183	1972	**£12**	

VINEYARD

Title	Format	Label	Cat. No.	Year	Price	Notes
Charlemaine	7"	Deram	DM420	1974	**£4**	

VINSON, EDDIE 'CLEANHEAD'

Title	Format	Label	Cat. No.	Year	Price	Notes
Backdoor Blues	LP	Riverside	3502	196-	**£15**	US
Cherry Red	LP	BluesWay	BL6007	1967	**£10**	US
Eddie Cleanhead Vinson Sings	LP	Aamco	312	196-	**£10**	US
Eddie Cleanhead Vinson Sings	LP	Bethlehem	BCP5005	196-	**£15**	US

VINSON, EDDIE 'CLEANHEAD' & JIMMY WITHERSPOON

Title	Format	Label	Cat. No.	Year	Price	Notes
Battle Of The Blues Vol.3	LP	King	634	1959	**£275**	US

VINTON, BOBBY

Title	Format	Label	Cat. No.	Year	Price	Notes
Corrine Corrina	7"	Fontana	H307	1961	**£4**	
Dancing At The Hop	LP	Epic	LN3727	1960	**£10**	US
Greatest Hits Of The Greatest Groups	LP	Epic	LN24049	1963	**£10**	US
I Love The Way You Are	7"	London	HLU9592	1962	**£4**	
Roses Are Red	7"	Columbia	DB4878	1962	**£4**	chart single
Songs Of Christmas	7" EP	Columbia	SEG8363	1964	**£6**	
Tell Me Why	LP	Columbia	33SX1649	1965	**£10**	
There I've Said It Again	7"	Columbia	DB7179	1963	**£4**	chart single
Young In Heart	7" EP	Columbia	SEG8212	1962	**£6**	
Young Man With A Big Band	LP	Epic	LN3780	1961	**£10**	US

VIOLENT THIMBLE

Title	Format	Label	Cat. No.	Year	Price	Notes
Gentle People	7"	Polydor	56217	1967	**£4**	

VIOLENTS

Title	Format	Label	Cat. No.	Year	Price	Notes
Ghia	7"	HMV	POP1130	1963	**£4**	

VIPERS SKIFFLE GROUP

Title	Format	Label	Cat. No.	Year	Price	Notes
Coffee Bar Session	LP-10"	Parlophone	PMD1050		**£30**	
Cumberland Gap	7"	Parlophone	R4289	1957	**£6**	chart single
Don't You Rock Me Daddyo	7"	Parlophone	R4261	1957	**£6**	chart single
Homing Bird	7"	Parlophone	R4351	1957	**£4**	
Jim Dandy	7"	Parlophone	R4286	1957	**£8**	
Make Ready For Love	7"	Parlophone	R4435	1958	**£4**	
No Other Baby	7"	Parlophone	R4393	1958	**£5**	
Pick A Bale Of Cotton	7"	Parlophone	R4238	1956	**£8**	
Skiffle Music Vol.1	7" EP	Parlophone	GEP8615	1957	**£10**	
Skiffle Music Vol.2	7" EP	Parlophone	GEP8626	1957	**£10**	
Skiffle Party	7"	Parlophone	R4371	1957	**£5**	
Skiffling Along With The Vipers	7" EP	Parlophone	GEP8655	1957	**£10**	
Streamline Train	7"	Parlophone	R4308	1957	**£4**	chart single
Summertime Blues	7"	Parlophone	R4484	1958	**£8**	

VIPPS

Title	Format	Label	Cat. No.	Year	Price	Notes
Wintertime	7"	CBS	202031	1966	**£20**	

VIRGIL BROTHERS

Title	Format	Label	Cat. No.	Year	Price	Notes
Good Love	7"	Parlophone	R5802	1969	**£4**	
Temptation 'Bout To Get Me	7"	Parlophone	R5787	1969	**£8**	

VIRGIN PRUNES

Title	Format	Label	Cat. No.	Year	Price	Notes
In The Grey Light	7"	Rough Trade	RT072	1981	**£10**	
New Form Of Beauty	7"	Rough Trade	RT089-91	1981	**£20**	3 records, boxed
Pagan Love Song	7"	Rough Trade	RT106	1982	**£10**	
Slow Children	12"	Rough Trade	RT099		**£6**	
Twenty Tens	7"	Baby	001	1981	**£12**	

VIRGIN SLEEP

Title	Format	Label	Cat. No.	Year	Price	Notes
Love	7"	Deram	DM146	1967	**£20**	
Secret	7"	Deram	DM173	1968	**£15**	

VIRGINIA WOLVES

Title	Format	Label	Cat. No.	Year	Price	Notes
Stay	7"	Stateside	SS563	1966	**£20**	

VIRTUES

Title	Format	Label	Cat. No.	Year	Price	Notes
Guitar Boogie Shuffle	7"	HMV	POP621	1959	**£8**	
Guitar Boogie Shuffle	LP	Strand	SL1061	1960	**£10**	US
Guitar Boogie Shuffle	LP	Wynne	WLP111	1960	**£10**	US
Shuffling Along	7"	HMV	POP637	1959	**£5**	

VIRTUES (2)

Title	Format	Label	Cat. No.	Year	Price	Notes
Your Wife And Your Mother	7"	Island	WI196	1965	**£10**	

VIRTUOSA, FRANK

Title	Format	Label	Cat. No.	Year	Price	Notes
Rollin' And Rockin'	7"	Melodisc	MEL1386	195-	**£4**	

VISAGE

Title	Format	Label	Cat. No.	Year	Price	Notes
Pleasure Boys	7"	Polydor	POSP523	1982	**£4**	
Pleasure Boys	12"	Polydor	POSPX523	1982	**£15**	
Tar	7"	Radar	ADA48	1979	**£4**	

VISCONTI, TONY

Title	Format	Label	Cat. No.	Year	Price	Notes
I Remember Brooklyn	7"	Regal Z.	RZ3089	1974	**£5**	

VISCOUNTS

The Viscounts were a vocal trio, whose easy harmonies were typical of the kind of thing the Beatles blew away. One of the group, however, was Gordon Mills, who later made himself a very comfortable living as manager of both Tom Jones and Engelbert Humperdinck.

Title	Format	Label	Cat. No.	Year	Price	Notes
Chug A Lug	7"	Top Rank	JAR388	1960	**£4**	
Harlem Nocturne	LP	Amy	8008	1965	**£15**	US
Harlem Nocturne	7"	Top Rank	JAR254	1959	**£4**	
Night Train	7"	Top Rank	JAR502	1960	**£4**	
Viscounts	LP	Madison	1001	1960	**£40**	US
Viscounts' Rock	7" EP	Top Rank	JKP3005	1961	**£20**	

VISCOUNTS (2)

Title	Format	Label	Cat. No.	Year	Price	Notes
Shortnin' Bread	7"	Pye	7N15287	1960	**£4**	chart single
Viscounts' Hit Parade	7" EP	Pye	NEP24132	1960	**£5**	
Who Put The Bomp	7"	Pye	7N15379	19961	**£4**	chart single

VOAG, L.

Way Out	LP	Axis	No.9	1979	**£10**	

VOGUES

Five O'Clock World	7"	London	HLU10014	1966	**£4**	
You're The One	7"	London	HLU9996	1965	**£4**	
Younger Girl	7"	Columbia	DB7985	1966	**£4**	

VOICE

Train To Disaster	7"	Mercury	MF905	1965	**£35**	

VOICE OF THE BEEHIVE

Just A City	7"	Food	FOOD9	1987	**£4**	
Just A City	7"	Food	FOODX9	1987	**£4**	
Just A City	12"	Food	SNAK9	1987	**£8**	

VOICES

Rock And Roll Hit Parade	7"	Beltona	BL2667	1956	**£4**	

VOIGHT, WES

I'm Moving In	7"	Parlophone	R4586	1959	**£5**	

VOKES, HOWARD COUNTRY BOYS

Howard Vokes Country Boys	7" EP	Starlite	GRK508	1966	**£5**	
Howard Vokes Country Boys	7" EP	Starlite	STEP27	196-	**£6**	
Mountain Guitar	7" EP	Starlite	STEP37	196-	**£6**	

VOLCANOES

Polaris	7"	Philips	BF1246	1963	**£4**	
Ruby Duby Du	7"	Philips	PB1098	1961	**£4**	
Tightrope	7"	Philips	PB1113	1961	**£4**	
Volcanoes	7" EP	Philips	BBE12432	1960	**£8**	

VOLUMES

Dreams	7"	Fontana	270109TF	1962	**£5**	
I Can't Help Myself	7"	Pama	PM755	196-	**£120**	un-released
Sandra	7"	London	HL9733	1963	**£4**	

VON TRAPP FAMILY

Brand New Thrill	7"	Woronzow	WOO1	1980	**£20**	

VONTASTICS

Lady Love	7"	Stateside	SS2002	1967	**£10**	

VOOMINS

If You Don't Come Back	7"	Polydor	56001	1965	**£8**	

VOXPOPPERS

Last Drag	7"	Mercury	7MT202	1958	**£10**	
Voxpoppers	7" EP	Mercury	MEP9533	1958	**£25**	

VULCAN'S HAMMER

True Hearts And Sound Bottoms	LP	Brown		1973	**£200**	

W

W. GIMMICS

Hot Rods	7" EP	Polydor	EPH27125	1965	**£4**	

W.A.S.P.

9.5 N.A.S.T.Y.	7"	Capitol	CLP432	1986	**£5**	pic disc
Animal	7"	Music For N.	PKUT109	1984	**£6**	shaped pic disc, 2 different designs
Animal	12"	Music For N.	12KUT109	1984	**£6**	white vinyl
Animal	12"	Music For N.	PIG109	1985	**£6**	pic disc
Blind In Texas	7"	Capitol	CLP374	1985	**£5**	pic disc
Blind In Texas	12"	Capitol	12CLP374	1985	**£6**	pic disc
I Don't Need No Doctor	7"	Capitol	CL469	1987	**£6**	blood pack
I Don't Need No Doctor	7"	Capitol	CLB469	1987	**£4**	with backstage pass
I Don't Need No Doctor	7"	Capitol	CLP469	1987	**£5**	shaped pic disc
I Don't Need No Doctor	7"	Capitol	CLS469	1987	**£5**	poster sleeve
I Wanna Be Somebody	12"	Capitol	12CLP336	1984	**£6**	pic disc
Mean Man	7"	Capitol	CLM521	1989	**£4**	purple vinyl, badge
Schooldaze	7"	Capitol	CL344	1985	**£4**	poster sleeve
Scream Until You Like It	12"	Capitol	12CLP458	1987	**£6**	pic disc
Wild Child	7"	Capitol	CLD388	1986	**£5**	double

WACKERS

Girl Who Wanted Fame	7"	Piccadilly	7N35210	1964	**£6**	
I Wonder Why	7"	Oriole	CB1902	1964	**£8**	
Love Or Money	7"	Piccadilly	7N35195	1964	**£6**	

WADE, ADAM

Adam And Evening	LP	Coed	LPC903	1961	**£12**	US
And Then Came Adam	LP	Coed	LPC902	1960	**£15**	US
And Then Came Adam	7" EP	HMV	7EG8620	1960	**£4**	
For The Want Of Your Love	7"	HMV	POP807	1960	**£4**	
Four Film Songs	7" EP	Columbia	SEG8316	1964	**£4**	
Take Good Care Of Her	7"	HMV	POP843	1961	**£4**	chart single

WADE, WELLINGTON

Let's Turkey Trot	7"	Oriole	CB1857	1963	**£6**	

WAGNER, ADRIAN

Distance Between Us	LP	Atlantic	K50082	1974	**£12**	

WAGNER, ROBERT

Almost Eighteen	7"	London	HLU8491	1957	**£4**	

WAGONER, PORTER

Little Slice Of Life	7" EP	RCA	RCX7157	1964	**£6**	
Satisfied Mind	LP	RCA	LPM1358	1956	**£20**	US
Slice Of Life	LP	RCA	LPM2447	1962	**£10**	US
Y'All Come	7" EP	RCA	RCX7158	1964	**£5**	

WAH!

Forget The Down	7"	Eternal	SLATE1	1981	**£4**	
Some Say	12"	Eternal	SIMEY1	1981	**£6**	

WAH! HEAT

Better Scream	7"	Inevitable	INEV100	1980	**£4**	
Seven Minutes To Midnight	7"	Inevitable	INEV004	1980	**£4**	

WAILERS

And I Love Her	7"	Ska Beat	JB230	1966	**£25**	
Bend Down Low	7"	Island	WI3043	1967	**£8**	
Concrete Jungle	7"	Island	WIP6164	1973	**£4**	
Dancing Shoes	7"	Rio	R116	1967	**£25**	

Title	Format	Label	Cat. No.	Year	Price	
Donna	7"	Island	WI216	1965	**£25**	
Down Presser	7"	Punch	PH77	1971	**£8**	
Dreamland	7"	Upsetter	US371	1971	**£10**	
Get Up Stand Up	7"	Island	WIP6167	1973	**£4**	
Good Good Rudie	7"	Doctor Bird	DB1021	1966	**£25**	
He Who Feels It Knows It	7"	Island	WI3001	1966	**£20**	
I Made A Mistake	7"	Ska Beat	JB226	1965	**£30**	
I Need You	7"	Island	WI3035	1967	**£10**	
I Stand Predominant	7"	Studio One	SO2024	1967	**£20**	
It Hurts To Be Alone	7"	Island	WI188	1965	**£30**	
Jailhouse	7"	Bamboo	BAM55	1970	**£10**	
Jumbie Jamboree	7"	Island	WI260	1966	**£20**	
Let Him Go	7"	Island	WI3009	1966	**£20**	
Lonesome Feelings	7"	Ska Beat	JB211	1965	**£30**	
Lonesome Track	7"	Ska Beat	JB249	1966	**£25**	
Love And Affection	7"	Ska Beat	JB228	1965	**£30**	
Maga Dog	7"	Island	WI212	1965	**£25**	
Mr.Chatterbox	7"	Jackpot	JP730	196-	**£20**	
Nice Time	7"	Doctor Bird	DB1091	1967	**£25**	
Playboy	7"	Island	WI206	1965	**£25**	
Put It On	7"	Island	WI268	1966	**£20**	
Rasta Put It On	7"	Doctor Bird	DB1039	1966	**£25**	
Reggae On Broadway	7"	CBS	8144	1972	**£12**	
Rude Boy	7"	Doctor Bird	DB1013	1966	**£25**	
Shame And Scandal	7"	Island	WI215	1965	**£25**	
Simmer Down	7"	Ska Beat	JB186	1965	**£30**	
Stop The Train	7"	Summit	SUM8526	1972	**£5**	
What's New Pussycat	7"	Island	WI254	1965	**£20**	

WAILERS (2)

Title	Format	Label	Cat. No.	Year	Price	
At The Castle	LP	Etiquette	ALB01	1962	**£15**	US
Fabulous Wailers	LP	Golden Crest	CR3075	1959	**£20**	US
Mau Mau	7"	London	HL8994	1959	**£20**	
Out Of Our Tree	LP	Etiquette	ALB026	1966	**£12**	US
Outburst	LP	United Artists	UAL3557	1966	**£10**	US
Tall Cool One	LP	Imperial	LP9262	1964	**£10**	US
Tall Cool One	7"	London	HL8958	1959	**£8**	
Tall Cool One	7"	London	HL9892	1964	**£4**	
Wailers And Company	LP	Etiquette	ALB022	1963	**£15**	US
Wailers Wailers Everywhere	LP	Etiquette	ALB023	1965	**£12**	US
Walk Thru The People	LP	Bell	6016	1968	**£10**	US

WAINER, CHERRY

Title	Format	Label	Cat. No.	Year	Price	
Cherry Wainer	7" EP	Pye	NEP24099	1959	**£6**	
I Walk The Line	7"	Top Rank	JAR253	1959	**£4**	
Itchy Twitchy Feeling	7"	Pye	7N15161	1958	**£4**	
Money	7"	Columbia	DB4528	1960	**£4**	

WAINMAN, PHIL

Title	Format	Label	Cat. No.	Year	Price	
Hear Me A Drummer Man	7"	Columbia	DB7615	1965	**£6**	

WAINWRIGHT III, LOUDON

Title	Format	Label	Cat. No.	Year	Price	
Album 1	LP	Atlantic	K40107	1971	**£10**	
Album 2	LP	Atlantic	K40272	1972	**£10**	

WAKE

Title	Format	Label	Cat. No.	Year	Price	
23.59	LP	Carnaby		1970	**£30**	
Linda	7"	Carnaby	6151001		**£8**	
Live Today Little Girl	7"	Carnaby	CNS4010	1970	**£8**	
Noah	7"	Carnaby	CNS4016	1971	**£8**	

WAKE (2)

Title	Format	Label	Cat. No.	Year	Price	
On Our Honeymoon	7"	Scanlist	SCN1		**£4**	

WAKELY, JIMMY

Title	Format	Label	Cat. No.	Year	Price	
Are You Mine?	7"	Vogue Coral	Q72125	1956	**£4**	
Are You Satisfied?	7"	Brunswick	05542	1956	**£6**	
Christmas On The Range	LP-10"	Capitol	H9004	195-	**£20**	US
Country Million Sellers	LP	Shasta	SHLP501	1959	**£12**	US
Enter And Rest And Pray	LP	Decca	DL8680	1957	**£15**	US
Folsom Prison Blues	7"	Brunswick	05563	1956	**£10**	
Jimmy Wakely Sings	LP	Shasta	SHLP505	1960	**£12**	US

Merry Christmas .... LP .... Shasta .... SHLP502 .... 1959 ...... **£12** .... US
Santa Fe Trail .... LP .... Decca .... DL8409 .... 1956 ...... **£15** .... US
Songs Of The West .... LP-10" .. Capitol .... H4008 .... 195- ...... **£20** .... US

WAKEMAN, RICK

Those critics who dismiss Rick Wakeman's music as no more than musak will be delighted if they hear the scarce "Piano Vibrations", as this really is a musak LP. Nevertheless, the modest value achieved by this rarity reflects not its paucity of musical imagination, but Rick Wakeman's limited status as a collectable artist. Many records as bland as this do attain high values!

Journey To The Centre Of The Earth ..... LP .... A&M .... QU53621 .... 1975 ...... **£10** .... US quad
Myths And Legends Of King Arthur .... LP .... A&M .... QU54515 .... 1975 ...... **£10** .... US quad
Piano Vibrations .... LP .... Polydor .... 2460135 .... 1971 ...... **£12** ....
Six Wives Of Henry VIII .... LP .... A&M .... QU54361 .... 1973 ...... **£10** .... US quad

WALHAM GREEN EAST WAPPING C.C.R.B.E. ASSOCIATION

Sorry Mr.Green .... 7" .... Columbia .... DB8426 .... 1968 ...... **£6** ....

WALKER BROTHERS

Scott Engel, John Morse, and Gary Leeds were not called Walker and were not brothers. Gary Leeds did not even seem to do very much - he had no voice to match the rich tones of the other two, and so he sat behind a drum kit and pretended (very unconvincingly) that drumming was a vital ingredient in the group's music. The cult interest in Scott Walker's solo music has extended very little towards the Walker Brothers, whose music was too popular to everaquire the attraction of exclusivity and which has none of the disturbing quality of Scott's best work.

Another Tear Falls .... 7" .... Philips .... BF1514 .... 1966 ...... **£4** .... chart single
Deadlier Than The Male .... 7" .... Philips .... BF1537 .... 1966 ...... **£4** .... chart single
Electrician .... 7" .... GTO .... GT230 .... 1978 ...... **£4** ....
I Need You .... 7" EP .... Philips .... DE12596 .... 1966 ...... **£4** ....
Images .... LP .... Philips .... BL7770 .... 1967 ...... **£10** .... chart LP
Love Her .... 7" .... Philips .... BF1409 .... 1965 ...... **£4** .... chart single
Make It Easy On Yourself .... 7" .... Philips .... BF1428 .... 1965 ...... **£4** .... chart single
My Ship Is Coming In .... 7" .... Philips .... BF1454 .... 1965 ...... **£4** .... chart single
No Regrets .... LP .... GTO .... GTLP007 .... 1975 ...... **£10** ....
Portrait .... LP .... Philips .... BL7732 .... 1966 ...... **£10** .... chart LP
Pretty Girls Everywhere .... 7" .... Philips .... BF1401 .... 1965 ...... **£4** ....
Shutout .... 7" .... GTO .... GT295 .... 1981 ...... **£4** ....
Stay With Me Baby .... 7" .... Philips .... BF1548 .... 1967 ...... **£4** .... chart single
Sun Ain't Gonna Shine Anymore .... 7" .... Philips .... BF1473 .... 1966 ...... **£4** .... chart single
Take It Easy .... LP .... Philips .... BL7691 .... 1965 ...... **£10** .... chart LP
Walker Brothers .... 7" EP .... Philips .... BE12603 .... 1967 ...... **£4** ....
Walking In The Rain .... 7" .... Philips .... BF1576 .... 1967 ...... **£4** .... chart single
You Don't Have To Tell Me .... 7" .... Philips .... BF1497 .... 1966 ...... **£4** .... chart single

WALKER, BILLY

Certain Girl .... 7" .... Columbia .... DB7724 .... 1965 ...... **£6** ....
My Heart Cries For You .... 7" .... Decca .... F11917 .... 1964 ...... **£4** ....

WALKER, CLINT

Inspiration .... 7" EP .... W. Bros .... WEP6006 .... 1960 ...... **£6** ....

WALKER, GARY

Here's Gary .... 7" EP .... CBS .... EP5742 .... 1966 ...... **£4** ....
Spooky .... 7" .... Polydor .... 56237 .... 1968 ...... **£6** ....
Twinkie Lee .... 7" .... CBS .... 202081 .... 1966 ...... **£5** .... chart single
You Don't Love Me .... 7" .... CBS .... 202036 .... 1966 ...... **£6** .... chart single

WALKER, JACKIE

Oh Lonesome Me .... 7" .... London .... HLP8588 .... 1958 ...... **£15** ....

WALKER, JERRY JEFF

Bein' Free .... LP .... Atco .... SD33336 .... 1970 ...... **£10** .... US
Driftin' Way Of Life .... LP .... Vanguard .... VSD6521 .... 1969 ...... **£10** .... US
Jerry Jeff Walker .... LP .... Atco .... SD33297 .... 1969 ...... **£15** .... US
Mr.Bojangles .... LP .... Atco .... SD33259 .... 1968 ...... **£10** .... US
Mr.Bojangles .... 7" .... Atlantic .... 584200 .... 1968 ...... **£4** ....

WALKER, JOHN

Annabella .... 7" .... Philips .... BF1593 .... 1967 ...... **£4** .... chart single
Cottonfields .... 7" .... Carnaby .... CNS4012 .... 1970 ...... **£4** ....
Everywhere Under The Sun .... 7" .... Carnaby .... CNS4004 .... 1969 ...... **£4** ....
I'll Be Your Baby Tonight .... 7" .... Philips .... BF1655 .... 1968 ...... **£4** ....
If I Promise .... 7" .... Philips .... BF1612 .... 1967 ...... **£4** ....
If You Go Away .... LP .... Philips .... BL7829 .... 1967 ...... **£15** ....

Kentucky Woman	7"	Philips	BF1676	1968	**£4**	
Over And Over Again	7"	Carnaby	CNS4017	1971	**£4**	
This Is John Walker	LP	Carnaby	CNLS6001	1969	**£20**	
True Grit	7"	Carnaby	CNS4009	1969	**£4**	
Woman	7"	Philips	BF1724	1968	**£4**	
Yesterday's Sunshine	7"	Philips	BF1758	1969	**£4**	

WALKER, JOHN & SCOTT

Solo John - Solo Scott	7" EP	Philips	BE12597	1966	**£12**	

WALKER, JUNIOR & THE ALL STARS

Cleo's Mood	7"	T. Motown	TMG550	1966	**£10**	
Cleo's Mood	7"	T. Motown	TMG550	1966	**£50**	demo
Come See About Me	7"	T. Motown	TMG637	1968	**£4**	
Come See About Me	7"	T. Motown	TMG637	1968	**£25**	demo
Do The Boomerang	7"	T. Motown	TMG520	1965	**£20**	
Do The Boomerang	7"	T. Motown	TMG520	1965	**£70**	demo
Do You See My Love	7"	T. Motown	TMG750	1970	**£4**	
Do You See My Love	7"	T. Motown	TMG750	1970	**£10**	demo
Gasss	LP	T. Motown	STML11167	1970	**£10**	
Gotta Hold On This Feeling	7"	T. Motown	TMG894	1974	**£4**	
Gotta Hold On This Feeling	7"	T. Motown	TMG894	1974	**£10**	demo
Greatest Hits	LP	T. Motown	STML11120	1969	**£10**	
Hip City	7"	T. Motown	TMG667	1968	**£5**	
Hip City	7"	T. Motown	TMG667	1968	**£30**	demo
Holy Holy	7"	T. Motown	TMG872	1973	**£8**	demo
Home Cookin'	LP	T. Motown	STML11097	1969	**£10**	
Home Cookin'	7"	T. Motown	TMG682	1969	**£5**	
Home Cookin'	7"	T. Motown	TMG682	1969	**£15**	demo
How Sweet It Is	7"	T. Motown	TMG571	1966	**£6**	chart single
How Sweet It Is	7"	T. Motown	TMG571	1966	**£50**	demo
Live	LP	T. Motown	STML11152	1970	**£15**	
Money	7"	T. Motown	TMG586	1966	**£8**	
Money	7"	T. Motown	TMG586	1966	**£40**	demo
Pucker Up Buttercup	7"	T. Motown	TMG596	1967	**£8**	
Pucker Up Buttercup	7"	T. Motown	TMG596	1967	**£40**	demo
Road Runner	7"	T. Motown	TMG559	1966	**£10**	
Road Runner	7"	T. Motown	TMG559	1966	**£50**	demo
Road Runner	7"	T. Motown	TMG691	1969	**£4**	chart single
Road Runner	LP	T. Motown	STML11038	1966	**£12**	
Road Runner	7"	T. Motown	TMG691	1969	**£15**	demo
Shake And Fingerpop	7" EP	T. Motown	TME2013	1966	**£12**	
Shake And Fingerpop	7"	T. Motown	TMG529	1965	**£12**	
Shake And Fingerpop	7"	T. Motown	TMG529	1965	**£50**	demo
Shotgun	LP	T. Motown	TML11017	1965	**£15**	
Shotgun	7"	T. Motown	TMG509	1965	**£12**	
Shotgun	7"	T. Motown	TMG509	1965	**£50**	demo
Soul Session	LP	T. Motown	TML11029	1966	**£15**	
Take Me Girl I'm Ready	7"	T. Motown	TMG840	1973	**£4**	chart single
Take Me Girl I'm Ready	7"	T. Motown	TMG840	1973	**£12**	demo
These Eyes	7"	T. Motown	TMG727	1970	**£4**	
These Eyes	LP	T. Motown	STML11140	1970	**£10**	
These Eyes	7"	T. Motown	TMG727	1970	**£12**	demo
Walk In The Night	7"	T. Motown	TMG824	1972	**£4**	chart single
Walk In The Night	7"	T. Motown	TMG824	1972	**£12**	demo
Way Back Home	7"	T. Motown	TMG857	1973	**£4**	chart single
Way Back Home	7"	T. Motown	TMG857	1973	**£10**	demo
What Does It Take To Win Your Love?	7"	T. Motown	TMG712	1969	**£4**	chart single
What Does It Take To Win Your Love?	7"	T. Motown	TMG712	1969	**£12**	demo

WALKER, LUCILLE

Best Of...	LP	Checker	1428	1957	**£20**	US

WALKER, RONNIE

Magic's In The Air	7"	Polydor	2066578	1975	**£4**	

WALKER, SCOTT

Scott Walker has followed an unusual musical course. He has the voice and the musical inclinations of a cabaret singer, yet he writes much of his own material in a style which is too unsettling and too idiosyncratic to fit comfortably into a cabaret setting. His tendency towards hermit-like behaviour has added to his enigma and created a climate within which his cult following is steadily increasing. As a result, the LPs he made in the years following the demise of the Walker Brothers are becoming more and more collectable.

Any Day Now	LP	Philips	6308148	1973	**£15**	
Delta Dawn	7"	CBS	2521	1974	**£4**	
Fire Escape In The Sky	LP	Zoo	ZOO2	1981	**£20**	
Great Scott	cass	Philips	MCP1006	1967	**£20**	
I Can Still See You	7"	Philips	6006168	1972	**£4**	
Jackie	7"	Philips	BF1628	1967	**£4**	chart single
Joanna	7"	Philips	BF1662	1968	**£4**	chart single
Lights Of Cincinnati	7"	Philips	BF1793	1969	**£4**	chart single
Looking Back With...	LP	Ember	EMB3393	1968	**£20**	
Moviegoer	LP	Philips	6308127	1972	**£15**	
Romantic Scott Walker	LP	Philips	6850013	197-	**£15**	
Scott	LP	Philips	BL7816	1967	**£15**	chart LP
Scott 2	LP	Philips	BL7840	1968	**£20**	chart LP
Scott 3	LP	Philips	SBL7882	1969	**£30**	chart LP
Scott 4	LP	Philips	SBL7913	1969	**£50**	
Sings Songs From His TV Series	LP	Philips	SBL7900	1969	**£12**	chart LP
Spotlight On Scott Walker	LP	Philips	6625017	1976	**£20**	double
Stretch	LP	CBS	65725	1973	**£15**	
Terrific	LP	Philips	6856022	197-	**£15**	
Till The Band Comes In	LP	Philips	6308035	1970	**£15**	
We Had It All	LP	CBS	80254	1974	**£15**	
Woman Left Lonely	7"	CBS	1795	1973	**£4**	

WALKER, T-BONE

Blue Rocks	LP	Bluestime	29010	1968	**£10**	US
Classics In Jazz	LP	Capitol	T370	1956	**£50**	US
Classics In Jazz	LP-10"	Capitol	H370	1953	**£75**	US
Funky Town	LP	Stateside	SSL10265	1969	**£10**	
Hustle Is On	78	London	HL8087	1954	**£15**	
I Get So Weary	LP	Imperial	9146	1961	**£25**	US
I Want A Little Girl	LP	Delmark	DS633	1967	**£10**	US
Party Girl	7"	Liberty	LIB12018	1965	**£10**	
Singing The Blues	LP	Imperial	9116	1960	**£25**	US
Sings The Blues	LP	Imperial	9098	1959	**£25**	US
Stormy Monday Blues	LP	Stateside	SSL10223	1968	**£10**	
T B Walker	LP	Capitol	T1958	1963	**£15**	
T-Bone Blues	LP	Atlantic	SD8020	1959	**£35**	US, black label
T-Bone Blues	LP	Atlantic	SD8020	196-	**£15**	US, red label
T-Bone Blues	LP	Atlantic	SD8256	1970	**£10**	US
Travellin' Blues	7" EP	London	REP1404	1963	**£8**	
Truth	LP	MCA	MUPS331	1968	**£10**	

WALKIE TALKIES

Rich And Nasty	7"	Sire	SIR4023	1979	**£8**	

WALKS, DENNIS

Billy Lick	7"	Blue Cat	BS144	196-	**£10**	
Drifter (with I Roy)	7"	Moodisc	HM104	197-	**£4**	
Time Will Tell	7"	Moodisc	HM101	197-	**£4**	

WALLACE BROTHERS

I'll Step Aside	7"	Sue	WI4036	1967	**£10**	
Lover's Prayer	7"	Sue	WI355	1965	**£10**	
Precious Words	7"	Sue	WI334	1964	**£8**	
Soul Connection	LP	Sue	ILP950	1967	**£20**	

WALLACE COLLECTION

Daydream	7"	Parlophone	R5764	1969	**£5**	
Fly Me To The Earth	7"	Parlophone	R5793	1969	**£4**	
Walk On Out	7"	Parlophone	R5844	1970	**£4**	

WALLACE, JERRY

Shutters And Boards	7"	London	HLH9630	1962	**£4**	
With This Ring	7"	London	HL8719	1958	**£4**	
You're Singing Our Love Song	7"	London	HLH9110	1960	**£4**	chart single

WALLER, GORDON

Every Day	7"	Columbia	DB8440	1968	**£5**	
Gordon	LP	Vertigo	6360069	1972	**£60**	spiral label
I Was A Boy When You Needed A Man	7"	Bell	BLL1059	1969	**£4**	
Rosecrans Boulevard	7"	Columbia	DB8337	1968	**£8**	

Weeping Analeah	7"	Columbia	DB8518	1968	**£5**	
You're Gonna Hurt Yourself	7"	Bell	BLL1106	1970	**£4**	

WALLER, JIM & THE DELTAS

Surfin' Wild	LP	Arvee	A432	1963	**£15**	US

WALLY

Wally	LP	Atlantic	K50051	1974	**£10**	
Wally Gardens	LP	Atlantic	K50180	1975	**£10**	

WALRUS

Never Let My Body Touch Ground	7"	Deram	DM323	1971	**£5**	
Walrus	LP	Deram	SML1072	1971	**£15**	
Who Can I Trust	7"	Deram	DM308	1970	**£5**	

WALSH, JOE

Smoker You Drink...	LP	ABC	COQ40016	1974	**£10**	US quad

WALTON, DAVE

Love Ain't What It Used To Be	7"	CBS	202057	1966	**£4**	

WAMMACK, TRAVIS

Scratchy	7"	Atlantic	AT4017	1965	**£20**	

WANDERERS

Ready To Snap	7"	Polydor	POSP239	1981	**£5**	
Times Are A-Changin'	7"	Polydor	POSP284	1982	**£5**	

WARD, BILLY & THE DOMINOES

Billy Ward And His Dominoes	LP	Decca	DL8621	1958	**£75**	US
Billy Ward And His Dominoes	LP	Federal	395548	1956	**£300**	US
Billy Ward And His Dominoes	LP-10"	Federal	29594	1954	**£700**	US
Billy Ward And His Dominoes	LP	King	LP548	1956	**£150**	US
Billy Ward And His Dominoes Feat. Clyde McPhatter And Jackie Wilson	LP	King	LP733	1961	**£100**	US
Billy Ward And The Dominoes	7" EP	London	REU1114	1958	**£60**	
Billy Ward And The Dominoes	LP-10"	Parlophone	PMD1061		**£150**	
Clyde McPhatter With Billy Ward	LP	Federal	395559	1957	**£300**	US
Clyde McPhatter With Billy Ward	LP	King	LP559	1956	**£150**	US
Deep Purple	7"	London	HLU8502	1957	**£12**	chart single
Don't Thank Me	78	Parlophone	R3789	1953	**£20**	
Evermore	7"	Brunswick	05656	1957	**£15**	
Jennie Lee	7"	London	HLU8634	1958	**£12**	
Pagan Love Song	LP	Liberty	LRP3113	1959	**£25**	US
Please Don't Say No	7"	London	HLU8883	1959	**£12**	
Sea Of Glass	LP	Liberty	LRP3056	1959	**£30**	US
Sixty Minute Man	78	Vogue	V9012	1951	**£20**	
St.Theresa Of The Roses	7"	Brunswick	05599	1956	**£20**	
Stardust	7"	London	HLU8465	1957	**£12**	chart single
Three Coins In A Fountain	7"	Parlophone	MSP6112	1954	**£50**	
Twenty-Four Songs	LP	King	LP952	1966	**£25**	US
Yours Forever	LP	London	HAU2116	1958	**£50**	

WARD, CHRISTINE

Face Of Empty Me	7"	Decca	F12339	1966	**£10**	

WARD, CLIFFORD T.

Singer Songwriter	LP	Dandelion	2310216	1972	**£10**	

WARD, DALE

Letter from Shirley	7"	London	HLD9835	1964	**£4**	

WARD, ROBIN

Wonderful Summer	LP	Dot	DLP3555	1963	**£20**	US
Wonderful Summer	7"	London	HLD9821	1963	**£4**	

WARDS OF COURT

All Night Girl	7"	Deram	DM127	1967	**£8**	

WARHORSE

Red Sea	LP	Vertigo	6360066	1972	**£40**	spiral label
St.Louis	7"	Vertigo	6059027	1970	**£10**	

Warhorse .... LP .... Vertigo .... 6360015 .... 1970 .... **£30** .... spiral label

WARLEIGH, RAY

First Album .... LP .... Philips .... SBL781 .... 1969 .... **£25** ....

WARLOCK, OZZIE & THE WIZARDS

Juke Box Fury .... 7" .... HMV .... POP635 .... 1959 .... **£5** ....

WARM DUST

And It Came To Pass .... LP .... Trend .... TNLS700 .... 1970 .... **£20** ....
Peace For Our Time .... LP .... Trend .... 6480001 .... 1971 .... **£15** ....

WARM EXPRESSION

Let No Man Put Asunder .... 7" .... Columbia .... DB8672 .... 1970 .... **£8** ....

WARM SOUNDS

Birds And Bees .... 7" .... Deram .... DM120 .... 1967 .... **£6** .... chart single
Nite Is A-Comin' .... 7" .... Deram .... DM174 .... 1968 .... **£12** ....
Sticks And Stones .... 7" .... Immediate .... IM058 .... 1967 .... **£12** ....

WARMAN, JOHNNY

Walking Into Mirrors .... LP .... **£12** ....

WARPIG

Warpig .... LP .... Fonthill .... 1971 .... **£80** .... Canadian

WARREN OF GHANA, GUY

African Soundz .... LP .... Regal Z. .... SLRZ1031 .... 1972 .... **£30** ....
Afro-Jazz .... LP .... Columbia .... SCX6340 .... 1969 .... **£30** ....

WARRIORS

The collectability of the Warriors' single derives from the fact that the group's singer was Jon Anderson. The drummer, however, was Ian Wallace, who has played on numerous records since, most notably LPs made by King Crimson and Bob Dylan.

You Came Along .... 7" .... Decca .... F11926 .... 1964 .... **£40** ....

WARSAW PAKT

Needletime .... LP .... Island .... ILPS9515 .... 1977 .... **£20** ....
Safe And Warm .... 7" .... 1978 .... **£4** ....

WARWICK, DEE DEE

Dee Dee Warwick .... LP .... Mercury .... SR61221 .... 1969 .... **£10** .... US
Do It With All Your Heart .... 7" .... Mercury .... MF860 .... 1965 .... **£4** ....
Gotta Get A Hold Of Myself .... 7" .... Mercury .... MF890 .... 1965 .... **£4** ....
I Want To Be With You .... LP .... Mercury .... MG21100 .... 1967 .... **£10** .... US
I Want To Be With You .... 7" .... Mercury .... MF937 .... 1965 .... **£4** ....
I'll Be Better Off .... 7" .... Mercury .... MF1061 .... 1968 .... **£6** ....
I'm Gonna Make You Love Me .... 7" .... Mercury .... MF953 .... 1965 .... **£4** ....
Lover's Chant .... 7" .... Mercury .... MF909 .... 1966 .... **£6** ....
We're Doing Fine .... 7" .... Mercury .... MF867 .... 1965 .... **£4** ....
We're Doing Fine .... 7" EP .... Mercury .... 10036MCE .... 1966 .... **£6** ....
When Love Slips Away .... 7" .... Mercury .... MF974 .... 1967 .... **£4** ....

WARWICK, DIONNE

Alfie .... 7" .... Pye .... 7N25424 .... 1967 .... **£4** ....
Always Something There To Remind Me .... 7" .... Pye .... 7N25474 .... 1968 .... **£4** ....
Another Night .... 7" .... Pye .... 7N25395 .... 1966 .... **£4** ....
Anyone Who Had A Heart .... 7" .... Pye .... 7N25234 .... 1964 .... **£4** .... chart single
Are You There .... 7" .... Pye .... 7N25338 .... 1965 .... **£4** ....
Dionne .... 7" EP .... Pye .... NEP44044 .... 1965 .... **£4** ....
Do You Know The Way To San Jose? .... 7" .... Pye .... 7N25457 .... 1968 .... **£4** .... chart single
Do You Know The Way To San Jose? .... 7" EP .... Pye .... NEP44090 .... 1968 .... **£4** ....
Don't Make Me Over .... 7" EP .... Pye .... NEP44026 .... 1964 .... **£4** ....
Don't Make Me Over .... 7" .... Stateside .... SS157 .... 1963 .... **£4** ....
Forever My Love .... 7" EP .... Pye .... NEP44046 .... 1965 .... **£4** ....
Here I Am .... LP .... Pye .... NPL28071 .... 1966 .... **£10** ....
Here I Am .... 7" .... Pye .... 7N25316 .... 1965 .... **£4** ....
Here I Am .... 7" EP .... Pye .... NEP44051 .... 1966 .... **£4** ....
I Just Don't Know What To Do With Myself .... 7" EP .... Pye .... NEP44077 .... 1966 .... **£4** ....
I Love Paris .... 7" EP .... Pye .... NEP44083 .... 1967 .... **£4** ....
I Say A Little Prayer .... 7" .... Pye .... 7N25435 .... 1967 .... **£4** ....
In Between The Heartaches .... 7" .... Pye .... 7N25357 .... 1966 .... **£4** ....
In Paris .... LP .... Pye .... NPL28076 .... 1966 .... **£10** ....

Title	Format	Label	Cat. No.	Year	Price	Notes
It's Love That Really Counts	7" EP	Pye	NEP44024	1964	£4	
Looking With My Eyes	7"	Pye	7N25310	1965	£4	
Make The Music Play	7"	Pye	7N25223	1963	£4	
Make The Music Play	7"	Stateside	SS222	1963	£5	
Make Way For...	LP	Pye	NPL28046	1964	£10	
Message To Michael	7"	Pye	7N25368	1966	£4	
Message To Michael	7" EP	Pye	NEP44067	1966	£4	
Odds And Ends	7"	Pye	7N25497	1969	£4	
People Got To Be Free	7"	Pye	7N25491	1969	£4	
Presenting	LP	Pye	NPL28037	1964	£10	chart LP
Promises Promises	7"	Pye	7N25496	1969	£4	
Reach Out For Me	7"	Pye	7N25265	1964	£4	chart single
Sensitive Sound Of...	LP	Pye	NPL28055	1965	£10	
This Girl's In Love With You	7"	Pye	7N25484	1969	£4	
Trains And Boats And Planes	7"	Pye	7N25378	1966	£4	
Valley Of The Dolls	7"	Pye	7N25445	1968	£4	chart single
Walk On By	7"	Pye	7N25241	1964	£4	chart single
Who Can I Turn To	7" EP	Pye	NEP44049	1965	£4	
Window Wishing	7" EP	Pye	NEP44073	1966	£4	
Windows Of The World	7"	Pye	7N25428	1967	£4	
Wishin' And Hopin'	7" EP	Pye	NEP44039	1965	£4	
Wishin' And Hopin'	7"	Stateside	SS191	1963	£4	
You Can Have Him	7"	Pye	7N25290	1965	£4	chart single
You'll Never Get To Heaven	7"	Pye	7N25256	1964	£4	chart single
You've Lost That Lovin' Feelin'	7"	Pye	7N25505	1969	£4	

WASHINGTON, BABY

Title	Format	Label	Cat. No.	Year	Price	Notes
Breakfast In Bed	7"	Atlantic	584316	1970	£4	
Get A Hold Of Yourself	7"	United Artists	UP2247	1968	£8	
I Can't Wait Until I See My Baby	7"	Sue	WI321	1964	£10	
I Don't Know	7"	Atlantic	584299	1969	£4	
Only Those In Love	7"	London	HLC9987	1965	£4	
That's How Heartaches Are Made	LP	Sue	LP1014	1963	£20	US
That's How Heartaches Are Made	7"	Sue	WI302	1963	£12	
With You In Mind	LP	Veep	16528	1968	£10	US

WASHINGTON, ELLA

Title	Format	Label	Cat. No.	Year	Price	Notes
He Called Me Baby	7"	Monument	MON1030	1969	£4	

WASHINGTON, GENO & THE RAM JAM BAND

Title	Format	Label	Cat. No.	Year	Price	Notes
Different Strokes	7" EP	Pye	NEP24293	1968	£5	
Hand Clappin', Foot Stompin'	LP	Piccadilly	NPL38026	1966	£15	chart LP
Hi	7" EP	Piccadilly	NEP34054	1966	£5	
Hi Hi Hazel	7"	Piccadilly	7N35329	1966	£4	chart single
Hipsters And Flipsters	LP	Piccadilly	NSPL38032	1967	£12	chart LP
I Can't Quit Her	7"	Pye	7N17570	1968	£4	
Michael	7"	Piccadilly	7N35359	1967	£4	chart single
Que Sera Sera	7"	Piccadilly	7N35346	1966	£4	chart single
Running Wild	LP	Pye	NSPL18219	1968	£10	
Shake A Tail Feather	LP	Piccadilly	NSPL38029	1968	£10	
She Shot A Hole In My Soul	7"	Piccadilly	7N35392	1967	£4	
Small Package Of Hipsters	7" EP	Pye	NEP24302	1968	£5	
Tell It Like It Is	7"	Piccadilly	7N35403	1967	£4	
Water	7"	Piccadilly	7N35312	1966	£4	chart single

WASHINGTON, SHERI

Title	Format	Label	Cat. No.	Year	Price	Notes
I Got Plenty	7"	Vogue	V9070	1957	£30	

WASHINGTON, TONY

Title	Format	Label	Cat. No.	Year	Price	Notes
Show Me How	7"	Sue	WI327	1964	£8	

WASHINGTON, TONY & THE DC'S

Title	Format	Label	Cat. No.	Year	Price	Notes
But I Do	7"	Black Swan	WI459	1965	£10	
Dilly Dilly	7"	Black Swan	WI460	1965	£10	

WASP (BRIAN BENNETT)

Title	Format	Label	Cat. No.	Year	Price	Notes
Melissa	7"	EMI	EMI2253	1975	£8	

WASTED YOUTH

Title	Format	Label	Cat. No.	Year	Price	Notes
I'll Remember You	7"	Bridgehouse	BHS10	1980	£4	
Jealousy	7"	Bridgehouse	BHS5	1980	£4	

WATCH COMMITTEE

Title	Format	Label	Cat. No.	Year	Price	Notes
Throw Another Penny In The Well	7"	Philips	BF1695	1968	**£5**	

WATER INTO WINE

Title	Format	Label	Cat. No.	Year	Price	Notes
	LP	Harvest		197-	**£100**	
Hill Climbing For Beginners	LP	Myrrh		1974	**£50**	

WATERBOYS

Title	Format	Label	Cat. No.	Year	Price	Notes
Big Music	7"	Ensign	ENY508	1984	**£8**	
Big Music	12"	Ensign	12ENY508	1984	**£15**	
December	7"	Ensign	ENY506	1984	**£8**	
December	12"	Ensign	12ENY506	1984	**£15**	
Girl Called Johnny	7"	Chicken Jazz	CJ1	1983	**£8**	
Girl Called Johnny	12"	Chicken Jazz	CJ1	1983	**£15**	
Whole Of The Moon	7"	Ensign	ENY520	1985	**£10**	
Whole Of The Moon	12"	Ensign	12ENY520	1985	**£15**	

WATERPROOF CANDLE

Title	Format	Label	Cat. No.	Year	Price	Notes
Electronically Heated Child	7"	RCA	RCA1717	1968	**£10**	

WATERS, MUDDY

Title	Format	Label	Cat. No.	Year	Price	Notes
After The Rain	LP	Chess	CRL4553	1969	**£12**	
At Newport	LP	Chess	CRL4513	1965	**£20**	
At Newport	LP	Pye	NJL34	1961	**£20**	
Back In The Good Old Days	LP	Synd. Chap.	SC001	1970	**£10**	
Best Of...	LP	London	LJZ-M15152	1959	**£30**	
Blues From Big Bill's Copacabana	LP	Chess	LP1533	1968	**£15**	US
Blues Man	LP	Polydor	236574	1969	**£12**	
Can't Get No Grindin'	LP	Chess	6310129	1973	**£10**	
Down On Stovall's Plantation	LP	Bounty	BY6031	1968	**£15**	
Electric Mud	LP	Chess	CRL4542	1968	**£12**	
Fathers And Sons	LP	Chess	CRL4556	1969	**£15**	
Folk Singer	LP	Pye	NPL28038	1964	**£20**	
Honey Bee	78	Vogue	V2372	1956	**£20**	
I Got A Rich Man's Woman	7"	Chess	CRS8019	1965	**£8**	
I'm Ready	7" EP	Chess	CRE6006	1965	**£8**	
Let's Spend The Night Together	7"	Chess	CRS8083	1969	**£5**	
London Revisited	LP	Chess	CH60026	1974	**£10**	US
London Sessions	LP	Chess	6310121	1972	**£10**	
Long Distance Call	78	Vogue	V2273	1954	**£20**	
McKinley Morganfield AKA...	LP	Chess	6671001	1971	**£12**	
Mississippi Blues	7" EP	London	REU1060	1956	**£25**	
More Real Folk Blues	LP	Chess	LP1511	1966	**£20**	US
Muddy Sings Big Bill	LP	Marble Arch	MAL723	1967	**£10**	
Muddy Waters	LP	Pye	NPL28040	1964	**£25**	
Muddy Waters	7" EP	Pye	NEP44010	1963	**£8**	
Muddy Waters Live	LP	Chess	CH50012	1972	**£10**	US
Muddy Waters With Little Walter	7" EP	Vogue	EPV1046	1955	**£40**	
Muddy, Brass And The Blues	LP	Chess	CRL4525	1967	**£15**	
My John The Conqueror Root	7"	Chess	CRS8001	1965	**£10**	
Real Folk Blues	LP	Chess	CRL4515	1966	**£20**	
Real Folk Blues Vol.4	7" EP	Chess	CRE6022	1966	**£6**	
Rollin' Stone	78	Vogue	V2101	1952	**£20**	
Sail On	LP	Chess	LPS1539	1969	**£12**	US
Sings Big Bill Broonzy	LP	Pye	NPL28048	1964	**£20**	
They Call Me Muddy Waters	LP	Chess	LPS1553	1971	**£10**	US
Unk In Funk	LP	Chess	CH60031	1974	**£10**	US
Vintage Mud	LP	Sunnyland	KS100	1969	**£15**	

WATERS, MUDDY / BO DIDDLEY & HOWLIN' WOLF

Title	Format	Label	Cat. No.	Year	Price	Notes
Super Super Blues Band	LP	Chess	CRL4537	1968	**£15**	

WATERS, MUDDY / BO DIDDLEY & LITTLE WALTER

Title	Format	Label	Cat. No.	Year	Price	Notes
Super Blues	LP	Chess	CRL4529	1966	**£15**	

WATERS, ROGER

Title	Format	Label	Cat. No.	Year	Price	Notes
5:06 am (Every Stranger's Eyes)	7"	Harvest	HAR5230	1984	**£10**	
Pros And Cons Of Hitch-Hiking	LP	Harvest	SHVL2401051	1984	**£12**	banded promo
Radio K.A.O.S.	LP	EMI	KAOSDJ1	1987	**£20**	banded promo, no dialogue
Radio Waves	CD-s	EMI	CDEM6	1987	**£8**	

Sunset Strip	7"	EMI	EM20	1987	**£10**	

WATERSON, LAL & MIKE

Bright Phoebus	LP	Trailer	LES2076	1972	**£15**	

WATERSONS

Frost And Fire	LP	Topic	12T136	1965	**£12**	
Watersons	LP	Topic	12T142	1966	**£15**	
Yorkshire Garland	LP	Topic	12T167	1966	**£15**	

WATERSONS, HARRY BOARDMAN / MAUREEN CRAIK

New Voices	LP	Topic	12T125	1965	**£15**	

WATSON, JOHN L.

Mother's Love	7"	Deram	DM285	1970	**£6**	
White Hot Blue Black	LP	Deram	SMLR1061	1970	**£15**	

WATSON, JOHNNY GUITAR

Bad	LP	OKeh	OKM4118	1967	**£10**	US
Blues Soul	LP	Chess	1490	1965	**£25**	US
I Cried For You	LP	Cadet	LP4056	1967	**£10**	US
In The Fats Bag	LP	OKeh	OKM4124	1967	**£10**	US
Johnny Guitar Watson	LP	King	LP857	1963	**£50**	US

WATTS 103rd STREET RHYTHM BAND

Do Your Thing	7"	W. Bros	WB7250	1969	**£4**	
Express Yourself	7"	W. Bros	WB7417	1970	**£4**	
Love Land	7"	W. Bros	WB7365	1970	**£4**	
Till You Get Enough	7"	W. Bros	WB7298	1969	**£4**	

WATTS, NOBLE THIN MAN

Hard Times	7"	London	HLU8627	1958	**£15**	
Noble's Theme	7"	Sue	WI347	1964	**£8**	

WATTS, NOBLE THIN MAN & WILD JIMMY SPURRILL

Noble Thin Man Watts & Wild Jimmy Spurrill	7" EP	XX	MIN717		**£5**	

WAVE CRESTS

Surftime USA	LP	Viking	VKS6606	1963	**£15**	US

WAY WE LIVE

Candle For Judith	LP	Dandelion	DAN8004	1971	**£60**	

WAY, DARRYL WOLF

Bunch Of Fives	7"	Deram	DM395	1973	**£4**	
Canis Lupus	LP	Deram	SDL14	1973	**£12**	
Night Music	LP	Deram	SML1116	1974	**£10**	
Saturation Point	LP	Deram	SML1104	1973	**£12**	
Two Sisters	7"	Deram	DM401	1973	**£4**	
Wolf	7"	Deram	DM378	1973	**£4**	

WAYBURN, NANCY

World Goes On Without Me	7"	W. Bros	WB5646	1965	**£8**	

WAYNE, ALVIS

Don't Mean Maybe Baby	7"	Starlite	ST45104	1963	**£60**	

WAYNE, CARL

Carl Wayne	LP	RCA		1971	**£12**	
Take My Hand For A While	7"	RCA	RCA2257	1972	**£4**	
Way Back In The Fifties	7"	Polydor	2058527	1975	**£4**	

WAYNE, CARL & THE VIKINGS

This Is Love	7"	Pye	7N15824	1965	**£15**	
What's A Matter Baby	7"	Pye	7N15702	1964	**£15**	

WAYNE, FRANCES

Frances Wayne	LP	Brunswick	BL54022	1957	**£12**	US
Songs For My Man	LP	Epic	LN3222	195-	**£12**	US
Warm Sound Of...	LP	Atlantic	1263	1956	**£15**	US
Half Hearted Love	7"	Vogue	V9169	1960	**£5**	

WAYNE, PAT & THE BEACHCOMBERS

Brand New Man	7"	Columbia	DB7417	1964	**£6**	
Bye Bye Johnny	7"	Columbia	DB7262	1964	**£8**	
Come Dance With Me	7"	Columbia	DB7603	1965	**£5**	
Jambalaya	7"	Columbia	DB7121	1963	**£8**	
My Friend	7"	Columbia	DB7739	1965	**£4**	
Night Is Over	7"	Columbia	DB7944	1966	**£5**	
Roll Over Beethoven	7"	Columbia	DB7182	1963	**£6**	

WAYNE, RICKY

Chick A Roo	7"	Top Rank	JAR432	1960	**£4**	
Chick A Roo	7"	Triumph	RGM1009	1960	**£20**	
Make Way Baby	7"	Pye	7N15289	1960	**£4**	

WAYNE, TERRY

All Mama's Children	7"	Columbia	DB4067	1958	**£8**	
Matchbox	7"	Columbia	DB4002	1957	**£8**	
Oh Lonesome Me	7"	Columbia	DB4112	1958	**£5**	
She's Mine	7"	Columbia	DB4312	1959	**£4**	
Slim Jim Tie	7"	Columbia	DB4035	1957	**£8**	
Terrific	7" EP	Columbia	SEG7758	1958	**£20**	
Where My Baby Goes	7"	Columbia	DB4205	1958	**£4**	

WAYNE, THOMAS

Tragedy	7"	London	HLU8846	1959	**£12**	

WAYNE, WEE WILLIE

Travellin' Mood	LP	Imperial	LP9144	1961	**£35**	US

WAYS AND MEANS

Little Deuce Coupe	7"	Columbia	DB7907	1966	**£6**	
Sea Of Faces	7"	Pye	7N17217	1966	**£6**	

WE FIVE

Let's Get Together	7"	Pye	7N25346	1966	**£4**	
Let's Get Together	7" EP	Pye	NEP44056	1966	**£5**	
You Were On My Mind	LP	A&M	LP111	1965	**£10**	US
You Were On My Mind	7"	Pye	7N25314	1965	**£4**	

WE THE PEOPLE

He Doesn't Go About It Right	7"	London	HLH10089	1966	**£10**	

WEASELS

Liverpool Beat	LP	Wing	MGW12282	1964	**£10**	US

WEATHER REPORT

When the time comes to assess the major innovators of late twentieth century music, then the name of Weather Report is likely to loom large. Marketed as jazz, Weather Report's music is of equal appeal to progressive rock fans for the way in which it blends improvisation with composed passages, setting up frequently elaborate structures in which the textures and timbres available to electronic instruments are exploited to the full. Under Josef Zawinul's fingers, the synthesiser begins to achieve some of the potential of which it is obviously capable, but which is so seldom realised. The double Japan-only release "Live In Tokyo" contains the complete concert that was presented in excerpt on the UK album "I Sing The Body Electric".

Live In Tokyo	LP	CBS Sony	40AP942-3	1972	**£25**	Japanese double

WEAVERS

Best Of...	LP	Decca	DL8893	1959	**£12**	US
Best Of...	LP	Decca	DXB173	1963	**£12**	US
Folk Songs Around The World	LP	Decca	DL8909	1959	**£12**	US
Reunion At Carnegie Hall	LP	Fontana	TFL6032	1963	**£10**	

WEB

Baby Won't You Leave Me Alone	7"	Deram	DM217	1968	**£8**	
Fully Interlocking	LP	Deram	SML1025	1968	**£15**	
Hatton Mill Morning	7"	Deram	DM201	1968	**£8**	
I Spider	LP	Polydor	2383024	1970	**£60**	
Monday To Friday	7"	Deram	DM253	1969	**£8**	
Theraphosa Blondi	LP	Deram	SML1058	1970	**£15**	

WEBB, DEAN

Hey Miss Fanny	7"	Parlophone	R4549	1959	**£10**	
Streamline Baby	7"	Parlophone	R4587	1959	**£6**	

WEBB, DON

Title	Format	Label	Cat. No.	Year	Price	Notes
Little Ditty Baby	7"	Coral	Q72385	1960	**£20**	

WEBB, JIMMY

Jimmy Webb is a songwriter of genius - "By The Time I Get To Phoenix", "Didn't We", "MacArthur Park", and "Wichita Lineman" are early landmarks in his career. His own records reveal him to be a limited but effective singer, with "Land's End" containing some particularly fine material.

Title	Format	Label	Cat. No.	Year	Price	Notes
And So On	LP	Reprise	6448	1971	**£10**	US
I Keep It Hid	7"	CBS	3672	1968	**£4**	
Jim Webb Sings Jim Webb	LP	Epic	26401	1968	**£15**	US
Land's End	LP	Asylum	SYL9014	1974	**£10**	
Letters	LP	Reprise	K44173	1972	**£10**	
Words And Music	LP	Reprise	K44101	1970	**£10**	
Dig	7"	Columbia	DB3805	1956	**£4**	

WEBB, ROGER TRIO

Title	Format	Label	Cat. No.	Year	Price	Notes
All My Loving	7"	Parlophone	R5176	1964	**£4**	

WEBB, SONNY & THE CASCADES

Title	Format	Label	Cat. No.	Year	Price	Notes
You've Got Everything	7"	Oriole	CB1873	1963	**£8**	

WEBBER SISTERS

Title	Format	Label	Cat. No.	Year	Price	Notes
My World	7"	Island	WI3109	1967	**£8**	

WEBSTER, DEENA

Title	Format	Label	Cat. No.	Year	Price	Notes
Scarborough Fair	7"	Parlophone	R5738	1968	**£4**	

WEDDING PRESENT

Title	Format	Label	Cat. No.	Year	Price	Notes
Anyone Can Make A Mistake	cass-s	Reception	REC006C	1987	**£5**	with badge
Brassneck	7"	RCA	PB43403	1990	**£15**	handpainted cover
Don't Try And Stop Me Mother	12"	Reception	REC002/12	1986	**£15**	
Go Out And Get 'Em Boy!	7"	City Slang	CSL001	1985	**£40**	
Go Out And Get 'Em Boy!	7"	Reception	REC001	1985	**£50**	
Katrusyu	7"	Reception		1988	**£15**	promo only
Million Miles	7"	Reception		1987	**£30**	promo only
My Favourite Dress	7"	Reception	REC005	1987	**£4**	
My Favourite Dress	7"	Reception	REC005	1987	**£15**	white vinyl
Nobody's Twisting Your Arm	7"	Reception	REC009	1988	**£5**	gatefold PS
Once More	7"	Reception	REC002	1986	**£25**	
This Boy Can Wait	7"	Reception	REC003	1986	**£10**	
This Boy Can Wait	12"	Reception	REC003/12	1986	**£15**	
Why Are You Being So Reasonable Now?	Cass-s	Reception	REC011C	1988	**£5**	

WEDGE

Title	Format	Label	Cat. No.	Year	Price	Notes
No One Left But Me	LP	Private		197-	**£40**	US

WEEDON, BERT

Title	Format	Label	Cat. No.	Year	Price	Notes
$64,000 Question	7"	Parlophone	R4256	1957	**£4**	
Apache	7"	Top Rank	JAR415	1960	**£4**	chart single
Big Beat Boogie	7"	Top Rank	JAR300	1960	**£4**	chart single
Big Note Blues	7"	Parlophone	R4446	1958	**£4**	
Boy With The Magic Guitar	7"	Parlophone	MSP6242	1956	**£6**	
China Doll	7"	HMV	POP946	1961	**£4**	
Dark Eyes	7"	HMV	POP1216	1963	**£4**	
Demonstration Record With David Gell	7" EP	Selmer		1959	**£6**	
Fifi	7"	Saga	SAG2906	1959	**£4**	
Ghost Train	7"	Top Rank	JAR582	1961	**£4**	
Gin Mill Guitar	7"	HMV	POP1302	1964	**£4**	
Ginchy	7"	Top Rank	JAR537	1961	**£4**	chart single
Guitar Boogie Shuffle	7"	Top Rank	JAR117	1959	**£5**	chart single
Guitar Man	7" EP	HMV	7EG8856	1964	**£4**	
High Steppin'	7"	HMV	POP1485	1965	**£4**	
Honky Tonk Guitar	LP	Top Rank	35101	1961	**£10**	
It Happened In Monterey	7"	HMV	POP1248	1964	**£4**	
Jealousy	7"	Top Rank	JAR210	1959	**£4**	
Kick Off	7"	HMV	POP1535	1966	**£4**	
King Size Guitar	LP	Top Rank	BUY026	1960	**£15**	chart LP
Lady Is A Tramp	7"	Top Rank	JAR121	1959	**£4**	
Mr.Guitar	7"	Top Rank	JAR559	1961	**£4**	chart single
Nashville Boogie	7"	Top Rank	JAR221	1959	**£4**	chart single
Night Cry	7"	HMV	POP1141	1963	**£4**	

Title	Format	Label	Cat. No.	Year	Price	Notes
Petite Fleur	7"	Top Rank	JAR122	1959	£4	
Play That Big Guitar	7"	Parlophone	R4381	1957	£4	
Rockin' At The Roundhouse	7"	Fontana	6007012	1970	£4	
Soho Fair	7"	Parlophone	R4315	1957	£4	
Some Other Love	7"	HMV	POP1043	1962	£4	
Sorry Robbie	7"	Top Rank	JAR517	1960	£4	chart single
South Of The Border	7"	HMV	POP1077	1962	£4	
Stardust	7"	Top Rank	JAR211	1959	£4	
Stranger Than Fiction	7"	HMV	POP1592	1967	£4	
Teenage Guitar	7"	Top Rank	JAR136	1959	£4	
Time To Say Goodnight	7"	Top Rank	JAR123	1959	£4	
Tokyo Melody	7"	HMV	POP1355	1964	£4	
Tune For Two	7"	HMV	POP1039	1962	£10	demo only
Twelfth Street Rag	7"	Top Rank	JAR360	1960	£4	chart single
Twelve String Shuffle	7"	HMV	POP1387	1965	£4	
Twist A Napoli	7"	HMV	POP989	1962	£4	
Watch Your Step	7"	Grosvenor	GRS1015		£4	
Waxing The Winners	7" EP	Esquire	EP56	1956	£8	
Weedon Winners	7" EP	Top Rank	JKP3008	1961	£5	

WEEDON, BERT & MAX JAFFA

Title	Format	Label	Cat. No.	Year	Price	Notes
Dancing Duck	78	Columbia	DB3343	1953	£4	
Sally	78	Columbia	DB3484	1954	£4	

WEEDON, BERT & OTHERS

Title	Format	Label	Cat. No.	Year	Price	Notes
Roulette	7" EP	Top Rank	TR5004	1959	£6	

WEIR, BOB

Title	Format	Label	Cat. No.	Year	Price	Notes
Ace	LP	W. Bros	K46165	1972	£15	

WEIR, NORRIS

Title	Format	Label	Cat. No.	Year	Price	Notes
Reggay Revolution	7"	Dragon	DRA1030	1974	£4	

WEIRDOS

Title	Format	Label	Cat. No.	Year	Price	Notes
We Got The Neutron Bomb	7"	Dangerhouse	SP1063	1978	£15	

WEISSBERG, ERIC

Title	Format	Label	Cat. No.	Year	Price	Notes
Duelling Banjos	LP	W. Bros	K46214	1973	£10	

WELCH, BOB

Title	Format	Label	Cat. No.	Year	Price	Notes
French Kiss	LP	Capitol	EST11663	1977	£50	US pic disc

WELCH, BRUCE

Title	Format	Label	Cat. No.	Year	Price	Notes
Please Mr., Please	7"	EMI	EMI2141	1974	£5	

WELCH, LENNY

Title	Format	Label	Cat. No.	Year	Price	Notes
Are You Sincere	7"	London	HLA9810	1963	£4	
Breaking Up Is Hard To Do	7"	Major Minor	MM707	1970	£4	
Darling Take Me Back	7"	London	HLR9981	1965	£4	
Ebb Tide	7"	London	HLA9880	1964	£4	
If You See My Love	7"	London	HLA9910	1964	£4	
Rags To Riches	7"	London	HLR10031	1966	£4	
Run To My Lovin' Arms	7"	London	HLR10010	1965	£4	
Since I Fell For You	LP	Cadence	CLP5068	1963	£10	US
Taste Of Honey	7"	London	HLA9601	1962	£4	
Two Different Worlds	7"	London	HLR9991	1965	£4	
When There's No Such Thing As Love	7"	Mainstream	MSS307	1975	£4	
You Don't Know Me	7"	London	HLA9094	1960	£4	

WELCH, TIM

Title	Format	Label	Cat. No.	Year	Price	Notes
Weak In The Knees	7"	Columbia	DB4529	1960	£4	

WELLINGTON, WADE

Title	Format	Label	Cat. No.	Year	Price	Notes
Let's Turkey Trot	7"	Oriole	CB1857	1963	£4	

WELLS, BOBBY

Title	Format	Label	Cat. No.	Year	Price	Notes
Let's Coppa Groove	7"	Beacon	BEA102	1968	£5	yellow label

WELLS, HOUSTON

Title	Format	Label	Cat. No.	Year	Price	Notes
Anna Marie	7"	Parlophone	R5099	1964	£4	
Blowing Wild	7"	Parlophone	R5069	1963	£4	
Blue Of The Night	7"	Parlophone	R5226	1965	£4	

Just For You	7" EP	Parlophone	GEP8878	1963	**£8**	
Livin' Alone	7"	Parlophone	R5141	1964	**£8**	
Only The Heartaches	7"	Parlophone	R5031	1963	**£4**	chart single
Ramona	7" EP	Parlophone	GEP8914	1964	**£10**	
Shutters And Boards	7"	Parlophone	R4980	1962	**£4**	
This Song Is Just For You	7"	Parlophone	R4955	1962	**£4**	
Western Style	LP	Parlophone	PMC1215	1963	**£50**	

WELLS, JOHNNY

Lonely Moon	7"	Columbia	DB4377	1959	**£4**	

WELLS, JUNIOR

Blues Hit Big Town	LP	Delmark	640	1969	**£10**	US
Blues With A Beat	7" EP	Delmark	DJB1	1966	**£10**	
Coming At You	LP	Vanguard	SVRL19011	1968	**£12**	
Girl You Lit My Fire	7"	Mercury	MF1056	1968	**£4**	
Hoodoo Man Blues	LP	Delmark	612	1966	**£15**	US
It's My Life Baby	LP	Fontana	TFL6084	1966	**£15**	
It's My Life Baby	LP	Vanguard	SVRL19028	1966	**£10**	
Junior Wells	7" EP	XX	MIN715		**£5**	
Southside Blues Jam	LP	Delmark	628	1967	**£10**	US
You're Tuff Enough	LP	Mercury	SMCL20130	1968	**£12**	

WELLS, KITTY

After Dark	LP	Decca	DL8888	1959	**£12**	US
Country Hit Parade	LP	Decca	DL8293	1956	**£15**	US
Dust On The Bible	LP	Decca	DL8858	1959	**£12**	US
Kitty Sings	7" EP	Brunswick	OE9149	1955	**£5**	
Kitty Wells Story	LP	Decca	DXB174	1963	**£10**	US, with booklet
Kitty's Choice	LP	Decca	DL8979	1960	**£10**	US
Winner Of Your Heart	LP	Decca	DL8552	1956	**£15**	US

WELLS, MARY

Ain't It The Truth	7"	Stateside	SS372	1965	**£15**	
Bye Bye Baby	LP	Oriole	PS40051	1963	**£40**	
Dear Lover	7"	Atlantic	AT4067	1966	**£10**	
Greatest Hits	LP	Motown	616	1964	**£20**	US
Greatest hits	LP	T. Motown	TML11032	1966	**£15**	
He's A Lover	7"	Stateside	SS439	1965	**£12**	
Laughing Boy	7"	Oriole	CBA1829	1963	**£30**	
Live On Stage	LP	Motown	611	1963	**£25**	US
Love Songs To The Beatles	LP	20th Century	TFM3178	1965	**£20**	US
Mary Wells	7" EP	T. Motown	TME2007	1965	**£12**	
Mary Wells	LP	20th Century	TFM3171	1965	**£12**	US
Me And My Baby	7"	Atlantic	584054	1966	**£4**	
Me Without You	7"	Stateside	SS463	1965	**£12**	
My Baby Just Cares For Me	LP	T. Motown	TML11006	1965	**£25**	
My Guy	LP	Stateside	SL10095	1964	**£40**	
My Guy	7"	Stateside	SS288	1964	**£8**	chart single
My Guy	7"	Stateside	SS288	1964	**£40**	demo
My Guy	7"	T. Motown	TMG820	1972	**£4**	chart single
My Guy	7"	T. Motown	TMG820	1972	**£10**	demo
Never Never Leave Me	7"	Stateside	SS415	1965	**£12**	
Nothing But A Man	LP	Motown	630	1965	**£15**	US
One Who Really Loves You	LP	Motown	605	1962	**£40**	US
Ooh	LP	Movietone	71010	1966	**£12**	US
Servin' Up Some Soul	LP	Stateside	SL10266	1968	**£12**	
Set My Soul On Fire	7"	Atlantic	584104	1967	**£4**	
Two Lovers	LP	Oriole	PS40045	1963	**£40**	
Two Lovers	7"	Oriole	CBA1796	1963	**£30**	
Two Sides Of	LP	Atlantic	587049	1966	**£10**	
Use Your Head	7"	Stateside	SS396	1965	**£12**	
Vintage Stock	LP	Motown	653	1966	**£20**	US
You Beat Me To The Punch	7"	Oriole	CBA1762	1962	**£30**	
You Lost The Sweetest Boy	7"	Stateside	SS242	1963	**£15**	
Your Old Standby	7"	Oriole	CBA1847	1963	**£30**	

WERLWINDS

Winding It Up	7"	Columbia	DB4650	1961	**£4**	

WERTH, HOWARD

Lucinda	7"	Charisma	CB225	1974	**£4**	

WERTH, HOWARD & THE MOONBEAMS

King Brilliant	LP	Charisma	CAS11004	1975	**£10**	

WESLEY, FRED & THE JB'S

Breakin' Bread	LP	Polydor	2391161	1975	**£15**	
Going It To Death	7"	Polydor	2066322	1973	**£4**	
JB Shout	7"	Mojo	2093025	1974	**£4**	

WEST COAST DELEGATION

Reach The Top	7"	Deram	DM113	1967	**£6**	

WEST COAST POP ART EXPERIMENTAL BAND

Child's Guide To Good And Evil	LP	Reprise	RSLP6298	1968	**£25**	
Part One	LP	Reprise	R6247	1967	**£20**	US
Volume 2	LP	Reprise	R6270	1967	**£20**	US
West Coast Pop Art Experimental Band	LP	Fifo	M101	1966	**£300**	US
Where's My Daddy	LP	Amos	AAS7004	1969	**£25**	US

WEST FIVE

But If It Doesn't Work Out	7"	HMV	POP1513	1966	**£8**	
Congratulations	7"	HMV	POP1396	1965	**£8**	
Just Like Romeo And Juliet	7"	HMV	POP1428	1965	**£10**	

WEST INDIANS

Never Gonna Give You Up	7"	Dynamic	DYN413	197-	**£4**	

WEST POINT SUPERNATURAL

Time Will Tell	7"	Reaction	591013	1967	**£8**	

WEST, ADAM & BURT WARD

Batman	LP	20th Century	TF4180	1966	**£30**	US

WEST, BRUCE & LAING

The connection between Mountain and Cream was made even tighter when Mountain's bass player, Felix Pappalardi, left to be replaced by Jack Bruce. Unfortunately, the newly constituted West, Bruce, & Laing chose to concentrate on the more bombastic elements of Cream's style and their records are much less interesting than those of either of the group's predecessors.

Dirty Shoes	7"	RSO	2090113	1973	**£4**	
Live And Kicking	LP	RSO	2394128	1974	**£10**	
Whatever Turns You On	LP	RSO	2394107	1973	**£10**	
Why Don'tcha	LP	CBS	65314	1972	**£10**	

WEST, DODIE

Going Out Of My Head	7"	Decca	F12046	1964	**£4**	chart single

WEST, KEITH

Keith West was the singer with Tomorrow, and his solo singles featured at least some of the members of that group. Certainly guitarist Steve Howe can be heard on West's hit, "Excerpt From A Teenage Opera". The opera from which this song was supposedly taken never did appear, if indeed it ever existed in the first place. The single works brilliantly in any case as a tantalising glimpse of something much larger, but invisible.

Excerpt From A Teenage Opera	7"	Parlophone	R5623	1967	**£4**	chart single
Havin' Someone	7"	Deram	DM410	1974	**£4**	
On A Saturday	7"	Parlophone	R5713	1968	**£6**	
Riding For A Fall	7"	Deram	DM402	1973	**£4**	
Sam	7"	Parlophone	R5651	1967	**£6**	chart single

WEST, LESLIE

Great Fatsby	LP	RCA	RS1009	1975	**£10**	US
Leslie West Band	LP	Phantom	701	1975	**£10**	US
Mountain	LP	Windfall	4500	1969	**£20**	US

WEST, MAE

Great Balls Of Fire	7"	MGM	2006203	1973	**£4**	
Twist And Shout	7"	Stateside	SS2021	1967	**£4**	

WEST, SPEEDY

Guitar Spectacular	LP	Capitol	T1835	1962	**£15**	US
Steel Guitar	LP	Capitol	T1341	1960	**£20**	US
West Of Hawaii	LP	Capitol	T956	1958	**£25**	US

WEST, SPEEDY & JIMMY BRYANT

Two Guitars Country Style	LP	Capitol	T520	1956	**£40**	US

Two Guitars Country Style	LP-10"	Capitol	H520	1954	**£75**	US
Two Guitars Country Style Part 1	7" EP	Capitol	EAP1520	1955	**£6**	
Two Guitars Country Style Part 2	7" EP	Capitol	EAP2520	1955	**£6**	

WESTBROOK, MIKE

Celebration	LP	Deram	SML1013	1967	**£50**	
Citadel/Room 315	LP	RCA	SF8433	1975	**£15**	
Life Of Its Own	7"	Deram	DM234	1969	**£8**	
Live	LP	Cadillac	SGC1001	1972	**£20**	
Love Songs	LP	Deram	SML1069	1970	**£40**	
Love, Dream And Variations	LP	Transatlantic		1976	**£20**	
Marching Song Vol.1	LP	Deram	SML1047	1969	**£50**	
Marching Song Vol.2	LP	Deram	SML1048	1969	**£50**	
Metropolis	LP	Neon	NE10	1971	**£30**	
Metropolis/Citadel/Room 315	LP	RCA		1979	**£20**	double
Original Peter	7"	Deram	DM311	1970	**£8**	
Release	LP	Deram	SML1031	1968	**£50**	
Requiem	7"	Deram	DM286	1970	**£8**	
Tyger	LP	RCA	SER5612	1971	**£30**	

WESTFAUSTER

In A King's Dream	LP	Nasco		1970	**£25**	US

WESTLAKE, CLIVE

Hundred Days	7"	Fontana	TF940	1968	**£4**	

WESTLAKE, KEVIN

Stars Fade	LP	Utopia	1388	1976	**£12**	US

WESTMINSTER FIVE

Railroad Blues	7"	Carnival	CV7017	1964	**£8**	
Sticks And Stones	7"	Carnival	CV7019	1965	**£6**	

WESTON, KIM

Danger Heartbreak Dead Ahead	7"	Major Minor	MM683	1970	**£4**	
For The First Time	LP	MGM	E4477	1967	**£10**	US
Helpless	7"	T. Motown	TMG554	1966	**£25**	
Helpless	7"	T. Motown	TMG554	1966	**£70**	demo
I Got What You Need	7"	MGM	MGM1338	1967	**£4**	
I'm Still Loving You	7"	T. Motown	TMG511	1965	**£25**	
I'm Still Loving You	7"	T. Motown	TMG511	1965	**£60**	demo
Kim Weston	7" EP	T. Motown	TME2005	1965	**£30**	
Little More Love	7"	Stateside	SS359	1964	**£25**	
Little More Love	7"	Stateside	SS359	1964	**£60**	demo
Nobody	7"	MGM	MGM1382	1968	**£6**	
Rock Me A Little While	7" EP	T. Motown	TME2015	1966	**£30**	
Take Me In Your Arms	7"	T. Motown	TMG538	1965	**£25**	
Take Me In Your Arms	7"	T. Motown	TMG538	1965	**£70**	demo
That's Groovy	7"	MGM	MGM1357	1967	**£4**	

WESTWIND

Westwind	LP	P. Farthing		1971	**£40**	

WET WET WET

Sweet Little Mystery	12"	Precious	JEWEL412	1987	**£6**	'wet' cover
Wishing I Was Lucky	12"	Precious	JWLD3	1987	**£6**	double

WET WILLIE

Wet Willie	LP	Capricorn	K40281	1971	**£10**	
Wet Willie II	LP	Capricorn	0109	1972	**£10**	US

WHALEFEATHERS

Whalefeathers	LP	Blue Horizon	2431009	1971	**£20**	
Whalefeathers Declare	LP	Nasco	9003	1969	**£25**	US

WHAM!

Bad Boys	7"	Innervision	WA3143	1983	**£8**	pic disc
Club Tropicana	7"	Innervision	WA3613	1983	**£10**	pic disc
Final	LP	Epic	WHAM2	1986	**£15**	2 gold vinyl discs, inserts, boxed
Freedom	7"	Epic	QA4743	1984	**£10**	shaped pic disc
Freedom	7"	Epic	WA4743	1984	**£12**	shaped pic disc

I'm Your Man	12"	Epic	WTA6716	1985	**£8**	pic disc
Last Christmas	7"	Epic	GA4949	1984	**£6**	gatefold sleeve
Last Christmas	12"	Epic	GTA4949	1984	**£8**	gatefold sleeve

WHEELER, KENNY

Windmill Tilter	LP	Fontana		1968	**£40**	

WHEELS

Herbie Armstrong has enjoyed a lengthy and varied career - gaining chart hits as a member of Fox and of Yellow Dog, playing on several Van Morrison LPs, and doing much other session work besides. His roots, however, go back to Belfast and an R&B group called Wheels. The group made two singles, then changed its name to Wheels-A-Way for a third.

Bad Little Woman	7"	Columbia	DB7827	1966	**£70**	
Gloria	7"	Columbia	DB7682	1965	**£50**	
Kicks	7"	Columbia	DB7981	1966	**£40**	

WHEELS-A-WAY

Kicks	7"	Columbia	DB7918	1966	**£50**	

WHICHWHAT

I Wanna Be Free	7"	Beacon	BEA144	1971	**£5**	
In The Year 2525	7"	Beacon	BEA133	1971	**£5**	
Vietnam Rose	7"	Beacon	BEA169	1971	**£5**	
Whichwhat's First	LP	Beacon		1970	**£20**	
Why Do Lovers Break Each Other's Hearts	7"	Beacon	BEA131	1971	**£5**	

WHIRLWIND

Blowing Up A Storm	LP-10"	Chiswick	4	1978	**£12**	
Hang Loose I've Gotta Rock	7"	Chiswick	NS25	1978	**£5**	

WHIRLWINDS

The Whirlwinds were led by Graham Gouldman, of later song-writing and Ten CC fame.

Look At Me	7"	HMV	POP1301	1964	**£20**	

WHISKY, NANCY & THE SKIFFLERS

Bowling Green	7"	Fontana	TF612	1965	**£4**	
He's Solid Gone	7"	Oriole	CB1394	1957	**£4**	
Hillside In Scotland	7"	Oriole	CB1452	1958	**£4**	
Old Grey Goose	7"	Oriole	CB1485	1959	**£4**	

WHISPERS OF TRUTH

Whispers Of Truth	LP	Key			**£30**	

WHISTLER

Ho-Hum	LP	Deram	SML1083	1971	**£20**	

WHITCOMB, IAN

Good Hard Rock	7"	Capitol	CL15431	1966	**£4**	
Mod, Mod Music Hall	LP	Stateside	SL10200	1966	**£10**	
N-N-Nervous	7"	Capitol	CL15418	1965	**£4**	
This Sporting Life	7"	Capitol	CL15382	1965	**£4**	
You Turn Me On	7"	Capitol	CL15395	1965	**£6**	
You Turn Me On	LP	Tower	T5004	1965	**£12**	US

WHITE DUCK

Billy Goat	7"	Uni	UN541	1972	**£5**	
Carry Love	7"	Uni	UN555	1973	**£4**	
In Season	LP	Uni	73140	1972	**£10**	US
White Duck	LP	Uni	73122	1971	**£10**	US

WHITE LIGHT

White Light	LP	Century	39955	196-	**£70**	US

WHITE MULE

Looking Through Cats' Eyes	7"	Uni	UNS523	1970	**£4**	

WHITE NOISE

Electric Storm	LP	Island	ILPS9099	1969	**£10**	

WHITE PLAINS

When You Are A King	LP	Deram		1971	**£10**	
White Plains	LP	Deram		1970	**£12**	

WHITE TRASH

Title	Format	Label	Catalogue	Year	Price	Notes
Road To Nowhere	7"	Apple	6	1969	**£12**	

WHITE, BUKKA

Title	Format	Label	Catalogue	Year	Price	Notes
Memphis Hot Shots	LP	Blue Horizon	763229	1969	**£35**	

WHITE, CHRIS

Title	Format	Label	Catalogue	Year	Price	Notes
Mouth Music	LP	Charisma	CAS1118	1976	**£10**	

WHITE, DANNY

Title	Format	Label	Catalogue	Year	Price	Notes
Keep My Woman Home	7"	Sue	WI4031	1967	**£8**	

WHITE, DUKE

Title	Format	Label	Catalogue	Year	Price	Notes
It's Over	7"	Island	WI084	1963	**£10**	
Sow Good Seeds	7"	Black Swan	WI444	1965	**£10**	

WHITE, IAN

Title	Format	Label	Catalogue	Year	Price	Notes
Ian White	LP			1970	**£30**	

WHITE, JEANETTE

Title	Format	Label	Catalogue	Year	Price	Notes
Music	7"	A&M	AMS761	1969	**£12**	

WHITE, JOE

Title	Format	Label	Catalogue	Year	Price	Notes
Downtown Girl	7"	Island	WI166	1965	**£10**	
Hog In A Coco	7"	Island	WI159	1964	**£10**	
I Need A Woman	7"	Doctor Bird	DB1090	1967	**£10**	
If It Don't Work Out	7"	Gayfeet	GS202	1973	**£8**	
Irene	7"	Island	WI201	1965	**£10**	
Kenyatta	7"	Dynamic	DYN440	197-	**£4**	
King Solomon	7"	R&B	JB137	1964	**£10**	
Lonely Nights	7"	Doctor Bird	DB1080	1967	**£10**	
Punch You Down	7"	Ska Beat	JB180	1965	**£10**	
Rudies All Around	7"	Doctor Bird	DB1069	1966	**£10**	
Try A Little Tenderness	7"	Blue Cat	BS119	1968	**£10**	
When You Are Young	7"	Island	WI145	1964	**£10**	

WHITE, JOSH

Title	Format	Label	Catalogue	Year	Price	Notes
Ballads	LP-10"	Decca	DL5082	195-	**£20**	US
Ballads Vol.2	LP-10"	Decca	DL5247	195-	**£20**	US
Blues And... Pt.1	7" EP	Pye	NJE1057	1957	**£4**	
Blues And... Pt.2	7" EP	Pye	NJE1058	1957	**£4**	
Blues And... Pt.3	7" EP	Pye	NJE1059	1957	**£4**	
Chain Gang Songs	LP	Golden Guin.	GGL0205	1962	**£10**	
Empty Bed Blues	LP	Golden Guin.	GGL0160	1962	**£10**	
Josh	LP	Elektra	EKL114	195-	**£10**	US
Josh At Midnight	LP	Elektra	EKL102	195-	**£10**	US
Josh White	LP	Ace Of H.	AH65	1964	**£10**	
Josh White	LP	Decca	DL8665	1957	**£15**	US
Josh White	LP-10"	London	338	195-	**£15**	US
Josh White	7" EP	Mercury	10006MCE	1964	**£4**	
Josh White Program	LP-10"	London	341	195-	**£15**	US
Josh White Sings	LP-10"	Mercury	MG25015	195-	**£15**	US
Josh White's Blues	LP	Mercury	MG20203	1956	**£12**	US
Singer Supreme	LP	W. Rec. Club	T298	196-	**£10**	
Southern Blues	7" EP	Mercury	YEP9504	1956	**£4**	
Storyville Blues Anthology Vol.8	7" EP	Storyville	SEP388		**£5**	
Twenty-Fifth Anniversary Album	LP	Elektra	EKL123	195-	**£10**	US

WHITE, JOSH & BEVERLY

Title	Format	Label	Catalogue	Year	Price	Notes
Beverly And Josh White Jnr.	7" EP	Realm	REP4003	1964	**£4**	

WHITE, JOSH & BIG BILL BROONZY

Title	Format	Label	Catalogue	Year	Price	Notes
Josh White And Big Bill Broonzy	LP	Period	1209	196-	**£12**	US

WHITE, K.C.

Title	Format	Label	Catalogue	Year	Price	Notes
Man No Dead	7"	Dynamic	DYN434	197-	**£4**	

WHITE, KITTY & DAVID HOWARD

Title	Format	Label	Catalogue	Year	Price	Notes
Jesse James	7"	London	HL8102	1954	**£10**	

WHITE, LOUISIANA JANE

Title	Format	Label	Catalogue	Year	Price	Notes
When the Battle Is Over	7"	Philips	BF1810	1969	**£4**	

WHITE, TAM

Title	Format	Label	Cat. No.	Year	Price	Notes
Girl Watcher	7"	Decca	F12849	1968	**£4**	
Tam White	LP	Middle Earth		1970	**£20**	
That Old Sweet Roll	7"	Deram	DM261	1969	**£4**	
What In The World's Come Over You	7"	RAK	RAK193	1975	**£4**	

WHITE, TERRY

Title	Format	Label	Cat. No.	Year	Price	Notes
Rock Around The Mailbag	7"	Decca	F11133	1959	**£20**	

WHITE, TONY JOE

Title	Format	Label	Cat. No.	Year	Price	Notes
Best Of	LP	W. Bros	K56149	1973	**£10**	
Black And White	LP	Monument	SMO5027	1968	**£12**	
Continued	LP	Monument	SMO5035	1969	**£12**	
Groupie Girl	7"	Monument	MON1043	1970	**£4**	chart single
Home-Made Ice Cream	LP	W. Bros	K46229	1973	**£10**	
I've Got A Thing About You Baby	7"	W. Bros	K16411	1974	**£4**	
Polk Salad Annie	7"	Monument	MON1031	1969	**£5**	
Roosevelt And Ira Lee	7"	Monument	MON1040	1969	**£4**	
Save Your Sugar For Me	7"	Monument	MON1048	1970	**£4**	
Soul Francisco	7"	Monument	MON1024	1968	**£4**	
Tony Joe	LP	Monument	SMO5043	1970	**£10**	chart LP
Tony Joe White	LP	W. Bros	K46068	1971	**£10**	
Train I'm On	LP	W. Bros	K46147	1972	**£10**	
Willie And Laura	7"	Monument	MON1036	1969	**£4**	

WHITEHORN, GEOFF

Title	Format	Label	Cat. No.	Year	Price	Notes
Whitehorn	LP	Stateside	ISS80164	1974	**£15**	Japanese

WHITEHOUSE

Title	Format	Label	Cat. No.	Year	Price	Notes
Buchenwald	LP	Come Org		1981	**£50**	
Dedicated To Peter Kurten	LP	Come Org		198-	**£50**	
Erector	LP	Come Org	WDC881007	1980	**£50**	
Live Action	LP	Come Org		198-	**£50**	
New Britain	LP	Come Org	WDC881017	1982	**£100**	
Total Sex	LP	Come Org		1980	**£50**	

WHITESNAKE

Title	Format	Label	Cat. No.	Year	Price	Notes
Bloody Mary	7"	EMI	INEP751	1978	**£5**	PS, white vinyl
Breakdown	7"	Purple	PUR136	1978	**£4**	
Fool For Your Loving	7"	United Artists	BP352	1980	**£5**	luminous sleeve
Guilty Of Love	7"	Liberty	BP420	1983	**£5**	pic disc
Here I Go Again (2 versions)	7"	Liberty	BP416DJ	1982	**£5**	promo
Here I Go Again	7"	Liberty	BP416	1982	**£5**	pic disc
Hole in The Sky	7"	Purple	PUR133	1977	**£4**	
Is This Love	7"	EMI	12EMP3	1987	**£4**	shaped pic disc
Live At Hammersmith	LP	Polydor	MPF1288	1980	**£12**	Japanese
Long Way From Home	7"	United Artists	BP324DJ	1979	**£5**	promo
Saints And Sinners	LP	United Artists	UAC5728	1983	**£10**	pic disc
Standing In The Shadow	7"	Liberty	BPP423	1984	**£4**	pic disc
Still Of The Night	12"	EMI	12EMIP5606	1987	**£6**	pic disc
Take Me With You	12"	Liberty		1982	**£6**	1 sided promo
Trouble	LP	Sunburst	INS3022	1978	**£10**	
Victim Of Love	7"	Liberty	BP418	1982	**£10**	

WHITFIELD, WILBUR & THE PLEASERS

Title	Format	Label	Cat. No.	Year	Price	Notes
Heart To Heart	7"	Vogue	V9097	1958	**£20**	
P.B.Baby	7"	Vogue	V9078	1957	**£20**	
Plaything	7"	Vogue	V9091	1957	**£20**	

WHITLEY, RAY

Title	Format	Label	Cat. No.	Year	Price	Notes
I've Been Hurt	7"	HMV	POP1473	1965	**£25**	

WHITLOCK, BOBBY

Title	Format	Label	Cat. No.	Year	Price	Notes
Bobby Whitlock	LP	CBS	65109	1972	**£10**	
One Of A Kind	LP	Capricorn	0160	1975	**£10**	US
Raw Velvet	LP	CBS	65301	1972	**£10**	
Rock Your Sox Off	LP	Capricorn	2429139	1976	**£10**	

WHITMAN, SLIM

Title	Format	Label	Cat. No.	Year	Price	Notes
All Time Favorites	LP	Imperial	LP9252	1964	**£10**	US
America's Favorite Folk Artist	LP-10"	Imperial	LP3004	1954	**£30**	US
And His Singing Guitar	LP-10"	London	HAPB1015	1954	**£30**	

Title	Format	Label	Number	Year	Price	Notes
And His Singing Guitar Vol.2	LP	London	HAU2015	1956	**£20**	
Annie Laurie	LP	Imperial	LP9077	1959	**£15**	US
Beautiful Dreamer	7"	London	HL8080	1954	**£12**	
Candy Kisses	7"	London	HLP8642	1958	**£4**	
Curtain Of Tears	7"	London	HLP8416	1957	**£4**	
Dear Mary	7"	London	HLU8327	1956	**£6**	
Favorites	LP	Imperial	LP9003	1956	**£25**	US
First Visit To Britain	LP	Imperial	LP9135	1960	**£10**	US
Gone	7"	London	HLP8420	1957	**£10**	
Haunted Hungry Heart	7"	London	HL8141	1955	**£8**	
Heart Songs And Love Songs	LP	London	HAP8059	1963	**£10**	
I Never See Maggie Alone	7"	London	HLP8835	1959	**£4**	
I'll Hold You In My Heart	7"	Liberty	LIB66040	1964	**£4**	
I'll Never Stop Loving You	7"	London	HLU8167	1955	**£8**	
I'll Take You Home Again Kathleen	7"	London	HLP8403	1957	**£6**	chart single
I'll Walk With God	LP	Imperial	LP9088	1960	**£12**	US
I'm A Fool	7"	London	HLU8252	1956	**£8**	chart single
I'm A Lonely Wanderer	LP	Imperial	LP9226	1963	**£10**	US
I'm Casting My Lasso	7"	London	HLU8350	1956	**£6**	
Indian Love Call	7"	London	L1149	1954	**£12**	chart single
Irish Songs The Slim Whitman Way	7" EP	Liberty	LEP4018	1964	**£4**	
Irish Songs The Whitman Way	LP	Imperial	LP9245	1963	**£10**	US
Just Call Me Lonesome	LP	London	HAP2392	1961	**£10**	
Lovesick Blues	7"	London	HLP8459	1957	**£4**	
Many Times	7"	London	HLP8434	1957	**£4**	
Million Record Hits	LP	Imperial	LP9102	1960	**£12**	US
My Heart Is Broken In Three	78	London	L1206	1953	**£5**	
My Love Is Growing Stale	78	London	L1191	1953	**£5**	
North Wind	7"	London	L1226	1954	**£12**	
Once In A Lifetime	LP	Imperial	LP9156	1961	**£10**	US
Reminiscing	7"	Liberty	LIB66103	1965	**£4**	
Restless Heart	78	London	L1194	1953	**£5**	
Roll River Roll	7"	London	HLP9103	1960	**£4**	
Rose Marie	7"	London	HL8061	1954	**£12**	chart single
Satisfied Man	7" EP	Liberty	LEP4046	1966	**£4**	
Secret Love	7"	London	HL8039	1954	**£12**	
Serenade	7"	London	HLU8287	1956	**£8**	chart single
Singing Hills	7"	London	HL8091	1954	**£12**	
Sings	LP	Imperial	LP9064	1959	**£15**	US
Slim Whitman	LP	Imperial	LP9056	1958	**£15**	US
Slim Whitman	LP	London	HAP2343	1961	**£12**	
Slim Whitman And His Singing Guitar	7" EP	London	REP1006	1954	**£20**	
Slim Whitman Sings	LP	Imperial	LP9026	1957	**£25**	US
Slim Whitman Sings	LP	London	HAP2139	1959	**£15**	
Slim Whitman Sings	7" EP	London	REP1199	1959	**£8**	
Slim Whitman Sings And Yodels	LP-10"	RCA	LPM3217	1954	**£30**	US
Slim Whitman Sings More Irish Songs	7" EP	Liberty	LEP4027	1965	**£4**	
Slim Whitman Sings No.2	7" EP	London	REP1258	1960	**£6**	
Slim Whitman Sings Vol.2	LP	London	HAP2199	1959	**£12**	
Slim Whitman Sings Vol.3	LP	London	HAP2443	1962	**£10**	
Slim Whitman Sings Vol.3	LP	London	SAHP6232	1962	**£15**	stereo
Slim Whitman Sings Vol.4	LP	London	HAP8013	1962	**£10**	
Slim Whitman Vol.2 Pt.1	7" EP	London	REP1064	1956	**£10**	
Slim Whitman Vol.2 Pt.2	7" EP	London	REP1070	1956	**£10**	
Slim Whitman Vol.2 Pt.3	7" EP	London	REP1100	1957	**£10**	
Song Of The Wild	7"	London	HLU8196	1955	**£8**	
Song Of The Wild	7" EP	London	REP1042	1955	**£10**	
Stairway To Heaven	7"	London	HL8018	1954	**£12**	
There's A Rainbow In Every Tear	7"	London	L1214	1954	**£12**	
Tumbling Tumbleweeds	7"	London	HLU8230	1956	**£8**	chart single
Unchain My Heart	7"	London	HLP8518	1957	**£4**	
Vaya Con Dios	7"	London	HLP9302	1961	**£4**	
Very Precious Love	7"	London	HLP8590	1958	**£4**	
Wayward Wind	7" EP	London	REP1360	1963	**£6**	
When I Grow Too Old To Dream	7"	London	HL8125	1955	**£8**	
Wherever You Are	7"	London	HLP8708	1958	**£4**	
Yodeling	LP	Imperial	LP9235	1963	**£10**	US

WHITREN, JAKI

Title	Format	Label	Number	Year	Price	Notes
Raw But Tender	LP	Epic	65465	1973	**£10**	

WHITSETT, TIM

Title	Format	Label	Cat. No.	Year	Price	Notes
Macks By The Tracks	7"	Sue	WI318	1964	**£8**	

WHO

The Who's status as one of the world's most popular rock groups has inevitably led to a considerable interest in their early recordings, which fetch respectable prices even where they were chart hits. The three different B sides for the original issues of "Substitute" are the result of a dispute between Brunswick and Reaction as to the ownership of the track "Circles". "Instant Party" is the same track, whose change of title did not fool anyone, but "Waltz For A Pig", credited to the Who Orchestra, is actually a Graham Bond Organisation instrumental. The 1976 reissue of "Substitute" has the distinction of being the first twelve inch single ever made. Meanwhile, the most expensive rarities include a withdrawn mail order compilation, "Who Did It", and scarce picture sleeves for the singles "Anyway,Anyhow,Anywhere" and "My Generation".

Title	Format	Label	Cat. No.	Year	Price	Notes
5.15	7"	Polydor	WHO3	1980	**£4**	PS
5.15	7"	Track	2094115	1972	**£20**	demo
5.15	7"	Track	2094115	1973	**£4**	chart single
Acid Queen	7"	Track	PRO3	1969	**£20**	promo
Anyway, Anyhow, Anywhere	7"	Brunswick	05935	1965	**£10**	chart single
Anyway, Anyhow, Anywhere	7"	Brunswick	05935	1965	**£100**	demo
Anyway, Anyhow, Anywhere	7"	Brunswick	05935	1965	**£100**	PS
Athena	7"	Polydor	WHOP6	1982	**£5**	pic disc
Athena	12"	Polydor	WHOPX6	1982	**£6**	pic disc
Athena	12"	Polydor	WHOX6	1982	**£6**	promo
Athena/Why Did I Fall For That?	12"	Polydor	WHOPX6	1982	**£15**	pic disc
Christmas	7"	Track	PRO4	1969	**£30**	promo
Circles	7"	Brunswick		1966	**£100**	
Direct Hits	LP	Track	613006	1969	**£20**	
Dogs	7"	Track	604023	1968	**£6**	chart single
Dogs	7"	Track	604023	1968	**£40**	demo
Excerpts From Tommy	7" EP	Track	2252001	1970	**£10**	
Face Dances	LP	Mobile Fid.	MFSL1115	1984	**£12**	US audiophile
Filling In The Gaps	LP	Polydor	WHOT1	1981	**£30**	double interview promo
Go To The Mirror	7"	Track	PRO2	1969	**£20**	promo
Happy Jack	LP	Decca	DL4892	1967	**£20**	US
Happy Jack	7"	Reaction	591010	1966	**£5**	chart single
Happy Jack	7"	Reaction	591010	1966	**£60**	demo
I Can See For Miles	7"	Track	604011	1967	**£5**	chart single
I Can See For Miles	7"	Track	604011	1967	**£50**	demo
I Can't Explain	7"	Brunswick	05926	1965	**£100**	demo
I Can't Explain	7"	Brunswick	05926	1965	**£8**	chart single
I'm A Boy	7"	Reaction	591004	1966	**£5**	chart single
I'm A Boy	7"	Reaction	591004	1966	**£60**	demo
I'm Free	7"	Track	PRO1	1969	**£20**	promo
It's Hard	LP	W. Bros	237311	1982	**£20**	US audiophile promo
Join Together	7"	Polydor	2094102	1972	**£15**	export, PS
Join Together	7"	Track	2094102	1972	**£4**	chart single
Join Together	7"	Track	2094102	1972	**£20**	demo
Kids Are Alright	7"	Brunswick	05956	1966	**£25**	
Kids Are Alright	7"	Brunswick	05965	1966	**£12**	chart single
Kids Are Alright	7"	Brunswick	05965	1966	**£60**	demo
La La La Lies	7"	Brunswick	05968	1966	**£20**	
La La La Lies	7"	Brunswick	05968	1966	**£60**	demo
Last Time	7"	Track	604006	1967	**£20**	chart single
Last Time	7"	Track	604006	1967	**£50**	demo
Legal Matter	7"	Brunswick	05956	1966	**£10**	chart single
Legal Matter	7"	Brunswick	05956	1966	**£60**	demo
Legal Matter	7"	Decca	AD1002	1968	**£35**	export
Let's See Action	7"	Track	2094012	1971	**£4**	chart single
Let's See Action	7"	Track	2094012	1971	**£20**	demo
Live At Leeds	LP	Track	2406001	1970	**£12**	12 inserts, chart LP
Long Live Rock	7"	Polydor	WHO2	1979	**£4**	
Magic Bus	LP	Decca	DL75064	1968	**£20**	US
Magic Bus	7"	Track	604024	1968	**£5**	chart single
Magic Bus	7"	Track	604024	1968	**£40**	demo
Making Of Tommy	LP	Polydor	SA010	1975	**£25**	US interview promo
My Generation	LP	Brunswick	LAT8616	1965	**£35**	chart LP
My Generation	7"	Brunswick	05944	1965	**£6**	chart single
My Generation	7"	Brunswick	05944	1965	**£100**	demo
My Generation	7"	Brunswick	05944	1965	**£150**	PS
My Generation	LP	Decca	DL4664	1966	**£25**	US
My Generation	7"	Decca	AD1001	1968	**£25**	export
Pictures Of Lily	7"	Track	604002	1967	**£5**	chart single
Pictures Of Lily	7"	Track	604002	1967	**£50**	demo

Title	Format	Label	Number	Year	Price	Notes
Pinball Wizard	7"	Track	604027	1969	**£4**	chart single
Pinball Wizard	7"	Track	604027	1969	**£40**	demo
Quadrophenia	LP	Track	2657013	1973	**£12**	double
Quick One	LP	Reaction	592002	1966	**£25**	mono, chart LP
Quick One	LP	Reaction	593002	1966	**£20**	chart LP
Ready Steady Who	7" EP	Reaction	592001	1966	**£30**	
Relay	7"	Track	2094106	1972	**£4**	chart single
Roger Daltrey And Pete Townshend Talk About Quadrophenia	LP	Polydor	PRO114	1979	**£20**	US interview promo
See Me Feel Me	7"	Track	2094004	1970	**£10**	
Seeker	7"	Track	604036	1970	**£4**	chart single
Seeker	7"	Track	604036	1970	**£25**	demo
Substitute	12"	Polydor	2058803	1976	**£6**	no PS
Substitute	7"	Reaction	591001	1966	**£75**	demo
Substitute/Circles	7"	Reaction	591001	1966	**£15**	
Substitute/Instant Party	7"	Reaction	591001	1966	**£10**	
Substitute/Waltz For A Pig	7"	Reaction	591001	1966	**£8**	chart single
Summertime Blues	7"	Track	2094002	1970	**£4**	chart single
Summertime Blues	7"	Track	2094002	1970	**£20**	demo
Tommy	LP	Track	613013/014	1969	**£15**	double, book, chart LP
Who Are You?	LP	MCA		1978	**£20**	US interview promo
Who Are You?	LP	MCA	P14950	1978	**£10**	US pic disc
Who Are You?	7"	Polydor	WHO2DJ1	1978	**£10**	promo
Who Are You?	7"	Polydor	WHO2DJ2	1978	**£20**	1 sided promo
Who Are You?	7"	Polydor	WHO2DJ3	1978	**£8**	1 sided promo
Who Are You?	LP	Superdisk	SD166108	1981	**£20**	US audiophile
Who Did It	LP	Track	2856001	1971	**£200**	
Who Sell Out	LP	Decca	DL4950	1967	**£20**	US, mono
Who Sell Out	LP	Decca	DL74950	1967	**£15**	US, stereo
Who Sell Out	LP	Track	612002	1967	**£25**	mono, chart LP
Who Sell Out	LP	Track	613002	1967	**£20**	chart LP
Won't Get Fooled Again	7"	Track	2094009	1971	**£20**	demo
Won't Get Fooled Again	7"	Track	2094009	1971	**£8**	PS
Won't Get Fooled Again	7"	Track	A4112	1971	**£15**	1 sided promo
Won't Get Fooled Again	7"	Track	2094009	1971	**£4**	chart single

WHO & STRAWBERRY ALARM CLOCK

Title	Format	Label	Number	Year	Price	Notes
Who/Strawberry Alarm Clock	LP	Decca	DL734568	1969	**£30**	US

WICHITA FALL

Title	Format	Label	Number	Year	Price	Notes
Life Is But A Dream	LP	Liberty	LBS83208	1969	**£10**	

WIG

Title	Format	Label	Number	Year	Price	Notes
Live At The Jade Room	LP	Texas Archive		1982	**£25**	US

WIGGINS, PERCY

Title	Format	Label	Number	Year	Price	Notes
Book Of Memories	7"	Atlantic	584113	1967	**£4**	

WIGGINS, SPENCER

Title	Format	Label	Number	Year	Price	Notes
I'm A Poor Man's Son	7"	Pama	PM794	196-	**£6**	
Uptight Good Woman	7"	Stateside	SS2024	1967	**£4**	

WIGGONS

Title	Format	Label	Number	Year	Price	Notes
Rock Baby	7"	Blue Beat	BB29	1961	**£10**	

WIGGY BITS

Title	Format	Label	Number	Year	Price	Notes
Wiggy Bits	LP	Polydor	16081	1976	**£12**	US

WIGWAM

Title	Format	Label	Number	Year	Price	Notes
Being	LP	Love	LRLP92	1974	**£20**	Swedish
Dark Album	LP	Love	LRLP227	1978	**£20**	Swedish
Fairyport	LP	Love	LRLP44/55	1971	**£30**	Swedish double
Hard And Horny	LP	Love	LRLP9	1969	**£20**	Swedish
Live From The Twilight Zone	LP	Love	LXPS517/8	1975	**£25**	Swedish double
Lucky Golden Stripes And Starpose	LP	Virgin	V2051	1976	**£10**	
Nuclear Nightclub	LP	Virgin	V2035	1975	**£10**	
Rumours On The Rebound	LP	Virgin	VD3503	1979	**£15**	double
Tombstone Valentine	LP	Love	LRLP19	1970	**£20**	Swedish
Wicked Ivory	LP	Love	LRLP52	1972	**£20**	Swedish
Wigwam	LP	Love	LRLP511	1972	**£20**	Swedish

WILBURN BROTHERS

Title	Format	Label	Cat. No.	Year	Price	Notes
Livin' In God's Country	LP	Decca	DL8959	1959	**£10**	US
Side By Side	LP	Brunswick	LAT8291	1958	**£10**	
Silver Haired Daddy Of Mine	7"	Brunswick	05799	1959	**£4**	
Wilburn Brothers	LP	Decca	DL8576	1957	**£12**	US
Wonderful Wilburn Brothers	LP	King	746	1961	**£20**	US

WILD & WONDERING

Title	Format	Label	Cat. No.	Year	Price	Notes
2000 Light Ales From Home	12"	Iguana	VYK14	1986	**£40**	

WILD ANGELS

Title	Format	Label	Cat. No.	Year	Price	Notes
Beauty School Dropout	7"	Decca	F13356	1972	**£4**	
Jo Jo Ann	7"	Decca	F13308	1972	**£4**	
Live At The Revolution	LP	B&C	BCM101	1970	**£12**	
Out At Last	LP	Decca	SKL5134	1972	**£10**	
Red Hot 'N' Rockin'	LP	B&C	BCM102	1970	**£12**	
Running Bear	7"	Decca	F13374	1973	**£4**	

WILD OATS

Title	Format	Label	Cat. No.	Year	Price	Notes
	7" EP			196-	**£120**	

WILD ONES

Title	Format	Label	Cat. No.	Year	Price	Notes
Bowie Man	7"	Fontana	TF468	1964	**£10**	

WILD SILK

Title	Format	Label	Cat. No.	Year	Price	Notes
Help Me	7"	Columbia	DB8611	1969	**£8**	
Plaster Sky	7"	Columbia	DB8534	1969	**£4**	

WILD SWANS

Title	Format	Label	Cat. No.	Year	Price	Notes
Revolutionary Spirit	12"	Zoo	CAGE009	1982	**£8**	

WILD THING

Title	Format	Label	Cat. No.	Year	Price	Notes
Old Lady	7"	Elektra	EKSN45076	1969	**£4**	
Wild Thing	LP	Polydor			**£15**	

WILD TURKEY

Title	Format	Label	Cat. No.	Year	Price	Notes
Battle Hymn	LP	Chrysalis	CHR1002	1971	**£15**	
Good Old Days	7"	Chrysalis	CHS2004	1972	**£4**	
Turkey	LP	Chrysalis	CHR1010	1972	**£15**	

WILD UNCERTAINTY

Title	Format	Label	Cat. No.	Year	Price	Notes
Man With Money	7"	Planet	PLF120	1966	**£10**	

WILDCATS

Title	Format	Label	Cat. No.	Year	Price	Notes
Bandstand Record Hop	LP	United Artists	UAL3031	1958	**£15**	US
Gazachstahagen	7"	London	HLT8787	1959	**£4**	

WILDE THREE

Title	Format	Label	Cat. No.	Year	Price	Notes
I Cried	7"	Decca	F12232	1965	**£8**	
Since You've Gone	7"	Decca	F12131	1965	**£10**	

WILDE, KIM

Title	Format	Label	Cat. No.	Year	Price	Notes
Rage To Love	7"	MCA	KIMP3	1985	**£4**	shaped pic disc
Touch	7"	MCA	KIMP2	1984	**£4**	shaped pic disc

WILDE, MARTY

Title	Format	Label	Cat. No.	Year	Price	Notes
Abergavenny	7"	Philips	BF1669	1968	**£4**	
All Night Girl	7"	Magnet	MAG11	1974	**£4**	
All The Love I Have	7"	Philips	BF1753	1969	**£4**	
Bad Boy	LP	Epic	LN3686	1960	**£25**	US
Bad Boy	7"	Philips	PB972	1959	**£5**	chart single
Busker	7"	Philips	6006126	1971	**£4**	
By The Time I Get To Phoenix	7"	Philips	BF1632	1968	**£4**	
Bye Bye Birdie	LP	Philips	SBL3383	196-	**£10**	
Bye Bye Birdie	7" EP	Philips	BBE12472	1961	**£5**	
Bye Bye Birdie No.2	7" EP	Philips	BBE12473	1961	**£5**	
Bye Bye Birdie No.3	7" EP	Philips	BBE12474	1961	**£5**	
Come Running	7"	Philips	BF1206	1961	**£4**	
Come Running	7" EP	Philips	BBE12517	1962	**£8**	
Diversions	LP	Philips	SBL7877	1968	**£10**	
Donna	7"	Philips	PB902	1959	**£5**	chart single

Endless Sleep	7"	Philips	BF1783	1969	**£4**	chart single
Endless Sleep	7"	Philips	PB835	1958	**£5**	
Ever Since You Said Goodbye	7"	Philips	326546BF	1962	**£4**	chart single
Fight	7"	Philips	BF1022	1960	**£4**	chart single
Hide And Seek	7"	Philips	PB1161	1961	**£4**	
Honeycomb	7"	Philips	JK1028	1958	**£20**	
Honeycomb	7"	Philips	PB750	1957	**£8**	
I Love You	7"	Magnet	MAG15	1974	**£4**	
I Wanna Be Loved By You	7"	Philips	BF1037	1960	**£4**	
I've Got So Used To Loving You	7"	Philips	BF1490	1966	**£4**	
Jezebel	7"	Philips	PB1240	1962	**£4**	chart single
Johnny Rocco	7"	Philips	PB1002	1960	**£4**	chart single
Kiss Me	7"	Columbia	DB7285	1964	**£4**	
Little Girl	7"	Philips	BF1078	1960	**£4**	chart single
Lonely Avenue	7"	Columbia	DB4980	1963	**£4**	
Love Bug Crawl	7"	Philips	PB781	1958	**£8**	
Marty	7" EP	Philips	433638BE	1963	**£8**	
Marty Wilde Favourites	7" EP	Philips	BBE12422	1960	**£8**	
Mexican Boy	7"	Decca	F11979	1964	**£4**	
More Of Marty	7" EP	Philips	BBE12200	1958	**£12**	
My Lucky Love	7"	Philips	PB850	1958	**£6**	
No One Knows	7"	Philips	PB875	1958	**£6**	
No Trams To Lime Street	7"	Philips	BF1839	1970	**£4**	
No! Dance With Me	7"	Philips	326579BF	1963	**£4**	
Oh Oh, I'm Falling In Love Again	7"	Philips	PB804	1958	**£8**	
Presenting Marty Wilde	7" EP	Philips	BBE12164	1957	**£15**	
Rock And Roll Crazy	7"	Magnet	MAG2	1973	**£4**	
Rubber Ball	7"	Philips	PB1101	1961	**£4**	chart single
Save Your Love For Me	7"	Columbia	DB7145	1963	**£4**	
Sea Of Love	7"	Philips	PB959	1959	**£4**	chart single
Sea Of Love	7" EP	Philips	BBE12327	1959	**£10**	
Shelley	7"	Philips	BF1815	1969	**£4**	
Showcase	LP	Philips	BBL7380	1960	**£20**	
Teenager In Love	7"	Philips	PB926	1959	**£5**	chart single
Tomorrow's Clown	7"	Philips	BF1191	1961	**£4**	chart single
Versatile Mr.Wilde	LP	Philips	BBL7385	1960	**£15**	
Versatile Mr.Wilde	7" EP	Philips	BBE12385	1960	**£8**	
When Does It Get To Be Love	7"	Philips	PB1121	1961	**£4**	
Wilde About Marty	LP	Philips	BBL7342	1960	**£25**	

WILDER BROTHERS

I Want You	7"	HMV	POP365	1957	**£8**	

WILDING-BONUS

Pleasure Signals	LP	DJM	DJF20553	1978	**£10**	
Pleasure Signals	LP	Visa	7003	1978	**£15**	US pic disc

WILDWEEDS

It Was Fun While It Lasted	7"	Chess	CRS8065	1967	**£4**	
Wildweeds	LP	Vanguard	VSD6552	1970	**£10**	US

WILFRED & MILLIE

Vow	7"	Island	WI190	1965	**£10**	

WILLETT, SLIM

Slim Willett	LP	Audio Lab	AL1542	1961	**£25**	US

WILLIAMS JR., HANK

Your Cheatin' Heart	LP	MGM	C996	1965	**£10**	

WILLIAMS, BIG JOE

Big Joe Williams	LP	W. Pacific	21897	1969	**£10**	US
Big Joe Williams	7" EP	XX	MIN700		**£5**	
Blues For Nine Strings	LP	Bluesville	BV1056	1963	**£12**	US
Blues On Highway 49	LP	Delmark	D604	1962	**£12**	US
Classic Delta Blues	LP	CBS	63813	1964	**£15**	
Hand Me Down My Old Walking Stick	LP	Liberty	LBL83207	1968	**£15**	
Hell Bound And Heaven Sent	LP	Folkways	31004	1967	**£10**	US
Live At Folk City	LP	XTRA	XTRA5059	1968	**£10**	
Mississippi's Big Joe Williams	LP	Folkways	F3820	1962	**£12**	US
On The Highway	7" EP	Delmark	DJB4	1966	**£5**	
Starvin' Chain Blues	LP	Delmark	D609	1966	**£10**	US

Studio Blues	LP	Bluesville	BV1083	1964	**£12**	US

WILLIAMS, BILLY

Billy Williams	LP	Coral	CRL57184	1957	**£20**	US
Billy Williams Quartet	LP	MGM	E3400	1957	**£20**	US
Billy Williams Revue	LP	Coral	CRL57343	1960	**£20**	US
Billy Williams Singing Oh Yeah	LP	Mercury	MG20317	1958	**£20**	US
Butterfly	7"	Vogue Coral	Q72241	1957	**£6**	
Crazy Little Palace	7"	Vogue Coral	Q72149	1956	**£5**	
Don't Let Go	7"	Coral	Q72303	1958	**£4**	
Follow Me	7"	Vogue Coral	Q72222	1957	**£6**	
Goodnight Irene	7"	Coral	Q72369	1959	**£4**	
Got A Date With An Angel	7"	Vogue Coral	Q72295	1957	**£4**	
Half Sweet, Half Beat	LP	Coral	CRL57251	1959	**£20**	US
I Cried For You	7"	Coral	Q72402	1960	**£4**	
I'll Get By	7"	Coral	Q72331	1958	**£4**	
I'm Gonna Sit Right Down	7"	Vogue Coral	Q72266	1957	**£6**	chart single
Love Me	7"	Vogue Coral	Q2039	1954	**£6**	
Nola	7"	Coral	Q72359	1959	**£4**	
Pray	7"	Vogue Coral	Q72180	1956	**£4**	
Steppin' Out Tonight	7"	Coral	Q72316	1958	**£4**	
Telephone Conversation	7"	Coral	Q72377	1959	**£4**	
Vote For Billy Williams	LP	Wing	MGW12131	1959	**£20**	US

WILLIAMS, BOBBY

Baby I Need Your Love	7"	Action	ACT4509	1968	**£12**	demo

WILLIAMS, CHRIS & HIS MONSTERS

Monster	7"	Columbia	DB4383	1959	**£5**	

WILLIAMS, DANNY

Everybody Needs Somebody	7"	Deram	DM199	1968	**£4**	
Moon River	7"	HMV	POP932	1961	**£4**	chart single
Never My Love	7"	Deram	DM149	1967	**£4**	
Wonderful World Of The Young	7"	HMV	POP1002	1962	**£4**	chart single

WILLIAMS, EDDIE & LITTLE SONNY WILLIS

Going To California	7" EP	XX	MIN707		**£5**	

WILLIAMS, GRANVILLE ORCHESTRA

Hi-Life	LP	Island	ILP971	1968	**£50**	
Hi-Life	7"	Island	WI3062	1967	**£10**	

WILLIAMS, HANK

Authentic Sound Of The Country Hits	7" EP	MGM	MGMEP770	1963	**£8**	
Beyond The Sunset	LP	MGM	E4138	1961	**£12**	US
Blue Love	7"	MGM	MGM931	1956	**£12**	
Crazy Heart	7"	MGM	SP1085	1954	**£12**	
First, Last And Always	LP	MGM	E3928	1961	**£15**	US
Greatest Hits	LP	MGM	E3918	1961	**£12**	US
Hank Williams And His Drifting Cowboys	7" EP	MGM	MGMEP[illegible]	[illegible]	**£12**	
Hank Williams	7" EP	MGM	MGMEP551	1956	**£15**	
Hank Williams Favorites	7" EP	MGM	MGMEP757	1961	**£10**	
Hank Williams Sings	LP-10"	MGM	D105	1952	**£30**	
Hank Williams Story	LP	MGM	E4267	1966	**£20**	US
Hank Williams With Strings Vol.3	LP	MGM	C8075	1968	**£10**	
Hank's Laments	7" EP	MGM	MGMEP675	1958	**£10**	
Honky Tonk Blues	7" EP	MGM	MGMEP614	1957	**£12**	
Honky Tonkin'	LP	MGM	E3412	1957	**£30**	US
Honky Tonkin'	LP-10"	MGM	E242	1954	**£35**	US
Honky Tonkin'	7" EP	MGM	MGMEP582	1957	**£12**	
I Ain't Got Nothing But Time	7"	MGM	SP1102	1954	**£12**	
I Saw The Light	LP	MGM	E3331	1956	**£30**	US
I Saw The Light	LP-10"	MGM	E243	1954	**£35**	US
I Saw The Light No.1	7" EP	MGM	MGMEP569	1956	**£12**	
I Saw The Light No.2	7" EP	MGM	MGMEP608	1957	**£12**	
I Wish I Had A Nickel	7"	MGM	MGM921	1956	**£12**	
I Won't Be Home No More	LP	MGM	C8057	1968	**£10**	
I'll Never Get Out Of This World Alive	7"	MGM	SP1016	1953	**£15**	
I'm Blue Inside	LP	MGM	C8021	1966	**£12**	
I'm Blue Inside	LP	MGM	E3926	1961	**£12**	US
I'm So Lonesome I Could Cry	7"	MGM	MGM1309	1966	**£8**	

Immortal Hank Williams	LP	MGM	E3605	1958	**£20**	US
Immortal...	LP-10"	MGM	D154	1958	**£25**	
In Memory Of...	LP	MGM	C8020	1966	**£12**	
Jambalaya	7"	MGM	2006106	1972	**£4**	
Kaw Liga	7"	MGM	SP1034	1953	**£15**	
Kaw-Liga	7"	MGM	MGM1322	1966	**£6**	
Leave Me Alone With The Blues	7"	MGM	MGM966	1957	**£10**	
Legend Lives Anew	LP	MGM	C8031	1967	**£10**	
Let Me Sing A Blue Song	LP	MGM	E3924	1961	**£12**	US
Lives Again	LP	MGM	E3923	1961	**£12**	US
Lonesome Sound Of...	LP	MGM	C811	1960	**£20**	
Love Songs, Comedy And Hymns	LP	MGM	C8040	1967	**£12**	
Low Down Blues	7"	MGM	MGM942	1957	**£12**	
Luke The Drifter	LP	MGM	C8022	1966	**£12**	
Luke The Drifter	LP	MGM	E3267	1955	**£35**	US
Luke The Drifter	LP-10"	MGM	D119	1953	**£30**	
Many Moods Of...	LP	MGM	C8023	1966	**£12**	
May You Never Be Alone	LP	MGM	C8019	1966	**£12**	
Memorial Album	LP	MGM	E3272	1955	**£30**	US
Memorial Album	LP-10"	MGM	D137	1955	**£25**	
Moanin' The Blues	LP	MGM	E3330	1956	**£30**	US
Moanin' The Blues	LP-10"	MGM	D144	1956	**£30**	
More Greatest Hits	LP	MGM	E4040	1961	**£10**	US
More Greatest Hits Vol.3	LP	MGM	E4140	1962	**£10**	US
More Hank Williams And Strings	LP	MGM	C8038	1967	**£10**	
My Bucket's Got A Hole In It	7"	MGM	SP1048	1953	**£15**	
On Stage Recorded Live	LP	MGM	C893	1962	**£20**	
Ramblin' Man	LP	MGM	E3219	1955	**£30**	US
Ramblin' Man	LP-10"	MGM	E291	1954	**£35**	US
Ramblin' Man	7"	MGM	SP1049	1954	**£15**	
Rootie Tootie	7"	MGM	MGM957	1957	**£12**	
Sing Me A Blue Song	LP	MGM	E3560	1958	**£20**	US
Sing Me A Blue Song	LP-10"	MGM	D150	1958	**£25**	
Someday You'll Call My Name	7"	MGM	SP1163	1956	**£12**	
Songs For A Broken Heart	7" EP	MGM	MGMEP639	1958	**£12**	
Songs For A Broken Heart No.2	7" EP	MGM	MGMEP649	1958	**£12**	
Spirit Of...	LP	MGM	C956	1963	**£15**	
Thirty-Six Greatest Hits	LP	MGM	3E2	1957	**£50**	US, triple
Thirty-Six More Greatest Hits	LP	MGM	3E4	1958	**£50**	US, triple
Unforgettable Hank Williams	LP	MGM	C784	1959	**£20**	
Unforgettable Hank Williams	7" EP	MGM	MGMEP710	1960	**£10**	
Unforgettable Hank Williams No.2	7" EP	MGM	MGMEP726	1960	**£10**	
Unforgettable Hank Williams No.3	7" EP	MGM	MGMEP732	1960	**£10**	
Wait For The Light To Shine	LP	MGM	C834	1960	**£15**	
Wanderin' Around	LP	MGM	E3925	1961	**£12**	US
Weary Blues	7"	MGM	SP1067	1954	**£15**	

WILLIAMS, HANK & HANK WILLIAMS JR.

Singing Together	LP	MGM	C1008	1965	**£12**	

WILLIAMS, JEANETTE

Hound Dog	7"	Action	ACT4557	1969	**£4**	
Stuff	7"	Action	ACT4534	1969	**£10**	demo

WILLIAMS, JERRY

If You Ask Me	7"	Pye	DDS102	1974	**£4**	

WILLIAMS, JIMMY

Walking On Air	7"	Atlantic	AT4042	1965	**£4**	

WILLIAMS, JOHN

Changes	LP	Fly	HIFLY5	1971	**£10**	
Height Below	LP	Fly	HIFLY16	1973	**£10**	

WILLIAMS, KENNETH

Ballad Of The Woggler's Moulie	7"	Parlophone	R5638	1967	**£4**	Credited to Rambling Syd Rumpo
Extracts From Pieces Of Eight	7" EP	Decca	DFE8548	1963	**£4**	
In Season	7" EP	Decca	DFE8671	1966	**£4**	
On Pleasure Bent	LP	Decca	LK4856	1967	**£10**	
Rambling Syd Rumpo In Concert No.1	7" EP	Parlophone	GEP8965	1967	**£4**	

Rambling Syd Rumpo In Concert No.2	7" EP	Parlophone	GEP8966	1967	**£4**	

WILLIAMS, LARRY

Baby Baby	7"	London	HLM9053	1960	**£8**	
Bony Moronie	7"	London	HLU8532	1958	**£12**	chart single
Dizzy Miss Lizzy	7"	London	HLU8604	1958	**£15**	
Greatest Hits	LP	OKeh	OKM2123	1967	**£12**	US
Here's Larry Williams	LP	Speciality	SP2109	1959	**£50**	US
I Can't Stop Loving You	7"	London	HLU8911	1960	**£8**	
Larry Williams	7" EP	London	REU1213	1959	**£25**	
Larry Williams Show	LP	Decca	LK4691	1965	**£15**	
On Stage	LP	Sue	ILP922	1965	**£20**	
She Said Yeah	7"	London	HLU8844	1959	**£12**	
Short Fat Fannie	7"	London	HLN8472	1957	**£15**	chart single
Strange	7"	Sue	WI371	1965	**£8**	
Turn On Your Lovelight	7"	Sue	WI381	1965	**£10**	

WILLIAMS, LARRY & JOHNNY GUITAR WATSON

Mercy Mercy Mercy	7"	Columbia	DB8140	1967	**£20**	
Sweet Little Baby	7"	Decca	F12151	1965	**£5**	
Too Late	7"	Epic	EPC4421	1976	**£6**	
Two For The Price Of One	LP	OKeh	OKM4122	1967	**£12**	US

WILLIAMS, LITTLE JERRY

Baby You're My Everything	7"	Cameo Park	C100	1962	**£10**	

WILLIAMS, LLOYD

Sad World	7"	Doctor Bird	DB1051	1966	**£10**	

WILLIAMS, LORETTA

Baby Cakes	7"	Atlantic	584032	1966	**£8**	

WILLIAMS, LUTHER

Early In The Morning	7"	Limbo	XL101	195-	**£4**	

WILLIAMS, MARY LOU

At The Piano	7" EP	Parlophone	GEP8567	1956	**£10**	
Chug A Lug Jug	7"	Sue	WI311	1964	**£10**	

WILLIAMS, MASON

Classical Gas	7"	W. Bros	WB7190	1968	**£4**	chart single
Hand Made	LP	W. Bros	WS1838	1970	**£10**	US
Improved	LP	W. Bros		1971	**£10**	
Mason Williams Ear Show	LP	W. Bros	WS1766	1969	**£10**	US
Music	LP	W. Bros	WS1788	1969	**£10**	US
Phonogram Record	LP	W. Bros	WS1729	1969	**£10**	US
Sharepickers	LP	W. Bros	K46120	1971	**£10**	

WILLIAMS, MAURICE & THE ZODIACS

At The Beach	LP	Snyder	5586	196-	**£20**	US
Come Along	7"	Top Rank	JAR563	1961	**£5**	
I Remember	7"	Top Rank	JAR550	1961	**£5**	
Stay	LP	Herald	HLP1014	1961	**£50**	US
Stay	LP	Sphere Sound	SSR7007	1964	**£15**	US
Stay	7"	Top Rank	JAR526	1960	**£6**	chart single
Stay	7" EP	Top Rank	JKP3006	1961	**£20**	

WILLIAMS, MEL & JOHNNY OTIS

All Through The Night	LP	Dig	103	1955	**£50**	US

WILLIAMS, MIKE

Lonely Soldier	7"	Atlantic	584027	1966	**£5**	

WILLIAMS, OTIS & THE CHARMS

Hearts Of Stone	7"	Parlophone	MSP6155	1955	**£60**	
I'm Waiting Just For You	7"	Parlophone	R4293	1957	**£30**	
It's All Over Now	7"	Parlophone	R4210	1956	**£30**	
Ivory Tower	7"	Parlophone	MSP6239	1956	**£50**	
Secret	7"	Parlophone	R4495	1958	**£15**	
Their All Time Hits	LP	Deluxe	750	1957	**£150**	US
Their All Time Hits	LP	King	560	1957	**£50**	US
This Is...	LP	King	614	1959	**£50**	US

Two Hearts	7"	Parlophone	R4860	1961	**£12**	

WILLIAMS, PAUL

Gin House	7"	Columbia	DB7421	1964	**£12**	
My Sly Sadie	7"	Decca	F12844	1968	**£6**	

WILLIAMS, PAUL (2)

Delta Blues Singer	LP	Sonet	SNTF654	1973	**£12**	

WILLIAMS, PAUL & ZOOT MONEY

Many Faces Of Love	7"	Columbia	DB7768	1965	**£10**	

WILLIAMS, POOR JOE

Man Sings The Blues	7" EP	Collector	JEN3	196-	**£6**	
Man Sings The Blues Vol.2	7" EP	Collector	JEN4	196-	**£6**	

WILLIAMS, SMITTY

Cure	7"	MGM	MGM1167	1962	**£4**	

WILLIAMS, SONNY

Bye Bye Baby Goodbye	7"	London	HLD8931	1959	**£4**	

WILLIAMS, TEX

All Time Greats	7" EP	Brunswick	OE9147	1955	**£6**	
Be Sure You're Right	7"	Brunswick	05516	1956	**£4**	
Country Music Time	LP	Decca	DL4295	1962	**£10**	US
Dance-O-Rama	LP	Decca	DL5565	1955	**£30**	US
Keeper Of Boot Hill	7"	Top Rank	JAR330	1960	**£4**	
Money	7"	Brunswick	05393	1955	**£4**	
River Of No Return	7"	Brunswick	05327	1954	**£5**	
Smoke! Smoke! Smoke!	LP	Capitol	T1463	1960	**£10**	US
Talking To The Blues	7"	Brunswick	05684	1957	**£8**	
Tex Williams' Best	LP	Camden	CAL363	1958	**£12**	US

WILLIAMS, TEX & REX ALLEN

This Ole House	7"	Brunswick	05341	1954	**£8**	

WILLIAMS, TONY

Girl Is A Girl Is A Girl	LP	Mercury	MG20454	1959	**£10**	US

WILLIAMSON, DUDLEY

Coming On The Scene	7"	Doctor Bird	DB1117	1967	**£10**	

WILLIAMSON, ROBIN

American Stonehenge	LP	Criminal	STEAL4	1978	**£10**	
Journey's Edge	LP	Flying Fish	033	1977	**£10**	US
Myrrh	LP	Island	HELP2	1972	**£12**	

WILLIAMSON, SONNY BOY

Blues Of	LP	Storyville	SLP170	196-	**£15**	
Bring It On Home	7"	Chess	CRS8030	1966	**£4**	
Bummer Road	LP	Chess	1536	1969	**£10**	US
Down And Out Blues	LP	Marble Arch	MAL662	1967	**£10**	
Down And Out Blues	LP	Pye	NPL28036	1964	**£20**	chart LP
From The Bottom	7"	Blue Horizon	451008	1966	**£20**	
Help Me	7" EP	Chess	CRE6001	1965	**£6**	
Help Me	7"	Pye	7N25191	1963	**£5**	
In Memoriam	LP	Chess	CRL4510	1965	**£15**	
In Memoriam	7" EP	Chess	CRE6013	1966	**£6**	
Lonesome Cabin	7"	Pye	7N25268	1964	**£5**	
More Real Folk Blues	LP	Chess	1509	1966	**£20**	US
No Nights By Myself	7"	Sue	WI365	1965	**£10**	
Portraits In Blues	LP	Storyville	SLP158	196-	**£15**	
Real Folk Blues	LP	Chess	1503	1966	**£20**	US
Real Folk Blues Vol.2	7" EP	Chess	CRE6018	1966	**£6**	
Sonny Boy Williamson	LP	Checker	1437	1959	**£50**	US
Sonny Boy Williamson	7" EP	Pye	NEP44037	1964	**£6**	

WILLIE & THE RED RUBBER BAND

We're Coming Up	LP	RCA	LSP4193	1969	**£15**	US
Willie And The Red Rubber Band	LP	RCA	LSP4074	1968	**£15**	US

WILLING, FOY & THE RIDERS OF THE PURPLE SAGE

Title	Format	Label	Number	Year	Price	Notes
Cowboy	LP	Roulette	R25035	1958	**£12**	US

WILLIS, CHUCK

Title	Format	Label	Number	Year	Price	Notes
Betty And Dupree	7"	London	HLE8595	1958	**£15**	
C.C.Rider	7"	London	HLE8444	1957	**£20**	
Chuck Willis Wails The Blues	LP	Epic	LN3425	1958	**£75**	US
I Remember Chuck Willis	LP	Atlantic	8079	1963	**£20**	US
King Of The Stroll	LP	Atlantic	8018	1958	**£75**	US, black label
King Of The Stroll	LP	Atlantic	8018	1959	**£30**	US, red label
My Life	7"	London	HLE8818	1959	**£12**	
That Train Has Gone	7"	London	HLE8489	1957	**£20**	
Tribute To Chuck Willis	LP	Epic	LN3728	1960	**£50**	US
What Am I Living For	7"	London	HLE8635	1958	**£12**	
Willis Wails The Blues	7" EP	Fontana	TFE17138	1959	**£50**	

WILLIS, RALPH

Title	Format	Label	Number	Year	Price	Notes
Mad Rooster	7"	Press. Beat	PB5502		**£6**	
Ralph Willis	7" EP	Esquire	EP241	196-	**£6**	
Ralph Willis	7" EP	XX	MIN703		**£6**	
Ralph Willis	7" EP	XX	MIN711		**£6**	

WILLIS, SLIM

Title	Format	Label	Number	Year	Price	Notes
Running Around	7"	R&B	MRB5004	1965	**£5**	

WILLOWS

Title	Format	Label	Number	Year	Price	Notes
Church Bells May Ring	7"	London	HLL8290	1956	**£80**	

WILLS, BOB

Title	Format	Label	Number	Year	Price	Notes
Best Of...	LP	Harmony	HL7304	1963	**£10**	US
Bob Wills And His Texas Playboys	LP	Decca	DL8727	1957	**£30**	US
Bob Wills Sings And Plays	LP	Liberty	LRP3303	1963	**£10**	US
Bob Wills Special	LP	Harmony	HL7036	1957	**£15**	US
Dance-O-Rama	LP-10"	Decca	DL5562	1955	**£50**	US
Great Bob Wills	LP	Harmony	HL7345	1965	**£10**	US
Keepsake Album #1	LP	Longhorn	LP001	1965	**£25**	US
Living Legend	LP	Liberty	LRP3182	1961	**£10**	US
Mr.Words And Music	LP	Liberty	LRP3194	1961	**£10**	US
Old Time Favorites	LP-10"	Antones	LP6000	195-	**£50**	US
Old Time Favorites	LP-10"	Antones	LP6010	195-	**£50**	US
Ranch House Favorites	LP	MGM	E3352	1956	**£50**	US
Ranch House Favorites	LP-10"	MGM	E91	1951	**£50**	US
Round Up	LP-10"	Columbia	HL9003	195-	**£50**	US
San Antonio Rose	LP	Starday	SLP375	1965	**£10**	US
Western Swing Band	LP	Vocalion	VL3735	1965	**£10**	US

WILLS, BOB & TOMMY DUNCAN

Title	Format	Label	Number	Year	Price	Notes
Bob Wills And Tommy Duncan	LP	Liberty	LRX1912	1961	**£10**	US
Together Again	LP	Liberty	LRP3173	1960	**£10**	US

WILMER & THE DUKES

Title	Format	Label	Number	Year	Price	Notes
Give Me One More Chance	7"	Action	ACT4500	1968	**£4**	
Wilmer And The Dukes	LP	Aphrodisiac	6001	1969	**£12**	US

WILSON, AL

Title	Format	Label	Number	Year	Price	Notes
Snake	7"	Liberty	LIB15121	1968	**£12**	

WILSON, BRIAN

Title	Format	Label	Number	Year	Price	Notes
Caroline No	7"	Capitol	CL15438	1966	**£10**	
Words And Music	LP	W. Bros	WBWM154	1988	**£15**	US promo

WILSON, BRIAN & MIKE LOVE

Title	Format	Label	Number	Year	Price	Notes
Gettin' Hungry	7"	Capitol	CL15513	1967	**£12**	

WILSON, CLIVE

Title	Format	Label	Number	Year	Price	Notes
Mango Tree	7"	R&B	JB144	1964	**£10**	

WILSON, DELROY

Title	Format	Label	Number	Year	Price	Notes
1-2-3	7"	Island	WI103	1963	**£12**	
Adis Ababa	7"	Spur	SP2		**£10**	
Dancing Mood	7"	Island	WI3013	1966	**£10**	
Easy Snappin'	7"	Studio One	SO2074	196-	**£10**	

Title	Format	Label	Cat. No.	Year	Price	Notes
Feel Good All Over	7"	Studio One	SO2057	196-	**£10**	
Get Ready	7"	Island	WI3050	1967	**£10**	
Give Me A Chance	7"	Doctor Bird	DB1022	1966	**£10**	
Good All Over	LP	Coxsone	CSL8016	196-	**£80**	
Goodbye	7"	Black Swan	WI420	1964	**£10**	
I Am Not A King	7"	Studio One	SO2031	196-	**£10**	
I Shall Not Remove	7"	Island	WI097	1963	**£12**	
I Shall Not Remove	LP	R&B	JBL1112	196-	**£50**	
Lion Of Judah	7"	R&B	JB108	1963	**£12**	
Lover Mouth	7"	R&B	JB148	1964	**£10**	
Mr.DJ	7"	Studio One	SO2040	196-	**£10**	
Never Conquer	7"	Studio One	SO2019	196-	**£10**	
Once Upon A Time	7"	Island	WI3127	1967	**£10**	
Pick Up The Pieces	7"	Island	WI205	1965	**£12**	
Prince Pharoah	7"	R&B	JB128	1963	**£10**	
Rain From The Skies	7"	Studio One	SO2046	196-	**£10**	
Riding For A Fall	7"	Island	WI3033	1967	**£10**	
Sammy Dead	7"	R&B	JB168	1964	**£10**	
Spit In The Sky	7"	Black Swan	WI405	1964	**£10**	
Spit In The Sky	7"	Blue Beat	BB172	1963	**£10**	
This Heart Of Mine	7"	Island	WI3099	1967	**£10**	
True Believer	7"	Coxsone	CS7064	196-	**£10**	
What Happen To The Youth Of Today	7"	Harry J	HJ6667	1974	**£4**	
Won't You Come Home Baby	7"	Studio One	SO2009	196-	**£10**	
You Bend My Love	7"	Island	WI116	1963	**£12**	

WILSON, DENNIS

Title	Format	Label	Cat. No.	Year	Price	Notes
Sound Of Free	7"	Stateside	SS2184	1970	**£20**	

WILSON, DOYLE

Title	Format	Label	Cat. No.	Year	Price	Notes
Hey Hey	7"	Vogue	V9117	1958	**£50**	

WILSON, EDDIE

Title	Format	Label	Cat. No.	Year	Price	Notes
Get Out On The Street	7"	Action	ACT4555	1969	**£6**	demo
Shing A Ling A Stroll	7"	Action	ACT4536	1969	**£5**	
Shing A Ling A Stroll	7"	Action	ACT4536	1969	**£15**	demo

WILSON, ERNEST

Title	Format	Label	Cat. No.	Year	Price	Notes
If I Were A Carpenter	7"	Studio One	SO2058	196-	**£10**	
Money Worries	7"	Studio One	SO2032	196-	**£10**	
Storybook Children	7"	Coxsone	CS7044	196-	**£10**	
Undying Love	7"	Coxsone	CS7059	196-	**£10**	

WILSON, FRANK

Title	Format	Label	Cat. No.	Year	Price	Notes
Do I Love You	7"	Motown	TMG1170	1979	**£25**	demo, PS
Last Kiss	7"	Fontana	TF505	1964	**£4**	
Last Kiss	LP	Josie	JS4006	1964	**£20**	US

WILSON, JACKIE

Title	Format	Label	Cat. No.	Year	Price	Notes
All My Love	7"	Coral	Q72407	1960	**£4**	chart single
Alone At Last	7"	Coral	Q72412	1960	**£4**	chart single
At The Copa	LP	Coral	LVA9209	1962	**£15**	mono
At The Copa	LP	Coral	SVL9209	1962	**£20**	stereo
Baby Workout	LP	Brunswick	BL54110	1963	**£12**	US
Baby Workout	7"	Coral	Q72460	1963	**£4**	
Big Boss Line	7"	Coral	Q72474	1964	**£4**	
Body And Soul	LP	Coral	LVA9202	1962	**£15**	
By Special Request	LP	Coral	LVA9151	1962	**£15**	mono
By Special Request	LP	Coral	SVL3018	1962	**£20**	stereo
Dogging Around	7"	Coral	Q72393	1960	**£6**	
Dynamic Jackie Wilson	7" EP	Coral	FEP2043	1960	**£12**	
Greatest Hurt	7"	Coral	Q72450	1962	**£4**	
He's So Fine	LP	Coral	LVA9087	1958	**£40**	
Helpless	7"	MCA	MU1105	1969	**£4**	
Higher And Higher	7"	Coral	Q72493	1967	**£5**	
Higher And Higher	LP	MCA	MUP304	1967	**£10**	
Higher And Higher	7"	MCA	BAG2	1969	**£4**	chart single
Higher And Higher	7"	MCA	MU1131	1970	**£4**	
I Believe I'll Love On	7"	Coral	Q72482	1965	**£4**	
I Get The Sweetest Feeling	7"	MCA	MU1160	1972	**£4**	chart single
I Just Can't Help It	7"	Coral	Q72454	1962	**£4**	
I'll Be Satisfied	7"	Coral	Q72372	1959	**£4**	

Title	Format	Label	Cat. No.	Year	Price	Notes
I'm Coming Back To You	7"	Coral	Q72434	1961	**£4**	
I'm Wandering	7"	Coral	Q72332	1958	**£4**	
Jackie Sings The Blues	LP	Coral	LVA9130	1960	**£20**	
Lonely Teardrops	LP	Coral	LVA9108	1959	**£35**	
Lonely Teardrops	7"	Coral	Q72347	1958	**£5**	
Lonely Teardrops	7" EP	Coral	FEP2016	1959	**£12**	
Merry Christmas	LP	Brunswick	BL54112	1963	**£12**	US
My Golden Favorites Vol.2	LP	Brunswick	BL54115	1964	**£12**	US
My Golden Favourites	LP	Coral	LVA9135	1960	**£20**	
My Heart Belongs To Only You	7"	Coral	Q72444	1961	**£4**	
New Breed	7"	Coral	Q72467	1963	**£4**	
No Pity In The Naked City	7"	Coral	Q72481	1965	**£4**	
Please Tell Me Why	7"	Coral	Q72430	1961	**£4**	
Reet Petite	7"	Vogue Coral	Q72290	1957	**£10**	chart single
Shake A Hand	LP	Brunswick	BL54113	1963	**£12**	US
Shake Shake Shake	7"	Coral	Q72465	1963	**£6**	
Since You Showed Me How To Be Happy	7"	Coral	Q72496	1967	**£5**	
Since You Showed Me How To Be Happy	7"	MCA	BAG7	1969	**£4**	
Since You Showed Me How To Be Happy	7"	MCA	MU1104	1969	**£4**	
Sing	7"	Coral	Q72453	1962	**£4**	
So Much	LP	Coral	LVA9121	1960	**£25**	
Somethin' Else	LP	Brunswick	BL54117	1964	**£12**	US
Soul Galore	LP	Coral	LVA9232	1966	**£12**	mono
Soul Galore	LP	Coral	SVL9232	1966	**£15**	stereo
Soul Time	LP	Brunswick	BL54118	1965	**£12**	US
Spotlight On Jackie Wilson	LP	Coral	LVA9231	1965	**£12**	
Squeeze Her, Tease Her	7"	Coral	Q72476	1964	**£4**	
Talk That Talk	7"	Coral	Q72384	1959	**£4**	
Tears Of The Year	7"	Coral	Q72424	1961	**£4**	
Tenderly	7"	Ember	JBS705	1962	**£15**	
That's Why	7"	Coral	Q72366	1959	**£4**	
To Be Loved	7"	Coral	Q72306	1958	**£5**	chart single
To Make A Big Man Cry	7"	Coral	Q72484	1966	**£4**	
We Have Love	7"	Coral	Q72338	1958	**£4**	
Whispers	LP	Coral	LVA9235	1967	**£12**	
Whispers Gettin' Louder	7"	Coral	Q72487	1966	**£4**	
Woman, A Lover, A Friend	LP	Coral	LVA9144	1961	**£20**	
World's Greatest Melodies	LP	Coral	LVA9214	1962	**£15**	mono
World's Greatest Melodies	LP	Coral	SVL9214	1962	**£20**	stereo
Years From Now	7"	Coral	Q72439	1961	**£4**	
You Ain't Heard Nothing Yet	LP	Coral	LVA9148	1961	**£15**	
You Better Know	7"	Coral	Q72380	1959	**£4**	

WILSON, JACKIE & COUNT BASIE

Title	Format	Label	Cat. No.	Year	Price	Notes
For Your Precious Love	7"	MCA	MU1014	1968	**£4**	

WILSON, JACKIE & LINDA HOPKINS

Title	Format	Label	Cat. No.	Year	Price	Notes
Shake A Hand	7"	Coral	Q72464	1963	**£4**	
Yes Indeed	7"	Coral	Q72480	1965	**£4**	

WILSON, JOE

Title	Format	Label	Cat. No.	Year	Price	Notes
Sweetness	7"	Pye	7N25550	1971	**£4**	

WILSON, MARTY & THE STRATOLITES

Title	Format	Label	Cat. No.	Year	Price	Notes
Hey Eula	7"	Brunswick	05750	1958	**£4**	

WILSON, MAYNELL

Title	Format	Label	Cat. No.	Year	Price	Notes
Crazy Baby	7"	Carnival	CV7002	1963	**£6**	
Hey Hey Johnny	7"	Carnival	CV7014	1964	**£6**	

WILSON, MURRY

At least John Lennon's father only got to make a single: they let the father of the Beach Boys make a whole album! The result consists of light instrumental music that would be of marginal interest were it not for Mr. Wilson's superstar connections.

Title	Format	Label	Cat. No.	Year	Price	Notes
Many Moods Of...	LP	Capitol	ST2819	1967	**£15**	
Plumber's Tune	7"	Capitol	CL15525	1967	**£5**	

WILSON, NANCY

Title	Format	Label	Cat. No.	Year	Price	Notes
Face It Girl It's Over	7"	Capitol	CL15547	1968	**£12**	
Uptight	7"	Capitol	CL15466	1966	**£4**	

WILSON, PEANUTS
Cast Iron Arm .... 7" .... Coral .... Q72302 .... 1958 .... **£100** ....

WILSON, SMILEY
Running Bear .... 7" .... London .... HLG9066 .... 1960 .... **£4** ....

WILSON, TIMOTHY
Phoney People .... 7" .... Decca .... F13432 .... 1973 .... **£5** ....

WILSON, TREVOR
You Couldn't Believe .... 7" .... Ska Beat .... JB207 .... 1965 ...... **£10** ....

WILTSHIRE, JOHNNY
If The Shoe Fits .... 7" .... Oriole .... CB1494 .... 1959 .... **£8** ....

WIMPLE WINCH
Rumble On Mersey Square South .... 7" .... Fontana .... TF781 .... 1967 ...... **£50** ....
Save My Soul .... 7" .... Fontana .... TF718 .... 1966 ...... **£50** ....
What's Been Done .... 7" .... Fontana .... TF686 .... 1966 ...... **£50** ....

WINCHESTER, JESSE
Jesse Winchester .... LP .... Ampex .... A10104 .... 1970 ...... **£10** .... US

WIND
Wind .... LP .... CBS .... **£70** ....

WIND IN THE WILLOWS
Lead singer with the Wind In The Willows was Debbie Harry. The folky music played by the group is as different from that of Blondie as is Debbie Harry's own appearance from that of the blonde bombshell she decided to become.

Moments Spent .... 7" .... Capitol .... CL15561 .... 1968 ...... **£15** ....
Wind In The Willows .... LP .... Capitol .... SKAO2956 .... 1968 ...... **£20** .... US, gatefold

WINGS
Wings .... LP .... Dunhill .... DS50046 .... 1968 ...... **£10** .... US

WINSTON & GEORGE
Keep The Pressure On .... 7" .... Pyramid .... PYR6002 .... 1966 ...... **£10** ....

WINSTON'S FUMBS
Real Crazy Appartment .... 7" .... RCA .... RCA1612 .... 1967 ...... **£40** ....

WINSTON, JIMMY & HIS REFLECTIONS
Jimmy Winston was the original organist with the Small Faces and plays on their first single. His own singles, however, recorded as Winston's Fumbs and as Jimmy Winston and his Reflections, were not at all successful.

Sorry She's Mine .... 7" .... Decca .... F12410 .... 1966 ...... **£30** ....

WINSTONE, NORMA
Edge Of Time .... LP .... Argo .... ZDA148 .... 1971 ...... **£60** ....

WINSTONS
Colour Him Father .... 7" .... Pye .... 7N25493 .... 1969 .... **£4** ....
Love Of The Common People .... 7" .... Pye .... 7N25500 .... 1969 .... **£4** ....

WINTER CONSORT
Winter Consort .... LP .... A&M .... 1969 ...... **£12** ....

WINTER, EDGAR
Entrance .... LP .... Epic .... 64083 .... 1970 ...... **£10** ....
Jasmine Nightdreams .... LP .... Blue Sky .... PZQ33483 .... 1975 ...... **£10** .... US quad
Road Work .... LP .... Epic .... 67244 .... 1972 ...... **£10** ....
Shock Treatment .... LP .... Epic .... PEQ32461 .... 1974 ...... **£10** .... US quad
They Only Come Out At Night .... LP .... Epic .... EQ31584 .... 1973 ...... **£10** .... US quad
White Trash .... LP .... Epic .... 64298 .... 1971 ...... **£10** ....
With Rick Derringer .... LP .... Blue Sky .... PZQ33798 .... 1975 ...... **£10** .... US quad

WINTER, JOHNNY
About Blues .... LP .... Janus .... 3008 .... 1969 ...... **£10** .... US
Before The Storm .... LP .... Janus .... 3056 .... 1970 ...... **£10** .... US
First Winter .... LP .... Buddah .... 2359011 .... 1970 ...... **£10** ....
I'm Yours And I'm Hers .... 7" .... CBS .... 4386 .... 1969 .... **£4** ....
John Dawson Winter III .... LP .... Blue Sky .... PZQ33292 .... 1974 ...... **£12** .... US quad
Johnny Winter .... LP .... CBS .... 63619 .... 1969 ...... **£10** ....

Johnny Winter And...	LP	CBS	64117	1971	**£10**	chart LP
Johnny Winter And...Live	LP	CBS	64289	1971	**£10**	chart LP
Progressive Blues Experiment	LP	Liberty	LBS83240	1969	**£10**	
Saints And Sinners	LP	Columbia	CQ32715	1974	**£12**	US quad
Second Winter	LP	CBS	66231	1970	**£12**	3 sides, chart LP
Still Alive And Well	LP	Columbia	CQ32188	1973	**£12**	US quad

WINTERS, DON

Someday Baby	7"	Brunswick	05827	1960	**£8**	

WINTERS, LIZ & BOB CORT

Liz Winters And Bob Cort	7" EP	Decca	DFE6409	1957	**£10**	
Love Is Strange	7"	Decca	F10878	1957	**£8**	
Maggie May	7"	Decca	F10899	1957	**£6**	

WINTERS, LOIS

Japanese Farewell Song	7"	London	HLD8266	1956	**£6**	

WINTERS, RUBY

Baby Lay Down	7"	Creole	CR171	1979	**£4**	
Back To Love	7"	Creole	CR174	1979	**£4**	
I Want Action	7"	Stateside	SS2090	1968	**£4**	

WINWOOD, STEVE

Conversation With Steve Winwood	LP	Island	SWCLP1	1986	**£15**	promo
Time Is Running Out	12"	Island		1977	**£6**	promo, no PS
Winwood	LP	United Artists	UAS9950	1971	**£12**	US, with booklet

WIPERS

Better Off Dead	7"	Trap	810X44	1978	**£30**	
Is This Real	LP	Park Avenue		1979	**£15**	US
Over The Edge	LP	Trap		1983	**£10**	US
Youth Of America	LP	Park Avenue	PA82802	1981	**£15**	US

WIRE

154	LP	Harvest	SHSP4105	1979	**£10**	with 7" (PSR444)
Chairs Missing	LP	Harvest	SHSP4093	1978	**£10**	lilac inner
Dot Dash	7"	Harvest	HAR5161	1978	**£6**	
I Am The Fly	7"	Harvest	HAR5151	1978	**£4**	
Mannequin	7"	Harvest	HAR5144	1977	**£12**	
Mannequin	12"	Harvest	HAR5144	1977	**£15**	
Map Ref 41N 93W	7"	Harvest	HAR5192	1979	**£4**	
Our Swimmer	7"	Rough Trade	RTO79	1981	**£4**	
Outdoor Miner	7"	Harvest	HAR5172	1979	**£4**	chart single
Outdoor Miner	7"	Harvest	HAR5172	1979	**£8**	white vinyl
Question Of Degree	7"	Harvest	HAR5187	1979	**£5**	

WIRTZ, MARK

Caroline	7"	CBS	4539	1969	**£5**	
He's Our Dear Old Weatherman	7"	Parlophone	R5668	1968	**£8**	
Mrs.Raven	7"	Parlophone	R5683	1968	**£6**	

WISDOM, NORMAN

Follow A Star	7"	Top Rank	JAR246	1959	**£4**	
Norman Wisdom	7" EP	Columbia	SEG7612	1956	**£8**	
Up In The World	7"	Columbia	DB3864	1957	**£4**	
Wisdom Of A Fool	7"	Columbia	DB3903	1957	**£4**	chart single

WISE GUYS

Big Noise	7"	Top Rank	JAR271	1960	**£4**	

WISEMAN, MAC

Beside The Still Waters	LP	Dot	DLP3135	1959	**£10**	US
Fireball Mail	LP	Dot	DLP3408	1961	**£10**	US
Fireball Mail	7"	London	HLD8259	1956	**£15**	
Great Folk Ballads	LP	London	HAD2217	1960	**£10**	
Keep On The Sunny Side	LP	Dot	DLP3336	1960	**£10**	US
Kentuckian Song	7"	London	HLD8174	1955	**£12**	
My Little Home In Tennessee	7"	London	HLD8226	1956	**£15**	
Songs From The Hills	LP-10"	London	HBD1052	1956	**£20**	
Songs From The Hills	7" EP	London	RED1056	1956	**£10**	
Songs From The Hills Vol.2	7" EP	London	RED1147	1958	**£10**	

Title	Format	Label	Cat. No.	Year	Price	Notes
Songs From The Hills Vol.3	7" EP	London	RED1242	1960	**£10**	
Step It Up And Go	7"	London	HLD8412	1957	**£40**	
Tis Sweet To Be Remembered	LP	Dot	DLP3084	1958	**£10**	US

WISHBONE ASH

Title	Format	Label	Cat. No.	Year	Price	Notes
Blind Eye	7"	MCA	MK5061	1970	**£5**	
Come In From The Rain	7"	MCA	PSR431	1977	**£4**	
Evening Program With Wishbone Ash	LP	Decca		1972	**£15**	US promo
Hometown	7"	MCA	MCA165	1974	**£4**	
LIve From Memphis	LP	MCA	L331922	1974	**£20**	US promo
No Easy Road	7"	MCA	MKS5097	1972	**£5**	
Outward Bound	7"	MCA	MCA261	1976	**£4**	
Silver Shoes	7"	MCA	MCA176	1975	**£4**	
So Many Things To Say	7"	MCA	MUS1210	1973	**£4**	
Wishbone Ash	LP	MCA	MKPS2014	1970	**£10**	chart LP

WISHFUL THINKING

Title	Format	Label	Cat. No.	Year	Price	Notes
Alone	7"	Decca	F22742	1968	**£8**	
Clear White Light	7"	B&C	CB184	1971	**£4**	
Count To Ten	7"	Decca	F12598	1967	**£5**	
Hiroshima	LP	B&C	CAS1038	1971	**£15**	
It's So Easy	7"	Decca	F12760	1968	**£4**	
La La La Lee	7"	B&C	CB169	1971	**£4**	
Live	LP	Decca	SKL4900	1967	**£20**	
Meet The Sun	7"	Decca	F22673	1967	**£8**	
Peanuts	7"	Decca	F12627	1967	**£5**	
Step By Step	7"	Decca	F12499	1966	**£4**	
Turning Round	7"	Decca	F12438	1966	**£6**	

WITHERSPOON, JIMMY

Title	Format	Label	Cat. No.	Year	Price	Notes
All That's Good	7"	Vogue	V2420	1964	**£8**	
At The Monterey Jazz Festival	LP	Hi Fi	421	1959	**£12**	US
At The Renaissance	LP	Hi Fi	426	1959	**£12**	US
Blue Point Of View	LP	Verve	V5007	1966	**£10**	US
Blue Spoon	LP	Stateside	SL10139	1965	**£12**	
Blues Around The Clock	LP	Stateside	SL10105	1965	**£12**	
Blues Singer	LP	Stateside	SL10289	1969	**£12**	
Come And Walk With Me	7"	Stateside	SS429	1965	**£4**	
Evening Blues	LP	Stateside	SL10088	1964	**£15**	
Feeling The Spirit	LP	Hi Fi	422	1959	**£12**	US
Feeling The Spirit Vol.1	7" EP	Vocalion	VEH170158	1964	**£5**	
Feeling The Spirit Vol.2	7" EP	Vocalion	VEH170159	1964	**£5**	
Goin' To Kansas City Blues	LP	RCA	LPM1639	1958	**£15**	US
Hey Mrs.Jones	LP	Reprise	R6012	1962	**£10**	US
Highway To Happiness	7"	Parlophone	MSP6125	1954	**£10**	
I Done Told You	7"	Parlophone	MSP6142	1954	**£8**	
I Never Will Marry	7"	Stateside	SS325	1964	**£4**	
If There Wasn't Any You	7"	Stateside	SS503	1966	**£4**	
It's All Over But The Crying	7"	Verve	VS538	1966	**£4**	
Jimmy Witherspoon	7" EP	Vocalion	EPVH1278	1964	**£5**	
Jimmy Witherspoon At Monterey No.1	7" EP	Vocalion	EPV1269	1962	**£8**	
Jimmy Witherspoon At Monterey No.2	7" EP	Vocalion	EPV1270	1962	**£8**	
Live	LP	Stateside	SL10232	1968	**£12**	
Love Me Right	7"	Stateside	SS461	1965	**£5**	
Money Is Getting Cheaper	7"	Stateside	SS304	1964	**£4**	
New Orleans Blues	LP	Atlantic	1266	1956	**£25**	US
No Rolling Blues	7"	Vogue	V2060	1968	**£8**	
Outskirts Of Town	7" EP	Vocalion	EPVH1284	1965	**£5**	
Past Forty Blues	7"	Verve	VS553	1967	**£4**	
Roots	LP	Reprise	R6059	1962	**£10**	US
Singin' The Blues	LP	W. Pacific	1267	1959	**£15**	US
Sings The Blues	LP	Society	SOC986	1964	**£10**	
Some Of My Best Friends...	LP	Stateside	SL10114	1965	**£12**	
Spoon	LP	Reprise	R2008	1961	**£10**	US
Spoonful Of Soul	LP	Verve	V65050	1968	**£10**	US
Take This Hammer	LP	Constellation	M1422	1964	**£12**	US
There's Good Rockin' Tonight	LP	Fontana		196-	**£10**	
You're Next	7"	Stateside	SS362	1964	**£4**	

WIZARD

Title	Format	Label	Cat. No.	Year	Price	Notes
Original Wizard	LP	Peon	1069	1971	**£50**	US

WIZARDS FROM KANSAS

Wizards From Kansas	LP	Mercury	SR61309	1970	**£20**	US

WIZZARD

I Wish It Could Be Christmas Every Day	7"	W. Bros	K16336	1973	**£4**	gatefold PS

WOLFMAN JACK

And The Wolf Pack	LP	Bread		1963	**£30**	US
Fun And Romance	LP	Columbia		1975	**£15**	US
Through The Ages	LP	Wooden N.		1973	**£10**	US

WOLVES

At The Club	7"	Pye	7N17013	1965	**£6**	
Journey Into Dreams	7"	Pye	7N15676	1964	**£8**	
Lust For Life	7"	Parlophone	R5511	1966	**£8**	
Now	7"	Pye	7N15733	1964	**£8**	

WOMACK, BOBBY

Across 110th Street	LP	United Artists	UAS29451	1973	**£10**	
Across 110th Street	7"	United Artists	UP35512	1973	**£4**	
Broadway Talk	7"	Minit	MLF11001	1968	**£6**	
California Dreamin'	7"	Minit	MLF11012	1969	**£4**	
Check It Out	7"	United Artists	UP35859	1975	**£4**	
Communication	LP	United Artists	UAS29306	1973	**£10**	
Daylight	7"	United Artists	UP36098	1976	**£4**	
Facts Of Life	LP	United Artists	UAG29456	1973	**£10**	
Fly Me To The Moon	7"	Minit	MLF11010	1968	**£4**	
Harry Hippie	7"	United Artists	UP35456	1973	**£4**	
I Can Understand It	LP	United Artists	UAS29715	1975	**£10**	
I Don't Know What The World Is Coming To	LP	United Artists	UAG29762	1975	**£10**	
Lookin' For A Love	7"	United Artists	UP35644	1974	**£4**	
Lookin' For A Love Again	LP	United Artists	UAS29574	1974	**£10**	
Nobody Wants You...	7"	United Artists	UP35565	1973	**£4**	
Safety Zone	LP	United Artists	UAG29907	1976	**£10**	
That's The Way I Feel About 'Cha	7"	United Artists	UP35339	1972	**£4**	
Understanding	LP	United Artists	UAS29365	1972	**£10**	
What Is This?	7"	Jayboy	BOY75	1974	**£8**	
What Is This?	7"	Minit	MLF11005	1968	**£5**	
Where There's A Will There's A Way	7"	United Artists	UP36042	1976	**£4**	
Woman's Got To Have It	7"	United Artists	UP35375	1972	**£4**	

WOMB

Overdub	LP	Dot	DLP25959	1969	**£10**	
Womb	LP	Dot	DLP25933	1968	**£10**	

WONDER STUFF

Give Give Give Me More More More	7"	Polydor	GONE3	1988	**£6**	
Give Give Give Me More More More	12"	Polydor	GONEX3	1988	**£10**	
Unbearable	7"	Farout	GONE002	1987	**£20**	
Wish Away	7"	Polydor	GONE4	1988	**£5**	
Wish Away	12"	Polydor	GONEX4	1988	**£8**	
Wonderful Day	7"	Farout	GONE ONE	1987	**£60**	

WONDER WHO

Don't Think Twice It's Alright	7"	Philips	BF1440	1965	**£6**	
Lonesome Road	7"	Philips	BF1600	1967	**£6**	
On The Good Ship Lollipop	7"	Philips	BF1504	1966	**£6**	

WONDER, STEVIE

12 Year Old Genius	LP	Oriole	PS40050	1963	**£40**	
Blowin' In The Wind	7"	T. Motown	TMG570	1966	**£8**	chart single
Blowin' In The Wind	7"	T. Motown	TMG570	1966	**£50**	demo
Castles In The Sand	7"	Stateside	SS285	1964	**£20**	
Castles In The Sand	7"	Stateside	SS285	1964	**£50**	demo
Down To Earth	LP	T. Motown	STML11045	1967	**£20**	
Eivets Rednow	LP	Gordy	GS932	1968	**£15**	US
Fingertips	7"	Oriole	CBA1833	1963	**£50**	demo
Fingertips	7"	Oriole	CBA1853	1963	**£20**	
For Once In My Life	LP	T. Motown	STML11098	1969	**£10**	
For Once In My Life	7"	T. Motown	TMG679	1968	**£5**	chart single
For Once In My Life	7"	T. Motown	TMG679	1968	**£15**	demo

Title	Format	Label	Cat. No.	Year	Price	Notes
Greatest Hits	LP	Tamla	TS282	1968	**£10**	US
Heaven Help Us All	7"	T. Motown	TMG757	1970	**£4**	chart single
Heaven Help Us All	7"	T. Motown	TMG757	1970	**£10**	demo
Hey Harmonica Man	LP	Stateside	SL10108	1965	**£50**	
Hey Harmonica Man	7"	Stateside	SS323	1964	**£20**	
Hey Harmonica Man	7"	Stateside	SS323	1964	**£50**	demo
Hi Heel Sneakers	7"	T. Motown	TMG532	1965	**£10**	
Hi Heel Sneakers	7"	T. Motown	TMG532	1965	**£50**	demo
Higher Ground	7"	T. Motown	TMG869	1973	**£8**	demo
I Call It Pretty Music	7" EP	Stateside	SE1014	1964	**£20**	
I Don't Know Why	7"	T. Motown	TMG690	1969	**£15**	demo
I Was Made To Love Her	LP	T. Motown	STML11059	1968	**£15**	
I Was Made To Love Her	7"	T. Motown	TMG613	1967	**£4**	chart single
I Was Made To Love Her	7"	T. Motown	TMG613	1967	**£30**	demo
I'm Wondering	7"	T. Motown	TMG626	1967	**£5**	chart single
I'm Wondering	7"	T. Motown	TMG626	1967	**£25**	chart single
If You Really Love Me	7"	T. Motown	TMG798	1972	**£4**	
If You Really Love Me	7"	T. Motown	TMG798	1972	**£10**	demo
Jazz Soul Of Little Stevie	LP	Stateside	SL10078	1964	**£40**	
Kiss Me Baby	7"	T. Motown	TMG505	1965	**£15**	
Kiss Me Baby	7"	T. Motown	TMG505	1965	**£50**	demo
Live	LP	T. Motown	STML11150	1970	**£10**	
Live At The Talk Of The Town	LP	T. Motown	STML11164	1970	**£10**	
My Cherie Amour	LP	T. Motown	STML11128	1970	**£10**	chart LP
My Cherie Amour	7"	T. Motown	TMG690	1969	**£4**	chart single
Never Dreamed You'd Leave Me In Summer	7"	T. Motown	TMG779	1971	**£4**	
Never Dreamed You'd Leave Me In Summer	7"	T. Motown	TMG779	1971	**£10**	demo
Never Had A Dream Come True	7"	T. Motown	TMG731	1970	**£4**	chart single
Never Had A Dream Come True	7"	T. Motown	TMG731	1970	**£10**	demo
Nothing's Too Good For My Baby	7"	T. Motown	TMG558	1966	**£15**	
Nothing's Too Good For My Baby	7"	T. Motown	TMG558	1966	**£60**	demo
Place In The Sun	7"	T. Motown	TMG588	1966	**£6**	chart single
Place In The Sun	7"	T. Motown	TMG588	1966	**£40**	demo
Shoo-Be-Doo-Be-Doo-Da-Day	7"	T. Motown	TMG653	1968	**£4**	chart single
Shoo-Be-Doo-Be-Doo-Da-Day	7"	T. Motown	TMG653	1968	**£15**	demo
Signed Sealed Delivered I'm Yours	7"	T. Motown	TMG744	1970	**£4**	chart single
Signed Sealed Delivered I'm Yours	7"	T. Motown	TMG744	1970	**£10**	demo
Someday At Christmas	LP	T. Motown	STML11085	1969	**£20**	
Stevie Wonder	7" EP	T. Motown	TME2006	1965	**£15**	
Superstition	7"	T. Motown	TMG841	1973	**£4**	chart single
Superstition	7"	T. Motown	TMG841	1973	**£10**	demo
Superwoman	7"	T. Motown	TMG827	1972	**£4**	
Superwoman	7"	T. Motown	TMG827	1972	**£10**	demo
Talking Book	LP	EMI	5CP06293880	1979	**£15**	Dutch pic disc
Travelling Man	7"	T. Motown	TMG602	1967	**£4**	
Travelling Man	7"	T. Motown	TMG602	1967	**£30**	demo
Tribute To Uncle Ray	LP	Oriole	PS40049	1963	**£40**	
Uptight	LP	T. Motown	STML11036	1966	**£15**	
Uptight	7"	T. Motown	TMG545	1966	**£10**	chart single
Uptight	7"	T. Motown	TMG545	1966	**£50**	demo
We Can Work It Out	7"	T. Motown	TMG772	1971	**£4**	chart single
We Can Work It Out	7"	T. Motown	TMG772	1971	**£10**	demo
With A Song In My Heart	LP	Tamla	T250	1964	**£40**	US
Workout Stevie Workout	7"	Stateside	SS238	1963	**£20**	
Workout Stevie Workout	7"	Stateside	SS238	1963	**£50**	demo
Workout Stevie Workout	LP	Tamla	TS248	1963	**£40**	US
Yester-me Yester-you Yesterday	7"	T. Motown	TMG717	1969	**£10**	demo
Yester-me, Yester-you, Yesterday	7"	T. Motown	TMG717	1969	**£4**	chart single
You Are The Sunshine Of My Life	7"	T. Motown	TMG852	1973	**£8**	demo
You Met Your Match	7"	T. Motown	TMG666	1968	**£4**	
You Met Your Match	7"	T. Motown	TMG666	1968	**£20**	demo

WONG, ROYCE

Title	Format	Label	Cat. No.	Year	Price	Notes
Everything's Gonna Be Alright	7"	Blue Beat	BB301	1964	**£10**	

WOOD, ANITA

Title	Format	Label	Cat. No.	Year	Price	Notes
Dream Baby	7"	Sue	WI328	1964	**£8**	
I'll Wait Forever	7"	London	HLS9585	1962	**£4**	

WOOD, BRENTON

Baby You Got It	LP	Double Shot	1003	1967	**£10**	US
Gimme Little Sign	LP	Liberty	LBL83088E	1967	**£10**	
Gimme Little Sign	7"	Liberty	LBF15021	1967	**£4**	chart single

WOOD, DEL

Ragtime Annie	7"	London	HL8036	1954	**£10**	
Ragtime Piano	7" EP	London	REP1007	1954	**£6**	

WOOD, ROY

On The Road Again	LP	W. Bros	BSK3247	1980	**£10**	US
On The Road Again	7"	W. Bros	K17459	1979	**£4**	pic disc
When Grandma Plays The Banjo	7"	Harvest	HAR5048	1972	**£4**	

WOOD, ROY & ANNIE HASLAM

I Never Believed In Love	7"	W. Bros	K17028	1977	**£5**	

WOODEN HORSE

Wooden Horse	LP	York		1972	**£30**	
Wooden Horse II	LP	York		1973	**£50**	

WOODEN O

Handful Of Pleasant Delites	LP	Middle Earth	MDLS301	1969	**£50**	

WOODPECKERS

Hey Little Girl	7"	Oriole	CB311	1965	**£4**	
Woodpecker	7"	Decca	F11835	1964	**£4**	

WOODS, TERRY & GAY

Backwoods	LP	Polydor	2383322	1975	**£15**	
Renowned	LP	Polydor	2383406	1976	**£10**	
Tenderhooks	LP	Rockburgh	ROC104	1978	**£10**	
Time Is Right	LP	Polydor	2383375	1976	**£12**	
Woods Band	LP	Greenwich	GSLP1004	1971	**£25**	
Woods Band	LP	Rockburgh	CREST29	1977	**£10**	

WOOFERS

Dragsville	LP	Wyncote	9001	196-	**£20**	US

WOOLEY, SHEB

Blue Guitar	7"	MGM	MGM1263	1965	**£4**	
Hootenanny Hoot	7"	MGM	MGM1257	1965	**£4**	
I Flipped	7"	MGM	SP1130	1955	**£5**	
Jest Plain, Wild And Wooley	7" EP	MGM	MGMEP540	1956	**£15**	
Laughing The Blues	7"	MGM	MGM1162	1956	**£4**	
Luke The Spook	7"	MGM	MGM1081	1960	**£5**	
Meet Mr.Lonely	7"	MGM	MGM1147	1961	**£4**	
More	7"	MGM	MGM1017	1959	**£4**	
Purple People Eater	7"	MGM	MGM981	1958	**£5**	2 different B sides, chart single
Santa And The Purple People Eater	7"	MGM	MGM997	1958	**£5**	
Sheb Wooley	LP	MGM	E3299	1956	**£20**	US
Songs From The Day Of Rawhide	LP	MGM	C859	1961	**£10**	
That's My Ma And That's My Pa	LP	MGM	C903	1962	**£10**	
Wayward Wind	7"	MGM	MGM1132	1961	**£4**	

WOOLIES

Basic Rock	LP	Split	96452001	1970	**£12**	US
Live At Lizard's	LP	Split		1973	**£20**	US

WOOLLY

Golden Golden	7"	RCA	RCA2297	1972	**£5**	

WORD

Nazz	7"	Charisma	CB345	1979	**£4**	

WORK, JIMMY

Country Songs	7" EP	London	RED1039	1955	**£10**	
When She Said You All	7"	London	HLD8270	1956	**£15**	
You've Got A Heart Like A Merry-Go-Round	7"	London	HLD8308	1956	**£10**	

WORLD

Title	Format	Label	Cat. No.	Year	Price	Note
Angelina	7"	Liberty	LBF15402	1970	**£5**	
Lucky Planet	LP	Liberty	LBS83419	1970	**£20**	

WORLD OF OZ

Title	Format	Label	Cat. No.	Year	Price	Note
King Croesus	7"	Deram	DM205	1968	**£8**	
Muffin Man	7"	Deram	DM187	1968	**£8**	
Willow's Harp	7"	Deram	DM233	1969	**£10**	
World Of Oz	LP	Deram	SML1034	1969	**£25**	

WORTH, JOHNNY

Title	Format	Label	Cat. No.	Year	Price	Note
Just Because	7"	Columbia	DB3962	1957	**£5**	
Living Doll	7"	Embassy	347	1959	**£4**	
Nightmare	7"	Oriole	CB1545	1960	**£4**	
Nine Times Out Of Ten	7"	Embassy	413	1960	**£4**	
You Know What I Mean	7"	Columbia	DB4811	1962	**£4**	

WRANGLERS

Title	Format	Label	Cat. No.	Year	Price	Note
Liza Jane	7"	Parlophone	R5163	1964	**£20**	

WRAY, LINK

Title	Format	Label	Cat. No.	Year	Price	Note
Be What You Want To Be	LP	Polydor	2391063	1973	**£10**	
Beans And Fatback	LP	Virgin	V2006	1973	**£10**	
Fire And Brimstone	7"	Polydor	2066120	1971	**£4**	
Good Rockin' Tonight	7"	Stateside	SS397	1965	**£6**	
Great Guitar Hits	LP	Vermillion	1924	196-	**£25**	US
Jack The Ripper	7"	Stateside	SS217	1963	**£8**	
Jack The Ripper	LP	Swan	SLP510	1963	**£25**	US
Link Wray	LP	Polydor	2489029	1971	**£10**	
Link Wray And The Wraymen	LP	Epic	LN3661	1960	**£30**	US
Link Wray Sings And Plays Guitar	LP	Vermillion	1925	196-	**£25**	US
Mr.Guitar	7" EP	Stateside	SE1015	1964	**£15**	
Rumble	7"	London	HLA8623	1958	**£12**	
Rumble	LP	Polydor	2391128	1974	**£10**	
Stuck In Gear	LP	Virgin	V2050	1976	**£10**	
Sweeper	7"	Stateside	SS256	1964	**£6**	
There's Good Rockin' Tonight	LP	Union Pacific	UP002	1971	**£15**	
Yesterday And Today	LP	Rec. Factory	1929	196-	**£12**	US

WRAY, VERNON & LINK WRAY

Title	Format	Label	Cat. No.	Year	Price	Note
Wasted	LP	Vermillion	1972	196-	**£15**	US

WREN, JENNY

Title	Format	Label	Cat. No.	Year	Price	Note
Chasing My Dreams All Over Town	7"	Fontana	TF672	1966	**£15**	

WRIGGLERS

Title	Format	Label	Cat. No.	Year	Price	Note
Cooler	7"	Giant	GN26	1967	**£10**	
Get Right	7"	Blue Cat	BS106	196-	**£10**	

WRIGHT, BETTY

Title	Format	Label	Cat. No.	Year	Price	Note
Girls Can't Do What The Guys Do	7"	Atlantic	584216	1968	**£4**	

WRIGHT, DALE

Title	Format	Label	Cat. No.	Year	Price	Note
She's Neat	7"	London	HLH8573	1958	**£50**	
That's Show Biz	7"	Pye	7N25022	1959	**£15**	

WRIGHT, GARY

Title	Format	Label	Cat. No.	Year	Price	Note
Extraction	LP	A&M	AMLS2004	1970	**£10**	
Foot Print	LP	A&M	AMLS64296	1971	**£10**	
Ring Of Changes	LP	A&M	AMLH64362	1972	**£10**	
Stand For Our Rights	7"	A&M	AMS852	1971	**£4**	

WRIGHT, GINNY

Title	Format	Label	Cat. No.	Year	Price	Note
Indian Moon	7"	London	HL8119	1955	**£10**	

WRIGHT, GINNY & TOMMY CUTRER

Title	Format	Label	Cat. No.	Year	Price	Note
Wonderful World	7"	London	HL8093	1954	**£10**	

WRIGHT, O.V.

Title	Format	Label	Cat. No.	Year	Price	Note
8 Men 4 Women	7"	London	HLZ10137	1967	**£4**	
8 Men, 4 Women	LP	Island	ILP975	1968	**£30**	
Gone For Good	7"	Vocalion	VP9272	1966	**£4**	

I Want Everyone To Know	7"	Action	ACT4527	1969	**£10**	demo
If It's Only For Tonight	LP	Back Beat	61	1965	**£10**	US
Nucleus Of Soul	LP	Back Beat	67	1969	**£10**	US
O.V.Wright	7" EP	Vocalion	VEP170165	1965	**£12**	
Oh Baby Mine	7"	Action	ACT4505	1968	**£5**	
Oh Baby Mine	7"	Action	ACT4505	1968	**£12**	demo
Poor Boy	7"	Vocalion	VP9255	1966	**£5**	
What About You	7"	Sue	WI4043	1968	**£8**	
You're Gonna Make Me Cry	7"	Vocalion	VP9249	1965	**£5**	

WRIGHT, OTIS

It Will Soon Be Done	LP	Doctor Bird	DLM5006	196-	**£80**	
Over In Gloryland	LP	Coxsone	TLP1001	196-	**£80**	
Peace Perfect Peace	LP	Doctor Bird	DLM5005	196-	**£80**	

WRIGHT, RITA

I Can't Give Back The Love	7"	T. Motown	TMG643	1968	**£6**	
I Can't Give Back The Love	7"	T. Motown	TMG643	1968	**£20**	demo
I Can't Give Back The Love I Feel For You	7"	T. Motown	TMG791	1971	**£10**	
I Can't Give Back The Love I Feel For You	7"	T. Motown	TMG791	1971	**£25**	demo

WRIGHT, RUBEN

Hey Girl	7"	Capitol	CL15460	1966	**£4**	

WRIGHT, STEVE

Wild Wild Women	7"	London	HLW8991	1959	**£15**	

WRIGHT, WINSTON

Musically Beat	7"	Moodisc	HM106	197-	**£4**	
Musically Red	7"	Moodisc	MU3501	197-	**£4**	

WRIT

Did You Ever Have To Make Up Your Mind	7"	Decca	F12385	1966	**£4**	

WRITING ON THE WALL

Child On A Crossing	7"	Middle Earth	MDS101	1969	**£12**	
Power Of The Picts	LP	Middle Earth	MDLS308	1969	**£80**	

WYATT, ROBERT

End Of An Ear	LP	CBS	64189	1970	**£12**	
I'm A Believer	7"	Virgin	VS114	1974	**£4**	
Shipbuilding	7"	Rough Trade	RT115	1982	**£5**	fold-out PS
Shipbuilding	12"	Rough Trade	RT115T	1982	**£6**	
Yesterday Man	7"	Virgin	VS115	1977	**£6**	

WYLIE, POPCORN

Funky Rubber Band	7"	T. Motown	TMG932	1975	**£4**	

WYLIE, RICHARD

Brand New Man	7"	Columbia	DB7012	1963	**£6**	

WYMAN, BILL

Je Suis Un Rock Star	7"	A&M	AMS8144DJ	1981	**£4**	promo
Monkey Grip	LP	R. Stones	QD79100	1974	**£10**	US quad
Stone Alone	LP	R. Stones	QD79103	1976	**£10**	US quad

WYNNS, SANDY

Touch Of Venus	7"	Fontana	TF550	1965	**£25**	

WYNTER, MARK

Dream Girl	7"	Decca	F11323	1961	**£4**	chart single
Exclusively Yours	7"	Decca	F11354	1961	**£4**	chart single
Girl For Everyday	7"	Decca	F11380	1961	**£4**	
Go Away Little Girl	7"	Pye	7N15492	1962	**£4**	chart single
Heaven's Plan	7"	Decca	F11434	1962	**£4**	
I Love Her Still	7"	Decca	F11467	1962	**£4**	
Image Of A Girl	7"	Decca	F11263	1960	**£4**	chart single
It's Almost Tomorrow	7"	Pye	7N15577	1963	**£4**	chart single
It's Mark Time	7" EP	Pye	NEP24176	1962	**£6**	
Kickin' Up The Leaves	7"	Decca	F11279	1960	**£4**	chart single
Mark Time	7" EP	Decca	DFE6674	1960	**£8**	
Mark Wynter	LP	Ace Of Clubs	ACL1141	1962	**£15**	

Mark Wynter	LP	Golden Guin.	GGL0250	1963	**£15**	
Only You	7"	Pye	7N15626	1964	**£4**	chart single
Shy Girl	7"	Pye	7N15525	1963	**£4**	chart single
Venus In Blue Jeans	7"	Pye	7N15466	1962	**£4**	chart single
Wynter Time	7" EP	Pye	NEP24185	1964	**£6**	

X

Adult Books	7"	Dangerhouse	D88	1978	**£20**	
White Girl	7"	Slash	SRS106	1981	**£4**	

X MEN

Ghosts	7"	Creation	CRE006	1984	**£10**	
Spiral Girl	7"	Creation	CRE014	1985	**£10**	

X-CERTS

Together	7"	Recreational	PLAY1	1981	**£4**	with insert

X-DREAMYSTS

Right Way Home	7"	Good Vibs	GOT5	1978	**£5**	

X-O-DUS

English Black Boys	12"	Factory	FAC11	1979	**£6**	

X-RAY SPEX

Day The World Turned Day-Glo	7"	EMI	INT553	1978	**£4**	chart single
Day The World Turned Day-Glo	7"	EMI	INT553	1978	**£6**	orange vinyl
Germ Free Adolescents	LP	EMI	INS3023	1978	**£20**	chart LP
Highly Inflammable	7"	EMI	INT583	1979	**£5**	red vinyl
Identity	7"	EMI	INT563	1978	**£4**	chart single
Identity	7"	EMI	INT563	1978	**£6**	pink vinyl
Oh Bondage, Up Yours	7"	Virgin	VS189	1977	**£12**	
Oh Bondage, Up Yours	12"	Virgin	VS18912	1977	**£6**	no PS

X-RAYS

Out Of Control	7"	London	HLR8805	1959	**£8**	

XIT

I Was Raised	7"	Rare Earth	RES107	1972	**£4**	
Plight Of Redman	LP	Rare Earth	SREA4002	1972	**£10**	
Reservation Of Education	7"	Rare Earth	RES111	1973	**£4**	
Silent Warrior	LP	Rare Earth	R5451	1973	**£12**	US

XL5

XL5	7"	HMV	POP1148	1963	**£4**	

XMAL DEUTSCHLAND

Incubus Succubus II	7"	4AD	AD311	1983	**£4**	

XTC

3D EP (Science Friction)	7"	Virgin	VS188	1977	**£110**	
Are You Receiving Me	7"	Virgin	VS231	1978	**£4**	
Black Sea	LP	Virgin	V2173	1980	**£10**	with green paper sleeve
Chain Of Command	7"	Virgin	VDJ30	1979	**£4**	
Generals And Majors	7"	Virgin	VS365	1980	**£5**	double
Go 2	LP	Virgin	V2108	1978	**£10**	with Go+ 12"
Life Begins At The Hop	7"	Virgin	VS259	1979	**£4**	clear vinyl
Looking For Footsteps	7"	Lyntone	LYN11032	1982	**£4**	Flexipop flexi
Making Plans For Nigel	7"	Virgin	VS282	1979	**£5**	with game
Statue Of Liberty	7"	Virgin	VS201	1978	**£4**	
This Is Pop	7"	Virgin	VS209	1978	**£4**	
Towers Of London	7"	Virgin	VS372	1981	**£5**	double
White Music	LP	Virgin	V2095	1978	**£10**	chart LP
Wonderland	7"	Virgin	VSY606	1983	**£5**	pic disc

XXX

Live	LP	Private			**£80**	US

Y

Y & T

Struck Down	LP	London	PS711	1978	**£10**	US
Yesterday And Today	LP	London	PS677	1976	**£15**	US

YA HO WA

All Or Nothing At All	LP	Higher Key		1975	**£60**	US
Father Yod	LP	Higher Key		1974	**£40**	US
Golden Sunrise	LP	Psycho		1983	**£40**	
I'm Gonna Take You Home	LP	Higher Key	3309	1974	**£100**	US
Kahoutek	LP	Higher Key		1973	**£75**	US
Penetration	LP	Higher Key		1974	**£40**	US
Savage Sons Of Yo Ho Wa	LP	Higher Key	3306	1974	**£100**	US
To The Principles For The Children	LP	Higher Key		197-	**£500**	US
Ya Ho Wa	LP	Higher Key		1974	**£50**	US
Ya Ho Wa	LP	Higher Key		1974	**£250**	US, sheep shag cover, double
Ya Ho Wa 2	LP	Higher Key		197-	**£100**	US
Yod Ship Suite	LP	Father		1975	**£100**	US

YAKS

Yakety Yak	7"	Decca	F12115	1965	**£8**	

YAMASH'TA, STOMU

Japanese percussionist Stomu Yamash'ta came to Britain during the early seventies and amazed the classical music world with his virtuosity. The two LPs listed here contain works by some of the leading contemporary classical composers which allow Yamash'ta to show off his formidable technique - the L'Oiseau Lyre record has percussion as the only instrumentation. Interestingly, Yamash'ta discovered progressive rock and completely changed his musical policy with a number of jazz-rock albums. Perhaps he realised that this was where the most vital musical developments were taking place, although the cynic might argue that he merely realised that there was more money to be made out of rock music.

Henze/Takemitsu/Maxwell Davies	LP	L'Oiseau Lyre	DSLO1	1972	**£10**	
Takemitsu Ishii	LP	EMI	EMD5508	1973	**£10**	

YAMASUKIS

Yamasuki	7"	Dandelion	DAN7004	1971	**£5**	PS
Yamasuki	7"	Dandelion	K19003	1972	**£4**	

YANA

Climb Up The Wall	7"	HMV	POP252	1956	**£6**	
I Miss You Mama	7"	HMV	POP481	1958	**£4**	
Mr.Wonderful	7"	HMV	POP340	1957	**£6**	

YANCEY, JIMMY

Jimmy And Mama Yancey	LP-10"	Atlantic	130	195-	**£30**	US
Jimmy And Mama Yancey	LP-10"	Atlantic	134	195-	**£30**	US
Jimmy Yancey	7" EP	HMV	7EG8062	195-	**£4**	
Jimmy Yancey	7" EP	Vogue	EPV1203	195-	**£5**	
Pure Blues	LP	Atlantic	1231	1956	**£25**	US
Yancey Special	LP-10"	Atlantic	103	195-	**£30**	US
Yancey's Piano	7" EP	HMV	7EG8083	195-	**£4**	

YANKEE DOLLAR

Yankee Dollar	LP	Dot	DLP25874	1968	**£15**	US

YANOVSKY, ZALMAN

Alive And Well In Argentina	LP	Buddah	BDS5019	1968	**£12**	US
Alive And Well In Argentina	LP	Kama Sutra	2316003	1971	**£10**	
As Long As You're Here	7"	Kama Sutra	KAS212	1967	**£4**	
As Long As You're Here	7"	Pye	7N25438	1967	**£4**	

YARDBIRDS

All of the Yardbirds' innovative original records are now collectable - even the chart hits - although the rarest come from right at the start of the group's career and right at the end. The single "Goodnight Sweet Josephine" definitely does exist, despite occasional murmerings to the contrary, although possibly only as a demo. Meanwhile, the LP "Live Yardbirds", ruined, according to the group, by the engineers miking Jimmy Page's monitor speaker rather than the real thing, and also by its extravagant over-dubbed applause, was given two releases and rapidly withdrawn each time. Counterfeits exist, but these have black and white covers, rather than the colour of the originals.

Evil Hearted You	7"	Columbia	DB7706	1965	**£6**	chart single
Face And Place	LP	Direction		1964	**£50**	New Zealand
Five Live Yardbirds	LP	Columbia	33SX1677	1964	**£30**	
Five Yardbirds	7" EP	Columbia	SEG8421	1965	**£15**	
For Your Love	7"	Columbia	DB7499	1965	**£6**	
For Your Love	LP	Epic	LN24167	1965	**£30**	US
Good Morning Little Schoolgirl	7"	Columbia	DB7391	1964	**£12**	chart single
Goodnight Sweet Josephine	7"	Columbia	DB8368	1968	**£150**	
Greatest Hits	LP	Epic	LN24246	1966	**£20**	US
Happening Ten Years Time Ago	7"	Columbia	DB8024	1966	**£15**	chart single
Having A Rave Up	LP	Columbia	SCXC28	1966	**£50**	export
Having A Rave Up	LP	Epic	LN24177	1965	**£25**	US
Heart Full Of Soul	7"	Columbia	DB7594	1965	**£6**	chart single
I Wish You Would	7"	Columbia	DB7283	1964	**£15**	
Little Games	7"	Columbia	DB8165	1967	**£20**	
Little Games	LP	Epic	LN24313	1967	**£30**	US
Live Featuring Jimmy Page	LP	Columbia	P13311	1972	**£30**	US, colour cover
Live Featuring Jimmy Page	LP	Epic	KE30615	1971	**£40**	US, colour cover
Over Under Sideways Down	7"	Columbia	DB7928	1966	**£8**	chart single
Over Under Sideways Down	LP	Epic	LN24210	1966	**£25**	US
Paf Bum	7"	Ricordi Int	SIR20010	1966	**£20**	Italian
Shapes Of Things	7"	Columbia	DB7848	1966	**£8**	chart single
With Sonny Boy Williamson	LP	Fontana	858025	1967	**£15**	
With Sonny Boy Williamson	LP	Fontana	SFJL960	1968	**£20**	
With Sonny Boy Williamson	LP	ontana	TL5277	1964	**£60**	
Yardbirds	LP	Columbia	SCX6063	1966	**£30**	
Yardbirds	7" EP	Columbia	SEG8521	1966	**£70**	chart LP
Yardbirds	LP	Epic	EG30135	1970	**£20**	US
Yardbirds	LP	Epic	HE38455	1983	**£20**	US audiophile

YARDBIRDS & HERBIE HANCOCK

Blow-Up	LP	MGM	E4447	1967	**£15**	US

YATES, CHRIS

New Born	LP	ILSM		1977	**£60**	US

YEAR ONE

Eli's Comin'	7"	Major Minor	MM660	1969	**£5**	

YELLO

Bimbo	7"	Do It	DUN11	1980	**£4**	
Bostich	7"	Do It	DUN13	1982	**£4**	
Bostich	12"	Do It	DUNIT13	1982	**£6**	
I Love You	7"	Stiff	PBUY176	1983	**£4**	3-D pic disc
She's Got A Gun	7"	Do It	DUN18	1982	**£4**	
She's Got A Gun	12"	Do It	DUNIT18	1982	**£6**	

YELLOW BALLOON

Stained Glass Window	7"	Stateside	SS2124	1968	**£5**	
Yellow Balloon	LP	Canterbury	CLPM1502	1967	**£15**	US
Yellow Balloon	7"	Stateside	SS2008	1967	**£8**	

YELLOW PAGES

Here Comes Jane	7"	Page One	POF090	1968	**£5**	

YELLOW PAYGES

Little Woman	7"	Uni	UNS516	1970	**£4**	
Volume One	LP	Uni	73045	1969	**£12**	US

YELLOWSTONE & VOICE

Memories	7"	Regal Z.	RZ3073	1973	**£4**	
Philosopher	7"	Parlophone	R5965	1972	**£4**	
Thinking About You And Me	7"	Regal Z.	RZ3065	1972	**£4**	
Yellowstone And Voice	LP	Regal Z.		1972	**£10**	

YEMM AND YEMEN

Black Is The Night	7"	Columbia	DB8022	1966	**£10**	

YES

Title	Format	Label	Cat. No.	Year	Price	Notes
Classic Yes	LP	Atlantic	K50842	1980	**£25**	test pressing, different sleeve
Close To The Edge	LP	Mobile Fid.	MFSL1077	1980	**£15**	US audiophile
Going For The One	LP	Atlantic	DSK50379	1977	**£12**	3 x 12", boxed
Going For The One	7"	Atlantic	K10985	1977	**£6**	
Going For The One	12"	Atlantic	K10985	1977	**£10**	
Interview	7"	Atlantic	SAM7	1972	**£10**	promo
Interview/Five Songs	7"	Lyntone	LYN2536		**£10**	with 80 page songbook
Into The Lens	12"	Atlantic	SAM125	1980	**£6**	1 sided promo
Looking Around	7"	Atlantic	584298	1969	**£25**	
Roundabout	7"	Atlantic	K10407	1974	**£5**	
Roundabout	7"	Atlantic	SAM141	1981	**£4**	
Sweet Dreams	7"	Atlantic	2091004	1970	**£25**	
Sweetness	7"	Atlantic	584280	1969	**£25**	
Time And A Word	LP	Atlantic	2400006	1970	**£10**	lyric sheet, chart LP
Time And A Word	7"	Atlantic	584323	1970	**£25**	
Yes	LP	Atlantic	588190	1969	**£10**	lyric sheet
Yes Solos	LP	Atlantic	PR260	1976	**£20**	US promo compilation

YOBS

Title	Format	Label	Cat. No.	Year	Price	Notes
Rub-A-Dum-Dum	7"	Safari	YULE1	1981	**£4**	
Run Rudolph Run	7"	NEMS	NES114	1977	**£4**	
Silent Night	7"	Yob	YOB79	1978	**£4**	
Yobs' Christmas Album	LP	Safari	RUDE1	1979	**£10**	

YOLANDA

Title	Format	Label	Cat. No.	Year	Price	Notes
With This Kiss	7"	Triumph	RGM1007	1960	**£8**	

YORK BROTHERS

Title	Format	Label	Cat. No.	Year	Price	Notes
Country And Western	7" EP	Parlophone	GEP8736	1958	**£6**	
Country And Western No.2	7" EP	Parlophone	GEP8753	1958	**£6**	
Sixteen Great Country & Western Hits	LP	King	820	1963	**£12**	US
York Brothers	LP	King	586	1958	**£15**	US
York Brothers Vol.2	LP	King	591	1958	**£15**	US

YORK, PETE

Title	Format	Label	Cat. No.	Year	Price	Notes
Pete York Percussion Band	LP	Decca	TXS109	1972	**£12**	

YORK, RUSTY

Title	Format	Label	Cat. No.	Year	Price	Notes
Peggy Sue	7"	Parlophone	R4398	1958	**£40**	

YOU KNOW WHO GROUP

Title	Format	Label	Cat. No.	Year	Price	Notes
Roses Are Red My Love	7"	London	HLR9947	1965	**£4**	
You Know Who Group	LP	Int. Allied	420	1965	**£30**	US

YOULDEN, CHRIS

Title	Format	Label	Cat. No.	Year	Price	Notes
City Child	LP	Deram	SML1112	1974	**£10**	
Nowhere Road	LP	Deram	SML1099	1973	**£10**	
Nowhere Road	7"	Deram	DM377	1972	**£4**	

YOUNG BLOOD

Title	Format	Label	Cat. No.	Year	Price	Notes
Continuing Story Of Bungalow Bill	7"	Pye	7N17696	1969	**£4**	
Green Light	7"	Pye	7N17495	1968	**£5**	
I Can't Stop	7"	Pye	7N17627	1968	**£6**	
Just How Loud	7"	Pye	7N17588	1968	**£4**	

YOUNG BROTHERS

Title	Format	Label	Cat. No.	Year	Price	Notes
High Energy Rock	LP	GDM		1978	**£25**	US, gold vinyl

YOUNG FLOWERS

Title	Format	Label	Cat. No.	Year	Price	Notes
Blomsterpistolen	LP	Sonet		1968	**£80**	
Quiet Days In Clichy	LP	Vanguard		1969	**£80**	
Volume 2	LP	Polydor		1969	**£80**	

YOUNG GROWLER

Title	Format	Label	Cat. No.	Year	Price	Notes
Amy The Sunbather	7"	Columbia	DB7870	1966	**£4**	
V For Victory	7"	Columbia	DB7958	1966	**£4**	

YOUNG IDEA

Title	Format	Label	Cat. No.	Year	Price	Notes
Gotta Get Out The Mess	7"	Columbia	DB8067	1966	**£4**	
Mr.Lovin' Luggage Man	7"	Columbia	DB8284	1967	**£4**	

Title	Format	Label	Cat. No.	Year	Price	Notes
Peculiar Situation	7"	Columbia	DB8132	1967	**£4**	
With A Little Help From My Friends	7"	Columbia	DB8205	1967	**£4**	chart single
World's Been Good To Me	7"	Columbia	DB7961	1966	**£5**	

YOUNG JESSIE

Title	Format	Label	Cat. No.	Year	Price	Notes
Shuffle In The Gravel	7"	London	HLE8544	1958	**£40**	

YOUNG ONES

Title	Format	Label	Cat. No.	Year	Price	Notes
Baby That's It	7"	Decca	F11705	1963	**£8**	

YOUNG TRADITION

Title	Format	Label	Cat. No.	Year	Price	Notes
Chicken On A Raft	7" EP	Transatlantic	TRAEP164	196-	**£10**	
Galleries	LP	Transatlantic	TRA172	1968	**£20**	
So Cheerfully Round	LP	Transatlantic	TRA155	1967	**£20**	
Young Tradition	LP	Transatlantic	TRA142	1966	**£20**	
Young Tradition Sampler	LP	Transatlantic	TRASAM13	1969	**£10**	

YOUNG WORLD SINGERS

Title	Format	Label	Cat. No.	Year	Price	Notes
Ringo For President	7"	Brunswick	05916	1964	**£4**	

YOUNG, BRETT

Title	Format	Label	Cat. No.	Year	Price	Notes
Guess What	7"	Pye	7N15578	1963	**£4**	
You Can't Fool Me	7"	Pye	7N15641	1964	**£5**	

YOUNG, FARON

Title	Format	Label	Cat. No.	Year	Price	Notes
Every Time I'm Kissing You	7"	Capitol	CL14891	1958	**£4**	
Five Dollars And It's Saturday Night	7"	Capitol	CL14655	1956	**£6**	
Hello Walls	7" EP	Capitol	EAP11549	1961	**£5**	
I Can't Dance	7"	Capitol	CL14860	1958	**£10**	
I Hate Myself	7"	Capitol	CL14930	1958	**£4**	
If You Ain't Lovin'	7"	Capitol	CL14574	1956	**£6**	
Live Fast, Love Hard, Die Young	7"	Capitol	CL14336	1955	**£8**	
Long Time Ago	7"	Capitol	CL14975	1959	**£4**	
Moonlight Mountain	7"	Capitol	CL14762	1957	**£4**	
Object Of My Affection	LP	Capitol	T1004	1958	**£10**	
Shrine Of St.Cecilia	7"	Capitol	CL14735	1957	**£4**	
Snowball	7"	Capitol	CL14822	1958	**£4**	
Sweethearts Or Strangers	LP	Capitol	T778	1957	**£15**	US
Sweethearts Or Strangers Pt.1	7" EP	Capitol	EAP1778	1957	**£5**	
Sweethearts Or Strangers Pt.2	7" EP	Capitol	EAP2778	1957	**£5**	
Sweethearts Or Strangers Pt.3	7" EP	Capitol	EAP3778	1957	**£5**	
This Is Faron Young	LP	Capitol	T1096	1963	**£10**	
Vacation's Over	7"	Capitol	CL14793	1957	**£8**	

YOUNG, GEORGIE

Title	Format	Label	Cat. No.	Year	Price	Notes
Nine More Miles	7"	London	HLU8748	1958	**£4**	

YOUNG, JESSE COLIN

Title	Format	Label	Cat. No.	Year	Price	Notes
Soul Of A City Boy	LP	Capitol	T2070	1964	**£15**	US
Two Trips	LP	Mercury		1971	**£20**	US
Youngblood	LP	Mercury	MG21005	1965	**£15**	US

YOUNG, JIMMY

Title	Format	Label	Cat. No.	Year	Price	Notes
Chain Gang	7"	Decca	F10694	1956	**£4**	chart single
Jimmy Young	7" EP	Decca	DFE6404	1957	**£5**	
Jimmy Young Sings	7" EP	Pye	NEP24004	1955	**£5**	
Man From Laramie	7"	Decca	F10597	1955	**£4**	chart single
More	7"	Decca	F10774	1956	**£4**	chart single
Presenting Jimmy Young	7" EP	Decca	DFE6277	1956	**£5**	
Unchained Melody	7"	Decca	F10502	1955	**£4**	chart single

YOUNG, JOHNNY

Title	Format	Label	Cat. No.	Year	Price	Notes
Fat Mandolin	LP	Blue Horizon	763852	1970	**£30**	

YOUNG, KAREN

Title	Format	Label	Cat. No.	Year	Price	Notes
Too Much Of A Good Thing	7"	Major Minor	MM584	1968	**£6**	

YOUNG, KATHY & THE INNOCENTS

Title	Format	Label	Cat. No.	Year	Price	Notes
Happy Birthday Blues	7"	Top Rank	JAR554	1961	**£6**	
Innocently Yours	LP	Indigo	503	1961	**£50**	US
Sound Of Kathy Young	LP	Indigo	504	1961	**£50**	US
Thousand Stars	7"	Top Rank	JAR534	1961	**£6**	

YOUNG, LAMONTE

Title	Format	Label	Number	Year	Price	Notes
Tortoise, His Dreams And Journeys	LP	Shandar	83510		£12	

YOUNG, LEON STRINGS

Title	Format	Label	Number	Year	Price	Notes
Glad All Over	7"	Pye	7N15646	1964	£6	

YOUNG, MIGHTY JOE

Title	Format	Label	Number	Year	Price	Notes
Legacy Of The Blues Vol.4	LP	Sonet	SNTF633	1972	£10	
Why Don't You Follow Me	7"	Parlophone	R5794	1969	£10	

YOUNG, NEIL

Title	Format	Label	Number	Year	Price	Notes
After The Goldrush	LP	Reprise	RSLP6383	1970	£10	chart LP
Conversation With Neil Young	LP	W. Bros		1980	£20	US promo
Don't Be Denied	7"	Reprise	SAM15	197-	£6	1 sided promo
Don't Cry No Tears	7"	Reprise	K14431	1976	£4	
Down By The River	7"	Reprise	RS23462	1969	£5	
Everybody Knows This Is Nowhere	LP	Reprise	RSLP6349	1969	£10	
Everybody's Rockin'	LP	Geffen		1983	£20	US audiophile promo
Four Strong Winds	7"	Reprise	K14493	1978	£4	chart single
Harvest	LP	Nautilus		1981	£15	US audiophile
Hawks And Doves	7"	Reprise	K14508	1980	£4	
Heart Of Gold	7"	Reprise	K14140	1972	£4	chart single
Hey Hey My My	7"	Reprise	K14498	1979	£4	
Journey Through The Past	LP	Reprise	K64015	1972	£12	double
Like A Hurricane	7"	Reprise	K14482	1977	£4	
Loner	7"	Reprise	RS23405	1969	£4	
Looking For A Love	7"	Reprise	K14416	1976	£4	
Neil Young	LP	Reprise	RS6317	1968	£20	US, no title on cover front
Neil Young	LP	Reprise	RSLP6317	1969	£10	
Oh Lonesome Me	7"	Reprise	RS20861	1970	£5	
Old Man	7"	Reprise	K14167	1972	£4	
Only Love Can Break Your Heart	7"	Reprise	RS20958	1970	£4	
Southern Man	7"	Reprise	K14350	1974	£4	
Trans	LP	Geffen	GHS2018	1982	£20	US audiophile promo
Walk On	7"	Reprise	K14360	1974	£4	
When You Dance I Can Really Love	7"	Reprise	RS23488	1971	£4	

YOUNG, RALPH

Title	Format	Label	Number	Year	Price	Notes
Bible Tells Me So	7"	Brunswick	05466	1955	£4	
Legend Of Wyatt Earp	7"	Brunswick	05605	1956	£4	

YOUNG, ROGER

Title	Format	Label	Number	Year	Price	Notes
Sweet Sweet Morning	7"	Columbia	DB7869	1966	£5	

YOUNG, ROY

Title	Format	Label	Number	Year	Price	Notes
Big Fat Mamma	7"	Fontana	H200	1959	£10	
Bony Moronie	7"	MCA	MKS5098	1972	£4	
Devil's Daughter	7"	MCA	MU1175	1972	£4	
Dig A Hole	7"	MCA	MU1214	1973	£4	
Four And Twenty Thousand Kisses	7"	Ember	EMB128	1961	£4	
Granny's Got A Painted Leg	7"	RCA	RCA2031	1970	£4	
Hey Little Girl	7"	Fontana	H215	1959	£6	
I Hardly Know It	7"	Fontana	H237	1960	£5	
I'm In Love	7"	Fontana	H247	1960	£5	
Mr.Funky	LP	MCA	MKPS2022	1972	£10	
Plenty Of Love	7"	Fontana	H290	1961	£5	
Rag Mama Rag	7"	MCA	MKS5080	1972	£4	
Roy Young Band	LP	RCA	SF8161	1971	£10	
Wild Country Wine	7"	MCA	MK5071	1971	£4	

YOUNG, STEVE

Title	Format	Label	Number	Year	Price	Notes
Rock Salt And Nails	LP	A&M	4177	1969	£20	US

YOUNG, VICKI

Title	Format	Label	Number	Year	Price	Notes
Bye Bye Just For A While	7"	Capitol	CL14528	1956	£4	
Hearts Of Stone	7"	Capitol	CL14228	1955	£8	
Live Fast Love Hard Die Young	7"	Capitol	CL14281	1955	£8	
Vicki Young	7" EP	Capitol	EAP1593	1956	£8	

YOUNG-HOLT TRIO

Title	Format	Label	Number	Year	Price	Notes
Wack Wack	7"	Coral	Q72489	1967	£4	

YOUNGBLOODS

Darkness Darkness	7"	RCA	RCA1821	1969	**£4**	
Darkness Darkness	7"	RCA	RCA1955	1970	**£4**	
Earth Music	LP	RCA	LSP3865	1967	**£10**	US
Elephant Mountain	LP	RCA	LSP4150	1969	**£10**	US
Get Together	7"	RCA	RCA1877	1969	**£4**	
Ride The Wind	LP	W. Bros	K46100	1971	**£10**	
Se Qualcuno Mi Dira	7"	RCA-Italiana		1970	**£10**	Italian
Sunlight	LP	RCA	SF8218	1971	**£10**	
Two Trips	LP	Mercury	SR61273	1970	**£10**	US
Youngbloods	LP	RCA	LSP3724	1967	**£10**	US

YOUNGFOLK

Lonely Girl	7"	President	PT136	1968	**£4**	

YOUTH

Meadow Of My Love	7"	Deram	DM226	1969	**£4**	

YOUTH BRIGADE

Youth Brigade EP	7"	Dischord	6	1981	**£40**	

YURO, TIMI

Amazing...	LP	Mercury	MG20963	1964	**£12**	US
Best Of...	LP	Liberty	LBY1290	1963	**£12**	
Hurt	LP	Liberty	LBY1247	1965	**£15**	
Hurt	7"	London	HLG9403	1961	**£4**	
In The Beginning	LP	Liberty	LBL83128	1968	**£10**	
Let Me Call You Sweetheart	LP	Liberty	LBY1275	1962	**£12**	
Make The World Go Away	LP	Liberty	LBY1192	1963	**£12**	
Make The World Go Away	7" EP	Liberty	LEP2252	1966	**£5**	
Something Bad On My Mind	LP	Liberty	LBL83198	1968	**£10**	
Soul	LP	Liberty	LBY1042	1962	**£15**	
Soul	7" EP	Liberty	LEP2214	1965	**£5**	
Timi Yuro	LP	Sunset	SUM1107	1966	**£10**	US
What's A Matter Baby?	LP	Liberty	LBY1254	1965	**£12**	
What's A Matter Baby?	7"	Liberty	LIB55469	1962	**£6**	

Z

Z, ROMEO

Title	Format	Label	Cat. No.	Year	Price	Notes
Come Back Baby Come Back	7"	CBS	202645	1967	**£4**	

ZACHERLEY, JOHN

Title	Format	Label	Cat. No.	Year	Price	Notes
Dinner With Drac	7"	London	HLU8599	1958	**£12**	
Monster Mash	LP	Parkway	P7018	1962	**£20**	US
Scary Tales	LP	Parkway	P7023	1963	**£20**	US
Spook Along With Zacherley	LP	Elektra	EKL7190	1960	**£20**	US
Zacherley's Monster Gallery	LP	Crestview	CR803	1963	**£20**	US

ZAGER & EVANS

Title	Format	Label	Cat. No.	Year	Price	Notes
2525	LP	RCA	LSP4214	1969	**£10**	
In The Year 2525	7"	RCA	RCA1860	1969	**£4**	chart single

ZAKARRIAS

Title	Format	Label	Cat. No.	Year	Price	Notes
Zakarrias	LP	Deram		1971	**£150**	

ZAPPA, FRANK

Critics have never known quite what to make of Frank Zappa. He is such a vastly talented musician and produces such a variety of material that they tend to focus on just one of the things that he does (usually his satire) and then criticise the rest of his output for failing to measure up in this one area. The fact that Zappa tends to hide his art behind a smokescreen of vulgarity does not help, of course, nor does the fact that he is quite self-deprecating about works that are actually little short of being masterpieces. In ages past, many composers were virtuoso instrumentalists who wrote music which would enable them to display their prowess in public performance. Frank Zappa continues this tradition, and because he is working in the rock age and in America, his instrument is the electric guitar and the music he plays is easily categorised as rock music. His best work, however, (and much of his output qualifies) transcends all the usual categories, emerging as a classical music for our time that is far more relevant, and probably far more durable, than most of what is actually produced under that name. The proof is as close as a copy of "Studio Tan", or "Uncle Meat", or "Ship Too Late To Save A Drowning Witch", or "The Perfect Stranger", or "The Grand Wazoo", or...

Title	Format	Label	Cat. No.	Year	Price	Notes
200 Motels	LP	United Artists	UDF50003	1971	**£20**	with booklet
Absolutely Free	LP	Verve	2317034	1971	**£25**	
Absolutely Free	LP	Verve	VLP9174	1967	**£30**	
Apostrophe	LP	Discreet	K59201	1973	**£15**	
Apostrophe	LP	Discreet	MS42175	1973	**£20**	US quad
Baby Take Your Teeth Out	7"	EMI	EMI5499	1984	**£4**	
Big Leg Emma	7"	Verve	VS557	1967	**£30**	
Bongo Fury	LP	Discreet	DS2234	1975	**£15**	US
Bongo Fury	LP	Discreet	K59209	1975	**£70**	test pressing only
Burnt Weeny Sandwich	LP	Reprise	K44083	1971	**£15**	
Burnt Weeny Sandwich	LP	Reprise	RSLP6370	1969	**£20**	chart LP
Burnt Weeny Sandwich/ Weasels Ripped My Flesh	LP	Reprise	K64024	1979	**£15**	double
Chunga's Revenge	LP	Reprise	K44020	1971	**£12**	
Chunga's Revenge	LP	Reprise	RSLP2030	1970	**£20**	green cover
Chunga's Revenge	LP	Reprise	RSLP2030	1970	**£15**	red cover, chart LP
Clean Cuts From Sheik Yerbouti	LP	Zappa	MK78	1980	**£20**	US promo
Clean Cuts From Tinseltown Rebellion	LP	Barking P.	AS995	1981	**£20**	US promo
Clean Cuts From You Are What You Is	LP	Barking P.	AS1294	1981	**£20**	US promo
Cosmic Debris	7"	Discreet	K19201	1973	**£10**	
Dancin' Fool	7"	CBS	7261	1979	**£4**	
Don't Eat The Yellow Snow	7"	Discreet	K19205	1973	**£10**	
Drafted	7"	CBS	8625	1980	**£5**	
Fillmore East 1971	LP	Reprise	K44150	1971	**£15**	
Frank Zappa & The Mothers Of Invention	LP	Verve	2352057	1975	**£20**	
Freak Out	LP	Verve	2683004	1971	**£30**	double
Freak Out	LP	Verve	V5005	1966	**£50**	US, with map insert
Freak Out	LP	Verve	VLP9154	1966	**£35**	
Grand Wazoo	LP	Reprise	K44209	1972	**£15**	
Hot Rats	LP	Reprise	K44078	1971	**£10**	
Hot Rats	LP	Reprise	RSLP6356	1969	**£15**	chart LP
Hot Rats	LP	Reprise	RSLP6356	1969	**£60**	with Zappa/Beefheart argument

Title	Format	Label	Cat. No.	Year	Price	Notes
It Can't Happen Here	7"	Verve	VS545	1966	**£40**	
Joe's Garage Act 1	LP	CBS	86101	1979	**£15**	with lyric sheet, chart LP
Joe's Garage Acts 2/3	LP	CBS	88475	1979	**£20**	double, lyric sheets, chart LP
Just Another Band From L.A.	LP	Reprise	K44179	1972	**£15**	
Lather	LP	Columbia	41500	1976	**£1000**	4 LPs, test pressings
Live In New York	LP	Discreet	K63204	1977	**£20**	double, chart LP
Live In New York	LP	Discreet	K63204	1977	**£60**	double, with 'Punky's Whips'
Lumpy Gravy	LP	Verve	2317046	1971	**£25**	
Lumpy Gravy	LP	Verve	VLP9223	1968	**£35**	
Man From Utopia	LP	CBS	25251	1983	**£10**	with lyric sheet, chart LP
Man From Utopia	7"	CBS	XPS180	1983	**£10**	promo only
Mothermania	LP	Verve	2317047	1971	**£20**	
Mothermania	LP	Verve	SVLP9239	1969	**£25**	
Mothers Of Invention	LP	MGM	GAS112	1970	**£20**	US
One Size Fits All	LP	Discreet	K59207	1974	**£15**	
Orchestral Favourites	LP	Discreet	K59212	1979	**£12**	
Overnight Sensation	LP	Discreet	K41000	1973	**£15**	
Overnight Sensation	LP	Discreet	MS42149	1973	**£20**	US quad
Roxy And Elsewhere	LP	Discreet	K69201	1974	**£20**	double
Ruben And The Jets	LP	Verve	2317069	1971	**£25**	
Ruben And The Jets	LP	Verve	SVLP9327	1968	**£30**	stereo
Ruben And The Jets	LP	Verve	V65055	1968	**£50**	US, with three inserts
Ruben And The Jets	LP	Verve	VLP9327	1968	**£35**	mono
Sheik Yerbouti	LP	CBS	88339	1979	**£15**	double, chart LP
Ship Arriving Too Late....Sampler	LP	Barking P.	AS1569	1982	**£15**	US promo
Shut Up And Play Your Guitar	LP	CBS	66368	1981	**£20**	triple
Shut Up And Play Your Guitar	7"	CBS	XPS147	1981	**£6**	
Sleep Dirt	LP	Discreet	K59211	1978	**£12**	
Studio Tan	LP	Discreet	K59210	1978	**£12**	
Tears Began To Fall	7"	Reprise	K14100	1971	**£20**	
Thingfish	LP	EMI	2402943	1985	**£20**	with libretto
Tinseltown Rebellion	LP	CBS	88516	1981	**£12**	double, chart LP
Uncle Meat	LP	Bizarre	MS2024	1969	**£15**	double
Uncle Meat	LP	Transatlantic	TRA197	1969	**£30**	double
Uncle Meat	LP	Transatlantic	TRA197	1969	**£40**	double, booklet
Valley Girl	7"	CBS	A2412	1982	**£4**	
Waka Jawaka	LP	Reprise	K44203	1972	**£15**	
We're Only In It For The Money	LP	Verve	2317035	1971	**£25**	
We're Only In It For The Money	LP	Verve	VLP9199	1967	**£30**	chart LP
We're Only In It For The Money	LP	Verve	VLP9199	1967	**£40**	with insert
Weasels Ripped My Flesh	LP	Reprise	K44019	1971	**£12**	
Weasels Ripped My Flesh	LP	Reprise	RSLP2028	1970	**£15**	chart LP
Welcome To Joe's Garage	LP	Zappa	MK129	1981	**£20**	US promo
What Will This Evening..	7"	United Artists	UP35319	1971	**£20**	
Worst Of The Mothers	LP	MGM	SE4754	1971	**£20**	US
XXXX Of The Mothers Of Invention	LP	Verve	V65074	1969	**£20**	US
You Are What You Is	12"	Barking P.	111622	1981	**£6**	pic disc
You Are What You Is	LP	CBS	88560	1982	**£12**	double, with lyric sheet, chart LP
You Are What You Is	7"	CBS	1622	1981	**£5**	
You Are What You Is	7"	CBS	A1622DJ	1981	**£10**	promo
Zapped	LP	W. Bros	PRO368	1969	**£25**	US, collage cover
Zapped	LP	W. Bros	PRO368	1969	**£15**	US, photo cover
Zoot Allures	LP	W. Bros	K56298	1976	**£15**	

ZARATHUSTRA

Title	Format	Label	Cat. No.	Year	Price	Notes
Zarathustra	LP	Metronome		1971	**£50**	

ZEITGEIST

Title	Format	Label	Cat. No.	Year	Price	Notes
Shake	7"	Enchaine	ENC1	1980	**£5**	

ZENITH SIX

Title	Format	Label	Cat. No.	Year	Price	Notes
At The Royal Festival Hall	7" EP	Decca	DFE6255	1956	**£4**	
Zenith Six	7" EP	Tempo	EXA42	195-	**£4**	
Zenith Six	7" EP	Tempo	EXA58	195-	**£4**	

ZEPHYR

Title	Format	Label	Cat. No.	Year	Price	Notes
Going Back To Colorado	LP	W. Bros	BS1897	1971	**£20**	US

Sunset Ride .... LP .... W. Bros .... BS2603 .... 1972 .... **£20** .... US
Zephyr .... LP .... Probe .... SPB1006 .... 1970 .... **£25** ....

ZEPHYRS

I Just Can't Take It .... 7" .... Columbia .... DB7571 .... 1965 .... **£10** ....
Little Bit Of Soap .... 7" .... Columbia .... DB7324 .... 1964 .... **£10** ....
She's Lost You .... 7" .... Columbia .... DB7481 .... 1965 .... **£8** .... chart single
Sweet Little Baby .... 7" .... Columbia .... DB7199 .... 1964 .... **£10** ....
What's All That About .... 7" .... Decca .... F11647 .... 1963 .... **£10** ....
Wonder What I'm Gonna Do .... 7" .... Columbia .... DB7410 .... 1964 .... **£8** ....

ZERO BOYS

Living In The 80's .... 7" .... Z Disc .... 6 .... 1981 .... **£70** ....
Vicious Circle .... LP .... Nimrod .... 1982 .... **£25** ....

ZERO FIVE

Dusty .... 7" .... Columbia .... DB7751 .... 1965 .... **£5** ....

ZEROS

Hungry .... 7" .... Small Wonder. SMALL2 .... 1977 .... **£4** ....
Something's Happening .... 7" .... Do It .... DUN5 .... 1978 .... **£4** ....
What's Wrong With A Pop Group .... 7" .... The Label .... ROK15/16 .... 197- .... **£4** ....

ZEVON, WARREN

I'll Sleep When I'm Dead .... 7" .... Asylum .... K13060 .... 1976 .... **£4** ....
Night Time In The Switching .... 7" .... Asylum .... K13124 .... 1978 .... **£4** ....
Wanted Dead Or Alive .... LP .... Imperial .... LP12456 .... 1969 .... **£15** .... US
Werewolves Of London .... 7" .... Asylum .... K13111 .... 1978 .... **£4** ....
Werewolves Of London .... 12" .... Asylum .... AS11386 .... 1978 .... **£10** .... US pic disc

ZIMMERMAN, TUCKER

Red Wind .... 7" .... Regal Z. .... RZ3020 .... 1969 .... **£4** ....

ZIMMERMANN, TUCKY

Ten Songs By... .... LP .... Regal Z. .... 1969 .... **£15** ....

ZIOR

Cat's Eyes .... 7" .... Nepentha .... 6129003 .... 1973 .... **£10** ....
Zior .... LP .... Nepentha .... 6437005 .... 1971 .... **£40** ....

ZIPPER

Zipper .... LP .... Whizeagle .... 1975 .... **£20** .... US

ZITRO

Zitro .... LP .... ESP .... 1967 .... **£20** .... US

ZOMBIES

With sixties rock music keenly seeking wider credibility within the arts generally, much used to be made of the Zombies' educational qualifications. In fact, the Zombies brand of pop-R&B was particularly distinctive, but this had rather more to do with Rod Argent's skilfull keyboard playing and Colin Blunstone's attractive, breathy singing than with any qualifications. "Odyssey and Oracle", recorded as the group was breaking up, is something of a pop masterpiece, inspired by the Beatles no doubt, but nevertheless retaining the Zombies stamp.

Begin Here .... LP .... Decca .... LK4679 .... 1965 .... **£60** ....
Bunny Lake Is Missing .... LP .... RCA .... LOC1115 .... 1965 .... **£30** .... US
Care Of Cell 44 .... 7" .... CBS .... 3087 .... 1967 .... **£8** ....
Friends Of Mine .... 7" .... CBS .... 2960 .... 1967 .... **£8** ....
Goin' Out Of My Head .... 7" .... Decca .... F12584 .... 1967 .... **£8** ....
Gotta Get A Hold Of Myself .... 7" .... Decca .... F12495 .... 1966 .... **£6** ....
I Love You .... 7" .... Decca .... F12798 .... 1968 .... **£6** ....
Indication .... 7" .... Decca .... F12426 .... 1966 .... **£8** ....
Is This The Dream .... 7" .... Decca .... F12296 .... 1965 .... **£5** ....
Leave Me Be .... 7" .... Decca .... F12004 .... 1964 .... **£5** ....
Odyssey And Oracle .... LP .... CBS .... 63280 .... 1968 .... **£30** ....
Remember You .... 7" .... Decca .... F12322 .... 1966 .... **£5** ....
She's Coming Home .... 7" .... Decca .... F12125 .... 1965 .... **£6** ....
She's Not There .... 7" .... Decca .... F11940 .... 1964 .... **£4** .... chart single
Tell Her No .... 7" .... Decca .... F12072 .... 1965 .... **£5** .... chart single
Time Of The Season .... 7" .... CBS .... 3380 .... 1968 .... **£8** ....
Time Of The Zombies .... LP .... Epic .... 65728 .... 1973 .... **£25** .... double
Whenever You're Ready .... 7" .... Decca .... F12225 .... 1965 .... **£5** ....
Zombies .... 7" EP .... Decca .... DFE8598 .... 1965 .... **£25** ....

ZONES

Stuck With You	7"	Zoom	ZUM4	1978	**£4**	

ZOO

I Shall Be Free	LP	Riviera	521147	1971	**£15**	
Zoo	LP	Barclay	521172	1971	**£12**	
Zoo	LP	Major Minor	SMLP74	1970	**£25**	

ZOO (2)

Zoo Presents The Chocolate Mouse	LP	Sunburst	7500	1968	**£15**	US

ZOOKIE

Bubbles	7"	DJM	DJS10866	1978	**£5**	
Judie Judie Hold On	7"	DJM	DJS10796	1977	**£5**	

ZYGOAT

Zygoat	LP	Polydor	2383270	1974	**£12**	

ZZ TOP

Arrested For Driving While Blind	7"	London	HLU10547	1977	**£12**	
Beer Drinkers And Hell Raisers	7"	London	HLU10458	1974	**£12**	
Eliminator	LP	W. Bros	W3774P	1985	**£10**	pic disc
Fandango	LP	London	SHU8482	1975	**£10**	chart LP
First Album	LP	London	PS584	1970	**£10**	US
Francene	7"	London	HLU10376	1972	**£12**	
Gimme All Your Lovin'	7"	W. Bros	W9693P	1983	**£15**	shaped pic disc
It's Only Love	7"	London	HLU10538	1976	**£10**	
La Grange	7"	London	HLU10475	1975	**£12**	
Rio Grande Mud	LP	London	SHU8433	1972	**£10**	
Rough Boy	7"	W. Bros	W2003FP	1986	**£4**	interlocking shaped pic disc
Sleeping Bag	7"	W. Bros	W2001P	1985	**£5**	interlocking shaped pic disc
Sleeping Bag	7"	W. Bros	W2001P	1985	**£10**	shaped pic disc
Stages	7"	W. Bros	W2002BP	1986	**£4**	interlocking shaped pic disc
Tejas	LP	London	LDU1	1976	**£12**	
Tres Hombres	LP	London	SHU8459	1973	**£10**	
Tush	7"	London	HLU10495	1975	**£10**	

ZZEBRA

Panic	LP	Polydor	2383326	1975	**£12**	
Zzebra	LP	Polydor	2383296	1974	**£10**	

MUSIC MASTER DISTRIBUTORS WORLDWIDE

RECORD TRADE DISTRIBUTION

Record trade orders for Music Master should be sent to the following companies:-

Canada:
RECORD PEDDLER, 12 Brant Street, Toronto, Canada. M5 2MI. Telephone: 416 364 5507.

France:
WOTRE MUSIC DISTRIBUTION, Les Carreaux, Route de Niort, 79410 St. Gelais, France. Telephone: 49 33 45 64. Fax: 49 24 97 47.

Germany:
BELLA MUSICA TONTRAEGER GmbH, Rheinstrasse 26, 7580 Buhl, Germany. Telephone: 7223 27009. Fax: 7223 30109.

Greece:
MUSI COMPACT, Shopping Centre 'Phinikas', 293 Kifissias Avenue, Athens, Greece. Telephone: 01 8015 794. Fax: 01 8016 425.

Holland:
HOME ENTERTAINMENT SERVICES, BV, Klokhoek 1, 3833 GW, Leusden, Netherlands. Telephone: 33 948300. Fax: 33 948709.

Indonesia:
INDY PARAMADELLE, Prince Centre II, 3rd Floor, Room 306, J1 Jenderal Sudirman 3-4, Jakarta, Indonesia. Telephone: 583901. Fax: 5704544.

Italy:
SOUND & VISION, P.O. Box 3196 00121, Ostia, Rome, Italy. Telephone: 06 561 11088.

Japan:
UNITED PUBLISHERS SERVICES LTD, Kenkyu-sha Building, 9 Kanda Surugadi 2-chrome, Chiyodaku, Tokyo, Japan. Telephone: 03 292 7160/03 291 4541. Fax: 03 292 8610.

Norway:
AKERS MIC 2A/S, Kongensgi 25, N-0153, Oslok Norway. Telephone: 472 33 0330.

Singapore:
AUDIO MUSICAL PTE LTD, 162 Rangoon Road, Singapore 0821. Telephone: 292 9896. Fax: 291 6009.

South Africa:
MUSICA CAPE, Techno Square 42, Morningside, Ndabeni, Capetown. Telephone: 21 531 1150.
MUSIC TEAM, 33 Scott Street, Waverly, Johannesburg, South Africa. Telephone: 11 887 7317. Fax: 11 887 7357.

Spain and Portugal:
DISCOBI, Luchana 1-4 Dpt 2, 48008 Bilbao, Spain. Telephone: 416 42 31. Fax: 443 00 24.
DISCOBI, Rafael Harrera 11, 28036, Madrid. 341-314-2114.

Sweden:
BLITZ RECORDS AB, PO Box 347, S-10124, Stockholm 1, Sweden. Telephone: 8 28 28 90. Fax: 8 29 01 22.

United Kingdom:
ARABESQUE RECORDS LTD, Network House, 29-39 Stirling Road, London, W3 8DJ. Telephone: UK Sales: 081 992 7732. International Sales: 081 992 0098. Fax: 081 992 0340.
CAROLINE EXPORTS, 56 Standard Road, London. NW10 6ES. Telephone: 081 961 2919.
MUSIC MASTER, Music House, 1 De Cham Avenue, Hastings, East Sussex, TN37 6HE. Telephone: 0424 715181. Fax: 0424 422805.
LASGO LTD, Unit 2, Chapmans Park Industrial Estate, 378-388 High Road, Willesden, London, NW10 2DY. Telephone: 081 459 8800.
WINDSONG INTERNATIONAL LTD, Election House, Cray Avenue, St. Mary Cray, Orpington, Kent, BR5 3RJ. Telephone: 0689 890392.

United States of America:
MUSIC/NH, WAYNE GREEN ENTERPRISES, Hancock, New Hampshire, 003449, USA. Telephone: 603 525 4201.

BOOK TRADE DISTRIBUTION

Book trade orders for Music Master should be sent to the following companies:-

All countries (except United States of America):
HARRAP PUBLISHING GROUP LTD, Chelsea House, 26 Market Square, Bromley, Kent. BR1 1NA. Telephone: 081 313 3484. Fax: 081 313 0702.

United States of America:
LAST GASP OF SAN FRANCISCO, 2180 Bryant Street, San Francisco, California, CA 94110, USA. Telephone: 415 824 6636. Fax: 415 824 1836.

LIST OF PLATES

The details below are of all the illustrations featured in the various sections within this book. The plate number refers to the plate number on the page in question. Most pages feature 12 different illustrations, the lists start from left to right, with the first row, second row and so on. For example, the left-hand illustration on plate 1 is Rhythm & Blues Showcase Vol 1, a Various Artists' recording. The middle illustration on row one is Singing the Blues E.P., another Various Artists' récording, and so on.

Plate 1

ARTIST	TITLE
Various Artists	Rhythm & Blues Showcase Vol. 1
Various Artists	Singing The Blues E.P.
Liitle Richard	And His Band E.P.
Brown, Ruth	Queen Of R & B
Berry, RIchard	Rhythm & Blues Vol. 3
Allen, Lee	Walkin With Mr. Lee
Jordan, Louis	Let The Good Times Roll
Coasters	Greatest Hits
Hawkins, Screamin' Jay	I Put A Spell On You
Little Richard	Here's Little Richard
Charles, Ray	Ray Charles In Person
Price, Lloyd	The Exciting Lloyd Price

Plate 2

ARTIST	TITLE
Nelson, Ricky	Ricky No.1
Haley, Bill	Rock And Roll E.P. (London)
Haley, Bill	Rock And Roll E.P. (Brunswick)
Cochran, Eddie	C'mon Everybody E.P.
Vincent, Gene	Race With The Devil E.P.
Vincent, Gene	Hot Rod Gang
Diddley, Bo	Hey Bo Diddley
Lewis, Jerry Lee	Jerry Lee Lewis No.6
Diddley, Bo	Rhythm & Blues With Bo Diddley
Lee, Brenda	Love You Till I Die
Berry, Chuck	R & B With Chuck Berry
Lewis, Jerry Lee	Jerry Lee Lewis No. 2 EP

Plate 3

ARTIST	TITLE
Everly Brothers	Rock 'N' Soul Vol. 2
Hawkins, Ronnie	Rockin' With Ronnie
Knox, Buddy	Rock-A-Buddy Knox
Champs	Everybody's Rockin' With The....
Haley, Bill	Rock 'N' Roll Stage Show
Valens, Ritchie	I Remember Ritchie Valens
Berry, Chuck	Chuck Berry Juke Box Hits
Berry, Chuck	On Stage
Vincent, Gene	Gene Vincent & The Blue Caps
Cochran, Eddie	Singin' To My Baby
Holly, Buddy	Buddy Holly
Vincent, Gene	A Gene Vincent Record Date

Plate 4

ARTIST	TITLE
Newley, Anthony	Idle On Parade
Steele, Tommy	Young Love
Fury, Billy	Sound Of Fury
Donegan, Lonnie	Lonnie Donegan Showcase
Weedon, Bert	King Size Guitar
Steele, Tommy	Get Happy With Tommy
Richard, Cliff	Summer Holiday
Marvin, Welch & Farrar	Second Opinion
Richard, Cliff	Good News
Richard, Cliff	Cliff
Richard, Cliff	Listen To Cliff
The Shadows	Shadows

Plate 5

Presley, Elvis	Good Rockin' Tonight
Presley, Elvis	Love Me Tender
Presley, Elvis	Best Of Elvis
Presley, Elvis	Rock 'N' Roll
Presley, Elvis	Rock 'N' Roll No. .2
Presley, Elvis	Loving You
Vincent, Gene	Bird Doggin'
Witherspoon, Jimmy	There's Good Rocking Tonight
Presley, Elvis	Flaming Star & Summer Kisses
Lewis, Jerry Lee	Greatest Live Show On Earth
Moore, Scotty	The Guitar That Changed The World
Ochs, Phil	Phil Ochs Greatest Hits

Plate 6

Little Richard	The Explosive Little Richard
Foxx, Inez & Charlie	Mocking Bird
Domino, Fats	Million Sellers By Fats Domino
James, Etta	The Soul Of Etta James
Chandler, Gene	Duke Of Earl
Baker, Lavern	See See Rider
Supremes	Meet The Supremes
Various Artists	Sound Of The R & B Hits
Martha & The Vandellas	Heatwave
Various Artists	On Stage
Van Dyke, Earl	That Motown Sound
Various Artists	R & B Chartmakers

Plate 7

Contours	Do You Love Me
Miracles	Hi We're The Miracles
Campbell, Choker	Hits Of The Sixties
Wells, Mary	Two Lovers & Other Great Hits
Clark, Chris	Soul Sounds
Monitors	Greetings! We're The Monitors
Various Artists	Shades Of Gospel Soul
Holloway, Brenda	Every Little Bit Hurts
Clark, Chris	C. C. Rides Again
Twisting Kings	Twistin' The World Around
McNair, Barbara	Here I Am
Holland, Eddie	Eddie Holland

Plate 8

Gaye, Marvin	In The Groove
Detroit Spinners	The Detroit Spinners
Elgins	Darling Baby
Gaye, Marvin & Kim Weston	Take 2
Knight, Gladys & The Pips	Feelin' Bluesy
Martha & The Vandellas	Watchout!
Gaye, Marvin	A Tribute To Nat King Cole
Wells, Mary	Mary Wells Greatest Hits
Supremes	I Hear A Symphony
Isley Brothers	This Old Heart Of Mine
Walker, Junior & The All Stars	Shotgun
Temptations	The Temptations Sing Smokey

Plate 9

Supremes	A Go-Go
Gaye, Marvin	Moods Of Marvin Gaye
Four Tops	Four Tops On Top
Ruffin, Jimmy	The Jimmy Ruffin Way
Walker, Junior & The All Stars	Roadrunner
Supremes	Supremes Sing Motown
Reeves, Martha & The Vandellas	Dancing In The Street
Terrell, Tammi	Irresistible Tammi Terrell

Johnson, Marv	I'll Pick A Rose For My Rose
Starr, Edwin	Soul Master
Marvelettes	The Marvelettes In Full Bloom
Eckstine, Billy	Gentle On My Mind

Plate 10

Pickett, Wilson	In The Midnight Hour
Franklin, Aretha	Lady Soul
Sam & Dave	Hold On, I'm Comin'
King, Ben E.	What Is Soul?
Redding, Otis	The Soul Album
Redding, Otis & Carla Thomas	King & Queen
Last Poets	This Is Madness
Davis, Miles	Black Beauty
Brown, James	I Got You (I Feel Good)
Peebles, Ann	I Can't Stand The Rain
Pickett, Wilson	The Wicked Pickett
Sly & The Family Stone	There's A Riot Going On

Plate 11

Milligan, Spike	Milligan Preserved
Markham, Pigmeat	Here Come The Judge
Goons	Best Of The Goon Shows
Sellers, Peter	Songs For Swingin' Sellers
Goons	Unchained Melodies
Flanders & Swann	At The Drop Of Another Hat
Shannon, Del	Handy Man
Orbison, Roy	Roy Orbison Sings Lonely & Blue
Cascades	Rhythm Of The Rain
Brown, Joe	A Picture Of You
Dee, Joey & His Starliters	Doin' The Twist
Dean, Jimmy	Big Bad John

Plate 12

Merseybeats	On Stage
Big Three	At The Cavern E.P.
Searchers	Meet The Searchers
Gerry & The Pacemakers	How Do You Like It
Various Artists	This Is Mersey Beat Vol. 2
Billy J. Kramer & The Dakotas	Listen
Poole, Brian & The Tremeloes	Twist And Shout
Poole, Brian & The Tremeloes	It's About TIme
Clake, Dave Five	Catch Us If You Can
Clake, Dave Five	Weekend In London
Clake, Dave Five	Session With The Dave Clark Five
Clake, Dave Five	Try Too Hard

Plate 13

Korner's, Alexis Blue's Incorporated	R & B From The Marquee
Money, Zoot	Zoot Money's Big Roll Band
Fame, Georgie	Sweet Things
Mayall. John	John Mayall Plays John Mayall
Bond, Graham	Solid Bond
Washington, Geno	Hand Clappin', Foot Stompin', ...LIVE
Yardbirds	Yardbirds
Kinks	Kinda Kinks
Animals	The Animals
Downliners Sect	Country Sect
Rolling Stones	Rolling Stones
Them	Angry Young Them

Plate 14

Rolling Stones	Get Off My Cloud
Yardbirds	Five Yardbirds E.P.
Four Pennies	Four Pennies E.P.
Bennett, Cliff & The Rebel Rousers	Bennett, Cliff & The Rebel Rousers
Fontana, Wayne & The Mindbenders	Um Um Um Um Um Um

Who	Ready Steady Who
Fame, Georgie	Rhythm & Blues
Fame, Georgie	Rhythm & Bluebeat
Searchers	Sweets For My Sweet
Mayall, John	John Mayall...With Paul Butterfield E.P
Fleetwood Mac	The Green Manalishi (Single)
Kinks	Kwyet Kinks

Plate 15

Arnold, P.P.	Kafunta
Troggs	Trogglomania
Animals	The Most Of The Animals
Faithfull, Marianne	Come My Way
Merseybeats	Merseybeats (Wing)
Gerry & The Pacemakers	Ferry Cross The Mersey
Zombies	Begin Here
Honeycombs	The Honeycombs
Troggs	Trogglodynamite
Dave Dee, Dozy, Beaky, Mick & Tich	Dave Dee, Dozy, Beaky, Mick & Tich
Mindbenders	Mindbenders
Freddie & The Dreamers	Freddie & The Dreamers

Plate 16

Rolling Stones	Aftermath
Kinks	Face To Face
Creation	'66-'67
Who	A Quick One
Small Faces	Small Faces
Move	Shazam
Ryan, Paul & Barry	Two Of A Kind
Proby, P.J.	P.J. Proby
Walker, Scott	Scott 3
Walker, Scott	Scott 2
Whitcomb, Ian	Mad Mad Music Hall
Murphy, Mark	Who Can I Turn To

Plate 17

Beatles	Yeaterday And Today
Beatles	6th Christmas Record
Beatles	4th Christmas Record
Beatles	Another Beatles Xmas Record
Beatles	Tony Sheridan With The Beatles
Beatles	Off The Beatle Track
Beatles	Beatles Box
Beatles	Long Tall Sally
Beatles	Twist & Shout E.P.
Beatles	All My Loving
Beatles	Magical Mystery Tour
Beatles	Strawberry Fields (Acetate)

Plate 18

McCartney, Paul	CHOBA B CCCP
Harrison, George & Others	The Concert For Bangladesh
Starr, Ringo Etc.	Scouse The Mouse
Ono, Yoko	Feeling The Space
Harrison, George	Wonderwall
Lennon, John & Yoko Ono	Life With The Lions
Various Artists	Walls Ice Cream Presents
Radha Krishna Temple	Hare Krishna Mantra
Badfinger	Straight Up
Ono, Yoko	Approximately Infinite Universe
Spector, Phil	Christmas LP
Elliot, Bill & The Elastic Oz Band	God Save Us

Plate 19

Beatles	Sgt. Pepper Pic Disc
Hollies	Evolution

Bee Gees	1st
Idle Race	Birthday Party
Donovan	Sunshine Superman
Rolling Stones	Their Satanic Majesties Request
Pink Floyd	A Saucerful Of Secrets
Family	Music In A Doll's House
Traffic	Mr. Fantasy
Incredible String Band	5000 Spirits Or The Layers Of The....
Brown, Arthur	The Crazy World Of Arthur Brown
Donovan	A Gift From A Flower To A Garden

Plate 20

Burdon, Eric & The Animals	Winds Of Change
Morrison, Van	Astral Weeks
Manfred Mann	Chapter Three
Animals	Animalization
Them, with Van Morrison	Them Again
Manfred Mann	Five Faces Of Manfred Mann
Davis, Spencer Group	Autumn '66
Hollies	Stay With The Hollies
Pretty Things	The Pretty Things
Davis, Spencer Group	With Their New Face On
Hollies	Butterflies
Pretty Things	S. F. Sorrow

Plate 21

Dylan, Bob	Bob Dylan
Farina, Richard & Mimi	Memories
Seeger, Pete	We Shall Overcome
Baez, Joan	Farewell Angelina
Ochs, Phil	I Ain't Marching Anymore
Dylan, Bob	Mr. Tambourine Man
Collins, Judy	In My Life
Ian & Sylvia	Best Of...
Simon, Paul	The Paul Simon Song Book
Kingston Trio	Close Up
Paxton, Tom	Outward Bound
Lind, Bob	Don't Be Concerned

Plate 22

Eddy, Duane	Because They're Young
Epps, Preston & Sandy Nelson	Rushin' For Percussion E. P.
Wilson, Murry	The Many Moods Of Murry Wilson
Beach Boys	Pet Sounds
Ventures	The Horse
Beach Boys	Surfin' USA
Ronettes	The Ronettes
Byrds	Mr. Tambourine Man
Shangri-Las	Leader Of The Pack
Buffalo Springfield	Last Time Around
Cooper, Alice	Pretties For You
Fugs	Virgin Fugs

Plate 23

Turtles	Happy Together
Revere, Paul & The Raiders	Hard N' Heavy
Lovin' Spoonful	Daydream
Monkees	Monkees
Lewis, Gary & The Playboys	Hits Again
Jan & Dean	Jan & Dean Meet Batman
Harpers Bizarre	The Secret Life Of Harpers Bizarre
Left Banke	Walk Away Renee / Pretty Ballerina
Beau Brummel's	Triangle
Mama's & The Papa's	If You Can Believe Your Eyes & Ears
Association	Birthday
Peanut Butter Conspiracy	The Great Conspiracy

Plate 24

Old And In The Way	Old And In The Way
Kaukonem, Jorma	Quah
Hunter, Robert	Tales Of The Great Rum Runners
Grateful Dead	Anthem Of The Son
Jefferson Airplane	After Bathing At Baxters
Jefferson Airplane	Takes Off
Quicksilver Messenger Service	Quicksilver Messenger Service
Country Joe & The Fish	Vanguard
Spirit	Spirit
Love	Love
Love	Four Sail
Doors	The Doors

Plate 25

Miller, Steve Band	Children Of The Future
Steppenwolf	Early Steppenwolf
Insect Trust	Insect Trust
It's A Beautiful Day	It's A Beautiful Day
Spence, Alexander	Oar
Fever Tree	Fever Tree
Ultimate Spinach	Behold And See
West Coast Pop Art Experimental Band	A Child's Guide To Good And Evil
H.P. Lovecraft	H.P. Lovecraft 2
13th Floor Elevators	13th Floor Elevators Live
Fifty Foot Hose......	Cauldron
Beacon Street Union	The Clown Died In Marvin Gardens

Plate 26

Amboy Dukes	Migration
Seeds	Future
Standells	Why Pick On Me
Various Artists	Nuggets
Knickerbockers	Lies
Blues Magoos	Blues Magoos
Nova, Ars	Sunshine & Shadows
Clear Light	Clear Light
Skin Alley	Skin Alley
Autosalvage	Autosalvage
New York Rock'n'Roll Ensemble	Reflections
Sons Of Champlin	Loosen Up Naturally

Plate 27

Endle St. Cloud	Thank You All Very Much
Hapshash & The Coloured Coat	Human Host & Heavy Metal Kids
Electric Prunes	I Had Too Much To Dream
Magic Carpet	Magic Carpet
Dr.John	Gris Gris
Tangerine Dream	Kaleidoscope
Mandrake Material	Mandrake Material
Saint Steven	Saint Steven
Quill	Quill
Tea Company	Come And Have Some Tea With....
Serpent Power	Serpent Power
Last Ritual	Last Ritual

Plate 28

Buckingham Nicks	Buckingham Nicks
Flaming Youth	Ark II
Great Society	Conspicious In Its Absence
Giles, Giles & Fripp	The Cheerful Insanity Of Giles, Giles...
Gods	Genesis
Graduate	Acting My Age
Barock And Roll Ensemble	Eine Kleine Beatlemusic E.P.
Dr. Marigold's Prescription	Pictures Of Life

Pepper, Billy & The Pepperpots	Beat!! More Merseymania
Brunning Sunflower Blues Band	Bullen St. Blues
First Impression/Good Earth	Swinging London
Funky Junction	Play A tribute To Deep Purple

Plate 29

Williamson, Sonny Boy	Down And Out Blues
Shakey Jake & The All Stars	Further On Up The Road
Various Artists	R & B All Stars
Fuller, Jesse	San Francisco Bay Blues
Leadbelly	Leadbelly 2
Sunnyland Slim	Slim's Got His Thing Goin' On
Notes, Freddie & The Rudies	Unity
Dekkar, Desmond	This Is Desmond Dekkar
Upsetters	Return & Django
Perry, Lee	Scratch The Upsetter Again
Count Ossie	Grounation
Various Artists	A Gift From Pama

Plate 30

Scott, Jack	I Remember Hank Williams
Elliott, Ramblin' Jack	Ramblin' Jack Elliott In London
Williams, Hank	Luke The Drifter
Williams, Hank	Moanin' The Blues
Cash, Johnny	Original Sun Sound Of Johnny Cash
Robbins, Marty	Marty's Big Hits
Area Code 615	Trip In The Country
Byrds	Sweet Heart Of The Rodeo
Flying Burrito Brothers	Gilded Place Of Sin
Nitty Gritty Dirt Band	Symphonian Dream
International Submarine Band	Safe At Home
Parsons, Gene	Kindling

Plate 31

Smokestack Lightnin'	Off The Wall
Westbound 9	Flaming Ember
Rascals	See
Rascals	The Young Rascals
Delaney & Bonnie & Friends	On Tour
Ryder, Mitch & The Detroit Wheels	Take A Ride
Hotlegs	Thinks School Stinks
Sweet	Fanny Adams
Move	Move
Royal Guardsmen	Snoopy Vs The Red Baron
Rutles	Rutles
Sonny & Cher	The Best Of Sonny & Cher

Plate 32

Dunbar, Aynsley	Dr. Dunbar's Prescription
Ckicken Shack	OK Ken
Groundhogs	Blues Obituary
Savoy Brown Blues Band	Shake Down
Brunning Sunflower Blues Band	Trackside Blues
Fleetwood Mac	Mr. Wonderful
Vick, Shakey	Little Woman Your So Sweet
Dummer, John	John Dummers Famous Music Band
Love Sculpture	Blues Helping
Fernbach, Andy	If You Miss Your Conexion
Bennett, Duster	Smiling Like I'm Happy
Dharma Blues	Dharma Blues

Plate 33

Colosseum	Those Who Are About To Die Salute...
Cream	Disraeli Gears
Fleetwood Mac	Fleetwood Mac
Hartley, Keef	Little Big Band
Mark-Almond	Mark-Almond

Dunbar, Aynsley	Retaliation
Dada	Dada
Jackson, J.J.	Greatest Little Soul Band In The Land
Chicago	IV At Carnegie Hall
Colosseum	Daughter Of Time
Mayall's, John Bluesbreakers	Barewires
Airforce	Airforce 2

Plate 34

Beck, Jeff	Truth
Cream	On Top
Hendrix, Jimi	Band Of Gypsies
Bloomfield, Mike, Al Kooper & Steve Stills	Super Session
Led Zeppelin	Led Zeppelin
Fleetwood Mac	Then Play On
Hendrix, Jimi	Axis Bold As Love
Miles, Buddy	Expressway To Your Skull
Cox, Billy	Nitro Function
Ramatam	Ramatam
Fat Mattress	Fat Mattress
Hendrix, Jimi	Are You Experienced

Plate 35

Bevis Frond	Miasma
Blue Phantom	Distortions
High Tide	High Tide
T.I.M.E.	Smooth Ball
Zior	Zior
Hawkwind	Hawkwind
Canned Heat	Boogie With Canned Heat
Mandel, Harvey	Feel The Sound Of Harvey Mandel
Gun	Gun
Clark-Hutchinson	A=MH\2
Ten Years After	Undead
Love Sculpture	Forms And Feelings

Plate 36

Faithfull, Marianne	Marianne Faithfull
Cilla Black	Cilla
Francis, Connie	The Exciting Connie Francis
Springfield, Dusty	Ev'rythings Coming Up Dusty
Lee, Brenda	All The Way
Shapiro, Helen	Tops With Me
Melanie	Four Sides Of Melanie
Velez, Martha	Fiends And Angels
Peacock, Annette	I'm The One
Driscoll, Julie	Open
Nyro, Laura	Eli And The Thirteenth Confession
Cher	With Love

Plate 37

Carthy, Martin	Byker Hill
Graham, Davy	Folk, Blues & Beyond
Renbourn, John	Another Monday
Pentangle	Pentangle
Jansch, Bert	It Don't Bother Me
Briggs, Anne	The Time Has Come
Bellamy, Peter	Oak, Ash And Thorn
Young Tradition	Galleries
Woods, Gay & Terry	Backwoods
Watersons	Watersons
Collins, Shirley & Dolly	Anthems In Eden
MacColl, Ewan, Peggy Seeger & Charles Parker	Big Hewer

Plate 38

Various Artists	Electric Muse

Hart, Tim & Maddy Prior	Folk Songs Of Old England
Denny, Sandy & The Strawbs	All Our Own Work
Fairport Convention	Fairport Convention
Eclection	Eclection
Sandy & Johnny	Sandy & Johnny
Fotheringay	Fotheringay
Collins, Shirley & The Albion Country Band	No Roses
Fairport Convention	Live At The L.A. Troubadour
Matthews, Ian	Matthews Southern Comfort
Thompson, Richard	Strict Tempo
Denny, Sandy	Like An Old Fashioned Waltz

Plate 39

Famous Jugband	Chameleon
Tir Na Nog	Tir Na Nog
Strawbs	Strawbs
Incredible String Band	Incredible String Band
C.O.B.	Spirit Of Love
Accolade	Accolade
Andrews, Harvey	Writer Of Songs
Christmas, Keith	Pigmy
Cousins, Dave	Two Weeks Last Summer
Martyn, John	The Tumbler
Chapman, Michael	Rainmaker
Blatting, Bob	You've Got To Go Down This Way

Plate 40

Pisces	Pisces
Dulcimer	Dulcimer
Bread, Love & Dreams	Bread, Love & Dreams
Forest	Forest
Trees	The Garden Of Jane Delawney
Spirogyra	St. Radiguards
Johnson, Bob & Pete Knight	The King Of Elfland's Daughter
Plainsong	In Search Of Amelia Earhart
C.O.B	Moyshe McStiff & The...........
J.S.D. Band	Country Of The Blind
Sallyangie	Children Of The Sun (2nd Issue)
Village Thing	The Sun Also Rises

Plate 41

Brett, Paul	Phoenix Future
Evans, Dave	Elephantasia
Brierley, Marc	Hello
Cartwright, Dave	Back To The Garden
Pegg, Bob & Nick Strutt	The Ship Builder
Ellington, Marc	Marc Ellington
Gryphon	Midnight Mushrumps
Gryphon	Gryphon
Harvey, Richard	Divisions On A Ground
Evensong	The Amazing Blondel
Pert, Morris	Luminos/Chromosp're/4 Jap'se Verses
Pert, Morris	B'k Of Love/Fragmenti I/Ult'me Decay

Plate 42

Hardin, Tim	Tim Hardin 1
Fahey, John	Transfiguration of Blind Joe Death
Holy Modal Rounders	Holy Modal Rounders
Buckley, Tim	Goodbye & Hello
Koerner, Spider John & Willie Murphy	Running Jumping Standing Still
Cleanliness & Godliness Skiffle Band	Greatest Hits
Cockburn, Bruce	Sunwheel Dance
White, Tony Joe	Continued
Buckley, Tim	Lorca
Henske, Judy & Jerry Yester	Farewell Aldebaran
Darrow, Chris	Under My Own Disguise
Keith	Ain't Gonna Lie

Plate 43

Strickland, William R.	Is Only The Name
Geesin, Ron	A Raise Of Eyebrows
Geesin, Ron	As He Stands
Dr.Wests Medicine Show And Junk Band	The Eggplant That Ate Chicago
Sutch, Screaming Lord	Lord Sutch & Heavy Friends
Sutch, Screaming Lord	Hands Of Jack The Ripper
Cutler, Ivor	Who Tore Your Trousers?
Tiny Tim	God Bless Tiny Tim
Fischer, Wild Man	An Evening With Wild Man Fischer
Bonzo Dog Doo Dah Band & Others	Alberts, Bonzo Dog Band & Temp. 7
Stanshall, Vivian	Sir Henry At Rawlinson End
Flo & Eddie	Phlorescent Leech And Eddie

Plate 44

Grand Funk Railroad	Good Singin' Good Playin'
Cooper, Alice	Love It To Death
Zappa, Frank	The Grand Wazoo
Zappa, Frank	Mothermania
Zappa, Frank	Lumpy Gravy
Zappa, Frank	We're Only In It For The Money
Reed, Lou	Metal Machine Music
Tucker, Maureen	Playin' Possum
Cale, John & Terry Riley	Church Of Anthrax
Captain Beefheart	Strictly Personal
Suicide	Suicide
United States Of America	United States Of America

Plate 45

Peel, John	Archive Things
Various Artists	Package Tour
Various Artists	Blues Anytime Vol. 1
Raven, Mike	The Mike Raven Blues Show
Various Artists	Rhythm & Blues
Various Artists	Thank Your Lucky Stars
Various Artists	Glastonbury Fayre
Various Artists	Hope And Anchor Front Row Festival
Various Artists	The Sue Story Vol. 3
Various Artists	Groovy Baby
Various Artists	Greasy Truckers Live At Dingwall's....
Various Artists	Greasy Truckers Party

Plate 46

Manfred Mann	Manfred Mann Go Up The Junction
Davis, Spencer Group & Traffic	Here We Go Round The Mulberry....
Various Artists	Just For Fun
Electric Flag	The Trip
Jagger, Mick & Others	Ned Kelly
Yardbirds & Herbie Hancock	Blow Up
Coxhill, Lol	Murder In The Air
Grimms	Grimms
Bonzo Dog Doo Dah Band	The Doughnut In Granny's Gr'nhouse
Barrow Poets	Outpatients
Principle Edward's Magic Theatre	Soundtrack
Liverpool Scene	Amazing Adventures Of...

Plate 47

Mahal, Taj	The Natchil Blues
Steamhammer	Mark II
Black Widow	Black Widow
Gantry, Elmer	Elmer Gantry's Velvet Opera
Electric Flag	A Long Time Comin'
Flock	Dinosaur Swamps
Gods	To Samuel A Son
Savoy Brown	Blue Matter

Blossom Toes	If Only For A Moment
Blossom Toes	We Are Ever So Clean
Galliard	Strange Pleasure
Morgan, John	Spirit Of John Morgan

Plate 48

St. John, Bridget	Ask Me No Questions
Coxhill, Lol	Ear Of Beholder
Beau	Beau
Medicine Head	Heavy On The Drum
Hart, Mike	Mike Hart Bleeds
Ward, Clifford T.	Singer Songwriter
Cooper, Mike	Machine Gun Co.
Fruupp	Future Legends
McAuley, Jackie	Jackie McAuley
Noir	We Had To Let You Have It
Jonesy	Keeping Up
McLaughlin, John & Others	Where Fortune Smiles

Plate 49

Bunch	Rock On
Patto	Roll 'Em, Smoke 'Em Put Another....
Heads, Hands & Feet	Tracks
Kossoff, Kirke, Tetsu & Rabbit	Kossoff, Kirke, Tetsu & Rabbit
Bronco	Country Home
Blodwyn Pig	Head Rings Out
Mott The Hoople	Mott The Hoople
Quintessence	Quintessence
Drake, Nick	Bryter Layter
Dr. Strangely Strange	Kip Of The Serenes
Free	Tons Of Sobs
Spooky Tooth	Spooky Two

Plate 50

Gentle Giant	Three Friends
Warhorse	Warhorse
Still Life	Still Life
Legend	Moonshine
Jackson Heights	The Fifth Avenue Bus
Warrior, Jade	Last Autumn's Dream
Ramases	Space Hymns
Tudor Lodge	Tudor Lodge
Downes, Bob	Open Music
Matthews, Ian	If You Saw Thro' My Eyes
Gracious	Gracious
Gentle Giant	Acquiring The Taste

Plate 51

Affinity	Affinity
Assagai	Assagai
Jade Warrior	Jade Warrior
Juicy Lucy	Juicy Lucy
Nirvana	Local Anaesthetic
Nucleus	Solar Plexus
Pink Floyd	A Nice Pair
Collins, Shirley & Dolly	Love, Death & The Lady
Greatest Show On Earth	Going's Easy
Brown, Pete	A Meal You Can Shake Hands With....
Harper, Roy	Valentine
Broughton, Edgar Band	Wasa Wasa

Plate 52

Gibbs, Michael	Tanglewood 63
Ardley, Neil, Ian Carr, Don Rendell	Greek Variations
Centipede	Septober Energy
McGregor, Chris	Brotherhood Of Breath
Westbrook, Mike	Marching Song Vol. 1

Westbrook, Mike	Celebration
Garrick, Michael Sextet	The Heart Is On Lotus
Beck, Gordon Trio	Gyroscope
Collier, Graham Septet	Deep Dark Blue Centre
McGregor, Chris	Very Urgent
Lowther, Henry Band	Child Song
Russell, Roy	Turn Circle

Plate 53

Spontaneous Music Ensemble	Karyobin
Harriott, Joe Quintet	Abstract
Amalgam	Prayer For Peace
Ovary Lodge	Overy Lodge
Oxley, Tony	Ichnos
Surman, John	Conflagration
Tippett, Keith	Dedicated To You But You Weren't....
Winstone, Norma	Edge Of Time
Gibbs, Michael	Michael Gibbs
Westbrook, Mike	Love Songs
Ardley, Neil	Symphony Of Amaranths
Carr, Ian	Belladonna

Plate 54

Harriott, Joe & Amancio D'Silva Quartet	Hum Dono
Dean, Elton	Elton Dean
Surman, John	John Surman
Coxhill, Lol	Toverbal Sweet
Skidmore, Alan Quintet	Once Upon A Time
Osbourne, Mike	Outback
Coryell, Larry	Offering
Weather Report	Live In Tokyo
Tony Williams' Lifetime	Turn It Over
Davis, Miles	Panagaea
Hancock, Herbie	Crossings
Bley, Carla	Escalator Over The Hill

Plate 55

Glass, Philip	Music In Similar Motion
Riley, Terry	Happy Ending
AMM	AMMMusic
Musica Elettronica Viva	Musica Elettronica Viva
Reich, Steve	Four Organs Phase Patterns
Stockhausen, Karlheinz	Trans
Various Artists	Three Pieces For Blues Band & Orch.
Taverner, John	The Whale
Bedford, David	Nurses Song With Elephants
Stockhausen, Karlheinz	Stimmung
Nitzsche, Jack	St. Giles Cripplegate
Yamash'ta, Stomu	Henze/Maxwell Davies/Takemitsu

Plate 56

Peacock, Annette & Paul Bley	Revenge
Tomita	Planets
Subotnick, Morton	The Wild Bull
Beaver & Krause	Gandharva
Tonto's Expanding Headband	Zero Time
Stockhausen, Karlheinz	Gesang Der Junglinge/Kontakte
Can	Ege Bamyasi
Conrad, Tony & Faust	Outside The Dream Syndicate
Kraftwerk	Ralf & Florian
Organisation	Tone Float
Faust	Faust
Can	Soon Over Babaluma

Plate 57

Soft Machine	Soft Machine Vol. 2
Hatfield & The North	Afters

Ayers, Kevin	Joy Of A Toy
Soft Machine	Soft Machine
Wyatt, Robert	End Of An Ear
Caravan	Caravan
Slapp Happy	Sort Of
Allen, Daevid	Obsolete
Moore, Anthony	Secrets Of The Blue Bag
Lady June	Linguistic Leprosy
Gong	Magick Brother
Clearlight	Forever Blowing Bubbles

Plate 58

Second Hand	Death May Be Your Santa Claus
Egg	The Polite Force
Gong	Camembert Electrique
Khan	Space Shanty
East Of Eden	Snafu
Far East Family Band	Parallel World
Clouds	Watercolour Days
Bardens, Peter	The Answer
Greenslade, Dave	Pentateuch
Fields	Fields
Grind, Jody	Far Canal
Rare Bird	Rare Bird

Plate 59

Genesis	In The Beginning
Audience	Audience
Renaissance	Illusion
Hannibal	Hannibal
Gnidrolog	In Spite Of Harry's Toe-Nail
McDonald & Giles	McDonald & Giles
Procol Harum	Shine On Brightly
Tonton Macoute	Tonton Macoute
Continuum	Continuum
Frupp	Modern Masquerades
Ekseption	Ekseption
Pulsar	The Strands Of The Future

Plate 60

Comus	Comus
Jones, Nigel Mazlyn	Ship To Shore
Mellow Candle	Swaddling Songs
Kaleidoscope	Faintly Blowing
Arcadium	Breathe Awhile
Nirvana	Songs Of Love And Praise
Godfrey, Robert John	Fall Of Hyperion
Baker, Glenn	Brief Encounter
Enid	The Liverpool Album
Enid	The Enid
Enid	The Stand

Plate 61

Gabriel, Peter	Ein Deutsches Album
Abrahams, Mick	Mick Abrahams
Harrison, Mike	Mike Harrison
Green, Peter	In The Skies
Heckstall-Smith, DIck	A Story Ended
Laine, Denny	Ahh.....Laine
Kingdom Come	Kingdom Come
Silk	Smooth As Raw Silk
Stackridge	Stackridge
Granny's Intentions	Honest Injun
Badger	One Live Badger
Darien Spirit	Elegy To Marilyn

Plate 62

Iguana	Iguana
Fair Weather	Beginning From An End
Auger, Brian	A Better Land
Grimes, Carol	Fools Meeting
Ashton, Gardner & Dyke	Ashton, Gardner & Dyke
Atomic Rooster	In Hearing Of Atomic Rooster
Gypsy	Gypsy
Stray	Stray
Cochise	So Far
Deviants	The Deviants
Help Yourself	Return Of Ken Whaley/Happy Days

Plate 63

Mohogany Rush	Child Of The Novelty
Tear Gas	Piggy Go Getter
UFO	Flying
Tempest	Tempest
Tea	Tea
Windfall	Mountain Climbing
Buzzard	Tucky Buzzard
Grand Funk	We're An American Band
Scarecrow	Scarecrow
Paladin	Paladin
Leaf Hound	Leaf Hound
May Blitz	May Blitz

Plate 64

Bolan, Marc	The Beginning Of Doves
Haskell, Gordon	It Is & It Isn't
Pembroke, Jim	Pigworm
Bowie, David	Fashions
Newman, Tom	Fine Old Tom
Friedman, Dean	Well, Well Said The Rocking Chair
Lee, Arthur	Vindicator
Cocker, Joe	With A Little Help From My Friends
Seger, Bob	Brand New Morning
Durham, Terry	Crystal Telephone
Jobriath	Jobriath
Nelson, Bill	Northern Dream

Plate 65

Undertones	Teenage Kicks
Buzzcocks	Spiral Scratch
Adverts	Gary Gilmore's Eyes
Stranglers	Peaches
Slits	Cut
X-Ray Spex	Highly Inflammable
Birthday Party	Mr. Clarinet
Fire Engines	Big Old Dream
Fall	It's The New Thing
Fall	Fiery Jack
Soft Cell	A Man Can Get Lost
Jesus & Mary Chain	Upside Down

Plate 66

Wedding Present	Go Out And Get 'Em Boy
Wedding Present	Once More
Cure	Jumping Someone Else's Train
Cure	Forest
Cure	Killing An Arab
Wedding Present	Brassneck
Residents	Santa Dog '78
Tubeway Army	Are Friends Electric
Bush, Kate	Man With The Child In His Eyes

Def Leppard	Photograph
Iron Maiden	Running Free

Plate 67

Throbbing Gristle	United
Psychic TV	Those Who Do Not
Throbbing Gristle	In The Shadow Of The Sun
Throbbing Gristle	Journey Through A Body
Throbbing Gristle	Heathen Earth
Gadgets	Gadgetree
Lemon Kittens	Spoofed And Writhing
The The	Cold Spell Ahead
The The	Controversial Subject
Johnson, Matt	Burning Blue Soul
The The	Sweet Bird Of Truth

Plate 68

Fire Engines	Fire Engines
Blue Sunshine	The Glove
Warsaw Pakt	Needle Time
Various Artists	Shoet Circuit Live At The Electric....
Sisters Of Mercy	Dominion
Joy Division & Others	Earcom 2
Saints	Prehistoric Sounds
Cramps	Gravest Hits
Bauhaus	The Sky's Gone Out
Bishops	Cross Cuts
Mothmen	Pay Attention
Residents	Finger Prince

Plate 69

Moore, R. Stevie	Phonography
Martyn, John	Live At Leeds
Eno, Brian	Music For Films
Justified Ancients Of Mu Mu	1987
Big Black	Sound Of Impact
Harvey, Richard	A New Way Of Seeing
Motorhead	No Remorse
Public Image Ltd.	Metal Box
Jethro Tull	Thick As A Brick
Small Faces	Ogdens Nut Gone Flake
McCartney, Paul	Press
Horslips	Happy To Meet

Plate 70

AC/DC	Live From The Atlantic Studios
Crosby, Stills, Nash & Young	12 Tracks From Their Best Selling....
Any Trouble	Live At The Revue
Bee Gees	Short Cuts
Sonic Youth	Daydream Nation Promo Pack
Winwood, Stevie	A Conversational With Stevie......
Various Artists	BBC Transcription Disc - 70's Issue
Various Artists	BBC Transcription Disc - 80's Issue
Waters, Roger	Radio KAOS - Radio Version
Costello, Elvis	Live At The Mocambo
Various Artists	US West'd 1 Boxed Radio Transc'pt....
Wilson, Brian	Brian Wilson

Plate 71

Springsteen, Bruce	Darkness On The Edge Of Town
Kansas	Point Of Know Return
Costello, Elvis	My Aim Is True/This Years Model
Oldfield, Mike	Tubular Bells
Curved Air	Airconditioning
Saturnalia	Magical Love
ZZ Top	Eliminator
Iron Maiden	Aces High

Iron Maiden	Flight Of Icarus
Def Leppard	Hysteria
Marillion	Fugazi
Meat Loaf	Dead Ringer

Plate 72

Various Artists	The Label Sofa
Frankie Goes To Hollywood	Welcome To the Pleasure Dome
Simple Minds	Once Upon A Time
Cramps	Off The Bone
Sex Pistols	Never Mind The Bollocks Here's The...
Bauhaus	Burning From The Inside
Chameleons	Script Of The Bridge
Psychic TV	Pagan Day
Moore, Gary	Run For Cover
Parker, Ray Jnr.	Ghostbusters
Psychic TV	Album 10
Eurythmics	Sweet Dreams

Plate 73

Marillion	Garden Party
Springsteen, Bruce	Cover Me
Motorhead	Killed By Death
Wedding Present	This Boy Can Wait
Bauhuas	Telegram Sam
Soft Cell	The Twelve Inch Singles
Frankie Goes To Hollywood	Two Tribes
Smiths	The Charming Man
Residents	Diskomo

Plate 74

Madonna	Like A Virgin
Madonna	Angel
Madonna	Borderline
Madonna	Holiday
Madonna	Papa Don't Preach
Madonna	La Isla Bonita
Prince	Girls And Boys
Prince	Purple Rain
Prince	Paisley Park

Plate 75

Elektra up to 1971	Silver & Orange
Warner Brothers 1960's	Grey
Warner Brothers up to 1971	Orange
Atlantic Special 1960's	Orange
Atlantic up to 1971	Red & Plum
Reprise up to 1971	Yellow & Pale Green
Parlophone up to 1963	Gold & Black
Parlophone 1963-69	Yellow, Silver & Black
Parlophone from 1969	Silver & Black
Columbia up to 1963	Gold & Green
Columbia 1963-69	Blue, Silver & Black
Columbia from 1969	Silver & Black

Plate 76

Decca up to 1968	Red
Decca 1968-70	Dark Blue
Decca from 1970	Dark Blue
Deram	Light Brown & Red
Deram Nova	Red
Decca Nova	Light Blue
Immediate	Grey
Island 1967-69	Pink, Red & Black Logo
Island 1969	Pink, Black Logo
Island 1969-70	Pink, White Logo
Island 1970-74	Pink Rim, Multi-coloured Picture

Charisma 1970-71	Deep Pink

Plate 77

Miles, Buddy Express	Expressway To Your Skull
Walker, Scott	Best Of Scott Walker
Country Joe & The Fish	I Feel Like I'm Fixin' To Die
Vertigo Spiral	Black & White
Vertigo Spiral	Black & White
Nepentha	Black & White
Noir	We Had To Let You Have It
Cox, Billy	Nitro Function
Donovan	Donovan In Concert
Lovin' Spoonful	Daydream
Washington, Geno & The Ram Jam band	Hand Clapping, Foot Stompin',....LIVE
Trifle	First Meeting

Plate 78

Ian & Sylvia	The Best Of Ian & Sylvia
Davis, Spencer Group	With Their New Face On
Hardin, Tim	Tim Hardin 1
Various Artists	Here We Go Round The Mulberry....
Canned Heat	Boogie With Canned Heat
Zappa, Frank	Mothermania
Charles, Roy	Greatest Hits
Whitcomb, Ian	Mad Mad Music Hall
Martha & The Vandellas	Vandella's Greatest Hits
Miller, Steve Band	Sailor
Beach Boys	Pet Sounds
Lightin', Smokestack	Off The Wall

Plate 79

Various Artists	Marmalade 100 proof
Redding, Otis & Carla Thomas	King & Queen
Jefferson Airplane	Crown Of Creation
Neon	(Label Design, Multicoloured)
Presley, Elvis	Flaming Star & Summer Kisses
Presley, Elvis	G.I. Blues
Second Hand	Death May Be Your Santa Claus
Principle Edwards Magic Theatre	Soundtrack (Label Design to 1970)
Bennett, Duster	Smiling Like I'm Happy
Dylan, Bob	The Times They Are A Changin'
Dandelion	Label Design '71 onwards
Soft Machine	Soft Machine

Plate 80

Pentangle	The Pentangle
Procol Harum	Shine On Brightly
Troggs	Best Of The Troggs
King, Mike & John Hilary, Gary Compton	Dharma Blues
Beatles	All You Need Is Love (Reissue)
Beatles	All You Need Is Love (Original)
Bolan, Marc	The Wizard
Domino, Fats	Why Don't You Do Right
Factotums	You're So Good To Me
Kinks	Set Me Free
Rockin' Berries	Mr. Blue
Fame, Georgie & The Blue Flames	Do The Dog